THE WESTMINSTER
DICTIONARY OF THE BIBLE

WESTMINSTER AIDS TO
THE STUDY OF THE SCRIPTURES

—

THE WESTMINSTER DICTIONARY OF THE BIBLE
Edited by John D. Davis
Fifth edition revised and rewritten by
Henry S. Gehman

THE WESTMINSTER HISTORICAL ATLAS
TO THE BIBLE
Edited by G. Ernest Wright
and Floyd V. Filson

THE WESTMINSTER STUDY EDITION OF
THE HOLY BIBLE

THE WESTMINSTER

DICTIONARY OF

THE BIBLE

BY JOHN D. DAVIS, Ph.D., D.D., LL.D.

Late Professor of Oriental and Old Testament Literature,
Princeton Theological Seminary

Revised and Rewritten

BY HENRY SNYDER GEHMAN, Ph.D., S.T.D.

Professor of Old Testament Literature and Chairman of
the Department of Biblical Literature, Princeton Theological Seminary,
and Lecturer in Semitic Languages, Princeton University

The Westminster Press

PHILADELPHIA

PREFACE

SEVERAL years ago Dr. Park Hays Miller, editor of the Board of Christian Education of the Presbyterian Church in the U.S.A., and the editor of this dictionary were discussing the merits of Davis' Bible Dictionary and the possibility of revising that work. That book had first appeared in 1898, and subsequent revised editions were issued in 1903, 1911, and 1924. Both Dr. Miller and the editor agreed that it had fulfilled a useful purpose for many years for pastors, church workers, and Bible teachers and that its tradition of sound and conservative scholarship should be continued. At that time the editor was challenged to undertake the revision and rewriting of the volume, and after a preliminary survey of the fourth edition it was obvious that it was impossible to achieve a respectable revision without making numerous corrections on every page besides completely rewriting many of the important articles. So many advances have been made in Biblical studies since the time of Dr. Davis that the book had become thoroughly antiquated in philology, archaeology, the history of the ancient Near East, Biblical geography, and Old and New Testament criticism. The editor, as successor to the chair formerly occupied by Dr. Davis in Princeton Theological Seminary, was interested in continuing this form of practical Biblical studies and in giving new life to a well-known handbook, and accordingly he accepted the responsibility of revising and rewriting the work of his predecessor.

Each article has been approached objectively, and every statement has been scrutinized with great care. In all instances the editor preserved a conservative attitude in scholarship; in cases where reputable scholars differ he took cognizance of their views, but concluded with a preferred opinion which is consistent with the Bible itself. Theories that are purely subjective, in most cases, have not even been mentioned, not only to save space, but also to keep the book primarily a dictionary of the Bible. The editor, however, made no attempt to imitate a tradition, and while conserving the meritorious features of the fourth edition, he did not retain anything for the sole reason that it came from Dr. Davis, whom, by the way, he had never known. He has relied upon the best authorities of our time, and his object has been to produce a work which within his limitations will be accurate and authoritative in statement and content, and of constructive value for students of the Bible. Naturally many restrictions of space were imposed upon the editor, but as far as was possible within the brief compass of this volume he has included the most important results of recent developments in Biblical studies in order to bring the dictionary up to date.

In exercising economy of space, a consistent policy was adopted. In etymologies transliterations are employed only in special cases where it seemed necessary to represent the original language. The editor, with his linguistic interests,

v

naturally would have preferred to transliterate every foreign word in connection with the etymology, but that would have increased the size of the volume unduly beyond its modest proportions. Accordingly, if no language is mentioned in an etymology, it is understood that the original language is Hebrew. Other languages have always been indicated in order to avoid confusion on this point. In case of differences of opinion on derivations, the most probable one has always been chosen, and for the sake of brevity the others generally had to be ignored. In writing the etymologies, the standard lexicons of Latin, Greek, Sanskrit, Iranian, Sumerian, Egyptian, Coptic, and Semitic languages were consulted.

In transliterating ב, ג, ד, כ, פ, ת without *dagesh* (i.e., where they follow a vowel directly and are not doubled) there have been kept in mind the needs of those who do not know Hebrew. Thus b̲, g, d̲, k̲, p, t̲ would be rather meaningless to one who is not a Semitist; bh, gh, dh, kh, ph, th, except for the last two, do not suggest the proper pronunciation to the English reader. Practical considerations led the editor to be governed by the form or pronunciation that Hebrew proper names assume in the English Bible. Accordingly, ב, ג, ד, כ with or without *dagesh* are always written as b, g, d, k; פ and ת are represented by p and t, but פ and ת are written ph and th respectively. For convenience *shin* is written *sh* instead of š. In this way accuracy has not been sacrificed, and the needs of the non-Hebraist are better met. Long vowels are indicated by the macron over the vowel; short vowels are unmarked; the three reduced vowels ă, e, ŏ, are marked with the breve, but the vocal *schwa* is written as a small e above the line.

The pronunciation of proper names has received due consideration. In his work Dr. Davis had indicated only the syllabic divisions and the accent, but this was felt to be inadequate. In this edition every proper name is phonetically transcribed and provided with diacritical marks in order that there may be no doubt about the correct pronunciation. The editor recognizes that in many cases a Biblical proper name has several accepted pronunciations, but in order to save space only one could be given. The preferred usage of Webster's New International Dictionary, Second Edition, 1934, has been followed; in a few cases, however, where Webster's second pronunciation seemed better, that was adopted. It was not deemed necessary to indicate the pronunciation of ordinary English words.

Dr. Miller and the reviser also felt that a number of articles should be included on words which had not been treated in the previous editions. The addition of these articles, it is hoped, will add to the usefulness of the book.

Biblical quotations have been taken from the American Standard Version. The Authorized Version (King James Version) still is the best-known Bible of the English-speaking world, and its spellings of proper names have all been included; it has also been quoted in certain important cases, where it differs from the American Standard Version. In a few cases, references have needs been made to the English Revised Version, and the Jewish Version (*The Holy Scrip-*

tures According to the Masoretic Text—a New Translation, Jewish Publishing Society of America) has received due recognition in various important interpretations.

For economy of space no bibliography has been given in this dictionary, and only a few direct citations have been made. It would be well-nigh impossible for the reviser to refer to all the works he has consulted in the preparation of this new edition. In his own studies in the past he used Hastings' four works: *A Dictionary of the Bible* (the five-volume and the one-volume editions), *A Dictionary of Christ and the Gospels, Dictionary of the Apostolic Church;* the *Encyclopaedia Biblica;* and the *International Standard Bible Encyclopaedia,* and gleaned many facts from them. He has also found helpful suggestions in E. Kalt's *Biblisches Reallexikon,* 1938, and K. Galling's *Biblisches Reallexikon,* 1937, and the *Cambridge Ancient History.* Needless to say, he frequently consulted the standard commentaries in English and German on various books of the Bible, as well as works on Old and New Testament Introduction in the same languages. For a number of years he has been taking notes from scientific Biblical periodicals in English, German, Dutch, French, and Italian, and now many of these have found their way into this work. Of the utmost importance, however, in bringing this work up to date have been the publications of the American Schools of Oriental Research: the *Annual,* the *Bulletin,* and the *Biblical Archaeologist;* in fact, these were indispensable in the preparation of this edition.

For the geography of the Holy Land the editor leaned heavily upon Père F. M. Abel's *Géographie de la Palestine,* 2 vols., Paris, 1933–1938, although the writings of George Adam Smith, Alt, Dalman, and Albright were also consulted.

Unfortunately, the editor was unable to make use of the new Westminster Atlas of the Bible in the preparation of his articles. This very competent work, edited by Dr. George Ernest Wright and Dr. Floyd Vivian Filson, of McCormick Theological Seminary, was not begun until after he had completed most of his work on this dictionary. He is happy, however, to include in this volume a number of the maps prepared for Drs. Wright and Filson by Dr. Georges A. Barrois and Mr. Harold Arbo. These maps are not revisions of previous works but have been specially prepared on the basis of modern research. They are the most recent and authentic maps which we have of Bible lands. The full use which has been made in them of the newer techniques in map-making adds greatly to their accuracy and usefulness.

The English spelling of modern Palestinian place names is often inconsistent and shows much variation, but the better-known spellings as in the works of the American Schools of Oriental Research generally have been followed. Here the editor kept in mind the English reader and not the specialist in Arabic.

For a number of years, scholars of the United States of America and of Canada have taken an active leadership in Biblical and Semitic studies, and since the close of the First World War their labors have been especially productive.

In the preparation of this dictionary the editor has drawn extensively from the published works of his contemporaries and colleagues, especially from the following: Professor James Alan Montgomery, his preceptor at the University of Pennsylvania and the Divinity School of the Protestant Episcopal Church in Philadelphia; the late Professor George Aaron Barton, of the same institutions; Professor William F. Albright, Johns Hopkins University; the late Professor James H. Breasted and Professor A. T. Olmstead, both of the University of Chicago; Professor Charles C. Torrey and Professor Millar Burrows, both of Yale University; Professor Ephraim A. Speiser, University of Pennsylvania; Professor Philip K. Hitti, Princeton University; Professor Theophile J. Meek, University of Toronto; Dr. Robert H. Pfeiffer, Harvard University; Dr. Nelson Glueck, Hebrew Union College and American School of Oriental Research, Jerusalem; Dr. Cyrus H. Gordon, formerly of Smith College; and Dr. Georges A. Barrois, Princeton Theological Seminary.

In revising and rewriting the New Testament articles of the late Professors G. T. Purves and B. B. Warfield, the editor has had the co-operation of Dr. Bruce Manning Metzger, instructor in New Testament at the Princeton Theological Seminary, with whom he discussed many problems of New Testament criticism. For various articles Dr. Metzger also furnished much excellent material which has been incorporated into the dictionary. While the editor assumed responsibility for these articles in their final form, every one was checked by Dr. Metzger before it was submitted to the press. At the end of these articles the reviser retained the initials G. T. P. and B. B. W. for historical reasons, but, to indicate that they were revised and rewritten he appended his own initials, H. S. G.; he also signed whatever additional material he introduced on the New Testament. The rest of the articles in this book bear no signature. Every entry was carefully revised and generally rewritten. Much old material was completely eliminated, and the editor made extensive original contributions. This edition in form and content is an entirely new work, and to have signed all the new information and additions would have meant a continuous repetition of the editor's initials. He has, to all intents and purposes, made this dictionary his own, and accordingly he lets his name on the title page cover both his responsibilities and his original contributions.

The editor is grateful to Dr. Park Hays Miller for many helpful suggestions in the early days of this undertaking, to Miss Wilhelmina D'Arcy Stephens and her competent assistants for preparing the manuscript for the printer and for reading the proof, to Miss Jean Woodward Steele for her researches in finding suitable illustrations for the dictionary, and to Mr. John Ribble for the efficient manner in which he has seen the book through the press.

Princeton, New Jersey,   HENRY SNYDER GEHMAN.
February 7, 1944

ACKNOWLEDGMENTS

The Westminster Press is indebted to the following persons, organizations, and publishers for permission to use illustrations that appear in this book:

American Schools of Oriental Research for:
The Areopagus (Mars' Hill) with the Acropolis Beyond
Assyrian Soldier
Camel
Captives, Probably Israelite, Playing Lyres
Early Sling Stones, Found in Palestine
The Great High Place at Petra
A Papyrus Letter
Part of a Lachish Letter Written on Pottery

American Sunday-School Union for:
Philistines, from a Relief (*Archaeology and the Bible*, by George A. Barton)

Trustees of the British Museum for:
Design of a Sheep's Liver in Terra Cotta (*Cuneiform Texts*, Vol. XV)

Funk & Wagnalls Company for:
Altar of Burnt Offering (*Jewish Encyclopedia*, Vol. I)

Ewing Galloway for:
The Dome of the Rock
The Garden of Gethsemane
Modern Bethlehem

Keystone View Co., Inc., of N. Y., for:
A City Gate
A Modern Palestinian Wedding

The Macmillan Company for:
A Potter Working at His Wheel (*The Story of the Old Testament*, by W. K. L. Clarke)

The Metropolitan Museum of Art for:
The Obelisk of Shalmaneser
Statue of Ramesses II

J. Lane Miller for:
Eastern Gate of the Street Called Straight
The Head of the Kidron Valley
The Mount of Olives
The Obelisk at Heliopolis
The Sacred Mosque at Hebron
Statue of Diana of Ephesus
The Village of Magdala

Orient and Occident Photos for:
St. Paul's Gate, Tarsus
A Street Scene in Antioch in Syria
The Treasury at Petra

A View of Modern Jaffa (Joppa)
The Village of Nablus, the Ancient Shechem

The Oriental Institute of the University of Chicago for:
The Moabite Stone
A Sacrificial Altar of the Second Millennium B.C.

Palestine Exploration Fund for:
A Baking Tray from Gezer
A Weight Found at Lachish

Princeton University Press for:
The Scheide Papyrus of the Greek Text of Ezek. 20:8–14 (*The John H. Scheide Biblical Papyri*, Ezekiel)

Publishers' Photo Service, N.Y., for:
Mary's Well at Nazareth
A Shepherd Outside Herod's Gate, Jerusalem

Scott, Foresman and Company for:
Diagram of a Roman Table and Couches (*Private Life of the Romans*, by H. W. Johnston)
Plan of a Greco-Roman House (*ibid.*)

Charles Scribner's Sons for:
Plan of Ezekiel's Temple (*The International Critical Commentary*, The Book of Ezekiel, II)

Emetta A. Simons for:
Remains of the Synagogue at Capernaum

Underwood-Stratton for:
Jacob's Well
Mount Hermon as Seen from Lebanon
The Plain of Jezreel
Ruins of the Babylon of Nebuchadnezzar
Sebastiyeh, the Site of Ancient Samaria
A Threshing Floor in Samaria

The University Museum, Philadelphia, for:
A Clay Tablet and Envelope
Goat Statuette from the Royal Cemetery at Ur
Mirror, Probably of the First Century A.D.
Restoration of a Babylonian Temple Tower
The Royal Cemetery at Ur
Silver Harp Found in the Royal Cemetery at Ur
Sumerian Soldier

ABBREVIATIONS

A.D., *Anno Domini* (in the year of our Lord)
Akkad., Akkadian
Ann., Annales (*Annals*, Tacitus)
Antiq., Antiquities (Josephus)
Apol., (*Apology,* Justin Martyr)
Arab., Arabic
Aram., Aramaic
Assyr., Assyrian
A.R.V., American Revised Version (i.e., American Standard Version)
A.U.C., *ab urbe condita* (from the founding of the city, i.e., Rome) ; *anno urbis conditae* (in the year of the founding of the city, i.e., Rome)
A.V., Authorized Version (King James Version)

Bab., Babylonian
B.B.W., Benjamin Breckinridge Warfield
B.C., Before Christ

c., *circa* (about)
cf., *confer* (compare)

Dial. c. Tryph., Dialogus cum Tryphone, (*Dialogue with Trypho,* Justin Martyr)
Dyn., Dynasty

e., east, eastern
e.g., *exempli gratia* (for example)
Egypt., Egyptian
Epis., Epistulae (*Letters,* Pliny the Younger)
Epist. ad Nepotianum (*Letter to Nepotianus,* Jerome)
E.R.V., English Revised Version
Eth., Ethiopic
ety., etymology
E.V., English Version (of the Bible)

fem., feminine
fl., floruit (flourished) ; the period during which a person flourished ; used especially when exact dates cannot be given
Fr., French

Georg., Georgics (Virgil)
Gr., Greek
G.T.P., George Tybout Purves

Haer., Adversus Haereses (*Against the Heresies,* Irenaeus)
H.E., Historia Ecclesiastica (*Ecclesiastical History,* Eusebius)
Heb., Hebrew
Herod., Herodotus
Hist., Historiae (*Histories,* Tacitus)
Hist. Nat., Historia Naturalis (*Natural History,* Pliny)

H.S.G., Henry Snyder Gehman

ibid., ibidem (in the same place)
i.e., *id est* (that is)

Jos., Josephus
J.V., Jewish Version (Jewish translation of O.T. into English, 1917)

Lat., Latin
Legat. ad Gaium, De Legatione ad Gaium (*On the Embassy to Gaius,* Philo)
Luc., Lucian

marg., margin
masc., masculine
MS., MSS., manuscript(s)

n., north, northern
N.T., New Testament

O.T., Old Testament

Pers., Persian
pl., plural
Pro. Flac., Pro Flacco (*In Defense of Flaccus,* Cicero)
Ptol., Ptolemy
q.v., quod vide (which see)

rev., revised
R.V., Revised Version (American Standard Version, when there is no need to distinguish it from the English Revised Version)

s., south, southern
Sans., Sanskrit
Sat. (*Satires,* Horace)
seq., sequens (the following)
sing., singular
Sympos. (*Symposium,* Plato)
Syr., Syriac

Tim., Timaeus (Plato)

Vit. Apol. (*Life of Apollonius,* Philostratus)
viz., *videlicet* (namely)

w., west, western

Xen., Xenophon

*An asterisk with an etymology means that the word before which it is placed is a hypothetical reconstruction.

†A dagger with a numeral signifies the year of death.

GUIDE TO PRONUNCIATION

THE diacritical marks and letters used for phonetic transcription are the same as those employed in Webster's New International Dictionary of the English Language, Second Edition, 1934.

ā as in fāte

ā as in vâ-ca'tion

â as in câre

ă as in ădd

ă as in in'fănt

ä as in ärm

a̍ as in a̍sk

a̤ as in so'fȧ

ch as in church

dû for du as in ver'dûre

ē as in mēte

ẹ as in hẹre

ė as in ė-vent'

ĕ as in mĕt

ĕ as in si'lĕnt

ē as in ma'kēr

g as in go

gz for x as in ex-ist'

I as in īce

I as in ĭll

ĭ as in char'ĭty

ks for x as in vex

ō as in nōte

ô as in ô-bey'

ô as in ôrb

ŏ as in ŏdd

ô as in sôft

ŏ as in cŏn-nect'

oi as in oil

o͞o as in mo͞on

o͝o as in bo͝ok

ou as in out

s (voiceless) as in so

sh as in she

th (for voiced th) as in then

th (voiceless) as in thin

tû for tu as in na'tûre

ū as in cūbe

û as in û-nite'

û as in ûrn

ŭ as in ŭp

ŭ as in cir'cŭs

z as in zone; also for voiced s as in wise

zh for z as in azure

' as in pardon (pär'd'n), eaten (ēt"n), evil (ē'v'l)

The sound of other letters or phonetic transcriptions will be self-evident to the English speaker and reader.

A hyphen is used in Biblical compound proper names whenever it is found in the spelling of the American Standard Version. All other syllabic divisions for the sake of pronunciation are indicated by a dot (·).

Two accent marks have been used. A heavy one (′) denotes the primary accent or chief stress in a word. Many trisyllables and most polysyllables have a secondary or weaker accent, which is indicated by a light mark (′). Generally, if the reader pronounces the word with the primary accent on the correct syllable, the secondary accent will automatically take care of itself.

THE WESTMINSTER
DICTIONARY OF THE BIBLE

A

Aar'on (âr'ŭn) [Heb. *'Ahărōn*, ety. doubtful]. The brother of Moses and his senior by 3 years (Ex. 7:7). He was a descendant of Levi through Kohath and Amram (Ex. 6:14–27). As we do not read of perils attending his infancy it may be inferred that he was born before the promulgation of the nefarious Egyptian edicts dooming the Hebrew male children to death. He was younger than his sister Miriam (*q.v.*). He married Elisheba, daughter of Amminadab and sister of Nahshon, of the tribe of Judah, who bore him 4 sons, Nadab, Abihu, Eleazar, and Ithamar (Ex. 6:23; Num. 3:2). When Moses at Horeb was called to stand forth as the deliverer of his oppressed countrymen, and, wishing to escape the mission, complained that he was "slow of speech, and of a slow tongue," God repelled the objection, and said, "Is there not Aaron thy brother the Levite? I know that he can speak well." Aaron was forthwith instructed to go out and meet Moses in the wilderness. He did so, and the brothers came together (Ex. 4:10–16, 27). Returning to Egypt, they gathered together the elders of Israel and intimated to them the approaching deliverance (Ex. 4:29–31). Aaron acted as the spokesman and agent of Moses and carried the rod in the first interviews with the elders and with Pharaoh, and during the first 3 plagues (Ex. 4:30; 7:2, 9, 19 [by the command of Moses and hence Moses' act, Ex. 17:5]; 8:5, 16). But soon afterward Moses partly dispensed with the agency of Aaron, and thenceforth, whenever the rod was used symbolically, it was in the hand of Moses himself (Ex. 9:23; 10:13, and cf. v. 22; 14:16, 21; 17:5; Num. 20:11). Aaron and Hur supported Moses' arms during the battle with Amalek (Ex. 17:12). When the covenant between Jehovah and Israel was entered into at Mount Sinai, the ceremony of its ratification was concluded, as usual, by a common meal spread for the contracting parties. Aaron and 2 of his sons with Moses and 70 elders of Israel were appointed to partake of this meal as the legal representatives of the nation and to behold the vision of the God of Israel at the ceremony (Ex. 24:1, 9, 10). During the prolonged stay of Moses in the mount, the people became impatient at the absence of their leader and turned to Aaron with the demand that he make them gods to go before them. Aaron weakly yielded and made the golden calf (Ex., ch. 32). According to instructions which Moses received, Aaron and his sons were to fill the office of priest.

THE PRIESTHOOD ESTABLISHED

Accordingly, after the tabernacle had been completed, and was ready for actual services to begin, Aaron and his 4 sons were solemnly consecrated to the priesthood by being anointed with oil and clothed in splendid typical official vestments (Ex., chs. 28; 40:13–16; Lev., ch. 8). Aaron was thus the first high priest, an office which he filled for nearly 40 years. Shortly after leaving Sinai, he joined with Miriam in finding fault with Moses for having married a Cushite woman (Num. 12:1–16). The rebellion of Korah was directed as much against the exclusive priesthood of Aaron and his sons as against the civil authority of Moses. The divine appointment of Moses and Aaron to their respective offices was attested by the destruction of the rebels; and Aaron's right to the priesthood was further and specially vindicated by the budding of the rod taken for Levi and inscribed with Aaron's name (Num., chs. 16; 17). Toward the close of the journey in the wilderness, when the people were encamped for the 2d time at Kadesh, Aaron and Moses dishonored God by their conduct when Moses smote the rock. For this sin they were denied the privilege of entering the Promised Land (Num. 20:1–13). Soon afterward, when the Israelites were encamped at Moserah, by divine direction Aaron was led by Moses up Mount Hor and stripped of his sacred vestments, which were transferred to his son Eleazar. There he died, at the age of 123 years. The nation publicly mourned for him 30 days (Num. 20:23–29; 33:37–39; Deut. 10:6). See PRIEST and HIGH PRIEST.

Aar'on·ites (âr'ŭn-īts), in the Hebrew text simply Aaron, the name being used collectively. The priesly descendants of Aaron (I Chron. 12:27; 27:17, A.V.).

Ab (ăb) [Heb. *'ăb*, from Akkad. *abu*, name of 5th month of the Babylonian and Jewish year. The bulrushes were cut in that month for building purposes]. See YEAR.

A·bad'don (a-băd'ŭn) [destruction, ruin]. 1. Destruction, ruin (Job 31:12); the place of the dead, synonymous with the grave (Ps. 88:11), Sheol (Job 26:6; Prov. 15:11), and death (Job 28:22).
2. A name of the angel of the abyss, who is called in Greek Apollyon (Rev. 9:11).

A·bag'tha (a-băg'thà). One of the 7 chamberlains of the Persian king Ahasuerus (Esth. 1:10). These chamberlains, guardians of the harem, ministered in the presence of the king (vs. 10, 11). They were eunuchs, as the Hebrew title denotes and custom required; and hence were probably foreigners and likely to bear foreign names.

Ab'a·nah (ăb'à-nà), in A.V. **Ab'a·na** (ăb'à-nà); in marg. of R.V. Amanah, of A.V. Amana (*q.v.*) [the name probably means stony]. One of the 2 rivers of Damascus; presumably the more important, for Naaman, of that city, mentions it first (II Kings 5:12). It is the modern Barada, the Chrysorrhoas of classical writers, which rises in a large blue pool of unfathomable depth on the high plain south of Zebedāny on Anti-Lebanon, 23 miles from Damascus, rushes in a s.e. course down the mountain, and then, turning e., runs along the n. wall of the city, to be lost finally in an inland lake, the middle lake of 3 existing. It flows sluggishly through the plain, but on its passage through Damascus it has a rapid

1

course. Nine or 10 branches are taken from it, yet it flows on, deep and broad. It is the chief cause of the beauty and fertility of the plain of Damascus.

Ab'a·rim (ăb'á-rĭm) [those beyond]. A region e. of the Jordan, so named by people living w. of the river. Jeremiah mentions Lebanon, Bashan, and Abarim in this order, from n. to s. (Jer. 22:20; in A.V., "passages"). The Israelites encamped in this region shortly before crossing the Arnon (Num. 21:11). In it the Reubenites were granted lands (Num. 32:2–37). The mountains of Abarim denote the bluffs which overlook the Dead Sea and Jordan Valley from the e., extending from Wadi Kefrein in n. to Wadi Zerḳā Māʿīn or even to Wadi el-Ḥesā, which flows into the s. part of the Dead Sea. On these heights the Israelites encamped before they moved down to Shittim by the Jordan (Num. 33:47–49). From a peak of the range Moses looked across at the Promised Land (Num. 27:12; Deut. 32:49; 34:1).

Ab'ba (ăb'á) [Aram., father]. A term borrowed from childhood's language to express filial address to God (Mark 14:36; Rom. 8:15; Gal. 4:6). The corresponding Hebrew word is Ab.

Ab'da (ăb'dá) [probably, servant (of God)]. 1. The father of Adoniram (I Kings 4:6). 2. A Levite, the son of Shammua (Neh. 11:17). See OBADIAH 12.

Ab'de·el (ăb'dĕ-ĕl) [servant of God]. The father of Shelemiah (Jer. 36:26).

Ab'di (ăb'dī) [perhaps, contraction of servant of Jehovah]. 1. A Levite of the family of Merari. He was the son of Malluch, and father of Kishi (I Chron. 6:44). The Abdi of II Chron. 29:12 seems to be the same man. See KISH 4. 2. Son of a certain Elam (Ezra 10:26).

Ab'di·el (ăb'dī-ĕl) [servant of God]. A Gadite, resident in Gilead (I Chron. 5:15).

Ab'don (ăb'dŏn) [servile]. 1. The son of Hillel, a native of Pirathon, in the tribe of Ephraim. He judged Israel, or a portion of it, 8 years, and is the 11th judge in the order of enumeration. He had 40 sons and 30 sons' sons, who rode on as many ass colts—a sign of rank in days when the Hebrews did not yet have horses. He was buried in his native place (Judg. 12:13–15). 2. Head of a father's house of Benjamin, a son of Shashak, dwelling in Jerusalem (I Chron. 8:23, 26, 28). 3. A Benjamite, the first-born of Jeiel of Gibeon and an ancestor of King Saul (I Chron. 8:30; 9:35, 36). See KISH 2. 4. An official of King Josiah (II Chron. 34:20); see ACHBOR. 5. A town in the territory of Asher, given, with its suburbs, to the Levites of the Gershon family (Josh. 21:30; I Chron. 6:74). Abdon is perhaps identical with Khirbet ʿAbdeh, 4 miles n.n.e. of Acre.

A·bed'-ne·go (á-bĕd'nē-gō) [servant of Nego, probably a deliberate change from Nebo, the Babylonian god of wisdom]. The name given by the prince of the eunuchs at Babylon to Azariah, one of the 3 faithful Jews afterward miraculously saved from the fiery furnace (Dan. 1:7; 3:12–30; I Macc. 2:59).

A'bel, I (ā'bĕl) [Heb. *Hebel,* breath; applied to Abel from the shortness of his life; some derive it from Akkad. *ablu,* son]. A younger son of Adam, and by calling a shepherd. Abel was a righteous man (Matt. 23:35; I John 3:12); one of the Old Testament worthies whose conduct was controlled by faith (Heb. 11:4). He offered to God a lamb from his flock, which was accepted. It was not the kind of offering, but the character of the offerer, that God respected. As brought by Abel, the offering showed the surrender of the heart to God. The offering of the best further revealed the sense of obligation and gratitude to God as the sole bestower of the good, to whom all thanks were due. It expressed the consciousness in the offerer of entire dependence upon God for daily blessing and the desire for the continuance of God's favor. In one in whom the sense of sin was deep, it set forth the entire dependence of the sinner upon God's unmerited mercy. Cain's character was different from Abel's; the former was rejected, and, at the promptings of envy, slew Abel (Gen., ch. 4).

A'bel, II (ā'bĕl) [a grassy place, a meadow]. 1. The same as Abel-beth-maacah (II Sam. 20:14, 15, 18). 2. In I Sam. 6:18 it is apparently an erroneous reading for *'Eben,* stone.

A'bel-beth-ma'a·cah (ā'bĕl-bĕth-mā'á-ká) and **A'bel of Beth-ma'a·cah** (ā'bĕl of bĕth-mā'á-ká), in A.V. written Ma'a·chah [Abel, i.e., meadow, near Beth-maacah]. A fortified town in the tribe of Naphtali (II Sam. 20: 15; I Kings 15:20), famous for prudence, or for its adherence to Israelite customs (II Sam. 20:18; cf. Gr. text). Sheba fled thither when his revolt against David failed. Joab prepared to assault the town to capture him, but a "wise woman," after conference with Joab, agreed to have the rebel slain, and thus saved the town (II Sam. 20:14–22). Benhadad seized it and other towns when Asa of Judah sought his aid against Baasha of Israel (I Kings 15:20). In 734 B.C. Tiglathpileser cap.ured it, and carried off its inhabitants to Assyria (II Kings 15:29). Its site is probably marked by Tell Abil, a village w. of the Jordan on a knoll overlooking the valley, 12 miles n. of Lake Ḥūleh and opposite Dan. Girded by a well-watered, fertile plain, it merits its name Abel-maim, meadow of waters (II Chron. 16:4).

A'bel-cher'a·mim (ā'bĕl-kĕr'á-mĭm) [meadow of vineyards]. A place e. of the Jordan to which Jephthah pursued the Ammonites (Judg. 11:33); perhaps Khirbet es-Sūḳ on the way from ʿAmmān to Ḥesbān.

A'bel-ma'im (ā'bĕl-mā'ĭm). See ABEL-BETH-MAACAH.

A'bel-me·ho'lah (ā'bĕl-mē-hō'lá) [meadow of dancing]. A town, apparently in the Jordan Valley, where Elisha was born (Judg. 7:22; I Kings 4:12; 19:16). It was fixed by Jerome 10 Roman miles s. of Scythopolis (Bethshean). Conder places it at ʿAin Ḥelweh, 9½ miles s. of Bethshean. The primitive site probably was in this neighborhood at Tell Abu Sifreh, a spur formed by the junction of the wadies el-Māliḥ and el-Ḥelweh.

A'bel-miz'ra·im (ā'bĕl-mĭz'rá-ĭm). See ATAD.

A'bel-shit'tim (ā'bĕl-shĭt'ĭm) [meadow of acacias]. See SHITTIM.

A'bez (ā'bĕz). See EBEZ.

A'bi (ā'bī). See ABIJAH 7.

A·bi'a (á-bī'á). See ABIJAH.

A·bi'ah (á-bī'á). See ABIJAH.

A'bi-al'bon (ā'bī-ăl'bŏn) [the component "albon" may be a scribal confusion from Shaalbonite, II Sam. 23:32]. One of David's mighty men (II Sam. 23:31). The LXX supports the reading Abiel in this passage, which is the name he bears in I Chron. 11:32.

A·bi'a·saph (á-bī'á-săf), or **E·bi'a·saph** [the Father has gathered, or added]. A descendant of Levi through Korah (Ex. 6:16, 18, 21, 24; I Chron. 6:23; 9:19).

A·bi'a·thar (*à-bī'à-thár*) [the Father is pre-eminent]. A priest, the son of Ahimelech, of the line of Eli. On the slaughter by Doeg at the instance of King Saul of the priests at Nob, Abiathar escaped, carrying the ephod with him; and, as was natural, cast in his lot with David (I Sam. 22:20–23). When David at length ascended the throne, Zadok and Abiathar apparently shared the high priesthood between them (cf. I Chron. 15:11, 12; II Sam. 15:24 *seq.*, 35, etc.). The mention of Ahimelech, son of Abiathar, as priest with Zadok in II Sam. 8:17, is regarded by some as a copyist's error, whereby the names of father and son were transposed. But the number of allusions to Ahimelech, the son of Abiathar, as priest, is so great that an error is improbable (I Chron. 18:16, LXX; 24:3, 6, 31). A simpler explanation is that, since Abiathar was becoming quite old (he was about 70 years of age at the time of Absalom's revolt), his son and legal successor assumed the burdensome priestly functions and was called priest, as Hophni and Phinehas served during the lifetime of Eli and were called priests (I Sam. 1:3; 2:11). The aged Abiathar remained faithful to the king during Absalom's rebellion, and rendered the fugitive monarch great service (II Sam. 15:24, 29, 35, 36; 17:15; 19:11); but when later Adonijah sought to wrest the succession to the throne from Solomon, Abiathar cast his priestly influence with the military influence of Joab, another old man, in favor of the attractive aspirant (I Kings 1:7). Though this attempt failed, he again favored Adonijah after David's death (I Kings 2:12–22). For this he was deposed from the high priesthood, and Zadok, a priest of approved loyalty, but of the other branch of the Aaronic family, was put into his place (I Kings 2:26, 35). His deposition involved that of his sons, Ahimelech and Jonathan; and thus the rule of the house of Eli came to an end, according to prophecy (I Sam. 2:31–35). The passage in I Kings 4:4 probably refers to the time immediately prior to his deposition. Abiathar is alluded to by our Lord in the New Testament (Mark 2:26).

A'bib (*ā'bĭb*) [an ear of corn]. The month that the Hebrews were directed to make the first of the year in commemoration of their departure from Egypt (Ex. 12:1, 2; 13:4). Harvest began in it. The feast of unleavened bread or the passover fell during the month (Ex. 12:1 *seq.*; 23:15; Deut. 16:1). The Jewish months following the moon, and ours being fixed, the two cannot be made exactly to correspond. Abib most nearly approaches our month of March, though in some years its end moves some distance into our April. After the Captivity the name Abib gave place to Nisan (Neh. 2:1; Esth. 3:7). See YEAR.

A·bi'da (*à-bī'dà*), in A. V. once **A·bi'dah** (*à-bī'dà*) (Gen. 25:4) [the Father knows]. A descendant of Abraham through Midian (Gen. 25:4; I Chron. 1:33).

A·bi'dan (*à-bī'dăn*) [the Father is judge]. The representative prince of the tribe of Benjamin in the wilderness. His father's name was Gideoni (Num. 1:11; 2:22; 7:60, 65; 10:24).

A'bi·el (*ā'bĭ-ĕl*) [God is a father]. 1. A Benjamite, the father of Kish and of Ner, and the grandfather of Saul and of Abner (I Sam. 9:1; 14:51). See KISH 2.
2. An Arbathite, one of David's mighty men (I Chron. 11:32), called in II Sam. 23:31 Abialbon (*q.v.*).

A'bi·e'zer (*ā'bĭ-ē'zẽr*) [the Father is help]. 1. A descendant of Manasseh through Machir, and founder of a family (Josh. 17:2; I Chron. 7:18); abbreviated in Num. 26:30 to Iezer (A. V. Jeezer). The judge Gideon belonged to this family (Judg. 6:11).

2. Collectively, the family of Abiezer (Judg. 6:34; 8:2).
3. One of David's heroes (II Sam. 23:27; I Chron. 11:28; 27:12).

A'bi·ez'rite (*ā'bĭ-ĕz'rīt*). One belonging to the family of Abiezer (Judg. 6:11, 24; 8:32). In Num. 26:30 abbreviated. A.V. has Jeezerite, but the spelling should rather be Iezrite to accord with the Hebrew and be consistent with Abiezrite.

Ab'i·gail (*ăb'ĭ-gāl*) once **Ab'i·gal** (*ăb'ĭ-găl*) [perhaps, the Father is rejoicing]. 1. The wife of Nabal. She was a woman of good understanding, and of a beautiful countenance, and on the death of her first husband became one of David's wives (I Sam. 25:3, 14–44; 27:3; II Sam. 2:2). When the Amalekites captured Ziklag they took her captive, but she was rescued by David after he had defeated the enemy (I Sam. 30:5, 18). She bore him a son called Chileab (II Sam. 3:3) or Daniel (I Chron. 3:1).
2. A sister of David (I Chron. 2:16); not, however, a daughter of Jesse, but of Nahash (II Sam. 17:25, in R.V. Abigal). She was the mother of Amasa.

Ab'i·hail (*ăb'ĭ-hāl*) [the Father is strength]. In the Hebrew text the *h* is a different letter in the name of the men (*ḥ*), and in that of the women (*h*). The difference is commonly attributed to an early misreading of the text. 1. A Levite of the family of Merari (Num. 3:35).
2. Wife of Abishur (I Chron. 2:29).
3. A Gadite (I Chron. 5:14).
4. Wife of King Rehoboam and a descendant of Eliab, David's brother (II Chron. 11:18).
5. Father of Queen Esther (Esth. 2:15).

A·bi'hu (*à-bī'hū*) [the Father is He]. A son of Aaron. He shared in the privileges, in the sin, and in the fate of Nadab, the eldest son, and like him died childless (Ex. 6:23; 24:1; 28:1; Lev. 10:1–7; Num. 3:2).

A·bi'hud (*à-bī'hŭd*) [the Father is majesty]. A descendant of Benjamin through the family of Bela (I Chron. 8:3).

A·bi'jah (*à-bī'jà*), in A. V. of O. T. 4 times **A·bi'ah** (I Sam. 8:2; I Chron. 2:24; 6:28; 7:8), in A.V. of N.T. **A·bi'a** [Jehovah is a father]. 1. The wife of Hezron, a man of the tribe of Judah (I Chron. 2:24).
2. A descendant of Aaron. His family had grown to a father's house in the time of David, and was made the 8th of the 24 courses into which David divided the priests (I Chron. 24:1, 6, 10). See 8 below.
3. A descendant of Benjamin through Becher (I Chron. 7:8).
4. The younger son of Samuel, who was appointed by his father a judge in Beer-sheba but proved corrupt (I Sam. 8:2; I Chron. 6:28).
5. A son of Jeroboam. While yet a child he fell dangerously sick. Jeroboam sent his queen in disguise to the Prophet Ahijah, who had predicted that he should obtain the kingdom, to inquire what the issue of the sickness would be. The prophet recognized the queen, notwithstanding her disguise, pronounced judgment against Jeroboam for his apostasy from Jehovah, and added that the child would die at once, and that alone of all that household he would obtain honorable burial, because in him was found some good thing toward the Lord God. All came to pass as the seer had foretold (I Kings 14:1–18).
6. The name given in Chronicles to the son and successor of Rehoboam (II Chron. 12:16; 13:1 to 14:1). See ABIJAM.
7. The mother of Hezekiah (II Chron. 29:1). In II Kings 18:2 she is called with great brevity Abi.

8. A chief of the priests who returned with Zerubbabel from Babylon (Neh. 12:4, 7). Possibly he was a representative of the old course of Abijah, but the connection cannot be established, and in view of Ezra 2:36 seq. is not probable. In the next generation, a father's house among the priests bore this name (Neh. 12:17). The father of John the Baptist belonged to this family (Luke 1:5).

9. A priest who, doubtless in behalf of a father's house, signed the covenant in the days of Nehemiah (Neh. 10:7).

A·bi'jam (a-bī'jăm), variant of Abijah. The son and successor of Rehoboam on the throne of Judah. His mother's name was Maacah, a descendant of Absalom (I Kings 15:2; II Chron. 13:2). See MICAIAH 1. He sinned after the manner of his father, and had not a heart true to Jehovah. The kings of Judah had not yet become reconciled to the revolt of the ten tribes, and Abijam continued the war with Jeroboam which his father had waged (I Kings 15:6, 7). According to II Chron. 13:3, compared with II Sam. 24:9, the whole population "able to go forth to war" was under arms. In the slaughter which accompanied the warfare, 500,000 men of Israel were slain (II Chron. 13:16–20). Abijam had 14 wives, 22 sons, and 16 daughters (II Chron. 13:21). He reigned 3 years, and died, leaving his son Asa to succeed him in the kingdom (I Kings 15:1–8; II Chron. 14:1).

Ab'i·le'ne (ăb'ĭ-lē'nê) [Gr. *Abilēnē*, so called from Abila, its capital, and that again probably from Heb. *'ābēl*, meadow]. A tetrarchy near Anti-Lebanon. Its capital Abila lay upon the Barada, 18 or 20 miles n.w. from Damascus, in part upon the site of the modern village of es-Suk. There is a romantic gorge, with a Roman road cut in the cliff, a cemetery, a number of tall pillars, a stream below, and the so-called "tomb of Abel" above. The local tradition that Abel was buried here doubtless originated in the similarity of sound between Abel and Abila. Of the formation of the tetrarchy Josephus makes no mention. In Luke 3:1 it is referred to as separate from the tetrarchy of Philip, and as governed by Lysanias in the 15th year of Tiberius. Likewise an inscription at Abila, dating from the reign of Tiberius, mentions Lysanias as tetrarch of Abilene at that time. Some years later the 2 tetrarchies were still distinct; for Caligula, A.D. 37, bestowed the "tetrarchy of Philip," then dead, and the "tetrarchy of Lysanias" upon Herod Agrippa, the Herod of The Acts (Jos. *Antiq.* xviii. 6, 10), and Claudius confirmed to him "Abila of Lysanias" (Jos. *Antiq.* xix. 5, 1).

There was an Abila in Perea, e. of Gadara, but it is not mentioned in Scripture.

A·bim'a·el (a-bĭm'a-ĕl) [El (God) is Father]. A name in the genealogy of Joktan. It may denote a person, a tribe, or a locality, and is to be sought in Arabia (Gen. 10:28; I Chron. 1:22).

A·bim'e·lech (a-bĭm'ĕ-lĕk) [the Father is king]. 1. The personal name or official title of a king of Gerar, at whose court Abraham attempted to pass off Sarah as his sister (Gen. 20:1–18). The king and the patriarch at a later period entered into a covenant with each other (Gen. 21:22–34).

2. A king of the Philistines at Gerar, at whose court Isaac attempted to pass off Rebekah as his sister, and with whom he also, like his father, at last formed a covenant (Gen. 26:1–33).

3. The son of the judge Gideon by a concubine. This woman was a native of Shechem, where her family had influence. One natural penalty of polygamy is that the sons by one mother tend to quarrel fiercely with those by another; and Abimelech, obtaining assistance from his mother's relatives, killed 70 sons of his father on one stone at Ophrah, the native city of the family. One son only, Jotham, escaped from the massacre. Then Abimelech was elected king of Shechem. Before he had ruled 3 years, he and his subjects were at variance, and his throne, founded in blood, had begun to totter. A plot against him was formed by Gaal. It came to the ears of Zebul, Abimelech's second in command. Gaal was defeated and driven out of Shechem, the city being afterward destroyed and sown with salt. A thousand men and women who had taken refuge in its tower were burned to death. When Abimelech shortly afterward was besieging Thebez, he was mortally wounded by a millstone dropped on his head from the city wall by a woman. Regarding it as dishonorable to be killed by a female, he ordered his armor-bearer to draw his sword and slay him, which he did (Judg., ch. 9).

4. See ACHISH.

5. A priest, a son of Abiathar (I Chron. 18:16). The spelling is doubtless a copyist's error for Ahimelech. The LXX reads Ahimelech; see also I Chron. 24:6, etc.

A·bin'a·dab (a-bĭn'a-dăb) [the Father is generous]. 1. A man of Kiriath-jearim, who, when the Ark was sent back by the Philistines, gave it accommodation in his house, where it remained until the reign of David. A son of Abinadab was consecrated to act as its custodian (I Sam. 7:1, 2; II Sam. 6:3; I Chron. 13:7).

2. The 2d son of Jesse and an elder brother of David (I Sam. 16:8; 17:13).

3. A son of Saul, killed with his father in the battle of Gilboa (I Sam. 31:2).

4. Father of a son-in-law of Solomon (I Kings 4:11, A.V.). See BEN-ABINADAB.

A·bin'o·am (a-bĭn'ō-ăm) [the Father is pleasantness]. The father of Barak (Judg. 4:6; 5:12).

A·bi'ram (a-bī'răm), variant of Abram [the Father is exalted]. 1. A Reubenite, a brother of Dathan and fellow conspirator with Korah (Num., ch. 16).

2. The first-born son of Hiel, who rebuilt Jericho (I Kings 16:34). His death, when its foundations were laid, in part fulfilled a curse pronounced by Joshua (Josh. 6:26).

Ab'i·shag (ăb'ĭ-shăg) [perhaps, father has wandered, erred]. A beautiful girl from Shunem, employed to attend upon King David when he was old and declining in vitality (I Kings 1:1–4). Adonijah wished to marry her after David's death, and made application for the needed permission to Solomon, who not merely refused his request but interpreted it to mean an insidious claim for the crown and put him to death (I Kings 2:13–25).

A·bish'a·i (a-bĭsh'a-ī) and **Ab'shai** (I Chron. 18:12 marg.) A son of David's sister Zeruiah, and brother of Joab and Asahel (II Sam. 2:18; I Chron. 2:15, 16). When David found Saul and his followers asleep, Abishai asked permission to kill the king; but David would not sanction his doing harm to "Jehovah's anointed" (I Sam. 26:5–9). He served under Joab in David's army (II Sam. 2:18; 10:10). When Abner, fleeing from the battle at Gibeon, was compelled to kill Asahel, the two brothers of the latter, Joab and Abishai, pursued the homicide, but without effect (II Sam. 2:18–24). He was loyal to David during the revolts of Absalom and Sheba (II Sam., chs. 16; 20). He desired to slay Shimei for cursing David, even when Shimei asked forgiveness (II Sam. 16:9; 19:21). He was one of David's mighty men who had lifted up his spear against 300 and slain them (II Sam. 23:18; I Chron.

4

11:20). He defeated the Edomites also in the Valley of Salt, slaying 18,000 of them and garrisoning their country (I Chron. 18:12, 13). He succored David in the fight with Ishbibenob (II Sam. 21:16, 17).

A·bish'a·lom (ă-bĭsh'ā-lŏm). See ABSALOM.

A·bish'u·a (ā-bĭsh'û-ā) [the Father is salvation]. 1. A Benjamite of the family of Bela (I Chron. 8:4).
2. The son of Phinehas the priest (I Chron. 6:4, 5, 50; Ezra 7:5).

A·bi'shur (ă-bī'shēr) [the Father is a wall]. A man of Judah, family of Hezron, house of Jerahmeel (I Chron. 2:28, 29).

A·bi'tal (ă-bī'tăl) [the Father is dew, perhaps in the sense of refreshment]. One of David's wives. Her son was Shephatiah (II Sam. 3:4; I Chron. 3:3).

A·bi'tub (ă-bī'tŭb) [the Father is goodness]. A Benjamite, son of Shaharaim by his wife Hushim (I Chron. 8:8–11).

A·bi'ud (ă-bī'ŭd) [the Gr. form, probably, of Heb. Abihud, q.v.]. A member of the royal line of Judah (Matt. 1:13). The name is omitted in I Chron. 3:19.

Ab'ner (ăb'nẽr) [the Father is a lamp]. A variant, Abiner, is used in the Heb. text of I Sam. 14:50. The son of Ner, King Saul's uncle. During the reign of that monarch Abner was commander in chief of the army (I Sam. 14:51). He first became acquainted with David when that youth offered to meet Goliath in combat (I Sam. 17:55–58). On the death of Saul, Abner availed himself of the tribal feeling adverse to Judah, and turned it to the advantage of the house to which he was related by blood, and to which he had owned allegiance. He proclaimed Saul's son Ish-bosheth king at Mahanaim (II Sam. 2:8). During the war between the house of Saul and David which followed, in an interview which he held at Gibeon with Joab, David's commander in chief, Abner proposed what he seems to have intended for a tournament between 12 young men picked from Ish-bosheth's supporters and as many taken from the followers of David, but mutual animosities converted the mimic combat into a real battle; and the 2 armies being drawn into the struggle, that which Abner led was defeated with great slaughter (II Sam. 2:12–32). During the retreat from this battle Abner was pursued with hostile intent by Asahel, one of Joab's brothers, and, after repeatedly warning him off, had at last to strike him dead in self-defense (II Sam. 2:18–24). Soon afterward Abner had a serious charge brought against him by Ish-bosheth, which so irritated him that he intimated his intention of transferring his allegiance to David, and was as good as his word. First he sent messengers to David, and then sought an interview with him, and was graciously received. But Joab, believing or pretending to believe that Abner had come simply as a spy, went after him, invited him to a friendly conversation, and stabbed him dead. The ostensible reason for this assassination was revenge for the death of Asahel, who, however, had died in fair fight. An unavowed motive probably was fear that Abner might one day displace him from the command of David's army. The king was justly incensed against the murderer, and conspicuously showed the people that he had no complicity in the crime. He attended the funeral, lamented the unworthy fate of the prince and great man who had fallen in Israel, and finally left it in charge to his successor to call Joab to account for the crime (II Sam. 3:6–39; I Kings 2:5). Abner had at least one son, Jaasiel (I Chron. 27:21). He seems to have had a regard for the house of God, for he dedicated to it some of the spoils which he had taken in battle (I Chron. 26:28).

A·bom'i·na'tion of Des'o·la'tion. Idolatry, with its blighting effect upon man, its degradation of the divine ideal, and its violent outward, as well as its less visible insidious, opposition to the Kingdom of God. To Daniel was revealed: "In the midst of the week he shall cause the sacrifice and the oblation to cease; and upon the wing of abominations shall come one that maketh desolate" (Dan. 9:27); "and they shall profane the sanctuary, even the fortress, and shall take away the continual burnt-offering, and they shall set up the abomination that maketh desolate" (Dan. 11:31); and "from the time that the continual burnt-offering shall be taken away, and the abomination that maketh desolate set up, there shall be a thousand two hundred and ninety days" (Dan. 12:11). These prophecies depict outstanding features of the development of the Kingdom of God, which are typical for all time. A notable fulfillment of Dan. 11:31, which the Jews were quick to discern, was the stoppage of the daily sacrifice by Antiochus Epiphanes in June, 168 B.C., and the erection on the brazen altar of an idolatrous one, on which sacrifices were offered to Jupiter Olympius (I Macc. 1:54; 6:7; II Macc. 6:2; Jos. Antiq. xii. 5, 4; 7, 6). But the prophecy of the abomination of desolation was not exhausted by this fulfillment. The prophecy belongs to Messianic times (Dan. 9:27), and yet more generally to the conflict of the Kingdom of God until its final triumphant establishment (cf. Dan. 12:7, 11, with ch. 7:25–27; cf. ch. 12:2). Christ re-iterated the prophecy, enjoining to flee to the mountains those who should see the abomination of desolation, spoken of by Daniel the prophet, standing in the Holy Place (Matt. 24:15, etc.).

A'bra·ham (ā'brā-hăm), at first **A'bram** [Abram in Heb. means "the Father is high." Abraham has the same meaning. In S. Arab. h denotes the presence of a vowel. When h was understood as a consonant, it was vocalized, and thus arose two a's in -rāhăm]. Son of Terah, progenitor of the Hebrews, father of the faithful, and the friend of God (Gen. 11:26; Gal. 3:7–9; James 2:23).

Is Abraham a tribal name? Is he the personification of a tribe? The justification for raising this question is the fact that many names in the genealogical registers of the Hebrews denote tribes and not individuals (Gen., chs. 10; 25:1–4). It is not always easy—at times it is impossible—to decide whether a people or a person is meant. But it is important to note, further, that a tribal name and history often include persons whose deeds are recorded in the name of the tribe and as the acts of the tribe (see CHRONOLOGY, I. 3). Noah, for example, may be the name of a tribe; but, if so, in the narrative of the flood it denotes likewise an individual member of that tribe, who was saved with his family in the ark. In the case of Abraham, Gen. 11:26, 27; 12:1–10 might readily be read as the story of a tribe's origin and migration; in fact, it does recount the movement of a sheik and his people; the separation of Abram and Lot might also be tribal, and so too the treaty with Abimelech. But though the tribal element may enter into the narrative, the history is not exclusively tribal. The majority of the deeds recorded in it cannot be explained as tribal movements without violence and improbable interpretations. They are the acts of an individual (Gen. 15:1–18; 16:1–11; 18:1 to 19:28; 20:1–17; 22:1–14; ch. 24), and during all the centuries that followed the Hebrews themselves regarded Abraham as an individual (Isa. 29:22; 41:8; 51:2; Jer. 33:26; Ezek. 33:24; Matt. 8:11).

I. *Chronology.* 1. *His life before his arrival in Canaan,* 75 years. In his early life Abraham dwelt with his father and his brethren in Ur of the Chaldees. He married Sarai, his half sister. See SARAH 1. After the death of his brother Haran, he, his wife, and Lot his nephew migrated, under the headship of Terah, from Ur to go to the Land of Canaan (Gen. 11:27–31). The motive which led the family to change its habitation is not stated in Gen., ch. 11. Josephus inferred from the narrative that Terah was actuated by a desire to escape from associations which reminded him of the son who had died (Jos. *Antiq.* i. 6, 5). It has also been suggested that the migration of the family may have been prompted by the wish to better their condition in a new and freer country, or have been incited by political disturbances in Sumer, such as an invasion of the Elamites. Stephen understood Gen. 12:1 to refer back to this time, and to be the initial command, given while the family was yet in Ur, for he says: "The God of glory appeared unto our father Abraham, when he was in Mesopotamia, before he dwelt in Haran" (Acts 7:2). Stephen's interpretation is countenanced by Gen. 15:7 and Neh. 9:7, although these passages might refer to God's providence. All the various causes suggested may have co-operated; and the natural motives may have been the means providentially employed by God to persuade the party to obey the heavenly vision. The family departed from Ur and, taking the customary route, followed the Euphrates toward the n.w. On reaching Haran, the party temporarily abandoned the purpose of journeying to Canaan and took up residence where they were.

When Abraham was 75 years old, he departed from Haran to go to Canaan. This move may have been due to God's will as revealed by him in Ur, or to a command now first received. Stephen, as already said, adopts the former interpretation and the wording of the details in Gen. 12:1 well suits, with our present meager knowledge of the community at Haran, this explanation. The departure is related after the record of Terah's death. It does not follow, however, from this that Abraham tarried at Haran until his father died. The narrator as usual concludes what he has to say of Terah before taking up the detailed history of Abraham. Still it is a plausible conjecture that Abraham did tarry so long, for the same party that left Ur now, with the exception of Terah, leaves Haran, and this also is the interpretation of Stephen. But if so, Abraham was born when Terah was at least 130 years old, and not 70, as is often unnecessarily inferred from Gen. 11:26. In this passage Abraham is mentioned first, either because he was the first-born and born in Terah's 70th year, or else, if he was a younger son and born after Terah's 70th year, because he was the progenitor of the chosen people (cf., for a similar interpretation, Gen. 5:32 with 9:22, 24). From Haran Abraham went to Canaan. He may have left Mesopotamia on his way to Palestine in the late 20th century, but the date is uncertain. What route did he take? Probably the road by way of Damascus, for a great highway led from Mesopotamia past that city to Canaan; and later mention is made of Abraham's steward, Eliezer of Damascus. Abraham did not stop long at any place along the way, but properly speaking journeyed continuously; for he was 75 years old when he left Haran, and he spent ten years in Canaan before he took Hagar to wife (Gen. 16:1–3), and he was 86 years old when Hagar bore Ishmael (v. 16); so that not more than a year elapsed between the departure from Haran and the arrival in Canaan.

I. 2. *Unsettled life in Canaan,* at most 10 years. He encamped at Shechem (Gen. 12:6), at Beth-el (v. 8), journeyed to the south country (v. 9), and was driven by famine into Egypt. In Egypt, through fear for his life, he represented Sarah merely as his sister (vs. 10–20). He returned to the south country (Gen. 13:1), was again at Beth-el (v. 3). He and Lot now separated on account of their increasing possessions. Lot chose the plain of the Jordan (vs. 5–12). Abraham afterward moved his tent to the oaks of Mamre at Hebron (v. 18).

I. 3. *Residence at the oaks of Mamre,* at least 15, perhaps 23 or 24 years. Abraham was in treaty with the Amorite chieftains of the vicinity (Gen. 14:13), pursued Chedorlaomer (vs. 1–16), was blessed by Melchizedek (vs. 17–24). The promise of an heir was given him and was believed; the promise of Canaan as an inheritance was confirmed by covenant (Gen., ch. 15). Ishmael was born (Gen., ch. 16). After an interval of 13 years (Gen., chs. 16; 17:1), the promise was unfolded. Man's attempt to fulfill God's promise did not alter God's intention: not the bondwoman's child, but the free woman's; not the child of the flesh, but the child of promise. On this occasion the covenant sign of circumcision was appointed, and the name Abram was changed to Abraham (Gen., ch. 17). Sodom was destroyed (Gen., chs. 18; 19).

I. 4. *Residence in the south country,* some 15 years during the childhood of Isaac. Sarah was taken to the court of Abimelech (Gen., ch. 20). When Abraham was 100 years old, Isaac was born, and a little later Ishmael was expelled (Gen. 21:1–21). At a well owned by Abraham, Abimelech and he concluded a treaty, and Abraham named the well Beersheba (vs. 22–34). When Isaac was somewhat grown (Gen. 22:6; Josephus conjectures 25 years, Jos. *Antiq.* i. 13, 2), Abraham's faith was put to an open test by the command to sacrifice his only son. In obedience to this command, he and Isaac repaired to the mountains of Moriah, where a ram was graciously substituted for Isaac. They returned to Beersheba (Gen. 22:1–19).

I. 5. *Again at Hebron,* after an uneventful interval of some 20 years. Here Sarah died, aged 127 years (Gen., ch. 23).

I. 6. *Probably in the south country with Isaac,* about 38 years. After the death of Sarah, when Abraham was 140 years old (Gen. 24:67; 25:20), he sent to Mesopotamia to obtain a wife from his own people for Isaac. Rebekah was brought back and met Isaac at Beer-lahai-roi (Gen., ch. 24). That Abraham took Keturah to wife is next recorded (see KETURAH). Abraham died, aged 175 years, and was buried in the cave of Machpelah (Gen. 25:1–9).

II. *The size of the community under Abraham.* Abraham departed from Haran with his wife, his nephew, and the souls that they had acquired (Gen. 12:5), and in Canaan he obtained additional servants by purchase, by gift, and doubtless by birth (Gen. 16:1; 17:23, 27; 18:7; 20:14). He was rich in flocks and herds, and their necessary accompaniment, menservants and maidservants (Gen. 12:16; 13:2, 7; 24:32, 35, 59; 26:15). He led 318 trained men, born in his house, to the rescue of Lot (Gen. 14:14). He was recognized by the neighboring chieftains as a mighty prince (Gen. 23:6), with whom they would do well to make alliances and conclude treaties (Gen. 14:13; 21:22 *seq.*). Yet when deprived of the aid of his allies, as when he went to sojourn in Egypt, his sense of insecurity triumphed over his better self, and he repressed part of the truth in regard to Sarah. He desired peace and was a man of peace (Gen. 13:8), yet like many other hardy settlers would in time of need brave hardship and danger and do battle for relatives and friends (Gen., ch. 14).

III. *The religious belief of Abraham.* His nearer ancestors served other gods (Josh. 24:2). Their worship was at least corrupted by the prevalent animism of Babylonia, which assigned a spirit to every object in nature, and which led to the conception of 11 great gods besides innumerable minor deities. The great gods were the deities of the majestic and impressive objec s in nature: of the sky; of the earth; of the ocean and all subterranean waters; of the moon, the sun, and the storm; and of the 5 planets visible to the naked eye. Various Sumerian cities had their special divinities. The religion of Ur was a polytheism of the grossest sort. The patron of that city was the moon-god Nannar, who was also recognized as the king of Ur and the lord of heaven. His sanctuary occupied a considerable area in the city. On a terrace stood the ziggurat, which was the chief glory of the city. It was a tower of solid brickwork and was already old in Abraham's day. In front of it were the twin temples of Nannar and his wife Ningal. At the top of the ziggurat was a shrine of Nannar.

Abraham's faith was distinguished from the belief of the great majority of his contemporaries of whom we have any knowledge, in that Abraham believed in God as the almighty (Gen. 17:1), the everlasting (ch. 21:33), the most high (ch. 14:22), the possessor or maker of heaven and earth, i.e., the actual and lawful Lord of all (ch. 24:3), the righteous judge, i. e., the moral governor of all the earth (ch. 18:25); Abraham believed in this God as the disposer of events, who sees and takes knowledge of what occurs on earth, and who gives and withholds as he will. In this faith Abraham obeyed, worshiped, and guarded the honor of God. How came Abraham by this faith? 1. Reason lent its aid, as it still helps the intelligent Christian. Polytheists have often arrived at henotheism; and there are traces of henotheism among Abraham's countrymen in Babylonia. A clear, logical mind, such as Abraham exhibits, would tend to pass from henotheism to monotheism. Melchizedek had come to worship the most high God, possessor of heaven and earth; and his religious conceptions and practices called forth profound recognition from Abraham. Evidence seems to show that occasionally an individual among the Egyptians, Assyrians, and Babylonians arrived at a speculative belief in the unity of God, but without influencing the people at large. 2. The religious inheritance which he received from his forefathers aided Abraham. In support of this source of religious information may be urged: (*a*) the reasons for believing in a primitive revelation; (*b*) the existence of the line which began with Adam and included such true worshipers of God as Seth (see Gen. 4:26), Enoch, and Noah. 3. Special revelation was granted to Abraham by dreams, visions, and theophanies (Gen. 12:7; 15:1, 12, 17; 17:1; 18:1, 2; 22:1, 2). Theophanies are as conceivable in Abraham's time as is the manifestation of Christ at a later age.

IV. *Harmony between the Hebrew record and contemporary history.* With our present knowledge it is impossible to fix exact dates for Abraham. According to Bishop Ussher's chronology, Abraham was born 1996 B.C. The route taken by the invading armies (Gen., ch. 14) was southward along the e. edge of Gilead and Moab. The explorations of Albright and Glueck have shown that there was a line of important cities along this route before 2000 B.C. and for a century or two thereafter, but not in later periods. According to Genesis (chs. 18; 19) Sodom and Gomorrah not only flourished, but were also destroyed, in the time of Abraham. About the 20th century B.C there was a great pilgrimage shrine at a place now called Bāb ed-Ḍra', near the s. end of the Dead Sea, not far from the probable site of Sodom and Gomorrah. Glueck's explorations in Edom and Moab show that, although those regions were thickly settled at that time, shortly thereafter there began a gap lasting until the 13th century B.C. in their sedentary occupation. Archaeological evidence thus favors dating Abraham c. 2000 B.C., and Bishop Ussher's date of the birth of Abraham and that of the destruction of Sodom and Gomorrah (1898 B.C.) seem quite reasonable.

Genesis, ch. 14, appears to refer to a loose control over Palestine which was exercised by the Elamite dynasty at Larsa. Rim-Sin, the last king of this dynasty, was defeated by Hammurabi (1792–1750). The name Chedorlaomer seems to be an Elamite formation, *Kudur-Lagamar*, servant of the god Lagamar, but this king has not been identified. One conjecture is that he is the Elamite king Kuter-Naḫḫunte I (c. 1625–1610 B.C.). The most we can say now is that he represents the power of Elam. It may be that Arioch represents the dynasty of Kudur-Mabuk, who placed his son Warad-Sin on the throne of Larsa; the latter was succeeded by his brother Rim-Sin. Even though the names of the invading kings cannot be positively identified with any of the royal names on extant records, it is certain that the author of Gen., ch. 14, did not invent these names or recount an imaginary incident. From early times the kings of Sumer and Akkad invaded the w. Thus Lugal-zaggisi, king of Erech, maintains that he conquered the land from the Persian Gulf to the Mediterranean. Sargon, who (c. 2425) deposed Lugal-zaggisi and founded the dynasty of Agade, also exercised dominion as far as the Mediterranean and perhaps made a voyage across a part of it. It is not certain whether he reached Cyprus. Naram-Sin, too, of the same dynasty, had an empire which extended to the w. Gudea (late 22d century B.C.), king of Lagash, had contacts with the w. and procured cedars, juniper wood, and boxwood from Syria. We have, accordingly, evidence that certain kings of Sumer and Akkad made expeditions w. and often held Canaan in subjection. Even though we cannot identify the kings against whom Abraham fought, the Hebrew record (Gen., ch. 14) gives an accurate and somewhat detailed picture of the political conditions in Canaan and Babylonia during the time of Abraham.

A'bra·ham's (ā'brȧ-hămz) **Bos'om.** The Jews fondly thought of being welcomed by Abraham, Isaac, and Jacob to paradise (IV Macc. 13:17); and of having fellowship with Abraham, even resting, as it were, on his breast (Luke 16:22). In the rabbinical speech of the 3d century A.D., to say that a person was sitting in Abraham's bosom meant that he had entered paradise.

A'bram (ā'brăm) (Gen. 11:26 to 17:5). See ABRAHAM.

A·bro'nah (ȧ-brō'nȧ), in A. V. **E·bro'nah** [a passage, or a place opposite]. A station of the Israelites in the wilderness (Num. 33:34, 35), an oasis, modern 'Ain Defiyeh, 7½ miles n. of Ezion-geber.

Ab'sa·lom (ăb'sȧ-lŏm) and **A·bish'a·lom** (I Kings 15:2, 10) [the Father is peace; cf. Salem (peace), the name of a deity in the Ras Shamra literature]. 1. The third son of David, king of Israel. He was born in Hebron, and had for his mother Maacah, the daughter of Talmai, king of Geshur, in Aram (II Sam. 3:3). He was of faultless form, and had long, fine hair, of which he was inordinately proud His beauty was shared by his sister Tamar, who so fascinated her half brother Amnon that he criminally dishonored her, for which two years afterward he was treacherously assassinated at the instance of Absalom, whose guest he was at the time. Though Absalom was his father's favorite, his crime was too gross to be overlooked even by his indulgent parent. He had to go into exile, and remained three years with his maternal relatives in Geshur, and two more at Jerusalem, before he was allowed to return to the court or see his royal father. He soon afterward deliberately set himself to win the hearts of the people away from the king his father, and when the plot was ripe, repaired, under false pretenses, to Hebron, and raised the standard of rebellion. Probably he had heard that Solomon was to succeed David, and considered the arrangement unfair to himself, as he was the older of the two brothers, and, unlike Solomon, was of royal blood by the mother's as well as the father's side. Whether or not he was aware that it was by the divine choice, as recorded in I Chron. 22 :7-10, that Solomon was designated to the sovereignty, is less certain ; if he did know it, then the enormity of his rebellion was heightened. It is noticeable, in connection with this point, that the priests and Levites sided with David, and brought him much moral as well as material support ; but the mass of the people seem to have gone against the king, and he had to escape with a few faithful followers from Jerusalem to save his life. Of David's two chief counselors, the abler one, Ahithophel, had gone over to Absalom ; the other, Hushai, was faithful to David, and went after the fugitive king. David sent him back to Jerusalem to pretend adherence to Absalom, and thwart the counsel of Ahithophel. When the time arrived for offering advice to Absalom, Ahithophel astutely recommended that he should be allowed to take 12,000 men that very night and follow David before David recovered from his depression. He would kill only the king, and the people would then come over to Absalom. Before the scheme was carried out, Hushai was asked if he adhered to it, and of course he raised objections, and proposed a rival scheme of his own, so preposterous that it does not say much for Absalom's penetration that he did not see that it was meant to effect his ruin. Hushai counseled long delay, a course that would really tend to make Absalom weaker and David stronger. He flattered Absalom's self-conceit by proposing that he should be commander, which would give the army a poor leader. When victory was achieved, which he assumed to be a certainty, he provided that there should be extensive and unnecessary bloodshed, a serious political blunder as well as a great crime. Hushai's absurd scheme, however, recommended itself to Absalom and the people, and Ahithophel, seeing that it was all over with the rebellion, went home and committed suicide. Hushai, understanding that the danger was not yet over, sent David counsel immediately to cross the Jordan, which he did. Absalom and the rebel army were beginning to revert to the policy of Ahithophel ; and ultimately a compromise was made between his plan and that of Hushai, i.e., hostilities should be immediate, but Absalom should be the commander in chief. The battle took place in the wood of Ephraim, apparently near Mahanaim, where David was then residing. The rebel host, undisciplined and badly led, went down at once before David's veterans, handled by three skillful commanders. When the rout took place, Absalom, riding furiously on a mule, got his head entangled among the spreading branches of an oak, great disservice being done him by the long hair of which he was so proud. The animal ran away, leaving him hanging helpless but alive. Joab, one of the three commanders, thrust three darts through the heart of the unhappy prince, and ten of Joab's immediate followers, surrounding him, completed the slaughter. David had given express directions that Absalom should not be injured, and on hearing of his son's death he gave himself up to excessive grief (II Sam. 13 :1 to 19 :8). Absalom was buried near the place where he died, in a pit under a great cairn of stones. He had reared for himself a pillar at Jerusalem to keep his name in remembrance (II Sam. 18 :17, 18). What is now called Absalom's tomb is in the valley of the Kidron. In the beginning of the 4th century A.D., however, it seems to have been regarded as the tomb of Hezekiah (Bordeaux Pilgrim), but scarcely in agreement with II Chron. 32 :33. The decorations of the monument date from the Greco-Roman period, but the chamber itself may be older. According to the title, Psalm 3 was composed by David during Absalom's rebellion.

2. Father of Mattathias and probably of Jonathan, captains of the Jewish army under the Maccabees, Jonathan and Simon (I Macc. 11 :70 ; 13 :11 ; Jos. *Antiq.* xiii. 5, 7 ; 6, 4).

Ab′shai (ăb′shī). See ABISHAI.

A·bu′bus (*a*-bū′bŭs). Father of that Ptolemy who was the governor of the district about Jericho (I Macc. 16 :11, 15).

A·byss′ [Lat. *abyssus*, from Gr. *abyssos*, bottomless]. Hades, the place of the dead (Rom. 10 :7) ; in particular, the dwelling of evil spirits, presided over by Apollyon, that is, Satan (Rev. 9 :11 ; 17 :8 ; 20 :1–3, in A.V. "bottomless pit" ; cf. Luke 8 :31, in A.V. "the deep").

A·ca′cia. See SHITTAH TREE.

Ac′cad (ăk′ăd), **Ak′kad** (ăk′ăd). An ancient city in the land of Shinar and one of 4 towns which constituted the original kingdom of Nimrod (Gen. 10 :10). The name was extended to denote a district called the land of Akkad. This district embraced n. Babylonia, the region between the Tigris and the Euphrates, where the 2 rivers are close together and almost parallel, and included within its bounds the cities of Babylon and Cutha. See BABYLONIA.

Ac′co (ăk′ō), in A.V. **Ac′cho** (ăk′ō) [sultriness, hot sand]. A city on a small promontory of the coast of Palestine, about 25 miles s. of Tyre. The town looks across the bay of its own name to Mount Carmel, about 8 miles to the s. It was assigned to the tribe of Asher, but was not occupied by the Hebrews (Judg. 1 :31). In the time of Hoshea it submitted to Shalmaneser, king of Assyria (Jos. *Antiq.* ix. 14, 2), and again in 701 to Sennacherib. It was chastised by Ashurbanipal in 640, who deported a part of its population. About the close of the 3d century B.C., its name was changed to Ptolemaïs, in honor of one of the early Ptolemies. It acquired importance politically as the key of Galilee and as a seaport at the end of commercial routes to Decapolis and Arabia (I Macc. 5 :15, 21, 55 ; 10 :1 ; Jos. *Antiq.* xiii, 12, 2 *seq.*). Jonathan Maccabaeus was treacherously slain there (I Macc. 12 :48 ; Jos. *Antiq.* xiii. 6, 2). A large number of Jews found a home within its walls (Jos. *War* ii. 18, 5), and a Christian community early grew up here. On his last journey to Jerusalem, Paul spent a day here with the brethren (Acts 21 :7). Later the town became the seat of a Christian bishop. The Arabs restored the old name, which the Franks corrupted into Acre. It fell into the hands of Saladin in 1187, but was taken in 1191 by Philip Augustus, king of France, and Richard I, king of England. From 1229 it was held by the Knights of St. John, and was often called in consequence St. Jean d'Acre. Prior to 1799 it was strongly fortified by Jezzar Pasha, who ruled with energy, but with such cruelty that he was nicknamed "the Butcher."

In that year it was attacked by Napoleon, who was baffled, and at once began his retreat from Syria. Jezzar's victory was largely due to English sailors, who had been landed to give him aid. In 1832 it was wrested from the Turkish sultan by one of his subjects, Ibrahim Pasha, son of Mohammed Ali, the ruler of Egypt. On November 3, 1840, it was bombarded by the British and Austrian fleets, until the day was decided by the explosion of the powder magazine, which caused the death of from 1,700 to 2,000 Egyptian soldiers. The place was given back to the sultan, but in World War I it was captured by Allenby in 1918.

Ac'cos (ăk'ŏs) [Gr. form of Hakkoz (I Chron. 24:10)]. Probably the priestly family Hakkoz (I Macc. 8:17).

Ac'curs'ed. Anything on which a curse has been pronounced, devoting it to destruction (Josh. 6:18; 7:1, 11, 13, 15; 22:20). See ANATHEMA.

A·cel'da·ma (á-sĕl'dá-má). See AKELDAMA.

A·cha'ia (á-kā'yá). Originally a state of Greece situated in the n. part of the Peloponnesus (now the Morea). After Greece had been conquered by the Romans, the Emperor Augustus divided that country with the adjacent regions into two provinces, Macedonia and Achaia. The latter comprehended the whole of the Peloponnesus, with continental Greece s. of Illyricum, Epirus, and Thessaly. Corinth was the capital, and was the residence of the proconsul by whom the province was ruled. It is in the second or comprehensive sense that the word Achaia is used in the New Testament (Acts 18:12, 27; 19:21; Rom. 15:26; II Cor. 1:1; 9:2; I Thess. 1:7, 8).

A·cha'i·cus (á-kā'i-kŭs) [Lat. from Gr., belonging to Achaia]. A Christian who came with two others from Corinth to Paul (I Cor. 16:17).

A'chan (ā'kăn) and **A'char** [trouble or troubler, cf. Heb. 'âkar, to trouble]. A son of Carmi, of the house of Zimri, family of Zerah, tribe of Judah. At the capture of Jericho he appropriated to his own use and hid in his tent a Babylonian garment and a wedge of gold, part of the spoil of Jericho, which had been devoted to utter destruction. He thereby troubled Israel. His transgression led to the defeat of the Israelites before Ai. Lots were then cast to discover the culprit who had brought on the catastrophe, and Achan was pointed out as the individual. He made confession of his guilt, but this did not avert his fate. He was stoned to death in the valley of Achor (Josh. 7:1–26; 22:20; I Chron. 2:7).

A'char (ā'kär). See ACHAN.

A'chaz (ā'kăz). See AHAZ.

Ach'bor [a mouse]. 1. The father of Baal-hanan, king of Edom (Gen. 36:38; I Chron. 1:49).

2. The son of Michaiah and father of Elnathan. He was a trusted officer at the court of Josiah (II Kings 22:12, 14; Jer. 26:22; 36:12). Called Abdon in II Chron. 34:20.

A'chim (ā'kĭm) [Gr., from Heb. Jachin or Jakim, He, i.e., God, raises or establishes]. An ancestor of Jesus in the line of Joseph, who lived after the Exile (Matt. 1:14).

A'chish (ā'kĭsh). The son of Maoch and king of Gath, to whom David twice fled during the time that he was persecuted by Saul (I Sam. 21:10–15; 27:1–12; 28:1, 2; 29:1–11). He is probably the Achish who was king of Gath at the beginning of Solomon's reign: for the latter was the son of Maachah, a name which is radically identical with Maoch, the father of the Achish already known. The reign of about 50 years required by this assumption is not

extraordinary (cf. among many others the reigns of Uzziah and Manasseh). Achish survived his contemporary, David, at least 3 years (I Kings 2:39). In the title of Psalm 34 he is called Abimelech, which may have been an official designation of the Philistine kings as Pharaoh was a title of the Egyptian monarchs.

Ach'me·tha (ăk'mē-thá) [Aram. from Old Pers. Hagmatāna]. A city in the province of the Medes. When the Jews asserted that Cyrus had issued a decree permitting them to build the Temple, their adversaries sent to Babylon to inquire if the document were in existence. Darius ordered an investigation. The house of the archives in Babylon was first searched, but in vain. The quest was continued in Achmetha, in the province of the Medes, and the decree was found in the palace (Ezra 5:6 to 6:2). Achmetha was Ecbatana, the capital of Media, the summer residence of the Persian kings, and a treasure city (Herod. i. 98; iii. 64; Xen. Cyropaedia viii. 6, 22). It is the modern Hamadan.

A'chor (ā'kôr) [trouble]. The valley near Jericho where the unhappy Achan was stoned to death (Josh. 7:24–26; Isa. 65:10; Hos. 2:15). It lay s. of Jericho, for it formed part of the n. boundary of Judah (Josh. 15:7), whereas Jericho was a city of Benjamin.

Ach'sah (ăk'sá), in A. V. once **Ach'sa** (ăk'sá) (I Chron. 2:49) [an anklet]. A daughter of Caleb, son of Jephunneh, who promised her in marriage to anyone who should capture Kiriath-sepher. Othniel, his younger brother or half brother, took the town, and received the maiden. At her request her father gave her the upper and nether springs (Josh. 15:16–19; Judg. 1:12–15; I Chron. 2:49). See DEBIR 2.

Ach'shaph (ăk'shăf) [sorcery]. A royal city of Canaan (Josh. 11:1), captured by Thutmose (Thothmes) III; also by Joshua (Josh. 12:20). It stood on the boundary of the territory of Asher (Josh. 19:25).

Ach'zib (ăk'zĭb) or **Che'zib**, as it was with equal correctness pronounced by the Hebrews [deceitful]. 1. A town of s. Palestine (Josh. 15:44; Micah 1:14); probably the same as Cozeba (I Chron. 4:22). Elliger identifies it with Tell el-Beiḍa on the road from Adullam ('Aid el-Mā) to Tell el-Judeiyideh. Chezib (Gen. 38:5), a place near Adullam, is commonly identified with 'Ain el-Kezbeh, with which Achzib also has been equated.

2. A town on the seacoast of Asher (Josh. 19:29), from which the Canaanite inhabitants were not driven out (Judg. 1:31). It yielded to Sennacherib in 701 B.C. It was known as Ekdippa to the Greeks and Romans (Jos. War i. 13, 4); and has been identified as ez-Zib, 8½ miles n. of Acre.

Acts, The, in A.V. **Acts of the A·pos'tles, The.** The common title, which is as old as the 2d century, does not mean that the book relates all the acts of the apostles. Its purpose was to show the establishment of Gentile Christianity by the Spirit through the apostles. At first Peter and afterward Paul is most prominent; but frequently the apostles as a body are represented as taking action (Acts 1:23–26; 2:42; 4:33; 5:12, 29; 6:2; 8:1, 14; 15:6, 23). The book is addressed to a certain Theophilus, probably a Gentile Christian who occupied some official position under the Roman Empire. The author refers (Acts 1:1) to a previous treatise by himself concerning the life and teachings of Christ, which was clearly our Third Gospel, because 1. it was addressed to Theophilus; 2. it consists of a narrative of Christ's life and teaching until his ascension (Luke 24:51); 3. it presents the ministry of Christ with special reference to its universal mission, which would naturally be the point of view adopted by the author of The Acts; 4. the

9

vocabulary and style of the two books are notably alike. Further, while the author does not name himself in either book, he uses the first person plural in certain portions of the narrative of Paul's journeys (the "we" sections, Acts 16 :10–17 ; 20 :5 to 21 :18 ; 27 :1 to 28 :16), and by this intimates that he was a companion of the apostle ; that he joined him on his Second Journey at Troas and accompanied him to Philippi, again rejoined him at Philippi in the Third Journey and went with him to Jerusalem, and traveled with him from Caesarea to Rome.

The earliest tradition of the postapostolic age assigns both the Third Gospel and The Acts to Luke, and the allusions to Luke in Paul's epistles accord with the above references to his movements in The Acts, while no other of Paul's known companions will fit into them. From Col. 4 :14, Philemon 24, we learn that Luke was with Paul in Rome, and no mention of him occurs in epistles written when, according to The Acts, its author was not with the apostle. His language is in accord with that of Greek medical writers, and the classical elements in his style, as well as his evident acquaintance with the Roman world, indicate that the author was an educated man such as a physician would be likely to be.

Analysis. Chapter 1 recounts Christ's last interviews with the apostles through 40 days, his promise of the Spirit, and his command to preach to all the world (v. 8), followed by his ascension and the actions of the disciples until Pentecost. Then follows an account of the church in Jerusalem after Pentecost (chs. 2 :1 to 8 :3), in which certain representative facts are described : the first conversions, the first opposition, the first discipline, the first persecution, the first organization, the first martyrdom), and, after each, a brief notice of its effect upon the Church (chs. 2 :41–47 ; 4 :23–37 ; 5 :11–16, 41, 42 ; 6 :7 ; 8 :1–3). Here Peter is most prominent, though the first martyr and the man who prepared for the following period was Stephen. Next we have an account of the transition of the Church to a missionary religion, offering salvation by faith alone to all men (chs. 8 :4 to 12 :25). Here five significant events are described : 1. Philip's work in Samaria and the Ethiopian steward's conversion (ch. 8 :4–40) ; 2. Saul's conversion and earliest preaching (ch. 9 :1–30) ; 3. Peter's missionary work in Syria, leading to the conversion of Cornelius and the conviction of the Church that the gospel was for Gentiles (chs. 9 :31 to 11 :18) ; 4. the founding of the Gentile church of Antioch, a new center for further Gentile work (ch. 11 :19–30) ; 5. the Herodian persecution, whereby the Jews finally repudiated Christianity (ch. 12). Then follows the establishment of Christianity, chiefly through Paul, in the principal centers of the empire (ch. 13 to the end). This was done in 3 great journeys: the 1st, to Cyprus and the interior of Asia Minor (chs. 13 ; 14), led to the Council of Jerusalem (ch. 15 :1–35), when the standing in the Church of uncircumcised Gentiles was formally recognized ; the 2d, to Macedonia and Greece (chs. 15 :36 to 18 :22) ; the 3d, to Ephesus as well as Greece (chs. 18 :23 to 20 :3), followed by Paul's last visit to Jerusalem (chs. 20 :4 to 21 :26), where he was arrested, and, after defending himself before the Jews, Felix, Festus, and Agrippa, and after 2 years' imprisonment in Caesarea (chs. 21 :27 to 26 :32), was sent, on his appeal to the emperor, to Rome (chs. 27 :1 to 28 :16), where he preached for 2 years (ch. 28 :17–31).

Various dates have been assigned to The Acts. A few would place the composition of the book at about A.D. 100, while others prefer 75–85. Many, more plausibly, think that The Acts was written just at the close of the "two years," i.e., A.D. 63 (ch. 28 :30). Some think

that Luke ended there because his object was attained in bringing Paul, as an apostolic preacher, to Rome, and because he knew no more. Accordingly The Acts should be dated at least before Paul's martyrdom, which took place about A.D. 67. The remarkable historical accuracy of The Acts has been verified (see, e.g., Ramsay's *Church in the Roman Empire*). Its harmony with Paul's epistles has been much debated and successfully defended. It is written with much artistic power, and supplies the information necessary to explain the rise of Christianity as a universal religion during the 33 years from the death of Christ covered by its narrative. G. T. P. (rev. H. S. G.)

Ad'a·dah (ăd'ȧ-dȧ) [holiday, festival]. A town on the extreme s. of the tribe of Judah (Josh. 15 :22). It has not been identified, unless Adadah is a misreading of 'Ar'āra, about 12 miles s.e. of Beer-sheba. See AROER 3.

A'dah (ā'dȧ) [Heb., ornament, but since Lamech's other wife was named Zillah (shadow), Adah may signify brightness. Cf. Arab. *ghudwat, ghadāt* (dawn, morning)]. 1. One of Lamech's wives, and mother of Jabal and Jubal (Gen. 4 :19–21, 23).
2. One of Esau's wives, daughter of Elon, the Hittite (Gen. 36 :2, 4) ; in Gen. 26 :34 the daughter of Elon, whom Esau took to wife, is named Basemath (*q.v.*).

A·da'lah (ȧ-dā'yȧ) [Jehovah has adorned]. 1. A man of Bozkath, father of Josiah's mother (II Kings 22 :1).
2. A Levite descended from Gershom (I Chron. 6 :41, 42).
3. A priest, descended through Jeroham from Malchijah (I Chron. 9 :12 ; Neh. 11 :12).
4. A Benjamite, son of Shimei (I Chron. 8 :21).
5 and 6. Two men descended from Bani, each of whom was induced to put away his foreign wife (Ezra 10 :29, 39).
7. A son of Joiarib (Neh. 11 :5).
8. Father of Maaseiah (II Chron. 23 :1).

A·da'li·a (ȧ-dā'lĭ-ȧ). One of Haman's ten sons (Esth. 9 :8).

Ad'am (ăd'ăm) [human being, mankind ; meaning, etymologically, ruddy from Heb. *'ādām* (red) ; another suggestion is that it means formed, i.e., a creature, from Akkad. *adāmu* (make, produce) ; cf. also Akkad. *admu* (child)]. 1. The first human being. Mankind was made, as were all other created things, by God (Gen. 1 :26) ; and was made male and female (Gen. 1 :27 ; Matt. 19 :4–6), the man being first formed, then the woman (Gen. 2 :7, 20–23 ; I Tim. 2 :13). Like all other living beings, his body was formed of the ordinary materials of the universe and life was granted by God (Gen. 2 :7 ; cf. v. 19 ; 6 :17 ; 7 :22 ; Job 10 :8–12 ; 27 :3 ; 33 :4). He was made in the image of God (Gen. 1 :26, 27). Paul describes the similarity as consisting in knowledge, or, more completely, in knowledge, righteousness, and true holiness (Eph. 4 :22–25 ; Col. 3 :9, 10). Mankind was invested with dominion over the inferior animals (Gen. 1 :26–28) ; was exhorted to be fruitful and multiply, to replenish the earth and subdue it (v. 28) ; and shared in the approval when God pronounced everything he had made very good (v. 31). Adam, the first of mankind, was placed with Eve in the Garden of Eden to dress it and keep it in order. A command was laid upon him, in the nature of a covenant of life and death (Gen. 2 :16, 17). On his transgression, sentence of death was passed upon him, toil and undesired results were annexed to labor, and he was expelled from the garden (Gen., ch. 3 ; II Esdras 3 :4–7, 21, 22). Afterward he had children, Cain, Abel, and, when he was 130 years old, Seth. He lived 800 years more, at last dying at the age of 930. See CHRONOLOGY, I.

10

Paul draws a double parallel between Adam and Christ, calling our Lord the last Adam (Rom. 5 :12–21 ; I Cor. 15 :22, 45).

2. A city in the Jordan Valley beside Zarethan (Josh. 3 :16). Its identification with Tell ed-Dāmieh on the e. bank of the river, less than a mile below the mouth of the Jabbok and 18 miles above Jericho, is assumed by many scholars.

Ad'a•mah (ăd'á-má) [soil]. A fenced city of Naphtali (Josh. 19 :36). The Palestine surveyors place it at ed-Dāmyeh, 5 miles s.w. of Tiberias, but the context favors a location n.w. of the Sea of Tiberias.

Ad'a•mant [in Gr., unconquerable]. An extremely hard metal or mineral, especially the diamond. It is the traditional rendering of the Hebrew *shāmîr,* a hard substance compared with flint and the stony heart (Ezek. 3 :9 ; Zech. 7 :12), and used to point graving tools (Jer. 17 :1, where it is rendered "diamond").

Ad'a•mi-ne'keb (ăd'á-mī-nĕ'kĕb) [perhaps, Adami of the pass], in A. V. **Ad'a•mi** (ăd'ámī) [human]. A frontier town of Naphtali (Josh. 19 :33), called Adam of the pass, in distinction probably from Adam of the ford (cf. Josh. 3 :16) ; perhaps Khirbet ed-Dāmiyeh, five miles s.w. of Tiberias, at the mouth of a pass on the old caravan route from Gilead to Acre. See NEKEB.

A'dar, I (ā'där) [perhaps, amplitude, magnificence]. A town of Judah, better written Addar (*q.v.*).

A•dar', II (á-där') [Akkad. *adaru, addaru,* probably, dark, cloudy]. The later name of the 12th month of the Jewish year, borrowed by the Jews from the Babylonian calendar during the Exile (Ezra 6 :15 ; Esth. 3 :7, 13 ; 9 :15). It extended from the new moon in February to that in March. See YEAR.

Ad'a•sa (ăd'á-sá). A town near Beth-horon (I Macc. 7 :40, 45, cf. v. 39 ; Jos. *Antiq.* xii. 10, 5), at the junction of two main lines of advance on Jerusalem ; modern Khirbet 'Addāseh, about 5 miles n. of the city.

Ad'be•el (ăd'bĕ-ĕl) [perhaps El (God) has invited, or disciplined. Cf. Arab. *'adaba,* to invite, discipline]. A tribe descended from Ishmael (Gen. 25 :13 ; I Chron. 1 :29). In the 8th century B.C. a tribe called Idiba'il dwelt in n. Arabia, at no great distance from the frontier of Egypt.

Ad'dan (ăd'ăn) or **Ad'don.** A place in Babylonia from which people who could not prove their Israelitish descent went to Palestine after the Captivity (Ezra 2 :59 ; Neh. 7 :61).

Ad'dar (ăd'är) [perhaps, amplitude, magnificence]. 1. A town of Judah, on the s. boundary line of Palestine (Josh. 15 :3, in A.V. written Adar). In Num. 34 :4, it is called Hazaraddar. See HEZRON 1.

2. A Benjamite. See ARD.

Ad'der. The rendering of 4 Hebrew words, referring probably to 4 distinct species of venomous snake. 1. *Shᵉphîphōn,* the creeper. Probably the *Vipera cerastes,* the horned sand snake of Arabia and Egypt. At Thebes it was regarded as sacred (cf. Herod. ii. 74). It is a venomous viper, 3 to 6 feet long, of a gray color, and with a horn above each eye. It hides in the sand, and may well be the serpent which bites the horses' heels so that the rider falls backward (Gen. 49 :17).

2. *Pethen,* a species of serpent incapable of being affected by the voice of the snake charmer, and therefore called the deaf adder (Ps. 58 :4, 5). It is very venomous (Ps. 91 :13). It is the asp of Deut. 32 :33 ; Job 20 :14, 16 ; and Isa. 11 :8. Probably the *Naja haje* of Egypt ; see ASP.

3. *'Akshûb* (Ps. 140 :3). In the LXX and in the quotation in Rom. 3 :13 it is translated

"asp." Bochart considers it the common adder (*Pelias berus*), and Colonel Hamilton Smith the puff adder of the Cape colonists, *Vipera arietans,* but there is as yet no certainty as to the identification.

4. *Ṣepha', ṣiph'ōnî* (Prov. 23 :32), translated in Isa. 11 :8 ; 14 :29 ; 59 :5, cockatrice (*q.v.*).

Ad'di (ăd'ī) [a Greek form of Iddo]. An ancestor of Christ who lived several generations before Zerubbabel (Luke 3 :28).

Ad'don (ăd'ŏn). See ADDAN.

A'der (ā'dĕr). See EDER.

Ad'i•da (ăd'ī-dá). See ADITHAIM and HADID.

A'di•el (ā'dī-ĕl) [El (God) is an ornament]. 1. A Simeonite (I Chron. 4 :36).

2. A priest, son of Jahzerah (I Chron. 9 :12).

3. Father of the supervisor of David's treasuries (I Chron. 27 :25).

A'din (ā'dĭn) [soft, delicate]. Founder of a family, members of which returned from Babylon with Zerubbabel (Ezra 2 :15) and Ezra (Ezra 8 :6). Its chief signed the covenant made by Nehemiah to serve Jehovah (Neh. 10 :16).

Ad'i•na (ăd'ī-ná) [delicate]. A Reubenite, one of David's military officers (I Chron. 11 :42).

Ad'i•no (ăd'ī-nō). One of David's mighty men, an Eznite ; the same as Josheb-basshebeth (II Sam. 23 :8). Adino the Eznite, it seems, was originally not intended to be a proper name, and the present Hebrew text is doubtless corrupt. In accordance with the parallel passage in I Chron. 11 :11, Luther and most modern commentators change the text, altering the words "Adino the Eznite" to "He lifted up his spear." The same expression occurs also in II Sam. 23 :18 and thus favors this interpretation.

Ad'i•tha'im (ăd'ī-thā'ĭm) [perhaps, double crossing]. A town in the lowland of Judah (Josh. 15 :36). Identified with a place called el-Ḥaditheh, 2½ miles n. of Aijalon.

Ad'la•i (ăd'lá-ī) [Jehovah is justice ; cf. Arab. *'adala,* to act equitably]. Father of a herdsman of David (I Chron. 27 :29).

Ad'mah (ăd'má) [perhaps, redness]. One of the cities of the plain (Gen. 10 :19 ; 14 :2, 8) which was destroyed with Sodom and Gomorrah (Gen. 19 :25, 28, 29 ; Deut. 29 :23 ; Hos. 11 :8).

Ad'ma•tha (ăd'má-thá) [Persian name, probably meaning unconquered]. One of the 7 princes of Persia and Media under Ahasuerus (Esth. 1 :14). See PRINCE.

Ad'na (ăd'ná) [pleasure]. 1. A priest, head of the father's house Harim in the 2d generation after the Exile (Neh. 12 :15).

2. A son of Pahath-moab, induced by Ezra to divorce his foreign wife (Ezra 10 :30).

Ad'nah (ăd'ná) [pleasure]. 1. A Manassite who joined David at Ziklag (I Chron. 12 :20).

2. A man of Judah, of high military rank under Jehoshaphat (II Chron. 17 :14).

A•do'ni•be'zek (á-dō'nĭ-bē'zĕk) [lord of Bezek]. A king of Bezek, conquered by the warriors of the tribe of Judah, who cut off his thumbs and great toes. This he regarded as a divine requital for similar cruelties perpetrated by him on 70 kings (Judg. 1 :4–7).

Ad'o•ni'jah (ăd'ō-nī'já) [Jehovah is Lord]. 1. A son of David by Haggith, one of his wives. He was the 4th son born to the king at Hebron (II Sam. 3 :2, 4). He was a goodly young man, and apparently his father's next favorite after Absalom. Blinded by foolish fondness, David never rebuked him for a misdeed. When David was stricken in years Adonijah attempted to seize the throne. He was doubtless aware of his father's intention that Solomon should be king (I Kings 1:13; I Chron. 23:1; 28:5); but since the first- and third-born sons of David, and probably the second-born also, were dead, Adonijah as the eldest remaining son doubtless felt that he had a claim to the crown, although neither law nor custom required the succession to go to the eldest. He won Joab to his cause, who, he hoped, would bring with him the army; and Abiathar, the priest, who, he expected, would bring with him the priests and the Levites. But Zadok the priest, Benaiah, commander of the royal bodyguard, and Nathan the prophet he did not gain. He invited his partisans to a great open-air feast at the stone of Zoheleth by the fountain of Rogel, and had himself proclaimed king. But Solomon had been divinely chosen to be the successor to David; and Bathsheba, Solomon's mother, supported by Nathan the prophet, waited on the aged king to remind him of his promise concerning Solomon, reported the proceedings of Adonijah, and asked instructions. Promptly, by David's order, Solomon was proclaimed king; the open-air feast came to an abrupt termination, the guests took to flight, and Adonijah sought asylum at the altar (I Kings 1:5–50). Solomon pardoned him for the time; but when Adonijah asked that the maid Abishag be given him to wife and thereby justified the belief that he was again aiming at the kingdom, Solomon ordered that he be put to death (I Kings 1:51–53; 2:13–25).

2. One of the Levites whom Jehoshaphat sent to instruct the people of Judah (II Chron. 17:8).

3. For Neh. 10:16, see ADONIKAM.

Ad'o·ni'kam (ăd'ō-nī'kăm) [the Lord is risen]. Founder of a family, members of which returned from Babylon both with Zerubbabel and with Ezra (Ezra 2:13; 8:13; Neh. 7:18). The head of this family, apparently, sealed the covenant in Nehemiah's time (Neh. 10:16), but is called Adonijah.

Ad'o·ni'ram (ăd'ō-nī'răm) [the Lord is exalted]. An officer who was over the tribute during the reigns of David and Solomon. He was the son of Abda, and was called also Adoram (II Sam. 20:24) and Hadoram (II Chron. 10:18). When the 10 tribes revolted, Rehoboam sent him to treat with the rebels, who, however, instead of listening to him, stoned him to death (II Sam. 20:24; I Kings 4:6; 12:18; II Chron. 10:18).

A·do'ni-ze'dek (à-dō'nī-zē'dĕk), in A.V. **A·do'ni-ze'dec** (à-dō'nī-zē'dĕk) [the Lord is righteousness]. A king of Jerusalem who, on learning that Ai had been captured by the Israelites, and that the Gibeonites had made peace with Joshua, formed a confederacy with four other Amorite kings to punish Gibeon. He and his confederates were defeated, taken, and slain (Josh. 10:1–27). In the LXX called Adonibezek.

A·dop'tion. The act of taking a stranger to be one's own child, as in the case of Moses and Esther (Ex. 2:10; Esth. 2:7). In the N. T. the word is used to denote: 1. The choice by Jehovah of the Jewish nation to be his special people (Rom. 9:4).

2. The reception of all true Christians to be in a special sense the sons of God (Gal. 4:5; Eph. 1:4). The spirit of adoption enables us to feel to God as children to a loving father. It is distinguished from the spirit of bondage, which compels one to feel to him as a slave to a master (Rom. 8:14–21).

3. The redemption of the body; its deliverance from sin, pain, and death in the glorified state (Rom. 8:23).

A·do'ra (à-dō'rà). See ADORAIM.

Ad'o·ra'im (ăd'ō-rā'ĭm) [perhaps, two mounds]. A city of Judah fortified by Rehoboam (II Chron. 11:9). It is probably identical with Adora, shortened into Dora (I Macc. 13:20; Jos. Antiq. xiii. 9, 1; 15, 4; xiv. 5, 3; War i. 2, 5). It is identified with Dura, a village on a hillside about 5 miles w. by s. of Hebron.

A·do'ram (à-dō'răm). See ADONIRAM.

A·dram'me·lech (à-drăm'ĕ-lĕk) [Adar is king]. 1. A deity to whom the colonists of Samaria, who had been brought from Sepharvaim, burned their children in the fire (II Kings 17:31). At that time this god was worshiped in n.w. Mesopotamia under the name of Adad-milki, a form of the Syrian god Hadad.

2. A son of Sennacherib. With another brother he murdered his father, and afterward escaped to Armenia (II Kings 19:37; Isa. 37:38).

Ad'ra·myt'ti·um (ăd'rà-mĭt'ĭ-ŭm). A maritime city in Mysia. Under the Romans it belonged to the province of Asia. The vessel in which Paul embarked at Caesarea for Rome was a ship of Adramyttium, about to sail to the places on the coast of Asia (Acts 27:2).

A'dri·a (ā'drĭ-à). The name was derived from the commercial town of Adria on the lower Po, and in the narrowest sense it denoted only the neighboring part of the Adriatic Sea. But the name was extended to include the Tarentine Gulf, the Sicilian Sea, the Ionian Sea, the Corinthian Gulf, and even the waters between Crete and Malta, as in Acts 27:27.

A'dri·el (ā'drĭ-ĕl) [(my) help is God]. A Meholathite, to whom Saul gave his daughter Merab in marriage, though he had previously promised her conditionally to David (I Sam. 18:19).

A·dul'lam (à-dŭl'ăm) [retreat, refuge]. A town in the Shephelah, in the territory of Judah, mentioned between Jarmuth and Socoh (Josh. 15:35). It was in existence, inhabited by Canaanites, as early as the time of Jacob (Gen. 38:1, 2). A petty king ruled over it at the time of the conquest (Josh. 12:15). It was fortified by Rehoboam (II Chron. 11:7), continued to flourish in the time of Micah the prophet (Micah 1:15), and was inhabited after the Exile (Neh. 11:30; II Macc. 12:38). In its vicinity was the cave which David at one period of his wanderings made his headquarters, and whither his father and his brethren and many other adherents went down to join him (I Sam., ch. 22; II Sam. 23:13; Jos. Antiq. vi. 12, 3). An echo of the name probably still lingers in 'Aid el-Mīyeh (Mā), but the primitive site is at Tell Sheikh Madhkūr about 9⅗ miles e.n.e. of Beit Jibrīn (Eleutheropolis). This hill dominates the wadi eṣ-Ṣūr and the roads leading into the region of Beth-zur. It is not far from the place where David and Goliath fought.

A·dul'ter·y. 1. In a special sense, sexual intercourse of a married man with a female not his wife, or that of a married woman with a man not her husband. Polygamy, with inferior wives and concubines, is not adultery. Under the Mosaic Law adultery was punished with death (Lev. 20:10).

2. In a general sense, all sexual impurity in thought, word, or deed, or whatever tends thereto. This is the sense in the Seventh Commandment, interpreted on the principles of the Sermon on the Mount (Ex. 20:14; Deut. 5:18; Matt. 5:27, 28).

3. Figuratively, the worship of false gods or other infidelity to the covenant with Jehovah (Jer. 3:8, 9; Ezek. 23:37, 43; Hos. 2:2–13), God claiming our undivided affections, as a husband does the undivided regard of the woman who has sworn him fidelity.

A·dum′mim (*ă-dŭm′ĭm*) [red objects]. The ascent of Adummim is a pass leading up from the Jordan Valley to the hill country. The boundary between Judah and Benjamin passed near it (Josh. 15:7; 18:17), and the shortest and most traveled road from Jerusalem to Jericho ran through it. It is the scene of our Saviour's parable of the Good Samaritan. Jerome ascribes the origin of the name to the blood frequently spilled there by robbers (cf. Luke 10:30); but it more probably arose from the red marl of the neighborhood. An echo of the name is still heard in Ṭal′at ed-Dumm, ascent of blood, the name given to a hill and fortress halfway between Jerusalem and Jericho, and to the wadi which the road follows downward.

Ae·ne′as (*ê-nē′ăs*) [Lat. from N. T. Gr. *Aineas*, classical Gr. *Aineias*; the name of a Trojan hero]. A man at Lydda bedridden 8 years with palsy. His restoration by the power of the risen Jesus resulted in large increase of the Church in that region (Acts 9:32–35).

Ae′non (*ē′nŏn*) [Gr. probably from Aram. *'ēnāwān*, fountains]. A village, or merely a locality of perennial springs, near Salim, where John at one time at least baptized because there was there much water (or, as in Gr., many waters) (John 3:23). The site has not been identified. But according to Jerome, Aenon and Salim were situated in the Jordan Valley, 8 Roman miles s. of Scythopolis. The names have ceased to be heard. Measurement indicates either the place now called ed-Deir, in the neighborhood of which are 7 springs and extensive ruins, or Umm el-'Amdān, hard by on the e., or the ruins and spring at the base of Tell Ridghah, which, however, is only 7 Roman miles from Scythopolis.

The modern map can, indeed, show villages bearing the names of 'Ainūn and Salim. A town called Salim is situated 4 miles e. of Shechem, on an extensive plateau s. of Wadi Fâr'ah. 'Ainūn is a ruin on the e. slope of Wadi Tubas, about 10 miles n.e. of Shechem and 4 miles n. of the Fâr'ah Valley. The objection to identifying 'Ainūn with Aenon mentioned by John is that 'Ainūn is not near Salim. The villages are distant from each other about 8 miles, and Wadi Fâr'ah lies between. 'Ainūn is but little farther from the important city of Shechem than from Salim, and is more closely connected with Shechem by road. Rejecting 'Ainūn, one thinks of the plentiful waters of the Fâr'ah Valley but 3 miles distant from Salim, or even the 2 living springs which supply Salim with water; but a place of fountains near this Salim would be in Samaria, and it is scarcely probable that John the Baptist was laboring among the Samaritans (cf. Matt. 3:5; 10:5; Luke 3:3). Another site proposed is Shilhim (in LXX Seleeim), in the wilderness in the extreme s. of Judah, near which was a place called Ain (Josh. 15:32); but Ain is constantly connected with Rimmon and not with Shilhim. More probable as a Judean site for Aenon is another Wadi Fâr'ah, a secluded valley with copious springs about 6 miles n.e. of Jerusalem. The name Aenon has not survived in connection with these springs, but within 2 miles of them is another valley, Wadi Saleim.

Ag′a·bus (*ăg′ă-bŭs*). A Christian prophet of Jerusalem. He went to Antioch and predicted a great famine which took place in the days of the emperor Claudius (Acts 11:28; see Jos. *Antiq.* xx. 2, 6; 5, 2). When Paul passed through Caesarea on his last journey to Jerusalem, Agabus, who was there, bound his own hands and feet with Paul's girdle, and announced that this would be done also to the owner of the girdle when he reached the capital (Acts 21:10, 11).

A′gag (*ā′găg*) [perhaps, flaming or violent]. Whether Agag was a title of the kings of Amalek, as Pharaoh was for those of Egypt, or was a recurring name in the royal line, is unknown. Specially: 1. A king of Amalek whose greatness was alluded to by Balaam (Num. 24:7).
2. The king of Amalek slain by Samuel, after he had been spared by Saul (I Sam. 15:9–33).

Ag′ag·ite (*ăg′ă-gīt*). An appellation given to Haman, the great enemy of the Jews (Esth. 3:1, 10; 8:3–5). Its reference to his Amalekite descent (Jos. *Antiq.* xi. 6, 5, and see AGAG) is extremely doubtful.

A′gar (*ā′gär*). See HAGAR.

Ag′ate [Gr. *achatēs*, so named from a river in Sicily near which the agate abounded]. A precious stone composed of various kinds of colored quartz, especially of amethyst, chalcedony, and jasper. Two Hebrew words are so rendered: 1. *Kadhôd*, which means sparkling (Isa. 54:12; Ezek. 27:16, both A.V.). This characteristic ill accords with the agate, which in its natural state is wanting in luster; hence the R.V. translates it rubies, and the margin of the A.V., chrysoprase.
2. *Shebô*; perhaps a loan word, Akkad. *šubû*, a precious stone, or derived from Psephō, an island s. of Meroë noted for its gems. It was the middle stone in the 3d row of gems on the high priest's breastplate (Ex. 28:19; 39:12).

Age. 1. The time counted by years, or more precisely by years, months, and days, that one has lived in the world. Extraordinary age is ascribed to men in the registers of Gen., chs. 5; 11; dwindling as the genealogy approaches Abraham; see CHRONOLOGY. Abraham died at the age of 175 (Gen. 25:7), and his wife Sarah at 127 (Gen. 23:1), Isaac at 180 (Gen. 35:28), Jacob at 147 (Gen. 47:28), Joseph at 110 (Gen. 50:26), Moses at 120 (Deut. 34:7), and Joshua at 110 (Josh. 24:29). The ordinary length of human life is reckoned at 70 years, or, by reason of strength, 80 years, in the prayer of Moses (Ps. 90:10). David died an old man at 70 (II Sam. 5:4; I Kings 2:11). Veneration for old age is inculcated in the Bible (Lev. 19:32; Prov. 20:29), and old age itself is considered a blessing (Ex. 20:12; Deut. 5:16).
2. A frequent rendering in the N. T. of the Gr. *aiōn*, whence Lat. *aeon:*
(*a*) A certain specified period of the world's history, past or future (I Cor. 10:11, in A.V. world; Eph. 2:7; 3:9; Col. 1:26; Heb. 6:5). More frequently it signifies an indefinitely long period of time, eternity past or to come; "unto the ages" being equivalent to "forever" (cf. text and marg., Luke 1:33; Rom. 1:25; 9:5; 11:36; Heb. 13:8), or "for evermore" (II Cor. 11:31). "The age of the ages" is "for ever and ever" (Eph. 3:21). "Unto the ages of ages" is also "for ever and ever" (Gal. 1:5; Phil. 4:20; Rev. 1:18).
(*b*) The world, literally (Heb. 1:2 marg.); or figuratively (Matt. 13:22; Luke 16:8; 20:34; Rom. 12:2; I Cor. 1:20; 2:6, 7, 8; II Cor. 4:4; Gal. 1:4; II Tim. 4:10; Titus 2:12— all marg.). The connecting link between (*a*) and (*b*) appears when "the world" means the duration of this world (Matt. 12:32; 13:40; 24:3), and of that to come (Mark 10:30; Luke 18:30; Heb. 2:5).
(*c*) The course of the world (Eph. 2:2 and marg.).

A′gee (*ā′gē*) [*'āgĕ'*, perhaps, a fugitive]. A Hararite, the father of one of David's mighty men (II Sam. 23:11).

Ag′ri·cul′ture. The word does not occur in
Scripture, but the idea does; and the analogous term "husbandry" is found in both O. T.
and N. T., while husbandman is common.
Adam was expected to dress the Garden of
Eden (Gen. 2:15); Cain cultivated the soil
(ch. 4:2); Noah planted a vineyard (ch.
9:20); and Isaac sowed (ch. 26:12). Agriculture was in an advanced stage among the
ruling race in the delta of the Nile at the time
of the sojourn of the Israelites in Egypt. Cereals of various kinds were cultivated and
exported (Gen. 41:49, 57; 43:2). Wheat, rye,
or rather spelt, and barley, are mentioned, besides which there were crops of flax (Ex. 9:31,
32). The crops cultivated by the Israelites
were sometimes summed up as corn and wine
(Gen. 27:37; Ps. 4:7). If a third agricultural
product was named it was generally olives
(Deut. 6:11). When the enumeration was
more ample, the list was increased to wheat,
barley, vines, fig trees, pomegranates, and
olives (Deut. 8:8), not to speak of honey,
which was from wild bees (cf. also Deut.
11:14; 12:17). To this list Isaiah adds fitches
(Isa. 28:25, 27), and Ezekiel beans, lentils,
and millet (Ezek. 4:9). The Israelites had
plows drawn by oxen (I Kings 19:19; Isa.
2:4), and pruning hooks, sickles, etc. (*ibid.*;

Now, however, appeared the most formidable
prophet known in the history of Israel, Elijah
the Tishbite. He was sent to Ahab to predict
years of drought and famine as the punishment of Ahab's sin. Toward the close of the
drought, which lasted 3 years and 6 months
(I Kings 18:1; Luke 4:25; James 5:17),
Elijah, by divine command, again confronted
Ahab, and demanded that the prophets of Baal
and he should meet on the top of Mount Carmel and submit the question between them to
a decisive test. The meeting took place; Jehovah vindicated himself by sending fire from
heaven to consume Elijah's sacrifice. By direction of the prophet the people who had witnessed the event and acknowledged Jehovah
took the 450 prophets of Baal and 400 prophets of the Asherah down to the brook Kishon,
and slew them. Jezebel, on learning what had
been done, uttered imprecations against herself if Elijah were alive by the morrow. The
prophet, fearing for his life, fled to Mount
Horeb. God sent him back with the charge to
anoint Hazael to be the king of Damascus and
the scourge of idolatrous Israel, Jehu to be the
king of Israel to supplant the family of Ahab
and put down the worship of Baal by the
power of the state, and Elisha to be prophet
to destroy idolatry by moral suasion. The cup

An Ancient Plow

Deut. 16:9; Joel 3:13, etc.). The purpose now
effected by rotation of crops was carried out
by letting the land lie fallow every 7th year
(Ex. 23:10, 11). Agriculture and the keeping
of flocks and herds continued, through all the
period of Scriptural history, the staple industries of Palestine, which was not to any considerable extent a commercial land.

A·grip′pa (*a·grĭp′a*). See HEROD.

A′gur (*ā′gûr*) [garnered, hireling, or col-
lector]. Son of Jakeh, and author of the maxims contained in Prov., ch. 30 (see v. 1).

A′hab (*ā′hăb*) [father's brother]. 1. A king
of Israel, and son and successor of Omri. He
began to reign about 875 B.C., in the 38th year
of Asa, king of Judah (I Kings 16:29). He
married an idolatress, Jezebel, the daughter
of Ethbaal, king of Sidon. She worshiped
Baal, and since her husband was weak and
irresolute, she ruled over him, and made him
also a Baal worshiper (I Kings 16:30–33).
This was a revolution in the national religion
of Israel. When Jeroboam set up the two
golden calves, he still desired to worship Jehovah nominally, using them as helps for the
purpose. But Ahab, under Jezebel's influence,
wholly gave up the adoration of Jehovah in
favor of Baal. The intolerant Jezebel did not
stop with Ahab's perversion, but attempted to
force the whole people to adopt her faith. The
prophets of Jehovah were sought out and
slain. Only a remnant escaped, being hidden
in a cave by a high functionary, Obadiah.

of iniquity of Ahab and Jezebel was made full
to overflowing by the affair of Naboth's vineyard. About this time Ahab had won a victory
over King Ben-hadad of Damascus, and had
permitted that potentate, who had been captured, to escape with a treaty. The approach
of Shalmaneser, king of Assyria, led to an
alliance between the king of Damascus, Ahab
of Israel, and other neighboring kings, to resist the invader. Ahab furnished 2,000 chariots and 10,000 infantry. The allies were defeated at Karkar, in the district of Hamath,
in (854) 853 B.C. The war with Damascus was
soon afterward renewed, and Ahab, taking advantage of a visit from Jehoshaphat, king of
Judah, proposed a joint expedition for the recovery of Ramoth-gilead, beyond Jordan. The
prophets of Baal spoke well of the enterprise.
Micaiah, the only prophet of Jehovah obtainable, foreboded the death of Ahab. The man
of doom resolved to go into the battle disguised, and he proposed that the king of Judah
should put on his royal robes, thus becoming
a mark for every missile. But a certain man
drew a bow at a venture and smote Ahab between the joints where the plates of his armor
met. Ahab died that evening, and the siege
of Ramoth-gilead was raised. Ahab's chariot
and armor were washed in the pool of Samaria, the dogs, as Elijah had predicted, licking his blood. Ahab died after a reign of 22
years, and was succeeded by his son Ahaziah
(I Kings 16:29 to 22:40; II Chron. 18:1–34).
2. A lying and immoral prophet, a son of

Kolaiah. Jeremiah predicted that Nebuchadnezzar, king of Babylon, would roast him in the fire (Jer. 29:21–23).

A·har'ah (*à-här'à*). See AHIRAM. A son of Benjamin, probably the founder of a family (I Chron. 8:1), who is called Ehi (Gen. 46:21) and Ahiram (Num. 26:38).

A·har'hel (*à-här'hĕl*) [ety. doubtful: strength has tarried; or bro.her of Rachel]. A son of Harum, founder of a family which was enrolled in the tribe of Judah (I Chron. 4:8).

A·ha'sai (*à-hā'sī*). See AHZAI.

A·has'bai (*à-hăs'bī*) [ety. uncertain; perhaps, I seek refuge with Jehovah]. A Maacathite, the father of Eliphelet, one of David's heroes (II Sam. 23:34). See UR, II.

A·has'u·e'rus (*à-hăz'û-ē'rŭs*) [Old Pers. *Xšayāršan*, the chief of rulers]. 1. The father of Darius the Mede (Dan. 9:1). See DARIUS 1. 2. A Persian king, the husband of Esther (Esth. 1:2, 19; 2:16, 17). Ahasuerus, through the Greeks, is better known to us as Xerxes. The Book of Esther tells of his sensuality, his fickleness, his lack of forethought, his despotism, and his cruelty. Greek history presents essentially the same picture of Xerxes (Herod. vii. 35, 37; ix. 107). He was the son of Darius Hystaspis, whom he succeeded on the Persian throne, 486 B.C. His mother was Atossa, the daughter of Cyrus. In the 2d year of his reign he subdued the Egyptians, who had revolted against his father Darius. After about 4 years' preparation, he led an immense host to invade Greece; but fled back to Persia on seeing his great fleet defeated (480 B.C.) by a much smaller number of Greek ships at Salamis. The next year (479 B.C.) his general, Mardonius, whom he had left behind with an army, allowed his camp at Plataea to be forced by the Greeks, when such a slaughter ensued as rendered the Persian invasion hopeless. In 465 Xerxes was murdered by a courtier, and was succeeded on the throne by his son, Artaxerxes Longimanus. Xerxes is probably again mentioned as Ahasuerus in Ezra 4:6, where the author completes the history of Samaritan machinations at the Persian court against the Jews, resuming in v. 24 the narrative which he interrupted at v. 5. Ezra 4:7–23 obviously is out of chronological sequence and as regards the contents probably should follow ch. 10.

A·ha'va (*à-hā'và*). A locality in Babylonia, doubtless to the n. of Babylon (Ezra 8:15). It serves to indicate the river or canal in its vicinity on which Ezra assembled the people who proposed to go to Jerusalem with him (cf. Ezra 7:28 with ch. 8:31). It appears to have been distant about 9 days from Babylon (chs. 7:9; 8:15, 31). On mustering the Jews who were present and finding no Levites, except priests, among them, Ezra sent for and secured a number of these ministers for the house of God. Here also a fast was kept, and the protection of God supplicated for the journey.

A'haz (*ā'hăz*), in A. V. of N. T. **A'chaz** [He, i.e., Jehovah, has seized]. 1. A king of Judah who was proclaimed king when 20 years old, in succession to his father Jotham, about 736 B.C. He was an idolater, causing his son to pass through the fire, and sacrificing and burning incense on high places and under green trees (II Kings 16:3, 4). He was unsuccessfully besieged in Jerusalem by the army of Rezin, king of Syria, and Pekah, king of Israel (II Kings 16:5; Isa. 7:1). In connection with this crisis, before the invading force arrived, Isaiah was sent to exhort him to rely upon Jehovah and not to call in foreign aid. He did not believe, and refused to ask a sign. Thereupon the prophet uttered the celebrated prophecy relative to the birth of Immanuel (Isa. 7:1–16); see IMMANUEL. Ahaz turned to Tiglath-pileser, king of Assyria, and purchased his aid with the treasures of the Temple and the palace. Tiglath-pileser marched to his assistance. The approach of the Assyrians seems to have led Rezin and Pekah to raise the siege of Jerusalem. Tiglath-pileser attacked Philistia, overran Samaria, took Damascus and slew Rezin, and connived at the murder of Pekah and enthronement of Hoshea as king of Israel. With other vassals of Assyria, Ahaz went to Damascus to do homage to Tiglath-pileser (II Kings, ch. 16; II Chron., ch. 28). While there he admired a heathen altar, and had a facsimile of it made at Jerusalem. Ahaz died about the year 721 B.C., after reigning 16 years, and left his son Hezekiah to ascend the throne. Hosea, Micah, and Isaiah prophesied during the whole of Ahaz's reign, zealously witnessing for Jehovah (Isa. 1:1; 7:1–16; Hos. 1:1).

Ahaz is mentioned on the Assyrian monuments by the name *Yauḥazi*, which corresponds to Heb. Jehoahaz, the full form of Ahaz. Ahaz means, "He has seized," while Jehoahaz signifies, "Jehovah has seized."
2. A descendant of Jonathan (I Chron. 8:35, 36; 9:42).

A'ha·zi'ah (*ā'hà-zī'à*) [Jehovah has seized]. 1. A king of Israel who succeeded his father Ahab on the latter's death. His entire reign lasted only 2 years (I Kings 22:40, 51). He joined with Jehoshaphat in fitting out ships of Tarshish to go to Ophir for gold; but the vessels were wrecked at Ezion-geber. Ahaziah proposed a second attempt; but Jehoshaphat, warned by a prophet, declined (I Kings 22:48, 49; II Chron. 20:35–37). After the death of Ahab, Moab, under King Mesha, rebelled; but Ahaziah took no steps to reduce it to subjection (II Kings 1:1; 3:5). Ahaziah fell through a lattice in his palace, and was seriously injured. He sent to consult Baal-zebub, the god of Ekron, as to the result. Elijah intercepted the messengers, and sent them back with the message that the injury would prove fatal (II Kings 1:2–17). Ahaziah left no son to succeed him, so the throne passed over to his brother Jehoram (v. 17).
2. A king of Judah, who began to rule the kingdom about 843 B.C. (II Kings 9:29), apparently during his father's sickness (II Chron. 21:18, 19), and succeeded his father Joram or Jehoram the next year (II Kings 8:25). He was then 22 years old, and reigned only a year. His mother, Athaliah, was his evil genius (II Chron. 22:3). He went with Joram, king of Israel, to fight with the Syrians at Ramoth-gilead. Joram returned to Jezreel wounded, Ahaziah paid him a visit, was with him during the revolt of Jehu, and was killed with him by that ruthless soldier (II Kings 8:25–29; 9:16–29; II Chron. 22:1–10). By a reversal of the constituent parts of his name, he is called Jehoahaz in II Chron. 21:17. "Azariah" in II Chron. 22:6 (where 15 Hebrew manuscripts have Ahaziah) has probably arisen from Ahaziah through corruption of the text.

Ah'ban (*ā'băn*) [the brother has discerned, given heed]. A man of Judah, family of Hezron, house of Jerahmeel (I Chron. 2:29).

A'her (*ā'hĕr*) [another]. A Benjamite (I Chron. 7:12). Margin identifies him with Ahiram. See AHARAH.

A'hi (*ā'hī*), probably contraction of Ahijah. 1. Chief of the Gadites in Gilead in Bashan (I Chron. 5:15).

2. An Asherite, son of Shamer, of the family of Beriah (I Chron. 7:34).

A·hi'ah (a-hī'ȧ). See AHIJAH.

A·hi'am (ȧ-hī'ăm) [perhaps, mother's brother]. One of David's mighty men (II Sam. 23:33).

A·hi'an (ȧ-hī'ăn) [perhaps, little brother]. A Manassite of the family of Shemida (I Chron. 7:19).

A'hi·e'zer (ā'hĭ-ē'zẽr) [the (divine) brother is help]. 1. Son of Ammishaddai, and head of the tribe of Dan in the wilderness (Num. 1:12; 2:25; 7:66).
2. A man of Gibeah who joined David at Ziklag (I Chron. 12:3).

A·hi'hud (ȧ-hī'hŭd) [the (divine) brother is majesty]. 1. The prince representing the tribe of Asher on the commission to divide the land (Num. 34:27).
2. Head of a father's house in Geba of Benjamin (I Chron. 8:7).

A·hi'jah (ȧ-hī'jȧ), in A.V. sometimes **A·hi'ah** (viz. 1, 3, 6) [Jehovah is a brother]. 1. A Benjamite who assisted in carrying off inhabitants of Geba (I Chron. 8:7). See AHOAH.
2. A man of Judah descended through Jerahmeel (I Chron. 2:25).
3. A son of Ahitub, and great-grandson of Eli. He at one time in the reign of Saul performed the functions of high priest at Gibeah (I Sam. 14:3, 18). He is probably to be identified with Ahimelech, the son of Ahitub, but he may have been his elder brother.
4. A Pelonite, one of David's mighty men (I Chron. 11:36).
5. A Levite who in David's reign was over the treasures of the tabernacle and the dedicated offerings (I Chron. 26:20; but see marg.).
6. A scribe in Solomon's reign (I Kings 4:3).
7. A prophet belonging to Shiloh, who, meeting Jeroboam, rent his own garment in 12 pieces, and directed Jeroboam to take 10, as an indication that he should be king over 10 tribes (I Kings 11:29–39). After Jeroboam had become king, he sent his queen disguised to the now aged and half-blind prophet to inquire whether their child who was sick would recover. Ahijah recognized her under her disguise, and predicted that the child would die (I Kings 14:1–18). He committed his prophecies to writing (II Chron. 9:29).
8. The father of Baasha, king of Israel (I Kings 15:27, 33).
9. A chief of the people who set his seal to the covenant to keep the law of God (Neh. 10:26, in R.V. irregularly Ahiah).

A·hi'kam (ȧ-hī'kăm) [the (divine) brother is risen]. Son of Shaphan and a prince of Judah (II Kings 22:12). He protected Jeremiah when priests and false prophets demanded Jeremiah's death (Jer. 26:24). He was the father of Gedaliah (II Kings 25:22).

A·hi'lud (ȧ-hī'lŭd) [a brother is born, or child's brother]. Father of the recorder Jehoshaphat (II Sam. 8:16; 20:24; I Kings 4:3), and quite likely the same as the father of Solomon's purveyor Baana (I Kings 4:12).

A·him'a·az (ȧ-hĭm'ȧ-ăz) [the brother is wrath]. 1. Father of Ahinoam, Saul's wife (I Sam. 14:50).
2. A son of Zadok, high priest in David's time. He and Jonathan, Abiathar's son, maintained communication between David and the loyal party in Jerusalem during Absalom's rebellion (II Sam. 15:27, 36; 17:20). He was the first to bring David intelligence of the victory over Absalom (II Sam. 18:19–30). It may have been he who was afterward Solomon's purveyor in Naphtali (I Kings 4:15).

A·hi'man (ȧ-hī'măn) [the brother is fortune]. 1. A son of Anak, and probably founder of a family of Anakim (Num. 13:22), the Nephilim (Num. 13:33; see GIANT), driven from Hebron by Caleb (Josh. 15:14; Judg. 1:10).
2. A Levite who acted as porter of the house of God (I Chron. 9:17).

A·him'e·lech (ȧ-hĭm'ĕ-lĕk) [the (divine) brother is king]. 1. A son of Ahitub, and chief priest at Nob. David, fleeing from Saul, but pretending to be on the king's business, being in great want of food, received from him the showbread, which, by the law, was a perquisite of the priests. He also obtained the sword which had formerly belonged to Goliath (I Sam. 21:1–9; in Mark 2:26 the event is dated in the time of Abiathar, Ahimelech's son). Doeg the Edomite reported the occurrence to Saul, who, interpreting it as a proof that Ahimelech and the other priests were treacherous, gave orders that they should be slain. One inhabitant of Nob—Abiathar, a son of Ahimelech—escaped from the massacre (I Sam. 21:7; 22:7–23; title of Psalm 52).
2. The son of the Abiathar who escaped from the slaughter at Nob, and the grandson of Ahimelech, son of Ahitub. He was one of 2 high priests during David's reign (II Sam. 8:17; I Chron. 24:3, 6, 31). Abimelech in I Chron. 18:16 is probably a copyist's error for Ahimelech.
3. A Hittite, and follower of David (I Sam. 26:6).

A·hi'moth (ȧ-hī'mŏth) [the brother is death]. A Levite, a son of Elkanah (I Chron. 6:25).

A·hin'a·dab (ȧ-hĭn'ȧ-dăb) [the (divine) brother is generous]. Solomon's purveyor in Mahanaim (I Kings 4:14).

A·hin'o·am (ȧ-hĭn'ō-ăm) [the (divine) brother is pleasantness]. 1. Saul's wife, a daughter of Ahimaaz (I Sam. 14:50).
2. A woman of Jezreel, one of David's wives (I Sam. 25:43; 27:3), taken captive at Ziklag by the Amalekites (I Sam. 30:5). She was the mother of Amnon (II Sam. 3:2).

A·hi'o (ȧ-hī'ō) [little brother]. 1. A son of Abinadab and brother of Uzzah. The two drove the cart on which David was taking the Ark to Jerusalem (II Sam. 6:3, 4).
2. A Benjamite, son of Elpaal (I Chron. 8:14).
3. A Benjamite, son of Jehiel by his wife Maachah (I Chron. 8:29, 31; 9:35, 37).

A·hi'ra (ȧ-hī'rȧ) [ety. uncertain; the brother is evil or Ra (an Egyptian sun-god) is a brother]. A son of Enan, and head of the tribe of Naphtali during the early journeyings in the wilderness (Num. 1:15; 2:29; 7:78; 10:27).

A·hi'ram (ȧ-hī'răm) [the (divine) brother is exalted]. A Benjamite, founder of a family (Num. 26:38). Aharah (I Chron. 8:1) doubtless represents the same name; and Ehi (Gen. 46:21) is probably a corruption, as the last syllable of Ahiram was easily overlooked by a copyist by reason of the recurrence of similar Hebrew letters in the two following names.

A·his'a·mach (ȧ-hĭs'ȧ-măk) [the (divine) brother has supported, sustained]. A Danite, the father of the craftsman Aholiab (Ex. 31:6).

A·hish'a·har (ȧ-hĭsh'ȧ-här) [the (divine) brother is the dawn]. A man descended from Benjamin through Jediael and Bilhan (I Chron. 7:10).

A·hi'shar (ȧ-hī'shär) [the (divine) brother is a singer or is straight, upright]. An official who was over Solomon's household (I Kings 4:6).

A·hith'o·phel (*à*-hĭth'ŏ-fĕl) [ety. uncertain; perhaps, the brother is folly]. A resident of Giloh in s.w. Judah, one of David's counselors (II Sam. 15:12), father of one of David's mighty men (II Sam. 23:34), and perhaps the grandfather of Bath-sheba (cf. II Sam. 11:3 with ch. 23:34). So unerring was his sagacity that his advice was "as if a man inquired at the oracle of God" (II Sam. 16:23), but he was morally untrustworthy. Absalom found him ready to betray David, and to point out how he might be destroyed. When Absalom preferred the absurd counsel of Hushai, who was secretly in David's interest, Ahithophel, foreboding that it was therefore all over with the rebellion, committed suicide (II Sam. 15:12, 31–34; 16:15; 17:23).

A·hi'tub (*à*-hī'tŭb) [the (divine) brother is goodness]. 1. A son of Phinehas, and grandson of Eli (I Sam. 14:3), and father of Ahimelech, the priest (I Sam. 22:9).

2. A son of Amariah, and father of Zadok, the priest (II Sam. 8:17; I Chron. 6:7, 8).

3. A later priest in the same family, son of another Amariah, and grandfather of another Zadok, also a priest (I Chron. 6:11, 12; Neh. 11:11).

Ah'lab (ä'lăb) [a fat, fruitful place]. A town within the territory of Asher, from which that tribe did not drive out the Canaanite inhabitants (Judg. 1:31). Probably the names Ahlab and Helbah are a doublet and are equivalent to Assyr. *Maḥaliba*, modern Khirbet el-Maḥalib, about 4 miles n.e. of Tyre.

Ah'lai (ä'lī) [O that!]. 1. A descendant (daughter?) of Sheshan (I Chron. 2:31, 34), but the name may be gentilic and not the name of an individual.

2. Father of Zabad (I Chron. 11:41).

A·ho'ah (*à*-hō'*à*). A Benjamite of the family of Bela (I Chron. 8:4); perhaps Ahijah (1). See AHOHITE.

A·ho'hite (*à*-hō'hīt). A descendant of Ahoah (II Sam. 23:9, 28; I Chron. 11:12, 29).

A·ho'lah (*à*-hō'lá). See OHOLAH.

A·ho'li·ab (*à*-hō'lǐ-ăb). See OHOLIAB.

A·hol'i·bah (*à*-hŏl'ĭ-bá). See OHOLIBAH.

A·hol'i·ba'mah (*à*-hŏl'ĭ-bä'má). See OHOLIBAMAH.

A·hu'mai (*à*-hū'mī) [perhaps, brother of water]. A descendant of Judah (cf. I Chron. 4:2 with ch. 2:18, 19, 50).

A·huz'zam (*à*-hŭz'ăm), in A. V. **A·hu'zam** (*à*-hū'zăm) [possession]. A man of Judah, son of Ashhur, of the family of Hezron (cf. I Chron. 4:5, 6 with ch. 2:24).

A·huz'zath (*à*-hŭz'ăth) [possession]. A friend of Abimelech, king of Gerar, in Isaac's time (Gen. 26:26). See FRIEND OF THE KING.

Ah'zai (ä'zī), in A. V. **A·ha'sai**, contraction of Ahaziah. A priest descended from Immer through Meshillemoth (Neh. 11:13); probably the person called Jahzerah in I Chron. 9:12.

A'i (ä'ī), in A. V. in Genesis **Ha'i**, which includes the Hebrew article [ruins]. Aijah and Aiath (Neh. 11:31; Isa. 10:28) are feminine forms of the word.

1. A town e. of Beth-el and near Beth-aven, with a valley on its n. (Gen. 12:8; Josh. 7:2; 8:11). It lay n. of Michmash, if Aiath is the same as Ai, as it probably is. Its site was apparently near the modern Deir Diwan, on the ancient road between Michmash and Beth-el, about midway between the two places. Three quarters of a mile n.w. of Deir Diwan is the ruin et-Tell, the heap (cf. Josh. 8:28). At

first Ai was unsuccessfully attacked by Joshua (Josh. 7:2–5). When it was found that the defeat was caused by the sin of Achan, and when he had suffered for it, Ai was again attacked, and this time was taken by stratagem. Its inhabitants, numbering about 12,000, were slaughtered, its king was hanged on a tree, and the city was burned (Josh., chs. 7; 8). It lay in ruins until some time after the account in Joshua was written (Josh. 8:28), but ultimately was rebuilt (Isa. 10:28; Ezra 2:28).

2. A city of the Ammonites, apparently not far from Heshbon (Jer. 49:3).

A·i'ah (*à*-ī'á), in A. V. once **A'jah** [falcon]. 1. A Horite, son of Zibeon and brother of Anah (Gen. 36:24; I Chron. 1:40).

2. The father of Rizpah, Saul's concubine (II Sam. 3:7; 21:8, 10, 11).

A·i'ath (*à*-ī'äth). See AI.

A·i'ja (*à*-ī'já), **A·i'jah** (*à*-ī'já). See AI.

Ai'ja·lon (ä'já-lŏn), in A.V. occasionally **Aj'a·lon** [place of harts]. 1. A village of the Shephelah, near a valley (Josh. 10:12; II Chron. 28:18), mentioned as Aialuna in the Tell el-Amarna letters. It corresponds to Yalo, a village 14 miles n.w. of Jerusalem, on a low spur, looking n. over a beautiful plain. It was assigned to the tribe of Dan, which did not expel the Amorite inhabitants (Judg. 1:34, 35). Aijalon was designated to be a Levitical city for the Kohathites (Josh. 21:20, 24; I Chron. 6:69). After the secession of the 10 tribes, it was included in Benjamin, and was fortified by Rehoboam (I Chron. 8:13; II Chron. 11:10); but in the time of Ahaz it was captured by the Philistines (II Chron. 28:18).

2. A place in the tribe of Zebulun, where the judge Elon was buried (Judg. 12:12). Exact site unknown, but Khirbet el-Lōn and Tell el-Buṭmeh in the Sahel el-Baṭṭauf (Plain of Asochis) have been proposed.

Ai'je·leth hash-Sha'har (ä'jĕ-lĕth hăsh-shä'här) in A. V., with omission of the Heb. article, **Ai'je·leth Sha'har** (ä'jĕ-lĕth shä'här) [hind of the dawn]. Probably a tune, to which the chief musician was directed to set the Twenty-second Psalm (Psalm 22, title).

A'in (ä'ēn). See AYIN.

A'jah (ä'já). See AIAH.

Aj'a·lon (ăj'á-lŏn). See AIJALON.

A'kan (ä'kăn). See JAAKAN.

A·kel'da·ma (*à*-kĕl'dá-má), in A.V. **A·cel'da·ma** [Gr. from Aram., field of blood]. A parcel of ground known as the potter's field. The priests purchased it with the 30 pieces of silver which Judas cast down in the Temple. They designed it to be a burial place for strangers (Matt. 27:7). The Greek spelling Akeldama represents Aram. *ḥăḳēl dᵉmā*, field of blood. The better attested Greek reading (H)akeldamach is from the same Aramaic source with the addition in Greek of *ch*, which shows the noun as indeclinable. Cf. *Iōsēch* (Luke 3:26) and *Seirach* (Ecclus. 50:27). The plot of ground, which was bought with the price of blood, and which was the place where Judas hanged himself, was accordingly well called the field of blood (Matt. 27:8; Acts 1:19). Peter alludes to Judas as acquiring the field (Acts 1:18, 19). Probably he does not mean that it was purchased by Judas in person, but by the priests with Judas' ill-gotten money. The traditional site, dating from the time of Jerome in the 4th century, is on the s. side of the Valley of Hinnom. This identification is not improbable, for the locality is one which can furnish potter's clay, and has long been surrendered to burial purposes. Many crusaders were subsequently buried there. Its modern name is Ḥaḳḳ ed-Dumm.

Ak'kad (ăk'ăd). See ACCAD.

Ak′kub (ăk′ŭb) [follower, cunning]. 1. A descendant of Shecaniah through Elioenai (I Chron. 3:21, 24).

2. A Levite who founded a family of Temple porters known by his name (I Chron. 9:17; Ezra 2:42; Neh. 11:19; 12:25).

3. The head of a family of the Nethinim (Ezra 2:45).

4. A Levite who helped to expound the Law (Neh. 8:7).

Ak′ra·bat·ti′ne (ăk′rȧ-bȧ-tī′nė). A place in Idumaea (I Macc. 5:3), probably Akrabbim.

Ak·rab′bim (ăk-răb′ĭm), in A.V. once **Ac·rab′bim** (ăk-răb′ĭm) (Josh. 15:3) [scorpions]. An ascent on the s.e. frontier of Judah near the s. point of the Dead Sea, and not far from the desert of Zin (Num. 34:4; Josh. 15:3; Judg. 1:36).

Al′a·bas′ter [Gr. *alabastros, alabastos,* which is of uncertain origin]. The material of which the cruse was made from which Jesus was anointed at Bethany (Matt. 26:7; Mark 14:3; cf. Luke 7:37). Alabaster commonly denotes massive gypsum of a fine-grained variety, white in color, and delicately shaded. Being more easily worked than marble, it can be made into columns or turned on the lathe into cups, boxes, basins, or vases. Anciently, alabaster denoted any stone suitable for working into such utensils. Most of the extant ancient ointment flasks are made of a light-gray translucent limestone.

Al′a·meth (ăl′ȧ-měth). See ALEMETH.

A·lam′me·lech (ȧ-lăm′ė-lĕk). See ALLAMELECH.

Al′a·moth (ăl′ȧ-mŏth) [maidens]. A musical term (I Chron. 15:20; Psalm 46, title). It probably refers to maiden or soprano voices, but the meaning is very uncertain.

Al′ci·mus (ăl′sĭ-mŭs) [Gr., strong; probably for Heb. Eliakim]. A high priest appointed by Antiochus Eupator (II Macc. 14:3, 7; Jos. *Antiq.* xii. 9, 7), confirmed by Demetrius I in 162 B.C. (I Macc. 7:5–9), and installed by Bacchides at the head of an army (vs. 10–20). He was entirely Greek in sympathy, and was abhorred by the Jews. He was driven out of Palestine by Judas Maccabaeus (I Macc. 7:21–25); but was brought back by Bacchides (ch. 9:1), and destroyed the inner wall of the Temple, 160 B.C. (v. 54). His sudden death soon afterward was regarded by the Jews as a punishment for the impious act (vs. 55, 56).

Al′e·ma (ăl′ė-mȧ). A town in Gilead (I Macc. 5:26), conjectured to be 'Almā or 'Ilmā, 10 miles s. w. of Buṣr el-Ḥarīrī.

Al′e·meth (ăl′ė-měth), in A.V. once **Al′a·meth**; the Hebrew pronunciation, in the latter instance, due merely to the fact that the name stands in pause in the sentence (I Chron. 7:8) [concealment]. 1. A Benjamite, descended through Becher (I Chron. 7:8).

2. A descendant of King Saul (I Chron. 8:36; 9:42).

3. A town (I Chron. 6:60); R.V. **Al′le·meth.** See ALMON.

A′leph (ä′lĕf) [ox]. The 1st letter of the Hebrew alphabet. Greek *alpha,* whence English *a,* is derived from this letter, but Hebrew *aleph* is a consonant, having no representative in English. In the spelling of Hebrew names in the English Bible it does not appear. It is the initial letter, for example, in the original of the words Edom, Ophir, and Ur. In transliteration it is represented by the apostrophe (').

Aleph stands at the head of the first section of Psalm 119, since in the original each verse of the section begins with this letter.

Al′ex·an′der (ăl′ĕg-zăn′dĕr) [Gr., defending men]. 1. Alexander the Great, king of Macedonia, who followed his father Philip. He began to reign 336 B.C. After quelling disturbances at home, he crossed the Hellespont to attack the Persians, whom he met and defeated at the Granicus, and again at Issus on the n.e. corner of the Mediterranean Sea. After the Battle of Issus, Alexander took Damascus, which contained great treasure, and laid siege to Tyre. From there he sent to the Jewish high priest Jaddua, demanding his allegiance and supplies for his army. Jaddua refused on the ground of being subject to the Persian king. Angry at this answer, Alexander set out in person for Jerusalem as soon as he had reduced Tyre. According to Josephus, the Jews were in terror at his approach, but Jaddua threw open the gates and went in full priestly robes to meet the conqueror, who fell at his feet in worship of the God whom Jaddua represented. He explained that before he left Macedonia he

Head of Alexander the Great

had seen in a dream the Deity in the garb o. this high priest, and had been promised victory over Persia. He granted the Jews many special privileges (Jos. *Antiq.* xi. 8, 5). From Palestine he went on to Egypt, where he founded Alexandria; he then returned through Palestine to Persia, where he overthrew the Persian king Darius Codomannus. After further conquests he died in Babylon in 323 B.C., aged 33. After his death, dissensions soon arose among the generals, and all the members of Alexander's family were made away with. Finally 4 generals ruled separate provinces: Ptolemy in Egypt, Seleucus in Babylonia, Cassander in Macedonia, and Lysimachus in Thrace.

Antigonus had attempted to maintain the unity of the empire, but he was defeated by these 4 men in the Battle of Ipsus in 301 B.C., where he lost his life. The empire was then split into a number of parts, the 3 most important of which were Syria, with all the eastern provinces and a portion of Asia Minor; Egypt; and Macedonia. The Seleucidae, or dynasty of Seleucus, established themselves in Syria; the Ptolemies, or Lagidae, ruled Egypt; Macedonia, of which Greece was a dependency, became, after much strife and bloodshed, the kingdom of the Antigonidae, the descendants of Antigonus.

2. Alexander Balas, a pretender, who claimed to be the son of Antiochus Epiphanes. By the help of Ptolemy, king of Egypt, whose daughter Cleopatra he married, he reigned over Syria 150–146 B.C. He proved incapable of holding the kingdom and, betrayed by Ptolemy, was easily driven out by Demetrius II. He appointed Jonathan Maccabaeus high

priest and sued for the help of the Jews (I Macc. 10:1, 18–20; Jos. *Antiq.* xiii. 2, 1; 4, 8).

3. A son of Simon of Cyrene (Mark 15:21).

4. A member of the high priestly family at Jerusalem when Peter and John were tried there (Acts 4:6).

5. A defender brought forward by the Jews during the tumult at Ephesus (Acts 19:33).

6. One who "made shipwreck concerning the faith," blasphemed, and was excommunicated by Paul (I Tim. 1:19, 20).

7. Alexander the coppersmith, who did the apostle and his associates much injury (II Tim. 4:14, 15).

Al'ex·an'dri·a (ăl'ĕg-zăn'drĭ-á) [named after its founder]. A city founded by Alexander the Great, in the year 332 B.C., on the n. coast of Egypt, of which it was designed to be the Greek metropolis. A site was fortunately selected w. of the mouths of the Nile, and the Mediterranean current which sweeps from the w. carries the mud of the river away from the harbor and prevents silting. The city was built on a tongue of land lying between the Mediterranean Sea and Lake Mareotis, and connected by a mole with the Isle of Pharos, on which there was a celebrated lighthouse. The city was admirably situated for commercial purposes. It became the great port for the export of Egyptian wheat, cargoes destined for Rome being carried direct to Puteoli, unless unfavorable winds compelled the vessels to coast along Asia Minor (Acts 27:6; 28:11–13). It was also the mart of interchange between the Orient and the Occident. The city flourished greatly under the Ptolemies, and subsequently under the Romans, until it extended along the coast 15 miles by a breadth of one. During the time that the old Roman Empire was dominant, Alexandria was considered the 2d city of the empire, having a population of 600,000 or 700,000. Its inhabitants were drawn from many nationalities—Greeks, Egyptians, Jews, Romans—who used the Greek language as the medium of communication. The different peoples occupied, as a rule, different quarters of the city. The Jews resided in the n.e. part, enjoyed equal rights with the other citizens, and were governed by their own ethnarch (Jos. *Antiq.* xix. 5, 2; *War* ii. 18, 7). The Ptolemies founded a museum with a renowned library of several hundred thousand volumes, and the city was looked upon as one of the greatest intellectual centers in the world. The translation of the Hebrew Scriptures into Greek was begun in Egypt, probably in this city, in the 3d century, and completed by the 2d century, B.C. Here, too, the spirit of Greek philosophy permeated Judaism, and exegetes like Philo arose who excessively allegorized Scripture. The Jews of Alexandria had their own synagogue in Jerusalem, and were among the persecutors of Stephen (Acts 2:10; 6:9); but the teaching of John the Baptist and the knowledge of Jesus also gained entrance into Alexandria, and under God produced such men as Apollos (Acts 18:24, 25). Tradition ascribes the planting of the Christian Church in Alexandria to the Evangelist Mark. In the early Christian ages the city was the seat of a celebrated Christian catechetical school, with such teachers as Clement and Origen, and the home of bishops like Hesychius and Athanasius.

Al'gum. See ALMUG.

A·li'ah (á-lī'á). See ALVAH.

Al'i·an (ăl'ĭ-ăn). See ALVAN.

Al·lam'me·lech (ăl-lăm'ĕ-lĕk) in A.V. **A·lam'me·lech** [perhaps, oak of Melech (the king)]. A village of Asher (Josh. 19:26). The wadi el-Melek, which drains the waters of the plain

of el-Baṭṭôf into the Kishon opposite Mount Carmel, may possibly echo the name.

Al'le·lu'ia. See HALLELUJAH.

Al'le·meth (ăl'ĕ-mĕth). See ALMON.

Al'lon (ăl'ŏn) [an oak]. A Simeonite, descended from Shemaiah (I Chron. 4:37).

In Josh. 19:33 Allon is not a proper name, as in A.V., but a common noun, the oak or terebinth of Bezaanannim. In Judg. 4:11, A.V., plain should be oak or terebinth. See ZAANANNIM, BEZAANANNIM.

Al'lon-bac'uth (ăl'ŏn-băk'ŭth), in A.V. **Al'lon-bach'uth** (ăl'ŏn-băk'ŭth) [oak of weeping]. An oak near Beth-el under which Deborah, Rebekah's nurse, was buried (Gen. 35:8).

Al·mo'dad (ăl-mō'dăd) [LXX *Elmōdad*, God is a friend; cf. Arab. *wadda*, to love]. A people descended from Shem through Joktan (Gen. 10:26; I Chron. 1:20). They doubtless settled in the s. of Arabia.

Al'mon (ăl'mŏn) [something hidden]. A village within the territory of Benjamin, assigned to the priests (Josh. 21:18). In I Chron. 6:60 it is called Allemeth (Alemeth). Both names have the same root. Its site is Khirbet 'Almît, a mound between Geba and Anathoth.

Al'mon-dib'la·tha'im (ăl'mŏn-dĭb'lá-thā'ĭm). A station of the Israelites between the Arnon and Shittim (Num. 33:46); probably same as Beth-diblathaim. It has been identified with Deleilat el-Gharbiyeh, a town commanding 3 roads, 2½ miles n.e. of Libb.

Al'mond. A tree and its fruit (Gen. 43:11; Eccl. 12:5), called in Hebrew *shāḳēd*, the awakening one, probably because it is the first tree to awake from the sleep of winter, i.e., to blossom in the spring. It is the *Amygdalus communis* of botanists. In Palestine it is found

Almond Tree

on Lebanon, Hermon, and in most of the region beyond Jordan. The town of Luz in the hill country of Ephraim derived its name from the almond. The tree grew also in Mesopotamia (Gen. 30:37, R. V.). There are two varieties, the bitter and the sweet; the former has white flowers, the latter roseate. Almonds were sent by Jacob to the Egyptian dignitary (Gen. 43:11). The cups on the branches of the golden candlestick were modeled after almond blossoms (Ex. 25:33, 34). When the rod marked with Aaron's name budded it brought forth almond blossoms (Num. 17:8). The rod of an almond tree, which Jeremiah saw in his earliest vision, signified symbolically Jehovah's wakefulness (Jer. 1:11, 12). The white hairs on the head of the aged are

ALPHABET

Proto-Sinaitic	Phoeni-cian	Hebrew	Greek	Arabic*
ᴤ ᴪ ᴴ	ⴿ ⵜ	א aleph ʼ (like Gr. smooth breathing)	A α alpha a	ا alif ʼ
▯ ⬭ ▭	૬ ૭	ב beth b	B β beta b	ب bā' b
		ב (postvocalic b, pronounced v)		ت tā' t
∟ ∟ ⟩	٦ ٦	ג gimel g	Γ γ gamma g	ث thā' th
		ג (postvocalic g, pronounced as g in German Wagen)		ج jīm j
▯ ⤙ ⸖	◁ ▵	ד daleth d	Δ δ delta d	ح ḥā' ḥ
		ד (postvocalic d, pronounced as th in though)		خ ḫā'(khā') ḫ(kh)
ᛘ		ה he h	E ε epsilon ĕ	د dāl d
Υ Υ	Υ	ו waw (vav, vau) w		ذ dhāl dh
ⲙ = ‖	I ⵎ	ז zayin (zain) z	Z ζ zeta z	ر rā' r
ᛉ ⵕ	ꟼ ᴴ	ח ḥeth (cheth, hheth), ḥ, a strong h as ch in German ach	H η eta ē	ز zāy z
⟶⚬	⊕ ⊗	ט teth ṭ	Θ θ theta, th as in thin	س sīn s
ⵕ ⵣ	٤ ⵤ	י yodh (jod) y	I ι iota i	ش shīn š(sh)
ⵝ (ⵣ)	Ψ ⵗ ⵎ	כ kaph (caph) k	K κ kappa k	ص ṣād ṣ
		כ (postvocalic k, pronounced as ch in German ich)		ض ḍād ḍ
		(ך form of letter at end of word)		
ℓ ૬ ⸴ℓ	◠	ל lamedh (lamed) l	Λ λ lambda l	ط ṭā' ṭ
ⵯⵯⵯ ⵯ	૬ ⵚ	מ mem m	M μ mu m	ظ ẓā' ẓ
		(ם form of letter at end of word)		
⟩ ⟨ ⟝ ⵜ	ⵛ ⵛ	נ nun n	N ν nu n	ع ʻayn ʻ

*In order to preserve the order of the Arabic letters no attempt has been made to correlate the Arabic alphabet with the first 4 columns.

probably compared to the white flower of the bitter almond tree (Eccl. 12:5).

Al'mug, in II Chron. **Al'gum** [perhaps from Sans. *valgu, valgum*]. A timber brought in abundance by sea from Ophir during the reign of Solomon. It was used to make pillars or balustrades, as also harps and psalteries (I Kings 10:11, 12; II Chron. 9:10, 11). It is generally supposed to be red sandalwood (*Pterocarpus Santalinus*). According to Josephus, it resembles the wood of the fig tree, but is whiter and shines more (Jos. *Antiq.* viii. 7, 1). It may accordingly be the *Santalum album* of botanists. The tree is a native of India and the Eastern islands. If found on Lebanon (II Chron. 2:8) it must have been introduced there. The wood, which is odoriferous, is burned to perfume temples and private houses both in India and in China.

Al'oes. Not the botanical genus *Aloe,* consisting of succulent plants belonging to the order *Liliaceae,* and furnishing a bitter purgative medicine. The chief value of the Scriptural plant is evidently its fragrance (Ps. 45:8; Prov. 7:17; S. of Sol. 4:14). It seems to be *Agallocha,* called by a name derived from an Indian dialect: cf. Sans. *aguru,* Pali *agaru, agalu.* From one of these words, or a cognate, the Heb. *'ăhālim* and *'ăhālōth* are probably a corruption. The species *Aquilaria agallocha* grows in Sylhet, in the e. of Bengal, and at Tennasserim, in the Eastern Peninsula. It is

ALPHABET—Continued

Proto-Sinaitic	Phoeni-cian	Hebrew	Greek	Arabic*
		ך form of letter at end of word)		غ ghayn gh
			Ξ ξ xi x(ks)	
𝕎 𝕮	‡	ס samekh (samech) s	Ο ο omicron ŏ	ڤ fā' f
⊘○○○	c	ע ayin (ain) ', a deep guttural or glottal sound, which has no equivalent in English		ق qāf ḳ(q)
□	) ʔ	פ pe p	Π π pi p	ك kāf k
		פ (postvocalic p, pronounced as ph)		
		(ף form of letter at end of word)		ل lām l
○δ δ	ᒥ ᒥ	צ sadhe (tsadhe, tzaddi) ṣ, pronounced as a strong or sharp s		م mīm m
				ن nūn n
		(ץ form of letter at end of word)		ه hā' h
⊸	ᵠ	ק qoph (koph) ḳ (q), a strong k formed at the back of the palate		و wāw w
𝕽𝕽𝕽	𝟡 𝟥	ר resh r	Ρ ρ rho r	ي yā' y
᾽ᴡ ᴡ	w	שׂ sin ś (pronounced as s)	Σ σ ς sigma s	
		שׁ shin š (sh) (pronounced as sh)		
✛ ✛	✛ ×	ת taw (tau, tav) t	Τ τ tau t	
		ת (postvocalic, t, pronounced as th in *thin*)		
			Υ υ upsilon y (pronounced as German ü or French u)	
			Φ φ phi ph	
			Χ χ chi ch (pronounced as ch in German *Buch* or Scottish *loch*)	
			Ψ ψ psi ps	
			Ω ω omega ō	

a large tree, having alternate lanceolate leaves, a leathery calyx, no petals, ten stamens, and a two-celled seed vessel. The wood contains a resin, and an essential oil, which constitutes the perfume for which it is prized in the East. It is the lignaloes of Num. 24:6, and the aloes of John 19:39, one of the kinds of spice with which Nicodemus designed to anoint the body of our Lord.

A'loth (ā'lŏth). The name of a place (A.V. and R.V. marg.) known only as constituting with Asher one of the 12 districts from which Solomon drew provisions (I Kings 4:16). This reading understands *b* in *bᵉʿālŏth* as the preposition *in*, while R.V. regards the expression as one word, Bealoth, *q.v.*

Al'pha (ăl'fà). The first letter in the Greek alphabet; derived from the Phoenician, and corresponding to the Hebrew letter *aleph. Omega* is the last letter of the Greek alphabet. "I am Alpha and Omega" means "I am the first and the last" of beings (Rev. 1:8, 11; 21:6; 22:13; cf. Isa. 44:6).

Al'pha·bet [from *alpha+beta*, the first two letters of the Greek alphabet]. The history of writing holds a very important place in the development of civilization. Even in prehistoric times man gave concrete expression to his thoughts by drawing pictures. Thus he was able to depict a great number of ideas. In the course of time, these pictures lost their original form and became conventionalized.

but in many cases the outline of the earlier picture remained obvious. From these more or less standardized pictograms were developed sense signs or ideograms, sound signs or phonograms or syllabic signs, and determinatives, all of which are grouped under the term of hieroglyphs in Egyptian writing.

Modern scholars trace the origin of our alphabet from the Egyptian hieroglyphs. Sometime before 3000 B.C. the Egyptians had evolved 24 letters or uniconsonantal signs, which constituted an incipient alphabet. It was used, however, only as a supplement to the cumbersome hieroglyphic system.

In 1904–1905 some inscriptions were discovered at Serābit el-Khādem on the Sinai peninsula, about 50 miles from Mount Sinai; these are known as the proto-Sinaitic inscriptions and date from the end of the 19th or the beginning of the 18th century B.C. There is a fairly unanimous agreement among scholars that the language of these inscriptions is Semitic and that the characters are a pure alphabet. It is believed that the proto-Sinaitic characters are derived from the Egyptian hieroglyphs by the principle of acrophony: each sign was given a phonetic value corresponding to the initial sound of its Semitic name. Thus *beth*, house, represents the sound of *b*; *gimel*, camel, *g*, etc. The proto-Sinaitic alphabet apparently is the link between the Egyptian hieroglyphs and the Phoenician alphabet.

A number of inscriptions from the 17th to the 12th century B.C. show the development from the proto-Sinaitic to the Phoenician. In the Ras Shamra tablets we have a type of cuneiform which had been adapted to alphabetic purposes before the 14th century B.C. on the analogy of the Phoenician alphabet. The famous Aḥiram epitaph from Byblos (Gebal) in the early Phoenician alphabet is dated about 1100 B.C. The inscription on the Mesha or Moabite stone (c. 850 B.C.) is written in a similar alphabet. The Siloam inscription (c. 700 B.C.) shows slight variations in the formation of some of the characters. The Lachish letters contemporary with the final siege of Jerusalem by Nebuchadnezzar furnish us with valuable epigraphic material; a schoolboy's scratching of the first five letters of the Hebrew-Phoenician alphabet on a step in Lachish shows that the alphabet was studied in its conventional order as early as the 7th century B.C. The Elephantine papyri written in Aramaic date from the 5th century B.C. The Samaritans retained an alphabet which resembles the Phoenician or Old Hebrew, while the Jews between the 6th and 4th century B.C. gradually adopted the Aramaic alphabet, which had grown out of the Phoenician. From the Aramaic script developed the square characters in which Hebrew Bibles are now printed.

The Greek alphabet was derived from the Phoenician; the tradition that Cadmus brought letters into Greece from Phoenicia has therefore a historical basis. The Greek alphabet developed into two types: the Eastern and the Western. From the latter was derived the Latin alphabet, which is what we now use in English. See table of alphabets.

Al·phae′us (ăl-fē′ŭs) [Lat. from Gr., probably from Aram. *Ḥilpai*, or *'Ilpā*, *'Ilpai;* meaning uncertain]. 1. The husband of one of the Marys, and father of James the Less and Joses (Matt. 10:3; Mark 15:40); often identified with Clopas, in A.V. Cleophas (John 19:25; Mark 15:40). While their identification has the support of tradition and appears probable, it remains doubtful and cannot be proved. See JAMES 2.

2. The father of Levi or Matthew (Mark 2:14; cf. Matt. 9:9).

Al′tar. An elevated structure on which incense is burned or sacrifice offered to the deity. It might be a mound of earth; or a huge stone or a platform built of several stones, dressed or undressed; or an object of similar shape made of metal. In patriarchal times, worshipers reared altars wherever they pitched their tents or had special occasion to sacrifice to

Worshiping at an Altar of Stones

God (Gen. 8:20; 12:7; 22:9; 35:1, 7; Ex. 17:15; 24:4). The fundamental law of the Hebrew altar, which was embodied in the theocratic covenant and was given at Sinai before the tabernacle was built, enjoined the erection of an altar of earth or stone wherever Jehovah should manifest himself. This law was the primary warrant for the altars at the tabernacle and Temple, where Jehovah's presence continually was, and for the transient altars and sacrifices on occasions of theophanies (Judg. 2:5, etc.).

The tabernacle had two altars: 1. The *brazen altar* or *altar of burnt offering,* which stood in the outer court and directly in front of the door of the tabernacle. It was 5 cubits square and 3 high. It consisted of a hollow frame of acacia wood overlaid with brass, and it was furnished with rings and staves that it might be transported from place to place. On its upper corners were projections called horns. It was without steps, but had a ledge around it, midway between the bottom and the top for the priests to stand on. It was probably intended to be filled with earth. All sacrifices were offered at this altar. Its position at the very threshold taught distinctly that man has no access to Jehovah except as a sinner atoned for by blood (Ex. 27:1–8; 30:28; 38:30; 40:29; cf. I Kings 1:50; Ps. 118:27). 2. The *golden altar*, or *altar of incense,* which stood in the Holy Place before the veil that hung before the mercy seat. It was a cubit square and 2 cubits high, and was made of acacia wood overlaid with gold, with a border of gold about its top, horns at its corners, and 2 golden rings at each side for staves. Incense of prescribed ingredients, lighted by fire from the brazen altar, was burned on it morning and evening when the light of the candlestick was seen to. It symbolized the obligatory and acceptable adoration of God by his people (Ex. 30:1–10, 28, 34–37; 40:5; cf. Heb. 9:4 and I Kings 6:22; Lev. 16:18, 19). When Solomon's Temple was built, the new brazen altar had nearly 4 times the dimensions of the old (I Kings 8:64; II Chron. 4:1). A new golden altar was also made (I Kings 7:48; II Chron. 4:19).

These were the only permanent altars on which sacrifices or incense could be acceptably offered (Deut. 12:2, 5, 6, 7). But the rearing of altars and offering of sacrifice in other places where God manifested himself was authorized by the fundamental law; and the privilege was embraced, as for example, by the Israelites at Bochim, by Gideon, by Manoah (Judg. 2:1–5; 6:20–25; 13:15–23). And Joshua erected an altar on Mount Ebal to serve for a single occasion. As the 12 tribes of Israel were assembled there for a national function, and the Ark of the Covenant was present, this altar was for the time being the national altar (Josh. 8:30–35), and quite in the spirit of the Deuteronomic legislation (Deut. 27:5–8). The law of the altar was necessarily in abeyance twice: 1. When God forsook the tabernacle and the Ark was in the hands of the Philistines, or in dreaded seclusion at Kiriath-jearim, there was no place where Jehovah manifested himself (Ps. 78:59–64; I Sam. 6:20 to 7:4). Samuel, as the prophet and representative of Jehovah, erected an altar at Ramah and sacrificed in several places (I Sam. 7:9, 17). Out of the confusion of worship caused by the capture of the Ark, the domination of the Philistines, and the political complications connected with Saul and David, there arose and continued for a time 2 high priests and 2 altars, the original altar at the original tabernacle and a new altar near the Ark in Jerusalem (I Kings 3:2, 4, 15; II Chron. 1:3–6). 2. When the 10 tribes revolted, the pious Israelites of the n. who were debarred from the pilgrimage to Jerusalem were compelled either to abstain from worshiping Jehovah by sacrifice, or else to erect local altars. They chose in some instances the latter alternative (I Kings 18:30, 32; 19:10).

After the Exile, at a time when the insistence of Deuteronomy upon one central, national altar had long been known, the Jews who were living at Yeb (Elephantine) in Upper Egypt in the 6th century B.C., and in the 2d century B.C. those Jews dwelling near Leontopolis, ventured to build in each of these places a local temple to Jehovah and to erect an altar and offer sacrifices on it to the God of heaven (Elephantine papyri; Jos. *Antiq.* xiii. 3, 1; *War* vii. 10, 2 and 3).

Altars were not always intended for sacrifices or for the burning of incense; the 2½ tribes who settled e. of the Jordan built an altar designed to be a memorial of their affinity in blood to the other tribes, who crossed the river (Josh. 22:10–34).

Al·tash′heth (ăl-tăsh′hĕth), in A.V. less accurately **Al·tas′chith** (ăl-tăs′kĭth) [do not destroy]. A compound word occurring in the titles of Psalms 57; 58; 59; 75. It probably refers to the name of some Hebrew melody to the tune of which those psalms were to be sung. Cf. Isa. 65:8: "Destroy it not."

A′lush (ā′lŭsh). An encampment of the Israelites between Egypt and Mount Sinai (Num. 33:13, 14).

Al′vah (ăl′và) or **A·li′ah** [high, tall]. Spelling implies a confusion of *waw* and *yod.* A duke of Edom, descended from Esau (Gen. 36:40; I Chron. 1:51). He probably bears the name of his district (Gen. 36:43).

Al′van (ăl′văn) or **A·li′an** [high, tall]. For spelling, see ALVAH. A Horite (Gen. 36:23; I Chron. 1:40).

A′mad (ā′măd) [people of duration or, better, station, domicile]. A frontier village of Asher (Josh. 19:26). Not identified.

A′mal (ā′măl) [labor, sorrow]. An Asherite, son of Helem (I Chron. 7:35).

Am′a·lek (ăm′à-lĕk). Son of Eliphaz, Esau's son, by his concubine Timna (Gen. 36:12); or, collectively, the Amalekites (Ex. 17:8; Num. 24:20; Deut. 25:17; Judg. 5:14, etc.).

Am′a·lek·ites (ăm′à-lĕk-īts). Descendants of Esau (Gen. 36:12). For a long time they were centered about Kadesh-barnea. In this neighborhood they dwelt at the time of the Exodus (Num. 13:29; 14:25). The territory occupied by them was visible from the mountains of Abarim (Num. 24:20; Deut. 34:1–3). They were among the foremost people of their time in that part of the world (Num. 24:20), but in the days of Saul they were somewhat weakened through the secession of the Kenites (I Sam. 15:6). From their center near Kadesh, the people roamed and their camps radiated. They harassed the rear of the Israelites soon after the Hebrews had left Egypt and entered the wilderness; and at Rephidim on the w. of Sinai they engaged with Israel in battle and were defeated. Because of their hostility to Israel, their utter destruction was authorized (Ex. 17:8–16; Deut. 25:17–19). A year later, when Israel had reached Kadesh, and in defiance of God attempted to push n. into Canaan, the Amalekites opposed and repulsed them (Num. 14:43–45). About that date perhaps or later, their name became attached to a hill district in Ephraim (Judg. 12:15; cf. ch. 5:14). Soon after the time of Moses and Joshua, they aided Eglon, king of Moab, to wrest Jericho from the Israelites; and a few generations later they were allied with the Midianites in oppressing northern Israel (Judg. 3:13; 6:3, 33). Evidently they had been working their way e., in friendly intercourse with other inhabitants of the desert; and in Saul's time their bands were found roaming through a stretch of perhaps 500 or 600 miles of wilderness from the border of Egypt, near their original seat, to Havilah, a designation which includes northern central Arabia (I Sam. 15:7; 27:8). They suffered crushing defeat from Saul; their king, Agag, was captured and later slain by Samuel. In David's time, Amalekite robbers took Ziklag, but were overtaken by David, who so severely smote them that they seem never to have recovered (I Sam., chs. 15; 30). During the reign of Hezekiah, the sons of Simeon "smote the remnant of the Amalekites that escaped" and dispossessed them of Mount Seir (I Chron. 4:43).

A′mam (ā′măm). A village of Judah in the southland (Josh. 15:26) upon the wadi eṣ-Ṣīni.

A·ma′na (à-mā′nà) [faith, firmness, a treaty]. The mountains of Anti-Lebanon, doubtless those in which the Abanah or, as it is also called, Amanah has its source (S. of Sol. 4:8).

Am′a·ri′ah (ăm′à-rī′à) [Jehovah has said], 1. Son of Meraioth, a priest descended from Phinehas (I Chron. 6:7).

2. A priest in the same high-priestly line of descent, a son of Azariah (I Chron. 6:11; Ezra 7:3).

3. A chief of the priests, who returned from Babylon with Zerubbabel (Neh. 12:2, 7). A father's house bore his name in the next generation (v. 13).

4. A priest, doubtless head of a father's house, who sealed the covenant in Nehemiah's time (Neh. 10:3).

5. A man who had taken a foreign wife, whom Ezra made him divorce (Ezra 10:42).

6. A man of Judah, family of Perez (Neh. 11:4).

7. A son of Hezekiah (A.V., Hizkiah) and

an ancestor of the Prophet Zephaniah (Zeph. 1:1).

8. A chief priest in Jehoshaphat's time (II Chron. 19:11).

9. A Levite, descended through Kohath and Hebron (I Chron. 23:19; 24:23).

10. An assistant distributor of the freewill offerings of God in Hezekiah's time (II Chron. 31:14, 15).

Am'a·sa (ăm′á-sá), probably a variant of Amasai. 1. The son of David's half sister Abigail and Jether an Ishmaelite (I Chron. 2:17). He was Joab's cousin (II Sam. 17:25). Absalom appointed Amasa captain of his army (*ibid.*). After Absalom's defeat and death, Amasa was forgiven by David and appointed commander in chief in place of Joab (II Sam. 19:13). On the breaking out of the revolt headed by Sheba, Amasa received orders to have an army in readiness to start in 3 days. He was behind his time; and Abishai was sent after Sheba with troops, among whom was Joab. The 2 companies united at Gibeon; and Joab, under pretext of greeting Amasa with a kiss, stabbed him (II Sam. 20:1–13). See AMASAI 2.

2. A prince of Ephraim and son of Hadlai. When captives from Judah were being carried off by the Israelite army under Pekah, he aided in securing their release (II Chron. 28:12).

A·mas'a·i (á-măs′â-ī) [Jehovah has borne]. 1. A Levite of the Kohathite family, descended through Abiasaph and an ancestor of Heman the singer (I Chron. 6:35). Amasai in v. 25 is perhaps a different person of the same family and name, but descended from the brother of Abiasaph (Ex. 6:24).

2. A chief who early joined David and at one time was a prominent captain (I Chron. 12:18). Perhaps he was David's nephew Amasa.

3. A Levite who blew a trumpet before the Ark in David's reign (I Chron. 15:24).

4. A Kohathite whose son aided in the religious revival in Hezekiah's reign (II Chron. 29:12).

A·mash'sa·i (á-măsh′sâ-ī) in A.V. **A·mash′a·i** (á-măsh′â-ī), perhaps two variant spellings of Amasai combined. A priest, the son of Azareel. He lived in Jerusalem, at Nehemiah's request (Neh. 11:13). See MAASAI.

Am'a·si'ah (ăm′á-sī′á) [Jehovah has borne]. A son of Zichri, and high military officer under Jehoshaphat (II Chron. 17:16).

Am'a·zi'ah (ăm′á-zī′á) [Jehovah is strong]. 1. A king of Judah who, about 799 B.C., at the age of 25 years, undertook the conduct of the government in behalf of his father Joash, who had become incapacitated. On the murder of his father, he succeeded to the throne (II Kings 14:1; II Chron. 24:25–27). When he found himself firmly established in power, he put the murderers of his father to death; but spared their children, in conformity with the principle laid down on the subject in the Mosaic Law (Deut. 24:16). He hired 100,000 Israelitish mercenaries to accompany him on an expedition against the Edomites, but at the command of a man of God he dismissed them and, taking the forces of Judah alone, defeated the Edomites in the Valley of Salt and captured their capital, Sela. But he brought back idols of the Edomites, and set them up for his gods. The dismissed Israelites on their way home plundered the cities of Judah n. of Beth-horon. Amaziah, following bad advice, challenged Jehoash, king of Israel, to fight, but he was defeated in a battle at Beth-shemesh, taken prisoner, and carried to Jerusalem. Part of the wall of Jerusalem, his capital, was broken down by Jehoash, and treasure and hostages were taken by him

to Samaria. About the year 782 B.C. a conspiracy was formed against Amaziah in Jerusalem. He fled to Lachish, but 12 years later was sought out there and murdered. He reigned 29 years (II Kings 14:1–20; II Chron. 25:1–27).

2. A Simeonite (I Chron. 4:34).

3. A Levite of the family of Merari (I Chron. 6:45).

4. Priest of Beth-el, who tried to silence the Prophet Amos (Amos 7:10–17).

Am'ber. The hardened or fossilized resin of a now extinct pine tree (*Pinus succinifer*) allied to the Norway spruce or to the silver fir. That it was originally fluid is plain from the fact that it is found to enclose numerous remains of plants and of insects. The pines producing it grew in the s.e. part of what is now the bed of the Baltic Sea, and it is still picked up on the s. shore of that sea. It was regarded as a gem, and early became an object of commerce over regions very remote from the Baltic Sea. It is generally yellow, and that is the color of amber referred to in Ezek. 1:4, 27; 8:2, R. V. marg., and A. V. See HYACINTH 2 and ELECTRUM.

A'men (ā′mĕn′, ä′mĕn′) [firm, established]. 1. Jesus, as the faithful and true One (Rev. 3:14; cf. Isa. 65:16, R.V. marg.).

2. An interjection, "So be it," "May it be" as has been asked, said, promised, or threatened (Matt. 6:13, R.V. marg.; Deut. 27:16–26; II Cor. 1:20). To render it more emphatic, it is sometimes redoubled (Num. 5:22). Jesus begins many of his sayings with this word, which is then translated "verily." This idiom is peculiar to him.

Am'e·thyst. A precious stone, believed to be intended by the Hebrew name for the last gem in the third row on the Jewish high priest's breastplate (Ex. 28:19; 39:12). The amethyst formed the twelfth foundation of the New Jerusalem (Rev. 21:20). It is a glassy, clear, purple or bluish violet variety of quartz, the color, it is believed, being produced by manganese.

A'mi (ā′mī). See AMON, I. 3.

A·min'a·dab (á-mĭn′á-dăb). See AMMINADAB.

Am·i'non (ăm-ī′nŏn), a diminutive used in a contemptuous sense for Amnon (II Sam. 13:20 marg.).

A·mit'tai (á-mĭt′ī) [truthful]. The father of Jonah the prophet (II Kings 14:25; Jonah 1:1).

Am'mah (ăm′á) [mother, beginning, foundation]. A hill near Giah, on the road from Gibeon through the wilderness to the Jordan (II Sam. 2:24; cf. vs. 16, 29).

Am'mi (ăm′ī) [my people] (Hos. 2:1).

Am'mi·el (ăm′ī-ĕl) [God is a paternal uncle or kinsman]. 1. Son of Gemalli, and representative of the tribe of Dan on the commission to spy out Canaan (Num. 13:12).

2. A man of Lo-debar, and father of Machir (II Sam. 9:4, 5; 17:27).

3. A son of Obed-edom (I Chron. 26:5).

4. Father of Bath-shua (I Chron. 3:5); see ELIAM.

Am·mi'hud (á-mī′hŭd) [the (divine) uncle or kinsman is majesty]. 1. An Ephraimite, descended through Tahan, and father of Elishama (Num. 1:10; I Chron. 7:26).

2. A man of Simeon, and father of Shemuel (Num. 34:20).

3. A man of Naphtali, and father of Pedahel (Num. 34:28).

4. Father of Talmai, king of Geshur (II Sam. 13:37, R.V. marg., and A.V.). In the Hebrew text the name is written with *ḥ* and *r*

instead of *h* and *d*, but is traditionally pronounced Ammihud.

5. A descendant of Judah through Perez (I Chron. 9 :4, R.V.).

Am·mi'hur (ă-mī'hûr). See AMMIHUD 4.

Am·min'a·dab (ă-mĭn'ă-dăb), in A.V. of N.T. **A·min'a·dab** [the (divine) uncle or kinsman is generous]. 1. A man of Judah, family of Hezron, house of Ram (I Chron. 2 :10). He was the father of Nahshon, the prince of Judah (Num. 1 :7), father-in-law of Aaron the priest (Ex. 6 :23), and an ancestor of David (Ruth 4 :19 ; Matt. 1 :4 ; Luke 3 :33).

2. A Levite, family of Kohath, house of Uzziel. He was head of his father's house in David's reign (I Chron. 15 :10, 11 ; cf. Ex. 6 : 18, 22).

3. A Levite, family of Kohath (I Chron. 6 :22). The genealogies of Kohath, however, regularly have the name Izhar in this place (I Chron. 6 :37, 38 ; Ex. 6 : 18, 21, 24), so that Amminadab is probably either another name of Izhar or a corruption of the genealogy.

Am·min'a·dib (ă-mĭn'ă-dĭb) [the (divine) uncle or kinsman is generous, noble]. If a proper name, which is doubtful, then it is someone famous for his chariots (S. of Sol. 6 :12 ; cf. text and marg.).

Am·mi·shad'dai (ăm'ĭ-shăd'ī) [an uncle or kinsman is the Almighty]. A Danite, father of Ahiezer (Num. 1 :12 ; 2 :25).

Am·miz'a·bad (ă-mĭz'à-băd) [the (divine) uncle or kinsman has endowed]. A son of David's mighty man Benaiah (I Chron. 27 :6).

Am'mon (ăm'ŏn) [cf. Heb. *'am*, Arab. *'amm*, paternal uncle, kinsman ; or perhaps Heb. *'am*, people, and Arab. *'amm*, crowd, multitude]. Same as Ben-ammi, Lot's younger son, ancestor of the Ammonites (Gen. 19 :38).

Am'mon·ites (ăm'ŏn-īts). A people descended from Ben-ammi, Lot's second son (Gen. 19 :38). They dispossessed the Zamzummim of the territory between the Arnon and the Jabbok (Deut. 2 :20, 21 ; 3 :11) ; but were in turn driven out by the Amorites and compelled to keep on the border of the e. desert, with the upper Jabbok as their w. boundary (Num. 21 :24 ; Deut. 2 :37 ; Judg. 11 :13, 22). For having joined the Moabites in hiring Balaam to curse the Israelites, they were excluded from the congregation of the Lord to the 10th generation (Deut. 23 :3–6). They aided Eglon, king of Moab, in subjugating a portion of the Israelites (Judg. 3 :13). In the time of Jephthah they again oppressed the Israelites e. of Jordan (Judg. 10 : 6, 9, 18). Just before Saul became actual king, Nahash, the Ammonite king, besieged Jabesh-gilead. Saul came to the assistance of the beleaguered citizens, and totally defeated Nahash (I Sam. 11 : 1–11). Nahash befriended David ; doing this, perhaps, because both were enemies of Saul. On the death of Nahash, David sent an embassy to his son, Hanun ; but the ambassadors were insulted, and war supervened. In the first campaign, the confederate Syrians and Ammonites were defeated by the Israelites, led by Joab and Abishai (II Sam., ch. 10 ; I Chron., ch. 19). In the second, the Israelites captured Rabbah, the Ammonite capital (II Sam., chs. 11 ; 12 ; I Chron. 20 :1–3). Solomon took several Ammonite women as wives (I Kings 11 :1). In the time of Jehoshaphat Moabites, Ammonites, and Edomites unsuccessfully invaded Judah (II Chron. 20 : 1–30). To Uzziah and Jotham the Ammonites sent tribute (II Chron. 26 :8 ; 27 :5). Ammonites joined with others in vexing Jehoiakim (II Kings 24 :2) ; and after the Fall of Jerusalem, they frustrated the attempt of the Jews to form a new community (II Kings 25 :25 ; Jer. 40 :11–14). As inveterate enemies of Is-

rael, they were denounced by the prophets (Jer. 49 :1–6 ; Ezek. 21 :20 ; 25 :1–7 ; Amos 1 13–15 ; Zeph. 2 :8–11). They opposed the rebuilding of the walls of Jerusalem by the returned exiles (Neh. 4 :3, 7) ; yet intermarriages between them and the Israelites took place, which were censured by Ezra and Nehemiah (Ezra 9 :1, 2 ; Neh. 13 :23–31). Judas Maccabaeus, under strong provocation, made war against them (I Macc. 5 :1–8). Their chief deity was Milcom, another designation of Molech (I Kings 11 :7, 33). In the time of Jephthah they were worshiping Chemosh, the Moabite god (Judg. 11 :24).

Am'non (ăm'nŏn) [faithful]. 1. A son of David by Ahinoam, the Jezreelitess ; born at Hebron while that was his father's capital. He dishonored Tamar, his half sister, and was in consequence murdered by her full brother Absalom (II Sam., chs. 13 ; 3 :2 ; I Chron. 3 :1).

2. A son of Shimon, registered with the tribe of Judah (I Chron. 4 :20).

A'mok (ā'mŏk) [deep, inscrutable]. A chief of the priests who returned from Babylon with Zerubbabel (Neh. 12 :7). In the next generation, a father's house bore this name (Neh. 12 :20).

The Egyptian God Amon

A'mon, I (ā'mŏn) [faithful or master workman]. 1. Governor of the city of Samaria under Ahab (I Kings 22 :10, 26).

2. A king of Judah who at the age of 22 succeeded his father Manasseh. He followed his father's bad example. It has been suggested that his name is the same as that of the Egyptian god Amon and thus reflects the heathenism of his father. In two years his servants murdered him in his palace. The people of the land put the murderers to death, and placed his son Josiah on the throne (II Kings 21 :19–26 ; II Chron. 33 :21–25).

3. One of the class known as the children of Solomon's servants (Neh. 7 :57–59) ; called Ami in Ezra 2 :57.

A'mon, II (ā'mŏn) [Egypt. *Amŭn*, the hidden one]. Originally a local god of Thebes, or No-amon, the capital of Upper Egypt (Jer.

46:25, R.V.; Nahum 3:8, R.V.). With the rise of that city during the Middle Kingdom, he assumed national importance and was often identified with Re under the name of Amon-Re. See EGYPT, II. 3 (4); II. 4.

Am'o·rites (ăm'ô-rīts) [Akkad. *Amurru*]. The early history of the Amorites is obscure, but they played an important part in the Fertile Crescent. Amurru, the land of the Amorites, extended from Palestine to Mesopotamia. During the 3d millennium B.C. the Babylonians called Syria and Palestine the land of the Amorites. Dyn. I of Babylon, founded by Sumu-abu c. 1894 B.C., was Amorite; its most important king was Hammurabi. This dynasty came to an end about 1595 B.C., when the Hittites sacked Babylon.

The Amorites occupied Canaan before the conquest by the Hebrews (Gen. 10:16; 15:21; Ex. 3:8). At the time of Abraham, they dwelt at least on the w. shore of the Dead Sea and back on the mountain (Gen. 14:7, 13). Even then they were the most powerful tribe in the hill country, and their name was practically synonymous with that of the inhabitants of that region (Gen. 15:16), if not, as later when their power had further increased, with that of the inhabitants of Canaan generally (Gen. 48:22; cf. Josh. 7:7; 9:7; 11:19 with II Sam. 21:2; Judg. 6:10; Amos 2:10). At the time of the Exodus they were still in the hill country (Num. 13:29; Deut. 1:7, 19, 20, 44); but before this date they had carried their conquests to the e. of the Jordan (Num. 21:26–30), and taken possession of the land from the Arnon to Mount Hermon and from the wilderness to the Jordan (Deut. 3:8; 4:48; Josh. 2:10; 9:10; Judg. 11:22). At this time they occupied the entire hill country w. of Jordan from Jerusalem to Hebron, and w. to and inclusive of the Shephelah (Josh. 10:5, 6) as far n. as Aijalon and even the territory of Ephraim (Judg. 1:35; Josh. 11:3; 13:4). For their wickedness they were devoted to destruction; but a strong remnant remained in the land after the conquest (Judg. 1:35; 3:5), with whom in Samuel's day there was peace (I Sam. 7:14), and who with other survivors of the earlier races were made bondservants by Solomon (I Kings 9:20, 21; II Chron. 8:7). See OG and SIHON; also HAMMURABI.

A'mos (ā'mŏs) [burden; burden bearer]. 1. A prophet from Tekoa, in the territory of Judah, about 6 miles s. of Bethlehem (Amos 1:1). He belonged to the humbler class. He was a herdsman; one of a number of shepherds who made their homes at Tekoa, but doubtless spent their lives out in the wilderness that extends from the village e. to the Dead Sea. In some sheltered spot in this wild region, down on the lower level toward the sea, he found further humble employment as a dresser of sycamore trees (Amos 1:1; 7:14, 15). From the acquaintance which he displays with distant places and events, it seems probable that he had driven sheep or carried hides and wool as far as Egypt and Damascus. Although a man of Judah, he was called to prophesy in the Northern Kingdom. He appeared at Beth-el, then the king's sanctuary and a royal house, which still probably had within it one of the two golden calves reared by Jeroboam I as objects of worship (Amos 8:14; cf. Hos. 8:5, 6; 10:5). Amos spoke with such boldness and faithfulness against the sins of the king and the people that Amaziah, the idolatrous priest at Beth-el, sent word to King Jeroboam II that Amos was conspiring against him in his own kingdom (Amos 7:10). The time and circumstances of Amos' death are unknown.

Amos was a monotheist; he knew God as omnipotent, the God of creation and providence, the sovereign ruler of individuals and nations, inflexible in justice, whose power reaches unto Sheol and who knows the thoughts of men. Amos was also a shrewd observer of men and manners, and able to reflect upon what he saw, and to generalize and look at it in its relation to God.

The prophecy of Amos is a fine example of pure Hebrew style. The diction is simple, and yet the speech is dignified and impressive. The prophet uses imagery with moderation, but with effect. Amos is not so tender in his entreaty or so full of feeling as Hosea, who belonged to the people among whom he labored; there is a certain air of aloofness about Amos, natural enough in a prophet from another tribe and kingdom.

The Book of Amos is the 3d of the Minor Prophets. Amos prophesied after the time of Hazael and Ben-hadad (Amos 1:4), in the days of Uzziah, king of Judah, and in the days of Jeroboam, son of Joash, king of Israel, 2 years before the earthquake (Amos 1:1; 7:10; cf. Zech. 14:5), and probably while the kingdom was at its greatest extent (Amos 6:14; cf. II Kings 14:25). Amos' prophetic ministry accordingly belongs to the period about 760–746 B.C.

The theme of the prophecy is the judgment of the Lord (Amos 1:2); and the book consists of 3 parts: 1. Introductory (chs. 1; 2). 2. Three discourses (chs. 3 to 6), followed by a series of 5 visions (chs. 7:1 to 9:7). These 1st 2 parts of the book are denunciatory, and each subdivision ends with the announcement of judgment to come. 3. Promissory (ch. 9:8–15). 1. In the introductory section (chs. 1:2 to 2:16) the prophet denounces judgment upon 6 neighboring Gentile nations, then upon Judah, and finally upon Israel. The 1st 7 denunciations are embraced in 7 stanzas of precisely the same structure, are opened and closed in the same way, and are linked to the introductory denunciation of Israel, to which they lead up, by the familiar opening formula. The argument seems to be: If these heathen nations are to be punished, how much more should Judah be, which has sinned against the law of God; and if Judah is punished, how much more should Israel be, which has sinned more deeply. 2. Denunciation of Israel occupies the body of the book (chs. 3:1 to 9:7). There are 3 discourses, each beginning with the formula, "Hear this word" (chs. 3:1; 4:1; 5:1), followed by 5 visions. In the 1st vision devouring locusts are seen; but at the prayer of the prophet God forgives Israel and ends the work of devastation. In the 2d vision fire is seen, which devours the waters and would have destroyed the land; but again at the prophet's prayer God makes the evil to cease. Perhaps an actual invasion of locusts occurred during the ministry of the Prophet Amos, and was followed by a season of intense heat and the resulting drought (see JOEL). Most probably Amos sees in these visions calamities which were sent to warn Israel and were checked by God's grace but failed to bring the nation to repentance (ch. 4:6–11). Therefore the people must prepare to meet their God in judgment (ch. 4:12); and the 3d vision, that of the plumb line, shows that a desolating judgment is certain to come and is according to the undeviating standard of righteousness (ch. 7:7–9). At this point the prophet is interrupted by the priest of Beth-el, and forbidden to prophesy; but he resumes his recital. In the 4th vision a basket of summer fruit is seen, indicating that Israel is ripe for judgment, yea, in God's sight is already plucked (ch. 8:1–3); Amos here uses a pun: ḳāyiṣ (summer fruit) suggests ḳēṣ (end). In the 5th vision Jehovah is seen standing beside the altar, doubtless that at Beth-el (cf. ch. 3:14), and commanding to smite and slay; showing that the order is being issued for the judgment to begin (ch. 9:1-4). 3. Epilogue. The prophecy concludes with promises (ch. 9:8-15): the Exile only a sifting (vs. 8-10); restoration of the royal house of David to its former glory (v. 11); extension of the kingdom over Edom and other heathen nations (v. 12); restoration of Israel from captivity (vs. 13-15). Here a beautiful picture of abundance and perfection in the realm of nature gives the proper background for visualizing spiritual happiness and perfection.

Of the promises of good, with which the book closes, ch. 9:8b-15, it has been asserted that the passage can scarcely have been the original conclusion of Amos' vision of judgment, because it differs from the rest of the prophecy in phraseology, conception, and outlook. It is, of course, a matter of small moment whether it was written by Amos at the time he penned the visions or later. No ground has been found for rejecting its genuineness. The prophets frequently annexed to the prediction of judgment a prophecy of hope. There was a purpose in the doom, which is followed by restoration. The godly needed encouragement, and it was necessary to show the congruity between the overwhelming judgment and God's long-standing promise of the stability of David's throne and the perpetuity and triumph of God's Kingdom on earth.

Permanent lessons of The Book of Amos: In this book we find truths which can never become superfluous or obsolete. The truths that justice between man and man is one of the divine foundations of society; that privilege implies responsibility, and that failure to recognize responsibility will surely bring punishment; that nations, and by analogy individuals, are bound to live up to that measure of light and knowledge which has been granted to them; that the most elaborate worship is but an insult to God when offered by those who have no mind to conform their wills and conduct to his requirements—these are elementary but eternal truths.

2. An ancestor of Christ (Luke 3:25).

A'moz (ā'mŏz) [strong]. The Prophet Isaiah's father (Isa. 1:1, etc.).

Am·phip'o·lis (ăm-fĭp'ō-lĭs) [Gr., a city pressed on all sides]. A city of Thrace, situated at the mouth of the Strymon on a bend of the river. It was founded by the Athenians in the 5th century B.C., and called Amphipolis because nearly surrounded by the river. Under the Romans it was the chief town of Macedonia Prima. It was on the Via Egnatia, 33 miles s.w. of Philippi, and Paul accordingly passed through it while traveling by that road from Philippi to Thessalonica (Acts 17:1).

Am·pli·a'tus (ăm'plĭ-ā'tŭs), in A.V. **Am'pli·as** (ăm'plĭ-ăs) [Lat., enlarged]. A Christian of Rome to whom Paul sent salutation (Rom. 16:8).

Am'ram, I (ăm'răm) (I Chron. 1:41). See HEMDAN.

Am'ram, II (ăm'răm) [the (divine) paternal uncle or kinsman is exalted]. 1. A Levite, son of Kohath, husband of Jochebed and founder of the father's house of the Amramites, who in the time of Moses numbered approximately 2,000 males (Num. 3:17, 19, 27, 28). He was an ancestor of Aaron and Moses, and lived to the age of 137 years (Ex. 6:20; for form of expression cf. Gen. 46:16-18, 19-22, 23-25; Matt. 1:5, 6, 8, 11).
2. A son of Bani, induced by Ezra to put away his foreign wife (Ezra 10:34).

Am'ram·ites (ăm'răm-īts). The descendants of Amram, constituting a subdivision of the Levites (Num. 3:27; I Chron. 26:23).

Am'ra·phel (ăm'rà-fĕl). King of Shinar, ally of Chedorlaomer in the invasion of the w. (Gen. 14:1, 9); formerly quite generally identified with Hammurabi by considering Amraphel a corruption of Hammurabi, thus Amrabi. The final l is a difficulty, and the equivalence is now seriously questioned by a number of leading scholars. See HAMMURABI.

Am'u·let. Anything worn as a protection against sorcery. It often serves at the same time as an ornament (Isa. 3:20, R.V.; cf. Gen. 35:4).

Am'zi (ăm'zī), perhaps a contraction of Amaziah. 1. A Levite, a descendant of Merari (I Chron. 6:46).
2. A priest of the course of Malchijah (Neh. 11:12).

A'nab (ā'năb) [grapes]. A town in the mountains of Judah (Josh. 11:21; 15:50), Khirbet 'Anāb, about 3 miles w. of Debir (Dāhariyeh), which is 13 miles s.w. of Hebron.

A'nah (ā'nà) [possibly, hearkening to]. 1. A daughter of Zibeon, and mother of Oholibamah, one of Esau's wives (Gen. 36:2, 14, 18, 25, R.V.). The LXX (vs. 2, 14) reads son instead of daughter, which presupposes Heb. bn, son, instead of bt, daughter, of the Masoretic text. The Samaritan Hebrew and the Peshitta have son only in v. 2. The LXX would identify this Anah with number 2.
2. A son of Zibeon (Gen. 36:24; I Chron. 1:40); he is said to have discovered hot springs in the wilderness.
3. A son of Seir and brother of Zibeon, a Horite chief (Gen. 36:20, 29; I Chron. 1:38).
If we follow the LXX and regard Anah as a tribal name rather than a personal name and think of relationships between clans or tribes rather than individuals, it is quite possible to consider the above 3 references as signifying the same Horite group.

A·na'ha·rath (à-nā'hà-răth) [possibly, nostril or pass]. An ancient town on the frontier of Issachar (Josh. 19:19). Possibly en-Na'ūrah, 5 miles n.e. of Jezreel, echoes the name.

A·nai'ah (à-nī'à) [Jehovah has answered]. One who stood by Ezra when he read the book of the Law to the people (Neh. 8:4), and who afterward sealed the covenant to serve God (Neh. 10:22).

A'nak (ā'năk) [cf. Arab. 'unḳ, neck]. Collective name of the Anakim (cf. Num. 13:22 with Deut. 1:28), who possibly, though not necessarily, were descended from Arba (cf. Josh. 14:15 with 15:13). The word Anak is properly a race name, and since it is often used with the article in Hebrew (Num. 13:22, 28, but not v. 33), it is really an appellative and probably means the long-necked (people).

An'a·kim (ăn'à-kĭm); A.V. has **An'a·kims** (ăn'à-kĭmz), formed by adding Eng. plural ending s to the Heb. plural. A stalwart race, connected with the Rephaim (Num. 13:33; Deut. 2:10, 11, 21). Three families of them settled at Hebron (Num. 13:22), and others were found in neighboring towns and elsewhere throughout the hill country (Josh. 11:21; 15:14; cf. Rephaim, ch. 17:15, R.V.). They were cut off by the Israelites in the general campaign under Joshua (Josh. 10:36-39; 11:21), and particularly at Hebron, on the allotment of the land by Judah under Caleb (Josh. 14:12; 15:13-19; Judg. 1:10-15). A remnant was left in Gaza, Gath, and Ashdod, in the Philistine country (Josh. 11:22). The giant Goliath, of Gath, was probably one of the Anakim.

An'a·mim (ăn'à-mĭm). An Egyptian tribe, of which nothing is known (Gen. 10:13; I Chron. 1:11).

A·nam′me·lech (ȧ-năm′ĕ-lĕk) [Anu is king]. One of the deities worshiped by the people of Sepharvaim, a city of Babylonia (II Kings 17:31). Anu was god of the sky. When Sepharvites were brought to colonize Samaria, they burned their children in the fire to him, worshiping Anu as Molech was worshiped.

A′nan (ā′năn) [a cloud, or probably a contraction of Ananiah]. One who with Nehemiah sealed the covenant to worship Jehovah (Neh. 10:26).

A·na′ni (ȧ-nā′nī), contraction of Ananiah. A son of Elioenai (I Chron. 3:24).

An′a·ni′ah (ăn′ȧ-nī′ȧ) [Jehovah has appeared]. 1. The father of Maaseiah (Neh. 3:23).
2. A town of Benjamin (Neh. 11:32). Formerly identified with Beit Hanīna, but probably Bethany, e. of Jerusalem.

An′a·ni′as (ăn′ȧ-nī′ăs), Gr. form of Hananiah. 1. A disciple of Jerusalem who, with his wife Sapphira, sold a piece of land, and taking a portion of the price, laid it at the apostles' feet (Acts 5:1 seq.). The Christian community held all things common. "Neither was there among them any that lacked: for as many as were possessors of lands or houses sold them, . . . and laid . . . [the prices] at the apostles' feet: and distribution was made unto each, according as any one had need." No one was under obligation to do this (v. 4), and the end proposed did not demand that all property be sold, but forbade it. Property was sold as need required. Ananias brought part of the proceeds, and laid it at the apostles' feet ostensibly as the whole. Peter rebuked him for having lied to the Holy Spirit, and he fell down and expired, as did his wife Sapphira, who came in three hours afterward; in ignorance of what had taken place, she repeated her husband's falsehood, and had the same doom foretold for her by Peter.
2. A Christian at Damascus who was informed in a vision of Saul's conversion, and sent to restore his sight and admit him to the Christian Church by baptism (Acts 9:10–18).
3. A high priest appointed by Herod, king of Chalcis, about A.D. 48 (Jos. Antiq. xx. 5, 2). Four years later he was sent to Rome by the governor of Syria to answer for violence done by the Jews to the Samaritans, but he was acquitted through the influence of Agrippa, and returned to Jerusalem (Jos. Antiq. xx. 6, 2 and 3; War ii. 12, 6 and 7). Jonathan, former high priest, was politically associated with him. In the year 58, Paul was arraigned before Ananias, and he appeared against the apostle before the procurator Felix (Acts 23:2; 24:1). Jonathan, his colleague, was now murdered, and about the year 59, toward the close of Felix' administration, Ananias himself was deposed by Agrippa (Jos. Antiq. xx. 8, 5 and 8; War ii. 13, 3). He appears to have resided on the s.w. hill of Jerusalem, in the upper city, near the palace of the Hasmonaeans. He was murdered in the year 67 (Jos. War ii. 17, 6 and 9).

A′nath (ā′năth) [a n. Semitic goddess of war, represented with helmet, shield, spear, and battle-ax]. Father of the judge Shamgar (Judg. 3:31; 5:6).

A·nath′e·ma [Gr., anything devoted]. In the N. T., a person or thing devoted to destruction. It corresponds to the Heb. ḥerem (Rom. 9:3, R.V.; I Cor. 12:3, R.V., and A.V. marg.; Gal. 1:8, 9, R.V.; see Lev. 27:28, 29; Josh. 6:17; 7:1, R.V.).

A·nath′e·ma Mar′a·nath′a (ȧ-nāth′ĕ-mȧ măr′ȧ-nāth′ȧ) [Gr., one devoted to destruction, and Aram. Māranā thā, O our Lord, come!]. Formerly interpreted as one ac-

cursed at the coming of the Lord (I Cor. 16:22, A.V.), with the sense of a double imprecation. Maranatha is, however, a distinct sentence consisting of two Aramaic words. E.R.V. divides Maran atha, Our Lord is come or comes; A.R.V. analyzes better: Marana tha, O our Lord, come! Cf. Rev. 22:20, "Amen: come, Lord Jesus."

An′a·thoth (ăn′ȧ-thŏth) [probably the plural of Anath, a goddess (cf. Beth-anath, and the plural, Ashtaroth)]. 1. Head of a father's house of Benjamin, family of Becher (I Chron. 7:8).
2. Head and representative of the men of Anathoth, who in their name sealed the covenant to worship Jehovah (Neh. 10:19).
3. A city in the territory of Benjamin assigned to the priests (Josh. 21:18; I Chron. 6:60). It was the home of Abiathar the high priest (I Kings 2:26), and the birthplace of Jeremiah, and the prophet's life was also endangered here (Jer. 1:1; 11:21). The town was repeopled after the Exile (Ezra 2:23). Its site is represented by the modern 'Anâta, which is 2½ miles n.e. of Jerusalem. It was once a fortified town.

An′a·thoth·ite (ăn′ȧ-thŏth-īt), in A.V. An′e·thoth·ite, An′e·toth·ite, and An′toth·ite. A native or inhabitant of Anathoth (II Sam. 23:27; I Chron. 11:28; 27:12).

An′drew (ăn′drōō) [Gr. Andreas, manly]. The brother of Simon Peter, of Bethsaida on the Sea of Galilee (John 1:44). By vocation he was a fisherman like his brother (Matt. 4:18; Mark 1:16–18), and with his brother had a house at Capernaum (Mark 1:29). He was a disciple of John the Baptist, but being directed by John to Jesus as the Lamb of God, he obtained an interview with Jesus and became convinced that Jesus was the Messiah. Forthwith he found his brother and induced him to visit Jesus (John 1:35–42). He was afterward called to permanent fellowship with Jesus (Matt. 4:18, 19; Mark 1:16, 17; cf. John 6:8), and appointed an apostle (Matt. 10:2; Mark 3:18; Luke 6:14; Acts 1:13). He joined with his brother and James and John in inquiring regarding the destruction of the city and Temple, and the Second Advent of Christ (Mark 13:3, 4), and with Philip he presented the request of the Greeks to Jesus (John 12:22). Nothing trustworthy is known of his subsequent life. According to tradition, he suffered martyrdom at Patrae in Achaia by crucifixion on a cross shaped like the letter X. This is now called St. Andrew's Cross. It is also related that a ship bearing two relics of him was wrecked in a bay of Scotland, afterward called St. Andrew's Bay. The mariners who reached the shore introduced the gospel into the region. Andrew, therefore, became the patron saint of Scotland, and gave name to St. Andrew's town. His festival is kept by the Greek and Roman Churches on November 30. In the Church of England it has become customary on that day to preach on the subject of missions. The Acts of St. Andrew, an alleged Gospel from his pen, is spurious.

An′dro·ni′cus (ăn′drō-nī′kŭs) [Gr., conquering men]. A Jewish Christian, and once fellow prisoner of Paul, to whom at Rome Paul sent greeting (Rom. 16:7).

A′nem (ā′něm) [two fountains]. A town in the territory of Issachar, given with its suburbs to the sons of Gershom (I Chron. 6:73). Probably a corruption of the text out of Engannim (Josh. 21:29; cf. 19:21).

A′ner (ā′nẽr). 1. An Amorite, resident at Mamre, and one of Abraham's confederates in the battle with the eastern kings (Gen. 14:13, 24).
2. A town of Manasseh w. of the Jordan. It was given with its suburbs to the Kohathites

28

(I Chron. 6:70). In Josh. 21:25, Taanach (A.V., Tanach) appears in its stead and is considered by many scholars as the correct reading for Aner.

An'e·thoth·ite (ăn'ē-thŏth-ĭt) or **An'e·toth·ite** (ăn'ē-tŏth-ĭt). See ANATHOTHITE.

An'gel [Gr. *angelos*, messenger, envoy]. 1. A celestial being a little higher in dignity than man. Angels are spiritual beings (Heb. 1:14), and they neither marry nor are given in marriage (Matt. 22:30). From their worship of God as well, probably, as from their nature, they are called, at least in poetry, sons of God (Job 1:6; 38:7); and from their character, holy ones (Job 5:1, R.V.; Ps. 89:5, 7, R.V.). Their office is denoted by the term angel (messenger). In the later books differences among angels in rank and dignity are implied, for there are archangels (chief angels), as well as those of a more ordinary kind (I Thess. 4:16; Jude 9). This twofold distinction does not seem to be all. Both among fallen angels and angels unfallen there are thrones, dominions, principalities, and powers (Rom. 8:38; Eph. 1:21; 3:10; Col. 1:16; 2:15). Cherubim and seraphim seem also to belong to the angelic order. The inanimate powers of nature, by which the ordinary economy of the universe is carried on, may be personified as God's messengers (Ps. 104:4, R.V.); but pestilence and death, when acts of the divine government, are represented as under angelic charge (II Sam. 24:16; Zech. 1:7–17). Unseen they encamp round about them that fear God (II Kings 6:17; Ps. 34:7; Isa. 63:9). The angel of the Lord came in human form to Abraham, Hagar, and Lot, to Moses and Joshua, to the Israelites at Bochim, to Gideon and Manoah. An angel came to Elijah and to Daniel. Angels are fittingly prominent in the history of Jesus, announcing his birth and that of his forerunner, heralding his advent to the shepherds, ministering unto him after his victory over temptation and in the Garden (Luke 22:43, a passage omitted in many ancient authorities), and bearing tidings to his disciples at the resurrection and ascension. An angel also aided Peter and stood by Paul. The names of some angels or archangels are mentioned, namely, Gabriel (Dan. 8:16; 9:21; Luke 1:19, 26), and Michael (Dan. 10:13, 21; 12:1; Jude 9; Rev. 12:7). The Apocrypha adds Raphael and Uriel; see MICHAEL 11. The ancient Persians recognized the existence of angels of different rank and many scholars maintain that the later Hebrew conception of angels was influenced by Zoroastrianism.

While any angel sent to execute the commands of God might be called the angel of the Lord (II Sam. 24:16; I Kings 19:5, 7), yet mention is made of an angel under circumstances that justify one in always thinking of the same angel, who is distinguished from Jehovah, and yet is identified with him (Gen. 16:10, 13; 18:2–4, 13, 14, 33; 22:11, 12, 15, 16; 31:11, 13; Ex. 3:2, 4; Josh. 5:13–15; 6:2; Zech. 1:10–13; 3:1, 2), who revealed the face of God (Gen. 32:30), in whom was Jehovah's name (Ex. 23:21), and whose presence was equivalent to Jehovah's presence (Ex. 32:34; 33:14; Isa. 63:9). The angel of the Lord thus appears as a manifestation of Jehovah himself, one with Jehovah and yet different from him. See THEOPHANY.

2 The representative of a church; but whether this is the presbyter or bishop, or the pastor of the local church, or a celestial being of the angelic order watching over the church, is by no means clear. For the interpretation that the angel is a preacher, cf. the meaning of the name Malachi. Another view is that these angels are personifications of their churches (Rev. 1:20; 2:1, 8, 12, 18; 3:1, 7, 14).

A·ni'am (*à*-nī'ăm [I am a paternal uncle or kinsman, or perhaps from the root *nā'ēm*, to be pleasant, agreeable]. A Manassite, family of Shemida (I Chron. 7:19; cf. Num. 26:32).

A'nim (ā'nĭm) [fountains]. A town in the hill country of Judah, mentioned immediately after Eshtemoh (Josh. 15:50). It is apparently identical with Khirbet Ghuwein, about 11 miles s. of Hebron and 3 s. of es-Semū'a, i.e., Eshtemoa.

An'ise. An umbelliferous plant (*Pimpinella anisum*) somewhat like caraway in appearance, occasionally cultivated in the East for its seeds, which are used as a seasoning and as a carminative. The English versions render the Greek word *anēthon* (Matt. 23:23) in the text by anise, on the marg. by dill. The latter is *Anethum graveolens* of the same order (umbelliferous) as anise, resembles anise in appearance and properties, and is more commonly grown in gardens.

An'kle Chain. A chain binding together the two ankles of a woman, so as to compel her to take short steps, and, especially when combined with anklets, to make a tinkling sound when she walked (Num. 31:50; Isa. 3:20, both R.V.; in A.V. called simply chains and ornaments of the legs).

An'klet. An ornament for the ankles, consisting of metallic or glass rings, and corresponding to bracelets on the wrists. Anklets are often worn by boys as well as women in the East (Isa. 3:18, R.V.; in A.V., called tinkling ornaments about the feet). See ANKLE CHAIN.

An'na (ăn'à), Gr. form of Hannah [grace]. A widow, daughter of Phanuel of the tribe of Asher. Her married life had lasted 7 years. At the age of 84 she visited the Temple daily, and was there when the Infant Jesus was brought to be dedicated. A prophetess, she recognized and proclaimed him to be the Messiah (Luke 2:36–38).

An'nas (ăn'ăs), Gr. for Hanan, contraction of Hananiah [Jehovah has been gracious]. A high priest at Jerusalem, named as Caiaphas, in the year when John the Baptist began his ministry (Luke 3:2), it is thought about A.D. 26. He is called Ananos by Josephus. He was appointed high priest about A.D. 6 by Quirinius, governor of Syria, and was deposed by the procurator of Judea, Valerius Gratus, about A.D. 15. Each of his 5 sons became high priest, and he was father-in-law of the high priest Caiaphas (Jos. *Antiq.* xviii. 2, 1 and 2; John 18:13). Although Annas was no longer officiating high priest when Jesus was arrested, he was yet the most influential priest and still bore the title (Luke 3:2; Acts 4:6), and to him Jesus was first taken (John 18:13), and after being examined by him was sent bound to Caiaphas (John 18:24). When Peter and John were subsequently arrested, Annas was prominent among their examiners (Acts 4:6).

An·nun'ci·a'tion [Lat. *annuntiatio*, announcement]. The announcement by the angel Gabriel to the Virgin Mary that she was to give birth to the Son of God (Luke 1:26–38). Annunciation or Lady Day is celebrated March 25.

A·noint'. To pour oil upon the head, or in any other way apply it to a person or to a thing. Among the Jews there were an ordinary, a sacred or official, and a medical or surgical anointing. The ordinary one was simply a matter of the toilet (II Sam. 12:20; Dan. 10:3; Matt. 6:17). The anointing of the head with oil in the time of Jesus was extended, as an act of courtesy, also to guests (Luke 7:46). The official anointing was conferred on prophets, priests, and kings. Elijah the prophet was directed to anoint Elisha, his successor (I Kings 19:16). Aaron the high priest, and those who followed him in the same office, were anointed with a holy consecrating oil (Ex. 28:41; 29:7; 30:30; 40:13, 15). Saul (I Sam. 9:16; 10:1), David (I Sam. 16:1, 12, 13; II Sam. 2:7; 3:39, etc.), Solomon (I Kings 1:34), Hazael of Syria (I Kings 19:15), Jehu (I Kings 19:16), Jehoash (II Kings 11:12), and others were anointed kings. Messiah and Christ mean the Anointed One. Jesus the Christ was anointed by the Spirit to be Prophet, Priest, and King. Of things, the altar (Ex. 29:36; 40:10), and the tabernacle (Ex. 30:26; 40:9), the laver, etc. (Ex. 40:9–11), were also anointed. The medicinal or surgical anointing, not necessarily with oil, was a customary remedy applied to the sick and wounded (Isa. 1:6; Luke 10:34; Rev. 3:18). The Christian places reliance, not in the natural means in themselves, but in God who works through the means and renders them effectual (James 5:14, 15).

Ant. Any hymenopterous insect of the family *Formicidae.* Ants are social insects like bees and wasps, to which they are not remotely akin. The species are numerous and widely diffused, the larger members, however, occurring in the tropics. The ant is held up as an example of industry and forethought, industriously providing food in summer and gathering grain in harvest (Prov. 6:6–8; 30:24, 25). That the ants of Palestine store food on which to live in winter is not expressly asserted in Proverbs, but it is clearly stated in similar Arabic maxims.

An′te·lope. An animal (Heb. *teʾō*) mentioned in Deut. 14:5 and Isa. 51:20, both R.V. It was captured in nets, and was ceremonially fit for food. Targum, followed by A.V., renders wild ox; probably meaning the bubale, *Antilope bubalis,* of Egypt and Arabia, classed by the Arabs with wild oxen. In the Greek versions and the Vulgate, the word is generally rendered oryx, which refers to the *Antilope leucoryx.* This animal has horns which are long, slender, conical, and with ringlike ridges round. The animal is white, with the exception of a long tuft of hair under the throat, which is black. It is a native of Sennaar, Upper Egypt, and Arabia, and is said to be found in Syria.

An′tho·thi′jah (ăn′thō-thī′já), in A.V. **An′· to·thi′jah.** A Benjamite descended through Shashak (I Chron. 8:24).

An′ti·christ′ [Gr. *antichristos,* against or instead of Christ]. The word antichrist may mean, as the etymology shows, an enemy of Christ or a usurper of Christ's name and rights. The former was probably its primary meaning, though the other idea was also attached to it. In the N.T. John alone uses the term (I John 2:18, 22; 4:3; II John 7). From I John 2:18, R.V., we learn that the Christians had been taught that "Antichrist" would appear in "the last hour," i.e., before the Second Advent of Christ. While not denying that Antichrist would be a single person, John lays stress on the spirit to be embodied in him, and declares that already many antichrists had come. The substance of the antichristian spirit, he says, is denial that Jesus is the Christ or the real incarnation of the Son of God, by which is meant not only denial of the doctrine, but moral antagonism to its religious implications. This opposition was already appearing in the Church in the persons of false teachers and false disciples, for Antichrist arises out of nominal Christianity itself. But while John alone uses the term, the doctrine is taught elsewhere. Jesus himself not only warned his apostles of "false Christs" (Matt. 24:5, 23, 24; Mark 13:21, 22)—by which, however, he meant primarily Jewish Messianic pretenders —but plainly intimated that apostasy would

arise within the Church (see parables of Tares, Ten Virgins, Matt. 7:22, 23; 24:12, etc.). Paul more fully teaches (II Thess. 2:3– 12) that before the Second Advent "the man of lawlessness" (R.V. marg.) must be revealed, "he that opposeth and exalteth himself against all that is called God or that is worshipped," and "in the temple of God" (probably the Church) claims to be God (to usurp the place of God). Paul too, like John, represents this as the culmination of a process of apostasy (II Thess. 2:7; cf. I Tim. 4:1). Many interpreters also see in the "beast" of Rev., ch. 13, a further description of Antichrist. Thus the N.T. declared that Christian history would not be a pure development of goodness and truth, but that within Christendom apostasy would arise, develop, have many representatives, and finally culminate in Antichrist proper (either a person or an institution, perhaps both), of which the essential spirit would be antagonism to Christ and the impious claim of that allegiance from man's mind and life which is alone due to God and his Son. In different periods, various apostasies have seemed to believers to be Antichrist, and have more or less embodied the antichristian principle; but doubtless the full manifestation of Antichrist is yet to come, and will precede and be destroyed at the Second Advent of the Lord.   G. T. P.

An′ti·och (ăn′tĭ-ŏk) [Gr. *Antiocheia*]. 1. The metropolis of Syria under the Macedonian Greek dynasty (I Macc. 3:37 *et passim*), founded about 300 B.C. by Seleucus Nicator,

A Street Scene in Antioch in Syria

and named by him after Antiochus, his father. It was situated on the s. side of the Orontes, about 15 miles from its mouth, the river being navigable up to the city. Mount Casius approached it closely on the s., and the Amanus mountains were not far off on the w., while in front lay the valley of the Orontes, 5 or 6 miles across. The city became large and numerously inhabited. It remained the capital when the Roman province of Syria was erected in 64 B.C. Its population was mixed, with not a few Jews. Christians who fled from Jerusalem to avoid the persecution which arose upon the martyrdom of Stephen preached the gospel here, addressing at first only Jews who spoke the Aramaic tongue, then those who spoke Greek. Barnabas was despatched from Jerusalem to aid the work. After laboring there for a while he fetched as a coadjutor Paul from Tarsus. For a whole year these two great evangelists made the city the sphere of their labors and taught much people. The disciples were called Christians first in Antioch (Acts 11:19–26). Further reinforcements arrived in the persons of prophets (ch. 11:27). This city also became the birthplace of foreign missions. From Antioch Paul and Barnabas were sent on a missionary journey (ch. 13:2). On its completion they returned to the city (ch. 14:26). The disciples at Antioch kept up active intercourse with the brethren at Jerusalem. In time of famine, they sent relief to them (ch. 11:28–30), and they submitted the question regarding the circumcision of Gentile converts to a council at Jerusalem (ch. 15). The Second Missionary Journey of Paul, like the first, commenced with a departure from Antioch (ch. 15:35, 36), to which Paul returned, this time by way of Caesarea (ch. 18:22). At Antioch Paul withstood Peter to the face because of his vacillating conduct with regard to the Gentile converts (Gal. 2:11). In apostolic days it was a great city of over 500,000 inhabitants and known as "Antioch the Beautiful," "The Queen of the East," and "The Third Metropolis of the Roman Empire" (after Rome and Alexandria). In A.D. 538 Chosroes, the Persian king, took and destroyed it. It was rebuilt by the Roman emperor Justinian. In A.D. 635 it was taken by the Moslems, from whom it passed in 1084 to the Turks. Except between 1098 and 1269, when it was the seat of a Christian kingdom founded by the crusaders, it has remained in Mohammedan hands. The place, still called Antakiya, is now unimportant.

2. A town in Asia Minor, also founded by Seleucus Nicator and named after his father, Antiochus. It was situated in Phrygia, near the borders of Pisidia, and was accordingly designated Antioch toward Pisidia and Pisidian Antioch to distinguish it from Antioch in Syria. It was included within the Roman province of Galatia, and was the center of the civil and military administration of the s. part of the province. Jews dwelt there, and had a synagogue (Acts 13:14). Barnabas and Paul visited it on their First Missionary Journey (Acts 13:14–52; 14:19–21; II Tim. 3:11). In 1833 Arundel identified the ruins of this Antioch near the modern town of Yalvatch.

An·ti'o·chus (ăn-tī'ô-kŭs) [Gr., withstander]. 1. Antiochus III, surnamed the Great, king of Syria and 6th ruler of the Seleucidan

Head of Antiochus Epiphanes

dynasty, father of Seleucus IV and Antiochus Epiphanes (I Macc. 1:10; 8:6–8). He reigned from 223 to 187 B.C. He attempted to wrest Coelesyria, Phoenicia, and Palestine from Ptolemy IV, but was defeated at Raphia 217 B.C. After the death of Ptolemy he renewed the attempt and was successful, gaining the decisive battle of Paneas in 198. He invaded Europe, but his victorious career was terminated at Thermopylae. On his retreat he was decisively defeated at Magnesia in Asia in 190. By the terms of peace he was obliged to send 20 hostages to Rome, including his son, and pay an enormous tribute. While plundering a temple in Susiana he was murdered by a mob. The Seleucidian line was continued as follows:

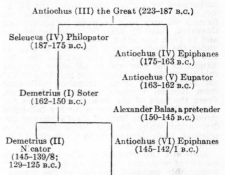

Antiochus (III) the Great (223-187 B.C.)

- Seleucus (IV) Philopator (187-175 B.C.)
- Antiochus (IV) Epiphanes (175-163 B.C.)
- Antiochus (V) Eupator (163-162 B.C.)
- Demetrius (I) Soter (162-150 B.C.)
- Alexander Balas, a pretender (150-145 B.C.)
- Demetrius (II) Nicator (145-139/8; 129-125 B.C.)
- Antiochus (VI) Epiphanes (145-142/1 B.C.)

Antiochus (VII) Sidetes (139/8-129 B.C.)

2. Antiochus E·piph'a·nes (ê-pĭf'á-nēz), the 8th ruler of the house of Seleucidae, 175–163 B.C. (I Macc. 1:10; 6:16). He passed 15 years of his life as a hostage at Rome (I Macc. 1:10). He was an energetic prince who extended and strengthened his kingdom, but enraged his subjects by religious intolerance. He stirred up the Jews by robbing the Temple and setting up a statue of Jupiter in the Holy of Holies. He also pulled down the walls of Jerusalem, commanded the sacrifice of swine, forbade circumcision, and destroyed all the sacred books that could be found. It was these outrages which induced the revolt of the Maccabees (I Macc. 1:41–53). He died between Elymais and Babylon, shortly after receiving news of the Jewish revolt (I Macc. 6:1–16).

3. Antiochus Eu'pa·tor, son of the above. As a minor he reigned 2 years under the regency of Lysias (I Macc. 6:17–63). He was slain and succeeded by Demetrius Soter.

4. Antiochus VI, the young child of the pretender Alexander Balas. He was set up as king by the general Tryphon, who used him merely as a cloak for his own ambition, and slew him as soon as he felt himself established, 142/1 B.C. (I Macc. 11:39, 40, 54; 13:31, 32).

5. Antiochus VII, brother of Demetrius II, who reigned in the stead of Demetrius during his imprisonment by Arsaces, 138–129 B.C. He defeated Tryphon (I Macc. 15: 1, 10–14), made first a treaty with Simon Maccabaeus, but afterward repudiated his help and tried to rob the Temple. His attempt was frustrated by Simon's sons Judas and John Hyrcanus. Later Simon and 2 of his sons, Mattathias and Judas, were assassinated. Antiochus besieged Jerusalem and again established Syrian suzerainty over Judea (I Macc. 16:1–10).

6. A Jew known only as being the father of the councilor Numenius (I Macc. 12:16).

An'ti·pas (ăn'tĭ-păs), contraction of Antipater. 1. A Christian who suffered martyrdom

at Pergamum, in Asia Minor (Rev. 2:12, 13).
2. Son of Herod the Great; see HEROD 2.

An·tip'a·ter (ăn-tĭp'*à*-tẽr) [Lat., from Gr., in place of the father]. 1. A Jew, son of Jason. He was a councilor, and one of two ambassadors sent by Jonathan and the elders to Rome to renew the alliance (I Macc. 12:16; 14:22; Jos. *Antiq.* xiii. 5, 8). His father was perhaps the Jason who had formerly gone on a similar mission (Jos. *Antiq.* viii. 17).
2. Father of Herod the Great (Jos. *Antiq.* xiv. 7, 3).

An·tip'a·tris (ăn-tĭp'*à*-trĭs) [Gr., belonging to Antipater]. A town founded by Herod the Great, in the fertile plain of Caphar Saba, on the site of that village, near the mountains, and called after Antipater, his father. It was surrounded by a river (Jos. *Antiq.* xiii. 15, 1; xvi. 5, 2; *War* i. 4, 7; 21, 9). It lay on the Roman military road between Jerusalem and Caesarea, about 39 miles from the former city and 24 from the latter. The old name lingers under the modern form Kefr Saba, and its site was sought at this village; but the conditions of the site are in all other respects fulfilled at Rās el 'Ain, at the junction of the old Roman road from Jerusalem with that from Ramleh through Lydda to Caesarea. From the base of the mound that covers the site the River 'Aujah gushes forth a full-sized stream. It was the limit of Paul's journey the first night while he was being taken as a prisoner from Jerusalem to Caesarea (Acts 23:31). See APHEK 3.

An·to'ni·a (ăn-tō'nĭ-*à*), **Tow'er of.** A castle connected with the Temple at Jerusalem. It presumably occupied the site of the stronghold Birah, which appertained to the Temple and was restored by Nehemiah (Neh. 2:8). John Hyrcanus built the tower, and he generally dwelt in it and kept the priestly vestments there, for he was entitled to wear them (Jos. *Antiq.* xv. 11, 4; xviii. 4, 3). Until the time of Herod the Great it was known as the Baris, but Herod repaired it at vast expense, and fortified it more firmly than before in order that it might guard the Temple, and named it Antonia in honor of Mark Antony (Jos. *War* i. 21, 1; v. 5, 8). It was situated at the n.w. corner of the Temple area, on a rock 50 cubits in height, the highest point in the neighborhood. Its presence there prevented the area from being foursquare (Jos. *War* vi. 5, 4). The fortress had the amplitude and form of a palace, with chambers, courts, barracks, and baths. Its walls rose 40 cubits above the rock on which they rested. At the corners were turrets, 3 of which were 50 cubits high, while the 4th, which overlooked the Temple, was 70 cubits. It was separated by a deep trench from the hill Bezetha (Jos. *War* v. 4, 2), but was connected with the n. and w. cloisters, at the junction of which it stood, with gates for the guards and a staircase (cf. Acts 21:35 with v. 37; v. 40 with ch. 22:24), and with the inner Temple at its e. gate by a subterranean passage (Jos. *Antiq.* xv. 11, 7), which seems to have existed in the Baris as built by Hyrcanus (*ibid.* xiii. 11, 2). Over the Temple end of this underground passage Herod erected a tower. The arrangement was intended to afford him a way of escape in case of a popular sedition. In the castle a Roman legion was stationed, which stood on guard in the cloisters, especially during the Jewish festivals, to prevent any excesses on the part of the populace (Jos. *Antiq.* xviii. 4, 3; *War* v. 5, 8). The castle was finally demolished by order of Titus in A.D. 70.

The most tragic event in the history of the castle occurred during the reign of Aristobulus, son of Hyrcanus. The king lay sick in one of its chambers. His beloved brother Antigonus, returning from the war, hastened clad in armor and accompanied by his military escort to the Temple to offer prayers for the recovery of the king. The act was misrepresented to Aristobulus; but he summoned his brother to his bedside, with the request that he come unarmed, and ordered soldiers to lie in the underground passage and slay him if he appeared in armor. The queen suppressed the message in part, and contrived to have Antigonus informed that the king desired to see his splendid armor. Suspecting nothing, he entered the passage clad in mail and was murdered. The deed was reported to the king, and the shock brought on a hemorrhage. A slave bore away the vessel in which the blood had been caught, but stumbled on the spot where Antigonus had been slain. The blood of the two brothers mingled on the floor. A cry of horror ran through the palace, and roused the king to inquire the cause. When he learned what had occurred he was filled with an agony of remorse and instantly expired (Jos. *Antiq.* xiii. 11).

Paul, when rescued from the infuriated mob that had dragged him out of the Temple, was carried into this castle, and on the way was allowed to address the people from the stairs (Acts 21:30 *seq.*).

An'to·thi'jah (ăn'tô-thī'já). See ANTHOTHIJAH.

An'toth·ite (ăn'tŏth-ĭt). See ANATHOTHITE.

A'nub (ā'nŭb) [ety. uncertain, perhaps, joined together]. A man of Judah, son of Hakkoz (I Chron. 4:8, R.V.).

Ape. The Hebrew word *ḳôph*, derived from Sans. *kapi*, is rendered ape, and probably includes both apes, which are without tails, and monkeys, which possess them. There is a Greek word *kēbos* or *kēpos* (long-tailed monkey), but the LXX uses *pithēkos*, which according to Aristotle is tailless. There is no genuine ape either in Malabar or in any other part of India. If the animals that were brought to Palestine by the vessels that went to Ophir for gold (I Kings 10:22; II Chron. 9:21) came from India, they were a species of tailed monkey, perhaps that called *Hanuman* (*Semnopithecus entellus*), which is common throughout India, and is worshiped as a god. There is no reason to believe that any one kind, or even family, of apes is intended.

A·pel'les (*à*-pĕl'ēz). An approved Christian at Rome to whom Paul sent a salutation (Rom. 16:10).

A·phaer'e·ma (*à*-fĕr'ê-m*à*). A government district which in the time of Jonathan Maccabaeus was separated from Samaria, annexed to Judea, and placed under the authority of the high priest (I Macc. 11:34; cf. ch. 10:30, 38). The name is probably a Greek form of Ephraim, and designates the most s. part of Samaria (cf. John 11:54).

A·phar'sach·ites (*à*-fär'săk-ĭts or **Aph'ar·sath'chites** (äf'är-säth'kits). A tribe from beyond the Euphrates, settled by Asnapper in Samaria (Ezra 4:9; 5:6).

A·phar'sites (*à*-fär'sĭts). An eastern tribe, transplanted by Asnapper to Samaria (Ezra 4:9).

A'phek (ā'fĕk) [strength, fortress]. 1. A city apparently n. of Zidon (Josh. 13:4), and hence commonly identified with Afka, the ancient Aphaca, 23 miles n.e. of Beirut, at the source of the River of Byblos, the Adonis or Nahr Ibrāhīm.
2. Aphek, variant Aphik, situated within the territory of Asher, but not cleared of its Canaanite inhabitants (Josh. 19:30; Judg. 1:31). It is located by Alt at Tell Kurdāneh, near the sources of the Na'mein River, which flows into the Mediterranean a little to the s.e. of Acco.

3. A town in the Plain of Sharon (Josh. 12:18, cf. Greek text of Rahlfs), at the source of the 'Aujeh, at Rās el-'Ain (Jos. *War* ii. 19, 1). Perhaps it was here that the Philistines encamped before the first battle with Israel at Ebenezer. Shiloh was within 25 miles (I Sam. 4:1, 12). See ANTIPATRIS.

4. A town apparently between Shunem and Jezreel. The Philistines pitched at Shunem, but soon discovered that the Israelites had occupied the heights of Gilboa. From Shunem they advanced to Aphek, and thence to Jezreel, where they attacked the Israelites who had descended to the spring at Jezreel, forcing them back to their former position on Gilboa and completing the slaughter on that mountain (I Sam. 28:4; 29:1, 11; 31:1). It may also be the town of Aphek to which Benhadad advanced with the intention of giving battle to Ahab, and to which he and his army retreated after his defeat, and where a wall fell and 27,000 of his soldiers were killed (I Kings 20:26–30); and it may also be the town where Joash, king of Israel, should, according to prophecy, smite the Syrians till they were consumed (II Kings 13:14–19). The situation presupposed in the narratives is limited met by a town w. of the Jordan in the Plain of Jezreel. Still the Aphek referred to in these two passages may be the town of that name beyond Jordan in Golan, about 3 miles e. of the Sea of Galilee, on the highway between Damascus and Beth-shean, and now represented by the village of Afīk or Fīk.

A·phe′kah (*á-fē′ká*) [strong place, fortification]. A town in the hill country of Judah (Josh. 15:53); probably the same as Aphek 1.

A·phi′ah (*á-fī′á*). An ancestor of King Saul (I Sam. 9:1).

A′phik (ā′fĭk). See APHEK 2.

Aph′rah (ăf′rá), in R.V. **Beth′-le-aph′rah** [dust]. A town (Micah 1:10), site unknown.

Aph′ses (ăf′sēz). See HAPPIZZEZ.

A·poc′a·lypse (*á-pŏk′á-lĭps*) [Gr., disclosure, revelation]. A name frequently given to the last book of the Bible. See REVELATION.

A·poc′ry·pha (*á-pŏk′rĭ-fá*) [Gr. *apokrypha*, hidden things, used by ecclesiastical writers for: 1. matters secret or mysterious; 2. of unknown origin, forged, spurious; 3. unrecognized, uncanonical]. The name generally given to the following 16 books: I and II Esdras, Tobit, Judith, The Rest of Esther, The Wisdom of Solomon, Ecclesiasticus, Baruch with The Epistle of Jeremy, The Song of the Three Holy Children, The History of Susanna, Bel and the Dragon, The Prayer of Manasses, I, II, III, and IV Maccabees. Sometimes the number is limited to fourteen, III and IV Maccabees being omitted.

Unlike the books of the O.T., which are in Hebrew, with some portions in Aramaic, the apocryphal productions are in Greek, though at least Judith, Ecclesiasticus, Baruch, chs. 1:1 to 3:8, and I Maccabees were originally written in Hebrew. The Jewish Church considered them uninspired, and some of their writers disclaim inspiration (Prologue to Ecclesiasticus; II Macc. 2:23; 15:38). The Apocrypha and Pseudepigrapha were produced between about 250 B.C. and somewhere in the early Christian centuries. They are not found in the Hebrew canon; they are never quoted by Jesus; and it cannot with certainty be affirmed that the apostles ever directly allude to them. The early churches permitted them to be read for edification, and recommended them to the catechumens for study, but rejected them from the canon, their decision carrying authority during the Middle Ages, as it does now with the various Protestant Churches. Thus the Church of England in the 6th of the Thirty-nine Articles published in 1562 calls the apocryphal treatises books which "the Church doth read for example of life and instruction of manners; but yet doth it not apply them to establish any doctrine." The Westminster Confession of 1643 declares, as a matter of creed, that "the books, commonly called Apocrypha, not being of divine inspiration, are no part of the canon of Scripture, and therefore are of no authority in the Church of God, or to be any otherwise approved or made use of than other human writings." The Council of Trent at its sitting on April 8, 1546, declared the following apocryphal books to be canonical: Tobit, Judith, The Wisdom of Solomon, Ecclesiasticus, Baruch (The Epistle of Jeremy being ch. 6), and I and II Maccabees, and adding The Rest of Esther to the canonical Esther, and incorporating The History of Susanna, The Song of the Three Holy Children, and Bel and the Dragon with Daniel. The Council pronounced an anathema against anyone who ventured to differ from it in opinion. This has since regulated the belief of the Roman Catholic Church. The Apocrypha was introduced into the English version by Coverdale in 1535, and was included in the King James Version, but began to be omitted as early as 1629. When inserted, it was placed between the O.T. and the N.T. A controversy on the subject was carried on between the years 1821 and 1826, which resulted in the exclusion of the Apocrypha from all Bibles issued by the British and Foreign Bible Society.

1. I Es′DRAS [*Esdras*, Gr. for Ezra]. The book narrates in Greek the decline and fall of the Kingdom of Judah from the time of Josiah, the destruction of Jerusalem, the Babylonian Captivity, the Return of the exiles, and the share taken by Ezra in reorganizing the Jewish polity. In some respects it amplifies the Biblical narrative; it probably is a translation from a Hebrew or Aramaic original. It is followed by Josephus in the legend of the three courtiers (cf. I Esdras 3:1 to 4:44 with Jos. *Antiq.* xi. 3, 2–8, etc.). The date of the book lies between 300 B.C. and A.D. 100. The work is known as III Esdras in the Vulgate, where it appears as an appendix to the N.T.;

Codex Vaticanus (4th Century), I Esdras 2:1, 2

no authority is attributed to it by the Church of Rome.

2. II Es'DRAS. This is in quite a different style from I Esdras, which it follows, under the name of IV Esdras, in the Vulgate in the appendix to the N.T. It is not a history, but a religious treatise, much in the style of the Hebrew prophets, and is apocalyptic in character. Its kernel, consisting of chs. 3 to 14, purports to record 7 revelations granted to Ezra in Babylon, several of which took the form of visions: the woman that mourned (chs. 9:38 to 10:56), the eagle and the lion (chs. 11:1 to 12:39), the man that rose from the sea (ch. 13:1–56). The author of these chapters is unknown; but he was evidently a Jew, full of affection for his people (Jesus in ch. 7:28 is wanting in the Oriental versions). Since the vision of the eagle, which is expressly based on the prophecy of Daniel (II Esdras 12:11), seems to refer to the Roman Empire, a date from about A.D. 88 to about A.D. 117 is generally accepted. A date later than A.D. 200 is precluded by the citation of II Esdras 5:35 in Greek by Clement of Alexandria, with the preface, "Esdras the prophet says." The first 2 and the last 2 chapters of II Esdras (chs. 1; 2; 15; 16) are additions. They are lacking in the Oriental versions and in a majority of the best Latin manuscripts. They date from a time after the LXX was in circulation, for the Minor Prophets are arranged in the order of the Greek version (ch. 1:39, 40). Chapters 1 and 2 abound in reminiscences of the New Testament and justify the rejection of Israel and the substitution of the Gentiles (chs. 1:24, 25, 35–40; 2:10, 11, 34); and accordingly were written by a Christian, not unlikely a Christian Jew.

3. To'BIT. This is a narrative of a certain pious Naphtalite, Tobit by name, who has a son Tobias. The father loses his eyesight. The son, dispatched to obtain payment of a debt to Rages in Media, is led on by an angel to Ecbatana, where he makes a romantic marriage with a widow, who had still remained a virgin, though she had been married to seven husbands, all of whom had been killed by Asmodeus, the evil spirit, on their marriage day. Tobias, however, is encouraged by the angel to become the eighth husband of the virgin-widow, and escapes death by burning the inner parts of a fish, the smoke of which puts the evil spirit to flight. Then he cures his father's blindness by anointing the darkened eyes with the gall of the fish which had already proved so useful. Tobit is manifestly a moral tale, and not serious history. The book was probably written in Aramaic toward the close of the 3d century B.C.

4. JU'DITH. A thrilling narrative of how Judith, a Jewish widow, in order to deliver her people, insinuated herself into the good graces of Holofernes, an Assyrian commander, then besieging Bethulia. She seized his sword when he was asleep and cut off his head. The narrative contains misstatements, anachronisms, and geographical absurdities. It is doubtful if there is any truth in the story, which may possibly have been suggested to the author by the narrative of Jael and Sisera (Judg. 4:17–22). The first distinct reference to the book is in an epistle of Clement of Rome, about the end of the 1st century A.D., but it may have existed as early as 175 to 100 B.C., say 400 or 600 years after the event it professed to record. By that time to say that Nabuchodonosor (Nebuchadnezzar) reigned in Nineveh, instead of Babylon (Judith 1:1), would not look so erroneous as it would to a contemporary of the great king. It is believed that the Greek text goes back to a lost Hebrew original.

5. THE REST OF ES'THER. The Hebrew canonical Esther ends with a short 10th chapter of 3 verses. The apocryphal production adds 10 verses more, and 6 chapters (chs. 11 to 16). In the LXX this supplementary matter is distributed in 7 portions through the text, and does not interrupt the history. It amplifies parts of the Scripture narrative by supplying a religious element, though it often contradicts the history as contained in the Hebrew. These Greek additions may be the work of different authors, and are by some supposed to have been interpolated by an Egyptian Jew, who wrote about the time of Ptolemy Philometor, 181–145 B.C. Some authorities, however, date the additions to a period between 125 B.C. and A.D. 90.

6. THE WIS'DOM OF SOL'O·MON. This pseudepigraph is an ethical treatise in commendation of wisdom and righteousness, and in denunciation of iniquity and idolatry. The passages which point out the sin and folly of image worship recall those on the same theme in The Psalms and Isaiah (cf. Wisd. of Sol. 13:11–19 with Psalms 115; 135:15–18; and Isa. 40:19–25; 44:9–20). It is remarkable to what extent the author, in referring to historical incidents illustrative of his doctrine, limits himself to those recorded in the Pentateuch. He writes in the person of Solomon; says that he was chosen by God as king of his people, and was by him directed to build a temple and an altar, the former on the model of the tabernacle. He was a man of genius and of piety, his religious character being sustained by his belief in immortality. He wrote in Greek, and probably was an Alexandrian Jew, who lived apparently between 150 and 50 B.C.; some would date the book as late as between 50 B.C. and A.D. 10. Though never formally quoted or in any way referred to in the N.T., yet occasionally both the language and the trains of thought in the N.T. somewhat resemble those in The Wisdom of Solomon (cf. Wisd. of Sol. 5:18–20 with Eph. 6:14–17; Wisd. of Sol. 7:26 with Heb. 1:2–6; and Wisd. of Sol. 14:13–31 with Rom. 1:19–32).

7. EC·CLE'SI·AS'TI·CUS, called also The Wisdom of Jesus, the Son of Sirach. This is a comparatively long work, extending to 51 chapters. In ch. 50:1–21 great commendation is bestowed on Simon, the high priest, the son of Onias, probably the 2d of that name (c. 218–198 B.C.). The work may, therefore, have been written in the 1st quarter of the 2d century B.C. (200–175). It was originally in Hebrew. The author, Jesus, son of Sirach, of Jerusalem (ch. 50:27), was the grandfather of the translator, who arrived in Egypt "in the eight and thirtieth year of Euergetes the king." The reference is probably to Ptolemy Physcon, surnamed Euergetes (II), who reigned as coregent from 169 to 164 and as sole king from 145 to 116 B.C. This would give 132 B.C. as the date of the grandson's arrival in Egypt, soon after which the translation was made. The great theme of the work is wisdom. It is a valuable ethical treatise, in places reminding one of the books of Proverbs, Ecclesiastes, and parts of Job, in the canonical Scriptures, and of The Wisdom of Solomon in the Apocrypha.

8. BAR'UCH, with The Epistle of Jeremy (Jeremiah). A pseudepigraph. Baruch was Jeremiah's friend. The first 5 chapters are made nominally to emanate from Baruch, while the 6th is headed "The Epistle of Jeremy." After an introduction describing the origin of the work (Baruch 1:1–14), the book of Baruch falls naturally into 3 divisions: 1. Israel's confession of sin and prayer for forgiveness and restoration to favor (chs. 1:15 to 3:8). This part bears evidence of having been written originally in Hebrew. It possibly belongs to the early decades of the 2d century B.C., although it may date from the times of

the Persian supremacy. 2. Exhortation to return to the fountain of wisdom (chs. 3:9 to 4:4). 3. Encouragement, and promise of deliverance (chs. 4:5 to 5:9). Opinion is divided whether these 2 latter sections were written originally in Hebrew or in Greek. It is disputed whether the similarity between ch. 5 and Psalm of Solomon 11 indicates that the chapter was based upon the psalm, and hence written after the middle of the 1st century B.C., or that both writings rest independently on the LXX. The Epistle of Jeremy warns the Jews in exile against Babylonian idolatry.

9. THE SONG OF THE THREE HO'LY CHIL'-DREN was designed to fit into the canonical Daniel between ch. 3:23 and v. 24. It was probably written in the 1st century B.C., and may have been composed originally in Hebrew. (Cf. Song of Three Childr. 35–68 with Psalm 148).

10. THE HIS'TO·RY OF SU·SAN'NA. This is also an apocryphal addition to Daniel, showing how the prophet sagaciously discovered an accusation against Susanna, a godly woman, to be a malignant slander. The book probably goes back to a Hebrew original which may have been written 80–50 B.C. In the LXX it precedes Daniel, while in the Vulgate it directly follows it.

11. BEL AND THE DRAG'ON. Another apocryphal addition to The Book of Daniel; the prophet proves that the priests of Bel and their families ate the food offered to the idol; and he kills a dragon, for which, a second time, he is put into a lions' den. The original may have been written in Hebrew in the 1st century B.C. In the LXX it directly follows Daniel, while in the Vulgate it comes after Susanna.

12. THE PRAYER OF MA·NAS'SES, king of Judah, when he was held captive in Babylon (cf. II Chron. 33:12, 13). Not in Roman canon, but appended to N.T. Author unknown; date very uncertain, but earlier than the 3d century A.D.

13. I MAC'CA·BEES. A historical work of great value, giving an account of the Jewish war of independence under the Maccabee family of Levites in the 2d century B.C.; see ANTI-OCHUS 2 and MACCABEE. Its author, whose name is unknown, was evidently a Palestinian Jew who wrote perhaps between 105 and 63 B.C. It was translated into Greek from a Hebrew original which survived as late as the time of Jerome.

14. II MAC'CA·BEES is professedly an abridgment of the large work of Jason of Cyrene. It is concerned chiefly with Jewish history from the reign of Seleucus IV, 175 B.C., to the death of Nicanor in 161 B.C. It is much less valuable than the First Book, and the author has a love of the marvelous which diminishes the credibility of his narrations, though they contain a good deal of truth. The book was written after 125 B.C., and before the destruction of Jerusalem in A.D. 70.

15. III MAC'CA·BEES professes to record events from the reign of Ptolemy (IV) Philopator (221–203 B.C.). After his victory at Raphia (217), Ptolemy tries to enter the Temple in Jerusalem but, struck from heaven, he falls to the ground. Upon his return to Alexandria, he seeks to massacre the Jews of Egypt, but all his attempts are miraculously thwarted. In the end he frees them and gives them a banquet lasting 7 days. The book was written shortly before or shortly after the beginning of the Christian Era. It is extant in Greek, but not in the Vulgate.

16. IV MAC'CA·BEES is a moral treatise advocating the mastery of the passions, and illustrating its teaching by examples of constancy under suffering, drawn from Maccabaean times. It was written after II Maccabees and

before the destruction of Jerusalem. It is extant in Greek, but not in the Vulgate.

Ap'ol·lo'ni·a (ăp'ŏ-lō'nĭ-á) [Gr., pertaining to Apollo]. A town of Macedonia, on the Egnatian Way, 28 miles w. of Amphipolis. Paul passed through it as he journeyed to Thessalonica (Acts 17:1).

Ap'ol·lo'ni·us (ăp'ŏ-lō'nĭ-ŭs) [Lat., from Gr., pertaining to Apollo] 1. An official under Antiochus Epiphanes, who, sent to Judea to collect tribute, treacherously ordered a massacre at Jerusalem (I Macc. 1:29–32; II Macc. 5:24–26; cf. ch. 4:21). He became governor of Samaria (Jos. Antiq. xii. 5, 5). He was defeated and slain by Judas Maccabaeus (I Macc. 3:10; Jos. Antiq. xii. 7, 1).

2. Governor of Coelesyria, whom Demetrius II made general of his army. He was defeated in battle by Jonathan Maccabaeus at Ashdod (I Macc. 10:69–85). Less credibly, Josephus speaks of him as on the side of Alexander Balas (Jos. Antiq. xiii. 4, 3 and 4).

A·pol'los (á-pŏl'ŏs), modification of Apollonius, Apollodorus, or Apollonides. A Jew born at Alexandria, eloquent and learned, and deeply versed in the O.T. Scriptures. He became a disciple of John the Baptist, and zealously taught concerning the Messiah, though knowing only the baptism of repentance. While itinerating in Asia Minor for this purpose, he met, at Ephesus, Aquila and Priscilla, who instructed him more fully; and the brethren wrote letters of introduction for him to the brethren in Achaia. On arriving in Greece, he helped the Christians, publicly confuting the Jews, and showing from the Scriptures that Jesus is the Christ (Acts 18:24–28). The disciples with whom Paul soon afterward fell in at Ephesus, who knew only John's baptism, and had never heard that there was a Holy Spirit, were probably converts of Apollos (Acts 19:1–7). Apollos' preaching at Corinth raised a party in the church at that place (I Cor. 1:12; 3:4, 5, 6, 22; 4:6). But Paul had all confidence in him, and urged him to revisit Corinth (I Cor. 16:12). He also enjoined Titus to help Apollos, apparently then in or on his way to Crete (Titus 3:13). It is thought by many scholars that Apollos was the writer of The Epistle to the Hebrews.

A·pol'lyon (á-pŏl'yŭn) [Gr., destroying, a destroyer]. The angel of the abyss (Rev. 9:11). The Greek synonym of Hebrew Abaddon.

A·pos'tle [Gr., one sent forth, a messenger, an ambassador (John 13:16, R.V. marg.)]. 1. One of the men selected by Jesus to be eyewitnesses of the events of his life, to see him after his resurrection, and to testify to mankind concerning him (Matt. 10:2–42; Acts 1:21, 22; I Cor. 9:1). They were chosen in succession at a very early period of the Saviour's public life. First came Andrew and his brother Simon, the well-known Simon Peter (Matt. 4:18–20; 10:2; Mark 1:16–18; Luke 6:14; John 1:35–42); then apparently James and John, sons of Zebedee (Matt. 4:21, 22; 10:2; Mark 1:19, 20; Luke 6:14); then seemingly Philip and Nathanael, named also Bartholomew (John 1:43–51); and subsequently 6 more, viz., Matthew, called also Levi (Matt. 9:9–13; Mark 2:14–17; Luke 5:27–32); Thomas; James the son of Alphaeus; Simon the Zealot or Cananaean; Judas, the brother of James; and Judas Iscariot (Matt. 10:1–4; Mark 3:16–19; Luke 6:13–16; Acts 1:13, all R.V.). The apostles were regarded as illiterate men by the higher Jewish dignitaries who had before them Peter and John (Acts 4:13). All they seem to have meant was that the apostles had received elementary rather than higher education. Jesus gave great attention to their spiritual training: yet to the last they failed to understand his mission, believing that he was about to set up a temporal rather than a spiritual kingdom (Matt. 20:20–28; Mark 10:35–45; Acts 1:6); they slept in the hour of his agony in the Garden (Matt. 26:40), and held aloof all the day of his death on the cross (Matt. 26:56; Mark 14:50). They were often called disciples or pupils (Matt. 11:1; 14:26; 20:17; John 20:2). Peter, James the son of Zebedee, and John, seem to have possessed a clearer comprehension of the Teacher's instructions and a higher appreciation of him than the others. On three different occasions they were singled out from the rest for special privilege. They were in the room at the raising from the dead of Jairus' daughter (Mark 5:37; Luke 8:51); they were present at the transfiguration (Matt. 17:1; Mark 9:2; Luke 9:28), and were in the Garden of Gethsemane during the agony (Matt. 26:37; Mark 14:33). Peter, though rash and impetuous in speech, was constitutionally the best fitted to lead. He is generally mentioned first, but not always (Gal. 2:9). John was the disciple whom Jesus peculiarly loved (John 19:26; 20:2; 21:7, 20). Thomas was scrupulous as to evidence, but yielded when the proof he sought was complete. Judas proved a traitor, who, betraying his divine Lord to death for the sake of lucre, and then repenting, committed suicide. The step taken to fill his place showed that the number of the apostles, fixed originally at 12, required, for a time at least, to be kept at that figure; the reason probably was that there might be as many apostles as there were tribes of Israel. Two men possessing the necessary qualifications were put forward, the one Joseph, called Barsabbas and surnamed Justus, and the other Matthias. The lot fell upon Matthias, who was consequently elected in Judas' room (Acts 1:15–26). The descent of the Holy Spirit on the Day of Pentecost produced a spiritual transformation of the apostles, fitting them for the great work to which they were called—the evangelization of the world (Acts, ch. 2). To this they at once addressed themselves, Peter and John taking the lead (Acts, chs. 3 to 5; 9:32 to 12:18). James was also zealous, for he became so obnoxious to the Jewish authorities that they slew him with the sword (Acts 12:2). Paul was divinely chosen and called for the arduous work of preaching the gospel to the Gentiles (Acts 9:1–31; 22:5–16; 26:1–20). He had not itinerated with Jesus while our Lord was on the earth; but he possessed the apostolic qualification of having seen Jesus after his resurrection. On the way to Damascus Jesus appeared to him and spoke to him, changing his hostility into passionate devotion. He was able to say: "Am I not an apostle? have I not seen Jesus our Lord?" (I Cor. 9:1). Paul was a highly educated man, and able to address cultured audiences of the Gentiles at Athens, Rome, and elsewhere. Nor did his intellectual acquirements lead him away from his proper work. His labors were so abundant that the record of them fills about half the book called The Acts. Where the several apostles labored, how they lived, and how they died is in most cases known only by the doubtful evidence of tradition. One matter, however, and an all-important one, is placed by tradition on a secure foundation, namely, that no second Judas appeared among them; all were faithful to the end; and some at least, if not even the majority, sealed their testimony to Jesus with their blood.

2. The word is occasionally applied in a less restricted sense in the N.T. to men of apostolic gifts, graces, labors, and successes. It is so notably of Barnabas, who was sent forth with Paul (Acts 13:3; 14:4, 14). Similarly one still meets with such expressions, as Judson, the apostle of Burma. The name is applied also to Jesus, in Heb. 3:1.

Ap'pa·im (ăp'ȧ-ĭm) [nostrils; cf. Lat. *naso*]. A man of Judah, family of Hezron, house of Jerahmeel (I Chron. 2:30, 31).

Ap'phi·a (ăf'ĭ-ȧ). A Christian woman, probably the wife of Philemon (Philemon 2).

Ap'pi·i Fo'rum (ăp'ĭ-ī fō'rŭm) [Lat., market place of Appius]. A town in Italy, about 39½ miles from Rome, on the celebrated Appian Way from Rome to Capua. Paul was met at this town by Christians from Rome, when he was being brought a prisoner to the capital (Acts 28:15).

Ap'ple. A tree and its fruit (S. of Sol. 2:3; 8:5; Prov. 25:11), the rendering of the Hebrew *tappûaḥ*, which is akin to Arabic *tuffākh* (apple). The one referred to in the O.T. is probably our apple tree *Pyrus malus*, which Thomson found growing splendidly at Askelon in the Philistine country. The name may have included the quince as well. Tristram believes that the apricot is meant. The apple tree is enumerated with the vine, the fig tree, the pomegranate, and the palm tree, as one of the chief trees cultivated (Joel 1:12). There were several towns called Tappuah—in the lowland (Josh. 15:34), near Hebron (v. 53), and on the border of Ephraim and Manasseh (ch. 17:8), where doubtless many apple trees grew.

The apple of the eye refers to the eyeball or the pupil (Deut. 32:10; Ps. 17:8; Zech. 2:8). For apple of Sodom, see VINE.

Aq'ui·la (ăk'wĭ-lȧ) [Lat., eagle]. A Jew, born in Pontus, who with his wife, Priscilla, lived for a time at Rome, but had to leave that city when the Emperor Claudius commanded all its Jewish inhabitants to depart. He removed to Corinth, where he worked at his craft, tentmaking. Paul, who was of the same occupation, lodged with him at Corinth, and formed a high opinion of him and his wife (Acts 18:1–3). They were his fellow passengers from Corinth as far as Ephesus, on his way to Syria (Acts 18:18, 19). In the First Epistle to the Corinthians, they join Paul in sending salutations from Asia, i.e., probably from Ephesus (I Cor. 16:19). At Ephesus they met Apollos, and instructed him more completely in Christian doctrine (Acts 18:26). Afterward they seem to have returned to Rome, for Paul sends them salutations in his letter to that church (Rom. 16:3). But they must again have left it, for in the apostle's Second Epistle to Timothy, written from Rome, salutations are sent them anew (II Tim. 4:19).

Ar (är) [city]. One of the chief cities of Moab, more fully called Ar of Moab (Isa. 15:1). It lay on the n. boundary of Moab (Num. 21:15; Deut. 2:18), in the Arnon Valley (Num. 22:36; Deut. 2:36; Josh. 13:9). The Greeks connected the name with Ares, the god of war, the Roman Mars, and called it after him Areopolis. The Jews and others in the early Christian centuries named it Rabbath Moab; it is now known as Khirbet er-Rabbah, about 13¾ miles s. of the Arnon.

A'ra (ā'rȧ). A man of Asher (I Chron. 7:38).

A'rab (ā'răb) [ambuscade]. A village in the hill country of Judah (Josh. 15:52), modern er-Rabiyeh, a ruin e. of Dumah (Dōmeh), not far from 'Umm el-'Amad. See ARBITE.

Ar'a·bah (ăr'ȧ-bȧ) [arid region, desert]. 1. The geographical name of that great depression of the land in which are found the Sea of Galilee, the Jordan, and the Dead Sea (Josh. 11:2; 12:3, R.V.). The name apparently belonged also to the extension of the valley to the Gulf of 'Aḳabah at the head of the Red Sea (Deut. 2:8, R.V.). In A.V. the word is translated, being generally rendered by plain, but also by desert or wilderness (Ezek. 47:8; Amos 6:14).

2. The same as Beth-arabah (Josh. 18:22).

A·ra′bi·a (*á*-rā′bĭ-*á*) [Lat., from Gr. *Arabia*, from Heb. *'árāb*, probably waste, desert. Cf. Ethiopic *'abra*, to be dry, waste, and Arab. *'arab*, Arab. See also ARABAH]. The most westerly of the 3 great peninsulas in s. Asia. Arabia, the largest peninsula in the world, is bounded on the e. by the Persian Gulf and the Gulf of Oman, on the s. by the Indian Ocean, and on the w. by the Red Sea. Northward it projects triangularly and passes into the Syrian desert, which is bounded on 3 sides by the Fertile Crescent. The length of the w. coast line is about 1,800 miles, while the width of the land is about 600 miles from the Red Sea to the Persian Gulf. Its area is about ¼ that of Europe and ⅓ that of the United States. The n. central plateau is called Nejd; it is separated from the w. coast by a low-lying sandy region which is called the Hejaz, s. of which is Asir. Yemen occupies the s.w. corner of the peninsula. Hadramaut is on the s. coast. Oman constitutes the s.e. corner. On the e. coast are Kuweit and al-Ḥasa (ancient al-Baḥrayn). Arabia lies athwart the enormous belt of desert, commencing near the Atlantic Ocean with the Sahara, and extending through Chinese Turkestan, almost to the Pacific Ocean. Arabia is consequently largely desert. Among the Hebrews the name Arabian denoted the inhabitants of the desert portion (Jer. 3:2), whether near Babylonia or Ethiopia (Isa. 13:20; II Chron. 21:16), often as distinguished from the prominent settled tribes (Jer. 25:24; Ezek. 27:21). Eventually Arabia came to denote the entire peninsula. Ptolemy, the geographer of Alexandria who wrote in the 2d century A.D., divided the country into 3 regions: Arabia Felix, the Happy or Fertile; Arabia Petraea, the Stony; and Arabia Deserta, the Desert. Arabia Felix was of indefinite extent. Arabia Petraea, having for its capital Petra, was the district between the Red and the Dead Seas; and Arabia Deserta, the Syrian desert. The streams are few and small, none navigable. The geology is little known, but gold and precious stones were obtained. The feature of the botany is the prevalence of aromatic plants, some of them furnishing valuable spices. Of its birds the most noted is the ostrich; of its quadrupeds the camel, the Arab horse, and the wild ass.

Scholars regard Africa as the probable Semito-Hamitic home and Arabia as the cradle of the Semitic people and the center of their distribution. South Arabia had an ancient civilization, but the dates are somewhat uncertain. According to one chronology, the Minaean Kingdom flourished from c. 1300 to 650 B.C., and in its heyday embraced most of s. Arabia. The capital was at Ḳarnāw, modern Ma'īn; the names of 26 kings have been identified. The Sabaean period extends from 950 to 115 B.C. About 650 B.C. the Sabaeans succeeded to the power of the Minaeans. Their capital was at Ma'rib, about 60 miles e. of Ṣan'ā'. This is the most glorious era of s. Arabian history. Ḳatabān, with its capital at Tamna', and Ḥaḍramaut, with the capital at Shabwah, had their own kings during a part of this period. The 1st Ḥimyarite Kingdom extends from 115 B.C. to c. A.D. 300. During this period s. Arabian colonists laid the basis of the Abyssinian Kingdom and civilization. The 2d Ḥimyarite Kingdom extends from A.D. 300 to 525. This was interrupted by a brief Abyssinian rule (c. 340–378). Both Judaism and Christianity were well established in s. Arabia. The last king of the Ḥimyarite dynasty was a Jew, who in 523 massacred the Christians. In consequence the Abyssinians invaded the land and remained in control (525–575). This great civilization finally disintegrated and decayed, and in 575 the region

became a Persian satrapy. In 628 the 5th Persian satrap embraced Islam. See SHEBA, I.

Arab tribes often came into contact with the Hebrews (Gen. 37:28, 36; Judg., chs. 6 to 8). Solomon bought from the Arabs gold, silver, and spices (II Chron. 9:14). Jehoshaphat received tribute from them in flocks of sheep and goats (II Chron. 17:11). In the reign of Jehoram, Arabs with other marauders plundered Jerusalem (II Chron. 21:16). They were afterward defeated by Uzziah (II Chron. 26:7). Isaiah and Jeremiah denounced judgments against their race (Isa. 21:13–17; Jer. 25:24), and both used the wandering Arab in their poetic illustrations (Isa. 13:20; Jer. 3:2). Arabs were hired allies of the Syrians against Judas Maccabaeus (I Macc. 5:39). There were Arabs (perhaps Jews from the Nabataean Kingdom) present on the Day of Pentecost (Acts 2:11), and Paul sojourned for a time in Arabia, before commencing his apostolic work (Gal. 1:17). The scantiness of water, the courage of the Arabs, and their wandering life, prevented even the greatest of the ancient empires from conquering Arabia and holding it in subjection. Both Judaism and Christianity had rooted themselves in Arabia when, in the 7th century of the Christian Era, Mohammed arose and founded Islam. Before his death (A.D. 632) his faith was well established throughout the peninsula, and in a century more the Arabs had built an empire extending from the Pyrenees across Spain and n. Africa to Transoxiana and Sind and the s. Punjab. See SELA and TADMOR.

A·ra′bi·an (*á*-rā′bĭ-*ăn*). One of the Arab race; a native or inhabitant of Arabia (II Chron. 17:11).

A′rad (ā′răd) [wild ass]. 1. A town on the border of the s. country and the wilderness of Judah (Num. 21:1; Josh. 12:14; Judg. 1:16). The site is marked by Tell 'Arād, on a barren-looking eminence 17 miles s. of Hebron. Its king fought against the Israelites when they were at Mount Hor and took some of them captive; but the Israelites roused themselves to new trust in God, and devastated the territory of the king, and eventually he himself or his successor was vanquished by Joshua (*ibid.*).

2. A Benjamite, descended through Beriah (I Chron. 8:15).

Ar′a·dus (ăr′á-dŭs). See ARVAD.

A′rah (ā′rá) [wayfarer, traveler]. 1. Founder of a family, members of which returned from Babylon with Zerubbabel (Ezra 2:5; Neh. 7:10).

2. An Asherite, a son of Ulla (I Chron. 7:39).

A′ram (ā′răm). 1. A person, or, collectively, the Aramaean people, descended from Shem, who inhabited the region known as Aram (Gen. 10:22, 23; I Chron. 1:17).

2. The plain occupied by the Aramaeans, extending from the Lebanon Mountains to beyond the Euphrates, and from the Taurus Mountains on the n. to Damascus and beyond on the s. The contact between the Hebrews and the Aramaeans goes back to the patriarchal period (Gen. 31:47), where is given the earliest citation of an Aramaic phrase. The maternal ancestry of Jacob's children is accordingly Aramaic, a tradition preserved in Deut. 26:5. About contemporaneously with the rise of the Hebrew monarchy appear the Aramaean states n. and e. of Canaan. Several districts were distinguished:

(1) A′RAM-NA′HA·RA′IM, i.e., Aram of the Rivers, referring either to the Euphrates and Tigris, or, more probably, to the Euphrates and Khabur. It is commonly believed that in this region Paddan-aram was situated (Gen. 28:5; 24:10). This is the Aram where the

patriarchs dwelt before they went to Canaan, where the ancient cities of Haran and Nisibis stood, where later Edessa, the noted seat of Syrian culture, arose; the Aram which the Hebrews speak of as, "Beyond the River" (II Sam. 10:16).

(2) A'RAM-DA·MAS'CUS. The Hebrews during almost, if not quite, the entire period of their kingdom, found Aramaeans in Damascus (II Sam. 8:5; I Kings 15:18). The city became eventually the center of Aramaean influence w. of the Euphrates, and waged intermittent warfare with the n. Israelites during almost their entire existence as a separate kingdom.

(3) A'RAM-ZO'BAH. In the days of Saul, David, and Solomon, another powerful Aramaean kingdom flourished w. of the Euphrates, namely the Kingdom of Zobah (I Sam. 14:47; II Sam. 8:3; cf. II Chron. 8:3), called Aram-Zobah by Hebrew writers (II Sam. 10:6). At one time its dominion extended as far as the borders of Hamath on the n.w. (I Chron. 18:3; II Sam. 8:10); it had Damascus to the s. or s.w., for one of its towns, Berothai, was situated between Hamath and Damascus (cf. II Sam. 8:5, 8 with Ezek. 47:16), and during this prosperous period probably exercised sway well toward the Euphrates on the e. and the Hauran on the s.

(4) A'RAM-MA'A·CAH lay e. of the Jordan within the contemplated bounds of Israel, hard by Mount Hermon (Josh. 12:5; 13:11). From the description of Abel, which belonged to the tribe of Naphtali, as "Abel [in the neighborhood] of Beth-maacah," it may be inferred that Maacah extended as far w. as the Jordan.

(5) GE'SHUR in Aram was a small kingdom not far from Maacah, and like it e. of the Jordan, near Mount Hermon, and within the territory allotted to Manasseh (Deut. 3:14; cf. II Sam. 15:8, R.V. marg., with ch. 13:37).

(6) A'RAM-BETH-RE'HOB (II Sam. 10:6). The location is uncertain. If identical with the place mentioned in Num. 13:21 and Judg. 18:28, it was near both Maacah and Dan.

3. A descendant of Asher (I Chron. 7:34).

4. A Greek form of Ram, the father of Amminadab (Matt. 1:3; Luke 3:33, R.V. marg.). See ARNI.

Ar'a·ma'ic (ăr'à-mā'ĭk) or the Ar'a·mae'an (ăr'à-mē'ăn) or Ar'a·me'an (ăr'à-mē'ăn) Lan'guage. A North Semitic language. Since this language was put into the mouth of the Chaldaeans (Dan. 2:4), it came to be called Chaldee, or Chaldaic. This inaccurate term has been discarded, since we now know that the Chaldaeans spoke Akkadian. The Greeks called Aram Syria (abbreviated from Assyria). Consequently the people are in the Bible often called Syrians and their language Syrian (Ezra 4:7) or "Syriack" (Dan. 2:4, A.V.). The term Syriac, however, is now restricted to the dialect of Edessa and its developments.

From the 14th century B.C. reference is found in the Assyro-Babylonian literature to the Arimi, or Aḫlamē, who as nomads wandered in the wilderness w. of Mesopotamia. For the early undivided Aramaic language we have: (a) monumental inscriptions from Syria and Asia Minor from c. 800 B.C. into the Persian period; (b) dockets, weights, etc., from Assyria and Babylonia from the 8th century to the 5th B.C.; (c) papyri, chiefly from one deposit at Elephantine in Upper Egypt, dating from 500–400 B.C.

The Aramaic ultimately divided into 2 groups, the Eastern and the Western. The former, occupying the Euphrates Valley, includes the Aramaic of the Babylonian Talmud; Mandaic, the language of the Mandaeans, a gnostic sect; and Syriac, the dialect of Edessa, which, with local variations, became the language of the Aramaic-speaking churches of Syria and Mesopotamia. For the dialects of Western Aramaic, we may make the following divisions (with the caution that the distinctions are often only chronological and literary): 1. Biblical Aramaic, found in Ezra 4:8 to 6:18; 7:12–26; Dan. 2:4b to 7:28; Jer. 10:11 (a gloss); Gen. 31:47 (a cited phrase of two words). 2. Post-Biblical Jewish Aramaic: (a) words and phrases in N.T., Josephus, etc.; (b) the Targums; (c) passages in the Mishnah, the Gemara, and the Midrashim; the Fast Calendar. 3. Samaritan Aramaic. 4. Nabataean of the century before and the century after Christ. 5. Palmyrene of Tadmor (Palmyra) of the 2d and 3d centuries A.D. 6. Christian Palestinian, going back possibly to the 5th century, contained in Biblical translations and Christian literature of Greek origin.

Aramaic was used by Laban (Gen. 31:47, R.V.); it is seen in the proper names Tabrimmon and Hazael (I Kings 15:18, R.V.; 19:15). It is found in inscriptions on weights as early as the time of Shalmaneser V and Sargon II, showing that it was used by traders at Nineveh. It became the international language of business and diplomacy (II Kings 18:26, R.V. marg.). With the rise of the Persian Empire we find its administration using Aramaic as the lingua franca over its Semitic territories from the e. to the upper end of Egypt. The official documents in The Book of Ezra appear in Aramaic. The Jews spoke the new language both in the Babylonian Diaspora and in Palestine, where the corruption of Hebrew was fast proceeding, as the Bible testifies (Neh. 13:23 seq.). The process went on apace, and the patent testimony is found in the Aramaic portions of the Books of Ezra and Daniel, as well as in the extensive Aramaic influence in the Hebrew language of the later Biblical literature. Aramaic became the vernacular of the Jews, while Hebrew was reserved for the synagogue and school, at the most surviving as a vehicle of intercourse in the speech of cultivated circles.

A'ram-Beth-re'hob (ā'răm-bĕth-rē'hŏb). See ARAM 2 (6).

Ar'a·mit'ess (ăr'à-mīt'ĕs). A woman of Aram (I Chron. 7:14).

A'ram-ma'a·cah (ā'răm-mā'à-kà). See ARAM 2 (4).

A'ram-na'ha·ra'im (ā'răm-nā'hà-rā'ĭm). See ARAM 2 (1).

A'ram-Zo'bah (ā'răm-zō'bà). See ARAM 2 (3).

A'ran (ā'răn) [mountain goat]. A descendant of Dishan or offshoot of that Horite tribe (Gen. 36:28; I Chron. 1:42).

Ar'a·rat (ăr'à-răt) [Heb. for Akkad. or Assyr: Uraṛṭu]. A mountainous country n. of Assyria, centering about the elevated plateau of the Araxes. In the time of Jeremiah it was the seat of a kingdom apparently adjacent to those of Minni and Ashkenaz (Jer. 51:27). When the sons of Sennacherib killed their father they escaped into the land of Ararat, which is Armenia (II Kings 19:37). On one of the mountains of Ararat the ark of Noah rested (Gen. 8:4). According to the Babylonian account of the Flood, the ark rested on Nizir, a mountain e. of Assyria. Traditions with respect to the resting place of the ark attach themselves to various mountains in w. Asia; but by Mount Ararat is now meant a noble mountain almost midway between the Black Sea and the Caspian, near the junction of Turkey, Armenia, and Iran (Persia). It has 2 peaks, one higher than the other. The loftier one rises 16,916 feet above the level of the ocean, more than 10,000 feet above the tableland on which it stands, and 3,000 above the line of perpetual snow. The ascent is so difficult and laborious that the Turks call Ararat Aghri Dagh, or the Painful Mountain. Its summit was long deemed inaccessible, but it was at length reached by Parrot in 1829, and in 1850 by Col. Khoelzko and his party of 60, while they were engaged on the trigonometrical survey of Trans-Caucasia.

Ar'a·rite (ăr'á-rīt). So R.V., following the present Hebrew text, once in II Sam. 23:33, where A.V. has Hararite as in the corresponding passage, I Chron. 11:35.

A·ra'thes (á-rā'thēz), in A.V. **Ar'i·a·ra'thes** (ăr'ĭ-á-rā'thēz). King of Cappadocia (163-130 B.C.), surnamed Philopator (I Macc. 15:22).

A·rau'nah (á-rô'ná). A Jebusite who possessed a threshing floor on Mount Moriah. David purchased the floor in order to erect there an altar to Jehovah that the plague then raging might be stayed (II Sam. 24:18-25; I Chron. 21:15-28). The place afterward became the site of Solomon's Temple (II Chron. 3:1). Araunah is called Ornan in Chronicles, Ornah in the Hebrew text of II Sam. 24:16, and yet differently in v. 18. It is difficult to determine which was the original form of the name.

Ar'ba (är'bá), in A.V. once **Ar'bah** (är'bá) [four]. Father or greatest man of Anak (Josh. 14:15; 15:13). He founded, or gave name to, Kiriath-arba, the city later known as Hebron, or else he derived his title from the town (Josh. 14:15; Judg. 1:10). See HEBRON 2.

Ar'ba·thite (är'bá-thīt). An inhabitant of Beth-arabah (II Sam. 23:31; I Chron. 11:32).

Ar·bat'ta (är-băt'á), in A.V. **Ar·bat'tis** (är-băt'ĭs). A locality near Galilee (I Macc. 5:23). The readings of the name vary greatly in the manuscripts, perhaps to be identified with Arubboth.

Ar·be'la (är-bē'lá). A place (I Macc. 9:2); according to Josephus, the well-known town of the name in Galilee (Jos. Antiq. xii. 11, 1), now Irbid. See BETH-ARBEL.

Ar'bite (är'bīt). A native of Arab, in the hill country of Judah (II Sam. 23:35; a variant reading is found in I Chron. 11:37).

Ar'che·la'us (är'kē-lā'ŭs) [Gr., leader of people, chief]. The elder of 2 sons whom Malthace, a Samaritan wife, bore to Herod the Great, the younger one being Antipas, afterward Herod the Tetrarch (Jos. Antiq. xvii. 1, 3). With his brother Antipas and his half brothers Herod and Philip, he received his education at Rome. While there Antipater, a half brother of his, falsely accused him and Philip of plotting to murder their common father; but Archelaus and Philip were acquitted, and the accuser was put to death (Jos. Antiq. xvi. 4, 3; xvii. 7, 1; War i. 31, 2 to 32, 7). Herod died immediately afterward, 4 B.C.; and when his will, which had been altered a few days previously, was opened, it was found that the greater part of the kingdom was left to Archelaus, though tetrarchies had been cut out of it for Antipas and Philip, and some cities reserved to Herod's sister Salome (Jos. Antiq. xvii. 8, 1). But at that time the Jewish kingdom stood to imperial Rome in the relation of a protected state. Archelaus therefore prudently abstained from ascending the throne till he had solicited permission from Augustus, the Roman emperor, and he resolved to start at once for the metropolis to urge his suit in person (Jos. Antiq. xvii. 8, 4). But before he could leave, an unhappy incident occurred. A number of people, who conceived that they had a grievance, wished it redressed by strong measures then and there. Their demand was

clearly premature, but they would take no denial; and when they could not have their way, they rioted at the passover, till, sorely against his will, for he wished to gain popularity, Archelaus had to put down the sedition by military force, and 3,000 people lost their lives. In consequence of this, a deputation of Jews was dispatched to Rome, to urge the emperor not to allow Archelaus to obtain the kingdom. His younger brother, Herod Antipas, also appeared as his rival, petitioning that he, in place of Archelaus, might be made king. The emperor confirmed Herod's will in its essential provisions. Archelaus obtained the larger portion of the kingdom, but only with the title of ethnarch, or ruler of a people, which was inferior to that of king (Jos. Antiq. xvii. 8, 1; 9, 7; 11, 5). His rival Antipas was given only a tetrarchy. Soon after this, Joseph and Mary returned with the Infant Jesus from Egypt. They might consider that the queller of the passover riot was not a man overtender of human life, and that it was only common prudence for them to turn aside to Galilee so as to keep out of his jurisdiction (Matt. 2:22). A parable of our Lord himself seems to refer to the circumstances attending the accession of Archelaus. "A certain nobleman," we read, "went into a far country, to receive for himself a kingdom, and to return" (Luke 19:12). "But his citizens hated him, and sent an ambassage after him, saying, We will not have this man to reign over us" (Luke 19:14). If the reference is really to Archelaus, then another verse may be history rather than parable. "But these mine enemies, that would not that I should reign over them, bring hither, and slay them before me" (Luke 19:27). Quite in keeping with this view, Josephus says that Archelaus used not only the Jews but the Samaritans barbarously, out of resentment for their old quarrels with him. Both nationalities, therefore, sent embassies to Rome to complain of his cruelty. They succeeded in their object. In the 9th year of his government, about A.D. 6, he was deposed, and banished to Vienne, in Gaul, while his wealth was put into the emperor's treasury (Jos. War ii. 7, 3).

Ar'che·vites (är'kē-vīts). Babylonians, inhabitants of Erech. A body of them were settled by Asnapper in Samaria after the ten tribes had been carried captive (Ezra 4:9).

Ar'chi (är'kī). See ARCHITE.

Ar·chip'pus (är-kĭp'ŭs) [Gr., master of the horse]. A Christian at Colossae who approved himself as a champion of the gospel, was intimate with Philemon, and an office-bearer in the church (Col. 4:17; Philemon 2).

Ar'chite (är'kīt), in A.V. once (Josh. 16:2) **Ar'chi**, the Hebrew form. A member of a Canaanite tribe of the same name, or else a native or inhabitant of a village known as Erech. The border of the Archites was on the boundary between Ephraim and Benjamin, w. of Beth-el, where is the modern 'Ain 'Arîk (Josh. 16:2). Hushai, David's faithful counselor, was an Archite (II Sam. 15:32).

Arc·tu'rus (ärk-tū'rŭs) [Lat., from Gr., the Bear ward]. A large and bright star, which the Greeks and Romans called by this name, meaning the keeper of the Bear, because in its course through the heavens it always kept behind the tail of Ursa Major, or the Great Bear. In the A.V. of Job 9:9 and 38:32 it is the translation of the Hebrew 'āsh or 'ayish. But 'āsh is not Arcturus, the Bear keeper, but probably the Bear itself, and is so rendered in the R.V.

Ard (ärd) [hump, humpbacked; cf. Aram. 'ardā, truffle]. A son of Bela and grandson of Benjamin (Gen. 46:21; cf. Num. 26:38, 41 with 40). He gave name to a family of the tribe of Benjamin (ibid.). The person called

Addar in I Chron. 8:3 is probably he. The variation in form is probably due to a copyist's transposition of two letters very similar in Hebrew, or to his confusion of Hebrew *daleth* and *resh*.

Ar'don (är'dŏn) [humpbacked; see ARD]. A man of Judah, family of Hezron, house of Caleb (I Chron. 2:18).

A·re'li (*à*-rē'lī). A son of Gad, and founder of a family (Gen. 46:16; Num. 26:17).

Ar'e·op'a·gite (är'ē-ŏp'*à*-jīt). A judge of the court of Areopagus (Acts 17:34).

Ar'e·op'a·gus (är'ē-ŏp'*à*-gŭs) [Gr., hill of Ares]. 1. One of the lower hills on the w. of the Acropolis of Athens. It was consecrated to Ares, the god of war. It is a narrow, naked

The Areopagus (Mars' Hill) with the Acropolis Beyond

ridge of limestone rock, running from n.w. to s.e., and terminating abruptly over against the Acropolis, or citadel of Athens. This s.e. end was crowned by several altars; and rises 50 or 60 feet above the valley separating it from the Acropolis, which is much the higher of the 2 hills. Ares corresponds to the Roman Mars, and Areopagus is the same as Mars' Hill.

2. The supreme court of Athens, which met on the hill called Areopagus to pass sentence. It was constituted of venerable and eminent citizens. The seats of the judges and others connected with the court are still seen hewn in the rock; and toward the s.w. there is a flight of steps descending to the market place. It was before the Areopagus that Paul pleaded his own cause and that of Christianity, and the philosophic character of his discourse arose from his vivid consciousness that he was addressing some of the most intellectual men in the most intellectual city in the world.

During judicial trial the court sat in the Stoa Basileios, its official chamber, in the Agora (market place), and adjourned to the hill to pass formal sentence. It has been argued that Paul made his defense in the chamber of justice and not on the hill, before the Areopagus and not on the Areopagus (Curtius). Or perhaps Paul appeared before the council of the Areopagus for the purpose of having his qualifications examined by a court which apparently had the power to admit foreign lecturers (Ramsay). The narrative in The Acts militates against the supposition that Paul's discourse was a formal defense in a trial before the court (Conybeare and Howson). It appears more probable that Paul addressed an informal gathering of philosophers on the Areopagus (Acts 17:16 *seq.*).

Ar'e·tas (är'ē-tăs) [Gr., from Nabataean Arab. *Ḥārithath; cf.* Arab. *Ḥārith*]. More than one king of Arabia Petraea, during the time that it was occupied by the Nabataean Arabs, bore this name. Among others, 1. A contemporary of the high priest Jason, about 170 B.C (II Macc. 5:8).

2. Aretas IV (9 B.C.–A.D. 40), father-in-law of Herod the Tetrarch. When Herod prepared to divorce his daughter in order to marry Herodias, Aretas declared war against Herod and totally defeated his army in A.D. 36. The Romans took Herod's part, and Vitellius was dispatched to chastise Aretas, but the death of the Emperor Tiberius put an end to the expedition (Jos. *Antiq.* xviii. 5, 1–3). It was about A.D. 39 or 40, during the reign of Caligula, or perhaps in 36, that Aretas for a brief period held Damascus (II Cor. 11:32). See NABATAEANS, SELA.

A·re'us (*à*-rē'ŭs). See ARIUS.

Ar'gob (är'gŏb) [region of clods, glebe]. 1. A region of Bashan, included within the dominions of Og, and bordering on Geshur and Maacah. It contained 60 fenced cities, besides the nomad encampments taken by Jair (Deut. 3:4, 13, 14; Josh. 13:30; I Kings 4:13); see HAVVOTH-JAIR. The Targum indicates the district of Trachonitis, but this region lies too far to the e. Josephus identifies a portion of it with Gaulonitis (cf. Jos. *Antiq.* 8:2, 3 with I Kings 4:13). The precise location, except that it lay in Bashan, is uncertain.

2. A man assassinated along with Pekahiah, king of Israel, by Pekah, who aspired to the throne (II Kings 15:25).

Ar'i·a·ra'thes (är'ĭ-*à*-rā'thēz). See ARATHES.

A·rid'a·i (*à*-rĭd'*à*-ī). A son of Haman (Esth. 9:9).

A·rid'a·tha (*à*-rĭd'*à*-thá). A son of Haman (Esth. 9:8).

A·ri'eh (*à*-rī'ĕ) [lion]. A man assassinated along with King Pekahiah, Argob, and others, by Pekah, the son of Remaliah (II Kings 15:25).

A'ri·el (âr'ĭ-ĕl) [Heb. *'ărī'ēl:* ety. uncertain; generally explained as (1) lion of God; (2) altar hearth. Probably from Akkad. *Arallu* (*Arallū*), which has a double sense of "underworld" and "mountain of the gods," the cosmic mountain in which according to an Assyrian text the gods were born and reared. Heb. *har'ēl* means "mountain of God" and is thus a popular ety. of the Akkad. loan word]. 1. A Moabite (II Sam. 23:20, R.V.).

2. An ominous name applied to Jerusalem (Isa. 29:1, 2, 7). The same word occurs 3 times in Ezek. 43:15, 16, first as *har'ēl* and in the other 2 instances as *'ărī'ēl;* each of these 3 examples is preceded by the definite article. The Targum defines this word in both Isaiah and Ezekiel as altar, and from the context in Isaiah this seems to be the preferable explanation of the word as applied to the city. R.V. translates the last 2 cases of the word in Ezekiel as altar hearth. Cf. Isa. 29:1, R.V. marg.

3. A chief of the Jews who were with Ezra at the River Ahava (Ezra 8:16).

Ar'i·ma·thae'a (är'ĭ-m*à*-thē'*à*) [Lat. from Gr. modification of Ramah]. The town from which the councilor Joseph came, who obtained permission of Pilate to take away the body of Jesus and give it honorable interment in his own new sepulcher (Matt. 27:57–60; Mark 15:43; Luke 23:51–53; John 19:38). Arimathaea is the Greek form of Ramah, but which town of that name is intended is uncertain. Ramleh near Lydda is out of the question; for it was not built until the beginning of the 8th century A.D. The name occurs in I Macc. 11:34 (cf. Jos. *Antiq.* xiii. 4, 9) as belonging at that period to Samaria.

Ar'i·och (är'ĭ-ŏk) [perhaps Sumerian *êriaku*, servant of the moon-god]. 1. King of Ellasar, who was confederate with Chedorlaomer on his invasion of the Jordan Valley (Gen. 14:1, 9). Some scholars have identified this king with one of the sons of Kudur-Mabuk, kings of Larsa: Warad-Sin (c. 1836–1824 B.C.) or Rim-Sin (c. 1824–1763 B.C.). The chronology of the period has not been definitely established. See BABYLONIA.

2. Captain of the king's guard at Babylon under Nebuchadnezzar (Dan. 2:14, 15). It pertained to the office to execute sentences of death (Dan. 2:24).

A·ris'a·i (à-rĭs'à-ī). A son of Haman (Esth. 9:9).

Ar'is·tar'chus (är'ĭs-tär'kŭs) [Gr., best ruling]. A Macedonian of Thessalonica who was with Paul at Ephesus, and in the riot was seized by the mob and probably dragged into the theater; but he seems not to have been seriously injured (Acts 19:29). On the apostle's return from Greece, whither he had gone from Ephesus, Aristarchus accompanied him from Troas to Asia (Acts 20:4, 6). He was subsequently his fellow voyager to Rome (Acts 27:2; cf. Philemon 24), as also at one time his fellow prisoner (Col. 4:10).

A·ris'to·bu'lus (à-rĭs'tô-bū'lŭs) [Gr., best advising]. 1. A celebrated Jewish philosopher at Alexandria (II Macc. 1:10b).

2. A Christian, to whose household at Rome Paul sent salutations (Rom. 16:10).

A·ri'us (à-rī'ŭs), in A.V. **A·re'us.** King of Sparta (I Macc. 12:20; Jos. *Antiq.* xiii. 5, 8), probably the first of the name, who reigned from 309 to 265 B.C.

Ark. A chest, box, or vessel of similar shape. 1. Noah's ark was the rude vessel which Noah was divinely ordered to construct, and in which he floated about when the Deluge was on the earth. If the cubit, in terms of which the dimensions of the ark are stated, was the ordinary cubit of 18 inches, then the length of the ark was 450 feet, the breadth 75 feet, and the height 45 feet. The ark was made of gopher, probably cypress, wood, and rendered watertight by being daubed inside and outside with bitumen. It had lower, 2d and 3d stories. A door in the side afforded ingress and egress. A window, probably a cubit in height, extended, with slight interruptions, all around the vessel. A rooflike covering protected the inmates from rain and sun (Gen. 6:14 to 8:19). The ark was designed for the accommodation of Noah, his family, and the animals which were selected to be preserved.

2. The infant Moses' ark, made for his reception when he was exposed upon the Nile, was a basket composed of papyrus leaves or stems, or both, plaited together, and rendered watertight by a coat of bitumen (Ex. 2:3–6).

3. The Ark of the Covenant or Testimony was the central object of the tabernacle. It was a chest 2½ cubits long, 1½ cubits broad, and the same in depth; made of acacia wood, and overlaid within and without with pure gold. A rim or molding of gold encircled it at the top. At the bottom were 2 golden rings on each side, through which poles of acacia wood overlaid with gold were put for the purpose of carrying the Ark about. It was covered by a lid of solid gold which was called the mercy seat. Two cherubim of gold stood on this cover, of one piece with it, one at each end, spreading their wings on high so as to overshadow it, and facing each other, but looking down toward the mercy seat. They were symbols of the presence and unapproachableness of Jehovah who, as King of Israel in the midst of his people, dwelt between the cherubim, uttered his voice from between them, and met the representative of his peo-

ple there (Ex. 25:10 *seq.*; 30:6; Num. 7:89; I Sam. 4:4). It was made specially as a receptacle for the testimony, which was written on the tables of stone (Ex. 25:21; 31:18; Deut. 10:3, 5), and it was placed in the Holy of Holies (Ex. 26:34). Afterward a pot of manna, Aaron's rod that blossomed, and the book of the Law were put beside the Ark (Ex. 16:34; Num. 17:10; Deut. 31:26; Heb. 9:4), but apparently were removed during the times of confusion (I Kings 8:9). The Ark was placed in charge of the Kohathite Levites (Num. 3:29–31; 4:4–15). The priests, who were Levites and of the family of Kohath, bore it themselves on occasions of special solemnity (Josh. 3:3; 6:6; 8:33; II Sam. 15:24, 29; I Kings 8:3). It went before the Israelites when they left Mount Sinai (Num. 10:33): either in the van or, as the expression may denote, like a king in the midst of his troops, leading and directing the march, while the priests who accompanied it signaled the orders of Jehovah (Num. 10:5, 6, 8; and for the phraseology Ex. 32:1; Deut. 3:28; 10:11; 31:3b). It went in advance of the people into the Jordan and halted, where the stream ceased to flow, until the tribes had done crossing to the other side (Josh. 4:9–11). It was carried in the midst of the host for 7 days around Jericho before the walls of the city fell down (Josh. 6:1–20). From Gilgal by Jericho it was removed to Shiloh (I Sam. 3:3). Having been taken in Eli's time to the field of battle, as a talisman which was expected to work wonders in the contest with the Philistines, it was captured by the enemy (I Sam., ch. 4), but was soon afterward sent back into the Hebrew territory (I Sam. 5:1 to 6:11). It was successively at Beth-shemesh, where the inhabitants looked into it and were punished (I Sam. 6:12–20; see BETH-SHEMESH); at Kiriath-jearim (I Sam. 7:1, 2); and at Perezuzzah, where Uzzah was struck dead for touching it (II Sam. 6:1–11; I Chron. 13:1–14; cf. Num. 4:15, 19, 20). See OBED-EDOM. Thence it was taken by David to Jerusalem (II Sam. 6:12–23), being now borne by men (v. 13) who, if the custom in Israel before and during the reign of David was followed, were priests or priests assisted by other Levites (Josh. 3:3, 13; 4:9; 6:4, 6; II Sam. 15:24, 25, 29), as the Chronicler states (I Chron. 15:1–15). At Jerusalem it was put in a temporary tabernacle erected for it by David (II Sam. 6:17; 7:1, 2; I Chron. 16:1, 4–6, 37–43). Later it was placed in the Holy of Holies in Solomon's Temple (I Kings 8:1–9). Josiah refers to it (II Chron. 35:3), but the meaning is obscure. It disappeared when Jerusalem was destroyed by Nebuchadnezzar, and has not been reported since.

Sacred chests were in use among other peoples of antiquity. They were employed by the Greeks and Egyptians, and served as receptacles for the idol, or for symbols of the deities, or for other sacred objects.

Ar'kit (är'kīt). A tribe descended from Canaan (Gen. 10:17; I Chron. 1:15). Modern 'Arka is about 12 miles n. of Tripolis in Syria. Arkantu mentioned by Thutmose III (1482–1450 B.C.) may be the same place. It is called Irkata in the Amarna tablets. It was captured by Tiglath-pileser III in 738 B.C.

Ar'ma·ged'don (är'má-gĕd'ŭn). See HAR-MAGEDON.

Ar·me'ni·a (är-mē'nĭ-á). See ARARAT.

Arm'let. An ornament like a bracelet, but surrounding the arm higher up than the wrist (Ex. 35:22, R.V.). There were armlets among the spoil of the Midianites (Num. 31:50, R.V.). In parts of the East an armlet, generally studded with jewels, is worn by kings as one of the insignia of royal authority (cf. II Sam. 1:10).

Ar·mo'ni (är-mō'nī) [pertaining to the palace]. One of Saul's sons by his concubine Rizpah. He was slain by the Gibeonites to satisfy justice (II Sam. 21:8–11).

Ar'mor. Covering worn to protect the person against offensive weapons (Eph. 6:11). It consisted of: 1. The shield. Shields were used by all nations of antiquity. The Israelites employed a larger and a smaller kind (I Kings 10:16, 17). The larger kind, translated shield, buckler, target, belonged to the heavy armed spearmen and lancers (I Chron. 12:8, 24, 34; II Chron. 14:8). The smaller shield, rendered shield or buckler, was carried by archers (I Chron. 5:18; II Chron. 14:8). Shields were of various shapes—round, oval, and oblong. They were commonly made of several thicknesses of leather or of wood covered with leather (cf. Ezek. 39:9), which was oiled to keep it glossy and pliable, and to protect it against the wet (Isa. 21:5). They were sometimes covered with brass (Jos. *Antiq.* xiii. 12, 5), or made entirely of brass (I Kings 14:27, probably), or even of beaten gold (I Kings 10:17; II Chron. 9:16; I Macc. 6:2, 39). Bronze shields were often 2 or 3 feet in diameter. Sometimes a shield-bearer accompanied a warrior into battle (I Sam. 17:7). 2. Helmets were made of leather and eventually of

Left, Assyrian Soldier, from an Assyrian Relief
Right, Sumerian Soldier, from a Battle Standard Found at Ur

iron and brass (I Macc. 6:35). They were known to Egyptians, Philistines, Assyrians, Babylonians, Persians (I Sam. 17:5; Jer. 46:4; Ezek. 23:23, 24; 27:10). Helmets of brass were in occasional use among the Israelites and Philistines as early as the time of Saul (I Sam. 17:5, 38). Uzziah armed his troops with helmets and coats of mail (II Chron. 26:14). 3. The breastplate or properly coat of mail, as it is sometimes rendered, covered the breast, back, and shoulders. It was made of leather, quilted cloth, linen (Herod. iii. 47), brass, or iron (I Sam. 17:5; Rev. 9:9), and even gold (I Macc. 6:2). There were joints in it or between it and the adjacent armor (I Kings 22:34). Scale-armor coats were worn by Goliath, and chain coats by the soldiers of Antiochus Eupator (I Sam. 17:5, Heb.; I Macc. 6:35, Gr.). 4. Greaves, consisting of thin plates of metal, were occasionally worn to protect the front of the leg below the knee (I Sam. 17:6); and sometimes, 5. Laced boots set with nails (Isa. 9:5, R.V. marg.). For offensive weapons, see the several articles.

Ar'my. The army of Israel consisted originally of infantry only (Num. 11:21; I Sam. 4:10; 15:4), composed of spearmen, slingers, and archers. It included all the able-bodied

men of the nation—all the males from 20 years old and upward, able to go forth to war, being enrolled for service (Num., ch. 1; II Sam. 24:9). The Levites were not numbered in the wilderness for military service; but they might bear arms, if the occasion arose (Num. 1:48–50; cf. I Chron. 12:26–28 with v. 23). The number of men reported as participating in various battles is sufficiently large to include the greater part of the adult male population of the region. For military operations of no great magnitude, each tribe furnished its quota of warriors (Num. 31:4; Josh. 7:3; Judg. 20:10); but inroads of the enemy were naturally met by all the manly spirits seizing their weapons to defend their firesides. In time of national peril messengers were sent throughout all the coasts of Israel to summon the men of war by the sound of the trumpet, by proclamation, or by symbolic act, to come to the rescue (Judg. 6:34, 35; 19:29; I Sam. 11:7).

The militia of Israel was organized on the basis of the political divisions. The unit, both military and political, was the thousand, a term apparently interchangeable with father's house, family, or clan (Ex. 12:37; Num. 1:2, 3, 16, 46; Judg. 6:15; I Sam. 10:19, 21; 17:18). A chieftain of Judah was accordingly often an *'alluph* or chiliarch (Zech. 9:7; 12:5), as were the chiefs of Edom (Gen., ch. 36; Ex. 15:15). For both political and military purposes the thousands were divided into hundreds (Ex. 18:25; Num. 31:14, 48; II Sam. 18:1; II Chron. 25:5), and fifties (Ex. 18:25; I Sam. 8:12; II Kings 1:9; cf. Num. 1:25), and tens (Ex. 18:25; cf. Num. 26:7). The actual number composing a father's house or thousand necessarily varied constantly, according to natural law; and it is probable that the "thousand" was usually very much smaller than the technical name indicates (cf. the varying numbers in legion and regiment). Each of these divisions was under its own officer (Num. 31:14; Judg. 20:10; I Sam. 8:12; II Kings 1:9; 11:4; II Chron. 25:5). The commander in chief and the officers formed a council of war (I Chron. 13:1; cf. II Kings 9:5, 13).

The first traces of a standing army in Israel are found in the reign of Saul. He retained 3,000 men of all Israel to hold the Philistines in check (I Sam. 13:2), and impressed any men of marked valor whom he saw (I Sam. 14:52). David increased the army, and organized it into 12 divisions of 24,000 footmen each (I Chron., ch. 27), and Solomon added a large force of chariots and horsemen, which he distributed in the cities throughout his kingdom (I Kings 9:19; 10:26; cf. ch. 4:26; II Chron. 9:25). The successors of these 3 kings of all Israel continued to bestow attention on the organization and equipment of the host, as Jehoshaphat (II Chron. 17:13–19), Amaziah (II Chron. 25:5, 6), Uzziah (II Chron. 26:11–15), Judas Maccabaeus (I Macc. 3:55). See WAR.

Ar'nan (är'năn) [Arab., quick, lively]. Founder of a family, presumably of the lineage of David (I Chron. 3:21).

Ar'ni (är'nī). Ram, the father of Amminadab (Luke 3:33, R.V.; cf. Ruth 4:19). The Hebrew name Ram generally appears in the LXX as Arran or Aram; Arni, Arnei, which is found in the better texts of Luke, may be a mere corruption.

Ar'non (är'nŏn) [rushing, roaring stream]. A river which anciently formed the boundary between the Amorite country on the n. and that of the Moabites on the s. (Num. 21:13, 26), and at a later period between the tribe of Reuben on the n. and again Moab on the s. (Deut. 3:8, 16; Josh. 13:16). It had fords (Isa. 16:2). Its valley is the deep chasm of the wadi el-Mōjib. The stream is perennial, formed by the junction of 3 smaller tributaries, and falls into the Dead Sea. It is fringed by oleanders, the vegetation of its banks is exuberant, and its waters are full of fish.

A'rod (ā'rŏd) or **Ar'o·di** (är'ō-dī) [humpbacked ; see ARD]. A son of Gad, and founder of a family (Gen. 46 :16 ; Num. 26 :17).

A·ro'er (à-rō'ēr) [naked, nakedness ; or juniper thicket]. 1. A town on the right or n. bank of the river Arnon. It was the s. point of the Amorite kingdom ruled by Sihon (Deut. 2 :36 ; Josh. 12 :2 ; Judg. 11 :26), and afterward of the tribe of Reuben (Josh. 13 :16) ; but it was fortified and occupied by Gadites (Num. 32 :34). It was fortified by Mesha, king of Moab (*Moabite Stone*, 26 ; see MOABITE STONE). It fell into the hands of Hazael, king of Syria (II Kings 10 :33 ; I Chron. 5 :8). In the time of Jeremiah it belonged to Moab (Jer. 48 :19). It is now called 'Arā'ir, and is a desolate heap just s. of Dibon and a little e. of the Roman road which runs n. and s. through Moab.

2. A city in Gilead on the frontier of Gad ; before, that is, e. of, Rabbah, doubtless Rabbath Ammon (Josh. 13 :25 ; and perhaps Judg. 11 :33). It may be sought to the n.w. of 'Ammān at 'Arjān or about 4¼ miles to the e. at Khirbet eṣ-Ṣafra.

3. A village of Judah, to which David sent spoil after his victory over the Amalekites who had pillaged Ziklag (I Sam. 30 :28). Its ruins lie in the wadi 'Ar'āra, 12 miles s.e. of Beersheba. See ADADAH.

If Aroer in Isa. 17 :2 is a proper and not a common noun meaning nakedness, ruin, the phrase in which it stands may be rendered, "The cities of Aroer," and interpreted as dependencies of the Gadite Aroer ; or, "The cities Aroer," the 2 Aroers e. of the Jordan being used representatively for all the cities of the region. The reading of the LXX (Damascus), deserted forever, suggests that the word is not to be taken as a proper noun.

A·ro'er·ite (à-rō'ēr-īt). A native or inhabitant of Aroer (I Chron. 11 :44, where the reference is probably to Aroer 3).

Ar·pach'shad (är-păk'shăd), in A.V. **Ar·phax'ad**. A son of Shem (Gen. 10 :22, 24 ; I Chron. 1 :17, 18, both R.V.). He was a remote ancestor of Abraham, was born 2 years after the Flood, at the age of 35 begat Shelah, and died 403 years afterward, at the age of 438 (Gen. 11 :10–13). Arpachshad is not necessarily a person. The structure of these genealogical registers, as is apparent, is such that the name may be that of a tribe or land, of which the people were descended from that son of Shem born 2 years after the Flood. Arpachshad was long identified with the mountainous country on the upper Zab n. and n.e. of Nineveh, called by the Greek geographers Arrapachitis. Some scholars consider the word as a compound : *Arpach* (=Arrapachitis)+ *Chesed* (Chaldea).

Ar'pad (är'păd), in A.V. twice **Ar'phad** (är'făd). A city, generally coupled in the O.T. with Hamath, from which, consequently, it was not far distant (II Kings 18 :34 ; 19 :13 ; Isa. 10 :9 ; Jer. 49 :23). It has been placed at Tell Erfād, 13 miles n. of Aleppo. It was a place of importance, and was subjected to repeated visitations from the Assyrians. It saw the army of Adad-nirari in 806 B.C., and of Ashurnirari in 754 ; it was besieged and taken by Tiglath-pileser (742–740) ; and an uprising of cities which included Arpad was suppressed by Sargon in 720.

Ar·phax'ad (är-făk'săd). See ARPACHSHAD.

Ar'sa·ces (är'sà-sēz). King of Persia and Media (I Macc. 14 :2, 3 ; 15 :22), from 174 to 136 B.C. He was the 6th of the name, but is better known as Mithridates I of Parthia. His rule extended far beyond the bounds of Media and Persia. He conquered Asia from the Hindu Kush to the Euphrates and raised the Parthian kingdom to an empire.

Ar'tax·erx'es (är'tăk-sûrk'sēz) [Old Persian *Artaxšathra*, he who gives the lordship to holy law]. The 3d son of Xerxes and his successor on the Persian throne, 465 B.C. He is called Longimanus (Longhanded). This epithet is generally interpreted literally, but some scholars take it figuratively as meaning only that Artaxerxes had a widely extended dominion. He was led to forbid building at Jerusalem (Ezra 4 :7), but afterward permitted it (ch. 6 :14). In the 7th year of his reign (458 B.C.) Artaxerxes let Ezra lead a great multitude of exiles back to Jerusalem (Ezra 7 :1, 11, 12, 21 ; 8 :1). In the 20th year of his reign (445 B.C.) he permitted Nehemiah to make his 1st journey to the Jewish capital, and rebuild the walls of the city (Neh. 2 :1, etc.). In the 32d year of his reign (433 B.C.) he allowed Nehemiah, who had returned for a little to Persia, to revisit Jerusalem, and become governor of the restored city and the adjacent country (Neh. 13 :6). Artaxerxes died in the year 424 B.C.

Ar'te·mas (är'tĕ-măs) [Gr., contraction of Artemidōros, gift of Artemis]. A companion whom Paul thought of sending on an errand to Titus (Titus 3 :12).

Ar'te·mis (är'tĕ-mĭs). The Greek goddess of hunting, corresponding to the Roman Diana (Acts 19 :24, R.V. marg.) ; see DIANA.

A·rub'both (à-rŭb'ŏth), in A.V. **A·ru'both** (à-rōō'bŏth) [the lattices]. A place mentioned (I Kings 4 :10) in connection with Socoh and Hepher ; probably to be identified with 'Arrābeh near Dothan. Alt places it to the n.w. in the region of Tell el-Asāwar.

A·ru'mah (à-rōō'má) [perhaps, a height]. A village near Shechem, once the residence of Abimelech (Judg. 9 :41). It has been supposed to be identical with Rumah (II Kings 23 :36), and has been placed doubtfully at el-'Ormeh, 6 miles s.e. of Shechem.

Ar'vad (är'văd) [perhaps, wandering]. The most n. of the Phoenician cities, modern Ruwād. In Ezekiel's time, it furnished mariners and valiant defenders of the stronghold of Tyre (Ezek. 27 :8, 11). It is the island of Aradus (I Macc. 15 :23), about 2 miles from the mainland, and 30 miles n. of Tripolis and 125 miles n. of Tyre.

Ar'vad·ite (är'văd-īt). One of the inhabitants of Arvad. They were reckoned to Canaan (Gen. 10 :18 ; I Chron. 1 :16).

Ar'za (är'zà) [delight]. The steward of King Elah's house in Tirzah (I Kings 16 :9).

A'sa (ā'sà) [physician, or perhaps a contraction for Jehovah has healed ; cf. Arab. *'asā*, to heal ; Aram. *'āsā, 'assā*, physician]. 1. A Levite, son of Elkanah who lived in a village of the Netophathites (I Chron. 9 :16).

2. A king of Judah, who ascended the throne in the twentieth year of Jeroboam, king of Israel. He was son of Abijam and grandson of Rehoboam. His mother (actually his grandmother) was Maacah, daughter of Absalom (I Kings 15 :9–10, cf. v. 2). His reign began with 10 years of peace (II Chron. 14 :1). He took away the male prostitutes out of the land, abolished the idols of his predecessors, and removed his grandmother from her position of queen mother, because she had made an abominable image for an Asherah (I Kings 15 :9–13 ; cf. ch. 14 :22–24 ; II Chron. 14 :1–5 ; 15 :16). He also destroyed the strange altars, the high places, and the sun images throughout Judah (II Chron.

14:3–5) as fully as he was able (cf. I Kings 22:46; II Chron. 19:4); but, though his own heart was perfect with Jehovah, the people still occasionally sacrificed to Jehovah on high places (I Kings 15:14; II Chron. 15:17). His kingdom was invaded by the Ethiopian Zerah, at the head of an enormous host of Africans, but by the help of Jehovah he defeated them, and drove them from the land (II Chron. 14:9–15). In the 15th year of his reign, encouraged by the Prophet Azariah, he completed the religious reformation, restored the altar of burnt offering at the Temple, and induced the people to renew the covenant with Jehovah (II Chron. 15:1–15). In the 36th (probably, 16th) year of his reign (see CHRONOLOGY, IV), Baasha, king of Israel, invaded Benjamin and fortified Ramah on the main road from Jerusalem to the n. Asa, finding himself too weak to capture Ramah and reopen the road, took the Temple treasures, and hired Ben-hadad, king of Damascus, to attack Baasha. Ben-hadad invaded the n. portion of the Israelite kingdom, compelling Baasha to withdraw from Ramah. Asa took the building materials which Baasha had gathered at Ramah and fortified Geba and Mizpah. The Prophet Hanani reproved the king for his worldly policy, after his experience of God's help at the time of the Ethiopian invasion. Asa resented the interference of the prophet, and put him in prison (I Kings 15:16–22; II Chron. 16:1–10). In the 39th year of his reign he became diseased in his feet. In his distress he sought help from the physicians, but not from Jehovah (I Kings 15:23; II Chron. 16:12). In his latter days he was not so true to Jehovah as in his earlier life. He died in the 41st year of his reign, and was buried with royal honors in a sepulcher which he had made for himself in the city of David.

As'a·hel (ăs'ȧ-hĕl) [God has made]. 1. Son of David's sister Zeruiah, and brother of Joab and Abishai (I Chron. 2:16); noted for valor and fleetness (II Sam. 2:18; 23:24). He was in the army of David; and in the rout of Ishbosheth's troops at Gibeon, he pursued Abner, their commander, in the desire to kill him. Abner, after vainly warning him to desist, in self-defense gave him a mortal thrust (II Sam. 2:12–23). His death occurred before David became king of all Israel; yet when David organized the army in 12 divisions, the 4th was assigned to Asahel and Zebadiah his son after him (I Chron. 27:7). The form of the statement is peculiar. It may denote that the command of the division for the 4th month was vested in the house of Asahel, being exercised by his son who was now the head of the house. Perhaps the new organization perpetuated an earlier arrangement, only on a larger scale.
2. One of the Levites employed by Jehoshaphat to teach the people the Law (II Chron. 17:8).
3. An overseer of the Temple in the reign of Hezekiah (II Chron. 31:13).
4. Father of a certain Jonathan (Ezra 10:15).

A·sa'iah (ȧ-sā'yȧ), in A.V. twice **As'a·hi'ah** (ăs'ȧ-hī'ȧ) (II Kings 22:12, 14) [Jehovah has made]. 1. A Simeonite prince (I Chron. 4:36).
2. A Levite, head of the family of Merari in David's time (I Chron. 6:30; 15:6, 11).
3. A man of Judah, son of Baruch, and head of the family of Shelah (Shilonites) at the time of the return from the Captivity (I Chron. 9:5). He was known also by the synonymous name Maaseiah (Neh. 11:5).
4. An officer whom Josiah sent with others to the Prophetess Huldah to inquire of Jehovah about the things which he had heard

from the Law found by Hilkiah (II Kings 22:12, 14; II Chron. 34:20).

A'saph (ā'săf) [collector; or perhaps, Jehovah has gathered]. 1. A Levite, the son of Berachiah, of the Gershomite family (I Chron. 6:39, 43). With Heman and Ethan, he sounded cymbals before the Ark during its removal from the house of Obed-edom to the city of David (I Chron. 15:16–19). He was then assigned the permanent office of sounding cymbals at the service (I Chron. 16:4, 5, 7); and when the service was finally and fully arranged, his family, with him at the head, was one of the three families permanently charged with the music and song and instructed in the art (I Chron. 25:1–9). Their position was on the right (ch. 6:39). The family often receives mention (II Chron. 20:14; 29:13). A hundred and twenty-eight, all of them singers, came back from Babylon (Ezra 2:41; Neh. 7:44), and conducted the psalmody when the foundations of Zerubbabel's Temple were laid (Ezra 3:10). Twelve psalms— Psalms 50; 73 to 83—are attributed in the titles to the family of Asaph (cf. II Chron. 29:30). Psalm 50 belongs to the 2d book of psalms; the others constitute the bulk of the 3d book. In them the usual name of the deity is God, rather than Jehovah. Asaph, like the other chief singers, is called a seer (II Chron. 29:30; cf. ch. 35:15 and I Chron. 25:5).
2. Father of Hezekiah's recorder (II Kings 18:18).
3. Keeper of the king's park in Palestine under Artaxerxes Longimanus, king of Persia (Neh. 2:8).
4. In I Chron. 26:1 read Ebiasaph (cf. ch. 9:19).

A·sar'a·mel (ȧ-săr'ȧ-mĕl), in A.V. **Sar'a·mel**. Perhaps a title of Simon Maccabaeus, śar 'am 'ēl, prince of the people of God; since the word is preceded by the preposition in, some think it represents a place, standing for ḥaśar 'am 'ēl, the court of the people of God, the forecourt of the Temple (I Macc. 14:28). If the 2d interpretation be correct, we have to assume that the translator mistook Hebrew w (and) for b (in) and then regarded the word as a place name. Or the preposition in may have been inserted by a copyist who supposed that the word was the name of a place.

As'a·rel (ăs'ȧ-rĕl), in A.V. **A·sa're·el** (ȧ-sā'-rē̇-ĕl) [God has bound]. A son of Jehallelel (I Chron. 4:16).

As'a·re'lah (ăs'ȧ-rē'lȧ). See ASHARELAH.

As'ca·lon (ăs'kā-lŏn) (I Macc. 10:86). See ASHKELON.

As·cen'sion [Lat. ascensio, ascending]. Forty days after Easter the risen Christ finally parted from his disciples (Acts 1:1–12; Mark 16:19; Luke 24:50, 51) and returned to the Father. The record indicates a bodily disappearance by an upward movement into the sky. The event took place at the Mount of Olives as the apostles were discussing the Kingdom with Christ. The ascension is the point of contact between the Jesus of the Gospels and the mystical Christ of the Epistles and thus preserves the historical character of the former and the universality of the latter in true continuity.

As·cents', A.V. **De·grees'**. A word occurring in the titles of 15 psalms, Psalms 120 to 134, which are called Songs of Ascents. It is the rendering of Heb. ma'ălôth, ascents or goings up (Ezra 7:9), steps (Ex. 20:26; I Kings 10:19). A Jewish tradition tells that the 15 Songs of Ascents were sung as an ascent was made by 15 steps from the court of the women to that of the men, a view not now generally entertained. The common opinion is that they were sung by the pilgrims during the ascent to

Jerusalem (cf. I Sam. 1:3; Ps. 42:4; 122:4; Isa. 30:29).

As'e·nath (ăs'ê-năth) [Egypt. *ns-N.t*, belonging to the goddess Neith]. Daughter of Poti-phera, priest of On, wife of Joseph and mother of Manasseh and Ephraim (Gen. 41:45, 50–52; 46:20).

A'ser (ā'sẽr). See ASHER.

Ash. The rendering in the A.V. of the Hebrew *'ōren* in Isa. 44:14. The wood of the tree was suitable for use in making idols. A tree which the Arabs call *'arān* is said by one of their writers to grow in Arabia Petraea, and is described as having thorns and producing bunches of bitter berries. But by *'ōren* the LXX understood the fir tree. Jerome renders it pine. R.V. translates the word by fir tree, and places ash in the margin. Perhaps the Syrian fir (*Pinus halepensis*) is meant, which flourishes on the mountains of Palestine, and is occasionally found as far s. as Hebron. See FIR.

A'shan (ā'shăn) [smoke]. A town in the lowland, allotted to Judah, afterward transferred to Simeon and assigned with its suburbs to the Levites (Josh. 15:42; 19:7; I Chron. 4:32; 6:59). In the present text of Josh. 21:16 or I Chron. 6:59 Ashan and Ain have become confounded through the misreading of one letter. Ashan is apparently identical with Borashan (smoking pit) of A.R.V. (I Sam. 30:30). Cf. A.V. Chor-ashan, E.R.V. Corashan (smoking furnace). For similarity of Hebrew *b* and *c* (*k*), see table of ALPHABET.

Ash'a·re'lah (ăsh'à-rē'là), in A.V. **As·a·re'lah** [perhaps, God has fulfilled with joy; cf. Arab. *'ashira*, to be cheerful. The preferred Hebrew text has *s* instead of *sh*.] A son of Asaph (I Chron. 25:2). Called, in v. 14, Jesharelah, *q.v.*

Ash'be·a (ăsh'bē-à) [let me call as witness]. A descendant of Shelah, of the tribe of Judah. The members of the family wrought fine linen (I Chron. 4:21). Beth-Ashbea may, however, be the name of a place.

Ash'bel (ăsh'běl) [perhaps, a secondary form of Eshbaal, man of the Lord]. A son of Benjamin and founder of a tribal family (Gen. 46:21; Num. 26:38; I Chron. 8:1). Apparently represented by Jediael in I Chron. 7:6.

Ash'che·naz (ăsh'kê-năz). See ASHKENAZ.

Ash'dod (ăsh'dŏd), in N.T. **A·zo'tus** [perhaps, strength, fortress]. One of the 5 chief Philistine cities, ruled over by a lord, and seat of the worship of Dagon (Josh. 13:3; I Sam. 5:1 *seq.*; 6:17; I Macc. 10:83; 11:4). Anakim remained in it after the conquest of Canaan by the Hebrews (Josh. 11:22). It was assigned to Judah (Josh. 15:46, 47), but was not possessed by that tribe. The Ark of God was carried to Ashdod by the Philistines after they captured it at Ebenezer, and was placed in the temple of Dagon (I Sam. 5:1–8). A judgment falling on the inhabitants, the Ark was transferred to Gath (I Sam. 5:6–8). Uzziah broke down the walls of Ashdod (II Chron. 26:6). The Tartan or Assyrian commander in chief under Sargon besieged it with success (Isa. 20:1). In the time of the Assyrian kings, from Sargon to Esarhaddon, Ashdod was ruled by an official called king by the Assyrians. According to Herodotus (ii. 157), Psammetichus, king of Egypt, besieged it for 29 years. Only a remnant survived (Jer. 25:20; cf. Zeph. 2:4; Zech. 9:6). Its inhabitants were among those who opposed the rebuilding of the walls of Jerusalem, and they spoke a different language from the Israelites of that day; nevertheless some of the returned Jews married women of Ashdod (Neh. 4:7; 13:23, 24). The city was twice besieged and partially destroyed by the Maccabees (I Macc.

5:68; 10:84), but was rebuilt by the Romans about 55 B.C. In N.T. times it was called Azotus (Acts 8:40).

Philip preached the gospel from this place as far as Caesarea (Acts 8:40). The city became the seat of a bishop in the 4th century A.D. Its approximate site is the mud village of Esdūd on the e. slope of a low, round knoll, 9 miles n.e. from Ascalon, 3 from the Mediterranean, and about midway between Jaffa and Gaza, about 18 miles from the latter place.

Ash'dod·ite, in A.V. once **Ash'·doth·ite.** A native or inhabitant of Ashdod (Josh. 13:3; Neh. 4:7).

Ash'doth·ite (ăsh'dŏth-īt). See preceding article.

Ash'doth-pis'gah (ăsh'dŏth-pĭz'gà). See PISGAH.

Ash'er (ăsh'ẽr), in A.V. of N.T. **A'ser,** following the Greek form [happy]. 1. The 8th son of Jacob, and the 2d by Zilpah, Leah's maidservant (Gen. 30:12, 13; 35:26). His blessing given by Jacob on his deathbed is thus worded:

"Out of Asher his bread shall be fat,
　And he shall yield royal dainties" (Gen. 49:20).

That of Moses:

"Blessed be Asher with children;
　Let him be acceptable unto his brethren,
　And let him dip his foot in oil.
　Thy bars shall be iron and brass;
　And as thy days, so shall thy strength be" (Deut. 33:24).

He had 4 sons, Jimnah, Ishuah, Isui, and Beriah; and a daughter named Serah (Gen. 46:17; I Chron. 7:30).

2. The tribe of which Asher, the son of Jacob, was the progenitor. As assigned, its territory extended on the n. to the n. boundary of Palestine, and on the s. reached to the s. of Carmel, a length of about 60 miles. On the e. it was bounded by the territories of Zebulun and Naphtali, and on the w. by the Mediterranean (Josh. 19:24–31). But from Tyre, Sidon, Accho, and other strong places the Asherites did not expel the Canaanite inhabitants (Judg. 1:31, 32). The failure of the Asherites to capture and occupy the Phoenician plain along the sea left them only the inland hill country, except near Carmel. This was well adapted for the culture of the olive, so that the inhabitants might dip their feet in oil (cf. Deut. 33:24).

3. Asher may possibly denote a town also, e. of Shechem (Josh. 17:7); perhaps Teyāsīr, about 11 miles n.e. of Shechem on the road to Beth-shean.

A·she'rah (à-shē'rà), pl. **A·she'rim** (masc.), and **A·she'roth** (fem.). The Hebrew form of the name of an Amorite or Canaanite goddess 'Ashirtu ('Ashratu), who is mentioned in the Amarna tablets. She appears in the Ras Shamra literature as Lady 'Asherat ('Athirat) and is known also as Lady of the Gods and Mistress of the Gods, being the mother of 70 *elim* (gods). Her most peculiar designation is 'Aserat, Lady of the Sea. In s. Arabia 'Athirat was a solar divinity.

A.V., following the LXX and the Vulgate, wrongly renders the word as grove. When not the name of a deity, Asherah refers to a wooden pole or mast which stood at Canaanite places of worship (Ex. 34:13); originally it was, perhaps, the trunk of a tree with the branches chopped off, and was regarded as the wooden symbol of the goddess Asherah, who like Ashtoreth, was the type of fertility (Ex. 34:13, R.V. marg.). It was erected beside the altar of Baal (Judg. 6:25, 28, R.V.). For the use of the word as the name of a goddess, see R.V., Judg. 3:7; I Kings 18:19; II Kings 21:7. The prophets of the Asherah in Ahab's time were, with those of Baal, slain by Elijah at the river Kishon (I Kings 16:33, R.V.). Women wove hangings for an Asherah in the Temple (II Kings 23:7, R.V.), and Josiah, as part of his religious reformation, brought out the idolatrous symbol and burned it at the Brook Kidron (v. 6).

A·she′rim (á-shē′rĭm). See ASHERAH.

Ash′er·ite (ăsh′ēr-ĭt). A member of the tribe of Asher (Judg. 1:32).

A·she′roth (á-shē′rŏth). See ASHERAH.

Ash′hur (ăsh′ēr), in A.V. **Ash′ur** (ăsh′ēr) [ety. uncertain; man of Horus; or blackness]. Son of Hezron by his wife Abiah. He was enrolled with the house of Caleb, was head or ancestor of the inhabitants of Tekoa, and had 2 wives and 7 children (I Chron. 2:24; 4:5–7).

A·shi′ma (á-shī′má). A divinity worshiped by the people of Hamath (II Kings 17:30).

Ash′ke·lon (ăsh′kĕ-lŏn), in A.V. sometimes **As′ke·lon** (ăs′kĕ-lŏn). One of the 5 leading Philistine cities each ruled by a lord (Josh. 13:3); it is mentioned in the Tell el-Amarna correspondence. It was situated in a valley on the Mediterranean seashore (Jer. 47:5, 7), 12 miles n. of Gaza, and was the seat of the worship of Derceto, a goddess with the body of a fish, whose temple and lake lay to the e. of the city. It was captured by the tribe of Judah in the time of the Judges (Judg. 1:18), but soon reverted to its old rulers (Judg. 14:19; I Sam. 6:17). It was Philistine in the days of David (II Sam. 1:20), Amos (Amos 1:8), Zephaniah (Zeph. 2:4, 7), and Jeremiah (Jer. 25:20; 47:5, 7); cf. also Zech. 9:5. Ashkelon was twice taken by Jonathan Maccabaeus (I Macc. 10:86; 11:60). It was the birthplace of Herod the Great, and the residence of his sister Salome. In the conflicts during the procuratorship of Florus the city was attacked by the Jews and set on fire (Jos. War ii. 18, 1); but not long afterward the citizens retaliated and butchered 2,500 in their midst (War ii. 18, 5). Its site lies within a natural amphitheater formed by a ridge of rock, with the open side to the sea. The wall ran along the top of the ridge. The soil is fertile, producing large apples, sycamore figs, etc. The onion of Ascalon called scallion, shallot, or eschalot, came at first from Ashkelon; hence its name.

Ash′ke·lon·ite (ăsh′kĕ-lŏn-ĭt), in A.V. **Esh′·ka·lon·ite.** An inhabitant of Ashkelon (Josh. 13:3).

Ash′ke·naz (ăsh′kĕ-năz), in A.V. twice **Ash′·che·naz** (ăsh′kĕ-năz). The eldest son of Gomer (Gen. 10:3; I Chron. 1:6). The name, whether originally that of a person or country or tribe, denoted a people of the race of Gomer. In the time of Jeremiah they dwelt in the neighborhood of Ararat and Minni, that is, near e. Armenia (Jer. 51:27).

Ash′nah (ăsh′ná) [hard, firm]. 1. A village in the lowland of Judah near Zorah (Josh. 15:33); probably ʽAslin, a village built upon its ruins at the foot of Deir Abu Ḳābûs near Eshtaol.

2. Another village of Judah, but farther s. (Josh. 15:43); identified with Idhna, a village on the way from Hebron to Eleutheropolis (Beit Jibrîn).

Ash′pe·naz (ăsh′pĕ-năz). The master of the eunuchs at Babylon during Nebuchadnezzar's reign (Dan. 1:3).

Ash′ri·el (ăsh′rĭ-ĕl). See ASRIEL.

Ash′ta·roth (ash′tá-rŏth) [plural of Ashtoreth (q.v.)]. 1. In connection with the plural of Baal, a general designation for the female divinities of the Canaanites; or perhaps, to judge from Gen. 14:5 and I Sam. 31:10, the plural of majesty, whereby the goddess Ash-

toreth was honorably spoken of in the plural number.

2. An ancient town of Bashan, seat of the worship of the goddess Astarte, and capital of Og (Deut. 1:4; Josh. 9:10). Some of the ancient inhabitants were giants, Og himself being of the number (Josh. 12:4; 13:12). The place fell to the lot of Machir, the son of Manasseh (Josh. 13:31), but became a Levitical city, inhabited by the children of Gershom (I Chron. 6:71). Uzzia, one of David's mighty men, was connected with the town (I Chron. 11:44). Its site is commonly identified with Tell ʽAshtarah, 21 miles e. of the Lake of Galilee. This tell stands on a hill in the midst of a well-watered, grassy plain. See ASHTE-ROTH-KARNAIM.

Ash′te·rath·ite (ăsh′tĕ-răth-ĭt). A native of Ashtaroth (I Chron. 11:44).

Ash′te·roth-kar·na′im (ăsh′tĕ-rŏth-kär-nā′-ĭm) [two-horned Ashtaroth]. In A.V. written as two words. A place smitten by Chedorlaomer on his expedition against the cities of the plain (Gen. 14:5, R.V.). Its name suggests that perhaps there was an Ashtoreth represented with the horns of a cow or a sheep. Probably Ashteroth-karnaim is the full name of Ashtaroth, and it may be the place known centuries later as Karnaim (Carnaim), which is mentioned in connection with cities of Gilead and in which Atargatis was worshiped (I Macc. 5:26, 36, 43; II Macc. 12:26). However, the physical features ascribed to Carnion in II Macc. 12:21 do not agree with Tell ʽAshtarah, the commonly accepted site of Ashtaroth. It has accordingly been proposed to identify this place with Tell ʽAshʽarī, which is 4 miles s. of Tell ʽAshtarah. The whole question is obscure.

Ash′to·reth (ăsh′tô-rĕth) [S. Arab. ʽathara, to be rich, to irrigate, whence, perhaps, the reflexive ʽathtar, the self-waterer, a spring]. Astarte, a goddess of the Phoenicians and Canaanites. The name occurs in South Arabic as ʽAthtar, a god identified with the planet Venus. In the Ras Shamra tablets are found the masculine ʽAthtar and the feminine ʽAthtart. In the Amarna letters this goddess is known as Ashtartu. In Babylonia Ishtar, whose name is cognate with Astarte (Ashtart), was identified with Venus. She was the goddess of sexual love, maternity, and fertility. Prostitution as a religious rite in the service of this goddess under various names is widely attested. The identification of ʽAshtart with Aphrodite is evidence of her sexual character. She also appears as a war-goddess in Assyria and Babylonia; cf. placing the armor of Saul as a trophy in the temple of the Philistine Ashtaroth (I Sam. 31:10). Her worship was early established at Sidon, hence she is called the goddess or the abomination of the Sidonians (I Kings 11:5, 33; II Kings 23:13). It was in vogue e. of the Jordan in the days of Abraham (Gen. 14:5). As early as the times of Judges it had spread to the Hebrews (Judg. 2:13; 10:6). Solomon in his old age gave it the support of his great name (I Kings 11:5; II Kings 23:13). The pronunciation of the name as Ashtoreth instead of Ashtareth is believed to express the loathing felt for idolatry, by conforming the sound to that of bōsheth (shame). See ISHBOSHETH.

Ash′ur (ăsh′ēr). See ASHHUR.

Ash′ur·ite (ăsh′ēr-ĭt). A people belonging to the kingdom of Ishbosheth (II Sam. 2:3). They are enumerated between Gilead and Jezreel. Vulgate and Syriac have Geshurites.

Ash′vath (ăsh′văth). An Asherite, family of Heber, house of Japhlet (I Chron. 7:33).

A′sia (ā′zhá). The continent e. of Europe and Africa. The name was employed in a narrower sense for the kingdom of the Seleucidae (I Macc. 8:6; 11:13), which embraced Syria and extensive regions w. of the river Halys. When the Romans transferred most of these w. districts, Mysia, Lydia, and Phrygia, to Eumenes II, king of Pergamos, the name was used by them for the kingdom of Pergamos, and when this kingdom was appropriated by them in 133 B.C., they added Caria and a strip of coast to it and formed the province of Asia (Acts 6:9; 27:2; I Peter 1:1; Rev. 1:4, 11). Pliny, however, distinguishes between Phrygia and Asia (*Hist. Nat.* v. 28). So do Paul and others (Acts 2:9, 10; 16:6). The names of the incorporated districts were not abandoned; and Paul, who was traveling along but outside of the borders of Asia, mentions being at a point over against Mysia (Acts 16:7, R.V.), in which Pergamos was situated, one of the cities of Asia (Rev. 1:4, 11). The province was at first governed by propraetors, but in 27 B.C. it was made senatorial and so continued for 300 years, being governed by proconsuls (cf. Acts 19:38, R.V.). Its capital was Ephesus. In the N.T. Asia always denotes the Roman province (Acts 19:10, 22, 26, 27; 20:4, 16, 18; 21:27; 24:18; 27:2; I Cor. 16:19; II Cor. 1:8; II Tim. 1:15).

A'si·arch (ā'shĭ-ärk) [Gr., chief of Asia]. Member of a college of deputies who were annually appointed by various towns of the province of Asia to conduct a festival and games in honor of the Roman emperor. The festivities took place yearly at one of the several cities which had the honor in succession. The Asiarchs were chosen each year, but in time formed an influential body in the towns, and often secured the re-election of their members. The Asiarchs of Ephesus were friends to Paul (Acts 19:31, R.V. marg.).

A·si·de'ans (ă-sĭ-dē'ănz). See HASIDAEANS.

A'si·el (ā'sĭ-ĕl) [God has made]. A Simeonite (I Chron. 4:35).

As'ke·lon (ăs'kĕ-lŏn). See ASHKELON.

As'mo·nae'an (ăz'mô-nē'ăn). See HASMONAEAN and MACCABEE.

As'nah (ăs'nà) [a bramble, thornbush]. One of the Nethinim, some of whose descendants returned from the Captivity at Babylon (Ezra 2:50).

As·nap'per (ăs-năp'ẽr). See OSNAPPAR.

Asp. The rendering of Heb. *pethen* in Deut. 32:33; Job 20:14, 16; and Isa. 11:8, and of Gr. *aspis* in Rom. 3:13. With some inconsistency *pethen* is rendered not asp but adder in Ps. 58:4 and 91:13. *Pethen* is a species of snake (Ps. 58:4), venomous (Deut. 32:33), dwelling in holes (Isa. 11:8); probably *Naja haje*, which is found in Egypt and Palestine, is the asp of the Greeks and Romans, is of the same genus as the deadly cobra of India, and is generally used by the snake charmers in their performances. It has a hood which it dilates when about to strike its prey.

As·pa'tha (ăs-pā'thà). A son of Haman (Esth. 9:7).

As'phar (ăs'fär). A pool in the wilderness of Tekoah (I Macc. 9:33).

As'ri·el (ăs'rĭ-ĕl), in A.V. once **Ash'ri·el** [ety. uncertain; perhaps, God striveth]. A descendant of Manasseh and founder of a family (Num. 26:31; Josh. 17:2).

Ass. The genus called by zoologists *Asinus*, containing the several species and varieties of asses, wild or domesticated. The ass genus belongs to the family *Equidae* or horses. Three asses are mentioned in Scripture. 1. The wild ass, called in Heb. '*ārōd*, the fugitive. It is poetically described in Job 39:5–8, where, however, there is mention also of the common wild ass of Syria, and is named also in Dan. 5:21. If distinct in species from the common

wild ass, it is probably *Asinus onager,* which is found in the Sahara and in Arabia, where it was once common, but is now more rare. It occasionally visits the Hauran. It is the progenitor of the domestic ass.

2. The wild ass of Syria (*Asinus hemippus*); Heb. *pere'*, the leaper, occurring in Job 24:5; 39:5; Ps. 104:11; Isa. 32:14, and Jer. 14:6. It is rather smaller than the onager. Tristram mentions that enormous herds of them often enter the Armenian mountains in summer. They are found at all times in n. Arabia, Mesopotamia, and Syria, occasionally entering n. Palestine. They are the species represented on the Ninevite sculptures.

3. The domestic ass (*Equus asinus*), Heb. *ḥămōr.* It is a subspecies descended from the onager. It is obstinate and typical of stupidity. But on the other hand the ass is strong, easily fed, patient, and forgiving. Its faults are mainly produced by the cruel bondage imposed upon it by its human taskmaster. The ass was early domesticated. Abraham had asses (Gen. 12:16) on which he rode (ch. 22:3), so had Jacob (ch. 30:43). They were used also for burden-bearing (Gen. 49:14; Isa. 30:6), for plowing, etc. (Deut. 22:10). White asses were deemed fit for persons of rank (Judg. 5:10), as they still are in Palestine. Jesus showed his lowliness, and at the same time the spirit of the earlier kings, by rejecting horses and riding on an ass in his triumphal entry into Jerusalem (Zech. 9:9; Matt. 21:5).

As·sas'sins. Ruffians (Gr. *sikarioi,* dagger men) who terrorized Judea, A.D. 50–70. Their organization was formed in order to assert liberty from the Romans and recognize no master save God. They carried a small sword hidden beneath the cloak; and, mingling with the multitude at the festivals, stabbed those who were marked for destruction. They even formed bands and pillaged villages (Acts 21:38, R.V.; Jos. *Antiq.* xx. 8, 10; *War* vii. 10, 1). See ZEALOT.

As'shur (ăs'shoor), in A.V. twice **As'sur** [Heb. *'Ashshūr,* Assyria; the land was named from the city of Ashur, which probably derived its name from the god Ashur, the chief deity of the Assyrian pantheon, the god of military prowess]. A people descended from Shem (Gen. 10:22), and the country which they inhabited (Ezra 4:2, A.V.; Ezek. 27:23). See ASSYRIA.

As·shu'rim (ă-shōō'rĭm). A people, doubtless of Arabia, descended from Dedan, and more remotely from Abraham by Keturah (Gen. 25:3).

As'si·de'ans (ăs'ĭ-dē'ănz). See HASIDAEANS.

As'sir (ăs'ẽr) [captive; sometimes derived from Egyptian *wsyr*, Osiris]. 1. A descendant of Levi through Korah, born in Egypt (Ex. 6:24; I Chron. 6:22).

2. A descendant of the preceding (I Chron. 6:23, 37).

3. A son of King Jeconiah (I Chron. 3:17). The name does not appear in the text of R.V., but is in the margin. The revisers regard it as an adjective descriptive of Jeconiah, and translate it "the captive"; but there is no definite article in the present Hebrew text, and there was none in the text used by the LXX. His name suggests that Assir was born in captivity. This accords with other indications. Jeconiah was 18 years old when carried off to Babylon, and in the enumeration of the members of his family deported with him, no children are mentioned (II Kings 24:8–15). Assir did not succeed to the royal title; the right to the throne passed to Shealtiel (*q.v.*).

As'sos (ăs'ŏs). A seaport town of Mysia, now called Behram, not far from Troas (Acts 20:13, 14).

As·sur (ăs'ẽr). See ASSHUR.

As·syr'i·a (ă-sĭr'ĭ-á) [Gr. *Assyria* from Heb. *'Ashshūr*, Akkad. *Ashshur*]. A country e. of the middle Tigris between 35° and 37° n. latitude. The only town w. of the Tigris was the old capital Ashur (Assur, Asshur, Ashshur), from which the whole land takes its name. With the growth of the city's power, the name came to denote the region compassed by the mountains of Armenia on the n., the ranges of Media on the e., and the Lower Zab River on the s. Westward it extended a short distance from the Tigris into Mesopotamia. This district is the Assyria proper of history, but the name is often applied to the extensive empire conquered and ruled by the Assyrians. Since Assyria proper was a highland region, it had a more invigorating climate than that of Babylonia.

The population in the region n. of Babylonia was not purely Semitic, and the origin of the Assyrians themselves is still wrapped in mystery. Undoubtedly they were an amalgam of many stocks, among which the Hurrians are of special importance, but ultimately the Semitic element prevailed. By 2900 B.C. there was a settlement of Sumerians at Ashur. The name Nineveh also suggests Sumerian influence. Later Assyria became a part of the Akkadian empire. In fact the language of Ashur is closely related to that of Akkad, and was also written in cuneiform. The Assyrian culture was deeply indebted to that of the Babylonians, the Hittites, and the Hurrians. Colonies were established in e. Asia Minor in the 20th century B.C. by a dynasty of Akkadian princes of Ashur which rose to power after the fall of Ur (c. 2000). This brief Assyrian commercial expansion was made possible by the fact that the Amorite nomads had cut the old route from Babylonia up the Euphrates by way of Mari and Ibla and that the Assyrians developed a new one up the Tigris through Hurrian territory. From the descendants of the colonists have come thousands of business documents (the Cappadocian tablets, c. 1920–1870 B.C.).

From c. 1950 to c. 1850 Assyria was under Babylonian rule, but Shamshi-Adad at the end of that period made it independent and extended its territory. About 1800 Ashur was occupied by an Amorite chieftain. Assyria was hard-pressed (c. 1800–1380) by the Hittites, the Egyptians under Thutmose III, and the Hurrians of Mitanni, but Ashur-uballit (1380–1341) revived its former power. Through campaigns in all directions Assyria consolidated its position (1341–1232). During this period Shalmaneser I (1280–1260) was a great conqueror and builder, who made Calah (Kalhu) his capital, about 40 miles s. of Nineveh. His son Tukulti-Ninurta (1260–1232) ruled Babylonia for 7 years, but he lost his life in a revolt led by his own son. There followed a period of weakness; the fall of the Hittite kingdom seriously affected trade, and Babylonian power revived. Assyria, however, recovered and waxed strong under Ashur-dan I (1175–1140). During the reign of Tiglath-pileser I (c. 1115–1102) there was a great era of conquests and national improvements; through successful campaigns he gained control of the main trade routes of w. Asia. Ashur once more was the capital. Under his successors the kingdom greatly declined, and from c. 1100 to c. 900 Assyria suffered at the hand of Aramaean nomads. As the fortunes of Assyria were at such a low ebb, the time was favorable for the kingdoms of David and Solomon to reach their widest limits.

Around 900 Assyria once more embarked upon an era of conquests. Tukulti-Ninurta II (890–885) conducted brilliant campaigns, and

was succeeded by his son Ashur-nasir-pal (885–860), who was a ruthless warrior and left a record of his cruelties. He rebuilt Calah. He campaigned successfully in the n. e. and the n. w. and reached the Mediterranean, where the Phoenician cities paid him tribute. His son Shalmaneser III (860–825) succeeded him. For 26 years he led every campaign in person. He is the first Assyrian king to come into contact with the Israelites. He waged war against Urartu (Armenia), captured Carchemish in 857, and in (854) 853 B.C. fought at Karkar a coalition of Ben-hadad, of Damascus, Ahab, of Israel, and their allies. In 842 he defeated Hazael, of Damascus, but did not take the city. In that year he received tribute from Tyre and Sidon and from Jehu, of Israel; he thus gained control of the Mediterranean trade routes. His son Shamshi-Adad V was married to Sammura-mat (Semiramis), who became famous as queen mother during the reign of her son Adad-nirari III (812–782). After the latter's death until 746 Assyria was in a period of decay.

With the advent of Tiglath-pileser III (746/5–728/7) there is a restoration and the beginning of the 2d empire. His successors are Shalmaneser V (728/7–722); Sargon (722–705); Sennacherib (705–681); Esar-haddon (681–669); Ashurbanipal (669–626). See separate articles on the first 5 of these kings and on Nineveh.

Ashurbanipal was succeeded by his son Ashur-etil-ilani. At the latter's death Sin-shum-lishir, an official of the king, seized the throne and held it for a few months. The last ruler was Sin-shar-ishkun, another son of Ashurbanipal. Nabopolassar, king of Babylonia, and his ally, Cyaxares, king of the Medes, attacked Nineveh in 612 and destroyed it; the king perished in the flames. A few Assyrians under the leadership of Ashur-uballit escaped to Harran where they set up a government. This city was taken in 610 by Nabopolassar and Cyaxares. After the battle of Carchemish (605) the Assyrians as a nation ceased to exist.

The Assyrian religion was borrowed from that of Babylon, except that Ashur, the presiding god of the city of Ashur, became the chief deity of Assyria. It was animistic nature worship. Every object and phenomenon in nature was believed to be animated by a spirit. The great gods, after Ashur, were the prominent objects of nature. They were 11 in number, in 2 triads and a pentad. Chief were Anu, heaven; Bel, the region inhabited by man, beast, and bird; and Ea, terrestrial and subterranean waters. Next in order were Sin, the moon; Shamash, the sun; and Ramman, god of the storm. Then came the 5 planets. There were innumerable other deities, some of whom were merely different aspects of the foregoing. Subordinate gods often attained eminence as patrons of important towns.

Excavations in the Assyrian palaces, begun by the Frenchman Botta in 1843, followed immediately by the Englishman Layard, and then, after a time, by George Smith of the British Museum, Rassam, and others, have made the Assyrian Empire, which was little more than a myth to the classic nations of antiquity, to us a great reality.

As'ta·roth (ăs'tá-rŏth) [Deut. 1:4, A.V.]. See ASHTAROTH 2.

As·tar'te (ăs-tär'tē). See ASHTORETH.

As·trol'o·gers. 1. The rendering of the Heb. words *hōbᵉrē shāmayim*, dividers of the heavens. They are mentioned with stargazers (Isa. 47:13). There is no question that these were astrologers who divided the heavens into certain mansions, with the view of tracing the course of the planets through each of them, in the vain hope of being able to tell fortunes and predict future events. Though their failure was complete, yet the careful study of the heavens which astrologers found needful led to the gradual growth of the sublime science of astronomy.

2. The rendering in A.V. of the Heb. and Aram. words *'ashshāphim* (Dan. 1:20), *'āsh*e*phîn* (ch. 2:27), and *'āsh*e*phayyā* (chs. 4:7; 5:7), all translated in the R.V. "enchanters." See ENCHANTMENT and ENCHANTER.

A·sup'pim (*a̍-sŭp'ĭm*) [collections, stores]. A building for storing Temple goods, which stood near the s. gate of the outer court (I Chron. 26:15, 17); hence R.V. renders the word by storehouse.

A·syn'cri·tus (*a̍-sĭng'krĭ-tŭs*) [Gr., incomparable or unlike]. A Christian at Rome to whom Paul sent a salutation (Rom. 16:14).

A'tad (*ā'tăd*) [thorn, bramble]. The great company which was bearing the body of Jacob from Egypt to the sepulcher at Hebron, after making a detour, perhaps to avoid the Philistines and Edomites, halted at the threshing floor of Atad, e. of the Jordan, and made a mourning for 7 days. The Canaanites saw and called the place Abel-mizraim, Meadow, or with slightly altered pronunciation, Mourning of Egypt. The procession afterward entered Canaan (Gen. 50:9–13).

At'a·rah (*ăt'a̍-rä*) [a crown, a diadem]. A wife of Jerahmeel (I Chron. 2:26).

A·tar'ga·tis (*a̍-tär'ga̍-tĭs*) [Gr. *Atargatis* from Aram. *'Atār* or *'Attār* (Astarte)+*'Atāh*, *'Atēh* (probably fem. form of Phrygian Attis, a god of vegetation)]. The great goddess of the Aramaeans, a goddess of fertility often confused with Astarte. The worship of this Syrian divinity is not mentioned in the canonical books, but in II Macc. 12:26 reference is made to her temple at Carnion in Gilead. In Palestine her principal seat of worship was at Ashkelon, where she was probably identified with the Heavenly Aphrodite. Another famous shrine of this goddess was at Hierapolis or Bambyce (Mabug) in Syria. According to Lucian's very full description of her cult (*De Dea Syria*), its general features were those found in the worship of the Semitic mother goddess.

At'a·roth (*ăt'a̍-rŏth*) [crowns, diadems]. 1. A town e. of the Jordan, rebuilt by the tribe of Gad (Num. 32:3, 34). It was taken from the men of Gad by Mesha, king of Moab (*Moabite Stone*, 10, 11; see MOABITE STONE). Its name is generally supposed to be preserved in Khirbet 'Aṭṭārūs, on the w. slope of Jebel 'Aṭṭārūs, 3 miles n.e. of Machaerus, where John the Baptist was confined and murdered. The mountain is some miles s. of Heshbon, which is in the tribe of Reuben; but the territories of Reuben and Gad, like those of Judah and Simeon, were much commingled.

2. The same as Ataroth-addar (Josh. 16:2).

3. A town on the border of Ephraim, on the edge of the Jordan Valley. Apparently different from Ataroth-addar (Josh. 16:7). Tell Sheikh ed-Dhiab, n.e. of Phasaelis, has been proposed by Elliger.

4. A village, apparently in Judah (I Chron. 2:54), near Bethlehem. The name should include the 4 words that follow in A.V. and be written as in R.V., Atroth-beth-joab.

At'a·roth-ad'dar (*ăt'a̍-rŏth-ă'där*), in A.V. once **At'a·roth-a'dar** (*ăt'a̍-rŏth-ā'där*) [crowns of Addar]. A village on the s. frontier of Ephraim (Josh. 16:5), on the boundary line between that tribe and Benjamin, w. of Luz and near the hill that lies on the s. side of the nether Beth-horon (ch. 18:13). Modern Tell

en-Naṣbeh, 7 miles n. of Jerusalem, is the most probable identification.

A'ter (*ā'tẽr*) [probably, closing, a binder]. 1. A man called, by way of distinction, Ater of Hezekiah, 98 of whose descendants returned from Babylon after the Captivity (Ezra 2:16; Neh. 7:21).

2. A porter (Ezra 2:42; Neh. 7:45).

A'thach (*ā'thăk*) [a lodging place]. A village in the s. of Judah, to which David sent some of the spoil of Ziklag (I Sam. 30:30). Perhaps it is Ether (Josh. 15:42; 19:7), *k* (*kaph*) and *r* (*resh*) being confused by a scribe.

A·tha'iah (*a̍-thā'ya̍*) [S. Arab., Jehovah is exalted; or perhaps, Jehovah has shown himself as surpassing; cf. Arab. *'atā*, to be proud]. A man of Judah, son of Uzziah, of the family of Perez (Neh. 11:4); by many identified with Uthai (I Chron. 9:4).

Ath'a·li'ah (*ăth'a̍-lī'a̍*) [Jehovah is exalted; cf. Akkad. *etlu*, great, lofty; *etellu*, lord]. 1. The wife of Jehoram, king of Judah, a daughter of Ahab and granddaughter of Omri (II Kings 8:18, 26; II Chron. 21:6; 22:2). She possessed the masculine courage of her mother Jezebel, and was equally unscrupulous in shedding blood. When her son, King Ahaziah, was slain by Jehu, she killed all the sons of the murdered monarch excepting one infant, Joash, who was stolen away by his aunt, Jehosheba. Then seizing the throne, she reigned 6 years, at the end of which a priestly insurrection took place in favor of Joash. Attempting to quell it, she was dragged from the Temple courts and killed at the horses' entry to the king's house (II Kings 11:1–16; II Chron., chs. 22; 23).

2. A Benjamite of the house of Jeroham (I Chron. 8:26).

3. A man of the father's house of Elam (Ezra 8:7).

Ath'a·rim (*ăth'a̍-rĭm*) [cf. Arab. *'athar*, track]. The way of the Atharim was not far from the town of Arad, and was the route followed by the Israelites as they journeyed from Kadesh by way of Mount Hor in order to enter Canaan (Num. 21:1, R.V.).

Ath'e·no'bi·us (*ăth'ê-nō'bĭ-ŭs*). A commissioner sent by Antiochus Sidetes to Simon Maccabaeus. He belonged to the privileged class known as friends of the king (I Macc. 15:28).

Ath'ens (*ăth'ĕnz*) [named after the patron goddess Athene]. The capital of Attica, one of the Greek states. The city became the center of enlightenment in science, literature, and art for the ancient world. It grew up around the rocky hill called Acropolis (top or highest point of the city), and covered the smaller hills and intervening valleys on the n.e. side of the Gulf of Aegina, between the small river Ilissus on the e. and s., and the Cephisus a little to the w. Athens was about 4½ miles from the sea. Its commercial port was Piraeus, with which the city when in its glory was connected by long walls. The navy anchored close by at Phaleron. The early history of Athens is involved in obscurity. Tradition says that the city was founded by Cecrops about 1581 B.C., that it sent 50 ships to the Trojan War, and that it was ruled by kings until about 1068 B.C. The supreme authority was afterward vested in archons. Two celebrated legislators are spoken of: Draco, about 621 B.C., whose name has become proverbial for pitiless severity; and Solon, about 594 B.C., a wiser man, whose laws were more humane. In 490 B.C. the Athenians, supported by the Plataeans, gained the great victory at Marathon against the generals of Darius Hystaspis, king of Persia. In 480 Athens had to be abandoned to his son and successor, Xerxes, but the great naval battle at Salamis gained by the Greeks compelled the invader to withdraw. The city was, however, burned in 479 B.C. by his general, Mardonius. The glory gained by the Athenians in the Persian War led to the establishment of a small empire, with Athens for its capital and a powerful fleet rather than a large army for its support. From 459 to 431 B.C. the power of Pericles, an able democratic leader, was very great. The good feature of his enlightened government was the erection of many beautiful public buildings in Athens. Literature also greatly flourished under his administration. In 431, while he yet lived and ruled, the Peloponnesian War began, which ended by the surrender of Athens to the Spartans in 404. The city afterward went through various political vicissitudes, though the intellect and knowledge of its inhabitants rendered them influential, whatever changes took place. Four great schools of philosophy—Platonic, Peripatetic, Epicurean, and Stoic—flourished here and attracted numerous students, not only from Greece, but also later from Rome. The city was taken by the Roman general Sulla in 86 B.C., and was still subject to the Romans when Paul was there. Altars "to an Unknown God" were found in the city and at the harbor Phaleron (Acts 17:23; Pausanias i. 1, 4; Philostratus Vit. Apol. 6, 2). Mars' Hill, on which Paul delivered his celebrated discourse, was a short distance w. of the Acropolis (Acts 17:15 to 18:1; cf. also I Thess. 3:1). Athens subsequently came into the hands of the Goths, the Byzantines, and other temporarily dominant races, ending with the Turks. The modern Greek kingdom was established in A.D. 1830 and Athens became the capital in 1835.

Ath'la·i (ăth'lā-ī), probably contraction of Athaliah. A man who was induced by Ezra to divorce his foreign wife (Ezra 10:28).

A·tone'ment [Eng. at-one-ment, a setting at one of those who before were at variance]. 1. Reconciliation between persons or beings at variance (Rom. 5:11, A.V.). As applied to the relation between God and man, it was effected through the death of Jesus Christ upon the cross.

2. That which produces this reconciliation, as well as the satisfaction or propitiation effected through the expiatory sacrifice designed to have that effect (Ex. 30:16; Lev. 4:20, 26, 31, 35). This is the sense in which the word atonement is now commonly used.

A·tone'ment, Day of. The annual day of humiliation and expiation for the sins of the nation, when the high priest offered sacrifices as an atonement for the sanctuary, the priests, and the people (Lev., chs. 16; 23:26–32; Num. 29:7–11). It was observed on the 10th day of the 7th month by abstinence from daily labor, by a holy convocation, and by fasting. It was the only fast enjoined by the law. It was "the Fast" (Acts 27:9; Jos. Antiq. xiv. 4, 3). On that day the high priest laid aside his official ornaments, and clad in simple white linen sacrificed a bullock as a sin offering for himself and the priests. Taking a censer of live coals from off the altar, he entered the Holy of Holies and burned incense that the smoke might cover the mercy seat above the law. He then fetched the blood of the slain bullock and sprinkled it on the mercy seat and on the floor. This completed the atonement for the priesthood. He took the two goats provided by the nation and cast lots upon them. One he slew as a sin offering for the people, brought its blood within the veil, and sprinkled it as before to make atonement for the Holy of Holies. By similar rites he made atonement for the Holy

Place and the altar of burnt offering. He now took the remaining goat, placed his hands on its head, and confessed over it the sins of the people. Typically the sins of the people were "laid on its head," it was made the sin bearer of the nation, and laden with guilt not its own was sent away into the wilderness; see AZAZEL. The high priest resumed his official raiment, offered his burnt offering and that of the people, and likewise the fat of the sin offering. The flesh of the bullock and the goat were carried without the camp and burned. The Epistle to the Hebrews points out that this entry of the high priest into the Most Holy Place, once a year, and not without blood, foreshadowed the entrance of Jesus, the great High Priest, once for all into heaven, having purchased for us eternal salvation (Heb. 9:1–12, 24–28).

At'roth (ăt'rŏth). See ATROTH-SHOPHAN.

At'roth-beth·jo'ab (ăt'rŏth-bĕth-jō'ăb) [the crowns of the house of Joab]. A village, apparently in Judah (I Chron. 2:54, R.V.). In A.V. the name is rendered "Ataroth, the house of Joab."

At'roth-sho'phan (ăt'rŏth-shō'făn) [crowns of Shophan]. A town rebuilt by the Gadites (Num. 32:35, R.V.). Site unknown. In A.V. incorrectly represented as 2 towns.

At'ta·i (ăt'á-ī) [perhaps, timely, opportune]. 1. A man of Judah whose descent through his mother was from Jerahmeel and Hezron, but whose father was an Egyptian slave (I Chron. 2:34–36).
2. A Gadite who came to David at Ziklag (I Chron. 12:11).
3. A son of Rehoboam by his queen Maacah (II Chron. 11:20).

At·ta·li'a (ăt'á-lī'á) [Gr., pertaining to Attalus]. A city on the seacoast of Pamphylia, built by Attalus Philadelphus, king of Pergamos, 159–138 B.C. Paul sailed thence to Antioch on his First Missionary Journey (Acts 14:25).

At'ta·lus (ăt'á-lŭs). King of Pergamos, either Attalus II, Philadelphus, or his nephew Attalus III, Philometor (138–133 B.C.) (I Macc. 15:22).

Au·gus'tan Band, in A.V. Au·gus'tus' Band. A cohort of Roman soldiers, apparently named after the Roman emperor Augustus (Acts 27:1).

Au·gus'tus (ô-gŭs'tŭs) [Lat., venerable, majestic]. An honorific title bestowed upon Octavian, the 1st Roman emperor, called Caesar Augustus (Luke 2:1). See CAESAR 1.

A'va (ā'vá). See AVVA.

A'ven (ā'vĕn) [emptiness, nothingness, an idol]. 1. The Egyptian city On, called by the Greeks Heliopolis (Ezek. 30:17). The Hebrew consonants of On and Aven are the same, though the vowels differ. The pronunciation has been intentionally modified by the prophet to express his contempt for the idolatries of the city.
2. A name applied by Hosea to Beth-el as no longer the house of God, but now a house of idolatry (Hos. 10:8); see BETH-AVEN 2.
3. A town which served to designate a valley in the kingdom of Damascus (Amos 1:5); probably Awaniyeh near Jerûd on the road to Palmyra.

A·veng'er of Blood. One who inflicts punishment on a murderer, thus vindicating the majesty of the law, "Whoso sheddeth man's blood, by man shall his blood be shed" (Gen. 9:5, 6; Num. 35:31). When civil life is regulated, this duty is undertaken by courts of justice. Of old, however, the Semitic nations, like the ancient Greeks, Germans, and Slavs, acted to a large extent on the system of each injured man being his own avenger. When murder or accidental homicide took place, the nearest relative of the victim was expected to avenge his death, and was called the avenger of blood. He slew the murderer or the unintentional homicide, without any preliminary trial to settle the actual facts of the case. Then, very probably, the nearest relative of the second man slain murdered the avenger of blood, and a blood feud was established. The Mosaic legislation introduced modifications into the system which destroyed its worst features. Cities of refuge were established, and anyone killing a man and fleeing to one of those cities was granted a fair trial, and was not put to death unless he had committed actual murder (Num. 35:19, 21, 24, 27; II Sam. 14:11). The A.V. reads, "Revenger of blood." See CITY OF REFUGE.

A'vim (ā'vĭm) and **A'vims** (ā'vĭmz). See AVVIM.

A'vites (ā'vīts). See AVVITES.

A'vith (ā'vĭth) [ruins]. An Edomite city, the native place of King Hadad (Gen. 36:35; I Chron. 1:46). Père Abel (1938) identifies it with Khirbet el-Jiththeh, between Ma'ān and el-Basṭa.

Av'va (ăv'à), in A.V. **A'va**. A city of the Assyrian Empire from which people were brought to help to colonize Samaria. Their gods were Nibhaz and Tartak (II Kings 17:24, 31). It is doubtless the place called Ivvah in II Kings 18:34; 19:13, R.V. It has been identified with Tell Kafr 'Aya on the Orontes, s.w. of Homs.

Av'vim (ăv'īm), in A.V. **A'vims** and **A'vites** and, as name of the town, **A'vim**. 1. The aborigines of the Philistine country about Gaza. All save a small remnant were destroyed by the Caphtorim, afterward called Philistines (Deut. 2:23; Josh. 13:3).
2. A town of Benjamin (Josh. 18:23); identified with Khirbet Ḥaiyān, s. of Ai.

Av'vites (ăv'īts), in A.V. **A'vites**. 1. The same as Avvim (Josh. 13:3).
2. People of Avva (II Kings 17:31).

A'yin (ā'yĕn), in A.V., **A'in** ['ayin, an eye, a spring]. 1. The 16th letter of the Hebrew alphabet, originally in outline an eye. Greek *omicron*, whence English *o*, comes from the same source, but is used as a vowel, whereas *ayin* is a consonant of peculiar guttural sound. In Anglicizing Hebrew names which contain *ayin*, the letter is sometimes not represented at all; at other times is expressed as *g*, through the Greek as in Gaza. In the original, *ayin* stands at the beginning of the words Ai, Amalek, Eli, Gomorrah. It heads the 16th section of Psalm 119, in which section each verse of the Hebrew begins with this letter.
2. A place on the n. boundary line of Palestine w. of Riblah (Num. 34:11).
3. A town in the territory of Judah, toward Edom and near Rimmon (Josh. 15:32; I Chron. 4:32), and, as it were, forming one town with it (Neh. 11:29). It was transferred with Rimmon to Simeon, and assigned to the priests who resided with that tribe (Josh. 19:7; 21:16; but see ASHAN). It is generally identified with Umm er-Ramāmīn, 9 miles n.e. of Beer-sheba.

Ay'yah (ăy'à) [heap, ruin]. This reading occurs in the margin of I Chron. 7:28, R.V. and is found ('*Ayyāh*) in the Heb. text of the editions of Baer and Delitzsch, Kittel, and Ginsburg. The Bomberg Bible (1524–1525) and many MSS. have '*Azzāh*. See GAZA 2. It is probably to be identified with Turmus 'Ayya, which lies in a small fertile plain between Sinjil and Seilūn (Shiloh).

A'zal (ā'zăl). See AZEL.

Az'a·li'ah (ăz'à-lī'à) [perhaps, Jehovah has shown himself distinguished; cf. Arab. '*aṣula*, to be rooted fast, to be excellent, of firm character]. Son of Meshullam and father of Shaphan the scribe (II Kings 22:3).

Az'a·ni'ah (ăz'à-nī'à) [Jehovah has given ear]. A Levite, father of Jeshua (Neh. 10:9).

Az'a·rel (ăz'à-rĕl), in A.V. **A·za're·el** (à-zā'rė-ĕl), once **A·za'ra·el** (à-zā'rà-ĕl) (Neh. 12:36) [God has helped]. 1. A Levite who joined David at Ziklag (I Chron. 12:6).
2. A singer in David's time (I Chron. 25:18). In v. 4 he is called Uzziel (as King Azariah was also known as Uzziah), and is recorded as of the lineage of Heman.
3. A son of Jeroham, the chief of the tribe of Dan (I Chron. 27:22).
4. A man whom Ezra persuaded to divorce his foreign wife (Ezra 10:41).
5. A priest of the father's house of Immer (Neh. 11:13).
6. A musician of priestly descent (Neh. 12:36).

Az'a·ri'ah (ăz'à-rī'à) [Jehovah has helped]. 1. A man of Judah, family of Zerah, house of Ethan (I Chron. 2:8).
2. A Levite, family of Kohath, line of Izhar, and an ancestor of Samuel the prophet and Heman the singer (I Chron. 6:36; perhaps, II Chron. 29:12).
3. One of Solomon's officials, son of the high priest Zadok (I Kings 4:2) and brother of Ahimaaz.
4. Grandson of Zadok and son of Ahimaaz. He was in the line of high-priestly succession (I Chron. 6:9).
5. Son of Nathan, and hence probably Solomon's nephew (II Sam. 5:14), who was over Solomon's 12 tax collectors (I Kings 4:5).
6. A prophet, son of Oded, who encouraged King Asa to persevere in national religious reformation (II Chron. 15:1–8).
7. Two sons of King Jehoshaphat (II Chron. 21:2). The recurrence of the same name in the family is surprising; but there is a slight difference of spelling of the names in Hebrew: '*azaryāh* and '*azaryāhū*. It may be due to an early corruption of the text; or, if the text is correct, to a difference of mother, the 2 boys being half brothers (cf. the Herods). It cannot be explained by the theory that the younger was named after a deceased elder brother, for the two seem to have been alive together and to have been put to death at the same time.
8. A man of Judah, family of Hezron, house of Jerahmeel (I Chron. 2:38, 39). His grandfather was Obed (v. 38); hence he was perhaps the captain Azariah, son of Obed, who assisted in overthrowing Athaliah and placing Joash on the throne (II Chron. 23:1).
9. Another captain, son of Jeroham, who aided in overthrowing Athaliah (II Chron. 23:1).
10. A prince of Ephraim, son of Johanan, who aided in persuading the soldiers of Pekah's army to release the captives of Judah (II Chron. 28:12).
11. A king of Judah, known also as Uzziah (cf. II Kings 15:1 with II Chron. 26:1); see UZZIAH 3.
12. A high priest (I Chron. 6:10), probably he who rebuked Uzziah for encroaching on the priest's office (II Chron. 26:17–20). Perhaps he was still officiating in Hezekiah's reign (II Chron. 31:10, 13), but probably the pontiff of the latter reign was another priest of the name Azariah. See HIGH PRIEST.
13. A Levite, family of Merari, who assisted in purifying the Temple in Hezekiah's reign (II Chron. 29:12).
14. A high priest, son of Hilkiah and father of Seraiah, not long before the Exile (I Chron. 6:13, 14; perhaps 9:11). See SERAIAH 11.

51

15. A son of Hoshaiah and an opponent of the Prophet Jeremiah (Jer. 43:2).

16. The Hebrew and original name of Abednego (Dan. 1:7; I Macc. 2:59).

17. A prominent person, probably prince of Judah, who marched in the procession at the dedication of the wall of Jerusalem (Neh. 12:32, 33).

18. A son of Maaseiah, who had a house at Jerusalem in Nehemiah's time, and repaired the wall in its immediate vicinity (Neh. 3:23, 24).

19. One of those, apparently Levites, who explained to the people the Law which Ezra read (Neh. 8:7).

20. A priest, doubtless head of a father's house, who in the days of Nehemiah sealed the covenant to keep separate from foreigners and observe the law of God (Neh. 10:2).

21. A descendant of Hilkiah who was ruler of the house of God after the Exile (I Chron. 9:11); see, however, SERAIAH 11.

Besides these, a king of Israel (not Uzziah) is called Azariah in II Chron. 22:6, but this seems a copyist's error for Ahaziah, which is given in the next verse (II Chron. 22:6, 7; cf. II Kings 8:29).

Az·a·ri′as (ăz′à-rī′ăs) [Gr. form of Azariah]. One of 2 men appointed by Judas Maccabaeus to chief authority in Judea during his absence (I Macc. 5:18), but who were defeated by Gorgias (vs. 56–60).

A′zaz (ā′zăz) [strong, perhaps contraction of Azaziah]. A Reubenite, line of Joel (1 Chron. 5:8).

A·za′zel (à-zā′zĕl) [ʿăzāʾzēl, probably for ʿazalzēl, in the sense of entire removal; cf. Arab. ʿazala, remove]. The word occurs in one passage only (Lev. 16:8, 10, 26, R.V.); see ATONEMENT, DAY OF. The data for determining its meaning are meager and insufficient. Numerous interpretations have been proposed, but they are conjectures more or less satisfactory. The word has been interpreted both impersonally and personally, as meaning: 1. Solitary desert place. 2. The departing goat (Jewish revisers of the LXX; caper emissarius, Vulgate); scapegoat, the goat that is allowed to escape (A.V.). 3. An abstract noun: removal (A.R.V. marg.) or dismissal (E.R.V. marg.). 4. A personal being: (a) some demon of the wilderness (Stade); (b) a fallen angel who seduces men to evil (Book of Enoch 8:1; 10:4); (c) an epithet applied to the Devil (Origen, Hengstenberg, Oehler, Kurtz, Keil; see Milton, Paradise Lost 1).

One of 3 interpretations is satisfactory: 1. To regard the word as the name of the spirit supposed to have his abode in the wilderness, remote from human habitation, to whom the goat laden with the sins of the people was sent. In Azazel may be the trace of illicit worship of demons or satyrs. If this be the case, the Pentateuch recognizes such a demon only as an evil spirit to whom belong the sins of the people. 2. To regard the word as an abstraction. "Aaron shall cast lots upon the two goats; one lot for Jehovah, and the other lot for Azazel [removal or dismissal]," and shall send the goat, upon which the latter lot falls, away as a removal (dismissal) "into the wilderness." The idea of the escaped goat is virtually preserved by this interpretation. 3. To regard the word as an epithet of the Devil, the Apostate One. Those who are laden with sin belong to the Devil. The objection to this interpretation is that Satan is nowhere mentioned in any part of the Pentateuch. The serpent indeed is, but it is not certain that the Devil was as yet recognized as the possessor and actuator of the serpent of the temptation.

Az′a·zi′ah (ăz′à-zī′à) [Jehovah is strong].
1. A harper for religious service during the reign of David (I Chron. 15:21).

2. Father of a prince of Ephraim in David's reign (I Chron. 27:20).

3. An overseer of the Temple in the reign of Hezekiah (II Chron. 31:13).

Az′buk (ăz′bŭk). Father of a certain Nehemiah, contemporary, but not identical with the celebrated governor of that name (Neh. 3:16).

A·ze′kah (à-zē′kà) [a place dug up with a hoe]. A town in the lowland, near Socoh, to which the kings besieging Gibeon were driven by Joshua (Josh. 10:10, 11). It was assigned to Judah (Josh. 15:35). Goliath and the Philistines encamped near it (I Sam. 17:1). It was fortified by Rehoboam (II Chron. 11:9), besieged by Nebuchadnezzar (Jer. 34:7), and it existed after the Exile (Neh. 11:30) between Eleutheropolis and Jerusalem, almost 9 miles from the former town, at Tell Zakariyeh.

A′zel (ā′zĕl); in A.V. once **A′zal** (Zech. 14:5), a Hebrew pronunciation sometimes employed when the word stands at a pause in the sentence (as in Heb. of I Chron. 8:38, and in the second occurrence in ch. 9:44) [perhaps, noble; cf. Arab. ʾaṣīl, well-rooted, noble. The name may be a contraction of Azaliah]. 1. A descendant of Jonathan, Saul's son (I Chron. 8:37, 38; 9:43, 44).

2. A place near Jerusalem (Zech. 14:5). LXX Iasol suggests Wadi Yaṣūl, a tributary of the Kidron.

A′zem (ā′zĕm). See EZEM.

Az′gad (ăz′găd) [the god Gad is strong, or fate is hard]. Founder of a family, members of which returned from Babylonia with both Zerubbabel and Ezra (Ezra 2:12; 8:12). Its representative sealed the covenant (Neh. 10:15). The name appears as Astad (I Esdras 5:13), Astath (I Esdras 8:38).

A′zi·el (ā′zĭ-ĕl). See JAAZIEL.

A·zi′za (à-zī′zà) [strong, robust]. A man whom Ezra induced to divorce his foreign wife (Ezra 10:27).

Az·ma′veth (ăz-mā′vĕth) [death is strong].
1. A Barhumite, one of David's mighty men (II Sam. 23:31).

2. A Benjamite, whose sons came to David at Ziklag (I Chron. 12:3).

3. The son of Adiel. He was over David's treasures (I Chron. 27:25).

4. A son of Jehoaddah and descendant of Jonathan, Saul's son (I Chron. 8:36).

5. A village in the vicinity of Jerusalem. Forty-two of its inhabitants returned from the Babylonian Captivity (Ezra 2:24). Some singers resided on its fields (Neh. 12:29). Called also Beth-azmaveth (Neh. 7:28). Its site is perhaps Hizmeh, midway between Geba and Anathoth.

Az′mon (ăz′mŏn) [strong, robust]. A place on the s. boundary of Canaan, to the w. of Kadesh-barnea and near the brook of Egypt (Num. 34:4, 5; Josh. 15:4, R.V.). Exact site unknown.

Az′noth-ta′bor (ăz′nŏth-tā′bôr) [the ears, i.e., slopes or peaks, of Tabor]. A place on the boundary of Naphtali, evidently near Mount Tabor (Josh. 19:34).

A′zor (ā′zôr). An ancestor of Christ who lived after the Exile (Matt. 1:13, 14).

A·zo′tus (à-zō′tŭs). See ASHDOD.

Az′ri·el (ăz′rĭ-ĕl) [God is a help]. 1. A chief man of the half tribe of Manasseh, e. of the Jordan (I Chron. 5:24).

2. A Naphtalite of David's time, father of Jerimoth (I Chron. 27:19).

3. Father of Seraiah of Jeremiah's time (Jer. 36:26).

Az·ri·kam (ăz'rĭ-kăm) [my help has arisen]. 1. A son of Neariah (I Chron. 3:23).

2. A son of Azel, and descendant of Jonathan, Saul's son (I Chron. 8:38; 9:44).

3. A Levite, descended from Merari (I Chron. 9:14).

4. The governor of the palace under King Ahaz. He was killed by an Ephraimite, Zichri (II Chron. 28:7).

A·zu'bah (á-zū'bá) [forsaken]. 1. A wife of Caleb (I Chron. 2:18, 19).

2. A daughter of Shilhi and mother of Jehoshaphat (I Kings 22:42).

A'zur (ā'zẽr). See AZZUR.

Az'zah (ăz'á). See AYYAH and GAZA.

Az'zan (ăz'ăn) [strong]. Father of Paltiel, prince of Issachar in the days of Moses (Num. 34:26).

Az'zur (ăz'ẽr), in A.V. twice **A'zur** [helpful]. 1. Father of Hananiah the false prophet (Jer. 28:1).

2. Father of Jaazaniah (Ezek. 11:1).

3. One of those who, with Nehemiah, sealed the covenant (Neh. 10:17).

B

Ba'al (bā'ăl) [lord, possessor, husband]. 1. Originally the word was not a proper noun, but later came to be so used, as is seen in the O.T. Baal worship apparently had its origin in the belief that every tract of ground owed its productivity to a supernatural being, or *baal*, that dwelt there. The farmers probably thought that from the Baalim, or fertility gods, of various regions came the increase of crops, fruits, and cattle. The name Baal occurs in the Hyksos period, and to the Egyptians of Dyn. XIX he was a well-known Semitic deity. In the Amarna letters Baal seems to be identical with Adad (Hadad). In the Ras Shamra texts the word is applied to gods as possessors of particular places, sanctuaries, or attributes; it is, however, also used as the name of a distinct god Baal.

Baal was adored on high places in Moab as early as the days of Balaam and Balak (Num. 22:41). In the time of the Judges he had altars in Palestine (Judg. 2:13; 6:28–32), and when Ahab married Jezebel, the daughter of Ethbaal, king of the Sidonians, the worship of Baal almost supplanted that of Jehovah. The struggle between the two religions culminated on Mount Carmel when the Prophet Elijah met the priests of Baal (I Kings 16:31, 32; 18:17–40). Though it ended in the slaughter of the priests of Baal, yet the cult soon recuperated until crushed by Jehu (II Kings 10:18–28). About this time, the worship of Baal received new impulse in Judah through Jezebel's daughter, Athaliah, wife of Jehoram (II Chron. 17:3; 21:6; 22:2). On her overthrow, the temple of Baal at Jerusalem was pulled down, the altars and images were destroyed, and Mattan, the chief priest, was slain before the altar (II Kings 11:18). After a time the worship of Baal was revived in both Israel (Hos. 2:8) and Judah. Ahaz made molten images for the Baalim (II Chron. 28:2). Hezekiah, indeed, wrought a reformation, but Manasseh erected altars to Baal (II Kings 21:3). Josiah removed from the Temple at Jerusalem and destroyed the vessels of Baal, and made the public worship of Baal for the time to cease (II Kings 23:4, 5). Jeremiah frequently denounced it, as did other prophets (Jer. 19:4, 5). The worship of Baal was ac-

companied with lascivious rites (cf. I Kings 14:24), the sacrifice of children in the fire by parents (Jer. 19:5), and kissing the image (I Kings 19:18; Hos. 13:2). Baal was often associated with the goddess Ashtoreth (Judg. 2:13), and in the vicinity of his altar there was often an Asherah (Judg. 6:30; I Kings 16:32, 33, R.V.). See BAALIM, BAALI, and ISHI, I.

Baal in compounds denoting place names implies the omission Beth (house of, abode of).

2. A Reubenite, house of Joel, who lived before the Captivity of the ten tribes (I Chron. 5:5, 6).

3. A Benjamite, son of King Saul's ancestor Jeiel (I Chron. 8:30; 9:35, 36, 39, R.V.).

4. A village of Simeon (I Chron. 4:33); the same as Baalath-beer (*q.v.*).

Ba'al·ah (bā'á-lá) [mistress]. 1. A town better known as Kiriath-jearim (Josh. 15:9).

2. A hill in Judah, between Ekron and Jabneel (Josh. 15:11).

3. A town in the s. of Judah (Josh. 15:29); apparently the same as the Simeonite town Balah (Josh. 19:3) or Bilhah (I Chron. 4:29). Probably modern Tulul el-Medhbaḥ near Khirbet el-Meshash.

Ba'al·ath (bā'ăl-ăth) [mistress]. A village of the original territory of Dan (Josh. 19:44), near Gezer (Jos. *Antiq.* viii. 6, 1). Solomon fortified it (I Kings 9:18; II Chron. 8:6).

Ba'al·ath-be'er (bā'á-lăth-bē'ẽr) [mistress of a well]. A town on the boundary line of the tribe of Simeon. Called simply Baal (I Chron. 4:33), and apparently known also as Ramah and Ramoth of the South (Josh. 19:8; I Sam. 30:27, R.V.). It may be located on the elevation between Khalaṣa and Biyâr Aslûj.

Ba'al-be'rith (bā'ăl-bē'rĭth) [lord of a covenant]. A designation under which in the time of the Judges Baal was worshiped at Shechem, where he had a temple (Judg. 8:33; 9:4). Sometimes he was spoken of as Elberith, the god of a covenant (Judg. 9:46, R.V.; where A.V. partly translates the name: "the god Berith").

Ba'al·e (bā'á-lē). See BAALE-JUDAH.

Ba'al·e-ju'dah (bā'á-lē-jōō'dá) [probably for Baalah of Judah]. A town of Judah, the same as Baalah and Kiriath-baal and Kiriath-jearim (II Sam. 6:2; cf. I Chron. 13:6; Josh. 18:14). See KIRIATH-JEARIM.

Ba'al-gad (bā'ăl-găd) [Gad is Baal]. A place at the foot of Mount Hermon, in the valley of Lebanon, where apparently Gad, the god of fortune, was worshiped. It constituted the extreme n. limit of Joshua's conquests (Josh. 11:17; 12:7; 13:5): perhaps it is Ḥáṣbeya in the *couloir* of the wadi et-Teim.

Ba'al-ha'mon (bā'ăl-hā'mŏn) [Baal of Hamon (multitude)]. A place where Solomon had a vineyard (S. of Sol. 8:11). Its identity with Balamon, a town near Dothan (Judith 8:3), is extremely doubtful in view of the variant spellings in Greek: Belbaim, Belmain, Bailmain, Abelmain (Judith 4:4; 7:3).

Ba'al-ha'nan (bā'ăl-hā'năn) [Baal is gracious]. 1. Son of Achbor and king of Edom (Gen. 36:38; I Chron. 1:49).

2. Custodian of the olive and sycamore trees under King David (I Chron. 27:28).

Ba'al-ha'zor (bā'ăl-hā'zŏr) [Baal of Hazor (enclosure)]. A place beside Ephraim (II Sam. 13:23). Gesenius suggested Hazor in Benjamin (Neh. 11:33). Probably it is Jebel el-'Aṣûr, 4½ miles n.e. of Beth-el and 15 miles n.n.e. of Jerusalem.

Ba'al-her'mon (bā'ăl-hûr'mŏn) [Baal of Hermon]. A place marking the n.w. limit of the half tribe of Manasseh e. of Jordan (Judg.

3:3; I Chron. 5:23). Baal-hermon denotes the sacred places of Mount Hermon, or is a place on its e. slope.

Ba'al·i (bā'á-lī) [my lord, my master]. Hosea represents the relation of Jehovah to Israel as that of husband to wife. After the conquest of Canaan, Jehovah was often identified with Baal. To avoid this further degradation Hosea writes (Hos. 2:16): "[Thou] shalt call me no more Baali." See ISHI, I.

Ba'al·im (bā'ăl-īm) [Heb. pl. of Baal]. Baalim (or Baal under different aspects) were worshiped by the nations neighbor to Israel (Judg. 2:11; 3:7; 8:33; 10:10; I Sam. 7:4; 12:10). Often coupled with Ashtaroth or Asheroth. There were various Baalim, as Melkart, the Baal of Tyre; Baal-shāmīm (lord of heaven) of Phoenicia and Palmyra; and Baal Sāphōn of the Ras Shamra texts. The O.T. also differentiates between Baalim, as Baal-berith, Baal-peor, and Baal-zebub.

Ba'a·lis (bā'á-lĭs). A king of the Ammonites who reigned shortly after Nebuchadnezzar's capture of Jerusalem (Jer. 40:14).

Ba'al-me'on (bā'ăl-mē'ŏn) [Baal of Meon (habitation)]. An old Amorite city on the frontiers of Moab, known fully as Beth-baalmeon (Num. 32:38; Ezek. 25:9; both forms on *Moabite Stone*, 9, 30; see MOABITE STONE). It was assigned to the Reubenites and rebuilt by them (Num. 32:38; in v. 3 called Beon; Josh. 13:17; I Chron. 5:8). It was held by Mesha, king of Moab (*Moabite Stone*, 9, 30; see MOABITE STONE), and was in the possession of the same people in the 6th century B.C. (Ezek. 25:9; and Jer. 48:23, where it is abbreviated to Beth-meon). In Jerome's day it was still a considerable town, about 9¾ miles from Heshbon. The ruins, now called Ma'īn, lie in the n. Moabite territory, 4 miles s.w. of Medeba.

Ba'al-pe'or (bā'ăl-pē'ôr) [Baal of Peor]. A Moabite deity, probably Chemosh, worshiped with immoral rites on the top of Mount Peor. The Israelites, when encamped at Shittim, felt attracted by it, and so sinned that a plague broke out among them, and was not stayed till a slaughter had been ordered of the chief transgressors (Num. 25:1–9; Ps. 106:28; Hos. 9:10). See PEOR 2.

Ba'al-pe·ra'zim (bā'ăl-pê-rā'zĭm) [Baal of the burstings]. A place near the valley of Raphaim where David gained a victory over the Philistines (II Sam. 5:18–20; I Chron. 14:9–11; cf. Isa. 28:21); located at Rās en-Nādir.

Ba'al-shal'i·shah (bā'ăl-shăl'ĭ-shá), in A.V. **Ba'al-shal'i·sha** (bā'ăl-shăl'ĭ-shá) [Baal of Shalishah (a third part)]. A village from which bread and corn of the firstfruits were brought to Elisha when he was at Gilgal, on the mountains, 7½ miles n. of Beth-el (II Kings 4:42–44). The gift was brought to Gilgal because a school of the prophets was there. Conder locates it at the present village of Kefr Thilth on the lower hills of Ephraim, 16 miles n.e. of Lydda and 13½ miles n.w. of Gilgal (Jiljilia). Cf. I Sam. 9:4.

Ba'al-ta'mar (bā'ăl-tā'mär) [Baal of the palm). A place in Benjamin, near Gibeah and Beth-el, where the Israelite army took its stand when about to attack Gibeah (Judg. 20:33), identified with Rās eṭ-Ṭawīl, a peak n.e. of Tell el-Fûl.

Ba'al-ze'bub (bā'ăl-zē'būb) [Baal (lord) of the fly]. The name under which Baal was worshiped at Ekron as the producer of flies, and consequently able to defend against this pest. Ahaziah, king of Judah, applied to him for a revelation (II Kings 1:6, 16). See BEEL-ZEBUB.

Ba'al-ze'phon (bā'ăl-zē'fŏn) [lord of the North, i.e., north point; or lord of the watchtower: cf. Migdol (tower) which was near by]. A place which was over against the Israelites while they were encamped beside Pi-hahiroth, between Migdol and the sea, just before they crossed through the sea (Ex. 14:2, 9). So also in Num. 33:7 Pi-hahiroth is said to be before Baal-zephon. See MIGDOL 1.

Ba'a·na (bā'á-ná); once **Ba'a·nah** (I Kings 4:16, A.V.) [perhaps derived from Baal]. 1. Solomon's purveyor for the s. district of the Plain of Jezreel from Megiddo to the Jordan. He was a son of Ahilud and probably brother of Jehoshaphat the recorder (I Kings 4:12; cf. v. 3).
2. Solomon's purveyor for Asher and vicinity. He was a son of Hushai, not unlikely of that Hushai who was the friend and adviser of David (I Kings 4:16).
3. A certain Zadok's father (Neh. 3:4).

Ba'a·nah (bā'á-ná) [perhaps derived from Baal]. 1. A Benjamite, brother of Rechab, and leader of a predatory band. Although the brothers belonged to the tribe of Saul, they nevertheless murdered his son Ish-bosheth, and thus were partly instrumental in turning the kingdom to David. They carried the head of the murdered man to David at Hebron in expectation of a reward; but David had them put to death as criminals (II Sam., ch. 4).
2. A Netophathite, father of Heled, one of David's worthies (I Chron. 11:30).
3. One of Solomon's purveyors. See BAANA.
4. A Jew who returned from Babylon with Zerubbabel (Ezra 2:2; Neh. 7:7). It was probably the representative of his family who sealed the covenant in Nehemiah's time (Neh. 10:27).

Ba'a·ra (bā'á-rá). A wife of Shaharaim (I Chron. 8:8).

Ba'a·se'iah (bā'á-sē'yá) [perhaps for Maaseiah, as is suggested by *Maasai* of Codex Vaticanus]. A Levite, descendant of Gershom and ancestor of Asaph the singer (I Chron. 6:40).

Ba'a·sha (bā'á-shá) [perhaps a contraction of Baal-shemesh (the sun is Baal or lord)]. Son of Ahijah, of the tribe of Issachar, who conspired against Nadab, the son and successor of Jeroboam I, king of Israel. When Nadab was directing the siege of Gibbethon, then in the hands of the Philistines, Baasha murdered him and all Jeroboam's descendants, thus fulfilling the judgment pronounced against his house (I Kings 16:7). Then the assassin ascended the throne of Israel in the 3d year of Asa, king of Judah, and fixed his capital at Tirzah (I Kings 15:25 to 16:4). He carried on a long war with Asa. He began to fortify Ramah to blockade the n. frontier of Judah, but was diverted from his purpose by the invasion of his kingdom by Ben-hadad, king of Damascus, whom Asa hired (I Kings 15:16–21; II Chron. 16:1–6). Baasha continued the calf worship begun by Jeroboam, and the Prophet Jehu threatened him and his house with Jeroboam's fate. He died after a reign of 24 years, and was buried in Tirzah. His son Elah succeeded him (I Kings 15:34 to 16:6).

Ba'bel (bā'bĕl) [Akkad. *bāb-ilu*, gate of God]. A city dating from prehistoric times in the plain of Shinar. It was the beginning of Nimrod's kingdom, i.e., probably the earliest and chief seat of his power (Gen. 10:10). In the English versions the word Babel occurs only in this passage and 11:9, being rendered Babylon in all other places.

While the phrase "Tower of Babel" is not used in the O.T., it has been applied to the structure built in the plain of Shinar, as recounted in Gen., ch. 11. The expression 'whose top may reach unto heaven" may be interpreted as signifying "a very high tower." The author of the chapter had an accurate knowledge of the building materials of Babylonia. There is neither building stone nor lime on the alluvial plain of Shinar, and so bricks were used for stone. Instead of mortar, slime (bitumen) was employed, of which abundant supplies were found in ancient times at Hit, about 140 miles up the Euphrates from Babylon. In connection with the incident of the unfinished tower, the Hebrew writer accounts for the origin of the various languages; here the original unity of the human race is taken for granted. By a popular etymology, the Hebrew author derives Babel from the root *bālal* (confuse, confound): "because Jehovah did there confound the language of all the earth." Here we have a play upon two words of similar sound, but this derivation should not be regarded as a scientific etymology. According to Gen. 11:9 this confusion of tongues was followed by the dispersion of mankind. Cf. Peleg (Gen. 10:25). Thus from the earliest times Babylon

who did much for it, rendering it the largest and most splendid capital of his time (cf. Dan 4:30). The old palace, which stood on the e bank of the Euphrates, was repaired and enlarged by Nebuchadnezzar, who built a summer palace a mile and a half to the n. of the older one. The old palace consisted of a number of structures and courtyards connected with monumental gateways. At the n.e. corner was a vaulted building consisting of a series of arches, some of which were superimposed upon a lower tier. On this structure were the famous hanging gardens. Herodotus states that Babylon was a square, each side being 120 stades, or about 14 miles, in length. This measurement yields an area of nearly 200 square miles, and includes Borsippa in the city limits. Ctesias, also an eyewitness, who flourished in the 5th century, makes each side of the square about 90 stades, or the length of the 4 sides together 42 miles. The city was surrounded by a wall (Jer. 51:58), or rather double walls (Herod. i. 181). A deep and broad moat ran around the city, and beyond that was a great wall 200 royal cubits

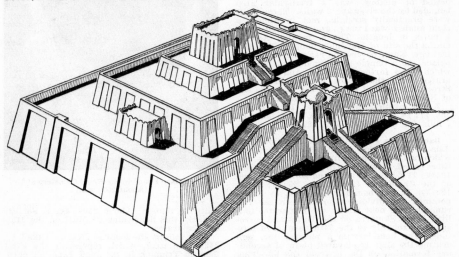

Restoration of a Babylonian Temple Tower (Ziggurat of Ur-Nammu, Dynasty III of Ur)

was conceived of as the emblem of human pride and ambition and was destined to fall.

The author of Gen., ch. 11, undoubtedly had in mind a Babylonian temple tower, or ziggurat. This type of structure is found in primitive Sumerian times. There was in Babylon an ancient ziggurat, which is known to have existed already in the 2d millennium B.C. It was called E-temen-ana-ki (house of the foundation stone of heaven and earth) and stood a short distance to the n. of E-sagila, the temple of Marduk. Including the foundation and the shrine on the top, this ziggurat had eight stories. It was like a step pyramid, 300 ft. square at the base and about 300 ft. high above the foundation. The top was reached by a stairway leading from terrace to terrace.

Bab'y·lon (băb'ĭ-lŏn) [Babel, Akkad. *Bābilu*, with the Greek ending *on*]. 1. The capital of the Babylonian Empire. The city became the mistress of Babylonia under King Hammurabi and henceforth was the political and religious center of the country. See HAMMURABI. It reached the height of its glory in the 6th century B.C., under Nebuchadnezzar,

(about 344 ft.) high and 50 royal cubits (about 86 ft.) wide. On top of this rampart was room enough for a 4-horse chariot to pass, and even to turn, in addition to space enough for chambers facing each other. There was also a strong inner wall. Quintus Curtius, about A.D. 40, gives the breadth at about 32 feet; and Clitarchus (as reported by Diodorus Siculus) and Strabo make the height 75 feet. These writers state the circuits variously, from 365 to 385 stades. The city had 100 gates of bronze, 25 on each side. From these there ran broad streets at right angles to the walls, thus dividing the whole area into squares. Procession Street began slightly n. of the Great Ishtar Gate, proceeded s., turned w. at a right angle to pass between E-sagila and E-temen-ana-ki, and continued to the bridge that crossed the Euphrates. The Euphrates flowed through the midst of the city, dividing it into 2 portions. Along each bank of the river there was a continuous quay. A wall separated the quay from the city; but it was pierced by 25 gateways, from each of which a sloping descent led to the water's edge. The walls, quays, palaces, temples, and private edifices were built of brick; the cement or mortar was bitumen (cf. Gen. 11:3). The timber of the houses, which were 2, 3, and 4 stories high, was of palm wood (Herod. i. 178–186).

In 521 B.C., and again in 514, Babylon revolted against Darius Hystaspis, but on both occasions it was subdued, and the last time was dismantled. Its decay was hastened by Seleucus Nicator, who conquered the city in 312 B.C., and made large use of its materials in building the new capital, Seleucia, on the banks of the Tigris.

The Scripture prophecies regarding Babylon have been fulfilled (Isa., chs. 13; 14:1–23; 21:1–10; 46:1, 2; 47:1–3; Jer., chs. 50; 51). Jeremiah (Jer. 51:37; cf. ch. 50:26) said that it should become heaps, and mounds are all that remain of it now. They commence about 3½ miles above the village of Hillah, and extend n. slightly above 3 miles, by 2 from e. to w., lying chiefly on the e. side of the river. The 3 most notable mounds are now called by the Arabs the Babil, the Kasr, and the Amran mounds. They lie e. of the river, and in a section of the old city which, at some period of history, was a triangular area bounded by the river and 2 walls. These walls were practically straight, met in almost a right angle toward the e., and measured 2 and 3 miles in length. The s. mound, Amran, marks the site of Marduk's temple. The central one, Kasr, covers the remains of the old palace and a temple of the goddess Ninmach, which stood farther to the e. and was separated from the palace by the Procession Street. The mound Babil, in the n., is the site of Nebuchadnezzar's summer palace.

2. The mystic Babylon of Rev. 14:8; 16:19; chs. 17; 18, is the city of Rome, which stood on 7 hills (cf. ch. 17:3, 5, 6, 9, 18).

Bab′y·lo′ni·a (băb′ĭ-lō′nĭ-á). A region of w. Asia at the e. end of the Fertile Crescent, which had Babylon for its capital. It is sometimes called, in whole or in part, Shinar (Gen. 10:10; 11:2; Isa. 11:11), and sometimes land of the Chaldeans (Jer. 24:5; 25:12; Ezek. 12:13). It was bounded on the n. by Mesopotamia, the dividing line between the two running from near Ḥit on the Euphrates to a little below Sāmarrā on the Tigris and corresponding roughly to the 34th parallel of latitude. The boundary is a natural one, separating the slightly elevated plain of secondary formation on the n. from the low-lying alluvium brought down by the Euphrates and the Tigris on the s. Babylonia is bounded on the e. by the mountains of Elam, on the s. by the Persian Gulf, and on the w. by the Arabian desert. It is rarely more than 40 miles wide and probably contained less than 8,000 square miles, roughly equal to the State of New Jersey or Wales. The deep, rich, alluvial soil, artificially irrigated, was of almost matchless fertility.

The land originally consisted of 2 political divisions, Sumer and Akkad. Sumer, the s. part, extended from the Persian Gulf to a line slightly n. of 32° latitude; Akkad occupied the rest of the land to 34° latitude. The principal cities of Akkad were Babylon, Borsippa, Dilbat, Kish, Kuthah, Opis, Sippar, and Agade (Accad); those of Sumer were Nippur, Adab, Lagash, Umma, Larsa, Erech (Uruk), Ur, and Eridu. Most of these cities were on or near the Euphrates.

Little is known of the earliest inhabitants of Babylonia that preceded the Sumerians and the Semites. During the 4th millennium B.C. the Sumerians were in Sumer and Semites occupied Akkad. The Sumerians spoke an agglutinative language, but their race and place of origin are unknown. They probably entered the Plain of Shinar before 4000 B.C. and developed a high civilization. Their sexa-

gesimal system (soon combined with the decimal) still survives. Out of pictographs they developed cuneiform writing. Originally each city had its own god or goddess, but eventually there was developed a triad pantheon: Anu (sky), Enlil (atmosphere and earth), and Ea (waters).

At first the cities were independent kingdoms. Authorities differ a great deal about the dates of the age of the city-kingdoms, but approximate dates may be set (c. 3000–c. 2600 B.C.). In this period falls Dyn. I of Ur. Dynasty I of Lagash was founded (c. 2600) by Ur-Nanshe or Zur-Nanshe (Ur-Nina). Eannatum, his grandson, defeated the city of Umma. Urakagina (c. 2450), of this dynasty, instituted important social reforms, but was defeated by Lugalzaggisi, founder of Dyn. III of Erech. There was now a certain sense of

Silver Harp Found in the Royal Cemetery at Ur
(About 2600 B.C.)

unity in Sumer. About 2600 B.C. a Semitic dynasty was flourishing at Mari on the Middle Euphrates.

Now follows the Semitic Dyn. of Akkad (c. 2425–2245 B.C.), which represents the First Semitic Triumph in the land (another chronology begins this period at c. 2550). Sargon, a great Semitic leader, defeated Lugalzaggisi and conquered all the Sumerian cities. He founded Agade and created an empire in the true sense for the first time in history. It extended from Elam and Assyria as far w. as the Mediterranean. During the reign of Naram-Sin, his grandson, the empire was prosperous. Later the Semitic power began to decay and the barbaric Gutians coming from the e. hills (c. 2250) ruled Babylonia for 125 years. Lagash, however, flourished under Gudea (late 22d century B.C.).

The Gutian period was followed by a renascence of the Sumerians, who remained in power from c. 2135 to c. 2025. Ur-Nammu or Zur-Nammu (Ur-Engur) is the 1st king of the brilliant Dyn. III of Ur. He was the founder of a Sumerian code of laws; his son Shulgi (Dungi) also codified the laws. Their domain extended from Ashur and Arbela to the Persian Gulf, from Susa to the Lebanons.

From c. 2025 on the Sumerians declined and lost their national identity. After the fall of Ur (c. 2025), Isin and Larsa were the dominant states and took over the heritage of Dyn. III of Ur. The Elamites furthermore invaded Sumer from the e., and the Amorites from the w. Dynasty I of Babylon, which was Amorite, was established c. 1894. This city became so important that it gave its name to the Plain of Shinar, which we may thenceforth properly call Babylonia. Now began a three-cornered fight involving Larsa, Isin, and Babylon, and the latter city became supreme. The 6th king of this dynasty was Hammurabi. In the past authorities have modified his dates from time to time, some placing him 2123–2081, 2067–2025, or 1955–1913, but according to the latest chronology his reign extended from 1792 to 1750 or 1749. He defeated Rim-Sin, an Elamite king of Larsa, and unified Sumer and Akkad. Now we can for the first time speak of Babylonia in a political sense; he conquered all Mesopotamia, carried out extensive public works, introduced an excellent administration, and made an extensive code of laws. See HAMMURABI.

Partly contemporary with the Dyn. I of Babylon was the Dyn. I of the Sea Country (c. 1880–c. 1513 B.C.) on the Persian Gulf. Hammurabi's dynasty came to an end in a raid (c. 1595) by the Hittites, who slew the last king, Samsu-ditāna. The Kassites (Cossaeans), who had been invading the land from the highlands to the e. and n.e. (c. 1746), made themselves masters of the country and remained dominant c. 1169 B.C. During the 15th and 14th centuries there was extensive correspondence with Egypt, as is seen in the Tell el-Amarna letters.

Finally Tukulti-Ninurta, king of Assyria (1260–1232), invaded Babylonia and ruled the land for 7 years. In the end the Assyrians were driven out. With the fall of the Kassites, a new dynasty arose in Babylonia, the Dyn. II of Isin. The kings were all native Babylonians; among them Nebuchadrezzar I (1146–1123) is the most famous. He defeated the Elamites and the Hittites, but was routed by the Assyrians. This dynasty came to an end in 1039 B.C. During that period Aramaic tribes (c. 1100–900) invaded Babylonia. Assyria again began to interfere in Babylonian affairs. In 729 Tiglath-pileser III (under the name of Pul) became king of Babylon. The city revolted against Sennacherib, who in 689 sacked Babylon and burned it to the ground; it was rebuilt by Esarhaddon. Until 625 Babylonia remained a part of the Assyrian Empire.

A new nation, the Chaldeans, had been developing around the head of the Persian Gulf and working northward. Merodach-Baladan, one of their kings, secured the support of the Aramaean tribes and made an alliance with Elam. In 721 he proclaimed himself king of Babylon; he sent an embassy to Hezekiah, king of Judah, in 712, but was defeated by Sennacherib in 703. Thereupon he fled to Elam, where he died.

Ashurbanipal, of Assyria, died in 626, and the following year Nabopolassar became king of the Chaldeans and thus founded the Neo-Babylonian or Chaldean Empire. With his ally Cyaxares, king of the Medes, he destroyed Nineveh in 612. His son Nebuchadnezzar (Nebuchadrezzar) totally defeated Necho at Carchemish in 605 and pursued him to the border of Egypt, but was recalled on account of the death of his father. The Chaldeans were now in control of the whole Fertile Crescent. Nebuchadnezzar (605–562) had one of the longest and most brilliant reigns of human history. He took Jerusalem twice (597 and 586) and destroyed it. The buildings and city walls of Babylon, admired by Greek historians, were erected by Nebuchadnezzar. His son Amel-Marduk (Evil-merodach), who reigned from 562 to 560, befriended the captive Jehoiachin (II Kings 25:27). He was assassinated, and Nebuchadnezzar's son-in-law, Neriglissar (560–556), succeeded to the throne; the latter's son,

Lābāshi-Marduk, reigned for 9 months and then was assassinated. A Babylonian, Nabonidus, became king in 556, who appointed his son, Belshazzar, as coregent. See BELSHAZZAR, NABONIDUS, CYRUS, DANIEL.

In 539 Gobryas, a general under Cyrus, king of Persia, took Babylon. The country remained under Persian rule from 539 to 332 B.C.; then it was under Alexander the Great until 323. The Seleucidae ruled Babylonia 312–171 B.C.; they were succeeded by the Parthians (Arsacid Dynasty), who ruled from 171 B.C. to A.D. 226. The Sassanian Dynasty remained in control from A.D. 226 to 641, when Babylonia was conquered by the Moslem Arabs.

After the fall of Jerusalem in A.D. 70 Babylonia became, and for centuries remained, a seat of Jewish schools devoted to the study and interpretation of the law.

Ba'ca (bā'kà) [a balsam tree, perhaps so named from its exuding tears of gum]. A valley in Palestine (Ps. 84:6), possibly so called from the balsam trees in it; cf. the valley of Rephaim, where such trees were found (II Sam. 5:22, 23, R.V. marg.). Perhaps, however, the expression is figurative, with a play upon bākāh (weep). Or by contrast with well, it may mean drought; cf. Arab. baka'a (to have little water).

Bac'chi·des (băk'ĭ-dēz). A Syrian general sent by Demetrius I at the close of 162 B.C. to place Alcimus in the high priesthood, and to subjugate Judah (I Macc. 7:8–20). The next year he defeated Judas and Jonathan Maccabaeus; but his 3d campaign, undertaken in 157 B.C., failed (I Macc. 9:1–57, 59–72).

Badg'er. The rendering of Heb. taḥash in the A.V. (Ex. 26:14; 35:7; Num. 4:25; Ezek. 16:10). The skin of the animal was used for the outer covering of the tabernacle, and for sandals. Tristram says that the common badger, Meles vulgaris, is not rare in the hilly and wooded parts of Palestine, but it does not seem to be alluded to in the Bible. See SEAL 1.

Bae'an (bē'ăn). A tribe, otherwise unknown, which was destroyed by Judas Maccabaeus (I Macc. 5:4).

Bag'pipe'. The rendering on the margin of R.V. of Aram. sūmpōnyā in Dan. 3:5, 10, 15. The texts of A.V. and R.V. translate dulcimer. Sūmpōnyā is apparently from the Greek symphōnia, symphony, unison of sounds. The instrument is used also in Egypt and Arabia, where it consists of a leathern bag in which two pipes are inserted, one for inflating the bag, the other for playing upon with the fingers.

Ba·ha'rum·ite (bà-hā'rŭm-īt). An inhabitant of Bahurim (I Chron. 11:33).

Ba·hu'rim (bà-hū'rĭm) [young men]. A village near the Mount of Olives, on the road from Jerusalem to the Jordan (II Sam. 16:5). It is mentioned repeatedly in the history of David. Thence came Shimei, who cursed him, and in a well there Jonathan and Ahimaaz hid when pursued by the partisans of Absalom (II Sam. 3:16; 16:5; 17:18; 19:16; I Kings 2:8). It has been identified with Rās et-Tmīm, e. of the Mount of Olives.

Ba'jith (bā'jĭth). See BAYITH.

Bak·bak'kar (băk-băk'ēr) [perhaps, investigator]. A Levite (I Chron. 9:15).

Bak'buk (băk'bŭk) [a flask]. One of the Nethinim, and founder of a family, members of which returned from the Captivity (Ezra 2:51; Neh. 7:53).

Bak·bu·ki'ah (băk'bû-kī'à) [flask; or perhaps, Jehovah has poured out]. 1. A Levite resident of Jerusalem, and in high office immediately after the Exile (Neh. 11:17).

2. A Levite, who served as gatekeeper of the Temple in Nehemiah's time (Neh. 12:25).

Ba'laam (bā'lăm) [perhaps, devouring]. A diviner (Josh. 13:22; cf. Num. 24:1), son of Beor, and resident at the town of Pethor, on the Euphrates (Num. 22:5), in Aram, in the hill country of the e. (ch. 23:7). The Hebrew text of Num. 22:5 describes Balak as sending to Balaam "to the land of the children of his people," meaning Balak's native land or, better, Balaam's. The Samaritan, Vulgate, and Syriac have "land of the children of Ammon"; but Balaam is nowhere else connected with the Ammonites, not even in Num. 31:8. This diviner recognized Jehovah as the God of Israel (Num. 23:21), and as one at least of his own gods (ch. 22:18; but the LXX reads merely "Lord God"). Balak, king of Moab, sent an embassy to him, consisting of elders of Moab and Midian, offering him reward to curse the Israelites (Num. 22:5-7). He answered that he could not do so without the consent of Jehovah. Balak dispatched more honorable negotiators, not elders, but princes. Balaam replied that not for a house full of gold and silver would he go beyond the word of Jehovah. He was allowed by God to go with the men, on condition of uttering only the words that God put into his mouth. On the way an angel of the Lord with drawn sword, visible to the ass on which Balaam rode, but not to its rider, thrice disputed his progress. The ass refused to go forward. When beaten it spoke (Num. 22:28-30; II Peter 2:15, 16). Finally, Balaam himself was permitted to see the angel, and learn the peril he was in. He offered to turn back, but was allowed to go forward, on the same stringent condition as before. Balak met him on the banks of the Arnon, and conducted him to Kiriath-huzoth, probably the same as Kiriathaim, on the conspicuous eminence near by, n. of the Arnon. The next morning the two, accompanied by the princes of Moab, went n. to the high places of Baal, from which lofty spot part of the camp of Israel at Shittim was visible (Num. 22:8-41). After sacrifices on 7 altars, Balaam went alone to a bare height. There the word of the Lord came to him. He returned to Balak, and under the irresistible power of God blessed the people he had been invited to curse (Num. 23:1-12). Balak was disappointed, but held to the idea that, as long as Balaam saw but a part of the camp, perhaps he might be able to curse the Israelites. He took Balaam to the top of Pisgah and sacrificed as before; but the only result was fresh blessing instead of cursing (vs. 13-26). A 3d attempt was made from the top of Peor, on the ridge n. of Nebo. Not merely was there blessing, but the utterance ended with the prophecy of a star out of Jacob, and a scepter out of Israel that should sway over Moab and Edom. Balak in anger dismissed Balaam without conferring on him the intended honor (Num. 23:27 to 24:25). Balaam, however, apparently before quitting the country, suggested that if the Israelites could be seduced into the idolatry and the impurity of the worship practiced at Baal-peor, they would come under Jehovah's curse (Num. 31:16). The evil counsel was followed. In the war waged by the Israelites to execute vengeance on the Midianites for this deed, Balaam was slain (Num. 31:8). Various other books of the Bible refer to Balaam's character and fate (Deut. 23:4, 5; Josh. 24:9, 10; Neh. 13:2; Micah 6:5; Jude 11; Rev. 2:14).

Ba'lac (bā'lăk). See BALAK.

Bal'a·dan (băl'á-dăn) [Akkad., (Marduk) has given a son]. Father of Merodach-baladan (II Kings 20:12; Isa. 39:1).

Ba'lah (bā'lả). See BAALAH 3.

Ba'lak (bā'lăk), in A.V. of N.T. **Ba'lac** [perhaps, devastator]. A Moabite king, son of Zippor, who hired Balaam to curse Israel.

Bald Lo'cust. The rendering of Heb. *sol'ām*, a species of edible locust or grasshopper (Lev. 11:22). There is nothing in the Hebrew etymology to suggest a bald appearance.

Balm, Balm of Gil'e·ad. The rendering of Heb. *ṣŏrī*, a resin perhaps obtained in Gilead (Gen. 37:25; Jer. 8:22; 46:11), and exported from Palestine (Gen. 37:25; Ezek. 27:17). It seems that Gilead was at least the entrepôt for it. It was used as an ointment for the healing of wounds (Jer. 51:8). It was once believed, and still is by many, that the balm of Gilead was opobalsamum, a greenish-yellow oily resin of the consistency of honey, to which wonderful healing virtues were attributed. It comes from a tree, *Balsamodendron opobalsamum* or *gileadense*, belonging to the order *Amyridaceae* (*Amyrids*). It is from 6 to 8 feet high. But the identification of the opobalsamum with the balm of Gilead is rendered doubtful by the fact that the tree producing it is not now found in Gilead, even in gardens, and there is no proof that it ever existed in that locality. It is a native of Arabia and Nubia, and its product is often called the balm of Mecca. In R.V. marg. (Gen. 37:25) the word is rendered by mastic, i.e., the resin yielded by the mastic tree, *Pistacia lentiscus*, a bushy evergreen tree, about 12 feet high, which grew in Palestine. The transparent, pale yellow, fragrant gum was used for incense and, when dissolved in water, as an ointment; while oil obtained from the bark, leaves, and berries was used as a medicine.

Bal'sam Tree. The rendering of Heb. *bākā'* in R.V. marg. of Ps. 84:6; II Sam. 5:22-24; I Chron. 14:14, 15. The Arabs apply the name to a bush which grows near Mecca, resembles the balsam, and has a white, acrid sap. See BACA, BALM, and MULBERRY TREE.

Ba'mah (bā'mä) [high place]. Ezekiel (Ezek. 20:29), in a contemptuous derivation, plays upon the two syllables, *bā* (go) and *māh* (what). See HIGH PLACES.

Ba'moth (bā'mŏth) [high places]. An encampment of the Israelites n. of the Arnon, probably an abbreviation of Bamoth-baal (Num. 21:19).

Ba'moth-ba'al (bā'mŏth-bā'ăl) [high places of Baal]. A place n. of the Arnon, probably that at which the Israelites temporarily encamped, to which Balak took Balaam, and whence the plains of Moab were visible (Num. 21:19; 22:41, R.V. marg.). It is called Bethbamoth on the Moabite Stone (27). See MOABITE STONE. It was within the limits of the tribe of Reuben (Josh. 13:17; where it is named between Dibon and Beth-baal-meon), and is probably to be identified with Khirbet el-Ḳueiḳiyeh, about 2½ miles s. of Mount Nebo.

Ba'ni (bā'nī) [builder, or perhaps a contraction of Benaiah]. 1. A Gadite, one of David's mighty men (II Sam. 23:36); cf. I Chron. 11:38, which seems to have undergone textual corruption.

2. A descendant of Judah through Perez (I Chron. 9:4, R.V.).

3. Founder of a family, members of which returned from Babylonia with Zerubbabel (Ezra 2:10). Some of them took foreign wives (Ezra 10:29). The family's representative sealed the covenant (Neh. 10:14). Called also Binnui (Neh. 7:15).

4. A Levite of the family of Merari (I Chron. 6:46).

5. A Levite who lived before the Return from Exile, of the sons of Asaph and hence of the family of Gershom (Neh. 11:22).

6. A Levite, father of Rehum (Neh. 3:17); perhaps he who took a prominent part at the

feast of tabernacles in Ezra's time (Neh. 8:7; 9:4, 5), and in behalf of his house sealed the covenant (Neh. 10:13).

7. A Levite (Neh. 9:4). As the name is mentioned twice in v. 4 and only once in v. 5, it is perhaps once corrupt in v. 4.

8. Founder of house or family (Ezra 10:34), among whose descendants was a person also named Bani (Ezra 10:38).

Bank and **Bank'er.** Not only was money lent by a man to his neighbor as a private transaction, but money-lending was a regular business. The banker sat at his table (Luke 19:23), received money on deposit, allowed interest on it (*ibid.*; Matt. 25:27), and lent it to others on pledge or mortgage (cf. Neh. 5:3, 4). A branch of the banking business was money-changing. For a small commission the broker exchanged money of one denomination for that of another, as shekels for the half shekels needed to pay the Temple tax; or gave coins current in the country for foreign money, as a Hebrew shekel for Roman denarii and Greek drachmas (Mark 11:15; John 2:15). See LOAN.

Bap'tism. The rite of washing with water as a sign of religious purification and consecration. Among the Jews, as elsewhere, such washings were frequent; some prescribed in the O.T. (Ex. 29:4; 30:20; 40:12; Lev., chs. 15; 16:26, 28; 17:15; 22:4, 6; Num. 19:8) and others the product of later custom (Mark 7:3, 4; Heb. 6:2). Many believe also that in Christ's time, as certainly was the case later, proselytes to Judaism were baptized. Hence John, the Forerunner, when sent to call Israel to repentance, was directed by God (John

Ancient Representation of the Baptism of Christ, from a Church in Ravenna
John stands on the riverbank, our Lord in the water. The river Jordan is symbolized by the sitting figure

1:33) to administer baptism to those who accepted his message. His rite is called "the baptism of repentance unto remission of sins" (Mark 1:4). Recipients of it thereby acknowledged their sins and professed their faith that through the coming Messiah they would be forgiven. Jesus sought baptism partly to express his sympathy with John's work, partly to dedicate himself to his own work, and partly to express his assumption of the sins of men. The mode of John's baptism is not described, but, as Jesus entered into the Jordan (Mark 1:9, 10), it was probably by affusion or by immersion. At first Christ's disciples continued to baptize the people as John had done (John 4:1, 2), thus carrying on John's work, but after Christ's Galilean ministry began, we read of this no more. But in his parting instructions (Matt. 28:19). Christ made bap-

tism the initiatory rite of his Church, one of the two sacraments to be observed by his followers. Hence we find it from the first required and administered by the apostles and their colaborers (Acts 2:38, 41; 8:12, 38; 9:18; 10:48; I Cor. 1:14, 16, etc.). It signifies and seals a believer's union with Christ through repentance and faith; the removal of his sins by Christ's death and the Spirit's operation in him; and his engagement to be the Lord's (Rom. 6:4; Gal. 3:27; Col. 2:11, 12; I Peter 3:21). Christians have differed, even from early times, as to the mode of baptism. While the word is derived from a verb, *baptizō*, which means, etymologically, to immerse, this does not prove that immersion was the mode always practiced, nor that it is necessary. In fact, instances occur where the word plainly does not mean immerse: (e.g., Luke 11:38, in A.V., wash [R.V., bathe], and probably Mark 7:4). The Scriptures nowhere describe, much less prescribe, the mode. In the postapostolic times both immersion and affusion were used. The Eastern Churches and the Protestant Baptists still practice immersion, the Latin Church generally uses affusion, while most Protestants use affusion or aspersion (sprinkling). Probably the mode varied even in apostolic times. According to Christ's command, it is to be administered in the name of the Trinity. Modern Baptists contend that baptism should be administered only to adult believers. The Church, however, from the earliest time has administered it also to children who have sponsors to care for their Christian nurture. It is certainly Scriptural to do this to children of believers, since Paul expressly teaches (Gal. 3:15–29) that believers in Christ are under the gracious provisions of the covenant which God made with Abraham. Under that covenant circumcision was administered to children as a sign of their participation in the relation in which their parents stood to God. The children of Christian believers have therefore a similar right to the ordinance which has replaced circumcision.

The phrase "baptized for the dead" (I Cor. 15:29) is difficult to explain. It probably either means "baptized with a view to the world of the dead into which we are going," or refers to a custom of baptizing one person in place of another who has died, a custom which Paul might cite for his argument without approving.

G. T. P.

Bar·ab'bas (bär-ăb'ăs) [Gr. from Aram., son of the father (master, teacher) or of Abba]. A robber who in an insurrection had committed murder. He was a notable prisoner when Jesus was arrested. Pilate, anxious to release Jesus, offered the Jews the option of releasing Jesus or Barabbas, and they chose Barabbas (Matt. 27:16–26).

Bar'a·chel (bär'á-kĕl) [God has blessed]. A Buzite, father of Elihu, Job's friend (Job 32:2, 6).

Bar'a·chi'ah (bär'á-kī'á) in A.V. **Bar'a·chi'as** (bär'á-kī'ăs), Gr. modification of Heb. name [Jehovah has blessed]. Father of that prophet, Zachariah, who was slain between the Temple and the altar (Matt. 23:35). See ZACHARIAH 3.

Bar'ak (bâr'ăk) [lightning]. An Israelite of the city of Kedesh-naphtali, who at the command of Deborah the prophetess, called together 10,000 men of Naphtali and Zebulun, with whom he routed Sisera, Jabin's commander in chief. (Judg., chs. 4; 5:1; 12; Heb. 11:32).

Bar·bar'i·an. 1. Originally one who did not speak Greek. "Greeks and . . . Barbarians" embraced all nations (cf. Rom. 1:14). There being nothing offensive in the word, the Romans and the Jews were content to be called barbarians.

2. Later, one who did not belong to the cultivated Hellenic race (cf. Col. 3:11).

3. One who spoke an unintelligible foreign tongue (I Cor. 14:11).

Bar·hu'mite (bär-hū'mĭt). Probably a misreading of Baharumite (cf. II Sam. 23:31 with I Chron. 11:33).

Ba·ri'ah (bả-rī'ả) [fugitive]. Son of Shemaiah, a descendant of David (I Chron. 3:22).

Bar'-Je'sus (bär'jē'zŭs) [Gr. from Aram., son of Jesus]. See ELYMAS.

Bar'-Jo'nah (bär'jō'nả), in A.V. **Bar'-jo·na** (bär'jō'nả) [Aram.]. A surname of the Apostle Peter (Matt. 16:17); probably meaning "son of John" (John 1:42; 21:15-17, R.V.), for the Hebrew word from which John is derived is occasionally written in Greek in a form not distinguished from the name of Jonah (cf. various Greek texts of II Kings 25:23; I Chron. 6:9, 10; 12:12; 26:3; Ezra 8:12; I Esdras 9:1, 23).

Bar'kos (bär'kŏs) [probably Aram., son of the Edomite god Kos]. One of the Nethinim, who founded a family, members of which returned from the Captivity (Ezra 2:53; Neh. 7:55); called Barchus in I Esdras 5:32.

Bar'ley. A cereal grain, called by the Hebrews śeʻōrāh, the hairy, bristling thing, and largely cultivated in Palestine (Ruth 1:22).

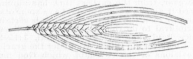

Head of Barley (*Hordeum distichon*)

Egypt (Ex. 9:31) and the adjacent regions, and made into cakes or loaves (Judg. 7:13; John 6:9). The several barleys belong to the genus *Hordeum*. For barley harvest see YEAR.

Bar'na·bas (bär'nả-băs) [Gr. from Aram. Explained in Acts 4:36b as son of exhortation or consolation, which favors Aram. *Bar-nebŭ'ăh,* son of prophecy, especially as it takes the form of exhortation or consolation (cf. I Cor. 14:3); the name may have been originally *Bar-Nebō,* son of (the Babylonian god) Nebo, and later by a popular etymology explained as above]. The surname of Joseph, a Levite of Cyprus, who, early converted to Christianity, sold his land and laid the price at the feet of the apostles in Jerusalem (Acts 4:36, 37). When the Christians of Jerusalem were afraid to receive the new convert Paul, Barnabas spoke in his behalf, and removed their apprehensions (Acts 9:27). When the report reached Jerusalem that Christians of Cyprus and Cyrene had been proclaiming the gospel with great success to Greeks as well as to Jews at Antioch of Syria, the Church sent Barnabas thither, and he aided in the work (Acts 11:19-24). From Antioch he went to Tarsus and brought back Saul (Acts 11:22-26). Later the two were dispatched to carry alms to their brethren at Jerusalem, who were suffering from famine (vs. 27-30). Returning with John Mark to Antioch (ch. 12:25), they were sent forth by the Church on a mission to the Gentiles (ch. 13:2). They visited Cyprus, and went thence to Perga, Antioch in Pisidia, Iconium, Lystra, and Derbe. At Lystra at Paul's command a cripple walked; and the inhabitants concluded that Barnabas was their supreme god Jupiter, and that Paul, since he was the chief speaker, was Mercury, the messenger of the gods (Acts 13:3 to 14:28). Having returned to Syria, they were sent by the church of Antioch to the council of Jerusalem. Barnabas spoke, as did Paul (ch. 15:1, 2, 12). At the close the two were commissioned to carry the decrees of the council to the churches in Syria and Asia Minor (vs. 22-31). After further labors at Antioch (v. 35), Paul proposed a 2d missionary journey. Barnabas desired to have with him his relative, John Mark (Col. 4:10). Paul objected, as John Mark had withdrawn from the work on the former tour. In sharp contention, the two evangelists separated and went different ways. Barnabas with Mark sailed again to Cyprus, while Paul went on to Asia Minor (Acts 15:36-41). But their mutual affection did not cease. Paul, in his epistles, speaks in a friendly way of Barnabas (I Cor. 9:6; Gal. 2:1, 9, 13; Col. 4:10), and yet more so of John Mark, about whom the quarrel arose (II Tim. 4:11).

Bar·sab'bas (bär-săb'ăs), in A.V. **Bar'sa·bas** (bär'sả-băs) [Gr. from Aram., son of Sabbas, Sabba(?); perhaps, son of, i.e., born on, the Sabbath]. 1. The surname of the Joseph who stood candidate for the apostleship against Matthias (Acts 1:23).

2. The surname of the Judas who was sent to Antioch as a delegate of the metropolitan church with Paul, Barnabas, and Silas (Acts 15:22).

Bar·thol'o·mew (bär-thŏl'ō-mū) [Gr. from Aram., son of Tolmai; cf. Heb. *telem,* furrow]. One of the 12 apostles (Matt. 10:3; Mark 3:18; Luke 6:14; Acts 1:13). As in the first 3 of these passages the name of Bartholomew immediately follows that of Philip, and nearly does so in the 4th. Bartholomew was probably the surname of Nathanael, who was led to Christ by Philip (John 1:45, 46).

Bar·ti·mae'us (bär'tĭ-mē'ŭs) [Lat. from Gr. from Aram., son of Timaeus]. A blind man healed by Jesus at Jericho (Mark 10:46).

Bar'uch (bâr'ŭk) [blessed]. 1. A scribe, son of Neriah, and a friend of Jeremiah (Jer. 36:26, 32; cf. Jos. *Antiq.* x. 9, 1). In the 4th year of Jehoiakim, he wrote from dictation the prophecies of Jeremiah (Jer. 36:1-8). In the following year he read them publicly on the fast day (Jer. 36:10), and afterward before the princes, who took the roll (vs. 14-20). The king, on hearing the opening sentences, burnt the roll and ordered the seizure of the prophet and the scribe, but they escaped (vs. 21-26). Baruch made a new copy with additions (vs. 27-32). In the 10th year of Zedekiah, during the siege of Jerusalem, Jeremiah bought a field at Anathoth from his uncle and, being at the time a prisoner, placed the deed in the charge of Baruch and testified that the land should again be possessed by Israel (Jer. 32:6-16, 43, 44). Baruch was taken with Jeremiah to Egypt (Jer. 43:1-7). For the book bearing the name of Baruch, see APOCRYPHA 8.

2. Son of Zabbai. He repaired part of the wall of Jerusalem (Neh. 3:20). He is perhaps the person of that name who sealed the covenant (Neh. 10:6).

3. A man of Judah, of the Shilonite family (Neh. 11:5).

Bar·zil'la·i (bär-zĭl'ȧ-ī) [made of iron]. 1. A wealthy Gileadite of Rogelim, e. of the Jordan. He showed David princely hospitality, sending him and his army food and other necessaries while the fugitive king was at Mahanaim during Absalom's rebellion (II Sam. 17:27-29). After the victory, Barzillai escorted David over the Jordan, and was invited to become a member of the king's household and court at Jerusalem, but he excused himself on account of his great age—80 years. It was therefore arranged that his son Chimham should go in his stead (II Sam. 19:31-40).

2. A Meholathite, whose son Adriel married Saul's daughter Michal (II Sam. 21:8).

3. A priest who married a daughter of Barzillai the Gileadite, and assumed his father-in-law's name (Ezra 2:61; Neh. 7:63).

Bas'ca·ma (băs'ká·må). A town in Gilead near which Jonathan Maccabaeus was put to death, and where for a time he was buried (I Macc. 13:23; and Jos. *Antiq.* xiii. 6, 6, where it is called Basca).

Bas'e·math (băs'ê·măth), in A.V. **Bash'e·math**, once **Bas'math** (I Kings 4:15) [fragrance; but cf. Arab. *basama*, to smile]. 1. One of Esau's wives, daughter of Elon the Hittite (Gen. 26:34); in Gen. 36:2 called Adah. See ADAH 2.

2. One of Esau's wives, a daughter of Ishmael and sister of Nebaioth (Gen. 36:3, 4, 13, 17); in Gen. 28:9 called Mahalath.

3. A daughter of Solomon and wife of his tax collector for Naphtali (I Kings 4:15).

Ba'shan (bā'shăn) [even and smooth land]. A region e. of the Jordan. Its location and extent in O.T. times is best learned from its cities. Within its bounds were Golan, n. of the Yarmuk (Deut. 4:43), Edrei and Ashtaroth (Deut. 1:4), Salecah on the s. slope of the Jebel Hauran (Deut. 3:10; Josh. 13:11, R.V.). That is to say, it extended s.e. from the neighborhood of the upper Jordan to the border of the Arabian desert s. of the Hauran mountain. On the n. it bordered upon Geshur and Maacah (Josh. 12:5), and contained "the region of the Argob," famous for 60 cities high-walled (Deut. 3:4, 5; I Kings 4:13). Josephus identifies Bashan with Gaulonitis and Batanea (cf. Jos. *Antiq.* iv. 5, 3 with I Kings 4:13; and *Antiq.* ix. 8, 1 with II Kings 10:33). In the days of Abraham it was occupied by a people of especially large and powerful build, known as Rephaim (Gen. 14:5). The last king of this race was Og, who was defeated and slain at Edrei by the Israelites in the time of Moses (Num. 21:33–35; Deut. 3:1–7). Bashan was assigned to the half tribe of Manasseh (Deut. 3:13). It is a broad, fertile plateau, of volcanic formation, and well adapted for pasture. It was celebrated for its cattle (Ps. 22:12; Ezek. 39:18; Amos 4:1), and for its breed of sheep (Deut. 32:14). It was known also for its oak trees (Isa. 2:13; Ezek. 27:6; Zech. 11:2). Forests of evergreen oak still survive.

Ba'shan·ha'voth·ja'ir (bā'shăn-hā'vŏth-jā'ĭr); rightly separated by R.V., which renders, "He called them, even Bashan, after his own name, Havvoth-jair" (Deut. 3:14). See HAVVOTH-JAIR.

Bash'e·math (băsh'ê·măth). See BASEMATH.

Ba'sin, formerly spelled **Ba'son**. A portable vessel for holding water for washing and other purposes (John 13:5). The word is used for bowls and dishes of various kinds, especially for:

1. A small vessel, in Heb. *'aggān* (Isa. 22:24, rendered cup), used for wine (S. of Sol. 7:2, rendered goblet) and other liquids (Ex. 24:6).

2. A shallow vessel, in Heb. *saph*, used for domestic purposes (II Sam. 17:28) and to receive the blood of sacrifices (Ex. 12:22). They were employed in the Temple (Jer. 52:19, R.V. cups; II Kings 12:13, A.V. bowl, R.V. cup).

3. A large bowl, in Heb. *mizrāk̦*, used in the tabernacle and Temple, especially in ministrations at the great altar (Num. 4:14), to hold the meal offering (Num. 7:13, rendered bowl), and to receive the blood of sacrifices (Zech. 9:15; 14:20, rendered bowl). It was made of gold, silver, or brass, and burnished (Ex. 27:3; Num. 7:84, rendered bowl; I Kings 7:45, 50). Revelers sometimes drank wine from such vessels (Amos 6:6, rendered bowl).

Bas'ket. Baskets of different sizes, shapes, and construction were in use, and various names were employed for them. As ancient sculptures and relics show, and as the etymology denotes, they were woven open or close, were made of the fiber or leaves of the palm tree or of rushes, reeds, twigs, or ropes, tapered at the top or at the bottom, were shallow or deep, ornamented with colors or plain, small enough to be carried in the hand, or so large that they were carried on the shoulder or head or borne on a pole between 2 men. They were employed for carrying fruit (Deut. 26:2; Jer. 6:9; 24:2; Amos 8:2, where in each passage a different Hebrew word is used); for carrying bread, cakes, and flesh (Gen. 40:17; Ex. 29:2, 3; Lev. 8:2; Judg. 6:19; Mark 8:19, 20, where still another Hebrew and 2 Greek names occur); for carrying clay to the brickyard and earth for the building of embankments (Ps. 81:6, R.V.).

Bas'math (băs'măth). See BASEMATH.

Bat. The rendering of Heb. *'ăṭallēph.* It was classed with fowls, and was ceremonially unclean (Lev. 11:13, 19; Deut. 14:11, 12, 18). The bat is not a bird, but is a quadruped, covered with hair instead of feathers, having teeth instead of a bill, and suckling its young. Nor is its "wing" a flying apparatus of the bird type; it is an unfeathered membrane connecting the fore and hind legs.

Bath. A Hebrew measure of capacity used for measuring liquids (I Kings 7:26, 38; II Chron. 2:10; 4:5; Ezra 7:22). It was 1/10 of a homer, and corresponds to the dry measure ephah in capacity (Ezek. 45:10, 11, 14); it equals about 9.8 gal. in the U.S.A. In the excavations at Lachish there were found 2 broken jars dating from the reign of Zedekiah, but both have been reconstructed. One bears a seal BTLMLK, which may be rendered, "Royal bath"; it contains 2,764.353 cubic inches, or 11.966 gals., U.S. standard. The other bears a private seal and has a capacity of 2,847.84 cubic inches, or 12.328 gals., U.S. standard. No doubt both jars were intended to hold the same quantity, and they give us an approximate idea of the bath in the 6th century B.C.

Bath'ing. In the warm climate of the East frequent bathing is a necessity. The daughter of Pharaoh bathed in the Nile (Ex. 2:5). The Egyptians wore linen garments, constantly fresh-washed, and their priests washed themselves in cold water twice every day and twice every night (Herod. ii. 37). Egyptians, Hebrews, and Syrians washed the dust of the road from their feet when they tarried at a house (Gen. 18:4; 19:2; 24:32; 43:24; John 13:10). If the Israelites contracted ceremonial defilement, they bathed the body and washed the raiment (Lev. 14:8; 15:5; 17:15; Num. 19:7, 8), either in running water (Lev. 15:13), at a fountain (Judith 12:7, 9; cf. John 9:7), in a river (II Kings 5:10), or at home in court or garden (II Sam. 11:2, 4; cf. Susanna 15). They washed and anointed themselves and put on their best garments for gala and court attire and on putting away mourning (Ex. 40:12, 13; Ruth 3:3; II Sam. 12:20; Judith 10:3; Matt. 6:17). The priests washed their hands and feet before entering the sanctuary or burning an offering on the altar (Ex. 30:19–21). The high priest bathed at his inauguration and on the day of atonement before each act of propitiation (Lev. 8:6; 16:4, 24). In the time of Christ, the Jews washed their hands before eating, and washed or sprinkled themselves on coming from the market (Mark 7:3, 4). At this time also, when Greek and Roman customs had gained entrance among the Jews, there were public baths. The warm springs at Tiberias, Gadara, and Callirrhoe, near the e. shore of the Dead Sea, were resorted to for health (Jos. *Antiq.* xvii. 6, 5;

xviii. 2, 3). The fish ponds connected with the palace at Jericho were used for bathing and swimming (Jos. *Antiq.* xv. 3, 3).

Bath'-rab'bim (băth'răb'ĭm) [daughter of multitudes]. Probably one of the gates of Heshbon (S. of Sol. 7:4).

Bath-she'ba (băth-shē'bá) [probably daughter of an oath; or, rather, daughter of the 7th day, i.e., of the Sabbath]. Daughter of Eliam, and wife of Uriah the Hittite. She is the woman with whom David so shamefully sinned, and who, after the removal of her husband, became the wife of David and mother of Solomon (II Sam. 11:3, 4; 12:24; I Kings 1: 11). When Adonijah was preparing to usurp the kingdom, Bath-sheba, supported by the Prophet Nathan, appealed to David in favor of her own son Solomon; the result was that Adonijah's enterprise was thwarted (I Kings 1:11–53), and he himself was ultimately put to death (I Kings 2:13–25).

Bath'-shu'a (băth'shōō'á) [daughter of opulence, or daughter of Shua]. 1. The daughter of Shua and wife of Judah (I Chron. 2:3, where E.R.V. reads Bath-shua; see Gen. 38: 2, 12).

2. The text of I Chron. 3:5 calls the mother of Solomon Bath-shua, the daughter of Ammiel. Bath-shua is probably a misreading of Bath-sheba, due to a partial effacement of the Heb. letter *beth*. The LXX has here the usual form for Bath-sheba.

Bav'va·i (băv'á-ī), in A.V. **Bav'a·i** (băv'á-ī). A son of Henadad, who superintended the repair of part of the wall of Jerusalem (Neh. 3: 18).

Ba'yith (bā'yĭth), in A.V. **Ba'jith** [house]. The Heb. text has the definite article. A Moabite town or temple (Isa. 15:2).

Bay Tree. The rendering in the A.V. of Heb. *'ezrāḥ* in Ps. 37:35. The R.V. more plausibly renders *'ezrāḥ* "a green tree in its native soil," which, of course, tends to flourish better than a transplanted and, perhaps, a sickly exotic. The same Heb. word is used in Lev. 16:29; 18:26, for a native as distinguished from a man from another country.

Baz'lith (băz'lĭth) or **Baz'luth** (băz'lŭth) [stripping]. One of the Nethinim and founder of a family, members of which returned from Captivity (Ezra 2:52; Neh. 7:54).

Bdel'li·um. The rendering of Heb. *bedōlaḥ*, a substance of the same color as manna (Num. 11:7), and found like gold and the onyx stone or the beryl in the land of Havilah (Gen. 2: 12). The Greeks gave the name *bdellion* to a transparent, waxy, fragrant gum obtained from a tree in Arabia, Babylonia, India, and Media. The best came from Bactria. As gold, the onyx, and the beryl, belong to the mineral kingdom, *bedōlaḥ* may perhaps also. The LXX translates it in Gen. 2:12 *anthrax*, the carbuncle, ruby, and garnet; and in Num. 11:7, *krystallos*, rock crystal.

Be'a·li'ah (bē'á-lī'á) [Jehovah is Lord]. A Benjamite warrior who came to David at Ziklag (I Chron. 12:5).

Be'a·loth (bē'á-lŏth) [mistresses, possessors]. 1. A village in the extreme s. of Judah (Josh. 15:24). See BAALATH-BEER.

2. A locality in the vicinity of the tribe of Asher, perhaps known by this name (I Kings 4:16, R.V.). See ALOTH. In Heb. *bealōth* it is uncertain whether we have one word or whether *be* is the preposition in.

Bean. Beans were used for food (II Sam. 17:28), and occasionally, especially during famine, were mixed with grain and made into a coarse bread (Ezek. 4:9).

Bear. The Syrian bear is of a yellowish-brown color, and, unless pressed by necessity,

lives chiefly on vegetable food. But all bears are dangerous when meddled with (Isa. 11:7; Amos 5:19), especially when robbed of their whelps (II Sam. 17:8; Prov. 17:12; Hos. 13:8). Though now almost confined to Lebanon, on the w. of the Jordan, and Hermon, Gilead, and Bashan, on the e. of the river, it anciently roamed over the land. David killed one in the vicinity of Bethlehem (I Sam. 17: 34), and near Beth-el two she bears, which came out of the woods, tore in pieces 42 young persons who mocked Elisha (II Kings 2:24).

The bear of Dan. 7:5, commissioned to devour much flesh, probably was Media. The 4 beasts of Daniel are combined in one beast in Rev. 13:2, to symbolize all the power of the world. The feet are bear's feet.

For the constellation Bear, see ARCTURUS.

Beard. The beard was cherished as the badge of manly dignity. Its neglect was an outward sign of mental aberration (I Sam. 21: 13) or of affliction (II Sam. 19:24). As a mark of mourning it was customary to pluck it out or cut it off (Ezra 9:3; Isa. 15:2; Jer. 41:5; Herod. ii. 36). The king of the Ammonites grievously insulted David's ambassadors when, among other acts, he shaved off one half of their beards (II Sam. 10:4, 5; cf. Herod. ii. 121, 4). The ancient Egyptians shaved the head and the face, but often wore a false beard. They let the hair and beard grow as a sign of mourning (Herod. ii. 36). Hence Joseph, when released from prison, shaved the beard in order to appear before Pharaoh (Gen. 41:14). The practice of shaving off the corners of the beard (Lev. 19:27; Jer. 9:26; 25:23, both R.V.) was probably a heathenish sign, as the Arabs shaved the side of the face between the ear and the eye in honor of their god Orotal (Herod. iii. 8).

Beast. 1. A mammal, not man, as distinguished from a fowl of the air and a creeping thing (Gen. 1:29, 30). The wild beasts are distinguished from domesticated animals (Lev. 26:22; Isa. 13:21, 22; 34:14; Jer. 50:39; Mark 1:13).

2. Any of the inferior animals, including reptiles and birds, as distinguished from man (Ps. 147:9; Eccl. 3:19; Acts 28:5). In this sense there was a distinction drawn under the Mosaic Law between ceremonially clean and unclean beasts.

3. Figuratively, a fierce destructive power. Four successive empires, beginning with Babylonia, are thus symbolized in Dan., ch. 7. The 4 beasts, combined into a composite monster, represent the power of the world in Rev. 13: 1–10, with its seat transferred from Babylon to Rome, Rev. 17:3–18. A beast with lamb's horns represents false prophecy (Rev. 13:11– 18), which is a ravening wolf in sheep's clothing. The beasts of Rev. 4:6–9 of the A.V. are very properly altered to "living creatures" in the R.V.

Be·at'i·tudes [Lat. *beatitudo*, blessedness]. This word does not occur in the English Bible. The primary meaning of beatitude is blessedness, whence it developed into the signification of a declaration of blessedness. In the latter sense the term Beatitudes has been applied to the sayings of Jesus which introduce the Sermon on the Mount (Matt. 5:3–12; Luke 6:20– 23). In regard to the number in Matthew, opinions differ; if vs. 10–12 are counted as one beatitude, there are 8. Augustine speaks of a heptad of Beatitudes, with the 8th returning upon the 1st. Luke records 4, and adds 4 woes which are not given by Matthew. The Beatitudes in Matthew are in the 3d person, while those of Luke are in the 2d; the more spiritual words which occur in Matthew are omitted in Luke. The 8 Beatitudes are an analysis of perfect spiritual well-being and correct all low and carnal views of human happiness. They do not necessarily describe 8 different classes of people, but 8 different elements of excellence which may all be combined in the same individual.

Be'ba·i (bē'bá-ī). The founder of a family, some of whose members returned from the Captivity (Ezra 2:11; 8:11; Neh. 7:16).

Be'cher (bē'kẽr) [cf. Arab. *bakr*, young camel]. 1. A son of Benjamin (Gen. 46:21; I Chron. 7:6). His descendants were apparently too few at the beginning to form a tribal family, at least they found no place in the registry of families (Num. 26:38; I Chron. 8:1–6), but they ultimately increased to 9 fathers' houses, inhabiting Anathoth and other towns in the territory of Benjamin and mustering 20,200 men (I Chron. 7:8, 9).
2. A son of Ephraim, and founder of a family (Num. 26:35). In I Chron. 7:20 the name appears as Bered.

Be·co'rath (bē-kō'răth), in A.V. **Be·cho'rath** (bē-kō'răth) [primogeniture]. A Benjamite, an ancestor of King Saul (I Sam. 9:1).

Bed. An article of domestic furniture to sleep upon. The poor and travelers often slept on the ground, using their upper garment as a covering (Gen. 28:11; Ex. 22:26). A bed might be no more than a rug or mat, easily bundled up and carried away (Matt. 9:6). But beds raised from the ground were early in existence (II Kings 1: 4, 6; 4:10), with bedsteads of wood, or of iron (Deut. 3:11), or among the wealthy of ivory (Amos 6:4), with silken cushions (Amos 3:12, R.V.) and rich coverings (Prov. 7:16; Judith 10:21).

Be'dad (bē'dăd) [separation]. The father of Hadad, king of Edom (Gen. 36:35; I Chron. 1:46).

Be'dan. (bē'dăn). Apparently a Hebrew judge, mentioned between Gideon and Jephthah, but the order cannot be pressed (I Sam. 12:11). He is not mentioned in The Book of Judges. Various theories have been proposed in explanation, but it is best to regard Bedan as an early misreading for Abdon (Judg. 12: 13) or for Barak, which is found in the LXX and the Peshitta (I Sam. 12:11; cf. Heb. 11: 32).

Be·de'iah (bē-dē'yá). A son of Bani, who was induced by Ezra to put away his foreign wife (Ezra 10:35).

Bee. An insect which makes honey (Judg. 14:8, 18). It is compared to an army (Isa. 7: 18) chasing man (Deut. 1:44), or surrounding him (Ps. 118:12). As Canaan was a land flowing with milk and honey (Ex. 3:8), bees must have been there in large numbers. Their nests were in rocks (Ps. 81: 16) and in woods (I Sam. 14:25), especially in Judah (Ezek. 27:17; cf. Matt. 3:4).

Be'e·li'a·da (bē'ē-lī'á-dá) [the Lord has known]. A son of King David, born at Jerusalem (I Chron. 14:7). During his lifetime he may also have been called by the alternate name Eliada (God has known); at any rate, when the word Baal became distasteful on account of idolatrous associations, the Hebrew historians wrote Eliada instead of Beeliada (II Sam. 5:16; I Chron. 3:8).

Be·el'ze·bub (bē-ĕl'zĕ-bŭb). The prince of the demons (Matt. 10:25; 12:24; Mark 3:22; Luke 11: 15, 18, 19), whom Jesus identifies with Satan (Matt. 12:26; Mark 3:23; Luke 11:18). The spelling Beelzebub differs but slightly from Baalzebub, god of Ekron. The Gr. text, however, has Beelzebul. Heb. *zᵉbûl* means habitation, and Baalzebul signifies lord of the habitation, which is pertinent to the argument in Matt. 10:25; 12:29; Mark 3:27. In the Ras Shamra literature occurs *zᵉbûl Ba'al* (abode of Baal), where *zᵉbûl* may be personified as deity. Ras Shamra shows the

antiquity of the form Beelzebul. In the component *-zebul* may also be a play upon late Heb. *zebel* (dung) to show disdain for the heathen god.

Be'er (bē'ẽr) [a well]. 1. A station of the Israelites on the confines of Moab, at which a well was dug by the leaders of Israel with their staves or under their official supervision (Num. 21:16–18); possibly the same as Beer-elim. A suggestion was made that it be identified with eth-Thamad at the head of Wadi el-Wāleh.
2. A place to which Jotham fled from his brother Abimelech (Judg. 9:21). Site unknown, but often identified with Beeroth. Eusebius locates it about 7½ miles n. of Eleutheropolis. El-Bīreh, n. of Beisan and s.e. of Mount Tabor, has also been accepted by some scholars. Josephus says that Jotham fled to the mountains (Jos. *Antiq.* v. 7, 2).

Be·e'ra (bē-ē'rá) [a well]. An Asherite, family of Heber (I Chron. 7:37).

Be·e'rah (bē-ē'rá) [a well]. A prince of the Reubenites, carried off by Tiglath-pileser (I Chron. 5:6).

Be·er-e'lim (bē'ẽr-ē'lĭm) [well of heroes or of terebinths]. A village of Moab (Isa. 15:8); see BEER 1.

Be·e'ri (bē-ē'rī) [belonging to the well]. 1. A Hittite, father of Judith, one of Esau's wives (Gen. 26:34).
2. Father of the Prophet Hosea (Hos. 1:1).

Be'er-la·hai'-roi (bē'ẽr-là-hī'roi) [the well of the Living One who sees me]. A well in the wilderness, between Kadesh and Bered on the road to Shur, where Hagar learned that Je-

A Well in the Desert

hovah watched over her (Gen. 16:7, 14). The Bedouins identify it with 'Ain Muweileh, about 12 miles n.w. of Kadesh ('Ain Ḳadais) and about 50 miles s.w. of Beer-sheba.

Be·e'roth (bē-ē'rŏth) [wells]. 1. A Gibeonite town (Josh. 9:17), assigned to the Benjamites (Josh. 18:25). The inhabitants were Hivites (Josh. 9:7) or Horites (LXX), who fled to Gittaim and settled there (II Sam. 4:3). The murderers of Ish-bosheth, and an armorbearer of Joab's, were Beerothites (II Sam. 4:2; 23:37); and men of Beeroth returned from Babylonia after the Exile (Ezra 2:25). The common identification is with el-Bīreh, a village on a rocky hill with copious flowing water at its foot, about 9 miles n. of Jerusalem.
2. Beeroth Bene-jaakan (of the children of Jaakan); wells on the borders of Edom, belonging to the tribe of Jaakan (Deut. 10:6); probably to be identified with el-Bīrein, about 6¼ miles s. of el-'Aujā. See JAAKAN.

Be·e'roth·ite (bē-ē'rŏth-īt), once **Be'roth·ite** (bē'rŏth-īt). A native or inhabitant of Beeroth (II Sam. 4:2; 23:37; I Chron. 11:39).

Be'er-she'ba (bē'ẽr-shē'bá) [well of seven, or well of an oath]. A place in the wilderness of s. Judah, where Abraham dug a well and where he and Abimelech, the king of Gerar, made a covenant not to molest each other. This well had already been an object of strife between their respective herdsmen. Accordingly Abraham gave Abimelech 7 ewe lambs as a witness of the Hebrew title, and to preserve the memory of the transaction, he called the place Beer-sheba (Gen. 21:22–32). He also planted there a tamarisk tree, and called on the name of Jehovah, the everlasting God (Gen. 21:33). Abraham resided for many years at this place. Then he went to Hebron, and afterward sojourned at Beer-lahai-roi. During the absence of the Hebrews from this part of the wilderness, the Philistines filled up the wells; but when Isaac came into authority, he began to reopen them. While he was at Beer-sheba, Abimelech, the king of Gerar, came and made a covenant with him, as he or his predecessor had done with Abraham. That same day Isaac's servants announced that they had reached water. As in former like cases, Isaac piously revived the old name, calling the well Shibah, the feminine form of the numeral *sheba'*, thus confirming and preserving the name Beer-sheba (Gen. 26:32, 33, R.V.). It was from this well that Jacob started on his journey to Haran (ch. 28:10), and there he sacrificed on his way to Egypt (ch. 46:1–5). A town ultimately rose in the vicinity of the well (Josh. 15:28). It was situated in the extreme s. of Judah (Josh. 15:28; II Sam. 24:7; II Kings 23:8), though allotted to the Simeonites (Josh. 19:1, 2; I Chron. 4:28), and was also the s. limit of Palestine, so that the expression became proverbial, "From Dan to Beer-sheba," i. e., from the extreme n. to the extreme s. of the Holy Land (Judg. 20:1 etc.). Samuel's sons were judges in Beersheba (I Sam. 8:2). Elijah passed through it on his way to Horeb (I Kings 19:3). It was a sanctuary in the 8th century and frequented by n. Israel (Amos 5:5; 8:14). It was inhabited after the Captivity (Neh. 11:27, 30). It is represented by the modern Bîr es-Seba' (28 miles s.w. of Hebron) on the n. side of the wadi es-Seba'. Seven wells are at this place. The larger of the wells described by Robinson was found to be 12½ feet in diameter and 44½ deep, to the surface of the water, 16 feet at the lower part being cut through solid rock.

Be·esh'te·rah (bĕ-ĕsh'tē-rȧ) [house or temple of Astarte]. The same place as Ashtaroth (cf. Josh. 21:27 with I Chron. 6:71). This contraction of Beth-ashterah is like that of Beth-shan to Beisan.

Bee'tle. See CRICKET.

Be·he'moth [pl. of Heb. *bᵉhēmāh* (beast), an intensive plural to denote magnitude]. A large animal described by Job which eats grass like an ox. It is amphibious, sometimes feeding with other beasts upon the mountains, and sometimes lying in fens, among reeds, or under willows, or apparently in flooded rivers (Job 40:15–24; R.V. marg., hippopotamus). It is probably the hippopotamus of the Nile (*Hippopotamus amphibius*). This has an unwieldy body 11 or 12 feet long, a large clumsy head, short stout legs, with 4 feet bearing toes. The gape of its mouth is enormous and the tusks of formidable size. It feeds on green corn, grass, and young shrubs. In ancient times it descended the Nile; but it was hunted for its valuable skin, teeth, and flesh, and it was also taken in considerable numbers to Rome for exhibition in the circus. Now, therefore, these animals are extinct in Egypt, though found on the Upper Nile.

Be'ka, in A.V. **Be'kah** [division, half]. Half a shekel (Ex. 38:26). It was used for weighing the precious metals (Gen. 24:22). See WEIGHTS.

Bel (bāl) (Akkad. *bēlu*, cognate of Heb. *ba'al* (lord)]. The patron god of Babylon (Isa. 46:1; Jer. 50:2; 51:44; Bel and Dragon 3–22), whose proper name was Marduk or, as called by the Hebrews, Merodach. He was a sun-god, the sun of early day and of spring; and he was regarded as the son of Ea, god of the ocean and other terrestrial waters. His festival was celebrated in the spring, at the beginning of the year. Because the sun in this aspect exerts such potent influence in nature, and because he was their tutelary divinity, the men of Babylon paid him supreme worship and ascribed to him the loftiest attributes. Marduk was not originally numbered among the chief gods by the people on the lower Tigris and Euphrates, but with the supremacy of Babylon (c. 1950) he became the head of the Babylonian pantheon.

Another Bel (En-lil), god of the region between earth and sky, and grouped in a triad with Anu, heaven, and Ea, was one of the 11 great gods.

Be'la (bē'lȧ), in A.V. once **Be'lah** (bē'lȧ) (Gen. 46:21) [devouring, destruction]. 1. A king of Edom, whose father's name was Beor (Gen. 36:32).

2. A Reubenite chief (I Chron. 5:8).

3. A son of Benjamin, and founder of a family (Gen. 46:21; Num. 26:38).

4. One of the cities of the plain, the same as Zoar (Gen. 14:2, 8).

Be'li·al (bē'lĭ-ăl) [worthlessness, wickedness]. Ungodliness (Ps. 18:4, R.V.). The phrase "sons of belial" is an expression meaning vile scoundrels or ungodly men (Deut. 13:13; Judg. 19:22). A wicked woman is called in Hebrew a daughter of Belial (I Sam. 1:16). Belial is personified in II Cor. 6:15.

Bell. Small golden bells, alternating with ornaments in the form of pomegranates, were attached to the lower part of the official blue robe of the high priest in order to send forth a sound that might be heard when he went into the Holy Place before Jehovah (Ex. 28:33–35; Ecclus. 45:9). A string of flat pieces of brass was hung around the neck of a horse, or a single bell was suspended from its throat (Zech. 14:20; cf. Judg. 8:21).

Bel'lows. An instrument for blowing the fire of a smelting furnace (Jer. 6:29). As used by the ancient Egyptians, the bellows consisted of a pair of leather bags, fitted into a frame, from each of which a pipe extended to the fire. They were worked by the feet, the operator standing upon them with one bag under each foot and pressing them alternately while he pulled up the exhausted skin with a string which he held in his hand. A double pair was used for each furnace.

Bel'ma·im (bĕl'mà-ĭm), **Bel'men** (bĕl'mĕn). See BILEAM, IBLEAM.

Bel·shaz'zar (bĕl-shăz'ẽr) [Akkad. *Bēl-shar-uṣur*, Bel protect the king]. According to contemporary Babylonian records, the first-born son and coregent of Nabonidus, the last king of the Neo-Babylonian Empire. The Babylonian records in a remarkable manner supplement the Biblical references (Dan., chs. 5; 7:1; 8:1, and Baruch 1:11, where he is called Baltasar). He is referred to (Dan. 5:11, 13) as the son of Nebuchadnezzar; a reasonable interpretation of this statement is that his mother was the daughter of that king. He may have been the Belshazzar who in 560 performed the functions of a chief officer of the king. According to Babylonian records, he became coregent of Nabonidus in the 3d year of his reign (553) and continued in that capacity until 539. Even though Nabonidus was absent for long periods at Taima, he never relinquished the kingship until Cyrus conquered Babylon. Whenever Nabonidus and

Belshazzar are mentioned together, the former receives the precedence; in the cuneiform records Belshazzar is always called not the king, but the son of the king.

Several texts record the business transactions of Belshazzar in Babylon. He did not engage in minor financial activities, but was represented by subordinates who looked after his affairs. Apparently he was interested in business, but not dependent upon it for a livelihood. A number of texts dating from the 5th to the 13th year of the reign of Nabonidus show that Belshazzar made offerings of silver, gold, and sacrificial animals to Babylonian sanctuaries. In the 5th year of Nabonidus he donated 60 shekels of silver to the temple in Erech; in the 9th year he gave the same weight of gold to Shamash (the sun-god). On one occasion, in the 9th year of Nabonidus, he presented 35 animals to the temple of Shamash in Sippar. In that case the sheep were taken from the king's maintenance supply, which was brought to the palace. The following year he gave 27 animals to Shamash and the other gods in Sippar. From his generous attitude toward these sanctuaries it may be inferred that shrines in other Babylonian cities benefited from his devotion.

When Nabonidus set out, in the 3d year of his reign, on a campaign against Taima, he divided the rule with Belshazzar. After the place was taken, the father adorned the city with the glory of Babylon and made it his residence. Contact with the capital was maintained across the desert by means of camels. In the 17th year of his reign, Nabonidus returned to Babylon, and the New Year's festival was celebrated. Cyrus entered Babylon on the 3d day of Marcheswan, and according to a broken tablet a certain Ugbaru died on the night of the 11th of that month; in the next line is mentioned the death of someone (the word is mutilated) "of the king." Probably it refers to the mother of Belshazzar. According to Dan., ch. 5, the death of Belshazzar occurred in connection with the actual capture of Babylon; this is also intimated by Xenophon (*Cyropaedia* vii. 5, 30). Belshazzar's feast, with the sacrilegious drinking of wine out of the holy vessels (Dan., ch. 5), must have preceded the fall of the city. See BABYLONIA, CYRUS, DANIEL, NABONIDUS.

Bel′te·shaz′zar (bĕl′tē-shăz′ẽr) [Akkad., *Balāṭsu-uṣur*, protect his life]. The name is abbreviated by omitting the name of the deity invoked. The name given by the prince of the Babylonian eunuchs to the Prophet Daniel (Dan. 1:7). The Hebrew vocalization in this name suggests the god Bel.

Ben (bĕn) [son]. A Levite (I Chron. 15:18), but probably the name has erroneously crept into the text; cf. vs. 20, 21, where it is lacking.

Ben′-a·bin′a·dab (bĕn′ȧ-bĭn′ȧ-dăb) [son of Abinadab]. Son-in-law of Solomon and his purveyor in the region of Dor (I Kings 4:11, R.V.).

Be·na′iah (bē-nā′yȧ) [Jehovah has built]. 1. A Levite, the son of Jehoiada, of Kabzeel, in Judah (II Sam. 23:20). His father was a priest (I Chron. 27:5). If the title here denotes a minister at the altar, Benaiah's father was probably the leader of the priests who joined the army which placed David on the throne (I Chron. 12:27). Benaiah was a valiant man, celebrated for having descended into a pit and killed a lion, for having slain two lionlike men of Moab, and, when armed only with a staff, for having met an Egyptian giant, wrested away his spear, and killed him with his own weapon (II Sam. 23:20, 21; I Chron. 11:22, 23). He was over the Cherethites and Pelethites. David's bodyguard (II Sam. 8:18), and also commanded the military

division for the 3d month (I Chron. 27:5, 6). He with the bodyguard remained faithful to David during Absalom's rebellion (cf. II Sam. 15:18; 20:23) and that of Adonijah (I Kings 1:10). By David's order he, at the head of the guard, escorted Solomon to Gihon, to be anointed king (I Kings 1:38), and as chief of the guard he executed Adonijah (I Kings 2:25), Joab (vs. 29–34), and Shimei (v. 46). The death of Joab left the office of commander in chief vacant, and Benaiah was promoted to the same (I Kings 2:35).

2. A Pirathonite, one of David's 30 mighty men of the 2d rank (II Sam. 23:30; I Chron. 11:31). He commanded the military division for the 11th month (I Chron. 27:14).

3. A Levite of the 2d degree who played the psaltery before the Ark when it was escorted to Jerusalem, and afterward in the tabernacle erected by David (I Chron. 15:18, 20; 16:5).

4. A priest who blew a trumpet in the company which escorted the Ark to Jerusalem and afterward in David's tabernacle (I Chron. 15:24; 16:6).

5. A Levite, descended from Asaph, and living before the reign of Jehoshaphat (II Chron. 20:14).

6. A Simeonite, possibly a contemporary of Hezekiah (I Chron. 4:36; cf. v. 41).

7. A Levite, an overseer of dedicated offerings in Hezekiah's reign (II Chron. 31:13).

8. Father of Ezekiel's contemporary, Prince Pelatiah (Ezek. 11:1, 13).

9–12. Four men, sons of Parosh, Pahathmoab, Bani, and Nebo, respectively, who were induced by Ezra to put away their strange wives (Ezra 10:25, 30, 35, 43).

Ben′-am′mi (bĕn′ăm′ī) [son of my kinsman]. Son of Lot's younger daughter, from whom sprang the Ammonite tribe (Gen. 19:38).

Ben′-de′ker (bĕn′dē′kẽr) [son of Deker]. Solomon's purveyor in Beth-shemesh and some other towns (I Kings 4:9, R.V.).

Ben′e·be′rak (bĕn′ē-bē′răk) [sons of Berak (lightning)]. A town of Dan (Josh. 19:45), now Ibn Ibrāḳ, 4 miles e. of Jaffa.

Ben′e·ja′a·kan (bĕn′ē-jā′ȧ-kăn). See JAAKAN.

Ben′-ge′ber (bĕn′gē′bẽr) [son of Geber]. Solomon's purveyor in Ramoth-gilead (I Kings 4:13, R.V.).

Ben′-ha′dad (bĕn′hā′dăd) [Heb. form of Aram. Bar-Hadad (son of the god Hadad)]. 1. King of Damascus, son of Tabrimmon and grandson of Hezion (Rezon?). When Baasha built Ramah to blockade the entrance into Judah from the n., Asa, king of Judah, hired Ben-hadad to break his treaty with Baasha and invade the Kingdom of Israel. The army of Ben-hadad entered the territory of the 10 tribes, captured the cities of Ijon, Dan, and Abel-maacah, and ravaged the land w. of the lake of Gennesaret. The diversion caused Baasha to withdraw from Ramah and terminate the blockade of the Kingdom of Judah: Asa gave Ben-hadad costly treasures from the Temple and royal palace (I Kings 15:18–21; II Chron. 16:1–6).

2. King of Damascus. He besieged Samaria, but drove Ahab to desperation and forced him to battle by insulting demands, and was defeated. The next year Ben-hadad renewed the war, but sustained a still heavier defeat; but Ahab granted him conditions of peace (I Kings 20:1–34). The arrival of a common enemy, Shalmaneser III, king of Assyria (860–825), in the w. necessitated the preservation of peace, which continued 3 years (I Kings 22:1).

Ben-hadad's name was probably Ben-hadadezer, by the Israelites shortened to Ben-hadad, by the Assyrians to Adadidri (Hadadezer). Or else in 854 B.C. Ben-hadad was succeeded by Hadadezer, and the latter about 845 by another Ben-hadad. Hence the king of Syria in I Kings 22:2 to II Kings 6:23, where his personal name is not given, may be Hadadezer. In 853 the king of Syria (Damascus), aided by Ahab and other allies, stopped the Assyrian advance at Karkar. In the following year, as is probable, in early spring Ahab lost his life in an attempt to wrest Ramoth-gilead from the king of Syria (I Kings 22:1–36). For some time the Syrians waged predatory warfare with the Israelites (II Kings 5:2; 6:8–23). These hostilities were repeatedly interrupted by Shalmaneser's operations against Damascus in the years 850, 849, and 846.

If Hadadezer is Ben-hadad II, as is generally believed, he was a contemporary of Ahab's son Jehoram (Joram). Between 846 and 843 B.C., there being no Assyrians in the w. to harass him, he invaded the territory of Israel and laid siege to Samaria; but his army, hearing a noise as of troops on the march, became panic-stricken and fled (II Kings 6:24 to 7:20). Shortly afterward he was murdered and succeeded by Hazael (842) (II Kings 8:15).

3. A son of Hazael. In the reign of Jehoahaz, king of Israel, Hazael and then Ben-hadad oppressed the 10 tribes (II Kings 13:3–13). But Joash, son of Jehoahaz, thrice defeated Ben-hadad and recovered the cities which the king of Damascus had wrested from Israel (II Kings 13:22–25; cf. ch. 10:32, 33).

The palaces of Ben-hadad are the palaces of Damascus (Jer. 49:27; Amos 1:4).

Ben'-ha'il (bĕn'hā'ĭl) [son of strength]. One of the princes sent by Jehoshaphat to teach in the cities of Judah (II Chron. 17:7).

Ben'-ha'nan (bĕn'hā'năn) [son of a gracious one]. A son of Shimon, registered with the tribe of Judah (I Chron. 4:20).

Ben'-he'sed (bĕn'hē'sĕd) [son of grace, loving-kindness]. Solomon's purveyor in Aruboth (I Kings 4:10, R.V.).

Ben'-hur' (bĕn'hûr') [son of Hur]. Solomon's purveyor in Mount Ephraim (I Kings 4:8, R.V.).

Ben·ni'nu (bĕ-nī'nū) [perhaps, our son]. A Levite who with Nehemiah and others sealed a covenant with Jehovah (Neh. 10:13).

Ben'ja·min (bĕn'jà-mĭn) [son of the right hand (of happiness) or son of the South]. 1. The youngest of Jacob's 12 sons and full brother of Joseph. As Jacob was approaching Bethlehem, Rachel gave birth to Benjamin, but, dying, named him Benoni (son of my sorrow). Jacob called him Benjamin (Gen. 35:16–20); and was deeply attached to him, especially after losing Joseph, as son of his old age and child of beloved Rachel. Only reluctantly did he allow Benjamin to go to Egypt with the brothers; and Judah expressed the fear that if evil should befall Benjamin too, their father would die of grief (Gen. 43:1–17). Joseph also felt much affection for Benjamin (Gen. 43:29–34; 44:1–34). Ultimately Benjamin had, besides other descendants, 5 sons and 2 grandsons, through whom he became the founder of families and a tribe in Israel (Gen. 46:21; Num. 26:38–41; I Chron. 7:6–12; ch. 8).

2. The tribe to which Benjamin gave origin, and the territory that it obtained. In the distribution of land at Shiloh, after Judah and Ephraim had received territory, the first lot came to Benjamin, who was assigned the district lying between those of Judah and Ephraim. Its n. boundary ran from Jordan through Beth-el to Ataroth-addar, s. of nether Beth-horon. Its w. border ran from this point to Kiriath-jearim. Its s. boundary went thence through the valley of the son of Hinnom, immediately s. of Jerusalem, to the n.

point of the Dead Sea. Its e. limit was the Jordan (Josh. 18:11–20). The territory thus marked out extended from w. to e. about 28 miles, and from n. to s. about 12 miles. It was a hilly country, but extremely fertile (Jos. Antiq. v. 1, 22) and it was studded with towns, the chief of which were Jerusalem, Jericho, Beth-el, Gibeon, Gibeath, and Mizpeh (Josh. 18:21–28). The tribe early furnished Israel with a deliverer from foreign oppression (Judg. 3:15). The tribe was nearly exterminated for protecting the guilty inhabitants of Gibeah (Judg., chs. 19 to 21). Later it gave the first king to Israel, and long clung to the house of Saul (II Sam. 2:9, 15; I Chron. 12:29). Even after David had become king of all Israel, Benjamites occasionally showed dissatisfaction (II Sam. 16:5; 20:1–22; Psalm 7, title); but a large part of the tribe remained true to the house of David when the 10 tribes separated under Jeroboam (I Kings 12:21), and shared the fortunes of Judah to the end (Ezra 4:1). From this tribe sprang the Apostle Paul (Phil. 3:5).

Two gates at Jerusalem bore the name of Benjamin. The upper or high gate of Benjamin was in the Temple (Jer. 20:2). For the other gate of Benjamin, see JERUSALEM, II. 3.

3. A Benjamite, a son of Bilhan, family of Jediael (I Chron. 7:10).

4. A son of Harim, who had taken a foreign wife (Ezra 10:18, 31, 32).

Be'no (bē'nō) [his son]. A descendant of Merari through Jaaziah (I Chron. 24:26, 27), if Beno is a proper name, as it seems to be in v. 27.

Ben'-o'ni (bĕn'ō'nī) [son of my sorrow]. The name given by Rachel to the son at whose birth she died. Jacob changed it to Benjamin (Gen. 35:18).

Ben'-zo'heth (bĕn'zō'hĕth) [son of Zoheth]. A descendant of Ishi, registered with the tribe of Judah (I Chron. 4:20).

Be'on (bē'ŏn). See BAAL-MEON.

Be'or (bē'ôr) [a burning]. 1. Father of Bela, king of Edom (Gen. 36:32; I Chron. 1:43).

2. Father of Balaam (Num. 22:5). Called in A.V. of II Peter 2:15 Bosor.

Be'ra (bē'rà) [cf. Arab. bara'a, ascend, excel]. A king of Sodom, defeated by Chedorlaomer and his confederates (Gen. 14:2).

Ber'a·cah (bĕr'à-kä), in A.V. **Ber'a·chah** (bĕr'à-kä) [blessing]. 1. A Benjamite who joined David at Ziklag (I Chron. 12:3).

2. A valley in Judah near Tekoa. Jehoshaphat gave it its name because he and his army there returned thanks to God for a great victory over the Ammonites, Moabites, and Edomites (II Chron. 20:26). The name still lingers as Bereikūt, a ruin about 4 miles n.w. of Tekoa, 6 miles s.w. of Bethlehem, and a little e. of the road from the latter village to Hebron.

Ber'a·chi'ah (bĕr'à-kī'à). See BERECHIAH.

Ber'a·i'ah (bĕr'à-ī'à) [Jehovah has created]. A son of Shimei (I Chron. 8:21, R.V.), descendant of Shaharaim who had his registry with Benjamin (vs. 8, 11–13).

Be're·a (bē'rē-à). A town in Judea near which Judas Maccabaeus was slain, 161 B.C. (I Macc. 9:4); probably modern el-Bīreh, about 10 miles n. of Jerusalem.

For Be-re'a, a city of Macedonia (Acts 17:10, A.V.), see BEROEA.

Ber'e·chi'ah (bĕr'ĕ-kī'à), in A.V. once **Ber'a·chi'ah** (I Chron. 6:39) [Jehovah has blessed]. 1. A Levite, the father of Asaph, descended from Gershom (I Chron. 6:39; 15:17).

2. A Levite, one of the 4 doorkeepers for the Ark in David's reign (I Chron. 15:23, 24).

3. One of the chief men of Ephraim in the reign of Pekah. He took the part of the captives from Judah. He was a son of Meshillemoth (II Chron. 28:12).

4. A son of Zerubbabel (I Chron. 3:20).

5. A Levite, descended from Elkanah of Ne ophah (I Chron. 9:16).

6. A son of Meshezabel. His son repaired part of the wall of Jerusalem (Neh. 3:4, 30).

7. Father of the Prophet Zechariah (Zech. 1:1, 7).

Be'red (bē'rĕd) [hail]. 1. A place in the wilderness of Shur, to the w. of Kadesh, and not far from Beer-lahai-roi (Gen. 16:7, 14).

2. An Ephraimite, of the family of Shuthelah (I Chron. 7:20).

Be'ri (bē'rī) [belonging to a well]. An Asherite, son of Zophah, family of Heber (I Chron. 7:36).

Be·ri'ah (bĕ-rī'à) [perhaps, prominent; cf. Arab. bara'a, excel]. 1. A son of Asher, and founder of a family (Gen. 46:17; Num. 26:44).

2. A son of Ephraim (I Chron. 7:23), with a play upon berā'āh (with or in evil).

3. A Benjamite, head of a father's house among the inhabitants of Aijalon (I Chron. 8:13).

4. A Levite, a son of Shimei, the Gershonite (I Chron. 23:10). His sons were united with the children of his brother Jeush into one father's house (v. 11).

Be'rite (bē'rīt). Apparently a people living near Abel-beth-maacah (II Sam. 20:14), but the text may be corrupt.

Be'rith (bē'rĭth). See BAAL-BERITH.

Ber·ni'ce (bĕr-nī'sē) [Macedonian Berenikē for Gr. Pherenikē, victorious]. The eldest daughter of Herod Agrippa I. She was married to her uncle, Herod, ruler of Chalcis, who soon afterward died. She was so much with her brother Agrippa that scandal arose in consequence. She tried to allay it by a marriage with Polemo, king of Cilicia. She soon became tired of him, and, deserting him, returned to her brother Agrippa (Jos. Antiq. xx. 7, 3; War ii. 11, 5). She was with him when Paul made his defense before him (Acts 25:23; 26:30). She afterward became the mistress, first of Vespasian and then of Titus.

Be·ro'dach-bal'a·dan (bē-rō'dăk-băl'à-dăn). See MERODACH-BALADAN.

Be·roe'a (bē-rē'à), in A.V. Be·re'a. 1. A city of Macedonia, about 50 miles w. of Thessalonica and 23 or 24 miles from the sea, where Paul preached on his 1st journey to Europe (Acts 17:10–14; 20:4). It is now called Verria.

2. Modern Aleppo, a Syrian city between Antioch and Hierapolis (Bambyce), where Menelaus, the former high priest, was put to death (II Macc. 13:4). The designation Berea was given by Seleucus Nicator.

3. See BEREA.

Be·ro'thah (bē-rō'thà) or Be·ro'thai (bē-rō'thī) [wells]. Berothah was a town situated between Hamath and Damascus (Ezek. 47:16). It is probably identical with Berothai, a city which was once subject to Hadadezer, king of Zobah, but was captured by David and yielded him large booty in brass (II Sam. 8:8; in I Chron. 18:8 called Cun [A.V. Chun]). Identified with 'Ain Berdai or Bereitān, s. of Ba'albek.

Ber'yl. 1. The rendering of Heb. tarshīsh, a precious stone (S. of Sol. 5:14; Ezek. 1:16; 10:9; 28:13; Dan. 10:6). It was the 1st stone of the 4th row on the Jewish high priest's breastplate (Ex. 28:20; 39:13). In R.V. marg., S. of Sol. 5:14, tarshīsh is rendered topaz, and in Ex. 28:20, chalcedony. The LXX renders the word by chrysolite in

Ex. 28:20; 39:13; Ezek. 28:13; and by anthrax (carbuncle) in Ezek. 10:9.

2. Greek beryllos (Rev. 21:20), the 8th foundation of the wall of the New Jerusalem. The beryl is a silicate of beryllium and aluminum. It occurs in hexagonal prisms, commonly green or bluish green, but also yellow, pink, or white with varieties in aquamarine and emerald.

Be'sai (bē'sī). One of the Nethinim and founder of a family (Ezra 2:49; Neh. 7:52).

Bes'o·de'iah (bĕs'ô-dē'yà) [in intimacy with Jehovah]. Father of Meshullam, who helped to repair a gate of Jerusalem (Neh. 3:6).

Be'sor (bē'sôr). A brook s. of Ziklag (I Sam. 30:9, 10, 21), perhaps the wadi Ghazzeh, which rises near Beer-sheba and empties into the Mediterranean s.w. of Gaza.

Be'tah (bē'tà) [trust, confidence]. A city of Aram-zobah (II Sam. 8:8) called Tibhath in I Chron. 18:8. See TEBAH.

Be'ten (bē'tĕn) [belly, valley]. A village of Asher (Josh. 19:25). Eusebius identified it with a village Beth-beten, about 7½ miles e. of Acre.

Beth (bĕth) [house]. The second letter of the Hebrew alphabet. Originally it was a rude representation of a dwelling, whence it derives its name. It became Greek beta and Latin and English B. As a Hebrew numeral it signifies 2.

Beth'ab'a·rah (bĕth'ăb'à-rà), R.V. marg.; in A.V. Beth'ab'a·ra (bĕth'ăb'à-rà) [house of the ford]. A place beyond Jordan at which John baptized (John 1:28, A.V.). The oldest MSS. have Bethany, as now the R.V.; but Origen, not being able to find a place of this name, decided in favor of the reading Bethabara. If the correct reading be Bethabara, then the site is evidently at one of the numerous fords of the Jordan, of which one is now called 'Abārah, about 12 miles s. of the outlet of the Sea of Galilee, n.e. of Beth-shean. The traditional site of the baptism of Jesus is Maḥāḍet el-Ḥajlah, near Beth-hoglah.

Beth'-a'nath (bĕth'ā'năth) [house of the goddess Anath]. An ancient fenced town in Naphtali (Josh. 19:35, 38), from which the Canaanites were not expelled (Judg. 1:33). Modern el-Ba'neh, about 12 miles e. of Acre on the way to Ṣafed.

Beth'-a'noth (bĕth'ā'nŏth) [house of the goddess Anath]. A town in the mountains of Judah (Josh. 15:59); Beit 'Ainūn, 1½ miles s.e. of Halḥūl.

Beth'a·ny (bĕth'à-nĭ) [Aram., house of the poor or afflicted one, or house of poverty; it may also mean house (place) of unripe figs]. 1. A small town on the Mount of Olives (Mark 11:1; Luke 19:29), about 1⅝ miles from Jerusalem (John 11:18) on the road to Jericho. Our Lord often lodged there (Matt. 21:17; 26:6; Mark 11:11, 12; 14:3). It was the town of Lazarus, of Martha, and of Mary (John 11:1; 12:1), as well as of Simon the leper, in whose house one of the anointings of Jesus took place (Matt. 26:6–13; Mark 14:3). From near the town Jesus ascended to heaven (Luke 24:50, 51). It has been generally identified as the village of el-'Azarīyeh (Lazarus' village) on the s. slope of the Mount of Olives, s.e. of Jerusalem. Today it is a small, wretched village, but its fig, olive, and almond trees give one at first a pleasant impression.

2. A place e. of the Jordan, where John was baptizing when Jesus returned from the temptation (John 1:28, R.V.; cf. ch. 10:40). See BETHABARAH.

Beth'-ar'a·bah (bĕth'ăr'à-bà) [house of the Arabah]. A village in the wilderness of

Judah, on the boundary between Judah and Benjamin (Jos. 15:6, 61; 18:22). Called simply Arabah in ch. 18:18; unless the reading of the LXX be correct, Beth-arabah instead of "the side over against the Arabah." It is situated near 'Ain el-Gharba in the wadi el Ḳelt.

Beth'-a'ram (bĕth'ȧ'răm). See BETH-HARAN.

Beth'-ar'bel (bĕth'är'bĕl) [house of Arbel]. A town destroyed by Shalman (Hos. 10:14). It has been identified with Arbela of Galilee (Jos. *Antiq.* xii. 11, 1; xiv. 15, 4; cf. I Macc. 9:2), now Irbid, 4 miles w.n.w. of Tiberias. The caverns of this place were the abode of robbers, whom Herod the Great rooted out (Jos. *War* i. 16, 2–4). Eusebius identified it with another Irbid (Arbela) in Gilead, 12 miles s.e. of Gadara.

Beth'-a'ven (bĕth'ȧ'vĕn) [house of nothingness or idolatry]. 1. A town in the territory of Benjamin, near Ai, e. of Beth-el (Josh. 7:2), w. of Michmash (I Sam. 13:5; cf. ch. 14:23), and on the border of a wilderness (Josh. 18:12).

2. Applied contemptuously by Hosea probably to Beth-el after it had become a seat of idolatry (Hos. 4:15; 5:8; 10:5).

Beth'-az-ma'veth (bĕth'ăz-mā'vĕth). See AZMAVETH 5.

Beth'-ba'al-me'on (bĕth'bā'ȧl-mē'ŏn). See BAAL-MEON.

Beth'-bar'ah (bĕth'bär'ȧ). A place on the Jordan, by some supposed to be the same as Bethabarah; probably s. of Beth-shean facing the wadi Fâr'a (Judg. 7:24).

Beth'ba'si (bĕth'bā'sī). A place in the wilderness (I Macc. 9:62), probably the wilderness of Tekoa (v. 33). Josephus calls it Bethalaga (Jos. *Antiq.* xiii. 1, 5); it is the modern Khirbet Beit Baṣṣa, e.s.e. of Bethlehem.

Beth'-bir'i (bĕth'bĭr'ī), in A.V. **Beth'-bir'e·i** (bĕth'bĭr'ē-ī). A Simeonite town (I Chron. 4:31). The name may be a corruption of Beth-lebaoth (cf. Josh. 19:6).

Beth'-car' (bĕth'kär') [house of a lamb]. A place, probably a height, to which the Philistines were pursued by the Israelites after the 2d and decisive battle of Ebenezer (I Sam. 7:11). 'Ain Kârim, 4⅜ miles w. of Jerusalem, is a possible site. See BETH-HACCHEREM.

Beth'-da'gon (bĕth'dā'gŏn) [house of Dagon]. 1. A village in the lowland of Judah (Josh. 15:33, 41) It has been identified with Khirbet Dajūn, but there may have been more than one Beth-dagon on the borders of Philistia.

2. A town of Asher, on the frontier toward Zebulun (Josh. 19:27). Probably Jelamet el-'Aṭîḳa, at the foot of Carmel.

Beth'-dib'la·tha'im (bĕth'dĭb'lȧ-thā'ĭm) [house of fig cakes]. A town on the tableland of Moab, territory once in possession of Israel (Jer. 48:21, 22; *Moabite Stone*, 30). Probably the same as Almon-diblathaim, which has been identified with the double ruin Deleilet el-Gharbiyeh, 2½ miles n.e. of Khirbet Libb.

Beth'-e'den (bĕth'ē'dĕn). See EDEN 2.

Beth'-el (bĕth'ĕl) [house of God]. 1. A town of Palestine, w. of Ai, s. of Shiloh (Gen. 12:8; Judg. 21:19), and near Michmash (I Sam. 13:2). Abraham on his 1st journey into Palestine, and subsequently, pitched his tent near it (Gen. 13:3). The town was called Luz by the Canaanites; but Jacob called the place close by, where he passed the night sleeping on the ground, Beth-el, on account of the vision which he saw there, and he erected a pillar to mark the spot (Gen. 28:18, 19;

31:13). The two are distinguished (Josh. 16:2); but the name Beth-el soon supplanted Luz as designation of the town. On the return of Jacob from Paddan-aram he went to Beth-el, built an altar, and reaffirmed the name (Gen. 35:1–15). The people of the town helped those of Ai in the 2d battle with Joshua (Josh. 8:9–17). Later it was taken and its king slain (Josh. 12:9, 16). It was assigned to Benjamin, and stood on the boundary line between that tribe and Ephraim (Josh. 16:1, 2; 18:11, 13, 21, 22). It was entered and its Canaanite inhabitants were slain by the men of Ephraim when they were engaged in securing their recently acquired territory (Judg. 1:22–26). Its villages on the n. of the boundary line belonged to Ephraim, and so perhaps did the town, as a result of this extermination of the Canaanites within its walls (I Chron. 7:20, 28). When the Israelites were gathered at Mizpah near Gibeah to war against Benjamin, the Ark was brought from Shiloh, 18 miles distant, to Beth-el, 8 miles off (Judg. 20:1, 18, 26, 27). Thither the men of Israel repaired to ask counsel of God, and there they built a temporary altar and offered sacrifices (Judg. 20:18, 26, R.V.). At the end of the war they came again to Beth-el, sat there before the Lord, built a new altar or repaired the old one, and offered sacrifices (Judg. 21:2–4, R.V.). When the regular services of the sanctuary at Shiloh were suspended during the loss and seclusion of the Ark, Beth-el was one of the places where Samuel judged Israel, and whither men went with their offerings to God (I Sam. 7:16; 10:3). Jeroboam fixed one of his calves there (I Kings 12:29–33), and Beth-el became a great center of idolatry (I Kings 13:1–32; II Kings 10:29). It was taken and temporarily held by Abijah (II Chron. 13:19). Elijah passed through it (II Kings 2:1–3), and it was from Beth-el that the youths came who mocked Elisha (II Kings 2:23, 24). The prophets denounced it for its idolatries (Jer. 48:13; Hos. 10:15; Amos 3:14; 4:4; 5:5, 6), and called it Beth-aven, house of nought (Hos. 4:15; 5:8; 10:5). Amos was in danger in Beth-el for his bold preaching (Amos 7:10–13). Josiah broke down its altars and its high places, and, as foretold, burned the bones of the priests taken from its sepulchers (I Kings 13:1–3; II Kings 23:4, 15–20). Some of its inhabitants returned from Babylon with Zerubbabel (Ezra 2:28; Neh. 7:32), and the place again reverted to the Benjamites (Neh. 11:31). In Maccabean times it was fortified by the Syrian Bacchides (I Macc. 9:50). In the Jewish war it was captured by Vespasian, later Roman emperor (Jos. *War* iv. 9, 9). The ruins, called Beitîn, lie on the watershed of Palestine, about 11 miles n. from Jerusalem. They are on the summit of a hill sloping to the s.e., and cover 3 or 4 acres. A range of hills trends to the s.e. (cf. I Sam. 13:2). The country around is of gray stone or white chalk, with scant vegetable mold.

2. A town in the territory of Simeon (I Sam. 30:27). See BETHUEL 2.

Beth'-e'mek (bĕth'ē'mĕk) [house of the valley]. A town within the territory of Asher (Josh. 19:27). Probably Tell Mîmâs, near the village of 'Amḳâ, 6½ miles n.e. of Acre.

Be'ther (bē'thẽr) [separation, division]. Probably a common noun, describing certain mountains as cleft and rugged (S. of Sol. 2:17; cf. chs. 4:6; 8:14); the LXX renders it, "Mountains of hollows or ravines." Not the town in Judah called Baithẽr (Josh. 15:59, Codex Alexandrinus), now Bittîr, 6 miles s.w. of Jerusalem, where on the height above the village the Jews under Bar-cocheba made their last stand against the Romans, 135 B.C.

Be·thes′da (bē-thĕz′då) [Gr., from Aram. *bĕth ḥesdā*, house of grace, loving-kindness]. Earlier MSS. of the N.T. have other spellings, as *Bēthsaida* (house of fishing) and *Bēthzatha* (house of the olive).

A pool at Jerusalem, which was near the sheep gate and had 5 porches, that were sufficiently ample to accommodate a great multitude (John 5:2, 3). Its waters were supposed to possess healing virtue. The 4th verse of the A.V., which mentions a periodic troubling of the waters wrought by an angel, is omitted in R.V. as being insufficiently supported by early texts. E. Robinson and Conder prefer to identify the pool with the Virgin's Fount (Gihon) at the foot of the Ophel slope, s.e. of the Temple; this spring is intermittent and is still credited with healing virtue. Tradition, however, located Bethesda at the Birket Israel, n. of the Temple, or at an adjacent pool. The tradition was well founded, even if it ultimately went astray. 1. In A.D. 333 the Bordeaux pilgrim stated that there were 2 pools and 5 porches. 2. Early MSS., e.g., the Sinaitic, have Bethzatha, abbreviated Bezatha, instead of Bethesda. These words suggest variations of Bezetha, the name of the quarter of the city n. of the Temple hill, and imply that the pool was in the Bezethan section of the city. 3. The pool was near the sheep gate, and the natural explanation of Neh., ch. 3, determines the location of this gate to have been n. of the Temple area. 4. In 1888 excavation in the n.e. part of Jerusalem, in connection with the repair of the church of Saint Anne, laid bare 100 feet n.w. of that building a pool with 5 porches. A faded fresco on the wall depicts an angel and water, and shows that in the early Christian ages this pool was regarded as Bethesda.

Beth′-e′zel (bĕth′ē′zĕl) [place near]. A town of s. Judah (Micah 1:11), identified with Deir el-ʿAṣal, about 2 miles e. of Tell Beit Mirsim.

Beth′-ga′der (bĕth′gā′dēr) [house or place of a wall]. A town of Judah (I Chron. 2:51). See GEDER.

Beth′-ga′mul (bĕth′gā′mŭl) [house of recompense]. A Moabite town (Jer. 48:23), Khirbet Jemeil, 6 miles e. of Dibon, between the Arnon and Umm er-Raṣāṣ.

Beth′-gil′gal (bĕth′gĭl′găl). See GILGAL 1.

Beth′-hac·che′rem (bĕth′hă-kē′rĕm), in A.V. **Beth′-hac′ce·rem** (bĕth′hăk′sē-rĕm) [house of the vineyard]. A town of Judah (Neh. 3:14; Jer. 6:1), probably ʿAin Kārim, 4⅜ miles w. of Jerusalem. On top of Jebel ʿAli above this village are cairns which once may have served as beacons.

Beth′-ha′ran (bĕth′hā′răn) and **Beth′-ha′ram** (bĕth′hā′răm), in A.V. **Beth′-a′ram**. A town in the Jordan Valley, rebuilt by the children of Gad (Num. 32:36; Josh. 13:27). It is identified with Tell er-Rāmeh at the mouth of Wadi Ḥesbān, 2½ miles w. of el-Ḥammam, the source of the celebrated warm springs, and 6 miles e. of the Jordan; also known as Betharamphtha, where Herod had a palace (Jos. *Antiq.* xviii. 2, 1; *War* ii. 4, 2; 9, 1); the place was called Livias by Herod Antipas in honor of the wife of Augustus.

Beth′-hog′lah (bĕth′hŏg′lå), in A.V. once **Beth′-hog′la** (bĕth′hŏg′lȧ) [house of the partridge]. A village of Benjamin on the boundary line between that tribe and Judah, and near the River Jordan (Josh. 15:6; 18:19, 21). The name and site are found at ʿAin Ḥajlah, 4 miles s.e. of Jericho.

Beth′-ho′ron (bĕth′hō′rŏn) [house or place of the hollow]. Upper and Lower Beth-horon, twin towns of Ephraim, with a difference of almost 800 feet in altitude, on the boundary between Ephraim and Benjamin, built by a woman of Ephraim called Sherah (Josh. 16:3, 5; 18:13; I Chron. 7:24). One of them was assigned as residence to the Levites of the family of Kohath (Josh. 21:22; I Chron. 6:68). The towns lay in a mountain pass on the highway between Jerusalem and the plain; the upper town is about 11 miles n.w. of the capital, while the lower one lies 1¾ miles farther n.w. They controlled the pass, and were fortified by Solomon (II Chron. 8:5); but especially did the upper town engage military attention, for it occupied the more strategic position (I Kings 9:17; I Macc. 9:50). The Amorites fled down this pass before Joshua (Josh. 10:10 *seq.*). The Philistines ascended it to make war with Saul (I Sam. 13:18). Judas Maccabaeus fought two battles here (I Macc. 3:15 *seq.*; 7:39 *seq.*), and the army of Cestius Gallus, governor of Syria, was almost annihilated here by the Jews (Jos. *War* ii. 19, 8). The towns still exist under the names Beit ʿUr et-Taḥta and el-Fōka.

Beth′-jesh′i·moth (bĕth′jĕsh′ĭ-mŏth), in A.V. once **Beth′-jes′i·moth** (bĕth′jĕs′ĭ-mŏth) [house of the wastes]. A town e. of the Jordan, near Pisgah and the Dead Sea (Josh. 12:3; 13:20). When the Israelites encamped at Shittim, it formed the s. limit of the camp (Num. 33:49). It was 9¼ miles s.e. of Jericho and is probably to be identified with Suweimeh near the n.e. end of the Dead Sea. It was assigned to the Reubenites, but in the time of Ezekiel was in the hands of the Moabites (Josh. 13:20; Ezek. 25:9).

Beth′-le-aph′rah (bĕth′lē-ăph′rȧ). See APH-RAH.

Beth′-le-ba′oth (bĕth′lē-bā′ŏth) [house of lionesses]. A town in the s. of Judah, assigned to the Simeonites (Josh. 15:32; 19:6); see BETH-BIRI. Probably at the ruins between Wadi Shenek and Wadi Imleiḥ, in the region dominated by Tell el-Fārʿah, Biblical Sharuhen.

Beth′-le·hem (bĕth′lē-hĕm) [house of bread; or perhaps, rather, house of the god Laḥmu or of the goddess Laḥamu]. 1. A town in the hill country of Judah, originally called Ephrath; hence, to distinguish it from a place of the same name in Zebulun, called also Beth-lehem-judah and Beth-lehem Ephrathah (Gen. 35:19; Judg. 17:7; Micah 5:2). Bethlehem is not mentioned among the cities assigned to Judah (Josh., ch. 15; but given in v. 59, LXX). As a village it existed as early as the time of Jacob. Rachel died and was buried in its vicinity (Gen. 35:16, 19; 48:7). Its citizens were hospitable to the Levites (Judg. 17:7; 19:1). A branch of Caleb's family settled in the town and attained to great influence (I Chron. 2:51, 54; cf. Ruth 4:20). It was the residence of Boaz, of Ruth (Ruth 1:19; 4:9–11), doubtless of Obed (Ruth 4:21, 22), and of Jesse, the father of David (Ruth 4:11, 17; I Sam. 16:1, 4). As the birthplace and ancestral home of David, it was the city of David (Luke 2:11). It was a walled town as early as the time of David. It fell temporarily into the hands of the Philistines (II Sam. 23:14, 15). Rehoboam strengthened its fortifications (II Chron. 11:6). Bethlehemites returned from Captivity with Zerubbabel (Ezra 2:21; Neh. 7:26). It was looked to as the place where the Messiah should be born (Micah 5:2; Matt. 2:5), and accordingly when the fullness of time was come Jesus became incarnate at Bethlehem. In its vicinity the annunciation to the shepherds took place (Luke 2:1–20). Thither the Magi went to salute the newborn Babe, and it was the infants of Bethlehem "and in all the borders thereof, from two years old and under," who were murdered by Herod to make sure that among them he had cut off the future king (Matt. 2:1-18). There has never been any doubt as to its site. It is 5 miles s. of Jerusalem, at the modern village of Beit Laḥm, on the e. and n.e. slope of a long ridge, which to the w. is higher than the village. A little e. of the town is the church built by Helena, the mother of Constantine, over the cave said to be the stable in which the Nativity took place. Half a mile to the n. of the town is the traditional tomb of Rachel. On the s. side of the town a valley running to the Dead Sea, while almost at the walls on the e. a valley begins which joins the wadi eṣ-Ṣurar or vale of Sorek, and near by is also an upper branch of the wadi es-Sunt or vale of Elah (cf. I Sam. 17:2).

2. A town with dependent villages within the territory of Zebulun (Josh. 19:15). Probably this Bethlehem was the home of the judge Ibzan (Judg. 12:8-11). It is the modern Beit Laḥm, a small village 7 miles n.w. of Nazareth.

Beth'-ma'a·cah (bĕth'mā'á-ká), in A.V. **Beth'-ma'a·chah** (bĕth'mā'á-ká) [house of Maacah]. A town (II Sam. 20:14, 15). See ABEL-BETH-MAACAH.

Beth'-mar'ca·both (bĕth'mär'ká-bŏth) [house of the chariots]. A town of the Simeonites (Josh. 19:5; I Chron. 4:31). Probably Madmannah (Josh. 15:31), modern Umm Deimneh, 11¼ miles n.e. of Beer-sheba.

Beth'-me'on (bĕth'mē'ŏn). See BAAL-MEON.

Beth'-mer'hak (bĕth'mēr'hăk) [house of removal]. Probably only a house beside the Brook Kidron, between Jerusalem and the Mount of Olives (II Sam. 15:17, R.V.). R.V. margin renders it the Far House; A.V., a place that was far off.

Beth'-nim'rah (bĕth'nĭm'rá) [house of limpid fresh water, or house of leopardess]. A town in the valley e. of the Jordan, assigned to Gad and rebuilt by that tribe (Num. 32:36; Josh. 13:27). Eusebius and Jerome locate it 4⁹⁄₁₀ miles to the n. of Livias, near Tell er-Rāmeh. The Bronze Age sites were at Tell Bileibil and Tell el-Mustaḥ at the end of the gorge of the wadi Sha'īb; the later site was at Tell Nimrīn, to the w. at the edge of the plain.

Beth'-pa'let (bĕth'pā'lĕt). See BETH-PELET.

Beth'-paz'zez (bĕth'păz'ĕz) [house of dispersion]. A town within the territory of Issachar (Josh. 19:21), modern Kerm el-Hadetheh.

Beth'-pe'let (bĕth'pē'lĕt); in A.V. **Beth'-phe'let** and **Beth'-pa'let** [house of escape]. A town in the most southerly part of Judah (Josh. 15:27; Neh. 11:26), probably el-Meshash.

Beth'-pe'or (bĕth'pē'ôr) [house of Peor]. A town near Pisgah. In the valley opposite to it the Israelites had their main encampment, elsewhere referred to as in the mountains of Abarim, when their army was warring with Sihon and Og (cf. Deut. 3:29; 4:46 with Num. 21:20; 23:28; 33:47-49). In this valley Moses was afterward buried (Deut. 34:6). The town was assigned to the Reubenites (Josh. 13:20). According to Eusebius, it lay almost 6 miles above, that is, in the mountains e. of, Livias (near Tell er-Rameh); Khirbet esh-Sheikh Jāyel best corresponds to this description.

Beth'pha·ge (bĕth'fá-jē) [Aram., house of unripe figs]. A village near Bethany, on or near the road from Jericho to Jerusalem (Mark 11:1; Luke 19:29). It probably stood between Bethany and Jerusalem, not far from the descent of the Mount of Olives (Matt. 21:1; John 12:1, 12), and near the old road that crosses the mountain at the summit.

Beth'-phe'let (bĕth'fē'lĕt). See BETH-PELET.

Beth'-ra'pha (bĕth'rā'fá) [perhaps, house of Rapha, or of a giant]. A family of Judah, or a town whose inhabitants belonged to that tribe (I Chron. 4:12).

Beth'-re'hob (bĕth'rē'hŏb) [house of a street]. A town in the n. of Palestine, by the valley of the upper Jordan (Num. 13:21, where it is called simply Rehob; Judg. 18:28). It was inhabited by Aramaeans (Syrians), who joined the Ammonites in a great war with David (II Sam. 10:6). It gave its name to the hollow valley in which Laish (Dan) was located and may be the original settlement of Bāniyās.

Beth'sa'i·da (bĕth'sā'ĭ-dá) [Gr. from Aram. *bĕth ṣaydā*, house or place of fishing]. A town on the Lake of Gennesaret, near the Jordan, rebuilt by Philip the tetrarch, and named Julias in honor of the daughter of the emperor Augustus (Jos. *Antiq.* xviii. 2, 1; *Life* 72). To this town, which was on the other side of the sea (actually at the n. end), Jesus withdrew on receiving news of the murder of John the Baptist (Luke 9:10; cf. Matt. 14:13; John 6:1). Going forth to a desert grassy place, apparently about 2 miles down the e. side of the lake, he was followed by the multitude. In the evening he miraculously fed them. The disciples then entered into a boat to precede him "unto the other side to [or toward] Bethsaida" (Mark 6:45). During the evening and night, the disciples were in the midst of the sea distressed in rowing, for the wind was contrary unto them. Jesus came walking on the water, and was taken into the boat. When they had crossed over they came to the land unto Gennesaret (Mark 6:53). Do these statements, taken in connection with John's mention of "Bethsaida of Galilee" (John 12:21), imply another Bethsaida? Some scholars think so, and locate it, among other places, at 'Ain et-Ṭābighah, about 3 miles s.w. of the mouth of the Jordan. But the existence of 2 towns of the same name on the same lake, and at most only a few miles apart, is so improbable that the words of the Evangelists must be carefully considered to see whether they require this assumption; and: 1. The ultimate destination of the disciples was Capernaum (John 6:17); but it was determined that they should sail "toward Bethsaida," keeping nearer the shore than the direct course to Capernaum would require (Thomson). 2. Even if their purpose was to make a stop at Bethsaida, it was proper to speak of going "to the other side to Bethsaida," for Josephus uses a similar expression for proceeding by boat from Tiberias 3¾ miles to Taricheae, both of which were on the w. shore of the lake. He "sailed over to Taricheae" (Jos. *Life* 59). 3. Peter, Andrew, and Philip were Galileans and of Bethsaida (John 1:44; 12:21). Thomson suggests that any city built at the mouth of the narrow Jordan, as Bethsaida-Julias admittedly was, would almost necessarily have part of its houses or a suburb on the w. bank of the river, which would be in Galilee. He also suggests that probably the whole city on both banks of the river was ordinarily attached to Galilee. G. A. Smith affirms that "the province of Galilee ran right round the lake." His opinion is based on Josephus' mention of a certain Judas, who belonged to Gamala in Gaulanitis, as a Galilaean (Jos. *War* ii. 8, 1; *Antiq.* xviii. 1).

Beth'-she'an (bĕth'shē'ăn), **Beth'-shan'** (bĕth'shăn') [house of quiet; but rather of the Babylonian god Shaḥan (Phoenician Sha'an), the Sumerian serpent-god]. Tell el Huṣn near modern Beisân in the throat of the valley of Jezreel, situated on the s. side of the Nahr Jālūd that flows from the great spring

MODERN BETHLEHEM

71

near Jezreel and at the point where the valley drops down 300 feet to the level of the Jordan. The town was founded in the chalcolithic period, i.e., before 3000 B.C. After the Battle of Megiddo (c. 1482 B.C.) it fell into the hands of the Egyptians, who garrisoned it for almost 300 years. It commanded the important route running e. from the Plain of Esdraelon into Trans-Jordan. At Beisân were found two steles of Sethi I and one of Ramesses II. From the one dated in the 1st year of Seti (1318 B.C.) it is inferred that he made a campaign to strengthen Egyptian prestige and to restore order on account of the Hittite pressure from the n.

The inhabitants of town and valley made themselves formidable by the use of chariots of iron (Josh. 17:16). Beth-shean with its dependent villages fell within the area of Issachar, but was given to the Manassites (Josh. 17:11; I Chron. 7:29). They failed, however, to drive out the Canaanites, but were strong enough to make them pay tribute (Josh. 17:12–16; Judg. 1:27, 28). At the Battle of Gilboa the town apparently sided with the Philistines, for after the defeat of Israel, the Philistines fastened the bodies of Saul and his sons to the wall of Beth-shean (I Sam. 31:10–13; II Sam. 21:12–14). In the reign of Solomon the city gave its name to a district (I Kings 4:12). It was called Scythopolis as early as the time of Judas Maccabaeus. In several instances this name is written *Skythôn polis*, city of the Scythians (Judg. 1:27, LXX; Judith 3:10; II Macc. 12:29); and it has been supposed that a remnant of the Scythian hordes settled here, who are said to have advanced through Palestine against Egypt in the latter half of the 7th century B.C. (Herod. i. 103, 105; Pliny *Hist. Nat.* v. 16). It is very doubtful whether any historical conclusions can be deduced from this name.

In the 1st century A.D. the population of the city was predominantly Gentile (II Macc. 12:30; Jos. *War* ii. 18, 1, 3, 4; *Life* 6), and the Jews consequently sacked it during the war with the Romans. The citizens retaliated by massacring the Jewish residents. Josephus says that it was the largest of the 10 cities called Decapolis, apparently disregarding Damascus, possibly because the city on the Abanah was not at this moment a member of the league (Jos. *War* iii. 9, 7). It was the only one of the 10 cities that lay w. of the Jordan. It figured in history as late as the crusades.

Beth'-she'mesh (bĕth'shē'mĕsh) [house of the sun]. 1. A town in the vale of Sorek (Wadi eṣ-Ṣarār), identified with Tell er-Rumeileh, near the Byzantine ruins of 'Ain Shems, on the main road from Ashkelon and Ashdod to Jerusalem, from which it is about 23¾ miles distant. The name indicates a seat of the worship of the sun. The ceramic finds in the funerary caverns under the rampart belong to all periods of the Bronze Age since the chalcolithic period. It was overthrown by the Hyksos about 1800 B.C., but enjoyed great prosperity in the 15th century, as is shown by the walls and the s. gate. The town was conquered by the Egyptians in the 15th century and flourished until the arrival of the Philistines, who seized and occupied it. From that time on it had a dull existence until its destruction by Nebuchadnezzar in 587 B.C.

It was allotted to Judah, and stood on the boundary line of Judah and Dan (Josh. 15:10; 19:41, where the synonymous name Ir-shemesh is used; cf. Mount Heres [Judg. 1:35], which is probably the same place). The Danites did not occupy it; and when provision was made for the tribe of Levi, it was given to the priests, the sons of Aaron, and reckoned as set apart from the tribe of Judah (Josh.

21:16, cf. v. 9; I Chron. 6:59). After the formation of the kingdom it was within Judah (II Kings 14:11). The people of Beth-shemesh, whither the kine brought the Ark from Ekron, were largely of priestly family, and offered sacrifice; but profanely looking into the Ark, they were smitten by a plague which carried off 70 persons (Jos. *Antiq.* vi. 1, 4). After the words "seventy men" there is the strange insertion in the Hebrew text, rendered suspicious by the absence of the conjunction, of the further words "fifty thousand men" (I Sam. 6:19, R.V.). At Beth-shemesh Joash, king of Israel, defeated Amaziah of Judah (II Kings 14:11; II Chron. 25:21). The Philistines took the town in the reign of Ahaz (II Chron. 28:18) during the Syro-Ephraimitic war.

2. A Canaanite city in Naphtali (Josh. 19:38; Judg. 1:33). It may be Ḥāris, s.w. of Tibnîn, but if it is identical with the following (3), it must be sought on the borders of Issachar toward the Jordan.

3. A city in Issachar (Josh. 19:22) which by some was identified with 'Ain esh-Shemsi-yeh. Modern scholars prefer Khirbet Shemsîn or el-'Abeidiyeh, on the Jordan a short distance s. of the Sea of Galilee.

4. An Egyptian city where the sun was worshiped (Jer. 43:13); probably Heliopolis, i.e., On.

Beth'-she'mite (bĕth'shē'mīt). A native of Beth-shemesh (I Sam. 6:14, 18).

Beth'-shit'tah (bĕth'shit'á) [house of the acacia]. A town between the valley of Jezreel and Zererah in the Jordan Valley (Judg. 7:22, R.V.). The fact that it is coupled with Zererah, and not with Beth-shean, excludes its identification with Shutta.

Beth'su'ra (bĕth'sū'rá). See BETH-ZUR.

Beth'-tap'pu·ah (bĕth'tăp'û-á) [house of apples]. A town in the hill country of Judah (Josh. 15:53), the modern village of Taffûḥ, about 5 miles w. of Hebron (cf. I Chron. 2:43).

Be·thu'el (bē-thū'ĕl) [perhaps, abode of God]. 1. Son of Nahor by his wife Milcah. He was the father of Laban and Rebekah, and nephew of Abraham (Gen. 22:20, 22, 23; 24:15, 29; 25:20; 28:2, 5).

2. A town of the Simeonites (I Chron. 4:30; in Josh. 19:4, Bethul). David sent thither part of the recaptured spoil of Ziklag (I Sam. 30:27). In this lat er passage it is called Beth-el; it seems to be the Chesil of Josh. 15:30. Probably Khirbet er-Rās, between Beer-sheba and Khuweilifeh.

Beth'ul (bĕth'ŭl). See BETHUEL 2.

Beth'zach·a·ri'as (bĕth'zăch-a-rī'ás) [house of Zechariah]. A town (I Macc. 6:32, 33), according to Josephus (Jos. *Antiq.* xii. 9, 4), 70 stades from Bethsura. It is identified with modern Beit Zakâriya, about 9 miles s. of Jerusalem and 6¼ n. of Beth-zur.

Beth·za'tha (bĕth-zā'thá) [Aram. house or place of the olive tree]. R.V. marg. John 5:2 for Bethesda.

Beth'-zur' (bĕth'zûr'), in Maccabees **Beth'-su'ra** [house of a rock]. A town in the hill country of Judah (Josh. 15:58). It was fortified by Rehoboam (II Chron. 11:7). In Nehemiah's time half its district was subject to Azbuk (Neh. 3:16). In the Greek period the name was written Bethsura, and it was important as a frontier town toward Idumaea. Here Judas Maccabaeus gained a great victory over the Syrian general Lysias (I Macc. 4:29; II Macc. 11:5; 13:19, 22). The patriot leader afterward fortified it (I Macc. 4:61; 6:7, 26, 31). Want of food compelled the garrison to surrender it to the Syrians (I Macc. 6:49, 50). Its defenses were strengthened by

Bacchides (ch. 9:52), but it was recaptured by Simon (chs. 11:65, 66; 14:7) and refortified (ch. 14:33). The name lingers in the ruins Beit Ṣūr, 4 miles n. of Hebron, but the ancient site was at Khirbet eṭ-Ṭabeiḳa.

Bet'o·nim (bĕt'ô-nĭm) [pistachio nuts]. A town of Gad (Josh. 13:26), probably Khirbet Baṭneh or Baṭana, 3 miles s.w. of es-Salṭ.

Beu'lah (bū'lȧ) [married]. A name prophetically applied to the once forsaken land of Palestine when it was restored to God's favor and repeopled after the Captivity (Isa. 62:4).

Be·za·a·nan'nim (bē-zā-ȧ-năn'ĭm). This name occurs in Josh. 19:33, R.V. marg. The question is whether Heb. beth (b) is the preposition "in" ("in Zaanannim") or the first letter is a proper name "Bezaanannim." Many scholars accept the latter view. J.V., considering the oak (or, terebinth) as a part of the proper name, renders: "from Elon-bezaanannim." See ALLON, ZAANANNIM.

Be'za·i (bē'zȧ-ī). Founder of a family, some of whom returned from Babylon with Zerubbabel (Ezra 2:17; Neh. 7:23). A representative of the family signed the covenant of fidelity to Jehovah (Neh. 10:18).

Bez'a·lel (bĕz'ȧ-lĕl), in A.V. **Be·zal'e·el** (bē-zăl'ê-ĕl) [in the shadow (protection) of God]. 1. A man of Judah, family of Hezron, house of Caleb, and a grandson of Hur (I Chron. 2:20); a skillful artificer raised up of God and appointed to work in gold, silver, copper, in the setting of precious stones, and the carving of wood; the chief architect of the tabernacle (Ex. 31:1–11; 35:30–35).
2. A son of Pahath-moab, induced by Ezra to put away his foreign wife (Ezra 10:30).

Be'zek (bē'zĕk) [scattering, sowing]. A town in central Palestine, not a great distance from Jabesh-gilead (I Sam. 11:8–11). Twin villages of this name existed in Eusebius' time about 16 miles from Shechem toward Beth-shean; identified with Khirbet Ibzīḳ, 13 miles n.e. of Shechem. With this town may be identified Bezek mentioned in Judg. 1:4, 5, on the assumption that Adoni-bezek advanced s. with his forces to unite with the s. Canaanites, was met and repulsed by Judah and Simeon, and pursued to his capital; Ganneau proposes Khirbet Bezḳa, about 3 miles n.e. of Gezer, as the site of the latter Bezek.

Be'zer (bē'zẽr) [fortress]. 1. An Asherite, son of Zophah (I Chron. 7:37).
2. A city within the territory of Reuben. It was given to the Levites, and was a city of refuge (Deut. 4:43; Josh. 20:8; 21:36). Later it was held by Moab, whose king, Mesha, fortified it (Moabite Stone, 27, see MOABITE STONE); probably Umm el-'Amad, about 5½ miles e. of Heshbon and 8¾ miles n.e. of Mādaba.

Be'zeth (bē'zĕth) [Gr. Bēthzaith, Bēzeth, Baithzēth, from Heb., house of the olive]. A place where Bacchides pitched his camp (I Macc. 7:19); modern Beit Zeita, about 3 miles n. of Beit Ṣūr, near Khirbet Kūfīn.

Bi'ble [Old French from Lat. biblia from Gr. biblia, pl. of biblion, diminutive of biblos (book), from byblos (papyrus) after the Phoenician city Byblos (Jubayl), whence papyrus was exported]. The names used in the O.T. and the Apocrypha for the Scriptures are: "the books" (LXX bibloi, Dan. 9:2), "the holy biblia" (books, I Macc. 12:9), "the biblia of the law" (I Macc. 1:56; sing., biblion, in ch. 3:48), "biblion of the covenant" (I Macc. 1:57). In the Prologue to Ecclesiasticus, the translator of the book from Hebrew into Greek, the author's grandson, refers to "the law, the prophets, and the other biblia

(books) of our fathers." The Second Epistle of Clement (2d century A.D.) applies the term biblia (ch. 14:2) to the O.T.; by about the 5th century this word was applied as a title of the whole Christian Scriptures by the Greek church fathers. The word passed to the w., and in Latin biblia, which is really a plural neuter noun, finally came to be used as a feminine singular. In the N.T. the usual term for the O.T. is "the scriptures" (Matt. 21:42; 22:29; Luke 24:32; John 5:39; Acts 18:24). The singular, "scripture," stands for the whole O.T. in Acts 8:32 and Gal. 3:22, but in Mark 12:10, it denotes only a portion of the O. T. Other expressions are "holy scriptures" (Rom. 1:2; II Tim. 3:15, A.V.) and "sacred writings" (II Tim. 3:15, R.V.).

Etymologically viewed, the Bible means "the Books," and that no qualifying adjective stands before the noun implies that these writings were regarded by those who used the term as forming a class by themselves and as superior to all other literary productions. They are uniquely and pre-eminently the books. The term Bible is absent from the sacred page; it is of ecclesiastical origin. The plural term Biblia marks the important fact that the Bible is not a single book, but a great many. The words Bible and Scripture, on the other hand, being both in the singular number, emphasize the fact that, under the diversity of human authorship, there lies a wonderful unity, pointing to the operation of one directing Mind, which acted during more than a thousand consecutive years when these writings were being produced.

The claims to divine authority made by Scripture are investigated by the science of apologetics. The word is used in a Greek rather than in an English sense, and must, therefore, not be misunderstood. It is related that when George III was told that Bishop Watson had published an Apology for the Bible, he dryly remarked that he did not know before that the Bible required an apology. The bishop used the word "Apology" like the Greek apologia, to mean defense; and the science of apologetics defends the Bible. A second science is that of Biblical criticism. This is divided into higher criticism, which inquires into the origin and character of the several books, and seeks to determine by whom, under what circumstances, and with what design they were written; and lower, or textual, criticism, which seeks, by the aid of the ancient manuscripts and versions, to bring the text of these books to the highest practicable level of accuracy. See APOCRYPHA, CANON. The science of hermeneutics investigates the principles of interpretation, while exegesis applies them. The contents of the Bible are then methodically arranged. It will be found when this is done that they touch language and philology, geography, history, science, philosophy, ethics—in fact, nearly every department of human thought. Further, Biblical theology investigates the doctrines of the Bible in their historical development, and dogmatic or systematic theology seeks to arrange the doctrines into the system which is contained in Scripture, show their relation to each other and to other truths, and to state them with precision.

The Bible embraces the Old and the New Testaments or covenants. The O.T. was written in Hebrew, except a few passages in Aramaic, and the N.T. in Greek. For the several books of the O.T. and N.T., see the articles which bear their names; and for the versions of the Scripture to other tongues, see SAMARITAN PENTATEUCH and VERSIONS.

The sacred books originally had no chapters. Formerly these divisions were ascribed to Hugues de St. Cher (Hugo a S. Caro), who died 1263, but the credit with more probabil-

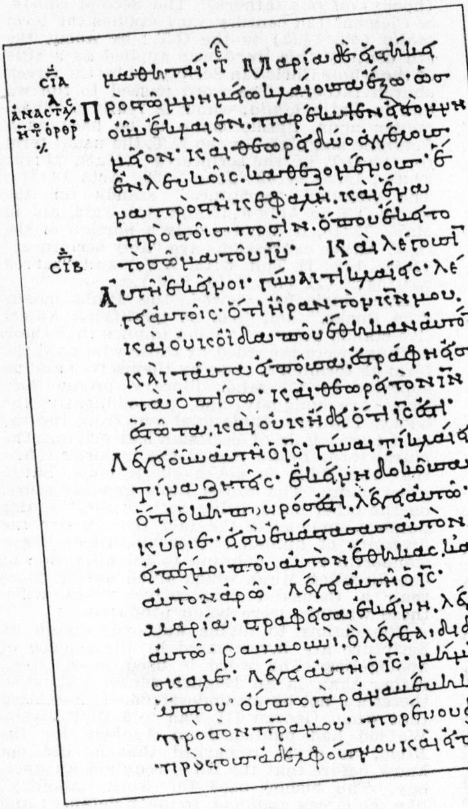

A Greek Gospel (9th or 10th Century),
John 20:11–17
(Left)

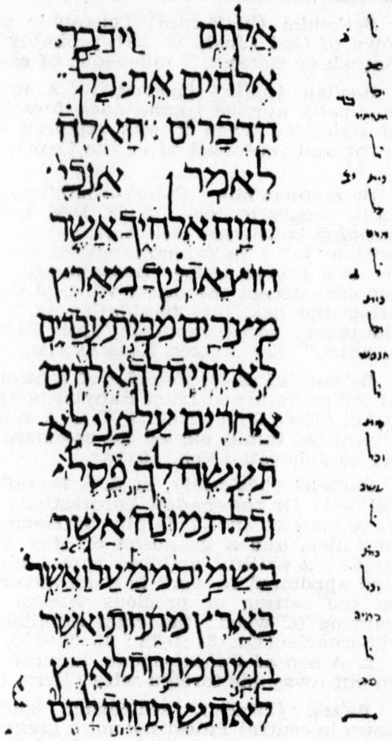

The Hebrew Pentateuch,
Ex. 20:1–5

אלהם וידבר
אלהים את־כל
הדברים האלה
לאמר אנכי
יהוה אלהיך אשר
הוצאתיך מארץ
מצרים מבית עבדים
לא יהיה לך אלהים
אחרים על פני לא
תעשה לך פסל
וכל תמונה אשר
בשמים ממעל ואשר
בארץ מתחת ואשר
במים מתחת לארץ
לא תשתחוה להם

Codex Alexandrinus (5th Century),
Luke 12:54 to 13:1

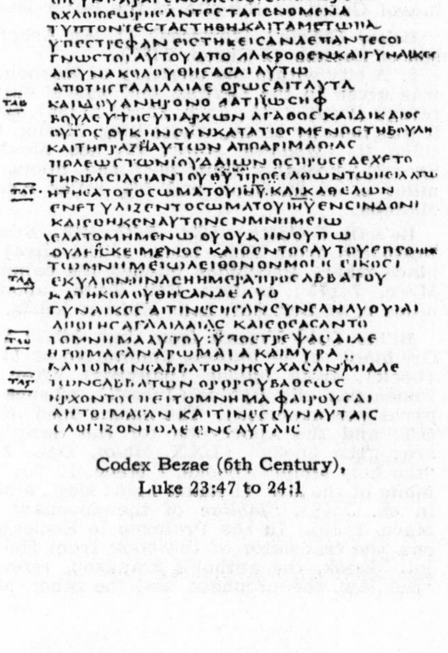

Codex Bezae (6th Century),
Luke 23:47 to 24:1

74

ity goes to Stephen Langton, archbishop of Canterbury, who died 1228. The Jewish Masoretes, however, divided the O.T. into verses. The division of the N.T. into its present verses is due to Robert Stephens, who introduced them into the Greek and Latin N.T. which he published at Geneva in 1551; and they were adopted in the English version of the N.T. printed at Geneva in 1557. The whole Bible first appeared with its present chapters and verses in Stephens' edition of the Vulgate in 1555. The first English Bible to be thus divided was the Genevan edition of 1560 (see NEW TESTAMENT). The verses are indispensable for the purpose of reference, but they often tend to break the sense of the text. R.V. accordingly prints the text in paragraphs, but retains the chapter and verse numbers.

The Bible has already been translated, in its entirety or in part, into more than 1,000 languages or dialects.

Bich′ri (bĭk′rī) [first-born]. Father of the rebel Sheba (II Sam. 20:1).

Bid′kar (bĭd′kär) [probably Baal+Deker, q.v.]. A captain under Jehu (II Kings 9:25).

Big′tha (bĭg′thá) [Old Pers. baga+dā, gift of God or giving good luck]. A chamberlain who ministered in the presence of Xerxes (Esth. 1:10).

Big′than (bĭg′thăn) or **Big·tha′na** (bĭg-thă′ná) [Old Pers.; see BIGTHA]. A chamberlain, keeper of the palace door, who conspired against King Xerxes (Esth. 2:21; 6:2).

Big′va·i (bĭg′vá-ī) [Old Pers., fortunate, happy, from baga, good luck; cf. Bagoi (I Esdras 5:14) and Bago (ch. 8:40)]. 1. One of the leaders of the exiles who returned from Babylon with Zerubbabel (Ezra 2:2).
2. Founder of a family, of which some 2,000 returned from Babylon with Zerubbabel (Ezra 2:14; Neh. 7:19), and several score afterward with Ezra (Ezra 8:14).

Bil′dad (bĭl′dăd) [probably, Bel has loved]. A Shuhite, one of Job's friends (Job 2:11), who made three speeches to the patriarch (chs. 8; 18; 25).

Bil′e·am (bĭl′ē-ăm) [perhaps, greed, destruction]. A town of Manasseh, w. of the Jordan, assigned to the Levites of the family of Kohath (I Chron. 6:70); modern Bel′āmeh, ½ mile s. of Jenīn, some 13 miles n.n.e. of Samaria. See IBLEAM. In its stead there appears in the present Hebrew text of Josh. 21:25 Gath-rimmon, which probably is a scribal error from the preceding verse. The LXX favors this view.

Bil′gah (bĭl′gá) [brightness, cheerfulness]. 1. A descendant of Aaron. His family had grown to a father's house in the time of David, and was made the 15th course of the priests (I Chron. 24:1, 6, 14).
2. A chief of the priests, perhaps representing the priestly course of this name, who returned from Babylon with Zerubbabel (Neh. 12:5, 7). In the next generation a father's house among the priests bore this name (v. 18); see BILGAI.

Bil′ga·i (bĭl′gá-ī) [brightness, cheerfulness]. One of the priests who, doubtless in behalf of a father's house, sealed the covenant in the days of Nehemiah (Neh. 10:8); see under the similar name BILGAH.

Bil′hah (bĭl′há) [foolish, simple; cf. Arab. baliha, to be unconcerned or stupid]. 1. Rachel's maidservant, who, at her mistress' desire, became one of Jacob's secondary wives. She was the mother of Dan and Naphtali (Gen. 30:1-8; I Chron. 7:13). Ultimately she committed sin with Reuben (Gen. 35:22).

2. A Simeonite town (I Chron. 4:29). See BAALAH 3.

Bil′han (bĭl′hăn) [foolish, simple; cf. Arab. baliha]. 1. A Horite, son of Ezer (Gen. 36:27).
2. A Benjamite, family of Jediael, and himself the ancestor of several father's houses (I Chron. 7:10).

Bil′shan (bĭl′shăn) [inquirer; or perhaps from Akkad. Bēlshun (their lord)]. One of the 12 chief men who returned from Babylon with Zerubbabel (Ezra 2:2; Neh. 7:7).

Bim′hal (bĭm′hăl) [perhaps, with patience; cf. Arab. mahl (slowness, leisure)]. An Asherite, family of Beriah, house of Japhlet (I Chron. 7:33).

Bin′e·a (bĭn′ē-á). A son of Moza, a descendant of Jonathan, Saul's son (I Chron. 8:37; 9:43).

Bin′nu·i (bĭn′ū-ī) [built]. 1. The head of a family, of which several hundred returned from the Captivity. His name is also pronounced Bani (Ezra 2:10; Neh. 7:15).
2 and 3. Two men, a son of Pahath-moab and a son of Bani, each of whom was induced by Ezra to put away his foreign wife (Ezra 10:30, 38).
4. A Levite who went from Babylon with Zerubbabel (Neh. 12:8). He was a son of Henadad (Neh. 10:9). His son was one who received the silver and gold brought from Babylon to the Temple by Ezra (Ezra 8:33), and his family was represented at the building of the wall (Neh. 3:24), and its representative sealed the covenant (Neh. 10:9).

Birds. The Hebrews classed as birds all animals which fly, including the bat and winged insects. Tristram enumerates 348 species of birds as either indigenous or visitants to Palestine. Of these 271 belong to the Palaearctic zone of Sclater—that to which most of the European birds belong; 40 to the Ethiopian, and 7 to the Indian zone; while 30, as far as is known, are peculiar to Palestine itself. The Ethiopian and Indian types are almost exclusively confined to the Dead Sea basin, but it is so depressed beneath the level of the ocean that it is really a small tropical region located in the midst of the temperate zone. In the Mosaic Law 20 or 21 birds and, in the case of 4 of them, their kind are expressly named as unclean (Lev. 11:13–19; Deut. 14:11–20). The only birds used for sacrifice were turtledoves and young pigeons (Lev. 1:14). Doves were domesticated (Isa. 60:8), and later, chickens. The cock is mentioned (Matt. 26:34), and the hen (Matt. 23:37; Luke 13:34). Wild fowl were hunted, among other ways, by decoy birds (Ecclus. 11:30), with snares (Amos 3:5), and with nets (Prov. 1:17). The migration of birds is referred to (Jer. 8:7).

Bir′sha (bĭr′shá) [perhaps, with (or in) wickedness]. A king of Gomorrah who was defeated by Chedorlaomer and his confederates (Gen. 14:2, 8, 10).

Birth′day′. The birth of a child, especially of a son, was a glad occasion, and was often celebrated by a feast (Jer. 20:15; Jos. Antiq. xii. 4, 7). The anniversary of one's birth was celebrated by the Egyptians and Persians (Gen. 40:20; Herod. i. 133). Herod the tetrarch kept the anniversary of his birth (Matt. 14:6; Mark 6:21).

Birth′right′. A certain right or privilege considered to belong to the first-born son in a family, and not shared by his younger brothers. The eldest son ordinarily succeeded to his father's rank and position, as head of the family or tribe and as representative of its prerogatives. He also inherited a double portion of his father's property, a right guaranteed to the first-born even when his mother was the less loved of two wives (Deut. 21: 17; cf. II Kings 2:9). A birthright might be sold to a younger brother, as Esau sold his birthright to Jacob (Gen. 25:29, 34; Heb. 12: 16). It might also be forfeited on account of misconduct (I Chron. 5:1).

Birth′stool′, in A.V. **Stool.** A chair of peculiar form, upon which the patient sat during parturition. It was denominated ′obnáyim, double stones, by the Hebrews (Ex. 1:16).

Bir·za′ith (bĭr-zā′ĭth), in A.V. **Bir·za′vith** (bĭr-zā′vĭth) [olive well]. The form in R.V. without v is favored by the Kere, the LXX, and the Vulgate. The Kethib has the letter waw which is represented by v in A.V.

An Asherite, family of Malchiel; or possibly a town (I Chron. 7:31), Bîrzeit, about 4⅝ miles n. of Ramallah.

Bish′lam (bĭsh′lăm) [perhaps, in peace]. A Persian who joined in the complaint to Artaxerxes that the Jews were rebuilding Jerusalem (Ezra 4:7); called Belemus in I Esdras 2:16.

Bish′op [Lat. episcopus, from Gr. episkopos, an overseer]. The Greek word is used in the LXX for an official overseer, whether civil or religious, as Eleazar the priest (Num. 4:16), and officers of the army (Num. 31:14). In the N.T. the word occurs first in the exhortation of Paul to the elders (marg., presbyters) of the church at Ephesus, when he said, "Take heed unto yourselves, and to all the flock, in which the Holy Spirit hath made you bishops [marg., overseers]" (Acts 20:17, 28). Here and elsewhere Paul identifies elders, presbyters, and bishops (Titus 1:5-7). The terms are different designations for the incumbent of the same office. Elsewhere he distinguishes simply between bishop and deacon (Phil. 1:1; I Tim. 3:1-8). Peter, using the verb episkopeō, exhorts the elders to tend the flock of God, "exercising the oversight, not of constraint, but willingly"; but some ancient authorities omit "exercising the oversight" (I Peter 5:2). In the Church of the N.T. the duties of the bishop were to care for the flock of God (Acts 20:28; I Peter 5:2). He was the shepherd, bearing rule and watching in behalf of souls, admonishing, encouraging, and supporting (I Thess. 5:14; Heb. 13:17), and some among them labored in the word and in teaching (I Tim. 5:17). His qualifications are enumerated in I Tim. 3:1-7 and Titus 1:7-9. A plurality of them existed in the church at Philippi, as in that of Ephesus (Phil. 1:1); and the college of presbyter-bishops ordained by the laying on of hands (I Tim. 4:14). In the church at Jerusalem the elders and apostles consulted together, and the decision of the council was given in the name of the apostles and elders (Acts 15:6, 22; 16:4; 21: 18); see ELDER. The name is applied figuratively to Jesus (I Peter 2:25). A distinction, however, grew up very early in the Church between elder or presbyter and bishop. It appears in the 2d century in the epistles of Ignatius, who died between 107 and 117. According to the Roman Catholic Council of Trent in the 16th century, bishops, being the successors of the apostles, are placed by the Holy Spirit to govern the Church of God, and to be superior to their presbyters or priests. Roman Catholic opinion assumes that the apostles had a general supervision of the congregation, while the elders whom they had ordained had the local oversight; but as the congregations increased in number, the apostles ordained assistants whom they appointed their successors, to be overseers of the congregation in a district. According to one interpretation such were the angels of the 7 churches (Rev. 1:20); see ANGEL. High An-

glicans find the institution implied in the position of Jesus' brother James in the church at Jerusalem, in the angels of the 7 churches, and in the work of Timothy and Titus. Paul did indeed exhort Timothy to tarry at Ephesus, order public worship, exhort and teach (I Tim. 1:3 seq.); and Titus, whom Paul had before employed as a messenger to the Corinthians (II Cor. 12:18), he left in Crete to set in order things that were wanting, and to appoint elders (bishops) in every city (Titus 1:5-7). But it is to be noted that Timothy was in the 1st instance ordained by presbytery (I Tim. 4:14), and there is not a trace in the N.T. of the apostles' appointing any man to succeed them.

Bi·thi′ah (bĭ-thī′à) [daughter, i.e., worshiper, of Jehovah]. A daughter of Pharaoh and wife of Mered, a man of Judah (I Chron. 4:18). Her name indicates that she was a convert to the worship of Jehovah.

Bith′ron (bĭth′rŏn) [cut, ravine, gorge]. A region, doubtless a valley, n. of the Jabbok near Mahanaim (II Sam. 2:29).

Bi·thyn′i·a (bĭ-thĭn′ĭ-à). A country in the n.w. part of Asia Minor, bounded on the n. by the Black Sea, on the s. by Phrygia and Galatia, on the e. by Paphlagonia, and on the w. by Mysia and Propontis. But its boundaries varied at different times. Under the Persian Empire it constituted a satrapy. Nicomedes III bequeathed it to the Romans in 74 B.C. Paul and Silas attempted to enter Bithynia, but the Spirit "suffered them not" (Acts 16:7). The gospel was carried thither by other means. Peter was able to address Christians of Bithynia in his 1st letter (I Peter 1:1), and at the beginning of the 2d century Pliny the younger reported numerous Christians there. Later still, in 2 of its towns, Nicaea and Chalcedon, great councils of the Church were held. It is a fertile country, in which the vine is largely cultivated. In various parts, especially in the chain of Mount Olympus, which runs along its s. boundary, there are forests of oak, interspersed with beech trees, chestnuts, and walnuts.

Bit′tern. The rendering in A.V. of Heb. ḳippōd, the one contracting or rolling itself together; an animal frequenting ruins (Isa. 14:23; 34:11), which ascended to the top of ruined doors or to window sills (perhaps fallen), and thence made its voice heard (Zeph. 2:14). The bittern (Botaurus stellaris) is a long-necked and long-legged wading bird, habitually frequenting pools of water. The R.V. considers the animal to be the porcupine and has the support of the LXX and the Vulgate (hedgehog).

Bi·tu′men. Mineral pitch. There are 3 varieties of it: 1. earthy bitumen; 2. elastic bitumen (elaterite or mineral caoutchouc); 3. compact bitumen or asphalt, asphaltum, or Jew's pitch. It sinks in water, is easily melted, and is very inflammable. It has been described as petroleum hardened by evaporation and oxidation, and it may vary from a solid to a semiliquid condition. Bitumen or asphalt exists at or near the Dead Sea, called, in consequence, by the Greeks and Romans, Lake Asphaltitis. It is found also at Hit, on the Euphrates, above Babylon, and in other places. Bitumen was the slime with which the bricks used for the erection of the Tower of Babel were cemented (Gen. 11:3). The slime pits in which the defeated kings of Sodom and Gomorrah fell were bitumen pits (Gen. 14:10).

Biz′i·o·thi′ah (bĭz′ĭ-ô-thī′à), in A.V. **Biz·joth′·Jah** (bĭz-jŏth′jà) [contempt of Jehovah]. A town in the most s. portion of Judah (Josh. 15:28). The text is suspicious. Almost the same consonants (benôthehā) would mean "its daughters or suburbs" (LXX; cf. Neh. 11:27).

Biz'tha (bĭz'thȧ) [probably from Avestan *biz-dā* (double gift, giving double)]. A chamberlain at the court of Xerxes (Esth. 1:10).

Blain. The rendering of Heb. *'ăba'bu'ōth.* It signifies a bleb, a bubble of matter, a blister full of serum arising upon the skin. Blains accompanied by boils is the disease which constituted the 6th of the 10 plagues of Egypt (Ex. 9:8–11).

Blas'phe•my [Gr. *blasphēmia*, abusive or scurrilous language]. Defamatory or other wicked language directed against God (Ps. 74:10–18; Isa. 52:5; Rev. 16:9, 11, 21). Under the Mosaic Law it was punished by stoning (Lev. 24:16). The charge of blasphemy was falsely brought against Naboth (I Kings 21:9–13), Stephen (Acts 6:11), and our Lord (Matt. 9:3; 26:65, 66; John 10:36).

Blasphemy against the Holy Spirit consisted in attributing the miracles of Christ, which were wrought by the Spirit of God, to satanic power (Matt. 12:22–32; Mark 3:22–30).

Blas'tus (blăs'tŭs) [Gr., a sprout or shoot]. A palace functionary who had charge of Herod Agrippa's bedchamber (Acts 12:20).

Bless. The three leading meanings which the verb bless has in Scripture are:
1. To bestow divine favor and confer divine benefits (Gen. 1:22; 2:3; 9:1–7).
2. To adore God for his goodness and return thanks (Ps. 103:1; Matt. 26:26; cf. Mark 14:22 with Luke 22:19 and I Cor. 11:24).
3. To invoke God's favor on a person (Gen. 27:4, 27–29; I Chron. 16:2; Ps. 129:8), including salutation and even the ordinary greeting, "Peace be to you" (I Sam. 25:5, 6, 14; II Kings 4:29).

Bless'ing. Any advantage conferred or wished for. Specially:
1. Favors, advantages, conferred by God, and bringing pleasure or happiness in their train (Gen. 39:5; Deut. 28:8; Prov. 10:22, etc.).
2. The invocation of God's favor upon a person (Gen. 27:12).
3. A present, a token of good will (Gen. 33:11; Josh. 15:19; II Kings 5:15).

Blind'ness. Blindness is extremely prevalent in the East. Its main causes are smallpox, and especially ophthalmia, aggravated by peculiar conditions, such as the perpetual glare of the sun, the quantity of fine dust in the air, and flies. Children are also sometimes born blind (John 9:1). Consequently blind beggars are frequent (Matt. 9:27; 12:22; 20:30; 21:14). Total or partial blindness may result from old age (Gen. 27:1; I Sam. 4:15; I

Assyrian King Piercing the Eyes of Captives

Kings 14:4). The eyes of captives taken in war were frequently put out by barbarous victors, as by the Ammonites, Philistines, Assyrians, and Babylonians (Judg. 16:21; I Sam. 11:2; II Kings 25:7). In a few instances men were miraculously smitten with temporary blindness (Gen. 19:11; II Kings 6:18–22; Acts 9:9; 13:11). The Mosaic Law inculcated the exercise of humanity toward the blind (Lev. 19:14; Deut. 27:18).

Blood. The vital fluid circulating through the body. The life is in the blood (Lev. 17:11, 14); or the blood is the life (Deut. 12:23), though not exclusively (Ps. 104:29, 30). The blood represented the life, and so sacred is life before God that the blood of murdered Abel could be described as crying to God from the ground for vengeance (Gen. 4:10); and immediately after the Flood the eating of the blood of the lower animals was forbidden, although their slaughter for food was authorized (Gen. 9:3, 4; Acts 15:20, 29), and the law was laid down, "Whoso sheddeth man's blood, by man shall his blood be shed" (Gen. 9:6). The loss of life is the penalty for sin, and its typical vicarious surrender was necessary to remission (Heb. 9:22), and so, under the Mosaic Law, the blood of animals was used in all offerings for sin, and the blood of beasts killed on the hunt or slaughtered for food was poured out and covered with earth, because withheld by God from man's consumption and reserved for purposes of atonement (Lev. 17:10–14; Deut. 12:15, 16). The "blood of Jesus," the "blood of Christ," the "blood of Jesus Christ," or "the blood of the Lamb," are figurative expressions for his atoning death (I Cor. 10:16; Eph. 2:13; Heb. 9:14; 10:19; I Peter 1:2, 19; I John 1:7; Rev. 7:14; 12:11).

For revenger, or rather avenger, of blood, see AVENGER OF BLOOD.

Blood'y Flux. See DYSENTERY.

Blood'y Sweat. See SWEAT.

Bo'a•ner'ges (bō'ȧ-nûr'jēz) [Gr., from Aram., sons of thunder, or of tumult, wrath: cf. Aram. *r°gōshā*, noise; *riggūshā* (Syriac *regshā*), tumult; *rugzā*, anger; cf. also Arab. *rajasa*, to rumble (thunder)]. A name given by Jesus to James and John on account of their impetuosity (Mark 3:17; cf. Luke 9:54, 55).

Boar. The rendering of Heb. *hăzīr*, when it refers to wild swine, and especially to the male of wild swine (Ps. 80:13). When the reference is to the domesticated animal, it is rendered swine. The wild boar is 3 or more feet long, not counting the tail. The canine teeth project beyond the upper lip, constituting formidable tusks, with which it seeks to rip up its assailants. The animal is still found in Palestine, especially in the ravines e. of the Jordan, in the valley near Jericho, in the swamps of the waters of Merom, on Tabor, Lebanon, and Carmel, and in the Plain of Sharon.

Bo'az (bō'ăz), in A.V. of N.T. Bo'oz [ety. uncertain; probably for *Ba'al 'ōz*, lord of strength. Another possibility is that it means quick-witted; cf. Arab. *baghz*, sprightliness].
1. A wealthy and honorable Bethlehemite, kinsman to the husband of Ruth the Moabitess. He respected the memory of the dead by marrying Ruth after the decease of her husband, and became ancestor of David and of Christ (Ruth, chs. 2 to 4; Matt. 1:5).
2. [ety. uncertain; often interpreted as "In him (or in it) is strength." It may be an abbreviation of an inscription like: "In the strength of Jehovah shall the king rejoice."]. One of 2 pillars, the one on the left or n. side, set up in the porch of Solomon's Temple (I Kings 7:15–22).

Bo'che·ru (bō'kĕ·rōō) [first-born]. A son of Azel and a descendant of Jonathan, Saul's son (I Chron. 8:38).

Bo'chim (bō'kĭm) [weepers]. A place near Gilgal, where the Israelites repented and wept under the rebuke of the angel of the Lord for their disobedience of God's commands (Judg. 2:1–5).

Bo'han (bō'hăn) [thumb]. 1. A son of Reuben (Josh. 15:6; 18:17), unless Bohan is a common noun in these passages.

2. The stone of Bohan, son of Reuben, or the stone known as the Reubenite's thumb, was a landmark on the boundary between Judah and Benjamin, not a great distance from the Jordan (Josh. 15:6; 18:17).

Boil. An inflamed ulcer. It was inflicted along with blains as the 6th plague of Egypt (Ex. 9:8–11; cf. Deut. 28:27, 35). It was a prominent symptom in leprosy (Lev. 13:18–20). It constituted the main feature of Hezekiah's disease, which brought his life into imminent danger (II Kings 20:7; Isa. 38:21). Job was smitten by Satan with boils from head to foot (Job 2:7). Ordinary boils are common, in the warmer parts of the East, during the rainy season. One type of boil, the carbuncle, may lead to pyemia and be fatal. This was probably Hezekiah's disease. The application of a poultice of figs would do it good, but the rapid cure was due to God.

Bol'ster. The word appears 6 times in A.V. (I Sam. 19:13, 16; 26:7, 11, 12, 16) and renders a Hebrew word meaning "the place at the head" or "head place." R.V. rightly translates "head" in all these cases. Jacob, sleeping in the open field, took a stone to support his head (Gen. 28:11, 18). Jesus probably placed the leather cushion of the steersman's seat under his head when he lay down to sleep in the stern of the boat (Mark 4:38). Michal put some article of goats' hair at the head of the teraphim which she laid in the bed to deceive the messengers who were sent to take David (I Sam. 19:13).

Bon'net. With the exception of Isa. 3:20, where it refers to female attire, this is the A.V. designation of the special headdress of the priests (Ex. 28:40; 29:9; 39:28; Lev. 8:13; Ezek. 44:18). In the last passage R.V. renders "tires," while in the others, "headtires." See TIRE.

Book. At an early time records were inscribed on stone or clay. The Egyptians invented papyrus probably in predynastic times. Skin or parchment was also used in antiquity. When written on skin, a long document took the form of a roll with writing on one or both of its sides. Of this type of book there is a trace in the word volume, Lat. *volumen* (something rolled up) (Ps. 40:7; Jer. 36:2; Ezek. 2:9). Books are 1st mentioned as written by the Hebrews after the sojourn in Egypt, where written literature had existed for centuries (Ex. 17:14). The 39 books of the O.T. and the 27 of the N.T., which constitute the canon of Scripture, do not represent the entire literary activity of the Hebrews during the time embraced by the canon. There were, for example, the books of the Apocrypha. Later there were memoirs of Jesus (Luke 1:1). In the O.T. period there were 2 poetical books at least, the Book of the Wars of Jehovah and the Book of Jashar (Num. 21:14; Josh. 10:13). The events of the reigns of David and Solomon were recorded in the History of Samuel the Seer, the History of Nathan the Prophet, the History of Gad the Seer, and in the Prophecy of Ahijah (I Chron. 29:29; II Chron. 9:29), and also in the Chronicles of King David, which apparently mark the beginning of the custom of keeping royal annals (I Chron. 27:24). The reigns of Solomon and Jeroboam found record in the Visions of Iddo the Seer (II Chron. 9:29); and Rehoboam's reign in the History of Shemaiah the Prophet and in the History of Iddo the Seer (II Chron. 12:15). The Chronicles of the Kings of Israel and the Chronicles of the Kings of Judah recorded the history of the 2 kingdoms from the time of Rehoboam and Jeroboam, until as late as the reign of Jehoiakim (I Kings 14:19, 29; II Kings 24:5); see KINGS. In addition to these works, there was quite a library in existence at the time when the books of Chronicles were written, consisting largely of monographs, of which not a few titles are cited (II Chron. 13:22; 20:34; 24:27; 26:22; 32:32; 33:18, 19; 35:25; see also Prov. 25:1; I Kings 4:32, 33). See PAPYRUS.

Booth. A rude habitation designed in most cases for a longer occupation than a tent, but not for permanence like a house. It was often formed with branches of trees. Jacob made booths at Shechem for his cattle, the place in consequence being afterwards called Succoth (Gen. 33:17). The keeper of a vineyard occupied a booth (Job 27:18; Isa. 1:8, R.V.), which during the vintage sheltered the owner and his friends. The Israelites were required to form booths of branches of trees, palm leaves, etc., and dwell in them for 7 days at the feast of tabernacles. The booths at this harvest festival were a reminder of the vintage life; but with this recollection there was also to be associated the memory of their deliverance from Egypt, when they sojourned in the wilderness without permanent habitation (Lev. 23:39–43; Neh. 8:14).

Boo'ty. The plunder of a conquered district or town. It consisted of everything of value—household goods, gold, silver, cattle, and captives to be used as slaves (Gen. 14:11, 12, 16; Num. 31:9, 26–52; Josh. 7:21). At the conquest of Canaan the Israelites were required to slay everything that breathed and to destroy all idols and places of idolatrous worship, but in foreign conquests they were bidden to slay the men only, and were authorized to take the remaining spoil (Num. 33:52; Deut. 20:14–16). Exceptions were occasionally made when everything was devoted, the living to destruction, the goods to the treasury of the sanctuary, or when a certain portion of the spoil was dedicated to the Lord (Num. 31:26–47; Josh. 6:19; I Sam. 15:2, 3). David made a law that the troops detailed to guard the baggage should share equally with those who engaged in the battle (I Sam. 30:23–25).

Bo'oz (bō'ŏz). See BOAZ.

Bor'row. To get in loan. Did the Israelites, when the Egyptians urged them to leave the country, borrow goods from the Egyptians or obtain them as gifts? Heb. *shā'al*, rendered borrow in A.V. (Ex. 3:22; 11:2; 12:35), means simply ask (R.V.) or request, whether the object desired was to be returned (II Kings 6:5) or not (Judg. 5:25; 8:24); and the word translated lend (Ex. 12:36, A.V.) is a form of the same verb, and means to grant a request or let one have what one asks (R.V.; cf. I Sam. 1:28).

Bos'cath (bŏs'kăth). See BOZKATH.

Bo'sor (bō'sôr). 1. A town of Gilead, Gilead being doubtless used in a broad sense (I Macc. 5:26, 36); identified with Buṣr el-Ḥariri, 12½ miles e. of Sheikh Miskin.

2. See BEOR 2.

Bos'o·ra (bŏs'ô·ră). A town of Gilead (I Macc. 5:26, 28), Bostra in Hauran, at an important junction of caravan roads leading to the Mediterranean, Damascus, the Red Sea, and the Persian Gulf; modern Buṣra eski Shăm.

Botch. The rendering in A.V. of Deut. 28:
27, 35 of Heb. *sh^eḥin,* elsewhere translated
boil.

Bot'tle. 1. A hollow vessel of leather, or the
hollow nide of an animal, used for holding

Wineskins

liquids (Job 32:19; Matt. 9:17); wine-skin
in R.V. See BUTTER.

2. A small vessel of earthenware formed by
potters, which was capable of being broken
(Jer. 19:1, 10, 11).

Bow. A weapon used for shooting arrows
(II Kings 6:22; I Chron. 12:2). It was made
of a strip of elastic wood or metal (II Sam.
22:35; Job 20:24), with a cord stretched between its 2 ends (Ps. 11:2), and was held in
the left hand (Ezek. 39:3). It was used both
in hunting and in war (Gen. 27:3; 48:22).
Its use was general among the nations of antiquity (I Sam. 31:3; I Kings 22:34; Jer.
46:9; 49:35). There were archers among the
soldiers of Reuben, Gad, the half tribe of
Manasseh, Ephraim, and especially Benjamin
(I Chron. 5:18; II Chron. 14:8; Ps. 78:9).
The bow was carried by officers and soldiers
on foot, in chariots, or on horseback (II
Kings 9:24). The archers carried the little
shield and a sword (I Sam. 18:4; I Chron.

writing tablets (II Esdras 14:24, A.V.). The
box, fir, and pine were the glory of Lebanon
(Isa. 60:13; cf. Isa. 41:19). The box tree of
Lebanon is *Buxus longifolia,* a small evergreen tree about 20 ft. high.

Bo'zez (bō'zĕz) [perhaps, shining; cf. Arab.
bāḍa, to exceed in whiteness]. Of 2 crags
near Gibeah, the northernmost, in front of
Michmash (I Sam. 14:4, 5). It overlooked
the wadi eṣ-Ṣuweiniṭ.

Boz'kath (bŏz'kăth), in A.V. once **Bos'cath**
[cf. Arab. *baṣḳah,* elevated, stony ground].
A town in the extreme s. of Judah (Josh.
15:39). Josiah's maternal grandfather, Adaiah, was the place (II Kings 22:1); near
Lachish, perhaps at Dawā'imeh.

Boz'rah (bŏz'rá) [fortified place, sheepfold].
1. An important city of Edom (Gen. 36:33;
I Chron. 1:44; Isa. 34:6; 63:1). Amos predicted that its palaces should be destroyed
(Amos 1:12); and Jeremiah foretold its utter
destruction (Jer. 49:13, 22). It was noted for
its sheep (Micah 2:12). Identified with
Buṣeirah, about 20 miles s.s.e. of the Dead
Sea and about 35 miles n. of Petra.

2. A city of Moab mentioned with Kerioth,
Beth-meon, Dibon, and other towns of the
plateau (Jer. 48:24); probably the same as
Bezer (in LXX, Bosor).

Brace'let. An ornament for the wrist or for
the arm, worn by both sexes (Ezek. 16:11).
One was put on Rebekah's wrist by Abraham's servant (Gen. 24:22). Bracelets were

Egyptian Bracelets

given by the Israelites in the wilderness to
furnish gold or silver for the construction of
the vessels of the tabernacle (Num. 31:50).
Saul wore one, unless what he had on was
rather an armlet (II Sam. 1:10). For brace-

The Bow Used in Battle Between Assyrians and Their Foes]

5:18; II Chron. 14:8), and with the slingers
constituted the light-armed troops.

The arrows were of cane or polished wood,
and were carried in a quiver (Lam. 3:13; Isa.
49:2; Ezek. 39:9). Their heads were made of
iron, copper, or stone, and were sometimes
poisoned (Job 6:4).

Bowl. See BASIN 3.

Box. 1. A small case or vessel with a cover.
In Scripture times boxes were used to hold
oil, ointment, etc. (II Kings 9:1; Matt. 26:7,
A.V.).

2. The rendering of Heb. *t^eashshur.* Boat
seats were made of it (Ezek. 27:6, R.V.), and

let in A.V. in Gen. 38:18, 25, R.V. substitutes
cord; in Ex. 35:22, brooches; and in Isa.
3:19, marg., chains.

Bram'ble. The rendering of Heb. *'āṭād* in
Judg. 9:14, 15. The plant is named from its
firmness. R.V. marg. renders it by thorn,
and both versions so translate the word in
Ps. 58:9. It is doubtless a variety of *Rhamnus.* The LXX and Vulgate render it by
Rhamnus. This thorn is quite common in the
warmer parts of Palestine, especially in the
vicinity of the Dead Sea, in the Jordan Valley,
and about the Sea of Galilee. It is also found
at Jerusalem. The *Rhamnus* is still called by

the Arabs *'aṭad* or *nabḳ*, applying the name not only to Christ's Thorn (*Zizyphus spina Christi*), which takes its name from the tradition that the crown placed on Christ's head was made from its twigs, but apparently also to *Rhamnus paliurus*.

Branch. A title applied to the Messiah as the offspring of David (Jer. 23:5; 33:15; Zech. 3:8; 6:12).

Brass. The rendering of Heb. *neḥôsheth* and Gr. *chalkos*. R.V. marg., however, at Gen. 4:22 gives copper as a constant alternative. Copper is supposed to have been discovered by the Egyptians at Sinai about 5000 B.C. It was smelted from the ore dug from the ground (Deut. 8:9; Job 28:2). Traces of ancient copper works exist in Lebanon and in Edom. It was obtained notably in the peninsula of Sinai, in Cyprus, and in Meshech and Tubal (Ezek. 27:13). Copper refineries of the time of Solomon have been discovered at Eziongeber (Tell el-Kheleifeh). They are elaborate structures with many flues and depended for their draft upon the strong winds blowing constantly from the n.

Brass is an alloy of copper and zinc, the general use of which is comparatively modern. In ancient times its place was supplied by bronze, an alloy of copper and tin. Brass in the English Bible means either bronze or copper itself. From copper and its alloys utensils were made: pots, shovels, basins, pans, spoons, snuffers (Ex. 38:3; Lev. 6:28; Num. 16:39; Jer. 52:18); armor, such as helmets, coats of mail, greaves, shields, spear points, and even bows (II Sam. 21:16; 22:35, R.V.; II Chron. 12:10); fetters, mirrors, city gates, musical instruments, idols, and in later times coins (Ex. 38:8; II Kings 25:7, 13; Isa. 45:2; Matt. 10:9; I Cor. 13:1; Rev. 9:20). Where casting is spoken of, the metal was bronze. Thus were made the plating and railing for the altar, the lavers and the sea with its pedestal of oxen, and two magnificent pillars for the Temple (I Kings 7:41–46; II Chron. 4:1–17). See BRONZE.

Bra'zen Ser'pent. The figure of a serpent made of bronze and erected by Moses on a pole in the wilderness, that the Israelites who were bitten by fiery serpents might look at it with faith in God's promise to heal those who looked (Num. 21:8, 9). In after years the Israelites began to use it as an idol, and Hezekiah had it broken into pieces, contemptuously calling it *Nehushtan*, i.e., only a piece of brass (II Kings 18:4). R.V. marg. and J.V., however, translate: "And it was called Nehushtan." This rendering, preferred by many commentators, can also be defended from the Hebrew and finds support in Lucian, the Peshitta, and the Targum, which have the verb in the plural. A statement regarding the real or popular name of the idol is more to be expected than one as to what Hezekiah called it in the act of destroying it. Nehushtan may be a play upon *naḥāsh* (serpent) and *neḥôsheth* (copper, bronze); cf. Num. 21:9, where the two words are used together. Jesus, in foretelling his crucifixion, explained its spiritual significance by comparing it with the rearing of the brazen serpent (John 3:14, 15).

Bread. The bread in use among the Israelites consisted generally of small flat cakes of wheaten flour or, among the poor, of barley flour. The grain was ground daily in a hand mill, and fresh bread baked every day. When this bread was to be eaten at once, it was often unleavened (Gen. 19:3; I Sam. 28:24), but the art of making leavened bread was also understood. The showbread which was edible after eight days was evidently leavened. The flour was made into a paste or dough by mixing with water, and might be leavened some

time after mixing; for example, at the 1st passover the dough was already mixed in the troughs, but not yet leavened, when the order came to march (Ex. 12:34).

The oven used by private families was a portable jar in which, after it had been heated, the loaves were laid or were stuck against the sides, the cakes baked in this fashion being very thin.

Besides the bread baked in the oven (Lev. 2:4), cakes something like pancakes (Lev. 2:5) were baked on a pan put over a fire.

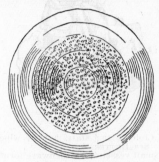

A Baking Tray from Gezer

Bread was also baked on the heated hearth or on any hot stones after the ashes were swept aside (I Kings 19:6). This kind was made especially when food was wanted in a hurry (Gen. 18:6). The Bedouins at present commonly bake by placing their loaves in a hole in the ground which has previously held a fire and then been cleared out. The hole is carefully covered and the bread allowed to bake all night. This method was probably well known to the Israelites. Baking was ordinarily done by the women (Gen. 18:6; I Sam. 8:13; Lev. 26:26; cf. Judg. 6:19), and in large households by the slaves, but in the cities there were also bakers who sold bread (Jer. 37:21). In Lev., ch. 2, is given a list of the different kinds of bread which were acceptable as offerings. In some places the word is applied to all kinds of food (Luke 11:3).

Breast'plate'. 1. A sacred article of dress worn by the Jewish high priest (Ex. 28:15–30). See HIGH PRIEST.

2. Armor designed to protect the body in battle (Rev. 9:9); see ARMOR. Figuratively, righteousness (Isa. 59:17; Eph. 6:14; Wisd. of Sol. 5:18), or faith and love, constitute a spiritual breastplate (I Thess. 5:8).

Breth'ren of the Lord. Their names are given in the Gospels as James, Joseph or Joses, Simon, and Judas (Matt. 13:55, R.V.; Mark 6:3). They appear in company with Mary (Matt. 12:47–50; Mark 3:31–35; Luke 8:19–21), moved to Capernaum with her and Jesus and the latter's disciples at the beginning of Christ's ministry (John 2:12), but are said not to have believed in Jesus even toward the close of his life (John 7:4, 5). After the resurrection, however, they are found united with the disciples (Acts 1:14), and are afterward mentioned as Christian workers (I Cor. 9:5). One of them, James (Gal. 1:19), became a distinguished leader of the Jerusalem church (Acts 12:17; 15:13; Gal. 2:9), and was the author of the epistle which goes by his name. In what sense they were Christ's "brethren" has been much disputed. In very early times they were regarded as the children of Joseph by a former marriage. The disappearance of Joseph from the Gospels suggests that he had died, and may have been much older than Mary, and may have been previously married. This view (Origen, 3d century and Epiphanius, 4th century) is a possible one, but, in view of Matt. 1:25 and Luke 2:7, not probable. In the 4th century Jerome proposed another view; viz., that they were Christ's cousins on his mother's side, the children of Alphaeus (or Clopas) and Mary's sister of the same name. This is inferred mainly from a combination of Mark 15:40 and John 19:25 (the latter being thought to mention but three women), and from the identity of the names Alphaeus and Clopas. On this view one (James the son of Alphaeus) and perhaps more (Simon and Judas) of the apostles were Christ's brethren. But the apostles are distinguished from his brethren; the latter did not believe in him, and it is unlikely that two sisters had the same name. Another very old view was that they were cousins on Joseph's side, and some have even supposed they were the children of the widow of Joseph's brother (Deut. 25:5–10). But all these theories appear to have originated from a wish to maintain the perpetual virginity of Mary. That they were the children of Joseph and Mary, born after Jesus, is the natural view, and that Mary had other children is implied in Matt. 1:25; Luke 2:7. This view (Tertullian, c. end of 2d century, and Helvidius, 4th century) explains also the constant association of "the brethren" with Mary.   G. T. P. (rev., H. S. G.)

Brick. A mass of clay made rectangular in shape and hardened either by burning in a kiln or by drying in the sun. Bricks were of course sun-dried when the clay was mixed with straw (Ex. 5:7). Both bricks and tiles are often found stamped with names and in-

Brick Bearing Name and Inscription of Nebuchadnezzar

scriptions, from which we have derived much of our knowledge of those ancient times, as well as from the tablets of burnt clay specially prepared as documents.

Brick'kiln'. A kiln for enclosing bricks while they are being burned (II Sam. 12:31 and Nahum 3:14, where R.V. marg. translates "brick-mould"; Jer. 43:9, in R.V. brickwork).

Bri'er. The rendering of 6 distinct Hebrew words and of one Greek word. 1. *Barkân* (Judg. 8:7, 16).

2. *Shâmîr*, thorn, adamant, flint (Isa. 9:18; 10:17; 27:4; 32:13), such as springs up in abandoned vineyards (chs. 5:6; 7:23).

3. *Sirpad* (Isa. 55:13). The LXX renders it fleabane, and the Vulgate, nettle.

4. *Sârâb*, refractory (Ezek. 2:6).

5. *Sillôn* (Ezek. 28:24; in ch. 2:6 rendered thorn).

6. *Hêdek* (Micah 7:4), used in hedges (Prov. 15:19, where it is rendered thorn).

7. Gr. *tribolos*, caltrop, burr, thistle (Heb. 6:8, brier, A.V.; thistle, R.V.). In Matt. 7:16

the same word is rendered thistle by A.V. and R.V.

Brig'an·dine. A coat of mail (so R.V.), composed of light, thin-jointed scales, or of thin, pliant plate armor (Jer. 46:4; 51:3).

Brim'stone'. Sulphur (Gen. 19:24; Deut. 29:23).

Bronze. See BRASS. In Palestinian archaeology we speak of these bronze periods:

Early Bronze	I	Centuries	32–29 B.C.
Early Bronze	II	Centuries	29–27 B.C.
Early Bronze	III	Centuries	27–24 B.C.
Early Bronze	IV	Centuries	24–22 B.C.
Middle Bronze	I	Centuries	22–21 B.C.
Middle Bronze	II	Centuries	21–16 B.C.
Late Bronze	I	Centuries	16–14 B.C.
Late Bronze	II	Centuries	14–13 B.C.

The Bronze Age is preceded by the Chalcolithic and followed by the Iron Age. The dates are all approximate.

Brook. A small perennial stream, as the Kishon (I Kings 18:40) and the Jabbok (Gen. 32:22, 23, A.V.). Generally, however, in Scripture the word is used for a stream (wadi) which flows in the rainy, winter season but is dry in summer, as the brook of Egypt (Num. 34:5, R.V.; see RIVER), the Zered (Deut. 2:13), and the Kidron (II Sam. 15:23; John 18:1, R.V.).

Broom. A much-branched bush, with twiggy, nearly leafless branches, and clusters of pinkish-white flowers, which grows in the Jordan Valley and Arabia, and is common in the peninsula of Sinai (Job 30:4; I Kings 19:4). Its large root stalk is made into charcoal (Ps. 120:4). In the text of the last 2 passages in the R.V., and in all the 3 in the A.V., it is rendered juniper, but Heb. *rôthem* corresponds to modern Arab. *ratam* (broom).

Broth'er. 1. A male person considered in his relation to another person or other persons of either sex born of the same parents (Gen. 27:6), or at least of the same father (Gen. 28:2) or the same mother (Judg. 8:19).

2. A man of the same near ancestry (as a nephew, Gen. 14:16), or of the same race or of a kindred nation (Deut. 23:7; Neh. 5:7; Jer. 34:9).

3. An ally (Amos 1:9) or coreligionist (Acts 9:17; I Cor. 6:6; II Cor. 2:13); often in the plural applied to Christian disciples (Matt. 23:8; Rom. 1:13).

4. One of the male sex greatly beloved or politely addressed by the person who calls him brother (II Sam. 1:26; I Kings 20:32).

5. Any man whatever, the common brotherhood of the human race being recognized (Gen. 9:5; Matt. 5:22; 18:35).

Buck'ler. See ARMOR.

Buk'ki (bŭk'ī) [abbreviation of Bukkiah]. 1. Prince of the tribe of Dan and member of the commission for allotting the land (Num. 34:22).

2. A descendant of Aaron, in the highpriestly line of Phinehas (I Chron. 6:5, 51; Ezra 7:4).

Buk·ki'ah (bŭ-kī'à) [perhaps, Jehovah has tested; cf. Aram. *bᵉkā'* (try)]. A Levite, son of Heman, and head of the 6th of the 24 companies of 12 musicians each which David appointed for the service of the sanctuary (I Chron. 25:4, 13).

Bul (bōōl) [probably, rain month]. The 8th month of the Jewish year (I Kings 6:38). See YEAR.

Bull. The male of the species called by naturalists *Bos taurus* (Job 21:10; Ps. 68:30; Isa. 34:7; Jer. 52:20); see Ox.

The word *te'ō*, rendered wild ox and wild bull in A.V. (Deut. 14:5; Isa. 51:20), is translated in R.V. by antelope (*q.v.*).

Bull'ock. A young bull, though the Heb. word is used once of an animal 7 years old (Judg. 6:25). Bullocks were used as draft animals bearing a yoke (Jer. 31:18, A.V.), and were offered in sacrifice (Ex. 29:1; I Chron. 29:21).

Bul'rush'. 1. Heb. *gōme'* (Ex. 2:3; Isa. 18:2, A.V.); papyrus (*q.v.*).
2. Heb. *'agmōn.* The etymology suggests that it grows in swamps; it is a low plant (Isa. 9:14; 19:15), bows the head (ch. 58:5), and was twisted into ropes (Job 41:2, R.V. marg.).

Bu'nah (bū'nȧ) [intelligence]. A descendant of Judah through Jerahmeel (I Chron. 2:25).

Bun'ni (bŭn'ī) [perhaps, built, erected].
1. A Levite who lived before the Exile (Neh. 11:15).
2. A Levite, contemporary of Nehemiah (Neh. 9:4).
3. Representative of a family or father's house who sealed the covenant (Neh. 10:15).

Bur'den. 1. A heavy load to be borne; used in a literal or a figurative sense (Ex. 23:5; Num. 11:11, etc.).
2. An utterance or prophecy, in almost every instance pronouncing heavy judgment on a place or people (Isa. 14:28; 15:1; Ezek. 12:10; Hos. 8:10; Nahum 1:1).

Bur'i·al. Interment in Bible lands followed speedily after death. Among Oriental Jews at the present time burial takes place, if possible, within 24 hours after death. The rapidity of decomposition in that climate requires that the survivors immediately bury their dead out of their sight (Gen. 23:3, 4). With few exceptions the Hebrews did not cremate (cf. I Sam. 31:11–13; II Sam. 21:12–14; and Amos 6:10, an emergency). When a death occurred, friends, especially women, hurried to the house and made loud lamentation (Mark 5:38). Mourners were even hired (Jer. 9:17). The body was washed (Acts 9:37), and wrapped in a cloth or closely bound in bands (Matt. 27:59; John 11:44). The wealthy added spices and perfumes (John 12:7; 19:39) or burned fragrant materials (Jer. 34:5). The body was carried upon a bier to the grave (II Sam. 3:31; Luke 7:14). Burial was generally in a cave or in a sepulcher scooped horizontally in the rock (Gen. 25:9, 10; Matt. 27:60). See Mourning and Sepulcher.

Burnt Of'fer·ing. See Offerings.

Burnt Sac'ri·fice, the same as burnt offering. See Offerings.

Bush. 1. Heb. *sᵉneh* and Gr. *batos,* a thorny bush (Luke 6:44), which Moses saw burning and from which Jehovah spoke (Ex. 3:2, 3; Deut. 33:16; Mark 12:26). Tristram believes it to have been the *Acacia vera* or *nilotica,* the Egyptian thorn. It is a withered-looking thorny tree, 12 feet high, with bipinnate leaves and white flowers. It grows throughout a large part of Africa, also in the Sinai Peninsula, and, in Palestine, on the shores of the Dead Sea. The identification, however, is not certain.
2. Heb. *śīaḥ* (Job. 30:4, 7; and Gen. 2:5, where it is rendered plant); a shrub large enough to afford some shade (Gen. 21:15, where it is rendered shrub).
3. Heb. *nahălōl* (Isa. 7:19), rendered in the text of R.V. by pasture, and in A.V. marg. by commendable trees.

Bush'el. The rendering of Gr. *modios,* a dry measure containing almost 2 gallons (Matt. 5:15; Mark 4:21). See Measure, III.

But'ler. See Cupbearer.

But'ter. *Hem'āh,* curdled milk or curds (Gen. 18:8; Deut. 32:14; Prov. 30:33; Isa. 7:15, 22). R.V. marg. of Isa. 7:15 translates curds. Thomson says that neither the ancient nor the modern Orientals have made butter in our sense of the word. The butter given to Sisera by Jael was sour milk, called in Arab. *laban* (Judg. 5:25). The butter of Prov. 30:33 is a production corresponding to the Arab. *samn,* which is made in the following manner: A bottle formed by stripping off the entire skin of a young buffalo is filled with milk and then perseveringly kneaded or shaken by women. Then the contents are taken out, boiled or melted, and put into bottles of goats' skins. In winter it resembles candied honey, and in summer is mere oil.

Buz (bŭz) [contempt; perhaps the same as Bāzu, a desert region and tribe, of the Assyrian inscriptions]. 1. An Aramaean tribe, descended from a son of Nahor (Gen. 22:20, 21), and probably dwelling in Jeremiah's time near Dedan and Tema in Arabia (Jer. 25:23).
2. A Gadite, founder of a tribal family or house (I Chron. 5:14).

Bu'zi (bū'zī) [descendant of Buz]. Father of the priest and prophet Ezekiel (Ezek. 1:3).

Buz'ite (bū'zīt). One belonging to the Arabian tribe of Buz (Job 32:2).

C

Cab'bon (kăb'ŏn) [cf. Aram. *kᵉban,* wrap around, surround]. A village of Judah in the lowland (Josh. 15:40). Perhaps identical with Machbena (I Chron. 2:49).

Ca'bul (kā'bŭl) [perhaps, fettered land, i.e., hard, dry, unproductive land; cf. Heb. *kebel,* a fetter]. 1. A town of Asher (Josh. 19:27; Jos. *Life* 43, 45), still known as Kābūl, a village 9 miles s.e. of Acre.
2. A district of Galilee, that is, of the n. part of the territory of Naphtali. It contained 20 towns, which Solomon presented to Hiram, king of Tyre, in return for services rendered in the building of the Temple. Hiram was displeased with the gift, and therefore called the region Cabul (I Kings 9:13), perhaps intending a pun: *Kābūl* and *kᵉbal* (like not= good as nothing). Hiram thus rejected the proffered compensation and returned the district to Solomon, who thereupon fortified the cities and caused Israelites to dwell in them (II Chron. 8:2; Jos. *Antiq.* viii. 5, 3).

Cae'sar (sē'zẽr). The family name of a branch of the Julian house or clan in Rome; its most illustrious representative was Gaius Julius Caesar, who was assassinated in 44 B.C. The name Caesar was assumed by his grandnephew Octavius, later the emperor Augustus. Tiberius, who succeeded Augustus, and Caligula, Claudius, and Nero, who followed in succession, were all entitled by relationship to the great dictator to bear the family name; the 6 succeeding emperors— Galba, Otho, Vitellius, Vespasian, Titus, and Domitian complete the number 12 in Suetonius' *Lives of the Caesars.* From having been the name of one mighty conqueror, and then of a series of emperors, the name Caesar became the type or symbol of the civil power in general, and it is continually used in this sense in discussions as to the relative domains of civil and ecclesiastical rulers (cf. Matt. 22:17, 21; Mark 12:14, 16, 17; Luke 20:22, 24, 25).

The name Caesar is applied in the N.T. to:
1. Au·gus'tus Cae'sar (ô-gŭs'tŭs sē'zẽr), the 1st Roman emperor (Luke 2:1). In 43 B.C. he was named one of the Second Triumvirate, Mark Antony and Lepidus being the

other members. Lepidus was found incompetent and forced to retire; and after the defeat of Antony at Actium in 31 B.C. Augustus was sole ruler of the Roman world, and was given the title of emperor. It was in consequence of a decree of Augustus that Joseph and Mary went to Bethlehem to be taxed, at the time of Christ's birth. Although Augustus was not fond of the Jews, he favored them from policy, and caused sacrifices to be made daily in the Temple at Jerusalem at his expense. He was friendly to Herod, recognizing that in him he had a valuable ally. Caesarea Philippi and Caesarea by the Sea were built in his honor by Herod. Augustus died A.D. 14, in the 67th year of his age.

2. Ti·ber'i·us Cae'sar (tī-bẽr'ĭ-ŭs sē'zẽr), the 2d Roman emperor (Matt. 22:17; Mark 12:14; Luke 3:1; 20:22; John 19:12), born 42 B.C., the adopted son, also stepson and son-in-law, of Augustus. During his reign Judea was governed by Valerius Gratus and Pontius Pilate. At one time he banished the Jews from Rome, but later recalled the edict, and

Bust of Tiberius

gave them redress for the severity of the provincial governors. Tiberias, on the Sea of Galilee, was built in his honor by Herod Antipas. His death (A.D. 37) was hastened by Caligula, who succeeded him and reigned until 41.

3. Clau'di·us (klō'dĭ-ŭs), the 4th Roman emperor, a weak, vacillating man, a nephew of Tiberius. He became emperor in A.D. 41, but left the real power in the hands of unprincipled favorites. Herod Agrippa I had been in Rome, and had assisted in his coronation, and in consequence was given the whole of Palestine as a mark of favor. In the beginning of his reign Claudius favored the Jews, and reinstated the Alexandrian Jews in their former privileges, but later he banished all Jews from Rome (Acts 18:2). He died A.D. 54, in the 14th year of his reign.

4. Ne'ro (nē'rō), the 5th Roman emperor (Acts 25:12, 21; 26:32; Phil. 4:22), the adopted son of his predecessor Claudius, who secured his own position by poisoning his stepbrother Britannicus. Nero was a monster of lust and cruelty, though, perhaps, his crimes have been exaggerated. In the 10th year of his reign, A.D. 64, a great fire broke out at Rome, in large measure destroying 3 of the 14 districts into which the city was divided. The emperor was believed, apparently on insufficient evidence, to have been

himself the incendiary, and was in consequence in danger of his life. To screen himself, he falsely accused the Christians of having caused the fire, and put many of them to cruel deaths, tradition adding that both Paul and Peter were among the sufferers. Finding that he was deserted by his troops, and that he would soon be put to death, he anticipated his fate. Like Saul, he attempted suicide,

Coin with Head of Claudius

and, failing, induced one of his supporters to complete the act of slaughter. He died A.D. 68, in the 32d year of his age and the 14th of his reign.

5. Ti'tus (tī'tŭs), son of Vespasian, and 10th Roman emperor. In A.D. 66, Vespasian was sent to Palestine to quell a revolt of the Jews, and Titus accompanied him. In 69, when Vespasian hurried from Judea to Rome to secure the imperial office for himself, he

Coin with Head of Titus

left Titus in command of the army, and Titus conducted the siege of Jerusalem in A.D. 70 (Jos. War iii. 1, 3 to vii. 3, 1). Titus became emperor in 79, and died in 81, in the 40th year of his age.

Caes'a·re'a (sĕs'à-rē'à) [pertaining to Caesar]. A city on the coast of Palestine, about 23 miles s. of Mount Carmel and 64 from Jerusalem. It was built by Herod the Great, on the site of a town called Straton's Tower. Twelve years, from 25 to 13 B.C., were spent in its erection. A sea mole was built of huge stones; it was 200 feet wide, stood in 20 fathoms of water, and enclosed a harbor as large as that at Athens. The entrance to the artificial port was on the n., where there was a tower. The city was provided with a temple, a theater, and an amphitheater, and had a complete system of drainage. Herod named the place Caesarea, after his patron Augustus Caesar (Jos. *Antiq.* xv. 9, 6; *War* i. 21, 5, *seq.*). It was sometimes called Caesarea of Palestine, or Caesarea by the Sea, to distinguish it from Caesarea Philippi. It became the Roman capital of Palestine. The gospel was carried thither by Philip the evangelist, who made it his residence (Acts 8:40; 21:8). When Paul, soon after his conversion, was in danger of being murdered by the Jews of Jerusalem, his Christian brethren brought him down to Caesarea, whence he sailed to his birthplace, Tarsus, in Asia Minor (Acts 9:30). It was at Caesarea that the Roman centurion Cornelius lived, to whom Peter preached Christ, and the calling of the Gentiles took place (Acts 10:1, 24; 11:11). Herod Agrippa died at Caesarea in A.D. 44 (Acts 12:19, 23; Jos. *Antiq.* xix. 8, 2). Paul twice revisited the city, and found a church existing (Acts 18:22; 21:8, 16). He was afterward taken thither as a prisoner (Acts 23:23, 33), and it was there that his trial before Festus and Agrippa took place (ch. 25:1–4, 6–13). The population of the city was mixed, and race jealousies existed to such an extent that in the reign of Nero the Syrians made a wholesale massacre of the Jews, commencing the troubles which culminated in A.D. 70 in the destruction of Jerusalem by Titus (Jos. *War* ii. 18, 1). In the 2d century A.D. Caesarea became the residence of a bishop, who down to 451 was metropolitan of Palaestina Prima. In 195 a council was held there. A Christian school was established in the city, in which Origen taught and where Eusebius, afterward bishop of Caesarea, was educated. In 548 the Jews and Samaritans joined in assaulting the Christians. In 640 the city was captured by the Mohammedans. In 1101 it was taken by the crusaders, led by Baldwin I. Saladin retook it from them in 1189; the crusaders recovered it in 1191, but lost it to the sultan Baybars in 1265. Caesarea is still called Ḳaysārîyeh.

Caes′a·re′a Phi·lip′pi (sĕs′à-rē′à fĭ-lĭp′ī) [Caesarea of Philip]. A city at the foot of Mount Hermon, at the main source of the Jordan, and in the angle of a small plain, with hills on all sides except on the w. No spot in Palestine can compare with this in romantic beauty. The worship of the Roman god Pan long prevailed here, and, Herod the Great having built a temple of fine marble near the sacred spot, the place was called Paneas (Jos. *Antiq.* xv. 10, 3). The town was afterward enlarged and adorned by Philip the tetrarch, and its name altered to Caesarea in honor of the Roman emperor Tiberius Caesar (Jos. *Antiq.* xviii. 2, 1; *War* ii. 9, 1). Jesus and his disciples visited it at least once, and it was there that the remarkable conversation took place between him and Peter arising out of the question, "Who do men say that I am?" (Matt. 16:13; Mark 8:27). Agrippa II still further embellished it, and changed the name to Neronias, to compliment the emperor Nero; but on the emperor's death the name speedily lapsed (Jos. *Antiq.* xx. 9, 4). After the destruction of Jerusalem, Titus exhibited gladiatorial shows in this town also, one part of the spectacle being Jewish captives thrown to the wild beasts, or compelled to encounter each other in deadly warfare (Jos. *War* vii. 2, 1; 3, 1). The town has dwindled to a small village called Bāniās, an alteration of its early name Paneas.

Cage. A box or basket, Heb. $k^e l \bar{u} b$, in which birds were kept, especially for purposes of decoy (Jer. 5:27; Ecclus. 11:30). Sennacherib boasts of having shut up Hezekiah in Jerusalem like a bird in a cage.

Ca′ia·phas (kā′yà-făs) [Gr. from Aram.; probably, physiognomist]. Joseph Caiaphas, who was appointed to the high priesthood c. A.D. 18 by Valerius Gratus, the Roman procurator and immediate predecessor of Pontius Pilate (Jos. *Antiq.* xviii. 2, 2). Caiaphas and his father-in-law Annas (John 18:13) were high priests when John the Baptist began his ministry (Luke 3:2). Caiaphas proposed the death of Jesus, and, speaking of its import more significantly than he was aware, said, "It is expedient for you that one man should die for the people, and that the whole nation perish not" (John 11:49–53; 18:14). At his palace the council of chief priests, scribes, and elders was held to devise measures for the arrest of our Lord (Matt. 26:3–5). When Jesus was apprehended, he was taken first to the palace of Annas, who sent him bound to Caiaphas (John 18:24), whence he was led to the *praetorium* of Pilate (v. 28). Deeply responsible for the judicial murder of the innocent prisoner, Caiaphas afterward took part in the trial of Peter and John (Acts 4:6). In A.D. 36 he was deposed by Vitellius, the Roman president of Syria (Jos. *Antiq.* xviii. 4, 2).

Cain (kān) [smith, spear]. 1. The elder brother of Abel, a farmer by occupation. He brought of the fruits of the ground an offering to God, an implied acknowledgment of gratitude to God for the produce of the earth. But the heart of Cain was not right, and his offering was rejected. Then his character was revealed. He showed envy and anger, refused the exhortation to strive against sin, committed murder, denied his guilt; and when judgment was pronounced, gave no evidence of repentance for his sin, but only of fear of the punishment. Sent into exile, he lived in the land of Nod, eastward of Eden. He had a wife, one of the unnamed daughters or granddaughters of Adam. In early ages no impropriety existed or was felt in such a marriage (cf. Gen. 11:27, 29; 20:12). In his exile Cain built a fortified hamlet, and became the progenitor of a race which made considerable progress in the mechanical arts (Gen. 4:1–25).

2. The progenitor of the Kenites. See KAIN 2.

3. A village in the mountains of Judah (Josh. 15:57, A.V.), Khirbet Yaḳîn, 3 miles s.e. of Hebron.

Ca·i′nan (kà-ī′năn). See KENAN.

Ca′lah (kā′là). A city of Assyria, built by Nimrod or by people from his country (Gen. 10:11, 12). According to Ashurnaṣirpal (885–860 B.C.) it was built or rebuilt, embellished, and fortified by Shalmaneser I (1280–1260 B.C.). Early in the 9th century B.C. it had fallen into decay, but was restored by Ashurnaṣirpal, who erected a palace and made the city the place of royal residence. Calah remained the favorite dwelling place of the Assyrian kings for more than 150 years. Its ruins, now called Nimrûd, lie about 20 miles s. of Nineveh.

Cal′a·mus [Gr. *kalamos*, a reed]. The rendering of Heb. $k^e neh$ *bōsem*, reed of fragrance, and *ḳaneh*, cane, reed, when an odorous variety is intended. The plant was sweet-smelling (S. of Sol. 4:14), a constituent of the anointing oil (Ex. 30:23), and used in connection with sacrifice (Isa. 43:24 and Jer. 6:20, R.V. marg.). It was brought from a far country (Jer. 6:20). The Tyrians obtained it apparently from Javan, the regions of w. Asia Minor, and Greece (Ezek. 27:19). What came from Europe was probably the *Acorus calamus,* or common sweet sedge. The rhizome, or underground stem, is aromatic. If an Indian plant is permissible, then the calamus was probably the *Andropogon calamus aromaticus,* a genuine grass, which, like its near ally, the lemon grass, *A. schoenanthus,* is highly scented.

Cal'col (kăl'kŏl), in A.V. once **Chal'col** [cf. Arab. *kulkul,* short and nimble]. One of 3 sons of Mahol, each of whom was celebrated for wisdom (I Kings 4:31; I Chron. 2:6).

Cal'dron. See POT.

Ca'leb (kā'lĕb) [dog]. 1. Son of Hezron, and brother of Jerahmeel (I Chron. 2:18, 42). A variant form of the name is Chelubai (I Chron. 2:9). In tribal registration, his posterity constituted a subdivision of the house of Hezron, family of Perez, tribe of Judah (I Sam. 25:3; I Chron. 2:3 *seq.,* R.V.). Among his more immediate descendants were Hur, Aaron's associate, and Hur's grandson, the skilled artificer Bezalel (I Chron. 2:19, 20, R.V.).

2. Son of Jephunneh the Kenizzite and an elder brother of Othniel (Num. 32:12, R.V.; Josh. 15:17; I Chron. 4:15, cf. v. 13). He was the head of a father's house of the tribe of Judah; was one of the 12 men sent to spy out the land of Canaan; was one of the 2 members of this commission who kept their faith in Jehovah, and 40 years later took part in the conquest of Canaan; was, in fact, the first to speak for this minority of 2 (Num., chs. 13; 14; Josh. 14:6–14). He was on the commission appointed by Moses before the conquest to distribute the land, and he represented, as before, the tribe of Judah (Num. 34:19). He was 85 years old when the conquest was completed (Josh. 14:7, 10). He received as his portion the town of Hebron (Josh. 14:14), from which he expelled the Anakim by whom it had been previously occupied (ch. 15:13, 14); see HEBRON 2. He had also to do with the taking of the adjacent town of Kiriath-sepher, or Debir (Josh. 15:15–19). The s. of Caleb mentioned in I Sam. 30:14 was probably the s. of the Hebron district or the vicinity of Debir.

In I Chron. 2:49 (cf. vs. 19, 42, 46) Achsah, the well-known daughter of Caleb the spy, is registered as daughter or descendant of Caleb the brother of Jerahmeel. To judge from this register, Caleb the son of Jephunneh and father of Achsah was descended from the elder Caleb, and perhaps his concubine Maacah, and hence through Hezron and Perez from Judah. There are many details to be accounted for, and the ordinary difficulty of interpreting an ancient Hebrew genealogy is in this case greatly increased by the imperfect state of the text in I Chron., chs. 2; 4. The general explanation probably is that a member of the tribe of Kenizzites became identified with the Israelites by taking service with Judah before the Israelites went into Egypt, and he or his descendant married a woman descended from Judah through Perez. Various modifications of this general theory are possible. All genealogical and historical references and the peculiarities of the register are satisfied by the assumption that shortly before the Exodus Jephunneh the Kenizzite married a woman of the household of Caleb the brother of Jerahmeel and by her had a first-born son to whom was given the family name Caleb. This youth inherited the prerogatives of the family, and in time became head of the house and a chief of Judah. Jephunneh the Kenizzite took a 2d wife, by whom he had Othniel and Seraiah. Hence they are called sons of Kenez or Kenizzites, and are enrolled loosely with the tribe of

Judah, and reckoned like Jephunneh as Kenizzites.

Ca'leb-eph'ra·thah (kā'lĕb-ĕf'rȧ-thȧ), in A.V. **Ca'leb-eph'ra·tah** (kā'lĕb-ĕf'rȧ-tȧ). Named in I Chron. 2:24 as the place where Hezron died, but the accuracy of the Masoretic text has been doubted in this passage. The Vulgate, which except for the proper names follows the LXX, reads: "Now when Hezron was dead, Caleb went in unto Ephrath. Hezron also had Abijah to wife, who bore him Ashhur, the father of Tekoa." On the basis of the LXX some commentators have emended the Hebrew text to read: "And after Hezron was dead, Caleb went in to Ephrath [v. 19] his father Hezron's wife, and she bare him," etc. The taking of a father's wife signified a claim to the father's possessions (cf. II Sam. 16:22; I Kings 2:13–25), and thus, according to this interpretation, was expressed the legitimacy of Caleb's residence in n. Judah (cf. I Chron. 2:18–24 with vs. 42–55).

Cal'en·dar. See YEAR.

Calf. A young bull or cow, *Bos taurus.* Calves were killed for food and for sacrifice. Aaron made a golden image of a male calf that the people might worship Jehovah under this form (Ex. 32:4; cf. Neh. 9:18). The young bull symbolized vigor, strength, and

Image of Apis, the Sacred Bull of Egypt

endurance (cf. Num. 23:22); and the choice of this animal rather than another to represent God was favored also by the pomp of the bull worship in Egypt. On the division of the kingdom, Jeroboam instituted the calf worship anew, setting up 2 calves, one at Beth-el and one at Dan (I Kings 12:29). He probably had seen the bull Apis worshiped in Egypt while he was a refugee at the court of Shishak (I Kings 11:40), but he was influenced more by the desire to adhere to ancient traditions, for in recommending the calves he quoted the words of Ex. 32:4. Among the Canaanites, Aramaeans, and Hittites we find gods nearly always represented as standing on the back of an animal or as seated on a throne borne by animals. It is better, therefore, to suppose that Jeroboam represented Jehovah as an invisible figure standing on a young bull of gold.

Cal'neh (kăl'ně). 1. A city of Babylonia, belonging to the kingdom of Nimrod (Gen. 10:10), not identified. Kulunu, the early name of an important city near Babylon, may be meant. Nippur has also been suggested. It may be that Calneh stands for -*kalama* in Hursagkalama, a twin city of Kish.

2. Calneh, linked with Hamath and Gath (Amos 6:2), is probably Kullani, modern Kullanhu, 6 miles from Arpad.

Cal'no (kăl'nō). A city which the Assyrians cited as an example of the futility of offering resistance to Assyria (Isa. 10:9), probably same as Calneh 2.

Cal'va·ry (kăl'vȧ-rĭ) [Lat. *calvaria*, skull]. A place close to Jerusalem, but outside the city walls, where Christ was crucified, and in the vicinity of which he was buried (John 19:17, 20, 41; Heb. 13:11–13). It appears to have been a conspicuous spot (Mark 15:40; Luke 23:49), and was perhaps near a highway (Matt. 27:39). The name is derived from Lat. *calvaria*, (Luke 23:33), translating Gr. *kranion*, skull, which is the rendering of Golgotha (Aram. *Gulgulthā*; Heb. *Gulgōleth*, skull). (Matt. 27:33; Mark 15:22; John 19:17, 41.) Jerome supposed that the name arose from uncovered or unburied skulls; others have thought rather of a place of execution. The common explanation is that the name was due to the cranial shape of the rock or hillock, although the expression "Mount Calvary" is modern.

The question of the site of the crucifixion is involved with that of the location of the sepulcher. Two sites contend for acceptance: 1. The Church of the Holy Sepulcher, within the walls of the modern city. 2. The Green Hill, or Gordon's Calvary, in which is Jeremiah's Grotto, about 250 yards n.e. of the Damascus Gate. The Church of the Holy Sepulcher has ancient tradition in its favor. Eusebius, born in Caesarea about A.D. 264, is the earliest historian who gives any information on the subject. He states that impious men had covered the sepulcher with earth and built a temple to the goddess Venus over it, and that the place had long been given over to forgetfulness and oblivion. Constantine erected a church where the temple of Venus stood, and the site of Constantine's building is occupied by the present Church of the Holy Sepulcher. While this site has the support of tradition, we cannot tell definitely whether the 2d wall ran n. or s. of the spot on which this church stands. Josephus (Jos. *War* v. 4, 2) has been interpreted as implying that the n. wall ran to the s. of this site. The whole region lies under the modern city where excavation has been impossible.

The theory that the hill above Jeremiah's Grotto marks the site of Calvary was suggested by Otto Thenius in 1849 and has been adopted or independently reached by other scholars, and greatly elaborated. According to modern Jewish tradition, criminals were here stoned to death. The hill in which is Jeremiah's Grotto admittedly rises beyond the course of the 2d wall. The rounded summit of the hill, and the 2 hollow cave entrances beneath, present a striking resemblance to a skull. Its commanding position renders it visible from a distance. Near it was the great highway to the n. In the neighborhood are gardens and rock-hewn tombs. But no ancient tradition connects the crucifixion with this place, and the arguments are not conclusive.

Cam'el [Lat. *camelus*, from Gr. *kamēlos*, from Heb. and Phoenician *gāmāl*]. The one-humped camel, the dromedary, has two well-marked varieties: the camel properly so called, which is a slow-going draft animal (II Kings 8:9), and the dromedary in the restricted sense, which is swift of foot (cf. Isa. 66:20, R.V.) and can cover 8 to 10 miles an hour and keep going for 18 hours out of the 24. The Bactrian or two-humped camel comes from the plateau of central Asia. The camel has been called the ship of the desert, and its whole organization fits it to cross sandy wastes. It is a ruminating animal, but does not have a cloven hoof; the foot is enveloped in a hardened skin, enclosing the cushionlike soles, which are adapted to walking over the sand without sinking deeply. Another adaptation is that in the walls of the paunch or 1st stomach there are 2 collections of water cells on which the animal can draw when no other water is procurable. Yet another adaptation is its ability to subsist on the poorest food. Even the hump is another adaptation. It is a storehouse of food, and becomes larger or smaller according as the animal is in good or in bad condition. The camel is stupid, ill-tempered, and sometimes vindictive; but its passive obedience and power of endurance render it very valuable. It is not now anywhere found wild, nor has it been known wild in historical times. Abraham and Jacob had camels (Gen. 12:16; 30:43), and so had later nomads in the s. of

Camel

Palestine (I Sam. 27:9; II Chron. 14:15). The Ishmaelites who bought Joseph also had camels (Gen. 37:25). The camel was not, however, so much at home in Palestine, which is a hilly country, as in the Arabian and the African deserts (Ex. 9:3; Judg. 6:5; I Kings 10:2; I Chron. 5:18–21). But it is still bred abundantly on the plains of Moab and in the s. of Judea. The milk was used (cf. Gen. 32:15), but the animal was ceremonially unclean (Lev. 11:4). From its hair a coarse cloth was woven, which was sometimes made into clothing (Matt. 3:4) and used for tents. The burden was borne on the hump (Isa. 30:6). When the camel is ridden, a saddle is commonly used, and sometimes a palanquin (cf. Gen. 31:34). The Arabs commonly deck their camels' necks with ornaments (cf. Judg. 8:21, 26).

Ca'mon (kā'mŏn). See KAMON.

Camp. The station of an army or other body of people, where temporary structures are erected for their accommodation (Ex. 14:19; I Sam. 4:5; 17:4; II Kings 7:7). Strict regulations were prescribed for the army of Israel in order to secure cleanliness in their camp (Deut. 23:9–14). The arrangement of the camp of the migrating Hebrew nation, which was adopted for the journey through the wilderness, is described in Num. 1:47 to 2:34; 3:14–39; cf. ch. 10:11–28, and see SHITTIM 1. It was, of course, absolutely regular only when the people were encamped on a broad, level plain. For the encampments of Israel during the journey through the wilderness, see WILDERNESS OF THE WANDERING.

Cam'phire [variant of English camphor; Fr. *camphre*, from Medieval Lat. *camphora*, from Arab. *kāfūr*, from Malay *kāpūr*]. The rendering of Heb. *kōpher* in S. of Sol. 1:14; 4:13, A.V. See HENNA.

Ca'na (kā'nȧ) [Gr. *Kana*, probably for Heb. *Ḳānāh*, place of reeds; cf. Heb. *ḳāneh*, reed]. A village, more fully named Cana of

Galilee, where Jesus wrought his first miracle, making water wine (John 2:1–11), and healed the nobleman's son at Capernaum (ch. 4:46). Nathanael was of Cana (John 21:2). Possibly the words, "Of Galilee," are added to this Cana to distinguish it from another in Coelesyria (Jos. *Antiq.* xv. 5, 1). Josephus also mentions Cana of Galilee (Jos. *Life* 16, 71). The traditional site is Kefr Kenna, a village about 3¾ miles n.e. of Nazareth, on the road to Tiberias. It is more probably to be identified with Khirbet Ḳānā or Ḳānā el-Jelīl, about 8 miles n. of Nazareth.

Ca'naan (kā'năn), in A.V. of N.T. twice **Cha'naan** [Heb., probably from Hurrian, belonging to (the land of) Purple]. 1. Son of Ham and grandson of Noah; or better, the descendants of Ham who occupied Canaan and took their name from that country (Gen. 9:18, 22; 10:6). This expresses the domination of Egypt over the land, as was the case especially during Dyns. XVIII and XIX; the Egyptians, however, had penetrated the land long before that time.

which is found a fully developed ceramic art of definitely Chalcolithic type. The Neolithic period is dated approximately in the 6th and 5th millenniums B.C.; the Sub-Chalcolithic probably falls in the late 5th millennium, while the Lower Chalcolithic begins about the 1st quarter of the 4th millennium, and the Upper Chalcolithic about the 3d quarter of that millennium. The Early Bronze period begins about the 32d century B.C. and continues to the 22d. Middle Bronze extends from this period to the 16th century. The Late Bronze periods continue from this point to the 13th century B.C. and are followed by the Iron Age. See BRONZE.

The political situation in Syria and Palestine during the 3d millennium B.C. is still very obscure. There were contacts with Babylonia in the days of Lugal-zaggisi and Sargon; Gudea secured building material from Syria. See BABYLONIA. During the 3d Dyn. of Egypt, Zoser and Snefru procured cedars from Lebanon. In the 12th Dyn., Sinuhe fled from Egypt to Palestine and gave an excel-

Camp of Dan
including
Dan, Asher, Naphtali.

Merarites

Camp of Ephraim including Ephraim, Manasseh, Benjamin.

Gersbonites

ARK

Altar of Burnt Offering

Moses Aaron Aaron's Sons

Camp of Judah including Judah, Issachar, Zebulon.

Kohathites

Camp of Reuben
including
Reuben, Simeon, Gad.

Arrangement of the Camp of the Israelites in the Wilderness Journey

2. Canaan, the old and native name of Palestine, is of doubtful origin. In the Amarna correspondence of the 14th century B.C., "Land of Canaan" is applied to the Phoenician coast; the Egyptians called all W. Syria by this name. According to Josh. 11:3, Canaanites dwelt both in the e. and w. part of the land; according to Judg. 1:9, 10, they were everywhere, in the hill country, the Negeb, the Shephelah, and Hebron. The language of Canaan (Isa. 19:18) refers to the group of W. Semitic languages of which Hebrew, Phoenician, and Moabite were dialects.

The land of Canaan formed the geographical center of the great Egypto-Mesopotamian civilization, within whose domain there was always an active movement of cultural elements which tended to create an almost imperceptible synthesis. Remains of the Paleolithic Age are found in Canaan, and we can trace the principal steps in the evolution of human culture from degenerate Mesolithic through an Early Neolithic stage without pottery to a Late Neolithic phase in which the first crude pottery was made. During the Neolithic period men dwelt in caves, which in the Bronze Age became tombs or were converted into storehouses or cisterns. After the Neolithic Age comes a period in

lent account of the country. He found a home with Ammi-enshi, an Amorite, and met other Egyptians, who were either exiles or traders. He maintains that he urged submission to Sesostris I. Both Sesostris II (1906–1887) and III (1887–1849) invaded Syria.

The most important historical problem connected with the Middle Bronze period is that of the Hyksos, who seem to have been Canaanites. Although they were Semites, some of them may have been Hittites, Luvians, and Hurrians. The Hyksos names, for the most part, are Semitic. The Hyksos were loosely organized in a kind of feudal state with an aristocracy of equestrian knights. After their expulsion from Egypt, Syria and Canaan were included in the Empire of Egypt, which was founded by Thutmose III (alone, 1482–1450). Amenhotep III (1412–1375) had a long and peaceful reign, but the Egyptian power in Canaan began to wane. Under Amenhotep IV (Akhnaton, 1387–1366), long a coregent with his father, the decay set in when the Hittites came in from the n. and the Habiru invaded the whole e. border of Syria. See HEBREW.

The Hebrews conquered Canaan under the leadership of Joshua after the death of Moses.

The date of the Israelite conquest still remains obscure and from the present available data cannot be fixed precisely. According to the view of some archaeologists, the main wave of destruction fell in the 13th century; thus Canaanite Lachish fell about 1230 B.C. Garstang dates the fall of Jericho c. 1400, while others favor between c. 1360 and c. 1320. The plan of the campaign included the establishment of a fixed camp at Gilgal. The site was on the e. of Jericho, in the plain (Josh. 4:19; 5:10). From it the Israelites *went up* to Ai and Gibeon (Josh. 7:3; 8:1, 3; 10:9). The advantages of this location for the camp of Israel were great. At Gilgal, Joshua had no enemies in his rear, had water in abundance for the people, could draw supplies from the 2½ tribes which had settled in the country e. of the Jordan, and had a safe place for hoarding spoil. The characteristic objects in this camp were the tabernacle (Josh. 6:24; cf. 9:23; 18:1; 22:19); the Ark (chs. 3:17; 6:11, etc.; 7:6); the altar (ch. 9:27; cf. ch. 22:19, 28, 29); Eleazar the priest (ch. 14:1), besides other priests (chs. 6:6, 12, etc.; 8:33); 12 stones which had been taken out of the bed of the Jordan and set up as a memorial of the passage of the river (ch. 4:20). Joshua's plan further included a preliminary campaign for the overthrow of the enemies which threatened the camp. He took Jericho, the outpost of Canaan, and then he marched into the mountain, directly to the w., and overthrew Ai. This town lay at the head of the valley which emerged opposite Gilgal, and from it troops might be poured down against the camp. After this preliminary campaign he fulfilled the injunction of Moses to erect an altar on Ebal (Josh. 8:30–35; Deut., ch. 27). According to Josephus, this solemnity was performed after the conquest of the entire country (Jos. *Antiq.* v. 1, 19). At this juncture ambassadors from the town of Gibeon appeared, with whom Joshua made a treaty without asking counsel of the Lord. It was an unfortunate step, as will be shown presently. Having obtained secure foothold in the country, Joshua proceeded to conquer Canaan in 2 campaigns. The alliance of the 5 kings determined the s. expedition (Josh., ch. 10). The king of Jerusalem summoned the kings of Hebron, Lachish, Eglon, and Jarmuth to war against Gibeon; and Joshua was obliged to help those with whom he was in treaty. The 5 kings were routed, and fled down the pass of Beth-horon. Following up the victory, Joshua captured Makkedah, in or near the maritime plain, and pitched a temporary camp there; took Libnah, which was likewise in the plain; Lachish, where the king of Gezer also was defeated; Eglon, where another temporary camp was fixed; and Hebron. From Hebron he turned and smote Debir, in the hill country. Thus the entire region included between Gibeon, Gaza, and Kadesh-barnea was smitten, and Joshua returned to Gilgal.

It was during this campaign that Joshua bade the sun stand still (Josh. 10:12–15). This event is cited from the Book of Jashar, a book of poems or songs. See SUN.

Having conquered the central region and the s., Joshua determined as a matter of expediency, or under compulsion of the n. confederacy, to neglect the inconsiderable towns on the coast n. of the Philistine country, and to strike at the populous and powerful n. (Josh., ch. 11). With this end in view, he undertook a n. campaign. The king of Hazor was head of a confederacy of petty monarchs, and on hearing of the Israelitish victories in the s. he summoned the remaining kings of the country to a united attempt to crush Joshua. The allied armies met at the waters of Merom. Joshua had reached the same neighborhood, and he attacked them. He routed them, pursued the fugitives as far as Sidon toward the n.w. and e. to Mizpeh. He then returned, captured and burned the town of Hazor, and took the capitals of the other petty kingdoms which had been in alliance. In Josh. 11:16 to 12:24 a summary of the conquest is given.

The power of the Canaanites was broken by these campaigns, but the inhabitants were not wholly exterminated. Many of the natives remained. Important towns were left in the possession of the Canaanitish population (Josh. 11:13; 15:63; 16:10, etc.); and even where the destruction was most complete, not a few of the people had escaped by flight or hiding and, when the army of Israel withdrew (ch. 10:43), they returned, rebuilt ruined towns, and placed the wasted fields once more under cultivation. Years afterward, when the tribes of Israel scattered over the country in order to settle, they met with sporadic resistance (Judg., ch. 2; see HEBRON 2, JOSHUA 1).

The time occupied in the conquest of Canaan was long, because not a city made peace with Israel save the 5 cities of the Gibeonites (Josh. 11:18, 19). It may be calculated with a considerable degree of accuracy. From the sending forth of the spies in the 2d year (Num. 13:17–20) to the time of assigning the reconquest of Hebron to Caleb when the land was about to be distributed was 45 years (Josh. 14:7, 10); from the sending forth of the spies to the crossing of the Zered was 38 years (Deut. 2:14); leaving for the conquest of the country, both e. and w. of the Jordan, about 6 or 7 years. From this is to be deducted the time consumed in the conquest of the e. country and by the events at Shittim. The death of Aaron (Num. 33:38) occurred in the 40th year, 5th month, 1st day, and the crossing of Jordan (Josh. 4:19) in the 1st month, 10th day; leaving for the conquest of the country of Sihon and Og, and for the events at Shittim, nearly 8 months, 9 days, of which period the events at Shittim occupied about 2 months (cf. Deut. 1:3, 4, with Josh. 4:19; Deut. 34:8; Josh. 2:22, etc.; Jos. *Antiq.* iv. 8, 49 and iv. 8, 1), leaving for the conquest of w. Palestine 5 or 6 years. Josephus assigns 5 years to this conquest (Jos. *Antiq.* v. 1, 19).

Three political blunders were committed by Joshua: making a treaty with the Gibeonites; allowing the Jebusites to hold Jerusalem (Josh. 15:63); and failing to dispossess the Philistines and control the country to the sea. A study of the map shows that, as a result of these mistakes, Judah and Simeon were isolated from the rest of the nation. The main road from Judah to the n. was commanded by the Jebusite stronghold at Jerusalem, and was skirted for 10 miles on the w. by the settlements of the Gibeonites. Between Jerusalem and Jericho on the e. was a tract of wild, rocky, uninhabited mountain land crossed e. and w. by impassable gorges. From Jerusalem to the Mediterranean Sea stretched a strip of country which was occupied by foreigners: first Gibeonites, next Canaanites in Dan, then Philistines as far as the sea. The consequences of this isolation of Judah and Simeon were serious, distinctly affecting the course of history in the years that followed.

Was the extermination of the Canaanites by the Israelites a justifiable act? The mere matter of their dispossessing the Canaanites presents no moral difficulties. This procedure accorded with the spirit of the age. The Israelites doubtless had as much right to Canaan as had the inhabitants whom they drove out. Nor does the manner of warfare present moral difficulties, for the conduct of the Hebrews in war compares favorably with the practices of the time. Judged by the standards of their own age, they were not bloodthirsty or cruel. The Assyrians have pictured their own wars. It was not infrequent for them to decapitate the inhabitants of captured cities, and pile the heads in heaps; to crucify or impale prisoners, pierce their eyeballs with a spear, or flay them alive. In the battles of Israel with the Canaanites there is record of death, but not of torture. The moral difficulty connected with the extermination of the Canaanites is that God commanded it. God's character is involved. But it is to be remembered that God had a twofold end in view in the utter extermination by death and expulsion which he commanded. It was punitive (Gen. 15:16; Lev. 18:25; Deut. 9:3, 4; 18:12) and preventive (Ex. 23:31–33; 34:12–16; Deut. 7:2–4). It was to punish the Canaanites for their outrageous wickedness, and to prevent them from contaminating the people of God. It is not asserted that the Canaanites were sinners above all men that ever lived. Their personal morals were perhaps not worse than those of other heathen as described in Rom., ch. 1. The Canaanites were idolaters, they indulged in shameful and abominable vice, they went beyond other nations in practicing human sacrifice. God holds nations as well as individuals responsible, and deals with them accordingly. He doomed the nations of Canaan to extermination as a punishment for their wickedness, and to prevent them from seducing the people of God. He had exterminated the wicked race of men in the days of Noah by the Flood; he had swept away the iniquitous cities of the Plain by an eruption, it would seem, of burning naphtha; he had overthrown Pharaoh and his host in the Red Sea; he had destroyed Korah and his rebellious crew by an earthquake and by fire. Now, instead of using the forces of nature to effect his punitory ends, he employed the Israelites as the ministers of his justice, as the public executioner, employed by the civil tribunal, is the minister of human justice. This truth was taught to the Israelites. They were informed that they were the instruments of divine justice. For these reasons the extermination of the Canaanites by the Israelites was just; the employment of the Israelites for the purpose was right; and in connection with the righteous judgment was an intention to benefit the world. The failure of the Israelites to carry out God's command fully was one of the great blunders which they committed, as well as a sin, and it resulted in lasting injury to the nation.

The distribution of the conquered territory on the w. of the Jordan was made partly at Gilgal and partly at Shiloh, whither the tabernacle was removed (Josh. 14:1, 2, 6; 18:1, 2). It was conducted by Eleazar the priest, Joshua, and 10 heads of fathers' houses (Josh. 17:4; cf. Num. 34:17, 18), and was made by lot (Josh. 18:6). The law to govern the distribution had already been enacted; namely, to the more numerous a larger inheritance, and wheresoever the lot fell to any man (Num. 26:52–56; 33:54). The rabbis state that 2 urns were used: in one were placed tickets with the names of the tribes, and in the other were tickets with the names of the districts. A tribe was drawn and the district which it should possess. The size of the territory was then determined by the populousness of the tribe. Probably, however, the commission selected a district without narrowly defining its boundaries, and merely determined by lot what tribe should possess it; for: 1. Compare the form of the question in Judg. 1:1. 2. This theory satisfies

Num. 33:54. 3. Compare Josh. 18:1–10, where the land is first described in 7 portions, and Joshua then cast lots for the tribes. 4. This theory also satisfies Josh. 19:1, etc., where it is stated that at the final allotment the 2d lot came out for Simeon, the 3d for Zebulun, etc. 5. The districts were assigned for occupation, not as though determined by lot, but in regular order, building up the nation compactly as the allotment proceeded, and not leaping hither and thither. 6. Much was evidently left to the discretion of the supervisors. Caleb must have Hebron whether the lot of the main body of the tribe of Judah allowed it to settle in that neighborhood or not. Jacob's last wishes would be observed so far as the lot permitted (Gen., ch. 49), though the lot did not permit Zebulun to possess the seacoast, but his possession was doubtless adjusted as nearly as possible to the patriarch's desire. Mistakes were made and rectified. Before the allotment was completed—and it was not carried out in a day or a week—Judah reported that it had been granted too much territory. The surplus was accordingly added to the undistributed domain. The children of Joseph, on the other hand, informed Joshua that they had received too little land, and they asked for and received more. It was intended, in accordance with Jacob's wish, that Ephraim and Manasseh should dwell side by side; hence the lot was not cast for them separately, but for them unitedly as the children of Joseph (Josh. 16:1, 4). In this manner the nation was compactly built up, the territory which lay nearest the camp being distributed first.

1. Southern hill country.	To Judah, 4th son of Leah.
2. Central hill country.	To Joseph, first-born of Rachel.
3. Intervening hill country.	To Benjamin, 2d son of Rachel.
4. Part of the surplus of the s. hill country which Judah gave back.	To Simeon, 2d son of Leah.
5, 6. Territory bounding central hill country on the n.	To Zebulun, 6th son of Leah. To Issachar, 5th son of Leah.
7. Adjoining seacoast.	To Asher, 2d son of Leah's maid.
8. Territory n. of Issachar and Zebulun.	To Naphtali, 2d son of Rachel's maid.
9. Remaining part of Judah's surplus.	To Dan, 1st son of Rachel's maid.

The tribes of Reuben, first-born of Leah, and Gad, son of Leah's maid, and the half tribe of Manasseh, descendant of Rachel, had obtained lands e. of the Jordan. These with the tribe of Levi, son of Leah, did not participate in the distribution.

Ca'naan·ite (kā'năn-īt). 1. An inhabitant of Canaan, of Semitic stock. On account of the long domination of the land of Canaan by Egypt, Canaan is called a son of Ham (cf. Gen. 10:6, 15–20). The Canaanites were doomed to destruction on account of their sins (Deut. 20:17). But the Israelites to a certain extent failed to carry out the injunction. They in many cases contented themselves with putting the Canaanite inhabitants to tribute (Judg. 1:27–36). Solomon levied on them a tribute of bond service; in other words, he made them perform forced labor (I Kings 9:20, 21). The Canaanites eventually devoted themselves extensively to trade, and their name became synonymous with trader (Isa. 23:8).

2. A member of a Jewish patriotic party. See CANANAEAN.

89

Ca'naan·it'ess (kā'năn-ĭt'ĕs). A woman of Canaan (I Chron. 2:3).

Ca'na·nae'an (kā'nà-nē'ăn), in A.V. **Ca'· naan·ite** [Lat. from Gr. *Kananaios*, prob. for *Kannaios*, from Aram. *ḳannā'āh, ḳan'ānā, ḳannay,* zealot, zealous; but it may be from Aram. *Ḳānānay,* one from Cana (of Galilee)]. A member of a Jewish patriotic party, also known by the synonymous Greek name Zealot (*q.v.*). Simon the apostle bore this epithet to distinguish him from Simon Peter (Matt. 10:4; cf. Mark 3:18; cf. Luke 6:15; Acts 1:13).

Can'da·ce (kăn'dà-sē). A queen of Ethiopia, probably of Meroë, in s. Nubia. A eunuch of great authority at her court, when returning home from a visit to Jerusalem, where he had gone to worship, was converted to Christianity through the instrumentality of Philip the evangelist (Acts 8:26–39). Strabo, Dion Cassius, and Pliny, all concur in stating that Meroë in the first century of the Christian era was governed by a succession of queens, each called Candace.

Can'dle. See LAMP.

Can'dle·stick'. A stand for a candle. That in the tabernacle was for lamps. It consisted of a base and a shaft with 6 branches, beaten out of solid gold, and it supported 7 lamps. It stood on the s. side of the sanctuary (Ex. 25:31–40; 40:24; Lev. 24:2–4). Pure olive oil was used in the lamps, and the light burned from evening to morning (Ex. 27:20, 21; 30:7, 8; I Sam. 3:3). According to Josephus, 3 of the lamps were allowed to burn by day (Jos. *Antiq.* iii. 8, 3). This continu-

The Seven-branched Candlestick of Herod's Temple
(Based on the Arch of Titus)

ous burning apparently symbolized the uninterrupted worship, even by night, the unceasing emission of light, by the people of God (cf. Zech., ch. 4). This candelabrum was perhaps deposited in the Temple (I Kings 8: 4). Solomon made 10 candlesticks, 5 for the right and 5 for the left of the oracle (I Kings 7:49; II Chron. 4:7). They were carried away to Babylon (Jer. 52:19). Zerubbabel had but one; this was carried off by Antiochus Epiphanes (I Macc. 1:20, 21). Replaced (I Macc. 4:49), it continued in use till the capture of Jerusalem by Titus, when it was

taken to Rome, figured in Titus' triumph, and was sculptured on his arch (Jos. *War* vii. 5, 5).

Cane [Lat., *canna*, from Gr. *kanna*, of Semitic origin; cf. Heb. *ḳăneh*, reed]. The rendering of Heb. *ḳăneh* in Isa. 43:24 and Jer. 6:20. In both places R.V. marg. renders it "calamus," and so it is elsewhere translated in both versions, where a specific odorous cane is intended.

Can'ker·worm'. The rendering of Hebrew *yeleḳ* in Joel and Nahum, and in R.V. of Jer. 51:27; also in E.R.V. Ps. 105:34. In the two latter passages A.V. has "caterpillers." It is very destructive to growing crops. As it is mentioned with the typical locust (Joel 1:4; Nahum 3:15), which it resembles also in the numbers in which it appears (Joel 2:25), it is probably a locust of some species or the locust in the larva or pupa stage of development.

Can'neh (kăn'ĕ). A place, evidently in Mesopotamia, perhaps the same as Calneh (Ezek. 27:23).

Can'on [Gr. *kanōn*, from Phoenician *ḳănā'* or Heb. *ḳăneh*, stalk, reed]. The meaning of the word was extended to denote: 1. any straight rod, such as a measuring rod or rule used in building; 2. figuratively, a norm or standard which serves to regulate or determine other things, especially classical books; a guide or model (II Cor. 10:13–16; Gal. 6:16); 3. a type of Christian doctrine, the orthodox as opposed to the heterodox; 4. the Scriptures viewed as a rule of faith and conduct. The word is Greek and was first used in this 4th sense by the early fathers, but the idea denoted was ancient. A book entitled to a place in the Bible is called canonical; one not so entitled, uncanonical; and title to a place, canonicity.

The Old Testament canon. Authoritative literature grew up by degrees and was carefully preserved. The Ten Commandments, written on tables of stone, Israel's constitution, were deposited in the Ark (Ex. 40:20). The statutes were recorded in the Book of the Covenant (Ex. 20:23 to 23:33; 24:7). The Book of the Law, written by Moses, was put by the side of the Ark (Deut. 31:24–26). Joshua made his addition to the collection (Josh. 24:26). Samuel wrote "the manner of the kingdom . . . in a book, and laid it up before Jehovah" (I Sam. 10:25). In the days of Josiah the Book of the Law of Jehovah was found in the Temple and recognized by king, priests, prophets, and people, as authoritative and ancient (II Kings 22:8–20). Copies of the Law were made (Deut. 17:18–20). Prophets committed their words to writing (e.g., Jer. 36:32), and they were acquainted with each other's writings and quoted them as authority (cf. Isa. 2:2–4 with Micah 4:1–3). The Law and the words of the prophets were recognized as authoritative, inspired by the Spirit of God, and jealously guarded by Jehovah (Zech. 1:4; 7:7, 12).

Eventually there were three parts of the O.T.: the *Tōrāh* (Law or Pentateuch); the *Nᵉbī'īm* (Prophets); and the *Kᵉthūbīm* (Writings, or Hagiographa). These divisions are fixed in the Hebrew canon, and no book may be transferred from one section to another. In the Hebrew canon the Pentateuch has the same order of books as in the English Bible. The Prophets are divided into the Former and the Latter. The Former, according to the Hebrew order, contain 4 books: Joshua, Judges, I and II Samuel, I and II Kings. The Latter consist of the Major (3 books: Isaiah, Jeremiah, Ezekiel) and the Twelve or the Minor, which follow directly after Ezekiel and have the same order as in the English Bible. The Major Prophets are so called because their books are larger than those of the Minor. In reckoning the number of books in the Hebrew Bible, the Twelve are counted as one book. The Prophets are followed by the Writings, the 11 books of which have the following order: Psalms, Proverbs, Job, Song of Solomon, Ruth, Lamentations, Ecclesiastes, Esther, Daniel, Ezra-Nehemiah, I and II Chronicles. This gives a total of 24 books in the Hebrew canon.

The canon of the O.T. in the English Bible contains the same books as the Hebrew Bible, but by counting each of the double books as 2 instead of one and the Twelve as actually 12 separate books, the number is raised to 39. Ruth (1:1) follows Judges, and Lamentations, which is ascribed to Jeremiah, is put after that prophet's book. It is especially noteworthy that Daniel is reckoned with the Prophets, and placed directly after Ezekiel. With the exclusion of the Apocryphal works, the order of books in the English Bible follows that of the Vulgate, which in turn was influenced by the LXX. The O.T. canon in the English Bible accordingly may be divided into 4 parts: the Pentateuch, historical books (Joshua to Esther); poetical books (Job to Song of Solomon, of which 3, Job, Proverbs, and Ecclesiastes, are wisdom literature); and the Prophets (Isaiah to Malachi). Daniel here occupies a place between the Major and the Minor Prophets.

The Law of Moses, comprising the five books of Moses, circulated as a distinct portion of the sacred literature in the time of Ezra. It was in Ezra's hand (Ezra 7:14), and he was a ready scribe in it (vs. 6, 11). At the request of the people, he read the book publicly to them (Neh. 8:1, 5, 8). About this time also, before the schism between the Jews and Samaritans had become final, the Pentateuch was taken to Samaria. The arrangement of the Minor Prophets into a group of 12 is attested by Jesus, son of Sirach, as in vogue c. 200 B.C. (Ecclus. 49:10). His language further suggests the great group of books—Joshua, Judges, Samuel, Kings, Isaiah, Jeremiah, Ezekiel, and the Twelve—which constitute the 2d division of the Hebrew canon. The existence of the threefold division of all the Scriptures into "the law, the prophets, and the others that have followed in their steps," or "the law, the prophets, and the other books," or, "the law, the prophecies, and the rest of the books," is attested as early as 132 B.C., by the grandson of Jesus, son of Sirach (Ecclus. Prologue). Reference is made in a passage which dates from c. 100 B.C. to "the sacred books which are now in our hands" (I Macc. 12:9). Philo Judaeus, who was born at Alexandria c. 20 B.C., and died there in the reign of Claudius, had the present canon, and quotes from nearly all the books while he cites nothing from the Apocrypha.

The N.T. refers to "the Scriptures" as a body of authoritative writings (Matt. 21:42; 26:56; Mark 14:49; John 10:35; II Tim. 3: 16), as holy (Rom. 1:2; II Tim. 3:15), and as the oracles of God (Rom. 3:2; Heb. 5:12; I Peter 4:11); mentions a threefold division into "the law of Moses, and the prophets, and the psalms" (Luke 24:44); and quotes from or refers to all the books except Obadiah and Nahum, Ezra and Nehemiah, Esther, Song of Solomon, and Ecclesiastes. Josephus, a contemporary of the Apostle Paul, writing about A.D. 100, and speaking for his nation, says in substance: "We have but twenty-two books, containing the history of all time, books that are justly believed in," or, according to the usual reading, "believed to be divine," and he speaks in the strongest terms of the exclusive authority of these

writings, continuing: "From the days of Artaxerxes to our own times every event has indeed been recorded; but these recent records have not been deemed worthy of equal credit with those which preceded them, on account of the failure of the exact succession of the prophets. There is practical proof of the spirit in which we treat our Scriptures; for although so great an interval of time has now passed, not a soul has ventured either to add or to remove or to alter a syllable, and it is the instinct of every Jew, from the day of his birth, to consider these Scriptures as the teaching of God, and to abide by them and, if need be, cheerfully to lay down his life in their behalf" (Jos. Apion i. 8). Josephus states the contents of Scripture under three heads: 1. "Five belong to Moses, which contain his laws and the traditions of the origin of mankind till his death." 2. "From the death of Moses to Artaxerxes, the prophets who were after Moses wrote down what was done in their time in thirteen books." Josephus probably followed the arrangement of LXX and the enumeration of the Alexandrians. The 13 books are probably Joshua, Judges with Ruth, Samuel, Kings, Chronicles, Ezra with Nehemiah, Esther, Job, Daniel, Isaiah, Jeremiah with Lamentations, Ezekiel, the Twelve, or the Minor, Prophets. 3. "The remaining four books contain hymns to God and precepts for the conduct of human life." These were doubtless Psalms, Song of Solomon, Proverbs, Ecclesiastes.

So far facts. There was also a tradition current that the canon was arranged in the time of Ezra and Nehemiah. Josephus, as already cited, expresses the universal or traditional belief of his countrymen that no books had been added since the time of Artaxerxes—that is, since the time of Ezra and Nehemiah. An extravagant legend of the latter part of the 1st century of the Christian Era (II Esdras, ch. 14) grew out of the current tradition that Ezra restored the Law and even the entire O.T. (vs. 21, 22, 40), of which the Temple copies had been lost. It attests that the Jews of Palestine in that age reckoned the canonical books at 24 (24+70=94; vs. 44–46, R.V. The 70 were not published). A passage of doubtful date and authenticity, perhaps penned about 100 B.C. (II Macc. 2: 13), alludes to Nehemiah's activity in connection with the 2d and 3d divisions of the canon. Irenaeus transmits the tradition thus: "After the sacred writings had been destroyed in the Exile under Nebuchadnezzar, when the Jews after seventy years had returned to their own country, he [i.e., God] in the days of Artaxerxes inspired Ezra the priest, of the tribe of Levi, to rearrange all the words of the prophets who had gone before, and to restore to the people the legislation of Moses." Elias Levita, writing in 1538, states the belief of his people in this wise: "In Ezra's time the twenty-four books were not yet united in a single volume. Ezra and his associates united them together and divided them into three parts, the Law, the Prophets, and the Hagiographa." This tradition contains truth. Whether it can be accepted in toto depends on the settlement of the date when certain books were written, such as Nehemiah and Chronicles; a number of critical problems in other books must also be considered.

The Pentateuch as the work of Moses, and as embodying the fundamental law of the nation, formed one division of the canon, and with chronological fitness occupied the first place in the collection. To the 2d division were assigned the Prophets, as noted above. For Joshua, regarded as a prophet, see Ecclus. 46:1. It is erroneous to suppose that all the writings included in the 3d division were composed after the 2d, or prophetic, collection had been closed. The books of this section form a group distinct in subject matter from those of the Law and the Prophets; its nucleus consists of the books of wisdom and poetry. These works attracted to themselves other authoritative literature, especially books late in composition or different in content from the Law and the Prophets. Although the distinction between lawgiver, priest, prophet, and wise man is ancient and the tripartite division of Scripture is logical and early, it must be admitted that the 3d division may have been longest in closing.

Lamentations, though ascribed to a prophet, yet being poetry, found its place in the 3d division of the Hebrew canon. An additional reason existed for separating it from Jeremiah. It was read on the anniversary of the destruction of both Temples, and hence was put with 4 other short books which were read on 4 other anniversaries, Song of Solomon, Ruth, Ecclesiastes, and Esther. They constitute the 5 rolls or Megilloth. Daniel was placed here because written by a man who, although gifted with prophecy, was not by office a prophet. In all probability Chronicles was written, not by a prophet, but by a priest; hence it belonged in the 3d division of the canon. The mere fact of its late authorship does not account for its place in this division, for books and sections of books in this division were in existence before Zechariah and Malachi, which were put in the 2d division. It is proper to add that while the contents of the several divisions of the canon were fixed, the order of the books in the 3d section varied from time to time; and even in the 2d part the Talmud knew Isaiah as standing between Ezekiel and the Minor Prophets.

It may be concluded that the Law was canonized c. 444 B.C.; the Prophets, c. 200 B.C.; and the Writings, c. 100 B.C. The canon, however, was determined by long and approved usage of books and not by the formal action of an assembly. As late as the close of the 1st century A.D., and even later, the right of several books (such as Ezekiel, Proverbs, Song of Solomon, Ecclesiastes, Esther) to remain in the canon was discussed. The books were in the canon—none questioned that. The discussions concerned the contents of the books and difficulties in reconciling them with other books; but the debates were probably merely academic. By the time of the Council of Jamnia (A.D. 90) the canon without doubt was in its present form and approved by the rabbis.   J. D. D. (rev. and rewritten, H. S. G.)

Canon of the New Testament. The Apostolic Church received from the Jewish the belief in a written rule of faith. Christ himself confirmed this belief by appealing to the O.T. as the written word of God (e.g., John 5:37–47; Matt. 5:17, 18; Mark 12:36, 37), and by instructing his disciples out of it (Luke 24:45); and the apostles habitually refer to the O.T. as authoritative (e.g., Rom. 3:2, 21; 15:4; I Cor. 4:6; II Tim. 3:15–17; II Peter 1:21). In the next place, the apostles claimed for their own teaching, oral and written, like authority with the O.T. (I Cor. 2:7–13; 14:37; I Thess. 2:13; Rev. 1:3), and directed the public reading of their epistles (I Thess. 5:27; Col. 4:16; II Thess. 2:15; II Peter 1:15; 3:1, 2), while revelations, given to the Church through inspired prophets (Acts 11:27, 28; 15:32; cf. I Cor., ch. 14), were considered to form, with apostolic instruction, the foundation of the Church (Eph. 2:20). It was therefore both natural and right that the N.T. literature should be added to the O.T., and thus the written canon of faith be enlarged. In the N.T. itself we may perhaps see the beginning of this process (I Tim. 5:

18; II Peter 3:1, 2, 16), and in the generations which followed the Apostles, the writings which were known to have apostolic authority were gradually collected into the second half of the Church's canon, and finally called the New Testament.

In discussing the history of the N.T., it is important, however, to observe the distinction between authorship and circulation of writings and their ultimate reception into the canon. At first the Christians regarded the O.T. as an authoritative book, while the words of Jesus were the teaching of an authoritative person. It is not known precisely when the teachings of our Lord were collected into book form, but probably no step had been taken before the end of the 1st century to transfer the authority of our Lord and his teaching to documents describing him and his work. Such an assignment of authority to writings, or canonization, began to be made in the subapostolic period, but proceeded very slowly. The evidence for the existence of several books and the authority attached to them near the end of the 1st century and the first half of the 2d is found in the Epistle of Clement of Rome to the Corinthians, the Epistles of Ignatius and Polycarp, the Didache (Teaching of the Apostles), the Epistle of Barnabas, the Shepherd of Hermas, Papias, Justin Martyr, and Tatian's *Diatessaron* (Harmony of the Four Gospels). The four Gospels were everywhere received from the beginning of the 2d century, while II Peter 3:16 shows that its readers were already familiar with a collection of Paul's Epistles. The heretic Marcion (c. 140) undertook to restore what he thought was the simplicity of Christianity on the basis of Paul, whom he regarded as the only true apostle. He rejected the O.T., and of the N.T. he retained only Luke in mutilated form and the 10 Epistles of Paul, omitting the Pastoral Epistles. The idea of a new canon is found from 180 to 200 in the works of 3 great representatives: Irenaeus, of Asia Minor and Gaul; Tertullian, of N. Africa; and Clement of Alexandria, in Egypt. The Church at that time was fully conscious that it had documents of the Apostolic Age, and regarded the teaching of the apostles as the rule of faith. The Muratorian fragment gives us the canon of the Church of Rome about 200. At this time seven books still lacked general recognition: Hebrews, James, II Peter, II and III John, Jude, and Revelation. Other books, as the Epistle of Barnabas, the Shepherd of Hermas, and the Didache, were on the fringe of the canon.

The second period of the canon may be reckoned from c. 200 to 325, during which the work of Origen and Eusebius is of special importance. There was a sifting of books on the fringe, and Origen classified the literature which laid claim to apostolic authority into genuine, rejected, and doubtful. He considered James, II Peter, II and III John, and Jude doubtful, but accepted Revelation. Eusebius followed closely in Origen's footsteps.

The third period begins in 325 and is marked by authoritative pronouncements, first by bishops of provincial Churches and later by councils or synods. In 367 Athanasius put forth a list of 27 N.T. books, which corresponds to the present canon. At the synods of Hippo Regius (393) and Carthage (397, 419), our N.T. of 27 books was accepted. Augustine supported this canon, which through the Vulgate eventually came into vogue throughout the West. The canon of the Eastern Church was ultimately the same as that of the Western. The Syrian Church, however, accepted only 22 books; II Peter, II and III John, Jude, and Revelation were lacking. With the separation of the Nestorians at the Council of Ephesus (431), the Eastern Syriac Church lost contact with the rest of the Church, and so in some Nestorian circles the 5 remaining books probably were never adopted. In W. Syria acceptance of these books was slow, although they were included in Bibles of the 6th and 7th centuries.

In view of these facts it should be noted: 1. That while the collection of the N.T. into one volume was slow, the belief in a written rule of faith was primitive and apostolic. The history of the formation of the collection should not be thought to give the rise into authority of a written rule of faith. It only shows the stages by which the books rightly belonging to the canon were recognized and brought together. 2. Differences of opinion and usage, as to what books were canonical, and as to the degree of certainty with which a book could be received, appear in the writers and Churches even of the 2d century. This fact, however, again only marks the stages by which the evidence for the books was gradually accepted by the Church as a whole, and the carefulness of the primitive Christians in receiving books as apostolic. In like manner the occasional acceptance of spurious writings was corrected in due time. 3. The proof on which *we* should accept the several N.T. books as canonical is *historical evidence*. As to this, the judgment of the Early Church that our 27 books are apostolic is entitled to acceptance unless it can be proved false. We should not, however, receive them merely because ecclesiastical councils decreed them canonical; nor, on the other hand, because of their contents. The question is one of historical evidence alone. 4. Finally, we note that the name "canon" is not known to have been applied to the collection of sacred books until the 4th century, when it was employed by Amphilochius (c. 380). But while this term, now universal, was not at first used, the thing denoted by it—viz., that the sacred books were the rule of faith—was, as we have seen, an apostolic doctrine.

G. T. P. (rev. and rewritten, H. S. G.)

Can'ti·cles. See SONG OF SOLOMON.

Ca·per'na·um (ká-pûr'ná-ŭm) [Gr. from Heb. *kefar Naḥûm*, village of Nahum]. A town on the n.w. shore of the Sea of Galilee, in the region of Zebulun and Naphtali (Matt. 4:13-16; cf. Luke 4:31; John 6:17-24). It was the seat of a tax collector (Mark 2:1, 14), and was apparently a Roman military post (Matt. 8:5-13; Luke 7:1-10). Our Lord at an early period of his ministry removed thither from Nazareth and made it so continually his headquarters that it came to be called his own city (Matt. 9:1; cf. Mark 2:1). It was there that he healed the centurion's palsied servant (Matt. 8:5-13; Luke 7:1-10), Peter's wife's mother when she was prostrate with fever (Matt. 8:14-17; Mark 1:29-31), a demoniac (Mark 1:21-28; Luke 4:31-37), a man sick of the palsy borne of four (Mark 2:1-13; cf. Matt. 9:1-8), a nobleman's son (John 4:46-54), and a number of other diseased people (Matt. 8:16, 17; Mark 1:32-34; Luke 4:23, 40, 41). The discourse recorded in John 6:24-71, which followed on the feeding of the 5,000, with many other addresses, was delivered at Capernaum (Mark 9:33-50). It was here also that Jesus called to the apostleship Matthew, or Levi, as he was sitting at the receipt of custom (Matt. 9:9-13; Mark 2:14-17; Luke 5:27-32; cf. Matt. 17:24). Notwithstanding the teaching and works of Jesus, its people did not repent, and Jesus predicted the utter ruin of the place (Matt. 11:23, 24; Luke 10:15).

Capernaum is not mentioned in the O.T., and perhaps did not arise till after the Captivity. Josephus was carried with bruised wrist from near Julias (not far from the spot where the Jordan enters the Sea of Galilee) into a village named Cepharnome, or Capernaum (Jos. *Life* 72).

Two spots, about 2½ miles apart, contend for the distinction of being the site. The more northerly is called Tell Ḥum, which is about 2½ miles s.w. of the mouth of the Jordan and 2 miles s. of Chorazin; the more southerly is Khân Minyeh. Each of them marks the site of a former town. The fountain of Capernaum, from which the plain of Gennesaret was in part irrigated, and where coracine are found (Jos. *War* iii. 10, 8) was doubtless the abundant 'Ain eṭ-Ṭâbighah, midway between Khân Minyeh and Tell Ḥum. While the site has not been definitely determined, the present trend of opinion is in favor of Tell Ḥum.

Caph (käf), A.R.V. **Kaph** [*kaph*, palm of hand]. The 11th letter of the Hebrew alphabet, which through the Greek *kappa* became Latin and English K. In anglicized Hebrew names *kaph* is represented by C, except final and before e and i, where Ch is employed. Caph stands at the head of the 11th section of Psalm 119; here each verse begins with this letter in the original.

Caph'ar·sal'a·ma (käf'är-săl'á-má) [village of Salem]. A town (I Macc. 7:31; Jos. *Antiq.* xii. 10, 4), perhaps the later Carvasalim, near Ramleh, or Selmeh, 3 miles e. of Joppa.

Ca·phen'a·tha (ka-fĕn'á-thá). See CHAPHENATHA.

Caph'tor (käf'tôr). An isle or seacoast, from which the Philistines originally came (Jer. 47:4; Amos 9:7). By one theory Caphtor was W. and S. Asia Minor from Lydia to Cilicia; support for this may be found in LXX's Cappadocia for Caphtor in Deut. 2:23 and Amos 9:7. Egyptian Keftiu and Caphtor, however, have been generally identified with Crete, and the Kefti(u)ans accordingly with the Minoan Cretans. This identification is not without its difficulties, and so the designation Caphtor must be extended to mean Crete and, in general, the other islands and lands in its vicinity, Caria and Lycia included. It should also be noted that the Cherethites are mentioned in synonymous parallelism with the Philistines in Ezek. 25:16 and Zeph. 2:5, where LXX renders the former word Cretans. Cf. also I Sam. 30:14. Genesis 10:14 lists Caphtorim as a descendant of Mizraim (Egypt), but this statement probably must be interpreted in a political, not racial, sense.

Caph'to·rim (käf'tô-rĭm); in A.V. once **Caph'to·rims** (käf'tô-rĭmz) and once **Caph'·tho·rim** (käf'thô-rĭm). People from Caphtor (Deut. 2:23); in Gen. 10:14 (cf. I Chron. 1:12), "whence went forth the Philistines" probably should follow Caphtorim. (Cf. Amos 9:7 and Jer. 47:4.)

Cap'i·tal, in A.V. **Chap'i·ter.** The head or uppermost part of a column, pillar, or pilaster (I Kings 7:16). It can be varied in form and ornamentation, according to the order of architecture used in the building (Ex. 36:38; 38:17, 19; I Kings 7:19, 20).

Cap'pa·do'ci·a (kăp'á-dō'shǐ-á). A highland province in the e. of Asia Minor; it was formed into a Roman province by Tiberius in A.D. 17 on the death of King Archelaus. In A.D. 70 Vespasian united it with Armenia Minor as one of the great frontier provinces of the empire. It produced excellent wheat and horses. Worshipers from Cappadocia were at the feast of Pentecost, rendered memorable by the descent of the Holy Spirit (Acts 2:9). Some of the Dispersion, to whom Peter wrote, lived in Cappadocia (I Peter 1:1).

Cap'tain. As a military title, captain is generally in O.T. the rendering of Heb. *şar*. It is a broad designation for an official, whether he be commander in chief (Gen. 21:22; Judg. 4:2; I Sam. 14:50; II Sam. 10:16), or the commander of a division of the army (II Sam. 18:2, 5), or part of a division (I Kings 16:9); an officer over 1,000 men or 100 men or 50 men (Num. 31:14, 48; I Sam. 8:12; 17:18; 18:13; 22:7; II Sam. 18:1; II Kings 1:9; Isa. 3:3); the commander of the king's body guard (Gen. 37:36; II Kings 25:8; Dan. 2:14, where the word is *rab*), or of a post of sentries (Jer. 37:13, in Heb. *ba'al*). The word rendered captain in A.V. of Num., ch. 2 is *nāśî'*, and denotes a tribal prince. *Ķāşin* is thrice rendered captain in A.V. (Josh. 10:24; Judg. 11:6, 11), where it refers to leaders of the host; but the word is a general term for one with whom decision rests, and it is applied to civil rulers (Isa. 3:1; Micah 3:1, 9), whose duties included that of judging (Isa. 1:10; 3:6; Prov. 6:7; 25:15, R.V. marg.).

In N.T. the chief captain was a *chiliarchos*, a term which originally denoted the commander of 1,000 men, but was used broadly for the commandant of a garrison, and as the equivalent of the Roman military tribune (John 18:12, R.V. marg.). He was one of the general officers of a legion, and higher in rank than a centurion (Acts 21:31, 32, R.V. marg.; 22:25, 26). The captain of the Temple was not a military officer, but the priest in command of the guard of Levites who kept watch at the Temple (Acts 4:1; 5:24, 26; cf. Jos. *Antiq*. xx. 6, 2 with *War* ii. 12, 6; vi. 5, 3). Under him were subordinate officers of the several divisions of the guard (Luke 22:4, 52).

Cap'tiv'i•ty. The state of being in bondage to enemies, especially in a foreign land. In O.T. times the Assyrians introduced, and the Chaldeans adopted, the practice of making a wholesale deportation of at least the leading men belonging to each country which they conquered, and locating them in districts where they would be removed from familiar associations and patriotic memories, and would be under the eye of the central government. Deportation was generally resorted to as an extreme measure when other means failed. The stronger state was usually content with imposing tribute. The withholding of the customary tribute was treated as rebellion, and was punished by a military invasion and pillage of the country. If these harsh measures proved ineffective, resort was had to deportation.

Two principal captivities are mentioned in the Bible:

I. The Captivity of the Ten Tribes

As early as 842 B.C. Jehu paid tribute to Shalmaneser, king of Assyria. It was not until the reign of Tiglath-pileser, 746/5-728/7, that the Assyrians began emptying the land of the Ten Tribes of Israel of its inhabitants. That king received tribute from Menahem. In the reign of Pekah he captured cities of Naphtali and carried off the inhabitants to Assyria (II Kings 15:29). He overran the country e. of the Jordan and deported the Reubenites, Gadites, and half-tribe of Manasseh to Mesopotamia (I Chron. 5:26). By his connivance Pekah was slain and Hoshea placed on the throne. His successor, Shalmaneser, besieged Samaria; the city was taken in the accession year of Sargon, 722 (721) B.C.; a large number of the inhabitants were deported to Mesopo-

tamia and Media (II Kings 17:5, 6, 18); the rest were placed under tribute. The gaps in the population were filled with colonists from other regions who brought in their own religious beliefs. Jehovah worship was once more introduced, but a mixed religion resulted. The later Samaritans descended from this heterogeneous people (II Kings 17:19-41). Some of the Israelites eventually returned to Jerusalem (Luke 2:36), but most of them remained in the countries whither they had been carried, preserving their racial distinctions and religious observances and visiting Jerusalem from time to time (Acts 2:9; 26:7).

II. The Captivity of Judah

Sennacherib recorded that he removed 200,-150 captives from Judah (cf. II Kings 18:13). But by the captivity of Judah is meant the deportation of the people to Babylonia. Judah's captivity was predicted a century and a half before its occurrence (Isa. 6:11, 12; 11:12), and Babylonia as the place was foretold by Micah (Micah 4:10) and Isaiah (Isa. 11:11; 39:6). The Prophet Jeremiah announced that it should continue 70 years (Jer. 25:1, 11, 12). It was effected by Nebuchadnezzar. In 605 B.C., in the 3d or 4th year of Jehoiakim, according to the method of reckoning which one adopts, he came unto Jerusalem, took the vessels of the Temple to Babylon, and carried off certain of the seed royal as captives (II Chron. 36:2-7; Jer. 45:1; Dan. 1:1-3). In 597 he carried off Jehoiachin and his mother and wives, and 3,000 princes, 7,000 men of might, and 1,000 artisans (II Kings 24:14-16). Eleven years later (586) his army burned the Temple, destroyed Jerusalem, and carried off the residue of the people, leaving only the poorest of the land to be vinedressers and husbandmen (II Kings 25:2-21). Five years after the destruction of the city, another group was deported to Babylonia (Jer. 52:30). In their exile the Jews enjoyed many privileges. They were permitted to build and occupy houses, keep servants, and engage in business (Jer. 29:5-7; Ezra 2:65), and there was nothing to hinder them from rising to the highest positions in the state (Dan. 2:48; Neh. 1:11). Their priests and teachers were with them (Jer. 29:1; Ezra 1:5), and they had the instructions and encouragement of Ezekiel (Ezek. 1:1). In 539 B.C. Babylon fell into the hands of Cyrus the Great, who issued a decree authorizing the Jews to return to the land of their fathers and rebuild the Temple (Ezra 1:1-4). In c. 538 about 43,000 of them embraced the opportunity (Ezra 2:64). Many, however, preferred to remain in Babylonia and the e., and with the Israelites in Mesopotamia and Media formed part of what became known as the Diaspora (Zech. 6:10; Acts 2:9). See DISPERSION.

Car'bun•cle. 1. The rendering of Heb. *bāreḳeth* and *bāreḳath*, shining like lightning. It denotes a gem (Ezek. 28:13), and was the 3d stone in the 1st row of the high priest's breastplate (Ex. 28:17). In both cases R.V. marg., following the LXX, the Vulgate, and Josephus, makes it an emerald.

2. The rendering of Heb. *'ekdāḥ*, a precious stone (Isa. 54:12).

Car'cas (kär'kas). One of 7 chamberlains who served in the presence of King Ahasuerus (Esth. 1:10).

Car'che•mish (kär'ke-mĭsh), in A.V. once **Char'che•mish** (II Chron. 35:20). The e. capital of the Hittites, w. of the Euphrates, at a ford of the river, and n. of the confluence with the Sājūr. Admirably situated for commercial purposes, it became very wealthy. The Assyrian king, Ashur-nasir-pal (885-860 B.C.), received from it rich tribute. In 717 B.C. it was captured by Sargon, and with it fell the Hittite empire (Isa. 10:9). Necho, king of Egypt, was decisively defeated at Carchemish by Nebuchadnezzar in 605 B.C. (II Chron. 35:20; Jer. 46:2). Its site is called Jerâbîs or Jerablus.

Ca·re′ah (kȧ-rē′ȧ). See KAREAH.

Ca′ri·a (kā′rĭ-ȧ). A country at the s.w. point of Asia Minor. It was part of the territory which the Romans took from Antiochus the Great. The Roman senate bestowed it on the Rhodians, but released it again in 168 B.C. (I Macc. 15:23), but it was finally incorporated in the province of Asia.

Car′ites (kär′īts). See CHERETHITES.

Car′mel (kär′mĕl) [garden land]. 1. A range of hills, about 15 miles long, connected by a chain of lower hills with the mountainous region of central Palestine and terminating in a promontory which juts into the Mediterranean (Jer. 46:18), and constitutes the s. boundary of the bay of Acre. Near its s.e. end it is 1,742 feet high, a little farther onward it is 1,715, and it gradually falls more and more, until at the n.w. top, which constitutes the promontory, it is only 556 feet high. The range constitutes the s.w. boundary of the valley of Esdraelon, through which the Kishon runs, and at one place that brook washes the n. slope of Carmel (I Kings 18:20, 40). The summit of the range consists of a series of eminences with tablelands on their tops, sometimes bare and rocky, and sometimes covered with shrubs, especially the prickly oak and the juniper. The strata are of limestone, and there are caves on the sides of the mountain chain, though not on its summit. The view from its higher parts is fine. Carmel, now called Jebel Kurmul, was on the s. boundary of Asher (Josh. 19:26), within the limits of that tribe. On the top of Carmel, Elijah brought to a decisive issue the question between Jehovah and the worship of Baal (I Kings 18:17–40), and from the top of the same range his servant saw the ascent from the Mediterranean of the little cloud like a man's hand which heralded the rainstorm and the termination of the drought (I Kings 18:41–46). Carmel was visited by Elisha (II Kings 2:25; 4:25). It is believed to have been anciently cultivated to the summit, with fruit trees in orchards or gardens, as its name imports, and as the fruitfulness ascribed to it indicates (Isa. 33:9; 35:2; Jer. 50:19). A forest, probably consisting chiefly of fruit trees, was in its midst (Micah 7:14). When in S. of Sol. 7:5 the lover says to the object of his affection, "Thy head upon thee is like Carmel," he probably means covered with luxuriant hair, as Carmel is with fruit trees. Amos prophesied, "The top of Carmel shall wither" (Amos 1:2). There has long been a convent on Mount Carmel, after which the Carmelite monks are named.

2. A town in the mountainous part of Judah (Josh. 15:55; cf. I Sam. 15:12; 25:2). The churlish Nabal's possessions lay in the vicinity (I Sam. 25:2–40). The name is still retained in the modern Kermel, a ruin about 7 miles s.s.e. of Hebron. From this town one of David's wives hailed (I Sam. 30:5), and also one of his mighty men (II Sam. 23:35).

Car′mi (kär′mī) [vinedresser]. 1. A son of Reuben, and founder of a tribal family (Gen. 46:9; Ex. 6:14; Num. 26:6).

2. A descendant of Judah and father of Achan (Josh. 7:1; I Chron. 2:6, 7).

Car′na·im (kär′nà-ĭm). See ASHTEROTH-KARNAIM.

Car′pen·ter. The first mention of carpentry in the Bible as a distinct occupation is on the occasion when carpenters were brought from Tyre to build David a palace (II Sam. 5:11). Among the carpenters' tools were the ax, saw (Isa. 10:15), measuring line, plane, compass (Isa. 44:13), iron nails, hammers (Jer. 10:4; I Chron. 22:3). Joseph, husband of Mary, was a carpenter (Matt. 13:55), and Jesus in his youth worked at the same calling (Mark 6:3).

Car′pus (kär′pŭs) [Gr., fruit; wrist]. A resident at Troas, with whom Paul left his cloak, for which he afterward sent (II Tim. 4:13).

Car′riage. That which is carried; baggage (I Sam. 17:22; Isa. 10:28; I Macc. 9:35, 39; Acts 21:15), heavy matters or goods (Judg. 18:21), a burden (Isa. 46:1). The place of the carriage (I Sam. 17:20; 26:5, 7, A.V. marg.) was the enclosure formed by the carts which were used to transport goods for the army, and which were drawn up in a circle around the camp. In all passages R.V. has abandoned this obsolete sense of carriage and substituted the appropriate modern word.

Car′she·na (kär′shĕ-nȧ) [probably Old Persian, plowman]. A prince of Persia at the court of King Ahasuerus (Esth. 1:14). See PRINCE.

Cart. A wheeled vehicle employed in peaceful occupations, and distinguished from the chariot, which was used for state and war. It was made of wood (I Sam. 6:14), was either covered or uncovered (Num. 7:3, where the Hebrew word is rendered wagon), was drawn by cattle (Num. 7:7; I Sam. 6:7; II Sam. 6:6), though horses occasionally dragged the

Ancient Egyptian Cart

threshing cart, it would seem (Isa. 28:28), and was used in threshing in lieu of a sledge (Isa. 28:27), for transporting goods (II Sam. 6:3), hauling grain (Amos 2:13), and conveying persons (Gen. 45:19, rendered wagon). In Egypt a cart was used like that which is now employed universally in western Asia, with 2

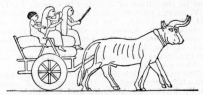

Cart with Captive Women of Lachish

wheels of solid wood. Asiatic carts, including the one in which Jewish captive women of Lachish are riding on sacks of grain, are represented in Assyrian bas-reliefs as having two wheels with 8, 6, or 4 spokes each and drawn by oxen. They are also depicted as drawn by mules, or by 2 men.

Carv′ing. The art of cutting letters, images, or ornamental designs in wood, stone, ivory, or other material. Bezalel, a man of Judah, and Oholiab, a Danite, were gifted for this work, and wrought the carving for the tabernacle (Ex. 31:1–7; 35:30–35). There was carved work in Solomon's Temple—flowers, palm trees, and cherubim (I Kings 6:18, 29); and in the superior kind of domestic architecture (Prov. 7:16, A.V.).

Case'ment. A sash which moves on a hinge; or part of a window, made movable by a hinge, so that it may be opened while the rest of the window remains shut (Prov. 7:6, A.V.). But in Judg. 5:28, A.V., and in R.V. of both passages, the Hebrew word is rendered "lattice."

Ca·siph'i·a (kȧ-sĭf'ĭ-ȧ). A place not far from the route between Babylon and Jerusalem, and in or near Babylonia (Ezra 8:17).

Cas'lu·him (kăs'lû-hĭm). A people descended from the Egyptians (or possibly only conquered and incorporated with them), and standing somewhere in the ancestral line of the Philistines (Gen. 10:14; I Chron. 1:12). See CAPHTORIM.

Cas'phor (kăs'fôr). A fortified town e. of the Jordan, captured by Judas Maccabaeus (I Macc. 5:26, 36). In the latter verse A.V. gives the name as Casphon. Josephus calls it Casphoma (Casphom) (Jos. Antiq. xii. 8, 3).

Cas'si·a. 1. The rendering of the Hebrew word ḳiddāh (Ezek. 27:19). It denotes an aromatic wood, and was an ingredient of the anointing oil (Ex. 30:24). The translation "cassia" is supported by the Syriac version, the Targum, and the Vulgate. If correct, the word probably denotes a species of the wood. R.V. marg. has "costus."
2. The rendering of Heb. ḳeṣī'āh. It is fragrant (Ps. 45:8). Cassia bark is derived from various species of Cinnamomum. See CINNAMON.

Cas'ta·net'. In the plural the rendering of Heb. mᵉnaʻanᵉʻīm, moving to and fro (II Sam. 6:5), a musical instrument which David and his subjects played. R.V. marg., following the Vulgate, has "sistra," and the A.V. "cornets." Castanets are a pair of small spoon-shaped cymbals fastened to the thumb and beaten together by the middle finger. The word castanets is derived from castanea, a chestnut, two of these fruits being anciently attached to the fingers and beaten together. Castanets were employed in Greece and Rome as an accompaniment to hymns in honor of the goddess Artemis or Diana.

Cas'tle. A fortified building or stronghold (Prov. 18:19). David took the Jebusite castle and converted it into his residence; and it was afterward called the city of David (I Chron. 11:5, 7, A.V.). Jehoshaphat built castles in the cities of Judah (II Chron. 17:12; A.V. marg., palaces), and Jotham in its forests (II Chron. 27:4). The habitations of the descendants of Aaron (I Chron. 6:54), and probably those of the Ishmaelite chieftains and of the Midianites (Gen. 25:16; Num. 31:10), were encampments (R.V.) and not castles (A.V.).
The castle which Nehemiah erected was presumably succeeded by the stronghold eventually known as Antonia, and in which Paul was confined at Jerusalem. See ANTONIA, TOWER OF.

Cas'tor (kăs'tẽr) **and Pol'lux** (pŏl'ŭks). Two Greek and Roman divinities, born of the same mother, Leda, but by different fathers. Castor's father was Tyndareus, a Spartan king, while that of Pollux was Zeus, the Greek supreme god. By another account, however, Castor was also the son of Zeus. Castor was a great charioteer and horse master, who was eventually killed in a fight. Pollux was a highly distinguished pugilist. His father Zeus

offered him immortality, but he begged to be allowed to share it day and day about with the deceased Castor. The request was granted, and both brothers were worshiped, especially at Sparta, under the name of the Dioscuri (Gr. Dioskouroi). They were regarded as the special protectors of distressed mariners. The Alexandrian vessel in which Paul sailed from Melita to Puteoli had for its sign or figurehead Dioskouroi. This the R.V. renders "The Twin Brothers" and the A.V., with more latitude, "Castor and Pollux" (Acts 28:11). The constellation Gemini (the Twins) is called after the affectionate brothers, and its two leading stars are named Castor and Pollux.

Cat'er·pil'lar. The rendering of Heb. ḥāsil, devourer. It is associated with the locust, and is a destroyer of vegetation (I Kings 8:37; II Chron. 6:28; Ps. 78:46; Isa. 33:4; Joel 1:4; 2:25). Probably a species of locust, or the common migratory locust in one stage of development (cf. Joel 1:4; 2:25, R.V. marg.). For Ps. 105:34, E.R.V., and Jer. 51:27 of A.V., see CANKERWORM.

Cat'tle. A comprehensive term used in the O.T. for domestic animals, large and small, for camels, horses, sheep, goats, oxen, and asses (Gen. 13:2; 26:13, 14; 30:32, A.V.; 31:9; 47:16–18).

Cau'da (kô'dȧ). See CLAUDA.

Caul. 1. A net worn over the hair by Hebrew women (Isa. 3:18); rendered "networks" on the margin of both R.V. and A.V.
2. The lesser omentum, a layer of the inner lining of the cavity of the belly, partly enveloping the liver, as the greater omentum does the stomach (Ex. 29:13, 22; Lev. 3:4, 10, 15).

Cave. A hollow place or cavern in the side of a hill or cliff. Caves are most numerous and largest in limestone countries, of which Palestine is one. They served as dwelling places in the Neolithic period; in the Bronze Age they became tombs or were converted into storehouses or cisterns. Even in later times they were used as temporary abodes, as by Lot and his daughters after the destruction of Sodom (Gen. 19:30), and by Elijah (I Kings 19:9). They often served as stables for cattle. They were natural tombs, and were constantly employed for burial purposes; for example, the cave of Machpelah (Gen., chs. 23; 49:29) and the tomb of Lazarus (John 11:38). In times of war and oppression they afforded a place of refuge (Judg. 6:2; I Sam. 13:6; 24:3–10; II Macc. 6:11), the most noted being the caves at Makkedah (Josh. 10:16–27) and Adullam (I Sam. 22:1; II Sam. 23:13).

Ce'dar. A famous tree of Lebanon (I Kings 5:6), tall and stately (Isa. 2:13; Ezek. 17:22; 31:3). It furnished a timber much prized in the construction of palaces and temples (II Sam. 5:11; I Kings 5:5, 6; 7:1–12; Ezra 3:7). From its pillars, beams, and planks were cut (I Kings 6:9, 10, 18; 7:2, 7); idols were hewn (Isa. 44:14); masts were made for ships (Ezek. 27:5). It is fragrant (S. of Sol. 4:11), and it was used in ceremonial purifications (Lev. 14:4; Num. 19:6). The tree is evidently the cedar of Lebanon (Abies cedrus or Cedrus libani), called 'erez in Hebrew. It is a large tree of dome-shaped form, with long, spreading, contorted branches, evergreen leaves, and cones 3" to 5" long. The Cedrus libani still survives in the mountains of Syria and flourishes in much greater numbers in the Taurus Mountains.

Ce'dron (sē'drŏn). See KIDRON.

Ce'lo·syr'i·a (sē'lô-sĭr'ĭ-ȧ). See COELESYRIA.

Cen'chre·ae (sĕn'krē-ȧ), in A.V. **Cen'chre·a** (sĕn'krē-ȧ) [Gr., millet]. A harbor of Corinth, about 7 miles e. of the city, on the Saronic Gulf. It was visited by Paul (Acts 18:18); and it possessed a Christian church, of which Phoebe was a servant or deaconess (Rom. 16:1).

Cen'de·bae'us (sĕn'dĕ-bē'ŭs), in A.V. **Cen'·de·be'us** (sĕn'dĕ-bē'ŭs). A general placed in command of the seacoast of Judea by Antiochus VII (I Macc. 15:38). He was routed by Judas and John, sons of Simon Maccabaeus (ch. 16:1–10).

Cen'ser. A vessel for holding incense while it is being burned (Num. 16:6, 7, 39). The censers of the tabernacle were of brass (Lev. 16:12; cf. Ex. 27:3, fire pans); those of the Temple were of gold (I Kings 7:50; II Chron. 4:22; Heb. 9:4). The censers of the book of Revelation (ch. 8:3, 5) were also of gold.

Cen'sus. An enumeration and registration of a people, conveniently made among the Hebrews according to tribe, family, and house (Num. 1:18), and in the wilderness probably based on the reports of the officers over thousands, hundreds, fifties, and tens (Ex. 18:25; cf. round numbers, Num. 1:21, 23, etc.). Besides enumerations of classes of the people, like that of the first-born (Num. 3:43), a formal census of all the Israelites of military age is recorded in the O.T. as having been taken on three different occasions. The first was taken at Mount Sinai in the 2d month of the 2d year after they had left Egypt (Num., ch. 1). Omitting the Levites (vs. 47–54), there were of males above 20 years of age, and capable of bearing arms, 603,550 (chs. 1:45–47; 11:21). The records of those who had recently paid tribute were probably used in making up the lists (Ex. 38:26). The Levites from one month old and upward were counted separately, and numbered 22,000 (Num. 3:39). The 2d census was taken 38 years later at the camp at Shittim in the Moabite country near the close of the 40 years' wandering. The number of men had altered but slightly and now was 601,730 (Num. 26:1–51), Levites 23,000 (v. 62). The 3d census was made by order of David, who found that there were of fighting men in Israel 800,000, in Judah 500,000 (II Sam. 24:1–9; cf. I Chron. 21:1–6). About the same time the Levites, from 30 years old and upward, numbered 38,000 (I Chron. 23:3). An enumeration was made of the exiles who returned to Jerusalem from Babylonia with Zerubbabel (Ezra, ch. 2), and an enrollment was ordered by the emperor Augustus for the Roman Empire shortly before the birth of Christ (Luke 2:1; see QUIRINIUS and THOUSAND).

Cen·tu'ri·on [from Lat. *centum*, 100]. An officer in the Roman army (Acts 21:32; 22:26), who at first commanded 100 soldiers and afterward about that number (cf. Acts 23:23). Two are mentioned by name in the N.T.: Cornelius, stationed at Caesarea, through whom it was made evident that the Holy Spirit is given to Gentile believers no less than to Jewish (Acts, ch. 10), and Julius, who conducted Paul and other prisoners to Rome and treated Paul kindly (Acts 27:1, 3, 43). Two centurions, besides Cornelius, believed—one at Capernaum (Matt. 8:5–13), the other at the cross (Matt. 27:54).

Ce'phas (sē'făs) [Gr. *Kēphās*, from Aram. *Kēphā*, rock or stone]. An appellation given by Jesus to the Apostle Simon (John 1:42; I Cor. 1:12; 3:22; 9:5; 15:5; Gal. 2:9); Peter is the Greek equivalent of Cephas.

Chal·ced'o·ny [from Gr. *Chalkēdōn*, a town in Asia Minor]. A precious stone, the 3d foundation of the wall of the New Jerusalem (Rev. 21:19). Chalcedony is a variety of quartz. It is hard, its largest ingredient being silica. It is of a waxy luster, and therefore much duller than typical quartz. It is white-gray, brown, blue, etc. It is not perfectly crystallized, but often coats crystals of quartz. It occurs in massive form in veins, in nodules of botryoidal form (i.e., resembling a cluster of grapes), or in stalactites. This stone, however, did not receive the name chalcedony, it is believed, until the Middle Ages, so that John, it would seem, had a different stone of Chalcedon in mind, perhaps the Chalcedonian emerald or the Chalcedonian jasper which are mentioned by Pliny (*Hist. Nat.* xxxvii. 18, 37).

Chal'col (kăl'kŏl). See CALCOL.

Chal·de'a (kăl-dē'ȧ) [Gr. *Chaldaia* from Akkad. *Kaldū*; cf. Heb. *Kaśdim*, Chaldeans, Chaldea]. Originally the s. portion of Babylonia, at the head of the Persian Gulf, but the designation was ultimately extended to the whole of the alluvial plain stretching from above Hit to the gulf. See BABYLONIA.

The people called Chaldeans in the mountains of Kurdistan during the retreat of the 10,000 under Xenophon (*Anabasis* iv. 3, 4, etc.), and others in Pontus mentioned by Strabo (549) are non-Semitic and are the Haldians (Khaldians), the inhabitants of Urartu (Ararat, Armenia).

Roman Centurion of the Time of Christ

Chal·de'an (kăl-dē'ăn), in N.T. **Chal·dae'an** (kăl-dē'ăn). A native or inhabitant of Chaldea. See BABYLONIA. In the Neo-Babylonian Empire the Chaldeans were the dominant race, and doubtless possessed themselves of all offices of influence. So exclusively did they fill ecclesiastical positions at the capital that at Babylon their name became synonymous with priests of Bel-marduk (Herod. i. 181, 183). These priests were esteemed as possessors of wisdom and equated with magicians, enchanters, sorcerers, and diviners (Dan. 1:4; 2:2, 4).

Chal·dees' (kăl-dēz'). A variant form of Chaldeans used in the expression "Ur of the Chaldees" (Gen. 11:31; Neh. 9:7), and also sometimes in A.V. when there is no mention of Ur (II Kings 24:2; 25:4–26; II Chron. 36:17; Isa. 13:19).

Chalk'stone'. A stone taken from the limestone rocks which constitute a marked feature of Palestine (Isa. 27:9).

Chal'phi (kăl'fī), in A.V. **Cal'phi** (kăl'fī). Father of Judas, one of the two captains who stood by Jonathan Maccabaeus at Hazor (I Macc. 11:70).

Cham'ber·lain. One who looks after the private chambers of a palace or mansion; as Blastus, who was over Herod's bedchamber (Acts 12:20); or one who has charge of the treasure chamber, as Erastus, the treasurer of the city of Corinth (Rom. 16:23, A.V.; in R.V. "treasurer"). In the O.T. the word rendered "chamberlain" signifies eunuch, and is often translated so; see EUNUCH.

Cha·me'le·on [Gr. *chamaileōn,* on the ground, dwarf,+lion]. A reptile which belongs to the same order as lizards (Lev. 11:30). In R.V. the name is the rendering of Heb. *tinshemeth,* breathing (A.V. mole), whereas in A.V. it represents Heb. *kŏaḥ* (R.V. land crocodile; see LIZARD). The lungs of the lizard are very large and, when expanded, render it semi-transparent. Its eyeballs protrude from the head, and are independent in their action, so that it can turn one eye up and the other down, or look in different directions and at different objects at the same time. It has also the faculty of changing its hue in accordance with the color of the objects about it or with its temper when disturbed. This power is due to the presence of clear or pigment-bearing cells in the skin, their contractions and dilations being controlled by the nervous system. It lives in trees. Its feet are fitted for use as hands and its tail is prehensile, so that it is able to cling to the branches. It feeds upon insects which it captures by means of its long tongue covered at the end with a viscous substance.

Cham'ois. The rendering of Heb. *zemer.* The animal is ruminant (Deut. 14:5). It is not the real chamois, which is a native of the European mountains from the Pyrenees to the Caucasus, but does not occur in Palestine.

Cham·paign'. In Deut. 11:30, A.V., meaning open country. R.V. has Arabah (*q.v.*).

Cha'naan (kā'năn). See CANAAN.

Cha·phen'a·tha (kȧ-fĕn'ȧ-thȧ), in A.V. **Caphen'a·tha.** Apparently a portion of the e. wall of Jerusalem, perhaps one of the towers or other mural fortifications (I Macc. 12:37).

Chap'i·ter. See CAPITAL.

Chap'man (A.V.). Originally a merchant; then a peddler (II Chron. 9:14, A.V.); in A.R.V. trader. In I Kings 10:15, A.V. renders the same expression by "merchantmen."

Char'a·shim (kăr'ȧ-shĭm). See GE-HARASHIM.

Char'che·mish (kăr'kĕ-mĭsh). See CARCHEMISH.

Charg'er. The word is used in A.V. for the dish (platter, A.R.V.) on which the head of John the Baptist was brought to Herodias' daughter (Matt. 14:8), and for the silver dishes of 130 shekels' weight presented by the tribal princes at the dedication of the altar (Num. 7:13). Hebrew *kˈeʿārāh,* rendered "charger" in the last passage, denotes the golden dishes which stood on the table of showbread (Ex. 25:29; 37:16; Num. 4:7).

Char'i·ot. A two-wheeled vehicle of various forms, drawn by horses (II Sam. 8:4), and used for military (Ex. 14:9; I Sam. 13:5), state (Gen. 41:43; II Sam. 15:1; I Kings 1:5), and private purposes (Gen. 46:29; II Kings 5:9; Acts 8:28). The bed was open behind, and rested on the axle without springs. The wheels were not clumsy, but consisted of fellies, spokes, and naves, and were often of metal (I Kings 7:33). Chariots were but poorly adapted to the hills of Palestine, and were not much used, but they were common among the Canaanites in the valley (Josh. 17:16; Judg. 4:3), and among the Egyptians (Isa. 31:1), Ethiopians (II Chron. 16:8), Syrians (II Kings 5:9), Hittites (II Kings 7:6), and Assyrians (Nahum 2:3, 4; 3:2). The war chariots commonly carried a driver (II Chron. 18:33), and occasionally a shield-bearer, besides the warrior himself. Probably among the Hebrews a 3d person, perhaps shield-bearer, sometimes occupied the chariot (II Kings 9:25). The war chariot was at times constructed of iron or covered with iron plates (Josh. 17:16, 18; Judg. 1:19; 4:3). The Persians armed the axles and sometimes the tongue with scythes; chariots of this sort were seen in Palestine in the Seleucidan period (II Macc. 13:2). A four-wheeled vehicle (Gr. *redē*) is intended in Rev. 18:13, A.V.

Royal Assyrian Chariot

Char'i·ty. Love, often manifested by almsgiving. The charity described in I Cor., ch. 13 is not almsgiving, as is evident from v. 3; it is love, charity in the broad sense, love toward all. It is so rendered by the R.V.

Char'ran (kăr'ăn). See HARAN, II.

Che'bar (kē'bär). A river in the land of the Chaldeans, on the banks of which some of the Jewish exiles, including the Prophet Ezekiel, were settled. It was there that the prophet saw several of his visions (Ezek. 1:1, 3; 3:15, 23; 10:15, 20). It is not the river Khabur, called by the Greeks Chaboras, which rises near Nisibis in upper Mesopotamia, and flows into the Euphrates. The Chebar was a great canal, s.e. of Babylon. These streams are known by the name *nāru,* river.

Ched'or·la·o'mer (kĕd'ŏr-lȧ-ō'mẽr) [Elamite, servant of the god Lagamar]. A king of Elam, who evidently held the sovereignty over Babylonia. In the days of Abraham, in alliance with Amraphel, king of Shinar; Arioch, king of Ellasar; and Tidal, king of Goiim, he made an expedition to the w. and subjugated the country about the Dead Sea. The people of the plain served him 12 years and then revolted. The next year Chedorlaomer came with his allies and smote the region e. of the Jordan from Bashan southward, the land of Edom to the head of the Red Sea, the country afterward inhabited by the Amalekites, and the plain about the Dead Sea. This conquest gave him control of the caravan routes from Arabia past the head of the Red Sea to Egypt, Canaan, and the n. But he carried off Lot from Sodom. This induced Abraham to lead his numerous servants and his allied chieftains in pursuit. They fell upon Chedorlaomer by night at Dan, put him and his followers to flight, and recovered the captives and the spoil (Gen. 14:1–16). It was not strange, even in those early days, for a Babylonian monarch to make an expedition to the countries on the Mediterranean Sea. See ABRAHAM, IV.

Cheese. The curd of milk, coagulated, separated from the whey, and pressed (Job 10:10; cf. I Sam. 17:18; II Sam. 17:29). A valley at Jerusalem bore the name Tyropoeon (Jos. *War* v. 4, 1), which in Greek means the Valley of the Cheese Makers.

Che'lal (kē'lăl) [completion, perfection]. A son of Pahath-moab, whom Ezra induced to divorce his foreign wife (Ezra 10:30).

Che'lub (kē'lŭb) [basket; bird's cage]. 1. A brother of Shuah, whose lineage is not traced, but who was entitled to registry in the tribe of Judah (I Chron. 4:11).
2. The father of David's officer over the cultivators (I Chron. 27:26).

Che·lu'bai (kē-lōō'bī). See CALEB 1.

Che·lu'hi (kē-lōō'hī), in A.V. **Chel'luh** (kĕl'ū). A son of Bani, whom Ezra induced to divorce his foreign wife (Ezra 10:35); R.V. marg., Cheluhu.

Chem'a·rim (kĕm'á-rĭm), in the text of A.V. **Chem'a·rims** (kĕm'á-rĭmz). Priests of the high places (II Kings 23:5, marg.), of the calves at Beth-el (Hos. 10:5, marg.), and of Baal (Zeph. 1:4).

Che'mosh (kē'mŏsh). The god of the Moabites (Num. 21:29; Jer. 48:46; *Moabite Stone*, 3), worshiped in the same manner as was Molech, by the sacrifice of children as burnt offerings (II Kings 3:27). His identity with Molech, god of the Ammonites (I Kings 11:7), has been assumed by some on the basis of Judg. 11:24, but here the historical argument applies to Moab, whom the speaker has in mind. Solomon erected a high place for him near Jerusalem (I Kings 11:7), which was afterward defiled by Josiah (II Kings 23:13).

Che·na'a·nah (kē-nā'á-nä) [toward Canaan; or fem. of Canaan in tribal sense]. 1. A Benjamite, family of Jediael (I Chron. 7:10).
2. The father of the false prophet Zedekiah, who deluded Ahab (I Kings 22:11; II Chron. 18:10).

Che·na'ni (kē-nā'nī) [contraction of Chenaniah]. A Levite who assisted in bringing the returned exiles to such a frame of mind that they agreed to enter into a covenant to worship Jehovah (Neh. 9:4).

Chen·a·ni'ah (kĕn'á-nī'á) [Jehovah has established]. A chief of the Levites in David's reign, of the house of Izhar, who was appointed superintendent of the outward business, such as judging (I Chron. 26:29), and the transportation of the Ark (ch. 15:22, 27, marg.; in text, song).

Che'phar·am'mo·ni (kē'fär-ăm'ô-nī), in A.V. **Che'phar·ha·am'mo·nai** (kē'fär-hȧ-ăm'ô-nī) [village of the Ammonite]. A village of Benjamin (Josh. 18:24), probably Khirbet Kafr 'Ana.

Che·phi'rah (kē-fī'rá) [village]. A city of the Gibeonites (Josh. 9:17), allotted to the Benjamites (ch. 18:26). It continued to exist after the Captivity (Ezra 2:25; Neh. 7:29). Its site is Kefīreh, 8 miles w.n.w. of Jerusalem.

Che'ran (kē'răn) [cf. *kar*, lamb]. A Horite, a son of Dishon (Gen. 36:26; I Chron. 1:41).

Cher'eth·ites (kĕr'ĕ-thīts), in A.V. once **Cher'e·thims** (kĕr'ĕ-thīmz) [probably Cretans]. A nation or tribe inhabiting the Philistine country or its s. portion (I Sam. 30:14; cf. Ezek. 25:16; Zeph. 2:5, where LXX renders the word by Cretans). They may be identical with the Philistines who came from Caphtor (*q.v.*), or may represent a direct emigration from Crete. Some of them were members of David's bodyguard (cf. II Sam. 8:18 with chs. 23:23; 15:18). In 3 places the name Carites appears instead (II Sam. 20:23, marg.; II Kings 11:4, 19, both R.V.).

Che'rith (kē'rĭth) [cut, gorge]. A brook before Jordan, by which Elijah sojourned (I Kings 17:3, 5), probably in Gilead, e. of the Jordan.

Cher'ub, plural **Cher'u·bim**; in A.V. **Cher'u·bims.** 1. Guardians placed e. of the Garden of Eden to prevent the approach of our first parents to the tree of life after their expulsion from the garden (Gen. 3:24). When the Ark was constructed for the tabernacle, cherubim wrought of gold were placed facing each other, one at each side of the mercy seat, overshadowing it with their wings (Ex. 25:18–20; 37:7–9). They symbolized the presence and unapproachability of Jehovah, whose glory was manifested between them (Lev. 16:2), who thus dwelt in the midst of his people, and was present in the tabernacle to receive worship (Ex. 25:22; Lev. 1:1). Frequent reference is made to Jehovah's dwelling between or above the cherubim (Num. 7:89; I Sam. 4:4; II Sam. 6:2; II Kings 19:15; Ps. 80:1; 99:1; Isa. 37:16). The conception underlying this designation is well illustrated by representations of a king seated on a throne supported on each side by cherubim, which have been found at Byblos, Hamath, and Megiddo, all dating between 1200 and 800 B.C. King Hiram of Byblos is represented as seated on a cherub throne. Cherubim were also embroidered on the hangings of the tabernacle (Ex. 26:1). For the grander Temple Solomon had two gigantic cherubim made. Their height was 10 cubits, or about 15 feet, and the expansion of their wings as many more. They were of olive wood, and were overlaid with gold (I Kings 6:23–28; 8:7; II Chron. 3:10–13; 5:7, 8; Heb. 9:5). Cherubim, with palm trees and open flowers, were also carved all round the walls of the Temple (I Kings 6:29). In a poem David represented Jehovah as riding upon a cherub and flying (II Sam. 22:11; Ps. 18:10). Ezekiel had a vision of cherubim by the river Chebar. Each had 4 faces and 4 wings (Ezek., ch. 10; cf. 9:3), and since they seem to be identical with the 4 living creatures previously seen by the prophet, these 4 faces were those of a man, a lion, an ox, and an eagle (cf. ch. 1:5–12 with ch. 10:20, 21). They carried the throne of Jehovah (chs. 1:26–28; 9:3). Finally the Apostle John in the Apocalypse describes 4 living creatures, who had faces like those of the same 4 animals (Rev. 4:6, 7).

The winged, man-headed bulls of Babylonia and Assyria have a certain external physical resemblance to cherubim as sometimes described in the Hebrew Scriptures; and they performed the same function, being placed at the entrance of palaces and temples where majesty dwelt. Archaeological discoveries have shown that in Syria and Palestine the winged sphinx is dominant in art and religious symbolism.

The varying forms assumed by the cherubim in art and poetic imagery show that they were symbols. The flaming sword (Gen. 3:24), and the darkness under Him who rode upon a cherub and flew upon the wings of the wind (Ps. 18:10), have been cited as the main support of the theory that the cherub is in ultimate analysis the storm cloud. It is true that the cherubim might represent some power of nature, or all the powers of nature, as the servants of Jehovah and guardians of his abode. But the Biblical writers represent the cherubim, symbolically at least, as animate beings with the intelligence of man, the strength of an ox, the courage of the lion, and the free motion of the eagle through the air. The facts at present obtainable indicate an order of angels.
2. A place in Babylonia, from which certain persons came who could not prove their Israel-

ite descent (Ezra 2:59; Neh. 7:61). Situation unknown. Pronounced kḗ'rŭb.

Ches'a·lon (kĕs'á-lŏn) [trust, hope]. A town on the boundary line of Judah, on Mount Jearim (Josh. 15:10), commonly identified with the village of Keslā, 10 miles w. of Jerusalem.

Che'sed (kē'sĕd) [sing. of *Kasdim*, Chaldeans]. A son of Nahor by his wife Milcah (Gen. 22:22).

Che'sil (kē'sĭl) [a fool]. A village, probably Khirbet er-Rās, in the most southerly region of Judah (Josh. 15:30); apparently called also Bethul and Bethuel (Josh. 19:4; I Chron. 4:30).

Chest'nut. See PLANE.

Che·sul'loth (kĕ-sŭl'ŏth) [loins or slopes]. A town on the boundary line of Issachar (Josh. 19:18), the same as Chislothtabor (*q.v.*), modern Iksal, about 3¾ miles s.e. of Nazareth.

Cheth (kāth), in R.V. **Heth, Hheth** (hāth) [*Ḥēth*]. The 8th letter of the Hebrew alphabet. English H, descended from *ḥēth*, and Ch, though neither is pronounced with the guttural sound of *ḥeth*, represent it in Anglicized Hebrew names, as Haran, Chezib. It stands at the beginning of the 8th section of Psalm 119 in which section each verse (in the Hebrew) begins with this letter.

Che'zib (kē'zĭb). See ACHZIB.

Chi'don (kī'dŏn) [a javelin]. A name for the threshing floor at which Uzza was struck dead for touching the Ark (I Chron. 13:9), in II Sam. 6:6 called Nachon. Exact site unknown.

Chil'e·ab (kĭl'ē-ăb). David's 2d son (II Sam. 3:3; cf. the LXX, Dalouia), born at Hebron. His mother was Abigail. In I Chron. 3:1 he is called Daniel.

Chil'i·on (kĭl'ĭ-ŏn) [wasting away]. The younger son of Elimelech and Naomi (Ruth 1:2, 5).

Chil'mad (kĭl'măd). A place which traded with Tyre, mentioned in connection with Sheba and Asshur (Ezek. 27:3, 23).

Chim'ham (kĭm'hăm) [of a livid countenance or blind; cf. Arab. *kamiha*, to be blind, dim, dark, to become pallid]. The son of Barzillai the Gileadite. When the father was invited by David to Jerusalem, and declined the honor on account of his advanced age, Chimham was sent in his place (II Sam. 19:37, 38). He seems to have settled near Bethlehem and erected a caravansary (Jer. 41:17, R.V. marg.).

Chin'ne·reth (kĭn'ê-rĕth) and **Chin'ne·roth** (kĭn'ê-rŏth), in A.V. once **Cin'ne·roth** (I Kings 15:20) [lute, harp]. 1. A fortified city of Naphtali (Josh. 19:35; Deut. 3:17), at Tell el-ʻOreimeh on n.w. shore of the Lake of Gennesaret.
2. The region around the city of Chinnereth (I Kings 15:20; cf. also Josh. 11:2), commonly identified with the plain of Gennesaret (Matt. 14:34).
3. The sheet of water adjacent to the fortified city and region of Chinnereth (Num. 34:11; Josh. 12:3; 13:27; I Kings 15:20). In later times known as the Lake of Gennesaret (Luke 5:1) and Sea of Galilee or Tiberias (John 6:1).

Chi'os (kī'ŏs). An island in the Greek Archipelago, at the entrance of the Gulf of Smyrna, s. of Lesbos. Paul's vessel passed it on his last voyage to Palestine (Acts 20:15).

Chis'lev (kĭs'lĕv), in A.V. **Chis'leu** (kĭs'lū) [Heb. *kislēw* from Akkad. *kis(i)limu*]. The 9th month of the Hebrew year (Neh. 1:1; Zech. 7:1; I Macc. 1:54). See YEAR.

Chis'lon (kĭs'lŏn) [trust, hope]. Father of the prince of Benjamin in the time of Moses (Num. 34:21).

Chis'loth·ta'bor (kĭs'lŏth-tā'bĕr) [the flanks of Tabor]. A locality hard by Mount Tabor, and a landmark on the boundary of Zebulun (Josh. 19:12); probably the same as Chesulloth, a town on the border of Issachar (v. 18). The two names have the same Hebrew consonants and differ only in the vocalization. See CHESULLOTH.

Chith'lish (kĭth'lĭsh), in A.V. **Kith'lish**. A village in the lowland of Judah (Josh. 15:40). *Maachōs* of Codex Vaticanus suggests modern Khirbet el-Mak-haz, e. of Tell en-Nejileh.

Chit'tim (kĭt'ĭm). See KITTIM.

Chi'un (kī'ŭn) [*Kiyyūn*]. A word occurring but once in the Hebrew Bible (Amos 5:26). It should probably be vocalized *Kaiwān* or *Kēwān*, for Akkad. *Kaiwānu* (Ninib or Saturn). It seems that the Masoretes gave the consonants *kyn* the vocalization of *shikkūṣ* (a detestable thing), whence *Kiyyūn*. A.R.V. translates it shrine. See REPHAN; SICCUTH.

Chlo'e (klō'ē) [Gr., first shoot of green grass]. A Christian woman, apparently of Corinth (I Cor. 1:11).

Chor'-ash'an (kŏr'ăsh'ăn). See ASHAN.

Cho·ra'zin (kô-rā'zĭn). A town mentioned along with Bethsaida and Capernaum, and probably, like them, near the Sea of Galilee. Like the two other places, Chorazin had at times been the scene of the Saviour's preaching and beneficent miracles; but it failed to turn its spiritual privileges to account, and was doomed to suffer the penalty of its neglect (Matt. 11:21; Luke 10:13). Eusebius, in the 4th century, said that it was 2 Roman miles from Capernaum. It is identified with Kerāzeh (or Kerāzieh), n. of Tell Ḥūm. It is a little inland, in a side valley branching off from another one which goes down to the lake. The spot is marked by extensive ruins, including a synagogue.

Cho'sen Peo'ple. A term applied to the Israelites as the people to whom God made a special revelation and through whom he made his purposes known to man (Deut. 14:2; I Kings 3:8; I Chron. 16:13; Ps. 33:12; 105:6, 42–45; 106:5; Isa. 41:8, 9; 43:10, 20; Amos 3:2). The conception starts with the call of Abraham and the covenant made with him (Neh. 9:7, 8; Acts 13:17). The choice of this nation was an act of grace on the part of God (Deut. 4:37, 38; 7:6–8; 10:15) and implied no immunity from hardships; on the contrary, through suffering the nation was visibly disciplined. The position of the chosen people was an exalted one in the spiritual realm (John 4:22); there was laid upon them moral responsibility and leadership. In knowing the one true God they enjoyed a unique religious privilege in antiquity. Genesis begins with creation, but in the choice of Israel in accordance with God's eternal purposes there is a gradual narrowing down of the line in the genealogies: Shem, Terah, Abraham, Isaac, Jacob (Israel) who begets twelve sons, who in turn become the founders of twelve tribes, which together constitute the nation of Israel. In the fullness of time Jesus Christ was born from the line of David in the tribe of Judah.

Cho·ze'ba (kô-zē'bá). See COZEBA.

Christ (krīst) [Gr., anointed]. The Anointed One, a title corresponding to Heb. and Aram. Messiah, which denoted the anointed king of Israel, and, after Saul's reign, the royal son of David. The term was borrowed from the LXX, especially from Ps. 2:2; Dan. 9:25 (Theodotion). When used in the N.T. it generally has the word "the" prefixed, and means the Messiah of O.T. prophecy (Matt. 16:16,

20; 26:63; Mark. 8:29; Luke 3:15; A.V., John 1:41). Sometimes the word the is omitted (Matt. 26:68; John 4:25).

Christ, though really used in the primary sense, is so constantly appended to Jesus, the distinctive personal name of our Lord, given from his birth, as virtually to constitute part of the proper name (John 1:17; Acts 11:17; Rom. 1:1; 5:1; A.V., Philemon 1, etc.).

Chris′tian (krĭs′chăn). A follower of the Lord Jesus Christ. The name was first given at Antioch, about A.D. 43, and apparently by foes rather than friends (Acts 11:26). Though destined ultimately to become universal, yet it took root so slowly that it is found only twice again in the N.T., once in the mouth of Agrippa II, when Paul preached repentance and remission of sins through Jesus and testified to the resurrection of Christ (Acts 26:28), and once in a letter from Peter to comfort the faithful whose adherence to Christ brought persecution upon them (I Peter 4:16).

Chron′i·cles, The Books of the. Two historical books of the O.T. They are evidently the work of a single author, generally called the Chronicler; they have unity of plan and purpose, and formed one book in the old Hebrew canon. The LXX translators divided them into two, and this division was finally admitted into printed editions of the Hebrew canon. The Hebrew name of the books is Acts of the Days, i.e., Annals. The LXX calls them *paraleipomena* (things left over). This title implies that the book was intended as a supplement to Samuel and Kings, but in reality it has an independent aim. The name Chronicles is derived from the title *Chronicon* applied to these writings by Jerome, who describes them as "a chronicle of the whole of sacred history."

The work naturally divides itself into 4 parts: (1) Introductory genealogies (I Chron., chs. 1–9); (2) Death of Saul, the kingdom under David (chs. 10–29); (3) Solomon (II Chron., chs. 1–9); (4) Division of the Kingdom, Kings of Judah to the Exile, edict of Cyrus (chs. 10–36).

Many parts of Chronicles are in close or literal agreement with the corresponding sections of the earlier historical books from Genesis to Kings, thus showing that the Chronicler extensively used these books as sources. The lists in I Chron., chs. 1–9, are mainly derived from these Biblical authorities, while I Chron., ch. 10, to II Chron., ch. 36, follows for the most part I Sam., ch. 31, to II Kings, ch. 24. The Chronicler, however, goes beyond Samuel-Kings (cf. I Chron. 11:10–47 with II Sam. 23:8–39; II Chron. 11:5–12, 18–23; 26:5–10); apparently he had access to other documents now lost. He quotes under various titles what appears to be one work, a history of both kingdoms (II Chron. 16:11; 20:34; 25:26; 27:7; 28:26; 33:18; 35:27; 36:8), which was not the canonical Book of Kings. Whether "the commentary [midrash] of the book of the kings" (II Chron. 24:27) is the same as the book of the kings of Judah and Israel remains uncertain. The Chronicler also quotes the works of seers and prophets (I Chron. 29:29; II Chron. 9:29; 12:15; 13:22; 20:34; 26:22; 32:32; 33:19). For other authorities, see I Chron. 5:17; 27:24; 28:19; II Chron. 35:25; much material from various documents accordingly was interwoven into what was taken from Samuel-Kings.

The Books of Samuel-Kings are written from the prophetic point of view; Chronicles, from the priestly. Great prominence is naturally given to genealogies. Events are presented with a didactic purpose and referred to moral and religious causes (I Chron. 10:13,

14; II Chron. 12:1–12; 16:7–12; 20:35–37; 24:17–25; 25:14–28; 26:16–23; ch. 33). The Chronicler believes in direct divine intervention in human affairs (II Chron. 13:13–20; 14:8–14; 20:1–30). In dealing with the history of the kings, the priestly Chronicler omits the history of Saul and the Northern Kingdom as not germane to his purpose. The death of Saul and his sons is introduced as a transition from the genealogies to David; the history of the Northern Kingdom offered no material for the development of the true worship of Jehovah at Jerusalem. The Chronicler, however, gives a fuller account than do The Books of the Kings of all those matters pertaining to the organization of public worship, religious ceremonies, the part taken by Levites and singers, and the relation of the kings of David's dynasty to the worship of Jehovah in Jerusalem. This priestly character of the book, however, does not lessen its historical value.

Ancient opinion was that Chronicles was written by Ezra. This tradition cannot be proved, and it is not vital that it should be. Chronicles, with Ezra-Nehemiah, forms a historical unit which embraces the history of the Kingdom of Judah, beginning with Adam and concluding with the re-establishment of the kingdom by Ezra and Nehemiah. II Chron. 36:22, 23 agrees almost verbatim with Ezra 1:1–3, and this has been adduced as evidence that originally Ezra-Nehemiah followed Chronicles. Some critics maintain that Ezra and Nehemiah are a compilation made by an author identical with the Chronicler; linguistically Chronicles and Ezra-Nehemiah belong to the late period of Biblical Hebrew, and they are similar in diction and ideas. As an explanation of the present Hebrew order of the books, it has been suggested that Ezra-Nehemiah was accepted as canonical before Chronicles, because the latter duplicated much of Samuel-Kings; when Chronicles found a place in the canon, the original and logical order of the books was not restored. Others have supposed that the opening of Ezra-Nehemiah was repeated at the end of Chronicles to ensure the connection of the former with the latter. It may also be that II Chron. 36:22, 23 was added to the book to avoid closing it with the desolation of Jerusalem; similarly, Kings ends with a gleam of hope (II Kings 25:27–30). The order—Chronicles, Ezra, Nehemiah—of the English Bible goes back to the LXX.

It is evident that the Chronicler was acquainted with the Pentateuch. On account of the connections with Ezra-Nehemiah, c. 450–425 B.C. has been accepted by some as the date of the Chronicler. As a *terminus a quo* c. 432 B.C., Nehemiah's 2d visit to Jerusalem, has been suggested (Neh. 13:6). Eliashib (ch. 12:10) was a contemporary of Nehemiah (chs. 3:1; 13:4, 7, 28). It is more difficult to find a *terminus ad quem*. Jaddua (ch. 12:11), the 5th generation from Jeshua, was high priest at Jerusalem in 332 B.C. Although there are difficulties in the Hebrew text in v. 21, I Chron. 3:19–24 is generally interpreted as citing 6 generations after Zerubbabel; reckoning 25 years to a generation, this would bring Anani (v. 24) to c. 400 B.C., or, calculating a generation at 30 years, the date would come to c. 350 B.C. On the other hand, the LXX, which is followed in this passage by the Vulgate, places Anani in the 11th generation; this rendering would give c. 250 B.C. as the *terminus ad quem*. In view of the Hebrew text of this passage, the Chronicler can be dated c. 400 B.C.

Chronicles stands among the Hagiographa. In the printed editions of the Hebrew Bible, it follows Ezra-Nehemiah, and is the last book in the canon. This position it probably occupied at the time of Christ, for Zechariah is cited as the last [named] prophet who suffered a violent death (Matt. 23:35; Luke 11:51; cf. II Chron. 24:20–22).

Chro·nol'o·gy. The nations of antiquity did not have a uniform system of chronology; nor did they entertain the same notions and feel the same need of an exact and unvarying chronological method as does the modern world. The Assyrians and Babylonians appear to have been confident of their ability to date events of remote antiquity; but, so far as known, they did not have an era serving as a fixed standard from which to reckon all occurrences, but named each year after a public official (eponym or limmu). A list of these annual eponyms was kept. When an event had been dated by the eponymy in which it happened, its remoteness was readily ascertained by counting on the list, or canon, the number of eponyms that had intervened. In Babylonia, Assyria, Palestine, and Egypt, documents were frequently dated by the regnal year of the reigning monarch. Unfortunately the scribes did not always reckon uniformly; but under the same king some regarded the accession year as the 1st regnal year, while others considered the civil twelvemonth which followed the accession as the 1st year of the reign. Furthermore, a son was not infrequently associated with his father on the throne, and some scribes treated the 1st year of association with the father, and others the 1st year of sole reign, as the 1st regnal year. The deficient sense of chronology, estimated by modern conceptions, is seen in the fact that Josephus determines the duration of the Kingdom of Israel by simply adding together the number of years that each king ruled, regardless of the fact that the reigns regularly overlapped one year, since the death of a king and the accession of his successor fell in the same year, and this year was apt to be reckoned to both reigns. Pursuing this method, he states that the Kingdom of Israel lasted 240 years, 7 months, and 7 days (Jos. *Antiq.* ix. 14, 1); yet by other calculations, which he makes on the basis of the reigns of the kings of Judah, he implies that the period was 263 years (cf. Jos. *Antiq.* x. 8, 5; viii. 7, 8; x. 9, 7). The same lack of a nice chronological sense appears in the fact that Josephus estimates the number of years that elapsed from the Exodus to the founding of the Temple at 592 (Jos. *Antiq.* viii. 3, 1), at other times at 612 (Jos. *Antiq.* xx. 10; *Apion* ii. 2), the Hebrew writer at 480 (I Kings 6:1), and Paul apparently at about 574 (Acts 13:18–21 and I Kings 2:11; 6:1). These diverse statements appear contradictory to the modern reader who lacks a historical sense and cannot divest himself of modern chronological conceptions; but they are accurate in the sense in which they were intended, and in which they were understood.

The era, as it is used in modern chronology, came into use at a comparatively late date. The Exodus served the Hebrews for a brief time as a point from which to reckon (Ex. 16:1; Num. 9:1; 10:11; 33:38). The Romans dated all documents by the name of the consul in office, and later they added the regnal year of the emperor. Their historians began to date from the foundation of the city of Rome (A. U. C.), but the custom did not arise until some centuries after the event. Varro's date for the founding of the city, 753 B.C., is generally accepted as the commencement of this era. The Greeks reckoned by periods of 4 years called Olympiads, the 1st of which began in 776 B.C. The Syrians used the Seleucidan era, beginning with October 312 B.C. It was used by the Jews in Maccabaean times (I Macc. 1:10). The era of Diocletian, known also as that of

the Martyrs, begins A.D. 284. The Mohammedans date from the Hegira, or flight of Mohammed from Mecca, A.D. 622. The Jews since the 15th century A.D. have used a mundane era, dating from creation, which they place in the year 3760–3761 B.C. The Christian era is computed from the birth of Christ. At the beginning of the 6th century, the Roman abbot Dionysius in his Easter tables counted from the incarnation of the Lord; he erred in his calculation of the date of Christ's birth, but the year which he fixed upon, A. U. C. 754, has been accepted as the commencement of the Christian era. The actual year of the Nativity is supposed to be 4 B.C. The Christian era began, not with no year, but with a 1st year. Events which occurred within the civil year which included Christ's birth are dated in the 1st year.

Dates were placed in the margin of A.V. in 1701. They represent the chronological scheme of Ussher, archbishop of Armagh, which he published in his *Annales Veteris et Novi Testamenti* in 1650–1654. His work was careful and scholarly, and served a useful purpose for 2½ centuries. It gives only one of several possible arrangements. It is based in crucial points on Ussher's private interpretation of disputed passages, in some of which he clearly erred, as has been proved in recent years. His system was worked out from the standpoint of modern chronological conceptions, and fails to do justice to the different notions which prevailed in antiquity. It was constructed without the invaluable aid of data which have been brought to light by modern research. But although Ussher's system is obsolete, it cannot as yet be superseded by a complete and final scheme. A few dates are fixed, and the chronology of certain periods is established. Other dates are still under investigation or are awaiting further definite evidence. Much is tentative and is useful only for observing the sequence of events.

I. FROM THE CREATION OF THE WORLD TO THE BIRTH OF ABRAHAM.

The data are furnished by the Hebrew records in Gen., chs. 5; 7:11; 11:10–26. There are several possible methods of interpreting them, among which may be mentioned:

I. 1. *The genealogy was constructed* by the ancient writers in the same manner as it would be framed by people of the present day.

Adam,	having lived	130	years,	begat	
Seth,	who, "	"	105	"	"
Enosh,	" "	"	90	"	"
Kenan,	" "	"	70	"	"
Mahalalel,	" "	"	65	"	"
Jared,	" "	"	162	"	"
Enoch,	" "	"	65	"	"
Methuselah,	" "	"	187	"	"
Lamech,	" "	"	182	"	"
Noah, in whose			600th	year the Flood	
From the Creation to				came.	
the Flood,			1,656	years.	

Noah,	having lived	500	years,	begat	
Shem,	who, "	"	100	"	"
Arpachshad,	" "	"	35	"	"
Shelah,	" "	"	30	"	"
Eber,	" "	"	34	"	"
Peleg,	" "	"	30	"	"
Reu,	" "	"	32	"	"
Serug,	" "	"	30	"	"
Nahor,	" "	"	29	"	"
Terah,	" "	"	70	"	"
Abram, Nahor, and					
Haran,			890	years after birth of Noah.	
			290	" after the Flood.	
			1,946	" after the Creation.	

The 2 years of Gen. 11:10 are added to this result by Ussher, according to whom Terah begat his sons 1,948 years after the Creation. On this interpretation Shem was not the eldest son of Noah, as is generally believed, born when his father was 500 years old (Gen. 5:32). But ch. 11:10 has another explanation. Interpreting the data of the genealogy as before, Noah, having lived 500 years, begat Shem, who, having lived 100 years, begat Arpachshad. Arpachshad was thus born in the 601st year of Noah's life. He was born in the 2d civil year after the Flood year, counting it the 1st. The Flood year was the 600th of Noah's life (ch. 7:6, 11), the flood itself prevailing during 5 months of that year. Noah lived 350 full years after the Flood year, counting it the 1st (ch. 9:28). In the Flood year he was 599 years and some months old. As he lived 350 years longer, he died when he was 949 years and some months old, in the 950th year of his age (ch. 9:29). There are discrepancies between the Hebrew and the LXX, and the Samaritan Pentateuch. The Hebrew (Masoretic) text is evidently the most accurate one with respect to dates. The LXX, probably on the ground that the long-lived antediluvians were not likely to beget sons while they were less than 150 years old, took the liberty of adding a century to the Hebrew date, where it was said that they had done so, as in the case of Adam, Seth, Enosh, Kenan, Mahalalel, and Enoch. The minor variations are that to Lamech the LXX assigns 188+565=753 years; Lucian divides Methuselah's life into 167+802=969 years. The Samaritan Pentateuch, on the contrary, apparently on the ground that an antediluvian was not likely to have lived 150 years without begetting his 1st son, finding by the Hebrew text that Jared did so at 162, Methuselah at 187 and Lamech at 182, cut the figures down to 62, 67, and 53. This reduced the total length of their lives, whereas the LXX had carefully balanced its additions to the 1st part of the lives by corresponding subtractions from the later part, so that the total length of each life was the same in that version as in the Hebrew original, except in the case of Lamech. Similarly, in the case of the postdiluvian patriarchs who preceded Abraham, the LXX hesitates to allow them to beget a son until they are 100 years old. It adds 100 years to the ages at which sons were begotten by Arpachshad, Shelah, Eber, Peleg, Reu, and Serug, and 50 to the time of life when Nahor begat Terah. After Arpachshad it inserts Kenan, and states that he begat Shelah when 130 years old. The Samaritan Pentateuch allows them to beget a son after 50; and in the case of Arpachshad, Shelah, Eber, Peleg, Reu, and Serug adds 100 years to the age assigned by the Hebrew text, and 50 years in the case of Nahor.

I. 2. *Or many links are omitted.* As in other Hebrew genealogies, each member is said to have begotten his successor, although the latter may be a grandson or even remoter descendant; as in the royal genealogy given in Matthew, the 3 kings, Ahaziah, Joash, and Amaziah are passed over and Joram is said to have begotten Uzziah, his great-great-grandson (Matt. 1:8, R.V.; cf. the use of the verb "bare" in Gen. 46:15, 18). Only prominent members of the line are enumerated, or else, as an aid to memory, a definite number is chosen: in Matthew groups of twice 7, in Genesis groups of 10.

Adam at the age of 130 begat
Seth, who at the age of 105 begat
 Ancestor of Enosh or Enosh himself.
Enosh at the age of 90 begat
 Ancestor of Kenan or Kenan himself.
Kenan at the age of 70 begat

Ancestor of Mahalalel or Mahalalel himself.

According to this theory, the Hebrew records afford no basis for a chronology from Adam to Abraham. It assumes furthermore that the age assigned to the patriarchs is that of their natural life. Adam lived 930 years. This extraordinary longevity is accounted for by the fact that sin, which has a physical effect and works disease and death, had only begun its malign influence on the race, and had not reached its normal hereditary power. The balance between man in a sinless state and man in the condition of sinner had not been attained.

I. 3. *Or the names denote an individual* and his family spoken of collectively; as Israel denotes a patriarch and his descendants, Kain is used for the Kenites (Num. 24:22, R.V.), David for the royal house (I Kings 12:16). Sometimes the family takes its name from its progenitor or later leading member of the tribe; sometimes the name of the tribe or of the country it inhabits is applied to its chief representative, as today men are constantly addressed by their family name, and nobles are called by the name of their duchy or county. In Gen., ch. 10, the names in the genealogy are sometimes individuals, sometimes peoples, sometimes cities, sometimes countries; and in the pedigree of Abraham given in this chapter Arpachshad, whom Shem begat (Gen. 10:22), is apparently a country whose inhabitants were descendants of Shem, and this country produced Shelah (cf. bear, beget, first-born in Gen. 25:2, 3, 12–16). The longevity is the period during which the family had prominence and leadership.

Adam.	1
Family of Seth originated when Adam was 130 years old (ch. 5:3).	130
Adam and his direct line were at the head of affairs for 930 years (v. 5), when they were superseded by	
Family of Seth.	930
In Seth, 105 years after it attained headship, the family of Enosh took its rise (v. 6).	1,035
After being at the head of affairs for 912 years (v. 8), Seth was succeeded by	
Family of Enosh.	1,842
Ninety years after Enosh attained to headship there sprang from it the family of Kenan (v. 9).	1,932
After Enosh had held the leadership 815 years longer (v. 10), Enosh gave place to	
Family of Kenan.	2,747
Family of Lamech.	6,848
Family which took its name from Noah originated.	7,030
Lamech is succeeded by	
Family of Noah.	7,625
Shem, Ham, and Japheth born about	8,125
Flood.	8,225
Arpachshad originates.	8,227
The race of Shem, as distinct from the other descendants of Noah, become pre-eminent.	8,575

Hence the years from the creation of Adam to the flood were 8,225, and from Adam to the death of Terah may have been 11,571. This outline exhibits one application of the theory; but it must be remembered that at different points in the genealogy various interpretations are possible.

II. From the Birth of Abraham to the Exodus.

How long after the Flood Abraham was born cannot be determined from the Biblical record, not even by the 1st method enumerated above and employed by Ussher in interpreting the genealogy from Adam to Abraham, for the age of Terah at the birth of Abraham is not so stated in Gen. 11:26, 32 as to be unquestionable; see ABRAHAM. According to Ussher, Abraham's birth occurred in 1996 B.C. The period from the birth of Abraham to the descent into Egypt can be measured:

Birth of Abraham to—
" " Isaac 100 years (Gen. 21:5).
" " Jacob 60 years (Gen. 25:26).
Jacob's age at descent into Egypt 130 years (Gen. 47:9).
　　　　　　　　　　　　　　290 years.

The sojourn of the Children of Israel in Egypt was 430 years (Ex. 12:40, 41). But from what initial date is this period reckoned? From the covenant with Abraham (Gen., ch. 15), when he was between 75 and 85 years old (chs. 12:4; 16:3), as Ussher and many others believe, or from the descent into Egypt? Probably from the latter event. See EGYPT, III. 3; 8.

III. FROM THE EXODUS TO THE FOUNDATION OF SOLOMON'S TEMPLE.

This interval was doubtless reckoned as 12 periods of 40 years each (I Kings 6:1), of which the 1st covered the sojourn in the wilderness (Ex. 16:35; Num. 14:33), 6 certainly, and probably 8, were allowed for the time of the Judges proper, the oppression and rest being frequently included in the statement (Judg. 3:11, 30—double period; 5:31; 8:28; 13:1; and probably 10:1–4 and 12:7–14), the high priesthood of Eli counted as one (I Sam. 4:18), Saul's reign probably as another (Acts 13:21), while David's reign made the 12th (I Kings 2:11). But the 40 years are a round number, and not always exact. The periods enumerated were sometimes in whole or in part contemporary; see JUDGE. Jephthah speaks of the Israelites' having occupied the country about Heshbon for 300 years (Judg. 11:26), some 7 periods of 40 years. Josephus, reckoning in a different manner, estimates the time from the Exodus to the Temple at 592 or 612 years (Jos. *Antiq.* viii. 3, 1; xx. 10). For the difference of 20 years, cf. I Kings 6:38 to 7:1, 7+13 years. Paul, according to the received text (used by A.V.), refers to the period of the Judges as lasting about 450 years (Acts 13:19, 20); the text of R.V., which follows the better MSS., apparently reckons from the promise to Abraham up to the Judges. As already pointed out, these diverse results do not contradict each other, although they do not agree. The variations are due to the different methods employed in calculating. The sum was not supposed to represent the exact duration of the period, as would a modern chronological statement. The exact length of the period cannot be determined until new data come to light.

IV. FROM THE FOUNDATION OF THE TEMPLE TO THE EXILE AND RETURN.

The Temple was founded in the 4th year of Solomon (I Kings 6:1). Solomon reigned 40 years, and was succeeded by Rehoboam, on whose ascension to the throne ten tribes revolted. The data obtained from both Hebrew and other sources may be arranged according to the following scheme. In general it may be remarked that this scheme recognizes the existence of coreigns. They were common in the neighboring monarchies, and are proved in individual cases for the Hebrews. David, when incapacitated by age for government, and in danger of having his throne usurped, had Solomon made king (I Kings, ch. 1). When Uzziah was compelled to seclude himself because he had become a leper, Jotham assumed the duties of royalty (II Kings 15:5). The scheme further recognizes that among the Hebrews, as among neighboring nations, no fixed rule existed as to whether the accession year of a king or the civil year which followed should be counted as the first regnal year. Some recorders followed one method, others another. Examples might be multiplied; one will suffice. In Ptolemy's canon 604, the civil year following accession, is treated as the 1st regnal year of Nebuchadnezzar. So it is by Josephus, Daniel, and Babylonian scribes, and in the record whence Jer. 52:28–30 is taken. But Jeremiah himself and other Palestinian writers of the day numbered the accession year of Nebuchadnezzar his 1st year, synchronizing Jehoiakim 4 with Nebuchadnezzar 1, and Zedekiah 11 with Nebuchadnezzar 19. It will be observed, finally, that 2 events, the slaughter of Ahaziah of Judah and Jehoram of Israel by Jehu and the fall of Samaria, divide the history of the divided monarchy into 3 periods, each chronologically complete in itself. The dates of these 2 events are established. The chronology, therefore, of each of these periods must be settled by itself. Difficulties which arise in matters of adjustment affect only their own period, not the others.

This scheme is not offered as final in every particular, but it can be used as a working basis for the dates of the kings of Israel and Judah. Many of these dates must be considered merely as approximate. Slightly different arrangements of the data are possible at several points, but they do not affect the chronology as a whole. It would be very desirable to have a scheme consistent in all details, but with our present knowledge that is impossible. The unqualified figures in parentheses after a king's name denote the length of his reign in years.

JUDAH, OR SOUTHERN KINGDOM				ISRAEL, OR NORTHERN KINGDOM, AND OTHER NATIONS		
Reference	Ruler and Events	Year of Reign	Date B.C.	Year of Reign	Ruler and Events	Reference
I Kings 14:21	**Rehoboam** (17) 931–915	1	931*	1	**Jeroboam** (22) 931–910	I Kings 14:20
		2		2		
II Chron. 11:17	Three years' godliness	3		3		
		4		4		
I Kings 14:25	Shishak's invasion	5		5		
		6		6		
		17	915	17		
I Kings 15:1,2 II Chron. 13:1,2	**Abijam** (3) 915–912	1		18		
		2		19		

*The exact date of the death of Solomon is unknown. According to different systems of chronology this event is variously dated: 945, 936, 935, 932, 931, 930, 926, 925. With our present knowledge we cannot be positive, and the above chronological scheme could be modified in various places.

IV. From the Foundation of the Temple to the Exile and Return — *Continued*

JUDAH, OR SOUTHERN KINGDOM					ISRAEL, OR NORTHERN KINGDOM, AND OTHER NATIONS		
Reference	Ruler and Events	Year of Reign	Date B.C.	Year of Reign	Ruler and Events	Reference
I Kings 15:9,10	**Asa** (41) 912–871; ascends throne	1	912	20		
	1st regnal yr.	1		21		
		2	910	1 [22]	**Nadab** (2) 910–909	I Kings 15:25
II Chron. 14:1	Land quiet 10 yrs.	3		2 [1]	**Baasha** (24) 909–886	I Kings 15:28–33
		4		2		
		10		8		
		11		9		
II Chron. 14:9–15	War with Zerah between yrs. 11 and 14	12		10		
		13		11		
		14		12		
II Chron. 15:10	Reformation	15		13		
II Chron. 15:19 } †	Buys aid of Ben-hadad against Baasha	16		14		
II Chron. 16:1,2 }		25		23		
		26	886	1 [24]	**Elah** (2) 886–885	I Kings 16:8
		27		2 / 1	**Zimri** (7 days)	I Kings 16:10,15
		28		2	**Omri** (12) 885–874	I Kings 16:15,16
		29		3		
		30		4		
		31		5	Civil war between Omri and Tibni. Omri prevails and reigns with undisputed authority	I Kings 16:22,23
		36	876	10		
LXX, I Kings 16:28a	Jehoshaphat associated		875	11		
		2 38	874	12 [1]	**Ahab** (22) 874–852	{ I Kings 16:29; Heb. text, 38th yr of Asa; LXX, 2d yr. of Jehoshaphat
II Chron. 16:12	Asa diseased	3 39		2		
		4 40		3		
I Kings 22:41,42	**Jehoshaphat** (25) 875–850	5 41		4		
	1st yr. of sole reign	1	870	5		
		2		6		
II Kings 8:16–26 } II Chron. 21:6; } 22:1,2 }	Married his first-born, Jehoram, to daughter of Ahab	3		7		
		4		8		
		5		9		
		15		19		
		16		20		
					Ahab, allied with Damascus, Arabs, and others, meets Shalmaneser at Karkar, (854) 853; battle indecisive	
	Jehoram (Joram) associated	17		1 [21]	**Ahaziah** (2) 852–850	I Kings 22:51
		2 18		2 [22]	**Jehoram (Joram)** (12) 850–842, perhaps associated with the government in some capacity before 850	II Kings 1:17; 3:1
		3 19		2	War with Moab	II Kings 3:4,5
		4 20		3		
		5 21	850	4		
					Shalmaneser at war with Damascus	
II Kings 8:16,17	**Jehoram** sole king (8) 850–843	1		5		
		4		8	Ben-hadad besets Samaria	II Kings 6:24
		5		9		
II Chron. 21:18,19	Sorely diseased, hence	6		10	Ben-hadad murdered and succeeded by Hazael between 845–843	
II Kings 9:29	Ahaziah made regent	7		11		

†The dates 35th and 36th yr. of the reign of Asa given in these vs. in the Heb. text were explained by the older com mentators as reckoned from the commencement of the Kingdom of Judah. The numbers are then correct. Modern interpreters generally regard the Heb. text as corrupt, and read 15 or 25 and 16 or 26 for 35 and 36 respectively. They are doubtless right in doing so, for the text of Chronicles has not been transmitted so carefully as it should have been, and the phrase "year of Asa," or other king, always refers to his regnal yr., and Baasha died in the 26th yr. of Asa (I Kings 16:8–10). The 15th and 16th yrs. of Asa correspond respectively to the 35th and 36th yrs. of the division of the kingdom.

105

IV. From the Foundation of the Temple to the Exile and Return — *Continued*

JUDAH, OR SOUTHERN KINGDOM				ISRAEL, OR NORTHERN KINGDOM, AND OTHER NATIONS		
Reference	Ruler and Events	Year of Reign	Date B.C.	Year of Reign	Ruler and Events	Reference
II Kings 8:25,26 II Chron. 22:1	Ahaziah, king (1)	8	842	12	Jehoram slain by Jehu Jehu seizes the throne (28) 842–814 Jehu and Hazael pay tribute to Shalmaneser	
II Kings 11:1–3	Slain by Jehu Joash (Jehoash), sole surviving heir and legitimate king In concealment for 6 yrs. from Athaliah, who usurped the power (842–836)			1 2 3 4 5 6 7	Shalmaneser at war with Hazael	
II Kings 11:4; 12:1	Joash, king (40) 836–797 Athaliah slain		836		On account of Jehu's increasing age and incapacity for war,	
				1 2	Jehoahaz associated	Jos. *Antiq.* ix.8,5, and II Kings 13:10, correcting v.1 (total 17)
II Kings 12:6 II Kings 12:17	Renewed attempt to repair Temple Hazael against Gath and Jerusalem. When he departs, he leaves		814	3 (28)	Hazael against Israel Jehoahaz alone 814–800 Hazael continues to oppress Israel all the days of Jehoahaz	II Kings 10:32 II Kings 10:36 II Kings 13:3,22
II Chron. 24:25	Joash sorely diseased	37	800	1 17	Jehoash (Joash) (16) 800–785	II Kings 13:10
II Kings 14:1	Amaziah undertakes government; 79?–782?; but (29) 799–771, total	1 2	799	2 3	[Bin-addu]-mari, king of Damascus, besieged by Ramman-nirari	
	Joash slain and Amaziah sole king	(40) 3	797	4 15	Moabites invade Israel Jehoash victorious over Ben-hadad	II Kings 13:20 II Kings 13:25
II Kings 14:21	Uzziah or Azariah (52) c. 785–c. 734, total	15 16 17	785 784	16 1 2	Jeroboam II (41) 785–745 1st regnal yr.	II Kings 14:23
II Kings 14:19	Conspiracy against Amaziah (782?)	18	782	3		
II Kings 14:21	Uzziah or Azariah. Actual reign c. 782 ? -c. 751		782 781	4		
II Kings 14:17 II Chron. 25:25 II Kings 14:19 II Chron. 25:27, 28	Amaziah survives Jehoash 15 yrs. Amaziah slain (29) and Uzziah supreme		771	14		Jos. *Antiq.* ix.10,3
II Kings 14:22	Builds Elath after death of Amaziah			15		
II Kings 15:1	In special sense "reigns"		758	27 28		
II Kings 15:5 II Kings 15:32,33	Becomes leprous and Jotham conducts the government (16) 751–736		751	34 39 40 41	Tiglath-pileser III, 746/5–728/7, king of Assyria	
		38 39 39	745		Zechariah (6 mo.) Shallum (1 mo.) Menahem ascends (10) 744–735 1st regnal yr.	II Kings 15:8 II Kings 15:13 II Kings 15:17
II Kings 17:1	Ahaz associated		742 738	1 2 3 8 9	Menahem pays tribute to Pul	II Kings 15:19
II Kings 16:1,2	Ahaz (16) 736–721	(50)	736 735	10 1 2	Pekahiah (2) 735–734	II Kings 15:23

IV. From the Foundation of the Temple to the Exile and Return — *Continued*

JUDAH, OR SOUTHERN KINGDOM				ISRAEL, OR NORTHERN KINGDOM, AND OTHER NATIONS		
Reference	Ruler and Events	Year of Reign	Date B.C.	Year of Reign	Ruler and Events	Reference
	Uzziah dies*	(52)	734	1	**Pekah** (20) 734–730	II Kings 15:27†
				2	Receives tribute from Ahaz	
			733	3	Tiglath-pileser against Damascus	
			732		Fall of Damascus. Tiglath-pileser captures Gaza	
II Kings 15:30 / II Kings 17:1	20th yr. of Jotham / 12th yr. of Ahaz		730	1	**Hoshea** (9) 730–722	II Kings 15:30 / II Kings 17:1
				2		
II Kings 18:1,2 / Jos. *Antiq.* ix.13,1	**Hezekiah** ascends / 1st regnal yr.	1		3		
				4	**Shalmaneser V,** 728/7–722, king of Assyria	
		2		5		
		3		6		
		4		7	Hoshea seeks an alliance with Sib'e (So) of Egypt	II Kings 17:4
		5		8		
II Kings 18:10	Ahaz dies	6	722–1	9	**Fall of Samaria‡**	
II Kings 18:9 / Jos. *Antiq.* ix.14,1	Hezekiah sole king (29) 721–693	7 (1)	721		**Sargon,** 722–705	
			720		Defeats Sib'e (So) of Egypt at Raphia	
		13	715		Assyrian troops in Samaria and Arabia. Tribute from Egypt	
II Kings 18:13 / II Chron. 32:1–8 / Isa. 36:1	Sennacherib invades Judah	14	714		Philistia in revolt against Assyria. Judah, Moab, and Ammon in coalition	
II Kings 20:1–6 / Isa. 38:1–8	Hezekiah sick					
			713			
II Kings 20:12 / Isa. 39:1	Receives embassy from Merodach-baladan about this date		712		Judah tributary to Assyria. Merodach-baladan incites neighboring nations against Assyria	
Isa. 20:1	Siege of Ashdod		712		Sargon besieges Ashdod	
			710		Sargon dethrones Merodach-baladan	
			705		**Sennacherib,** 705–681	
II Kings 18:14 *seq.*	Besieged by Sennacherib		701		Against Hezekiah and Jerusalem	
					Defeat of Egyptians at Eltekeh	
					Siege of Lachish and Jerusalem	
					Hezekiah pays tribute	II Kings 18:14–16
					Discomfiture of Assyrians	II Kings 19:35
	Hezekiah dies		693			
II Kings 21:1 / II Kings 19:37	**Manasseh** (55) 693–639		681		**Esarhaddon,** 681–669	
					Receives tribute from Manasseh of Judah	
					Invasion of Egypt (675–671)	
					Fresh colonists settled in Samaria by Esarhaddon and Ashurbanipal	Ezra 4:2,10
			669		**Ashurbanipal,** 669–626	
					Invasion of Egypt (667–663)	
II Chron. 33:11	Carried in chains to Babylon by the Assyrians, probably at this time				Ashurbanipal captures Babylon and dethrones (652)	
					Shamash-shum-ukin, his brother, who had incited peoples from	
		55	639		Elam to the Mediterranean to revolt against Assyria	
					Receives tribute from Manasseh of Judah	

*"In the year that king Uzziah died" (Isa. 6:1) is often given as about 740 B.C.

†Ussher and the older chronologists assumed that anarchy prevailed for several yrs. between the death of Pekah and the accession of Hoshea. Both the Hebrew and the Assyrian records, however, clearly indicate that no interregnum occurred, but that Hoshea slew Pekah and succeeded him on the throne. For the 20 yrs. assigned to the reign of Pekah, see Pekah.

‡Dated by many authorities in the early months of 721 B.C.

IV. From the Foundation of the Temple to the Exile and Return — *Continued*

JUDAH, OR SOUTHERN KINGDOM					ISRAEL, OR NORTHERN KINGDOM, AND OTHER NATIONS	
Reference	Ruler and Events	Year of Reign	Date B.C.	Year of Reign	Ruler and Events	Reference
II Kings 21:19	**Amon** (2) 639–638					
II Kings 22:1	**Josiah** (31) 638–608	1	638			
II Chron. 34:3	Seeks Jehovah	8	631			
II Chron. 34:3	Begins to purge nation	12	627			
Jer. 1:1,2	Jeremiah begins	13	626		**Nabopolassar,** 626–605 Chaldeans independent of Assyria	
Jer. 25:1,3	13th Josiah to 4th Jehoiakim inclusive= 23 yrs.	18	621			
II Kings 22:23	Reformation by Josiah		621			
II Chron. 34:8						
			609		Necho, king of Egypt, 609–593	
II Kings 23:29	Battle of Megiddo; death of Josiah					
II Kings 23:31	**Jehoahaz** king 3 mos.	31	608			
II Kings 23:36	**Jehoiakim** (11) 608–597	1				
Jer. 25:1; 46:2	He and Necho subjugated	4	605		Battle of Carchemish (605)	
Jos. *Antiq.* x.6,1	by Nebuchadnezzar				**Nebuchadnezzar (Nebuchadrezzar)** 605–562	
Jer. 36:9	9th mo., public fast Jeremiah's roll burned	5	604			
Jos. *Antiq.* x.10,3	Two yrs. *after* the defeat of Egypt					
Dan. 2:1	Nebuchadnezzar dreams	6	603		3d or 2d yr.	
II Kings 24:1	Having paid tribute to Neb. 3 yrs., rebels	7	602		4th yr.	
	Jehoiakim dead before surrender of Jerusalem	11				
II Kings 24:8–12	**Jehoiachin,** 3 mos.		597		8th or 7th yr.	
II Chron. 36:10	Goes captive to Babylon					
Jer. 52:28	toward close of yr.					
II Kings 24:18	**Zedekiah** (11) 597–586	1	597			
Jer. 51:59	Visits Babylon	4	594			
					Psamtik (Psammetichus) II, king of Egypt, 593–588	
II Kings 25:1	Jerusalem besieged	9	c.588		**Apries (Hophra),** king of Egypt, 588–569	
Jer. 32:1		10	587		18th (or 17th) of Nebuchadnezzar	
II Kings 25:8,9	Temple burned in 5th mo.	11	586		19th (or 18th) of Nebuchadnezzar Zedekiah captured, taken to camp of Nebuchadnezzar at Riblah, where he was blinded; deported to Babylon Ezek. 12:13	
Jer. 52:12–16,29						
Jos. *Antiq.* x.8,5						
Jos. *Apion* i.21						
Ezek. 33:21	News reaches Ezekiel					
Jer. 44:30	Hophra, i.e., Apries, mentioned					
Jer. 52:30	Captives carried to Babylon 5th yr. *after* destruction of Jerusalem=23d Neb.		582–1		23d yr. of Nebuchadnezzar	
Jos. *Antiq.* x.9,7						
			568		Nebuchadnezzar invades Egypt in 37th yr. of his reign	
			562		**Evil-merodach (Amel-Marduk)**	
II Kings 25:27	37th yr. of Jehoiachin's captivity		561			
			539		**Cyrus** takes Babylon	
II Chron. 36:22,23	Rebuilding of Temple authorized		538		1st yr.	
Ezra 3:8	Rebuilding begun in 2d mo., having remained waste for 50 yrs.—i.e., 49 yrs. and 9 mos.		537		2d yr.	
Jos. *Apion* i.21						

V. From the Return from Exile to the Birth of Christ.

Judah, or Southern Kingdom	Date B.C.	Israel, or Northern Kingdom, and Other Nations
Ruler and Events		**Ruler and Events**
Judea under Persian rule	539	**Cyrus** on throne of Babylon
Ezra 1:8, 11; 5:14–16 Sheshbazzar* (Zerubbabel) leads back 42,360 Jews to Jerusalem	538	
Foundation of the Temple laid, but the work is soon interrupted	537	
	529	**Cambyses,** 529–522
Decree of Darius and return of Zerubbabel(?); cf. I Esdras 3:13 to 5:3	521	**Darius Hystaspis,** 521–486
Haggai and Zechariah exhort the people to resume work on the Temple	520	
Temple completed in 12th mo. of 6th yr., in the early spring	515	
	490	Persians defeated by the Greeks at Marathon
	486	**Xerxes I (Ahasuerus),** 486–465
	480	Persians victorious at Thermopylae but defeated at Salamis
	479	Persians defeated at Plataea
	465	**Artaxerxes (I) Longimanus,** 465–424
Ezra leads back 1,755 Jews to Jerusalem	458	
Nehemiah hears evil tidings	445	
Nehemiah sent by Artaxerxes to Jerusalem in mo. Nisan	444	
Repair of city wall begun on 3d day of 5th mo., and completed on 25th of Elul, the 6th mo.		
Reading of law by Ezra	444	
Nehemiah recalled to the Persian court, but returns to Jerusalem	433–2	
	424	**Darius (II) Nothus,** 423–404
		Artaxerxes (II) Mnemon, 404–359/8
	359	**Artaxerxes (III) Ochus,** 359/8–338/7
	338	**Arses,** 338/7–336/5
	336	**Darius (III) Codomannus,** 336/5–331
		Alexander ascends throne of Macedon
	334	Alexander victorious at the Granicus
	333	Alexander victorious at Issus
Alexander the Great visits Jerusalem, and is met by the high priest Jaddua	332	
	331	Foundations of Alexandria
		Alexander defeats Darius at Arbela
	330	Darius assassinated
	323	Death of Alexander
Judea annexed to Egypt by Ptolemy Soter	320	
	312	**Seleucus Nicator** (312–280) founds the kingdom of the Seleucidae
	223	**Antiochus the Great,** 223–187
After the battle of Raphia, 217 b.c., Ptolemy Philopator sacrifices at Jerusalem. Being prevented from entering the Holy of Holies he attempts to destroy the Jews in Alexandria		
Antiochus takes Jerusalem	203	
Scopas recovers Judea for Egypt	201–0	
Judea annexed to Syria, being finally wrested by Antiochus from Egypt at the battle of Paneas (Panion)	200	
	189	Defeated by the Romans at Magnesia (probably January, 189)**
	175	**Antiochus Epiphanes,** 175–163
The high priest Onias removed, and Jason, of the Grecian party, put in office	174	
Antiochus takes Jerusalem, massacres citizens, and defiles the Temple	170	
Antiochus orders an idolatrous altar to be erected on the Temple altar and heathen sacrifices to be offered	168	
The priest Mattathias raises the standard of revolt		
The Maccabees. Judas placed in command	166	
Defeats Gorgias	165	
Defeats Lysias, and on 25th Chislev rededicates the Temple	165	
	163	Death of Antiochus and accession of **Antiochus Eupator,** 163–162
	162	**Demetrius I,** 162–150
Falls in battle, and is succeeded by Jonathan	160	
	150	**Alexander Balas,** 150–145
	145	**Antiochus VI,** ascends the throne with the aid of his general, Tryphon. Demetrius II his rival
Jonathan Maccabaeus murdered by Tryphon, and succeeded by Simon	143	

*According to a widely held view, Sheshbazzar is identical with Zerubbabel. Many historians, however, regard them as two different persons; in that case Zerubbabel, in accordance with a decree of Darius, returned to Jerusalem in 521.

**190 b.c., however, is the date generally given for the battle of Magnesia.

V. From the Return from Exile to the Birth of Christ.—*Continued*

JUDAH, OR SOUTHERN KINGDOM		ISRAEL, OR NORTHERN KINGDOM, AND OTHER NATIONS
Ruler and Events	Date B.C.	Ruler and Events
1st yr. of the freedom of Jerusalem and of Simon, high priest and captain	142	Murder of Antiochus (142/1)
	138	**Antiochus VII,** 139/8–129
Simon murdered; succeeded by John Hyrcanus	134	
Pompey takes Jerusalem	63	
C. Julius Caesar appoints Antipater procurator of Judea	47	
	44	Assassination of C. Julius Caesar
Assassination of Antipater	43	
	42	Battle of Philippi
Parthians take Jerusalem and place Antigonus, the Maccabee, on the throne. The Roman senate, however, toward the end of the yr. appoints Herod to be king of Judea	40	
Herod takes Jerusalem, slays Antigonus, the last of the Maccabaean priest-kings, and becomes king of Judea	37	
	31	{ Battle of Actium { **Augustus** becomes Roman emperor
Rebuilding of the Temple begun	19	
Birth of Jesus Christ. Close of	5	
or beginning of	4	
Death of Herod and division of the kingdom among his 3 sons, Archelaus receiving Judea		

VI. From the Death of Herod to the Destruction of Jerusalem.

The chronology of the life of Christ and of Paul is treated under the respective articles. The chronology of Paul's life hinges on the date of Festus' appointment to the procuratorship.

Ruler and Events	Date B.C.	Ruler and Events
On the death of Herod the Great his kingdom is divided among his 3 sons: Archelaus becomes king of Judea; Herod Antipas, tetrarch of Galilee and Perea; Philip, tetrarch of Ituraea and Trachonitis	4	
Deposition of Archelaus; Judea and Samaria incorporated with the province of Syria, and placed under procurators. Coponius procurator	A.D. 6	
Marcus Ambivius procurator	10	
	13	Tiberius associated with Augustus, receiving from the senate *imperium proconsulare* in all provinces
Valerius Gratus 4th procurator	14	Augustus dies Aug. 19, and **Tiberius** is emperor
Pontius Pilate procurator	26	
Jesus begins his public ministry (Luke 3:1, 23; cf. John 2:20) probably early in	27	
Death of Philip the tetrarch. His tetrarchy is annexed to Syria	33	
Pontius Pilate deposed by Vitellius, governor of Syria, and sent to Rome	36	
Herod Antipas attends passover at Jerusalem; Caligula appoints Herod Agrippa to be king of the tetrarchies of Philip and Lysanias, and sends Marullus to be procurator	37	Tiberius smothered March 16, and **Caligula** is emperor
Herod Antipas banished to Gaul, and his tetrarchy given to King Herod Agrippa	39	
Claudius makes Herod Agrippa king of Judea and Samaria	41	Caligula assassinated Jan. 24, and **Claudius** becomes emperor
Death of Herod Agrippa. Judea again placed under procurators. Cuspius Fadus procurator	44	
Tiberius Alexander, apostate Jew of Alexandria, procurator	46	
Ventidius Cumanus procurator, probably jointly with Felix	48	
Antonius Felix procurator	52	Claudius expels the Jews and sorcerers and astrologers from Rome
	54	Claudius dies of poison Oct. 13, and **Nero** becomes emperor
Porcius Festus succeeds Felix; but if the procuratorship of Felix be reckoned from A.D. 48, it is possible to date Festus' appointment in 55 or 56	59 or 60	
Albinus procurator	62	
Gessius Florus procurator (64–66)	64	Persecutions under Nero begin
Outbreak of the Jewish war	66	
	68	Nero ends his life. **Galba** and **Otho** become emperors successively and die violent deaths
	69	**Vitellius** obtains the empire and is slain **Vespasian** becomes emperor
Destruction of Jerusalem	70	

Chrys′o·lite, in A.V. **Chrys′o·lyte** [Gr. gold stone]. A magnesium, iron silicate, usually olive-green. It is disputed whether the chrysolite of Pliny and of the N.T. was a gold-colored chrysolite or a topaz. It constitutes the 7th foundation of the New Jerusalem (Rev. 21:20).

Chrys′o·prase, in A.V. **Chrys·op′ra·sus** [Gr. golden-green stone]. An apple-green chromium-colored variety of chalcedony. It constitutes the 10th foundation of the New Jerusalem (Rev. 21:20). See AGATE 1.

Chub (kŭb). See CUB.

Chun (kŭn). See BEROTHAH.

Church [Mid. Eng. *chirche*, from Anglo-Saxon *circe*, from Gr. *kyriakon*, the Lord's house]. The rendering in the N.T. of the Greek *ekklēsia*, which in the states of Greece meant the assembly of citizens summoned for legislative or other purposes (Acts 19:32, 41, assembly). The sacred writers use the word *ekklēsia* to denote an organized community acknowledging the Lord Jesus Christ as their supreme ruler, and meeting statedly, or as opportunities offered for religious worship (Matt. 16:18; 18:17; Acts 2:47, A.V.; 5:11; Eph. 5:23, 25). As followers of Jesus arose in many different cities, the plural, "churches," began to be employed, the Christian community in each separate locality being considered a church (Acts 9:31; 15:41; Rom. 16:4; I Cor. 1:17; I Thess. 2:14). Church is nowhere unequivocally used in the N.T. for the building in which any particular Christian community met. The Protestant doctrine of the Church is that the Church may exist without a visible form, because it is both invisible and visible. The invisible Church is composed of all who are really united to Christ (I Cor. 1:2; 12:12, 13, 27, 28; Col. 1:24; I Peter 2:9, 10). The visible Church consists of all who profess to be united to Christ.

The apostles occupied a peculiar position of authority (Acts 5:2; 6:6; I Cor. 12:28; Eph. 2:20; II Peter 3:2); but they were not the sole governing body: the elders or bishops also exercised rule (Acts 15:2, 4, 6, 22, 23; I Tim. 4:14; 5:17; I Peter 5:1). The officers of the local churches were elders or bishops and deacons (Acts 6:3; 14:23; 20:17; I Tim. 3:1, 8; Titus 1:5–9). The apostles sometimes appointed commissioners for special work (I Tim. 1:3; Titus 1:5).

The public worship of the church was engrafted upon the synagogue service. It consisted of preaching (Matt. 28:20; Acts 20:7; I Cor. 14:19, 26–36), reading of Scripture (James 1:22; Col. 4:16; I Thess. 5:27; cf. Acts 13:15), prayer (I Cor. 14:14–16), singing (Eph. 5:19; Col. 3:16; and cf. the hymns Eph. 5:14; I Tim. 3:16), administration of the sacraments of baptism and the Lord's Supper (Matt. 28:19; Acts 2:41; I Cor. 11:18–34), and almsgiving (I Cor. 16:1, 2). When the spiritual gift was present, there were also prophesyings and tongues.

Chu′shan-rish′a·tha′im (kū′shän-rĭsh′a-thā′-ĭm). See CUSHAN-RISHATHAIM.

Chu′zas (kū′zăs), in A.V. **Chu′za** (kū′za) [perhaps Aram. *kūzā′*, jug]. Herod the tetrarch's steward, whose wife Joanna ministered to the wants of Jesus (Luke 8:3).

Ci·li′ci·a (sĭ-lĭsh′ĭ-a). A district in the s.e. corner of Asia Minor, separated on the n. by the Taurus Mountains from Cappadocia, Lycaonia, and Isauria, and on the e. by Mount Amanus from Syria; bounded on the s. by the Mediterranean, and on the w. by Pamphylia. It was anciently divided into two portions, the western one, which was mountainous, called the Rugged, and the eastern one, which was level, the Plain Cilicia. The chief town in the latter was Tarsus, the birthplace of Paul (Acts 21:39; 22:3; 23:34). Cilicia formed part of the kingdom of Syria; and when in 148–147 B.C. Demetrius II landed on its shores and set himself up as king of Syria, the bulk of its inhabitants supported him (I Macc. 11:14; Jos. *Antiq.* xiii. 4, 3). Jews from Cilicia disputed with Stephen (Acts 6:9). The gospel reached it very early (ch. 15:23), planted apparently by Paul (ch. 9:30; Gal. 1:21). Afterward, passing through it, he confirmed the churches which had been founded (Acts 15:41). Subsequently on his voyage as a prisoner to Rome he sailed over the sea of Cilicia (ch. 27:5).

Cin′na·mon. A fragrant wood (S. of Sol. 4:14; Rev. 18:13). It was an ingredient in the sacred anointing oil used in the consecration of Aaron and his successors (Ex. 30:23). It was used in after times to perfume beds (Prov. 7:17). It is the aromatic bark of a tree, *Cinnamomum zeylanicum,* belonging to the laurel order, and cultivated in Ceylon, of which it is a native. The bark of the tree yields an oil, which is a golden-yellow color, has an agreeable smell, and is used in perfumery. The tree has been grown in Arabia.

Cin′ne·roth (sĭn′ĕ-rŏth). See CHINNERETH.

Cir′cum·ci′sion [Lat., a cutting around]. The initiatory rite into the covenant privileges of the family of God represented by Abraham and his descendants through Isaac, and the token of the covenant (Gen. 17:1–10, 21). As a rite of the religion of this people, it was instituted by God and enjoined upon Abraham, who was himself to be circumcised, as were all his male children and his male slaves, whether born in his house or bought with money. The act consists in removing the foreskin, and it was performed on the child by the father of the house or some other Israelite, and even by the mother (Ex. 4:25; I Macc. 1:60). The proper time to carry out the rite was when the boy was 8 days old, but those born before the institution of the ordinance were to be circumcised at any time of life. Abraham was circumcised when he was 99, and Ishmael when 13 (Gen. 17:11–27). The rite was observed during the bondage in Egypt, but was neglected in the wilderness. Before the entry into Canaan, however, Joshua made knives of flint and circumcised the people (Josh. 5:2–9). By this time metal was known, but there is a strong conservatism in religion, and antique arrangements tend to remain after the necessity for them has passed away; so flint held its own against metal for centuries after the time that the former might have been superseded (cf. Ex. 4:25). Foreigners who wished to become members of the commonwealth of Israel were required to submit to the rite, whatever their age might be (Gen. 34:14–17, 22; Ex. 12:48). Shortly before the Christian era, the conquered Edomites and Ituraeans were by force added thus to the Jewish nation (Jos. *Antiq.* xiii. 9, 1; 11, 3).

Circumcision seems to have been a primitive Semitic institution. From an early time Egyptian priests also were circumcised, and in prehistoric times it was known in Egypt and its environs (Herod. ii. 36–37; 104; Jos. *Antiq.* viii. 10, 3; *Apion* i. 22; ii. 13). The Philistines were not circumcised, and the word "uncircumcised," as a term of reproach, meant almost practically (not etymologically) the same as heathen (Gen. 34:14; Judg. 14:3; 15:18; I Sam. 17:26, 36; 31:4; II Sam. 1:20; I Chron. 10:4; Ezek. 28:10; 31:18; 32:19–32). "The circumcision," on the contrary, used in the N.T. meant the Jewish Church and nation (Gal. 2:8; Col. 4:11). Circumcision in its full significance betokened the putting away of carnal lust (Col. 2:11). To circumcise the heart is so to regenerate it that its irreligious obstinacy will disappear (Deut. 10:16; Jer. 4:4; 9:25, 26), and it will be able and willing to love God with all its powers (Deut. 30:6; Rom. 2:28, 29). Circumcision is universal among the Mohammedans as well as the Jews.

Cis (sĭs). See KISH.

Cis'tern. A small artificial reservoir dug in the earth and enclosed by stone or brick work, or scooped in a rock to collect and retain rain water (Deut. 6:11; Jer. 2:13). Cisterns were very numerous in Palestine, as the populace was largely dependent upon rain water. In the cities they were constructed on the top of the towers of the city wall (Jos. *War* v. 4, 3). They were also excavated under the houses and in the courtyards (cf. II Sam. 17:18; Jer. 38:6), and supplied with water conducted to them from the roof; some were supplied with water by a conduit from a spring at a distance. In the open country the mouth is closed with a large stone and frequently, especially in the wilderness, is covered with earth to conceal it.

Cit'y. In Hebrew usage a collection of permanent human habitations, whether few or numerous, especially if surrounded by a wall (Gen. 4:17; 18:26; 19:20; Num. 13:19; Josh. 10:39; 13:17; Judg. 20:15; Luke 2:4; 23:51). Walled and unwalled cities are distinguished (Deut. 3:5; Esth. 9:19). Cities were built on hills (I Kings 16:24; Matt. 5:14), where the situation rendered defense easy; and in fertile spots, where water and soil invited man to dwell. They were usually fenced with high walls, gates and bars (Num. 13:28; Deut. 3:5; Josh. 2:5, 15; 6:5; Neh. 3:3; Acts 9:24, 25), and further defended by towers (Neh. 3:1, 11, 25). Walls of the thickness of 20 to 30 feet were not unusual. The gate was a massive structure, with a room over the gateway (II Sam. 18:33). In time of need a guard was posted at the gate (II Kings 7:10; Neh. 13:19), and a watchman was stationed on the roof of gatehouse or tower (II Sam. 18:24; II Kings 9:17). In open places at the gate public business was transacted, cases at law adjudicated, and markets held (Gen. 23:10; Ruth 4:1–11; II Sam. 15:2; I Kings 22:10; II Kings 7:1; Neh. 8:1). The streets were as a rule narrow (Jos. *Antiq.* xx. 5, 3; *War* ii. 14, 9; 15, 5; v. 8, 1), but not always (S. of Sol. 3:2; Nahum 2:4); some streets were devoted to bazaars (I Kings 20:34; Jer. 37:21).

Cit'y of Da'vid (dā'vĭd). See DAVID, CITY OF.

Cit'y of Mo'ab (mō'ăb) (Num. 22:36) [Heb. *'ir-Mō'āb*]. See AR.

Cit'y of Ref'uge. Six Levitical cities were designed to shelter one who had accidentally committed manslaughter from the pursuit of the avenger of blood (Num. 35:9–14; Ex. 21:13); see AVENGER OF BLOOD. Moses appointed the 3 e. of the Jordan: Bezer in Reuben, Ramoth-gilead in Gad, and Golan in Bashan in the tribe of Manasseh (Deut. 4:41–43). After the conquest of Canaan, Joshua and the heads of the tribes designated the 3 w. of the river, setting apart Kedesh in Naphtali, Shechem in Ephraim, and Kiriath-arba (Hebron) in the mountain of Judah (Josh. 20:7). No part of Palestine was far from a city of refuge. To the nearest the manslayer fled. He might be overtaken on the way and slain by the avenger; but if he reached a city of refuge he was received into it and obtained a fair trial. If guilty of willful murder he was delivered to death. If he had slain a fellow creature by accident or in self-defense, actual or constructive, he was granted asylum in the city. If he left the city before the death of the high priest, he did so

at his own risk. On the death of the high priest he was at liberty to return to his home and enjoy the protection of the authorities (Num., ch. 35; Deut., ch. 19; Josh., ch. 20). The matter was between man and God; and the death of the high priest, who represented the people before God, closed a period of theocratic life (cf. the release at the year of jubilee).

Clau'da (klō'dȧ). A small island off the s.w. coast of Crete. Paul's ship ran under its lee when caught by the tempest off Crete (Acts 27:16). It was also called Cauda (R.V. text) and Gaudos (Pliny *Hist. Nat.* iv. 42).

Clau'di·a (klō'dĭ-ȧ). A Christian woman who joined Paul in sending a salutation to Timothy (II Tim. 4:21).

Clau'di·us (klō'dĭ-ŭs). See CAESAR 3.

Clau'di·us Lys'i·as (klō'dĭ-ŭs lĭs'ĭ-ăs). A chiliarch (commander of 1,000 men), who seems to have been the military tribune in charge of the whole garrison at Jerusalem. His 2d name shows him to have been a Greek, but he had bought Roman citizenship (Acts 22:28). He resided in the Castle of Antonia, and sent soldiers to rescue Paul from fanatical Jewish rioters. He gave orders that this unknown Jew be examined by scourging, but had him unbound on being informed of his Roman citizenship. Soon afterward he frustrated a plot against Paul's life by sending him by night under military escort to Caesarea to Felix, the Roman procurator (Acts 22:24 to 23:35).

Clean. See UNCLEAN ANIMALS, UNCLEANNESS.

Clem'ent (klĕm'ĕnt) [Lat. *clemens*, mild, merciful]. A Christian who labored along with Paul, apparently at Philippi (Phil. 4:3).

Cle'o·pas (klē'ō-păs) [probably contraction of Gr. *Kleopatros*]. One of the 2 disciples who journeyed to and from Emmaus on the evening of the resurrection day (Luke 24:18). Apparently not the same as Clopas or Cleophas, though some Christian fathers, not of early date, assumed the identity of the two.

Cle'o·pa'tra (klē'ō-pā'trȧ). A name borne by many Egyptian princesses. One was daughter of Ptolemy VI and wife of Alexander Balas (I Macc. 10:57, 58). Her father afterward took her from Balas and married her to Demetrius Nicator when he invaded Syria (ch. 11:12; Jos. *Antiq.* xiii. 4, 7). During the captivity of Demetrius in Parthia, she married his brother Antiochus VII (Jos. *Antiq.* xiii. 7, 1; 9, 3; 10, 1). She had two sons by Demetrius; the elder she murdered, and then raised to the throne the younger, Antiochus VIII, called Grypus. As he was unwilling to gratify her ambitious designs, she attempted to make away with him by offering him a cup of poison, but was compelled to drink it herself, 120 B.C.

Clo'pas (klō'păs), in A. V. **Cle'o·phas** (klē'ō-făs) [cf. Palmyrene *Klōpā'*]. Often identified with Alphaeus. See ALPHAEUS 1. According to Hegesippus this name was borne by a brother of Joseph, the husband of the Virgin Mary.

Cloth'ing. Man at first went naked (Gen. 2:25). The first clothing consisted of the skins of beasts (ch. 3:21). Subsequently the materials used for clothing were wool (Gen. 31:19; Lev. 13:47), linen (Ex. 9:31; Lev. 16:4), byssus, a fabric made of cotton or flax (Gen. 41:42; Luke 16:19), silk (Ezek. 16:10, 13), and camel's hair (Matt. 3:4). The essential articles of the apparel of men and women were 2: 1. An undergarment or tunic, commonly called coat, less frequently garment, in the English versions. It usually had short sleeves and reached nearly to the knees, though a longer form, with sleeves of full length, was in use (Gen. 37:3; II Sam. 13:18, R.V. marg.). This tunic was sometimes woven without seam (John 19:23, 24). It was confined at the waist by a girdle. 2. An upper garment or mantle (Ruth 3:15, R.V.; I Kings 11:30; Acts 9:39), a large, square piece of cloth, provided with tassels (Num. 15:38; Matt. 23:5). It was thrown over the left shoulder and brought over or under the right arm. The pendant ends were called skirts (Hag. 2:12; Zech. 8:23). The garment of hair worn by prophets (II Kings 1:8; Zech. 13:4) may have consisted of a sheepskin or goatskin (cf. Heb. 11:37), but was more probably made of coarse camel's hair (cf. Matt. 3:4). The girdles, which confined the undergarments at the waist to prevent them as far as possible from impeding the action of the limbs, were made of leather, linen, or byssus (II Kings 1:8; Jer. 13:1; Ezek. 16:10); often elaborately wrought and richly decorated (Ex. 28:39; 39:29; Dan. 10:5; Rev. 1:13). The sword was worn in the girdle and money was carried there (Judg. 3:16; I Sam. 25:13; Matt. 10:9, R.V. marg.). When outside a room people wore sandals, an imperfect shoe consisting of a sole of wood or leather (Ezek. 16:10), fastened to the bare foot by straps passing over the instep and around the ankle (Gen. 14:23; Isa. 5:27; Acts 12:8). Probably people commonly went bareheaded; still turbans were on occasion worn by both sexes (Job. 29:14, R.V. marg.; Isa. 3:20; Ezek. 23:15). The veil was worn by women in the presence of strangers (Gen. 24:65; S. of Sol. 5:7); but it was not uncommon for them to go with face unveiled (Gen. 24:16; Judith 10:7, 14). By the Mosaic Law a man was forbidden to wear a garment that pertains to a woman, and a woman to wear that belonging to a man (Deut. 22:5; cf. I Cor. 11:6, 14).

Cloud. As agents in connection with rain, clouds are the bearers of moisture (II Sam. 22:12; Job 26:8; 37:11; Eccl. 11:3), and discharge it upon the earth (Judg. 5:4; Ps. 77:17). A cloud in the w. was a harbinger of rain (I Kings 18:44; Luke 12:54).

The pillar of cloud was a miraculous cloud taking the form of a pillar, which moved in front of the Israelites in the wilderness to indicate to them the way along which God wished them to advance (Ex. 13:21, 22). When the evening was too far advanced for it to be seen, it shone with light as a pillar of fire. When God designed to show his presence to the Israelites he did it in the pillar of cloud (Num. 12:5; Deut. 31:15), and when he designed to discomfit the Egyptians at the Red Sea he looked at them through the pillar of cloud (Ex. 14:24).

Cni'dus (nī'dŭs). A city of Caria, on the s.w. coast of Asia Minor, over against the isle of Cos, which is about 10 miles away. It was a Dorian colony. Paul's vessel passed near it during the voyage to Rome (Acts 27:7). It had Jewish inhabitants as early as the 2d century B.C. (I Macc. 15:23) and was a free city.

Coal. In Scripture this refers to charcoal made by burning wood. Hence we read of coals of juniper (Ps. 120:4). It was used to furnish warmth in winter (Isa. 47:14; John 18:18), for culinary purposes (Isa. 44:19; John 21:9), and by the smith (Isa. 44:12; 54:16). In 2 cases (Isa. 6:6; I Kings 19:6) the Heb. word denotes a hot stone (cf. R.V. marg.).

Coat. See CLOTHING and HIGH PRIEST.

Coat of Mail. See ARMOR.

Cock. The male of the well-known domestic fowl *Gallus domesticus*. The cock is men-

tioned in the N.T. (Matt. 26:34, 74, 75). Cockcrow, as a portion of time, is the 3d watch of the night, just before the dawn (Mark 13:35). See NIGHT.

Cock'a·trice. A fabulous monster with deadly glance, reputed to be hatched by a serpent from a cock's egg. The A.V. so renders Heb. *şiph'ōnī* (Isa. 11:8; 59:5; Jer. 8:17), and *şepha'* (Isa. 14:29); but in Prov. 23:32 it translates the word by adder. In all these passages A.R.V. reads "adder"; in the first 3, E.R.V. has basilisk in the text and adder in the marg., but interchanges these words in the last case.

Cock'le. The rendering of Heb. *bo'shāh*, malodorous plant (Job 31:40). The margin has "noisome weeds," which is a more exact rendering.

Coel'e·syr'i·a (sĕl'ē-sĭr'ĭ-ȧ), in A.V. **Ce'lo·syr'i·a** [Gr., hollow Syria]. The valley between the Lebanon and Anti-Lebanon Mountains. It is watered by the 2 streams Orontes and Litany, which rise in the vicinity of Baalbek and flow in opposite directions. The term had, however, a wider application (I Macc. 10:69). It included the w. side of the Jordan Valley as far as Beth-shean (Jos. *Antiq.* xiii. 13, 2) and the region extending from Damascus s. through Trachonitis, Perea, and Idumaea to include Moab and Ammon (cf. Jos. *Antiq.* i. 11, 5). It was distinct from Phoenicia (I Esdras 2:17; II Macc. 3:5) and extended from the Euphrates to Egypt (Jos. *Antiq.* xiv. 4, 5).

Col·ho'zeh (kŏl-hō'zĕ) [all-seeing one]. Father of Shallun and perhaps one with the father of Baruch (Neh. 3:15; 11:5).

Col'lege. A mistranslation of Heb. *mishneh* in A.V. of II Kings 22:14, and II Chron. 34:22. The word is correctly rendered "the second" in Zeph. 1:10. In these passages R.V. has "the second quarter."

Col'o·ny. A settlement of Roman citizens authorized by the senate, in conquered territory. They retained their Roman citizenship, and formed the aristocracy of every town in which they were located. Under the Empire the colonists generally were Roman citizensoldiers, settled on a military road to hold the enemies of the Roman Empire in check. Their constitution was on the model of Rome. Philippi was a colony (Acts 16:12).

Col'ors. In Biblical Hebrew there are few real color terms; the words denote rather a contrast between light and darkness, brightness and dimness. The abstract idea of color is expressed in Hebrew by *'ayin* (eye, with a derived sense of appearance). In Babylonia different clays were employed to produce orange, red, and yellow bricks. Bricks of blue were obtained by vitrifaction. The ancient Egyptians prepared colors from various metallic and earthy substances. The Hebrews dyed skins in various colors (Ex. 25:5), and wove and embroidered cloth out of threads of various hues (Ex. 27:16). A reddish-purple dye (I Macc. 4:23; Acts 16:14) was obtained from the secretion of a species of shellfish, *Murex trunculus*, found in the Mediterranean. Blue (Num. 4:7; Ezek. 23:6) was obtained from another shellfish, *Helix ianthina*. Scarlet or crimson was made from an insect (Ex. 25:4; Isa. 1:18). They used a vermilion pigment for decorating walls, beams, idols, and the like (Jer. 22:14; Ezek. 23:14). In addition to these artificial coloring matters, allusion is made in the Bible to white (Gen. 49:12; Isa. 1:18), black, including brown (Gen. 30:32; S. of Sol. 1:6; Micah 3:6, R.V.), red (Gen. 25:25, 30; II Kings 3:22; Prov. 23:31), reddish (Lev. 13:19), sorrel (Zech. 1:8; in A.V., speckled;

marg., bay), greenish (Ps. 68:13, E.R.V., yellow; Lev. 13:49).

Symbolism was connected with colors. In the Scripture white is the constant emblem of purity (Mark 16:5; Rev. 3:4; 19:11, 14) and joy (Eccl. 9:8). The white horse signifies victory in Rev. 6:2. The black horse is typical of famine and death (vs. 5, 6). Red commonly typifies blood, in which is life, or war and carnage (v. 4). Blue is the familiar color of the sky, and purple was worn by princes and the rich in their magnificence (Judg. 8:26; Esth. 8:15; Luke 16:19).

Co·los'sae (kŏ-lŏs'ē), in A.V. **Co·los'se** (kŏ-lŏs'ē). A city of s.w. Phrygia, in Asia Minor, lying on the river Lycos not far e. of its confluence with the Meander. It was originally on the trade route from w. to e. and was a place of much importance (Herod. vii. 30; Xen. *Anabasis* i. 2, 6). But the road system was changed, and the neighboring cities of Laodicea and Hierapolis (Col. 2:1; 4:13), distant 10 and 13 miles respectively, surpassed it in position and wealth, and the importance of Colossae declined. It was, however, like Laodicea, famous for its fine wool, and it retained municipal independence under the Romans. A Christian community grew up at Colossae under the ministrations of Epaphras and later of Archippus (Col. 1:7; 4:17; Philemon 2). Of this church Philemon was an active member, and also Onesimus (Col. 4:9).

Co·los'sians (kŏ-lŏsh'ănz), **The E·pis'tle of Paul to the.** An epistle written when the Apostle Paul was a prisoner (Col. 4:3, 10, 18) probably at Rome during the 2 years of his 1st imprisonment there (Acts 28:30, 31), though some believe that it was written from Caesarea (Acts 23:35; 24:27) or even Ephesus. From Col. 2:1 it appears evident that he had never himself preached at Colossae; and ch. 1:7 seems to imply that Epaphras had been the founder, or at least had assisted in the establishment of the Colossian church. The church may have been founded while Paul was laboring in Ephesus (Acts 19:1, 10). Epaphras had recently joined the apostle (ch. 1:8), and his report of the condition of the church prompted the writing of the letter. It was sent by the hand of a certain Tychicus (ch. 4:7, 8), who was also intrusted with the letter to the Ephesians (Eph. 6:21), probably written at the same time. With him went Onesimus (Col. 4:9), who also bore the letter to Philemon, a resident of Colossae, whose slave Onesimus had formerly been. The Archippus mentioned in Philemon 2, probably Philemon's son, is also mentioned in Col. 4:17. The salutations which the letter contains (ch. 4:10–17) indicate that while Paul had not labored in Colossae his friends had, and that he himself was well acquainted with some of the Colossians. In fact, Philemon was one of his converts (Philemon 19), made, perhaps, in Ephesus. The reports of Epaphras had shown that the Colossian Christians were threatened by false teachers, who seemed to have combined ritualistic, ascetic, and speculative tendencies. That they were Jewish appears from Col. 2:11, 16. But they were also ascetic (vs. 16, 20–23), a feature which may have come from the Jewish sect of Essenes. With this they united a mystic philosophy (v. 8), which seems to have claimed superior knowledge of divine things (v. 18) and to have introduced the worship of angels (v. 18), thus infringing on the all-sufficiency and the supremacy of Christ. These false teachers, therefore, were different from the Judaizers whom Paul opposed in The Epistle to the Galatians. They represent a new form of error, that of religious syncretism with pagan cultus, and in certain respects appear as the forerunners of the Gnostics. They united with ritualism that theosophical tendency which was almost characteristic of Oriental thought, and therefore demanded an immediate refutation by the apostle.

The epistle naturally falls into 4 parts: 1. the introduction and thanksgiving (ch. 1:1–8); 2. the doctrinal section (chs. 1:9 to 3:4); 3. practical exhortations (chs. 3:5 to 4:6); 4. concluding salutations (ch. 4:7–18). The doctrinal section is of great importance. Beginning with a prayer for their growth in knowledge and holiness, Paul rises to a description of the pre-eminence of Christ in his relation to God, the universe, and the Church. Then in ch. 2 he sets forth Christ's pre-eminence as against the errorists, assuring believers of their completeness in him, since he has once for all triumphed over their spiritual foes, and nothing but union with him by faith is requisite for the full experience of salvation. As against asceticism he further urges, in his practical exhortations, to a spiritual morality and to social order. The epistle is, therefore, Christological in character. It assumes the doctrines of salvation taught in previous epistles, but more explicitly states the pre-eminence of Christ's person and the sufficiency of his work. This epistle, together with Philemon and Ephesians, was probably written toward the middle or end of Paul's Roman imprisonment, perhaps in A.D. 62. The Epistle to the Ephesians has many remarkable coincidences of language and thought with that to the Colossians, though their differences are equally noteworthy; see EPHESIANS. While evidently written at the same time, Ephesians presents a further unfolding of the truths which the specific needs of his Colossian readers led Paul to write to them.   G. T. P. (rev., H. S. G.)

Com'men·tar'y. Translation of Heb. *midrash*, from root *dărash* (search out, investigate, and so discover or develop a thought not apparent on the surface). A midrash denotes a didactic or homiletic exposition or an edifying religious story such as that of Tobit. It may also be applied to a religious interpretation of history, as the Prophet Iddo's commentary on the acts, ways, and sayings of King Abijah (II Chron. 13:22, R.V.), and the commentary of the Book of the Kings, in which were set forth the burdens laid upon King Joash and his rebuilding of the Temple (II Chron. 24:27, R.V.).

Com·mun'ion. See LORD'S SUPPER.

Con'a·ni'ah (kŏn'à-nī'à), in A.V. twice **Con'o·ni'ah** [Jehovah has established]. 1. A Levite who had charge of the tithes and offerings in Hezekiah's reign (II Chron. 31:12, 13).

2. A Levite of high station in the reign of Josiah (II Chron. 35:9).

Con'cu·bine. A secondary wife under the system of polygamy. Concubines were commonly taken from among the purchased slaves or captives; as Hagar (Gen. 16:2, 3), Bilhah (ch. 29:29), Gideon's concubine (Judg. 8:31). They could be more easily put away than a wife (Gen. 21:10–14), yet their rights were recognized and guarded by the Mosaic Law (Ex. 21:7–11; Deut. 21:10–14).

Co'ney. The coney of England is the rabbit; that of Scripture is probably the rock badger (Lev. 11:5, R.V. marg.). See ROCK BADGER.

Con'gre·ga'tion. In Scripture the word is used mainly for: 1. The body politic of Israel, including men, women, and children (Ex. 12:3, 19, 47; 16:1, 22; Lev. 4:13; 24:14; Num. 1:2; Judg. 20:1).

2. An assemblage of the people, especially for religious purposes (A.R.V., assembly, I Kings 8:14, 65; II Chron. 30:2, 4; Ps. 22:22, 25), or the community regarded as ever summoned and assembled for worship. A.R.V. and E.R.V. often agree in using the word assembly (Num. 10:7; 16:3; 19:20; 20:4; Josh.

8:35; also sometimes in A.V., Judg. 20:2); in Acts 13:43 synagogue has the same meaning.

3. In A.V. the tabernacle of the congregation designates the tent of meeting (R.V.), the appointed place where Jehovah and his people met (Ex. 27:21; cf. 25:22; 29:42; 30:36).

Co·ni'ah (kō-nī'a). See JECONIAH.

Con'o·ni'ah (kŏn'ō-nī'á). See CONANIAH.

Con'quest. See CANAAN.

Con'se·cra'tion. The act whereby a person or thing is dedicated to the service and worship of God. It includes ordination to a sacred office (Ex. 29:9), ordination to sacred service (Lev. 8:33; I Chron. 29:5; II Chron. 29:31), and the setting apart of things from a common to a sacred use (Josh. 6:19; II Chron. 31:6).

Con'ver·sa'tion. The word conversation in its archaic sense denotes manner of life. 1. The rendering in the A.V. of the Greek words *politeuō* and *politeuma* (Phil. 1:27; 3:20). The words refer to civil life, as is recognized by R.V. Christians are citizens of the heavenly Kingdom and their daily civil conduct should correspond with the teachings of the gospel of the Kingdom.
2. The rendering, in many passages of the A.V., of various words, especially of the Greek *anastrophē*. It means conduct, or mode of life, especially with respect to morals (Ps. 37:14; Eph. 4:22; Heb. 13:5; I Peter 1:15).

Con'vo·ca'tion. A festival on which the Israelites were summoned to assemble together and when no servile work was allowed to be done. The holy convocations were every Sabbath (Lev. 23:1–3, the 1st and 7th days of the feast of unleavened bread (Ex. 12:16; Lev. 23:6, 7; Num. 28:18, 25), Pentecost (Lev. 23:15–21), the 1st and 7th days of the 7th month, the latter being the great Day of Atonement (Lev. 23:24–28; Num. 29:1), and the 1st and 8th days of the feast of tabernacles, which began on the 15th of the 7th month (Lev. 23:34–36; Neh. 8:18).

Co'os (kō'ŏs). See Cos.

Cop'per. See BRASS.

Cor. See MEASURE, III.

Cor'al. A rendering of Hebrew *rā'mōth*. It was highly prized (Job 28:18), and was brought to the markets of Tyre by Aramaean traders (Ezek. 27:16). It was obtained in the Mediterranean and Red Seas, and was made into beads and charms. Coral is properly the calcareous skeleton of certain animals of low organization, popularly but erroneously called coral insects. They are radiated animals, with a central mouth surrounded by fleshy limbs; and are either attached singly to a rock, or so bud from parents as to make a compound being of many half-distinct, half-united individuals. The carbonate of lime of which the coral skeleton is made is obtained from the sea water. The coral is often beautifully branched like a tree or shrub, whence these animals are often called zoophytes (plant animals). Some species form great reefs.

Coral is also a rendering (R.V. marg.) of Hebrew *penînim*, rendered "rubies" in the text (Lam. 4:7; Job 28:18; Prov. 3:15).

Cor'-a'shan (kŏr'ā'shăn). See ASHAN.

Cor'ban [Heb. *korbān*, offering]. An offering or oblation, either of a bloody or an unbloody sacrifice, given to God (Lev. 1:2, 3; 2:1; 3:1; Num. 7:12–17; where the word occurs in the Hebrew text). An Aramaic word *korbanās*, from the same root, is rendered in Matt. 27:6 "treasury," and on the margin of the R.V. "sacred treasury." Corban is used for money or service dedicated to God (Mark 7:11). The reprehensible practice arose of

children's giving no aid to parents needing their support, on the pretense that the money or service which would otherwise have been available for the parents had been dedicated to God and that it would be sacrilege to divert it from this sacred purpose. Josephus (*War* ii. 9, 4) relates that a clamorous mob beset the tribunal of Pontius Pilate when he took the sacred money called corban and expended it on aqueducts designed to improve the water supply of Jerusalem. This doubtless was a public benefit, but the Jews evidently thought that money once dedicated to God could never again be lawfully used for a secular purpose, however conducive to the public welfare.

Co're (kō'rē). See KORAH.

Co'ri·an'der. A plant, called in Hebrew *gad*, which had white seeds (Ex. 16:31; Num. 11:7). It was the *Coriandrum sativum*, a branched annual, with cut leaves, umbels of pink or white flowers, and a small globular fruit used to season dishes. It has a carminative action upon the stomach.

Cor'inth (kŏr'ĭnth). A city of Greece, on the narrow isthmus between the Peloponnesus and the mainland. At an early date a town grew up at the s. end of this neck of land on the plateau at the n. foot of the Acro-Corinthus. This mountain is 1,800 feet high, and its summit served as a citadel and as the site for a temple. The land traffic between the peninsula and the mainland was obliged to pass the town, and much of the commerce between Asia and the w. was brought to its harbors, Cenchreae, 8½ miles to the e. on the Saronic Gulf, and Lechaeum, 1½ miles to the w. on the Corinthian Gulf. The latter city was connected with Corinth by the Long Walls. Another harbor on the e. is Schoenus. Small ships and the cargoes of larger ones were hauled across the isthmus on a made track called the *diolkos*. The town attracted Phoenician settlers, who made a purple dye from fish of the neighboring waters, introduced the manufacture of cloth, pottery, and armor, and established the impure worship of the Phoenician deities. At a later time emigrants from Attica became dominant. About 1074 B.C. the political supremacy passed to the Dorians. But the character of the inhabitants remained unchanged; they were commercial in spirit, unwarlike, luxurious, and licentious. Their immoral life gave rise and meaning to a verb "to corinthianize."

Except during the years 243–222 B.C., the Macedonians held the citadel from 335–197 B.C., when in 196 B.C. Greece was declared independent by the Romans. In 146 B.C., in consequence of rebellion against Rome, the Roman consul Mummius burned the city to ashes. The city was rebuilt by Julius Caesar in 44 B.C., became the capital of the Roman province of Achaia, and was ruled by a proconsul. Paul reached Corinth probably in A.D. 52 and labored there for a year and a half. He lodged with Aquila and Priscilla, supported himself by tentmaking, and preached Christ, first in the synagogue and then in the house of Justus. At length he was dragged before the tribunal of the proconsul Gallio, but was dismissed (Acts 18:1–18). After Paul's departure, Apollos continued the work (vs. 24–28). On 4 several occasions later the apostle sent letters to the Corinthian church (I Cor. 5:9). The 3 months (Acts 20:3) when Paul was in Greece were doubtless spent at Corinth, probably during the winter of 57–58. The Christian community continued to increase; and by the 2d century its bishop possessed great influence in the Church.

Co·rin'thi·ans (kō-rĭn'thĭ-ănz), **The E·pis'·tles of Paul to the.** The First Epistle of Paul to the Corinthians was written during the apostle's long sojourn in Ephesus (I Cor. 16:8, 9, 19; Acts, ch. 19), probably early in A.D. 57. He had had much anxiety over the state of the Corinthian church, which he had founded a few years before.

Because of disquieting news from Corinth, Paul wrote a letter, no longer extant, in which he warned the Corinthians against associating with immoral persons (I Cor. 5:9 *seq.*). Scholars call this epistle "the previous letter" and believe that a fragment of it is preserved in II Cor. 6:14 to 7:1, a section which interrupts the thought of the passage in which it now stands. This hypothesis may be correct, since these verses would fit very well into the context of "the previous letter."

The evidence as to the circumstances under which Paul wrote I Corinthians is contained within the epistle itself. While at Ephesus, he was informed about the condition of the church at Corinth by those of the household of Chloe (I Cor. 1:11); by a deputation from Corinth, Stephanas, Fortunatus, and Achaicus (ch. 16:17); and in a letter from the church asking Paul's judgment on various questions (ch. 7:1). Sometime before this, Paul had sent Timothy to Corinth by way of Macedonia, and he was anxious about the reception he would receive there (I Cor. 4:17; 16:10; Acts 19:22), but the later news moved him immediately to write this epistle. It is generally accepted that Paul himself made a brief unrecorded visit to Corinth from Ephesus for the purpose of exercising discipline in the church. This is inferred from II Cor. 2:1; 12:14; 13:1, where he speaks of being about to visit the Corinthians a 3d time; Acts (ch. 18:1) speaks of only one previous visit. The unrecorded visit should be placed between I and II Corinthians.

In I Corinthians he takes up in order the practical and doctrinal points on which they needed instruction. The epistle combines cogent doctrinal discussion and skillful dealing with moral and ecclesiastical problems, clearly reflecting the conditions of the churches among the Gentiles. In chs. 1:12 to 6:20 Paul deals mainly with matters of which he had heard oral reports, while in ch. 7:1 he begins to answer the letter he had received from Corinth. The subjects discussed are, after the introductory salutation (I Cor. 1:1–9):

1. The divisions in the church (chs. 1:10 to 4:21). Factions had arisen, claiming to follow particular leaders, and doubtless characterized by special theological tendencies. He mentions a Paul party, an Apollos party, a Cephas party, and a Christ party. Against them all he sets forth the dependence of all believers on Christ crucified, the inspired authority with which the gospel had first been preached to them, and the subordinate character of every one by whom it was administered, even though he were an apostle; so that none should be made the head of a party, but glory given to God in Christ alone.

2. The duty of exercising and honoring church discipline (chs. 5; 6), especially in the case of offenders against purity, of which there had been one conspicuous example.

3. Directions on the subject of marriage and divorce (ch. 7).

4. Directions concerning practical questions arising from contact with heathen society (chs. 8:1 to 11:1). These pertained especially to the eating of food which had been offered to idols; in regard to which self-denial should control their liberty (ch. 8), even as he sought to have it do in his own life (ch. 9). While not needlessly inquiring as to the origin of the food they bought or ate, they should be careful not to seem to participate in recognition of the idol (ch. 10).

5. Warnings against certain abuses in public worship (ch. 11:2–34) with respect to the prophesying of women and the administration of the Lord's Supper.

6. Directions as to the estimate, exercise, and regulation of miraculous gifts (chs. 12 to 14).

7. Instruction concerning the doctrine of the resurrection of the dead, which some were disposed to doubt (ch. 15).

8. Directions about the collections being made for the saints in Judea, and concluding remarks about his own movements and other personal matters (ch. 16).

Apparently Timothy's mission was unsuccessful, and I Corinthians did not have the desired effect. I Cor. 1:14 *seq.* and ch. 4 show premonitory signs of a definite refusal to accept Paul's authority. Seemingly his unrecorded visit was so distressing that he returned to Ephesus much troubled. Evidence is present (II Cor. 2:4; 7:8) that he wrote a "severe" or "sorrowful" letter, of which II Cor., chs. 10 to 13, is regarded by many scholars as a fragment. Probably Titus was the bearer of this epistle. Then, after Paul had left Ephesus (Acts 20:1) and was met in Macedonia by Titus, who gave a good account of affairs at Corinth (II Cor. 2:12–17; 7:5–7), the apostle in a cheerful spirit wrote what is now II Cor., chs. 1 to 9, his 4th letter to the Corinthians. In support of this proposed reconstruction there should be noticed three pairs of parallel passages (chs. 10:6 and 2:9; 13:2 and 1:23; 13:10 and 2:3), which exhibit a phenomenon that is strange on the supposition that II Corinthians is a literary unit. In each pair the same thing is referred to twice; the verses from the section chs. 10 to 13 have the present or future tense, while those from the section chs. 1 to 9 have the past tense. This was in the summer or early autumn of A.D. 57. Timothy was now with Paul again (ch. 1:1). Titus and another had recently been sent from Ephesus to Corinth (chs. 2:13; 7:6, 7, 13, 15; 12:18) with directions to have the church immediately discipline an offender, perhaps the incestuous person of I Cor. 5:1, who had openly defied the apostle's authority and whose continued sin threatened the very stability of the church. Titus was to rejoin Paul at Troas, but the apostle, not finding him there, had gone on to Macedonia in great distress of mind. At last, however, Titus came with the good news that the Corinthians had disciplined the offender, and that the latter had humbly acknowledged his sin. Thereupon this epistle (or, according to the critical view, chs. 1 to 9 minus chs. 6:14 to 7:1) was written, and Titus, with 2 others (ch. 8:16–24), was sent back with it to Corinth. It is the least methodical and most personal of Paul's epistles.

It falls into three main divisions: 1. Chs. 1 to 7, in which, after grateful recognition of God's goodness to him even amid trial (ch. 1:1–14), he vindicates himself from the charge of vacillation (chs. 1:15 to 2:4), bids them not carry too far their zeal against the offender (ch. 2:5–11), and describes the spiritual (ch. 3), honest (ch. 4:1–6), suffering (vs. 7–18), hopeful (ch. 5:1–9), solemn (vs. 10,11), Christ-impelled (vs. 12–17) ministry of reconciliation (vs. 18–21) with which, as a co-worker with God, he had been intrusted (chs. 5:18 to 6:2), in which he had appeared himself (ch. 6:3–10), on the ground of which he appealed to them (vs. 11–18), and in their acknowledgment of which he found boldness and joy (ch. 7). 2. Chs. 8; 9, in which he treats of the collections for the Judean saints and urges liberality. 3. Chs. 10 to 13, in which he gives a pathetic but confident testimony to his apostolic office and authority. The epistle closes with a renewed warning against their besetting sins, and declares that if, when he comes to them, he find these sins uncor rected, he will exercise his authority unsparingly.

The problem of literary analysis does not affect the genuineness of the Pauline authorship or the inspiration of the documents. It suggests, however, that Paul's correspondence with Corinth was more voluminous than has previously been supposed. The view which segregates II Cor. 6:14 to 7:1 and regards chs. 10 to 13 as earlier than chs. 1 to 9 is a hypothesis. Some scholars still maintain that II Corinthians is a unit in the form in which we now have it. G. T. P. (rev., H. S. G.)

Cor'mo·rant. 1. The rendering of Heb. *shālāk*, plunger; a bird ceremonially unclean (Lev. 11:17; Deut. 14:17). It is probably the common cormorant (*Phalacrocorax carbo*), a large swimming bird of the pelican family, but

Common Cormorant

distinguished from the pelican by not having a pouch below the lower mandible. The common cormorant is widely distributed. In Palestine it lives on the Mediterranean coast and on the Sea of Galilee. Its appetite is proverbial; and Tristram describes it as sitting on the snag of a tree where the Jordan enters the Dead Sea, and catching the fish while they are stupefied by being carried into the briny water. Another species, *Phalacrocorax pigmaeus*, the pygmy cormorant, is found sparingly on the streams which flow through Palestine to the Mediterranean.

2. The rendering of Heb. *kā'āth* in text of A.V. (Isa. 34:11; Zeph. 2:14); see PELICAN.

Corn. The generic name for the several cereal grasses cultivated in Palestine, and so staple that corn and wine stand figuratively for the entire vegetable produce of the fields (Gen. 27:28; Deut. 7:13, etc.). In this sense A.R.V. almost invariably substitutes "grain" for "corn." The chief were wheat, barley, spelt, and millet (Deut. 8:8; and R.V. of Isa. 28:25 and Ezek. 4:9).

Cor·nel'i·us (kôr-nēl'yŭs) [Lat.]. A centurion of the Roman cohort called the Italian band. He lived at Caesarea; and was a devout, charitable, God-fearing Gentile. On the ground of visions received by him and Peter, and the descent of the Holy Spirit upon him and his household when they believed, Peter baptized him. The descent of the Holy Spirit upon him was an event of prime importance in the Early

Church. It marked the beginning of the calling of the Gentiles and revealed that the Spirit is given to believers irrespective of nationality (Acts, ch. 10).

Cor'ner·stone'. A stone placed at the angle where two walls of a building meet, and helping to bind them together. Any stone in this position, from the foundation (Job 38:6; Isa. 28:16) to the roof (Ps. 118:22; Zech. 4:7), is a cornerstone. Figuratively, Christ is the chief cornerstone at the foundation (Rom. 9:33; Eph. 2:20; I Peter 2:6) and also the head of the corner (Matt. 21:42; I Peter 2:7).

Cor'net. 1. The rendering of Heb. *shôphār* in I Chron. 15:28; II Chron. 15:14; Ps. 98:6; Hos. 5:8. Elsewhere, as in Lev. 25:9, it is translated trumpet (*q.v.*).

2. The rendering of Heb. *mena'an'im* in II Sam. 6:5, A.V. R.V. renders it "castanets" (*q.v.*).

3. The rendering of Aram. *karna'*, corresponding to Heb. *keren* in Dan. 3:5, 7, 10, 15. It means a horn, and is so rendered in ch. 8:20. This instrument originally consisted of the hollow horn of some mammal; but later it was generally made of metal, and was curved, like many animals' horns.

Cor·rup'tion, Mount of. A hill to the e. of Jerusalem (II Kings 23:13; cf. I Kings 11:7). Solomon built altars on its s. side to the gods worshiped by his heathen wives. By common consent it is the s. portion of the Mount of Olives and is known in tradition as the Mount of Offense.

Cos (kŏs), in A.V. **Co'os.** An island in the archipelago off the coast of Caria in Asia Minor, in a gulf between Cnidus and Halicarnassus. It lies between Miletus and Rhodes, about a day's sail from the latter city (Acts 21:1). It is about 21 miles long by 6 broad. The Jews there were favored by the Romans in 139–138 B.C. (I Macc. 15:23). Cos was celebrated for its wines, its ointments, and its purple dyes.

Co'sam (kō'săm). A descendant of David through Nathan and an ancestor of Zerubbabel and Christ (Luke 3:28).

Cot'ton. The correct rendering of Heb. *karpas* in R.V. marg., Esth. 1:6. In the court of the royal palace at Shushan were hangings of fine cotton. Heb. *karpas* goes back to Sans. *karpāsa* (cotton tree, cotton); Indian cotton (*Gossypium herbaceum*) was early cultivated in Persia, and was probably that of The Book of Esther.

Coun'cil. 1. The Jewish governing body. The Persians granted to the Jews jurisdiction over their own affairs (Ezra 7:25, 26; 10:14). After the fall of the Persian Empire similar privileges were enjoyed by the Jews. A governing body arose and became known as *gerousia* or senate (Jos. *Antiq.* xii. 3, 3), and more fully as the senate of the nation (I Macc. 12:6). It was composed of elders (cf. ch. 14:20). It represented the nation (ch. 12:3), and united with Jonathan, the high priest and leader, in making offensive and defensive alliance with the Spartans. Jonathan also called the elders of the people together and consulted with them about building strongholds in Judea and increasing the height of the walls of Jerusalem (v. 35; cf. also chs. 13:36; 14:20, 28, 47). Under Gabinius, proconsul of Syria, 57–55 B.C., Judea was divided into 5 districts, each under a *synedrion* or *synodos*—i.e., assembly or sanhedrin (Jos. *Antiq.* xiv. 5, 4; *War* i. 8, 5). Henceforth the highest body at Jerusalem was called *synedrion*, though not to the exclusion of *gerousia* or *boulē*. The arrangement, however, did not last long. In 47 B.C., Caesar extended the jurisdiction of the sanhedrin of Jerusalem once more over all Judea (cf. Jos. *Antiq.* xiv. 9, 3–5; *War* i. 10, 7). Under the Roman procurators, A.D. 6–66, its powers were extensive. According to Jewish authorities, it was composed of 71 members (cf. the mock council, Jos. *War* iv. 5, 4), and only Israelites whose descent was above question were eligible to membership. The 70 ordinary members corresponded, probably, to the 70 elders appointed by Moses to assist him as judges. The 71st member was the high priest, the official president of the body. It was the highest court, with power of life and death (Jos. *Antiq.* xiv. 9, 3 and 4; Matt. 26:3, 57; Acts 4:5, 6, 15; 5:21, 27, 34, 41; 6:12, 15; 7:1; 23:2), though apparently it had no recognized authority to execute its sentence of death, but had to submit its action to the review of the Roman authorities. It had the general administration of the government and of justice, so far as this was not exercised by the procurator and subordinate officials (cf. Acts 22:30). In the time of Florus, at least, the revenue was collected by the rulers and councilors, who dispersed themselves among the villages for that purpose (Jos. *War* ii. 17, 1). It had police at command and could make arrests on its own authority (Matt. 26:47; Mark 14:43). Jesus was tried before the council (Matt. 26:59; Mark 14:55; 15:1; Luke 22:66; John 11:47). It was before the council that Peter, John, and the other apostles were brought (Acts 4:5, 6, 15; 5:21, 27, 34, 41). Stephen was taken before the council (ch. 6:12), so also was Paul (ch. 22:30; 23:15; 24:20). The sanhedrin was swept away at the destruction of Jerusalem (A.D. 70).

2. A body of advisers selected by the highest Roman official of a province, in Judea the procurator, to assist him in the administration of justice, before whom, with the official as president, cases were tried (Acts 25:12; Jos. *Antiq.* xvi. 11, 1 *seq.*; *War* ii. 16, 1).

Coun'cil House. A building in Jerusalem w. of the Temple, near the gymnasium and adjoining the innermost city wall (Jos. *War* v. 4, 2). It was burned by the Romans under Titus in the course of their struggle for the possession of the city (Jos. *War* vi. 6, 3). The council house was probably the place where the sanhedrin met, for: (1) Its name in Greek was *bouleutērion*, and a member of the sanhedrin was called *bouleutēs* (Luke 23:50, 51; cf. Jos. *War* ii. 17,1). (2) The council is called by Josephus *synedrion*—i.e., sanhedrin—and *boulē* indifferently (cf. Jos. *Antiq.* xiv. 9, 3 and 4, with xx. 1, 2; *War* ii. 15, 6). (3) According to Jewish authorities, the sanhedrin met in the *lishkath haggāzîth*, or chamber of the *gāzîth*, which probably denoted a chamber by the gymnasium. According to the Mishnah, it is true, the *lishkath haggāzîth* was situated at the e. corner of the court of the Temple. But *gāzîth* means hewn, especially hewn stone (Ex. 20:25; I Kings 6:36); and as the chambers of the Temple were largely constructed in this manner, the name *gāzîth* could not distinguish one from another. Now the council house stood near or adjoined the *xystos* or gymnasium; but *xystos* is the Greek equivalent of *gāzîth*, and is one of the words used in the LXX to translate *gāzîth* (I Chron. 22:2; Amos 5:11). It can scarcely be doubted, therefore, that the *xystos* was called the *gāzîth* by one who chanced to be speaking Hebrew, and that the name *lishkath haggāzîth* meant the hall by the *xystos*.

Probably, as the Mishnah states, the meetings originally were held in one of the chambers of the inner court of the Temple in order that the discussions might have more religious authority. The account of Josephus refers to the last years of the Jewish state, and by that time conditions were changed. It may be that at that time the Pharisees would not permit the secular sanhedrin to hold its sessions in the sanctuary.

Coun'se·lor. The 7 counselors of Artaxerxes (Ezra 7:14) were probably the 7 princes of Media and Persia "who saw the king's face, and sat first in the kingdom," and from whom the king sought advice (Esth. 1:14).

Court. An enclosed but uncovered area either connected with a private house and often containing a well (II Sam. 17:18; Neh. 8:16); or in a palace (I Kings 7:8, 9, 12; Jer. 32:2), in front of the royal apartments (Esth. 4:11; 5:1; 6:4) and sometimes containing a garden (ch. 1:5); or around the tabernacle and Temple (Ex. 27:9; 40:8; I Kings 6:36). As the area about the Temple was divided (II Kings 21:5), the word is generally used in the plural (Ps. 65:4; 84:2).

Cov'e·nant. An agreement between 2 or more persons. Various covenants between man and man are mentioned in Scripture (Gen. 21:27, 32; I Sam. 18:3; 23:18; I Kings 20:34). More important are those in which God condescended to be a covenanting party. His covenant with man is a free promise on his part, generally based upon the fulfillment of certain conditions by man. He made a promise of continued life and favor to man on condition of obedience, coupled with a penalty for disobedience (Gen. 2:16, 17). He established a covenant with Noah, that Noah should be saved when the old world perished (Gen. 6:18), and that there should be no other great deluge, the rainbow being the token of the covenant (Gen. 9:12, 15, 16); with Abraham and his posterity, of which circumcision was to be the sign, to be their God and to give them the land of Canaan for an inheritance (Gen. 13:17; 15:18; 17:2, 4, 7, 11, 13, 14, 19; II Kings 13:23; I Chron. 16:15–18; Ps. 105:9–11; Acts 7:8; Rom. 4:13, 17); with the Israelites as a nation, to continue to be their God and to grant national protection, of which a sign was to be the Sabbath (Ex. 31:16), and the keeping of the Ten Commandments its condition (Deut. 4:13, 23). This covenant was made at Horeb (Deut. 5:2; 29:1) and was renewed with the next generation on the plains of Moab (Deut. 29:1). There was a covenant with the Levites (Mal. 2:4, 8), and one specially with Phinehas to give him and his descendants an everlasting priesthood (Num. 25:12, 13). There was a covenant with David that his posterity should forever occupy his throne (Ps. 89:20–28, 34; cf. II Sam., ch. 7 and I Chron., ch. 17; II Chron. 7:18; Jer. 33:21). In contrast with the covenant at Sinai, there was to be a new covenant, also with the Israelites, which was to be of a more spiritual character than its predecessors (Jer. 31:31–34; Heb. 8:8–11), administered by the Spirit (John 7:39; Acts 2:32, 33; II Cor. 3:6–9), based on faith (Gal. 4:21–31), and designed for all nations (Matt. 28:19, 20; Acts 10:44–47). Of this Christ is the Mediator (Heb. 8:6 to 9:1; 10:15–17; 12:24). With reference to it the Old and New Testaments would, perhaps, better have been called the Old and New Covenants.

The 2 tablets of stone on which were engraved the Ten Commandments, which were the fundamental law of God's covenant with Israel, were called the Tables of the Covenant (Deut. 9:11), and the Ark, in which these tables were deposited, was designated the Ark of the Covenant (Num. 10:33). The Book of the Covenant, prefaced perhaps by the Ten Commandments, consisted of the ordinances contained in Ex. 20:22 to 23:33, which were written by Moses in a book, formally accepted by the Israelites, and ratified as a covenant between the Lord and his people (Ex. 24:

3–8) ; see THEOCRACY. Later the term is used as synonymous with the Book of the Law (cf. II Kings 23 :2 with 22 :8, 11) and included Deuteronomy (Deut. 31 :9, 26 ; cf. II Kings 14 :6 with Deut. 24 :16).

Cow. Cows were early domesticated. Egypt, Philistia, and Palestine afforded excellent pasturage, and cows were kept in these lands (Gen. 41 :2 ; Deut. 7 :13 ; I Sam. 6 :7). Cows were herded by Abraham and his descendants (Gen. 12 :16 ; 32 :15). Their milk served for food (II Sam. 17 :29). They were used in concluding a covenant (Gen. 15 :9), in the ceremony attending the profession of innocence of a death caused by an undiscoverable murderer (Deut. 21 :1–9), for a peace offering (Lev. 3 :1), for a sin offering for uncleanness arising from contact with the dead (Num. 19 :2, 9 ; Heb. 9 :13), and in exceptional cases for a burnt offering (I Sam. 6 :14).

Coz (kŏz). See HAKKOZ.

Coz′bi (kŏz′bĭ) [untruthful]. A daughter of Zur, prince of Midian. In the idolatrous rites to which the Midianites seduced Israel the woman was publicly taken by a prince of the Simeonites. Both were thrust through by Phinehas, son of the high priest, and shortly afterward her father also was slain (Num. 25 : 6–8, 14, 15, 18 ; 31 :8).

Co·ze′ba (kō-zē′bá), in A.V. **Cho·ze′ba** [untruthful]. A village in Judah, peopled chiefly by descendants of Shelah (I Chron. 4 :22). It is generally believed to be the same as Achzib and Chezib.

Crane. Hebrew *'āgūr,* a migratory bird which has a note like a chatter (Isa. 38 :14 ; Jer. 8 :7). The crane is the type of a family of long-legged wading birds. It is a large and elegant bird, breeding in the n. of Europe and of Asia, and migrating s. at the approach of winter. On these flights cranes go in large flocks of wedge-shaped form or in long lines. See SWALLOW 3.

Cre·a′tion. The act or operation of God whereby he calls into existence what did not before exist. The verb always has God for its subject, and the result is an entirely new thing. God created the heavens and the earth (Gen. 1 :1), aquatic and aërial life (v. 21), man (v. 27), the stars (Isa. 40 :26), the wind (Amos 4 :13). He creates the clean heart (Ps. 51 :10). Jehovah commanded, and the heavens, with all their hosts, angels, sun, moon, and stars, and the waters that be above the heavens, were created (Ps. 148 :5). He spoke and it was done. Upon him all living creatures depend ; his hand provides for them, his look preserves them, the hiding of his face destroys them, and his creative breath renews animate life on earth (Ps. 104 :27–30). God created the worlds by the Word, who is the Son (John 1 :3 ; Eph. 3 :9 ; Col. 1 :16 ; Heb. 1 :2).

The designation "Creation" is used specially for the original formation of the universe by God. In Genesis a general account of the creation of the universe is first given (chs. 1 :1 to 2 :3), which is followed by a particular account of the formation of man and his surroundings (ch. 2 :4–25). These two accounts are not contradictory, but supplementary. All Hebrew history is written from a theistic point of view. God controls human affairs, and everything is so, because it is a part of his divine plan. In Genesis we find an attempt to glorify God and to set Hebrew history into the scheme of the universe. The author of Genesis begins with creation, proceeds to man, and gradually narrows down the narrative to his main theme, viz., Israel.

The recital of the facts of creation is obviously not a literal historical record, but rather a series of general statements written by an inspired writer. The Babylonian parallels show a resemblance to the O.T. account and a common Semitic background. Gen., chs. 1 ; 2, is distinguished by reasonableness and dignity ; the Babylonian account is often offensive, childish, and grossly materialistic. In the description of the various stages of creation according to Gen., ch. 1, a remarkable though superficial agreement with the conclusions of modern scientific research may be detected. But it must be borne in mind that the author of Genesis had no intention of furnishing us with a textbook on geology or biology ; his purpose was not scientific. His views are general and written from the point of view of his age ; but when we consider the theological and philosophical aspects of Gen., chs. 1 ; 2, we are dealing with inspired insight. No discovery has yet been made which invalidates the belief that the world was created by a personal God. The existence of God is taken for granted, and his creative power is represented as active *"in the beginning."*

Before the Reformation scholars were uncertain whether the days of Gen., ch. 1, denote succession of time or are merely the distribution into logical groups of things created by one divine fiat (Augustine *De Civitate Dei* xi. 6, 7). During the next 300 years the narrative was understood to mean that God created the universe in one week of 7 consecutive days of 24 hours each. But geologists and astronomers alike became convinced that myriads of years had been required to produce the solar system and bring about the changes which the earth itself had undergone. When it became apparent that the geological claim for extended time rested on substantial grounds, Dr. Thomas Chalmers adopted the result and publicly declared in 1804 that "the writings of Moses do not fix the antiquity of the globe." Afterward, in his *Evidences of Christianity,* published in 1813, he explained that many ages may have elapsed between the 1st act of creation described in Gen. 1 :1, and the others commencing with v. 2. But was not a long period involved in the work of the 6 days themselves?

The order in which the various kinds of animals are described as having been created corresponds roughly to that in which by the evidence of geology they actually appeared on the earth. Accordingly some have assumed that *day* means a geological period. In 1857 Hugh Miller in his *Testimony of the Rocks* interpreted the six days, as Cuvier of Paris had already interpreted them in 1798 in the preliminary discourse to his *Ossements Fossiles,* as being six geological ages ; and traced the correspondence between the successive stages of creation as told in Gen., ch. 1, and as written in the rocks. But such a view creates more difficulties than it solves. Nothing is gained by making a desperate attempt to force science into the Bible. Nor does Ps. 90 :4 assist in the matter :

"For a thousand years in thy sight
Are but as yesterday when it is past."

God rested on "the sabbath day" and "hallowed" it (cf. also Ex. 20 :8–11). Obviously the author was thinking of literal days ; he also uses the terms *evening* and *morning.* Furthermore in Gen. 1 :16 the word day is used in a literal sense. It is far more logical to assume that the author of Genesis refers to 6 literal days than that in some cryptic manner he is hinting at geological periods.

There is no conflict between genuine science and the Bible, nor between science and religion. If science does not seek the truth impartially, it is no longer science. Scientists admit that many of their hypotheses are tentative, subjective, and liable to change. It is unreasonable to expect the sacred writer to give us in 2 chapters all the facts of astronomy, geology, and biology. If we turn to Gen., chs. 1; 2, for a confirmation of science, we do not understand the purpose of Scripture, for which see II Tim. 3:16, 17. It is a mistake to go to science for religion or to the Bible for science; their spheres and purposes are different. Men err when they refuse to listen to the scientific affirmations of nature because they *seem* to disagree with what is found in the Bible; on the other hand, it is just as serious an error to suppose that nature and science can tell us all we need to know about ourselves, the world, and God. Gen., chs. 1; 2, is not written from the scientific point of view of any age or period; on account of the continual growth of scientific studies and changes in scientific theories, any scientific description in the course of time would have become antiquated. The sacred writer does not commit himself to any definite limits of time; but simply speaks of creation as taking place *in the beginning,* and this phrase is elastic enough to cover the modern scientific position. His scientific knowledge may be bounded by the horizon of the age in which he lived, but the religious truths he teaches are irrefutable and eternal. Gen., chs. 1; 2, accordingly will never become out of date; this religious account has remained as true today as it was in antiquity.

Science observes natural phenomena and discovers or deduces from them the laws of nature; it cannot create life or establish new laws of nature. It is limited to study and observation and may form hypotheses and theories, but it cannot answer the question how the universe was created. Genesis gives a better answer.

In view of various interpretations of Gen., chs. 1; 2, shall we consider it literally, as an allegory, or as symbolism? It may also be regarded as a grand epic of creation, the culmination of which is the creation of man in the image of God, who breathed into man the breath of life. Whatever view we take, God is a person; God created the world and all that is in it; God is the author of everything; God works according to definite plans and laws. Our faith in a transcendent God goes beyond the limitations of science. Throughout this narrative we find the truths of divine personality, divine unity, and divine goodness. All belief in creation involves a belief in God's personality. Creation is not impersonal, nor spontaneous, nor the result of an accident; it is the work of an intelligent, almighty personality. God speaks, creation follows. We have monotheism, not polytheism, in Gen., chs. 1; 2. There is anthropomorphism in Gen. 2:7, 8, 15–22, but it is never grotesque. God is the Creator; he is interested in his work; he establishes laws that govern the universe; and he is an ethical being. We may grant that the description of creation in Genesis is only general and does not attempt to be scientific. Yet the scientist in the end must come to the same conclusion as does the author of Gen., chs. 1; 2: God is a personality and the source of all life and physical laws. This inspired writer has solved a problem which is beyond the limits of the scientist.

The Hebrew narrative is marked by a symmetry and grouping, which may be plausibly explained as intentional arrangement. The chronological order has been observed in the main at least, but it remains to be discovered whether it has been followed in every detail. At any rate the works of the 6 days were more than 6 acts; God spoke, to use a significant Biblical term, 8 times (Gen. 1:3, 6, 9, 11, 14, 20, 24, 26), and on the 3d day the command went forth for both dry land and vegetation, on the 5th day for fish and for fowl, and on the 6th day for beast and for man. Moreover, the 6 days form 2 interrelated groups: the 1st day saw light, and the 4th day, the 1st of the 2d group, saw the luminaries; on the 2d day the waters were divided and the sky appeared, and on the 2d day of the other group fish were divinely willed in the waters and fowl to fly in the expanse of the sky; on the 3d day dry land and vegetation were decreed, and on the corresponding day of the 2d group land animals, including man, were made, and vegetation was granted them for food.

The Babylonian epic known as the *Enuma elish,* from the first 2 words of the poem, was found written on 7 tablets in Ashurbanipal's library, but the original goes back to a much earlier period. The poem begins with a period:

"When above the heaven was not named,
    And beneath, the earth bore no name."

Apsu (the abyss) and Tiāmat (the salt sea) are mentioned, but none of the gods had been born. Tiāmat corresponds etymologically to Hebrew $t^e h\bar{o}m$ ("deep," Gen. 1:2). Then gods were created; apparently they descended from chaos. Ea killed Apsu, whom Tiāmat determined to avenge. Mother Khubur (world-encircling stream of salt water) spawned various monsters whose bodies were filled with poison instead of blood; among them was Kingu. All the gods except Marduk were afraid to attack Tiāmat and her allies. In the ensuing conflict he slew Tiāmat and took Kingu prisoner. With the death of Tiāmat creation began. In the words of the epic,

"The flesh of the monster he [Marduk] divided; he formed a cunning plan,
He split her open like a flat fish into two halves,
One half of her he established and made a covering of the heavens,
He drew a bolt, he established a guard,
And not to let her waters come out, he commanded."

Cf. the "firmament" in Gen. 1:6–8. We may assume that the other half of Tiāmat became the earth, although the poem does not expressly say so. Then Marduk ordained the stations of the great gods: "The stars, their images, as the stars of the zodiac he fixed." He ordained the year and the 12 months. "The moon-god he caused to shine; the night he entrusted to him." No creation of the sun is mentioned, because Marduk is the sun-god. Cf. Gen. 1:14–18.

Then Marduk said:

"Blood will I bind, bone will I fashion,
    I will produce a man; 'man' is his name;
    I will create the man 'man.'"

Kingu was accordingly brought before Ea, who laid a curse upon the monster, whose blood burst forth. From this Ea created man. Thus the Babylonians expressed man's kinship to divinity. Cf. Gen. 1:27; 2:7. There was a purpose in Marduk's creation; he made mankind for the service of the gods.

This epic of creation is mythological and polytheistic and has no exalted conception of divinity. The gods love and hate, scheme and plot, fight and destroy. Marduk conquers only after a severe struggle. Before the discovery of cuneiform tablets, the Babylonian story of creation was known only from Berossus, who says that at Bel's command one of the gods cut off Bel's head and mixed his blood with clay to create man. The original of Berossus is not extant, and he may have referred to the head of Tiāmat. In a Sumerian account, man is created from the blood of Lamga, the god of carpenters. Clay in creation was also used when the goddess Aruru created Engidu as a rival of Gilgamesh: she washed her hands, took a piece of clay, and spat upon it.

The resemblances between Gen., chs. 1; 2, and the Babylonian parallels suggest a common background, but this does not imply that Genesis is borrowed from the epic. In Genesis we have monotheism: God is master of the elements. The majesty of God is supreme. We have a dignified and exalted account of creation which has permanent spiritual values.

Creep'ing Thing. Any animal which creeps (Gen. 1:24, 25), whether a land or a water reptile (Gen. 6:7; Ps. 104: 25), and whether crawling on the belly or creeping on 4 or more feet (Lev. 11:41, 42).

Cres'cens (krĕs'ĕnz) [Lat., growing, increasing]. A Christian, who was for a time at Rome while Paul was a prisoner there, and then departed to Galatia or Gaul (II Tim. 4:10).

Crete (krēt). A large island in the Mediterranean, lying s.e. of Greece, and also known as Candia. It is about 160 miles long by 6 to 35 broad. It is traversed from e. to w. by a chain of mountains, of which Mount Ida, near the center, is 8,065 ft. high. Homer speaks of its fair land, its countless men of different races, and its hundred cities (*Iliad* ii. 649; *Odyssey* xix. 174). The half-mythic legislator, Minos, lived in Crete, and the fabulous Minotaur also was said to dwell there. Crete was conquered by the Romans, 68–66 B.C. Many Jews settled in the island (Acts 2:11; cf. I Macc. 15:19–23, Gortyna being in Crete). Christianity was early introduced; and Titus was left there to arrange the affairs of the churches and to counteract Judaizing doctrine (Titus 1:5, 14). Paul sailed along its whole s. coast on his voyage to Rome (Acts 27:7, 12, 13, 21). The Cretans were famous bowmen; but their moral reputation was bad, their unchastity and untruthfulness were proverbial (Titus 1:12, and R.V. note).

Crib. See MANGER.

Crick'et. The rendering in the text of R.V. of Hebrew *ḥargōl*, which belongs with grasshoppers and locusts, and which does not creep but leaps, is winged, and can be eaten (Lev. 11:22). The chief leaping insects belong to 3 families of *Orthoptera* (the grasshoppers, the locusts, and the crickets). The *ḥargōl* almost certainly belongs to one of the 3, though to which of them cannot now be determined. Among the few known species are the house cricket (*Gryllus domesticus*) and the field cricket (*G. campestris*). The A.V. renders *ḥargōl* "beetle," but the most typical species of the *Coleoptera*, or beetle order, are not leaping insects.

Cris'pus (krĭs'pŭs) [Lat., curled]. The ruler of the Jewish synagogue at Corinth. After listening to Paul's reasonings, he, with all his household, believed in Jesus (Acts 18:8), and was one of the few persons whom Paul personally baptized (I Cor. 1:14).

Croc'o·dile. See LEVIATHAN and LIZARD.

Cross. This word does not occur in the O.T., but crucifixion was common among various nations of antiquity; see CRUCIFIXION. Cross is used in a figurative sense by Jesus (Matt. 10:38; 16:24). From the narrative of the crucifixion it is evident that the cross was of wood, and was heavy, but still not too much so to be borne by a strong man (Matt. 27:32; Mark 15:21; Luke 23:26; John 19:17), and can scarcely, therefore, have been one of the massive structures which some painters depict. It was raised from the earth either before or after the victim had been affixed to it; probably, in most cases, before. Crosses are of three leading types: one, generally called the St. Andrew's cross, like the letter X; another like the letter T; and the third of the

dagger form, †, known as the Latin cross. The cross of Christ was, probably, as artists believe, of the last-named type, which more easily than the others allowed the name, title, or crime of the victim to be affixed to the upper part (Matt. 27:37; Mark 15:26; Luke 23:38; John 19:19). Up to the death of Christ, and even after, the cross was evidently a name of horror and loathing (John 19:31; I Cor. 1:23; Gal. 3:13; Phil. 2:8; Heb. 12: 2; 13:13), so that to bear the cross meant to incur great reproach and obloquy; but after the crucifixion the more zealous followers of Jesus regarded the cross with wholly altered feelings. Paul gloried in the cross of Christ (Gal. 6:14), by which he meant the atonement resulting from his crucifixion (Eph. 2: 16; Col. 1:20).

Crown. 1. An ornamental headdress worn as a badge of authority or dignity; especially: (1) The royal crown. It was generally a circlet of gold (Ps. 21:3), and was often studded with gems (II Sam. 12:30; Zech. 9:16). Sometimes several crowns were combined or intertwined (Zech. 6:11; I Macc. 11:13). The crown which David took at Rabbah from the Ammonites probably belonged to the idol Malcam (II Sam. 12:30, R.V. margin). Its weight was a talent of gold, and in it were precious stones. The ordinary headdress of the Persian king (Esth. 1:11; 6:8) was a stiff cap, probably of felt or of cloth, encircled by a blue and white band, which was the diadem

Crowns of Egypt and Assyria and the Common Radiated Diadem

proper. The royal crown of Assyria was a conical cap, sometimes tapering in a compound curve, but more frequently shaped like the modern fez or tarboosh only higher and ending in a round, blunt point. It was adorned with bands of wrought gold and jewels. The king is also represented wearing a simple fillet, and it is probable that this was a common custom, the crown royal being reserved for state occasions. In Egypt there were two royal crowns. The one for Upper Egypt was a high, round white cap, tapering to a knob; the crown for Lower Egypt was a flat-topped red cap, rising in a high point at the back and having a projection with a curled end springing diagonally toward the front. When the 2 kingdoms were united under one sovereign, he wore the 2 crowns combined, the crown of Lower Egypt being superimposed upon that of Upper Egypt. The Egyptian king is also frequently depicted with a band or diadem. The royal headdress generally bears just over the forehead of the king the Uraeus, the sacred serpent of the Egyptians, symbolizing sovereignty. The radiated diadem was a form of crown familiar to the Greeks and Romans and to the peoples under their influence. A crown or garland of some thorny plant was placed by the Roman soldiers around the temples of Jesus, with the twofold intention of torturing him and mocking his kingly claims (Matt. 27:29). (2) The high priest's crown. It consisted of a golden plate (Lev. 8:9), inscribed with the legend "Holy to Jehovah," and fastened on a lace of blue to the forefront of the miter (Ex. 28:36, 37; 29:6). (3) The crown of victory (II Tim. 2:5; 4:8; Heb. 2:9). It might consist merely of a wreath of leaves or be made of metal.

2. Anything resembling a crown, as the border or molding round about the Ark, the table, and the altar (Ex. 25:11, 24, 25; 30:3, 4).

Cru'ci·fix'ion. The act of fixing a victim to a cross for the purpose of capital punishment. This was done either by tying his hands and feet to it, or in the more cruel way of fixing them to it by nails driven through their fleshy portions. This method of punishment existed in many ancient nations. Alexander the Great crucified 1,000 Tyrians. According to Josephus, Cyrus introduced into his edict for the return of the Jews from Babylon a threat of crucifying anyone who attempted to prevent the missive from being carried into execution (Jos. *Antiq.* xi. 1, 3; 4, 6). Darius the Persian threatened this death, apparently, to those who refused obedience to his decrees (Ezra 6:11). Antiochus Epiphanes crucified faithful Jews who would not abandon their religion at his bidding (Jos. *Antiq.* xii. 5, 4), and Alexander Jannaeus crucified his enemies (Jos. *War* i. 4, 6; 5, 3). Among the Romans crucifixion was a penalty inflicted only on slaves, or on other persons who had committed the most heinous crimes; the ordinary Roman citizen was exempted from it by express legal enactment, but under the Empire crucifixion was imposed on citizens until Constantine put an end to it on religious grounds. The preliminary cruelties of scourging the victim (Matt. 27:26; Mark 15:15; John 19:1), and then, when his body was lacerated, compelling him to bear his cross (John 19:17), were not rare (cf. the proverb, Matt. 10:38). Thus the Roman procurator Florus (Jos. *War* ii. 14, 9) and Titus, at least on one occasion, had those scourged first who were afterward to be crucified. If the victim was simply tied to the cross, death did not take place till thirst and hunger had done their work; and this was sometimes the case even when the hands and feet were pierced by nails. If it was expedient on any ground to get rid of the victims before natural death had released them from their tortures, the end was sometimes hastened by breaking their legs, as was done in the case of the robbers crucified with Jesus (John 19:31–33). Many Jews were crucified after Titus took Jerusalem (Jos. *Life* 75). Constantine abolished punishment by crucifixion in the Roman Empire.

Cruse. A small pot or jug used for carrying water during a journey (I Sam. 26:11; I Kings 19:6) and for holding oil (I Kings 17:12; Judith 10:5); a flask, such as were made of alabaster and used for holding ointment (Matt. 26:7, R.V.). For cruse of honey (I Kings 14:3), a different word in Hebrew, the margin substitutes bottle; and the cruse of salt (II Kings 2:20) was rather a dish.

Crys'tal. 1. The rendering of Hebrew *gābish*, ice and crystal, another reputed product of cold (Job 28:18; in A.V., pearl).

2. The rendering of Hebrew *ḳeraḥ* (Ezek. 1:22), which R.V. marg. renders "ice," which is an established meaning of the word (Job 6:16; 38:29; Ps. 147:17).

3. The rendering of Greek *krystallos* (Rev. 4:6; 22:1). It is either ice or rock crystal, which is quartz, transparent, and when pure colorless.

4. The rendering of Hebrew *zᵉkŭkīth*, in A.V. of Job 28:17. R.V. makes it glass, since crystal occurs in the next verse. The cognate in Syriac is used for glass in Rev. 4:6.

Cub (kŭb), in A.V. **Chub.** A people mentioned with Ethiopia, Put, and Lud (Ezek. 30:5). "Libyans" of LXX suggests Lub.

Cu'bit [Latin *cubitum*, elbow, cubit]. A measure of length based on the length of the forearm, about 18 inches. The Egyptian cubit (17.72 inches) contained 6 handbreadths or palms (Herod. ii. 149). The royal cubit was a palm longer and was equal to 20.67 inches, as appears from measuring sticks found in the tombs. The Hebrews also had 2 cubits, the common and perhaps older cubit (Deut. 3:11; II Chron. 3:3) and a cubit which was a handbreadth longer than the common one (Ezek. 40:5; 43:13). The table of Hebrew lineal measure is 4 fingers=1 handbreadth or palm; 3 handbreadths=1 span; 2 spans=1 cubit (cf. Ex. 25:10 with Jos. *Antiq.* iii. 6, 5). It is not unlikely that the royal Egyptian cubit and the cubit of Ezekiel were theoretically equal, so that the common Hebrew cubit was 17.72 inches and the long cubit 20.67 inches.

Cuck'ow. See SEA MEW.

Cu'cum·ber. The rendering of Heb. *kisshū'*, a vegetable which the Israelites obtained while they were slaves in Egypt, and longed for when they could not have it in the wilderness (Num. 11:5). It is *Cucumis chate*, which is very common in Egypt and somewhat sweeter than the common cucumber, *Cucumis sativus*. The cucumber was raised in gardens in Palestine (Isa. 1:8), and both the species mentioned are grown there today.

Cum'min [Gr. *kyminon* from Heb. *kammōn*]. A cultivated plant sown broadcast and, when ripe, beaten with a rod to detach its seeds (Isa. 28:25, 27). It was one of the trifles of which the Pharisees were particular in paying tithes (Matt. 23:23). Cummin is the *Cuminum cyminum* of botanists, a fennel-like plant bearing umbels of small white flowers. It was cultivated in Palestine for its seeds, which were eaten as a spice or relish with food. They are not in large measure superseded by caraway seeds, which are more agreeable to the taste and more nutritious.

Cun (kŭn), in A.V. **Chun.** See BEROTHAH.

Cup. 1. A small drinking vessel (II Sam. 12:3), of earthenware or metal (Jer. 51:7), held in the hand (Gen. 40:11), and used for water (Mark 9:41), or wine (Ps. 75:8; Jer. 25:15). See BASIN.

2. Figuratively, the contents of the cup, whether pleasant or bitter; that which falls to one's lot (Ps. 23:5; Isa. 51:17; Jer. 16:7; Matt. 26:39).

Cup'bear'er. The official who poured drink into the cup and gave it to the king (Gen. 40:9–14, where the Hebrew word is rendered butler; Neh. 1:11; 2:1, 2). The office was one of the most dignified in an Oriental kingdom, and required moral trustworthiness in its occupant, lest he be bribed to present poisoned wine to the king (Jos. *Antiq.* xvi. 8, 1). It said much for the character of Nehemiah that he, a stranger and a foreigner, should have been appointed to such an office at the Persian court.

Cush (kŭsh) [Heb. *Kūsh*, Ethiopia]. 1. A son of Ham and his descendants collectively. They constituted 5 principal peoples, Seba, Havilah, Sabtah, Raamah, Sabteca, and were located in central and s. Arabia, except Seba, which is probably to be sought on the neighboring African coast (Gen. 10:6–8; 1 Chron. 1:8–10).

2. The land of the Cushites. In most passages it designates Ethiopia (II Kings 19:9; Esth. 1:1; Ezek. 29:10). In Gen. 2:13, R.V. (cf. ch. 10:8) the term denotes territory drained by the Tigris and Euphrates and so probably stands for Kassites (Cossaeans). Herodotus describes Asiatic Ethiopians in the army of Xerxes, who were different from the African Ethiopians (Herod. vii. 70).

3. A Benjamite, perhaps of Ethiopian descent (LXX, *Chousi* for Heb. *Kûshi*), who was a foe to David (Psalm 7, title).

Cu′shan (kū′shăn) [belonging to Cush]. A country or its inhabitants mentioned in connection with Midian, and hence probably Arabia as occupied by Cushites (Hab. 3:7).

Cu′shan-rish′a·tha′im (kū′shăn-rĭsh′a-thā′-ĭm), in A.V. **Chu′shan·rish′a·tha′im** [Cushan of double wickedness]. A king of Mesopotamia, who held the Israelites in subjection for 8 years. Deliverance was achieved under the leadership of Othniel, Caleb's younger brother (Judg. 3:5–11).

Cu′shi (kū′shī) [an Ethiopian]. 1. An ancestor of that Jehudi who lived in Jeremiah's time (Jer. 36:14).

2. Father of the Prophet Zephaniah (Zeph. 1:1).

3. According to A.V., one of the 2 men who carried David the news of the victory over his rebellious son Absalom; but the Heb. has "the Cushi," evidently meaning, as R.V. renders it, "the Cushite," i.e., the Ethiopian. The actual name of the runner is unknown (II Sam. 18:21–23, 31, 32).

Cush′ite (kŭsh′īt). Ethiopian (Num. 12:1, R.V. and A.V. marg.; II Sam. 18:21, R.V.).

Cuth (kŭth) and **Cu′thah** (kū′thȧ). A city of Babylonia, often mentioned in connection with Babylon and Borsippa, and whose tutelary deity was Nergal. Colonists were brought from this place, among others, to Samaria after the deportation of the 10 tribes of Israel (II Kings 17:24, 30). Its site is at Tell Ibrāhīm, n.e. of Babylon.

Assyrian Cupbearer

Cym′bal [Gr. *kymbalon* (I Cor. 13:1)]. A musical instrument (II Sam. 6:5; I Chron. 16:5), Heb. *şelşĕlim, meşiltayim,* from the root *şālal* (to tinkle or clang). One form of the name is in the dual number, which implies that the instrument is of 2 distinct parts. This undoubtedly suggests cymbals, as the

LXX renders the word, which are concave plates of brass (I Chron. 15:19), one form of them being nearly flat, another consisting of hollow cones designed to be clashed together for their sound. See MUSIC.

Eastern Cymbals

Cy′press [Lat. *cupressus, cypressus,* from Gr. *kyparissos*]. 1. E.R.V. marg. for Heb. *te′ashshūr* in Isa. 41:19; 60:13. The text of both versions has "box."

2. Rendering of *berōsh,* A.R.V. marg., Isa. 41:19. See FIR. The cypress, *Cupressus sempervirens,* is the type of the suborder *Cupresseae,* ranking under the order *Pinaceae* (conifers). About 10 species of the genus *Cupressus* are known. The common cypress is an evergreen running into 2 well-marked varieties, one a tall tree 60 feet high with erect closely appressed branches, and the other smaller, with the branches spreading. The cypress is a native of Persia and the Levant. It is extensively planted in cemeteries of the East.

3. The rendering in A.V. of Isa. 44:14 of Heb. *tirzāh* (cf. Arab. *taraza,* to be hard). See HOLM TREE.

Cy′prus (sī′prŭs). An island celebrated in the earliest ages for the richness of its mines of copper. It is situated in the n.e. part of the Mediterranean Sea, about 41 miles from the coast of Cilicia and 60 from Syria. The more compact part of the island is 110 miles in length by 30 to 50 or 60 in breadth; besides which there runs from its n.e. extremity a narrow strip of land, 40 miles long by 5 or 6 broad, projecting from the rest of the island like a bowsprit from a ship. The area of Cyprus is about 3,584 square miles. The island is mountainous, with intermediate valleys, which are at certain seasons unhealthy. The mountains yield copper, and the mines were at one time farmed to Herod the Great (Jos. *Antiq.* xvi. 4, 5). Its ancient inhabitants were Kittim, probably akin to the pre-Hellenic population of Greece (Gen. 10:4), but Phoenicians from the coast of Syria colonized the island. They built as their capital the town of Kition or Citium. Later other bodies of Greeks reinforced the original stock (cf. Herod. vii. 90), so that to this day about ¾ of the population belong to that race. In 58 B.C. Cyprus was seized by Rome and joined with Cilicia for administrative purposes; after the battle of Actium it was made an imperial Roman province (27–22 B.C.). In the year 22 B.C. Augustus handed it over to the senate, and henceforth it was under a proconsul. Many Jewish communities existed in the island (I Macc. 15:23; Acts 4:36). There were Christians connected with it before Stephen's martyrdom; and during the persecution which followed some of them returned to it, preaching the gospel (Acts 11:19, 20). It was visited for missionary purposes, first by Barnabas and Paul (Acts 13:4), and afterward by Barnabas and Mark (ch. 15:39). Paul sailed past it at least twice without landing (chs. 21:3; 27:4). See KITTIM.

Cy·re′ne (sī-rē′nê). An important Greek colonial city in North Africa, beautifully situated on a tableland about 2,000 feet above the sea level, and a few miles distant from the Mediterranean. It constituted one of 5 Greek cities called Pentapolis, situated in Libya Cyrenaica, now Tripoli. It is believed that it was founded by Dorians about the year 632 B.C. During the time of the Ptolemies, in the 3d century B.C., many Jews became resident in Cyrene (Jos. *Apion* ii. 4; *Antiq.* xiv. 7, 2). Simon, who was compelled to carry the cross of Jesus, seems to have been a Cyrenian Jew (Matt. 27:32). Cyrenians joined with Libertines and others in forming a synagogue at Jerusalem (Acts 6:9). Men of Cyrene early became converts and preachers (ch. 11:20). Among them was a certain Lucius, a prominent man in the church at Antioch (ch. 13:1).

Cy·re'ni·us (sĭ-rē'nĭ-ŭs). See QUIRINIUS.

Cy'rus (sī'rŭs) [Gr. *Kyros* from Old Persian *Kûrush*]. A Persian king twice named in The Book of Isaiah (ch. 44:28; 45:1–14). Daniel, referring to the conquest of Babylonia by the Medes and Persians, records that during the night which followed a great feast, Belshazzar, who had been regent at Babylon for his father Nabonidus, was slain (Dan. 5:30). Ezra relates that Cyrus, king of Persia, in the 1st year of his reign issued a proclamation permitting the Jews to return to their own land and rebuild the Temple, for the use of which he restored the sacred vessels taken by Nebuchadnezzar (Ezra, chs. 1; 5:13, 14; 6:3). Many of the Jews embraced the privilege and returned to Jerusalem (538 B.C.); but the work of rebuilding the sanctuary was greatly hindered by adversaries.

According to the Babylonian inscriptions, Cyrus was a son of Cambyses, grandson of Cyrus, great-grandson of Teispes (Chispis), all of whom reigned as kings of Anshan, a designation which appears to denote e. Elam with Susa as its capital. This royal line was founded by Achaemenes, father of Teispes. About the year 550 B.C., Astyages (Ishtumegu), king of the Medes, marched against Cyrus, but was betrayed by his own army and delivered into the hands of Cyrus. Cyrus then took Ecbatana and carried its spoil to his own city. In 547 B.C., Cyrus, now called king of Persia, led the Persian army across the Tigris near Arbela and carried his conquest into the w. He conquered Lydia about this time, taking Sardes and making a prisoner of Croesus, its king (546). Next the Ionian Greeks were subdued, and before the end of 545 the entire peninsula of Asia Minor was a part of the Persian Empire. In 539 B.C., the 17th year of Nabonidus, in the month Tishri, Cyrus met and defeated the Babylonians at Opis; on the 14th day he took Sippar, and Nabonidus fled. Two days later, on the 16th, Gobryas (Ugbaru), governor of Gutium, at the head of a detachment of Cyrus' army, entered Babylon without fighting. Nabonidus was afterward captured at Babylon. On the 3d of Marheshvan Cyrus himself formally entered Babylon, his governor Gobryas proclaimed peace to the province, governors were appointed, and an order issued for the restoration of many captive foreign idols to their several native sanctuaries.

Cyrus was succeeded by Cambyses in 529 B.C. According to Herodotus (i. 190, 191), Cyrus captured Babylon by turning the waters of the Euphrates temporarily into a lake excavated for the purpose, and then entering from the nearly dry bed of the river by the gates which had been left open on the night of a festival while the inhabitants were engaged in revelry. Historians now universally reject the tradition of a forcible capture of Babylon; according to the plain record of the Nabonidus-Cyrus Chronicle, Cyrus' troops under Gobryas peacefully occupied the city

and captured Nabonidus in it. The account given by the Babylonian priest Berossus, who lived about the time of Alexander the Great, is as follows: "In the 17th year of Nabonidus, Cyrus came out of Persia with a great army, and, having conquered all the rest of Asia, came hastily to Babylonia. When Nabonidus perceived that he was advancing to attack him, he assembled his forces and opposed him; but he was defeated and fled with a few of his troops and was shut within the city of Borsippa [the twin of Babylon]. Hereupon Cyrus took Babylon and gave order that the outer walls should be demolished, because the city had proved very troublesome to him and difficult to take. He then marched to Borsippa to besiege Nabonidus; but as Nabonidus delivered himself into his hands without holding out the place, he was at first kindly treated by Cyrus, who sent him out of Babylonia but gave him a habitation in Carmania, where he spent the remainder of his life and died" (Jos. *Apion* i. 20).

D

Dab'a·reh (dăb'á-rĕ). See DABERATH.

Dab'be·sheth (dăb'ĕ-shĕth), in A.V. **Dab'·ba·sheth** (dăb'á-shĕth) [hump of a camel]. A town on the boundary line of Zebulun (Josh. 19:11). Probably Tell esh-Shemmâm opposite Tell Ḳaimûn (Jokneam), s. of the Kishon.

Dab'e·rath (dăb'ĕ-răth), in A.V. once **Dab'·a·reh** (dăb'á-rĕ) erroneously (Josh. 21:28) [probably, pasture land]. A city within the territory of Issachar, given with its suburbs to the Gershonites (Josh. 19:12; 21:28; I Chron. 6:72; Jos. *War* ii. 21, 3). It has been identified as the village of Deburieh at the w. base of Mount Tabor.

Da'gon (dā'gŏn) [*dāgān*, grain; cf. *dāg*, fish]. The national god of the Philistines. At Gaza, at Beth-dagon, and especially at Ashdod, he had a temple (Judg. 16:21, 23; I Sam. 5:1–7; I Chron. 10:10). Jonathan Maccabaeus, after defeating the Philistines, drove them into the temple of Dagon in Ashdod, and set fire both to the city and the temple (I Macc. 10:84; 11:4). Dagon was worshiped at an early time in Phoenicia. According to the Ras Shamra texts Dagan (Dagon) was the father of Aleyan (Baal), who was a corn god. The temples of both gods are similar and date from the beginning of the 12th dyn. of Egypt. The idol is considered to have had the head, arms, and upper parts of a human form (I Sam. 5:4), while the lower parts tapered away into the tail of a fish. Diodorus Siculus (ii. 4) mentions a goddess called Derceto, of similar form, as having existed at Ashkelon, another Philistine town. Leaping over the threshold of Dagon's temple may have been a part of Philistine ritual (cf. I Sam. 5:5, LXX; Zeph. 1:9).

Dal'a·i'ah (dăl'á-ī'á). See DELAIAH.

Da'leth (dā'lĕth). The 4th letter of the Hebrew alphabet. From Phoenician *daleth* is derived the Greek *delta*, whence Latin and English *d*. It stands at the head of the 4th section of Psalm 119, in which section each verse of the Hebrew begins with this letter.

The two Hebrew letters, *daleth* and *resh* (*r*), are somewhat similar now, and at certain stages of their development were distinguishable only when carefully written. This similarity caused difficulty to readers and copyists, and occasionally misled them as to the true spelling of words (cf. Gen. 10:4, Dodanim, and I Chron. 1:7, Rodanim).

Dal'ma·nu'tha (dăl'ma-nū'tha). A place situated probably on the w. shore of the Sea of Galilee in the vicinity of Magdala (Mark 8:10; cf. Matt. 15:39 A.V.). Dalmanutha may originate in an error for Heb. pl. *migdā-lôth* read as *Dalmagôth* (-*noutha*). It has also been suggested that Mark originally had Magada, which a scribe wished to correct to Magdal with a marginal gloss *dal ou da* (*dal*, not *da*); when this was introduced into the text *Dalmanoutha* resulted. At any rate, the place is not otherwise known. See MAGDALA, MAGADAN.

Dal·ma'ti·a (dăl-mā'shǐ-a). A region on the e. shore of the Adriatic Sea, with the small but numerous adjacent islands. The mountain tribes were subdued in A.D. 9 by the Romans under Augustus Caesar and Tiberius and the province of Dalmatia was erected. It was regarded as part of Illyricum, which constituted the limit of Paul's missionary journeys in that direction (Rom. 15:19). His associate Titus, after being for a time with Paul in the Italian capital, departed to Dalmatia, perhaps to plant the gospel among its wild inhabitants (II Tim. 4:10).

Dal'phon (dăl'fŏn). A son of Haman (Esth. 9:7).

Dam'a·ris (dăm'a-rǐs). A woman converted through Paul's preaching at Athens (Acts 17:34).

Dam'a·scene (dăm'a-sēn). A native or inhabitant of Damascus (II Cor. 11:32).

Da·mas'cus (da-măs'kŭs). A city of Syria, on a plateau watered by the rivers Abanah and Pharpar (II Kings 5:12). The tableland is about 2,200 feet above the level of the sea, at the e. foot of the Antilibanus chain of mountains, and contains about 500 square miles. Where watered by channels from the rivers, it is exceedingly fertile, so that the city is embosomed in gardens and orchards, in refreshing contrast to the neighboring desert. Three great trade routes center at Damascus; one leads s.w. to the Mediterranean seacoast and Egypt, another runs s. to Arabia, and the third crosses the desert to Bagdad. The city is very ancient. It is mentioned as early as the time of Abraham (Gen. 14:15). In the days of David, Damascus was one of several petty states of s. Syria. It was captured and garrisoned by David (II Sam. 8:5, 6; I Chron. 18:5, 6). After he smote the Syrian kingdom of Zobah, a man called Rezon, a former subject of the king of Zobah, collected a band of men, seized Damascus, and founded the Syrian kingdom, which henceforth was so often in conflict with Israel (I Kings 11:23, 24). Damascus was the capital of Hezion, Tabrimmon, and the Ben-hadads (I Kings 15:18, 20; 20:34; II Kings 8:7), of Hazael (I Kings 19:15, 17; II Kings 8:8–15), and of Rezin (II Kings 16:5). Tabrimmon and the first Ben-hadad were in league with the king of Judah (I Kings 15:18, 19; II Chron. 16:2, 3). Ahab agreed to a covenant, obtaining the right to establish streets of bazaars in Damascus (I Kings 20:34). At this period Damascus took a leading part among the w. nations in resistance to Assyria. In alliance with kings of the seacoast and Ahab of Israel it met Shalmaneser at Karkar in (854) 853 B.C., and, though defeated, checked the Assyrian advance. But in 842, Shalmaneser defeated Hazael, king of Damascus, at Mount Hermon and forced him to pay tribute. When, in 734, Rezin of Damascus and Pekah of Israel planned to assault Jerusalem, Ahaz of Judah called in Tiglath-pileser, king of Assyria, who captured Damascus (732 B.C.), carried the inhabitants captive to Kir, and killed Rezin (II Kings 16:5–9; Isa. 7:1 to 8:6; Amos 1:3–5). But Damascus soon regained its prosperity (Ezek.

27:18). From the Assyrians Damascus passed to the Chaldeans, from them to the Persians, and then to the Macedonian Greeks. It was one of the 10 cities originally forming the Decapolis. Damascus was taken in 64 B.C. by the Roman general Metellus, and in 63 Syria became a Roman province. Many Jews dwelt in Damascus, and supported several synagogues (Acts 9:2; Jos. *War* ii. 20, 2). Near Damascus, Saul of Tarsus, when on his way to persecute the Christians of the city, was smitten to the earth and heard the heavenly voice (Acts 9:2, 3, 8–10; 22:6, 10–12; 26:12); and from the walls he was let down to escape the fury of the Jews (Acts 9:24, 25; cf. ch. 26:20; Gal. 1:17). The traditional street

Eastern Gate of the Street Called Straight

called Straight is about 2 miles long, and runs from n.e. to s.w., almost through the center of the city. It is a poor street now, but in the time of Paul it was a magnificent thoroughfare, flanked with Corinthian columns. At its e. end is the e. gate of the city. In Paul's time the city was in the hands of Aretas, king of Arabia Petraea, but it soon reverted to the Romans (II Cor. 11:32).

Dan (dăn) [a judge]. 1. A son of Jacob by Bilhah (Gen. 30:5, 6). He had one son, Hushim (Gen. 46:23) or Shuham (Num. 26:42). The future destiny of his descendants was thus predicted by Jacob:

"Dan shall judge his people,
    As one of the tribes of Israel.
Dan shall be a serpent in the way,
    An adder in the path,
    That biteth the horse's heels,
So that his rider falleth backward"
                (Gen. 49:16, 17);

meaning that his tribe would contend with the foes of Israel as earnestly and craftily as would any of the tribes. Speaking on the same subject, Moses compared Dan to a lion's whelp "that leapeth forth from Bashan" (Deut. 33:22).

2. The tribe to which Dan gave origin, and the territory in Canaan which it obtained by allotment (Num. 1:12, 38, 39). Its assigned territory contained, among other towns, Zorah, Aijalon, Ekron, Eltekeh, and ended opposite Joppa (Josh. 19:40–46; 21:5, 23, 24; cf. Judg. 5:17). The Danites, however, did not possess themselves of all this region, but were restricted by the Amorites to the hill country (Judg. 1:34, 35). Cramped for room, they sent spies to the extreme n. of Palestine to look for a new location; they found what they desired in the town of Laish, occupied by foreigners. The Danites sent an expedition, seized the place, slew its inhabitants, and rebuilt it under the new name of Dan (Josh. 19:47; Judg., ch. 18). Oholiab and Samson were Danites (Ex. 31:6; Judg. 13:2, 24).

3. A town in the extreme n. of Palestine, the phrase "from Dan even to Beer-sheba" or "from Beer-sheba even to Dan" denoting the land in its entire extent from n. to s. (Judg. 20:1; I Chron. 21:2). The town was originally called Laish or Leshem. The name Dan

have Greek dancing girls in mind when he warns against a woman that is a singer (Ecclus. 9:4). Salome, the daughter of Herodias, danced before an assembly of men (Matt. 14:6; Mark 6:22); probably her performance was derived from the pantomime solo dance of the Greek hired female dancers. Dancing as part of a religious ceremony or as an act of worship seems to have been common among the Hebrews. It was practiced chiefly by women (Ex. 15:20; Judg. 21:21, 23), but occasionally by men, as in the well-known instance of David's dancing before the Ark (II Sam. 6:14–23; I Chron. 15:29). Dancing before images was common among idolaters (Ex. 32:19; I Kings 18:26).

Dan′iel (dăn′yĕl) [God has judged]. 1. Son of David and Abigail, born at Hebron (I Chron. 3:1). He is called Chileab in II Sam. 3:3.

2. A priest who, doubtless in behalf of a father's house, signed the covenant in the days of Nehemiah (Ezra 8:2; Neh. 10:6). Chronologically he is the 3d of the name mentioned in the Old Testament.

3. A hero Danel (Daniel) in the Ras Shamra texts who renders justice to the widow and orphan. It has been supposed by some that Ezek. 14:14, 20; 28:3 refers to this ancient hero. It is noteworthy that in

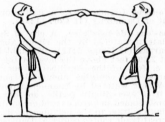

Two Steps in an Ancient Egyptian Dance

was given to it after its capture by the Danites (Josh. 19:47; Judg., ch. 18). Abraham pursued Chedorlaomer as far as Dan (Gen. 14:14); thought by some to be Dan-jaan (*q.v.*). But Dan-jaan may be Laish, i.e., Dan; if so, the familiar name Dan has supplanted the older designation in Genesis (cf. Deut. 34:1). At Dan Jeroboam fixed one of his golden calves (I Kings 12:28–30; II Kings 10:29; Amos 8:14). Ben-hadad destroyed the town with other places in its vicinity (I Kings 15:20; II Chron. 16:4). Dan was in a fertile valley by Beth-rehob (Judg. 18:9, 28), near Lebanon, at the sources of the lesser Jordan (Jos. *Antiq.* v. 3, 1; viii. 8, 4), near the marshes of the waters of Merom (Jos. *War* iv. 1, 1), and about 3 miles w. of Bāniyās. The site is at Tell el-Ḳāḍi, which in Arabic signifies "mound of the judge," and thus preserves the sense of the old name Dan. At the base of this mound are 2 springs, whose waters presently unite and form the river Leddan, the shortest but most abundant in water of the 3 streams which flow together a few miles below and form the Jordan.

Dance. On joyous occasions of a secular or semisecular character, dancing, accompanied by music, was practiced among the Hebrews by women, either singly or in groups, especially in welcoming a victor home (Judg. 11:34; I Sam. 18:6, 7; 29:5; cf. Jer. 31:4, 13). Children, apparently of both sexes, took part in dances (Job 21:11; Matt. 11:16, 17; Luke 7:32). Dancing is a sign of joy (Ps. 30:11; Eccl. 3:4; Lam. 5:15; Luke 15:25).

Some of the customs of Hellenism were dangerous morally to the Jews. Ben Sira may

these 3 verses the kethib of the Hebrew text like Ras Shamra omits *yod*.

4. The celebrated Jewish prophet at the Babylonian court. He sprang from the princely family of the tribe of Judah (Dan. 1:3–7). When a youth, he was carried off with other captives by Nebuchadnezzar, in the 3d or, reckoning accession year as 1st year, the 4th of Jehoiakim, 605 B.C. (Dan. 1:1; Jer. 25:1). At Babylon the boy was selected with other young captives of good birth and parts to be trained for the state service. He and 3 companions obtained leave from the master of the eunuchs, under whose charge they were, to substitute simple food for the viands assigned them by the king which were likely to be contrary to the Mosaic Law and defiled by heathen rites (Dan. 1:8). The 4 young exiles all became proficient in Babylonian learning, while the grace of God enabled them to manifest uncompromising principle, even when it brought them face to face with death. The period of tutelage ended in the 3d year (v. 5), when they were given service at court; and Daniel continued in it with varying prominence until 538 B.C., the 1st year of Cyrus (v. 21). In Nebuchadnezzar's 2d year, 603 B.C., doubtless toward its close (cf. vs. 5 and 18), Daniel interpreted the king's dream of the great image (ch. 2:1–45). This success led to the prophet's being made ruler over the province of Babylon, and head over its wise men (vs. 46–49). He afterward interpreted the vision which revealed the approaching madness of Nebuchadnezzar (ch. 4). About this time Ezekiel cited Daniel as a notable example of righteousness and wisdom (Ezek. 14:14;

28:3); but see DANIEL 3. In the 1st year of Belshazzar Daniel himself had a vision and saw, under the figure of animals, 4 successive empires reaching to the time when the ancient of days should sit, and one like a son of man come with the clouds of heaven to set up a spiritual kingdom which should endure eternally (Dan., ch. 7). The scene of the vision of the 3d year of Belshazzar was at Shushan (ch. 8:2), the Elamite capital, and residence of Cyrus, king of Persia. The prophet himself was probably at Babylon (for a similar case, cf. Ezek. 8:1–3). In this vision he saw a ram trampled by a goat, and from the head of the latter, when its power was in turn broken, 4 horns appearing, from one of which a little horn sprang and wrought proudly, especially toward the glorious land and its sanctuary; whereby were symbolized the Persian and Macedonian empires, the division of the latter into 4 kingdoms, the rise of a fierce king and his desecration of the sanctuary (Dan., ch. 8).

On the fall of the Neo-Babylonian Empire, Darius the Mede appointed 120 satraps over the new kingdom, with 3 presidents over them, Daniel being one of the 3 (ch. 6:1, 2). Jealousy of Daniel on account of his ability and eminence led to a plot against him, and he was cast into the den of lions (vs. 3–23; I Macc. 2:60). In the 1st year of Darius, Daniel concluded from the statements of Jeremiah (Jer. 25:11, 12; 29:10) that the Captivity was approaching its close (Dan. 9:1, 2). He humbled himself, confessed the sins of the nation and prayed. In consequence there was revealed to him the prophecy of the 70 weeks (v. 24). In the 3d year of Cyrus, king of Persia, he had a vision of the final conflict between the powers of the world and the Kingdom of God (chs. 10 to 12). Daniel is referred to in Matt. 24:15; Mark 13:14; Heb. 11:33; II Esdras 12:11; I Macc. 2:60.

The Book of Daniel in the LXX, the Vulgate, and the English versions follows Ezekiel, but in the Hebrew canon is placed in the Writings or Hagiographa. It was not put with the Prophets because Daniel, although called a prophet (Matt. 24:15; Jos. *Antiq.* x. 11, 4 and 6), and one of the greatest of them (Jos. *Antiq.* x. 11, 7), and although he was marvelously gifted by the spirit of prophecy, was not regarded as officially a prophet. He had the *donum propheticum*, but not the *munus propheticum:* the prophetic gift, not the prophetic vocation. He was officially a statesman, and his life was passed in the business of the state. He does not use the common prophetic declaration, "Thus saith the Lord," and he does not exhort his contemporaries, as it was the function of the prophets to do. The book is in Hebrew, except chs. 2:4b to 7:28, which is in Aramaic. The book may be divided into 2 sections:

I. *Six anecdotes of his life* in company with 3 compatriots (chs. 1 to 6): (*a*) the preparation of Daniel and his 3 companions for their work (ch. 1); (*b*) witness borne by God through the 4, at a foreign court and largely to foreigners, of his omnipotent and omniscient control of the powers of the world in their development and in their relation to the Kingdom of God (chs. 2 to 6). It includes Nebuchadnezzar's dream of the image made of 4 metals, together with clay in the feet, and its destruction (ch. 2); the attempt against Daniel's 3 companions and their deliverance from the fiery furnace (ch. 3); Nebuchadnezzar's dream of the tree hewn down (ch. 4); the writing on the wall at Belshazzar's feast (ch. 5); the plot to destroy Daniel, and his deliverance from the lions' den (ch. 6).

II. *The visions of Daniel:* (*a*) the 4 beasts and the being "like unto a son of man" (ch. 7); (*b*) visions having the fortunes of God's people especially in view (chs. 8 to 12), comprising 3 visions: 1. concerning the cessation of sacrifice, desolation of the sanctuary, opposition to the prince of princes (ch. 8; cf. vs. 13, 25). 2. In view of the near completion of the predicted 70 years of exile, Daniel prepared for the great event by confessing national sins and supplicating forgiveness. From prophecies gone before, it might be supposed that the Kingdom of the Messiah would be established immediately at the expiration of the Captivity; but in a vision Daniel is informed that 70 weeks must elapse after the decree to rebuild Jerusalem is issued before reconciliation is made and everlasting righteousness brought in (ch. 9). 3. He is further informed by a vision in the 3d year of Cyrus in regard to the overthrow of the Persian Empire, the persecution of God's people that shall ensue, and the final relief of the saints and the resurrection to glory (chs. 10 to 12).

The prophecy of the image broken by the stone (ch. 2:31–45), and that of the 4 beasts replaced by a being "like unto a son of man" (ch. 7), depict 4 worldly powers yielding place to the Kingdom of God. The 1st of these kingdoms symbolized in parallel is Babylonia as it is incarnated in Nebuchadnezzar (ch. 2:37, 38). The 2d is Media, which according to ancient historiography was one of the great monarchies of the Orient. That Media and Persia are the 2 horns of the ram (ch. 8:20) cannot be used as an argument against this identification, for a distinction between Medes and Persians is also maintained: "Darius the Mede" (ch. 5:31), "seed of the Medes" (ch. 9:1); "Cyrus the Persian" (ch. 6:28), "Cyrus, king of Persia" (ch. 10:1). Cf. also the prophecy of the destruction of Babylon by the Medes and note the reference to the king of the Medes (Isa. 13:17; 21:2; Jer. 51:11, 27–29). The 3d kingdom is Persia, and the 4th is Greece (the empire of Alexander the Great). The 4th beast had 10 horns (Dan. 7:7); the horn is a type of aggressive strength. Antiochus Epiphanes, the little horn (v. 8), had 7 predecessors in the Seleucid Dynasty: Seleucus (I) Nicator, Antiochus (I) Soter, Antiochus (II) Theos, Seleucus (II) Callinicus, Seleucus (III) Ceraunus, Antiochus (III) Magnus, Seleucus (IV) Philopator. There is no agreement about the 3 subsequent kings whom Antiochus Epiphanes displaced, but it is not necessary to insist on exact identification. Some include Alexander in the series. In that case, the 3 are: Antiochus' brother, whom he displaced by natural cause; Heliodorus, Philopator's prime minister, whom he got rid of; and the rightful heir, Demetrius, whose rights he usurped. Another solution, confining itself to the Seleucid Dyn., accepts a historical tradition of another son of Philopator, whom Antiochus caused to be put out of the way. By this interpretation, Alexander would not be included in the 7.

The 2-horned ram (ch. 8:3, 20) is the symbol of Media and Persia. The he-goat with the conspicuous horn between his eyes (v. 5) stands for the Greek Empire; the great horn, Alexander the Great, was broken (v. 8). The 4 horns which came in place of the great horn are the kingdoms of the Diadochi: Macedonia (under Cassander), Thrace and Asia Minor (under Lysimachus), Syria (under Seleucus), and Egypt (under Ptolemy). The little horn (v. 9) is Antiochus Epiphanes (cf. ch. 7:8). Some commentators, however, maintain that the Medo-Persian Empire is the 2d world power; in that case, Rome is the 4th empire. This view involves more difficulties than the explanation adopted above and seems less logical.

The prophecy of the 70 weeks also concerns the sufferings of the people of God (ch. 9:24–27). The prophetic era from which the weeks are reckoned is a decree for restoring and building Jerusalem (v. 25). "The anointed one," a prince (v. 25), is variously interpreted, as referring to Cyrus (Isa. 45:1), Zerubbabel (Hag. 1:14; Zech. 4:8–10; 6:12, 13), or better Joshua, the high priest, the contemporary of Zerubbabel (Zech. 3:8). "The anointed one" (Dan. 9:26) probably is the high priest Onias III, who was murdered at Antioch, c. 171 B.C. (II Macc. 4:33–35). It is accordingly reasonable to attribute the title (Dan. 9:25) to one of the priestly line, i.e., Joshua. The main interest of the writer lies in the maintenance of the cult. The rites were suspended in 586 B.C., but resumed in 538 upon the return from Babylon, making c. 49 years. The word "week" must be interpreted as a year-week. For a sabbath of years, see Lev. 25:2–4, 8.

The 70 weeks (Dan. 9:24) fall into 3 periods (vs. 25 seq.): 7+62+1. A.V., E.R.V. (marg.), and A.R.V. (text) read: "Seven weeks, and threescore and two weeks," agreeing with the Vulgate, which follows Theodotion. This, however, obscures the sense of the original. In the Hebrew text (v. 25) the main division of the verse falls after "seven weeks." E.R.V. (text), A.R.V. (marg.), and J.V. follow the punctuation of the Hebrew.

The prophecy of Jeremiah (Jer. 25:1, 11, 12; cf. II Chron. 36:21) concerning the 70 years was fulfilled with the return under Cyrus in 538 B.C.; by that time, as noted above, 7 year-weeks after the destruction of the Temple were completed. Sixty-two year-weeks equal 434 years. If this number be deducted from 605 B.C., the result is the period of Antiochus Epiphanes, but the 62 weeks should follow directly upon the 1st 7, i.e., after 538 B.C. It seems, therefore, better to assume that the writer is following no exact chronology from 538 to the Maccabaean period. The last week (7 years) is introduced by the cutting off of an anointed one, who probably is Onias III; "the people of the prince that shall come shall destroy the city and the sanctuary," and he will make a league with the majority. The half-week (3½ years) of Dan. 9:27, when the tyrant shall cause the cult to cease, corresponds closely to the 3 years (168–165 B.C.) during which the Temple suffered sacrilege under Antiochus Epiphanes (I Macc. 1:54–64; 4:52–58); this 2d half of the week equals approximately the 2,300 mornings and evenings (Dan. 8:14). The week terminates with the purification of the Temple in 165 B.C. By this interpretation the 1st half of the week corresponds to Antiochus' earlier treatment of the Jews (I Macc. 1:10–15). The abomination of desolation (Dan. 9:27, LXX, and Vulgate; cf. Dan. 11:31; 12:11) is the heathen altar and its accompaniment which Antiochus set up in the Temple (I Macc. 1:54).

I Maccabees was written in Hebrew about the end of the 2d century B.C., and so shows an early traditional interpretation of the 70 weeks. The 2d of the dream visions of Enoch (Book of Enoch, 85–90) presents a series of 70 shepherds extending from the destruction of Jerusalem to the Messianic Kingdom; the last 12 are assigned to the Syrian period. The visions are generally regarded as among the earliest parts of Enoch, and since they are dated before the death of Judas Maccabaeus, they can be cited as a contemporary interpretation of the 70 weeks of Daniel.

Josephus made direct application of this passage from Daniel to the destruction of Jerusalem in A.D. 70 (Jos. Antiq. x. 11, 7). Subsequent Jewish interpretation made the destruction of Jerusalem, either under Titus or under Hadrian, the terminus ad quem. Occasionally there is an apocalyptic or Messianic interpretation.

There developed also a specifically Christian interpretation which assumed various forms.

One combination which coincides with known history throughout starts with the decree of Artaxerxes in his 7th year, 458 B.C. A period of 7 weeks or 49 years came to a close about 408 B.C., and the reformation under Ezra and Nehemiah was conducted during this period and characterized this period as a whole. When this reform ceased to be the dominating feature of God's Kingdom is unknown, but Nehemiah's successor, who was a Persian and naturally not a maintainer of the exclusiveness of Jehovah's religion, was in office in 411 B.C., before the close of the 7th week. Then follow 62 weeks or 434 years, coming down through A.D. 26 to the time when Jesus began his public ministry, A.D. 27, probably early in that year. After these threescore and 2 weeks an anointed one was cut off (Dan. 9:26), making, it may well be, the reconciliation for iniquity and bringing in the everlasting righteousness, spoken of in v. 24; and in the midst of this last week one caused the sacrifice and oblation to cease, not by forbidding them, but by the one sacrifice on Calvary that rendered all others henceforth unnecessary. Nevertheless, notwithstanding the coincidence of the prophecy with the known events in the history of God's Kingdom, and the significance of this correspondence, yet quite probably the 70, and the 7 separated from it at the beginning, and the one week marked off from it at the end, are all symbolical, and measure symbolically, not mathematically, a vast period in the history of God's Kingdom on earth.

The largeness of the outlook and the comprehensiveness of the prophecies of Daniel are realized in the light of the use made of this book by the men of the Bible. 1. Our Lord chose the title Son of Man, by which he referred to himself more often than by any other title, from ch. 7:13, 14; and thus placed that aspect of his mission and Kingdom, which this title denotes, in the forefront. See SON OF MAN. 2. An apocalyptic interpretation of the prophecy of Daniel appears in the N.T.; Christ warned men that the abomination of desolation should yet stand in the Holy Place (Dan. 9:27; 11:31; 12:11; Matt. 24:15; Mark 13:14; cf. II Thess. 2:1–12). Evidently, on Christ's explanation, the content of the prophecies was not exhausted when the idolatrous altar was erected on Jehovah's altar by Antiochus Epiphanes (I Macc. 1:54). The prophecy could thus be made to fit the prospect of any great calamity which should threaten the Jewish religion; or the "abomination of desolation" embodies an idea which will come to manifestation in concrete form whenever the idea itself is present as a potent principle in history. Likewise the apostles understood that the little horn of the 4th beast (Dan. 7:7, 8, 24), and the king that speaks marvelous things against God (ch. 11:36), belong to the future and are yet to be revealed (II Thess. 2:4; Rev. 13:5, 6). Characteristic features of the conflict between the world and God's Kingdom undoubtedly belonged to the bitter struggle in the time of Antiochus Epiphanes, but not to that time only; and Christ and the apostles saw in these prophecies of Daniel an apocalypse of the future. These revelations were not exhausted by the events of the reign of Antiochus; they are big with meaning for the latter days of God's Kingdom. 3. The beast which John saw coming up out of the sea (Rev. 13:1) is a composite picture of the 4 beasts which Daniel saw emerging from the sea (Dan. 7:3–7). Daniel saw a lion with eagle's wings, a bear, a leopard with 4 wings and 4 heads, and finally a beast with 10 horns. On combining these 4 beasts as one animal, the beast that John saw is produced: like a leopard, but with the feet of a bear and the mouth of a lion, having 10 horns and 7 heads. Daniel describes 4 kingdoms of this world which rise successively, and are as fierce and terrible as wild beasts in their antagonism to the Kingdom of God. John does not view the kingdoms individually, but all the kingdoms of this world collectively. He gazes upon them as one, notwithstanding external differences. And John sees the dragon, the tempter serpent of Eden (Rev. 12:3, 9), conformed in appearance to the beast, because the dragon is the animating and molding spirit in the kingdom of the world. To neither Daniel nor John are the world powers presented in their political aspect, but solely as representatives of the world in its antagonism to the Kingdom of God. It is not the fortunes of the nations, but their relation to God's Kingdom, that is the prime object of the prophecy. This fact is important, and furnishes a clue to the final revelation, Dan., chs. 10 to 12, which may be divided into: prologue, chs. 10 to 11:2a; the revelation, chs. 11:2b to 12:4; epilogue, ch. 12:5–13. The last 2 chapters contain a presentation of universal history and may be interpreted and analyzed as follows: (a) ch. 11:2b, the Persian age; (b) vs. 3, 4, Alexander and the division of his empire; (c) vs. 5–20, the conflicts of the Lagidae and Seleucidae prior to Antiochus Epiphanes, with these episodes: v. 5, Ptolemy (I) Soter and Seleucus (I) Nicator; vs. 6–9, the tragedy of Laodice and Berenice and revenge taken by Ptolemy (III) Euergetes; vs. 10–19, Antiochus the Great; v. 20, Seleucus (IV) Philopator; (d) vs. 21–45, Antiochus (IV) Epiphanes; (e) ch. 12:1–3, final triumph of the righteous; (f) v. 4, injunction as to the book. It suggests that in these chapters also the aim is not to unfold political history, but is mainly to sketch apocalyptically great movements of the world in relation to the Kingdom of God. The enemies of Zion came, and had always come, from the n. and s. Developing that historical circumstance apocalyptically, the vision pictures a struggle between the contending world powers, a war of varying fortunes; the gradual overthrow of the king of the s. and the ultimate triumph of the king of the n., and his final mortal conflict with the Kingdom of God. The picture is a companion piece to Ezek., chs. 38; 39. 4. Daniel speaks of the time of the end, that is, the final time. It is "the latter time of the indignation" [of God] (Dan. 8:19; cf. ch. 11:36), when judgment is being executed upon the kingdoms of the world and the eternal Kingdom of God is being established (cf. ch. 10:14), to be followed by the consummation (ch. 12:1c–3). It is the final period of the conflict between the powers of the world and the Kingdom of God, ending in the complete victory of the Kingdom. The apostles also speak of this period, calling it the last hour, the last time, or the last days; and they allude to it as already begun in their day and not ended, and destined to witness a manifestation of Antichrist (II Thess. 2:2–4; II Tim. 3:1; I John 2:18; Jude 18). These men of the N.T. clearly saw the scope and meaning of Daniel's prophecies concerning the final time, and they had a sense of living in that predicted period.

There is no doubt that The Book of Daniel has a unity of thought. The use of 2 languages, however, has caused some difficulty, and various theories have been offered in explanation. Some have supposed that a portion of the Hebrew text was lost and that it was filled in from an Aramaic version of the book. But the question may be raised why the Aramaic begins at the proper place (Dan. 2:4b). Others have held the opposite view that the whole book was originally composed in Aramaic, then translated into Hebrew, and when portions of the Hebrew were lost the gap was supplied from the Aramaic original. The 2 divisions of the book (chs. 1 to 6 and chs. 7

to 12), however, correspond roughly to the limits of the 2 languages. It has accordingly been assumed that chs. 1 to 6 were originally in Aramaic, and the latter 6 chapters in Hebrew. By this theory, a redactor turned chs. 1 to 2:4a into Hebrew and then rendered Hebrew 7 into Aramaic, thus bonding the 2 into one. The Hebrew at both ends of the book would facilitate recognition of the work as eligible for the sacred canon.

The date of authorship has not been definitely settled. Some excellent modern scholars continue to date the book in the time of Daniel in the 6th century. Among the church fathers Jerome is a famous commentator on this book and presents the traditional Jewish exegesis of his time. He opposed the Neoplatonist Porphyry, who attacked the historicity of the work and maintained that it was Maccabean. Commentators now generally accept the date assigned by Porphyry and contend that it was written under the name of Daniel c. 168 B.C. to support the faith of the Jews under the dreadful persecution then raging under Antiochus Epiphanes. In its contributions to apocalyptic and eschatology the book holds an important place in O.T. theology.

The problems of authorship do not disturb the unity of the book. The contents of the work and its veracity must not be confused with the linguistic problems and the formation of the book. It is universally accepted that the Hebrew of Daniel is that of Chronicles, Ezra, Nehemiah, and Esther. The literary use of Ezekiel is generally regarded as a terminus a quo for the book. Many scholars maintain that the great turning point in Hebrew style falls in the age of Nehemiah, and not in the Captivity. Linguistically Hebrew can hardly be earlier than the 5th century. In comparison with other Biblical literature, Daniel belongs to the late period and could very easily be assigned to the 2d century B.C. It is difficult to determine an exact date from the linguistic evidence. The Aramaic of Daniel, according to Professor J. A. Montgomery, "is not earlier than within the 5th century, is more likely younger, certainly is not of the 6th century." Not counting ancient borrowings, there are about 15 Akkadian loan words and about 17 Persian words, all except 3 of which are found in the Aramaic section. Since Daniel lived from the days of Nebuchadnezzar to the fall of the Chaldean Empire under Nabonidus and Belshazzar, this number of Persian words may be rather surprising and may argue for Persian influence after the Exile. There are 3 words of Greek origin (ch. 3:5), which refer to musical instruments: ḳithrōs (ḳithārōs, ḳathrōs) for Greek kitharis; peʿsantērin for psalterion; and sŭmpônyāh for symphōnia. Rather plausible arguments have been presented for early Hellenic influences in the Near East, but in view of the Persian loan words the Greek words also may point to a late date. In fact, the character of the Hebrew, the Aramaic, which seems later than that of the 6th century papyri, and the Persian elements may all point to the Persian period and even perhaps to the Hellenistic. In the light of this evidence, Montgomery presents the view that chs. 1 to 6, which he assigns roughly to the 3d century, were composed in Babylonia, while chs. 7 to 12 belong to the early years of the Maccabees, 168–165 B.C.

The spiritual lessons of the book are more important than questions of authorship. God rules, and his purposes will be vindicated. One must differentiate between the historicity of Daniel and the authenticity of the prophecies and visions on the one hand and the recording of the events and the redaction of the book in its final form on the other.

The asserted historical inaccuracies in Daniel are not statements which are disproved by history, but only statements which have seemed difficult to harmonize with the meager accounts of secular historians. The asserted historical inaccuracies have, moreover, been steadily diminishing before the increasing knowledge of the times of Cyrus. The existence of King Belshazzar was scouted; but now the records contemporary with the capture of Babylon have made him a well-known historical character; they have explained why he raised Daniel to the 3d place of power in the kingdom instead of the 2d, for his father and he already occupied the 2 higher places of authority; and they have made clear why he and not Nabonidus is mentioned as king at Babylon on the night of the capture of the city (see BELSHAZZAR). They do not yet clear up the reference to Darius the Mede's receiving the kingdom, but they show that the appointment of a regent for Babylonia by Cyrus was in accord with his policy. The allusions to Belshazzar as a descendant of Nebuchadnezzar agree with a custom of the time (see BELSHAZZAR). The growth of our knowledge of this period shows how cautious one should be in doubting the historical accuracy of the Biblical records.

The prophecy of Daniel is quoted by Christ as genuine and certain of fulfillment (Matt. 24:15). Josephus, who speaks of Daniel as a great prophet (Jos. Antiq. x. 11), believed that the prophecies of Daniel were in existence before the time of Alexander the Great, 330 B.C. (Jos. Antiq. xi. 8, 5), in fact, before the days of Artaxerxes (Jos. Apion i. 8). The deliverance of Shadrach, Meshach, and Abednego from the fiery furnace and of Daniel from the lions' den are cited in I Macc. 2:59, 60 · cf. also ch. 1:54 with Dan. 9:27; 11:31.

Dan'-ja'an (dăn'jā'ăn). A place between Gilead and Sidon (II Sam. 24:6). It may be identical with Dan, the conventional extreme n. of the country (cf. the connection with Sidon, Judg. 18:28, 29). The text may be corrupt, and this has been suggested: "And they came to Dan and Ijon [I Kings 15:20] and went round about to Sidon," or, "And they came to Dan and went round to Sidon."

Dan'nah (dăn'ȧ). A village in the hill country of Judah (Josh. 15:49), modern Deir esh-Shemsh or Sĭmya. LXX has Renna.

Da'ra (dâr'ȧ). See DARDA.

Dar'da (där'dȧ) [probably, thorn, thistle, for Heb. dardar]. A son of Mahol, family of Zerah, tribe of Judah, who was celebrated for wisdom (I Kings 4:31). In I Chron. 2:6 the name appears as Dara.

Dar'ic. A gold coin current in Persia, worth about $5.50, which had on one side a king with a bow and a javelin, while on the other was a somewhat square figure; see MONEY. The chronicler reckons the value of the gold contributed by the princes in David's reign for the Temple in darics (I Chron. 29:7), because at the time of writing the daric was familiar to his readers and a common standard. The daric was current in the Persian period (Ezra 2:69; 8:27; Neh. 7:70-72; in A.V., dram).

Da·ri'us (dȧ-rī'ŭs) [Old Pers. Dārayavaush, possessing the good]. 1. Darius the Mede, son of Ahasuerus (Dan. 5:31; 9:1). When about 62 years old he was made king over the realm of the Chaldeans after the capture of Babylon by the army of Cyrus, and he reigned a part of one year at least before Cyrus (ch. 6:28). He set 120 satraps over the kingdom (ch. 6:1). The satraps were subject to 3 presidents, of whom Daniel was one (v. 2). Presi-

dents and satraps were at the court of Darius (v. 6), and he had authority to write unto "all the peoples, nations, and languages, that dwell in all the earth" or land (v. 25). He was inveigled into issuing the foolish decree, for violating which Daniel was cast into the lions' den (ch. 6:1-27). In his 1st year Daniel saw the vision of the 70 weeks (ch. 9). He has not been identified with certainty, but was probably sovereign of the Babylonian Empire ad interim until Cyrus, who was pressing his conquests, was ready to assume the duties of king of Babylon. Josephus says that he was son of Astyages, but was known to the Greeks by another name (Jos. Antiq. x. 11, 4). Perhaps, then, he was Cyaxeres, son and successor of Astyages and father-in-law and maternal uncle of Cyrus (Xen. Cyropaedia i. 5, 2; viii. 5, 17-20); more frequently he is identified with Gobryas (Ugbaru), governor of Gutium, apparently a province in w. Media or on its borders, who led the detachment of Cyrus' army which captured Babylon and held the city until Cyrus arrived. Subsequently he was governor of that province.

2. A king of Persia (521-486 B.C.), known as Darius Hystaspis, i.e., Darius, son of Hystaspes. When he came to the throne, the building of the Temple had been suspended owing to complaints from the jealous neighboring tribes; but Darius, on being applied to, caused a search to be made at Achmetha, the Median capital, where the edict of Cyrus permitting the work to be undertaken was found (Ezra 6:1-12). The erection of the sacred edifice accordingly recommenced in his 2d year, 6th month, and 24th day (Ezra 4:24; Hag. 1:15; 2:18), and on the 3d day of the 12th month of his 6th regnal year (516) was completed (Ezra 6:15). The prophets Haggai and Zechariah prophesied during the reign of this monarch (Hag. 1:1; 2:1, 10, 18; Zech. 1:1, 7; 7:1). Through his father Darius belonged to the family of the Achaemenidae, which was already represented on the throne by Cyrus and Cambyses; but he was not in the line of succession. The leading events of his life are detailed in an inscription of Darius' own on a rock at Behistun, 65 miles s.w. of Hamadan. It is in 3 languages, Old Persian, Babylonian, and Elamite. Cambyses, Cyrus' son, put his brother Bardes (Bardiya, Smerdis) to death, and some time afterward committed suicide. Then a Magian Gomates or Gaumata started up, pretending to be Bardes, who he alleged had not really been slain. The fraud was discovered and a conspiracy formed against Gomates by 7 men of rank, one of whom was Darius Hystaspis. In 522 B.C. they slew the Magian and saluted Darius king. Susiana rose against the new monarch, but was temporarily subdued. Babylon followed under a leader called Nidintu-Bel, who was defeated in 521. There was a general revolt throughout the empire, and Darius says: "While I was in Babylon these provinces rebelled against me: Persia, Susiana, Media, Assyria, Armenia, Parthia, Margiana, Sattagydia, and the Sacians." But he and his lieutenants subdued them all, generally ending by impaling the rebel leader. Darius now ruled over an empire extending e. into India and w. to the Grecian Archipelago. He administered it, on the whole, wisely and well. After an unsuccessful campaign against the Scythians near the river Don, in what is now Russia, and a quarrel with the Greeks, in which his generals Datis and Artaphernes were defeated in 490 B.C. at Marathon, Darius died at the age of 73 (Ctesias) in 486 B.C., after a reign of 36 years.

3. The last king of Persia, who reigned from 336/5 to 331 B.C. His true name was Codomannus. He was defeated by Alexander the Great (I Macc. 1:1; Jos. Antiq. xi. 8, 3), first

at Issus in 333, when he fled into Persia, and again at Arbela in 331. He died about 4 months later at the hands of his servants.

Dar'kon (där'kŏn) [cf. Arab. *daraḳa*, to hasten]. Founder of a family, among the children of Solomon's servants (Ezra 2:56; Neh. 7:58).

Date. The fruit of the date palm or *Phoenix dactylifera* (II Chron. 31:5, A.V. marg.), from which honey was made (Jos. *War* iv. 8, 3). The text and the R.V., like the Hebrew original, use the general name honey, without specifying the kind.

Da'than (dā'thăn) [cf. Akkad. *datnu*, strong]. A son of Eliab, a Reubenite, who with Abiram, his brother, and On, a man of the same tribe, were prominent leaders in the rebellion of Korah the Levite. Their grievance was different from his. They thought that the leadership of Israel should have gone to the tribe to which they belonged, for Reuben was Jacob's eldest son. Then, again, they complained that Moses had taken them from a country where there was plenty, under the promise of leading them into "a land flowing with milk and honey," while in fact all that he had done was to march them up and down amid naked rocks and barren sands (Num. 16:1–35, cf. vs. 13, 14; 26:7–11; Deut. 11:6; Ps. 106:17).

Dath'e•ma (dăth'ē-mà). A fortress in Gilead, into which the faithful Israelites fled for safety in the time of Judas Maccabaeus (I Macc. 5:9, 10). They were relieved by Judas and his brother Jonathan. Probably the ancient site of Tell Ḥamad, near Sheikh Miskīn, in the plain of Hauran.

Daugh'ter. Besides corresponding to the several senses in which son is used, especially for child or remoter female descendant or as an expression of tender sympathy for a woman (Gen. 30:21; Ex. 2:1; Matt. 9:22; Luke 13:16), daughter denotes a female inhabitant of a country or town (Gen. 24:3; Judg. 21:21), a female worshiper of a god (Isa. 43:6; Mal. 2:11), the suburb of a city (Num. 21:25 marg.), the collective body of the citizens of a town or country (Ps. 9:14; 137:8; Lam. 4:21; Zech. 2:10). See HEIR, MARRIAGE, SLAVE.

Da'vid (dā'vĭd) [beloved]. Son of Jesse and 2d king of Israel. His life falls into several distinct periods:

I. *His youth*, which was passed at Bethlehem of Judah. He was the youngest of 8 brothers (I Sam. 16:10, 11; 17:12–14). In the registry of the tribe of Judah (I Chron. 2:13–15) only 7 of these sons of Jesse are named, probably because one died without issue. David's mother was tenderly remembered for her godliness (Ps. 86:16; 116:16). His ancestral history was picturesque, inspiring, and generally praiseworthy, yet at times tainted by sin (Gen. 37: 26, 27; 38:13–29; 43:8, 9; 44:18–34; Josh. 2:1–21; Ruth 4:17–22). In person he was ruddy and beautiful to look upon (I Sam. 16:12). As youngest son, he was charged with the care of his father's sheep, and he displayed his fidelity and courage in this occupation by slaying both a lion and a bear which attacked the flock (chs. 16:11; 17:34–36). He possessed musical gifts of high order, at this period playing skillfully on the harp and later composing psalms. When King Saul had been rejected by God, the Prophet Samuel was sent to Bethlehem and directed to anoint David as Saul's successor. There was no public proclamation of David, lest the hostility of Saul should be aroused. At most, the act was performed in the presence of the elders of the town, and, so far as appears, no word concerning the purpose of the anointing was

spoken to the audience (ch. 16:4, 5, 13), though Jesse and David were doubtless informed. It was a crisis in David's history. "The Spirit of Jehovah came mightily upon David." Still he did not despise his humble, daily work.

II. *His service under Saul*. Saul, forsaken by God, distressed by an evil spirit, and subject to melancholy and insanity, was advised by his attendants to attach a harper to his person to soothe him by music when disturbed; and one recommended David as a cunning musician, a man of valor and ready for war by reason of age, skill, and courage, even though perhaps not as yet experienced in battle, discreet, comely, pious (ch. 16:14–18). Saul summoned him, was benefited by his music and pleased with his character, asked Jesse that he might remain, and appointed him one of his armor-bearers (vs. 19–23). The service thus begun proved a school for David. He learned war and government, had intercourse with able men, and saw the dark and bright side of court life. David did not, however, as yet remain continuously with Saul. The king's condition evidently improved, and David returned frequently to Bethlehem to have an oversight over his father's sheep (ch. 17:15). While he was on a visit home the Philistines invaded Judah and encamped about 15 miles w. of Bethlehem. Saul led forth the army of Israel to meet them. The 3 eldest brothers of David were with the army, and after they had been absent from home about 6 weeks, their father sent David to inquire about their welfare. Goliath's challenge stirred his spirit. He felt certain that God through him would remove the reproach from Israel, and he asked who the Philistine was that defied the armies of the living God. His words were reported to Saul, who perceiving the spirit by which the young man was animated intrusted the single combat to him. David put off the armor with which Saul had armed him, urging that he had not proved it. He showed true genius. Goliath was rendered slow of motion by weight of armor; the kind of weapon he carried obliged him to fight at close quarters; and he was vulnerable only in the face, which under the circumstances was out of reach. David approached him, unhampered in movement by any armor, with a sling, in the use of which he was proficient, with 5 stones that could be hurled from a distance, with the consciousness of the righteousness of his cause and with implicit confidence in God. The taunts between the 2 champions are characteristic of ancient battle. Goliath fell, struck by a stone from David's sling. After the combat, David, on his way to Gibeah of Benjamin where Saul held court or to the tabernacle at Nob, displayed the head of the giant at Jerusalem, apparently in defiance to the Jebusites, who held the stronghold, and put the armor in the tent which he thenceforth occupied (ch. 17:54). The sword was deposited in the tabernacle (ch. 21:9). When David had gone forth to meet Goliath Saul, amazed at his spirit, asked Abner whose son such a youth could be; and when David returned triumphant the king put the same question to him, only to receive the simple answer, "I am the son of thy servant Jesse the Beth-lehemite." This reply formed the sum and substance of the interview (chs. 17:55 to 18:1); David's ancestors were not notable for heroic achievement. The question of the king had also reference to the rank and material condition of the family, for Saul had promised to accept the victor as son-in-law and to free his father's family from taxation (chs. 17:25; 18:18). He found that he had no occasion to be ashamed of the birth of his son-in-law. The victory over Goliath was a second crisis in David's life. The valor, modesty, and piety, which he displayed won for him the disinterested and enduring love of Jonathan (ch. 18:1). He was no longer permitted to repair periodically to his father's house, but he remained continuously at court (v. 2). The ovation which he received aroused the jealousy of Saul, who thenceforth was David's enemy (vs. 6–9). Saul saw that Samuel's prediction of the transfer of the kingdom from him to one better than he (ch. 15:17–29) approached fulfillment in David, and he attempted to prevent it. He endeavored to slay David with his spear (ch. 18:10, 11). Failing in this, he reduced David in military rank and power (v. 13). He gave his daughter, whom he had promised to David for a wife, to another (vs. 17–19). He endeavored to entrap him to death through his love for Michal (vs. 20–27). As David grew in favor (vs. 29, 30) Saul's fear increased, and he no longer concealed his purpose to slay David (ch. 19:1). This purpose was never after allowed by Saul's adherents to be abandoned, but was fostered by a party at court (ch. 24:9; Psalm 7, title). Appeased for a time, jealousy soon revived, and he again attempted to smite David with his spear (ch. 19:4–9). Then he would have arrested David, who, however, escaped through Michal's subtlety (vs. 10–17). David wrote Psalm 59 at this time. He fled to Samuel at Ramah, whither Saul sent to seize him (I Sam. 19:18–24); fled next to Jonathan, who inquired and informed him that there was no longer safety for him at court (ch. 20).

III. *The fugitive hero.* Without confidence in God and sunk in despair David fled from Saul. Stopping at Nob, without faith, he told a lie (ch. 21:1–9); then hurried to Gath and sought protection of Saul's enemy Achish (v. 10). The lords of the Philistines, however, refused to harbor him who had formerly humiliated them, and they seized David (v. 14; Psalm 56, title). He feigned madness and made himself despicable, and Achish drove him away (cf. Psalm 34, title, but no doubt Abimelech=Achish). He regained his faith in Jehovah (Psalm 34), returned to Judah, and abode in the cave of Adullam (I Sam. 22:1), but placed his parents in Moab (vs. 3, 4). A motley company, mostly of unemployed and desperate men, numbering 400 at first, increasing eventually to 600, began to join him. Among these were Abiathar, the surviving priest of Nob, who brought an ephod with him, and the Prophet Gad, whom David had probably met at Ramah (vs. 5, 20; ch. 23:6). David thus had religious aid and companionship. From Adullam he went to the relief of Keilah and delivered the town out of the hands of the Philistines (ch. 23:1–5). On Saul's preparing to attack him there, he fled to the wilderness of Judah (v. 14; Psalm 63), whither Saul, at the instigation of the Ziphites, pursued him until compelled to desist by an incursion of the Philistines (I Sam. 23:14–29). That trouble being settled, Saul sought David in the wilderness near Engedi, but was for the time conquered by the kindness of David, who had the king in his power in the cave, but spared his life (ch. 24; Psalms 57; 142). David and his band of armed followers protected the exposed property of the Israelites from thieving marauders (I Sam. 23:1; 25:16, 21; 27:8), and naturally enough expected some return in gifts of food. He did not levy tax or demand regular contributions of provisions. Nabal's scornful rejection of his request incensed him, and he was saved from shedding blood in his fury only by the wisdom and address of Nabal's wife (ch. 25), whom David married after the death of her husband. David again came into the neighborhood of Ziph, and the Ziphites

again informed Saul, who marched against David. David showed his magnanimity by not slaying the sleeping king, but merely carrying away from his side his spear and cruse of water (ch. 26). Despairing of always escaping Saul, David left Judah and obtained permission from Achish to occupy Ziklag, a frontier town toward the southern desert. Here he remained a year and 4 months, protecting the Philistines by warring with the desert tribes, yet sometimes wasting a remote village even of Philistia (ch. 27). When the Philistines went to Gilboa to war with Saul, David was prevented from accompanying them by the lords of the Philistines (chs. 28: 1, 2; 29). Upon his return he found Ziklag in ruins. He pursued the retreating invaders and recovered the spoil (ch. 30). When he heard the result of the battle of Gilboa, he mourned the fate of Saul and Jonathan in an elegy (II Sam., ch. 1.)

IV. *King of Judah.* On the death of Saul the tribe of Judah, to which David belonged, elected him king, and he began to reign in Hebron (II Sam. 2:1–10), being then about 30 years old (ch. 5:4). The rest of the tribes, under the leadership of Abner, one of the ablest men of the time, set up Ish-bosheth, Saul's son, at Mahanaim, and for the next 2 years civil war raged between his partisans and those of David. It ended by the assassination, sorely against David's will, both of Abner and of Ish-bosheth (chs. 2:12 to 4:12). David's reign at Hebron continued for 7 years and 6 months (ch. 5:5). He had already several wives, and among the sons born to him at Hebron were Amnon, Absalom, and Adonijah (ch. 3:1–5).

V. *King of all Israel.* On the death of Ish-bosheth, David was elected king over all the tribes, and he at once set to work to establish the kingdom (ch. 5:1–5). Various towns in the territory of Israel were garrisoned by the Philistines, and others were held by the Canaanites. David began a siege of the Jebusite stronghold at Jerusalem. It was deemed impregnable by its inhabitants, but David took it by storm. He wisely made it his capital, and erected a palace there by the skill of Tyrian artificers. The new capital stood on the border of Judah and Israel. Its situation tended to allay the jealousy between n. and s. Its deliverance from the hands of the Canaanites opened the highway between Judah and the n., facilitated intercourse, and tended further to cement the kingdom. The Philistines twice invaded the land, and twice suffered defeat near Jerusalem (ch. 5:17–25; I Chron. 14:8–17). The king followed up the 2d victory by invading the country of the Philistines, took Gath, and by this conquest and by brief campaigns later (II Sam. 21: 15–22) so completely subjugated the Philistines that these hereditary enemies ceased to trouble Israel for centuries. The kingdom being established, David turned his attention to religious affairs. He brought the Ark, with ceremony, sacrifices, and rejoicing, from Kiriath-jearim (Josh. 15:9; II Chron. 1:4), and placed it within a tabernacle which he had pitched for it in the city of David (II Sam., ch. 6; I Chron., chs. 13; 15:1–3). Next he organized the worship on a magnificent scale (I Chron., chs. 15; 16), and planned a splendid temple (II Sam., ch. 7; I Chron. chs. 17; 22:7–10). Through the divine favor he now became very prosperous. To insure the safety of the nation, to keep it from idolatrous contamination, and to avenge insult offered to it, he waged war with surrounding nations, and subdued the Moabites, the Aramaeans of Zobah and Damascus, the Ammonites, the Edomites, and the Amalekites (II Sam., chs. 8; 10; 12:26–31), thus extending his kingdom to the limits long before promised to Abraham (Gen. 15:18). It was during the Ammonite war that David committed his great sin in the matter of Uriah the Hittite, for which God rebuked him through Nathan the prophet, and imposed the penalty that the sword should never depart from his house (II Sam. 11:1 to 12:23). David sincerely repented (Psalm 51), but the child of the union died (II Sam. 12:19). Lawless lust and lawless vengeance were manifested in his own family (ch. 13). Lawless and unfilial ambition triumphed for a time in his family and led to civil war (chs. 14 to 19). The spirit of dissatisfaction and tribal jealousy fomented by Absalom showed itself after the suppression of Absalom's rebellion once more in the revolt of Sheba (ch. 20). David solemnly satisfied justice, according to the ideas of that age, in avenging Saul's bloody violation of the treaty rights of the Gibeonites (ch. 21). He committed a sin of pride in numbering the people, and was punished by a pestilence (ch. 24; I Chron., ch. 21). David was much occupied during his reign with the organization of internal affairs and with the preparation of material for the erection of the Temple. He closed his reign by securing the succession to Solomon (I Kings, ch. 1), and by providing that the guilt of some who had escaped justice in his day should not go unpunished (ch. 2:1–11). He died in his seventy-first year, after having reigned 40 (or, more precisely, 40½) years, 7½ at Hebron and 33 at Jerusalem (II Sam. 2:11; 5:4, 5; I Chron. 29:27).

David was early regarded as the sweet singer of Israel (II Sam. 23:1). Ancient Hebrew tradition, much of which was unquestionably current about David's own time and shortly after, ascribed the composition of psalms to him both directly and indirectly. His fondness for music is recorded in the historical books; he played skillfully on the harp (I Sam. 16:18–23; II Sam. 6:5), and he arranged the service of praise for the sanctuary (I Chron. 6:31; 16:7, 41, 42; 25:1). He composed a lament over Saul and Jonathan, and over Abner, and a song of deliverance and last words (II Sam. 1:17–27; 3:33, 34; chs. 22; 23:1–7). His musical activity is referred to by Amos, Ezra (Ezra 3:10), Nehemiah (Neh. 12:24, 36, 45, 46; Amos 6:5), and the son of Sirach (Ecclus. 47:8, 9). Such work on the part of David accorded with the times, for poetry and music had long been cultivated by the Hebrews as well as by the Egyptians and Babylonians (Num. 21:14; Judg., ch. 5). Seventy-three psalms are designated as David's in their Hebrew titles; and as in many cases the intention is to indicate that he is the author (cf. Psalms 3; 7; 34; 51 et cetera), it is possibly always the intention. Psalm 59 and perhaps Psalm 7 are assigned to the time of his sojourn at Saul's court; Psalms 34; 52; 54; 56; 57; 63; 142 to the period of distress when he was a fugitive; and Psalms 3; 18; 30; 51; 60 to the years of varied experiences when he was king.

Though at times David committed deep-dyed sins, for which the early and comparatively dark period of the Church's history in which he lived and his own deep penitence are his only defense, yet his general fidelity to Jehovah was such that he was called the man after God's own heart (I Sam. 13:14). Speaking generally, he did that which was right in the eyes of the Lord, save in the matter of Uriah the Hittite (I Kings 15:5). He served his generation by the will of God, and then fell asleep (Acts 13:36). His influence on mankind can scarcely be overestimated. He, rather than his predecessor Saul, was the founder of the Jewish monarchy. His psalms, sung throughout Christendom century after

century, revive his spiritual influence. He was an important link in the chain of ancestry of Him who was at once David's son and David's Lord (Matt. 22:41–45).

Da′vid (dā′vĭd), **Cit′y of.** 1. The Jebusite stronghold of Zion captured by David's men, and called by him the city of David, because he made it his royal residence (II Sam. 5: 6–9; I Chron. 11:5, 7). It stood on the ridge, s. of the later site of the Temple. It was early settled, and was a walled town in the 3d millennium B.C. The Ark was taken thither by David, and stayed there until the Temple was built (II Sam. 6:12, 16; I Kings 8:1; I Chron., ch. 15; II Chron. 5:2). David was buried there (I Kings 2:10). Solomon's queen, Pharaoh's daughter, dwelt there for a time (I Kings 3:1), though he afterward erected a palace for himself and her (chs. 7:1; 9:24; II Chron. 8:11). He was buried in the city of David (I Kings 11:43; II Chron. 9:31), as were Rehoboam (I Kings 14:31; II Chron. 12:16) and many other kings (I Kings 15:8, 24; 22:50; II Kings 8:24; 9:28; 12:21; 14: 20; 15:7, 38; 16:20; II Chron. 14:1; 16:14; 21:1, 20; 24:16, 25; 27:9). Jehoiada, the high priest, was also interred there (II Chron. 24: 16). Hezekiah brought the upper watercourse of Gihon to the w. side of the city of David (ch. 32:30; cf. ch. 33:14). Millo was apparently within its limits (ch. 32:5). In Nehemiah's time there was a descent from the city of David by means of stairs (Neh. 3:15; 12:37). It was fortified and garrisoned by the Syrians and Greeks during the Maccabean war (I Macc. 1:33; 2:31; 14:36, 37). See JERUSALEM.

2. Bethlehem, the birthplace or at least the home of David (Luke 2:4).

Day. 1. An interval of time comprising the period between two successive risings of the sun (Gen. 7:24; Job 3:6). The Hebrews reckoned it from evening to evening (Ex. 12:18; Lev. 23:32; Jos. *War* iv. 9, 12). This custom was probably due to the use of lunar months, which began with the appearance of the new moon. The exact designation of the civil day accordingly was evening-morning or night-day (Dan. 8:14, A.V. marg.; II Cor. 11:25). But although the evening properly introduced a new day, it was often reckoned in connection with the natural day which, strictly speaking, it followed—e.g. the evening which began the 15th of Nisan is designated by the expression "the fourteenth day . . . at even" (Ex. 12:18; cf. II Chron. 35:1). The days of the week were numbered, not named. The only exception was the 7th day, which was also called Sabbath.

2. The interval between dawn and darkness (Gen. 1:5; 8:22). It was divided into morning, noon, and evening (Ps. 55:17; cf. Dan. 6:10); or its time was indicated by reference to sunrise, heat of the day, cool of the day, sunset, and the like. After the Exile the use of hours became common, and the day from sunrise to sunset was divided into 12 hours (Matt. 20:1–12; John 11:9); the 6th hour being noon (John 4:6; Acts 10:9), the 9th hour the hour of prayer (Acts 3:1; Jos. *Antiq.* xiv. 4, 3).

3. Any period of action or state of being (Zech. 12:3 seq.); as day of trouble (Ps. 20: 1), day of his wrath (Job 20:28), day of the Lord (Isa. 2:12; 13:6, 9; in the N.T. specially of the 2d advent of Christ, I Cor. 5:5; I Thess. 5:2; II Peter 3:10). So also in the Hebrew phrase translated, "In the day that," which is equivalent to "when" (Gen. 2:4, 17; Lev. 14:2), and is often rendered so in the English versions (Lev. 14:57; Num. 6:13; I Sam. 20:19; Ps. 20:9).

Day of the Lord. An eschatological term; it is the day of Jehovah's self-revelation to judge evil and to bring his work of redemption among men to completion. In that day Jehovah manifests himself in triumph over his foes and interposes in behalf of his people to deliver them. This deliverance will be primarily from external hostile oppression, but there may also be included release from social miseries. As such it was a day to be desired; apparently the term is older than written prophecy, for Amos (Amos 5:18) puts it into the mouth of the people. There will be a national dissolution, but only in order to usher in reconstruction. The popular idea of a day of deliverance was misleading to a people who depended more upon form and correct ritual than upon an ethical religion. Amos accordingly gave the term a new significance, when he spoke of the day of the Lord as God's judgment upon Israel (Amos 5:18–20; cf. also chs. 2; 3; 4:12 *seq.*; 5:10 to 6:14; 9:1–10). The day of the Lord, as understood by Amos, becomes a figure which is afterward often used by the prophets to portray impending doom. While the day is a judgment primarily on Israel, it also includes the Gentiles (cf. Ezek. 30:1 *seq.*; Obad. 15–17). The prophets in adopting the figure develop it partly according to the occasion and partly under the influence of the imagination. Isaiah (Isa. 2:12–21) represents it as directed against various objects of pride and strength; Joel (Joel 2:1 *seq.*) derives his imagery from a plague of locusts (cf. also Isa., chs. 2; 3; 13; 24; 34:8; Hos. 2:18 *seq.*; 4:3; 10:8; Joel, chs. 1 to 3; Micah, chs. 3; 4; Zeph., chs. 1 to 3; Zech., ch. 14; Mal., chs. 3; 4). The day of the Lord is the final and universal judgment. Although that day fills men with terror and anguish, it is also a cause of universal rejoicing, for then begins the reign of God (cf. Ps. 97:1; 98:9).

In the N.T. it is the day of Christ, the day of his coming in the glory of the Father. It is a day of wrath (Rom. 2:5 *seq.*), a day of judgment (Matt. 10:15; Rom. 2:16), a great day (Jude 6). Sometimes it is called "that day" (Matt. 7:22; I Thess. 5:4) or simply "the day" (I Cor. 3:13); also "the day of our Lord Jesus" (II Cor. 1:14); "the day of Jesus Christ" or "Christ" (Phil. 1:6, 10). The epistles of Paul are suffused with the longing for the day of Christ's glorious manifestation. The conception of the day centers in Christ and points to the establishment of the Kingdom of heaven.

Days'man (A.V.). One who has set a day for hearing a cause; a mediator or an arbitrator (Job 9:33, A.V.).

Day'star'. See LUCIFER.

Dea'con [Gr. *diakonos;* in classical writers a servant, a waiting man, a messenger. It is used in this sense in Matt. 20:26, where it is translated "minister," and is distinguished from *doulos*, bond servant or slave in the next verse]. A Christian officer, whose spiritual and moral qualifications are laid down in I Tim. 3:8. It is justly assumed that the 7 men chosen to relieve the apostles of the secular care of the widows and other poor people in the Early Church were deacons (Acts 6:1–6; cf. the words ministration, *diakonia*, and serve, *diakoneō*, in vs. 1 and 2). Their charge of the needy did not debar them from the privilege of speaking publicly for Christ, for Stephen and Philip labored also as preachers and evangelists. They did so, however, in the exercise of a personal gift rather than of an official duty. A plurality of deacons existed in the church at Philippi, and shared with the bishops the duties of the church (Phil. 1:1).

Dea'con·ess. A female deacon; like Phoebe, servant or *diakonos* of the church at Cenchreae

(Rom. 16:1, R.V. marg.). Deaconesses are probably referred to in I Tim. 3:11. They existed in the churches of Bithynia as early as A.D. 100, for Pliny, in his celebrated letter to the emperor Trajan regarding the Christians, reports having examined "two old women" of the Christian community "who were called ministers" (*ministrae*).

Dead Sea. The name now given to the sheet of water called in the Bible the Salt Sea (Gen. 14:3; Num. 34:12; Deut. 3:17; Josh. 3:16), the sea of the Arabah or Plain (Deut. 3:17; Josh. 3:16), and the e. or eastern sea (Ezek. 47:18; Joel 2:20; R.V., Zech. 14:8). Josephus calls it Asphaltites (Jos. *Antiq.* i. 9, 1). It was named the Dead Sea by the Greeks as early as the latter half of the 2d century of the Christian Era (Pausanias). It is situated in the deep volcanic rent or fissure which runs through Palestine from n. to s.; and is fed chiefly by the river Jordan, which empties into it on an average 6,000,000 tons of water every 24 hours. Its surface was ascertained by the officers of the ordnance survey to be 1,292 feet lower than the ocean level. The sea is like a long rectangle with the angles beveled off; but its regularity of form is interrupted by a projection into its s.e. side of a great promontory or peninsula called Lisan (the Tongue). The length of the sea from n. to s. is on an average about 47 miles, but it varies, a large portion of the s. shore being sometimes dry and sometimes covered with water. The breadth a little n. of En-gedi is 9½ miles, and it is nearly as much everywhere n. of the Lisan. Ancient watermarks indicate that the area, especially the length, was formerly much larger (Jos. *War* iv. 8, 4). The Lisan is about 9 miles long from n. to s. Its banks are from 40 to 60 feet high; while, according to Tristram, its highest point is about 300 feet above the water. Lieutenant Lynch, who in 1848 led an expedition for the exploration of the Jordan and the Dead Sea, found the maximum depth of the latter, as ascertained by sounding, to be 1,278 feet; this was at a point near the mouth of the Arnon. Soundings farther n. yield 1,300 feet. South of the Lisan, on the contrary, the sea is quite shallow. Except on the n. side, where the Jordan enters, the Dead Sea is nearly surrounded by a rampart of cliffs, which in some places leave a narrow beach between them and the water, while in others they themselves constitute the coast line. These rise in successive terraces, which also exist along the lower part of the Jordan Valley. On the w. side, at En-gedi, the height from the seashore to the top of the cliffs is 1,950 feet; a little farther n. at Rās esh Shufk, the top is 2,519 feet above the Dead Sea, i.e., 1,227 above the Mediterranean. Farther n. the elevation gradually decreases till it reaches 1,400 feet above the Dead Sea. These w. cliffs contain deposits of bitumen in both liquid and solid state. On the e. side the precipitous mountains of Moab rise from 2,500 to 3,000 feet above the shore.

The Dead Sea is one of the most remarkable sheets of water on the face of the earth. No other is known to occupy so deep a hollow on the surface of the globe. Its waters are much salter than those of the ocean, for while in the latter 100 lbs. of water contain 6 lbs. of salt, in the former 100 lbs. of water contain from 20 to 27.8 lbs. of salt. In consequence of this, eggs will float on its surface. A bather, too, finds himself buoyant, and when he comes ashore there is a greasy deposit of salt upon his skin, which tortures him if there happens to be a scratch on his body. The saltness of the water is due to the nature of the soil, which abounds in the chlorides of sodium, magnesium, and calcium.

These substances are carried into the sea by the river and the brooks; and there being no outlet, the salt remains and accumulates year by year, while the water with which it comes goes off to a large extent in vapor, evaporation being immense, since the air comes dry and thirsty from the desert.

The Scripture name, Salt Sea, has been superseded by the name Dead Sea. The old belief, however, that there is a total absence of life in and around the sea is erroneous. Organic life scarcely exists in its waters; neither shellfish nor corals are found. But vegetation flourishes on its shores at the mouth of wadies and by springs of fresh water; and birds frequent its strand or fly over its surface. According to Lartet, fish are found in small numbers s. of the Lisan. As a symbol of life in the new Kingdom of God, Ezekiel pictures the healing of the waters of the Dead Sea, and the multiplication of fish till the species rival in number those of the Mediterranean (Ezek. 47:6–12).

Dearth. See FAMINE.

De'bir (dē'bẽr). 1. A king of Eglon, ally of Adoni-zedek; defeated, captured, and executed by Joshua (Josh. 10:3, 23, 26).

2. A city in the hill country of Judah, yet in the Negeb or southland. It was also called Kiriath-sepher (city of books); and Kiriath-sannah, city of a palm branch (Josh. 15:15, 19, 48, 49). In the time of Joshua it was inhabited by Anakim, had a king, and was head of other towns. Joshua captured it and slew its inhabitants (Josh. 10:38, 39; 11:21; 12:13); but it was reoccupied by returned fugitives, and had to be recaptured by Othniel (Josh. 15:15–17; Judg. 1:11, 12). It was assigned to the priests (Josh. 21:13, 15; I Chron. 6:57, 58). Dhāharīyeh, about 12 miles s.w. of Hebron, has been accepted by many as the site. A more probable identification is Tell Beit Mirsim about 13 miles w.s.w. of Hebron and about 3 miles n.n.w. of Shamir.

3. A town on the boundary of the tribe of Judah, near the valley of Achor (Josh. 15:7). The name is perhaps preserved in Thoghret ed-Debr, near ed-Dumm (Adummim), on the road between Jerusalem and Jericho.

4. A place e. of the Jordan, near Mahanaim (Josh. 13:26). R.V. marg. has Lidebir. Perhaps Lodebar (q.v.).

Deb'o·rah (dĕb'ō-ra) [a bee]. 1. Rebekah's nurse, who accompanied her from Mesopotamia and lived until Jacob's return from Paddan-aram. She had perhaps returned to her kindred in Haran after the death of Rebekah and accompanied Jacob back to Canaan, or she had gone to him when he was sojourning at Shechem. At any rate she was with him at Beth-el. There she died at the age of about 155 years, for she could not have been much younger than Isaac. She was buried at the foot of the hill on which the town stood and under an oak, called in consequence Allon-bacuth, oak of weeping (Gen. 24:59; 35:8).

2. A prophetess, the wife of Lappidoth. She dwelt under a palm tree, called after her name, between Ramah and Beth-el, in Mount Ephraim, and there judged the Israelites. She summoned Barak to undertake the contest with Sisera, and accompanied him to the rendezvous of his army (Judg. 4:4–14). Afterward she composed a song of triumph for the victory (ch. 5; cf. v. 7).

Debt'or. One who owes another money. To foster the spirit of brotherhood and mutual helpfulness, the Mosaic Law ordained that the creditor release his brother Israelite from all obligations at the year of release, which recurred every 7 years (Deut. 15:1–4). In the intervening years custom permitted the

seizure and enslavement of a debtor, his wife, and his children (II Kings 4:1; Neh. 5:5, 8; Isa. 50:1). In the time of Jesus, in accordance with Roman law, imprisonment was sometimes inflicted on a debtor (Matt. 5:25; 18:25, 30; Luke 12:58).

Dec'a·logue. See TEN COMMANDMENTS.

De·cap'o·lis (dē-kăp'ō-lĭs) [Gr., league of 10 cities]. A district, beginning where the Plain of Esdraelon opens into the Jordan Valley and expanding e., which was dominated by 10 associated Greek cities. The Greek population had come in the wake of Alexander's conquest. The 10 cities originally included in the association were Scythopolis (Beth-shean), Hippos, Damascus; Gadara, Raphana, Kanatha; Pella, Dion, Gerasa, and Philadelphia (Rabbath Ammon). Other towns were afterward added. Ptolemy enumerates 18. Three roads connect Esdraelon with the commercial highway which runs between Damascus and Arabia along the margin of the desert. The 10 towns stood on these 3 roads and on the highway. The district is called "Decapolita regio" by Pliny (*Hist. Nat.* v. 16). Multitudes from Decapolis followed Jesus at an early period of his ministry (Matt. 4:25). The Gadarene demoniac, when the evil spirit was expelled, published his deliverance in Decapolis (Mark 5:20). Jesus traveled through its midst on his way from Tyre and Sidon to the Sea of Galilee, approaching the lake from the e. side (ch. 7:31).

De'dan (dē'dăn). A Cushite people (Gen. 10:7), but also related to Abraham through Keturah (ch. 25:3). They were an important commercial people (Ezek. 27:15, 20; 38:13) of Arabia (Isa. 21:13), in the neighborhood of Edom (Jer. 25:23; 49:8; Ezek. 25:13), where caravan routes from southern, eastern, and central Arabia converged. The name lingers in Daidān, to the w. of Taima (Taymā') and s.e. of Ailah. The Dedanites came from s. Arabia and dwelt near Raamah (Gen. 10:7), which is located in s.w. Arabia. N. Arabian Dedan, an emporium of the s. Arabian trade, was located at al-'Ula, in the once fertile Wadi el-Kura, in n. al-Ḥijāz. This Liḥyānite capital was once a Minaean colony on the great trade route which carried the merchandise of Yemen and India to the Mediterranean ports. In Ezek. 25:13 and Jer. 49:7 *seq.* Dedan refers to the extreme s. of Edom, as Teman does to the n. of that land. On the basis of this it may be necessary to assume that another Dedan was on the s. border of Edom, but it may mean simply that the Dedanites constituted the s. border of Edom.

Ded'i·ca'tion, Feast of. An annual festival instituted by Judas Maccabaeus in 165 B.C. to celebrate the purification and renewal of the Temple, exactly 3 years after it had been desecrated by the introduction of Greek idolatry and other pollutions by order of Antiochus Epiphanes (I Macc. 4:52–59; cf. ch. 1:54, 59). The festival, called also lights (Jos. *Antiq.* xii. 7, 7), and celebrated much after the manner of the festival of tabernacles (II Macc. 10:6, 7), lasted 8 days, beginning on the 25th of Chislev (approximately December), and falling consequently in winter. Jesus was present at least once at Jerusalem during the festival, and delivered a discourse to the assembled multitude (John 10:22). The Jews still keep the festival.

Deer (A.V.). The English name of the genus *Cervus*, or of the family *Cervidae*. The word occurs only in A.V. in the name fallow deer (Deut. 14:5; I Kings 4:23), but the hart is frequently mentioned. Tristram enumerates 2 species of the genus *Cervus* as still occurring in Palestine, the roebuck (*Cervus capreolus*) and the fallow deer (*Cervus* *dama*) ; while the teeth and bones of 3 others, the red deer (*Cervus elaphus*), the reindeer (*Cervus tarandus*), and the elk (*Cervus alces*), are found in bone breccia in caves in the Lebanon Mountains.

De·grees'. See ASCENTS.

De·ha'ites (dḗ-hā'īts), in A.V. **De·ha'vites** (dḗ-hā'vīts). One of the tribes brought over to Samaria from the Assyrian Empire to replace the 10 tribes carried captive (Ezra 4 :9). Rawlinson believes that they were the Dai, a nomad tribe of Aryan descent mentioned by Herodotus (i. 125).

De'ker (dē'kĕr), A.V. **De'kar** (dē'kär) [piercing, mattock]. The father of Solomon's purveyor, Ben-deker (I Kings 4 :9, R.V.).

De·la'iah (dḗ-lā'yȧ), in A.V. once **Dal'a·i'ah** (dăl'ȧ-ī'ȧ) (I Chron. 3 :24) [Jehovah has drawn out, i.e., delivered]. 1. A descendant of Aaron. His family, grown to a father's house by the time of David, was made the 23d course of the priests (I Chron. 24 :18).
2. A prince, son of Shemaiah, and one of those who urged King Jehoiakim not to burn the roll containing the prophecies of Jeremiah (Jer. 36 :12, 25). Perhaps it is he or his grandson who is incidentally mentioned later (Neh. 6 :10).
3. One of the Nethinim, and founder of a family (Ezra 2 :60 ; Neh. 7 :62).
4. A son of Elioenai (I Chron. 3 :24).

De·li'lah (dḗ-lī'lȧ) [coquette ; cf. Arab. *dalla*, to make gestures of love, to play the coquette]. The Philistine woman from the valley of Sorek who lured Samson to his ruin (Judg. 16 :4–22).

De'los (dē'lŏs), in A.V. **De'lus** (dē'lŭs). A small island in the Aegean, celebrated as the birthplace of Apollo and Diana. The Roman consul Lucius wrote to Delos concerning a pact of friendship established between the Romans and the Jews (I Macc. 15 :23). It was at that time the center of an extensive commerce.

Del'uge. See FLOOD.

De'mas (dē'măs). A fellow laborer of Paul, who sent salutations from Rome to the Colossians and to Philemon (Col. 4 :14 ; Philemon 24). Afterward he deserted the apostle from unwillingness to suffer, and went to Thessalonica (II Tim. 4 :10).

De·me'tri·us (dḗ-mē'trĭ-ŭs) [Lat. from Gr., belonging to Demeter, the goddess of agriculture]. 1. Demetrius I, surnamed Soter, king of Syria 162–150 B.C., nephew of Antiochus Epiphanes. He had been kept as a hostage at Rome ; but on hearing of his uncle's death he made his escape, and arriving safely in Antioch made himself master of the kingdom, and put to death Lysias and the young Eupator (I Macc. 7 :1–4). In war with him Judas Maccabaeus lost his life (ch. 9 :1–19). In 152 B.C. Alexander Balas, with the consent of the Roman senate, claimed the throne. The rivals met in a decisive battle in 150 B.C., and Demetrius was defeated and slain (I Macc. 10 : 48–50 ; Jos. *Antiq.* xiii. 2, 4).
2. Demetrius II, surnamed Nicator, son of Demetrius I. In 148–147 B.C. he raised the standard of revolt against Alexander Balas, aided by Ptolemy VI, defeated him (145 B.C.). Alexander fled into Arabia, where he was murdered, and Demetrius became king of Syria (I Macc. 11 :15–19). But Alexander's general Tryphon almost immediately proclaimed Alexander's young son Antiochus king (vs. 39, 40). The struggle lasted until 139/8 B.C., when Demetrius, during a plundering expedition in Persia, was taken prisoner by King Arsaces and kept in bonds for 10 years. Before his departure on this expedition he gave the

Jews their independence (I Macc. 13 :36–42, Jos. *Antiq.* xiii. 4, 9). Demetrius regained liberty and the throne in 129 B.C. An Egyptian pretender, supported by Ptolemy VII, took the field against him. Demetrius was defeated near Damascus, fled to Ptolemais, and took ship to Tyre, where he was murdered (Jos. *Antiq.* xiii. 9, 3).
3. A silversmith at Ephesus, who made for sale silver models of the celebrated temple of Diana. Believing his craft to be in danger from Christianity, he excited his fellow workmen against Paul, and stirred up the riot in which the mob cried for two hours, "Great is Diana of the Ephesians" (Acts 19 :24–41).
4. An approved Christian, commended by John also (III John 12).

De'mon [Gr. *daimōn:* (1) a god or deity in general ; (2) one's genius ; (3) one's fortune ; (4) the soul of some man belonging to the golden age, now acting as a tutelary divinity ; a god of inferior rank]. An evil spirit (Luke 8 :29 ; 10 :17–20). The designation is applied especially to the gods of the heathen (Deut. 32 :17 ; Ps. 106 :37 ; I Cor. 10 :20 ; cf. Rev. 9 :20 ; all R.V.), and to inferior evil spirits, subject to the Devil (A.R.V., Matt. 12 :24–27 ; Luke 4 :33 ; James 2 :19 ; Rev. 16 :14) ; see DEMONIAC.

The Jews held various notions on the subject ; such as, the demons were the spirits of the wicked dead (Jos. *War* vii. 6, 3), and could be exorcised by means of roots and the name of Solomon (Jos. *Antiq.* viii. 2, 5), or driven away by fumes from the roasting heart and liver of a fish (Tobit 6 :7, 16, 17).

De·mo'ni·ac [Lat., possessed by a demon]. A person possessed and ruled by a demon (Matt. 4 :24, R.V. marg.). The inhabitation of such a being in some cases affected the person physically, and produced certain ordinary diseases. Thus one possessed boy is described as having a deaf and dumb spirit and as being affected at intervals with morbid symptoms resembling those of epilepsy (Mark 9 :14–29 ; cf. Matt. 17 :15, 18 ; Luke 9 :37–42). Hence the opinion of many was that possession was simply a Jewish hypothesis to account for bodily and mental diseases and for the visible effects on body and will of enslavement to sin. But this view takes no note of the fact that the demons speak (Mark 1 :23, 24 ; 3 :11, 12 ; 5 :7) ; that they possessed at times knowledge beyond that of men ; as, for example, of the divinity of Christ (ch. 1 :24) ; that they recognized their own distinct individuality independent of Jesus and independent of the person possessed (Matt. 8 :31) ; that the distant herd of swine became frenzied when the demons were cast out of the demoniac of Gadara and allowed to enter into them (vs. 30–32) ; that Jesus apparently recognized them as actually existing beings, and instructed his disciples, saying : "This kind can come out by nothing, save by prayer" (Mark 9 :29) ; and that later, when the disciples reported that even the demons were subject unto them in his name, Jesus replied : "I beheld Satan fallen as lightning from heaven. . . . Nevertheless in this rejoice not, that the spirits are subject unto you ; but rejoice that your names are written in heaven" (Luke 10 :17–20). Man was himself responsible for his hideous visitor. Probably not until a person was degraded and weakened by sin, personal or inherited, might he be taken captive by a demon (cf. I Sam. 16 :14 with chs. 13 :8–14 ; 15 :10–31).

Dep'u·ty. One empowered to act for another, generally of higher rank than himself ; as a regent ruling in place of a king (I Kings 22 :47) ; an official invested with the powers and rank of a Roman consul (Acts 13 :7 ; 18 :12 ; 19 :38, A.V.) ; see PROCONSUL.

Der′be (dûr′bē). A city in the s.e. part of Lycaonia, in Asia Minor. Paul was stoned and left for dead at Lystra, on his First Missionary Journey. On reviving, he went to Derbe (Acts 14:6, 20). On his Second Journey he again passed through it, and either there or at Lystra made the acquaintance of Timothy (ch. 16:1). Gaius was a native of Derbe (ch. 20:4). Sterrett located it at Zosta, but Ramsay more accurately fixed it in that neighborhood at the mound of Gudelissin in the plain about 3 miles n.w. of Zosta and 45 miles s. of Konia (Iconium).

Des′ert. 1. A rendering of Heb. *midbār* and Gr. *erēmos*, an unenclosed, uncultivated plain, where wild beasts roam at will (Job 24:5); often terrible in its solitude and desolateness (Deut. 32:10; A.V., Isa. 21:1), yet also capable of affording pasturage (Ex. 3:1, A.V.). The words are usually rendered wilderness (Gen. 16:7; 21:20; I Sam. 17:28; 25:21; Matt. 3:1; Mark 1:13; Luke 15:4).

2. A rendering of Heb. *‘ărābāh*, arid region (Isa. 35:1, 6; 51:3). With the definite article the word specially denotes the plain of the Jordan and Dead Sea (Ezek. 47:8; II Sam. 2:29), and is rendered in R.V. as a proper name, Arabah.

3. A rendering of Heb. *yeshīmōn*, a waste, a desolation (Ps. 78:40; 106:14; Isa. 43:19, 20). When the definite article is prefixed it is rendered as a proper name, Jeshimon (Num. 21:20, A.V. and marg. R.V.).

4. A rendering of Heb. *ḥărābōth*, waste, desolate places (Isa. 48:21). R.V., Ps. 102:6; Ezek. 13:4, waste places.

Deu′el (dū′ĕl) [knowledge of God; or invocation of God; cf. Arab. *da‘ā*, call aloud]. A Gadite, the father of Eliasaph (Num. 1:14; 7:42; 10:20). Called in ch. 2:14 Reuel, which means "friend of God." It is uncertain which of these 2 forms is correct. The Samaritan text has "Deuel" everywhere, whereas the LXX and the Peshitta read "Reuel"; see DALETH, REUEL.

Deu′ter·on′o·my (dū′tĕr-ŏn′ō-mĭ) [Lat., from Gr., repetition of the law]. The name, derived from the LXX, of the 5th book of the Pentateuch. The Gr. word, of which Deuteronomy is the English form, is used in the LXX to translate "copy of this law" in Deut. 17:18. But this book is not merely the repetition or copy of laws already given. It is a rehearsal under peculiar circumstances and for a special purpose. In Exodus, Leviticus, and Numbers, the legislation is represented as in process of enactment, the occasion or the time when the successive installments were received is commonly stated, and each body of statutes is severally declared to proceed from God. In Deuteronomy, on the other hand, the law is represented, not as being enacted, but as being rehearsed and expounded. Thirty-eight years have elapsed since the greater part of the old legislation was given. The new generation, on the eve of taking possession of Canaan, is summoned to hear the law of the nation, to be instructed in the application of its principles to the new circumstances which await them, to have their apprehension of its spirituality quickened, and then to renew intelligently the covenant made with their fathers. Instead of the Lord speaking unto Moses, it is now Moses, at the command of God, speaking to the people (chs. 1:1–4; 5:1; 29:1). The book consists first and mainly of an address delivered in 3 installments, committed to writing, and solemnly ratified as a covenant (chs. 1 to 30).

First Address, chs. 1:6 to 4:40; with supplementary statement, vs. 41–49: Rehearsal of the history of the people since the covenant was made with the preceding generation at Sinai as a motive for obedience to Jeho-

vah's laws. The speaker is declared to be Moses (ch. 1:1, 3, 5, 9, 15, 16, 19, etc.). The date is the 40th year, 11th month, 1st day; after the smiting of Sihon and Og, and after the sin in the matter of Baal-peor (chs. 1:3, 4; 4:3) beyond Jordan in the land of Moab (ch. 1:5; cf. Num. 33:48; 35:1), in the wilderness, in the Arabah (Deut. 1:1; cf. Num. 23:28; 24:1). The phrase "beyond Jordan" or "other side of Jordan" was ambiguous and required precise definition. To Abraham and the Canaanites it meant the country e. of the river; and as an established geographical term it meant the same to Abraham's descendants. They had arrived there; but they still called the place where they were by the old inherited designation "the other side of Jordan," just as they called the neighboring bluffs Abarim or "mountains of the other side." And the people felt, too, that they were on the other side of Jordan, outside of the Promised Land. But with the river in front of them the phrase was ambiguous, hence its repeated elucidation by some expression like "in the land of Moab."

Second Address, chs. 5 to 26: Rehearsal of statutes which concerned the people, with emphasis on the spirituality of the laws and urgent insistence upon their observance. These statutes are generally either substantive laws, that is, rights and duties (the procedure not being rehearsed), or else laws which natural depravity might lead men to ignore and where the appeal must be to religious motives: such as, asylum for the unintentional murderer, banishment of idolatry, and consideration for the weaker members and dependent classes of the community. The speaker is Moses (ch. 5:1, 5, 22); the date is at the end of the forty years, on the eve of crossing the Jordan, after Balaam's prophecy (chs. 8:2; 9:1; 11:31; 23:4).

Third Address, chs. 27; 28: Conclusion of the preceding: 1. Provision for writing the law on plastered stones on Mount Ebal. 2. Blessings and curses annexed to obedience and disobedience respectively. This great address is closely followed by a brief address (chs. 29;30) at the ratification of the covenant as thus proclaimed (chs. 29:1; 30:1). This covenant, like the words of the former one made at Horeb, was recorded in a book (chs. 29:20, 21, 27; 30:10; cf. Ex. 24:4–8). The place and date are alluded to in Deut. 29:1, 5, 7, 8.

After delivering the address which forms the body of the book of Deuteronomy, Moses publicly appointed Joshua to be his successor and gave a formal charge to him (ch. 31:1–8). Moses delivered the written Law to the priests with a charge regarding its public reading (vs. 9–13). He repaired with Joshua to the tabernacle that Joshua might be charged by Jehovah, and was there instructed to prepare a song for the people (vs. 14–23). He prepared and wrote the song (v. 22), charged the Levites who bore the Ark to put the completed book, which contained law and song, beside the Ark for a witness (vs. 24–29), ordered an assembly called to hear and learn the song (v. 28), and repeated it publicly (chs. 31:30 to 32:47). Moses' farewell (chs. 32:48 to 33:29) and death (ch. 34).

The distinctive feature of Deuteronomy is the evident preparation for the settlement in Canaan. 1. It affects the language. For example, the people are about to live a settled life; hence the camp which figures so largely, though of course not exclusively, in the former legislation disappears from Deuteronomy, except where reference is made to future war or to the encampment at Shittim where they then are. The speaker mentions houses, towns, city gates. 2. It leads to minor modifications of existing laws to adapt them to the new mode of life. For example, the law which required animals that were slain for food to be brought to the door of the tabernacle is changed to permit the people to slay for food in the town where they reside (cf. Deut. 12:15, 21 with Lev. 17:3, 4); and for the same reason the firstling of animals need no longer be offered to God on the 8th day, but the sacrifice may be postponed until the owner comes up from his distant home to the sanctuary at the annual feasts (cf. Deut. 15:20 with Ex. 22:30); and in the case of the Hebrew bondman who wishes to remain attached to the household of his master, rather than claim his legal freedom, the ceremony at the doorpost suffices, and there is no longer insistence upon appearance before God (cf. Deut. 15:17 with Ex. 21:6). 3. It leads to the attempt to safeguard the interests of the dependent classes, the Levites, widows, orphans, strangers, and to protect them from the evils which evidently threatened to befall them in the future, in view of the spirit of self-seeking and indifference to others that had been manifested by the people time and again during the sojourn in the wilderness. 4. It leads to insistence upon one altar for the nation in the place where Jehovah shall record his name. The unity of the altar was intended to counteract the tendency to lapse into idolatry, by preventing the people from worshiping at the numerous local sanctuaries of the Canaanites; to render the worship of Jehovah a grander spectacle and of greater pomp than the rites of the idols of the Canaanites by uniting the numbers and the wealth of the Hebrews; and to give strength to the communal feeling and aid in binding the nation together. The spirit of jealousy between individuals and between tribes, the popular proneness to idolatry, and the willingness of large sections of the people to separate from their brethren and settle in attractive pastoral regions had already become manifest. The old law of the one altar is emphatically insisted upon at this crisis. It was essential to the unity of the nation and continuance of the theocracy. See ALTAR.

It has been urged that no distinction is made in Deuteronomy between priests and Levites such as appears in the legislation of Leviticus and Numbers. The priests are frequently called "the priests the Levites," and the passage Deut. 18:1–8, if it be isolated, may be interpreted to mean that any Levite might become a priest. But: 1. The tribe of Levi is indeed assigned priestly functions (Deut. 10:6; 18:1–8; 33:8, 9). That is correct, for the tribe as a whole was called to holy service, especially to priestly service. Even when the distinction between the priests and the lower order of the Levites was firmly established, the tribe as a whole is spoken of as priestly (I Kings 12:31; Mal. 2:1–4; 3:3; cf. Heb. 7:11). 2. The title "the priests the Levites" occurs in writings which were composed after the legislation of Leviticus was in full force. It is used by Ezekiel (Ezek. 43:19; 44:15) and by the Chronicler (II Chron. 23:18; 30:27). It should also be remembered that Jeremiah uses the expression (Jer. 33:18, 21). 3. Deuteronomy is based on previous priestly legislation, for it presupposes the technical laws of the ritual. The speaker explicitly refers to former laws on the subject of which he is speaking, and these laws are known only from the books of Leviticus and Numbers (cf. Deut. 18:1, 2 with Num. 18:20; Deut. 24:8, 9 with Lev., chs. 13; 14; Num., ch. 12), or he makes allusions which imply these laws (cf. Deut. 12:15 with Lev. 17:3 seq.). 4. The passage Deut. 18:1–8 may be readily interpreted on the assumption that the laws of Leviticus were in force. Levi was to have no inheritance with Israel, but

was to enjoy certain perquisites (Lev. 6:17, 18; Num. 18:20, 21, 24, 26). The speaker presses this law with earnestness. The priests the Levites, the whole tribe of Levi, have no inheritance; they shall eat the offerings (Deut. 18:1). The dues of the priests, without the epithet "the Levites," are next spoken of. It is an urgent matter. The people must not defraud the priests of their income (cf. Deut. 18:3, 4 with Ex. 29:27, 28; Lev. 7:34; Num. 18:11, 12, where slight changes are introduced). Finally, the rights of the Levites at the sanctuary are dwelt upon. If a Levite —not necessarily a Levite of lower rank— come from any part of the country to the sanctuary, he shall minister in the name of the Lord as all his brethren the Levites do, which stand before the Lord, and he shall fare as they do (Deut. 18:6–8). The kind of service which he shall perform is not the matter at issue. The language covers both priestly service and the labors rendered by the lower order of the Levites (Deut. 17:12; 18:5; I Sam. 2:11, 18; 3:1; II Chron. 23:6; 29:4, 5, 11). The point insisted upon is that all Levites shall receive full recognition at the sanctuary and be accorded their prerogatives. It goes without saying that if the Levite be a priest, he shall serve and fare like his brethren the priests; if he be not a priest, he shall enjoy the privileges that belong to his brethren who are Levites but not priests. Those in power shall not deprive him of his prerogatives because he is obscure and from a distant part of the country. See PRIEST.

Dev'il (Gr. diabolos, slanderer]. 1. An evil spirit (A.V. of Mark 1:34; Luke 4:33; 8:29). A.V. and E.R.V. (text) do not observe the distinction made in the Greek original between a demon and the Devil. Demons take possession of wicked men and are subject to the Devil (Matt. 4:24; 12:24); see DEMONIAC.

2. The Evil One, Satan, the greatest of all the fallen spirits (Rev. 12:9; Matt. 4:8–11; 13:38, 39; 25:41; cf. Jude 6). The general opinion is that the sin into which he fell was pride (I Tim. 3:6). He is the great enemy of God and man (I Peter 5:8; I John 3:8), who tempted Christ and incites men to sin (Matt. 4:1; John 13:2). He is that old "serpent" who tempted Eve (II Cor. 11:3; Rev. 12:9; 20:2). Perhaps with reference to this transaction he is called a murderer from the beginning, and a liar, and the father of lies (John 8:44; cf. I John 3:8). When the good seed of truth is sown the Devil either steals it away (Luke 8:12) or sows tares (Matt. 13:38). He is continually going about like a roaring lion seeking whom he may devour (I Peter 5:8). He lays snares or practices wiles to injure the children of God (Eph. 6:11; II Tim. 2:26), and seduces them by his subtilty (II Cor. 11:3); but the person tempted is not to yield to him, but to resist him, and he will flee (Eph. 4:27; James 4:7). He had power to produce demoniacal possession (Acts 10:38), and he instigated the imprisonment of martyrs (Rev. 2:10). He is finally to be cast into a lake of everlasting fire prepared for the Devil and his angels (Matt. 25:41; cf. Jude 6). Pre-eminently sinful, unrighteous men, also those imbued with the spirit of lying and murder, are figuratively called children of the Devil (John 8:44; I John 3:8, 10). Judas was even called by Jesus a devil (John 6:70). His works Christ came to destroy (I John 3:8). Jude alludes to a dispute of the Devil with Michael for the body of Moses (Jude 9; cf. Rev. 12:7). Jude has been thought to quote an authoritative teaching of the Jewish Church, or a familiar interpretation of Zech., ch. 3, according to which the high priest represents Mosaism. More

probably he drew this information from the apocryphal work, the Assumption of Moses.

De·vote'. See ANATHEMA.

Dew. Moisture condensed from the atmosphere upon cold bodies. Used in Scripture figuratively for whatever comes noiselessly and even invisibly, but proves a refreshment and a blessing, as dew does to vegetation (Deut. 32:2; Ps. 110:3; Prov. 19:12; Micah 5:7).

Di'a·dem. 1. The rendering of Heb. *ṣānīph, ṣānūph,* something bound round. It was a headdress for man and woman (Job 29:14, R.V. marg., turban; Isa. 3:23, in A.V. hoods, R.V. turbans). A royal diadem of this type was worn by kings (Isa. 62:3), and is once mentioned as worn by the high priest (Zech. 3:5), where it is translated miter, but R.V. marg., turban (also, diadem, E.R.V.).
2. A rendering of Heb. *miṣnepheth,* a name applied specially to the miter of the Jewish high priest (Ezek. 21:26, A.V.), and regularly translated so.
3. The rendering of Heb. *ṣᵉphīrāh,* circlet, crown (Isa. 28:5).

Di'al. An instrument consisting of a surface which is graduated into hour lines, and furnished with a projecting gnomon to cast a shadow as the sun advances in its daily course, and thus indicate the hours. The dial of Ahaz (II Kings 20:11; Isa. 38:8) may have been such an instrument, with either flat or concave dial and with graduated lines called steps or degrees, which Ahaz had in-

Ancient Dial

troduced from Babylonia, where the sundial was in use before the time of Herodotus (Herod. ii. 109), and at least as early as the 8th century B.C. It may, however, have been a flight of steps (Jos. *Antiq.* x. 2, 1) at the palace of Ahaz, so designed and arranged that the shadow of an obelisk near by passed over the steps and thus indicated the time of day. Heb. *ma'ălōth,* translated dial, is the same word as is rendered "steps" 5 times in II Kings 20:9–11 (R.V. text) and 3 times in Isa. 38:8 (R.V. text). The recession of the shadow on the dial of Ahaz may be explained as caused by refraction of the sun's rays, or by a solar eclipse. II Chron. 32:31 ("the wonder that was done in the land") seems to treat it as a local marvel.

Di'a·mond. A mineral of unequaled hardness and luster, transparent or translucent, and capable of taking a splendid polish. It is simply crystallized carbon.

Diamond is the rendering of:
1. Heb. *yahălōm,* a precious stone (Ezek. 28:13), one of those in the breastplate of the high priest (Ex. 28:18, R.V. marg., sardonyx; 39:11).
2. Heb. *shāmīr,* a hard stone used to point graving instruments (Jer. 17:1); elsewhere rendered "adamant" (Ezek. 3:9; Zech. 7:12).

Di·an'a (dī-ăn'a). The Roman goddess of the moon. She corresponded to the Greek Artemis, who was twin sister of Apollo, and

huntress of the sky. She was the ideal of chastity and virginity, and is generally represented as a tall and beautiful maiden, with a quiver on her shoulder and a bow or a javelin in her right hand, and as engaged in hunting deer. The Asiatic Artemis, Diana of Ephesus, had no connection with the Diana (or Artemis) of classical mythology, but was the mother-goddess of Asia Minor, known as Cybele, Magna Mater, and Ma. See ASHTORETH and ATARGATIS. Her image was supposed to have fallen from heaven (Acts 19:35), and it may have been originally a meteoric stone. Its form is known from ancient coins as the rude figure of a woman with crowned head, many breasts, and ex-

Coin Showing the Temple of Diana

tended arms supported by props. Her primitive shrine near the sea, at the mouth of the Cayster, became eventually an imposing temple (see EPHESUS). Demetrius the silversmith and his fellow craftsmen made silver models of it (Acts 19:24).

Di·as'po·ra (dī-ăs'pô-ra). See DISPERSION.

Dib'lah (dĭb'la), in A.V. **Dib'lath** [rounded mass, cake]. A place in Palestine (Ezek. 6:14), which has not been located. The name probably should be changed to Riblah, a reading which has the authority of some MSS. quoted by Ginsburg in his edition of the Hebrew O.T. The expression "from the wilderness toward Diblah" should accordingly be understood as "from the wilderness to Riblah," i.e., from the farthest s. to the ideal boundary in the n. The latter has been described as "the entrance of Hamath" (cf. Ezek. 47:16; 48:1). In this case, Riblah, which is about 50 miles s. of Hamath, is used perhaps on account of its painful associations (II Kings 23:33; 25:6 *seq.*, 20 *seq.*). For possible confusion of *R* and *D,* see the table of the alphabet.

Dib·la'im (dĭb-lā'ĭm) [twin fig cakes]. A parent-in-law to Hosea, if the transaction was real and not typical (Hos. 1:3).

Dib'lath (dĭb'lăth). See DIBLAH.

Di'bon (dī'bŏn) [a wasting away]. 1. A town n. of the Arnon, wrested from Moab by the Amorites, taken by the Israelites (Num. 21:30; 32:3), rebuilt by the Gadites (ch. 32:34), and hence called Dibon-gad (ch. 33:45, 46), afterward given over to the tribe of Reuben (Josh. 13:9, 17). It reverted to the Moabites (*Moabite Stone,* 21, 28, see MOABITE STONE; Isa. 15:2; Jer. 48:18, 22). It still exists, as a heap of ruins, retaining its old name Dhībān, 3 miles n. of the Arnon, n.w. of 'Ara'ir. It was among the ruins of Dibon that in 1868 the Moabite Stone was found (*q.v.*).
2. A village in the territory of Judah (Neh. 11:25). See DIMONAH.

Di'bon-gad' (dī'bŏn-găd'). See DIBON 1.

Dib'ri (dĭb'rī) [loquacious]. A Danite, ancestor of him who was stoned to death in the days of Moses for blaspheming the Name (Lev. 24:11–14).

Did'y·mus (dĭd'ĭ-mŭs) [Lat. from Gr., a twin]. See THOMAS.

Dik′lah (dĭk′lä) [cf. neo-Heb. *deḳel*; Aram. *diḳlā*, palm tree; Arab. *daḳal*, a species of poor dates]. A people descended from Joktan (Gen. 10:27; I Chron. 1:21), and who doubtless dwelt in Arabia.

Dil′e•an (dĭl′ē-ăn), in E.R.V. and J.V. **Dil′an** (dĭl′ăn). A town in the lowland of Judah (Josh. 15:38); identified with Tell en-Nejileh.

Dill. See ANISE.

Dim′nah (dĭm′nä). See RIMMON, I. 3.

Di′mon (dī′mŏn) [probably a variant of Dibon]. A place in Moab (Isa. 15:9); apparently Dibon, by an interchange of labials. Jerome states that in his day both names were common for the town. The form with m is chosen for the sake of an alliteration with *dam* (blood) used in the same verse. The waters of Dibon are best regarded as the Arnon, as the waters of Megiddo are the Kishon (Judg. 5:19).

Di•mo′nah (dī-mō′nà). A town in the Negeb, near Edom (Josh. 15:22), probably the same as Dibon (Neh. 11:25), and is to be sought near Ḳebāb, n.e. of ‘Ar′ara and e. of Tell el-Milḥ.

Di′nah (dī′nà) [judgment or, perhaps, judged]. A daughter of Jacob by his wife Leah (Gen. 30:21). Going out apparently unprotected to see the Canaanite daughters of the land, she was either led astray or outraged by Shechem, the son of Hamor the Hivite. The young prince afterward wished to take her in honorable marriage, and her brothers apparently consented, on condition that the Hivites should be circumcised. These acquiesced in the stipulation, and carried it out; but an attack on their town was suddenly made by Simeon and Levi, 2 of Dinah's full brothers, who slew all the males in the place, Hamor and Shechem among the rest (Gen. 34:1–29). Jacob took no part in the treacherous and cruel deed, regarded it as inexpedient (v. 30), and denounced it with horror on his deathbed (ch. 49:5–7). By this act of his sons, however, the conquered district fell to him as head of the tribe, and he bequeathed it, not to those who were answerable for the abhorred deed, but to Joseph (Gen. 48:22).

Di′na•ites (dī′nà-īts). One of the foreign tribes settled in Samaria to replace the 10 tribes carried into captivity (Ezra 4:9). Probably the Armenian people who were known to the Assyrians as Dayani.

Din′ha•bah (dĭn′hȧ-bä) [perhaps, give judgment]. The city of Bela, king of Edom (Gen. 36:32; I Chron. 1:43). Location uncertain. Jerome identified it with Dannaia, modern Khirbet ed-Denn, a town in Moab, a little s. of the Arnon.

Din′ner. See MEALS.

Di′o•ny′si•us (dī′ō-nĭsh′ĭ-ŭs) [Lat. from Gr., belonging to the god Dionysos]. A member of the Athenian supreme court, or Areopagus, who was converted through the preaching of Paul on Mars' Hill, where the court held its sittings (Acts 17:34).

Di•ot′re•phes (dī-ŏt′rė-fēz) [Gr., nurtured by Zeus]. A member of the church of which Gaius, to whom John sent his Third Epistle, was a member. He loved to have the preeminence in the church to which he belonged, refused to receive the Apostle John or the brethren who went forth for the sake of the Name, and excommunicated those who entertained them (III John 9, 10).

Di′phath (dī′făth). See RIPHATH.

Dis•ci′ple. A pupil or scholar (Matt. 10:24); especially the follower of a public teacher, like John the Baptist (ch. 9:14). A person taught of God (Isa. 8:16). It is used

of all of whatever age who in faith received the divine Master's instructions (Matt. 10:42; Luke 14:26, 27, 33; John 4:1; 6:66), and especially of the 12 apostles (Matt. 5:1; 8:23; 10:1; 12:1, etc.).

Dis•eas′es. Disease arises from the violation of physical or mental laws. The observance of these laws is often a moral act, and their transgression is sin (Prov. 23:29–32); so that disease is in certain cases the punishment imposed by the Creator for sin. God, moreover, sometimes smites a sinner with disease where no natural cause can be traced (Ex. 9:8 *seq.*; Num. 11:33; 12:9–11; Deut. 28:21–60; II Sam. 21:1; 24:15; II Kings 5:27). From the connection between sin and various diseases, the latter are sometimes attributed to Satan, who seduced the race to its fall into sin and who is still the great tempter to sin (Luke 13:16); but the inference is not legitimate that every disease is caused directly by sin or that Satan is the immediate cause of our maladies (Job, chs. 3 to 42; John 9:1–3). Various human diseases are mentioned, such as fever (Deut. 28:22; Matt. 8:14; John 4:52; Jos. *Antiq.* xiii. 15, 5), cutaneous disease (Lev. 13:6–8, 30, 39), dysentery (II Chron. 21:15, 18; Acts 28:8, R.V.), ophthalmia (Rev. 3:18; Tobit 2:10; 6:8; 11:13), boils (Ex. 9:9; I Sam. 5:6), paralysis (I Macc. 9:55; Matt. 8:6; 9:2; Acts 9:33).

Di′shan (dī′shăn) [pygarg, antelope]. A Horite tribe (Gen. 36:21, 28) under a chief (v. 30).

Di′shon (dī′shŏn) [pygarg, antelope]. A Horite tribe (Gen. 36:21, 26, 28; I Chron. 1:38), organized under a chief (Gen. 36:30), and descended through Anah from Zibeon (vs. 24, 25). Many interpreters, however, discover 2 persons of this name: one in vs. 20, 26, 30, the other in v. 25.

Dis•per′sion. Translation of Gr. *diaspora*; the body of Israelites scattered abroad in other lands than their own (Jer. 25:34; John 7:35; James 1:1). Dispersion was threatened as a penalty if the people departed from the Mosaic Law (Lev. 26:14, 33; Deut. 4:27; 28:64–68). The captivity of the 10 tribes and that of the 2 largely helped to fulfill these prophecies; for the mass of the 10 tribes were never restored to their own land, and of the 2 a very large number chose to remain in the region to which they had been taken rather than return to their own country. A very considerable immigration of Jews took place into the cities and towns of Alexander the Great's empire, and into the kingdoms of Egypt, Syria, etc., into which it was afterward divided; and later when the Roman Empire established its sway over these and other regions, colonies of Jews sought a settlement in all the important places. Agrippa, in a letter to Caligula preserved by Philo, says: "Jerusalem is the capital not alone of Judea but, by means of colonies, of most other lands also. These colonies have been sent out at fitting opportunities into the neighboring countries of Egypt, Phoenicia, Syria, Coelesyria, and the farther removed Pamphylia, Cilicia, the greater part of Asia as far as Bithynia and the most remote corners of Pontus. In the same manner also into Europe: Thessaly, Boeotia, Macedon, Aetolia, Attica, Argos, Corinth, and the most and finest parts of the Peloponnesus. And not only is the mainland full of Israelitish communities, but also the most important islands: Euboea, Cyprus, Crete. And I say nothing of the countries beyond the Euphrates, for all of them, with unimportant exceptions, Babylon and the satrapies that include the fertile districts lying around it, have Jewish inhabitants." Thus the Dispersion, with synagogue and doctrine, was found in all parts of the known world (Acts 2:5–11; I Peter 1:1; Jos. *War* vii. 3, 3).

Div'i·na'tion. The attempt to read the future and utter soothsaying either by a kind of inspiration or afflatus (Acts 16:16), or else by means of signs. In the latter sense, it includes augury or foretelling the future by means of natural signs, such as the flight of birds, the disposition of the liver (Ezek. 21:21); hydromancy or foretelling from the appearance of water poured into a vessel or of objects dropped into the water (Gen. 44:5); foretelling by casting lots (Ezek. 21:21); and astrology or the determination

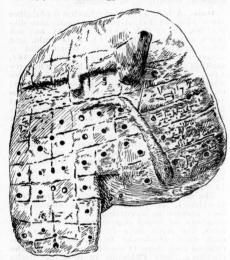

Design of a Sheep's Liver in Terra Cotta, Used for Instruction in Babylonian Divination Methods

of the supposed influence of the stars on the destiny of a person or a nation (cf. Isa. 47:13). The Hebrews also included in divination necromancy or foretelling the future by calling up the spirits of the dead and conversing with them (I Sam. 28:8). The Babylonians were famous for liver divination (hepatoscopy). The diviner sometimes pronounced blessing or cursing (Num. 22:6) as prophecy revealed by the afflatus or familiar spirit or the sign (vs. 12, 13).

Di·vin'er. A soothsayer; a practicer of divination. They were numerous among heathen nations (Deut. 18:9–12; I Sam. 6:2; Isa. 19:3; Ezek. 21:21; Dan. 2:2; Acts 16:16), and also at various times among the Israelites, who were informed of the diviner's imposture, warned against placing reliance in him, and threatened with punishment for the sin of consulting him (Lev. 19:31; 20:6, 27; Deut. 18:10; I Sam. 28:8; Isa. 2:6; 3:2, R.V.; Jer. 27:9; 29:8; Ezek. 13:23; 22:28; Micah 3:6, 7, 11; Zech. 10:2). He practiced his art for hire (Num. 22:7,17,18; Acts 16:16).

Di·vorce', Di·vorce'ment. Annulment of the bonds of matrimony. Under the Law of Moses a man could divorce his wife if he found some unseemly thing in her. She might then be married to another man. If her second husband also divorced her, the first one was not allowed to take her again. The process of divorce, when once resolved upon, was easy. All the husband had to do was to give his partner a bill of divorcement, and send her away (Deut. 24:1–4; cf. Isa. 50:1; Jer.

3:8). Our Lord explained that this enactment was framed only on account of the Israelites' hardness of heart. He added that the original and just law, that of nature, is that a man cleave to his wife and they twain become one flesh, marriage being a permanent compact; and that a wife should not be divorced except for fornication, including what is now technically called adultery. If a man puts away his wife on other grounds and marries another, he commits adultery. If anyone marries a divorced woman, he also has committed the same sin (Matt. 5:31, 32; 19:3–9; Mark 10:2–12; Luke 16:18; cf. I Cor. 7:10–17).

Di'-za·hab (dī'zȧ-hăb), A.V. **Di'za·hab** [having gold]. A place cited to indicate the locality and circumstances connected with the farewell addresses of Moses (Deut. 1:1). Location uncertain. Edh-Dheibeh, e. of Heshbon, has been proposed; near el-'Al there is Rujm Umm edh-Dhahab. Perhaps Di-zahab was a district in Edom identical with Me-zahab (Gen. 36:39; cf. LXX of Num. 21:14, which has Zahab for Vaheb of R.V.).

Do'dai (dō'dī). See DODO 2.

Do'da·nim (dō'dȧ-nĭm) [Dodanites]. Fourth son of Javan (Gen. 10:4). The LXX and the Samaritan text (Gen. 10:4), as well as the Hebrew (Masoretic) text in I Chron. 1:7, have Rodanim, which seems to be the correct reading. See RODANIM.

Do'da·va'hu (dō'dȧ-vā'hū), in A.V. **Do'da·vah** (dō'dȧ-vȧ) [beloved of Jehovah, or Jehovah is a Friend]. A man from Mareshah, father of that Eliezer who prophesied the destruction of Jehoshaphat's ships (II Chron. 20:37).

Do'do (dō'dō) [contraction of Dodavahu]. 1. A man of Issachar, ancestor of the judge Tola (Judg. 10:1).
2. An Ahohite, and the father of Eleazar, one of David's 3 mighty men of the 1st rank (II Sam. 23:9, R.V., following the Kethib of the Hebrew text, Dodai; I Chron. 11:12). David appointed Dodai (or probably his son) as military commander over the course of the 2d month (I Chron. 27:4).
3. A man of Bethlehem, father of Elhanan, one of David's mighty men (II Sam. 23:24; I Chron. 11:26).

Doe. A female deer or antelope. In Prov. 5:19, R.V., it is the female ibex or wild goat of Sinai (*Capra beden*), in Hebrew *ya'ălāh.* See ROE, GOAT.

Do'eg (dō'ĕg) [timid]. An Edomite, the chief of Saul's herdsmen (I Sam. 21:7). He was at Nob at the tabernacle, detained before the Lord on account of a vow or uncleanness or signs of leprosy (Lev. 14:4, 11, 21), or was perhaps in sanctuary for some crime (cf. I Kings 1:50), when David, a fugitive from Saul's court, arrived at Nob and obtained food and a sword from Ahimelech, who did not know that he was fleeing from the king (Psalm 52, title). Doeg subsequently told Saul what had occurred, which so excited the king that he summoned Ahimelech and fellow priests and demanded an explanation. Not considering it satisfactory, he ordered the guard to kill the priests. They would not. The king then bade Doeg do the deed. He did so, slaying 85 men. He subsequently fell upon the village, massacred the women and children, and destroyed even the cattle (I Sam. 22:7–23).

Dog. During the earlier period of Bible history the dog is described as prowling about the streets and suburbs of cities (Ps. 59:6, 14), feeding on what was thrown out to it (Ex. 22:31), licking up blood when it was shed (I Kings 22:38; Ps. 68:23), or devouring dead bodies (I Kings 14:11; 16:4; II

Kings 9:35, 36); even sometimes congregating in packs, to surround and attack human beings (Ps. 22:16, 20). It was early trained sufficiently to aid the shepherd in protecting the flock against beasts of prey and thieves (Job 30:1). It was at length sometimes domesticated, accompanied its master from place to place (Tobit 5:16; 11:4), and was in the house with him and picked up the crumbs from under his table (Mark 7:28). Moreover, dogs licked the sores of beggars at the rich man's gate (Luke 16:21). The dog was also widely used by the ancients for hunting. But the great mass of dogs ran wild. On account of their food and habits, they were deemed unclean; and to call one a dog was a gross insult (I Sam. 17:43; II Kings 8:13). The term dog is applied in a figurative sense to those who are incapable of appreciating what is high or holy (Matt. 7:6), who introduce false doctrines with cynical effrontery (Phil. 3:2), who, like a dog returning to its vomit, go back to sins which nominally they had renounced forever (II Peter 2:22; cf. Prov. 26:11), or who are so vile as to submit to lust like dogs (Deut. 23:18). The later Jews were accustomed to call the heathen dogs because ceremonially unclean; and even Jesus once employed the term in order vividly to express his doctrine of grace (Matt. 15:26; Mark 7:27).

Dok (dŏk), in A.V. **Do'cus** (dō'kŭs) [cf. Syriac *dûk*, observe]. A little stronghold near Jericho, built by Ptolemy (I Macc. 16:15), son-in-law of Simon Maccabaeus (vs. 11, 12); Josephus calls it Dagon. Into this castle he received Simon and 2 of his sons, and then treacherously slew them (v. 16). The murder was avenged by John Hyrcanus, a 3d son of Simon. He besieged Dok, and after a time Ptolemy fled beyond Jordan (Jos. *Antiq.* xiii. 8, 1; *War* i. 2, 3). The name seems to remain in 'Ain Duk, a copious spring about 4 miles n.w. of Jericho.

Doph'kah (dŏf'kȧ). A station of the Israelites on the route to Sinai between the Red Sea and Rephidim (Num. 33:12, 13). Serābīt el Khādem or a place near the wadi Megharet has been suggested.

Dor (dōr) [habitation]. A town of the Canaanites on the Mediterranean (Josh. 11:2; I Macc. 15:11), about 8 miles n. of Caesarea. Joshua defeated its king (Josh. 12:1, 23). It lay in the territory of Asher; but was given to the tribe of Manasseh (ch. 17:11), which, however, did not expel the Canaanites (Judg. 1:27). About 1190 it fell into the hands of the Zakkalu, a people with the Philistines included in the "Peoples of the Sea"; they were still there in the days of Ramesses XII. The region about Dor was one of Solomon's tax districts (I Kings 4:11). In the latter half of the 4th century B.C. Sidon obtained Dor and Joppa. In 217 B.C. Antiochus the Great besieged it (Polybius 566); and about 138 B.C. Antiochus VII invested it by land and sea (I Macc. 15:11–14; Jos. *Antiq.* xiii. 7, 2). In the days of Alexander Jannaeus it was held for a time by the tyrant Zoïlus (Jos. *Antiq.* xiii. 12, 2). In 64 B.C. Pompey granted it autonomy (Jos. *Antiq.* xiv. 4, 4). In 56 B.C. it was rebuilt by Gabinius (Jos. *Antiq.* xiv. 5, 3). Remains of Dor are found at el-Burj, a short distance n. of eṭ-Ṭanṭūra.

Dor'cas (dôr'kăs) [Gr. for Aram. *ṭᵉbīthā*, gazelle]. Tabitha, a Christian woman of Joppa, a friend and helper of the poor. At her death, Peter was sent for, who, after prayer, bade her arise, and her life returned. The fame thereof spread, and many believed on the Lord (Acts 9:36–43). Dorcas societies are sewing circles for the poor, named from her.

Do'than (dō'thăn) [possibly wells]. A town, known also as Dothain and Dothaim, not far from Shechem and Samaria, hard by a caravan route (Gen. 37:14, 17, 25; II Kings 6:13), near the Plain of Esdraelon and a pass into the hill country of Judah (Judith 4:6, 7). Joseph was cast into a pit in the vicinity, whence he was taken out and sold to the Midianites (Gen. 37:17–28). Elisha was once besieged in the town by the Syrians; but the soldiers of the beleaguering army were miraculously struck with blindness, led to Samaria, had their vision restored, and were finally sent home without molestation (II Kings 6:8–23). Its site is Tell Dōthān, near a well 9½ miles n., slightly e., of Samaria.

Dove. A bird (Ps. 55:6) having a plaintive voice (Isa. 38:14), a gentle, affectionate disposition (S. of Sol. 2:14; 5:2; 6:9), but not much sagacity (Hos. 7:11). It is timid, and when frightened trembles. When wild it sometimes frequents valleys (Ezek. 7:16), making its nest in the side of holes or fissures (Jer. 48:28). When domesticated it flies when alarmed to windows or cotes (Isa. 60:8; cf. Gen. 8:8–12). Jesus refers to it as proverbially harmless (Matt. 10:16). It was bought and sold within the Temple courts (Matt. 21:12; Mark 11:15; John 2:14), for it was used in sacrifice (Luke 2:24). The dove is a symbol of the Holy Spirit (Luke 3:22).

Dove is but another name for pigeon, though in popular usage it is usually restricted to the smaller species. It is frequently translated pigeon in the English versions (Gen. 15:9; Lev. 1:14; 5:7, 11; 12:6, 8; 14:22, 30; 15:14, 29; Num. 6:10).

The doves constitute a family of birds (*Columbidae*), of which Tristram enumerates four species as occurring in Palestine: the ringdove or wood pigeon (*Columba palumbus*), the stock dove (*Columba oenas*), the rock dove (*Columba livia*), and the ash-rumped rock dove (*Columba schimperi*). The ringdove visits Palestine in immense flocks in spring and autumn during its annual migrations; individuals also remain all the winter. The stock dove is found chiefly e. of the Jordan, or in the valley of that river. The rock dove is abundant on the coast and in the highlands w. of the Jordan. The ash-rumped rock dove is exceedingly abundant in the interior of the country and in the Jordan Valley, taking refuge in caves and fissures. It is the species described in Jer. 48:28.

Dove's Dung. A substance which rose to famine prices during the siege of Samaria by Ben-hadad (II Kings 6:25). Dung was also eaten during the siege of Jerusalem (Jos. *War* v. 13, 7).

Dow'ry. Among the Israelites and neighboring nations a bridegroom or his father paid a dowry to the bride's father to induce him to give her in marriage (Gen. 29:15–20; 34:12; Ex. 22:17; I Sam. 18:25). The lowest legal amount seems to have been 50 shekels (Deut. 22:29). Occasionally the bride's father gave his daughter a wedding present (Josh. 15:19; I Kings 9:16).

Drag'on [Gr. *drakōn*, dragon]. In the O.T. the word dragon is often used to translate *tannîn*. *Tannîn* denotes a land serpent (Ex. 7:9; cf. 4:3, 4; Ps. 91:13; and doubtless Deut. 32:33), great sea animals (plural, Gen. 1:21, in A.V. whales, in R.V. sea monsters; Ps. 74:13; 148:7), and the crocodile of the rivers of Egypt (Ezek. 29:3). The last is described as having jaws, and scales to which fish could stick (v. 4), and feet with which it disturbed the waters (ch. 32:2), as lying in the sea and in the branches of the Nile (ch. 29:3; 32:2), as swimming (v. 6), and as taken with great hooks (ch. 29:4) and with nets (ch. 32:3). It is used as a symbol for Egypt (Isa. 51:9; and probably 27:1).

The R.V. recognizes that *tan,* rendered "dragon" in A.V. of Job 30:29; Ps. 44:19; Isa. 13:22; 34:13; 35:7; 43:20; Jer. 9:11; 10:22; 14:6; 49:33; 51:37; Micah 1:8, and "sea monster" in Lam. 4:3, should be translated "jackal" and that, on the basis of certain Hebrew MSS., the Hebrew text of Ezek. 29:3; 32:2 should be emended to read "dragon," where A.V. has once properly "dragon" and once "whale."

The dragon of N.T. imagery is "the old serpent," the Devil (Rev. 12:9; 20:2), who is symbolically portrayed as in color red and having 7 heads, 10 horns, an enormous tail, and a huge mouth, from which he was able to cast forth water like a river after those whom he would destroy (ch. 12:3, 4, 15; 16:13). He was hurled from the heavens to the earth, where he persecuted the Church, but was finally chained and imprisoned in the abyss (ch. 12:7–17; 20:2, 3). In certain features the dragon bears resemblance to the beast of ch. 13. This beast is a combination of Daniel's 4 beasts, and represents the combined powers of earth in opposition to the Kingdom of God (Dan., ch. 7). The picture of the dragon was conformed to that of the beast, because the dragon, that old serpent, is the animating and molding spirit in the kingdom of this world, and when he was portrayed in ch. 12, features of the world power familiarized by Daniel were combined with the distinguishing feature furnished by the serpent of Gen., ch. 3.

Drag'on's Well, in A.V. **Drag'on Well.** A well at Jerusalem, apparently between the Valley Gate and Dung Gate (Neh. 2:13; cf. ch. 3:13, 14); called Jackal's Well in A.R.V.

Dream. Ideas present to the mind during sleep. They may be classified as: 1. Vain dreams (Job 20:8; Ps. 73:20; Isa. 29:8). 2. Dreams employed by God for the purposes of his Kingdom. In producing them God works according to the laws of mind, and perhaps always employs secondary causes. They are (*a*) intended to affect the spiritual life of individuals. A Midianite's dream discouraged the enemy, and encouraged Gideon, who providentially heard it (Judg. 7:13). Perhaps such was the dream of Pilate's wife (Matt. 27:19). Many such providential dreams have been sent in modern times. John Newton, concerned about his soul's salvation, had a dream which made the way of salvation clear to him. (*b*) Directive and prophetic dreams, used when revelation was incomplete. They seem to have carried with them credentials of their divine origin. Divine communications were made in dreams to Abimelech (Gen. 20:3), to Jacob (ch. 28:12; 31:10), to Laban (ch. 31:24), to Joseph (ch. 37:5, 9, 10, 20), to Pharaoh's butler and baker (ch. 40:5), to Pharaoh (ch. 41:7, 15, 25, 26), to Solomon (I Kings 3:5), to Nebuchadnezzar (Dan. 2:1, 4, 36; 4:1, 2), to Daniel (ch. 7:1, 2), to Joseph the betrothed husband of Mary (Matt. 1:20), to the Magi (ch. 2:12). The power of accurately interpreting prophetic dreams was granted to certain favored people, as to Joseph (Gen. 41:16, 25) and to Daniel (Dan. 2:25–28, 47). Dreams offered as revelations to the Church were subjected to tests to determine their character. If they inculcated immoral conduct, they were by that very fact proclaimed false; and any man who sought by their means to lead Israel from the worship of Jehovah was to be put to death (Deut. 13:1–5; cf. Jer. 23:25–32; 29:8; Zech. 10:2). See VISIONS.

Dress. See CLOTHING.

Drink. The usual beverage of the Hebrews was water (Gen. 21:14; Ex. 23:25; I Sam. 25:11; I Kings 13:8; II Kings 6:22), though they also frequently used milk (Judg. 5:25), sour wine (Num. 6:3; Ruth 2:14), ordinary wine (Gen. 14:18; 27:25; Judg. 19:19; Neh. 5:15), and, more rarely, strong drink (Lev. 10:9).

Drink Of'fer·ing. See OFFERINGS.

Drom'e·dar'y [Lat. *dromedarius,* from Gr. *dromas,* running]. 1. The rendering of Hebrew *rekesh* in A.V. of I Kings 4:28; but in Micah 1:13, "swift beast," and in Esth. 8:10, "mule." R.V. everywhere translates it "swift steed."

2. The rendering of Heb. *rammāk* (Esth. 8:10) in A.V. text and R.V. marg. R.V. text translates it "steed." Gesenius understands it to mean a mare.

3. The rendering of Heb. *bēker* (Isa. 60:6; Jer. 2:23). Arab. *bakr* denotes a young, vigorous he-camel. R.V. margin accordingly renders its "young camels."

The dromedary is a variety of the Arabian or one-humped camel (*Camelus dromedarius*) bred for speed and endurance. It can travel about 125 miles a day.

Drop'sy. A disease marked by an unnatural accumulation of watery liquid in any cavity of the body or in the tissues (Luke 14:2).

Dru·sil'la (drōō-sĭl'á). The youngest daughter of Herod Agrippa I and his wife Cypros (born c. A.D. 38). Before the death of her father in A.D. 44, and when not yet 6 years old, she was promised in marriage to a certain Epiphanes, son of Antiochus, king of Commagene. The bridegroom promised to accept Judaism, but later refused, and the proposed alliance fell through. Azizus, king of Emesa, was next applied to, the condition offered being the same as in the former case. He accepted, and Drusilla became his wife. She had great beauty, and was in consequence persecuted by her elder sister Bernice, who was plain in appearance. Felix, procurator of Judea, was captivated by Drusilla's beauty and employed one Simon, a Cypriote, to gain her for his wife. She responded all the more readily because Bernice's petty tyranny over her made her unhappy. In defiance of Jewish law, she left her husband and married Felix, a Gentile and an idolater (c. 53). They had a son called Agrippa, who grew up to manhood and married, but perished in an eruption of Mount Vesuvius (Jos. *Antiq.* xviii. 5, 4; xx. 7, 1 and 2). One can well understand that when Paul, then a prisoner, reasoned before Felix and Drusilla of righteousness, temperance, and judgment to come, Felix trembled (Acts 24:24, 25).

Dul'ci·mer. The rendering of Aram. *sŭmpōnyāh(-ā')*, *simpōnyāh(-ā')* (Dan. 3:5, 10, 15), probably meaning bagpipe, as R.V. marg. and J.V. make it. The real dulcimer is quite a different instrument. The list of instruments in which this word occurs begins with 2 wind instruments, followed by 3 stringed instruments, and closes with a wind instrument (bagpipe).

Du'mah (dū'má) [silence]. 1. A tribe descended from Ishmael (Gen. 25:14; I Chron. 1:30). Its territory was probably the region called Doumaitha by Ptolemy, and Domata by Pliny, on the confines of the Syrian and Arabian deserts. It is the oasis Dūmat al-jandal (modern al-Jauf), in the n.w. part of the Arabian peninsula.

2. A symbolic designation of Edom, chosen on account of its assonance with Edom and in allusion to the desolation in store (Isa. 21:11).

3. A town in the hill country of Judah (Josh. 15:52). Its site is ed-Dōmeh, about 10 miles s.w. of Hebron and 2½ miles n. of Dhahariyeh.

Dung. Dung was used for manuring plants (Luke 13:8; Ps. 83:10). A dunghill, with straw trodden in it by the cattle, is referred to (Isa. 25:10). In the East dried cow dung is constantly used for fuel (Ezek. 4:12, 15). Beggars often lay on dunghills and ash heaps (I Sam. 2:8; Lam. 4:5). As a punishment, the house of a man was sometimes made a dunghill (Dan. 2:5), that is, probably, was converted into a draughthouse (II Kings 10:27). The passage in Daniel, however, is better rendered, "And your houses shall be made ruins."

Dung Gate. See JERUSALEM, II. 3.

Du'ra (dū'rȧ) (Akkad. *dūru*, circuit, wall]. A plain in the province of Babylon where Nebuchadnezzar's golden image was set up (Dan. 3:1). Several localities in Babylonia were called Duru; there is a river Dūra with Tulūl Dūra near by.

Dys'en·ter'y. A disease characterized by inflammation and ulceration of the lower part of the intestines, with hemorrhage from the bowels. It is so constantly attended by fever that it is often called fever and dysentery. The father of Publius, chief man of the island of Melita while Paul was there, suffered from this complaint, but was miraculously cured by the apostle (Acts 28:7, 8, R.V.; in A.V., bloody flux).

E

Ea'gle. A bird of prey (Job 9:26; 39:27-30; Hab. 1:8), large (Ezek. 17:3, 7), swift of flight (II Sam. 1:23), seeing at a great distance, and building its nest on lofty rocks (Job 39:27-29; Jer. 49:16). It was currently believed to bestow great care upon its young while training them to act for themselves, stirring up the nest and forcing them out, hovering over them and under them when they made their first weak attempts to fly (Deut. 32:11; Ex. 19:4, 5). Sir Humphrey Davy relates witnessing a pair of golden eagles similarly engaged above the crags of Ben Nevis. There is also probably an allusion to an ancient popular belief that the eagle, at the end of a certain period molts and renews its youth (Ps. 103:5). The story was that the eagle, on reaching old age, flew upward toward the sun until its feathers were singed and it fell into the sea. Thence it emerged in the strength of youth. The allusion may, however, be to the great age to which the eagle lives and retains the vigor of youth. As a carnivorous bird, feeding on reptiles and occasionally on carrion, it was unclean (Lev. 11:13). The Hebrews, like the Arabs, applied the name which they used for eagle to birds that eat carrion, probably, like the Greek and Roman naturalists Aristotle and Pliny, including certain larger varieties of the vulture among the eagles (Matt. 24:28; cf. Prov. 30:17). In alluding to the baldness of the eagle (Micah 1:16), the prophet, if he does not refer to molting, which is an inconspicuous process in the eagle, has some vulture in mind, whose head is bald and neck but scantily feathered.

Ear'nest. Part payment in advance of a wage, a sum of money, or anything else promised, this being intended as a pledge or guarantee to the recipient that the bargain, contract, or promise will in due time be carried out. Blackstone says that the prepayment of a penny in England will legally bind

a contract, and the handing over of the smallest quantity of goods ordered will bind the engagement for the remainder. The earnest, as a rule, is the same in kind as the ultimate payment, of which it is the pledge. The Spirit in the hearts of Christians is the earnest of their inheritance (II Cor. 1:22; 5:5; Eph. 1:13, 14).

Ear'ring. Earrings were worn by the Israelites, men, women, and children (Ex. 32:2), especially by the women (Ezek. 16:12; Judith 10:4). They were also worn by the Midianites (Num. 31:50), Assyrians, Egyptians, and other peoples. The custom was innocent in itself. But the earrings sometimes served as an amulet (cf. Isa. 3:20, R.V., amulet). As used in idolatrous worship, earrings were worn by the men and women of Jacob's household, until he ordered the strange gods to be put away (Gen. 35:4). They were made of gold (Ex. 32:2; cf. Prov. 25:12) or other precious metal. It is often not clear from the narrative whether earrings or nose rings are intended (Gen. 24:22, 30; Ex. 35:22).

Earth. 1. The world in which we dwell as distinguished from the heavens overhead (Gen. 1:1).
2. The dry land, as distinguished from the sea (Gen. 1:10); the habitable world (Gen. 1:28; 10:25; 18:18). It is frequently described in poetry. The earth is referred to as standing on pillars, on which it had been placed by God (I Sam. 2:8; Job 9:6; Ps. 75:3). The psalmist speaks of the inhabited earth as founded upon the seas and established on the floods (Ps. 24:2; 136:6; cf. Ex. 20:4). Others speak literally or figuratively of the foundations of the earth (Ps. 102:25; 104:5-9; Prov. 3:19; 8:29; Isa. 48:13).
3. Vegetable soil (Gen. 27:28; Ex. 20:24; Ps. 104:14).
4. The inhabitants of the world or of any region in it (Gen. 11:1; Ps. 98:9).

Earth'quake'. A shaking or trembling of the earth. In severe earthquakes, at the point where the force is greatest, the hills move to and fro (Jer. 4:24) and the foundations of the mountains, as it were, tremble (Ps. 18:7); clefts appear in the earth's crust (Zech. 14:4, 5) and chasms, into which men may fall, open and close (Num. 16:31-33); buildings are shaken down and their inhabitants often buried in the ruins; and if the sea is near, it may leave its bed for a few minutes nearly dry, and then bring in a wave upon the land which will sweep over it with destructive effect. Judea was visited by a severe earthquake in the days of Uzziah and Jeroboam II (Amos 1:1; Zech. 14:5; Jos. *Antiq.* ix. 10, 4). Another notable earthquake occurred in the 7th year of Herod the Great, which destroyed much cattle and upward of 10,000 lives (Jos. *Antiq.* xv. 5, 2). An earthquake, accompanied by darkness, signalized the death of Christ (Matt. 27:45, 51-54), and another heralded his resurrection (ch. 28:2). One occurred in Macedonia when Paul and Silas were in the jail at Philippi (Acts 16:26).

East. The direction toward the sunrise (as is denoted by the Hebrew and Greek words employed in Josh. 11:3; 12:3, etc.; Matt. 2:1). The Hebrews faced the point of the rising sun when they determined direction; hence the e. was the front (as is denoted by the Hebrew word in Gen. 2:8). The orientation of the e. gate of the Temple at Jerusalem was important; it was so built that on the days of the spring and fall equinoxes the first rays of the rising sun, heralding the advent of the glory of God, could penetrate into the Holy of Holies.

East, Chil'dren of the, or **Men of,** or **Peo'ple of.** A general designation of the tribes occupying the e. country, who inhabited the region bordering on Ammon and Moab (Ezek. 25:4, 10), dwelt as far n. as a district where people of Haran pastured their flocks (Gen. 29:1, 4), and extended far southward into Arabia.

East Coun'try. The region lying e. of Palestine (Zech. 8:7), especially the Arabian and Syrian deserts (Gen. 25:1–7).

East Sea or **East'ern Sea.** See DEAD SEA.

East Wind. A wind blowing, broadly speaking, from the e. In Egypt it blasts the ears of corn (Gen. 41:23, 27), and in Palestine the vines and vegetation generally (Ezek. 17: 7–10; 19:10–12). The e. wind in these lands is hot and sultry, and deleterious to vegetation, because it has been blowing over the Arabian or Syro-Arabian Desert (Hos. 13: 15). Doubtless this same wind is meant in Jonah 4:8, although the Ninevites themselves would not have called it an e. wind.

East'er. Originally the spring festival in honor of the Teutonic goddess of light and spring known in Anglo-Saxon as Eastre. As early as the 8th century the name was transferred by the Anglo-Saxons to the Christian festival designed to celebrate the resurrection of Christ. In A.V. it occurs once (Acts 12:4), but is a mistranslation. The original is *pascha*, the ordinary Greek word for passover. R.V. properly employs the word passover.

E'bal (ē'băl). 1. A son of Shobal, and a descendant of Seir the Horite (Gen. 36:23; I Chron. 1:40).

2. The same as Obal (cf. I Chron. 1:22 with Gen. 10:28).

3. A mountain separated only by a narrow valley from Mount Gerizim (Deut. 27:12, 13), w. of the w. highway and near the oaks of Moreh (ch. 11:30), which were near Shechem (Gen. 12:6; 35:4). When the Israelites passed the Jordan they were to set up great stones, plastered, on which the words of the Law were to be written. An altar also was to be built (Deut. 27:1–8). Representatives of 6 tribes, those of Reuben, Gad, Asher, Zebulun, Dan, and Naphtali, were to stand on Mount Ebal and pronounce curses on those who were guilty of certain heinous sins. The representatives of the remaining 6 tribes standing on Mount Gerizim were to pronounce blessings (Deut. 11:29; 27:9–26). These directions were carried out by Joshua (Josh. 8:30–35). Mount Ebal lies on the n. side of Nablus, the ancient Shechem, whilst Mount Gerizim lies on its s. side (Jos. *Antiq.* iv. 8, 44). Both are w. of the road from the s. to the n., and the branch road to Samaria and En-gannim passes between them. Ebal rises 3,077 feet above the sea, and is steep, rocky, and barren. In some places a few stunted olive trees may be discovered on its lower part, and prickly pear above; in others it is destitute of vegetation.

E'bed (ē'bĕd) [servant]. 1. Father of Gaal (Judg. 9:28, 30).

2. A chief of the father's house of Adin, who returned from Babylon with 50 males under the leadership of Ezra (Ezra 8:6).

E'bed-me'lech (ē'bĕd-mē'lĕk) [servant of the King, i.e., God]. An Ethiopian, a eunuch of the palace, who heard that Jeremiah had been cast into a dungeon where he would probably have soon died of hunger, and, having obtained the king's permission, drew him out by cords let down, and rags to protect the prophet's armpits against their sharpness (Jer. 38:7–13). Jeremiah was subsequently commissioned to inform him that, on account

of the service he had rendered, he should be preserved when Jerusalem was taken (ch. 39:15–18).

Eb'en·e'zer (ĕb'ĕn-ē'zēr) [stone of help]. A commemorative stone set up by Samuel, seemingly near Mizpah, between Mizpah and Shen, where the Lord discomfited the Philistines (I Sam. 7:10, 12). Twenty years previously the Israelites themselves had been defeated at this place by the Philistines and had lost the Ark (ch. 4:1–11; where the place is mentioned by its later name).

E'ber (ē'bēr), in A.V. thrice **He'ber** (I Chron. 5:13; 8:22; Luke 3:35) [other side, region beyond]. 1. A descendant of Shem through Arpachshad (Gen. 10:22, 24); and progenitor of a group of peoples (v. 21), embracing the Hebrews (ch. 11:16–26), the Joktanide Arabs (ch. 10:25–30), and certain Aramaean tribes descended from Nahor (chs. 11:29; 22:20–24). The name is used for these peoples collectively (Num. 24:24). Originally Eber belonged to the region beyond or e. of the Euphrates, perhaps also of the Tigris, with respect to the later Hebrews (cf. Josh. 24:2, 3, 14, 15), and to the Joktanide Arabs, and not unlikely with respect to his descendants, the ancestors of Abraham and Nahor, in Ur (Gen. 11:28).

2. A priest, head of the father's house of Amok in the days of the high priest Joiakim (Neh. 12:20).

3. A Gadite, head of a father's house in Gilead in Bashan (I Chron. 5:13).

4 and 5. Two Benjamites, a son of Elpaal and a son of Shashak (I Chron. 8:12, 22, 25).

E'bez (ē'bĕz), in A.V. **A'bez** (ā'bĕz) [tin]. A town of Issachar (Josh. 19:20). 'Ain el-Ḥbuṣ, or el-'Abuṣ, between 'Aulam and Sirîn, may be considered as the place.

E·bi'a·saph (ê-bī'à-săf). See ABIASAPH.

Eb'on·y. Wood of various species of the genus *Diospyros,* of the Ebenaceae family. The inner wood is black, very hard, and heavy. Ebony is used for inlaying and ornamental turnery. The men of Dedan traded with it in the markets of Tyre, having obtained it apparently from India or Ceylon (Ezek. 27:15). The Greeks recognized 2 kinds of ebony, one variegated, from India, and the other black, from Ethiopia.

E'bron (ē'brŏn), in A.V. **He'bron.** A town on the boundary line of Asher (Josh. 19:28). Perhaps identical with Abdon.

E·bro'nah (ê-brō'nà). See ABRONAH.

Ec·bat'a·na (ĕk-băt'à-nà). See ACHMETHA.

Ec·cle'si·as'tes (ĕ-klē'zĭ-ăs'tēz) [Gr. *ekklēsiastēs,* one who sits and speaks in an assembly or church, a preacher]. The name borrowed from the LXX and applied to the O.T. book called in Heb. *Ḳôheleth. Ḳôheleth* is etymologically related to the Heb. word for assembly or congregation. Originally it was a feminine abstract, which on account of its transference to a concrete male person became masculine. The English Bible follows the Greek and Latin versions in rendering it "the Preacher" (Eccl. 1:1). The Preacher is distinctly represented as Solomon, "son of David, king in Jerusalem" (v. 1), excelling all his predecessors in Jerusalem in wisdom and wealth (chs. 1:16; 2:7, 9). The book may be regarded either as a writing of Solomon himself in his old age or as words which, though not actually uttered by Solomon, accurately sum up his completed experience, are spoken from the standpoint of his finished course, teach the great lesson of his life as he himself learned it, and express the sentiments which he might rightly be supposed to entertain as he looked at life in the retrospect. The meaning of ch. 1:12–14 in the Hebrew may be either: "As for me, during my reign [which still continues] I have applied my heart to seek wisdom and have discovered that all is vanity," or "When I was king [as I am not now] I applied my heart to seek wisdom and discovered that all is vanity." The latter explanation is doubtless correct, for the language smacks everywhere of the vocabulary and grammar of the later post-exilic Hebrew Scriptures and of the Aram. portions of Daniel and Ezra. The book recounts the feelings, experiences, and observations which would be unavoidable to the wise man situated as was Solomon.

The message concerns solely the present life on earth. The question is raised whether any real profit accrues to man from toil (ch. 1:3). The method of investigation is that of the sage (v. 13). By observation and experience the Preacher finds that man's one source of satisfaction lies in himself, in the normal and healthy exercise of his powers of mind and body in harmony with the physical and moral laws of the universe in which he is placed (chs. 2:24; 3:12, 22; 5:18; 9:7–10). Vain are wisdom (ch. 1:12–18) and pleasure (ch. 2:1–11). Still they have value; hence the Preacher compares wisdom and folly (vs. 12–23). He concludes that the homely rewards of labor excel (chs. 2:24; cf. 5:12). The conclusion is strengthened by the fact that man's activities are bound to the stages of his growth. There is a time fixed and unalterable for the exercise of each power of mind and body, and everything is beautiful in its season (ch. 3:1–11). And other joy is often rendered impossible by injustice and oppression (chs. 3:16 to 4:3). Formalism and dishonesty are unwise; and wealth is often injurious, and is less desirable than health (chs. 5:1 to 6:9). The Preacher speaks of the value of a good name and the means of obtaining it (ch. 7:1–10); and of the value of wisdom as a safeguard (vs. 11–22), and in dealing with kings (ch. 8:1–8); and he insists on the general truth that godliness is the best policy (vs. 10–15). Death comes alike to all; let man find pleasure, then, in the common, humble joys of life. They are his portion (ch. 9:2–10). After sundry other shrewd observations, the Preacher is led again to his main theme; exhorts young men to rejoice in their powers, but to use them mindful of being under moral government; makes his great appeal to youth to remember God, and sums up the matter in the pithy sentence: "Fear God, and keep his commandments; for this is the whole duty of man. For God will bring every work into judgment [even now, whatever the Judge may do in the world to come]" (chs. 11:9 to 12:14).

In his argument the writer appeals to man's relation to God in so far only as God is known in nature and experience. His references to God are thus in accordance with the methods of that philosophical school to which he belonged (see WISDOM), and are indispensable in a complete discussion of the means of adjusting oneself to the conditions which one learns by experience to be imposed upon him and under which he lives.

The startling character of some statements in Ecclesiastes led certain Jews to question its right to place among inspired books. At last, however, its right to remain in the canon was universally accorded. There is no direct quotation from it or unequivocal allusion to it in the N.T.

Ed (ĕd) [a witness]. A word inserted in A.V. and R.V. of Josh. 22:34. It or a similar word was doubtless originally in the Heb. It is found in some Hebrew MSS. and in the Peshitta, though it may be an insertion in

them as it is in the English version. It is needful to the full meaning of the passage, which tells how the 2½ tribes e. of the Jordan reared an altar as a witness that they were of common descent and religion with those w. of the river. These latter, taking the altar to be the commencement of apostasy from Jehovah, were preparing to make war upon those who had erected it, when explanations were given and accepted as satisfactory (Josh., ch. 22).

E'dar (ē'dẽr). See EDER.

E'den (ē'd'n) [Heb. *'ēden*, delight, pleasantness; cf. Neo-Heb. *'iddēn*, to delight, make agreeable, and Arab. *ghudnah*, delicacy; or perhaps Akkad. from Sumerian *edinu*, plain, steppe, cultivated or arable land]. 1. A country in which God caused trees to grow from the ground and in this manner planted for Adam a garden, called from its situation the Garden of Eden. A river went out of the country of Eden to water the garden, and being thence parted, became 4 heads, called Pishon, Gihon, Hiddekel, and Euphrates. Of these 4 rivers, the Euphrates is well known. Hiddekel is the Tigris; the other two are doubtful. The Pishon surrounded or meandered through the land of Havilah, where there is gold; and the Gihon surrounded the land of Cush.

The main theories as to the site of the garden may be classed in two groups:

I. *Those which, while proposing to identify* the 4 streams with still existing rivers, fail to find a geographical counterpart of the one stream divided into 4. The site is, by many, sought in Armenia. The sources of the Tigris and Euphrates are in this region. The Pishon is supposed to be either the Phasis (modern Rion) or the Kur, the large tributary of the Araxes. The Gihon is identified with the Araxes, in Arabic known as *Gaiḥun er-Ras*. Objections to this theory are: (*a*) the difficulty in explaining the one river; (*b*) the absence of proof that the land of Cush ever extended to this region; (*c*) Havilah, as located by the Biblical writers, did not lie in Armenia. By others the garden is thought of as situated between the Nile and India or between India and the Oxus. Havilah is identified with a portion of India, where gold was obtained; and Cush with either Ethiopia, which is called Cush in the Scriptures, or the plateau of central Asia which was inhabited by the Kassites (Cossaeans). The Gihon, the river of Cush, is hence either the Nile, called by the Ethiopians *Gēwŏn* or *Gēyŏn*, or the Oxus. The same objections, *mutatis mutandis,* lie against the 2d theory as against the 1st. It may be added that the identification of the Gihon with the Nile is traceable as far back as Josephus, who identified the Pishon with the Ganges. In his case it probably rests on a misconception. The only land of Cush in the geographical knowledge of the later Israelites was Ethiopia; and accordingly Josephus understood the Nile by the Gihon, because it is the great river of the land of Cush. Some, accepting the Gihon as the Nile, have also identified the Pishon with the Persian Gulf.

II. *Theories which seek an exact geographical* counterpart to the Biblical description and identify not only the 4 rivers, but also the one. Calvin observed that the Tigris and Euphrates are actually united for a short distance as one stream, the Shatt al-Arab, which then divides and enters into the Persian Gulf by several mouths; and he concluded that the district watered by the united streams was the site of the garden. The annual deposit of silt at the head of the Persian Gulf through the centuries, however, is evidence that this particular spot was formerly submerged and that once the Tigris and the Euphrates emptied directly into the Persian Gulf. But the general locality indicated has much in favor of its being the site of the garden. Friedrich Delitzsch thinks that the river of Eden is the Euphrates. Its channel being higher than the Tigris, its superabundant waters on entering the alluvial plain n. of Babylon flowed from its banks and found their way across the plain to the Tigris. The district thus watered was extremely fertile, and here the Garden of Eden is to be sought. The word *edinu* in Sumerian and Babylonian means plain; and the two river bottoms of s. Mesopotamia and the alluvial lowland form a plain, and were spoken of as an *edinu*. A descendant of Cush reigned in the Babylonian plain (Gen. 10:8–10); and Kassites (Cossaeans) early descended upon Babylonia and for a time held the political power (c. 1746–1169). Hence the land of Cush may be satisfactorily regarded as having designated at one period Babylonia or its s. portion. Havilah was situated n.w. of the Persian Gulf, according to Scripture notices, and may be assumed to have extended to the Euphrates and bordered on Babylonia. Under these circumstances, the Pishon may reasonably be identified with the Pallakopas canal, which was probably a natural channel originally; and the Gihon with a great Babylonian canal which branched from the Euphrates e. at Babylon, and on which two of Nimrod the Cushite's cities, Babylon and Erech, stood. It may be the canal near Babylon whose name was Kaḥana or Guḥana, corresponding to Gihon. This scholarly theory still lacks proof. According to another explanation, Eden was an island not far from the head of the Persian Gulf, near the mouths of the Euphrates, Tigris, Kerkha (Choaspes), and Karūn. Sayce proposed that the Garden of Eden is to be identified with the sacred garden of Ea at Eridu, once a seaport on the Persian Gulf; he makes the river which waters it (Gen. 2:10) the Persian Gulf, while in one of his views (1906) the Pishon is the Pallakottas and the Gihon the Shatt al-Ḥai. He maintains that an oblong was formed by the 4 rivers, which are given in this order of directions: s., e., n., w.

The site of the Garden of Eden is most probably to be sought about the head of the Persian Gulf, but the exact spot cannot be definitely determined. The locality is e. of Palestine, as Gen. 2:8 may mean. The Tigris and Euphrates Rivers are there. Havilah was a district of northern central Arabia. A land of Cush corresponded approximately to Elam, where the names Kashshu and Cossaean long lingered. The plain of Babylonia could be and evidently was called an *edinu*, as Delitzsch has shown. Possibly the fact that the Persian Gulf was called a river may also have some bearing on the solution of the problem. The Garden of Eden is referred to in Isa. 51:3; Ezek. 28:13; 31:9, 16–18; 36:35; Joel 2:3; cf. Gen. 13:10.

2. A region in Mesopotamia; mentioned in connection with Gozan, Haran, Reseph, Telassar (II Kings 19:12; Isa. 37:12), and with Haran and Canneh (Ezek. 27:23, 24). Apparently the locality is called in Amos 1:5 (marg.) Beth-eden. The region is mentioned in Assyrian documents by the name Bīt-Adini, situated on both sides of the Euphrates n. of the Balikh River.

3. A Gershonite Levite, a son of Joah (II Chron. 29:12; 31:15).

E'der (ē'dẽr), in A.V. once **E'dar** (Gen. 35:21) and once **A'der** (I Chron. 8:15) [flock]. 1. A tower, beyond which Jacob on one occasion spread his tent (Gen. 35:19, 21, 27), between Bethlehem and Hebron.

2. A town in the s. of Judah (Josh. 15:21); el-'Adar, about 4⅓ miles s. of Gaza on the right bank of the wadi Ghazzeh.

3. A Benjamite, son of Elpaal (I Chron. 8:15).

4. A Levite, son of Mushi, of the family of Merari (I Chron. 23:23; 24:30).

Ed'na (ĕd'nȧ) [Gr. from Heb. 'ednāh, delight]. Wife of Raguel and mother of Sarah, who became the wife of Tobias (Tobit 7:2; 10:12; 11:1).

E'dom (ē'dŭm); in A.V. of O.T. 4 times **Id'u•me'a** [red]. 1. A name of Esau, given in memory of his having sold his birthright for red pottage (Gen. 25:30; 36:1, 8, 19).

2. The Edomites collectively (Num. 20:18, 20, 21; Amos 1:6, 11; 9:12; Mal. 1:4).

3. The region occupied by the descendants of Edom, i.e., Esau. It was originally called the land of Seir (Gen. 32:3; 36:20, 21, 30; Num. 14:18). In the mind of the Israelites, Edom as the name of the country was doubtless associated with the settlement of their kinsman Edom in that region. It is a mountainous and extremely rugged country, about 100 miles long, extending s. from Moab on both sides of the Arabah, or great depression connecting the s. part of the Dead Sea with the Gulf of 'Aḳabah (Gen. 14:6; Deut. 2:1, 12; Josh. 15:1; Judg. 11:17, 18; I Kings 9:26). The summit of Mount Seir is believed to rise about 3500 feet above the adjacent Arabah. The lower part of the chain is of red Nubian sandstone, with dikes of red granite and porphyry; the summit is of a chalky limestone, probably of cretaceous age. Edom is not nearly so fertile as Palestine (cf. Mal. 1:2–4); but in the time of Moses it had fields, vineyards, wells, and a highway (Num. 20:17, 19). The Edomite capital in the times of the Hebrew monarchy was Sela, probably later Petra. Other important towns were Bozrah and Teman. In the Greek period the name was modified to Idumaea (*q.v.*).

The wilderness of Edom was the Arabah at the s. extremity of the Dead Sea (II Kings 3:8, 20).

E'dom•ites (ē'dŭm-īts). The descendants of Edom, i.e., Esau (Gen. 36:1–19), and others incorporated with them. As early as the return of Jacob from Mesopotamia, Esau had occupied the land of Edom (Gen. 32:3; 36:6–8; Deut. 2:4, 5; Josh. 24:4), having driven out the aboriginal Horites (cf. Gen. 14:6; 36:20–30; Deut. 2:12, 22). The Edomites appear to have been first ruled by tribal chiefs (A.V., dukes), who were probably like Arab sheiks (Gen. 36:15–19, 40–43; I Chron. 1:51–54); but before the rise of the Hebrew monarchy they were governed by kings (Gen. 36:31–39; I Chron. 1:43–51). When the Israelites were approaching Canaan, they sought permission from the king of Edom to pass through his territory, giving assurance that the privilege would not be abused. He refused the request, and was prepared to fight if the Israelites had persisted in moving forward (Num. 20:14–21). Notwithstanding this hostility, an Edomite was regarded in the Mosaic Law as a brother of the Israelites, and the posterity of the former were allowed in the 3d generation to become incorporated with the Hebrew people (Deut. 23:7, 8), while it was not till the 10th generation that the descendants of a Moabite or an Ammonite could share the same privilege (vs. 3–6). Saul fought against the Edomites (I Sam. 14:47); and David put garrisons in Edom after conquering the country (I Chron. 18:13; and II Sam. 8:13, 14, where 'ărām [Syrians] is doubtless the error of a copyist who misread *daleth* [d] as *resh* [r]). This

conquest had been predicted by Balaam
(Num. 24:18). Joab, David's commander in
chief, remained in Edom for 6 months, cutting off every male (I Kings 11:15, 16); but
Hadad, one of the royal family, escaped with
some others of his countrymen to Egypt and
became an active enemy of Solomon (vs. 14–
22). After the death of Ahab of Israel, and
during the reign of Jehoshaphat of Judah,
Edomites, Ammonites, and Moabites invaded
Judah (II Chron. 20:1; see MEUNIM), but
perished in internecine strife caused by Jehovah (vs. 22, 23). About this time, and perhaps during years previously, a deputy or
appointee was "king" in Edom (I Kings 22:
47), perhaps the person called king in II
Kings 3:9. Edomites aided Israel and Judah
in the contest with Mesha, king of Moab (vs.
4–27); but in the reign of Jehoshaphat's son
Joram they revolted. Joram vanquished them
in the field, but could not reduce them to subjection (II Kings 8:20–22; II Chron. 21:8–
10). Amaziah was more successful. He slew
10,000 Edomites in the Valley of Salt, took
Sela, the capital, and put 10,000 Edomites to
death by flinging them from the top of the
rock (II Kings 14:7; II Chron. 25:11, 12).
In the reign of Ahaz, when Judah was attacked by Pekah and Rezin, the Edomites
invaded Judah, and carried off captives (II
Chron. 28:17). For a number of years, under Tiglath-pileser III, Sargon, Sennacherib,
Esarhaddon, and Ashurbanipal, Edom was a
vassal state of Assyria, but would join coali-
tions in revolt (711 and 701 B.C.). The Edomites rejoiced when Nebuchadnezzar destroyed
Jerusalem (Ps. 137:7). The prophets foretold the calamities that should befall Edom
for its inveterate enmity toward Israel (Ezek.
35:5, 6), but announced its ultimate incor-
poration into the Kingdom of God (Jer. 49:
7–22; Lam. 4:21, 22; Ezek. 25:12–14; 35:
15; Joel 3:19; Amos 9:12; Obadiah). When
the captivity of the 2 tribes rendered the
territory of Judah somewhat destitute of inhabitants, the Edomites seized on it as far
as Hebron, and were themselves supplanted
in Mount Seir by the Nabataeans. The political power of Edom was really completely
at an end when Nabonidus made Taima his
place of residence. Judas Maccabaeus retook
Hebron and the other towns which the Edomites had occupied (I Macc. 5:65; Jos. Antiq.
xii. 8, 6). John Hyrcanus compelled the
Edomites to submit to the rite of circumcision, and incorporated them with the Jewish
people (Jos. Antiq. xiii. 9, 1). The Herods
were Idumaeans, i.e., Edomites.

Ed're·i (ĕd'rê-ī). 1. The capital city of
Bashan (Deut. 3:10; Josh. 12:4; 13:12, 31).
There the Israelites fought the great battle
with Og, which deprived him of his dominions
and his life (Num. 21:33–35; Deut. 1:4; 3:1,
10). Edrei has been identified with Der'ā,
about 27 miles e. of Gadara and about 22
n.w. of Bosora, modern Buṣra eski Shām.
2. A fenced city of Naphtali (Josh. 19:37),
perhaps Tell Khureibeh, s. of Kedesh.

E'glah (ĕg'lȧ) [heifer]. One of David's
wives, and mother of Ithream (II Sam. 3:5;
I Chron. 3:3).

E'gla·im (ĕg'lȧ-ĭm) [perhaps, 2 ponds; cf.
Arab. 'ajala, to collect itself (water)]. A
Moabite town (Isa. 15:8). Eusebius men-
tions Agallim, 8 Roman miles s. of Areopolis
(Rabba); cf. also the town Agalla (Jos.
Antiq. xiv. 1, 4). About 7½ miles s. of Rabba
is Kerak, near which is Rujm el-Jilimeh which
preserves the name of Byzantine Aegallim.
Another suggestion is Khirbet Jaljūl, which
lies about 4⅓ miles farther s.

Eg'lath-shel'i·shi'yah (ĕg'lăth-shĕl'ĭ-shī'yȧ)
[third Eglath]. A place in Moab (Isa. 15:5;

Jer. 48:34, R.V.). J.V. follows A.V. in rendering, "A heifer of three years old."

Eg'lon (ĕg'lŏn) [perhaps, vituline]. 1. A
king of Moab, who captured Jericho, held it
for 18 years, and exacted tribute from Israel.
He was assassinated by Ehud, the bearer of
the tribute, who obtained a private interview
with him on the pretext of bringing secret
tidings (Judg. 3:12–30).
2. A town in the lowland and assigned to
Judah (Josh. 15:39). Its king was one of the
5 allies who made war on Gibeon, but were
defeated, captured, and executed by Joshua
(Josh. 10:3–23, 34–37; 12:12). Khirbet 'Ajlān,
16 miles n.e. of Gaza, preserves the name, but
the site is not ancient. Tell el-Ḥeṣi, which is
a few miles distant, has been proposed as
more appropriate; Tell en-Nejīleh, fully 3
miles s.e. of Tell el-Ḥeṣi, has also been suggested.

E'gypt (ē'jĭpt). I. The country. 1. Its names.
The country was named Aigyptos by the
Greeks as early as the time of Homer. This
name was apparently derived from Amarna
ḥikuptaḥ, which represents Egyptian Ḥa(t)-
ka-ptaḥ, a designation of Memphis. The ancient Egyptians, however, called their native
land Kemet (the black land), from its dark
soil of Nile mud in contrast with the red land
of the deserts. The most common designation
was Touï (the two countries), meaning Upper
and Lower Egypt. According to the Amarna
tablets, the Canaanites called the land Miṣri.
The Hebrew name, Miṣrayim, which has the
same root, has generally been explained as a
dual, but this view is not accepted by all grammarians. The modern Arab. name for Egypt
is Miṣr.
I. 2. The territory and its divisions. In ancient times Egypt was the country watered by
the Nile from the Mediterranean Sea as far
as the First Cataract. In addition it included
a series of oases in the w. desert, and also the
territory between the e. mouth of the Nile and
the wadi el-'Arish (the river of Egypt). The
country is divided by nature into two tracts:
a narrow valley running from s. to n., sunken
in the midst of a desert; and the prolongation
of the valley into a delta. These geographical
divisions formed political boundaries also:
Upper Egypt to coincident with the valley,
and Lower Egypt with the Delta. The length
of the Nile country from the sea to the First
Cataract is 550 miles, and its breadth, from
the head of the Delta to the cataract, averages
about 12 miles. The cultivable tract thus
formed between the cataract and the sea is
somewhat less than 13,000 square miles, being
about equal to the area of Connecticut and
Massachusetts. Ancient Egypt was a small
country, but at the same time, in proportion
to its width, it was the longest country in the
world. This long, narrow valley of the Nile,
as far as the First Cataract, was in geologic
times an estuary of the sea. In the strictest
sense, Egypt, as the ancient Greeks said, is
"the gift of the Nile." The soil varies from
33 to 38 ft. in depth; although the annual inundation of the Nile (June to October) fer-
tilizes and softens the ground, irrigation is
indispensable. Agriculture was and remained
the foundation of the economic life. See NILE.
I. 3. The adjacent region. Egypt is bounded
on either side by desert land. The waste country gradually rises from the Sahara in the w.
toward the e., and terminates in a chain of
mountains which skirt the Red Sea. The
desert region on the e. of the river, extending
to the Red Sea, was virtually uninhabited, and
its scanty resources were worked by the Egyptians. The mountains form a broad and massive range of crystalline rock, running parallel
with the coast of the Red Sea and sending
forth numerous ramifications into the interior

of the country. It was in these mountains, at Hammāmāt, on the caravan route between Koṣēr and Thebes, that the ancient Egyptians quarried the hard, dark-colored stone which they used for sarcophagi; and at Jebel Dukha, nearly opposite the extremity of the Sinaitic peninsula, they mined copper and emerald. Green and blue malachite, turquoise, and lapis lazuli, as well as copper, were also procured in the Sinaitic peninsula. Extensive masses of limestone stretch from the mountains to the Nile, yielding the alabaster with which the ancient Egyptians embellished their buildings. The desert on the w. of the Nile belongs to Libya. It presents an entirely different aspect from the region e. of the river, for it consists of an immense, monotonous, and stony tableland, 650 to 1,000 feet above the level of the Nile. The utter desolation of this desert is relieved at only 5 points within the Egyptian territory by oases.

Ancient Egypt was thus an isolated land—sea on the n., desert and sea on the e., and the Libyan Desert on the w. In the s. the valley is very narrow and the navigation of the Nile is obstructed by the cataracts.

Nubia, which finally became a part of the empire, extends from the First Cataract to the Sixth, a short distance north of the 16th parallel of latitude. During Dyn. XII the region between the First and Second Cataracts was conquered. Under Dyn. XVIII the frontier was extended to the Fourth Cataract.

II. *The people.* 1. *Their origin.* According to the Bible, Mizraim (Miṣrayim) was the son of Ham and the brother of Canaan, Put, and the Ethiopian Cush (Gen. 10:6). This statement can be interpreted in a political sense, since Egypt controlled Canaan for many centuries. The ancient Egyptians were Hamites and belonged to the white race. In prehistoric times a Hamitic race migrated in successive waves into Egypt and supplanted the aborigines. Later on, another invasion from Babylonia, largely of Semitic stock, entered the country and left its influence upon the language; at the same time a Nubian element was also injected into the Egyptian mixture. At a later date the country was divided into 42 nomes (provinces), or 20 in Lower Egypt and 22 in Upper Egypt, the great majority of which go back to prehistoric times.

II. 2. *Their language.* The Egyptian language offers an unusual philological history of about 5,000 years; its earliest records begin with Dyn. I, and the language, in one form or another, lived on continuously until Coptic, its lineal descendant, became practically extinct as a spoken language in the 16th century A.D.

Egyptian belongs to the Hamitic group of languages, but because it is closer to the Semitic than the other 2 main divisions of the Hamitic languages (the North African and the Ethiopian or Cushite), it may properly be called a Hamito-Semitic or Semito-Hamitic language. It is now generally believed that the Hamitic and Semitic families of languages are descended from a common stock. We may roughly distinguish the following linguistic stages: (1) Old Egyptian, of Dyns. I-VIII, which includes the language of the pyramid texts; (2) Middle Egyptian, the literary tongue of Dyns. IX-XVIII, and the vernacular of the early two thirds of the period (This became the classical norm and was imitated in later times.); (3) Late Egyptian of Dyns. XVIII-XXIV, exhibited chiefly in business documents and letters, but also in some literary works; (4) Demotic, a term applied loosely to the language used in books and documents written in the demotic script from Dyn. XXV to late Roman times (700 B.C. to A.D. 470); (5) Coptic, from the 3d century A.D. onward. This is the language of the Copts, the Christian descend-

ants of the ancient Egyptians. The Bible has been translated into various dialects of Coptic, which is still, in the Bohairic dialect, used for liturgical purposes.

Originally there was used a kind of conventionalized picture writing known as hieroglyphic writing. It consisted chiefly of representations of objects, such as birds, beasts, plants, and implements, together with various geometric symbols. Two classes of hieroglyphic signs need to be distinguished here: (1) ideograms or sense signs, which signify either the actual object depicted or some closely connected notion; (2) phonograms or sound signs, which originally were ideograms and are in many cases still employed as such, but now have acquired sound values. These, when combined, yield a new word, which may have no connection with the original meaning of the symbols. Long before 3000 B.C. the Egyptians had evolved 24 letters, or uniconsonantal signs, which constituted an incipient alphabet, but it was used only to supplement the hieroglyphs. In the Egyptian characters vowels were not written, and even though the Egyptians had an adequate alphabet of consonants, they conservatively clung to the hieroglyphs as the basis of their writing. Hieroglyphs survived down to Christian times. Already under the Old Kingdom, the scribes began to dispense with the details of the pictures in order to write more rapidly, and thus arose hieratic writing, which was employed whenever ornamentation was not an object. About the 8th century B.C., the demotic, or popular, writing came into vogue. It was used in social and commercial intercourse, and was a cursive form of the hieratic.

With the spread of Christianity, the knowledge of the old native scripts and lore rapidly fell into oblivion. In the 3d century A.D. demotic was no longer used for documents, though there are demotic inscriptions at Philae as late as 473, more than two centuries after the final disappearance of the hieroglyphs. The Egyptian inscriptions, accordingly, long remained a mystery. In 1799 some French soldiers found at Rosetta a black basalt stone bearing an inscription in hieroglyphic, demotic, and Greek. It was a decree in honor of Ptolemy Epiphanes, erected by the priests (196 B.C.). This stone, now in the British Museum, became famous as the real key to the reading of the Egyptian language, and is known as the Rosetta Stone. In 1815 there was discovered at Philae an inscription in Greek and hieroglyphic in honor of Ptolemy Physicon and the two Cleopatras. From a study of the proper names on these two inscriptions, and a careful comparison of the Egyptian texts with the Greek, gradual steps were made in the decipherment of Egyptian, which was brought to a successful conclusion by Champollion in 1822.

II. 3. *Their history.* The basic economic, social, and political institutions of ancient Egypt were developed in the predynastic period. Reckoning by the Sothic cycle, Breasted calculated that in 4236 B.C. the Egyptians introduced the solar year of 365 days (12 months of 30 days each plus 5 feast days at the end of the year). To some scholars, however, this date seems too early, and they have taken 2773 B.C. as the year of the invention of the calendar.

Already in prehistoric times there were two kingdoms, Upper and Lower Egypt, which were united under one king; the capital was at Heliopolis. This consolidation, however, did not endure, but c. 3000 B.C. Menes, a king of Upper Egypt, restored the union. His capital was at Thinis. Manetho, a priest of Sebennytos, who flourished under Ptolemy I (305–285 B.C.), wrote a history of his country in the Greek language. He divided the long succession of pharaohs as known to him into 30 royal houses or dynasties from Menes to 332 B.C., when Egypt fell into the hands of Alexander the Great.

(1) *The Old Kingdom.* This early period is followed by the Old Kingdom, Dyns. III–VI (2600–2250 B.C.) ; during this period the capital was at Memphis. In Dyn. III (c. 2600–2550) expeditions were sent to Phoenicia for cedars. King Zoser, of Dyn. III, built a step pyramid and had as his vizier Imhotep, a distinguished physician, philosopher, and architect. Dynasty IV (c. 2550–2450) was the age of pyramid-building. There are three great pyramids at Gizeh, of which the largest was erected by Khufu (Cheops). Its original height was 482 ft. ; it is 755 ft. square at the

XII (2000–1780) the first pharaoh, Amenemhet I, moved the capital northward to Ithtouï (Captor of the Two Lands), on the w. side of the river, some miles s. of Memphis. In the latter part of this dynasty the pharaohs lived in the Fayyūm. This was the classical age of Egyptian literature. Amenemhet I wrote a series of maxims for his son. The romance of Sinuhe gives us an excellent picture of conditions in Syria and Palestine during this period. The great conqueror Senwosret (Sesostris) III established the frontier at the Second Cataract and invaded Syria. It was an era of great commercial activity ; a canal was dug from the n. end of the Red Sea westward to the nearest branch of the Nile in the eastern Delta.

The Pyramids at Gizeh, Egypt

base and covers almost 13 acres. It is a solid mass of limestone, consisting of some 2,300,-000 blocks, each of which weighs on the average 2½ tons. Herodotus relates a tradition that the labor of building this structure required 100,000 men for 20 years. Smaller pyramids were erected by Khafre and Menkure. The Sphinx is supposed to go back to Khafre. Dynasties V and VI extend from c. 2450 to c. 2250. In Dyn. V, Sahure built the first navy in the history of the world. He invaded Syria and sent expeditions to Punt for spices which were used in mummification. At this time Egypt controlled the trade routes in Egypt and the Sudan. Ptah-hotep composed some *wisdom* literature in this dynasty.

In Dyn. VI, the local governors began to assert themselves as landed barons, and the dissolution of the kingdom resulted. The nomes regained their independence, and thus Egypt was politically almost as it was before the accession of Menes. The Old Kingdom collapsed, and Dyns. VII and VIII are unimportant. In Dyns. IX and X a succession of 18 men at Heracleopolis succeeded in maintaining order. Dynasties VII–XI constitute the First Intermediate Period, which closed c. 2000 B.C. Dynasty XI built a centralized state at Thebes.

(2) *The Middle Kingdom.* Now follows the Middle Kingdom (Dyn. XII). The s. had triumphed over the n., and during Dyn. XI the capital was established at Thebes. In Dyn.

(3) *Second Intermediate Period (1780–1546), including the Hyksos.* The brilliant period of the Middle Kingdom was followed by the internal conflicts of the feudatories in Dyns. XIII–XIV, upon which succeeded the conquest by the Hyksos (rulers of the foreign lands), popularly called the Shepherd Kings, who reigned about 175 years (Dyns. XV–XVI, c. 1730–c. 1555). The Hyksos seem to have been Canaanites ; recent evidence thus supports Manetho who calls them "Phoenicians." Their personal names for the most part are Semitic. Although most of the Hyksos were Semites, some may have been Hittites, Luvians and Hurrians. It has been supposed that Joseph was vizier under one of the Hyksos rulers. Not much is known of this foreign domination ; the capital of the Hyksos was located at Avaris in the Delta. Toward the end of the Hyksos period there maintained itself at Thebes Dyn. XVII, the last king of which was Ahmose (Amosis), who died c. 1546. He completed the expulsion of the Hyksos. While this invasion by the Hyksos was regarded by the Egyptians as a calamity, its influence was epoch-making and had much to do with transforming a peaceful people into a military nation. The Hyksos brought the horse and the chariot into the Nile valley, and the Egyptians learned war on a grand scale.

(4) *The Empire (1546–1085 B.C.).* With the expulsion of the Hyksos began the period of the Empire, or New Kingdom, with the capital

at Thebes. All Egypt was now practically the personal estate of the pharaoh. The feudal lords had almost disappeared. Under the Empire, there were two viziers, one for the n. and one for the s.; the various departments of government were well organized. It was an era of great building projects, as is evident from the great temple at Karnak. Amenhotep I (1546–1525) was succeeded by Thutmose (Thothmes, Thutmosis) I (1525–1508). At the death of Thutmose II (1508–1504), the power was usurped by Hatshepsut (1504–1482), the daughter of Thutmose I; she was an aggressive ruler, and for 22 years kept the throne from Thutmose III. The greatest of all empire builders was Thutmose III (alone 1482–1450 B.C.), who conducted 17 campaigns and extended the empire to its widest limits. His domains included Palestine, Syria, and the region of the Upper Euphrates and reached to the Fourth Cataract, while his influence extended much farther. One of his most important battles took place at Megiddo, where, c. 1482, he defeated the Hittites. This great empire soon began to decay under the weak successors of Thutmose III. Amenhotep (Amenophis) III reigned from c. 1412 to c. 1375 and was followed by his son, Amenhotep IV (c. 1375–c. 1366), who had been coregent since c. 1387. He is better known as Akhnaton (Ikhnaton), and was interested more in religion than in the empire. He gave to the worship of Aton (the sun disk), a religion which was an approach to monotheism, official support against the well-established religion of Amun (Amon), the sun-god of Thebes. He moved the capital to a new city, Akhetaton (modern Tell el-Amarna), nearly 300 miles below Thebes. The frontiers of the empire were now neglected, and the Hittites and the Habiru were gradually encroaching upon Syria and Palestine. The Tell el-Amarna letters of this period contain many earnest pleas from Akhnaton's vassals in Byblos and Jerusalem for aid against the invaders, but he sent no effective help. Under Tutankhamun (Tutenkhamon) the capital was once more at Thebes. During Dyn. XVIII Amen-em-apt wrote his proverbs, which have many resemblances to those of Solomon.

Dynasty XIX (1353–1205) marks the restoration of the worship of Amun, the resumption of the old order, and the beginning of the new epoch. Harmhab (1353–1319) was the first ruler of this dynasty, and at once he proceeded with the work of reorganization. Ramesses (Ramses) I reigned from 1319 to 1318 and was succeeded by Sethi I (1318–1299); he began the conquest of Palestine and was succeeded· by his son, Ramesses II (1299–1232), who c. 1295 fought with the Hittites at Kadesh on the Orontes in an indecisive battle. C. 1279, Ramesses, who could not regain the n. territory of Thutmose III, made a treaty on terms of equality with the Hittites, regaining control of Palestine and a great deal of Syria. Merenptah (Merneptah) (1232–1222) succeeded Ramesses II; during his reign Egypt was threatened with a desperate attack by the Libyans and the "Peoples of the Sea." The movement of these Aegean peoples is connected with the Homeric war against Troy and brought about the end of the Hittites. The empire was now on the defensive, and decay was not far off. At the end of Dyn. XIX a Syrian usurper held the throne for 5 years.

Dynasty XX (1200–1085) had 10 rulers bearing the name of Ramesses. During the reign of Ramesses III (1198–1167) another land and sea attack by the "Peoples of the Sea" was made upon Egypt, which was successfully repulsed.

(5) *The Decline* (*1085–332* B.C.). During Dyn. XXI (1085–945), the Tanite-Amonite period, the high priests of Amun at Thebes (Hri-

hor and his line) and the nobles of Tanis (Smendes and his line) strove for the royal power. In the meantime the Libyans were peacefully penetrating the country, and Sheshonk I, a Libyan, succeeded to the throne, thus establishing Dyn. XXII (945–745). See SHISHAK (SHESHONK) and ZERAH (OSORKON) under PHARAOH. The capital was now at Bubastis in the e. Delta. Dynasties XXIII (745–718) and XXIV (718–712) were also Libyan.

Lower Nubia had been dominated by the Egyptians for over 1,800 years, and the region between the Second and Fourth Cataracts had been under Egyptian control for about 1,000 years. By the middle of the 8th century B.C., a fully developed Nubian kingdom appeared, with the seat of government at Napata, just below the Fourth Cataract. By 722 or 721 Piankhi, a Nubian king, was in the possession of Upper Egypt as far as Heracleopolis; he captured Memphis, and received the submission of the lords of the Delta. See So (SIB'E). Dynasty XXV (712–663), known as the Nubian or Ethiopian Dyn., was founded by Shabaka, a brother of Piankhi; the 3d and last ruler was Taharka (Tirhakah), a son of Piankhi. See PHARAOH.

Both Libyans and Nubians were largely Egyptianized and ruled as Egyptian pharaohs. Next came the Assyrians. In 671, Esarhaddon conquered the Delta, and Taharka abandoned Lower Egypt. Twenty lords of the Delta swore fealty to the new ruler, but with the withdrawal of the Assyrian forces Taharka once more became ruler of the whole country. Under Ashurbanipal a new conquest (667) was made and the Assyrians penetrated as far as Thebes. In a 2d campaign by Ashurbanipal, Thebes was taken and sacked (663). Cf. Nahum 3:8–10.

With Psamtik (Psammetichus) I began the 26th or Saïte Dyn. (663–525); the capital was then at Saïs in the Delta. He was placed under Assyrian suzerainty until about 651, when the Assyrian garrisons were withdrawn on account of the revolt of Babylon under Shamashshum-ukin; accordingly Psamtik, who had built up an army of Anatolian and Ionian mercenaries, was left independent. Another view is that the mercenaries were sent by Gyges, king of Lydia, and that the Assyrian garrisons were driven out. During this period the nation once more flourished, and an attempt was made to emulate the glories of the past. He was succeeded by his son Necho II (609–593). See PHARAOH 5, 6. Psamtik II, who saw no hope of conquest in Asia, turned his attention to Nubia; his son Hophra (Apries) once more directed longing eyes to the ancient dominions of Egypt in Asia. Hophra lost his life in a civil war with Ahmose (Amasis) II (569–525), who succeeded him. During the reign of Ahmose II, Naucratis, a Greek city, was founded on the Canopic mouth of the Nile. Egypt's naval strength of this period was the foundation of the sea power which under the Ptolemies made Egypt the dominant state on the Mediterranean.

In 525 B.C., Egypt was conquered by Cambyses (Dyn. XXVII) and became a Persian satrapy. In 404 Amyrtaeus made himself king and reigned for 6 years, Dyn. XXVIII. In 398, Nepherites revolted against Persia and founded Dyn. XXIX. Twenty years later, the last king of the dynasty, Hakori, died, and there followed Dyn. XXX, the last dynasty of native Egyptian kings to rule the whole land. The first king was Nectenabo I; in this late period the course of events was dependent on the kaleidoscopic change of politics in Greece. Artaxerxes Ochus sent an expedition which conquered the land (343–342). In 332 the country submitted to Alexander the Great, whom the people regarded as their deliverer. After his death, it was ruled by the Ptolemies.

In 30 B.C. it became a Roman province and was governed by the Romans until A.D. 395. Then it was under Byzantine rule until A.D. 639, when the Arabs conquered Egypt.

II. 4. *Their religion.* In the earliest period each town had its own deity. The religion of the Egyptians for the most part centered about the veneration of the sun and of the Nile, as sources of life. In the Egyptian religion primitive conceptions of various ages and places were retained; apparently nothing was given up, and a conglomeration resulted. Osiris, the god of the Nile, consequently became the god of fertility; he was also god of the underworld. Re, the sun-god, was worshiped at Heliopolis (On). With the rise of Thebes, the local god Amun received prominence and was finally identified with Re under the compound name Amun-Re. The moon, as the measurer of time, the god of reckoning, of letters, and of wisdom, was worshiped at Hermopolis. Ptah, a god of Memphis, was known as the

and 2 grandsons were already in Egypt; and his 2 sons by Rachel's maid, with 5 grandsons (Gen. 46:8–25). "All the souls that came with Jacob into Egypt, that came out of his loins" (even though some perhaps were still unborn, cf. Heb. 7:9, 10), were 66 souls (Gen. 46:26). "All the souls of the house of Jacob" which came into Egypt first and last, including the head of the house and Joseph with his 2 sons who were born in Egypt, were 70 souls (v. 27). This is also the enumeration of Ex. 1:5 (as in Gen. 46:15, apparently exclusive of Jacob, but in reality inclusive of him) and Deut. 10:22. The LXX, however, and Stephen, who follows the Greek version (Acts 7:14), reckon 75. This result is due to the addition in Gen. 46:20 of 3 grandsons and 2 great-grandsons of Joseph, whose names are obtained from Num. 26:29 and 35 *seq.* according to the text of the LXX. The numerical correspondences of the register, a total of 70, and the descendants of each maid precisely half those of her

Judgment Scene from the Papyrus of Ani (About 1400 B.C.)

"Great Chief of Artificers." The Egyptians also had a number of sacred animals, such as the bull, cow, cat, baboon, jackal, crocodile, etc. Some of the deities had human bodies and animal heads. Anubis, the guide of the dead, had a jackal head; Thoth, the scribe of the gods, that of an ibis; Horus, the sun-god, that of a hawk. With the growth of the empire there developed the idea of a universal god in Egypt; Aton is clearly distinguished from the material sun. The religion fostered by Akhnaton was a short-lived solar monotheism. A remarkably clear knowledge of ethical and religious truths was possessed from very early times—truth in regard to human conduct, sin, justification, immortality, and, with all the nature worship, even in regard to God. Of special interest is the Egyptian conception of immortality.

III. *The Sojourn of the Israelites in Egypt.* 1. *The descent into Egypt.* A grievous famine prevailed throughout the whole known world, or at least throughout that region about the e. and s.e. shores of the Mediterranean Sea. During this distress Joseph, who had risen to authority at the court of Pharaoh second only to that of the king, urged his father and brethren to leave Canaan and settle temporarily in Egypt (Gen. 45:9–11; 47:4, 29, 30; 48:21; 50:24). Accordingly Jacob migrated with his tribe. It consisted of the patriarch himself, his 6 sons and 1 daughter by Leah, with 23 grandsons and 2 great-grandsons; his 2 sons by Leah's maid, with 11 grandsons, 1 granddaughter, and 2 great-grandsons; his 2 sons by Rachel, with 12 grandsons, of whom 1 son

mistress (Leah 32, Zilpah 16, Rachel 14, Bilhah 7), suggest design, and can scarcely be altogether accidental. A comparison with Num., ch. 26, leads to the belief that regard was had to the subsequent national organization in constructing this table, and that its design was to include those descendants of Jacob from whom permanent tribal divisions sprang. The tribe of Israel settled in Goshen, and remained in and about this fertile region until the Exodus (Gen. 47:6, 11; Ex. 8:22; 9:26; 12:37).

III. 2. *The sojourn as embedded in the national consciousness.* The descent of Jacob and his family into Egypt, their subsequent increase and enslavement, their sufferings and their exodus in a body, were recorded in their earliest historical document (Gen. 46:4, 28–34; 47:27; Ex. 1:9, 11, 15–22; 2:11; 12:31–37; 13:21). The feast of the passover, and to a less degree that of the tabernacles, bore testimony to the events, and kept the knowledge of them alive among the people. A historical sojourn and the Exodus are accepted as facts in the experience of the nation by both psalmists and prophets. The standing types of the grievous oppression of the Church and of God's redemptive power and love are Israel's bondage in Egypt and deliverance from that affliction. The tradition is not peculiar to one tribe, as though but a portion of the Hebrew folk had endured Egyptian slavery; it is not exclusively Judean, but it is Ephraimite as well. The prophets of both kingdoms voice it —Isaiah, Micah, and Jeremiah, among the hills of Judah (Isa. 11:16; Micah 6:4; 7:15;

Jer. 2:6; 7:22), and Hosea and Amos in the kingdom of Samaria (Hos. 2:15; 8:13; 9:3; 11:1; 12:9, 13; Amos 2:10; 3:1; 9:7). The tradition is the common property of all Israel. The people as a whole had suffered Egyptian bondage.

III. 3. *The duration of the sojourn.* The Biblical data are stated in the following terms: "He said unto Abram, . . . Thy seed shall be a stranger in a land that is not theirs, and shall serve them; and they shall afflict them four hundred years. . . . But in the fourth generation they shall come hither again" (Gen. 15:13-16, A.V.). "Now the time that the children of Israel dwelt in Egypt was four hundred and thirty years" (Ex. 12:40, R.V.); according to the LXX and Samaritan Pentateuch in this passage, the sojourning "in Egypt *and in the land of Canaan* was four hundred and thirty years." God spake to Abraham "that his seed should sojourn in a strange land; and that they should bring them into bondage, and treat them ill four hundred years" (Acts 7:6). "The law . . . came four hundred and thirty years after" the covenant (Gal. 3:17).

These statements are interpreted to mean: (1) The Children of Israel dwelt in Egypt 215 years. For the LXX, either to remove an ambiguity or because the Hebrew MSS. differed from the present Hebrew text, adds the words, "And in the land of Canaan," to the statement in Ex. 12:40. Now from the date of the covenant with Abram, shortly after his arrival in Canaan, to the migration of his descendants into Egypt was about 215 years (cf. Gen. 12:4; 21:5; 25:26; 47:9), leaving 215 years for the sojourn of the Children of Israel in Egypt. This statement is also made by Josephus (Jos. *Antiq.* ii. 15, 2): "The Hebrews left Egypt 430 years after our forefather Abraham came into Canaan, but 215 years only after Jacob removed into Egypt." In this statement he is following the LXX, but he nullifies his statement by saying elsewhere, "Four hundred years did they spend under these labors" (Jos. *Antiq.* ii. 9, 1; *War* v. 9, 4; manifestly incorrect, for the Israelites were not *oppressed* for 400 years). But however Josephus may vacillate, Paul dates the law at Sinai 430 years after the covenant with Abram, and the genealogies give 4 generations between Jacob and the Exodus, which may cover 215 years, but scarcely 400 years (Ex. 6:16-20).

(2) The Children of Israel dwelt 430 years in Egypt. (*a*) The natural interpretation of Gen. 15:13-16 requires this. (*i*) The statement is not that the Israelites should be afflicted 400 years, but that the entire sojourn as strangers in a land not theirs, where they shall be eventually brought into bondage, is 400 years. (*ii*) The event is not to take place until after Abraham's death (v. 15). (*iii*) The 4 generations are equivalent to the aforementioned 400 years. In this passage, generation does not mean each succession of persons from a common ancestor, as it does in Ex. 20:5; Job 42:16, but the age or period of a body of contemporaries, and this not in our modern sense of the average lifetime of all who pass the age of infancy, but the average period of the activity of any generation, and this is determined by the normal span of life. The generation lasts while any of its members survive (Ex. 1:6; Num. 32:13; Judg. 2:10; Eccl. 1:4). The period of a generation's activity may be judged from the length of the life of Isaac, 180 years; of Jacob, 147 years; of Levi, 137; of Kohath, 133; of Amram, 137; of Aaron, 123; of Moses, 120 (Gen. 35:28; 47:28; Ex. 6:16, 18, 20; Num. 33:39; Deut. 34:7). Or the period of a generation's activity may be estimated from the record of 3 generations between the birth of Abraham and the descent

into Egypt, when Jacob was still active, a period of 290 years. A generation was about 100 years. But are not just 4 generations registered—namely, Levi and Kohath, who came into Egypt with Jacob, Amram, Moses, and Moses' sons? A consecutive genealogy in Levi, Kohath, and Amram is admitted; but was Moses the son of Amram and Jochebed (Ex. 6:20; I Chron. 6:1-3)? A difficulty arises if the passage be so interpreted. In the first place, Amram and his brothers gave rise to the Amramites, Izharites, Hebronites, and Uzzielites; and these one year after the Exodus amounted to 8,600 males; that is, the grandfather of Moses had 8,600 male descendants in the days of Moses, of whom 2,750 were between the ages of 30 and 50 (Num. 3:27; 4:36). Furthermore, in the parallel genealogy of the contemporaries of Moses Bezalel is 7th from Jacob and Joshua apparently 11th (I Chron. 2:18-20; 7:23-27). The language of Ex. 6:20 does not necessarily, nor even evidently, mean that Amram and Jochebed were the immediate parents of Moses and Aaron. In Gen. 46:18, great-grandsons of Zilpah are mentioned with others as sons which she bore to Jacob. In Matt. 1:8 Joram is said to have begotten his great-great-grandson Uzziah. According to Gen. 10:15-18 Canaan begat nations. Where the birth of Moses is narrated in detail, he is not said to be the child of Amram and Jochebed (Ex., ch. 2). The reason for registering only 4 names in the genealogy of Moses and others (Ex. 6:16-22) is that the first 3 names are official and give the tribe, family, and father's house to which Moses and Aaron belonged. The 3 names properly and at once classify Moses and Aaron. (*b*) Four hundred and thirty years for the sojourn is also the record of Ex. 12:40. The statement does not include the sojourn of the patriarchs in Canaan, for (*i*) Abraham and Isaac were not sons of Israel, and (*ii*) the verse in the Heb., Targum, etc., except the LXX and Samaritan, makes no reference to Canaan. (*c*) Paul's statement in Galatians can be explained on the interpretation of the data as meaning that the sojourn lasted 430 years. It is not his object to measure the exact time between the covenant and the law. His argument only requires him to prove that the law was given long after the covenant, and hence cannot disannul it. He proves it by citing the well-known period of the sojourn which intervened between the two events, the largest and most familiar single sum of years in the interval. He does not mean to state that the law came exactly 430 years after the covenant, but he rather refers in a general way to a great period in Hebrew history. The length which elapsed is immaterial to the argument. It seems, however, that Paul in this passage had the chronology of the LXX in mind, but this is indifferent.

III. 4. *The multiplication of the Israelites during the sojourn.* (1) It has been pointed out (Keil) that if from the 70 souls who went down into Egypt there be deducted the patriarch Jacob, his 12 sons, Dinah, and Serah daughter of Asher, and also the 3 sons of Levi, the 4 grandsons of Judah and Asher, and those grandsons of Jacob who probably died without male offspring, inasmuch as their descendants are not named among the families of Israel (see Num., ch. 26), there will remain 41 grandsons of Jacob (besides the Levites) who founded families; and if, furthermore, there be allowed but 10 generations for the 430 years, nevertheless the 41 men would increase to 478,224 males if each family averaged 3 sons and 3 daughters during the first 6 generations, and 2 sons and 2 daughters during the last 4 generations. These, with the survivors of the 9th generation, would amount to more than 600,000 men above 20 years of age. (2) It is a mistake to overlook the fact that the household of the patriarch included numerous servants (Gen. 30:43; 32:5; 45:10), who were circumcised (Gen. 17:12, 13) and enjoyed full religious privileges (Ex. 12:44, 48, 49, etc.), and with whom intermarriage was no degradation (Gen. 16:1, 2; 30:4, 9; Num. 12:1; I Chron. 2:34, 35).

III. 5. *The change of occupation during the sojourn.* When the Israelites settled in Goshen they were a comparatively small tribe, independent, and herdsmen. But after Joseph and the men of that generation died, a new king arose who knew not Joseph (Ex. 1:6–8). He saw the increasing numbers of the Israelites, and, fearing that they might ally themselves with the enemies of Egypt, took measures to render them a subject people and to check their increase. Taskmasters were placed over

Pharaoh sufficient evidence at the outset of the divine authority of Moses, without inflicting unnecessary sufferings upon the Egyptians; and when he refuses to let the Hebrews go, they become more intense, and bring increasing pressure upon his obdurate heart until he finally yields. Even though the first 9 plagues can be explained as natural phenomena, the rapid succession of events and the definite purpose constitute a miracle. (2) A distinction was made, between the people of God and the Egyptians (Ex. 8:22, 23; 9:4, 25, 26; 10:22, 23; 11:5–7; and cf. chs. 9:11; 10:6). (3) A pestilence might have slain a great number of the Egyptians in one night, but the 10th plague is a pestilence with a method, and cannot under any circumstances be explained as a mere phenomenon of nature. We have here a direct intervention by

Egyptian Brickmakers, from a Wall Painting in a Tomb

them, and rigorous service was exacted from them in the form of agriculture, brickmaking, and building (Ex. 1:11, 14; 5:6–8), while they still provided at least some of their own support by herding (chs. 9:4, 6; 10:9, 24; 12:38).

III. 6. *The miracles wrought by Moses at the end of the sojourn.* The oppression of the Israelites lasted 80 years or more (Ex. 7:7; cf. ch. 2:2 *seq.*). At length their cry came up unto God and he sent Moses to deliver them (ch. 2:23 *seq.*). The humble ambassador of heaven was provided with miracles as his credentials. They were actual miracles—in Scripture parlance, signs, wonders, and powers. They were wonderful, unusual, and intended to enforce attention. They were signs accrediting Moses as the messenger of God to the Israelites (chs. 4:8, 9, 30, 31; 6:7) and to Pharaoh (chs. 3:20; 4:21; 7:3–5; 8:22, 23). They were powers, not mere natural phenomena; for (1) design is apparent in them. Even though the first 9 plagues are in the realm of nature, God controls nature and uses natural phenomena to accomplish his purposes. The plagues form an orderly series; each one is in logical, but not causal, relation to its successor; they increase in severity, affording

God. It is not a promiscuous death: the firstborn of every family of the Egyptians dies.

These signs, wonders, and powers belong to the first group of miracles recorded in Scripture. See MIRACLE, PLAGUE.

III. 7. *The organization of the Israelites at the end of the sojourn.* The forefathers of the Children of Israel had descended into Egypt as a family of 12 households, and had settled together in Goshen. As is quite natural in itself, and as appears from the narrative, they retained their organization despite their enslavement. They did not amalgamate with the master race, but remained a distinct people and preserved the 12 great family divisions. By the end of the 430 years, the families of the 12 sons had become 12 tribes, and the sons' sons, and in a few instances the sons' remoter descendants, had grown into large family connections. Accordingly at the time of the Exodus there was a people, Israel, divided into 12 tribes; and each tribe was subdivided into families or connections, which derived their names for the most part from the grandsons of Jacob (cf. Ex. 6:14 with Gen. 46:9, and Num., ch. 26 with Gen., ch. 46) and at the time of the 2d census numbered 57, without Levi; and each family connection, into fathers' houses (Num. 1:2, 18, 20). Authority of various kinds was vested in: (1) princes by birth (Ex. 16:22), heads of the tribes or family connections (Num. 1:4, 16); (2) elders, who were probably heads of tribes and families, and aged (Ex. 4:29; 12:21; 17:5, 6); (3) apparently also in priests (Ex. 19:22, 24; perhaps cf. Ex. 24:5). They were probably men out of the various tribes who performed priestly functions for the Israelites, as Abraham, Isaac, and Jacob as heads of the family had offered sacrifice. (4) The Egyptians had imposed further organization on the Israelites by setting over them officers (Ex. 5:6, 10, 19), Hebrews (vs. 15, 16), who had undoubtedly been appointed on their ability to direct. Through these various representatives, Pharaoh and Moses communicated their will to all the people with dispatch. The Children of Israel, grouped in tribes, families, and fathers' houses, officered and accustomed to obedience, were not an unwieldy horde, but a multitude with the organization of an army. They were fittingly called the hosts or armies of the Lord, and it is significantly said that they went out of Egypt by their hosts (Ex. 12:41).

III. 8. *The Pharaohs of the Oppression and the Exodus.* For many years Ramesses II was commonly regarded as the pharaoh of the oppression, and Merenptah as the pharaoh of the Exodus. The whole matter is, however, still in a state of uncertainty. On the basis of archaeological evidence some authorities have fixed upon c. 1400 B.C. as the year of the destruction of the city of Jericho. This agrees well with the Biblical chronology. The 4th year of Solomon's reign was c. 968 B.C., which according to I Kings 6:1 was the 480th year after the Children of Israel were come out of Egypt. Making allowance for approximate dates, this brings the year of the Exodus to a date not far from 1450 B.C., the year in which Thutmose III died. Accordingly he would be the pharaoh of the oppression, and Amenhotep II (1450–1425), his successor, the pharaoh of the Exodus. According to Judg. 11:26, 300 years intervened between Israel's occupation of the East Jordan and Jephthah's day, which would favor the earlier date of the Exodus. According to one of the steles of Sethi I, '*Apiru* (Hebrews) were found in the vicinity of Beisan. Sethi I and Ramesses II mention the tribe of '*sr*, identified by most scholars with Asher, as settled in n. Palestine in the 15th century. On the Merenptah stele there appears the word "Israel" as the name of a people of Palestine raided by the Egyptians, which is naturally clear evidence for the presence of the Israelites there at that time. This is against the theory which makes Merenptah the pharaoh of the Exodus.

Some archaeologists, however, maintain that Jericho did not fall as early as 1400 B.C., but contend for a date between c. 1375 and c. 1300; while Ai slightly later in the early 13th century, and Kiriath-sepher and Lachish around 1230, fell into Israelite hands. Naturally this interpretation of the fall of Jericho and other cities would place the Exodus at a date between c. 1415 and c. 1340.

From the Amarna letters we learn that during the reigns of Amenhotep III and IV, nomads known as the Habiru (or Hapiru) were invading Syria along the whole frontier. Habiru (Hapiru), which corresponds to Egyptian '*Apiru*, may be equated philologically with Hebrew '*Ibrî* (Hebrew), which means, "One from the other side," and perhaps, "One who passes (from place to place), a nomad." Some think that the invasion of the Habiru is that of the Israelites under Joshua, since the conditions reflected in the Amarna tablets correspond so accurately to those depicted in The

Book of Joshua. A Joshua appears in both accounts, but we have not sufficient grounds for identifying the 2 men.

There are, however, some historians who still consider Ramesses II as the pharaoh of the oppression and Merenptah (Mernephtah) as the pharaoh of the Exodus. In Ex. 1:11 it is stated that the Children of Israel built for the pharaoh store cities, Pithom and Raamses. The inference is that the latter city was named for the reigning pharaoh. But this name hardly proves anything. It is now known that Avaris, the Hyksos capital; Raamses, the capital of Dyn. XIX; and Tanis were all successive phases of the same city.

The Amarna tablets, which come to an end before 1360 B.C., and the Egyptian lists do not mention the fortified towns n. of the Arnon. It has therefore been suggested that Sihon's kingdom was founded after the Amarna period. It is also maintained for archaeological reasons that the regions of Moab and Edom to the s. were almost entirely unoccupied by

Storehouse for Grain in Ancient Egypt

a sedentary population between the 19th and 13th centuries B.C. It has accordingly been concluded that the Israelites may have occupied Sihon's territory shortly before 1250 B.C., and thus ⁺he Exodus would be dated c. 1290 B.C. or a few years earlier. The date 1290 for the Exodus is not certain, but reckoning 430 years (Ex. 12:40) from the era of Tanis (c. 1720), we obtain the date 1290 B.C., but this agreement may be accidental. At any rate, if this date be correct or approximately so, Ramesses II was the pharaoh of the Exodus. The date of the Exodus cannot be definitely determined on the present evidence available.

E'hi (ē'hī). See AHIRAM.

E'hud (ē'hŭd) [probably contraction of Abihud]. 1. A Benjamite, descended through Jediael (I Chron. 7:10).

2. A left-handed Benjamite, descended through Gera. He assassinated Eglon, king of Moab, then the oppressor of Israel. Fleeing to the hill country of Ephraim, he summoned the Israelites by sound of trumpet, put himself at their head, descended to the valley of the Jordan, seized the ford of the river, and slew 10,000 Moabites as they attempted to cross. He judged Israel for the remainder of his life, and kept the people true to Jehovah (Judg. 3:15 to 4:1).

E'ker (ē'kẽr) [offshoot, stock; cf. Lev. 25:47]. A man of Judah, a son of Ram, of the house of Jerahmeel (I Chron. 2:27).

Ek'ron (ĕk'rŏn) [rooting out]. The most n. of the 5 chief Philistine cities (Josh. 13:3; I Sam. 6:16, 17). It was assigned to Judah (Josh. 15:45, 46), and afterward to Dan (ch. 19:43); but the boundary line of Judah ran past it (ch. 15:11), and it was taken and possessed by the men of that tribe (Judg. 1:18). After a time it was recovered by the Philistines. When the people first of Ashdod and then of Gath became afraid to retain the Ark of God, they sent it to Ekron, whence it was returned to Israel (I Sam. 5:10, 11). Samuel recovered Israel's border as far as Ekron (I Sam. 7:14); and the Philistines, fleeing when Goliath fell, were pursued to its gates (ch. 17: 52). Baal-zebub was worshiped there, a god Ahaziah, king of northern Israel, sought to consult (II Kings 1:2–16). Judgment was denounced against it and the other Philistine cities by the prophets (Jer. 25:15–20; Amos 1:8; Zeph. 2:4; Zech. 9:5, 7). In 701 B.C. it closed its gates against Sennacherib, but in vain. Alexander Balas, king of Syria, gave Ekron to Jonathan Maccabaeus (I Macc. 10: 89). It is believed to be represented by the village of 'Aḳir, 6 miles w. of Gezer and 12 n.e. from Azotus.

El'a (ē'lȧ), in A.V. **E'lah** [probably hypocoristic, *El* (God)+*a* (meaning uncertain, perhaps an element of greatness)]. The father of one of Solomon's purveyors (I Kings 4:18).

El'a·dah (ĕl'ȧ-dȧ). See ELEADAH.

E'lah (ē'lȧ) [terebinth]. 1. A valley near Socoh in which Saul and the Israelites pitched, confronting the Philistines, just before the combat between David and Goliath (I Sam. 17:2, 19; 21:9). Probably the wadi es-Sunt, which is formed by the junction of 3 other valleys, and is about 14 or 15 miles w. by s. from Bethlehem. It is fertile and traversed by a stream. Wadi es-Sunt means the valley of the acacia (*Acacia vera*).
2. A duke of Edom, named from his habitation (Gen. 36:41; I Chron. 1:52). See ELATH.
3. A son of Caleb, the son of Jephunneh (I Chron. 4:15).
4. A Benjamite, son of Uzzi (I Chron. 9:8).
5. The father of one of Solomon's purveyors. See ELA.
6. The son and successor of Baasha in the kingdom of Israel. He reigned part of 2 years. As he was drinking himself drunk in the house of his steward in Tirzah, his capital, he was assassinated, with all his house, by Zimri, who commanded half his chariots. This fulfilled the prophecy made by Jehu, the son of Hanani, to Baasha (I Kings 16:6, 8–10).
7. The father of Hoshea, king of Israel (II Kings 15:30; 17:1; 18:1).

E'lam (ē'lăm) [Heb. *'ēlām*, Akkad. *elamtu*, highland]. 1. Elam was a region beyond the Tigris, e. of Babylonia. It was bounded on the n. by Assyria and Media, on the s. by the Persian Gulf, on the e. and s.e. by Persia. The name is preserved in Gr. and Lat. *Elymais*. Its capital was Shushan or Susa, which gave rise to the name Susiana, though sometimes Elymais and Susiana are made the names of adjacent instead of identical regions.
Elam was the seat of an ancient empire. See BABYLONIA, HAMMURABI, ABRAHAM, IV, CHEDORLAOMER. The first known historical ruler to mention Elam in a contemporary inscription is Eannatum of Lagash, who boasts that he conquered Elam. This victory did not have a prolonged effect, since under one of his successors, Enetarsi, the Elamites plundered Lagash. Affairs took a different turn under Sargon of Agade, who calls himself "smiter of Elam and Barahsi" (a district on the n.w. border of Elam). His successors all were victorious, and Naram-Sin was master "of the land of Elam, all of it." As a result of the blows dealt by the dynasty of Agade, Babylonia had rest from Elamite invasions for 300 years, but was held in subjection by the Gutians for 125 years to c. 2125 B.C. Under Ibi-Sin, the brilliant Sumerian 3d Dyn. of Ur came to an end (c. 2025) and he was carried in fetters to Anshan. The stage was now set for a ruler of Elamite origin to be-

come king of Sumer and Akkad. Kudur-Mabuk, near the end of the 2d millennium, became master of Larsa; he was not a barbarian, but a statesman and an organizer. He was succeeded by his sons, Warad-Sin and Rim-Sin. Under their reign the land was prosperous, and there was cultural activity. After having reigned for 60 years, Rim-Sin was defeated by Hammurabi. The way for Hammurabi's brilliant rule was clearly paved by the Elamites. Later on an Elamite conqueror carried the stone on which was inscribed the Code of Hammurabi to Susa, where it was found in A.D. 1901–1902. In the time of Abraham, Chedorlaomer, king of Elam, was recognized as sovereign by Babylonian states, and laid even the country on the Jordan under tribute (Gen. 14:1–11). In the 8th and 7th centuries B.C., when Assyria was the dominant power in western Asia, Elam was its doughty opponent; but was subjugated after repeated campaigns of the Assyrians under Sargon, Sennacherib, and Ashurbanipal. Shushan was at length taken about 645 B.C. Elamites rendered military service to the Assyrians in the invasion of Judah (cf. Isa. 22:6). But before the close of the century, Elam was relieved of the Assyrian yoke through the fall of Nineveh. When Ezekiel prophesied the invasion of Egypt by Nebuchadnezzar, he mentioned a prior slaughter of the Elamites, perhaps by Nebuchadnezzar (Ezek. 32:24). But Elam, joining with Media, was ultimately to capture Babylon (Isa. 21:2; cf. v. 9). The following prophecies regarding Elam seem to refer to conquest and restoration (Jer. 49:34–39; Ezek. 32:24, 25). Elam was a province and Shushan a capital of the Persian Empire (Dan. 8:2; Herod. iii. 91; iv. 83; v. 49). On the return of the Jews from Babylon, Elamites, who had long before been forcibly settled in Samaria, joined with others in attempting to prevent the rebuilding of the Temple and city of Jerusalem (Ezra 4:9). Elamites were present on that day of Pentecost which was notable for the descent of the Holy Spirit (Acts 2:9). Elam or Susiana, now Khūzistān, is a province of modern Iran.
2. The 5th son of Meshelemiah, a Korahite Levite, in the reign of David (I Chron. 26:3).
3. A Benjamite, a son of Shashak (I Chron. 8:24, 25).
4. The head of a family of which 1,254 individuals returned from Babylon with Zerubbabel (Ezra 2:7; Neh. 7:12), and 71 more with Ezra (Ezra 8:7). Its representative signed the covenant in Nehemiah's time (Neh. 10:1, 14).
5. The other Elam, of whom just as many descendants returned as of No. 4 (Ezra 2:31; Neh. 7:34).
6. A priest who took part in the dedication of the wall of Jerusalem (Neh. 12:42).

E'lam·ites (ē'lăm-īts). Inhabitants of Elam. They were not a Semitic people, but were the easternmost neighbors of the Semites. At an early period they had settled in the Tigris-Euphrates Valley; in fact the Elamites or a people closely related to them constituted an important element in the pre-Sumerian population of Babylonia. Probably on account of these ancient contacts they were listed among the sons of Shem (Gen. 10:22; I Chron. 1: 17). Their language has some relations to the Caucasian or Japhetic group and was in use for at least 4,000 years.

El'a·sa (ĕl'ȧ-sȧ), in A.V. **El'e·a'sa**. A place at which Judas Maccabaeus once camped (I Macc. 9:5) probably Khirbet Il'asa, which lies midway between the 2 Beth-horons.

El'a·sah (ĕl'ȧ-sȧ) [God has made]; see ELEASAH. 1. A son of Shaphan. He and Gemariah carried a letter from Jeremiah in Jerusalem to the exiles in Babylon (Jer. 29:1–3).

2. A son of Pashur, induced by Ezra to put away his foreign wife (Ezra 10:19, 22).

E'lath (ē'lăth) and **E'loth**, the singular or plural being used indifferently; cf. **E'lah** [terebinth or other large tree]. A town on the Gulf of 'Aḳabah (Deut. 2:8; I Kings 9:26), on the e. border of the wilderness of Paran (Gen. 14:6). The caravan routes between s. Arabia and Egypt and Phoenicia passed its gates, making its possession valuable to an exactor of tribute. It was taken by Chedorlaomer from the Horites (Gen. 14:5, 6). In it dwelt a chief of Edom (ch. 36:41), and it constituted the s. limit of the Edomites (Deut. 2:8). It doubtless fell into the hands of David (II Sam. 8:14; cf. I Kings 9:26; II Chron. 8:17). After a time it reverted to the Edomites. Uzziah rebuilt it and restored it to Judah (II Kings 14:22; II Chron. 26:2). It was afterward captured by the Syrians and long remained in their power (II Kings 16:6). Elath, called in the Greek and Roman period Aila and Aelana, gave the name Aelanitic to the Gulf of 'Aḳabah, at the n.e. corner of which it was situated. It was long the station of a Roman legion, and was once the seat of a Christian bishopric. An Early Iron Age Elath may be detected at Aila. Ezion-geber lay w. of Elath, but, from the time of Uzziah, Elath is to be identified with Ezion-geber. It is now called Aila and 'Aḳabah.

El-be'rith (ĕl-bē'rĭth). See BAAL-BERITH.

El'-beth'-el' (ĕl'bĕth'ĕl') [God of Beth-el]. The name given by Jacob to an altar which he reared at Beth-el, after his return from Mesopotamia. It commemorated the appearance of God to him there in a dream when he was fleeing to escape the consequences of his brother's wrath (Gen. 35:7; cf. 28:10 *seq.*). The sanctuary was named after the God to whom it was dedicated. See EL-ELOHE-ISRAEL.

El·da'ah (ĕl-dā'à) [perhaps, God has called; cf. Arab. *da'ā*, to call]. A son or tribe descended from Midian and related to Abraham (Gen. 25:4; I Chron. 1:33).

El'dad (ĕl'dăd) [God has loved]. An elder and officer of the Israelites who was summoned with 69 others to assist Moses in bearing the burden of government. Eldad and Medad for some reason failed to present themselves with the others at the tabernacle; nevertheless they too, although absent in the camp, were filled like the others with the divine Spirit, who works when and where he will. Joshua was jealous for Moses' honor, which he feared would suffer because they had received the gift without the intervention of Moses; but Moses rejoiced, and only wished that the Lord would put his Spirit upon all his people (Num. 11:26–29).

Eld'er. An official who, so far as can be judged, had by virtue of his right as first-born succeeded to the headship of a father's house, of a tribal family, or of the tribe itself (I Kings 8:1–3; Judg. 8:14, 16). When he was the head and representative of a tribe or of the larger tribal families the elder was an important prince. Ordinarily, only men of mature age came into these positions; hence the designation "elder." Other peoples which were organized on the tribal system had elders, as the Midianites and Moabites (Num. 22:4, 7). The title designates high officials generally in Gen. 50:7. They exercised authority over the people (Deut. 27:1; Ezra 10:8), and represented the nation in affairs of state (Ex. 3:18; Judg. 11:5–11; I Sam. 8:4), in extending honor to a distinguished guest (Ex. 18:12), in concluding covenants (II Sam. 5:3), and in

religious acts (Lev. 4:13–15; Josh. 7:6). A body of 70 elders assisted Moses in the government of the Israelites (Num. 11:16, 24). Each town had its elders, who were probably the heads of the several family connections in the place and who administered its civil and religious affairs (Deut. 19:12; 21:2; Ruth 4:2–11); I Sam. 11:3; Ezra 10:14). These functions were still performed by the elders at the time of the Roman government of Judea (Matt. 21:2; 21:23; 26:3, 47). See SYNAGOGUE and SANHEDRIN.

In the churches founded by the apostles, elder or presbyter and bishop were interchangeable designations (cf. Acts 20:17 with v. 28, R.V.; Titus 1:5, 7), though not strictly synonymous. The former had primary reference to the dignity of the office, the latter to its duties. The distinction between elder or presbyter and bishop, as 2 separate orders of ministers, dates from the 2d century. The origin of the office of elder is not recorded, but elders existed practically from the beginning. In A.D. 44 they already existed in the church at Jerusalem (Acts 11:30); Paul on his First Missionary Journey appointed elders in every church (ch. 14:23), and they held office in churches not founded by Paul (James 5:14; I Peter 5:1). The office of elder in the Christian Church was evidently suggested by the office of elder among the Jews, and was invested with similar authority. Elders were associated with the apostles in the government of the Church (Acts 15:2, 4, 6, 22, 23; 16:4; cf. 21:18). They were the bishops or overseers of the local churches (ch. 20:17, 28; Titus 1:5), having the spiritual care of the congregation, exercising rule and giving instruction (I Tim. 3:4, 5; 5:17; Titus 1:9; James 5:14; I Peter 5:1–4; cf. Heb. 13:17), and ordaining to office (I Tim. 4:14). There were several bishops (Phil. 1:1) or elders (Acts 11:30) in a local church. There is no intimation of any division of labor among them. As in the synagogue, so in the Christian Church of apostolic times, preaching was not the peculiar function of the elders, nor was it restricted to them. They were, indeed, the regular pastors and teachers. Aptness to teach was an essential qualification for the office (I Tim. 3:2; Titus 1:9). But any man who possessed the gift of prophecy or teaching exhorted (I Cor. 12:28–30; 14:24, 31).

In the government of Reformed Churches the teaching elder is the minister, and the ruling elder is a layman who is an elder. The arrangement is convenient, but its existence in apostolic times is not universally admitted. Calvin interpreted I Tim. 5:17 as teaching two kinds of elders: first, those who both teach and rule, and secondly, those who rule only. But there is a wide dissent from this interpretation. It is urged that the apostle is speaking of two functions of the same office, the primitive elder having been, it is contended, both teacher and ruler.

In the Apocalypse the elders are 24 in number, possibly with reference back to the 12 founders of tribes under the Jewish economy, and the 12 apostles under the Christian Church (Rev. 4:4, 10; 5:5, 6, 8, 14; 7:11–13; 11:16; 19:4).

El'e·ad (ĕl'ē-ăd) [God has testified]. A descendant, perhaps son, of Ephraim. He and his brother were killed by the people of Gath when attempting to carry away the cattle belonging to that Philistine town. Ephraim, who was alive at the time, greatly mourned his loss (I Chron. 7:20–22).

E·le·a'dah (ē-lê-ā'dà), in A.V. **El'a·dah** [God has adorned].

A descendant of Ephraim (I Chron. 7:20).

El'e·a'leh (ĕl'ē-ā'lē). A town rebuilt by the Reubenites (Num. 32:3, 37). Later it fell into the hands of the Moabites (Isa. 15:4; 16:9; Jer. 48:34). The ruins, now called el-'Al, are on top of a hill, scarcely 2 miles n.n.e. of Heshbon.

El'e·a'sa (ĕl'ê-ā'sà). See ELASA.

El'e·a'sah (ĕl'ê-ā'sà) [God has made]. In Hebrew it is the same word as Elasah. 1. A descendant of Judah through Jerahmeel, but with Egyptian blood in his veins (I Chron. 2:33, 39).

2. A descendant of Saul and Jonathan (I Chron. 8:33–37; 9:43).

El'e·a'zar (ĕl'ê-ā'zēr) [God has helped; see LAZARUS]. 1. The 3d son of Aaron (Ex. 6:23; Num. 3:2) and father of Phinehas (Ex. 6: 25). With his brothers and his father he was consecrated a priest, and afterward acted as such (Ex. 28:1; Num. 3:4; 16:39; 19:3). He was not allowed to mourn when his elder brothers, Nadab and Abihu, were killed for offering strange fire (Lev. 10:1–7). He then became chief of the Levites, and 2d only to Aaron in priestly authority (Num. 3:32). Before Aaron died on Mount Hor, Eleazar, who had been directed to ascend the mountain with him, was invested with his sacred garments, and succeeded him in the high priesthood (Num. 20:25–28; Deut. 10:6). He held this office during the remainder of Moses' life and the leadership of Joshua. He took a prominent part in distributing Canaan by lot among the several tribes (Josh. 14:1). He was buried in a hill belonging to his son Phinehas in Mount Ephraim (Josh. 24:33), and was succeeded by Phinehas (Judg. 20:28).

2. A Levite, family of Merari, house of Mahli. He died without sons; his daughters were taken to wife by their cousins (I Chron. 23:21, 22; 24:28; cf. Num. 36:6–9).

3. A son of Abinadab. He was consecrated by the men of Kiriath-jearim to keep the Ark when they nobly received it from Beth-shemesh after its restoration by the Philistines (I Sam. 7:1).

4. One of David's mighty men, a son of Dodo (Dodai in R.V.), the Ahohite (II Sam. 23:9; I Chron. 11:12; cf. 27:4 perhaps).

5. A priest, son of Phinehas. He assisted the high priest in the time of Ezra (Ezra 8: 33).

6. A son of Parosh, who was induced by Ezra to put away his foreign wife (Ezra 10: 18–25).

7. A priest, one of those who acted as musicians at the dedication of the wall of Jerusalem in the time of Nehemiah (Neh. 12:27–42).

8. Surnamed Avaran, of priestly descent, a son of Mattathias and brother of Judas the Maccabee (I Macc. 2:5). In the battle between Judas and the Syrians at Beth-zacharias, he boldly ran into the ranks of the enemy, crept under an elephant whose trappings indicated that it carried a royal rider, and thrust it in the belly. The beast in its fall crushed Eleazar to death (ch. 6:43–46).

9. An ancestor, perhaps great-grandfather, of Joseph, the husband of Mary (Matt. 1:15).

E·lec'trum [Lat. from Gr. ēlektron, a pale-yellow alloy of gold and silver; also amber, as in Homer]. Rendering of Hebrew ḥashmal in the LXX and Vulgate (Ezek. 1:4, 27; 8:2), followed by J.V. (text) and E.R.V. marg. A.V. translates "amber," and A.R.V. (text), "glowing metal."

El'-E·lo'he-Is'ra·el (ĕl'ê-lō'hĕ-ĭz'rà-ĕl) [God, the God of Israel]. The name given by Jacob to an altar which he erected near Shechem (Gen. 33:20).

E'leph (ē'lĕf) [an ox]. A village of Benjamin (Josh. 18:28). Site unknown, but near Jerusalem.

El'e·phant. A genus of animals containing two recent species—Elephas indicus, the Indian, and Elephas africanus, the African elephant, with several others now extinct. Their tusks furnish ivory (I Kings 10:22, A.V. marg.). The elephant was used in war (I Macc. 1:17; 3:34), each beast being in charge of an Indian driver, and bearing on its back a tower from which 2, 3, or 4 soldiers fought (I Macc. 6:37, where 32 is an obvious error; Livy xxxvii. 40). The entire body of elephants was under a master (II Macc. 14:12). Before they entered battle, it was customary to inflame them by the sight and even taste of wine (I Macc. 6:34; III Macc. 5:2).

El'e·phan·ti'ne (el'ê-făn-tī'nê). See SEVENEH.

E·leu'ther·us (ê-lū'thēr-ŭs) [Lat. from Gr., free]. A river (I Macc. 11:7; Jos. Antiq. xiii. 4, 5) which flows from Lebanon and empties into the Mediterranean Sea n. of Tripoli, and which formed the boundary between Palestine and Syria (I Macc. 12:30; Jos. Antiq. xv. 4, 1). It is now called Nahr el-Kebir.

El·ha'nan (ĕl-hā'năn) [God has been gracious]. 1. A son of Jair and perhaps a Bethlehemite, who slew [the brother of] Goliath of Gath (cf. II Sam. 21:19 with I Chron. 20: 5). The text of at least one passage, perhaps of both, has become corrupt. The Hebrew letters of "Beth-lehemite Goliath," with the particle 'ēth between them in the text of Samuel, closely resemble those of "Lahmi the brother of Goliath."

2. A Bethlehemite, a son of Dodo, and one of David's 30 heroes of the 2d rank (II Sam. 23:24; I Chron. 11:26).

E'li, I (ē'lī) [Heb., my God, but occasionally also used in Aramaic]. A word in the utterance of Jesus on the cross, spoken in Aram.. 'ēlî, 'ēlî, lᵉmā(h) shᵉbaḵtānî: "My God, my God, why hast thou forsaken me?" (Matt. 27:46; cf. Ps. 22:1). In Mark 15:34, instead of Eli, we have Eloi, which is for Aram. 'ĕlāhî (ā being transliterated as ô).

E'li, II (ē'lī) [high; perhaps contraction for "God is high"]. A high priest of the family of Ithamar (I Sam. 1:9; cf. I Kings 2:27 and I Chron. 24:3, 6). He is said to have been the first of Ithamar's line to receive the office (Jos. Antiq. v. 11, 5; viii. 1, 3), but it is uncertain which priest of the other line he succeeded. Eli was also active as a judge of Israel. Being deeply pious, he had an essential qualification for his exalted offices. But there was one serious defect in his conduct: he did not deal firmly with his two sons, Hophni and Phinehas, when their behavior in the priestly office was scandalous (I Sam. 2:23–25; 3:13). Divine judgment was therefore denounced against him and his house by a prophet: Eli should see evil befall the sanctuary, his descendants should die in the flower of their age, his 2 sons should perish in one day, and a faithful priest should supersede Eli's descendants, from whom they should seek for subordinate priestly appointments that they might be fed (ch. 2:27–36). The message was confirmed by a similar revelation to young Samuel, which Eli received with resignation (ch. 3:11–18). Soon afterward Hophni and Phinehas, as custodians of the Ark, carried it to the field of battle, to aid the Israelites against the Philistines. Eli, now 98 years old and blind, being anxious for the Ark, took his seat by the wayside to watch. A runner arrived from the scene of strife with the news of Israel's defeat, the death of Hophni and Phinehas, and the capture of the Ark of God. On hearing that the Ark of God had been taken by the enemy, Eli fell backward from the seat and broke his neck and expired (ch. 4:1–18). He had judged Israel 40 years. With the death of Eli, the office lost for a long time its importance, for the Ark was in captivity and seclusion, and the tabernacle was no longer the place of Jehovah's gracious presence. Samuel the prophet was the religious leader of the people. The judgment against Eli's posterity was executed when Solomon deposed Eli's descendant Abiathar from the high priesthood, substituting Zadok in his room (I Kings 2:35).

E·li'ab (ē-lī'ăb) [God is a father]. 1. The son of Helon, and the head of the tribe of Zebulun in the wilderness (Num. 1:9; 2:7; 7:24, 29; 10:16).
2. A Reubenite, son of Pallu and father of Dathan and Abiram (Num. 16:1, 12; 26:8, 9).
3. A Levite, an ancestor of Samuel (I Chron. 6:1, 27, 28). See ELIHU 1.
4. David's eldest brother. He was so tall and had so kingly a countenance that on seeing him Samuel exclaimed, "Surely Jehovah's anointed is before him." But, judged by the heart, he was not worthy of the kingdom (I Sam. 16:6, 7; 17:13). One defect which he had was his inability to appreciate the larger soul of David, his youngest brother (ch. 17: 28, 29). His daughter Abihail married a son of David (II Chron. 11:18).
5. A Gadite, of the heroic type who joined David at Ziklag (I Chron. 12:1, 8, 9).
6. A Levite, musician in the sanctuary in David's reign (I Chron. 15:12, 16, 20).

E·li'a·da (ē-lī'à-dà), in A.V. once **E·li'a·dah** (ē-lī'à-dà) (I Kings 11:23) [God has known —i.e., kindly regarded]. 1. A son of David, born at Jerusalem (II Sam. 5:13–16; I Chron. 3:8). Called also Beeliada (q.v.).
2. Father of Rezon of Zobah (I Kings 11: 23).
3. A Benjamite, one of Jehoshaphat's chief captains (II Chron. 17:17).

E·li'ah (ē-lī'à). See ELIJAH 2 and 4.

E·li'ah·ba (ē-lī'à-bà) [God conceals (i.e., defends)]. A Shaalbonite, one of David's mighty men (II Sam. 23:32; I Chron. 11:33).

E·li'a·kim (ē-lī'à-kǐm) [God will establish]. 1. An ancestor of Christ. He lived before the Captivity, and was descended from David through Nathan (Luke 3:30, 31).
2. Son of Hilkiah. He was over King Hezekiah's household; and when Jerusalem had closed its gates against the Assyrians, he was one of 3 representatives of the king who were sent to confer with the Rabshakeh of Sennacherib (II Kings 18:18, 26, 37; Isa. 36:3, 11, 22). Next they were dispatched to lay the answer of the Rabshakeh before Isaiah, and desire him to obtain divine direction in the great crisis which had arisen (II Kings 19:2; Isa. 37:2). The prophet so highly commended Eliakim, and made him such promises from God, as to suggest that he must be regarded as a type of the Messiah (Isa. 22:20–25).
3. One of Josiah's sons, made king by Pharaoh-necho, who changed his name to Jehoiakim (II Kings 23:34; II Chron. 36:4).
4. One of the priests who officiated at the dedication of the wall of Jerusalem (Neh. 12: 27, 41).
5. A descendant of Zerubbabel and an ancestor of Christ (Matt. 1:13).

E·li'am (ē-lī'ăm) [God is a kinsman]. Father of Bath-sheba (II Sam. 11:3); by transposition of the constituent parts of the name called Ammiel (I Chron. 3:5). Perhaps he was David's mighty man of this name, the son of Ahithophel (II Sam. 23:8, 34).

E·li'as (ē-lī'ăs). See ELIJAH.

E·li'a·saph (ē-lī'à-săf) [God has added]. 1. The head of the tribe of Gad in the wilderness (Num. 1:4, 14; 2:14; 7:42).

2. A Levite, the son of Lael, and prince of the Gershonites during the wilderness wandering (Num. 3:24).

E·li'a·shib (ē-lī'à-shĭb) [God will restore]. 1. The ancestor from whom the 11th priestly course took its name (I Chron. 24:1, 12).
2. A Levite and singer whom Ezra induced to put away his foreign wife (Ezra 10:10, 19, 24).
3 and 4. Two men, a son of Zattu and a son of Bani, similarly persuaded by Ezra (Ezra 10:27, 36).
5. The high priest, the 2d in succession from Jeshua (Neh. 12:10). He lived in the time of Nehemiah, and with the priests rebuilt the sheepgate of Jerusalem (ch. 3:1, 20, 21). As high priest he could assign chambers in the Temple to whomsoever he pleased (Ezra 10: 6). He was allied by marriage with Tobiah the Ammonite, and his grandson was son-in-law of Sanballat (Neh. 13:4, 28). Not being strict in regard to the separation of Jew and Gentile, he even assigned a chamber of the Temple to Tobiah (v. 5).
6. A son of Elioenai, a descendant of Zerubbabel (I Chron. 3:24).

E·li'a·thah (ē-lī'à-thà) [God has come]. A son of Heman, and a musician in the reign of David (I Chron. 25:1, 4, 27).

E·li'dad (ē-lī'dăd) [God has loved]. A prince of the tribe of Benjamin at the time when the Israelites were encamped at Shittim on the eve of entering the Promised Land. He was appointed a member of the commission to divide the land among the tribes (Num. 24:17, 21).

E·li'e·ho·e'nai (ē-lī'ē-hō-ē'nī), in A.V. **El'i·ho·e'nai** [to Jehovah are my eyes]. See also ELIOENAI. 1. A Korahite porter, the son of Meshelemiah (I Chron. 26:2, 3). A.V. has the variant Elioenai.
2. A son of Zerahiah. He, with 200 followers, accompanied Ezra from Babylon (Ezra 8:1, 4).

E'li·el (ē'lĭ-ĕl) [El (God) is God]. 1. A Levite, family of Kohath, and an ancestor of Samuel the prophet (I Chron. 6:1, 34). See ELIHU.
2. A Mahavite, one of David's mighty men (I Chron. 11:26, 46).
3. Another of David's heroes (v. 47).
4. One of the Gadites who came to David at Ziklag (I Chron. 12:1, 8, 11).
5. A Levite, a son of Hebron. He lived in David's time (I Chron. 15:9, 11).
6. A Benjamite, a son of Shimei (Shimhi) (I Chron. 8:1, 20, 21).
7. Another Benjamite, a son of Shashak (I Chron. 8:22, 25).
8. A chief man of the half tribe of Manasseh e. of the Jordan (I Chron. 5:24).
9. An overseer of the tithes and offerings in the reign of Hezekiah (II Chron. 31:13).

El'i·e·nai (ĕl'ĭ-ē'nī). Probably a contraction of Elihoenai. A Benjamite, a son of Shimei (Shimhi) (I Chron. 8:1, 20).

El'i·e'zer (ĕl'ĭ-ē'zẽr) [God is a helper]. 1. A man of Damascus, the steward of Abraham (Gen. 15:2; cf. 24:2).
2. The younger son of Moses (Ex. 18:4; I Chron. 23:15, 17).
3. A Benjamite, family of Becher (I Chron. 7:8).
4. A son of Zichri. He was a captain over the Reubenites in David's reign (I Chron. 27:16).
5. A priest who blew the trumpet before the Ark in David's reign (I Chron. 15:24).
6. A prophet, son of Dodavahu of Mareshah. He predicted the shipwreck of Jehoshaphat's vessels because he had joined with Ahaziah. of Ahab's family (II Chron. 20:37).

7. One of those whom Ezra sent for Levites, when it was found that there were few of them among the returning exiles (Ezra 8:16).

8, 9, and 10. Three men, one a priest, one a Levite, and one a son of Harim, whom Ezra induced to put away their foreign wives (Ezra 10:10, 18, 23, 31).

11. An ancestor of Christ who lived between the time of David and the Captivity (Luke 3:29).

El'i·ho·e'nai (ĕl'ĭ-hō-ē'nī). See ELIEHOENAI.

El'i·ho'reph (ĕl'ĭ-hō'rĕf) [perhaps, God is (the giver of) autumn (fruit)]. One of Solomon's scribes (I Kings 4:3).

E·li'hu (ė-lī'hū) [El (God) is He, or He is God]. 1. An Ephraimite, son of Tohu and an ancestor of Samuel the prophet (I Sam. 1:1), apparently called also Eliab and Eliel (I Chron. 6:27, 34).

2. David's eldest brother, called also Eliab (cf. I Sam. 16:6 with I Chron. 27:18). See JESSE.

3. A Manassite captain who with others joined David on his way to Ziklag (I Chron. 12:20).

4. A doorkeeper during David's reign, of the family of Obed-edom (I Chron. 26:1, 7).

5. One of Job's friends, a Buzite, the son of Barachel (Job, chs. 32 to 37).

6. A forefather of Judith; A.V., Eliu (Judith 8:1).

E·li'jah (ė-lī'jȧ); in A.V. twice **E·li'ah** (I Chron. 8:27; Ezra 10:26); in A.V. of N.T. **E·li'as,** the Gr. form of the name [Jehovah is God]. 1. One of the greatest of the prophets. He was a Tishbite, having been born perhaps at Tishbeh in Galilee; but he dwelt in Gilead (I Kings 17:1); see TISHBITE. He wore a garment of skin or of coarse camel's hair, which was girt about his loins with a leather girdle (II Kings 1:8; I Kings 19:13). When Ahab, influenced by his wife, Jezebel of Tyre, had given himself to the worship of the Tyrian god Baal, Elijah suddenly appeared upon the scene. He presented himself before the erring king, and predicted a drought of indefinite duration as a penalty for the rejection of Jehovah. On account of the famine he retired

first to the brook Cherith, where he was providentially fed by ravens; see RAVEN. When the brook became dry he went to Zarephath on the coast of the Mediterranean, n. of Tyre. A widow trusted God and shared her last cake with Elijah. God saw to it that her jar of meal and cruse of oil did not fail until the famine was ended; and when her son died he was restored to life at the prayer of the prophet (I Kings, ch. 17). After many days, in the 3d year (I Kings 18:1), Elijah was directed to show himself to Ahab. Then followed the scene at Mount Carmel. The priests of Baal endeavored to secure evidence of Baal's divinity, but failed. Then Elijah gathered the people about an ancient altar of the Lord; he repaired it, taking 12 stones for the purpose, thus silently testifying that the division of the 12 tribes into two kingdoms was at variance with the divine will. To obviate every possibility of fraud, he made the people drench the sacrifice and the altar with water. Then he cried to the Lord. Fire fell, and consumed the sacrifice and destroyed the altar. Jehovah had attested his existence and his power. Baal's prophets, proved to be impostors, were taken down to the brook Kishon, at the foot of the mountain, and slain at Elijah's bidding (I Kings 18:1–40; cf. Deut. 17:2–5; 13:13–16). The people had acknowledged Jehovah and obeyed his prophet, and the token of God's returning favor was seen in the gathering clouds of rain; and the prophet, to do honor to the king as ruler of a realm now professedly the kingdom of God, girded up his loins and ran before the chariot of Ahab to the gate of Jezreel (I Kings 18:41–46); see FORERUNNER. But Jezebel, furious at the destruction of her prophets, vowed the death of Elijah, who fled to Mount Horeb. There, like Moses, he was divinely sustained for 40 days and nights (Ex. 24:18; 34:28; Deut. 9:9, 18; I Kings 19:8), a foreshadowing of the similar incident in the life of Jesus (Matt. 4:2; Luke 4:2). Elijah was rebuked, sent back to duty, and told to anoint Hazael as king of Syria and Jehu as king of Israel, that they might be the scourge of God to idolatrous Israel, and Elisha as his successor. Elijah cast his mantle upon Elisha, calling

A Sacrificial Altar of the Second Millennium B.C., Excavated in Megiddo, Palestine

him to the work, and entrusted to him the further execution of the commission (I Kings, ch. 19).

When Jezebel had Naboth judicially murdered in order to obtain his vineyard for Ahab, Elijah met the king in the coveted plot of ground and denounced Jehovah's vengeance for the crime (ch. 21). The death of Ahab in the battle of Ramoth-gilead was the beginning of the judgment which Elijah had uttered against the royal house (ch. 22:1–40). When Ahab's son and successor, Ahaziah, injured by a fall from a window, sent messengers to the idol temple at Ekron to ask whether he should recover from his hurt, Elijah stopped them and turned them back; and twice when a captain with 50 men was sent apparently to arrest him, he called fire from the sky which consumed them. The 3d captain begged for his life, and Elijah went with him to the king (II Kings 1:1–16). Finally the prophet obtained the honor, bestowed before only on Enoch (Gen. 5:24), of being translated to heaven without dying. A chariot and horses of fire appeared to him when he had gone with his attendant Elisha to the e. of the Jordan, and, parting them asunder, took Elijah up in a whirlwind to heaven (II Kings 2:1–12). The event seems to have occurred just before Jehoram of Israel ascended the throne (II Kings, ch. 2; cf. chs. 1:18; 3:1) and during the reign of Jehoshaphat of Judah (ch. 3:11); yet Elijah wrote a document in which he addressed Jehoram of Judah, who indeed was a coregent with Jehoshaphat, and threatened him with divine judgment, not only for sins committed during the lifetime of Jehoshaphat, but for murder which he committed after Jehoshaphat's death (II Chron. 21:12–15; cf. v. 13 with v. 4). If Elijah was translated at the time indicated, he prophesied during his lifetime concerning future deeds of Jehoram, just as he foretold future acts of Hazael and Jehu (I Kings 19:15–17). Less in accordance with the language of II Kings 3:11 is the explanation that the account of Elijah's translation is inserted where it is in II Kings simply to complete the narrative of his public activity, and that Elijah was still alive when Elisha was with the army of Jehoshaphat in southern Judah, and was living when Jehoram became sole king. The last 2 verses of the O.T. predict that God will send Elijah before the coming of the great and dreadful day of the Lord (Mal. 4:5, 6). The N.T. explains that the reference is to John the Baptist, who was like the Tishbite in humble dress and appearance (Matt. 3:4; Mark 1:6), in fidelity and in work (Matt. 11:11–14; 17:10–12; Mark 9:11–13; Luke 1:17).

There are those, however, who contend that while John appeared in the spirit and power of Elijah, the O.T. prophet is yet to come, in person, before the Second Advent of Christ. Elijah appeared on the Mount of Transfiguration as the representative of the O.T. prophecy to do honor to Jesus (Matt. 17:4; Mark 9:4; Luke 9:30); and Elijah's ascension, to which there was nothing analogous in the history of John the Baptist, doubtless foreshadowed that of our risen Lord.

The miracles which were wrought during the ministry of Elijah belong to the 2d of the 4 miracle periods of redemptive history, the period of the life-and-death struggle between the religion of Jehovah and Baal worship, when the adherence of the people of northern Israel to the faith of their fathers was at issue, and all other questions regarding religious observances sank to minor importance. See MIRACLE.

2. A Benjamite, a son of Jeroham, resident at Jerusalem (I Chron. 8:27, R.V.).

3. A priest, a son of Harim. He married a Gentile wife (Ezra 10:18, 21).

4. An Israelite induced by Ezra to put away his foreign wife (Ezra 10:19, 26, R.V.).

E·li'ka (ê-lī'kä) [perhaps, God has spewed out (rejected)]. A Harodite, one of David's mighty men (II Sam. 23:8, 25).

E'lim (ē'lĭm) [large trees, such as oaks, terebinths, palms]. The 2d encampment of the Israelites after the passage of the Red Sea. It was between Marah and the desert of Sin, and had 12 springs of water and 70 palm trees (Ex. 15:27; 16:1; Num. 33:9, 10). It is identified with the oasis of Wadi Gharandel, 63 miles from Suez; here there is a permanent discharge of about 84 quarts (U.S. measure) of water per second. The vegetation consists of palm trees, tamarisks, and acacias.

E·lim'e·lech (ê-lĭm'ê-lĕk) [God is king]. A man of Bethlehem of Judah, the husband of Naomi (Ruth 1:1–3).

E·li'o·e'nai (ê-lī'ô-ē'nī) [my eyes (are turned) toward Jehovah]. Variant of Elioenai. 1. A descendant of Simeon (I Chron. 4:24, 36).

2. A Benjamite, family of Becher (I Chron. 7:8).

3. A Levite (I Chron. 26:3, A.V.). See ELIEHOENAI.

4 and 5. Two Hebrews, each of whom was induced by Ezra to put away his foreign wife (Ezra 10:10, 19, 22, 27).

6. A man of Judah, descended from Shecaniah (I Chron. 3:22–23).

E·li'phal (ê-lī'făl) [God has judged]. One of David's mighty men, a son of Ur (I Chron. 11:26, 35). Apparently called Eliphelet, the son of Ahasbai (II Sam. 23:34). See UR, II.

E·liph'a·let (ê-lĭf'ä-lĕt). See ELIPHELET.

El'i·phaz (ĕl'ĭ-făz) [possibly, God is fine gold]. 1. A son of Esau, by Adah, one of his wives (Gen. 36:4).

2. A Temanite, one of Job's friends (Job 2:11; 4:1; 15:1; 22:1; 42:7, 9). Probably a descendant of No. 1, who had a son Teman (Gen. 36:11).

E·liph'e·le'hu (ê-lĭf'ê-lē'hū), in A.V. E·liph'e·leh (ê-lĭf'ê-lĕ) [may God distinguish him]. A Levite, a singer and a harper, who acted also as a porter when David brought up the Ark from the house of Obed-edom (I Chron. 15:15–21).

E·liph'e·let (ê-lĭf'ê-lĕt), in A.V. twice E·liph'a·let [God is deliverance]. 1. A son born to David in Jerusalem (I Chron. 3:5, 6). A correct Hebrew alternate form is Elpalet, in A.V.; Elpelet, in R.V. (ch. 14:5).

2. Another son of David's, born also at Jerusalem, probably after the death of the former (II Sam. 5:16; I Chron. 3:8; 14:7).

3. A son of Ahasbai, and one of David's mighty men (II Sam. 23:34). Apparently called Eliphal in I Chron. 11:35.

4. A descendant of Jonathan and of Saul (I Chron. 8:33, 39).

5. A son of Adonikam. He returned with Ezra from Babylon (Ezra 8:13).

6. A son of Hashum. Ezra induced him to put away his foreign wife (Ezra 10:33).

E·lis'a·beth (ê-lĭz'ä-bĕth) [Lat. from Gr. Elisabet(h), from Heb. 'elisheba', God is an oath, i.e., the absolutely faithful One or a covenant maker]. A godly woman, a daughter of the house of Aaron, and bearing the name of Aaron's wife (Ex. 6:23, Elisheba). She became the wife of the priest Zacharias and the mother of John the Baptist. She bore him when she was of advanced years, his birth and mission having been communicated beforehand by an angel to her husband. Though of different tribes, she and Mary of Nazareth were kinswomen, and Mary visited Elisabeth at a village in the hill country of Judea. Elisabeth, inspired by the Holy Spirit welcomed Mary as the mother of the Lord (Luke 1:5–45).

E·li′sha (ê-lī′shà), in A.V. (Luke 4:27) **El′i·se′us** (ĕl′ĭ-sē′ŭs) for *Elisaios*, the Greek form of the name [God is salvation]. The successor of Elijah in prophetic work in the Northern Kingdom. He was the son of Shaphat, dwelt at Abel-meholah in the Jordan valley, and belonged to a family of means; 12 yoke of oxen plowed his father's fields. God appointed him to succeed Elijah (I Kings 19:16, 19). Elijah found him plowing and cast his mantle over him. Elisha understood the significance of the act; he went home, gave a farewell feast to the people, and returned to be the follower and assistant of Elijah (vs. 19–21). When Elijah went beyond the Jordan to be translated to heaven, Elisha kept by him and, when told to ask a parting gift, he had the wisdom to petition for a double portion of Elijah's spirit. He saw the fiery chariot bear his master away and, taking the mantle which had fallen from Elijah, he struck the Jordan with it, which divided and permitted him to cross to its w. side (II Kings 2:1–18). His subsequent life was marked by a series of miracles, some of knowledge, others of power, expressly wrought in the name of the Lord. They belong to the 2d group of miracles in redemptive history. See MIRACLE. They occurred at a time when the religion of Jehovah was engaged in a desperate struggle for existence against Baal worship, and, like the miracles wrought by Elijah, were intended to accredit the prophet and to attest Jehovah to be the living God. The miraculous power was so much under Elisha's control that apparently he could exercise it at discretion; and he used it largely, as did Christ, in simple deeds of kindness. In the name of the Lord he healed with salt the waters of the spring at Jericho (vs. 19–22). He pronounced Jehovah's curse on lads who mocked in him the prophet of the Lord, and 2 bears presently tore 42 of them (vs. 23–25). He foretold the success of the expedition against Moab (ch. 3:11–27), secured the increase of a widow's oil (ch. 4:1–7), predicted to a Shunammite woman the birth of a son, and at his prayer that son was restored to life when he had died (vs. 8–37). He named an antidote to a poisonous plant in the pot in which food was being cooked for the prophets (vs. 38–41). As prophet of the Lord, he fed 100 men with 20 barley loaves and a few ears of corn (vs. 42–44), told Naaman to wash in the Jordan and he would be healed of his leprosy (ch. 5:1–19), and foretold its transference to Gehazi as a punishment for lying and covetousness (vs. 20–27). He made an iron axhead, which had fallen into the river, float to the surface (ch. 6:1–7). He informed the king of Israel of the movements and intentions of his Syrian rival (vs. 8–12). At his prayer, the Lord revealed to the prophet's servant horses and chariots of fire surrounding them for their protection (vs. 13–17), and caused blindness to fall on the Syrian emissaries sent to arrest them (vs. 18–23). He intimated, without being told it, that a messenger from the king of Israel was at the door to take his life (vs. 32, 33). He predicted great plenty and consequent cheapness of food in Samaria, while it was at famine prices during a siege, adding, however, that an unbelieving lord who discredited the prediction should not participate in the boon, and he did not, for he was trampled to death in a crowd (ch. 7). He informed Ben-hadad, king of Syria, of his approaching death (ch. 8:7–15). He declared the destruction of Ahab and his whole house, and sent a young prophet to anoint Jehu to execute the threatened judgment (chs. 9:1 to 10:28). He predicted 3 victories over the

Syrians (ch. 13:14–19). Finally, after his death, a man hastily cast into the same sepulcher was at once restored to life on touching the prophet's bones (vs. 20, 21).

E·li′shah (ê-lī′shà). The descendants of Javan collectively, who inhabited the country of Elishah (Gen. 10:4). This country was maritime and exported blue and purple dye stuffs (Ezek. 27:7). It has been variously explained as Hellas, Elis, Aeolis, Italy, and Carthage. Philological objections weigh against the first 4; and there is no proof that Carthage was ever called Elissa, which is another name for its queen, Dido. Alishiya, a country near Cilicia, whose king exchanged correspondence with the pharaohs of the 18th Egyptian dynasty, has been suggested. This identification commends itself.

E·lish′a·ma (ê-lĭsh′à-mä) [God has heard]. 1. Son of Ammihud, and prince of the Ephraimites at the beginning of the sojourn in the wilderness (Num. 1:10; 2:18), and ancestor of Joshua (I Chron. 7:26).
2. A man of Judah, descended through Jerahmeel and Sheshan (I Chron. 2:33–41).
3. A son of David, born at Jerusalem (I Chron. 3:1, 5, 6). See ELISHUA.
4. Another son of David (II Sam. 5:16; I Chron. 3:8).
5. A priest, one of those sent by Jehoshaphat to teach in the cities of Judah (II Chron. 17:7, 8).
6. A prince and scribe in the reign of King Jehoiakim (Jer. 36:9, 12, 20, 21), and probably identical with the grandfather of Ishmael of the seed royal who murdered Gedaliah, the governor of Judea under the Babylonians (II Kings 25:25; Jer. 41:1).

E·lish′a·phat (ê-lĭsh′à-făt) [God has judged]. One of the captains of hundreds who supported Jehoiada in the revolt against Athaliah (II Chron. 23:1).

E·lish′e·ba (ê-lĭsh′ê-bä) [God is an oath]. Daughter of Amminadab, and sister of Nahshon. She became the wife of Aaron, and the mother of Nadab, Abihu, Eleazar, and Ithamar (Ex. 6:23).

El′i·shu′a (ĕl′ĭ-shū′à) [God is salvation]. A son of David, born at Jerusalem (II Sam. 5:15; I Chron. 14:5). In the corresponding position in the 3d list of David's sons (ch. 3:6) the name Elishama appears. In view of the reading of the other catalogues, and since the name Elishama was borne by another of David's sons, mentioned farther on in all 3 lists, it is reasonable to believe that Elishama in I Chron. 3:6 is a misreading of Elishua.

E·li′ud (ê-lī′ŭd) [Lat. from Gr. *Elioud*, probably from Heb. *'ĕlīhōd*, God is majesty]. Son of Achim, and father of Eleazar, in the ancestry of Christ (Matt. 1:14, 15).

El′i·za′phan (ĕl′ĭ-zā′făn) or **El·za′phan**, the forms being interchangeable in Hebrew [God has concealed]. 1. Son of Uzziel, and chief of the Kohathites in the wilderness (Ex. 6:18, 22; Num. 3:30). He assisted in removing the bodies of Nadab and Abihu from the camp (Lev. 10:4). A new father's house was derived from him (I Chron. 15:8; II Chron. 29:13).
2. Son of Parnach, and prince of the tribe of Zebulun in the wilderness (Num. 34:25).

E·li′zur (ê-lī′zẽr) [God is a rock]. The prince of the Reubenites in the wilderness, the son of Shedeur (Num. 1:5; 2:10).

El·ka′nah (ĕl-kā′nà) [God has created or acquired]. 1. A Levite, family of Kohath, house of Izhar, division of Korah. He was brother of Assir and Abiasaph (Ebiasaph) (Ex. 6:24; I Chron. 6:23, 36).
2, 3, and 4. Three Levites, links in one genealogy, one the son of Joel, the 2d the son

of Mahath, and the 3d the son of Jeroham. Like the preceding, they were of the family of Kohath, house of Izhar, Korahite division; but they were descended from Abiasaph (I Chron. 6:36, son of Joel; vs. 26, 35, of Mahath; vs. 27, 34, and I Sam. 1:1, of Jeroham). The last of the 3 belonged to the hill country of Ephraim, lived at Ramathaim of the Zophites, was the husband of Hannah and Peninnah, and the father of Samuel (I Sam. 1:1; 2:11, 20).

5. Another Korahite who had dwelt in Benjamin, perhaps because the Korahites were doorkeepers of the tabernacle which was pitched in Benjamin (I Chron. 9:19), and who joined David at Ziklag (ch. 12:1, 6).

6. A doorkeeper for the Ark during the reign of David (I Chron. 15:23).

7. A high dignitary at the court of Ahaz, 2d only to the king (II Chron. 28:7).

8. A Levite who dwelt in a village of the Netophathites (I Chron. 9:16).

El'kosh·ite (ĕl'kŏsh-īt). A citizen of Elkosh (Nahum 1:1). The tradition that Alkush, 2 days' journey n. of Nineveh, was the birth and burial place of Nahum is late, being unknown to early Arabian and Syrian writers; and the contents of The Book of Nahum are against it. A credible, but unproved, identification is with the town Elcesi, or Helcesaei, in Galilee, which was pointed out to Jerome. According to another tradition, preserved by Epiphanius, Elkosh lay to the s. of Begabar, in Syriac *Bēt Gabrē*, that is, Beit Jibrin, in the lowland of Judah.

El·la'sar (ĕl-lā'sär). A place in Babylonia, probably Larsa (Gen. 14:1, 9). See ARIOCH.

Elm. An erroneous rendering of Heb. *'ēlāh* in Hos. 4:13, A.V.; R.V. renders "terebinth." The word is translated "oak" in Gen. 35:4 and Judg. 6:11, 19, with terebinth in R.V. marg.

El·ma'dam (ĕl-mā'dăm), in A.V. **El·mo'dam** (ĕl-mō'dăm). An ancestor of Christ, who lived before the Exile (Luke 3:28).

El·na'am (ĕl-nā'ăm) [God is pleasantness]. The father of certain valiant men in David's army (I Chron. 11:26, 46).

El·na'than (ĕl-nā'thăn) [God has given]. 1. The father of Nehushta, mother of King Jehoiachin (II Kings 24:8). He dwelt at Jerusalem, and was probably the prince Elnathan, son of Achbor (Jer. 26:22; 36:12, 25).

2, 3, and 4. Three Levites, the first 2 chief men and the 3d a teacher, sent for by Ezra to the brook Ahava (Ezra 8:15, 16).

E·lo'i (ē-lō'ī) [Aram., my God]. See ELI, I.

E'lon (ē'lŏn) [oak or terebinth]. 1. A Hittite, whose daughter Esau married (Gen. 26:34; 36:2).

2. A son of Zebulun, and founder of a tribal family (Gen. 46:14; Num. 26:26).

3. A Zebulunite who judged Israel for 10 years, and was buried at Aijalon, in Zebulun (Judg. 12:11, 12).

4. A village of Dan (Josh. 19:43). Probably 'Alein, w. of Beit Maḥṣīr, or Khirbet Wadi 'Alīn, between Deir Aban and 'Ain Shems (Beth-shemesh).

E'lon-beth-ha'nan (ē'lŏn-bĕth-hā'năn) [Elon of Beth-hanan]. A town in Dan, to judge from its associates (I Kings 4:9), perhaps identical with Elon.

E'loth (ē'lŏth). See ELATH.

El·pa'al (ĕl-pā'ăl) [God has wrought]. A man of Benjamin, son of Shaharaim, and head of a father's house (I Chron. 8:1, 8, 11, 12, 18).

El·pa'ran (ĕl-pā'răn). See ELATH. El-paran (Gen. 14:6) may possibly be identified with an early Elath, perhaps one situated farther e., approximately on the site of modern 'Akabah.

El·pe'let (ĕl-pē'lĕt), in A.V. **El·pa'let** (ĕl-pā'lĕt). See ELIPHELET.

El Shad'dai (ĕl shăd'ī). The etymology of this word is doubtful, but the correctness of the Masoretic pointing is shown by LXX *Saddai* (Ezek. 10:5). *Shaddai* is preceded by *El* in seven cases (Gen. 17:1; 28:3; 35:11; 43:14; 48:3; Ex. 6:3; Ezek. 10:5), where R.V. marg. reproduces the Hebrew. The traditional English rendering is "God Almighty"; this is based on interpreting *Shaddai* as One furnished with violent power, hence almighty, from Hebrew *shâdad* (deal violently with, devastate). Cf. Isa. 13:6, "destruction [Heb. *shōd*] from the Almighty [Heb. *Shaddai*]." The Vulgate has *"Deus omnipotens"* in the above Gen. and Ezek. passages. The LXX has "Almighty" only in Job, where in 16 out of 31 instances it renders *Shaddai* by *Pantokratōr* (Almighty) (Job 5:17; 8:5, etc.).

By another interpretation *Shaddai* means the One who is sufficient; this is based upon a division: *sha* (who)—*ddai* (sufficiency). The LXX renders by *"hikanos"* (sufficient) in Ruth 1:20, 21; Job 21:15; 31:2; 40:2.

There has also been proposed a connection with Akkad. *shadū* (mountain), *shaddā'ū* (mountaineer), whence *shaddāya*, which came into Hebrew as *Shaddai*. This implies a mountain deity and suggests a N. Mesopotamian origin of the name before it was brought to Palestine. Although the meaning of the name is obscure, the rendering "Almighty" includes all the ideas suggested by these etymologies and does justice to God's nature.

El'te·ke (ĕl'tĕ-kē), in A.V. **El'te·keh** (ĕl'tĕ-kē). A town of Dan assigned to the Levites (Josh. 19:40, 44; 21:20, 23). In 701 B.C. Sennacherib destroyed the town, and in its vicinity the decisive battle between the Assyrians and Egyptians was fought. Probably Khirbet el-Muḳanna', about 6 miles s.s.e. of 'Aḳir (Ekron) and 7 miles n.n.w. of Khirbet Tibneh (Timnah).

El'te·kon (ĕl'tĕ-kŏn) [perhaps, God is firmness]. A village in the hill country of Judah (Josh. 15:59), probably to be identified with Khirbet ed-Deir, about 1⅞ miles s. of Ḥauṣān and about 4 miles w. of Bethlehem.

El·to'lad (ĕl-tō'lăd) [birth, race; el is by some taken as the definite article, as in Arabic]. A town in the extreme s. of Judah (Josh. 15:21, 30), assigned to the Simeonites (ch. 19:4); called in I Chron. 4:29 Tolad. Probably to be identified with Khirbet Erḳa Saḳra, about 13 miles s.e. of Beer-sheba.

E·lul' (ē-lōōl') [Heb. *'ĕlūl* from Akkad. *ulūlu*]. The 6th month of the year (Neh. 6:15; I Macc. 14:27), approximately September.

E·lu'za·i (ē-lū'ză-ī) [God is my strength]. One of the valiant men who came to David to Ziklag (I Chron. 12:1, 5).

El'y·ma·is (ĕl'ĭ-mā'ĭs). This name, which represents O.T. Elam, was applied to a region of Persia on the s. spurs of Mount Zagros, s. of Media and n. of Susiana. See ELAM.

El'y·mas (ĕl'ĭ-măs) [ety. uncertain]. A Jewish impostor, Bar-Jesus by name, which means son of Jesus or Joshua, who pretended to learn the future through sorcery. Paul encountered him in Paphos, a town of Cyprus, during his First Missionary Journey. He sought to turn from the faith Sergius Paulus, the Roman deputy or proconsul of the island, who seemed disposed to accept the doctrine of Paul and seek for baptism. The apostle, therefore, severely rebuked the sorcerer and struck him with temporary blindness, the miracle removing the last doubt which the proconsul had as to the claims of Christian truth on his acceptance (Acts 13:6–12).

El·za'bad (ĕl-zā'băd) [God has bestowed].
1. One of the valiant Gadites who came to
David (I Chron. 12:8, 12).

2. A Levite of the family of Obed-edom,
and a doorkeeper at the house of the Lord
(I Chron. 26:1, 4, 7).

El·za'phan (ĕl-zā'făn). See ELIZAPHAN.

Em·balm'. The Hebrews seldom embalmed
their dead (Gen. 50:2, 26; cf. II Chron. 16:14;
John 19:39), but the art of embalming was
practiced by the Egyptians from very early
times. The embalmers were a numerous guild,
who dwelt at the cemeteries. They were divided into 3 classes—the 1st made the incision
in the body, the 2d handled the spices, and the
3d conducted the religious ceremonies when
the body was placed in the tomb. By the time
of the 18th Dyn. they had brought their art
to great perfection. The brain was drawn
through the nose with an iron hook and replaced with spices. The entrails were removed,
and the abdominal cavity was washed out by
the injection of palm wine, and then filled

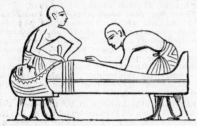

Egyptian Embalming

with bruised myrrh, cassia, cinnamon, and
other spices. Next the whole body was plunged
in natron and left in it for 70 days. Then it
was rolled in linen bandages only 3 or 4 inches
wide, but of the extraordinary length of 700
or even 1,000 yards. Gum arabic was used to
keep the bandages in their place, and finally
the corpse, now mummified, was placed in a
case of wood or cartonnage, made in the shape
of a man, and carved and painted to represent the deceased person. It was often enclosed in a 2d or outer case of wood or in a
stone sarcophagus. A less expensive method
required no incision; the intestines were dissolved by an injection of oil of cedar. In the
case of the poor, the abdomen was merely
purged and steeped in natron (Herod. ii. 85–
88). According to the historian Diodorus
Siculus, the interment of a rich man cost the
relatives the equivalent of about $1,200. A
second-rate embalmment cost about $400, and
there was a much cheaper kind for the common people. Embalming ceased about A.D.
700. Many mummies are in the British and
other museums. Occasionally one is unrolled,
but it tends to fall to pieces when exposed to
the air.

Em·broi'der·y. Ornamentation by raised figures of needlework, executed with colored
silks, gold or silver thread, or any similar material differing from that of the original cloth.
Bezalel and Oholiab were able to practice,
among other arts, that of embroidering in
blue, purple, scarlet, and fine linen (Ex. 35:30–
35; 38:23). The screens for the door of the
tabernacle and the gate of the court (chs.
26:36; 27:16) and the girdle of the high
priest (chs. 28:4–39; 39:27–29) were embroidered. The wealthy often wore embroidered
garments (Judg. 5:30; Ps. 45:14).

E'mek-ke'ziz (ē'mĕk-kē'zĭz), in A.V. valley
of Ke'ziz [a vale cut off or vale of fissure]. A
town of Benjamin, evidently in a valley and

apparently near Jericho and Beth-hoglah
(Josh. 18:21).

Em'er·ald [Gr. *smaragdos*]. 1. The rendering of Heb. *nŏphek*. It was the 1st stone in the
2d row of those on the Jewish high priest's
breastplate (Ex. 28:4, 15, 18; 39:11). The
Syrians brought precious stones of this kind
into Tyre (Ezek. 27:2, 3, 16), and the Tyrians
used them for ornaments (Ezek. 28:13). The
exact stone intended is doubtful. It may be
the carbuncle (R.V. marg.; cf. LXX, and Vulgate).

2. The rendering of Gr. *smaragdos*, a
precious stone of a light green color. The
name was perhaps applied to any green crystallized mineral. It was used for signets
(Ecclus. 32:6); a rainbow is likened to it
(Rev. 4:3); it was to be the 4th foundation
in the New Jerusalem (Rev. 21:19; cf. Tobit
13:16). The emerald is a variety of beryl,
distinguished by its color, which is bright
green, from typical beryl, which is pale green,
passing into light blue, yellow, or white. While
the beryl is colored by iron, the emerald is
colored by chromium. Anciently it was found
in Cyprus, in Egypt, and in the mountains of
Ethiopia.

Em'er·ods. Hemorrhoids (Deut. 28:27).
They were inflicted on the Philistines of Ashdod and Ekron, to compel them to send back
the Ark which they had captured (I Sam. 5:1,
6, 10, 12; 6:11).

E'mim (ē'mĭm), in A.V. **E'mims** (ē'mĭmz),
a double plural. The ancient inhabitants of
territory afterward occupied by the Moabites.
They were tall as the Anakim, and were once
a numerous and powerful people (Deut. 2:9–
11). Chedorlaomer smote them in the plain of
Kiriathaim (Gen. 14:5).

Em·man'u·el (ĕ-măn'ū-ĕl). See IMMANUEL.

Em·ma'us (ĕ-mā'ŭs). 1. A village 60 furlongs from Jerusalem, a distance which could
be traversed on foot between the hour for
supper and the time of an evening meeting
(Luke 24:13, 29, 33; cf. Mark 16:14; John
20:19). Vespasian located 800 veterans at
"Emmaus distant 30 [according to another
reading, 60] furlongs from Jerusalem" (Jos.
War vii. 6, 6). The Talmud states that Moza
is Colonia. Kubeibeh, 7 miles n.w. of Jerusalem on the Roman road, was pointed out to
the Crusaders as the site of Emmaus. In the
vicinity was the town of Mozah (Josh. 18:26).
Three miles to the s. of Kubeibeh is Kulonieh
(colony), whose distance from Jerusalem is 4
miles or more according to the road followed.
Probably, therefore, the site of Emmaus is to
be found either at Kubeibeh or Kulonieh, or
in the intervening country. The distance and
tradition since the time of the Crusaders point
to Kubeibeh; the Roman colony to which Emmaus was assigned may have left its name
attached to a village in the s. part of its
possessions.

2. A walled town about 20 miles from Jerusalem by a circuitous Roman road (I Macc.
3:40; 9:50; Jos. *War* ii. 20, 4). Now 'Amwâs.

Em'mor (ĕm'ôr). See HAMOR.

E·na'im (ĕ-nā'ím) [two springs]. A town
on the road from Adullam to Timnah (Gen.
38:14, 21, R.V.).

E'nam (ē'năm). A village in the lowland of
Judah (Josh. 15:20, 34); probably identical
with Enaim.

E'nan (ē'năn) [having fountains; or having
eyes, i.e., keen-eyed]. The father of the prince
of the tribe of Naphtali in the days of Moses
(Num. 1:15).

En·camp'ment. See CAMP.

En·chant'er. In Daniel (ch. 2:2, 10, R.V.) it
is the rendering of Heb. *'ashshâph*, Aram.

'ashaph. It denotes conjurors and exorcists who used incantations and pronounced spells for the purpose of securing the aid of evil spirits or of freeing the supposed victims of evil spirits from their torments.

En·chant'ment. The practice of magical arts or the utterance of certain words whereby the aid of evil spirits is invoked, in order to produce supernatural effects over human beings, dangerous animals, or nature generally. Enchantment is not always distinguished from divination in the English versions (Num. 23:23; 24:1; II Kings 17:17; Jer. 27:9, A.V.). Under enchantment are properly included magic (Ex. 7:11), conjuration, exorcism (Dan. 2:2, A.V., astrologer), sorcery (Acts 8:9, 11; 13:8, 10). The practicing of enchantments was forbidden by the Mosaic Law (Deut. 18:10). Charming practiced to prevent a venomous snake from biting (Eccl. 10:11; cf. Ps. 58:5; Jer. 8:17) belongs, of course, to a different category.

En'-dor (ĕn'dôr) [fountain of habitation]. A town belonging to the tribe of Manasseh (Josh. 17:11). Fugitives from Sisera's defeated army, fleeing home to the n., perished in its vicinity (Ps. 83:9, 10). Here dwelt the woman with a familiar spirit, whom King Saul consulted (I Sam. 28:7). It has been identified with modern Endôr (Indûr) on the n. shoulder of Little Hermon, 6 miles s.e. of Nazareth.

En·eg'la·im (ĕn-ĕg'lâ-ĭm) [fountain of two calves]. A place on the Dead Sea (Ezek. 47:10); identified with 'Ain Ḥajlah, n. of the Dead Sea and w. of the Jordan. Same as Beth-hoglah, *q.v.*

En-gan'nim (ĕn-găn'ĭm) [fountain of gardens]. 1. A village in the lowland of Judah (Josh. 15:20, 34). It has been identified with Umm Jîna, s.w. of Beth-shemesh, but 'Ain Faṭîr, e. of Beit el-Jemal, in the neighborhood, has been suggested as the more probable site.
2. A town on the boundary line of Issachar (Josh. 19:17, 21), assigned to the Gershonite Levites (ch. 21:29). It seems to be the Ginaea of Josephus (Jos. *Antiq.* xx. 6, 1; *War* iii. 3, 4). It is the modern Jenîn, a village of about 3,000 inhabitants, on the s. margin of the Plain of Esdraelon, 5 miles n.e. of Dothan, about 7 s.w. from Mount Gilboa, and about 68 miles n. of Jerusalem.

En-ge'di (ĕn-gē'dī) [fountain of a kid]. A fountain and town originally called Hazazon-tamar, meaning pruning of a palm (II Chron. 20:2), on the w. shore of the Dead Sea, in the tribe of Judah (Josh. 15:62), about 35 miles from Jerusalem. A difficult caravan route, crowded between mountain and sea, passed the spot. In the time of Abraham it was occupied by Amorites, who were smitten at the spot by Chedorlaomer (Gen. 14:7). David took refuge in the strongholds of the vicinity (I Sam. 23:29). In one of the caves where he was hiding he cut off the skirt of Saul's robe (I Sam., ch. 24). The fountain, which still bears the name of 'Ain Jidî, is a copious hot spring of fresh water, bursting forth about 300 or 400 feet above the base of a vast cliff, midway between the mouth of the Jordan and the s. point of the sea. The hot water created an oasis, rich with semitropical vegetation and celebrated for palms, vineyards, and balsam (S. of Sol. 1:14; Jos. *Antiq.* ix. 1, 2). The ancient site seems to have been at Tell el-Jurn, near 'Ain Jidî. See HAZAZON-TAMAR.

En-had'dah (ĕn-hăd'à) [swift fountain]. A frontier village of Issachar (Josh. 19:17, 21), probably el-Ḥadetheh, about 6 miles e. of Mount Tabor.

En-hak'ko·re (ĕn-hăk'ô-rē) [spring of the partridge, or of the caller]. A spring in Lehi which burst forth when Samson cried to the Lord (Judg. 15:18, 19).

En-ha'zor (ĕn-hā'zôr) [fountain of Hazor]. A fenced city of Naphtali (Josh. 19:32, 37). identified with Khirbet Haṣîreh, w. of 'Ain Ibl. not far from the ruin of Hazzûr.

En-mish'pat (ĕn-mĭsh'păt) [fountain of judgment]. The same as Kadesh-barnea (Gen. 14:7).

E'noch (ē'nŭk), in A.V. once **He'noch** (I Chron. 1:3) [initiated, dedicated]. The same name, borne by others, is rendered Henoch and Hanoch. 1 and 2. A son of Cain, and the city which Cain built and named after him (Gen. 4:17).
3. A descendant of Jared, and progenitor of Methuselah. He lived 365 years, and walked with God. He is the only one of the line of whom it is not said that he died. "He was not; for God took him" (Gen. 5:18–24). He was translated, and did not see death (Heb. 11:5; Ecclus. 44:16; 49:14). In Jude 14, 15 there is a prophecy of Enoch's in which he declares God's just judgment of the unrighteous. The words of this prophecy are found in the pseudepigraphical Book of Enoch.

E'nosh (ē'nŏsh), in A.V. **E'nos** (ē'nŏs), except in I Chron. 1:1 [man]. The son of Seth (Gen. 4:26; 5:6–11; I Chron. 1:1; Luke 3:38, Enos).

En-rim'mon (ĕn-rĭm'ŏn) [fountain of Rimmon or of the pomegranate]. A town of Judah, inhabited after the Captivity (Neh. 11:29), usually identified with Umm er-Rumāmîn 9 miles n. of Beer-sheba. See RIMMON, I. 2.

En-ro'gel (ĕn-rō'gĕl) [perhaps, fuller's spring]. A fountain just outside Jerusalem (II Sam. 17:17), near the valley of Hinnom and on the boundary line between Judah and Benjamin (Josh. 15:1, 7; 18:11, 16). According to Josephus, it was in the king's garden (Jos. *Antiq.* vii. 14, 4). During Absalom's rebellion Jonathan and Ahimaaz took up their abode there, to be able to collect and send news to David (II Sam. 17:17). Near by was the stone Zoheleth, where Adonijah instituted festivities when he conspired to seize the kingdom (I Kings 1:9). The traditional situation of the fountain, almost universally accepted, is Bîr Eyyûb (Job's well), just below the junction of the valleys of Hinnom and the Kidron, s. of Jerusalem. This is a well, 125 feet deep, walled half way down and sunk the rest of the distance into the solid rock. That it is a well and not a fountain is scarcely a serious objection to the traditional identification (cf. Gen. 16:7 with v. 14). The identification of En-rogel with the Fountain of the Virgin in the side of Ophel has a few advocates, especially Grove, Conder, and Clermont-Ganneau.

En·she'mesh (ĕn-shē'mĕsh) [fountain of the sun]. A fountain and town on the boundary line between Judah and Benjamin (Josh. 15:1, 7; 18:11, 17). It is commonly identified with 'Ain el-Ḥaud, a little e. of Bethany, on the road between Jerusalem and Jericho, and the last spring until the Jordan Valley is reached.

En-tap'pu·ah (ĕn-tăp' û-ä) (Josh. 17:7). See TAPPUAH 2.

E·pae'ne·tus (ê-pē'nê-tŭs) [Gr., praiseworthy]. A convert belonging to Achaia, and the first fruits of that region to Christ. Paul called him beloved (Rom. 16:5).

Ep'a·phras (ĕp'à-frăs) [contraction of Epaphroditus]. A Christian who, coming to Paul whilst he was a prisoner at Rome, gave a highly favorable account of the Colossian church, with which he was connected, perhaps as its minister. He joined the apostle in sending it salutations (Col. 1:7, 8; 4:12). He remained in Rome, and was in some sense Paul's fellow prisoner in Christ (Philemon 23).

E·paph'ro·di'tus (ê-păf'rô-dī'tŭs) [Gr., lovely, charming]. A Christian whom the church at Philippi sent with a present to the Apostle Paul, then a prisoner at Rome. Soon afterward he became seriously ill. It grieved him that the news of this sickness reached Philippi and created anxiety among his friends there. On this account Paul sent him back to Philippi as soon as his health permitted (Phil. 2:25–30; 4:18), making him the bearer of the Epistle to the Philippians. Epaphroditus and Epaphras hardly were the same person, for the former seems clearly connected with the church at Philippi, and the latter with that at Colossae.

E'phah, I (ē'fà). A measure of capacity containing 10 omers (Ex. 16:36), and used for such articles as flour (Judg. 6:19) or barley (Ruth 2:17). It was equivalent to a bath or ¹⁄₁₀ of a kor (Ezek. 45:11, 14), and contained one Attic metretes or 72 sextaries (Jos. Antiq. viii. 2, 9; xv. 9, 2, where read metretes for medimnoi), and it contained 1.05 bushels, American measure. See MEASURE, III.

E'phah, II (ē'fà) [darkness]. 1. A branch of the Midianites (Gen. 25:4; I Chron. 1:33), rich in camels and dromedaries (Isa. 60:6). They lived in n.e. Arabia.
2. A concubine of Caleb (I Chron. 2:46).
3. A man of Judah, a son of Jahdai (I Chron. 2:3, 47).

E'phai (ē'fī) [Heb. 'ēphai, fatigued, gloomy (kere); 'ôphai, flying, bird, or gloomy, dark (kethib)]. A Netophathite whose sons came with others to the Babylonian governor of Judea after the fall of Jerusalem and were promised protection (Jer. 40:8). All were subsequently massacred by Ishmael (Jer. 41:3).

E'pher (ē'fēr) [young deer or gazelle] 1. A branch of the Midianites (Gen. 25:4; I Chron. 1:33).
2. A man of Judah descended from Ezrah (I Chron. 4:1, 17).
3. A chief man in the half tribe of Manasseh, e. of the Jordan (I Chron. 5:23, 24).

E'phes·dam'mim (ē'fēs-dăm'ĭm) [end or boundary of Dammim (blood)]. A place within the territory of Judah, between Socoh and Azekah (I Sam. 17:1); called Pas-dammim in I Chron. 11:13. Commonly identified with the ruins Damūn, about 4 miles n.e. of Socoh. Abel prefers Beit Faṣed, s.e. of Socoh.

E·phe'si·ans (ê-fē'zhănz), **The E·pis'tle of Paul to the.** This epistle was written by the Apostle Paul when he was a prisoner (Eph. 3:1; 4:1; 6:20), probably at Rome A.D. 62, though some have assigned it to the Caesarean imprisonment (Acts 24:27). It is addressed "to the saints that are at Ephesus, and the faithful in Christ Jesus," R.V. notes, however, that some very ancient authorities omit the words "at Ephesus." The 2 chief N.T. manuscripts (Sinaiticus and Vaticanus) omit them, as does also the Chester Beatty papyrus, dating from the early 3d century (the oldest known MS. of Paul's letters). From very early times a difference of opinion appears as to its intended readers, though the tradition of the Church called it "to the Ephesians." The most probable explanation is that it was a circular letter intended for all the churches of the province of Asia, and that, since Ephesus was the chief of these, the epistle naturally came to be considered as addressed to it. Perhaps the address was blank,

and copies left in each city with the blank filled. Its circular character seems to be confirmed by the absence from it of local allusions and discussions. It is a doctrinal and ethical treatise in the form of an epistle. Like that to the Colossians, it was sent by Tychicus (Eph. 6:21), and the similarity of language and thought shows that the two were written at the same time. Compare, for example:

Eph. 1:1, 2 with Col. 1:1, 2.
Eph. 1:3, 20; 2:6; 3:10; 6:12 with Col. 1:5; 3:1–3.
Eph. 1:6, 7 with Col. 1:13, 14.
Eph. 1:9; 3:9; 6:19 with Col. 1:26; 2:2; 4:3.
Eph. 1:10 with Col. 1:20, 25.
Eph. 1:11 with Col. 1:12.
Eph. 1:17 with Col. 1:10.
Eph. 1:19, 20 with Col. 2:12.
Eph. 1:20 with Col. 3:1.
Eph. 1:22 with Col. 1:18.
Eph. 1:23 with Col. 2:9.
Eph. 4:22–24 with Col. 3:8–10.
Eph. 4:32 with Col. 3:13.

These are but examples, to which even the reader of the English Bible can add many more.

The two epistles were evidently the product of the apostle's mind acting under the same circumstances; and Ephesians seems to have been written just after Colossians. In it the thought is carried farther. The theme of Colossians is the pre-eminence of Christ's person and work. That of Ephesians is the establishment of the Church, considered as the entire number of the redeemed. Ephesians, in fact, may be said to sum up all Paul's previous teaching in order to state the purpose of God in the mission of his Son, which was the redemption of his chosen people, a redemption which was to manifest to all the universe the riches of his grace. Hence, assuming salvation through faith, the divinity and finished work of Jesus and the calling of the Gentiles, it advances to a complete theodicy.

In Eph., ch. 1, we have what may be called the divine side of the Church's history, which originated in God's sovereign and eternal purpose (vs. 3–6), was effected by Christ's work (vs. 7–12), and is certified by the sealing of the Spirit (vs. 13, 14). Paul prays that they may understand the hope of Christ's calling, of which the risen and exalted Saviour is the first fruit and pledge (vs. 15–23). In ch. 2 we have the human side of the history, being taught that the elect are delivered out of sin and condemnation by unmerited grace (vs. 1–10), and are united, Jew and Gentile, through Christ into one spiritual temple (vs. 11–22). In ch. 3 the apostle states his own position as the minister to the Church of this divine mystery (vs. 1–13), and prays that they may realize and enjoy what God has prepared for them (vs. 14–21). Chs. 4 to 6 are an extended exhortation to walk worthily of their high calling in all the relations of the present life.

Before the Epistle to the Ephesians was written, Paul had seen a new spiritual community arise in the world, composed of persons of different races; he had been teaching that this community, the Church, is the body of Christ; and he had been emphasizing the importance of harmony among its members (Rom. 12:4–8; I Cor. 12:12–30; Col. 1:18; 2:19). In writing at this time to the churches in the province of Asia, whose membership was composed of the most diverse racial elements and among whom speculative theories were rife which tended to subordinate Christ, it was natural for the apostle to give prominence to the conception of Christ as the head of the body, the Church (Eph. 1:22, 23), "from whom all the body fitly framed and knit together through that which every joint supplieth, according to the working in due measure of each several part, maketh the increase of the body unto the building up of itself in love" (ch. 4:16, R.V.; cf. ch. 2:11–22).

The Epistle to the Romans, addressed from the East to the West, was Paul's complete statement of the way of salvation. The Epistle to the Ephesians, addressed from the West to the East, was his complete statement of the whole purpose of God in human history. It may be said to mark the climax of his theological instruction.

G. T. P. and J. D. D. (rev., H. S. G.)

Eph'e·sus (ĕf'ē-sŭs). A city of Lydia on the w. coast of Asia Minor, at the mouth of the Cayster, nearly midway between Miletus on the s. and Smyrna on the n. It was situated at the junction of natural trade routes, and was on the main route from Rome to the East. Here was located the famous temple to Artemis (Diana), who was represented as a

Statue of Diana of Ephesus

many-breasted mother goddess. See DIANA. In the 11th century B.C. the town was seized by the Ionians, a section of the Greek race. Ephesus became one of the 12 cities belonging to their confederation, and itself the capital of Ionia. About 555 B.C. the city submitted to Croesus, king of Lydia, whose capital was at Sardis, but it soon fell under the Persian domination. With the victories of Alexander the Great, Ephesus came under Macedonian-Greek rule. Hitherto it had been confined to a low, alluvial plain liable to be flooded. About 286 B.C. Lysimachus extended it to an adjacent eminence beyond the reach of the water. By this change of location the temple of Artemis was left outside the city

walls. In 190 B.C. the Romans, after defeating Antiochus the Great at Magnesia, took Ephesus from him, and gave it to Eumenes II, king of Pergamos. On the death of Attalus III of Pergamos in 133 B.C. it reverted to them, and eventually became the capital of the Roman province of Asia. In A.D. 29 the city was much damaged by an earthquake, but was rebuilt by the emperor Tiberius.

Many Jews with Roman citizenship resided at Ephesus, and maintained a synagogue (Acts 18:19; 19:17; Jos. *Antiq.* xiv. 10, 11, and 13); and Paul, on his way to Jerusalem, toward the end of his Second Missionary Journey, paid a short visit to the place, preached in the synagogue, and left Aquila and Priscilla there, who continued the work (Acts 18:18–21). On his Third Journey he labored at Ephesus at least 2 years and 3 months, leaving the city after the riot which was stirred up by Demetrius, a maker of small silver models of the temple, who found his craft endangered by the preaching of the apostle (Acts, ch. 19; cf. I Cor. 15:32; 16:8; II Tim. 1:18). Paul left Timothy behind to prevent the church from being corrupted by false doctrine (I Tim. 1:3). Subsequently, returning from Europe and unable to revisit Ephesus, he summoned the elders of the church to him at Miletus (Acts 20:16, 17). Tychicus was afterward sent to Ephesus with the Epistle to the Ephesians (Eph. 1:1; 6:21; II Tim. 4:12). The church at Ephesus was one of the 7 churches of Asia addressed in The Revelation of John (ch. 1:11; 2:1–7), and according to tradition the Apostle John spent the last years of his life in that city. The 3d general council of the Church was held at Ephesus, A.D. 431, and defined the doctrine of the person of Christ so far as affirming that Christ has two natures and one person. The silting up of the harbor by mud brought down by the Cayster led to the decay of the city. Among its remains are the ruins of the wall and a gate, the stadium, a fine theater, Roman baths, and a library. The site of the great temple is a swamp.

An earlier Ionic temple was set on fire by Herostratos in 356 B.C. and destroyed; but it was rebuilt within a few years. The new structure was a magnificent work of Ionic architecture, 4 times as large as the Parthenon at Athens, and ranked as one of the 7 wonders of the world. It stood on a platform about 425 feet in length and 239½ feet in width, measured from the lowest step. A flight of 10 steps led to the pavement of the platform, and 3 more steps to the pavement of the temple. The temple itself was 342½ feet in length and 164 feet in width. It consisted of 2 rows of 8 columns each in front and rear, and 2 rows of 20 columns each on either side of the sanctuary. These with 2 columns at each entrance of the sanctuary made 100 in all. Each was a monolith of marble 55 feet in height, and the 18 at each end were sculptured. The roof was covered with large white marble tiles. The cella, or inner sanctuary, which these columns surrounded, was 70 feet wide and 105 long. Its internal ornamentation was of surpassing splendor, adorned with works of art by Phidias and Praxiteles, Scopas, Parrhasius, and Apelles. It was destroyed by the Goths about A.D. 260.

The theater was one of the largest known of all that have remained to modern times. The auditorium was semicircular, 495 feet in diameter, and the orchestra was 110. The stage was 22 feet wide. The theater contained 66 rows of seats, and afforded room for an audience of 24,500 persons.

Eph'lal (ĕf'lăl) [judicious]. A man of Judah of the family of Jerahmeel (I Chron. 2:3, 25, 37).

E'phod (ē'fŏd) [a covering]. 1. An upper garment worn by the Jewish high priest. It was one of 6 sacred vestments which he was required to put on when about to conduct the worship of God (Ex. 28:4), and was of gold, blue, purple, scarlet, and fine twined linen. The ephod went closely round the body; it was supported by 2 straps, which passed over the shoulders and were attached in front and behind to its top edges (vs. 6, 7). There was a hole in the top, doubtless for the head, with a woven border of the same materials around, to render the cloth less likely to tear (v. 8; cf. v. 32). On top of each of the shoulder straps was an onyx stone, enclosed in a filigree setting of gold and engraved with the names of 6 tribes of Israel (chs. 28:9; 39:6, 7). In front, to rings attached underneath close to the coupling, the breastplate was bound with a lace of blue, so that the breastplate itself might be supported (chs. 28:25, 27, 28; 39:19–21). The robe of the ephod was a garment distinct from the ephod, was blue, and was sleeveless, fringed at the bottom with alternate bells of gold and pomegranates of blue, purple, and scarlet (Ex. 28:31–35; 29:5; 39:22–26).

A more simple ephod of linen, probably without the ornamentation, was worn by ordinary priests. The 85 priests whom Doeg slew all wore the linen ephod (I Sam. 22:18). Samuel, also, wore an ephod while he was a child in charge of Eli, the high priest (ch. 2:18). David wore one when officiating before the Ark as king (II Sam. 6:14).

David, desiring to ask counsel of the high priest, had the ephod brought near (I Sam. 23:9–12; 30:7, 8), for with it were the Urim and Thummim (Ex. 28:30). An ephod might thus readily become an object of adoration or be used in the worship of an idol (Judg. 8:27; 17:5).

It has been supposed that ephod does not everywhere denote a priestly linen waistcoat, but may also refer to some kind of idol or image. Thus if an ephod were the covering or casing of an image (cf. Isa. 30:22; 40:19), the term could finally be applied to the image itself. Thus with some plausibility Gideon's ephod (Judg. 8:26 *seq.*) has been explained as an idol. The ephod also figures as a part of the equipment of a sanctuary, as in the case of Micah (Judg. 17:5; 18:14–20). The mention of ephod in those passages in connection with teraphim (cf. Hos. 3:4) does not prove that it was an image. It has also been suggested that perhaps the ephod was an instrument of divination, an ark in which were the teraphim. On the whole, we do not have enough data to settle with confidence the difficulties involved in the cases where the ephod may not have been a garment.

2. The father of Hanniel, prince of Manasseh in the time of Moses (Num. 34:23).

Eph'pha·tha (ĕf'à-thà). An Aramaic imperative signifying, "Be opened" (Mark 7:34).

E'phra·im (ē'frà-ĭm) [double fruitfulness]. 1. The younger son of Joseph and Asenath, daughter of Potipherah, priest of On. He was born while Joseph was prime minister of Egypt (Gen. 41:45–52). When the two sons were brought to Jacob on his sickbed, to receive their grandfather's blessing, Jacob intentionally laid his right hand (the hand of greater honor) on the head of Ephraim, the younger grandson, and his left on that of Manasseh, the elder. Being remonstrated with by Joseph, he explained that both should become a people, but Ephraim should be the greater and should be the ancestor of a multitude of peoples or tribal families (ch. 48:8–20). Ephraim and Manasseh, though only grandchildren of Jacob, were treated as if they were his children, and their descendants were

consequently regarded as two tribes instead of one. Ephraim had the sorrow of losing 2 of his sons, Ezer and Elead, who were slain while making a raid on the cattle of the Philistines (I Chron. 7:20–22).

2. The tribe of which Ephraim was the progenitor (Josh. 16:4, 10; Judg. 5:14). The growth of the tribe was for a time retarded by the death of his sons in the above-mentioned raid. At the 1st census in the wilderness the Ephraimites numbered 40,500, being the lowest in number of the tribes excepting only Manasseh and Benjamin (Num. 1:33). They fell off during the wanderings, and at the 2d census numbered only 32,500, being now the lowest of all the tribes except Simeon (ch. 26:37); still the double tribe of Joseph was the largest of the tribes, and numbered 85,200 men, besides women and children (vs. 34, 37; cf. Deut. 33:17). When Joshua was the leader of Israel, the tribe rose rapidly in reputation, for he was himself an Ephraimite (Josh. 19:50; 24:30). The tribe was allotted territory west of the Jordan. Its s. boundary line ran from the Jordan at Jericho to Beth-el, Luz, Ataroth-addar, Upper Beth-horon, Lower Beth-horon, Gezer, and the sea (ch. 16:1–3, 5). The n. line ran through Michmethath, near Shechem, eastward to Taanath-shiloh, Janoah, Ataroth, and Naarah, reached Jericho and the Jordan (vs. 6, 7), and passed w. from Michmethath to En-tappuah, the river Kanah and the Mediterranean (v. 8; cf. 17:7). It had the territory of the half tribe of Manasseh, w. of the Jordan, on the n., and Benjamin on the s.; it reached the Mediterranean on the w. and to the Jordan on the e. Shechem was within the territory of Ephraim (Josh. 21:20, 21; I Kings 12:25; I Chron. 6:67). The Ephraimites failed to expel the Canaanites from Gezer, which was within the lot of Ephraim; but, either alone or in conjunction with the Manassites, they captured Beth-el (Judg. 1:22–29). They acted patriotically in the fight celebrated in song by Deborah (ch. 5:14). They quarreled with Gideon, who was a Manassite, for not having called them to aid him in expelling the Midianites from Canaan (ch. 8:1–3). They resolutely encountered in battle Jephthah, the deliverer of Israel, for not having summoned them to assist him in the Ammonite War, 42,000 of the tribe falling in the struggle (ch. 12:1–6). Micah, of graven image notoriety, resided in Mount Ephraim (ch. 17:1); and the Levite, the ill-treatment of whose concubine led to the hostilities against Benjamin, sojourned there (ch. 19:1). Jeroboam was a man of Ephraim, and after he had become king over the revolted 10 tribes, he rebuilt Shechem in Mount Ephraim to be his capital (I Kings 12:25).

The hill country of Ephraim, or Mount Ephraim, as it is sometimes called, was the part of the central range of Palestine occupied by the tribe of Ephraim. It did not include the towns of Taanach, Megiddo, Beth-shean, and Abel-meholah, on the n. and e. (I Kings 4:8, 12), nor Kiriath-jearim, Gibeah, or the territory of Benjamin on the s. (Judg. 18:12, 13; 19:16; I Sam. 9:4). If it included territory n. of Shechem (cf. I Chron. 6:66, 68, with I Kings 4:12), it was thus bounded on 3 sides by the s. border of the Plain of Esdraelon, the Jordan Valley, and the territory of Benjamin. The term did not properly designate any part of the district occupied by Benjamin. Even Judg. 4:5 and II Sam. 20:1, 21 do not necessarily imply any broader use of the term. But after the establishment of the Northern Kingdom with its shifting s. frontier, the s. limits of the hill country of Ephraim were no longer clearly defined.

The wood of Ephraim, in which the battle took place between the forces of David and those of the rebel Absalom (II Sam. 18:6; cf.

17:22, 24, 26, 27), was evidently e. of the Jordan, and near Mahanaim, but its exact situation is unknown. It probably took its name either from the defeat of the Ephraimites in the time of Jephthah (Judg. 12:1 *seq.*), or because it was opposite to the territory and mountain of Ephraim.

For the gate of Ephraim, see JERUSALEM, II. 3.

3. The 10 tribes of which Ephraim became the head. Used in this sense especially by the prophets (Isa. 7:2, 5, 9, 17; 9:9; 17:3; 28:3; Hos. 4:17; 5:3; 9:3–17).

4. A city to which Baal-hazor was adjacent (II Sam. 13:23), probably the same place as Ephraim near the wilderness (John 11:54), and Aphaerema, which at one time belonged to Samaria (I Macc. 11:34). The Roman general Vespasian took Ephraim and Beth-el during his advance on Jerusalem (Jos. *War* iv. 9, 9). It has been identified with Ophrah of Benjamin, at the modern village of Taiyibeh, on a conical hill standing on high land 4 miles e.n.e. of Beth-el.

E'phra·im·ite (ē'frā-ĭm-īt). A member of the tribe of Ephraim (Judg. 12:5). More frequently Ephrathite, as in the original.

E'phra·in (ē'frā-ĭn). See EPHRON 2.

Eph'ra·thah (ĕf'rá-thȧh), in A.V. **Eph'ra·tah** (ĕf'rá-tá) [fruitfulness, fruitful land]. A shorter form, occasionally used in the Hebrew text and preserved in the versions, is Ephrath.
1. The original name of Bethlehem in Judea (Gen. 35:19; 48:7; Ruth 4:11). It is sometimes called Bethlehem Ephrathah (Micah 5:2).
2. A wife of Caleb, son of Hezron. She was the mother of Hur (I Chron. 2:19, 50; 4:4).
3. The territory of Ephraim (Ps. 132:6; see EPHRATHITE 2); or better, Kiriath-jearim, which belonged to Caleb-ephrathah (I Chron. 2:24, 50), and where the Ark had been kept for a long time.

Eph'rath·ite (ĕf'rá-thīt). 1. A native or inhabitant of Ephrath, i.e., Bethlehem (I Sam. 17:12; Ruth 1:2).
2. An Ephraimite, one belonging to the tribe of Ephraim (I Sam. 1:1; I Kings 11:26, both A.V.).

E'phron (ē'frŏn) [fawn]. 1. A Hittite, resident at Hebron, and owner of the cave of Machpelah, which he sold to Abraham (Gen. 23:8, 9; 25:9).
2. A city which was taken from Jeroboam by Abijah (II Chron. 13:19). The kethib is 'Ephrōn, but the kere 'Ephrayin is reproduced as Ephrain in A.V. and R.V. marg. Commonly identified with the town of Ephrain or Ophrah.
3. A city e. of the Jordan in the territory of Manasseh, in a pass on the road between Karnaim and Beth-shean. It was captured by Judas Maccabaeus (I Macc. 5:46–52; II Macc. 12:27, 29; Jos. *Antiq.* xii. 8, 5). It has been identified with et-Taiyibeh, n. of the wadi et-Taiyibeh.
4. A mountain ridge between Nephtoah and Kiriath-jearim, on the boundary between Judah and Benjamin (Josh. 15:1, 9).

Ep'i·cu·re'ans (ĕp'ĭ-kû-rē'ǎnz). One of the leading philosophic sects of Greece and Rome. It derived its name and its existence from the great philosopher Epicurus. He was born 341 B.C. in the island of Samos, but was of Athenian descent, and made Athens the scene of his lifework. In 306 B.C. he founded a school or college with a garden attached, in which he taught for the next 36 years, till his death in 270 B.C. He is said to have written about 300 philosophic books, nearly all of which are lost. In physics he, like Democritus, attributes all nature to changes among atoms in themselves eternal. He does not recognize a Creator; but, with curious inconsistency, finds a place in his system for a multitude of gods, who, however, supremely happy in themselves, take no part in human affairs. With regard to his ethics, a popular misconception prevails. He desires that pleasure shall be pursued and pain avoided; but the notion that by pleasure he meant only sensual gratification is erroneous. He included under the term the pleasure derived from the exercise of the intellect and the moral faculty. Personally he was so pure that some thought he was destitute of passions. The Epicureans were mostly men of soft temperament, the very opposite of the Stoics, who were cast in an iron mold. Both philosophic sects rejected Paul's doctrine at Athens, but both showed their tolerance by taking the apostle to the Areopagus to have his teaching examined.

Ep'i·lep'tic. A person affected with the falling sickness, a disease which in its severe form is characterized by recurrent attacks of loss of consciousness with spasms (Matt. 17:15, in A.V. "lunatick"; Mark 9:18). In this case the disease was occasioned by demoniacal possession.

E·pis'tles. The name given to 21 books of the N.T. The earliest of them antedate the Gospels, Paul having written his Epistles to the Thessalonians about A.D. 50. They are letters which were written by the apostles, or which received apostolic sanction; and they are addressed to particular churches, and deal with doctrinal and practical questions, or to individuals, yet contain matter of wide import, or to Christians generally, and not to any one person or church. With the exception of The Epistle to the Hebrews and I John, the epistles, according to the custom of the time, begin with the name or title of the writer and that of the person or church addressed; then follow words of greeting.

The epistles are classed in 3 groups, but the groups are neither exhaustive nor mutually exclusive: 1. Pauline; for the first 13 begin with the statement that the letter was sent by Paul or by him in conjunction with other Christian workers, as Sosthenes (I Cor. 1:1), Timothy (II Cor. 1:1; Phil. 1:1; Col. 1:1; Philemon 1), or Silvanus and Timothy together (I Thess. 1:1; II Thess. 1:1). Paul, as a rule, employed an amanuensis to write from his dictation (Rom. 16:22), the apostle adding the salutation in his own hand, which he says was the token in every epistle (I Cor. 16:21; Col. 4:18; II Thess. 3:17). In the case of the Epistle to the Galatians, however, he departed from his rule, and wrote the whole letter with his own hand (Gal. 6:11). 2. Within the group of Pauline Epistles are 3 known as the Pastoral Epistles, namely, I and II Timothy and Titus. They are addressed to the persons whose names they bear, and contain directions for the training and governing of churches and the proper treatment of individual members. 3. Five epistles are called General in the titles prefixed to them in the A.V.: James, I and II Peter, I John, and Jude. In the Early Church, however, 7 were classed as Catholic, II and III John being included (Eusebius *H.E.* ii. 23), although these 2 are simple personal letters addressed to individuals. The word "catholic" was probably used in its sense of "general," to denote an encyclical letter to the Church at large; and the elect lady and Gaius, to whom II and III John respectively are addressed, were probably understood to represent the Church Universal.

The epistolary form was not a mere literary device, chosen for a doctrinal treatise. Usually at least the epistles were written in the way of ordinary correspondence. They were prompted by personal motives and were due to the writer's own initiative (Philemon, II John) ; or they were penned in reply to letters, or were based on information otherwise obtained, concerning matters requiring attention in any particular church (I Cor. 1:11; II Cor. 7:5-7 ; I Thess. 3:5, 6). But they are adapted to all persons in like circumstances ; Paul requested that certain of his epistles be read by others than by those only to whom they were addressed (Col. 4:16). The apostles claimed that these epistles are the word of God (I Thess. 2:13 ; I Peter 1:12), and from the beginning they ranked with the other Scriptures. Peter spoke of Paul's epistles as part of the Scriptures (II Peter 3:15, 16), and Polycarp in A.D. 115 quoted The Psalms and Ephesians side by side as equally Scripture. See CANON.

The titles of the epistles were not part of the original composition, but were prefixed afterward. They are lacking in early manuscripts, and are no part of Scripture. Most of them are founded on the 1st verse of the epistle ; but that prefixed to The Epistle to the Hebrews in A.V. is not derived from the letter itself, and is of doubtful accuracy. The notices appended to the epistles in the A.V. regarding the place where the letter was penned were likewise no part of the original composition.

Er (ûr) [watching]. 1. A son of Judah who died in Canaan by a judgment of God for his wickedness (Gen. 38:1-7 ; 46:12 ; I Chron. 2:3).

2. A descendant of Judah, of the family of Shelah (I Chron. 4:21).

3. An ancestor of Christ, about midway between David and Zerubbabel (Luke 3:28).

E'ran (ē'răn) [watchful]. A descendant of Ephraim through Shuthelah, and founder of a tribal family (Num. 26:36).

E-ras'tus (ē-răs'tŭs) [Gr., beloved]. A Christian, one of those who ministered to Paul. He was sent with Timothy from Ephesus into Macedonia just before the riot at the former place (Acts 19:22). He is probably the person mentioned in II Tim. 4:20 as having abode at Corinth, who perhaps was the Christian in high official position, treasurer of Corinth, who joined with Paul in sending salutations to the Roman converts (Rom. 16:23).

E'rech (ē'rĕk) [Akkad. *Uruk* and *Arku*]. A city of Shinar (Sumer), one of those constituting part of Nimrod's kingdom (Gen. 10:10). It is now represented by the mounds of Warka, a considerable distance s. of Babylon, in a marshy region, e. of the Euphrates. Archevites were settled in Samaria by Asnapper (Ezra 4:9).

E'ri (ē'rī) [watching]. A son of Gad and founder of a tribal family (Gen. 46:16 ; Num. 26:16).

E·sa'ias (ē-zā'yăs). See ISAIAH.

E'sar·had'don (ē'sär-hăd'ŏn) [Ashur has given a brother]. The favorite, though not the eldest, son of Sennacherib, king of Assyria. This partiality so annoyed 2 other brothers, Adrammelech and Sharezer, that they assassinated their father (681 B.C.), escaping afterward into Armenia (II Kings 19:36, 37; II Chron. 32:21; Isa. 37:37, 38). When this base murder was perpetrated, Esarhaddon was himself conducting a campaign in the n.w., probably in Armenia. Sennacherib was killed in the month of Tebeth, and Esarhaddon set out for Nineveh at the beginning of Shebat. The civil war came to an end in Assyria in Adar of 681.

Esarhaddon was equally eminent as a military general and a political ruler. In his 1st year he defeated the son of Merodach-baladan in s. Babylonia. Later he commenced the restoration of the city of Babylon which Sennacherib, provoked by its continual revolts against the Assyrian domination, had destroyed. Esarhaddon also waged war against the Cimmerian barbarians who had descended upon Assyria from beyond the Caucasus, against the mountaineers of Cilicia, and against the children of Eden who were in Telassar (cf. Isa. 37:12). In his 4th year he captured and pillaged Sidon, deported its inhabitants, razed the city to the ground, and erected a new town on the old site. Its king had escaped by sea, but he was pursued, taken, and beheaded. The same fate befell his 2 royal allies. Afterward 12 tribes on the mainland and 10 in Cyprus submitted to the Assyrian dominion. Among others were Manasseh, king of Judah, and the kings of Edom, Moab, Ammon, Gaza, Ashkelon, Ekron, and Ashdod. Esarhaddon successfully accomplished 2 most difficult military enterprises, the penetration of the Arabian desert and of far-off Media. He turned his attention to a yet greater undertaking, the conquest of Egypt, 675-674, but he was for a time diverted from his purpose, being compelled in his 8th year to war with a tribe at the head of the Persian Gulf and near Ur. At length in 671 he made his great expedition against Egypt. Marching past Tyre, he left the city under siege. He entered Egypt, captured Memphis, and conquered the entire country. He died in 669 B.C., and was succeeded by his eldest son, Ashurbanipal. Another son, Shamash-shum-ukin, was made ruler of Babylon under the suzerainty of Ashurbanipal.

E'sau (ē'sô) [hairy]. Son of Isaac and Rebekah, and elder twin brother of Jacob. Esau was so named because he was "all over like a hairy garment" (Gen. 25:21-26). As he grew up he became a skillful hunter, and was accustomed to bring home venison, doubtless the flesh of various antelopes, to his father Isaac. On one occasion he returned from the chase famishing, and asked for some red pottage which Jacob had just made ready. Jacob asked from him his birthright as payment ; and Esau, esteeming the higher blessings lightly, and caring more for present gratification, sold his birthright rather than wait for the preparation of food. From the red pottage, which was its price, Esau obtained a 2d name, Edom (Red) (vs. 27-34 ; Heb. 12:16, 17). When he was 40 years old he married 2 wives, Judith or Oholibamah and Basemath or Adah, both Hittites (Gen. 26:34, 35 ; 36:1, 2). Afterward he wedded Mahalath, called also Basemath, the daughter of Ishmael (chs. 28:9 ; 36:3). When Isaac was old and nearly blind, he designed to confer the covenanted blessing on Esau, who was his favorite son. But Jacob was Rebekah's favorite, and she induced him to personate Esau and obtain the blessing by fraud. Esau resolved to kill his selfish brother, but did not like to carry out the murder while his father was living (ch. 27:1-41). To give time for Esau's anger to cool, Jacob fled to Mesopotamia, and for 20 years was an exile (chs. 27:42 to 31:55). On his return he took means to appease his justly offended brother ; and Esau, who was of a generous nature, dismissed his vindictive feeling, and gave Jacob a fraternal reception (chs. 32:3 to 33:15). Prior to this, Esau had taken up his abode in Mount Seir, to which he at once returned (ch. 33:16). The reconciliation between the brothers was permanent, and both met to bury their father (ch. 35:29). Esau's descendants increased and ultimately dispossessed the original inhabitants of Mount Seir and became the Edomite people (Deut. 2:4, 12, 22). Mount Seir could, accordingly, be called the Mount of Esau (Obad. 8, 9, 19, 21). For the election of

Jacob to be the child of promise and the rejection of Esau, see Gen. 25:23; Mal. 1:2, 3; Rom. 9:12, 13.

Es'dra•e'lon (ĕs'drå-ē'lŏn). See JEZREEL.

Es'dras (ĕz'drăs). See APOCRYPHA and EZRA.

E'sek (ē'sĕk) [contention]. A well dug by Isaac in the valley of Gerar, which the Philistine herdsmen claimed (Gen. 26:20).

E'shan (ē'shăn), in A.V. **Esh'e•an** [support]. A village in the mountains of Judah, grouped with Dumah and Hebron (Josh. 15:52). LXX has Soma; hence it may be identical with Khirbet Sam'a, w. of Dōmeh, and about 10 miles s.w. of Hebron.

Esh'ba'al (ĕsh'bā'ăl) [for 'ĭsh-ba'al, man of Baal (Lord)]. See ISHBOSHETH.

Esh'ban (ĕsh'băn). A son of Dishon, descended from Seir the Horite (Gen. 36:26; I Chron. 1:38, 41).

Esh'col (ĕsh'kŏl) [a cluster, especially of grapes]. 1. One of 3 Amorite brothers, residing near Hebron and confederate with Abram (Gen. 14:13, 24).
2. A valley near, probably n. of, Hebron (Num. 13:22, 23; Deut. 1:24). The region round about Hebron is celebrated for its large clusters of luscious grapes. It is uncertain whether the valley bore this name before the time of Moses or not. At any rate the name henceforth suggested to the Israelites the spot where the spies, whom Moses had sent to spy out the land, cut the famous cluster which 2 of them carried suspended on a pole between them (Num. 13:24).

Esh'e•an (ĕsh'ē-ăn). See ESHAN.

E'shek (ē'shĕk) [violence, oppression]. A Benjamite, a descendant of Saul (I Chron. 8:1, 33, 39).

Esh'ka•lon•ite (ĕsh'kå-lŏn-īt). See ASHKELONITE.

Esh'ta•ol (ĕsh'tå-ŏl). A town in the lowland of Judah (Josh. 15:20, 33), eventually allotted to the Danites (ch. 19:40, 41). It is commonly mentioned in connection with Zorah (Judg. 13:25; 16:31; 18:2, 8, 11; I Chron. 2:53). It has been identified as the village of Eshwa', about 1½ miles e. by n. from Zorah, and 13 miles w., slightly n. from Jerusalem.

Esh'ta•o'lite (ĕsh'tå-ō'līt), in A.V. **Esh'ta•u'lite** (ĕsh'tå-ū'līt). An inhabitant of Eshtaol (I Chron. 2:53).

Esh'te•mo'a (ĕsh'tĕ-mō'å), once **Esh'te•moh** (ĕsh'tĕ-mō) (Josh. 15:50) [obedience]. 1. A town in the hill country of Judah, given with its suburbs to the priests (Josh. 15:20, 50; 21:14; I Chron. 6:57). David sent it some of the spoils obtained on the recapture of Ziklag (I Sam. 30:28). The site has been found at es-Semū'a, 9 miles s. of Hebron.
2. A Maacathite, son of Hodiah (I Chron. 4:19, R.V.).

Esh'ton (ĕsh'tŏn) [possibly, uxorious]. A descendant of Chelub, reckoned in the genealogy of Judah (I Chron. 4:1, 11, 12).

Es'li (ĕs'lī) [Gr., perhaps from Heb., Jehovah has reserved; cf. Heb. 'āṣal, reserve, set apart]. An ancestor of Christ who lived after the Captivity (Luke 3:25).

Es'rom (ĕs'rŏm). See HEZRON.

Es•senes' (ĕ-sēnz'). An order of men among the Jews in the time of Christ, who numbered about 4,000, and devoted themselves to a more or less ascetic life. Hoping by isolation to escape ceremonial defilement, they formed colonies by themselves. The wilderness of Judea near En-gedi was a favorite place for their settlements, but there were colonies in various towns of Judea also. Each colony had its own synagogue, a common hall for meals and assemblies, and provision for daily bathing in running water. Whoever became a member of the order gave up all that he possessed to it. They read the Law of Moses daily and nightly, and endeavored to regulate their lives in every detail according to it. Their habits were simple. Their food and clothing were plain. They passed the day in husbandry and other useful industry. Money was almost unnecessary, as they supplied their needs by their own labor; and when they traveled, they found lodging and food free of cost among their brethren. They had no slaves, as they recognized no distinction between men save that of clean and unclean. They did not deny the fitness of marriage; but they abstained from wedlock, except one party among them. Their morality was lofty. They promised "to honor God, to be righteous toward man, to injure no one, either at the bidding of another or of their own accord, to hate evil, to promote good, to be faithful to every one, especially those in authority, to love the truth, to unmask liars, and to keep the hand from theft and the conscience from unrighteous gain" (Jos. Antiq. xviii. 1, 5; War ii. 8, 2–13).

Es'ther (ĕs'tēr) [Heb. 'Estēr, probably from Persian; cf. Avestan star (star); or perhaps from Akkad. Ishtar, which equals Heb. 'Ashtōreth]. A beautiful maiden, daughter of Abihail, and probably of the tribe of Benjamin (Esth. 2:15; and cf. v. 5 with v. 7). Her Hebrew name was Hădassāh (myrtle). Early left an orphan, she was brought up at Susa, the Persian metropolis, by Mordecai, her cousin, who adopted her. Ahasuerus, king of Persia, who is identified with Xerxes, when in wine, ordered Vashti the queen to be brought into the banquet hall and displayed to the revelers. Angered by her refusal to submit to such indignity, he followed the advice of his obsequious courtiers and decreed her permanent seclusion, and had his realm searched for a fair maiden to take her place. Eventually, in the 7th year of the king, Esther was selected and installed in the palace as queen. It was not known at the time that she was a Jewess. She came to the throne at a critical time. The royal favorite was Haman. Five years after Esther's elevation (Esth. 2:16; 3:7), Haman, annoyed by Mordecai's refusal to do him obeisance, wished to revenge himself by the massacre, not simply of Mordecai, but of all the large Jewish population scattered throughout the empire. He secured the king's consent by the offer of a heavy bribe and by allusion to the stubborn adherence of the Jews to their own laws and customs; and he sought to get the aid of the rabble in the work of slaughter by an appeal to their greed (chs. 2:5 to 3:15). Mordecai urged Esther to

Xerxes Holding the Staff of Authority

interfere for the protection of her race. She was afraid; but, on being solemnly addressed by her guardian, she, after fasting and prayer, risked her life by coming unbidden into the king's presence. With great prudence and tact she made a favorable opportunity for bringing to the king's attention the fact that Haman's plot invaded the palace and included her; and, since the edict of destruction could not be recalled, she gained permission for the Jews to defend themselves, and even to take the offensive against their foes.

The time and manner of Esther's death are unknown. If Ahasuerus is Xerxes, as is believed, Esther was one of Xerxes' wives, of whom one was Amestris, the daughter or granddaughter of Otanes, first definitely reported as already Xerxes' wife in 479 B.C., his 7th or 8th regnal year (Herod. ix. 109; cf. vii. 61). Vashti was the reigning wife in Xerxes' 3d year (Esth. 1:3, 9), and Esther was put into her place in the 10th month of the 7th year (Esth. 2:16, 17), and was queen in the 12th year also (chs. 3:7; 5:3).

The Book of Esther is the last O.T. historical book in the English Bible. In the Hebrew canon it stands among the Hagiographa, and is grouped with 4 other rolls which were used on 5 solemn anniversaries. The last of these anniversaries is Purim; hence Esther is placed last among the Five Rolls (Megilloth). Long after the completion of the canon, the right of Esther to its place in that canon was called in question by the Jews—probably, however, not seriously, but to afford opportunity for intellectual display in its defense. The Jews now regard it with special honor. Christians have been more divided on the subject of its merits. Melito of Sardis and Gregory of Nazianzus omitted it from their lists of canonical books; Athanasius classed it with noncanonical books, and Luther denounced it. Opposition to it was based mainly on the fact that the name of God does not occur in it even once. But ch. 4:14 implies the existence of Providence; ch. 4:16 recognizes fasting as a religious practice, and ch. 9:31 not merely fasting, but a cry or prayer. The great lesson of the book is, in fact, the overruling power of Providence.

Investigators who seek for a possible mythological or legendary origin for certain narratives of the O.T. argue that The Book of Esther springs from such a source; they would make it of Babylonian origin. In its principal form this theory rests its claim for acceptance mainly on the evidence that Esther is a late form of the name of the Babylonian goddess Ishtar; and that Esther's other name Hadassah is the Babylonian word *ḥadashatu* (bride, originally myrtle), and is used as a title of goddesses. Mordecai is the same as Marduk, the patron deity of Babylon. He is the cousin of Esther, and it is possible thus to relate Marduk to Ishtar. Haman, the adversary of Mordecai, represents Hamman or Humman (Humban), a chief god of the Elamites, in whose capital, Susa, the scene is laid; and Zeresh, the wife of Haman, may be the same as Kirisha, an Elamite goddess, presumably the consort of Hamman. Vashti is also an Elamite deity, presumably a goddess. The successful resistance of Mordecai and Esther to Haman, Zeresh, and Vashti is the conflict of the gods of Babylonia with the gods of Elam; in other words, it is the struggle between Babylonia and Elam for supremacy, which lasted for a thousand years and ended in the victory of Babylonia (Jensen, *Wiener Zeitschrift f. d. Kunde des Morgenlandes*, vi. 47 ff., 209 ff.; Gunkel, *Schöpfung und Chaos*, 310–314, who admits that the basis is lacking so long as the word Pur remains unexplained, 314). If this theory were established, it might show that the Jews of the Dispersion, feeding their hopes on the prophecies of deliverance, instituted a joyous feast and made use of the contest of Marduk and Ishtar with Hamman and Vashti to illustrate or typify the certain victory of the Jews over all their foes.

This theory has serious weaknesses, and many critics have regarded the book as a historical romance written to glorify the Jews in a period when they were hated and envied by their neighbors, and to explain the origin of Purim. This feast has been variously assigned to a Persian or Babylonian origin.

It is easier and more satisfactory, however, to regard the book as historical. The narrative claims to be historical and refers to the chronicles of Persia as containing a record of the events in question (chs. 2:23; 6:1; 10:2). It gives the origin of Purim, which in the time of Josephus was observed in all parts of the world (Jos. *Antiq.* xi. 6, 13); the connection of the book with such an ancient Jewish feast still forms a considerable presumption in favor of its being founded on facts. This book gives a lifelike representation of Persian manners and customs, especially in connection with the palace at Susa (chs. 1:5, 10, 14; 2:9, 21, 23; 3:7, 12, 13; 4:6, 11; 5:4; 8:8). Furthermore, the character of Ahasuerus is in harmony with that of Xerxes as he is known in history. It appears that Xerxes held a great council of war in the 3d year of his reign before setting out for Greece and that he returned to Susa in the spring of his 7th year (cf. Herod. vii. §; ix. 108). This agrees with the dates assigned to the great feast and the choice of a successor to Vashti (chs. 1:3; 2:16).

The narrative is minute and circumstantial, containing many names of courtiers and princes (ch. 1:10, 14). The Book of Esther tells more about Haman than his name. It knows him as the son of Hammedatha and an Agagite (chs. 3:1, 10; 8:5; 9:24), and gives the name of his 10 sons (ch. 9:7–10). Concerning the Hebrews who figure in this narrative, Esther is known in the book as the daughter of Abihail and a queen of Ahasuerus. Mordecai either means "belonging to Marduk" or is a diminutive form of Marduk. The form cf the name, however, points to a man, not a god. Such names were not wanting among godly Hebrews: cf. Apollos, Henadad, Shenazzar. The name Mordecai itself was borne by another Jew of the Exile besides the cousin of Esther (Ezra 2:2). The narrative takes Mordecai's lineage back through several ancestors to the tribe of Benjamin (Esth. 2:5).

No substantial ground has been found for regarding Esther, Mordecai, Haman, and Vashti as deities; in the narrative they are human beings. Against the heathen origin of Purim is the acceptance of the event by the Jews as historical. Furthermore, against the theories which assume a heathen festival as the origin of Purim, the grand objection is that no heathen celebration has yet been discovered for the 14th and 15th days of Adar, the 12th month of the year. See MORDECAI, PROVINCE, VASHTI.

The language of The Book of Esther is the Hebrew of the late period, but with many Persian words. From ch. 10:2 it would seem that Xerxes was dead when it was penned. By some, the date of composition is fixed in the reign of Artaxerxes Longimanus (465–425 B.C.); materials, however, do not exist for definitely dating the book. By the majority of critics it is assigned either to the early years of the Greek period (which began 332 B.C.) or to the 3d century B.C. Some favor c. 300 B.C. The book is not quoted in the N.T., nor alluded to. Certain additions to it appear in the LXX. Jerome separated them and put them at the end of the book, and they now find place in the Apocrypha.

E'tam (ē'tăm) [perhaps, place of birds of prey]. 1. A village on the border of the s. country and the lowland, transferred from Judah to Simeon (I Chron. 4:32; cf. Josh. 15:32, 42); identified with 'Aiṭūn, about 11 miles w.s.w. of Hebron.

2. Samson dwelt for a time in the cleft of the rock of Etam (Judg. 15:8, 11), having gone there from Timnah. Conder locates this cleft at Beit 'Aṭāb, 5 miles s.e. by e. of Zorah. Others favor 'Arāḳ Isma'īn, in Wadi Isma'īn, 2½ miles e.s.e. of Zorah.

3. A town in the neighborhood of Bethlehem, fortified by Rehoboam for the defense of Judah after the secession of the 10 tribes (I Chron. 4:3; II Chron. 11:6; and Josh. 15:59a in LXX). According to the Talmud, the Temple at Jerusalem was supplied with water conducted from the spring of Etam, and an ancient aqueduct extends for 7 miles from the Temple hill, past Bethlehem, to 3 pools, the lowest of which is fed by a neighboring spring, situated on the s., called 'Ain 'Aṭān. Josephus relates that Solomon was fond of driving out in the early morning to Etan (written also Etam), distant 2 *schoinoi* or 7 miles from Jerusalem, where there was a delightful prospect of gardens and rivulets (Jos. *Antiq.* viii. 7, 3). Here, at Khirbet el-Khoḥ, near 'Ain 'Aṭān, near the village of Urṭās and about 2 miles s.w. of Bethlehem, was the site of Etam. The 3 reservoirs were discovered by pilgrims at quite a late date and named the pools of Solomon. The aqueduct is ancient, antedating the Christian era and the Roman period. Pontius Pilate probably used it as the last section of the great conduit which he undertook to build for the purpose of bringing water to Jerusalem from a distance of 200 stadia or 23 miles (Jos. *Antiq.* xviii. 3, 2), or 400 stadia (Jos. *War* ii. 9, 4).

E'tham (ē'thăm). The 1st encampment of the Israelites after leaving Succoth, on their departure from Egypt. It was on the edge of the wilderness (Ex. 13:20; Num. 33:6). It apparently did not lie on the direct road from Egypt to the Philistine country (Ex. 13:17). The name was extended to a portion of the wilderness of Shur, requiring at least 3 days to cross it, and apparently reaching to or even including Marah (Num. 33:8; cf. Ex. 15:22). Apparently it was located at the e. end of the wadi Ṭūmīlāt, n. of Lake Timsāḥ.

E'than (ē'thăn) [perennial; permanent]. 1. A descendant of Judah, belonging to the tribal family of Zerah (I Chron. 2:6). He seems to have been the person of this name who was celebrated for his wisdom (I Kings 4:31; Psalm 89, title).

2. A Levite, of the family of Gershom, house of Libni (I Chron. 6:42, 43; cf. v. 20 and Num. 26:58).

3. A Levite, of the family of Merari, house of Mushi. He was a son of Kishi or Kushaiah, and was appointed a singer in the time of David (I Chron. 6:44, 47; 15:17, 19). His name, it appears, was changed to Jeduthun, "praising one," after his appointment to service in the tabernacle at Gibeon (ch. 16:38–41; cf. 15:17, 19 with 25:1).

Eth'a·nim (ĕth'à-nĭm) [incessant rains]. The 7th month (I Kings 8:2), called also Tishri. It was approximately October. Within it fell the feast of trumpets, the great Day of Atonement, and the feast of tabernacles. See YEAR.

Eth'ba·al (ĕth'bā'ăl) [with Baal; Gr. *Itho-balos* suggests "With him is Baal"]. A king of the Tyrians and Sidonians, and father of Jezebel (I Kings 16:31; Jos. *Antiq.* viii. 13, 1 and 2; ix. 6, 6). He was priest of Ashtoreth, but slew his brother and seized the throne (Jos. *Apion* i. 18).

E'ther (ē'thĕr) [abundance]. A village in the lowland of Judah (Josh. 15:42), but allotted to the tribe of Simeon (ch. 19:7). It is called Tochen in I Chron. 4:32; identified with Khirbet el-'Ater, about a mile n.w. of Beit Jibrin.

E'thi·o'pi·a (ē'thĭ-ō'pĭ-à) [Greek *Aithiōpia*]. A country called in Hebrew *Kūsh* (Cush), which is continually mentioned in connection with Egypt (Ps. 68:31; Isa. 20:3–5; Ezek. 30:4, 5; Dan. 11:43; Nahum 3:9) and sometimes with Libya or the Libyans (II Chron. 16:8; Ezek. 30:5; 38:5; Dan. 11:43; Nahum 3:9), and must certainly have been in e. Africa. It ran s. from Syene, the s. point of Egypt (Ezek. 29:10, R.V. marg.; cf. Judith 1:10). It was manifestly the upper region of the Nile, the Sudan, Nubia with Kordofan, Sennaar, and n. Abyssinia, a region in large measure desert. though in places fertile. The rivers of Ethiopia (Isa. 18:1; Zeph. 3:10) were probably the White and Blue Niles, with the Atbara and Takkaze. The topazes of Ethiopia were celebrated (Job 28:19). Its inhabitants were tall (Isa. 45:14). They were colored men, probably black (Jer. 13:23). They engaged in mercantile transactions, selling the productions of their country in foreign lands (Isa. 45:14), and as a consequence became wealthy (ch. 43:3). When the Ethiopians, led by Zerah, invaded Judah, they were signally defeated by King Asa (II Chron. 14:9–15; 16:8). An Ethiopian dynasty, the 25th, established itself in Egypt; to it belonged that Tirhakah who met Sennacherib in battle at Eltekeh (II Kings 19:9; Isa. 37:9). Isaiah (ch. 20:1–6) and Zephaniah (ch. 2:12) prophesied against the Ethiopians, while the psalmist predicted that Ethiopia would "haste to stretch out her hands unto God" (Ps. 68:31; cf. Ps. 87:4). The prophecy was fulfilled in the conversion of the Ethiopian eunuch (Acts 8:26–40) and the introduction of the gospel into Abyssinia.

Eth'·ka'zin (ĕth'kā'zĭn), in A.V. **It'tah·ka'·zin** (ĭt'à-kā'zĭn), with ending, *-āh*, which denotes direction. A place on the boundary line of Zebulun (Josh. 19:13), near Sepphoris; Kefr Kenna has been suggested as the site.

Eth'nan (ĕth'năn) [gift, hire]. A man of Judah, family of Hezron (I Chron. 4:7; cf. ch. 4:5 *seq.* and ch. 2:24).

Eth'ni (ĕth'nĭ) [cf. Ethnan]. A Gershonite Levite (I Chron. 6:41). In v. 21 he is called Jeatherai. The main difference is found in the last consonant and may have arisen from a scribal confusion of Heb. *nun* (*n*) and *resh* (*r*).

Eu·bu'lus (û-bū'lŭs) [Gr., well-advised, prudent]. A Roman Christian (II Tim. 4:21).

Eu'me·nes (û'mē-nēz) [Gr., well-disposed]. King of Pergamos, 197–159 B.C. When the Romans defeated Antiochus the Great at Magnesia in 190 B.C., they assigned the greater part of the defeated king's realm n. of the Taurus Mountains to Eumenes in return for the services which he had rendered them (I Macc. 8:6–8; Livy xxxvii. 44). They bestowed Lycia and Caria on the Rhodians. The report, which Judas Maccabaeus heard, that the Romans had taken India and Media also was not true.

Eu·ni'ce (û-nī'sê) [Gr., blessed with victory]. A pious Jewess, mother of Timothy (Acts 16:1; II Tim. 1:5).

Eu'nuch [Gr., keeping or guarding the couch]. Properly a chamberlain; but in the East persons who had been rendered impotent were employed for this office, hence an impotent man (Isa. 56:3; Matt. 19:12). There is scarcely a doubt that the word is used in this sense throughout Scripture, even when it is rendered into English by some other term. There have been, and still are, married eunuchs (Gen. 39 :1, rendered "officer," and v. 7). Eunuchs often obtained high position and great authority. The captain of the guard of Pharaoh and his chief butler and his chief baker were eunuchs (Gen. 37 :36 ; 40 :2, 7, translated "officer"). Eunuchs ministered at the court of Babylon (Dan. 1 :3). They served in the presence of the Persian king, and acted as doorkeepers of his palace (Esth. 1 :10 ; 2 :21) ; a eunuch was over his harem (ch. 2 :3, 14), and a eunuch was deputed to attend his queen (ch. 4 :5). They served also at the court of Ahab and his son Jehoram, and they waited upon Jezebel (I Kings 22 :9 ; II Kings 8 :6 ; 9 :32). Even in Judah, although eunuchs were legally excluded from the congregation of the Lord (Deut. 23 :1), they were employed at David's court (I Chron. 28 :1), and, in the last days of the monarchy, at the degenerate court of the successors of Josiah (cf. II Kings 24 :15 with Jer. 29 :2 ; II Kings 25 :19). The eunuchs in Judah were probably in most, if not in all, cases foreigners (Jer. 38 :7). The cupbearer of Herod the Great was a eunuch, as were also the official who brought him his food and the one who assisted him to bed ; and his favorite wife Mariamne was served by a eunuch (Jos. Antiq. xv. 7, 4 ; xvi. 8, 1). A eunuch was over the treasure of Queen Candace of Ethiopia, and he was admitted to baptism (Acts 8 :27, 37 ; cf. Isa. 56 :3).

Eu·o′di·a (û-ō′dĭ-á), in A.V. **Eu·o′di·as** (û-ō′dĭ-ăs) [Gr., fragrance]. A Christian woman at Philippi blemished by bickering with Syntyche (Phil. 4 :2).

Eu·phra′tes (û-frā′tēz) [Gr. of Heb. Peꞧāth]. One of the great rivers of w. Asia. It is formed by the junction of two streams : the Murad Su, rising in Armenia, between Lake Van and Mount Ararat, being the more easterly ; and the Frat or Kara Su, rising n.e. of Erzurum (Erzerum), the more westerly. Sometimes the name Frat, cognate with Heb. Peꞧāth, is applied to both of these streams. They run in a w. direction to about latitude 39° N., and longitude 39° E., after which the combined waters turn s., break through the s. chain of the Taurus Mountains. Then the river bends s.e., constituting the w. boundary of Mesopotamia. About latitude 31° N., longitude 47° E., the Tigris unites with the Euphrates, to constitute what is now called the Shattal-Arab, which, after a course of about 90 miles more, falls into the Persian Gulf. The whole length of the Euphrates is about 1,800 miles. It was one of the rivers of paradise (Gen. 2 :14). It was familiarly known to the Hebrews as "the great river" or simply "the river." It formed the n.e. limit of the Hebrew dominion when its extension was at the greatest (Gen. 15 :18 ; cf. II Sam. 8 :3 ; I Chron. 18 :3 ; I Kings 4 :21, 24). It was a boundary between e. and w., between Egypt and Assyria-Babylonia, each power desiring to possess the country between the brook of Egypt and the Euphrates. In the Persian period also it separated e. from w. (Ezra 4 :10, 11 ; 5 :3 ; 6 :6 ; Neh. 2 :7). It was a boundary of the Seleucidan kingdom (I Macc. 3 :32 ; 8 :8), and it was regarded as the e. limit of the Roman Empire. The greatest city on its banks was Babylon. Another important place was the old Hittite capital Carchemish, the scene of various battles, especially of one (605 B.C.) between the Chaldeans led by Nebuchadnezzar and the Egyptians under Necho (Jer. 46 :2). In the book of Revelation certain angels are described as being "bound at the great river Euphrates" (Rev. 9 :14), and the 6th vial was poured out upon the Euphrates itself (ch. 16 :12).

Eu·pol′e·mus (û-pŏl′ĕ-mŭs) [Gr., good at war]. Son of that John who obtained special privileges for the Jews from Antiochus the Great (I Macc. 8 :17 ; II Macc. 4 :11). Eupolemus was one of two ambassadors sent by Judas Maccabaeus to Rome to make a treaty with the Romans (Jos. Antiq. xii. 10, 6). Some think that he is the Jewish historical writer Eupolemus whom Alexander Polyhistor quotes so frequently.

Eu·raq′ui·lo (û-răk′wĭ-lō) [Gr. Eurakylon (e.n.e. wind), from Gr. euros (e. wind)+ Lat. aquilo (n.e. wind) ; cf. Vulgate euroaquilo]. A tempestuous n.e. wind of the Mediterranean (Acts 27 :14). The wind from that quarter, now called gregale, blows generally in early spring, and is the most violent wind on the Mediterranean.

Eu·roc′ly·don (û-rŏk′lĭ-dŏn) [Gr. euroklydōn, from Gr. euros (e. or e.s.e. wind)+Gr. klydōn (wave)]. A tempestuous wind which blows from the s.e. or the e. It brought the vessel in which Paul was sailing toward Rome first into danger and then to shipwreck (Acts 27 :14, A.V.). R.V. prefers the reading Eurakylōn, which has better MS. authority, and accordingly renders "Euraquilo."

Eu′ty·chus (û′tĭ-kŭs) [Gr., fortunate]. A young man of Troas who, falling asleep while Paul was preaching there, fell from the 3d loft or floor. He was taken up dead, but was miraculously restored to life by the apostle (Acts 20 :9, 10).

E·van′ge·list [Gr., euangelistēs, a messenger of good tidings]. An order of men in the primitive Church distinct from apostles, prophets, pastors, and teachers (Eph. 4 :11). Their name implied that their special function was to announce the glad tidings of the gospel to those before ignorant of them, and, as they were not pastors of particular churches, they were able to go from place to place preaching to those who as yet were without the Christian pale. Philip, who was the means of converting and baptizing the Ethiopian eunuch, was an evangelist (Acts 21 :8), and we find him successively at Jerusalem (ch. 6 :5), in Samaria (ch. 8 :5), on the road between Jerusalem and Gaza (v. 26), in the cities n. of Azotus (Ashdod) (v. 40), and finally at Caesarea (v. 40 ; ch. 21 :8). Timothy was also commanded by Paul to do the work of an evangelist (II Tim. 4 :5). At a later date the name was given to the writers of the 4 Gospels.

Eve (ēv) [Heb., Hawwāh, life]. The name given by Adam to the first woman because she was the mother of all living (Gen. 3 :20). Soon after his creation, she was brought into being to be a help meet for him. The narrative has been variously interpreted as meaning that : 1. Woman was formed from the rib of man, Adam being in a deep sleep (trance), which produced anesthesia (there may be the additional idea that divine working cannot take place under human observation) ; 2. Woman was not actually formed from man's rib, but Adam had a vision by which he was taught his oneness of nature with woman and her rights and privileges ; 3. Woman's relation to man is set forth in allegory. The two human beings were placed in the Garden of Eden ; and in order to test their obedience they were forbidden to touch or taste the fruit of one particular tree. But the serpent under Satanic influence led Eve to question the goodness of God and then to eat the forbidden fruit. She afterward persuaded Adam to eat, who thus shared her guilt. The result was the fall of man (Gen. 3 :1–24 ; II Cor. 11 :3 ; I Tim. 2 :14). After the expulsion of the guilty pair from the garden, Eve became successively the mother of Cain, Abel, Seth, and other sons and also daughters (Gen. 4:1, 2, 25, 26; 5:1–5).

E'vi (ē'vī). One of the 5 kings of Midian, allies or vassals of Sihon, slain in the war waged by Moses against the Midianites because they seduced the Israelites to licentious idolatry (Num. 31:8; Josh. 13:21).

E'vil. The origin of evil is a problem which has perplexed speculative minds in all ages and countries. God is not the author of sin, but he permits it. He has permitted it, because the revelation of his infinite perfection is the highest conceivable good and the ultimate end of all his works, and there could be no manifestation of certain of his attributes if sin were not permitted. Were there no misery, there could be no mercy shown by God; and there could be no revelation of his grace and justice, if there were no sin (Rom. 9:22, 23). Sin is permitted that God's justice may be known in its punishment, and his mercy in its forgiveness.

E'vil-Me·ro'dach (ē'vĭl-mê-rō'dăk) [Akkad. *Amēl-Marduk*, man of Marduk]. Son and successor of Nebuchadnezzar. He became king in 562 B.C., and reigned until 560. In the first of these 2 he took Jehoiachin, the captive king of Judah, from his prison and placed him above all the other rulers whom he had in thrall, giving him a daily allowance of food during the remainder of his life (II Kings 25:27–30; Jer. 52:31–34). A conspiracy was formed against Evil-Merodach, his own brother-in-law, Neriglissar or Nergalsharuṣur, being at its head. The king was accused of lawlessness and intemperance, and was put to death in 560 B.C. Neriglissar, the chief conspirator, then ascended the throne (Jos. *Antiq.* x. 11, 2).

E'vil Spir'it. See DEMON.

Ex·e·cu'tion·er. See GUARD.

Ex'ile. See CAPTIVITY and DISPERSION.

Ex'o·dus (ĕk'sŏ-dŭs) [Gr., a going out, a way out]. 1. The departure of the Israelites from Egypt, after they had been divinely emancipated from bondage in that land. There is great difficulty in settling the exact route of the Exodus. The miracles by the hand of Moses were wrought at Zoan, i.e., Tanis (Ps. 78:12), and Raamses was a suburb of that capital. Thence the Israelites journeyed to Succoth (Ex. 12:37), a site which is the same as, or near, Pithom; it is marked by Tell el-Maskhutah in the wadi Tumilat, 32 miles s.s.e. of Tanis and 11 miles w. of Isma'iliya. They did not take the shortest route to Palestine, which lay through the land of the Philistines, but went by way of the wilderness by the Red Sea (Ex. 13:17, 18). Their first encampment after leaving Succoth was Etham. The site has not been identified; but it was on the edge of the wilderness (v. 20). Thence they turned back and encamped before Pi-hahiroth, between Migdol and the sea, before Baal-zephon (Ex. 14:2; Num. 33:7). This camp has not been definitely located. It was, however, w. of the Red Sea. From this place they marched through the Red Sea into the wilderness of Shur (Ex. 15:4, 22; Num. 33:8), and thence along the coast of the Red Sea toward Mount Sinai (Ex. 15:10, 15). For the date of the Exodus, see EGYPT, III. 8.

2. The book of Exodus, the 2d book of the Pentateuch. In the Hebrew Scriptures the title consists of the opening words, "And these are the names." The name Exodus was appropriately given to the book by the Greek translators, because it narrates the departure from Egypt, which was a turning point in Israel's history.

The book is a continuous narrative and may be divided into 3 sections: 1. In Egypt (chs.

1:1 to 12:36). The period of several centuries immediately following the descent of Jacob into Egypt is passed over with a single remark about the increase of the people after the death of Joseph (ch. 1:7). Oppression of the Israelites (v. 8 *seq.*). Birth, earlier life, and call of Moses (chs. 2 to 4). Struggle with Pharaoh and infliction of the plagues; in connection with the last plague, institution of the passover (chs. 5:1 to 12:36). 2. From Egypt to Sinai (chs. 12:37 to 19:2). Departure from Raamses (ch. 12:37–42). Supplementary regulation respecting the passover, stating the condition upon which foreigners could partake of it (ch. 12:43–51). Sanctification of the first-born enjoined upon Moses (ch. 13:1, 2); announcement to the people of a 7 days' festival to be observed henceforth in connection with the passover, and of God's command to sanctify the first-born (vs. 3–16). Passage of the Red Sea (ch. 14), song of deliverance (ch. 15:1–19), bitter water at Marah, manna and quails (chs. 15:20 to 16:36). At Rephidim: water from rock in Horeb, victory over Amalek, and visit of Jethro (chs. 17; 18). 3. At Sinai (chs. 19:3 to 40:38 and uninterruptedly to Num. 10:10). Establishment of the theocracy: theocratic covenant proposed by God on condition of obedience (Ex. 19:3–6), approval of the terms by the elders of the people (vs. 7, 8), the Ten Commandments and subsidiary laws enacted and written in the Book of the Covenant (chs. 20 to 23; 24:4; for analysis and form of these laws, see THEOCRACY). Ratification of the covenant by the nation (ch. 24:1–8), and the covenant meal of the contracting parties (vs. 9–11). Moses in the mount; architectural specifications for the tabernacle and its furniture, tables of stone (chs. 24:12 to 31:18; for analysis, see TABERNACLE). The golden calf (chs. 32; 33). Moses' 2d sojourn in the mount, with summarizing urgent repetition of covenant laws (ch. 34). Construction and erection of the tabernacle (chs. 35 to 40). See PENTATEUCH.

Ex'or·cist. One who professes by using words and ceremonies to eject evil spirits and deliver from their malign influence. Certain impostors of this sort, vagabond Jews, were encountered by Paul at Ephesus (Acts 19:13–19).

E'zar (ē'zẽr). See EZER, I.

Ez'ba·i (ĕz'bâ-ī). Father of one of David's mighty men (I Chron. 11:26, 37, possibly merely a variant reading for Arbite of II Sam. 23:35).

Ez'bon (ĕz'bŏn). 1. A son of Gad (Gen. 46:16). See OZNI.
2. The head of a father's house, family of Bela, tribe of Benjamin (I Chron. 7:6, 7).

Ez'e·ki'as (ĕz'ê-kī'ăs). See HEZEKIAH.

E·zek'iel (ê-zēk'yĕl) [El (God) strengthens]. One of the greater Jewish prophets, a son of Buzi, and of priestly family (Ezek. 1:3). He grew up, until beyond the years of childhood, in the homeland, probably at Jerusalem in the environment of the Temple, during the ministry of the Prophet Jeremiah. He was carried captive from Judah with Jehoiachin (597 B.C.), 8 years after Daniel's deportation (chs. 33:21; 40:1; cf. II Kings 24:11–16). Josephus says that he was a youth at the time (Jos. *Antiq.* x. 6, 3). He was not a child but was under the age when Levites assumed their duties and were reckoned in the census as men. He lived with the Jewish exiles on the Chebar, a canal in Babylonia, probably at Tel-abib (Ezek. 1:1, 3; 3:15); married probably as early as the 6th, at least by the 9th year of the Captivity, and had a house (chs. 8:1; 24:1, 18).

His prophetic ministry began in the 5th year of Jehoiachin's captivity, 7 years before the destruction of the Temple at Jerusalem, while he was dwelling on the Chebar (ch. 1:1, 2). He was then in his 30th year (ch. 1:1), the age at which Levites entered upon service (Num. 4:3). The theory that the 30th year does not refer to Ezekiel's age, but is a date reckoned either from the accession of Nabopolassar, Nebuchadnezzar's father, or from the reforms of Josiah, fails in view of Jer. 25:1, 3; II Kings 23:36; 25:2–6; Ezek. 1:2. Though an exile in a foreign land, Ezekiel had freedom to utter his prophecies and was resorted to for advice by the elders of the people (chs. 8:1; 14:1; 20:1); but his words were not followed faithfully (ch. 33:30–33).

It is evident from the affinities of thought and language that he was quite familiar with Jeremiah's teaching. He takes up brief doctrinal remarks, or suggestive allegories, or short speeches of Jeremiah, and develops and expands them, and often gives to them a literary finish: as the caldron (Jer. 1:13–15; Ezek. 11:2–11; 24:3–14); the two sisters (Jer. 3:6–11; Ezek., ch. 23); forgiveness for the condemned, when penitent (a nation, Jer. 18:5–12, an individual, Ezek. 18:21–32); the evil shepherds replaced by the Davidic king (Jer. 23:1–6; Ezek. 34:1–24); individual responsibility in view of the proverb about the fathers eating sour grapes (Jer. 31:29, 30; Ezek. 18:2–31); the new spiritual nature (Jer. 31:33, 34; Ezek. 11:19, 20; 36:25–29); the exiles, not the Jews in Jerusalem, the hope of the future (Jer., ch. 24; Ezek. 11:15–21; 37:1–14). Ezekiel's prophetic activity extended over a period of at least 22 years (cf. ch. 1:2 with 29:17). The time and manner of his death are unknown.

The Book of Ezekiel stands in the English Bible between Lamentations and Daniel. As these 2 books are placed among the Writings or Hagiographa in the Hebrew canon, Ezekiel's place in the Hebrew Scriptures is directly after Jeremiah. The prophecies are arranged nearly, though not quite, in chronological order, and they are dated according to the years of Jehoiachin's captivity in which they were delivered. The book falls into 3 divisions:

I. *Prophecies delivered before the capture* of Jerusalem, foretelling its overthrow for its sins. In the 5th year the priest is called to the prophetic office and prepared for his work by a vision (chs. 1:1 to 3:21), and then is directed to prophesy, by symbolical actions and their interpretation, the destruction of the city (chs. 3:22 to 7:27). In the 6th year, are denunciations of Judah for idolatry (ch. 8); symbolical departure of Jehovah from the Temple because of its profanation (chs. 9:1 to 11:13); comfort, the exiles are still God's people, he will be a sanctuary to them (v. 16), restore them to the land of Israel (v. 17), give those that reform their lives a new heart (vs. 18–21). Unbelief and adherence to false prophets are the reasons for Jehovah's forsaking his city (chs. 12 to 14); the event is certain (chs. 15 to 17), but the repentant shall enjoy God's favor (ch. 18). Lamentation for the princes of Israel (ch. 19). In the 7th year, it is prophesied that, because Jehovah's name has been profaned in the sight of the heathen, he will punish the people, but will afterward restore them for his name's sake (ch. 20:1–44); the doom is certain, the transgressions are come to remembrance before God (chs. 20:45 to 23:49). In the 9th year, the siege of Jerusalem and the dispersion of the people are symbolized by a caldron (ch. 24).

II. *Prophecies of judgment* against the nations: in the 9th year, against Ammon, Moab, Edom, and Philistia (ch. 25); in the 11th year, against Tyre and Sidon (chs. 26 to 28);

and in the 10th, 27th, and 11th years, against Egypt (chs. 29 to 32).

III. *Prophecies concerning the Restoration*, delivered after the capture and destruction of Jerusalem by Nebuchadnezzar. In the 12th year, the evening before the news of the fall of the city reached the prophet, the hand of the Lord was upon him, and the actual reception of the news marks the opening of a new activity on the part of Ezekiel (ch. 33:1–22). He is taught that, after the judgment, the people shall recognize that Jehovah is God, and that a true prophet has been among them (ch. 33:23–33); a good shepherd, even David, shall be raised up (ch. 34), their present foes punished (ch. 35), the people sanctified and restored to their land (ch. 36), revived as from the dead, their 12 tribes reunited (ch. 37), and their foes finally overthrown (chs. 38; 39). In the 25th year, the re-establishment of God's Church is disclosed, being symbolically exhibited in the vision of the Temple enlarged and holy throughout, and the people cleansed and accepted by Jehovah (chs. 40 to 43), its holy services (chs. 44 to 46), the river of life issuing from it and making the desert to rejoice (ch. 47), and the distribution of the land among the tribes, and their common city known as the place where Jehovah is (ch. 48).

In this vision the Temple that Ezekiel had known so well in his younger days is quite changed in appearance. Instead of the little hill of Zion, he beholds a high mountain, crowned by the buildings of a new and grander sanctuary. An angel, with a measuring rod and line, is standing at the gate. The new Temple is modeled, indeed, after the old in its general arrangements, but it is so located with reference to the habitations of men, and its courts and chambers are so disposed, as to safeguard the holiness of Jehovah, who is soon to dwell there, and impress upon the worshipers Jehovah's separateness from both moral and ceremonial impurity. Many years earlier Ezekiel had seen in vision Jehovah leaving the old, desecrated Temple (chs. 10:18, 19; 11:22–24); now the prophet beholds Jehovah returning by the same gate into the Temple and the glory of Jehovah filling the house, and he hears a voice from within saying: "This is the place of my throne, . . . where I will dwell in the midst of the children of Israel for ever. And the house of Israel shall no more defile my holy name" (ch. 43:1–7). In the inner court, before the holy house, Ezekiel sees the altar of atonement provided for the new Israel and hears the declaration, "And I will accept you, saith the Lord Jehovah" (vs. 13–27).

The worship of accepted Israel is now described to the prophet. In the new theocracy the reality will correspond to the divine ideal. The uncircumcised in heart or flesh will not enter into the sanctuary. The Levitical families who proved unfaithful of old will not be allowed to officiate at the altar; yet they will be given a place, albeit a humble one, in the Temple. The priests, the sons of Zadok, whose very name means righteous, that had remained faithful, will alone fill the high office of priest before Jehovah (ch. 44). An oblation unto Jehovah will be made of a portion of the land for the support of the services and ministry of the sanctuary (ch. 45:1–6). For the prince also suitable provision will be made from the oblation-land, enabling him to maintain the public services in the name of the people, and he shall not abuse his power by oppressing the people or encroaching on the prerogatives of the priests (chs. 45:7–12; 46:2, 16–18). The people likewise shall assemble in their own appointed place in the Temple, when they worship (v. 9). All members of the theocracy, official and lay, know

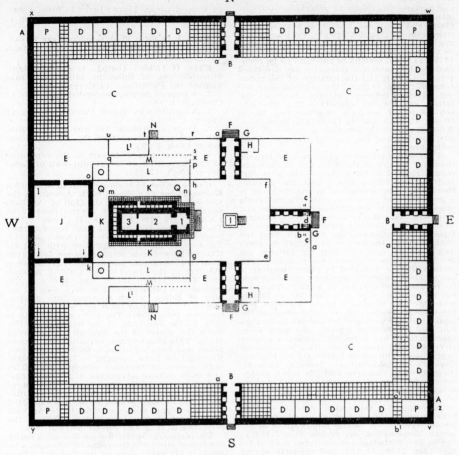

PLAN OF EZEKIEL'S TEMPLE

A. The outer wall encompassing the Temple area
B. The three outer gates
C. The outer court
D. The thirty chambers or cells
E. The inner court
F. The inner gates
G. Eight steps leading to the inner gates
H. Chambers for the singers in the inner court
I. Altar of burnt offerings
J. The building in the inner court behind the Temple
K. A court or passage called "The Separate Place"
L. Longer chambers (Ezek. 42:1, 8)
L¹. Shorter chambers (Ezek. 42:7, 8)
M. Walk between the blocks of chambers
N. Steps facing eastward and leading into the shorter chamber or block of rooms
O. Priests' kitchens
P. People's kitchens
x. The place where Ezekiel stood, according to ch. 42:2

The checkered space within the outer wall is the pavement.

Q. The Temple building
1. The porch (Ezek. 40:48, 49)
2. "The Temple" or the Holy Place (Ezek. 41:1, 2)
3. The Most Holy Place or the Holy of Holies

The checkered space around the Temple building represents "a raised basement round about" (Ezek. 41:8); i.e., it corresponds to a pavement.

a-a	Chapter 40:19-23, 27.
b	Chapter 40:38.
cc	Chapter 40:39.
d	Chapter 40:41, 42.
e f g h	Chapter 40:47.
i-j	Chapter 41:12.
i-k	Chapter 41:12.
j-l	Chapter 41:12.
m-n	Chapter 41:13.
m-l	Chapter 41:13.
g-h	Chapter 41:14.
k-o	Chapter 41:15.
p-q	Chapter 42:2, 4, 8.
h-r	Chapter 42:2.
p-s	Chapter 42:4, 11.
r-t	Chapter 42:7.
t-u	Chapter 42:8.
v-w	Chapter 42:16.
w-x	Chapter 42:17.
v-y	Chapter 42:18.
y-x	Chapter 42:19.
v-y, y-x	Chapter 42:20.
z-a¹	Chapter 46:22.
a¹-b¹	Chapter 46:22.

and perform the duties in reference to atonement which belong to them in their several places and relations. Ezekiel is next shown a river issuing from the Temple, swelling into a mighty stream, and bringing life and health to the regions of barrenness and death (ch. 47:1–12). The bounds of the land to be occupied by the restored community are described (ch. 47:13–20), and the location of the tribes (chs. 47:21 to 48:29); the oblation-land being divided between priests, Levites, the prince, and the city (ch. 48:8–22). The city belongs to all Israel in common (vs. 15–20, 30–34; cf. v. 19 and ch. 45:6), and its name is Jehovah-shammah, Jehovah is there (ch. 48:35), symbolizing the central thought of the entire prophecy.

What was Ezekiel's contribution to Israel's thought? Critics of the school of Wellhausen regard Ezekiel as the father of the later formal Judaism. They assert that the description of the new Jerusalem in chs. 40 to 48 is a program, and gave rise to the characteristic priestly regulations contained in Leviticus and Numbers. This theory is rejected by scholars who take the Biblical view of the origin of Israel's institutions; they maintain that the characteristic legislation of Leviticus antedates Ezekiel, and also that the prophet did not intend these chapters as a program. The picture that is unfolded in these chapters is not an ideal which the prophet expected would be realized literally, but is purely symbolic; for in no other way is it possible to understand the high mountain of the new Zion, and the measurements, and the allotments of the land which are geometrical and not geographical, and the healing waters that issue from the sanctuary and presently become a mighty river, and the trees whose fruit is produced every month and whose leaves are for healing. Ezekiel's enrichment of Israel's thought, through these chapters and his other prophecies, is found in his spiritual teaching. Among other things he contributed: 1. To the thought of God. He removes as far as possible an anthropomorphic conception of God; cf. "the appearance of the likeness of the glory of Jehovah" (ch. 1:28). While others speak of Jehovah shepherding his people (Gen. 48:15; Psalm 28), gathering the scattered flock of Israel (Jer. 23:3; 31:10), and tenderly caring for them (Isa. 40:11), Ezekiel represents God as seeking his lost sheep (Ezek. 34:11–16; cf. Matt. 18:12–14; Luke 19:10). 2. To the vision of the new Jerusalem: the high mountain (Ezek. 40:2; Rev. 21:10), the holy city, God's tabernacle among men (Ezek. 37:27; Rev. 21:3), the glory of God in it (Ezek. 43:2–5; Rev. 21:11), the city foursquare (Ezek. 48:16, 30; Rev. 21:16), having 12 gates (Ezek. 48:30–34; Rev. 21:12, 13), the river of life (Ezek. 47:1; Rev. 22:1), and the trees on either side of the river, whose leaves are for healing (Ezek. 47:7, 12; Rev. 22:2). As in Ezekiel, so in John the vision is symbolical. 3. But above all Ezekiel contributed to the spiritual conception of the Jerusalem of the future. Taking up a germinal teaching of Jeremiah, he lays the emphasis on individual responsibility (Ezek., chs. 18; 33:1–20) and on the renewed nature of the people and the holiness of the kingdom as the crowning glory of the coming time (chs. 11:19, 20; 36:24–29). The spiritually regenerate Zion is henceforth definitely before the minds of God's people as a noble idea and the great hope.

E'zel (ē'zĕl) [departure]. The place where David hid until Jonathan could inform him of Saul's disposition toward him (I Sam. 20:19).

E'zem (ē'zĕm), in A.V. twice **A'zem** [mighty]. A village near the border of Edom in that part of the territory allotted to the tribe of Judah, which was afterward assigned to Simeon (Josh. 15:29; 19:3; I Chron. 4:29). It has been identified with Khirbet Umm el 'Azam.

E'zer, I (ē'zēr), in A.V. once **E'zar** [treasure]. A Horite tribe and its chieftain (Gen. 36:21, 30; I Chron. 1:38).

E'zer, II (ē'zēr) [help]. 1. A descendant, probably son, of Ephraim, killed in a raid against the Philistines (I Chron. 7:21).

2. A man of Judah, descended from Hur (I Chron. 4:1, 4).

3. A Gadite who joined David at Ziklag (I Chron. 12:9).

4. A son of Jeshua. He was ruler of Mizpah, and repaired part of the wall of Jerusalem (Neh. 3:19).

5. A priest who took part in the ceremony at the dedication of the rebuilt wall of Jerusalem (Neh. 12:42).

E'zi·on-ge'ber (ē'zĭ-ŏn-gē'bēr), in A.V. often **E'zi·on-ga'ber** (ē'zĭ-ŏn-gā'bēr). A town on the Red Sea, at the n. end of the Gulf of 'Akabah, near and probably w. of Elath (Deut. 2:8; I Kings 9:26; 10:22; 22:48; II Chron. 8:17). The Israelites encamped by the town as they journeyed in the wilderness (Num. 33:35). Ezion-geber has been identified with Tell el-Kheleifeh, which is situated some 500 yards from the seashore, about halfway between 'Akabah at the e. end of the Gulf of 'Akabah and Mrashrash at the w. end. It lies in the bottom of a curve banked on the e. side by the hills of Edom, which continue into Arabia, and on the w. side by those of Palestine, which continue into Sinai. The town accordingly is open to the full fury of the winds that blow down the center of the Arabah like a forced draft. This phenomenon explains why Ezion-geber was founded at such an inclement site. Excavations have brought to light an elaborate system of furnaces equipped with flues and built to take advantage of the draft furnished by the winds from the n. Here were smelted, refined, and wrought into semifinished and finished products the ores extracted from the copper and iron mines in the Arabah. This discovery is interesting in view of the reference to iron and copper in Deut. 8:9.

The place apparently did not become a really important site until the reign of Solomon, who made it his naval base on the Red Sea. That king controlled the overland trade route to Arabia and the sea route from Ezion-geber to Ophir. For about 200 years Judah and Edom were engaged in a bitter struggle for the domination of these routes. After Solomon's death the sea traffic from Ezion-geber to Ophir seems to have ceased. Apparently the sea trade with Arabia remained quiescent until Jehoshaphat became king of Judah; it seems that he attempted to revive it, but failed. Ahaziah, the son of Ahab, offered to co-operate, but Jehoshaphat refused his aid (I Kings 22:48, 49; but cf. II Chron. 20:36, 37). During the reign of Joram, son of Jehoshaphat, Edom revolted against Judah and regained its independence (II Kings 8:20–22; II Chron. 21:8–10). Amaziah, king of Judah, however, waged a successful war against Edom (II Kings 14:7; II Chron. 25:11, 12) and his son Uzziah (Azariah) "built Elath, and restored it to Judah" (II Kings 14:22; II Chron. 26:1, 2). From the time of Uzziah Elath apparently is to be identified with Ezion-geber. If the reading of R.V. marg. in II Kings 16:6 (according to the LXX) is adopted, Ezion-geber (Elath) in 735 B.C. passed into the control of the Edomites and out of Biblical history. See ELATH.

Ez'nite (ĕz'nīt). See ADINO.

Ez'ra (ĕz'rá), in R.V. once **Ez'rah** [help]. 1. A man who is registered with Judah (I Chron. 4:1, 17); R.V. spells Ezrah as in Heb.

2. One of the chief priests who returned from Babylon with Zerubbabel (Neh. 12:1, 7). A father's house bore his name in the next generation (v. 13).

3. A priest descended from Zadok and from Phinehas (Ezra 7:1-6). He was a ready scribe in the Law of Moses, making the written law, which was in his hand (v. 14), the subject of study and teaching (vs. 10, 11). In the 7th year of Artaxerxes Longimanus, king of Persia from 464 to 424 B.C., he was commissioned by the king to go to Jerusalem to inquire into the civil and religious condition of the Jewish community and conform it to the teaching of God's law (v. 14). He was given orders to the authorities in the province "beyond the River" for money and goods for the Temple and for the exemption of the Temple officials from taxation (vs. 21, 24). He was authorized to lead a fresh company of Jewish exiles to Palestine, in addition to those who had accompanied Zerubbabel and the high priest, Jeshua, 80 years before (538 B.C.). On gathering together those who proposed to return, and mustering them, he found no Levites of the lower order; but on sending word to their chief, a few were persuaded to join him. After fasting and seeking God's guidance for the journey, the party, numbering over 1,700 men, set forth on the 12th day of the 1st month, in the 7th year of Artaxerxes, 458-457 B.C. (Ezra 8:1-23, 31). On reaching Jerusalem 4 months later, on the 1st day of the 5th month (ch. 7:8), Ezra gave over the vessels he had received for the Temple, offered sacrifice, and presented the king's orders to the neighboring governors (ch. 8: 33-36). He was grieved to discover that Jews of Palestine, including even some of the priests, contrary to the Law of Moses, had married heathen wives; but he succeeded in inducing most of them to divorce these foreign women (chs. 9; 10). Thirteen years later, after Nehemiah had come to Jerusalem and repaired its walls, Ezra took the leading part in reading the Law of Moses to the people of the colony (Neh., ch. 8). He died, according to Josephus, about the time of Eliashib's succession to the high priesthood (Jos. *Antiq.* xi. 5, 5). He was certainly for a while contemporary with Eliashib (Neh. 3:1; 13:4, 7, 28). For his relation to the Law and to the O.T. books, see CANON.

The Book of Ezra consists of 2 parts: 1. A narrative of the return of the Jews from Babylonia under Zerubbabel in the year 538 B.C., the restoration of divine service, and the erection of the Temple in the face of Samaritan opposition (chs. 1 to 6). 2. Without reference to a gap of 58 years in the chronology, the narrative continues with an account of the return of a second body of exiles under Ezra in the year 458-457 B.C., and of Ezra's energetic and successful measures to put a stop to the marriage of Israelites with foreigners (chs. 7 to 10).

The book is largely composed of copies of public records and official documents. The provincial documents and history are written in Aram. (chs. 4:8 to 6:18; 7:12-26); namely, copies of the letters sent to the Persian kings by officials of the province "beyond the River" (chs. 4:8-16; 5:7-17; 6:6-12), the royal replies and decrees imposing commands on these officials (chs. 4:17-22; 6:3-5; and ch. 7:12-26, cf. vs. 21, 24), and the brief connecting history referring primarily to provincial affairs (chs. 4:23 to 5:5; 6:1, 2, 13-18). Aramaic had been for several centuries the language of international commerce and diplomacy. The remainder of the book, written in Heb., records the proper domestic history of Judah and is based on various historical documents. It includes the royal edict issued in behalf of the Jews (ch. 1:2-4), the list of the

vessels of the Temple (ch. 1:7-11), copies of Jewish archives (chs. 2:1-67; 8; 10:18-44), and the connecting history. The personal memoirs of Ezra are distinguished by the use of the first person pronoun, sing. and pl. (chs. 7:27 to 8:34; 9). The "we" sections also come from the records of Ezra, who in those verses speaks for the returned exiles as well as for himself.

Some scholars have assumed that the whole book was written by Ezra, but its historical value does not depend on such a hypothesis. While there is no doubt about the reliability of the historical contents, the majority of critics believe that the present form of Ezra-Nehemiah is the work of an editor, better known as the Chronicler, who has been conservatively dated at c. 400 B.C. See CHRONICLES. If the Chronicler actually compiled this book, he had access to official documents and to the personal memoirs of Ezra or to a reliable edition of such works. He himself may have supplied some of the connecting historical material and references to the Temple, cult, and music. If he was a contemporary of Ezra, this material came from his own observations; if he lived later than Ezra, he had access to reliable tradition or records.

The order of the Persian kings of the period is Darius (521-486 B.C.), Xerxes (486-464), and Artaxerxes (464-424). In view of this succession, ch. 4:6-23 is out of chronological order and properly belongs after chs. 4:24 to 6:18 (or v. 24). A reasonable explanation of this is that the Chronicler depended for Ezra, chs. 1 to 6, upon two main sources: one in Heb., represented by chs. 1:1 to 4:5; and another in Aram., represented by chs. 4:6 to 6:18. In this 2d source, chs. 4:24 to 6:18 probably stood before ch. 4:6-23, and thus the correct order of the Persian kings was preserved. The Chronicler, however, may have considered a sequence of content more important than a chronological order. Thus there are brought together the successful attempts of the enemies of the Jews to hinder the building of the Temple and the city walls. Chapter 4:5 refers to the opposition toward building the Temple in the days of Cyrus and Darius, and this is followed by a protest against restoring the city and its walls in the days of Xerxes and Artaxerxes (ch. 4:6-23). In ch. 4:6-8 the verses are disjointed, and it seems reasonable to suppose that each of these 3 verses presents a separate instance of Samaritan opposition. In fact, the Heb. text has a break between vs. 6 and 7 and one between vs. 7 and 8. In v. 7 there is no more than a bare reference to an Aram. letter; but the letter of v. 8, which seems to be a different one, is quoted in Aram. (ch. 4:11-16). Chapters 4:24 to 6:18 resumes the narrative which had been interrupted at ch. 4:5. Regardless of the sources used by the Chronicler, the hindrances raised by the Samaritans are thus grouped together.

Ezra and Nehemiah constitute a historical unit and linguistically belong to the same period as Chronicles. In the Heb. Bible, the books of Ezra and Nehemiah are counted as one, and the Talmud follows the same tradition. Originally they were one in the LXX, as they are in codices Vaticanus, Sinaiticus, and Alexandrinus. Esdras is the Gr. form of Ezra. Esdras A of the LXX is an apocryphal work, and Esdras B is our Ezra-Nehemiah. The Vulgate divides Ezra-Nehemiah, calling the former The First Book of Esdras and the latter The Book of Nehemias, which is also called the Second of Esdras. In the Eng. Bible, Ezra and Nehemiah are counted as 2 books. This separation probably began in the Christian Church; the 2 sections were doubtless regarded originally as 2 parts of the same book, as in the case of Samuel, Kings, and

Chronicles. Since the 16th century, however, printed Heb. Bibles mark a division either as a concession to Christian usage or to facilitate reference; but in counting the total number of books, Ezra and Nehemiah are reckoned as one in the Heb. Scriptures.

In the Eng. Apocrypha I Esdras represents Esdras A of the LXX or III Esdras of the Appendix to the Vulgate; II Esdras is the Ezra Apocalypse or IV Esdras of the Appendix to the Vulgate. Thus in English Protestant usage the name Esdras is relegated to the Apocrypha.

For the relation of Ezra-Nehemiah to Chronicles, see CHRONICLES. See also NEHEMIAH.

Ez'rah (ĕz'rȧ). See EZRA 1.

Ez'ra·hite (ĕz'rȧ-hīt) [alternate form of Zarhite]. A descendant of Zerah, belonging to the tribe of Judah, as Ethan (I Kings 4:31; Psalm 89, title; cf. I Chron. 2:6) and Heman (Psalm 88, title; cf. I Chron. 2:6).

Ez'ri (ĕz'rī) [probably, (God is) a help]. Overseer of the laborers who tilled David's fields (I Chron. 27:26).

F

Fair Ha'vens (fâr hā'vĕnz). A harbor on the s. coast of Crete, near the city of Lasea, where Paul's ship touched (Acts 27:8). It is located about 5 miles e. of Cape Matala, just w. of which the coastline turns n.

Faith. As far as a difference exists between belief and faith, belief is assent to testimony. and faith is assent to testimony united with trust. Faith is an active principle; it is an act of both the understanding and the will. The distinction between belief and faith is that between "believe me" and "believe on me." The verb believe thus does service for the two nouns faith and belief. In the Bible faith or belief is confidence in the absolute truthfulness of every statement which comes from God (Gen. 15:6; Mark 11:22; Rom. 4:3–5). In this faith the heroes of Scripture acted (Heb., ch. 11). In a special sense, faith is reliance on God's testimony regarding the mission and atoning death of his Son, the Lord Jesus Christ (John 5:24), and on the testimony of Jesus regarding himself (cf. John 3:18; Acts 3:16; 20:21; Rom. 3:25). Faith in the Redeemer, whereby a sinner rests upon him alone for salvation, is essential to salvation (John 3:15, 16, 18; Eph. 2:8, etc.). Belief in his historical existence and in the truth of his claims may be produced by evidence, but faith in him, reliance upon him for salvation, cannot be. It is the gift of God (Eph. 2:8); the Spirit applies the truth to the soul. Human means should be used, in co-operation with his Spirit, for its production (Rom. 10:17). It may exist in larger or in smaller measure (Rom. 4:19, 20; 14:1). The apostles when they deplored the weakness of their faith prayed to Jesus for its increase (Luke 17:5). It works by love (Gal. 5:6), and overcomes the world (I John 5:4). But with all its importance it is not the greatest of the 3 primary Christian graces, that position being occupied by love (I Cor. 13:13).

The system of doctrine given by revelation of God is termed the faith (Acts 6:7; 24:24; Rom. 1:5, etc.).

Fal'con. A diurnal bird of prey other than a vulture. The family includes among its genera falcons strictly so-called, hawks, kites, eagles. The word is used in R.V. to render Heb. 'ayyāh (Job 28:7; in A.V. vulture), an unclean bird (Lev. 11:14; Deut. 14:13; in A.V. kite).

Fall, The [translation of Gr. *paraptōma*, trespass, as applied to Adam's transgression (Wisd. of Sol. 10:1; cf. Rom. 5:15, etc.)]. The account of the fall of man (Gen., ch. 3) cannot be dismissed as an allegory or as a purified Semitic myth. In a Babylonian story Ea warned his son Adapa not to partake of food or drink offered him by the gods in Anu's heaven:

"Food of death they will offer thee to eat;
   Thou shalt not eat. Water of death they
     will offer thee to drink;
Thou shalt not drink. A garment they will
     show thee;
Put it on. Oil they will set before thee;
     anoint thyself.
The command which I give thee, forget
     not. The word
Which I have spoken, hold fast."

As it turned out, they offered him the food and drink of immortality, but Adapa obeyed his father and thus lost eternal life. The resemblance to Gen., ch. 3, is remote and suggests no borrowing from the Babylonian.

The fall of man is narrated in Gen., ch. 3, as a fact, and the whole narrative is psychologically faithful to human experience. The Scriptural view of sin and redemption takes the Fall for granted. God created man, male and female, "endued them with living, reasonable, and immortal souls; made them after his own image, in knowledge, righteousness, and holiness, having the law of God written in their hearts and power to fulfill it, . . . yet subject to fall" (Larger Catechism, 17). But upon being left to the freedom of their will, they yielded to temptation and thus transgressed the commandment of God (Gen. 2:16, 17; 3:1–8). Through their disobedience they fell from the state of innocency and sinlessness. The result of the Fall is original sin, which has been conveyed to posterity by natural generation so that all human beings are conceived and born in sin (Ps. 51:5; John 3:6; Rom. 5:12). Death—spiritual, temporal, and eternal—is the consequence of sin. Many exegetes see in Gen. 3:15 the protevangelium or the first announcement of the gospel of redemption. The narrative includes also much symbolism of human suffering connected with the Fall (Gen. 3:16–19).

Paul assumes as not needing any proof that man's sinfulness is the result of Adam's fall. Just as Adam is related to the race as the author of sin and death, so Christ is the author of righteousness and life. At one end are Adam and sinful humanity; at the other, Christ and redeemed humanity (Rom. 5:12–21; I Cor. 15:21, 22, 45–49).

Fal'low Deer. The rendering of Heb. *yaḥmūr* in A.V. of Deut. 14:5; I Kings 4:23. R.V. has roebuck (*q.v.*). The genuine fallow deer (*Dama vulgaris*) has horns, with their upper part palmated. The hair in summer is yellowish-brown all over, with spots; in winter the tints are less bright. The male is about 3 feet high at the shoulder. Its native country seems to be the Mediterranean region. It occurs sparingly in Galilee and Mount Lebanon.

Fa·mil'iar Spir'it. The spirit of a dead person which professed mediums claimed to summon to consultation (Deut. 18:11), and which appeared to speak from the earth (Isa. 29:4), or to dwell in the controlling medium (Lev. 20:27, in Heb.). The medium was called the possessor or lord of a spirit (I Sam. 28:7, in Heb.). It revealed the future (Isa. 8:19). It was either a special spirit which was believed to respond always to the summons of the medium, as the English rendering would lead one to suppose, and who might raise other ghosts; or it was any spirit whom the medium desired.

I Sam. 28:8 is capable of either interpretation, "Divine ... by the familiar spirit" in you or "whomsoever I shall name." To consult familiar spirits was apostasy from Jehovah (Lev. 19:31; Isa. 8:19). Under the Mosaic Law a person pretending to possess the power of consulting a familiar spirit was to be put to death (Lev. 19:31; 20:6, 27; Deut. 18:11). Saul carried out this enactment, but when sorely troubled about his fate, he sought out a woman of En-dor who had a familiar spirit, asked her to bring back Samuel to the world, and believed her statement that she had succeeded (I Sam. 28:3, 5–25). Manasseh favored them that professed to have familiar spirits (II Kings 21:6; II Chron. 33:6). His grandson Josiah carried out the Mosaic Law against them (II Kings 23:24). They probably included ventriloquists, as the rendering of the LXX implies, and the voice of the spirit accordingly merely appeared to come in a whisper from the ground.

Fam'ine. Deficiency of food, generally produced either by failure of rain leading to the withering of the crops, or by the prevention of the entrance of food into a beleaguered city. Famine compelled Abraham to leave Canaan and sojourn in Egypt (Gen. 12:10). It was the first of a series of famines connected with the history of the patriarch and his descendants, and which led the Hebrews to withdraw temporarily from Palestine (chs. 26:1; 41:27–56; 47:13). Other famines occurred in the days of the Judges which made Elimelech remove to Moab (Ruth 1:1), in David's reign (II Sam. 21:1), in the time of Elijah (I Kings 17:1 *seq.*), in Elisha's time (II Kings 4:38; 8:1), and in the reign of Claudius, A.D. 41–54, when severe local famines swept in succession from Judea in his 4th year to Greece in his 9th year and Italy in his 11th year (Acts 11:28; Jos. *Antiq.* xx. 2, 5; 5, 2; Tacitus *Ann.* xii. 43). Among famines produced in besieged cities by the foe who prevented provisions from entering are those during the siege of Samaria by Ben-hadad (II Kings 6:24 to 7:20) and during the sieges of Jerusalem by Nebuchadnezzar (II Kings 25:1–3; Jer. 52:4–6) and by Titus (Jos. *War* v. 10, 2 and 3).

Fan. The winnowing fan, in Heb. *mizreh,* was a fork with 6 prongs, with which grain, after it had been threshed, was thrown up against the air to clear it of the chaff (Isa. 30:24; Jer. 15:7). A shovel was also used for the same purpose. See THRESHING.

Far'thing. 1. A Roman *quadrans,* a small brass coin equal to the 4th part of an *as.* The Greeks used the Roman name, calling the coin *kodrantēs.* In the time of Christ its value was about one half of an English farthing, or one quarter of a cent (Matt. 5:26; Mark 12:42).
2. An *assarion,* diminutive of the Lat. *as,* a copper coin equal to about 1 cent (Matt. 10:29).

Fast. Abstinence from food, or the period during which it takes place. 1. *Involuntary,* arising from the fact that nothing to eat is procurable. Of this type were apparently the 40 days' fast of Moses on Mount Sinai (Ex. 34:28; Deut. 9:9), of Elijah on his journey to Horeb (I Kings 19:8), and of our Lord during his temptation in the wilderness (Matt. 4:2; Mark 1:13; Luke 4:2); also of Paul (II Cor. 6:5).
2. *Voluntary,* from religious motives. In this sense it is often used regarding prescribed periods of abstinence. There do not appear to be any injunctions regarding fasting in the Mosaic Law, and neither the verb "to fast," nor the nouns "fast" and "fasting," occur in the Pentateuch. If fasts are prescribed at all, it is in the ambiguous language "Ye shall

afflict your souls" (Lev. 16:29; 23:27; Num. 29:7). The 1st mention of voluntary fasting is in connection with King David, who refused food when he supplicated God for the life of the child borne to him in sin by the wife of Uriah (II Sam. 12:22). Many instances of the same unprescribed fasting are found in the later books of the O.T. (Ezra 8:21; Neh. 9:1; Esth. 4:3; Ps. 35:13; 69:10; 109:24; Dan. 6:18; 9:3). Sometimes fasts were proclaimed at periods of calamity (Jer. 36:9; Joel 1:14), the object being to chasten the soul (Ps. 35:13; 69:10) and make the voice heard in heaven (Isa. 58:3, 4). The public fast signified that a load of guilt was resting on the people, for which they humbled themselves before God (I Sam. 7:6). True fasting must not be confined to externals, but involves abstinence from iniquity and illicit pleasures (Isa., ch. 58). In Zechariah's days there were stated fasts in the 4th, 5th, 7th, and 10th months (Zech. 8:19), to commemorate the commencement of the siege of Jerusalem in the 10th month (II Kings 25:1), its capture in the 4th month (II Kings 25:3, 4; Jer. 52:6, 7), the destruction of the Temple in the 5th month (II Kings 25:8, 9), and the murder of Gedaliah and the Jews that were with him in the 7th month (v. 25). Anna served God with fasting (Luke 2:37). The Pharisee did so twice in the week (Luke 18:12). When religious formalists fasted, they sometimes ostentatiously put on a sad countenance. This practice was denounced in the Sermon on the Mount (Matt. 6:16–18). The disciples of John the Baptist fasted; those of our Lord did not, at least while he was among them (Matt. 9:14, 15; Mark 2:18–20; Luke 5:33–35), but afterward in certain circumstances they did so (Acts 13:3; 14:23).

There are no injunctions laid upon Christians to fast; and the revisers, on the ground of textual criticism, have removed the word from Matt. 17:21; Mark 9:29; Acts 10:30; I Cor. 7:5.

Fat. 1. Abel offered the fat of the firstlings of his flock to Jehovah (Gen. 4:4; cf. Num. 18:17). The principle was laid down in the Mosaic Law that to the Lord belongs all the fat of sacrificial animals (Lev. 3:16; 7:23, 25). Neither it nor the blood was eaten (ch. 3:17), but was burned as an offering to Jehovah (Ex. 29:13, 22; Lev. 3:3–5; 4:8–10); for a sweet savor unto Jehovah (ch. 4:31). In view of the settlement in Canaan and the remoteness of the majority of the people from the altar, this provision was apparently abolished with respect to animals slain solely for food (Deut. 12:15, 16, 21–24), the animals of the flock and herd being eaten as were nonsacrificial animals.
2. A wine vat (A.V., Joel 2:24; Isa. 63:2).

Fa'ther. 1. The immediate progenitor of a person (Gen. 42:13), or grandfather (ch. 28:13), or more remote ancestor (ch. 17:4). See PARENTS.
2. The founder of an occupation or a social group (Gen. 4:20). The ancestor or head, or one of the heads, of the inhabitants of a town (I Chron. 2:51; 4:14, 18).
3. One who acts toward another with paternal kindness and wisdom (Gen. 45:8; Judg. 17:10; 18:19). A title of respect and honor bestowed upon an authorized teacher, especially when aged (I Sam. 10:12; II Kings 2:12), and upon royal advisers and prime ministers (Gen. 45:8).
4. God, either as the Creator of the human race (Mal. 2:10; Jos. *Antiq.* iv. 8, 24; cf. Acts 17:28), or as the begetter and loving guardian of his spiritual children (Rom. 8:15; Gal. 4:6), or as standing in a more mysterious relation to Jesus (Matt. 11:26; Mark 14:36; Luke 22:42). See GOD.

Fath'om. A measure much used in reckoning depth of water (Acts 27:28). It is the rendering of Gr. *orguia*, which denotes the length of the outstretched arms, and was estimated at 4 cubits or 24 palms (Herod. ii. 149). The English fathom is 6 feet.

Feast. 1. A sumptuous meal attended by mirth and joyfulness (Dan. 5:1).

2. A time set apart by the canons of some religions for sacred joy. Besides the appointed seasons, called feasts or set feasts in the Eng. versions (Lev. 23:2, R.V. marg.), which included the weekly Sabbath, the memorial of trumpet-blowing on the 1st day of the 7th month, and the Day of Atonement on the 10th day of that month (Lev. 23:3, 24, 27), the Mosaic Law enjoined 3 annual celebrations called feasts or festivals. They were the passover on the evening of the 14th day of the 1st month, with the accompanying feast of unleavened bread commencing on the 15th and lasting 7 days (Lev. 23:5-8); the feast of weeks, called also feast of harvest and day of first fruits (Ex. 23:16; 34:22; Num. 28:26), and in later times, because celebrated on the 50th day after the passover, Pentecost (Acts 2:1); and the feast of tabernacles or ingathering, which commenced on the 15th day of the 7th month and continued for 7 or 8 days (Lev. 23:34-44). These 3 annual festivals were deemed so important that when they came every adult male not incapacitated by disease or infirmity was required to appear before the Lord at the sanctuary (Ex. 23:17; Deut. 16:16). For further description of these feasts, see the appropriate articles. As Jesus desired "to fulfil all righteousness," it may be assumed that he was customarily present at Jerusalem 3 times a year, on the occasions of the 3 festivals (Matt. 26:17; Mark 14:12; Luke 22:8; John 2:23; 7:2-37; 13:1). In addition to the festivals prescribed by the law, a festival called Purim was instituted to commemorate annually, on the 14th and 15th of Adar, the deliverance of the Jews from the plot of Haman (Esth. 9:21-28). Later still the festival of dedication was appointed, which was instituted by Judas Maccabaeus, to be celebrated annually for 8 days, from the 25th day of Chislev, in commemoration of the rededication of the Temple after its pollution by the agents of Antiochus Epiphanes (I Macc. 4:41-59; John 10:22). The Lord's Supper, instituted by Christ, or more broadly the Christian's life of faith, is also a feast (I Cor. 5:8).

Fe'lix (fē'lĭks) [Lat., happy]. A freedman of the emperor Claudius, who was appointed procurator of Judea. The date of his appointment to office in Palestine is disputed. Cumanus succeeded the procurator Tiberius Alexander in A.D. 48 (Jos. *Antiq.* xx. 5, 2). According to Tacitus, Cumanus governed Galilee, and Felix ruled part of Samaria until, on the deposition of Cumanus, he was appointed procurator of the whole province by Quadratus, governor of Syria. Josephus, who was a boy in Jerusalem in A.D. 48, and became historian of the Jews, represents Cumanus as procurator of Judea, and states that Felix was sent as successor of Cumanus by the emperor Claudius to administer the affairs of Judea in 52 (Jos. *Antiq.* xx. 7, 1; *War* ii. 12, 8). Probably Cumanus and Felix exercised a joint procuratorship, with Cumanus higher in authority. In this article A.D. 52 is assumed as the date of his sole procuratorship in Judea. He seems to have obtained this appointment partly through the influence of his brother Pallas, who was a great man at the court of Claudius. Nero, the successor of Claudius, transferred 4 Galilean cities from Felix to Agrippa. Felix was cruel and tyrannical, and in the exercise of power showed the disposition of a slave (Tacitus *Hist.* v. 9; *Ann.* xii.

54). Jonathan, the high priest, had supported the appointment of Felix to the procuratorship, but displeased Felix by the fidelity with which he counseled him regarding his government of the Jews. Jonathan was murdered by the robbers, the so-called Assassins, who according to Josephus were encouraged by Felix. Felix undertook to suppress the robbers, who had become the terror of Judea. He captured many of them and crucified the ordinary sort. Their leader, Eleazar, however, had been sent to Rome before the assassination of Jonathan (Jos. *Antiq.* xx. 8, 5; *War* ii. 13, 2). Next, false prophets arose and led people in multitudes into the wilderness, where they were told God would show them the signals of liberty. Felix, believing these gatherings in the wilderness to be the commencement of revolt, attacked the people present and slew them in large numbers (Jos. *War* ii. 13, 4). An Egyptian soon afterward made his appearance as a prophet and led out a great mob to the Mount of Olives, under the pretense that they would see the walls of Jerusalem fall down, allowing them to enter the city. Felix attacked them with troops, slew about 400 and took about 200 prisoners. The Egyptian escaped. His insurrection was in A.D. 55; and when about 5 years later the riot about Paul arose, the Roman commandant at Jerusalem suspected that the apostle was the Egyptian back again to excite fresh troubles (Acts 21:38; Jos. *Antiq.* xx. 8, 6). Paul, arrested on the false charge of profaning the Temple, was sent for protection from Jewish violence to Caesarea, the seat of the Roman government for Judea (Acts 23:26, 33), and the trial took place before Felix (ch. 24:1-23). Felix' wife Drusilla, a Jewess, whom he had seduced from her lawful husband (Jos. *Antiq.* xx. 7, 1, 2), was present at an interview when Paul reasoned of righteousness, temperance, and judgment to come, with such power that Felix trembled. He did not repent, however. Nor did he set Paul free, for he hoped that his prisoner would buy freedom (Acts 24:24-26). On going out of office he left the apostle bound in order to please the Jews (Acts 24:27). This favor did not, however, prevent them from complaining of him after he had ceased to be procurator and returned to Rome, about A.D. 60. They represented that he had not acted well in the recent riots between Jews and Syrians at Caesarea, and he would have been punished by Nero had not the powerful intercession of his brother Pallas, who was a favorite with the reigning emperor, been exerted in his favor (Jos. *Antiq.* xx. 8, 9; cf. 8, 7; *War* ii. 13, 7). He was succeeded in the procuratorship by Porcius Festus.

Fenced Cit'ies. See FORTIFIED CITIES.

Fer'ret. See GECKO.

Fes'tus (fĕs'tŭs) [Lat., festal, joyful]. Porcius Festus, who succeeded Felix as procurator of Judea in the reign of Nero, while Pallas was still the emperor's favorite and Burrus was still alive (Jos. *Antiq.* xx. 8, 9). Pallas was put to death in A.D. 62, and Burrus died not later than February of the same year. Two years before the arrival of Festus, Paul could say that Felix had been for many years a judge unto the nation (Acts 24:10, 27). If the procuratorship of Felix be reckoned from A.D. 48 (see FELIX), he would have been many years in office in Palestine in A.D. 54 or 55, and Festus may have succeeded him in 55 or 56, the 2d and 3d years of Nero respectively. This date is adopted by some authorities, with the result of putting the dates of important events in Paul's life, among others his imprisonment, 4 or 5 years earlier than the date generally accepted by leading investigators who date Felix' accession in 52 and Festus' appointment in 60. Festus fell on troublous times. The Assassins were murdering and pillaging. An impostor led a crowd of adherents into the wilderness, where the forces of Festus routed them with great slaughter. King Agrippa built a dining room in the royal palace of Jerusalem, and its windows overlooked the courts of the Temple. The Jews were annoyed, and built a wall to block the view. But the wall prevented the Roman guards also from seeing the inner courts, and Festus ordered its demolition. On appeal to Nero, however, it was allowed to remain (Jos. *Antiq.* xx. 8, 11). The character of Festus contrasts favorably with that of Felix (Jos. *War* ii. 14, 1). He reinvestigated Paul's case, and was satisfied of his innocence; but, in attempting to please the Jews, he suggested that the apostle be tried at Jerusalem. It was against this injudicious proposal that Paul appealed to Caesar (Acts, chs. 25 ; 26). Festus died at his post, and was succeeded, about A.D. 62, by Albinus, who is not mentioned in the Scripture narrative (Jos. *Antiq.* xx. 9, 1).

Fe'ver. A disease, or rather a genus of diseases, attended by dryness and heat of the body, with consequent thirst, a high pulse, and other symptoms. Fever is the rendering of Heb. *ḳaddaḥath*, burning (Lev. 26 :16, in A.V. burning ague ; Deut. 28 :22). In the latter passage it is associated with inflammation and fiery heat, both febrile symptoms. Fever is likewise the correct rendering of Gr. *pyretos*, from *pyr,* fire (Matt. 8 :15 ; Luke 4 :38 ; John 4 :52 ; Acts 28 :8). Galen and the Greek physicians divided fevers into greater and lesser. Luke in the passage quoted does so also, as might be expected from one who was himself a medical man. When the sword, the famine, and the pestilence are mentioned in this order of succession, the pestilence was probably typhus fever.

Field. In Biblical usage, unenclosed ground, whether pasture or tillage (Gen. 37 :7, 14–16), of whatever extent, from a small area to the territory of a people (Gen. 14 :7, R.V. marg. ; 23 :9 ; Ruth 1 :6, rendered country ; Matt. 6 :28 ; 13 :24). Boundaries, when artificially marked, were indicated by stones (cf. Deut. 19 :14).

Fig and **Fig Tree.** A tree producing good fruit (Judg. 9 :10) and the fruit itself (Num. 13 :23), both called *te'ēnāh* in Heb., while in Gr. the tree is *sykē* and the fruit *sykon*. The tree is native in w. Asia. The young tree does not bear fruit unless the ground is cultivated (Luke 13 :6–9), and old trees speedily degenerate and fail when neglected (Prov. 27 :18). The young fruit appears in spring before the

Branch of a Fig Tree

leaves open, on branches of the last year's growth ; it is the green fig (S. of Sol. 2 :13). If blown from the tree (Rev. 6 :13), it is eaten, though immature. If green fruit is not on the tree when the leaves have opened, no figs will be borne. The first ripe fruit is ready in June, in favored localities earlier (Isa. 28 :4 ; Jos. *War* iii. 10, 8). The late figs grow on the new wood, keep appearing during the season, and are ripe from August onward. They are dried for preservation, pressed into cakes, and form a staple article of food (I Sam. 25 :18 ; 30 :12). The tree was highly prized, and is often mentioned along with the vine (Deut. 8 :8 ; Ps. 105 :33 ; Jer. 5 :17 ; Joel 1 :12), and to sit under one's vine and one's fig tree was the symbol of prosperity and security (I Kings 4 :25 ; Micah 4 :4 ; Zech. 3 :10). The barren fig tree of our Lord's parable meant the Jewish nation. Figs were used in medicine, and there is mention of their employment as a poultice (II Kings 20 :7).

Fir and **Fir Tree.** The rendering of Heb. *berōsh,* Aram. *berōth* (II Sam. 6 :5 ; S. of Sol. 1 :17) ; R.V. marg., cypress. The tree grew with the cedar in Lebanon (I Kings 5 :8, 10 ; Isa. 14 :8 ; 37 :24 ; 60 :13 ; Zech. 11 :2). It was used for the woodwork of Solomon's Temple along with cedar (I Kings 5 :8, 10 ; 6 :15, 34 ; II Chron. 2 :8 ; 3 :5), for the planks of ships (Ezek. 27 :5), for spears (Nahum 2 :3), and for musical instruments (II Sam. 6 :5). It belongs to the *Coniferae* or pine family. The only true fir of the region is *Abies cilicica*. It grows on the higher parts of Lebanon and in the mountains n., attaining a height of from 30 to 75 feet. The cypress (*Cupressus sempervirens*) is a tall tree, from 20 to 60 or 75 feet. The wood is reddish yellow, pleasant to the smell, and durable. It was much used for cabinet work. It is extensively planted in burial grounds in the East, for which its slender pyramidal form and gracefulness render it well-adapted. See CYPRESS 2. The Syrian or Aleppo pine (*Pinus halepensis*) is found in the mountains of w. Palestine, and is one of the characteristic trees of the lower Lebanon. It is inferior in size to the fir and the cypress. The stone pine (*Pinus maritima*) grows on the coast and in sandy plains, but is not common. In Gilead there are extensive forests of *Pinus carica* on the highest mountains above the line where the evergreen oaks cease. A tall, fragrant juniper (*Juniperus excelsa*) grows abundantly on Lebanon. For Isa. 44 :14, see ASH.

Fire. Fire was found to be indispensable (Ecclus. 39 :26). It was used in the arts (Gen. 4 :22), in the preparation of food (Ex. 16 :23 ; Isa. 44 :16), and for warmth (Jer. 36 :22 ; John 18 :18 ; Acts 28 :2). Offerings were made to Jehovah by fire (Gen. 8 :20). The fire carried, as it were, the sacrifice to God, who took delight in the offering, or, to speak figuratively, smelled a sweet savor (Gen. 8 :21). The offerer kindled the fire himself (ch. 22 :6). Moses offered burnt offerings on the great altar newly erected (Ex. 40 :29), but at the conclusion of the consecration of Aaron and his sons to the priesthood, fire came forth from the presence of Jehovah and consumed the sacrifice (Lev. 9 :24). God accepted and appropriated the offering. This fire was not allowed to go out (ch. 6 :9–13). Likewise at the dedication of the Temple and the new altar, fire came from heaven and consumed the sacrifice (II Chron. 7 :1). On other occasions also God indicated his acceptance of a sacrifice by causing it to kindle (Judg. 6 :21 ; I Kings 18 :23, 24 ; I Chron. 21 :26). Among the heathen there were fire worshipers (Wisd. of Sol. 13 :2). The worshipers of Molech and some other idolaters burnt their children in the fire as an act of piety (II Kings 16:3; 21:6; Jer. 7:31; Ezek. 16:20, 21).

Fire Pan. A pan made of brass, gold, or silver (Ex. 27:3; I Kings 7:50; II Kings 25:15), and used for carrying fire (Lev. 16:12, censer).

Fir'kin. A measure of capacity (John 2:6), the rendering of Gr. *metrētēs*, which held approximately 9 gallons, American standard.

Fir'ma·ment. The sky or heaven (Gen. 1:8), an expanse beaten out as it were, if we employ the figure embodied in the Heb. word (cf. Ezek. 1:22), which divided the primeval watery mass (Gen. 1:6), so that part of the waters were above it and others were below it (ch. 1:7; Ps. 148:4). The stars and planets were placed in it (Gen. 1:14, 17). The heavens, and presumably the firmament, are compared to a tent spread above the earth (Ps. 104:2; Isa. 40:22), are likened in strength to a molten mirror (Job 37:18), and are spoken of as if having windows, through which the rain pours and God's blessings descend (Gen. 7:11; II Kings 7:2; Ps. 78:23). This conception was current in ancient Semitic thought.

First'-born' or **First'ling,** the former being used chiefly of men, the latter always of beasts. To the first-born offspring of men and animals God the giver has the first claim (cf. Gen. 4:4). Among the Israelites an additional reason existed in the fact that Jehovah had freed the people from Egyptian bondage. In the 10th and last plague of Egypt the first-born of the Egyptians were slain, while the first-born of the Israelites were preserved by sprinkling blood on the lintels and doorposts of the houses within which they resided (Ex. 12:12, 13, 23, 29). Saved in this manner, they became consecrated to Jehovah. Every first-born male of man and beast was holy to the Lord (chs. 13:2; 34:19), and could not be used by man (Lev. 27:26), but belonged to the sanctuary for sacrifice; the first-born of man, however, was redeemed (Ex. 13:13, 15; 34:20; cf. Lev. 27:6). On this occasion he was brought to the sanctuary and presented to Jehovah (Luke 2:22; cf. Num. 18:15). The Levites were afterward substituted for the Israelite first-born (Num. 3:12, 41, 46; 8:13–19; cf. Ex. 32:26–29) and served at the sanctuary. Those of animals also, against which the 10th plague was partly directed, became similarly consecrated to Jehovah, but there were distinctions among them. The firstling of clean animals was sacrificed. Unclean animals, of which the ass is named as representative, either had the neck broken or were replaced by a lamb (Ex. 13:13, 15; 22:29, 30; 34:20). On the establishment of the priesthood at Sinai, the disposition of these animals was specified. The fat of the clean animal was burned and the flesh was given to the priest. The unclean animal was redeemed or sold (Lev. 27:27; Num. 18:15–18). Later, in view of the new circumstances in which it was foreseen that the people would be placed in Palestine, and the inconvenience and expense of the journey to the sanctuary, a delay was authorized in presenting the firstling at the house of God. The firstling might be kept beyond the 8 days originally prescribed until the time of an annual festival; and the flesh, instead of falling as a perquisite to the priest, was given to the pilgrim who brought the animal, and to his family, to eat at the sanctuary (Deut. 15:19, 20). But defective animals were eaten at home without religious ceremony (vs. 21–23).

For the legal privileges of the first-born son, see BIRTHRIGHT.

First Fruits. The fruits first ripe, the plucking of which was an earnest of the coming harvest. First fruits were to be given as an offering to Jehovah: on behalf of the nation, a sheaf at the feast of unleavened bread and two loaves at the feast of weeks (Lev. 23:10, 17); and by individuals (Ex. 23:19; Deut. 26:1–11). The term is used figuratively in Rom. 8:23; 11:16; 16:5; I Cor. 15:20, 23; 16:15; James 1:18; Rev. 14:4. See FIRSTBORN.

Fish'ing. There was fishing in Egypt in the main channel of the Nile and in the several branches into which it separates before reaching the Mediterranean (Isa. 19:8), and the Israelites when in bondage in Egypt ate fish freely (Num. 11:5). The fishing along the

Fishing with the Hook in Ancient Egypt

Mediterranean coast of Palestine was largely in the hands of the Tyrians and Sidonians in the n. (Neh. 13:16) and the Philistines in the s. To the Israelites belonged the Sea of Galilee, which was their chief fishing ground. Tristram enumerates 22 species of fish in its

Fishing with a Net

waters, many of which pass down the Jordan also; but any that reach the Dead Sea die in its briny water. Fish were on sale in Jerusalem (II Chron. 33:14; Neh. 13:16). For fishing, lines, hooks, and spears were used (Job 41:1, 7; Isa. 19:8; Amos 4:2; Matt. 17:27), and nets were cast from boats (Luke 5:4–7).

Fitch [variant of Eng. vetch]. A tare (*Vicia*), an herb much cultivated as a forage

plant (Isa. 28:25, 27, Heb. *ḳeṣaḥ*). The plant
so designated was sown broadcast; and when
its fruits were ripe, they were beaten out with
a staff to separate the seeds. R.V. marg.
prefers black cummin (*Nigella sativa*), and
considers the plant to have been what is now
called, from its fennel-like leaves, fennel
flower. It is of the crowfoot or buttercup order (*Ranunculaceae*). It is a foot and a half
high, with yellow or, more rarely, blue petals,
many stamens, and several seed vessels, with
numerous black acrid and aromatic seeds,
which are used in the East for seasoning
dishes and as a carminative.

Hebrew *kussemeth* is likewise translated
fitch in Ezek. 4:9, A.V.; but elsewhere in A.V.
is rendered rye. Everywhere in R.V. it is
translated spelt.

Flag. 1. The rendering of Heb. *'āḥū* in Job
8:11. R.V. marg. translates it reed-grass, and
also in the text of Gen. 41:2, where A.V. renders it meadow. It was a water plant and
grew, among other places, on the edge of the
Nile. It is not likely that it was the flag,
which is an iris, with 3 brightly colored
petals. It seems to have been the Egyptian
designation for the crowded mass of water
plants, rushes, reeds, sedges found along the
margin of the Nile.

2. The rendering of *sûph* (Ex. 2:3, 5; Isa.
19:6), a plant growing by the brink of the
Nile. It also grew in salt water (Jonah 2:5,
where it is rendered "weeds"). The Red Sea in
Heb. is called the Sea of Suph. The word denotes aquatic vegetation, whether seaweeds or
fresh water reeds and sedges.

Flag'on. 1. A vessel for holding liquids (Isa.
22:24, in Heb. *nēbel*).

2. The rendering in A.V. of Heb. *'ashīshāh*,
something pressed closely together (II Sam.
6:19; I Chron. 16:3; S. of Sol. 2:5; Hos. 3:1).
R.V. correctly translates it cake of raisins.

Flax. The rendering of Heb. *pēsheth* and
pishtāh and of Gr. *linon* (cf. Isa. 42:3 with Matt.
12:20). It was a plant cultivated in Egypt
and elsewhere (Ex. 9:31). It had stalks,
which were spread on flat roofs of houses and
dried by exposure to the heat of the sun (Josh.
2:6). Its fibers were fine (Isa. 19:9), and
were woven like wool (Prov. 31:13; cf. Hos.
2:5). It is undoubtedly the flax plant (*Linum
usitatissimum*), the type of the botanical order *Linaceae*, or flaxworts. It is a small plant,
with solitary erect stems, 5 sepals, 5 fugitive
petals, with 5 perfect and as many rudimentary stamens. It is now found only in a state
of cultivation. The woody fiber of the bark
furnishes the flax fiber of which linen is
woven, and the seeds constitute the linseed of
commerce, valued on account of its oil.

Flea. An insect, called in Heb. *par'ōsh* (I
Sam. 24:14; 26:20). The species is a universal pest in Palestine; so much so that it has
become a popular saying that the king of the
fleas has his court at Tiberias.

Flesh. 1. The muscles of the animal body,
whether of man, beast, bird, or fish; or, less
precisely, all its softer parts (Gen. 40:19; Ex.
12:8; 16:8; Lev. 21:5; Job 10:11; Luke 24:
39; I Cor. 15:39). It is distinct from the
spirit (Job 14:22; Isa. 10:18, Heb.; 31:3;
Matt. 26:41; Col. 2:5).

2. All beings possessed of flesh, man and
the inferior animals, especially man (Gen.
6:13, 19; 8:17; Acts 2:17; Rom. 3:20; I Cor.
1:29).

3. Human nature deprived of the Spirit of
God, dominated by the appetites and obeyed
by the mind (Rom. 7:5; 8:5–7; II Cor. 7:1;
Gal. 5:16–21; II Peter 2:10), thus including
the whole unregenerated and unsanctified nature of man (Rom. 8:8, 9; cf. John 3:6).

Flint. In Scripture, any hard or intractable
rock (Deut. 8:15; 32:13; Ps. 114:8); and
hence figuratively, uncompromising firmness
in the discharge of duty (Isa. 50:7; Ezek.
3:9). In it the miner sinks his shaft in quest
of gold (Job 28:9, R.V.). Broken fragments
were used as rude knives (R.V., Ex. 4:25;
Josh. 5:2, where in Heb. the generic word for
rock is used).

Flood. A stream, especially a great stream
(Job 14:11; 28:11, A.V.), as the Nile in its
inundations (Jer. 46:7; Amos 8:8, A.V.), the
Euphrates (Josh. 24:2, A.V.), the Jordan (Ps.
66:6, A.V.). An inundation (Dan. 9:26;
Nahum 1:8; Matt. 7:25, 27; Luke 6:48). A
great restless mass of water; the sea and its
currents (Ps. 24:2; Jonah 2:3).

Specially, the Deluge in the time of Noah.
It was sent as a divine judgment on the antediluvians for their wickedness (Gen. 6:5–13).
Secondary causes were employed to bring on
the catastrophe. Two are mentioned: the
fountains of the great deep were broken up,
and the windows of heaven were opened. Thus
part of the water was that of the ocean, the
rest was produced by a downpour of rain continuing 40 days and nights (ch. 7:11, 12).

Coin of Apamea, Representing Noah and the Ark

All the high mountains under the whole
heaven were covered, 15 cubits upward the
waters prevailed, and all flesh died that moved
on the earth, man, bird, beast, and creeping
thing. Noah only was left and they that were
with him in the ark (ch. 7:19–23); see ARK 1.
The waters prevailed 150 days, until at length
the ark rested on the mountains of Ararat.
Two and a half months later the tops of the
mountains were seen (ch. 8:3–5). Three
months later, after investigating the state of
the water by means of birds which he sent
forth, on the 1st day of the 1st month Noah
removed the covering from the ark and saw
that the face of the ground was dried; but
8 weeks more elapsed before God gave
command to go forth from the ark (ch. 8:13–
15). The chronology of the flood according to
Genesis is given on the following page.

As is now generally known, the account of
the Flood was handed down by tradition. The
description originated with eyewitnesses. Its
language must be understood in the sense
which it bore to the authors and promulga-
tors of the narrative centuries before the days
of Moses. The extent of the Flood cannot be
determined from the account of it which has
been transmitted. The Deluge may have been
universal and covered the globe, or it may
have been confined to a locality of greater
or less extent. All the mountains under the
whole heaven, that is within the horizon of the
inmates of the ark as they drifted on the
waters, were covered (cf. the employment of
similar language in Col. 1:23). The explanation of a local flood in the Tigris-Euphrates
valley would satisfy the Biblical account, since

Gen. 7:4, 10.	COMMAND TO BEGIN EMBARKING THE ANIMALS.	2d mo.	10th day.
7:11.	ENTRANCE OF NOAH INTO THE ARK, and in the evening, as related by the Babylonian tradition, bursting of the storm.	2d mo.	17th day.
7:12.	Rain 40 days and 40 nights, so that RAIN CEASED toward evening.	3d mo.	27th day.
7:24.	The waters prevailed on the earth		
8:3.	150 days, so that the		
8:4.	ARK STRANDED.	7th mo.	17th day.
	The waters decreased continually until		
8:5.	TOPS OF THE MOUNTAINS VISIBLE.	10th mo.	1st day.
8:6.	After seeing the mountaintops, Noah waited 40 days; expecting that, as the rain had fallen 40 days, the waters would perhaps abate from the ground in 40 days; and then (or on the following day) the		
8:7.	RAVEN RELEASED, which returned not.	11th mo.	11th (or 12th) day.
	After 7 days (cf. "yet other," v. 10) a		
8:8.	DOVE RELEASED, which returned.	11th mo.	18th (or 19th) day.
	After yet other 7 days, the		
8:10.	DOVE RELEASED, which returned with olive leaf. So Noah knew that the waters were abated from off the earth.	11th mo.	25th (or 26th) day.
	After yet other 7 days, a third time the		
8:12.	DOVE RELEASED, which did not return, since food and shelter were now found outside the ark.	12th mo.	2d (or 3d) day.
	Notwithstanding these favorable indications, Noah did not leave the ark, but waited for God's command. After nearly a month, on the 1st day of the 1st month		
8:13.	NOAH REMOVED THE COVERING OF THE ARK, and saw that the waters were dried up and the face of the ground was dried.	1st mo.	1st day.
	But Noah still awaited God's bidding, and 8 weeks later, the earth being dry, God gave the		
8:14, 15.	COMMAND TO GO FORTH FROM THE ARK.	2d mo.	27th day.

the first home of man was in that region and the Deluge is recorded in the early chapters of Genesis. The purpose of the Flood was to destroy the corrupt race of man (Gen. 6:7, 13, 17; 7:4), and with man all animals dependent upon the existence of dry land were involved in destruction. This was also the result as discerned by those who were saved in the ark (ch. 7:21–23), and as confirmed by their descendants when they migrated in the earth. They met no survivors. They found the world uninhabited. Noah had been instructed to take male and female of every kind of animal, and to gather food for them (ch. 6:20, 21). The language of the command was intended to be understood in its usual sense, as any man of that age would understand it. Noah doubtless took specimens of every animal of which he had knowledge and food suitable for them; but there is no evidence that he believed himself to be commanded to seek for species as yet unknown, or if under supernatural impulse the animals unsought came to him (as some would unnecessarily interpret ch. 7:8, 9), to gather peculiar food and provide peculiar shelter for strange animals of different kinds and from different climes.

The tradition of the Flood was current among the people from whom the Hebrews sprang. In the ancestral home of Abraham (Sumer and Akkad) the Flood was remembered as a great crisis in human history. Eight rulers are mentioned in the Sumerian list of kings. Then follows this statement: "The flood swept thereover. After the flood had swept thereover, when the kingship was lowered from heaven, the kingship was in Kish." Thereupon the list of kings is resumed.

Archaeological excavations have shown the destruction wrought by floods in Sumer and Akkad to be a fact. At Kish a flood sediment (averaging a thickness of 1 foot) covered uniformly all that constituted the civilization of that city. The foundations of the buildings, however, were not affected by the overflow of the river, and the remains below and above the flood deposit reveal a continuous Sumerian civilization. Kish, it seems, was temporarily abandoned. When the civil and religious classes returned to the site of the city, they possessed the new stage of culture represented in the finds above the flood level. The Kish flood deposit lies shortly above the Jemdet Nasr period (toward the end of 4th millennium B.C.). There is also evidence of a deluge at Shuruppak during the same period. There is, however, more spectacular evidence of a flood at Ur. During 1927–1929 Woolley worked on a prehistoric graveyard at Ur. In the course of this excavation, there was found a layer of clay 8 feet thick, the texture of which showed that it had been deposited there by the water. Below this clay were definite remains of an earlier civilization. It certainly may be inferred that a flood of unusual magnitude was required to leave such a deposit. This deluge was not the same as that of Kish and Shuruppak, but took place at an earlier period, between al-Ubaid I and II. Although all these discoveries have been very interesting, we do not have sufficient evidence to equate any one of these floods with that of Genesis; they prove, however, that civilization was interrupted at several places and at different periods by floods.

The Sumerians, Babylonians, and Assyrians had slightly divergent traditions. The story, as current in Babylonia in the time of Alexander the Great, was recorded by Berosus (Jos. Antiq. i. 3, 6; Apion i. 19), and is quoted in full by the church historian Eusebius. Berosus lists 10 antediluvian kings. Two of his names are corruptions of one Sumerian name, En-men-lu-Anna. The last one in his list is Xisouthros, the hero of the flood, who lived at Sippar. Xisouthros was commanded to build a boat, into which he took his family and near friends and fowls and quadrupeds, together with provisions. After the rain had ceased, he released some birds which returned to the ship. After some days he let them go again, and they returned with their feet soiled with clay. After the 3d release the birds did not return. The ship had been grounded in Armenia, and so Xisouthros removed a part of the side of the ship and left with his wife, daughter, and the pilot. An altar was erected and sacrifice was offered. The rest of the persons in the ship left after these 4 had departed.

The oldest account of the flood is recorded in a Sumerian version, which has been preserved in fragmentary form. It probably was written in the time of the dynasty of Isin, but not later than the 1st dynasty of Babylon (i.e., somewhere between 1894 and 1595 B.C.). According to this narrative "the deluge swept over the land for seven days and seven nights." The hero of the flood was Zi-u-sud-ra, who had found safety in a ship, sacrificed after it was all over, and finally was made immortal by the gods.

The most complete Babylonian account is found in the Gilgamesh epic. The text, as we have it, comes from the library of Ashurbanipal (669-626 B.C.) but it was copied from much older originals. This epic was written on 12 tablets, of which the 11th is devoted to the flood.

Gilgamesh was a king of Uruk (Erech). His friend Engidu died and he was anxious to find a means of restoring him to life. He knew that Ut-napishtim, who survived the flood, had attained immortality, and so with Ur-Shanabi, the sailor of Ut-napishtim, he crossed in 3 days the sea, which under ordinary circumstances required a month and a half. Gilgamesh asked Ut-napishtim how he attained endless life, and in the ensuing conversation is related the history of the deluge. There was a city Shuruppak on the Euphrates, and the gods resolved to send a flood. So the god of wisdom, Ea, repeated their decision to a reed hut:

"O reed hut, reed hut, O wall, wall,
  O reed hut hearken, O wall attend!
  O man of Shuruppak, son of Ubar-Tutu,
  Pull down thy house, build a ship,
  Leave thy possessions, take thought for thy life . . ."

It seems that Ut-napishtim was sleeping at the time in the hut and that he received the warning in a dream (cf. Gen. 6:8, 13, 14, 17). So he built a boat in the form of a cube, with 120 cubits as each of its 3 dimensions; it was 6 stories high (cf. Gen. 6:15, 16). He divided it on the outside into 7 parts and in its interior into 9 parts; he pitched it with 3 sars of bitumen on the outside and with the same amount on the inside (cf. ch. 6:14). Oil was brought in for food and for the libation (cf. ch. 6:21). He filled the ship with gold and silver, and he also took in his family and household, craftsmen, and the beasts of the field (cf. chs. 6:18–22; 7:1–3, 7–9, 13–16). When the appointed time approached, in the evening there appeared a heavy rainstorm. Ut-napishtim embarked and closed the door (cf. ch. 7:16b). At dawn there came a black cloud up from the horizon, and Adad thundered within it. While some gods went as messengers over mountains and valleys, the rain descended (cf. ch. 7:11). The flood covered the mountains, and no more were people recognized in heaven (cf. ch. 7:18, 19). At this point the gods became afraid:

"The gods were frightened at the deluge,
  They fled, they climbed to the highest heaven;
  The gods crouched like a dog, they lay down by the walls.
  Ishtar cried like a woman in travail. . . .
  The gods sat bowed and weeping."

The wind blew for 6 days and nights, and the tempest overwhelmed the land, but abated on the 7th (cf. chs. 7:4, 10, 12, 17, 24; 8:1 seq.). Ut-napishtim says:

"I looked upon the sea, the roaring was stilled,
  And all mankind was turned to clay"

(cf. ch. 7:21–23). He then opened the window (cf. chs. 6:16; 8:6) and looked in all directions (cf. ch. 8:13). After 12 days an island appeared, and finally the ship was grounded upon Mount Nisir (cf. ch. 8: 4, 5). Seven days later Ut-napishtim sent forth a dove which came back; then he released a swallow, which also returned. Finally he let go a raven. In telling about this, he says:

"The raven went out, the diminution of the waters it saw;
  It alighted, it waded about, it croaked, it did not come back"

(cf. ch. 8:7–12).

Thereupon Ut-napishtim sent everything forth to the 4 quarters of heaven (cf. ch. 8: 14–19) and sacrificed upon the mountain peak (cf. v. 20). He arranged the sacrificial vessels by sevens and piled beneath them reeds, cedar wood, and myrtle. The gods apparently were pleased, for he says:

"The gods smelled the savor,
  The gods smelled the sweet savor,
  The gods gathered like flies over the sacrificer"

(cf. ch. 8:21). In the end it seems that the gods did not approve of the deluge; Ishtar says about Enlil:

"For he was not wise; he sent the deluge,
  And numbered my people for destruction."

And Ea said to Enlil:

"How, how couldest thou without thought send a deluge?
  On the sinner let his sin rest,
  On the wrongdoer rest his misdeed.
  Forbear, let it not be done, have mercy [that men perish not]"

(cf. chs. 8:21, 22; 9:11–17).

Then Ea, having gone on board the ship, brought forth Ut-napishtim and his wife. He blessed them (cf. ch. 9:1–3, 7) and bestowed immortality upon them.

It is quite apparent that the Hebrew account has much in common with the Babylonian, and perhaps both go back to a common source. Yet the name Noah has its closest parallel in a Hurrian fragment, where he is called Naḫ-molel. The origin of viticulture (cf. ch. 9:20), which has no counterpart in Babylonia, is appropriate to a Hurrian source. While the similarities are apparent, the differences are still more remarkable. Although we are dealing with a prehistoric period and therefore with traditions, a spirit which is unique in literature breathes through this O.T. account. The Babylonian account is polytheistic, materialistic, and in many respects crude; it reflects a low conception of divinity. In the O.T. narrative, on the other hand, we have monotheism and a God who hates iniquity, transgression, and sin. The incident of the Flood, as related in Genesis, has ethical and spiritual meaning. God works among men; he is interested in humanity and is merciful. In this early tradition are depicted the reward of righteousness and the possibility of fellowship with God. The inspiration of the O.T. account becomes self-evident in contrast with the Babylonian.

Flute. A musical instrument (Dan. 3:5); called in Aram. mashrôḳithâ, pipe. Pipes consisting of 1, 2, or more reeds were in use.

A flute or pipe, in Gr. aulos, was played in the house of mourning (Matt. 9:23, R.V.) and on occasions of joy (Rev. 18:22). See PIPE.

Flux. See DYSENTERY.

Fly. 1. A two-winged insect, one of the order *Diptera*, specially the domestic fly (*Musca domestica*). So troublesome are flies of various kinds in hot countries (Isa. 7:18; Eccl. 10:1) that the Ekronites worshiped a god Baal-zebub, lord of flies, who was supposed to avert them (II Kings 1:2).

2. The rendering of Heb. *'ārōb,* a voracious, biting insect of Egypt (Ex. 8:21; Ps. 105:31). It devoured (Ps. 78:45) and destroyed (Ex. 8:24 marg.). According to the LXX, the dog fly.

Fol'ly. The absence of wisdom, disregard of the true nature of things in their relation to man and God. Hence injudicious action or conduct (Prov. 15:21; Eccl. 1:17; 10:1; II Cor. 11:1, A.V.), and wickedness (Gen. 34: 7; Deut. 22:21; Josh. 7:15; Judg. 19:23; 20: 6).

Food. The food of the Hebrews, when they lived a simple nomadic life, consisted largely of bread and the products of the herd, such as milk, curds, and occasionally meat (Gen. 18:7, 8; Judg. 5:25). Wild honey was also eaten (Judg. 14:8, 9). When they adopted a settled life in Palestine, the products of garden, vineyard, and olive yard were added, such as lentils, cucumbers, beans (II Sam. 17:28), pomegranates, figs, grapes (Num. 13: 23; 20:5; Matt. 7:16). Sweet and sour wine were important articles of food. Fish were eaten, locusts also, and fowl and eggs (I Kings 4:23; Neh. 13:16; Matt. 4:18; Luke 11:12). A simple repast consisted of bread and lentils (Gen. 25:34) or other pottage (II Kings 4:38), or bread and wine (Gen. 14:18), or roasted grain and sour wine (Ruth 2:14). Abraham honored his unexpected guests with a more pretentious meal, consisting of butter and milk, cakes made of fine flour, and the flesh of a calf (Gen. 18:3–8). A greater variety of foods came on the tables of the rich and great (I Kings 4:22, 23; Neh. 5:18). See MEALS.

Fool. One destitute of understanding or wisdom (II Cor. 11:16), especially a wicked man; the idea is that nothing shows a greater want of understanding than for a man to commit wickedness. The greater the talents, the greater the responsibility, and consequently the folly of misusing them for evil ends (I Sam. 26:21; II Sam. 3:33; 13: 13; Ps. 14:1; cf. vs. 2, 3, etc.; Prov. 26:10; Matt. 5:22). See FOLLY, PHILOSOPHY, and WISDOM.

Fool'ish·ness. The same as folly (II Sam. 15:31; Prov. 22:15).

Foot'man. 1. A soldier who marches and fights on foot, in contradistinction to one on horseback (Num. 11:21; II Kings 13:7; I Chron. 18:4).

2. A runner (I Sam. 22:17, A.V.), one of the king's bodyguard. See RUNNERS.

For'eign·er, in A.V. usually stranger. A Gentile; a person belonging to another people than Israel and owning other allegiance than to Israel and Israel's God (Deut. 29:22), as the Egyptians (Ex. 2:22), Jebusites (Judg. 19:12), Philistines (II Sam. 15:19), Moabites, Ammonites, Edomites, Sidonians, Hittites (I Kings 11:1). As a technical term foreigner does not include: 1. Slaves bought with money and captives taken in war; for they were in the power of their masters and subject to the laws of Israel (Gen. 17:12; Ex. 21:20, 21. 2. Proselytes to the religion of Israel (Gen. 34:14–17; Isa. 56:6–8; Acts 2:10). 3. The so-called sojourners or strangers. See STRANGER. Israel was Jehovah's peculiar people (Deut. 14:1, 2); therefore idolatrous Canaanites specifically were not to be received into covenant relations of any sort (Ex. 23:32), and all foreigners were debarred from eating the passover (Ex. 12:43), entering the sanctuary (Ezek. 44:9; Acts 21:28; cf. Deut. 23:3, 7, 8), and ascending the throne as king (Deut. 17: 15). Intermarriage with them on equal terms was forbidden (Ex. 34:12, 16; Deut. 7:3; Josh. 23:12, specifically Canaanites; cf. Gen. 24:3, 4; 26:34, 35; 28:1; 34:14–17; Judg. 14: 3; Ezra 10:2; Neh. 13:26, 27; Tobit 6:12). The flesh of animals that died, which the Israelites were not allowed to eat, might be sold to foreigners (Deut. 14:21); money might be lent to them on interest (ch. 23:20; cf. Ex. 22:25); and debts could be collected from them even in the year of release, when they were remitted to Israelites (Deut. 15:3). In later times strict Jews abstained from even eating and drinking with Gentiles (Acts 11: 3; Gal. 2:12). Yet access into Judaism was always open to the Gentiles (Gen. 17:27; 34: 14–17; Matt. 23:15); and their ultimate engrafting into the Kingdom was Israel's expectation.

Fore·run'ner. A precursor; as: 1. A runner who immediately precedes the horse or chariot of high officials in order to clear the way or make proclamation (I Sam. 8:11; II Sam. 15: 1; I Kings 1:5; 18:46; Esth. 6:9). 2. Descriptive of a herald (Herod. i. 60). 3. The advance guard of an army (Wisd. of Sol. 12: 8; Herod. iv. 121, 124; cf. ix. 14). 4. First fruits (Num. 13:20, LXX).

As a forerunner Christ has entered on our behalf into heaven, the Holy of Holies, into the immediate presence of God (Heb. 6:20).

For'est. One was on Lebanon, famed for its cedars and firs (I Kings 7:2); another stretched from the Mediterranean Sea well into the hill country of Ephraim (Josh. 17: 15, 18); a 3d was in Judah (I Sam. 22:5); and a 4th, the forest of Ephraim, generally supposed to have been e. of the Jordan near Mahanaim (II Sam. 18:6).

For'ti·fied Cit'ies. Towns fortified by walls, towers, gates, and bars (Deut. 3:5; II Chron. 8:5; Neh., ch. 3). Such were the cities of the Canaanites and the Amorites when the Israelites warred against them (Num. 13:28; Deut. 3:5; Josh. 14:12). After the Israelites had occupied Canaan, they, like their predecessors, had fenced cities (Deut. 28:52; II Sam. 20:6; II Kings 14:13; II Chron. 12:4; Jer. 5:17; Hos. 8:14; Zeph. 1:16).

For·tu·na'tus (fôr-tû-nā'tŭs) [Lat., fortunate]. One of 3 messengers, apparently from Corinth, who reached Paul and supplied what was lacking on the part of the church in that city (I Cor. 16:17).

Foun'tain. A spring arising from under a rock or a bank, or welling up from the ground (Deut. 8:7). Strong fountains are numerous in Palestine. They are the permanent source of rivers, and give life and fertility to the soil. Many towns are named from them, as En-dor and the other compounds of En. Figuratively, fountain symbolizes the permanent and inexhaustible source of spiritual blessings (Ps. 36:9; Jer. 2:13; Rev. 7:17; 21: 6). Children are also described as a fountain proceeding from the parents (Deut. 33: 28).

Foun'tain Gate. See JERUSALEM, II. 3.

Fowl. Any bird. (Gen. 1:26; Lev. 11:13–19).

Fowl'er. One who catches birds by a net or other snare (Ps. 124:7; Prov. 6:5); hence figuratively one who ensnares the innocent or unwary and takes their life, or lures them to moral and spiritual ruin (Ps. 91:3; 124:7; Hos. 9:8).

Fox. An animal which dwells in holes (Matt. 8:20), especially among solitary ruins

(Lam. 5:18), and is sly and careful for its own safety (Ezek. 13:4; Luke 13:32). Tristram enumerates two species as occurring in Palestine, the Egyptian fox (*Vulpes nilotica*), and the tawny fox (*Vulpes flavescens*). The former is abundant in central and s. Palestine, as well as e. of the Jordan, and the latter, which is somewhat larger and may perhaps be only a variety of the common fox (*Vulpes vulgaris*), in the wooded parts of the country.

Under the general name of fox, *shū'āl*, the Hebrews appear to have comprehended the jackal, which belongs to the dog family, although they had a special name for the jackal. The jackal is perhaps intended in Judg. 15:4, R.V. marg.; for it abounds in the lowland of Philistia, goes about by night in bands, and spends the day as a pack in some cave. It is thus easily caught; whereas the fox is a solitary animal and difficult to capture. The jackal also devours carrion (Ps. 63:10, R.V. marg.), which the fox is loath to do. The jackal eats fruit as well as flesh, and may be intended in S. of Sol. 2:15, yet the fox tramples and destroys vineyards.

Frank'in·cense. A fragrant gum of a tree (Ecclus. 50:8; S. of Sol. 3:6). It is white in color, as its Heb. name *lᵉbōnāh* denotes. It was an ingredient in the holy anointing oil with which priests were consecrated to their sacred functions (Ex. 30:34). It was added with oil to the meal offerings (Lev. 2:1, 2, 15, 16), and ultimately burned (ch. 6:15). No

Frankincense (*Boswellia Carteri*)

frankincense was added to sin offerings (Lev. 5:11) and offerings of jealousy (Num. 5:15). Pure frankincense was poured upon the 12 loaves of showbread (Lev. 24:7; cf. I Chron. 9:29; Neh. 13:5). The dromedaries of Midian, Ephah, and Sheba, brought it to Palestine from Arabia (Isa. 60:6; Jer. 6:20, R.V.). The hill of frankincense (S. of Sol. 4:6) was probably a retired spot in the palace gardens, among exotic frankincense trees (cf. Eccl. 2:5; Jos. *Antiq.* viii. 6, 6; ix. 1, 2). The frankincense of antiquity, the olibanum of European commerce, comes from *Boswellia floribunda*, one of the *Amyridaceae* (Amyrids), growing in India, or from other species of

the genus, especially *B. Carteri*, *B. Frereana*, and *B. serrata*, of which there are 2 varieties, *B. serrata* proper, the *B. thurifera* of Roxburgh, and the variety *B. glabra*. The 1st and 4th species are Indian; the 2d and 3d occur on the Somali coast of Africa and on the s. coast of Arabia. The frankincense itself is gum resin, which is dry, consists of tears often an inch long, with a balsamic odor, especially when burnt. A poor quality, reddish in color, is obtained in the spring; the best is got later, and is white.

Friend of the King. A high court official (Gen. 26:26; I Kings 4:5), probably the king's confidential adviser. Under the Syro-Macedonian kings there was a specially privileged class known as the king's friends (I Macc. 2:18; 3:38; 6:10). See PRIEST.

Frog. An amphibious animal (Ex. 8:3; Rev. 16:13); in the O.T. probably *Rana punctata*, the dotted frog of Egypt.

Front'let. A band for the forehead; then, figuratively, the constant public exhibition of a trait or obedience to a command (Ex. 13:16; Deut. 6:8; 11:18; cf. Prov. 3:3). The injunction was interpreted literally by the later Jews. See PHYLACTERY.

Full'er. One who cleanses undressed cloth from oil and grease and renders it thick or compact by the application of pressure, or else one who thoroughly cleanses soiled garments (Mark 9:3). The clothing was steeped in soap and water (Mal. 3:2) and trodden, as the Heb. word denotes. A fuller's field lay outside of Jerusalem and was a well-known landmark at the time of the monarchy. It had a highway and the conduit of the upper pool (Isa. 7:3; 36:2), and was so near the city that the Assyrian ambassadors standing in the field and speaking were heard and understood by the people on the city wall (II Kings 18:17). An old view placed these events somewhere on the w., near the present Jaffa Gate, as here runs an aqueduct from the Birket Mamilla, in the upper Hinnom valley, into the city. Another view favors a n. location, since the n. was the usual side for attack. Josephus (*War* v. 4, 2) places a Monument of the Fuller at the n.e. corner. It is more probable, however, that the conduit referred to is the tunnel connecting the Fountain of the Virgin with the Pool of Siloam; in that case the fuller's field was in the valley of the Kidron.

Fur'long. The rendering of Gr. *stadion* (Luke 24:13; John 6:19; 11:18; Rev. 14:20). The Gr. *stadion* was 600 Greek and 606⅞ English feet, or about ⅛ of a Roman mile. It is a little less than an English furlong, which is 660 English feet, or ⅛ of an English mile. See MEASURE, I.

Fur'nace. 1. An oven for smelting iron from the ore (Deut. 4:20; I Kings 8:51). See IRON, I.

2. A crucible for refining gold and silver, and for melting gold, silver, brass, tin, and lead (Prov. 17:3; Ezek. 22:20). See SMITH.

3. A bake oven; so in Neh. 3:11; Isa. 31:9. See BREAD.

G

Ga'al (gā'ăl) [loathing; but cf. Arab. *ju'al*, beetle]. A son of Ebed. With a band of followers he came to Shechem and began to vilify Abimelech, the absent king, and to assume authority. Zebul, the governor, sent word to Abimelech of what was going on and advised him to lie in wait by night and advance against the town at dawn. He did so. Gaal went forth and gave him battle, but was put to flight (Judg. 9:26–41).

Ga′ash (gā′ăsh) [trembling, earthquake]. A hill in the hill country of Ephraim, s. of Timnath-serah (Josh. 24:30; Judg. 2:9; II Sam. 23:30; I Chron. 11:32).

Ga′ba (gā′bá). See GEBA.

Gab′ba·i (găb′á-ī) [tax gatherer]. A Benjamite who consented to live in Jerusalem after the Captivity (Neh. 11:8).

Gab′ba·tha (găb′á-thá) [Aram. *gabbethā*, back, ridge, hill, height; or perhaps *gabbaḥtā*, bald forehead]. The equivalent in Aram. of Gr. *lithostrōton*, a pavement of tessellated work (John 19:13). On it stood the public tribunal on which Pontius Pilate sat to decide cases. Probably it was an open space in front of Herod's palace (cf. Jos. *War* ii. 14, 8).

Ga′bri·el (gā′brĭ-ĕl) [man of God, or probably, God has shown himself mighty]. An angel of high rank sent to interpret a vision to the Prophet Daniel (Dan. 8:16–27). He was commissioned again to visit the prophet to give him skill and understanding, and reveal to him the prophecy of the 70 weeks (ch. 9:21–27). At a long subsequent period he was dispatched to Jerusalem to announce to Zacharias the birth of John the Baptist (Luke 1: 11–22), and to Nazareth to hail the Virgin Mary as chosen to the high privilege of being mother of the Messiah (vs. 26–38). Gabriel described himself as habitually standing in the presence of God (Luke 1:19).

Gad (găd) [good fortune]. 1. A son of Jacob by Zilpah, Leah's handmaid. At his birth Leah said, "With fortune [or Fortunate!]" and she called his name Gad (Gen. 30:10, 11; cf. v. 13, R.V.). By another interpretation of the text (kere), it may mean "Fortune is come." Jacob prophesied:

"Gad, a troop shall press upon him;
But he shall press upon their heel"

(Gen. 49:19, R.V.). Moses blessed God who enlarged Gad, and praised the valor of the tribe and its fidelity to duty (Deut. 33:20, 21). Gad had 7 sons (Gen. 46:16), each of whom, with the possible exception of Ezbon, founded a tribal family (Num. 26:15–18).
2. The tribe of which Gad was the progenitor, the Gadites (Num. 1:14; Deut. 27: 13; Ezek. 48:27, 28, 34). At the 1st census in the wilderness the Gadites capable of bearing arms were 45,650 (Num. 1:24, 25); at the 2d there were 40,500 (ch. 26:15–18). Valiant Gadites joined David at Ziklag (I Chron. 12: 8). The territory occupied by the tribe was e. of the Jordan and was assigned them by Moses, but with the proviso that, before finally settling down in it, the warriors of the tribe should cross the river with their brethren, and give assistance in the conquest of Canaan (Num. 32:20–32). The territory of the Gadites was situated between that of Reuben on the s. and the half tribe of Manasseh on the n. It included the s. part of Mount Gilead from the Jabbok s. to Heshbon, and from the vicinity of Rabbath-ammon on the e. westward to the Jordan Valley. In the valley it took in the entire e. bank from Bethnimrah, near the n. end of the Dead Sea, to the Lake of Gennesaret (Josh. 13:24–28; Deut. 3:12, 16, 17). The country was adapted to pasturage (Num. 32:1–4). Ramoth in Gilead was in the territory of Gad, and was appointed a city of refuge (Josh. 20:8). II Sam 24:5 probably means that the enumerators passed from the Arnon toward Gad and unto Jazer.
3. A prophet, David's seer, who, when David was in the cave of Adullam, advised him to quit that place of refuge and seek safety elsewhere (I Sam. 22:5), and who later gave the king the option from God of 3 kinds of punishment for his having numbered the people (II Sam. 24:11–14). He aided in arranging the musical service of the sanctuary (II Chron. 29:25), and he wrote an account of David's reign (I Chron. 29:29).
4. A heathen deity was known by the name of Gad. The Israelites are represented as engaging in idolatrous worship and setting a table for Fortune (Gad) and filling up mingled wine unto Destiny (Meni) (Isa. 65:11, R.V.).

Gad′a·renes′ (găd′á-rēnz′). Natives or inhabitants of Gadara, which Josephus describes as a Greek city (Jos. *Antiq.* xvii. 11, 4). Eusebius places it e. of the Jordan, nearly opposite to Tiberias and Scythopolis. It has been identified as Umm Keis, on a bold headland about 5½ English miles s.e. from the s. side of the Sea of Galilee, with the sea in full view and the river Yarmūk between. The hot springs belonging to Gadara are n. of the Yarmūk, while Umm Keis lies to the s. of that river. Gadarenes is the reading approved by textual criticism in Matt. 8:28 (cf. Mark 5:1; Luke 8:26, 37, A.V.). See GERGESENES. If Josephus is correct in giving Pella as the n. boundary of Perea (Jos. *War* iii. 3, 3), there probably was a 2d Gadara, the metropolis of Perea, a place of strength, which had wealthy inhabitants (Jos. *War* iv. 7, 3). It is probably represented by Tell Jadūr, near es-Salṭ.

Gad′di (găd′ī) [cf. Gaddiel]. The spy from the tribe of Manasseh in the exploration of Canaan (Num. 13:11).

Gad′di·el (găd′ī-ĕl) [Gad (fortune) is God]. The spy representing Zebulun in the exploration of Canaan (Num. 13:10).

Ga′di (gā′dī) [a Gadite]. Father of King Menahem (II Kings 15:14).

Ga′ham (gā′hăm) [cf. Arab. *jaḥm*, burning]. A son of Nahor and Reumah (Gen. 22:24).

Ga′har (gā′här) [cf. Arab. *jaḥir*, weak]. Head of a family of Nethinim who returned from captivity (Ezra 2:47; Neh. 7:49).

Ga′i (gā′ī) [valley]. A locality near Ekron, probably Gath (I Sam. 17:52, R.V. marg., as in LXX, Codex Vaticanus).

Ga′ius (gā′yŭs). 1. A Macedonian, one of Paul's companions who was dragged into the amphitheater during the riot at Ephesus (Acts 19:29).
2. A man of Derbe, who accompanied Paul on his last journey to Asia (Acts 20:4).
3. A Christian of Corinth, baptized by Paul, noted for hospitality to his fellow Christians (Rom. 16:23; I Cor. 1:14). Perhaps he was the person to whom John addressed his 3d epistle (III John 1).

Gal′a·ad (găl′á-ăd). See GILEAD.

Ga′lal (gā′lăl) [rolling, or perhaps, for the Lord has rolled]. 1. A Levite (I Chron. 9:15).
2. Another Levite, the son of Jeduthun (I Chron. 9:16; Neh. 11:17).

Ga·la′ti·a (gá-lā′shĭ-á). A district of central Asia Minor, bounded on the n. by Bithynia, Paphlagonia, and Pontus, on the e. by Pontus and Cappadocia, on the s. by Cappadocia, Lycaonia, and Phrygia, on the w. by Phrygia and Bithynia. Its name was derived from the fact that certain Gallic tribes, after having invaded Macedonia and Greece (278–277 B.C.), migrated to Asia Minor and received this territory from Nicomedes, king of Bithynia, in return for services rendered him in war. The Gauls were commonly called *Galatai* by the Greeks. The chief cities of Galatia were Pessinus, Ancyra, and Tavium. The territory, however, varied in size at different times according to the fortunes of war. In 189 B.C. the Galatians were subdued by the Romans, but retained their self-government, and were favored by their conquerors, since they were valuable allies. Hence under their last king, Amyntas, their territory was much extended to the s., so as to include part of Phrygia, Pisidia, Lycaonia, and Isauria; and, after the death of Amyntas (25 B.C.), this enlarged region became the Roman province of Galatia. In 7 B.C. Paphlagonia and part of Pontus were added on the n., and after A.D. 63 other territorial changes were frequently made. During the travels of Paul, therefore, the term Galatia was applicable both to the original Galatic territory and to the large Roman province. It is disputed in which sense it is used in Acts 16:6 (R.V., "they went through the region of Phrygia and Galatia," but which Ramsay translates "they went through the Phrygo-Galatic region"), and in Acts 18:23 (which translation is open to similar differences of opinion), and in Paul's epistle to the "churches of Galatia." If Galatia meant the Roman province, then Paul evangelized it on his First Missionary Journey (Acts, chs. 13; 14) in company with Barnabas. If it meant the old territory of Galatia, then he evangelized it on his Second Journey (Acts 16:6). The churches of Galatia are also mentioned in I Cor. 16:1. In II Tim. 4:10 we read that Crescens had gone to Galatia, which, however, many think meant Gaul (now France). I Peter was addressed to the Christians of Galatia among others (ch. 1:1), and there Galatia clearly means the Roman province. There are, however, serious difficulties in so understanding it in The Acts and in the Epistle to the Galatians.   G. T. P. (rev., H. S. G.)

Ga·la'tians (gȧ-lā'shᾰnz), **The E·pis'tle of Paul to the.** A letter addressed to the churches of Galatia (ch. 1:2), showing that there were a number of them in different parts of the territory. What churches are thus described depends on the meaning we attach to the term Galatia (*q.v.*). The date of the epistle also turns on this point. If Galatia be the Roman province and the churches of Galatia those founded on Paul's First Journey (Acts, chs. 13; 14), then the epistle was probably written toward the latter part, or at the close, of Paul's Second Journey, since Gal. 4:13 ("the first time," R.V.) implies that he had visited them twice, and since for various reasons it seems necessary to date the epistle later than those to the Thessalonians. If, however, Galatia means Galatia proper, and if it was evangelized on the Second Journey (Acts 16:6), then the epistle could not have been written before the apostle's sojourn in Ephesus, since Acts 18:23 mentions his 2d visit, on this interpretation, to Galatia. In conformity with this latter view are the facts, 1st, that the apostle appeals to his readers as if he alone had been their spiritual father (Gal. 4:13-20), whereas on his First Missionary Journey Barnabas was associated with him; and, 2d, that Paul's description of his reception as an angel of God (ch. 4:14) hardly comports with any known experience of his on his 1st journey. Many scholars take this latter view, conclude that Galatia proper was evangelized on the 2d journey, and date the epistle in A.D. 55 or 56. Others, however, put it still later, thinking that its resemblance to Romans shows that it was written shortly before that epistle, say in the winter of 57-58. Whatever its readers and date, it was occasioned by the operations of certain Judaizing teachers among the Galatians, who assailed Paul's authority, and taught the necessity of observing the Mosaic laws. They declared that Paul, not being one of the original apostles, was dependent on others for his knowledge of the gospel. They seem also to have charged him with being himself inconsistent in his preaching of Gen-

tile freedom from the Law. They also attacked his doctrine, and persuaded his converts to adopt Jewish observances. The very gospel being thus at stake, Paul wrote this epistle with great intensity of feeling and vigorous argument.

This epistle is the Magna Charta of Christian liberty. After the introduction (ch. 1:1-10), in which the apostle opens the subject of their error in listening to false teachers, and vehemently asserts the divineness of the gospel he had preached, he defends his apostolic authority (chs. 1:11 to 2:21) as given directly by Christ and not dependent on man. He also shows that the Jerusalem church and the original apostles agreed with his position (ch. 2:1-10), and that (ch. 2:11-21) he had never changed his teaching, even when Peter at Antioch had seemed by his conduct to oppose it. In ch. 3 he defends his doctrine of justification by faith alone, appealing in proof to their own experience of salvation through faith (ch. 3:1-5), to the teaching of Scripture regarding the original Abrahamic way of salvation (vs. 6-9) and to certain facts, fully taught in Scripture, concerning the Law, namely, that the Law, since it requires perfect obedience as the condition of salvation, brings only a curse or penalty (vs. 10-12); that Christ has redeemed us from the curse, having become a curse for us (vs. 13, 14); that God ratified his covenant of salvation by faith with Abraham and his seed, and hence the Law, which came later, cannot disannul the original compact (vs. 15-18), but was intended as a temporary discipline to make men realize that sin is a transgression of God's commandments (vs. 19, 20), that the Law was therefore a tutor to bring sinners to Christ (vs. 21-24). In ch. 4 the apostle advances 3 more reasons for their fidelity to his gospel, namely, the analogy of sonship and its rights under the civil law (ch. 4:1-11), their personal affection for himself (vs. 12-20), and the illustration which the narrative of Genesis provided in the account of Hagar and Sarah and their sons (vs. 21-31). In chs. 5:1 to 6:10 he applies the doctrine of freedom from the Law, bidding them to maintain, yet not to abuse, their liberty, and to exercise it with meekness and a sense of responsibility. The closing verses (ch. 6:11-18), form the conclusion, probably in the apostle's own handwriting (see v. 11 in R.V.), in which he summarizes the substance of his instruction.

The Epistle to the Galatians is of immense value. 1. It is important for the details it gives about the apostle's life. Its harmony with the account in The Acts of Paul's life, and of his relation to the church, has been much contested but may be completely proved (see PAUL and the remarks, made at the proper chronological point in the article, concerning Paul's 1st visit to Jerusalem after his conversion, Gal. 1:18, 19; Acts 9:26-29, and concerning the Council at Jerusalem, Gal. 2:2-10 and Acts, ch. 15). 2. The epistle proves also that the older apostles were in accord with Paul, though to him was allotted the work among the Gentiles. 3. It gives in briefer outline, and with special application, the same scheme of salvation and the same view of the Hebrew dispensation which is more elaborately and calmly presented in The Epistle to the Romans. All men being under the Law, and condemned as sinners by the Law, salvation is impossible by the works of the Law. Christ alone can save, since he has by his death met the claims of the Law against those who believe. The Law was never intended to save, but to be a tutor or schoolmaster (i.e., a slave who led children to school) to bring us to Christ. By faith Abraham was saved, and by faith alone do we become children of Abraham, partakers of the blessing and heirs of the promise. Judaism, as a method of salvation, was therefore a misinterpretation even of the O.T. itself, and the distinction between Jew and Gentile has been done away. The declaration of these truths made Christianity a world religion instead of a Jewish sect.

G. T. P. (rev., H. S. G.)

Gal'ba·num. A fragrant spice (Ex. 30:34; Ecclus. 24:15), in Heb. *ḥelbᵉnāh*, in Gr. *chalbanē*. The Gr. and Rom. *Galbanum* was a gum brought from Persia. It is generally supposed to have come from 2 umbelliferous plants, *Ferula galbaniflua* and *F. rubricaulis*.

Gal'e·ed (găl'ê-ĕd) [heap of witness]. A cairn erected by Jacob in Mount Gilead, n. of the Jabbok. The exact situation is unknown. It was between the respective homes of Laban and Jacob, and was intended as a memorial of the covenant concluded between them there, that neither would pass that place to do the other injury (Gen. 31:45–54); see MIZPAH 1.

Gal'ga·la (găl'gȧ-lȧ). A place (I Macc. 9:2), presumably one of the towns known as Gilgal; mentioned in connection with Arbela. It may be for Galilee, since Josephus (*Antiq.* xii. 11, 1) does not mention it, but refers simply to Arbela of Galilee. See GILGAL.

Gal'i·lae'an (găl'i-lē'ăn), in A.V. **Gal'i·le'an** (găl'i-lē'ăn). A native or inhabitant of Galilee (Mark 14:70; Acts 13:1).

Gal'i·lee (găl'i-lē) [Lat. *Galilaea*, from Gr. *Galilaia*, from Heb. *Gālīl*, circle, region, district]. Originally a district in the hill country of Naphtali (II Kings 15:29; I Chron. 6:76), Kedesh being one of its cities (Josh. 20:7; 21:32). The 20 unimportant towns given by Solomon to Hiram were in the land of Galilee (1 Kings 9:11). In this region many of the Canaanites remained (Judg. 1:30–33; 4:2), and the expression "Galilee of the nations" or "Gentiles" implies that the district or region so called was inhabited chiefly by a non-Jewish population (Isa. 9:1; cf. I Macc. 5:15 and Matt. 4:15). The name Galilee gradually extended until it included the country as far s. as the Plain of Esdraelon (I Macc. 5:55; 10:30; 12:47, 49). Many of its inhabitants had been carried away, especially during the Assyrian wars (II Kings 15:29), and the few Jews who settled in Galilee after the Return were taken to Judea by Simon Maccabaeus about 164 B.C. (I Macc. 5:23); but Galilee soon afterward became thoroughly Jewish. It formed part of the kingdom of Herod the Great, and on his death passed under the authority of Herod the tetrarch. It was the most n. of 3 provinces w. of the Jordan into which (if Phoenicia be ignored) Palestine was divided in the times of the Romans. At the period of the Jewish war, A.D. 70, it was divided into Upper and Lower Galilee; and was bounded on the n. by Tyrian territory, on the s. by the n. boundary line of Samaria and Scythopolis to the Jordan, on the e. by Hippene, Gadaris, Gaulonitis, and the kingdom of Agrippa, that is, by the Jordan and its lakes, and on the w. by Phoenicia. Lower Galilee lay to the s. of Upper Galilee and extended from Tiberias to near Ptolemais, now Acre, on the Mediterranean Sea (Jos. *War* iii. 3, 1; *Life* 13, 14, 37; cf. Judith 1:8). It was at that time densely populated. It furnished an army of 100,000 men (Jos. *War* ii. 20, 6). There were 240 cities and villages within the limits of the two Galilees (Jos. *Life* 45). The smallest of these villages, according to Josephus (Jos. *War* iii. 3, 2), had 15,000 inhabitants, but this probably is an exaggeration. The largest city was Sepphoris, and the largest village Japha (Jos. *Life* 45). The mixture of races tended to produce a distinct accent or even dialect (Mark 14:70; Luke 22:59; cf. Acts 2:7). The people also was supposed to be one which never would produce a prophet (John 7:41, 52). Nevertheless, nearly all the apostles of Jesus were natives of Galilee, and he himself was brought up in it and made it the chief scene of his ministry, laboring on its e. limits by the Sea of Galilee, and within its area at Chorazin, Bethsaida, Capernaum, Nain, Cana, and Nazareth.

Galilee is about 60 miles long by 25 broad. It is generally mountainous with fertile valleys between. Its scenery is picturesque. Lower Galilee is divided from Upper Galilee on a line running almost due w. from the n. end of the lake to Acre. It is a grain-growing region, with a less elevation above the sea level than Upper Galilee, its mountains being all under 1,850 feet high. Upper Galilee has summits of 2,000, 3,000, and 4,000 feet altitude.

Gal'i·lee (găl'i-lē), **Sea of.** A fresh-water lake, fed by the river Jordan. It was called originally Sea of Chinnereth (Num. 34:11), later Lake of Gennesaret (Luke 5:1; Jos. *Antiq.* xviii. 2, 1; cf. xiii. 5, 7; I Macc. 11:67), and Sea of Galilee or Tiberias (John 6:1; 21:1). The latter name is preserved in Arab. Bahr Tabariya.

It is enclosed by hills, except where the Jordan enters and leaves. The hills on the e. side rise to the height of 1,000 feet and more; those on the w. side toward the s. end of the lake are of like character, but toward the n.w. they are lower and less steep. It is designated a sea, from its considerable extent, though its water is fresh. Its length from the entrance to the exit of the Jordan is 12¾ miles; its greatest breadth, which is opposite to Magdala, is 7½ miles. Its e. side is destitute of conspicuous indentations, while on the w. side there is a swelling bay extending from Tell Hum on the n. to Tiberias on the s. The surface of the lake is 682 feet below the level of the Mediterranean. Lying so low, it has a semitropical climate, and since ice-crowned Hermon is not far away, sudden and violent storms at times rush down the mountain slope and terminate on the lake.

The water abounds in fish, and in Christ's day fishing in this lake apparently was a profitable industry. Thus Zebedee employed men to help him (Mark 1:20). Tristram enumerates 22 species; 2 of *Blenniidae*, 7 of *Chromidae*, 1 of *Siluridae*, and 12 of *Cyprinidae*. Some are called after Biblical personages, viz., *Chromis Andreae*, *C. Simonis*, and *C. Magdalenae*. The best for the table of all fish now in the lake are the sheatfish (*Clarias macracanthus*) and the barbel (*Barbus longiceps*). The sheatfish, called by Josephus *Coracinus* (*War* iii. 10, 8), belongs to the same family as the American catfish, and attains a length of 3 feet. The most abundant fish is *Chromis tiberiadis*. Tristram saw them in shoals of over an acre in extent, so closely packed that it seemed impossible for them to move. Their dorsal fins, rising above the water, gave it at a distance an appearance as if a heavy shower were pattering on one spot of the glassy lake. Of course, the same kinds of fish are found in the Jordan and its tributaries also.

Gall. 1. The bitter secretion of the liver, bile (Job 16:13; 20:25); in Heb. *mᵉrērāh* and *mᵉrōrāh*, as being bitter. Venomous, malignant feeling against what is good was called the gall of bitterness (Acts 8:23).

2. A poisonous, bitter herb (Deut. 29:18; 32:32, 33; Ps. 69:21), called in Heb. *rōsh*, in Gr. *cholē*. It grew up spontaneously in the furrows of fields (Hos. 10:4, where the Eng. Bible translates it hemlock); hemlock, colo-

cynth, and the poppy have all been suggested as the equivalent of *rōsh*. It was associated in rhetorical language with wormwood. A sore punishment was likened to a drink of gall water (Jer. 8:14 ; 9:15 ; 23:15).

The wine to drink mingled with gall, *cholē* (Matt. 27:34), doubtless is derived from the LXX of Ps. 69:21, where *rōsh* is rendered by *cholē*. According to Mark 15:23, it was myrrh. It is well known that the Romans gave wine with frankincense to criminals before execution to alleviate their sufferings ; in Jesus' case myrrh was used.

Gal'ler·y. A long room or corridor, or a partial story in a building (Ezek. 41:15, 16 ; 42:3, 5). A different Heb. word, rendered galleries in A.V. of S. of Sol. 7:5, doubtless means tresses, as it is translated in R.V.

the case. He remained equally indifferent when the crowd took Sosthenes, the ruler of the synagogue, and beat him before the judgment seat (Acts 18:12–17).

Gal'lows. Haman had a gallows (tree, R.V. marg.) made 50 cubits high, on which to hang Mordecai (Esth. 5:14). Hanging by strangulation was not a Persian method of punishment. Haman no doubt intended to impale Mordecai (cf. Esth. 2:23 ; Herod. iii. 159) ; the "tree" probably was a pole or stake.

Ga·ma'li·el (ga-mā'li-ĕl) [God has rewarded]. 1. Son of Pedahzur and head of the tribe of Manasseh in the wilderness (Num. 1:10 ; 2:20 ; 7:54, 59).

2. A member of the Jewish sanhedrin, a Pharisee, and a doctor of the Law, held in

Fishermen Mending Their Nets by the Sea of Galilee

Gal'ley. A low flat-built vessel with one or more banks, i.e., rows of oars (Isa. 33:21 ; II Macc. 4:20).

Gal'lim (găl'ĭm) [heaps]. 1. A village near Gibeah of Saul and Anathoth (Isa. 10:29, 30), apparently not a great distance from Bahurim (I Sam. 25:44 ; II Sam. 3:13–16) ; probably Khirbet Ka'kūl.

2. A town of Judah called Gallim, mentioned by the LXX in a group with Tekoa, Bethlehem, Etam, and especially in connection with towns s.w. of Jerusalem, between Karem and Baither ; probably Beit Jāla, near Bethlehem (Josh. 15:59a).

Gal'li·o (găl'ĭ-ō). Roman proconsul of Achaia at the time of Paul's 1st visit to Corinth. His original name was Marcus Annaeus Novatus ; but he was adopted into the family of Lucius Junius Gallio and took the name Junius Annaeus Gallio. He was the brother of the Roman philosopher Seneca, and, like him, was put to death by the emperor Nero. When the Jews, maddened by the success of Paul at Corinth, dragged him before the proconsul's tribunal, Gallio refused to take notice of religious questions and summarily dismissed

high reputation by the Jewish people. He advised against persecuting the apostles on the ground that if their work were simply man's it would eventually fail, while if it were from God opposition to it was wicked and vain (Acts 5:34–39). Gamaliel had Paul for one of his pupils in the Law (ch. 22:3). According to the Talmud, Gamaliel was the grandson of the celebrated rabbi Hillel. Gamaliel died about A.D. 50.

Games. In the N.T. there are numerous allusions to the games of ancient Greece. The most important of these were 4 : the Olympic, at Olympia, in the district of Elis, in the Peloponnesus ; the Pythian, at Delphi, in Phocis ; the Nemean, at Argos, in Argolis, in the Peloponnesus ; and the Isthmian, on the isthmus of Corinth. The contests were in chariot, horse, and foot racing, quoiting, boxing, wrestling, hurling the spear. The competitors went through a long course of severe training. Immense multitudes were spectators of their skill, and though the reward of the victor was but a crown of leaves (wild olive at Olympia, pine at the Isthmus, laurel at Delphi, parsley at Nemea), the honor given to him by his fellow citizens and countrymen was great beyond measure. Similar games were introduced into Judea by hellenizing Jews in the reign of Antiochus Epiphanes, and were fostered by Herod the Great (I Macc. 1:10, 14; Jos. *Antiq.* xv. 8, 1). As the Isthmian games were held in the vicinity of Corinth, and the other 3 at no great distance, it is natural for Paul's 2 epistles to the Corinthians to contain metaphors or comparisons borrowed from the games. In I Cor. 9:24–27 there is allusion to the training of a competitor in the games, to running, and to fighting, the object in view being to gain a prize. There are scattered allusions of a similar kind through other epistles (Gal. 2:2; 5:7; Phil. 2:16; 3:14; II Tim. 2:5). In Hebrews there is a notable passage (ch. 12:1, 2). The vast multitude of men and women who have borne testimony to their faith in God is likened to the immense concourse of spectators at a foot race. The competitor lays aside every weight to make himself lighter, and the long, flowing garment, which else would beset him and perhaps throw him down. He requires patience to go forward perseveringly, but obtains it by looking at the umpire seated at the end of the course,

(Jos. *Antiq.* viii. 7, 3; cf. S. of Sol. 6:11; Eccl. 2:5), another in the palace at Shushan (Esth. 1:5). To protect gardens against depredators they were enclosed with a wall or hedge (S. of Sol. 4:12; Isa. 5:2, 5), and occasionally a lodge was placed within them, attended by a watcher (Isa. 1:8). In the seclusion and coolness of gardens people walked (Susanna 1:7), sometimes bathed (v. 15), spread repasts (Esth. 1:5), engaged in devotion (Matt. 26:36), practiced idolatrous rites (Isa. 1:29; 65:3; 66:17; cf. II Kings 16:4), and occasionally buried their dead (John 19:41).

Ga'reb (gā'rĕb) [late Heb. *gārāb*, jug, but cf. Arab. *jirāb*, scabby; Heb. *gārāb*, leprosy]. 1. An Ithrite, one of David's mighty men (II Sam. 23:38; I Chron. 11:40).

2. A hill near Jerusalem on the w. (Jer. 31:39; cf. vs. 38, 40). Exact situation unknown.

Gar'lic. A bulbous plant resembling the onion, and in Heb. called *shūm*. It was much eaten in Egypt (Herod. ii. 125), and the Israelites when there used it for food (Num. 11:5). It is *Allium sativum*, of the same genus as the onion but with more taste and scent than

Grecian Games of Pulling and Wrestling

ready to confer the prize if it be fairly won. Every one of these details had a distinct spiritual reference, which would come home with great power to every reader of the epistle who had seen any of the Grecian games.

Gam'ma·dim (găm'*à*-dĭm), in A.V. double pl. **Gam'ma·dims** (găm'*à*-dĭmz) [valorous men, A.R.V.]. Brave people who manned the towers of Tyre (Ezek. 27:11, A.V.). A proper name is expected in the context, and these men may come from Kumidi, a place in n. Syria, mentioned in the Tell el-Amarna letters.

Ga'mul (gā'mŭl) [recompensed]. A descendant of Aaron whose family in David's reign was made the 22d course of the priests (I Chron. 24:17).

Gar'den. The first garden or park of Scripture is that of Eden, which God caused to grow for man in his state of innocence (Gen. 2:8 to 3:24; Ezek. 28:13; 31:8, 9). Gardens were watered in Egypt (Deut. 11:10) with water raised from the Nile by sweep and bucket, or by wheel from wells, and poured into the irrigation ditch. By opening or closing this furrow with the foot the water was led to the spot desired. Irrigation was practiced in Palestine also (Eccl. 2:6; Isa. 58:11; Jer. 31:12). Herbs were cultivated in gardens (I Kings 21:2); so also were lilies and other flowers (S. of Sol. 5:1; 6:2), and fruit trees (Jer. 29:5, 28; Amos 9:14). The Garden of Gethsemane seems to have been an olive grove and to have had a press in it wherewith to express the oil from the fruit. There was a royal garden at Jerusalem (II Kings 25:4), another at Etam near Bethlehem

that esculent. It is a native of central Asia, is grown largely in the Mediterranean region, and is eaten by the common people as a relish to their bread.

Gar'ment. See CLOTHING.

Gar'mite (gär'mīt) [pertaining to Gerem, or bony]. A gentilic name applied to Keilah (I Chron. 4:19).

Gar'ner. A place for storing grain, a granary (Ps. 144:13; Joel 1:17; Matt. 3:12).

Gar'nish. To adorn, to decorate with ornamental additions (II Chron. 3:6; Job 26:13; Matt. 12:44; 23:29; Luke 11:25; Rev. 21:19, A.V.).

Gar'ri·son. A military post; a body of troops stationed in a fort (I Sam. 13:23; 14:1, 4, 6, 11, 15; II Sam. 23:14; II Cor. 11:32, A.V.). In the O.T. passages, Heb. *maṣṣab* is rendered garrison.

A different Heb. word, *neṣīb*, is used in I Sam. 10:5; 13:3, 4, but the Eng. Bible also renders it garrison. This word has caused some difficulty in commentators, since in Gen. 19:26 it signifies pillar. In I Kings 4:19 *neṣīb* means officer, and could very well have this translation in II Sam. 8:6, 14, where the Eng. Bible has garrison. II Sam. 23:14 reads *maṣṣab*, garrison, while the corresponding section, I Chron. 11:16, has *neṣīb*, which must accordingly be rendered garrison. It may, to some commentators, seem desirable to limit, in the Books of Samuel, the meaning of *neṣīb* to officer. Thus the Targum translates the word in I Sam. 10:5; 13:3, 4; the smiting of a Philistine officer by Jonathan would naturally be regarded as a cause of war. The Eng. rendering, however, makes sense in the context and has the support of the Vulgate.

Gash'mu (găsh'mū). See GESHEM.

Ga'tam (gā'tăm) [cf. Arab. *ja'tham*, lean and weak]. A descendant of Eliphaz (Gen. 36:11; I Chron. 1:36), and chief of a tribe of the sons of Esau (Gen. 36:16).

Gate. Every city or palace had a gate. It was often protected by a strong tower (II Chron. 26:9), and the gateway frequently led through the tower. Bars were placed across the gates to render them stronger against assault (Deut. 3:5; I Kings 4:13; II Chron.

A City Gate

8:5; 14:7). The gate was a place of public concourse where business was carried on (I Kings 22:10; II Kings 7:1; Ezek. 11:1); legal transactions conducted and witnessed (Gen. 23:10, 18; Ruth 4:1-11); cases tried and judgment pronounced (Deut. 21:19; 22:15; 25:7-9; Job 31:21; Amos 5:15). There were gates in the enclosures connected with the mansions of the aristocracy (Luke 16:20), where love of magnificence and display found expression (Prov. 17:19).

Gath (găth) [wine press]. One of the 5 great Philistine cities (I Sam. 6:17; 7:14). It was noted as the residence of a remnant of the Anakim, men of great stature (Josh. 11:22; cf. Num. 13:33; Deut. 2:10, 11). To this race Goliath and the other gigantic warriors probably belonged (I Sam. 17:4; II Sam. 21:15-22; I Chron. 20:4-8). The town was captured by David (I Chron. 18:1). During Solomon's reign, it had a king of its own who was probably subject to the king at Jeru-

salem (I Kings 2:39, 42). It was fortified by Rehoboam (II Chron. 11:8), but soon again reverted to the Philistines. It was captured by Hazael (II Kings 12:17). Uzziah broke down its wall (II Chron. 26:6); and henceforth it drops out of history. Micah names it, but he may be quoting an old expression (Micah 1:10; cf. II Sam. 1:20). When afterward the Philistine cities are mentioned, Gath is missing (Jer. 25:20; Zeph. 2:4; Zech. 9:5); and it is not referred to in Maccabees, nor by Josephus when he relates events subsequent to the year 750 B.C. It is probably to be located at Tell 'Arak el-Menshiyeh, 6½ miles w. of Beit Jibrîn (Eleutheropolis).

Gath'-he'pher (găth'hē'fĕr), in A.V. once through misapprehension **Git'tah-he'pher** [wine press of digging]. A town on the boundary line of Zebulun (Josh. 19:13). It was the birthplace of the Prophet Jonah (II Kings 14:25). In Jerome's day it existed as a small village, 2 Roman miles e. of Sepphoris. This location corresponds with el-Meshhed, 3 miles n.e. of Nazareth. The original site was s. of this village at Khirbet ez-Zurra'. Here one of Jonah's tombs exists, its chief rival being at the site of ancient Nineveh.

Gath'-rim'mon (găth'rĭm'ŭn) [pomegranate press]. 1. A town of the tribe of Dan (Josh. 19:45), assigned to the Kohathite Levites (ch. 21:24; I Chron. 6:69). It may have been at Tell Abu Zeitûn, e. of Jerisheh in the plain of Joppa.

2. A town in Manasseh w. of the Jordan, assigned to the Kohathite Levites (Josh. 21:25); probably an erroneous transcription of Ibleam or Bileam (*q.v.*).

Gauls (gôlz). See GALATIA.

Ga'za (gā'zà), thrice **Az'zah** in A.V. and once in R.V. (I Chron. 7:28) [Heb. *'azzäh*, Gr. *Gaza*, Arab. *Ghazzah* has preserved the ancient name]. 1. The most s. of the 5 Philistine cities (Josh. 13:3; I Sam. 6:17; Jer. 25:20), and very ancient (Gen. 10:19; el-Amarna letters, 15th century B.C.). It stood on the main road, between Mesopotamia and Egypt, at the edge of the desert and at the junction of a trade route from s. Arabia. Assigned to Judah (Josh. 15:47), it was captured by the men of that tribe (Judg. 1:18), but reverted to the Philistines (cf. Judg. 6:4). Samson carried off the doors of the city gate (Judg. 16:1-3). In prison and blinded he ground grain there (v. 21). The tutelary god of Gaza, as of Ashdod, was Dagon. The last act of Samson's life was to throw down the 2 middle pillars of the temple of Dagon from their place (vs. 23-31). Gaza was the limit of Solomon's dominion toward the s.w. (I Kings 4:24). Hezekiah smote the Philistines as far as Gaza's gate (II Kings 18:8). The city was taken by Sargon in 720 B.C. Necho took the city (Jer. 47:1), probably after the battle of Megiddo in 608 B.C. (Herod. ii. 159). Judgment was denounced against it and the other Philistine cities by the prophets (Jer. 25:20; 47:1, 5; Zeph. 2:4; Zech. 9:5). One sin specified was its sale of captured Hebrews to the Edomites (Amos 1:6). It held out against Alexander the Great for 5 months, and when it fell its inhabitants were massacred. Jonathan Maccabaeus was shut out of Gaza and burnt its suburbs; but he eventually made peace without storming the place (I Macc. 11:61, 62). It was afterward captured by his brother Simon (ch. 13: 43-48; Jos. *Antiq.* xiii. 5, 5). About 96 B.C., after a year's siege, it was devastated by Alexander Jannaeus (Jos. *Antiq.* xiii. 13, 3). In 62 B.C. Pompey placed it under the jurisdiction of Syria (Jos. *Antiq.* xiv. 4, 4). Gabinius, the Roman governor of Syria, built it in 57 B.C., probably on a new site, and the old town perhaps became known as Desert Gaza (Jos. Antiq. xiv. 5, 3; Strabo xvi. 2, 30; cf. Acts 8:26). About A.D. 65 the Jews destroyed Gaza, but it rose again, and coins are extant belonging to it which were struck in honor of Titus and Hadrian. Later it became the seat of a Christian bishopric; in A.D. 634 it was captured by the Arabs. It is situated 44½ miles s. of Jaffa and 2½ miles from the Mediterranean.

2. A town of Ephraim (I Chron. 7:28, A.V.); R.V. reads Azzah, but Ayyah in marg., which is the better Heb. reading. It is probably to be identified with Turmus 'Ayya in a small fertile plain between Sinjil and Seilūn (Shiloh).

Ga'za'ra (gȧ-zā'rȧ). See GEZER.

Ga'zath·ite (gā'zăth-īt). See GAZITE.

Ga·zelle'. A small antelope, called in Heb. ṣebī. Where A.V. renders this word by roebuck, R.V. substitutes gazelle; and where A.V. renders it by roe, R.V. generally places gazelle on the marg. There is no doubt that the gazelle (Gazella dorcas) is intended. It was ceremonially clean (Deut. 12:22; 14:5), was hunted (Prov. 6:5; Isa. 13:14), and was swift-footed (II Sam. 2:18; I Chron. 12:8). Its beauty and grace rendered it a term of endearing comparison (S. of Sol. 2:9, 17; 8:14). It is about 3 feet 6 inches long by 1 foot 9 inches high. The horns are larger in the male than in the female; the limbs and whole form in both sexes graceful; the fur mostly fawn colored about the head, more fulvous on the other parts. It is found in Syria, Egypt, and Arabia, mostly in small groups or nearly solitary. It is timid and flees from a pursuer rapidly and with great bounds. Tristram found a 2d species of gazelle (Gazella arabica), larger than the common one, e. of the Jordan.

Ga'zer (gā'zẽr) and **Ga·ze'ra** (gȧ-zē'rȧ). See GEZER.

Ga'zez (gā'zĕz) [shearer]. A son and perhaps also a grandson of the elder Caleb (I Chron. 2:46).

Ga'zite (gā'zīt), in A.V. once **Ga'zath·ite.** A native or inhabitant of Gaza (Josh. 13:3; Judg. 16:2).

Gaz'zam (găz'ăm) [devourer, destroyer; cf. late Heb. gāzam, to cut off]. Founder of a family of Nethinim who returned with Zerubbabel (Ezra 2:48).

Ge'ba (gē'bȧ), in A.V. thrice **Ga'ba** [a hill]. A city of Benjamin (Josh. 18:24; I Chron. 8:6), allotted to the priests (Josh. 21:17). It must be distinguished from Gibeah of Saul (Isa. 10:29). Geba was the n. extreme of the Kingdom of Judah (II Kings 23:8; Zech. 14:10). A village bearing the old name marks the site, 6 miles n.n.e. of Jerusalem and 2 miles s.w. of Michmash.

Ge'bal (gē'băl) [mountain]. 1. A city on the Mediterranean (Josh. 13:5; I Kings 5:18, R.V.; Ezek. 27:9), 42 miles n. of Sidon; called Byblos by the Greeks and Jubayl in Arab. It was a dependency of Egypt in the 15th century B.C., and the correspondence of its governor Rib-Addi with the pharaoh has been preserved in the Tell el-Amarna letters.

2. The n. portion of the mountains of Edom (Jos. Antiq. ii. 1, 2; ix. 9, 1; Ps. 83:7); known also as Teman.

Ge'bal·ites (gē'băl-īts), in A.V. **Gib'lites.** The people of the town and kingdom of Gebal (Josh. 13:5; I Kings 5:18; in text of A.V. stonesquarers).

Ge'ber (gē'bẽr) [a man, a hero]. Solomon's purveyor for the territory of s. Gilead (I Kings 4:19), and probably father of the purveyor for n. Gilead and Argob (v. 13).

Ge'bim (gē'bīm) [cisterns]. A village n. of Jerusalem (Isa. 10:31); identified by various scholars with Khirbet ed-Duweir, but Bâṭn el-Baṭṭāsh has also been suggested with good reason.

Geck'o. The rendering of Heb. 'ănāḳāh, a ceremonially unclean animal classed with creeping things (Lev. 11:30, R.V.). The gecko is a wall lizard. It has white spots on its back; and it emits a plaintive wail, whence the Heb. name. The common gecko or fanfoot (Ptyodactylus gecko) is very common in Palestine. It frequents houses, running over the walls and ceiling. It is able to do this by reason of the peculiar construction of its toes, which are provided with plates under which a vacuum is created when the animal walks, thus causing it to adhere.

Ged·a·li'ah (gĕd'ȧ-lī'ȧ) [Jehovah is great]. 1. A harper, son of Jeduthun (I Chron. 25:3), and head of the 2d of the 24 companies of 12 musicians each which David appointed for the service of the sanctuary (v. 9).

2. An ancestor of the Prophet Zephaniah (Zeph. 1:1).

3. A son of Pashhur in Jeremiah's time (Jer. 38:1).

4. A man of Judah of high birth, son of Ahikam, son of Shaphan. He was appointed by Nebuchadnezzar governor of Judah after the capture of Jerusalem. He fixed his residence at Mizpah, where he was treacherously assassinated by Ishmael of the seed royal (II Kings 25:22–26; Jer. 39:14; 40:5 to 41:18).

5. A priest whom Ezra induced to divorce his foreign wife (Ezra 10:18).

Ged'e·on (gĕd'ė-ŭn). See GIDEON.

Ge'der (gē'dẽr) [a wall]. A town in the extreme s. of Judah (Josh. 12:13), but exact site unknown. It may be the same as Bethgader or Gedor, 3.

Ge·de'rah (gė-dē'rȧ) [wall, enclosure, sheepfold]. 1. A town in the lowland of Judah (Josh. 15:36), identified with Jedīreh, 4 miles and 4½ miles respectively to the n.w. of Zorah and Eshtaol (v. 33).

2. A village of Benjamin (cf. I Chron. 12:4), identified with Jedīreh, about 6 miles n. by w. of Jerusalem.

Ge·de'rite (gė-dẽr'īt). A man of Geder or Gederah (I Chron. 27:28; cf. Josh. 15:36).

Ge·de'roth (gė-dē'rŏth) [enclosures, sheepfolds]. A town in or near the lowland of Judah (Josh. 15:41). In Ahaz' reign it was taken by the Philistines (II Chron. 28:18). Its site is commonly fixed at Kaṭrah, called in I Macc. 15:39 Kidron, in the maritime plain about 4 miles s.w. of Ekron.

Ged'e·ro·tha'im (gĕd'ė-rô-thā'ĭm) [2 enclosures]. A town within the territory of Judah (Josh. 15:36), otherwise unknown. The LXX regards it as a common noun and translates it "its cattle shelters." One thing is in favor of this rendering; while the towns are reckoned up as but 14, 15 names are given. The name may have come into the text by dittography of the preceding Gederah.

Ge'dor (gē'dôr) [wall, fortress, walled enclosure]. 1. A son of Jehiel, and a brother of Ner, the ancestor of Saul (I Chron. 8:30, 31; 9:35–37).

2. A town in the hill country of Judah (Josh. 15:58; I Chron. 4:4, 18). Its site is marked by Khirbet Jedūr, about 7 miles n. by w. of Hebron.

3. A town, apparently in the territory of Simeon, not far from the s.w. boundary of Palestine (I Chron. 4:39); see GEDER. The LXX, however, reads Gerar.

4. A village in Benjamin (I Chron. 12:7; cf. v. 1); Khirbet el-Judeira, between Beit 'Anān and Beit Liḳya.

Ge'·ha·ra'shim (gē'hả-rā'shǐm) [valley of craftsmen], in A.V. **Char·a·shim** [craftsmen]. A valley in Judah (I Chron. 4:14), inhabited after the Exile by the tribe of Benjamin (cf. Neh. 11:35). It may perhaps be identified with Ṣarafand el-Kharāb, about 5 miles s.w. by w. of Lydda (Lod) in a dale that slopes into the valley of the Nahr Rūbīn. See CHARASHIM.

Ge·ha'zi (gē-hā'zī) [valley of vision]. Elisha's servant. He told the prophet of their hostess' desire for a son; but when the lad that was given her died and the mother cast herself at Elisha's feet, Gehazi would have thrust her away (II Kings 4:14, 27). To teach that it is not magic but faith and prayer which avail, Elisha sent Gehazi to lay the prophet's staff on the dead child. He did so, but without effect (vs. 29–37). When Naaman the Syrian followed the directions of Elisha and was cured of leprosy, he wished to make the prophet a present. The man of God refused, but Gehazi ran after him and told him that Elisha asked a talent of silver and 2 changes of raiment for needy friends. As penalty for his avarice and lying, and for bringing the prophetic office into contempt, the leprosy of Naaman cleaved to him (II Kings 5:20–27). More sayings and doings of Elisha's servant are subsequently reported, but the person referred to was probably Gehazi's successor.

Ge·hen'na (gē-hěn'ả). See HELL 2.

Ge·li'loth (gē-lī'lŏth) [circles, regions]. Apparently the same place as Gilgal, opposite the ascent of Adummim (cf. Josh. 15:7 and 18:17).

Ge·mal'li (gē-măl'ī) [probably, camel owner]. Father of the spy Ammiel (Num. 13:12).

Gem·a·ri'ah (gĕm'ả-rī'ả) [Jehovah has accomplished]. 1. A son of Hilkiah. He was one of two messengers sent by Zedekiah to Nebuchadnezzar. Jeremiah took advantage of the opportunity to send by them a letter to the captives in Babylon (Jer. 29:3).
2. A prince, son of Shaphan the scribe, and brother of Ahikam. He occupied a chamber in the Temple. He joined in requesting Jehoiakim not to burn Jeremiah's writings (Jer. 36:10, 12, 25).

Gen·e·al'o·gy. The tracing backward or forward of the line of ancestry of an individual or a family. The regulations of the commonwealth of Israel necessitated this being done to a large extent. Succession to the royal sovereignty, the high priesthood, the headship of tribe, tribal family, and father's house, depended upon lineage. There was general knowledge on the subject from the earliest period. There was interest in genealogy by reason of the constitution of tribes, which were divided on the lines of growth into great families, and these in turn into smaller families and so-called houses. Birth in a household declared one's relation to the several divisions of the tribe as distinctly as the native place determined one's classification according to the geographical divisions and subdivisions of a kingdom. Definite genealogical records are traceable from the beginning of the Hebrew nation (Num. 1:2, 18; I Chron. 5:7, 17). Claimants in the days of Ezra sought their register among those that were reckoned by genealogy, but since they could not find it, they were expelled from the priesthood as being polluted (Ezra 2:61, 62; Neh. 7:63, 64).

Two genealogies of Christ are given: 1 by Matthew in the direct, and 1 by Luke in the reverse, order of descent (Matt. 1:1–16; Luke 3:23–38). Matthew's purpose is to show Christ's legal title to the throne of David and to the covenant with Abraham (Matt. 1:1). Luke begins with the 2d Adam, the eternally begotten Son of God, and ascends to the 1st Adam, the son of God by creation (Luke 3:38). Apparently to help the memory, either Matthew or the official record from which he quoted made $3 \times 14 = 42$ generations for the period between Abraham and Jesus; viz., 14 generations between Abraham and David, 14 between David and the Babylonian Captivity, and 14 more between the Babylonian Captivity and Jesus Christ. To carry out this artificial division Ahaziah, Joash, and Amaziah are omitted between Joram and Uzziah in the second 14. There may be similar omissions in the last 14. In Luke there are 41 names in the line of descent from David to Jesus, against 28, or, with the omitted 3, 31 in Matthew. If the Shealtiel and Zerubbabel of Matthew are the same as those of Luke, as can scarcely be questioned, the difficulty arises that in Matthew Shealtiel is the son of Jechoniah, but in Luke the son of Neri; indeed, the 2 lines of descent from David to Jesus are different in the 2 evangelists. They diverge from David; one line passes through Solomon and the other through his brother Nathan. Putting both in the direct order of descent, they stand thus:

From Matthew's Genealogy	From Luke's Genealogy
David	David
Solomon	Nathan
	Mattatha
Rehoboam	Menna
Abijah	Melea
Asa	Eliakim
	Jonam
Jehoshaphat	Joseph
Joram	Judas
	Symeon
	Levi
	Matthat
Uzziah	Jorim
Jotham	Eliezer
Ahaz	Jesus
Hezekiah	Er
Manasseh	Elmadam
Amon	Cosam
Josiah	Addi
Jechoniah	Melchi
	Neri
Shealtiel (Salathiel)	Shealtiel (Salathiel)
Zerubbabel	Zerubbabel
	Rhesa
	Joanan
Abiud	Joda
	Josech
	Semein
Eliakim	Mattathias
	Maath
Azor	Naggai
	Esli
Sadoc	Nahum
	Amos
Achim	Mattathias
	Joseph
Eliud	Jannai
	Melchi
Eleazar	Levi
Matthan	Matthat
Jacob	Heli
Joseph, the husband of Mary	Joseph, the husband of Mary

Two explanations of these divergent genealogies are possible.

I. *The Early Church generally explained* both tables as recording the genealogy of Joseph. Julius Africanus (A.D. 220), the first known investigator of the question, adopted the theory that Joseph's grandfathers in the 2 genealogies, Melchi [Africanus has a corrupt text] and Matthan, had married successively the same woman, and that consequently Heli and Jacob were half brothers, having the same mother but different fathers. Heli married and died childless; and Jacob, according to the law of Levirate marriage (Deut. 25:6), took the widow to wife and raised up seed to his brother Heli by begetting a son Joseph. Hence Matthew can say, "Matthan begat Jacob, and Jacob begat Joseph"; and Luke can say, "Joseph, the son of Heli, the son of Matthat."

A readier solution of the problem on the lines of this theory is that the table in Matthew contains the legal successors to the throne of David, while that in Luke gives the paternal ancestors of Joseph. The line of Solomon became extinct in Jechoniah, otherwise known as Jehoiachin; and the succession passed over to the collateral line of David which sprang from David's son Nathan. The representative of this line was Shealtiel. For a brief space the royal line and the natural lineage of Joseph were identical; but after Zerubbabel the two lines separated. The family of the elder son, in whom the title to the throne inhered, at length became extinct, and the descendants of the younger son succeeded to the title. Matthat of this line (by some identified with Matthan) became heir apparent. He is supposed to have had 2 sons, Jacob and Heli. The elder, Jacob, had no son, but probably a daughter, the Virgin Mary. The younger, Heli, had a son Joseph; and Joseph, since his uncle Jacob had no male descendant, became heir to his uncle and to the throne. Broad genealogical terminology enables Matthew to say "Jacob begat Joseph," and Luke to say "Joseph, the son of Heli."

II. *Since the Reformation* a different conception of the 2 genealogies has won wide favor. According to this opinion, the table in Matthew gives the genealogy of Joseph and exhibits him as heir to the throne of David, while the table in Luke gives the genealogy of Mary and shows Jesus to be the actual son of David. With the clear declaration of Luke that Jesus had no human father, with the customary Heb. usage of the word son for descendant however remote, and on the basis of the approved Gr. text, the advocates of this view render Luke 3:23, Jesus, "being the son (as was supposed) of Joseph the son of Heli," etc. Jesus, according to Luke, is grandson of Heli, Mary's father, and thus a lineal descendant of David. A difficulty, not however peculiar to this theory, but lying equally against the first-mentioned hypothesis, is Matthew's record that Shealtiel was begotten by King Jechoniah, whereas Luke makes Shealtiel the son of Neri. Perhaps the simplest solution is the following: Jechoniah, who spent years in captivity, appears to have been the surviving nominal king of Judah in the year 562 B.C., 25 years after the fall of Jerusalem (II Kings 25:27). He apparently had no sons when carried off captive in 597. He was comparatively young, and children are not mentioned in the enumeration of his family (II Kings 24:8, 12, 15). Jeremiah prophesied that no son of his should occupy the throne (Jer. 22:30; cf. what is said of his father, ch. 36:30). In the genealogy as given in Matt., ch. 1, appears the entry, "After the carrying away to Babylon, Jechoniah begat Shealtiel." The 2 genealogies are intelligible, if this notice in Matthew be understood as a broad declaration in genealogical form denoting legal succession to the throne. The title passed from Jechoniah on his death to Shealtiel, a lineal descendant of David. There may of course have been close kinship between Jechoniah and Shealtiel. If Jechoniah had no son surviving him, but only a daughter, the inheritance passed to her children according to the Law (Num. 27:8–11). The phraseology of the genealogies is therefore explained on the assumption that Neri married the daughter of Jechoniah and begat Shealtiel by her. Shealtiel's lineage was reckoned as usual through his father back to Nathan and David, but his title to the throne

was reckoned through his maternal grandfather Jechoniah to Solomon and David.

In I Chron. 3:17 is the record: "The sons of Jeconiah, the captive: Shealtiel his son, and Malchiram," etc. The epithet "his son" is peculiar to Shealtiel, peculiar also in that it is deemed necessary to apply it to one of a group already designated as sons of Jeconiah. It marks Shealtiel as the king's successor. He could be called his son, if his daughter's son, just as Abiezer, son of the sister of Gilead, son of Manasseh, is reckoned among the sons of Manasseh, and apparently even among the sons of Gilead (I Chron. 7:14, 18; Num. 26:30).

Hebrew genealogical tables are apt to differ in the principles of construction from modern registers of pedigree. 1. Symmetry is often preferred to the exhibition of the unbroken descent from father to son. Hence links were freely omitted, and the enumeration was otherwise left incomplete: ten in the genealogy from Adam to Noah, and 10 from Shem to Abraham; seventy sons of Noah's sons, and 70 souls of the house of Jacob (Gen. 46:27). 2. The genealogy may be tribal rather than personal; and son may denote the inhabitants of a country, a people or tribe (Gen. 10:2–22), a town (v. 15), rarely an individual (vs. 8–10). Similar phenomena are found elsewhere (Gen. 25:2–4; I Chron. 2:50–55; see Son). 3. The words bear and beget and father are used with a corresponding breadth of meaning; as bear or beget a grandchild (cf. Gen. 46:12 with vs. 15, 18, 25), or great-grandchild (v. 12 and probably vs. 21, 22), or grandchild's grandchild (Matt. 1:9), or country (Gen. 25:2, 3).

Gen′er·a′tion. 1. A begetting or producing, and then the person or thing produced (Gen. 2:4; 5:1); in Heb. only pl. *tōlĕdōth.*

2. Each succession of persons from a common ancestor (Gen. 50:23; Ex. 20:5; Deut. 23:2); in Heb. expressed by a modification of the proper numeral or by *dōr* with an ordinal number.

3. The age or period of a body of contemporaries, not in the modern sense of the average lifetime of all who survive infancy, but the average period of the activity of any body of contemporaries as determined by the normal span of life. The generation lasts as long as any of the members survive (Ex. 1:6; Num. 32:13; Judg. 2:10; Eccl. 1:4); in Heb. *dōr.*

Gen′e·sis (jĕn′ê-sĭs) [Gr. *genesis,* origin]. The name, borrowed from the LXX, of the first O.T. book, called by the Hebrews from its initial word *Bĕrēshith* (In the beginning). It naturally divides itself into 3 sections: 1st, the history of the universe, showing God's relation to it, and introducing human history (chs. 1:1 to 2:3); 2d, a sketch of human history before Abraham, showing God's relation to the human race, and introducing the history of the chosen people (chs. 2:4 to 11:26); and 3d, the history of the covenant people down to the descent into Egypt (chs. 11:27 to 50:26). The 2d section, which deals with prehistoric times, includes the creation of man and his original condition (ch. 2:4–25), the Fall (ch. 3), the progress of sin (ch. 4:1–15), the worldly race (vs. 16–24), the godly line (chs. 4:25 to 5:32), the increase of wickedness (ch. 6:1–8), the flood (chs. 6:9 to 9:17), the re-peopling of the earth (chs. 9:18 to 10:32), the building of the tower of Babel (ch. 11:1–9), and the Semitic race in its earliest germs (ch. 11:10–26). The 3d section includes the early history of Abraham, his call, and his sojourn in Canaan (chs. 11:27 to 25:10), the life of Isaac from his father's death to the departure of Jacob for Mesopotamia (chs. 25:11 to 27:40), the life of Jacob from his departure for Mesopotamia to the death of Isaac (chs.

27:41 to 35:29), the descendants of Esau (ch. 36), the early history of Joseph to the time when he was sold into Egypt (ch. 37), Judah's sin and shame (ch. 38), Joseph in Egypt (chs. 39 to 45), Jacob and his whole household with Joseph in Egypt (chs. 46 to 49), and the death of Jacob and Joseph (ch. 50).

In this book 10 successive sections begin with the formula, "These are the generations of" (chs. 2:4; 5:1; 6:9; 10:1; 11:10; 11:27; 25:12, 19 ; 36:1 ; 37:2).

Gen·nes'a·ret (gĕ-nĕs'á-rĕt) ; in A.V. of I Macc. **Gen·ne'sar** (gĕ-nē'sär), in R.V. of same **Gen·nes'a·reth** (gĕ-nĕs'á-rĕth). A land adjacent to the Lake of Gennesaret, on its n.w. shore (Matt. 14:34 ; Mark 6:53) ; described by Josephus as a fertile plain, 30 stades in length by 20 in breadth, watered by a fountain called Capharnaum, and producing walnuts, palms, fig trees, olives, and grapes (Jos. *War* iii. 10, 8). It is the plain now called el-Ghuweir, formed by a recession of the hills from the shore just n. of Magdala, and measuring about 3 miles by 1½ miles.

The Lake of Gennesaret (Luke 5:1 ; Jos. *Antiq.* v. 1, 22 ; xviii. 2, 1 and 3) or Gennesar (Jos. *War.* ii. 20, 6), or the water of Gennesareth or Gennesar (I Macc. xi. 67 ; Jos. *Antiq.* xiii. 5, 7), was a common name for the Sea of Galilee.

Gen'tiles (jĕn'tīlz). All nations of the world other than the Jews (Isa. 49:6 ; Rom. 2:14 ; 3:29). The Jews were the chosen people of God ; their religion was sublime and stood in strong and favorable contrast to the Gentile religions ; strict laws were enacted to prevent the corruption of manners and of the true religion through contact with idolaters. These things led the Jews, though unjustly, to feel contempt for the Gentiles. The Israelites had been chosen for a purpose. They were to be "a light to the Gentiles" (Isa. 49:1–6), who were embraced in the promises (Isa. 2:2–4 ; Amos 9:12 ; Zech. 9:7). When Peter, taught by the vision at Joppa, broke through caste restriction, visiting and eating with the Gentile Cornelius, it gave offense even to Christian Jews (Acts 10:28 ; 11:3) ; and when Paul, speaking from the steps of the castle of Antonia, declared that God had commissioned him to preach to the Gentiles, the audience of Jews in the Temple court cried out for his death (ch. 22:21, 22). The early churches consisted largely of Gentiles, and the first Council of Jerusalem declined to impose on the former the burden of the Mosaic Law (ch. 15:1–29).

Ge·nu'bath (gĕ-nū'băth) [theft]. The son of the Edomite prince Hadad and the Egyptian queen's sister (I Kings 11:20).

Ge'ra (gē'rá) [probably hypocoristic; Heb., *gēr*, sojourner, and a divine element]. 1. A son of Bela and grandson of Benjamin (Gen. 46:21 ; I Chron. 8:3).

2. Another descendant of Bela, perhaps remoter than son (I Chron. 8:3, and probably v. 7).

3. A Benjamite, father of Ehud (Judg. 3:15).

4. A Benjamite, father of that Shimei who cursed David (II Sam. 16:5).

Perhaps 3 and 4 denote the founder of the family to which Ehud and Shimei belonged and are identical with the grandson of Benjamin.

Ge'rah (gē'rá). See WEIGHTS.

Ge'rar (gē'rär) [cf. Arab. *jarrah*, earthenware pot]. An ancient city on the s. border of Palestine near Gaza (Gen. 10:19 ; II Chron. 14:13), and early occupied by Philistines (Gen. 26:1). The country subject to it ex-

tended toward Kadesh and Shur (cf. ch. 20:1, 9 with ch. 26:6, 17, 18). It is commonly identified with Tell Jemmeh (near Khirbet Umm Jerrār) on the s. side of the wadi Ghuzzeh about a mile above the point at which the wadi esh-Sheri'ah enters it, about 8 miles s.s.e. of Gaza. Some scholars, however, prefer Tell esh-Sheri'ah, about 19 miles s.w. of Eleutheropolis (Beit Jibrīn).

Ger'a·senes (gĕr'á-sēnz). The people of Gerasa (R.V. of Mark 5:1 and Luke 8:26, 37 ; MSS. vary between Gerasenes, Gadarenes, Gergesenes) ; the name Gerasa is probably still echoed by Kersa, a ruin on the e. shore of the Sea of Galilee, opposite Magdala, 5 miles from the entrance of the Jordan into the lake. A short distance s. of the site is the only place on this coast where the steep hills come down close to the water (Luke 8:32). The city of the Decapolis, known as Gerasa, now Jerash, does not meet the conditions of the narrative, being 37 miles s.e. of the Sea of Galilee and 32 miles s.e. of Gadara.

Ger'ge·senes (gûr'gĕ-sēnz'). The people of Gergesa (Matt. 8:28, A.V., but in R.V., Gadarenes). The introduction of the name Gergesenes into the text is ascribed to Origen, who is said to have felt that Gadara was too far from the lake and to have been told by people acquainted with the region that an old town named Gergesa existed near the declivity down which the swine rushed. The ruin Kersa is probably this old town. See GERASENES.

Ge·ri'zim (gĕ-rī'zĭm) [a pl., Gerizites]. A steep rocky mountain forming the s. boundary of the valley in which Nablus, the ancient Shechem, lies, and facing the more elevated Mount Ebal, on the n. side of the valley. Mount Gerizim rises 2,849 feet above the level of the Mediterranean, and 700 feet above the town. When the Israelites conquered central Palestine, Joshua carried out the direction given to Moses and placed half of the tribes in front of Mount Gerizim to pronounce blessings and the other half over against Mount Ebal to pronounce curses (Deut. 11:29 ; 27:12, 13 ; Josh. 8:33–35). Jotham, the son of Gideon, standing on Mount Gerizim, proclaimed his parable to the men of Shechem (Judg. 9:7). Josephus (*Antiq.* xi. 8, 2, 7) says that Manasseh, brother of Jaddua, the high priest in the time of Alexander the Great, had married the daughter of a foreigner, Sanballat. The elders at Jerusalem commanded him either to divorce her or no longer to approach the altar. Manasseh thought of divorcing her, though she was still dear to him ; but her father, Sanballat, promised to build for his son-in-law, if he retained his wife, a rival temple to that of Jerusalem. He kept his word, erecting one on Mount Gerizim. This was the origin of the Samaritan temple on that mountain and must be dated before 330 B.C. If Sanballat was the Samaritan of that name who was an opponent of the Jews in the time of Nehemiah, about 445 B.C. (Neh. 4:1 ; 13:28), and not an official sent by Darius Codomanus (Jos. *Antiq.* xi. 7, 2 ; xii. 5, 5), the temple was built considerably before 330 B.C., perhaps c. 432. It was destroyed by John Hyrcanus, 128 B.C. The erection of the edifice made Gerizim the Samaritan sacred mountain. It was to it that the woman of Samaria and Jesus referred as "this mountain" (John 4:20, 21 ; cf. Jos. *Antiq.* xii. 1) ; and Jacob's Well, at which they were conversing, was at the foot of Mount Gerizim. Gerizim, now called Jebel et-Ṭūr, is a high tableland stretching far toward the e. and s.e. of Nablus. From the days of Benjamin of Tudela, a Jewish rabbi who traveled in Palestine about A.D. 1160, on to recent times, the view was held that Gerizim, the mountain of blessings, was fertile, and Ebal, that of curses, barren. But with the exception of a small ravine coming down from Gerizim near Nablus, both mountains are equally barren. See SHECHEM.

Ger'shom (gûr'shŏm) [By a popular ety. in Ex. 2:22; 18:3, interpreted as "sojourner there." "Banishment" has been suggested from Heb. *gārash* (drive out); also defined as "bell" from Arab. *jaras*. In both these cases *-om* is a suffix]. 1. Gershom, the son of Levi (I Chron. 6:16, 17, 20, 43, 62, 71). See GERSHON.
2. The elder son of Moses, born to him in Midian (Ex. 2:22; 18:3). He gave rise to a father's house which was reckoned among the Levites, not among the priests (I Chron. 23: 14-16).
3. A descendant of Phinehas the priest, and head of a father's house in that line in the time of Ezra (Ezra 8:2).

Ger'shon (gûr'shŏn) [banishment, but cf. Arab. *jaras* (bell); here the suffix is *-on*]. A son of Levi, and founder of the Gershonite family (Gen. 46:11; Ex. 6:16; Num. 3:17). He is sometimes called Gershom, which has a different suffix with the same meaning. His 2 sons, Libni and Shimei, gave rise to 2 subdivisions of the greater tribal family (Ex. 6:17; Num. 3:18; I Chron. 6:17).

Ger'shon·ites (gûr'shŏn-īts). The children and descendants of Gershon, constituting one of the 3 great divisions of the Levitical body. In the wilderness they encamped on the w. side of the tabernacle and had charge of the tabernacle itself, the tent with its hangings, and those of the courtyard (Num. 3:23-26; 4:21-28). To aid them in moving the tabernacle there were assigned to them 2 wagons and 4 oxen (ch. 7:7). The Gershonites consisted of 2 families, the Libnites and the Shimeites, and at the first census in the wilderness numbered 7,500 males (ch. 3:21, 22). Of the 13 cities assigned to them, 2 were in the half-tribe of Manasseh beyond the Jordan, 4 were in Issachar, 4 in Asher, and 3 in Naphtali (Josh. 21:27-33). The Gershonites were reorganized by David (I Chron. 23:7-11).

Ge'ruth Chim'ham (gē'rōōth kĭm'hăm) [the lodging place of Chimham]. Probably a khan (Jer. 41:17, R.V.). See CHIMHAM.

Ger'zites (gûr'zīts). See GIRZITE.

Ge'shan (gē'shăn), in A.V. **Ge'sham** (gē'shăm). A man of Judah, a son of Jahdai (I Chron. 2:47).

Ge'shem (gē'shĕm) and **Gash'mu** [rain; but cf. Arab. *jasuma*, to be bulky]. An Arabian, a great opponent of the Jews after their return from captivity. He ridiculed the proposal of Nehemiah to rebuild the wall of Jerusalem, as if this were tantamount to rebellion (Neh. 2:19). Not succeeding in deterring the Jew by this means, he joined with others in plotting violence, if not even actual murder, against him. Failing in this purpose also, he allowed the report to be circulated far and wide on his authority that Nehemiah was fortifying the city preparatory to rebelling against Persia and proclaiming himself king (Neh. 6:1 *seq.*).

Ge'shur (gē'shẽr) [a bridge]. A district lying between Hermon and Bashan and bordering on Argob (Deut. 3:14; Josh. 12:5; 13:11, 13; I Chron. 2:23). Evidently it was situated to the e. of Maacah, for Maacah bordered on Naphtali. It probably extended across Jauban from the Sea of Galilee to Bashan. It constituted an Aramaean kingdom (II Sam. 13:37; 15:8). Here David obtained a wife, and hither his son Absalom fled after the murder of Amnon (II Sam. 3:3; 13:37).

Gesh'u·rites (gĕsh'û-rīts); in A.V. twice **Ge·shu'ri** (gē-shōō'rĭ), as in Heb. 1. The people of Geshur (Deut. 3:14; Josh. 12:5; 13:11, 13).

2. A people in the country s. of Philistia in the direction of Egypt (Josh. 13:2; I Sam. 27:8).

Ge'ther (gē'thẽr). A family of the Aramaeans (Gen. 10:23; I Chron. 1:17). Their locality is uncertain.

Geth·sem'a·ne (gĕth-sĕm'a-nē) [Gr. from Aram., an oil press]. A garden, presumably of olives and furnished with a press to squeeze oil from the fruit. It was e. of Jerusalem, a little beyond the brook Kidron, and at or near the foot of the Mount of Olives (cf. Matt. 26:30 with v. 36; cf. Mark 14:26 with v. 32; John 18:1). It was a favorite spot with our Lord, who often resorted to it for retirement (Luke 22:39; John 18:2), and it is now forever sacred as having been the scene of his agony and of his betrayal and arrest (Matt. 26:36-56; Mark 14:32-52; Luke 22:39-53; John 18:1-12). The traditional site of Gethsemane lies a little e. of the bridge by which the road from St. Stephen's gate of Jerusalem crosses the Kidron. The Garden is situated at the angle made by the division of the road into 2 branches, one, the most n., leading directly up the face of the Mount of Olives, while the more s. one winds gently around the s. brow of the hill. The Garden is nearly square, measuring about 150 by 140 feet, and the Franciscans in 1848 enclosed it with a wall. Eight venerable olive trees are within, on which it is said the tax levy can be traced back to the occupation of Jerusalem by the Arabs in the 7th century; and many equally old are outside on the slope of the mount. These trees, however, did not witness our Lord's agony, for all the trees around Jerusalem were cut down during the siege of the city by Titus (Jos. *War* v. 12, 4). Robinson thinks that the spot is the same as that described by Eusebius as at the Mount of Olives, and afterward more definitely by Jerome at the foot of the mount, but he is doubtful if it is the genuine Gethsemane. Thomson regards the position as too near the city and too close to the great thoroughfare e. to have served as a place for retirement on that dangerous and dismal night. He believes Gethsemane to have been in a secluded vale several hundred yards n.e. of the traditional site. Barclay thinks it evident that the present enclosure, from its narrow dimensions, can occupy only in part the site of the ancient garden, and finds a better position higher up in the valley. The Greeks enclosed an adjacent piece of ground to the e., on the slope of the mountain, as being the Garden.

Ge·u'el (gē-ū'ĕl) [majesty of God; or perhaps, redeemed of God]. The spy from the tribe of Gad (Num. 13:15).

Ge'zer (gē'zẽr), in A.V. twice **Ga'zer** [portion]. In A.V. of I Macc. the Gr. forms Gazara and Gazara are used. An ancient Canaanite town, going back to c. 3000 B.C., not far from Lachish and the lower Beth-horon (Josh. 10: 33). It was on the boundary line of Ephraim (Josh. 16:3; cf. I Chron. 7:28), and with its suburbs was assigned to the Kohathite Levites (Josh. 21:21; I Chron. 6:67). The Ephraimites failed to expel the Canaanite inhabitants, and occupied the city with them at least for a time (Josh. 16:10; Judg. 1:29). More than one battle in David's reign was fought at or near Gezer (II Sam. 5:25; I Chron. 14:16; 20:4). One of the pharaohs captured Gezer from the Canaanites (I Kings 9:16). After burning it, he gave the ruins over to Solomon as a dowry with his daughter when she was married to the Hebrew king. The city was at once rebuilt. It was an important place in the wars of the Maccabees. Bacchides strengthened its fortifications (I Macc. 9:52). It was besieged and taken by Simon, and made

THE GARDEN OF GETHSEMANE

Ancient Olive Trees in the Garden of Gethsemane

stronger than before (chs. 13:43, R.V., 48, 53; 14:34). It is now called Tell Jazer and is situated about 18 miles w.n.w. of Jerusalem and 5⅔ e. of Ekron.

Gez′rite (gĕz′rīt). See GIRZITE.

Gi′ah (gī′à) [breaking forth, as of a spring]. A village somewhere between Gibeon in Benjamin and the ford of the Jordan near the Jabbok (II Sam. 2:24).

Gi′ant. A man of abnormally tall stature; like Og, king of Bashan, whose bedstead or sarcophagus was 9 cubits long by 4 broad (Deut. 3:11), Goliath of Gath, whose height was 6 cubits and a span (I Sam. 17:4), and the man whom Benaiah slew, whose height was 5 cubits (I Chron. 11:23). A stalwart race of men like the Anakim and other early nations of Canaan e. of the country e. of the Jordan (Deut. 1:28; 2:10, 11, 20, 21; 9:2). When Hebron was captured by the Hebrews, the Anakim who escaped destruction took refuge in the Philistine towns. Goliath of Gath, Ishbi-benob, and other huge Philistines were probably of this expelled race of the Anakim (I Sam. 17:4; II Sam. 21:15–22). The valley of the Rephaim or giants near Jerusalem was a perpetual reminder, by its name, of the early stalwart race which long inhabited it (Josh. 15:8; 18:16). The exact meaning of *nephilim*, the word rendered giants in Gen. 6:4; Num. 13:33 A.V., is uncertain, and accordingly it is left untranslated in R.V.

Gib′bar (gĭb′är) [mighty man, hero]. A man whose children, or a place of whose former inhabitants some descendants, returned from captivity with Zerubbabel (Ezra 2:20). In the parallel passage in Neh. 7:25 Gibeon stands in place of Gibbar.

Gib′be•thon (gĭb′e-thŏn) [mound, height]. A town of Dan (Josh. 19:44) assigned to the Levites of the family of Kohath (ch. 21:20–23). The Philistines gained possession of it. Nadab was assassinated there while laying siege to the place (I Kings 15:27). Omri before he ascended the throne also besieged the town (I Kings 16:15, 17). It is probably to be identified with Tell el-Melāt, ⅝ of a mile s. of Na′aneh and directly e. of Ekron (′Aḳir).

Gib′e•a (gĭb′e-à) [a hill]. A grandson of Caleb, but probably a village (I Chron. 2:49); see GIBEAH 1.

Gib′e•ah (gĭb′e-à) [a hill]. 1. A village in the hill country of Judah (Josh. 15:57); it has been identified with el-Jeba′ about 10 miles n.n.w. of Hebron, and about 11 n.e. of Eleutheropolis, and about 7½ s.w. of Bethlehem, but on account of the list of places in vs. 55–57 its location is to be sought s.e. of Hebron. 2. A town of Benjamin near Ramah (Judg. 19:13, 14); called also Geba, the masculine form of the same name (cf. ch. 20:10, R.V. marg., with v. 4). It is designated Gibeah of Benjamin (*ibid.*; cf. I Sam. 13:2), and Gibeah of the children of Benjamin (II Sam. 23:29); and appears to be identical with Gibeah of Saul (I Sam. 11:4; II Sam. 21:6; Isa. 10:29). Its inhabitants by their misbehavior brought down punishment, not merely on themselves, but on the whole tribe of Benjamin (Judg., chs. 19; 20). Gibeah was Saul's place of residence when he was called to be king (I Sam. 10:26), and it remained his home and served as the political capital of his kingdom (chs. 15:34; 22:6; 23:19). It existed in the days of Isaiah and of Hosea (Isa. 10:29, distinguished from Geba; Hos. 9:9; 10:9). The town was situated on the highway from Jerusalem to the n., about midway between Jerusalem and Ramah (Judg. 19:13; Jos *Antiq.* v. 2, 8, cf. viii. 12, 3; *War* v. 2, 1). Its site is Tell el-Fūl, about 4 miles n. of Jerusalem.

3. A hill or town in the hill country of Ephraim, belonging to Phinehas, where Eleazar the high priest, the son′ of Aaron, was buried (Josh. 24:33; Jos. *Antiq.* v. 1, 29). Generally identified with Jībia, 8½ miles w.s.w. of Seilun (Shiloh), and 3½ miles e. by s. of Tibneh (Timnath); but Nebi Sāleḥ about 1½ miles n.e. of Tibneh seems a better site. The tradition of the Samaritans, which locates the grave at ′Awertah, 4½ miles s. of Shechem, is late.

4. Gibeah or hill of God (I Sam. 10:5, R.V. marg.). Often identified with Gibeah of Saul, for it appears to have been Saul's home (ch. 10:10–14). On account of the name (v. 5, R.V. marg.) its identity with Ram Allah (height of God), 4 miles n.w. by n. of Ramah, has been proposed. Much depends upon the identification of Rachel's sepulcher and Zelzah (cf. ch. 10:2–5 with ch. 13:3).

Gib′e•ath (gĭb′e-ăth) [a hill]. A town of Benjamin (Josh. 18:28). Generally identified with Gibeah, 2.

Gib′e•ath•ite (gĭb′e-ăth-īt). A native or inhabitant of Gibeah (I Chron. 12:3).

Gib′e•on (gĭb′e-ŭn) [pertaining to a hill]. The chief city of the Hivites, a people of Canaan (Josh. 11:19), included in the general designation Amorite (II Sam. 21:2). They possessed also Chephirah, Beeroth, and Kiriath-jearim (Josh. 9:17). They obtained a treaty with Joshua by false pretenses. The deceit was discovered and they were made slaves of the Israelites (ch. 9). But the treaty was respected: the Gibeonites were aided against their enemies (ch. 10:1–11); and several centuries later, when Saul violated its provisions by a massacre of Gibeonites, the sense of justice was satisfied by the execution of 7 of Saul's sons (II Sam. 21:1–9). Gibeon was within the territory assigned to the Benjamites (Josh. 18:25); and was given, with its suburbs, to the family of Aaron (ch. 21:17). Saul's ancestors dwelt for a time in the town and were men of influence (I Chron. 8:29; 9:35). In the contest between Ish-bosheth and David, a battle took place here (II Sam. 2:8–17, 24; 3:30). Here David gained a victory over the Philistines (I Chron. 14:16; in II Sam. 5:25, Geba). In its vicinity Joab murdered Amasa (II Sam. 20:8). There also, in David's reign and in the early part of Solomon's reign, before the Temple was built, stood the tabernacle and the brazen altar; and there Solomon sacrificed and in a dream received a message from God (I Kings 3:4–15; I Chron. 16:39, 40; 21:29; II Chron. 1:3, 6, 13). Gibeonites returned from the Exile (Neh. 7:25), and aided in rebuilding the wall of Jerusalem (ch. 3:7). According to Josephus, Gibeon was 40 or 50 stadia (about 4½ to 6 miles) from Jerusalem (Jos. *Antiq.* vii. 11, 7; *War* ii. 19, 1). Its site is found at the modern village of el-Jīb, 5½ miles n.w. by n. of Jerusalem. An oblong or oval hill stands in the midst of a basin consisting of broad valleys in a high state of cultivation. The hill is steep of ascent, being composed of horizontal layers of limestone rock that form great steps from the plain upward.

S.e. of the village, and quite a distance down the hill, is a fine fountain of water, which flows into a subterranean reservoir artificially cut. Not far from it, among olive trees, is an open reservoir about 59 feet long by 36 feet broad; it was doubtless intended to receive the superfluous waters of the cavern. On the w. is a tank, 11 by 7 feet in size, cut in the rock, and called el-Birkeh, the pool. In the plain a little lake, 6 to 8 acres in extent, is formed during the winter. One or other of these was doubtless the pool or great waters of Gibeon (II Sam. 2:13; Jer. 41:12).

The wilderness of Gibeon was perhaps simply the uncultivated plateau between Gibeon and Ramah. If a desert is meant, it was at considerable distance e. from the city (II Sam. 2:24).

Gib'e·on·ites (gĭb'ê-ŭn-īts). The inhabitants of Gibeon or of that city with its 3 dependent towns (II Sam. 21:1-4; cf. Josh. 9:3, 7, 17).

Gib'lites (gĭb'lîts). See GEBALITES.

Gid·dal'ti (gĭ-dăl'tī) [I have magnified (God)]. A singer, a son of Heman (I Chron. 25:4), and head of the 22d of the 24 companies of 12 musicians each which were appointed in David's reign for the service of the sanctuary (v. 29).

Beginning with Hananiah the names in I Chron. 25:4, read in their present sequence, but variously divided and conjoined and changed in vocalization, form a prayer. The sequence, however, is not preserved in vs. 23-31.

Gid'del (gĭd'ĕl) [(God) has increased, or reared]. 1. Head of a family of Nethinim (Ezra 2:47; Neh. 7:49).
2. Head of a family of Solomon's servants (Ezra 2:56; Neh. 7:58).

Gid'e·on (gĭd'ê-ŭn), in A.V. of N.T. **Ged'e·on** after the Gr. [hewer, feller]. A son of Joash, family of Abiezer, tribe of Manasseh, who dwelt at Ophrah (Judg. 6:11). While threshing wheat in the wine press at Ophrah, to hide it from the Midianite pillagers, he was called by the angel of Jehovah to deliver his people (vs. 12-24). At once he offered sacrifice (cf. Ex. 20:24). That night he threw down his father's altar of Baal and built an altar of Jehovah (Judg. 6:25-27). The townspeople demanded his death, but his father urged that Baal be allowed to contend for himself. Gideon thus acquired the name Jerubbaal, "Let Baal contend," and later, when the word Baal was shunned as abominable, Jerubbesheth, "Let the shameful thing contend" (Judg. 6:28-32; II Sam. 11:21; see ISH-BOSHETH). Having summoned the men of Manasseh, Asher, Zebulun, and Naphtali (Judg. 6:35), he yet hesitated until his call had been confirmed by the miracle of the fleece (vs. 36-40). With his followers intentionally reduced to 300, that the glory of the victory might be not with man but with Jehovah, he made a night attack on the Midianite camp, which was pitched in the valley of Jezreel (v. 33), by the hill of Moreh (ch. 7:1). The Midianites were thrown into confusion, fought each other and fled. The flight was to the Jordan and their own country beyond. Ephraimites, summoned by couriers from Gideon, seized the fords of the river to intercept fugitives, and captured and slew 2 princes of Midian and took their heads to Gideon, already across the river (chs. 7:24 to 8:3). Continuing the pursuit, he and his band drove the Midianites to the confines of the desert and brought back the 2 kings of Midian captive and put them to death (ch. 8:4-21). This victory was the celebrated day of Midian (Isa. 9:4; 10:26; Ps. 83:11). A movement now set in to make Gideon and his house royal, but he refused the crown because Jehovah was their king (Judg. 8:22, 23). However, he had the earrings of the Midianites made into an ephod, which he put in his own city, Ophrah. His act was unwise as the event proved, and the ephod became a snare to Gideon and his family and a means of seduction to Israel (Judg. 8:24-27; cf. Lev. 20:6). Gideon had many wives and 70 sons, besides a son Abimelech, a concubine's child, who made himself king on the death of his father. Gideon died in a good old age (Judg., chs. 6 to 8; Heb. 11:32).

Gid'e·o'ni (gĭd'ê-ō'nī) [cf. Gideon]. Father of the prince of the tribe of Benjamin in the time of Moses (Num. 1:11).

Gi'dom (gī'dŏm) [a cutting off]. A village apparently in Benjamin, between Gibeah and the rock of Rimmon (Judg. 20:45).

Gier'-ea'gle. 1. The rendering in A.V. of Heb. *rāḥām*, so named from its affection for its young. In R.V. the word is translated vulture, which is the meaning of gier. It was ceremonially unclean (Lev. 11:18; Deut. 14:17). Undoubtedly the Egyptian vulture, Pharaoh's hen or chicken (*Neophron percnopterus*), is meant, which the Arabs still call *raḥam*. Its general color is white but the primary feathers of the wings are black. The young are brown. The length of the adult is a little over 2 feet. It ranges in summer from the s. of France, by s. Europe and n. Africa, to the w. of India, where it is replaced by a closely allied species. The Egyptian vulture is common in Palestine during its n. migration, and breeds in that country.
2. The rendering in R.V. of Heb. *peres* (Lev. 11:13; Deut. 14:12). See OSSIFRAGE.

Gifts. Gifts were given by fathers to sons (Gen. 25:6), or as dowry to daughters on their marriage (Judg. 1:15), or by the bridegroom to the bride's father (Gen. 34:12), or by people present by invitation at a wedding (Ps. 45:12). They were bestowed upon fellow men out of good will (Esth. 9:22) or to secure favor (Prov. 18:16). It was forbidden to offer them to judges for the purpose of bribery (Ex. 23:8; Deut. 16:19; Prov. 29:4). Monarchs bestowed them as a reward for service (Dan. 2:48), or as a gracious favor to cause public rejoicings (Esth. 2:18). They were brought by subjects as tribute (II Sam. 8:2, 6; II Chron. 26:8; Ps. 45:12; 72:10; Matt. 2:11). Gifts were required for the expenses of religious worship (Matt. 5:23, 24; 8:4; Luke 21:5). Essentially the same customs as to gifts still prevail throughout the East.

The gift of God is eternal life through Jesus Christ (John 4:10; Rom. 6:23). Christ gave gifts unto men (Eph. 4:8). He not only opened up a way for them to God, and enables them to stand before the just and holy One, but he has obtained for them the gift of the Holy Spirit (John 14:16; 16:7; Acts 2:38) and all the manifestations of the Spirit in the hearts and lives of believers: repentance (Acts 5:31), faith (Eph. 2:8), love (Rom. 5:5), joy, peace, long-suffering, gentleness, goodness, meekness, temperance (Gal. 5:22). All Christian virtues are graces, that is, gifts. God bestows various gifts upon men, qualifying them severally as he will for different forms of work in the Kingdom (Rom. 12:6; I Cor. 7:7; 12:4, 9; Eph. 4:7-16). See MIRACLE, TONGUE.

Gi'hon (gī'hŏn) [bursting forth, as a fountain]. 1. One of the 4 rivers of paradise (Gen. 2:13). See EDEN.
2. A spring in a valley outside the walls of Jerusalem from which the city obtained part of its water supply (II Chron. 32:30; 33:14; Jos. *Antiq.* vii. 14, 5). It was not in sight of the stone of Zoheleth, near En-rogel; but the sound of the trumpet and the noise of the shouting at Gihon were heard at En-rogel (I Kings 1:40-45). On Ophel the Jebusites (c. 2000 B.C.) cut a passage through the rock to a chamber. Thence a channel descended for 125 ft. to a spot where buckets could be let down a 40-ft. shaft. At the bottom was the water which had been carried back 50 ft. from Gihon; the spring had been dammed up, and so its water flowed into this underground conduit. It was probably up this water passage that Joab climbed to admit

the armies of David into the city. There was an upper and presumably a lower Gihon, as early as the time of Hezekiah at least. The upper Gihon is to be identified with St. Mary's Well or the Virgin's Fount, which is situated in the Kidron Valley on the e. side of Ophel and s. of the Temple area. From Gihon Hezekiah made his aqueduct, the Siloam tunnel (II Kings 20:20; II Chron. 32:30), which led to the Siloam pool within the city walls to the s.w. of the spring (cf. John 9:7).

Gil'a·lai (gĭl'á-lī) [perhaps, Jehovah has rolled away]. A Levite, a musician who took part in the dedication of the wall of Jerusalem (Neh. 12:36).

Gil·bo'a (gĭl-bō'á). The mountain on which Saul was defeated by the Philistines and met his death (I Sam. 28:4; 31:1, 8; II Sam. 1:6, 21; 21:12; I Chron. 10:1, 8). It is the n.e. spur of Mount Ephraim, and forms the watershed between the Kishon basin and the Jordan Valley. The ridge forms an arc e. of the Plain of Esdraelon and runs first s.e. and then s. It is about 8 miles long and 3 to 5 miles in breadth, and is divided by ravines into several plateaus. The highest point, which is at Sheikh Burkān, is 1,696 feet above sea level. The w. slopes of the range are gradual, but those facing n. are steep and rugged, with precipices in many places. The e. slopes over the Jordan Valley are also steep, in places precipitous, especially toward the s. On the tablelands and gentle w. slopes pasture land is found, wheat and barley grow, and olives and figs are cultivated. The rest of the ridge is naked rock, or is covered with wild grass and brushwood. The modern name is Jebel Fukū'a, but a village, Jelbōn, suggests the name Gilboa.

Gil'e·ad (gĭl'ē-ăd), in A.V. of Maccabees **Gal'a·ad** [cf. Arab. jal'ad, hard, rough]. 1. The son of Machir and grandson of Manasseh. He founded a tribal family (Num. 26:29, 30; Josh. 17:1).

2. Father of Jephthah (Judg. 11:1).

3. A Gadite (I Chron. 5:14).

4. The mountainous country e. of the Jordan, extending from the tableland of Moab n. at least to the Yarmuk (Deut. 3:16, 17; I Sam. 31:11), and perhaps farther, since the ruggedness of the land continues unchanged n. of that river. It is divided by the Jabbok into 2 parts (Josh. 12:2). The s. half was assigned to the tribe of Gad, and the n. half was included in the territory of half Manasseh (Deut. 3:12, 13; Josh. 13:24–31). The name is still connected with a mountain s. of the Jabbok in its designation Jebel Jele'ād. The last interview between Laban and Jacob took place in Mount Gilead (Gen. 31:21, 25). It was a place well suited for cattle (I Chron. 5:9, 10); and the sight of Gilead and the land of Jazer (cf. I Chron. 26:31) suggested to the Reubenites and the Gadites, who had large flocks and herds, the expediency of applying to Moses for permission, which was conditionally granted them, of settling permanently on the e. side of the Jordan (Num., ch. 32; Josh. 13:8–11). Within the limits of Gilead grew the celebrated balm (Jer. 8:22; cf. Gen. 37:25). In an extended sense the term Gilead includes the whole region e. of the Jordan (Deut. 34:1; Josh. 22:9; Judg. 20:1; II Sam. 2:9; I Macc. 5:17, 24–27, 36; Jos. Antiq. xii. 8, 3; in ix. 8, 1, Gilead and Bashan are distinguished).

5. A mountain abutting on the valley of Jezreel (Judg. 7:3; cf. v. 1 and ch. 6:33). While Gilead in this passage may be a misreading for Gilboa, it should be borne in mind that the LXX agrees with the Heb. text in this name. The spring of Harod beside which Gideon encamped is generally identified with 'Ain Jālūd, and the stream in the vale of

Jezreel is now called Nahr Jālūd, in which may be an echo of Gilead. There is perhaps better evidence than the present name. Gilead was part of Naphtali (II Kings 15:29). It may be that Naphtali extended across the Jordan to the e., but it is quite possible that Gilead denoted a rugged district of Naphtali w. of the Jordan; and if so, the correctness of the text of Judg. 7:3 is confirmed.

6. A city in the region of Gilead (Hos. 6:8; cf. ch. 12:11).

Gil'gal (gĭl'găl) [a circle, a cromlech]. 1. The first encampment of the Israelites after crossing the Jordan, and their headquarters during the conquest of Canaan; 12 memorial stones taken from the bed of the river were erected here (Josh. 4:19–24). By a wordplay the name Gilgal (rolling) is connected with the rolling away of their reproach by their circumcision after long neglect of the ordinance in the wilderness (Josh. 5:7–9). The camp was pitched between the Jordan and Jericho, and on its site arose a town, which was on the n. border of Judah (ch. 15:7). It is uncertain whether this town or another place of the same name was on Samuel's circuit (I Sam. 7:16), and where, it may be inferred, Saul was made king and the kingdom renewed (ch. 11:15). At any rate, it was at Gilgal in the Jordan Valley where a muster of the people took place to form an army which should encounter the Philistines then oppressing the land, when Saul, finding it difficult to hold the people together until Samuel should come and offer sacrifice, himself offered burnt offerings (ch. 13:4–15). By this disobedience he forfeited the privilege of founding a dynasty (vs. 13, 14). There, too, for his obstinacy in sparing Agag he was rejected from being king and God's spirit withdrew from him (chs. 15:20–23; 16:14). To Gilgal the representatives of the tribe of Judah went to welcome David back after the death of Absalom (II Sam. 19:15, 40). Like other holy places it became a focus of idolatry under the kings who succeeded Jeroboam, and it was in consequence denounced by the prophets (Hos. 4:15; 9:15; 12:11; Amos 4:4; 5:5). It is probably the house of Gilgal or Beth-gilgal mentioned after the Captivity (Neh. 12:29). The site of Khirbet al-'Athlah, near which is a pool called Birket Jiljūliyeh, about 1½ miles e. of Jericho fulfills the requirements of Biblical data and tradition.

2. A village from which Elijah and Elisha went down to Beth-el (Deut. 11:30; II Kings 2:1–4; 4:38[?]). It was probably the present village of Jiljilia, 7 miles n. by w. of Beth-el.

3. A town associated with Dor and Tirzah (Josh. 12:23); probably Jiljūlieh, a little n. of the brook Ḳānah, and 5 miles n.e. by n. of Antipatris, on the edge of the plain of Sharon.

Gi'loh (gī'lō) [probably for original Gilōn]. A village in the hill country of Judah (Josh. 15:51); Khirbet Gāla, 1¼ miles w. of Beit Ummar and 5 miles n.n.w. of Hebron.

Gi'lo·nite (gī'lō-nīt). A native or inhabitant of Giloh, as Ahithophel (II Sam. 15:12; 23:34).

Gim'el (gĭm'ĕl) [camel]. The 3d letter of the Heb. alphabet, to which corresponds Gr. gamma; it is pronounced like Eng. g. Gimel stands at the head of the 3d section of Psalm 119, since each verse of the section begins with this letter in the original.

Gim'zo (gĭm'zō) [abounding in sycamores; cf. Arab. jummaiz, sycamore]. A town with dependent villages situated in Judah. It was taken by the Philistines during the reign of Ahaz (II Chron. 28:18); identified with Jimzu, on an eminence about 3 miles s.e. of Lydda.

Gin. A noose or trap, laid on the ground, in which birds, beasts, and even men are caught (Job 18:9; Amos 3:5). The 2 words *môḳesh* and *paḥ*, of which it is the translation, are usually rendered by snare.

Gi'nath (gī'năth). Father of Tibni (I Kings 16:22).

Gin'ne·tho'i (gĭn'ê-thō'ī), in A.V. **Gin'ne·tho** (gĭn'ê-thō) [gardener]. A chief of the priests who returned with Zerubbabel from Babylon (Neh. 12:4, 7). In the next generation, a father's house among the priests, which occupies the same position in the corresponding catalogue, bore the name Ginnethon (v. 16). The difference is merely that between a *yodh* (y) and a final *nun* (n). Probably Ginnethon stood originally in v. 4.

Gin'ne·thon (gĭn'ê-thŏn) [gardener]. 1. A father's house among the priests in the days of the high priest Joiakim (Neh. 12:16); see GINNETHOI.

2. A priest who, doubtless in behalf of a father's house, sealed a covenant to worship Jehovah (Neh. 10:6).

Gir'dle. See CLOTHING and HIGH PRIEST.

Gir'ga·shite (gûr'gȧ-shīt), in A.V. pl., but once **Gir'ga·site** (gûr'gȧ-sīt). A tribe of Canaan (Gen. 10:15, 16; 15:21; Deut. 7:1; Josh. 3:10; 24:11; Neh. 9:8). They must not be confounded with the Gergesenes.

Gir'zites (gûr'zīts); in A.V. **Gez'rites**, in marg. **Giz'rites** and **Ger'zites** respectively. A people living s. of the Philistine country and mentioned with the Amalekites and Geshurites (I Sam. 27:8).

Gis'pa (gĭsh'pȧ), in A.V. **Gis'pa** (gĭs'pȧ). An overseer of the Nethinim in Nehemiah's time (Neh. 11:21).

Git'tah-he'pher (gĭt'ä-hē'fẽr). See GATH-HEPHER.

Git'ta·im (gĭt'ȧ-ĭm) [perhaps, a dual, 2 wine presses]. A village of Benjamin (Neh. 11:31, 33), to which the Beerothites fled probably at the time of Saul's cruelty (II Sam. 4:3). Identified with Gamteti of the Tell el-Amarna tablets and located at or near Ramleh.

Git'tite (gĭt'īt) [of Gath]. A native or inhabitant of Gath (II Sam. 6:10, 11; 15:18, 19, 22).

Git'tith (gĭt'īth) [Gittite]. A musical term (Psalms 8; 81; 84, titles). It is the feminine form of the Heb. adjective for Gittite, and it denotes a musical instrument in use in Gath, or a vintage song to the tune of which the psalm should be sung, or a march of the Gittite guard (II Sam. 15:18).

Gi'zo·nite (gī'zō-nīt). The designation of Hashem, one of David's mighty men (I Chron. 11:34), pointing either to his paternity or to his birthplace. But neither man nor place with a name like Gizoh is found in the Bible; and perhaps Gizonite is a corruption of Gunite (cf. *Gennouni*, text of Rahlf's LXX; cf. Num. 26:48).

Giz'rite (gĭz'rīt). See GIRZITE.

Glass. 1. A mirror (Ex. 38:8; Job 37:18; I Cor. 13:12, all A.V.); see MIRROR.

2. The rendering of Heb. *zᵉḳuḳith* (Job 28:17, R.V., where A.V. has crystal) and of Gr. *hyalos* and its adjective (Rev. 4:6; 15:2; 21:18, 21). It is probably real glass. Glass was known to the Greeks as early as the time of Herodotus, and to the Egyptians long before the Exodus.

Glean'ing. Gathering the grain which the reapers have failed to remove, or the grapes which remain after the vintage (Judg. 8:2; Ruth 2:2, 16; Isa. 17:6). For the benefit of the poor, the fatherless, the widow, and the stranger, the owner was instructed by the Law not to glean his harvest field or vineyard, nor return for a forgotten sheaf, nor gather fallen fruit (Lev. 19:9, 10; 23:22; Deut. 24:19).

A Gleaner

Glede. The common kite (Deut. 14:13); the word used to render Heb. *rā'āh*, which is a copyist's error for *dā'āh*; see DALETH. A later scribe seems to have written *dayyāh* on the marg. as a correction, which afterward crept into the text (for it is not mentioned in the corresponding list in Lev., ch. 11), and is rendered kite in R.V., vulture in A.V.

Gnat. The rendering of Gr. *kōnōps*, a small insect (Matt. 23:24), abounding in marshes and vexatious by reason of its bite, from which the Egyptians protected themselves at night by sleeping under nets (Herod. ii. 95). It is evidently some species of *Culex*, a genus known by its hairy antennae, plumed in the males, its proboscis, its slender body, its 2 gauzy wings, its long legs, and its blood-sucking propensities. "To strain *at*" in the A.V. is a misprint in the original edition of 1611 for "strain *out*." The earlier Eng. versions have "out," and the R.V. corrects the error of A.V., and translates to "strain out the gnat, and swallow the camel." To strain out anxiously any small insect which has accidentally fallen into the water one is about to drink, but unconcernedly to swallow a camel, is to be particular about minute points of ceremony or of duty, while practicing gross violations of the moral law.

Goad. A long pole sharpened at the point or iron-tipped, used to urge cattle forward (I Sam. 13:21). With a goad Shamgar slew 600 Philistines (Judg. 3:31). "It is hard for thee to kick against the pricks" (Acts 9:5, A.V.) is the metaphor of a recalcitrant animal injuring itself against the oxgoad. The words of the wise are compared to goads (Eccl. 12:11).

Go'ah (gō'ȧ), in A.V. **Go'ath** [lowing]. A place near Jerusalem to the w. or s. (Jer. 31:39).

Goat. The rendering of a number of Heb. words in the O.T., and of more than one Gr. word in the N.T.: *'attud*, he-goat, probably as leader of the flock; *tayish*, he-goat; *ṣaphir*, he-goat, as the leaper; *'ēz*, she-goat, also a goat without regard to sex; *śā'ir*, he-goat, and *śᵉirāh*, she-goat, as shaggy; and the Gr. words *tragos*, he-goat; *aix*, goat; *eriphos*, goat, and *eriphion*, a young goat, kid. Goats were tended with the sheep by the same shepherd (Gen. 27:9; 30:32), but in separate companies (Matt. 25:32). Their hair was woven into cloth (Ex. 25:4; 35:26), the flesh and milk were used for food (Lev. 7:23; Deut. 14:4; Prov. 27:27), and in extremity their hairy skin served as clothing (Heb. 11:37). They were an important item of a cattle owner's wealth (Gen. 30:33, 43; 31:1; I Sam. 25:2; II Chron. 17:11). The goat was a sacrificial animal, used for burnt offering and sin offering (Gen. 15:9; Ex. 12:5; Lev. 1:10; 4:24; Num. 7:17; 15:27; Ezra 6:17; 8:35; Heb. 9:12). The domestic goat (*Capra hircus*) belongs to the great family of *Bovidae*, or hollow-horned ruminants. The closest affinity is believed to be to the sheep, and there is a series of connecting links between the 2 animals. One of the few points of difference is that in the goat the horns are simply curved backward. Their habits are different. In Palestine the sheep may be seen grazing the tender herbage and grass, while the goats browse tender twigs and leaves. Every flock of goats has its own stately leader (cf. Jer. 50:8). The goat was very abundant in ancient Palestine, as was to be expected in a hilly and somewhat dry country. The ordinary goat of Syria is black in color and has pendant ears a foot long hanging down below the recurved horns. It is Linnaeus' *Capra mambrica*. His *Capra hircus*, variety *angorensis*, the Mohair goat, is also occasionally bred in the n. of Palestine.

Goat, Wild. An animal, in Heb. *yāʻēl*, eminent. Its refuge is among the high hills (Ps. 104:18) and rocks (Job 39:1), En-gedi being its special haunt in Palestine (I Sam. 24:2). It is a species of ibex (*Capra beden*), called by the Arabs *badan* (*beden*). It is of a much lighter color than the European ibex. Its horns are more slender and recurved, wrinkled, and knotted on the front face only. It is found in Egypt, Arabia, Persia, Moab, and in the wilderness of Judea near the Dead Sea. Tristram met with it twice at its favorite spot, En-gedi, and found its teeth fossil in cave breccia on Lebanon, where it does not now occur. Wild goat is also the rendering of Heb. *'akkō* (Deut. 14:5). It may be the same species.

Go'ath (gō'ăth). See GOAH.

Gob (gŏb) [Heb. *gēb*; Aram. *gubbā*; pit, cistern]. A place at which war was waged with the Philistines twice in the reign of David (II Sam. 21:18, 19). Site unknown. The text is uncertain. In I Chron. 20:4 the seat of war is Gezer.

God (gŏd). The Eng. word God is derived from a root meaning to call, and indicates simply the object of worship, one whom men call upon or invoke. The Gr. word which it translates in the pages of the N.T., however, describes this object of worship as Spirit; and the O.T. Heb. word, which this word in turn represents, conveys, as its primary meaning, the idea of power. On Christian lips, therefore, the word God designates fundamentally the almighty Spirit who is worshiped and whose aid is invoked by men. This primary idea of God, in which is summed up what is known as theism, is the product of that general revelation which God makes of himself to all men, on the plane of nature. The truths involved in it are continually reiterated, enriched, and deepened in the Scriptures; but they are not so much revealed by them as presupposed at the foundation of the special revelation with which the Scriptures busy themselves—the great revelation of the grace of God to sinners. On the plane of nature men can learn only what God necessarily is, and what, by virtue of his essential

attributes, he must do; a special communication from him is requisite to assure us what, in his infinite love, he will do for the recovery of sinners from their guilt and misery to the bliss of communion with him. And for the full revelation of this, his grace in the redemption of sinners, there was requisite an even more profound unveiling of the mode of his existence, by which he has been ultimately disclosed as including in the unity of his being a distinction of persons, by virtue of which it is the same God from whom, through whom, and by whom are all things, who is at once the Father who provides, the Son who accomplishes, and the Spirit who applies, redemption. Only in the uncovering of this supernal mystery of the Trinity is completed the revelation of what God is. That there is no hint of the Trinity in the general revelation made on the plane of nature is due to the fact that nature has nothing to say of redemption, in the process of which alone are the depths of the divine nature made known. That the Trinity is explicitly revealed only in the N.T. is due to the fact that not until the N.T. stage of revelation was reached was the redemption which was being prepared throughout the whole O.T. actually accomplished. That so ineffable a mystery was placed before the darkened mind of man at all is due to the necessities of the plan of redemption itself, which is rooted in the trinal distinction in the Godhead, and can be apprehended only on the basis of the Trinity in Unity.

The nature of God has been made known to men, therefore, in 3 stages, corresponding to the 3 planes of revelation, and we will naturally come to know him, first, as the infinite Spirit or the God of nature; then, as the Redeemer of sinners, or the God of grace; and lastly, as the Father, Son, and Holy Ghost, or the Triune God.

I. *God, the Infinite Spirit.* The conviction of the existence of God bears the marks of an intuitive truth in so far as it is the universal and unavoidable belief of men, and is given in the very same act with the idea of self, which is known at once as dependent and responsible and thus implies one on whom it depends and to whom it is responsible. This immediate perception of God is confirmed and the contents of the idea developed by a series of arguments known as the "theistic proofs." These are derived from the necessity we are under of believing in the real existence of the infinitely perfect Being, of a sufficient cause for the contingent universe, of an intelligent author of the order and of the manifold contrivances observable in nature, and of a lawgiver and judge for dependent moral beings, endowed with the sense of duty and an ineradicable feeling of responsibility, conscious of the moral contradictions of the world and craving a solution for them, and living under an intuitive perception of right which they do not see realized. The cogency of these proofs is currently recognized in the Scriptures, while they add to them the supernatural manifestations of God in a redemptive process, accompanied at every stage by miraculous attestation. From the theistic proofs, however, we learn not only that a God exists, but also necessarily, on the principle of a sufficient cause, very much of the nature of the God which they prove to exist. The idea is still further developed, on the principle of interpreting by the highest category within our reach, by our instinctive attribution to him, in an eminent degree, of all that is the source of dignity and excellence in ourselves. Thus we come to know God as a personal Spirit, infinite, eternal, and illimitable alike in his being and in the intelligence, sensibility, and will which belong to him as personal Spirit. The attributes which are thus ascribed to him, including self-existence, independence, unity, uniqueness, unchangeableness, omnipresence, infinite knowledge and wisdom, infinite freedom and power, infinite truth, righteousness, holiness and goodness, are not only recognized but richly illustrated in Scripture, which thus puts the seal of its special revelation upon all the details of the natural idea of God.

II. *God, the Redeemer of Sinners.* While reiterating the teaching of nature as to the existence and character of the personal Creator and Lord of all, the Scriptures lay their stress upon the grace or the undeserved love of God, as exhibited in his dealings with his sinful and wrath-deserving creatures. So little, however, is the consummate divine attribute of love advanced, in the Scriptural revelation, at the expense of the other moral attributes of God, that it is thrown into prominence only upon a background of the strongest assertion and fullest manifestation of its companion attributes, especially of the divine righteousness and holiness, and is exhibited as acting only along with and in entire harmony with them. God is not represented in the Scriptures as forgiving sin because he really cares very little about sin; nor yet because he is so exclusively or predominatingly the God of love that all other attributes shrink into desuetude in the presence of his illimitable benevolence. He is rather represented as moved to deliver sinful man from his guilt and pollution because he pities the creatures of his hand, immeshed in sin, with an intensity that is born of the vehemence of his holy abhorrence of sin and his righteous determination to visit it with intolerable retribution; and by a mode which brings as complete satisfaction to his infinite justice and holiness as to his unbounded love itself. The Biblical presentation of the God of grace includes thus the richest development of all his moral attributes, and the God of the Bible is consequently set forth, in the completeness of that idea, as above everything else the ethical God. And that is as much as to say that there is ascribed to him a moral sense so sensitive and true that it estimates with unfailing accuracy the exact moral character of every person or deed presented for its contemplation, and responds to it with the precisely appropriate degree of satisfaction or reprobation. The infinitude of his love is exhibited to us precisely in that while we were yet sinners he loved us, though with all the force of his infinite nature he reacted against our sin with illimitable abhorrence and indignation. The mystery of grace resides just in the impulse of a sin-hating God to show mercy to such guilty wretches; and the supreme revelation of God as the God of holy love is made in the disclosure of the mode of his procedure in redemption, by which alone he might remain just while justifying the ungodly. For in this procedure there was involved the mighty paradox of the infinitely just Judge himself becoming the sinner's substitute before his own law and the infinitely blessed God receiving in his own person the penalty of sin.

III. *God, the Father, Son, and Holy Ghost.* The elements of the plan of salvation are rooted in the mysterious nature of the Godhead, in which there coexists a trinal distinction of persons with absolute unity of essence; and the revelation of the Trinity was accordingly incidental to the execution of this plan of salvation, in which the Father sent the Son to be the propitiation for sin, and the Son, when he returned to the glory which he had with the Father before the world was, sent the Spirit to apply his redemption to men. The disclosure of this fundamental fact of the divine nature, therefore, lagged until

the time had arrived for the actual working out of the long-promised redemption; and it was accomplished first of all in fact rather than in word, by the actual appearance of God the Son on earth and the subsequent manifestations of the Spirit, who was sent forth to act as his representative in his absence. At the very beginning of Christ's ministry the 3 persons are dramatically exhibited to our sight in the act of his baptism. And though there is no single passage in Scripture in which all the details of this great mystery are gathered up and expounded, there do not lack passages in which the 3 persons are brought together in a manner which exhibits at once their unity and distinctness. The most prominent of these are perhaps the formula of baptism in the triune name, put into the mouths of his followers by the resurrected Lord (Matt. 28:19), and the apostolic benediction in which a divine blessing is invoked from each person in turn (II Cor. 13:14). The essential elements that enter into and together make up this great revelation of the Triune God are, however, most commonly separately insisted upon. The chief of these are the 3 constitutive facts: (1) that there is but one God (Deut. 6:4; Isa. 44:6; I Cor. 8:4; James 2:19); (2) that the Father is God (Matt. 11:25; John 6:27; 8:41; Rom. 15:6; I Cor. 8:6; Gal. 1:1, 3, 4; Eph. 4:6; 6:23; I Thess. 1:1; James 1:27; 3:9; I Peter 1:2; Jude 1); the Son is God (John 1:1, 18; 20:28; Acts 20:28; Rom. 9:5; Heb. 1:8; Col. 2:9; Phil. 2:6; II Peter 1:1); and the Spirit is God (Acts 5:3, 4; I Cor. 2:10, 11; Eph. 2:22); and (3) that the Father, Son, and Holy Ghost are personally distinct from one another, distinguished by personal pronouns, able to send and be sent by one another, to love and honor each the other, and the like (John 15:26; 16:13, 14; 17:8, 18, 23; 16:14; 17:1). The doctrine of the Trinity is but the synthesis of these facts, and, adding nothing to them, simply recognizes in the unity of the Godhead such a Trinity of persons as is involved in the working out of the plan of redemption. In the prosecution of this work there is implicated a certain relative subordination in the modes of operation of the several persons, by which it is the Father that sends the Son and the Son who sends the Spirit; but the three persons are uniformly represented in Scripture as in their essential nature each alike God over all, blessed forever (Rom. 9:5); and we are therefore to conceive the subordination as rather economical, i.e., relative to the function of each in the work of redemption, than essential, i.e., involving a difference in nature.

B. B. W.

Gog (gŏg). 1. A Reubenite (I Chron. 5:4). 2. The prince of Rosh, Meshech, and Tubal (Ezek. 38:2, R.V.), who is prophetically described as invading the land of Israel in the last times, and being defeated on the mountains with immense slaughter (Ezek., chs. 38; 39). He and his people and his allies serve the prophet as a type of heathenism contending against the Kingdom of God. The name may have been taken from Gyges, the chief of a Lydian princely family called the Mermnadae; he is called Gûgu by Ashurbanipal. He belonged to the royal bodyguard and was the confidant of the king. About 700 B.C. he murdered his sovereign, of the rival house of the Heraclidae, and took possession of the throne of Lydia. He had great wealth and made notable gifts to the temple of Apollo at Delphi. But he warred against the Greek cities in Asia Minor (Herod. i. 7–15). In his old age his country was invaded by the Cimmerians. He defeated them in battle and captured several of their chiefs. But fearing renewed invasion, he sent presents to Ashurbanipal, the Assyrian king. For a long time no one could be found among the Assyrians who understood the Lydian language spoken by the ambassadors. At length a man was obtained who comprehended what they said, and the friendship of Gyges was accepted. In a short time, however, Gyges aided Egypt in its revolt against Assyria. In retaliation the Assyrian king stirred up the Cimmerians to a fresh invasion of Lydia, in which, about 662 B.C., Gyges was killed, leaving his son Ardys to ascend the throne. See GOMER, II, and MAGOG.

3. A mystic personage, akin in character to the Gog of Ezekiel, to appear immediately before the close of the present dispensation (Rev. 20:8–15).

Goi'im (goi'ĭm) [gôyĭm, nations, Gentiles]. Generally identified with Gutium, modern Kurdistan. See TIDAL.

Go'lan (gō'lăn) [cf. Arab. jaul, coast, side; jaulān, dust and sand; jawabān, going around, traveling through]. A city of Bashan, within the territory of the half-tribe of Manasseh e. of the Jordan. It was assigned, with its suburbs, to the Gershonite Levites (Josh. 21:27; I Chron. 6:71), and was one of the cities of refuge (Deut. 4:43; Josh. 20:8; 21:27). Alexander Jannaeus sustained a severe defeat near this place, and on a later campaign demolished the town (Jos. War i. 4, 4 and 8). The town gave name to the small province of Gaulanitis, or Gaulonitis, as the name was also pronounced (Jos. Antiq. viii. 2, 3, various Gr. texts). This region was situated between Hermon and the Yarmuk, and extended from the neighborhood of the Jordan e. The e. border has not been determined. The district is divisible into a southern and more arable, and a northern and more rocky half. It was surveyed by Schumacher, who with other authorities considers that the site of the town was at Sahem el-Jaulān, about 17 miles e. of the Sea of Galilee, where there are extensive ruins. Gaulonitis is now known as Jaulān. It is a tableland watered by streams from Hermon and by numerous springs, and with pastures which are among the richest in Syria; yet it lies desolate.

Gold. A precious metal anciently obtained in Havilah (Gen. 2:11, 12); Sheba (I Kings 10:2; Ps. 72:15); and Ophir (I Kings 22:48; II Chron. 8:18). It was lavishly used for overlaying the furniture of the tabernacle and the Temple, and ornamenting the latter edifice itself (Ex. 25:18; I Kings 6:22, 28). It was made into idols (Ex. 20:23; 32:31; Isa. 40:19; Acts 17:29), crowns (Ps. 21:3), chains (Gen. 41:42), rings (S. of Sol. 5:14), earrings (Judg. 8:26). It was used for coinage at a comparatively early date (Ezra 2:69, R.V.; cf. Acts 3:6; 20:33). It serves as a symbol for a thing of genuine worth and great value (Lam. 4:2; Rev. 3:18).

Gol'go·tha (gŏl'gŏ-thȧ) [Gr. from Aram. gulgultā; cf. Heb. gulgōleth, skull]. See CALVARY.

Go·li'ath (gō-li'ăth) [exile, or an exile]. The giant from the Philistine city of Gath who was slain by David (I Sam., chs. 17; 21:9, 10); probably one of the Anakim (cf. Num. 13:33; Josh. 11:22). Perhaps another giant of Gath, besides the one slain by David, bore the name of Goliath (II Sam. 21:19; cf. I Chron. 20:5). See ELHANAN.

Go'mer, I (gō'mẽr) [perhaps, (God) accomplishes (it), i.e., the birth of a child]. Daughter of Diblaim and wife of Hosea the prophet (Hos. 1:3).

Go'mer, II (gō'mẽr). A people descended from Japheth, and inhabiting the n. (Gen.

10:2, 3; I Chron. 1:5, 6; Ezek. 38:6); probably the Cimmerians of classical history, mentioned by Homer as people of the far n. (Odyssey xi. 14). They came into Asia from the regions beyond the Caucasus (Herod. iv. 11, 12), settled in Cappadocia, and threatened the Assyrian empire, but were defeated by Esarhaddon. Turning w., they overran part of Asia Minor, fighting more than one battle with Gyges, king of Lydia, whom they killed and whose name is probably preserved in the Scripture Gog. They were afterward driven out of Asia (Lydia) by Alyattes (Herod. i. 16).

Go·mor'rah (gô-mŏr'ȧ), in A.V. of N.T. **Go·mor'rha** (gô-mŏr'ȧ) [submersion; cf. Arab. ghamara, to overflow]. A city in the plain of the Jordan (Gen. 10:19; 13:10). Like Sodom its king was defeated by Chedorlaomer and his allies and the city plundered (ch. 14:8–11). Soon afterward it was destroyed by fire from heaven on account of wickedness (Gen. 18:20; 19:24–28; Deut. 29:23; Isa. 1:9; Amos 4:11; Jer. 23:14; 49:18; Zeph. 2:9; Matt. 10:15). Various locations have been proposed, but by many scholars the site of Gomorrah is supposed to be submerged by the waters of the Dead Sea. Some would accordingly place it on the s.e. shore, s. of the Lisān, probably in the region of the mouth of the wadi el-'Esāl.

For the vine of the fields of Gomorrah (Deut. 32:32), see VINE OF SODOM.

Go'pher Wood. The wood of which the ark was made (Gen. 6:14). The view that Heb. gōpher is related to Heb. kōpher, Akkad. kupru, Arab. kufr, pitch, suggests trees of the pine family, perhaps the cypress.

Gor'gi·as (gôr'jĭ-ăs). A Syrian general under Antiochus IV. In 166 B.C. he led a detachment of troops from Emmaus, in the Philistine plain, where the main army was encamped, to make a night attack on Judas Maccabaeus; but Judas, having learned of the plan, withdrew his forces and led them to a successful attack on Gorgias' own camp. When Gorgias returned, his followers saw their camp in flames and fled (I Macc. 3:38 to 4:25). A little more than a year later Gorgias was commanding at Jamnia, and he met and defeated Joseph and Azarias, who in the absence of Judas had charge of the troops in Judea, and were advancing to attack the town (ch. 5:55–62).

Gor·ty'na (gôr-tī'nȧ). An important city in the southern part of Crete (I Macc. 15:23).

Go'shen (gō'shĕn) [probably, mound of earth]. 1. A district of Egypt, adapted for flocks and herds, situated in the delta, a few miles to n.e. of On. It belonged to the nome called Arabia (Gen. 46:34, LXX), and formed part of the land of Ramesses (Gen. 46:28; 47:11, 27, LXX). Thither Joseph went up in his chariot to meet his father who was coming from Canaan (ch. 46:28, 29). The Hebrews were allowed to settle there (ch. 47:6), and the mass of the people were still there at the time of their oppression (Ex. 8:22).

2. A region in the s. of Judah (Josh. 10:41; 11:16); name probably derived from following (3).

3. A town in the hill country of Judah (Josh. 15:51); Dahariyeh corresponds to this location.

Gos'pel. The Eng. word gospel is derived from Anglo-Saxon gōd-spell, good tidings. Later it was interpreted as godspell, godspel, meaning God-story, i.e., the story about God, i.e., Christ. The word as now used describes both the message which Christianity announces and the books in which the story of Christ's life and teaching is contained. A similar transition in meaning was experienced by the Gr. *euangelion* (whence Lat. *evangelium* and our evangel) rendered gospel (good tidings). In the N.T. it never means a book, as it may in English, but the message or "good tidings" which Christ and his apostles announced. It is called the gospel of God (Rom. 1:1; I Thess. 2:2, 9; I Tim. 1:11); the gospel of Christ (Mark 1:1; Rom. 1:16; 15:19; I Cor. 9:12, 18; Gal. 1:7); the gospel of the grace of God (Acts 20:24); the gospel of peace (Eph. 6:15); the gospel of your salvation (Eph. 1:13); and the glorious gospel (II Cor. 4:4). It was preached by our Lord (Matt. 4:23; 11:5; Mark 1:14; Luke 4:18; 7:22) and called the gospel of the Kingdom; it was also preached by the apostles (Acts 16:10; Rom. 1:15; 2:16; I Cor. 9:16), and by evangelists (Acts 8:25). But in the Post-apostolic Age (c. A.D. 150, Justin Martyr, *Apol.* i. 66) the term was also applied to the writings in which the apostolic testimony to Jesus was contained. Each one of them was called a gospel and likewise the 4 together were called the gospel. Our present English usage, therefore, exactly corresponds with that of the early Christians of the age immediately succeeding the Apostolic.

The Four Gospels. Historical evidence shows that our 4 Gospels have been attributed from the earliest times to Matthew, Mark, Luke, and John, respectively, and that from the very beginning of the post-Apostolic Age they were received by the Church as authoritative documents and as containing the apostolic testimony to the life and teachings of Christ. In the 2d century they were quoted, commented upon, and described; so that there need be no doubt of their authenticity. An examination of the N.T. epistles also shows that our Gospels describe Jesus as the same kind of person, doing the same kind of works, and having the same history to which the epistles allude. They may, therefore, be confidently accepted as trustworthy reports.

The first 3 have much in common and, in general, present the life of the Lord from the same point of view. They are called the Synoptic Gospels (from Gr. *synopsis*, a seeing together), and in particular are quite different from John's. The Synoptics take for their chief theme Christ's ministry in Galilee; the Fourth Gospel gives prominence to his labors in Judea; though his betrayal, arrest, trial, crucifixion, and resurrection are so important that they are narrated by all. The only prior incident recorded by all the Evangelists is the feeding of five thousand. The Synoptics also say comparatively little, in so many words, of the divinity of Christ, while John especially records the Lord's self-testimony to it. They present mainly Christ's teaching about the Kingdom of God, his parables, his instruction of the common people; while John records his teaching about himself and this usually in the form of extended discourses. At the same time the Fourth Gospel assumes and implies the other 3, while they in turn are often made intelligible only by the facts which John records. Thus John 1:15 implies the fact recorded in Matt. 3:11, etc.; John 3:24 the fact given in Matt. 4:12; John, chs. 6:1 to 7:9, the whole Synoptic story of the Galilean ministry, etc. So in turn Christ's reception in Galilee and the willingness of Peter, Andrew, James, and John to leave all and follow him are only explicable by such events as are recorded in John, chs. 1 and 2; and the sudden rise of the Sabbath controversy in the Synoptics (see Mark 2:23, etc.) is likewise to be explained by the events of John, ch. 5.

Moreover, while the Synoptics have the same general point of view, each has its individual characteristics, determined by the writer's purpose and the readers whom he had in mind. Matthew, writing from the Jewish point of view, sets Jesus forth as the royal Messiah. He constantly cites in proof O.T. prophecies, and is interested to give Christ's teaching concerning the true Kingdom of God in contrast to the false views of current Judaism. Mark, writing evidently for Gentiles, and possibly for the Romans in particular, represents mainly Christ's power to save as shown in his miracles. Luke, long the companion of Paul, sets the Lord forth as the gracious Saviour, and is fond of exhibiting his favor to the fallen, the outcast, and the poor. So John has his special purpose, which is to represent Jesus as the incarnate, divine Word, revealing the Father to those who would receive him. None of the Gospels, however, aims at being a complete biography of our Lord. They are collections of his acts and words, made for the purpose of practical and doctrinal instruction. The student must construct his conception of the history of Jesus out of the materials furnished by the Gospels. They themselves were prepared with other objects in view (John 20:30, 31; cf. ch. 21:25).

The question has often been asked from what sources the 4 Evangelists derived their information. Matthew and John were apostles and therefore possessed personal knowledge of the events they record or were in a position to obtain it from those who had it. But Mark also was a companion of Paul and Peter, and is said, by very early tradition, to have embodied in his Gospel the preaching of Peter about Jesus. Luke himself assures us (ch. 1:1-4) that his knowledge was obtained from "eyewitnesses . . . . of the word" and that he had made himself well acquainted with the facts. Thus the Gospels give us the testimony of the apostles. The many coincidences of language in the Synoptics confirm this. If any itinerant speaker or preacher, such as a foreign missionary home on furlough, relates at different places incidents of his experience abroad, he gradually settles into a fixed narrative through his very desire to be accurate, repeating the same stories in the same form, though now and then adding particulars which he had omitted elsewhere. It is probable that the apostles and early evangelists acted in much the same way; so that their recital became largely stereotyped. After a while parts of this narrative were put into writing for use in the newly founded churches. Thus a gospel narrative became current which, while doubtless differing in extent in different places, had much of its matter, even to the very words, in common. The verbal coincidences, therefore, of our Synoptic Gospels attest that they give us the common apostolic testimony to Jesus. The Fourth Gospel, on the other hand, contains material which at first was not so widely called for, but which John finally wrote, out of his own knowledge, when the needs of the Church seemed to demand it.

The coincidences between the Synoptics have raised, however, the further question whether any of them have directly utilized the material in the others. This question is often called the Synoptic problem. The facts which enter into its solution are very many and complex. While the 3 have much in common, Matthew and Luke have much that is not in Mark, and each of the 3 has much that is not in the others. Moreover, even in the sections which are in common the language of one Evangelist often differs as remarkably as in other points it agrees with that of his colleagues.

Many modern writers think that Matthew and Luke drew from Mark his historical narrative, making its language fundamental to their own account, arranging its material to conform to their own purposes in writing, and adding matter from other sources oral and written. In support of this view they point to the following facts: 1. There is very little in Mark apart from details that is not in Matthew or in Luke. 2. When Mark and Luke differ in order, Matthew agrees with Mark; but when Mark and Matthew differ in order, Luke agrees with Mark. 3. Matthew and Luke never agree in order against Mark; this seems to indicate that Matthew and Luke are in some way dependent upon Mark. And it is quite customary to combine with this explanation the theory that a collection of the sayings of Jesus early existed, from which also the 2 Evangelists Matthew and Luke drew. Scholars designate this collection of sayings by the symbol Q and call the theory that Matthew and Luke depended upon Mark and Q the two-document hypothesis. A further development is the four-document hypothesis, which holds that Matthew depended upon Mark, Q, and a special document, M; and that our Gospel of Luke can be traced to Mark and Proto-Luke (i.e., an earlier edition of Luke made from Q and a special source, L).

These theories concern themselves with literary criticism; a new method of investigating the N.T., form criticism (in German called *Formgeschichte*), seeks to go behind the written Gospels to a period of oral tradition. It is supposed that the various units which later were woven into documents were circulated for a while by word of mouth. The form critics classify these assumed units according to their form, such as pronouncement stories (e.g., Mark 3:31–35), miracle stories, parables, stories about Jesus, etc.; they suppose that the preservation and inevitable modification of these separate and self-contained fragments were secured by the practical needs and interests of the earliest communities and preachers. Not a few form critics would hold that the framework of chronological and geographical details represents a later accretion imposed upon the detached incidents and sayings. Many advocates of this method of Gospel criticism, however, overemphasize the part played by the Christian community and its leaders in originating and formulating oral tradition. Too often form critics disregard the very real factors that tended to preserve faithfully the reports of our Lord's sayings and of the events of his life.

Papias (early 2d century) says that Matthew wrote the *logia* (discourses, oracles, which may mean Gospel) in Heb. (i.e., Aram.). Various scholars (e.g., C. F. Burney and J. A. Montgomery) have suggested an Aram. origin of the Gospels, but the most complete presentation of this theory has been worked out by C. C. Torrey (*The Four Gospels, A New Translation,* 1933), who maintains that the Aramaisms in the Gospels and the first half of The Acts are not due to bilingual authors who thought in Aram. and wrote barbarous Gr., but that they are due to translations from Aram. documents no longer extant. He believes that accounts of the life, words, and works of Christ were put into writing almost immediately after the crucifixion (cf. Luke 1:1, 2). According to this theory, everything in the Gospels could have been written within 20 years of the death of Jesus, and the 4 were probably written before A.D. 70. Accordingly Mark in Aram. is dated A.D. 40. Q is believed to be an Aram. document. Matthew, who depends upon Mark, i's sources, and other material, is dated slightly later. Next, somewhat earlier than Luke, comes John, who was acquainted with

the Aram. sources of Matthew and Mark, if not with their actual Gospels. Luke, c. A.D. 60, used a Heb. narrative of the Nativity and infancy of Jesus and Aram. sources. According to this theory, the translator of Matthew had access to the Gr. Mark. Luke, who apparently was his own translator, had at hand the Gr. of the first 2 Gospels.

With the exception of Luke, chs. 1; 2, and John, ch. 21, the Aram. idiom is everywhere present in the Gospels; various difficulties can be clarified by turning the Gr. into Aram., and in many cases the interpretation of a word or passage is simplified by considering the meaning of the supposed Aram. original. Jesus and his disciples spoke Aram., and the Gospels reflect the atmosphere of Palestine.

To the literary critics this theory of the Aram. origins is revolutionary. Yet it is a refreshing contribution to N.T. studies, because it is based on sound philology and does not lead into the involved study of interior sources or documents. While it definitely throws light upon difficult passages, it has a special merit in projecting the written sources to a period very close to the time of our Lord and thus supporting the impression of authenticity and, by inference, the trustworthiness of the records.

In attempting to trace the history of the Synoptics we should not forget the promise made by Christ to the apostles, and meant doubtless for others who might be employed in the proclamation of the gospel. "But the Comforter, even the Holy Spirit, whom the Father will send in my name, he shall teach you all things, and bring to your remembrance all that I said unto you" (John 14:26, R.V.).

To obtain a clear idea of the life of Christ it is necessary to construct a harmony of the Gospels. This, of course, should be done with fidelity to the chronological indications, few though they are, which the Gospels contain. But it should also be remembered that the indications of time and relation are not only few, but also often doubtful of interpretation, and that, therefore, a harmony must be regarded in many points as merely approximate. Matthew's method is mainly topical, and, therefore, he seldom provides a basis for a harmony. Mark appears to be much more chronological, and his order may generally be followed; but there is much that he does not give at all. Luke follows in the 1st half of his work nearly the order of Mark, though with important differences, and he, too, is often topical in his method. But John's Gospel, by noting successive feasts which Jesus attended, provides the general framework into which the other material should be fitted. It is on this basis that the following outline and harmony have been prepared: We believe that the feast of John 5:1 was a passover; that therefore Christ's ministry included 4 passovers (John 2:13; 5:1; 6:4; 13:1), at the last of which he died. The ministry was thus three and a quarter years in length, since John, ch. 1, shows that Christ was baptized a few months before his 1st passover. Others however, denying that John 5:1 was a passover, make the ministry two and a quarter years in length. On this, as on many similar points, absolute demonstration is impossible. In the following table, moreover, the dates assigned to some of the events must likewise be regarded as open to question. It appears clear to most scholars that Herod the Great died about April 1, 4 B.C. If so, Christ was probably born in December, 5 B.C., or January, 4 B.C. We assume the date to be December 25, 5 B.C., without, however, meaning to affirm that there is any evidence for the exact day of the month. If then, when he was baptized, he was about 30

(Luke 3:23), his baptism is probably to be assigned to the latter part of A.D. 26 or the beginning of A.D. 27. We assume for it January A.D. 27. If his ministry included 4 passovers, he died at the passover of A.D. 30. Many complex calculations tend to confirm these dates, though they are not capable of perfect demonstration. Our view assumes

that "the fifteenth year of Tiberius Caesar" (Luke 3:1) is to be dated from the time when Tiberius became coregent with Augustus in the empire (A.D. 11–12). At that time he became in the provinces the practical ruler. It is well known that our common Christian calendar dates the birth of Christ too late. See JESUS CHRIST.

HARMONY OF THE FOUR GOSPELS

Incidents	Time	Place	Matthew	Mark	Luke	John
1. Introductory verses	. . .	. . . .	. . .	. . .	1: 1–4	
2. Prologue to the Fourth Gospel	. . .		. . .	. . .	. . .	1: 1–18
3. The genealogy of Christ	. . .	. . . .	1: 1–17	. . .	3: 23ᵇ–38	
4. Annunciation to Zacharias of John the Baptist's birth	B.C. 6	The Temple	. . .	. . .	1: 5–25	
5. Annunciation to Mary of Christ's birth	B.C. 5	Nazareth			26–38	
6. Mary's visit to Elisabeth	B.C. 5	A city of Judah	. . .	. . .	39–56	
7. Birth of John the Baptist	B.C. 5	A city of Judah	. . .	. . .	57, 58	
8. Circumcision and naming of John	B.C. 5	A city of Judah	. . .	. . .	59–79	
9. Annunciation to Joseph of Christ's birth	B.C. 5	Nazareth	18–23			
10. The birth of Jesus	B.C. 5	Bethlehem	24, 25	. . .	2: 1–7	
11. Annunciation to the Shepherds	B.C. 5	Near Bethlehem	. . .		8–14	
12. Visit of the shepherds to adore Christ	B.C. 5	Bethlehem	. . .		15–20	
13. Circumcision of Jesus	B.C. 4	Bethlehem	. . .	. . .	21	
14. Presentation in the Temple; prophecies of Simeon and Anna	B.C. 4	Jerusalem	. . .	. . .	22–38	
15. Visit of the Magi	B.C. 4	Bethlehem	2: 1–12			
16. Flight into Egypt	B.C. 4	Bethlehem to Egypt	13–15		●	
17. Slaughter of the children by Herod	B.C. 4	Bethlehem	16–18			
18. Return from Egypt to Nazareth	B.C. 4	Egypt to Nazareth	19–23	. . .	39	
19. Life of Jesus at Nazareth for 30 years, but with 1 recorded visit to Jerusalem at the feast of the passover when 12 years of age; John in retirement in the desert	B.C. 4– A.D. 26 A.D. 9	Nazareth	. . .	. . .	2: 40–52 1: 80	
20. The public ministry of John the Baptist	A.D. 26	At the Jordan	3: 1–12	1: 1–8	3: 1–18	19–28
21. Jesus baptized and witnessed to by John	A.D. 27	At the Jordan	13–17	9–11	21–23ᵃ	29–34
22. The temptation of Jesus	A.D. 27	Wilderness of Judea(?)	4: 1–11	12, 13	4: 1–13	
23. John (?), Andrew, and Peter meet Jesus	A.D. 27	Near the Jordan	. . .	. . .	. . .	35–42
24. Philip and Nathanael called	A.D. 27	On the way to Galilee	. . .	. . .	. . .	43–51
25. The first miracle; water changed to wine	A.D. 27	Cana of Galilee	. . .	. . .	. . .	2: 1–11
26. Christ goes to Capernaum	A.D. 27	Capernaum	. . .	. . .	. . .	12
Early Judean Ministry						
27. **The 1st passover;** money-changers driven from the Temple	April A.D. 27	Jerusalem	. . .	. . .	. . .	2: 13–25
28. Instruction of Nicodemus	A.D. 27	Jerusalem	. . .	. . .	. . .	3: 1–21
29. Jesus preaches in Judea	A.D. 27	Judea	. . .	. . .	. . .	22
30. Renewed testimony of John to Jesus	A.D. 27	Judea	. . .	. . .	. . .	3: 23–36
31. Jesus goes to Galilee	A.D. 27	Judea to Galilee	. . .	. . .	. . .	4: 1–3
32. Interview with woman of Samaria	A.D. 27	Near Sychar	. . .	. . .	. . .	4–42
33. Cure of nobleman's son	A.D. 27 or 28	Cana	. . .	. . .	. . .	43–54
34. Imprisonment of John the Baptist	. . .	Fortress of Machaerus	14: 3–5	6: 17–20	3: 19, 20	
Early Galilean Ministry						
35. Commencement of Christ's public work in Galilee	A.D. 28	Galilee	4: 12–17	1: 14, 15	4: 14, 15	
36. First rejection at Nazareth	A.D. 28	Nazareth	. . .	. . .	16–30	

HARMONY OF THE FOUR GOSPELS—*Continued*

Incidents	Time	Place	Matthew	Mark	Luke	John
37. Call of Simon, Andrew, James, and John	A.D. 28	Near Capernaum	18–22	16-20	5: 1–11	
38. Cure of demoniac in the synagogue	A.D. 28	Capernaum	. . .	21–28	4: 31–37	
39. Cure of Peter's wife's mother	A.D. 28	Capernaum	8: 14, 15	29–31	38, 39	
40. Cure of many on the same evening	A.D. 28	Capernaum	16, 17	32–34	40, 41	
41. Circuit through Galilee	A.D. 28	Galilee	4: 23–25	35–39	42–44	
42. Cure of a leper	A.D. 28	A city of Galilee	8: 2–4	40–45	5: 12–16	
43. Healing of paralytic	A.D. 28	Capernaum	9: 1–8	2: 1–12	17–26	
44. Call of Matthew (Levi); his feast	A.D. 28	Capernaum	9–13	13–17	27–32	
45. **The 2d passover;** healing of impotent man at pool of Bethesda, and discussion with the Jews	April A.D. 28	Jerusalem	. . .	. . .	. . .	5: 1–47
46. Plucking ears of corn leads to discussion of the Sabbath question	Early Summer A.D. 28	On way to Galilee (?)	12: 1–8	23–28	6: 1–5	
47. Cure on Sabbath of man with withered hand	A.D. 28	Capernaum	9–13	3: 1–6	6–11	
48. Plots against Jesus; extraordinary enthusiasm of the people; many follow him from all the land	A.D. 28	Near Capernaum	14–21	7–12	17–19	
49. Selection of the 12 apostles	A.D. 28	Near Capernaum	10: 2–4	13–19	12–16	
50. Sermon on the Mount	A.D. 28	Near Capernaum	5: 1 to 8: 1	. . .	20–49	
51. Healing of centurion's servant	A.D. 28	Capernaum	8: 5–13	. . .	7: 1–10	
52. Circuit through Galilee	A.D. 28	Galilee	11: 1			
53. Raising of widow's son	A.D. 28	Nain	. . .	. . .	7: 11–17	
54. Inquiry of John the Baptist about Jesus, and the latter's reply, etc.	A.D. 28	Galilee	11: 2–19	. . .	18–35	
55. Jesus anointed by a sinful woman	A.D. 28	Galilee	. . .	. . .	36–50	
56. A further circuit through Galilee with his disciples	A.D. 28	Galilee	. . .	. . .	8: 1–3	
57. Cure of a demoniac; blasphemy of Pharisees reproved	A.D. 28	Capernaum	12: 22–37	3: 20–30	11: 14, 15, 17–23	
58. Pharisees' desire for a sign commented on	A.D. 28	Capernaum	38–45	. . .	16, 24–26, 29–36	
59. Christ's mother and brethren desire to see him	A.D. 28	Capernaum	46–50	31–35	27, 28; 8: 19–21	
60. Woes against Pharisees	A.D. 28	Capernaum	. . .	. . .	11: 37–54	
61. Discourses to the people on trust in God, against worldliness, etc.	A.D. 28	Capernaum	. . .	. . .	12: 1–59	
62. Remarks on the slaughter of the Galileans	A.D. 28	Capernaum	. . .	. . .	13: 1–5	
63. Parables of the Sower, the Tares, the Seed Growing Secretly, the Mustard Seed, the Leaven, the Hid Treasure, the Pearl, the Dragnet, and other sayings	A.D. 28	Capernaum	13: 1–53	4: 1–34	8: 4–18; 13: 18–21	
64. The 3 inquirers	A.D. 28	Near Sea of Galilee	8: 18–22	. . .	9: 57–62	
65. The tempest stilled	A.D. 28	Sea of Galilee	23–27	35–41	8: 22–25	
66. The demoniacs of Gadara (or Gerasa)	A.D. 28	East shore of Sea of Galilee	28–34	5: 1–20	8: 26–39	
67. Inquiry of John's disciples and the Pharisees about fasting	A.D. 28	Capernaum	9: 14–17	2: 18–22	5: 33–39	
68. Raising of Jairus' daughter, and cure of woman with bloody issue	A.D. 28	Capernaum	18–26	5: 21–43	8: 40–56	
69. Cure of 2 blind men	A.D. 28	Capernaum	27–31			
70. Cure of a dumb demoniac	A.D. 28	Capernaum	32–34			
71. Second rejection at Nazareth	A.D. 28	Nazareth	13: 54–58	6: 1–6ᵃ		
72. The Twelve sent out	A.D. 28	Galilee	9:35 to 10:1; 10: 5–11: 1	6ᵇ–13	9: 1–6	

HARMONY OF THE FOUR GOSPELS — *Continued*

	Incidents	Time	Place	Matthew	Mark	Luke	John
73.	Herod's inquiry about Jesus, with which is connected the account of the recent murder of John the Baptist	A.D. 29(?)	Galilee	14: 1, 2, 6–12	14–16, 21–29	7–9	
74.	The Twelve return; Jesus retires with them across the sea; 5,000 fed	A.D. 29	N. e. coast of Sea of Galilee	13–21	30–44	10–17	6: 1–14
75.	Jesus walks on the water	A.D. 29	Sea of Galilee	22–33	45–52	. . .	15–21
76.	Triumphal march through Gennesaret	A.D. 29	Gennesaret	34–36	53–56		
77.	Discourse on the bread of life at the time of the **3d passover**	April A.D. 29	Capernaum	. . .	. . .	. . .	22–71
78.	Reproof of Pharisaic traditions	A.D. 29	Capernaum	15: 1–20	7: 1–23		

Later Galilean Ministry

	Incidents	Time	Place	Matthew	Mark	Luke	John
79.	Daughter of Syrophoenician healed	A.D. 29	Region of Tyre and Sidon	15: 21–28	7: 24–30		
80.	Deaf and dumb man and others healed	A.D. 29	The Decapolis	29–31	31–37	. . .	7: 1
81.	The 4,000 fed	A.D. 29	The Decapolis	32–38	8: 1–9		
82.	The Pharisees and Sadducees again require a sign	A.D. 29	Near Magadan [A. V. Matt. Magdala]; in Mark, the parts of Dalmanutha	39 to 16: 4	10–12		
83.	Disciples warned against the leaven of the Pharisees, etc.	A.D. 29	Sea of Galilee	5–12	13–21		
84.	Blind man healed	A.D. 29	Bethsaida	. . .	22–26		
85.	Peter's confession	A.D. 29	Region of Caesarea Philippi	13–20	27–30	18–21	
86.	Christ foretells his death and resurrection	A.D. 29	Region of Caesarea Philippi	21–28	31 to 9: 1	22–27	
87.	The transfiguration	A.D. 29	Region of Caesarea Philippi	17: 1–13	2–13	28–36	
88.	Healing of the demoniac boy	A.D. 29	Region of Caesarea Philippi	14–21	14–29	37–43a	
89.	Christ again foretells his death and resurrection	A.D. 29	Galilee	22, 23	30–32	43b–45	
90.	The tribute money	A.D. 29	Capernaum	24–27			
91.	Instructions to disciples on humility, etc.	A.D. 29	Capernaum	ch. 18	33–50	46–50	

The Last Journeys to Jerusalem
(Judean and Perean Ministry)

	Incidents	Time	Place	Matthew	Mark	Luke	John
92.	Final departure from Galilee; rejected in Samaria	A.D. 29	From Galilee to Judea	19: 1a	10: 1a	9: 51–56	
93.	The Seventy instructed and sent out	A.D. 29	From Galilee to Judea	11: 20–24	. . .	10: 1–16	
94.	Christ attends the **feast of tabernacles**	Oct. A.D. 29	Jerusalem	. . .	. . .		7: 2–52
95.	[The woman taken in adultery] *bracketed in R. V.*	Oct. A.D. 29	Jerusalem	. . .	. . .		[53 to 8: 11]
96.	Discussion with the Jews during the feast	Oct. A.D. 29	Jerusalem	. . .	. . .	. . .	8: 12–59
97.	Jesus apparently retires from Jerusalem and the Seventy return to him	A.D. 29	Judea	25–30	. . .	17–24	
98.	A lawyer instructed; parable of the Good Samaritan	A.D. 29	Judea	. . .	. . .	25–37	
99.	Jesus at the house of Martha and Mary	A.D. 29	Bethany			38–42	
100.	The disciples taught how to pray	A.D. 29	Judea	. . .	. . .	11: 1–13	
101.	**The feast of dedication**; blind man healed; parable of the Shepherd; conflict with the Jews; Jesus retires to Perea, beyond Jordan	Dec. A.D. 29	Jerusalem	. . .	. . .	. . .	9: 1 to 10: 39
102.	Ministry in Perea	A.D. 30	Perea	19: 1b, 2	10: 1b	. . .	39–41
103.	Parable of the Barren Fig Tree	A.D. 30	Perea	. . .	. . .	13: 6–9	
104.	Healing infirm woman on the Sabbath	A.D. 30	Perea	. . .	. . .	10–17	

HARMONY OF THE FOUR GOSPELS — *Continued*

Incidents	Time	Place	Matthew	Mark	Luke	John
105. Teaching and journeying toward Jerusalem; warned against Herod	A.D. 30	Perea	. . .	. . .	22–35	
106. Dines with a Pharisee; healing of man with dropsy; parable of the Great Supper	A.D. 30	Perea	. . .	. . .	14: 1–24	
107. Requirements of true disciples	A.D. 30	Perea	. . .	. . .	25–35	
108. Parables of the Lost Sheep and Coin and the Prodigal	A.D. 30	Perea	. . .	. . .	ch. 15	
109. Parable of the Unjust Steward	A.D. 30	Perea	. . .	. . .	16: 1–13	
110. Pharisees reproved; parable of the Rich Man and Lazarus	A.D. 30	Perea	. . .	. . .	14–31	
111. Instructs disciples in forbearance, faith, and humility	A.D. 30	Perea	. . .	. . .	17: 1–10	
112. The ten lepers	A.D. 30	Between Samaria and Galilee (R.V. marg.)	. . .	. . .	11–19	
113. The suddenness of his advent	A.D. 30	Perea	. . .	. . .	20–37	
114. Parable of the Importunate Widow	A.D. 30	Perea	. . .	. . .	18: 1–8	
115. Parable of the Pharisee and the Publican	A.D. 30	Perea	. . .	. . .	9–14	
116. **The raising of Lazarus**	A.D. 30	Bethany	. . .	. . .	. . .	11: 1–46
117. Counsel of Caiaphas; Jesus again retires	A.D. 30	Jerusalem, Ephraim	. . .	. . .	. . .	47–54
118. Precepts concerning divorce	A.D. 30	Perea (?)	19: 3–12	10: 2–12		
119. Christ blesses little children	A.D. 30	Perea	19: 13–15	10: 13–16	18: 15–17	
120. The rich young ruler, etc.	A.D. 30	Perea	16–30	17–31	18–30	
121. Parable of the Laborers in the Vineyard	A.D. 30	Perea	20: 1–16			
122. Third prediction of his death and resurrection	A.D. 30	Perea	17–19	32–34	31–34	
123. **Ascent to Jerusalem;** request of James and John	A.D. 30	Perea	20–28	35–45		
124. Two blind men healed near Jericho	A.D. 30	Jericho	29–34	46–52	35–43	
125. Conversion of Zacchaus	A.D. 30	Jericho	. . .	. . .	19: 1–10	
126. Parable of the Pounds	A.D. 30	Jericho	. . .	. . .	11–28	
127. Arrival at Bethany 6 days before the passover	A.D. 30	Bethany	. . .	. . .	. . .	11: 55 to 12: 1

The Last Week

Incidents	Time	Place	Matthew	Mark	Luke	John
128. Supper at Bethany; anointed by Mary; hostility of rulers	Saturday, April 1, A.D. 30	Bethany	26: 6–13	14: 3–9	. . .	2–11
129. Triumphal entry into Jerusalem; spends night at Bethany	Sunday, April 2	Mount of Olives, Jerusalem, and Bethany	21: 1–11	11: 1–11	19: 29–44	12–19
130. Cursing of barren fig tree; cleansing of Temple; praises of the children; miracles	Monday, April 3	Near and in Jerusalem	12–19	12–19	45–48; 21: 37, 38	
131. Lesson of the fig tree	Tuesday, April 4	On the way to Jerusalem	20–22	20–25 [26]		
132. The sanhedrin demand Christ's authority; his reply and parables of the Two Sons, the Wicked Husbandmen, and the Marriage of the King's Son	" " "	Jerusalem	23–32, 33–46; 22: 1–14	27–33; 12: 1–12	20: 1–8, 9–19	
133. Question of the Pharisees (tribute to Caesar); of the Sadducees (the resurrection); of the lawyer (the Great Commandment); Christ's question (David's Lord)	" " "	Jerusalem	15–22, 23–33, 34–40, 41–46	13–17, 18–27, 28–34, 35–37	20–26, 27–40, 41–44	
134. Warnings against scribes and Pharisees	" " "	Jerusalem	ch. 23	38–40	45–47	
135. The widow's mite	" " "	Jerusalem	. . .	41–44	21: 1–4	

HARMONY OF THE FOUR GOSPELS—*Continued*

Incidents	Time	Place	Matthew	Mark	Luke	John
136. Visit of the Greeks; last teachings	Tuesday, April 4	Jerusalem	. . .	. . .	. . .	12: 20–50
137. Christ's prediction of the fall of Jerusalem, the future of the Church, and the Second Advent	Tuesday evening, April 4	Mount of Olives	24: 1–31	13: 1–27	21: 5–28	
138. Instructions to watch: parables of Ten Virgins and Talents; the Last Judgment	" " "	Mount of Olives	32 to 25: 46	28–37	29–36	
139. Conspiracy of the rulers; treachery of Judas	Tuesday evening, Apr. 4, or Wednesday, April 5	Jerusalem	26: 1–5, 14–16	14: 1, 2, 10, 11	22: 1–6	
140. Preparations for the passover	Thursday, April 6	Bethany and Jerusalem	17–19	12–16	7–13	
141. **The last passover;** strife of the disciples	Thursday evening, April 6	The upper room in Jerusalem	26: 20	14: 17	22: 14–18, 24–30	
142. The feet washing	" " "	" " "	. . .	. . .	. . .	13: 1–20
143. The traitor announced; Judas withdraws	" " "	" " "	21–25	18–21	21–23	21–35
144. The Lord's Supper	" " "	" " "	26–29	22–25	19, 20	(cf. I Cor. 11: 23–25)
145. Prediction of Peter's fall, and other warnings	" " "	" " "	. . .	. . .	31–38	36–38
146. Last discourses with the disciples and prayer	" " "	" " "	. . .	. . .	. . .	14 to 17: 26
147. Renewed prediction of Peter's fall and of the scattering of the disciples	" " "	On the way to Gethsemane	30–35	26–31		
148. The agony in the Garden	" " "	Gethsemane	36–46	32–42	39–46	18: 1
149. The arrest of Christ; dispersion of the disciples	Thursday night, April 6–7	Gethsemane	47–56	43–52	47–53	2–12
150. Preliminary examination before Annas	" " "	High-priest's palace in Jerusalem	. . .	. . .	. . .	13, 14, 19–24
151. Examination before sanhedrin; mockery of Jesus	" " "	" " "	57, 59–68	53, 55–65	54, 55, 63–65	
152. Peter's denials	" " "	" " "	58, 69–75	54, 66–72	56–62	15–18, 25–27
153. Final condemnation of Jesus by the sanhedrin	Early Friday morning, Apr. 7	" " "	27: 1	15: 1a	66–71	
154. Jesus led to Pilate, who seeks to secure his release	" " "	The governor's residence in Jerusalem	2, 11–14	1b–5	23: 1–5	28–30
155. Jesus before Herod	Friday, April 7	Jerusalem	. . .	. . .	6–12	
156. Pilate further seeks to release Jesus; the Jews demand Barabbas	" " "	Governor's residence	15–26a	6–15a	13–25	39, 40
157. Pilate delivers Jesus to death; scourging	" " "	Governor's residence	26b–30	15b–19	. . .	19: 1–3
158. Pilate again seeks to release Jesus	" " "	Governor's residence	. . .	. . .	. . .	4–16a
159. Judas' remorse and suicide	" " "	Jerusalem	3–10	(cf. Acts 1: 18, 19)		
160. Jesus led to crucifixion	" " "	Jerusalem	31–34	20–23	26–33a	16b, 17
161. The crucifixion	" " "	Near Jerusalem	35–38	24–28	33b, 34, 38	18–24
162. Incidents at the cross	" " "	Near Jerusalem	39–49	29–36	35–37, 39–45a	25–29
163. The death of Jesus	Friday, 3. P.M., April 7	Near Jerusalem	50	37	46	30
164. Incidents following his death	Friday, April 7	Jerusalem and vicinity	51–56	38–41	45b, 47–49	
165. Taking down from the cross; burial	" " "	Near Jerusalem	57–61	42–47	50–56	31–42
166. The watch at the sepulcher	. . .	Near Jerusalem	62–66			
The Resurrection						
167. Visit of the women	Sunday. April 9	Jerusalem and vicinity	28: 1–10	16: 1–8	24: 1–11	
168. Visit of John and Peter; return of Mary Magdalene to sepulcher and Christ's appearance to her	" " "	Jerusalem and vicinity	. . .	[16: 9–11*]	12	20: 1–18

*The last 12 verses of Mark are in R.V. spaced from the preceding because of doubt whether they originally formed part of Mark's Gospel.

Harmony of the Four Gospels—*Continued*

Incidents	Time	Place	Matthew	Mark	Luke	John
169. Report of the watch	Sunday, April 9	Jerusalem and vicinity	11–15			
170. Interview with 2 disciples on the way to Emmaus	" " "	Jerusalem and vicinity	. . .	[12, 13*]	13–35	
171. Christ appears to the Eleven, Thomas being absent	Sunday, April 9	Jerusalem	. . .	[16: 14*]	24: 36–49	20: 19–24
172. Christ again appears to them, Thomas being present	Sunday, April 16	Jerusalem	. . .	. . .	. . .	25–29
173. Appearance to 7 disciples; Peter's restoration, etc.	A.D. 30	Sea of Galilee	. . .	. . .	. . .	21: 1–23
174. The Great Commission. See I Cor. 15:6	A.D. 30	Mountain in Galilee	28: 16–20	[15–18*]		
175. The ascension. See Acts 1: 1–11	Thursday, May 18, A.D. 30	Mount of Olives toward Bethany	. . .	[19, 20*]	50–53	
176. John's closing words	. . .	. . . .	. . .	. . .	. . .	20: 30, 31; 21: 24, 25

G. T. P. (rev., H. S. G.)

Index for Finding Any Passage in the Harmony

Matthew

Chapter and Verse		Section	Chapter and Verse		Section	Chapter and Verse		Section	Chapter and Verse		Section
1:	1–17	3	9:	35 to 10: 1	72	16:	13–20	85	26:	17–19	140
	18–23	9	10:	2–4	49		21–28	86		20	141
	24–25	10		5 to 11: 1	72	17:	1–13	87		21–25	143
2:	1–12	15	11:	1	52		14–21	88		26–29	144
	13–15	16		2–19	54		22, 23	89		30–35	147
	16–18	17		20–24	93		24–27	90		36–46	148
	19–23	18		25–30	97	18:	1–35	91		47–56	119
3:	1–12	20	12:	1–8	46	19:	1a	92		57	151
	13–17	21		9–13	47		1b, 2	102		58	152
4	1–11	22	12:	14–21	48		3–12	118		59–68	151
	12–17	35		22–37	57		13–15	119		69–75	152
	18–22	37		38–45	58		16–30	120	27:	1	153
	23–25	41		46–50	59	20:	1–16	121		2	154
5:	1 to 8: 1	50	13:	1–53	63		17–19	122		3–10	159
8:	2–4	42		54–58	71		20–28	123		11–14	154
	5–13	51	14:	1, 2	73		29–34	124		15–23a	156
	14, 15	39		3–5	34	21:	1–11	129		26b–30	157
	16, 17	40		6–12	73		12–19	130		31–34	160
	18–22	64		13–21	74	21:	20–22	131		35–38	161
	23–27	65		22–33	75		23 to 22: 14	132		39–49	162
	28–34	66		34–36	76	22:	15–46	133		50	163
9	1–8	43	15:	1–20	78	23:	1–39	134		51–56	164
	9–13	44		21–28	79	24:	1–31	137		57–61	165
	14–17	67		29–31	80		32 to 25: 46	138		62–66	166
	18–26	68		32–38	81	26:	1–5	139	28:	1–10	167
	27–31	69		39 to 16: 4	82		6–13	128		11–15	169
	32–34	70	16:	5–12	83		14–16	139		16–20	174

Mark

Chapter and Verse		Section	Chapter and Verse		Section	Chapter and Verse		Section	Chapter and Verse		Section
1:	1–8	20	6:	1–6a	71	10:	2–12	118	14:	26–31	147
	9–11	21		6b–13	72		13–16	119		32–42	148
	12, 13	22		14–16	73		17–31	120		43–52	149
	14, 15	35		17–20	34		32–34	122		53	151
	16–20	37		21–29	73		35–45	123		54	152
	21–28	38		30–44	74		46–52	124		55–65	151
	29–31	39		45–52	75	11:	1–11	129		66–72	152
	32–34	40		53–56	76		12–19	130	15:	1a	153
	35–39	41	7:	1–23	78		20–25 [26]	131		1b–5	154
	40–45	42		24–30	79		27 to 12: 12	132		6–15a	156
2:	1–12	43		31–37	80	12:	13–37	133		15b–19	157
	13–17	44	8:	1–9	81		38–40	134		20–23	160
	18–22	67		10–12	82		41–44	135		24–28	161
	23–28	46		13–21	83	13:	1–27	137		29–36	162
3:	1–6	47		22–26	84		28–37	138		37	163
	7–12	48		27–30	85	14:	1,2	139		38–41	164
	13–19	49		31 to 9: 1	86		3–9	128		42–47	165
	20–30	57	9:	2–13	87		10, 11	139	16:	1–8	167
	31–35	59		14–29	88		12–16	140		9–11	168
4:	1–34	63		30–32	89		17	141		12, 13	170
	35–41	65		33–50	91		18–21	143		14	171
5:	1–20	66	10:	1a	92		22–25	144		15–18	174
	21–43	68		1b	102					19, 20	175

*The last 12 verses of Mark are in R.V. spaced from the preceding because of doubt whether they originally formed part of Mark's Gospel.

INDEX FOR FINDING ANY PASSAGE IN THE HARMONY — *Continued*

Luke

Chapter and Verse	Section	Chapter and Verse	Section	Chapter and Verse	Section	Chapter and Verse	Section
1: 1-4	1	6: 12-16	49	11: 24-26	58	21: 5-28	137
5-25	4	17-19	48	27, 28	59	29-36	138
26-38	5	20-49	50	29-36	58	37, 38	130
39-56	6	7: 1-10	51	37-54	60	22: 1-6	139
57, 58	7	11-17	53	12: 1-59	61	7-13	140
59-79	8	18-35	54	13: 1-5	62	14-18	141
80	19	36-50	55	6-9	103	19, 20	144
2: 1-7	10	8: 1-3	56	10-17	104	21-23	143
8-14	11	4-18	63	18-21	63	24-30	141
15-20	12	19-21	59	22-35	105	31-38	145
21	13	22-25	65	14: 1-24	106	39-46	148
22-38	14	26-40	66	25-35	107	47-53	149
39	18	41-56	68	15: 1-32	108	54-62	152
40-52	19	9: 1-6	72	16: 1-13	109	63-65	151
3: 1-18	20	7-9	73	14-31	110	66-71	153
19, 20	34	10-17	74	17: 1-10	111	23: 1-5	154
21-23a	21	18-21	85	11-19	112	6-12	155
23b-38	3	22-27	86	20-37	113	13-25	156
4: 1-13	22	28-36	87	18: 1-8	114	26-33a	160
14, 15	35	37-43a	88	9-14	115	33b, 34	161
16-30	36	43b-45	89	15-17	119	35-37	162
31-37	38	46-50	91	18-30	120	38	161
38, 39	39	51-56	92	31-34	122	39-45a	162
40, 41	40	57-62	64	35-43	124	45b	164
42-44	41	10: 1-16	93	19: 1-10	125	46	163
5: 1-11	37	17-24	97	11-28	126	47-49	164
12-16	42	25-37	98	29-44	129	50-56	165
17-26	43	38-42	99	45-48	130	24: 1-11	167
27-32	44	11: 1-13	100	20: 1-19	132	12	168
33-39	67	14, 15	57	20-44	133	13-35	170
6: 1-5	46	16	58	45-47	134	36-49	171
6-11	47	17-23	57	21: 1-4	135	50-53	175

John

Chapter and Verse	Section	Chapter and Verse	Section	Chapter and Verse	Section	Chapter and Verse	Section
1: 1-18	2	5: 1-47	45	12: 12-19	129	19: 1-3	157
19-28	20	6: 1-14	74	20-50	136	4-16a	158
29-34	21	15-21	75	13: 1-20	142	16b, 17	160
35-42	23	22-71	77	21-35	143	18-24	161
43-51	24	7: 1	80	36-38	145	25-29	162
2: 1-11	25	2-52	94	14: 1 to 17: 26	146	30	163
12	26	53 to 8: 11	95	18: 1	148	31-42	165
13-25	27	8: 12-59	96	2-12	149	20: 1-18	168
3: 1-21	28	9: 1 to 10: 38	101	13, 14	150	19-24	171
22	29	10: 39-42	102	15-18	152	25-29	172
23-36	30	11: 1-46	116	19-24	150	30, 31	176
4: 1-3	31	47-54	117	25-27	152	21: 1-23	173
4-42	32	55 to 12: 1	127	28-38	154	24, 25	176
43-54	33	12: 2-11	128	39, 40	156		

Gourd. The rendering of Heb. *ḳĭḳāyŏn* in Jonah 4 :6-10, the marg. of R.V. substituting Palma Christi. The plant so designated grew up in a night, sheltering the Prophet Jonah from the fierce heat of the sun ; but its decay was as rapid as its growth. The LXX translates the Heb. by Gr. *kolokynthē*, meaning the pumpkin (*Cucurbita pepo*), which may be considered the type of the gourd family (*Cucurbitaceae*). A native of Astrakhan, along the n.w. coast of the Caspian Sea, it may well have been introduced into the Ninevite region before the time of Jonah. It is in favor of the identification that it is a plant of rapid growth. But the Heb. *ḳĭḳāyŏn* is very like the Greco-Egyptian *kiki*, which means the castor-oil plant (*Ricinus communis*), sometimes called Palma Christi (Christ's palm). It is not, however, a palm, but a euphorbiaceous plant, like the little milky weeds called spurges. It is a native of India, but was cultivated in s. Asia and Egypt (Herod. ii. 94). It attains a height of from 8 to 10 feet, growing to a considerable height in a few days. The stem is purplish-red and covered with a pearl-like bloom, the leaves are peltate and palmate, the flowers are in racemes, the seed vessel has 3 two-valved cells, each one-seeded. If this was the plant which shaded Jonah, its rapid growth was miraculous.

Gourd, Wild. The rendering of Heb. *paḳḳŭʻōth*, splitters, bursters (II Kings 4: 39). It is the fruit of a wild plant growing in Palestine which flourishes when other vegetation is dead or dying through excessive drought. A son of the prophets gathered a lapful of the gourds near Jericho and put them into a pot to be cooked, but the moment the pottage of which they constituted the chief ingredient was put to the mouth the taste betrayed that there was death in the pot : in other words, the fruit was poisonous (II Kings 4:38-41). The plant was pretty clearly one or other of 2 species of the gourd order, the colocynth, or the squirting cucumber, probably the former. The colocynth (*Citrullus colocynthis*) is a prostrate gourd-like vine with tendrils ; in Palestine it is wild on the maritime plain and in the Jordan Valley. It bears gourds which are 3 or more inches in diameter. If the traveler plucks the smooth gourdlike fruits and cuts them across with his penknife, he will find that they both look and smell like the cucumber. If he puts them to his lips, he will feel as if he had touched fire. The colocynth is a cathartic and is a valuable but dangerous medicine. The other claimant, the squirting cucumber (*Ecballium elaterium*) is a stiff and upright plant and has no tendrils; it bears little gourds, 1½ to 2 inches long, which when ripe fall suddenly when touched or shaken. Then the bitter irritating juice is squirted out and the seeds are thrown all around. It is a drastic cathartic. The squirting cucumber grows in waste places and by the roadside throughout Palestine, and its unfitness for food would probably be known to the young companion of Elisha.

Gov'er·nor. One who governs a land by authority of a supreme ruler to whom he is subordinate. Joseph when prime minister of Egypt was called its governor (Gen. 42:6; 45:26). When Nebuchadnezzar, after capturing Jerusalem, departed, he left a governor, Gedaliah, behind to rule the conquered people (Jer. 40:5; 41:2, etc.). After the Captivity, the Israelites were ruled by Persian governors: Zerubbabel, Nehemiah, and others, though Jews by birth, were Persian officials (Neh. 5:14, 18; Hag. 1:14). Pontius Pilate was governor of Judea when our Lord was crucified, and is so called (Matt. 28:14), though his specific Roman title was procurator (*q.v.*).

For governor of a feast, see RULER.

Go'zan (gō'zăn). A town and district in Mesopotamia on the river Habor, or Khabur (II Kings 17:6; 18:11; 19:12; I Chron. 5:26; cf. Isa. 37:12). Gozan was called Guzanu by the Assyrians and is the Gauzanitis of Ptolemy, a province of Mesopotamia, on the upper reaches of the Khabur River, and along the s. slopes of Mount Masius. Ptolemy mentions a town of Media called Gauzania in its vicinity.

Grape. See VINE.

Grass. A plant belonging to the endogenous order *Graminaceae*, of which the ordinary grasses of the fields, or the cultivated cereals, may be considered as typical representatives. Popularly, the term grass is extended to many other endogenous plants, and even to various exogens, especially those possessing linear leaves. In Gen. 1:11, 12 the vegetable kingdom is divided into 3 great classes: grass, herbs, and trees. The word grass is used in a more limited sense when man's brief life on earth is compared to grass, which in the morning flourishes and in the evening is cut down and withers (Ps. 103:15, 16; cf. also Ps. 37:2; 90:5, 6; 92:7; 102:11; Isa. 40:6, 7; Matt. 6:30; Luke 12:28).

Grass'hop'per. 1. The rendering of Heb. *'arbeh*, the numerous or gregarious, in A.V. of Judg. 6:5; 7:12; Job 39:20; Jer. 46:23. It is undoubtedly the migratory locust, as the R.V. makes it, and as even the A.V. has it in Ex. 10:4; Joel 1:4. See LOCUST.

2. The rendering of Heb. *ḥāgāb* in Lev. 11:22; Num. 13:33; Eccl. 12:5; Isa. 40:22. It is very small (Num. 13:33) and voracious (II Chron. 7:13, locust). It perhaps derived its name from its covering the ground or hiding the sun. In Lev. 11:22, R.V. marg., it is admitted that it is unknown whether the animal was a grasshopper or a locust. The grasshopper family, now called *Acridiidae*, consists of leaping orthopterous insects, with four-jointed tarsi, wing cases in repose placed like the two sloping sides of a roof, and long, tapering antennae. The type is the great English grasshopper (*Locusta viridissima*).

3. The rendering of Heb. *gōb* and *gōbay*, creeper from the earth (Nahum 3:17). It devours the grass (Amos 7:1, R.V., locust). It

was probably an insect of the locust family; but of which species is unknown.

Grave. The cavity in the ground in which a body is interred. The Jews were sometimes buried in graves dug in the earth (Tobit 8:9, 18), but more commonly in caves scooped out in rocks or naturally existing (Gen. 23:9; Matt. 27:60; John 11:38). See SEPULCHER.

Grav'en Im'age. An image of wood, stone, or metal fashioned by means of a sharp cutting instrument as distinguished from one cast in a mold (Isa. 30:22; 44:16, 17; 45:20; cf. Hab. 2:18, 19). Sometimes, however, the image was first cast and then finished by the graver (Isa. 40:19; 44:10). Graven im-

Statuette of a Canaanite God, Found at Ras Shamra

ages were in use among the Canaanites before the Israelites entered the country (Deut. 7:5; 12:3). They were also used in Babylon and elsewhere (Jer. 50:38; 51:47, 52). The Second Commandment expressly forbade the people of God to make them (Ex. 20:4; Deut. 5:8; cf. also Lev. 26:1; Deut. 27:15; Isa. 44:9; Jer. 10:14; 51:17).

Greaves. See ARMOR.

Gre'cians (grē'shănz). 1. The people of Greece (Joel 3:6).

2. Jews who spoke Greek as distinguished from those who used Aramaic, which in N.T. times was popularly called by the Jews Hebrew (Acts 6:1; 9:29, in R.V. Grecian Jews; cf. ch. 11:20, A.V. and R.V. marg.). See HELLENIST.

Greece (grēs), in A.V. of Daniel **Gre'ci·a** (grē'shǐ·à) [Lat. *Graecia*, from *Graeci*, from Gr. *Graikoi*, an old name of a tribe in Epirus. The Greeks called their land *Hellas* and themselves, usually, *Hellênes*]. A small but highly celebrated country in the s.e. of Europe. Its n. limit was never perfectly defined; it may, however, be placed at the Olympian chain of mountains. On the s. it was bounded by the Mediterranean; on the e. by the Aegean Sea; and on the w. by the Ionian Sea and the Adriatic Sea. Its position during the time when the Mediterranean was the highway of civilization gave it unequaled advantages.

The authentic history of Greece with its first written records dates from the first Olympiad, 776 B.C. Previous to that time, and including the period known as the heroic age, history is so mingled with legend that it is difficult to separate truth from myth. It seems certain, however, that the Greeks were descended from 4 tribes, which in turn claimed descent from a common ancestor,

Hellen. Of these tribes, the Aeolians and the Achaeans played a prominent part during the heroic age, Homer sometimes speaking of the whole Greek people as Achaeans. The other 2 tribes, the Dorians and the Ionians, became more important in historic times, the Athenians and the Spartans being descended from them respectively.

The early historic period, from 776 to 500 B.C., may be regarded as a period of individual growth by the different states comprising the nation. These states were theoretically independent of one another, but were united by a common language and literature, by national games, and a general national development. There were also frequent though changing political alliances. During this period the foundations of Grecian architecture, art, literature, and philosophy were laid. Greece was early within the geographical knowledge of the Hebrews, who called it Javan, that is, Ionia (Gen. 10:4); but it was known merely as a country at the ends of the earth (Isa. 66:19; Ezek. 27:13; Joel 3:6).

About the year 500 B.C. Greece came into prominent notice on account of her struggle with Persia, at that time the great world power. As early as 546 Cyrus captured Sardis, the capital of Lydia. The fall of this city was followed by the subjection of the Greek cities of Asia to the Persian yoke. The Hellespont was crossed by the Persians in the reign of Darius, and Macedonia submitted in 510. But the Greek cities of Asia rose and maintained determined revolt against their conquerors during the years 500 to 495; and the Greeks of Europe defeated the Persians at Marathon in 490, and, after suffering reverses at Thermopylae, inflicted crushing defeats upon them at Salamis in 480, and at Plataea and Mycale in 479. The struggle with Persia resulted in drawing the entire nation together under the leadership of one state. The first state to attain this supremacy was Athens. After the Persian wars she held the leadership from 479 to 431 B.C. Then followed the Peloponnesian War (431–404 B.C.), which began in a quarrel between Corinth and her colonies, but finally drew into the struggle the whole naval and military strength of Greece; it was led on one side by Sparta and on the other by Athens. The war resulted in the downfall of the Athenian power and the period of Spartan supremacy (404–371 B.C.). There followed in turn the Theban supremacy, which lasted until 362 B.C. Finally (338) all Greece fell under the power of Philip of Macedon, and became thenceforth a part of the Macedonian empire.

It is under the rule of Alexander the Great that Greece comes into direct contact for the first time with Judea. On his march to Persia Alexander passed through Judea, which fell into his hands without a struggle. See ALEXANDER 1. From this time Greek influence spread rapidly and took firm hold in the countries situated around the e. end of the Mediterranean Sea; this is the Hellenistic period. Even after the Roman conquest the influence of the Greek language, culture, and philosophy remained paramount, and even influenced the Jewish religion itself. In the time of Christ the Greek language was spoken throughout the civilized world. After the death of Alexander, his empire fell into the hands of his generals, who parceled it out among themselves. At first Greece proper was held in the name of his infant son, but soon he, as well as all members of Alexander's family, were put to death, and the country became the prey of anyone strong enough to take it, until it finally fell under the dominion of Rome. The last struggle against Rome resulted in the destruction of Corinth under Mummius, 146 B.C. Now Greece

was annexed to Macedonia, but later it was declared a Roman province under the name of Achaea. The division of the Roman power into the Eastern and Western empires revived Greek influence for a time. The Eastern empire survived long after the Western empire fell, but finally it came to an end in the capture of Constantinople by the Turks in 1453.

Some of the Apostle Paul's most earnest labors took place in Greece, notably in Athens and Corinth, besides his general travels through Achaia, the name at that time for ancient Greece.

Greek (grēk). 1. A native of Greece, or one of the Greek race (Acts 16:1; 17:4). When Jew and Greek are contrasted in the N.T., the term Greek is used for a foreigner in general, the Greek being looked on as the highest type of Gentile (Rom. 1:14, 16; 10:12).

2. After the Macedonian conquest of the East and the establishment of the kingdoms of Syria and Egypt, the name Greek was applied, especially by Orientals, to all who spoke the Greek language in ordinary life and enjoyed the privileges of Greek settlers in the kingdoms ruled by Alexander's successors. The Greeks who wished to see Jesus (John 12:20) were foreigners, but it is not certain that they were of the Greek race.

3. The language of the ancient Greeks. It belongs to the Indo-European family of tongues, having affinities with Sanskrit, Avestan and Old Persian, Slavonic, Teutonic, Latin, and Celtic. It excels in power of full and precise expression. Jews who spoke Greek (Acts 21:37) used the common idiom (koine) of their day. The O.T. was translated into Greek before the advent of Christ (see VERSIONS, I. 1); the N.T. is written in Greek.

Grey'hound'. The rendering of Heb. *zarzir*, well girt or well knit in the loins, in Prov. 30:31. The greyhound is figured on the Assyrian monuments. The word may, however, denote the war horse (R.V. marg.) as ornamented with girths and buckles about the loins; or the starling, as the cognate word in Arab., Syr., and post-Biblical Heb. denotes.

Grind'ing. See MILL.

Grove. A group or clump of trees. In the A.V. it is uniformly a mistranslation of: 1. Heb. *'ēshel* (Gen. 21:33; cf. I Sam. 22:6). R.V. renders this a tamarisk tree. See TAMARISK TREE.

2. Heb. *'ăshērāh*, with its 2 plurals *'ăshērîm* and *'ăshērôth* (Ex. 34:13, and elsewhere except Gen. 21:33). See ASHERAH.

Guard. In Oriental countries, where the king, as a rule, is despotic, it is necessary that he should be continually defended by a bodyguard; such a military organization is worse than useless unless complete dependence can be placed on its fidelity. Hence, service in the bodyguard is considered specially honorable, and its captain is a high officer. Such an appointment was filled by Potiphar (Gen. 37:36; 41:12), by Benaiah (II Sam. 23:22, 23; I Chron. 18:17), by Nebuzaradan (II Kings 25:8; Jer. 39:9, 10), by Arioch (Dan. 2:14), and others. The captain of the guard and his men were often employed to inflict capital punishment on political or other offenders. In Mark 6:27, the Gr. is *spekoulatōr*, spy. Such spies constituted a division in each Roman legion, and under the empire acted as the bodyguard of a general and were employed as messengers and to seek out persons proscribed or sentenced to death.

Gud·go'dah (gŭd-gō'dȧ). See HOR-HAGGIDGAD.

Guest. One temporarily entertained in the house of another, even though it be only for a few hours at a feast (I Kings 1:41; Zeph. 1:7; Matt. 22:10, 11). Complete strangers were received as guests and shown great consideration (Gen. 18:1–8; 19:3; Ex. 2:20; Judg. 13:15; 19:20, 21; Job 31:32). Important houses had a guestchamber (Mark 14:14; Luke 22:11; cf. also II Kings 4:10), and at Jerusalem these rooms were freely placed at the disposal of Jews visiting the city at the annual festivals. Hospitality is enjoined in the N.T. (Heb. 13:2; cf. Matt. 25:43). Ordinary morality dictates that one should not be guest in the house of a notorious sinner; but prominent Pharisees went so far as to apply this principle indiscriminately to the acceptance of hospitality from people of the publican class (Luke 5:27–32; 19:7).

Guilt Of'fer·ing. See OFFERINGS.

Gu'ni (gū'nī) [cf. Arab. *jaun*, black, white, or light red]. 1. A son of Naphtali, and founder of a tribal family (Gen. 46:24; Num. 26:48; I Chron. 7:13).

2. A Gadite (I Chron. 5:15).

Gur (gûr) [lion's whelp or other young animal]. An ascent near Ibleam, where Ahaziah, king of Judah, was smitten by order of Jehu and mortally wounded (II Kings 9:27). Exact situation unknown.

Gur'-ba'al (gûr'bā'ăl) [sojourn of Baal]. A place inhabited by Arabs (II Chron. 26:7); perhaps in the desert s. of Beer-sheba, at Huleh Ghurri.

Gym·na'si·um, in A.V. **Place of Ex'er·cise.** A public place in Jerusalem for athletic exercise and exhibitions, below the w. cloister of the Temple (Jos. *War* iv. 9, 12; vi. 3, 2; 6, 2), below the palace of the Asmonaeans (Jos. *Antiq.* xx. 8, 11; *War* ii. 16, 3), below the citadel or acropolis (II Macc. 4:12, 27; not the Syrian fortress called the Acra, which was erected later, I Macc. 1:33). It was situated near the council house, by the first or innermost wall, and at the end of the bridge which led from the Temple across the Tyropoeon Valley (Jos. *War* v. 4, 2; cf. vi. 6, 2). It was erected by hellenizing Jews, under the leadership of Jason, by permission of Antiochus Epiphanes (I Macc. 1:10, 14; II Macc. 4:7 *seq.*). The essential features of a gymnasium were: 1. An open court for boxing, wrestling, pitching quoits, and throwing the javelin (II Macc. 4:14, palaestra, discus); 2. A stadium or course for the foot race; 3. A colonnade for a place of recreation and for athletic exercises in winter (Jos. *Antiq.* and *War, passim, xystos*); 4. A bathroom. The gymnasium at Jerusalem was condemned by strict Jews because it introduced heathen customs; led Jewish youth to wear the hat of Hermes, to exercise stark naked in public, and to be ashamed of the mark of their religion; and infected even the priests and caused them to neglect their official duties (I Macc. 1:14, 15; II Macc. 4:13–17). It existed until the overthrow of the city by Titus; and was not only resorted to for athletic sports, but was also occasionally used for popular assemblies (Jos. *War* ii. 16, 3).

H

Ha'a·hash'ta·ri (hā'ȧ-hăsh'tȧ-rī) [the Ahashtarite]. A Hezronite, son of Ashhur (I Chron. 4:6; cf. ch. 2:24).

Ha·ba'iah (hȧ-bā'yȧ), and **Ho·ba'iah** (hō-bā'yȧ) [Jehovah has hidden]. Father of certain Jews claiming sacerdotal descent. Their names not being found in the register, they were put out of the priesthood (Ezra 2:61; Neh. 7:63; cf. R.V.); called Obdia in I Esdras 5:38.

Ha·bak'kuk (hȧ-băk'ŭk) [embrace; or perhaps the name of a garden plant: cf. Akkad. *ḥambaḳūḳu*]. A prophet of Judah. It is inferred from his psalm (Hab., ch. 3) and from the directions to the chief musician (v. 19) that he was of the tribe of Levi and one of the Temple singers; but the evidence proves nothing.

The Book of Habakkuk is the 8th of the Minor Prophets. It consists of: 1. A first complaint: his cry to God against violence and wickedness is unheeded (Hab. 1:2–4); iniquity is triumphant. The Lord's response: God is raising up the Chaldeans (vs. 5–10), but as guilty the Chaldeans shall be punished (v. 11). 2. A second complaint: God's Kingdom indeed shall not perish, and the Chaldeans shall be visited with judgment (v. 12); but yet a moral problem remains: God allows the Chaldeans to waste and destroy those who are more righteous than they. Shall this go on (vs. 13–17)? The Lord's response: the Chaldeans are puffed up and unrighteous [that fact to the eye of faith is sufficient; it dooms them (cf. Hab. 1:11; Isa. 10:12–16), and dooms all like them]; but the just shall live by his faith (Hab. 2:1–4). That truth, rightly understood, solves the problem. Moreover, faith in the certainty that God will punish wickedness enables the prophet to pronounce 5 woes against the great world power for 5 forms of wickedness (vs. 5–20). 3. A prayer of praise (ch. 3:1–19), in which after an invocation and a petition that God in wrath remember mercy (v. 2), the prophet describes God's appearance in majesty and the ensuing consternation of his enemies (vs. 3–15), and expresses the quiet confidence of faith in God (vs. 16–19).

The book is not dated, but was evidently a production of the Chaldean period. 1. The Temple is still standing (ch. 2:20), and musical service is conducted (ch. 3:19). 2. The rise of the Chaldeans to a formidable power among the nations occurs during that generation (ch. 1:5, 6), and the slaying of the nations by the Chaldeans had already begun (vs. 6, 17).

The Chaldeans had been long known to the Hebrews. They attracted renewed attention by their successful revolt from the Assyrians in 626 B.C.; and they began their great career of subjugation and attained to the leading place among the powers of the world on the fall of Nineveh in 612 B.C., and by their victory over the Egyptians at Carchemish in 605. From internal evidence it is supposed that Habakkuk prophesied during the reign of Jehoiakim (607–597 B.C.), but it is difficult to fix the precise period. Most critics date the prophecy in the early part of that reign, about the time of the battle of Carchemish. It may, however, antedate the fall of Nineveh by some years; for not only had the Chaldeans bestirred themselves in 626 B.C. but military events before the collapse of Nineveh indicated the Chaldeans as the coming world power; their subjugation of Judah had long been predicted by the Hebrew prophets (Isa. 11:11; 39:6, 7; Micah 4:10); and their fierce, warlike character, their habitual cruelty and rapacity in war, and their method of battle were known to all nations. There was thus, even before their victory at Carchemish, full justification for the declarations made in Hab. 1:5–10. If the prophecy was uttered before the Chaldean success at Carchemish, Habakkuk in ch. 1:2–4 is lamenting the carnival of wickedness which he witnessed in Israel or in the world at large.

Hab'az·zi·ni'ah (hăb'ȧ-zĭ-nī'ȧ), in A.V. **Hab'·a·zi·ni'ah** (hăb'ȧ-zĭ-nī'ȧ). A Rechabite who lived long before Jeremiah (Jer. 35:3).

Hab'er·geon. A coat of mail to defend the breast and neck (II Chron. 26:14; Neh. 4:16; in R.V., coat of mail). In Job 41:26, R.V. on good grounds substitutes pointed shaft in the text, and places coat of mail in the marg. Habergeon, or coat of mail, is also used to translate a different Heb. word of uncertain meaning in Ex. 28:32; 39:23.

Ha'bor (hā'bōr). A river of Mesopotamia to which captives from the 10 tribes were carried (II Kings 17:6; 18:11; I Chron. 5:26). It has been identified as the Khabur, which, flowing s. through Mesopotamia, after a course of 190 miles, meets the e. branch of the Euphrates at Ḳarḳīsiyā, the ancient Circesium.

Hac'a·li'ah (hăk'à-lī'à), in A.V. Hach'a·li'ah (hăk'à-lī'à) [ety. uncertain; perhaps, wait for Jehovah, or Jehovah is dark (from displeasure?). Cf. Arab. ḥakala, to be dark]. The father of Nehemiah (Neh. 1:1).

Ha·chi'lah (hà-kī'là) [dark, gloomy]. A hill in the wilderness of Ziph (I Sam. 26:1–3), s.e. of Hebron, and on the s. of the desert, not far from Maon (ch. 23:19, 24–26). David concealed himself there whilst fleeing from Saul, and there Saul afterward encamped when engaged in his pursuit.

Hach'mo·ni (hăk'mō-nī) [wise]. The founder of the Hachmonite family, the members of which are called sons of Hachmoni (I Chron. 11:11; 27:32), or simply Hachmonites (cf. II Sam. 23:8).

Ha'dad, I (hā'dăd) [sharpness, fierceness]. A son of Ishmael (Gen. 25:15; in A.V., following a variant Heb. reading, Hadar; I Chron. 1:30).

Ha'dad, II (hā'dăd). 1. A deity worshiped by the Aramaeans. It occurs in proper names, as in Ben-hadad, Hadadezer. The Assyrian scribes identified Hadad with their own weather-god Ramman, i.e., Rimmon.

2. A king of Edom, son of Bedad, and of the city of Avith. He smote Midian in the field of Moab (Gen. 36:35, 36; I Chron. 1:46, 47).

3. A king of Edom, whose city was Pau or Pai (I Chron. 1:50). In Gen. 36:39 he is called Hadar. See DALETH.

4. An Edomite prince, who escaped from his country when Joab, at the head of the Israelite army, was engaged for 6 months in the cruel task of cutting off every male in Edom. Hadad was then a little child and was taken by his guardians to Egypt. The king of Egypt received him with much kindness, assigned him a house and land, provided him with food, and gave him an Egyptian princess, sister of the queen, to wife. But after the death of David and Joab, the great foes of his race, he returned to Edom and became an adversary to Solomon (I Kings 11:14–22).

Had'ad·e'zer (hăd'ăd-ē'zēr) [Hadad is a help]. Son of Rehob and king of Zobah, in Syria (II Sam. 8:3). He is frequently called Hadarezer, the latter form being doubtless an early misreading of daleth; see DALETH. When going to recover his border at the river Euphrates, he was met and defeated by King David. The Syrians of Damascus, who afterward arrived to assist him, shared his fate. From Betah and Berothai, cities of Hadadezer, David took much brass or copper. Toi, king of Hamath, probably a Hittite by race, had formerly been at war with Hadadezer, and he congratulated David on his victory (II Sam. 8:3–13; I Chron. 18:3–10). Hadadezer renewed the war with David, became confederate with the Ammonites, and sent his army, led by his general, Shobach, to try another engagement with their common foe. David was victorious and Shobach, was among the slain.

The dependent kings who had served Hadadezer now made peace with David, and Hadadezer is heard of no more (II Sam. 10:6–19; I Chron. 19:16–19). See BEN-HADAD 2.

Ha'dad·rim'mon (hā'dăd-rĭm'ŏn) [Hadad and Rimmon, 2 Syrian divinities]. A city in the plain of Jezreel, near Megiddo (Zech. 12:11). Jerome says that it was the place in his day called Maximianopolis. This is now called Rummāneh, and is about a mile n.w. by w. of Taanach.

Ha'dar (hā'där). See HADAD, I and II.

Had'a·re'zer (hăd'à-rē'zēr). See HADADEZER.

Ha·dash'ah (hà-dăsh'à) [new]. A village in the lowland of Judah (Josh. 15:37); it may be located at Khirbet el-Judeideh between 'Araḳ el-Menshiyeh and Khirbet 'Aglān.

Ha·das'sah (hà-dăs'à) [a myrtle]. The original Jewish name of Queen Esther (Esth. 2:7).

Ha·dat'tah (hà-dăt'à). See HAZOR-HADATTAH.

Ha'des (hā'dēz). See HELL 1.

Ha'did (hā'dĭd) [sharp, pointed; a point]. A town of Benjamin, mentioned in connection with Lod, i.e., Lydda (Ezra 2:33; Neh. 11:34). It is commonly identified with Adida, a town built upon a hill of the Shephelah and overlooking the plain (I Macc. 12:38; 13:13; Jos. Antiq. xiii. 6, 5). Its site is located at Ḥadītheh, 3 miles e.n.e. of Lydda.

Had'lai (hăd'lī) [ceasing, forbearing]. A man of Ephraim (II Chron. 28:12).

Ha·do'ram (hà-dō'răm). 1. An Arabian tribe descended from Joktan (Gen. 10:27; I Chron. 1:21).

2. A son of the king of Hamath (I Chron. 18:10). See JORAM 1.

3. An officer over Rehoboam's levy (II Chron. 10:18). See ADONIRAM.

Ha'drach (hā'drăk). A country mentioned in connection with Damascus and Hamath (Zech. 9:1). It lay on the Orontes, s. of Hamath.

Ha'gab (hā'găb) [a locust, grasshopper]. Founder of a family of Nethinim (Ezra 2:46).

Hag'a·bah (hăg'à-bä) or **Hag'a·ba** (hăg'-à-bä) [Aram., a locust]. Founder of a family of Nethinim, distinct from that of Hagab (Ezra 2:45; Neh. 7:48).

Ha'gar (hā'gär), in A.V. of N.T. both times **A'gar**, like the Gr. [if Heb., flight; cf. Arab. hijrah, emigration, flight]. An Egyptian bondwoman of Sarah, perhaps obtained during Abraham's sojourn in Egypt (Gen. 16:1; cf. ch. 12:10). After Abraham had been 10 years in Canaan, and the promised son had not been born to him, Sarah, now 76 years old, despaired of sharing in the promise, and proposed earthly means to secure a son to Abraham and obtain the name of mother. In accordance with a custom of the times, she gave her maid to Abraham. When Hagar perceived herself to be with child she despised her mistress, and, being treated by her harshly, fled into the wilderness. There the angel of the Lord found her at a fountain between Shur and Bered, revealed to her the future of the child she was to bear, and bade her return to her mistress. Hagar called the name of the place "the well of the living one who seeth me" (Gen. 16:1–16). She then returned to her mistress and in due time gave birth to Ishmael. Some 15 years later the youth Ishmael mocked at the child Isaac. For this offense Hagar, with a skin of water on her shoulder, and Ishmael were expelled with God's approval from the family of Abraham. They wandered in the wilderness of Beer-sheba until the water was spent. The exhausted boy, whom Hagar had been supporting, was placed under the shade of a bush, and she sat down a bowshot off that she might not see him die. Again the angel of the Lord intervened, directing her to a well in the vicinity and reminding her of the promise concerning the boy. The last we hear of Hagar is her taking a wife for her son out of the land of Egypt, whence she herself had originally come (Gen. 21:1–21). For Gal. 4:21–31, see ISHMAEL.

Hag'a•rene' (hăg'á-rēn'), **Ha'gar•ite** (hă'-gär-īt), and **Ha'ger•ite** (hă'gĕr-īt). See HAGRITE.

Hag'ga•i (hăg'á-ī) [festal, i.e., born on a feast day]. A prophet, contemporary with Zechariah (cf. Hag. 1:1 with Zech. 1:1). He prophesied after the return from Babylon. The work on the Temple had ceased for 15 years, and Haggai was largely instrumental in arousing the people to proceed with the building (Ezra 5:1, 2; 6:14).

The Book of Haggai is the 10th of the Minor Prophets. It consists of 4 prophecies delivered within the space of 4 months in the 2d year of Darius Hystaspis, 520 B.C.

1. On the 1st day of the 6th month the prophet reproaches those who left the Temple in ruins and built ceiled houses for themselves, and he points out that God's blessing is withheld from their ordinary labor. In consequence of this exhortation, work on the Temple was resumed on the 24th day of the same month (ch. 1).

2. In the 7th month, 21st day, he encourages those who mourn over the humble character of the new building as compared with the splendor of the old edifice. He predicts that the latter glory of the house shall be greater than the former glory, for God will shake the nations and the desirable things of all nations, their silver and gold, shall come and fill the house with glory, and God will give peace in that place (ch. 2:1–9; Heb. 12:26–28).

3. In the 9th month, 24th day, he adds a sequel to the 1st prophecy. As the touch of the unclean pollutes the clean, so their former neglect of God polluted their labor and God did not bestow his blessing. But their revived zeal for God will be accompanied by fruitful seasons from the Lord (Hag. 2:10–19).

4. On the same day he adds a sequel to the 2d prophecy. When the Lord shakes the nations, he will establish Zerubbabel, who represents the royal line of David (ch. 2:20–23).

Hag'ge•ri (hăg'ĕ-rī). See HAGRI.

Hag'gi (hăg'ī) [festal, i.e., born on a feast day]. A son of Gad, and founder of a tribal family (Gen. 46:16; Num. 26:15).

Hag•gi'ah (hă-gī'á) [a festival of Jehovah]. A Levite, a descendant of Merari (I Chron. 6:30).

Hag'gith (hăg'ĭth) [festal]. One of David's wives, the mother of Adonijah (II Sam. 3:4; I Kings 1:5).

Hag'i•og'ra•pha (hăg'ĭ-ŏg'rá-fá). See CANON.

Hag'ri (hăg'rī), in A.V. **Hag'ge•ri**. Rather an adjective, Hagrite, than a proper name (I Chron. 11:38). The parallel passage (II Sam. 23:36) reads "Bani the Gadite"; see MIBHAR.

Hag'rite (hăg'rīt); in A.V. **Ha'gar•ite**, and once **Ha'ger•ite**, and once, in Ps. 83:6, **Hag'-a•renes'**, in which passage R.V. in its text follows A.V. A nomad people who dwelt throughout all the land e. of Gilead, and were rich in camels, sheep, and asses. During the reign of Saul they were vanquished by the Israelite tribes e. of the Jordan (I Chron. 5:10, 18–22). A Hagrite had charge of David's flocks (I Chron. 27:31). They are the *Agraioi* of the Greek geographers.

Ha'i (hā'ī). See AI.

Hail. Hail falls not merely in cold and temperate climates, but also in hot and even tropical latitudes, where snow and ice are not to be found except at great elevations. The most destructive hailstones are those which accompany a violent thunderstorm. In all places 2 or more hailstones can unite so as to make an irregularly shaped mass of ice, which, when large, becomes formidable by the momentum with which it descends. Hail occasionally falls in Egypt (Ex. 9:22–25) between December and April. It is more frequent in Palestine (Josh. 10:11; Hag. 2:17). The area affected by a hailstorm is generally a long, narrow line, so that of 2 places near each other, one may be in and the other out of the storm. Thus Goshen might escape it, whilst the adjacent district of Egypt to the w. might be in its track and suffer severely (Ex. 9:26); and a pursuing army might be untouched by the storm and yet see their fleeing foes beaten down by the falling stones (Josh. 10:11).

Hair. The natural covering and ornament of the head. In Egypt men ordinarily shaved the head, but when mourning let the hair grow (Herod. ii. 36; iii. 12). The Assyrians wore it long (Herod. i. 195), falling to the shoulders. The Israelites also wore it tolerably long; but cut it to prevent its reaching an extreme length (cf. Num. 6:5; II Sam. 14:26; Jos. *Antiq.* xiv. 9, 4), and the services of the barber were sometimes employed (Ezek. 5:1); but they were forbidden to cut off the edge of the hair from about the temples, so as to round it (Lev. 19:27), for that was a significant heathen custom (Herod. iii. 8). Hebrew women wore the hair long (S. of Sol. 7:5; Rev. 9:8; cf. I Cor. 11:15), binding it up or braiding it (Judith 10:3; 16:8; I Tim. 2:9; I Peter 3:3). Oil was used for the hair by both men and women (Ps. 23:5; Matt. 6:17). Herod the Great, in order to conceal his age, dyed his hair black (Jos. *Antiq.* xvi. 8, 1). The priests were forbidden to make any baldness upon the head (Lev. 21:5), and none of the Israelites was allowed to make a baldness between the eyes for the dead (Deut. 14:1), since this was a heathen custom. The captive woman who was chosen by a Hebrew for his wife and the leper in the day of his cleansing were required to shave the head for purposes of purification (Lev. 14:8, 9; Deut. 21:12). The Nazirite also, when the time of his service was ended, shaved his head as a sign of the fulfillment of his vow (Num. 6:18). See BEARD.

Hak'ka•tan (hăk'á-tăn) [the small or the younger one]. Father of a certain Johanan (Ezra 8:12).

Hak'koz (hăk'ŏz), in A.V. sometimes **Koz**, once **Coz**, the first syllable (the Heb. definite article) being omitted [thorn]. 1. A descendant of Aaron. His family had grown to a father's house in the time of David and was made the 7th of the 24 courses into which David distributed the priests (I Chron. 24:1, 6, 10). Perhaps it was members of this family who returned from Babylon with Zerubbabel, but, failing to find their register and establish their genealogy, were put from the priesthood (Ezra 2:61, 62; Neh. 7:63, 64). They appear to have eventually succeeded, however, in establishing their right to the office (Neh. 3:21; cf. Ezra 8:33).

2. A man of Judah (I Chron. 4:8).

Ha•ku'pha (há-kū'fá) [bent; bowed; cf. Arab. *ḥaḳafa*, to be curved]. Founder of a family of Nethinim (Ezra 2:51; Neh. 7:53).

Ha'lah (hā'lá). A district of the Assyrian empire to which captives from the 10 tribes were carried (II Kings 17:6; 18:11; I Chron. 5:26). Probably the district known later as Chalkitis, in Mesopotamia, near Gozan, in the basin of the Habor and the Saokoras.

Ha'lak (hā'lăk) [smooth, bare]. A mountain in the s. of Palestine on the way to Mount Seir (Josh. 11:17; 12:7). It is l cated n.n.e. of 'Abdea, which is on Wadi el-Marra.

Half Shek'el. See MONEY, TRIBUTE 2.

Hal'hul (hăl'hŭl). A village in the hill country of Judah (Josh. 15:58). The Arabs still call the village Ḥalḥul, about 4 miles n. of Hebron. Tradition has located the tomb of Jonah and also that of the Prophet Gad in this place.

Ha'li (hā'lī) [ornament, necklace]. A village on the boundary line of Asher (Josh. 19:25). Khirbet 'Alia, 13 miles n.e. of Acre, has been suggested, but Tell el-'Aly, s. of Ḥaritiyeh, seems to fit better into the context.

Hal'i·car·nas'sus (hăl'ĭ-kär-năs'ŭs). A city of Caria, renowned as being the birthplace of Herodotus and as containing the mausoleum erected by Artemisia, which was reckoned one of the 7 wonders of the world. Alexander captured and almost totally destroyed the city in 334 B.C. It contained a colony of Jews (I Macc. 15:23; Jos. *Antiq.* xiv. 10, 23).

Hall. A building, or large room in a building, devoted to public use. In A.V. it denotes:
1. The court of the high priest's palace (Luke 22:55; in R.V. court).
2. The official residence of the provincial governor, with its court where he sat in judgment. It was called the *praetorium* (Matt. 27:27; Mark 15:16; John 18:28, 33; 19:9; Acts 23:35, where R.V. has palace or *praetorium*). See PRAETORIUM.

Hal'le·lu'jah, in A.V. of N.T. **Al'le·lu'ia,** like the Gr. [praise ye Jehovah]. A compound word used by the writers of various psalms to invite all to join them in praising Jehovah (R.V. marg. of Ps. 104:35; 105:45; 106:1, 48; 111:1; 112:1; 113:1, 9; 115:18; 116:19; 117:2; 135:1, 21; 1st and last vs. of Psalms 146 to 150; cf. A.V. marg. also). From these psalms John borrowed the term Alleluia (Rev. 19:1, 3, 4, 6).

Hal·lo'hesh (hă-lō'hĕsh), in A.V. once **Ha·lo'hesh** (hă-lō'hĕsh) [the whisperer, the enchanter]. Father of a certain Shallum (Neh. 3:12). With Nehemiah he or the representative of his family sealed the covenant to worship Jehovah (ch. 10:24).

Ham, I [perhaps, Heb. *ḥām*, hot; but cf. S. Arab. *ḥam*, protection. Hardly Egypt. *km*, black]. The youngest son of Noah, born after the latter's 500th year (Gen. 5:32; 6:10; 9:24). At the time of the Deluge he was married but apparently had no children (Gen. 7:7; I Peter 3:20). On the occasion of his father's drunkenness he behaved undutifully and incurred a curse to descend upon Canaan (Gen. 9:22–27). The list of peoples of s. Arabia, Ethiopia, Egypt, and Canaan (ch. 10:6–14) includes both his descendants and those acquired by conquest and political annexation.

Ham, II (hăm). Egypt. Used in the Bible only in poetry (Ps. 78:51; 105:23, 27; 106:22).

Ham, III (hăm) [ety. unknown; initial letter is *h*, but in I and II is *ḥ*]. A place between Ashteroth-karnaim in Bashan and the Moabite country, where Chedorlaomer defeated the Zuzim (Gen. 14:5; cf. Deut. 2:10). The order of enumeration makes it probable that Ham was n. of Kiriathaim and the Arnon; it is no. 118 on the list of Thutmose III and is to be identified with modern Hăm about 5 miles s.s.w. of Irbid on the 'Ajlūn.

Ha'man (hā'mǎn) [probably from name of Elamite divinity, Hamman, Humman, Humban]. Son of Hammedatha (Esth. 3:1). His father bore a Persian name, but he is called the Agagite (ch. 3:1; 9:24). Josephus (*Antiq.* xi. 6, 5), who is followed by some commentators, understands this appellation to mean that Haman was descended from Agag, king of Amalek, thus making him a descendant of Saul's conquered foe. The term Agagite, however, may denote a spiritual descent from an enemy of Israel, or it may refer to a place or family otherwise unknown. Exalted by the Persian king to the highest official position, he received ostentatious reverence from time-servers. But on account of his unprincipled character, perhaps also for other reasons, the Jew Mordecai deliberately withheld from him the customary signs of respect. Haman planned revenge, plotting the destruction not of Mordecai only but of all Jews in the empire. His plan was frustrated by Esther, who was prompted by Mordecai; and Haman and his sons perished (Esth. 7:10; 9:7–10). See ESTHER.

Ha'math (hā'măth), in A.V. once **He'math** (Amos 6:14), and once **Am'a·this** (ăm'ȧ-thĭs) (I Macc. 12:25) [fortification, citadel]. 1. A city on the Orontes, n. of Hermon (Josh. 13:5), about 120 miles n. of Damascus. It was a Hittite city as is shown by a large number of Hittite inscriptions. Toi, its king, congratulated David on his victory over Hadadezer, their common enemy (II Sam. 8:9, 10; I Chron. 18:3, 9, 10). Solomon took Hamath and built store cities in the region (II Chron. 8:3, 4). It soon, however, reverted to its old inhabitants, but Jeroboam II, king of Israel, captured Damascus and Hamath, which had formerly belonged to Judah, and kept them for the 10 tribes (II Kings 14:28). About this time Amos (Amos 6:2) called the city Hamath the great. At the battle of Karkar, Hamath was allied with Ben-hadad (Adadidri) of Damascus and Ahab against Shalmaneser III, king of Assyria; but later it was conquered by the Assyrians (II Kings 18:34; 19:13). After the capture of Samaria by the Assyrians, it joined with the remnant of the inhabitants of that city in revolt, 720 B.C. But the uprising was quickly suppressed by Sargon. Colonists from Hamath, who brought with them Ashima, their god, were placed by the Assyrians in Samaria (II Kings 17:24, 30), while some of the exiles of Israel seem to have been located in Hamath (Isa. 11:11). Afterward its history becomes merged in that of Syria, and it seems to have become subordinate to Damascus (Jer. 49:23). Ezekiel prophesied that the restored land of Israel should still extend n. to Hamath (Ezek. 47:16, 17, 20; 48:1). Hamath was known as Epiphania during the period of Grecian supremacy (Jos. *Antiq.* i. 6, 2), but is now called Ḥamāh.
2. The district ruled by the city (I Macc. 12:25). One of its towns was Riblah (II Kings 23:33).

The entrance of Hamath was regarded as the n. border of Israel (Num. 13:21; 34:8; I Kings 8:65). To people on the s. the term may have had special meaning and denoted the long valley of Coelesyria, between Lebanon and Anti-Lebanon, through which the road to Hamath lay. Some consider it as the pass between Lebanon and the Nusairiyeh Mountains, leading from Ḥoms to Tripoli and thus connecting the inland region of Syria with the Mediterranean coast. Another view is that Heb. *lᵉbō'* (at, upon entering) is a proper name and accordingly there is assumed a place Lebo Hamath (modern Lebweh), located 14 miles n.n.e. of Baalbek and thus commanding the watershed between the Orontes and the Leontes.

Ha'math·ites (hā'măth-ĭts). The people of Hamath (Gen. 10:18).

Ha'math-zo'bah (hā'măth-zo'bȧ). The neighbor kingdoms of Hamath and Zobah, or some small place called Hamath, belonging to the Syrian kingdom Zobah. It was captured by Solomon (II Chron. 8 :3).

Ham'math (hăm'ăth), in A.V. once **He'math** (I Chron. 2 :55) [hot spring]. 1. A fenced city of Naphtali (Josh. 19 :35). Probably one with Hammothdor and Hammon, which was assigned to the Levites (Josh. 21 :32; I Chron. 6 :76), and to be identified with Emmaus, a village with warm baths at a little distance from Tiberias (Jos. *Antiq.* xviii. 2, 3; *War* iv. 1, 3); now called Ḥammām on the w. shore of the Sea of Galilee, about 1¼ miles s. of Tiberias. The water is sulphurous and medicinal.

2. The founder of the house of Rechab, a family of the Kenites (I Chron. 2 :55).

Ham·me'ah (hȧ-mē'ȧ). See MEAH.

Ham'me·da'tha (hăm'ê-dā'thȧ) [Avestan, *hama,* equal, +*dātā,* giver]. Father of Haman (Esth. 3 :1).

Ham'me·lech (hăm'ê-lĕk) [the king]. Fathers of Jerahmeel and Malchijah (Jer. 36: 26; 38 :6, A.V. and R.V. marg.).

Ham'mer. A tool, called in Heb. *paṭṭīsh,* and used for smoothing metals and for breaking rocks (Isa. 41 :7; Jer. 23 :29). It serves as a figure for any crushing power. Babylon was the hammer of the whole earth (Jer. 50 :23). God's word is like a hammer that breaks the rock in pieces (ch. 23 :29). Another name for an implement of the same class is *makkebeth,* used for driving the tent pin (Judg. 4 :21), in building operations (I Kings 6 :7), and in the manufacture of idols (Isa. 44 :12; Jer. 10 :4).

Ham·miph'kad (hăm-mĭf'kăd), in A.V. **Miph'kad,** without the Hebrew article [appointed place]. A gate at Jerusalem, probably of the Temple (Neh. 3 :31); see JERUSALEM, II. 3.

Ham'mol·e'cheth (hă-mŏl'ê-kĕth), in A.V. **Ham·mol'e·keth** (hă-mŏl'ê-kĕth) [the queen]. A sister of Gilead (I Chron. 7 :18). Several tribal families of Manasseh sprang from her.

Ham'mon (hăm'ŏn) [glowing, warm]. 1. A frontier village of Asher (Josh. 19 :28). About 10 miles s. of Tyre, n. of Cape Naķūra, near Wadi el-Ḥamūl, ¾ of a mile from Umm el-'Amūd, where Baal Hammon was worshiped.

2. A town of Naphtali. See HAMMATH 1.

Ham'moth·dor' (hăm'ŏth-dōr') [warm springs of Dor]. See HAMMATH 1.

Ham'mu·el (hăm'û-ĕl), in A.V. **Ham'u·el** [perhaps, warmth of God]. A Simeonite, son of Mishma, probably of the family of Shaul (I Chron. 4 :26).

Ham'mu·ra'bi (hăm'ōō-rä'bê). Formerly thought to be Amraphel (Gen., ch. 14), but this identification is no longer generally accepted. Hammurabi is the 6th king of Dyn. I of Babylon, and his reign has been variously dated: 2123–2081, 2067–2025, 1955–1913, and 1870–1830 B.C. According to more recent evidence, however, his reign extended from 1792 to 1750 or 1749 B.C. At first he held sway over a small district only; but he wrested Larsa from the Elamites and made himself lord of all Babylonia. See BABYLONIA. He sought the welfare of his subjects; repaired old canals and cut new ones in order to bring fertility to both n. and s. Babylonia, strengthened fortifications, embellished and erected temples, superintended the administration of justice, and codified the laws of the land. He had forerunners in reform and in the codification of law among the Sumerian kings: Urukagina of Lagash (c. 2450 B.C.); Ur-Nammu (Ur-Engur) and Shulgi (Dungi) of Dyn. III of Ur. He was doubtless himself a legislator; but

beyond enacting legislation, he discerned the importance of collecting the laws of the realm which pertained to the social life of the people, grouping the related ones, and giving them the widest publicity. Two hundred and eighty-two sections of his code have been preserved on a block of black diorite nearly 8 feet high.

These ancient laws of Babylonia bear a close resemblance to the enactments in the Book of the Covenant by which justice was administered in Israel (Ex. 20 :23 to 23 :33; cf. ch. 24 :7). Not only are they codified like the later body of Hebrew legislation, but they are like many of those Hebrew statutes in beginning with the word "if." Hammurabi and Moses often reflect the same Semitic psychology, as for example in the *lex talionis* (Deut. 19 :21). In a number of instances the 2 bodies of legislation treat of the same injury to person or property. This coincidence is, of course, not surprising, since just these mishaps and misdeeds occur in every community of men and must receive notice in any code of laws dealing with civil life. It is more remarkable that in so many instances the same classes of people, particularly the less fortunate members of society, were regarded by both Babylonians and Israelites as possessing rights that could be recognized by the state. But what is most remarkable is that in at least 14 instances the Babylonian and Hebrew laws impose the same, or practically the same, penalty for the same offense. To a remarkable degree the 2 peoples shared the same conception of justice. The Hebrew legislator hardly had the laws of Hammurabi before him; but it is probable that the Babylonian influence in the Fertile Crescent left some impression upon the Israelites. The 2 codes have a common Semitic background, which may perhaps be traced to primitive Semitic times. See MOSES.

Ha·mo'nah (hȧ-mō'nȧ) [multitude]. Symbolical name of the city near which Gog is to be defeated (Ezek. 39 :16).

Ha'mon·gog' (hā'mŏn-gŏg') [multitude of Gog]. A name to be given to a certain valley where the hosts which Gog brings with him shall be slain and buried (Ezek. 39 :11, 15).

Ha'mor (hā'môr), in A.V. of N.T. **Em'mor,** following the Gr. [an ass]. The prince of Shechem (Gen. 34 :20; Josh. 24 :32; Judg. 9 :28); a Hivite (Gen. 34 :2). His son Shechem ruined Dinah, and both father and son fell victims to the vindictiveness of her brothers Simeon and Levi (ch. 34 :1–31).

Ham'ran (hăm'răn). See HEMDAN.

Ham'u·el (hăm'û-ĕl). See HAMMUEL.

Ha'mul (hā'mŭl) [pitied, spared]. Younger son of Perez, and founder of a tribal family of Judah (Gen. 46 :12; Num. 26 :21; I Chron. 2 :5).

Ha·mu'tal (hȧ-mū'tăl) [probably, father-in-law is dew]. Daughter of Jeremiah of Libnah, wife of King Josiah, and mother of the kings Jehoahaz and Zedekiah (II Kings 23 :31; 24: 18; Jer. 52 :1).

Han'a·mel (hăn'ȧ-mĕl), in A.V. **Han'a·meel** (hăn'ȧ-mēl) [perhaps, God has pitied]. Son of Shallum, and cousin of the Prophet Jeremiah (Jer. 32 :7).

Ha'nan (hā'năn) [gracious, merciful]. 1. One of David's mighty men (I Chron. 11 :43).

2. A Benjamite, son of Shashak (I Chron. 8 :23).

3. A son of Azel, a descendant of Jonathan (I Chron. 8 :38; 9 :44).

4. A prophet, son of Igdaliah. His sons had a chamber in the Temple (Jer. 35 :4).

5. Founder of a family of Nethinim, members of which returned from Babylon with Zerubbabel (Ezra 2 :46; Neh. 7 :49).

6. A man, probably a Levite, whom Ezra employed with others to make the people understand the Law (Neh. 8:7). He seems to have sealed the covenant (ch. 10:10).

7 and 8. Two chiefs of the people, who also sealed the covenant (Neh. 10:22, 26).

9. A son of Zaccur, appointed assistant treasurer by Nehemiah (Neh. 13:13).

Han'a·nel (hăn'à-nĕl), in A.V. **Ha·nan'e·el** (hà-năn'ē-ĕl) [God has been gracious]. A tower at Jerusalem (Jer. 31:38; Zech. 14:10), near the sheep gate and the tower of Meah (Neh. 3:1; 12:39); see JERUSALEM, II. 3.

Ha·na'ni (hà-nā'nī) [gracious, or contraction of Hananiah]. 1. A son of Heman and head of the 18th of the 24 courses of musicians appointed by David for the sanctuary (I Chron. 25:4, 25).

2. Father of the Prophet Jehu (I Kings 16:1) and himself a seer. He rebuked Asa, and was by the king's orders committed to prison (II Chron. 16:7–10).

3. A brother of Nehemiah who brought him news regarding Jerusalem (Neh. 1:2). He and the governor of the castle were afterward given charge of the city (ch. 7:2).

4. A priest, son of Immer, induced by Ezra to put away his foreign wife (Ezra 10:20).

5. A Levite who played an instrument at the dedication of the wall of Jerusalem by Nehemiah (Neh. 12:36).

Han'a·ni'ah (hăn'à-nī'à) [Jehovah has been gracious]. 1. A Benjamite, son of Shashak (I Chron. 8:24).

2. A son of Heman and head of the 16th of the 24 courses of musicians formed by David for the sanctuary (I Chron. 25:4, 23).

3. One of King Uzziah's captains (II Chron. 26:11).

4. Father of Jeremiah's contemporary, the prince Zedekiah (Jer. 36:12).

5. Son of Azzur of Gibeon. In the 4th year of Zedekiah's reign he prophesied a return of the captives after 2 years' captivity. Jeremiah had given forth a different prediction. As a penalty the false prophet was doomed to death, his decease occurring 2 months later (Jer., ch. 28).

6. Grandfather, or remoter ancestor, of Irijah, the captain of the watch who arrested Jeremiah on the charge of intending to desert to the Chaldeans (Jer. 37:13–15).

7. The Heb. name of the captive called by the Chaldeans Shadrach (Dan. 1:6, 7; I Macc. 2:59).

8. A son of Zerubbabel, and father of Pelatiah and Jeshaiah (I Chron. 3:19, 21); perhaps the ancestor of Christ called, by transposition of the constituent parts of the name, Joanan (Luke 3:27, R.V.).

9. A son of Bebai, induced by Ezra to put away his foreign wife (Ezra 10:28).

10. An apothecary who helped to rebuild the wall of Jerusalem (Neh. 3:8).

11. A priest who blew a trumpet at the dedication of the wall (Neh. 12:41).

12. A chief of the people, who with Nehemiah sealed the covenant (Neh. 10:23).

13. The governor of the castle and joint ruler with Hanani, Nehemiah's brother, over Jerusalem (Neh. 7:2).

14. A priest, head of the father's house of Jeremiah, in the days of the high priest Joiakim, a generation after the Exile (Neh. 12:12).

Hand'breadth'. The breadth of the hand, a palm (Ex. 25:25; in A.V., Ezek. 40:43, a hand broad); see CUBIT. It is used by the psalmist figuratively of human life, especially when life closes prematurely (Ps. 39:5).

Hand'ker·chief. A small cloth used by the Romans for wiping the hands and face. The Jews adopted it in the Roman period. They bound it about the head of their dead (John 11:44; 20:7; A.V., R.V., napkin). Once in Ephesus handkerchiefs were carried from the body of the Apostle Paul to the sick, and their diseases departed (Acts 19:12). The man who received 1 pound from his lord hid it in such a cloth (Luke 19:20; A.V., R.V., napkin).

Ha'nes (hā'nĕz). A city of Egypt (Isa. 30:4) about 50 miles s. of Memphis, on the w. bank of the Nile, and still known as Ahnas. In the Greco-Roman period it was known as Heracleopolis Magna.

Hang'ing. A form of punishment in which, after the criminal was put to death, his body was suspended from a tree or post. It was in vogue in Egypt (Gen. 40:19, 22), among the Israelites (Deut. 21:22; Josh. 10:26; II Sam. 4:12), and the Persians (Herod. iii. 125). The hanging intensified the disgrace. Among the Israelites, the elevation of the body on the tree was a call to God to witness that the guilty one had paid just and sufficient penalty, and was a testimony of God's abhorrence of sin. But while the body remained exposed, it proclaimed that sin had been committed in Israel. It was therefore buried out of sight at nightfall (Deut. 21:23; Josh. 8:29; cf. Gal. 3:13). Suicide was sometimes committed by hanging which caused strangulation (II Sam. 17:23; Matt. 27:5). See GALLOWS.

Han'i·el (hăn'ĭ-ĕl). See HANNIEL.

Han'nah (hăn'à) [grace, compassion]. One of the 2 wives of Elkanah. She was her husband's favorite and was in consequence subjected to petty annoyances by the rival wife. She vowed that if she gave birth to a man-child, she would devote him to the service of Jehovah. Her wish was gratified; she became the mother of the Prophet Samuel, and carried out her vow (I Sam., ch. 1). Her song of triumph is highly poetic and was probably in the mind of the Virgin Mary when she expressed her gratitude in similar poetic strains on learning that she was to give birth to the Son of God (I Sam. 2:1–10; Luke 1:46–55).

Han'na·thon (hăn'à-thŏn) [regarded with favor]. A frontier town of Zebulun (Josh. 19:14), on a road from Megiddo to Acco (El-Amarna letters), and probably to be located at Tell Harbaj on the wadi el-Melek.

Han'ni·el (hăn'ĭ-ĕl), in A.V. **Ha'ni·el** in I Chron. 7:39 [God has been gracious]. 1. Prince of the Manassites who, when the Israelites were about to enter Canaan, was appointed on the committee to divide the land (Num. 34:23).

2. An Asherite, son of Ulla (I Chron. 7:39).

Ha'noch (hā'nŏk), in A.V. once **He'noch** (I Chron. 1:33) [initiated, dedicated]. Exactly the same Heb. word as that rendered Enoch. 1. A son of Midian, and a descendant of Abraham by Keturah (Gen. 25:4; I Chron. 1:33).

2. A son of Reuben, and founder of a tribal family, Hanochites (Gen. 46:9; Ex. 6:14; Num. 26:5; I Chron. 5:3).

Ha'nun (hā'nŭn) [favored]. 1. A king of the Ammonites, son and successor of David's friend Nahash. The Hebrew king sent to condole with him on his father's death, and congratulate him on his own accession. Evil counselors suggested that the real object of the embassy was to spy out the Ammonite capital, and so Hanun grossly ill-treated the ambassadors, shaving off half their beards and cutting off their garments in the middle. Knowing that the outrage would be resented, he prepared for war. He obtained the Syrians as his allies, but was defeated (II Sam. 10:1 to 11:1; I Chron. 19:1 to 20:3).

2 and 3. Two Jews who repaired portions of the wall of Jerusalem under Nehemiah (Neh. 3:13, 30).

Haph'a·ra'im (hăf'ȧ-rā'ĭm), in A.V. **Haph·ra'im** (hăf-rā'ĭm) [two pits, double pit]. A frontier town of Issachar (Josh. 19:19), by some identified with Khirbet el-Farrīyeh, 5½ miles n.w. of Megiddo, but more probably to be identified with eṭ-Ṭaiyibeh, n.w. of Beth-shan, in the heart of Issachar.

Hap'piz·zez (hăp'ĭ-zĕz), in A.V. **Aph'ses** [the shattering]. A descendant of Aaron. His family became the 18th of David's 24 courses of the priests (I Chron. 24:1).

Ha'ra (hā'rȧ). A place in Assyria to which captives from the 10 tribes were carried (I Chron. 5:26). In the corresponding passages (II Kings 17:6; 18:11) the expression "the river of Gozan" directly follows "the Habor," with which it is in apposition. In both cases the verse concludes with "and in the [*'ārē Mādāy*] cities of the Medes"; instead of "cities" the LXX reads "mountains," which presupposes Heb. *hārē mādāy*. The reading of Chronicles apparently is due to textual corruption: a phrase has been transposed, and, with the omission of *Mādāy*, *hārē* (mountains of) became a proper name *Hārā'*.

Ha·ra'dah (hȧ-rā'dȧ) [trembling, fear]. An encampment of the Israelites in the wilderness, after being turned back from Rithmah (Num. 33:24).

Ha'ran, I (hā'răn). 1. A son of Terah, and brother of Abraham. He died early, in his native place, Ur of the Chaldees; but left a son, Lot, and 2 daughters, Milcah and Iscah (Gen. 11:29).
2. A Gershonite Levite, son of Shimei (I Chron. 23:9).

Ha'ran, II (hā'răn), in A.V. of N.T., **Char'·ran** [cf. Akkad. *ḫarrānu*, road, caravan, business]. 1. A city of Mesopotamia, on the Belīkh, an affluent of the Euphrates, about 240 miles w. by n. from Nineveh and 280 n.n.e. of Damascus. It was a commercial center, being on one of the main trade routes between Babylonia and the Mediterranean; and, like Ur of the Chaldees, had the moon-god for its patron deity. Terah and Abraham sojourned in it for a time, and Terah died there (Gen. 11:31, 32; 12:4, 5). The family of Nahor settled there, and Jacob for a time resided there (chs. 28:10; 29:4, 5). The Assyrians hunted in its vicinity as early as 1100 B.C.; and they long held sway over it. A capture of the city by them is mentioned (II Kings 19:12). In 53 B.C. the Roman triumvir Crassus, the colleague of Pompey and of Julius Caesar, was defeated near Haran by the Parthian general Surena, by whose representatives he was soon afterward barbarously slain. It is now a small Arab village, still retaining the name of Ḥarrān.
2. Son of Caleb and Ephah, of the family of Hezron (I Chron. 2:46).

Ha'ra·rite (hȧ'rȧ-rīt) [perhaps, mountaineer]. An epithet applied to several of David's heroes (II Sam. 23:11, 33; I Chron. 11:34, 35). Probably, to judge from the context of II Sam. 23:33, it means an inhabitant of a hamlet called Harar (mountain) from its location on some peak. See ARARITE.

Har·bo'na (här-bō'nȧ) and **Har·bo'nah** (här-bō'nȧ) [Avestan, the bald man]. A chamberlain of Ahasuerus (Esth. 1:10; 7:9).

Hare. An animal (Heb., *'arnebeth*) said to chew the cud, but not to part the hoof, and therefore unclean (Lev. 11:6; Deut. 14:7). The opinion of the Hebrews that the animal chewed the cud was founded on a peculiar movement of its mouth. Physiologically it is not a ruminating animal but a rodent. The common hare of Palestine (*Lepus syriacus*) is 2 inches shorter than the European hare (*L. europaeus*) and has slightly shorter ears. It

frequents wooded and cultivated places. The common hare of s. Judea and the Jordan Valley (*L. judeae* of Gray) has very long ears and light tawny fur. Tristram enumerates 3 other species of the s. frontier: *L. aegyptiacus*, the Egyptian hare, in the s.e. part of Judea; *L. isabillinus*, in the sandy deserts of s.e. Palestine; and *L. sinaiticus*, with fur of a reddish hue.

Har'el (här'ĕl). A portion of the altar described by Ezekiel (Ezek. 43:15). In the text of the A.V. it is rendered altar, and in that of the R.V. upper altar. See ARIEL.

Ha'reph (hā'rĕf) [reproaching; but cf. Syriac *harīf*, sharp, keen]. A son of Caleb, and ancestor of the inhabitants of Beth-gader (I Chron. 2:51).

Ha'reth (hā'rĕth). See HERETH.

Har·ha'iah (här-hā'yȧ). Father of the goldsmith Uzziel (Neh. 3:8).

Har'has (här'hăs). An ancestor of Shallum, husband of Huldah the prophetess (II Kings 22:14). Called Hasrah in II Chron. 34:22.

Har'hur (här'hûr) [violent heat, fever]. The founder of a family of Nethinim, some of whom returned from Babylon with Zerubbabel (Ezra 2:51; Neh. 7:53).

Ha'rim (hā'rĭm) [consecrated, inviolable; or having a slit nose]. 1. A descendant of Aaron. His family had grown to a father's house in the time of David and constituted the 3d course of the priests (I Chron. 24:1, 6, 8). Probably they were members of this family who returned from Babylon (Ezra 2:39; Neh. 7:42). A father's house among the priests in the next generation after the Exile bore this name (Neh. 12:15); see REHUM. At a later period some of this family were among those who had married foreign wives (Ezra 10:21). And later still a priest of this name, doubtless head of a father's house, signed the covenant to observe the law of God and to endeavor to prevent intermarriages with foreigners (Neh. 10:5).
2. Founder of a nonpriestly family, members of which returned from Babylon with Zerubbabel (Ezra 2:32; 10:31; Neh. 3:11; 7:35).

Ha'riph (hā'rĭf) [autumnal, harvested; cf. Heb. *hōreph*, Arab. *ḥarīf*, autumn]. Founder of a family, members of which returned from Babylon with Zerubbabel (Neh. 7:24). A prince of this name sealed the covenant, doubtless as representative of the family (ch. 10:19). The same as Jorah (Ezra 2:18), which also means autumnal rain.

Har'lot. A prostitute (Gen. 38:15; Lev. 21:7; Deut. 23:18; Josh 2:1; Judg. 16:1). To play the harlot or to go a whoring after, often means, in Scriptural usage, to go with or after a paramour; in a figurative sense, to depart from Jehovah and give the affections and worship to other gods (Jer. 2:20; 3:1; Ezek. 16:15, 16; 23:5).

Har'·Ma·ged'on (här'mȧ-gĕd'ŭn), in A.V. **Ar'ma·ged'don** [Gr., from Heb., mountain of Megiddo]. A prophetic battlefield where the kings of the whole world gather together unto the war of the great day of God (Rev. 16:16). The name is framed with evident reference to the sanguinary contests which took place near the town of Megiddo; the 1st, that in which Sisera and the Canaanites were defeated at the waters of Megiddo (Judg. 5:19), the 2d, that which resulted in the death of Ahaziah, king of Judah, at Megiddo (II Kings 9:27), and the 3d, that in which King Josiah was killed when in conflict with the army of Necho (II Kings 23:29; Zech. 12:11). The historical associations with Megiddo in the past were seized upon by the prophet to supply a name appropriate in a description of the future sorrows and triumphs of God's people.

Har'ne·pher (här'nĕ-fẽr) [perhaps, Egypt., Horus is good]. An Asherite, son of Zophah (I Chron. 7:36).

Ha'rod (hā'rŏd) [trembling, terror]. A well near which Gideon pitched while his adversaries, the Midianites, were by the hill of Moreh, in the valley (Judg. 7:1). It is commonly identified with 'Ain Jālūd, on the n.w. side of Mount Gilboa, about a mile e. by s. of Jezreel.

Ha'rod·ite (hā'rŏd-īt). An inhabitant of the town of Harod (II Sam. 23:25), probably to be identified with Khirbet Khareidān about 3¾ miles s.e. of Jerusalem.

Ha·ro'eh (há-rō'ĕ). See REAIAH.

Ha'ro·rite (hā'rŏ-rīt). Rather Harodite (q.v.) (I Chron. 11:27; cf. II Sam. 23:25). The second r (resh) probably arose through confusion with d (daleth).

Ha·ro'sheth (há-rō'shĕth) [carving]. A town more fully called Harosheth of the Gentiles or nations. Sisera had his residence there (Judg. 4:2, 13, 16). It is Tell 'Amār below el-Harithīyeh, located at a small village on the n. bank of the Kishon, at the point where the stream passes through a narrow gorge to enter the plain of Acre; it is 16 miles n.n.w. of Megiddo.

Harp. Rendering of Heb. kinnōr; and in the N.T. of Gr. kithara (lyre, lute). It was a stringed musical instrument of the harp kind, small enough to be carried about (Isa. 23:16), and was played with the fingers (I Sam.

Ancient Egyptian Harp

16:23; Jos. Antiq. vii. 12, 3), or with a plectrum. It was played by Jubal, an antediluvian, of the race of Cain (Gen. 4:21), was known to Laban (ch. 31:27), was the instrument with which David soothed Saul during his fits of melancholy madness (I Sam. 16:16). The prophets and others used it for

sacred purposes (I Sam. 10:5; Ps. 43:4; 49:4), and it was played in the Temple orchestra (I Chron. 25:1, 3); see MUSIC. It was employed also in festive entertainments (Job 21:12). Harlots sometimes carried it about with them (Isa. 23:15, 16). It was the instrument which the captive Jews hung on the Babylonian willows (Ps. 137:2). Two kinds were in use in Egypt: a larger, of the height of a man, and a smaller, which was easily carried. The Hebrews were acquainted with the harp, but it is not certain that the word kinnōr really means harp. The Seventy regarded it rather as a lyre or lute, than a harp, for they render the Heb. word by kithara.

Har'row. An agricultural implement consisting of a wooden frame armed with teeth of wood or iron (II Sam. 12:31). It is drawn over plowed land to level it and break the clods preparatory to sowing the seed, and to cover the seed when sown. It may be that the Heb. word in II Sam. 12:31 denotes threshing-sledges (cf. Amos 1:3). The Israelites broke the clods in some manner (Job 39:10; Isa. 28:24; Hos. 10:11), but it is doubtful whether they used a harrow.

Har'sha (här'shá) [dumb, silent]. Founder of a family of Nethinim, some of whom returned from Babylon with Zerubbabel (Ezra 2:52; Neh. 7:54).

Hart. A stag, or male deer, 5 years old, and which has developed its sur-royal or crown antler. It is the rendering of Heb. 'ayyāl (deer), a wild, clean animal (Deut. 12:15; 14:5; I Kings 4:23; Ps. 42:1; S. of Sol. 8:14). See DEER.

Ha'rum (hā'rŭm). A man of Judah, father of Aharhel (I Chron. 4:8).

Ha·ru'maph (há-rōō'măf) [having a slit nose]. Father of a certain Jedaiah (Neh. 3:10).

Ha·ru'phite (há-rōō'fīt). The designation of Shephatiah, a Benjamite, who joined David at Ziklag (I Chron. 12:5). The kere has ū, as above, but the kethib has ĭ, making the word Hariphite, a member of the family of Hariph (cf. Neh. 7:24).

Ha'ruz (hā'rŭz) [gold; but cf. S. Arab., covetous, eager]. Father-in-law of King Manasseh (II Kings 21:19).

Har'vest. The period of harvest in ancient Palestine may be divided into 2 portions: that of barley and that of wheat harvest, the former preceding the latter by about a fortnight (Ruth 2:23). Its beginning was consecrated by the bringing of the sheaf of first fruits (Lev. 23:10). It began in the lowlands before the crops were ripe on the hills. In the hot Jordan Valley barley harvest commenced in April, when the Jordan was full (Josh. 3:15; cf. ch. 5:10), directly after the rainy season (I Sam. 12:17, 18; Prov. 26:1). Wheat harvest lingered in the uplands to the month of June. It was a hot time of the year (Prov. 25:13; Isa. 18:4). When the harvest was

Harvest in Ancient Egypt

completed and the produce gathered in, there were great rejoicings (Isa. 9:3). The feasts of unleavened bread, of weeks or harvest, and of ingathering, had all a relation to the season of reaping. See YEAR.

Has'a·di'ah (hăs'à-dī'à) [Jehovah has been gracious]. A son of Zerubbabel (I Chron. 3:20).

Has'e·nu'ah (hăs'ê-nū'à). See HASSENUAH.

Hash'a·bi'ah (hăsh'à-bī'à) [Jehovah has reckoned, devised, imputed]. 1. A Merarite Levite, descended through Amaziah, and an ancestor of Jeduthun [Ethan] (I Chron. 6:44, 45). Perhaps he is the descendant of Bunni mentioned as ancestor of Shemaiah (I Chron. 9:14; Neh. 11:15).
2. A Merarite Levite, son of Jeduthun and head of the 12th company of musicians appointed by David for the sanctuary (I Chron. 25:3, 19).
3. A Kohathite Levite of the family of Hebron, and inspector for the country w. of Jordan (I Chron. 26:30; cf. ch. 23:12).
4. A Levite, son of Kemuel, prince of the tribe of Levi in David's reign (I Chron. 27:17).
5. A chief of the Levites during the reign of Josiah (II Chron. 35:9).
6. A Merarite Levite, who joined Ezra at the river of Ahava, and was apparently one of the 12 who were entrusted with the treasure which was being conveyed to Jerusalem (Ezra 8:19, 24). Probably it was he who sealed the covenant (Neh. 10:11), and who was a chief Levite and one of the Temple musicians (Neh. 12:24).
7. The ruler, in Nehemiah's time, of half Keilah. He repaired part of the wall of Jerusalem (Neh. 3:17).
8. A Levite, descended from Asaph (Neh. 11:22).
9. A priest, head of the father's house of Hilkiah, in the time of Joiakim the high priest (Neh. 12:21).

Ha·shab'nah (hà-shăb'nà) [perhaps for Hashabneiah]. One of those who with Nehemiah sealed the covenant (Neh. 10:25).

Hash'ab·ne·i'ah (hăsh'ăb-nê-i'à), in A.V. **Hash'ab·ni'ah** (hăsh'ăb-nī'à) [perhaps, Jehovah has taken account of me]. 1. Father of a certain Hattush (Neh. 3:10).
2. One of those Levites who by their exhortations prepared the returned exiles for sealing the covenant with Jehovah (Neh. 9:5).

Hash·bad'da·nah (hăsh-băd'à-nà), in A.V. **Hash·bad'a·na** (hăsh-băd'à-nà). One of those who stood beside Ezra when he addressed the returned exiles (Neh. 8:4).

Ha'shem (hā'shĕm). A Gizonite, mentioned in the catalogue of David's mighty men (I Chron. 11:34). See JASHEN.

Hash·mo'nah (hăsh-mō'nà). A camping ground of the Israelites in the wilderness (Num. 33:29, 30).

Ha'shub (hā'shŭb). See HASSHUB.

Ha·shu'bah (hà-shōō'bà) [esteemed; consideration]. A son of Zerubbabel (I Chron. 3:20).

Ha'shum (hā'shŭm) [cf. Arab. ḫathim, flat-nosed]. Founder of a family, members of which returned from Babylon with Zerubbabel (Ezra 2:19; 10:33; Neh. 7:22). The representative of the family, or a person of this name, stood beside Ezra while the latter addressed the people (Neh. 8:4), and then sealed the covenant (ch. 10:18).

Ha·shu'pha (hà-shōō'fà). See HASUPHA.

Has'i·dæ'ans (hăs'ĭ-dē'ănz), in A.V. **As'i·de'ans** and **As'si·de'ans** [Gr. Asidaioi from Heb. Ḥăsīdīm, pious]. A party among the Jews

who held strenuously to the old faith (I Macc. 2:42). They joined Mattathias, and later co-operated with Judas Maccabaeus in most of his plans (I Macc. 2:42; II Macc. 14:6), although contrary to his judgment they sought peace from the Syrians (I Macc. 7:13).

Has'mo·nae'an (hăz'mô-nē'ăn) [Gr. Asamōnaios, from Heb. Ḥashmōnay, probably the family name of the house of Mattathias). A descendant of Hashman, a priest of the family of Joarib (Jehoiarib) and ancestor of the Maccabees (Jos. Antiq. xii. 6, 1; cf. I Macc. 2:1; I Chron. 24:7). The title Hasmonaean is commonly employed in Jewish literature to designate the family from Mattathias to Herod the Great and Aristobulus (Jos. Antiq. xiv. 16, 4; xx. 8, 11).

Has'mo·nae'ans (hăz'mô-nē'ănz), **Pal'ace of the.** A palace in Jerusalem erected by the Hasmonaean princes, opposite the w. court of the Temple, on an elevation which commanded a view of the city and the sanctuary (Jos. Antiq. xx. 8, 11). It stood near the Xystus and overlooked it (Jos. War ii. 16, 3). It is probably the royal palace that was reckoned 1 of the 2 fortresses of Jerusalem, the Baris being the other, and in which Herod the Great resided before the erection of his palace in the upper city (Jos. Antiq. xiv. 13, 9; xv. 3, 7; 8, 4 and 5). This latter building excelled it in magnificence and as a fortress. So late as A.D. 60 the last prince of the Herodian house used it as a residence, Agrippa II, the King Agrippa of Acts 25:13 (Jos. Antiq. xx. 8, 11; War ii. 16, 3). It was probably the palace burned by the seditious Jews at the beginning of the war with the Romans (Jos. War ii. 17, 6).

Has'rah (hăz'rà) [perhaps, want]. See HARHAS.

Has'se·na'ah (hăs'ê-nā'à), and without the definite article **Se·na'ah** [perhaps, hated]. The sons of Hassenaah rebuilt the fish gate of Jerusalem (Neh. 3:3). Of the children of Senaah, some 3,000 returned from Babylon with Zerubbabel (Ezra 2:35; Neh. 7:38). The context suggests that it is the name of a place; Eusebius and Jerome identified it with Magdalsenna, about 7 miles n. of Jericho. About 7 miles from Jericho on the side of the mountain is a stronghold Khirbet el-'Auja el Fōka which commands the road from the Jordan Valley to Baal-hazor; near by is Sheikh-Terūni with which Senaah may probably be identified.

Has'se·nu'ah (hăs'ê-nū'à), in A.V. **Has'e·nu'ah**, and without the article, **Se·nu'ah** [perhaps, hated]. 1. A Benjamite, father of Hodaviah (I Chron. 9:7).
2. Parent of a certain Judah (Neh. 11:9).

Has'shub (hăsh'ŭb), in A.V. of Nehemiah **Ha'shub** [perhaps, hypocoristic, thought of (by God)]. 1. A son of Pahath-moab. He repaired part of the wall of Jerusalem (Neh. 3:11).
2. A Jew who repaired part of the wall of Jerusalem opposite to his house (Neh. 3:23). It was probably either he or No. 1 who signed the covenant (ch. 10:23).
3. A Merarite Levite, father of Shemaiah (I Chron. 9:14; Neh. 11:15).

Has'so·phe'reth (hăs'ô-phē'rĕth). See SOPHERETH.

Ha·su'pha (hà-sū'fà), in A.V. once **Ha·shu'pha** [made bare]. Founder of a family of Nethinim, members of which returned from captivity with Zerubbabel (Ezra 2:43; Neh. 7:46).

Hat. The rendering of Aram. karbelā (Dan. 3:21; in R.V. mantle). See CLOTHING.

Ha'thach (hā'thăk), in A.V. **Ha'tach** (hā'-tăk) [Avestan, *hat* (good)+*ka*]. A chamberlain of King Ahasuerus, who was appointed to attend Esther (Esth. 4:5, 10).

Ha'thath (hā'thăth) [terror]. A son of Othniel (I Chron. 4:13).

Ha·ti'pha (há-tī'fá) [Aram., captive]. One who founded a family of Nethinim, members of which returned from Babylon with Zerubbabel (Ezra 2:54; Neh. 7:56).

Ha·ti'ta (há-tī'tá) [Aram., dug up, furrowed]. A porter who founded a family, members of which returned from Babylon with Zerubbabel (Ezra 2:42; Neh. 7:45).

Hat'til (hăt'ĭl) [cf. Arab. *ḥaṭila*, to be talkative]. One of Solomon's servants, who founded a family, the members of which returned from Babylon with Zerubbabel (Ezra 2:55, 57; Neh. 7:57–59).

Hat'tin (hăt'tēn), **Horns of** [Arab. *Ḳarn Ḥaṭṭîn*, horn of depressions or hollows]. A two-peaked hill on the road from Tiberias on the Sea of Galilee to Cana and Nazareth. According to a tradition of the Latin Church dating from the 13th century, it was the scene of the delivery of the Sermon on the Mount, but we have no means of confirming so late a tradition.

Hat'tush (hăt'ŭsh). 1. A man of Judah, son of Shemaiah, and family of Shecaniah (I Chron. 3:22).

2. A chief of the priests, who returned with Zerubbabel from Babylon (Neh. 12:2, 7).

3. Head of a father's house, of the sons of David, who returned with Ezra to Jerusalem (Ezra 8:2).

4. A son of Hashabneiah. He repaired part of the wall of Jerusalem (Neh. 3:10).

5. A priest who with Nehemiah sealed the covenant (Neh. 10:4).

Ha'u·ran' (hā'ōō-rän') [probably, black land (as basaltic region); cf. Arab. dialect *ḥawr*, black]. A region s. of Damascus and bordering on Gilead (Ezek. 47:16, 18). In the Greco-Roman period it designated a smaller district. It was then known as Auranitis, and was one of 4 provinces, having Trachonitis on the n. and Gaulonitis and apparently Batanea toward the n.w. (Jos. *Antiq.* xvii. 11, 4; xviii. 4, 6; *War* i. 20, 4; ii. 6, 3; 17, 4). Thus it probably consisted of the plain lying between Gaulonitis and the present Jebel Ḥaurān, perhaps including the latter. About the year 23 B.C. Auranitis with Trachonitis and Batanea was bestowed on Herod the Great by Augustus. When Herod's kingdom was divided, these districts constituted the major part of Philip's tetrarchy (Luke 3:1; Jos. *Antiq.* xvii. 11, 4). The surface is flat, broken only by a few volcanic mounds. The soil is so fertile that the Hauran is the granary for the whole region round. Many towns and villages, mostly deserted, exist within its limits, some of them "the giant cities of Bashan," built of basalt.

Hav'i·lah (hăv'ĭ-lä) [sandy; cf. Heb. *ḥôl*, sand]. A district of Arabia, peopled in part by Cushites and in part by Joktanites, a Semitic people (Gen. 10:7, 29; I Chron. 1:9, 23). The association of Havilah with Hazarmaveth and other places points to a locality in central or s. Arabia. To Havilah belonged the river Pishon; and the region was rich in gold, aromatic gum, and precious stones (Gen. 2:11, 12). Some prefer to identify it with Haulan (Khawlān), in the w. part of Arabia, n. of Yemen. How far n. Havilah extended is not clear. From the record of Saul's warfare with the Amalekites it may be inferred that the Arabian desert for several hundred miles n. of al-Yamāmah bore the name Havilah (I Sam. 15:7; cf. Gen. 25:18).

Hav'voth-ja'ir (hăv'vŏth-jā'ĭr), in A.V. **Ha'·voth-ja'ir** (hā'vŏth-jā'ĭr) [tent villages or encampments of Jair]. Unwalled towns in the n.w. part of Bashan, in the region of the Argob, where this tract approaches the country of the Geshurites and Maacathites, and where the boundaries between the rugged land, Gilead, and the open, sandy land, Bashan, insensibly merge into each other (Deut. 3:4, 14). They were captured by Jair, a Manassite. Their number was liable to fluctuation because they lay in a debatable land (I Chron. 2:23, R.V. marg.). They are to be carefully distinguished from the 60 walled cities in the heart of Bashan, and likewise in the Argob (Deut. 3:4, 5; I Kings 4:13). Since the boundary between Gilead and Bashan was not clearly defined by nature, it never was conventionally, and places on this undefined border are referred to as in Gilead or in Bashan according to the momentary point of view of the narrator. The conquest of Bashan by the Israelites included the capture of the unwalled towns in the Argob on this indefinite border; and when their capture by Jair is related in connection with the conquest of Og's kingdom, which was carried on from Edrei in Bashan as the center, the Havvoth-jair are described as in Bashan (Deut. 3:14; Josh. 13:30). When, however, the e. country is before the mind of a sojourner in the Jordan Valley or in Canaan w. of the river, he naturally speaks first of Gilead, and sometimes even uses that designation broadly for the entire highland e. of the river, or he may speak of a conquest of Gilead which was not narrowly confined to the distinctively rugged land. From this point of view he is apt to refer to the towns on the undefined border of Gilead and Bashan as in Gilead (I Chron. 2:21–23; indefinitely, Num. 32:40, 41; I Kings 4:13). It is clear that the Havvoth-jair and the Argob were not the same.

Hawk. The rendering of Hebrew *nēṣ* (Job 39:26). It was ceremonially unclean (Lev. 11:16; Deut. 14:15), and included more than one species of the smaller predatory birds, as the sparrow hawk (*Accipiter nisus*) and the kestrel (*Falco tinnunculus*). The former abounds in Lebanon and the hilly parts of Galilee in summer, and in Judea and the Arabah in winter; the latter, which is properly a falcon instead of a genuine hawk, is abundant in every part of Palestine throughout the year.

Haz'a·el (hăz'á-ĕl) [God has seen]. A Syrian courtier whom Elijah was directed by Jehovah to anoint king over Syria (I Kings 19:15). Some years later, between 845 and 843 B.C., Ben-hadad, who then reigned over that country, with Damascus for his capital, hearing that Elisha was in the city, sent Hazael to ask the prophet whether he should recover from a serious illness from which he then suffered. Elisha told Hazael that his master would not recover and that he himself would be king of Syria and would perpetrate great cruelties on the people of Israel. When Hazael returned to Ben-hadad, he told him that the prophet foretold his recovery, and next day assassinated him and reigned in his stead (II Kings 8:7–15, R.V.). In 842 the Assyrian king Shalmaneser warred against Hazael and exacted tribute. In 838 Shalmaneser again warred with him. Toward the close of Jehu's reign over Israel, Hazael smote the country of the Hebrews e. of the Jordan (II Kings 10:32); and in the succeeding reign, crossing the river, he mightily oppressed the Israelites (ch. 13:4–7), invaded the country of the Philistines, took Gath, and was only deterred from attacking Jerusalem by a rich present consisting of the dedicated treasures of the Temple (ch. 12:17, 18). The house of Hazael (Amos 1:4) is Damascus.

Ha·za'iah (hȧ-zā'yȧ) [Jehovah has seen]. A man of Judah, family of Shelah (Neh. 11:5).

Ha'zar-ad'dar (hā'zär-ăd'är). See ADDAR.

Ha'zar-e'nan (hā'zär-ē'năn) and **Ha'zar-e'non** (hā'zär-ē'nŏn) [village of fountains]. A village on the n. boundary of Palestine (Num. 34:9; Ezek. 47:17; 48:1), probably Ḳiryatein on the route from Damascus to Palmyra.

Ha'zar-gad'dah (hā'zär-găd'ȧ) [village of good fortune]. A town in the extreme s. of Judah (Josh. 15:27), perhaps Khirbet Ghazza, s.w. of Rās Zuweira.

Ha'zar-hat'ti·con (hā'zär-hăt'ĭ-kŏn). See HAZER-HATTICON.

Ha'zar·ma'veth (hā'zär-mā'vĕth) [village of death]. A body of Joktanites who peopled a district in Arabia (Gen. 10:26; I Chron. 1:20). A region in Arabia Felix, in the s. of the peninsula, is still called by the Arabs Had(h)ramaut, which corresponds etymologically to Hazarmaveth.

Ha'zar-shu'al (hā'zär-shōō'ăl) [fox village]. A town in the extreme s. of Judah, assigned to the Simeonites (Josh. 15:28; 19:3; I Chron. 4:28). It was occupied after the Captivity (Neh. 11:27); perhaps to be identified with el-Waṭan, between Beer-sheba and Tell es-Saba', s.e. of the former.

Ha'zar-su'sah (hā'zär-sū'sȧ), in pl. **Ha'zar-su'sim** (hā'zär-sū'sĭm) [village of a mare, mares]. A village belonging to the Simeonites (Josh. 19:5; I Chron. 4:31). As a possible site Sblat Abū Sūsein near Tell el-Far'a has been suggested, but perhaps Sūsĭyeh (near Tell Mā'ĭn) 2 miles e. by n. of Eshtemoa is better.

Haz'a·zon-ta'mar (hăz'ȧ-zŏn-tā'mēr), in A.V. once **Haz'e·zon-ta'mar** [Hazazon (sandy surface) of the palm tree]. Cf. En-gedi (II Chron. 20:2). It has also been identified with Tamar (Ezek. 47:19; 48:28) or Thamara, whose site probably is marked by Kurnūb, 20 miles w.s.w. of the s. end of the Dead Sea on the road from Hebron to Elath.

Ha'zel. The rendering in Gen. 30:37, A.V., of Heb. *lūz*, better translated in R.V., the almond tree.

Haz'e·lel·po'ni (hăz'ē-lĕl-pō'nĭ). See HAZZELELPONI.

Ha'zer-hat'ti·con (hā'zĕr-hăt'ĭ-kŏn), in A.V. **Ha·zar-hat'ti·con** [the middle Hazer or village]. A town on the border of the Hauran (Ezek. 47:16).

Ha·ze'rim (hȧ-zē'rĭm) [villages]. Habitations of the Avvim (Deut. 2:23); in the R.V. properly translated by villages.

Ha·ze'roth (hȧ-zē'rŏth) [enclosures, courts]. An encamping ground of the Israelites in the wilderness beyond Kibroth-hattaavah (Num. 11:35) and on this side of Paran (Num. 12:16; 33:17; Deut. 1:1). It was there that Miriam and Aaron murmured against Moses (Num., ch. 12). 'Ain Ḥuḍra (or Khuḍra), about 36 miles n.e. of Mount Sinai, was suggested by Burckhardt, and adopted by Robinson and others, as the site.

Haz'e·zon-ta'mar (hăz'ē-zŏn-tā'mēr). See HAZAZON-TAMAR.

Ha'zi·el (hā'zĭ-ĕl) [probably contraction of Jahaziel]. A Gershonite Levite, son of Shimei (I Chron. 23:9).

Ha'zo (hā'zō). A son of Nahor and Milcah (Gen. 22:22). The name is probably preserved in the hilly region Hazū, which Esar-

haddon traversed, not remote from the Hauran.

Ha'zor (hā'zōr) [an enclosure]. 1. The capital of the Canaanite kingdom in the n. of Palestine, ruled over in Joshua's time by Jabin. According to Josephus, it was situated above the waters of Merom (Jos. *Antiq.* v. 5, 1). The town was taken by Joshua and burnt (Josh. 11:1–13; 12:19). It was rebuilt, and was assigned to the tribe of Naphtali (Josh. 19:36). In the days of Deborah and Barak it was ruled by another King Jabin. On the defeat of his general, Sisera, he attempted to continue the war against the Israelites, but was ultimately overcome and slain (Judg. 4:1–24; I Sam. 12:9). It is doubtful whether this or some other Hazor was the town fortified by Solomon (I Kings 9:15), but it was certainly the place so named whose inhabitants were carried into captivity to Assyria by Tiglath-pileser (II Kings 15:29). In the neighboring plain Jonathan defeated Demetrius (I Macc. 11:67; in A.V. Nasor; Jos. *Antiq.* xiii. 5, 7). Robinson identified Hazor with Tell Khūreibeh, 3½ miles w. of the waters of Merom, but more recent evidence favors Tell Waḳḳāṣ or Tell el-Ḳedaḥ, about 3¾ miles w. of the Bridge of Jacob's Daughters.

2. Hazor, in the extreme s. of Judah, near Kedesh (Josh. 15:23), may be identified with el-Jebariyeh upon the wadi Umm Ethnān near Bīr el-Hāfir, which is about 8¾ miles s.e. of el-'Aujā.

3. Kerioth-hezron (Josh. 15:25, R.V.). Generally identified with Khirbet el-Karyathein about 4½ miles s. of Tell Mā'ĭn. A.V. and J.V. do not have the compound name, which Père Abel also rejects.

4. A village of Benjamin (Neh. 11:33). Conder identifies it with Khirbet Hazzur, 4 miles n.n.w. of Jerusalem, and between Beit Hanīna and Nebi Samwīl.

5. A region in the Arabian desert, e. of Palestine. Jeremiah prophesied its plundering by Nebuchadnezzar (Jer. 49:28–33). Berosus states that Nebuchadnezzar conquered Arabia (Jos. *Apion* i. 19). The name is probably a collective and refers to the settled village life of the community in contrast to that of the nomads.

Ha'zor-ha·dat'tah (hā'zōr-hȧ-dăt'ȧ), in A.V. punctuated as 2 places, **Ha'zor, Ha·dat'tah** (hā'zōr, hȧ-dăt'ȧ) [if the 2d word is Aram., the name means new village]. A town in the s. of Judah (Josh. 15:25), apparently near Hazor 3; perhaps at el-Huḍeira, s.e. of Tuwāni toward the Dead Sea.

Haz'ze·lel·po'ni (hăz'ē-lĕl-pō'nĭ), in A.V. **Haz'e·lel·po'ni** [give shade, thou who turnest toward me]. A woman of Judah, daughter of the ancestor of the men of Etam (I Chron. 4:3).

He (hā). The 5th letter of the Heb. alphabet; pronounced like English *h*. It stands at the head of the 5th section of Psalm 119, since each verse in the section begins with this letter in the original.

Head'band'. The rendering of Heb. *ḳishshūr*, (Isa. 3:20, in R.V. a sash; Jer. 2:32, attire).

Heath. The rendering of the Heb. words *'ar'är* (Jer. 17:6; but R.V. marg., following the LXX, has tamarisk), in Arab., juniper, *J. oxycedrus* (Post), and *'ărō'ēr* (Jer. 48:6); both of which involve the idea of nakedness. Heath is a shrub, with minute, narrow, rigid leaves. The species *Erica verticillata*, a low shrub with racemed, pink, sweet-scented flowers, grows on the w. slopes of Lebanon (Post).

Hea'then [Anglo-Saxon, dweller on the heath]. The word suggests the fact that the gospel first rooted itself in towns, the inhabitants of which became Christians, while the dwellers on heaths remained worshipers of false divinities. The word pagan, from Lat. *paganus*, belonging to a village, rustic, has a somewhat similar connotation.

One of a people who do not worship the God of the Bible, especially if they are addicted to idolatry. It is a frequent rendering of Heb. *gōy* and Gr. *ethnos*, each of which means nation or people. E.R.V. employs the word heathen only in O.T. and then only when the character of the Gentile nations is clearly referred to; as in speaking of the abominations of the heathen (II Kings 16:3; Ezek. 23:30), their filthiness (Ezra 6:21), their ignorance of the truth, opposition to the true religion, barbarous trampling upon it and upon the people of God, and consequent exposure to the righteous indignation of Jehovah (Ps. 79:1, 6, 10, but not Ps. 115:2; also in Jer. 10:25; Lam. 1:3, 10; Ezek. 34:28, 29; 36:6, 7, 15; in these passages A.V. has heathen, and A.R.V. nations).

Heav'en, often **The Heav'ens.** 1. The sky, the expanse around the earth. It embraces all that is apart from the earth (Gen. 2:1); hence heaven and earth comprehend the universe (Gen. 1:1; 14:19; 24:3; Jer. 23:24; Matt. 5:18). Beyond the visible firmament was the primeval watery mass (Gen. 1:7, 8; Ps. 148:4); which is not further referred to in the account of creation, but out of which it is reasonable to believe the heavenly bodies were formed. These upper waters remained in Hebrew thought along with other Babylonian conceptions. In the visible heavens are the stars and planets (Gen. 1:14–17; Ezek. 32:7, 8). In the part of it next the earth is the atmosphere, in which clouds float, through which birds fly, and from which rain descends (Gen. 1:20; 7:11; 8:2; 27:28; II Sam. 21:10; Ps. 147:8; Lam. 4:19; see FIRMAMENT. The Hebrews, by a familiar idiom, spoke of the heaven of heavens (Deut. 10:14; I Kings 8:27), meaning the heavens in their widest extent. The later Jews were fond of dividing the heavens into 7 different strata. No fixed, definite conception of these several regions prevailed. The highest was regarded as God's dwelling place. Paul describes Christ as ascending far above all the heavens (Eph. 4:10); and he relates an experience, whether in vision or reality he knew not, in which he was caught up into the 3d heaven and into paradise (II Cor. 12:1–4).

2. The place where God's immediate presence is manifested (Gen. 28:17; Ps. 80:14; Isa. 66:1; Matt. 5:12, 16, 45, 48; 23:9), where the angels are (Matt. 24:36; 28:2; Mark 13:32; Luke 22:43), and where the redeemed shall ultimately be (Matt. 5:12; 6:20; 18:10; Eph. 3:15; I Peter 1:4). Christ descended from heaven (John 3:13), and ascended thither again (Acts 1:11), where he maketh intercession for the saints and whence he shall come to judge the quick and the dead (Matt. 24:30; Rom. 8:34; I Thess. 4:16; Heb. 6:20; 9:24).

3. The inhabitants of heaven (Luke 15:18; Rev. 18:20).

Heave Of'fer•ing. Every hallowed thing which the Israelites heaved, i.e., took up, took away, from a larger mass and set apart for Jehovah (Lev. 22:12; Num. 5:9; 18:8; 31:28, 29). In general it comprehended: 1. From the most holy things, the portions of the meal offerings, sin offerings, and guilt offerings which were not required to be burned on the altar. These parts were perquisites of the priests, and were eaten by them in the precincts of the sanctuary (Num. 18:9, 10; cf. Lev. 6:16). 2. From the holy gifts, Num. 18:11–19: (a) The heave offering of all wave offerings. It was assigned to the priest's fam-

ily, for use as food by all the members, male and female, provided they were ceremonially clean (v. 11). (b) The first fruits of the oil, wine, and grain (Num. 18:12; cf. vs. 24, 30; Deut. 18:4; Neh. 10:39). A basketful of these first fruits was presented to Jehovah by the offerer and then spread as a feast for the offerer and his family as the guests of the Lord (Deut. 26:2, 10, 11; cf. ch. 12:6–12). Except this basketful the whole of the first fruits belonged to the priestly families, but could be eaten only by those members of the household who were ceremonially clean (Num. 18:13; Deut. 18:4). (c) Every devoted thing (Num. 18:14). (d) The flesh of every unredeemed firstling (Num. 18:15–18). 3. The tithe (Num. 18:21–24), which was assigned as a perquisite to the Levites.

Particular heave offerings were: 1. From peace offerings the right thigh and 3 cakes, 1 out of each oblation (Lev. 7:14, 32–34). 2. From the ram of consecration, used at the induction of the priests into office, the right thigh (Ex. 29:27). It belonged to a peace offering, and accordingly was given to the priests (v. 28); but at the induction of Aaron, the first of the priestly line, it was burnt (Ex. 29:22–25; Lev. 8:25–28). 3. From the first dough, made from the new meal of the year, a cake (Num. 15:20, 21).

He'bel (hē'bĕl) [rope, territory]. In marg. of R.V. and text of J.V. (Josh. 19:29); according to this interpretation, a place mentioned in connection with Hosah and Achzib.

He'ber (hē'bĕr) [fellowship, associate]. 1. A son of Beriah, grandson of Asher, and founder of a tribal family (Gen. 46:17; Num. 26:45).

2. A Kenite, descendant of Moses' brother-in-law or father-in-law Hobab, and the husband of Jael, who slew Sisera (Judg. 4:11–24).

3. A man registered with Judah, descended from Ezra, and ancestor of the men of Socoh (I Chron. 4:18).

4. A Benjamite, descended from Shaharaim through Elpaal (I Chron. 8:17).

For 2 others bearing this name in A.V., see EBER.

He'brew (hē'brōō) [one from the other side, a crosser, a nomad; or pertaining to Eber]. 1. According to Biblical history, the Hebrews were men from the other side of the Euphrates (cf. Gen. 12:5 with ch. 14:13; Josh. 24:2, 3). The name may have denoted this, or it may have been originally a patronymic formed from Eber, and have designated all his descendants, including the Israelites (Gen. 10:21), until the increasing prominence of the Israelites led to restricting its use to them; see EBER.

The Heb. word *'ibri* (Hebrew) is regarded by many scholars as cognate with Akkadian *ḫabiru*, or *ḫapiru* (pl., *ḫabirū*), which occurs in the cuneiform literature from one end of the Near East to the other from about the last quarter of the 26th century B.C. to the 11th. It also appears in Egypt as *'apiru*. The Habirū were aliens and soldiers of fortune. In Babylonia they were mercenaries; among the Hurrians of Nuzu (Nuzi) they had to sell themselves into virtual slavery in order to make a living. Originally the name seems to have been not an ethnic term, but an appellative. According to the Tell el-Amarna letters, the Habirū were invading Palestine, and Abdi-Hiba of Jerusalem made frantic appeals to Akhnaton (alone, c. 1375–c. 1366 B.C.) for help. The situation corresponds in general to that of the time of the invasion under Joshua. Doubtless the Israelites belonged to the group called Habirū, but not all Habirū were Israelites. See EGYPT, III. 8.

Hebrews in the plural was applied to the

Israelites (Gen. 40:15; I Sam. 4:6; 13:3; II Cor. 11:22) In N.T. times it was used specially of those Jews who spoke Hebrew or rather Aramaic in distinction from the Hellenists, their fellow countrymen who spoke Greek (Acts 6:1). A Hebrew of the Hebrews was a thorough Hebrew; as, for example, a person of Hebrew parentage on both the father's and the mother's side (Phil. 3:5).

2. The language spoken by the Hebrews (II Kings 18:26, 28; Isa. 36:11, 13), and called the lip (language) of Canaan (Isa. 19:18), is a member of the Semitic group. Abraham found it in Canaan upon his arrival in the land. The tablets from Tell el-Amarna, the Moabite stone, and Phoenician inscriptions have shown that at least the Canaanites, the Phoenicians, and the Moabites, if not even the adjacent tribes, spoke a language not very different from Hebrew. A form of proto-Hebrew written in a cuneiform alphabet is found in the Ras Shamra tablets of the 14th or 15th century B.C.

The Heb. alphabet consists of 22 consonants. Originally the language was written without vowel points, these not being introduced earlier than the 6th century A.D., or perhaps even a little later. They were the work of certain Jewish scholars called Masoretes, whose headquarters were at Tiberias. With the exception of portions of the books of Daniel and Ezra and a few verses elsewhere in Aramaic, the whole of the O.T. was written originally in Hebrew.

Languages have their periods of growth, and likewise there was a development previous to Biblical Hebrew and during O.T. times. Furthermore there were dialects in ancient Hebrew (cf. Shibboleth and Sibboleth, Judg. 12:5, 6). The Biblical language before the Babylonian Captivity is comparatively pure; during the Exile and in postexilic times Aramaic exerted a decided influence on Hebrew and finally superseded it as the spoken vernacular. Hebrew, however, remained the language of religion and of the schools. The Mishnah (c. A.D. 200) is written in the later Hebrew of antiquity. A further development is Rabbinic Hebrew, the language used by the Jewish theologians on Talmudic subjects and in Biblical exegesis. Thus Hebrew continued through the Middle Ages as a learned tongue. Its final form is Modern Hebrew, which is now spoken in Palestine and recognized as an official language in that land.

The Aramaic in the time of our Lord had taken the place of Hebrew as the colloquial language (Mark 5:41), and had usurped its name; accordingly Aramaic is meant by the Hebrew language, or the Hebrew tongue, or the Hebrew, or simply Hebrew, in John 5:2; 19:13, 17, 20; Acts 21:40; 22:2; 26:14; Rev. 9:11.

He'brews (hē'brōoz), **The Epistle to the.** The 14th of the N.T. epistles as they are arranged in the Eng. Bible. That it was addressed to Jewish Christians is quite generally accepted. They were in danger of returning to Judaism through the pressure of outward trial and opposition (Heb. 2:1; 3:12; 4:1, 11; 5:12; 6:6; 10:23-25, 29). They had been early converts (ch. 5:12) and had received the gospel from its first preachers (ch. 2:3). They had long ago been persecuted (ch. 10:32-34) and had often ministered to the saints (ch. 6:10; 10:34). There is no reference to Gentile members in their churches, and their danger lay in a return not so much to the Law as to the ritual. These allusions best suit the Hebrew Christians of Palestine, and to them doubtless, with perhaps other Jewish believers of the East, the epistle was addressed. Some critics, however, maintain that it was directed to Gentile Christians, or to

Christians regardless of their origin, or even to a small group in Rome.

Its authorship has always been disputed. Even in the ancient Church opinion was divided, though the canonicity and authority of the book were recognized. The early Eastern Church received it as Pauline, though it was felt to be unlike the rest of Paul's epistles, and theories were advanced to explain the difference. Clement of Alexandria thought that perhaps Luke translated it from a Heb. original written by Paul. In the early Western Churches its Pauline authorship was doubted and denied, and Tertullian attributed it to Barnabas. Origen in the 3d century said that only God knows who wrote it, but finally the Eastern opinion, though uncritical, became the universally accepted one. The book is anonymous. Ch. 2:3, however, seems to imply that the author was not an apostle. It certainly implies that he was not one of the original apostles, and it is unlike Paul to represent himself as receiving the gospel from others (cf. Gal. 1:11-24). From Heb. 13:18, 19 we may infer that the writer was well known to his readers and was unhappily separated from them. In ch. 13:23 the reference to Timothy is not sufficient to indicate the author, nor does the expression "they of Italy" (ch. 13:24) prove his locality, though the natural inference is that he was in Italy.

The evidence of the contents and style also impresses different minds in different ways. It certainly is not a translation of a Heb. original. Its doctrine has much in common with Paul, though the truth is put in a slightly different way. Its language has a large classic element in it, and its style has seemed to most critics unlike the apostle's, being smoother, often more elegant, and less impetuous. The omission of any address also is unlike Paul's usage elsewhere; and the author seems to have used exclusively the LXX, while Paul constantly shows his familiarity with the Hebrew as well. Since no good evidence points to Paul as the author, many suggestions as to authorship have been advanced. Because of the literary elegance of the epistle, Luther ascribed it to Apollos (Acts 18:24). Another plausible view is that which attributes it to Barnabas, who has at least some ancient testimony in his favor, and who in The Acts appears as the mediator between the Jewish Christians and Paul. No early MS. attributes it to Paul, and consequently A.R.V. has the heading "The Epistle to the Hebrews." The following analysis will exhibit the thought of the epistle:

I. *The author begins by stating the superiority* of Christianity to all previous and possible revelation because of the superior dignity of Christ to all previous and possible organs of revelation (ch. 1), a fact which should warn us not to forsake the gospel (ch. 2:1-4). Nor should the humiliation of Christ appear a difficulty, since just by it he becomes our Saviour and high priest (ch. 2:5-18). Christ, therefore, is of superior dignity even to Moses (ch. 3:1-6), and the warnings against unbelief in the older revelation which were addressed to Israel are doubly applicable against unbelief in the final revelation of the gospel (chs. 3:7 to 4:13).

II. *The epistle then unfolds the value* of Christ's high-priestly office (ch. 4:14-16); explaining its nature and showing that Christ did, and that it was predicted he would, exercise it (ch. 5); and, after gently, yet vigorously, rebuking them for their failure to grasp the full truth of the gospel (ch. 6), unfolding the superiority of Christ's priesthood, as typified in Melchizedek, to the Levitical, the consequent abrogation of the latter with its ritual, and the all-sufficiency of Christ's (ch. 7).

THE SACRED MOSQUE AT HEBRON

This is the supposed site of the Cave of Machpelah, where Abraham and Sarah were buried.

III. *Then the epistle shows that Christ's priesthood* must now be necessarily exercised in heaven, so that his invisibility should be no difficulty to them. In this heavenly ministry Christ fulfills the types, realizes the promises and remedies the imperfections of the earthly ritual (chs. 8:1 to 10:18).

IV. *The 4th section* (chs. 10:19 to 12:29) *urges* them to live up to these truths by an enduring faith. The writer exhorts to renewed confidence in Christ and to the maintenance of their Christian associations (ch. 10:19–25); depicts the hopelessness which would follow apostasy (ch. 10:26–31); incites them by recalling their former zeal (ch. 10:32–39), the examples of the Hebrew heroes of faith (ch. 11) and of Christ himself (ch. 12:1–3); and bids them consider their trials as but the chastening of the Lord preparatory to a glorious salvation (ch. 12:4–29).

V. *In ch. 13 are added some specific exhortations.*

This epistle is the only one in which the title of priest is applied to Christ, though of course the substance of the doctrine is elsewhere taught; it represents Christianity as the completion and goal of the old dispensation; the clear announcement of that way of salvation previously taught by type and ritual. It gives the argument, therefore, most likely to establish Hebrews in the faith, and without it the N.T. teaching would be obviously incomplete.

Internal evidence bearing upon the date of composition in all probability favors c. A.D. 65–68, for the present tense used to describe the Levitical ritual (chs. 9:6 *seq.,* 9, 22, 25; 10:1, 8; 13:11) implies a date prior to the destruction of the Temple in A.D. 70. Some scholars, however, who date the book c. 80–90, maintain that the author wrote of that ritual from an idealized point of view, basing his description solely upon the Pentateuch. At any rate, the epistle was known to Clement of Rome (A.D. 96); and Timothy, who was born probably c. A.D. 25, was still living (ch. 13: 23).   G. T. P. (rev., H. S. G.)

He'bron (hē'brŏn) [union, league]. 1. A Levite, son of Kohath and founder of a tribal family (Ex. 6:18; I Chron. 6:2); see HE-BRONITES.

2. A town in the hill country of Judah (Josh. 15:48, 54), called originally Kiriath-arba (fourfold city, or Tetrapolis) (Gen. 23:2; Josh. 20:7); see ARBA. It was built 7 years before Zoan, in Egypt (Num. 13:22), and existed at least as early as the days of Abraham, who for a time resided in its vicinity, under the oaks or terebinths of Mamre (Gen. 13:18; 35:27). Sarah died there, and Abraham bought the cave of Machpelah for a sepulcher. He purchased it from the Hittites who then occupied the town (ch. 23:2–20). Isaac and Jacob for a time sojourned at Hebron (Gen. 35:27; 37:14). It was visited by the spies, who found Anakim among its inhabitants (Num. 13:22). Its king, Hoham, was one of the 4 kings who allied themselves with Adoni-zedek against Joshua, but who were defeated, captured, and slain (Josh. 10:1–27). Hebron itself was afterward taken and its inhabitants destroyed (vs. 36–39). This account is supplemented by ch. 11:21, 22, where it is recorded that at that time Joshua cut off the Anakim from Hebron, Debir, Anab, and all the hill country, and utterly destroyed their cities. After this 1st general campaign, however, the survivors of the old population gradually returned from their hiding places and retreats, and in the course of a few years rebuilt many of the ruined towns. Among those who thus returned were remnants of the 3 families of Anakim who had dwelt at Hebron. Here they

were found re-established after the conquest of Canaan (Josh. 14:12). Caleb claimed that district as his own; and when the tribe of Judah took possession of its allotted territory after the death of Joshua, Caleb retook Hebron (Judg. 1:10, 19, 20; and, apparently by anticipation, Josh. 15:13–19). Hebron had dependent villages (Josh. 15:54), was assigned to the priests, and was one of the cities of refuge (Josh. 20:7; 21:10–13; I Chron. 6:54–57). David sent thither part of the recaptured spoil of Ziklag (I Sam. 30:31), and afterward reigned in it for 7½ years (II Sam. 2:1–3, 11, 32; 5:1–5; I Kings 2:11; I Chron. 29:27), several of his sons being born there (II Sam. 3:2–5; I Chron. 3:1–4). Abner was buried there (II Sam. 3:32), and the head of Ish-bosheth was placed in the same grave (ch. 4). It was at Hebron that Absalom raised the standard of rebellion (ch. 15:7–10). It was fortified by Rehoboam (II Chron. 11:5, 10). During the Captivity, when the Edomites occupied the s. of Judah, Hebron, among other places, fell into their hands. It was recaptured from them by Judas Maccabaeus. At that time it had a fortress with towers and was the head of other towns (I Macc. 5:65). It is not mentioned in the N.T. Hebron is now called el-Khalil. It is one of the oldest towns in the world which is still inhabited, instead of being simply a ruin. Hebron is situated in a valley and on an adjacent slope, 3,040 feet above the level of the ocean. It is 19 miles s.s.w. of Jerusalem, and 13½ s.s.w. of Bethlehem. There are 25 springs of water and 10 large wells near Hebron, with vineyards and olive groves.

3. A town of Asher (Josh. 19:28, A.V.), but R.V. Ebron is closer to the Heb. original; see EBRON.

He'bron·ites (hē'brŏn-īts). The descendants of Hebron, the Kohathite (Num. 3:27; I Chron. 26:30, 31).

Heg'a·i (hĕg'á-ī) and **He'ge** (hē'gē) [perhaps, the sprinkler, from Avestan *haēk,* to sprinkle]. One of the chamberlains of King Ahasuerus. He was the keeper of the women (Esth. 2:3, 8, 15, A.R.V. marg., Hegee).

Heif'er. A young cow (Gen. 15:9; Deut. 21:3; I Sam. 16:2); see Cow and PURIFICATION.

Heir. Inheritance early became a custom. Abraham was acquainted with it (Gen. 15:3, 4). Only sons of a legal wife, not those of a concubine, had the right of inheritance. Ishmael, son of the bondwoman, might not inherit with the son of the free woman (ch. 21:10); and Abraham dismissed with presents the sons whom he had begotten by concubines (ch. 25:5, 6). Still, all Jacob's sons were accorded equal rights. Daughters sometimes inherited like sons (Job 42:15). By the Mosaic Law a man's property was divided on his death among his sons, the eldest obtaining double the portion assigned to his younger brothers (Deut. 21:15–17). When there were no sons, the property went to the daughters (Num. 27:1–8), who, however, were required to abstain from marrying out of their own tribal family (Num., ch. 36; Tobit 6:10–12). If circumstances demanded that a man of other family marry a sole heiress, the children of such a marriage appear to have taken the name of the mother's father (I Chron. 2:34–41; Ezra 2:61). Failing both sons and daughters, the inheritance went to the father's brother, and after him to the nearest of kin (Num. 27:9–11). Greek and Roman rule introduced new customs and made testaments and testators familiar to the Jews (Heb. 9:16, 17). In a figurative sense, believers are heirs of God and joint heirs with Christ (Rom. 8:17).

He'lah (hē'lä) [ornament, necklace]. One of the 2 wives of Ashhur, the ancestor of the men of Tekoa (I Chron. 4:5, 7).

He'lam (hē'lăm). A place e. of Jordan, where David defeated Hadarezer, king of Syria (II Sam. 10:16-19). Probably to be iden.ified with Alema (I Macc. 5:26), which is 'Alma in the plain of Hauran.

Hel'bah (hĕl'bă) [fatness, a fertile region]. A city within the territory of Asher, from which the Canaanites were not driven out; probably the same as Ahlab (Judg. 1:31). Identified with Maḥalliba of the Assyrians, which is Khirbet el-Maḥālib, n.e. of Tyre. Cf. Josh. 19:29, R.V. marg., "from Hebel," which in Heb. is meḥebel and may stand for a place Mahalab.

Hel'bon (hĕl'bŏn) [fat, fertile]. A city of Syria, celebrated for its wines (Ezek. 27:18). It is commonly identified with Khalbūn, 13 miles n.n.w. of Damascus. The village is situated in a narrow valley shut in by steep, bare cliffs and long, shelving banks 2,000 to 3,000 feet high. The bottom of the glen is occupied by orchards, and far up the mountain slopes are terraced vineyards. Along the terraces and in the valley below are extensive ruins. The wine was celebrated in Assyria, Babylonia, and Persia.

Hel'da·i (hĕl'dā-ī) [durable, transitory]. 1. A Netophathite, descended from Othniel. He was David's captain for the 12th month (I Chron. 27:15) Doubtless the person called Heled in I Chron. 11:30 (cf. Heleb, II Sam. 23:29).
2. An exile who returned from Babylon (Zech. 6:10), called also Helem (v. 14).

He'leb (hē'lĕb) [fatness]. The name given to Heled (II Sam. 23:29).

He'led (hē'lĕd) [duration, world]. The son of Baanah, a Netophathite, and one of David's mighty men (I Chron. 11:30). See HELEB and HELDAI.

He'lek (hē'lĕk) [portion, lot]. A son of Gilead, and founder of a tribal family of Manasseh (Num. 26:30; Josh. 17:2).

He'lem, I (hē'lĕm) [health, strength]. An Asherite, brother of Shamer (I Chron. 7:35), and probably the person called Hotham in v. 32.

He'lem, II (hē'lĕm). The same as Heldai 2 (Zech. 6:10, 14).

He'leph (hē'lĕf) [permutation, change]. A frontier town of Naphtali (Josh. 19:33). Van de Velde identified it with Beit Līf, in the mountains of Galilee, midway between Kadesh and Rās el-Abiad.

He'lez (hē'lĕz) [perhaps, strength; or (God) has delivered]. 1. A Paltite or Pelonite, David's captain for the 7th month (I Chron. 27:10).
2. A man of Judah, descended from Hezron (I Chron. 2:39).

He'li (hē'lī) [Gr. form of Eli]. The father of Joseph, the husband of Mary, but by another view he is the father of Mary, the mother of Jesus. The latter interpretation is reached by punctuating the Gr. differently and understanding Jesus as "being son (as was supposed of Joseph) of Heli" (Luke 3:23). See GENEALOGY.

Hel'ka·i (hĕl'kā-ī) [probably contraction of Hilkiah]. A priest, head of the father's house Meraioth (Neh. 12:15).

Hel'kath (hĕl'kăth) [portion, a field]. A town on the boundary line of Asher (Josh. 19:25), assigned, with its suburbs, to the Gershonite Levites (ch. 21:31). Called in I Chron. 6:75 Hukok, which is probably a corruption of the text. Formerly identified with

Yerḳā, 8½ miles e.n.e. of Acre, but Alt favors Tell el-Harbaj.

Hel'kath-haz'zu·rim (hĕl'kăth-hăz'ū-rīm) [field of sharp flints or sword-edges]. A name given to the scene of the combat, at the pool of Gibeon, between 12 Benjamites of Ishbosheth's party and the same number of David's men (II Sam. 2:16).

Hell. 1. The place of the dead. It is one rendering of Heb. Sheʾōl and Gr. Haidēs. A.R.V. of O.T. places Sheol in the text in Deut. 32:22; Ps. 55:15; 86:13, while A.V. has hell. In N.T. R.V. puts Hades in the text (cf. Ps. 16:10 with Acts 2:27). The two words are also rendered grave in A.V. (Gen. 37:35; Isa. 38:10, 18; Hos. 13:14; and A.V. of I Cor. 15:55; in R.V., death). The etymology of the words is in doubt. Sheol is represented as insatiable (cf. Prov. 27:20, R.V.; 30:15, 16). Hades, when pronounced without the aspiration, means the unseen. Both words denote the place of the dead. The evidence is not clear, but it may be safely affirmed that for centuries the Hebrews shared the common Semitic conception of Sheol. This conception was vague and undefined. There was consequently room for the imagination to play, and fancy was fond of supplying all manner of details; and care must be taken not to confound fancies with faith. The ancient Hebrews, like other Semites, thought of Sheol as beneath the earth (Num. 16:30-33; Isa. 31:17; Amos 9:2). They pictured it as entered through gates (Isa. 38:10), a dark, gloomy region, where the inhabitants pass a conscious, but dull, inactive existence (II Sam. 22:6; Ps. 6:5; Eccl. 9:10). They regarded it as the place whither the souls of all men without distinction go (cf. Gen. 37:35; Ps. 31:17; Isa. 38:10), where punishments may be suffered and rewards enjoyed, and from which a return to earth was not an impossibility (I Sam. 28:8-19; Heb. 11:19). It is important to note, however, that in authoritative Hebrew doctrine Sheol was open and naked to God (Job 26:6; Prov. 15:11), that God was even there (Ps. 139:8), and that the spirits of his people, and their condition in that abode, were ever under his watchful eye. This doctrine of God's knowledge of his people after death, presence with them, and unceasing love for them, involved the blessedness of the righteous and the woe of the wicked after death, and 2 places oι abode for them, the righteous being with the Lord and the wicked being banished from his presence. This doctrine lay also at the basis of the related teaching of the eventual resurrection of the body, and the life everlasting. The doctrine of future glory, and even of the resurrection of the body, was cherished in O.T. times (Job 19:25-27; Ps. 16:8-11; 17:15; 49:14, 15; 73:24; Dan. 12:2, 3). A foundation for it was early afforded by the translation of Enoch and Elijah; it is not certain to what extent, if any, the Hebrews were influenced by the Egyptians, who had definite teaching regarding the future life and the relation of morality in the present life to happiness beyond the grave. But it remained for Christ to bring immortality to full light, and, by revealing the bliss of the saved soul even out of the body in his presence, to dispel all gloom from the future abode of his saints (Luke 23:43; John 14:1-3; II Cor. 5:6-10; Phil. 1:23). See PARADISE.
2. The place of woe. In this sense it is the rendering of Gr. Geenna in Matt. 5:22, 29, 30; 10:28; 18:9; 23:15, 33; Mark 9:47; Luke 12:5, and James 3:6. This word is the Gr. form of Heb. Gê Hinnōm, valley of Hinnom, where children were burnt to Molech. From the horrible sins practiced in it, its pollution by Josiah, and perhaps also because offal was

burnt in it, the valley of Hinnom became a type of sin and woe, and the name passed into use as a designation for the place of eternal punishment (Matt. 18:8, 9; Mark 9:43). From the scenes witnessed in the valley, imagery was borrowed to describe the Gehenna of the lost (Matt. 5:22; cf. ch. 13: 42; Mark 9:48). In II Peter 2:4, "to cast down to hell" is the rendering of the verb *tartaroō*, meaning "to cast down to Tartarus." The *Tartarus* of the Romans, the *Tartaros* of the Greeks, was their place of woe, situated as far below Hades as Hades was below heaven. Gehenna and Tartarus are both the place of punishment for the lost.

Hel'len·ist (hĕl'ĕn-ĭst). One, not of the Greek nation, who spoke Greek. The term is used specially of Jews who had adopted the Greek tongue, and with it often Greek practices and opinions (R.V., marg., Acts 6:1 and 9:29). The text calls them Grecian Jews; the A.V. simply Grecians.

Hel'met. See ARMOR.

He'lon (hē'lŏn) [strong, valorous]. Father of Eliab, prince of Zebulun (Num. 1:9; 2:7; 7:24, 29; 10:16).

Hem. The edge, border, or margin of a garment (Ex. 28:33, 34; 39:24–26, in the R.V. skirts; and Matt. 9:20; 14:36, in the R.V. borders). The Jews attached a certain sacredness to the hem, fringe, or border of their garments.

He'mam (hē'măm). See HOMAM.

He'man (hē'măn) [faithful]. 1. A sage whose reputation for wisdom was high in Solomon's reign (I Kings 4:31). He belonged to the tribe of Judah (I Chron. 2:6). He composed a meditative psalm (Psalm 88, according to its 2d title).
2. A singer in David's reign, a son of Joel, a grandson of the Prophet Samuel, of the Levite family of Korah (I Chron. 6:33; 15:17). He was also appointed to sound a brazen cymbal (v. 19). He rose to prominence among David's musicians (ch. 16:41, 42).
3. A.R.V. (Gen. 36:22) for Hemam (A.V. and E.R.V., which agree with the Heb.); cf. Vulgate *Heman* and LXX *Haiman*.

He'math (hē'măth). See HAMATH for Amos 6:14, A.V., and HAMMATH for I Chron. 2:55, A.V.

Hem'dan (hĕm'dăn) [pleasant, desirable]. A Horite, the eldest son of Dishon (Gen. 36:26). In the parallel passage, I Chron. 1:41, the Heb. text and R.V. have Hamran, which A.V. erroneously represents by Amram. The 2 Heb. words differ only in the 3d consonant. The difference is undoubtedly due to a scribe who confused *r* (*resh*) and *d* (*daleth*). Hemdan probably is the original form.

Hem'lock. See GALL 2 and WORMWOOD.

Hen (hĕn) [grace, favor, kindness]. A son of Zephaniah (Zech. 6:14). But in R.V. marg. Hen is translated, "For the kindness of the son of Zephaniah," in which case that son's name disappears.

He'na (hē'nȧ). A city captured by the Assyrians (II Kings 18:34; 19:13; Isa. 37:13). It is mentioned with Sepharvaim and Ivvah, and is commonly identified with the town of ānah on the Euphrates, at 42° E. longitude from Greenwich. The Targum understands Hena and Ivvah as verbs: "He has driven away and overturned." But Ivvah, if the same as Avva (II Kings 17:24), was a town. See AVVA.

Hen'a·dad (hĕn'ȧ-dăd) [probably, favor of Hadad]. Founder of a Levitical family, whose sons supported Zerubbabel at the time the foundations of the Temple were being laid

(Ezra 3:9), and assisted in rebuilding the wall of Jerusalem (Neh. 3:18).

Hen'na [Arab. *hinnā'*]. The rendering of Heb. *kōpher* in the LXX and in R.V. of S. of Sol. 1:14 and ch. 4:13. It is translated in the A.V. camphire. Henna is a plant of the *Lythrarieae* or looses.rife order (*Lawsonia alba* or *inermis*), with opposite entire leaves, and fragrant yellow and white flowers in corymbs or clusters (S. of Sol. 1:14). The Greeks called it *kypros*, from the island of Cyprus, where it grew. In Palestine its special seat was the virtually tropical region of En-gedi (S. of Sol. 1:14) and Jericho (Jos. *War* iv. 8, 3). The leaves and young twigs are made into a fine powder, converted into paste with hot water, and used by Oriental women and wealthy men to dye the finger and toe nails and the soles of the feet a reddish orange color.

He'noch (hē'nŭk). See ENOCH for I Chron. 1:3, A.V., and HANOCH for I Chron. 1:33, A.V.

He'pher (hē'fēr) [pit, well]. 1. A town west of the Jordan (Josh. 12:17). The name belonged to a district also, probably near Socoh (I Kings 4:10). Maisler identifies it with Tell Ibshār on the wadi el-Ḥawārith in the plain of Sharon.
2. A son of Gilead, founder of a tribal family of Manasseh (Num. 26:32; 27:1; Josh. 17:2).
3. A man of Judah, son of Ashhur of Tekoa (I Chron. 4:6).
4. A Mecherathite, and one of David's worthies (I Chron. 11:36). See, however, remarks under UR, II.

Heph'zi·bah (hĕf'zĭ-bá) [my delight is in her]. 1. Mother of King Manasseh (II Kings 21:1).
2. A symbolical name to be given to Zion (Isa. 62:4).

He'res (hē'rēz) [sun]. 1. An eminence in the district of Aijalon (Judg. 1:35). The meaning and a comparison with Josh. 19:41, 42 render the opinion probable that Mount Heres is identical with the town Ir-shemesh, that is, Beth-shemesh.
2. The ascent of Heres (Judg. 8:13, R.V.); the spot e. of the Jordan from which Gideon returned after the defeat of Zebah and Zalmunna.
3. An Egyptian city; Isa. 19:18, marg. of A.V. and R.V., "city of the sun," i.e., Heliopolis. See ON, II.

He'resh (hē'rĕsh) [dumb, silent]. A Levite (I Chron. 9:15).

Her'e·sy. 1. A party, sect, or faction (Acts 5:17; 15:5); strong party spirit, even when this is not produced on one side or the other by departure from sound doctrine (I Cor. 11:19, A.R.V. factions; Gal. 5:20, A.R.V. parties).
2. A doctrine or a sect consequent upon departure from sound doctrine (II Peter 2:1, R.V. marg., sects of perdition).

He'reth (hē'rĕth), in A.V. **Ha'reth**, the Heb. pausal form. A forest in Judah, in which David for a time lurked while his life was being sought by Saul (I Sam. 22:5).

Her'mas (hûr'măs). A Christian at Rome to whom Paul sent his salutations (Rom. 16:14).

Her'mes (hûr'mēz). 1. The Greek god corresponding to the Roman Mercury (Acts 14: 12, R.V. marg.). See MERCURY.
2. A Christian (not the same as Hermas) at Rome, to whom Paul sent his salutations (Rom. 16:14).

Her·mog'e·nes (hûr-mŏj'ē-nēz) [Gr., sprung from Hermes]. An inhabitant of the Roman province of Asia, who finally, with many others, turned away from the Apostle Paul (II Tim. 1:15).

Her'mon (hûr'mŏn) [sacred mountain]. A mountain called by the Sidonians Sirion, and by the Amorites Senir or Shenir (Deut. 3:8, 9). The last name belonged especially to a part of the mountain (I Chron. 5:23). Another name for it was Sion (Deut. 4:48). It constituted the n.e. limit of the Israelite conquests under Moses and Joshua (Deut. 3:8, 9; Josh. 11:3, 17; 12:1; 13:5, 11; I Chron. 5:23). It figures in Hebrew poetry, being coupled with Tabor (Ps. 89:12), Zion (Ps. 133:3), and Lebanon (S. of Sol. 4:8), really, however, overtopping them all. It constitutes the s. end of the Anti-Lebanon chain, and rises to the elevation of 9,166 feet above the sea. It may be seen from many parts of Palestine. The view from the top is magnificent; from it one can see Lebanon, the plain around

father's nor by the mother's side was Herod a real Jew, though the Idumaeans, who had been conquered 125 B.C. by John Hyrcanus, and compelled to be circumcised and adopt Judaism, had now become nominally Jews.

Antipater was made procurator of Judea by Caesar in 47 B.C. (Jos. *Antiq.* xiv. 8, 3 and 5). He had 5 children, Phasaëlus, Herod, Joseph, Pheroras, and a daughter Salome (Jos. *Antiq.* xiv. 7, 3). Phasaëlus, the eldest son, was made governor of Jerusalem and vicinity by his father, and Galilee was committed to Herod, who was then 25 years old (Jos. *Antiq.* xiv. 9, 2). After the murder of Antipater, 43 B.C., Mark Antony visited Syria and appointed the 2 brothers tetrarchs, committing the public affairs of the Jews to them (Jos. *Antiq.* xiv. 13, 1). They were afterward sorely pressed by Antigonus, last king of the Maccabaean family, and by the Parthians. Phasaëlus fell into the hands of the latter and committed

Mount Hermon as Seen from Lebanon

Damascus, Tyre, Carmel, the mountains of Upper Galilee, the plains of Lower Galilee, Lake Ḥûleh and the Sea of Galilee. The summit has 3 peaks, that on the s.e. being the highest. Having these peaks it is described as the Hermons (Ps. 42:6, R.V.); but the word in this passage may denote the Hermon range in general. The summit of the mountain is covered with snow all the year round, wavy white furrows descending from the crest in the lines of the several valleys. The proper source of the Jordan is in Hermon. Some one of its solitary recesses may have been the scene of our Lord's transfiguration, but this is disputed. Hermon is now called Jebel esh-Sheikh.

Her'mon·ites (hûr'mŏn-īts). Natives or inhabitants of Mount Hermon (Ps. 42:6, A.V.; in R.V., the Hermons).

Her'od (hĕr'ŭd). The name of several rulers over Palestine and the adjacent regions or portions of them. Three are mentioned in the N.T. by the name of Herod and 1 by the name of Agrippa.

1. HEROD THE GREAT. He was the 2d son of the Idumaean Antipas, or Antipater, by his wife Cypros, who was of the same race (Jos. *Antiq.* xiv. 1, 3; 7, 3). Thus, neither by the

suicide to avoid being put to death by them (Jos. *Antiq.* xiv. 13, 10). The Romans were now induced by Antony to espouse the cause of Herod; and war ensued with Antigonus and the Parthians, in the course of which Herod's brother Joseph was slain in battle (Jos. *Antiq.* xiv. 15, 10), Jerusalem was captured and Herod became king of Judea in 37 B.C.

The surviving children of Antipater were now Herod, Pheroras, and Salome. Salome married her uncle Joseph (Jos. *Antiq.* xv. 3, 5; *War* i. 22, 4). After he had been put to death for adultery, 34 B.C., she married Costobarus, an Idumaean of good family whom Herod made governor of Idumaea and Gaza (Jos. *Antiq.* xv. 7, 9; *War* i. 24, 6). She divorced him (Jos. *Antiq.* xv. 7, 10), and against her will was married to Alexas, a friend of Herod's (Jos. *War* i. 28, 6). During the whole of Herod's reign, she engaged in intrigues against members of his family; but she was faithful to him, and he bequeathed to her Jamnia, Ashdod, and Phasaëlis near Jericho (Jos. *Antiq.* xvii. 6, 1; 8, 1; 11, 5). She accompanied Herod's son Archelaus to Rome, when he went thither to obtain imperial sanction to ascend the throne. Her ostensible purpose was to assist him in prosecuting his claim, but her real object was to thwart him (Jos.

War ii. 2, 1–4). She died about A.D. 10, when Marcus Ambivius was procurator (Jos. *Antiq.* xviii. 2, 2). Pheroras, the youngest of the 4 sons of Antipater (Jos. *Antiq.* xiv. 15, 4), lived nearly as long as Herod. He was partner in the kingdom, had the title of tetrarch, and enjoyed the revenue accruing from the country e. of the Jordan (Jos. *War* i. 24, 5). He was more than once accused of plotting the death of Herod, and matters came to a crisis shortly before the latter's death; but Pheroras died without being brought to trial (Jos. *Antiq.* xvii. 3, 3).

Herod the Great had 10 wives from first to last (Jos. *Antiq.* xvii. 1, 3; *War* i.; xxviii. 4). His 1st wife was Doris, a woman of an obscure family in Jerusalem. She bore him 1 son, Antipater, who took an active part in the events of Herod's reign, plotting against his younger half-brothers to secure the kingdom for himself. Herod, just before the capture of Jerusalem, by which he became king, married his 2d wife, the beautiful and chaste Mariamne (I), granddaughter of Hyrcanus. She bore him 3 sons, Alexander, Aristobulus, and the youngest son who died without issue, and 2 daughters, Cypros and Salampsio. Mariamne was put to death in 29 B.C. (Jos. *Antiq.* xv. 7, 4). About 24 B.C. he married Mariamne (II), daughter of Simon, whom he raised to the high priesthood (Jos. *Antiq.* xv. 9, 3; xviii. 5, 4). Herod also took to wife his 2 nieces, whose names are not given and who died childless, Malthace a Samaritan, Cleopatra of Jerusalem, Pallas, Phaedra, and Elpis. With the 2 unnamed nieces and last 3 of known name history is not specially concerned. The descendants of the others are more important. Of Mariamne (II), Herod (Philip) was born (cf. Matt. 14:3; Mark 6:17; Luke 3:19; Jos. *Antiq.* xviii. 5, 4); Malthace became mother of Archelaus, Herod Antipas, and a daughter Olympias; and Cleopatra bore Herod and Philip.

came the father of 5 children, several of whom played an important part later in the history. Of these 2 young men, sons of the beloved Mariamne (I), Antipater, the first-born of Herod, was jealous. His jealousy was aroused against his half-brothers by the evident intention of his father to overlook his right as first-born in their favor (Jos. *War* i. 22, 1), and he and his clique at court poisoned the mind of Herod against them. At length, about 7 B.C., Herod had them put to death, named Antipater his heir and appointed Herod, son of Mariamne II, next in succession (Jos. *Antiq.* xvi. 11, 7; xvii. 3, 2; *War* i. 29, 2). This order conformed to birth, his sons Archelaus and Antipas, Herod and Philip, being doubtless younger than Herod, son of Mariamne II. Antipater next accused Herod's sister, Salome, and his sons, Archelaus and Philip, who were in Rome being educated, of plotting the murder of Herod; but the crime charged against Salome was brought home to himself. He and his uncle Pheroras, Herod's brother, were accused of seeking the king's life. Pheroras died, but Antipater was cast into prison. Herod's suspicions were thereby aroused that Antipater had falsely accused Alexander and Aristobulus, who had already been executed, and he altered his will, appointing Antipas to be his successor, and passed over Archelaus, the elder brother, and Philip, as he still held them in suspicion (Jos. *War* i. 32, 7). Soon afterward he ordered Antipater to be slain and altered his will again, giving the kingdom to Archelaus, making Antipas tetrarch of Galilee and Perea, and Philip tetrarch of Batanea, Trachonitis, and Auranitis, and bestowing several cities on his sister Salome (Jos. *Antiq.* xvii. 8, 1; *War* i. 33, 7). Herod's disposition of his affairs was observed at his death, except that Archelaus was finally confirmed by the emperor Augustus not as king but as ethnarch of Judea (Jos. *Antiq.* xvii. 11, 4 and 5).

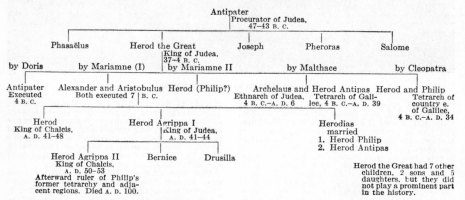

The domestic troubles of Herod began early in his reign in the hatred which he incited in the beloved Mariamne (I) toward himself; and they culminated in the last decade of his reign, when his sons had reached manhood. The domestic history eventually revolves about the 8 young men: Antipater, son of Doris; Alexander and Aristobulus, sons of Mariamne (I); Herod (Philip) son of Mariamne (II); Archelaus and Antipas, sons of Malthace; and Herod and Philip, sons of Cleopatra. Alexander married Glyphyra, daughter of Archelaus, king of Cappadocia. Two sons were born to them whose history is not important (Jos. *Antiq.* xvi. 1, 2; *War* i. 24, 2). Aristobulus married his 1st cousin, Bernice, daughter of Herod's sister, Salome, and be-

Herod, son of Mariamne (II), married, or had married, Herodias, daughter of his half-brother, the dead Aristobulus. She, however, left him and married another half-brother of his, Herod the tetrarch, and her former husband disappears from history. So does Herod, son of Cleopatra and brother of Philip, the tetrarch. See HERODIAS and PHILIP 5, Aristobulus, as already mentioned, had married his cousin, Bernice, daughter of Salome, and had begotten 5 children (Jos. *War* i. 28, 1). They were Herod, Agrippa, Aristobulus, Herodias, and Mariamne (III). Herod married Mariamne (IV), daughter of Olympias, daughter of Herod the Great and the Samaritan Malthace; Agrippa married Cypros, daughter of Salampsio and Phasaëlus the younger, son of Herod the Great's brother, Phasaëlus; Aristobulus married Jotape, daughter of a king of Emesa; Herodias married 2 uncles in succession, as already noted; and, it may be inferred, Mariamne III married Antipater, son of Doris (Jos. *Antiq.* xviii. 5, 4; *War* i. 28, 5; cf. 4). Three of these children of Aristobulus are persons of note—namely, Herod, Agrippa, and Herodias. Herodias was the woman who crowned her infamies by telling her daughter to demand the head of John the Baptist on a charger. Herod was made king of Chalcis, and after his wife's death took his niece, Bernice, Agrippa's daughter, to wife. Agrippa became King Agrippa I. He married, had 1 son and 3 daughters. Three of these children are mentioned in Scripture, Agrippa II and the 2 notorious women, Bernice and Drusilla.

Besides this domestic history of the rise of the family to power and the intrigues among its members, there is the political history of Herod's reign. Soon after he had been made ruler in Galilee, which was in 47 or 46 B.C., he came in contact with the sanhedrin through his summary execution of some robbers without the sanhedrin's formal permission. He was summoned for trial and appeared with an armed bodyguard, intimidating the council. He was acquitted for lack of evidence. Herod sought to be, for his own interest, on good terms with the successive representatives of the warring factions into which the Roman people were then divided. He obtained a generalship from Sextus Caesar, president of Syria, a relative of the great Julius Caesar; and then, after a time, gained the favor of Cassius, the most malignant of the great dictator's assassins. Then he cast in his lot with Mark Antony, one of the murdered man's chief avengers; nor was even this his last change of sides. About 41 B.C. Herod was made tetrarch of Galilee by Antony. When after fresh vicissitudes, he went to Rome in 40 B.C., as a fugitive rather than a visitor, his patron induced the Roman senate to appoint him king of the Jews. It was not, however, till 37 B.C. that, with the assistance of Sosius, a general of Antony's, he succeeded in taking Jerusalem and commencing his actual reign. By his marriage at this time with Mariamne, granddaughter of Hyrcanus and daughter of Alexander, son of Aristobulus, he became allied with the royal Hasmonaean family (Maccabees). He now endeavored further to strengthen his position by the removal of possible rivals. The principal members of the party of Antigonus, 45 in number, were sought out and put to death. Soon afterward Mariamne's brother, Aristobulus, a boy of 17, whom Herod had just raised to the high priesthood, was drowned in a bath by Herod's orders, within a year after his elevation to the pontificate; and about 31 B.C. her grandfather, although 80 years old, was put to death (Jos. *Antiq.* xv. 1, 2; 3, 3; 6, 2). Herod's attention was called from these atrocities by the new crisis which had arisen. His patron Antony was totally defeated by Octavius (Augustus) in the sea fight at Actium on Sept. 2, 31 B.C. The position of Herod was now critical, but he made a manly and judicious speech to the victorious Octavius, and was forgiven for his partisanship toward Antony. He was given the friendship of the man he had offended and retained it through most of his life, besides having his dominions increased (Jos. *Antiq.* xv. 6, 5–7; 10, 3). The murder of a wife's brother and her grandfather did not tend to increase her attachment to her husband, and by and by variance arose between Herod and Mariamne. It increased, till it culminated at length in the queen's being falsely accused and executed. Remorse followed in due course and almost, if not altogether, deprived the king of reason (Jos. *Antiq.* xv. 7, 7; *War* i. 22, 5).

Partly to divert his mind from gloomy remembrances, partly to please Octavius, now the emperor Augustus, he built theaters and exhibited games, although both of these acts were inconsistent with Judaism. He also rebuilt, enlarged, and beautified a place named Strato's Tower, calling it, after his imperial patron, Caesarea. It ultimately became the Roman capital of Palestine (Jos. *Antiq.* xv. 8, 5; 9, 6; cf. Acts 23:23, 24). Then to conciliate the Jews, between 19 and 11 or 9 B.C., he rebuilt and beautified the Temple.

The birth of Jesus Christ took place at the close of Herod's life, after he had removed his rivals from other families by violent deaths and when his domestic troubles were at their height. He had slain his sons Alexander and Aristobulus, and more recently Antipater, for plotting against his life; and now he was told that a child of David's line had just been born to be king of the Jews. The slaughter of the infants who came into the world about the same time and place was such a method of meeting the difficulty as would suggest itself to one with Herod's propensity to bloodshed (Matt., ch. 2). It was one of the last acts of his life. Seized at length with loathsome and mortal disease, he repaired to Callirhoe, the hot sulphur springs of the Zerka, the water from which runs into the e. part of the Dead Sea. They came to be called, in consequence, by many, the baths of Herod; but they did not do the king much good (Jos. *Antiq.* xvii. 6, 5). He felt that he was dying and that there would be rejoicing when he passed away. He therefore told his sister Salome and her husband Alexas to shut up the principal Jews in the circus at Jericho, and put them to death whenever he expired, that there might be mourning at, though of course not for, his death. Then, about 4 B.C., he passed away, in the 70th year of his age and the 34th of his reign, counting from the time when he actually obtained the kingdom. When news of his demise arrived, the circus prisoners were set free, and the death of the tyrant was welcomed as a relief instead of being attended by mourning, lamentation, and woe (Jos. *Antiq.* xvii. 6, 5; 8, 2; *War* i. 33, 5).

2. HEROD THE TETRARCH. A son of Herod the Great by his Samaritan wife called Malthace. He was, therefore, half Idumaean and half Samaritan, perhaps without a single drop of Jewish blood in his veins. He was called indifferently Antipas and Herod (Jos. *Antiq.* xvii. 1, 3; xviii. 5, 1; 6, 2; *War* ii. 9, 1), and it is customary to distinguish him from the other Herods of the family as Herod Antipas. He was the full brother of Archelaus, and was younger than Archelaus (Jos. *Antiq.* xvii. 6, 1; *War* i. 32, 7; 33, 7). He was educated with him and his half-brother Philip at Rome (Jos. *Antiq.* xvii. 1, 3). By the 2d testament of his father, the kingdom was bequeathed to him (Jos. *Antiq.* xvii. 6, 1); but by his father's final will he was appointed tetrarch of Galilee and the kingdom was given to Archelaus (Jos. *Antiq.* xvii. 8, 1). On his father's death he competed with his brother for the kingdom, but received only the tetrarchy of Galilee and Perea (Jos. *Antiq.* xvii. 11, 4; Luke 3:1). He erected a wall around Sepphoris and made it his metropolis. Betharamphtha in Perea he walled, and built a palace there. It was named Livias and Julias, after the wife of Augustus (Jos. *Antiq.* xviii. 2, 1; *War* ii. 9, 1); see BETH-HARAN. He also built Tiberias (Jos. *Antiq.* xviii. 2, 3). He married a daughter of Aretas, king of the Nabataean Arabs, whose capital was Petra; but afterward, while lodging at Rome with Herod Philip, his half-brother, he indulged a guilty passion for his entertainer's wife, Herodias, and arranged to divorce his lawful consort and take Herodias instead. This immoral transaction was carried

into effect. Herodias was Herod's evil genius, and she made a tool of him, as Jezebel had done of Ahab. Aretas resented the injury inflicted upon his daughter, and he commenced a war against Herod and waged it successfully (Jos. *Antiq.* xviii. 5, 1). Herodias was the prime mover in the murder of John the Baptist (Matt. 14:1–12; Jos. *Antiq.* xviii. 5, 2). Because of his cunning, the tetrarch was described by our Lord as "that fox" (Luke 13:31, 32). But the tetrarch had a following, for mention is made of the leaven of Herod (Mark 8:15); see HERODIANS. When the fame of Jesus began to spread abroad, the uneasy conscience of Herod made him fear that John had risen from the dead (Matt. 14:1, 2). He was present at Jerusalem at the time of the crucifixion, and Jesus was sent to him by Pilate. He thought that now he would have the opportunity of seeing a miracle performed, but he was disappointed. The same day he was reconciled to Pilate, whereas they had before been at variance (Luke 23:7–12, 15; Acts 4:27). The advancement of Herodias' brother Agrippa to be king, while her husband remained only tetrarch, aroused the envy of this proud woman, and she prevailed upon Herod to go with her to Rome and ask for a crown. Agrippa, however, sent letters after them to the emperor Caligula, accusing Herod of being secretly in league with the Parthians, and Herod was in consequence banished to Lyons in Gaul, A.D. 39, where he died (Jos. *Antiq.* xviii. 7; but according to *War* ii. 9, 6, Spain was the place of exile).

3. HEROD THE KING. Josephus calls him simply Agrippa. Both names are generally combined, and he is designated Herod Agrippa I, to distinguish him from Herod Agrippa II, before whom Paul was tried. Agrippa I was the son of Aristobulus, son of Herod the Great and Mariamne, granddaughter of Hyrcanus. He was educated in Rome with Drusus, son of the emperor Tiberius, and Claudius (Jos. *Antiq.* xviii. 6, 1 and 4); but the death of Drusus and lack of funds led to his return to Judea (Jos. *Antiq.* xviii. 6, 2). In A.D. 37 he made another journey to Rome to bring accusations against Herod the tetrarch (Jos. *Antiq.* xviii. 5, 3; *War* ii. 9, 5). He did not return when his business was transacted, but remained in the metropolis, cultivating the acquaintance of people who might be of use to him in the future. Among others, he ingratiated himself with Caius, son of Germanicus, who shortly became the emperor Caligula (Jos. *Antiq.* xviii. 6, 4; *War* ii. 9, 5). For rash words spoken in favor of Caius, Tiberius cast him into chains; but 6 months later Caius became emperor and appointed Agrippa to be king of the tetrarchy which his late uncle Philip had governed, and also of the tetrarchy of Lysanias (Jos. *Antiq.* xviii. 6, 10). In A.D. 39 the emperor banished Herod the tetrarch and added his tetrarchy, which was Galilee, to the kingdom of Agrippa (Jos. *Antiq.* xviii. 7, 2). Agrippa left his kingdom for a time, and resided at Rome (Jos. *Antiq.* xviii. 8, 7). During this sojourn at the capital he prevailed upon the emperor to desist from his determination to erect his statue in the Temple at Jerusalem (Jos. *Antiq.* xviii. 8, 7 and 8). When Caligula was assassinated, and Claudius, against his own will, chosen in his place, Agrippa, who was then at Rome, acted as negotiator between the senate and the new emperor, whom he persuaded to take office. As a reward, Agrippa had Judea and Samaria added to his dominions, which now equaled those of Herod the Great (Jos. *Antiq.* xix. 3–5; *War* ii. 11, 1–5). He commenced to build a wall about the n. suburb of Jerusalem, so as to include it in the city, but was ordered to abandon the work (Jos. *Antiq.* xix. 7, 2). He slew James, the brother of John, with the

sword (Acts 12:1, 2), imprisoned Peter (vs. 3–19, and at Caesarea, immediately after he had accepted divine honor, was miserably eaten up of worms (Acts 12:20–23; Jos. *Antiq.* xix. 8, 2). He died A.D. 44, in the 54th year of his age, leaving 4 children, of whom 3 are mentioned in Scripture, Agrippa, Bernice, and Drusilla (Jos. *War* ii. 11, 6).

4. AGRIPPA, commonly known as Herod Agrippa II. He was son of Herod Agrippa I, and consequently great-grandson of Herod the Great, and was the brother of the notorious women Bernice and Drusilla (Jos. *War* ii. 11, 6). At the time of his father's death, A.D. 44, he was 17 years old, and residing at Rome, where he was being brought up in the imperial household (Jos. *Antiq.* xix. 9). The emperor Claudius was dissuaded from appointing him to the throne of his father on account of his youth, and Judea was placed under a procurator. Agrippa remained in Rome. He successfully seconded the efforts of the Jewish ambassadors to obtain the imperial permission to retain the official robes of the high priest under their own control (Jos. *Antiq.* xx. 1, 1). When his uncle Herod, king of Chalcis, died about A.D. 48, Claudius presently bestowed his small realm on the w. slope of Anti-Lebanon on Agrippa (Jos. *Antiq.* xx. 5, 2; *War* ii. 12, 1), so that he became King Agrippa. He espoused the cause of the Jewish commissioners who had come to Rome to appear against the procurator Cumanus and the Samaritans, and he prevailed upon the emperor to grant them an audience (Jos. *Antiq.* xx. 6, 3; *War* ii. 12, 7). In A.D. 52 Claudius transferred him from the kingdom of Chalcis to a larger realm formed of the tetrarchy of Philip, which contained Batanea, Trachonitis, and Gaulonitis, the tetrarchy of Lysanias, and the province of Abilene (Jos. *Antiq.* xx. 7, 1; *War* ii. 12, 8). His constant companionship with his sister Bernice about this time began to create scandal (Jos. *Antiq.* xx. 7, 3). In A.D. 54 or 55 Nero added the cities of Tiberias and Taricheae in Galilee and Julias in Perea with its dependent towns to his dominion (Jos. *Antiq.* xx. 8, 4). When Felix had been succeeded by Festus as procurator of Judea, Agrippa went to Caesarea to salute him, accompanied by Bernice. Paul was then in confinement. Festus laid his case before the king, and on the morrow the apostle was permitted to plead his cause before the procurator, the king, and Bernice. He was entirely successful in clearing himself (Acts 25:13 to 26:32). Soon afterward Agrippa built an addition to the palace of the Hasmonaeans at Jerusalem (Jos. *Antiq.* xx. 8, 11). Later still he enlarged and beautified Caesarea Philippi, and established theatrical exhibitions at Berytus (Jos. *Antiq.* xx. 9, 4). When the troubles which culminated in the Jewish war began, Agrippa endeavored to dissuade the Jews from making armed resistance to Florus the procurator and the Romans (Jos. *War* ii. 16, 2–5; 17, 4; 19, 3). When the war broke in its fury, he fought by the side of Vespasian and was wounded at the siege of Gamala (Jos. *War* iii. 9, 7 and 8; 10, 10; iv. 1, 3). After the capture of Jerusalem he removed with Bernice to Rome, where he was invested with the dignity of praetor. He died A.D. 100.

Her'od (hĕr'ŭd), **Pal'ace of.** A palace-fortress erected by Herod the Great about the year 24 or 23 B.C. (Jos. *Antiq.* xv. 9). It stood at the n.w. corner of the upper city, adjoined the towers of Hippicus, Phasaëlus, and Mariamne on their s., and formed with them a stronghold which excited the admiration of even the Romans (Jos. *War* v. 4, 4; 5, 8; vi. 8, 1; 9, 1). Its site is the modern citadel by the Jaffa Gate. The 3 towers were built of white stone. Hippicus was square, with sides

25 cubits in length. To the height of 30 cubits it consisted of solid masonry; over this was a reservoir, 20 cubits deep; and over this again a two-story house, 25 cubits in height, surmounted by battlements 2 cubits high with turrets 3 cubits higher. The entire altitude of the tower was 80 cubits. Phasaëlus was larger. Its stock was a cube of solid masonry measuring 40 cubits in each direction, surmounted by a cloister, and that in turn by a palatial tower. Its entire height was about 90 cubits. It was completed about the year 10 B.C. (Jos. *Antiq.* xvi. 5, 2). Mariamne had half the dimensions of Phasaëlus, save that it was 50 cubits high. It was magnificently adorned by Herod as befitted a tower named in honor of his wife. The palace proper on the s. of these towers was entirely walled about to the height of 30 cubits, and was further protected by turrets which surmounted the wall and stood at equal distances from each other. Within were open courts with groves of trees and numerous apartments, among which 2 were conspicuous for size and beauty, and were called Caesareum and Agrippium, after Herod's friends (Jos. *Antiq.* xv. 9, 3; *War* i. 21, 1; v. 4, 4). The palace was occupied by Sabinus, the procurator of Syria (Jos. *Antiq.* xvii. 10, 2 and 3; *War* ii. 3, 2 and 3). In it Pilate erected golden shields in honor of the emperor Tiberius; and it is expressly called the house of the procurators (Philo *Legat. ad Gaium* xxxviii. and xxxix.). The procurator Florus took up his quarters in this building, erected his tribunal before it, and sentenced men to scourging and crucifixion (Jos. *War* ii. 14, 8 and 9). It was burned by the seditious Jews at the beginning of the war with the Romans. The 3 mighty towers, however, withstood the flames and were allowed by the conqueror to stand as a witness to the kind of city the Romans had overthrown (Jos. *War* ii. 17, 8; vii. 1, 1).

He·ro'di·ans (hê-rō'dĭ-ănz). Various views have been expressed about the Herodians, but according to the present evidence it seems clear that they were not a religious sect or a political party. In Galilee they had joined with the Pharisees in plotting against Jesus' life (Mark 3:6; cf. ch. 8:15). It does not seem probable that they were members of the domestic staff of Herod, for the Pharisees would hardly seek their associates from among the menials of the court. Once the Pharisees and the Herodians combined at Jerusalem to entangle our Lord about paying tribute to Caesar (Matt. 22:16; Mark 12:13). From this connection it may be inferred that they were not court officers; the Pharisees would doubtless have felt that officials would serve rather to intimidate than to entrap Jesus. Court officers in the East are not accustomed to inquire of those beneath them about the legality of the taxes which are levied. The Herodians probably were Jews of influence and standing who were well disposed to the Herodian rule and consequently also to that of the Romans, who supported the Herods. They were on the side of Herod in a land where many people were definitely opposed to that regime.

He·ro'di·as (hê-rō'dĭ-ăs). Daughter of Aristobulus, and half-sister of Herod Agrippa I. She was married to Herod, the son of Herod the Great by Mariamne, the high priest Simon's daughter. This husband is called Philip in the N.T., but is not entitled to a tetrarch (Matt. 14:3; Mark 6:17). He was a different person from Philip the tetrarch. It is customary to speak of him as Herod Philip, which was probably his full name. See PHILIP 4. His half-brother, Herod the tetrarch, indulged a guilty passion for Herodias, and divorcing his wife, a daughter of King Aretas of Arabia, married Herodias while her first husband was still alive (Jos. *Antiq.* xviii. 5, 1, 4; 6, 2; 7, 2; *War* ii. 9, 6). John the Baptist reproved the guilty pair, on which Herodias plotted his death. When her daughter Salome had gained Herod's favor by dancing before him at a gathering of the dignitaries of his tetrarchy, she extorted from him a promise to give her the head of John the Baptist. The king was sorry but, for his oath's sake, complied with her wishes (Matt. 14:3–12; Mark 6:17–29; Luke 3:19, 20). On the banishment of the tetrarch, Herodias went with him into exile (Jos. *Antiq.* xviii. 7, 2; *War* ii. 9, 6).

Herodias' daughter Salome married Philip the tetrarch, son of Herod the Great. After his death she married her first cousin, Aristobulus, son of King Agrippa's brother Herod and great-great-grandson of Herod the Great (Jos. *Antiq.* xviii. 5, 4).

He·ro'di·on (hê-rō'dĭ-ŏn). A Christian at Rome whom Paul called his kinsman, and to whom he sent a salutation (Rom. 16:11).

Her'on. The rendering of Heb. *'ănāphāh* (Lev. 11:19, in marg. of R.V. ibis; Deut. 14:18). The bird so designated was held to be typical of a family, for it is followed by the words "after its kind." The heron family (*Ardeidae*) is placed under the *Grallatores* or Waders. The birds which it includes are generally of large size. They have a long bill, long bare legs adapted for wading, a large hind toe, and large wings, their flight, however, being comparatively slow. Their food is principally fish and reptiles. The buff-backed heron (*Ardea bubulcus*), often called the white ibis, is the most abundant. These birds live and breed in vast numbers in the swamps of Lake Ḥūleh, and they associate with cattle in the pastures, where several purple ibises may usually be seen with them. The common heron (*Ardea cinerea*) occurs on the Jordan and its lakes, on the Kishon, and on the seacoast of Palestine. With it are found also the purple heron (*Ardea purpurea*) and several egrets.

He'sed (hē'sĕd) [mercy, grace]. Father of Ben-hesed, one of Solomon's purveyors (I Kings 4:10).

Hesh'bon (hĕsh'bŏn) [reckoning, account]. The city of Sihon, the Amorite king, but apparently taken originally from the Moabites (Num. 21:25–30, 34). It was assigned by Moses to the Reubenites, and after the conquest was rebuilt by the men of that tribe (Num. 32:37; Josh. 13:17). But it stood on the boundary line between Reuben and Gad (Josh. 13:26), came to be possessed by the latter, and was assigned as a town of Gad to the Levites (Josh. 21:39; I Chron. 6:81). The Moabites held it in Isaiah's and Jeremiah's times (Isa. 15:4; 16:8, 9; Jer. 48:2, 33, 34). Later still it was in the possession of Alexander Jannaeus and Herod the Great (Jos. *Antiq.* xiii. 15, 4; xv. 8, 5). It is still known as Ḥesbân, a ruined city standing on an isolated hill, between the Arnon and the Jabbok, about 7½ miles n. of Mādabā. A great reservoir, a little e. from the ruins of Heshbon, is probably one of the pools which were outside the town walls (S. of Sol. 7:4).

Hesh'mon (hĕsh'mŏn). A town in the extreme s. of Judah (Josh. 15:27).

Heth (hĕth). See CHETH and HITTITES.

Heth'lon (hĕth'lŏn). A place on the n. boundary of Palestine, as prophesied by Ezekiel, near the entering in of Hamath (Ezek. 47:15; 48:1; cf. Num. 34:8). It may be identified with Heitela, n.e. of Tripoli.

Hez'e·ki (hĕz'ē-kī). See HIZKI.

Hez·e·ki'ah (hĕz'ē-kī'à), in A.V. once **Hiz·ki'ah** (Zeph. 1:1), once **Hiz·ki'jah** (Neh. 10:17), in A.V. of N.T. **Ez·e·ki'as**, the Gr. form

241

[Jehovah has strengthened or is strength].
1. Son of Ahaz, king of Judah. He was associated with his father in the government in 728 B.C. Since Ahaz was incapacitated for active participation in the affairs of state, Hezekiah was made active ruler. Hezekiah is said to have begun to reign at the age of 25 (II Kings 18:2; II Chron. 29:1). He was a devoted servant of Jehovah and commenced his reign by repairing and cleansing the Temple, reorganizing its religious services and its officers, and celebrating a great passover, to which he invited not merely the 2 tribes, but the 10 (II Chron. 29:1 to 30:13). He removed the high places, cast down the images, and broke in pieces the brazen serpent which Moses had made, but which had become an object of idolatrous worship.

Hezekiah gained a victory over the Philistines and in other ways became great and prosperous. In his 4th regnal year, 724 B.C., Shalmaneser commenced, and in 722 B.C. Sargon completed, the siege of Samaria, carrying the 10 tribes into captivity (II Kings 18:9, 10). In 714 B.C., according to the method of reckoning already employed by the Hebrew annalist, began the series of Assyrian invasions which formed a marked feature of Hezekiah's reign and terminated disastrously for Assyria. The Biblical account of these events is presented as a connected narrative. It falls into 3 sections: the beginning of the invasions about 714 (II Kings 18:13; Isa. 36:1; probably II Chron. 32:1-8; cf. invasion of Philistia in 712-711, Isa. 20:1); the main campaign of 701, in its 1st stage (II Kings 18:14-16), and in its final stage (II Kings 18:17 to 19: 35; II Chron. 32:9-21; Isa. 36:2 to 37:36); and the end of the troubler in 681 (II Kings 19:36, 37; Isa. 37:37, 38). Sargon was still on the throne of Assyria in 714, but he had placed his son Sennacherib in high military position before that date, and Sennacherib may have led the troops of his father which in 720 or 715 and the beginning of 714, probably at the latter date, "subjugated Judah" according to the Assyrian account, when the main army of Assyria was waging war to the n. and e. of Assyria. Apparently immediately after the beginning of these invasions, in 714, Hezekiah was sick, probably from a carbuncle, and nigh unto death, but was granted a new lease of life for 15 years (II Kings 20:1-11; Isa., ch. 38). To inquire into the sign which Hezekiah received at this time was the ostensible object of an embassy from Merodach-baladan, king of Babylon. The real object was to persuade Judah's king to join the great confederacy which was being secretly formed against the Assyrian power. Hezekiah was quite elated by the coming of the Babylonian ambassadors and displayed to them his financial resources; but the Prophet Isaiah warned him that the people of Judah would be carried captive to that same place from which the ambassadors had come (II Kings 20:12-19; II Chron. 32:31; Isa., ch. 39). Hezekiah joined the confederacy. Sargon, who was an able general, broke in upon the allies before their plans were matured. His expedition against Ashdod, conducted by his tartan (Isa. 20:1), took place in 712 and was occasioned by the refusal of Philistia, Judah, Edom, and Moab to pay tribute. In 710 he dethroned Merodach-baladan and made himself king of Babylonia.

In 705 Sargon was murdered and his son Sennacherib ascended the Assyrian throne. This change of rulers was the signal for new uprisings. To quell revolt in the w., Sennacherib advanced as far as the country of the Philistines in 701, conquering Phoenicia on the way and receiving envoys from Ashdod, Ammon, Moab, and Edom, suing for peace. Many towns still held out, and Sennacherib

proceeded against Joppa, Beth-dagon, Ashkelon, and other places. Turning e., he captured Lachish, pitching his camp there and receiving tribute from the terrified Hezekiah. This tribute consisted of 30 talents of gold, 300 or, according to the Assyrian scribe who perhaps computes by a lighter standard, 800 talents of silver. Besides this, according to the Assyrian report, were precious stones, costly woods, articles of ivory, daughters of Hezekiah, women of the palace, and others. To obtain the precious metals, Hezekiah stripped the doors and pillars of the Temple of their plating. News, however, reached Sennacherib while still at Lachish of an alliance between the Philistine towns and Egypt and Ethiopia (II Kings 18:21, 24), and, unwilling to have so strong a fortress as Jerusalem in his rear, he sent a detachment from his army to garrison the city. Hezekiah had heard of the advance of the southern army and of the sturdy resistance of Ekron to the Assyrians. His faith in Jehovah also revived under the exhortations of Isaiah, and he refused to admit the Assyrian troops into the city. In the meantime the Assyrian king had broken camp at Lachish and fallen back on Libnah (II Kings 19:8). Hearing of Hezekiah's new attitude of defiance, he dispatched messengers with threatening letters to him, vowing future vengeance; and, not daring to meet the Egyptians and Ethiopians while Ekron and Jerusalem were in his rear, he retreated to Eltekeh, where a battle took place. The Egyptians were repulsed, but the spoils of victory were inconsiderable. Sennacherib now turned his attention to the hostile towns in the vicinity. His devastation and his advance toward Jerusalem were only terminated by the sudden plague which smote his army, whereby in one night 185,000 of his warriors perished (II Kings 19:35, 36). See SENNACHERIB.

Besides Isaiah, Hosea and Micah were contemporaries of Hezekiah (Hos. 1:1; Mic. 1:1). The king died about 693 B.C., leaving his son Manasseh to ascend the throne (II Kings 20: 21; II Chron. 32:33).

2. An ancestor of the Prophet Zephaniah (Zeph. 1:1; in A.V. Hizkiah).

3. A son of Neariah, akin to the royal family of Judah (I Chron. 3:23, A.V.; in R.V. Hizkiah).

4. A man some of whose descendants through Ater returned with Zerubbabel (Ezra 2:16; Neh. 7:21). Probably it was the representative of his family who signed the covenant under Nehemiah's rule (Neh. 10:17; in A.V. Hizkijah).

He′zi·on (hē′zĭ-ŏn) [vision]. Father of Tabrimmon and grandfather of Ben-hadad, king of Syria (I Kings 15:18).

He′zir (hē′zẽr) [swine, boar]. 1. A descendant of Aaron. His family had grown to a father's house in the time of David and became the 17th course of the priests (I Chron. 24:15).

2. A chief of the people who with Nehemiah sealed the covenant (Neh. 10:20).

Hez′ra·i (hĕz′rá-ī). A Carmelite, one of David's mighty men (II Sam. 23:35, A.V.; Hezro, R.V.); here A.V. follows the kere. The difference is due to a scribal confusion of yodh (y) and waw [vav] (w). In I Chron. 11:37 both A.V. and R.V. have Hezro.

Hez′ro (hĕz′rō). See HEZRAI.

Hez′ron (hĕz′rŏn), in A.V. of N.T. **Es′rom** (Matt. 1:3), which follows the Gr. [enclosure]. 1. A place on the s. boundary of Judah, not far from Zin and Kadesh-barnea (Josh. 15:3; Num. 34:4). It was very near Addar, if not the same site. Probably to be located at Khirbet el-Ḳedeirāt on a wadi bearing the same name. It was a station between Jerusalem and Ezion-geber. For Kerioth-hezron (Josh. 15:25, R.V.), see Hazor 3.

2. A son of Reuben, and founder of the Hezronite family (Gen. 46:9; Ex. 6:14; Num. 26:6; I Chron. 5:3).

3. Son of Perez, of the tribe of Judah, and founder of a tribal family (Gen. 46:12; Num. 26:21; Ruth 4:18; I Chron. 2:5).

Hid'da·i (hĭd'á-ī) [cf. Heb. *hôd*, splendor, majesty]. A man from the brooks of Gaash. He was one of David's heroes (II Sam. 23:30). Called in I Chron. 11:32, Hurai, probably by confusion of *resh* (r) for *daleth* (d).

Hid'de·kel (hĭd'ê-kĕl) [Heb. *Ḥiddekel*, Akkad. *Idiḳlat*, Sumerian *Idigna*; Old Pers. *Tigrā*, Gr. *Tigris*]. The river Tigris (Gen. 2:14; Dan. 10:4). It is called *Dijlah* in modern Arabic. Its principal sources in central Armenia spring from the s. slope of Anti-Taurus. The w. source flows by Diarbekr, winding for above 150 miles. The 2 e. sources, known as Bitlis Chai and Bohtan Chai, rise s. of Lake Van, and are about 100 miles long. After the junction of these streams the river proceeds nearly e.s.e., through the Kurdistan Mountains, gradually increased by various affluents, especially the greater and lesser Zab and the Diyalah from the e. side, with smaller feeders from the w. side, finally joining the Euphrates. In antiquity it emptied through its own mouth into the Persian Gulf. In its course it passes the ruins of Nineveh, which lie on the left or e. bank, nearly opposite Mosul on its right side. Lower down it separates Bagdad into 2 portions; and afterward passes the ruins, first of Ctesiphon, the Parthian capital, and then those of Seleucia, which, under the Greek dynasty, became the rival of Babylon. The whole course of the Tigris to the junction with the Euphrates is 1,146 miles, only a little more than half the length of the sister stream.

Hi'el (hī'ĕl) [probably, God liveth]. A native of Beth-el, who, in Ahab's reign, fortified Jericho, bringing down on himself the fulfillment of Joshua's imprecation. His eldest son died, perhaps was sacrificed, when the foundation of the city was laid, and his youngest son when the gates were set up (I Kings 16:34; Josh. 6:26).

Hi'er·ap'o·lis (hī'ĕr-ăp'ó-lĭs) [Gr., sacred city]. A city in Asia Minor, in the valley of the Lycos near the confluence with the Meander. Not far distant were Colossae and Laod-

icea (Col. 4:13). It was a seat of worship of the Syrian goddess Atargatis, and was celebrated for its warm baths.

Hig·ga'ion (hĭ-gā'yŏn) [a deep sound; meditation]. A musical term occurring in Ps. 9:16. The word is used elsewhere in the sense of solemn sound, meditation (Ps. 19:14; 92:3; Lam. 3:63).

High Pla'ces. Localities selected as shrines for the worship of God or of false divinities, or the shrines themselves. They were established on lofty heights (Num. 22:41; I Kings 11:7; 14:23), within or near towns (II Kings 17:9; 23:5, 8), and even in valleys (Jer. 7:31; cf. Ezek. 6:3). The Canaanites possessed them, and the Israelites were strictly enjoined to destroy them when they entered Canaan (Num. 33:52; Deut. 33:29). The Moabites also had high places (Num. 21:28; 22:41; Josh. 13:17, see the name Bamoth-baal; Isa. 15:2; Jer. 48:35). Licentiousness was often connected with the worship on the high places (Hos. 4:11–14), and immorality was common on the way to those shrines (Jer. 3:2; cf. II Chron. 21:11).

A suitable area, of a size determined by circumstances, was prepared by leveling the ground. On it stood an altar (I Kings 12:32), which, as at Petra, might be a part of the living rock left standing, with steps to approach it, when the spot was leveled. Near the altar was a wooden Asherah; and not far off was a pillar or a row of pillars, consisting of unhewn stones, 6 feet or more in length, set on end, as at Gezer and Petra (I Kings 14:23; Jer. 17:2; see Asherah and Pillar). Houses were often connected with these sanctuaries (I Kings 12:31; II Kings 23:19), for sheltering the idol (II Kings 17:29, 32), and presumably for other purposes also. Benches around the sides of the area or a chamber afforded a place for the worshipers to sit and partake of the sacrificial feast (I Sam. 9:12, 13, 22). Priests were attached to the high place (I Kings 12:32; II Kings 17:32), who burned incense and offered sacrifice (I Kings 13:2; cf. chs. 3:3; 11:8).

At times the worship of Jehovah was conducted by the Israelites on high places; but this was forbidden by law, which insisted upon one altar for all Israel. The purpose of this law was to foster the national spirit and guard against schism, to prevent the people from worshiping at idolatrous shrines and losing or corrupting the religion of Jehovah, and to secure the support of a national sanctuary

The Great High Place at Petra

which would enable the worship of Jehovah to be conducted on a scale of magnificence commensurate with his glory and equal, if not superior, to the pomp displayed at the heathen temples. The worship of Jehovah at other altars was legitimate only during the time that the national sanctuary had temporarily ceased, during the period when Jehovah had forsaken Shiloh and the Temple was not yet erected (Ps. 78:60, 61, 67–69; I Kings 3:2, 4; II Chron. 1:3). Altars and sacrifices elsewhere than at Jerusalem were also legitimate in the Northern Kingdom when the pious were precluded from attendance at Jerusalem, and could not worship Jehovah at all, unless according to the earlier custom (I Kings 18:30–32; see ALTAR. Solomon, sinfully complying with the wishes of his heathen wives, erected high places in the mount of corruption for Ashtoreth, Chemosh, and Milcom or Molech (II Kings 23:13). Jeroboam, to counteract the influence of the national sanctuary at Jerusalem, made a house of high places at Beth-el and ordained priests (I Kings 12:31, 32; 13:33), purposing the adoration of Jehovah, but by idolatrous symbols (chs. 12:28–33; 13:2). These places were denounced by the prophets (I Kings 13:1, 2; Hos. 10:8). Schismatic high places existed not merely at Beth-el, but also at other cities in Samaria (I Kings 13:32; II Kings 17:32; II Chron. 34:3). The action of Asa and Jehoshaphat in the Kingdom of Judah with regard to high places was ineffective (I Kings 15:14; 22:43; II Chron. 14:3; 15:17; 17:6). Jehoram, Jehoshaphat's son, made high places in the mountains of Judah (II Chron. 21:11). So did Ahaz, and that too for the worship of false divinities, where he sacrificed and burned incense (ch. 28:4, 25). Hezekiah broke them down (II Kings 18:4, 22), but they were re-erected by Manasseh (II Kings 21:3; II Chron. 33:3), and again removed by Josiah (II Kings 23:5, 8, 13). The high places were denounced by the prophets (Ezek. 6:3), and emphasis was laid on the fact that Zion was Jehovah's dwelling place, his sanctuary and holy mountain (Isa. 2:2, 3; 8:18; 18:7; 33:20; Joel 2:1; 3:17, 21; Amos 1:2; Micah 4:1, 2).

High Priest. The supreme pontiff and the representative of the nation before Jehovah. Aaron was appointed to this office after the establishment of the covenant at Sinai and after the erection of the tabernacle had been authorized (Ex. 27:21; ch. 28). The reference in Ex. 16:33, 34, where Moses bids Aaron lay up a pot of manna before the Lord, is not an anticipation of this call; for the command was probably issued by Moses at a later time, at least it was obeyed by Aaron at a later time, and is recorded here because the entire story of the manna is related here (vs. 31–35). The first hint that it was important for the sons of Aaron to be admitted to the privilege enjoyed by the elders of Israel was given after the covenant had been proclaimed (Ex. 24:1, 9). The distinction accorded them, however, did not suggest the national priesthood to them. Aaron was not the priest of the nation at this time; he was the prophet of Moses. The addition of his sons to the commission appointed to witness a manifestation of God's glory might suggest that Aaron's present office was to be inherited by his sons. At any rate it foreshadowed their call to future work. The legal head of the house of Aaron held the office of high priest; and the succession was probably determined by primogeniture, unless legal disabilities interfered (Lev. 21:16–23). Political considerations, also, not infrequently played a part in his selection (I Kings 2:26, 27, 35). His age when he might assume office was 20, accord-

ing to tradition. Aristobulus, however, officiated when he was 17 (Jos. *Antiq.* xv. 3, 3). He must govern his conduct by special laws (Lev. 21:1–15). His duties were the oversight of the sanctuary, its service, and its treasure (II Kings 12:7 *seq.*; 22:4); the performance of the service on the Day of Atonement, when he was obliged to enter the Holy of Holies; and the consultation of God by Urim and Thummim. Besides these distinguishing duties, he was qualified to discharge any priestly function; and it was customary for him to offer sacrifices on Sabbaths, new moons, and annual festivals (Jos. *War* v. 5, 7). He presided also over the sanhedrin when religious questions were before that body (Matt. 26:57; Acts 5:21). His official garments, besides the raiment of white linen which he wore in common with other priests (see PRIEST), were: 1. Breastplate: square, made of gold, and blue, purple, scarlet, and

A Jewish High Priest

fine twisted linen, set with 4 rows of precious stones, 3 in a row, each inscribed with the name of a tribe. Within the breastplate were the Urim and Thummim (*q.v.*). 2. Ephod: an embroidered vestment of the same rich materials as the breastplate. It was intended for the front and back of the body, and was made in 2 parts clasped together at the shoulder by onyx stones. Each stone bore the names of 6 tribes. The ephod carried on its front the breastplate, and was bound about the waist by a girdle of gold, blue, purple, scarlet, and fine twisted linen. 3. Robe of the ephod: which was longer than the ephod, and worn underneath it, entirely blue, sleeveless, and adorned below with a fringe of alternate pomegranates and golden bells; see BELL. 4. Miter: a cap or turban, made of linen and surmounted, in later times at least, by another of blue, and this in turn by a triple crown of gold. A gold plate, bearing the inscription "Holiness to Jehovah," was fastened to the front by a blue ribbon (Ex., ch. 28: Ecclus. 45:8–13; Jos. *Antiq.* iii. 7, 1–6; cf. I Macc. 10:20).

The high priest wore this official garb when discharging his peculiar duties, except that on the Day of Atonement he laid it aside while he entered the Holy of Holies to make atonement for the priesthood and the sanctuary. The mode of consecration is described in Ex., ch. 29. Among other ceremonies the sacred oil was poured upon his head (Ex. 29:7; Lev. 8:12; Ps. 133:2), and hence by way of distinction he is designated the anointed priest (Lev. 4:3, 5, 16; 21:10; Num. 35:25). There is some uncertainty concerning the difference of consecrating the high priests and the common priests (Ex. 29:21; Lev. 8:30); but rabbinical tradition makes the distinction consist in the quantity of oil used. It was poured abundantly on the head of the high priest and sparingly upon the heads of the ordinary priests. At first the high priesthood was for life, but Herod, and afterward the Romans, jealous of the power which a life tenure of the office gave to the high priest, made and unmade the pontiffs at will. Jesus is the High Priest of our profession, of whom the Jewish dignitary of the same designation was only the type (Heb. 3:1-3; 8:1-6; 9:24-28). For the chief priests of the N.T., see PRIEST, end of the article.

THE LINE OF THE HIGH PRIESTS

I. *From the establishment of the Aaronic priesthood to the Exile.* The Biblical catalogues are 2 (I Chron. 6:1-15; Ezra 7:1-5), each of which omits links of the genealogy, as is quite usual in Hebrew genealogical tables.

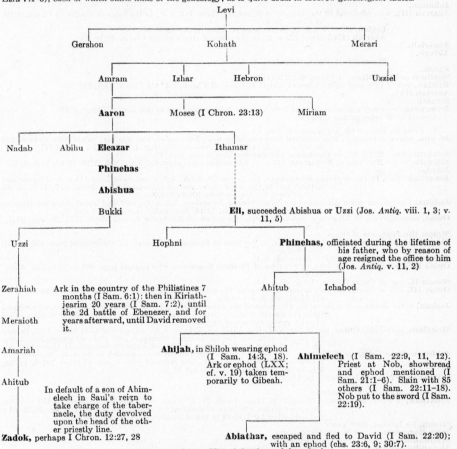

245

THE LINE OF THE HIGH PRIESTS — *Continued*

Zadok is loyal to David (I Kings 1:8).   Abiathar favors Adonijah (I Kings 1:7).
                    Zadok and Ahimelech, son of Abiathar, superin-
                    tend the division of the priests into courses (I
                    Chron. 24:3, 6, 31). They do this as the active
                    heads of their respective fathers' houses. In conse-
                    quence of a 2d conspiracy in favor of Adonijah,
                    made after Solomon had ascended the throne,
Zadok is put into the place of Abiathar (I Kings 2:26, 35).
                    By the deposition of Abiathar, the house of Eli
                    falls (I Kings 2:27), and
Zadok is sole high priest.
Ahimaaz.
Azariah (I).
          Amariah, chief priest in the reign of Jehoshaphat, about 853 B. C. (II Chron. 19:11).
          Jehoiada, in the reigns of Athaliah and Joash, dying in the reign of Joash at the age of 130 years
                    (II Kings 11:4–19; 12:2; II Chron. 22:10 *seq.*; 24:15).
          Zechariah, son of Jehoiada, perhaps high priest, slain by Joash between 819 and 805 B. C. (II
                    Chron. 24:20, 22).
Johanan.
Azariah (II), who officiated in the Temple at Jerusalem about 750 B. C., in the reign of Uzziah (I Chron. 6:10;
          II Chron. 26:17).
          Urijah, about 732 B. C., in the reign of Ahaz (II Kings 16:10).
          Azariah (III), about 727 B. C., in the reign of Hezekiah (II Chron. 31:10, 13).
Amariah.
Ahitub.
          Meraioth (I Chron. 9:11; Neh. 11:11).
Zadok.
Shallum or **Meshullam** (I Chron. 6:12; 9:11).
Hilkiah, in the 18th year of the reign of Josiah, 621 B. C. (I Chron. 9:11; II Chron. 34:8, 9).
Azariah (IV).
Seraiah.
Jehozadak, who was carried captive to Babylonia by Nebuchadnezzar in 586 B. C. (I Chron. 6:15).
          Interval of 50 years during the Exile.

II. *From the Exile to the Maccabaean priests.*
Jeshua, son of Jehozadak, who returned from captivity with Zerubbabel, and was high priest from at least 538
          to 520 B. C. (Ezra 2:2; 3:2; Neh. 12:10; Hag. 1:1; Zech. 1:7; 3:1; 6:11).
Joiakim (Neh. 12:10, 12), in the days of [Arta]xerxes (Jos. *Antiq.* xi:5, 1).
Eliasib, in the 20th year of Artaxerxes, 445 B. C., and still in office after 433 B. C. (Neh. 3:20; 12:10; 13:4, 6, 7).
Joiada.
Jonathan (Neh. 12:11), or rather Johanan (vs. 22, 23), in Gr. John, high priest, as early as 411 B. C. (Elephantine
          papyri) and in the reign of Artaxerxes [Mnemon] (Jos. *Antiq.* xi. 7, 1; cf. 5, 4),
          who occupied the throne from 404 to 359/8 B. C.
Jaddua, high priest when Alexander the Great visited Jerusalem, 332 B. C., and died about the same time as
          Alexander, 323 B. C. (Neh. 12:11; Jos. *Antiq.* xi. 8, 4 and 5 and 7).
Onias, contemporary of Arius, who was king of Sparta from about 309 to 265 B. C. (I Macc. 12:7, 20; Jos. *Antiq.*
          xi. 8, 7).
Simon the Just, son of Onias.
Eleazar, son of Onias and brother of Simon, in the time of Ptolemy Philadelphus, who reigned from 285 to 246
          (Jos. *Antiq.* xii. 2, 5).
Manasseh, uncle of Eleazar (Jos. *Antiq.* xii. 4, 1).
Onias II, son of Simon the Just, in the time of Ptolemy Euergetes, who reigned from 246 to 221 (Jos. *Antiq.*
          xii. 4, 1).
Simon II, son of Onias II (Jos. *Antiq.* xii. 4, 10).
Onias III, son of Simon II, in the time of Seleucus IV, called Philopator, who reigned from 187 to 175 B. C.
          (II Macc., ch. 3; Jos. *Antiq.* xii. 4, 10).
Joshua, in Gr. **Jesus**, son of Simon II, who assumed the name **Jason**, induced Antiochus Epiphanes, who reigned
          from 175 to 163 B. C., to depose Onias (II Macc. 4:7–26). After holding office
          about 3 years, Jason was supplanted, about 171 B. C., by
Menelaus, called also **Onias**, son of Simon II (Jos. *Antiq.* xii. 5, 1; xv. 3, 1). According to II Macc. 4:23, he was
          the brother of Simon the Benjamite. Menelaus held office 10 years (Jos. *Antiq.*
          xii. 9, 7), and was put to death in the time of Judas Maccabaeus (II Macc. 13:1–8).
Jakim, with the Gr. name of **Alcimus**, who was not of the high priestly line, although of the stock of Aaron, put
          in office by Demetrius, 161 B. C., and retained office 3 years (I Macc. 7:5–9, 12–25;
          9:1, 54–56; Jos. *Antiq.* xii. 9, 7; xx. 10, 1).
          Vacancy of 7 years (Jos. *Antiq.* xx. 10, 1).

III. *The Maccabaean priest-kings.*
Jonathan, of the priestly family of Joarib (I Macc. 10:20, 21; I Chron. 24:7), made high priest in 152 B. C. by
          Alexander Balas, who was contending for the Syrian throne (I Macc. 10:18–21),
          and held office for 7 years in round numbers (Jos. *Antiq.* xx. 10, 1).
Simon, his brother, for 8 years.
John Hyrcanus, son of Simon, for 30 years.
Aristobulus, son of Hyrcanus, for 1 year.
Alexander Jannaeus, son of Hyrcanus, for 27 years.
Hyrcanus II, son of Alexander, for 9 years.
Aristobulus, son of Alexander, for 3 years, 3 months.
Hyrcanus II, a 2d time, for 24 years, from 63 B. C.
Antigonus, son of Aristobulus, for 3 years, 3 months, until Herod the Great took possession of Jerusalem in 37
          B. C. (Jos. *Antiq.* xiv. 16, 4; xx. 10, 1).

IV. *From the accession of Herod the Great until Jerusalem was taken by Titus.* During this period there were 28
high priests (Jos. *Antiq.* xx. 10, 1), one being generally removed to make way for his successor.
Appointed by Herod the Great, king from 37 to 4 B. C.:
          Hananel, in Latinized Gr. **Ananelus** (Jos. *Antiq.* xv. 2, 4).
          Aristobulus, grandson of Hyrcanus, for 1 year, about 35 B. C. (Jos. *Antiq.* xv. 3, 1 and 3).
          Hananel, a 2d time (Jos. *Antiq.* xv. 3, 3).
          Jesus, son of Phabet (Jos. *Antiq.* xv. 9, 3).
          Simon, son of Boethus (Jos. *Antiq.* xv. 9, 3), from about 24 to 5 B. C.
          Matthias, son of Theophilus and son-in-law of Boethus (Jos. *Antiq.* xvii. 4, 2) [**Joseph**, son of
                    Ellemus, high priest for 1 day as his assistant (Jos. *Antiq.* xvii. 6, 4)].
          Joazar, son of Boethus (Jos. *Antiq.* xvii. 6, 4; 13, 1).

THE LINE OF THE HIGH PRIESTS — *Continued*

Appointed by Archelaus, who ruled from 4 B. C. to A. D. 6:
    Eleazar, son of Boethus, who did not abide long in office (Jos. *Antiq.* xvii. 13, 1).
    Jesus, son of Sie (Jos. *Antiq.* xvii. 13, 1).
Appointed by Quirinius, president of Syria:
    Annas, or Ananus, son of Seth, who obtained the office in A. D. 6 or 7, Joazar, whom the multitude had made high priest, being put down (Jos. *Antiq.* xviii. 2, 1; cf. 1, 1).
Appointed by Valerius Gratus, procurator of Judea A. D. 14–25:
    Ismael, son of Phabi, who held office but a short time (Jos. *Antiq.* xviii. 2, 2).
    Eleazar, son of Annas, for 1 year (Jos. *Antiq.* xviii. 2, 2).
    Simon, son of Camithus, for 1 year (Jos. *Antiq.* xviii. 2, 2).
    Joseph Caiaphas, son-in-law to Annas, from about A. D. 18 to 36 (John 18: 13; Jos. *Antiq.* xviii. 4, 3).
Appointed by Vitellius, president of Syria:
    Jonathan, son of Annas, in A. D. 36 (Jos. *Antiq.* xviii. 4, 3; cf. xix. 6, 4; xx. 8, 5).
    Theopailus, son of Annas, in A. D. 37 (Jos. *Antiq.* xviii. 5, 3).
Appointed by King Herod Agrippa I, who reigned from A. D. 41 to 44:
    Simon Cantheras, son of Boethus (Jos. *Antiq.* xix. 6, 2).
    Mattuias, son of Annas (Jos. *Antiq.* xix. 6, 4).
    Elionaeus, son of Cantheras (Jos. *Antiq.* xix. 8, 1).
Appointed by Herod, king of Chalcis, who died in A. D. 48:
    Joseph, son of Camydus (Jos. *Antiq.* xx. 1, 3).
    Ananias, son of Nedebaeus (Jos. *Antiq.* xx. 5, 2), sent in bonds to Rome during the procuratorship of Cumanus, but acquitted and still in office in A. D. 57, 2 years before Felix was succeeded by Festus (Acts 23:2; 24:1, 27).
Appointed by King Agrippa II:
    Ismael, son of Phabi (Jos. *Antiq.* xx. 8, 8), about A. D. 59, who went to Rome and was detained there as hostage (Jos. *Antiq.* xx. 8, 11).
    Joseph, called **Cabi,** son of the former high priest Simon (Jos. *Antiq.* xx. 8, 11).
    Annas, son of Annas, for 3 months in A. D. 62 (Jos. *Antiq.* xx. 9, 1).
    Jesus, son of Damnaeus (Jos. *Antiq.* xx. 9, 1).
    Jesus, son of Gamaliel (Jos. *Antiq.* xx. 9, 4; cf. *War* iv. 5, 2).
    Mattnias, son of Theophilus, appointed about A. D. 64 (Jos. *Antiq.* xx. 9, 7).
Made high priest by the people during the war:
    Phanas, or Phannias, son of Samuel (Jos. *War* iv. 3, 8; cf. *Antiq.* xx. 10, end).

Hi'len (hī'lĕn). See HOLON 1.

Hil·ki'ah (hĭl-kī'á) [Jehovah is the portion (cf. Ps. 16:5)]. 1. A Levite, son of Amzi, descended from Merari (I Chron. 6:45, 46).

2. Another Merarite Levite, son of Hosah (I Chron. 26:11).

3. Father of Eliakim, who was over the household in Hezekiah's reign (II Kings 18: 18, 26; Isa. 22:20; 36:3).

4. A priest, father of Jeremiah (Jer. 1:1).

5. Father of Jeremiah's contemporary Gemariah (Jer. 29:3).

6. The high priest contemporary with Josiah, who aided the king in his reformation of religion and found the Book of the Law (II Kings 22:4–14; 23:4; I Chron. 6:13; II Chron. 34:9–22). See JOSIAH 1.

7. A chief of the priests who returned from Babylon with Zerubbabel (Neh. 12:7). In the next generation a father's house bore this name (v. 21).

8. One of those who stood by Ezra when he read the Law to the people (Neh. 8:4).

Hill. The name is generally applied to a natural eminence smaller than a mountain and larger than a mound; but the terms are relative, the same height being sometimes known by both names (Isa. 31:4), or called a mountain in one locality and a hill in another (Rev. 17:9). Hill is chiefly the rendering of Heb. *gib'āh* and Gr. *bounos*. Not infrequently it is also employed in the A.V., and much less frequently in the R.V. (Ps. 2:6; 3:4; 15:1; 24:3; 42:6; Matt. 5:14; Luke 4:29), to translate Heb. *hār* and Gr. *oros*, which are usually rendered mountain.

Hil'lel (hĭl'ĕl) [he has praised]. Father of Abdon the judge (Judg. 12:13, 15).

Hin. A Hebrew liquid measure, containing in early times 1.62 gallons, later 1.78 gallons, U. S. wine measure (Ex. 29:40; Jos. *Antiq.* iii. 8, 3). See MEASURE, III.

Hind. A female stag, in Heb. *'ayyālāh* (Gen. 49:21; Job 39:1; Ps. 18:33; Prov. 5: 19; S. of Sol. 2:7; Jer. 14:5). See HART.

Hinge. In ancient times in the East heavy doors turned on pivots, which were constructed on the upper and lower corners of one side and inserted in sockets. The socket is probably more especially referred to in I Kings 7:50. See also Prov. 26:14.

Hin'nom (hĭn'ŏm), **Val'ley of**; known also as the valley of the son of Hinnom or of the children of Hinnom. A valley at Jerusalem, near the gate of potsherds (Jer. 19:2, R.V. marg.; not east gate as in A.V.). The boundary between Judah and Benjamin passed from En-rogel by the valley of the son of Hinnom to the s. side of Jerusalem, and thence to the top of the mountain which faces the valley of Hinnom from the w., and is at the outermost part of the vale of Rephaim (Josh. 15:8; 18:16). If the term "shoulder of the Jebusite (the same is Jerusalem)" includes the hill on the w. of the Tyropoeon Valley, and not merely the Temple hill; in other words, if the term denotes the plateau which juts out s. between the great encircling wadies, and which was not only crowned by the citadel of the Jebusites, but also occupied by their dwellings without the walls and by their fields, then the description in The Book of Joshua identifies the valley of Hinnom with at least the lower part of the valley which bounds Jerusalem on the s., and is now known as the wadi er-Rabābi, near its junction with the ravine of the Kidron. At the high place of Tophet, in the valley of Hinnom, parents made their children pass through the fire to Molech. Ahaz and Manasseh were guilty of this abomination (II Chron. 28:3; 33:6). Jeremiah foretold that God would visit this awful wickedness with sore judgment, and would cause such a destruction of the people that the valley would become known as the valley of slaughter (Jer. 7:31–34; 19:2, 6; 32:35). Josiah defiled the high place to render it unfit for even idolatrous rites and thus to stop the sacrifices (II Kings 23:10). From the horrors of its fires, and from its pollution by Josiah, perhaps also because offal was burnt there, the valley became a type of sin and woe, and the Heb. name *Gē ben-Hinnōm* (*Gē-Hinnōm*), corrupted into Gehenna, passed into use as a designation for the place of eternal punishment.

Hip·po·pot'a·mus [Gr., river horse]. See BEHEMOTH.

Hi'rah (hī'rá) [cf. Arab. *ḥīr*, nobility]. An Adullamite, a friend of Judah (Gen. 38:1, 12).

Hi′ram (hī′răm) ; in Chronicles **Hu′ram**, except in the Heb. text of II Chron. 4 :11b ; 9 :10, where the kere has *ŭ*, and the kethib *î*. In Heb. the name is also written Hirom (I Kings 5 :10, 18 ; 7 :40, R.V. marg.) [probably for *'ăḥirăm* (Heb. and Phoenician), the Brother is exalted]. 1. A king of Tyre. According to the citation which Josephus makes from the Phoenician historian Dios, and from the Tyrian annals which Menander translated, Hiram succeeded his father Abibaal, reigned 34 years, and died at the age of 53 (Jos. *Antiq.* viii. 5, 3 ; *Apion* i. 17, 18). He enlarged the city of Tyre by constructing an embankment on the e. side, built a causeway to connect the city with the island on which the temple of Jupiter or Baal-samem stood, dedicated a golden pillar in this temple, rebuilt old sanctuaries, roofing them with cedars cut on Lebanon, and erected temples to Hercules and Astarte. He was a friend of both David and Solomon (I Kings 5 :1 ; II Chron. 2 :3). Sometime after David had captured the stronghold of Zion, Hiram sent an embassy to him ; and, when David desired a palace, Hiram furnished the cedar timber and the masons and carpenters (II Sam. 5 :11). This was evidently before the birth of Solomon (II Sam. 7 :2, 12 ; 11 :2). When Solomon ascended the throne, Hiram sent congratulations. For a consideration he furnished cedar and fir for building the Temple, and skilled workmen to assist in preparing the timber and stone (I Kings 5 :1– 12 ; II Chron. 2 :3–16). He also advanced 120 talents of gold (I Kings 9 :14), and joined Solomon in sending to Ophir for the precious metal (I Kings 9 :26–28 ; II Chron. 9 :21). In partial payment for his contributions, he was offered 20 towns in Galilee, which however he refused (I Kings 9 :10–12 ; II Chron. 8 :1, 2) ; see CABUL 2. The chronological statements of Josephus and the Bible have never been reconciled. Josephus' statement that the Temple was begun in Hiram's 11th year (Jos. *Antiq.* viii. 3, 1) or 12th (Jos. *Apion* i. 18) need not receive serious consideration ; for it is probably a calculation of his own and not a citation from the archives. Either the 34 years assigned as the duration of Hiram's reign or the text of I Kings 9 :9–12 may be corrupt. The passage in Kings is parallel to II Chron. 8 :1, and this latter passage does not require the assumption that Hiram lived to the end of the 20 years wherein the Temple and the royal palace were built.

2. An artificer, whose father was a Tyrian ; his mother was a widow of Naphtali (I Kings 7 :13, 14) but by birth a woman of Dan (II Chron. 2 :14). He extended the bronze or copper work in connection with Solomon's Temple, as the pillars, the laver, the basins, the shovels (I Kings 7 :13–46 ; II Chron. 2 :13, 14). The title father (II Chron. 2 :13 ; 4 :16) probably denotes a master workman or a counselor.

His′to•ry. Biblical history is the record of that series of events which form the basis for the religion of the Bible. It may be divided into 4 periods : I. An account of the creation of the universe, showing God's relation to the world, and introducing human history. II. A sketch of human history, showing God's relation to the human race, and introducing the history of the chosen people. III. The history of the chosen people, showing God's dealing with them and the preparation for the Advent of Christ. IV. The history of the establishment of the Christian Church, which is to reach all nations. Inter-Biblical history falls between sections III and IV.

I. *An account of the creation* of the universe, showing God's relation to the world, and introducing human history (Gen. 1 :1 to 2 :3). See CREATION and SABBATH. The great doctrine is that God is the Creator and Lord of all things. This account, which teaches monotheism, denies materialism and polytheism. In taking for granted that God is personal and omnipotent, it makes reasonable his supernatural manifestation in human history.

II. *A sketch of human history,* showing God's relation to the human race, and thus laying a foundation for introducing the history of the chosen people (Gen. 2 :4 to 11 :26). The events of this period fell almost entirely into the prehistoric period. The period is divided into 2 parts by the Flood. The narrative is symmetrical ; 10 generations before the Flood, from Adam to Noah inclusive, and 10 generations after the Flood, from Shem to Abraham inclusive (chs. 5 ; 11 :10–26). The postdiluvian period is divided into 2 parts at Peleg, in whose days the earth was divided. From Shem to Peleg inclusive are 5 generations, and from Reu to Abraham inclusive are 5. In the antediluvian period are detailed the covenant with Adam, its failure through man's disobedience, the downward course of man in sin, his punishment by a flood, and the deliverance of Noah. In the postdiluvian period are related the new and unconditioned covenant with Noah, the new command laid upon man, the increasing population, the growing independence of men from God, their punishment by confusion of speech and dispersion. The genealogy of the Sethitic-Semitic line to Abraham is recorded, and at the same time its common origin with the other families of the earth is made plain. The locality where the recorded events occurred was the basin of the Tigris and Euphrates Rivers ; at least, every definite geographical reference is to this region (chs. 2 :14 ; 8 :4 ; 10 :10 ; 11 :2, 28). From this center the people spread on all sides, especially toward the w. and s.w., where the course of migration was not blocked by great mountains (ch. 10). By the close of the period the inhabited world, so far as it was within the sphere of history, extended from the Caspian Sea, the mountains of Elam and the Persian Gulf on the e., w. to the isles of Greece and the opposite shore of Africa, and from the neighborhood of the Black Sea on the n. to the Arabian Sea on the s. The length of the period from Adam to Abraham was at the lowest calculation 1,946 years, but it must have been much longer ; see CHRONOLOGY, I. With the personal history of man began those theophanies, rare indeed though they were (Gen. 3 :8 *seq.*), which are important in the history of revelation. During this period man made progress in civilization. He had been created with capacity, and was commanded to subdue nature. He advanced from the unclothed state, passing beyond rude garments of leaves and afterward of skins (ch. 2 :25 ; 3 :7, 21) to woven clothing ; from a food of fruits that grew of itself to food obtained by agriculture and herding (chs. 1 :29 ; 4 :2) ; from uncertain abodes to movable tents, settled habitations (ch. 4 :17, 20), and large cities built of brick (ch. 11 :3, 4) ; from the family to the tribe and the kingdom (ch. 10 :10) ; from no implements to tools of metal and instruments of music (ch. 4 :21, 22). In this period also simple speech became diversified dialects and languages (chs. 10 :5 ; 11 :1, 6, 9). Man recognized the duty of walking before God in holiness of life (chs. 3 :2, 3, 10 ; 4 :7 ; 5 :22 ; 6 :9) ; distinguished between clean and unclean animals (chs. 7 :2 ; 8 :20) ; erected altars and worshiped God by bloody and bloodless offerings (chs. 4 :3, 4 ; 8 :20) ; and prayed to God in his character of Jehovah (ch. 4 :26). Religion, however, suffered decadence (ch. 6 :2, 5), and idolatry became widespread (Josh. 24 :2). See especially GENESIS, EDEN, ADAM 1, SATAN, SERPENT 1, ABEL, I, CAIN 1, ENOCH 3, FLOOD, NOAH, I, BABEL.

III. *The history of the chosen people,* showing God's dealing with them and the preparation for the Advent of Christ. This period differs from the preceding in the shifting of the central locality from the valley of the Tigris and Euphrates to Palestine. Canaan becomes the center of the history. The duration of the period, regarded as having begun with Abraham's birth, was reckoned by Ussher at 1,996 years, and so stands on the margin of many editions of the A.V. There are certainly errors in this calculation; but whether they equalize themselves, or whether the total length should be several centuries more or less, cannot be determined as yet from the Biblical and other data. At the beginning of this period, and on several occasions later, besides the ordinary ways in which God reveals himself to man and to the prophets, he appeared in theophanies. This period also embraces 3 of the 4 great miracle epochs; namely, at the deliverance of the people from Egypt and their establishment in Canaan under Moses and Joshua, during the mortal struggle between the worship of Jehovah and Baal worship in the time of Elijah and Elisha, and during the Babylonian Captivity. These miracle epochs were separated from each other by centuries during which there were, with extremely rare exceptions, no miracles. This period may conveniently be divided into sections according to the progressive stages in the outward development of the people of God.

III. 1. *An independent tribe in Canaan under Abraham, Isaac, and Jacob.* The patriarch was the priest and responsible ruler of the tribe. The history is reviewed in the articles on ABRAHAM, VISIONS, THEOPHANY, MELCHIZEDEK, ISAAC, JACOB.

III. 2. *A folk of 12 tribes for a long time in Egyptian bondage.* See EGYPT, III, JOSEPH 1, MIRACLE, EXODUS, MARAH, MANNA, QUAIL, REPHIDIM.

III. 3. *A nation, constituted at Sinai, and independent.* Led to Sinai the people became a nation by accepting the covenant which God proposed, and which was contained in ten commandments, and formed the constitution of the nation. Jehovah is king, who henceforth dwells in the tabernacle in the midst of his people, reveals his will to prophet and priest, and exercises the legislative, judicial, and executive offices through laws which he reveals, judgments which he pronounces, and officials whom he raises up. The nation was (a) *A brotherhood of 12 tribes under a religious constitution, and with a common sanctuary* (Ex., ch. 19 to I Sam., ch. 7). The high priest was the chief representative and was aided by prophets and occasional leaders, like Moses. See SINAI, THEOCRACY, TENT OF MEETING, TABERNACLE, LEVITES, LEVITICUS, CAMP.

Leaving Sinai the Israelites journeyed to Kadesh. On account of their lack of faith, they were turned back into the wilderness, where they sojourned 38 years; see NUMBERS, WILDERNESS OF THE WANDERING, KORAH 4. At length they encompassed the land of Edom and found a crossing at the head of the Arnon Valley. The conquest of the country e. of the Jordan followed; see SIHON, OG. The camp was then pitched in the Jordan Valley; see SHITTIM 1, BALAAM, BAAL-PEOR, MIDIAN 2, DEUTERONOMY. On the death of Moses, the Jordan was crossed and Canaan conquered and possessed; see JOSHUA 1, CANAAN, SHILOH. After the settlement of the Israelites in Canaan, Joshua died, and was succeeded at intervals by other persons of ability and influence, 15 in number, who led the people against their enemies and exercised governmental functions; see JUDGES, BOOK OF, SAMUEL. Unifying forces were at work during the times of the Judges, and a national feeling existed and sometimes manifested its strength;

but still the people too often allowed natural barriers and petty jealousies and local interests to separate them. There are bright examples of godliness and filial piety, but along with these is the spectacle of a people easily seduced to idolatry; see JUDGES, BOOK OF. During this entire period the weaknesses and defects of the human parties to the covenant were disclosed. At the very beginning of the period lack of faith in God was shown at Kadesh, the existence of tribal jealousy was manifested in the rebellion of Korah and his company against the high priesthood of Aaron and the political supremacy of Moses, and the readiness of the people to lapse into idolatry became apparent in the affair of the golden calf and in their ensnarement by the seductions of Baal-peor. The great political blunders of the period were the league made by Joshua with the Gibeonites, and the failure of Israel to occupy Jerusalem. These defects and blunders were of far-reaching consequence in the history of Israel.

(b) *A monarchy of 12 tribes.* The people had failed to foster the centralizing influences which their religion designedly provided, allowed senseless tribal jealousies to sunder them, and accustomed themselves to turn from God to idols. The threatening attitude of neighboring nations made them realize the need of organization, a strong government, and a military leader. Samuel was old. They turned away from the good provision which God had made, but which they had neglected, and demanded an earthly king. By the side of the high priest and the prophet there was now a permanent earthly ruler, with supreme political power, instead of the Judges whom God was wont to raise up. Saul was the first king, but on account of his overestimate of his position, his failure to recognize the superior functions of the high priest and prophet, he was denied the privilege of founding a dynasty; and finally his willful transgression of God's explicit command led to the rejection of him from being king, and to the withdrawal of God and God's prophet from him. David was then chosen; see SAMUEL, BOOKS OF, SAUL 2, DAVID. Under David the 12 tribes were reunited after 7 years of civil war, Jerusalem was taken from the Jebusites and made the political and religious capital, the borders of the kingdom were extended by conquest far to the n.e. of Damascus, and the acquired country was laid under tribute. Deputies were placed in Edom also. See JERUSALEM, III. 1; 2. David was succeeded by Solomon, under whom the Temple was erected, Jerusalem greatly embellished and its fortifications extended, and the fame of Israel enhanced. But his exactions made the people discontented, and on his death the failure of his son to discern the gravity of the situation incited 10 tribes to revolt from the house of David; thus Judah and Benjamin constituted the Southern Kingdom. See SOLOMON, REHOBOAM, ISRAEL 3.

(c) *A monarchy consisting chiefly of the tribe of Judah,* 10 tribes having revolted and formed a rival schismatic apostate kingdom. The causes which led to this revolt were long standing and many; see ISRAEL 3. The Kingdom of Judah possessed the greater strength. It had material strength: the stronger natural position, the capital, the organized government, and the worship to which the people were accustomed. It had moral strength: the consciousness of adhering to the legitimate line of kings, which has ever been a mighty force in history, the true religion with its elevating influence, the sense of loyalty to Jehovah, and a line of godlier kings. It had the providential care of God, who was preserving the knowledge and worship of himself among men and was preparing the way for his Messiah. The religious history of Judah during this period was marked by a decline in the days of Rehoboam (I Kings 14:22), and again in the days of his son Ab.jam (ch. 15:3), and yet again in the days of Jehoram and Ahaziah (II Kings 8:27). The cause of this religious deterioration was the corruption introduced by Solomon and intermarriage with idolaters. Rehoboam's mother was an Ammonites, for whom Solomon had built a high place to Milcom, and who had sacrificed to this abomination of her people. Jehoram was son-in-law of Ahab and Jezebel. Each of these periods of religious decay was followed by reformation, the 1st under King Asa and the 2d under Jehoash, but Jehoash himself afterward turned away from the Lord, and another religious revival became necessary, only to be followed by the dominance of idolatry later under the pernicious influence of Ahaz. The encroachments of the Assyrians on the Hebrew people began in this period. The divided nation, largely degenerate in religion, was not in condition to offer effective resistance; and by slow but steady advance, which began in the days of Ahab, the Assyrians pushed their conquest until they had overthrown the Northern Kingdom. See ISRAEL 3, SAMARIA, SARGON.

(d) *The monarchy of Judah sole survivor.* The Southern Kingdom was now exposed to the attacks of the Assyrians, and later of their successors, the Chaldeans (Babylonians); see HEZEKIAH 1, SENNACHERIB, MANASSEH 4, NEBUCHADNEZZAR. The religious condition also of the people was not good, although great prophets like Isaiah, Jeremiah, and Micah were laboring to advance the truth. Its kings, with the exception of Hezekiah and Josiah, did not render true and steadfast allegiance to Jehovah, and the people were like-minded. There was an idolatrous party in the state which had been triumphant in the reign of Ahaz. Idolatry was deep-rooted among the people, and the reforms of any king affected the nation only superficially. Foreign idolaters were also in the land. The nation drifted to destruction. The army of Nebuchadnezzar visited Jerusalem at brief intervals during the course of 2 decades, several deportations of Jews to Babylonia took place, and the city was taken and burned in 586 B.C. The Hebrew people had failed to conserve the elements of national strength, and to ab:de under the shadow of the Almighty, and they fell. See JUDAH 2.

III. 4. *A subject people.* (1) *Judah in the Babylonian Exile.* See CAPTIVITY, II.

(2) *Judah in Palestine.* In the 1st year of his reign over Babylon, 539–538 B.C., Cyrus issued an edict which permitted the Jews to re urn to Palestine and rebuild the Temple. Forty-three thousand embraced the opportunity and returned under Zerubbabel. This colony was

(a) *A province of the Persian empire, subordinated to the province Beyond-the-river.* It remained such for 200 years. Twice it enjoyed local governors of its own, appointed by the Persian monarch; see ZERUBBABEL and NEHEMIAH 3. But for the greater part of the time its civil affairs were subject to the jurisdiction of the Persian satrap beyond the river. He had authority to appoint a deputy for Judah and to call on the Jews for men or money. But the local administration was left to the high priest, and he gradually came to be regarded as the political as well as the religious head of the nation. Immediately on the Return of the exiles from Babylon the foundations of the Temple were laid. The work was pushed on under the exhortations of the prophets Haggai and Zechariah despite interruptions and opposition, and the building was completed in 515 B.C. The walls were erected under the supervision of Nehemiah by authority of Artaxerxes in 444 B.C.; see JERUSALEM, III. 2. At this time also Ezra the priest was in the city,

zealous for the Law of God, and successfully laboring for the purity of religion; see EZRA 3 and CANON. About 365 B.C. there was a dispute between 2 brothers about the high priesthood, which ended by one killing the other within the precincts of the Temple. In connection with this affair Bagoses, general of the army of Artaxerxes Mnemon, entered the Temple (Jos. *Antiq.* xi. 7, 1). In March or April, 334 B.C., Alexander of Macedon crossed the Hellespont, defeated the Persian satraps, then marched on, and the next year gained a victory over the Persian monarch Darius Codomannus at Issus, a defile near the n.e. angle of the Mediterranean Sea, laid Syria at his feet, and entered Jerusalem. After an almost uninterrupted career of conquest, extending e. as far as the Punjab, Alexander died at Babylon in June, 323 B.C. See ALEXANDER 1.

(b) *Judea subject to Egypt.* Ptolemy Soter wrested Palestine from Syria, to which it had fallen after Alexander's death, in 320 B.C., and the Ptolemies retained it, except for occasional brief periods, until 198 B.C., when Antiochus the Great defeated the Egyptian general Scopas near Paneas (Bānias); see PTOLEMY. During these 122 years the Jews were governed by their high priest subject to the king of Egypt. At this time the Hebrew Scriptures were translated into Greek at Alexandria in Egypt. See VERSIONS, I. 1.

(c) *Judea subject to Syria.* Antiochus the Great wrested Pales'ine from Egypt in 198 B.C. by his victory over Ptolemy V (Epiphanes) at Paneas. The Syrians not only supported the Grecian party among the Jews which attempted to Hellenize the nation, but they also endeavored by force to impose idolatry upon the Jews. The sacrilegious tyranny of the Syrians became intolerable to the pious portion of the nation, and led to the Maccabaean revolt in 166 B.C. See GYMNASIUM, JASON 2, ANTIOCHUS 1, 2.

A period of independence under the Maccabaean priest-kings followed; see MACCABEE. It lasted from 166 B.C. until Pompey took Jerusalem in 63 B.C.; but the Maccabees were allowed to hold the throne until 40 B.C., when Herod the Great was appointed king of Judea by the Roman senate. He began his actual reign by the capture of Jerusalem in 37 B.C. During this period the Pharisees and Sadducees became recognized parties, exerting great political and religious influence. See PHARISEES, SADDUCEES, COUNCIL.

(d) *Under the Romans.* During this period the affairs of Judea were administered by appointees of the Romans; first by Herod the Great, then by Archelaus, and afterward by procurators, except from A.D. 41–44, when Herod Agrippa I reigned as king; see JUDAEA, HEROD, PROCURATOR. The maladministration of these officials exasperated the people and drove them to revolt. Obstinate war raged from A.D. 66 until the fall of Jerusalem in A.D. 70. The remnant of the Jewish people who remained in Palestine were denied access to their capital and had no longer a national existence. While the Jews still constituted a nation under the Romans, in the days of Herod the king, Jesus of Nazareth was born and a new period of Biblical history began.

IV. *The history of the establishment* of the Christian Church, which is to reach all nations. 1. *Christ's preparation for the establishment of his Church,* by example, teaching, and redemption. See JESUS CHRIST, GOSPEL, APOSTLE.

2. *The Church among the Jews.* The Church was founded by the risen Chr'st. On the Day of Pentecos', the promised Spirit was given, and the Church's work was initiated by Peter's sermon, increase of believers, and baptism; see WEEKS, FEAST OF, HOLY SPIRIT, TONGUE, BAPTISM, CHURCH. During the next

few years, 6 perhaps, the Church experienced the difficulties incident to the imperfections of believers and to persecution; but it grew steadily in purity and numbers. See ANANIAS 1, DEACON, STEPHEN. The persecution which arose on the death of Stephen scattered the brethren abroad, and the evangelization of the Jews in Palestine and Syria began. The gospel was carried to Samaria and to the cities on the seacoast from Gaza to Caesarea. See PHILIP 7. For the purpose of persecuting the believers who were now found in the Jewish colony in Damascus, Saul went thither, and was converted, and was told that he was to be a teacher of the Gentiles. The vision of Peter at Joppa, and its complement in the conversion of Cornelius and his baptism with the Holy Spirit, opened the eyes of the Church to the truth, already theoretically known, that the Holy Spirit is for all believers, Jew and Gentile. See CORNELIUS. At Antioch Jewish believers from the West, who had been driven from Jerusalem by the persecution which had arisen on the death of Stephen, began to preach Jesus to the Greeks also (Acts 11:20, R.V.), and now the followers of Jesus began to be called Christians, no longer being identified with the Jews. The Church was now ready to undertake the evangelization of the Gentiles; the truth of the equality of all believers was known, a man had been raised up to work among the Gentiles, and the first beginnings had been made.

3. *The Church among Jews and Gentiles.* Paul and Barnabas, called by the Holy Ghost, began the evangelization of Jews and Gentiles in Asia Minor. The question about the obligations of Gentile converts arose. The Council at Jerusalem took a firm stand for Christian liberty, refused to impose circumcision and the observance of the Mosaic Law upon Gentile converts, and only insisted upon certain moral duties and certain matters of expediency which it was necessary to emphasize on account of the state of public opinion. The rights of Gentile Christians were now secure. On a Second Missionary Journey, Paul, under the direction of the Spirit, came to Troas, and was called by a vision to extend his labors to Europe, and the evangelization of Europe from Philippi to Rome ensued. See PAUL, JOHN 7, PETER.

Hit'tites (hĭt'īts) [Heb. *Ḥittî*, pl., *Ḥittîm*; also Heb. *Ḥēth*]. For a number of years Orientalists reckoned with 2 centers of great empires: the valley of the Nile and that of the Tigris-Euphrates. From 1871, when inscriptions were found at Carchemish which represented a new element, the Hittites began to be recognized as the founders of a 3d great Oriental empire, which flourished in Asia Minor between c. 1900 and c. 1200 B.C.

The racial affinities of the Hittites are not clearly understood. One type frequently seen on the monuments of Egypt has the large nose; it seems that the modern Armenians are the lineal descendants of 1 group of this nation. The Hittites were short and stocky and had thick lips. The large nose and retreating forehead are also represented on the Hittite monuments. The Hittites were not Semites. According to the monuments they wore heavy clothing, coats that reached down to the knees, and high woolen headdress. They wore shoes which were turned up at the toes, which suggests that they came from the snowy mountains. It is inferred from their appearance that they were a people from a cold climate. In fact, the plateau of Anatolia varies from 4,000 to 3,000 feet above sea level.

Historically a sharp distinction must be made between the Hittite Empire and the Hittite states of n. Syria and s.e. Asia Minor. Archaeologically the word Hittite applies to

remains of the remarkable and unique culture found in Asia Minor, n. Syria, and n. Mesopotamia. In spite of all the similarity between the Asia Minor Hittite monuments and those from n. Mesopotamia and n. Syria (including the Taurus region), there are some factors that suggest a general separation of the 2 groups. The Anatolian Hittite culture seems to have centered in Cappadocia, the pottery of which shows many affiliations with Troy.

Probably as early as 2500 B.C. the Hittites (Nasians) came into Asia Minor, where they met the Anatolian aborigines, who spoke Hattic, a non-Indo-European tongue. It may be that they were preceded in this invasion by a people (Luwi, Luwians) that spoke Luian or Luish, a language related to Indo-European. The Luwians occupied most of s. Asia Minor, entering not later than the early part of the 3d millennium; in the 18th century B.C. a Luwian dynasty was ruling as far e. as Carchemish. The name Hittite is derived from Hatti (i.e., Anatolia), the capital of which was Hattushash. In the 20th century B.C. colonies were established by an Akkadian dynasty of Ashur (Assur) in Asia Minor, but this influence was rather short-lived. The expansion of the Hittites (Nasians), who had been in Cappadocia before 2000 B.C., may explain this decadence of Assyrian power.

It is now generally agreed that Hittite is somehow related to the Indo-European languages. It seems that Hittite and primitive Indo-European are connected by virtue of a common descent from a parent speech, which may be called Indo-Hittite. This language developed into 2 branches: pre-Hittite, the forerunner of Hittite, and pre-Indo-European, out of which developed Indo-European, which in turn is the parent language of Sanskrit, Iranian, Armenian, Greek, Latin, Celtic, Slavonic, and Teutonic.

The real key to the Hittite problem was discovered by Hugo Winckler of Berlin, who in 1906–1907 and 1911–1912 discovered at Boghazköi (the site of ancient Hattushash) about 10,000 clay tablets inscribed in cuneiform characters. Here were represented a number of languages: Sumerian, Akkadian, Hattic, Hittite (Nasi or Nesi), Luian or Luish (the tongue of Arzawa and closely related to Hittite), Palaic, and Hurrian. The inscriptions on the Hittite monuments are written in Hittite hieroglyphs.

The word Hittite (sing. and pl.) occurs 47 times in the O.T., while Heth, which means the same thing, is found 14 times. Probably these words do not always refer to the same group within this extensive confederation of peoples. The Hittites are often mentioned in the list of nations inhabiting Canaan before the Conquest (cf. Gen. 15:20; Ex. 3:8; Deut. 7:1; 20:17; Josh. 3:10; 11:3; 24:11). Abraham purchased the cave of Machpelah from Ephron the Hittite (Gen. 23:10–18). Esau took Hittite wives (Gen. 26:34), and later the Israelites intermarried with the Hittites (Judg. 3:5, 6). When Ezekiel addressed the unfaithful Jerusalem, he said (ch. 16:3): "Thy birth and thy nativity is of the land of the Canaanite; the Amorite was thy father, and thy mother was a Hittite" (cf. ch. 16:45). David had Hittite associates (I Sam. 26:6), and he married Bath-sheba, the wife of Uriah the Hittite (II Sam. 11:2–27). Solomon had Hittite women in his harem (I Kings 11:1). Solomon impressed Hittites, among other peoples of his realm, into his system of forced labor (I Kings 9:20–22; II Chron. 8:7–9).

Apparently the Hebrew did not regard the Hittites as a homeless, nondescript people; they recognized a land of the Hittites (Josh. 1:4). The kings of the Hittites are mentioned in the same sentence with those of Aram (I Kings 10:29; II Chron. 1:17). As a sign of their greatness they are placed in the same category with the Egyptians (II Kings 7:6).

The Hittite kingdom was essentially a feudal aristocracy; the king was crowned by the nobles during the Old Kingdom or First Empire (c. 1900–1650 B.C.). King Pitḫanas ruled (c. 1900 B.C.) in Kushshara or Kussaras (modern Giaour Kalesi, s.w. of Angora); he captured Nēsas (Nyssa) to the s. of the Halys River. His son Anittas, who succeeded him, waged 2 successful wars against the city of Hattushash. Then Piiustis (Bijustis), king of Hatti, whose capital was at Hattushash, formed a new coalition against Anittas, and all the countries between the Black and Mediterranean Seas joined Hatti. Again Anittas was successful, and he conquered all of Asia Minor. Nēsas was his capital, and Kushshara was a 2d capital merely in name.

Later a great conqueror Labarnash (c. 1680) ruled in Kushshara and undertook expeditions beyond Asia Minor. He was succeeded by Hattushilish I (1650), who in turn was followed by Murshilish I (1620). The latter transferred the capital to Hattushash and conquered Halpa (Aleppo). In a raid he plundered Babylon and put an end to the Amorite dynasty of Hammurabi (c. 1595). But there were also internal disorders and finally, c. 1570, a great king Telepinush tried to reorganize the shattered kingdom. He came to the throne after 3 usurpers and fixed the royal succession on a hereditary basis. Probably Hittite law was codified at this time.

There followed a dark period in Hittite history; in 1482 Thutmose III of Egypt defeated the Hittites at Megiddo, and they had to pay him tribute. He went as far as Aleppo and crossed the Euphrates. The Taurus Mountains were now the s. boundary of the Hittite territory.

The New Kingdom or Second Empire extended from c. 1450 to c. 1200 B.C. The government remained a hereditary monarchy. About 1430 the Hittites again entered international politics. During the reigns of Tudḫalijash II, Hattushilish II, and Tudḫalijash III, the Mitannians still had the upper hand, but Shuppiluliumash (c. 1395–1355), the son of Tudḫalijash III, reconquered Anatolia and made n. Syria between the Euphrates and the Mediterranean to the Lebanons again a part of the empire. Except for a small buffer state e. of the Euphrates, Mitannu became subject to the Hittites, who now were a first-rate military and political power. By 1350 the Hittite empire was the most powerful state in w. Asia. Murshilish II, the son of Shuppiluliumash, was one of the most enterprising and warlike rulers of the ancient East.

During Dyn. XIX the Egyptians under Sethi I again came into clash with the Hittites in Syria. Muwatallish fought the battle of Kadesh with Ramesses II c. 1295, and the Egyptians were forced to evacuate n. Syria. In c. 1279 Hattushilish III (c. 1295–1260) concluded a treaty with Ramesses II on terms of equality. The Hittite king visited Egypt to celebrate the marriage of his eldest daughter to Ramesses II.

Already under Shuppiluliumash there were contacts between the Hittite empire and Aḫḫijā (Aḫḫijawā), the Achaean empire on the Greek mainland with its capital at Orchomenos. At first the Achaean kings appear as allies or even vassals of the Hittite Great King; in other words they were also rulers of a region in s. Asia Minor. But more and more they seem to have opposed the Hittite rule in that land, until under Tudḫalijash IV (1260–1230) and Arnuwandash II (c. 1230–1215), they openly defied Hittite rule. About 1200 B.C. the Hittite empire fell at the hands of an invasion by an Aegean people, probably the Thracians and the Phrygians.

The Hittites not in Asia Minor were now grouped around Carchemish as their capital, where they came into contact with the Assyrians. Tiglath-pileser I fought with them and other peoples of w. Asia. Ashur-nasir-pal (885–860) received tribute from Sangara, king of Carchemish. Finally, 717 B.C., Carchemish fell into the hands of Sargon II. Thus n. Syria and e. Asia Minor were gradually absorbed by Assyria. The Hittites had been the cultural link between the Tigris-Euphrates Valley and Europe.

Hi'vites (hī'vīts) [cf. Heb. *ḥawwāh*, tent-village; Arab. *ḥiwā'*, collection of tents]. One of the races of Canaan before the conquest of the country by the Hebrews (Gen. 10:17; Ex. 3:17; Josh. 9:1). They scattered into several communities. A body of them dwelt at Shechem in the time of Jacob (Gen. 33:18; 34:2), and their descendants still had influence in the city several generations after the conquest (Judg. 9:28). A body of them also dwelt in Gibeon and its vicinity. They obtained a treaty of peace from Joshua by stratagem, but on their deceit being discovered, they were made hewers of wood and drawers of water (Josh., ch. 9). They had also an extensive settlement, probably their principal one, at the foot of Lebanon, from Mount Hermon to the entering in of Hamath (Josh. 11:3; Judg. 3:3). In these n. mountain regions they had villages of their own as late as the time of David (II Sam. 24:7). Those of Palestine proper were, with the other Canaanites who remained in the land, required to render bond service to Solomon in connection with his extensive building operations (I Kings 9:20–22; II Chron. 8:7, 8).

It may be asked, however, whether the Hivites as a people ever had a real or separate existence. It is an established fact that Horites or Hurrians lived in central Palestine and Syria at an early date. There is a confusion between Hivite and Horite in the Heb. text of Gen., ch. 36; v. 2 makes Zibeon a Hivite, but in vs. 20 and 29 he is a Horite. Gen. 34:2 reads Hivite, for which the LXX has Horite. The same is true in Josh. 9:7 (LXX, v. 13). Except for 1 letter, Heb. *Ḥiwwī* (Hivite) and *Ḥōrī* (Horite) look alike in the unpointed text, and it is possible that we have a scribal confusion between *resh* (*r*) and *waw* [*vav*] (*w* [*v*]). If this be the case, Horite is the original name. It is possible, however, that there was a Horite subdivision known as the Hivites, whose name supplanted the general designation on account of a popular etymology which considered the Horites as cave dwellers.

Hiz'ki (hĭz'kī), in A.V. **Hez'e·ki** [my strength, or a contraction of Hezekiah (*q.v.*)]. A Benjamite, son of Elpaal (I Chron. 8:17).

Hiz·ki'ah (hĭz-kī'á). See HEZEKIAH 2.

Hiz·ki'jah (hĭz-kī'já). See HEZEKIAH 4.

Ho'bab (hō'băb) [beloved]. The father-in-law of Moses, according to the Heb. (Masoretic) text (Judg. 4:11, A.V., J.V.). But the father-in-law of Moses was Reuel, or Jethro (Ex. 3:1; 4:18; 18:1, 2, 5, 6). Hobab is definitely stated to have been the son of Reuel (Num. 10:29; Raguel, A.V.), and if the Masoretic vocalization is ignored, and regard paid to the Heb. consonants only, the Heb. words may equally well be translated "Hobab the brother-in-law of Moses" (Judg. 1:16; 4:11, R.V.). Moses' father-in-law Reuel, or Jethro, visited Moses in the camp at Rephidim and returned to his own land (Ex. 18:1, 5, 27). A year later, when the Israelites were about to advance from Sinai, Moses urged Hobab, the son of Reuel, to accompany them and aid them with his knowledge of the desert. Hobab finally consented (Num. 10:29; Judg. 1:16;

4:11). It seems, therefore, that Hobab is not the same person as Reuel. After the conquest of Canaan, his family settled in Judah, s. of Arad, and were still there in the time of Saul and David (Judg. 1:16; I Sam. 15:6; 27:10; 30:29). Hobab belonged to the Kenites (Judg. 1:16; 4:11), a family of the Midianites.

Ho'bah (hō'bȧ). A town to the n. of Damascus. Hobah was the extreme limit to which Abraham pursued the defeated e. kings (Gen. 14:15). Wetzstein mentions a place of this name between Tadmor and Homs, about 50 miles n. of Damascus.

Hod (hŏd) [majesty]. An Asherite, son of Zophah (I Chron. 7:37).

Hod'a·vi'ah (hŏ'dȧ-vī'ȧ), in A.V. once **Ho·da'iah** (hō-dā'yȧ) (I Chron. 3:24) [praise ye, or thank ye Jehovah]. 1. A son of Elioenai, descended through Shecaniah from David (I Chron. 3:24).
2. One of the heads of the half tribe of Manasseh e. of the Jordan (I Chron. 5:24).
3. A Benjamite (I Chron. 9:7).
4. A Levite, founder of a family, some members of which returned from Babylon (Ezra 2:40). He is called Judah (ch. 3:9), probably from the same root (cf. Gen. 29:35; 49:8); and the kethib of the Heb. text in one place is Hodevah, and the kere Hodeiah (Neh. 7:43 and R.V. marg.).

Ho·de'iah (hō-dē'yȧ). See HODAVIAH 4.

Ho'desh (hō'dĕsh) [new moon]. A wife of Shaharaim (I Chron. 8:9).

Ho·de'vah (hō-dē'vȧ). See HODAVIAH 4.

Ho·di'ah (hō-dī'ȧ), in A.V. of Nehemiah **Ho·di'jah** (hō-dī'jȧ) [Jehovah is majesty, or praise (thou) Jehovah]. 1. A man who was reckoned as belonging to the tribe of Judah, perhaps because of his marriage with the sister of Naham (I Chron. 4:19, R.V.). A.V. does not give a correct rendering of the Heb. text.
2. One of the Levites employed by Ezra to explain the Law to the people (Neh. 8:7), and to assist on the day of penitence and prayer (ch. 9:5). He was probably one of the 2 Levite Hodiahs who sealed the covenant (ch. 10:10 or 13).

Hog'lah (hŏg'lȧ) [cf. Arab. ḥajal, partridge]. A daughter of Zelophehad (Num. 26:33).

Ho'ham (hō'hăm). A king of Hebron, who entered into a league against Joshua, and was defeated, captured, and executed (Josh. 10:1–27).

Holm Tree. The evergreen oak (Quercus ilex), the rendering of Heb. tirzāh, in the only passage where it occurs (Isa. 44:14; in A.V. cypress); the Vulgate renders it by ilex.

Ho'lon (hō'lŏn) [probably sandy]. 1. A town in the hill country of Judah (Josh. 15:51), given, with its suburbs, to the priests (ch. 21:15). Called also Hilen (I Chron. 6:58). Not identified.
2. A Moabite town (Jer. 48:21), perhaps Horon.

Ho'ly. The ordinary Heb. word for holy is ḳādōsh, separated, consecrated. It is represented in the N.T. by the Gr. word hagios. It is used for what is set apart from a common to a sacred use, as the utensils and ministers of the sanctuary, and certain days (Ex. 20:8; 30:31; 31:10; Lev. 21:7; Num. 5:17); for what is separated from ceremonial defilement (Ex. 22:31; Lev. 20:26) or immorality (II Cor. 7:1; I Thess. 4:7), including false worship and heathen practices (Lev. 20:6, 7; 21:6). In a larger sense God is holy, for he is separated from all other beings by his infinite perfections, by his being, wisdom, power, holiness, justice, goodness, and truth, the glory of which fills the earth (Isa. 6:3). Even holy angels ascribe holiness to him (Isa. 6:3).

Ho'ly Ghost. See HOLY SPIRIT.

Ho'ly Place. See TABERNACLE, TEMPLE.

Ho'ly Spir'it. The Spirit of God, the third person of the Trinity. The word spirit now more correctly expresses the idea than does the term ghost, which has narrowed its meaning, and commonly denotes a disembodied spirit wandering on earth. The name Holy Spirit is used 3 times only in the O.T. (Ps. 51:11; Isa. 63:10, 11), but there are numerous references to his work. The Spirit of God is the divine principle of activity everywhere at work in the world, executing the will of God. The Spirit is sent forth by God (Ps. 104:30) and given by God (Num. 11:29; Isa. 42:1, 5). The Spirit brooded over chaotic matter in the beginning and is everywhere present (Gen. 1:2; Ps. 139:7), and is thus immanent and the energy in cosmical processes; is the source of physical, intellectual, and moral life (Gen. 6:3; Job 32:8; 33:4; 34:14; Ps. 104:30; cf. Isa. 42:5); is able to produce supernatural effects (I Kings 18:12; II Kings 2:16). He abides with the people of God (Isa. 63:11; Hag. 2:5), and bestows varied powers for the work of the Kingdom: strength (Judg. 3:10; 14:6, 19; 15:14; I Sam. 11:6; 16:13; I Chron. 12:18), skill (Ex. 31:3), wisdom (Num. 27:18), in short, everything needful for the work of the kingdom (Isa. 11:2; Zech. 4:6). He instructed the people of God (Neh. 9:20) by inspiring the prophets (Num. 24:2; I Sam. 10:6; Micah 3:8; Zech. 7:12). He works upon the heart of the individual child of God. It was foretold that this work would be especially powerful and widespread in the Messianic period, when the Spirit shall be poured out on the people of God (Isa. 44:3), will give to them a new heart and a new spirit (Ezek. 36:26), produce sorrow for sin (Zech. 12:10), and even be poured out on all flesh (Joel 2:28). The Spirit is grieved when men resist his holy work (Isa. 63:10; cf. Ps. 106:33). Jesus promised that on his departure the Spirit should come and dwell with every believer, clothe with power, guide and teach the Church, bear witness of Christ and glorify him, convict the world of sin, righteousness, and judgment (Luke 24:49; John 7:37–39; 14:25, 26; 15:26; 16:7–14; Acts 1:8). The Holy Spirit is known as the Comforter in John 14:16, 26; 15:26; 16:7 (cf. R.V. marg., Advocate, Helper, Paraclete).

The N.T. treats of Messianic times and the dispensation of the Spirit, and consequently the Spirit is mentioned much oftener in the N.T. than in the O.T. All the attributes of the Spirit revealed in the O.T. are more fully disclosed in the N.T. in operation. The doctrine of the Spirit advances beyond the teaching of the O.T. chiefly in becoming more definite in respect to his personality. Though the word spirit is neuter in Gr. and fem. in Heb., yet the Spirit is sometimes called who, not which, the masc. form of the pronoun being used (Eph. 1:13, 14; cf. John 16:13). The Spirit further speaks in the 1st person, using the pronouns I and me (Acts 10:19, 20; 13:2); is associated with the Father and the Son in the baptismal formula and the apostolic benediction (Matt. 28:19; II Cor. 13:14); can be grieved (Eph. 4:30).

Memorable acts of the Spirit at the beginning of the Christian dispensation are the miraculous conception of Jesus by the Holy Spirit (Matt. 1:18–20); the descent of the Spirit upon Jesus at his baptism, in the form of a dove visible to him and to John the Baptist (Matt. 3:16; Mark 1:10; John 1:32), and the effusion of the Holy Spirit in the likeness of tongues of fire on the Day of Pentecost, and the accompanying gift of languages (Acts

2:2–4). See GOD, INSPIRATION, WEEKS, FEAST OF.

Ho'mam (hō'măm) [cf. Heb. *hāmam*, make a noise, confuse, discomfit]. Son of Lotan, and grandson of Seir (I Chron. 1:39). The name appears in Gen. 36:22 as Hemam. The difference in the Heb. is slight, and is doubtless due to a misreading. The latter name has *yodh* where the former has *waw* (*vau, vav*). The LXX has Haiman in both places, thus favoring *yodh*.

Ho'mer [a heap]. A measure for dry substances and liquids. It contained 10 baths or ephahs (Ezek. 45:11, 14) and 100 omers (Ex. 16:36). It held 10.48 bushels in early times, but later 11.49 bushels, U.S. measure. See EPHAH, I, MEASURE, III.

Hon'ey. A sweet, thick fluid collected by bees from flowers and fruit and deposited in the cells of a comb (Judg. 14:8; Ps. 19:10); much esteemed as an article of food (Gen. 43:11; II Sam. 17:29), and eaten as found in the comb or as prepared in various ways (Ex. 16:31; I Sam. 14:26). Wild honey was deposited by bees in rocks, trees, and other places (Deut. 32:13; Judg. 14:8; I Sam. 14:25; Matt. 3:4). Because it acts like a leaven, producing fermentation, honey might not be used in offerings made by fire unto the Lord (Lev. 2:11). An artificial honey or syrup was prepared from dates (Jos. *War* iv. 8, 3). Canaan was described as flowing with milk and honey (Ex. 3:8, 17).

Hook. The Hebrews and contemporary peoples used hooks of various kinds: 1. Curtains were hung by means of hooks, those employed about the tabernacle being made of gold and silver (Ex. 26:32, 37; 27:10).

2. By means of fleshhooks meat was lifted from the pot (Ex. 27:3; I Sam. 2:13, 14), and on firmly fixed hooks slain animals were hung up (Ezek. 40:43, but the word rendered hook in this passage may rather mean ledge or slab (cf. R.V. marg. and J.V.).

3. Hooks resembling thorns, and sometimes called so in Hebrew (Amos 4:2), were used in fishing (Job 41:1; Hab. 1:15). See FISHING.

4. A large hook was thrust through the mouth of a fish or other aquatic animal, and attached by a cord to a stake, when it was desired to keep it alive (Job 41:2; Ezek. 29:4). A similar hook was used for leading about lions and other beasts (II Kings 19:28; Ezek. 19:4, in A.V. chains; cf. ch. 38:4), and for a like purpose were inserted in the lips of captives (II Chron. 33:11, R.V. marg.). See illustration under BLINDNESS.

5. Pruning hooks were used by vinedressers (Isa. 2:4; 18:5).

Hoo'poe. See LAPWING.

Hoph'ni (hŏf'nī) [cf. Heb. *ḥōphen*, hollow of hand, and Arab. *ḥafnah*, handful]. A son of Eli. He and his brother Phinehas discharged the priest's office in the old age of Eli, but showed themselves unworthy of the sacred office by scandalous behavior. Eli mildly remonstrated when summary proceedings were required; and, in consequence, the divine judgment was pronounced against him and his house. When it was resolved that the Ark of God should be taken to the battlefield, Hophni and Phinehas, who as officiating priests were its custodians, accompanied it, and were both slain in the disastrous battle which followed (I Sam. 2:22 to 4:22).

Hor (hōr) [mountain]. 1. A mountain on the border of the Edomite country, where Aaron died and was buried (Num. 20:22–29; 33:37–39; Deut. 32:50). Josephus says that it was one of the mountains surrounding Petra (Jos. *Antiq.* iv. 4, 7). Tradition has settled on

Jebel Hārūn, meaning Aaron's Mountain, a great two-topped eminence of sandstone, about 4,800 feet high, on the e. side of the Arabah, nearly midway between the s. extremity of the Dead Sea and the n. end of the Gulf of 'Aḳabah. It is the highest and wildest of the whole Edomite range. Petra is close by, to the w.; but the ruined city is not visible from the summit. On its summit stands a tomb, nominally that of Aaron; but the upper part of it, at least, is only a modern Mohammedan mosque. The tradition, however, is open to serious question. Jebel Hārūn is in the midst of Edom and not on its border, as was Hor. If Edom extended to the Gulf of 'Aḳabah, the Israelites could not reach the traditional mountain without crossing Edom, which they were forbidden to do (Deut. 2:8). Jebel Maderah, about 15 miles n.e. of Kadesh, is a more likely site, being on the direct route from Kadesh across Edom to Moab. The solemn transaction (Num. 20:22–29) carried out "in the sight of all the congregation" could have been done on Jebel Maderah, while Jebel Hārūn is too high for the people to see what took place.

2. A mountain on the n. boundary of Palestine, between the Mediterranean Sea and the entering in of Hamath (Num. 34:7, 8). It was probably a prominent peak of Lebanon.

Ho'ram (hō'răm). A king of Gezer, defeated and slain by Joshua (Josh. 10:33).

Ho'reb (hō'rĕb) [drought, desert]. The mount of God in the peninsula of Sinai (Ex. 3:1; 18:5), where the Law was given to Israel. The names Horeb and Sinai refer to the same mountain (for example, Horeb in Ex. 17:6; 33:6; Deut. 1:2, 6, 19; 4:10, 15; 5:2; 9:8; 18:16; 29:1; I Kings 8:9; 19:8; II Chron. 5:10; Ps. 106:19; Mal. 4:4; but Sinai in Ex. 19:11, 18, 20, 23; 24:16; 31:18; 34:2, 4, 29, 32; Lev. 7:38; 25:1; 26:46; 27:34; Deut. 33:2; Judg. 5:5; Neh. 9:13). In Ecclus. 48:7 the 2 are equated in Hebrew parallelism. According to critical scholars the use of the 2 names in the Pentateuch goes back to variations in the documentary sources (Horeb in E and D; Sinai in J and P).

Ho'rem (hō'rĕm) [enclosed, sacred]. A fenced city of Naphtali (Josh. 19:38); probably a ruin like Khirbet Katamūn near Jebel Haramūn, s. of Yārūn in Upper Galilee.

Ho'resh (hō'rĕsh) [forest]. A locality, probably at the time overgrown with bush, where David lurked (I Sam. 23:16, R.V. marg.). It may be identified with Khirbet Khoreisa, about 2 miles s. of Tell Zīf.

Hor'hag·gid'gad (hŏr'hă-gĭd'găd), in A.V. **Hor'ha·gid'gad** (hŏr'hă-gĭd'găd) [hollow or cavern of Gidgad]. An encampment of the Israelites in the wilderness (Num. 33:32). The same as Gudgodah (Deut. 10:6, 7; cf. Num. 33:31–33). It may be located on Wadi Ghaḍagheḍ, a tributary of Wadi Jerāfi, n. of Kuntilet el-Jerāfi, n.n.w. of the Gulf of 'Aḳabah.

Ho'ri (hō'rī) (see HORITE). 1. A Horite tribe descended from Lotan, and called by the general name of the stock to which it belonged (Gen. 36:22).

2. Father of Shaphat the spy (Num. 13:5).

Ho'rite (hō'rīt), in A.V. of Deut. **Ho'rims** (hō'rĭmz). The inhabitants of Mount Seir, and hence called the children of Seir (Gen. 36:20). They were defeated by Chedorlaomer and his allies (Gen. 14:6). They were governed by chieftains (ch. 36:29, 30). They were subsequently destroyed by the posterity of Esau (Deut. 2:12, 22).

Formerly the word was derived from Heb. *ḥōr* (hole, cave), and the name was explained as meaning troglodytes or cave dwellers. This popular ety. no longer meets with general acceptance since the discovery of the Hurrians (Kaurrians) as an ethnic element in the Near East. The Hurrians were a non-Semitic people from the mountains, who probably about the beginning of the 2d millennium migrated into n. and n.e. Mesopotamia. Later they spread into the fertile lowlands of Mesopotamia and Syria, eventually reaching Palestine and the borders of Egypt. They preceded the Israelites in Palestine, and the middle Euphrates was one of the centers of their culture. The kingdom of Mitannu or Hanigalbat on the upper Euphrates was really Hurrian, although the rulers were at first Indo-European and later Hittites. The Assyrian culture of the early 1st millennium is the heir of that of the Hurrians of the 2d. Hurrian Nuzu was destroyed by the Assyrians between 1425 and 1375 B.C., probably c. 1400.

Hor'mah (hôr'má) [a devoted place, destruction]. The town Zephath, called Hormah after its destruction. It was situated in the s. country, toward the border of Edom, near Ziklag. When the Israelites after their loss of faith presumed to advance from Kadesh toward Canaan, the Amalekites and Canaanites came down, smote them, and drove them as far as Hormah, as the district was called from its devastation some 38 years later (Num. 14:45; Deut. 1:44). On the 2d departure of the Israelites from Kadesh, after the lapse of these 38 years, while they were encamped at Mount Hor, the Canaanites under the king of Arad again attacked them and made some captives. Israel vowed their destruction if Jehovah would aid, devastated their cities, and called the wasted region Hormah, desolation (Num. 21:1–3).

It was allotted to Judah, but was afterward transferred to Simeon (Josh. 15:30; 19:4). After the death of Joshua, Judah assisted Simeon to take the town. It was inhabited by Canaanites; and had either escaped destruction when the region was first devastated in fulfillment of the vow (Num. 21:2), or it had been rebuilt by fugitives who returned. At any rate, it was still included in the old vow; and it was now devoted to destruction, man and beast were slain, and the town was henceforth called Hormah (Judg. 1:17). Joshua had already defeated its king, who probably was absent from his city, assisting men of his own race at Hebron at the time of his defeat. Joshua had similarly defeated the king of Jerusalem and the king of Gezer when they were away from their cities (Josh. 12:14; cf. ch. 10:10, 33). After the town had been destroyed, it was inhabited by Simeonites (I Chron. 4:30). It was hospitable to David when he lived as an outcast, and to his friends there David sent of the spoils of Ziklag (I Sam. 30:30). It is probably to be located at Tell es-Seba' (also called Tell el-Mshâsh), about 3 miles e. of Beer-sheba.

Horn. Since Palestine, especially its s. portion, was a pastoral country, the Israelites were very familiar with the horns of animals. In early times they converted them into trumpets (Josh. 6:13), or into flasks for such substances as oil (I Sam. 16:1, 13; I Kings 1:39). When God exalts the horn of an individual, the meaning is that he confers great power and prosperity (I Sam. 2:10; Ps. 89: 24); but when one exalts or lifts up the horn, it means that he indulges in arrogance and insolence (Ps. 75:4, 5). The horn is the emblem of strength and denotes political power, the image being drawn from bulls which push with their horns (Ps. 132:17; Jer. 48:25), and in prophetic language signifies a kingdom or kings (Dan. 7:8, 11, 21; Zech. 1:18, 19; Rev. 17:12, 16).

Horns of the altar were projections resembling horns placed at the corners of the altar of burnt offering (Jos. *War* v. 5, 6). They were smeared with the blood of the sacrifice (Ex. 29:12; Lev. 4:7), and the bodies of the victims offered in sacrifice appear to have been bound to them (Ps. 118:27), and offenders clung to them for safety from punishment (I Kings 2:28).

Horn was also used to denote a peak (Isa. 5:1 marg.). The Horns of Hattin are the traditional Mount of Beatitudes. See HATTIN, HORNS OF.

Hor'net. The rendering of Heb. ṣir'āh, according to the ancient versions. The hornet (*Vespa crabro*) is of the same genus as the wasp, but larger and more formidable. Either the common hornet or a closely allied species is common in Palestine. Hornets were to be sent to drive out the Canaanite nations before the Israelites (Ex. 23:28; Deut. 7:20; Josh. 24:12; Wisd. of Sol. 12:8). It is doubtful whether hornet is here used in a literal or a figurative sense. Probably the solution to the difficulty is to be found in the Egyptian hieroglyphs. The sovereignty of the Pharaoh over united Egypt was expressed by a hieroglyphic combination n-sw-byt (king of Upper and Lower Egypt), which means literally "he who belongs to the sedge of Upper Egypt and the bee of Lower Egypt." The sign for byt is a bee, which, however, resembles a hornet and is thus interpreted by some scholars. At any rate, the hornet may with good reason refer to Egypt, which had penetrated Palestine at an early time, under Thutmose III had conquered the land, but had temporarily lost it through the invasion of the Habiru and the Hittites. During the period of the Judges it seems that the Israelites were oppressed by their foes when Egypt was weak, but that the land had rest when Egyptian power was strong. By this interpretation the Egyptian conquest and spoliation of Palestine with the subsequent breakdown of authority facilitated the conquest by the Israelites under Joshua.

Hor'o•na'im (hôr'ō-nā'ĭm) [2 caverns or ravines]. A Moabite city at the foot of a declivity, and apparently not far from Zoar (Isa. 15:5; Jer. 48:3, 5, 34; *Moabite Stone*, 31, see MOABITE STONE). Doubtless the town Oronae, which Alexander Jannaeus took from the Arabians, and his son Hyrcanus restored to Aretas (Jos. *Antiq.* xiii. 15, 4; xiv. 1, 4). It may be el-'Arâk, which is about 1,640 feet below the level of the plateau and provided with springs, gardens, and numerous grottos.

Hor'o•nite (hôr'ō-nīt). A native or inhabitant of Horonaim or, more probably, of Bethhoron (Neh. 2:10, 19).

Horse. The horse was domesticated in early antiquity somewhere e. of the Caspian Sea by Indo-European nomads. Later the Kassites and the Hittites imported it on a large scale and introduced it into w. Asia. Horses were used for military purposes c. 1900 B.C., and horse-drawn chariots were known c. 1800 in Asia Minor and Syria. Mention is made of its rider in the time of Jacob (Gen. 49:17). Mountainous Palestine was not well adapted for its use, and in early times it was principally employed in the maritime plain and in the valley of Jezreel. The horse was found in Egypt (Gen. 47:17; Ex. 9:3), whither it was introduced by the Hyksos. When the Exodus took place, Pharaoh's pursuing army was equipped with chariots and horses (Ex. 14:9; 15:19). They existed also in the force of the n. Canaanites led by Sisera, Jabin's commander-in-chief (Judg. 4:15; 5:22). In Deut. 17:16, the king who was to be elected when monarchy was established among the Israelites was forbidden to multiply horses; however Solomon imported them in great numbers from Egypt, paying for each animal 150 shekels of silver. He afterward exported them to the kings of the Hittites and those of the Syrians (I Kings 10:28, 29; II Chron. 1:16, 17; 9:28). Horses later became common in Israel and Judah (I Kings 9:18; Isa. 2:7), and were used in battle (I Kings 22:4; II Kings 3:7; 9:33). Foreign kings rode on horseback (Esth. 6:8), while it was considered lowly in a sovereign to sit upon an ass (Zech. 9:9), and accorded with the simple manners of the early Hebrew patriarchs, judges, and kings (Gen. 22:3; Judg. 10:4; 12:14; I Kings 1:33). Horses were sometimes dedicated to the sun for the purpose of drawing the chariots of the sun-god (II Kings 23:11). They are frequently mentioned in the prophecies of Zechariah (Zech. 1:8; 6:2, 3; 10:5; 14:20), and in the book of Revelation (Rev. 6:2, 4, 5, 8; 19:11, etc.). See LINEN 6.

Horse'leech'. A large leech (*Haemopsis sanguisuga*), common in Palestine. The leech was known to the Hebrews by the name '*ălûḳâh* (Prov. 30:15); in Arab. it is called '*alaḳah*, because it clings to the flesh. It is noted for its insatiable appetite for blood. In the proverb it is used figuratively. Its 2 insatiable daughters are perhaps named in the 1st line of v. 16. The marg. of the R.V. substitutes vampire, which refers to certain female specters that are superstitiously believed to haunt graves and suck human blood. The ground for this interpretation is that in Arab. '*aulaḳ* is the name of a demon or goblin, and '*alûk* is equivalent to ghoul.

Ho'sah (hō'sá) [refuge, seeking refuge].
1. A porter in the time of David (I Chron. 16:38; 26:10).
2. A village on the frontier of Asher, and apparently s. of Tyre (Josh. 19:29). Probably to be identified with Palaetyros, or Tyre on the mainland.

Ho·san'na [Gr. *hōsanna*, from Heb. *hōshî'āh nnā'* (Ps. 118:25, *hiph'îl* imperative), save, now; or save, pray. The imperative form *hōsha'* (Ps. 86:2; Jer. 31:7), however, seems to be the basis of Gr. *hōsanna*]. An acclamation of the multitude on the occasion of Jesus' triumphal entry into Jerusalem. It occurs 6 times in the Gospels: twice absolutely (Mark 11:9; John 12:13); twice followed by the dative "to the son of David" (Matt. 21:9, 15); and twice by the phrase "in the highest" (Matt. 21:9; Mark 11:10). The derivation of the word from the imperative plus *nnā'* is favored by the fact that the 3 Gospels in this connection quote Ps. 118:26. Verse 25 of this psalm is said to have been repeated once on each of the 1st 6 days of the feast of tabernacles, during the solemn procession around the altar of burnt sacrifice, and 7 times on the 7th day. The word originally had a supplicatory sense, but, as the context in the Gospels shows, it had become an ejaculation of joy or a shout of welcome. Augustine accordingly regards it as an interjection of admiring joy, and the Anglo-Saxon versions render it "Hail." A Scottish note defines it: "Alss mekill as to say, Gyff health, prosper, gud lucke."

Ho·se'a (hŏ-zē'á), in A.V. of N.T. **O'see** (ō'zē), like the Gr. form; the same word as Oshea or Hoshea (Num. 13:8, 16, A.V. and R.V.), the 1st name of Joshua, and as Hoshea, king of Israel (II Kings 15:30) [save, salvation; or a short form of Hoshaiah]. A prophet, son of Beeri, whose predictions were uttered in the reigns of Uzziah, Jotham, Ahaz, and Hezekiah, kings of Judah, and Jeroboam II, king of Israel (Hos. 1:1). The dating by Jeroboam (Hos. 1:1) is supported by internal evidence (ch. 1:4), which clearly states that the house of Jehu (to which Jeroboam belonged)

is still on the throne. References to the disorders and assassinations in the Northern Kingdom which followed the death of Jeroboam may be detected in chs. 7:3, 16; 8:4, and the conditions depicted in chs. 5:8 to 6:6 may reflect the Syro-Ephraimitic War (734–733 B.C.; cf. II Kings 15:29 to 16:9; I Chron. 5:26; II Chron., ch. 28; Isa. 7:1–9). It has been assumed by some critics that the chronology of the kings of Judah (Hos. 1:1) has been added to represent Hosea as a contemporary of Isaiah (Isa. 1:1), and that the work of Hosea was closed c. 734–733. Yet the dates (Hos. 1:1) are reasonable and within the limits of possibility. Assuming that Hosea prophesied during as many as 12 or 13 years of Jeroboam's reign, and that he lived to see the overthrow of Samaria in 722 B.C., his ministry extended over a period of 40 years. Hosea was doubtless a citizen of the Northern Kingdom, for he speaks of "our king" and "the land," meaning Northern Israel, without feeling the need of a restrictive adjective (chs. 1:2; 7:5); and he prophesied to the people of that kingdom. He was a contemporary of Isaiah, who labored in Judah (cf. Hos. 1:1 with Isa. 1:1); he began his prophetic activity in the reign of Jeroboam II, when Jeroboam and Uzziah were contemporaries, that is, before 746 B.C., or c. 750. Hosea was also a contemporary of Amos in the Northern Kingdom and of Micah who prophesied in Judah.

The Book of Hosea is the 1st of the Minor Prophets in the order of their arrangement. It consists of 2 portions, chs. 1 to 3 and 4 to 14. The 1st part belongs to the earlier period of the prophet's ministry; for ch. 1 at least dates from the reign of Jeroboam II, or within 6 months after its close, before the destruction of the house of Jehu (ch. 1:2–4). These first 3 chs. furnish the key to the whole book, in which the unfaithfulness of Israel to Jehovah during the entire national history is pressed home on the conscience (chs. 4:1 to 5:7; 6:4 to 7:16; 8 to 11), the necessity of chastisement is shown, and the unquenchable love of Jehovah for his erring people is earnestly taught (chs. 6:1–3; 12 to 14). In chs. 1 to 3 the unfaithfulness of Israel and the Lord's patience and forbearance are set forth under the analogy of an adulterous wife. The logical order of thought of chs. 1 to 3 is: chs. 1:1–9; 3:1–5; 2:2–23; 1:10 to 2:1.

Regarding the account of the prophet's marriage interpreters have been divided in opinion from ancient times.

I. *Some say that it was all a vision,* a transaction in a trance or a dream but never carried out in real life.

II. *Closely allied to the preceding,* and like it based on an objection to a literal interpretation, is the view which makes it a parable, or an allegory, or a figurative mode of speech. It has been argued that we are dealing with an allegorical and not a real incident, for the following reasons: 1. It is impossible that God would have commanded a prophet to enter into such a revolting alliance, and one that was apt to lessen his influence with the better part of the people as a marriage with a harlot would do. 2. The Law of Moses (Lev. 21:7) forbade a priest to marry an unchaste woman, and although the prophets were not priests, it has been assumed that God would hardly direct a prophet to marry an unclean woman. 3. The action of the first chapter, if real, would require years for its performance, involving not only the prophet's marriage but also the birth of several children, and the symbolic lesson would be lost. This 3d objection, however, cannot be taken too seriously. A prophet's call may be progressive; years of experience would fortify him in certain convictions; or his sorrow, which extended over a number of years, would give him more time to make a comparison between the unfaithfulness of Gomer to himself and that of Israel to God.

Now against the preceding views (I and II) we may present the following reasons: 1. What is morally and religiously objectionable in actual practice becomes no more defensible by being presented as a vision or a parable. 2. If this had not been a real incident in Hosea's life, his parable would have put a blot upon the life of his children, defamed the character of Gomer, who was innocent of adultery, and have brought ridicule upon the prophet and misunderstanding at home. 3. Hosea gives no indication that he is giving us an allegory or a parable. 4. The name Gomer bath-Diblaim gives no symbolical meaning. 5. No symbolism can be attached to the fact that the 2d child is a girl and not a boy. 6. Realism was used by the earlier prophets (cf. Ahijah, I Kings, ch. 11, and Zedekiah, ch. 22:11). 7. Prophets were accustomed to give symbolical names to real children (cf. the names of Isaiah's children, Isa. 7:3; 8:3). 8. Hosea 1:2-4, 6 refers to Hosea in the 3d person, while in ch. 3:1-3 the prophet speaks in the 1st person; the narrative of an actual happening could reasonably be presented in this form, but it is difficult to see why an allegory or a parable should be thus divided. 9. An experience such as that of Hosea furnishes the best explanation of his message: *it was the outcome of the sufferings of his own heart.*

III. *Another view is that an actual marriage took place,* but within this theory there are many divergent views. How shall we justify the 1st word of God to Hosea, "Go, take unto thee a wife of whoredom and children of whoredom"? The older supporters of the literal theory maintained that such a thing may be justified by the express command of God, or that it was well worth the end, viz., the salvation of a lost soul. But it would be a rather horrible thing to have God command Hosea against his own desire to marry an impure woman for whom the prophet has no love. We can in this case, however, reconcile the idea of God's plan with that of the freedom of choice. At the time of his marriage Hosea had not known the impure tendencies of Gomer. Later, when he discovered her real nature, it seemed to him as if he had married her in obedience to a call from God. In other words, he understands his impulse for her as a command from God, of which, however, at the time he was not conscious. According to this view, he would have to understand the command (Hos. 1:2) in a proleptic sense. Although he exercised his freedom of choice when he fell in love with Gomer and married her, in the end he realized that this bitter experience was all a part of God's plan. Education and piety do not always govern a man in the right choice of a wife. Hosea may have erred to his later regret, but subsequently he saw in what was his own choice the plan of God through which he became a messenger unto Israel.

Although there are various views within the theory of a real marriage, it seems most reasonable to assume that the disposition toward adultery in Gomer did not manifest itself until after her marriage. This explanation has a number of advantages: 1. It accepts the narrative as being the simple recital of biographical facts, while at the same time it does away with all the moral difficulties involved in views which regard Gomer as an acknowledged harlot or a devotee of Baal worship previous to her marriage. 2. It furnishes a reasonable basis for Hosea's love for Gomer. 3. It most easily explains the processes through which Hosea came to a realization of the mutual relationship of Jehovah and Israel. 4. It is supported by ch. 3, where Hosea takes back his wife who had been guilty of adultery;

if the prophet had married her with full knowledge of an immoral life on her part, he would not have been justified in holding her conduct against her.

The question may be raised as to when Hosea found out about his wife's infidelity: before the birth of Jezreel or after the event. Probably before, for he foretells doom for Israel on the basis of the 1st child's name. The 1st child belonged to Hosea (ch. 1:3), but we have no positive evidence to determine the paternity of the other 2. Even though ch. 1 contains a he-account and ch. 3 has an I-account of the prophet's domestic life, there is no doubt that in both cases the woman is Gomer. The I-account goes back to the prophet himself, while the he-account may have been composed by one of his disciples on the basis of documents or of knowledge of the circumstances.

The names of the children are significant. Jezreel means "El (God) soweth," and has in this connection (ch. 1:4, 5) an ominous import of sowing destruction based on a historical background. In this plain Sisera was defeated (Judg. 4:13 *seq.*); in the same region Gideon fought the Midianites and the Amalekites (Judg. 6:33 *seq.;* 7:1 *seq.*). Here also conflicts took place between the Philistines and the Israelites (I Sam. 29:1 *seq.*). Most ominous of all was the fact that it was the scene of the massacre of the house of Ahab by Jehu; here also Ahaziah, king of Judah, was mortally wounded by Jehu's men (II Kings, chs. 9; 10). Now it will be the scene of vengeance upon the house of Jehu (Hos. 1:4, 5). Lo-ruhamah (v. 6) means literally, "She will not be shown compassion." Lo-ammi (v. 9) signifies, "Not my people." Just as Gomer had been unfaithful to Hosea, so Israel had been unfaithful to the covenant that God had made with it, and figuratively speaking was guilty of adultery. The love of Hosea for Gomer is a symbol of the abiding love of God for his people. Just as Gomer was disciplined when Hosea took her back, so faithless Israel had to undergo discipline (ch. 3:3-5). The period of punishment, however, is a means of reformation (ch. 2:14-23), and Israel will again know God and return to him. The name Jezreel, although still to be understood literally, now refers in a good sense to sowing the people anew in the land (ch. 2:23). In the other 2 names the negative prefix is dropped (ch. 2:1, 23), and now they signify: "She has been shown compassion" and "My people." Harmony then exists between God and Israel, and this is extended even to the realm of nature (ch. 2:21-23).

The 2d part of The Book of Hosea, consisting of chs. 4 to 14, is not a series of discourses, nor even one continuous sermon, but is a summary of his prophetic teaching, prepared by him toward the close of his ministry or by one of his disciples after his death. The prophecy thus consists the gist of his public addresses. The prophecies of chs. 4 to 14 were for the most part uttered originally when Assyria was filling Israel with great dread. There are occasional indications of date; ch. 10:14 may refer to Shalmaneser V, king of Assyria (728-722 B.C.). The frequent references of the prophet to the dallying of the government, now with Assyria and now with Egypt, may be interpreted as representing Israel's politics at the time of Pekah and Hoshea (chs. 5:13; 7:11; 8:9; 14:3; cf. Hos. 12:1 with II Kings 17:3, 4); accordingly it may be that the rebuke of Israel for its foreign policy was uttered during the reigns of its last 2 kings. At any rate, the superscription (Hos. 1:1) should not be rejected.

The paragraphs into which chs. 4 to 14 are divided in the R.V. form units of thought complete in themselves, as follows:

1. Chs. 4:1 to 6:3. The thought that binds the various utterances together is sin and the need of repentance. The people are arraigned for gross iniquity (ch. 4), and the princes and priests as being the leaders in sin (ch. 5). The arraignment is followed by a beautiful exhortation to repentance and the promise of God's return in favor (ch. 6:1-3).

2. Chs. 6:4 to 10:15. The unifying thought is the grievous punishment that must come for heinous sin. Halfhearted repentance does not satisfy God (ch. 6:4-11). The immoral life and shameless excess of the mighty is manifest to God (ch. 7:1-7). Israel's stupidity and folly in seeking aid from the powers of the world; for its foolishness it shall be chastised (vs. 8-16). The invader is near because of Israel's idolatry and schism (ch. 8:1-7). Israel has drawn judgment upon itself by dallying with Assyria, by religious abuses, and by trusting in human means (vs. 8-14). Israel's infidelity (ch. 9:1-9), and consequent punishment (vs. 10-17). Israel, flourishing like a vigorous vine, only increases its idolatry; but judgment shall spring up as abundant and as destructive as the noxious weed (ch. 10:1-8). Israel's sin compared to that of Gibeah (vs. 9-11). Whatsoever one sows, that shall one also reap (vs. 12-15).

3. Chs. 11 to 13. A passage characterized by yearning and expostulation. Jehovah's love for Israel is the unquenchable love of a father for his child, even for a wayward child (ch. 11:1-11). Jacob relied upon his own strength and shrewdness at first, but finally importuned God and prevailed; therefore turn from earthly alliances to thy God (ch. 11:12 to 12:6). Ephraim is a dishonest tradesman, and, having become rich, excuses himself of sin; but Jehovah will cast him out of his home, he who saved Israel from Egypt will now punish (ch. 12:7-14). Ephraim's idolatry condemned (ch. 13:1-8), and its consequence declared (vs. 9-16).

4. Ch. 14. Exhortation to repentance, confession, and humble supplication, and the promise of Jehovah's gracious acceptance of the penitent and bestowal of richest blessings.

It may be observed that chs. 4:1 to 9:9, which inveigh against the heathenish cult and the political conditions of the time, are brought together without a definite principle of order. But the rest of the book (chs. 9:10 to 14:9), in historical retrospect derives the sinfulness of Israel out of the past. The prophet recognizes the fact that the religion of Israel is a historical religion and that it has its roots in the past. This section may be summarized as follows: ch. 9:10-14 recalls Israel's defection to Baal of Peor (Num., ch. 25); ch. 9:15-17 traces the evil conditions of the time to Gilgal, where was inaugurated the kingdom under Saul (I Sam. 11:14, 15; 13:7-15; 15:10-35); ch. 10:1-8 is directed against the cultic and political errors which began with Israel's prosperity and found expression in the worship of the calves and in the Northern Kingdom; ch. 10:9-15 inveighs against the Kingdom of Israel, which began at Saul's residence in Gibeah (I Sam. 11:4) and the threat of the dire results of war; ch. 11:1-11 goes back to the Exodus, accuses Israel of ingratitude, but closes with divine mercy; chs. 11:12 to 12:14, in assailing Israel, draws illustrations from the life of Jacob, beginning with his prenatal state, and shows how the sins of the time were typified in the patriarch (reference is made again to the Exodus and the simplicity of ancient life); ch. 13:1-11, Ephraim has fallen through the worship of Baal and of images, but the God of the time of the Exodus is unchanging; ch. 13:12-16, the iniquity of Israel and the threat of terrible punishment; ch. 14:1-8, an appeal to repentance and the promise of divine grace; ch. 14:9, a final exhorta-

tion to take to heart the words of the book. Although the order of events from antiquity is not chronological, the appeal to history by the prophet plays an important part in his teaching.

In chs. 4 to 14 the text in many places is corrupt, which produces difficulties in interpretation. Some critics have denied to Hosea the genuineness of the references to Judah, to the restoration of Israel to God's favor and its return to its native land (e.g., chs. 1:10 to 2:1), and to the sole legitimacy of the Davidic monarchy (chs. 1:4; 3:5; 8:4). Concerning the 3 classes of passages to which exception has been taken: 1. The references to Judah. An occasional side glance at Judah, a people so intimately connected with his own, must not be denied to the prophet; especially since he saw the moral conditions in Judah becoming similar to those of Ephraim. For example, the elimination of Judah from chs. 5:8 to 6:6 would completely destroy the sense of the passage. 2. The references to a restoration of Israel to God's favor and the return of the people to their own country. (a) A reference to restoration to God's favor is demanded by the symmetry, since each section of chs. 1 to 3, and greater sections of the book as a whole, end with promises (chs. 1:10 to 2:1; 2:14-23; 3:5). (b) It is the custom of prophecy not to close with the threatening of doom and leave the people to despair, but to let the light of hope break through the dark clouds and irradiate the great future. (c) Continuing the picture of the destruction of Israel in battle for its sins, the verses of hope (chs. 1:10 to 2:1) represent the victory of united Israel and Judah over their foes. (d) Thought was turned to the possibility of a return both by the prospect of imminent exile for the nation, and also presently by the knowledge that many Israelitish captives were in Assyria (II Kings 15:29; I Chron. 5:26; Isa. 9:1). 3. The references to the legitimacy of the Davidic monarchy and the illegitimacy of northern Israel's kings. (a) To question these it is necessary to reject the genuineness not only of these prophecies in Hosea, but also of the prediction of the universal dominion of the Davidic king which was uttered in northern Israel by a contemporary prophet of Judean birth (Amos 9:11). (b) To the believer in the moral government of the universe the failure and fall of one dynasty after another in the n., during the preceding 2 centuries, was conclusive evidence of their rejection by God; and the continuance of the Davidic monarchy confirmed the prophetic words, spoken in the Southern Kingdom concerning that line, and was itself independent proof that God had chosen the house of David.

Hosea strikes a modern note when he deplores the ignorance of the people: "My people are destroyed for lack of knowledge: because thou hast rejected knowledge, I will also reject thee" (ch. 4:6; cf. chs. 4:1; 5:4; 6:3, 6; 11:3). If we remember that Hosea means by the knowledge of God an impression of facts implying a change of both temper and conduct, it is very easy to pass to his doctrine of repentance. According to Hosea, repentance is a turning around and going back to God; it is the effect of a knowledge of God —a knowledge not of new facts, but of facts which have been present for a long time and which ought to have been appreciated before. Because Hosea's doctrine of God's love is so rich, so fair, and so tender, his doctrine of repentance is so full and gracious. His appreciation of God's love is presented in such a way that sin appears the more heinous since it really implies sinning against God's love.

Amos is the prophet of justice and social righteousness; Hosea, the prophet of love. They are not contradictory, rather supplementary. We need both in the economy of revelation. Yet the prophet, who so beautifully depicts the love of God (Hos. 14:4–8), also shows his wra'h and threatens dire punishment (cf. chs. 5:10, 14; 7:12–16; 8:5, 13; 9:7–17; 11:5, 6; 13:7, 8). In ch. 11:8, 9, Hosea presents the exhaustless mercy of God which no sin of man can bar or wear out. The master thought of Hosea's message is that God's mighty and inextinguishable love for Israel will not rest satisfied until it has brought all Israel into harmony with itself.

Ho·sha'iah (hŏ-shā'yå) [Jehovah has saved]. 1. Father of Jezaniah and Azariah (Jer. 42:1; 43:2).

2. A m n, doubtless a prince of Judah, who walked immediately behind the chorus of t'ose who gave thanks in the procession at the dedication of the 2nd Temple (Neh. 12:32).

Hosh'a·ma (hŏsh'å-må) [probably for Jehoshama, Jehovah has heard]. One of the family or descendants of King Jeconiah (I Chron. 3:18).

Ho·she'a (hŏ-shē'å), in A.V. of Num. 13:8, 16 **O·she'a** (ŏ-shē'å) [save]. 1. The earlier name of Joshua, the son of Nun, which was changed by Moses into Joshua (Num. 13:8, 16). See JOSHUA 1.

2. Son of Azaziah and prince of Ephraim in David's reign (I Chron. 27:20).

3. A son of Elah. With the connivance of Tiglath-pileser, king of Assyria, he conspired against Pekah, king of Israel, slew him, and ascended the throne (II Kings 15:30). His reign lasted about 9 years, from about 730 to 722 B.C. He did evil in the sight of Jehovah, but still was better than the average of the preceding kings. Shalmaneser, king of Assyria, made an expedition against him. Not being able to repel the invader, Hoshea paid tribute (ch. 17:3); but knowing that the powerful kingdom of Egypt looked with jealousy on the approach of the Assyrians to its frontiers, he soon sought assistance from Egypt. Trusting that aid would be forthcoming, he withheld the annual tribute from Assyria (v. 4). Shalmaneser again invaded the Israelite territory, took Hoshea captive, and laid siege to Samaria. See SHALMANESER 3. The city was reduced to great straits, but it held out 3 years. At t e end of the 3 years Shalmaneser died and was succeeded by Sargon, who claims the honor of capturing the city. He carried the leading inhabitants into captivity, and placed them in Halah and in Habor, by the river of Gozan, and in the cities of the Medes (vs. 5, 6). This event is known as t e captivity of the 10 tribes. It was not any special wickedness on the part of Hoshea that brought it on. The cup of Israel's iniquity had been filling for centuries, and Hoshea's iniquities only added the last drop which made the cup full to overflowing (vs. 7–23). See SAMARIA 1, SARGON, ISRAEL 3.

4. One of those who sealed the covenant (Neh. 10:23).

5. The Hebrew name of the Prophet Hosea. See HOSEA.

Host. A multitude, especially when organized; an army (Gen. 21:22; Judg. 4:2) or the division of an army (Ex. 7:4, in A.V. armies; 12:41; Num. 2:3, in A.V. armies; I Kings 2:5); the angels, constituting a heavenly host (I Kings 22:19; Ps. 148:2; Luke 2:13); and the stars (Deut. 4:19; II Kings 23:5). The Semites comprehended heaven and all its forces and beings, heaven and all that is therein, in the phrase host of heaven; and in the phrase host of the earth, they included the earth and all that is therein, the forces of nature like wind, lightning, heat and cold, and things animate and inanimate (Gen. 2:1; Ps. 33:6).

The title Lord of hosts has sometimes been explained as meaning that Jehovah is the God of the armies of Israel. In proof, David's words to Goliath are cited: "Thou comest to me with a sword, and with a spear . . . : but I come to thee in the name of Jehovah of hosts, the God of the armies of Israel" (I Sam. 17:45). The Prophet Isaiah is also quoted, who says: "Jehovah of hosts will come down to fight upon mount Zion" (Isa. 31:4). But this does not comprehend the full meaning of the term. Jehovah did fight for his people; he was indeed "Jehovah strong and mighty, Jehovah mighty in battle." But the Lord of hosts was more than the war-god of Israel. The Greek translators grasped the true meaning of the title and rendered it *Pantokratōr*, the Almighty. The word hosts which is used in the title refers to the armies of the universe. The designation pictures the universe, in its spiritual and material aspects, as forming a vast army, in numerous divisions, of various kinds of troops, in orderly array under the command of Jehovah. One division consists of the angels. It was the Lord, the God of hosts, who appeared to Jacob at Beth-el when he beheld the ladder and the angels of God ascending and descending (Gen. 28:12, 13; Hos. 12:4, 5).

"Who in the skies can be compared unto Jehovah?
Who among the sons of the mighty is like unto Jehovah,
A God very terrible in the council of the holy ones,
And to be feared above all them that are round about him?
O Jehovah God of hosts,
Who is a mighty one, like unto thee, O Jehovah?"

(Ps. 89:6–8; cf. A.V.). Another host consists of the stars, in their beautiful order and wonderful array. Jehovah is their commander. Isaiah bids those who would know God to go forth, and lift up their eyes on high and see (Isa. 40:26; 45:12). Yet another host consists of all the forces of nature; they stand at the bidding of Jehovah, worshiping and serving him (Neh. 9:6). The Lord of hosts sends sword, famine, and pestilence (Jer. 29:17). "The Lord, which giveth the sun for a light by day and the ordinances of the moon and of the stars for a light by night, which stirreth up the sea that the waves thereof roar, the Lord of hosts is his name" (Jer. 31:35). The Greeks, looking at the heavens above them, and at the earth around them, called what they saw "cosmos," the beauty of harmony. The Romans, discovering the same harmonious relations and movements, named the entirety of creation a "universe," combined as one. To the poetic imagination of the Hebrews, with their knowledge of the omnipotent reigning God, the regularity and order everywhere apparent suggested an army in vast, numerous, and varied divisions, acting under the command of one will. The Lord of hosts, he is the king who alone commands. See SABAOTH.

Ho'tham (hō'thăm) [seal, signet ring]. 1. An Asherite, son of Heber, family of Beriah (I Chron. 7:32).

2. An Aroerite, 2 of whose sons were among David's mighty men (I Chron. 11:44); A.V., Hothan.

Ho'than (hō'thăn). See HOTHAM 2.

Ho'thir (hō'thēr). A son of Heman, David's seer and singer (I Chron. 25:4).

Hour. See DAY 2 and NIGHT.

House. In Palestine and other parts of the East the houses of the common people, who constitute more than ¾ of the population, have only 1 story, and sometimes only 1 room. The interior is frequently divided into 2 portions, 1 several feet higher than the other.

The door from the outside leads into the lower portion, which is occupied by the cattle. Troughs for their feed are arranged along the side of the platform where the family dwells. This higher floor is reached by a short flight of steps. Sometimes there is a loft above the stable for guests. These several apartments are not walled off from each other. The walls of the house are often of mud or sun-dried brick, even when, as in Palestine, stone is procurable (cf. Job 24:16; Ezek. 13:10–16). The roofs are made of branches of trees, canes, palm leaves, etc., covered with a thick stratum of earth. Materials so flimsy cannot long re-

An Oriental House

sist the heavy rains which at certain seasons fall in warm countries.

The houses of the better class are generally built, as of old, in a quadrangle. around a central courtyard, which in certain cases may contain a fountain, or even a well (II Sam. 17:18). The upper chamber is an important room in the 2d story, sometimes constituting all there is of a 2d story, being built above the general level of the roof (Judg. 3:20; I Kings 17:19; II Kings 4:10; Mark 14:15; Acts 1:13; 9:37). The roofs of the houses are flat and are generally surrounded by battlements according to Mosaic Law (Deut. 22:

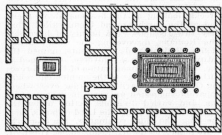

Plan of a Greco-Roman House

8). They are well adapted for storing and drying agricultural produce (Josh. 2:6), for walking to and fro (II Sam. 11:2), for conversation (I Sam. 9:25, 26), for idolatrous worship (II Kings 23:12), or for religious meditation and prayer (Acts 10:9). There is a staircase outside the house, by which the roof can be reached without entering the building (cf. Matt. 24:17; Mark 13:15). Although roofs for the most part are flat, there have been discovered cases of gabled roofs. The windows are generally narrow, and mostly open into the courtyard instead of facing the street.

Ho'za·i (hō'za-ī) [perhaps, (Jehovah) is seeing]. Writer of a history which treated of King Manasseh (II Chron. 33:19). In A.V., following the LXX, Heb. Hōzăy has been translated as if it were a common noun, and the book cited appears as a collection of sayings by the seers (cf. v. 18). The LXX seems to be based on a Heb. form haḥozīm.

Huk'kok (hŭk'ŏk) [hewn in, decreed]. A town on the boundary line of Naphtali (Josh. 19:34). Yaḳūḳ, about 6 miles w. by n. of Tell Ḥūm, is generally accepted as the site.

Hu'kok (hū'kŏk). See HELKATH.

Hul (hŭl) [circle, circuit]. The 2d son of Aram (Gen. 10:23; I Chron. 1:17). As a geographical region, the name may possibly be identified with Hūli'a which is mentioned by Ashur-nasir-pal in connection with Mount Masius.

Hul'dah (hŭl'dà) [weasel, mole]. A prophetess, who lived in the 2d quarter of Jerusalem (II Kings 22:14). She was the wife of Shallum, keeper of the wardrobe, and was held in the highest esteem. She lived during the reign of Josiah, and prophesied the destruction of Jerusalem, but added that on account of Josiah's piety he should die before the coming of the catastrophe (II Kings 22:12–20; II Chron. 34:20–28).

Hum'tah (hŭm'tà) [place of lizards or, perhaps, fortress]. A town in the hill country of Judah (Josh. 15:54). Site unknown.

Hunt'er and Hunt'ing. Hunting was a favorite pastime of ancient kings (Gen. 10:9). The Babylonian and Assyrian monarchs delighted in it and were proud of their achievements, recording their success in inscriptions, and depicting their deeds in sculpture to adorn the walls of their palaces. In Palestine game existed during the entire Biblical period in certain localities, as in the wilderness of Judah, the thickets of the Jordan, the more notable forests, and the s. country (Gen. 25:27; Jos. Antiq. xvi. 10, 3). Many of the animals recognized as clean and fit for food were wild and could be obtained only by hunting. When the animal was slain, its blood was poured out upon the earth and not eaten (Deut. 12:15, 16,22). Hunting was practiced in order to exterminate noxious beasts (Ex. 23:29; I Kings 13:24), to secure food (Gen. 27:3; Ecclus. 36:19), and as sport (Jos. War i. 21, 13). People hunted alone or in companies (Jer. 16:16), on foot or on horseback (Jos. War i. 21, 13), and on the great plains in chariots. The hunter used bow and arrows (Isa. 7:24) and the spear (Jos. Antiq. xvi. 10, 3). Decoys were employed (Jer. 5:26, 27), and nets and traps (Job 18:10; Ecclus. 27:20) and pits (II Sam. 23:20; Ezek. 19:4, 8). Babylonians, Assyrians, and Persians kept dogs trained for the chase.

Hu'pham (hū'făm). A son or more remote descendant of Benjamin, and founder of a tribal family (Num. 26:39). Called Huppim (Gen. 46:21; cf. I Chron. 7:12, 15), and perhaps Huram (I Chron. 8:5). Huram would seem to be descended from Bela or Gera. Huppim is not registered with either Bela, Becher, or Jediael in I Chron. 7:12, unless he is descended from Bela through Ir or Iri (v. 7).

Hup'pah (hŭp'à) [perhaps, (Jehovah is) a covering]. A descendant of Aaron. His family became the 13th course of the priests (I Chron. 24:13).

Hup'pim (hŭp'ĭm). See HUPHAM.

Hur (hŭr) [whiteness, splendor]. 1. A man of Judah, family of Hezron, house of Caleb (I Chron. 2:18, 19). He was the grandfather of Bezaleel (I Chron. 2:20; Ex. 31:1, 2). With Aaron, he supported the arms of Moses during the fight with the Amalekites (Ex. 17:10–12). He was associated with Aaron in the government of the Israelites while Moses was absent in Mount Sinai (ch. 24:14). Josephus, writing many centuries after the event, calls Hur the husband of Miriam, Moses' sister (Jos. Antiq. iii. 2, 4). The O.T. is silent on the subject.

2. One of 5 kings of Midian slain by Moses (Num. 31:8; Josh. 13:21).

3. Father of Solomon's purveyor in Mount Ephraim (I Kings 4:8).

4. Father of a certain Rephaiah (Neh. 3:9).

Hu′ra·i (hū′rå-ī). One of David's mighty men from the brooks of Gaash (I Chron. 11:32). Called Hiddai in II Sam. 23:30.

Hu′ram (hū′răm). 1. A king of Tyre (II Chron. 2:3). See Hiram.

2. A Tyrian artificer (II Chron. 4:11, 16). See Hiram.

3. A Benjamite, perhaps a son of Bela (I Chron. 8:5). See Hupham.

Hu′ri (hū′rī). A Gadite (I Chron. 5:14).

Hu′shah (hū′shå) [haste, emotion]. A town of Judah, to judge from I Chron. 4:4; 27:11; probably Hūsan, s.w. of Bethlehem.

Hu′shai (hū′shī) [hasty, hastening]. An Archite, one of David's 2 leading counselors. He remained faithful to his sovereign during Absalom's rebellion, and effectually defeated the counsel of Ahithophel (II Sam. 15:32–37; 17:5–16). See Ahithophel and Baana 2.

Hu′sham (hū′shăm) [haste]. A man of the land of the Temanites, who succeeded Jobab as king of Edom (Gen. 36:34, 35; I Chron. 1:45, 46).

Hu′shath·ite (hū′shăth-īt). An inhabitant of Hushah (II Sam. 21:18; 23:27).

Hu′shim (hū′shĭm). 1. The son of Dan (Gen. 46:23). Called in Num. 26:42, Shuham. The difference is due to a transposition of the consonants.

2. A Benjamite family, sons of Aher (I Chron. 7:12).

3. One of the 3 wives of the Benjamite Shaharaim (I Chron. 8:8, 11).

Husk. A kind of food eaten by swine, and which the Prodigal Son in his poverty was glad to share (Luke 15:16). It is the pod of the carob tree (Ceratonia siliqua), and is also called locust bean and St. John's bread. The tree is a handsome evergreen, attaining a height of 30 feet, thornless, and with leaves like the ash. The legumes are borne in great

Pod and Branch of the Carob Tree

profusion, and are often a foot long. When green they are used for cattle and swine and in times of great famine are eaten by people. A sirup is made of the pulp of the pods.

Huz (hŭz). See Uz.

Huz′zab (hŭz′ăb). According to the interpretation of A.V. the name of the queen or a poetic term for Nineveh (Nahum 2:7). The Targum understands it to mean "the queen," and so it is rendered by J.V. But in A.V. marg. it is rendered, "That which was established," or, "There was a stand made." A.R.V. translates, "And it is decreed." Both these renderings make Huzzab simply a part of the Heb. verb yāṣab, to place or establish.

Hy′a·cinth, or in modified form **Ja′cinth.** 1. The name of a color (Rev. 9:17).

2. A precious stone, constituting the 11th foundation of the New Jerusalem (Rev. 21:20; R.V. marg., sapphire) and one of the 12 jewels in the high priest's breastplate (Ex. 28:19, R.V.; marg., amber).

Hy·e′na. An animal which feeds on offal (Ecclus. 13:18). The striped hyena (Hyaena striata) is common in every part of Palestine, living in caves and tombs, coming forth after dark to rifle graves or otherwise seek after prey. The valley of Zeboim in I Sam. 13:18 means the valley of hyenas.

Hy′me·nae′us (hī′mĕ-nē′ŭs) [Gr., pertaining to Hymen, the god of marriage]. One who made shipwreck of his faith, blasphemed, and was excommunicated by Paul (I Tim. 1:20). He declared that the resurrection was already past. Philetus was associated with him in this error (II Tim. 2:17, 18).

Hymn. A spiritual meditation designed, or at least suitable for, singing or chanting in the worship of God. The book of Psalms is the earliest hymnbook in existence. Other magnificent Hebrew religious odes are the songs of Moses (Ex. 15:1–19; Deut. 32:1–43), Deborah (Judg., ch. 5), Hannah (I Sam. 2:1–10), Mary (Luke 1:46–55), and Zacharias (Luke 1:68–79). The last 2 are known as the Magnificat and the Benedictus respectively, from the 1st word of the Lat. translation. The Hebrew psalms were often sung to the accompaniment of music (II Chron. 29:27, 28; cf. I Chron. 16:42). In the N.T. 3 terms are used for Christian songs: psalms, hymns, and spiritual songs or odes (Eph. 5:19; Col. 3:16). The hymn which Christ and his disciples sang after supper on the night of the betrayal (Matt. 26:30) was doubtless the hallel (Psalms 113 to 118), which was sung by the Jews at the celebration of the passover. The early Christians sang hymns in public worship and privately as a means of worshiping God and of edification and comfort (Acts 16:25; I Cor. 14:26; Eph. 5:19; Col. 3:16). Fragments of early Christian hymns, known as such from the meter in the Gr. text, are preserved in Eph. 5:14; I Tim. 3:16; cf. Rev. 15:3, 4. At the beginning of the 2d century, in the reign of Trajan, the Christians of Bithynia were reported by Pliny the Younger as singing songs to Christ as God (Pliny Epis. x. 96).

Hys′sop [Gr. hyssōpos, hyssōpon, from Heb. 'ēzōb]. A plant of Egypt and Palestine (Ex. 12:22), well adapted for sprinkling. It springs out of walls, and is small in comparison with the cedar of Lebanon (I Kings 4:33). It is aromatic, and was largely used, under the Law, often in bunches, with cedar wood and wool, for ceremonial purification (Lev. 14:4, 6, 49–52; Num. 19:6, 18; Ps. 51:7; Heb. 9:19). A sponge filled with vinegar was put upon hyssop and raised to the lips of Jesus when he was on the cross (John 19:29). The common hyssop (Hyssopus officinalis) is a sweet-smelling plant, belonging to the order

Lamiaceae or *Labiatae*, or Mints. It is a small bushy herb which grows to a height of 12 or 18 inches, and has small, hairy, lanceolate leaves. But Tristram states that its area is the s. of Europe, the Danubian province, and Siberia. Moreover, the statement of 2 of the Evangelists (Matt. 27:48; Mark 15:36) that the sponge of vinegar offered to Jesus was put upon *kalamos*, a reed which the common hyssop does not produce, has led some interpreters to think that a different plant from the common hyssop is intended, perhaps the caper plant (*Capparis spinosa*), but this view has little to commend it.

Rabbinic tradition identifies Heb. *'ēzōb* with Arab. *ṣa'tar* (*Origanum*, marjoram, or thyme), which may be *Origanum maru*. This

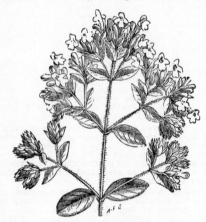

Common Hyssop

plant is common in Palestine, growing on walls and rocks. Its thick, hairy leaves and hairy branches can be made into a bunch, and would hold liquids for sprinkling. The leaves and head of this plant have a pungent, aromatic flavor. Like peppermint, at first it tastes hot, but this is followed by a cooling, refreshing feeling. The addition of this herb to the vinegar or sour wine on the sponge would aid in alleviating the suffering of one on the cross. A bunch of hyssop may have accompanied the sponge upon the reed. This plant seems to fulfill the requirements of both the O.T. and the N.T. passages. One MS. reads *hyssōi* for *hyssōpōi* (John 19:29); in that case the passage means: "So they put a sponge full of vinegar upon a javelin."

I

Ib'har (ĭb'här) [He (God) chooses]. One of King David's sons born at Jerusalem (II Sam. 5:15; I Chron. 14:5).

I'bis. A bird (Lev. 11:19, R.V. marg.), allied to the herons and storks. It was formerly venerated by the Egyptians. See HERON.

Ib'le·am (ĭb'lē-ăm). A city in the territory of Issachar, given to the tribe of Manasseh; but the Canaanite population was not expelled (Josh. 17:11, 12; Judg. 1:27). Near it Ahaziah, king of Judah, was mortally wounded by the followers of Jehu (II Kings 9:27). Zechariah, king of Israel, was slain there (II Kings 15:10, text of Lucian). It is generally identified with Bileam, a town of Manasseh given to the Levites (I Chron. 6: 70); Bel'ameh, a ruin 1¼ miles s. of Jenin

and about 13 miles e. of n. of Samaria (cf. Belmen, Belma:m, Judith 4:4; 7:3).

Ib'ne·iah (ĭb'nē'yȧ) [Jehovah builds up]. A Benjamite, son of Jeroham and head of a father's house (I Chron. 9:8).

Ib·ni'jah (ĭb-nī'jȧ) [Jehovah builds up]. A Benjamite, father of Reuel (I Chron. 9:8).

Ib'ri (ĭb'rī) [a Hebrew]. A son of Jaaziah (I Chron. 24:27).

Ib'sam (ĭb'săm), in A.V. **Jib'sam** [fragrant, balsam]. A man of Issachar, family of Tola (I Chron. 7:2).

Ib'zan (ĭb'zăn) [cf. Arab. *'abūṣ*, swift (of a horse)]. A judge who ruled over Israel, or part of it, for 7 years. He was a native of Bethlehem, apparently that in Zebulun, was buried in his native place, and was succeeded by a Zebulunite. He had 30 sons and 30 daughters (Judg. 12:8–10).

Ich'a·bod (ĭk'ȧ-bŏd) [inglorious, no glory]. Son of Phinehas and grandson of Eli. The name commemorated the fact that the glory had departed from Israel, for the Ark of God was taken (I Sam. 4:19–22).

I·co'ni·um (ī-cō'nĭ-ŭm). A city of Asia Minor, which is described by Xenophon as the last city in Phrygia to one traveling e. (*Anabasis* i. 2, 19). Under the Roman and Greek empires Iconium was considered the capital of Lycaonia. It was situated in a fertile spot in the high, waterless plain of Lycaonia. Barnabas and Paul visited it on the First Missionary Journey both going and returning (Acts 13:51; 14:1–6, 19–22; cf. 16:2; II Tim. 3: 11). It has had an unbroken history and is now known as Konya (Konia).

Id'a·lah (ĭd'ȧ-lȧ). A border town of Zebulun (Josh. 19:15), Khirbet el-Ḥuwāra, about ⅝ of a mile s. of Beit Laḥm.

Id'bash (ĭd'băsh) [honey-sweet]. A man of Judah (I Chron. 4:3).

Id'do, I (ĭd'ō) [Heb. *'iddō*; cf. Arab. *'adda*, to happen unexpectedly, to overwhelm]. The chief at Casiphia through whom Ezra, when conducting a company of exiles from Babylonia to Jerusalem, obtained the contingent which was lacking of Levites and Nethinim for the service of the Temple (Ezra 8:17–20).

Id'do, II (ĭd'ō) [Heb. *Yiddō*, probably, loving, beloved]. 1. Son of Zechariah, and a chief in David's reign of the half tribe of Manasseh e. of the Jordan (I Chron. 27:21). 2. A man induced by Ezra to put away his foreign wife (Ezra 10:43). In A.V. the name is written Jadau, a form arising from the translators' pronouncing the consonants of the kethib (but only one *d*) with the vowels of the kere. Jaddai (text of J.V., and marg. of R.V.) is the kere.

Id'do, III (ĭd'ō) [Heb. *'iddō'*, *'iddō*, *ye'dō*, *ye'dī*, decked, adorned]. 1. A Levite, a descendant of Gershom (I Chron. 6:21). Apparently called Adaiah synonymously (v. 41). 2. Father of Ahinadab, Solomon's purveyor at Mahanaim (I Kings 4:14). 3. A seer who wrote a book of visions concerning Jeroboam and in which events of Solomon's reign were related (II Chron. 9:29), a book on genealogies, in which deeds of Rehoboam were recorded (ch. 12:15), and a history which treated of King Abijah's acts (ch. 13:22). 4. Grandfather of the Prophet Zechariah (Zech. 1:1, 7; cf. Ezra 5:1; 6:14). He is not unreasonably believed to be identical with Iddo, a chief of the priests who returned with Zerubbabel to Jerusalem and whose name is that of a father's house in the next generation. The head of this house at the time mentioned is a priest named Zechariah (Neh. 12: 4, 16).

I'dol. An image, a sculpture, or other representation of any person or being, intended as an object of worship, or as the embodiment and efficient presence of a deity (Ex. 20:4, 5, 23; Judg. 17:3; I Sam. 5:3, 4; Rom. 1:23). Idols were made of silver, gold (Ps. 115:4; 135:15), wood, or other material (Isa. 44:13–17). When metallic, they were fashioned by running melted metal into a mold, in which case they were called molten images; or they consisted of plates of metal over a wooden core fashioned with a graving tool. When of wood or stone, they were made by graving tools or other instruments, and were called graven images. The process of manufacture is described in Isaiah and Jeremiah (Isa. 40:19, 20; 44:9–20; Jer. 10:9). Some were small, especially those designed as household gods or teraphim (Gen. 31:34; 35:1–4); some were as large as a human being (I Sam. 19:16); some, such as that erected by Nebuchadnezzar in the plain of Dura, were colossal (Dan. 3:1).

About A.D. 300 images were introduced into some Christian churches for instruction and ornament only. In 736 the Eastern emperor Leo issued edicts against them. In 780 the empress Irene introduced image worship into the Eastern Church, and in 787 the Second Council of Nice gave them ecclesiastical sanction.

I·dol'a·try. Idolatry was practiced at a comparatively early period of man's history. The immediate ancestors of Abraham worshiped other gods (Josh. 24:2) in addition to Jehovah, it may be believed, and doubtless by means of idols. Laban had images, which Rachel was too justly accused of stealing (Gen. 31:30, 32–35). The Egyptians made figures of the gods to serve as objects of worship, and in the innermost sanctuary of their temples lay the symbol of a god (Herod. ii. 63, 138). The Canaanite nations had idols which the Israelites, on succeeding to the land, were ordered to destroy (Ex. 23:24; 34:13; Num. 33:52; Deut. 7:5). The Second Commandment was directed against idolatry (Ex. 20:4, 5; Deut. 5:8, 9), forbidding man to bow down to images, sculptures, statues, and pictures. And the teachers of Israel followed up this injunction by pointing out and ridiculing the impotency of idols (Ps. 115:2–8; Isa. 2:8, 18–21; 40:19, 20; 44:9–20; Jer. 10:3–5). Their helplessness was discovered when the Ark of the Lord was in the Temple of Dagon (I Sam. 5:3–5). The apocryphal book of Bel and the Dragon treats of the deceitful practices of the priests in the idol temples. Of the nations with whom the Israelites were brought into contact during Scripture times, all but the Persians were idolaters, and they did not worship Jehovah. When the Israelites borrowed idolatrous practices from the neighboring nations, 2 well-marked stages were traceable in the progress of error. At first they attempted to worship Jehovah by means of images; see JEROBOAM 1. Then they departed entirely from Jehovah, and the idols they made were designed to represent other divinities; see BAAL 1. In N.T. times church members who lived in heathen communities were required to take precautions to avoid compromising themselves with idolatry. The Council of Jerusalem enjoined that they should abstain from the flesh of animals that had been sacrificed to idols (Acts 15:29). Paul gave the same injunction, but explained that in the case of those who had no faith in idols, abstinence was designed to avoid casting a stumbling block in the path of the weaker brethren (I Cor. 8:4–13). If receiving hospitality at any house, and meat which might possibly have been offered to an idol was set on the table, the Christian guest was not required to ask any questions for conscience' sake; but if he was expressly told that the food had been offered to an idol, then he was to abstain. The same rule was to be carried out with regard to food purchased for the household in the ordinary market (I Cor. 10:18–33).

Id'u·mae'a (ĭd'ụ̄-mē'ā́), in A.V. of O.T. and Apocrypha **Id'u·me'a** (ĭd'ụ̄-mē'ā́) [Gr., pertaining to Edom]. The name used by Greeks and Romans, in slightly different spelling, for the country of Edom (Mark 3:8; and in A.V. only, Isa. 34:5, 6; Ezek. 35:15; 36:5). After the fall of Jerusalem, in 586 B.C., the Edomites began to press n. (Ezek. 36:5). They themselves were driven from Petra w. by the Nabataeans, who were established there by 312 B.C. and who before the middle of the 2d century B.C. were occupying, not only s. Judah, but also Hebron and the country to its n. as far as Bethzur (I Macc. 4:29; 5:65). Judas Maccabaeus warred against them successfully; and John Hyrcanus, about 126 B.C., completely subjugated them and placed them under a Jewish governor (Jos. *Antiq.* xiii. 9, 1).

I·e'zer (ī-ē'zēr). See ABIEZER 1.

I·e'zer·ite (ī-ē'zēr-īt). See ABIEZERITE.

I'gal (ī'găl), in A.V. once **I'ge·al** (I Chron. 3:22) [he (God) redeems]. 1. The spy sent forth by the tribe of Issachar to search out the Land of Canaan (Num. 13:7).

2. One of David's mighty men, the son of Nathan (II Sam. 23:36). He occupies the same position in the catalogue as does Joel in I Chron. 11:38, and it is natural to identify the 2. But the relation of the 2 lists at this point is difficult to determine; and as Igal and Joel are differently described, they may be different persons, nephew and uncle. 3. A son of Shemaiah, a descendant of King Jeconiah (I Chron. 3:22).

Ig'da·li'ah (ĭg'dá-lī'á) [great is Jehovah]. Father of the Prophet Hanan (Jer. 35:4).

I'ge·al (ī'gē-ăl). See IGAL.

I'im (ī'ĭm) [heaps, ruins]. 1. A town e. of the Jordan (Num. 33:45, A.V.; in R.V. Iyim); it may be the Moabite fortress Maḥaiy, about 7 miles e. of Dhat Rās. See IYE-ABARIM.

2. A town in the extreme s. of Judah (Josh. 15:29); Deir el-Ghawi, near Umm Deimneh.

I'je-ab'a·rim (ī'jê-ăb'á-rĭm). See IYE-ABA-RIM.

I'jon (ī'jŏn) [a ruin]. A fortified city of Naphtali, one of those captured by Ben-hadad, king of Syria, at the instigation of Asa (I Kings 15:20; II Chron. 16:4). Its inhabitants were subsequently carried into captivity by Tiglath-pileser (II Kings 15:29). Robinson located it at Tell Dibbīn, a hill 110 feet high, on the e. border of Merj 'Ayūn, meadow of springs. The site is about 8 miles n.n.w. of Banias.

Ik'kesh (ĭk'ĕsh) [crooked, perverse]. Father of David's captain and mighty man Ira (II Sam. 23:26; I Chron. 11:28).

I'la·i (ī'lā-ī). One of David's mighty men (I Chron. 11:29), called Zalmon in II Sam. 23:28.

Il·lyr'i·cum (ĭ-lĭr'ĭ-kŭm). A country bounded on the n. by Pannonia, on the s. by Epirus, on the e. by Macedonia, and, when it included Dalmatia, on the w. by the Adriatic Sea. It is traversed from n.w. to s.e. by the Noric, Carnic, and Julian Alps, constituting the most e. portion of the great Alpine chain. Along the coast are excellent harbors and numerous islands. The Illyrian race inhabiting the region were wild mountaineers, who were a thorn in the side of their neighbors, the Macedonians; and, when they descended to the seacoast, they so practiced piracy as to bring them into collision with the Romans, who, in 229 B.C., began to conquer them, and finally made Illyricum, or Illyria, a province of the empire. The Apostle Paul preached the gospel "from Jerusalem, and round about even unto Illyricum" (Rom. 15:19). In the later years of the Roman Empire the name Illyricum gained a much wider meaning.

Im'age. See IDOL.

I·mal·cu'e (ĭ-măl-kū'ē), in A.V. **Si·mal·cu'e.** An Arabian who brought up the young Antiochus, son of Alexander Balas (I Macc. 11:39); in Jos. *Antiq.* xiii. 5, 1 called Malchus. The name doubtless contains the Arab. word *malik,* king.

Im'la (ĭm'lȧ) or **Im'lah** (ĭm'lȧ) [he (God) is full, or fills (fulfills)]. Father of the Prophet Micaiah (I Kings 22:8, 9; II Chron. 18:7, 8).

Im·man'u·el (ĭ-măn'ū-ĕl), in A.V. of N.T. **Em·man'u·el,** the Gr. form [God with us]. A son whom "the maiden" should bear (Isa. 7:14, R.V. marg.). Before the son is born, or at the time of his birth, historical events will justify naming him "God with us"; before he attains to years of moral determination, the land of n. Israel and Damascus will be forsaken, and unexampled punishment will be inflicted on Judah (Isa. 7:16,17); and hence during the years of his moral maturity, he shall eat the products of a land that has been wasted by the nations (vs. 15, 18 *seq.*). Isaiah had in mind that worthy son of David about whom prophecy had begun to cluster, for: 1. He foretells the birth of a son, not simply of a child. 2. He utters this prophecy to the house of David in view of God's rejection of the faithless successor of David who then occupied the throne. 3. On the natural interpretation of ch. 8:8, which observes the previous use of Immanuel as the name of the son, which does justice to the pronoun of the 2d person in the clause preceding Immanuel, and which affords an easy transition to the succeeding verse, Immanuel is a person; and if so, he is a native of Judah and sufficiently great to be singled out as a representative, for Judah is spoken of as the land of Immanuel; and he is a powerful personage, for because of him the rage of the nations is vain (v. 9 *seq.*). 4. The Messiah is definitely before the prophet's mind in ch. 9:6, 7 and ch. 11:1; and violence is required to separate these prophecies from that of ch. 7. The Messianic hope was awake at this period of history. 5. The use of the article with maiden is adequately explained. Isaiah uses it to designate the young woman, unknown by name, yet definite, who is to be the mother of the Messiah (cf. Micah 5:3). 6. Looking back, Matthew (Matt. 1:22, 23) sees the fulfillment of this prophecy in the birth of Jesus.

The prophet is, therefore, thinking of David's son who might appear at any time. But he is not predicting the birth of Hezekiah and expecting him to be the Messiah for: 1. Hezekiah was already born. This prophecy was delivered in 734 B.C., and Hezekiah was on the throne, a vigorous ruler in 727 B.C. 2. After the lapse of a year and when Hezekiah was a youth, the prophet still continues to look forward to the future for the going forth of the shoot out of the root of Jesse. 3. Hezekiah did not eat curds and honey; the processes which issued in the spoliation and subjection of the land had only begun in Hezekiah's time. If vs. 18–25 of Isa., ch. 7, are included in the prophecy, the fly of Egypt did not come upon Judah in Hezekiah's day. Even v. 17 presents a picture which belongs to the remoter future. Days such as had not been were not brought upon Ahaz and his people;

only the beginning of the process which resulted in the predicted calamity was seen.

Immanuel was a sign. Before the child reached moral self-determination, the lands of Rezin and Pekah were to be forsaken (Isa. 7:16). Immanuel was not a sign to compel faith in Ahaz, but one that called for faith. Like many other signs of the O.T., it called for present faith and occurred only when the prophecy was fulfilled (e.g. Ex. 3:12).

The birth, infancy, and youth of the Messiah are described as actually passing before the prophet's sight; but the prophet himself did not understand that the Messiah was necessarily to be born immediately, for when the Messiah did not appear within a year, Isaiah shows no signs of disappointment, loses no faith in the prophetic revelation, continues his activity, makes still greater disclosures regarding Immanuel, and enjoys the continued confidence of his fellow countrymen.

The promise of immediate deliverance from the advancing enemy (Isa. 7:3–11) is confirmed by an appeal to an event which might occur sooner or later. But whether occurring at once or long subsequently, it is confirmatory, because it implies the deliverance promised to Ahaz. The assurance already given by God (II Sam. 7:11–17), that the Messiah should be born of the royal family of David was a sign to the house of David, including Ahaz, that the purpose of Rezin and Pekah to destroy the kingdom and place a new king over the people should not stand (Isa. 7:13, 14). And the remoter the sign, that is the remoter the birth of the Messiah, the stronger was the guarantee of the long continuance of the royal family of Judah.

The birth and infancy of Immanuel measure the progress of the predicted events. "I see his birth, who is God's guarantee of the continued existence and deliverance of Judah, as though it is already at hand. I do not know the times and the seasons, but it is revealed to me as a sign to you, and as though about to occur. As such it contains a measure of time for the immediate future. Before the child comes to the years when one chooses between right and wrong, the northern land shall be forsaken. At the time of life when one's moral faculties have matured, he, the scion of the royal house of Judah, will dwell in a wasted land." Any child would serve for measuring the time; but the child chosen is the Messiah because the prophecy of deliverance rested upon the promises which centered in the Messiah.

Now let us consider the period. 1. Before the child attained the age when man's moral faculties are mature the Northern Kingdom was desolate. In fact, before a child born in the year of this meeting between Isaiah and Ahaz could have reached moral maturity the land of the north was desolate. The meeting is known to have taken place in 734 B.C.. In 732 Damascus and the district governed by it fell into the hands of the Assyrians. The 2½ tribes of Israel e. of the Jordan and Naphtali were carried off at the close of the Syro-Ephraimitic War (734–733), Samaria fell, and a large body of its inhabitants were deported in 722 (721). At Christ's appearance, the 10 tribes no longer existed as a nation, and no longer occupied the land of their fathers. 2. Ahaz himself had gone to Damascus, had done homage to the Assyrian king, and had acknowledged that Judah was a tributary state to Assyria. Judah itself was not actually devastated, but it had bowed itself down to the foreign yoke. From this time onward, with the exception of short intervals, it was in a sense subject to the dominant world power, and it was looked upon by the great empire of each period as a dependency; whenever Judah claimed independence it was visited sooner or later by the imperial power, which claimed sovereignty, and was punished and wasted. Its nationality was not blotted out and the royal family was not destroyed nor overlooked; but Judah was, generally speaking, a dependency. When Christ actually appeared, Judah was still acknowledging a foreign sovereign. In other words, all the processes foretold by Isaiah began in the lifetime of Ahaz, and their results were in full force when the Messiah actually appeared.

Im'mer (Im'ẽr) [sheep, lamb]. 1. A descendant of Aaron. His family had become a father's house in the time of David, and was made the 16th course of priests (I Chron. 24:1, 6, 14). The ruler of the house of God in the days of Jeremiah, and an antagonist of the prophet, apparently belonged to this house (Jer. 20:1), and doubtless they were members of this family who returned from Babylon with Zerubbabel (Ezra 2:37; Neh. 11:13). Two priests of this house were among those who about a century after the Return were guilty of marrying foreign wives (Ezra 10:20). A little later another son of Immer took part in the honorable work of rebuilding the walls of Jerusalem (Neh. 3:29).
2. A person or a place in Babylonia whence exiles returned. He or the exiles failed, however, to prove their genealogy (Ezra 2:59; Neh. 7:61).

Im'na (Im'nȧ) [he (God) keeps off, i.e., defends; cf. Arab. *mana'a*]. An Asherite, a son of Helem (I Chron. 7:35).

Im'nah (Im'nȧ), in A.V. once **Jim'na** (Num. 26:44), and once **Jim'nah** (Gen. 46:17) [probably, good fortune; cf. Arab. *yumnah*, good luck, happiness]. 1. Son of Asher and founder of a tribal family (Num. 26:44; I Chron. 7:30; Gen. 46:17).
2. A Levite, father of Kore, in Hezekiah's reign (II Chron. 31:14).

Im'rah (Im'rȧ) [he (God) resists]. An Asherite, son of Zophah (I Chron. 7:36).

Im'ri (Im'rī) [contraction of Amariah]. 1. A man of Judah, son of Bani, and a descendant of Perez (I Chron. 9:4).
2. Father of the Zaccur who rebuilt part of the wall of Jerusalem after the Captivity (Neh. 3:2).

In·car·na'tion [Late Lat. *incarnatio*, from *incarnari*, to be made flesh]. The union of divinity with humanity in Christ. He was conceived by the power of the Holy Spirit and was born without sin, of the Virgin Mary. The Son of God became man by taking to himself a true body and a rational soul. In assuming a true human body and proper human nature, he became subject to the limitations of the flesh; but he is at once truly God and truly man, and although he has two distinct natures, he is only one person.

While the mediator between God and man (I Tim. 2:5), on the one hand had to be God in order to be perfect, it was requisite that he should be man "that he might advance our nature, perform obedience to the law, suffer and make intercession for us in our nature, have a fellow-feeling for our infirmities; that we might receive the adoption of sons, and have comfort and access with boldness unto the throne of grace. . . . It was requisite that the Mediator, who was to reconcile God and man, should himself be both God and man, and this in one person; that the proper works of each nature might be accepted of God for us, and relied on by us, as the works of the whole person" (Larger Catechism, 39, 40). (Cf. Matt. 1:18 to 2:21; Luke 1:26 to 2:52; John 1:1–14; Matt. 26:38; John 11:33; II Cor. 8:9; Gal. 4:4; Phil. 2:6–8; I

John 5:20; Rom. 3:24–26; 8:34; Eph. 1:6; Titus 2:14).

In'cense. Fragrant substances as gums and spices designed to be burned, especially in religious worship. Sweet incense was used extensively as an element in the Israelite ritual (Ex. 25:6; 35:8, 28; 37:29). The ingredients were stacte or opobalsamum, onycha, galbanum, and pure frankincense in equal proportions, tempered with salt. It was not allowed to be made for ordinary purposes (Ex. 30:34–38; Lev. 10:1–7). An altar of incense was fashioned of acacia wood overlaid with pure gold. It belonged to the oracle (I Kings 6:22), but was set in the Holy Place, just outside the veil which concealed the Holy of Holies; and each morning when the high priest dressed the lamps, he burned incense on it (Ex. 30:1–9; Luke 1:8–10); see ALTAR. Once a year on the great Day of Atonement, he brought the incense within the veil, and, burning it on a fire in a censer in the Most Holy Place, enveloped the mercy seat in a cloud of the odoriferous smoke which it sent forth (Lev. 16:12, 13). When the altar was dedicated, each of the princes brought a gift of incense carried in a spoon (Num. 7:14, 20, etc.). Where so many animal sacrifices were offered as there were in the courts, both of the tabernacle and the Temple, the smell of blood must have polluted the atmosphere, and doubtless burning of incense effected a sanitary influence. But it had also a symbolic reference. It availed to make atonement (Num. 16:46, 47), for it was typical of the intercession of the appointed high priest. The psalmist requested that his prayer might be set forth before Jehovah as incense (Ps. 141:2); the worshipers prayed outside the Temple while Zacharias offered incense within its walls (Luke 1:10); and in an apocalyptic vision an angel burned incense on the golden altar, the smoke ascending with the prayers of saints (Rev. 8:3–5). The worshipers of false divinities, no less than those who adored the true God, burned incense (II Chron. 34:25; Jer. 48:35). It seems that the so-called sun images (Lev. 26:30; II Chron. 14:5; 34:4, 7; Isa. 17:8; 27:9; Ezek. 6:4, 6) really were pagan altars of incense.

In'di·a (In'dĭ-ȧ) [Heb. *Hōddū*, from Old Pers. *hindav*, Avestan *hindav*, *hṯdav*, India; cf. Sans. *Sindhu*, Indus River]. A district on the lower Indus, conquered by Darius the Great and incorporated with the Persian empire (Herod. iii. 94; iv. 44; Persepolis inscription). It formed the e. limit of the Persian empire (Esth. 1:1; 8:9; cf. Herod. iv. 40). Alexander the Great crossed the Indus on his career of conquest. The occurrence of the name in I Macc. 8:8 is suspicious, and so Luther substituted Ionia. At any rate Judas Maccabaeus was misinformed if he was told that the Romans had taken India from Antiochus.

In'gath'er·ing, Feast of. See TABERNACLES, FEAST OF.

In·her'it·ance. See HEIR.

Ink'horn'. A horn or anything similar for holding ink. It was carried at the side (Ezek. 9:2). The inkhorn is still in use in the East. It consists of a case of wood, horn, or metal, with a head at one end for holding the ink, and a long shaft in which the reeds for writing are kept. The case is worn stuck in the girdle.

Inn. An Oriental inn bears little resemblance to an Occidental hotel. The inn was not so necessary in primitive times. Travelers readily found reception in the houses of the hospitable (Ex. 2:20; Judg. 19:15–21; II Kings 4:8; Acts 28:7; Heb. 13:2). The public inn was a mere place of shelter for man and beast.

Like the modern khans, it was probably a large, quadrangular court, with a well in the center and rooms around the sides for travelers, chambers for goods, and stalls for cattle. The rooms were destitute of furniture. The traveler spread his mat on the floor, if he had one; if not, then his shawl-like mantle sufficed for mattress and covering. He also provided food for himself and fodder for his cattle. Free lodging places of this sort were erected by liberal wealthy men for the benefit of wayfarers (cf. Jer. 41:17). Rarely was there a host from whom food could be purchased (Luke 10:34, 35).

In'spi•ra'tion [Lat. *inspirare,* to breathe into]. The terms inspiration and inspired are used in English with great latitude of meaning, and this latitude is reflected to some extent in their usage in the English Bible. The word inspiration occurs, however, only twice

written Scriptures, by virtue of which they are the word of God, and are clothed with all the characteristics which properly belong to the word of God. In accordance with the teaching of this classical passage, Scripture is uniformly recognized, throughout the N.T., as the very word of God, and is treated as possessing all the qualities which would naturally flow from its divine origin. Thus it is currently cited by the exclusive titles Scripture, the Scriptures, the Oracles of God (Rom. 3:2) or the Living Oracles (Acts 7:38, R.V.), and its words are ordinarily adduced by the authoritative formula, "It is written." Its divine character is explicitly expressed in the constant ascription of the words cursorily quoted from it to God as their author (Matt. 1:22; 2:15; Acts 13:34; Rom. 1:2; I Cor. 6:16), or more specifically to the Holy Spirit (Acts 1:16; 4:25, R.V.; 28:25; Heb. 3:7; 9:8; 10:

Courtyard of an Oriental Inn

in the English Bible, and in both cases in a religious sense (Job 32:8, A.V.; breath, R.V.; II Tim. 3:16). In the former passage the word is used loosely to give expression to the broad fact that men are not independent of God as intellectual beings, but that for small and great, old and young, alike, it is "the breath [or inspiration] of the Almighty [that] giveth them understanding." In the latter passage the word inspired is used in its more proper and specific sense as a direct predicate of the written Scriptures, affirming that quality of divinity in them by virtue of which they are "profitable" for the great ends for which they are given. The Scriptures which the apostle had particularly in mind in this passage were the sacred books of the Jews, what we call the O.T.; but the affirmation he makes will naturally hold good of all writings which rightly share the high title of Scripture with them. The quality which he thus makes the fundamental characteristic of Scripture is expressed in the original Greek not by the simple word inspired, but by a compound word, God-inspired, possibly of his own coinage, by which the divine source of the inspiration is emphasized. He adduces this fundamental quality of Scripture as the ground on which the unique value of the Scriptures rests: "All scripture," he says, "is given by inspiration of God, and is [therefore] profitable," etc. (A.V.), or, "Every scripure [seeing that it is] inspired of God is also profitable," etc. (R.V.). Inspiration, according to the apostle, is, therefore, the fundamental quality of the

15); and that, even when they are not ascribed to God in the original passages, but are spoken of or even addressed to him, and can be thought his only because they are part of the Scripture text (Matt. 19:5; Acts 4:24, 25; 13:34, 35; Heb. 1:6–10; 4:4, 7; 7:21; 10:30). While on the other hand the human writers of Scripture are said to have spoken "in" the Holy Spirit (Matt. 22:43; Mark 12:36, both R.V.), and are treated as merely the media through whom God the Holy Spirit speaks (Matt. 1:22; 2:15; Acts 1:16; 4:25; 28:25; Rom. 1:2). Accordingly, the very words of Scripture are accounted authoritative and "not to be broken" (John 10:34, 35; Gal. 3:16); its prophecies sure (John 19:36, 37; 20:9; Acts 1:16; II Peter 1:20); and its whole contents, historical as well as doctrinal and ethical, not only entirely trustworthy, but designedly framed for the spiritual profit of all ages (Rom. 4:23; 9:17; 15:4; I Cor. 9:10; 10:11; Gal. 3:8, 22; 4:30; II Tim. 3:16; I Peter 2:6; cf. II Chron. 17:9; Neh. 8:1). That the books of the N.T. are given to the Church as equally Scripture with those of the O.T., and share with them in all their divine qualities, is shown by the equal claim to authority which is made for them (I Cor. 7:40; 14:37; Gal. 1:8; II Thess. 3:4, 14); the similar representation of their authors as the organs of God (I Cor. 2:13, 16; 7:40; I Thess. 2:13; 4:2); and the inclusion of N.T. books along with those of the O.T. under the common sacred title of Scripture (I Tim. 5:18; II Peter 3:16).   B. B. W. (rev., H. S. G.)

In'stant and **In'stant·ly.** As an adjective or adverb, used in A.V., in the obsolete sense of earnest or steadfast (Luke 7:4; Acts 26:7; Rom. 12:12; II Tim. 4:2).

Iob (yōb), in A.V. **Job.** See JASHUB 1.

Iph·de'iah (ĭf-dē'yȧ), in A.V. **Iph'e·de'iah** (ĭf'ė-dē'yȧ) [Jehovah redeems]. A Benjamite, son of Shashak (I Chron. 8:25).

Iph'tah (ĭf'tȧ), in A.V. **Jiph'tah** [he (God) opens or sets free]. A town of Judah (Josh. 15:43). Site unknown.

Iph'tah·el (ĭf'tȧ-ĕl), in A.V. **Jiph'thah·el** [God opens or sets free]. A valley on the boundary line between Zebulun and Asher (Josh. 19:14, 27). The name is perhaps found in Jotopata, the modern Tell Jefāt, 9 miles n. by w. of Nazareth.

Ir (ĭr). See IRI.

I'ra (ī'rȧ) [perhaps, watchful, but cf. Heb. *'ayir*, young ass]. 1. Priest or chief minister to David; a Jairite (II Sam. 20:26) or a man of Jattir (Syriac text and suggested by Lucian's).
2. One of David's mighty men, a Tekoite, son of Ikkesh (II Sam. 23:26; I Chron. 11:28).
3. An Ithrite, one of David's mighty men (II Sam. 23:38; I Chron. 11:40).

I'rad (ī'răd). A descendant of Cain (Gen. 4:17, 18).

I'ram (ī'răm) [perhaps, watchful, aroused]. A chieftain of Edom (Gen. 36:43; I Chron. 1:54).

I'ri (ī'rī) and probably **Ir** [perhaps, watchful, or, my watchman]. A Benjamite, family of Bela (I Chron. 7:7, 12).

I·ri'jah (ī-rī'jȧ) [Jehovah sees or provides]. A captain of the guard. During the temporary departure of the Chaldeans from the siege of Jerusalem, he arrested Jeremiah, who was going out at the gate of Benjamin, on the charge of attempting to desert to the enemy (Jer. 37:13).

Ir'-na'hash (ĭr'nā'hăsh) [city of a serpent; probably originally, city of copper]. A town listed with the tribe of Judah (I Chron. 4:12). The marg. renders city of Nahash (cf. II Sam. 17:25). Ge-harashim (valley of craftsmen), in I Chron. 4:14, suggests that Ir-nahash means city of copper. If that valley be Wadi 'Arabah with its many copper and iron mining and smelting sites, it is probable that Ir-nahash is to be identified with the large Iron Age mining and smelting site of Khirbet Naḥas (Copper Ruin), located near the n. end of Wadi 'Arabah.

I'ron, I. Tubal-cain, of the race of Cain, worked in brass and iron (Gen. 4:22). As early as the Mosaic period there were axes and other instruments of iron (Num. 35:16; Deut. 19:5 marg.). Og's bedstead was made of iron (Deut. 3:11). In the time of Joshua, vessels were made of the metal (Josh. 6:19, 24); and chariots of iron for war purposes were in use (Josh. 17:16), continuing through the period of the Judges, and on to later times (Judg. 1:19; 4:3, 13). Of iron were made armor and weapons, as spearheads and breastplates (I Sam. 17·7; Rev. 9:9); agricultural implements, as harrows and threshing instruments (II Sam. 12:31; Amos 1:3); builder's tools and nails (I Kings 6:7; I Chron. 22:3); graving tools (Job 19:24; Jer. 17:1); barbed irons for fishing (Job 41:7); gates, bars, fetters (Ps. 105:18; 107:10, 16; 149:8; Isa. 45:2; Acts 12:10); idols (Dan. 5:4). Iron was imported from Tarshish, Greece, and the n., doubtless from the vicinity of the Black Sea (Jer. 15:12; Ezek. 27:12, 19). It was obtainable in Palestine (Deut. 8:9), being abundant on the Lebanon mountains. According to available evidence, the first smelting of iron took place c. 1400 B.C., possibly in the Hittite highlands of Asia Minor. The ore was reduced in furnaces (Deut. 4:20; I Kings 8:51) which, to judge from those in use in Lebanon, were built of stone, about 10 feet in height and 3 in diameter. Charcoal was used in them, and the fire was blown by bellows (Ezek. 22:20; cf. Jer. 6:29). It would seem that the Philistines had learned the use of iron in the n. and closely guarded the methods of working it (I Sam. 13:19-22). It was only after Saul and David had broken the Philistine power that the metal came into common use in Israel. See SMITH, EZION-GEBER.

I'ron, II (ī'rŏn) [perhaps, possessing a view, conspicuous]. A fortified city of Naphtali (Josh. 19:38); probably the present village of Yārūn, 10 miles w. from the Lake of Ḥuleh.

Ir'pe·el (ĭr'pė-ĕl) [God heals]. A town of Benjamin (Josh. 18:27). Conder thinks it probably the village Rāfāt, 6½ miles n. by w. of Jerusalem.

Ir'-she'mesh (ĭr'shē'mĕsh) [city of the sun]. A town of Dan (Josh. 19:41), the same as Beth-shemesh.

I'ru (ī'rōō) [perhaps, watchful]. A son of the celebrated Caleb (I Chron. 4:15); probably to be read Ir, the -*u* being the Heb. conjunction *and*.

I'saac (ī'zȧk) [he (God) laughs; perhaps, may El (God) smile (favorably upon me in my distress); cf. Ras Shamra literature, where El laughs]. The son of Abraham and Sarah, born in the s. country, doubtless at Beer-sheba (Gen. 21:14, 31), when his father was 100 years old and his mother about 90 (chs. 17:17; 21:5). When the promise was made that Sarah should bear him a son, Abraham laughed questioningly (ch. 17:17-19). Later when Sarah heard the promise from the mouth of the stranger stopping at the camp, she laughed incredulously (ch. 18:9-15); and when the child was born she joyfully confessed that God had prepared laughter for her and her friends (ch. 21:6). To commemorate these events and the faithfulness of God, Abraham called the boy's name Isaac, "one laugheth" (v. 3). He was circumcised on the 8th day (v. 4); and being the child of promise and legal heir he had higher privileges than Ishmael, Abraham's son by the handmaid (chs. 17:19-21; 21:12; 25:5, 6). To exhibit and develop Abraham's faith, God commanded him to offer Isaac as a burnt offering. Isaac was then a youth (ch. 22:6), perhaps 25 years old, as Josephus says; but he filially acquiesced in the purpose of his father. When Abraham had laid him upon the altar, and thus shown his readiness to give all that he possessed to God, the angel of the Lord forbade the sacrifice and accepted a ram instead, thus testifying against child sacrifices, practiced by the Canaanites and many other idolatrous peoples, and teaching to all men that human sacrifices are an abomination to the Lord (ch. 22:1-18).

Isaac dwelt in the s. country, at Beer-lahai-roi (ch. 24:62). In disposition he was retiring and contemplative, affectionate also, and felt his mother's death deeply (vs. 63, 67). He married at the age of 40 years, but his 2 sons were not born until he was 60 (ch. 25:20, 26). Because of a famine he moved 50 miles n., to Gerar (ch. 26:1, 6). There Jehovah appeared to him, telling him not to go to Egypt and reaffirming the Abrahamic covenant (vs. 2-5). It had been the settled policy of Abraham, whenever he was in foreign parts (ch. 20:13), to represent Sarah as his sister; and Isaac, in similar peril at Gerar, likewise tried to pass off Rebekah as his sister, but without success (ch. 26:6–11; cf. ch. 12:10–20). Leaving Gerar, Isaac pitched his camp in the valley of Gerar (ch. 26:17), and opened again the wells that his father had dug. Thence he removed to Beer-sheba (Heb. *be'ēr-sheba'*), which long remained his headquarters (chs. 26:23; 28:10). Jehovah appeared to him during the night and encouraged him; and he erected an altar, as his father had done (ch. 26:24, 25). Abimelech, the king of Gerar, visited him and entered into a treaty with him (vs. 26–31). This sworn agreement gave a new occasion for linking the memory of an oath with the name of the place; cf. Heb. *sheba'* (seven), *shâba'* (to swear), *shebû'āh* (oath); Shibah (Heb. *shib'āh*) (ch. 26:33; cf. ch. 21:31).

Esau, the elder of Isaac's 2 sons, was his favorite, although God had declared that the elder should serve the younger. Jacob was Rebekah's favorite (ch. 25:28). When Isaac was much over 100 years old (cf. ch. 27:1 with chs. 25:26; 26:34), Rebekah and Jacob took advantage of his age and blindness. Thus deceived as to the identity of person, Isaac transferred the Abrahamic blessing to the younger son. Soon after, at the instigation of Rebekah, who wished to save Jacob from the murderous wrath of Esau, but feigned a different reason, Isaac sent Jacob to Laban in Paddan-aram to get a wife (chs. 27:46 to 28:5).

Some 20 years later Isaac was residing near Hebron, where he had sojourned in his father's later life (ch. 35:27; cf. ch. 23:2). There he died at the age of 180 years (ch. 35:28, 29), and was buried by his 2 sons beside his parents and his wife in the cave of Machpelah (ch. 49:30, 31). The N.T. alludes to Isaac as a child of promise (Gal. 4:22, 23), and cites his tent life and his blessing Esau and Jacob as evidences of his faith (Heb. 11:9, 20).

I·sa′iah (ī-zā′yà), in A.V. of N.T. **E·sa′ias,** the Gr. form [Jehovah has saved]. A prophet of Judah in the reigns of Uzziah, Jotham, Ahaz, and Hezekiah, kings of Judah (Isa. 1:1; cf. chs. 6:1; 7:3; 14:28; 20:1, 2; 36 to 39). He was the son of Amoz, who must not be confounded with the Prophet Amos. He lived in Jerusalem, and prophesied concerning Judah and Jerusalem; his prophecies concerning Samaria, Damascus, Philistia and other nations being subordinate to those which directly concerned Jerusalem, and being introduced because of their relation to Zion and the people of God. It is now generally acknowledged that the vision which he saw in the year that King Uzziah died (ch. 6) marked his call to the prophetic office. By the year 734 B.C. Isaiah was a married man (Isa. 8:3), with a son named Shear-jashub, which means "A remnant shall return" (ch. 7:3, R.V. marg.). A 2d son was afterward born to him, whom by divine direction he called Maher-shalal-hash-baz, which means "The spoil speedeth, the prey hasteneth" (ch. 8:1, R.V. marg.). The names of both sons enshrine prophecies. Isaiah's wife is called a prophetess (ch. 8:3), probably merely because she was the wife of a prophet.

Isaiah spoke much on the relations of Israel, both as a church and as a body politic, to the world. In regard to political relations he urged king and people to put trust in Jehovah and avoid entangling alliances with earthly powers (ch. 8:12–14; etc.). In 734 B.C., when Syria and Israel joined forces in order to capture Jerusalem, and put an appointee of their own upon the throne, Isaiah declared Jehovah's purpose that the attempt should fail, and he vainly endeavored to persuade Ahaz to rely on Jehovah and not put confidence in heathen princes (ch. 7). Ahaz unwisely re-

jected this advice, called in Tiglath-pileser, king of Assyria, and became his vassal (II Kings 16:7–10); see Tiglath-pileser. Under Hezekiah the prophet's counsel was treated with more respect. The Assyrians invaded Judah in Hezekiah's 14th year, about 714 B.C. (II Kings 18:13; Isa. 36:1). Shortly afterward, in the same year, Hezekiah fell dangerously sick, and Isaiah foretold his recovery (II Kings 20:1–11). Then followed the embassy of Merodach-baladan, 712 B.C. (Isa., ch. 39; II Kings 20:12, 13), the conquest of Ashdod by Sargon's army, 711 B.C. (Isa., ch. 20), and the expeditions sent against Jerusalem by Sennacherib, 701 B.C. (II Kings 18:14). During the last-named crisis, Isaiah's prophecies and encouraging words nerved the government to refuse the Assyrian demands (II Kings 18:13 to 19:36).

The time and manner of Isaiah's death are not known with certainty. Hezekiah died c. 693 B.C. The murder of Sennacherib and accession of Esarhaddon, which occurred in 681 and 680, are recorded (Isa. 37:38). Doubtful Jewish tradition affirms that Isaiah was martyred by Manasseh, having been sawed asunder, and some have supposed that Heb. 11:37 alludes to the manner of his death. The date involved is not impossible, for Isaiah may have begun his ministry about or after 740 B.C., prophesied in the reigns of the 4 kings, Uzziah, Jotham, Ahaz, and Hezekiah, survived Hezekiah, and written his acts (II Chron. 32:32), heard of the murder of Sennacherib, and have suffered martyrdom in or after the 18th year of Manasseh, at the age of not more than 80 years. At any rate, in writing his history of Uzziah's reign (II Chron. 26:22), Isaiah probably used records and other authoritative sources for the earliest part of the reign.

The Book of Isaiah is divisible as follows:

I. Chs. 1 to 12, *prophecies* relating to the Kingdoms of Judah and Israel and belonging to various occasions from c. 740 to 701 B.C. 1. Introduction (ch. 1). 2. A prophecy against Jerusalem (chs. 2 to 4), with a continuation or closely related prophecy (ch. 5). The denunciation culminates in ch. 4 with the effect of the Judgment and a picture of the glory of Messianic times. This prophecy may have been delivered during the prosperous times of the joint reign of Uzziah and Jotham. 3. The vision of ch. 6, which stands in close relation to the Book of Immanuel (chs. 7 to 12).

II. Chs. 13 to 23, *10 burdens on the nations,* divided by ch. 20, which is of international import, into 2 series of 5 burdens each.

III. Chs. 24 to 27. *These chapters are intimately connected* and present a vivid picture of a great judgment upon the whole world (ch. 24), and followed by Judah's triumph and blessedness (chs. 25 to 27).

IV. Chs. 28 to 33, *a group of discourses* dealing for the most part with the relation of Judah to Assyria. The earlier ones insist on the shortsightedness of revolting from Assyria and trusting to Egypt for aid; the latter foretell the trouble in which, through neglect of Isaiah's warnings, Judah and Jerusalem would be involved, and their subsequent deliverance.

V. Chs. 34; 35, *the contrasted future* of Edom and of Israel.

VI. Chs. 36 to 39, *a historical section,* differing (except for the addition of ch. 38:9–20) only verbally from II Kings 18:13, 17 to 20:19. This passage narrates certain important events in which Isaiah was concerned: 1. Sennacherib's double demand (chs. 36:2 *seq.*; 37:7 *seq.*) for the surrender of Jerusalem, Isaiah's prediction of its deliverance followed by fulfillment (chs. 36; 37). 2. Hezekiah's sickness, his prayer and cure, song of thanksgiving (ch. 38). 3. Embassy from Merodach-baladan, Isaiah's reproof of King Hezekiah, and prediction of spoliation by the Babylonians.

VII. *The Book of Consolation* (chs. 40 to 66), which treats of Israel's restoration from exile in Babylon. The prominent figure in these chapters is the servant of the Lord (see SERVANT OF JEHOVAH).

Some critics have attempted to treat chs. 1 to 35 according to a threefold scheme or pattern such as is found in The Book of Ezekiel and in the LXX of Jeremiah: 1. threats against the prophet's own people; 2. threats against foreign nations; 3. promises for his own people. The outlines of such a scheme may be discerned: chs. 1 to 12 contain threats against Judah and Jerusalem; chs. 13 to 23 (or 27), mainly threats against foreign nations; within chs. 24 (or 28) to 35, promises are found in chs. 33 to 35, but chs. 28 to 32 also contain many promises. It must be admitted, however, that this scheme is not so definite as it is in Ezekiel and in the LXX of Jeremiah, and it does not aid us in understanding the process of the formation of these chapters.

Critics differ a great deal in their views of the growth or formation of chs. 1 to 39, especially since they consider some passages as later than Isaiah's time, and they also make room for the work of redactors. Without endorsing the views of these scholars, it may be of interest to note that they doubt the genuineness of some of the passages of promise or of the ideal commonwealth (chs. 11:10–16; 14:1, 2; 29:16–24; 30:18–26; 32:1–8). It has been argued that the ideas of these sections correspond to a time subsequent to that of Isaiah. There is also dispute concerning ch. 2:2–4, which is parallel to Micah 4:1–4. It is not certain which prophet is the author, and both may have drawn from an anonymous source. While critics do not agree about ch. 9:1–6, the better works regard it as genuine; in the case of ch. 11:1–9 there is also considerable disagreement.

Critics have regarded the following as later additions to the work of Isaiah: chs. 13:2–22 (which they date shortly before 539 B.C.); 14:4b–21; 15; 16; 21:1–10; 24 to 27; 33 to 35. It should be borne in mind, however, that critics are far from unanimous in their opinions and that they differ greatly in their reasons and in the dates they assign to these passages.

The last 27 chapters of The Book of Isaiah have to be considered separately. The traditional view, which is still held by some scholars, ascribes them to Isaiah, but at the present time the great majority of even conservative critics ascribe them to Deutero-Isaiah, or chs. 40 to 55 to Deutero-Isaiah and chs. 56 to 66 to Trito-Isaiah.

In favor of unity of authorship, the following arguments have been presented: 1. There has not been shown a single word of known late date, nor a single foreign element which there is any reason to believe was not current in Jerusalem in the days of Isaiah. Every word, phrase, and form is found in earlier Hebrew literature or may be explained by the history of the times. As to the style being peculiar, change of style is consistent with unity of authorship. The style of Shakespeare changed. His literary activity lasted but 25 years, yet 4 distinct periods are discernible in his plays, marked by differences of style. The literary activity of Isaiah was continued through at least 40 years and perhaps 60. And is the style so peculiar after all? Those who deny the Isaianic authorship find it incumbent upon them to explain the similarity of style. 2. To the argument that the allusions, which are made in these chapters to the condition of Jews and Gentiles,

reveal the time of the Exile, it is replied: (*a*) The prophets frequently transport themselves to the future and describe what they are predicting as already past; for instance, although Zebulun and Naphtali had been ravaged and their inhabitants carried into captivity, Isaiah says of them: "The people that walked in darkness have seen a great light" (ch. 9:2). (*b*) The explicit references to Babylon, the Exile, and the restoration are few. (*c*) Isaiah and his contemporary prophets were already living in anticipation of the Babylonian Exile. There is scarcely an event connected with the Exile, to which the author refers, but was known to the Israelites in the time of Isaiah. The prophets of the time predicted the destruction of Jerusalem and the Temple (Amos 2:5; Micah 3:12; Isa. 3:8; 6:11), the desolation of the land of Judah (Hos. 8:14; Amos 9:11, 14; Isa. 3:25, 26; 6:11, 12; 32:13), the captivity of the people of Judah (Isa. 11:12; Micah 1:14–16). This captivity was to be in Babylon (Isa. 39:6, 7; cf. ch. 11:11; Micah 4:10). There should be a return from exile (Joel 3:1; Isa. 11:11). Jerusalem and the Temple should be rebuilt (Micah 4:2; although the destruction of Jerusalem had been foretold, Micah 3:12; cf. Joel 3:16–20), and many people would come to Jerusalem to worship (Isa. 2:2–4; 11:10; 18:7; Micah 4:1–3). (*d*) The spiritual condition of the people, as exhibited in these chapters, is that of the time of Isaiah; idolatry under every green tree (Isa. 57:5; 1:29; II Kings 16:4) and among the oaks (Isa. 57:5; 1:29; Hos. 4:13) and in gardens (Isa. 65:3; 66:17; 1:29); the slaying of children in the valleys (Isa. 57:5; II Chron. 28:3; 33:6; II Kings 23:10); ascending a high mountain to offer sacrifice (Isa. 57:7; II Chron. 28:4; Hos. 4:13; cf. Ezek. 6:13); hypocrisy (Isa. 58:2–4; 29:13); Sabbath-breaking (Isa. 58:13; Amos 8:5; Jer. 17:19–27); bloodshed and violence (Isa. 59:3, 7; 1:15; Micah 7:2); falsehood, injustice, and oppression (Isa. 59:3, 4, 6, 7, 9; 5:7, 23; 10:1, 2; Micah 2:1, 2; 7:3); neglect of the Temple worship (Isa. 43:23, 24; II Chron. 28:24; 29:27; II Kings 15:4; II Chron. 27:2; II Kings 15:35). Burning incense upon bricks (Isa. 65:3) was appropriate to a worship derived from either Egypt, Assyria, or Babylonia, and was practiced in Jerusalem before the Exile (II Kings 23:12; Jer. 19:13). Swine's flesh was offered and eaten (Isa. 65:4) by the Egyptians on the festival of Selene and Dionysus (Herod. ii. 47, 48) and commonly enough by the Babylonians. 3. To the argument that the statements concerning the condition of the people agree with the historical facts, whereas those which relate to the future have fallen far short of fulfillment, it is replied that the assertion applies with equal force to the acknowledged writings of the Prophet Isaiah. He foretold the destruction of the cities, the utter desolation of the land, and the removal of the inhabitants far hence (Isa. 6:11, 12). This was fulfilled to the letter. But he prophesied also the flocking of the Gentiles to the standard of Jesse's son, the return of the captive people of God from all parts of the world, the drying up of rivers which were obstacles in the course of the march, a highway from Assyria for the remnant of the people, the wolf dwelling in peace with the lamb (Isa. 11:6–16; see also Amos 9:11–15; Micah 5:4; 7:12). These are the same predictions as those which in the latter portion of the book are pointed to as the extravagant utterances of an enthusiast and as having fallen short of fulfillment. Unless there be numerous passages be excised, the acknowledged Isaiah, and often his contemporaries also, living 2 centuries before the fall of Babylon and the hopes which that event are supposed to have awakened, wrote in precisely the same manner as the author of the last section.

A special ground on which the denial of the genuineness of the last 27 chapters rests is the mention of Cyrus by name (ch. 44:28; 45:1; cf. also Ezra 1:1; II Chron. 36:22, 23). So also Josiah was foretold by name (I Kings 13:2). Unusual conditions obtained when Isaiah wrote these closing chapters. With the Exile impending, the faithful needed some special proof of the prophet's assurance of return. This assurance was in Cyrus. When Cyrus should actually arise, Israel would know that their redemption drew nigh. Calvin says that when Cyrus would be informed of the prediction of his name, it would make a profound impression upon him and induce him to permit the exiles to return to Palestine. If predictive prophecy is possible, if it was ever uttered by holy men taught by the Holy Spirit, then the name of Cyrus could have been penned by Isaiah. Otherwise the words, as they stand, were not uttered until nearly 200 years after Isaiah.

It has further been urged that these chapters are known only as a part of Isaiah and that it seems strange that the author of such noble literary and religious passages should have been forgotten. The fact that chs. 40 to 66 are joined to Isa., chs. 1 to 39, may point to a common authorship. The oldest literary witness (Ecclus. 48:24, 25) ascribes this section to Isaiah. It may also be said that the author of chs. 40 to 66 does not show the familiarity with the land or religion of Babylonia which we should expect from a man living among the exiles. This ignorance of detail shows that the prophet's standpoint among the captives is ideal rather than real. The Bible Commission of the Roman Catholic Church, June 29, 1908, was opposed to the critical-rationalistic exegetes and concluded that the philological argument is not convincing and that the prophet does not address the people in exile as contemporaries.

Fairness in scholarship, however, demands that the theories of divided authorship receive due consideration, especially since recent commentaries and books on O.T. Introduction generally recognize a Deutero-Isaiah (Second Isaiah) and in many cases a Trito-Isaiah (Third Isaiah).

Toward the close of the 11th century A.D. a Jewish commentator of Cordova in Spain, Moses ibn Chiquitilla, suggested that the 2d half of The Book of Isaiah (chs. 40 to 66) was the work of a prophet near the end of the Babylonian Exile. The Masoretes also felt that some important transition took place at ch. 40:1, since the verse begins with a capital nun (n). In 1782 Eichhorn came to the conclusion that chs. 40 to 66 were not written by Isaiah, but would have to be ascribed to a prophet of the 6th century. Döderlein had already, in 1775, begun a new book with ch. 40. Since that time the critical explanation has gained favor among O.T. scholars and is today the prevailing one.

A number of allusions in chs. 40 to 66 clearly indicate that the writer's *apparent* position is in the period of the Exile, and it seems reasonable to assume that such was also his *actual* position. Predictive prophecy must be admitted on various occasions, but a prophet to be understood must address himself to his contemporaries in the 1st instance. If Isaiah wrote these chapters, he transported himself about 200 years, or at the least 160 years, into the future, gathered around himself all the elements of a definite and complex historical situation, and forecast from it a future still more distant. If Isaiah is the author of this section, he ignored his contemporaries and alluded to circumstances of

which they were not cognizant. The interpretation is simplified and seems more reasonable if a later authorship for these chapters is accepted.

The circumstances outlined in these chapters suggest a period of affliction. Jerusalem and the cities of Judah lie in ruins (chs. 44:26; 51:3; 52:9; 58:12; 61:4; 63:18; 64:9-11). The nation is subject to foreigners, is in captivity, and this state of affairs has been existing for some time (chs. 42:14, 22, 24, 25; 52:2-5; 58:12; 63:19). In the first 39 chs., the name of Assyria or Assyrian occurs about 40 times, but only once in the 2d half of the book (ch. 52:4), and then in connection with Egypt; in contrast Babylon comes to the front, whose rulers, the Chaldeans, are the oppressors (chs. 43:14; 47:1, 5; 48:14, 20). Cyrus the Persian, who destroyed the kingdom of the Medes (cf. ch. 41:25), will conquer Babylon (chs. 44:28; 45:1). In contrast to the predicted Babylonian Exile (ch. 39:5-7), the people will be delivered from oppression (ch. 52:2, 3) through the conquest of Babylon (chs. 43:14; 48:14); this takes place under a definite personality (chs. 41:2, 3, 25; 46:11; 48:14), whose name is Cyrus (chs. 44:28; 45:1). After the conquest of Babylon there follows a return through the wilderness (ch. 43:19-21), and Jerusalem and the Temple are rebuilt (chs. 44:26-28; 49:8; 51:3; 58:12; 60:10; 61:4). There is renewed prosperity of the nation (chs. 40:9-11; 41:27; 46:13; 66:22-24), which is typical of the future Messianic period.

Some critics think that the section chs. 40 to 55 consists of 2 parts: 1. Chs. 40 to 48, in which Cyrus is the central point of interest. 2. Chs. 49 to 55, in which we hear nothing of the Persian king and the capture of Babylon. Accordingly they would date the 1st section directly before or after the capture of Sippar in 539 B.C. and chs. 49 to 55, after the capture of Babylon in the same year, when Deutero-Isaiah was disappointed and the hope of immediate return was not realized. Others, however, assume that chs. 49 to 55 were written not merely after the edict for the Return, but actually in Palestine. Cyrus' edict for the return of the Jews to Palestine was issued from Ecbatana and not from Babylon. Yet it does not seem wise to make this division in chs. 40 to 55. The language is poetical, and we are hardly justified in drawing a line of demarcation between ch. 48 and ch. 49. The close of the section (ch. 55:8-13) seems to go back to the beginning (ch. 40:3-5), and this suggests that the section is a unit. The best that can be done is to date these chapters between c. 550, the rise of Cyrus, and 539, when Babylon fell into his hands. It cannot be determined where the author lived, but most probably he was among the exiles. There is no allusion to Deutero-Isaiah as a speaker, and it has been suggested that he wrote for an unseen public. Some scholars also see the work of a redactor in chs. 40 to 55. These suggestions, however, lie in the realm of conjecture. Within this section (chs. 40 to 55) fall the so-called Songs of the Servant of Jehovah: chs. 42:1-4(7); 49:1-6; 50:4-9; 52:13 to 53:12.

Even though there is a trend among critics to find a unity of authorship in chs. 40 to 55, the problem in Trito-Isaiah (chs. 56 to 66) is more complicated. While these scholars recognize the dependence of these latter chapters upon chs. 40 to 55, the question is whether they all hail from Trito-Isaiah or from several writers. It seems that chs. 60 to 62; 57:14-19; 66:6-16 show such a strong relationship that they must come from one poet, Trito-Isaiah. The problem, however, seems different in chs. 56:1-8; 58; 65; 66:5, 17-24, and likewise chs. 56:9 to 57:13 are regarded as not belonging to the imitator of Deutero-Isaiah; the same is asserted to be the case in chs. 59; 63:1 to 64:11; 66:1–4.

The language is poetical, and it is difficult to determine a date from internal evidence. Eissfeldt names 2 periods: the middle of the 5th century, the time of Malachi; or the last 3d of the 6th century, the time of Haggai and Zechariah; he gives decided preference to the latter period. Yet he doubts whether all the poems can be dated from that era. Thus he says that chs. 63:7 to 64:11 may be decades older and have been composed shortly after 587; ch. 57:7–13 may be older than 587, and likewise ch. 57:1–6. On the other hand, since foreign cults were practiced by the population remaining in Palestine, the latter passage may be later. Eissfeldt concludes that the passages of chs. 60 to 62; 57:14–19; 66:6–16, which were written by an imitator of Deutero-Isaiah, i.e., Trito-Isaiah, fit especially well into the time of Haggai and Zechariah and give us the background for their Messianic hopes. Critics have to admit, however, that their views are only possibilities, and they cannot answer how the poems in the collection of chs. 56 to 66 were combined. Those who argue for the unity of chs. 56 to 66 also have difficulties both in chronology and in the order of the contents. So critics find refuge in a redactor without being able to discover his principle of order. Driver, however, maintains that chs. 40 to 66 form a continuous prophecy dealing throughout with a common theme: Israel's restoration from exile in Babylon.

The question may be raised how these sections, chs. 40 to 55 and chs. 56 to 66, were appended to the work of Isaiah. One may propose a mechanical theory, that the anonymous sections were written on the same roll with Isaiah and thus finally joined to Isaiah. According to the Babylonian Talmud (Baba Bathra, 14b) this was the order of the prophets: Jeremiah, Ezekiel, Isaiah, the Twelve; and this may favor such a mechanical theory. On the other hand, it is more probable that chs. 40 to 55 were joined to chs. 1 to 35 (39) and chs. 56 to 66 joined to chs. 40 to 55; the similarity of style and subject matter would facilitate ascription to 1 author. Chs. 1 to 39 and chs. 40 to 66 have in common the experience of a heroic faith in God and, in consequence, a similarity of language (cf. the Holy One of Israel, chs. 1:4; 5:19, etc., with ch. 41:14, 16, 20, etc.). It has been assumed by some that Deutero-Isaiah (chs. 40 to 55) and the parts of chs. 56 to 66 which are based on his work were issued as a pseudepigraph under Isaiah's name, but this is all conjecture.

In 1928, C. C. Torrey maintained that there never was a time when chs. 40 to 66 formed a separate book. On the other hand, he holds that chs. 34; 35; 40 to 66 constitute a collection of 27 poems, which are the work of a single author, the Second Isaiah, who wrote in Palestine near the end of the 5th century B.C. His theory, however, requires him to delete ch. 44:28 as an interpolation; he also excises Babylon and Chaldeans in chs. 43:14; 48:14, 20. In ch. 45:1 he omits Cyrus as a probable interpolation, because it disturbs the meter in Hebrew. He believes that the second Temple was in existence at the time of the Second Isaiah and that the majority of his contemporaries were lukewarm in their faith. But the prophet had 3 supports for his confidence: Jehovah's omnipotence; Jehovah's choice of Israel as the servant of the Lord; the prophet's vision of the possibility, through divine help, of arousing the Jewish people and through them all mankind to a living faith and better life.

If anyone favors the views of a Deutero-Isaiah and a Trito-Isaiah, he can hold that opinion without lowering his conception of Scripture. The ancient Hebrews did not make very much of authorship. The name Isaiah may be applied to the whole book in a general sense without implying that Isaiah is the author of all. The point that is most important is not who wrote all the parts of the book, but what are its contents? Does it have spiritual values? Does it reveal God's dealings with man? It should also be borne in mind that Deutero-Isaiah and Trito-Isaiah may have been divinely inspired just as much as Isaiah. The later writers in the book may have been pupils of Isaiah's thought and therefore have been identified ideally and spiritually with Isaiah. At any rate, there is a unity in The Book of Isaiah which cannot be overlooked.

Is'cah (Is'kà). A daughter of Haran and sister of Milcah (Gen. 11:29), and consequently sister of Lot (v. 27). Iscah has been regarded as another name of Sarai (Jos. Antiq. i. 6, 5; Targum of Jonathan); but in that case Sarai would have been Abraham's niece and not his half-sister (Gen. 20:12).

Is·car'i·ot (ĭs-kăr'ĭ-ŏt) [Gr., probably from Heb. man of Kerioth]. A designation of Judas the traitor (Matt. 10:4; Luke 6:16), which belonged to his father Simon before him (John 6:71; 13:26, R.V.). It was used to distinguish him from the other apostle called Judas (Luke 6:16; Acts 1:13, 16). It seems to mean that Judas was a native of Kerioth in the s. of Judah (Josh. 15:25); some favor Koreae, on the n.e. border of Judea (Jos. Antiq. xiv. 3, 4; War i. 6, 5). In the Codex Bezae the word is written apo Karyōtou everywhere in the Fourth Gospel, and is so written in John 6:71 in Codex Sinaiticus. Accordingly Judas was probably a Judean. Thus he would be the only apostle from Judea, for the rest were Galileans.

Ish'bah (ĭsh'bà) [he praises, or may he (God) be calm, allay (his wrath)]. A man of Judah, ancestor or head of the inhabitants of Eshtemoa (I Chron. 4:17).

Ish'bak (ĭsh'băk) [he leaves behind: cf. Aram. shᵉbak̲, to leave behind; or he outruns: cf. Arab. sabak̲a, to precede, outstrip, overcome]. An Arab tribe descended from Abraham through Keturah (Gen. 25:2).

Ish'bi-be'nob (ĭsh'bĭ-bē'nŏb). A Philistine giant who was on the point of killing David, but was himself slain by Abishai (II Sam. 21:16, 17). There is a textual difficulty in this name. The kethib has, "And they abode [or tarried] in Nob" (perhaps for Gob, v. 18), but by that interpretation the name of the giant is lost.

Ish'-bo'sheth (ĭsh'bō'shĕth) [man of shame]. One of Saul's younger sons, originally called Esh-baal (the Lord's man, or man of Baal), which was changed to Ish-bosheth, either during his lifetime when the glory of his house departed, or rather in later times when the name Baal fell into disrepute through its idolatrous associations (cf. II Sam. 2:8 with I Chron. 8:33; 9:39). He was not present at the battle of Gilboa; or, if present, he escaped the slaughter on that disastrous day. On the death of Saul, David obtained the sovereignty over Judah, but the other tribes refused him allegiance and proclaimed Ish-bosheth king as successor to his father Saul. Ish-bosheth was then aged about 40, and reigned 2 troubled years (II Sam. 2:8–10). His capital was at Mahanaim, e. of the Jordan (ch. 2:8, 12). He was unsuccessful in the war which he waged with David to secure the undisputed sway over the 12 tribes (chs. 2:12 to 3:1). He brought a serious charge against his main supporter, Abner, who thereupon offered his services to David and, on David's making demand on Ish-bosheth, conducted David's wife Michal back to him (ch. 3:6–21). When Abner was murdered at Hebron, Ish-bosheth lost heart (ch. 3:27; 4:1). He was soon afterward assassinated and his head carried in triumph to David. But by David's order the severed head was honorably interred in Abner's tomb at Hebron, and the assassins were put to death for their crime (ch. 4:5–12). With the death of Ish-bosheth the dynasty of Saul came to an end, although a grandson of Saul's remained (ch. 4:4).

Ish′hod′ (ĭsh′hŏd′), in A.V. **I′shod** [man of majesty]. A Manassite whose mother was Hammoleketh (I Chron. 7:18).

Ish′i, I (ĭsh′ī) [Heb. *'ishî*, my husband]. A name by which the Israelites call Jehovah, when they return to their allegiance. It supersedes the synonymous one Baali (my lord or husband), since the word Baal had come into ill repute because it suggested a heathen god or an identification of Jehovah with Baal (Hos. 2:16, 17).

Ish′i, II (ĭsh′ī) [Heb. *yish'î*, saving, salutary]. 1. A man of Judah, son of Appaim, house of Jerahmeel (I Chron. 2:31).
2. A man of Judah, father of Zoheth (I Chron. 4:20).
3. A Simeonite whose sons led a band which overcame the Amalekites of Mount Seir and seized on their settlements (I Chron. 4:42).
4. Head of a father's house of the half tribe of Manasseh e. of the Jordan (I Chron. 5:24).

I·shi′ah (ĭ-shī′á). See Isshiah.

I·shi′jah (ĭ-shī′já). See Isshijah.

Ish′ma (ĭsh′má) [perhaps contraction of Ishmael]. A man of Judah, descended from Hur (I Chron. 4:3, 4).

Ish′ma·el (ĭsh′má-ĕl) [God hears]. 1. The son of Abraham by Hagar the Egyptian maid; born when Abraham was 86 years old, after he had been 10 full years in Canaan (Gen. 16:3, 15; cf. ch. 12:4). He was the child of worldly wisdom, not of faith; he was born of parents who, in the face of God's promise, were blinded by seeming impossibilities and sought by earthly means to enable God to fulfill his engagements. When the rite of circumcision was instituted for the family of Abraham, Ishmael, then 13 years of age, was circumcised (ch. 17:25). The next year Isaac was born, when his mother was past age, the child of promise, a rebuke to unbelief (ch. 21:5). At his weaning, the customary feast was made, when Ishmael was seen to be mocking. This was the first occasion in the family of Abraham that those born after the flesh in doubt of God's way mocked at the heirs of promise; and Paul seizes upon the allegory in the incident (Gal. 4:22–31). This misbehavior of Ishmael led to the expulsion of him and his mother. They wandered in the wilderness of Beer-sheba till both were nearly perishing with thirst. The angel of the Lord directed Hagar to some water among the shrubs, and the life of herself and her son was preserved. Ishmael grew up in the wilderness of Paran, s. of Canaan, where he lived by his bow. Eventually he married a wife from Egypt, his mother's ancestral home (Gen. 21:3–21). In fulfillment of a promise made by God to Abraham, Ishmael became the progenitor of 12 princes (chs. 17:20; 25:12–16); see ISHMAELITE. He had also a daughter, who was married to Esau (ch. 28:9; 36:10). Ishmael took part with Isaac in burying their father Abra-

ham (ch. 25:9). He himself died at the age of 137 (ch. 25:17).
2. A descendant of Jonathan (I Chron. 8:38; 9:44).
3. A man of Judah, father of the high judicial functionary Zebadiah (II Chron. 19:11).
4. A son of Jehohanan. He took part in the successful conspiracy against Athaliah (II Chron. 23:1).
5. A son of Nethaniah, who belonged to the seed royal of Judah. When Nebuchadnezzar departed from Palestine, after the capture of Jerusalem, he left behind him as governor of Judah a certain Jew called Gedaliah, who promised protection to any of the conquered people who placed themselves under his rule. Among others Ishmael came, but with hostile intent. Instigated by the king of the Ammonites, he assassinated Gedaliah, massacring at the same time the people with him. After further murders he carried off captives, including the king's daughters, and finally attempted to make his way to the Ammonite country. Johanan, son of Kareah, and others went forth to fight with him. They found him at Gibeon. His captives turned to Johanan, but he himself succeeded in escaping with 8 men to the king of Ammon, who had instigated his crimes (II Kings 25:25; Jer. 40:7–16; 41:1–18).
6. A son of Pashhur, who was induced by Ezra to put away his foreign wife (Ezra 10:22).

Ish′ma·el·ite (ĭsh′má-ĕl-īt), in A.V. often **Ish′me·el·ite**, an orthography true to the Hebrew. A descendant of Ishmael. The Ishmaelites had Egyptian blood, as well as the blood of Abraham, in their veins. Twelve princes sprang from Ishmael (Gen. 17:20; 25:12–16). He may have had more sons, and possibly some of those enumerated were grandsons. Twelve was an approved number and was carefully preserved as the number of the tribes of Israel. The Ishmaelites in their twelvefold division dwelt in settlements and in movable camps in the desert of n. Arabia, in the region included between Havilah, Egypt, and the Euphrates (Gen. 25:18; Jos. *Antiq.* i. 12, 4). Occasionally 1 of their tribes acquired permanent residence and civilization, as the Nabateans; but they mostly possessed the character of their ancestor and dwelt like "a wild ass" of the desert (Gen. 16:12). Like Ishmael, too, they were celebrated for their skill with the bow (Isa. 21:17). To Ishmaelites traveling as carriers between Gilead and Egypt, or, more definitely, to "certain Midianites, merchants," in the caravan, Joseph was sold by his brethren (Gen. 37:25–28). In Ps. 83:6 they are mentioned with Edomites, Moabites, and Hagarenes.

In a wider sense, the nomadic tribes of n. Arabia generally; either because the Ishmaelites were the chief people of the desert, and their name came to be used as a synonym for any nomad of the region, or because an Ishmaelite confederacy had been formed which included tribes of other blood (Judg. 8:24; cf. chs. 7:25; 8:22, 26; Judith 2:23). All the Arabs, after the example of Mohammed, claim descent from Ishmael.

Ish·ma′iah (ĭsh-mā′yá), in A.V. once **Is·ma′iah** (I Chron. 12:4) [Jehovah hears]. 1. A Gibeonite who joined David at Ziklag (I Chron. 12:4).
2. Son of Obadiah and head in David's reign of the Zebulunites (I Chron. 27:19).

Ish′me·el·ite (ĭsh′mė-ĕl-īt). See ISHMAELITE.

Ish′me·rai (ĭsh′mė-rī) [Jehovah keeps]. A Benjamite, son of Elpaal (I Chron. 8:18).

I′shod (ī′shŏd). See ISHHOD.

Ish'pah (ĭsh'pà), in A.V. **Is'pah** [cf. Heb. *shāphāh*, to sweep or lay bare, bald]. A Benjamite, son of Beriah (I Chron. 8:16).

Ish'pan (ĭsh'păn). A Benjamite, son of Shashak (I Chron. 8:22).

Ish'tob (ĭsh'tŏb) [men of Tob]. See TOB.

Ish'u·ah (ĭsh'û-à). See ISHVAH.

Ish'u·ai (ĭsh'û-ī) and **Ish'u·i** (ĭsh'û-ī). See ISHVI.

Ish'vah (ĭsh'và), in A.V. **Ish'u·ah** and **Is'u·ah** [probably, he is equal (of birth) or worthy]. The 2d son of Asher (Gen. 46:17; I Chron. 7:30). He probably died childless; or, if he had descendants, they did not constitute a tribal family or perpetuate his name (cf. Num. 26:44).

Ish'vi (ĭsh'vī), in A.V. **Ish'u·ai**, **Ish'u·i**, **Is'u·i**, and **Jes'u·i** [probably for Heb. *yishyō= 'ishyāhū*, man of Jehovah, a change from Esh-baal; but cf. Ishval]. 1. The 3d son of Asher, and founder of a tribal family (Gen. 46:17; Num. 26:44; I Chron. 7:30).
2. A son of Saul (I Sam. 14:49).

Isle, Is'land. The rendering of Heb. *'ī*, meaning: 1. Habitable land, as opposed to water (Isa. 42:15). 2. An island in the ordinary sense of the word (Jer. 47:4). 3. A maritime country, even when constituting part of a continent; the coast land of Palestine and Phoenicia (Isa. 20:6, in R.V. coast land; cf. ch. 23:2, 6), and the coasts and islands of Asia Minor and Greece (Gen. 10:5). 4. The remotest regions of the earth and their inhabitants (Isa. 41:5; Zeph. 2:11). This employment of the term may have arisen: (*a*) By synecdoche, the isles of the Mediterranean being remote and scarcely known. (*b*) From the current belief that the world was surrounded with water, so that the most distant region was the coast land of the world ocean.

Is'ma·chi'ah (ĭs'mà-kī'à) [Jehovah supports]. An overseer connected with the Temple in Hezekiah's reign (II Chron. 31:13).

Is·ma'iah (ĭs-mā'yà). See ISHMAIAH.

Is'pah (ĭs'pà). See ISHPAH.

Is'ra·el (ĭz'rā-ĕl) [popularly, he strives with God; but rather, God strives or let God rule (or God rules)]. 1. The name given to Jacob when he was returning from Mesopotamia and just about to cross the brook Jabbok, where he expected to meet Esau (Gen. 32:22–32); see JACOB.
2. The whole body of the descendants of Jacob at any one time. This use of the word began in his own lifetime (Gen. 34:7). It was common during the wilderness wanderings (Ex. 32:4; Deut. 4:1; 27:9), though the designation Children of Israel was yet more frequent both during this and the former period. Down to the death of Saul, Israel and the Children of Israel, when used as a national designation, comprehended the Hebrews generally, without distinction of tribes. There were, however, geographical and other causes already at work which tended to separate Judah from the rest of Israel; and the distinction had come to be recognized before the actual division of the people into 2 kingdoms took place (I Sam. 11:8; 17:52; 18:16); see JUDAH. It was used also under the united monarchy (I Kings 11:42). In the parallelism of Hebrew poetry it often corresponds in the 2d line of the couplet to Jacob in the 1st (Num. 23:7, 10, 21; 24:5; Ps. 14:7). After the Exile the reference is frequently to the people of the various tribes who returned to Jerusalem (Ezra 9:1; 10:5; Neh. 9:2; 11:3).
3. The tribes which acted independently of Judah. The split of the Hebrew people into 2

kingdoms occurred on the death of Saul. The n. and e. tribes recognized Saul's son Ish-bosheth as king, and the tribe of Judah followed David. From this time onward Israel is frequently used to denote the 10 tribes. Ish-bosheth reigned 2 years and was assassinated, but 7 years elapsed before the breach was healed and David was anointed king of all Israel (II Sam. 2:10, 11; 5:1–5). The jealousies, however, remained, and on the death of Solomon the rupture became final. Ten tribes followed Jeroboam and one cleaved to the house of David. The 10 tribes which were rent from the house of David were Reuben, Gad, and half Manasseh e. of the Jordan, and w. of the river half Manasseh, Ephraim, Issachar, Zebulun, Naphtali, Asher, Dan, and lastly Benjamin, which belonged in part to the Northern Kingdom, Beth-el, Gilgal, and Jericho, chief places in the tribe of Benjamin, being within the bounds of the Northern Kingdom.

The causes which led to the schism were:
1. The isolation of Judah caused by nature.
2. The ancient jealousy between the 2 powerful tribes of Ephraim and Judah. It had caused a temporary disruption of the kingdom after Saul's death; it broke out again after the defeat of Absalom because Judah was the first to welcome the king back (II Sam. 19:15, 40–43). It had been freshly provoked by Solomon's lavish adornment of Jerusalem, and at his death resulted in permanent separation. 3. Discontent caused by the excessive luxury of the throne. The people were groaning under oppressive burdens. Solomon's love of splendor had led to taxation to support his enormous household and maintain his display, and to enforcement of labor to carry out his great works (I Kings 4:22, 23, 26; 5:13–16). The reasonable request of the people for relief was perversely refused by Rehoboam. 4. Idolatry, fostered by foreign marriages (I Kings 11:1–13). A subtle corruption spread through all ranks owing to the encouragement given to false religions, attachment to the worship of Jehovah was weakened, and one great unifying force was destroyed. 5. The folly of Rehoboam in refusing the request of the people for relief intensified the disintegrating forces and precipitated the catastrophe (I Kings 12:3–5, 12–16).

As compared with Judah in respect to strength the Northern Kingdom had 10 tribes, twice the population, and nearly 3 times the extent of territory. But it was more exposed to war and less easy of defense than Judah. It was the apostate nation, and defection from God is weakness and inevitably undermines the stability of a state. It had an inferior religion with its lower moral tone, and many of its best spirits forsook it; the priests and Levites migrated into Judah (II Chron. 11:13, 14).

The capital of the Northern Kingdom was at Shechem at first. It was soon removed to Tirzah, and then Omri founded Samaria and transferred the seat of government to the new city (I Kings 12:25; 14:17; 15:21; 16:23, 24).

Jeroboam, the 1st king, was afraid that if his people visited Jerusalem for worship, they would be won over to their old allegiance; he therefore established 2 shrines, one at Dan in the extreme n., and the other at Beth-el, in the s. of the kingdom. At each of these places he erected a golden calf, which he designed as an aid to the worship of Jehovah. Judgment was threatened against him and his race for this partial apostasy, and after his son, Nadab, had reigned 2 years, the dynasty was swept away. Nineteen kings in all sat upon the throne. See CHRONOLOGY, IV. Their united reigns covered a period of about

210 years; 7 of them reigned but 2 years or less; 8 were slain or committed suicide and the throne was transferred to another family, and in only 2 instances was the royal power held by as many as 4 members of the same family in succession. None of the kings removed the calves from Beth-el and Dan; indeed, under Ahab, who was influenced by his wicked heathen wife, Jezebel, the apostasy was rendered complete by the introduction of the worship of Baal instead of Jehovah. But God raised up prophets who contended steadfastly for the worship of Jehovah, at whatever risk to themselves. The most notable were Elijah and Elisha (*q.v.*). After the suppression of Baal worship, other prophets, especially Hosea and Amos, labored for the reformation of the moral life of the nation. The n. Israelites were frequently at war with Judah. Indeed, the 2 kingdoms were in hearty alliance only while the house of Omri held the throne of Israel, when the royal families of Israel and Judah were united by intermarriage. When the Syrian kingdom of Damascus rose to power, it necessarily affected the politics of the adjacent Kingdom of Israel. Often the 2 were at war. They united, however, in making common cause against the Assyrians in the days of Ahab; and 120 years later they were again in alliance, their common object being the capture of Jerusalem. It was this danger that led Ahaz, king of Judah, terrified for his throne and life, and having no faith in Jehovah, to act contrary to the exhortations of Isaiah and to call in Tiglath-pileser, king of Assyria, at the price of independence. Judah became tributary to Assyria, and its king did homage to the Assyrian monarch at Damascus (II Kings 16:8–10). Tiglath-pileser relieved Judah of the invaders, ravaged northern Israel, struck a blow at the Philistines, besieged and ultimately captured Damascus and slew Rezin, deported Naphtali and the Israelites from the country e. of the Jordan, connived at the death of Pekah or actually ordered it, and placed Hoshea on the throne c. 730 B.C. Hoshea rebelled against Assyria after Tiglath-pileser's death. The Assyrian armies returned. In 722 (721) Samaria fell and a large number of the inhabitants were carried off to Assyria. See CAPTIVITY, I and SARGON. The place of the deported Israelites was supplied by colonists from 5 districts in the Assyrian empire, who, mingling with the remaining Israelite population of central Palestine, laid the foundations of what afterward became the Samaritan nation.

The captivity of Israel was a punishment because the people had sinned against the Lord their God and had feared other gods, walking in the statutes of the nations and of the kings of Israel (II Kings 17:7, 8). They were apostate. They had broken the covenant (II Kings 17:15; cf. Ex., chs. 20 to 22; Hos. 6:7; 8:1), rejecting the statutes of the Lord. Their apostasy had manifested itself in 2 directions: they walked in the statutes of the nations whom the Lord cast out (II Kings 17:8, 15, 17; cf. Hos. 2:13; 4:2, 11, 15; Amos 2:6–9), and they walked in the statutes of the kings of Israel, especially in the matter of the calf worship and its attendant ceremonies and ordinances, and in the general idolatry that followed in its train (II Kings 17:8, 16; Hos. 8:4–6; 10:5, 8; 13:2–4). They had sinned despite the fact that the Lord had testified unto them by prophets and by mighty acts (II Kings 17:13; Hos. 12:10; Amos 2:9–11; 4:6–13). Their sin issued in separation and degradation and paved the way for punishment. They separated from Judah and thus weakened were overthrown. Their idolatry, drunkenness, and licentiousness weakened the manhood of the nation, deprived it

of sturdiness, and made its soldiery no better in character and moral purpose than the warriors of Egypt, Assyria, and Babylonia.

Is'ra·el·ite (ĭz'rĭ-ĕl-it). A descendant of Israel, i.e., of Jacob (Ex. 9:7); and consequently, by implication, the possessor of true religious knowledge, a faithful servant of Jehovah, and an heir of the promises (John 1:47; Rom. 9:4–13; II Cor. 11:22).

Is'sa·char (ĭs'à-kär) [there is hire, or man of hire; or perhaps he (God or the child) causes to have or procures hire]. 1. The 9th son of Jacob, the 5th by Leah (Gen. 30:17, 18; 35:23). His sons were Tola, Phuvah or Pua, Job or Jashub, and Shimron (Gen. 46:13; Num. 26:23, 24; I Chron. 7:1). With them he went down with Jacob into Egypt (Gen. 46:13; Ex. 1:3). Jacob, shortly before death, with keen and prophetic insight into character, described Issachar and his children as a strong ass, couching down between the sheepfolds, who submits to the burdens imposed by foreign masters, provided they permit him to remain in his pleasant land (Gen. 49:14, 15).

The descendants of Issachar formed a tribe, consisting of 5 great tribal families, the posterity of his 5 sons (Num. 26:23, 24). Its prince in the early period of the wanderings was Nethanel, son of Zuar (Num. 1:8; 2:5; 7:18; 10:15), and at a later period Paltiel, son of Azzan (ch. 34:26). At the 1st census in the wilderness it numbered 54,400 fighting men (ch. 1:28, 29); at the 2d 64,300 (ch. 26:25); while in David's reign it reached 87,000 (I Chron. 7:5). Igal, son of Joseph, was the spy from the tribe (Num. 13:7). The men of Issachar were among those who stood on Mount Gerizim to bless the people (Deut. 27:12). Moses, in predicting the future of the tribes, foretold Issachar's joyous and quiet life (ch. 33:18). One of the judges, Tola, belonged to the tribe of Issachar (Judg. 10:1); so did King Baasha (I Kings 15:27). The princes of Issachar had the political insight to discern the fit moment for turning from Saul's family and accepting David as the king of all Israel (I Chron. 12:32). About that time Omri, son of Michael, was head of the tribe (ch. 27:18). Many men of Issachar, although they belonged to the Northern Kingdom, attended Hezekiah's passover (II Chron. 30:18). In the apocalyptic vision 12,000 of the tribe of Issachar were sealed (Rev. 7:7), this being the normal number.

When the Land of Canaan was distributed by lot, the 4th lot taken after the Ark was removed to Shiloh came forth for the tribe of Issachar. Its territory was bounded on the n. by Zebulun and Naphtali, on the e. by the Jordan, on the s. and w. by Manasseh and probably Asher. Jezreel and Shunem lay within its limits, while Chesulloth and Mount Tabor were on its n. border, and En-gannim near the s. line (Josh. 19:17–23); but towns within it were held by Manasseh (ch. 17:10, 11) and others by the Gershonite Levites (Josh. 21:6, 28, 29; I Chron. 6:62–72). The tribe of Issachar occupied the greater part of the plain of Jezreel, or Esdraelon, constituting the low, level, and fertile plain of the Kishon. The character of their territory combined with the tribal traits explains why the people of Issachar, in accordance with Jacob's prophecy, were so ready to submit to servitude. They had much to lose, and lived on ground well adapted for the action of the war chariots of their enemies, while the tribes located among the mountains could not so readily be attacked in this manner. That the people of Issachar were not exceptionally cowardly is plain from their conduct in the battle with Sisera, which elicited the commendation of Deborah (Judg. 5:15).

2. A Levite, appointed doorkeeper in David's reign (I Chron. 26:5).

Is'shi'ah (ĭs'shī'á), in A.V. once **I·shi'ah** (I Chron. 7:3) and twice **Je·si'ah** (I Chron. 12:6; 23:20) [Jehovah forgets; cf. Jer. 23:39)]. 1. A man of Issachar, family of Tola (I Chron. 7:3).

2. One of those who came to David at Ziklag (I Chron. 12:6).

3. A Levite, descended from Moses, and head of the house of Rehabiah (I Chron. 24:21; cf. ch. 23:14–17).

4. A Levite, family of Kohath, house of Uzziel (I Chron. 23:20; 24:25).

Is·shi'jah (ĭs-shī'já), in A.V. **I·shi'jah** [Jehovah forgets]. A son of Harim, induced by Ezra to put away his foreign wife (Ezra 10:31).

Is'sue. A man's disease, probably blennorrhea or perhaps gonorrhea (Lev. 15:2–15; cf. Jos. *War* v. 5, 6; vi. 9, 3). An issue of blood is a female complaint (Lev. 15:25–30; Matt. 9:20).

Is'u·ah (ĭs'û-á). See ISHVAH.

Is'u·i (ĭs'û-ī). See ISHVI.

It'a·ly (ĭt'á-lĭ). A geographical name which, in the 5th century B.C., meant only a small district in the extreme s. of what is now called Italy; but which gradually extended its signification, till in the 1st century of the Christian era it began to be used in the same sense as we now attach to the word. In the days of the apostles Italy, and, indeed, the greater part of the civilized world, was ruled from Rome (*q.v.*). A cohort called the Italian was stationed in Syria (Acts 10:1). Aquila and Priscilla, who were of Jewish descent, resided for a time in Italy (ch. 18:2). Paul's appeal to Caesar involved his sailing into Italy (ch. 27:1,6), and his ship coasted along Italy from Rhegium to Puteoli (ch. 28:13–16). The salutation in The Epis le to the Hebrews, "They of Italy salute you" (Heb. 13:24), indicates the presence of Christians, not only in Rome, but in other parts of the country (cf. Acts 28:14).

Ith'a·i (ĭth'á-ī). See ITTAI 1.

Ith'a·mar (ĭth'á-mär) [ety. uncertain; perhaps, palm-coast]. The youngest son of Aaron (Ex. 6:23; I Chron. 6:3; 24:1). With his father and his 3 elder brothers he was consecrated to the priestly office (Ex. 28:1; I Chron. 24:2). Upon him devolved the duty of enumerating the materials gathered for the tabernacle (Ex. 38:21). The Gershonites and the Merarites acted under his superintendence (Num. 4:21–33). He founded a priestly family (I Chron. 24:4, 5, 6), which continued after the Captivity (Ezra 8:2). To this family belonged Eli and his descendants, who held the office of high priest for several generations. See HIGH PRIEST.

Ith'i·el (ĭth'ĭ-ĕl) [perhaps, God is with me]. 1. One of the 2 persons to whom Agur addressed his prophecy (Prov. 30:1); but see R.V. marg. for another interpretation.

2. A Benjamite, son of Jesaiah (Neh. 11:7).

Ith'lah (ĭth'lá), in A.V. **Jeth'lah** [a hanging or lofty place]. A town of Dan (Josh. 19:42), identified by Conder with Beit Thûl (Beithûl), about 3 miles e. of Yalo (Aijalon).

Ith'mah (ĭth'mä) [bereavement, orphanhood]. A Moabite, one of the valiant men of David's army (I Chron. 11:46).

Ith'nan (ĭth'năn) [perhaps, perennial]. A town in the extreme s. of Judah (Josh. 15:23), el-Jebariyeh on the wadi Umm Ethnan.

Ith'ra (ĭth'rá) [abundance, excellence]. An Israelite, or rather Ishmaelite, who married Abigail, David's sister, and became the father of Amasa (II Sam. 17:25; I Kings 2:5, 32; I Chron. 2:17). In the last 3 passages he is called Jether.

Ith'ran (ĭth'răn) [abundance, excellence]. 1. A Horite, son of Dishon (Gen. 36:26; I Chron. 1:41).

2. An Asherite, son of Zophah (I Chron. 7:37); apparently the same as Jether (v. 38).

Ith're·am (ĭth'rê-ăm) [the (divine) kinsman has been liberal, or is abundance]. The 6th son born to David at Hebron. His mother was Eglah (II Sam. 3:5; I Chron. 3:3).

Ith'rite (ĭth'rīt). A family who dwelt at Kiriath-jearim (I Chron. 2:53). Two of David's mighty men were Ithrites (II Sam. 23:38; I Chron. 11:40). The word is derivable from Jether or from Jattir.

It'tah·ka'zin (ĭt'á-kā'zĭn). See ETH-KAZIN.

It'ta·i (ĭt'á-ī) [perhaps, with me (is Jehovah)]. 1. A son of Ribai, from Gibeah of Benjamin. He was one of David s mighty men (II Sam. 23:29). Called in I Chron. 11:31, Ithai.

2. An inhabitant of Gath, the commander of 600 men, who followed David from that Philistine city. He was faithful to the king through all vicissitudes, and led a 3d part of the royal army in the battle which resulted in the death of Absalom (II Sam. 15:18–22; 18:2, 5).

It'u·rae'a (ĭt'û-rē'á) [pertaining to Jetur]. A region occupied by a people called Jetur, who were descended from Ishmael (Gen. 25:15; I Chron. 1:31). The tribe of Jetur was at war with the Israelitish tribes e. of the Jordan (I Chron. 5:19). In Hasmonaean times Aristobulus conquered a portion of Ituraea and, annexing it to Judea, compelled the vanquis..ed inhabitants to adopt the rite of circumcision (Jos. *Antiq.* xiii. 11, 3). It was a mountainous country, including part of Anti-Lebanon. Its prince, Ptolemy, son of Mennaeus, had territory in Coelesyria, with Chalcis as stronghold, and proved a bad neighbor to Damascus (Strabo xvi. 2, 18, 20; Jos. *Antiq.* xiii. 16, 3). In 66 B.C. he purchased immunity from Pompey (Jos. *Antiq.* xiv. 3, 2). His son Lysanias was put to death by Antony (Jos. *Antiq.* xv. 4, 1), and the country was farmed to Zenodorus (Jos. *Antiq.* xv. 10, 1; for Zenodorus' domain cf. also 2 and 3). Part of Ituraea and Trachonitis constituted the tetrarchy of Philip (Luke 3:1). Josephus enumerates the constituent parts of Philip's tetrarchy differently, and he is not careful always to enumerate in one and the same way (Jos. *Antiq.* xvii. 8, 1; 11, 4, where part of the house of Zenodorus is included; xviii. 4, 6; *War* ii. 6, 3).

I'vah (ī'vá). See IVVAH.

I'vo·ry. A substance derived from the tusk of the elephant, or of the hippopotamus, the walrus, and other animals. In Heb. it is called *shēn*, tooth, or *shenhabbīm*, a compound word in which *habbīm* probably denotes elephants. It is first mentioned in the Bible as having been brought from abroad by Solomon's ships (I Kings 10:22; II Chron. 9:21). It seems to have come from India, and was made into a throne for the king (I Kings 10:18). Afterward, when luxur.y had established itself to a larger extent in Jerusalem, beds (Amos 6:4) and even houses were made or overlaid with the precious material (I Kings 22:39; Amos 3:15; Ps. 45:8). The Tyrians inlaid benches for rowers with it (Ezek. 27:6). Ethiopia also supplied ivory to the ancient world (Herod. iii. 97, 114).

Iv'vah (ĭv'á), in A.V. **I'vah.** A city which the representative of Sennacherib could boast that the Assyrians had captured (II Kings 18:34; 19:13; Isa. 37:13). It is probably the same as AVVA (*q.v.*).

I'ye-ab'a·rim (ī'yê-ăb'á-rĭm), in A.V. I'Je-ab'a·rim [ruins of Abarim]. A halting place of the Israelites in the wilderness, on the border of Moab (Num. 21:11; 33:44). In v. 45 the place is called simply Iyim, in A.V. Iim, because the context sufficiently defined the locality to be in Abarim. See IIM 1.

I'yar (ē'yär) [Heb. 'iyyār, from Akkad. ayaru, a-a-ru, āru, blossom, offspring, from root meaning to go forth]. Same as Ziv (Zif), the 2d month of the year.

I'yim (ī'yĭm). See IYE-ABARIM.

Iz'har, I (ĭz'här), in A.V. once Iz'e·har (Num. 3:19) [probably Heb. Yiṣhār, (the deity) shines, or let (the deity) shine]. A Levite, son of Kohath, and founder of a tribal family (Ex. 6:18, 19; Num. 3:19, 27; I Chron. 6:18, 38). From him descended the rebel Korah (Num. 16:1).

Iz'har, II (ĭz'här), in A.V. Je·zo'ar [Heb. Yiṣhār; cf. Arab. ṣaḥrā', fawn-colored, reddish-white]. A man of Judah, family of Hezron, son of Ashhur (I Chron. 4:5–7). The kere weṣōḥar means "and Zohar" (q.v.).

Iz·li'ah (ĭz-lī'á), in A.V. Jez·li'ah [cf. Arab. yazalīy, unceasing, eternal]. A Benjamite, son of Elpaal and descended from Shaharaim (I Chron. 8:18).

Iz'ra·hi'ah (ĭz'rá-hī'á) [Jehovah arises (cf. Isa. 60:2)]. A man of Issachar, family of Tola, and son of Uzzi (I Chron. 7:3).

Iz'ra·hite (ĭz'rá-hīt). A member of the family, or an inhabitant of the town, of Izrah (I Chron. 27:8), perhaps the same as Ezrahite.

Iz'ri (ĭz'rī) [fashioner, or perhaps contraction for Jehovah has formed]. A Levite, son of Jeduthun, and head of the 4th course for the musical service of the sanctuary (I Chron. 25:11). Called in v. 3 Zeri (q.v.).

Iz·zi'ah (ĭz-ī'á), in A.V. Je·zi'ah [perhaps, Jehovah sprinkles]. A son of Parosh. He was induced by Ezra to put away his foreign wife (Ezra 10:25).

J

Ja'a·kan (jā'á-kăn), in A.V. of I Chron. 1:42 Ja'kan. Written A'kan in Gen. 36:27. A descendant or prominent branch of the Horites of Mount Seir, who were eventually dispossessed by the Edomites (Gen. 36:20, 21, 27; I Chron. 1:38, 42; Deut. 2:12). At the time of the Exodus sons of Jaakan constituted a tribe which occupied a district on the borders of Edom near Mount Hor, where Aaron died. The Israelites encamped at certain of their wells (Deut. 10:6; Num. 20:21–23; 33:31, 32, Bene-jaakan.) See BEEROTH 2.

Ja'a·ko'bah (jā'á-kō'bá) [probably, he (God) protects; cf. S. Arab. and Ethiopic 'aḳaba, to guard]. A Simeonite prince (I Chron. 4:36).

Ja'a·lah (jā'á-lá), or Ja'a·la (jā'á-lá) [ibex]. The founder of a family, ranked among the children of Solomon's servants (Ezra 2:56; Neh. 7:58).

Ja'a·lam (jā'á-lăm). See JALAM.

Ja'a·nai (jā'á-nī). See JANAI.

Ja'ar (jā'är) [forest]. A proper name (Ps. 132:6, R.V. marg.). It is believed to be the same as Kiriath-jearim.

Ja'a·re-or'e·gim (jā'á-rē-ôr'ê-jĭm). See JAIR, II.

Ja'a·re·shi'ah (jā'á-rē-shī'á), in A.V. Jar'e·si'ah [Jehovah plants; cf. Akkad. erēshu, Arab. gharasa, to plant]. A Benjamite, son of Jeroham (I Chron. 8:27).

Ja'a·sai (jā'á-sī) and Ja'a·sau (jā'á-sō). See JAASU.

Ja·a'si·el (jā-ā'sī-ĕl), in A.V. once Ja'si·el (jā'sī-ĕl) (I Chron. 11:47) [El (God) makes]. 1. A Mezobaite, one of David's mighty men (I Chron. 11:47).
2. A son of Abner (I Chron. 27:21).

Ja'a·su (jā'á-sū), in A.V. Ja'a·sau, in R.V. marg. Ja'a·sai [Jehovah makes]. A son of Bani. He was induced by Ezra to put away his foreign wife (Ezra 10:37).

Ja·az'a·ni'ah (jā-ăz'á-nī'á) [Jehovah hearkens]. 1. Son of a Maacathite (II Kings 25:23). See JEZANIAH.
2. A Rechabite, son of a certain Jeremiah, not the prophet of that name (Jer. 35:3).
3. A son of Shaphan. He was a leader of idolatry in Ezekiel's time (Ezek. 8:11).
4. A son of Azzur and prince of Judah, who was seen by Ezekiel in vision (Ezek. 11:1; cf. chs. 8:1, 3; 11:24).

Ja'a·zer (jā'á-zēr). See JAZER.

Ja·a·zi'ah (jā'á-zī'á) [Jehovah strengthens]. A Levite, registered as head of a father's house with the family of Merari (I Chron. 24:26, 27), and perhaps called his son or descendant (benō, his son); this Heb. word is rendered as a proper name, Beno. There is a textual difficulty in this passage. No hint is elsewhere given of Merari's having a 3d son. Can Jaaziah represent the house of the dead Eleazar (ch. 24:28; cf. ch. 23:22), or is the passage ch. 24:26b, 27 an interpolation?

Ja·a'zi·el (jā-ā'zī-ĕl) or A'zi·el [God strengthens]. A Levite of the 2d rank, one of the musicians who played on the psaltery at the removal of the Ark from the house of Obed-edom, and afterward as a regular duty in the tent at Jerusalem (I Chron. 15:18, 20; and probably ch. 16:5). In the last passage the form Jeiel is probably a copyist's error.

Ja'bal (jā'băl). Son of the Cainite Lamech, by his wife Adah. He was the father of such as dwell in tents and have cattle (Gen. 4:20).

Jab'bok (jăb'ŏk) [cf. Arab. baḳḳa, to give abundantly, to split]. An e. tributary of the Jordan. Jacob forded it on his way back from Mesopotamia (Gen. 32:22). Rising near Rabbath Ammon, it flows for 12 miles from that town toward the n.e. and then sweeps around toward the n.w. After holding this course for about 15 miles it turns w. and for 17 miles flows through a valley which separates Gilead from Ammon. On emerging into the valley of the Jordan it bends toward the s.w. and enters the Jordan at a point about 43 miles s. of the Sea of Galilee and 23 miles n. of the Dead Sea. It is now known as the Nahr ez-Zerḳā. The Jabbok was a recognized frontier. It formed the w. boundary of the Ammonites, and separated them from the Amorite kingdom of Sihon and later from the tribe of Gad. It divided Mount Gilead into 2 parts, of which the s. was held by Sihon before the Israelite conquest, and afterward was assigned to Gad, while the n. was possessed by Og and passed from him to the half tribe of Manasseh (Num. 21:24; Deut. 2:36, 37; 3:12, 13, 16; Josh. 12:2–6).

Ja'besh (jā'bĕsh) [dry]. 1. A town. See JABESH-GILEAD.
2. Father of King Shallum (II Kings 15:10).

Ja'besh-gil'e·ad (jā'bĕsh-gĭl'ê-ăd) [Jabesh of Gilead]. A town of Gilead. It is believed to have stood at or near ed-Deir, 9½ miles s.e. of Beth-shean on the other side of the Jordan. Ed-Deir is on the wadi el-Yābis, which seems to preserve the old name Jabesh. In the war waged against Benjamin in the days of the Judges on account of the matter of the Levite and his concubine, none of the men of Jabesh-gilead took part. For this indifference to a national sin, they were condemned to utter destruction. Only 400 unmarried girls were saved alive and given for wives to 400 of the remaining men of Benjamin (Judg. 21:8–15). The place was soon reoccupied. Shortly after Saul had been chosen king, Nahash, king of the Ammonites, besieged Jabesh-gilead. The town was sore pressed; and the Ammonite king doomed every man to the loss of the right eye on the surrender of the town. This was intended as an insult to the whole Israelite nation. Saul raised the siege by defeating the besieging army (I Sam. 11:1–11). The men of the town remembered their deliverer with gratitude, and when, after the battle of Gilboa, his headless body, with those of his sons, was fastened to the wall of Beth-shean, they crossed the Jordan, carried off the corpses, burned them and buried the bones in the vicinity of Jabesh-gilead (I Sam. 31:11–13; I Chron. 10:11, 12) from which they were ultimately removed to the sepulcher of Kish (II Sam. 21:12–14). David sent the men of Jabesh his personal thanks for what they had done (II Sam. 2:4–7).

Ja'bez (jā'bĕz) [he makes sorrow; with metathesis of last 2 radicals of Heb. 'āṣab, to pain, grieve]. 1. A man of Judah, whose mother gave him the name Jabez, because she bore him in sorrow. He was more honorable than his brethren. He prayed that God would enlarge the boundary of his possessions, besides keeping him from evil. God granted his request (I Chron. 4:9, 10). 2. A place, doubtless in Judah, where families of scribes dwelt (I Chron. 2:55).

Ja'bin (jā'bĭn) [he (God) perceives]. 1. A Canaanite, king of Hazor in Galilee and its dependent towns and the head of the confederacy of n. and central kings whom Joshua defeated at the waters of Merom. After the battle the Israelites took and burned Hazor and slew its king (Josh. 11:1–14). 2. Another king of Canaan who reigned at Hazor, probably a lineal descendant of the 1st (Judg. 4:2). He, too, had kings fighting under him (ch. 5:19). He oppressed the Israelites 20 years; but at length his commander in chief Sisera was defeated by Barak at the river Kishon and afterward murdered. Jabin continued the war but was ultimately destroyed (ch. 4:2–24).

Jab'ne·el (jăb'nē-ĕl) [God causes to be built]. 1. A town on the n. border of Judah (Josh. 15:5, 11). It is the same place as the Philistine city of Jabneh, the wall of which was broken down by Uzziah (II Chron. 26:6); and it was known later as Jamnia (I Macc. 4:15; 5:58; II Macc. 12:8, 9). It is represented by the village of Yebnah, about 4 miles inland from the Mediterranean, and 9 n.e. by n. of Ashdod. 2. A frontier town of Naphtali (Josh. 19:33). Conder identifies it with the ruin Yemma, about 7 miles s. by w. of Tiberias.

Jab'neh (jăb'nĕ) [he (God) causes to be built]. See JABNEEL 1.

Ja'can (jā'kăn), in A.V. **Ja'chan** (jā'kăn). A Gadite, probably head of a father's house (I Chron. 5:13).

Ja'chin (jā'kĭn) [he (God) establishes]. 1. A son of Simeon, and founder of a tribal family (Gen. 46:10; Ex. 6:15; Num. 26:12). Called Jarib in I Chron. 4:24, which is doubtless due to a copyist's error. 2. A descendant of Aaron. In the time of David, his family was made the 21st of the courses into which the sacerdotal body was divided (I Chron. 24:17). It dwelt at Jerusalem, according to the probable meaning of I Chron. 9:10; but it is not at all certain that

the priest Jachin, who was resident at Jerusalem afer the Captivity, was of this family (Neh. 11:10). 3. The righthand pillar of 2 set up in the porch of Solomon's Temple (I Kings 7:15–22), probably as a symbol of firmness. The name may be an abbreviation of an inscription like: "He (Jehovah) will establish the throne of David, and his kingdom to his seed forever." See BOAZ 2.

Ja'cinth. See HYACINTH and LIGURE.

Jack'al. The rendering in the R.V. of the Heb. plurals tannîm and tannôth, which in the A.V. are regularly translated by dragon (q.v.). The creature intended is a mammal (Lam. 4:3, in A.V. sea monsters) and dwells in the wilderness (Isa. 35:7; 43:20) and in deserted places (Isa. 34:13, 14; Jer. 49:33; 51:37).

The jackal (Canis aureus) belongs to the dog genus Canis. It differs from the dog in its long and pointed muzzle. The name aureus, golden, refers to the color of the under fur, which is brownish yellow, mottled with black, gray, and brown hairs. Its length is about 30 inches, and its height at the shoulder 17. It hunts in packs, and feeds chiefly on carrion, though it carries off and devours children when opportunity arises. It has been called the lion's provider, the opinion being entertained that when its voice is heard, the lion, following on, tries to claim his share of the prey. It raises the most unearthly yell of all of its compeers. It is found throughout Palestine, especially frequenting ruins. See also FOX; and for the Jackal's Well, see DRAGON'S WELL.

Ja'cob (jā'kŭb) [popular ety., one that takes by the heel or supplants; the heeler. But probably rather, he (God) guards, or protects; cf. S. Arab. and Ethiopic 'aḳaba, to guard]. A son of Isaac and Rebekah, a twin with Esau, but born a short time after him and therefore considered the younger brother (Gen. 25:21–26). He was born when his father was 60 years old (v. 26). He became a quiet, inoffensive man, dwelling in tents (v. 27). He was his mother's favorite, while the father preferred Esau (v. 28). As Esau came in from hunting, faint with hunger, Jacob chanced to have pottage of lentils ready boiled, but relieved his brother's necessities only after he had compelled him first to surrender his birthright (vs. 29–34). Positive fraud followed. When Isaac was about 137 years old and nearly blind, Rebekah induced Jacob to dress himself in Esau's raiment, make his neck and hands artificially hairy, and, passing himself off as Esau, obtain from Isaac, who thought himself near death, the blessing belonging to the birthright. Esau recalled the 1st wrong when this 2d was perpetrated, and resolved that when his father died, he would kill his brother (ch. 27:1–41). Rebekah heard the threat and, to give time for Esau's wrath to cool, sent Jacob away to her relatives in Haran, on the pretext of seeking a wife. While on this journey he had the night vision in which a ladder connected earth and heaven, angels ascended and descended, and God standing above assured him of the covenant blessings (chs. 27:42–46; 28:1–22).

Jacob sojourned in Paddan-aram at least 20 years, while he was in Laban's employ, serving him 14 years for his 2 daughters, Leah and Rachel, and 6 for a payment in cattle. During this period in Haran there were born to him 11 sons: by Leah 6, Reuben, Simeon, Levi, Judah, Issachar, and Zebulun (besides a daughter, Dinah); by Bilhah, Rachel's maid, 2, Dan and Naphtali; by Zilpah, Leah's maid, 2, Gad and Asher; and by Rachel 1, Joseph (chs. 29; 30). The last was born when Jacob was 90 or 91 years of age (cf. ch. 47:9 with chs. 41:46, 47, 54; 45:11). Six years later, perceiving that Laban and his sons, envying his prosperity, were turning against him, he became alarmed. While pasturing his flocks, probably 3 days from Haran (chs. 30:36; 31: 22) on the Euphrates, he sent for his wives (ch. 31:4), crossed the river, and fled with his family and possessions toward Canaan (v. 21). Three days later Laban was informed of Jacob's flight; he presently gathered his male relatives, started in pursuit of the fugitives, and after a week's journey by forced marches overtook them on Mount Gilead, apparently between the Yarmuk and the Jabbok, scant 300 miles from the Euphrates, at least 10 days after Jacob's departure and probably longer, for Laban was busy shearing sheep when he received information of the flight and was unprepared for the journey. God shielded Jacob from injury, and a reconciliation and a treaty of amity between the alienated parties took place. A heap of stones was erected and a covenant meal eaten to establish the agreement that neither party should pass that point to attack the other (ch. 31).

Jacob had manifestations of the divine favor at Mahanaim and on the Jabbok, where a man wrestled with him until break of day, showed his superiority to Jacob by disabling him by a touch, and before departing blessed him, saying: "Thy name shall be called no more Jacob, but Israel; for thou hast striven with God and with men, and hast prevailed." And Jacob called the name of that place Peniel, face of God, for he said: "I have seen God face to face, and my life is preserved" (Gen. 32:22–32; cf. the names in Gen. 33:20; Hos. 12:4). This event proved a crisis in the life of Jacob. Heretofore he had been trusting to his own strength and shrewdness for success. He now learns that his own strength is of no avail in wrestling with God and that he must resort to prayer for the blessing which he cannot do without. Henceforth the record of his worshiping becomes frequent. Before he crossed the Jordan, he met Esau and obtained forgiveness for the wrongs which had so long made him an exile. Then the brothers parted, Esau returning to Mount Seir and Jacob going to Canaan (Gen. 33:1–18).

Jacob sojourned in Canaan at Shechem, where he bought a parcel of ground from the chief of Shechem, on which he pitched his camp and erected an altar (ch. 33:18–20). While here his daughter Dinah was violated by the chief's son. The deed was avenged by 2 of Jacob's sons, Simeon and Levi, and the other sons joined in spoiling the town. Jacob feared the consequences of this act; but since his sons had captured the place, slain the males, appropriated the wealth, and made captive the women and children, he recognized the conquest of the place and the consequent ownership of it by his tribe (ch. 48:22; cf. ch. 37: 12). From Shechem Jacob removed to Beth-el. There Deborah died and was buried (ch. 35:6–8); see DEBORAH 1. There also, at the place where God had appeared to him as he went to Paddan-aram, God appeared to him again when he came back from Paddan-aram (chs. 35:9; 28:10–22), emphasized the change of his name to Israel, and confirmed the blessing of the Abrahamic covenant to him. As he drew near to Bethlehem on his way to Hebron, his 12th and last son, Benjamin, was born, and his beloved Rachel died (ch. 35:9–20). At length Jacob came to his father Isaac at Mamre (v. 27). Isaac died about 23 years later, and was buried by Esau and Jacob (vs. 28, 29). Jacob seems to have dwelt at Mamre during the next 33 years; for he was at Hebron about 10 years after his return (ch. 37:14; cf. v. 2), and he was evidently still there when he was summoned to go down to Egypt (ch. 46:1).

Jacob was 130 years old when he went to Egypt (ch. 47:9), and he lived there 17 years. He gave a special blessing, 1st to Joseph's children and then to his own, after which he died at the age of 147 (chs. 47:28; 48; 49). His body was embalmed, taken to Canaan with much pomp, and interred in the cave of Machpelah (ch. 50:1–14). Jacob had glaring faults of character. For his sins he suffered severely, and in his old age he was sorely chastened by the loss of Joseph. In his later life he acknowledged, at least tacitly, the sinfulness of his earlier career and his failure to walk before God, and he spoke only of God's grace (ch. 48:15, 16). He was animated also in his latter days by unwavering faith in God (Gen. 48:21; Heb. 11:21).

The Hebrew nation, as descended from Jacob, is often called in Scripture the Children of Israel (Ex. 14:16, 29; 15:1, etc.). The prophets often use Jacob and Israel as parallel names in their poetic couplets (Deut. 33:10; Isa. 43:1, 22; 44:1). See ISRAEL 2.

Jacob's Well, beside or on the edge of which Jesus sat when conversing with the woman of Samaria, was at Sychar, near the parcel of ground that Jacob gave to his son Joseph. "Jacob," the woman of Samaria said, "drank

Jacob's Well

thereof himself, and his sons, and his cattle" (John 4:5, 6, 12; cf. Gen. 33:18–20; 37:12). A tradition going back as far as the time of the Bordeaux pilgrim, A.D. 333, and accepted by Jews, Samaritans, Christians, and Mohammedans, identifies Jacob's Well with the Bir Ya'kūb. It is situated at the e. mouth of the valley between Mount Ebal on the n. and Mount Gerizim on the s., about 2 miles e.s.e. from Nablus, the modern Shechem, and half a mile s.s.w. of 'Askar, believed by many to be Sychar. Maundrell, generally very accurate, made its diameter 9 feet and its depth 105. Dr. John Wilson, measuring a line with which a boy was let down into it with a light in 1843, determined it to be 75 feet deep. Conder reported its depth in 1875 as 75 feet. It is less deep now than formerly, because somewhat choked with rubbish. The water is good, but is not easy to reach (John 4:11). The shaft is lined with masonry in the upper part. The lower part is cut through soft limestone. A low subterranean vault, 20 feet long from e. to w. and 10 broad, the crypt of an ancient Christian church, is built over the well, the mouth of which is contracted and covered with one or more large stones. There is a fine fountain a little to the w., and many others in the valley. The well, however, was dug, perhaps, because these fountains sometimes were dry in the summer. The water from the well is superior to that of the adjacent springs and streams. For Jacob-el and Joseph-el, see JOSEPH 1.

Ja'da (jä'dȧ) [knowing]. A son of Onam, a man of Judah, family of Hezron, house of Jerahmeel (I Chron. 2:28, 32).

Ja'dau (jä'dō). See IDDO, II. 2.

Jad·du'a (jă-dū'ȧ) [known]. 1. One of the chiefs of the people who, with Nehemiah, sealed the covenant (Neh. 10:21).
2. A high priest, son of Jonathan and the 5th in descent from the high priest Jeshua, who returned with Zerubbabel from Babylon (Neh. 12:11, 22). He was probably a youth in the reign of Darius Nothus, and survived Darius Codomannus, the Persian sovereign defeated by Alexander the Great at Arbela in 331 B.C. See HIGH PRIEST.

Ja'don (jä'dŏn) [he rules, judges, or abides]. A Meronothite, who repaired part of the wall of Jerusalem after the Captivity (Neh. 3:7).

Ja'el (jä'ĕl) [wild goat, ibex]. The wife of Heber the Kenite (Judg. 4:17). Sisera, Jabin's general, trusting to the peace subsisting between his royal master and Heber, fled to her tent after he was defeated by Barak. On his approach Jael went out, invited him to enter, and gave him milk to relieve his thirst. But as he lay sleeping in the tent, she took a hammer and drove a tent pin through his temples, fixing his head to the ground. When the victorious Barak passed, she called him in to see what she had done (Judg. 4:11–22). Deborah highly commended the deed of Jael (ch. 5:6, 24–27), though it was cruel and treacherous. It reveals a rudeness of manners and a hardness of character which found frequent exemplification in those early times.

Ja'gur (jä'gẽr) [cf. Heb. *gūr*, to sojourn]. A town in the extreme s. of Judah (Josh. 15:21), probably Tell Ghurr, n. of Bîr el-Meshâsh.

Jah (jä). A form of Jehovah occurring in poetry (Ps. 68:4, A.V., R.V. marg.; R.V. of Ps. 89:8) In various other places Jah, or, rather, Heb. *yāh* is rendered Lord in the A.V. and R.V.
In the Heb. sometimes Jah and Jehovah stand together, Jah first (Isa. 12:2 and ch. 26:4, marg. of R.V.).

Ja'hath (jä'hăth) [perhaps, he (God) will snatch up]. 1. A man of Judah, family of Hezron, descended through Shobal (I Chron. 4:2; cf. ch. 2:19, 50).
2. A son of Libni, a Levite, family of Gershom (I Chron. 6:20, 43).
3. A Levite, family of Gershom and head of a subdivision of the house of Shimei (I Chron. 23:10).
4. A Levite, family of Kohath, house of Izhar (I Chron. 24:22).
5. A Merarite Levite, an overseer of the workmen engaged in repairing the Temple during Josiah's reign (II Chron. 34:12).

Ja'haz (jä'hăz) and **Jah'zah**, in A.V. once **Ja·ha'za** (jȧ-hā'zȧ) (Josh. 13:18), and twice **Ja·ha'zah** (jȧ-hā'zȧ) (Josh. 21:36; Jer. 48:21) [a place trodden under foot, an open space]. A place in the plain of Moab (Jer. 48:21) where Sihon, king of the Amorites, was defeated by the Israelites (Num. 21:23; Deut. 2:32; Judg. 11:20). It was assigned to the Reubenites (Josh. 13:18), and set apart for the Merarite Levites (Josh. 21:36; I Chron. 6:78). It was taken from Israel by Mesha, king of Moab (*Moabite Stone*, 18–20, see MOABITE STONE), and it was held by Moab in

the time of Isaiah and Jeremiah (Isa. 15:4; Jer. 48:21, 34). Umm el-Walîd has been suggested; Khirbet Iskander, n. of the wadi el-Wâleh, if it had remains of the Iron Age, would be an admirable identification.

Ja'ha·zi'ah (jä'hȧ-zī'ȧ). See JAHZEIAH.

Ja·ha'zi·el (jȧ-hā'zĭ-ĕl) [El (God) sees].
1. A Levite, family of Kohath, house of Hebron (I Chron. 23:19).
2. One of the Benjamite warriors who joined David at Ziklag (I Chron. 12:4).
3. A priest in David's reign who was employed to sound a trumpet in the sanctuary (I Chron. 16:6).
4. A Levite, son of Zechariah of the Asaph family, who prophesied in the time of Jehoshaphat (II Chron. 20:14).
5. Father of a chief of the people who returned from Babylon (Ezra 8:5).

Jah'da·i (jä'dȧ-ī) [(Jehovah) leads]. A man of Judah, enrolled with Caleb's posterity (I Chron. 2:47).

Jah'di·el (jä'dĭ-ĕl) [God makes glad]. A leading man in the half tribe of Manasseh e. of the Jordan (I Chron. 5:24).

Jah'do (jä'dō) [cf. Jahdiel]. A Gadite, son of Buz (I Chron. 5:14).

Jah'le·el (jä'lē-ĕl) [probably, may God show himself well-disposed; cf. Neo-Heb. *ḥālāh*, Arab. *ḥalā*, to be sweet, agreeable]. A son of Zebulun, and founder of a tribal family (Gen. 46:14; Num. 26:26).

Jah'ma·i (jä'mȧ-ī) [(God) protects; cf. Arab. *ḥamā*, to protect, and S. Arab. *yaḥmi'il*, *ḥamay'il*]. A prince of Issachar, of the family of Tola (I Chron. 7:2).

Jah'zah (jä'zȧ). See JAHAZ.

Jah'ze·el (jä'zĕ-ĕl) and **Jah'zi·el** [God divides, distributes]. A son of Naphtali, and founder of a tribal family (Gen. 46:24; Num. 26:48; I Chron. 7:13).

Jah·ze'iah (jä-zē'yȧ), in A.V. **Ja'ha·zi'ah** [Jehovah sees]. A son of Tikvah who opposed the proposition that the Jews put away their foreign wives (Ezra 10:15, R.V.; but see marg.).

Jah'ze·rah (jä'zĕ-rȧ) [prudent; cf. Arab. *ḥadhir*, cautious, prudent]. A priest descended from Immer (I Chron. 9:12). See AHZAI.

Jah'zi·el (jä'zĭ-ĕl). See JAHZEEL.

Ja'ir, I (jä'ẽr) [Heb. *yā'ir*, he enlightens].
1. A son of Segub and grandson of Hezron, of the tribe of Judah, and his wife, who was of the family of Machir, of the tribe of Manasseh (I Chron. 2:21, 22). He was reckoned with the tribe of Manasseh (I Chron. 5:23; Num. 32:41; Deut. 3:14). At the time of the conquest by the Israelites under Moses of the country e. of the Jordan, he took villages in the Argob, on the border of Bashan and Gilead, and called them Havvoth-jair (*q.v.*).
2. A Gileadite who judged Israel 22 years, succeeding or surviving Tola in office. Each of his 30 sons had an ass for riding purposes, which in that age was an indication of standing in the community. They also had 30 cities, called Havvoth-jair. He may have belonged to the family of the earlier Jair (see JAIRITE), and have inherited prerogatives connected with the Havvoth-jair, or have used his influence to place his sons over these encampments (Judg. 10:3–5).
3. A Benjamite, Mordecai's father or remoter ancestor (Esth. 2:5).

Ja'ir, II (jä'ẽr) [Heb. *yā'ir*, he arouses]. Father of Elhanan (I Chron. 20:5); called in II Sam. 21:19, Jaare-oregim, where -oregim doubtless came into the text by error from Heb. *'ōreḡîm* (weavers) in the line below.

Ja'ir·ite (jā'ẽr-īt). A descendant of some Jair or other, whose name was written as is that of Jair, I (II Sam. 20:26).

Ja'i·rus (jā'i-rŭs) [Gr. *Iaeiros*, for Jair]. A ruler of the synagogue (Mark 5:22; Luke 8:41), probably at Capernaum. His young daughter lay at the point of death; and he went to Jesus, beseeching him to heal her. On the way to the house word reached them that the child was dead (Mark 5:23, 24, 35; Luke 8:42, 49); but the father, with confidence in Jesus' power, still entreated (Matt. 9:18), and Jesus told him to put away all fear and to trust him (Mark 5:36; Luke 8:50). Entering the house with Peter, James, and John (Mark 5:37; Luke 8:51; cf. Matt. 9:19) he found it full of noisy professional mourners and rebuked them and said: "The damsel is not dead, but sleepeth" (Matt. 9:24; Mark 5:39; Luke 8:52). Taking the 3 disciples and the parents (Mark 5:40), he went into the chamber where the dead child lay (Mark 5:40; Matt. 9:25), took her by the hand, and said in Aram. *Tᵉlīthā ḳŭm*(ī), "Damsel, ... Arise" (Mark 5:41; cf. Matt. 9:25; Luke 8:54). She obeyed, and he bade the parents not to tell what had taken place (Mark 5:43; Luke 8:56). But such a miracle could not be kept from public knowledge (Matt. 9:26).

Ja'kan (jā'kăn). See JAAKAN.

Ja'keh (jā'kĕ) [pious; cf. Arab. *waḳā*, to guard, preserve, be pious]. The father of that Agur whose words are recorded in Prov., ch. 30. In the Heb. Bible his name is followed by *ham-massā'*, translated in the A.V. the prophecy, and in the R.V. the oracle. The marg. of the R.V. translates the title Jakeh of Massa, and refers to Gen. 25:14, where Massa, a son of Ishmael, represents a North Arabian tribe.

Ja'kim (jā'kĭm) [he (God) raises up]. 1. A descendant of Aaron. His family grew to a father's house and was made the 12th of the 24 courses into which David divided the priests (I Chron. 24:12).
2. A Benjamite (I Chron. 8:19).

Ja'lam (jā'lăm), in A.V. **Ja'a·lam**. A son of Esau by his wife Oholibamah. He became a chieftain of Edom (Gen. 36:5, 18; I Chron. 1:35).

Ja'lon (jā'lŏn). A son of Ezrah, registered with the tribe of Judah (I Chron. 4:17).

Jam'bres (jăm'brēz) [cf. Heb. root *mārăh*, to be refractory, rebellious]. One of 2 Egyptian magicians who attempted to counterwork Moses (II Tim. 3:8). See JANNES.

Jam'bri (jăm'brī). Founder of a family which dwelt at Medeba (I Macc. 9:36, 37; Jos. *Antiq.* xiii. 1, 2).

James (jāmz) [a form of the name Jacob]. 1. James the son of Zebedee (Matt. 4:21; 10:2; Mark 1:19; 3:17), and brother of the Apostle John (Matt. 17:1; Mark 3:17; 5:37; Acts 12:2), one of the earliest disciples (Matt. 4:21; Mark 1:19, 29; cf. John 1:40, 41) and most trusted apostles (Matt. 17:1; Mark 5:37; 9:2; 13:3; 14:33; Luke 8:51; 9:28) of our Lord. Of his birthplace or early home we are told nothing. His occupation as a fisherman on the Sea of Galilee, in partnership with Peter and Andrew (Luke 5:10), might seem to suggest a contiguous locality. But the fishery of the Sea of Galilee was expressly kept free for every Israelite, and a social difference between the sons of Zebedee and the sons of Jonas may be implied in the facts that the former kept hired servants (Mark 1:20), and that John at least was known to the high priest (John 18:16) and may have had a house in Jerusalem (ch. 19:27). His father, Zebedee, appears only once in the pages of the Gospels (Matt. 4:21; Mark 1:19), where he raises no obstacle to his sons' following Jesus. From

Matt. 27:56, compared with Mark 15:40; 16:1 and with John 19:25, it seems reasonable to infer that his mother was named Salome and was sister to the mother of Jesus; in which case James would be a near kinsman of Jesus, and like him of Davidic descent. His name occurs only in the Synoptic Gospels and the book of The Acts, although he is alluded to twice in the Gospel of John (chs. 1:40, 41; 21:2). It never occurs apart from that of John, which it ordinarily precedes (Matt. 4:21; 10:2; 17:1; Mark 1:19, 29; 3:17; 5:37; 9:2; 10:35, 41; 13:3; 14:33; Luke 5:10; 6:14; 9:54), while John is designated as the brother of James (Matt. 4:21; 10:2; 17:1; Mark 1:19; 3:17; 5:37). From this it has been inferred that he was the older brother; while the occasional reverse usage in Luke (chs. 8:51, R.V.; 9:28) and Acts (chs. 1:13, R.V.; 12:2 only) is supposed to arise from John's greater prominence in the apostolic circle. Along with John, he received from Christ the surname Boanerges or son of thunder (Mark 3:17), and along with him earned his Master's rebuke for the fierceness of his anger against the Samaritan village which would not receive Jesus (Luke 9:55), and the indignation of his fellow apostles for his ambitious self-seeking (Mark 10:41). After the crucifixion we find him with the other apostles in Galilee (John 21:2), and in Jerusalem (Acts 1:13), and his record closes with his death by the sword at the hands of Herod Agrippa I, probably A.D. 44 (Acts 12:2). He was the first of the apostolic band to seal his testimony with his blood.

2. James the son of Alphaeus and 1 of the apostles of our Lord (Matt. 10:3; Mark 3:18; Luke 6:15; Acts 1:13). Nothing further is certainly known of him. It is natural, however, as it has been usual, to assume that the James of Matt. 27:56; Mark 15:40; 16:1; Luke 24:10 is this James; in which case we may learn that he bore the surname of "the little" (R.V. marg.), possibly with reference to his stature (Mark 15:40); that his mother was called Mary, and was 1 of the women who accompanied Christ; and that he had a brother named Joses. Levi, or Matthew, who, according to Mark 2:14, was son of Alphaeus, may be another brother, but it is far more probable that 2 different men bore the name of Alphaeus.

It is possible to fill in the ellipsis of Luke 6:16; Acts 1:13 (cf. A.V. and R.V. marg.) so as to make the Apostle Judas another brother. It is possible further to identify the Mary of Clopas of John 19:25 with Mary the mother of James; and it is then possible, though scarcely natural, to read John 19:25 as declaring that Mary of Clopas was Jesus' mother's sister. By this combination, James, the son of Alphaeus, would be made out to be the cousin-german of our Lord. It is common, on this assumption, to take still another step, and, on the ground of the similarity between the names of the Lord's brethren and those of the sons of Alphaeus, so obtained, to suppose that this near relative of our Lord's is intended by "James the Lord's brother." The whole construction, however, involves many insecure assumptions and scarcely satisfies the Biblical facts.

3. James, the Lord's brother (Matt. 13:55; Mark 6:3; Gal. 1:19), and the head of the Church at Jerusalem in the apostolic age (Acts 12:17; 15:13; 21:18; Gal. 1:19; 2:9, 12). This James is mentioned by name only twice in the Gospels (Matt. 13:55; Mark 6:3), but the outlines of his life may be traced by means of the notices of the "brethren of the Lord," who constituted a distinct class, both during our Lord's life, when they did not believe on him (John 7:5), and after his resurrection, when they are found among his followers (Acts 1:14). The exact relationship

which these "brethren" bore to our Lord has always been a matter of dispute. Some, identifying them with the sons of Alphaeus, represent them as his cousins. Others think of them as his half-brothers, children of Joseph by a former marriage. As they always appear with Mary, living and journeying with her and holding just such relations with her as would naturally be borne by her children (Matt. 12:46, 47; Luke 8:19; John 2:12), there is no reason to question the natural implication that they were Jesus' own brothers. As James's name stands first in the lists (Matt. 13:55; Mark 6:3), it is probable that he was the oldest of our Lord's brothers. He doubtless shared their unbelief (John 7:5), and doubtless also their natural anxieties in his behalf (Mark 3:31 seq.). When or how the change was wrought in him by which he became a servant of Christ (Acts 1:14; James 1:1) we are not told: possibly, as in the case of Paul, his conversion was due to a special appearance of the risen Lord (I Cor. 15:7). From the very first organization of the Church in Jerusalem, James appears as its head (Acts 12:17; 15:13; 21:18; Gal. 1:19; 2:9, 12). As early as c. A.D. 37, when Paul first visited Jerusalem after his conversion, James's position was such that Paul felt it necessary to name him along with Peter as having been seen by him (Gal. 1:19). The reference of Acts 12:17 (A.D. 44), where James is clearly the official head of "the brethren," as well as that of ch. 21:18 (A.D. 58), where he seems to stand at the head of the elders of the Church (cf. ch. 15:6), enable us to estimate wherein his preeminence consisted. Since he was not an apostle (the R.V. marg. gives the correct translation of Gal. 1:19), we cannot be far wrong in assuming that he was the head of the board of elders of the Church at Jerusalem; that is, what we should call the "pastor" of that Church. See ELDER. As such, his name stands for the Church of Jerusalem (Gal. 2:12), of which he was the natural representative (Acts 12:17; 15:13; 21:18); and visitors to the Church made themselves known in the first instance to him and laid their errand before him (Acts 12:17; 21:18; Gal. 1: 19; 2:9). In his position, James's lifework was naturally to smooth the passage of Jews over to Christianity. That he stood on the same platform of faith with Paul is apparent not only from Paul's assertion in Gal. 2:9, but also from James's remarks recorded in Acts 15:13-21. But on both occasions he speaks also in behalf of the Jewish-Christian conscience, and it is equally apparent that, as Paul became as all men to all men because he was sent to all, James became as a Jew to Jews because he was sent to Jews. The use of his name by intense Judaizers (Gal. 2:12, and the later Clementine literature) is thus explicable, as also the admiration which is said to have been conceived for him by the Jews themselves, who are reported to have given him the surname of "the Just" (Eusebius H. E. ii. 23). After Acts 21:18 (A.D. 58) we meet no further reference to this James in the N.T. Secular history tells us, however, that he was martyred in a popular outbreak of the Jews in the interregnum between the death of the procurator Festus and the appointment of his successor, i.e., A.D. 62 (Jos. Antiq. xx. 9, 1).

4. James, the father or, less probably, brother of the Apostle Judas (Luke 6:16; Acts 1:13). Nothing further is known of him.

B. B. W. (rev., H. S. G.)

James (jāmz), **The Epistle of.** This letter does not announce itself as the production of an apostle, but describes its author simply as James, a bond servant of God and of the Lord Jesus Christ (ch. 1:1, R.V. marg.). It is most

natural to think of James, the Lord's brother, as meant, and all the characteristics of the letter agree with this attribution. Although some scholars place the date of its composition near the end of the 1st century or at the beginning of the 2d, the following considerations bear witness to its primitiveness: the Christian place of worship is still spoken of as a synagogue (ch. 2:2); Christians are not sharply discriminated from Jews (ch. 1:1); the sins rebuked and errors corrected are such as would naturally spring up in a Jewish soil; while there is not a trace of the controversies which already in the 6th decade of the 1st Christian century were distracting the whole Church. It may, therefore, be reasonably dated c. A.D. 45 and considered the earliest of the N.T. writings. The letter is addressed to the 12 tribes which are of the Dispersion (ch. 1:1), that is, not to the dispersed Jews, nor yet to the whole Christian Church, considered as the spiritual Israel, but, probably, to the Christians (chs. 2:1, 5, 7; 5:7) among the Jewish Dispersion, as the Jews dwelling outside the Holy Land were technically called (John 7:35; cf. II Macc. 1:27). The object of its writing was to reform and correct those sins and errors to which its lately Christianized Jewish readers continued to be liable, and to encourage them in the sore trials to which they were exposed.

After the address (ch. 1:1), James first consoles his readers in their trials and exhorts them to steadfastness, pointing out at the same time the source of the temptation to apostasy (ch. 1:2-21). He proceeds then to warn them against mere word-service, explaining what is meant by true faith (ch. 1: 22-27), what will be the effect of true faith on the prevalent sin of respect of persons (ch. 2:1-13), and how a true faith evinces itself (ch. 2:14-26). Exhortations against hasty assumption and misuse of the functions of religious teachers and exposure of their root in a jealous heart follow (ch. 3); and then reproofs of contentiousness (ch. 4:1-12) and self-sufficiency (chs. 4:13 to 5:6). The epistle closes with exhortations to patience in suffering (ch. 5:7-12) and to prayer as the sufficient resource of the Christian in every need (ch. 5:13-18), along with a final declaration of the joy of Christian propagandism (ch. 5:19-20). To this end the author sees fit to employ over 50 imperatives in a document of only 108 vs.

The linguistic and rhetorical character of the epistle is very high. It is written in excellent Greek, in a strikingly elevated and picturesque style resembling that of the Hebrew prophets. It contains more imagery drawn from nature than all the epistles of Paul, in this recalling the manner of our Lord's Synoptic speeches, to which it presents numerous parallels. The tone and matter of its teaching are appropriate to its early date and the recent emergence of its readers from Judaism. The section on faith and works (ch. 2:14-26) has often been misapprehended as a polemic against Paul's doctrine of justification by faith, or at least as a corrective of perversions of that doctrine. It is really a rebuke of a prevalent Jewish notion—that mere intellectual assent to divine teaching is all that is necessary for salvation. James as pointedly as Paul makes faith the instrument of salvation (ch. 2:22, 23), and Paul as firmly as James insists that the only saving faith is the faith that works (Gal. 5:6).

The epistle reflects a Palestinian atmosphere and is a paraenetic document of Christian origin, which was influenced by the Gospel tradition, especially the words of Jesus, without implying literary dependence. The following passages may be compared as noteworthy: James 1:2 with Matt. 5:10-12; James

1 :4 with Matt. 5 :48 ; James 1 :5, 17 with Matt. 7 :7–11 ; James 1 :22 with Matt. 7 :21–27 ; James 2 :10 with Matt. 5 :19 ; James 3 :18 with Matt. 5 :9 ; James 4 :4 with Matt. 6 :24 ; James 4 :12 with Matt. 7 :1 and 10 :28 ; James 5 :1 *seq.* with Matt. 6 :19 and Luke 6 :24 ; James 5 :10 with Matt. 5 :12 ; James 5 :12 with Matt. 5 :34–37 ; James 1 :6 with Mark 11 :23 *seq.;* cf. also James 1 :9 *seq.;* 2 :5 *seq.;* 4 :4 *seq.,* 13 *seq.;* 5 :1 *seq.* with Luke 1 :46 *seq.;* 6 :20 *seq.,* 24 *seq.;* 12 :16 *seq.;* 16 :19 *seq.*

There is clear evidence of the use of this epistle by the Church from the very earliest times. Origen, however, writing early in the 3d century, is the first writer to quote it explicitly by name ; and there was a period during which the Latin writers seem to have used it little.   B. B. W. (rev., H. S. G.)

Ja'min (jā'mĭn) [the right hand, south, good fortune]. 1. A son of Simeon and founder of a tribal family (Gen. 46 :10 ; Ex. 6 :15 ; Num. 26 :12).

2. A man of Judah, family of Jerahmeel (I Chron. 2 :27).

3. One of the Levites who, under the direction of Ezra, read the Law of God to the people and caused them to understand it (Neh. 8 :7, 8).

Jam'lech (jăm'lĕk) [(God) gives, or let him (God) give dominion]. A Simeonite prince (I Chron. 4 :34).

Jam'ni·a (jăm'nĭ-à). See JABNEEL 1.

Ja'na·i (jā'nà-ī), in A.V. **Ja'a·nai** [Jehovah answers]. A Gadite chief (I Chron. 5 :12).

Ja'nim (jā'nĭm), in A.V. **Ja'num** (cf. Heb. *nūm,* to slumber, be drowsy). A village in the hill country of Judah (Josh. 15 :53) ; doubtless to the w. or s.w. of Hebron.

Jan'na·i (jăn'à-ī), in A.V. **Jan'na** (jăn'à). The father of Melchi in the ancestry of Christ (Luke 3 :24).

Jan'nes (jăn'ēz). One of 2 Egyptian magicians who attempted to counterwork Moses, Jambres being the other (II Tim. 3 :8). The reference is to the occurrences described in Ex. 7 :11, 12, 22 ; 8 :7, 18, 19 ; 9 :11, where, however, the names of the magicians are not given nor their number. They were known to late Jewish tradition being found in the Targum of the pseudo-Jonathan. The Talmud mentions Jōḥānā and Mamrē. Jambres is believed to be the Gr. form of Jamreh (Heb. *Yamreh,* he shows disobedience, rebelliousness). Mamre, from the same root, is used in the Talmud for one who resists the decisions of the sanhedrin. Jannes is perhaps a corruption of Johanan (Heb. *Yōḥānān,* John ; cf. Jannaeus), but in sound suggests Talmudic Heb. *yānāh,* Aram. *yᵉnī* (to oppress, vex).

Ja·no'ah (jà-nō'à), and **Ja·no'hah** (jà-nō'hà) in A.V. of Joshua [rest, quiet]. 1. A town of Naphtali, captured by Tiglath-pileser (II Kings 15 :29). Yānūh, 6½ miles e. by s. of Tyre, has been suggested.

2. A town on the boundary line of Ephraim (Josh. 16 :6, 7). It has been fixed at Yānūn, 7 miles s.e. of Shechem.

Ja'num (jā'nŭm). See JANIM.

Ja'pheth (jā'fĕth) [beauty, or let him make wide]. A son of Noah, and doubtless 1 of the 2 elder sons (Gen. 10 :21 ; cf. ch. 9 :24), born about Noah's 500th year (chs. 5 :32 ; 6 :10) ; see NOAH. At the time of the Deluge he was married, but had no children with him in the ark (Gen. 7 :7 ; I Peter 3 :20). On the occasion of Noah's drunkenness, Japheth acted to him in a dutiful manner and in consequence received a blessing, the essential part of which was that he should receive large territory and enjoy free action and that he should occupy

the tents of Shem, not in the sense of conquering the Semites, but of dwelling with them in peace and sharing their privileges (Gen. 9 :20–27). Japheth was the progenitor of the people who inhabited, or perhaps in some cases conquered and annexed, Gomer, Magog, Madai, Javan, Tubal, Meshech, and Tiras (Gen. 10 :2), extending from the high plateau s. of the Caspian Sea w. through the mountain region s. of the Black Sea to the islands and n. shores of the e. Mediterranean, with settlements farther w.

Ja·phi'a (jà-fī'à) [may he (God) cause to shine forth]. 1. A king of Lachish, defeated, captured, and executed by Joshua (Josh. 10 : 3–27).

2. A son of David, born at Jerusalem (II Sam. 5 :15).

3. A border town of Zebulun (Josh. 19 :12), identified with Yāfa, 1¼ miles s.w. of Nazareth.

Japh'let (jăf'lĕt) [may he (God) deliver, or he will deliver]. An Asherite, family of Heber (I Chron. 7 :32).

Japh'le·tite (jăf'lĕ-tīt), in A.V. **Japh'le·ti** (jăf'lĕ-tī). The descendants of a certain Japhlet, apparently not the same as the Asherite of that name. Their location was on the border of Ephraim, near Beth-horon (Josh. 16 :3).

Ja'pho (jā'fō). See JOPPA.

Jar. A vessel of earthenware, but occasionally of other material (John 2 :6), used for either dry articles or liquids. An earthen jar, generally having 1 or 2 handles, was used for drawing water and for bearing it home from the well or fountain (Eccl. 12 :6). Ordi-

Eastern Waterpots

narily women fetched the water for the household, carrying the jar on the head or the shoulder (Gen. 24 :13, 15, 16 ; John 4 :28), but men sometimes brought it (Mark 14 :13). Wine was stored in earthen jars (Herod. iii. 6 ; Xen. *Anabasis* vi. 1, 15), which were often of great size (Homer *Odyssey* ii. 340). Oil also was kept in them ; and they were used in the house for holding meal (I Kings 17 :12, in A.V. barrel).

Ja'rah (jā'rà) [honeycomb]. A descendant of King Saul (I Chron. 9 :42). Called Jehoaddah in ch. 8 :36.

Ja'reb (jā'rĕb) [contentious, or he will contend]. A king of Assyria whose name has not been identified (Hos. 5:13; 10:6), or rather Jareb is not a proper name at all, but a descriptive term, and Heb. *melek yārēb* is to be rendered, "The king who contends"; or it may be understood as equivalent to Akkadian *sharru rabū* (great king); cf. Ps. 48:2 *melek rāb* (great King).

Ja'red (jā'rĕd), in A.V. once **Je'red** (I Chron. 1:2) [perhaps, descent]. Son of Mahalaleel and father of Enoch (Gen. 5:16–20; (I Chron. 1:2; Luke 3:37). See CHRONOLOGY, I. 1.

Jar'e·si'ah (jăr'ē-sī'à). See JAARESHIAH.

Jar'ha (jär'hà). An Egyptian servant of a man of Judah called Sheshan. The master gave his daughter in marriage to Jarha (I Chron. 2:34, 35).

Ja'rib (jā'rĭb) [he (God) contends, pleads]. 1. A son of Simeon (I Chron. 4: 24); see JACHIN 1.

2. A chief man who was with Ezra the priest at the river of Ahava (Ezra 8:16).

3. A priest who was induced to put away his foreign wife (Ezra 10:18).

Jar'muth (jär'mŭth) [a height]. 1. A town in the lowland, whose king was defeated, captured, and slain by Joshua (Josh. 10:3–27; 12:11). It was assigned to Judah (ch. 1ɔ: 35), and was inhabited after the Captivity (Neh. 11:29). Eusebius identified it with a village known in his day as Iermochōs, 10 Roman miles from Eleutheropolis on the road to Jerusalem. The site is marked by Knirbet Yarmūk, 16 miles w. by s. from Jerusalem and 8 miles n.n.e. of Eleutheropolis (Beit Jibrīn).

2. A town of Issachar, assigned to the Gershonite Levites (Josh. 21:28, 29). It is called Ramoth (I Chron. 6:73) and Remeth (Josh. 19:21), synonyms of Jarmuth. Not identified. Albright suggests Kaukab el-Hawā, the Coquet or Belvoir of the Crusaders.

Ja·ro'ah (jà-rō'à) [cf. Arab. *wariḥa*, to be soft, thin]. A Gadite, descended through Buz (I Chron. 5:14).

Ja'shar (jā'shĕr), in A.V. **Ja'sher** [righteous, upright]. The Book of Jashar is quoted in Josh. 10:13; II Sam. 1:18; and in LXX of I Kings 8:53. From these citations, the book was evidently a collection of poems which were apparently accompanied by introductory, and perhaps also concluding, explanatory remarks in prose. It resembled in this respect the psalms with prose introductions, such as Psalms 18 and 51, or The Book of Job with its prose introduction (Job 1:1 to 3:1) and conclusion (ch. 42:7–17). In 1751 there appeared a volume which professed to be an English translation of The Book of Jashar, alleged to have been found, but the production was an impudent forgery.

Ja'shen (jā'shĕn) [sleeping]. A name in the catalogue of David's mighty men (II Sam. 23:32) occupying the place of Hashem in I Chron. 11:34. Perhaps the preceding Heb. letters *bni* rendered "the sons of" are a dittograph of the last 3 Heb. letters *bni* of Shaalbonite and so should be omitted. On the basis of this emendation and a comparison with the text of Chronicles and the Lucianic reading (Gr.), the verse may be rendered: "Eliahba the Shaalbonite, Jashen the Gunite, Jonathan the son of Shammah the Hararite."

Ja'sher (jā'shĕr). See JASHAR.

Ja·sho'be·am (jà-shō'bē-ăm) [let the people return]. 1. A man of the family of Hachmoni and chief of David's mighty men (I Chron. 11:11). He is reasonably identified with the son of Zabdiel, of the children of Perez, and consequently of the tribe of Judah, who was made military captain over the

course for the 1st month (I Chron. 27:2, 3). Called in II Sam. 23:8 Josheb-basshebeth (*q.v.*).

2. A Benjamite who joined David at Ziklag. He belonged to the family of the Korahites, probably the Levitical family of that name who kept the doors of the tabernacle (I Chron. 12:1, 2, 6).

Ja'shub (jā'shŭb) [he returns]. 1. A son of Issachar, and founder of a tribal family (Num. 26:24; I Chron. 7:1). Called Job in Gen. 46:13 A.V., probably through a copyist's omission of the Heb. letter *shin* (*sh*).

2. A son of Bani whom Ezra induced to put away his foreign wife (Ezra 10:29).

Ja·shu'bi·le'hem (jà-shōō'bĭ-lē'hĕm) [perhaps, bread returns]. Probably a man, and not a locality; a member of the family of Shelah, tribe of Judah (I Chron. 4:22).

Ja'si·el (jā'sĭ-ĕl). See JAASIEL.

Ja'son (jā'sŭn) [Gr. *Iasōn*, healing; adopted by Hellenizing Jews as a substitute for Joshua, Jeshua, or Jesus]. 1. One of the 2 envoys sent by Judas Maccabaeus to Rome (161 B.C.) to invoke aid against the Syrians (I Macc. 8:17). It was perhaps his son who was sent to renew this alliance (ch. 12:16).

2. A high priest, son of Simon II, who held office c. 174–171 B.C., and used his influence to Hellenize the Jews (II Macc. 4:7–26); see HIGH PRIEST.

3. A man of Cyrene and author of a history of the Jewish war for freedom, 175–160 B.C. (II Macc. 2:23); see APOCRYPHA 14.

4. A Christian, a relative of Paul (Rom. 16:21). He was probably the Jason who resided at Thessalonica, gave lodging to Paul and Silas in his home during their visit to the city, and was dragged by the Jews and their abettors before the rulers for this act of hospitality to objectionable men and was released only on giving bail (Acts 17:5–9).

Jas'per. The rendering of Heb. *yāshᵉpheh* and Gr. *iaspis*, a precious stone (Ex. 28:20; Ezek. 28:13; Rev. 4:3). Jasper is a variety of quartz, of a red, brown, yellow, green, or gray color, and opaque. Among the ancients the term was of broader meaning. It included, according to Pliny, a transparent or translucent green variety (cf. Rev. 21:11), and hence denoted a kind of chalcedony or agate. The LXX renders the Heb. word by onyx.

Jath'ni·el (jăth'nĭ-ĕl) [God bestows gifts]. A Korahite doorkeeper, son of Meshelemiah (I Chron. 26:2).

Jat'tir (jăt'ẽr) [pre-eminence]. A town in the hill country of Judah assigned to the priests (Josh. 15:48; 21:14; I Sam. 30:27; I Chron. 6:57). Robinson identified it with Khirbet 'Attīr, on a hill about 13 miles s.s.w. of Hebron.

Ja'van (jā'văn) [Heb. *yāwān*, Arab. *yūnān*, Greeks, Greece]. 1. A region settled by descendants of Japheth (Gen. 10:2). The name corresponds etymologically with Ionia, and denotes the Greeks; see GREECE. Javan was synonymous with the farthest w., where Jehovah's fame had not been heard (Isa. 66:19). From early days the country had commercial relations with Phoenicia (Ezek. 27:13; Joel 3:6, in Eng. version Grecians).

2. Heb. *wᵉyāwān* (and Javan) in Ezek. 27: 19 was read by the LXX as *wᵉyayin* (and wine). There are textual difficulties in the passage, but if the Heb. text is retained, Javan may refer to an Arab tribe or a Greek colony in Arabia.

Jave'lin. A smaller kind of spear, which was intended to be thrown (Job 41:29), was borne suspended between the shoulders (I Sam. 17:6), and could be stretched out in the hand (Josh. 8:18). The Heb. name for it was *kĭdŏn.* The A.V. never translates this word by javelin, but renders it by spear in Josh. 8:18, 26; Job 41:29; Jer. 6:23; by lance in Jer. 50:42; and by shield or target in I Sam. 17: 6, 45; Job 39:23. Wherever javelin occurs in A.V. the Revisers have properly substituted spear.

Ja'zer (jā'zēr), in A.V. twice **Ja'a·zer** [helpful]. A city e. of the Jordan in Gilead (II Sam. 24:5; I Chron. 26:31). The Israelites captured it and drove out the Amorite inhabitants (Num. 21:32). It stood in a region well fitted for pasturage (Num. 32:1, 3). It was assigned to the tribe of Gad (Josh. 13:25), who rebuilt the city (Num. 32:34, 35; II Sam. 24:5); and it was appointed to the Merarite Levites for residence (Josh. 21:39; I Chron. 6:81). It passed into Moabite hands (Isa. 16: 8, 9; Jer. 48:32); was taken by Judas Maccabaeus from the Ammonites (I Macc. 5:8). According to Eusebius, Jazer was situated 10 Roman miles to the w. of Rabbath Ammon, and 15 from Heshbon; and a considerable tributary of the Jordan took its rise near the town. Jerome mentions a village called Azor, 8 Roman miles to the w. of Rabbath Ammon. These various places are commonly identified with Wadi Şīr, an upper branch of Wadi Kefrein, and the ruins Şīr and Şār, on opposite sides of the valley. The distance from Rabbath Ammon approximately corresponds, but the names are radically different from Jazer and Azor. Père Abel prefers Khirbet Jazzir, s. of Şalţ, not far from 'Ain Hazîr on Wadi Sha'ib.

Ja'ziz (jā'zĭz). A Hagrite, the overseer of David's flocks (I Chron. 27:30).

Je'a·rim (jē'à-rĭm) [forests]. A mountain crossed by the boundary line of Judah (Josh. 15:10), and which, to judge from its connection with Chesalon (*q.v.*), was at that point about 8 miles to the n.e. of Beth-shemesh.

Je·ath'e·rai (jê-ăth'ê-rī), in A.V. **Je·at'e·rai** (jê-ăt'ê-rī). See ETHNI.

Je·ber'e·chi'ah (jê-bĕr'ê-kī'à) [Jehovah blesses]. Father of Isaiah's contemporary, Zechariah (Isa. 8:2).

Je'bus (jē'bŭs). The name borne by Jerusalem while the city was in the possession of the Jebusites (Josh. 15:63; Judg. 19:10; I Chron. 11:4). The area included within Jebus was, of course, small compared with the dimensions of Jerusalem in the time of Solomon. Its citadel was the stronghold of Zion (II Sam. 5:7; I Chron. 11:5).

Je'bu·site (jĕb'û-zīt), in A.V. twice **Jeb'u·si** (jĕb'û-sī) (Josh. 18:16, 28, the Heb. word being transliterated instead of being translated. A tribe of Canaan before the conquest of the country by the Hebrews (Gen. 10:16; 15:21; Ex. 3:8). At the date of the Exodus they were one of the mountain tribes (Num. 13:29; Josh. 11:3). They are known only as dwelling at Jebus, i.e., Jerusalem. Their king was slain by Joshua (Josh. 10:23–26), their territory was assigned to Benjamin (ch. 18: 28), and later their city was taken by the men of Judah, on the border of which tribe it stood, and set on fire (Josh. 15:8; Judg. 1:8); but the Jebusites either never lost the citadel (Jos. *Antiq.* v. 2, 2), or recovered the city in whole or in part. They dwelt with the children of Judah and Benjamin as strangers (Josh. 15:63; Judg. 1:21; 19:11). They still held the stronghold of Zion at the beginning of David's reign (II Sam. 5:6, 7); and even after he had captured it the old inhabitants were not wholly expelled, for Araunah, who had a threshing-floor on the site afterward occupied by Solomon's Temple, was a Jebusite by birth (II Sam. 24:16, 18; II Chron. 3:1).

Solomon subjected the remnant of the Jebusites to bond service (I Kings 9:20).

Jec'a·mi'ah (jĕk'à-mī'à). See JEKAMIAH.

Jech'i·li'ah (jĕk'ĭ-lī'à) and **Jech'o·li'ah** (jĕk'ō-lī'à). See JECOLIAH.

Jech'o·ni'ah (jĕk'ō-nī'à) and **Jech'o·ni'as** (jĕk'ō-nī'ăs). See JECONIAH.

Jec'o·li'ah (jĕk'ō-lī'à) and **Jech'i·li'ah**, in A.V. once **Jech'o·li'ah** (II Kings 15:2) [Jehovah has prevailed]. The mother of King Uzziah (II Kings 15:2; II Chron. 26:3).

Jec'o·ni'ah (jĕk'ō-nī'à), in R.V. of N.T. **Jech'o·ni'ah**, in A.V. of N.T. **Jech'o·ni'as** [Jehovah establishes]. A variant of the name of Jehoiachin, king of Judah, a cognate root being used and the constituent parts transposed (I Chron. 3:16, etc.). Contracted to Coniah (Jer. 22:24, 28; 37:1).

Je·da'iah, I (jê-dā'yà) [Jehovah has been beneficent; cf. Arab. *yadā*, to do good]. 1. A Simeonite (I Chron. 4:37).
2. A son of Harumaph, who repaired part of the wall of Jerusalem opposite to his house (Neh. 3:10).

Je·da'iah, II (jê-dā'yà) [Jehovah knows; Heb. root *yāda'*]. 1. A descendant of Aaron. His family had grown to a father's house in the time of David, and was numbered the 2d course when David distributed the priests into divisions (I Chron. 24:1, 6, 7). Members of the family returned from Babylon (Ezra 2: 36; Neh. 7:39); cf. the 2 following.
2. A chief of the priests who returned from Babylon with Zerubbabel (Neh. 12:6). In the next generation a father's house bore this name (v. 19).
3. Another chief priest with the same history (Neh. 12:7, 21).
4. One of those who came from the Captivity bringing gifts for the Temple in the days of the high priest Joshua (Zech. 6:10, 14).

Je·di'a·el (jê-dī'à-ĕl) [known of God]. 1. A son of Benjamin, and founder of a family (I Chron. 7: 6, 10, 11).
2. A Manassite who joined David at Ziklag (I Chron. 12:20).
3. One of David's mighty men, a son of Shimri (I Chron. 11:45).
4. A Korahite doorkeeper in the reign of David (I Chron. 26:1, 2).

Je·di'dah (jê-dī'dà) [beloved]. Wife of Amon and mother of King Josiah (II Kings 22:1).

Jed'i·di'ah (jĕd'ĭ-dī'à) [beloved of Jehovah]. A name which Nathan the prophet, by divine direction, gave to Solomon (II Sam. 12:25).

Je·du'thun (jê-dū'thŭn) [praising, praise]. 1. A Levite, one of the 3 chief singers or rather musicians appointed in the time of David, and founder of an official musical family (I Chron. 16:41; 25:1, 6; II Chron. 5:12; 35:15; Neh. 11:17). He or his family is mentioned in the title of 3 psalms (Psalms 39; 62; 77). He was evidently known earlier as Ethan; see ETHAN 3.
2. Father of Obed-edom the doorkeeper and apparently of the family of Korah, a division of the Kohathites (I Chron. 16:38; cf. ch. 26: 1, 4, and also vs. 8, 12, 15). Some interpreters, however, hold him to be Jeduthun, the singer, of the family of Merari.

Je·e'zer (jê-ē'zēr). See ABIEZER 1.

Je·e'zer·ite (jê-ē'zēr-īt). See ABIEZRITE.

Je'gar·sa'ha·du'tha (jē'gär-sā'hà-dū'thà) [Aram., heap of witness]. Laban's designation of the cairn Galeed (Gen. 31:47); see GALEED.

Je·hal′le·lel (jĕ-hăl′ē-lĕl), in A.V. **Je·ha·le′-le·el** (jē′hȧ-lē′lē-ĕl) and **Je·hal′e·lel** (jĕ-hăl′ē-lĕl) [God will flash forth light]. 1. A man registered with the tribe of Judah and founder of a family (I Chron. 4:16).

2. A Merarite Levite (II Chron. 29:12).

Jeh·de′iah (jĕ-dē′yȧ) [Jehovah will be glad]. 1. A Levite, family of Kohath, house of Amram (I Chron. 24:20).

2. A Meronothite who had charge of David's asses (I Chron. 27:30).

Je·hez′kel (jĕ-hĕz′kĕl), in A.V. **Je·hez′e·kel** (jĕ-hĕz′ē-kĕl) [God will strengthen]. A descendant of Aaron whose family was made the 20th course of the priests (I Chron. 24:16).

Je·hi′ah (jē-hī′ȧ) [Jehovah lives]. A doorkeeper for the Ark in David's reign (I Chron. 15:24).

Je·hi′el (jĕ-hī′ĕl) [God lives]. 1. A Levite of the 2d degree, who played a psaltery at the removal of the Ark to Jerusalem and afterward as a regular duty in its tent (I Chron. 15:18, 20; 16:5).

2. A Levite, family of Gershon and chief of the house of Laadan in David's reign (I Chron. 23:8). He gave rise to the father's house named from him Jehieli (ch. 26:21, 22).

3. A son of Hachmoni in David's reign (I Chron. 27:32).

4. A son of Jehoshaphat, placed by his father over one of the fenced cities of Judah, but slain with others of his brothers by Jehoram (II Chron. 21:2–4).

5. A Levite, family of Kohath and house of Heman the singer (II Chron. 29:14, in R.V. Jehuel). He aided Hezekiah in his religious reformation, and is perhaps the assistant overseer of the Temple revenues who served during the same reign (II Chron. 31:13).

6. A ruler of the Temple at the time of Josiah's religious reformation (II Chron. 35:8).

7. Father of Ezra's contemporary Obadiah (Ezra 8:9).

8. A son of Elam and father of Ezra's contemporary Shechaniah (Ezra 10:2. He may be the person of this name whom Ezra induced to put away his foreign wife (ch. 10:26).

9. A priest, of the course of Harim, induced by Ezra to put away his foreign wife (Ezra 10:21).

For others whose name is thus spelled in A.V. see JEIEL.

Je·hi′e·li (jĕ-hī′ē-lī). See JEHIEL 2.

Je·hiz′ki·ah (jē′hĭz-kī′ȧ) [Jehovah strengthens]. A son of Shallum, and one of the heads of the Ephraimite tribe in the reign of Pekah. He assisted in securing the release of the captives from Judah (II Chron. 28:12).

Je·ho·ad′dah (jē′hō-ăd′ȧ), in A.V. **Je·ho′a·dah** (jē-hō′ȧ-dȧ) [perhaps Jehovah has numbered; cf. Arab. '*adda*, to count]. A son of Ahaz, and a descendant of Jonathan, Saul's son (I Chron. 8:36). Called in ch. 9:42 Jarah.

Je·ho·ad′dan (jē′hō-ăd′ăn), in R.V. of Kings **Je·ho·ad′din** (jē′hō-ăd′ĭn) [perhaps, Jehovah is delight]. Mother of King Amaziah. She was from Jerusalem (II Kings 14:2; II Chron. 25:1).

Je·ho′a·haz (jĕ-hō′ȧ-hăz) and, contracted, **Jo′a·haz** [Jehovah has laid hold of]. 1. A variant form of the name of Ahaziah, youngest son of Jehoram, king of Judah (II Chron. 21:17; cf. ch. 22:1), the components of the name being transposed.

2. The son and successor of Jehu in the Kingdom of Israel. He began to reign c. 817 B.C., apparently as associate of his father, and reigned 17 years (II Kings 10:35; 13:1). He continued the calf worship established by Jeroboam. As a penalty for this apostasy, the Syrians, first under Hazael and then under Ben-hadad, were permitted to carry on successful hostilities against him, capturing city after city, till at length he had no force left but 50 horsemen, 10 chariots, and 10,000 footmen. In distress he called on Jehovah, who gave Israel a savior. This deliverer of Israel appeared after the death of Jehoahaz in the persons of his 2 successors Jehoash and Jeroboam. The former recovered the cities which the Syrians had taken from his father, and the latter restored the ancient boundaries of Israel. Probably Jehoash received unintended assistance from the king of Assyria, who, attacking the Syrians in the rear, compelled them to desist from the invasion of the Israelite kingdom and return to defend their own country. Jehoahaz was succeeded by his son Jehoash (II Kings 13:2–9, 22–25).

3. A younger son of Josiah, who, on the death of Josiah, was placed by the people of Judah on his father's throne. He was then 23, and reigned only 3 months, during which time his tendencies were evil rather than good. He was deposed and taken in chains to Riblah by Necho, king of Egypt, and afterward carried down into Egypt. Necho, as victor over Josiah, decided to dispose of the throne of Judah, and gave it to Jehoiakim, Jehoahaz' elder brother (II Kings 23:30–34; II Chron. 36:1–4). Jehoahaz was also called Shallum (I Chron. 3:15; Jer. 22:10–12), and he is the 1st of the lion's whelps (Ezek. 19:1–9). Although the 3d of Josiah's sons in point of age and the 1st to occupy the throne, he is enumerated 4th in I Chron. 3:15, perhaps by way of intentional degradation.

Je·ho′ash (jĕ-hō′ăsh). See JOASH, 1.

Je·ho′ha·nan (jē′hō-hā′năn) [Jehovah is gracious]. 1. A Korahite Levite, who had the 6th course of the doorkeepers in David's reign (I Chron. 26:3).

2. The 2d in honor of Jehoshaphat's captains. He had under him 280,000 men (II Chron. 17:15).

3. Father of Jehoiada's supporter, Ishmael, in the revolt against Athaliah (II Chron. 23:1).

4. A priest, head of the father's house of Amariah. He lived in the days of the high priest Joiakim (Neh. 12:13).

5. A son of Eliashib (Ezra 10:6, R.V.). See JOHANAN 9.

6. A son of Bebai, induced by Ezra to put away his foreign wife (Ezra 10:28).

7. A son of Tobiah the Ammonite (Neh. 6:18, R.V.). See JOHANAN 10.

8. A priest who officiated at the dedication of the wall of Jerusalem by Nehemiah (Neh. 12:42).

Je·hoi′a·chin (jĕ-hoi′ȧ-kĭn) [Jehovah establishes]. The son and successor of Jehoiakim in the Kingdom of Judah. He came to the throne in the year 597 B.C. According to II Kings 24:8, he was then 18 years old; according to II Chron. 36:9, his age was 8. The discrepancy exists in the LXX as well as in the Heb. text, but probably Kings is correct. He did that which was evil in the sight of the Lord, according to all that his father had done. But his reign continued only 3 months and 10 days. During this short period Nebuchadnezzar, king of Babylon, sent his generals to besiege Jerusalem, which surrendered after the 8th year of Nebuchadnezzar had begun (cf. II Kings 24:12; cf. Jer. 52:28); see CHRONOLOGY, IV. Jehoiachin, his wives, his mother, the palace servants, every dignitary in the city and the country, with all the skillful artisans, were carried into captivity (II Kings 24:8–16; II Chron. 36:9, 10). For a long period he seems to have been in actual confinement; but in the 37th year of his exile,

562 B.C., Evil-merodach ascended the throne of Babylon, released him from prison, and assigned him a daily allowance of, or for, food while he lived (II Kings 25:27-30; Jer. 52: 31-34). Jeremiah, who prophesied during, and after, the brief reign of Jehoiachin, frequently mentions him under the name Jeconiah or Coniah. On these modifications of the name, see JECONIAH.

Je·hoi′a·da (jĕ-hoi′à-dá) [Jehovah knows].
1. The father of that Benaiah who held high military office in the latter part of David's and in Solomon's reign (II Sam. 23:22; I Kings 4:4). Jehoiada was probably the priest (I Chron. 27:5, text; but not as in A.V. chief priest), and the leader of the Aaronites who brought 3,700 men to David at Ziklag (ch. 12:27).
2. A son of Benaiah, 2d to Ahithophel in David's counsels (I Chron. 27:34). Most commentators believe that some copyist accidentally wrote Jehoiada son of Benaiah for Benaiah son of Jehoiada. There is no reason, however, why a grandson of Jehoiada, bearing the same name, should not be occupying a position of influence at this time.
3. A high priest during the usurpation of Athaliah. His wife concealed in the Temple the young prince Joash, the only surviving direct representative of the royal line of David, and Jehoiada planned and successfully carried out the revolt which led to the slaughter of Athaliah and the proclamation of Joash as king. Jehoiada's wife was the daughter of King Joram and the sister of Ahaziah; the high priest was, therefore, the uncle of the young monarch whom he befriended and placed on the throne. So long as he lived he was instrumental in keeping the king true to the worship of Jehovah (II Kings 11:1 to 12: 16; II Chron. 22:10 to 24:14). He died at the age of 130, and, in recognition of his eminent services to church and state, he was buried in the city of David among the kings (II Chron. 24:15, 16). After his death Joash turned from the Lord and ungratefully put Jehoiada's son to death for rebuking the sins of the people (vs. 17-22).
4. A priest who was succeeded in Jeremiah's time by Zephaniah in the office of 2d priest and overseer of the Temple (Jer. 29:26; cf. 52:24).
5. A son of Paseah, who repaired a gate of Jerusalem (Neh. 3:6; in R.V. Joiada).

Je·hoi′a·kim (jĕ-hoi′à-kĭm) [Jehovah raises up]. A son of King Josiah by his wife Zebidah (II Kings 23:34, 36). He was called originally Eliakim (God raises up). On the death of Josiah the people placed Jehoahaz, 3d son of Josiah in age, on the throne; but 3 months afterward Necho put him in chains and carried him to Egypt, and made his elder brother Eliakim king in his stead, changing his name to Jehoiakim. He began to reign c. 608 B.C., at the age of 25 years. He was obliged to collect heavy tribute from the people for Pharaoh. He departed from Jehovah, whom his father had so faithfully served, and went back to idolatry. Jeremiah wrote a roll threatening the divine judgment unless repentance took place; but Jehoiakim treated the matter with contempt, and after listening to 3 or 4 leaves of the roll cut it up and committed it to the flames (Jer., ch. 36). Babylon under the Chaldeans was now the dominant Asiatic power. In the 4th year of Jehoiakim's reign, Nebuchadnezzar defeated Necho at Carchemish (605 B.C.) and advanced, probably afterward, against Jerusalem, and Jehoiakim became his servant (II Kings 24:1; Jer. 46:2; Dan. 1:1, 2; see CHRONOLOGY, IV. Three years later he rashly rebelled against Nebuchadnezzar. There were other troubles afflicting the kingdom. Syrians, Moabites, and

Ammonites made predatory incursions into its territories, as did bands of Chaldeans, whom Nebuchadnezzar probably dispatched on learning of the revolt (II Kings 24:2). The Babylonian king himself, or his army, eventually entered Jerusalem and bound the Jewish rebel with chains to carry him to Babylon (II Chron. 36:6). The purpose of carrying him to Babylon was apparently abandoned. He died or was murdered, and his body had the burial of an ass, being drawn and cast forth beyond the gates of Jerusalem (Jer. 22:19; 36:30; Jos. Antiq. x. 6, 3). He reigned 11 years and was succeeded by his son Jehoiachin (II Kings 23:36; 24:6).

Je·hoi′a·rib (jĕ-hoi′à-rĭb) [Jehovah pleads, or contends]. A descendant of Aaron. His family had grown to a father's house in the time of David and was numbered the 1st course when David distributed the priests into divisions (I Chron. 24:1, 6, 7), and it dwelt at Jerusalem (ch. 9:10).
For other persons of the name, see JOIARIB.

Je·hon′a·dab (jĕ-hŏn′à-dăb). See JONADAB.

Je·hon′a·than (jĕ-hŏn′à-thăn), variant form of Jon′a·than [Jehovah has given]. 1. Son of Uzziah, and an official appointed by King David. He was charged with the oversight of the royal treasures which were in various places outside of Jerusalem (I Chron. 27:25, in R.V. Jonathan).
2. One of the Levites sent by Jehoshaphat to teach in the cities of Judah (II Chron. 17:8).
3. A priest, head of the father's house of Shemaiah in the days of the high priest Joiakim (Neh. 12:18).

Je·ho′ram (jĕ-hō′răm) [Jehovah is high].
1. Son of Ahab and king of Israel (II Kings 3:1); see JORAM 3.
2. A priest, one of those sent by Jehoshaphat to instruct the people (II Chron. 17:8).
3. Son of Jehoshaphat and king of Judah (II Kings 8:16, A.V.); see JORAM 5.

Je·ho·shab′e·ath (jĕ-hŏ-shăb′ê-ăth). See JE-HOSHEBA.

Je·hosh′a·phat (jĕ-hŏsh′à-făt), in A.V. of N.T. Jos′a·phat [Jehovah has judged]. 1. Son of Ahilud and recorder under David and Solomon (II Sam. 8:16; 20:24; I Kings 4:3).
2. One of the priests appointed to blow a trumpet before the Ark when it was being brought up from the house of Obed-edom to the city of David (I Chron. 15:24, in R.V. Joshaphat).
3. Son of Paruah and Solomon's purveyor in the territory of Issachar (I Kings 4:17).
4. Son and successor of King Asa on the throne of Judah. He appears to have been associated with his father in the latter's 37th regnal year, the 11th of Omri (I Kings 16:28, 29, LXX), and to have become sole king on the death of his father 5 years later, about 871 B.C. (I Kings 22:41, 42; II Chron. 17:1). He reigned 25 years, including the time that he was associated with Asa. He was 35 years old at his accession. His mother was Azubah, daughter of Shilhi (I Kings 22:42). He was a good king. He worshiped Jehovah and "sought not unto the Baalim" (I Kings 22:43; II Chron. 17:3), although the people still sacrificed on high places (I Kings 22:43). Therefore the Lord greatly prospered him. In the 3d year of his reign, he took measures for instructing his people, sending princes and Levites, with the Book of the Law in their hands, to teach in the cities of Judah (II Chron. 17:7-9). The fear of the Lord fell upon the neighboring kingdoms. Philistines and Arabians paid tribute (vs. 10, 11). He garrisoned the fenced cities of his realm (vs. 12-19). He terminated the desultory warfare which had gone on between Israel and Judah since the

time of Rehoboam. He made peace with Israel and took Athaliah, daughter of Ahab, as a wife for his son (I Kings 22:44; II Kings 8:18, 26). When he found that Jehovah was thus blessing him, he was encouraged to remove the high places and the Asherim out of Judah (II Chron. 17:5, 6). He put away also the remnant of the sodomites out of the land (I Kings 22:46).

In 853 or 852 B.C. he went on a visit to King Ahab and was persuaded to join him, with the army of Judah, in the attempt to re-take Ramoth-gilead from the Syrians. Dressed in the royal robes of Ahab, he went into battle. Ahab was mortally wounded; Jehoshaphat, notwithstanding his exposure, survived (I Kings 22:1–38; II Chron. 18:1–34). On his return home he was reproved by the Prophet Jehu, son of Hanani, for having fraternized with such a king as Ahab (II Chron. 19:1, 2). He resumed his work of reformation in church and state, promoting the worship of Jehovah, and appointing judges in the walled towns of Judah, with a supreme court, consisting of Levites, priests, and laymen of high position, in Jerusalem (II Chron. 19:4–11). After this reform had begun, a great confederacy of Ammonites, Moabites, and Edomites invaded Judah from the s.e., making their headquarters at En-gedi on the w. side of the Dead Sea. Jehoshaphat claimed the promise of deliverance which Solomon had asked (cf. II Chron. 6:24–30 with ch. 20:9). Jahaziel prophesied deliverance, and Jehoshaphat went forth with thanksgiving and placed singers before the army to praise the Lord. Success was achieved without fighting. Hostilities broke out in the confederate army, the Ammonites and Moabites attacked and destroyed the Edomites, and they, quarreling among themselves, turned their weapons against each other (ch. 20:1–30). After this event, perhaps in late autumn during the time of peace, Jehoshaphat, who had been building ships at Ezion-geber, asked Ahaziah, king of Israel, to take part in a mercantile voyage. The Prophet Eliezer rebuked him for joining himself with Ahaziah, and the ships were wrecked. Ahaziah desired to share in a new venture, but Jehoshaphat refused (II Chron. 20:35–37; I Kings 22:48, 49). About 850 B.C., Jehoram, king of Israel, desired to render Moab again tributary to Israel, and sounded Jehoshaphat on his willingness to aid. Jehoram had exhibited signs of godliness by a considerable reformation (II Kings 3:2), and Jehoshaphat consented to join him. The expedition enjoyed partial success (II Kings 3:4–27). Jehoshaphat died at the age of 60, about the year 850 B.C., and was buried in the city of David, leaving his son Jehoram to ascend the throne (I Kings 22:50).

5. Son of Nimshi and father of Jehu, king of Israel (II Kings 9:2, 14).

Je·hosh'a·phat (jė-hŏsh'á-făt), **Val'ley of.** A valley where all nations shall be gathered by Jehovah for judgment (Joel 3:2, 12). At least as early as the time of Eusebius, in the 4th century A.D., the valley of Jehoshaphat was identified with the valley of the Kidron, so that now Jews, Roman Catholics, and Mohammedans fix the scene of the Last Judgment here. This identification is only a conjecture, based on the cited passages and Zech., ch. 14. So far as evidence goes, no valley actually bore this name. Joel doubtless chose this designation, which means "Jehovah hath judged," as symbolic of the event.

Je·hosh'e·ba (jė-hŏsh'ė-bá), **Je'ho·shab'e·ath** (jė'hŏ-shăb'ė-ăth) [Jehovah is an oath]. Daughter of Jehoram and sister of Ahaziah, kings of Judah, and wife of the high priest Jehoiada. On the murder of Ahaziah and the slaughter of the seed royal, Jehosheba rescued his infant son Joash and hid him in the Tem-

ple until he could be safely proclaimed king (II Kings 11:2; II Chron. 22:11).

Je·hosh'u·a (jė-hŏsh' û-á) and **Je·hosh'u·ah** (jė-hŏsh'û-á). See JOSHUA.

Je·ho'vah (jė-hō'vá). The common Eng. pronunciation of the Heb. tetragram YHWH, one of the names of God (Ex. 17:15). The original name was occasionally used even by so late a writer as Nehemiah (Neh. 1:5; 5:13; 8:1), in fact a form of it constitutes the latter part of his name. But it was not the favorite name of God with him; and it had ceased to be pronounced when the LXX was made, for the translators substituted Lord. It seems that, out of reverence for the divine name, there had grown up around 300 B.C. the custom among the Jews in reading to pronounce the word 'ădōnāy (my Lord, or LORD) in its stead or, when it follows 'ădōnāy, to pronounce 'ĕlōhīm, God (Gen. 15:2). When the vowel points were added to the Heb. consonantal text, the vowels of 'ădōnāy and 'ĕlōhīm were accordingly given to the tetragram. This pointing gave rise to the Eng. pronunciation, Jehovah, current since the days of Petrus Galatinus, confessor of Leo X, A.D. 1518. The substitution of the word Lord by the later Hebrews and by the translators of the LXX led to the like substitution in the A.V. (Gen. 2:4). In such instances Lord is printed in small capitals. The tetragram is generally believed to have been pronounced Yāhweh, because the divine name Jah (Ps. 89:8, R.V. marg.) and the forms Yᵉho, Yo and Yăh, Yāhū, which occur constantly in proper names, as in the Heb. of Jehoshaphat, Joshaphat, Shephatiah, can all be derived from Yāhweh. This pronunciation is also favored by Gr. transcriptions: Iabe, Iaoue, Iaouai, Iaē. Yāhweh is an archaic form. It is the Qal imperfect of the verb hāwāh, later hāyāh, to befall, come to pass, happen, become, be; cf. Arab. hawā, to fall. The name accordingly means "He who happens (upon us), he who befalls (upon us), he who in the absolute sense exists and who manifests his existence and his character" (Ex. 3:13–15). The creator, upholder, and moral governor of the universe is 'ĕlōhīm, God; the covenant God of Abraham, Isaac, and Jacob, the God in whom lay their present strength and their hope for their future existence, is El Shaddai ('ēl Shadday, God Almighty); but the God of revelation and grace, dwelling with his people, guiding and delivering them, and receiving their worship is Jehovah.

Whether the name was known to other peoples before it attained to celebrity through the Hebrews is still a question. Men began to call upon the name of Jehovah in the days of Enosh, the 3d from Adam (Gen. 4:26). It must not be inferred, however, that they necessarily used the name Jehovah. They worshiped the God of revelation and grace, whatever name they may have employed to denote the idea. Its 1st occurrence in recorded proper names is in Jochebed, an ancestress of Moses (see also I Chron. 2:8, 24). In the generation after the Exodus, it appears in Joshua (Num. 13:16). It then becomes frequent (I Chron. 6:6, 7, 36).

To know that God is Jehovah and to know the name of Jehovah do not denote a mere external acquaintance with the word Jehovah, but an experience of God manifesting himself to his people in grace and love (I Kings 8:43; Ps. 9:10; 91:14; Isa. 52:6; Jer. 16:21). In Ex. 6:2–8 God promises that the Children of Israel shall be delivered from bondage and have an experience of his gracious intervention and love such as their forefathers had not known. See PENTATEUCH.

Je·ho'vah-ji'reh (jė-hō'vá-ji'rĕ) [Jehovah will see or provide]. The name given by

Abraham to the place where God provided a ram to be offered in sacrifice, instead of Isaac (Gen. 22:14). Exact site unknown.

Je·ho'vah-nis'si (jė-hō'vȧ-nĭs'ī) [Jehovah is my banner]. The name given by Moses to an altar built by him at Rephidim as a memorial of Israel's victory over Amalek (Ex. 17:15, 16).

Je·ho'vah-sha'lom (jė-hō'vȧ-shā'lŏm) [Jehovah is peace]. An altar built by Gideon in Ophrah to commemorate the visit of Jehovah's angel, who summoned him to deliver Israel, and, when Gideon expected to die because he had seen the heavenly one, said to him: "Peace be unto thee; . . . thou shalt not die" (Judg. 6:23, 24).

Je·hoz'a·bad (jė-hŏz'ȧ-băd) [Jehovah has bestowed]. 1. A Korahite porter, son of Obed-edom (I Chron. 26:4).

2. Son of a Moabitess, and a servant of Joash and one of his assassins (II Kings 12:21; II Chron. 24:26). He was put to death for the deed (II Chron. 25:3).

3. A Benjamite, a high military captain under King Jehoshaphat (II Chron. 17:18).

Je·hoz'a·dak (jė-hŏz'ȧ-dăk). See JOZADAK.

Je'hu (jē'hū) [probably, Jehovah is He].
1. A Benjamite of Anathoth, who joined David at Ziklag (I Chron. 12:3).

2. A prophet, son of Hanani. He denounced judgment against Baasha and his house for continuing in the sin of Jeroboam I (I Kings 16:1–4, 7). He reproved Jehoshaphat for helping ungodly Ahab (II Chron. 19:2), and wrote a book in which the acts of Jehoshaphat were narrated (ch. 20:34).

3. The founder of the 4th dynasty of rulers in the Kingdom of Israel. He was a son of Jehoshaphat and grandson of Nimshi, but was often called the son of Nimshi (I Kings 19:16; II Kings 9:2). He was a soldier in the service of Ahab (II Kings 9:25), and when Ahab and Jezebel were rejected for their crimes, Elijah received a command from God to anoint Jehu king over Israel (I Kings 19:16, 17). The commission was executed by Elijah's successor, Elisha, who for that purpose sent a young prophet to Ramoth-gilead, where Jehu was with the army. The prophet anointed Jehu king over Israel and commissioned him to destroy the house of Ahab. On learning the purpose of the prophet's visit, Jehu's fellow officers resolved to support him. They went to Jezreel, where the reigning king, Jehoram, Ahab's son, was at the time. The watchman on the tower in Jezreel descried the party in the distance, and presently identified Jehu by his furious driving. Aha-

ziah, king of Judah, was visiting Jehoram; and the two kings, each in his chariot, went out to meet the advancing company. They met at the vineyard wh ch Ahab had wrongfully gotten through the judicial murder of Naboth. The parley was short, and Jehoram was killed by an arrow sent with great force from Jehu's bow, and his body was cast into the plot of ground which had been Naboth's. Ahaziah also, whose mother was Ahab's daughter, was smitten by Jehu's order. By his command also, Jezebel, the queen-mother, Ahab's heathen queen and evil genius, was flung from a window and killed (II Kings 9:1–37). Then he induced their guardians to slay the 70 princes of the royal house; and the heads were piled in 2 heaps at the gate of Jezreel. Jehu had been ordered to smite the house of Ahab (ch. 9:7); hence his deeds thus far, apart from their needless brutality, were acts of obedience. As such they are commended (ch. 10:30). But they were not wrought in singleness of heart, from a sense of duty and for the honor of Jehovah (v. 31); and the Prophet Hosea condemns the motive (Hos. 1:4). Next Ahab's great men and his familiar friends were slain, and then Ahaziah's 42 brothers. Finally the priests and worshipers of Baal were summoned to a festival of the god, and all who managed to get into Baal's temple were massacred (II Kings 10:12–28). But Jehu himself took no heed to walk in the law of God, and did not depart from the schismatic calf worship (II Kings 10:29, 31). He ascended the throne c. 842 B.C. In that year, according to Assyrian records, he paid tribute to Shalmaneser, king of Assyria, who came into the neighborhood to wage war against Hazael. He reigned 28 years (v. 36). About 821 B.C., on account of his advancing age and loss of his energy and military skill, his son Jehoahaz was probably associated with him. But the change did not prevent his reign from closing in disaster. Hazael cut Israel short (v. 32); see CHRONOLOGY, IV. A promise had been given that the dynasty of Jehu should continue for 4 generations; and it did so, the line of descent being Jehoahaz, Jehoash or Joash, Jeroboam II, and Zechariah (chs. 10:30; 15:8–12).

4. A man of Judah, family of Jerahmeel (I Chron. 2:38).

5. A Simeonite (I Chron. 4:35).

Je·hub'bah (jė-hŭb'ȧ) [kethib, *Yaḥbāh,* he (God) hides]. An Asherite, family of Beriah (I Chron. 7:34). J.V. follows the kere: "and Hubbah."

Je·hu'cal (jė-hū'kăl), **Ju'cal** [Jehovah is able]. A son of Shelemiah and prince of

Jehu Bringing Tribute to Shalmaneser, King of Assyria

Judah. King Zedekiah sent him and others to ask the prayers of Jeremiah, when the Babylonian siege of Jerusalem was imminent (Jer. 37:3). Afterward he wished the prophet to be put to death on the ground that his prediction of the capture of Jerusalem by the Babylonians discouraged its defenders (ch. 38:1-6).

Je′hud (jē′hŭd) [praise]. A town in the original territory of Dan (Josh. 19:45); modern Yazūr, about 5 miles s. e. of Joppa.

Je·hu′di (jē-hū′dī) [a man of Judah, a Jew]. A messenger sent by King Jehoiakim to ask Baruch for the roll written by Jeremiah. He was afterward employed to read it, which he did, till the king, enraged at its contents, cut it in pieces and cast it into the fire (Jer. 36:14, 21, 23).

Je·hu·di′jah (jē′hŭ-dī′jȧ) [Jewess]. One of the 2 wives of Mered, the other being Bithiah, an Egyptian princess (I Chron. 4:18, A.V.). Jehudijah is, however, not a proper name, but an adjective meaning Jewess; and it has the definite article (R.V.). She was called the Jewess to distinguish her from the Egyptian.

Je′hush (jē′hŭsh). See JEUSH.

Je·i′el (jē-ī′ĕl), in A.V. twice **Je·hi′el** (I Chron. 9:35; 11:44) [El (God) has gathered; cf. Arab. wa′ȧ, gather]. 1. Father of the inhabitants of Gibeon and an ancestor of King Saul (I Chron. 9:35, 36, 39); see KISH 2.
2. A son of Hotham, an Aroerite, in the reign of David (I Chron. 11:44). Perhaps he was the Reubenite chief (ch. 5:6, 7).
3. A Levite musician (I Chron. 16:5, first half); see JAAZIEL.
4. A Levite of the 2d degree, who was a doorkeeper and played the harp at the removal of the Ark to Jerusalem and afterward as a regular duty in the tent at Jerusalem (I Chron. 15:18, 21; 16:5).
5. A Levite of the sons of Asaph (II Chron. 20:14).
6. A scribe who recorded the number of soldiers in Uzziah's army (II Chron. 26:11).
7. A Hebrew who was induced by Ezra to put away his foreign wife (Ezra 10:43).
For others whose name is thus spelled in A.V., see JEUEL 3. Jehiel in R.V. is a different name.

Je·kab′ze·el (jē-kăb′zē-ĕl). See KABZEEL.

Jek′a·me′am (jĕk′ȧ-mē′ăm) [the (divine) kinsman will raise up]. A Levite, family of Kohath, house of Hebron (I Chron. 23:19; 24:23).

Jek′a·mi′ah (jĕk′ȧ-mī′ȧ), in A.V. once **Jec′a·mi′ah** (I Chron. 3:18) [Jehovah will raise up]. 1. A man of Judah, descended through Sheshan from Jerahmeel (I Chron. 2:41).
2. A son or descendant of Jeconiah (I Chron. 3:18).

Je·ku′thi·el (jē-kū′thĭ-ĕl) [El (God) will nourish; cf. Arab. ḳāta, to nourish, support]. A man of Judah, father of the inhabitants of Zanoah (I Chron. 4:18).

Je·mi′mah (jē-mī′mȧ), in A.V. **Je·mi′ma** (jē-mī′mȧ) [a pigeon, a dove]. The 1st of the 3 daughters born to Job after his great trial (Job 42:14).

Je·mu′el (jē-mū′ĕl). A son of Simeon (Gen. 46:10; Ex. 6:15). In Num. 26:12; I Chron. 4:24 he is called Nemuel. He founded a tribal family.

Jeph′thah (jĕf′thȧ), in A.V. of N.T. **Jeph′thae** (jĕf′thē) [he will open or set free; perhaps, will open (the womb)]. A Gileadite, in the twofold sense of having a certain man called Gilead for his father and the country of Gilead for his early home. He was an ille-

gitimate child, and his brothers born in wedlock expelled him from the paternal abode. He saw injustice in the treatment whica he received, and years later he charged the elders of Gilead, among whom were probably his brothers, with being party to the iniquity and animated by hatred. He fled to the land of Tob, probably in the Hauran, where life was free and where with trusty weapon abundant food was to be had. There he made a name for himself by his prowess, and attracted a band of the unemployed around him as their chief. He must not be thought of as a lawless freebooter, however, for he was a man with a conscience. He sought sufficient justification before undertaking an enterprise, he feared God and taught his daughter the fear of God, and he won her entire confidence and religious respect. About the time of Jephthah's expulsion, the Ammonites invaded the Israelitish territory e. of the Jordan and held it in subjection 18 years. In this extremity the elders of Gilead, who had driven Jephthah away, were compelled as a last resort to urge the fugitive to return and become their chief and deliverer. On assuming headship over the Gileadites, Jephthah informed the neighboring tribe of Ephraim of the distress of Gilead, but he exhorted them in vain to come to the help of their brethren. He also demanded of the king of the Ammonites the ground of his hostility, whose reply justified Israel for taking up arms. While yet the issue of the war was doubtful, Jephthah had vowed that if he were permitted to achieve victory, he would offer to God as a burnt offering whatever first came to him out of his house. On his return from the defeat of the Ammonites what first came was his only daughter, who, moreover, was his only child. He was greatly troubled when he saw her, but felt compelled to do with her according to his vow. Probably he sacrificed her (cf. II Kings 3:27), though many have thought that he may have redeemed her with money (Lev. 27:1-8) and doomed her to perpetual celibacy. The Israelite women were accustomed 4 times a year to mourn her sad fate. Hostilities breaking out between him and the Ephraimites, who complained that he had slighted them in making arrangements for his Ammonite campaign, he answered their false accusation and defeated them in battle. Jephthah judged Israel 6 years (Judg. 10:6 to 12:7). Samuel cited him as one proof of Jehovah's faithfulness to his promise to raise up a deliverer for Israel in time of need (I Sam. 12:11), and he is cited in The Epistle to the Hebrews as a man of faith (Heb. 11:32).

Je·phun′neh (jē-fŭn′ĕ) [it will be prepared]. 1. Father of Caleb, the representative spy from the tribe of Judah (Num. 13:6).
2. An Asherite (I Chron. 7:38).

Je′rah (jē′rȧ) [moon]. An Arabian tribe descended from Joktan (Gen. 10:26; I Chron. 1:20).

Je·rah′me·el (jē-rä′mē-ĕl) [may God have compassion, or God pities]. 1. A descendant of Judah through Perez and Hezron (I Chron. 2:9; cf. vs. 4, 5). Two wives are mentioned and a numerous progeny is registered (vs. 25-41).
2. Son of a Levite called Kish, not Saul's father (I Chron. 24:29).
3. One of the officers sent by King Jehoiakim to arrest Baruch (Jer. 36:26). He was probably of royal blood (R.V.). See HAMMELECH.

Je′red (jē′rĕd) [descent]. 1. Son of Mahalaleel (I Chron. 1:2, A.V.); see JARED.
2. A man of Judah and father of the inhabitants of Gedor (I Chron. 4:18).

Jer'e·mai (jĕr'ê-mī) [high]. A Hebrew who was induced by Ezra to put away his foreign wife (Ezra 10:33).

Jer'e·mi'ah (jĕr'ê-mī'à), in A.V. of N.T. **Jer'e·my** and **Jer'e·mi'as** (jĕr'ê-mī'ăs) (Matt. 2:17; 16:14) [Jehovah founds, establishes; or perhaps, lifts up, exalts]. 1–3. A Benjamite and 2 Gadites who joined David at Ziklag (I Chron. 12:4, 10, 13).

4. Head of a father's house in e. Manasseh (I Chron. 5:24).

5. A native of Libnah and the father of Hamutal, wife of King Josiah and mother of Jehoahaz (II Kings 23:30, 31).

6. Son of Habaziniah and father of Jaazaniah, a Rechabite (Jer. 35:3).

7. The great prophet, a son of Hilkiah, a priest of Anathoth, in the territory of Benjamin (Jer. 1:1). He was called to the prophetic office by a vision. He was young at the time, and felt his immaturity and inexperience and inability to speak to men; but Jehovah reached out a hand and touched Jeremiah's mouth, putting into it words, and setting him over nations and kingdoms, on the one hand to root out, overthrow, and destroy, and on the other to plant and to build. He was told, further, that he would meet with violent opposition from princes, priests and people, but that they should not prevail (ch. 1:4–10). He began to prophesy in the 13th year of the reign of Josiah, and continued his work till the capture of Jerusalem, in the 5th month of the 11th year of Zedekiah's reign (vs. 2, 3). Thus his public life extended through the last 18 years of Josiah's reign, the 3 months during which Jehoahaz ruled, the 11 years of Jehoiakim, the 3 months of Jehoiachin, and the 11 years and 5 months of Zedekiah, in all about 41 years. Nor did he, even then, cease from his prophetic functions (chs. 42 to 44).

The men of Anathoth, his paternal home, were among the first to oppose him, and threatened to kill him if he did not desist from prophesying. He persevered in his mission despite the persecution, but he felt keenly this opposition to the work of God from his countrymen, the chosen people of God, and he cried to God for judgment (Jer. 11:18–21; 12:3). The hostility to the prophet, which began at Anathoth, after a time became general, and again evoked a cry for judgment upon his opponents (ch. 18:18–23; cf. also ch. 20:12). But he remained faithful to his duty in spite of obloquy and persecution. In the 4th year of Jehoiakim's reign Jeremiah dictated the prophecies which he had been uttering during the preceding 20 years, and the scribe Baruch wrote them in the roll of a book. Knowing that he himself was hindered, for some reason not stated, and would doubtless still be hindered for a long time, from going to the house of God, the prophet told Baruch to take the roll to the sanctuary and read it before the people who would be coming to the Temple on occasion of a fast. The roll finally reached the king, who, after hearing a few leaves or columns read, cut the roll in pieces and flung it into the fire until the entire roll had been read and burned a section at a time (ch. 36:1–26). By divine direction the prophet at once prepared a 2d roll like the 1st, but with additions (vs. 27–32). A foe of his, the priest Pashhur, chief governor of the Temple, put him in the stocks; but he was released the next day (ch. 20:1–3).

During the siege of Jerusalem the Jewish authorities looked at Jeremiah's prophecies of the success of the Chaldeans and the subsequent captivity of Judah from the political or military, instead of from the religious, point of view; and they claimed that his unfavor-

able predictions discouraged the defenders of Jerusalem. And when the Chaldeans temporarily raised the siege to meet the Egyptians, and Jeremiah was about to take advantage of their absence to go to Anathoth on business, the charge was made against him that he was deserting to the Chaldeans, and he was thrown into prison (ch. 37:1–15). After many days King Zedekiah released him from his cell and committed him to the court of the guard (vs. 16–21); but the princes soon had him cast into the dungeon to die (ch. 38:1–6). An Ethiopian eunuch, however, took compassion on him and obtained the king's leave to take him from the miry pit and put him back in the court of the guard. The prophet was there when Jerusalem was taken (vs. 7–28). The Chaldeans looked upon him as one who had suffered much for them, and Nebuchadnezzar gave express orders for his kind treatment. Accordingly, Nebuzaradan, the Chaldean official, sent and had Jeremiah taken out of the court of the guard and brought to him with the other captives to

A Potter Working at His Wheel (Jer., ch. 18)

Ramah, set him free, and granted him leave to go to Babylon or stay in the home land. On his choosing the latter, Nebuzaradan gave him victuals and a present and sent him to the protection of Gedaliah, whom Nebuchadnezzar had made governor of Judah (ch. 39:11–14; 40:1–6). On the murder of Gedaliah, Jeremiah strongly urged the Jews not to flee to Egypt. It was in vain; they not merely went thither themselves, but they compelled the prophet to accompany them on their journey (chs. 41:1 to 43:7). He delivered his last predictions at Tahpanhes, in Egypt (chs. 43:8 to 44:30). The time and manner of his death are unknown.

Beyond most prophecies The Book of Jeremiah reveals the spiritual life of its author. His was a message of doom to his native land, and a message that brought the hatred of his fellow-countrymen upon him; and the burden of it forced from him the bitter lament that he had ever been born (chs. 15:10; 20:14–18). But he remained true to duty. He was a lone man, misunderstood, maligned, persecuted, his efforts for the moral welfare of his countrymen foredoomed to failure, without the solace of domestic life and social joys (ch. 16:1–9), often kept in ward, forced to turn for consolation and sympathy and companionship to God only. Being thus thrown much upon God, he came to realize the sense of individual responsibility to God (chs. 17:9; 31:29, 30). And so it comes to pass that in Jeremiah is notably exhibited the possibility and reality of communion between the individual soul and God.

Religion in the heart and in the life is a dominant note in Jeremiah's preaching. He was called to the prophetic office 5 years before the eventful discovery of the Book of the Law in the Temple, during repairs to the edifice; and he was in the midst of his work when King Josiah, under the profound impression made upon him by the words of the book, led the crusade against idolatry and inaugurated a revival in the national worship. Jeremiah, too, exhorted the people to hearken to the words of the covenant entered into at Mount Sinai; and he pointed out that God had visited them with the evils threatened therein for disobedience, and that to obey is the 1st requirement of the covenant (Jer. 11:1–8). Jeremiah would guard the people from limiting reform to things external. He would carry it into the inner life. In the spirit of the older prophets, of the familiar proverb, and of the covenant itself (I Sam. 15:22; Isa. 1:11–17; Amos 5:21–24; Micah 6:6–8; Prov. 15:8; Deut. 10:12), and using the rhetorical negation, frequently employed for emphatic antithesis (e.g. Deut. 5:3), he denied that God commanded sacrifice, and insisted that the one requirement is obedience. God commanded sacrifice indeed (Ex. 20:24; 23:14–19; Deut. 12:6), but did not speak of sacrifice. Sacrifice was not the theme; God spoke of moral conduct (Jer. 7:21–28; cf. chs. 6:20; 14:12). The sacrifices of the obedient are pleasing to God (chs. 17:24–26; 27:19–22; 33:10, 11, 18, the latter verse in a section lacking in the LXX); but the fasts and sacrifices of those who love to wander from him are not acceptable (ch. 14:10–12). Trust in the presence of Jehovah in the Temple in the midst of Israel is also vain; and equally vain is the mere possession of the Law of Jehovah. Obedience alone avails (chs. 7:4–7; 8:7–9). Eventually even the Ark will be no more remembered (ch. 3:16). God looks at the heart (chs. 11:20; 17:10; 20:12). To serve God man must remove carnal lust from the heart (Jer. 4:4; cf. Deut. 10:16), wash it of wickedness (Jer. 4:14), and return to God with the whole heart and not feignedly (chs. 3:10; 17:5). In due time Jeremiah foretold the new covenant when the people shall have a new heart and God's Law written in it (chs. 24:7; 31:33; 32:39, 40). His vision descried the true glory of the Kingdom of the future. Henceforth this truth holds a chief place in the mind of God's people.

Jeremiah committed some of his prophecies to writing in the reign of Jehoiakim, but the roll was destroyed by the king (ch. 36:1, 23). They were soon rewritten, however, with large additions (v. 32). The present book is a further enlargement, including the later prophecies; and is a rearrangement, prepared at the close of his ministry; for prophecies of different periods are placed together and those of the same period are often dispersed.

The Book of Jeremiah consists of an introduction narrating the prophet's call (ch. 1), 3 sections of prophecy, often recorded in connection with the event that called forth the prophetic utterance (chs. 2 to 51), and a historical appendix, added probably by a later writer (ch. 52; cf. ch. 51:64). The 3 prophetic sections are:

I. *Prediction of the approaching judgment* of Judah and the promise of restoration from exile (chs. 2 to 33). It includes a general denunciation of Judah (chs. 2 to 20), denunciation of the civil and religious rulers (chs. 21 to 23), an unfolding of the design and duration of the judgment (chs. 24 to 29), and prophecy of the blessings which will follow the judgment (chs. 30 to 33).

II. *History of the infliction of the judgment* (chs. 34 to 44), including denunciations of the corruption which prevailed immediately before the destruction of the city (chs. 34 to 38), an account of the destruction of the city (ch. 39), and of the wretched conditions of the remnant, and the prophecies spoken to them (chs. 40 to 44).

III. *Predictions respecting foreign nations* (chs. 46 to 51), introduced by an address to Baruch (ch. 45).

The Messiah is spoken of in ch. 23:5–8; 30:4–11; 33:14–26; and Jehovah's sure covenant with Israel is dwelt upon in chs. 31:31–40; 32:36–44; 33.

The text of the LXX differs considerably from the Heb.: chapters 46 to 51 are not only arranged in a different order among themselves, but the entire section has been inserted after ch. 25:13; chs. 29:16–20, and 33:14–26, and 39:4–13, and 52:28–30 are wanting in the Gr.; and in many other places the Gr. version presents a shorter text than the Heb. (e.g. chs. 2:1, 2; 7:1–3). This shorter text is often due to the absence of unimportant words, such as the customary lack of "the prophet" when Jeremiah is named (e.g. ch. 28:5, 11, 15), "the king," when the proper name is given (chs. 36:32; 37:17) and *vice versa* (e.g. chs. 26:22, 23; 37:18, 21), "of hosts" after Jehovah (e.g. ch. 6:6, 9), "of hosts, the God of Israel," the sufficient title Lord being used instead (e.g. chs. 7:21; 19:15), and "saith the Lord," where the expression is parenthetic (e.g., chs. 2:9; 3:10; 7:13).

In chronological order the prophecies and narratives, so far as they bear explicit dates, stand thus:

In Josiah's reign of 31 years:

In the 13th year.... ch. 1.

Between the 13th and 31st years.
{ chs. 2 to 6 (cf. 3:6), and probably chs. 7 to 12, and 14 to 20.

In Jehoahaz' reign of 3 months:

None.

In Jehoiakim's reign of 11 years:

In the beginning.... ch. 26, and probably ch. 22:1–19 (cf. vs. 10, 18, 19).

In the 4th year..... chs. 25; 36; 45; 46:1–12.

After the 4th year   ch. 35 (cf. vs. 1, 11).

In Jehoiachin's reign of 3 months:

Probably ch. 22:20–30, and perhaps ch. 13 (cf. ch. 13:18 with ch. 22:26 and II Kings 24:12).

In Zedekiah's reign of 11 years:

In the beginning... chs. 24; 49:34–39.

In his 4th year..... chs. 27 (cf. ch. 27:3, 12, with ch. 28:1); 28; 51:59–64.

In unnoted years....chs. 21; 29.

During the earlier part of the siege, while Jeremiah was yet free.
} ch. 34.

During the interruption of the siege.
} ch. 37 (cf. vs. 4, 5).

After the resumption of the siege, while Jeremiah was in ward.
} chs. 32 (in the 10th year); 33; 38; 39:15–18.

291

In Judah after the fall of Jerusalem:

chs. 39 :1–14 ; 40 :1 to
43 :7.

In Egypt ....chs. 43 :8–13 ; 44.

Undated, but not al-⎫ chs. 23 ; 30 ; 31 ; 45 ;
ways without indi- ⎬ 46 :13 to 48 :47 ; 49 :
cations of time. ⎭ 1 to 51 :58.

Appendix ....ch. 52.

8. A chief of the priests, who returned with Zerubbabel from Babylon (Neh. 12 :1, 7). A father's house bore his name in the next generation (v. 12).

9. A priest, doubtless head of a father's house, who set his seal to the covenant to keep separate from the foreigners and observe the Law of God (Neh. 10 :2).

Jer′e•moth (jĕr′ĕ-mŏth) and **Jer′i•moth** (jĕr′ĭ-mŏth) [swollen, thick, tall ; cf. Arab. *warima*, to be swollen, to shoot up high]. 1. A Benjamite, family of Becher (I Chron. 7 :8).

2. A Benjamite (I Chron. 8 :14), probably the person called Jeroham (v. 27).

3. A Levite, family of Merari, house of Mushi (I Chron. 23 :23 ; 24 :30).

4. A descendant of Heman and head of the 15th course among the musicians in David's reign (I Chron. 25 :4, 22).

5. A son of Azriel and prince of Naphtali in David's reign (I Chron. 27 :19).

6–8. Two descendants of Elam (Ezra 10 :26, 27) and a son of Bani (ch. 10 :29, in A.V. and J.V., which follow the kere : and Ramoth), who consented to put away their foreign wives.

For persons who bear the name Jerimoth only, see JERIMOTH.

Jer′e•my (jĕr′ĕ-mĭ). See JEREMIAH.

Je•ri′ah (jê-rī′a̤), once **Je•ri′jah** [Jehovah sees]. A Levite, family of Kohath, house of Hebron (I Chron. 23 :19 ; 24 :23 ; 26 :31).

Jer′i•bai (jĕr′ĭ-bī) [Jehovah contends, pleads]. A son of Elnaam, and one of David's mighty men (I Chron. 11 :46).

Jer′i•cho (jĕr′ĭ-kō) [moon city, or perhaps, place of fragrance]. An important city situated in the valley of the Jordan (Deut. 34 :1, 3), w. of the river about 5 miles from the n. end of the Dead Sea and about 17 miles from Jerusalem, at the foot of the ascent to the mountainous tableland of Judah. It was known as the city of palm trees (*ibid.* ; Judg. 3 :13). It is first mentioned in Scripture when the Israelites encamped at Shittim on the e. side of the Jordan (Num. 22 :1 ; 26 :3). As it was strongly fortified and commanded the valley of the lower Jordan and the passes into the w. mountains, its conquest by the Israelites was essential to their advance. Joshua accordingly sent spies to examine it (Josh. 2 :1–24), led the Israelites across the river, and pitched camp near the city. By divine command the men of war went round the city once a day for 6 consecutive days, with the Ark of the Covenant in their midst and 7 priests blowing on trumpets in front of the Ark. On the 7th day they compassed the city 7 times ; and on the 7th circuit, when the signal was given by a long blast with the horn, the host shouted, the walls fell, and the Israelites entered. It seems reasonable to suppose that God's purpose was accomplished by an earthquake which occurred at that time by divine intervention and threw down the walls. For date, see EGYPT, III. 8. The place had been put under the ban. Except Rahab, who had protected the spies, and her father's family, all living creatures were slain. The silver and the gold, with other valuables, were put into the treasury of the house of the Lord. Finally, Joshua foretold that if anyone ever fortified the town he should lose

his elder son when the foundations were being laid, and the younger one when the gates were being set up (Josh. 5 :13 to 6 :26). The place was assigned to Benjamin, and stood on the boundary between the tribes of Ephraim and Benjamin (chs. 16 :1, 7 ; 18 :12, 21). It was occupied as a royal residence by Eglon, king of Moab, when he oppressed the Israelites (Judg. 3 :13). David's ambassadors, returning from the Ammonite king by whom they had been insulted, stopped at Jericho until their beards grew (II Sam. 10 :5 ; I Chron. 19 :5). In Ahab's reign Hiel the Bethelite fortified the city, but lost or sacrificed his 2 sons as predicted by Joshua (I Kings 16 :34). During Elijah's lifetime there was a community of the prophets at the place (II Kings 2 :5). Elijah, when about to be translated to heaven, passed through it with Elisha, and Elisha returned to it after finally parting with Elijah (vs. 4, 15, 18). The captives of Judah, taken by the Israelite army under Pekah, were set free at Jericho (II Chron. 28 :15). In its vicinity Zedekiah was captured by his Babylonian pursuers (II Kings 25 :5 ; Jer. 39 :5 ; 52 :8). Three hundred and forty-five former inhabitants and their descendants returned from captivity with Zerubbabel (Ezra 2 :34 ; Neh. 7 :36). Some of its new populace helped to rebuild the wall of Jerusalem (Neh. 3 :2). Bacchides, the Syrian general, repaired the fortifications of Jericho during the Maccabaean period (I Macc. 9 :50). In the early years of Herod the Great the Romans plundered Jericho (Jos. *Antiq.* xiv. 15, 3). Subsequently Herod beautified it, established a royal palace, and on the hill behind the town built a citadel which he named Cyprus (Jos. *Antiq.* xvi. 5, 2 ; xvii. 13, 1 ; *War* i. 21, 4 and 9). There was also a hippodrome there at the time of Herod's death (Jos. *Antiq.* xvii. 6, 5 ; *War* i. 33, 6 and 8). The road from Jerusalem to Jericho was the scene of the action in the parable of the Good Samaritan (Luke 10 :30). At Jericho itself Jesus restored sight to blind Bartimaeus and his companion (Matt. 20 :29 ; Luke 18 :35). There also he brought salvation to Zacchaeus, whose home was in Jericho (Luke 19 :1, 2).

Jericho, lying 820 feet below the level of the Mediterranean, has a tropical climate. Palms, balsams, sycamores, and henna flourished (S. of Sol. 1 :14 ; Luke 19 :2, 4 ; Jos. *War* iv. 8, 3). The rose plant of Jericho was proverbially fine (Ecclus. 24 :14). Ancient Jericho stood close by the copious spring 'Ain es-Sultân, apparently the fountain healed by Elisha (Jos. *War* iv. 8, 3). The modern village called er-Riha is 1½ miles s.e. of the fountain.

Je′ri•el (jē′rĭ-ĕl) [El (God) sees]. A descendant of Tola, of the tribe of Issachar (I Chron. 7 :2).

Je•ri′jah (jê-rī′ja̤). See JERIAH.

Jer′i•moth (jĕr′ĭ-mŏth) [cf. Jeremoth]. 1. A Benjamite, family of Bela (I Chron. 7 :7).

2. A Benjamite who joined David at Ziklag (I Chron. 12 :5).

3. A son of David, and father of Mahalath, a wife of Rehoboam (II Chron. 11 :18).

4. A Levite, an overseer in connection with the Temple in Hezekiah's reign (II Chron. 31 :13).

For others whose name sometimes appears as Jeremoth, see JEREMOTH.

Jer′i•oth (jĕr′ĭ-ŏth) [(tent) curtains]. One of Caleb's wives (I Chron. 2 :18).

Jer′o•bo•am (jĕr′ô-bō′ăm) [the people become numerous]. 1. An Ephraimite, who founded the kingdom of the ten tribes. His father was an official under Solomon, named Nebat, of the village of Zeredah in the Jordan Valley; his mother's name was Zeruah, who was a widow at the time of his birth (I Kings 11:26). As a young man he showed industry and ability; and Solomon, who was engaged in building operations at Jerusalem, made him overseer of the heavy work assigned to the house of Joseph (vs. 27, 28). One day as Jeroboam was walking outside of Jerusalem he was met by a prophet, Ahijah of Shiloh, clad in a new garment, who rent the cloth in 12 pieces, and gave 10 to Jeroboam as a pledge that Jehovah destined him to be king over 10 out of the 12 tribes. News of the transaction reached Solomon, who sought to kill Jeroboam, but he escaped to Egypt and was kindly received by Shishak, its king (vs. 29–40). When the refugee was notified that Solomon was dead and that an assembly of the tribes was to take place at Shechem to make Solomon's son Rehoboam king, he returned to attend the meeting. He put himself forward as spokesman of the people, and urged the alleviation of their burdens. Rehoboam denied the petition, returning a foolish and exasperating answer. Ten tribes thereupon revolted from the house of David and elected Jeroboam king. The prophecy of Ahijah had come true; yet Jeroboam resolved to depart from the counsel by which it had been accompanied. The prophet had exhorted him to remain true to Jehovah, in which case the crown should descend permanently in his family (vs. 37, 38). But he was afraid that if the people went up at stated times to Jerusalem to worship they would be won back to the house of David and would reject and slay him. He therefore established a center of worship at each of the 2 extremities of his kingdom, Dan in the n. and Beth-el in the s. In defiance of the commandment which forbids the adoration of God by means of images, he set up a golden calf in each of the 2 places (I Kings 12:26–30; II Chron. 13:8), and recommended the worship as not altogether new by using the familiar words of Aaron (Ex. 32:4). It seems that his plan was to worship Jehovah under the image of the calf. Furthermore he established houses of high places, and he made israel us who were not of the tribe of Levi priests, doubtless because few or none of the lawful priests and other Levites consented to serve in the idolatrous and schismatic worship (I Kings 12:31; II Chron. 11:13–15; 13:9). He further decreed that the harvest festival, which was celebrated in Judah on the 15th day of the 7th month, should be observed in the Northern Kingdom on the 15th day of the 8th month (I Kings 12:32, 33). The mass of the people conformed. Thus Jeroboam made Israel to sin. This abhorrent worship continued until the fall of the kingdom. The successive kings, with the possible exception of Hoshea, supported it and are accordingly described as walking in the way of Jeroboam, the son of Nebat, who made Israel to sin (I Kings 15:26, 34; 16:19, 31; 22:52; II Kings 3:3; 10:29; 13:2, 11; 14:24; 15:9, 18, 24, 28). The idolatry established by Jeroboam was one cause which led to the carrying of the 10 tribes into captivity to Assyria (II Kings 17:16); for it kept the Hebrew nation divided and made 2 inferior kingdoms where there had been one strong united people; and, as it was a degradation of the lofty spiritual worship of Jehovah, it resulted in lowering the spiritual tone of the northern Israelites. Jeroboam was rebuked for his apostasy, first by an unnamed prophet from Judah, and then by Ahijah, the Shilonite, who had promised him the kingdom; but he continued to the end unrepentant (I Kings 13:1 to 14:18). He fortified Shechem and Penuel, both sacred places. The former he made his residence, but seems to have taken up his abode later

at beautiful Tirzah (I Kings 12:25; 14:17; S. of Sol. 6:4). There was a desultory warfare between Jeroboam and Rehoboam (I Kings 15:6), and a great battle was fought between Jeroboam and Rehoboam's son and successor, Abijam, in which the army of Israel was defeated with a great slaughter, and Beth-el, which was only 10 miles from Jerusalem, was captured by Abijam (I Kings 15:7; II Chron. 13:1–20; see ABIJAM. Jeroboam was made king c. 931 B.C., and reigned 22 years (I Kings 14:20). One son of his had died in infancy (vs. 1–17); another, Nadab, ascended the throne (v. 20).

2. The son of Joash, king of Israel, and his successor on the throne of the 10 tribes. He was of the dynasty of Jehu, and the 3d in descent from that ruler. He became king in Samaria c. 785 B.C., and reigned 41 years. He found the kingdom in a low state, but raised it again to prosperity, capturing Damascus, the capital of Syria, and Hamath in the valley of the Orontes, and restoring to Israel the country from the entrance of Hamath to the Dead Sea. These successes had been predicted by Jonah (II Kings 14:23–28; cf. Deut. 3:17). Amos prophesied in Jeroboam's reign (Amos 1:1), drawing a dark picture of the moral and religious state of Israel at the time (chs. 2:6 to 5:27; 8:4–6, etc.), and predicted judgment from God (chs. 7:1–9; 8:7–10). For these prophecies of doom the priest at Beth-el made a complaint against him to Jeroboam, but it does not seem to have brought any penalty on the prophet (Amos 7:10–17). Hosea also began his prophetic work in the Northern Kingdom during the lifetime of Jeroboam. The first 3 chapters pertain to that period. On the death of Jeroboam, his son Zechariah ascended the throne (II Kings 14:29).

Je·ro'ham (jê-rō'hăm) [may he be compassioned, or he is pitied (by God)]. 1. A Levite, an ancestor of the Prophet Samuel (I Sam. 1:1; I Chron. 6:27, 34).

2. A Benjamite, whose sons were chief men and dwelt at Jerusalem (I Chron. 8:27). See JEREMOTH 2. He may be identical with the following.

3. A Benjamite, father of Ibneiah who dwelt at Jerusalem (I Chron. 9:8).

4. A priest of the house of Malchijah (I Chron. 9:12; Neh. 11:12).

5. A Benjamite of Gedor, whose sons joined David at Ziklag (I Chron. 12:7).

6. Father of the chief of the tribe of Dan in the reign of David (I Chron. 27:22).

7. Father of one of the captains who aided Jehoiada in putting Joash on the throne of Judah (II Chron. 23:1).

Jer'ub·ba'al (jĕr'ŭb-bā'ăl) [let Baal contend; or perhaps, let Baal show himself great or master, or give increase]. See GIDEON.

Jer'ub·be'sheth (jĕr'ŭb-bē'shĕth). For Jerubbaal with -besheth (shame) instead of -ba'al (lord) to avoid the suggestion of identifying Baal with Jehovah, which would be offensive (II Sam. 11:21).

Je·ru'el (jê-rōō'ĕl) [probably, founded by God]. A wilderness in Judah, adjacent to the cliff of Ziz, and therefore in the vicinity of En-gedi (II Chron. 20:16).

Je·ru'sa·lem (jê-rōō'sȧ-lĕm) [ety. uncertain; foundation of peace, possession of peace]. The sacred city and well-known capital of Judah, of Judea, of Palestine, and of the Jews throughout the world. For the sake of convenient reference and clearness, the subject is presented under certain heads: I. Name. II. The city in itself: 1. Site; 2. Water supply; 3. Artificial defenses; 4. Notable buildings in the time of Christ. III. The history of the city: 1. The city of the Canaanites; 2. The city of the Hebrews; 3. The city since Titus.

I. *Name*. The earliest known name is *Urusalim*, i.e., Jerusalem. It was in use at the dawn of the 15th century B.C., before the Conquest of Canaan by the Israelites under Joshua, for it is found in letters from its subject prince to Amenhotep (Amenophis) IV, king of Egypt, his lord. Salem, of which Melchizedek was king, is a natural abbreviation of Jerusalem and not unlikely denoted this city. The place is mentioned as Jerusalem in the account of the Conquest of Canaan, but in that narrative it is also referred to as Jebus; in fact, this latter name is frequent after the Conquest during the occupation of the city by the Jebusites; but when David captured the city and made it his capital, the old name of Jerusalem, or abbreviated Salem (Ps. 76:2), became once more the sole designation. The pronunciation of the final syllable in Y*e*rūshālēm was in later times modified so that it resembles a dual, Y*e*rūshālá(y)im, and is so interpreted by some grammarians.

II. 1. *Site*. Jerusalem is situated on a tableland on the crest of the central ridge of Palestine and at one of its highest points. It has the same latitude as the n. end of the Dead Sea. The portion of the tableland occupied by the city is isolated from the rest of the plateau, except on the n. On the other sides it is encompassed by deep ravines. This jutting promontory is itself cut by another valley (Tyropoeon) which, followed upward from its mouth at the s.e. corner of the promontory at the junction of the s. and e. ravines (Hinnom and Kidron respectively), trends like the arc of a circle for nearly a mile n., midway sending a branch from its concave side due w. Such at least was the original configuration of the city's site; but in the course of centuries, through municipal improvements and the devastation of war, heights were lowered and valleys filled. As a result of these ramifications, there are 3 principal hills, an e., a s.w., and a n.w. The e. hill is a ridge extending for somewhat more than half a mile from n. to s., which rises to a height of from 200 to 300 feet above its encompassing valleys, tapers to a blunt point at its s. extremity, and at its n. end is almost separated (the reference is to the ancient topography) from the tableland, of which it is a part, by a branch of the e. ravine. This ridge attains a general altitude of 2,400 feet above sea level. There is some evidence that a slight depression or valley, about 100 feet wide and in places 40 feet deep, lay athwart it toward the s. end from the so-called fountain of the Virgin n.w. to the Tyropoeon valley. The s.w. hill is much the largest of the 3. In form it is oblong, with a spur thrown out on the n.e. corner toward the e. ridge. It rises abruptly from the encircling valleys. Its broad summit begins at an altitude of about 2,400 feet above the level of the sea and swells 150 feet higher, with its greatest elevation on the w. The 3d hill is rather a projection of the plateau than an isolated mound. It lies n. of the one just described. The present elevation of that part included in the ante-Christian city is about 2,450 feet. This triad of hills, with the protecting ravines, afforded a strong position for a city, although it is encircled beyond the ravines by hills which tower above it. "The mountains are round about Jerusalem."

The e. ravine is the valley of the Kidron. The hill to the e., which faces and overlooks the hills of the city, is the Mount of Olives. The long ridge which runs n. and s. is the Temple hill, called, at least in that portion of its extent where the sanctuary stood, Mount Moriah. Its s. tapering extremity was known as Ophel. The valley w. of this ridge is the Tyropoeon. The pool in the valley at the extreme s. point of the hill is Siloam. South of the city, running from n.w. to s.e. and w. to e. and joining the valley of the Kidron, is the valley of Hinnom. A pool n. of the Temple area is Bethesda.

Which height was Mount Zion? This question has received 3 principal answers: (1) Mount Zion was the s.w. hill. This view has prevailed since the 4th century. (*a*) Zion was the city of David (II Sam. 5:7–9), and Josephus says that the upper city, unquestionably the s. w. hill, was called the citadel by David (Jos. *War* v. 4, 1). Strangely enough, however, Josephus does not explicitly call it Zion. (*b*) Too much building is spoken of in Neh., ch. 3, for Zion to be part of the Temple hill. (*c*) The sanctity of Zion is accounted for by the fact that it was for many years the abiding place of the Ark, and was celebrated as such by David (II Sam. 6:12–18; I Kings 8:1–4; Ps. 2:6). The name Zion thus became the title for Jerusalem as a whole in its quality as a holy city (Psalms 48; 87; 133:3). (2) Mount Zion was the n.w. hill (Warren). This hill is identified with that quarter of the city called by Josephus the Acra, which in Gr. means citadel. It is, indeed, styled by him the lower city, for so it was in his day; but originally it was much higher, and was cut down by Simon Maccabaeus because it commanded the Temple (Jos. *Antiq*. xiii. 6, 7). It was originally a suitable site for the Jebusite fortress. (3) Mount Zion was a portion of the Temple hill. The main arguments for this view are: (*a*) The Temple hill is best adapted by nature for a stronghold. (*b*) The Temple could be reached by going from the fountain gate, up the stairs of the city of David, and past the water gate (Neh. 12:37), steps which may be those that have been discovered ascending the ridge from the pool at the s. end. (*c*) Zion is spoken of as holy in terms such as are never applied to Jerusalem, but are intelligible if Zion was the hill on which the Temple stood. Zion is called the hill of the Lord, the holy hill, the dwelling place of Jehovah (Ps. 2:6; 9:11; 24:3; 132:13). (*d*) In the First Book of the Maccabees Zion is the Temple hill (I Macc. 1:33–38). The invariable distinction of the city of David from Mount Zion and the sanctuary shows that the terms had undergone a change of meaning since II Sam. 5:7. The simplest explanation is that Mount Zion was part of the Temple hill, and by synecdoche often used for the whole of it, whereas the designation city of David, which denoted the municipality of Jerusalem (II Sam. 5:7; Jos. *Antiq*. vii. 3, 2), was extended, with the growth of population, beyond the bounds of Mount Zion and embraced the new suburbs on the neighboring hills, around which the protecting walls of the city were cast. The term city of David might then on occasion include the sanctuary or exclude it. The Syrians erected a fortress in the city of David, but Judas Maccabaeus came and took possession of the sanctuary on Mount Zion (I Macc. 1:33 *seq*.; 4:36 *seq*.).

The 3d opinion is correct. Zion, the stronghold of the Jebusites, had 4 gates and occupied the s. end of the e. ridge, s. of the Temple, s. also of the transverse ravine. Parts of the old walled town have been explored, traceable even into the 3d millennium B.C.

II. 2. *Water supply*. Although Jerusalem was often long and closely besieged, and suffered grievous famine from having its supplies of food cut off, there is no record of the inhabitants' having ever lacked water. In fact, it was the besiegers who were apt to want water, not the besieged. There is no spring n. of the city, and none is known at present e., w., or s., which was not commanded by the walls, except En-rogel. This is located in the s., below the junction of the valleys of Hinnom and the Kidron, on the wadi en-Nar. It is known also as Job's Well ('Ain 'Ayyūb), and probably is to be identified with the Dragon's or Jackal's Well (Neh. 2:13). A living fountain to supply the Māmillā pool and the pool of the Sultan on the w. has not been discovered. The s.w. hill is likewise without springs, so far as known. But the Temple hill is well supplied (Tacitus *Hist.* v. 12). East of the old city, in the Kidron valley, is a well-known living source: the Fountain of the Virgin (St. Mary's Well or Gihon); its abundant water was conducted to the pool of Siloam at the s. end of the hill. The water of Gihon was led originally by an ancient channel on the surface of the ground to the Old or Lower Pool, which is identified with the modern Birket el-Ḥamra, below 'Ain Silwān (Siloam). In anticipation of the coming of Sennacherib, Hezekiah stopped up this surface channel and diverted the water of Gihon from the Old or Lower Pool through a subterranean conduit to the New or Upper Pool (II Kings 18:17; 20:20; II Chron. 32:4, 30; Isa. 7:3; 8:6; 22:9, 11; 36:2). With Siloam may be identified the king's pool (Neh. 2:14); Solomon's pool apparently was e. of Siloam (Jos. *War* v. 4, 2). On the w. side of the ridge, directly w. of the Temple, are the so-called healing baths, Ḥammām esh-Shifā; and just n. of the ridge, Bethesda.

The springs were supplemented by cisterns. The towers, which were upon the city walls, contained immense reservoirs for rain water (Jos. *War* v. 4, 3); and numerous cisterns, of which not a few still exist, were found in all parts of the city (Tacitus *Hist.* v. 12).

Besides the supply afforded by the springs and cisterns of the city, water was brought from a distance. The Māmillā pool, cut out of the rock, is at the head of Wadi er-Rabābi, w. of the city. Lower down Hinnom, opposite the s.w. corner of the present walls, is Birket es-Sulṭān (pool of the Sultan), constructed in the 12th century A.D. Some have identified the Māmillā with the Serpent Pool of Josephus (Jos. *War* v. 3, 2). An aqueduct brought the water from Māmillā to the pool of the patriarch e. of the Jaffa gate. This is known to tradition as the pool of Hezekiah, and is probably the pool Amygdalon, i.e., pool of the almond or tower, mentioned by Josephus (Jos. *War* v. 11, 4). A reservoir was also constructed at a late period n. of the Temple area, in ground made where the small valley diverged w. from the Kidron. It was fed from the w. It is now known as the pool of Israel (Birket 'Isrā'īn). To the w. of this are the twin pools, which Clermont-Ganneau considers identical with the pool Strouthios (pool of the sparrow or of soapwort, which was used for cleansing wool), which existed when Jerusalem was besieged by Titus, and lay in front of the tower of Antonia (Jos. *War* v. 11, 4). But the most extensive aqueduct was that which brought water to Jerusalem from beyond Bethlehem; see ETAM 3. It is believed to antedate considerably the Christian era.

II. 3. *Artificial defenses.* Immediately after capturing Jerusalem, David took measures to enclose the city with a wall. The old Jebusite stronghold, henceforth called the city of David, already existed. David, in addition, fortified the city round about, "from Millo even round about" (II Sam. 5:9; I Chron. 11:8). David's Millo apparently was a castle which defended the old Jebusite city and doubtless was located at the n.w. end of the

s.e. hill. Solomon built Millo and the wall of Jerusalem, closing up the gap in the city of David (I Kings 9:15, 24; 11:27). It appears, however, that Millo does not always denote the same place. If the word denotes acropolis or citadel, Solomon's Millo may have been in the Temple and palace area. Succeeding kings made repairs and additions, until eventually at least the wall passed near the present Jaffa gate on the w. (II Chron. 26:9), approached the valley of Hinnom on the s. (Jer. 19:2), ran near the pool of Siloam (cf. II Kings 25:4), included Ophel (II Chron. 27:3; 33:14), and on the n. enclosed the suburb which grew up on the n.w. hill (II

The Tower of David, Jerusalem

Kings 14:13; II Chron. 33:14; Jer. 31:38). This wall was razed to the ground by Nebuchadnezzar (II Kings 25:10).

Nehemiah rebuilt the wall out of the old material (Neh. 2:13-15; 4:2, 7; 6:15). It began, so to speak, at the sheep gate (Neh. 3:1), which was near the pool of Bethesda (John 5:2). This pool has been discovered near the church of St. Anne, about 100 yards from the gate now called St. Stephen's, and on what was originally the n. side of that branch of the Kidron valley which was interposed between the Temple hill and the main plateau. The sheep gate stood, therefore, in this branch valley or on the slope of the plateau to the n. or n.w. Near the sheep gate, in the direction away from the Temple, were the towers of Hammeah (Meah) and Hananel (Neh. 3:1; 12:39). Then came the fish gate, in the new or 2d quarter of the city (Neh. 3:3; Zeph. 1:10), and next the old gate (Neh. 3:6; 12:39). Some distance on from the latter point was the broad wall (chs. 3:8; 12:38), and farther on the tower of the furnaces (chs. 3:11; 12:38). To this there succeeded the valley gate, the technical designation of the valley on the w. of the city being used (ch. 3:13; cf. ch. 2:13-15), then the dung gate (ch. 3:14), then the gate of the fountain, the wall of the pool of Siloam by the king's garden. at the s.e. corner of the city, and the stairs that go down from the city of David (v. 15); to the e. of this point was the water gate (of the Temple?), with a large open place before it (chs. 8:1–3; 12:37). The wall next went past the sepulchers of David, the pool that was made, and the house of the mighty (ch. 3:16); the ascent to the armory, at the turning of the wall (v. 19); the house of the high priest, Eliashib (v. 20); then various points indicated by other houses unto the turning of the wall, the corner (v. 24); the turning of the wall and the tower that stands out from the king's upper house, that was by the court of the guard (v. 25). Now the Nethinim dwelt here in Ophel from over against the water gate (of the Temple?) toward the e. and this tower that stands out (v. 26; cf. ch. 11:21). Then came a piece of wall from this tower to the wall of Ophel (ch. 3:27). The horse gate came next, above which the priests resided (v. 28). It was on the e. side of the city, overlooking the Kidron valley (Jer. 31:40), but it was not necessarily an outer gate. It may rather have been the connection between Ophel and the area to the n. where were located the Temple and the palace. Then came a portion of the wall over against the house of Zadok; then a section repaired by the keeper of the e. gate (of the Temple, probably) (Neh. 3:29); presently the house of the Nethinim; then a section from over against the gate of Hammiphkad (the Miphkad) (which was probably a gate of the Temple at the place where the sin offering was burned, called the Miphkad [appointed place], cf. Ezek. 43:21) to the upper chamber of the tower (Neh. 3:31); and, finally, the sheep gate, which was the starting point of the description (v. 32). The gate of Hammiphkad has also been rendered the muster gate and by some identified with the gate of the guard (ch. 12:39); this latter probably was an inner gate of the Temple area.

Two important gates of the former wall are not mentioned, though one at least existed at this time, the corner gate (II Kings 14:13; II Chron. 26:9; cf. Zech. 14:10) and the gate of Ephraim (Neh. 8:16; 12:39). The corner gate appears to have been the extreme n.w. point of the city (Jer. 31:38), and it was distant 400 cubits from the gate of Ephraim

The Damascus Gate, Jerusalem

(II Kings 14:13). Through this latter gate the road to Ephraim passed; presumably, therefore, it was in the n. wall of the city, and if so, then e. of the corner gate. It was certainly w. of the old gate (Neh. 12:39). Beginning with the sheep gate and following the n. wall w., the order of gates and towers is sheep gate, towers of Hammeah and Hananel, fish gate, old gate, gate of Ephraim, corner gate. Whether the broad wall and tower of furnaces were beyond the corner gate is difficult to determine. It is to be observed that the gates of the corner and Ephraim occur in that part of the wall where it is recorded that "they left Jerusalem" (ch. 3:8, R.V. marg.), as if the wall required no repairs at this point.

There was also a gate of Benjamin, through which the road to Benjamin passed (Jer. 37:13; 38:7; Zech. 14:10); this probably corresponds to the sheep gate. There is a great deal of uncertainty concerning the location of some of the gates, and authorities are not in agreement. The gate of Ephraim may be identified with the middle gate (Jer. 39:2), and attempts have been made to equate it also with the fish gate. It has also been assumed by some that the corner gate and the old gate are the same.

During the interval between Nehemiah and Christ the fortifications of Jerusalem suffered many vicissitudes. About 150 years after the building of Nehemiah's wall, the high priest, Simon the Just, found it necessary to fortify the Temple and the city so that they might be able to stand a siege (Ecclus. 50:1–4; for such a need, cf. Jos. *Antiq.* xii. 1, 1). In 168 B.C. Antiochus Epiphanes had the walls of Jerusalem thrown down and a fortress with a great and strong wall and mighty towers erected in the city of David, perhaps a broad designation meaning the city as distinct from the Temple (I Macc. 1:31, 33, 39; II Macc. 5:24–26). This fortress became celebrated as the Akra. It overlooked the Temple (Jos. *Antiq.* xiii. 6, 7), and for 25 years was a menace to the Jews. About 2 years after the demolition of the city walls, Judas Maccabaeus partly restored them, strengthening the outer wall of the Temple; but only to have his work undone (I Macc. 4:60; 6:18–27, 62). His brother and successor, Jonathan, however, renewed the work, proposing additional fortifications and rebuilding and repairing the walls, particularly around the Temple hill (I Macc. 10:10; 12:36, 37; Jos. *Antiq.* xiii. 5, 11). His brother Simon carried the work to completion (I Macc. 13:10; 14:37; Jos. *Antiq.* xiii. 6, 4). Under this great priest-king, not only were the walls of the city built, but the foreign garrison was forced in the year 142 B.C. to evacuate the Akra (I Macc. 13:49–51). After a time the fortress was demolished and the hill on which it had stood was graded down so as to be lower than the level of the Temple (I Macc. 14:36; 15:28; Jos. *Antiq.* xiii. 6, 7). Although Akra means citadel in Gr., it must not be confused with Baris or the Tower of Antonia, which lay n. of the n.w. corner of the Temple area. The Akra was w. of the Temple, and the term was applied to the lower city (Jos. *War* v. 6, 1).

Simon appears also to have taken up his residence in the fortress Baris, which protected the Temple on the n. (I Macc. 13:12; cf. Neh. 2:8). In the reign of John Hyrcanus a portion of the fortifications of the city was dismantled by Antiochus Sidetes, but the ruin seems to have been repaired by John (Jos. *Antiq.* xiii. 8, 3; I Macc. 16:23). John also remodeled and strengthened the fortress Baris (Jos. *Antiq.* xviii, 4, 3; cf. xv. 11, 4). Pompey found the defenses of Jerusalem strong. On finally capturing the city in 63 B.C., he demolished the walls (Tacitus *Hist.* v. 9; and next 2 references). Caesar allowed them to be rebuilt (Jos. *Antiq.* xiv. 8, 5; *War* i. 10, 3 and 4). On the n. they consisted of 2 walls which Herod and his Roman allies took in the year 37 B.C., but did not destroy (Jos. *Antiq.* xiv. 16, 2 and 4; cf. xv. 1, 2).

At the time of Christ, Jerusalem had the 2 walls aforementioned on the n., and shortly afterward 3. Josephus identifies the 1st and innermost wall as the work of David, Solomon, and succeeding kings. He describes it by reference to landmarks of his day as extending from the tower of Hippicus, which stood immediately s. of the modern Jaffa gate at the n.w. corner of the old city wall, e. to the w. cloister of the Temple and from the tower of Hippicus s. and e. by the pool of Siloam and Ophel to the e. cloister of the Temple (Jos. *War* v. 4, 2). It enclosed the s.w. and e. hills. The 2d wall encompassed the n. and principal business quarter of the city (Jos. *War* v. 4, 2; for bazaars in this section, 8, 1; i. 13, 2; *Antiq.* xiv. 13, 3). It began at the gate Gennath, that is, by interpretation, the garden gate, which belonged to the 1st wall and stood not far e. of the tower of Hippicus (Jos. *War* v. 4, 2; 3, 2 for gardens); and terminated at the Tower of Antonia, formerly called Baris, n. of the Temple (Jos. *War* v. 4, 2). Herod Agrippa I, who reigned over Judea from A.D. 41 to 44, undertook a 3d wall in order to include within the city limits the unprotected suburb of Bezetha, which had grown up outside the fortifications. After laying the foundations, however, he relinquished the work at the command of the emperor Claudius. It was finally completed by the Jews themselves. It began at the tower of Hippicus, extended n. to the tower of Psephinus, at the n.w. corner of the city (Jos. *War* v. 3, 5; 4, 3); turned e. and passed on to the monuments of Helena, queen of Adiabene (Jos. *War* v. 4, 2; *Antiq.* xx. 4, 3); included the traditional site of the camp of the Assyrians (Jos. *War* v. 7, 3); passed the caves of the kings; bent s. at the corner tower, near the monument of the fuller; and joined the old wall at the valley of the Kidron (Jos. *War* v. 4, 2). The circumference of the walls was 33 stadia, a little less than 4 miles (Jos. *War* v. 4, 3). The defenses of the city were augmented by the fortress of Antonia at the Temple, and by the palace of Herod with its adjacent towers on the w. wall. All these fortifications Titus razed to the ground on his capture of the city in A.D. 70. He left only the group of 3 towers, Hippicus, Phasaelus, and Mariamne, and so much of the wall as enclosed the city on the w. side. He spared this portion of the wall in order that it might afford protection to his garrison, and the towers that posterity might see what kind of city it was which Roman valor had taken (Jos. *War* vii. 1, 1).

II. 4. *Notable buildings in the time of Christ.* Besides the walls which have been already described, there were many structures to awaken conflicting emotions in the pious and patriotic Israelite. Foremost was the Temple. The n. side of Temple area is partly bounded by the great block of rock on which stood the fortress of Antonia, which was occupied by a Roman garrison; w. of it stood the council house, probably the place where the council of the nation or sanhedrin met; a little more to the w., at the farther end of the bridge which sprang from the w. cloister of the Temple and spanned the Tyropoeon valley, lay the gymnasium or *xystos*, an object of abhorrence on account of its heathenizing influence; above it, looking down into it and peering across the valley into the sanctuary, rose the palace of the Hasmonaeans, recalling the heroic achievements of the Maccabees. Or taking a wider circuit, to the n. of the Temple and e. of the fortress of Antonia was the pool

of Bethesda with its healing waters; away to the w., at the opposite side of the city from the Temple, stood the magnificent palace of Herod with its impregnable towers, the residence of the procurators when in Jerusalem; around toward the s. was the pool of Siloam, and not too far from it were the sepulchers of the kings. In this neighborhood may best be sought the very large amphitheater erected by Herod the Great in the plain (Jos. *Antiq.* xv. 8, 1). It was, perhaps, the same as the hippodrome, which lay s. from the Temple (Jos. *War* ii. 3, 1), for chariot races as well as wild beast fights and gladiatorial combats seem to have taken place in it (Jos. *Antiq.* xv. 8, 1), and in the hippodrome men were confined (Jos. *Antiq.* xvii. 9, 5; *War* i. 33, 6). Other buildings were the house of the high priest (Matt. 26:3; Luke 22:54; Jos. *War* ii. 17, 6); the house of records, near the Temple (Jos. *War* ii. 17; vi. 6, 3); the palace of the proselyte queen of Adiabene, Helena (*ibid.*).

III. 1. *The city of the Canaanites.* If the Salem of Melchizedek be Jerusalem, as is probable, the city first emerges in history in the days of Abraham, when it already had a king of the Semitic race, who was at the same time priest of the Most High God (Gen. 14: 18). Manetho, an Egyptian priest and historian of the 3d century before Christ, transmits a tradition, which may contain considerable truth, to the effect that the nation of the Shepherd Kings (or Hyksos) to the number of 240,000 were driven out of Egypt by Thoummosis [or Thmosis, perhaps for Amosis, i.e., Aahmes], and fled toward Syria; but fearing the Assyrians, who had dominion over Asia, they built a city in the country now called Judea of sufficient size to contain the multitude and named it Jerusalem (Jos. *Apion* i. 14, 15). This expulsion of the Hyksos took place 1580 B.C. The earliest mention of Jerusalem in extant original documents is in the Tell el-Amarna tablets, where Abdi-ḥiba (Abdi-khiba) of this city writes to Amenhotep IV (or Akhnaton), Pharaoh of Egypt (alone, 1375–1366 B.C.). When the Israelites entered Canaan, Jerusalem was ruled by a king, still a Semite, and occupied by Amorites, or more definitely by Jebusites. Joshua defeated its king and his allies at Gibeon, drove them down the pass of Beth-horon, and slew them in the lowland (Josh., ch. 10). But no attempt was made to enter the city. The Jebusites still dwelt in it. It was allotted to the tribe of Benjamin; but as it stood on the border of Judah, its castle commanded a portion of the territory of 2 tribes (Josh. 15:8; 18:28). In the war which was waged by the several tribes against the Canaanites within their own bounds after the death of Joshua, Judah fought against Jerusalem, took it, and set it on fire (Judg. 1:8). But apparently Judah did not capture the citadel. Neither did Benjamin (v. 21). Hence, when the city was rebuilt, it was still under the shadow of the Jebusite stronghold and its inhabitants were Jebusites. It was a city of foreigners and a reproach in the midst of the land (Josh. 15: 63; Judg. 1:21; 19:11, 12). Such was the state of affairs when David began his career. When he had slain Goliath, he returned from the field of battle by way of Jerusalem and brought the head of the Philistine thither (I Sam. 17:54). And when he became king of all Israel, and found a united and enthusiastic nation obedient to him, and the jealousy between Judah and Benjamin allayed, he at once led his troops against the border town, and in face of the derision of the inhabitants, who believed their walls to be impregnable, gained possession (II Sam. 5:6 *seq.*). Henceforth for many centuries Jerusalem was a city of the Hebrews.

III. 2. *The city of the Hebrews.* David made

Jerusalem the capital of his kingdom and took measures to make it the religious center also. The Ark, which had had no dwelling place of its own since Jehovah forsook Shiloh, he brought to Jerusalem, pitched a suitable tent for it, and began the collection of materials for a temple. The city shared in the prosperity of Solomon's reign. The walls were enlarged, the Temple was erected on a scale of great magnificence, and surrounded by a wall which gave it the appearance of a fortress, and a royal palace was built not inferior to the Temple in splendor. In the next reign, however, the army of Shishak, king of Egypt, entered the city and robbed the Temple and the palace of their treasures (I Kings 14:25-27), and about 80 years later bands of Philistines and Arabs gained brief admission to the city and carried off plunder (II Chron. 21:17). The population was in the meanwhile increasing, quarters of the city began to be distinguished (II Kings 20:4; 22:14), and before the beginning of the 8th century a suburb on the n.w. hill was enclosed by an addition to the city wall. This part of the city was the mercantile district, and continued to be such after the Exile and until the destruction of the city by Titus (Jos. War v. 8, 1). Here were the sheep gate and fish gate, and the quarter was skirted by the valley of the Tyropoeon (the cheesemongers). In the reign of Amaziah a portion of the city wall was broken down, and Temple and palace were despoiled of treasure by the northern Israelites (II Kings 14:13, 14). Uzziah and Jotham repaired the ruin, strengthened the walls, and erected new towers for defense (II Chron. 26:9; 27:3). But they had perhaps other ruins to care for than those wrought by war, for in Uzziah's reign the city was visited by a memorable earthquake (Amos 1:1; Zech. 14:5; Jos. Antiq. ix. 10, 4). Under Ahaz the city was besieged, but not taken, by the northern Israelites in alliance with the Syrians (II Kings 16:5), and shortly afterward, by reason of the king's inclination to heathenism, the lamps of the Temple were allowed to go out, the offering in the Holy Place ceased, and the Temple was closed (II Kings 16:14 seq.; II Chron. 28:24; 29:7). Hezekiah reopened the Temple and restored the service, but he was obliged to empty the royal and the sacred treasuries and to strip the plates of gold from the Temple doors in order to raise a sum sufficient to purchase exemption from a threatened raid by the Assyrians; and even this relief was but temporary, for eventually Assyrian troops stood before the walls (II Chron. 29:3; II Kings 18:15, 16). The city was, however, delivered by the providential outbreak of pestilence in the camp of the enemy (II Kings 19:35). When Manasseh returned from captivity he built walls for the city and strengthened the fortifications (II Chron. 33:14).

During the reigns of the sons and grandson of Josiah the city experienced its overwhelming calamities. Nebuchadnezzar besieged it in the days of Jehoiakim, entered it, bound but eventually released the king, and carried off a number of noble youth and costly vessels from the Temple (II Kings 24:1; II Chron. 36:6; Dan. 1:1). Again he came, emptied the royal and the sacred treasuries, seized the remaining vessels of gold and silver belonging to the Temple, carried King Jehoiachin a prisoner to Babylon, and deported the best and most useful citizens (II Kings 24:10–16). Nine years later, in the reign of Zedekiah, he laid siege to the city for the 3d time. The investment lasted 2 years. The misery within the walls was extreme. Finally a breach was made, the city was taken, the Temple and the palaces were burnt, the wall was broken down, and the remnant of the population, save the poorest, was deported (II Kings, ch. 25). The

city lay waste for 50 years. Zerubbabel and 50,000 followers returned to Jerusalem in 538 B.C., and at the beginning of the next year laid the foundation of the Temple (Ezra 2:64, 65; 3:8). The walls of the city were rebuilt under Nehemiah about 444 B.C. The supreme power was then in the hands of the Persians, from whom it passed, under Alexander the Great, to the Macedonian Greeks. The city was taken by Antiochus the Great 203 B.C., retaken by the Egyptians in 199, and opened its gates again to Antiochus coming as a friend in 198. In 170 B.C. Antiochus Epiphanes took Jerusalem, subsequently desecrating the Temple. But the Maccabees arose; and in 165 B.C. Judas retook the city and purified the Temple. The kings of the Hasmonaean race built near the Temple a citadel called Baris or the tower; see ANTONIA, TOWER OF. Pompey captured Jerusalem 63 B.C., breaking down part of the wall; Crassus despoiled the Temple in 54 B.C. and the Parthians plundered the city in 40 B.C. Jerusalem was taken again in 37 B.C. by Herod the Great, who repaired the walls, adorned the city with various edifices, and rebuilt the Temple on a scale of magnificence which markedly contrasted with the compara-

Reverse of Coin of Vespasian Commemorating the Capture of Jerusalem

tively humble character of Zerubbabel's Temple. The work began 20–19 B.C. and was not quite completed when our Lord was on earth. Herod also strengthened the citadel and called it Antonia (see ANTONIA, TOWER OF). When he passed away there were 2 walls, in whole or in part encompassing Jerusalem, against 1 in Solomon's time. A 3d wall was begun by Herod Agrippa (about A.D. 42 or 43) a dozen years after the crucifixion. In A.D. 70 the Romans, under Titus, took Jerusalem, the Temple and nearly all the city having been burnt or otherwise destroyed during the siege. He broke down all the walls, with the exception of part of the w. one and 3 towers, Hippicus, Phasaelus, and Mariamne, which he left so that future generations might see the nature of the defenses he had succeeded in capturing (Jos. War vii. 1, 1).

III. 3. The city since Titus. Under the emperor Hadrian the Romans commenced to refortify Jerusalem as a Gentile city, and hold it against its former inhabitants. This seems to have been one main cause of the Jewish revolt under Bar Cocheba (c. A.D. 132 to 135). On its suppression, the rebuilding of the city was resumed and completed. The old name Jerusalem was discarded. It was called Colonia Aelia Capitolina: Colonia to denote that it was a Roman colony, Aelia in honor of Hadrian, whose praenomen was Aelius, and Capitolina because it was dedicated to Jupiter Capitolinus. To this heathen deity a temple was dedicated on the spot where those of Solomon, Zerubbabel, and Herod had stood. The

THE DOME OF THE ROCK, JERUSALEM

Jews were forbidden, on pain of death, to enter within its walls. The Christians were, perhaps, by this time sufficiently distinguished from the Jews not to come under the prohibition. The name Aelia continued for many centuries. The emperor Constantine first partially, and then completely, removed the prohibition against the Jews' entering the Holy City; in 326 Helena, his mother, built a church on the Mount of Olives. In 333, by order of Constantine, the church of the Anastasis, marking the supposed site of the Holy Sepulcher, was begun; see CALVARY. In 614 Jerusalem was taken by storm by the Persians under Chosroes II, thousands of the inhabitants were massacred and other thousands were carried off prisoners to Persia, and the church of the Holy Sepulcher was burnt down. In 628, on the death of Chosroes, Jerusalem was retaken by the Roman emperor, Heraclius. In 638 it surrendered on conditions to the Arabs under Omar ('Umar). In 691 'Abd-al-Malik erected the magnificent Dome of the Rock (wrongly called by Europeans the Mosque of Omar), upon, or very near, the site of the Temple of Solomon. Near the Dome and in the s. section of the sacred area 'Abd-al-Malik built another mosque, possibly on the site of an earlier church; it is called al-Masjid al-Akṣa (the farther mosque), but the term is also applied to the whole collection of sacred buildings on that area. Al-Ḥaram al-Sharif (the noble sanctuary) is another name for this group. During the period when Jerusalem was ruled by the Moslems, the treatment of the Christian pilgrims who visited the sacred shrines varied. Once the church of the Holy Sepulcher was set on fire under a Fatimite ruler, but on the whole there was toleration. It was different when the Arabs were displaced by the Seljuk Turks in A.D. 1077. The insults and oppression practiced by the semi-savages who had now gained power, threw all western and central Europe into a ferment, and brought on the Crusades. In the 1st of these religious expeditions Jerusalem was taken by storm on July 15, 1099, and a Christian kingdom established, which continued 88 years. During the Christian occupation the buildings connected with the Holy Sepulcher were enlarged and made more splendid and other edifices erected in the city. In 1187 it had to be surrendered to Saladin, sultan of Egypt and Syria; in 1192 he repaired the walls, but in 1219 they were dismantled by orders of the sultan of Damascus. In 1229 Emperor Frederick II of Germany obtained the Holy City by treaty with the stipulation that the fortifications be not restored. Ten years later the inhabitants of the city broke these conditions, and vengeance was taken by the emir of Karak. In 1243, however, the city was restored to the Christians unconditionally. The following year the Khwārizm Turks captured Jerusalem and restored it to Islam. Three years later the invaders were driven out of Palestine by the Egyptians, who held the city until 1517, when it fell into the hands of the Ottoman Turks. The greatest of their sultans, Sulaymān the Magnificent, built the present walls in 1542. In World War I Palestine was conquered by the British under General Allenby, and Jerusalem surrendered Dec. 9, 1917.

Je·ru′sha (jê-rōō′shá) and **Je·ru′shah** (jê-rōō′shá) [possessed, i.e., married]. Wife of Uzziah, king of Judah, and mother of his successor, Jotham (II Kings 15:33; II Chron. 27:1).

Je·sha′iah (jê-shā′yá), in A.V. twice **Je·sa′iah** (jê-sā′yá) (I Chron. 3:21; Neh. 11:7) [Jehovah has saved]. 1. A son of Jeduthun, and a musician in the reign of David (I Chron. 25:3).

2. A Levite, son of Rehabiah; he also was in David s reign (I Chron. 26:25).

3. A son of Hananiah, and a descendant of Zerubbabel (I Chron. 3:21).

4. A son of Athaliah and head of the father's house of Elam, who, with 70 males, returned from Babylon with Ezra (Ezra 8:7).

5. A Merarite Levite who returned in the same company (Ezra 8:19).

6. A Benjamite, the father of Ithiel (Neh. 11:7).

Jesh′a·nah (jĕsh′á-ná) [old]. A city in the hill country of Ephraim, wrested by Abijah from the Northern Kingdom (II Chron. 13:19; cf. ch. 15:8). It is believed to be the village called Isanas, where Herod the Great defeated the general of Antigonus (Jos. Antiq. xiv. 15, 12). 'Ain Sînia, 3¼ miles n. of Beth-el may mark the site. See SHEN.

Jesh′a·re′lah (jĕsh′á-rē′lá) [since the Heb. has s instead of sh, the name may signify "toward Israel"]. See ASHARELAH.

Je·sheb′e·ab (jê-shĕb′ê-ăb) [uncertain; perhaps, may the father (not divine) tarry, i.e., continue to live]. A descendant of Aaron. His family became the 14th course of the priesthood (I Chron. 24:13).

Je′sher (jē′shēr) [uprightness]. A son of Caleb (I Chron. 2:18).

Je·shi′mon (jê-shī′mŏn) [a waste, a desert]. 1. A wilderness at the n.e. end of the Dead Sea, not far from Pisgah and Peor (Num. 21:20; 23:28). In both passages R.V. and J.V. render it desert. Beth-jeshimoth was situated in it; see BETH-JESHIMOTH.

2. A wilderness n. of the hill Hachilah and of Maon (I Sam. 23:19, 24; 26:1, 3). In these passages R.V. regards Jeshimon not as a proper name but renders it desert. J.V. considers it a proper name.

Je·shish′a·i (jê-shīsh′á-i) [old, venerable]. A Gadite, descended from Buz (I Chron. 5:14).

Jesh′o·ha′iah (jĕsh′ô-hā′yá). A Simeonite prince (I Chron. 4:36).

Jesh′u·a (jĕsh′û-á), in A.V. once **Jesh′u·ah** (jĕsh′û-á) (I Chron. 24:11) [a late form of Joshua, Jehovah is salvation]. 1. Joshua, the military leader in the wars of Canaan (Neh. 8:17).

2. A descendant of Aaron. His family had grown to a father's house in the time of David and was made the 9th of the 24 courses into which David divided the priests (I Chron. 24:1, 6, 11).

3. One of the Levites in Hezekiah's reign who had to do with the receipt and distribution of the freewill offerings in the Temple (II Chron. 31:15).

4. A high priest who returned with Zerubbabel from Babylon (Ezra 2:2; Neh. 7:7). He was the son of Jozadak. He built the altar of burnt offering, and encouraged the workmen and the people generally to rebuild the Temple (Ezra 3:2–9). In Zechariah's prophecies he is called Joshua, and stands as the priestly representative of the returned exiles to whom divine support is given (Zech., chs. 3; 6:11–13).

5. A man of the house of Pahath-moab, some of whose children returned with Zerubbabel and others from captivity (Ezra 2:6; Neh. 7:11).

6. A Levite, head of a Levitical family, who, with members of the family, returned from captivity with Zerubbabel (Ezra 2:40; Neh. 7:43; 12:8). He actively assisted Jeshua, the high priest, in stimulating the workmen and people to rebuild the Temple (Ezra 3:9). The representative of the house bearing his name affixed his seal to the covenant (Neh. 10:9). From the last passage, it appears that Jeshua was the son of Azaniah (v. 9). In Neh. 12:24

300

the word *ben*, the son of, after Jeshua is probably a corruption of the name Bani (cf. ch. 9:4, 5). Not unlikely it was this Levite Jeshua who was the father of the ruler of Mizpah, Ezer, who repaired a portion of the wall (ch. 3:19).

7. A Levite, probably of the aforementioned family, who aided Ezra in explaining the Law to the people (Neh. 8:7), and in preparing them for a more heartfelt worship of Jehovah (ch. 9:5, 26).

8. A village of s. Judah (Neh. 11:26), identified with Tell es-Sa'weh.

Jesh'u·run (jĕsh'û-rŭn), in A.V. once **Jes'-u·run** (Isa. 44:2) [upright one]. A name of endearment used in poetry for the nation of Israel with reference to the moral character which it was created to exhibit (Deut. 32:15; 33:5, 26; Isa. 44:2).

Je·si'ah (jė-sī'à). See ISSHIAH.

Je·sim'i·el (jė-sĭm'ĭ-ĕl) [God sets up, establishes]. A prince of the tribe of Simeon (I Chron. 4:36).

Jes'se (jĕs'ē) [Heb. *Yishay*; *'ishay* (I Chron. 2:13); ety. uncertain, but cf. Heb. *'ish*, man]. Son of Obed, family of Perez. He was descended from Nahshon, chief of the tribe of Judah in the days of Moses, and from Ruth the Moabitess (Ruth 4:18–22). He was father of 8 sons, the youngest of whom was David (I Sam. 17:12–14). To judge from I Chron. 2:15, 1 of them died without leaving posterity: unless, as is less probable, Elihu (ch. 27:18) has been lost from the register. Jesse had 2 daughters, but by a different wife from David's mother (ch. 2:16; cf. II Sam. 17:25). Jesse lived at Bethlehem, to which Samuel was sent to anoint a king from among his sons. After 7 of them had been passed before him in the order of their birth, David was called from the flock which he was tending, and on his arrival was anointed king (I Sam. 16:1–13). After Saul had become jealous of David he usually called him the son of Jesse (ch. 20:31; 22:7; 25:10), in order to emphasize David's humble origin. Saul ignored the fact that his own father was no more a king than was David's father. In the cave of Adullam David was joined by his father, his mother, and his brothers. He allowed his brothers to share the dangers of his wanderings, but placed his parents under the protection of the king of Moab, the native land of his ancestress Ruth, till he knew what God had in store for him in the future (ch. 22:1–4). It is uncertain when Jesse died. Although of good ancestry and himself an able man, yet his station in life was lowly. This humble position of the family is alluded to by the prophets (Isa. 11:1, 10; cf. Micah 5:2; Rom. 15:12), and was recalled by all who refused the rule of the house of David (II Sam. 20:1; I Kings 12:16; II Chron. 10:16).

Jes'u·i (jĕs'û-I). See ISHVI.

Jes'u·run (jĕs'û-rŭn). See JESHURUN.

Je'sus (jē'zŭs) [Lat. from Gr. *Iēsous*, which is for Heb. Jeshua, a late form of Jehoshua or Joshua (Jehovah is salvation)]. 1. Joshua, the military leader in the wars of Canaan (A.V. of Acts 7:45; Heb. 4:8); see JOSHUA.

2. An ancestor of Christ, who lived about 400 years after David (Luke 3:29). The A.V., following a different Gr. text, calls him Jose.

3. In the LXX the name occurs several times in the Apocrypha. It was borne by the author of Ecclesiasticus, and 12 persons with this name are mentioned by Josephus outside of his references to Joshua and to Christ. It was a common name among the Jews of the Greek-speaking period.

4. A Jewish Christian, also called Justus, associated with Paul (Col. 4:11).

5. The name of our Lord. See JESUS CHRIST.

Je'sus Christ (jē'zŭs krīst). Our Lord was named Jesus in accordance with the directions of the angel to Joseph (Matt. 1:21) and Mary (Luke 1:31). When given to ordinary children, the name expressed, if anything, the parent's faith in God as the savior of his people, or their faith in the coming salvation of Israel. When given to Mary's child, it was designed to express the special office he would fulfill: "Thou shalt call his name Jesus; for it is he that shall save his people from their sins" (Matt. 1:21). Christ is from Gr. *Christos* (anointed), a translation of Aram. M*e*shīḥā, Heb. *Māshīaḥ* (anointed, Messiah). Jesus, therefore, was our Lord's personal name and Christ was his title (the Christ); though the latter was early used also as a proper name, as it is by us, either alone or with Jesus.

It is the object of the following article to ske ch the progress of our Lord's life on earth so as to place its principal events in their probable order and relation.

I. *Chronology.* The exact dates of the birth, baptism, and death of Jesus cannot be absolutely demonstrated; but most scholars now agree within narrow limits. Our ordinary Christian calendar originated with Dionysius Exiguus, a Roman abbot who died sometime before A.D. 550. He first selected the year of the incarnation as that before and after which dates should be reckoned. He fixed, however, on the year of Rome 754, as that in which Christ was born, and that year consequently equals A.D. 1. But the statements of Josephus make it clear that Herod the Great, who died shortly after Jesus was born (Matt. 2:19–22), died several years before the year of Rome 754. His death occurred 37 years after he had been declared king by the Romans, which was in A.U.C. 714. This might be 751 or 750, according to whether Josephus counted fractions of a year as whole years or not. The year 750 is, however, made the more probable from the further statement of Josephus that shortly before Herod's death he put to death 2 Jewish rabbis, and that on the night of their execution there occurred an eclipse of the moon. Astronomical calculations show that in 750 there was a partial lunar eclipse on the night of March 12 or 13; but in 751 there was no eclipse. Josephus also narrates that Herod died shortly before the passover, which began in 750 on April 12. We may, therefore, with considerable confidence date Herod's death about April 1, in the year of Rome 750, which was 4 B.C. Before that date, therefore, we must place the events given in the Gospels which occurred between the birth of Jesus and the death of Herod, for which a period of 2 or 3 months is probably required. Christ's birth, therefore, is to be placed at the close of 5 B.C. or beginning of 4 B.C. The observance of December 25 did not arise until the 4th century, so that it has no authority. It may, however, be accepted as an approximation to the truth, and then Christ's birth would be assigned to December 25, 5 B.C. This puts it 5 years earlier than in the calendar of Dionysius, who assigned it to December 25, A.D. 1. The date of the opening of our Lord's public ministry is to be obtained principally from Luke 3:23, where it is said that at his baptism he was about 30 years of age. The expression is obviously indefinite; but, assuming that he was born December 25, 5 B.C., he would be 30 on December 25, A.D. 26. The traditional date of the baptism is January 6, and if we suppose at any rate that it occurred early in A.D. 27, Luke's expression, "about thirty years of age," would be correct. This date also is somewhat confirmed by the statement of the Jews (John 2:20), made shortly after his baptism: "Forty and six years was this temple in building." The rebuilding of the Temple by Herod was begun, as might be shown, in 20–19 B.C.; so that the 46 years, supposing them to have elapsed when the remark was made, would bring us again to A.D. 27. If, finally, "the fifteenth year of the reign of Tiberius" (Luke 3:1), when John the Baptist began his ministry, be reckoned, as it properly may be, from the time when Tiberius was associated with Augustus in the empire (A.D. 11 to 12), it coincides with A.D. 26 and further agrees with our other calculations. It is true that all these items of evidence contain in them points on which opinions may not unreasonably differ; yet the dates we have given appear to be the most probable and to support one another. The length of Christ's ministry and consequently the year of his death are to be fixed by the number of passovers which John notes in his Gospel. If we had only the Synoptic Gospels (see GOSPEL), we might infer that his ministry was only a year in length, and this was in ancient times a not uncommon opinion. But John's Gospel speaks of at least 3 passovers (chs. 2:13; 6:4; 13:1), and it is highly probable that the feast referred to in John 5:1 was also a passover. If so, Christ's ministry included 4 passovers, at the last of which he died; and, if he was baptized early in A.D. 27, his 1st passover was in April of that year, and he died in A.D. 30, when the passover festival began on April 7. Those who think that John 5:1 does not refer to a passover, date Christ's death in A.D. 29. We thus obtain as the probable leading dates in Christ's life: bir h, December 25 (?), 5 B.C.; baptism and beginning of his ministry, January (?), A.D. 27; death, April 7, A.D. 30.

II. *Political condition of the Jews.* When Jesus was born, Herod the Great, an able but cruel man, was king of the Jews. His kingdom included Samaria and Galilee as well as Judea. He was an Idumaean by descent, though professing the Jewish religion. His fa her, Antipater, had been made governor of Judea by Julius Caesar, and, after several changes of fortune, Herod had been declared king of the Jews by the Romans in 40 B.C. But, while an independent king in many ways, Herod ruled by the favor of and in dependence on the Romans, who had become the practical rulers of the world. On his death, 4 B.C., his kingdom was divided among his sons. Archelaus received Judea and Samaria. Herod Antipas received Galilee and Perea. Herod Philip received the territory n.e. of the Sea of Galilee (Luke 3:1). In the 10th year of his reign (A.D. 6), Archelaus was deposed by Augustus, and from that date Judea and Samaria were ruled by Roman governors (procurators) until the destruction of Jerusalem, with the exception of the years A.D. 41–44, when Herod Agrippa I was invested with the royal power (Acts 12:1). During the ministry of Christ, therefore, Galilee and Perea, where he spent most of his time, were under the rule of Herod Antipas (Matt. 14:3; Mark 6:14; Luke 3:1, 19; 9:7; 13:31; 23:8–12), while Samaria and Judea were ruled directly by the Romans through their governor, who at that time was Pontius Pilate. The rule of the Romans, whether direct or indirect, irritated the Jews exceedingly, and, during Christ's life, the land was in an almost constant state of political ferment. While the Romans sought to give the nation as much self-government as possible, so that their sanhedrin, or chief court, exercised jurisdiction in a very large number of cases; and while the conquerors granted many privileges to the Jews, especially in respect to their religious observances, yet the nation fretted under a foreign domination which was very positive, when it wished to be so, and which did not intend ever to grant them their old liberty. The Jewish aristocracy, however, including most of the Sadducees, were not unfriendly to the Romans. The Pharisees, who

comprised the strictest religionists, were disposed to devote themselves to the conservation of Judaism, while generally avoiding political complications. We read also of Herodians, who doubtless favored the claims of the Herodian family to the Jewish throne, while from Josephus we learn of political patriots who successively arose in the vain endeavor to throw off the Roman yoke. In such a condition of things, one who claimed to be the Messiah would easily be involved in political difficulties. We shall see that Jesus carefully and successfully avoided these in order that he might proclaim the true, spiritual Kingdom of God.

III. *Religious condition of the Jews.* As already implied, this was largely affected by the state of political affairs. So far as the official classes were concerned, the purely religious hopes of the O.T. had been almost forgotten, and even among the people the idea of an earthly kingdom had nearly displaced that of a spiritual one. We meet in the Gospels with 2 leading sects, the Pharisees and the Sadducees. The former were religious and had the greater influence among the people; but they had substituted theological and ceremonial tradition, as well as casuistic subtleties, for the word of God, and in their hands the religion of Moses and the prophets often became a narrow, barren, and unspiritual form. The Pharisees naturally opposed the spiritual and unconventional religion which Jesus taught, and especially his appeal from tradition to Scripture. The Sadducees, on the other hand, were the aristocrats. They included the high-priestly families. They were infected by Gentile cul ure, rejected the Pharisaic traditions, and were more interested in politics than in religion. They were led finally to oppose Jesus because they thought that his success would disturb the existing political relations (John 11:48). Meanwhile the ceremonies of God's worship were carried on wi h much magnificence in the Temple at Jerusalem, the people attended with fidelity and in great numbers the religious festivals, and the zeal of the nation for its religious privileges and traditions was never greater, while every now and then some outbreak of mingled patriotism and fanaticism fanned the embers of popular hope into a flame. Yet there were some who still preserved the spirit and faith of a pure religion. They were found mainly, though not wholly, among the humble classes. In them the expectation of a savior from sin had not died out, and from the bosom of one of these pious circles Jesus himself came. The Jewish people, therefore, in Christ's life ime were still a religious people. They knew the O.T., which was read in their synagogues and taught to their children. The nation was in a state of religious interest as well as of political unrest. These facts explain to us the popular excitement caused by the preaching of John the Baptist and of Jesus, the opposition of the ruling classes to both of them, and the success of the method which Jesus pursued in preaching his gospel, as well as the fate which he himself saw from the beginning to be, even humanly speaking, inevitable.

IV. *Life of Jesus.* 1. *Family, Birth, and Infancy of Jesus.* The circumstances of the birth of Jesus, as recorded in the Gospels, were in accord with his dignity and the predictions of the Messiah, yet such also as to harmonize with the lowly appearance which the Saviour was to make on earth. As Malachi (ch. 3:1; also ch. 4:5, 6) had prophesied that a herald, in the spirit and power of Elijah, should precede the Lord when he should come to his temple, so Luke tells us first of the birth of John the Baptist, the herald of the Christ. A certain pious priest, named Zacharias, who had no child and was far advanced in years, was discharging his duties at the Temple. He was chosen by lot. as the custom was, to offer the incense, representing the prayers of Israel, on the altar in the Holy Place. To him the angel Gabriel appeared and announced that he was to be the father of the promised forerunner of the Messiah. This was probably in October, 6 B.C. After his term of service in the Temple was over, he and his wife, Elisabeth, returned to their home in a city in the hill country of Judah (Luke 1:39), and awaited the fulfillment of the promise. Six months later the angel appeared to Mary, a maiden probably of Davidic descent, who lived in Nazareth and was betrothed to Joseph, who was certainly descended from the great king of Israel (Matt. 1:1–16; Luke 1:27); see GENEALOGY. Joseph was a carpenter by trade, a man of humble station though of high descent, and a devout Israelite. To Mary the angel announced that she was to become the mother of the Messiah (Luke 1:28–38) by the power of the Holy Spirit working in her, and that the child, who was to be called Jesus, should have the throne of his ancestor David. At that time she was also told of the pregnancy of Elisabeth, who was her kinswoman. When the angel left her, Mary hastened to Elisabeth. At their meeting, the spirit of prophecy came on these 2 women. While Elisabeth greeted Mary as the mother of her Lord, Mary, like Hannah of old (I Sam. 2:1–10), broke forth in a song of praise for the salvation of Israel that was coming and for the honor which had been conferred on her. When the time drew near for Elisabeth to be delivered of the child which she had conceived, Mary returned to Nazareth. Her further protection against reproach was, however, secured by God himself. Joseph, seeing her condition, was disposed quietly to put her away without public accusation, but even this gentle treatment was forestalled. An angel revealed to him in a dream the cause of Mary's condition; told him that he was to have the Messiah for his child; and that, as Isaiah had foretold, the latter was to be born of a virgin. With faith, equal to Mary's, Joseph believed the message and made Mary his legal wife. It was thus secured that Mary's child was born of a virgin, and at the same time that he had a legal human father, while his mother was protected by the love and respectability of a husband. There can be little doubt that these facts were later made known by Mary herself.

The fact that neither Christ nor his apostles appeal to his miraculous conception in proof of his Messiahship occasions no reason for doubting the narrative. The event was not one which could be used as public proof. But the narratives of Christ's birth beautifully harmonize with what we now know of his dignity and his mission upon earth. The Messiah was to be the perfect flower of Israel's spiritual life; and so Jesus was born in the bosom of this pious family circle where the pure religion of the O.T. was believed and cherished. The Messiah was to appear in lowliness; and so Jesus came from the home of the Nazarene carpenter. The Messiah was to be the son of David; and so Joseph, his legal father, and probably Mary, his actual mother, were descended from David. The Messiah was to be the incarnation of God, a divine person uniting to himself a human nature; and so Jesus was born of a woman but miraculously conceived by the power of the Holy Spirit.

After relating the birth of John and the prophetic song which burst from the long-sealed lips of his father Zacharias over the advent of the Messiah's forerunner, the Evangelist Luke (Luke 1:57–79; 2:1–6) explains how Jesus came to be born in Bethlehem. The emperor Augustus had ordered an enrollment of all the subjects of the empire, and although Palestine was under Herod, its inhabitants also were included in the decree. The enrollment of the Jews, however, evidently took place after the Jewish method, by which each father of a household was registered, not at his dwelling place, but at the place where his family belonged in view of its ancestry. Hence Joseph had to go to Bethlehem, the original home of David. Mary accompanied him. The lodging place, or khan, where strangers were permitted to sojourn, was already fully occupied when they arrived, and they found shelter only in a stable, which may have been, as early tradition affirms, in a cave near the town. Such caves were often used about Bethlehem for stables. We are not told that any cattle were occupying the stable. It may have been unused at the time. Nor would a stable in that country and among that people have seemed as offensive a lodging place as it might with us; but it was a lowly abode for the birthplace of the Messiah. Yet such it was destined to be, for there Mary's child was born, and she laid him in a manger (Luke 2:7). But though born so humbly, he was not to be without attestation. That night shepherds in a field near Bethlehem were visited by angels. who told them of the Messiah's birth and where he lay, and sang in the hearing of the shepherds: "Glory to God in the highest, and on earth peace among men in whom he is well pleased" (Luke 2:14, R.V.). The shepherds hastened to Bethlehem and saw the child. They related what they had seen and heard, and then returned again to their flocks. All this was again in striking harmony with the mission of the Messiah. Yet we should remember that the event occurred in a circle of humble peasants, and that it made no noise in the busy world. For a while Joseph and Mary lingered in Bethlehem. On the 8th day the child was circumcised (Luke 2:21) and the appointed name, Jesus, was given to him. Forty days after his birth his parents took him, as the Law directed (Lev., ch. 12) to the Temple and Mary offered her gifts of purification and presented her child unto the Lord. The first-born male child of a Hebrew mother was to be redeemed by the payment of 5 shekels (Num. 18:15, 16), and this is what is meant when it is said that they brought him "to present him to the Lord." The mother was also to offer her thanksgiving, and it is specially noted by Luke that Mary gave the offering of the poor, "a pair of turtle doves, or two young pigeons." The modest circumstances of the family are thus further attested. Yet the lowly Messiah was not to leave his Father's house without recognition. An aged saint, Simeon by name, came into the Temple and the spirit of inspiration fell upon him when he saw the child. He had been promised by God that he should not die till he had seen the Messiah. Taking the infant in his arms, Simeon gave thanks and predicted the glory and sorrow of his life (Luke 2:25–35). Anna also, a prophetess of great age, who continually dwelt in the Temple, bore witness to the advent of the Christ (Luke 2:36–38).

A more remarkable attestation was soon to follow. Some time after Joseph and Mary had returned to Bethlehem, certain Magi from the East appeared in Jerusalem and declared that they had seen the Messiah's star in the heavens and were come to worship him. They had doubtless learned from the Jews scattered throughout the East of the expectation of a coming king in Judea who would be man's great deliverer. They were doubtless also students of the stars, and God used their superstitious notions to make them witnesses to the Gentiles, who awaited in the half-light of natural religion the coming of the Saviour, of whom they felt the need, but whose real character they did not understand. In the e. the Magi had seen a star which for some reason they felt portended the birth of the Jewish king. Coming to Jerusalem, they inquired for him. Their message troubled the equally superstitious Herod and, summoning the scribes, he demanded where the Messiah was to be born. When told that he was to be born in Bethlehem, Herod sent the Magi there, but bade them promise to inform him if they found the child. On the way the Magi saw the star again over Bethlehem, and, having found Jesus, offered him rare gifts of frankincense, gold, and myrrh. We can imagine with what renewed awe Joseph and Mary must have received these unexpected and strange visitors. They were another sign of the high destiny of the child. The Magi, however, were warned of God not to return to Herod, for that wicked man only intended to use them to destroy the newly born king. They departed home, therefore, by another way.

Joseph also was warned by an angel of the impending danger and instructed to take Mary and the babe to Egypt, well out of Herod's reach. It was none too soon, for presently the cruel king, whose readiness to murder even his own sons is related by Josephus, sent soldiers to slay all the male children in Bethlehem who were 2 years of age and under. He hoped thus to accomplish the object in which he had been foiled by the departure of the Magi without informing him concerning the child they had sought. Bethlehem was a small place and the number of children slain may not have been large; but the act was cruel enough at the best. Jesus, however, had escaped. How long he was kept in Egypt we do not know. Probably it was for a few months. There were many Jews there, so that Joseph could easily find a refuge. But in due time the angel informed him of Herod's death and directed him to return. It was apparently his first purpose to rear the child in Bethlehem, David's city, but his fear of Archelaus, Herod's son, made him hesitate. Again God gave him instruc ions, and in accordance with them Joseph and Mary sought once more their old home in Nazareth. In consequence of this, Jesus appeared among the people, when his public life began, as the prophet of Nazareth, the Nazarene. Such are the few incidents preserved in the Gospels of the birth and infancy of Jesus. Wonderful as they appear to us, they attracted no attention at the time on the part of the world. The few persons concerned in them either forgot them or kept them to themselves. But when the Church was founded we may suppose that Mary told them to the disciples. Matthew and Luke have related them to us quite independently of each other, the former to illustrate the royal Messiahship of Jesus and his fulfillment of prophecy; the latter to explain the origin of Jesus and the historical beginnings of his life.

IV. 2. *Childhood and Youth.* After the return to Nazareth, nothing is told us of Jesus' life, except the 1 incident of his visit with his parents to the Temple when he had become 12 years of age (Luke 2:41–51). That incident, however, is instructive. It shows the continued piety of Joseph and Mary and the devout training which they sought to give the child. It shows also the early spiritual development of Jesus, for he was already mainly interested in those religious questions on which the Jewish rabbis gave instruction to their pupils. We are not to imagine the boy of 12 as instruc ing the teachers, but as a pupil in one of their Temple schools, and yet as showing by his questions a spiritual insight which amazed them. The incident also illustrates the natural, human life which Jesus led. He grew, we are told, "in wisdom and stature [or age], and in favor with God and men"

(Luke 2:52). The wonders of his infancy were doub less kept a secret by Joseph and Mary, and Jesus appeared to his companions and the family in no wise a supernatural being, but only remarkable for his mental force and moral purity. Putting together, however, other facts incidentally mentioned in the Gospels, we can form some idea of the circumstances in which the childhood and young manhood of Jesus were passed. He was a member of a family. He had 4 brothers and some sisters (Mark 6:3, etc.). Some have supposed that these were the children of Joseph by a former marriage; others that they were Christ's cousins. It seems to us most natural and Scriptural to believe that they were the children of Joseph and Mary, born after Jesus (see BRETHREN OF THE LORD and JAMES 3). But at any rate, Jesus grew up in a family, experiencing the pleasures and the discipline of family life. He became, like Joseph, a carpenter (Mark 6:3), so that he was accustomed to manual labor. But mental discipline also was not wanting. Jewish children were well instructed in the Scriptures, and our Lord's familiarity with them is evident from his teaching. His parables also reveal a mind sensitive to the teaching of nature, and which must always have delighted to ponder the evidence of God's mind in the works of his hand. Nazareth was on the edge of the busiest part of the Jewish world and not far from some of the most famous scenes of Israel's history. From the cliff back of the town the eye could contemplate many places associated with great events. Not far off was the Sea of Galilee, around which was gathered the varied life of the world in miniature. It was a period also, as has been said, of much political excitement, and Jewish homes were often agitated with the report of stirring events. There is no reason to suppose that Jesus grew up in isolation. We should rather imagine him keenly alive to the progress of events in Palestine. While the language spoken by him was Aramaic, which had displaced the older Hebrew among the later Jews, he must often have heard Greek used and may have been familiar with it. All this period of his life, however, the Evangelists pass over. Their books were writ.en not to give biographies of Jesus, but to report his public ministry. We can see enough, however, to prove the naturalness of our Saviour's human life, the fitness of his surroundings to prepare him for his future work, the beauty of his character, and thus the gradual unfolding of his humanity in expectation of the hour when he was to offer himself as God's Messiah to his people.

IV. 3. *Baptism.* That important hour drew nigh when, perhaps in the summer of A.D. 26, John, the son of Zacharias, who had hitherto led a life of ascetic devotion in the desert (Luke 1:80), received from God his commission to summon the nation to repentance for their sins in preparation for the Messiah's coming. John moved from place to place along the Jordan Valley and administered the rite of baptism to those who believed his message. He called both the nation and individuals to repentance for sin, spoke in the tone of the older prophets, especially of Elijah, and announced that the Messiah was at hand, that he would purify Israel with judgments and make expiation for the world's sin (Matt., ch. 3; Mark 1:1–8; Luke 3:1–18; John 1:19–36). The effect of his ministry was widespread and profound. Even from Galilee the people flocked to his preaching. The sanhedrin sent a deputation to inquire his au hority. While the ruling classes were unmoved by his appeal (Matt. 21:25), popular wonder and excitement were aroused, and the purely religious character of his message led the truly pious to believe that the long-deferred hope of Israel was at last to be fulfilled. After John's ministry had continued for some time, perhaps for 6 months or more, Jesus appeared amid the multitude and asked the prophet to baptize him. The inspired insight of the Baptist recognized in him one who had no need of repentance; saw in him, in fact, no less than the Messiah himself. "I have need," he said, "to be baptized of thee, and comest thou to me?" (Matt. 3:14). We are not to suppose that Jesus did not already know himself perfectly well to be the Christ. His reply rather shows the contrary: "Suffer it now: for thus it becometh us to fulfill all righteousness." The baptism meant for him, partly, self-dedication to the work which John had announced, and also the conscious taking upon himself of the sin of the people whom he had come to save. As he came from the baptism (Mark 1:10), John (John 1:33, 34) saw the heavens opened and the Spirit of God, in the form of a dove, descending and remaining on him, and a voice came from above: "This is my beloved Son, in whom I am well pleased" (Matt. 3:17). This was the full endowment of our Lord's human nature with spiritual power for his ministry. How truly human, as well as divine, he was through it all is shown by what immediately followed.

IV. 4. *The Temptation.* Jesus was not to enter on his work without adequate preparation. Realizing his vocation, he was led by the Spirit into the wilderness, doubtless for meditation. There Satan met him, and sought to pervert his purpose to selfish and worldly ends. Jesus himself must have related this experience to his disciples. While we are not to doubt the outward reality of the Tempter and the physical features of the scene as described to us (Matt. 4:1–11; Luke 4:1–13), we should not forget that the power of the temptation lay in the subtlety with which the world was presented to Jesus as more attractive than the life of stern obedience to God, with its probably fatal close. This temptation lasted for 40 days, and Jesus returned from it to the Jordan fully dedicated to the lowly, suffering lot which he knew to be God's will for his Messiah.

IV. 5. *Calling of Disciples.* Jesus inaugurated his work with no loud proclamation of his Advent. The Baptist pointed him out to some of his own disciples as the Lamb of God (John 1:29, 36). Two, Andrew and probably John, followed the new teacher. Simon was soon added to the number (vs. 35–42). The next day Philip and Nathanael were called (vs. 43–51). With his little band Jesus quietly returned to Galilee, and at Cana performed his first miracle, in which the disciples saw the first signs of his coming glory (ch. 2:1–11). We must be impressed with the absence of any attempt to make a public display. The new movement began with the faith of a few obscure Galileans. But John's account makes it clear that Jesus was fully sensible of who he was and what he had come to do. He was only waiting for the favorable moment to offer himself to Israel as the Messiah.

IV. 6. *Early Judean Ministry.* That opportunity was naturally found in the approaching passover (April, A.D. 27). From Capernaum, whither he and his family and disciples had gone (John 2:12), Jesus ascended to Jerusalem, and there proceeded to cleanse the Temple of the traders who profaned it. It was an act worthy of a prophet to reform the flagrant abuses of God's service; but Christ's words, "Make not my Father's house a house of merchandise," indicate that he claimed to be more than a prophet (v. 16). It was, in fact, a public summons of Israel to follow him in the work of religious refor-

mation, for only when the Jews had rejected him would he proceed to organize the new Church of the future; but he himself did not expect them to follow him. This is proved by his veiled prediction of his death at their hands (v. 19), while in the conversation with Nicodemus he clearly brought out the necessity of a new birth and of his own suffering (ch. 3:1–21), in order that any might enter the Kingdom which God's love had sent him to establish. For our knowledge of this early Judean ministry of Jesus we are indebted to John (chs. 2:13 to 4:3). It lasted apparently about 9 months. After the passover Jesus retired from the city to the Judean country, and having found the nation unwilling to follow him, he began to preach, as the Baptist was still doing, the necessity of repentance. For a while the 2 worked side by side. Jesus would not begin an independent work of his own until John's providential mission was plainly over. Both labored together for the spiritual quickening of the nation. Jesus began finally to attract more disciples than John did. This led him to terminate his Judean ministry, for he would not appear as a rival of his coworker (John 4:1–3).

IV. 7. *Galilean Ministry.* On the way through Samaria occurred Jesus' memorable meeting with the woman at Jacob's Well (John 4:4–42). But he hastened n. Arriving in Galilee, he found that his fame had preceded him (vs. 43–45). A nobleman from Capernaum sought out Jesus, who was tarrying in Cana, and secured from him the cure of his son (vs. 46–54). It was clear that Galilee was the place where he should labor and that the fields were white to harvest (v. 35). Then, it would seem, an event occurred which indicated that the hour for him to begin his proper work had indeed providentially arrived. The news came that John the Baptist had been cast into prison by Herod Antipas. The work of the herald was over. The old Jewish church had been sufficiently called to repentance and reformation, and it had refused to listen. Jesus began forthwith in Galilee to preach the Kingdom of God, to announce the germinal principles of the new dispensation, and to gather the nucleus of the future Church.

The *great Galilean ministry* of Jesus lasted about 16 months. He took for his center the busy mart of trade, Capernaum. In Galilee he was in the midst of a population prevailingly Jewish, yet in a region removed from interference by the religious authorities of the nation. His evident purpose was to set forth the true, spiritual Kingdom of God, and by mighty works to convince men of his own authority and of the character of the Kingdom. He asked for faith in himself. He unveiled the real character of God and his requirements of men. He did not apply to himself the name Messiah, for it would have been too easily misunderstood by carnal minds. He generally called himself the Son of Man. He did not at first speak of his death. The people were not ready to hear of that. He taught the principles of true religion, with himself as its authoritative expounder. His mighty works roused the greatest enthusiasm. He was thus enabled to attract wide attention, till the whole land was eager to see and hear him. But, as he foresaw, the final result was the disappointment of the people with his unworldly ideas. Only a little band faithfully followed him. Yet by his teaching he laid down truths which that band of disciples were to carry, after his death, throughout the world.

For the order of events in the lower or early Galilean ministry, see the harmony in the article GOSPEL. We can here only note the leading phases. The 1st was that of the opening of the work. This was marked by startling miracles, by the summons to believe the gospel, and by the awakening of enthusiastic interest in Jesus on the part of the Galileans. It included the events noted in the harmony, beginning with the 1st rejection at Nazareth and ending with Levi's feast. The close of this phase of his work, which lasted perhaps 4 months, found Jesus the center of universal interest in Galilee, and gathered about him a little company of devoted followers. We are not told much about his teaching as yet; but from what we are told and from the significant miracles he performed—such as the cure of the demoniac (Mark 1:23–27), the healing of the leper (vs. 40–45), the cure of the paralytic (ch. 2:1–12), the miraculous draught of fish (Luke 5:1–11)—it is clear that the burden of his message was substantially that which he announced in Nazareth (ch. 4:18–21), "The Spirit of the Lord is upon me, because he hath anointed me to preach the gospel to the poor; he hath sent me to heal the brokenhearted, to preach deliverance to the captives, and recovering of sight to the blind, to set at liberty them that are bruised, to preach the acceptable year of the Lord" (A.V.).

The aspect of affairs soon began to change, for opposition arose on the part of the Pharisees. This is the *second phase* of the *Galilean ministry*. Jesus visited Jerusalem (John 5: 1) and there healed the impotent man on the Sabbath. At once conflict with the rulers and rabbis broke out. Yet the conflict seems to have been purposely provoked by Jesus, in order that through it the difference between the spirit of his teaching and that of current Judaism might appear. We see in him now the spiritual interpreter of the O.T., bringing out its real meaning, and doing so (ch. 5) with express appeal to his own authority as the Son of God and the divinely appointed teacher of men. This phase included, besides John, ch. 5, the incidents of plucking the ears of corn and healing the man with the withered hand; see GOSPEL.

The conflict with the Pharisees and the continued advance of popular interest led next to the organization of his disciples, which constituted the *third phase* of this part of his ministry. He now appointed his 12 apostles, and gave in the Sermon on the Mount a description of the character and life of the true members of God's Kingdom. It is a sublime presentation of a genuinely religious life, in joyful unison with the heavenly Father, and consecrated to his service in the salvation of the world, the real fulfillment of the old Law, though utterly opposed to the formality and superficiality of Pharisaism, the ideal of trust and communion of man in relation to God. The Sermon on the Mount was not meant by Jesus to teach the way of salvation, nor did it constitute by any means his whole gospel. He, like the apostles, taught salvation through faith in himself. But in this sermon, over against Pharisaism and popular ignorance, he set forth that spiritual life which is the manifestation of the divine Kingdom. Faith in Jesus leads into this Kingdom.

The outlines of the new organization having thus been enunciated, we read, as the *fourth phase*, of a succession of miracles and tours through lower Galilee—Jesus being accompanied by his apostles—for the purpose of extending his influence. This phase extends in the harmony from the close of the Sermon on the Mount to the time when Herod inquired concerning the new teacher. During these months the popular interest in Jesus steadily increased, but the opposition of the Pharisees increased equally. The most notable point in the history just here is the great day of parables. The parable was a form of instruction

in which Jesus was unrivaled. It was intended to convey truth to receptive minds, and yet to avoid such open expression of it as would give his enemies a plea for interfering with him. The appearance of parables in his teaching just at this period shows the increasing gravity of the situation, necessitating a certain reserve on Christ's part. We must, at the same time, admire the incomparable skill with which he embodied in these simple stories the profoundest truths concerning the origin, progress, perils, and destiny of the spiritual Kingdom which he was establishing in the world. At length, however, the work in Galilee came to a crisis. Herod Antipas began to inquire concerning Jesus, and the fact was a warning that complications, such as had already led to John's imprisonment, and still more recently to his murder, might ensue. A sufficient opportunity had, moreover, been given to the people to test their relation to the truth. Just then an event occurred which decided the matter. Jesus had sought temporary retirement with the Twelve; but the multitudes had followed him to a desert place on the n.e. shore of the Sea of Galilee, and, in compassion for their needs, he had miraculously fed them, 5,000 in number, from 5 loaves and 2 fishes. The enthusiastic Galileans wished to take him by force and make him a king (John 6:15); but that very fact proved that they had wholly misunderstood his mission. It was time to bring his work to a close. From the beginning he had intimated that he had come to die, and that only by dying could he be their Saviour (ch. 3:14, 15). It was now time to prepare for the sacrifice. On the next day after the feeding of the 5,000 Jesus delivered in Capernaum the discourse, recorded in ch. 6:22–71, upon himself as the bread of life and on the necessity of eating his flesh and drinking his blood. Then, after some parting denunciation of the Pharisaic misrepresentations of religion (Mark 7:1–23), he brought his public ministry in Galilee to a close by retiring with his disciples from the region in which he had hitherto been working.

The next great period in Christ's life is called the *later Galilean ministry;* see harmony, in article GOSPEL. It lasted about 6 months. In it Jesus went, for the only time in his life, into Gentile territory, viz., the regions of Tyre and Sidon. Then, having apparently passed s. along the e. side of the upper Jordan and the Sea of Galilee, we find him in the region of Decapolis. Again he went far into the n. part of Galilee, and finally returned again to Capernaum. The period was mainly devoted to the preparation of his disciples for his death and for the extension of his gospel to all peoples. He preached little, and then mainly to Gentiles or to the half-heathen people on the s. and e. of the Sea of Galilee. Finally, near Caesarea Philippi, at the base of Mount Hermon, he elicited from Peter and the rest the full confession of his Messiahship, and, in connection therewith, he plainly told them of his coming death and resurrection, and of the necessity that every follower of his should be willing also to bear the cross. Shortly after occurred the transfiguration, in which 3 of his apostles beheld his glory, and in which, it would seem, he devoted himself finally, with sublime exaltation of spirit, to the sacrifice to which law and prophecy, as he was reminded by Moses and Elias (Elijah), had pointed. Afterward he repeated the prediction of his death, and, having returned to Capernaum, further instructed his disciples (Matt., ch. 18) in that conception of God's service as one of humility, self-sacrifice, and love, of which his own great act of self-devotion was to be the permanent example. It was now probably the early autumn of A.D. 29, and leaving Capernaum for the last time Jesus "stedfastly set his face to go to Jerusalem" (Luke 9:51).

IV. 8. *The Last Journeys to Jerusalem and the Perean Ministry.* It is impossible to follow in exact order our Lord s movements, for Luke, on whom we are mainly dependent for the record of this period, does not follow a precise chronological method of narration. But the main features of the period are clear enough. Jesus now sought to attract the public at ention of the whole land, including Judea. He sent out the seventy to announce his coming. He visited Jerusalem at the feast of tabernacles (John, ch. 7), and again at the feast of dedication (ch. 10:22), and on both occasions offered himself repeatedly to the people. He called himself the Light of the world and the Good Shepherd of God's flock, and boldly contended with the rulers who opposed his pretensions. He also moved back and forth through Judea and Perea, and explained in popular discourse and with more beauty of illustration than ever before the true religious life and the true idea of God and of his service. Here belong the parables of the Good Samaritan, the Wedding Feast, the Lost Sheep, the Lost Coin, the Prodigal Son, the Unjust Steward, the Rich Man and Lazarus, the Importunate Widow, the Pharisee and the Publican. Thus the announcement of the gospel became more complete, while the fierceness of the opposition of the rulers became more intense, until an event occurred which brought matters to a climax. Word was brought to Jesus of the sickness of his friend Lazarus in Bethany. Going to him, he found him already 4 days dead, and forthwith he eclipsed all his previous miracles by raising the dead man to life (John 11:1-46). The miracle was so stupendous and performed so near Jerusalem that it had a profound effect on the people of the capital; and the sanhedrin, under the lead of Caiaphas, the high priest, decided that the influence of Jesus could be des royed only by his death (vs. 47-53). Forthwith Jesus retired from the vicinity (v. 54), evidently determined that he should not die until the passover. As that drew near he began to approach the city through Perea (Ma t., chs. 19; 20; Mark, ch. 10; Luke 18:31 to 19:28), teaching as he went, but again predicting his death and resurrection, until he reached Bethany, 6 days before the feast (John 12:1).

IV. 9. *The Last Week.* At Bethany, Mary, the sister of Lazarus, anointed his head and feet as he was at supper, an event in which Jesus saw a prophecy of his coming burial. The next day he made the triumphal entry on an ass's colt into Jerusalem. By that he invited the anger of the rulers, offered himself publicly as the Messiah, and illustrated the peaceful character of the Kingdom he had come to found. The next day he returned again to the capital, on his way cursing the barren, though blooming, fig tree, which was so apt an emblem of the barren, though pretentious, Jewish church. Then, as 3 years before, he cleansed the Temple of the traders who profaned its courts, thus once more calling the nation to follow him in a purification of Israel. But though the pilgrims to the festival crowded about him and had hailed him at the triumphal entry as the Messiah, the rulers maintained their resolute enmity. On the next day (Tuesday) he again visited the city. Upon his arrival at the Temple, he was met by a deputation from the sanhedrin, which demanded his authority for his acts. This he refused to give, knowing that they were already resolved to destroy him, while, by the parables of the Two Sons, the Wicked Husbandmen, and the Marriage of the King's Son, he described their disobedience to God, the

infidelity of Israel to her high trust, and the certain desolation of the faithless church and city. For hwith he was questioned by a succession of parties who sought to find accusation against him or to weaken his reputation. The Pharisees and Herodians asked about the lawfulness of giving tribute to Caesar; the Sadducees about the resurrection; a lawyer about the Great Commandment; and he, having silenced each in turn, discomfited them by his questioning concerning David's address to the Messiah as Lord, for the psalmist's language clearly implied that his own claim to be the Son of God and equal with God was not blasphemous. It was a day of bitter conflict. Jesus vehemently denounced the unworthy leaders of the people (Matt. 23:1-38). When certain Greeks desired to see him, he saw in their coming a presage of the Jew's rejection of him, and that the Gentiles were to be his followers, and realized that the end was at hand (John 12:20-50). As he left the Temple he sadly remarked to his disciples that soon the splendid building would be in ruins, and later on the same evening he gave to 4 of them his prediction of the destruction of Jerusalem, the spread of the gospel, the sufferings of his followers, and his own Second Advent. This prediction shows to us that amid the lowering storm of Jewish hostility the vision of Jesus was clear, and that he moved on to his fate knowing it to be the appointed path to ultimate victory. It is probable that on that very night the plot was formed to destroy him. Judas, one of the Twelve, had, we may believe, long been alienated from the spiritual ideas of the Master. He was grieved also at Christ's refusal to seek a worldly kingdom; for Judas, John tells us, was an avaricious man. At the supper at Bethany he had become finally and fully conscious of his entire want of sympathy with Jesus, and as the disappointment which he felt over the failure of his hopes grew keener he resolved to wreak his anger on the Lord by betraying him to the rulers. His offer changed their plans. They had purposed to wait until the festival was over and the crowds had departed. But in the absence of any real charge against Jesus they were only too glad to avail themselves of the traitor's proposal. The next day (Wednesday) seems to have been spent by Jesus in retirement. He probably remained in Bethany. On Thursday afternoon the paschal lambs were to be slain, and after sunset the paschal supper, with which the seven-day feast of unleavened bread began, was to be eaten by all pious Israelites. On that day Jesus sent Peter and John into the city to prepare the passover for him and the Twelve. He sent them, no doubt, to the house of a disciple or friend (Matt. 26: 18); but, by the device of telling them to follow when they entered the city a man whom they would meet bearing a pitcher of water, he kept the place of assembly secret from the rest of the disciples, for the purpose no doubt of preventing Judas from betraying it to the rulers and thus possibly interfering with the last precious interview with the apostles. When evening came he observed with them the passover supper. For the order of events during the evening, see GOSPEL, harmony. The view of some that according to John's Gospel (chs. 13:1, 29; 18:28; 19:31) Jesus was crucified on Nisan 14th, the day on which the paschal lamb was slain, and therefore that he did not eat the passover supper at the regular time, but anticipated it by a day, appears to be quite inconsistent with the language reported by Matthew (ch. 26: 17-19), Mark (ch. 14:12-16), and Luke (ch. 22:7-13, 15), and the expressions appealed to in John may be explained on the hypothesis which we are following. [NOTE: John

13:1 does not mean that all that is recorded in ch. 13 was "before the feast of the passover," but is an introductory remark describing the loving spirit in which the fatal passover was entered upon by Jesus; ch. 13: 29, "buy what things we have need of for the feast," may refer to things necessary for the next day, on which the freewill offerings of the people were presented; ch. 18:28, "that they . . . might eat the passover," may mean simply "keep the paschal festival"; ch. 19:31, "the preparation," was not the preparation for the passover, but for the Sabbath.] It should be noted that in all probability Judas withdrew before the institution of the Eucharist, and that Jesus twice predicted the fall of Peter, once in the upper room and again while on the way to Gethsemane. John's Gospel does not relate the institution of the Eucharist, but it gives the Lord's last discourses with the apostles, in which he comforted them in view of his departure from them by revealing the unchangeable spiritual union between himself and them, and the mission of the Spirit which would bring to fruition their relation to him. It records also his sublime high-priestly prayer (ch. 17). On the way to Gethsemane Jesus further warned the disciples that they would soon be scattered, and appointed a meeting with him, after his resurrection, in Galilee. The agony in the Garden was his final and complete surrender of himself to the last great act of sacrifice. It was interrupted by the coming of Judas with a company of soldiers, obtained doubtless from the garrison near the Temple on the ground that a seditious person was to be arrested (John 18:3, 12), together with some of the Levitical guard and servants of the chief priests. Judas knew that Jesus was wont to resort to Gethsemane. Some suppose that he had first visited the upper room and, finding Jesus gone, followed to Olivet, at the base of which the Garden lay. Jesus, after a brief expostulation, submitted to arrest; whereupon his disciples fled.

The captors took him first to Annas (John 18:13), the father-in-law of Caiaphas, where he had a preliminary examination while the sanhedrin was being convened (vs. 13, 14, 19–24). It is not improbable that Annas and Caiaphas lived in the same palace, for Peter's denials are said to have occurred in the court of the palace, both while this examination before Annas and the later one before the sanhedrin were taking place. At the 1st examination Jesus refused to answer the inquiries and demanded that evidence against him be produced. He was sent bound, however, to the apartments of Caiaphas, where the sanhedrin had hastily assembled. No harmonious evidence of blasphemy, which was the crime they sought to prove against him, could be found; the high priest at last solemnly adjured him to say if he were the Messiah. Thereupon Jesus made the claim in the most explicit manner, and the angry court condemned him as worthy of death for blasphemy. The unjust spirit of his judges appeared in the ribald mockery to which he was subjected. It was, however, the law that the decisions of the sanhedrin must be made in the daytime. Hence very early in the morning the court convened again and the same formalities were gone through (Luke 22:66–71), and then, since permission of the governor was required for the execution of a criminal, they hastened with Jesus to Pilate. The indecent haste of the whole proceeding shows their fear that the people might prevent his destruction. Pilate probably resided in Herod's palace on the hill of Zion. But the distance from the high priest's house was not great, and it was still very early when the governor was summoned forth to hear their request. They wished him at first to grant permission for the execution without inquiring into the charges, but this he refused to do (John 18:29–32). Then they accused Jesus of "perverting our nation, and forbidding to give tribute to Caesar, saying that he himself is Christ a king" (Luke 23:2). After Jesus had acknowledged to the governor that he was a king (v. 3), Pilate examined him privately (John 18:33–38), and discovered the wholly nonpolitical and harmless character of his claims. He forthwith declared that he found no fault in him and that he would let him go. But the governor was in reality afraid to thwart the will of his intractable subjects, and when they fiercely demanded the crucifixion of Jesus he fell back on various weak expedients to shift the responsibility. Having learned that Jesus was from Galilee, Pilate sent him to Herod Antipas (Luke 23:7–11), who also was then in Jerusalem; but Herod refused to exercise jurisdiction. Meanwhile the crowd had increased, and the governor appealed to them to say what prisoner he should release, as his custom was, at the passover. He evidently hoped that the popularity of Jesus would rescue him from the chief priests. But the latter persuaded the rabble to ask for Barabbas. The message of his wife further increased Pilate's anxiety to release Jesus; but though he several times appealed to the multitude in his behalf, they were implacable and bloodthirsty. The governor was afraid to act on his own convictions and weakly gave permission for the execution. Yet while the scourging which always preceded crucifixion was in progress in the hall of his palace he could not rest. Again he sought to satisfy the Jews by the spectacle of Jesus bleeding and thorn-crowned, but they, made bold with success, cried out that he ought to die because he made himself the Son of God (John 19:1–7). This, however, increased Pilate's superstitions, so that again he examined Jesus privately and again sought to release him (vs. 8–12); but the Jews finally appealed to his political ambition and practically accused him of disloyalty to Caesar in abetting a rival king. This decided the matter. Pilate had the grim satisfaction of hearing the Jews proclaim their supreme allegiance to the emperor (vs. 13–15), and therewith he handed Jesus over for execution. Jesus thus died for no crime and without any real legal process. His death was literally a judicial murder. The execution was carried out by 4 soldiers (John 19:23) under the supervision of a centurion. With him also 2 common robbers were led to death. The victims usually carried their crosses, either the whole of them or the transverse portion. Jesus seems to have carried the whole (John 19:17), but it appears that his strength gave way and Simon of Cyrene was compelled to relieve him of the cross (Matt. 27:32; Mark 15:20; Luke 23:26). The place of crucifixion was a short distance outside the city; see CALVARY. The victim was usually nailed to the cross on the ground and then the cross was placed upright in the hole prepared for it. The crime of the offender was written on a tablet and placed over his head. In Jesus' case the accusation was in Hebrew (Aramaic), Greek, and Latin. Its longest form is given by John (ch. 19:19), "Jesus of Nazareth, the king of the Jews." Mark tells us that it was "about the third hour" (i.e., 9 A.M.) when the crucifixion was completed. If we remember that the proceedings began "as soon as it was day" (Luke 22:66), their completion about 9 o'clock will not seem incredible. It is moreover in accord with the haste which had characterized the action of the Jews from the beginning.

Into the incidents which the Gospels have preserved as occurring during the crucifixion we cannot go here. Such sufferers of en remained alive for several days; but the already exhausted frame of Jesus did not endure the agony so long. At the 9th hour, after 3 hours of miraculous darkness (from noon to 3 P.M.), he expired with a great cry. The words spoken from the cross, however, indicate that he retained his consciousness to the end, and that he fully realized the significance of all that happened. When he died there seem to have been but few present. The crowd which followed him at first had returned to the city. The mocking priests also had left him. A few disciples and the soldiers are all that we know to have been present at the end. The rulers were, therefore, not aware that he had died. Unwilling to have the bodies hanging on the cross over the Sabbath, the Jews went to Pilate and asked that their legs might be broken; but, when the soldiers came to Jesus for this purpose, they found him already dead. One, however, pierced his side to make sure, and John, who was near, saw blood and water issue from the wound (John 19:34). Jesus seems to have died literally of a broken heart. Meanwhile Joseph of Arimathaea, a secret disciple of Jesus, though a rich man and a member of the sanhedrin— who, however, had not consented to his Master's condemnation (Luke 23:51)—knowing that death had come, had begged for the body of Jesus. By him and a few others it was laid in a garden of Joseph's, in a new tomb hewn out of a rock.

IV. 10. *Resurrection and Ascension.* Now it is clear that the disciples were wholly disconcerted and overwhelmed by the sudden arrest and death of their Lord. Though he had on 3 recorded occasions forewarned them of his death and of his resurrection on the 3d day, they were too distressed to have any hope. Though he had told them to go to Galilee to meet him, they lingered in Jerusalem. Their conduct will not seem incredible nor the narrative doubtful to those who know the prostration which of en accompanies bitter disappointment and sorrow. Hence Jesus appeared to them in Jerusalem and its vicinity. The resurrection narratives in the Gospels are not intended, however, to be complete accounts of the events. They do not pretend to marshal the evidence for the reality of the resurrection. That consisted in the testimony of apostles to whom he repeatedly appeared (I Cor. 15:3–8). In the Gospels we have a number of incidents preserved either because of their intrinsic interest or for the sake of the spiritual instruction which they provided to believers. The order of events may very likely have been the following: Early in the morning of the 1st day of the week 2 companies of pious Galilean women proceeded to the sepulcher to anoint the body of Jesus for permanent burial. The one company consisted of Mary Magdalene, Mary the mother of James, and Salome (Mark 16:1). Joanna and other unnamed women were probably in the 2d party (Luke 24:10, which is a general statement, including the report of all the women). The former group saw the stone rolled away from the tomb, and Mary Magdalene, supposing that the body had been stolen, returned to Peter and John with the news (John 20:1, 2). Her companions went on, and entering the tomb heard from the angel the news of the resurrection and the message to the disciples (Matt. 28:1–7; Mark 16: 1–7). As they hastened away, we may suppose that they met the other company of women, and that all returned again to the tomb, but only to receive from 2 angels a more emphatic assurance and direction (Luke 24:1–8). The women then hastened toward the city with the news and on the way Jesus met them (Matt. 28:9, 10). Meanwhile Mary Magdalene had reported to Peter and John that the tomb was empty, and they had run thither and found it even so (John 20:3–10). She had followed them and, when they departed from the garden, she remained, and to her also did Jesus appear (vs. 11–18). All the women finally returned to the disciples and reported the wonderful news. It was not, however, on the testimony of these women that faith in the resurrection of Jesus was to rest. During the day he appeared to Simon Peter (Luke 24:34; I Cor. 15:5), later to 2 disciples journeying to Emmaus (Luke 24: 13–35), and in the evening, to all the Eleven except Thomas (Luke 24:36–43; John 20:19– 24). At that time he ate before them, proving the reality of his physical resurrection. Since, however, Thomas even yet would not believe, the disciples still lingered in Jerusalem, and on the following Sunday Jesus again appeared to them and proved to the doubting apostle that he had indeed risen (John 20:24–29). Then, it would appear, the apostles returned to Galilee. We next read of 7 of them fishing in the Sea of Galilee and of the Lord's appearance to them (John, ch. 21). By appointment also he met them on a mountain of Galilee and gave to them the Great Commission, with the assurance of his power and presence (Matt. 28:16–20). This may very probably have been the occasion when 500 disciples were present (I Cor. 15:6). Later on he appeared also to James (v. 7), but where we know not. Finally he brought the apostles again to Jerusalem, and leading them out to the Mount of Olives to a place where Bethany was in sight (Luke 24:50, 51) he was taken up into heaven and a cloud received him out of their sight (Acts 1:9–12). We have thus 10 appearances of the risen Saviour recorded in the New Testament, while Paul properly adds the appearance to him on the way to Damascus (I Cor. 15:8). There were doubtless, however, other appearances not recorded. Luke says (Acts 1:3) that "he also showed himself alive af er his passion by many proofs, appearing unto them by the space of forty days." Yet he did not continue with them in constant intercourse as he had done before. He rather manifested himself to them (John 21:1). The 40 days between his resurrection and ascension formed evidently a transitional period, intended to train the disciples for their future work. It was necessary to give them ample, repeated, and varied proof of the resurrection, and this was done as we have seen. It was essential to give them instruction concerning the necessity of his death and the character of the Kingdom which through their labors he was to establish. It was requisite to point out to them the fulfillment of Scripture by his death and resurrection, for thus alone would they see the continuity of the new dispensation with the old. For this instruction they had not been ready before his death, but it is repeatedly referred to as having been given during these 40 days (Luke 24:44–48; John 20:21–23; 21:15–22; Acts 1:3–8). And finally the experiences of the 40 days trained the disciples to think of their Master as absent and yet living; as invisible and yet near them; as risen to a new life and yet retaining the old nature and even the old, though now glorified, body, which they had loved; as exalted but still the same, so that they were prepared to go forth and proclaim him as the glorified Son of God and crowned King of Israel, yet also the Man of Nazareth and the Lamb of God who takes away the sin of the world. Meanwhile the Jews affirmed that his disciples had stolen his body. Fearing this, they had on the day of his death requested from Pilate a military watch to guard the tomb. When the resurrection occurred, accompanied, as we are told, by the descent of an angel who rolled the stone from the tomb, the soldiers were overcome with fright and afterward fled. Superstitious pagans as they were, they doubtless were little more affected by what they had seen than ignorant men usually are by what they consider ghostly appearances. But the Jewish rulers, who may possibly have accounted for the soldiers' report by supposing a trick on the part of the disciples, gave the men money to keep the matter quiet, and thus the report was given out that the body had been stolen while the soldiers slept (Matt. 28:11–15). When, however, the apostles began, on the Day of Pentecost, to give their testimony to the resurrection, and the number of believers in it grew rapidly (Acts, ch. 2, etc.), it was by force, not by proofs, that the chief priests tried to silence their witness and subdue the growing sect (Acts, ch. 4).

We have sought in this article to exhibit, not the teaching of Jesus, but the outward framework and historic movement of his life. In the latter there appears, as we gather it from the Gospels, a gradual, progressive revelation of himself and of his message, which constitutes one of the strongest evidences of the truthfulness of the accounts on which our knowledge is based. The reality of the humanity of Christ made it possible for him thus to appear as a real character of human history, related to a particular environment, and to present in his life a career which moved naturally, yet steadily, forward to a definite goal. His was a genuinely human life and, therefore, capable of historical treatment. At the same time Jesus knew and declared himself to be more than man (e.g. Matt. 11:27; John 5:17–38; 10:30; 17:5, etc.). As his self-revelation advanced his disciples realized his divine dignity (Matt. 16:16; John 20:28). Then later reflection and experience, under the illumination of the Spirit, made his divinity still more evident to them, until the last surviving apostle was led to become the 4th Evangelist and to present in his Lord's earthly career the incarnation of the personal divine Word. Yet John never forgot nor obscured the real humanity of Jesus. He gives us the full truth concerning the person of the great Master. "In the beginning was the Word, and the Word was with God, and the Word was God" (John 1:1), and "the Word became flesh, and dwelt among us, (and we beheld his glory, glory as of the only begotten from the Father), full of grace and truth" (v. 14). "These [things] are written," he concludes, "that ye may believe that Jesus is the Christ, the Son of God; and that believing ye may have life in his name" (John 20: 31).   G. T. P. (rev., H. S. G.)

Je'ther (jē'thẽr) [abundance, eminence, excellence]. 1. A descendant of Judah through Jerahmeel. He died childless (I Chron. 2:32; cf. vs. 26, 28).

2. A man registered among the descendants of Judah, but the lineage is not traced beyond his father, Ezrah (I Chron. 4:17).

3. An Asherite, apparently the same as Ithran, son of Zophah (cf. I Chron. 7:37 with v. 38).

4. A form of Jethro, Moses' father-in-law (Ex. 4:18 marg.).

5. The first-born son of Gideon. His father bade him fall upon the captives, Zebah and Zalmunna, and slay them; but the youth shrank from the deed, and they escaped the disgrace of dying at the hands of a boy (Judg. 8:20, 21).

6. The father of Amasa, Absalom's commander-in-chief (I Kings 2:5). See ITHRA.

Je'theth (jē'thĕth). A chieftain of Edom (Gen. 36:40; I Chron. 1:51).

Jeth'lah (jĕth'lá). See ITHLAH.

Jeth'ro (jĕth'rō) [pre-eminence, excellence]. A priest of Midian and Moses' father-in-law (Ex. 3:1). He is called Reuel (ch. 2:18; cf. Jos. Antiq. ii. 12, 1). Reuel, which means friend of God, seems to have been his personal name, and Jethro (excellence) to have been his honorary title. His 7 daughters tended his flocks; and Moses, who had fled from Egypt, rendered them a service which led to his introduction to Jethro's family and marriage with Zipporah, one of the daughters. Moses kept his father-in-law's flocks for about 40 years (Ex. 3:1, 2; Acts 7:30). When called by God to return to Egypt and achieve the emancipation of the Hebrews, Moses obtained Jethro's permission to depart, and took with him his wife Zipporah and his 2 sons (Ex. 4:18–20); but he afterward sent her and her 2 sons back temporarily to her father's house (chs. 4:24– 26; 18:2); see ZIPPORAH. After the passage of the Red Sea, which conducted the Israelites into the vicinity of Jethro's country, the Midianite priest brought his wife and her 2 sons back to Moses (ch. 18:1–7). He rejoiced in the deliverance of the Israelites, offered sacrifices to Jehovah, and suggested the appointment of judges when he saw that the Hebrew leader was wearing himself out by deciding even trivial cases personally (vs. 8– 27). See HOBAB.

Je'tur (jē'tẽr). A people descended from Ishmael (Gen. 25:15; I Chron. 1:31; 5:19). See ITURAEA.

Je·u'el (jê-ū'ĕl). 1. A man of Judah, family of Zerah. At one period he, with 690 of his clan, lived at Jerusalem (I Chron. 9:6).

2. A Levite, a descendant of Elizaphan. He took part in the reformation under Hezekiah (II Chron. 29:13, in A.V. Jeiel).

3. A contemporary of Ezra who with members of his family returned from Babylonia with the scribe (Ezra 8:13, in A.V. Jeiel).

Je'ush (jē'ŭsh), in A.V. once **Je'hush** (I Chron. 8:39) [He (God) comes to aid, or may he aid]. 1. A son of Esau by his wife Oholibamah (Gen. 36:5). He became a chieftain in Edom (v. 18).

2. A Benjamite, son of Bilhan (I Chron. 7: 10).

3. A Levite, family of Gershon and a son of Shimei (I Chron. 23:10, 11).

4. A descendant of Jonathan (I Chron. 8: 39).

5. A son of Rehoboam (II Chron. 11:19).

Je'uz (jē'ŭz) [counseling]. A Benjamite, son of Shaharaim by his wife Hodesh (I Chron. 8:10).

Jew (jōō) [Lat. Iudaeus, Gr. Ioudaios, Heb. Yᵉhūdī]. One belonging to the tribe or to the Kingdom of Judah (II Kings 16:6; 25: 25). Then the meaning was extended, and the word was applied to anyone of the Hebrew race who returned from the Captivity; and finally it comprehended all persons of that race throughout the world (Esth. 2:5; Matt. 2:2). Their language (II Kings 18:26; Neh. 13: 24) was Hebrew. For their history while they were in Palestine, see HISTORY, III. 4 (2). Dispersion among the nations, to the ends of the earth, was foretold as the doom of the people of the kingdom of God in case they forsook God and obeyed not his Law (Lev. 26:33, 39; Deut. 4:27; 28:25, 36, 37, 64–68; Isa. 6:12; 11:11, 12).

Jew'ess (jōō'ĕs). A woman of the tribe of Judah (I Chron. 4:18, R.V.) or of the Hebrew race (Acts 16:1; 24:24).

Jew'ry (jōō'rǐ). See JUDAEA.

THE PLAIN OF JEZREEL

311

Jez′a·ni′ah (jĕz′ȧ-nī′ȧ) ; in full **Ja·az′a·ni′ah** (II Kings 25:23) [Jehovah hearkens]. A captain of the forces, son of Hoshaiah, a Maacathite (II Kings 25:23; Jer. 40:7, 8; 42:1). He came with his men to pay his respects to Gedaliah, whom Nebuchadnezzar had appointed governor of Judah after the capture of Jerusalem. Jezaniah had no complici·y in the subsequent murder of Gedaliah, and seems to have taken a prominent part in attempting to bring the perpetrators to justice. He joined in appealing to Jeremiah, the prophet, to ask advice of God concerning the purpose of the remnant of the Israelites to migrate to Egypt (Jer., ch. 42). He was a brother of Azariah, or more probably Azariah is a corruption of Jezaniah (Jer. 43:2).

Jez′e·bel (jĕz′ē-bĕl) [ety. uncertain; perhaps, unexalted, unhusbanded]. 1. Daughter of Ethbaal, king of the Zidonians and former priest of Astarte (I Kings 16:31; Jos. *Apion* i. 18). She became the wife of Ahab, king of Israel. She was a woman of masculine temperament and swayed her husband at will. She was a devoted worshiper of Baal, and intolerant of other faiths. To please her, Ahab reared a temple and an altar to Baal in Samaria, and set up an Asherah (I Kings 16:32, 33). Though legally only the king's consort, and not the ruler of the country, yet she slew all the prophets of Jehovah on whom she could lay hands (ch. 18:4–13). When she planned the death of Elijah (ch. 19:1, 2), and afterward effected the judicial murder of Naboth, she similarly ignored the king's authority, though she condoned the deed (ch. 21:16–22). On account of these murders and other violations of the moral law, the divine sentence was pronounced against her that the dogs should eat Jezebel by the wall of Jezreel (ch. 21:23). The prophecy was fulfilled. When, 11 years after Ahab's death, Jehu executed pitiless vengeance on the royal household, Jezebel painted her face, attired her head, and, looking out at a window, called to him as he approached, "Is it peace, thou Zimri, thy master's murderer?" Jehu looked up at the window and said: "Who is on my side? who?" Two or 3 eunuchs looked out. "Throw her down," he cried, and they unhesitatingly obeyed. She fell in front of his chariot, which he intentionally drove over her, and her blood bespattered the horses and the wall. About an hour later, recalling that the dead woman was a king's daughter, he gave directions to bury her; but it was found that dogs, the scavengers of Oriental cities, had anticipated him, and had left of her nothing but the skull, and the feet, and the palms of the hands (II Kings 9:7, 30–37).
2. A woman at Thyatira who called herself a prophetess, and seduced some members of the Christian Church there to commit fornication and eat things sacrificed to idols. It is probable that Jezebel is a symbolic name. If so, it was given because of a resemblance between her and Ahab's idolatrous and wicked queen (Rev. 2:20, 23).

Je′zer (jē′zẽr) [form, purpose]. A son of Naphtali, and founder of a tribal family (Gen. 46:24; Num. 26:49; I Chron. 7:13).

Je·zi′ah (jê-zī′ȧ). See IZZIAH.

Je′zi·el (jē′zĭ-ĕl) [perhaps, God will sprinkle, or leap; cf. Arab. *nazā*, to leap]. A Benjamite, son of Azmaveth, who joined David at Ziklag (I Chron. 12:3).

Jez·li′ah (jĕz-lī′ȧ). See IZLIAH.

Je·zo′ar (jê-zō′ẽr). See IZHAR, II.

Jez′ra·hi′ah (jĕz′rȧ-hī′ȧ) [Jehovah will arise or shine]. An overseer of singers in Nehemiah's time (Neh. 12:42).

Jez′re·el (jĕz′rê-ĕl) [God sows]. 1. A fortified town (I Kings 21:23, wall; II Kings 9:17, tower; 10:7, 8, gate), in the territory of Issachar (Josh. 19:17, 18), not far from Mount Gilboa (cf. I Sam. 31:1–5 with ch. 29:1 and II Sam. 4:4). The Israelites encamped at a fountain in its vicinity just before the battle of Gilboa (I Sam. 29:1; cf. II Sam. 4:4), the Philistines following them to the same locality (I Sam. 29:11). Ish-bosheth ruled over Jezreel among other places (II Sam. 2:9); and it was one of the capitals of Ahab (I Kings 18:45), and also of his son (I Kings 8:29). Naboth was a Jezreelite, his vineyard was in close proximity to Ahab's palace, and he was stoned outside the city (I Kings 21:1, 13). Jezebel met her violent death in Jezreel (I Kings 21:23; II Kings 9:10, 30–35). The heads of Ahab's 70 sons were piled at the gate of Jezreel by order of Jehu (II Kings 10:1–11). The bloodshed in these sanguinary transactions is called by Hosea "the blood of Jezreel," and he prophesied that it should be avenged (Hos. 1:4). The crusaders correctly identified Jezreel with the Parvum Gerinum, now the village Zer′īn. Though in a plain, the site was an admirable one for a fortified city, standing as it does upon the brow of a very steep, rocky descent, of 100 feet or more, toward the n.e., with a splendid view all the way to the Jordan. The fountain of Jezreel, which is below the village, is copious and good. It is called 'Ain el-Meiyiteh. Another and yet more copious one, 'Ain Jālūd, is at no great distance. The ancient vineyards seem to have been to the e. of the city, where rock-cut wine presses now exist.

The term "valley of Jezreel" has been applied to the great plain intersecting Palestine immediately n. of Carmel, but this is better known as the Plain of Esdraelon (a Gr. modification of Jezreel) or the Plain of Megiddo (cf. Judi.h 1:8; 3:9; 4:6; 7:3). Jezreel is the gate to the valley of Jezreel, which is a broad deep vale e. of Jezreel descending to the Jordan (Josh. 17:16; Hos. 1:5). In the O.T. the valley of Jezreel is the vale down which Jezreel looks to the Jordan, and not the plain across which Jezreel looks to Carmel. In Gideon's days the Midianites and Amalekites pitched within its limits (Judg. 6:33). Through all bygone time it has been a battlefield of nations.
2. A town in the hill country of Judah (Josh. 15:56). It seems to have been from this place that David obtained his wife Ahinoam the Jezreelitess (I Sam. 25:43; 27:3). Probably Khirbet Terrāma in the plain of Dibleh.
3. A man of Judah, descended from Hur (I Chron. 4:3).
4. A son of the Prophet Hosea. So named because Jehovah had declared that he would avenge the blood of Jezreel on the house of Jehu (Hos. 1:4, 5).

Jib′sam (jĭb′săm). See IBSAM.

Jid′laph (jĭd′lăf) [he weeps]. A son of Nahor and Milcah (Gen. 22:22). It is not known where he settled.

Jim′na (jĭm′nȧ) and **Jim′nah** (jĭm′nȧ). See IMNAH.

Jiph′tah (jĭf′tȧ). See IPHTAH.

Jiph′tah·e′ (jĭf′thȧ-ĕl). See IPHTAH-EL.

Jo′ab (jō′ăb) [Jehovah is father]. 1. Son of Seraiah and descendant of Kenaz, who was reckoned with the tribe of Judah. He was the father of the inhabitants of the valley of craftsmen (I Chron. 4:13, 14).
2. A son of Zeruiah (II Sam. 8:16), David's half-sister (I Chron. 2:16; cf. II Sam. 17:25). Joab was, therefore, David's nephew. He was the 2d of 3 brothers, Abishai, Joab, and Asahel, all men of heroic type. He first appears in public life at the head of David's soldiers in

the war with Ish-bosheth. He commanded at the battle which followed the tournament at Gibeon, and was victorious (II Sam. 2:12–32). Abner, Ish-bosheth's commander-in-chief, after a quarrel with his royal master, had an interview with David. Joab reproved the king for allowing Abner to depart in peace, denounced Abner as a spy, recalled him, and, with the connivance of Abishai (ch. 3:30, 39; cf. ch. 2:24), assassinated him at a nominally friendly interview. Joab committed the murder in vengeance for the death of his younger brother Asahel at the hands of Abner at the battle of Gibeon (ch. 3:30); where, however, Abner had acted reluctantly and strictly in self-defense. Probably, also, a 2d reason was the apprehension of Joab and Abishai that Abner might be given the command of the army. David felt himself politically too weak to bring them to justice, yet he never condoned the crime (II Sam. 3:6–39). In the assault on the Jebusite stronghold on Mount Zion Joab was the first to enter the fortress, and as a reward was made the commander of the armies of all Israel (II Sam. 4:8; I Chron. 11:6). He soon afterward repaired a portion of the city (I Chron. 11:8). After David's conquest of the Edomites (II Sam. 8:13, 14; I Chron. 18:12), Joab remained in Edom with the army for 6 months, cutting off every male (I Kings 11:14–17). He commanded in the war with the confederate Syrians and Ammonites (II Sam. 10:1–14; I Chron. 19:1–19), and he pressed the siege of Rabbah so successfully that he could have taken the town by storm; but instead of doing so he sent for David that the king might have the credit of the victory (II Sam. 11:1; 12:26–29; cf. I Chron. 20:1–3). He obeyed David's order to put Uriah in the forefront of the battle that he might be slain (II Sam. 11:6–27). It was Joab who sent to David the wise woman of Tekoa to induce him to forgive Absalom (ch. 14:1–27); but he did not interfere further in the case until his barley field had been set on fire by the prince (vs. 28–33). When Absalom rebelled Joab remained loyal to David, and led 1 of the 3 divisions of the royal forces which defeated the rebels (ch. 18:1, 2). Then, in defiance of the king's command, he thrust 3 darts through the heart of the revolting prince, terminating his life (vs. 9–17), and afterward he spoke some plain though not unwise words to the king on his extravagant grief at the death of a rebellious son (ch. 19:1–8). David shortly afterward appointed Amasa to be captain of the host in place of Joab (v. 13), and when Sheba rebelled Amasa was employed to lead the forces sent to crush the revolt. Joab was overcome by jealous hate and, at an avowedly friendly interview, stabbed him dead just as he had killed Abner in similar circumstances; but this time there was no pretense of a blood feud between the parties. Then Joab and Abishai put down the rebellion (ch. 20:1–22). Joab thus again became commander-in-chief (II Sam. 20:23; cf. also I Kings 2:34, 35). He was opposed to David's numbering the people, and intentionally did the work imperfectly (II Sam. 24:1–9; I Chron. 21:1–6). When Adonijah set himself up for king, Joab went with him (I Kings 1:7), but, with his other supporters, deserted him on hearing that Solomon had been proclaimed king (vs. 28–49). David on his deathbed indicated his wish that Joab should be brought to justice for the murders of Abner and of Amasa. Solomon carried out the sentence. Joab, clinging to the horns of the altar in the court of the tabernacle, fell by the hand of Benaiah, chief of the bodyguard, and was buried in his own house in the wilderness (I Kings 2:5, 6, 28–34).

3. Founder of a family, members of which returned from captivity (Ezra 2:6; 8:9; Neh. 7:11).

For I Chron. 2:54, A.V., see ATAROTH 4.

Jo'ah (jō'á) [Jehovah is brother]. 1. A son of Obed-edom (I Chron. 26:4).

2. A Levite, son of Zimmah and a descendant of Gershom (I Chron. 6:21). Perhaps he was the Levite, son of Zimmah and descendant of Gershon, who assisted at the religious reformation under King Hezekiah (II Chron. 29:12).

3. A son of Asaph. He was the recorder under King Hezekiah (II Kings 18:18, 26; Isa. 36:3, 11, 22).

4. A son of Joahaz. He was recorder under King Josiah (II Chron. 34:8).

Jo'a·haz (jō'á-hăz) [Jehovah has laid hold of]. Father of King Josiah's recorder Joah (II Chron. 34:8). For others, see JEHOAHAZ.

Jo·a'nan (jō-ā'năn), in A.V. **Jo·an'na** [Gr. from Heb. Yōḥānān, Jehovah has been gracious]. An ancestor of Christ, who lived about 500 B.C. (Luke 3:27).

Jo·an'na (jō-ăn'á) [Gr. fem. of Heb. Yōḥānān, Jehovah has been gracious]. The wife of Chuza, steward of Herod the tetrarch. She was one of those women who ministered to Jesus of their substance (Luke 8:3), and one of the party who accompanied Mary Magdalene to the sepulcher of our Lord (ch. 24:10). For the man called Joanna in A.V., see JOANAN.

Jo·an'nan (jō-ăn'ăn). See JOHN 2.

Jo'a·rib (jō'á-rĭb). See JOIARIB 2.

Jo'ash. I (jō'ăsh) and **Je·ho'ash** [Heb. Yehō'āsh, Yō'āsh, Jehovah has given; cf. Arab. 'āsa ('awasa), to bestow]. The longer form is used in II Kings only, but the shorter form also occurs there frequently. 1. A man of Judah, family of Shelah (I Chron. 4:22).

2. A man of Manasseh, family of Abiezer and father of Gideon (Judg. 6:11, 15). He lived at Ophrah, and was apparently a man of substance. He had reared an altar to Baal and an Asherah. These Gideon was directed to throw down, and he did so. The idolaters demanded that Joash should surrender his son to be put to death for the sacrilege, but Joash shrewdly said: "If Baal is a god, let him plead for himself" (Judg. 6:11–32).

3. A Benjamite of Gibeah who came to David at Ziklag (I Chron. 12:3).

4. A son of Ahab (I Kings 22:26; II Chron. 18:25).

5. Son of Ahaziah, king of Judah. When Athaliah, the mother of Ahaziah, heard that her son had been slain, she massacred all the seed royal except Joash, and ascended the throne. Joash, then only an infant, escaped by the artifice of the late king's sister Jehosheba, wife of the high priest. He was hidden with his nurse for 6 years in the Temple. In the 7th year, Jehoiada, the high priest, summoned 5 captains of the royal bodyguard, put them under oath, and showed them the king. Five companies of armed men were arranged for (II Kings 11:5–7), probably consisting of 3 companies of the guard and 2 courses of Levites with spears from the Temple arsenal; on a certain Sabbath these 5 bodies were drawn up across the court of the Temple in front of the altar, representative men of the nation assembled by appointment, and the king was brought into their midst, crowned, and greeted with loud acclaim. Athaliah, hearing the noise, hurried into the Temple; but, by the high priest's orders, she was at once ejected and slain, leaving Joash now without a rival. Then Jehoiada framed 2 covenants: the one that the youthful ruler and his people should serve Jehovah, and the other that they should discharge their mutual duties as king and subjects. Then they proceeded to the house of Baal and broke it down, de-

stroying the images and killing the officiating priest (II Kings 11:1–20 ; II Chron. 23:10–21). Joash ascended the throne c. 836 B.C., but was the only legitimate king since 842. Joash was 7 years old at his coronation and he reigned 40 years. While a child the character of his rule depended wholly on his advisers. Happily, he was under the direc.ion of the high priest, Jehoiada, and as long as that wise and pious counselor lived, Joash did well, one notable measure of his being the repair of the Temple, though the people still continued generally to worship at the high places (II Kings 12:1–16). But on the death of Jehoiada both the king and his people apostatized from Jehovah and began to set up Asherim and other idols. Zechariah, the son of Jehoiada, denounced judgment upon the evildoers, whereupon Joash gave orders for his murder ; and the multitude, breaking out into riot, stoned him to death (II Chron. 24:15–22 ; Matt. 23:35). Soon afterward Hazael, king of Syria, having captured the Philistine city of Gath, threatened Jerusalem, and had to be bought off with the contents of the Temple treasury. When the invaders departed, Joash was suffering from sore diseases. Amaziah, his son, conduc.ed the government ; and in the course of 3 years, as it would appear, the servants of Joash slew him in his bed in revenge for the murder of Zechariah (II Kings 12:20 ; II Chron. 24:25) ; see CHRONOLOGY, IV. He was buried in the city of David, but not in one of the proper sepulchers of the kings. Joash was an infant in 842 B.C. and was 7 years old in 836 or 835 (II Kings 11:21), and his son Amaziah was 25 years old in c. 799 (ch. 14:2). The son was accordingly born in c. 824. The early marriage of Joash was desirable and was doubtless urged by the high priest Jehoiada, since Joash was the sole survivor of his family and in his offspring lay the only hope that so great a calamity would be averted as the extinction of the direct line of David.

6. Son of Jehoahaz, king of Israel. He began to reign c. 800 B.C., and reigned 16 years. He continued the worship of the 2 calves at Beth-el and Dan. Nevertheless he felt veneration for Elisha and sorrowed when the great prophet lay dying. Elisha told him to open the window e. and shoot out an arrow. He did so. The prophet then bade him take arrows and smite upon the ground. He did so, smiting the ground thrice. The arrows symbolized victories which he was to gain over the Syrians ; and had he struck 6 times instead of 3, the number of victories would have been doubled (II Kings 13:14–25). Afterward he furnished 100,000 mercenaries to Amaziah, king of Judah, for an Edomite expedition. A prophet directed them to be sent home. Though they had been paid in advance for the services which they were not allowed to render, yet they depar'ed in a rage and plundered the territory of Judah as they went along (II Chron. 25:6–10, 13). Perhaps on this account Amaziah sent Joash a challenge to fight. Joash remonstrated, but Amaziah would not forbear. A bat'le took place at Beth-shemesh, in which Joash was victorious ; and he followed up his success by breaking down a part of the wall surrounding Jerusalem and carrying off the treasures of the Temple and the palace, with hostages as guarantees against further disturbance of the peace. On the death of Joash, his son, Jeroboam II, ascended the throne (II Kings 14:8–16 ; II Chron. 25:17–24).

Jo'ash, II (jō'ăsh) [Heb. Yō'āsh, Jehovah has come to help]. 1. A Benjamite, family of Becher (I Chron. 7:8).

2. An officer who had charge of David's oil cellars (I Chron. 27:28).

Jo'a·tham (jō'á-thăm). See JOTHAM 2.

Job, I (jōb) (Gen. 46:13, A.V.). See JASHUB 1.

Job, II (jōb) [Heb. 'Iyyōb. Ety. uncertain ; cf. Arab. 'awwāb, one who comes back to God, a penitent ; or one persecuted, i.e., by Satan, his friends, or calamity, from Heb. 'āyab, to be hostile to]. A pious man of the O.T. who dwelt in the land of Uz (Job 1:1). He is mentioned for the 1st time elsewhere by Ezekiel (Ezek. 14:14, 16, 20). He lived under patriarchal conditions, in some district to the e. of Palestine and near the desert, at a time when the Chaldeans made raids in the w. (Job 1:17). There is no reason to doubt that he is a historical personage and that he passed through the remarkable experiences that are described, albeit with poetic license, in the book which bears his name. These experiences brought the question to the forefront, Why does God permit the righteous to suffer? and afforded the material for a magnificent philosophical poem.

The Book of Job, which belongs to wisdom literature, is a poetic book and gives an account of the sufferings of Job, of the argument carried on between himself and his friends concerning the reasons for his sufferings, and of the solution of the problem. The prologue (chs. 1:1 to 3:2), the introductions to the various speeches and especially to Elihu's speech (ch. 32:1–5), and the epilogue narrating the prosperity of Job in his latter days under Jehovah's blessing (ch. 42:7–17), are in prose.

The problem of the book is: Why do the righteous suffer? and the principal aim is to controvert the theory that suffering is a sign of the divine displeasure and that it presupposes sin on the part of the sufferer. The O.T. often observes that righteousness brings prosperity and that wickedness is the forerunner of misfortune (cf. Ex. 23:20 seq.; Lev., ch. 26 ; Deut., ch. 28 ; Psalms 1 ; 37 ; 73 ; Isa. 58:7–13 ; Jer. 7:5–7 ; 17:5–8, 19–27 ; 31:29, 30 ; Ezek., ch. 18). Apparent exceptions to the law of reward and punishment were accordingly a source of great perplexity. In the case of the sufferings of the righteous there was a tendency to conclude that because sin is followed by suffering, therefore all suffering is necessarily a consequence of antecedent sin. Naturally such a conclusion is far from logical, even though all men are born in sin and no one is free from error. Men are furthermore variously bound together in society, and the innocent may suffer through the ill deeds of the unrighteous or the guil.y ; or wickedness may not be detected, and apparently triumph, at least for a while, unchecked. In the argument Job does not claim sinlessness, but he maintains that his punishment is out of proportion to the magnitude of his sin.

In the opening of the book, Job is represented as being very prosperous, possessing many flocks and herds, a large number of servants, and a numerous family. Satan is permitted to try Job's faith in God, first by causing him to be despoiled of his possessions, and to be bereaved of his family ; when this means fails, Satan is further permitted to cause Job much suffering in body. Job's faith triumphs over all difficulties, and he is finally restored to more than his former prosperity.

The book between the introduction and conclusion may be divided into 3 main parts, each of which may be again divided into 3 minor parts. The introduction describes Job's prosperity and happy condition. In part 1, 1st subhead, we find Job's 1st affliction described, the loss of his property and family ; under the 2d head comes the 2d stage of the affliction, the attack on Job's person ; and under the 3d head, the coming of his 3 friends, Eliphaz the Temanite, Bildad the Shuhite, and Zophar the Naamathite, to condole with him. Part 2 contains the argument between Job and his 3 friends, this being threefold, each friend speaking 3 times (except the 3d, who speaks twice), and Job replying to each. This forms the principal part of the book. The 3 friends argue on the basis that affliction is always and necessarily a result of sin, and as Job accepts this general principle, but denies its application to himself, misunderstandings result, and the speakers are as far from a solution of the situation in the end as in the beginning. First, Eliphaz begins the argument by expressing in general the sinfulness of man and hinting at, rather than boldly asserting, Job's special sinfulness. Job answers, declaring his innocence. Secondly, Bildad continues in the same strain, insisting that the Lord cannot be unjust, therefore man must be at fault. Job answers as before that he is innocent, appealing to God to lighten his burden of affliction. Thirdly, Zophar follows with the same argument, implying more directly that Job must be a sinner. The 2d series of speeches (chs. 12 to 20) now begins. The same arguments are gone over by the speakers in the same order, the friends becoming more vehement and impatient of what they consider Job's obstinacy. In the 3d series (chs. 21 to 31) Eliphaz openly accuses Job of secret sin. After Job's earnest denial, Bildad falls back on the 1st position, and Zophar remains silent.

During the whole course of this argument Job has been profoundly conscious of his own uprightness, yet he cannot understand God's apparent harshness to him. His inward struggle becomes more intense as his outward situation appears more hopeless, but he remains firm in his determination that whatever befall him still will he trust in God. Then the thought bursts upon him that sometime, in God's own pleasure, he will be justified. It may not be in this life, but it will certainly come. That carries with it a conviction of immortality, and with the statement,

"I know that my Redeemer liveth,
And at last he will stand up upon the earth:
And after my skin, even this body, is destroyed,
Then without my flesh shall I see God,"

Job reaches a foundation from which nothing can afterward move him (ch. 19:25, 26).

In the 3d part of the book, Elihu, who until this time has been a silent listener, proposes to argue out the matter upon a different basis. Instead of regarding the afflictions of men as a punishment for sin, he declares that they are often sent as a means of strengthening and purifying the children of God. They are not, then, the expression of an angry and implacable God, but the chastening of a loving father. In this, Elihu appears as the messenger of the Lord, preparing the way for his coming, and offering an argument which Job could dispute or accept. Job accepts this view (chs. 32 to 37). Then Jehovah speaks and shows to Job that man knows far too little to justify him in attempts fully to explain the mysteries of God's rule; and Job humbles himself before the Lord (chs. 38:1 to 42:6). Finally, Job is restored to double his former prosperity, and his family is restored to the same number as before (ch. 42:7-17).

Many critics regard the prose introduction and conclusion of the book as an old source which the poet used as a framework into which to set his poetry. Moreover, the 4 Elihu speeches (chs. 32:6 to 33:33; 34; 35; 36 and 37) have received special consideration from critics, and the majority of scholars hold that they are not an original part of the poem, but were later incorporated into the work. The foreword in prose (ch. 32:1-5) and the introductory poetry (chs. 32:6-22; 33:8-11) are regarded as intended to introduce Elihu and to join these speeches to the dialogue between Job and his 3 friends. If Elihu's appearance on the scene be sufficiently explained by ch. 32:1-5, a difficulty remains in that he receives no consideration at the end of the book (ch. 42:7-9). A further argument produced is that the Elihu speeches seem to disturb the sequence between those of Job (chs. 29 to 31) and those of Jehovah (chs. 38:1 to 40:2; 40:6 to 41:26). At any rate, chs. 38:1, 2 and 40:6 seem to imply that the previous speaker had been Job, not Elihu. It has also been observed that chs. 32 to 37 have more Aramaisms than the rest of the book. Emphasis has been laid upon the teleological explanation of suffering that it should lead to knowledge of oneself on the part of the sufferer and become a source of blessing. This is held by some critics to be in direct contradiction to the view expressed in chs. 38:1 to 42:6: the power and wisdom of God are supreme, and man has to yield to this higher wisdom. On the other hand, it must be borne in mind that a number of first-class critics maintain that the Elihu speeches are original and that they present the only solution of the problem which the poet could give from his O.T. point of view.

Critics have also picked out certain passages in chs. 38 to 41 as from a later hand. Thus the description of behemoth (ch. 40:15-24) and of leviathan (chs. 40:25 to 41:26) are said not to fit well into the context. The genuineness of ch. 38 has also been questioned. Jehovah speaks twice out of the whirlwind (chs. 38:1; 40:6), and Job twice expresses his submission (chs. 40:3-5; 42:1-6). In this case, however, some notable scholars see no conflict or inconsistency; in chs. 38; 39 reference is made to the majesty and wisdom of God in nature, while the parallel passage (ch. 40:6-14) deals with God's rule in human affairs.

It should be noted, however, that the consistent progress of the argument is strong evidence for the literary unity of the book. The assumption of interpolations or supplements is needless so far as the dramatic development is concerned. But whether the poem has been supplemented by the addition of chs. 32 to 37 and 38 to 42, as many students of it contend, or not, these chapters are the work of a master mind and gifted poet, to whom God had spoken, and who with clear insight removed the errors of the popular doctrine that distorted the view of the moral question; also to the primary truths which Job had discovered they added a fuller disclosure of the truth, though not the final one (chs. 32 to 37), and directed attention to the humble position which it behooves ignorant and impotent man to take before God and the mysteries of the divine government (chs. 38 to 41). Behind the seen is the unseen (cf. chs. 1:6-12; 2:1-6), and the disputants had argued in total ignorance of the reasons for God's action and of the compensation for the sufferer which God had in store (as made known to the reader in the closing chapter, ch. 42). In fact this outcome of the argument (chs. 38:1 to 42:6) would seem to have been in the author's thought when he wrote the opening passage to his poem, for it accounts for his introduction of Satan into the plot and his intimation thereby that reasons may exist for God's procedure which lie beyond the ken of man.

According to William Henry Green, the 3 friends of Job "had really inculpated the providence of God by their professed defense of it. By disingenuously covering up and ignoring its enigmas and seeming contradictions, they had cast more discredit upon it than Job by honestly holding them up to the light. Their denial of its apparent inequalities was more untrue and more dishonoring to the divine administration, as it is in fact conducted, than Job's bold affirmation of them. Even his most startling utterances wrung from him in his bewilderment and sore perplexity were less reprehensible than their false statements and false inferences."

The scene of the poem is the steppe e. or s.e. of Palestine, where are located Uz, Teman, Shuah, and Naamah, but this does not prove that the author, whose name is unknown, came from that region. He probably was a native of Palestine. The date of the book cannot be fixed precisely; some critics have suspected the age of Jeremiah. Others maintain that the inner struggle of Job and the conflict between the theory of reward or retribution and actual experience point to a postexilic period. The language has an Aramaic or Arabic-Aramaic coloring, which also points to a late date. While some scholars say that the book was written during or shortly after the Babylonian Captivity, others more definitely place it in late postexilic times, probably around the 4th century B.C.

Jo'bab (jō'băb) [cf. Heb. *yābab*, to call loudly, shrilly; but cf. also S. Arab. *yuhaybib*, and Arab. *yabāb*, desert]. 1. An Arabian tribe descended from Joktan (Gen. 10:29; I Chron. 1:23). It is not known what district they occupied.

2. A king of Edom. He was the son of Zerah of Bozrah (Gen. 36:33; I Chron. 1:44, 45).

3. A king of Madon, who entered into the n. confederacy against Joshua, but, with his allies, was totally defeated at the waters of Merom (Josh. 11:1; 12:19).

4 and 5. Two Benjamites, a son of Shaharaim and a remoter descendant (I Chron. 8:9, 18).

Joch'e·bed (jŏk'ē-bĕd) [Jehovah is glory]. A daughter of Levi, who married her nephew Amram and became the ancestress of Miriam, Aaron, and Moses (Ex. 6:20; Num. 26:59); see EGYPT, III. 3.

Jod (jŏd). See YODH.

Jo'da (jō'dá). An ancestor of Christ, who lived near the time of the Exile (Luke 3:26). A.V., following a different reading, has Juda, i.e., Judah.

Jo'ed (jō'ĕd) [Jehovah is witness]. A Benjamite, descended from Jeshaiah (Neh. 11:7).

Jo'el (jō'ĕl) [Jehovah is God]. 1. A Levite, family of Kohath, and an ancestor of Samuel the prophet (cf. I Chron. 6:36 with vs. 34, 38). Probably he is not identical with Shaul (v. 24), but belongs to the collateral line descended through Zephaniah from Tahath.

2. The elder son of Samuel the prophet and father of Heman the singer (I Sam. 8:2; I Chron. 6:33; 15:17). Called once Vashni in the Heb. text, and so in A.V. (I Chron. 6:28). This name the R.V. relegates to the marg., placing Joel in italics in the text.

3. A Gershonite Levite, who with 130 of his brethren, of whom he was the head, aided in bringing up the Ark from the house of Obed-edom to the city of David (I Chron. 15: 7, 11, 12). He seems to have been the son of Ladan (I Chron. 23:8), and guardian of the treasures dedicated to God (ch. 26:21, 22).

4. A man of Issachar, and a chief of that tribe. He was descended through Uzzi (I Chron. 7:3).

5. One of David's valiant men, a brother of Nathan (I Chron. 11:38); see IGAL 2.

6. Son of Pedaiah and ruler of w. Manasseh in David's reign (I Chron. 27:20).

7. A chief of the Gadites in Bashan prior to the reigns of Jotham king of Judah and Jeroboam II king of Israel (I Chron. 5:12; cf. v. 17).

8. A Reubenite (I Chron. 5:4), probably he whose family had much cattle in Gilead (vs. 8, 9).

9. A Kohathite Levite, son of Azariah, who aided in cleansing the Temple during Hezekiah's reign (II Chron. 29:12).

10. One of the Simeonite princes who seized pasture land at Gedor (I Chron. 4:35–43).

11. A son of Nebo, induced by Ezra to put away his foreign wife (Ezra 10:43).

12. A Benjamite, son of Zichri, overseer at Jerusalem during the government of Nehemiah (Neh. 11:9).

13. Son of Pethuel, and the author of the 2d among the minor prophetic books (Joel 1:1). His history is unknown.

The Book of Joel opens with a description of dire distress caused by a plague of locusts and apparently aggravated by drought (Joel 1:4–12, 17–20; cf. Amos 7:1, 2, 4). Locusts are a natural figure for an invading army (Rev. 9:3–11); and the oldest interpreters of the prophecy regard them in it merely as symbols of Israel's foes. An actual devastation by these insects seems, however, to be intended in Joel, ch. 1; and probably in ch. 2 also, where they are likened to an army, for swarms of locusts occasionally come into Palestine from the n.e., and they quite frequently perish in the sea (cf. ch. 2:20). If locusts were actually wasting the country, the event served the prophet as a type of the dreadful day of the Lord and as an occasion for his message.

The book consists of a sublime address, comprising, 1st, a twice repeated tale of judgment, followed in each instance by a call to repentance and prayer (chs. 1:2 to 2:17), and, 2d, an announcement of the blessings, near and remote, material and spiritual, that follow upon repentance (chs. 2:18 to 3:21 [Heb. text, ch. 4:21]). The prophecy thus falls into 4 parts:

I. *The prophet depicts the distress* that has occurred or is impending, and calls upon the inhabitants to mourn (ch. 1:2–12) and to repent and cry unto Jehovah (vs. 13, 14).

II. *The prophet explains the event.* The day of Jehovah is at hand, and shall come as destruction from the Almighty (v. 15). A day of affliction: a people great and strong, like an irresistible army, executing the will of Jehovah (ch. 2:1–11). But even now repentance may avail (vs. 12–17).

III. *The result of repentance.* Jehovah, jealous for his land, promises to destroy the spoilers, to give seasons of plenty which shall make good the first suffering and loss, and not to allow that his people be again put to shame (vs. 18–27).

IV. *This deliverance is the herald* of deliverance "afterward." Having poured out the rain to make the earth bring forth abundantly, Jehovah will pour out his Spirit upon all flesh. The sun shall, indeed, be darkened, symbolical of the wrath of God, before the terrible day of Jehovah comes (as described in ch. 3:14–17); and whosoever shall call on the name of Jehovah shall be saved, for in Mount Zion shall be those that escape (ch. 2: 28–32). In those days, when Jehovah shall bring back the captivity of Judah, all enemies of the kingdom shall be brought to judgment. In one picture Joel exhibits God's successive judgments of the nations, and the final, universal judgment, culminating in the establishment of Zion forever (ch. 3:1–21 [Heb. text, ch. 4:1–21]).

The book bears no date, and so we have to rely upon internal evidence. The interpretation for an early date is given first.

1. Joel cites earlier prophecy (ch. 2:32). Part of the declaration is found verbally in Obadiah (Obad. 17), and Joel may have quoted from that book. He may, however, be alluding to a previous announcement of his own; or he may have had Isa. 4:2, 3 in mind, where both the thought and the several words occur. 2. The book mentions the scattering of Israel among the nations (ch. 3:2), but the reference is not to the 10 tribes specifically, but to the children of Abraham, Isaac, and Jacob, God's people and heritage, and is moreover a prophecy. So, too, the Captivity of Judah and Jerusalem is mentioned (ch. 3:1), but likewise prophetically in the spirit of Deuteronomy (Deut., ch. 28) or Hosea (Hos. 6:11) or Micah (Micah 3:12; 4:10). For the prophet and people are in Judah, Zion exists (Joel 2:1, 15), the Temple is standing (ch. 1:14; 2:17), and the service is regularly conducted, although the meal and drink offerings have been cut off by reason of the destruction of all the vegetation (ch. 1:9-13; cf. ch. 2:14). 3. The reference to past events begins with the last clause of ch. 3:2 [Heb. text, ch. 4:2], as the grammatical construction seems to indicate. Hostile nations had parted Jehovah's land among them, cast lots for the captives, plundered the Temple of its silver and gold, sold children of Judah to the Greeks, and shed innocent blood (vs. 2-6, 19). Some critics maintain that the allusions are not to the period after the Exile, nor to the time between the 1st deportation of the Jews and the fall of the city, nor to the earlier period when the Assyrians were invading the land, for: (a) Judgment is not pronounced against Assyria or Babylon or later enemies, but only against Judah's foes, Tyre and Sidon, Philistia, Edom, and Egypt (ch. 3:4, 19). Tyre and Sidon had forgotten the brotherly covenant (Joel 3:4; Amos 1:9), and had purchased Jewish captives from the Philistines and sold them to the remote Greeks. Philistia and Edom had done violence to Judah (Joel 3:4, 19; II Chron. 21:16, 17; 28:17, "again"). (b) There is no reference to Syria, from which Judah scarcely suffered before the reign of Ahaz (II Kings 12:17). During and after the reign of Ahaz, the prophets of Judah frequently refer to Syria as a hostile power (Isa. 7:8; 8:4; ch. 17; Jer. 49:23-27; Zech. 9:1). (c) Nor is any mention made of the Assyrians, who did not come into conflict with Judah until after the time of Ahaz, and who for a half century preceding Ahaz' reign had not been active in w. Asia. (d) There is reference to the Greeks, not as present in Palestine or as hostile to Judah, but simply as a nation afar off to whom the Phoenicians and Philistines had sold captive children of Judah, and as contrasted with the men of Sheba, a nation at another extremity of the earth, to whom Judah shall sell captives taken from Philistia and Phoenicia (Joel 3:1-8). Accordingly some commentators have come to the conclusion that the prophecy was uttered before the time of Ahaz. The position of the book as 2d among the Minor Prophets indicates that the belief was current at the time of forming the canon that Joel began to prophesy after Hosea had commenced his prophetic labors and before Amos had entered upon his. This factor, however, no longer receives consideration from critics. In fact, attempts have been made to date Joel anywhere from the death of Solomon to the time of Malachi.

There seems no doubt that chs. 1:1 to 2:27 (Heb. text, chs. 1; 2) refer to an actual plague of locusts, which is an omen of the approach of the day of the Lord (cf. chs. 1:15; 2:1, 2, 10, 11). In chs. 2:28 to 3:21 (Heb. text, chs. 3; 4) the theme is the day of the Lord.

The question is whether chs. 1:1 to 2:27 are to be understood in a predictive sense or whether the passage is to be explained either as a narrative of a past event or as a description of a contemporary calamity. If chs. 1:1 to 2:27 refer to a future event, some scholars have no trouble in deriving the whole book from one author. On the other hand, if this section alludes to a past or contemporary happening, these same critics feel that the book falls into 2 parts and so probably is to be ascribed to 2 authors. Yet it is to be observed that the words on the day of the Lord in chs. 1:1 to 2:27 refer to the future; Joel could easily have given future significance to a past or contemporary calamity. One proposed solution of the apparent difficulty is to suppose that chs. 2:28 to 3:21 were appended to the description of the locust plague in chs. 1:1 to 2:27, which was then adapted to the theme of the day of the Lord by the interpolation of chs. 1:15; 2:1b, 2a, 10a, 11b. The question, however, may be raised whether books were composed in that way in antiquity. The addition of the apocalyptic chapters (chs. 2:28 to 3:21) together with the supposed interpolation would be favored by understanding the locusts as a figure of the heathen nations. The locusts are compared to military forces (chs. 1:6; 2:2-9); the expression "the northern *army*" (ch. 2:20) or "the northern one" (J.V.) would facilitate such an interpretation, since the invasion of the heathen nations was expected from the n. (Ezek., chs. 38; 39). This view assumes that a plague of locusts was the occasion of Joel's calling the people to repentance and his receiving the words of the Lord (Joel 2:12, 13, 19, 20), but this calamity was interpreted in a different light by the addition of chs. 2:28 to 3:21. It should be borne in mind, however, that the acceptance of a late date of composition does not require a division of the book into 2 parts or a denial of authorship to Joel.

Recent scholarship quite generally interprets the evidence of the book as favoring a late date for Joel. Literary parallels with about 24 passages from other prophets (Isaiah, Ezekiel, Amos, Obadiah, Nahum, Zephaniah) may favor a late date. The language of ch. 3:1-3 hardly refers to any calamity less than that of the Babylonian Captivity. Ch. 3:17b seems to have more significance if spoken after the desecration of the Temple by the Chaldeans in 586 B.C. The foes of Judah are the nations collectively who are assembled for a signal defeat outside the walls of Jerusalem (ch. 3); this is a feature prominent in late prophets (cf. Ezek., chs. 38; 39; Zech., ch. 14). Joel mentions Tyre, Sidon, the Philistines, the Greeks, Sabeans, Egypt, and Edom but is silent about the Syrians, Assyrians, and Chaldeans; some consider this as evidence for a late date. There is no attack on the social and moral offenses of the time (except perhaps Joel 1:5) as we find in Amos, Hosea, Micah, and Isaiah. The book implies a nation united religiously: there are no denunciations of idolatry such as are found in the earlier prophets and even in Ezekiel. The one altar (ch. 1:13), the significance of the cult for the people and prophet (chs. 1:9; 2:14, 17), and the reference to the reproach of the heathen (ch. 2:17, 19) suggest a postexilic period. That there is no Northern Kingdom mentioned indicates that there was none, and Israel seems to be synonymous with Judah. No king is mentioned, but there are priests and elders, a condition best explained by the circumstances after the Exile. Edom's hostility to Judah cannot be limited to one particular period, and Egypt may be merely the type of a power hostile to Judah (ch. 3:19). There is no ground for limiting the slave trade to the time of Amos, and the reference to the Greeks may argue for a late date when Syrian slaves were in demand in Greece. The eschatological picture in Joel seems to be based on the work of previous prophets; cf. the calling of the nations to judgment (Zeph. 3:8; Ezek., chs. 38; 39) and the wonders of fire and blood (Ezek. 38:22). For the fertility of the land (Joel 3:18), cf. Amos 9:13; for the fountain coming forth from the house of Jehovah, cf. Ezek. 47:1–12 and Zech. 14: 8; for the outpouring of the Spirit, cf. Ezek. 39:29. Judah is dispersed among the nations (Joel 3:1, 2), and this favors a date subsequent to 586 B.C. Furthermore, the apocalyptic character of the book fits better into a postexilic period.

Since we have only internal evidences for dating Joel, it is not possible to give a precise date. Some critics, who divide the book, place the 1st part at c. 500 and the 2d part during the 1st half of the 4th century or even as late as the 3d century B.C. Others, who consider it a unit, date it c. 400 B.C.

Jo•e'lah (jō-ē'lȧ) [possibly, let him help]. A son of Jeroham of Gedor. He joined David at Ziklag (I Chron. 12:7).

Jo•e'zer (jō-ē'zẽr) [Jehovah is help]. A Korahite who joined David at Ziklag (I Chron. 12:6).

Jog'be•hah (jŏg'bē-hä) [lofty]. A town of Gad (Num. 32:35; Judg. 8:11). Its name still lives in Jubeihah, a village 6 miles n.w. of Rabbath Ammon on the road from es-Salt and the Jordan.

Jog'li (jŏg'lī) [led into exile]. Father of Bukki, of the tribe of Dan (Num. 34:22).

Jo'ha (jō'hȧ). 1. A Benjamite, son of Beriah (I Chron. 8:16).
2. A Tizite, son of Shimri and one of David's mighty men (I Chron. 11:45).

Jo•ha'nan (jō-hā'năn) [Jehovah is gracious]. 1. A Benjamite who joined David at Ziklag (I Chron. 12:4).
2. The 8th of the Gadites who joined David. He was made a captain in David's army (I Chron. 12:12, 14).
3. A member of the high-priestly line, who lived about 800 B.C. (I Chron. 6:10).
4. An Ephraimite (II Chron. 28:12).
5. The eldest son of King Josiah (I Chron. 3:15). He seems to have died young.
6. A captain, son of Kareah. He and his men made their submission to Gedaliah, whom Nebuchadnezzar set as governor over Judah (II Kings 25:22, 23; Jer. 40:8, 9). He warned Gedaliah of the plot to murder him (Jer. 40: 13, 14); and when the governor, neglecting the warning, was assassinated, he led the force which went to avenge his death (ch. 41: 11–15). He afterward counseled and carried out a removal of the Jewish remnant to Egypt, against the advice of Jeremiah (chs. 41:16 to 43:13).
7. A son of Elioenai (I Chron. 3:24).
8. A son of Hakkatan, of the clan of Azgad. With 110 males, he accompanied Ezra from Babylon (Ezra 8:12).
9. Son of Eliashib, but scarcely of the high priest Eliashib. Ezra went to Johanan's chamber and, refusing to eat or drink, mourned over the sin of those who had contracted foreign marriages (Ezra 10:6, in R.V. Jehohanan).
10. Son of Tobiah, the Ammonite, who married a Jewess in the days of Nehemiah (Neh. 6:18, in R.V. Jehohanan).
11. A high priest (Neh. 12:22), grandson of Eliashib (v. 23; cf. v. 11). In v. 11, the name appears as Jonathan, doubtless through corruption of the text. The Jews at Elephantine opposite Syene in Egypt, whose temple was destroyed in 411 B.C. by the command of a local official at the instigation of the Egyptian priests, at once sent word of the outrage to Johanan in the hope that he might be able

to secure them redress (Elephantine Papyri). Josephus, who correctly calls him John, says that he killed his brother Jesus in the Temple, believing that he was about to supersede him in the high priesthood. This murder was committed in the reign of Artaxerxes Mnemon, 405–362 B.C. (Jos. Antiq. xi. 7, 1; cf. 5, 4).

John (jŏn) [Gr. 'Iōannēs, from Heb. Yō-ḥānān, Jehovah has been gracious]. 1. Father of Mattathias, the instigator of the Maccabaean revolt (I Macc. 2:1).
2. Eldest son of Mattathias (I Macc. 2:2, in A.V. Joannan). He was surnamed Gaddis (in A.V. Caddis), a word of unknown meaning. He was slain by the children of Jambri, about 160 B.C. (I Macc. 9:36, 38, 42; and II Macc. 8:22, where he is erroneously called Joseph).
3. A man who obtained special privileges for the Jews from Antiochus the Great (II Macc. 4:11). He was son of Accos and father of Eupolemus (I Macc. 8:17).
4. Son of Simon, the Maccabee (I Macc. 13:53; 16:1). He became known as John Hyrcanus. About 142 B.C. he was appointed by his father commander-in-chief of the army (ch. 13:53). He met and defeated Cendebaeus in battle near Jamnia (ch. 16:1–10). When his father and two brothers were murdered in 135 B.C., and he himself was marked for destruction, he took the offensive against his adversary and drove him from Judea (Jos. Antiq. xiii. 8, 1). He exercised the office of high priest and civil governor from 135 to 105 B.C. Antiochus Sidetes, king of Syria, invaded Judea, and in the fall of 134 B.C. laid siege to Jerusalem. After a year, the Syrians took the city and dismantled its fortifications (Jos. Antiq. xiii. 8, 2 and 3). The death of Antiochus afforded John an opportunity to enlarge his domains, and he conquered Samaria and Idumaea. He also renewed the alliance with the Romans and thereby secured the restoration of Joppa and other towns to Jewish authority. He also repaired the walls of Jerusalem (I Macc. 16:23). The civil war which broke out in Syria in 125 B.C. and a succession of Syrian kings from whom, for one reason or another, he had nothing to fear, enabled John to maintain his independence without difficulty. He favored the Pharisees at the first, but when they unreasonably clamored for his resignation of the high priesthood, he went over to the Sadducees. With his death in 105 B.C. the power of the Maccabees and, with it, of Israel rapidly waned. See MACCABEE.
5. John the Baptist. The immediate forerunner of Jesus, whose way he was sent to prepare. John was born of godly parents, and was of full priestly descent, both his father Zacharias and his mother Elisabeth being descendants of Aaron (Luke 1:5). At the same time Elisabeth, the Levite, who belonged to the tribe of Judah (v. 36). The residence of John's parents was at a town in the hill country of Judea (v. 39), perhaps Juttah or the priestly city of Hebron. When Zacharias, in the performance of his priestly duties, was burning incense in the Temple at Jerusalem, the angel Gabriel appeared to him, promised that he should become the father of a son, directed that the child should be named John and be brought up as a Nazirite, like Samson and Samuel, and foretold that he should be filled with the Holy Spirit from birth and prepare the people for the Lord (Luke 1:8–17). John was born in the year 5 B.C. He spent his early years in seclusion in the wilderness near his home, w. of the Dead Sea (v. 80). In A.D. 26 he appeared as a preacher in the wilderness adjoining the Jordan. His ministry is believed to have been exercised during a Sabbatic year (ch. 3:1, 2), in which the people were relieved of labor in the fields and had leisure

to attend John's preaching. He came to announce a new dispensation, proclaiming the advent of the Kingdom of God and the baptism of the Holy Spirit (Matt. 3:2, 11), to prepare the people in intellect and heart for the reception of Christ (vs. 3, 8), to point out the Christ in the person of Jesus (John 1:15), and to show the union of the 2 dispensations in the Christ, as the Lamb of God (vs. 29, 36). He addressed himself with great earnestness and plainness of speech to the immense multitudes who repaired to him from all quarters. He urged the necessity of immediate and sincere repentance, the special reason assigned being that the Kingdom of heaven was at hand. The penitents, after confessing their sins, were baptized by John in the Jordan; and he became distinguished from others of the name by being called the Baptist. The baptism by water which he administered typified cleansing from sin. He did not regard it as enough, but directed his hearers to One who should come after him, whose shoe-latchet he was not worthy to unloose, and who would baptize them with the Holy Ghost and fire (Matt. 3:5–12). Notwithstanding this confession of inferiority to Jesus, our Lord sought baptism at John's hands. John remonstrated, which shows that he knew Jesus to be the Messiah; but he obeyed, for he recognized his own subordinate position (vs. 13–17). He knew Jesus from the teaching of his parents, and the correctness of this information was confirmed to him by the visible descent of the Holy Spirit upon Jesus at his baptism. By this sign he was authorized to declare Jesus to be the Christ (John 1:32, 33). Malachi had foretold the appearance of Elijah, the prophe , before the great and terrible day of the Lord, to turn the heart of the fathers to the children and the heart of the children to their fathers. John denied that he was Elijah in person (John 1:21); he defined his own mission and characteristics by simply quoting Isa. 40:3. But John came in the spirit and power of Elijah (cf. Mal. 4:5, 6; Luke 1:17), he was the messenger sent to prepare the way before Christ (cf. Mal. 3:1; Mark 1:2), and Jesus applied these predictions to John (Matt. 11:10, 14; 17:12, 13). There was a resemblance between the 2 men also in their cheap and coarse attire, which they wore to symbolize the renouncement of ease and luxury, and in their blunt manners, which rendered them fitter for the wilderness than for kings' courts (cf. II Kings 1:8; Matt. 3:4; 11:8; Mark 1:6). John had said of Jesus, "He must increase, but I must decrease"; and without jealousy he saw the fulfillment of his prediction (John 3:25–30). His public ministry was short, but his popular success was immense. At length, toward the close of A.D. 27 or in the early part of 28, having wi h his usual fidelity reproved Herod the tetrarch for living in sin with his brother Philip's wife, he was committed to prison (Luke 3:19, 20). While there, perplexed and impatient at Christ's method of developing his work, and perhaps feeling that he was forgotten while o hers were helped, he sent 2 of his disciples to ask if Jesus were the promised Messiah. In reply Jesus pointed to his works. When the 2 disciples departed, Jesus took the opportunity of passing a high panegyric on John (Matt. 11:2–15). John was the greatest of the prophets in that he was privileged to prepare the people for the Christ's appearance and to point out the Christ to them. The vindictiveness of the adulteress Herodias caused John's death. She persuaded her daugh·er, who had pleased Herod by her dancing, to ask the head of the Baptist. It was given her, and the headless body was soon afterward removed by John's disciples and buried. Finding their master gone, they

remembered his testimony to the Lamb of God, and became disciples of Jesus (Matt. 14:3–12; Mark 6:16–29; Luke 3:19, 20). Josephus at.ributes the death of John the Baptist to Herod's jealousy of his great influence with the people. He says also that the destruction of Herod's army in the war with Aretas, which soon after occurred, was generally considered a divine judgment on the tetrarch for the murder of John. Josephus makes the place of the Baptist's imprisonment and death the fort of Machaerus (Jos. *Antiq.* xviii. 5, 2). Machaerus, now called Mekaur (Mukawer), is situated in the mountains on the e. side of the Dead Sea, about 5 miles n. of the Arnon, and on the top of a conical hill 3,800 feet above the Dead Sea. The wall of circumvallation of the old stronghold still remains clearly traceable, while inside are a deep well and 2 dungeons. One of the latter may have been the prison in which John was confined.

6. Father of the Apostle Peter (John 1:42; 21:15–17, both R.V.). He is called Jonah in Matt. 16:17, R.V. See JONAH 2.

7. John the apostle. A son of Zebedee, and brother of that James who suffered martyrdom under Herod Agrippa I (Matt. 4:21; Acts 12:1, 2). It is reasonably inferred that he was younger than James, and that his mother was named Salome and was sister to the mother of Jesus; see JAMES 1. His father was a master fisherman on the Sea of Galilee, and his 2 sons aided him in his occupation (Mark 1:19, 20). John had attended the preaching of the Baptist at the Jordan, and was evidently the unnamed disciple with Andrew to whom John the Baptist pointed out Jesus as the Lamb of God (John 1:35–40). He doubtless accompanied Jesus back to Galilee, and attended the wedding at Cana (ch. 2: 1–11). But he had not been summoned yet to permanent fellowship with Jesus, and he resumed his work on the lake, sometimes together with his brother in partnership with Peter (Luke 5:10).

From their business Jesus called James and John to follow him (Matt. 4:21, 22; Mark 1: 19, 20). Later they were appointed apostles (Matt. 10:2). Jesus named them Boanerges, sons of thunder (Mark 3:17), evidently because of their vehemence. The impetuosity of their natural temperament, not yet fully chastened by grace, was shown when John rebuked one who cast out demons in Christ's name, but did not follow Christ in the company of the disciples (Luke 9:49); and when, finding their Master rejected in a Samaritan village, they wished to call down fire from heaven on the inhabitants (vs. 52–56). They showed selfishness once in joining with their mother to ask for the places of honor beside Jesus in his future kingdom; but at the same time their zeal was manifested, for they declared themselves ready to face death for him (Matt. 20:20–24; Mark 10:35–41). But the natural defects of their character were overcome, and their very vehemence, chastened by grace, became an element of strength and a glory.

John was a man of deep spiritual insight and loving disposition, and in consequence he was the disciple whom Jesus peculiarly loved. He was one of the three apostles whom Jesus chose to be with him at the raising of Jairus' daughter (Mark 5:37; Luke 8:51), at the transfiguration (Matt. 17:1; Mark 9:2; Luke 9:28), and at the agony in the Garden (Matt. 26:37; Mark 14:33). At the Last Supper he occupied the place next to Jesus at the table (John 13:23). He followed Jesus from Gethsemane into the palace of the high priest, to whom he was known, and to the place of crucifixion; and on the cross Jesus commended his mother Mary to John's loving care, and he accepted the trust (ch. 18:15; 19:27). When the tomb of Christ was reported to him to be empty, he ran with Peter to the sepulcher to investigate, and learned by what he saw that Christ had risen (ch. 20:1–10). With the other disciples he saw the risen Christ the same evening and again a week later (Luke 24:33–43; John 20:19–30; I Cor. 15:5), and like them John went to Galilee, as Jesus had directed, and again saw the Lord (Matt. 26:32; 28:10, 16; John 21: 1–7). While there, through a misunderstanding of an utterance of Jesus, the idea got abroad among the brethren that John was not to die (John 21:22).

After the ascension, he abode for some time with the ten other apostles in an upper room at Jerusalem (Acts 1:13), and after Pentecost he became Peter's colleague in active missionary work (ch. 3:1). Both were imprisoned by the Jewish authorities, and witnessed a good confession (ch. 4:19). Both were sent by their fellow apostles to Samaria to aid in the work begun by Philip (ch. 8:14). John was one of the apostles who remained in Jerusalem during the persecutions that soon assailed the infant Church, and he was still there, a pillar of strength, when Paul visited the city after his First Missionary Journey (Acts 15:6; Gal. 2:9). Five books of the N.T. are ascribed to him—the Fourth Gospel, 3 Epistles, and The Revelation. In the title of the last-named work the author is called John. Tradition fixes on Ephesus as the scene of his later ministrations, and it is probable that the 7 churches of Asia enjoyed his care (Rev. 1:11). When he penned The Revelation, probably c. A.D. 95, he was in the island of Patmos, an exile for the word of God and the testimony of Jesus (Rev. 1:9). The accession of Nerva (96) is said to have freed him from danger and enabled him to return to Ephesus. Polycarp, Papias, and Ignatius were his pupils. Polycarp's disciple Irenaeus states that he continued to reside at Ephesus until his death in the reign of Trajan (98–117).

8. **John Mark.** Mark the Evangelist. Mark, however, was only the surname; John was the proper, and probably the earlier, name (Acts 12:12, 25). See MARK.

9. A Jewish dignitary who took part with Annas, Caiaphas, Alexander, and as many as were of the kindred of the high priest, which perhaps he was himself, in calling the Apostles Peter and John to account for their preaching (Acts 4:6).

John (jŏn), **The E·pis'tles of.** THE FIRST EPISTLE OF JOHN is evidently by the author of the Fourth Gospel. For his identity, see JOHN, THE GOSPEL ACCORDING TO. The same characteristic phraseology is found in both works and the same way of constructing sentences. Both were evidently sent primarily to the same churches. This epistle bears none of the usual marks of a Greek letter: it lacks the author's name, its destination, the usual greetings at the end. Accordingly some scholars have called it a homily, but it is essentially a letter which was directed to the congregations of the province of Asia.

The opening words of the epistle suggest at once the Gospel's prologue, and parallels between the 2 books may be found in nearly every verse of the epistle. The epistle, moreover, has in view the world as the antagonist of the Church and the field of its operations (I John 2:2, 15–26; 4:3–5; 5:4, 5, 19), and warns against Antichrist and heresies which struck at the integrity of Christ's person. The writer probably had in mind a Gnostic movement which represented a Docetic Christology, i.e., that Christ had no real material body, but only an apparent body, or phan-

tom. Thus chs. 1:1–3; 2:22; 4:1–3 seem to be a polemic against Docetism. Together with this heresy went an ethical view which divided the firm bond between Christian faith and life, between piety and morality. The epistle seeks to apply to Christian life the truth whose historical revelation is recorded in the Gospel. The writer was one of those who had lived in personal contact with Christ (chs. 1:1–3, 5; 4:14) and writes in an authoritative manner (chs. 1:4; 2:1; 4:6, 14). How deeply he had absorbed the teaching of his Lord is proved by the similarity of phraseology and thought between the epistle and Christ's discourses in the Gospel. The Johannine authorship of the epistle is vouched for by Irenaeus and the Muratori Fragment; while earlier quotations by Polycarp, Papias, etc., prove its use in the Church in the early part of the 2d century.

Its train of thought may be outlined as follows: After the introduction (ch. 1:1–4), in which John declares the purpose of his ministry to be the declaration to men of the manifestation of the life-giving, divine Word, in order that they may have joyful fellowship in Him with the original apostles, he teaches that the character of God, as learned from Christ, must determine the character of the Christian's inward and outward life (chs. 1:5 to 2:6); hence he urges his readers to love the brethren, and warns against love of the world and heretical teaching (ch. 2:7–27). He next insists (chs. 2:28 to 3:24) on the necessity of doing righteousness, and so of abiding in God, in view of the coming Second Advent of Christ; since at it our divine sonship will be fully manifested and that sonship is distinguished by obedience and love. Then he reminds his readers (ch. 4) that the test of having the Spirit of God is to be found in the true confession of Christ as the incarnate Son of God, in adherence to apostolic teaching, and in love; and that right faith in Jesus is the condition of the whole spiritual life of love (ch. 5:1–12); I John 5:7, A.V., is a spurious interpolation deriving from Latin authors of the 5th century; no Greek MS. earlier than the 15th century and no independent Greek father has these words. In the conclusion (ch. 5:13–21) he tersely summarizes the purpose of the epistle as intended to confirm them in faith and communion with God, and solemnly recites the historical and spiritual facts on which their eternal life steadfastly reposes.

It can hardly be determined whether the epistle was written before or after the Gospel. It seems certain, however, that the epistle is close to the time and place of the Gospel.

THE SECOND EPISTLE OF JOHN. This is written in the form of a Hellenistic private letter and contains just the number of words (as does III John likewise) which could conveniently be written on a single sheet of papyrus. Quite in accord with the reserve shown by the Apostle John, the author of the Second Epistle calls himself "the elder," a designation used by Peter of himself (I Peter 5:1) and given by Papias to all the apostles. The author writes to "the elect lady and her children," expressing his joy at the Christian life of her children and warning her against heretical teachers, as in I John. The brevity of the epistle easily explains the paucity of references to it in the earliest writers. In fact, the external evidence is larger than would be expected. The most ancient historical testimony ascribes the epistle to the Apostle John. Clement of Alexandria was acquainted with at least one shorter epistle by the apostle, and Irenaeus quotes II John 11 as coming from John the disciple of the Lord. Moreover, the Johannine authorship is abundantly proved by the remarkable coincidences of language and thought with I John, and no motive can be imagined for its forgery.

It is generally supposed that by "the elect lady and her children" is meant a church and its spiritual children. Some consider her an individual named Kyria (Gr. for lady). It may perhaps seem strange that the writer feels it necessary to exhort the lady "that we love one another" (v. 5; cf. also 2d person plural in vs. 9, 10). If the lady is the church, the exhortation is natural. The children of the elect sister (v. 13) accordingly would be the members of a sister church.

THE THIRD EPISTLE OF JOHN. This too is in the form of a Hellenistic private letter. Another brief letter addressed to "the elder" to Gaius the well-beloved, expressing joy at the hospitality to the brethren which Gaius had shown, and urging his friend to continue to imitate that which is good. Reference is also made to a certain Diotrephes who had opposed the writer; and on the other hand to a Demetrius who is praised. It is impossible to identify this Gaius with any of that name mentioned in the N.T.; see GAIUS 3. He appears to have been a prominent man in one of the churches of Asia, but not an officer of the church. This epistle is remarkably like the first and second in style and thought, and there is no reason to doubt that the three were by the same writer. See JOHN, THE GOSPEL ACCORDING TO.

All John's epistles, with those of James, Peter, and Jude, are frequently included in the number of the so-called "catholic" or "general" epistles, i.e., those addressed not to particular churches or persons, but to large or many communities. I John was no doubt sent to the churches of Asia, among which the Fourth Gospel was first issued. To II and III John, however, this title does not apply, nor are they styled "general" in A.V. or R.V. They were probably placed among the "general" epistles simply because, being brief, they were attached to I John. G. T. P. (rev., H. S. G.)

John (jŏn), **The Rev′e·la′tion of.** See REVELATION.

John (jŏn), **The Gos′pel Ac·cord′ing to.** Like the other Gospels the Fourth does not mention the writer's name, but both internal and external considerations lend some support to the traditional belief that the work was written by the Apostle John.

I. *Internal evidence.* 1. The writer was one of the apostles. This appears from his use of the 1st person plural (ch. 1:14 and perhaps ch. 21:24) and from many items of minute description, especially concerning the impression made on the disciples by events in Christ's life, etc. (chs. 1:37; 2:11, 17; 4:27, 54; 9:2; 11:8–16; 12:4–6, 21, 22; 13:23–26; 18:15; 19:26, 27, 35; 20:8), and from the explicit statement in ch. 21:24. 2. He mentions a "disciple whom Jesus loved" (chs. 13:23; 19:26; 20:2; 21:7, 20, 21), who, in ch. 21:24, is said to be the author. All the apostles, however, are mentioned by name in the book except Matthew, James the son of Alphaeus, Simon Zelotes, and the sons of Zebedee. The 3 former did not belong to the narrower circle of intimate disciples, to one of whom this title would alone be applicable, and James the son of Zebedee died early (Acts 12:2). John, therefore, alone remains. 3. That the writer was a Jew is proved incontestably by the strongly Aramaic character of his style in writing Greek. 4. He shows intimate acquaintance with the geography, history, and customs of the Jews during Christ's ministry (e.g., chs. 1:21, 28, 46; 2:6; 3:23; 4:5, 27, R.V.; 5:2, 3; 7:40–52; 9:7; 10:22, 23; 11:18; 18:28; 19:31), and his book gives more personal details than the Gospels. The internal evidence thus harmonizes strik-

ingly with the tradition of Johannine authorship.

II. *External evidence* is of two kinds: (a) explicit mention of authorship and (b) implicit high regard for the Fourth Gospel shown by the use made of it in early documents. Irenaeus (bishop of Lyons c. 185), a disciple of Polycarp, who in turn had been a disciple of John, is explicit in his statement that John wrote this Gospel in Ephesus after the other Gospels had been issued. At the end of the 2d century and beginning of the 3d, Clement of Alexandria, Tertullian, and Origen bear witness to the same tradition.

The 2d type of external evidence attests the existence of the Fourth Gospel and the high regard in which it was held. The Didache (c. 110) seems to be indebted for some of its phrases to Johannine terminology. The Ignatian epistles (not later than 117) show that the Gospel was familiar and authoritative to Ignatius and probably as well to the churches of Asia Minor at the beginning of the 2d century. The earliest known fragment of any part of the N.T. is part of a leaf of a papyrus codex (dated paleographically c. 125), which bears a few verses of John, ch. 18. Inasmuch as the fragment was found in Egypt, it furnishes tangible evidence to the early and widespread dissemination of the Fourth Gospel. In addition, another papyrus fragment (dating from c. 150), relating incidents in the life of Jesus, uses the Fourth Gospel as one of its sources. Justin Martyr (c. 150) very likely alludes to it, and evidently considered it one of "the memoirs of the apostles," which he says were called Gospels and were written by the apostles and their companions. The apocryphal Gospel of Peter and Acts of John (both c. 150) show clear traces of the Johannine thought forms. Tatian's *Diatessaron* (c. 170) was a harmony of the same 4 Gospels that are recognized as canonical today. The Sinaitic MS. of the Old Syriac Gospels indicates that in the 2d century the Syrian Church accepted our four Gospels. Finally, it is certain that even the earliest Gnostic heretics of the 2d century (e.g. Basilides c. 120–140, Heracleon c. 160–180, and perhaps Valentinus c. 140–160) quoted and even commented upon the Fourth Gospel. Thus external evidence seems to confirm the impression given by internal evidence regarding the Apostle John as the author, and it indicates furthermore over how wide a geographic area the Fourth Gospel was received as authoritative in the early postapostolic Church.

It must be stated, however, that many scholars today do not feel the cogency of the above reasoning. They believe that the author of the Fourth Gospel was distinct from John the apostle, who was the *witness* to whose testimony the author and his followers appeal (John 19:35; 21:24). The Evangelist (the author proper) was, according to these scholars, a disciple and follower of John the son of Zebedee (the apostle), and wrote from the reminiscences and teaching of his master, an eyewitness. His name is either unknown to us or, more likely, was John the Presbyter or Elder (cf. II John 1 and III John 1). Thus, though the Apostle John was responsible for the Gospel, it was actually written by the pen of another; it is according to this view "the Gospel of John the Elder according to John the apostle."

No more likely explanation of the Fourth Gospel has been found than that it emanated from the Apostle John. Whether the Fourth Gospel was written directly or indirectly by John the apostle, evidence points to its composition in Asia Minor (tradition says Ephesus) in the last quarter of the 1st century. The opponents of Jesus are called simply the Jews (chs. 1:19; 2:18; 5:10; 7:15, etc.), explanations are given about the Jewish feasts (chs. 6:4; 7:2; 11:55; 19:31), the Sea of Galilee is explained by its Gentile name, Sea of Tiberias (ch. 6:1), and the designation in the prologue of Christ as the Word of God points to a period when Christianity was confronted with such philosophical tendencies as we know existed in Asia Minor. This explains also the apparent purpose of the book. It was to give Christ's testimony to himself as the incarnate Son of God and Saviour of the world (ch. 20: 30, 31). The author assumes that his readers are acquainted with many of the incidents that are recorded in the Synoptic Gospels; see GOSPEL. They had not given those great discourses of the Lord, in which he had replied to the attacks of the Jews upon his divine claims or had unfolded to his disciples the mysteries of his being and their spiritual relations to himself. This self-testimony of Jesus John determined to set down, especially since heresies had risen which denied some aspects of the person of Christ. With this he combined also, as was natural, many items of personal reminiscence. The result was to provide the Church with a complete portrayal of her divine-human Lord.

John's Gospel begins with a prologue (ch. 1:1–18), in which the apostle summarizes the great truth about to be shown in the life of Christ, viz. the existence of a 2d divine Person whose office it is to reveal God and who is, therefore, called the Word, who, besides being the universal source of life and light to creation, became incarnate as Jesus Christ, and thus to those who believed revealed God and imparted salvation. He then relates: 1. The opening testimonies to Jesus given by John the Baptist and by Jesus himself to his first disciples (chs. 1:19 to 2:11). 2. Christ's revelation of himself in a series of acts and, still more, of discourses addressed to inquirers or to his adversaries (chs. 2:12 to 12:50). This includes (a) his testimony at his first passover (ch. 2:12–25), and the discourse with Nicodemus (ch. 3:1–21), together with the renewed testimony of the Baptist (vs. 22–36); (b) the conversation with the woman of Samaria (ch. 4:1–42); (c) the 2d miracle in Galilee (vs. 43–54); (d) Christ's defense to the Jews of his divine dignity and authority (ch. 5); (e) his presentation of himself as the bread of life (ch. 6); (f) his renewed defense of his authority and dignity at the feast of tabernacles (chs. 7; 8) [NOTE: In all but one of the oldest MSS. chs. 7:53 to 8:11 is omitted and in others it is marked as doubtful, or assigned to a different place or to another Gospel altogether. It is to be regarded as a stray fragment of trustworthy tradition which the Church was unwilling to lose.]; (g) the healing of the blind man and parable of the Good Shepherd (chs. 9:1 to 10:21); (h) Christ's final testimony to the Jews (vs. 22–42); (j) the raising of Lazarus and its consequences (ch. 11); (k) the testimony given at Bethany, in the triumphal entry, and at the visit of the Greeks (ch. 12). 3. Christ's revelation of himself in connection with his death and resurrection (chs. 13:1 to 21:25). This includes (a) his last discourses with his disciples (chs. 13 to 17); (b) his arrest, trial, and crucifixion, in which he bore witness, particularly before Pilate, to his person and work (chs. 18; 19); (c) his resurrection and certain testimonies connected with it (chs. 20; 21; ch. 21 is evidently an addition by the author to his work, which was originally intended to close with ch. 20). The result is to show that in the human Jesus there was the eternal Son of God, who by his person, teaching, and redeeming work has revealed God and secured eternal life to those who receive him. John thus represents the mission of Jesus as the climax of God's self-revelation and as the pro-

curement for believers of that light which consists in knowledge of the highest truth and of that life which consists in spiritual union with God, which together constitute the perfect good and the everlasting salvation. "These [things]," he says, "are written, that ye may believe that Jesus is the Christ, the Son of God; and that believing ye may have life in his name" (ch. 20:31).

G. T. P. (rev., H. S. G.)

Joi'a·da (joi'å-då) [Jehovah has known]. 1. A son of Paseah, who repaired a gate of Jerusalem (Neh. 3:6; in A.V. Jehoiada).

2. A high priest, great-grandson of Jeshua (Neh. 12:10). One of his sons married a daughter of Sanballat, the governor of Samaria, and for thus defiling the priesthood was expelled, probably from Jerusalem, by Nehemiah (ch. 13:28).

Joi'a·kim (joi'å-kīm) [Jehovah raises up, establishes]. A high priest, son of Jeshua (Neh. 12:10, 12, 21–26), in the reign of [Arta]xerxes (Jos. Antiq. xi. 5, 1).

Joi'a·rib (joi'å-rīb) or **Je·hoi'a·rib** [Jehovah pleads, contends]. 1. A descendant of Aaron. See JEHOIARIB.

2. A chief of the priests who returned from Babylon with Zerubbabel (Neh. 12:6, 7). In the next generation a father's house bore this name (v. 19; cf. I Macc. 2:1, Joarib being the Greek form).

3. A man of understanding who was returning from Babylon with Ezra and was sent with others from the encampment on the river of Ahava to secure Levites and Ne hinim for the service of the Temple (Ezra 8:16, 17).

4. A man of Judah, descended from a certain Zechariah (Neh. 11:5).

Jok'de·am (jŏk'dē-ăm). A town in the mountains of Judah (Josh. 15:56). It may be Khirbet Raka', between Yatta and Tell Zif.

Jo'kim (jō'kĭm) [see JOIAKIM]. A man of Judah, family of Shelah (I Chron. 4:22).

Jok'me·am (jŏk'mē-ăm) [let the people arise]. A town of Ephraim (I Chron. 6:68), apparently near Abel-meholah (I Kings 4:12, where A.V., contrary to the Hebrew text, calls it Jokneam). The Kohathite Levites were given residence in it (I Chron. 6:66, 68). Instead of this town, Kibzaim is given in Josh. 21:22, and is commonly believed to be another name of the same place.

Jok'ne·am (jŏk'nē-ăm) [perhaps, let the people acquire]. 1. A town on or near Mount Carmel (Josh. 12:22). The boundary line of the tribe of Zebulun extended to the river that is before Jokneam (ch. 19:11). It was given with its suburbs to the Merarite Levites (ch. 21:34). It is identified with Tell Kaimūn, probably the Cyamon of Judith 7:3, on the s. margin of the Plain of Esdraelon, on the slopes of Carmel, a little s. of the Kishon, and about 15 miles n.w. by w. of Jezreel; it lies on the modern route from Jenin to Haifa.

2. A place mentioned in A.V. of I Kings 4:12; but see JOKMEAM.

Jok'shan (jŏk'shăn). A tribe and its progenitor descended from Abraham by Keturah (Gen. 25:1, 2). From Jokshan sprang Sheba and Dedan (v. 3). Exact place of settlement unknown.

Jok'tan (jŏk'tăn) [cf. Arab. wakaṭa, to beat unmercifully]. A person or rather tribe descended from Shem through Eber and from whom 13 tribes of Arabia sprang (Gen. 10: 25, 29; I Chron. 1:19–23).

Jok'the·el (jŏk'thē-ĕl). 1. A village in the lowland of Judah (Josh. 15:33, 38).

2. A name given by Amaziah, king of Judah, to Sela, now Petra, when he had taken it in war (II Kings 14:7, R.V.).

Jo'na (jō'nà). See JONAH 2.

Jon'a·dab (jŏn'à·dăb) and **Je·hon'a·dab** [Jehovah is bounteous]. 1. Son of David's brother Shimeah (II Sam. 13:3).

2. A son of Rechab, the Kenite (Jer. 35:6; cf. I Chron. 2:55). He became head of the tribe and gave character to it by his rule requiring his people to dwell in tents, refrain from agriculture, and abstain from wine (Jer. 35:6, 7) in order to preserve primitive simplicity of manners. Jehu, finding that Jonadab sympathized with his work of suppressing Baal worship, took him to Samaria, where he aided Jehu in putting out of Baal's temple all who were not priests of that god, in preparation for the massacre which was to ensue (II Kings 10:15, 23).

Jo'nah (jō'nà), in A.V. of N.T. **Jo'nas**, twice **Jo'na**, the Greek genitive case (Matt. 16:17; John 1:42) [a dove]. 1. A prophet of Israel, a son of Amittai, and citizen of Gath-hepher in Galilee, who before the close of the reign of Jeroboam II foretold Israel's recovery of its borders from the entering of Hamath to the sea of the plain (II Kings 14:25; Jonah 1:1).

The Book of Jonah is the 5th in order of the Minor Prophets. It differs from the other prophetical books in stressing the biographical element. It may be divided into 3 sections:

I. *Jonah's disobedience* (ch. 1). He was bidden to go to Nineveh and cry against it, but he was unwilling to go. Accordingly he took ship at Joppa to flee to Tarshish. A great storm arose. The ship was in danger. At length the sailors cast lots to ascertain on whose account the storm had been sent. The lot fell upon Jonah. He told them that he was a worshiper of Jehovah and that, if they would cast him overboard, the sea would become calm. They reluctantly obeyed. The sea became quiet, and the prophet, who had disappeared in the depths, was swallowed by a great fish which the Lord had prepared.

II. *Jonah's prayer* (ch. 2). Surprised at finding himself alive in the midst of the sea, the prophet gave thanks to God for his present escape from death and gratefully expressed the hope of ultimate deliverance. The fish at length vomited him upon the dry land.

III. *Jonah's message* and its results (chs. 3; 4). Bidden a 2d time to go to Nineveh, he obeyed and delivered his message. The Ninevites publicly repented and God spared the city. At this Jonah was displeased; not that his prophecy had been nullified by the repentance of the people, for he and his hearers expected that it would be (chs. 3:9; 4:2), but probably because he felt that with the sparing of Nineveh the doom of his own country was sealed. By the withering of a gourd, however, the Lord taught him the lesson of divine compassion on man and beast generally, irrespective of man's relation to the Church.

The motive that led Jonah to flee was probably a narrow and mistaken patriotism. He feared that Nineveh would repent and that God in his mercy would spare the city. Jonah wished Nineveh to perish (ch. 4:2, 4, 11); for it was a powerful foe of Israel and, if it were not destroyed, the doom of Israel was sealed.

The purpose of the book is primarily to teach that God's purposes of grace are not limited to the children of Abraham, but the Gentiles can receive mercy while still outside the pale of Israel's law. But besides this great lesson The Book of Jonah affords illustrations of truth, which from their nature may perhaps even be regarded as types teaching truth.

a. Nineveh repented at the preaching of one prophet; whereas Israel repented not, although many prophets were sent to it (cf. Matt. 12:41). This seems to be a type, to be

related to and look forward to a general truth—that the Gentiles yield a readier acquiescence to the doctrines of God than Israel had done, acquiescing not more readily to the moral law indeed, but to the revelation of God as a whole; for example, to his method of salvation as outlined in Hosea, ch. 14 (cf. Isa. 2:2–4 with v. 5).

b. Jonah, an Israelite and God's servant sent to preach to the Gentiles, is an evidence of God's will that the people of God's kingdom shall lead the Gentiles to repentance and to God. Jonah was not the only Israelite in whom this truth was exemplified: Elijah was sent to a woman of Zarephath (I Kings, ch. 17), Elisha cured Naaman the Syrian (II

Flowers and Huge Leaves of the Palma Christi (*Ricinus communis*), Believed by Many to Be the "Gourd" of Jonah 4: 6

Kings, ch. 5), Christ talked to a woman of Samaria about the things of God and healed the daughter of a Syrophoenician woman (Mark, ch. 7; John, ch. 4).

c. Jonah, an Israelite and God's servant fleeing from duty, is cast into the sea, but is delivered in order that he may fulfill his mission. This incident accordingly received an allegorical interpretation: Jonah symbolizes the nation Israel. Israel, as a nation, had been chosen to be a witness and upholder of divine truth, but Israel often apostatized and failed to execute its mission. It was in consequence swallowed up in the Exile by Babylonia (cf. Jer. 51:34) as was Jonah by the fish. In exile, however, the nation like Jonah (Jonah, ch. 2) sought the Lord. There followed a return from the Exile; in other words, the nation was disgorged (cf. Jer. 51:44) as was Jonah (ch. 2:10). Upon the Return from Babylon, many Jews were disappointed that the judgment uttered by the prophets did not at once take effect, just as

Jonah was displeased that God spared Nineveh. But God's purposes will be carried out, and the remnant survived to fulfill Israel's mission to the world (Isa. 42:1-4; 49:1-13; cf. ch. 2:2-4; 11:10).

d. Jonah, an Israelite and God's servant cast into the depths of Sheol and yet brought up alive out of the pit (Jonah 2:2, 6), as a type illustrates the death for sins not his own, and the burial and the resurrection of the Messiah, the representative Israelite and perfect servant of the Lord (Matt. 12:40).

e. The book may be regarded as a great work on foreign missions. It has been observed that The Book of Jonah nowhere claims to have been written by that prophet. It is further urged by critics that the book was written long after Jonah's time, because: 1. In the prayer ascribed to him are some quotations from late psalms (cf. Jonah 2:3 with Ps. 42:7; Jonah 2:5 with Ps. 69:1; Jonah 2:9 with Ps. 50:14). 2. The language contains Aramaic elements and grammatical constructions which are found in the late books. Some of these linguistic features might be compatible with a pre-exilic origin in n. Israel; but taken as a whole, they can be most consistently explained by the supposition that the book is a work of the postexilic period. 3. The failure to give the name of the Assyrian king indicates that it was unknown to the author, but the reference is merely to the ruler as such. Ordinarily, however, the Hebrews spoke of the king who ruled at Nineveh as the king of Assyria, but here he is singularly called the king of Nineveh. 4. From Jonah 3:3b it has been inferred that Nineveh was a thing of the past (the city was destroyed 612 B.C.). 5. It has been assumed that ch. 3:10 reflects the conditional nature of prophecy as taught by Jer. 18:5-12. When a divinely inspired judgment has been proclaimed by a prophet, repentance may avert its fulfillment, but God's mercy in such a case does not make his word of none effect. 6. It has also been suggested that the worldwide point of view of the book and the all-embracing fatherly love of God which has no respect for person or nation reflect the time of a writer who lived in postexilic times.

In view of all these considerations a postexilic date for the writer of The Book of Jonah seems the more probable. The date of composition has nothing to do with the historicity of Jonah the son of Amittai who prophesied in the reign of Jeroboam II. There is no evidence that Jonah wrote the book which bears his name.

The narrative has been variously regarded as myth, legend, parable, history. The chief interpretations are: 1. The allegorical or parabolical, which was discussed above. This conception of the prophecy is much in vogue, for it avoids the miracle or, if no miracle was involved in the escape of Jonah, the extraordinary nature of the event. 2. The historical. Modern instances have been quoted where a man was saved alive from the stomach of a whale or large fish, but such examples are not in themselves evidence of the historicity of Jonah's adventure. It should also be borne in mind that the spiritual lessons to be derived from the book are far more important than the question whether a large fish could have swallowed Jonah and whether he could have survived 3 days and 3 nights in the belly of the fish. The miraculous element is magnified or minimized according to individual judgment and knowledge. The conception of the narrative as historical has these supports: 1. The form of the book is historical and has left this impression on its readers. 2. Jonah himself was unquestionably a historical personage. 3. While it is conceivable that the words of Christ regarding

Jonah in the belly of the fish and at Nineveh do not imply his belief in the events, it is highly probable that they do, especially since Jonah was a real person (Matt. 12:39, 40; Luke 11:29, 30). 4. The narrative was regarded by the Jews as historical (Jos. *Antiq.* ix. 10, 2). 5. The repentance of the Ninevites is credible. National distress and a low state of the empire would dispose them to listen to a warning from God; the arrival from a foreign country of a strange prophet, of whose peculiar history they may have heard, was calculated to affect them; the Spirit of God works when and where he will. It is urged, indeed, against the historical character of the book that (a) permanent conversion of the Ninevites did not take place. That is quite true, but it is nowhere asserted that it did. The statement merely is that the men of that generation repented under the lead of their king. So the men of Judah in Hezekiah's and Josiah's reigns sanctified themselves under the leadership of those kings. (b) Against the historical character of the book is also urged the size ascribed to Nineveh (Jonah 3:3; 4:11). But see NINEVEH. (c) Also the rapid growth of the gourd or ricinus has been regarded with suspicion (ch. 4:10). Probably the words describe merely the ephemeral character of the plant. From the narrative itself, vs. 6-8, it does not appear that the growth was supernaturally rapid.

There are parallels to Jonah in Buddhist literature. Thus a certain Mittavindaka (*Jātaka,* 41) was upon a ship, which, after having sailed for 7 days, stood immovable upon the waters. The sailors cast lots, and for 7 successive times Mittavindaka was found guilty; thereupon the crew gave him a raft of reeds upon which he reached land. Another Mittavindaka's guilt (*Jātaka,* 439) was determined in 3 lots, and in his case the mariners gave him a board on which he reached an island. In both instances, the boat proceeded on its course. According to the *Peta-Vatthu* (IV, 11) a certain lady journeyed on a ship to Suvannabhūmi. A *peta* (departed spirit), who lived in a *vimāna* (a magical palace that floated in the air from place to place at the will of the occupant) stopped the boat on the ocean in order to gain possession of the woman. Three successive lots showed that the lady was the cause of the ship's failure to move, and so she was placed adrift upon a bundle of bamboo rods. The *peta* took her into his *vimāna* and in due time left her with her kinsfolk in Pataliputra. Although these tales have a superficial resemblance to the story of Jonah, no connection or borrowing is evident; they merely show community of feeling and action, under similar circumstances, of Hindu and Phoenician mariners.

2. Father of Simon Peter (Matt. 16:17; John 1:42 A.V.; 21:15 A.V.). In R.V. of John Simon's father is called John on the authority of manuscripts. See BAR-JONAH.

Jo'nam (jō'năm), in A.V. John (jō'năn) [perhaps a modification of Heb. *Yōḥānān,* Jehovah has been, or is, gracious]. An ancestor of Christ, who lived about two hundred years after David (Luke 3:30).

Jo'nas (jō'nás). See JONAH.

Jon'a·than (jŏn'á-thăn) [Jehovah has given]. 1. A Levite, son or remoter descendant of Gershom, son of Moses (Judg. 18:30, R.V.). He was doubtless the Levite who had sojourned at Bethlehem-judah, but had left that town to seek another residence, and, when passing through Ephraim, was hired by Micah to officiate as priest before an image of Jehovah (ch. 17:7-13). But Danites, on their way to found a settlement on the upper Jordan, seized Micah's idol and persuaded the mercenary priest to go with them, promising that he should be the priest, not of a single household, but of a tribe. Thus Jonathan became the first of a line of priests who officiated at the shrine of the stolen idol all the time that the tabernacle was in Shiloh, till the captivity of the land or district (ch. 18:3–6, 14–31). Jonathan had dishonored his descent from Moses, and accordingly the letter *nun* (n) was inserted in the Hebrew word for Moses, changing it to Manasseh (ch. 18:30, A.V., J.V., R.V. marg.). The inserted letter was not incorporated into the text, but was suspended above the line.

2. Eldest son of King Saul (I Sam. 14:49; cf. 20:31). His father gathered an army of 3,000 men and placed 1,000 of them at Geba under the command of Jonathan, who presently smote the Philistine garrison or deputy at Geba and thus provoked war (ch. 13:3). During its course, attended only by his armorbearer, he climbed the steep side of the gorge of Michmash to an outpost of the Philistines on its northern brink, and falling boldly upon them slew twenty men. The tumult at the outpost started a panic in the camp, and when Saul came to attack he found Philistines confusedly fighting each other. A rout ensued. Saul pronounced a curse on any who should eat food during the pursuit. Ignorant of the oath, Jonathan, seeing wild honey, ate a little, and for this act his father would have given him up to death. But the people intervened (I Sam., ch. 14). At the time of Goliath's defiance of Israel Jonathan discerned the nobility of David's soul, and loved him forthwith and remained steadfast in friendship for him, even when Saul suggested that David would someday be king in their stead. He kept David informed of the king's moods and purposes, till at length Saul, angered by what he considered Jonathan's unfilial conduct, threw a javelin at him, as he had more than once done at David (chs. 18 to 20). On this occasion Jonathan was seeking to discover whether a reconciliation of Saul with David was possible. David was lying in concealment in the fields waiting for word. The two friends anticipated the difficulty Jonathan might have in conveying this information to David, especially if Saul should show himself of evil mind toward the son of Jesse, for Saul and the party opposed to David would watch Jonathan to prevent him from communicating with David and again frustrating their plans. Accordingly, to disarm suspicion, Jonathan arranged to go out with company, and as though to hunt, and by means of arrows to give a sign to David. He did so, and then, finding that suspicion had been allayed and that he was no longer observed, he sent the boy back to the town with the bow and arrows, and remained for a final interview with David. The two friends met once after this in the wood of Ziph (I Sam. 23:16–18). Jonathan was killed, with two of his brothers and their father, at the battle of Gilboa, and his bones, like theirs, were affixed to the wall of Beth-shean, till the men of Jabesh-gilead removed them and gave them honorable burial (I Sam. 31:1, 11–13; I Chron. 10:2, 8–12). David deeply lamented his death (II Sam. 1:17–27). Jonathan left one son, called Mephibosheth and Merib-baal, who was lame (II Sam. 4:4). David showed him kindness for Jonathan's sake, and the line of his descendants is traceable for several generations in increasing numbers, as if all danger of its extinction had passed away (II Sam., ch. 9; I Chron. 8:33–40; 9:39–44).

3. Uncle of King David. He was a counselor, a man of understanding, and a scribe (I Chron. 27:32). Some expositors believe that in this passage the Hebrew word for uncle is used in a general sense for relation,

and they identify this counselor with David's nephew Jonathan (R.V. marg.).

4. Son of the high priest Abiathar. He was one of two young men who concealed themselves at En-rogel, near Jerusalem, during Absalom's rebellion, and sent David information of everything passing in the city (II Sam. 15:36; 17:15–22). When Adonijah attempted to usurp the throne and was celebrating a feast, Jonathan brought the news that Solomon had been proclaimed king, a piece of intelligence which led to the breaking up of the assemblage (I Kings 1:41–49).

5. A son of David's brother Shimei, and distinguished as the slayer of one of the gigantic men of Gath (II Sam. 21:21, 22).

6. One of David's mighty men, son of Shagee or, rather, Shammah the Hararite (I Chron. 11:34; cf. II Sam. 23:11). The text of II Sam. 23:32, 33 is to be emended by comparison with Chronicles.

7. An official under David (I Chron. 27:25). See JEHONATHAN.

8. A son of Kareah. After the capture of Jerusalem by Nebuchadnezzar, he placed himself under the protection of Gedaliah (Jer. 40:8). The name is not found in the corresponding passage (II Kings 25:23).

9. A scribe, in whose house Jeremiah was imprisoned (Jer. 37:15, 20).

10. A son of Jada (I Chron. 2:32).

11. A descendant of Adin (Ezra 8:6).

12. An opponent of Ezra's proposal that foreign wives should be put away (Ezra. 10:15, R.V.).

13. A Levite of the lineage of Asaph (Neh. 12:35; cf. ch. 11:15, 17).

14. A priest, head of a father's house in the days of the high priest Joiakim (Neh. 12:14).

15. A high priest, son of Joiada (Neh. 12:11). See JOHANAN 11.

16. Youngest son of the priest Mattathias (I Macc. 2:5). When his brother Judas Maccabaeus was slain in battle in 161 B.C., Jonathan was chosen his successor (ch. 9:23–31). The forces at his disposal were, however, too few for offensive operations against the Syrians, and he withdrew into the wilderness of Tekoa (v. 33). He was surnamed Apphus (ch. 2:5), which is thought by some to mean Dissembler, and to have been given him on account of his first exploit, in which he laid an ambush for the children of Jambri and slew them because they had killed his brother John (ch. 9:37–41). On a Sabbath Day in c. 161 B.C. he repulsed an attack of the Syrians under Bacchides on the Jordan, probably on the e. bank; but after the victory he and his followers leaped into the river and swam to the other side (ch. 9:43–48), where they remained (v. 58), outwitting the attempts which were made to assassinate their leader (vs. 60, 61). Jonathan and Simon afterward fortified themselves at Bethbasi in the wilderness, probably of Tekoa; and when Bacchides besieged the fortress, Jonathan left Simon to defend the place, while he himself ravaged the surrounding country (vs. 62, 66). Bacchides was so straitened that he made peace with Jonathan and withdrew from Judea (vs. 67–72). Jonathan took up his residence at Michmash, and began to judge the people (v. 73). When Alexander Balas revolted against Demetrius, king of Syria, the latter hastened to secure Jonathan as an ally, and gave him authority to gather troops. The Syrians who were still in the strongholds of Judea fled, and Jonathan entered Jerusalem in 153 B.C. (ch. 10:1–14). Alexander, equally desirous to have the support of Jonathan, appointed him high priest of the Jews and king's friend, and Jonathan put on the pontifical robes at the feast of tabernacles in 153 B.C. (vs. 15–21). Upon hearing of this event, Demetrius hastened to make further concessions to the

Jews (vs. 22–45). Jonathan, however, gave no credence to the words of Demetrius; and Alexander, when he secured the throne of Syria in 150 B.C., appointed him governor of Judea (vs. 46, 59–66). In 148–147 B.C. Demetrius II raised the standard of revolt against Alexander. Demetrius was assisted by Apollonius, who sent a threatening message to Jonathan. Jonathan seized Joppa and defeated Apollonius in the neighboring plain (vs. 67–87). When Alexander's father-in-law, Ptolemy, intervened in the war, Jonathan showed his friendship and accompanied him to the borders of Syria (ch. 11:1–7). Ptolemy proved treacherous to Alexander and placed Demetrius on the throne. Jonathan was able to secure the friendship of the new king, and rendered him great service by a contingent of 3,000 Jewish soldiers, who quelled an insurrection against Demetrius in Antioch. Demetrius proved false, and Jonathan sided with the young Antiochus and fought successfully with the troops of Demetrius near Kedesh in Galilee. Jonathan now sought the aid of the Romans and Spartans (ch. 12:1, 2); he also undertook aggressive operations against Demetrius, and defeated his troops and allies in the vicinity of Hamath (vs. 24–35). But Tryphon, who had championed the cause of the young Antiochus, now lifted up his hand against his master and sought to destroy Jonathan also. He persuaded the Jewish leader to come with but a small bodyguard to Ptolemaïs. When Jonathan entered, the gates of the city were closed, Jonathan's escort was put to the sword, he himself was seized and kept for a time a prisoner and finally slain in Gilead in 143 B.C. (chs. 12:39–48; 13:12–23). The bones of Jonathan were recovered and buried in the family sepulcher at Modin (ch. 13:25–27).

17. A general who, at the command of Simon Maccabaeus, took possession of Joppa. He was a son of Absalom (I Macc. 13:11).

Jo'nath e'lem re·ho'kim (jō'năth ē'lĕm rē-hō'kĭm), in A.V. **Jo'nath-e'lem-re·cho'k·m** (jō'-năth-ē'lĕm-rē-kō'kĭm) [the silent dove of them that are afar off or, by reading the middle word, in Heb. *'ēlīm* instead of *'ēlem*, the dove of the distant terebinths]. Probably the tune to which Psalm 56 was to be set (Psalm 56, title).

Jop'pa (jŏp'pá), in A.V. once **Ja'pho** (Josh. 19:46), and so twice in R.V. marg. of O.T., this being the Heb. form, while Joppa is derived from the Greek [beauty]. An ancient walled town (mentioned in the list of Thutmose III and in the Amarna letters), assigned to Dan (Josh. 19:46); about 35 miles from Jerusalem, of which it was the seaport, to which timber cut on Lebanon for the building of Solomon's Temple was floated from Tyre (II Chron. 2:16). Jonah embarked at Joppa in a ship about to sail to Tarshish, when he sought to flee from Jehovah (Jonah 1:3). When the Temple was being rebuilt, after the return of the Jews from Babylon, rafts of cedar trees were again floated from Tyre to Joppa (Ezra 3:7, R.V.). In Maccabaean times Joppa was garrisoned by the Syrians (I Macc. 10:75). The Jews of the town were induced to go aboard ships, and 200 of them were treacherously drowned. In retribution Judas set fire by night to the docks and boats in the harbor and slew the fugitives (II Macc. 12:3–6). Eventually Simon captured the town, garrisoned it, completed the harbor, and restored the fortifications (I Macc. 12:33, 34; 14:5, 34). The disciple Tabitha, a woman full of good deeds, lived at Joppa. Having died, she was raised to life at the prayer and word of Peter. As a result many believed (Acts 9:36–42). Peter remained at Joppa for some time, lodging with Simon a tanner (v. 43); and thither the servants of Cornelius came to invite Peter to Caesarea (ch. 10:5–48). Joppa, now called Jaffa, is built on a rocky mound 116 feet high at the edge of the sea. A small harbor is formed by a ledge of rocks lying parallel to the shore, but entrance to it from the s. is barred by rocks. The n. end is open but shallow, and the one passage through the reef is but 10 feet wide.

Jo'rah (jō'rá). See HARIPH.

Jo'ra·i (jō'rá-ī). A Gadite (I Chron. 5:13).

Jo'ram (jō'răm), **Je·ho'ram**, the forms interchangeable in Heb. [Jehovah is high]. 1. A son of Toi, king of Hamath, who was sent by his father to congratulate David on his victory over Hadadezer (II Sam. 8:10). Called in I Chron. 18:10 Hadoram, which in this case probably means "the god Addu (Adad) or Hadad is exalted."

A View of Modern Jaffa (Joppa) from the Air

2. A Levite, descended from Moses' son Eliezer (I Chron. 26:25; cf. ch. 23:15, 17).

3. Son of Ahab, king of Israel. He succeeded his elder brother, Ahaziah and reigned till 842 B.C. He put away the image of Baal which his father had made, but adhered to the calf worship instituted by Jeroboam. On the death of Ahab, Mesha, king of Moab, had rebelled and withheld tribute. To recover his dominion over Moab, Joram obtained the assistance of King Jehoshaphat of Judah, and of the Edomite ruler. As the confederates were marching around the s. portion of the Dead Sea, they were nearly perishing with thirst, but Elisha bade them dig trenches, and on the following morning water came rushing down the wadi and filled the trenches. Not only did the water supply the needs of the Israelites, but, looking ruddy under the rays of the morning sun, was mistaken by the Moabites for blood; and, supposing that the Israelites had fallen out among themselves, they rushed to the spoil. Joram and his allies rose against them when they were thus off their guard, and put them to flight, and then overran Moab, but without being able permanently to reduce it to subjection (II Kings 3:1–27); see MOABITE STONE. Joram was without doubt the king to whom the king of Syria sent Naaman to be cured of his leprosy (ch. 5:1–27); and to whom Elisha made known every movement of the Syrian invaders, and who had them in his power at Samaria, and by Elisha's advice sent them home unmolested (ch. 6:8–23); and who, during the famine, when Ben-hadad was besieging Samaria, vowed vengeance against Elisha for the distress (vs. 24–31; called in v. 32 the son of a murderer). His end was tragic. He was at Jezreel, seeking cure from wounds received at Ramoth-gilead, when a watchman announced the approach of Jehu. Mounting his chariot and accompanied by his nephew Ahaziah, the king of Judah, in another chariot, Joram drove forth to meet Jehu. They came up to him at the field which Joram's mother had got for his father by having its owner, Naboth, slain. Jehu shot Joram through the heart with an arrow and, recalling a prophecy to mind, had the body thrown from the chariot into the field of Naboth (ch. 9:14–26). With Joram the dynasty of Omri ceased, and that of Jehu began.

4. One of the priests sent by Jehoshaphat to instruct the people (II Chron. 17:8).

5. Son of Jehoshaphat. From c. 854 B.C. he was associated with his father in the government, and in 849 B.C., in the 5th year of Jehoram, king of Israel, the reins of government were transferred entirely to his hands (II Kings 8:16; cf. chs. 1:17; 3:1). No sooner did he feel himself secure on his throne than he murdered all his brothers and some other princes of Judah (II Chron. 21:1–4). He had for his wife a daughter of Ahab, who led him into gross forms of heathenism, as Jezebel had seduced Ahab (II Kings 8:18; II Chron. 21:6, 11). As in other cases, his departure from Jehovah brought with it adversity. The Edomites rose in rebellion, and though he gained a victory over them, yet this did not prevent their achieving their independence (II Kings 8:20–22; II Chron. 21:8–10). Philistine and Arab marauders entered Judah and plundered the palace, carrying off the king's wives and children, with the single exception of Jehoahaz, or Ahaziah, the youngest boy (II Chron. 21:16, 17; 22:1). A writing from the Prophet Elijah was handed to the king, denouncing his apostasy and his wickedness, and threatening him with painful disease and death; see ELIJAH 2. He was soon afterward seized with dysentery, which became chronic and continued for 2 years (II

Chron. 21:18, 19). During this sickness Ahaziah acted as regent (cf. II Kings 9:29 with ch. 8:25, 26). There was no pretense at lamentation when his death occurred. His sole reign, beginning in the 5th year of Jehoram of Israel, was 8 years. He died in 842 B.C., leaving his 1 surviving son Ahaziah to ascend the throne (II Kings 8:24; II Chron. 21:12 to 22:1).

Jor'dan (jôr'dăn) [descender]. The most important river in Palestine. It rises from various sources. The e. source is at Bāniās, the ancient Caesarea Philippi, where a copious stream, the Bāniās, issues from a cave in a lofty cliff. The central and largest source is at Tell el-Ḳāḍi, probably the ancient Dan, where from 2 great springs the abundant Leddan takes its rise. The 3d source, the most n. and highest perennial one, is the fountain, below Ḥasbeya, from which the river Ḥasbāny flows. Thomson says that the Ḥasbāny is the longest by 40 miles, the Leddan much the largest, and the Bāniās the most beautiful. From the source of the river at Bāniās to Lake Ḥūleh the distance is 12 miles; the junction of the Bāniās and the Leddan taking place about midway between these points, and the confluence with the Ḥasbāny a fraction of a mile lower. The lake itself is 4 miles long. The Jordan, emerging from it at its s. side, next makes its way 10½ miles more to the Sea of Galilee, which is 12½ miles long. After passing through this lake, it pursues a tortuous course, till it enters the Dead Sea, at a point 65 miles in a straight line from the s. part of the Sea of Galilee. Including the 2 lakes, and taking no note of the windings, the river from Bāniās to the Dead Sea is 104 miles long. As far as is known, it stands absolutely alone among the rivers of the world in the fact that throughout the greater part of its course it runs below the level of the ocean. When it issues from the cave at Bāniās it is 1,000 feet above the level of the Mediterranean. By the time it enters Lake Ḥūleh it has fallen to within 7 feet of sea level. At the Sea of Galilee it is 682 feet below the sea level, and when entering the Dead Sea 1,292 feet. The stream was appropriately named Jordan, the descender, and is tortuous also. Lieut. Lynch, of the U.S. Navy, who in 1848 sailed from the Sea of Galilee to the Dead Sea, wrote: "In a space of 60 miles of latitude and 4 miles of longitude the Jordan traverses at least 200 miles. . . . We have plunged down 27 threatening rapids, besides a great many of lesser magnitude."

The Biblical associations with the river proper attach mainly to the stretch from the Sea of Galilee to the Dead Sea. The river was fringed, as it is now, with a thicket of trees and shrubs, principally tamarisks, oleanders, and willows, among which lions lurked (Jer. 49:19; Zech. 11:3). The valley in its s. part, where the depression below sea level is greatest, is virtually a tropical country, and under irrigation produced crops of tropical luxuriance (Jos. War iv. 8, 3). On account of its fertility Lot, forgetful of moral considerations, chose it as the place of his residence (Gen. 13:8–13). The river was not bridged until Roman times, but was forded. The fords are frequent and easy in the upper stream and as far down as the mouth of the Jabbok, where Jacob crossed (Gen. 32:10; 33:18). Below that point the river is rarely fordable, and then only at certain seasons of the year. The current of the river is so rapid near Jericho that the numerous pilgrims who go thither to bathe are always in danger, and not infrequently are swept away.

For the Israelites to cross the Jordan under Joshua's leadership required the miracle or extraordinary providence of the checked waters (Josh. 3:1–17; 4:1–24; Ps. 114:3, 5). Adam or Adamah (modern Dāmieh) is 16 miles up the river from Jericho or Shittim. Its location is marked by a small Bronze Age tell, about ½ mile e. of the best ford of the middle Jordan. The river near this ford is liable to be blocked at intervals by great land-slides, of which several important instances are on record. In A.D. 1266 Sultan Baybars ordered a bridge to be built over the Jordan near Dāmieh, but the task was found to be difficult on account of the rising of the waters. But in the night preceding December 8, 1267, a lofty mound, which overlooked the river on the w., fell into it and dammed up the waters, which were held back for 16 hours. A similar case occurred in 1906. In 1927 a section of a cliff fell bodily across the river and completely dammed it. No water flowed down the river bed for 21½ hours, and people crossed and recrossed the bed of the river on foot. It may be that in Joshua's time a similar landslide made it possible for the Israelites to cross the Jordan from the e. into Palestine. If such be the case, it means that God uses the forces of nature to accomplish his purposes, and such an explanation is no attempt to explain away the miraculous element. The fullness of the Jordan, with the overflow of its water over its banks, during the time of harvest (March or April in that warm valley) is produced by the melting of the snow on Mount Hermon (Josh. 3:15). The fleeing Midianites, pursued by Gideon, crossed by the fords at and above the mouth of the Jabbok (Judg. 7:24; 8:4, 5). David, when fleeing from Absalom and on returning to his kingdom, crossed twice somewhere between Jericho and the Jabbok (II Sam. 17:22, 24; 19: 15–18). Elijah and Elisha, amidst the wonderful events at the close of Elijah's career, crossed at Jericho (II Kings 2:5–8, 13–15). Naaman the Syrian, as directed by the prophet, washed 7 times in the Jordan, somewhere in its upper reaches, either n. or s. of the Sea of Galilee, and was cured of his leprosy (II Kings 5:14). John the Baptist administered the special rite which gave him his designation, in the Jordan, and it was there that our Lord was baptized (Matt. 3:6, 13–17).

Jo'rim (jō'rĭm) [Gr. for Aram. Yᵉhōrim or Yōrim, Jehovah is high]. An ancestor of Christ, who lived about 350 years after David (Luke 3:29).

Jor'ke·am (jôr'kĕ-ăm), in A.V. **Jor'ko·am** (jôr'kŏ-ăm). A place peopled by members of the family of Hezron and house of Caleb (I Chron. 2:44). Some suppose it to be for Jokdeam (q.v.).

Jos'a·bad (jŏs'á-băd). See JOZABAD.

Jos'a·phat (jŏs'á-făt). See JEHOSHAPHAT.

Jo'se (jō'sĕ). See JESUS 2.

Jo'sech (jō'sĕch) [Gr. for Aram. Yōsē, contraction of Joseph]. An ancestor of Christ, who probably lived after the Exile (Luke 3:26). The A.V., following a different reading, calls him Joseph.

Jos'e·dech (jŏs'ĕ-dĕk). See JOZADAK.

Jo'seph (jō'zĕf) [may he (Jehovah) add, from Heb. root yāsaph]. The name has also the sound of a verb form of the root 'āsaph, meaning "he taketh away"; the Hebrew writer in Gen. 30:23, 24 plays upon the sound and upon both etymologies when he explains, not what the root of the word is, but the reason for bestowing the name.

1. The 11th of Jacob's 12 sons, and the elder son of Rachel, who, when she gave him birth, said, "The Lord add to me another son," and therefore called his name Joseph (Gen. 30:22–24). He was born in Paddan-aram, about 6 years before the return of Jacob to Canaan (v. 25; cf. ch. 31:41), when Jacob was 90 or 91 years old. He was his father's favorite child, because he was the son of his old age and Rachel's child; and he made him a coat such as was worn by young people of the better class (ch. 37:3). The father's favoritism aroused the envy of the elder brethren; and their ill will was increased by 2 dreams that Joseph related which foreshadowed the time when his father, his mother, and his brethren should bow down and do him obeisance. When Joseph was 17 years old (ch. 37:2), Jacob sent him to Shechem, where his brothers were feeding their flocks, to ask after their welfare. On reaching Shechem, he found that they had gone on to Dothan, and he followed them thither. As he was seen approaching, the brothers proposed to slay him and report to his father that a wild beast had devoured him. Reuben, however, prevailed upon them not to take Joseph's life, but to cast him alive into a pit, intending eventually to take the youth out and restore him to his father. In Reuben's absence a caravan of Ishmaelites, traveling on the great highway that led down into Egypt, drew near. To Midianite merchantmen of the company Joseph was sold. A kid of the goats being killed, Joseph's coat was dipped in the blood and the besmeared garment was sent to Jacob, who concluded that his son had been torn to pieces by some wild beast (Gen. 37:1–35).

Meanwhile the slave dealers took Joseph down into Egypt, and sold him to Potiphar, the captain of Pharaoh's guard. The young slave's ability was soon discovered, and Potiphar gave him charge of all his house. But on false accusations he was committed to prison, where he was confined for years. There he so gained the confidence of the jailer that all the prisoners were committed to his charge. God enabled him to interpret prophetic dreams of the chief butler and the chief baker of Pharaoh, who were confined with him in prison, and his interpretation in each instance was found correct. Two years later Pharaoh dreamed 2 prophetic dreams, which no one could interpret, and the chief butler, who had been restored to his royal master's favor, remembered Joseph and told of the occurrences in the prison. Joseph was immediately sent for, and interpreted the dreams, both of which had the same meaning. Seven years of great plenty were to be succeeded by 7 years of grievous famine. He ventured to recommend that someone should be appointed to collect the surplus produce during the 7 years of plenty, and store it against the years of famine. Pharaoh approved the plan; and, having had evidence of the wisdom of Joseph (ch. 41:9–13, 25–36), he appointed him superintendent of the royal granaries and as such the head of a department of the state and one of the officials next in rank to the king (ch. 41:39–44). Joseph was now 30 years of age (ch. 41:46). He had been chastened and humbled by the sufferings of 13 years. Pharaoh gave him Asenath, daughter of a priestly family at On, to wife; and before the famine began 2 sons were born to him, Manasseh and Ephraim (ch. 41:50–52). The famine came as predicted (see NILE), and affected all the known world, especially the w. part of it around the Mediterranean (ch. 41:54, 56, 57). In Egypt, however, there was a store of food, and Joseph's brothers went thither to buy grain. They did not recognize Joseph, but he knew them; and as they did obeisance to him, he saw that the dreams which brought him into such trouble had come to be verified. After testing their character in various ways, on their 2d visit he revealed himself to them, forgave them the wrong they had done him, and persuaded them and their father to settle in Egypt. The Pharaoh who welcomed them was doubtless of the Hyksos dynasty, and being himself a Semite, was the more ready to welcome men of a race identical with his own. With this agrees the fact that the Israelites were settled around the Hyksos capital of Egypt in the "plain of Tanis" (Zoan, Ps. 78:12, 43). The king who knew not Joseph (Ex. 1:8) and who oppressed the Israelites represents a Pharaoh who reigned after the expulsion of the Hyksos. Joseph died at the age of 110 years, and his body, in accordance with Egyptian custom, was embalmed and put in a coffin; but he had left strict injunctions that when the Exodus took place his remains should be removed to Canaan (Gen., chs. 42 to 50; Heb. 11:22). His wishes were carried out, and his remains were ultimately buried near Shechem in the very center of the Promised Land (Ex. 13:19; Josh. 24:32).

and a member of the priestly class, which kept apart from the laity. The Egyptians ate by themselves, for Egyptians held aloof from foreigners; the priests ate and drank nothing that was imported (Porphyrius, *De Abstinentia ab Esu Animalium* iv. 7), and the people generally considered it an abomination to use Greek knives and cooking utensils (Herod. ii. 41), and ostracized shepherds, swineherds, and cowherds, even when native Egyptians, because the occupation of tending cattle was incompatible with the refinement and cleanliness demanded by Egyptian standards (Gen. 46:34; Herod. ii. 47; cf. 164). This objection to herdsmen was probably the cause of Joseph's settling his kindred in the land of Goshen, where they would not come in contact with the natives of the land.

Egyptian *I'kbir* in the lists of Palestinian place names of Thutmose III and Ramesses II is equivalent to Jacob-el (God supplants). Egyptian *Išpir* from the same list of Thutmose

Migration of Asiatics Into Egypt

The particulars of Joseph's life, which involve Egyptian customs, are borne out by the monuments and the papyri. It is known from the Rosetta stone that at least in the Ptolemaic period it was the habit of the king to release prisoners at his birthday feast and on other great occasions. References to magicians and soothsayers are frequent, and great stress is laid on dreams as messages from the gods. When Joseph was sent for in the prison, although there is express mention of haste, yet he stayed to shave himself and put on clean raiment (Gen. 41:14). Shaving was particularly practiced and among the priests was a religious rite. The investiture of an official of high rank is frequently depicted and agrees with the description in Genesis, the signet ring, the linen vesture, and the chain about the neck being prominent. An economic change, whereby the land came to be owned entirely by the king and priests, took place some time before the rise of the Empire; see EGYPT, II. 3.

There is reference to Egyptian conceptions of propriety in the separate setting of bread for Joseph, for his brethren, and for the Egyptians present (Gen. 43:32). Joseph ate by himself, because he was a man of highest rank

III is by some regarded as representing Joseph-el (may God add, or God takes away); others interpret it as Jesheb-el (where God dwells). Whatever philological equivalence there be, with our present knowledge we cannot say whether they stand in any relation to the patriarch Jacob and his son Joseph. They may be names like Jiphthah-el or Iphtah-el, a valley in the territory of Zebulun (Josh. 19:14).

An Egyptian story, known as the Tale of the Two Brothers, recounts the temptation of a young man in the home of his elder brother, similar to the experience of Joseph in the house of Potiphar (Gen., ch. 39). The younger brother is saved from the wrath of the elder by the interposition of the sun-god, who makes a river full of crocodiles to flow as a barrier between the two. The further adventures of the twain, at length reconciled to each other, are equally fabulous. The story was transcribed in the reign of Sethi II, of Dyn. XIX, centuries after the time of Joseph; but when the tale was composed is not known. A similar incident is told in Greek mythology: Bellerophon, having rejected the advances of Antaea, wife of Proetus, king of Argos, was falsely accused by her to her husband of an attempt on her virtue (Homer *Iliad* vi. 155 ff.).

The 2 tribes of Manasseh and Ephraim descended from Joseph's 2 sons. The blessings pronounced on Joseph by the dying Jacob were designed for these tribes as well as for Joseph himself (Gen. 48:8–22; 49:22–26). In Ps. 80:1 Joseph is a poetic designation of the tribes of Manasseh and Ephraim.

2. Father of the spy from the tribe of Issachar (Num. 13:7).

3. A son of Asaph and head of a course of musicians in the reign of David (I Chron. 25:2, 9).

4. An ancestor of Christ, who lived between the time of David and the Exile (Luke 3:30).

5. A son of Bani, induced by Ezra to put away his foreign wife (Ezra 10:42).

6. A priest, head of the family of Shebaniah in the days of the high priest Joiakim (Neh. 12:14).

7. An ancestor of Christ who lived after the Exile (Luke 3:26, in R.V. Josech).

8. Son of Mattathias, in the ancestry of Christ (Luke 3:24, 25).

9. Son of Zacharias. When Judas Maccabaeus sent Simon to aid the Jews in Galilee and himself went to fight in Gilead, he left Joseph and Azarias in charge of the forces in Judea. They engaged in battle, contrary to the orders given by Judas, and were defeated (I Macc. 5:18, 55–62).

10. The husband of Mary, the mother of Jesus (Matt. 1:16; Luke 3:23). For his ancestry see GENEALOGY. When Mary was found with child before marriage, Joseph was minded to put her away without public exposure, for he was a just man. But an angel informed him in a dream that the child to be born had been miraculously conceived by the Holy Spirit. Thereupon he had no hesitation in carrying out his contract with her, and he made her his wife (Matt. 1:18–25). Being a descendant of David, he had to go to Bethlehem, the early home of his ancestors, for enrollment, according to the decree of the emperor Augustus, and was there with Mary when Jesus was born (Luke 2:4, 16). He was with Mary when, at the presentation of Jesus in the Temple, Simeon and Anna gave forth their prophetic utterances (v. 33). Warned by an angel in a dream that Herod plotted the murder of the Child, Joseph conducted the flight into Egypt (Matt. 2:13, 19). He returned to Nazareth when Herod was dead (vs. 22, 23). He was accustomed to go with Mary annually to the passover at Jerusalem, and he took Jesus also to the feast when our Lord was 12 years old (Luke 2:43), and he also safely reached Nazareth on the return journey (v. 51). He was a carpenter (Matt. 13:55), and was assisted in his work by the young man Jesus (Mark 6:3). Apparently Joseph was alive when Jesus' ministry had well begun (Matt. 13:55), but as we do not hear of him in connection with the crucifixion, it may be inferred that he died previously to that event. This was the reason why Jesus, when on the cross, commended Mary to the kindness of the Apostle John, which he would scarcely have done had her natural guardian still been alive (John 19:26, 27).

11. The same as Joses 1 (Matt. 13:55, R.V.). See BRETHREN OF THE LORD.

12. A Jew of Arimathaea, a member of the sanhedrin, a councilor of honorable estate, who looked for the Kingdom of God (Mark 15:43). He had not consented to the resolution of the sanhedrin to put Jesus to death, for he was a disciple of Jesus, although secretly, for, like Nicodemus, the only other member of the governing body who believed on our Lord, he was fearful of publicly committing himself. Both became more courageous

when they saw the crucifixion. Joseph went boldly to Pilate, begged the body of Jesus, and laid it in his own new tomb, which he had hewed out in a rock (Matt. 27:57–60; Luke 23:50–53; John 19:38).

13. A Christian called Barsabbas or son of Sabbas, and Justus. He had companied with Jesus and the disciples from the time of Jesus' baptism, and was one of 2 who were considered worthy to fill the vacancy among the apostolic 12 produced by the apostasy of Judas; but the lot fell upon Matthias (Acts 1:21, 26). He was probably a brother of Judas, called Barsabbas (Acts 15:22).

14. The personal name of Barnabas (Acts 4:36; in A.V. Joses).

Jo'ses (jō'sēz) [a Gr. form of Joseph]. 1. One of the brethren of the Lord (Mark 6:3). In Matt. 13:55, R.V. prefers the manuscripts which gave the name as Joseph.

2. The personal name of Barnabas, for a time the missionary colleague of Paul (Acts 4:36, in R.V. Joseph).

Jo'shah (jō'shà). A Simeonite, son of Amaziah (I Chron. 4:34).

Josh'a·phat (jŏsh'à-făt) [Jehovah has judged]. 1. A Mithnite, one of David's mighty men (I Chron. 11:43).

2. A priest, one of the trumpeters before the Ark during its removal to Jerusalem (I Chron. 15:24, in A.V. Jehoshaphat).

Josh'a·vi'ah (jŏsh'à-vī'à). One of David's mighty men (I Chron. 11:46).

Josh·be·ka'shah (jŏsh·bē-kā'shà) [perhaps, he (God) brings back hard fate]. A singer, son of Heman (I Chron. 25:4), and head of the 17th course of singers (v. 24).

Jo'sheb-bas·she'beth (jō'shĕb-băs-shē'bĕth), in A.V. marg. **Jo'sheb-bas·se'bet** (jō'shĕb-băs-sē'bĕt). A textual corruption in II Sam. 23:8, apparently for Ish-baal (man of Baal). Baal was altered, as was often done after it had acquired idolatrous associations, to *bōsheth*, shame. Apparently Ish-bosheth became Yishbosheth. The last Hebrew word in v. 7 is *bashshābeth*, which may have caught the eye of a copyist. Through an error of transcription *b* apparently was added to *Yish-* and the consonants of *bashshābeth* written instead of *b-sh-th* (*bōsheth*). With a change of vocalization the result was Josheb-basshebeth. His identity with Jashobeam is fairly established by comparison of this verse with I Chron. 11:11 and vs. 8, 9 with I Chron. 27:2, 4. This latter form is perhaps another mode of avoiding the name Baal.

Josh'i·bi'ah (jŏsh'ĭ-bī'à), in A.V. **Jos'i·bi'ah** [Jehovah causes to dwell (in peace and security)]. A Simeonite, family of Asiel (I Chron. 4:35).

Josh'u·a (jŏsh'ū-à), in A.V. once **Je·hosh'u·a** (Num. 13:16), and once **Je·hosh'u·ah** (I Chron. 7:27). Jehoshua developed into **Jesh'u·a** (Neh. 8:17), and this form was Hellenized and appears as **Je'sus** (Acts 7:45) [Jehovah is salvation]. 1. An Ephraimite, the son of Nun (Num. 13:8, 16). He commanded the Israelites in their successful conflict with the Amalekites at Rephidim (Ex. 17:8–16). A personal attendant on Moses, he was with him on Mount Sinai when the golden calf was made, and mistook the noise of idolatrous revelry in the camp for the shouting of hostile combatants (Ex. 24:13; 32:17, 18). He had charge of the first tent of meeting (Ex. 33:11). At the age of 40, as prince of Ephraim, he was a member of the commission of 12 sent to report on the Land of Canaan and its assailability, and he joined Caleb in seeking to persuade the people to go and possess the land (Josh. 14:7; Num. 13:8; 14:6–9). For this the two narrowly escaped being stoned to death (Num.

14:10), but God rewarded them for their fidelity and trust in Jehovah by keeping them alive to enter the Promised Land (vs. 2?, 38). At the end of the 40 years' sojourn in the wilderness by divine direction Moses placed Joshua before the high priest and the congregation in Shittim and publicly ordained him to be his successor (Num. 27:18-23; Deut. 1:38), and just before death the lawgiver took Joshua to the tabernacle to receive his charge from the Lord (Deut. 31:14, 23). On the death of Moses, Joshua began immediate preparations for crossing the Jordan. The people were allowed 3 days in which to prepare victuals (Josh. 1:10, 11), the 2½ tribes were reminded of their obligation to render their brethren armed assistance (vs. 12-18), and spies were dispatched to search out Jericho (ch. 2:1). The camp was then moved to the river and the people carefully instructed as to the order of march (ch. 3:1-6). Joshua showed his military skill in the plan of campaign which he adopted for the conquest of Canaan: a central camp, advantageously situated; the capture of the towns which commanded the approaches to his camp; great campaigns following up victories; see CANAAN 2). He blundered, however, in making a treaty with the Gibeonites and in not garrisoning the citadel of the Jebusites. By these two mistakes Judah was to a degree isolated from the n. tribes. He carried out the injunction to assemble the people on Ebal and Gerizim to hear the blessings and the cursings (ch. 8:30-35). His campaigns had broken the power of the Canaanites, but not exterminated them (see CANAAN 2). But, although the prospect of further fighting remained, the time had come to plan for the settlement of the country. Aided by the high priest and a commission, he superintended the allotment of the conquered country, beginning the distribution while the camp was at Gilgal (chs. 14:6 to 17:18), and completing it and assigning cities of refuge and the Levitical towns after he had removed the tabernacle to Shiloh (chs. 18 to 21). For himself he asked and obtained a town, Timnath-serah, in Mount Ephraim (ch. 19:50). When old, he convoked an assembly of the people at Shechem, because it was the place of Abraham's first altar on entering Canaan and the locality where the tribes had invoked blessings and cursings upon themselves. There he made them a powerful address, urging them not to forsake Jehovah (ch. 24:1-28). Soon afterward he died, at the age of 110, and was buried at the place of his choice, Timnath-serah (vs. 29, 30).

The Book of Joshua properly follows Deuteronomy in the Hebrew Scriptures and in the English Bible, for it continues the history from the death of Moses, which was the last event recorded in Deuteronomy. It is more intimately connected with the Pentateuch than with the books which follow it, for the spirit of the Mosaic times was still active in the history which it recounts and it is the sequel of Genesis in that it records the possession of the Promised Land for which Abraham waited, as related in Genesis. In scientific studies critics generally regard the Pentateuch and The Book of Joshua as forming a unit, which they call the Hexateuch. In the Hebrew Scriptures it is the first of the Prophets, and begins that division of them called the Former Prophets, which embraces all the books of the English Bible between Joshua and II Kings inclusive, except Ruth; see CANON. The book may be divided into 3 sections:

I. *The conquest of Canaan* (chs. 1 to 12), including: the preparation for crossing the Jordan and the passage of the river (chs. 1:1 to 4:18); the establishment of the camp and celebration of the passover (chs. 4:19 to 5:

12); the capture of Jericho and Ai, the confirmation of the covenant on Ebal, and the treaty with the Gibeonites (chs. 5:13 to 9:27); the s. and n. campaigns (chs. 10; 11); and the summary (ch. 12).

II. *The distribution of Canaan* (chs. 13 to 22), including: a description of the land which remained to be divided (ch. 13); its allotment, with the assignment of cities of refuge and the allotment of towns to the tribe of Levi (chs. 14 to 21); and the temporary misunderstanding about the altar on the Jordan, as though it were intended to divide the nation (ch. 22).

III. *Joshua's farewell address* and death (chs. 23; 24).

It is expressly stated that Joshua wrote "these words," including at least the account of the proceedings at Shechem (chs. 23:1 to 24:25) in the book of the law of God (ch. 24:26). The concluding verses of the book (ch. 24:29-33) were written after the death of Joshua, Eleazar, and the men of that generation. The conquest of Hebron, Debir, and Anab by Caleb (ch. 15:13-20) took place after the death of Joshua and is inserted in this place for the sake of completeness (cf. Judg. 1:10-20; see HEBRON 2). In ch. 12:14 Zephath is called by its later name Hormah (Judg. 1:17; see HORMAH). Apparently Josh. 19:47 records the migration of the Danites in the days of the Judges. It seems reasonable to conclude from the general character of the documents and casual statements in them that large portions of the book were in writing in the time of Joshua. At any rate, it may be concluded that such records were in final form while the town of Ai was still in ruins (ch. 8:28), before the reign of Solomon, while the Canaanites still dwelt in Gezer (cf. ch. 16:10 with I Kings 9:16), and before the reign of David, at a time when the Jebusites still occupied the stronghold of Jerusalem (ch. 15:63).

2. A native of Beth-shemesh, the owner of a field to which the kine drawing the cart which carried the Ark from the Philistine country made their way (I Sam. 6:14).

3. The governor of Jerusalem during the reign of Josiah (II Kings 23:8).

4. The high priest while Zerubbabel was governor of Judah (Hag. 1:1, 12, 14; 2:2-4; Zech. 3:1-9). Called in Ezra and Nehemiah Jeshua (*q.v.*).

Jo·si'ah (jō-sī'á), in A.V. of N.T. **Jo·si'as** (jō-sī'ǎs) [Jehovah heals; cf. Arab. *'asā*, to nurse, cure]. 1. Son and successor of Amon as king of Judah. He came to the throne c. 638 B.C., when 8 years old. In his youth his adviser seems to have been the high priest Hilkiah, and Josiah hearkened to him. In the 8th year of his reign he began the attempt to conform his own conduct as king, and the life of the court, to the laws of God. In his 12th regnal year he commenced to suppress idolatry and other unlawful worship, a work which he prosecuted for years, not only in Judah and Jerusalem, but after his 18th year in Israel also (II Kings 22:1, 2; II Chron. 34:1-7, 33). In his 18th year (621 B.C.) he took energetic steps to repair and adorn the Temple, and the workmen, entering with enthusiasm into his plans, acted with exemplary fidelity in using the money entrusted to them for the purpose. While the repairs of the Temple were being executed, Hilkiah, the high priest, found the book of the law in the house of the Lord, and handed it over to Shaphan, the scribe, who read it to the king. Josiah was deeply impressed by the prophecy that if the people departed from Jehovah dreadful consequences would ensue. He rent his clothes and humbled himself before God, who was pleased to give him the gracious assurance that the threatened calamity should not come in his time (II Kings 22:8-20; II Chron. 34:15-28).

The prophecy which so affected Josiah was Deut., chs. 28 to 30, especially ch. 29:25-28. The book found by Hilkiah must thus have contained Deuteronomy at least, and it may have been a copy of the Pentateuch. The sacred books had, doubtless, been generally destroyed and lost sight of during the apostasy and persecution in the long reign of Manasseh (II Kings 21:16; II Chron. 33:9), and the book found by Hilkiah was probably the Temple copy of the law, which had been hidden or thrown aside during the profanation of the sanctuary (Deut. 31:9, 26); or possibly it was a law book that had been placed in the wall, according to an ancient custom, when the Temple was first built. That Deuteronomy, or at any rate its basic document, was an old book at the time may be argued from the fact that it reflects the condition of Israel in early times and not in the reign of Josiah. It enjoins upon the people the extermination of the Canaanites and Amalekites (chs. 20:16-18; 25:17-19), but in Josiah's day there was no occasion for such a law. It contemplates foreign conquest on the part of the Israelites (ch. 20:10-15); but in Josiah's day and for nearly a century previously the question was not of conquest, but whether Judah could maintain its existence at all. It vests the supreme authority under Jehovah in a judge and the priesthood, but makes provision for a time when the Israelites should desire a king (chs. 17:8-20; 19:17); but in Josiah's day the Israelites had been ruled by kings for centuries. It discriminates against Ammon and Moab in favor of Edom (ch. 23:3-8); but in Josiah's day and for a long time previously Egypt was the representative foe of the people of God (Isa. 63:6; Joel 3:19; Obad.), and Jeremiah promises future restoration to Moab and Ammon, but denies it to Edom (Jer. 48:47; 49:6, 17, 18). The legislation of Deuteronomy was in force long before the time of Josiah; it was observed at the coronation of Joash c. 836 B.C. (II Kings 11:12), and was followed by Joash's son and successor, Amaziah (II Kings 14:6; cf. Deut. 24:16). The reading of the book to the people affected them as it had the king. So deep was the impression produced that a 2d assault upon idolatry was begun, more sweeping than the first. After the king and his subjects had together covenanted to worship Jehovah only, they proceeded to take the vessels of Baal, of the Asherim, and of the heavenly bodies, burn them, and cast the ashes into the brook Kidron. The Asherah in the house of the Lord was similarly burned, the residences of the sodomites were broken down, and the high places were destroyed, not merely through the Kingdom of Judah, but through the former territory of the n. tribes, now largely empty of its Israelitish inhabitants. The Valley of Hinnom and the shrine of Topheth, in which children had been made to pass through the fire to Molech, were defiled, and other sweeping reforms effected. When at Beth-el, Josiah took the bones of the idolatrous priests from their graves, and burned them on the altar, thus fulfilling the prophecy of a man of God in Jeroboam's time (I Kings 13:2). Nor did he scruple to slay the living idolatrous priests themselves on the altars on which they had been accustomed to sacrifice. Then he concluded by holding a passover, so well attended and so solemn that nothing like it had been celebrated since the time of Samuel (II Kings 23:1-25; II Chron. 34:29 to 35:19).

Thirteen years afterward Pharaoh-necho, king of Egypt, marched an army along the maritime portion of Palestine on his way to the Euphrates, where he designed to try his strength against the great Assyrian power. Situated as the small and comparatively feeble Kingdom of Judah was between the Assyrian and Egyptian Empires, then in mutual hostility, it was difficult for it to maintain neutrality; indeed, Josiah seems to have looked on himself as a vassal of the Assyrian king, legally and morally bound to give him military aid in war; and he gave battle to Pharaoh-necho at Megiddo in the plain of Jezreel, and in the fight was mortally wounded by an arrow. His attendants removed him from his war chariot to a second conveyance, which brought him to Jerusalem. He had, however, only reached that capital when he died. Great lamentations were made for him by Jeremiah, the singing men and the singing women, and the people generally. His loss to his country was irreparable. The religious reforms which he had commenced were assailed, and the partial independence which his country had enjoyed under his rule passed away. He had reigned 31 years, but was only 39 when he died, about 608 B.C. (II Kings 22:1; 23:29, 30; II Chron. 35:20-27; cf. Zech. 12:11). Jeremiah and Zephaniah prophesied during the latter part of his reign (Jer. 1:2; 3:6; Zeph. 1:1).

2. A son of Zephaniah, in Zechariah's days (Zech. 6:10). Perhaps the same as Hen of v. 14; but see HEN.

Jos′i·bi′ah (jŏs′ĭ-bī′á). See JOSHIBIAH.

Jos′i·phi′ah (jŏs′ĭ-fī′á) [Jehovah will add, increase]. Head of the house of Shelomith, who returned from exile with Ezra (Ezra 8:10).

Jot [Lat. *iota*, from Gr. *iōta*=i; cf. Heb. *yōd*, *yōdh*=y]. The discourse of which Matt. 5:18 forms a part undoubtedly was spoken in Aramaic, and jot accordingly refers to the Hebrew letter *yōd*, *yōdh* (y). In the Aramaic-Hebrew writing in vogue in the time of our Lord, *yōd* (*yōdh*) was already the smallest letter in the alphabet. Hence, figuratively, jot signifies a matter that seems to be of small moment.

Jot′bah (jŏt′bá) [pleasantness, goodness]. The town of King Amon's grandfather (II Kings 21:19), probably same as Jotapata, which is identified with Khirbet Jefât about 7 miles n. of Sepphoris.

Jot′ba·thah (jŏt′bá-thá), in A.V. once **Jot′·bath** (jŏt′băth) (Deut. 10:7) [goodness, pleasantness]. A station of the Israelites in the wilderness, apparently near Ezion-geber (Num. 33:33). The place abounded in brooks of water (Deut. 10:7), and is probably to be identified with eṭ-Ṭâba, about 22 miles n. of 'Akabah.

Jo′tham (jō′thăm), in A.V. once **Jo′a·tham** (Matt. 1:9), in imitation of the Gr. form [Jehovah is perfect, sincere]. 1. Youngest son of Gideon. He escaped when his 70 brothers (the offspring of polygamy) were massacred by their half brother Abimelech; and afterward, in contempt of the usurpation, standing on Mount Gerizim, he uttered the parable, audible to the Shechemites in the valley below, of the trees anointing a king (Judg. 9:1-21).

2. A king of Judah, who began to reign as regent of his father, Uzziah, while the latter was a leper (II Kings 15:5). His regency began while Jeroboam II was still king of Israel (I Chron. 5:17). Further evidence of the partial contemporaneousness of the regency of Jotham and the reign of Jeroboam exists, if the earthquake took place while Uzziah and Jeroboam were reigning (Amos 1:1; Zech. 14:5) and occurred coincidently with or

shortly after Uzziah's invasion of the priest's office (Jos. *Antiq.* ix. 10, 4). He followed Jehovah, but did not interfere with the high places at which the people worshiped other gods. He built the high gate of the Temple and worked on the wall on the hill of Ophel, s. of the holy house. He erected cities in the uplands of Judah and castles and towers in the forests. He gained a victory over the Ammonites and made them tributary. During his reign of 16 years Isaiah and Hosea continued to prophesy (Isa. 1:1; Hos. 1:1). At the close of his reign the allied Israelites and Syrians began their invasion of Judah. He died at the age of 41, surviving his father scarcely a year it seems. He left his son Ahaz to ascend the throne (II Kings 15:32–38; II Chron. 27:1–9). With Jotham, Hoshea is connected by a strange synchronism: "Hoshea . . . reigned . . . in the twentieth year of Jotham" (II Kings 15:30). This reference has been explained as meaning the 20th year since Jotham began to reign, his accession having been recorded (v. 5), but his reign and death not having been yet described by the author of Kings. Whatever be the true explanation, this strange synchronism goes far to bring the data of the Hebrew record into harmony with the Assyrian chronology.

3. A son of Jahdai (I Chron. 2:47).

Jour'neys of the Is'ra·el·ites (ĭz'rĭ-ĕl-īts). See WILDERNESS OF THE WANDERING.

Joz'a·bad (jŏz'á-băd), in A.V. once **Jos'a·bad** (I Chron. 12:4) [Jehovah has bestowed]. 1. A Gederathite who joined David at Ziklag (I Chron. 12:4).

2 and 3. Two Manassites who assisted David to pursue the Amalekites after their capture of Ziklag (I Chron. 12:20).

4. A Levite, one of the overseers of the tithes in Hezekiah's reign (II Chron. 31:13).

5. A chief of the Levites in the time of Josiah (II Chron. 35:9).

6. A Levite, son of Jeshua (Ezra 8:33). Perhaps he was the Jozabad who by order of Ezra took part in teaching the people the law (Neh. 8:7), and was the Levitical chief who had the oversight of the outward business of the house of God (Neh. 11:16); he may have been the Levite of the name, who was induced by Ezra to put away his foreign wife (ch. 10:23).

7. A priest, a son of Pashhur, induced by Ezra to put away his foreign wife (Ezra 10:22).

Joz'a·car (jŏz'á-kär), in A.V. **Joz'a·char** (jŏz'á-kär) [Jehovah has remembered]. Son of an Ammonitess and one of the 2 assassins of Joash, king of Judah (II Kings 12:21). Some Hebrew MSS. read Jozabad (Heb. *Yōzá-băd*), which is probably reflected in Zabad (II Chron. 24:26). This confusion of consonants was easy, since *kaph* (k) and *beth* (b) resemble each other; so also do *resh* (r) and *daleth* (d).

Joz'a·dak (jŏz'á-dăk) and **Je·hoz'a·dak**, in A.V. **Jos'e·dech** in Haggai and Zechariah [Jehovah is just]. Father of Jeshua, the high priest (Ezra 3:2, 8). He was carried captive to Babylonia by Nebuchadnezzar (I Chron. 6:15).

Ju'bal (jōō'băl). The younger son of Lamech, by his wife Adah. Jubal was the father of all such as handle the harp and pipe (Gen. 4:21).

Ju'bi·lee, Ju'bi·le [Late Lat. *jubilaeus,* from Gr. *iōbēlaios,* from Heb. *yōbēl,* ram's horn, trumpet]. The 50th year occurring after 7 times 7 years had been counted from the institution of the festival or from the last jubilee (Lev. 25:8–10); cf. the calculation of Pentecost. It derived its name from the custom of proclaiming it by a blast on the trum-

pet. As every 7th year was a Sabbatical year, the jubilee followed immediately after one of this character. On the 10th day of the 7th month (the great Day of Atonement), in the 50th year, the trumpet of the jubilee was sounded. It proclaimed liberty to all Israelites who were in bondage to any of their countrymen, and the return to their ancestral possessions of any who had been compelled through poverty to sell them. Even the ground for that year was allowed to remain fallow, though it had been so in the previous Sabbatical year. To prevent injustice to one who having purchased land could retain it only to the first jubilee, the practice (thoroughly in conformity with the principles of political economy) was to give for the purchased possession only the worth of the temporary occupation till the jubilee year. But one purchasing from another a house in a walled city retained it permanently; it did not revert to the original owner at the jubilee, since city lots were apparently not bound up with the several portions of Canaan as originally allotted to families. Those of the unwalled villages were regarded as belonging to the field and did so return; so also did the houses of Levites wheresoever situated (Lev. 25:8–55; 27:17, 18; Num. 36:4). There appears to be an allusion to the jubilee in Isa. 61:1–3 and Ezek. 46:17; cf. also Neh. 5:1–13.

There are considerable difficulties entailed in carrying out the regulations of the Sabbatical year; an abundant harvest, however, is promised for the 6th year, which will be ample until that of the 9th is gathered in (Lev. 25:20–22). Some scholars suppose that perhaps not all the land lay fallow simultaneously every 7 years, but that various portions had their Sabbatical year at different times; thus a serious interruption in agriculture would be avoided. A more difficult problem arises when the 7th Sabbatical year and the year of jubilee fall together, since that involves having the land lie fallow for 2 successive years. In that case, since nothing could be sown in the 49th and 50th years, only some summer fruit could be obtained in the 51st. The 7th Sabbatical year and the year of jubilee, however, cannot be identified. Historical evidence is lacking that the year of jubilee was ever strictly observed in actual practice. But even if it remained ideal legislation, its social values lay in teaching personal liberty, restitution of property, and the simple life.

Ju'cal (jōō'kăl). See JEHUCAL.

Ju'da (jōō'dá). See JUDAH, JUDAS, JODA.

Ju·dae'a (jōō-dē'á) in A.V. in canonical books once **Ju·de'a** (jōō-dē'á) (Ezra 5:8), and thrice **Jew'ry** (jōō'rĭ) (Dan. 5:13; Luke 23:5; John 7:1) [Lat. from Gr. *Ioudaia,* from Heb. *Yehūdāh*]. A geographical term first introduced in the Bible in Ezra 5:8, A.V., to designate a province of the Persian Empire. It is there the rendering of the Aramaic *Yehūd.* The R.V. translates it "the province of Judah." The land of Judea is mentioned in I Esdras 1:39, and the kings of Judea in v. 33. The land of Judea is also spoken of in Maccabaean times after the Persian had given place to the Macedonian-Greek dominion (I Macc. 5:45; 7:10, A.V.). On the banishment of Archelaus Judea was annexed to the Roman province of Syria; but it was governed by procurators appointed by the Roman emperor. The succession of procurators was interrupted for a brief period by the reign of Herod Agrippa I, A.D. 41–44. The procurator resided at Caesarea. His immediate superior was the proconsul, or president, of Syria, ruling from Antioch (Luke 3:1; Jos. *Antiq.* xvii. 13, 5; xviii. 1, 1). This arrangement obtained when our Lord carried out his ministry on earth, and Judea is often mentioned in the N.T. (Luke 23:5-7; John 4:3; 7:3; Acts 1:8). Its n. boundary may be considered as extending from Joppa on the Mediterranean to a point on the Jordan about 10 miles n. of the Dead Sea. Its s. boundary may be drawn from the wadi Ghuzzeh, about 7 miles s.w. of Gaza, through Beer-sheba, to the s. portion of the Dead Sea. The length from n. to s. is about 55 miles, and that from e. to w. the same. See HISTORY.

Ju'dah (jōō'dȧ), Hellenized Ju'das, Ju'da, once Anglicized Jude (Jude 1) [let him (God) be praised]. 1. The 4th son of Jacob and of Leah. He was not associated with his brothers Simeon and Levi, when by treachery and murder they avenged the wrong done to Dinah, who was the full sister of all 3 (Gen., ch. 34). He married a Canaanite, a daughter of Shua of Adullam, and had 2 sons, Er and Onan, who were slain by divine judgment for their sins (ch. 38:1-10). Prior to this he had had a 3d son, Shelah (v. 5). Afterward, by Tamar, the deceased Er's widow, Judah became the father of twin sons, Perez and Zerah (vs. 11-30; ch. 46:12; Num. 26:19). It was through Perez that Judah became the ancestor of David (Ruth 4:18-22), and when the fullness of time was come, of our Lord (Matt. 1:3-16). Judah saved Joseph's life by proposing that he should be sold instead of murdered (Gen. 37:26-28). When Joseph, whose relationship to his brother was not suspected, proposed to detain Benjamin in Egypt, Judah made a plea in a speech marked by great natural eloquence, and ended by offering himself to remain a prisoner provided Benjamin were set free (ch. 44:33, 34). The result of this splendid advocacy was that Joseph, without further delay, revealed himself to his brethren (ch. 45:1). When Jacob was on his way to Egypt he chose Judah, though not the eldest son, to go before him to Joseph, to show the way before him unto Goshen (ch. 46:28). On account of the sins of Reuben, Simeon, and Levi, they were passed over, and the blessing of the birthright was bestowed by Jacob on Judah (ch. 49:3-10).

2. A tribe sprung from Judah. It was divided into 5 tribal families which proceeded from his 3 sons and 2 grandsons (Num. 26:19-21; I Chron. 2:3-6). The prince of the tribe of Judah in the early period of the wanderings was Nahshon, the son of Amminadab (Num. 1:7; 2:3; 7:12-17; 10:14). Another prince was Caleb, son of Jephunneh (chs. 13:6; 34:19). At the 1st census in the wilderness it numbered 74,600 (ch. 1:26, 27); and at the 2d census, taken at Shittim on the eve of entering Canaan, 76,500 (ch. 26:22). It was one of the tribes that stood on Mount Gerizim to bless the people (Deut. 27:12). Achan, who brought trouble upon all Israel by his greed, belonged to the tribe of Judah (Josh. 7:1, 17, 18). After the death of Joshua, this tribe was the first one sent to take possession of its allotted territory; and its fighting men, with the aid of the Simeonites, captured such towns as were found occupied by the Canaanites, and drove out the inhabitants of the hill country (Judg. 1:1-20).

The tribe of Judah occupied the greater part of s. Palestine. The boundary drawn for it by Joshua commenced at the extreme s. point of the Dead Sea, passed thence, probably by Wadi el-Fiḳrah, s. of the ascent of Akrabbim, to the wilderness of Zin, thence by the s. of Kadesh-barnea and the brook of Egypt to the Mediterranean Sea. The e. border was the Dead Sea. The n. boundary started from the n. end of the sea, at the mouth of the Jordan, and passing by Beth-hoglah and near Jericho, went up by the ascent of Adummim, by En-shemesh, to En-rogel and the valley of the son of Hinnom, s. of Jeru-

salem, passed on to Kiriath-jearim, and thence by Beth-shemesh and Timnah, n. of Ekron, to Jabneel, and on to the Mediterranean. That sea itself constituted the w. boundary, but a portion of the area was almost always in the hands of the Philistines (Josh. 15:1-12; cf. also vs. 13-63; ch. 18:11-20). The length of the territory of the tribe of Judah from n. to s. was about 50 miles where most thickly inhabited, but about 95 miles from Jerusalem to Kadesh-barnea; and its breadth from the Jordan to the Philistine plain was about 45 miles. As to its physical features, it is naturally divided into 3 regions: the hill country of Judah (Josh. 15:48; Luke 1:39); the lowland or Shephelah (Josh. 15:33), and the plain near the Mediterranean Sea. The country about Beer-sheba was known as the Negeb or South. A great part of Judah is rocky and barren, but it is admirably adapted for the culture of the vine and for pasture (cf. Gen. 49:11, 12). The artificially terraced hills (now neglected) were once the scene of extensive cultivation. Parts of the territory were regarded as a wilderness, especially the region s. of Arad (Judg. 1:16) and that immediately w. of the Dead Sea (Psalm 63, title). The city of Judah (II Chron. 25:28) is the city of David (II Kings 14:20).

Soon after their conquest of Canaan the Israelites were oppressed by the king of Mesopotamia, but Othniel, of the tribe of Judah, delivered the nation from the foreign domination (Judg. 3:8-11). In the troublous times which now came upon the Israelites, due to their neglect of God, to tribal jealousies, and to failure to dispossess all the heathen, Judah, Dan, and Simeon became a group by themselves, separated from the other tribes to the n. by a strip of country several miles broad which was traversed with inconvenience, in part by reason of its Canaanite inhabitants, Amorites, Gibeonites, and Jebusites, and in part on account of its natural roughness and wildness, being cleft by deep transverse valleys between Jerusalem and Jericho. It was also separated from Gad and Reuben by the Jordan and the Dead Sea. The tribe had its own difficulties to contend with, being beset by the Philistines (Judg. 3:31; 10:7; 13:1), and took little part in the wars of the other tribes against oppressors. Boaz and Ruth lived in Bethlehem at this time. Judah, however, united with the other tribes to punish Benjamin (ch. 20:1, 18). In the time of Eli and Samuel, when the Philistines oppressed both Judah and Benjamin, intercourse with the n. tribes became closer, and Judah was included in the kingdom of Saul. After the death of Saul, the men of Judah supported the claims of their tribesman David to the throne, and for 7 years warred in his behalf. When his cause triumphed, Jerusalem on the border of Judah and Benjamin was made the capital of all Israel. The promise had been given to David that his posterity should forever occupy his throne (II Sam. 7:13-16; I Chron. 17:12, 14, 23), though chastisement would be inflicted if there were a departure from Jehovah. The promise was not intended to do away with the necessity for wisdom in the king, and when Rehoboam showed his ignorance of the first principles of democratic government, 10 tribes were lost to the house of David. See ISRAEL 3.

Judah and a large part of Benjamin remained loyal to David's line, and constituted the main elements of the Kingdom of Judah. This kingdom lasted from c. 935 B.C. until the fall of Jerusalem in 586 B.C. During this time 19 kings of David's line, exclusive of the usurping Queen Athaliah, occupied the throne; see CHRONOLOGY, IV. Its territory was nearly coincident with that of the tribes of Judah and Benjamin, save that the n. boundary fluctuated, Beth-el being sometimes held by Judah, especially after the fall of Samaria. An event which exercised the most powerful influence on the history and ultimate fate of the rival kingdoms was the construction of the 2 golden calves by Jeroboam, that the people of the Northern Kingdom might have local sanctuaries, and not have to visit Jerusalem for worship, and perhaps be there won over to their old allegiance. One effect this had was to make all who were faithful to Jehovah emigrate to the Kingdom of Judah, bringing it no mean accession of spiritual and even of political strength (I Kings 12:26–33; 13:33; II Chron. 10:16, 17). The first relations of the 2 rival kingdoms were naturally those of mutual hostility. This, doubtless, emboldened the neighboring nations to intermeddle in Jewish affairs, and in the 5th year of Rehoboam's reign Shishak, king of Egypt, plundered Jerusalem (I Kings 14:25–28; II Chron. 12:1–12). War between Judah and Israel went on intermittently during the first 60 years of their separate existence (I Kings 14:30; 15:7, 16; II Chron. 12:15; 13:2–20); after which, under Ahab and Jehoshaphat, not merely peace, but a political and family alliance took place between the 2 reigning houses. In consequence, the worship of Baal was introduced into Judah, and at last became a potent factor in the destruction of the kingdom. Two great parties were formed, the one attached to the worship of Jehovah, the other in favor of Baal and other foreign divinities. During the subsequent period of the Kingdom of Judah these parties were in continual conflict with each other, first one and then the other becoming temporarily dominant, according as the reigning monarch was its friend or its opponent. As at other periods of the theocracy, fidelity to Jehovah brought temporal as well as spiritual prosperity, while apostasy from him was attended by disaster. Among the good kings were Asa, Jehoshaphat, Hezekiah, and Josiah, while Ahaz, Manasseh, and some others were conspicuously the opposite.

The foreign relations of the kingdom were important. Egypt was Judah's neighbor on the s.w., and was frequently involved in the affairs of Judah. The Egyptian kings Shishak and Zerah and, after a long interval, Necho warred with Judah. On the other hand, Egypt was regarded as a valuable ally against the great empires on the Tigris and Euphrates; yet the glorious past of Egypt rather gave false hopes to Judah, and the pro-Egyptian party in Jerusalem thus contribued to the fall of the nation. Egypt in the period of its decadence is aptly described by Rabshakeh (Isa. 36:6) as a bruised reed which will pierce the hand of him who leans upon it. In the final attack upon Jerusalem by the Chaldeans, the siege was temporarily raised, but resumed upon the defeat of an approaching Egyptian army. On the capture of Jerusalem by the Chaldeans, a large body of Jews found refuge in the country of the Nile (Jer., chs. 42 to 44).

In respect to the powerful nations on the Tigris and Euphrates, there was, of course, an Assyrian and a Neo-Babylonian or Chaldean period. The Assyrian period began in 734 B.C., when Ahaz invoked the aid of Tiglath-pileser against the allied kings of Israel and Syria, and afterward did homage to him at Damascus. After the Assyrian conquest of the Northern Kingdom in 722, Judah was exposed for nearly a century and a quarter to the greed and fury of the Assyrians, until Nineveh was overthrown in 612 B.C. Sargon, Sennacherib, Esarhaddon, and Ashurbanipal, 4 successors on the Assyrian throne, mention more or less extensive conquests of Judah. Three of these 4 kings are mentioned in the Hebrew records (Isa. 20:1; 36:1; 37:38), and apparently the 4th also (see OSNAPPAR). The

Neo-Babylonian or Chaldean period began in 605, when Jehoiakim was subjugated by Nebuchadnezzar. In less than a score of years Jerusalem was in ruins and the people of Judah were deported to Babylonia. The divine promise to David did not preclude the temporary loss of the throne by his descendants.

The causes which led to the fall of Jerusalem and the Exile were: 1. Those causes which issued in the disruption of the kingdom and the fall of Samaria and left Judah solitary. See ISRAEL 3. 2. The neglect of God's command to exterminate the Canaanites. When the Israelites could not, or would not, utterly destroy the Canaanites, they preserved the leaven of corruption in their midst. 3. Social and political alliances with idolatrous peoples. 4. The loss of moral strength by apostasy and the loss of enthusiasm for a great cause on earth, the establishment of God's Kingdom. 5. Refusal to repent at the call of the prophets. 6. These agencies had wrought ruin to the state and to manhood; and when it was time for Judah to yield, the persistent resistance to the dominant empire made with the help of petty alliances was a short-sighted policy, and a mistaken estimate of the coming imperial power. Little Judah should not have been submissive to Assyria, but should have yielded to Babylon toward the last. Such was the exhortation of Jeremiah. From the very beginning of their national existence the Hebrew people needed to husband all their resources, physical and political, moral and spiritual, if their kingdom was to stand amidst the empires of the world. On the return from exile, Zerubbabel, a descendant of David, was the civil ruler; but he was only a local governor under the Persians. He was followed after a time by Nehemiah, also of the tribe of Judah. Except during the administration of these 2 men, the governor of the Persian province Beyond-the-river, of which Judah formed a part, was the responsible head. After the disruption of the empire of Alexander the Great, Judea belonged to Egypt and Syria in turn. The successful revolt of the Maccabees against the Syrians led to the establishment of a dynasty of priest-kings, who sprang from the tribe of Levi, but occupied the throne of David. See MACCABEE. They were succeeded by an Idumaean dynasty, beginning with Herod the Great, ruling under the authority of the Romans. See HEROD 1, HISTORY, III. 4 (2), JERUSALEM, III. 2. When the scepter reverted to the house of David the kingdom was no longer temporal but spiritual, and the sovereign no earthly potentate, but the Son of God.

3. A Levite, among whose descendants was Kadmiel (Ezra 3:9). See HODAVIAH 4.

4. A Levite who returned from Babylon with Zerubbabel (Neh. 12:8).

5. A Levite, induced by Ezra to put away his foreign wife (Ezra 10:23).

6. A Benjamite, son of Hassenuah, and second in command over the city of Jerusalem (Neh. 11:9).

7. One who took part in the dedication of the wall, probably a prince of Judah (Neh. 12:34).

Ju'das (jōō'dás), **Ju'da**; Gr. form of Heb. Judah. 1. Judah, son of Jacob (Matt. 1:2, 3, A.V.).

2. An ancestor of Jesus, who lived before the Exile (Luke 3:30, in A.V. Juda).

3. Judas Maccabaeus, 3d of the 5 sons of the priest Mattathias (I Macc. 2:1–5). His father, driven to desperation by the determination of Antiochus Epiphanes to force idolatry upon the Jews, began the struggle for religious liberty. On the death of Mattathias, in 166 B.C., Judas, in compliance with his father's wish, assumed the military leadership of the

faithful Jews (chs. 2:66; 3:1). He entered immediately upon a career of victory. A combined Syrian and Samaritan army, under the command of Apollonius, advanced against him. He routed it, slew Apollonius, and took his sword (vs. 10, 11). Judas fought with this sword during the remainder of his life (v. 12). He defeated another Syrian army under Seron near Beth-horon (vs. 13–24), and, in 165 B.C., won a decisive battle with Gorgias near Emmaus (v. 27 to ch. 4:25). In the following year Antiochus sent a large army into Judea under the command of Lysias, but it was defeated by Judas at Beth-zur (Bethsura, ch. 4:26–34). In consequence of these successes, the Jews recovered control of the Temple (164 B.C.), purified it, and consecrated it anew (vs. 36–53). This event was celebrated by the annual feast of dedication (John 10:22). This Syrian war was followed by offensive operations under Judas and his brother Simon against hostile neighboring nations (I Macc. 5:9–54). Antiochus Eupator succeeded his father Antiochus Epiphanes on the throne of Syria, and reigned from 163 to 162 B.C. Under the guidance of Lysias he renewed the war with the Jews. Lysias defeated Judas at Beth-zacharias (ch. 6:28–47), and laid siege to Jerusalem (vs. 48–54), but was compelled by complications at home to conclude a peace with Judas and return to Antioch. The Jews acknowledged the suzerainty of Syria, but were promised the free exercise of their religion (vs. 55–61). Demetrius Soter, who reigned from 162 to 150 B.C., again favored the Grecian party among the Jews, and put the Hellenizer Alcimus into the high-priesthood (ch. 7:1–20). Judas resisted the efforts of this high priest (vs. 23, 24), and Demetrius sent an army under Nicanor to support Alcimus; but Nicanor was defeated at Capharsalama and again at Adasa near Beth-horon (vs. 26–50). During the brief peace which ensued Judas began negotiations with the Romans, and obtained from them assurances of friendship and assistance (ch. 8); but probably before the answer of the senate was returned, Demetrius sent another army under Bacchides into Judea in 160 B.C. Judas offered valiant resistance to the invaders at Elasa, but his troops were worsted and he himself was slain (ch. 9:1–18). His body was recovered by his brothers, and buried in the family sepulcher at Modin (v. 19). It was some time before the patriotic party recovered from the demoralization caused by their defeat and the death of their leader, but at length they offered the command to Judas' brother Jonathan (vs. 23–31).

4. Son of Chalphi and one of the 2 captains who stood by Jonathan Maccabaeus at Hazor when all the rest had fled, and enabled him to retrieve the day (I Macc. 11:70).

5. A son of Simon Maccabaeus (I Macc. 16:2). His father devolved the command of the army upon him and his brother John, and sent them against Cendebaeus. The 2 brothers gained a great victory over the Syrian general near Kidron, not far from Ashdod (vs. 2–10). Judas was wounded in the battle (v. 9). In 134 B.C., about 3 years later, he and his brother Mattathias were treacherously murdered in the castle of Dok by a kinsman by marriage, either at a feast at the same time that their father Simon was assassinated (vs. 14–17) or a little later (Jos. Antiq. xiii. 7; 8, 1).

6. Judas of Galilee, who, in the days of the enrollment, raised a revolt; but he perished, and all, as many as obeyed him, were scattered abroad (Acts 5:37; cf. Luke 2:2). Josephus calls him several times a Galilean, but once a Gaulonite, of the city of Gamala, implying that he was from Gaulonitis, e. of the Jordan. It appears that, with the support of a Pharisee called Sadduc, Judas imbued his countrymen with the belief that the enrollment under Quirinius was the commencement of their reduction to a state of servitude. He founded a philosophic sect whose chief tenet was that their only ruler and lord was God (Jos. Antiq. xviii. 1, 1 and 6; War ii. 8, 1). Josephus states that Judas succeeded in making some of the Jews revolt, and implies, but does not directly mention, that he lost his life. He expressly states, however, that his sons were slain (Antiq. xx. 5, 2). The indirect consequence of this attempt was the rise of the party of zealots, who largely contributed to the disturbances which provoked the Jewish war of A.D. 66–70.

7. Judas Iscariot, son of Simon Iscariot (John 6:71, R.V.), and the apostle who betrayed his divine Lord. By being surnamed Iscariot he is distinguished from another of the Twelve who was named Judas (Luke 6:16; John 14:22). The surname is generally interpreted as signifying that he came originally from Kerioth (see ISCARIOT), and may thus indicate that he was not a Galilean. Judged by his character, he followed Jesus probably because he expected to derive earthly advantage from the establishment of Christ's Kingdom. Jesus, without naming any person, early referred to the future act of treason which one of the Twelve would commit (John 6:70). Judas was appointed to keep the bag, but he yielded to dishonesty, and appropriated part of the money to himself. When Mary of Bethany in her affection for Jesus broke the alabaster box of precious ointment and anointed him, Judas was the spokesman of himself and others in denouncing what he considered extravagance, not that he cared for the poor, but that he wished the price of the ointment to be put into the bag, whence he could help himself as he had done before (John 12:5, 6). Jesus mildly reproved him; but the rebuke aroused his resentment, and he went to the chief priests and offered to betray Jesus to them for a price. They agreed with him on 30 pieces of silver, about $19.50, an ordinary price for a slave. From that time Judas sought an opportunity to deliver Jesus to them (Matt. 26:14–16; Mark 14:10, 11; cf. Ex. 21:32; Zech. 11:12, 13). At the passover supper Jesus, in order to carry out his design of being crucified at the feast, pointed out the traitor. The Devil had already put into the heart of Judas to betray his Master (John 13:2). When Jesus solemnly said, "One of you shall betray me," each disciple asked, "Is it I, Lord?" Peter beckoned to John to ask Christ who it was. Jesus replied enigmatically that it was one of those that were dipping with him in the dish (Matt. 26:23; Mark 14:20), one to whom he would give the sop (John 13:26, R.V.): in other words, his own familiar friend, one who ate bread with him (v. 18; cf. Ps. 41:9). Jesus and Judas, it would seem, were dipping together in the dish, and Jesus dipped the sop that he then held in his hand and gave it to Judas (John 13:26). After the sop Satan entered into Judas (v. 27). He also asked: "Is it I, Rabbi?" Jesus answered: "Thou hast said," which was the equivalent of "yes" (Matt. 26:21–25, R.V.). Even yet the disciples did not know just what Jesus meant, and when he added, "What thou doest, do quickly," they supposed that this was a direction to the treasurer to lose no time in buying some articles of which they had need. The traitor went at once to the chief priests. He was present at the supper and partook of it with the Twelve (Matt. 26:20); but he went out immediately after receiving the sop (John 13:30). The Eucharist was instituted after the supper (Matt. 26:26–29; Mark 14:22–25; Luke 22:19, 20). Luke in narrating the events of the supper, changes the actual order that he may place the spirit of Christ and the spirit

of the disciples in contrast (ch. 22:15–20 and vs. 21–24). After the departure of Judas the tone of Jesus' conversation changes. When supper was ended he led the Eleven to the Garden of Gethsemane. Thither Judas came, accompanied by a great multitude with swords and staves, from the chief priests and elders. In accordance with a sign that had been agreed upon, in order to point out Jesus to the soldiers, Judas advanced and saluted Jesus with a kiss, and Jesus was seized (Matt. 26: 47–50). The next morning, when Judas, now in calmer mood, saw that Jesus was condemned and was likely to be put to death, he awoke to the enormity of his guilt and went to the chief priests with the confession, "I have sinned in that I betrayed innocent blood," and offered to return the money. His conscience was not so seared as the consciences of the chief priests, who, having seduced the erring apostle into his great sin, then turned round on him and said, "What is that to us? see thou to it." On which he cast down the silver pieces in the Temple, and went and hanged himself (Matt. 27:3–5), "and falling headlong, he burst asunder in the midst, and all his bowels gushed out" (Acts 1:18). Acts 1:20 quotes Ps. 69:25 and 109:8; Judas was the antitype of the man who requited love with treachery; the quotation from Scripture is the sanction for filling his office by the election of another apostle.

8. One of the 12 apostles, carefully distinguished from Judas Iscariot (John 14:22). He was son or perhaps brother of James (Luke 6:16; Acts 1:13; see R.V. text and margin). He was also called Thaddaeus, for this name is found in other lists in the place corresponding to his (Matt. 10:3; Mark 3:18). The received text of Matt. 10:3 has "Lebbaeus, whose surname was Thaddaeus."

9. One of the 4 brethren of the Lord (Matt. 13:55; Mark 6:3, in A.V. Juda), and probably the author of The Epistle of Jude. See BRETHREN OF THE LORD, JUDE.

10. A man who lived at Damascus, in the street called Straight, and with whom Paul lodged just after his conversion (Acts 9:11).

11. Judas, surnamed Barsabbas. He was a leading man in the church at Jerusalem, and was chosen with Silas to accompany Barnabas and Paul to Antioch, bearing the letter from the council at Jerusalem to the churches of Syria and Cilicia. He had prophetic gifts. His subsequent history is unknown (Acts 15:22, 27, 32). He bears the same surname as the disciple Joseph, who was proposed for the apostleship, and may have been his brother (ch. 1:23).

Jude (jōōd). An English form of the name Judas, given to the writer of The Epistle of Jude (v. 1). He describes himself simply as "brother of James," by whom the author of The Epistle of James and leader of the church in Jerusalem seems to be meant. In this case Jude should be a brother of the Lord, and not an apostle; and these inferences seem borne out by the presence of a Judas in the lists of our Lord's brethren (Matt. 13:55; Mark 6:3), and by the apparent implication of v. 17 of his epistle that its writer was not an apostle. Except his bare name, nothing is recorded of him beyond what we may infer from the facts that the brethren of the Lord did not believe on him during his life on earth (John 7:5) and that after his resurrection they were his followers (Acts 1:14). According to Hegesippus (c. 110–c. 180), who is quoted by Eusebius (*H.E.* iii. 20), 2 grandsons of Jude, the brother of the Lord, were brought before Domitian as descendants of David, but they were dismissed as harmless peasants. This story confirms the possible inference from I Cor. 9:5 that

Jude was married, and implies that he was dead before A.D. 80.

The Epistle of Jude names its author as Judas, a bondservant of Jesus Christ and brother of James (v. 1); that is probably Judas, the brother of the Lord (Matt. 13:55; Mark 6:3). Its address is quite general: "To them that are called, beloved in God the Father, and kept for Jesus Christ" (Jude 1). In the vocabulary of Jude there is the obvious Christian element; certain words, largely through the teaching and writings of Paul, had acquired a fixed and recognized meaning among Greek-speaking Christians. The author also knew the language of the LXX. A remarkable feature of this book is the use made of pseudepigraphical literature. Thus vs. 14 and 15 are an almost exact quotation from the Book of Enoch (ch. 1:9). In v. 9 Jude refers to an incident recorded in the Assumption of Moses. Certain parallels in thought also suggest an acquaintance with the Testament of Moses.

According to the generally accepted view, the letter was largely used by II Peter, ch. 2; vs. 4–18, with the exceptions of vs. 14 and 15, are represented in II Peter, chs. 2:1 to 3:3. So it must have been written before II Peter, but probably not much before, and it seems natural to date it about A.D. 66. Those scholars who hold the genuineness of II Peter, but contend for its priority to Jude, are apt to date The Epistle of Jude between the death of Peter, c. A.D. 68, and the accession of the Roman emperor Domitian in A.D. 81. The reason for fixing upon A.D. 81 as the limit is found in the ancient tradition, quoted above from Hegesippus, from which it appears that Jude, the Lord's brother, had died before or at latest early in the reign of Domitian.

The epistle was called out by the outbreak among Jude's readers of an alarming heresy with immoral tendencies, probably something like the incipient Gnosticism rebuked in the Pastoral Epistles and the Apocalypse (vs. 3, 4, 10, 15, 16, 18), and was designed to save the churches addressed from its inroads. Jude attempts to encourage Christians to hold the faith once for all delivered to them against those who, though appearing to be Christians, have in practice denied the Lord. After the address (vs. 1, 2) the letter assigns the reason for its writing (vs. 3, 4) and then announces the condemnation in store for the false teachers (vs. 5–16); afterward it divulges the duty of true Christians in the circumstances (vs. 17–23), concluding with a rich and appropriate doxology (vs. 24, 25). Owing doubtless to its brevity, there are no very clear traces of the use of Jude in the very earliest fathers of the Church. In the latter part of the 2d century, however, it is found in full use in the Greek and Latin churches alike. It is included in the Old Latin version, listed in the Muratorian fragment, quoted and referred to as Jude's by Clement of Alexandria and Tertullian and later by Origen, and was clearly from the beginning a part of the Christian canon.

B. B. W. (rev., H. S. G.).

Judge. 1. A civil magistrate (Ex. 21:22; Deut. 16:18). On the advice of his father-in-law, and in order to relieve himself of overwork, Moses organized the judiciary of Israel; henceforth he himself acted only in matters of great importance, and for the adjudication of cases of less moment he assigned a judge to each 1,000, to each 100, to each 50, and to each 10 (Ex. 18:13–26). All the tribal subdivision heads already existed, and were known as princes and elders, who possessed civil and religious authority. In the judicial system which he organized Moses included these officials, and they retained under the new regulations their hereditary function of judging (Deut. 1:15–17; cf. 21:2, and see THOUSAND). Before his death Moses gave directions that the Israelites, on settling in Canaan, should appoint judges and officers in all their towns, with instructions to refer matters too difficult for these magistrates to the priests (chs. 16:18–20; 17:2–13; 19:15–20; cf. Josh. 8:33; 23:2; 24:1; I Sam. 8:1). With the establishment of the kingdom the king became the supreme judge in civil matters (II Sam. 15:2; I Kings 3:9, 28; 7:7; cf. I Sam. 8:5). David assigned Levites to the judicial office, and appointed 6,000 as officers and judges (I Chron. 23:4; 26:29). Jehoshaphat organized the judiciary in Judah still further, setting judges in the fortified cities, with a supreme court at Jerusalem, consisting of Levites, priests, and the heads of fathers' houses under the presidency of the high priest in religious matters and of the prince of Judah in civil matters (II Chron. 19:5–8).

The judges' activities, however, were not limited to judicial functions. The word judges is often parallel to kings (cf. Ps. 2:10; 148:11; Prov. 8:15, 16; Isa. 33:22; 40:23; Amos 2:3). The chief magistrate of the Carthaginians, who corresponded to the Roman consul, was called in Latin *sufes* (pl. *sufetes*), which is cognate with Hebrew *shôphêṭ*, judge. This usage explains the meaning of JUDGE 2.

2. A man whom God raised up to lead a revolt against foreign oppressors and who, having freed the nation and shown thereby his call of God, was looked to by the people to maintain their rights. The judges numbered 12, not including Abimelech, who was a petty king (ch. 9). They were Othniel of Judah, deliverer of Israel from the king of Mesopotamia; Ehud, who expelled the Moabites and Ammonites; Shamgar, smiter of 600 Philistines and savior of Israel; Deborah, associated with Barak, who led Naphtali and Zebulun to victory against the n. Canaanites; Gideon, who drove the Midianites from the territory of Israel; Tola and Jair; Jephthah, subduer of the Ammonites; Ibzan, Elon, Abdon, and Samson, the troubler of the Philistines. Eli and Samuel also judged Israel (I Sam. 4:18; 7:15), but the former acted in his official capacity as high priest and the latter as a prophet of Jehovah. These judges did not form an unbroken succession of rulers, but appeared sporadically. They were often local heroes, discharging their duties in restricted districts. According to the chronology of The Book of Judges, the total of years listed amounts to 410. Obviously this is too high and is inconsistent with I Kings 6:1, which reckons 480 years from the Exodus to the 4th year of Solomon. It must be borne in mind that some of the oppressions and not a few of the judges were evidently contemporaneous and overlapped. Shamgar, for example, was contemporary with Ehud, for the account of his exploit is inserted in the midst of the narrative of Ehud's work (Judg. 3:31); and a Philistine oppression of Judah was coeval with the Ammonite domination e. of Jordan and attack on Judah, Benjamin, and Ephraim (ch. 10:7). See CHRONOLOGY, III.

These facts throw light on the distracted state of the nation during the period of the Judges. The political districts, moreover, are found to be those that were separated by the Jordan and by the heathen barrier between Judah and the n. The song of Deborah and the history of Jephthah show the laxity of the bonds which united the tribes, and make known what tribes were able and willing to join forces and fortunes (cf. chs. 6; 8:1–9; 12:1–6). The isolation of Judah is remarkable; see JUDAH. But there were centralizing influences at work. National feeling existed, for the war of extermination waged against Benjamin shows the sense of national guilt and national responsibility. There was one Ark for all the tribes in the national tabernacle at Shiloh (Josh. 18:1; Judg. 21:19; cf. Ex. 23:14–17). It was carried to Beth-el, where the tribes had gathered for battle and would worship the Lord and ask counsel of him (Judg. 20:18–29). Great oppressions united the people in common misery and called for united action; great deliverers united the hearts of the people in loyalty and pride about one head; and great deliverances, obtained by united action, bound tribes together in common glory.

The period of the Judges has been called Israel's iron age. It was a cruel, barbarous, and bloody epoch. In fact a state of anarchy is suggested (chs. 17:6; 21:25) in the statement: "In those days there was no king in Israel: every man did that which was right in his own eyes." The people frequently lapsed into idolatry, and worship at the sanctuary was rendered difficult by the distracted state of the country. Ruthlessness and cruelty were displayed in Jael's murder of Sisera, in Jephthah's foolish vow and sacrifice of his daughter, in Gideon's treatment of the men of Succoth, in the sin of the men of Gibeah. Against these shadows, however, there stand out brightly the trust and filial piety of Jephthah's daughter, the fidelity of Ruth to Naomi, and the kindly and upright character of Boaz.

Judg'es, The Book of. A historical book of the O.T. following The Book of Joshua. It continues the narrative from his death, and consists of 3 parts:

I. *Introduction:* departure of the tribes to occupy the districts allotted to them (see Josh., chs. 15 to 21), and a list of the towns left by them in the possession of the Canaanite idolaters (Judg., chs. 1 to 2:5).

II. *History of the judges* as saviors of Israel, from the death of Joshua to that of Samson (chs. 2:6 to 16:31). This section has its own introduction, which, in forming a connection with The Book of Joshua, summarizes the events of the period and points out the religious lesson (chs. 2:6 to 3:6); then follow the more or less detailed accounts of 6 judges and brief mention of other 6. The assumption of kingship by Abimelech, son of Gideon, is recorded as an integral part of the history, although he was a petty king rather than a judge, and was not a savior of Israel.

III. *An appendix* giving 2 incidents of the period, viz., Micah's image worship and its establishment among the Danites who migrated to the n. (chs. 17; 18), and the outrage of Gibeah and the consequent war of the Israelites against Benjamin for its punishment (chs. 19 to 21).

The date of the composition of The Book of Judges is difficult to determine. At any rate, the following facts must be considered. All schools of criticism at present acknowledge the great antiquity of the song of Deborah, and that it is practically contemporary with the event which it celebrates. This section, the 2d and main portion of the book, could not have been written until after the death of Samson (ch. 16:30, 31). In the appendix, the recurring expression, "In those days there was no king in Israel," points to the composition of these chapters at least after the establishment of the kingdom. The tabernacle was no longer at Shiloh (ch. 18:31) when they were written. The mention of the "captivity of the land" (ch. 18:30) has been interpreted as a reference to the ravages of Tiglath-pileser in the n. (II Kings 15:29), or to the deportation of the 10 tribes after the fall of Samaria. There arises a difficulty, however, in the parallel statement (Judg. 18:31), "All the time that the house of God was in Shiloh," and so from the time of David Kimchi (c. A.D. 1160–1235) many interpreters have understood the captivity of the land to refer to the capture of the Ark by the Philistines, when Jehovah forsook Shiloh. Several expositors have adopted the conjecture of Houbigant (1777) that the last letter in the phrase, "Captivity of the land," has become corrupt, and that the Hebrew text originally had *nun* (n) instead of *ṣādē* (ṣ), which would then read, "Captivity of the Ark." Keil thinks that the reference is to a conquest of the land of the n. Danites and enslavement of its population by the neighboring Syrians of Damascus. Any of these suppositions is beset by fewer difficulties than the assumption that Micah's image worship continued until the fall of Samaria. The expression, "From Dan even to Beer-sheba" (Judg. 20:1), was appropriate even in the times of the Judges. The indications of time found in the appendix point to the period before David's reign over all Israel. The general introduction to the book, or at any rate some of its source material, was written while the Jebusites still occupied the stronghold at Jerusalem (Judg. 1:21; cf. II Sam. 5:6, 7). According to Jewish tradition, the book was written by Samuel, but this view is not held by critical scholars. The 3 parts, as outlined above, represent clear divisions and indicate that documents were used by a redactor in compiling the present work or an earlier form of it. These documents, it is believed, were based on older oral and written sources, and thus the history of that period was preserved. It is generally held by critics that the editor of the 2d section was influenced by the teachings of Deuteronomy. It is not known who the final editor was that united the 3 parts into one book.

As the analysis of the work shows, these histories were gathered and placed in their present framework in order to exhibit their religious teaching and serve as an admonition to subsequent ages. In this book we learn that the various nationalities, who lived in Canaan, were not exterminated, but continued to live with the Israelites in the land. In consequence of pagan influences the worship of Jehovah was endangered, but enough Israelites remained loyal to God to preserve the true religion (ch. 10:10–16; for the neighboring peoples cf. chs. 1:19–36; 3:13, 31; 6:3–33). The song of Deborah and the national uprising to punish the perpetrators and abettors of the crime of Gibeah reveal the consciousness of the participants that they were engaged in sacred warfare. The book shows by stern precept and example the consequences of forsaking the true worship of God.

Judg'ment Hall. See PRAETORIUM.

Ju'dith (jōō'dĭth) [Heb., fem. of *Yᵉhūdī*, Judean, Jew]. 1. A wife of Esau and daughter of Beeri, the Hittite (Gen. 26:34). She was also called Oholibamah (ch. 36:2; see ANAH 1).
2. Heroine of the book of Judith; see APOCRYPHA 4.

Jul'i•a (jōōl'yá) [Lat., fem. of *Julius*]. A Christian woman at Rome (Rom. 16:15), not unlikely the wife of Philologus.

Jul'ius (jōōl'yŭs) [Lat., name of a Roman clan]. A centurion of the Augustan band, employed to conduct Paul and other prisoners to Rome (Acts 27:1). He showed courtesy to the apostle, allowing him to visit his friends at Sidon (v. 3). At Crete he did not believe Paul's prediction of the coming storm (v. 11), but after the tempest broke he heeded Paul's advice and kept the sailors from forsaking the ship (v. 31). When the vessel was wrecked, the guard wanted to kill the prison-

ers lest any should escape; but he forbade the butchery, desiring to save Paul (vs. 42, 43).

Ju'ni•as (jōō'nĭ-ăs), in A.V. **Ju'ni•a** (jōō'-nĭ-á). A Jewish Christian at Rome, a kinsman and fellow prisoner of Paul, and in Christ before him (Rom. 16:7).

Ju'ni•per. Not the coniferous tree of the genus *Juniperus,* of which several species occur in Lebanon, Galilee, and Bashan, but a leguminous plant (*Retama raetam*), an almost leafless broom (I Kings 19:4, 5; Job 30:4; Ps. 120:4); cf. J.V. and R.V. marg. See BROOM.

Ju'pi•ter (jōō'pĭ-tẽr). The supreme god of the Romans. He corresponded to the Zeus of the Greeks, and in the only part of the N.T. in which the name is introduced (Acts 14:12, 13) the Greek text has Zeus. Zeus had a noted temple at Olympia in Elis (Herod. ii. 7), from which he derived his designation of Olympius. Antiochus Epiphanes erected a temple to him under that title at Athens and dedicated the temple at Jerusalem to Jupiter Olympius. According to Josephus, at the request of the Samaritans he called the sanctuary on Gerizim by the name of Jupiter, the Protector of strangers (II Macc. 6:2; Jos. *Antiq.* xii. 5, 5). The worship of Jupiter, which Paul and Barnabas met with at Lystra, existed at the time over the whole Greek and Roman world. He had temples and a priesthood; garlands were presented to him, as were also offerings of other kinds, and oxen and sheep were sacrificed to propitiate his favor.

Ju'shab•he'sed (jōō'shăb-hē'sĕd) [loving-kindness is returned or requited]. A son of Zerubbabel (I Chron. 3:20).

Jus'tus (jŭs'tŭs) [Lat., just, righteous]. 1. A surname of Joseph, the unsuccessful candidate for the apostleship rendered vacant by the fall of the unworthy Judas (Acts 1:23).
2. A godly man of Corinth, whose house adjoined the synagogue, and with whom Paul lodged (Acts 18:7). His fuller name was Titus Justus (R.V.).
3. The surname of a Jew called Jesus, who joined Paul in sending salutations to the Colossians (Col. 4:11).

Ju'tah (jōō'tá) and **Jut'tah** (jŭt'á) [extended, inclined]. A town in the hill country of Judah, mentioned with Maon, Carmel, and Ziph, and doubtless in their vicinity (Josh. 15:55). With its suburbs it was assigned to the priests (ch. 21:16). It is now called Yaṭṭā (Yuṭṭā), and stands on a low eminence, about 5½ miles s. by w. of Hebron. It has been suggested that Jutah was the city of Judah in the hill country to which Mary went to visit Elisabe h (Luke 1:39), and that Judah (*Iouda*) has been substituted for Jutah (*Iouta*). The more common conjecture, however, is that Hebron was the city of Elisabeth, but we do not know the birthplace of John the Baptist.

K

Kab (kăb), in A.V. **Cab** [a hollow vessel]. A Heb. dry and liquid measure (II Kings 6:25). It held ⅙ of a seah or ¹⁄₁₈₀ of a homer and was equal to about 2 quarts. See MEASURE, III.

Kab'ze•el (kăb'zĕ-ĕl) [(whom) God gathers]. A city in the extreme s. of Judah (Josh. 15:21). It was the home of David's heroic supporter Benaiah (II Sam. 23:20; I Chron. 11:22). The town was inhabited after the Exile (Neh. 11:25; where it is once called by the synonymous name of Jekabzeel). Probably to be identified with Khirbet Ḥōra.

Ka'desh (kā'dĕsh) [consecrated], including **Ka'desh-bar'ne·a** (kā'dĕsh-bär'nē-á). 1. A fountain, city or town, and wilderness on the s. frontier of Judah and of Palestine (Num. 20:16; 34:4; Josh. 15:3; Ps. 29:8; Ezek. 47:19; 48:28); distinguished as Kadesh-barnea from other places bearing the name Kadesh (cf. Num. 13:26 with ch. 32:8; cf. Deut. 1:19 with ch. 46). At an early period it was called En-mishpat or Fountain of Judgment (Gen. 14:7). It was in the wilderness of Paran (Num. 13:3, 26), in the wilderness of Zin (ch. 20:1; 27:14), 11 days' journey from Sinai by way of Mount Seir (Deut. 1:2), in the uttermost of the border of Edom (Num. 20:16). It appears to have been not a great distance from the highway between Palestine and Egypt, for Hagar's well was situated between Kadesh and Bered, and on the road to Egypt (Gen. 16:7, 14; cf. ch. 20:1). The place was overrun by Chedorlaomer (ch. 14:7). Into the region adjacent Hagar fled (ch. 16:7, 14), and Abraham sojourned there for a time (ch. 20:1). The Israelites, during their wanderings, twice encamped at Kadesh. They arrived in the neighborhood in the 2d year about the 5th month (Num. 13:20; cf. 10:11), sent thence the spies into Canaan, received the discouraging report there about the difficulties of conquest (Gen. 13:26), refused to advance, and were condemned to remain in the wilderness, and abode at Kadesh many days (Deu.. 1: 46). They returned to Kadesh in the 1st month (Num. 20:1) of the 40th year (ch. 33:36, 38; cf. Deut. 2:7, 14). Here Miriam died and was buried (Num. 20:1); and here Moses smote the rock that water might gush out, as, in similar circumstances, it had done at Rephidim (ch. 20:1–13); see MERIBAH 1. But he and Aaron sinned in acting in their own name. From Kadesh ambassadors were sent to the king of Edom to ask permission for the Israelites to pass through his territory (ch. 20:14, 16, 22; Judg. 11:16, 17). The place has been identified with 'Ain Ḳadīs, which is about 77 miles to the s. of Hebron and 51 miles s. of Beer-sheba. The spring, which is of sweet water, issues from under a rugged spur of rock belonging to the n.e. mountain range w. of the 'Arabah. The stream is copious and is intercepted in its course by 2 or 3 wells built round with masonry. Then after traversing the oasis which it has created, it is finally lost in the desert beyond. See KEDESH 1.

2. The name is perhaps contained in "the land of Tahtim-hodshi" (II Sam. 24:6), corrected by means of Lucian's text (Greek) to "the land of the Hittites, toward Kadesh."

Kad'mi·el (kăd'mĭ-ĕl) [God is in front (as leader)]. A Levi.e, head of a tribal house, who returned from Babylon with Zerubbabel (Ezra 2:40; Neh. 7:43; 12:8). He helped to oversee the workmen engaged in rebuilding the Temple (Ezra 3:9). The representative of the house sealed the covenant (Neh. 10:9), perhaps being the same person who had previously assisted in the public confession (Neh. 9:4, 5).

Kad'mon·ites (kăd'mŏn-īts) [people of the east]. A tribe dwelling somewhere between Egypt and the Euphrates (Gen. 15:19), probably in the Syrian desert.

Kain (kān) [smith]. 1. The tribal name from which the more familiar Gentile adjective Kenite is derived (R.V. of Num. 24:22; Judg. 4:11 marg.). See KENITE.

2. A village in Judah, in A.V. spelled Cain (Josh. 15:57); perhaps it was an old settlement of the Kenites. See CAIN 3.

Kal'la·i (kăl'á-ī) [swift]. A priest, head of the father's house of Sallai in the time of Joiakim, the high priest (Neh. 12:20).

Ka'mon (kā'mŏn); in A.V. **Ca'mon**. The place where the judge Jair the Gileadite was buried (Judg. 10:5), probably Ḳamm in Gilead. Eusebius and Jerome locate it in the Plain of Esdraelon, between Megiddo and Acre; but presumably it was in Gilead, as Josephus states (Jos. *Antiq.* v. 7, 6). Polybius mentions a town Kamous which was taken by Antiochus in his war with Ptolemy Philopator, immediately after he had captured Scythopolis and at the same time that he took Pella, Abila, Gadara, and other places in Gilead (Polybius *Hist.* v. 70, 12).

Ka'nah (kā'ná) [place of reeds]. 1. A brook which formed part of the boundary line between Ephraim and Manasseh (Josh. 16:8; 17:9). Robinson identified it with the wadi Kānah, which rises s. of Shechem and joins the 'Aujah, the combined streams falling into the Mediterranean 4 miles n. of Joppa. This seems too far s., but the identity of the ancient and modern names is in its favor.

2. A town on the boundary of Asher (Josh. 19:28), probably modern Ḳānā, about 7 miles s.e. of Tyre.

Kaph (käf). See CAPH.

Ka·re'ah (ká-rē'á), in A.V. once **Ca·re'ah** [bald]. Father of the captains Johanan and Jonathan, who came to Gedaliah, the Babylonian governor of Judah (II Kings 25:23; Jer. 40:8).

Kar'ka (kär'ká), in A.V. **Kar'ka·a** (kär'ká-á), retaining the final syllable which denotes direction [floor, ground, bottom]. A place on the s. boundary of Judah (Josh. 15:3).

Kar'kor (kär'kôr) [cf. Arab. *ḳarḳar*, soft, even ground]. A place e. of the Jordan, where Zebah and Zalmunna encamped with their army (Judg. 8:10).

Kar'tah (kär'tá) [city]. A town of Zebulun given to the Merarite Levites (Josh. 21:34); identified with 'Athlīt, on the seacoast about 9 miles s. of the headland of Carmel.

Kar'tan (kär'tăn) [town, city]. A town of Naphtali, given to the Gershonite Levites (Josh. 21:32). Called in I Chron. 6:76 Kiriathaim, A.V. Kirjathaim. Identified with Khirbet el-Ḳureiyeh, n.e. of 'Ain Ibl.

Kat'tath (kăt'ăth). A town of Zebulun (Josh. 19:15); identified sometimes with Kitron of Judg. 1:30, and sometimes with Kartah.

Ke'dar (kē'dĕr) [probably, mighty; cf. Arab. *ḳadara* (to be able), but also to be considered is Heb. *ḳādar* (to be dark). A tribe descended from Ishmael (Gen. 25:13), children of the e., dwelling in black tents, possessing flocks and camels (S. of Sol. 1:5; Isa. 60:7; Jer. 49:28, 29), and having villages also in the wilderness (Isa. 42:11). They were an Arabian tribe (Isa. 21:13, 16; Ezek. 27:21). They were ruled by princes (*ibid.*), and were skillful in archery (Isa. 21:16, 17). They dwelt between Arabia Petraea and Babylonia, and are called the Cedrei by Pliny.

Ked'e·mah (kĕd'ē-má) [toward the east]. A tribe descended from Ishmael (Gen. 25:15; I Chron. 1:31).

Ked'e·moth (kĕd'ē-mŏth) [ancient places or eastern parts]. A city e. of the Jordan, near the wilderness (Deut. 2:26), allotted to the Reubenites (Josh. 13:18) and assigned to the Merarite Levites for residence (ch. 21:37; I Chron. 6:79). The preferred location is Ḳaṣr ez-Za'ferān, about 2½ miles n.w. of el-Medeiyineh, but consideration is also given to Khirbet er-Remeil, 2½ miles w.s.w. of el-Medeiyineh.

Ke'desh (kē'dĕsh) [sacred place, sanctuary]. 1. A town in the extreme s. of Judah

(Josh. 15:23), possibly Kadesh-barnea (v. 3), but Dillmann identifies it with Kādūs, s. of Hebron, 1 day's journey by caravan.

2. A town of the Canaanites taken by Thothmes III, later by Joshua after the defeat of its king (Josh. 11:12; 12:22), allot.ed to the tribe of Naphtali (ch. 19:37) and, to distinguish it from other towns of the name, called Kedesh-naphtali (Judg. 4:6; Tobit 1:2) and Kedesh in Galilee (Josh. 20:7), given to the Gershonite Levites for their residence, and made a city of refuge (Josh. 21:32). It was the residence of Barak (Judg. 4:6). Its inhabitants were removed to Assyria by Tiglath-pileser (II Kings 15:29). Jonathan defeated the army of Demetrius there (I Macc. 11:63, 73; Jos. *Antiq.* xiii. 5, 6). Identified with Ḳades in Upper Galilee, about 4½ miles n.w. of Lake of Ḥūleh and 26 miles e. of Tyre.

3. A city of Issachar given to the Gershonite Levites (I Chron. 6:72; in Josh. 21:28 Kishion, A.V. Kishon); identified with Tell Abū Ḳedeis, 2½ miles s.e. of Megiddo. See KISHION.

Ke'he·la'thah (kē'hê-lā'tha͘) [an assembly]. A station of the Israelites in the wilderness (Num. 33:22, 23), probably at Kuntilet Ḳrayeh, also called 'Ajrūd, near Bir el-Māyen.

Ke·i'lah (kê-ī'la͘). A town in the lowland of Judah (Josh. 15:44; I Chron. 4:19). The Philistines fought against it, but David attacked them and delivered the town. Nevertheless he did not remain in the town when Saul approached, lest the men of Keilah should surrender him to Saul (I Sam. 23:1–13). The town was inhabited after the Captivity (Neh. 3:17, 18). Probably to be identified with Khirbet Ḳīlā, 8½ miles n.w. of Hebron.

Ke·la'iah (kê-lā'ya͘). See KELITA.

Kel'i·ta (kĕl'ĭ-ta͘) [perhaps, dwarf; cf. Arab. ḳulāṭ]. A Levite, called also Kelailah, who was induced by Ezra to put away his foreign wife (Ezra 10:23). He was employed with others by him to read and interpret the law to the people (Neh. 8:7), and with Nehemiah sealed the covenant (ch. 10:10).

Kem'u·el (kĕm'ū-ĕl) [perhaps, congregation of God]. 1. Son of Nahor and Milcah, and head of a younger branch of the Aramaeans (Gen. 22:21).

2. A prince of the tribe of Ephraim and a commissioner for the allotment of Canaan (Num. 34:24).

3. A Levite, father of Hashabiah (I Chron. 27:17).

Ke'nan (kē'năn), in R.V. of O.T. and once in A.V. (I Chron. 1:2); in A.V., and R.V of N.T., **Ca·i'nan (Cai'nan)**. 1. Son of Enos (Gen. 5:9–14; I Chron. 1:2; Luke 3:37, 38).

2. Son of Arphaxad, and father of Shelah (Luke 3:36, R.V.). The corresponding genealogy of Gen. 10:24; 11:12 has no Cainan; the LXX, however, has, and Luke quotes from it.

Ke'nath (kē'năth) [possession]. A town on the w. slope of the Jebel Hauran, on the extreme n.e. border of Israelitish territory. It was the most easterly of the 10 cities of the Decapolis, and is generally identified with Ḳanawāt, 16 miles n.n.e. of Bostra (Boṣrah). It was taken by Nobah, probably a Manassite, who called it after his own name (Num. 32:42). The new name, however, did not permanently supplant the old one. The town passed again into Gentile hands (I Chron. 2:23). Herod the Great was defeated here by the Arabians (Jos. *War* i. 19, 2).

Ke'naz (kē'năz). 1. A descendant of Esau through Eliphaz (Gen. 36:9, 11). He became a chieftain in Mount Seir (v. 15), probably

taking his title from the clan which he ruled (vs. 40–43). The reference in Josh. 15:17; I Chron. 4:13 is probably likewise to the tribe. See KENIZZITE.

2. A descendant of Caleb, son of Jephunneh (I Chron. 4:15).

Ke'nez·ite (kē'nĕz-īt). See KENIZZITE.

Ke'nite (kē'nīt) [smith]. A tribe of which a branch dwelt in Canaan or vicinity in the time of Abraham, apparently closely allied to the Kenizzites and the Amalekites (Gen. 15:19; Num. 24:20–22); another portion of the same people was in Midian, and by the time of Moses had become incorporated with the Midianites (Judg. 1:16; 4:11; cf. Num. 10:29). Long before the advent of the Israelites, the presence of the mineral deposits in the wadi 'Arabah was known, and the mines in all probability were exploited by the Kenites and Edomites. As their name implies, the Kenites were smiths by occupation. Balaam's parable implies that the Kenites were at home in Edom and in the wadi 'Arabah (Num. 24:20–22). Apparently before the conquest of Canaan the Kenites dwelt in the rugged, rocky country n.e. of the Amalekites and to the e. and s.e. of Hebron. Hobab the Midianite, of the family of the Kenites, accompanied the Israelites on their march from Mount Sinai to Canaan to aid them with his knowledge of the country (Num. 10:29–32). When the Israelites crossed the Jordan, encamped at Gilgal, and took Jericho, Hobab's family pitched their tents at Jericho; but after the conquest of Canaan they cast in their lot with the tribe of Judah, and settled in the wilderness of Judah, s. of Arad and s.e. of Hebron (Judg. 1:16). This choice perhaps indicates that they were indeed a branch of the old Kenite tribe of Canaan and sought the home of their forefathers. One Kenite, however, did not care to dwell with his brethren in the s., but took up his abode near Kedesh in Naphtali (Judg. 4:11). The Kenites who settled in the s. of Judah were still there in friendly relations with the Israelites in the time of Saul and David (I Sam. 15:6; 27:10; 30:29). They had their registry with Judah (I Chron. 2:55). The presence of individual Kenites in Judah and Israel may be explained on the supposition that they were itinerant smiths. See AMALEKITES, KENIZZITE.

Ken'iz·zite (kĕn'ĭz-īt), in A.V. **Ke'nez·ite**, save once (Gen. 15:19). One of the tribes in or near Canaan in the time of Abraham (Gen. 15:19). Found settled in Mount Seir, it became subject to the victorious descendants of Esau, when they took possession of the country (Deut. 2:12), amalgamated with the conquerors, and looked to one of Esau's descendants as its head. This chieftain was known as Kenaz from the tribe which he ruled (Gen. 36:11, 15, 40–42). The name of one of the descendants of Kenaz, Ge-harashim (I Chron. 4:14), suggests that the Kenizzites lived in the Valley of Smiths, which may be identified with the wadi 'Arabah. See IR-NAHASH. Individuals of the tribe united with the sons of Jacob, Jephunneh the Kenizzite apparently taking to wife a woman of the tribe of Judah, and Othniel the Kenizzite becoming the first judge of Israel after the Conquest. See CALEB 2.

Ke·re' (kē-rā', kĕ-rē') [Aram. passive participle, ḳerē (what is to be) read]. A variant or official reading of a Hebrew word appearing in the margin of a MS. or an edition of the Hebrew Bible, which in the opinion of the Jewish critics (Masoretes) is to be substituted or read for what is in the text (the *kethib, q.v.*).

Ker'en-hap'puch (kĕr'ĕn-hăp'ŭk) [the horn of antimony (eye paint)]. The youngest of

Job's 3 daughters born after his great trial (Job. 42:14).

Ke'ri•oth (kĕr'ĭ-ŏth), in A.V. once **Kir'i•oth** (Amos 2:2) [cities]. 1. A town in the extreme s. of Judah, Kerioth-hezron (Josh. 15:25). The same as Hazor 3 (q.v.).

2. A town of Moab (*Moabite Stone*, 13, see MOABITE STONE; Jer. 48:24), apparently fortified (v. 41). It possessed palaces (Amos 2:2). It is supposed to be a synonym of Ar, the ancient capital of Moab, because it seems to be referred to as the capital (*ibid.*), and because in enumerations of the towns of Moab when Kerioth is cited Ar is omitted (Jer., ch. 48; *Moabite Stone*) and vice versa (Isa., chs. 15; 16; cf. Josh. 13:16–21). See AR. An identification with Kir of Moab has also been suggested.

Ke'ri•oth-hez'ron (kĕr'ĭ-ŏth-hĕz'rŏn). See KERIOTH 1 and HAZOR 3.

Ke'ros (kē'rŏs). Founder of a family of Nethinim, members of which returned from captivity (Ezra 2:44; Neh. 7:47).

Ke•thib' (kĕ-thēv'), **Ke•thiv'** (kĕ-thēv') [Aram. passive participle, kᵉthīb, written]. The word actually written or appearing in the text of the Hebrew Bible, for which according to the Masoretes the *kere* is to be substituted. The *kethib*, however, cannot always be rejected, since in some cases it represents an old tradition, may have the support of ancient versions, and may be the better reading. In many cases the differences between the *kethib* and the *kere* are not very serious, but in Biblical studies both must receive careful consideration.

Ket'tle. See POT.

Ke•tu'rah (kĕ-tū'rȧ) [incense]. Abraham's 2d wife (Gen. 25:1; 26:3). She became the ancestress of the tribes of Zimran, Jokshan, Medan, Midian, Ishbak, and Shuah (Gen. 25:1, 2; I Chron. 1:32). Her sons were not regarded as on the same level with Isaac, and their father gave them gifts and sent them away during his lifetime to the e. country (Gen. 25:6). A tribe Ḳaṭūrā is mentioned in late Arabian genealogies as dwelling near Mecca.

Ke•veh' (kĕ-vā'). See LINEN 6.

Key. An Oriental key (Judg. 3:25) consists of a piece of wood with pegs fastened on it corresponding to small holes in a wooden bar or bolt within. The action of such a key was rather to lift and push the bar inside the door; it was not turned like a modern key. See LOCK. It is generally carried in the girdle, but occasionally it is fastened to something else and borne over the shoulder (cf. Isa. 22:22). The key is the symbol of authority (*ibid.*; Matt. 16:19; Rev. 1:18; 3:7; 9:1; 20:1). It is also the symbol of access to that from which one would otherwise be shut out (Luke 11:52).

Ke•zi'ah (kĕ-zī'ȧ), in A.V. **Ke•zi'a** (kĕ-zī'ȧ) [cassia]. The 2d of Job's daughters born after his great trial (Job 42:14).

Ke'ziz (kē'zĭz). See EMEK-KEZIZ.

Kib'roth-hat•ta'a•vah (kĭb'rŏth-hă-tā'ȧ-vȧ) [the graves of lust]. A place in the Sinaitic peninsula, between Mount Sinai and Hazeroth, where the Israelites were buried who were slain by a plague for lusting after the flesh-pots of Egypt (Num. 11:33–35; 33:16, 17; Deut. 9:22). Identified with a caravan station, Rueis el-Ebeirig, which is a hill about 10 hours by foot n.e. of Jebel Mûsa in a wide place formed by the crossing of Wadis Sa'al, Khalif, Metūra, and Elleiga.

Kib•za'im (kĭb-zā'ĭm) [two heaps]. See JOKMEAM.

Kid. A young goat. It was highly esteemed as an article of food (Luke 15:29). The flesh was boiled and eaten (Judg. 6:19). It was forbidden to cook a kid in its mother's milk (Ex. 23:19), since that may have been a heathen fertility rite. A kid might be used as a burnt offering (Judg. 13:15, 19). The Hebrew words, *śā'īr*, he-goat, and *śᵉīrāh*, she-goat, modified by *'izzīm*, she-goats, are rendered "kid of the goats" in A.V., but translated by "goat" with the proper indication of gender in R.V. (Gen. 37:31; and wherever kid occurs in Leviticus, Numbers, and Ezekiel). See GOAT.

Kid'ron (kĭd'rŏn), in A.V. of I Maccabees and N.T. **Ce'dron** [perhaps, dark, turbid]. 1. A valley known today as the wadi Sittī Maryam, which lies between the e. walls of Jerusalem and the Mount of Olives. It is nearly 3 miles in length, commencing about 1¼ miles n. of the n.w. corner of the city as a wide open valley. It trends for a mile and a half toward the s.e. under the name of Wadi el-Jauz; then turns sharply to the s. and continues in this direction past the city as far as the Valley of Hinnom and En-rogel. Opposite St. Stephen's gate the depth is fully 100 feet and the width not more than 400 feet. Here it bends again to the s.e. and pursues a tortuous course to the Dead Sea. No stream flows in it except during continuous heavy rains in winter, and there is no evidence that its bed was ever occupied by a perennial brook. The word brook used with it in the English version represents Heb. *naḥal*, torrent, wadi, which either means a ravine occupied by the channel of a torrent dry during the hot season or denotes the winter torrent itself. By writers who use Greek, the Kidron is expressly called winter brook (John 18:1, R.V. marg.; I Macc. 12:37, LXX). The name may be derived from the turbid water of the winter torrents or from the gloominess of the valley, especially in its lower part. To speakers of the Greek language, the Greek form of the name suggested the word for cedar and the rivulet came to be frequently called the brook of the cedars (John 18:1, R.V. marg.; II Sam. 15:23, Codex Vaticanus). It separates Jerusalem from the Mount of Olives and had to be crossed by those going from the city to Bethany or Jericho (II Sam. 15:23). It was regarded as the e. boundary of the city (I Kings 2:37; Jer. 31:40). The portion of the valley lying near the s. part of the city was early used as a common burying ground (II Kings 23:6); and godly kings, who from time to time found it necessary to cleanse the Temple of idolatrous symbols, made the Kidron valley the dumping place for the ashes of these abominations (I Kings 15:13; II Kings 23:4; II Chron. 29:16; 30:14). Athaliah is reported to have been led away to the Kidron for execution that the Temple might not be defiled by her blood (Jos. *Antiq.* ix. 7, 3). See JEHOSHAPHAT, VALLEY OF.

2. A town near Jamnia and Ashdod (I Macc. 15:39; 16:9, 10), fortified by Cendebaeus and occupied by a detachment of his Syrian army because it commanded several roads into Judea (ch. 15:41). See GEDEROTH.

Ki'nah (kī'nȧ) [dirge, lamentation]. A village in the extreme s. of Judah (Josh. 15:22), at the head of Wadi el-Ḳeini, near Khirbet Samra.

Kine. See COW.

King. A male sovereign invested with supreme authority over a nation usually for life and by hereditary succession; he rules over that form of state which is specifically called a kingdom. Deep religious fervor was regarded as an essential characteristic of Baby-

THE HEAD OF THE KIDRON VALLEY

Showing the Jericho Road, the New Palestine Archaeological Museum, and the Walls of the City of Jerusalem

lonian and Assyrian kings. The ideal priest-king may be traced back to Sumerian times. Sovereignty upon earth included submission to the gods and loyalty to righteousness as well as support of justice and punishment of evil. Kings were deified in Sumerian times. Nimrod ruled over a kingdom in Babylonia containing several cities (Gen. 10:10). Chedorlaomer was king of Elam and head of a confederacy of kings (ch. 14:1, 5). Nebuchadnezzar of Babylon and Artaxerxes the Persian were each a king over kings (Ezra 7:12; Dan. 2:37; cf. II Kings 24:17). In Canaan in the time of Abraham the rule of a king was often over one town only (Gen. 14:2, 18; 20:2), as was the case of the early Sumerian city-states. Some centuries later Joshua enumerated 31 kings whom he had conquered within the bounds of Canaan (Josh. 12:7–24). It was not until centuries after the tribes and nations adjacent to Palestine had been ruled by kings that the Israelites demanded a visible monarch. Although the demand when made was prompted by unbelief and insofar was rebellion against Jehovah, yet it was not in itself at variance with the theocracy and the invisible rule of Jehovah; for the theocracy in its very institution contemplated the administration of the several offices of government by human agents; see THEOCRACY. Moses foresaw the need that would arise for a visible king and he provided for the event (Deut. 17:14–20), just as provision was made for prophets and priests to make known the will or legislation of Jehovah and for judges to represent the unseen Judge. When the king was chosen the theocracy was not abolished. The nominally uncontrolled sovereign was required to be the vicegerent of Jehovah; and when Saul, mistaking his position, sought to act independently, another was chosen to supersede him and his posterity on the throne. The same rule obtained with all Saul's successors; when they gave up fidelity to Jehovah, they forfeited their title to the kingdom (I Kings 11:31–36). For the succession of kings who ruled in Judah and Israel, see CHRONOLOGY, IV.

A man became king of a nation through appointment to the office by one higher in authority (I Sam. 9:16; 16:1, 13; II Kings 23:33, 34; 24:17), by the choice of the people (I Sam. 18:8; II Sam. 5:1–3; I Kings 12:20; II Kings 23:30), by usurping a throne (I Kings 15:27, 28), or by inheritance (ch. 11:36). The choice of a king by the people shows that the foundations of democracy are found in Israel and Judah. The ceremony of coronation among the Israelites consisted regularly in placing on the throne, putting the crown upon the head, anointing with oil, and proclamation (II Kings 11:12; cf. I Sam. 10:24; II Sam. 2:4; 5:3; I Kings 1:34; II Kings 23:30). It was doubtless regularly accompanied by sacrifice, and sometimes also by a solemn procession (I Sam. 16:2, 5; I Kings 1:25, 43–46). The king often led the army to battle in person (Gen. 14:5; Num. 21:23; I Sam. 8:20; 14:20), made treaties in behalf of himself and his people (Gen. 21:22–32; I Kings 15:19), enacted laws and executed them (Esth. 3:12, 13; 8:7–12; Dan. 3:1–6, 29; 6:6–9), exercised judicial functions (II Sam. 15:2; Isa. 33:22), and had the power of life and death (II Sam. 14:1–11; I Kings 1:51, 52; 2:24–34; Esth. 4:11; 7:9, 10). The restraints upon the king were the fear of God and man. The popular will might not always be ignored (I Sam. 14:45; 15:24). The endurance of the people might not be overtaxed with impunity (I Kings 12:4). There were officers of religion, both priests and prophets, who in religious matters were independent of the king and did not hesitate to rebuke misdemeanors (I Sam. 13:10–14; 15:10–31; II Sam. 12:1–15; I Kings 18:17, 18; 21:17–22; II Chron. 26:16–21). But a despotic king sometimes broke through these restraints (I Sam. 22:17–19; I Kings 12:12–16; Jer. 26:20–23). In view of the royal duties and prerogatives, the king required physical, mental, and moral qualities of a high order to rule well. Physical superiority is appreciated the moment it becomes visible. Thus, when Saul was presented to his future subjects, and they saw him tower head and shoulders above all the multitude present, they raised the shout, "God save the king" (I Sam. 10:23, 24; cf. ch. 16:7). In order to be an able judge the king must be a man of penetration, able to disentangle truth from falsehood, and punish, not the innocent, but the guilty. This is the reason why there was such emotion among the Israelites when Solomon, trying his first case, that of the 2 women and the child, so signally detected where the truth and where the falsehood lay (I Kings 3:28). But penetration was not enough; the moral element was requisite to make the sovereign give, without fear or favor, the verdict which he considered just. For the protection of his person and assistance in the discharge of his duties the king had a bodyguard, the captain of which generally acted as executioner (cf. II Sam. 15:18; 20:23 with I Kings 1:43, 44; 2:25, 29); see GUARD. Wealthy kings had magnificent palaces, surrounded themselves with luxury, and lived in state (I Kings, ch. 10).

God is compared to a king possessed of unlimited power, and using it under the influence of supreme beneficence (Ps. 5:2; 10:16). He is the King of kings (I Tim. 6:15). Christ is a King. He called himself so, but explained that his Kingdom is not of this world (John 18:33–37). He also is the King of kings (Rev. 19:16).

King'dom. 1. The territory or the people ruled over by a king (II Kings 15:19).

2. The sovereign rule of God over the universe (I Chron. 29:11; Ps. 22:28; 145:13; Matt. 6:13).

3. On the basis of the conception of God as the Creator rests the doctrine of his unlimited dominion in the natural and the spiritual realm. In consequence of the sinful state of humanity God's moral Kingdom will be brought into existence by grace. In the history of O.T. revelation is found the history of the development of the Kingdom of God. David is the type of the ideal King or Messiah, who will rule the Kingdom in strict subordination to the will and law of God. The Messiah, however, is not always mentioned in connection with the future Kingdom of perfection (cf. Isa. 2:2–4; Micah 4:1–5). The Book of Daniel gave definite shape and direction to the sovereignty which God will establish on earth, and which, when once set up, will remain forever. In distinction from the kingdoms of this world, which are exhibited under the figure of beasts, the Kingdom of God has for its representative a person "like unto a son of man" (Dan. 7:13, 14, R.V.). John the Baptist and our Lord declared that it was at hand (Matt. 3:2; 4:17). Jesus taught his disciples to pray for its coming (Matt. 6:10), instructed his apostles on their first mission to say that it was at hand (ch. 10:7), spoke of it afterward as having come (ch. 12:28), and illustrated its nature by parables. It is called the Kingdom of heaven and the Kingdom of God. Matthew prefers the former and Mark and Luke the latter designation (cf. Matt. 13:24, 31, 33, 44, 45 with Mark 4:11, 26, 30; Luke 14:15; 17:20, etc.). The Kingdom is spiritual in character, and no carnal weapons may be used

in its establishment (John 18:33–37). Commenced on earth with the royal ministry of Christ, it shall be consummated amid the bliss of the eternal world (Matt. 25:31–46; Luke 23:42, 43). The Kingdom of God is thus the "invisible Church." It is the whole spiritual commonwealth of God's children, the true company of all faithful people. It is represented by the organized or visible Church, but is more comprehensive and greater than the visible Church in any age or all ages.

King's Gar'den. See POOL.

King's High'way'. An ancient highway which led through Trans-Jordan from 'Aḳabah to Syria. Its entire length can be traced by the ruins of sites which may be dated approximately between the 23d and 20th centuries B.C. Probably the invasion of Chedorlaomer and his allies went down this road to El-paran, which may possibly be located on the n. shore of the Gulf of 'Aḳabah. In their request to pass through the land of Edom and that of Sihon, king of the Amorites, the Israelites promised to keep to the king's highway (Num. 20:17; 21:22). Trajan's Road followed the same course, which in modern times has become Emir Abdullah's Road.

King's Moth'er. See QUEEN.

King's Pool. See POOL.

King's Vale, A.V. **King's Dale.** See SHAVEH.

Kings, The Books of the. The 2 Books of the Kings were originally one book, but were divided in the LXX into 2. They are placed among the Prophets in the Hebrew canon, in that group of Scriptures which, because standing first among the Prophets, were known as Former Prophets. The writings of the Former Prophets form a continuous narrative which begins at the death of Moses and ends with the Exile. Joshua is the 1st book in the series and The Books of the Kings are the last. These latter were written to point out the religious teaching of the national history during the period of the kingdom from the accession of Solomon. The author or redactor, who was strongly influenced by Deuteronomy, shows the growth and decay of the kingdom, indicates the causes which worked to effect these results, and draws attention to the large part played by forces of a moral and religious character (cf. II Kings, ch. 17). His narrative covers a period of more than 400 years, and he is consequently dependent on former historians for his facts.

The Books of the Kings differ from the preceding historical books in the fact that the compiler refers habitually to certain sources for particulars not contained in his own work. These authorities are: (1) for the reign of Solomon, the "book of the acts of Solomon" (I Kings 11:41); (2) for the Northern Kingdom to the death of Pekah, the "book of the chronicles of the kings of Israel" (ch. 14:19); (3) for the Southern Kingdom to the death of Jehoiakim, "the book of the chronicles of the kings of Judah" (v. 29). These chronicles were originally, as the titles suggest, 2 separate works. Probably they were ultimately united into one and constituted the work quoted by the Chronicler as the "book of the kings of Judah and Israel" (II Chron. 16:11). These 2 chronicles contained more than the present Books of the Kings, for the writer of Kings refers his readers to them for further details (I Kings 14:19, 29), and the Chronicler quotes portions which the writer of Kings does not (II Chron. 27:7; 33:18). It is commonly held that these 2 chronicles were not the original public annals, but 2 independent historical works based upon them. This opinion is based on the fact

that writings of various prophets are mentioned as having been inserted in the book of the kings of Israel (II Chron. 20:34; cf. ch. 32:32), which could not have been done if the book were the state annals to which additions were made from day to day by the royal scribe. The double chronicles were written before the fall of Jerusalem; for the phrase "unto this day" refers, so far as can be determined, invariably to the time when the city and Temple were in existence (I Kings 8:8); at any rate it shows that the writer of the book which is quoted lived before the Exile. Whether the writer of the present Books of the Kings began the work before the destruction of Jerusalem or not, he did not complete it until after the middle years of the Babylonian Exile (II Kings 25:27). He perhaps finished it before the close of the Exile, since the work contains no allusion to the deliverance of the people from Babylon.

The author is chiefly concerned with the history of the Davidic monarchy, and accordingly he records events relating to Israel before giving the contemporaneous history of Judah. This leads him sometimes to narrate the same event in connection with both the Northern and the Southern Kingdoms (cf. I Kings 15:16 with v. 32; cf. II Kings 17:5, 6 with ch. 18:9).

The work is divided into 3 parts: I. The reign of Solomon (I Kings, chs. 1 to 11). II. A synchronistic account of the Kingdoms of Judah and Israel until the Captivity of Israel (ch. 12 to II Kings, ch. 17). III. The Kingdom of Judah until the Babylonian Exile (chs. 18 to 25).

Kir (kĭr) [Heb., wall; Moabite, city]. 1. The place from which the Aramaeans migrated to Syria (Amos 9:7), and to which those of them living in Damascus were carried on being conquered by the Assyrians (II Kings 16:9; Amos 1:5). Its inhabitants are represented as arrayed with Elam against Judah (Isa. 22:6), and while its location is very uncertain, it may probably be identified with the plain between the Tigris and the highland of Elam.

Kir of Mo'ab. (kĭr of mō'ăb). A fortified city of s. Moab (Isa. 15:1), identified with Kir-haraseth and Kir-heres (ch. 16:7, 11; Jer. 48:31, 36; in A.V. sometimes Kir-haraseth and Kir-haresh). It was strong enough to resist the combined forces of Israel, Judah, and Edom (II Kings 3:25). Its modern name, traceable back to the Targum, is Kerak. It is 11 miles e. from the s. bay of the Dead Sea, s. of the Lisan or tongue, and 18 s. of the Arnon River. It stands on an elevation of 3,370 feet above the Mediterranean, on a rocky platform which rises at its s.e. extremity to 3,720 feet. Except at one or two spots, the hill is isolated from the neighboring hills by precipices falling sheer down to the deep valleys below. Its weak point for military purposes is that it is commanded by adjacent hills 4,050 feet high. Kerak constitutes a triangle from 2,400 to 3,000 feet on each side. It is entered by 2 arched tunnels, probably of Roman age It dominated the great caravan road connecting Syria with Egypt and Arabia. Under King Fulco of Jerusalem a castle was built here in A.D. 1131, and the crusaders held the place from 1167 to 1188, when it was captured by Saladin. The Greek bishop of Petra has had his seat at Kerak since the time of the crusades.

Kir'-har'a•seth (kĭr'hăr'á-sĕth), **Kir'-har'e•seth** (kĭr'hăr'ĕ-sĕth), **Kir'-ha'resh** (kĭr'hā'-rĕsh), **Kir'he'res** (kĭr'hē'rĕs) [interpreted by Aquila, Symmachus, and the Vulgate as city of pottery; but in Isaiah the readings of LXX suggest that -d- was read instead of -r-, which would make it mean new city]. See KIR OF MOAB.

Kir'i•ath (kĭr'ĭ-ăth), in A.V. **Kir'jath** [city]. A town of Benjamin (Josh. 18:28), probably to be identified with Kiriath-jearim, as in Codex Alexandrinus.

Kir'i•a•tha'im (kĭr'ĭ-a-thā'ĭm), in A.V. sometimes **Kir'ja•tha'im** (kĭr'ja-thā'ĭm) [twin cities]. 1. An ancient city of the Emim (Gen. 14:5), rebuilt by the Reubenites (Num. 32:37; Josh. 13:19), which afterward fell into the hands of the Moabites (*Moabite Stone*, 10, see MOABITE STONE; Jer. 48:1, 23; Ezek. 25:9). Its site was at Khirbet el-Kureiyāt, n. of the Arnon, and 2½ miles s. by e. of Ataroth. The ruins are on 2 hills. 2. The same as Kartan (*q.v.*) (I Chron. 6:76).

Kir'i•ath-ar'ba (kĭr'ĭ-ăth-är'ba), in A.V. **Kir'jath-ar'ba** [city of Arba, or 4-fold city, tetrapolis]. An old name for the city of Hebron, pointing to the fact that it was the city of Arba, or the Arba, father of Anak. Perhaps he was its founder (Gen. 23:2; Josh. 14:15; 15:13, 54; 20:7; 21:11; Judg. 1:10). The old name was not obsolete even in the time of Nehemiah (Neh. 11:25). See HEBRON 2.

Kir'i•ath-a'rim (kĭr'ĭ-ăth-ā'rĭm), in A.V. **Kir'jath-a'rim** (kĭr'jăth-ā'rĭm). See KIRIATH-JEARIM.

Kir'i•ath-ba'al (kĭr'ĭ-ăth-bā'ăl), in A.V. **Kir'jath-ba'al** (kĭr'jăth-bā'ăl) [city of Baal]. See KIRIATH-JEARIM.

Kir'i•ath-hu'zoth (kĭr'ĭ-ăth-hū'zŏth), in A.V. **Kir'jath-hu'zoth** (kĭr'jăth-hū'zŏ.h) [city of streets]. A Moabite town near Bamoth-baal (Num. 22:39, 41). Location uncertain; Kiriathaim and Kerioth 2 have been suggested.

Kir'i•ath-je'a•rim (kĭr'ĭ-ăth-jē'a-rĭm), in A.V. **Kir'jath-je'a•rim** (kĭr'jăth-jē'a-rĭm) [city of woods]. A town belonging originally to the Gibeonites (Josh. 9:17). It was on the w. part of the boundary line between the tribes of Judah and Benjamin (Josh. 15:9; 18:14, 15), but pertained to Judah, being considered a town belonging in the hill country of the latter tribe (Josh. 15:48, 60; Judg. 18:12). After the Ark had been returned to the Israelites by the Philistines, it remained in safe custody in Kiriath-jearim for the next 20 years, until the 2d battle of Ebenezer, and longer (I Sam. 6:19 to 7:2). Some of its population returned from captivity (Neh. 7:29; in Ezra 2:25 the name appears as Kiriath-arim). It was called also Kiriath-baal (Josh. 15:60; 18:14), Baalah (Josh. 15:9, 11), or Baale (II Sam. 6:2; cf. I Chron. 13:6). Eusebius states that it was situated 9 or 10 Roman miles from Jerusalem on the road to Diospolis (Lydda), and accordingly it is commonly identified with Karyat el-'Inab (also known as Abū Ghōsh, after a brigand of the 19th century A.D. who is buried there), about 8⅓ miles w. by n. of Jerusalem.

Kir'i•ath-san'nah (kĭr'ĭ-ăth-săn'a), in A.V. **Kir'jath-san'nah** (kĭr'jăth-săn'a). See DEBIR 2.

Kir'i•ath-se'pher (kĭr'ĭ-ăth-sē'fẽr), in A.V. **Kir'jath-se'pher** (kĭr'jăth-sē'fẽr). See DEBIR 2.

Kir'i•oth (kĭr'ĭ-ŏth). See KERIOTH.

Kir'jath (kĭr'jăth). See KIRIATH.

Kir'jath-ar'ba (kĭr'jăth-är'ba), etc. See KIRIATH-ARBA, etc.

Kish (kĭsh), in A.V. of N.T. **Cis**, from Greek. 1. A Benjamite, son of Jeiel (I Chron. 8:30; 9:35, 36).

2. A Benjamite, father of King Saul and son of Abiel (I Sam. 9:1), but also registered as a son of Ner and a descendant of Jeiel of Gibeon (I Chron. 8:33; 9:36, 39). This latter genealogy may indeed merely register the fact that

Kish was a descendant of Ner, without implying that he was his immediate son; and allow of the insertion of Abiel and others between Kish and Ner.

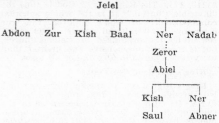

But perhaps only one Kish and one Ner descended from Jeiel. If so, the explanation of the genealogy is that Ner's descendants became 2 tribal houses, those of Kish and Ner. The former, the important royal family of Saul, looked to Ner's son Kish as its founder; but it was merely a younger branch of the older but less distinguished line of Ner. Both houses belonged to the family of Jeiel, and hence Kish as well as Ner is registered, according to the familiar principle, among Jeiel's sons (ch. 9:36). Saul's father, Kish, and Abner's father, Ner, are mentioned as sons of Abiel also (I Sam. 9:1; 14:51), and either Ner or Abner is stated to have been Saul's uncle (ch. 14:50). Abiel may be, as some expositors suppose, or may not be, another name for the uncorrupted form of Jeiel.

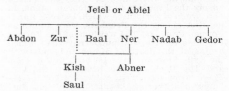

3. A Levite, in David's time, of the family of Merari, house of Mahli (I Chron. 23:21, 22; 24:29).

4. A Levite, family of Merari and son of Abdi, who aided in the revival under Hezekiah (II Chron. 29:12).

5. A Benjamite, an ancestor of Mordecai (Esth. 2:5).

Kish'i (kĭsh'ĭ). See KUSHAIAH.

Kish'i•on (kĭsh'ĭ-ŏn), in A.V. once **Ki'shon** (Josh. 21:28) [hardness]. A border town of Issachar (Josh. 19:20), given to the Gershonite Levites (ch. 21:28). In I Chron. 6:72 Kedesh appears in its stead, probably by a copyist's error. Conder identified it with Tell Abū Kedeis, but Père Abel locates it at Tell el-Ajjūl, about 12½ miles n.e. of Megiddo and almost 5 s.s.w. of Tabor. See KEDESH 3.

Ki'shon (kĭ'shŏn), in A.V. once **Ki'son** (kĭ'sŏn) (Ps. 83:9) [bending, curving; cf. Arab. kawisa, to be crookbacked]. 1. The most important river of Palestine next to the Jordan; now known as the Nahr el-Mukatta'. Its n. arm rises in springs w. of Mount Tabor, and its s. arm near Mount Gilboa; the two meet in the plain n.n.e. of Megiddo. "That ancient river, the river Kishon" swept away the soldiers of Sisera's beaten army when they fled n. from Taanach and attempted to cross the stream (Judg. 5:19–21; Ps. 83:9). The priests of Baal who had the contest with Elijah were slain on its s. bank (I Kings 18:40). As the name Kishon implies, the river is tortuous, making great curves as it proceeds in a generally n.w. direction through the Plain of Esdraelon. It looks an insignificant stream, of 15 or 18 feet across, but has treacherous banks and a muddy bottom, so much so that when the Turks and Arabs were defeated by the French in the battle of Mount Tabor, on April 16, 1799, the fate of the vanquished host was the same as that of Sisera's army. Toward Harosheth of the Gentiles, Jabin's city, the Kishon runs through a narrow gorge under the cliffs which constitute the n. side of Mount Carmel, the water at one place being nearly hidden by oleander bushes. Then the stream enters the Plain of Acre. Sand dunes, dotted with palm trees, interfere with it in the latter part of its course, and it is only when full of water that it can overcome the obstacle and make a proper entrance into the Mediterranean.

2. A town, so spelled in A.V. See KISHION.

Kiss. A salutation, common in the Orient from patriarchal times onward, between persons of the same sex and to a limited extent between individuals of different sexes. Fathers and mothers kissed their children and descendants (Gen. 31:28, 55; 48:10; II Sam. 14:33, etc.), and children their parents (Gen. 27:26, 27; 50:1; I Kings 19:20). Brother and sister kissed each other (S. of Sol. 8:1), and brother kissed brother (Gen. 45:15; Ex. 4:27). So did other relatives and kinsfolk (Gen. 29:11; Ex. 18:7; Ruth 1:9). Comrades kissed each other; so did friends (I Sam. 20:41; II Sam. 19:39; 20:9; Acts 20:37). In the time of our Lord, a guest invited to a house expected a kiss of welcome from his entertainer (Luke 7:45). It was in these circumstances that Christians were enjoined to salute each other with a holy kiss (Rom. 16:16; I Cor. 16:20; II Cor. 13:12; I Thess. 5:26), or with a kiss of love (I Peter 5:14), symbolical of Christian brotherhood. As kissing between friends, guests, and entertainers lapsed, the salutation enjoined by the apostle fell also into desuetude. In all the foregoing cases a kiss was, or at least professed to be, an expression of love. It therefore added to the baseness of Judas' treachery that he not merely betrayed his Lord, but did so by means of a kiss (Matt. 26:48, 49; Luke 22:47, 48; cf. Prov. 27:6). The feet of kings were kissed in token of great respect and to offer allegiance (Ps. 2:12), and the same idea was involved in the kiss given to idols (I Kings 19:18; Hos. 13:2). A kiss was sometimes thrown by the hand (Job 31:27). When women kissed the feet of our Lord, it indicated the unbounded respect and affection which they felt for his character and work (Luke 7:38, 45).

Kite. A bird of prey of the falcon family, with long, pointed wings and usually long, forked tail. The word is used in R.V. to render Heb. *dā'āh* and *dayyāh* (Lev. 11:14; Deut. 14:13; Isa. 34:15; in A.V. vulture) and twice in A.V. to render *'ayyāh* (Lev. 11:14; Deut. 14:13; in R.V. falcon). Both birds were ceremonially unclean (Lev. 11:14). Kites are of various kinds (Deut. 14:13). The black kite (*Milvus migrans* or *ater*) is found in central and s. Europe, n. Africa, and w. Asia. It appears in Palestine in March, gliding noiselessly in the air, looking down for its food, which consists of offal, for, being a somewhat cowardly bird, it does not molest poultry. It breeds in trees, ornamenting its nest with rags of different colors. The black-winged kite (*Elanus caeruleus*) also occurs in Palestine, but is rare.

Kith'lish (kĭth'lĭsh), in R.V. **Chith'lish.** A village in the lowland of Judah (Josh. 15:40); identified with Khirbet el-Mak-haz, e. of Tell en-Nejileh. See DILEAN.

Kit'ron (kĭt'rŏn). A town in the territory of Zebulun, but from which the Canaanites were not driven out (Judg. 1:30). Identified

by Alt with Tell el-Fär, which is 1 mile n. of Tell Harbaj, which in turn is on the wadi el-Melek, about 7½ miles s.e. of Haifa. See KATTATH.

Kit'tim (kĭt'ĭm) or **Chit'tim,** the latter being the more consistent, and in A.V. more frequent spelling. Descendants of Javan, who inhabited Cyprus and other islands and coasts of the e. Mediterranean (Gen. 10:4; Num. 24:24; I Chron. 1:7; Isa. 23:1, 12; Jer. 2:10; Ezek. 27:6; Dan. 11:30; Jos. *Antiq.* i. 6, 1). The name is connected definitely with Cyprus, chiefly through Kition, an ancient town on the s. coast of the island, but it was eventually greatly extended. In I Macc. 1:1 Alexander the Great is said to have come out of the land of Chittim, and in ch. 8:5 Perseus is called king of Chittim, meaning Macedonia.

Knead'ing Trough. A shallow vessel, usually of wood and portable, in which dough is worked into a well-mixed mass preparatory

Egyptians Kneading Dough in a Trough

to baking (Ex. 12:34). The Egyptians kneaded the dough with their feet (Herod. ii. 36) or with their hands.

Knife. The Hebrews used a knife which they called *ma'ăkeleth*, eating instrument, for slaughtering animals for food or sacrifice, and for cutting up the carcass (Gen. 22:6; Judg. 19:29; cf. Lev. 8:20; 9:13). Another word, *ḥereb*, which commonly signifies a sword, denotes a knife made of flint (Josh. 5:2), and perhaps a knife for shaving (Ezek. 5:1; in R.V. sword); see FLINT. The Egyptians also, when embalming a corpse, used a sharp stone knife for making an incision in the body (Herod. ii. 86). The Hebrew scribes sharpened the stylus with a small knife (Jer. 36:23). Herod the Great was accustomed to use a knife for paring fruit, and attempted to kill himself with it (Jos. *Antiq.* xvii. 7, 1).

Knop. 1. The rendering of Heb. *kaphtōr* in Ex. 25:33–36; 37:17–22, where it constitutes a part of the candlestick used in the tabernacle. In other passages the Hebrew word apparently denotes the capital of a column (Amos 9:1; Zeph. 2:14; cf. R.V. and A.V. marg.). It seems to have been some projecting support for the branches of the candlestick, and for the corollas of the ornamental flowers; but its precise nature is unknown; cf. Jos. *Antiq.* iii. 6, 7.

2. The rendering of Heb. *pᵉḳā'îm* (I Kings 6:18; 7:24), an ornament cut in cedar and associated with open flowers in the woodwork of Solomon's Temple. Since *paḳḳū'ōth* denotes gourds or colocynths, the R.V. places gourds in the margin of the first passage, as if the ornament was shaped like a gourd.

Ko'a (kō'à). A people (Ezek. 23:23) identified with Ḳutû or Ḳu, located e. of the Tigris, s. of the lower Zab.

Ko'hath (kō'hăth). A son of Levi and founder of the great Kohathite family (Gen. 46:11; Ex. 6:16, 18).

Ko'hath·ite (kō'hăth-īt). A member of the great Levite family founded by Kohath. This was subdivided into the families or houses of the Amramites, the Izharites, the Hebronites, and the Uzzielites (Ex. 6:18; Num. 3:27). Moses and Aaron were of the Kohathite family (Ex. 6:20). The Kohathites pitched on the s. side of the tabernacle in the wilderness (Num. 3:29). When the priests had covered the sanctuary and its vessels, the Kohathites carried the latter, but were not to touch any holy thing, lest they should die (Num. 4:15, 17–20; II Chron. 34:12). At the 1st census in the wilderness, the Kohathite males from a month old and upward were 8,600 (Num. 3:28), and those from 30 to 50 years old 2,750 (ch. 4:34–37). In the subsequent allotment of cities to the family, the priests, the descendants of Aaron, had shares with the other Kohathites, the former obtaining 13 cities out of the tribes of Judah, Simeon, and Benjamin, and the latter 10 cities out of the tribes of Ephraim, Dan, and Manasseh (Josh. 21:4, 5; I Chron. 6:61, 66–70).

Ko·hel'eth (kô-hĕl'ĕth). See ECCLESIASTES.

Ko·la'iah (kô-lā'yà) [perhaps, voice of Jehovah]. 1. Father of the false prophet Ahab (Jer. 29:21).

2. A Benjamite (Neh. 11:7).

Koph (kōf), in A.R.V. **Qoph**. The 19th letter of the Hebrew alphabet. English Q comes from the same source; but in Anglicized Hebrew names C or K represents it, as in Cain and Korah. It heads the 19th section of Psalm 119, in which section each verse of the original begins with this letter.

Ko'rah (kō'rà), in A.V. once **Ko're** (I Chron. 26:19) and once **Co're** (Jude 11) [bald]. 1. A son of Esau by his wife Oholibamah, born in Canaan (Gen. 36:5, 14), who became a tribe that dwelt in Edom and was ruled by a chieftain (v. 18).

2. A son of Eliphaz and grandson of Esau (Gen. 36:16). But the name apparently has crept into the text erroneously, not being found in Gen. 36:11, 12 or I Chron. 1:36.

3. A son of Hebron (I Chron. 2:43). See MARESHAH 2.

4. A Levite, family of Kohath, house of Izhar (Num. 16:1). In conjunction with the Reubenites Dathan, Abiram, and On, he rebelled against Moses and Aaron. He was jealous that Aaron, a Levite of the same family as he and only his equal in rank, should have the office of priest for all Israel. The Reubenites were discontented because the leadership in Israel, which belonged to Reuben as the first-born of Jacob, was possessed by the tribe of Levi, represented by Moses and Aaron. At length Korah and his company, sons of Levi (v. 7), who formed a large portion of the conspirators, but not all of them, for at least Dathan and Abiram were absent (v. 12), assembled against Moses and Aaron, publicly charged them with usurping the supremacy over the tribes, and claimed that all the congregation was holy and that anyone might officiate as a priest (v. 3). Moses replied that God would himself decide the matter, and he bade Korah and his company provide themselves with censers and be ready to offer incense on the morrow (vs. 6–11). Moses sent word to Dathan and Abiram to appear likewise on the morrow, but they refused on the ground that Moses had no right to summon them (vs. 12–15). Moses then turned to Korah, saying: "Be thou and all thy company

before Jehovah, thou, and they, and Aaron, to-morrow: and take ye every man his censer, and put incense upon them, and bring ye before Jehovah every man his censer, two hundred and fifty censers; thou also, and Aaron, each his censer" (vs. 16, 17). They did so, assembling at the tabernacle (v. 18). Korah gathered also the whole congregation of Israel there and incited them against Moses and Aaron (v. 19). God directed Moses and Aaron to separate themselves from the multitude that it might be destroyed, but Moses interceded for the people (vs. 20–22). Moses was then directed to bid the congregation remove from the district in the camp occupied by Korah, Dathan, and Abiram (v. 24). The division of the Levites to which Korah belonged was accustomed to pitch on the s. of the tabernacle in immediate proximity to the tribe of Reuben: see CAMP. Accordingly, followed by the elders of Israel, and certainly also by Korah, Moses went to the locality where the tents of Korah, Dathan, and Abiram were pitched and warned the congregation to leave the district (vs. 25, 26). The people obeyed. Dathan and Abiram, together with their families, appeared at the door of their tents (v. 27). The earth opened and swallowed them up with their households and Korah with his servants (vs. 32, 33; ch. 26:10). The sons of Korah, however, were not destroyed (v. 11). After the earthquake fire devoured the 250 men that offered incense (chs. 16:35; cf. v. 40). See KORAHITE.

Ko'rah·ite (kō'rà-īt) and **Ko'rath·ite** (kō'răth-īt). A descendant of that Korah who was swallowed up in the wilderness as a punishment for his rebellion. The Korahites constituted a father's house among the Kohathites. Heman the singer and Samuel the prophet were Korahites (I Chron. 6:33–38). The descendants of Heman were organized by David as singers (I Chron. 15:17; 16:41, 42; 25:4, 5). Psalms 42 (which probably once included 43); 44 to 49; 84; 85; 87; 88 bear the name of the family in the title. Korahites were gatekeepers (I Chron. 9:19; 26:19) and bakers for the sanctuary, preparing the showbread and sacrificial cakes (ch. 9:31, 32).

Ko're (kō'rê) [a partridge]. 1. The rebellious Levite, founder of a house (I Chron. 26:19); see KORAH 4.

2. A Levite of the house of Korah (I Chron. 9:19; 26:1).

3. A Levite, son of Imnah, appointed over the freewill offerings during the reign of Hezekiah (II Chron. 31:14).

Kor'hite (kôr'hīt). See KORAHITE.

Koz (kŏz). See HAKKOZ.

Ku·sha'iah (kû-shā'yà). A Levite of the family of Merari, house of Mushi (I Chron. 15:17), in ch. 6:44 called Kishi.

L

La'a·dah (lā'à-dà) [perhaps, having a fat neck; cf. Arab. lughd, the flesh at the throat and under the chin and ear]. A man of Judah, family of Shelah. He was the father of the inhabitants of Mareshah (I Chron. 4:21).

La'a·dan (lā'à-dăn). See LADAN.

La'ban (lā'băn) [white]. 1. Son of Bethuel, and grandson of Nahor, Abraham's brother. He lived at Haran in Paddan-aram (Gen. 24:10, 15; 28:5, 10; 29:4, 5). He was the brother of Rebekah. When he saw the valuable presents which Abraham's servant had given Rebekah, he readily allowed her to go to Canaan to become Isaac's wife (ch. 24). When Jacob fled from the vengeance of Esau he went to Laban his uncle. He found him the head of a household, father of several sons (chs. 30:35; 31:1) and at least 2 daughters (ch. 29:16), owner of slaves (vs. 24, 29), and the possessor of a flock of sheep and goats (v. 9; ch. 31:38). Jacob remained with him at least 20 years, serving him 7 for his daughter Rachel, and then, having Leah handed over to him in a fraudulent way, a 2d 7 to obtain the daughter for whom he really cared, and then 6 more for cattle. At the end of the 20 years, Jacob, perceiving that his prosperity had excited the enmity of Laban and his sons, fled with his wives, his children, and his cattle, in the direction of Canaan. He was overtaken by Laban in Mount Gilead; but the pursuer, warned by God not to molest Jacob, made a covenant with him, and the two parted to meet no more (Gen., chs. 29 to 31). Laban worshiped the God of his fathers, the God of Nahor (ch. 31:53), Jehovah (chs. 24:50; 30:27); but he combined idolatry with his worship, making use of household gods called teraphim (ch. 31:30; cf. 35:4) and practicing divination (ch. 30:27, R.V.).

2. An unidentified place in the Sinaitic peninsula (Deut. 1:1). It is mentioned with Hazeroth; hence some have thought that it may be the same as Libnah, the 2d station from Hazeroth (Num. 33:20).

La'chish (lā'kĭsh). A fortified city in the lowland of Judah (Josh. 15:33, 39), formerly identified with Tell el-Ḥesi, 16 miles e. by n.

Part of a Lachish Letter Written on Pottery in the Time of Jeremiah

of Gaza and 11 miles s.w. of Beit Jibrin, but now more appropriately located at Tell ed-Duweir, 5 miles s.s.w. of Beit Jibrin.

It seems that between the 27th and 24th centuries B.C. people were living in caves around the edge of the mound at Tell ed-Duweir. Here the Hyksos built a rectangular enclosure of earth which served both as a protection and as a place to keep horses and chariots. Of special importance in the history of the alphabet are an inscribed dagger of c. 1600 B.C., and a ewer and bowl with inscriptions of c. the 14–13th century B.C., all found at Tell ed-Duweir.

At the time of the conquest of Palestine, its king was defeated and slain by Joshua (Josh. 10:3–35; 12:11). Rehoboam strengthened its defenses (II Chron. 11:9); a double wall encircled the mound, buttressed at intervals by towers. Amaziah, king of Judah, having fled thither from conspirators at Jerusalem, was pursued and slain in the town (II Kings 14:19; II Chron. 25:27). Lachish was besieged by Sennacherib, king of Assyria (701 or perhaps 700), and it was from the camp in front of it that the rabshakeh was dispatched to demand the surrender of Jerusalem (II Kings 18:14, 17; cf. ch. 19:8, and II Chron. 32:9; Isa. 36:2; 37:8). Lachish is charged with being the beginning of sin to the daughter of

Zion, for the transgressions of Israel were found in her (Micah 1:13). Nebuchadnezzar besieged Lachish, with other fenced cities of Judah (Jer. 34:7). The archaeological evidence indicates that the city suffered 2 terrific destructions in the early 6th century, which may be connected with the sieges of Jerusalem (II Kings 24:10 *seq.*; 25:1 *seq.*). At the time of the 1st attack (597), the city was crowded with houses and very strongly fortified, but the Chaldeans razed it more or less completely. The inhabitants who remained were never able to rebuild it entirely. In both destructions the whole city seems to have been set on fire, and great portions of the city wall and gate towers collapsed. So hot was the fire that much of the mud-brick work was burned a bright red throughout. With the Exile Lachish never regained its former importance, but it was inhabited after the Captivity (Neh. 11:30).

In 1935 there were found at Tell ed-Duweir the Lachish letters, which are written in Hebrew and belong to the time of Jeremiah. They reflect the disturbed condition of the country just before the final destruction of Lachish at the end of Zedekiah's reign.

La'dan (lā'dăn), in A.V. **La'a·dan** [cf. Laadah]. 1. An Ephraimite in the ancestry of Joshua (I Chron. 7:26).

2. A Gershonite in whom several fathers' houses had their origin (I Chron. 28:7–9; 26:21).

La'el (lā'ĕl) [belonging to God]. A Gershonite, father of Eliasaph (Num. 3:24).

La'had (lā'hăd) [cf. Arab. *lahada*, to overburden, press down]. A son of Jahath, a man of Judah (I Chron. 4:2).

La·hai'-roi (là-hī'roi). See BEER-LAHAI-ROI.

Lah'mam (lä'măm), in R.V. marg., **Lah'mas** (lä'măs). A village in the lowland of Judah (Josh. 15:40), probably Khirbet el-Lahm, 2½ miles s. of Beit Jibrin.

Lah'mi (lä'mī). The brother of Goliath the Gittite. He was slain by Elhanan the son of Jair (I Chron. 20:5). The word Lahmi, however, corresponds to the last part of Bethlehemite (Heb. *Bêth hallaḥmî*) in II Sam. 21:19. See ELHANAN 1.

La'ish (lā'ish) [lion]. 1. A man of Gallim, father of Palti (I Sam. 25:44).

2. A Canaanite city in the extreme n. of Palestine, "in the valley that lieth by Beth-rehob." The Danites captured the city and rebuilt it, altering the name to Dan (Judg. 18:7–29). See DAN 3.

3. A village (Isa. 10:30, A.V.). See LAI-SHAH.

La'i·shah (lā'ĭ-shà), in A.V. **La'ish** [lion]. A village in Benjamin between Gallim and Anathoth (Isa. 10:30), el-'Isāwīyeh, n.n.e. of the Mount of Olives.

Lak'kum (lăk'ŭm), in A.V. **La'kum** (lā'kŭm) [obstruction; cf. Arab. *lakama*, to obstruct a road]. A town of Naphtali (Josh. 19:33), probably to be located at Manṣūra, near Tayyaret ed-Delakeh, at the head of Wadi Fejjās.

Lamb. The flesh of lambs was early used as food (cf. Lev. 3:7 with ch. 7:15; II Sam. 12:4; Amos 6:4); and lambs and kids were largely offered in sacrifice even before the promulgation of the Mosaic Law (Gen. 4:4; 22:7). When the passover was instituted in Egypt, a lamb or a kid of the 1st year was sacrificed and eaten (Ex. 12:3, 5). Under the Mosaic Law a male lamb of the 1st year was offered for a burnt offering every morning and every evening, while on the Sabbath there were 2 (Ex. 29:39–41; Num. 28:4). On the 1st day of each month (Num. 28:11), during the 7 days of the passover (vs. 16, 19), at the feast of weeks (vs. 26, 27), on the day of blowing of trumpets (ch. 29:1, 2), and on the Day of Atonement (vs. 7, 8), 7 male lambs of the 1st year formed part of the special burnt offering; while at the feast of tabernacles the lambs numbered 14 during each of the 1st 7 days and 7 on the 8th day (vs. 13–36). For all the principal sacrifices of ordinary occasions a lamb might be used, as: a male lamb for a burnt offering (Lev. 9:3; 23:12, 18; Num. 6:14; 7:15), a ewe lamb for a sin offering for others than the nation or rulers (Lev. 4:27, 32; Num. 6:14), and a male or female lamb for a guilt offering (Lev. 5:6; 14:12, 21; Num. 6:12) or for a peace offering (Lev. 3:6, 7; 23:19; Num. 7:17). In every case the lamb must be without blemish. All this points to our Lord. He resembled a lamb in his spotless purity (I Peter 1:19). He was like a lamb also in his gentleness and in his submission to unmerited suffering without murmur or complaint (cf. Isa. 53:7 with Luke 23:25; Acts 8:32; I Peter 2:21–23). Finally, he, like a lamb, was sacrificed for guilt not his own. Hence he is called the Lamb of God, "that taketh away the sin of the world" (John 1:29, 36), the Lamb slain "from the foundation of the world" (Rev. 13:8), or simply the Lamb (chs. 5:6, 8, 12; 7:14, 17; 14:1, 4). Both in the O.T. and in the N.T. the term lamb is at times used figuratively for child (Isa. 40:11; John 21:15).

La'mech (lā'mĕk). 1. A son of Methusael, of the race of Cain. He had 2 wives, Adah and Zillah. By Adah he was the father of Jabal and Jubal, and by Zillah he had a son, Tubal-cain, and a daughter, Naamah. His address to his wives is a fine specimen of Hebrew poetry. There are two principal interpretations of Gen. 4:23: 1. Lamech declares himself a murderer, saying, "I have slain a man." Stung by remorse, he confesses the rebuke of conscience. He had slain another to his own wounding and hurt. Or else he excuses himself for a murder committed in self-defense, having slain a man for wounding him. 2. Lamech utters a threat, "I will slay any man who wounds me," his words being a song of exultation on the invention of the sword by his son Tubal-cain, sung in anticipation of the advantage he would have in avenging wrongs done to him. The attempt has been made to explain the poem as simply an expression of Lamech's determination to put the new weapon to its lawful use; but expositors quite generally agree that Lamech is vaunting himself. If Cain, who slew a man, is under God's protection and shall be avenged sevenfold should one dare to slay him, surely Lamech with the new weapon, a visible and surer defense, shall be avenged seventy and sevenfold (Gen. 4:18–24).

2. An antediluvian patriarch of the race of Seth. He was son of Methuselah and father of Noah. He feared the Lord, rested in God's promise for the removal of the curse of sin, and on the birth of his son Noah gave expression to the hope that this child would lead men to a better and a happier life under God's blessing, saying, "This same shall comfort us in our work and in the toil of our hands, which cometh because of the ground which Jehovah hath cursed" (Gen. 5:25, 28–31).

La'med (lä'mĕd), in A.R.V. **La'medh** (lä'-mĕd) [oxgoad]. The 12th letter of the Hebrew alphabet, from which comes Gr. *lambda* (l), to which corresponds Latin and English l. It stands at the head of the 12th section of Ps. 119, in which section each verse of the original begins with this letter.

Lam•en•ta'tions. Mournful speeches or compositions, elegies such as the lament of David over Saul and Jonathan (II Sam. 1:17–27).

The Lamentations of Jeremiah are an O.T. book placed in the English Bible between Jeremiah and Ezekiel, but in the Hebrew Scriptures among the Hagiographa or Sacred Writings, between Ruth and Ecclesiastes. It should be noted that of the 5 chapters of The Lamentations, chs. 1; 2; 4; and 5 have each 22 verses, and ch. 3 has 22×3=66. There are 22 distinct letters in the Hebrew alphabet, and in chs. 1; 2; and 4 the verses are arranged alphabetically, v. 1 beginning with *aleph*, v. 2 with *beth*, v. 3 with *gimel*, and v. 4 with *daleth*, and so on to the end. In ch. 3 the 1st 3 verses begin with *aleph*, the 2d 3 with *beth*, and so on to the end. However, in chs. 2 to 4 the order of the letters *ayin* (*ain*) and *pe* is not the same as in ch. 1 and Ps. 119, but is reversed, *pe* preceding *ayin* (*ain*). The 5th chapter has not an alphabetical arrangement. The theme of the whole 5 elegies or lamentations is the capture and destruction of the Jewish capital, with dreadful suffering to i s defenders by famine, the sword, and outrage of every kind. The catastrophe, it is admitted, was brought on by the sins of the people, not omitting even the prophets and the pries s. In various places the Jewish state is personified, and bemoans its hard fate (chs. 1:9, 11, 12–22; 2:18–22), or the prophet, as representing the nation, speaks in the 1st person (chs. 2:11; 3:1–51, and also vs. 52–66). In the Hebrew this book is anonymous, being named only by its first word, "how," and is placed among the Hagiographa. In the LXX the following statement is prefixed to the book: "And it came to pass after Israel was led into captivity and Jerusalem laid waste, that Jeremiah sat weeping and lamented this lamentation over Jerusalem, and said." The ascription of the book to the prophet is thus ancient. This view is accepted by the Vulgate, the Targum, and the Talmud, and traditional scholarship accordingly has assigned the authorship to Jeremiah. Critical scholars, while not holding that Jeremiah is the author, believe that these elegies were written in his time, between 586 B.C. (the destruction of Jerusalem) and 538 B.C. (the Return from the Exile), but they do not pretend to know who was the author or authors. Some scholars would grant that Jeremiah wrote at least chs. 2 to 4. Although The Book of Jeremiah and The Lamentations have the same sensitive temper and sympathy in national sorrow and use many similar expressions, critics feel that the differences between the two books have greater weight than the resemblances. The prophet lamented for Josiah (II Chron. 35:25), but this has no connection with our present book of The Lamentations.

Lamp. A vessel designed to contain an inflammable liquid, to be burned for illuminating purposes, and a wick to lift the liquid by capillary attraction to feed the flame (Herod. ii. 62). The 7 lamps of the golden candlestick of the tabernacle and Temple were made of gold (Ex. 37:23; I Kings 7:49) and burned olive oil (Ex. 27:20). Tongs were used to trim the wick, and dishes to receive the snuff (Ex. 25:38). The ordinary lamp for domestic use was made of earthenware. It might have a cover which was either removable or made of one piece with the rest of the lamp. Near the center of the cover or top was a hole for introducing the oil. There was another opening at the margin of the cover, or else a spout for the wick.

The Hebrew word regularly rendered lamp is *nêr*. It is translated light in II Sam. 21:17, A.V., and candle in A.V. of Jer. 25:10 and Zeph. 1:12. In the latter passage, E.R.V. places lamp in the margin, while A.R.V. has lamp in these passages; and everywhere else in both O. and N.T. A.R.V. substitutes the word lamp in the text where A.V. has candle. Heb. *lappid* is also often rendered lamp in O.T.; for example, Judg. 7:16, 20, A.V., and Isa. 62:1; Dan. 10:6, A.V. But it is of more general meaning. It is translated firebrand in Judg. 15:4; and torch in Nah. 2:4; Zech. 12: 6; and in R.V. of Gen. 15:17; Judg. 7:16, 20; and lightning in Ex. 20:18. The Greek word rendered lamp in Matt. 25:1 and Rev. 4:5 is translated lights in Acts 20:8, and torches in John 18:3 and marg. of R.V. of Matt. 25:1.

Ancient Lamps

The extinction of the lamp of anyone means figuratively the destruction of his family (Prov. 13:9).

Lan'cet. See SPEAR.

Lan'guage. See TONGUE.

Lan'tern. Lanterns were carried by the band of Roman soldiers who were sent with Judas to arrest Jesus (John 18:3); it is possible that the reference here is to some form of torch. The Romans, however, made the sides of lanterns out of bladder or plates of translucent horn.

La·od'i·ce'a (lá-ŏd'ĭ-sē'á). A city founded probably by Antiochus II (261–247 B.C.), and named by him Laodicea, after his wife Laodice. It was the chief city of Phrygia Pacatiana, in Asia Minor, and was situated a little s. of Colossae and Hierapolis, on the River Lycos, a tributary of the Meander. It manufactured cloth and garments from the black wool produced by a breed of sheep in its vicinity; and it was the seat of a medical school, whose physicians prepared the Phrygian powder for the cure of ophthalmia. It numbered many Jews among its inhabitants (Jos. *Antiq.* xiv. 10, 20). Epaphras labored there (Col. 4:12, 13), and is regarded as the founder of its Christian church. Paul felt greatly desirous of spiritually benefiting the Laodiceans (Col. 2:1). He sent them salutations, and he wrote a letter of which perhaps a copy only was left at Laodicea (Col. 4:15, 16). It is believed to be the letter known as the Epistle to the Ephesians. Laodicea was one of the 7 churches in Asia addressed in the book of Revelation. It is sharply rebuked (Rev. 1:11; 3:14–22), and the words in which the rebuke is couched contain allusions to the products and the wealth for which the city was noted. About the year 65 of the Christian era, Laodicea, Colossae, and Hierapolis were destroyed by an earthquake. The citizens rebuilt Laodicea out of their own resources, without the customary aid from Rome. Its ruins still exist at a place called Eski Hissar, near Denizlu, about 56 miles e.s.e. of Smyrna.

Lap'pi·doth (lăp'ĭ-dŏth), in A.V. **Lap'i·doth** (lăp'ĭ-dŏth) [torches]. Husband of Deborah the prophetess (Judg. 4:4).

Lap'wing. The rendering of Heb. *dūkiphath* in A.V. of Lev. 11:19; Deut. 14:18. The lap-

wing (*Vanellus cristatus*), a member of the subfamily *Charadriidae*, or true plovers, is found in flocks in winter in Palestine. R.V., following the LXX and Vulgate, substitutes hoopoe (*Upupa epops*), the type of the *Upupidae*, a family of birds with deeply cleft bills. The hoopoe is a bird about a foot long, grayish-brown above, with the wings and shoulders black, barred with white, and a large crest of feathers upon the head. It is found in central and s. Europe, in Asia, and in n. and central Africa. Tristram says that it appears in Palestine in March, spreading in small parties over the whole country. On the approach of winter it makes a short migration to Egypt and the Sahara.

La·se'a (lá-sē'á). A seaport of Crete, about 5 miles e. of the Fair Havens, passed by the vessel which carried Paul (Acts 27:8).

La'sha (lā'shá). A place mentioned with the cities of the plain (Gen. 10:19). Jerome says it was at Callirrhoe, a ravine e. of the Dead Sea, notable for its hot springs, which were visited by Herod the Great during his last illness. The stream from Callirrhoe, now called the Zerḳa Ma'īn, enters the Dead Sea at the e. side, about 11 miles in a direct line from the mouth of the Jordan. The springs are about 3 miles up the stream.

Las·sha'ron (lá-shā'rŏn), in A.V. **La·sha'ron** (lá-shā'rŏn) [probably, of, or to, Sharon]. A town whose king was one of those slain by Joshua (Josh. 12:18). The Hebrew text may, however, be read "king over Sharon." The indications of the LXX are that the original text of the verse was "the king of Aphek [which belongs] to Sharon."

Las'the·nes (lăs'thê-nēz). A Cretan who raised an army of mercenary soldiers for Demetrius II, by which the latter effected a landing in Cilicia and set up the standard of revolt against Alexander Balas (Jos. *Antiq.* xiii. 4, 3). He was rewarded with high office, perhaps the governorship of Coelesyria. Demetrius calls him kinsman and father (I Macc. 11:31, in A.V. cousin; v. 32). The latter title implies that he was a man of considerable age; the former means either that he was related to Demetrius or that he held a high position at court. He was notified by letter of the terms of peace agreed upon between Demetrius and Jonathan Maccabaeus, and of the concessions made to the Jews (I Macc. 11:32–37).

Last Sup'per. See LORD'S SUPPER.

Latch'et. The thong with which the sandal was bound to the foot (Isa. 5:27; Mark 1:7; cf. Gen. 14:23).

Lat'in (lăt'ĭn). The language spoken by the Romans. Though from the 1st century B.C. on for some hundred years the supreme power in Palestine was in the hands of the Romans, whose language was Latin, yet it did not root itself in that country. Only a few words were adopted, as *praetorium* and *centurio*, which are written in Greek letters in Mark 15:16, 39, 45. But since Latin was the language of the Roman officials, the inscription over the cross of Christ was written in Latin as well as in Greek and Aramaic (John 19:20).

Lat'tice. A network formed of crossed laths and covering a window (Judg. 5:28; Prov. 7:6, in A.V. casement; II Kings 1:2; S. of Sol. 2:9).

La'ver. A basin or trough in which to wash. A laver of brass or copper was used in connection with the tabernacle services. It stood upon a base of brass in the court between the altar and the door of the tabernacle. Both laver and base were made of the mirrors given by the women who assembled to minister at the door of the tent of meeting (Ex.

38:8; cf. ch. 33:7). Women served at the door of the tabernacle (I Sam. 2:22, R.V.), as did the Levites (Num. 4:23; 8:24). They probably came at stated intervals, as did the Levites and priests (Deut. 18:6; Luke 1:8, 23), to render various kinds of service, such as the performance of sacred dances and instrumental and vocal music (Ex. 15:20; Judg. 21:21; Ps. 68:25). The priests washed their hands and their feet in the laver before ministering at the altar or entering the sanctuary (Ex. 30:17–21; Lev. 8:11). This ceremony symbolized the holiness that is required in the service of God. In Solomon's Temple there were a molten sea and 10 lavers instead of 1 (I Kings 7:23–26, 38–40, 43). Some of the arrangements were afterward altered by Ahaz (II Kings 16:17).

Law. Of the several meanings which the word law possesses, 2 are employed in Scripture:

1. A uniformly acting force which determines the regular sequence of events; any uniformly acting influence or motive which controls the will (Rom. 7:23).

2. A rule of conduct enjoined by a competent authority and, if need be, enforced by penalties. This is the principal meaning of the word in Scripture. Many laws have commenced as customs, which, arising naturally in the intercourse between members of the same society, ultimately gained such acceptance that the community finally resolved to enforce them as laws. But a law may be imposed by a ruler, human or divine, without any reference to previous custom or legislation. In the English version law is mainly the rendering of Heb. *tōrāh*, instruction, Aram. *dāth*, decree, law, and Gr. *nomos*, custom, law; and it denotes, except as noted under 1, an authoritative rule of conduct whether revealed from within or from without. It may be imposed by the constituted authorities of the state, which are ordained of God (Ezra 7:26; Esth. 1:19; Dan. 6:8), or proceed immediately from God, being revealed audibly in a supernatural manner as at Sinai or through the Spirit to prophets (Zech. 7:12) or made known in the constitution of our nature (Rom. 2:14, 15). They who fear God and keep his commandments are wise; and the godly wisdom which they have acquired from the study of the written law, from observation of the human heart, and from a life of holiness, when given forth in instruction is "the law of the wise" which is "a fountain of life" (Prov. 13:14), and when taught by parents to children is the law of father and mother which to them that obey is "a chaplet of grace" about the head (Prov. 1:8, 9).

The term "the law" with the definite article, but without any other qualifying word, occasionally refers to the whole O.T. in general (John 12:34; I Cor. 14:21; cf. John 10:34; 15:25), but it is employed much more frequently as the title of the Pentateuch (Josh. 1:8; Neh. 8:2, 3, 14; Matt. 5:17; 7:12; Luke 16:16; John 1:17). The Law of Moses was given by God through Moses (Ex. 20:19–22; Matt. 15:4; John 1:17). It is the law of God (Josh. 24:26; II Chron. 31:3). It was written in a book (Josh 1:7, 8), included the legislation contained in Exodus, Leviticus, Numbers, and Deuteronomy (cf. Mark 12:26 with Ex. 3:6; Mark 7:10 with Ex. 20:12; 21:17; Luke 2:22 and John 7:22, 23 with Lev. 12:2, 3; Matt. 8:4 with Lev. 14:3; Matt. 19:8; 22:24 with Deut. 24:1; 25:5), and was the title of the Pentateuch, the 1st division of the canon (Luke 24:44); see PENTATEUCH. The legal portion, consisting of the Ten Commandments, which form the fundamental law of the theocracy, and statutes based on them, was given at Sinai. The fundamental law was uttered within the hearing of the whole congregation. The body of statutes controlled the general form of worship, protected human rights, regulated personal conduct, and prescribed sacred seasons and sacrifice. It was given at the same time as the Ten Commandments, but through Moses. See THEOCRACY. When the tabernacle was erected, the legislation was enacted which in detail regulated approach to God. See LEVITICUS. Thirty-eight years later Moses rehearsed the Law publicly before the new generation, and introduced modifications which the prospective change in the circumstances of the people rendered necessary. See DEUTERONOMY. It is generally held that when all that is local and temporary is put away the remaining portion of the Commandments, constituting the essential part, was designed for the Christian as well as the Jewish dispensation, and will not become obsolete at any future time (cf. Ex. 20:12 or Deut. 5:16 with Eph. 6:2, 3). The Ten Commandments, being the fundamental law and a summary of the whole moral code, endure. They are founded in the immutable nature of God and in the permanent relations of men on earth. Of the Fourth Commandment Christ said: "The sabbath was made for man," hence its principles remain in force while man continues on earth. Regarding the Fifth Commandment, the Apostle Paul evidently considers both the precept and the essential part of the promise still in force, though the local or temporary portion, "the land" of Canaan, disappears, and "the earth" takes its place (Eph. 6:2, 3). The ceremonial law apparently referred to in Heb. 8:7 as the first covenant is there described as decaying and waxing old, and being ready to vanish away (v. 13; cf. also chs. 8 to 10). Hence the apostles declined to impose it on the Gentile converts (Acts 15:23–29, etc.). Its function has been to point, by means of its priesthood, its sacrifices, its ceremonies, and its symbols to Christ, our great High Priest, and his atoning sacrifice for sin. When the antitype came, the types were no longer needful, though the memory of what they had been rendered them objects of interest, and will do so through all future ages. The enactments constituting the civil and criminal code of the Israelites were admirably adapted to the state of civilization which the people had then reached; but these laws were freely modified as the circumstances contemplated by them changed.

Documents from Nuzu (Nuzi) in e. Mesopotamia of the 15th century B.C. show that the customs of the patriarchs in Genesis have important correspondences to Nuzian laws and social practice. There are also many resemblances between the Code of Moses and that of Hammurabi (*q.v.*). See PUNISHMENT.

Law'yer. One versed in the Law of Moses, of which he was the professional interpreter, a scribe (cf. Matt. 22:35 with Mark 12:28); see SCRIBE 3. In Luke 11:44 the words "scribes and Pharisees, hypocrites!" (A.V.) are omitted in R.V., and there is no contrast between scribes and lawyers (v. 45). The lawyers joined the Pharisees in rejecting the preaching of John the Baptist (Luke 7:30). They considered themselves above the need of instruction from Jesus; and when one of them did condescend to hold communication with him, it was to try to puzzle him by means of a difficult question (Matt. 22:35; Luke 10:25; cf. Luke 14:3). Jesus denounced them at last in severe language for laying heavy burdens on the people, and keeping back from them the key of knowledge (Luke 11:45–52).

Lay'ing On of Hands. An act symbolizing dedication to a special purpose. The Israelites placed their hands on the heads of the Levites, dedicating them to the service of the Lord at the tabernacle in the stead of the firs -born of all the tribes. They pressed down their hands upon the heads of the Levites, doubtless with the intention of signifying thereby that, with God s permission and by his authority, they transferred their own obligation to service to the Levites (Num. 8:5-20). The Israelite, who brought an animal to the sacrificial altar, placed his hands upon the victim's head, thereby dedicating it to God and making it his own representative and substitute (Lev. 1:4; 16:21). The aged Jacob laid his hands on the heads of Joseph's sons, giving them a place among his own sons, and bestowing upon them the covenant blessing, transferring it from himself as its past possessor to them (Gen. 48:5-20). The hands of presbytery were laid upon the head of Timothy. The young man was thereby set apart to official service and grace was bestowed (I Tim. 4:14). Imposition of the hands of presbytery denoted not only commission, but also the bestowal, by those divinely authorized, of official spiritual grace; or at least it signified the authoritative recommendation of the candidate to God as a recipient of grace.

Laz'a·rus (lăz'á-rŭs) [Lat. from Gr., for Heb. *Eleazar*, *q.v.*]. 1. The name of the beggar in the parable of the Rich Man and Lazarus. He was laid at the gate of the rich man, desiring to be fed with the crumbs which fell from the sumptuously furnished table. He was also afflicted with ulcers, and the dogs licked his sores. Nothing is said of his and nothing of the rich man's character; but when they died Lazarus was carried by angels into Abraham's bosom, while the rich man went to Hades. At first sight it might appear that the one was rewarded simply for being poor, and the other punished for being rich; but the hint that the rich man's brothers, who evidently lived exactly as he had done, did not believe Moses and the prophets, and needed repentance, shows that a moral element entered into the case, and that conduct, not position, decided their ultimate destiny (Luke 16:19-31). 2. A member of the family of Bethany, and brother of Martha and Mary. He was an object of deep affection not only to his sisters, but to Jesus, which speaks well for his character. He was chosen for the signal honor of being raised from the dead. When he had fallen sick with a grievous disease the sisters sent word to Jesus, who was beyond the Jordan, but he did not respond at once. Two days later, when Lazarus was dead, Jesus went to Bethany. Being met by Martha outside the village, he had an important conversation with her in which he called forth an expression of her faith in the resurrection and in his power to do all things, and declared himself to be the resurrection and the life. When Mary had come, Jesus went with the sisters and their friends to the sepulcher, which was of the usual kind then in use among the Jews—a cave, either natural or artificial, in the face of a rock. After the stone had been rolled away, Jesus prayed to the Father. He did this for the sake of the people that stood by, that in the miracle they might discern proof that the Father had sent him. Then he said in the hearing of all present, "Lazarus, come forth," and the dead awoke to life and came forth (John 11:1-44). The effect of this miracle was profound. It was the cause of the enthusiastic reception of Jesus at Jerusalem. It also brought the sanhedrin to their decision to put him to death; for the people were hailing him as king, and if they should accept him and his undisguised

doctrine of the spiritual nature of Christ's Kingdom, all hope of their rising against the Romans and endeavoring to restore the theocracy would vanish. The rulers decided that it was better for one man to perish, whether he were guilty or not, rather than for the whole nation to be lost (John 11:45-53; 12:9-19). Lazarus was present at a supper given in honor of his great Benefactor by Simon the leper at Bethany 6 days before the passover (Matt. 26:6; Mark 14:3; John 12:1, 2). The extent to which his restoration to life tended to bring new followers to Jesus so irritated the Jewish authorities that they plotted to put him also to death (John 12:10, 11). This is the last mention of Lazarus in Scripture. The plot to take his life does not seem to have been carried out, and in due time he doubtless died a second death, the time, the place, and the circumstances of which are all unknown.

Lead. One of the metals known to the ancients. It was taken as spoil from the Midianites (Num. 31:22), was used by the Egyptians (Jos. *Apion* i. 34), was obtained in large quantities in the peninsula of Sinai, was found in Egypt, and was imported from Tarshish (Ezek. 27:12). It was used for weights (Zech. 5:7), for sinkers on fish lines (Homer *Iliad* xxiv. 80), and for tablets on which inscriptions were written (Tacitus *Ann.* ii. 69; Pliny *Hist. Nat.* xiii. 21; Pausanias ix. 31, 4). Job 19:24 has been understood to refer to such tablets; but the words rather mean that, since a book (v. 23) is liable to perish, Job desires the letters to be cut in the rock and then, to render them more distinct and durable, to be filled with molten lead.

Leaf. 1. Foliage of a tree (Gen. 3:7; 8:11). 2. Part of the wing of a folding door, when each of the 2 wings was divided either lengthwise or crosswise (I Kings 6:34; Ezek. 41:24). In the former passage, the door of the Holy Place in Solomon's Temple is referred to. It was the 4th part of the wall (I Kings 6:33); and was probably oblong like the wall itself, and measured 5 cubits in width by 7½ in height (cf. v. 2). The measurement presumably includes the 2 doorposts and the lintel, leaving an opening at least 4 cubits wide by 7 high. This was closed by 2 doors, each of which was divided perpendicularly or horizontally into halves. If divided horizontally through the middle, the leaf measured 2 by 3½ cubits, or 3 by 5¼ feet, and was quite ample to afford ingress and egress to the priests in their daily ministrations, without requiring the entire door to be opened. The interpretation of the Hebrew text of I Kings 6:33, however, is difficult, and the words translated "out of a fourth part of the wall" should probably on the basis of the LXX and Vulgate be rendered "door-posts foursquare." 3. The page or column of a roll (Jer. 36:23; cf. v. 2).

Le'ah (lē'á) [probably, wild cow, as in Arab.]. The elder daughter of Laban. She was less attractive than her younger sister, Rachel, one chief defect being that her eyes were tender (weak, delicate). By a trick she was passed off on Jacob as his bride, when he had served 7 years for Rachel. Leah became the mother of Reuben, Simeon, Levi, Judah, Issachar, Zebulun, and their sister Dinah (Gen. 29:16-35; 30:17-21).

Leas'ing. Lying, falsehood (Ps. 4:2; 5:6, A.V.). As the word is now obsolete, R.V. substitutes "falsehood" and "lies."

Leath'er. The art of tanning and dyeing skins was understood by the Hebrews (Ex. 25:5; Acts 9:43). Leather was used by them and other nations of antiquity for numerous purposes: for articles of clothing (Lev. 13: 48; Num. 31:20), coverings of tents (Ex. 26:14), bottles (Judith 10:5), shields. The leather of the shield was oiled to keep it soft and shining (II Sam. 1:21; Isa. 21:5). Seal or porpoise skin was used for making a superior kind of sandal (Ezek. 16:10; in A.V. badgers' skin). Elijah and John the Baptist wore leather girdles (II Kings 1:8; Matt. 3:4).

Leav'en. A substance used to produce fermentation in dough and make it rise (Ex. 12:15, 19; 13:7). In Scripture times leaven generally consisted of a little old dough in a high state of fermentation. Its disadvantages were that the bread thus produced had a disagreeably sour taste and smell. To obviate these defects yeast or barm is now employed as leaven. The use of leaven was forbidden in all offerings made by fire to the Lord (Lev. 2:11). But when the offering was to be consumed by man, leaven might be used (Lev. 7:13; 23:17). The principal reason for the prohibition was that fermentation is incipient corruption, and was emblematic of corruption. It is used for corrupt doctrine (Matt. 16:11; Mark 8:15) and for wickedness in the heart (I Cor. 5:6–8; Gal. 5:9). The Israelites were forbidden to eat leavened bread or to have any leaven in their houses during the passover festival. The absence of leaven symbolized the incorruptness of life which God's service requires, reminded them of the haste in which they had fled out of Egypt, and suggested the affliction of Egypt by the insipidi y of the bread (Ex. 12:39; Deut. 16:3; I Cor. 5:7, 8). The word is used, however, in a good sense in the parable of the leaven, where its hidden but pervasive action is taken as a symbol of the growth of the Kingdom of heaven (Matt. 13:33; Luke 13:20, 21).

Le·ba'na (lê-bā'nȧ) and **Le·ba'nah** (lê-bā'-nȧ) [white]. Founder of a family, members of which returned from captivity (Ezra 2:45; Neh. 7:48).

Leb'a·non (lĕb'ȧ-nŏn) [white]. A snow-clad mountain range (Jer. 18:14), with hills of less elevation running from it in every direction (Hos. 14:5). Its streams rendered the rich soil of the valleys extremely productive. The lower zone was covered with vines (Hos. 14:6, 7), but the mountains were most noted for their forests of gigantic cedars. Fir trees or cypresses also abounded (I Kings 5:6–10; II Kings 19:23; Isa. 60:13; Zech. 11:1). Lions and leopards roamed in the woods (II Kings 14:9; S. of Sol. 4:8). The trees were felled, and the timber was used not only in the construction of palaces and temples, but also by the Phoenicians for the masts of ships (Ezra 3:7; Ezek. 27:5). Lebanon was the n.w. boundary of the Promised Land (Deut. 1:7; 11:24; Josh. 1:4; 11:17; 12:7; 13:5). It is of limestone formation. The mountains consist of 2 ranges, running n. and s., separated by the valley of the Litany and the Orontes. In the Greek period the name Lebanon became restricted to the w. range, while the e. received the name Anti-Lebanon. This distinction still exists. The intervening valley is called Coelesyria, that is, Hollow Syria, or the Bekā'. The chain may be considered to commence about 15 miles s.e. of Sidon, and to run to about 12 miles n.e. by n. of Tripoli, a distance of about 100 miles. The greatest elevation of Lebanon is at its n. end; of Anti-Lebanon, at its s. end in Mount Hermon. "For 10 miles the n. end of this ridge [of Lebanon] is over 10,000 feet above the sea. For another 10 miles it is between 7,500 and 8,000 feet. Then for 20 miles it sinks to an average of from 6,500 to 7,000 feet. Then it rises in the grand

truncated cone of Jebel Sunnīn to over 8,500 feet. Again it sinks to the plateau between Sunnīn and Kenīseh, to about 6,000 feet. The highest peak of Kenīseh rises again to nearly 7,000 feet. Then comes the pass of the Damascus road at Khan Muzhir, 5,022 feet. Then the ridge of Jebel Barūk and Jebel Nīha, over 40 miles long, about 6,500 feet, the latter ending in the picturesque Twins (To-māt Nīha). Finally, Jebel Rīhān, which sinks gradually to the level of the plateau of Merj 'Ayûn. Jebel Kenīseh, and Jebel Sunnīn, at the center of the chain, although not the highes', are from their isolation far the most imposing peaks" (Post). The highest peaks are Jebel Makmal and Kurnat es-Sauda, each about 10,200 feet.

Le·ba'oth (lê-bā'ŏth) [lionesses]. A town in the extreme s. of Judah (Josh. 15:32). See BETH-LEBAOTH.

Leb·bae'us (lĕ-bē'ŭs). See JUDAS 8.

Leb'-ka'mai (lĕb'kā'mī). An artificial name (Jer. 51:1, R.V.), which, when the consonants are exchanged according to the system called Athbash, yields KSDIM, that is, Chaldeans. The method is explained, and another instance is cited, in the article SHESHACH.

Le·bo'nah (lê-bō'nȧ) [incense, frankincense]. A town n. of Shiloh (Judg. 21:19), identified with Lubban, on the road between Shechem and Jerusalem, 3 miles w. by n. of Shiloh.

Le'cah (lē'kȧ). A village of Judah (I Chron. 4:21), to judge from the context. Site unknown.

Leek. The rendering in Num. 11:5, of Hebrew *ḥāṣîr*, which commonly denotes grass. The leek (*Allium porrum*) is probably intended in this passage, for it is mentioned, along with onions and garlic, as eaten in Egypt; the word is so rendered by the Targum of Onkelos, the LXX, Vulgate, and Peshitta.

Lees. Dregs or sediment deposited from wine or other liquor (Isa. 25:6). The liquor was allowed to stand on the lees that its color and body might be better preserved. To settle on one's lees is to settle down in contentment with one's character and circumstances (Jer. 48:11; Zeph. 1:12). To drink the lees of the cup of wrath means to drain the cup, enduring the punishment to the utmost (Ps. 75:8, rendered "dregs").

Le'gion. 1. The chief subdivision of the Roman army (Jos. *War* iii. 4, 2). It originally contained 3,000 foot soldiers with a contingent of cavalry of 300 men in 10 squadrons. From 100 B.C. to the fall of the empire the number varied from 5,000 to 6,200, while from Augustus to Hadrian or during the N.T. period 6,000 seems to have been the normal size besides the cavalry. At this time the legion consisted of 10 cohor's, each cohort of 3 maniples, and each maniple of 2 centuries (cf. Matt. 27:27, R.V. marg.); and was officered by tribunes and centurions (Jos. *War* iii. 5, 3; Acts 21:31, 32, R.V. marg.; 23:23), numbering 10 and 60 respectively. In Scripture legion is used to denote any large host (Matt. 26:53; Mark 5:9).

The military standard of the Romans was at first a bunch of straw attached to a pole. Later an eagle and 4 other animals formed the standards of a legion, but after 104 B.C. the eagle alone was employed (Pliny *Hist. Nat.* x. 4). It was committed to the custody of the chief centurion. In addition to the eagle, the standard also commonly bore a small image of the emperor, and the introduction of these images into Jerusalem by Pontius Pilate caused an insurrection of the Jews (Jos.

Antiq. xviii. 3, 1; *War* ii. 9, 2). But while the great standard of the whole legion was the eagle, each cohort and century had its own standard, and these minor ensigns assumed a variety of forms.

2. The name of an unclean spirit, or spirits (Mark 5:9, 15; Luke 8:30), so called in comparison with the multitude of men in a Roman legion.

Roman Soldier, from a Bas-relief of the First Century A.D.

Le'ha·bim (lê-hā'bĭm). A tribe sprung from or incorporated with the Egyptians (Gen. 10:13; I Chron. 1:11), probably the same as the Lubim (*q.v.*).

Le'hi (lē'hī) [jawbone, cheek]. A place in Judah (Judg. 15:9), elevated (vs. 11, 13), where the Philistines spread themselves when they advanced into Judah to seize Samson. It may have been a ridge. It received its name either from a series of jagged crags resembling a jawbone, or from Samson's exploit with the jawbone of an ass. At any rate, that part of it where Samson beat down the Philistines, who seem to have been fleeing, and cast aside the jawbone that had served him as a weapon, was remembered, and it was pointed out as Ramath-lehi, height of the jawbone (v. 17). Guérin locates Lehi at 'Ain el-Lehi, n.w. of Bethlehem, about 2 miles w.s.w. of Mālhah, and hence not far from E am (cf. v. 11), on the high plateau. But the existence of 'Ain el-Lehi appears doubtful. It may have been in Wadi eṣ-Ṣarār, not far from Zorah and Timnath.

Lem'u·el (lĕm'û-ĕl) [devoted to God]. The royal author of Prov., ch. 31, who reproduces what was taught him by his mother (v. 1).

Len'til. A plant (II Sam. 23:11), boiled as pottage (Gen. 25:29, 34) and in times of scarcity made into bread (Ezek. 4:9). The lentil (*Ervum lens*) is a papilionaceous plant, allied to the vetches. It has compound leaves, with 5 to 6 pairs of oblong leaflets, white

flowers striped with violet, and small broad legumes. Pottage made from it is red. It was this which was given to Esau when he was famishing, and it was from it (Gen. 25:30) that his 2d name Edom was derived (but cf. ch. 25:25). The plant is wild in Moab and is cultivated in all parts of Palestine. The seeds when boiled are thoroughly wholesome. It is from them that revalenta Arabica is made.

Leop'ard [Lat. *leopardus*, from Gr. *leopardos*, from *leōn*, lion, and *pardos*, pard]. A large and ferocious spotted (Jer. 13:23) cat of Africa and s. Asia. It was very swift (Hab. 1:8). Its appropriate food was the kid (Isa. 11:6), but it sometimes attacked man (Hos. 13:7, 8); lurking for the purpose in the vicinity of cities or villages (Jer. 5:6), though its ordinary habitation was among the mountains (S. of Sol. 4:8). The leopard (*Felis pardus* or *Leopardus*) was believed by the ancients and some moderns to be a hybrid between the lion and the panther; hence its name, as in the etymology above. In Palestine it now occurs chiefly in the region e. of the Jordan; but it was evidently more common in Scripture times than at present, in the country w. of the river.

In Dan. 7:6 it symbolizes a fierce nation and its king, doubtless the Persian Empire; in Rev. 13:2 the composite creature, which combines the four beasts of Daniel and typifies the united powers of this world, has the body of a leopard.

Lep'er. See LEPROSY 1.

Lep'ro·sy. 1. A dreadful disease, in Heb. *ṣāra'ath* (literally, scourge); the person afflicted with it is called a leper. The homiletic use of leprosy as a type of sin is not Biblical; Ps. 51:7 might approach this sense, but it may refer to Num. 19:18 instead of to the cleansing of a leper. The symptoms are described in Lev. 13:1-46. It was not a superficial, but a deep-seated malady. It often began as a rising, or a scab, or a bright spot, which tended to spread, turning white the

Lentils

hair covering the parts affected (Lev. 13:2, 3, 7, 8, 10, 24, 25, 27, 35, 36). Raw flesh tended to appear (vs. 10, 14–16, 24). Among the parts of the body specially liable to attack were the scalp of the head, the beard, the top of the head, or the forehead, after these had become bald; also any spot which had been accidentally injured by fire (vs. 24, 29, 30, 42). A leper was to be excluded from the camp; was required to let the hair of his head go loose and his clothes be rent; was to cover his upper lip, and cry, "Unclean! Unclean!" (vs. 45, 46); cf. II Kings 7:3–15; Luke 17:12 seq. He had to appear repeatedly before the priest, who was to pronounce on the character of the disease (Lev. 13:1–44); and in the event of the malady's departing, he was to go through an elaborate process of cleansing and sacrifice (Lev. 14:1–32). While the leprosy was spreading, the sufferer was unclean, but if it overspread the whole body, he was adjudged clean (Lev. 13:6, 12 seq.). In the description of the disease given in Lev., ch. 13, there is no mention of the leper's hue changing to a snowy white, as was the case with Miriam (Num. 12:10) and Gehazi (II Kings 5:27), and momentarily with Moses (Ex. 4:6). Not even those whose circumstances were comfortable were exempt from this disease. Thus, it affected Naaman, when commander in chief of the army of Syria (II Kings 5:1–14), and Uzziah during the later years of his reign over Judah (II Kings 15:5; II Chron. 26:21). In the cases of Miriam, Gehazi, and Uzziah the sudden infliction of leprosy was a divine judgment. The regulations about excluding the leper from society were carried out among the Hebrews (Num. 5:1–4; 12:10, 15; II Kings 7:3, 8, 10; 15:5; II Chron. 26:21; cf. also Luke 17:12); but the fact that the king of Syria seems to have depended on Naaman, even when he was a leper, and that Naaman dwelt with his family and was accompanied by servants, shows that leprosy, though loathsome, was not actually contagious (II Kings 5:2, 13).

The disease to which the English word leprosy is now confined is a formidable malady, technically called Elephantiasis Graecorum, elephant disease of the Greeks. It appears under 2 forms: the tubercular or nodular or black leprosy is at present the more common, and the name is restricted to it by some authorities. It affects primarily the skin and mucous membranes. The anesthetic or white leprosy affects the peripheral nerves principally and produces numbness. The symptoms of the 2 forms are often united, and one form frequently passes into the other. The coming of the disease is preceded by lassitude for months or years. Then circular spots or blotches of irregular form and varying extent appear on the forehead, the limbs, and the body. After a time, the central portion of the spots and blotches becomes white, and the parts affected contract a certain numbness. In the worst cases the joints of the fingers and toes fall off one by one, and injuries to the other parts produce mutilation and deformity. Thomson says: "The 'scab' comes on by degrees in different parts of the body; the hair falls from the head and eyebrows; the nails loosen, decay, and drop off; joint after joint of the fingers and toes shrink up and slowly fall away. The gums are absorbed, and the teeth disappear. The nose, the eyes, the tongue, and the palate are slowly consumed." Again, he says that when approaching the Jaffa Gate of Jerusalem he was startled by the sudden apparition of a crowd of beggars, without eyes, nose, or hair. They held up handless arms, and unearthly sounds gurgled through throats without palates. This loathsome and fatal disease is popularly believed to be identical with that of Leviticus and the other books of the Bible (cf. Num. 12:12).

But the disease mentioned in Scripture seems to have been curable (Lev. 14:3), whereas Elephantiasis Graecorum is not, except in the early stages. Sir Risdon Bennett and others believe that probably Lepra vulgaris, now merged in the genus Psoriasis, called Psoriasis vulgaris, the dry tetter, is the

Biblical leprosy. It is a noncontagious, scaly disease, generally commencing about the elbows and knees, as small circular patches of silvery-white scales, which spread till they become the size of a quarter or a half dollar, by which time the scales have fallen from the central portion of the circle, leaving it red: other circles arising coalesce. Afterward the abdomen, the chest, and the back become affected, and in rare cases the disease extends at last also to the head, face, and hands. The constitutional disturbance is trifling, and while the disease is apparently curable, it is liable to recur. It is simply a skin disease, in no way endangering life. Or, the white leprosy of the O.T. may have been Psoriasis guttata, in which the scattered patches are said to give an appearance to the skin as if it had been splashed with mortar. Perhaps Heb. ṣāra'ath was a generic term, and the elephantiasis and the psoriasis two of its species; and it is quite possible that different varieties prevailed at different times. If the leprosy of the Old and that of the New Testament were identical, then confirmation is given to the opinion that the former was psoriasis, for Luke (5:12, 13), himself a physician, employs Gr. lepra, which was technically used of psoriasis. With this Josephus' description of leprosy agrees, for (Jos. Antiq. iii. 11, 4) he defines a leper to be a man who has a misfortune in the color of his skin and makes no allusion to graver symptoms. He mentions also that among the Gentiles lepers were not excluded from society, but were competent to discharge important functions in the body politic.

2. The same word ṣāra'ath was applied to a greenish or reddish appearance in a garment and to hollow greenish or reddish streaks in the wall of a house (Lev. 13:47–59; 14:33–37). The leprosy in garments may be mildew; that of houses, mold or dry rot, or any fungus growth.

Le'shem (lē'shĕm. See DAN 3.

Le·tu'shim (lē-tū'shĭm). A tribe descended from Dedan (Gen. 25:3). They doubtless settled in Arabia.

Le·um'mim (lē-ŭm'ĭm) [peoples, nations]. A tribe descended from Dedan (Gen. 25:3). They doubtless settled in Arabia.

Le'vi (lē'vī) [joined, attached; following]. 1. Third son of Jacob and Leah (Gen. 29:34). He took part with Simeon, Leah's second son, in massacring Hamor, Shechem, and the men of their city, in revenge for the injury done by Shechem to their sister Dinah (Gen. 34:25–31). Jacob on his deathbed remembered with fresh abhorrence this deed of blood, and, referring to Simeon and Levi, said, "Cursed be their anger, for it was fierce; and their wrath, for it was cruel: I will divide them in Jacob, and scatter them in Israel" (Gen. 49:7). Levi had 3 sons: Gershon or Gershom, Kohath, and Merari (Gen. 46:11), and died in Egypt at the age of 137 (Ex. 6:16). See LEVITES.

2 and 3. Two ancestors of Christ, one the son of Symeon, and the other a son of Melchi (Luke 3:24, 29, 30).

4. Another name for the Apostle Matthew (cf. Matt. 9:9–13; Mark 2:14–17; Luke 5:27–32).

Le·vi'a·than [one spirally wound]. A great aquatic animal mentioned only in poetic passages. He was formed by God to play in the sea (Ps. 104:26). He has limbs, head, neck, eyes, nose, jaw, mouth, teeth, and tongue (Job 41:1, 2, 7, 12, 14, 18, 19, 22), and is covered with scales and an impenetrable hide (vs. 7, 15–17, 26–29). He lies upon the mire or makes the sea to boil like a pot (vs. 30, 31). He is too large to be taken by fishhook or harpoon (vs. 1, 26), is terrible of aspect (v. 9), and mighty in strength, but comely of proportion (v. 12). He is poetically described as breathing fire and smoke (vs. 19–21). When God worked salvation by dividing the sea, he destroyed the sea monsters which inhabited it, broke the heads of leviathan, and left his carcass to be eaten by the people of the desert (Ps. 74:14). As the sea is the type of the restless, surging nations of the earth, so leviathan which dwells therein, leviathan the flying serpent, leviathan the swift serpent, leviathan the crooked serpent, and the dragon symbolize the fierce and terrible powers of the world that have afflicted the people of God, but whom God will ultimately destroy (Isa. 27:1). Leviathan is commonly regarded as the crocodile (Job 41:1, R.V. marg.). Accordingly the imagery is apt. Egypt, his habitat, was the typical oppressor of the Kingdom of God, and Egypt's power was broken and its king thwarted when God divided the Red Sea for the deliverance of his people. Leviathan may, however, be merely a creation of the fancy, an imaginary sea monster, the inspired poets and prophets of Israel employing popular material to serve in the illustration of truth. In Job 3:8 leviathan may be a fabulous dragon which caused eclipses by swallowing sun and moon, and the cursers of the day may be conjurers who claimed the power to produce eclipses by his aid. Or in this passage leviathan may be the untamable, terrible crocodile which only conjurers of highest skill claimed ability to summon to their aid.

Le'vites (lē'vīts). 1. The descendants of Levi, the son of Jacob. He had 3 sons: Gershon or Gershom, Kohath, and Merari, each of whom founded a tribal family (Gen. 46: 11; Ex. 6:16; Num. 3:17; I Chron. 6:16–48). Moses and Aaron were Levites of the house of Amram and family of Kohath (Ex. 6:16–26).

2. The men of the tribe of Levi charged with the care of the sanctuary. It has been suggested that the Hebrew term Lewi (Levi, e) is derived from *lawiyu, a person pledged for a debt or a vow. Thus Samuel was vowed by his mother at Shiloh before he was born. Aaron and his sons were set apart for the priesthood and the office was made hereditary. But the tabernacle and its service had been projected on a noble scale. The care and transportation of the costly sanctuary and the preparation of materials for the elaborate service entailed labors which no one man or no one family was equal to. Helpers were needed. The charge of the tabernacle was an honorable work. Who should undertake it? The first-born belonged to God. This conviction was deepened by the circumstances connected with the deliverance from Egypt. When the first-born of the Egyptians were slain, blood on the lintel and side doorposts was needed to protect the Israelite first-born males from a similar fate. They had then become the special property of Jehovah and henceforth were consecrated to him as a memorial (Ex. 13:11–16). But instead of the first-born of all the tribes, the Levites were chosen for service in connection with the sanctuary; and the choice was made because, when the people had broken the covenant with Jehovah by making the golden calf, the Levites alone had voluntarily returned to their allegiance and shown zeal for God's honor (Ex. 32:26–29; Num. 3:9, 11–13, 40, 41, 45 seq.; 8:16–18). The first-born males of Israel, exclusive of the Levites, numbered 22,-273 in the census taken at Sinai (Num. 3:43, 46). There were 22,000 Levites (v. 39); but the items given in vs. 22, 28, and 34 total 22,300. Either an error has occurred some-

where in the transcription, or else 300 of these Levites were themselves first-born and therefore could not serve as substitutes for the first-born of the other tribes. The 22,000 were substituted. The remaining 273 first-born of Israel were redeemed by the payment of 5 shekels apiece (Num. 3:46–51).

It was the duty of the Levites to transport the tabernacle and its furniture when the camp moved; and when the camp rested to erect the tent, have care of it, and assist the priests in their varied work (Num. 1:50–53; 3:6–9, 25–37; 4:1–33; I Sam. 6:15; II Sam. 15:24). As the sons of Aaron were Levites as well as priests, they are frequently included under the designation Levite (Deut. 33:8–10; Josh. 14:3; 21:1, 4; Mal. 3:3); and also, either as higher officials or as Levites, they might, if they saw fit, discharge any service that pertained to the Levites.

The age at which the obligation of service began was 30 years (Num. 4:3; I Chron. 23:3–5, and 25 years (Num. 8:24), and 20 years (I Chron. 23:24, 27). The divergent practice at different periods of the history explains the peculiarity in part. It is even conceivable that a reduction in the age for entrance and a lengthening of the term of service was made by Moses himself sometime during the course of 40 years, and such a change is expressly stated to have been made by David. But it is noticeable that both in the book of Numbers and in the books of Chronicles the age of 30 years is forthwith followed by an earlier age. Also in Num., ch. 4, the service of the Levites who were 30 years old is defined by an explanatory clause: "Every one that entered in to do the work of service, and the work of bearing burdens in the tent of meeting" (vs. 47, 49); and, in fact, the particular service is defined by the specifications of the entire chapter. It is, therefore, not at all improbable that at 30 years of age the Levites became eligible to full service of every sort that pertained to Levites at the sanctuary, including the high and honorable offices of bearing the tabernacle and its sacred furniture in public procession and, at a later period, of serving in positions that brought distinction and called for wisdom and discretion (Num. 4:1–33; I Chron. 23:3–5); but the Levites began general service at first at 25 years of age, and performed the various duties belonging to their calling with the exceptions that have been noted; at least the higher duties are not mentioned in connection with the more youthful age (Num. 8:24–26; I Chron. 23:25–32). David, however, saw fit to make a further reduction in the age at which the simpler duties should be undertaken; he directed that the Levites should enter upon service at the same time of life as that at which the other Israelites became liable to military service, namely, at 20 years, seeing that the need of transporting the Ark no longer existed and the service of the sanctuary had become a routine, and a sort of apprenticeship was a useful preparation for the regular ecclesiastical duties. Twenty years was henceforth the legal age for the Levites to enter upon service (II Chron. 31:17; Ezra 3:8). At this age they commenced as assistants to the priests and chief Levites (I Chron. 23:28–31; cf. II Chron. 29:34; 35:11), but probably not until they reached 30 years were they regarded as experts or eligible for the higher offices of doorkeeper or member of the Temple orchestra or administrator or judge (I Chron. 23: 3–5). They retired from active service at 50, but were free to render assistance to the Levites who succeeded them in the work at the sanctuary (Num. 8:25, 26).

An official dress was prescribed for the Levites, but on great occasions they drew on

festal raiment (I Chron. 15:27; II Chron.
5:12). It was an innovation when the Levitical singers in the 1st century A.D. obtained
permission from King Agrippa, with the sanction of the sanhedrin, to wear linen garments
as constantly as did the priests (Jos. Antiq.
xx. 9, 6). They were not required to devote
their entire time to the sanctuary or to dwell
continually near it; but on the allotment of
Canaan they were distributed to various
towns (Josh. 21:20–40). Exclusive of the
towns allotted to the Levites who were
priests, all of which were in Judah, Simeon,
and Benjamin, the Levitical towns numbered
35 and were situated among the remaining
tribes on the n. and e. (Josh. 21:5–7). Since
the Levites as a tribe were "wholly given unto
the Lord in behalf of the children of Israel,"
and were appointed to service at the tabernacle, it was natural that in the n. districts,
where no Levitical priests dwelt, the lower
order of the Levites should be drawn upon
by the idolater Micah and after him by the
idolatrous migrating Danites to furnish a man
for priestly services (Judg. 17:8–13; 18:18–
20, 30, 31). In David's reign the Levites were
divided into 4 classes: 1. assistants to the
priests in the work of the sanctuary; 2.
judges and scribes; 3. gate keepers; 4. musicians. Each of these classes, with the possible exception of the 2d, was subdivided into
24 courses or families to serve in rotation (I
Chron., chs. 24 to 26; cf. ch. 15:16–24; II
Chron. 19:8–11; 30:16, 17; Ezra 6:18; Neh.
13:5). On the disruption of the monarchy,
many Levites and priests left the Northern
Kingdom and came to Judah and Jerusalem
(II Chron. 11:13–15).

Le·vit'i·cus (lĕ-vĭt'ĭ-kŭs) [Lat. from Gr., relating to the Levites]. The 3d book of the Pentateuch. When the tabernacle had been erected
and a priest appointed to minister at the altar,
the next step was to regulate access to God.
This is the object of the ordinances contained
in Leviticus. In approach to Jehovah, sacrifices and a priesthood were needed, and intercourse with God requires the attainment and
maintenance of purity, both ceremonial and
moral. To exercise a proper control over
these matters several manuals were prepared,
which were placed together and form the
book of Leviticus: 1. A directory of procedure
to be followed by the worshiper and the priest
at the offering of the various kinds of sacrifice (Lev. 1:1 to 6:7), and a book on the disposal of the sacrifice (chs. 6:8 to 7:36). The
directory of procedure was drawn up at Sinai
after the tabernacle had been erected, and the
book on the disposal of the sacrifice was written at the same general time, when "he commanded the children of Israel to offer their
oblations unto Jehovah" (ch. 1:1; cf. ch. 7:38
with ch. 1:2). 2. A record of the consecration
of Aaron and his sons to the priestly office
(chs. 8; 9), an official act prescribed during
Moses' first sojourn in Sinai (Ex., ch. 29),
which established the priesthood and was the
precedent for future ordinations. To this record an account of the punishment of Nadab
and Abihu for illegal approach was appended,
together with legislation which was enacted
to meet deficiencies revealed in the laws on
this occasion (Lev., ch. 10). 3. A directory
of ceremonial purity (chs. 11 to 16), containing laws concerning foods that defile, diseases or natural functions that render unclean, and the ceremonial national purification (already prescribed, Ex. 30:10). This
directory is ascribed to Moses as the repre-
sen'ative of Jehovah (Lev. 11:1, etc.), when
Israel was in the wilderness (chs. 14:34;
16:1). 4. The law of holiness (chs. 17 to 26),
statutes concerning holiness of life, given by
Moses (ch. 17:1, etc.), at Sinai (chs. 25:1;

26:46; cf. 24:10). These several collections
are followed by an appendix on vows, tithes,
and things devoted (ch. 27). Occasionally a
law is repeated in a new connection and for a
different purpose. At times also the legislation is interrupted by the narrative of events
that led to enactments (chs. 10:1–7, 12–20;
21:24; 24:10–23). Possibly some laws that
were framed after the departure from Sinai
were inserted for the sake of convenience in
their proper place among the laws relating to
the same subject. See PENTATEUCH.

Throughout the book but one sanctuary
(ch. 19:21 et passim) and one altar for all
Israel are recognized (chs. 1:3; 8:3; 17:8, 9),
and the sons of Aaron are the sole priests
(ch. 1:5). The Levites are only incidentally
mentioned (ch. 25:32, 33). Variations in the
laws or their statement as found in Leviticus
and Deuteronomy are intelligible when it is remembered that: 1. Leviticus is a manual for
the priests, to guide them through the tech-
nicalities of the ritual; while Deuteronomy
is primarily not a law book at all, but a
popular address to instruct the people in their
own duties and to exhort them to fidelity.
Deuteronomy omits matters of detail which
concern priests only. 2. The laws of Leviticus
are dated at Sinai an entire generation before the addresses contained in Deuteronomy
were delivered at Shittim. Accordingly the
legislation of Leviticus is presupposed in
Deuteronomy. This is the standpoint of the
Pentateuch.

The essentials of the legislation of Leviticus are reflected in the history in the early
recognition of the Aaronic priesthood. So far
as the evidence reaches, the priests were sons
of Aaron exclusively (Deut. 10:6; Josh. 14:1;
cf. ch. 21:4, 18 with I Kings 2:26; Judg. 20:27,
28; I Sam. 1:3; 2:27, 28; cf. I Sam. 21:6 with
I Chron. 24:3; I Sam. 22:11; and II Sam. 8:
17 with Ezra 7:3 and I Chron. 24:3). The Levites are sojourners and subordinate (Judg.
17:7–9; 19:1; I Sam. 6:15; II Sam. 15:24).
Compare also the one house of the Lord
(Judg. 18:31; 19:18; I Sam. 1:7, 24; 3:3;
4:3), and the feast of the Lord, at the tabernacle visited by all Israel (Judg. 21:19; I
Sam. 1:3); see further the articles PRIEST,
HIGH PRIEST, LEVITES, ALTAR, DEUTERONOMY.

Lib'er·tines [Lat., freedmen]. A section of
the Jewish community which had a synagogue at Jerusalem and were among the foes
of the first martyr, Stephen (Acts 6:9). They
were probably Jews, who, having been taken
prisoners in battle by Pompey and other Roman generals, had been bondsmen at Rome,
but were afterward restored to liberty.

Lib'nah (lĭb'nȧ) [whiteness]. 1. An encampment of the Israelites in the wilderness
(Num. 33:20). See LABAN 2.

2. A city in the lowland between Makkedah
and Lachish (Josh. 10:29–31), captured by
Joshua (vs. 30, 39; ch. 12:15). It was situated in the territory allotted to Judah (ch.
15:42), and was subsequently assigned to the
descendants of Aaron (ch. 21:13; I Chron.
6:57). When Jehoram, son of Jehoshaphat,
was king, Libnah revolted against Judah (II
Kings 8:22; II Chron. 21:10). Sennacherib,
king of Assyria, warred against it (II Kings
19:8; Isa. 37:8). The father of Hamutal, the
mother of Jehoahaz and Zedekiah, was from
this place (II Kings 23:31; 24:18; Jer. 52:1).
Probably to be located at Tell Bornâṭ, about
2 miles n.w. of Eleutheropolis (Beit Jibrîn);
Tell eṣ Ṣâfi (or Ṣâfiyeh) has also been suggested.

Lib'ni (lĭb'nī) [white, pure]. 1. Son of Gershon, and grandson of Levi. He was founder
of a minor tribal family or father's house
(Ex. 6:17; Num. 3:18, 21; 26:58).

2. A Levite, family of Merari, house of Mahli (I Chron. 6:29).

Lib'y•a (lĭb'ĭ-à), **Lib'y•ans** (lĭb'ĭ-ănz). A rendering of *Pūt* (Jer. 46:9; Ezek. 30:5; 38:5, A.V.) and *Lūbim* (Dan. 11:43). A country and its inhabitants in the w. part of Lower Egypt or on its borders. The Greeks first applied Libya to all Africa w. of Egypt; later the name was restricted to the part between Egypt and the Roman province of Africa, the w. frontier being at Philaenorum Arae in the middle of the Greater Syrtis The Romans divided the country into 2 parts, calling the e. district Libya Inferior (Marmarica) and the w., Libya Superior (Cyrenaïca). The s. limit at the desert was undefined. Cyrenaïca consisted of the Pentapolis of Cyrene, Barca with its port Ptolemaïs, Euesperides, Apollonia, and Teuchïra or Arsinoë. Cyrenaïca was formed with Crete into a province in 67 B.C. Its capital was Cyrene, and it was from this w. province that representatives were present at Jerusalem on Pentecost (Acts 2:10; cf. Jos. *Antiq.* xvi. 6, 1).

L'ce. The rendering of Heb. *kinnām* or *kinnīm* (Ex. 8:16-18; Ps. 105:31), referring to some small insect noxious to man. Josephus understood the word to mean lice (Jos. *Antiq.* ii. 14, 3). R.V. marg. translates it sandflies or fleas.

Lic'tor. See PRAETOR.

Lieu•ten'ant. See SATRAP.

Lign'al'oes. See ALOES.

Lig'ure. The rendering of Heb. *leshem*, a gem, the 1st stone in the 3d row of the high priest's breastplate (Ex. 28:19). This translation is derived from the LXX, Vulgate, and Josephus (Jos. *War* v. 5, 7); but it is impossible to identify the *ligurius* of the ancients with any known gem. The R.V. renders the Hebrew word by jacinth or amber.

L'k'hi (lĭk'hī). A Manassite, family of Shemida (I Chron. 7:19).

Lil'y. The rendering of the Hebrew words *shūshan*, *shōshān* (in pause), and *shōshannāh*. The plant so designated is found in pastures where sheep and gazelles feed (S. of Sol. 2:16; 4:5; 6:3), and among thorns (ch. 2:2), besides being cultivated in gardens (ch. 6:2). It was so much at home in valleys that it was designated the lily of the valleys (ch. 2:1). It was a sweet-scented plant, dropping a myrrhlike perfume (ch. 5:13). The Hebrew word was rendered *krinon* by the Greek translators. The *krinon* is a plant which grows beside the water (Ecclus. 50:8) and among the grass of the field (Matt. 6:28). It is often mentioned in connection with frankincense and the rose (Ecclus. 39:13, 14). It is the type of a life of beautiful deeds. The high priest, coming forth from the sanctuary is compared with it (ch. 50:8). It excels Solomon in his glorious array (Matt. 6:28 *seq.*; Luke 12:27 *seq.*).

The words *shūshan* and *krinon* were not always used with reference to the lily in its modern scientific sense, but included with the true lily various plants that resemble the lily. The lotus was known to the ancient Egyptians as *sshshn*, *sshn*, *sshnn* (cf. Bohairic Coptic *shōshen*, lily), and is called by Herodotus *krinon* (Herod. ii. 92). The ordinary word for a lily in Arabic is still *sausan*, *sūsan;* but it is used generically rather than specifically, including the tulip and even the anemone and ranunculus. What varieties of lily were anciently cultivated in the gardens of Palestine is not known. Besides the true lily, other genera of the order *Liliaceae*, as hyacinths and tulips, grow in profusion in the spring. A fine, dark-violet flower, known as *sūsan*, is found far and wide in the Hauran. Thomson describes a splendid iris, which he calls the Hu'eh lily, growing among the oak woods around the n. base of Tabor and on the hills of Nazareth. The flower is dark purple and white. He believes that it is the lily referred to by Jesus. Red anemones are so marked a feature of the valleys of Palestine in the spring that various travelers, Tristram included, have suggested that *Anemone coronaria*, the red variety of which is very common, was probably the lily of the N.T. G. E. Post thinks that Christ referred to some plant of the *Liliaceae*, *Iridaceae*, or *Amaryllidaceae*, all of which could popularly be cal'ed lilies. Various species of *Gladiolus* grow among the grain, often overtopping it and decorating the fields with various shades of pinkish purple to deep violet-purple and blue; the beautiful racemes of these flowers

Red Anemone (*Anemone coronaria*)

peer up in every direction above the standing grain. Beautiful irises are also found in swamps and pasture lands. It is doubtful whether our Lord had any particular lilies in mind, but more likely he refers to all the splendid colors and beautiful shapes of the numerous wild flowers included under the general designation of lily. See ROSE.

Lime. A material prepared by burning limestone, shells, and other calcareous substances (Isa. 33:12; Amos 2:1), and used for making mortar and plaster, and for whitewashing walls (Deut. 27:2; Matt. 23:27; Acts 23:3). See MORTAR, II.

Lin'en. 1. Fine linen is the rendering of Heb. *shēsh*, applied to a stuff of which vestments were made; it is a loan word from Egypt. *shś*. It was in it that Joseph was arrayed by Pharaoh's order (Gen. 41:42). Of this material also were made the curtains, veil, and door hangings of the tabernacle (Ex. 26:1, 31, 36), and the hangings for the gate of the court and for the court itself (ch. 27:9, 16, 18). The distinguishing attire of the high priest consisted of the ephod, breastplate, robe of blue, and the gold plate on the miter; and of these the ephod and breastplate contained fine linen (ch. 28:6, 15). Other official garments were common to the high priest and the ord'nary pries'—the tunic, girdle, breeches, and headdress (Ex. 28:40-42; 39:27-29; cf. Lev. 16:4). The headdress, however, of the high priest was a miter or turban, while a simple cap appears to have been worn by the ordinary priest. Of these 4 articles of priestly dress, the girdle was embroidered, consisting largely of linen (Ex.

39:29). The 3 other garments were made of fine white linen exclusively (chs. 28:39; 39:27, 28). In the margin of Gen. 41:42 and of Ex. 25:4 the R.V. substitutes cotton. In the margin of Ex. 28:39 the R.V., referring to the coat and miter of the high priest, substitutes silk.

2. Hebrew *bad* is a synonym for *shêsh*, but is more general in its meaning, hence it is rendered merely linen (cf. Ex. 28:42 with 39:28). It sufficiently described the material of the priest's raiment, when there was no need to state explicitly the quality of the stuff (*ibid.*; Lev. 6:10; 16:4). Of it was made the plain ephod worn by the boy Samuel, by the priests at Nob, and by David on the occasion of removing the Ark (I Sam. 2:18; 22:18; II Sam. 6:14). In it the man with the inkhorn in Ezekiel's vision and Daniel's heavenly comforter were clothed (Ezek. 9:2; Dan. 10:5).

3. The rendering of Heb. *pishteh*, flax, which here denotes the material of which the goods are made (Jer. 13:1). It is used in contrast to woolen clothing (Lev. 13:47; Deut. 22:11). It describes the material of the priestly garments, the headtires, breeches, and girdles (Ezek. 44:17, 18).

4. The rendering of Heb. *bûṣ*, which occurs only in the later books, and of Gr. *byssos*. Of this material were made the robe, not the ephod, which David wore at the removal of the Ark (I Chron. 15:27), the veil of the Temple in part, the other stuffs employed being blue, purple, and crimson (II Chron. 3:14), the clothing of the Levites who were musicians at the dedication of the Temple (ch. 5:12), the cords which fastened the hangings in Ahasuerus' palace (Esth. 1:6), the state dress of Mordecai (ch. 8:15), the garments of the rich man at whose gate Lazarus sat (Luke 16:19), and of the luxurious city of Babylon (Rev. 18:16), and the bright and pure raiment of the Lamb's wife (ch. 19:8).

Whether the words denote linen or fine cotton cloth, or comprehend both, is much debated. Linen and cotton were employed in Egypt from the earliest times for mummy cloths.

5. The rendering of Heb. *'êṭûn* (Prov. 7:16; in R.V. yarn). It was imported from Egypt, where the most skillful manufacturers of linen lived.

6. Linen yarn is the rendering of Heb. *miḳweh* in A.V. of I Kings 10:28; II Chron. 1:16. R.V. renders it "a drove." The LXX in Kings, "*ek Thekoue*" (from Thekoue) and the Vulgate in both passages, "*de Coa*" (from Coa) suggest a place name. Eusebius in the *Onomasticon* mentions *Kod*, which Jerome renders as *Coa*, which is near Egypt. Akkadian *Kue*, however, is Cilicia, or the region around the Gulf of Alexandretta. If this place be referred to, it may suggest the Hittite country as a source of horses. J.V. renders, "Out of Keveh" (Keve).

7, 8. The rendering of Gr. *sindōn*, a fine Indian cloth, muslin, later linen. A tunic or perhaps a sheet might be made of it (Mark 14:51), and in this material the body of Jesus was wrapped for burial (Matt. 27:59). It is a synonym of *othonion*, though more special in meaning (cf. Luke 23:53 with ch. 24:12; John 19:40; 20:5, 7). In classical Greek the latter word means linen and also sailcloth and bandage, lint for wounds.

9. The rendering of Gr. *linon*, linen (Rev. 15:6, A.V. and margin of R.V.). The text of R.V. has "precious stones," from another reading *lithon*.

Lin'tel. The transverse piece of wood or other material constituting the upper part of a doorway or casement (Ex. 12:22), called in Heb. *mashḳôph*. 1. Lintel is also the rendering of Heb. *'ayil*, a ram, in I Kings 6:31. It may denote a projecting lintel or post. The Hebrew word occurs 18 times in an architectural sense in Ezek., chs. 40; 41, where it is rendered post (v. 9, etc.), with jamb in the margin of R.V.

2. The rendering of Heb. *kaphtor*, in A.V. of Amos 9:1 and Zeph. 2:14, which is translated capital in R.V. In Ex., chs. 25 and 37, where it occurs 14 times, it is rendered "knop" in both versions.

Li'nus. (li'nŭs). A Christian at Rome who joined Paul in sending salutations to Timothy (II Tim. 4:21). According to Irenaeus and Eusebius, he was the first bishop of Rome. See BISHOP. No lofty pre-eminence was attached to the office, for he is mentioned without distinction between 2 other members of the church at Rome.

Li'on. The *Felis leo* of naturalists. The lion is diffused over the whole of Africa and portions of s. Asia, as far e. as the province of Gujarat in India. It was formerly found in Greece, but does not now occur wild in that country or anywhere in Europe. In Biblical times it was common in Palestine. The Hebrews had no fewer than 6 words to designate it in different states or at successive stages of growth. The ordinary words are *'aryêh* and *'ărî*, which occur 80 times in the O.T. Allusion is made to the lion's strength (II Sam. 1:23; Prov. 30:30) and courage (II Sam. 17:10; Prov. 28:1), to his teeth (Joel 1:6), to his tendency to crouch before springing on his victim (Gen. 49:9), to prey on sheep, calves, and other beasts (I Sam. 17:34; Isa. 11:6, 7), or upon man (I Kings 13:24; Jer. 2:30), and to his roaring (Job 4:10; Prov. 20:2; I Peter 5:8). He is represented as lurking in thickets (Jer. 4:7), forests (ch. 5:6), or other coverts (ch. 25:38). A special haunt of his appears to have been among the trees and bushes fringing the Jordan (ch. 49:19). Of the living creatures seen by Ezekiel in his vision each one had the face of a lion on the right side of the head (Ezek. 1:10; 10:14). The 1st of the 4 living creatures seen by John was like a lion (Rev. 4:7). Our Lord is called the Lion of the tribe of Judah (ch. 5:5; cf. Gen. 49:9).

Liz'ard. Any small lacertilian reptile. It was called *leṭâ'âh* in Hebrew, and was regarded as unclean (Lev. 11:30). The R.V. understands the 4 animals associated with it to be the gecko, the land crocodile, the sand lizard, and the chameleon; but states in the margin that the words are of uncertain meaning, but probably denote 4 kinds of lizards. Lizards abound in Palestine and the adjacent countries. The number of species is very great. In the woods and on cultivated ground the green lizards are the most beautiful, especially *Lacerta viridis* and *L. laevis*. Of the same family (*Lacertidae*) are the wall lizards, which appear in warm weather in multitudes, crawling over walls, rocks, and stony ground. Other families of eriglossate lacertilians are represented in Palestine, as the *Scincidae*, *Zonuridae*, *Agamidae*, and *Monitoridae*. The first of these contains the skinks or sand lizards (Lev. 11:30; A.V., snail). They chiefly inhabit desert districts, are generally small and of the yellowish color of the desert, are as common as the true lizard, but unlike it do not climb, and hide themselves under stones or by burrowing rapidly in the ground. The family of *Zonuridae* is represented by the glass snake (*Pseudopus pallasi*). Its hind legs are rudimentary, so that it looks much like a snake. It is black, and attains a length of 2 or 2½ feet, of which the tail forms two thirds. Closely related to this family are the *Agamidae*, containing *Uro-*

mastix spinipes. This reptile inhabits the sandy deserts of Africa and Arabia, and is common in the wilderness of Judea. It attains a length of 2 feet. Its body is green in color, spotted with brown. It has a powerful tail, encircled with rows of strong spines, which it uses as a weapon of defense. The Hebrew name, *ṣāb*, is rendered "great lizard" (Lev. 11:29; A.V., tortoise). The family of *Monitoridae* or *Varanidae* contains the monitors, of which the land crocodile of the ancients (Lev. 11:30; A.V., chameleon), commonly known as the land monitor, the *waran el-'ard* of the Arabs (*Psammosaurus scincus*), is common in s. Judea, the peninsula of Sinai, and the sandy parts of Egypt. It attains a length of 4 or 5 feet, and has a long snout, sharp, pointed teeth, and a long, tapering tail. The water monitor, *waran el-bahr* (*Hydrosaurus niloticus*), is slighly larger than its congener of the land, and is readily distinguished from it by the high keel along the whole length of its tail. Both reptiles are extremely rapid in their movements. They feed on small lizards and jerboas, and devour the eggs and young of the crocodile with avidity. They are eaten by the natives.

Loaf. A mass of bread. It was made of the flour of barley (II Kings 4:42; John 6:9) or wheat (cf. Lev. 23:17 with Ex. 34:22), round in shape (Ex. 29:23; Judg. 8:5, in Heb. *kikkār*, disk), and of a size convenient for baking and carrying with one (I Sam. 10:3; Matt. 14:17; John 6:9). See BREAD and SHOWBREAD.

Lo·am'mi (lō-ăm'ī) [not my people]. The symbolic name of the Prophet Hosea's 2d son by his wife Gomer (Hos. 1:8, 9).

Loan. Anything, especially money, that is lent. In the early ages of the Hebrew nation loans were not sought for the purpose of obtaining capital, but for the necessaries of life. The Israelites were commanded to open their hearts to their brother, who had fallen into poverty, and to lend him sufficient for his need (Deut. 15:7–11). They were forbidden to charge interest for any loan to a poor Israelite (Ex. 22:25; Lev. 25:35–37). But to a foreigner they might lend on interest (Deut. 23:20), and the poor Israelite might sell himself as a servant (Lev. 25:39; II Kings 4:1). If a pledge was asked from a poor Israelite for a loan, the creditor was not to go into the debtor's house to obtain it, but to remain outside and allow it to be brought out to him. If the pledge was a garment, it was to be returned to the owner before the evening, as probably it might be part of his sleeping attire (Ex. 22:26, 27). No one was to take the upper or nether millstone as a pledge, thus preventing the debtor and his family from grinding corn for their daily food (Deut. 24:6). Nor could anyone take a widow's garment (v. 17). Finally, when the 7th year, called the year of release, came, the debt was to be forgiven (ch. 15:1–11). The practice of suretyship, however, unfortunately grew up (Prov. 6:1; Ecclus. 8:13), and in later times interest was sometimes exacted for loans, although the practice was condemned by the prophets (Jer. 15:10; Ezek. 18:13). The beneficent regulations of the Law were systematically ignored after the Exile, and Nehemiah took vigorous measures to terminate the abuse (Neh. 5:1–13). The Roman law was a marked contrast in its severiy to that of Moses. By a law of the 12 tables a creditor could put his insolvent debtor in fetters and cords. Doubtless with allusion to the ordinary procedure Jesus describes the lord of a debtor as commanding that he, his wife, his children, and all that he had, be sold in liquidation of the debt (Matt. 18:25), and, when he had abused leniency

which was shown him on his appeal for mercy, be delivered to the torturers till he should pay all that was due (v. 34). In the time of Christ banking was a regular institution (ch. 25:27; Luke 19:23). A public building was provided in Jerusalem, where documents relating to loans, whether interest-bearing or not, might be deposited (Jos. *War* ii. 17, 6). See BANK.

Lock. A fastening for a door (Judg. 3:23), evidently consisting of a short bolt of wood, which slid through a groove in an upright piece attached to the door and entered a socket in the doorpost. Above the groove in the upright were holes containing small iron or wooden pins. When the bolt was thrust into the socket, these pins dropped into corresponding holes in the bolt and held it in place. The key is furnished with a like number of projections, and, when introduced into a hollow in the bolt underneath the pins, raised them and allowed the bolt to be shoved back.

Lo'cust. The rendering of Heb. *'arbeh* and Gr. *akris*. The insect referred to is evidently the migratory locust (*Oedipoda migratoria*), or in some cases possibly an allied insect, *Oedipoda cinerescens, Acridium peregrinum*, or other species. The locust is 2 inches or more in length. It is a winged, creeping thing. Like other insects of the order *Orthoptera*, it has 4 wings. Those of the anterior pair are narrow, while those of the posterior pair are broader, folded up when not in use, and trans-

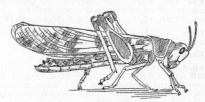

Locust (*Acridium peregrinum*)

parent. It has 6 legs, on 4 of which it walks, while the hindmost pair, which are much longer than the others and equal to the body in length, it uses for springing. The mouth is furnished with cutting jaws, by means of which it nips off leaves and blades of grass. Locusts were clean insects (Lev. 11:21, 22), and John the Baptist ate them, as many Orientals did before him and still do (Matt. 3:4). They are prepared by being slightly roasted, dried in the sun, and salted. When used the head, wings, legs, and intestines are commonly removed, and only the fleshy portion is eaten. The locust is exceedingly destructive to vegetation, and locusts blown into the valley of the Nile by the e. wind constituted the 8th Egyptian plague (Ex. 10:4, 5, 12, 15, 19). In some passages, as Judg. 7:12 and Jer. 46:23, the A.V. renders *'arbeh* "grasshopper"; the R.V. uniformly translates it "locust." The locust is distinguished from the grasshopper by the shortness of its antennae. It must not be confounded with the seventeen-year locust (*Cicada septendecim*), which is commonly called locust in the United States.

Many other words refer to different species of locusts difficult to identify, or some of them may mean the migratory locust in different stages of development (Lev. 11:22; Joel 1:4). The eggs of the various species of locust are deposited in April or May, in a cylindrical hole excavated in the ground by the female. They are hatched in June. The young insect emerges from the egg a wingless larva. It enters the pupa state, when it has rudimentary wings enclosed in cases. It is more voracious in this stage of its development than at any other period. In another month it casts the pupa or nymph skin, and has become the imago or perfect insect.

Lod (lŏd). A town of Benjamin, built by the sons of Elpaal, a man of Benjamin (I Chron. 8:12), and generally mentioned in connection with Ono (Neh. 11:35). It was inhabited after the Babylonian Captivity (Ezra 2:33; Neh. 7:37), and is believed to have been the Lydda of the New Testament (I Macc. 11:34); see LYDDA. It still exists as Ludd, about 11 miles s.e. of Joppa. In it are the remains of the church of St. George, the Christian martyr of Nicomedia and adopted in the 14th century as the patron saint of England, who was said to have been a native of the place.

Lo'de'bar (lō'dē'bär) [perhaps, without pasture]. A place in Gilead (II Sam. 9:4, 5; 17:27), probably the same as Lidebir (Josh. 13:26, R.V. marg.). Identified with Umm ed-Dabar, s. of Wadi el-'Arab, e. of the Jordan. See DEBIR 4.

Lodge. A shelter erected for the watchman of a garden for occupation during the time of ripe fruit (Isa. 1:8; in ch. 24:20, A.V. cottage, R.V. hammock). Not improbably the structure intended is the kind built among the branches of a tree or, where trees are lacking, upon posts, and consisting of a rude floor, a roof of mats or branches, and sides of branches.

Log [cf. Arab. *lujj*, depth]. A Hebrew measure of capacity used specially for oil (Lev. 14:10, 12, 15, 21, 24). See MEASURE, III.

Lo'is (lō'ĭs). Timothy's grandmother, a woman of unfeigned faith (II Tim. 1:5).

Look'ing Glass. See MIRROR.

Lord. When used of God and printed in small letters with only the initial a capital, it is usually the rendering of Heb. *'ādōn*, master (Ex. 23:17; Ps. 114:7), much more frequently of *'ădōnāy*, properly, my master (Ex. 4:10; Isa. 40:10), or of Gr. *Kyrios*, master, lord (Matt. 1:20). When printed in A.V. in small capitals, it represents the Hebrew YHWH, Jehovah, the most sacred and incommunicable name of God, used of himself alone (Gen. 2:4). See JEHOVAH.

Lord of Hosts. See HOST.

Lord's Day. The day specially associated with the Lord Jesus Christ. The expression occurs but once in the N.T., where John says, "I was in the Spirit on the Lord's day" (Rev. 1:10). Various interpretations have been offered: 1. John, it is said, is speaking of the Sabbath or 7th day of the week, which God himself has called, "My holy day" (Isa. 58:13). But if he intended the 7th day, it is strange that he did not use the customary designation. 2. It is contended that the expression Lord's Day is the same as the "day of the Lord" in II Peter 3:10, where it undoubtedly means the day of the Second Advent, and John would state that he was rapt, in vision, to the Day of Judgment. But John is apparently dating his vision. 3. John (Rev. 1:9) mentions the place where he was at the time he received the revelation, the Isle of Patmos, and declares the cause of his being on that island. In this sentence he states the day when he had the vision. It is also to be noticed that he does not speak of the day of the Lord, which is the constant designation of the day of the Second Advent (II Peter 3:10), but uses the adjective *kyriakē*, a distinction which was observed ever afterward between the day of the Second Advent and the first day of the week when Christ rose from the dead. 4. A special honor, however, was reserved by the apostles for Sunday or resurrection day. On the resurrection day itself our Lord appeared to his disciples (Luke 24:13–49; John 20:1–26). After 8 days, which in ordinary usage meant a week, Jesus a 2d time honored the first day of the week.

Since Pentecost occurred 50 days after the 2d day of unleavened bread (Lev. 23:11, 15; see WEEKS, FEAST OF), it probably fell on the first day of the week in the year of Christ's crucifixion; and so the effusion of the Holy Spirit took place on the first day of the week (Acts 2:1). The Christians at Troas in Paul's time seem to have regarded that day as the stated one on which they were to assemble to break bread (ch. 20:7). On the same day of the week the Christians were to lay by them in store the money which they designed to give in charity (I Cor. 16:2). These passages, aided by more general principles, have led the great majority of Christians to consider the Lord's Day a day set apart by the example of our Lord and his apostles for sacred purposes. The weekly observance of Sunday points back of Corinth to Jewish-Christian soil, but we cannot say when the custom began. The use of Sunday as the one distinctive day for worship was a matter of gradual development. At first Jewish Christians observed both the Sabbath and the Lord's Day, but the Gentile Christians were not bound to observe the Jewish Sabbath. Even though the Sabbath was not observed by the Gentile Christians, they were not ignorant of its deeper meaning, and gradually the essential principles of the Sabbath passed into the Christian sacred day of rest and worship. See SABBATH.

It may be added that some members of the primitive Church made no distinction between days, including Jewish festivals and Sabbaths and possibly the 1st day, rightly or wrongly esteeming every day alike. They were not to be harshly judged; they were acting out of the fear of God (Rom. 14:5). Some of the Jewish converts continued to keep the 7th day and the Jewish festivals. It was a matter of liberty (Col. 2:16), so long as the convert did not regard the observance as necessary to salvation (Gal. 4:10).

Lord's Prayer, The. The prayer which Christ taught his disciples. It is so called because it comes from our Lord. The form in Matthew (ch. 6:9–13) has been more influential in the later history of The Lord's Prayer, but Luke (ch. 11:1–4) seems to give it a more historical setting. The doxology which concludes the prayer (Matt. 16:13b, A.V.) is omitted in R.V., because it does not appear in the oldest and best MSS.; it seems not to have been an original part of the prayer, but represents a liturgical addition.

Lord's Sup'per. The name given by Paul to the commemorative ordinance instituted by our Lord on the evening preceding his crucifixion (I Cor. 11:20). Paul's account is the earliest record of the institution of the supper by at least 2 or 3 years. It was written probably early in A.D. 57, just 27 years after the supper was instituted. The apostle had introduced it 5 years earlier, when he organized the Corinthian church and "delivered" to them the ordinance (v. 23). He pledges his own truthfulness and authority for the correctness of his account by saying, "I received" and "I delivered"; and he refers to the source of his information: he had not been an eyewitness of the event, he had not been present at the institution of the supper, but he had received from the Lord what he had delivered to them. These words are capable of 2 interpretations: either Paul had been granted a special communication direct from the risen Lord or else he had received the account from the Lord through the Lord's apostles, participants in the first supper. Matthew, an eyewitness, and Mark, the companion of Peter who was present at the institution of the supper, also record the circumstances; and so does Paul's companion, Luke. Wishing to fulfill all righteousness and to honor the ceremonial law while it continued, Jesus made arrangements to eat the passover with his disciples (Matt. 26:17–19). Since the paschal lamb was killed in the evening, and its flesh eaten the same evening, the paschal feast necessarily took place in the evening (Matt. 26:20). Wine mixed with water had come into use on such occasions; the Greeks and Romans drank their wine diluted with water (cf. II Macc. 15:39). When, therefore, our Lord was about to follow up the supper by the Communion, there was wine mixed wi h water on the table. So also was there unleavened bread. He and his disciples were sitting (Matt. 26:20), by which is meant that, after the custom of that time, they half sat, half reclined on couches (Mark 14:18, R.V. marg.). When the paschal feast was finished, Jesus took bread and blessed it, at the same time rendering thanks for it, and, giving it to the disciples, said: "This is my body which is given for you: this do in remembrance of me." And the cup in like manner after supper, saying: "This cup is the new covenant in my blood, even that which is poured out for you" (Luke 22:19, 20, R.V.), "which is shed for many unto remission of sins" (Matt. 26:28, R.V.). The object for which the Lord's Supper was instituted was to keep him in remembrance (Luke 22:19). It was to show forth "the Lord's death till he come" (I Cor. 11:25, 26). The feast was not confined to the apostles or to the Jewish Christians, but was celebrated in the churches of the Gentiles also, for instance at Corinth (I Cor. 10:15–21). It was understood to be the privilege of the Church for all time. The table on which the bread was placed was known as the Lord's table (ch. 10:21); the cup of wine retained the old name which it bore at the Jewish passover, cup of blessing (v. 16), and was also called the cup of the Lord (chs. 10:21; 11:27).

Lo'-ru-ha'mah (lō'rōō-hä'má) [that has not been compassionated]. The symbolic name of the Prophet Hosea's daughter by his wife Gomer (Hos. 1:6, 8).

Lot, I (lŏt). The use of the lot to determine doubtful questions was much in vogue among the nations of antiquity (Esth. 3:7; Jonah 1:7; Matt. 27:35). Stones or inscribed tablets or the like were put into a vessel and, having been shaken, were drawn out or cast forth. The act was commonly preceded by prayer, and was an appeal to God to decide the matter (Acts 1:23–26; Homer *Iliad* iii. 316–325; vii. 174–181). In the early history of the Jewish people God was pleased to use the lot as a method of making known his will, so that the weighty statement was made in Prov. 16:33,

"The lot is cast into the lap;
But the whole disposing thereof is of Jehovah."

The Land of Canaan was divided among the twelve tribes by lot (Josh. 14:2; 18:6); for the method, see CANAAN. On one occasion Saul and Jonathan stood on one side and Jonathan cast lots against the people. The king and his son being thus singled out, they cast lots with each other, Jonathan being finally pointed out by this me hod of inquiry (I Sam. 14:40–45). The courses of the priests, etc., were settled by lot (I Chron. 24:5 seq.). By casting lots after prayer the question was decided whether Joseph Barsabbas or Matthias should be Judas Iscariot's successor in the apostleship (Acts 1:15–26). This method of selection was not repeated by the apostles after the descent of the Holy Spirit.

Lot, II (lŏt). Son of Haran, Abraham's brother, and consequently nephew to the patriarch himself, whom he accompanied from Mesopotamia to Canaan (Gen. 11:31; 12:5), and to and from Egypt (ch. 13:1). Like his uncle, he acquired much cattle; and his herdsmen and those of Abraham quarreled over the pasturage. Abraham proposed that he and Lot separate, and generously invited Lot to choose first. Lot, seeing that the hills were less fertile than the valley of the Jordan, chose the latter, and became a resident in Sodom. He did not take into account the character of the people among whom he was going to settle and the probable effect of their evil example on his family, though he maintained his own integrity among them and was distressed from day to day by the sight and the story of lawless deeds (II Peter 2:8). During the invasion of Chedorlaomer and his confederate kings, Lot was made prisoner, and owed his release to the courage and skill of Abraham (Gen. 13:2 to 14:16). When two angels were sent to Sodom to warn him of its approaching destruction, the conduct of the mob toward these strangers showed how ripe the city was for des ruc ion. Lot was saved from its overthrow; but his wife, looking back, became a pillar of salt. In looking back with regretful longings for the possessions left behind, she proved herself unworthy of the salvation offered her (cf. Luke 17:32). His sons-in-law, probably prospective ones (Gen. 19:14, R.V. margin; cf. v. 8), remained behind and perished (ch. 19:1–29; Wisd. of Sol. 10:6–9). Soon afterward, under the influence of wine, Lot unconsciously became guil.y of incest. The Moabites and Ammonites were his descendants (Gen 19:30–38).

Lo'tan (lō'tăn). A tribe of Horites, dwelling in Mount Seir (Gen. 36:20) and governed by a chieftain (v. 29).

Love Feasts. The rendering of Gr. *agapai* (cf. II Peter 2:13, R.V., marg.); the translation, deceivings, of A.V. and R.V. text is based upon a different Greek reading (*apatai*). In Jude 12 "feasts of charity" of A.V. is "love-feasts" in R.V. They were social meals held in churches in connection with the Lord's Supper (cf. Acts 2:46; 6:1; 20:7, 11). It seems that originally the sacrament of the Lord's Supper or Eucharist took place at the end of the *agapē* or love feast (cf. Matt 26:26–29; Mark 14:22–25; Luke 22:14–20; I Cor. 11:25). Apparently there were cases at Corinth where the meal was desecrated: instead of being an expression of brotherhood, it became an ordinary meal and an occasion for display and gluttony (I Cor. 11:17–34). Chrysostom states that after the early community of goods had ceased, the wealthier members brought contributions of food and drink to the church, of which, at the conclusion of the services and af er the celebration of the Lord's Supper, all partook, the poorest not excepted, by this means helping to promote the principle of love among Christians. In putting the Lord's Supper first, Chrysostom may reflect the custom of his own time. As the purity of the Church declined and ceremony increased, scandals arose in connection with these feasts. The council of Laodicea, (date uncertain; A.D. 320 or somewhere between 343 and 381), and that of Carthage, A.D. 397, forbade them to be held in churches; so did the council of Orleans, A.D. 541, that of Trullo, A.D. 692, and that of Aix-la-Chapelle, A.D. 816; but all these councils together did not quite succeed in extinguishing the love feasts' excessive tenacity of life in the Western Church, while in the Greek Church they still continue to exist. Of more modern religious denominations, love feasts were revived by the Moravians and the Dunkers. They exist also among the Sandemanians.

Low'land or **She·phe'lah**; variously rendered in A.V. by the vale, the valley, the low country, the plain. The region of low hills between the plain of Philistia and the high central range of Palestine. It is described by Eusebius (in his *Onomasticon* under *Sephela*) as "all the low country about Eleutheropolis [modern Beit Jibrïn] toward the n. and w."; but in O.T. times the term comprehended the low, hilly country lying to the e. and s. as well. The hills rise to a height of from 500 to 800 feet, with a few higher summits. On their slopes the olive flourishes. The district is separated from the central Judean range by a series of valleys which run n. and s. from Aijalon to near Beer-sheba; and it is itself cut by several wide, fertile valleys which lead from the Judean ridge to the sea. It was assigned, as part of their inheritance, to the tribe of Judah; and when they found that they had too much territory, a small portion of it in the n. was allotted to Dan (Josh. 15:33 *seq.*; 19:40 *seq.*). It included such notable places as Adullam, Beth-shemesh, Gezer, Eglon, Lachish, and part of the valleys of Aijalon, Sorek, and Elah (ch. 19:33 *seq.*; I Sam. 17:1, 2; II Chron. 28:18).

Lu'bim. (lū'bĭm). An African people, the Libyans, from whom Shishak, king of Egypt, drew part of his army for the invasion of Palestine (II Chron. 12:3; 16:8; cf. Dan. 11:43; Nahum 3:9).

Lu'cas (lū'kăs). See LUKE.

Lu'ci·fer (lū'sĭ-fẽr) [Lat., light bearer]. The planet Venus, as the morning star. With the exception of the sun and moon, Venus is the brightest object in the sky. It appears as a morning or an evening star according as it is w. or e. of the sun, returning to the same position about every 19 months. As the former, Venus is the harbinger of daylight. The prophet likened the splendor of the king of Babylon to Lucifer, son of the morning (Isa. 14:12; in R.V. day-star), and Jesus calls himself "the bright, the morning star" (Rev. 22:16; cf. II Peter 1:19). The application of the name Lucifer to Satan, the rebel angel hurled from heaven, has existed since the 3d century, especially among poets. It is based on the erroneous supposition that Luke 10:18 is an explanation of Isa. 14:12; cf. also Rev. 9:1; 12:7-10.

Lu'ci·us (lū'shĭ-ŭs). 1. A Roman official who in the year 174 of the Seleucidan era, 139-138 B.C., issued letters in favor of the Jews to various kings subject to Rome (I Macc. 15:16). He is entitled a consul, which identifies him with Lucius Calpurnius Piso, one of the consuls for the year 139 B.C. It is possible, however, that he was the praetor Lucius Valerius who conducted the proceedings in the Roman senate which led to their making a league of friendship with the Jews, to the issuance of the aforementioned letters, and, in the days of Hyrcanus II, to action favorable to the Jews (Jos. *Antiq.* xiv. 8, 5).
2. A Christian from Cyrene, who was a teacher in the church at Antioch (Acts 13:1). He is commonly supposed to have been the kinsman of Paul who at Corinth joined with the apostle in sending salutations to the brethren at Rome (Rom. 16:21).

Lud (lŭd), **Lu'dim** (lū'dĭm) (pl.). 1. A people classed among the Semites (Gen. 10:22); believed to be the Lydians (Jos. *Antiq.* i. 6, 4; compare order of enumeration in Genesis), occupying, however, a wider territory than Lydia in w. Asia Minor. In the 20th century B.C. colonies were established in e. Asia Minor

by a dynasty of Akkadian princes of Asshur which rose to power after the fall of Ur (c. 2000 B.C.). From the descendants of these colonists have come the Cappadocian tablets (c. 1920-1870). According to Herodotus (i. 7), their 1st king was a son of Ninus and grandson of Belus, that is, he was descended from the Assyrians.
2. A people connected with the Egyptians (Gen. 10:13), also the country which they inhabited. They are mentioned as bowmen in the armies of Egypt and Tyre (Jer. 46:9; Ezek. 27:10; 30:5). They may be Lydians as above (1), for there were Lydian troops in the army of Psamtik I of Egypt (663-609 B.C.). The Ludim may perhaps be sought in n. Africa, w. of the Nile, but there is no authority to emend the word to Lubim.

Lu'hith (lū'hĭth) [of tablets or planks]. A Moabite town approached by an ascent (Isa. 15:5; Jer. 48:5); according to Eusebius and Jerome, Loueitha, between Areopolis, that is, Rabbath of Moab, and Zoar; situated at Khirbet Fâs or Khirbet Medint er Râs, between Ghôr eṣ-Ṣâfiyeh and Khanzîreh.

Luke (lūk), in A.V. once **Lu'cas** (Philemon 24) [Lat. *Lucas*, from N.T. Gr. *Loukas*, probably a pet name for Lat. *Lucanus* or *Lucius*]. A friend and companion of Paul, who joined him in sending from Rome salutations to the Colossian church (Col. 4:14) and to Philemon (Philemon 24). In the former place he is described as "the beloved physician" and in the latter place as one of the apostle's fellow laborers. He was also with Paul in Rome at a later time when II Timothy was written (II Tim. 4:11), and then the apostle gives a touching tribute to his friend's fidelity in the words, "Only Luke is with me." These are all the notices of Luke by name in the N.T., for he must not be identified with the Lucius of Acts 13:1 or with the one mentioned in Rom. 16:21; see LUCIUS 2.
We find in the 2d century the tradition already established that Luke was the author of the Third Gospel and of The Acts, both of which were certainly written by the same hand (Acts 1:1). Accordingly we may learn more of him from The Acts, in which he intimates his presence with Paul during certain portions of the latter's Missionary Journeys by the use of "we" or "us" in the narrative (Acts 16:10-17; 20:5 to 21:18; 27:1 to 28:16). From these passages it appears that Luke joined Paul on the Second Missionary Journey at Troas and went with him to Philippi. Again on the Third Journey Luke rejoined the apostle at Philippi and went with him to Jerusalem. He appears to have remained in Palestine during the 2 years in which Paul was imprisoned at Caesarea, for he sailed with the apostle from Caesarea to Rome; see ACTS, THE. In Col. 4:14 Luke is plainly distinguished from Paul's Jewish companions (cf. v. 11). He was therefore a Gentile. Early tradition made him a native of Antioch in Syria, and this is quite probable. At any rate, his interest in and familiarity with the Church of Antioch is evident (Acts 6:5; 11:19-27; 13:1-3; 14:26-28; 15:1, 2, 30-40; 18:22, 23). The time and manner of his death are unknown.
The Gospel According to Luke is addressed to a certain Theophilus, probably a Gentile Christian; claims to be based upon careful investigation of the apostolic testimony; and was intended to furnish Theophilus, as well as other readers, with assured knowledge of the truth in which he had been instructed. Its material is doubtless derived both from earlier documents and from information obtained by Luke personally from the actors in the history. The narrative may be divided as follows: 1. Introductory verses (ch. 1:1-4). 2.

The immediate preparation for the appearance of Jesus, consisting of the annunciations and births of John the Baptist and Jesus, with some significant events from the latter's infancy and boyhood (chs. 1:5 to 2:52). 3. The inauguration of Christ's ministry, including (a) the ministry of John the Bap.ist, (b) the baptism of Jesus, to which is appended his genealogy, and (c) the temptation of Jesus (chs. 3:1 to 4:13). 4. The Lord's ministry in Galilee (chs. 4:14 to 9:50). In this part of his Gospel Luke often follows the same order as Mark, but not always. He also introduces more of the teaching of Jesus than Mark does, in this often corresponding with Matthew. Luke, moreover, has some material peculiar to himself in these chapters. The following analysis will bring out the progress of this portion of his narrative: (a) Introductory description (ch. 4:14, 15). (b) Opening of the Galilean work, including the first visit to Nazareth, miracles in Capernaum and tour through Galilee, the call of 4 disciples and the healing of the leper (chs. 4:16 to 5:16). (c) Rise of opposition, in the face of which Christ vindicated his teaching, including the cure of the paralytic, Levi's call and feast, discourse about fasting, and the Sabbath controversy (chs. 5:17 to 6:12). (d) Organization of the disciples, including the appointment of the Twelve and Christ's discourse on the characteristics of true discipleship (Sermon on the Mount) (ch. 6:13–49). (e) Incidents illustrative of the gracious ministry of Jesus, including the healing of the centurion's servant, the raising of the son of the widow of Nain, the inquiry of John the Baptist, and Christ's reply and discourse concerning John, the anointing of Jesus by a sinful woman (ch. 7:1–50). (f) The extension of Christ's work, including his tours through Galilee with a company of disciples; his teaching by parables; the visit of his mother and brethren; the four great miracles of stilling the tempest, healing the Gadarene demoniac and the woman with the issue of blood, and raising Jairus' daughter; the sending out of the apostles; Herod's desire to see Jesus and the latter's subsequent retirement, followed by the feeding of the 5,000 (chs. 8:1 to 9:17). (g) Christ's instructions to his disciples in view of the close of the Galilean ministry and his coming death, including Peter's confession, Christ's prediction of his death and resurrection, his transfiguration and the cure of the demoniac boy, warnings against pride (ch. 9:18–50). 5. The journeyings of Jesus to Jerusalem (ch. 9:51 to 19:48). This part of Luke contains a large amount of material peculiar to him. It is probably not arranged in exact chronological order, but rather in accordance with certain topics. Some of the material given here really belongs in the Galilean ministry (chs. 9:57–60; 13:18–21; probably chs. 11:14 to 13:5). But the section describes in the main a series of journeys toward Jerusalem, ending in the final ascent, with discourses appropriate to the situation. It may be subdivided as follows: (a) The departure from Galilee and instructions concerning the true spirit of disciples, including Christ's rejection by a Samaritan village, his replies to three inquirers, the mission of the Seventy and their return, the lawyer's question and the parable of the Good Samaritan, Christ in the house of Martha and Mary, instructions about prayer (chs. 9:51 to 11:13). (b) Denunciation of the Pharisees and instructions concerning the duty of confessing him, against covetousness, and concerning watchfulness, etc. (chs. 11:14 to 13:5). (c) Discourses illustrative of the true Israel and of the true service: the former including the parable of the Barren Fig Tree, the woman with the spirit of infirmity, the parables of the Mustard Seed and

Leaven, the warning against self-deception and the lamentation over Jerusalem; the latter including the healing of the dropsical man, and the beautiful parables of the Wedding Feast, the Great Supper, the Lost Sheep, the Lost Coin, the Lost Son, the Unjust Steward, the Rich Man and Lazarus, the Importunate Widow, interspersed with incidents and teachings on the same general subject (chs. 13:6 to 18:30). (d) The final ascent to Jerusalem, including a renewed prediction of death and resurrection, the healing of Bartimaeus, the conversion of Zacchaeus, the parable of the Pounds, and the triumphal entry (chs. 18:31 to 19:48). 6. The last week in Jerusalem, including the final teachings of Jesus in the Temple and to his disciples, his arrest, trials, crucifixion, and burial (chs. 20:1 to 23:56). 7. Appearances of Jesus after his resurrection, his last directions to his disciples to preach his gospel, and his final departure (ascension) from them (ch. 24).

Luke states (ch. 1:3) that his narrative is written "in order." This use of this phrase elsewhere (Acts 11:4; 18:23; and Greek text of Luke 8:1 and Acts 3:24) shows that he does not necessarily mean exact chronological order. While chronological in general outline, his arrangement is often topical. The book, however, is, like The Acts, a careful and systematic presentation of the life of the Founder of Christianity. Luke also expressly disclaims personal acquaintance with Jesus, and bases his work on the testimony of eyewitnesses (apostles) whose reports he had accurately studied. His Gospel shows a truly historical spirit. This appears, e.g., in the personal account of the origin of John the Baptist and of Jesus, in his dating by secular events the birth of Jesus and the public appearance of John (Luke 2:1, 2; 3:1, 2), and in his presentation of the ministry of Christ in such a manner as to bring out its leading religious ideas, its triumph over opposition, and the historical foundation which it laid for Christianity (see the analysis above). It shows also the Evangelist's fondness for those aspects of the Lord's teaching and work, whereby he revealed himself as the divine-human Saviour of men. Christ's gospel is here described as universal in its mission (Luke 2:32; 3:6; 4:24–27; 24:47, etc.), a gospel for the lost and the lowly (chs. 7:36–50; 15; 19:1–9, etc.), a message of salvation to the poor and distressed (chs. 6:20–26; 7:11–18; 12:32, etc.). It delineates the graciousness of Christ's personal character—his piety, compassion, charity, prayerfulness, holiness, tenderness. In recording the Lord's utterances about the rich, Luke uses more unqualified language than the other Evangelists do (chs. 6:24, 25; 16:25, etc.), though he also makes it clear that he did not understand Christ to denounce rich men as such, but only so far as they put their trust in riches and were not rich toward God (ch. 12:21). In what he reports about Samaritans also (chs. 10:33; 17:16) he doubtless wished to illustrate the destruction of national prejudices by the gospel. In short this Gospel presents Christ as establishing a religion which seeks to uplift and save suffering and sinful humanity.

From Paul's statement in Col. 4:14 we learn that Luke was a physician. It was natural, therefore, for scholars to examine minutely the style and language of Luke's writings to determine whether they supply evidence of his profession. These investigations have shown that it is unwise to attempt to prove by linguistic comparisons alone that Luke was a physician. But, given the knowledge that Luke was a physician, a few statements in his Gospel, when compared with parallel passages in Matthew and Mark, may be fairly interpreted as indicating a physician's point of view (cf.

Luke 4:38 with Matt. 8:14 and Mark 1:30; Luke 5:12 with Matt 8:2 and Mark 1:40; Luke 8:43 with Mark 5:26).

The material in Luke is derived from written and oral sources of Jesus' life and teaching. Luke certainly knew and used Mark's Gospel. It is likely that he also utilized a second source, available as well to the author of the present Gospel of Matthew, composed chiefly of sayings, which scholars designate by the symbol Q (for German *Quelle*, source). There is, in addition to these sources, a large body of material peculiar to the Third Gospel (e.g., 14 parables, and various sayings and narratives). Some scholars believe that Luke composed a preliminary book, designated as Proto-Luke (which they suppose began with the chronological data in ch. 3:1), from this material and Q. It is believed that later Luke learned of Mark's Gospel and incorporated considerable portions from it; then he added the material in chs. 1 and 2, so markedly Semitic in expression and sentiment. The result was our Third Gospel.

Scholars have suggested 3 dates for the composition of Luke's Gospel—before 63, 75–85, and after 94. The last date is highly improbable. It is held only by those who think that Acts 5:36 *seq.* is based on Jos. *Antiq.* xx. 5, 1, which appeared in 93–94, but this dependence has not been proved. Of the other 2 dates, the period 75–85 is urged by those who believe that an earlier date will not allow sufficient time for the writing of the many narratives of which Luke speaks in his preface (ch. 1:1). In addition, these scholars also regard Luke's report of Christ's prediction of the Fall of Jerusalem (chs. 19:43 *seq.*; 21:20 *seq.*) as manifesting a knowledge on the part of Luke of the occurrence of that event in A.D. 70. But Luke's language is more likely only an interpretation of Christ's words designed to make their meaning clear to Gentile readers (cf. Luke 21:20 with Matt. 24:15 and Mark 13:14) and therefore does not presuppose that the event had happened before Luke's writing.

The early date, before 63, is maintained by those who hold that if Luke had known the outcome of Paul's trial in Rome and of the apostle's martyrdom, he would surely have mentioned them; Acts therefore must have been written very shortly after the last events it recounts (c. A.D. 63). That Acts evidences no knowledge of the Pauline Epistles and makes no allusion to the Neronian persecution is confirmatory evidence for its early date. Since Acts presupposes the Third Gospel, this latter must have been written still earlier. Furthermore, there is a slight possibility that I Tim. 5:18 may contain a quotation from this Gospel (Luke 10:7); if so, this is evidence for the early date.

G. T. P. (rev., H. S. G.)

Lu′na·tic [Lat., insane, with lucid intervals]. The Greek word is derived from *selēnē*, moon, as the English word is from the Latin *luna*, moon, for it was believed that the disease is affected by the light or by the periodic changes of the moon. Lunacy is distinguished from demoniacal possession (Matt. 4:24), for it was often due to other causes. Yet possession by a demon might give rise to lunacy (cf. Matt. 17:15 with Mark 9:17). A comparison of these 2 passages has led to the opinion that the Greek word denotes epilepsy. Hence R.V. uses epileptic instead of lunatic.

Lute. See PSALTERY.

Luz (lŭz) [almond tree]. 1. A Canaanite town, afterward Beth-el (Gen. 28:19; 35:6; 48:3; Josh. 18:13; Judg. 1:23). In Josh. 16:2 it is distinguished from Beth-el and located to the w. See BETH-EL 1.

2. A town in the Hittite country, built by an inhabitant of Luz in Mount Ephraim, who betrayed that town to the Israelites and was allowed by them to depart with his family uninjured (Judg. 1:22–26). About 4½ miles w. by n. of Bāniâs is the ruin Luweiziyeh, which is proposed as the site by Conder.

Lyc′a·o′ni·a (lĭk′å-ō′nĭ-å). An elevated, rugged, inland district of Asia Minor, bounded on the n. by Galatia, on the s. by Cilicia and Isauria, on the e. by Cappadocia, and on the w. by Phrygia and Isauria. It was mainly suitable for pasturage only. Its peculiar dialect was still spoken when Paul visited the district and preached in 3 of its cities, Iconium, Derbe, and Lystra (Acts 13:51 to 14:23, especially v. 11).

Lyc′i·a (lĭsh′ĭ-å). A province of Asia Minor, jutting s. into the Mediterranean Sea, and bounded on the n. by Caria, Phrygia, Pisidia, and Pamphylia. Paul on his last voyage to Jerusalem passed Rhodes, an island off its w. coast, and landed at Patara, within its limits, where he took ship for Phoenicia (Acts 21:1, 2). On his voyage to Rome he landed at Myra, another city of Lycia, whence he sailed in an Alexandrian vessel bound for Italy (ch. 27:5, 6).

Lyd′da (lĭd′å). A town about 11 miles s.e. of Joppa (Acts 9:38; Jos. *Antiq.* xx. 6, 2); probably the Lod of the O.T. The gospel early took root in it (Acts 9:32). Shortly before 153 B.C. the town with the district about it formed a distinct government in connection with Samaria, but in 145 B.C. it was transferred to Judea (I Macc. 11:34; cf. v. 28; 10:30, 38). Peter visited it, and his cure of Aeneas through the name of Jesus resulted in a large increase of disciples (Acts 9:33–35). It was burned by Cestius in the time of Nero, but was soon rebuilt (Jos. *War* ii. 19, 1). See LOD.

Lyd′i·a (lĭd′ĭ-å). 1. A region on the w. coast of Asia Minor, with Sardis for its capital. Thyatira and Philadelphia were within its limits. It was very fertile and had a mild climate, and consequently it was densely populated. The state rose to power about 689 B.C., under Gyges, when the Greeks on the coast and the tribes of Asia Minor were subdued. In 549 B.C. Croesus, the last king, was defeated by Cyrus, and Lydia became a Persian province. It never regained independence. Antiochus III, of Syria, was forced to cede it to the Romans (cf. I Macc. 8:8). Many Jews dwelt there (Jos. *Antiq.* xii. 3, 4), and Christian churches were founded (Rev. 1:11).

2. A woman of Thyatira, a town of Lydia, though it is not known whether this was the origin of her name. Thyatira was noted for its dyeing, and Lydia made her living in Philippi, to which she had removed, by selling purple dyes or dyed goods. She was a worshiper of God before Paul arrived at Philippi. She received the gospel of Christ gladly, and became Paul's first convert in Macedonia and Europe. At her urgent invitation Paul and his missionary associates took up their abode with her; and when Paul and Silas were released from prison, to which they had been consigned after a riot of which they were the innocent cause, they returned to her house (Acts 16:14, 15, 40).

Ly·sa′ni·as (lī-sā′nĭ-ăs) [Gr., ending sadness]. A tetrarch of Abilene in the 15th year of Tiberius (Luke 3:1). Some critics have thought that Lysanias, son of Ptolemy, who ruled Chalcis in Coelesyria during the years 40 to 34 B.C. (Jos. *Antiq.* xiv. 13, 3; xv. 4, 1), gave name to this tetrarchy, and that Luke is in error. The facts, however, should be presented as follows: Lysanias who ruled Chalcis is never called tetrarch, and Abila nowhere appears in his dominions. From Jos. *Antiq.* xv. 10, 1–3, it appears that the house or territory of Lysanias was hired by Zenodorus about 25 B.C., became known as the country of Zenodorus, lay between Trachonitis and Galilee, chiefly about Paneas and Ulatha, and hence apparently did not include Chalcis in Coelesyria, and stric;ly speaking was distinct from Batanea, Trachonitis, and Auranitis. These districts were bestowed on Herod the Great and passed to his son Philip the tetrarch, Augustus confirming to him Batanea, Trachonitis, Auranitis, and part of the house of Zenodorus (Jos. *Antiq.* xvii. 11, 4) which included Paneas (8, 1). In A.D. 37 the emperor Caligula made Herod Agrippa king of the tetrarchy of Philip and added the tetrarchy of Lysanias (Jos. *Antiq.* xviii. 6, 10). This latter tetrarchy had its capital at Abila, some 18 miles n.w. of Damascus, and was distinct from the kingdom of Chalcis (Jos. *Antiq.* xix. 5, 1 ; xx. 7, 1 ; *War* ii. 11, 5). In the reign of the emperor Tiberius the region about Abila was ruled by a tetrarch named Lysanias (see ABILENE), in exact agreement with Luke's statement. Although far n., it may have been the remaining part of the country of Zenodorus, which after his death and the division of his land, as before mentioned, had been formed into a tetrarchy or kingdom under a younger Lysanias, perhaps of the same line as the former ruler of Chalcis.

Lys'i·as (lĭs'ĭ-ăs). 1. A general of the army of Syria during the reigns of Antiochus Epiphanes and Antiochus Eupator. When Antiochus Epiphanes went to Persia about 165 B.C., he appointed Lysias, who was of royal blood, viceroy during his absence, with the duty of quelling the Jewish insurrection under the Maccabees (I Macc. 3 :32–37). After operating through others, Lysias found it necessary to take the field himself ; but he was defeated by Judas with great loss (chs. 3 :38–40 ; 4 :1–22, 28–35). When the news of Antiochus' death arrived in 163 B.C., Lysias seized the reins of government and ruled in the name of the young Antiochus, although the late king had named Philip for regent during the minority of the heir to the throne (ch. 6 :14–17). In this capacity Lysias undertook another campaign against the Jews. He gained a victory over Judas and laid siege to Jerusalem ; but the news that Philip was on his way from Persia to claim the regency, compelled him to make terms of peace wi;h the Jews and return to Antioch (ch. 6 :28–63). He maintained himself successfully against Philip, but was put to death in 162 B.C. by Demetrius I (ch. 7 :1–4).

2. Roman commandant at Jerusalem, who rescued Paul from the mob of Jews (Acts 22 :24). See CLAUDIUS LYSIAS.

Lys'tra (lĭs'trȧ). A city of Lycaonia and a Roman colony, where Paul cured a man crippled from bir'h, and would have been worshiped as a god had he not refused. It was there also that he was stoned and left for dead (Acts 14 :6–21 ; II Tim. 3 :11). Either at Lystra or Derbe he first met Timothy (Acts 16 :1, 2). The colony was located on a hill, about 1 mile n.w. of Khatyn Serai, which is 18 miles s.s.w. of Iconium.

M

Ma'a·cah (mā'ȧ-kȧ), in A.V. often **Ma'a·chah,** and in R.V. of Josh. 13:13 **Ma'a·cath** (mā'ȧ-kăth) [oppression ; but cf. Arab. *ma'ik,* stupid]. 1. A place in Syria (II Sam. 10 :6, 8), sometimes called Aram-maacah or Syriamaachah (I Chron. 19 :6, 7) ; see ARAM 2 (4).

Its inhabitants were descended from Nahor (Gen. 22 :24).

2. Wife of Machir, the son of Manasseh (I Chron. 7 :15, 16).

3. A concubine of Caleb, the son of Hezron (I Chron. 2 :48).

4. Wife of Jehiel and ancestress of King Saul (I Chron. 8 :29 ; 9 :35).

5. Daughter of Talmai, king of Geshur. She became one of David's wives and mother of Absalom (II Sam. 3 :3).

6. Father of Hanan, one of David's mighty men (I Chron. 11 :43).

7. Father of the ruler of the Simeonites in David s reign (I Chron. 27 :16).

8. Father of Solomon's royal contemporary Achish of Gath (I Kings 2 :39) ; see ACHISH.

9. Wife of Rehoboam, and daughter, or in view of II Chron. 13 :2 perhaps the granddaughter, of Absalom (I Kings 15 :2 ; II Chron. 11 :20–22), and mother of King Abijah. After the death of the latter, she remained queen mother (*gᵉbîrāh*) ; but her grandson Asa took this position from her because she had made an abominable image for an Asherah (II Chron. 15 :16, R.V.). She is called Micaiah (A.V., Michaiah) in II Chron. 13 :2 ; but this is probably a textual corruption, for in the 7 other places where her name occurs it is Maacah.

Ma·ac'a·thite (mȧ-ăk'ȧ-thīt), in A.V. **Ma·ach'a·thite** (mȧ-ăk'ȧ-thīt), but in Deut. 3 :14 **Ma·ach'a·thi,** the Hebrew form. A descendant of a person named Maacah, or a native or inhabitant of the Syrian kingdom of Maacah or of the town of Beth-maacah in Naphtali (Josh. 12 :5 ; II Sam. 23 :34).

Ma·a·chah (mā'ȧ-kȧ). See MAACAH.

Ma·ach'a·thi (mȧ-ăk'ȧ-thī). See MAACATHITE.

Ma·a·da'i (mā'ȧ-dā'ī) [see MAADIAH]. A son of Bani, induced by Ezra to put away his foreign wife (Ezra 10 :34).

Ma·a·di'ah (mā'ȧ-dī'ȧ) [Jehovah is an ornament]. A chief of the priests who returned from the Babylonian Captivity (Neh. 12 :5, 7). In the next generation, a father's house among the priests, which occupies the same position in the corresponding ca.alogue, bears the name Moadiah (v. 17), apparently a variation.

Ma·a'i (mȧ-ā'ī). A priest who blew a trumpet at the dedication of the second Temple (Neh. 12 :36).

Ma'a·leh-a·crab'bim (mā'ȧ-lĕ-ȧ-krăb'ĭm) [ascent of Akrabbim, R.V.]. See AKRABBIM.

Ma'a·rath (mā'ȧ-răth) [a place bare of trees]. A town in the hill coun;ry of Judah (Josh. 15 :59). It may be Beit Ummar, almost 7 miles n. of Hebron.

Ma'a·reh-ge'ba (mā'ȧ-rĕ-gē'bȧ) [place destitute of trees at Geba]. A place adjacent to Geba (Judg. 20 :33, R.V.). In the margin it is translated the meadow of Geba or Gibeah ; in the text of A.V., the meadows of Gibeah. The correct reading probably is in Greek MS. A, "from the w. of Geba."

Ma'a·sai (mā'ȧ-sī), in A.V. **Ma·as'i·ai** [work of Jehovah]. A priest of the family of Immer (I Chron. 9 :12). The name may be an abbreviation of Maaseiah or another form of that word ; or perhaps it is an accidental transposition of the letters of Amasai (*q.v.*). See AMASHSAI.

Ma·a·se'iah (mā'ȧ-sē'yȧ) [work of Jehovah]. 1. A Levi;e of the 2d degree, who acted as por;er in the reign of David (I Chron. 15 :18), and played a psaltery (v. 20).

2. One of the captains of hundreds, who co-operated with the high priest Jehoiada in

overthrowing Athaliah and placing Joash on the throne of Judah (II Chron. 23:1).

3. An officer who seems to have acted with Jeiel the Levite in keeping a list of the military men in Uzziah's reign (II Chron. 26:11).

4. A prince of the royal house, a son of Jotham more probably than of Ahaz, since the latter was too young to have adult children. He was slain during Pekah's invasion of Judah (II Chron. 28:7).

5. The governor of Jerusalem in Josiah's reign (II Chron. 34:8).

6. Ancestor of Seraiah and Baruch (Jer. 32:12; 51:59, A.V.). R.V.'s spelling Mahseiah indicates that the root is not the same as that of the other occurrences of Maaseiah. See MAHSEIAH.

7. Father of the false prophet Zedekiah (Jer. 29:21).

8. A priest, father of the Temple official Zephaniah (Jer. 21:1; 29:25).

9. Son of Shallum and doorkeeper of the Temple (Jer. 35:4). He was doubtless a Levite (I Chron. 26:1). See SHALLUM 4.

10. A man of Judah, family of Shelah. He lived at Jerusalem after the Captivity (Neh. 11:5); see ASAIAH 3.

11. A Benjamite, whose descendants lived at Jerusalem after the Captivity (Neh. 11:7).

12–15. A man of the house of Pahath-moab and 3 priests, one a member of the house of the high priest Jeshua, one of the house of Harim, and the 3d of the house of Pashhur, each of whom put away his foreign wife (Ezra 10:18, 21, 22, 30).

16. Father of that Azariah who repaired the wall of Jerusalem beside his house (Neh. 3:23).

17. A chief of the people who signed the covenant with Nehemiah (Neh. 10:25).

18. A priest who marched in the procession at the dedication of the wall of Jerusalem (Neh. 12:41), perhaps one of the 6 who stood by Ezra when he read the law to the people (ch. 8:4).

19. A Levite, probably, who marched in the procession at the dedication of the wall (Neh. 12:42), perhaps one of the 13 who expounded the law as it was read to the people (ch. 8:7).

Ma·as'i·ai (mȧ-ăs'ĭ-ī). See MAASAI.

Ma'ath (mā'ăth). An ancestor of Christ, who lived after the time of Zerubbabel (Luke 3:26).

Ma'az (mā'ăz) [anger; cf. Arab. *ma'ida*, to be angry]. A descendant of Judah through Jerahmeel (I Chron. 2:27).

Ma'a·zi'ah (mā'ȧ-zī'ȧ) [Jehovah is a refuge].

1. A descendant of Aaron. His family had grown to a father's house by the time of David and was made the last of the 24 courses into which the priests were divided (I Chron. 24:1, 6, 18).

2. A priest who, doubtless in behalf of a father's house, sealed the covenant in the days of Nehemiah (Neh. 10:8).

Mac'ca·bee (măk'ȧ-bē).* A family, also called Hasmonaean (Asmonaean) from one of its ancestors, which ruled Judea from 166 B.C. to 37 B.C.; see HASMONAEAN. The title Maccabaeus, in A. V. Maccabeus, was first given to Judas, 3d son of Mattathias (I Macc. 2:4), but at an early date it was transferred to the entire family and to others who had a part in the same events. The origin and meaning of the term are uncertain. It is usually derived from Heb. *makkebeth*, Aram. *makkābā*, a hammer, probably in allusion to the crushing blows inflicted by Judas and his successors upon their enemies. It has also been explained as composed of the initials of the Hebrew words in the sentence, "Who is like to thee among the gods, Jehovah?" (Ex. 15:11), or in the sentence, "What is like my father?" Another derivation is from Heb. *makkebay*, a contraction of *makkabyāhū* (the naming of Jehovah), based upon Isa. 62:2, where is found the root *nākab*. The 1st of the family mentioned is Mattathias, an aged priest, who, driven to desperation by the outrages of Antiochus Epiphanes, raised a revolt against him and fled to the mountains, followed by those who were zealous for the faith of Israel. Mattathias died about 2 years afterward, but the revolt was carried on by his 5 sons. Judas, the 3d son, was the 1st military leader, 166 B.C. By avoiding pitched battles, and harassing the Syrians by vigorous and persistent guerilla warfare, he and his devoted band defeated and routed every detachment of the Syrian army sent against them. He retook Jerusalem, purified the Temple, and restored the daily sacrifice. A feast to celebrate this restoration was instituted and was kept annually thereafter. This was the winter feast of dedication alluded to in John 10:22. Judas fell in battle in 160 B.C., whereupon his younger brother Jonathan, who was already high priest, assumed command of the army. About this time John, the eldest brother, was captured and killed by the children of Jambri (I Macc. 9:36); and shortly before this another brother, Eleazar, had been crushed to death underneath an elephant which he had

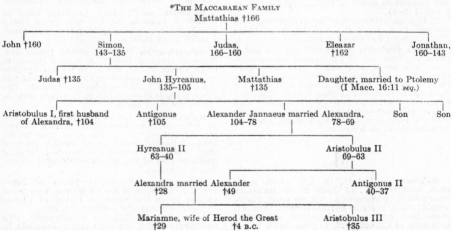

*THE MACCABAEAN FAMILY
Mattathias †166

John †160	Simon, 143–135	Judas, 166–160	Eleazar †162	Jonathan, 160–143
Judas †135	John Hyrcanus, 135–105	Mattathias †135	Daughter, married to Ptolemy (I Macc. 16:11 *seq.*)	
Aristobulus I, first husband of Alexandra, †104	Antigonus †105	Alexander Jannaeus married Alexandra, 104–78	Son	Son
	Hyrcanus II 63–40		Aristobulus II 69–63	
	Alexandra married Alexander †28 †49		Antigonus II 40–37	
	Mariamne, wife of Herod the Great †29 †4 B.C.		Aristobulus III †35	

wounded in battle. During the leadership of Jonathan the Syrians were occupied with civil war, so that not only was Judea left in peace, but the favor of the Jews was sued for, and Jonathan was able to strengthen his position. He made a treaty with the Romans and also with the Spartans. He was treacherously slain by Tryphon, a Syrian general, in 143 B.C. On his death the leadership fell to Simon, the last remaining son of Mattathias. The most important event that fell under his rule was the granting of Jewish independence by the Syrian king Demetrius II. Coins were struck bearing the name of Simon, and contracts were dated "in the first year of Simon high priest and governor." Simon and 2 of his sons were treacherously slain by his son-in-law Ptolemy, in Dok near Jericho, 135 B.C. The one son who escaped, John, assumed the power and was known as John Hyrcanus. He was a shrewd and vigorous ruler and enlarged his province. He conquered the Edomites and merged them in the Jewish people. After a long and prosperous reign he died a natural death, and was succeeded by his son Aristobulus, a cruel and unprincipled man who killed his mother and brother. He changed the theocracy into a kingdom, calling himself king, but retained at the same time the high priesthood. After a reign of 1 year he was succeeded by a brother, Alexander Jannaeus, during whose reign the country was torn by the dissensions of the Sadducees and Pharisees. He had a troubled reign of 27 years, and was followed by his widow Alexandra, who reigned for 9 years. She left 2 sons, Hyrcanus and Aristobulus, who quarreled about the succession. Hyrcanus was established as high priest while Aristobulus seized the civil authority. Civil war broke out. The Romans interfered, and at first upheld Aristobulus, but later deposed him and carried him to Rome. Hyrcanus was nominally king, but the real ruler was Antipas, or Antipater, an Idumaean, who had been appointed procurator of Judea under Hyrcanus by the Romans. A period of quarrels and dissensions among the members of the reigning family followed, during which time Antipater steadily grew in influence and power with the Romans, until, the Maccabaeans falling into disfavor, the crown of Judea was given to Antipater's son, Herod, who married Mariamne and thus united the family of the Herods with the Hasmonaeans.

For I, II, III, and IV Maccabees, see APOCRYPHA.

Mac'e·do'ni·a (măs'ĕ-dō'nĭ-à). A country lying immediately to the n. of Greece. Little is known of it prior to 560 B.C., and for more than 200 years afterward it possessed no special interest. But under Philip of Macedon (359–336 B.C.) and his yet more celebrated son Alexander the Great (336–323 B.C.), it rose to world-wide power and imperial importance; see PHILIP 1 and ALEXANDER 1. Under his successors the empire was divided, and the country declined, until in 168 B.C. it was conquered by the Romans, and in 142 B.C. became a Roman province. Macedonia is not mentioned by name in the O.T.; but the Macedonian empire is referred to in Dan. 8:5–8. In I Macc. 1:1 Chittim is Macedonia. Paul, summoned in a vision by a man of Macedonia, on his Second Journey, passed from Asia into Europe, and preached the gospel in that continent first on Macedonian soil. At this time he passed through the Macedonian towns of Neapolis, Philippi, Amphipolis, Apollonia, Thessalonica, and Berea (Acts 16:9 to 17:14). When Paul departed, Silas and Timothy continued the work (Acts 17:14, 15; 18:5). Paul revisited the region (Acts 19:21, 22; 20:1–3; cf. II Cor. 2:13; 7:5; I Tim. 1:3). Gaius and Aristarchus, Macedonians, were Paul's companions in travel, and were in danger on his account during the riot at Ephesus (Acts 19:29). Secundus, also a Macedonian, was one of those who waited for him at Troas, when for the last time he was to leave Philippi on his way to Jerusalem (Acts 20:4). Paul's converts in Macedonia made a collection for the poor Christians of the Jewish capital (Rom. 15:26). They also ministered to the wants of the apostle himself (II Cor. 8:1–5), the Philippians being the most prominent in the work of charity (Phil. 4:15).

Mach'ban·nai (măk'bá-nī), in A.V. Mach'·ba·nai (măk'bà-nī). One of the Gadite heroes who joined David at Ziklag (I Chron. 12:13).

Mach·be'na (măk-bē'ná), in A.V. Mach·be'·nah (măk-bē'ná). A town of Judah, to judge from the context (I Chron. 2:49). See CABBON.

Ma'chi (mā'kī). Father of the spy from the tribe of Gad (Num. 13:15).

Ma'chir (mā'kĭr) [sold]. 1. The first-born and only son of Manasseh (Gen. 50:23; Josh. 17:1). His mother was an Aramitess (I Chron. 7:14). He was the founder of the family of the Machirites, which would have been the sole family of Manasseh. But as posterity increased, new families were set apart from the main line through the first-born; and thus Machir became one among the families of Manasseh (Num. 26:29). The family, collectively called Machir, was warlike, and subjugated Gilead. This district was accordingly assigned to the family for its inheritance (Num. 32:39, 40; Josh. 17:1) and was given by Moses. The name of Machir was once used poetically for the whole tribe of Manasseh, w. as well as e. of the Jordan (Judg. 5:14).

2. A son of Ammiel, in Lo-debar, e. of the Jordan (II Sam. 9:4, 5), who brought provisions to David during the rebellion of Absalom (ch. 17:27).

Mach'mas (măk'măs). See MICHMASH.

Mach·nad'e·bai (măk-năd'ĕ-bī). A son of Bani, induced by Ezra to put away his foreign wife (Ezra 10:40).

Mach·pe'lah (măk-pē'lá) [probably, double]. A place before Mamre, where was a field with trees and a cave belonging to Ephron, a Hittite (Gen. 23:9, 17, 19). The place was purchased by Abraham for 400 shekels of silver in order to use the cave as a sepulcher for Sarah, his wife. He himself was buried there by his sons, Isaac and Ishmael (ch. 25:9, 10). There also Isaac and Rebekah were buried; so likewise were Leah and Jacob (chs. 49:29–33; 50:12, 13), and perhaps others of whom we have no record. There were monuments to the patriarchs at Hebron in the time of Christ (Jos. War iv. 9, 7). The cave is probably correctly identified as the one which undoubtedly lies beneath the great mosque at Hebron. Christians have all along been excluded from the mosque and the cavern beneath; but the Prince of Wales on April 7, 1862, the Crown Prince of Prussia in November, 1869, and the 2 sons of the Prince of Wales, one of whom later became King George V, on April 5, 1882, were permitted to make an imperfect examination. On the slope of the hill looking toward the w. stands the Haram, a sacred enclosure, in form an oblong lying n.w. and s.e., surrounded by walls of similar masonry to those of early date around the Temple area at Jerusalem, and measuring externally about 197 feet in length and 111 feet in breadth. The ancient Christian church, which completely filled the s.e. end of the enclosure, has been converted into a mosque. In the mosque, close to its n.w. wall and about 10 feet s.w. of the main entrance, is a round opening, about a foot in diameter, through the stone flooring. Through this hole a glimpse is had into a shaft about 12 feet square and 15 feet deep, with a door in the s.e. wall. This chamber is supposed to be an anteroom to the double cave situated immediately to the s.e. under the floor of the mosque. Two entrances to the cave are marked in the flagging of the mosque, but they cannot be opened without tearing up the pavement. Their position would indicate that they afforded access to the cave through its roof of rock. The floor of the mosque and the courtyard in front are 15 feet higher than the street which skirts the Haram on the long s.w. side. In the n.w. corner of the enclosure is a shrine sacred to Joseph, but he was buried at Shechem (Josh. 24 :32).

Mad'a·i (măd'á-ī). A people descended from Japheth (Gen. 10:2; I Chron. 1:5), doubtless the inhabitants of Media.

Ma'di·an (mā'dĭ-ăn). See MIDIAN.

Mad·man'nah (măd-măn'á) [dunghill]. A town in the extreme s. of Judah (Josh. 15:31; I Chron. 2:49); perhaps identical with Beth-marcaboth (q.v.), Umm Deimneh, about 13 miles n.e. of Beer-sheba.

Mad'men (măd'měn) [dunghill]. A town in Moab (Jer. 48:2), Khirbet Dimneh, 2½ miles n.w. of Rabba, at the head of Wadi Beni Hammad.

Mad·me'nah (măd-mē'ná) [dunghill]. A town near Jerusalem and on the n. (Isa. 10:31), probably near Sha'fāṭ.

Mad'ness. 1. Disorder of the mind which renders a person void of right reason (Deut. 28:28). David, when feigning to be mad, made marks on the doors of the gate and let the spittle fall down upon his beard (I Sam. 21:13, 14, where the 2 principal Hebrew synonyms are used). It may manifest itself in hallucinations (Acts 12:15), or in wild raving (I Cor. 14:23), or even in violence, such as hurling about firebrands and arrows (Prov. 26:18). Its symptoms are temporarily produced by drink (Jer. 25:16; 51:7).
2. A state of uncontrollable emotion, as infatuation (Jer. 50:38) or fury (Ps. 102:8; Luke 6:11; Acts 26:11).

Ma'don (mā'dŏn) [contention, strife]. A town of n. Canaan, whose king was in confederacy with the king of Hazor (Josh. 11:1–12; 12:19); probably Khirbet Madin, about ⅓ mile s. of Ḥaṭṭīn.

Mag'a·dan (măg'á-dăn). A locality into the borders of which Jesus went after crossing the Sea of Galilee (Matt. 15:39, in A.V. Magdala). It seems to have been on the w. shore of the lake and may have included Magdala (cf. Mark 8:10). See DALMANUTHA.

Mag'bish (măg'bĭsh) [cf. Akkad. gabshu, massive, strong]. A town (Ezra 2:30). Père Abel identifies it with Khirbet el-Maḥbiyeh, 3 miles s.w. of Adullam.

Mag'da·la (măg'dá-lá) [Heb. migdāl, Aram. migdelā, tower]. A town which, according to the Talmud, stood on the w. shore of the Sea of Galilee, near Tiberias and Hammath, and within less than a Sabbath-day's journey of the water. It exists in the wretched village el-Mejdel, scarcely 3 miles n. of Tiberias. In Matt. 15:39 the R.V., following the best manuscripts, substitutes Magadan (q.v.). See also MAGDALENE.

Mag'da·lene (măg'dá-lēn; măg'dá-lē'nĕ) [Gr., of Magdala]. Mag-da-le'ne has the accent as in Latin, which follows the Greek in having long e; Mag'da-lene is the more frequent English pronunciation. A designation of one of the Marys, implying that she came from some Magdala, probably from the village now called el-Mejdel, on the w. shore of the Sea of Galilee, about 3 miles n.n.w. of Tiberias. For modern use of magdalen see MARY 3.

Mag'di·el (măg'dĭ-ĕl) [God is excellence, glory]. A duke descended from Esau (Gen. 36:43; I Chron. 1:54).

Ma'gi (mā'jī) [Gr. Magoi, pl. of Magos, from Old Pers. magav]. The religious caste to which the Wise Men belonged who came from the e. to worship the Infant Jesus (Matt. 2:1, R.V. marg.). The Magi were a priestly caste, numerous enough to be regarded as one of the 6 tribes of Media (Herod. i. 101). When the Persians conquered the Medes, the Magi retained their influence in the new empire. An attempt on their part to seize the crown led to a dreadful slaughter of them, notwithstanding which their power soon revived (Herod. iii. 79). They worshiped the elements, fire, air, earth, and water, especially the first. The only temples they had were fire temples, generally on housetops, where they kept the sacred element burning night and day. What to do with the dead was a question which, with their views, involved much perplexity. The corpse could not be burned, buried, cast into water, or left to decay in the air without defiling an element. It was therefore exposed to be devoured by carrion-loving

The Village of Magdala, with Booths on the Housetops

birds or beasts (cf. Herod. i. 140; Strabo xv. 3, 20). To do this in the least offensive manner they erected towers called towers of silence, with transverse bars at the top, on which vultures and ravens might s_and while they did their melancholy work. The Magi wore as sacerdotal vestments a white robe, with a headdress consisting of a tall felt cap, with lappets at the side which concealed the jaws. They claimed to be mediators between God and man, intervening in all sacrifices (Herod. i. 132; vii. 43). They interpreted dreams and omens and claimed the gift of prophecy (Herod. i. 107, 120; vii. 19, 37, 113). They were diligent in killing such animals as were regarded as belonging to the bad creation (Herod. i. 140). The foreigner was apt to observe the religious doctrine and priestly functions of the Magi less attentively than their incantations, and in process of time the Greeks bestowed the epithet Magos on any sorcerer who employed the methods and enchantments of the East. The Jew Bar-Jesus was a Magus (Acts 13:6, R.V. marg.), and so was Simon, often called Magus, of Samaria (ch. 8:9).

Ma·gi'cian. A man who pretends to have preternatural powers, which he has obtained by the study of an occult science or the practice of a black art in connivance with evil spirits, and which he calls magic (cf. Acts 19:19); see SORCERER. In the Bible magician is the rendering of *ḥarṭōm*, one of the class of sacred scribes, who were skilled in writing and acquired vast information (Dan. 1:20), and who often claimed occult knowledge, practiced magic (Ex. 7:11), and undertook to interpret dreams (Gen. 41:8; Dan. 2:10). The Egyptian magicians who withstood Moses were 2 in number, and their names were Jannes and Jambres (II Tim. 3:8).

Ma'gog (mā'gŏg). A people descended from Japhe_h (Gen. 10:2), at one period inhabiting a n. land (Ezek. 38:2, 15). Josephus identified them with the Scythians (Jos. *Antiq.* i. 6, 1), and his identification is commonly accepted, but it may be a comprehensive term for n. barbarous peoples. The final struggle of heathenism with the Kingdom of God is prophetically portrayed by Ezekiel under the figure of an invasion of the land of Israel by the hordes of the king of Magog and their overthrow. Ezekiel's description is referred to and its imagery is borrowed by John (Rev. 20:8, 9). See GOG 2.

Ma'gor-mis'sa·bib (mā'gŏr-mĭs'á-bĭb) [terror on every side]. A prophetic name given to Pashhur, a priest and governor of the Temple who ill-treated the Prophet Jeremiah (Jer. 20:3).

Mag'pi·ash (măg'pĭ-ăsh) [cf. Magbish]. One of the chiefs of the people who with Nehemiah sealed the covenant (Neh. 10:20).

Ma·ha'lah (má-hā'lä). See MAHLAH 2.

Ma·ha'la·lel (má-hā'lá-lĕl), in A.V. and in R.V. of N.T. **Ma·ha'la·le·el** (má-hā'lá-lē'ĕl), in A.V. of N.T. **Ma·le'le·el** (má-lē'lĕ-ĕl) [praise of God, or probably, God shines forth]. 1. An antediluvian patriarch in the line of Seth (Gen. 5:12–17; Luke 3:37).

2. One of the tribe of Judah, family of Perez, who lived in Jerusalem after the Captivity (Neh. 11:4).

Ma·ha'lath (mā'há-lăth) [sickness]. 1. A musical term (Psalms 53; 88, titles), which judged by Heb. etymology refers to sickness (cf. Isa. 38:9 *seq.*). *Maḥălath* is probably the initial word of some well-known Hebrew song to the melody of which Psalm 53 was set. In Psalm 88 *'al maḥălath le'annōth* may mean "set to 'sickness to afflict, or to sing,'" which too was the name of a well-known song.

Le'annōth, however, may mean "for singing antiphonally." The meaning is quite uncertain.

2. Daughter of Ishmael and a wife of Esau (Gen. 28:9). Called also Basemath. See BASEMATH 2.

3. Daughter of Jerimoth and one of Rehoboam's wives (II Chron. 11:18).

Ma'ha·li (mā'há-lī). See MAHLI.

Ma·ha·na'im (mā'há-nā'ĭm) [two camps]. The name given by Jacob to a place e. of Jordan where the angels of God met him, apparently in 2 detachments, just after he had finally parted from Laban and before he crossed the Jabbok (Gen. 32:2). It was on the boundary line between the tribes of Gad and Manasseh (Josh. 13:26, 30). It was afterward assigned to the Merarite Levites (Josh. 21:38; I Chron. 6:80). Commencing as a sacred spot, it ultimately became a fortified city. It was Ish-bosheth's capital (II Sam. 2:8, 12, 29). David retired thither while his rebellious son Absalom was in possession of Jerusalem (II Sam. 17:24, 27; 19:32; I Kings 2:8). Ahinadab the son of Iddo was Solomon's purveyor in the region (I Kings 4:14). The site has not been identified. Robinson, and long before him the Jewish traveler Moses hap-Parchi, about 1315, suggested Khirbet Maḥneh, about 2½ miles n. of 'Ajlūn. Some have thought that Gerasa (Jerash) was built upon the site. Dalman prefers Tulul edh-Dhahab on the n. bank of the Jabbok, though others would locate Penuel at this place.

Ma·ha·neh·dan' (mā'há-nĕ-dăn') [camp of Dan]. A place behind, that is w. of Kiriath-jearim (Judg. 18:12), between Zorah and Eshtaol (ch. 13:25), so named when the Danite spies encamped at the spot.

Ma·har'a·i (má-hăr'á-ī) [swift, impetuous]. A Netophathite, one of David's mighty men (II Sam. 23:28; I Chron. 11:30). He was David's captain for the 10th month (ch. 27:13).

Ma'hath (mā'hăth) [seizing]. 1. A Kohathite Levite, descended by the line of Zephaniah, Tahath, and Abiasaph (I Chron. 6:35). He was an ancestor of Samuel (v. 33).

2. Another Levite, one of the overseers who looked after the tithes and freewill offerings in Hezekiah's reign (II Chron. 31:13). Probably he was the son of Amasai, a descendant of Kohath (ch. 29:12).

Ma·ha'vite (mā'há-vīt). A designation of unknown meaning appended to the name of Eliel, one of David's mighty men (I Chron. 11:46).

Ma·ha·zi·oth (má-ha'zī-ŏth) [visions]. A Levite, a descendant of Heman (I Chron. 25:4). He obtained the 23d lot among the singers (v. 30).

Ma'her-shal'al-hash'baz' (mā'hĕr-shăl'ăl-hăsh'băz') [spoil speeds, prey hastes]. The words which Isaiah was directed to display on a public tablet and have duly witnessed, and a year later was told to give as a name to his 2d son. They predicted the speedy conquest of Damascus and Samaria by the king of Assyria (Isa. 8:1–4). The preliminary formality drew public attention to the enigmatical words and attested that God was preparing and revealing the event a year before its occurrence.

Mah'lah (mä'lä), in A.V. once **Ma·ha'lah** (I Chron. 7:18) [disease]. 1. Daughter of Zelophehad (Num. 26:33; 27:1).

2. Another Manassite, whose mother was Hammoleketh (I Chron. 7:18).

Mah'li (mä'lī), in A.V. once **Ma'ha·li** (Ex. 6:19) [sick, weak]. 1. A Levite, son of Merari and brother of Mushi. He founded a tribal family or house (Ex. 6:19; Num. 3:20, 33; 26:58). His grandsons married their cousins (I Chron. 23:22).

2. A Levite, family of Merari, house of Mushi (I Chron. 6:47; 23:23; 24:30).

Mah'lon (mä'lŏn) [sickly]. Elder son of Elimelech and Naomi, and the 1st husband of Ruth (Ruth 1:2; 4:10).

Ma'hol (mä'hŏl) [dance]. Father of Heman, Chalcol, and Darda, 3 noted wise men (I Kings 4:31).

Mah·se'iah (mä-sē'yà), in A.V. **Ma'a·se'iah** [Jehovah is a refuge]. An ancestor of Jeremiah's friend, Baruch, and of the chief chamberlain, Seraiah (Jer. 32:12; 51:59).

Ma'kaz (mä'kăz) [a cutting off, end]. A town whence one of Solomon's purveyors drew supplies (I Kings 4:9).

Ma'ked (mä'kĕd), in A.V. once **Ma'ged** (mä'gĕd). A town of Gilead, in which Jews were shut up by the heathen (I Macc. 5:26). It was captured by Judas Maccabaeus, and the Jews were released (v. 36). It is located at Tell Miḳdad, almost 7 miles n. of Sheikh Miskīn.

Mak·he'loth (măk-hē'lŏth) [assemblies]. An encampment of the Israelites in the wilderness (Num. 33:25, 26); probably Kuntilet Ḳrayeh or 'Ajrūd.

Mak·ke'dah (mä-kē'dà) [place of shepherds]. A Canaanite town in the lowland, taken by Joshua (Josh. 15:41). Near it was a cave (ch. 10:16). Eusebius located it 8 Roman miles e. of Eleutheropolis. He may, however, mean n. (as he sometimes does by e.), and so the place would be located at Khirbet el-Kheishum.

Mak'tesh (măk'tĕsh) [a mortar, a trough, a hollow]. A locality at Jerusalem (Zeph. 1:11). The Targum identifies it with the Kidron valley; it probably was in the n. part of the city, and the name may have been derived from the hollowed-out form of that part of the Tyropoeon just n. of the walls, where foreign merchants congregated.

Mal'a·chi (măl'à-kī) [my messenger, or rather, messenger (of Jehovah); cf. II Esdras 1:40]. A prophet, the writer of the last book of the O.T. (Mal. 1:1). Nothing is known of his history except what may be learned from his book. Since the name may be interpreted as my messenger (so in ch. 3:1, but this may be a case of wordplay), some have supposed it to be, not the proper name, but the title of a prophet, perhaps of Ezra. But since each of the 11 preceding minor prophecies has its author's name prefixed, there is a strong presumption that it is so in the present case also, and that Malachi was the actual name of the author.

The book may be divided into the following sections: (1) God's peculiar love for Israel, shown in his choice of Jacob instead of Esau (ch. 1:2–5), was not requited: (a) The priests and people dishonored God by presenting blemished offerings (vs. 6–14); punishment threatened for this departure from the norm established by God for the priesthood and once realized (ch. 2:1–9); (b) The people dealt treacherously against their brethren, intermarrying with the heathen, putting away their own wives, and doing deeds of violence (ch. 2:10–16). (2) Judgment imminent. God's messenger is about to prepare the way; the Lord himself will suddenly come to his temple; the messenger of the covenant shall come as judge and purify Levi from dross and visit evildoers (chs. 2:17 to 3:6; cf. Ex. 23:20–23; Matt. 11:10). (3) Call to repentance. Then the Lord will come in blessing and judgment, putting to nought

the complaint that he makes no distinction between the good and the evil. Those who have turned from sin to God will be his peculiar treasure, but the wicked shall be burned as stubble (chs. 3:7 to 4:3). Exhortation to remember the Law of Moses, and announcement of the mission of Elijah to prepare for the terrible day of the Lord (ch. 4:4–6; Matt. 17:10–13; Luke 1:17).

When the prophecy was delivered the Jewish people were not under a king, but under a governor (Mal. 1:8), doubtless one appointed by the Persian emperor (Neh. 5:14). Zerubbabel's Temple was standing, as was the altar, and sacrifices were being offered as in the olden time (Mal. 1:7–10); hence Malachi is later than Haggai and Zechariah. But the outburst of religious life which had immediately followed the Return from Babylon, and had resulted in the rebuilding first of the sanctuary and then of the fortifications of Jerusalem, had had time to expend its force. Priests and people were corrupt. This condition suits the time of Nehemiah (Neh., ch. 13). Although the book reflects the age of Ezra and Nehemiah, it is not possible to determine the exact date of composition. While some date it before Ezra's return (458 B.C.) or before 444 B.C., a later date is more probable. In 433 Nehemiah was recalled to the Persian court, and on the whole the period of his absence may be the most probable date; it was hardly written while he was governor (cf. Mal. 1:8 with Neh. 5:15, 18).

Mal'cam (măl'kăm), in A.V. **Mal'cham** (măl'kăm) [(their) king]. 1. A Benjamite, son of Shaharaim and Hodesh (I Chron. 8:9).

2. Same as Milcom, the chief deity of the Ammonites (Jer. 49:1, 3, in A.V. and R.V. marg., their king; Zeph. 1:5). See MOLECH.

Mal'chi·el (măl'kĭ-ĕl) [God is king]. A son of Beriah and grandson of Asher, and founder of a tribal family (Gen. 46:17; Num. 26:45).

Mal·chi'jah (măl-kī'jà), in A.V. often **Mal·chi'ah**, once **Mel·chi'ah** (Jer. 21:1) [Jehovah is king]. 1. A Levite, family of Gershom, house of Shimei (I Chron. 6:40).

2. A descendant of Aaron. His family had grown to a father's house in the time of David, and became the 5th course when David distributed the priests into divisions (I Chron. 24:1, 6, 9). Apparently members of a subdivision of his family, viz., the house of Pashhur, returned with Zerubbabel from Babylon (Ezra 2:38). He is also probably referred to in I Chron. 9:12 and Neh. 11:12, where a priestly line is traced back through Pashhur to one of this name. The royal prince of Jer. 38:6 (and hence probably of v. 1) is a different person.

3. A royal prince, into whose dungeon the Prophet Jeremiah was cast (Jer. 38:6). It is natural to identify him with the father of Pashhur mentioned in v. 1 and ch. 21:1.

4, 5. Two sons of Parosh, both induced by Ezra to put away their foreign wives (Ezra 10:25).

6. A son of Harim, induced by Ezra to put away his foreign wife (Ezra 10:31). He joined with another Hebrew in repairing part of the wall of Jerusalem and the tower of the furnaces (Neh. 3:11).

7. A son of Rechab. He also repaired part of the wall of Jerusalem (Neh. 3:14).

8. A goldsmith who repaired part of the wall of Jerusalem (Neh. 3:31).

9. A priest who with others officiated at the dedication of the wall of Jerusalem (Neh. 12:42); perhaps one of those who assisted Ezra when the law was explained to the people (Neh. 8:4).

10. A priest who, doubtless in behalf of a father's house, signed the covenant (Neh. 10:3).

Mal·chi'ram (măl-kī'răm) [the king, i.e., God, is exalted]. A son of King Jehoiachin (I Chron. 3:18).

Mal'chi·shu'a (măl'kī-shŏŏ'á), in A.V. **Mel'·chi·shu'a** in I Samuel [the king, i.e., God, is salvation]. A son of King Saul (I Sam. 14:49; I Chron. 8:33; 9:39). He was killed at the battle of Gilboa (I Sam. 31:2).

Mal'chus (măl'kŭs) [Lat. from Gr. of Heb. *melek*, king]. The high priest's servant whose ear Peter cut off (John 18:10).

Ma·le'le·el (má-lē'lè-ĕl). See MAHALALEL.

Mal'lo·thi (măl'ō-thī). A son of Heman (I Chron. 25:4). He obtained by lot the leadership of the 19th course of singers (v. 26).

Mal'lows. The rendering of Heb. *Mallûaḥ*, salt plant (Job 30:4, A.V.). Since genuine mallows are mucilaginous and not saline, the R.V. alters the name of the plant to saltwort; see SALTWORT.

Mal'luch (măl'ŭk) [reigning, counselor]. 1. A Levite, family of Merari, house of Mushi (I Chron. 6:44).

2. A chief of the priests, who returned from Babylon with Zerubbabel (Neh. 12:2, 7). A father's house bore his name in the next generation (v. 14, R.V.). In the latter passage the form Malluchi is probably due to dittography; the final letter of Malluchi is the initial letter of the following word, and moreover is not found in the LXX. Malluchi represents the *kethib* of the Hebrew text, but Melicu (A.V. and marg. of R.V.) is the *kere*.

3, 4. A son of Bani and a son of Harim, each of whom was induced by Ezra to put away his foreign wife (Ezra 10:29, 32).

5, 6. A priest and a chief of the people who signed the covenant (Neh. 10:4, 27).

Mal'lu·chi (măl'ū-kī). See MALLUCH 2.

Mam'mon [Gr. *mamōnás*, from Aram. *māmōnā*, wealth, riches]. A personification of wealth (Matt. 6:24; Luke 16:9, 11, 13).

Mam're (măm'rē). 1. The town or more probably district of Hebron (Gen. 23:19; 35:27), to the w. of Machpelah (ch. 23:17). A grove was there, near Hebron, where Abraham several times resided (chs. 13:18; 14:13; 18:1, etc.). In Josephus' time an aged terebinth was pointed out as Abraham's tree, 6 stades or ⅔ of a mile from Hebron (Jos. *War* iv. 9, 7); in the 4th century, one at Rāmet el-Khalil, 2 Roman miles n. of Hebron, which Constantine enclosed within the walls of a basilica. The remains of this building are called the house of Abraham. The tree which now claims the honor of being Abraham's oak, and which was already celebrated as such in the 16th cen ury, is a genuine oak. Its trunk has a girth of 26 feet at the ground, and its branches extend over an area of about 1½ miles w.n.w. of modern Hebron.

2. An Amorite chieftain who dwelt at Mamre and who with his brothers, Eshcol and Aner, helped Abraham to retake the captives and the spoil carried off by Chedorlaomer (Gen. 14:13, 24). He was probably designated by the name of the district over which he ruled.

Man. See ADAM 1.

Man'a·en (măn'á-ĕn) [Gr. form of Menahem]. A Christian prophet or teacher in the church at Antioch. He had been brought up with Herod the tetrarch as his companion (Acts 13:1, A.V.), or was his foster brother, brought up at the same mother's breast (R.V.). He may have been a descendant, or at least a relative of Manahem, the Essene, who predicted to Herod the Great, when yet a schoolboy, that he would obtain the kingdom.

When the prophecy was fulfilled, Herod held him and his sect in high esteem (Jos. *Antiq.* xv. 10, 5).

Man'a·hath (măn'á-hăth) [resting place]. 1. A son of the Horite, Shobal (Gen. 36:23; I Chron. 1:40).

2. A place to which Benjamites of Geba were carried captive by their fellow tribesmen (I Chron. 8:6); probably Mālha, 3 miles s.w. of Jerusalem. Descendants of Salma, of the family of Caleb, tribe of Judah, probably formed half the population of it or of another place of the name (ch. 2:54); see MANAHATHITES.

Ma·na'hath·ites (má-nā'hăth-īts), in A.V. **Ma·na'heth·ites** (má-nā'hĕth-īts). The inhabitants of a place or the descendants of a man Manahath (I Chron. 2:54). To judge by the context, a place is intended. For Manahethites in v. 52, A.V., see MENUHOTH.

Ma·nas'seh (má-năs'ĕ), in A.V. of N.T. **Ma·nas'ses** (má-năs'ĕz), the Greek form [making to forget]. 1. The elder son of Joseph. He was born in Egypt, his mother being Asenath, daughter of Po.i-phera, priest of On. In race, therefore, he, like his brother Ephraim, was half Hebrew, half Egyptian (Gen. 41:50, 51). When Jacob desired to bless the 2 boys, Joseph took Ephraim in his right hand, toward Jacob's left, and Manasseh in his left, toward Jacob's right; but the dying patriarch crossed his arms, so as to lay his right hand on Ephraim's head and his left on that of Manasseh, intimating prophetically that while both sons should become ancestors of great peoples, Ephraim should excel (ch. 48:8–21).

2. The tribe which descended from Manasseh. It consisted of 7 tribal families, of which one was founded by his son Machir and the remaining 6 sprang from his grandson Gilead (Gen. 50:23; Num. 26:28–34; Josh. 17:1, 2). At the 1st census in the wilderness the tribe numbered 32,200 fighting men (Num. 1:34, 35); at the 2d, which was taken 38 years later, 52,700 (ch. 26:34). After Moses had defeated Sihon, king of Heshbon, and Og, king of Bashan, one half the tribe of Manasseh joined with the tribes of Reuben and Gad in requesting permission to settle e. of the Jordan and obtained the leave they sought, on condi.ion of going armed before their brethren, who had not yet obtained settlements, and aiding in the war w. of the Jordan (chs. 32:33–42; cf. vs. 1–32; 34:14, 15; Deut. 3:12, 13; 29:8; Josh. 12:4–6; 18:7). They observed the conditions laid down (Josh. 1:12–18; 4:12); and, when the war had been successfully fought out, were honorably dismissed to the territory they had chosen. A temporary misunderstanding about the building of an altar at one time threatened unpleasant consequences; but on explanation being given, matters were amicably arranged (ch. 22:1–34). The region given to the half tribe of Manasseh e. of the Jordan comprehended part of Gilead and all Bashan (Deut. 3:13–15), Mahanaim in one direction being on its boundary line (Josh. 13:29–33). It is between 65 and 70 miles from e. to w., by 40 or more from n. to s. It is mostly a tableland of 2,500 feet elevation, one of the richest parts of Palestine, and to this day the granary of a large part of Syria. It is studded with ruined towns. The other half of the tribe crossed the Jordan and had their inheritance in central Palestine, w. of the river. It was bounded on the s. by Ephraim, on the n.w. by Asher, and on the n.e. by Issachar. Its s. boundary ran by Janoah and Taanath-shiloh, near Shechem, and along the n. bank of the brook Kanah to its entrance into the Mediterranean (Josh. 17:5–10). But the children of Ephraim had cities in the midst of the inheritance of the children of Manasseh (ch. 16:9); and, on the

other hand, Manasseh had various towns, viz., Beth-shean, Ibleam, Dor, En-dor, Taanach, and Megiddo, within the territories of Issachar and Asher (ch. 17:11; cf. I Chron. 7:29). The Manassites, however, failed to expel the Canaanite inhabitants of the cities just named, but eventually put them to tribute (Josh. 17:12, 13; Judg. 1:27, 28). Levitical cities were allotted from Manasseh as from the other tribes, including Golan in Bashan in the region e. of the Jordan, one of the 6 cities of refuge (Josh. 20:8; 21:27). The hero and judge Gideon was a Manassite (Judg. 6:15). Some Manassites joined David at Ziklag (I Chron. 12:19, 20). No fewer than 18,000 offered him their services during his reign at Hebron (v. 31; cf. v. 37). The e. Manassites, in conjunction with the 2 tribes e. of the Jordan, waged war with the Hagrites and took possession of their country. They were themselves carried into exile by Tiglath-pileser (ch. 5:18–26). Some Manassites came to Asa when they saw that the Lord was with him (II Chron. 15:9); men of the same tribe also attended the great passover in Hezekiah's reign and also in Josiah's reign (chs. 30:1, 10, 11, 18; 31:1; 34:6, 9).

3. An intentional modification of the name Moses (Judg. 18:30, A.V.); see JONATHAN 1.

4. Son and successor of the good king Hezekiah. He ascended the throne about the year 693 B.C., when he was only 12 years of age. He undid the work of reformation which had been carried out in the former reign. He established the high places, built an altar to Baal, and reared an Asherah; made altars for the worship of the host of heaven within the 2 courts of the Temple, and caused one of his sons to pass through the fire. Prophets warned him, but he paid no attention to their threatenings. Instead of listening, he shed much innocent blood throughout every part of Jerusalem. The victims were doubtless chiefly those who, retaining their fidelity to Jehovah, opposed Manasseh's reactionary religious measures (II Kings 21:1–16). As a penalty for his wickedness, God left him to his enemies. Two kings of Assyria, Esarhaddon and Ashurbanipal, report receiving tribute from him. The Assyrian king by whose captains he was carried captive to Babylon (II Chron. 33:11) was probably Ashurbanipal. Manasseh repented, and was after a time restored to his kingdom. He put away the idols which had been his ruin, and restored the worship of Jehovah. He also added to the fortifications of Jerusalem (II Chron. 33:12–19). After a reign of 55 years, a longer one than any other king of Judah had enjoyed, he died about the year 639 B.C., leaving his son Amon to ascend the throne (II Kings 21:17, 18; II Chron. 33:20). For the Prayer of Manasses, see APOCRYPHA 12.

5 and 6. A son of Pahath-moab and a son of Hashum, each of whom was induced by Ezra to put away his foreign wife (Ezra 10:30, 33).

Man'drake. The rendering of Heb. *dūdā'īm,* by a popular etymology connected with Heb. *dōd* (beloved, love). The plants were supposed to act as a love philter (Gen. 30:14–16; in R.V. marg., love apples). They are odoriferous (S. of Sol. 7:13). The mandrake (*Mandragora officinarum*) is a handsome plant of the solanaceous (nightshade) order. It has wavy leaves and pale-violet, white, or deep-blue flowers. Its fruit is small and yellow. The forked root bears a slight resemblance to the human body. It is found in the Jordan Valley and along the rivers running into it, in the plains of Moab and Gilead, and in Galilee.

Ma'neh (mā'nĕ). See WEIGHTS.

Man'ger. A feeding place for cattle, a crib or trough, in Greek *phatnē* (Luke 2:7, 12;

13:15, R.V. marg.; cf. Isa. 1:3). Mangers are ancient (*Iliad* x. 568; xxiv. 280; Herod. ix. 70). In Palestine the stable is usually in the owner's house, a portion of the interior being set apart for the cattle and furnished with mangers built of small stones and mortar in the shape of a box.

Man'na [Gr. *manna,* from Aram. *mannā* from Heb. *mān* (manna); cf. popular etymology (Ex. 16:15) Heb. *mān hū'* (what is it?) and Arab. *mann* (gift, manna)]. A food on which the Israelites mainly subsisted during the 40 years' sojourn in the wilderness. It was first bestowed in the wilderness of Sin, in the 2d half of the 2d month, when the people murmured, owing to the deficiency of food. The descent of manna was described as a raining of bread from heaven (Ex. 16:1–4, 12). "In the morning . . . when the dew . . . was gone up," there lay "upon the face of the wilderness a small round thing, small as the hoar-frost on the ground. And when the children of Israel saw it, they said one to another [ch. 16:15], *mān hū,* What is it? [A.V., It is manna] for they knew not what it was. And Moses said unto them, It is the bread which Jehovah hath given" (ch. 16:13–15; Num. 11:9). It was white like coriander seed, with a yellowish tinge and resinous appearance like bdellium, and tasted like wafers made with honey or like fresh oil (Ex. 16:31; Num. 11:8). It was ground in mills, beaten in mortars, boiled in pots, and made into cakes (Num. 11:8). The people were directed to gather an omer a day (about 3.36 quarts) for each member of their households, and not to attempt to keep any till the morrow. Some of the people disobeyed this injunction, but the hoarded manna decayed and stank. On the 6th day 2 omers were gathered for each person, as none descended on the Sabbath (Ex. 16:22–30). An omerful, which evidently was preserved from decay, was kept by Aaron and his successors to show future generations the nature of the food on which the Israelites had subsisted in the wilderness (vs. 32–34); see HIGH PRIEST. A year after it was first given, at the same season, the people are mentioned as having it, and again toward the end of the 40 years. It is referred to because the people were murmuring against the food (Num. 11:

·Mandrake

4–9 ; 21:5), but the boon which they failed to appreciate was not withdrawn. It was continued during the whole of the 40 years' desert wanderings (Ex. 16:35 ; Deut. 8:3, 16 ; Neh. 9:20 ; Ps. 78:24), and did not cease till the day after the Israelites had crossed the Jordan, encamped at Gilgal, and begun to eat of the produce of Canaan (Josh. 5:10–12).

No substance is known which satisfies all the requirements of the O.T. references. The amount furnished during the journey of the Israelites is also miraculous. Various plants exude a mannalike substance, either emanating spontaneously from the plant itself or produced by the puncture of an insect. The *Tamarix gallica mannifera* does so, and grows in the peninsula of Sinai. The exudation is dirty yellow in color, but white when it falls on stones. It melts in the heat of the sun. It is produced during a period of from 6 to 10 weeks, the height of the season being June. *Alhagi maurorum* and *A. desertorum,* 2 species of camel's-thorn, also exude a mannalike substance, and there are other manna-bearing plants. The Arabs use plant manna of different kinds as butter and honey. Moreover, if taken in more than the most limited quantities it is purgative.

Insects (the *Trabutina mannipara* and the *Najacoccus serpentinus minor*), which suck the sap of the *Tamarix mannifera*, also are a source of manna ; they exude the substance in beads varying between the size of a pinhead and that of a pea. In a few days the beads of manna crystallize and in color become anything between milk-white and yellow-brown.

In 1932 a white substance resembling manna one morning covered a patch of 2,100 feet by 60 feet in the farm owned by a Mr. Botha in Natal, South Africa. It was gathered and eaten by the natives.

Ma·no'ah (ma-nō'a) [rest, quiet]. A Danite belonging to the village of Zorah, and father of Samson (Judg. 13:1–25).

Man'slay'er. See MURDER.

Man'tle. The large, sleeveless, outer garment or, as a rendering of Heb. *me'il,* an occasional garment worn between the tunic and the outer garment. See CLOTHING.

Ma'och (mā'ŏk) [perhaps, oppression]. Father of Achish, king of Gath (I Sam. 27:2). See ACHISH.

Ma'on (mā'ŏn) [dwelling, habitation, abode].
1. A town in the hill country of Judah (Josh. 15:55), the residence of Nabal (I Sam. 25:2), now Tell Ma'īn, about 1½ miles s. from Carmel of Judah, and 8½ s. of Hebron. In the wilderness in the vicinity of Maon David and his men for a time took refuge (I Sam. 23:24, 25).
2. Son of Shammai, of the tribe of Judah, and ancestor of the inhabitants of Beth-zur (I Chron. 2:45). Maon may indeed in this passage possibly be used collectively for the inhabitants of the town of this name (cf. Bethlehem, v. 54), and that Maon is immediately called the father of Beth-zur may be paralleled by I Chron. 1:8, 9, 11, 13.
3. A people that oppressed Israel (Judg. 10:12). The English versions translate, Maonites. See MEUNIM.

Ma'on·ites (mā'ŏn-īts). See MAON 3 and MEUNIM.

Ma'ra (mä'ra) [bitter, sad of spirit]. The name chosen by Naomi to express her bereavements (Ruth 1:20).

Ma'rah (mä'ra) [bitter, bitterness]. A fountain of bitter water in the wilderness of Shur on the route to Sinai, at which the Israelites halted when 3 days or a little more had elapsed after their passage of the Red Sea.

The badness of the water, and perhaps its scantiness, opened their eyes to the hardships which they might expect, and they murmured. Moses was directed by God to cast a certain tree into the waters, whereby they were rendered palatable, either miraculously or through the chemical and medicinal properties of the tree (Exod. 15:23–26 ; Num. 33:8, 9). Marah has been generally located at 'Ain Ḥawārah, about 47 miles from Suez, and a few miles inland from the Red Sea, from which it is separated by a range of hills. The well measures about 20 feet across, but is much wider at the bottom. Its depth is perhaps 25 feet. The soil of the region abounds in soda, and the water of the well is consequently salty and bitter.

Mar'a·lah (mär'a-lä). A frontier village of Zebulun toward the sea (Josh. 19:11) ; probably Tell Ghalta in the plain of the Kishon, s. of Jeida.

Mar'a·nath'a (mär'a-năth'a) (A.V.), **Mar'a·na tha** (mär'a-nä thá) (A.R.V.), **Mar'an ath'a** (mär'ăn ăth'a) (E.R.V.). See ANATHEMA MARANATHA.

Mar'ble. Limestone, especially in a crystalline condition, which is capable of taking polish. It was called in Hebrew *shayish* and *shēsh,* from its brightness, and in Greek *marmaros.* It was used for columns and costly pavements (Esth. 1:6 ; S. of Sol. 5:15), and was employed in Solomon's Temple (I Chron. 29:2). Josephus, in describing the walls of this edifice, mentions that they were built of white stone, but does not specify the kind of stone (Jos. *Antiq.* viii. 3, 2). White, yellow, and red marble is obtained in Lebanon, but a choicer variety came from Arabia. Red and white marble was employed in the Greco-Roman period for palatial buildings in Palestine, both e. and w. of the Jordan. In Herod's Temple the pillars of the cloisters were monoliths of white marble, 25 cubits high (Jos. *War* v. 5, 2).

Mar'cus (mär'kŭs). See MARK.

Ma·re'shah (ma-rē'sha) [perhaps, head place].
1. A town in the lowland of Judah (Josh. 15:44 ; cf. I Chron. 4:21). Rehoboam strengthened its fortifications (II Chron. 11:8). The great battle between King Asa and Zerah the Ethiopian was fought in its vicinity (ch. 14:9, 10). In the Greek period it was an important town, inhabited by Edomites, and known as Marissa (Jos. *Antiq.* xiii. 9, 1 ; xiv. 1, 4). It was plundered by Judas Maccabaeus (I Macc. 5:66 ; II Macc. 12:35 ; Jos. *Antiq.* xii. 8, 6). John Hyrcanus planted a Jewish colony there (Jos. *Antiq.* xiii. 9, 1 ; 10, 2) ; but Pompey made the town free in 63 (Jos. *Antiq.* xiv. 4, 4). Gabinius fortified it (Jos. *Antiq.* xiv. 5, 3). It was finally destroyed by the Parthians in 40 B.C. (Jos. *Antiq.* xiv. 13, 9). According to Eusebius, its ruins existed 2 Roman miles from Eleutheropolis ; and Bliss has located it at Tell Sandaḥannah, 1 mile s. by e. of Beit Jibrīn.
2. The father of Hebron (I Chron. 2:42). The form of expression, in the light of its context, suggests that Mareshah was the progenitor of the inhabitants of Hebron, but the mention of Hebron's sons in the following verse makes it probable that Hebron was a man. If so, he is not mentioned elsewhere.

Mar·hesh'van (mär-hĕsh'văn), **Mar·ches'·van** (mär-kĕs'văn) [Heb. *marḥeshwān,* from Akkad. *araḥ (warḥu) + samnu (shawna,* in Neo-Babylonian), eighth month]. Same as Bul. See BUL and YEAR.

Mark (märk), in A.V. of N.T. thrice **Mar'·cus** (Col. 4:10 ; Philemon 24 ; I Peter 5:13) [Lat. *marcus,* a large hammer]. The Evangelist to whom is traditionally assigned the Second Gospel. Mark was his surname (Acts 12:12, 25; 15:37); his 1st name was John, by which alone he is designated in Acts 13:5, 13. There are several instances in the N.T. of Jews with Latin surnames (Acts 1:23; 13:1, 9). His mother, Mary, was in comfortable circumstances, and her house in Jerusalem was one of the meeting places of the Christians (Acts 12:12–17); see MARY 5. Mark was also the cousin of Barnabas (Col. 4:10, R.V.; in A.V. sister's son). He accompanied Barnabas and Paul from Jerusalem to Antioch of Syria (Acts 12:25; 13:1) and afterward on their missionary journey (ch. 13:5); but, for some unstated reason, he left them at Perga (v. 13) and returned to Jerusalem. Whatever was the reason of Mark's conduct on that occasion, Paul disapproved of it so much that he refused to take him with them when a second journey was proposed (ch. 15:38). This caused a contention between the 2 missionaries, so that they separated and Barnabas, with Mark, sailed to Cyprus to resume his evangelistic work. After this Mark disappears from the history for about 10 years. We next find him in Rome with Paul and joining with the apostle in sending salutations (Col. 4:10; Philemon 24). It thus appears that the former cause of variance between the 2 men had been removed; and, at a still later period, Paul speaks of Mark in highly commendatory terms: "Take Mark, and bring him with thee; for he is useful to me for ministering" (II Tim. 4:11). This last reference further implies that Mark had been in the e., certainly in Asia Minor and perhaps still farther e. Peter calls Mark his son, which, if not a mere term of endearment, may mean that Mark had been one of Peter's converts. The fact that Peter, when released by the angel from prison, went to the house of Mark's mother (Acts 12:12) may indicate his intimacy with the family. Tradition varies on the point as to whether Mark had been an immediate follower of Jesus. Many think, however, that the young man who was present at the time of Christ's arrest (Mark 14:51, 52) was Mark himself. The incident is mentioned by no other Evangelist, and there would seem to be no motive for recording it except the wish to give a personal reminiscence. The time and place of Mark's death are unknown. Early tradition represents him as the interpreter of Peter. Among others, Papias of Hierapolis, who wrote about A.D. 140, quoting "the elder" as his authority, says: "Mark, having become Peter's interpreter, wrote down accurately, though not in order, as many as he remembered of the things said or done by the Lord. For he neither had heard the Lord nor followed him, but at a later time, as I said, [he followed] Peter, who delivered his instructions according to the needs [of the occasion], but not with a view to giving a systematic account of the Lord's sayings. So that Mark made no mistake, thus writing down some things as he remembered them; for of one thing he took forethought, [namely] not to leave out any one of the things he had heard or to state falsely anything in them" (Eusebius, *H.E.* iii. 39, 15). This reference to Mark as the interpreter of Peter may either mean that he accompanied Peter, in the later years of the apostle's life, on his missionary journeys and acted as his spokesman when he was addressing Gentile audiences, or may merely describe Mark's work in writing down the preaching of Peter in the Gospel which goes by his [Mark's] name. There can be little doubt that Mark was in Rome with both Paul and Peter. Tradition also made him the founder of the church in Alexandria, but the value of the tradition is uncertain. The main point to be observed is that Mark's early his-

tory and his later association with the chief apostles fitted him to become the writer of a Gospel.

The Gospel According to Mark is the 2d of our 4 Gospels, though not necessarily the 2d in order of composition. It is the shortest of the 4, but this brevity is not the result of condensation of the material. What Mark does give he generally describes with much detail. The story moves forward rapidly with pictorial power, and consists of a succession of descriptive scenes. These proceed in a more chronological order than in Matthew or Luke. Especial stress is laid on the deeds of Christ rather than on his formal instruction by word of mouth, only 4 full parables being related compared with 19 miracles and but one of Christ's longer discourses being given at any length (ch. 13). Christ is depicted as the mighty Son of God (chs. 1:11; 5:7; 9:7; 14:61; also chs. 8:38; 12:1–11; 13:32; 14:36), the conquering Saviour. These proceed in a more mainly with 2 themes: the ministry in Galilee (chs. 1:14 to 9:50), and the last week at Jerusalem (chs. 11:1 to 16:8). These sections are connected by a somewhat brief survey of the intervening period (ch. 10:1–52). Throughout the whole book the thought of suffering and the doctrine of the cross are stressed again and again. The account of the Passion occupies nearly a 3d of the record, and its shadows lie on some of the earliest pages of the Gospel (cf. chs. 2:20; 3:6). The way of discipleship is the way of cross-bearing (ch. 8:34 *seq.*), and implies a baptism of suffering and the drinking of a cup (ch. 10:38 *seq.*). No saying is more characteristic of the Marcan representation than the words of Jesus recorded in ch. 10:45.

In its entirety, it may be divided as follows: 1. Beginning of the gospel of Jesus Christ, including the ministry of John the Baptist and the baptism and temptation of Jesus (ch. 1:1–13). 2. The opening of the Galilean ministry, giving the place and the message, the call of the 1st 4 apostles, miracles in Capernaum and Galilee (ch. 1:14–45). 3. Christ's triumph over rising opposition, including the curing of the paralytic, Levi's feast and the discourse on fasting, and the Sabbath controversy (chs. 2:1 to 3:6). 4. Extension of Christ's work amid increasing opposition, including the description of the multitudes who followed him; the appointment of the Twelve; replies to the Pharisees; the visit of his mother and brethren; the parables of the Sower, the Seed Growing Secretly, and the Mustard Seed, with remarks; the great miracles of stilling the waves, the Gerasene demoniac, the woman with a bloody issue, and the raising of Jairus' daughter; the (2d) rejection at Nazareth; the sending out of the Twelve; Herod's inquiry about Jesus together with an account of the death of John the Baptist; the feeding of the 5,000; the walking on the sea; and Christ's denunciation of Pharisaic traditionalism (chs. 3:7 to 7:23). 5. A period of comparative retirement, embracing the later Galilean ministry (see GOSPEL), including: the healing of the Syrophoenician's daughter in the borders of Tyre and Sidon and of a deaf-mute in Decapolis; the feeding of the 4,000; the refusal to give the Pharisees a sign and the warning of the disciples against them; healing of a blind man near Bethsaida, followed by incidents near Caesarea Philippi, including the prediction by Christ of his death, Peter's confession, etc., the transfiguration, the cure of the demoniac boy, a renewed prediction of Christ's death and, on returning to Capernaum, special instructions to the disciples (chs. 7:24 to 9:50). This period is specially complete in Mark. 6. Christ's closing ministry in Perea, including the question of the Pharisees about divorce; the blessing of the children; the rich young ruler; explanations to the disciples; the ascent to Jerusalem, including a 3d prediction of his death, the request of James and John, the healing of Bartimaeus (ch. 10). 7. The last week, including the triumphal entry; the blasting of the barren fig tree; the (2d) cleansing of the Temple; the visit of the deputation from the sanhedrin; the parable of the Wicked Husbandmen; the questions of the Pharisees and Herodians, and of the Sadducees, and of the scribe (lawyer); Christ's question about the son of David; a brief report of his denunciations of the Pharisees and scribes (cf. Matt., ch. 23); the widow's gift; the discourse on the Mount of Olives; Judas' treachery and, in connection with it, the supper at Bethany; a brief account of the last evening with the disciples and the institution of the Lord's Supper; the agony in Gethsemane; the arrest; the trial of Jesus at night before the sanhedrin; Peter's denials; the trial before Pilate and the crucifixion; the burial; the announcement of Christ's resurrection to certain women by an angel seated in his empty tomb (chs. 11:1 to 16:8).

The last 12 verses of Mark's Gospel, as found in A.V. are not present in B and א, the oldest MSS. of the N.T.; therefore they are believed by most scholars not to have formed the original close of the book. Hence in R.V. they are separated by a space from the preceding verses. They were certainly added at a very early time, perhaps at the beginning of the 2d century. They seem to have been formed in part out of the other Gospels and they truthfully describe the beliefs of the apostolic churches on the subjects with which they deal. Chapter 16:8, however, is too abrupt an ending. The original close must have been lost at a very early time, soon after the book was finished. Some have supposed that Mark was prevented by death or some other cause from finishing.

This Gospel was in general circulation among the Christians as early as the middle of the 2d century, and was included by Tatian in his *Diatessaron*, or *Harmony of the Four Gospels*, c. A.D. 170. Irenaeus, writing in the last quarter of the 2d century, repeatedly quotes it, and quotes it as Mark's; and, as others before him (such as Papias), declares Mark to have been Peter's disciple and interpreter. Thus ancient and trustworthy tradition represents the Gospel of Mark as in some degree connected with Peter's preaching about Christ. This relation to Peter is confirmed by the many vivid particulars which it contains, which seem to be due to the reminiscences of an eyewitness (e.g. chs. 1:40; 2:1–4; 3:5; 5:4–6; 6:39, 40; 7:34; 8:33; 10:21; 11:20); by its superiority to the other Gospels in those sections where Peter alone was an eyewitness or competent to give a full account (cf. the account of Peter's denials); and, as Eusebius noticed, by its silence regarding matters which reflect credit on Peter (Matt. 16:17–19; Luke 5:3–10). This reported dependence on Peter must not be pressed, however, to the exclusion of other sources of information; for Mark had abundant opportunities to learn from other eyewitnesses besides Peter, and from other members of the primitive Christian community, such as his kinsman Barnabas and Paul and the disciples who frequented his mother's house (Acts 12:12, 17). These sources of the Second Gospel circulated partly in oral form, partly in written (as the Passion narrative). Much of the material discloses an Aramaic coloring that points to its early currency on Palestinian soil. Tradition states that Mark wrote his Gospel at Rome, either shortly before or shortly after Peter's death. If so, it must be dated A.D. 65–68. But if Luke's Gospel was written

prior to 63 (see LUKE), Mark must be dated still earlier, because Luke used Mark. Recent interpreters regard it as the Gospel for a persecuted Church (under Nero) called to a great missionary task, furnished with information as to the origins of the faith, with weapons for its defense and means for its world-wide dissemination.

Mark's Gospel was evidently written primarily for Gentiles. This appears, e.g., in his explanations of Palestinian places and Jewish customs and terms (chs. 3:17; 5:41; 7:3, 4, 11, 34; 12:42; 14:12; 15:22, 42, etc.). He uses also a good many Latin words in Greek form, which may indicate that his book was originally published, as tradition states, at Rome. Unlike Matthew, he says nothing of Christ's relation to the Mosaic Law, but few allusions to the fulfillment of prophecy are noted, and except in reporting Christ's words there is an almost total absence of quotation from the Old Testament.

G. T. P. (rev., H. S. G.)

Mar'ket of Ap'pi·us (ăp'ĭ-ŭs). See APPII FORUM.

Ma'roth (mā'rŏth) [bitterness, bitter fountains]. A town of Judah (Micah 1:12). Site unknown.

Mar'riage. Marriage is a divine institution, constituted at the beginning before the origin of human society. The Creator made man male and female, and ordained marriage as the indispensable condition of the continuance of the race (Gen. 1:27, 28). He implanted social affections and desires in man's nature. He made marriage an ennobling influence, powerfully contributing to the development of a complete life in man and woman. He declared it to be not good for man to be alone and provided a help meet for him (Gen. 2:18). Abstinence from marriage is commendable at the call of duty (Matt. 19:12; I Cor. 7:8, 26), but its ascetic prohibition is a sign of departure from the faith (I Tim. 4:3).

Monogamy is the divine ideal. The Creator constituted marriage as a union between one man and one woman (Gen. 2:18–24; Matt. 19:5; I Cor. 6:16). He preserves the number of males practically equal to the number of females.

Marriage is a permanent relation (Matt. 19:6). The Creator has indicated the permanence of the relation by making the growth of affection between husband and wife, as the years pass, to be a natural process, invariable under normal conditions. Moral ends require that the relation be permanent: the disciplining of husband and wife in obedience to the obligations which spring from their relations to each other, and the adequate training of children to obedience and virtue. It cannot be dissolved by any legitimate act of man. It is dissolved by death (Rom. 7:2, 3). It may be dissolved on account of adultery (Matt. 19: 3–9). Protestants, following Paul, teach that it may be dissolved by willful, deliberate, final desertion (I Cor. 7:15). It is probable, however, that in those times desertion was accompanied by adulterous or marital consorting with another person. The marriage of persons divorced on improper grounds is forbidden (Matt. 5:32; 19:9; Mark 10:11 *seq.*; Luke 16:18; I Cor. 7:10 *seq.*). In the sight of God, a civil tribunal cannot annul a marriage; it declares whether the marriage has been sinfully annulled by one or both of the persons concerned.

Among the antediluvians, Adam, Cain, Noah, and his 3 sons appear each as the husband of 1 wife. But polygamy was already practiced, Lamech having 2 wives (Gen. 4:19); and the purity of marriages was impaired by men allowing themselves to be governed by low motives in the choice of wives (ch. 6:2). Polygamy was unwisely adopted by Abraham, when he thought that he must needs help God to fulfill his promise (Gen. 16:4). Isaac had 1 wife. Jacob took 2 wives and their maids. Moses, who was correcting abuses, not suddenly abolishing them, did not forbid polygamy, but discouraged it. He regulated what he found; but the record of the primitive period showed that the state of things among the Israelites was not the ordination of the Creator. Moses' service to the cause of matrimony consisted in setting a higher ideal by establishing the degrees of consanguinity and affinity within which marriage is proper (Lev., ch. 18), discouraging polygamy (Lev. 18:18; Deut. 17:17), securing the rights of inferior wives (Ex. 21:2–11; Deut. 21:10–17), restricting divorce (Deut. 22:19, 29; 24:1), and requiring purity in the married life (Ex. 20:14, 17; Lev. 20:10; Deut. 22:22). Polygamy continued to be practiced more or less by wealthy individuals after the time of Moses, as by Gideon, Elkanah, Saul, David, Solomon, Rehoboam, and others (Judg. 8:30; I Sam. 1:2; II Sam. 5:13; 12:8; 21:8; I Kings 11:3). The evils of polygamy are exhibited in Scripture by the record of the jealousies of the wives of Abraham and Elkanah (Gen. 16:6; I Sam. 1:6), and beautiful pictures are presented of the felicity of marriage between one man and one woman (Ps. 128:3; Prov. 5:18; 31:10–29; Eccl. 9:9; cf. Ecclus. 26:1–27).

In the family to which Abraham belonged marriage was permitted with a half-sister and with 2 sisters (Gen. 20:12; 29:26). Marriage with a full sister was not rare in Egypt, and an exception was made for Cambyses in Persia (Herod. iii. 31). Marriage with a half-sister by the same father was permitted at Athens, and with a half-sister by the same mother at Sparta. The Mosaic Law prohibited alliance with persons so closely related by blood as these and with others less near of kin (Lev. 18:6–18); but in case a man died childless, his brother took the widow (Deut. 25:5). This was called a levirate marriage. Such marriage was ordained, but it was not compulsory. The Roman law was not unlike the Hebrew. It declared marriages to be incestuous "when the parties were too nearly related by consanguinity—that is, by being of the same blood, as brother and sister; or by affinity—that is, by being connected through marriage, as father-in-law and daughter-in-law."

The selection of a wife for a young man devolved on his relatives, especially on his father (Gen. 21:21; 24; 38:6; II Esdras 9:47), though sometimes the son made known his preference and the father merely conducted the negotiations (Gen. 34:4, 8; Judg. 14:1–10). Only under extraordinary circumstances did the young man make the arrangements (Gen. 29:18). Likewise it was the consent of the maid's father and eldest brother that was sought, and it was not necessary to consult her (Gen. 24:51; 34:11). Occasionally a parent looked out an eligible husband for a daughter or offered her to a suitable person in marriage (Ex. 2:21; Josh. 15:17; Ruth 3:1, 2; I Sam. 18:27). Presents were given to the parents, and sometimes to the maiden (Gen. 24:22, 53; 29:18, 27; 34:12; I Sam. 18:25). Between betrothal and marriage all communication between the affianced parties was carried on through a friend deputed for the purpose and termed the friend of the bridegroom (John 3:29).

The marriage itself was a purely domestic affair, without definite religious services, though probably the espousal was ratified by an oath (Ezek. 16:8; Mal. 2:14). After the Exile it became customary to draw up and seal a written contract (Tobit 7:14). When the day appointed for the wedding arrived, the bride bathed (cf. Judith 10:3; probably also Eph. 5:26 seq.), put on white robes, often richly embroidered (Rev. 19:8; Ps. 45:13, 14), decked herself with jewels (Isa. 61:10; Rev. 21:2), fastened the indispensable bridal girdle about her waist (Isa. 3:24; 49:18; Jer. 2:32), covered herself with a veil (Gen. 24:65), and placed a garland on her head. The bridegroom, arrayed in his best attire, with a handsome headdress and a garland on his head (S. of Sol. 3:11; Isa. 61:10), set out from his home for the house of the bride's parents, attended by his friends (Judg. 14:11; Matt. 9:15), accompanied by musicians and singers and, if the procession moved at night, by persons bearing torches (I Macc. 9:39; Matt. 25:7; cf. Gen. 31:27; Jer. 7:34). Having received his bride, deeply veiled, from her parents with their blessing and the good wishes of friends (Gen. 24:59; Ruth 4:11; Tobit 7:13), he conducted the whole party back to his own or his father's house with song, music, and dancing (Ps. 45:15; S. of Sol. 3:6–11; I Macc. 9:37). On the way back they were joined by maidens, friends of the bride and groom (Matt. 25:6). A feast was served at the house of the groom or of his parents (Matt. 22:1–10; John 2:1, 9); but if he lived at a great distance the feast was spread in the house of the bride's parents, at either their expense or the groom's (Gen. 29:22; Judg. 14:10; Tobit 8:19). The groom now associated with his bride for the first time. In the evening the bride was escorted to the nuptial chamber by her parents (Gen. 29:23; Judg. 15:1; Tobit 7:16, 17), and the groom by his companions or the bride's parents (Tobit 8:1). On the morrow the festivities were resumed, and continued for 1 or 2 weeks (Gen. 29:27; Judg. 14:12; Tobit 8:19, 20).

The spiritual relation between Jehovah and his people is figuratively spoken of as a marriage or betrothal (Isa. 62:4, 5; Hos. 2:19). The apostasy of God's people through idolatry or other form of sin is accordingly likened to infidelity on the part of a wife (Isa. 1:21; Jer. 3:1–20; Ezek., chs. 16; 23; Hos., ch. 2), and leads to divorce (Ps. 73:27; Jer. 2:20; Hos. 4:12). The figure is continued in the N.T.; Christ is the bridegroom (Matt. 9:15; John 3:29), and the Church is the bride (II Cor. 11:2; Rev. 19:7; 21:2, 9; 22:17). The love of Christ for the Church, his solicitude for her perfection, and his headship are held up as the standard for imitation by husbands and wives (Eph. 5:23–32).

Mar·se′na (mär-sē′na) [cf. Avestan *marshanā*, forgetful man]. One of the 7 princes of Persia who were permitted to see the king's face (Esth. 1:14). See PRINCE.

Mars' (märz) **Hill.** See AREOPAGUS.

Mar′tha (mär′tha) [Aram., lady, mistress]. Sister of Mary and Lazarus of Bethany (John 11:1, 2). The 3 were tenderly attached to Jesus. Martha loved him and desired to make him comfortable and show him respect in her house. Mary gave evidence of a deeper appreciation by her hunger for the words of truth that fell from his lips; and when Martha would have him rebuke Mary for not assisting her to attend to his external wants, Jesus taught that he himself regarded the inward craving of his followers for spiritual fellowship with him as more essential than their concern for his external honor (Luke 10:38–42). Both sisters were sincere believers (John 11:21–32). The house where Jesus was received is called Martha's (Luke 10:38); and the supper which was given to him at Bethany, at which Lazarus was present and Martha again served, where Mary anointed his

A MODERN PALESTINIAN WEDDING

The bride must draw water from the nearest well and give it
to the bridegroom.

379

feet (John 12:1-3) was at the house of Simon the leper (Matt. 26:6; Mark 14:3). Accordingly it has been suggested that Martha may have been the wife or widow of Simon.

Mar'y (mâr'ĭ) [Lat. *Maria*, from Gr. *Maria*, *Mariam*, from Heb. *Miryâm*. See MIRIAM]. Six women of the name mentioned in the New Testament. (1) Mary the (wife) of Clopas or Cleophas, a Mary so designated in John 19:25. "Wife," according to the idiom of the Greek language, is not found in the original Greek, but is properly supplied both by A.V. and R.V. Clopas of the R.V., Cleophas of the A.V., is apparently to be identified with Alphaeus (Matt. 10:3; Mark 3:18; Luke 6:15), the 2 names being variant forms of the same Aramaic original. He and Mary were thus the parents of the Apostle James the Less, who had also a brother Joses (Matt. 27:56; Mark 15:40; Luke 24:10). Those who understand the Lord's "brethren" to have been his cousins on his mother's side suppose that this Mary was a sister of the Virgin, and that John (ch. 19:25) mentions only 3 women at the cross. But it is unlikely that 2 sisters should have had the same name, and other considerations make the cousin theory improbable; see BRETHREN OF THE LORD. In that case John mentions 4 women at the cross. One of them was Mary the wife of Clopas; but, beyond the fact that her husband and sons were, like herself, disciples of Jesus and that probably one of her sons was an apostle, we know nothing more of her. Besides being at the cross, Mary was one of the women who followed the body of Jesus to the tomb (Matt. 27:61), and on the 3d day took spices to the sepulcher, and to whom the risen Saviour appeared (Matt. 28:1; Mark 15:47; 16:1; Luke 24:10). See section 2 of this article; also ALPHAEUS 1, JAMES 2.

2. Mary the Virgin; the Virgin Mary. All the authentic information about her comes from Scripture. We are told that, in the 6th month after the conception of John the Baptist, the angel Gabriel was sent from God to Nazareth, a city or village of Galilee, to a virgin named Mary, who was residing there and who was betrothed to a carpenter named Joseph (Luke 1:26, 27). Joseph is explicitly declared to have been a descendant of David. Mary is not so described; but many believe that she too was of Davidic lineage, because she was told that her child should receive "the throne of his father David," also because our Lord is said to have been of "the seed of David according to the flesh" (Rom. 1:3; II Tim. 2:8; cf. Acts 2:30), and again because, in the opinion of many scholars, the genealogy of Christ given by Luke (ch. 3:23-38) is through his mother, in which case Mary's father is supposed to have been Heli. However this may be, Gabriel hailed Mary as a highly favored one, and announced to her that she should have a son whose name she should call Jesus. "He," said the angel, "shall be great, and shall be called the Son of the Most High: and the Lord God shall give unto him the throne of his father David: and he shall reign over the house of Jacob for ever; and of his kingdom there shall be no end" (Luke 1:32, 33, R.V.). When Mary asked how this could be, since she was a virgin, she was told that it would be wrought by the power of the Holy Ghost, "wherefore also that which is to be born shall be called holy, the Son of God" (Luke 1:35, R.V.). These expressions revealed to Mary that she was chosen to be the mother of Messiah, and with humble piety she accepted the honor which God mysteriously chose to confer upon her. For her comfort she was informed by the angel that her kinswoman Elisabeth was also to become a mother,

whereupon Mary hastened to the village of Judah where Zacharias and Elisabeth lived. At her coming Elisabeth was made aware of the honor intended for Mary, and broke out into an inspired song of praise. Thereupon Mary also gave voice to a hymn of thanksgiving ("The Magnificat," Luke 1:46-55). We learn from all this the profound piety and solemn joy with which these holy women contemplated the power and grace of God which was through their offspring to fulfill the ancient promises to Israel and bring salvation to the world. Mary remained under the protection of Elisabeth until just before the birth of John, when she returned to Nazareth. The cause of her condition was revealed in a dream to Joseph, who at first had thought of quietly putting her away from him (Matt. 1:18-21). He was directed to marry her and to call the name of the child Jesus, "for it is he that shall save his people from their sins." Joseph reverently obeyed. He "took unto him his wife; and knew her not till she had brought forth a son: and he called his name Jesus" (Matt. 1:24, 25, R.V.). By this marriage Mary was protected, her mysterious secret was guarded, and her child was born as the legal son of Joseph, and therefore through him heir of David.

The birth, however, took place at Bethlehem. A decree of Augustus "that all the world should be enrolled" (Luke 2:1, R.V.) was being carried out in Palestine, and compelled Joseph, being of Davidic descent, to repair to David's city to be enrolled. Mary accompanied him. Finding no room in the inn, or khan, they were compelled to lodge in a stable, perhaps, however, one that was then not being used by cattle. There Jesus was born, and his mother "wrapped him in swaddling clothes, and laid him in a manger" (Luke 2:7). With reverent, trustful awe Mary heard the shepherds relate the vision of angels which they had seen and the song of peace which they had heard heralding the Saviour's birth. Of course, she did not know that her child was God made flesh. She only knew that he was to be Messiah, and with true piety she waited for God to make his mission clear. On the 40th day after the birth Mary went, with Joseph and Jesus, to Jerusalem to present the child to the Lord and to offer in the Temple the offering required by the Law (Lev., ch. 12) from women after childbirth. The fact that her offering is said to have been that required of poor people—a pair of turtledoves or 2 young pigeons—indicates the humble circumstances of the family. When, however, the parents brought in the child, they were met by the aged Simeon who rejoiced over the birth of Messiah, but foretold to Mary that she should have great sorrow because of what would happen to him (Luke 2:35). After this Joseph and Mary appear to have returned to Bethlehem and to have lived in a house (Matt. 2:11). There Mary received the Wise Men from the East who came to worship Jesus (Matt. 2:1-11). Shortly thereafter she fled with Joseph and the child to Egypt, and afterward by divine direction they returned to Nazareth. There she must have devoted herself especially to the rearing of the child of promise who had been committed to her care and of whose future she must have thought continually. One glimpse of Mary's character is given us when Jesus was 12 years old. She was in the habit piously of attending with Joseph the yearly passover (Luke 2:41), though this was not specifically required of Jewish women (Ex. 23:17). With like piety Joseph and Mary took Jesus with them, as soon as he reached the age when it was customary for children to attend, and his delay in the Temple and his words when his parents found him with the doctors were the occasion of increased awe to his parents. "His mother kept all these sayings in her heart" (Luke 2:51). Mary did not understand how great her child really was or how he was to fulfill his mission. It was hers reverently and trustfully to rear him for God's service, and this she did so long as he was under her. If the "brethren of the Lord" (see BRETHREN OF THE LORD) were, as is probable, the children of Joseph and Mary, born after Jesus, Mary was the mother of a large family. We read also of Christ's sisters (Mark 6:3). But nothing further is recorded of Mary until the beginning of Christ's public ministry. She then appears at the marriage in Cana (John 2:1–10). She evidently rejoiced in her son's assumption of Messianic office and fully believed in him. But she ventured improperly to direct his actions, and thus elicited from him a respectful but firm rebuke. Mary must understand that in his work she could share only as a follower. While as her son he gave her reverence, as the Messiah and Saviour he could only regard her as a disciple, needing as much as others the salvation he came to bring.

A similar truth was brought out on another occasion on which she appears (Matt. 12:46–50; Mark 3:31–35; Luke 8:19–21). While Jesus was teaching the multitudes, Mary with his brethren desired to see him. Perhaps they wished to restrain him from a course which seemed to be bringing upon him opposition and peril. His reply again declared that the spiritual bond between him and his disciples was more important than any human tie. "For whosoever shall do the will of my Father which is in heaven, he is my brother, and sister, and mother" (Matt. 12:50). While Christ pursued his ministry, Mary and his brethren appear to have still lived in Nazareth. As no mention is made of Joseph, it is natural to suppose that he had died. But at the crucifixion Mary appears with other women at the cross. Unlike his brethren (John 7:5) she had always believed in her son's Messiahship, and therefore it is not strange to find that she followed him on the last fatal journey to Jerusalem. With a mother's love, as well as with a disciple's sorrow, she beheld his crucifixion, and to her Jesus spoke in the hour of his suffering. He gave her to the care of his beloved disciple John, and "from that hour that disciple took her unto his own home" (John 19:25–27). After the ascension she was with the apostles in the upper room in Jerusalem (Acts 1:14), and this is the last notice of her in Scripture. We do not know the time or manner of her death. The tomb of the Virgin is shown in the valley of the Kidron, but there is no reason to believe in its genuineness. Later legends were busy with her name, but none contain trustworthy information. As presented in Scripture, she is simply a beautiful example of a devoted and pious mother.

3. Mary Magdalene. The designation given to this Mary (Matt. 27:56, 61; 28:1; Mark 15:40, 47; 16:1, 9; Luke 8:2; 24:10; John 19:25; 20:1, 18) doubtless indicates that she was a resident of Magdala, on the s. w. coast of the Sea of Galilee. Out of her Jesus had cast 7 devils (Mark 16:9; Luke 8:2), and she became one of his most devoted disciples. The old belief that she had been a woman of bad character, from which the current use of the word magdalen has arisen, rests merely on the fact that the first mention of her (Luke 8:2) follows closely upon the account of the sinful woman who anointed the Saviour's feet in a city of Galilee (Luke 7:36–50). This, however, is not sufficient proof, and we have no reason to identify her with the sinful woman, whose name has been withheld. What form her terrible malady had taken we do not know. She became a disciple during the early

Galilean ministry, and was one of those who joined the little company of Christ's immediate followers, and ministered to him of her substance (Luke 8:1–3). She was one of the women at the cross (Matt. 27:56; Mark 15:40; John 19:25) and observed the Lord's burial (Matt. 27:61). Early on the 3d day she, with Mary the wife of Clopas and Salome, went to the sepulcher to anoint the body of Jesus (Mark 16:1). Finding the stone rolled away she quickly returned to the city and told Peter and John that the body of Jesus had been taken away (John 20:1, 2). Then, following the apostles, she returned again to the garden and lingered there after they had gone. To her first Jesus appeared (Mark 16:9; John 20:11–17), and she reported his resurrection to the other disciples (John 20:18). Nothing further is known of her history.

4. Mary of Bethany. A woman who, with her sister Martha, lived in "a certain village" (Luke 10:38 seq.) which John reveals to have been Bethany (John 11:1; 12:1 seq.), about a mile e. of the summit of the Mount of Olives. On the first occasion when Jesus is recorded to have visited their house (Luke 10:38–42), Mary appears as eager to receive his instruction. Martha requested Jesus to bid Mary help her in serving the entertainment, but he replied: "But one thing is needful: for Mary hath chosen the good part, which shall not be taken away from her" (Luke 10:42, R.V.). John (ch. 11) further relates that Mary had a brother named Lazarus whom the Lord raised from the dead. When Jesus reached the house, after Lazarus had been 4 days dead, Mary at first "still sat in the house" (John 11:20, R.V.), but afterward was summoned by Martha to meet the Lord who had called for her (v. 28). As Martha had done, Mary exclaimed, "Lord, if thou hadst been here, my brother had not died," and the grief of the sisters deeply moved the sympathetic Saviour. Afterward, 6 days before his last passover (John 12:1), Jesus came to Bethany, and a supper was made in his honor in the house of Simon the leper (Mark 14:3). While it was in progress Mary brought an alabaster box of pure ointment, very costly, and, breaking the box, poured the ointment on the head of Jesus (ibid.), and anointed his feet, wiping them with her hair (John 12:3). It was an act of rare devotion, testifying both to her gratitude and to her sense of the high dignity of him whom she honored. Judas, and some others of the disciples, were disposed to find fault with the waste; but Jesus commended the act and declared that "wheresoever the gospel shall be preached throughout the whole world, that also which this woman hath done shall be spoken of for a memorial of her" (Matt. 26:6–13; Mark 14:3–9). He looked upon her act also as a loving, though doubtless unintentional, consecration of him to his approaching sacrifice (John 12:7, 8).

5. Mary the mother of Mark. The Christian woman in whose house the disciples had met to pray for the release of Peter, when he was imprisoned by Herod Agrippa, and to which Peter at once went when delivered by the angel (Acts 12:12). Her son was the author of our Second Gospel; see MARK. She was evidently in comfortable circumstances (v. 13), and her house is supposed to have been one of the principal meeting places of the early Jerusalem Christians. According to A.V. in Col. 4:10 she was the sister of Barnabas; but R.V. correctly translates "cousin" instead of "sister's son," and it does not appear whether Mark's relationship to Barnabas was on his father's or his mother's side. Nothing is told us of Mary's husband.

6. Mary of Rome. A Christian woman at Rome to whom Paul sent his salutation (Rom. 16:6). The A.V. reads "who bestowed much

labor on *us*," implying that Mary at one time
had greatly assisted the apostle. The R.V.,
however, properly reads "who bestowed much
labor on *you*." Mary had thus been an active
worker in the Christian cause at Rome. Beyond this reference we know nothing of her.

G. T. P. (rev., H. S. G.)

Mas'a·loth (măs'à-lŏth). See MESALOTH.

Mas'chil (măs'kĭl) [attentive, intelligent, or
rendering intelligent]. A Hebrew word occurring in the titles of Psalms 32; 42; 44; 45;
52; 53; 54; 55; 74; 78; 88; 89; 142. Although
the meaning is obscure, it probably signifies
a didactic psalm (cf. Ps. 32:8, "I will instruct," same root); or it may mean a meditation, a skillful psalm.

Mash (măsh). A branch of the Aramaeans
(Gen. 10:23). Called in I Chron. 1:17 Meshech (the LXX has *Mosoch* in both places).
This is due to its confusion by copyists with
the more familiar name; or else, if the original text, it points to an intermingling of
Japhetic and Semitic people in Meshech.

Ma'shal (mā'shăl). See MISHAL.

Ma'son. A workman skilled to hew and saw
stones into shape for building purposes and
erect walls (II Sam. 5:11; I Kings 7:9; I
Chron. 22:2; II Chron. 24:12). The art made

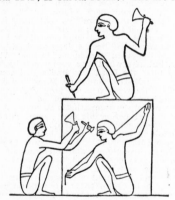

Masons at Work in Ancient Egypt

great progress among the ancient Egyptians;
as the pyramids, built under Dyn. IV, and
numerous temples show. The Hebrews served
in brick and mortar while they were in bondage in Egypt (Ex. 1:11, 14); but there is no
mention of their being employed in shaping
and laying stones. In Solomon's time the
Phoenicians had more skill in the art than the
Hebrews, who as yet had not had occasion to
erect great structures of stone, and Phoenician
masons were accordingly hired to build the
Temple and Solomon's palace. They managed
blocks of stone 12 and 15 feet in length and
even longer, and proportionately broad and
high (I Kings 7:10). But they were doubtless
Hebrew workmen who afterward erected walls
and fortresses, built aqueducts and reservoirs,
arches and bridges, and fashioned columns
(II Chron. 33:14; Ezra 3:10; S. of Sol. 5:15;
Jos. *Antiq.* xv. 11, 2). They also understood
the use of the plummet (Amos 7:7; Zech.
4:10; Isa. 28:17).

Ma·so'ra (mà-sō'rà), **Mas'o·retes** (măs'ō-
rĕts), **Mas'o·ret'ic** (măs'ō-rĕt'ĭk). See OLD
TESTAMENT.

Mas'pha (măs'fà). See MIZPEH 2 and 5.

Mas're·kah (măs'rê-kà) [perhaps, vine-
yard]. An Edomite city (Gen. 36:36; I Chron.

1:47); Jebel el-Mushrāk, about 22 miles s.s.w.
of Ma'ān.

Mas'sa (măs'à) [a load, a burden]. A tribe
descended from Ishmael (Gen. 25:14; I
Chron. 1:30; cf. Prov. 30:1 and 31:1, R.V.
marg.); generally identified with the Masani,
a tribe of the Arabian desert near the Persian
Gulf, n.e. of Dumah. The Assyrian inscriptions refer to Massa, Tema, and Nebaioth; cf.
Gen. 25:13–15.

Mas'sah (măs'à) [testing, temptation]. A
name given by Moses to the place at Horeb
where the smitten rock yielded water, because
the Israelites there in unbelief put Jehovah to
a test (Ex. 17:7; Ps. 95:8, 9, R.V.; and also
Deut. 33:8, where the thought is expressed
that Jehovah tested the fideli y of the Levites
in the person of Moses). In Ex. 17:7 the place
is called Meribah also; possibly so in the 2
other passages already cited, although there
2 distinct events and places may be in the
writer's mind. The name Massah alone is used
in Deut. 6:16; 9:22. Israel's rebelliousness
against Jehovah soon after leaving Egypt (ch.
9:7), and apparently before reaching Horeb
(v. 8), is dwelt upon; the event at Massah is
mentioned in the same breath with similar
even s that occurred in the immediate vicinity
of Horeb (v. 22). See MERIBAH 1.

Ma·thu'sa·la (mà-thū'sà-là). See METHUSE-
LAH.

Ma'tred (mā'trĕd) [perhaps, expulsion].
The mother-in-law of Hadar, king of Edom
(Gen. 36:39; I Chron. 1:50).

Ma'tri (mā'trī) [rainy]. A Benjamite family, from which sprang Kish and his son King
Saul (I Sam. 10:21).

Mat'tan (măt'ăn) [a gift]. 1. A priest of
Baal slain before the altar of that god during
the revolution which led to the death of Athaliah and the elevation of Joash to the throne
of Judah (II Kings 11:18; II Chron. 23:17).
2. Father of Shephatiah (Jer. 38:1).

Mat'ta·nah (măt'à-nà) [a gift]. One of the
stations of the Israelites in or near the Moabite territory (Num. 21:18 *seq.*); el-Medeiyineh, at the wadies Wāleh and eth-Themed.

Mat'ta·ni'ah (măt'à-nī'à) [gift of Jehovah].
1. A singer, son of Heman, in David's time
(I Chron. 25:4, 16).
2. A Levite, of the sons of Asaph, and
founder of a branch of the family (II Chron.
20:14). Probably he himself is mentioned in
I Chron. 9:15, and Neh. 13:13; and the representative of the house in Neh. 12:8; cf. Ezra
2:41; Neh. 11:17, 22; 12:25.
3. A Levite descended from Asaph. He was
one of those who aided King Hezekiah in his
work of religious reformation (II Chron.
29:13).
4. A son of King Josiah. He was placed on
the throne and his name was altered to Zedekiah by Nebuchadnezzar (II Kings 24:17);
see ZEDEKIAH 4.
5–8. Four Hebrews, a son of Elam, a son of
Zattu, a son of Pahath-moab, and a son of
Bani, who were induced by Ezra to put away
their foreign wives (Ezra 10:26, 27, 30, 37).

Mat'ta·tha (măt'à-thà) [gift (of God)]. A
son of Nathan and grandson of King David
(Luke 3:31).

Mat'ta·thah (măt'à-thà). See MATTATTAH.

Mat'ta·thi'as (măt'à-thī'ăs) [Greek form of
Mattithiah, gift of Jehovah (see LXX, I
Chron. 9:31; 25:3)]. 1 and 2. A name borne
by 2 ancestors of Christ, separated from each
other by 5 generations, who lived after the
time of Zerubbabel (Luke 3:25, 26).
3. A priest, founder of the Maccabee family
(I Macc., ch. 2). See MACCABEE.

4. Son of Absalom, and a captain in the army of Jonathan Maccabaeus. He distinguished himself at the bat le of Hazor by remaining at the side of Jonathan when all the other captains save one had fled (I Macc. 11:70). He was perhaps a bro.her of Jonathan, son of Absalom (ch. 13:11).

5. Son of Simon Maccabaeus. His father, his brother, and he were treacherously murdered by his brother-in-law in the castle of Dok (I Macc. 16:14–17). See JUDAS 5.

Mat'tat·tah (măt'ă-tä), in A.V. Mat'ta·thah [gift (of Jehovah)]. A son of Hashum, induced by Ezra to put away his foreign wife (Ezra 10:33).

Mat'te·na'i (măt'ē-nā'ī) [gift of Jehovah]. 1. A priest, head of the father's house Joiarib in the time of Joiakim (Neh. 12:19).

2 and 3. Two Hebrews, a son of Hashum and a son of Bani, each of whom was induced to put away his foreign wife (Ezra 10:33, 37).

Mat'than (măt'thăn) [gift (of God)]. A near ancestor of Joseph and, in law, of Christ (Matt. 1:15).

Mat'that (măt'thăt) [gift (of God)]. Two ancestors of Christ: the one near, the other quite remote (Luke 3:24, 29).

Mat'thew (măth'ū) [Gr. Maththaios, Mattaios, from Heb. Mattithyāh, gift of Jehovah]. A publican or taxgatherer, in the service either of the Roman or Herodian Government, stationed at Capernaum. While sitting at "the place of toll" (A.V., "the receipt of custom"), he was called by Jesus to become his follower and, leaving his business, he immediately obeyed (Matt. 9:9; Mark 2:14; Luke 5:27). He was afterward appoin ed one of the twelve apostles (Matt. 10:3; Mark 3:18; Luke 6:15). Mark and Luke give his name as Levi and state that his father was named Alphaeus. Either he had originally 2 names, as was not uncommon among the Jews, or he received the name Matthew when he became a Christian, as Simon did that of Peter. He is always called Matthew in the lists of apostles and as the author of our First Gospel. The acceptance by Jesus of a publican as a disciple evidently led others of the outcast classes to follow him and increased the opposition of the Pharisees. This appears at the feast which Matthew gave to Jesus soon after his conversion, when many "publicans and sinners" were present, and when, in answer to the criticism of the Pharisees, the Lord made the famous reply, "I am not come to call the righteous but sinners to repentance" (Matt. 9:10–13; Mark 2:15–17; Luke 5:29–32). Matthew himself does not say that the feast was in his house (Matt. 9:10), but Mark (ch. 2:15) and Luke (ch. 5:29) do, and Luke adds that it was a great feast. Some have identified Matthew's father Alphaeus with the father of James the Less; but Matthew and James are not joined together in the lists of apostles as other pairs of brothers are. The identification is therefore to be rejected. Matthew appears for the last time in the N.T. among the apostles after Christ's resurrection (Acts 1:13). Tradition sta es that he first preached among the Jews, and from the charac.er of his Gospel, this is not improbable.

The Gospel According to Matthew is the 1st of our 4 Gospels. Its contents may be arranged as follows:

1. The descent, birth, and infancy of the royal Messiah (chs. 1 and 2). The special object of this section is to set forth Jesus as the son of David and the Christ of prophecy.

2. Introduction to the public ministry of Christ (chs. 3:1 to 4:17), relating the preparatory work of the Baptist, the baptism and temptation of Jesus, and the latter's settlement in Capernaum in accordance with prophecy.

3. The Galilean ministry of Christ (chs. 4:18 to 9:35). This important section begins with Christ's call of the 4 leading disciples (ch. 4:18–22), and a summary description of his teaching and healing, and of his fame throughout Palestine (ch. 4:19–25). Then follows, as an example of his teaching, the Sermon on the Mount (chs. 5 to 7), to which is appended a collection of incidents, mostly miracles, which illustrated his teaching (chs. 8:1 to 9:34).

4. The mission of the apostles (chs. 9:36 to 10:42), beginning with an account of Christ's compassion on the shepherdless people, his appointment of the Twelve, and his instructions to them.

5. Christ in conflict with increasing opposition (chs. 11:1 to 15:20), comprising the inquiry of the Baptist and Christ's discourse concerning John, together with other remarks occasioned by popular unbelief; the opposition of the Pharisees, beginning with the Sabbath controversy and culminating in the charge that Jesus was in league with Beelzebub, together with Christ's reply and his refusal to give them a sign; the visit of his mother and brethren; a collection of the parables of Jesus spoken at this time; his (2d) rejection at Nazareth; Herod's inquiry and the death of the Baptist; the feeding of the 5,000 and walking on the water; Christ's final rupture with the Pharisees in Galilee and his denunciation of their formalism.

6. Chris.'s retirement from Capernaum and instruction of his disciples (chs. 15:21 to 18:35), comprising the healing of the daughter of the woman of Canaan, the feeding of 4,000, refusal of a sign and warning against the leaven of the Pharisees and Sadducees, the confession and rebuke of Peter, Christ's first prediction of his death, his transfiguration and the cure of the demoniac boy; the return to Capernaum, the provision of tribute money, and instruction of the disciples concerning the humble, self-denying, loving, and forgiving spirit of true discipleship.

7. The closing ministry of Christ in Perea and Judea (chs. 19; 20), comprising instructions about divorce, blessing the children, the rich young ruler, the parable of the Laborers in the Vineyard, the ascent to Jerusalem, with another prediction of his death, the request of James and John, and the healing of two blind men at Jericho; cf. Bartimaeus, Mark 10:46–52.

8. The last week of Christ's ministry (chs. 21 to 28), comprising the triumphal entry and the cleansing of the Temple; the withering of the barren fig tree; the deputation from the sanhedrin; the parables of the Two Sons, the Wicked Husbandmen, and the Marriage of the King's Son; the questions of the Pharisees, Sadducees, and a lawyer, with Christ's question in reply concerning the son of David; woes against the scribes and Pharisees; the eschatological discourse on Olivet, followed by the parables of the Virgins and of the Talents and a description of the Last Judgment. Then follow the treachery of Judas, the last passover, the agony in Gethsemane, the arrest and trial of Jesus before the sanhedrin, Peter's denials, the remorse of Judas, the trial before Pilate, and the crucifixion and burial. The last chapter relates the appearance of Jesus to the women, the report of the Roman watch, and the gathering of Christ with his disciples on a mountain in Galilee, when he gave them the commission to preach his gospel to the world and promised to be always with them.

The arrangement of this Gospel is chronological only in general outline. In the 2d half, indeed, beginning with ch. 14:6, it follows with seldom a deviation what is probably the true order of events, but this is because that order naturally agreed with the Evangelist's object. This orderly arrangement is manifested in numerical groupings of 3, 5, and 7 units. There are 3 sets of 14 generations each in the genealogy of ch. 1. Three kinds of hypocritical ostentation are warned against in ch. 6—in connection with almsgiving, prayer, and fasting. Chapter 13 has 7 parables. Furthermore the author deliberately calls attention to 5 great discourses of our Lord by concluding each with a formula such as: "And it came to pass, when Jesus had finished these words" (chs. 7:28; 11:1; 13:53; 19:1; 26:1). Thus the Sermon on the Mount (chs. 5 to 7), the charge to the apostles (ch. 10), the parabolic teaching concerning the Kingdom of heaven (ch. 13), the teaching concerning the Church and Christian relationship (ch. 18), and that concerning the end of the age (ch. 24 seq.) are plainly marked by this formula as key sections in the structure of the Gospel. He sets forth Jesus as the royal Messiah, who brought about the fulfillment of law and prophecy, and established in the Church, by his redeeming work and spiritual teaching, the true Kingdom of God, which is meant to embrace all nations. The fulfillment of prophecy is frequently noted (chs. 1:22, 23; 2:5, 6, 15, 17, 18, 23; 3:3; 4:14–16; 8:17; 11:10; 12:17–21; 13:14, 15, 35; 21:4, 5; 26:24, 31, 56; 27:9, 35), and there are about a hundred quotations, more or less formal, from the O.T. While Matthew wrote from the Hebrew point of view, he brings out the destination of the gospel for the Gentiles (e.g., chs. 8:10–12; 10:18; 21:43; 22:9; 24:14; 28:19), represents the opposition to Christ of current Judaism (e.g., chs. 5:20–48; 6:5–18; 9:10–17; 12:1–13, 34; 15:1–20; 16:1–12; 19:3–9; 21:12–16; 23, etc.), and shows by his explanations of terms (chs. 1:23; 27:33), places (chs. 2:23; 4:13), Jewish beliefs (ch. 22:23) and customs (ch. 27:15), that he wrote not merely for Jews, but for all believers.

The question of authorship is no easy problem. There is a strong and consistent tradition in the Early Church that Matthew was the author. This tradition is confirmed: (1) by the conclusive evidence, furnished by the contents, that the writer of this Gospel was a Jewish Christian emancipated from Judaism; (2) by the improbability that so important a book would have been attributed to so obscure an apostle without good reason; (3) by the likelihood that a publican would keep records; (4) by the modest way in which the writer speaks of the feast given by Matthew to Jesus (ch. 9:10; cf. Luke 5:29).

On the other hand, many scholars feel that internal evidence makes it difficult to accept this tradition of the Early Church. Matthew reproduces about 90 per cent of the subject matter of Mark in language very largely identical with that of Mark. Now it is highly improbable that an apostle would have used as a major source the work of one who in all likelihood had not been an eyewitness of the ministry of Jesus. Papias, bishop of Hierapolis in Phrygia, writing c. A.D. 140, may provide a key to this problem. Eusebius (H.E. iii. 39, 16) quotes him as saying, "Matthew collected the logia (sayings, or oracles) in the Hebrew language, and each one interpreted them as he was able." This brief sentence is probably to be interpreted as follows. The Apostle Matthew (c. A.D. 50) wrote down Jesus' sayings in Aramaic. These sayings, with a brief frame of historical narrative were translated into Greek and thus constituted the document that scholars designate by the symbol Q (for German Quelle, source). This document and material from Mark and other sources were woven into what is now our First Gospel. By this hypothesis, the name

Matthew, originally attached to the Aramaic source of Q, was transferred to the whole work which had incorporated it.

The date of the completed Gospel is difficult to determine. Many modern scholars date it variously from shortly after A.D. 70 to c. 85, but conservative scholars generally assign it to a date just prior to the Fall of Jerusalem in A.D. 70. The baptismal formula (Matt. 28:19), which has been regarded as evidence of a late date, is matched by a similar formula in a benediction (II Cor. 13:14); and the word church for an organized body (Matt. 18:17) was early used, being so employed by Stephen, Paul, and James (Acts 7:38; 20:28; James 5:14). The Fall of Jerusalem seems not to have occurred (Matt. 5:35; 24:16). The most ancient tradition, that of Irenaeus (c. A.D. 175), assigns it to the period when Peter and Paul were preaching the gospel in Rome (Haer. iii. 1, 1). The place of its composition is unknown; Jerusalem and Antioch in Syria have been suggested. The acquaintance with it shown by postapostolic writers in widely scattered localities proves that it obtained, as soon as it was published, general circulation.

G. T. P. (rev., H. S. G.)

Mat·thi·as (mă-thī′ăs) [probably a variant form of Mattathias, gift of Jehovah (see LXX, I Chron. 25:21, MS., A)]. One of those disciples who companied with the followers of Christ from the time of Christ's baptism and was a witness of the resurrection. He accordingly had qualifications for the apostleship. The question whether he or another disciple with similar qualifications should fill the place in the number of the Twelve made vacant by the treachery of Judas was submitted to God by prayer; and when lots were given, Matthias was chosen, and he was at once numbered with the apostles (Acts 1:21–26). Nothing more is known of his history.

Mat·ti·thi·ah (măt′ĭ-thī′ă) [gift of Jehovah].
1. A Levite, son of the singer Jeduthun (I Chron. 25:3), and himself one of the musicians of the sanctuary who played the harp (ch. 15:18, 21). He was afterward made head of the 14th of the courses into which the musicians were divided by David (ch. 25:21).
2. A Levite of the sons of Korah, family of Kohath. He was the eldest son of Shallum, and was placed in charge over the things that were baked in pans (I Chron. 9:31).
3. A son of Nebo, induced by Ezra to put away his foreign wife (Ezra 10:43).
4. A priest or Levite who supported Ezra when he addressed the returned exiles regarding the Law (Neh. 8:4).

Mat·tock. An instrument for loosening the soil, shaped like a pickax or hoe with two blades in different planes, the cutting edge of one resembling that of an ax, and the other that of an adz. It is used specially for grubbing up the roots of trees. In the O.T. mattock is the rendering of: 1. Heb. mahărēshāh, cutting instrument, in I Sam. 13:20, 21. Mahăresheth, a similar word from the same root, occurs in v. 20, and is believed to denote the plowshare. Both of these implements are made of metal. 2. The Hebrew ma'dēr, dressing instrument. It was used in digging and dressing vineyards (Isa. 7:25).

In II Chron. 34:6 the Hebrew is believed to be corrupt, and for mattock of the A.V., the R.V. substitutes ruins (axes, in the margin).

Maul. The rendering of Heb. mēphĭs, breaker, a weapon of war (Prov. 25:18).

Maz·za·roth (măz′ă-rŏth) [mazzārŏth]. A feature of the starry heavens (Job 38:32). The margin of both English versions interprets it as the signs of the zodiac, equivalent to Heb. mazzālŏth (II Kings 23:5 marg.). The parallel passage, Job 9:9, suggests that the *mazzārōth* are a constellation of the s. sky, a cluster among the stars that are chambered in the s.

Mead'ow. 1. The rendering of Heb. *'āhū* in A.V. of Gen. 41:2, 18. The word denotes reed grass or, as it is rendered in Job 8:11, flag.
2. The rendering of Heb. *ma'āreh* (Judg. 20:33, A.V.); see MAAREH-GEBA.

Me'ah (mē'*á*) [a hundred]. A tower at Jerusalem not far from that of Hananeel and the sheep gate (Neh. 3:1; 12:39); R.V. Hammeah; here *Ham-* is the Hebrew definite article. See JERUSALEM, II. 3.

Meal Of'fer·ing. See OFFERINGS.

Meals. The Israelites ate in the morning and in the evening (Ex. 16:12; I Kings 17:6; John 21:4, 5, 12). This custom did not forbid a morsel at other hours. Laborers partook of a light repast at noon (Ruth 2:14). Later the ascetic Essenes did with 2 meals, the 1st at the 5th hour or 11 o'clock in the morning, and the other in the evening (Jos. *War* ii. 8, 5). Among the stricter Jews of the time of Christ,

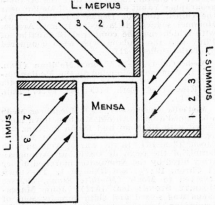

L. MEDIUS

MENSA

L. SUMMUS

L. IMUS

Diagram of a Roman Table and Couches
(*Mensa*, table; *Lectus summus*, highest couch; *Lectus medius*, middle couch; *Lectus imus*, lowest couch)

the fast of the night was not broken by a meal on an ordinary day before 9 o'clock, which was the hour of prayer (Acts 2:15); and on the Sabbath food was not served before 12 o'clock, when the service in the synagogue was over (Jos. *Life* 54). The chief meal of the day took place in the evening (Jos. *War* i. 17, 4; *Life* 44; cf. Gen. 19:1–3; Ex. 12:18). Feasts were sometimes spread at noon by the Egyptians and Syrians (Gen. 43:16; I Kings 20:16).

As to the posture at meals, the ancient Hebrews, like the ancient Egyptians and Greeks and modern Arabs, were in the habit of sitting, probably on mats spread on the floor or ground. Reclining on couches came into use later (Esth. 1:6; 7:8; Ezek. 23:41; John 21:20). Three couches were ordinarily placed about a table, being arranged so as to form 3 sides of a square and leave the 4th side open for the admittance of servants with the dishes. The couches were designated highest, middle, and lowest respectively, the highest being to the right of the servants as they approached the table. Generally, only 3 persons occupied a couch, but occasionally 4 or 5. The body lay diagonally on the couch, the head being near the table and the feet stretched out toward the back of the couch. The left elbow rested on a cushion and supported the upper part of the body. The right arm remained free. The head of the person reclining in front of another rested on or near the breast of him who lay behind (John 13:23; 21:20). The 3 positions on each couch were also termed highest, middle, and lowest, the highest person being the one who had nobody at his back. The position of honor (Matt. 23:6, R.V.) was the highest place on the highest couch. Women took their meals with men, occasionally at least (Ruth 2:14; I Sam. 1:4; Job 1:4).

The Hebrews and Greeks, like the modern Arabs, washed their hands before eating (Matt. 26:23), since generally there was a common dish into which the hand of each was dipped. This custom became a ritual observance with the Pharisees, and as such was condemned by Christ (Mark 7:1–13). A blessing was asked before the meal by Samuel (I Sam. 9:13), by Christ (Matt. 14:19; 15:36; 26:26), and by the early Christians (Acts 27:35). It was also customary among the Jews in the time of Christ (cf. Jos. *War* ii. 8, 5). A piece of bread served as a spoon and was dipped into the bowl of grease or meat, or the thick soup or po.tage was ladled with the hollow hand into a dish. Occasionally separate portions were served in the same manner to each (Ruth 2:14; I Sam. 1:4; John 13:26). Prayer after meals developed out of Deut. 8:10 (Jos. *War* ii. 8, 5).

At pretentious meals on festive occasions, when a large company of guests gathered about the table, greater ceremony was observed. It was courteous to receive the guest with a kiss (Luke 7:45), and indispensable to provide water for him to wash his feet and hands with (Gen. 18:4; 19:2; Luke 7:44; John 2:6). He came in his best attire, of course, and often with the hair, beard, feet, and sometimes clothes, perfumed (Amos 6:6; Wisd. of Sol. 2:7). Occasionally he was anointed at the house of the host (Luke 7:38; John 12:3). The participants at the feast sometimes wore a wreath on the head (Isa. 28:1; Wisd. of Sol. 2:7, 8; Jos. *Antiq.* xix. 9, 1). They were arranged according to rank (I Sam. 9:22; Luke 14:8; and so in Egypt, Gen. 43:33). Portions of food were placed before each (I Sam. 1:4), and the guest of honor received a larger or choicer share (chs. 1:5; 9:24; so in Egypt, Gen. 43:34). A ruler was sometimes appointed to preside at the feast, taste the viands, and direct the proceedings (Ecclus. 32:1, 2; John 2:9, 10). The banquet was rendered merrier by music (Isa. 5:12; Ecclus. 32:5, 6), singing (II Sam. 19:35; Amos 6:4–6), dancing (Matt. 14:6; Luke 15:25), and riddles (Judg. 14:12). These customs receive illustration from the manner of feasts among the Greeks. The guests were apt to be placed according to rank, and the guest of honor received the choicest food (Herod. vi. 57; Homer *Iliad* vii. 321). At the conclusion of the meal garlands and various kinds of perfumes were given to the guests, and wine was served. Ordinarily a governor, chosen from among the company (Xen. *Anabasis* vi. 1, 30), presided. His command was law. He tasted the food and drink before they were placed on the table, directed the servants, fixed the proportion in which the wine and water were mixed, and determined the quantity which each of the company should drink. He also proposed the amusements. The pleasure was heightened by songs, and by the spectacle of dancing (Pla.o *Sympos.* ii., *Leges* 671; Xen. *Anabasis* vi. 1, 3–13).

A gruesome custom existed among the Egyptians, according to Herodotus (ii. 78). At the banquets of the wealthy the image of a dead body in a coffin was carried round and shown to each of the company with the remark: "Look upon this, then drink and enjoy yourself; for when dead you will be like this."

Me·a'rah (mê-ā'rá) [a cave]. A place near Sidon (Josh. 13:4); commonly, but without certainty, identified with a district of caves, on the top of Lebanon, e. of Sidon, known as Mughār Jezzīn or caves of Jezzīn. Conder suggests Mogheirīyeh, 6 miles n.e. of Sidon.

Meas'ure.

I. MEASURES OF LENGTH.

The unit was the cubit, 18 inches or more; see CUBIT.

> 4 fingers = 1 handbreadth
> 3 handbreadths = 1 span
> 2 spans = 1 cubit

The finger, accordingly, was ¾ inch. In the Greco-Roman period distance was measured by miles and stades. 5,000 Roman feet = 1 Roman mile = about 1,482 meters = about 4,860 English feet. The Roman mile equaled about .92 of an English mile. The stadium (plural stadia; Luke 24:13, furlong) in the race course at Olympia equaled 630.8 English feet; the Attic and the Roman stadium measured 607 English feet.

II. MEASURE OF AREA.

In most countries it was the custom to state land area in terms of that which a yoke of oxen could plough in a day. A second ancient measure was the amount of seed required to sow an area. Acre is the rendering of Heb. ṣemed, yoke of oxen (I Sam. 14:14; Isa. 5:10). The Roman actus (furrow) was 120 Roman feet in length, and the unit of Roman land measure was the square actus. The jugerum (yokeland) was 2 actus long and 1 wide, i.e., it consisted of 2 square actus or .622 acre.

III. MEASURES OF CAPACITY.

Our knowledge of ancient measures is not exact, and there were variations in the standards at different periods. The equivalents in U.S. values given below are to be understood as representing merely approximate values. The unit was the ephah for dry substances and the bath for liquids, the ephah and the bath being of equal capacity (Ezek. 45:11), and containing 1.05 bushels, U. S. dry measure, or 9.8 gallons, U. S. wine measure. See BATH; EPHAH, I.

Liquid Measure

> 12 logs = 1 hin
> 6 hins = 1 bath
> 10 baths = 1 homer, or cor (Ezek. 45:14)

The log, accordingly, contained .54 quart, and the hin 1.62 gallons, U. S. measure. A 3d part, Heb. shālish (Ps. 80:5; Isa. 40:12, rendered measure) was probably the 3d of an ephah, and hence corresponded to a seah. The Greek measure metrētēs (John 2:6, rendered firkin) contained in Athens 39 liters or 10.3 U. S. gallons.

Dry Measure

> 4 logs = 1 kab
> 6 kabs = 1 seah
> 3 seahs or measures ⎫
> or ⎬ 1 ephah (Ex.
> 10 omers or tenth parts ⎭ = 16:36; Num.
> 10 ephahs = 1 homer (Ezek. 45:11)   15:4, LXX)

The kab was equivalent to 1.86 quarts, U. S. measure, and the seah to 1.4 pecks, U. S. measure. The Greek choinix (Rev. 6:6, rendered measure) is estimated at 1.08 liters or .98 quart. The Roman modius (Matt. 5:15, rendered bushel) contained .96 peck, or 7.68 U. S. dry quarts.

Meat Of'fer·ing. See OFFERINGS.

Me·bun'nai (mê-bŭn'ĭ) [built]. A Hushathite, one of David's mighty men (II Sam. 23:27). The name is probably to be read Sibbecai, in accordance with ch. 21:18 and I Chron. 11:29; 20:4; 27:11.

Me·che'rath·ite (mê-kē'rǎth-īt). A person related by birth or residence to Mecherah (I Chron. 11:36). No person or place called Mecherah is known; cf. Maacathite in II Sam. 23:34.

Me·co'nah (mê-kō'nȧ), in A.V. **Me·ko'nah** [foundation]. A town in the territory of Judah (Neh. 11:28), named in connection with Ziklag and other towns of the extreme s.

Me'dad (mē'dăd) [beloved, friend]. A man who, though not present at the tabernacle when the Spirit was imparted to the elders, yet received the gift (Num. 11:26–29). See ELDAD.

Me'dan (mē'dăn). A tribe descended from Abraham and Keturah and mentioned in connection with Midian (Gen. 25:2; I Chron. 1:32). We.zstein observes that the Arabian geographer Yakut mentions Wadi Medān near the ruined town of Dedān (cf. Gen. 25:3). Hommel suggests it is Bedan in n.w. Arabia, with which may be compared Badanatha of Pliny and the Badana who were conquered by Tiglath-pileser III.

Mede (mēd), in A.V. once **Me'di·an** (Dan. 5:31). A person belonging to the Median nationality; a native or an inhabitant of Media (II Kings 17:6; Esth. 1:19; Isa. 13:17; Dan. 5:28, 31).

Med'e·ba (mĕd'ê-bȧ), in I Maccabees **Med'a·ba** (mĕd'ȧ-bȧ). An old Moabite town mentioned with Heshbon and Dibon in Num. 21:30. It was allotted to the tribe of Reuben (Josh. 13:9, 16). In the war of Ammon with Israel, in the reign of David, an Aramaean army hired by the Ammonites marched hither (I Chron. 19:7); see RABBAH 1. The town reverted to Moab (Moabite Stone, 30, see MOABITE STONE; Isa. 15:2). John Maccabaeus was seized and slain here by sons of Jambri or Ambri, a powerful family of the town. The act was revenged by his brothers Jonathan and Simon (I Macc. 9:36–42; Jos. Antiq. xiii. 1, 2, 4). John Hyrcanus took the town after a siege lasting nearly 6 months (Jos. Antiq. xiii. 9, 1). The ruins today are called Mādabā and are situated about 16 miles e. by s. of the mouth of the Jordan and 6 to the s. of Heshbon. They are on an eminence, from which the city extended e. into the fertile plain. There are remains of a city wall, and of churches and other buildings, which date mainly from Christian times. Outside the walls are the remains of a fine tank or reservoir 108 yards by 103 yards; it was 12 feet deep, but is now dry.

Me'di·a (mē'dĭ-ȧ). A country in Asia lying e. of the Zagros Mountains, s. of the Caspian Sea, w. of Parthia, and n. of Elam. Its length was about 600 miles, its breadth about 250, and its area about 150,000 square miles. But when the empire was at the greatest it extended beyond these limits, especially in the n.w. A great part of Media proper was a tableland 3,000 feet high. The rest consisted of 7 parallel mountain chains running from the n.w. to the s.e., with fertile and well-watered valleys between. The pasturage was excellent, and the country was noted for its horses. The aborigines were conquered by an Indo-European people, the Madai of Gen. 10:2 (cf. Herod. vii. 62).

The history of Media begins to be known in the 9th century B.C. The name of the Medes is met for the 1st time in the inscriptions of Shalmaneser III of Assyria who c.

835 invaded their land; 27 petty kings of Parsua land paid him tribute. These invasions were continued by Shamshi-Adad (825–812) and by Adad-Nirari III (812–782); the latter made his expeditions against Media in 801, 795, 790, and 787. Tiglath-pileser III in 737 invaded and annexed districts of Media. When Sargon captured Samaria, 722 B.C., he placed Israelites in the cities of the Medes (II Kings 17:6; 18:11). About 710 the Medes themselves were more thoroughly subjugated by Sargon, who exacted from them a tribute of the fine horses for which Media was celebrated. Sennacherib also boasts of tribute received from Media, and Esarhaddon placed governors in the country. In all this there is no trace of the Medes' forming a united nation under one king (contrary to Herod. i. 96 *seq.*). Under Phraortes, 674–653 B.C., Media became a formidable power. About 625 his son Cyaxares allied himself with Nabopolassar of Babylon, besieged and captured Nineveh, and terminated the Assyrian Empire (cf. Jos. *Antiq.* x. 5, 1). The victors divided the spoil between them, the share of Cyaxares being Assyria proper and the countries dependent on it toward the n. and n.w. The marriage of Nebuchadnezzar, son of Nabopolassar, with Amyitis (Amuhea, Amuhia), daughter of Cyaxares, cemented the alliance between Babylonia and Media, and greatly strengthened both monarchies. Cyaxares (652–612) was succeeded by Arbaces (612–585). Astyages, son of Cyaxares, reigned from 584 to 550; in the year 550 the Persians, whose country lay s. and s.e. of Media, successfully rebelled, and Cyrus, king of Anshan, became king of Media and Pers.a. The conquerors and the conquered were both of the fine Aryan race, and they became a dual nation, Medo-Persia. In 330 B.C. Media became a part of Alexander's empire. Af.er this conqueror's death it was united to Syria (I Macc. 6:56), and later it formed a part of the Parthian Empire.

In the Hebrew Scriptures the Medes are introduced as one of the nationalities which should take part in the capture of Babylon (Isa. 13:17 *seq.*; cf. also Jer. 51:11, 28); and Elam and Media are named as the 2 countries from which the conquerors of Babylon should come (Isa. 21:2, 9). On the capture of the great city by the Medo-Persians under Cyrus in 539, Darius the Mede took the kingdom of Babylon (Dan. 5:31; cf. v. 28). The Median Empire is the 2d kingdom (Dan. 2:39), the bear (ch. 7:5); the two-horned ram (ch. 8: 3–7, 20) is the symbol of Media and Persia. One horn was higher than the other, and the higher came up last (v. 3); in other words, the Median power came first, but the Persian, which followed, surpassed it in strength.

Me′di·an (mē′dĭ-ăn). See MEDE.

Med′i·cine. Egypt was early renowned for medical knowledge and skill. Cyrus of Persia sent to Egypt for an oculist, and Darius had Egyptian physicians at Susa (Herod. iii. 1, 129). For each disease there was a practitioner (Herod. ii. 84). They embalmed (Gen. 50:2); they treated diseases of the eye and feet (Herod. iii. 1, 129); women practiced midwifery (Ex. 1:15). They had many medicines (Jer. 46:11). Hammurabi fixed the physicians' fees, which varied according to the social rank of the patient. Bronze lancets were used in performing operations. Surgeons must have had considerable skill, since they operated upon the eyes for cataracts. In Greece the physicians of Crotona enjoyed the highest reputation, while those of Cyrene in Africa stood next (Herod. iii. 131).

The physician and his coadjutor the apothecary are mentioned in the writings of the Hebrews, beginning as early as the Exodus

from Egypt (II Chron. 16:12; Jer. 8:22; Matt. 9:12; Mark 5:26; Jos. *War* ii. 8, 6; and Ex. 30:35; Neh. 3:8; Eccl. 10:1; Ecclus. 38:8). The means and medicines which they employed for effecting cures were bandages (Isa. 1:6), applications of oil and of oil mingled with wine, and baths of oil (Isa. 1:6; Luke 10:34; James 5:14; Jos. *War* i. 33, 5), salves and poultices (II Kings 20:7; Jer. 8: 22), roots and leaves (Ezek. 47:12; Jos. *War* ii. 8, 6), and wine (I Tim. 5:23). "The Lord created medicines out of the earth; and a prudent man will have no disgust at them" (Ecclus. 38:4).

Med′i·ter·ra′ne·an (mĕd′ĭ-tĕ-rā′nē-ăn) **Sea.** The sea which lies between Europe and Africa. In Scripture it is referred to simply as the sea, since it was the chief one in the current thought of the Hebrews (Num. 13:29; Acts 10:6); or it is called the great sea (Num. 34:6; Josh. 15:47), or the hinder or western sea (Deut. 11:24; Joel 2:20; in A.V. utmost and uttermost), or the sea of the Philistines (Ex. 23:31). Its length is 2,000 miles, and its narrowest part is between Sicily and the African coast, where it is only 79 miles in width. In O.T. times the Phoenician navigators were acquainted with it in its entire extent from Syria to the Straits of Gibraltar, or the Pillars of Hercules.

Me·gid′do (mê-gĭd′ō), once **Me·gid′don** (mê-gĭd′ŏn) (Zech. 12:11). An important town in Palestine, settled c. 3500 B.C.; it is mentioned as captured by Thothmes III of Egypt c. 1479 B.C. The site has now been cleared to bedrock. Many of its first inhabitants lived in caves. A pavement of the last half of the 4th millennium has been found. The city wall of colossal masonry was built about 2500 B.C.; it had an original width of 13 feet, which subsequently was doubled. When found it still had a height of 11½ feet (cf. Deut. 1: 28).

When the Israelites entered Canaan, Megiddo had a native king, who was slain by Joshua (Josh. 12:21). It was within the limits of the tribe of Issachar; but was assigned to the Manassites, who, however, failed to drive out the Canaanite inhabitants (ch. 17:11; Judg. 1:27; I Chron. 7:29). It had waters, doubtless some stream, in its vicinity (Judg. 5:19), and was not far from Taanach and Beth-shean (ch. 1:27; I Kings 4:12). Solomon strengthened its fortifications (chs. 9:15–19; 10:26). Archaeological excavations have shown that Solomon had built at Megiddo well-constructed stables with cement floors for at least 400, and perhaps many more, horses. Ahaziah, king of Judah, wounded by the partisans of Jehu, fled to Megiddo, and died there (II Kings 9: 27). In the plain near the city the battle was fought between Necho and Josiah, in which the latter was killed (ch. 23:29; II Chron. 35:22; I Esdras 1:29). A great mourning for the death of the good king took place (II Chron. 35:25; Zech. 12:11). The name Megiddo enters into the composition of Harmagedon (Armageddon, *q.v.*). Robinson, and 500 years before him Moses hap-Parchi, considered Megiddo to have been at el-Lejjūn, on the chief tributary of the Kishon, about 9 miles w. slightly n. of Jezreel. The site, however, has been located at Tell el-Mutesellim, less than a mile n. of el-Lejjūn. Recent excavation has shown that the citadel crowned the height marked by Tell el-Mutesellim; while the camp of the legion, which the Romans stationed at Megiddo, stood 5 minutes' walk distant at the hamlet known as el-Lejjūn, which perpetuates Lat. *legio* (legion) and where bricks have been found bearing the stamp of the 6th legion. The place had great strategic importance, since it commanded the pass through the mountains between the plains of Sharon and Esdraelon.

Me·gil'loth (mē-gĭl'ōth) [scrolls]. See CANON, OLD TESTAMENT.

Me·het'a·bel (mē-hĕt'á-bĕl), in A.V. once **Me·het'a·beel** (mē-hĕt'á-bēl) (Neh. 6:10) [God benefi.s]. 1. The wife of Hadar, king of Edom (Gen. 36:39; I Chron. 1:50).
2. Father of a certain Delaiah (Neh. 6:10).

Me·hi'da (mē-hī'dá). Founder of a family of Nethinim, members of which returned from captivity (Ezra 2:43, 52).

Me'hir (mē'hēr) [price, hire]. A man of Judah (I Chron. 4:11).

Me·ho'la·thite (mē-hō'lá-thīt). A native or inhabitant of a place called Meholah (I Sam. 18:19); perhaps Abel-meholah, Elisha's native village.

Me·hu'ja·el (mē-hū'já-ĕl). Son of Irad, and father of Methushael, of the race of Cain (Gen. 4:18).

Me·hu'man (mē-hū'măn) [trusty, eunuch; *Pu'al* participle based on Aram. m°hēman (*Haph°el* passive participle), reliable]. One of the 7 chamberlains who served in the presence of King Ahasuerus (Esth. 1:10). See ABAGTHA.

Me·hu'nim (mē-hū'nĭm), **Me·hu'nims** (mē-hū'nĭmz). See MEUNIM.

Me'jar'kon (mē'jär'kŏn) [waters of yellow color]. A spot in the territory of Dan near Joppa (Josh. 19:46). A place on the river 'Aujâh has been suggested. The river flows from a swamp, through canes, willows, rushes, and grass, and then in a deeply hollowed channel, whence it carries away vegetable soil enough to render the water yellow. The stream is never dry, and in win.er is unfordable. It falls into the Mediterranean, 3¾ miles n. of Joppa.

Me·ko'nah (mē-kō'ná). See MECONAH.

Mel'a·ti'ah (mĕl'á-tī'á) [Jehovah has set free]. A Gibeonite who helped to rebuild part of the wall around Jerusalem (Neh. 3:7).

Mel'chi (mĕl'kī) [N.T. Gr., probably contraction of Malchijah (*q.v.*)]. A name borne by two ancestors of Christ who lived, the one before, the other after, the time of Zerubbabel (Luke 3:24, 28).

Mel'chi'ah (mĕl-kī'á). See MALCHIJAH.

Mel'chis'e·dec (mĕl-kĭz'ĕ-dĕk). See MELCHIZEDEK.

Mel'chi·shu'a (mĕl'kī-shōō'á). See MALCHISHUA.

Mel'chiz'e·dek (mĕl-kĭz'ĕ-dĕk), in A.V. of N.T. **Mel'chis'e·dec** [king of righteousness or probably originally, the (divine) king is righteousness, cf. Ps. 4:2]. King of Salem and priest of the Most High God (Gen. 14:18 seq.). By Salem, Jerusalem is probably meant; for: 1. The city was in existence, bore the name of Jerusalem, and was under a king before the conquest of Canaan by the Israelites. 2. The name Jerusalem means city or, to the Hebrew ear, foundation of peace or safety, so that Salem is an appropriate abbreviation. 3. Salem is used as the name of Jerusalem in Ps. 76:2. 4. The comparison of David's Lord with Melchizedek in Ps. 110:4 appears most apt if Melchizedek was king of the same city as David. Jerusalem is on the rou e from Hobah and Damascus to Hebron, whither Abraham was going.
Melchizedek, as described in Heb. 5:10; 6:20; ch. 7, was without father, without mother, without genealogy. This statement means that his pedigree is not recorded (cf. Ezra 2:59, 62). This mode of expression is ancient. Thus Urukagina, king of Lagash (c.

2450 B.C.), who is famous for his economic reforms, said that he had neither father nor mo.her, but that the god Ningirsu appointed him; he probably was a usurper. Melchizedek is further described as having neither beginning of days nor end of life, of whom it is testified that he lives. He suddenly emerges from the unknown and as suddenly disappears; it is not known whence he came or whither he went; neither birth nor death is assigned to him; he is a type of undying priesthood.

Melchizedek was priest of God Most High. 'ēl 'elyôn appears late among the Phoenicians as a title of Saturn, the begetter of heaven and earth. If 'ēl 'elyôn is not in Melchizedek's conception the absolutely only God, he is the highest, the God of the gods; a lofty idea, even though not a pure monotheism. Melchizedek came forth from his royal city to welcome the returning benefactor of the peoples of Canaan; and Abraham recognized him as a priest of the true God and public'y testified to sharing the same or a kindred faith by paying tithes to him who was representative of God Most High, to the priest who had ascribed the victory to the Creator of heaven and earth (cf. Acts 10:35).

The author of The Epistle to the Hebrews shows how great a personage Melchizedek was, to whom even Abraham, and through him virtually Levi, paid tithes, thus admitting their inferiority. When thus our Lord was made a high priest after the order of Melchizedek, he held a higher office than the Aaronic priesthood.

Me'le·a (mē'lĕ-á). An ancestor of Christ, who lived shortly after David (Luke 3:31).

Me'lech (mē'lĕk) [a king]. A son of Micah, a descendant of Saul and Jonathan (I Chron. 8:35; 9:41).

Mel'i·cu (mĕl'ĭ-kū). See MALLUCH 2.

Mel'i·ta (mĕl'ĭ-tá). The island where Paul was shipwrecked (Acts 28:1). Two islands bore this name in ancient times. One, now called Meleda, lies in the Adriatic Sea off the coast of Dalmatia; the other is now known as Malta. The latter is now probably universally believed to be the island where the ship of Paul was wrecked. This opinion is strongly confirmed by the fact that Mr. Smith, of Jordanhill, who was accustomed to sail in a yacht on the Mediterranean, investigated first the direction from which the wind Euroclydon or Euraquilo blew, then the course in which the ship would drift, and her probable rate of progress while she lay to under storm sails. The result was that he found she would reach Malta just about the time which the narrative in The Acts requires. The vessel had been driven to and fro in the (sea of) Adria (Ac s 27:27); see ADRIA. The traditional site of the shipwreck is St. Paul's Bay, on the n.e. coast of the island. In The Acts the inhabitants of the island are called barbarians because they were neither Greeks nor Romans.

Mel'on. A succulent plant and its edible fruit, in Hebrew 'abațțiah, which the Hebrews ate when in Egypt (Num. 11:5). Melons of all sorts were cultivated in Egypt, among which was the watermelon (*Citrullus vulgaris*).

Mel'zar (mĕl'zär) [from Akkad. mașșar, watch, sentry]. A man whom the chief of the eunuchs set over Daniel and his companions (Dan. 1:11, 16, A.V.). But in Hebrew it has the article before it; the R.V., J.V., and the margin of the A.V. therefore more properly translate it steward.

Mem (mĕm). The 13th letter of the Hebrew alphabet, from which is derived Gr.

mu (m), whence Latin and English *m*. It stands at the head of the 13th section of Ps. 119, in which section each verse of the original begins with this letter.

Mem'phis (mĕm'fĭs) [Gr. *Memphis*, from Coptic (Sahidic) *Memphe*, (Bohairic) *Memphi*, from Egyptian *Mn-nfr*, good permanence (the name of the pyramids of Pepi II)]. An important Egyptian city, said by Herodotus to have been built by Menes, the first historical king of Egypt, on land reclaimed by him from the Nile. It stood in the plain on the w. side of the Nile, about 10 miles above the apex of the delta. It became the metropolis and capital of Lower Egypt, and the 3d, the 4th, the 5th, the 7th, and the 8th dynasties were considered Memphite by Manetho. The deity specially worshiped in the city was Ptah. Memphis remained a flourishing city even after the capital was transferred to Thebes, and did not lose its importance until Alexandria was founded. To the Hebrews Memphis was known as Noph (Isa. 19:13, A.V.) and Moph (Heb. text Hos. 9:6). After the fall of Jerusalem and murder of Gedaliah, the Jews left in the land fled to Egypt, and some of them settled at Memphis (Jer. 44:1). Judgment was threatened against the city by Jeremiah and Ezekiel (Jer. 46:19; cf. also chs. 2:16 and 46:14; Ezek. 30:13, 16; cf. also Isa. 19:13; Hos. 9:6). A considerable part of Memphis existed in the Middle Ages, but materials from it were continually carried away to be used for building purposes in Cairo. Now it is all but gone, 2 Arab villages occupying its site. But 20 pyramids, which constituted its necropolis, and the celebrated sphinx present the most impressive memorials of its former greatness.

Me·mu'can (mē-mū'kăn) [perhaps from Old Pers. *magav*, Magian]. One of the 7 princes of Persia and Media at the court of Ahasuerus who saw the king's face. Memucan's counsel was adverse to Vashti (Esth. 1:14, 16, 21).

Men'a·hem (mĕn'à-hĕm) [comforter]. A son of Gadi who, when the news reached Tirzah that Shallum had murdered King Zechariah, went to Samaria, slew Shallum, and reigned in his stead (II Kings 15:14). The town of Tiphsah refused to admit him within its gates, so he captured it, and perpetrated cruelties on the inhabitants (v. 16). His throne was unsteady, and when Tiglath-pileser III, king of Assyria, invaded the land, Menahem purchased exemption from devastation for his realm and support for his own tottering throne by the payment of 1,000 talents of silver. The money was raised by a tax on the wealthiest men in Israel, who had to pay 50 shekels each. There must, therefore, have been more than 60,000 Israelites able to contribute this amount under compulsion. Tiglath-pileser, as recorded in the Assyrian sculptures, claims Menahem of Samaria as one of his tributaries. In religion the Israelite king adhered to the calf worship of Jeroboam I. He reigned 10 years, from about 744 to 735 B.C. inclusive, and was succeeded on the throne of Israel by his son Pekahiah (II Kings 15:17, 22).

Me'nan (mē'năn). See MENNA.

Me'ne (mē'nē). The 1st word of the Aramaic inscription written by a hand on the wall at Belshazzar's feast: MENE, MENE, TEKEL, UPHARSIN (Dan. 5:25), rendered in the margin of R.V., "Numbered, numbered, weighed, and divisions." These words appear in Theodotion as three in number: *manē thekel phares*, with which agrees the Vulgate: *mane thecel phares*. From this and from PERES (v. 28) it may be inferred that the original Aramaic text was *mᵉnē', tᵉḳēl,*

pᵉrēs. Mᵉnē' is a passive participle of the *Pᵉ'al; tᵉḳīl* and *pᵉris* (passive participles, *Pᵉ'al*) accordingly are vocalized to conform to *mᵉnē'*. The inscription therefore means, "Numbered, weighed, divided." It seems probable, however, that they were understood as nominal forms, for Josephus (Jos. *Antiq.* x. 11, 3) renders, "Number, weight, fragment." The repeated MENE (*mᵉnē'*) and UPHARSIN (*ûpharsîn*) accordingly are secondary. Daniel's interpretation follows (Dan. 5:26–28): "God hath numbered thy kingdom and brought it to an end," or transferred it; "thou art weighed in the balances, and art found wanting." In the case of UPHARSIN, *û* is the conjunction *and* and *pharsin* is the plural of *pᵉrēs*. In the interpretation of this word, the singular, PERES, is used (v. 28): "Thy kingdom is divided, and given to the Medes and Persians." With a play upon *pāras* (Persia, Persians) a double meaning is given to the mystic word.

Professor James A. Montgomery says: "The terms may have been actual language of the countinghouse or of the law, used of the settling of a bargain, winding up of a contract, settling a bankrupt's affairs, or the like." Another interpretation of *mᵉnē', tᵉḳēl, pᵉrēs* is that the words represent a series of money values: mina, shekel, half mina. There were two difficulties in reading the inscription: first, intelligent vocalization, since the consonants alone were written and the vowels were not supplied in Aramaic script; secondly, the correct interpretation of the words after they had been correctly pronounced.

Me'ni (mē'nī) [Heb. *mᵉnī*, fate, destiny; cf. Arab. *maniyyah*, which has same meaning. MENE (Dan. 5:25) is from the same root]. The name of the god of destiny, whom idolatrous Hebrews worshiped (Isa. 65:11 marg.).

Men'na (mĕn'nä), in A.V. **Me'nan** (mē'năn). An ancestor of Christ, who lived shortly after the time of David (Luke 3:31).

Me·nu'hoth (mē-nū'hŏth) [the resting places]. A place, if the present Hebrew text is correct, of which half the inhabitants were descended through Shobal from Caleb of the tribe of Judah (I Chron. 2:52, R.V.). The name, if vocalized as in the present Hebrew text, would not give rise to the gentile adjective of v. 54, which is rendered Manahathites. Perhaps, therefore, Menuhoth should be read Manahath (*q.v.*).

Me·on'e·nim (mē-ŏn'ē-nĭm) [augurs]. The augurs' oak or terebinth stood near Shechem (Judg. 9:37; not plain, as in A.V.). See MOREH 1.

Me·on'o·thai (mē-ŏn'ō-thī) [my habitations]. A man of Judah, the father of the inhabitants of Ophrah (I Chron. 4:14).

Meph'a·ath (mĕf'à-ăth) [splendor]. A town of the Reubenites (Josh. 13:18), since given to the Merarite Levites (ch. 21:37; I Chron. 6:79). In Jeremiah's time it was in the hands of the Moabites (Jer. 48:21). Probably at Tell Jawa, about 6 miles s. of 'Ammān.

Me·phib'o·sheth (mē-fĭb'ō-shĕth) [one who scatters or disperses shame]. 1. Son of King Saul by Rizpah, the daughter of Aiah. He was executed at the instance of the Gibeonites (II Sam. 21:8, 9).

2. The son of Jonathan. He was 5 years old when the tidings came of his father's and his grandfather's death at Gilboa. Under the influence of panic, the nurse took him up in her arms and fled with him; but in her flight she let him fall, so that he became lame in both his feet (II Sam. 4:4). For a long time he lived at Lo-debar, e. of the Jor-

dan, whence David called him to court to show him kindness for his father Jonathan's sake, restoring to him the estates of Saul and appointing him a place at the royal table (ch. 9:1-13). During the rebellion of Absalom he remained at Jerusalem, and was accused by his servant Ziba of disloyalty. David believed the accusation and transferred Mephibosheth's estates to Ziba. After the return of David, Mephibosheth attempted to clear himself of the charge, and David restored half the estates to him; but he declared that he did not wish the property, since he had his desire in the restoration of the king (chs. 16: 1-4; 19:24-30). He had a son Mica (ch. 9: 12), through whom the race of Jonathan was perpetuated. In I Chron. 8:34; 9:40 Mephibosheth is called Merib-baal (*q.v.*). This was probably his original name, *bôsheth*, shame, being substituted for *ba'al*, lord, by later writers when the word Baal had become distasteful through association with idolatry.

Me′rab (mē′răb) [perhaps, increase]. Saul's elder daughter (I Sam. 14:49). Her father promised her in marriage to David, and then, breaking faith, gave her as a wife to Adriel the Meholathite (ch. 18:17-19). Their 5 sons were given up by David to the Gibeonites to be put to death for the sin of Saul (II Sam. 21:8 marg.; cf. Greek of Lucian, which reads *Merob*).

Me•ra′iah (mê-rā′yà) [rebellious]. A priest, head of the father's house Seraiah in the days of Joiakim, a generation after the Exile (Neh. 12:12).

Me•ra′ioth (mê-rā′yŏth) [rebellious]. 1. A priest, son of Zerahiah (I Chron. 6:6, 7, 52). He lived while the house of Eli had charge of the tabernacle.
2. A priest, son of Ahitub and father of the younger Zadok of the high-priestly line (I Chron. 9:11; Neh. 11:11). He seems to have lived about half a century before the Exile.
3. A father's house among the priests in the days of Joiakim (Neh. 12:15). See MEREMOTH 1.

Me•ra′ri (mê-rā′rī) [bitter, but perhaps from Egypt. *mrr*, beloved]. Son of Levi, and founder of one of the 3 Levitical families (Gen. 46:11; Ex. 6:16; Num. 26:57).

Me•ra′rites (mê-rā′rīts). One of the 3 great families of the tribe of Levi. They were descended from Merari. In the wilderness they encamped on the n. side of the tabernacle (Num. 3:35), had under their charge its boards, bars, pillars, sockets, and vessels (chs. 3:36; 4:29-33), and were under the direction of Ithamar, the youngest son of Aaron (ch. 4:28). To enable them to carry these materials there were assigned to them 4 wagons and 8 oxen (ch. 7:8). They were subdivided into the Mahlites and the Mushites (ch. 3:20, 33); and at the first census in the wilderness numbered 6,200 males from a month old and upward (vs. 33, 34), being fewer in total number than the other families of Levi. Of these, 3,200 were from 30 to 60 years old (ch. 4:42-45), a larger proportion than in the other families. The cities assigned to them numbered 12, of which 4 were in the tribe of Zebulun, 4 in that of Reuben, and 4 in that of Gad; one of them, Ramoth-gilead, being a city of refuge (Josh. 21:34-40; I Chron. 6:63, 77-81). They were reorganized by David (I Chron. 23:6, 21-23). They had a due part with their fellow Levites in the musical service of the sanctuary, holding 6 of the 24 offices (I Chron. 6:31, 44; 25: 3). Members of the family are mentioned among those who aided in cleansing the Temple in Hezekiah's reign (II Chron. 29:12), and a small but notable company of them re-

turned with Ezra to Jerusalem after the Exile (Ezra 8:18, 19).

Mer′a•tha′im (mĕr′à-thā′ĭm) [twofold rebellion]. A symbolical name for Babylon (Jer. 50:21); the name *Marrātim* (S. Babylonia) may have suggested this use.

Mer′cu•ry (mûr′kû-rĭ), in A.V. **Mer•cu′ri•us** (mûr-kū′rĭ-ŭs). A deity worshiped by the Romans and, under the name of Hermes, by the Greeks also. He was the herald of the gods, and specially attended upon Jupiter. He is generally represented as equipped with the *caduceus*, a winged rod entwined by two serpents, a winged cap, and winged sandals. Paul and Barnabas were looked upon as gods by the people of Lystra, when the cripple was

The Flying Mercury, by Giovanni di Bologna

healed at the apostle's word; and as Paul was the chief speaker, they took him for Mercury and Barnabas, whom he accompanied, for Jupiter (Acts 14:12).

Mer′cy Seat. The covering of the Ark; the Heb. word *kappōreth* (from the Heb. root *kāphar*, to cover over in a figurative sense, to make propitiation, to make atonement), means covering (especially, if not exclusively, in the sense of a onement), and in Greek *hilastērion*, propitiatory (Ex. 26:34; Heb. 9:5). Its name did not suggest a mere lid, but brought to mind the act and place of atonement and the accomplished atonement. The rendering "mercy seat" is therefore a happy one, adopted by Tyndale from Luther. It was made of pure gold; its length was 2½ cubits, and its breadth a cubit and a half. On each side of it and wrought as one piece with it stood a cherub, with its face toward the other cherub, but bent downward toward the mercy seat, and with outstretched wings, so that a wing of each extended over the mercy seat and that of the other cherub. Between these cherubim Jehovah's glory was manifested, and there Jehovah communed with his people (Ex. 25:17-22; 30:6; Num.

7:89). There was a similar arrangement in Solomon's Temple (I Kings 6:23–28; 8:6–11; I Chron. 28:11). Once a year, on the great Day of Atonement, the high priest, after he had offered a sin offering for himself, entered the Most Holy Place and burned incense, symbol of accepted worship, in the presence of Jehovah, which rose and enveloped the mercy seat in a cloud. He then sprinkled the blood of the sacrificed bullock on and before the mercy seat. Having sacrificed the goat that was the sin offering for the nation, he carried its blood also beyond the veil, into the Most Holy Place, and sprinkled it upon and before the mercy seat. He made atonement for the sins of himself and the nation in the presence of the covenant law, which was written on the tables of stone and was lying in the Ark, and of Jehovah, who dwelt between the cherubim (Lev. 16:2, 13–17).

Me'red (mē'rĕd) [rebellion]. Son of Ezrah, who was reckoned as belonging to the tribe of Judah. He had a daughter of Pharaoh to wife and probably also a Jewess (I Chron. 4:17, 18, R.V.).

Mer'e·moth (mĕr'ĕ-mŏth) [elevations]. 1. A chief of the priests, who returned from Babylon with Zerubbabel (Neh. 12:3, 7). In the next generation a father's house among the priests, enumerated in the corresponding position in the catalogue, bears the name Meraioth (v. 15), which probably arose out of an error in reading yodh (y) and waw (w) for mem (m).
2. A priest, son of Uriah. He was employed to weigh the silver and gold brought by Ezra from Babylon (Ezra 8:33). He repaired part of the wall of Jerusalem (Neh. 3:4, 21), and is probably the person of the name who sealed the covenant (Neh. 10:5).
3. A son of Bani, induced by Ezra to put away his foreign wife (Ezra 10:36).

Me'res (mē'rēz) [perhaps, the forgetful one, from Avestan marša]. One of the 7 princes of Persia and Media at the court of Ahasuerus (Esth. 1:14).

Mer'i·bah (mĕr'ĭ-bä) [contention, strife]. 1. A name used in addition to Massah to designate the place at Horeb, near Rephidim, where the people strove with Moses (Ex., ch. 17) for water, and God gave them drink from the rock (vs. 1–7). See MASSAH.
2. A 2d locality, namely, Kadesh-barnea in the wilderness of Zin, where also the people strove with Moses and with Jehovah and water was miraculously brought from the rock (Num. 20:3, 13, 24; 27:14; Deut. 32:51). The waters of this Meribah are the waters of strife, which are mentioned in the A.V. of Ps. 106:32 and Ezek. 47:19; 48:28. For strife the R.V. in its text of the first passage substitutes Meribah, in the 2d Meriboth-kadesh, and in the 3d Meribath-kadesh. This event may well be referred to in Ps. 81:7, where it is God who proves Israel; and in Deut. 33:8, where God proves Levi and where Meribah is mentioned with Massah; and in Ps. 95:8, R.V., where also Meribah is mentioned with Massah (see MASSAH). It is to be noted that there is nothing surprising, under the circumstances, in the outbreak of discontent at the scarcity of water, which was experienced more than twice or thrice. The localities are different and quite far apart.

Mer'ib-ba'al (mĕr'ĭb-bā'ăl) [Baal (i.e., the lord) contends; or, my lord is Baal; or, Baal rewards]. See MEPHIBOSHETH.

Mer'i·bath-ka'desh   (mĕr'ĭ-băth-kā'dĕsh) [contention at Kadesh] and **Mer'i·both-ka'desh** (mĕr'ĭ-bŏth-kā'dĕsh) [contentions at Kadesh]. A station of the Israelites in the

wilderness (Ezek. 47:19; 48:28, R.V.). See MERIBAH 2.

Me·ro'dach (mē-rō'dăk) [Akkad. Marduk]. The patron deity of Babylon (Jer. 50:2). See BEL.

Me·ro'dach-bal'a·dan (mē-rō'dăk-băl'ă-dăn), in II Kings 20:12 **Be·ro'dach-bal'a·dan** [Heb. for Akkad., Marduk has given a son]. Berodach may be a copyist's misspelling for Merodach, or represent the approximation of sound between m and b in Akkadian. A king of Babylon, son of Baladan (II Kings 20:12), from Bit-Yakin, which lay in the marshes near the mouth of the Euphrates, a district which was the ancestral home of the Chaldeans. He was a man of great ability, courage, and enterprise, and became the leader of the Chaldeans. About 731 B.C. he did homage to Tiglath-pileser III, king of Assyria; but when, in 722, the Assyrian army was absent carrying on the siege of Samaria, and news reached Babylonia that Shalmaneser V, king of Assyria, had died, Merodach-baladan seized the opportunity of becoming king of Babylon. Sargon, king of Assyria, recognized him in 721. He reigned 11 years. In 712, or thereabouts, Merodach-baladan sent the embassy to Hezekiah, which, traveling with the ostensible object of congratulating Hezekiah on his recovery (II Kings 20:12–19; II Chron. 32:31; Isa. 39:1–8), was really designed to invite him to join in a confederacy with the rulers of Babylon, Susiana, Phoenicia, Moab, Edom, Philistia, and Egypt for a grand attack on the Assyrian Empire. Sargon suspected what was going on, attacked his enemies individually before they had time to unite, and vanquished them one by one. In 710 Sargon took Babylon, and in 709 Bit-Yakin, capturing Merodach-baladan at the latter place. Apparently Merodach-baladan made a favorable impression on the Assyrians, for he was reinstated in his princedom of Bit-Yakin. In 703 he re-entered Babylon, and once again ruled in the capital city, making Borsippa his residence. But his 2d reign lasted less than a year. He was defeated and driven from Babylon to Bit-Yakin by Sennacherib, Sargon's son and successor. Belibni, who was left to govern Babylonia, proved to be incompetent, and so in 700 Sennacherib sent his son Ashur-nadin-shum to pacify the country. Bit-Yakin was conquered, and Merodach-baladan fled across the Persian Gulf into Elamite territory at Nagite-rakki. Many of the inhabitants of Bit-Yakin were deported, but those who had fled were safe under Elamite protection. In 694 Sennacherib determined to reduce the Chaldeans. Boats were built on the Tigris and floated down the river to Opis, whence they were conveyed by camels overland to the Euphrates. The Assyrians, who had Phoenician and Cyprian sailors, proceeded to the mud banks of the Persian Gulf and overpowered the remnants of Bit-Yakin and the adjoining districts of Elam. Though Merodach-baladan may have ultimately failed in his enterprises, yet he had not lived in vain. The Chaldeans, whose chief he was, became from his days the dominant caste in Babylon.

Me'rom (mē'rŏm) [a height, a high place]. By the waters of Merom Joshua defeated the kings of n. Canaan and their allies (Josh. 11:5, 7). Since Reland (1714) these waters are usually identified with a lake on the Jordan, 11 miles n. of the Sea of Galilee, or with the streams that flow through its basin. This lake is 4 miles long by 3½ broad, its surface lies 689 feet above the Sea of Galilee, and it is almost certainly the body of water called by Josephus the lake Semechonitis (Jos. Antiq. v. 5, 1; War iv. 1, 1). It occupies the s. portion of a very marshy basin about 15 miles long by 5 broad. The basin is now called the Ḥûleh and the lake Baḥret el-Ḥûleh or lake of the Ḥûleh. Ḥûleh, an Arabic name given also to the plain s. of Hamath, perhaps echoes the name of the district Ulatha, between Trachonitis and Galilee (Jos. *Antiq.* xv. 10, 3).

Scholars, however, are not unanimous in accepting the traditional interpretation. *Mrm* appears in the list of Thutmose III (c. 1482 B.C.), and this has been identified with modern Meirôn, situated at the foot of Jebel Jermak, w. of Ṣafed; near Meirôn an important spring gushes into a wadi. Some scholars consider this place to be Merom. Others, however, take Mārûn er-Rās; in this case the waters would be the perpe ual stream of Wadi 'Aubā. At Khirbet el-Bijar, near Mārûn er-Rās, are almost a hundred springs. If Meirôn be accepted, the battle took place on the relatively flat spaces of Ṣafṣāf and el-Jis; in the other case, those of Yārûn. An abundance of water for the armies would have been found in the springs which flow from the foot of the mountains on which are located Kedesh (of Naphtali), Mārûn er-Rās, and Meirôn; these springs may be the waters of Merom. If Merom refers to a region instead of a definite place, the traditional and the later views are not mutually exclusive.

Me·ron'o·thite (mĕ-rŏn'á-thīt). An inhabitant of Meronoth (I Chron. 27:30; Neh. 3:7). Meronoth has not been identified.

Me'roz (mē'rŏz). A town which gave no assistance in the fight with Sisera (Judg. 5:23); Khirbet Mārūs, about 7½ miles s. of Kedesh of Naphtali.

Mes'a·loth (mĕs'á-lŏth), in A.V. **Mas'a·loth** [perhaps, from Heb. *mᵉsillôth*, ascents, stairs]. A place in the district of Arbela (I Macc. 9:2). Josephus understood it to be the region of fortified caves at Arbela in Galilee, which were only to be reached by steps (Jos. *Antiq.* xii. 11, 1).

Me'sech (mē'sĕk). See MESHECH 1.

Me'sha, I (mē'shá). The limit in one direction of the region occupied by the descendants of Joktan (Gen. 10:30). In contrast to Sephar it seems to refer to a w. place, and so Hommel suggests Jebel Shammar and perhaps also the date region of Gôf.

Me'sha, II (mē'shá). A Benjamite, a son of Shaharaim by his wife Hodesh (I Chron. 8:8, 9).

Me'sha, III (mē'shá) [salvation]. 1. A man of Judah, family of Hezron, house of Caleb. He was ancestor of the inhabitants of Ziph (I Chron. 2:42).

2. A king of Moab, son of Chemosh-melech. He rendered to King Ahab the tribu e of 100,000 lambs and as many rams, namely their wool (II Kings 3:4). Ahab was slain at the battle of Ramoth-gilead c. 852 B.C., which probably took place in the early spring, "the time when kings go forth to war," and Ahaziah thereby became sole king. The discomfiture of Israel and Judah at Ramoth-gilead and the death of Ahab were the signal to Mesha to refuse the tribute of this year, the 2d of Ahaziah (Jos. *Antiq.* ix. 2, 1), to Israel (II Kings 1:1). Jehoshaphat, king of Judah, returned from Ramoth-gilead to Jerusalem and undertook a religious reformation of the nation (II Chron., ch. 19). After this work of reform had begun (ch. 20:1), the Ammonites and Moabites, in alliance with the Edomites, who had been persuaded to revolt, invaded Judah. Jehoshaphat defeated the allies and reduced Edom to its former subjection, and a time of peace ensued (v. 30). Upon the death of Ahaziah Jehoram his brother succeeded him (II Kings 1:17). Je-

horam, desiring to render Moab again tributary, asked aid of Jehoshaphat (ch. 3:7). The latter probably wished to chastise the Moabites still further for their invasion of Judah, and, therefore, although he had been rebuked for allying himself with ungodly Ahab and Ahaziah, consented, for Jehoram had exhibited signs of godliness by a considerable reformation (v. 2). Jehoram advanced with his confederates, Jehoshaphat and an unnamed Edomite king, round the s. end of the Dead Sea. The allied armies almost perished with thirst, but Elisha bade them dig trenches, predicting that water would come. It flowed into the valley early in the morning; and as the ruddy light of the sun shone on it, the Moabite king, doubtless Mesha, thinking it was blood and inferring that the 3 invading armies had quarreled and turned their swords against each other, carelessly advanced with his forces to take the prey. He was routed, and the Israelites entered his land and beat down his cities (vs. 24, 25). At Kir-hareseth, seeing that the battle was too sore for him and failing in a desperate attempt to break through the lines of the enemy, he took his eldest son and heir apparent and offered him as a burnt offering to Chemosh on the city wall. The besiegers thereupon in fear raised the siege and returned to the land of Israel without resubjugating Moab (vs. 25–27). The Moabite Stone was erected partly for the purpose of commemorating this revolt and its successful issue; see MOABITE STONE.

Me'shach (mē'shăk). The name given by the prince of the eunuchs at Babylon to Mishael, one of the 3 faithful Jews afterward saved from the fiery furnace (Dan. 1:7; 2:49; 3:13–30).

Me'shech (mē'shĕk), in A.V. once **Me'sech** (Ps. 120:5). 1. A people descended from Japheth (Gen. 10:2). They traded in the Tyrian markets in slaves and vessels of brass (Ezek. 27:13). They were allies of Tubal, and allies or subjects of Gog, the prince of Rosh, Meshech, and Tubal (Ezek. 32:26; 38:2, 3; 39:1, R.V.). In the days of Tiglath-pileser I c. 1115–1102 B.C., and Shalmaneser III, 860–825, the land of Musku, that is Meshech, lay in the mountains to the n. of Assyria and bordered on Tabal, that is Tubal, in the w. They were gradually driven n. to near the Black Sea. Herodotus calls the 2 races the Moschoi and Tibarenoi, and locates them in the mountains s.e. of the Black Sea (Herod. iii. 94; vii. 78). The Moschoi dwelt between the Phasis and Cyrus Rivers (Pliny *Hist. Nat.* vi. 4; Strabo xi. 2, 14–17).

2. Meshech (I Chron. 1:17). See MASH.

Me·shel'e·mi'ah (mĕ-shĕl'ĕ-mī'á) [Jehovah recompenses]. A Levite, family of Kohath, house of Izhar and Korah. He and his sons were doorkeepers of the sanctuary (I Chron. 9:21; 26:1). In ch. 26:14 he is called Shelemiah.

Me·shez'a·bel (mĕ-shĕz'á-bĕl), in A.V. **Me·shez'a·beel** (mĕ-shĕz'á-bĕl) [God delivers]. 1. Father of a certain Berechiah (Neh. 3:4).

2. One of those who sealed the covenant (Neh. 10:21).

3. A man of Judah, family of Zerah (Neh. 11:24).

Me·shil'le·mith (mĕ-shĭl'ĕ-mĭth) [recompense, retribution]. See MESHILLEMOTH 2.

Me·shil'le·moth (mĕ-shĭl'ĕ-mŏth) [acts of recompense]. 1. An Ephraimite, father of that Berechiah who urged the release of the captives brought from Judah by Pekah's army (II Chron. 28:12).

2. A priest descended from Immer (Neh. 11:13), called Meshillemith in I Chron. 9:12.

Me·sho'bab (mĕ-shō'băb) [restored]. One of the Simeonite princes who seized upon the pasture lands near Gedor (I Chron. 4:34–41).

Me·shul'lam (mĕ-shŭl'ăm) [recompensed, requited]. 1. A Benjamite, descended from Shaharaim through Elpaal (I Chron. 8:17).

2. A leading man among the Gadites in the reign of Jotham (I Chron. 5:13).

3. An ancestor of Shaphan the scribe (II Kings 22:3).

4. A priest, son of Zadok, and father of the high priest Hilkiah who lived in Josiah's reign (I Chron. 9:11; Neh. 11:11). See SHALLUM 7.

5. A Kohathite Levite who with others helped faithfully to superintend the workmen who repaired the Temple in Josiah's reign (II Chron. 34:12).

6. A priest, son of Meshillemith of the house of Immer (I Chron. 9:12).

7. A son of Zerubbabel (I Chron. 3:19).

8. A Benjamite, father of Sallu (I Chron. 9:7; Neh. 11:7).

9. Another Benjamite, son of Shephatiah (I Chron. 9:8).

10. A chief man whom, with others, Ezra sent from the river of Ahava to secure Levites to go to Jerusalem (Ezra 8:16).

11. One of those who were connected with the matter of inducing the Jews who had married foreign wives to put them away (Ezra 10:15). It is not certain from the Hebrew text whether they were opposed to the measure or not. (Cf. R.V. text and marg., also A.V.)

12. A son of Bani, induced by Ezra to put away his foreign wife (Ezra 10:29).

13. A son of Berechiah. He helped to repair 2 portions of the wall of Jerusalem, at the 2d of which he had a chamber (Neh. 3:4, 30). Johanan, son of Tobiah the Ammonite, married his daughter (ch. 6:18).

14. Son of Besodeiah. He with another returned exile repaired the old gate of the wall of Jerusalem (Neh. 3:6).

15. One of those who stood on Ezra's left hand while he read and explained the law to the people (Neh. 8:4).

16. A priest who, doubtless in behalf of a father's house, sealed the covenant (Neh. 10:7).

17. A chief of the people who sealed the covenant (Neh. 10:20).

18. One of the princes of Judah who marched in the procession at the dedication of the wall of Jerusalem (Neh. 12:33).

19. A priest, head of the father's house Ezra in the days of the high priest Joiakim (Neh. 12:13).

20. Another priest at the same date, head of the father's house Ginnethon (Neh. 12:16).

21. A porter who lived at the same date (Neh. 12:25).

Me·shul'le·meth (mĕ-shŭl'ĕ-mĕth) [fem. of Meshullam]. Wife of King Manasseh, and mother of King Amon (II Kings 21:19).

Me·so'ba·ite (mĕ-sō'bȧ-īt). See MEZOBAITE.

Mes'o·po·ta'mi·a (mĕs'ô-pô-tā'mĭ-ȧ) [Gr., land between rivers]. The rendering, borrowed from the LXX, for the Hebrew Aram-naharaim; see ARAM 2, (1). It is a Greek name which appears after the time of Alexander the Great. The Greek and Roman geographers used the term for the whole country between the Euphrates and Tigris Rivers, excluding the mountainous region where the rivers take their rise and ordinarily also the low-lying plain of Babylonia in the other direction. Thus limited, its upper portion is hilly and fertile and its lower part, especially toward the Tigris, is a salt desert.

Some of its inhabitants were present on that Day of Pentecost on which the Holy Spirit descended (Acts 2:9). Stephen in-

cludes Ur of the Chaldees in Mesopotamia (ch. 7:2), and the name is often used in that broad sense by modern scholars.

Mes·si'ah, in A.V. of N.T. **Mes·si'as** (John 1:41; 4:25), the Greek form [Aram. *mᵉshihȧ*, Heb. *māshiaḥ*, anointed one, of which Gr. *Christos* is a translation]. The term was applicable to any person anointed with the holy oil, as the high priest (Lev. 4:3, 5, 16; I Sam. 12:3, 5, Hebrew) or the king (II Sam. 1:14, 16). The title is given to the patriarchs Abraham and Isaac and to the Persian king Cyrus, as chosen ones to administer the kingdom of God (Ps. 105:15; Isa. 45:1). When God promised David that the throne and scepter should remain in his family forever (II Sam. 7:13), the title acquired a special reference and denoted the representative of the royal line of David (Ps. 2:2; 18:50; 84:9; 89:38, 51; 132:10, 17; Lam. 4:20; Hab. 3:13). And when prophecy began to tell of a king who should appear in this line and be the great deliverer of his people (Jer. 23:5, 6), "whose goings forth are from of old, from everlasting" (Micah 5:2–5), and who should uphold the throne and kingdom of David forever (Isa. 9:6, 7), the title of the Messiah, par excellence, naturally became attached to him (Dan. 9:25, 26; Targum of Onkelos, Num. 24:17–19), and ultimately became a customary designation of him, being as common as the title son of David (John 1:41; 4:25; and in the form Christ, Matt. 1:1 *et passim*). In Jewish and Christian belief the Messiah is the one anointed, i.e., empowered by God's resident spirit, to deliver his people and to establish his Kingdom.

The term Messianic prophecy denotes all prophecy which treats of the person, work, or Kingdom of Christ, and by extension it is often applied to passages which speak of the future salvation, glory, and consummation of God's Kingdom without mention of the Mediator. The term Messianic times does not refer exclusively to the period when Christ lived on earth. It generally comprehends the dispensation which Christ inaugurated and conducts as mediatorial king, whether viewed in its entirety or in some of its aspects.

Met'als. The metals used in ancient times were gold, silver, iron, copper, lead, and tin (Num. 31:22, *q.v.*). Perhaps antimony was employed for coloring the eyelids and eyebrows. See PAINT.

Me'theg·am'mah (mē'thĕg-ăm'ȧ) [bridle of the mother city, i.e., jurisdiction of the metropolis]. A town taken by David from the Philistines (II Sam. 8:1). The reference is doubtless to Gath and its suburbs (I Chron. 18:1).

Me·thu'sa·el (mĕ-thū'sȧ-ĕl). See METHUSHAEL.

Me·thu'se·lah (mĕ-thū'zĕ-lȧ), in A.V. of N.T. **Ma·thu'sa·la** [probably, man of a javelin]. Son of Enoch and father of the Sethite Lamech (Gen. 5:21–27). If the number of years which are assigned to him refer to his own individual life, he is notable for having lived to a greater age than any other man recorded in history. See CHRONOLOGY, I.

Me·thu'sha·el (mĕ-thū'shȧ-ĕl) in A.V. **Me·thu'sa·el** [man of God]. Son of Mehujael, and father of Lamech, of the race of Cain (Gen. 4:18).

Me·u'nim (mĕ-ū'nĭm), in A.V. also **Me·hu'nim** and **Me·hu'nims** [plural of the gentilic adjective from Maon, denoting the people of Maon]. A people whose capital was probably the city of Ma'ân, 12 miles s.e. of Petra. They inhabited Mount Seir (cf. II Chron. 20:1, emended text, R.V. marg., with v. 10; cf. Minaeans of LXX). A body of them were smitten by the Simeonites near Gedor, where they dwelt as strangers (I Chron. 4:39–41). They are mentioned in connecion with Philistines and Arabians (II Chron. 26:7). Some of them, probably captives of war and their descendants, served at the Temple in Jerusalem as Nethinim (Ezra 2:50; Neh. 7:52). They are mentioned in Judg. 10:12, where the LXX has *Madiam* (= Midian). The Meunim are identified by the LXX with the Minaeans. If the identification be correct, they are a n. settlement of that people.

Me·za·hab (mĕz'à-hăb), in A.V. **Mez'a·hab** (mĕz'à-hăb) [waters of gold]. An ancestress of the wife of Hadar, king of Edom (Gen. 36:39; I Chron. 1:50); or perhaps a district, of which Matred was a native.

Me·zo·ba·ite (mĕ-zō'bá-ĭt), in A.V. **Me·so'·ba·ite.** Apparently a gentilic adjective (I Chron. 11:47). The Hebrew text is evidently corrupt; perhaps for "from Zobah."

Me·zu'zah (mĕ-zōō'zä) [doorpost]. Among orthodox Jews a piece of parchment containing Deut. 6:4–9; 11:13–21 written in 22 lines. It is rolled up in a wooden, metal, or glass case or tube and attached to the doorpost as is commanded in these passages.

Mi·a·min (mī'à-mĭn). See MIJAMIN.

Mib'har (mĭb'här) [choice, elite]. One of David's mighty men, son of Hagri or better a Hagrite (I Chron. 11:38); see remarks about the text under BANI 1.

Mib'sam (mĭb'săm) [sweet odor, balsam].
1. A tribe descended from Ishmael (Gen. 25:13; I Chron. 1:29).
2. A Simeonite (I Chron. 4:25).

Mib'zar (mĭb'zär) [a fortification, a stronghold]. An Edomite chieftain (Gen. 36:42; I Chron. 1:53).

Mi'ca (mī'cà), in A.V. **Mi'cha,** once **Mi'cah** (I Chron. 9:15) [evidently, like Micah, an abbreviation of Micaiah, Who is like Jehovah? (cf. Micah 1:1 with Jer. 26:18, R.V., and II Chron. 34:20 with II Kings 22:12)]. A variant Hebrew spelling yields the English form Micah; cf. II Sam. 9:12 with I Chron. 8:34.
1. A son of Mephibosheth (II Sam. 9:12). The interchangeable form of the name, Micah, is given him in I Chron. 8:34, 35; 9:40, 41.
2. A Levite who sealed the covenant (Neh. 10:11).
3. A Levite descended from Asaph (I Chron. 9:15; Neh. 11:17, 22; 12:35, where the form Micaiah is used).

Mi'cah (mī'kà), in A.V. thrice **Mi'chah** (mī'kà) (I Chron. 24:24, 25) [who is like Jehovah?]. See MICA. 1. A Levite, family of Kohath, house of Uzziel (I Chron. 23:20; 24:24, 25).
2. An Ephraimite who stole from his mother 1100 shekels of silver, but afterward gave them back again. His mother dedicated 200 of them to the Lord for images. A graven and a molten image were made of them and placed in the house of Micah, and Micah consecrated his son to be priest. A Levite chanced to pass that way, and Micah embraced the opportunity to secure an accredited minister at the sanctuary by hiring the Levite, who, though not a priest, was better than the layman, Micah's son. Sometime afterward, migrating Danites passed that way, allured the Levite to go with them, and carried off Micah's images, despite his protestations (Judg., chs. 17; 18).
3. A son of Merib-baal (I Chron. 8:34, 35; 9:40, 41); see MICA 1.
4. A Reubenite who lived several generations before 734 B.C. (I Chron. 5:5).
5. Father of Abdon. He was born before

Josiah's reign (II Chron. 34:20; II Kings 22:12, where the form Micaiah is used); cf. ACHBOR 2.
6. A descendant of Asaph (I Chron. 9:15, A.V.); see MICA 3.
7. A Morashtite, a native apparently of Moresheth-gath (Micah 1:14), a town believed to have been in Judah, not far from Gath and for a time a dependency of the Philistine city. He prophesied in the reigns of Jotham, Ahaz, and Hezekiah (Micah 1:1; and Jer. 26:18, R.V. marg., Micaiah). He therefore began his career a little later than his contemporaries Hosea and Isaiah (cf. Micah 1:1 with Isa. 1:1 and Hos. 1:1). He spoke upon the same great themes as Isaiah and so similarly that, as Calvin has said, Micah was, as it were, Isaiah's colleague. Isaiah, however, writes as one acquainted with the society and manners of the capital; Micah is a "man of the people," who sympathized with the peasantry in their sufferings. He attacks (ch. 3:2–4) the wrongs to which the poor were exposed at the hands of the nobles and rich proprietors of Judah.

Micah's style is simple; not rugged, but elegant. He is plain-spoken in the rebuke of sin (Micah 1:5; 2:1, 2; 6:10–12). His transitions of thought are often abrupt, but a logical connection is seldom difficult to discern. He is fond of the interrogation (chs. 1:5; 2:7; 4:9; 6:3, 6, 7, 10, 11), uses irony (ch. 2:11), introduces a metaphor, and retains it and carries it forward (chs. 1:6; 3:2, 3, 6; 4:6–8, 13; 6:10, 11, 14, 15), and delights in paronomasia or play upon words, employing it largely in the 1st chapter and perhaps allowing it to determine the form of the concluding paragraph of the book. That paragraph is spoken in praise of Jehovah, and is based on the rhetorical question, "Who is a God like unto thee?" (ch. 7:18). The prophet closes his prophecy by publishing the claim which his own name makes. See etymology of the name Micah.

Micah drew confidence and strength from the character of God, as revealed in the Ten Commandments, in his dealing with Israel, and in individual experience (chs. 2:7; 6:3–5; 7:15). God himself does justice and loves mercy, and he requires these traits in his people. The promises of God were also a source of strength and sweet encouragement to the prophet. He knew that Israel's security lay in God's purpose to save his people according to the promise made to Abraham (ch. 7:20) and centered in the son of David (ch. 5:2–6; cf. Luke 1:72–75). The foes of the Kingdom cannot prevail. Chapter 5 is based on the same truth as Psalm 2; and, like the sweet message of forgiveness and restoration (Micah 7:8–20), rests upon God's word.

The Book of Micah is the 6th of the Minor Prophets. Its author prophesied in the reigns of Jotham, Ahaz, and Hezekiah (ch. 1:1). Its contents also show that it was written after the reigns of Omri and Ahab (ch. 6:16), at the time when Assyria was the power which the Israelites dreaded (ch. 5:5 *seq.*), and in part at least while Samaria and the Northern Kingdom were still in existence (ch. 1:6, 14); but how long before the fall of Samaria the words of ch. 1:5–7 were uttered cannot be determined, for from the time of Uzziah and Jotham the prophets were foretelling the approaching doom of Samaria (Hos. 1:6; 3:4; 5:9; Amos 2:6; 3:12; 5:1–3, 27; 6:1, 7–11, 14; Isa. 7:8, 9; 8:4) and the desolation of Judah (Hos. 5:10; Amos 2:4; Isa. 6:1, 11–13; 7:17–25). Micah 1:9–16 may contain a reference to the campaign of Sargon (711) or that of Sennacherib (701). The prophecy of ch. 3:12 was spoken during the reign of Hezekiah (Jer. 26:18), though Micah may have discoursed on this theme before.

The prophecies of Micah, although they refer especially to Judah and were spoken to the people of the Southern Kingdom, yet concern all Israel (Micah 1:1, 5-7, 9-16). The abrupt transitions indicate that the book is rather a summary of the prophet's teaching than a series of distinct discourses. The expression, "Hear ye," repeated 3 times, serves to mark the beginning of 3 divisions, each of which likewise ends with a message of hope.

1. *Prophecies of judgment.* The prophet begins (ch. 1:2-4) by describing, in impressive imagery, the approaching manifestation of Jehovah for judgment. He prophesies judgment upon Samaria for its incurable disposition toward idolatry (ch. 1:2-8), and upon Judah as involved in like guilt (vs. 9-16). Micah prophesies woe upon the oppressors of the people and the ruin and captivity of the nation (ch. 2:4, 5) as a punishment for the unrighteousness and injustice of its representative men (vs. 1-11). Yet a remnant shall be restored (vs. 12, 13).

II. *Denunciations passing into prophecies of salvation.* In contrast to, "And I said" (ch. 3:1), we have (v. 5), "Thus saith Jehovah." As opposed to the false prophets, Micah appears as a true prophet of God (v. 8). Here we have rebuke of the civil and religious authorities for heartless indifference to truth and right and for the mercenary character of their doctrine and government (ch. 3:1-11); and the consequent abandonment of Zion by Jehovah to the power of its foes (v. 12). This prophecy of v. 12 made such an impression that it was still remembered more than a hundred years later (Jer. 26:18). There follows the ultimate exaltation of Jehovah's Kingdom in moral influence among men and in peace, prosperity, and power (ch. 4:1-8). But at present the prophet sees dismay, helplessness, captivity (vs. 9, 10), followed by the overthrow of its enemies for their sinful opposition to Jehovah (vs. 11-13); now there is discomfiture for Zion (ch. 5:1), until he shall come forth unto God that is to be ruler in Israel, "whose goings forth are from of old, from everlasting" (vs. 2-4). This foreordination of God regarding the Messiah assures and secures the deliverance of Zion from the Assyrians (v. 5 *seq.;* cf. Isa. 7:4-16), and is the pledge and potency that guarantees the survival of God's people throughout the ages and their ultimate triumph over all foes and attainment of conformity to God's ideal (Micah 5:7-15).

III. *Jehovah's controversy* with the people as a whole, not with the wealthy and the official classes only (ch. 6:1-5), explaining the requirements of true religion (vs. 6-8; cf. Isa. 1:11-17), lamenting its absence and the presence of its very opposite (Micah 6:9 to 7:6), and closing with the prophet's own confidence in a glorious future due to the forgiving grace of Jehovah and his faithfulness to his covenant with Abraham (vs. 7-20).

The book may also be divided according to form and general arrangement of material as follows: chs. 1 to 3, threats; chs. 4:1 to 5:9, promise; chs. 5:10 to 7:6, threats; ch. 7:7-20, promise.

Chapter 4:1-3 is almost identical with Isa. 2:2-4, but is more closely connected than in the corresponding passage in Isaiah with the verses which immediately follow. Joel expresses a similar thought (Joel 3:10). It appears that both Isaiah and Micah are quoting an anonymous prophecy which was well-known in their time. The liturgical refrains (Isa. 2:5; Micah 4:5) suggest that both prophets quoted from a liturgical collection of hymns, or, in view of the difference in the refrains, from two different collections. At any rate God's people of old had authoritative prophecy upon which they relied, and favorite passages which they quoted, just as Christians of today have.

Eissfeldt maintains that Micah 7:7-20 is a unity of 4 parts (vs. 7-10, 11-13, 14-17, 18-20), all of which can with certainty be assigned to a later period, c. the 2d half of the 6th century B.C.; he sees a resemblance between this section of Micah and Isa., chs. 56 to 66. Micah 7:7-20 bears the same relation to chs. 5:10 to 7:6 as chs. 4:1 to 5:9+ch. 2:12 *seq.* to chs. 1 to 3. The Book of Micah accordingly has a twofold succession of threats and promises. According to this scholar, it is possible that there were 2 collections of Micah's prophecies of doom, which were each secondarily provided with a message of hope or release and later joined together. He sees, however, another possibility, that the prophecies of doom were mitigated by the addition of a prophecy of deliverance both in the middle and at the end, especially since the prediction of calamity (ch. 3:12) seemed to demand a more hopeful outcome. Eissfeldt supposes that perhaps ch. 4:1-15 was first introduced and that in consequence other prophecies of promise were added. He sees a condition similar to what is found in Isa., chs. 11; 12, where he proposes 2 possibilities: these 2 chapters either were inserted into a collection of Isa., chs. 1 to 35, or were added to a collection extending to ch. 10. By this theory Micah 2:12 *seq.;* 4:1 to 5:9; 7:7-20 are according to form and content not to be assigned to Micah, but are considered as valuable witnesses to the hope which inspired and sustained postexilic Judaism.

Several remarks that bear on the genuineness of chs. 6 and 7 may be thrown loosely together. The thought of the exiles scattered far and wide (Micah 7:12) is not surprising in a contemporary of Isaiah; and the hope that the walls of Jerusalem will be rebuilt (ch. 7:11) is natural after one has pictured the enemy treading down Zion as the mire of the streets (v. 10). Over against Ewald's assignment of chs. 6 and 7 to the time of Manasseh (a date which need not fall outside of Micah's lifetime) may be placed Cornill's opinion that everything in these chapters applies well to the time of Ahaz. The anticipation of exile (ch. 7:7-20), and the ravaging of the kingdom by its foes, yet their submission (chs. 6:13-16; 7:16, 17), and the transition from threatening to promise, characterize chs. 1 to 5 equally with chs. 6 and 7. Chapters 6 and 7 form a natural advance from the denunciation of the official representatives of the nation (chs. 1 to 3) to Jehovah's controversy with the people as a whole (chs. 6; 7). The figure of Jehovah in controversy with Israel was familiar to the prophets of this period (Hos. 4:1; 12:2; cf. Isa. 1:2-24); and to refer to events of Israel's early history, as in chs. 6:4, 5; 7: 15, 20, was a common practice with Micah (chs. 1: 15; 5:6), Hosea, and Isaiah. As the prophecies of chs. 1 to 5 resemble Isaiah's utterances, so ch. 6 resembles Isa., ch. 1.

It may be supposed that Micah uttered other prophecies which, however, have not been recorded. At any rate he is the prophet of the humble and the poor. The Messiah, he says, will not come from the capital, but from the small town (ch. 5:2). The passage, ch. 5:2-4, is especially dear to the Christian on account of the interpretation we have in Matthew (Matt. 2:5 *seq.*), who sees here a reference to Christ. We find in Micah a protest against formalism and a demand for an ethical religion (Micah 6:6-8); here is found (v. 8) the classic definition of a simple practical religion, which has not been surpassed. The book is brief, but its value and influence must not be judged by its size.

Mi·ca'iah (mī-kā'yȧ), in A.V. Mi·cha'iah except in I Kings 22:8–28; II Chron. 18:6–27 [who is like Jehovah?]. 1. Daughter of Uriel of Gibeah, wife of Rehoboam, and mother of King Abijah (II Chron. 13:2). According to II Chron. 11:20, Abijah's mother was Maacah, daughter of Absalom. Micaiah is probably a corruption of Maacah, for so Abijah's mother is always called elsewhere, and she was probably granddaughter of Absalom and daughter of Uriel by his wife Tamar, Absalom's daughter. See MAACAH 9.

2. A prophet, son of Imlah. Being desired by Ahab to concur in the favorable prediction given by the prophets of Baal regarding Ahab's expedition against Ramoth-gilead, he did what was required of him, but with such transparent insincerity that he was adjured to speak the truth, on which, in the name of Jehovah, he predicted the death of Ahab in the coming fight. The order was given to make him a prisoner till Ahab's expected victory should prove his unfavorable vaticination to be untrue (I Kings 22:8–28; II Chron. 18:6–27). As it turned out, Ahab lost his life at Ramoth-gilead.

3. One of Jehoshaphat's princes sent by him to teach in the cities of Judah (II Chron. 17:7).

4. The prophet, better known as Micah (Jer. 26:18, A.R.V. marg.).

5. Father of Achbor. He lived before Josiah's reign (II Kings 22:12); see MICAH 5.

6. A son of Gemariah, who reported to the Jewish princes in the reign of Jehoiakim the contents of Jeremiah's book as read by Baruch (Jer. 36:11–13).

7. A descendant of Asaph (Neh. 12:35); see MICA 3.

8. A priest, one of those who blew trumpets when the wall of Jerusalem was dedicated by Nehemiah (Neh. 12:41).

Mi'cha (mī'kȧ). See MICA.

Mi'cha·el (mī'kȧ-ĕl) [who is like God?]. 1. A man of Asher, father of the representative from that tribe on the commission to spy out Canaan (Num. 13:13).

2. A Gadite, descended from Buz and head of a father's house in Gilead (I Chron. 5:13; cf. vs. 11, 14, 16).

3. Another Gadite, ancestor of the preceding (I Chron. 5:14).

4. A Levite, family of Gershom and ancestor of Asaph (I Chron. 6:40).

5. A chief man of the tribe of Issachar, family of Tola, house of Uzzi (I Chron. 7:3).

6. A Benjamite, family of Beriah (I Chron. 8:16).

7. A Manassite captain who joined David at Ziklag (I Chron. 12:20).

8. Father of Omri, who ruled the people of Issachar in David's reign (I Chron. 27:18).

9. A son of King Jehoshaphat (II Chron. 21:2).

10. Father of Zebadiah, of the sons of Shephatiah (Ezra 8:8).

11. An archangel (Jude 9), one of the chief angelic princes who helped the man clothed in linen against the spiritual being, called the prince of the kingdom of Persia (Dan. 10:13); he also contended for Israel (Dan. 10:21; 12:1), and later with his angels warred victoriously against the enemies of the people of God (Rev. 12:7). When the doctrine of angels was wrought out by the Jews after the Exile, Michael was made one of 7 archangels (Tobit 3:17; 12:15), Gabriel being, of course, included in the number (Dan. 8:16; 9:21), and 5 others being added to make up 7, namely, Raphael, Uriel (II Esdras 4:1), Chamuel, Jophiel, and Zadkiel. The belief that Michael disputed with Satan about the body of Moses, to which Jude refers and upon which he bases a lesson (Jude 9; cf. II Peter

2:11) is derived from the pseudepigraph Assumption of Moses; cf. the Targum of Jonathan on Deut. 34:6, which ascribes the burial of Moses to Michael and other angels.

Mi'chah (mī'kȧ). See MICAH.

Mi·cha'iah (mī-kā'yȧ). See MICAIAH.

Mi'chal (mī'kăl) [perhaps, who is like El (God)?]. The younger daughter of King Saul (I Sam. 14:49). After Saul had failed to fulfill his promise to give his elder daughter Merab to David, he learned that Michal was in love with the young hero, and he gladly embraced the opportunity which this affection afforded him to expose David to the risk of death. He offered Michal to David on condition that he should slay a hundred Philistines. David accomplished the assigned task and received Michal to wife (I Sam. 18:27, 28). She aided David in escaping from her father's machinations, but after the former became a fugitive Saul married her to another man, regardless of her obligations to David (I Sam. 25:44). When Abner, Ish-bosheth's general, sought to make up matters with David, the king required that his wife Michal should be restored to him, which was done (II Sam. 3:15). But when David was bringing the Ark to Jerusalem and, in the intensity of his religious zeal, danced before the Lord, Michal thought the hero and king was acting in an undignified manner, and she despised him in her heart, and rebuked him. But David replied that he had humbled himself before the Lord and would continue to do so, and that he would be held in honor by those in whose sight she falsely insinuated he had acted in a lewd manner. After a time Michal died childless (II Sam. 6:14–23).

Mich'mash (mĭk'măsh) and twice Mich'mas (mĭk'măs) (Ezra 2:27; Neh. 7:31), and so in A.V. of I Macc. 9:73 [a hidden place]. A town near the mount of Beth-el (I Sam. 13:2), e. of Beth-aven (v. 5), and n. of Geba (I Sam. 14:5, in A.V. Gibeah; Isa. 10:28, 29). The Philistines encamped at Michmash to war with Saul; but through the valor of Jonathan and his armor-bearer at the craggy pass near by a slaughter was begun among them and they were routed by the army of Israel (I Sam. 13:5–7, 15 seq.; 14:1–23). Exiles from Michmash returned from the Captivity (Ezra 2:27; Neh. 7:31). They were Benjamites (Neh. 11:31). Jonathan Maccabaeus took up his residence at Michmash and exercised judgeship (I Macc. 9:73, in A.V. Machmas; Jos. Antiq. xiii. 1, 6). The pass of Michmash, still retaining the name of Mukhmās, is 7½ miles n. by e. of Jerusalem, 2 n.e. of Geba, and 3 s. by e. of Beth-el. The village of Mukhmās is one of a humble character; the pass is probably Wadi eṣ-Ṣuweiniṭ.

Mich'me·thath (mĭk'mĕ-thăth), in A.V. Mich'·me·thah (mĭk'mĕ-thȧ). A town on the boundary line between Ephraim and Manasseh. It lay "before Shechem" (Josh. 16:6; 17:7), and is to be identified with Khirbet Juleijil.

Mich'ri (mĭk'rī) [perhaps, purchase price]. A Benjamite (I Chron. 9:8).

Mich'tam (mĭk'tăm). A word of obscure meaning occurring in the titles of Psalms 16; 56 to 60. The LXX, followed by Theodotion, translates: "An engraved writing," "An inscription on a tablet," with or without the preposition for; cf. Targum: "A straight [or upright] inscription." From this has been deduced the explanation: a poem of epigrammatic character. Aquila, Symmachus, and Jerome render it as an epithet of David: "The humble and sincere [blameless]." The margin of A.V. reads: "A golden Psalm." It has also been understood as meaning a mysterious poem, poetry concerning problems, or a hitherto unknown composition. In connection with this last explanation, cf. Arab. *katama*, to hide, and Akkad. *katâmu*, to cover; the root may accordingly be understood in the sense of *to cover sin*. Michtam may therefore mean a song the object of which is to cover or atone for sin, uncleanness, or the consequences of sin.

Mid'din (mĭd'ĭn) [perhaps, extensions]. A village in the wilderness of Judah (Josh. 15: 61); perhaps, Khirbet Ḳumrân, almost 2 miles n. of 'Ain Feshkhah on the n.w. shore of the Dead Sea.

Mid'i·an (mĭd'ĭ-ăn), in A.V. of N.T. **Ma'· di·an** [place of judgment]. 1. A son of Abraham by Keturah, sent away with gifts into the wilderness, and in whom the Midianites were linked with Abraham. The person and tribe form one conception (Gen. 25:1–6).

2. A region in the Arabian desert near the Gulf of 'Aḳabah, occupied by the Midianites. It was bordered by Edom on the n.w. Its boundaries were never demarked, and doubtless shifted considerably at different periods; but all the region referred to in the O.T. as dominated by the Midianites is found within an area which measures about 175 miles from n. to s. About the time of the Exodus Midian controlled the pasture lands e. of Horeb in the peninsula of Sinai (Ex. 3:1). A district adjacent to Moab and near the Amorite kingdom, whose capital was Heshbon, was occupied by Midianites, who had been settled there for some time (Gen. 36:35; Num. 22:4; 25: 1, 6; Josh. 13:21). The intervening region e. of Edom to the Red Sea doubtless belonged to Midian. The Midianites who were routed in the valley of Jezreel fled in this direction, and Gideon in pursuing them passed Succoth and the Gadite town of Jogbehah (Judg. 8: 5, 10, 11; cf. Gen. 37:25, 28). In David's time a royal refugee from Edom found temporary asylum in Midian, probably s.e. of Edom, before he went into Egypt (I Kings 11:17, 18). The center of population was e. and s.e. of the Gulf of 'Aḳabah, where the name is still preserved in Madyan.

Mid'i·an·ites (mĭd'ĭ-ăn-īts). A people of the desert (Gen. 25:2, 6; Num. 10:29–31; Isa. 60:6; Hab. 3:7; Judith 2:26). Five families of them sprang from Midian, *q.v.* (Gen. 25: 4). Midianite merchants, who were with the caravan of Ishmaelites coming from Gilead, bought Joseph and carried him to Egypt (Gen. 37:25, 28, 36). The father-in-law of Moses was a Midianite (Ex. 3:1). Midianites joined with Moabites in hiring Balaam to curse the Israelites and afterward seduced the people to idolatry and licentiousness (Num. 22:4, 6; ch. 25). The Israelites were consequently directed to make war on them. They did so, killing the 5 kings of Midian with all the male population of the district and the married women (ch. 31). These kings were allies or vassals of Sihon, king of the Amorites (Josh. 13:21). In the period of the Judges, Midianites, in conjunction with the Amalekites and the children of the e., entered Canaan, with their cattle and their tents, like locusts for multitude, everywhere appropriating the crops, and reducing to the greatest distress those who had sown them. After the oppression had lasted for 7 years, God raised up Jerubbaal, or Gideon, to deliver the now repentant people. The decisive battle was fought in the Plain of Jezreel. It resulted in the complete defeat of the foreign oppressors. Their 2 princes, Oreb and Zeeb, were taken and put to death; and later their 2 kings, Zebah and Zalmunna, shared the same fate. The land had rest, then, for the normal period of 40 years (Judg., chs. 6 to 8; 9:17; Ps. 83:9–12; Isa. 9:4; 10:26).

Mid'rash. See COMMENTARY.

Mig'dal-el' (mĭg'dăl-ĕl') [tower of God]. A fortified city of Naphtali (Josh. 19:38). Its site may be at Mujeidil (on a hill n.w. of Tibnīn), 12½ miles n.w. of Kades (Kedesh) and 11 miles n.n.w. of Yârūn (Iron).

Mig'dal-gad' (mĭg'dăl-găd') [tower of Gad or fortune]. A town in or near the lowland of Judah (Josh 15:37), probably Khirbet el-Mejdeleh, 5 miles s. of Beit Jibrîn, near Dawâ'imeh.

Mig'dol (mĭg'dŏl) [tower]. 1. An encampment of the Israelites while they were leaving Egypt. It was near the Red Sea (cf. Ex. 15:4, 22; Deut. 11:4); before Pi-hahiroth and before Baal-zephon (Ex. 14:2; Num. 33:7). It may have been a watchtower or military post on the way.

2. After the capture of Jerusalem by Nebuchadnezzar, Jews fled to Egypt and took up their abode in a place called Migdol (Jer. 44:1; 46:14). The marginal reading of Ezek. 29:10; 30:6, from Migdol to Syene (which is the text of J.V.) seems to be the better interpretation of those 2 passages. Migdol was in the extreme n. of Egypt. It may be identified with *Magdali* of the Tell el-Amarna tablets and Egypt. *Mktr;* it corresponds to Magdolo of the Itinerarium Antonini, which is modern Tell el-Heir, about 11 miles s. of Pelusium.

Mig'ron (mĭg'rŏn) [probably, precipitous]. 1. A village of Benjamin, s. of Aiath and n. of Michmash (Isa. 10:28). The site may be at Makrūn n. of Michmash on the way to Ai.

2. Saul once camped at Migron in the outermost part of Gibeah (I Sam. 14:2). If the site of Gibeah is Tell el-Fūl, as is commonly believed, or perhaps even if Geba is intended, and if the text of I Sam. 14:2 is pure, there apparently were 2 Migrons, one n. and the other considerably s. of Michmash.

Mij'a·min (mĭj'à-mĭn), in A.V. sometimes **Mi'a·min** [from the right hand, i.e., side of good luck]. 1. A descendant of Aaron. His family had grown to a father's house by the time of David, and became the 6th of the 24 courses into which David distributed the priests (I Chron. 24:1, 6, 9).

2. A chief of the priests who returned with Zerubbabel from Babylon (Neh. 12:5, 7). In the next generation a father's house among the priests bore the name Miniamin (v. 17). There is no difference between these names: in one form the letter *nun* (n) is assimilated; in the other it is not.

3. A son of Parosh, induced by Ezra to put away his foreign wife (Ezra 10:25).

4. A priest who, doubtless in behalf of a father's house (cf. 2), sealed the covenant in the time of Nehemiah (Neh. 10:7). Perhaps it was he who was one of the trumpeters at the dedication of the wall (ch. 12:41); see MINIAMIN 3, and for form of the name see under 2 of this article.

Mik'loth (mĭk'lŏth) [rods]. 1. A military captain in David's reign, who was on duty with another captain in the 2d month (I Chron. 27:4).

2. A Benjamite, of the family of Jeiel of Gibeon (I Chron. 8:32; 9:37, 38).

Mik·ne'iah (mĭk-nē'yá) [possession of Jehovah]. A Levite of the 2d degree, a gatekeeper of the Ark, who played the harp in David's reign (I Chron. 15:18, 21).

Mil'a·la'i (mĭl'à-lā'ī) [perhaps, eloquent]. A Levite who played a musical instrument at the dedication of the wall of Jerusalem (Neh. 12:36).

Mil'cah (mĭl'kà) [counsel]. 1. A daughter of Haran and sister of Lot. She became the wife of Nahor and the mother of Huz, Buz, Kemuel, Chesed, Hazo, Pildash, Jidlaph, and

Bethuel (Gen. 11:29; 22:20–23). She was the grandmother of Rebekah (chs. 22:23; 24:15, 24).

2. A daughter of Zelophehad (Num. 26:33).

Mil'com (mĭl'kŏm). See MOLECH.

Mile [Lat. *milia*, thousand (paces)]. In the only passage of the Bible in which the word occurs (Matt. 5:41) the Roman mile is intended, containing 1,000 paces of 5 Roman feet each, and equivalent to 4,860 English feet, or about 12/13 of an English mile.

Mi·le'tus (mĭ-lē'tŭs), in A.V. once **Mi·le'tum** (mĭ-lē'tŭm). A seaport to which Paul came a day after he had been at Trogyllium (Acts 20:15). Thither he summoned the elders of the church at Ephesus, to give them exhortations and bid them farewell (vs. 17–38). At Miletus Trophimus was once left when he was sick (II Tim. 4:20, in A.V. Miletum). The city was on the seacoast of Ionia, about 36 miles s. of Ephesus, being located on the s. shore of the bay of Latmus into which flowed the Menander. It had a celebrated temple of Apollo, and was the birthplace of the philosophers Thales and Anaximander.

Milk. An important article of diet, especially in the East. The milk of cows, sheep (Deut. 32:14), goats (Prov. 27:27), and camels (cf. Gen. 32:15) was and is still used. The milk of the camel is excellent, being rich and strong, but not very sweet. Milk was used in its natural state and as curds and as cheese (Deut. 32:14; Judg. 5:25; II Sam. 17:29). It was kept in skin bottles, and served in dishes (Judg. 4:19; 5:25).

Mill. In Palestine and neighboring lands the mill was a simple machine, consisting of 2 round millstones (Deut. 24:6). In the mill in use among the people today, the stones are generally made of basalt, about a foot and a half in diameter and from 2 to 4 inches thick. The nether stone is slightly convex on the top. It has a peg in the center, about which the upper stone revolves. This upper stone is slightly concave on the under side in order to fit on the nether stone, and is pierced by a hole in the center which receives the peg and in o which the grain is dropped by hand. It is turned by means of an upright handle near the circumference. The meal falls over the edge of the nether stone into a cloth spread underneath or into a platter. The work of grinding is laborious and menial. It was performed by the women (Eccl. 12:3, R.V. marg.;

Women at the Mill

Matt. 24:41), slave women (Ex. 11:5; Isa. 47:2), and prisoners (Judg. 16:21). In ordinary Jewish households, however, it was not regarded as at all degrading for the women to grind meal every morning for a day's consumption, rising long before daybreak, at least in winter. If the millstone was taken away, the family was left without ground grain till it was returned, on which account it was forbidden by the Mosaic Law to take "the mill or the upper millstone to pledge; for he taketh a man's life to pledge" (Deut. 24:6). The cessation of the sound of grinding betokens utter desolation (Jer. 25:10; Rev. 18:22).

A larger mill, constructed on the same principle, but turned by an ass, was also in use (Matt. 18:6, R.V. marg.).

Mil'let. A cereal (*Panicum miliaceum*), Heb. *dōḥan*. Ezekiel was bidden to use it as an ingredient of the bread which he was ordered to prepare (Ezek. 4:9). It is extensively used in w. and s. Asia, n. Africa, and s. Europe. The stalks make an excellent fodder for cattle, while the grain is fed to poultry, and affords a nutritious and palatable food for man. It is possible that under the Hebrew *dōḥan* other allied species of cereals may be included, and especially *Sorghum vulgare*, the Indian millet, a taller grass much cultivated in India and s.w. Asia.

Mil'lo (mĭl'ō) [filling, terrace, artificial elevation, citadel]. 1. A house, probably a fortress, at Shechem (Judg. 9:6, 20).

2. A bastion at Jerusalem, in existence in the time of David, rebuilt by Solomon, and strengthened by Hezekiah as a precaution against the expected siege by the Assyrians (II Sam. 5:9; I Kings 9:15, 24; 11:27; II Chron. 32:5). See JERUSALEM, II. 3.

Mine. The operation of mining, by which gold, silver, iron, copper, and precious stones were obtained, is graphically described in Job 28:1–11. The Egyptians carried on mining operations from an early period. As early as the 4th dynasty they discovered copper in Wadi Maghārah, in the Sinai peninsula, and commenced mining and smelting operations, which continued for many years. They also worked the turquoise mines at Serabit el-Khadem on the Sinai peninsula, about 50 miles from the traditional site of Mount Sinai. The miners were criminals, prisoners of war, and slaves, working under the whip of the taskmaster and often in fetters. The mines had broad, low openings. The shaft penetrated to a consderable depth. The roof was supported by pillars of stone which the miners left and by timber of acacia wood. The gold and silver mines of Spain were celebrated (I Macc. 8:3). Canaan was described to the expectant Israelites as "a land whose stones are iron, and out of whose hills thou mayest dig copper" (Deut. 8:9); see EZION-GEBER. That the Hebrews unders'ood how to drive shafts is shown by the tunnel which they cut from the Fountain of the Virgin to the Pool of Siloam.

Min'ia·min (mĭn'yȧ-mĭn) [see MIJAMIN]. 1. One of those who, under the direction of a Levite, Kore, took charge of the freewill offerings in the Temple and distributed them to the Levites during Hezekiah's reign (II Chron. 31:15).

2. A father's house among the priests in the days of the high priest Joiakim (Neh. 12:17); see MIJAMIN 2.

3. A priest; one of those who blew trumpets at the dedication of the wall of Jerusalem (Neh. 12:41); see MIJAMIN 4.

Min'is·ter. 1. A personal attendant and helper, not a menial. Joseph, the slave, when raised to a position of honor and trust in his master's household, "ministered unto him"

(Gen. 39:4). Abishag was given honorable and influential place by David, and she ministered to him (I Kings 1:4, 15). Joshua attended Moses, took charge of the first tent of meeting, and succeeded Moses in office (Ex. 24:13; 33:11; Josh. 1:1). Elisha attended Elijah, poured water on his hands, and succeeded him (I Kings 19:21; II Kings 3:11). The attendant of the synagogue aided the officiating teacher in the service (Luke 4:20). The disciples attended Jesus and were eyewitnesses (Luke 1:2; Acts 26:16). John Mark attended Paul and Barnabas during a part of the First Missionary Journey (Acts 13:5).

2. A public functionary in the service of the state or of God (Heb. m⁰shārêth, Gr. leitourgos): as the priests and Levites in the performance of the duties of the sanctuary (Ex. 28:43; Num. 3:31; Deut. 18:5; Isa. 61:6; cf. LXX; Luke 1:23; Heb. 9:21); Christ as high priest in the heavenly sanctuary (Heb. 8:2); Paul in administering the gospel to the Gentiles (Rom. 15:16). The epithet is applied to the civil magistrate as a public official (Rom. 13:6). It designates an attaché of the royal court (I Kings 10:5), of en a person of high rank (II Chron. 22:8; Esth. 1:10), and it is used of the angels (Ps. 103:21; 104:4).

3. One engaged in the service of another, and regarded primarily as the master's own representative and servant, and not as acting in behalf of others (Gr. diakonos); for example, a magistrate as the representative of God, "an avenger for wra h to him that doeth evil" (Rom. 13:4). It is used especially for God's minister in the gospel: as Timothy (I Thess. 3:2), Paul and Apollos (I Cor. 3:5), Tychicus (Eph. 6:21), Epaphras (Col. 1:7). The term diakonos was also used in a restricted sense for deacon, a church officer with specified duties distinguishing him from a bishop.

Min'ni (mǐn'ī). A people of Armenia (Jos. Antiq. i. 3, 6) inhabiting the district near Lake Van, probably between that and Lake Urmia, and adjacent to the kingdom of Ararat on the Araxes. In 830 B.C. Shalmaneser, king of Assyria, pillaged the country of the Minni. In 716 B.C. and again in 715 the king of the Minni revolted against Assyria, but in 714 he was subdued anew. The Minni continued to give trouble at intervals, especially during the reign of the Assyrian king Ashurbanipal (669–626); till at length in 612 B.C. they took part with the Medes, Cimmerians, and other nationalities in capturing Nineveh and ending the Assyrian Empire. In Jer. 51:27, R.V., the kingdoms of Ararat, Minni, and Ashkenaz are described as uniting for the destruction of Babylon.

Min'nith (mǐn'ǐth). A town of the Ammonite country (Judg. 11:33). It exported wheat to Tyre (Ezek. 27:17). According to Eusebius, there was a village called Manith 4 Roman miles from Heshbon in the direction of Philadelphia.

Min'strel. A musician (Rev. 18:22, in A.V. musician); especially one who sings to the accompaniment of an instrument. 1. Hebrew m⁰naggēn, which is rendered minstrel in II Kings 3:15, signifies a player on a strin⁀ed instrument, as harp or lyre. Music was employed by the Hebrews to still excitement; and when Saul was troubled by an evil spirit, Da'id was summoned to the court to act as minstrel (I Sam. 16:14–23). Music, sometimes at least, formed part of the religious exercises of the prophets (I Sam. 10:5–10); and Elisha summoned a minstrel to play before him while he waited for God to speak to him (II Kings 3:15). The music calmed the prophet's mind, recalled his thoughts from the outside world, and gladdened his spirit.

"Prophecy," says Maimonides, "dwelleth not in the midst of melancholy nor in the midst of apathy, but in the midst of joy."

2. The minstrels hired by Jairus (Matt. 9:23, A.V.) were "flute-players" (R.V.), who with singers and wailing women were employed as professional mourners (II Chron. 35:25; Jer. 9:17–20; cf. ch. 48:31 with v. 36).

Mint. An herb of the genus Mentha, of which there are several species. It is called in Greek hēdyosmon, sweet-smelling (Matt. 23:23). Horsemint (Mentha sylvestris) is the most common species in Syria, and grows wild on all the hills. It is not known certainly which sort the ancient Israelites cultivated.

Miph'kad (mǐf'kǎd). See HAMMIPHKAD.

Mir'a·cle. Miracles are wonders, signs, types, powers, works of God (Deut. 11:3; 29:3; Ps. 78:7, 11, 12, 43; 95:9; Mark 9:39; Luke 23:8; John 2:11, 23; 9:3; Acts 2:22; 6:8; 8:13; see R.V.). They are not merely supernatural events, like the creation of the world; for God is not represented as bringing the universe into existence as a sign of attestation. The locusts which were blown into Egypt by the strong e. wind and blown away again by the w. wind (Ex. 10:13, 19), and the arrival of quails, which migrate in the spring and supplied the camp of Israel with meat for an evening (Ex. 16:13), were extraordinary providences, but with additional elements. They were foretold and were intended as signs. The plague of locusts was one of the signs and wonders wrought at Zoan (Ps. 78:43, 46), and the quails were sent that Israel might know that Jehovah is God and their God (Ex. 16:12). In the narrowest Biblical sense, miracles are events in the external world, wrought by the immediate power of God and intended as a sign or attestation. They are possible because God sustains, controls, and guides all things, and is personal and omnipotent. Perhaps the manner of working these deeds in the realm of the physical universe is illustrated by the power of the human will. Man wills, and muscular force is exerted which controls or counteracts nature's laws, as when one hurls a stone into the air against the law of gravitation.

Miracles are not to be credulously received, but their genuineness must be tested. The tests are: 1. They exhibit the character of God and teach truths concerning God. 2. They are in harmony with the established truths of religion (Deut. 13:1–3). If a wonder is worked which contradicts the doctrines of the Bible, it is a lying wonder (II Thess. 2:9; Rev. 16:14). 3. There is an adequate occasion for them. God does not work them except for great cause and for a religious purpose. They belong to the history of redemption, and there is no genuine miracle without an adequate occasion for it in God's redemptive revelation of himself. 4. They are established, not by the number of witnesses, but by the character and qualifications of the witnesses.

The miracles of the Bible are confined almost exclusively to 4 periods, separated from each other by centuries. The time of: 1. The redemption of God's people from Egypt and their establishment in Canaan under Moses and Joshua. 2. The life-and-death struggle of the true religion with heathenism under Elijah and Elisha. 3. The Exile, when Jehovah afforded proof of his power and supremacy over the gods of the heathen, although his people were in captivity (Daniel and his companions). 4. The introduction of Christianity, when miracles attested the person of Christ and his doctrine. Outside these periods miracles are rare indeed (Gen. 5:24). They were almost totally unknown during the many centuries from the Creation to the Exodus.

The working of miracles in the Apostolic Age, although not confined to the apostles (Acts 6:8; 8:5–7), were the signs of an apostle (II Cor. 12:12; Heb. 2:4; cf. Acts 2:43; Gal. 3:5).

Mir'a·cles of Our Lord. In the following list are considered the miracles wrought by our Lord during his life in the flesh, and one (No. 18) performed af·er the resurrection is included. For obvious reasons other miraculous events associated with the career of Jesus have been omitted: annunciation by the angels, Virgin birth, angels' song, appearances of angels to Joseph to protect the Child Jesus, the star of the Magi, descent of dove and voice at baptism of Jesus, transfiguration and voice heard in that connection, falling to ground of soldiers (John 18:6), opening of graves after death of Jesus, rending of veil of Temple, darkness over land, earthquake, the resurrection, entering a room through closed doors (John 20:26), and the ascension.

Num. 26:59). It was probably she who watched over the ark which contained the infant Moses (Ex. 2:4–8). After the passage of the Red Sea, she took a timbrel and led the Israelite women with timbrels and with dances, saying:

"Sing ye to Jehovah, for he hath triumphed gloriously;
The horse and his rider hath he thrown into the sea." (Ex. 15:20, 21.)

She was a prophetess, and she and her brothers were chosen by God to be leaders of the Hebrew people (Ex. 4:15, 29, 30; Micah 6:4); but she instigated Aaron, and they made Moses' marriage with a Cushite woman the occasion of murmuring against his superior position and influence. They claimed that God had spoken by them as well as by Moses. For this insubordination to the will of God, she was made a leper as white as snow, but owing to the intercession of Moses was speedily healed (Num. 12:1–16; Deut. 24:9). She

MIRACLES (ONLY FIRST VERSE OF EACH INCIDENT GIVEN)	MATT.	MARK	LUKE	JOHN
I. NARRATED IN ONE GOSPEL ONLY.				
1. Two blind men healed	9:27	....	....	......
2. A dumb demoniac cured	9:32	....	....	......
3. Tribute money in the mouth of fish	17:24	....	....	......
4. A deaf and dumb man healed	....	7:31	....	......
(Cf. Matt. 15: 29–31, healing lame, blind, dumb, maimed, and others.)				
5. The blind man of Bethsaida healed	....	8:22	....	......
6. Christ's escape from the hostile multitude	....	....	4:30	......
7. Draught of fishes	....	....	5:1	......
8. Raising of widow's son at Nain	....	....	7:11	......
9. Healing the bent woman	....	....	13:11	......
10. Healing the man of dropsy	....	....	14:1	......
11. Healing the ten lepers	....	....	17:11	......
12. Restoring the ear of Malchus	....	....	22:50	......
13. Turning water into wine	....	....	....	2:1
14. Healing the nobleman's son (of fever)	....	....	....	4:46
15. Healing the infirm man at Bethesda	....	....	....	5:1
16. Healing the man born blind	....	....	....	9:1
17. Raising of Lazarus	....	....	....	11:43
18. Second draught of fishes	....	....	....	21:1
II. NARRATED IN TWO GOSPELS.				
19. Demoniac in synagogue cured	....	1:23	4:33	......
20. Healing centurion's servant (of palsy)	8:5	....	7:1	......
21. A blind and dumb demoniac cured	12:22	....	11:14	......
(Luke uses only one adjective, but probably he refers to the same incident.)				
22. Healing the Syrophoenician woman's daughter	15:21	7:24	....	......
23. Feeding the four thousand	15:32	8:1	....	......
24. Blasting the fig tree	21:18	11:12	....	......
III. NARRATED IN THREE GOSPELS.				
25. Healing Peter's mother-in-law	8:14	1:30	4:38	......
26. The sick healed at evening	8:16	1:32	4:40	......
27. Healing the leper	8:2	1:40	5:12	......
28. Healing the man sick of palsy	9:2	2:3	5:18	......
29. Healing the man who had a withered hand	12:9	3:1	6:6	......
30. Stilling the storm	8:23	4:35	8:22	......
31. Legion of demons entering swine	8:28	5:1	8:26	......
32. Healing the woman suffering with an issue of blood	9:20	5:25	8:43	......
33. Raising Jairus' daughter	9:18,23	5:22,35	8:40,49	......
34. Walking on the sea	14:25	6:48	....	6:19
35. Healing an epileptic child	17:14	9:17	9:38	......
36. Healing blind Bartimaeus	20:30	10:46	18:35	......
(Two blind men according to Matthew.)				
IV. NARRATED IN FOUR GOSPELS.				
37. Feeding the five thousand	14:13	6:30	9:10	6:1

Approximate chronological sequence of our Lord's recorded miracles: first miracle, No. 13; Early Judean Ministry, No. 14; Early Galilean Ministry, Nos. 6, 7, 19, 25, 26, 27, 28, 15, 29, 20, 8, 21, 30, 31, 32, 33, 1, 2, 37, 34; Later Galilean Ministry, Nos. 22, 4, 23, 5, 35, 3; Judean and Perean Ministry, Nos. 16, 9, 10, 11, 17, 36; the Last Week, Nos. 24, 12; postresurrection, No. 18.   **H. S. G.**

Mir'i·am (mĭr'ĭ-ăm) [obstinacy, rebellion]. 1. Sister of Aaron and of Moses (Ex. 15:20;

died in Kadesh, and was buried there (Num. 20:1).

2. A man of Judah, descended from Ezrah (I Chron. 4:17).

Mir'mah (mûr'má), in A.V. **Mir'ma** (mûr'-má) [deceit]. A Benjamite, son of Shaharaim by his wife Hodesh (I Chron. 8:10).

Mir'ror. A polished surface intended to reflect objects, especially the face (Wisd. of Sol. 7:26; II Cor. 3:18; James 1:23). Ancient mirrors were made of molten brass or other alloy of copper (Ex. 38:8; Job 37:18), and were round, oval, and square, and often provided with a handle. If they acquired rust spots, they were polished anew (Ecclus. 12:11). They lacked the perfection of the modern glass, and the image in them was less clear and true (I Cor. 13:12). As the material was metal, R.V. substitutes mirror for glass, the rendering of A.V.

Later, in the West, mirrors were sometimes made of tin. Praxiteles, in the time of Pompey, is said to have been the first to make them of silver. They were even made of gold.

Mirror, Probably of the First Century, A.D.

Mis'gab (mĭs'găb) [high place, the high fort]. An unidentified Moabite city (Jer. 48:1), but it may not be a proper name (cf. R.V. marg.).

Mish'a·el (mĭsh'à-ĕl) [who is what God is?] 1. A Levite, family of Kohath, house of Uzziel (Ex. 6:22; Lev. 10:4).
2. One of Daniel's 3 companions, called by the Babylonians Meshach (Dan. 1:6, 7, 11, 19; 2:17; I Macc. 2:59).
3. One of those who stood by Ezra when he preached to the people (Neh. 8:4).

Mi'shal (mĭ'shăl), in A.V. once **Mish'e·al** (Josh. 19:26). A village of Asher (Josh. 19:26), given with its suburbs to the Levites of the Gershonite family (Josh. 21:30); called Mashal in I Chron. 6:74. Probably located in the plain s. of Acre toward Tell Naḥl.

Mi'sham (mĭ'shăm) [swift; cf. Arab. sa'ama, to walk swiftly (of a camel)]. A Benjamite, a son of Elpaal, who with his brothers built Ono and Lod (I Chron. 8:12).

Mish'e·al (mĭsh'ĕ-ăl). See MISHAL.

Mish'ma (mĭsh'mà) [hearing; but perhaps, mixed with black and white; cf. Arab. thamagha]. 1. A tribe descended from Ishmael (Gen. 25:14; I Chron. 1:30). The name perhaps lingers either in Jebel Misma', midway between Damascus and Jauf, or in the other Jebel Misma', about 150 miles due e. of Teima.
2. A descendant of Simeon (I Chron. 4:25).

Mish·man'nah (mĭsh-măn'à) [fatness, titbit]. One of the Gadites who came to David at Ziklag (I Chron. 12:10).

Mish'ra·ites (mĭsh'rà-īts). A family which was connected with Kiriath-jearim (I Chron. 2:53).

Mis'par (mĭs'pär), in A.V. **Miz'par** [a narrative, a number]. One of those who returned with Zerubbabel from captivity (Ezra 2:2). In Neh. 7:7 the feminine form, Mispereth, is used.

Mis'pe·reth (mĭs'pĕ-rĕth). See MISPAR.

Mis're·photh-ma'im (mĭs'rĕ-fŏth-mā'ĭm)[hot springs]. A place to which Joshua pursued the kings defeated at the waters of Merom (Josh. 11:8), on the frontier of the country of the Sidonians (Josh. 13:6). It is now commonly, and probably correctly, identified with Khirbet el-Musheirifeh, 11 miles n. of Acre, and ½ mile from the sea, at the foot of Rās en-Naḳûrah.

Mite. A small coin, worth about ⅛ cent (Mark 12:42). See MONEY.

Mi'ter. The headdress or turban, called in Hebrew mignepheth, which was worn by the high priest. It was made of fine linen. Its distinguishing characteristic was a golden plate inscribed with the words "Holiness to the Lord," and affixed in front by a blue-colored lace (Ex. 28:4, 36–39; Lev. 16:4; Ezek. 21:26, in A.V. diadem); see HIGH PRIEST, and for Zech. 3:5 see DIADEM 1, 2.

Mith'kah (mĭth'kà), in A.V. **Mith'cah** (mĭth'kà) [sweetness]. An encampment of the Israelites in the wilderness (Num. 33:28, 29); perhaps Wadi Abu Ṭaḳiyeh, which descends from Naḳb el-Arūd to Wadi Jerāfi.

Mith'nite (mĭth'nīt). Probably an inhabitant of a town called Methen (I Chron. 11:43).

Mith're·dath (mĭth'rĕ-dăth) [from Old Pers., gift of Mithra (Persian god of the light of the zone between heaven and hell, defender of the truth)]. 1. Treasurer under Cyrus, king of Persia, through whom the sacred vessels were restored to the Jews (Ezra 1:8).
2. One of those who in the reign of Artaxerxes Longimanus complained that the Jews were rebuilding the walls of Jerusalem (Ezra 4:7).

Mit·y·le'ne (mĭt-ĭ-lē'nĕ). A city on the island of Lesbos, visited by Paul in going from Assos to Chios (Acts 20:13–15).

Mi'zar (mĭ'zär) [small]. A hill on the e. side of the Jordan, probably within sight of the peaks of Hermon (Ps. 42:6).

Miz'pah (mĭz'pà) and **Miz'peh** [watchtower]. 1. The name given to the cairn n. of the Jabbok, called Galeed or heap of witness, to indicate the special thing to which it bore witness, namely, that God is the watcher between the covenanting parties (Gen. 31:44–49); see GALEED.
2. A town in Gilead, e. of the Jordan (Judg. 10:17; 11:11); probably identical with Mizpeh of Gilead (Judg. 11:29) and with Ramath-mizpeh or height of Mizpeh (Josh. 13:26), otherwise known as Ramoth in Gilead or Ramoth-gilead (Deut. 4:43; I Kings 4:13) and Ramah (II Kings 8:28, 29). It was situated in the territory of Gad, on the boundary (Josh. 13:26), assigned to the Levites (Josh. 21:38), and appointed a city of refuge (Deut. 4:43; Josh. 20:8). Jephthah dwelt here (Judg. 11:34), and it was the residence of the taxgatherer for one of the twelve districts into which Solomon divided the country (I Kings 4:13). To gain and hold possession of it battles were fought between Israel and the Syrians (I Kings 22:3 seq.; II Kings 8:28). It was taken and burned by Judas

Maccabaeus (I Macc. 5:35, A.V., Maspha).
According to Eusebius, it lay 15 Roman miles
w. of Philadelphia, on the Jabbok. It is supposed to have been at el-Ḥoṣn in 'Ajlūn, about
10 miles s.w. of er-Ramthah, but another
suggestion is that it was located at er-Ramthah.
3. A place at the foot of Mount Hermon
(Josh. 11:3). The land of Mizpah is probably the same as the valley of Mizpeh (v. 8).
Robinson located it 8 miles w.n.w. of Bāniās
at Muṭallah, at the s. end of the broad and
fertile plain, the Merj 'Ayūn, between the
Ḥaṣbāny and the Liṭāny, but this is considered by many as not far enough to the e.
Accordingly some prefer a height 2 miles n.e.
of Bāniās, where are now the ruins of the
castle Kal'at eṣ-Ṣubeibeh.
4. A village in or near the lowland of Judah
(Josh. 15:38). Eusebius located it n. of Eleutheropolis (Beit Jibrīn), in the direction of
Jerusalem. There are Khirbet Ṣāfiyeh about
2 miles n.e. of Beit Jibrīn and Ṣufīyeh 6 miles
n. of the same place; either may be the site.
5. A town of Benjamin (Josh. 18:26), not
far from Ramah (v. 25; I Kings 15:22) and
over against Jerusalem (I Macc. 3:46, A.V.,
Maspha). The tribes were summoned to it at
times for conferences (I Sam. 7:5–17; 10:17;
Judg. 20:1–3; 21:1, 5, 8). It was fortified by
Asa as a defense against the n. tribes (I
Kings 15:22; II Chron. 16:6). After the destruction of Jerusalem, the Babylonian governor fixed his residence here (II Kings 25:
23–25; Jer. 40:6–16; 41:1–16). It was inhabited after the Captivity (Neh. 3:7, 15,
19). Robinson located it at Neby Samwīl,
4½ miles n.w. of Jerusalem. The place is
2,935 feet above the sea level, and 500 feet
higher than the surrounding country. Many
scholars, however, follow Badé, who identifies
it with Tell en-Naṣbeh, the summit of an isolated hill between Wadi Jiliān and its tributary Wadi Duweiṭ, about 8 miles n. of Jerusalem and almost 2 s. of el-Bīreh.
6. A place in Moab (I Sam. 22:3), perhaps Rujm el-Meshrefeh, w.s.w. of Mādabā.

Miz'par (mĭz'pär). See MISPAR.

Miz'peh (mĭz'pĕ). See MIZPAH.

Miz'ra·im (mĭz'rā-ĭm). Egypt, the form
(probably a dual) pointing to the 2 countries
of Upper and Lower Egypt, settled by descendants of Ham (Gen. 10:6); see EGYPT,
I. 1; II. 1.

Miz'zah (mĭz'ȧ). The chief of a tribe in
the land of Edom, a descendant of Esau, and
also of Ishmael (Gen. 36:3, 4, 13, 17; I Chron.
1:37).

Mna'son (nā'sŏn). An early disciple from
Cyprus, who accompanied Paul on his last
journey from Caesarea to Jerusalem, and
with whom the apostle was to lodge (Acts
21:16).

Mo'ab (mō'ăb) [probably, desirable; perhaps, seed of a father]. 1. Son of Lot by an
incestuous union with his elder daughter
(Gen. 19:37).
2. The descendants of Moab, Lot's son,
closely related to the Ammonites (Gen. 19:37,
38). They had become numerous before the
time that the Israelites crossed the Red Sea
(Ex. 15:15); had taken possession of the
country from the plain of Heshbon unto the
Seil el-Ḳerāḥi, which emerges at the s. end of
the Dead Sea, and formed the boundary of
Moab toward Edom; and with their kindred
the Ammonites had absorbed and destroyed
the remnants of the stalwart race which had
previously occupied the country e. of the Jordan (Deut. 2:10, 11, 19–21; cf. Gen. 14:5).
Shortly before the arrival of the Israelites,
Sihon, king of the Amorites, had wrested from

them the pasture land n. of the Arnon, though
the country was still remembered as the land
of Moab, confining Moab for a time to the
country s. of the Arnon (Num. 21:13–15, 26–
30). The Moabites showed a commercial
friendliness to the migrating Israelites (Deut.
2:28, 29), but refused them permission to
pass through their land (Judg. 11:17; cf.
Deut. 23:4). Doubtless because of the kinship between the Moabites and Israelites,
Moses was forbidden to attack them (Deut.
2:9; cf. v. 19). Nevertheless, the king of
Moab, alarmed when the Israelites encamped
in his vicinity, sent for Balaam to curse them
(Num., chs. 22 to 24; Josh. 24:9). For this
hostile attitude the Israelites were commanded
to exclude them from the congregation to the
10th generation, and to maintain a coldness
and indifference toward them forever (Deut.
23:3–6; Neh. 13:1). The last encampment of
the Israelites before they crossed the Jordan
was at Shittim in the plains that lay within
the old bounds of Moab (Num. 22:1; Josh.
3:1). While they were there, Moabite and
Midianite women seduced them to licentious
idolatry (Num., ch. 25; Hos. 9:10).
Early in the time of the Judges Eglon,
king of Moab, invaded Canaan, established
his seat of government at Jericho, and oppressed the Israelites of the adjacent hill
country 18 years until he was assassinated by
Ehud (Judg. 3:12–30). Elimelech sojourned
in Moab, and thence came his 2 daughters-in-
law, Orpah and Ruth. Ruth married Boaz
and became the ancestress of David (Ruth
1:22; 4:3, 5, 10, 13–17; Matt. 1:5–16). Saul
warred with the Moabites (I Sam. 14:47),
and David, when a fugitive from Saul, put his
father and mother in charge of the king of
Moab (ch. 22:3, 4). After David became king,
he overcame the Moabites, laid them under
tribute, and doomed a large proportion of
them to death (II Sam. 8:2, 12; I Chron.
18:2, 11). The Moabites were subject to Omri
and his son; but on the death of Ahab they
rebelled, and neither of Omri's grandsons,
Ahaziah, who was incapacitated for the attempt by a fall, and Jehoram, was able to
subdue them (II Kings 1:1; 3:4–27; *Moabite
Stone*, see MOABITE STONE). Jehoshaphat was
king of Judah at that time, and the Moabites
formed a confederacy with the Ammonites,
Edomites, and others for the invasion of
Judah, but the allies turned their weapons
against each other, and Judah did not need
to strike a blow (II Chron. 20:1–30; cf. Ps.
60:8; 83:6; 108:9). The year that Elisha
died, bands of Moabites invaded the Kingdom
of Israel (II Kings 13:20). They paid tribute
to Tiglath-pileser and Sennacherib, kings of
Assyria. They entered Judah in the reign of
Jehoiakim (II Kings 24:2). Many of the
towns n. of the Arnon had reverted to Moab
(cf. Isa., ch. 15). The prophets denounced the
Moabites often as types of the enemies of the
Kingdom of God (Isa., chs. 15; 16; 25:10;
Jer. 9:26; 25:21; 27:3; ch. 48; Ezek. 25:8–
11; Amos 2:1, 2; Zeph. 2:8–11). Some of the
Jews, who fled from Jerusalem when Nebuchadnezzar invaded Judah, took refuge in
Moab, but returned when Gedaliah was appointed governor (Jer. 40:11 *seq.*). Nebuchadnezzar subjugated the Moabites (Jos.
Antiq. x. 9, 7). They disappear henceforth
from history as a nation, though still existing
as a race (Ezra 9:1; Neh. 13:1, 23; Jos.
Antiq. i. 11, 5). Alexander Jannaeus placed
them under tribute (Jos. *Antiq.* xiii. 13, 5)
3. The country occupied by the Moabites.
There was c. 1900 B.C. a thoroughgoing destruction visited upon all the great fortresses
and settlements of the land, which in consequence had no sedentary population until the
13th century B.C.; then a new agricultural
civilization appeared. Moab was bounded on

the w. by the Dead Sea; it was separated from Edom on the s. by the Seil el-Ḳerāḥi, known in its upper course as Wadi el-Ḥesā. This fact is learned from the towns which are mentioned as situated in Moabite territory. On the e. lay the desert (Num. 21:11). The n. boundary which the Amorites and Israelites recognized was the Arnon (Num. 21:13; Deut. 2:36; 3:12; Josh. 12:1; Judg. 11:18), but the Moabites at an early date possessed (Num. 21:26), and always regarded as theirs and frequently occupied, a considerable district n. of the river (Isa., ch. 15; *Moabite Stone*, 8–30, see MOABITE STONE). Moab is chiefly a rolling plateau, about 3,200 feet above the level of the sea, and is well adapted for pasturage. The w. edge descends abruptly to the Dead Sea, and the face of the bluff is cut by deep valleys. Machaerus, the place where John the Baptist was imprisoned and beheaded, lay in the land of Moab, e. of the Dead Sea and n. of the Arnon. The shore of the Dead Sea is comparatively fertile from the great abundance of springs.

The field of Moab was the territory of Moab (Gen. 36:35; Num. 21:20, R.V.). The plains of Moab were those parts of the Arabah or level valley of the Jordan which at one time were included within the bounds of Moab. They lay on the e. of the river, opposite Jericho, and along the e. shore of the Dead Sea (Num. 22:1; 33:48, 49).

Mo′ab·ite (mō′ăb-īt) **Stone.** An inscribed stone found within the territory of Moab and recording Moabite history. On the 19th of August, 1868, Rev. F. Klein, a German in the employ of the Church Missionary Society,

was encamped at Dhībān, the ruins of the ancient Moabite town of Dibon, when he was informed by a sheik that within 10 minutes' walk from his tent there lay an inscribed stone. Proceeding to the spot, he found lying on its back a slab of black basalt, 3 feet 10 inches high, 2 feet broad, and a foot and 2½ inches thick, rounded at the top and the bottom to nearly a semicircle. The inscription consisted of 34 lines of writing in an unknown character, running across the stone, about an inch and a quarter apart. He at once set on foot negotiations for its transfer to the Berlin Museum. Unhappily, M. Clermont-Ganneau, of the French Consulate, also attempted to obtain it for the Paris Museum. This ran it up to a nearly prohibitory price. Then the Arabs fell to fighting over the expected money. The dispute settled nothing, so, kindling a fire under the stone and pouring water on it when it was hot, they broke it into fragments, which they distributed among the several granaries to act as blessings to the grain. Prior to the destruction, a messenger from M. Clermont-Ganneau had obtained a squeeze of the inscription; but having to escape precipitately on horseback and crumpling up the paper while it was still wet, he broke it into seven pieces, and it was not of much use. Better squeezes of the two larger portions of the broken stone were afterward obtained by a messenger from Sir Charles Warren and by another from M. Clermont-Ganneau; finally many of the fragments were recovered and as far as possible placed together by M. Clermont-Ganneau. Although parts here and there are uncertain or missing, the inscription is in the main quite intelligible and clear. The stone with the missing parts supplied in plaster of Paris from the squeezes is now in the Museum of the Louvre in Paris. It was found that of about 1,100 letters, 669 in all, or less than ⅔, had been recovered, and that the language was akin to Hebrew. The inscription is as follows:

1. I am Mesha, son of Chemosh ... king of Moab, the D-
2. aibonite. My father reigned over Moab for thirty years, and I became king
3. after my father. And I made this high place for Chemosh in Ḳrhh with ... [Sal vation,
4. because he saved me from all the kings and because he let me see my desire upon all them that hated me. Omr-
5. i king of Israel, he afflicted Moab many days, because Chemosh was angry with his la-
6. nd. And his son succeeded him; and he too said: "I will afflict Moab." In my days he said. ...
7. But I saw my desire upon him and upon his house, and Israel perished with an everlasting destruction. Now Omri had taken possession of all the la-}
8. nd of Meheḍeba (Medeba), and dwelt in it during his days and half the days of his sons, forty years; but resto-
9. re it did Chemosh in my days. And I built Ba'alme'on and I made in it the reservoir (?) and I built
10. Ḳiriathan (Kiryathaim). And the men of Gad had dwelt in the land of 'Aṭaroth from of old, and had built for himself the king of I-
11. srael 'Aṭaroth. And I fought against the city and took it, and slew all the [people of]
12. the city, a gazingstock unto Chemosh and unto Moab. And I brought back from there the altar hearth of Daudoh (?) and drag-
13. ged it before Chemosh in Ḳeriyyoth (Kerioth). And I settled the men of Srn therein and the men of
14. Mhrth. And Chemosh said to me: "Go, take Nebo against Israel." And I
15. went by night and fought against it from break of dawn until noon, and to-
16. ok it and slew all of them, seven thousand men and ... and women and ...
17. and maidservants: for I had devoted it to 'Ashtar-Chemosh. And I took thence the a ltar-hear-]

18. ths of Jehovah and dragged them before Chemosh. Now the king of Israel had built
19. Yahaṣ; and he abode therein while he fought against me. But Chemosh drove him out from before me. And
20. I took of Moab two hundred men, all its chiefs; and led them against Yahaṣ and took it
21. to add to Daibon. I built Krhh, the wall of the Woods and the wall of
22. the Mound. And I built its gates and I built its towers. And
23. I built the king's palace, and made the sluices (?) of the reserv[oir (?) for wat]er in the midst of
24. the city. And there was no cistern in the midst of the city, in Krhh. And I said to all the people: "Make for
25. yourselves, each one a cistern in his house." And I cut out the cutting for Krhh with the help of prisoner-
26. s of Israel. I built 'Aro'er and made the highway by the Arnon.
27. I built Beth-bamoth, for it was pulled down. I built Beṣer, for ruins
28. . . . . [had it become . . . of] Daibon were fifty, for all Daibon was obedient. And I reigned
29. [over] one hundred in the cities which I added to the land. And I built
30. Mehĕdeba (Medeba) and Beth-diblathen and as for Beth-ba'alme'on, I took thither the [herdsmen]
31. . . . . . . the sheep of the land. And as for Hauronān, there dwelt in it the so n].... . And
32. . . . . . . Chemosh said to me: "Go down, fight against Hauronān"; and I went down and . . .
33. . . . . . . and Chemosh [resto] red it in my days. And I . . . thence ten (?)
34. . . . .

To judge from Mesha's own words, the stele was a memorial commemorative not merely of his recovery of independence for Moab from Israel, but of his glorious and successful reign as a whole (l. 4, 31); it was erected late in his reign, after the death of Ahab, after the humiliation of that house also, and not improbably after the extinction of the line of Omri by Jehu, and the entrance of Israel into its period of dire distress (l. 7). The Hebrew records date the revolt of Moab after the death of Ahab (II Kings 1:1; 3:5). See OMRI 4; MESHA, III. 2.

Mo'a·di'ah (mṓ'á·dī'á) [Jehovah summons (or promises, in Arabic)]. A father's house among the priests in the time of the high priest Joiakim (Neh. 12:17); see MAADIAH.

Mo'din (mṓ'dĭn) [informers or prognosticators, prognostication (cf. Isa. 47:13)]. The native town of the Maccabees (I Macc. 2:1), with the family tomb where Mattathias and 2 of his sons, Judas and Jonathan, were buried (I Macc. 2:70; 9:19; 13:25). It stood on the edge of the plain of Philistia (ch. 16:4, 5), and the tomb was visible from the sea (ch. 13:29 seq.). In Hebrew it was called Mṓdĭ'ĭm and Mṓdĭ'ĭth. The town was still in existence in the time of Eusebius and Jerome, in the vicinity of Diospolis (Lydda). The Talmud states its distance from Jerusalem at 15 Roman miles. The most probable location is el-Medyeh (or el-Midyah), a village about 7 miles e. of Lydda and about 16 from the sea. South of the village is a conical knoll, Er-Rās, from the top of which Joppa and the sea are visible; this may have been the site of Simon's tomb.

Mol'a·dah (mŏl'á-dá) [birth, origin]. A town in the extreme s. of Judah (Josh. 15:26), assigned to the Simeonites (Josh. 19:2; I Chron. 4:28). It was inhabited after the Captivity (Neh. 11:26). It is doubtless the town known in the Greek period as Malatha, in Idumaea, to which Herod Agrippa I, during the earlier and less prosperous period of his life, retired in debt and in depression of spirits (Jos. Antiq. xviii. 6, 2). The Onomasticon locates Malatha 4 Roman miles from Arad and on the road from Hebron to Aila, that is Elath; identified with Tell el-Milḥ, on the Roman road 7½ miles s.w. of Arad, where there are ves iges of an extensive town with important wells. It is about 14 miles e. by s. from Beer-sheba, and 22 s. by w. from Hebron.

Mole. 1. The rendering of Hebrew tinshemeth (Lev. 11:30, A.V.). See CHAMELEON.

2. The rendering of the Hebrew words ḥăphōr pērōth, digging of holes or digging of rats (Isa. 2:20). The 2 words are better regarded as one, ḥăpharpārōth, diggers. These may be rats or moles. It is believed that no species of Talpa, the genus to which the common mole (T. europaea) belongs, exists in Palestine, its place being taken by the mole rat (Spalax typhlus), which is probably the animal intended by Isaiah. This animal is very common in the Holy Land, living underground in small groups. It resembles the mole in appearance, but is not of the same order, being a rodent feeding on vegetables, chiefly bulbs, whereas the mole is insectivorous. It is larger than the mole, being 8 or more inches long. It is silverȳ gray in color, is tailless, and has only minute or rudimentary eyes.

Mo'lech (mō'lĕk), in A.V. twice **Mo'loch**, a spelling introduced into the English version through the LXX of Amos 5:26 and its quotation by Stephen in Acts 7:43. The Hebrew text and R.V. have "your king" in place of Moloch [Heb. melek, king, with the vowels of bōsheth, shame, in order to show contempt for the heathen god]. A deity worshiped by the children of Ammon (I Kings 11:7). The article is prefixed to his name where it occurs in Hebrew, indicating that the word is not a proper name, but an appellative preserving its meaning of "reigning one." He was known also as Milcom (I Kings 11:5, 33) and Malcam (Jer. 49:1, 3, R.V.; Zeph. 1:5; and R.V. marg., II Sam. 12:30; I Chron. 20:2), proper names formed by the familiar terminations ōm and ām. He was an aspect of Baal (Jer. 32:35), whose name is a common noun likewise and signifies lord. Baal was worshiped with human sacrifices at Tyre under the name of Melcarth, king of the city; and an exceedingly detestable feature of Molech's worship was the burning of children to him in the fire. The practice was in vogue early; and the Mosaic law was enacted that if any man made or permitted his children to "pass through the fire to Molech" he was to be put to death (Lev. 18:21; 20:1–5). Nevertheless Solomon in his old age erected an altar to Milcom, being led into this idolatry by his Ammonite wives; and in the following centuries children were burned to Molech in the valley of Hinnom at the high place of Topheth (Ps. 106:38; Jer. 7:31; 19:4, 5; Ezek. 16:21; 23:37, 39; cf. Isa. 30:33). Ahaz burned children of his there (II Chron. 28:3), and Manasseh made at least one of his sons pass through the fire (II Kings 21:6). The n. Israelites were also guilty of this hideous rite (II Kings 17:17; Ezek. 23:37). Josiah destroyed the altars which Solomon built on the mount of corruption to this false divinity and other heathen gods, and defiled the high place of Topheth (II Kings 23:10, 13).

Mo'lid (mō'lĭd) [begetter]. A man of Judah, family of Hezron, house of Jerahmeel (I Chron. 2:29).

Mo'loch (mō'lŏk). See MOLECH.

Mol'ten Sea or **Bra'zen Sea.** A great basin made by Solomon of brass which David had taken as booty (I Chron. 18:8). It stood in the inner court of the Temple between the altar of burnt offering and the sanctuary, somewhat toward the s., and was intended for the priests to wash their hands and feet in before entering the sanctuary or approaching the altar (I Kings 7:39; II Chron. 4:6; Jos. *Antiq.* viii. 3, 6; cf. Ex. 30:18–21). It was round, 10 cubits in diameter and 5 in height, and held 2,000 baths (I Kings 7:23, 26; in II Chron. 4:5 incorrectly 3,000). The brim curved outward like a cup, and the sides were ornamented with 2 rows of knops underneath the brim (I Kings 7:24, 26). It was not an exact hemisphere, but its sides bulged out like a tulip, as appears from the statement of its capacity and from the comparison of it to a lily. It stood upon 12 brazen oxen, in 4 groups of 3 each, facing the 4 quarters. Ahaz took it down from the oxen (II Kings 16:17); and finally, when Nebuchadnezzar captured Jerusalem, he broke the basin in pieces (II Kings 25:13, 16; Jer. 27:19–22).

Mon'ey. Barter was originally the method of exchange. Thus Latin *pecunia* (money) from *pecus* (cattle) shows that once cattle were the standard of value. Coins were probably first issued in the 8th century B.C., in Asia Minor, where lived the Lydians and Greeks. According to Herodotus (i. 94) the Lydians were the first to issue coins. Staters, made of an alloy of gold with silver called electron, were struck in Lydia in Asia Minor and silver coins at Aegina as early as 700 to 650 B.C. In the rest of w. Asia and in Egypt people were content to use gold and silver in bars, rings, and other forms, probably stamped with the value, but not issued by authority (Josh. 7:21; and cf. name of talent, *kikkār,* circle). In business transactions reliance was not placed on the stamp, but the quantity was determined by weighing (Gen. 23:16; 43:21); see WEIGHTS. Counting was rarely resorted to (II Kings 12:10 *seq.*), and then only to form a general estimate. Shekel in the early period does not mean a coin bearing an authoritative stamp, but a certain weight (*shekel*) of silver. The weights formed a series in the denomination of talent, maneh, shekel, gerah, and beka or half shekel; see WEIGHTS. References to shekels or other denominations of precious metal before the time of native Jewish coinage are to uncoined metal, not to coins. Darius Hystaspis, 521–486 B.C., is credited with the introduction of coinage into Persia (Herod. iv. 166), whereby the Jews became acquainted with coins. The ordinary daric (Ezra 2:69; in A.V. dram) was a thick gold coin, showing on one side the king, kneeling and holding a bow and a javelin. On the reverse was an irregular square, doubtless the mark of the punch with which the lump of metal was driven into the die. It was worth about $5.50; see DARIC. After the fall of the Persian Empire, the Greek system came into vogue in Palestine, and money was reckoned by talents and drachmas (I Macc. 11:28; II Macc. 4:19).

In the year 141–140 B.C., Simon Maccabaeus obtained the right to coin money for his nation with his own stamp (I Macc. 15:6), but apparently the privilege was soon withdrawn (v. 27). The small copper coin of John Hyrcanus bears on the obverse within a wreath of olive the inscription, "Jehohanan the high priest, and the community of the Jews." The reverse has a Greek symbol, the double cornucopia with a poppy head in the center. Herod the Great and his successors down to Herod Agrippa II issued copper coins, but only with Greek legends.

The money of the Greeks, however, continued to circulate along with the Jewish coinage. The coins consisted of drachmas and tetradrachmas. The silver drachma (Luke 15:8, R.V. marg.) in the time of the Herods and the procurators was equivalent to the Roman denarius and worth about 16 cents; the silver stater or tetradrachma (Matt. 17:27 marg.), struck by the Greek cities of Syria and Phoenicia, was worth about 66 cents, but soon afterward became much debased. The lepton was a small copper coin (Luke 12:59; 21:2, rendered mite), not the lepton of the Greek system, but the smallest copper coin in circulation, worth about ⅛ cent and equal to half the quadrans (Mark 12:42). It was a Jewish coin, for only Jewish money was allowed to be offered in the Temple; and it was probably a copper coin issued by John Hyrcanus or another Maccabaean prince. The didrachma, which corresponded to the half shekel (Matt. 17:24 marg.), was probably not in circulation or but little used in Palestine. The talent employed in Palestine (I Macc. 11:28; Matt. 18:24) was the Attic talent, which Alexander had made the lawful standard throughout his empire and which afterward maintained its supremacy. It was not a coin, but money of account; was divided into minas (I Macc. 14:24; Luke 19:13–25, Gr. *mnā,* mina, rendered pound); and it consisted of 60 minas or 6,000 drachmas. A mina consisted of 100 drachmas. It suffered great depreciation, the drachma falling off from about 67.5 grains to about 55 grains or 16 cents under the early Caesars. Pound (Gr. *mnā*=mina) as a sum of money was equivalent to 100 drachmas and worth about 16 dollars (Luke 19:13, R.V. marg.; cf. 15:8, R.V. marg.).

With the advent of the Romans in Palestine, the money of the Romans had also come into circulation. The denarius (Matt. 18:28; A.V., penny; R.V., shilling) was a silver coin. In the time of the empire its obverse almost invariably bore the head of the reigning sov-

Silver Denarius with Image and Superscription of Tiberius Caesar

ereign or of some member of the imperial family. From the time of Augustus to that of Nero, its standard weight was 60 grains, equivalent to about 17 cents. It was the tribute money payable by the Jews to the imperial treasury (Matt. 22:19). The assarion (Matt. 10:29; Luke 12:6, A.V., farthing; R.V., penny), the Greek name of the Roman as, was a small copper coin, the value of which was reduced in 217 B.C. to ¹⁄₁₆ of a denarius or

Copper Coin of Herod Antipas, Tetrarch of Galilee

to about 1 cent. The quadrans (Matt. 5:26; Mark 12:42, rendered farthing) was the 4th part of an as, or ¼ cent. The procurators of Judea were also accustomed to coin money. They issued copper pieces in the name of the imperial family and with the legend in Greek letters. One coin bears the name of Ti. Claudius Caesar Germanicus written in Greek on the margin, and in the center two palm branches laid crosswise with the date, "year 14," between them. The reverse contains the name of the emperor's wife, Julia Agrippina. It was struck in A.D. 54, during the procurator-ship of Felix.

The gold coin which was current in Palestine during the N.T. period was the Roman denarius aureus, generally termed simply aureus (Jos. *Antiq.* xiv. 8, 5, rendered pieces of gold), which passed for 25 silver denarii.

Silver Half Shekel of Year 1 of the First Revolt
(A.D. 66-70)

A national coinage of silver was struck by the Jews during the First Revolt (A.D. 66–70) and also during the Second Revolt (A.D. 132–135). On the suppression of the First Revolt and the capture of Jerusalem (A.D. 70), coins

Silver Shekel of Year 2 of the First Revolt
(A.D. 66-70)

such as that shown in the accompanying cut were struck in Rome with the image and name of the emperor Vespasian on the obverse, and a female captive under a palm tree, with the inscription "Judaea subdued" or "Judaea captive" on the reverse. Herod Agrippa II, king of part of Galilee and the region to the e., continued to issue copper coins after the fall of Jerusalem. Some dating from the reign of Titus bear the head of the emperor, his name and titles, on the obverse; on the reverse a winged victory holding a wreath and

Silver Coin of Vespasian, Commemorating the
Capture of Jerusalem (Struck at Rome)

a palm branch, and the date, "year 26 of King Agrippa."

During the Second Revolt, which was headed by Bar-cocheba, A.D. 132–135, shekels and quarter shekels of silver and also of copper, with old Hebrew inscriptions, were again coined. The shekel shows a tetrastyle temple on the obverse, probably a conventional representation of the Beautiful Gate of the Temple at Jerusalem. At the sides of it appears the word Simon, the personal name of the leader of the revolt; while above it a star is introduced, doubtless in allusion to the surname of the leader, Bar-cocheba, son of a star. To obtain quarter shekels the Roman denarius was restruck, which at this time so nearly equaled the quarter shekel in value that it could be substituted for it without inconvenience.

Mon'ey-chang'ers. When a census was taken every Israelite, whether rich or poor, who had reached the age of 20 years was required to pay half a shekel into the treasury of the Lord as an offering to make atonement (Ex. 30:13–15). Later it was customary, according to Maimonides, to pay this poll tax annually. Besides this tax, pious Israelites made freewill offerings, which they cast into chests placed in the court of the women (Mark 12:41). This money had to be in native coin since several currencies circulated in Palestine in the time of Christ, and as multitudes of Jews from foreign lands visited Jerusalem at the passover, bringing the coin of their country with them, need arose of facilities for exchanging foreign for native money. The business of the money-changer sprang up. These men had stalls in the city, and as the feast approached they were admitted to the precincts of the Temple and placed their tables in the Court of the Gentiles. The commission paid for half a shekel was, according to the Talmud, a *kollybos*, equal to 12 grains of silver and worth about 3 cents. From this premium the money-changer was called a *kollybistēs* (Matt. 21:12), and from the table at which he sat a *trapezitēs* (Matt. 25:27). On two different occasions Jesus overturned the tables of the money-changers and drove the cattle dealers from the court, because their presence and too often their dishonesty and avarice were incompatible with the sanctity of the place and with the quiet which is necessary for worship (John 2:14–16; Matt. 21:12, 13).

Month. In Egypt the Israelites were acquainted with a year of 12 months of 30 days each, with 5 additional days to produce conformity with the solar year of 365 days (Herod. ii. 4), and in the account of the Flood the months are reckoned at 30 days each (Gen. 7:11, 24; 8:3, 4). Afterward, however, the Hebrews appear to have used a lunar month. This may be gathered from: (1) the 2 words for month which denote respectively new moon and lunation and indicate the original measurement; (2) passages like Gen. 1:14; Ps. 104:19; Ecclus. 43:6–8; (3) the observance of the day of the new moon by special offerings to Jehovah (Num. 10:10; 28:11–14; II Chron. 2:4); and (4) the coincidence between the passover, which was always celebrated on the evening of the 14th day of the month, and the full moon (Ps. 81:3–5); see further Jos. *Antiq.* iii. 10, 3 and 5; iv. 4, 6, and article YEAR. A lunation requires a little more than 29½ days. The months would accordingly average 29 and 30 days alternately. When, however, a month is spoken of generally, 30 days are meant (cf. Num. 20:29; Deut. 34:8 with ch. 21:13). The months were commonly distinguished by number. The names of only 4 Hebrew months are found in Bible narratives relating to the period before the Captivity. They are the 1st month, Abib (Ex. 13:4, etc.); the 2d month, Ziv (I Kings 6:37); the 7th, Ethanim (I Kings 8:2); and the 8th, Bul (I Kings 6:38). After the Captivity the names in common use among the Babylonians and other Semites were employed. See YEAR.

Moon. The principal luminary of the night (Gen. 1:16; Ps. 136:9), relied upon to measure time, marking off moons or months, and regulating the day of the passover, and thus aiding in regulating the feasts of the year (Gen. 1:14; Ps. 104:19; Ecclus. 43:6, 7; Jos. *Antiq.* iii. 10, 5). Almost all the nations with which the ancient Hebrews came into contact worshiped the moon. Ur of the Chaldees, from which Abraham emigrated, and Haran, where he settled for a time and where Jacob dwelt for 20 years, were noted seats of the moon's worship. When Abraham removed to Canaan, he had neighbors who worshiped the moon. The Egyptians sacrificed the pig to the moon, when the disk was at its full (Herod. ii. 47). In the time of the Assyrian and Babylonian invasions of Palestine, the Hebrews came again into contact with people who regarded the moon as one of the great gods. At this time the worship of the moon and other heavenly bodies made serious inroads on the religion of Jehovah (II Kings 21:3; 23:4, 5; Jer. 7:18; 8:2). The moon was adored by a kiss of the hand (Job 31:26, 27), with the burning of incense (II Kings 23:5). In heathen temples the moon was often represented by the crescent as a symbol and by an image in the form of a human being. This heathenism had its check in the sublime doctrine of Jehovah. The sun and moon were made by the God of Israel, were created for the useful purpose of giving light, and were serviceable to man in affording a convenient measurement of time.

Different from the worship of the moon was the conception that the varying appearance of the moon from night to night at its rising, during its course across the sky, and at its setting, which are due to atmospheric and astronomic conditions, presaged political occurrences. The aspect of the moon may indicate weather probabilities, but the folly of basing predictions of national events on such phenomena was pointed out by the prophets (Isa. 47:13). The Hebrews seem to have shared in the widespread belief that the moon may affect the health and under circumstances produce evil consequences to muscles and nerves. But the child of God can safely entrust himself to the watchful care of Jehovah (Ps. 121:6).

As the months were lunar, the new moon marked the beginning of the month, and the day of the new moon, being the commencement of a natural division of time, was observed as a holy day. No set convocation seems to have been prescribed, but additional sacrifices were offered (Num. 28:11–14), trumpets were blown (Num. 10:10; Ps. 81:3), ordinary labor was suspended (Amos 8:5), and the day offered favorable opportunity for religious instruction (II Kings 4:23; Ezek. 46:1, 3). It was kept with joy and feasting (I Sam. 20:5; Judith 8:6). The new moon of the 7th month marked the beginning of the 7th recurrence of a fixed portion of time and consequently fell under the Sabbath law and was observed as such in addition to the usual worship on the day of the new moon (Lev. 23:24, 25; Num. 29:1–6). After the Exile this celebration assumed the character of a new year's festival.

The advent of the new moon was calculated at an early period (I Sam. 20:5, 18). The Babylonian astrologers watched for it on the evening when it was expected to be seen, in order to take note of its appearance. According to the Talmud, the sanhedrin assembled 7 times a year early in the morning of the 30th day of the month. Watchmen were stationed on the heights about Jerusalem to watch for the new moon and report it as soon as seen. When the evidence of its appearance was deemed sufficient, the sanhedrin pronounced the word Me'kuddash (consecrated), and the day became the 1st of the new month, leaving 29 days for the preceding month. If fogs or clouds prevented the moon from being discerned, the day was reckoned as the 30th and the new month began on the morrow. The announcement of the new moon was made to the country at large by lighting a beacon fire on the Mount of Olives, which was repeated by similar signals from other mountain tops. The Samaritans are said to have thwarted this plan by kindling fires prematurely. In consequence the signals were discontinued, and the announcement of the new moon was made by messengers.

Moph (mŏf). See MEMPHIS.

Mo·rash'tite (mō-răsh'tīt), in A.V. **Mo·ras'thite** (mō-răs'thit). A native or inhabitant of Moresheth, as was the Prophet Micah (ch. 1:1; Jer. 26:18); see MORESHETH-GATH.

Mor'de·cai (môr'dĕ-kī) [from Akkad. *Marduk*, chief god of Babylon]. 1. A Benjamite, son or descendant of Jair, son of Shimei, son of Kish (Esth. 2:5). The relative clause which as v. 6 follows this genealogy may refer to the last name of the series (cf. II Chron. 22:9), and state that Kish, a Benjamite, was carried into exile with King Jeconiah in 597 B.C.; or the clause may relate to an earlier name in the list, for example, to Jair, in which case Mordecai was a descendant of Jair, a Benjamite, who was carried away to Babylonia with Jeconiah. He brought up Hadassah or Esther, his uncle's daughter, adopting her as his own after her father and mother had died. She acted under his direction in the series of events which ended by making her queen of Persia as wife of Ahasuerus (Esth. 2:7–20). This king was Xerxes, who reigned from 486 to 464 B.C. Through Esther Mordecai informed the king of a plot against his life, and the 2 conspirators were executed (vs. 21–23). When Haman was the king's favorite, Mordecai declined to prostrate himself before him, refusing to pay the customary civility because of Haman's unprincipled character or perhaps because Haman was an Agagite. The insulted dignitary determined to wreak vengeance not on Mordecai alone, but on the entire Jewish people, and the king granted him leave (ch. 3:5–11). One night Ahasuerus could not sleep, and to relieve the tedium of his waking hours, he desired that the book recording the chronicles of the kingdom should be read to him by his attendants. The conspiracy came up in the part read, and the king remembered that he had done nothing for his deliverer. When morning dawned he requested Haman, who had come to ask permission to hang Mordecai, to take that faithful subject, array him in royal apparel, and conduct him through the streets of the city (Susa) mounted on a horse belonging to the sovereign, and to proclaim before him as he went along: "Thus shall it be done to the man whom the king delighteth to honor." This was the commencement of Haman's fall, and of a series of events which resulted in the death of Haman and his sons, and the promotion of Mordecai to be the 2d man in the empire (Esth., chs. 6 to 10).

2. A Jew who returned from Babylon with Zerubbabel (Ezra 2:2; Neh. 7:7).

Mo'reh (mō'rĕ) [teacher, soothsayer]. 1. A terebinth or oak tree and grove near Shechem (Gen. 12:6; Deut. 11:30), which most probably took its name from an archer or teacher who at one time or other dwelt there. Abraham encamped by it when he arrived in Canaan from Mesopotamia, and erected an altar there to Jehovah who appeared unto him. It was probably the tree under which Jacob buried the amulets and idols that his family had brought with them from Haran, and where Joshua erected a stone to commemorate the covenant which the people renewed there, and whither the men of Shechem went to make Abimelech king (Gen. 35:4; Josh. 24:26, though slightly different words are used for terebinth in these two passages from that employed in Gen. 12:6; Judg. 9:6).

2. A hill in the valley of Jezreel to the n. of the spring of Harod (Judg. 7:1), probably Jebel Dahy, or Little Hermon, about 8 miles n.w. of Mount Gilboa and 1 mile s. of Nain.

Mo'resh·eth-gath' (mō'rĕsh-ĕth-găth') [possession of Gath or of a wine press]. A town mentioned in connection with places in Judah, and therefore evidently situated in the same region (Micah 1:14). Jerome located it in the vicinity of Eleutheropolis, and it may be identified with Khirbet el-Baṣal, about 1¼ miles from that place. Gath in the name is generally supposed to denote the Philistine city and to indicate that Moresheth was near it. Perhaps the town was the home of the Prophet Micah (ch. 1:1).

Mo·ri'ah (mȯ-rī'ȧ). 1. A district, on one of whose hills Abraham prepared to sacrifice Isaac; probably the region lying round about the hill of the same name on which the Temple was afterward built, and taking its name from that hill or from some circumstance common to both it and the hill (Gen. 22:2; Jos. *Antiq.* i. 13, 1 and 2). The Samaritans, and after them a few modern scholars like Bleek, Tuch, Stanley, identify Moreh near Shechem with Moriah (see Samaritan text) and Gerizim with the scene of Abraham's sacrifice. The Samaritan identification doubtless rests on the fact that Abraham did build an altar at Moreh (Gen. 12:6, 7), and the identification was encouraged by the desire to enhance the religious glory of their country. But the etymology of Moreh and Moriah is different.

2. The hill on which was the threshing floor of Ornan the Jebusite. David purchased the floor and erected an altar on it, and Solomon made it the site of the Temple (II Sam. 24:18 *seq.;* II Chron. 3:1). The original hill has been much altered artificially and part of its slopes are hidden beneath accumulated rubbish and embankments, but its general contour has been determined. Mount Moriah stood between the Kidron and Tyropoeon valleys, and lifted its summit directly opposite the mouth of that ravine which forms the w. branch of the latter valley. On the n. a slight depression separated it from the narrow neck of land which connected it with the main plateau. It is difficult to state exact dimensions; to call its original area 600 feet from n. to s. by 300 from e. to w. may be not far from the truth. Its highest point is now, according to Warren, 2,448 feet above the ocean. Other platforms are 2,430 and 2,420 feet, from which the e. and w. slopes very rapidly fall.

Mor'tar, I. A vessel in which grain and spices are pounded with a pestle (Num. 11:8; Prov. 27:22).

Mor'tar, II. A substance used to bind bricks or stones together in a wall. Various materials were used: 1. Mud or clay without lime (Nahum 3:14), frequently employed by peasants in Palestine. 2. Mortar properly so called, consisting of sand and lime mixed with water, which was employed in building the better class of houses (cf. Ezek. 13:10). Palestine is a limestone country, and lime is easily obtained (Isa. 33:12). 3. Bitumen in regions like Babylonia where clay and lime are scarce (Gen. 11:3, R.V. marg.). The walls of houses were and still are daubed or plastered with mud or mortar, often mixed with straw and pebbles, to protect them against the weather (Lev. 14:42). The mortar used for this purpose in Egypt consists of ½ clay, ¼ lime, and the rest ashes and straw.

Mo·se'rah (mȯ-sē'rȧ), in A.V. **Mo·se'ra** (mȯ-sē'rȧ) [bond, fetter]. An encampment of the Israelites in the wilderness near Benejaakan (Deut. 10:6). In Num. 33:30, the plural form Moseroth is used as the name of the place. The site is unknown; but it was near Mount Hor, by the border of Edom (Num. 20:23; 33:37), in the country of the Horites (cf. Gen. 36:20, 27 with I Chron. 1:42). See HOR 1.

Mo·se'roth (mȯ-sē'rŏth). See MOSERAH.

Mo'ses (mō'zĕz) [from Egypt. *mś,* child, a son]. The great Hebrew leader and legislator. He was a Levite, family of Kohath, house of Amram (Ex. 6:18, 20). Jochebed is called the mother of Moses (v. 20); but this expression is doubtless to be understood in the sense of ancestress, Amram and Jochebed being founders of the tribal house into which Moses was born; see EGYPT. The edict requiring the Hebrew male children to be cast into the Nile brought Moses into imminent peril of his life. But his mother saw that he was a goodly child, or, as Stephen words it, "exceeding fair" (Acts 7:20), and she hid him 3 months in her house. When she could hide him no longer, she placed him within an ark of bulrushes, which had been daubed with bitumen and pitch to render it watertight; put it among the flags on the river's bank; and posted Miriam, then a young girl, to watch the result. By and by Pharaoh's daughter, attended by her maidens, came to the river to bathe. Her name was Thermuthis, according to Josephus (Jos. *Antiq.* ii. 9, 5). The rabbis identified her with Bithiah (I Chron. 4:18). She espied the ark, and had it opened. She saw by the features and color of the infant that he was a Hebrew. He wept and she was touched with pity. At this critical moment Miriam stepped forward, and with admirable tact asked: "Shall I go and call thee a nurse of the Hebrew women, that she may nurse the child for thee?" The princess bade her go, and the child's mother was called and the infant committed to her care. When he was weaned he was taken to Pharaoh's daughter, who adopted him and called him Moses. The name was doubly fitting, the child having been drawn from the water and being adopted as a son (Ex. 2:1–10); the Egyptian *mś* (son) by a popular etymology is connected with Heb. *māshāh,* to draw out.

The adopted son of a princess required a princely education, and Moses became instructed in all the wisdom of the Egyptians (Acts 7:22), who were then unsurpassed in civilization by any people in the world. This was designed to fit him for high office under the government, if not even for the Egyptian throne. But in God's intention it was to prepare him for the leadership of the Hebrews. He was possessed of great natural ability, and the training which he received schooled him for the great work for which he was destined. He became familiar with court life and intercourse with princes, with the grandeur and pomp of religious worship and with ritualistic conventionalities and symbolism, with letters and the literary ideas of the time. He witnessed the administration of justice, and he acquired a general acquaintance with the arts which were practiced in civilized life. He remembered, however, his origin, believed the promises which had been made to the Hebrew people, and before the close of his sojourn in Egypt he had discovered the call of God to him to be the judge and the deliverer of the Israelites. Going out to observe the state of his countrymen, he saw one of them struck by an Egyptian. Moses killed the oppressor, and hid his body in the sand. Another day he tried to reconcile 2 Hebrews who were striving together, on which the one who was in the wrong insolently asked: "Who made thee a prince and a judge over us? thinkest thou to kill me, as thou killedst the Egyptian?" Moses was alarmed to find that his deed of the previous day had become known, and, on learning that it had reached the ears of Pharaoh, who said that he would kill him for it, fled from Egypt to the land of Midian. He had thus refused to be called the son of Pharaoh's daughter; he had cast in his lot with the people of God, and was to assume the position of deliverer and judge (Ex. 2:11–15; Acts 7:24–28; Heb. 11:24, 25). He was now 40 years old (Acts 7:23).

On arriving in Midian, Moses aided the daughters of Jethro to water their flocks. This act introduced him to Jethro, who was a priest. Jethro showed him hospitality, furnished him with employment, and gave him one of his daughters to wife. She bore Moses 2 sons, Gershom and Eliezer (Ex. 2:22; 18:3, 4). He remained in Midian 40 years (Acts 7:30), intimately associated with a people who were descended from Abraham and perhaps worshiped the God of Abraham (cf. Ex. 18:10–12). This period was likewise a time of preparation. He enjoyed close fellowship with a leading man of the Midianites, a man of sound judgment (Ex., ch. 18) and a priest. Here Moses widened his acquaintance with religious thought and forms of worship. He learned the roads of the wilderness, its resources, climate, and mode of life of its inhabitants. Amid its solemn grandeur and in its deep solitude he had opportunity for reflection. At the close of this period he was astonished to see a bush burning and yet remaining unconsumed. As he turned aside to look more narrowly at a sight so unique, he received an authoritative call from Jehovah, and the objections which he raised on the ground of insufficiency for the work were overcome (Ex. 3:11): inability to tell the people in what character God would manifest himself for their deliverance (v. 13), lack of credentials to secure the recognition of the people (ch. 4:1), and lack of eloquence to persuade (v. 10). These difficulties were removed, and Moses acquiesced, but unwillingly. God was displeased, and promised that Aaron should help Moses (v. 14).

Moses took his wife Zipporah and his sons to return to Egypt (v. 20). Two sons had been born to him. One of them, doubtless the younger, he had not circumcised, because Zipporah regarded the rite as bloody. In yielding to her in this matter Moses had shown himself unfaithful in his own household and unfit for his high commission. God was displeased with this neglect of the sign of the covenant; and now, as Moses was returning to Egypt with his family, God brought him nigh unto death at the inn. But Zipporah discerned the cause and, desirous of saving her husband's life, at once took a knife and performed the operation, saying, "A bridegroom of blood art thou to me" (Ex. 4:24–26). Arriving in Egypt, Moses, in conjunction with Aaron, repeatedly conveyed to Pharaoh the divine commands, the rejection of which brought on the obstinate king and his people the succession of judgments known as the ten plagues (chs. 5 to 13:16). When the departure from Egypt took place, it was Moses who, under divine guidance, led the people. At Sinai he was admitted to intimate relations with God. God allowed all the people to hear his voice in articulate words; but he permitted Moses to see him manifested and he "spake unto Moses face to face, as a man speaketh unto his friend" (Ex. 24:9–11; 33:11, 17–23; 34:5–29), and he revealed his will to Moses from time to time for the instruction of his people, as he did afterward to the successive prophets. In communion with God Moses obtained the statutes based on the Ten Commandments (see THEOCRACY). Immediately afterward, during a sojourn of 40 days on the mount, he was made acquainted with the form, dimensions, and materials of the tabernacle and its furniture (see TABERNACLE 2), and received from God the two tables of stone; but on finding that in his absence the people had taken to worshiping a golden calf, he dashed the tablets to the ground as he neared the camp and broke them in his right-

eous indignation and in token of the fact that the covenant, of which they were the fundamental law, had been annulled by the sin of the people. He then inflicted punishment upon the people; and all who had not held aloof from the place of idolatrous worship, or had not retired when reminded of their sin by the act of Moses, in their obstinacy were exposed to death at the hands of the Levites who offered themselves as executioners. Having acted symbolically and judicially, Moses now acted mediatorially and interceded for the people, and God promised that his angel should accompany the host.

Moses was again called into the mountain, and the portions of the covenant respecting the service of God, which had been grossly violated in a fundamental principle, were singled out and emphasized, and he received two other tables inscribed like the first (Ex., chs. 19; 20; 32 to 34). On each of these occasions he fasted forty days and nights (Ex. 24:18; 34:28; Deut. 9:9, 18), as Elijah afterward did (I Kings 19:8), both in this respect foreshadowing the similar fast of our Lord (Matt. 4:2). The name of Moses is forever associated with the laws given at Sinai and during the subsequent desert wanderings (see LEVITICUS and NUMBERS).

When Moses came down from Mount Sinai, after the 2d sojourn of 40 days, with the tables of the law in his hand, the skin of his face shone, sending forth beams (Heb., horns), and the people were afraid to come near him (Ex. 34:29, R.V. marg.). Moses called to them, and they returned to him, and he spoke with them and gave them all that the Lord had spoken with him. "And till Moses had done speaking with them, he put a veil on his face. But when Moses went in before the Lord to speak with him, he took the veil off, until he came out" (Ex. 34:33, 34, A.V.). The R.V. and J.V., following the LXX and Vulgate and correctly rendering the Hebrew, say just the contrary: "And when Moses had done speaking with them, he put a veil on his face." He did not wear the veil while speaking either with the people or with the Lord. He wore the veil, not to hide the splendor (A.V.), but to conceal the vanishing away of the splendor (R.V.); and he wore it until he returned to the presence of the Lord, where the light of his countenance was rekindled. Moses "put a veil upon his face, that the children of Israel should not look stedfastly on the end of that which was passing away" (II Cor. 3:13, R.V., cf. v. 7).

In the 2d year of the sojourn of the Israelites in the wilderness, Moses is mentioned as having married a Cushite woman (Num. 12:1). Zipporah may have died during the preceding year, although her death is not recorded (cf. Ex. 18:2). Among the later Jews the story ran that the Cushite woman was an Ethiopian princess named Tharbis, who had fallen in love with Moses on the occasion of his leading an Egyptian army into Ethiopia, while he was still a member of Pharaoh's household (Jos. Antiq. ii. 10, 2). The tale is evidently a fabrication. The marriage took place in the wilderness, when Miriam and Aaron were jealous of Moses' superiority in public affairs. They were leaders of the host, directors of the national life, and prophets as well as Moses; and on this ground they claimed that their opposition to Moses' marriage with the foreigner should have been heeded by him. The Cushite woman was probably one of the mixed multitude which accompanied the Israelites in the flight from Egypt (Ex. 12:38).

Shortly after leaving Kadesh, Korah and other princes rebelled against the authority of Moses and Aaron, but were signally punished by God (Num., ch. 16); see KORAH 4.

At the 2d encampment at Kadesh, Moses and Aaron grievously sinned (Num., ch. 20). When bidden by God to speak to the rock that it give forth its water, Moses said to the assembled people: "Hear now, ye rebels; shall we bring you forth water out of this rock?" The brothers failed to observe their subordinate position. They claimed to be the leaders and providers of the people, whereas it was God who had led the Israelites from Egypt and had fed them for 40 years in the wilderness. They took to themselves the honor which belonged to God alone. When called upon to act for God, they acted in their own name, and used for their own glory the power delegated unto them. For this sin of treason they were denied the privilege of conducting the people into the Promised Land. It was a sore chastisement to Moses, but it made no change in the fidelity of this great servant of the Lord. After the condemnation he was faithful, as he had been before. He started the people once more on their march to Canaan. He led Aaron up Mount Hor, stripped him of his official robes, and transferred his office to Eleazar. When the people were bitten by the fiery serpents, he interceded with God for them, and at God's bidding erected the brazen serpent and bade his dying countrymen look and live. He led the armies of Israel into the territory of Sihon and Og, and conquered it for Israel. When the camp was pitched in a valley in the mountains of Abarim, and glimpses of the land of Abraham, Isaac, and Jacob were obtained, the pent-up emotions of Moses' soul again, as on other unrecorded occasions since his transgression found relief in prayer: "O Lord God, thou hast begun to show thy servant thy greatness, and thy strong hand: . . . . Let me go over, I pray thee, and see the good land that is beyond Jordan, that goodly mountain, and Lebanon." But the answer came: "Let it suffice thee; speak no more unto me of this matter . . . . for thou shalt not go over Jordan" (Deut. 3:24–27).

The camp was moved and pitched at Shittim in the valley, and Moses put his house in order that he might die. He delivered a parting address to the people; see DEUTERONOMY. He led Joshua, whom God had appointed to succeed him, before the high priest in the presence of the congregation, placed his hands upon him, and, giving him a charge, transferred to him the office which he himself had so honorably and efficiently filled for 40 years. He afterward led Joshua to the door of the tabernacle to receive a charge from God. Then he taught the people a song that they might have words of religious wisdom in their memory and on their tongues, bestowed his farewell blessing on the several tribes, ascended Mount Nebo and viewed the Promised Land from its summit, and died. He was 120 years old, yet "his eye was not dim, nor his natural force abated." God buried him near by (Deut., ch. 34).

It was during the 40 years in the wilderness that the principal literary work of Moses was done. He kept a record of the encampments (Num., ch. 33), made a note of events, such as the battle with Amalek (Ex. 17:14), committed the statutes founded on the covenant law to writing (Ex. 24:4–7), preserved a copy of his farewell address (Deut. 31:24). He had also the richness, vividness, and depth of thought requisite for writing Hebrew poetry, which is very simple in its structure and a ready vehicle for fervid utterance. The most spontaneous of his poems, written under the intense feeling of the moment, was the song which he uttered when Pharaoh was overthrown in the Red Sea (Ex. 15:1–18). Moses ascribes the glory to Jehovah (Ex. 15:1–3), describes the event (vs. 4–12), anticipates its

effect upon the enemies of Israel (vs. 13–15), and discerns in it a guarantee that Jehovah will bring Israel into the Promised Land (vs. 16–18). His farewell blessing of the tribes, like the farewell words of Jacob to his sons, was also cast in poetic form (Deut., ch. 33). Moses had literary ability; in these several forms of literature he had predecessors among the Egyptians; and especially did he have also the stimulus afforded by their literary ideas and the example of their histories, and the incentive of the awakened national life of the Hebrews, and the stirring events amid which he lived, to lead him to write a connected history of his people (or at least the basic facts), such as is found in the Pentateuch. See PENTATEUCH.

As the organizer of a nation Moses under the guidance of God provided Israel with civil and religious institutions. These institutions were timely in the sense that both kinds were regarded by the peoples of that day as normal and essential to a state, their character corresponded to the ideals of the age, and they represented the highest moral and religious truth possessed by men. The laws were not as a whole novel. The constitution consisted of ten commandments. It had long been known to Israel that idolatry, proscribed by the Second Commandment, was abhorrent to Jehovah (Gen. 35:2). There is evidence that the Sabbath day was instituted long before the Fourth Commandment was promulgated at Sinai (cf. Ex. 16:21–30). Long also before Israel heard the Law at Sinai, murder, adultery, theft, and false witness-bearing were universally held to be crimes punishable by man. The significance of Israel's constitution lay in the fact that recognized moral obligations were made the fundamental law of the kingdom, and that the Tenth Commandment probed back of the outward act into the inner nature of man and located the source of sin in the evil desires of the heart. The main portion of the Book of the Covenant consists of statutes based on the covenant law of the Decalogue (Ex. 21:1 to 23:19). In certain cases at least old laws were reaffirmed and ancient customs were made laws of the kingdom. The Code of Hammurabi (q.v.) enables the student to trace more of the ordinances back into the period before Moses than had previously been possible; and it shows also that the idea of codification, which is so marked a feature of the Book of the Covenant, had dawned upon man centuries before the time of Moses.

The ecclesiastical legislation of Moses was also timely, providing a sanctuary with the ground plan of the prevalent type of Egyptian temple, as an edifice stable, symmetrical in its proportions, and employing the approved symbolism of the day in its appointments and ritual, with a priesthood and priestly organization and priestly functions in general like those of contemporary nations. It was a sacred house and a worship that embodied the good in the religious thought and practice of the civilized world, which were intelligible alike to Israelite and Gentile, and were distinguished by monotheism and spirituality, and by the exhibition of the way in which the sinner may approach the holy God. Moses was inspired, but a body of laws and a form of worship entirely hidden from the foundation of the world were not revealed to him. Moses was a prophet, and was inspired as other prophets were inspired. Under the influence of the Holy Spirit he was made an infallible communicator to his fellow men of the mind and will of God. He spent days in personal communion with God, who enlightened his mind concerning God and the nature of the Kingdom. God led him infallibly to discern the laws appropriate to the condition of the people and adapted to discipline them in the spirit of the Kingdom; he prompted and controlled and enabled Moses to frame legislation and found institutions, more or less out of old materials and on old models indeed, yet distinguished from all analogies among contemporary peoples by the exhibition of the spiritual nature and holiness of God, by the extrication of man's conduct from merely civil relations and bringing it also into relation to God, and by the power to lift the secular life into the true service of God.

Moses had the wisdom of a statesman. He observed the opposition to him which was manifested in his own family (Num., ch. 12), the jealousy of other tribes and his own of the pre-eminence of himself and Aaron (Num., ch. 16), the worldly considerations by which the people were actuated (Num., ch. 32), their lack of faith in Jehovah at critical moments, and their readiness to lapse into idolatry. He meditated on these weaknesses which threatened the national existence; and when he came to prepare his farewell address he insisted upon the law of the one altar and upon the spirituality of religion as the great means under God of overcoming these defects by deepening the moral life on the one hand, and on the other hand by preserving purity of worship and doctrine, binding the people together as one nation, and making their own religion a grander spectacle than the ceremonies at heathen shrines; see ALTAR and DEUTERONOMY. After his death the greatness of Moses was universally recognized (Jer. 15:1; Heb. 3:2). He had, moreover, the distinguished honor of being permitted to reappear as the representative of O.T. law, with Elijah, the representative of O.T. prophecy, to hold converse with Jesus on the Mount of Transfiguration (Matt. 17:3, 4). See MICHAEL 11.

Moth. An insect proverbial for its destruction of clothing (Job 13:28; Matt. 6:19; James 5:2). Its larva feeds upon wool (Isa. 51:8), and out of the same substance builds itself a house or case, in which it lives (Job 27:18), protruding its head while eating. The clothes moth (*Tinea*) is intended, of which several species feed on fur and wool.

Mount. 1. A mountain. The word is now used almost exclusively in poetry or as part of a compound name, as Mount Carmel, Mount Tabor, Mount Zion, Mount of Olives (I Kings 18:19; Ps. 48:2; Zech. 14:4); see CARMEL, OLIVES, MOUNT OF, TABOR, ZION.
2. A mound, especially one raised against the wall of a besieged city by the assailing army (Jer. 6:6; Dan. 11:15; and R.V. of II Sam. 20:15; II Kings 19:32), and on which the battering-ram was placed (Ezek. 26:8, 9, R.V.).

Moun'tain. Of the mountains in or near Palestine the loftiest was Mount Hermon. Then followed the Lebanon range. Compared with those towering elevations such hills as Mount Zion, Mount Moriah, Mount Carmel, Mount Tabor, etc., were very inferior eminences (Deut. 3:25). Mountain is a natural image for eternal continuance (Deut. 33:15; Hab. 3:6), for stability (Isa. 54:10), for difficult, dangerous, wearisome paths in life (Jer. 13:16), for insurmountable obstacles (Zech. 4:7; Matt. 21:21).

Mount of Con'gre·ga'tion. A mountain in the farthest n. (Isa. 14:13); the reference probably being to a conception common in ancient mythology and current among the Babylonians that the gods assembled on a mountain of the n.

Mourn'ing. The mourning of the Oriental always has been ostentatious. Public expression was given to grief principally by removing ornaments and neglecting the person (Ex. 33:4; II Sam. 14:2; 19:24; Matt. 6:16–18), rending the clothes by slitting the tunic at the throat or tearing the coat or the outer mantle (Lev. 10:6; II Sam. 13:31; Joel 2:13), shaving the head or plucking out the hair (Ezra 9:3; Jer. 7:29), putting on sackcloth (Joel 1:8), sprinkling ashes or dust on the head (II Sam. 15:32), fasting (Ps. 35:13), weeping and lamenting (Joel 1:8, 13). Several of these modes were usually combined (Gen. 37:34; II Sam. 3:31, 32; 13:19; 15:32; Ezra 9:3, 5; Job 1:20; Jer. 41:5). Friends came to the house of mourning, and flute players and professional mourners, chiefly women, were employed, who made loud lamentations (Jer. 9:17, 18; Matt. 9:23; Acts 9:39); see MINSTREL. Feasts were provided for the crowds that assembled at the funeral (Jer. 16:7; Baruch 6:32). After the funeral women would come forth very early in the morning to visit the grave, as they are still accustomed to do, and to pray, weep, and sob or chant hymns or beat their breasts (Mark 16:1, 2). Many of them were professionals; but others were sincere mourners, relatives of the deceased and their sympathizing friends (John 11:31). Customs, in general similar, prevailed in Egypt, Persia, and Scythia (Herod. ii. 66, 85; iv. 71; viii. 99; ix. 24).

The period of mourning varied. It was 30 days for Aaron and Moses (Num. 20:29; Deut. 34:8), and 7 days for Saul (I Sam. 31:13). The Egyptians observed 70 days for Jacob, and 7 more days were devoted to public mourning for him at the threshing floor of Atad (Gen. 50:3, 10).

Mouse. A small rodent quadruped, *Mus musculus* and other allied species of the family *Muridae*. It was an unclean animal (Lev. 11:29), but was eaten by Israelites in Isaiah's time who gave themselves up to heathenism and paid no attention to the Mosaic Law (Isa. 66:17). The field mouse (*Arvicola arvalis*) was destructive to crops (I Sam. 6:5). The Hebrew word for mouse, '*akbār*, is a comprehensive one, including not merely the genus *Mus*, but most of the family *Muridae*, with many animals from other families having either an affinity or an analogy to the typical mice.

Mo'za (mō'za) [a going forth, sunrise]. 1. A man of Judah, family of Hezron, house of Caleb (I Chron. 2:46).
2. A descendant of Jonathan (I Chron. 8:36, 37).

Mo'zah (mō'za). A town of Benjamin (Josh. 18:26), probably to be identified with Ķālunya (or Ķolōniyeh), about 4⅔ miles n.w. of Jerusalem on the road to Jaffa.

Mul'ber'ry Tree. A tree of the genus *Morus*, of the family *Moraceae*. It is cultivated in Syria for the sake of its leaves, on which the silkworm feeds. A cooling drink is made from its berries, the juice being expressed, sweetened with honey, and flavored with spices. The juice of the berries was shown to elephants to prepare them for battle (I Macc. 6:34). A mulberry is mentioned in the N.T. under the name of sycamine (Luke 17:6).

Mulberry is the rendering of the Heb. *bākā'*, weeping, distilling; a tree which grew near Jerusalem and of which the leaves rustled in the wind (II Sam. 5:23 *seq.*; I Chron. 14:14, 15). In these passages and in Ps. 84:6 the margin of R.V. has balsam tree.

Mule. A graminivorous animal, called in Heb. *pered* (I Kings 18:5). The mule is a hybrid between the horse and the ass. It is often mentioned with horses (Ps. 32:9), and was much used for riding and for carrying burdens (II Sam. 13:29; II Kings 5:17; I Chron. 12:40). It is not mentioned before the time

of David, but was in common use from his
days onward. The Tyrians obtained mules in
Armenia (Ezek. 27:14).

In A.V. of Gen. 36:24 the Heb. plural *yēmim*
is translated mules; but it should rather be
rendered hot springs, as it is in the Vulgate
and in R.V. In A.V. of Esth. 8:10, 14 *rekesh*
is rendered mule; in I Kings 4:28, dromedary.
R.V. substitutes swift steed.

Mup'pim (mŭp'ĭm). A son of Benjamin
(Gen. 46:21); see SHEPHUPHAM.

Mur'der. Just after the deluge it was enacted that "whoso sheddeth man's blood, by
man shall his blood be shed: for in the image
of God made he man" (Gen. 9:6). The avenger of blood had the right to put the murderer
to death (Num. 35:19); but if the manslayer
reached a city of refuge he was temporarily
safe. The cities of refuge were not instituted
for the benefit of the deliberate murderer;
they were designed for the man who had accidentally committed manslaughter (Num., ch.
35). Even if the deliberate murderer had fled
for asylum to the altar, and probably taken
hold of its horns, he was to be taken from it
and put to death (Ex. 21:14; cf. I Kings 2:
28–34). At the city of refuge the manslayer
was given a trial. The concurrent testimony
of at least 2 witnesses was required to convict him of murder. Num. 35:30; Deut. 17:6).
If he was guilty of deliberate murder, no ransom was accepted (Num. 35:31), and he was
delivered to the avenger of blood to be slain
(v. 19; Deut. 19:12). If acquitted, he was
granted asylum in the city. See CITY OF REF-
UGE.

Mu'shi (mū'shī). A Levite, son of Merari,
and the founder of a tribal family or house
(Ex. 6:19; Num. 3:20; 26:58; I Chron. 6:19,
47; 23:21, 23; 24:26, 30).

Mu'sic. Music is ancient (Gen. 4:21). Among
the Hebrews, Miriam and her companions took
timbrels and danced and sang praises to the
Lord for his deliverance of the Israelites at
the Red Sea (Ex. 15:20). The people danced
and sang in idolatrous worship about the
golden calf (Ex. 32:6, 18). In family feasts
and religious festivals they sang, played on
musical instruments, and danced (Jer. 25:10;
I Macc. 9:39; Luke 15:25). Marriage processions, as they passed through the streets,
were accompanied with music and song (Jer.
7:34). Women and maidens welcomed the victorious warrior on his return home with
music, song, and dance (Judg. 11:34; I Sam.
18:6). Kings had their court musicians (II
Chron. 35:25; Eccl. 2:8). The accession of a
king and his marriage and his feasts were
made joyous with music (II Sam. 19:35; I
Kings 1:40; Ps. 45:8, R.V.). The shepherd
might have his harp (I Sam. 16:18). The
mind might be quieted and refreshed by music
(I Sam. 10:5; 16:16; II Kings 3:15). Psalms
might be sung to the accompaniment of the
harp (Ps. 92:1–3; 137:2; cf. Amos 6:5).

The musical instruments of the Hebrews
were of 3 classes: stringed instruments, wind
instruments, and instruments of percussion.
Stringed instruments consisted of a body of
wood with strings of gut, and were played
with the fingers of one or both hands or were
struck with a plectrum of wood, ivory, or
metal. They were chiefly the harp and psaltery. The harp was in general use among the
people both for worldly and sacred music; the
psaltery was commonly, though not exclusively, reserved for religious purposes. The
psaltery was tuned to the soprano register,
the harp an octave lower (I Chron. 15:20, 21).
The wind instruments were chiefly flutes or
pipes and horns. The pipe was often played
with other instruments (I Sam. 10:5; I Kings
1:40; Isa. 5:12; 30:29; Ecclus. 40:21), was
employed to lead dancing (Matt. 11:17), and

was played at weddings (I Macc. 3:45; Rev.
18:22). It was specially the instrument of
lamentation (Jer. 48:36; Matt. 9:23, R.V.;
Jos. *War* iii. 9, 5). The Bible does not mention its use in the Temple service, not even in
I Macc. 4:54; but it was used in sacred music
and was heard in processions of worshipers
marching to the house of God, and in the later
Temple it had an assigned place, especially at
the passover and feast of tabernacles. The
ram's horn, or an imitation of it, was sometimes used to increase the noise of other instruments (I Chron. 15:28; II Chron. 15:14;
Ps. 98:6, rendered trumpet), but was generally blown by itself. Its principal employment was not in music, but for military purposes and to make proclamations. Straight,
narrow, silver trumpets, about a cubit in
length, and called *hăṣōṣᵉrāh*, were used by the
priests to announce festivals, to call the congregation, and on advancing to battle (Num.
10:1–10). They were rarely blown by laymen
(Hos. 5:8; perhaps, II Kings 11:14 and II
Chron. 23:13). Of the instruments of percussion the timbrel or tabret was the popular
instrument; it was usually played by women

Captives, Probably Israelite, Playing Lyres, from
an Assyrian Relief

and was employed on festive occasions, especially to beat time at the dances and for singers (Gen. 31:27; Ex. 15:20; Judg. 11:34; Ps.
81:2). Cymbals of brass were used in the
Temple service (I Chron. 15:19).

Music was cultivated by the companies
which gathered about the prophets (I Sam.
10:5), various instruments being employed as
an orchestra. It is not mentioned as belonging to the service of the tabernacle in the
early period. David introduced it into the
worship at the sanctuary, and Solomon promoted it (II Sam. 6:5, 14; I Kings 10:12; I
Chron., chs. 15; 16). Hezekiah and Josiah
paid special attention to its restoration (II
Chron. 29:25; 35:15). David was assisted in
his work by Asaph, Heman, and Ethan or
Jeduthun, 3 masters of music. A choir of singers and musicians, with Asaph at its head, was
formed of Levites, and stationed before the
Ark at the tabernacle on Zion, while Heman
and Jeduthun, with their choirs, were assigned
to the old tabernacle at Gibeon (I Chron. 16:
4–6, 39–42). These 3 choirs were afterward
united in the Temple. In David's reign they
numbered 4,000 members (I Chron. 23:5), of
whom 288 were trained musicians, who were
depended upon to lead the less skilled body of
assistants (I Chron. 25:7, 8). They were divided into 24 courses, containing 12 trained
musicians each. Of these courses 4 belonged
to the family of Asaph, 6 to that of Jeduthun,
and 14 to that of Heman. The orchestra
which accompanied the singing consisted of
stringed instruments, but cymbals were also
used, being probably struck by the chief mu-

sician to beat time (I Chron. 15:19–21). It appears from this passage that the proportion of psalteries to harps was 8 to 6. In Herod's Temple there were ordinarily 2 psalteries, 9 harps, and 1 cymbal, and on certain days pipes were added. The participation of priests with trumpets in the orchestra of stringed instruments was exceptional (II Chron. 5:12, 13; 7:6). In the 2d Temple the trumpets, when blown in connection with the regular orchestra, were heard only in the pauses or as responsive music (Ezra 3:10, 11). The musicians stood on the e. of the great altar (II Chron. 5:12). In Herod's Temple they occupied a broad staircase, which led from the court of Israel to the court of the priests. In this later Temple a choir of boys, standing at the foot of the stairs, lent their higher voices to the song of the Levites.

Little is known of the character of the music. The Hebrews had a scale of 8 tones. Their sacred choirs probably sang in unison the same simple melody, divided into 2 parts, the one an octave higher than the other, and representing the male and female voices, and were accompanied by the instruments in the same tones (I Chron. 15:20, 21). Melodies are probably named in the titles of Psalms 9; 22; 45; 56; 57, and others. Antiphonal and responsive singing was practiced (Ex. 15:21; Neh. 12:31–43) and was often heard in the Temple service (Ezra 3:10, 11; Jer. 33:11); several psalms were arranged for this purpose, e.g., Ps. 24:7–10; 136. The congregation seldom, if ever, joined in the singing in the 1st Temple, but at its close they united in saying "Amen" (I Chron. 16:7, 36). In the Herodian Temple the people sometimes participated by singing responses.

Mus'tard. A garden herb (Luke 13:19), which in comparison with other herbs becomes a great tree (Matt. 13:32; Mark 4:32), on whose branches the birds rest for the sake of obtaining its seeds. Its seeds are, hyperbolically speaking, less than all seeds (Matt. 13:32). The largeness of the plant grown from seeds so small illustrates the increase of the Kingdom of heaven from a very small beginning. The mustard seed was employed proverbially by the Jews, just as it was by Jesus (Matt. 17:20; Luke 17:6), to denote anything very minute. The common mustard of Palestine is *Sinapis nigra* or black mustard. It grows wild, attaining the height of a horse and rider, as travelers have noticed. It is also cultivated in gardens for its seed, which is used as a condiment. Those who seek another identification generally consider the mustard of Scripture to have been *Salvadora persica*, the type of the natural order *Salvadoraceae* or Salvadorads, but this view is unlikely. Royle, who supported this view, says that it has a succulent fruit, tasting like garden cress. It is, however, small, and apparently confined to the low valley of the Jordan; and it is not an herb.

Muth'-lab'ben (mŭth'lăb'ĕn) [die for the son; death of the son; death whitens]. An expression of doubtful meaning in the title of Psalm 9. Probably the opening words of a well-known song to the melody of which the psalm was to be sung.

Myn'dos (mĭn'dŏs), in A.V. **Myn'dus** (mĭn'dŭs). A small town of Caria, situated on the seacoast (Herod. v. 33). It was not far from Halicarnassus, for Alexander led a detachment of troops across the intervening country in one night. In the time of Simon Maccabaeus it was subject to Rome (I Macc. 15:23). Its site is probably marked by the small sheltered port of Gumishlu.

My'ra (mī'ra). A city of Lycia, where Paul, when a prisoner on his way to Rome, changed ships (Acts 27:5, 6). Myra was one of the principal cities of Lycia. It stood some 2 miles from the sea, and was built on and about a cliff, at the mouth of the gorge leading into the interior mountain region. It is now called Dembre.

Myrrh. 1. A fragrant substance, called in Heb. *mŏr*, in Gr. *smyrna, myrrha*. It was an ingredient in the oil with which Aaron and his successors were anointed (Ex. 30:23). Beds and garments were perfumed with it (Ps. 45:8; Prov. 7:17; S. of Sol. 3:6), and an oil of myrrh was used in the purification of women (Esth. 2:12). The Magi brought it from the e. to present to the infant Jesus (Matt. 2:11). At the crucifixion it was offered to him in wine, probably to deaden pain (Mark 15:23), and was an ingredient in the spices designed for anointing his body (John 19:39). It was used for embalming the dead (Herod. ii. 86). The tree which produced it grew in Arabia and was probably the *Balsamodendron myrrha*. It is a small tree, with odoriferous wood and bark, short spiny branches, trifoliolate leaves, and plumlike fruit. The tree *Commiphora abyssinica* of e. Africa and Arabia furnishes the myrrh of modern commerce.

2. The rendering of Heb. *lŏṭ* (Gen. 37:25; 43:11). Myrrh is not a happy translation; it should have been ladanum (R.V. marg.), called by the Greeks *lēdon, lēdanon*, and *ladanon*. It is a highly fragrant resin, containing a volatile oil, and is produced by *Cistus creticus* and various other species of rock rose. It grows in parts of Syria.

Myr'tle. A tree, called in Heb. *hădas*. It grew in the mountains near Jerusalem, and booths were made of its branches at the feast of tabernacles (Neh. 8:15). It is mentioned also in Isa. 41:19; 55:13; Zech. 1:8–11. The tree is undoubtedly the common myrtle (*Myrtus communis*), which grows in Palestine.

Mys'i·a (mĭsh'ĭ-a). A province in the extreme n.w. of Asia Minor; bounded on the n. by the Propontis, now Sea of Marmora, on the s. by Lydia, on the e. by Bithynia, and on the w. by the Hellespont. The Troad lay within its limits. Paul and Silas passed through it to Troas, one of its cities (Acts 16:7, 8). Assos, to which Paul sailed to meet his associates, was another (Acts 20:13). A third was Pergamos, one of the 7 churches in Asia (Rev. 1:11; 2:12–17).

Mys'ter·y. A word taken over from heathen religion, in which a mystery was a secret and peculiar doctrine, which found expression in rites, ceremonies, and purifications to which only initiated persons were admitted. The purpose of the ceremonies was to better the worshipers in this life and to assure them of life after death through union with the god thus worshiped. The word does not imply that the doctrine is incomprehensible. In the N.T. it denotes a secret hidden from the world till the appointed time (Rom. 16:25), or until man has been prepared by the Spirit of God to receive and appreciate it (Mark 4:11), which forms a characteristic and essential doctrine and finds expression in the life (I Tim. 3:16).

N

Na'am (nā'ăm) [sweetness, pleasantness]. A son of the celebrated Caleb (I Chron. 4:15).

Na'a·mah (nā'a-ma) [sweet, pleasant]. 1. Daughter of Lamech, and sister of Tubal-cain (Gen. 4:22).

2. An Ammonitess, a wife of Solomon and the mother of King Rehoboam (I Kings 14:21, 31; II Chron. 12:13).

3. A town in the lowland of Judah (Josh. 15:41); probably Khirbet Fered near 'Arak Na'aman.

Na'a·man (nā'á-măn) [pleasant]. 1. A grandson of Benjamin, a son of Bela and founder of a family (Gen. 46:21; Num. 26: 40).

2. Commander of the army of Ben-hadad, king of Damascus. He was an able general, and had won deliverance for the Syrians, but he was a leper. In Syria leprosy did not exclude from human society, as it did in Israel, though it was a loathsome disease. In one of the Syrian raids on the Israelite territory, the soldiers had brought away a little maid, who became a slave to Naaman's wife. This girl expressed to her mistress the wish that Naaman were with Elisha in Samaria, because the prophet would heal him of his leprosy. The speech of the maiden was reported to her master, who resolved to seek a cure from Elisha. His sovereign, the king of Syria, wrote a letter of introduction for him, and sent him to the king of Israel to be cured. When the Israelite ruler received it he thought that the real intention of his correspondent was to pick a quarrel and declare war. Elisha reassured the king, and desired that Naaman should be sent to him, when he would learn that there was a prophet in Israel. When he came with his horses and chariot to Elisha's door, the prophet in order to humble his pride and teach him that he owed his cure not to man, but solely to the power of God, did not appear, but sent out a message that he should dip 7 times in the Jordan. Naaman, feeling affronted, and despising the means, started for home in a passion, saying, "Are not Abana and Pharpar, rivers of Damascus, better than all the waters of Israel? may I not wash in them and be clean?" But his servants soothed his temper, and urged him to dip in the Jordan. He did so, and was cured. Filled with gratitude, he wished to reward Elisha. The prophet desired to impress upon the Syrian the freeness of God's blessings, and refused all recompense; but Gehazi, his servant, acted in a very different spirit. Naaman renounced idolatry, and became a worshiper of Jehovah; and he carried home 2 mules' burden of earth to build an altar to Jehovah. He lived, however, in a heathen community and could not altogether escape outward participation in heathen customs. His king was an idolater, a worshiper of Rimmon; and it was Naaman's official duty to support him when he entered the Temple and bowed before the god. The prophet of Jehovah permitted Naaman to fulfill his secular duties, even though to do so involved his assisting his king to perform heathen worship (II Kings, ch. 5).

Na'a·ma·thite (nā'á-má-thīt). A native or inhabitant of Naamah; as Zophar, Job's friend (Job 2:11; 11:1; 20:1; 42:9). The place was probably in n. Arabia.

Na'a·rah (nā'á-rá) [a girl]. 1. A wife of Ashhur, the ancestor of the inhabitants of Tekoa (I Chron. 4:5, 6).

2. A town on the boundary line of Ephraim, e. of Beth-el, and not far from Jericho (Josh. 16:7). In A.V. the name is written Naarath. The town is doubtless one with Naaran (I Chron. 7:28). Archelaus diverted half the water supply of Neara to irrigate the palms of his palace at Jericho (Jos. Antiq. xvii. 13, 1). Eusebius mentions a village Noorath, 5 Roman miles from Jericho; probably to be identified with 'Ain Dûk.

Na'a·rai (nā'á-rī). One of David's valiant men (I Chron. 11:37; apparently a diverse reading, perhaps the correction, of Paarai, II Sam. 23:35).

Na'a·ran (nā'á-răn). See NAARAH 2.

Na'a·rath (nā'á-răth). See NAARAH 2.

Na·ash'on (ná-ăsh'ŏn). See NAHSHON.

Na·as'son (ná-ăs'ŏn). See NAHSHON.

Na'bal (nā'băl) [foolish, churlish]. A sheepmaster, resident in Maon, who pastured his flocks around the village of Carmel in Judah, on the confines of the wilderness. His wife's name was Abigail. David and his followers had dwelt for some time in the neighborhood, and had used their might to protect the property of the people from marauding bands of robbers. When Nabal was shearing his sheep, David sent 10 young men to solicit assistance for himself and his followers. Nabal sent back a churlish refusal, which so irritated David that he put his men in motion with the intention of cutting off Nabal and every other male belonging to the household. Abigail, who was a clever and judicious woman, made ready a present for David, and, starting promptly, apologized for her husband's conduct, allayed the resentment which it had caused, and prevented the gathering storm from breaking on her home. Returning to her abode, she found a great feast in progress, and her lord completely intoxicated. Next morning, when he was sober, she told him how narrowly he had escaped destruction. He was profoundly affected by the report, and from the shock which it caused died about 10 days later. After a time, Abigail became one of David's wives (I Sam. 25:1–42).

Nab'a·tae'ans (năb'á-tē'ănz); **Nab'a·thae'· ans** (năb'á-thē'ănz), in A.V. **Nab'a·thites** (năb'á-thīts). The Nabataeans were an Arabian people, who not only spoke Arabic, but also wrote and spoke Aramaic; many of them also knew Greek. They developed a remarkable civilization in the first 2 centuries B.C. and the first century of our era. At one time their power extended as far n. as Damascus and Coelesyria and as far s. as Madā'in Ṣāliḥ (al-Ḥijr) in n. al-Ḥijāz (cf. besides the inscriptions, I Macc. 5:25; 9:35; Jos. Antiq. xiii. 15, 2). The capital Petra was situated on the important trade routes between s. Arabia and Syria, and this location explains the spectacular rise and development of the Nabataean kingdom. The entire country from the Euphrates to the Red Sea was called Nabatene (Jos. Antiq. i. 12, 4). On the Arabian trade routes there were carried by numerous caravans the products of s. Arabia as well as merchandise from Africa, India, and even China. These commodities were distributed from Petra to Egypt, to Syria, and to Greece and Italy by way of Gaza. The Nabataeans became wealthy through the duties imposed on goods sent through their territory, and their trade routes were guarded by frontier posts, watchtowers, and fortresses. In art, architecture, engineering, and ceramics they were very gifted. They carved dwellings, temples, and tombs out of the native rock. No other people in the ancient Near East pushed agriculture as far into the desert as they did. When springs were available, water was carried by aqueducts long distances for irrigation purposes. In fact the Nabataean occupation of Edom and Moab was sustained both by trade and by agriculture.

In the 4th century B.C. the Nabataeans were nomadic Arabs, who did not engage in agriculture, but traded in the rich products of Arabia. They lived in tents and abhorred the use of wine. By c. 300 B.C. they had stone houses and also took up agriculture. Apparently the ban on wine was gone, judging from the motif of the grape, leaf, and vine in decoration.

A fertility religion developed out of their agricultural background. The best-known deity is dhu-al-Shara (Dushara, Dusares-

Dionysus). Other deities of which we have representatives are Zeus-Hadad and Atargatis. A winged Tyche-Nike at Khirbet Tannur, holding aloft a cornucopia, combines the characteristics of Tyche, the goddess of fortune, and those of Nike, the goddess of victory. Nabataean temples have been discovered at Khirbet Tannur, Petra, Mesheirfeh, Kerak, Khirbet Dherih, Dhat Ras, Aineh, Ḳasr Rabbah, and Ramm.

About 312 B.C. the Nabataeans were strong enough to resist 2 expeditions sent against them by Antigonus, one of the successors of Alexander the Great. The following kings are known: Aretas (Ḥārithath) I, 169 B.C.; Erotimus, 110–100 B.C.; Aretas II, 96 B.C.; Obedas ('Obīdath), 90 B.C.; Aretas III, c. 85–60 B.C.; Malchus (Mālik) I, c. 50–28 B.C.; Obedas II, c. 28–9 B.C.; Aretas IV, 9 B.C. to A.D. 40; Abias; Malchus II, c. A.D. 48–71; Rabel (Rabbīl), A.D. 71–106.

In the reign of Aretas III the Nabataeans first came into close contact with the Romans. In 47 B.C. Julius Caesar called on Malchus I to provide him with cavalry for the Alexandrian War. In the time of Obedas II there took place the Roman invasion of Arabia under Gallus (24 B.C.), in which the Nabataeans co-operated. Arabia Petraea reached its height under Aretas IV, whose ethnarch endeavored to arrest Paul at Damascus (II Cor. 11:32). In A.D. 105 Trajan put an end to Nabataean autonomy, and the following year their territory became a Roman province called Arabia Petraea (the Arabia of Petra). See ARETAS 1, SELA.

Nab'o·ni'dus (năb'ō-nī'dŭs) [Akkad. *Nabŭnā'id*, the god Nabū (Nebo) is exalted]. The last king of the Neo-Babylonian or Chaldean Empire (556–539 B.C.). His father, Nabūbalāṭsu-iḳbi, was an important prince known for his wisdom and great attainments. His mother probably was Shumūa-damḳa, a priestess in the temple of the moon-god at Harran; this may explain his ardent interest in the shrines of Sin (the moon-god) at Ur and Harran. From a reasonable interpretation of the evidence it appears that his wife Nitocris was the daughter of Nebuchadnezzar II; Belshazzar, their son, was the coregent of Nabonidus at Babylon from the 3d year of his reign to the fall of the city in 539, but during that time the father did not relinquish his position as first ruler of the land.

It seems that the social rank of his father and the religious prestige of his mother prepared the way for Nabonidus' early rise to eminence. He probably is the individual of this name who in the 8th year of Nebuchadnezzar's reign was a city administrator. The Labynetus (Herod. i. 74), who in 585 was Nebuchadnezzar's emissary associated with Syennesis of Cilicia to make peace between Alyattes of Lydia and Astyages the Mede, probably was Nabonidus.

Amel-Marduk, the son of Nebuchadnezzar, who reigned from 562 to 560, was slain as the result of a conspiracy; he was succeeded by Nebuchadnezzar's son-in-law, Neriglissar, who was king for four years (560–556). His young son Lābāshi-Marduk, after a reign of 9 months, was slain by conspirators, who then chose Nabonidus, already an old man, as king. Nabonidus was an archaeologist and a builder and restorer of temples. In rebuilding a temple, his workmen were instructed to dig for the original foundation stones. In finding inscriptions, which even at that time were ancient, and copying names and lists of kings, the work of Nabonidus has proved valuable for the historian in establishing dates. His own daughter, Bēl-Shalti-Nannar, was dedicated to the great temple of Sin at Ur. Nabonidus' devotion to Sin and the neglect of

Marduk evidently aroused priestly opposition to his religious program. When Cyrus invaded Babylonia, Nabonidus had the images of the different gods in the various temples brought to Babylon for safekeeping; subsequently they were restored by Cyrus to their original shrines.

He spent many years of his reign at Taima (Teima), a healthful region which had important commercial and military advantages in the w. On account of the threatening invasion by Cyrus, Nabonidus returned home in the 17th year of his reign (539). The only real battle was fought at Opis in the 7th month (Tishri), and on the 14th of that month Sippar was captured by Cyrus. Two days later Babylon fell into the hands of Ugbaru (Gobryas), the chief general of Cyrus; the latter entered the city 17 days later (the 3d of Marheshvan). Nabonidus was kindly treated by Cyrus, who gave him Carmania (in s. Persia) to rule or much more probably as a place of abode in a new land (Jos. *Apion* i. 20). World power had now passed from the Semites to an Indo-European people. Babylon for centuries had stood for Semitic power, civilization, and culture, and its glory was ended. See BABYLONIA, BELSHAZZAR, CYRUS.

Na'both (nā'bŏth) [perhaps, a sprout; cf. Arab. *nabata*, to grow, sprout]. An inhabitant of Jezreel, who had a vineyard at that town near one of Ahab's palaces. The king wished to buy it, but its owner would not sell it because it had descended to him from his ancestors. At the instance of Jezebel, Naboth's life was sworn away by suborned witnesses, he and his sons (II Kings 9:26), to whom the vineyard would have descended, were stoned to death, their bodies were left to be devoured by the dogs, and the vineyard was seized by Ahab. This act of violence called down the judgment of God on the guilty king and his yet guiltier wife (I Kings 21:1–24; 22:34–38; II Kings 9:30–37).

Na'chon (nā'kŏn). See NACON.

Na'chor (nā'kôr). See NAHOR.

Na'con (nā'kŏn), in A.V. **Na'chon** [firm, prepared]. The designation of a threshing floor at which Uzzah was struck dead for touching the Ark (II Sam. 6:6), and hence called Perezuzzah, i.e., breach of Uzzah (II Sam. 6:8); see CHIDON.

Na'dab (nā'dăb) [(God is) liberal]. 1. The eldest of Aaron's 4 sons (Ex. 6:23; Num. 3:2). With his brother Abihu, he was granted the privilege of a near approach to Jehovah at Sinai (Ex. 24:1), and was subsequently appointed to the priesthood (Ex. 28:1), but both of them afterward offered strange fire to God, and as a penalty were consumed by fire (Lev. 10:1–7; Num. 26:61). From the fact that a command was immediately thereafter given to Aaron not to drink wine or strong drink when he entered the tabernacle, it may be inferred that Nadab and Abihu had done so, and were under the influence of liquor when they committed the sin which cost them their lives (Lev. 10:9). They both died childless (Num. 3:4; I Chron. 24:2).

2. A man of Judah, family of Hezron, house of Jerahmeel (I Chron. 2:28, 30).

3. A Benjamite, a son of Gibeon and Maachah (I Chron. 8:30; 9:36).

4. Son of Jeroboam I, and his successor on the throne of Israel. He began to reign c. 913 B.C. He followed the evil example of his father with respect to calf worship. He led the forces of his kingdom to besiege Gibbethon, but was murdered with his relatives by Baasha, who then mounted the vacant throne. This massacre fulfilled the threatenings of Jehovah against Jeroboam and his house. Nadab

reigned less than 2 full years (I Kings 14:10, 11, 20; 15:25, 30).

Nad'a·bath (năd'á-băth), in A.V. **Na·dab'-a·tha** (ná-dăb'á-thá). A place e. of the Jordan (I Macc. 9:37; in Jos. *Antiq.* xiii. 1, 4 Gabatha); probably Khirbet el-Teim, about 1¼ miles s. of Mādabā.

Nag'gai (năg'ī), in A.V. **Nag'ge** (nă'gē). An ancestor of Christ (Luke 3:25).

Na·ha·lal (nā'há-lăl) and **Na·ha·lol** (Judg. 1:30), in A.V. once **Na·hal'lal** (Josh. 19:15) [drinking place for flocks]. A village of Zebulun (Josh. 19:15 *seq.*), from which, however, that tribe failed to drive out the Canaanite inhabitants (Judg. 1:30). It was assigned to the Merarite Levites (Josh. 21:35). It probably is the modern Tell en-Naḥl in the plain s. of Acre.

Na·ha'li·el (ná-hā'lĭ-ĕl) [torrent-valley of God]. An encampment of the Israelites, between Beer, in the desert e. of Moab, and Bamoth, which lay between Dibon and Baalmeon (Num. 21:19). It may be the wadi Wāleh, a tributary of the Arnon draining a wide area n.e. of that river, or the wadi Zerḳā Ma'īn farther to the n.

Na·hal'lal (ná-hăl'ăl). See NAHALAL.

Na·ha·lol (nā'há-lŏl). See NAHALAL.

Na'ham (nā'hăm) [solace, consolation]. Brother of Hodiah's wife (I Chron. 4:19, R.V.).

Na·ha·ma·ni (nā'há-mā'nī) [compassionate]. One of those who returned with Zerubbabel from Babylon (Neh. 7:7).

Na·ha·rai (nā'há-rī), in A.V. once **Na·ha·ri** (nā'há-rī) (II Sam. 23:37) [snorting]. A Beerothite, Joab's armor-bearer (II Sam. 23:37; I Chron. 11:39).

Na'hash (nā'hăsh) [serpent]. 1. Father of Abigail and Zeruiah, David's sisters (II Sam. 17:25; cf. I Chron. 2:16). Probably his widow, the mother of Abigail and Zeruiah, married Jesse and became the mother of David. This explanation is better than the assumption that Nahash was the name of Jesse's wife; or, as the later Jews interpreted the passage, that Nahash was another name of Jesse.
2. An Ammonite king who besieged Jabeshgilead, and when its inhabitants offered to surrender and become tributary, would not accept the proposal unless every man in the place consented to lose the right eye. He determined to put a reproach upon Israel. A week's time was given in which to seek help. Before it expired, Saul, just before elected king, appeared with a relieving army, totally defeated the Ammonites, and saved Jabesh-gilead and its defenders (I Sam. 11:1–11). Either this Nahash or a son of his bearing the same name treated David kindly, perhaps because he was at variance with Saul (II Sam. 10:2).
3. A man who lived in Rabbah of the Ammonites (II Sam. 17:27). He may have been the king aforementioned, or an Israelite who had settled in Rabbah after its capture by David (II Sam. 12:29).

Na'hath (nā'hăth) [descent or quiet]. 1. A descendant of Esau and also of Ishmael. He became a chieftain of Edom (Gen. 36:3, 4, 13, 17; I Chron. 1:37).
2. A Kohathite Levite (I Chron. 6:26); probably the person elsewhere called Tohu and Toah (I Sam. 1:1; I Chron. 6:34).
3. A Levite; one of those who had charge of the tithes and offerings under Hezekiah (II Chron. 31:13).

Nah'bi (nä'bī) [concealed; but cf. Arab. *naḫb*, fainthearted]. The representative spy from the tribe of Naphtali (Num. 13:14).

Na'hor (nā'hōr), in A.V. twice **Na'chor** (Josh. 24:2; Luke 3:34) [breathing hard, snorting]. 1. A son of Serug, and grandfather of Abraham (Gen. 11:24, 25).
2. A son of Terah, and brother of Abraham (Gen. 11:27). He married his niece Milcah, daughter of Haran and sister of Lot (Gen. 11:29). He is not mentioned as emigrating from Ur with Terah, Abraham, and Lot; but later he is found in Mesopotamia at Haran (Gen. 24:10; 27:43). Eight sons were born to him by Milcah, from whom sprang Aramaean tribes. Four others traced their descent from his concubine (Gen. 22:21–24). One of his sons by Milcah was Bethuel, who became the father of Rebekah and Laban (Gen. 24:15, 29).
The city of Nahor (Gen. 24:10) figures often as Nakhur (Naḫur) in the Mari tablets and also in the more recent Middle-Assyrian documents. It seems to have been located below Haran in the Balikh valley, and was ruled by an Amorite prince in the 18th century B.C.

Nah'shon (nä'shŏn), A.V. has once **Na·ash'on** (Ex. 6:23), and in N.T. **Na·as'son** [serpent]. A prince of the tribe of Judah in the early period of the wilderness wanderings (Num. 1:7; 2:3; 7:12, 17; 10:14). His sister was married to Aaron, who was of the tribe of Levi (Ex. 6:23). Nahshon was the grandfather or remoter ancestor of Boaz, Ruth's husband, and the 5th backward in the genealogy of David (Ruth 4:20–22; I Chron. 2:10–12). This placed him in the ancestry of our Lord (Matt. 1:4; Luke 3:32, 33).

Na'hum (nā'hŭm) [compassionate]. 1. A prophet born at Elkosh, doubtless a village of Palestine. He prophesied to Judah (Nahum 1:15), not to the 10 tribes in captivity. The prophet cites the destruction of No-amon (Thebes) in Egypt (ch. 3:8–10), which was overthrown by the Assyrians 663 B.C., and predicts the fall of Nineveh (v. 7), which occurred 612 B.C.; this narrows the limits within which the composition of the book must be sought to the years between these events. Kuenen suggested that the unsuccessful attack of Cyaxares upon Nineveh in 623 was the occasion of the prophecy.
The theme of the prophecy in The Book of Nahum is the burden of Nineveh (ch. 1:1). The prophet insists on the familiar truth that Jehovah is a jealous God, whose vengeance is certain to fall on his adversaries, but who is a stronghold to those that trust in him (vs. 2–8), urges the people to turn a deaf ear to the counsel of those who were speaking against Jehovah's tardiness and advising the abandonment of his service (vs. 9–11), declares the unalterable purpose of the Lord to deliver his people (vs. 12–14), and exhorts them to unswerving loyalty to their God and the faithful observance of his worship (v. 15). On the basis of this truth, the prophet proceeds to describe the overthrow of the worldly power which was then oppressing the kingdom of God. He pictures the siege of the city (ch. 2:1–10), and takes occasion to taunt the city which had been as a den of lions (vs. 11–13). Returning to the description of the siege, he attributes the judgment which befalls the city to its whoredoms (ch. 3:1–4). This allusion leads to a change of the figure, and he depicts the punishment as the punishment of a harlot (vs. 5–7). He draws attention to the fact that Nineveh is no better than No-amon, which went into captivity (vs. 8–10), and he predicts that like No-amon Nineveh shall be destroyed (vs. 11–19).
The prophecy opens with an address poetic in character and alphabetic in form (ch. 1:2–15; in Heb. text, chs. 1:2 to 2:1). But it is not an alphabetic psalm of the ordinary kind, in which the verses begin with the letters of the

alphabet in their conventional sequence (cf. Psalm 119). The prophet has done more. He has allowed the consecutive sounds to introduce topics rather than verses and to follow each other singly or in groups throughout the stately oration. He teaches the ear to listen for certain sounds and to hear them with satisfaction. Nahum's book falls into 2 parts. Chapter 1 describes the majesty of God; chapters 2 and 3 pronounce judgment upon Nineveh.

I. *The prophet enunciates a doctrine* of Jehovah, God of Israel (*aleph* ['] in the very first word, *'ēl*, God [v. 2]); the doctrine that forms the basal truth of his prophecy, namely, that Jehovah, though slow to anger, yet takes vengeance on his adversaries (ch. 1:2, 3; *aleph* beginning important words). Then the prophet describes the majesty and might of Jehovah in nature: he is in the whirlwind and in the storm, and the clouds are the dust of his feet (*beth* [b] being heard thrice in this part of v. 3); he rebukes the waters that they dry up and vegetation languishes (v. 4, which begins with *gimel* [g]); the mountains and hills tremble before him (v. 5; *he* [h] being heard 4 times in prominent words, and the conjunction and [*vav*, w] being used 4 times also, if that is intentional); the fierceness of his indignation none can withstand (v. 6; the significant words beginning once with *zayin* [z] and twice with *hheth* [ḥ] in proper order). The truth that has been set forth involves on the one hand the goodness of Jehovah to his people and his knowledge of them (v. 7; facts stated in words beginning with *teth* [t] and *yodh* [y]), and on the other hand, the overthrow of evil (v. 8; the principal word being *kālāh*, yielding the 2 sounds *kaph* [k] and *lamedh* [l] and followed twice by that of *mem* [m] in the word *mākōm*, place). The climax of doctrine has been reached.

II. *A new section of the exalted discourse opens,* in which the prophet bases prediction on the truth that has been set forth. He reiterates the impotence of opposition to Jehovah: first in the form of a question (v. 9; which in its main part begins with another *mem* [m] and ends with *nun* [n]; next as a declaration, repeating the conclusion of the doctrinal section (the consecution of sounds being allowed to recur, *kaph* [k] being heard once and *lamedh* [l] twice in the 2 words that dominate the thought, *kālāh* and *lō'*, and immediately afterward *mem* [m] thrice). Then the prophet foretells the destruction of God's foes (vs. 10–13; *samekh* [s] beginning 4 consecutive words and fairly hissing through v. 10, while *ayin* ['] snarls 4 times in consecutive words in v. 11 and 4 times in the second half of v. 12 and in the first word of v. 13). The prediction of the deliverance of God's people proceeds (v. 14; *tsadhe* [ṣ] beginning the verse, and *qoph* [k] being the initial letter of 2 words at its close). Finally, in view of the truth that has been presented, the prophet exhorts God's people to continue steadfast and undismayed in his service and worship (v. 15; *resh* [r] and *sin* [ś] and *shin* [sh] being prominent tones, repeatedly heard in the first half of the verse; and *tav* [t] being the last letter of the verse and the concluding sound of the prophecy which began with *aleph*). This last verse, both by its thought and rhythm, forms the transition to ch. 2.

Nahum concentrates his prophetic passion, not upon Jerusalem, but upon Nineveh. Relief from the hated oppressor, Assyria, is in sight; the prophet sees the directing hand of God in history. For centuries Assyria had oppressed all the peoples of w. Asia. Probably the feeling of despair and suffering which they as well as their neighbors had endured helped to develop among the Hebrews the idea of a common humanity. Amos, Hosea, and Isaiah had

told their hearers that they would be besieged and carried into captivity; in their inscriptions the Assyrian kings boasted of their sieges, conquests, and cruelties. Nahum prophesied how retribution would come to Nineveh and mark her end.

2. An ancestor of Christ, born scarcely 3 centuries earlier (Luke 3:25). A.V. uses the Greek form of the name, Naum.

Nail. 1. The horny scale at the end of the finger (Deut. 21:12; Dan. 4:33).

2. A tent pin (Judg. 4:21), which was of large size and commonly made of wood. Those used to fasten the curtains of the tabernacle were of brass (Ex. 27:19).

3. A pin, commonly of metal, used for driving into wood or other material to hold separate pieces together, or left projecting for hanging things on. It might be made of iron (I Chron. 22:3), or of gold, or be gilded (II Chron. 3:9). It was sometimes driven between the stones of a wall (Ecclus. 27:2). Idols were fastened securely in place by nails (Isa. 41:7; Jer. 10:4), and victims were often affixed to the cross by means of a nail driven through each hand and the feet (John 20:25).

Na'in (nā'ĭn). A town where our Lord raised to life the only son of a widow (Luke 7:11–17). It is still called Nein, and is in the n.w. corner of the eminence called Jebel ed-Duḥy, or Little Hermon, 2 miles w.s.w. of En-dor, and 5 miles s.s.e. of Nazareth. It is a small hamlet, little more than a cluster of ruins, with ancient sepulchral caverns s.e. of the village.

Nai'oth (nā'ŏth) [perhaps, habitations]. The quarter in Ramah where the prophets, who gathered about Samuel to work under his direction, dwelt as a community (I Sam. 19:18 to 20:1).

The word occurs in this passage only, and the exact meaning is obscure. It appears in the kere as *nāyŏth*, but as *nāweyath* in the kethib; LXX (Codex Vaticanus and Lucian) favors the latter form. Heb. *nāweh* (pasture, pastoral or nomadic abode, and then abode in general) may be related. On the basis of Arabic, *nāweyath* has also been explained as a place of study, a college, or school, but it is doubtful whether this meaning was developed so early. Accordingly, it is well to adhere to the common interpretation, habitation or habitations; see PROPHETIC ASSOCIATIONS.

Name. English names, such as James, Robert, Anne, have a meaning, but it is known only to those who have studied the etymology. In Biblical times it was different. The names of persons were not only significant, but as a rule everybody knew the meaning as soon as the name was heard. Sarah, Jacob, Miriam, Jehoshaphat, Martha, Rhoda, Dorcas were intelligible to all.

The name was probably given by the Hebrews on the 8th day after birth (Gen. 17:12; 21:3, 4; Luke 1:59; 2:21). The child might be given the name of a natural object, as: Terah, wild goat; Leah, wild cow; Jonah, dove; Tamar, palm tree; Tabitha, gazelle. It might receive a name expressive of its physical condition; for example, Shiphrah, beauty; or of the parents' hope regarding it, as Noah, rest (Gen. 5:29). Some names were given prophetically, as that of Jesus because he should be the Saviour (Matt. 1:21). Many names testified to the piety or gratitude of the parents, as: Simeon, hearing (Gen. 29:33); or Nethaniah, Jehovah has given; or Elizur, God is a rock. Others were commemorative of national events, as Ichabod (I Sam. 4:21); yet others were family names (Luke 1:59–61; cf. ch. 3:23–38). When character had developed, a new name was sometimes given as expressive of it, as Israel and Cephas. In the later period, when several languages were spoken in

Palestine, a name was often translated and the person was known by 2 names, as: Cephas after the Aramaic; Peter after the Greek; Thomas and Didymus, both names meaning twin; Messiah and Christ, both meaning anointed. At this time also names were transformed, the Hebrew Jehohanan became in Greek Joannes, and Joseph became Joses.

Surnames were lacking among the Hebrews; persons were designated by adding to the personal name the name of their city, as Jesus of Nazareth, Joseph of Arimathaea, Mary Magdalene, Nahum the Elkoshite; or by a statement of their descent, as Simon son of Jonah; by their disposition, trade, or other characteristic, as Simon Peter, Nathan the prophet, Joseph the carpenter, Matthew the publican, Simon the Zealot, and Dionysius the Areopagite. Every Roman had three names: a *praenomen*, which was his personal name and stood first, a *nomen*, which was that of his *gens* or house and stood second, and a *cognomen* or surname, which was that of his family and came last. Thus M. Antonius Felix, the procurator, was Marcus of the clan Antonia and the family called Felix. Frequently only the nomen and cognomen were given, the personal name being omitted; as Julius Caesar, Pontius Pilate, Claudius Lysias.

Name is often used in Hebrew in the sense of revealed character and essence. God swears by his great name to carry out his purpose (Jer. 44:26), that is, he swears by his attested power to accomplish his word. The name of God which is excellent in all the earth (Ps. 8:1) is that expression of his being which is exhibited in creation and redemption. The name of the God of Jacob which sets the king on high (Ps. 20:1) is the manifested power of Israel's God. The name of God was in the angel which led Israel through the wilderness (Ex. 23:21), because in him the revealed might and majesty of God himself dwelt. The name of God dwelt in his sanctuary (II Sam. 7:13), the place where he manifested himself. To know the name of God is to witness the manifestation of those attributes and apprehend that character which the name denotes (cf. Ex. 6:3 with v. 7; I Kings 8:43; Ps. 91:14; Isa 52:6; 64:2; Jer. 16:21).

Na′o·mi (nā′ô-mī ; nâ-ō′mī) [my sweetness or delight]. Wife of Elimelech. Elimelech went with her and his 2 sons to sojourn in Moab, because famine prevailed in Judah. The sons married Moabite women. Elimelech and his sons died, and Naomi accompanied by her daughter-in-law Ruth returned to Bethlehem of Judah (Ruth, chs. 1 to 4).

Na′phish (nā′fĭsh), in A.V. once **Ne′phish** (I Chron. 5:19). Son of Ishmael (Gen. 25:15; I Chron. 1:31), and founder of a clan with which the Israelite tribes e. of the Jordan were at one time in conflict (I Chron. 5:18–22).

Naph′ta·li (năf′tȧ-lī), in A.V. twice **Neph′·tha·lim** (Matt. 4:13, 15), once **Nep′tha·lim** (Rev. 7:6) [my wrestling]. 1. Sixth son of Jacob, and second by Bilhah, Rachel's maidservant. Rachel gave him this name because she had wrestled in prayer for God's favor and blessing (Gen. 30:8).

2. The tribe descended from Naphtali. It was subdivided into 4 great families which sprang from the 4 sons of Naphtali (Gen. 46:24; Num. 26:48, 49). The prince of the Naphtalite tribe early in the wilderness wanderings was Ahira, son of Enan (Num. 1:15; 2:29); at a later period it was Pedahel, son of Ammihud (Num. 34:28); its representative spy was Nahbi, son of Vophsi (ch. 13:14). At the 1st census in the wilderness its fighting men were 53,400 (ch. 2:29, 30); at the 2d they were 45,400 (ch. 26:50). The tribe of Naphtali pitched on the n. side of the tabernacle,

beside those of Dan and Asher (ch. 2:29). Upon their arrival in Canaan, they were one of the 6 tribes which stood upon Mount Ebal to pronounce curses on transgressors of the law (Deut. 27:13; cf. Josh. 8:33). The territory allotted to them was in n. Palestine. It was bounded on the e. by the upper Jordan and the Sea of Galilee, on the s. by Issachar and Zebulun, and on the w. by Zebulun and Asher (Josh. 19:34). It was a long, narrow strip of land, about 50 miles from n. to s. and varying from about 10 to 15 from e. to w. It is mostly mountainous (Josh. 20:7), and is quite fertile. Its boundary ran by Mount Tabor (ch. 19:34), and it numbered Ramah, Hazor, Kedesh, Iron, and Beth-anath among its fortified cities (vs. 36–38). The Gershonite Levites had 3 cities allotted them within its limits; they were Kedesh, Hammoth-dor, and Kartan. The first of them was a city of refuge (Josh. 20:7; 21:6, 32; I Chron. 6:62, 76).

Up to the early period of the Judges the Naphtalites had not succeeded in expelling the Canaanites from Beth-shemesh and Beth-anath; they had, however, made them tributary. The Naphtalites took a large share in the fighting under Deborah and Barak, being mentioned with Zebulun as having jeopardized their lives unto death in the high places of the field (Judg. 4:6, 10; 5:18). They also responded to the summons to arms issued by Gideon (Judg. 6:35; 7:23). A thousand captains, with 37,000 fighting men, came to David at Hebron, to aid him in the contest with Ish-bosheth (I Chron. 12:34; cf. v. 40). Their ruler some time afterward was Jerimoth, son of Azriel (I Chron. 27:19; cf. Ps. 68:27). Ahimaaz was Solomon's purveyor in Naphtali (I Kings 4:15). Hiram, not the Tyrian king, but the skillful worker in metal, was a widow's son of the tribe of Naphtali (I Kings 7:14). The land of Naphtali was ravaged by Ben-hadad, king of Syria (I Kings 15:20; II Chron. 16:4), and many of its inhabitants were subsequently carried into captivity by Tiglath-pileser, king of Assyria (II Kings 15:29). To these calamities Isaiah alludes, and comforts the afflicted people by intimating in the name of the Lord that the territory now ravaged should one day receive special privilege, so that they who walked in darkness should see a great light (Isa. 9:1–7). This prophecy was fulfilled when our Lord made the region on which the invasion had fallen the special seat of his ministry (Matt. 4:12–16). Chorazin, Capernaum, and Tiberias were within the limits of what had been Naphtali.

Naph·tu′him (năf-tū′hĭm). A tribe of Egyptian descent, mentioned between the Libyans of Lower and the Pathrusim of Upper Egypt (Gen. 10:13; I Chron. 1:11). It may be a designation for Lower Egypt or The Delta.

Nap′kin. See HANDKERCHIEF.

Nar·cis′sus (när-sĭs′ŭs) [Lat. from Gr.]. A Roman, whose household was in the Lord and was greeted by Paul in his letter to the church (Rom. 16:11).

Nard. See SPIKENARD.

Na′sor (nā′sôr). See HAZOR 1.

Na′than (nā′thăn) [he (i.e., God) has given]. 1. Son of Attai, and father of Zabad, belonging to the house of Jerahmeel, family of Hezron, tribe of Judah (I Chron. 2:36).

2. A distinguished prophet in the reign of David and Solomon. The proposal to build the Temple was submitted to him by David. At first he was favorable to the project, but afterward received a message from the Lord directing that not David, but his successor was to have the honor of building the holy house (II Sam., ch. 7; I Chron. 17:1–15). Nathan was afterward sent to David to bring him to a sense of his great sin in the matter of Uriah

the Hittite. This the prophet did by the parable of the ewe lamb (II Sam. 12:1–15; cf. Psalm 51, title). In his official capacity as prophet of the Lord he named the young Solomon Jedidiah (II Sam. 12:25). With his and Gad's concurrence, or possibly at their instigation, David arranged the musical service for the sanctuary (II Chron. 29:25). When Adonijah aspired to the throne in lieu of Solomon, he sent no intimation of his intention to Nathan, believing probably that the prophet was too loyal to David to be seduced from his allegiance (I Kings 1:8–10). Nathan advised Bath-sheba to go at once and tell David what had occurred, arranging that he would come in and confirm her words. The plan was carried out, and David gave orders to Zadok the priest, Nathan the prophet, and Benaiah, chief of the bodyguard, to proclaim Solomon (I Kings 1:11–45). Nathan wrote a history in which he described the reign of David and part at least of that of Solomon (I Chron. 29:29; II Chron. 9:29).

3. The father of one and brother of another of David's mighty men (II Sam. 23:36; I Chron. 11:38); see IGAL 2.

4. The 3d of those children of David who were born in Jerusalem (II Sam. 5:14). He, or possibly the prophet, was father of Solomon's officials, Azariah and Zabud (I Kings 4:5). His family is mentioned in Zech. 12:12. Through him David and Jesus Christ are connected by natural lineage (Luke 3:31); while it is through Solomon that Joseph, the husband of Mary, is connected with David (Matt. 1:6).

5. A chief man with Ezra at the brook of Ahava (Ezra 8:16).

6. A son of Bani, induced by Ezra to put away his foreign wife (Ezra 10:39).

Na·than′a·el (nȧ-thăn′ȧ-ĕl) [Gr. from Heb., God has given]. A native of Cana in Galilee, whom Jesus declared to be an Israelite indeed in whom was no guile. His attention was directed by Philip to Jesus as the Messiah of O.T. prophecy. But as Nazareth is not mentioned in O.T. prophecy and besides had a questionable reputation, he felt difficulty in accepting the Messianic claims of one who had been brought up in that town; but he at once yielded to the evidence which the superhuman knowledge of Jesus furnished (John 1:45–51). He was in the boat with Simon Peter when the miraculous draught of fishes was brought in (ch. 21:2). The name does not occur in the lists of the apostles given in the first 3 Gospels, but he was probably the same person as Bartholomew.

Other persons of the name are mentioned in the O.T., but there the original Heb. form is used. See NETHANEL.

Na′than-me′lech (nä′thăn-mē′lĕk) [the (divine) king has given]. A chamberlain who lived in Josiah's time within the precincts of the Temple (II Kings 23:11).

Na′um (nä′ŭm). See NAHUM 2.

Naz′a·rene′ (năz′ȧ-rēn′) [belonging to Nazareth]. 1. One born or resident in Nazareth (Matt. 2:23; Mark 16:6). In Isa. 11:1 the Messiah is called nēṣer or shoot out of the roots of Jesse; an offspring of the royal family indeed, but of that family shorn of its glory and reduced to its original humble condition. He is frequently called the branch also (Jer. 23:5; 33:15; Zech. 3:8; 6:12). On the most probable interpretation of Matt. 2:23, the Evangelist sees a fulfillment of Isaiah's prophecy in the providence which led the parents of Jesus to take up their residence in Nazareth again and resulted in Jesus' being a Nazarene. If Nazareth means protectress or guardian, Matthew finds the fulfillment merely in the similarity of sound and in the low esteem in which the town and its inhabitants were held; but if the name is derived from the same root as nēṣer (see NAZARETH), then Matthew finds the fulfillment chiefly in the meaning (Matt. 26:71, Gr. Nazōraios, of Nazareth, or Nazarene; cf. Mark 16:6, R.V.).

2. An adherent of the religion founded by Jesus; a Christian. It is used contemptuously (Acts 24:5).

Naz′a·reth (năz′ȧ-rĕth). A town of Galilee (Matt. 2:23), where Joseph and Mary lived (Luke 2:39), and where Jesus was brought up (ch. 4:16) and spent the greater part of 30 years (cf. Luke 3:23 with Mark 1:9). He was accordingly known as Jesus of Nazareth (Matt. 21:11; Mark 1:24). He was held in favor there (Luke 2:52; 4:16); but after he entered on his mission, he was twice rejected by his fellow townsmen (Luke 4:28–31; cf. Matt. 4:13; 13:54–58; Mark 6:1–6). Nazareth stood upon a hill (Luke 4:29). The town was either small and unimportant or of recent origin; for it is not mentioned in the O.T. or in the Apocrypha or by Josephus. It is still called en-Nāṣirah. It lies in a secluded valley in Lower Galilee, a little n. of the great Plain of Esdraelon, and is about 15 miles w.s.w. of Tiberias, 20 s.w. of Tell Ḥūm, the reputed site of Capernaum, and 19 s.e. of Acre; it is 88 miles n. of Jerusalem. The valley is about a mile from e. to w. and, on an average, a quarter of a mile from n. to s. The hill on the n.w. rises about 500 feet above the valley, and is cut into ravines on its e. slope. On that e. declivity stands the village of Nazareth. The houses are better than those in many other villages in Palestine, being made of the white limestone which is conspicuously displayed along all the higher parts of the investing hills. They are prettily situated among fig trees, olive trees, and some cypresses, while down below in the valley are gardens surrounded by hedges of prickly pear. In the midst of the gardens is the Fountain of the Virgin, from which Nazareth derives its water, and whither doubtless Mary frequently went to obtain water for her household. Nazareth now contains about 10,000 inhabitants, of whom 3,000 are Christians. There is a fine Franciscan convent. The monks point out many sacred sites in Nazareth, but only the Fountain of the Virgin rests on good evidence. The site of the place where Jesus' fellow townsmen attempted to cast him headlong from the brow of the hill (Luke 4:29) was probably near the Maronite church, where there are 2 or 3 bare scarps, 20, 30, 40, or 50 feet high.

The name Nazareth is written in several forms in the manuscripts of the N.T. Nazareth and Nazaret are the best attested, but there are also found Nazarath, Nazarat; in Matt. 4:13 and Luke 4:16 Westcott and Hort, and Nestle prefer the reading Nazara. The precise form of the word and its meaning are alike uncertain; the town may have been called in Aram. Nāṣerā, Nāṣerath, Nāṣartā, with the fem. ending t (th) retained, as was frequently the case in the names of towns (Zarephath, Daberath, Bozkath, Timnath). Accordingly, it may, under Heb. influence, have been pronounced Nāṣereth (cf. Aram. ᾽iggerā, ᾽iggartā, and Heb. ᾽iggereth, a letter). As thus explained, the word is a fem. participle. It is rare for the Semitic sound ṣ to be represented by z in Gr., as this explanation of Nazareth requires; but it is not unparalleled (cf. Zilpah; Heb. Ṣilpāh, Gr. Zelpha). The Syriac preserves ṣ, using the form Nāṣerath. The Arabs who conquered the country heard the emphatic sibilant and perpetuated the name in the form en-Nāṣirah. The Arabic name signifies helper or victor. The derivation of the original name is frequently sought in the Heb. root nāṣar (watch, protect,

MARY'S WELL AT NAZARETH

guard), so that Nazareth means protectress or guardian in the sense of a watchtower. A comparison of Matt. 2:23 with the Heb. text of Isa. 11:1 favors the derivation of the name Nazareth from the root which appears in Heb. *nēṣer* and Aramaic *niṣrā*, sprout; Nazareth accordingly would mean verdant place or offshoot. The name may also be explained as a passive from *nāṣar*, signifying protected, secluded. If considered as a *Niph'al* participle of the root *ṣur* or *ṣārar*, it would mean confined, shut in.

Naz'i•rite (năz'ĭ-rīt), in A.V. **Naz'a•rite** (năz'à-rīt) [separated, consecrated (to God)]. A person, male or female, who was specially consecrated to God. Nazirites probably existed of old among the Hebrews, but their mode of life was brought under the regulations of the Law at Sinai. The Nazirite vowed to separate himself unto the Lord for a certain specified period. He did not, however, become a hermit; he continued to live in human society. Nor was he necessarily an ascetic. By the Law he must not drink wine or strong drink nor eat any product of the vine during the days of his separation; for from the time of the nomadic patriarchs the vine was the symbol of a settled life and culture, which were quite right in themselves, but were removed from the ancient simplicity of life and manners. See JON-ADAB 2. Nor must the Nazirite shave his head. The long hair was the visible sign of his consecration to God; the hair was the glory of the head and the product of the body he had devoted to God; and the cutting of the hair, which God made grow, was popularly regarded as rendering the head in a measure common (cf. Ex. 20:25; Num. 19:2; Deut. 15:19). Finally, the Nazirite must not render himself ceremonially unclean by touching a dead body, even if the corpse should be that of a near relative. When the time approached for his vow to expire, he appeared before the priest, made certain prescribed offerings, and shaved off his hair and burned it, after which he might again drink wine (Num. 6:1–21). One might be a Nazirite for life instead of for a limited period, and might be dedicated to that mode of existence at or even before his birth. This was the case with Samson (Judg. 13:4, 5) and with Samuel (I Sam. 1:11, 28). Samson, however, permitted deviations not only from the law of the Nazirite, but at the same time from other laws and ancient customs and the dictates of refinement. In the time of Amos profane people tempted the Nazirites to break their vow of total abstinence from wine, even offering it to them to drink (Amos 2:11, 12). After the Exile Nazirites became comparatively numerous (I Macc. 3:49; Jos. *War* ii. 15, 1). John the Baptist was consecrated a Nazirite from his birth (Luke 1:15). The prophetess Anna was not unlikely a Nazirite (ch. 2:36, 37). It seems to have been the Nazirite vow that Paul was induced to take to allay the storm which his friends saw to be gathering against him on his last visit to Jerusalem (Acts 21:20–26). Wealthy persons often bore the legal expenses of poor Nazirites (Jos. *Antiq.* xix. 6, 1).

Ne'à (nē'à). A place on the boundary line of Zebulun (Josh. 19:13); probably Tell el-Wāwiyāt, one of the tells of Sahel el-Baṭṭôf.

Ne•ap'o•lis (nē-ăp'ŏ-lĭs) [Gr., new city]. The seaport of Philippi, and the 1st place in Europe at which Paul touched (Acts 16:11; implied also in ch. 20:6). It was situated on the Strymonian Gulf, 10 miles e.s.e. of Philippi.

Ne'a•ri'ah (nē'à-rī'à) [shield-bearer of Jehovah]. 1. A Simeonite captain, who took part in a successful war against the Amalekites near Mount Seir during the reign of Hezekiah (I Chron. 4:42).

2. A descendant of Shecaniah (I Chron. 3: 22, 23).

Ne'bai (nē'bī). See NOBAI.

Ne•ba'ioth (nē-bā'yŏth), in A.V. of Genesis **Ne•ba'joth** (nē-bā'jŏth) [cf. name of god Nebo]. An Arabian tribe descended from Ishmael (Gen. 25:13, 16; 28:9; 36:3); and rich in flocks (Isa. 60:7); not to be identified with the Nabataeans.

Ne•bal'lat (nē-băl'ăt). A town of Benjamin inhabited after the Captivity (Neh. 11:34), now Beit Nabāla, about 4 miles n.e. of Lydda and 1½ n. of el-Haditheh, i.e., Hadid, and w. by n. of Beth-el.

Ne'bat (nē'băt) [(God has) looked]. Father of Jeroboam I (I Kings 11:26).

Ne'bo (name of god, nā'bō; geographical name, nē'bō) [Heb. *Nebō*, from Akkad. *Nabū* (root meaning to call, announce), a Babylonian god; as a geographical name it may indicate that the place was a seat of Nebo's worship, or correspond to Arab. *naba'a* (to be high), and denote elevation]. 1. A Babylonian god (Isa. 46:1), who presided over knowledge and literature. The special seat of his worship was at Borsippa, near Babylon. In Isaiah's time images of Nebo were used as objects of worship.

2. A peak of the Abarim mountains over against Jericho (Num. 33:47; Deut. 32:49), and the summit, apparently, of Pisgah (Deut. 34:1). Its probable site is Jebel en-Nebā, 8 miles e. of the mouth of the river Jordan. From its summit, especially from the elevation called Rās Siāghah, there are visible in the clear atmosphere of spring Hermon, at the foot of which lay Dan, and the mountains of Naphtali, and the hill country of Ephraim and Judah, which are bounded and at Carmel washed by the hinder sea, and the depression which marks the south country, and the Dead Sea and the Jordan Valley.

3. A Moabite town near or on Mount Nebo (Num. 32:3). It was rebuilt by the Reubenites (Num. 32:37, 38; 33:47; cf. I Chron. 5:8), but came again into Moabite hands (*Moabite Stone*, 14, see MOABITE STONE; Isa. 15:2; Jer. 48:1, 22). The site is probably represented by Khirbet el-Mḥayieṭ, s. of Mount Nebo-Siāghah.

4. A town mentioned just after Beth-el and Ai (Ezra 2:29; Neh. 7:33); identified by Conder with Nūba, e. of Khirbet Kīla.

Neb'u•chad•nez'zar (nĕb'ů-kăd-nĕz'ẽr) and **Neb'u•chad•rez'zar** (nĕb'ů-kăd-rĕz'ẽr) [Akkad. *Nabū-kudurri-uṣur*, Nebo, defend the boundary. The form with -n- is due to dissimilation]. Son of Nabopolassar and king of Babylon. His father headed a successful revolt of the Chaldeans against Assyria and founded the Neo-Babylonian Empire in 625 B.C. Nineveh, the capital of Assyria, was taken by the Umman-Manda, the allies of Nabopolassar, 612 B.C., and the Egyptians had to reckon with the new claimants of the Assyrian dependencies. Necho II, who ascended the throne of Egypt in 609 B.C., invaded Palestine to protect Egyptian interests (II Kings 23:29; II Chron. 35:20) and fought Josiah, King of Judah, at Megiddo (608). Josiah was killed in battle. Necho returned home and came back with a large army in order to extend his empire beyond the Euphrates. Nabopolassar sent his son Nebuchadnezzar to meet the Egyptians. Nebuchadnezzar defeated them in 605 B.C. with great slaughter at the battle of Carchemish, drove them back to their own land, and subjugated the intervening regions (II Kings 24:7; Jer. 46:2). But news arrived that his father was dead. Committing affairs in the w. to his generals, he hastened back to Babylon and ascended the throne in 605 B.C. (Jos. *Apion* i. 19). Information regarding his reign is derived from the O.T. writers, including Nebuchadnezzar's contemporaries Jeremiah and Ezekiel. The Book of Daniel is also very important in this connection. The O.T. records are supplemented by notices on inscribed bricks, and the statements of the Babylonian historian Berosus, a priest of the 3d century B.C. After its subjection, Judah rendered tribute to Nebuchadnezzar for 3 years and then revolted (II Kings 24:1). He returned to Palestine after a while, suppressed the revolt, threw one king in fetters, presently ordered the new king to be carried captive to Babylon, and placed yet another king on the throne (II Chron. 36:6, 10); see JEHOIAKIM, JEHOIACHIN, ZEDEKIAH 4. Zedekiah remained professedly loyal for about 8 years; in the 9th year he struck for independence, being assisted by the advance of an Egyptian army (Jer. 37:5). The ultimate result was that Jerusalem was taken (586), and the Temple was burned, and the leading inhabitants of the capital and the country were carried into captivity (II Kings, chs. 24; 25; II Chron. 36: 5–21; Jer., chs. 39; 52). About this time (586–573), Nebuchadnezzar besieged Tyre (Ezek. 29:18; Jos. *Apion* i. 21; *Antiq.* x. 11, 1). In his 23d year, 582 B.C., he warred against Coelesyria, Moab, and Ammon, and deported several hundred Jews (Jer. 52:30; Jos. *Antiq.* x. 9, 7). In his 37th year, c. 567 B.C., he invaded Egypt (cf. Ezek. 29:19).

It is probable that Nebuchadnezzar carried on other military campaigns, though the record of them is lost. He acted on the policy of transporting the inhabitants of conquered countries to other parts of the empire, and thus had at his command much labor, which enabled him to carry out important works. He built the great wall of Babylon, erected a magnificent palace for himself, and repaired the great temple of Marduk at Babylon, the temple of Nebo at Borsippa, and many other sanctuaries. He is said to have built hanging gardens to remind his wife Amyitis (Amuhea, Amuhia) of her native Median hills (Jos. *Apion* i. 19; *Antiq.* x. 11, 1), and to have constructed near Sippara a huge reservoir for irrigation, reputed to have been 140 miles in

circumference and 180 feet in depth, besides canals across the land, and quays and breakwaters on the Persian Gulf. The form of madness from which he suffered when pride overthrew his reason was that called lycanthropy, in which the patient fancies himself one of the inferior animals and acts as such. Nebuchadnezzar imagined that he had become an ox, and went forth to eat grass like other cattle (Dan., ch. 4). He reigned more than 43 years and died after a brief illness in the year 562 B.C., leaving his son Evil-merodach to ascend the throne.

Neb'u·shaz'ban (něb'û-shăz'băn), in A.V. **Neb'u·shas'ban** (něb'û-shăs'băn) [Akkad., *Nabū-šēzibanni*, Nebo, save me]. A Babylonian prince who held the office of rab-saris under Nebuchadnezzar (Jer. 39:13).

Neb'u·zar·a'dan (něb'û-zăr-ā'dăn) [Akkad., *Nabū-zēr-iddina*, Nebo has given offspring]. The captain of the guard in the army of Nebuchadnezzar which captured Jerusalem. He was chief in command of the troops which completed the destruction of the city and burned the Temple (II Kings 25:8–11, 18–21; Jer. 39:9, 10; 52:12–30; cf. chs. 41:10; 43:6). To the Prophet Jeremiah, who had recommended his countrymen to submit to the Babylonians, he, by express orders from the victorious sovereign, showed all kindness (Jer. 39:11–14; 40:1–5). Five years later he deported a body of Jews (ch. 52:30).

Ne'co (nē'kō) and **Ne'coh** (nē'kō), in A.V. **Ne'cho** (nē'kō) and **Ne'choh** (nē'kō). See PHARAOH 5.

Nec'ro·man'cy. See FAMILIAR SPIRIT and WIZARD.

Ned'a·bi'ah (něd'à-bī'à) [Jehovah has been generous]. A son of King Jeconiah (I Chron. 3:18).

Nee'dle. A sharp instrument required for embroidering and sewing (cf. Ex. 35:35; Eccl. 3:7; Mark 2:21). The eye was called simply the hole (Matt. 19:24, Gr.). When Jesus speaks of a camel going through the eye of a needle, he uses a vivid figure of speech and aptly illustrates the difficulty, or rather impossibility, for them that trust in riches to enter into the Kingdom of God (Mark 10:24–26).

Neg'eb (něg'ĕb), **The** [dry]. The grazing region lying a few miles s. of Hebron (cf. Gen. 18:1 with ch. 20:1; Num. 13:22); called in R.V. the South (Gen. 12:9 marg.). As a physical division of the country, it contrasted with the hill country, the lowland, and tne Arabah (Josh. 10:40; 12:8). The n. part of it was allotted to the tribes of Judah and Simeon (Josh. 15:21–32; 19:1–9). Notable places in it were Kadesh-barnea (Gen. 20:1), Beer-lahai-roi (Gen. 24:62), Beer-sheba (Josh. 15:28), Ziklag (Josh. 15:31), and Arad (Num. 21:1).

Ne·gi'nah (nĕ-gē'nä), pl., **Neg'i·noth** (něg'ĭ-nŏth) [music of a stringed instrument; stringed instrument]. A musical term occurring in the title of many psalms, where it denotes a stringed instrument, and is so rendered in R.V. (Psalm 61). Elsewhere the word often means song, music.

Ne·hel'a·mite (nĕ-hĕl'à-mīt). The designation of the false prophet Shemaiah (Jer. 29:24). It may be derived from his native place Nehelam, but no such place is mentioned in the Bible. In A.V. marg. it is rendered dreamer.

Ne·he·mi'ah (nē'hĕ-mī'à) [Jehovah has comforted]. 1. One of the chief men who returned with Zerubbabel from Babylon (Ezra 2:2; Neh. 7:7).

2. Son of Azbuk and ruler of half the district of Beth-zur. He repaired part of the wall of Jerusalem (Neh. 3:16).

Ruins of the Babylon of Nebuchadnezzar

3. A Jew of the Captivity, son of Hachaliah (Neh. 1:1). He was discharging his duty of cupbearer to Artaxerxes Longimanus, king of Persia, when the king observed that he looked sad, and questioned him as to the cause of his sorrow. Nehemiah frankly told him it was the state of ruin in which the city of his fathers' sepulchers, Jerusalem, was lying. He therefore begged permission to go and build again the wall of the city (445 B.C.). The king accorded him an escort of cavalry for the journey, gave him letters commending him to the different Persian governors by the way, and appointed him governor of Judah, as Zerubbabel had been (chs. 1:1 to 2:9; 5:14). He arrived at Jerusalem in the 20th year of Artaxerxes' reign, 444 B.C. Ezra the priest was then at the Jewish capital, having come from Babylonia 13 years previously. Nehemiah, on reaching the capital, made a journey by night around the city and viewed the ruined walls. He now intimated to the people his intention of rebuilding the walls, and solicited their active aid. They gave it with good will, each notable man undertaking a part of the wall (ch. 3). The neighboring Gentile tribes did not like to hear that Jerusalem was being rebuilt, and 3 of their representatives, Sanballat, the Horonite, Tobiah, an Ammonite, and Geshem, an Arab, put forth active efforts to stop the building. But they could neither circumvent nor intimidate Nehemiah, who resolutely held on his course. The builders also guarded against sudden attack by working with one hand while with the other they carried a weapon (chs. 2:10; 4 to 6; Ecclus. 49:13). The wall was rebuilt in 52 days (Neh. 6:15), in the year 444 B.C. Attention was next turned to the instruction of the people (ch. 8), and a religious revival followed, which led to all the leading men, both of priests and people, sealing with Nehemiah a covenant to worship Jehovah (chs. 9; 10). After governing Judah for 12 years, Nehemiah, in 433–432 B.C., returned to Susa. He asked for further leave of absence (ch. 13:6), and, returning to Jerusalem, seems to have governed it for the remainder of his life, trying to enforce the Law of Moses against all who in any way departed from its provisions (ch. 13:8–31). Josephus states that he died at a great age (Jos. Antiq. xi. 5, 8). A successor, Bagohi (same name, but not same person as Bigvai, q.v.) by name, was in office in 411 B.C. (Elephantine papyri). For Nehemiah's connection with the formation of the canon, see CANON.

The Book of Nehemiah stands in the Hagiographa, or 3d division of the Hebrew Scriptures, immediately after Ezra and before Chronicles. In counting the books of Scripture, the Jews reckoned Ezra and Nehemiah as one book; see EZRA.

Nehemiah, informed of the wretched condition of Jerusalem (Neh., ch. 1), obtains permission of the Persian king Artaxerxes to visit Jerusalem temporarily as a royal commissioner (ch. 2; cf. v. 6). He incites the people to rebuild the walls (v. 17); the names of the builders are listed in ch. 3. He finds it necessary to arm the builders because of the opposition of the Samaritans (ch. 4). While the wall is in process of construction, he corrects abuses among the people (ch. 5). The wall is finished notwithstanding all attempts of Sanballat and Tobiah to terrify Nehemiah, and the secret aid furnished these foreigners by nobles of Judah (ch. 6). The city being large, but the population scanty, Nehemiah desires to increase the number of the inhabitants (ch. 7:4). To this end he gathers together the nobles, the rulers, and the people with the view 1st of reckoning them by genealogy and then of drafting some to dwell in Jerusalem. The register of them that came up at the 1st with Zerubbabel (ch. 7:6–73) is the register of Ezra, ch. 2. Before the registration had been accomplished, the 7th month arrived, which brought the populace to Jerusalem to the feast. The people asked that the Law of Moses be read. The reading resulted, 1st, in their building booths in which to dwell during the feast (Neh., ch. 8), and, 2d, in repentance of their sins and of their guilt in intermarriage with foreigners (ch. 9). They subscribed or sealed a covenant to obey God's Law and to abstain from intermarriage with the heathen. Chapter 10 gives a list of those who sealed. These religious acts having been performed, the original intention of making a registration of the people and securing additional inhabitants for the city was carried out. Lots were cast to draft 1 in 10 from the country people to dwell in Jerusalem in addition to those already inhabiting the city (ch. 11:1, 2). A list of the families who dwelt at Jerusalem (vs. 3–24). A list of the priests and Levites who returned at the first with Zerubbabel (ch. 12:1–9). List of high priests from Jeshua to Jaddua (vs. 10, 11). A list of the heads of the priestly houses in the generation after the Return (vs. 12–21). A list of the heads of the Levites at the same time and shortly after (vs. 22–26). The dedication of the wall (v. 27 seq.). In the interval during which Nehemiah was absent at the Persian court abuses had grown up: the Levites had been ill provided for (ch. 13: 10), the law of the Sabbath was observed with laxity (v. 15), and intermarriages with foreigners had not entirely ceased (v. 23). These abuses Nehemiah corrected.

The title assigns the authorship of the book to Nehemiah (ch. 1:1). Neh. 1:1 to 7:73a is an excerpt, apparently unaltered, from the memoirs of Nehemiah, as is clear from the use of the 1st person sing.; the register (ch. 7:6–73a) is expressly stated to have been an earlier document, which Nehemiah found and incorporated in his work. Ezra appears in chs. 7:73b to 10:39, and both Ezra and Nehemiah are mentioned in the 3d person (cf. ch. 8:1–9); in chs. 8:9; 10:1 Nehemiah receives the Persian title Tirshatha (so in A.V. and J.V., but governor in R.V.; cf. the same title applied to Zerubbabel, Ezra 2:63; Neh. 7:65, 70). Even though the register (Neh. 7: 6–73a; cf. Ezra 2:1–10) be segregated, there is a difficulty of connection; Neh. 7:73b to 8:18 is not the sequel to ch. 7:4, 5. This section (chs. 7:73b to 10:39), based upon a reliable contemporary source, is perhaps modified here and there by the compiler or Chronicler, who is supposed to have edited the historical material composing the book. Many critics suppose that this source comes from the memoirs of Ezra. The prayer in ch. 9:6–38 is ascribed by the LXX to Ezra. In ch. 10: 28–39 the 1st person pl. is employed.

Chapter 11 continues the material of ch. 7:4, but it is remarkable that there is no reference to Nehemiah's initiative, so prominent in ch. 7:1–5. It seems probable, however, that the facts contained in ch. 11 are based upon the materials left by Nehemiah himself, even though the 1st person does not occur here.

In chs. 12 and 13, ch. 12:27–43 and ch. 13: 4–31 constitute 2 additional extracts from Nehemiah's memoirs (cf. the 1st person sing., chs. 12:31, 38, 40; 13 passim); it may be that the former in the introductory and concluding verses (ch. 12:27–30, 42, 43) were somewhat altered by the compiler or Chronicler. The lists in ch. 12:1–7, 8, 9, 12–21 probably were derived from older sources by the compiler. Reference to a source is made in ch. 12:23. Ch. 12:10, 11, 22–26 refers to circumstances after the time of Nehemiah; the references to the days of Nehemiah (chs. 12:44–47; 13:1–3) as of the past may be ascribed to the Chronicler. Critics accordingly recognize as definitely belonging to the memoirs of Nehemiah the following passages: chs. 1:1 to 7:5; 11:1, 2; 12:27–43; 13:4–31. The rest of the book is also based upon historical sources.

It cannot be determined whether the Chronicler had predecessors in editing the works of Ezra and Nehemiah. Critics, however, favor the view that the books of Ezra and Nehemiah in their present form are substantially due to the work of the Chronicler, who may be dated c. 400 B.C. See CHRONICLES, EZRA.

Ne'hi·loth (ne̅'hĭ-lŏth [perhaps, wind instruments] (Psalm 5, title).

Ne'hum (ne̅'hŭm) [consolation]. One of those who returned from the Babylonian Captivity (Neh. 7:7). Called in Ezra 2:2 Rehum, for which Nehum may be a copyist's error.

Ne·hush'ta (ne̅-hŭsh'tà)[of bronze]. Daughter of Elnathan of Jerusalem. She became the wife of Jehoiakim and mother of Jehoiachin (II Kings 24:8).

Ne·hush'tan (ne̅-hŭsh'tăn) [piece of brass]. See BRAZEN SERPENT.

Ne·i'el (ne̅-ĭ'el). A frontier village of Asher (Josh. 19:27); probably Khirbet Ya'nīn, about 2 miles n. of Kabūl on the edge of the plain of Acre.

Ne'keb (ne̅'kĕb) [a hollow, a narrow pass]. A frontier village of Naphtali (Josh. 19:33, A.V.). The R.V. joins the name with the preceding word, calling the place Adami-nekeb. If one wishes to give it a separate location, it may be placed at el-Boṣṣa, s.e. of Dāmieh and e. of Kefr Sabt. But see ADAMI-NEKEB.

Ne·ko'da (ne̅-kō'dà) [dotted, speckled]. Founder of a family of Nethinim (Ezra 2:48, 60).

Nem·u'el (nĕm'ū-ĕl). 1. A Reubenite, brother of Dathan and Abiram (Num. 26:9). 2. A son of Simeon (Num. 26:12); see JEMUEL.

Ne'pheg (ne̅'fĕg). 1. A Levite, family of Kohath, house of Izhar (Ex. 6:21). 2. One of the sons born to David in Jerusalem (II Sam. 5:15; I Chron. 3:7; 14:6).

Neph'i·lim (nĕf'ĭ-lĭm). See GIANT.

Ne'phish (ne̅'fĭsh). See NAPHISH.

Ne·phi'sim (ne̅-fī'sĭm), or **Ne·phu'sim** (ne̅-fū'sĭm); while in **Ne·phish'e·sim** (ne̅-fīsh'ē-sĭm) or **Ne·phush'e·sim**, 2 spellings, 1 with sh, the other with s, are apparently combined in the same word [hackled ones]. A family of Nethinim (Ezra 2:50; Neh. 7:52), perhaps originally captives taken from the tribe Naphish (q.v.).

Neph'tha·lim (nĕf'thà-lĭm). See NAPHTALI.

Neph·to'ah (nĕf-tō'à) [an opening]. The fountain of the waters of Nephtoah was w. of Jerusalem, on the boundary between Judah and Benjamin (Josh. 15:9; 18:15). The place is usually identified with Liftā, 2 miles n.w. of Jerusalem.

Ne·phush'e·sim (ne̅-füsh'ē-sĭm) and **Ne·phu'sim** (ne̅-fū'sĭm). See NEPHISIM.

Nep'tha·lim (nĕp'thà-lĭm). See NAPHTALI.

Ner (nûr) [a lamp]. 1. A Benjamite, son of Abiel and father of Abner (I Sam. 14:51). He or Abner was Saul's uncle (v. 50). If Abner was Saul's uncle, Ner was Saul's grandfather and identical with the following. 2. A Benjamite, son of Jeiel and father or remoter ancestor of Saul's father, Kish (I Chron. 8:33; 9:35, 36). See KISH 2.

Ne'reus (ne̅'rūs) [Lat. from Gr., name of a sea god]. A Roman Christian to whom Paul sent a salutation (Rom. 16:15), not improbably the son of Philologus.

Ner'gal (nâr'găl). The Babylonian god of the sun in its burning destructive aspect (II Kings 17:30). The chief seat of his worship was Cuthah. He was ruler of the nether world, and god of war and pestilence.

Ner'gal·sha·re'zer (nûr'găl-shà-re̅'zĕr) [Akkad. Nergal-šar-uṣur, Nergal, protect the king]. One of Nebuchadnezzar's princes, who held the office of rab-mag (Jer. 39:3, 13). He is the Nergalsharuṣur, known to the Greeks as Neriglissar, who married a daughter of Nebuchadnezzar, murdered his brother-in-law Evil-merodach, and ascended the throne as the latter's successor (Jos. Apion i. 20), reigning from 560 to 556 B.C.

Ne'ri (ne̅'rī). An ancestor of Christ and somehow genealogically the father of Shealtiel (Luke 3:27).

Ne·ri'ah (ne̅-rī'à) [Jehovah is a lamp]. Son of Maaseiah, and father of Baruch and Seraiah (Jer. 32:12; 36:4; 51:59).

Net. The net was used by the Hebrews in fowling (Prov. 1:17). Doubtless, as in Egypt, the clap net was used, a familiar form of which consisted of 2 half hoops or frames covered with netting and attached to a common axis. The trap was spread open flat, and the bait placed in the center. The motion of the bird at the bait released a spring, the 2 sides closed suddenly, and the bird was caught.

The net was also used in hunting (Isa. 51:20). It was cast about the game (Job 19:6) or over it (Ezek. 12:13; 19:8), or laid to catch the feet (Ps. 9:15; 25:15; 57:6; Lam. 1:13). Throughout the ancient world, as sculpture and narrative reveal, it was usual to extend nets on stakes to inclose a large space as by a fence, a single opening being left as an entrance. Through this gateway various kinds of game were driven, such as hares, boars, deer; and once within the inclosure they were under control and easily dispatched. Small nets were used to close gaps between bushes or to bar a path. Purse nets were laid that animals might run into them as into a tunnel and find no exit.

In fishing both drag nets (Hab. 1:15; Matt. 13:47, 48) and casting nets (Matt. 4:18; John 21:6) were used. The Hebrews were acquainted with the common drag net of Egypt (Isa. 19:8). It was quite large, its cords were made of flax, the lower edge was weighted with lead and sunk to the bottom of the river or sea, and the upper edge was floated by pieces of wood.

Ne·ta'im (ne̅-tā'ĭm) [plantings]. A place in Judah with royal plantations (I Chron. 4:23).

Ne·than'el (ne̅-thăn'ĕl), in A.V. **Ne·than'e·el** (ne̅-thăn'ē-ĕl) [God has given]. The Gr. form is Nathanael. 1. Prince of the tribe of Issachar at an early period of the wilderness wanderings (Num. 1:8; 2:5; 7:18, 23; 10:15).
2. Jesse's 4th son, and David's brother (I Chron. 2:14).
3. One of the priests who blew trumpets when the Ark was brought up to the city of David (I Chron. 15:24).
4. A Levite, father of Shemaiah (I Chron. 24:6).
5. A son of Obed-edom in David's reign (I Chron. 26:4).
6. One of the princes whom Jehoshaphat sent to teach in the cities of Judah (II Chron. 17:7).
7. A chief of the Levites in Josiah's reign (II Chron. 35:9).
8. A son of Pashhur, induced by Ezra to put away his foreign wife (Ezra 10:22).
9. A priest, head of the father's house of Jedaiah in the days of the high priest Joiakim (Neh. 12:21).

10. A priest's son who blew a trumpet at the dedication of the wall of Jerusalem (Neh. 12:36).

Neth·a·ni'ah (něth'á-nī'á) [Jehovah has given]. 1. A son of Asaph (I Chron. 25:2), the head of the 5th course of singers (v. 12).
2. A Levite sent with others by Jehoshaphat to teach in the cities of Judah (II Chron. 17:8).
3. Father of Jehudi (Jer. 36:14).
4. Father of that Ishmael who assassinated Gedaliah (II Kings 25:23, 25).

Neth'i·nim (něth'ĭ-nĭm), in A.V. **Neth'i·nims** (něth'ĭ-nĭmz) [given (pl.)]. Temple servants or slaves given by David and the princes for the service of the Levites (Ezra 8:20). Prior to their appointment, similar functions seem to have been discharged by the Midianites, whom Moses gave over to the Levites (Num. 31:47), and at a subsequent period by the Gibeonites, whom Joshua assigned as hewers of wood and drawers of water for the house of God (Josh. 9:23). Even after the Nethinim were associated with them or superseded them, the number of the Nethinim may have been too small for the elaborate Temple services instituted by David's son and successor, and have been increased; for we find in the books of Ezra (ch. 2:55–58) and Nehemiah (ch. 7:57–60) the children of Solomon's servants, i.e., slaves, mentioned after the Nethinim. Although they were organized by David, it was probably under a different name; for the word Nethinim occurs only in the books of Ezra and Nehemiah, with a solitary passage in I Chronicles (ch. 9:2). They discharged the more menial duties required by the Temple worship. Of the Nethinim and the children of Solomon's servants, 392 returned from captivity with Zerubbabel (Ezra 2:58; Neh. 7:60), and 220 more with Ezra (Ezra 8:17–20). The Nethinim seem to have been naturalized foreigners rather than people of true Israelite descent (I Chron. 9:2; Ezra 2:59; Neh. 7:61), and several of the names on the list of their leading men have a foreign aspect (Ezra 2:43–54; Neh. 7:46–56). They were probably descendants of the Midianites and Gibeonites, who have already been mentioned, and of various bands of captives taken in war; they are designated by the name of their progenitor or that of the prince or tribe from whom they were taken, as the children of Sisera, of Rezin, of Meunim, and of Nephisim (cf. Ezra 2:48, 50, 53; with I Chron. 5:19–21; II Chron. 26:7). Some of them lived on Ophel, a s. prolongation of the Temple hill (Neh. 3:26, 31; 11:3, 21), others in the villages round about Jerusalem (Ezra 2:70; Neh. 7:73). Holding an official position at the Temple, although the office was menial, they were exempt from imperial taxation (Ezra 7:24). They seem to have adopted with some cordiality the covenant made at the instance of Nehemiah to worship Jehovah (Neh. 10:28, 29).

Ne·to'phah (ně-tō'fá) [dropping, falling in drops]. A town of Judah, evidently near Bethlehem (I Chron. 2:54; Ezra 2:21, 22; Neh. 7:26). It was the home of 2 of David's mighty men (II Sam. 23:28, 29). Netophathites with Seraiah at their head were among the men who assembled loyally about Gedaliah, whom Nebuchadnezzar had made governor of Judah on the fall of Jerusalem (II Kings 25:23; Jer. 40:8 *seq.*). Fifty-six of the town's people returned after the Exile (Ezra 2:22). It was not originally assigned to the Levites, but after the Return its dependent villages were occupied by certain of them, including singers (I Chron. 9:16; Neh. 12:28). It is identified with Khirbet Bedd Fālūḥ, about 3½ miles s. of Bethlehem at the junction of Wadi eṭ-Ṭaḥūneh and Wadi eḍ-Di', near the road to Tekoa.

Ne·toph'a·thite (ně-tŏf'á-thīt), in A.V. of Neh. 12:28 **Ne·toph'a·thi** (ně-tŏf'á-thī), the Heb. form being preserved. An inhabitant of Netophah (II Sam. 23:28).

Net'tle. 1. The rendering of Heb. *ḥārūl*. Men driven by want take refuge under it (Job 30:7). Along with another nettle, Heb. *ḳimmĕśōnîm* (pl.), it overspreads the sluggard's unweeded garden (Prov. 24:31). In fact it springs up everywhere when cultivation of the land is neglected (Zeph. 2:9). The plant cannot be identified. R.V. places wild vetches in the marg.
2. The rendering of Heb. *ḳimmōś* in Isa. 34:13 and Hos. 9:6. The Roman or pill nettle (*Urtica pilulifera*) is found everywhere in Palestine. A modification of the word is pl., *ḳimmĕśōnîm* (Prov. 24:31), which the Eng. versions render "thorns."

New Moon. See MOON.

New Tes'ta·ment. The 2d of the 2 portions into which the Bible is naturally divided. Testament represents the Lat. word *testamentum*, which is used to translate Gr. *diathēkē*, covenant (II Cor. 3:14). The N.T. embodies the new covenant of which Jesus was the Mediator (Heb. 9:15; cf. ch. 10:16, 17 and Jer. 31:31–34). The 1st covenant was dedicated with blood (Heb. 9:19, 20), but was in no sense a testament: the 2d, while primarily a covenant was also a testament; that is, it was not merely dedicated with blood, but it required the death of the testator to give it force. It would not have had proper efficacy had not Jesus its Mediator died an atoning death.

The language of the 27 books of the N.T. is the *koine* or common Greek. This language had taken deep root in Palestine during the more than 3 centuries which had elapsed since the conquest of the Holy Land by Alexander the Great; and the merits of the language itself, and that of the literature which it enshrined, had given it the widest currency among educated men throughout the Roman Empire, though Greece had now for a considerable time lost its political independence.

The original MSS. of the books of the N.T. and almost all the copies made during the first 3 centuries have disappeared. Papyrus, which was commonly used for letters (II John 12), soon wore out, and in the time of Diocletian, A.D. 303, it was customary for the persecutors of Christians to seek for copies of the Scriptures and destroy them. The art of printing was unknown, but transcribers laboriously multiplied copies. The 4 Gospels were most frequently transcribed, and after them the Epistles of Paul. The Revelation was copied least often. No fewer than 4,489 MS. copies of the N.T. in whole or in part exist, their abundance markedly contrasting with the small number of the classical writers which have come down to our own day.

Corruptions of the text soon crept in. Copyists were fallible, careless, and sometimes imperfectly acquainted with Greek. Men of the patristic age and later were not governed by the modern demand for scientific exactness, and they handled the text with considerable license. They attempted to improve the grammar and the style, to correct supposed errors in history and geography, to adjust the quotations from the O.T. to the Greek of the LXX, and to harmonize the Gospels. They incorporated marginal notes, and they added to the Gospel narratives incidents obtained from authentic sources, as John 7:53 to 8:1 and Mark 16:9–20. The various readings which thus originated are very numerous. If each variant in every MS. is reckoned, the total is about

200,000. Nineteen twentieths of these are, however, of no authority, being evidently not genuine, and only the merest fraction of the remainder are of any consequence as affecting the sense. The very number of these readings, and the fact that they were made originally in different parts of the world, and from a variety of MSS., enables Biblical students to detect and eliminate the errors, and to approximate the original text more closely than if the various readings were fewer. This tedious but necessary work has been carried out with untiring energy by textual critics. It is possible indirectly to gain access to the readings in MSS. which have perished, for there were early versions of the N.T. in different languages, such as the Syriac and Latin, and quotations from the N.T. are found in the writings of the early Christians, especially in Clement of Alexandria and Origen. In most cases these versions and citations were made from MSS. not now existing, but a translation generally shows what the original must have been.

The N.T. MSS. fall into 2 divisions: Uncials, in Gr. capitals, at first without breathings or accents and with no separation between the different words, except occasionally to indicate the beginning of a new paragraph; and Cursives, in small running hand, and with divisions of words. The change between the 2 kinds of Greek writing took place about the 9th century. Only 5 MSS. of the N.T. approaching to completeness are more ancient than this dividing date. The 1st, designated as A, is the Alexandrian MS. Though given to England by Cyril Lucar, patriarch of Constantinople, as a present to Charles I, it is believed that it was written, not in that capital, but in Alexandria, whence its title. It is dated in the 1st half of the 5th century. In addition to a large portion of the O.T. and the First Epistle of Clement and part of the Second, it contains the whole of the N.T. except that the leaves containing Matt. 1:1 to 25:5; John 6:50 to 8:52; II Cor. 4:13 to 12:6 are lost. The page is divided into 2 columns, and the text is marked off into chapters, Mark, e.g., containing 48. The 2d, known as B, is the Vatican MS. It has been in the Vatican library at Rome from 1481 or an earlier period, but not till 1857 was an edition of it published, and that one, by Cardinal Mai, when issued, was uncritical and of little value. But in 1889–1890 a facsimile of it came forth, so that now it is fully accessible to scholars. The Vatican MS. dates from the middle of the 4th century, if not even from an earlier period. Besides most of the O.T., it contains all the N.T. except Heb. 9:14 to 13:25; I and II Timothy; Titus, Philemon, and Revelation. It has 3 columns to the page, and is divided into short chapters, Matthew, e.g., having 170. The 3d, C, or the Ephraem MS., is a palimpsest. In the 12th century the original writing was removed to make room for the text of several ascetic treatises of Ephraem the Syrian. Traces of the older writing were, however, discernible, and most of the N.T. text was recovered and published by Tischendorf in 1843. It is believed that it belongs to the 5th century, and perhaps a slightly later period of it than the MS. A. It contains portions of the O.T. and five eighths of the N.T. The lines run across the page. The 4th, D, is the MS. of Beza, to whom it belonged after it was taken from the abbey of St. Irenaeus in Lyons at the sack of the city in 1562. It is commonly dated in the 6th century, though some scholars favor the 5th. It contains the greater part of the Gr. text of the Gospels and Acts, together with a Lat. translation. It is for the most part the only witness among Gr. MSS. to a type of text which was widely current as early as the 2d century, and of

which the other principal representatives are the Old Latin and the Old Syriac versions. It is written stichometrically, i.e., in single lines containing as many words as could be read at a breath, consistently with the sense. The 5th, called א (the Heb. first letter, *aleph*), is the Sinaitic MS., obtained in 1844 and 1859 by Tischendorf from the monks belonging to the convent of St. Catherine on Mount Sinai. Besides the major part of the O.T., it contains the whole N.T. without a break, together with the Epistle of Barnabas and a large part of the Shepherd of Hermas. The last 12 verses of Mark are lacking. It was made in the 4th century, a little later than B. It has 4 columns to the page.

Of the 53 papyrus fragments, some very small, of the N.T., the most important are the Chester Beatty papyri. Portions of 30 leaves of the Gospels and Acts have been preserved from a codex of originally about 220 leaves. Eighty-six leaves, all slightly mutilated, show that another codex originally contained Romans, Hebrews, I and II Corinthians, Ephesians, Galatians, Philippians, Colossians, and I and II Thessalonians, in this order. Both codices are dated early in the 3d century A.D. Ten leaves from a codex of Revelation, dating from the 3d century, comprise a 3d section of these famous papyri. The earliest known portion of the Greek N.T. is a tiny fragment of a papyrus codex dating from not later than A.D. 140; it contains part of John 18:31–33, 37 *seq*.

Cursive or minuscule MSS. are much more numerous, numbering some 2,429 as compared with 212 uncial MSS. The great majority of them, however, date from the late Middle Ages and possess little or no value in determining the early text. In addition to these, 1,678 lectionaries (medieval MSS. containing lessons from the N.T. prescribed to be read during the church year) have been catalogued, though very few have been critically examined.

The 1st printed edition of the Greek N.T. actually published was that of Erasmus, who issued it in 1516. It was reprinted in 1518, a 2d and more correct edition followed in 1519, a 3d in 1522, a 4th in 1527, and a 5th in 1535. Cardinal Ximenes, the Roman Catholic primate of Spain, had been engaged for some years in preparing an edition of the Greek N.T.; though it was printed in 1514, various causes of delay kept it back from the world till 1521 or 1522. From being made at Alcalá, called by the Romans Complutum, it is known as the Complutensian edition. Among other editions of the Greek N.T. which followed, none were more celebrated than those of Robert Stephanus (Estienne, Stephens) of Paris, which appeared in 1546, 1549, 1550, and 1551. Then Beza the reformer came upon the scene and issued 9 editions of the Greek N.T. between 1565 and 1604, based on Stephanus' 3d edition (1550), which in turn had been founded mainly on Erasmus' 4th or 5th edition. Stephanus' edition of 1550 is the *textus receptus* in England, but on the continent of Europe this designation and authority are generally given to the 1st Elzevir edition, printed at Leyden in 1624. This Elzevir text is mainly that of Stephanus' edition of 1550, from which it differs in 287 places, including merely orthographic variations. It was mainly from Beza's edition of 1598 that the A.V. of the English Bible was made.

The division of the O.T. and N.T. into our present chapters is probably due to Stephen Langton, later archbishop of Canterbury, who died in 1228. The division of the N.T. into our present verses was made by Robert Stephanus in the Greek N.T. which he published in 1551. The 1st English N.T. to be so divided was Whittingham's translation, Geneva, 1557, and the 1st English Bible so divided was the Geneva version of 1560.

Ne·zi'ah (nē-zī'á) [pre-eminent; cf. Arab., sincere]. Founder of a family of Nethinim, members of which returned with Zerubbabel from the Babylonian Captivity (Ezra 2:54; Neh. 7:56).

Ne'zib (nē'zīb) [pillar, garrison]. A town in the lowland of Judah (Josh. 15:43); Khirbet Beit Neṣīb (or Nāsīf), a little over 2 miles s. of Khirbet Ḳīla.

Nib'haz (nīb'hăz). An idol, 1 of 2 worshiped by the Avvites, a tribe brought with others from the Assyrian empire to colonize Samaria after the captivity of the ten tribes (II Kings 17:31). Hommel identifies Nibhaz with an Elamite divinity, *Ibna-ḫaza*; it has also been compared with Mandaic *Nᵉbaz*, the lord of darkness, who is a heavenly power.

Nib'shan (nīb'shăn). A town in the wilderness of Judah (Josh. 15:62).

Ni·ca'nor (nī-kā'nôr) [Gr., victorious]. 1. Son of Patroclus and one of the king's friends whom Lysias, regent in w. Syria during the absence of Antiochus Epiphanes, in 166 B.C. selected to lead the army to suppress the Judean revolt (I Macc. 3:38; II Macc. 8:9). The Syrians were defeated, Nicanor stood high in the favor of Demetrius I also, and was appointed governor of Judea by him (I Macc. 7:26; II Macc. 14:12). He professed friendship for Judas Maccabaeus, but the Jew was not deceived. Nicanor engaged in battle with Judas at Capharsalama, and was slain in battle with him near Beth-horon, 160 B.C. (I Macc. 7:27-49; II Macc. 15:1-36).

2. One of the 7 men who were chosen in the church at Jerusalem to look after the Greek-speaking widows and, apparently, the poor in general (Acts 6:5).

Nic'o·de'mus (nīk'ŏ-dē'mŭs) [Gr., victor over the people]. A Pharisee and a member of the sanhedrin. Convinced by the miracles which Jesus wrought that the Teacher of Nazareth had come from God, he sought an interview with him; but by night, to escape observation or because the hour was convenient. Jesus explained to him the nature of the new birth, and the love of God for the world which prompted him to give his only begotten Son that whosoever accepted him in faith might have eternal life (John 3:1-21). At a meeting of the sanhedrin, when the members began to denounce Jesus as an impostor, Nicodemus pointedly asked whether the Law condemned a man unheard (ch. 7:50-52). After the death of Christ Nicodemus took about 100 pounds' weight of myrrh and aloes and aided in preparing the body for burial (ch. 19:39).

Nic'o·la'i·tans (nīk'ŏ-lā'ĭ-tănz). A party or sect in the churches of Ephesus and Pergamos whose practice and doctrine were severely censured. Following the doctrine of Balaam, they taught that Christians were free to eat things offered to idols and to commit the excesses of heathenism (Rev. 2:6, 14, 15), contrary to the command issued by the apostolic council held at Jerusalem A.D. 50 (Acts 15:29). Presumably the Nicolaitans were the followers of some heresiarch called Nicolaus. But that he was the deacon of that name in the church at Jerusalem (ch. 6:5) lacks proof. The earliest trace of the theory that the sect originated in the teaching of the deacon is found in the writings of Irenaeus, about A.D. 175. A sect of Nicolaitans existed among the Gnostics of the 3d century. They, too, taught the freedom of the flesh; and they may have grown out of these corrupt Christians of the Apostolic Age.

Nic'o·la'us (nīk'ŏ-lā'ŭs), in A.V. **Nic'o·las** (nīk'ŏ-lás) [Gr., victor over the people]. A proselyte of Antioch, who was 1 of the 7 elected at the instance of the apostles to look after the interests of the Greek-speaking widows and, apparently, the Christian poor in general (Acts 6:5).

Ni·cop'o·lis (nĭ-cŏp'ŏ-lĭs) [Gr., city of victory]. A place at which Paul, when he wrote the Epistle to Titus, hoped to winter (Titus 3:12). The note appended to the epistle says it was sent from Nicopolis of Macedonia, but it is of no authority and is not found in the oldest MSS. The place referred to in this postscript was situated on both sides of the river Nestus, which was the boundary line between Thrace and Macedonia. The postscript of the epistle in the received text is wrong: it assumes that Paul wrote from Nicopolis in spite of the distinct *there*, which shows that he was not then at Nicopolis, and it imagines that the Macedonian city by that name is meant. The probability is that the Nicopolis at which Paul meant to winter was the town in Epirus, 4 miles from Actium, which Augustus founded in 30 B.C. to commemorate his victory. Herod the Great built a number of its public edifices (Jos. *Antiq.* xvi. 5, 3). Its ruins remain at Prevesa.

Ni'ger (nī'jēr) [Lat., black]. A Latin surname of Simeon, a prophet and a teacher in the church of Antioch (Acts 13:1).

Night. The period of darkness (Gen. 1:5). It was divided into 3 watches: sunset to midnight, midnight to cock-crow, cock-crow to sunrise (Ex. 14:24; Judg. 7:19; Lam. 2:19). The Greek and Roman division into 4 watches was in use in N.T. times (Mark 6:48; Luke 12:38). At this period the night, from sunset to sunrise, was divided into 12 hours (cf. Acts 23:23).

Night Hawk. The rendering of Heb. *taḥmās* (cf. *ḥāmas*, to treat violently); an unclean bird mentioned in Lev. 11:16; Deut. 14:15). It is doubtful what bird is meant. The Eng. versions make it the night hawk, which is another name for the night jar, better known as the goatsucker (*Caprimulgus europaeus*), or some species akin to it. The LXX and Vulgate identify it with the owl.

Night Mon'ster. The rendering of Heb. *lilith* (Isa. 34:14, R.V. marg.; in A.V. screech owl). The word in Heb. means simply nocturnal, and may denote any female nocturnal bird or beast. In Assyrian, it was applied to a nocturnal demon. See SATYR.

Nile (nīl). The great river of Egypt (Isa. 23:3, in A.V. Sihor; Jer. 2:18, marg. of R.V.); in Heb. *Shiḥōr* and *Yᵉōr* (river). Its waters covered so vast an expanse, especially during the inundation, that it is sometimes called a sea (Nahum 3:8). The ultimate sources of the river are the streams which feed the Victoria Nyanza, 3° S. latitude; the Nile thus attains a length of some 3,670 miles. But the Nile in a narrower sense, as it presents those peculiarities which have made it famous, is formed by the confluence of the White and the Blue Nile at Khartum; from which point to its principal mouths at Damietta and Rosetta, a distance of about 1,650 miles as the river winds, it traverses an absolutely barren country and receives only 1 tributary, the Atbara, on the e. side, about 140 miles below Khartum. The banks rise several hundred feet and at places to upwards of 1,000 feet, resembling 2 large canal embankments, and wall the valley all the way to Cairo, where they diverge abruptly toward the e. and n.w. and face the protruded Delta. At Khartum, or just below it, the Nile enters the tableland of Nubian sandstone and winds its course in the form of a huge S; in this winding way are 6 cataracts. A short distance above Assuan, the ancient Syene, a ridge of granite, extending for 180 miles from e. to w., lies athwart the river's course. The stream breaks through this barrier, plunges down the rocks of the last or, on ascending the river, First Cataract, and enters the bounds of ancient Egypt. All above that cataract was Ethiopia, which extended from the First Cataract to the Sixth Cataract. The granite of this transverse ridge is colored; it is the well-known light-brown stone of which so many of the polished statues of the Pharaohs are made. Below Cairo the river divides and seeks the sea by several great channels. These mouths are now 2, the Damietta and the Rosetta; but formerly they numbered 7 of which the most important were the e. or Pelusiac, the w. or Canopic, and the middle or Sebennytic (Herod. ii. 17).

As the river pursues its tortuous course through thirsty land, much of its water is consumed by evaporation and infiltration, and still more by the extensive system of irrigating canals, which are necessary for agriculture.

The annual overflow is the famous feature of the Nile. Its occurrence in a rainless region was mysterious to the ancients (Herod. ii. 19–25). The region of Lake Victoria Nyanza is watered by rains which fall almost daily; this steady water supply gives the Nile its constant volume. The Blue Nile rises in the lofty highlands of Ethiopia and is a considerable mountain torrent. In the dry season this stream dwindles almost to nothing; in the rainy season it is a turbid mountain torrent, which rushes impetuously onward, laden with loose soil from the land which it drains. The Atbara is a freshet not unlike the Blue Nile.

Egypt is flanked on each side by extensive barren deserts. If it were not for the annual overflow of the Nile, Egypt would be a part of this desert. It is the variation of the water supply from the Blue Nile and the Atbara which causes the overflow of the Nile. At the beginning of June the river begins slowly to swell; between the 15th and 20th of July the increase becomes very rapid. Toward the end of September the water ceases to rise and remains at the same height for 20 to 30 days. In October it rises again attaining its greatest height. It then decreases, and in January, February, and March the fields gradually dry off. In consequence of this inundation the soil is both softened and fertilized. During a good inundation the Nile reaches a height of 40 feet at Assuan and of 23 to 27 at Cairo.

Occasionally inundation does not take place. A certain Amenemhet (Ameni) of Dyn. XII under Sesostris I says that he did not collect arrears of the fields due after short payments during unfruitful years. The inundation failed for 7 years in the time of Joseph (Gen. 41:54); and it failed likewise for 7 years in the reign of the caliph el-Mustanṣir, the resulting famine reaching its height A.D. 1070. The ancient Egyptians kept records of the height of the inundation at different places in various years.

In the time of the Pharaohs the Egyptian agricultural year was divided into 3 seasons: the period of inundation (from the end of June to the end of October); spring (or winter), that of the growing of the crops (from the end of October to the end of February); summer, that of the harvest (from the end of February to the end of June).

Nim'rah (nĭm'rȧ). An abbreviation of Bethnimrah (cf. Num. 32:3 with v. 36); see BETH-NIMRAH.

Nim'rim (nĭm'rĭm) [perhaps, a pl. of Nimrah, limpid waters, or pl. meaning leopards]. A locality in Moab, noted for its waters (Isa. 15:6; Jer. 48:34). The name is still found in Wadi Nemeirah, near the s.e. end of the Dead Sea, where the ruins of a town Nemeirah exist. Tristram locates the site higher up the valley, where it is said there is

an old Moabite city with the name Springs of Nemeirah. It has many well-watered gardens still in cultivation.

Nim'rod (nĭm'rŏd). A Cushite, a mighty hunter and a potent monarch, the beginning of whose original kingdom embraced Babel, Erech, Accad, and Calneh, cities in the land of Shinar (Gen. 10:8–10; Micah 5:6). The only ancient king of Babylonia known, who fits this description, and was at the same time celebrated in tradition and song, was Gilgamesh. There is, however, no proof that Nimrod and Gilgamesh are identical. Nothing is known of Nimrod beyond what is recorded in the O.T.

Nim'shi (nĭm'shī) [ety. uncertain; drawn out, but cf. Arab. nims, ichneumon, weasel]. An ancestor of Jehu (I Kings 19:16; II Kings 9:2), who was generally designated the son of Nimshi.

Nin'e·veh (nĭn'ē-vĕ). The capital of the Assyrian empire. The Hebrews embraced the entire population which was collected about the capital, and occupied the district at the confluence of the Tigris and the Upper Zab under the designation of Nineveh the great city (Gen. 10:11, 12; Jonah 1:2; 3:3; Judith 1:1). Nineveh in the narrower sense stood on the e. bank of the Tigris, at the mouth of a small tributary which is now known as the Khosr, about 27 miles above the confluence of the Zab with the main stream. It was built by a people of Babylonian origin (Gen. 10:11). Its tutelary deity was the goddess Ishtar, to whom Manishtusu of the Semitic Dynasty of Akkad (c. 2425–2245 B.C.) built a temple. The cult of the Ishtar of Nineveh was carried by Hurrians and Hittites as far as Egypt and s.w. Asia Minor. Asshur, 60 miles s. of Nineveh and on the opposite bank of the river, was the ancient seat of government; but Shalmaneser erected a palace at Nineveh (1280–1260), and from that period it was looked upon as the chief city of Assyria. Ashurnaṣirpal and his successor Shalmaneser, whose united reigns extended from c. 885 to 825, had palaces in both Nineveh and Calah, and resided sometimes in one place, sometimes in the other. Their successors dwelt in Nineveh in the broad sense; but the palace was not always in Nineveh proper, but was often erected in one of the suburbs, as Calah or Dur-sharrukin or Tarbisu.

The Assyrians were great warriors, and the spoils of the conquered cities and nations were brought to the capital and used to embellish it. It was also the center of some literary activity. About 650 B.C. Ashurbanipal gathered a great library, consisting of documents inscribed on clay tablets, which related to history, ritual, incantation, astronomy, and mathematics. It was composed for the most part of copies of older works, which had been brought from Babylonia. The Prophet Nahum calls Nineveh the bloody city (Nahum 3:1), both because of the wars which it had waged for centuries with the surrounding nations, and because of the cruelty which was practiced by the victors. Ashurnaṣirpal, for example, was accustomed after his victories to cut off the hands and feet, and the noses and ears, and put out the eyes of his captives, and to raise mounds of human heads. In 625 B.C., when the Assyrian empire began to decline in vigor, Nabopolassar, governor of Babylon, declared himself independent, and in 612 B.C. the Umman-manda, acting in confederation with Nabopolassar, descended upon the plain and by their own might captured and destroyed Nineveh. They were greatly aided by a sudden rise of the Tigris, which carried away a great part of the city wall and rendered the place indefensible.

So complete was the desolation that in Greek and Roman times the departed Nineveh became like a myth. Yet all the while part of the city lay buried under mounds of apparent rubbish. In 1820 Rich, an English resident at Baghdad, inspected the mound called Kouyunjik, on the e. bank of the Tigris, and became convinced that it concealed the ruins of Nineveh. In 1843 Botta, French consul at Mosul, on the w. bank of the Tigris, began to make excavations. He was soon diverted to Khorsabad, 10 miles off, the site of Dur-sharrukin. Between 1845 and 1850 Layard commenced operations at Nimroud, 18 miles s. of Kouyunjik; then he made excavations at the latter place itself, which proved to be the site of Nineveh. George Smith conducted further excavations at the place from 1873 to 1876, and after his death the work was taken up and extended to other mounds by Rassam. The walls of Nineveh have been traced and indicate a city 3 miles in length by less than a mile and a half in breadth, containing an area of about 1,800 English acres. But, as already said, the Hebrews and perhaps other foreigners were accustomed to include under the name of Nineveh the complex of cities which included, besides Nineveh, Calah, 18 miles s., Resen between Calah and Nineveh, and Rehoboth-Ir, broad places or suburb of the city, which is perhaps identical with Rebit Nina, suburb of Nineveh, which lay to the n.e. of the city. These are the 4 places which are enumerated in Gen. 10:11, 12 as composing the great city. But they were not the only towns which sprang up in the environs of Nineveh. Yarimja, on the river directly s. of Nineveh, marks an ancient site, and near the Tigris, 3 miles above Nineveh, was Tarbiṣu, with a royal palace, beginning the imposing line of habitations and walled towns which extended along the river s. to Calah. Back from the river, n.e. of Nineveh and beyond Rebit Nina, at the foot of the e. mountains, was Dur-sharrukin or Sargon's burg, a town about as large as Calah, built about 707 B.C., and containing a great palace. Seven miles s.e., and also at the foot of the e. mountain, was another town scarcely inferior in size to Calah. Its ancient name is unknown, but it is situated hard by Baasheiḥah. It was 1 of a series of towns which extended to Calah. Birtelleh, 6 miles s., probably marks the site of an ancient town, and Keremlis, 3 miles farther on, is known to do so. Imgurbel, with its palace and temple which Ashurnaṣirpal adorned, was 6 miles s. of the latter place, and was 9 miles from Calah. Other towns and villages dotted the plain within the bounds which have been thus defined. It may be that Diodorus Siculus, of the 1st century B.C., is citing an authentic tradition when he states that Nineveh formed a quadrangle measuring 150 stadia by 90, or 480 in circuit, about 60 miles. Strabo, a few years later, says that it was much larger than Babylon.

Ni'san (nĭ'săn) [Heb. *nĭsān*, from Akkad. *nisannu*, opening, beginning]. The name given after the Captivity to Abib, the 1st month of the year (Neh. 2:1; Esth. 3:7). It nearly corresponds to March. See YEAR.

Nis'roch (nĭs'rŏk). A god worshiped by Sennacherib. It was in the temple of Nisroch at Nineveh that he was assassinated (II Kings 19:37; Isa. 37:38). The name has not been identified; attempts have been made to equate him with Nusku or to see in the name a composite containing Asshur. Perhaps it is an intentional perversion of the name Marduk.

Ni'ter. Saltpeter, potassium nitrate; but among the ancients sodium carbonate and potassium carbonate. It is an alkali (Prov. 25:20), and in solution was used in washing clothes (Jer. 2:22).

No (nō), once **No'-a'mon** (Nahum 3:8) [Egypt. *nw.t*, city, village]. The Egyptian

city of Thebes, often called by this name on the monuments. Herodotus found its distance from On to be a voyage of 9 days up the river (Herod. ii. 9). After the expulsion of the Hyksos from Egypt, Ahmose I, the founder of Dyn. XVIII, turned his attention to the reorganization and improvement of the kingdom, and among other works embellished Thebes. The city at once rose to chief importance as the capital of the new empire, and became large, splendid, and populous. Homer speaks of its hundred gates (*Iliad* ix. 381). Its tutelary divinity was Amon, and the high priest of Amon was 2d only to the king. It remained the center of Egyptian civilization and power until, 1st, Esarhaddon, king of Assyria, conquered Egypt, in 671 B.C., and, afterward, Ashurbanipal, his son and successor, made a new conquest (667) and the Assyrians got as far as Thebes. In a 2d campaign by Ashurbanipal Thebes was taken and sacked 663 B.C. (Nahum 3:8). But even after that disaster Thebes long remained a place of importance (Jer. 46:25; Ezek. 30:14—16; Herod. ii. 3; iii. 10). It was finally destroyed utterly by the Roman prefect, Cornelius Gallus, for its participation in the revolt of Upper Egypt in 30—29 B.C. against oppressive Roman taxation. Splendid remains of the city, consisting of temples, obelisks, sphinxes, etc., still exist at Luxor and Karnak, on the e., and Kurna and Medinet-Habu, on the w. side of the river. West of what was the site of the city there is a gorge cut into the lower limestone which contains the tombs of the ancient Theban kings.

No·a·di'ah (nō'á-dī'á) [Jehovah has met by appointment]. 1. Son of Binnui. He was one of those who took charge of the gold and silver vessels brought by Ezra and the returned captives from Babylon (Ezra 8:33).

2. A prophetess whose evil vaticinations were intended to frighten Nehemiah (Neh. 6:14).

No'ah, I (nō'á), in A.V. of Matthew and Luke No'e [rest]. Son of Lamech of the posterity of Seth (Gen. 5:28, 29). The reason for bestowing the name Noah is stated in words which bear some resemblance to the name in sound. Lamech called him Noah, saying: "This same shall comfort us [*yᵉnaḥămēnū*] in our work and in the toil of our hands, . . . because of the ground which Jehovah hath cursed." This method of wordplay is employed quite frequently by the Hebrew writers. The references to the years of Noah's life are capable of several explanations, in accordance with ancient methods of statement and of constructing genealogical registers. Several methods are mentioned in the article on chronology (*q.v.*). The application of the first 2 of these to the data referring to Noah is simple and needs no explanation. The 3d method is more intricate, but is also applicable. According to it, in the family of Lamech, 182 years after it succeeded to the position of prominence among the children of Seth and became the family through which the Church descended, a son was born whom his father called Noah, saying: "This same shall comfort us." Long afterward, among the descendants of this child of hope, who are collectively called Noah, just as the descendants of Israel were frequently called Israel, appeared one in whom the hopes were realized, who proved a comforter, whose conduct and worship were rewarded by God's promise not to curse the ground again for wicked man's sake or to smite any more everything living, who built the ark and who was the family's head and representative. He is referred to by the tribal name. His eldest son was about 100 years old when the Flood came. This event occurred in the 600th year of Noah, that is, 600 years after the family which was spoken of as Noah had attained to leadership. If the 3d method is the true one, such is its application to the record concerning Noah.

Noah was a just man and, like Enoch, walked with God (Gen. 6:9). But it was a time of almost universal apostasy. It was an age of religious indifference, when even the sons of God had become worldly and in contracting marriage chose by the outward appearance rather than by the disposition of the heart (ch. 6:2), and when men generally were living for the present moment, eating and drinking, marrying and giving in marriage (Matt. 24:38). It was also an age that was defiant of God: there was secret hostility of the heart; men formed their plans without regard to God, every imagination and device of man's heart was evil (Gen. 6:5); there was open defiance also; the earth was filled with violence, the strong oppressed the weak (v. 11). The age was so corrupt that God purposed to destroy mankind; but a respite apparently of 120 years was given (v. 3). By his exemplary life at least, Noah was a preacher of righteousness (II Peter 2:5). To him God, the Creator and Judge of all, revealed his purpose to destroy man, and commanded him to build an ark to save himself and his family and keep alive the various kinds of animals, for a flood of waters was to overwhelm the land. Noah did so. When the ark was finished, Jehovah, God of redemption, bade Noah enter the ark with his family and provide for their use the clean animals which they needed for food and sacrifice; and he who had created the beasts and the birds had them also go by pairs into the vessel for the preservation of their species. The same God of redemption shut Noah in. Then the flood broke in all its violence. See FLOOD. When at length the judgment purposed by the Creator and Governor of the universe was accomplished, he remembered Noah and made the waters to assuage. After catching the first glimpse of the mountain tops, Noah waited the same length of time as the storm had raged and then sent forth birds to discover whether the waters were abated from the surface of the earth. When he learned that they were, he tarried yet in the ark, waiting until God should bid him disembark. On the 1st day of the 1st month, he removed the covering and saw that the ground was dry, but it was 8 weeks longer before God bade him go forth. Then he built an altar and offered burnt offerings to the God of his redemption, who accepted the worship and purposed in his heart not to curse the ground again and smite every living thing on account of man's wickedness. God proceeded to reveal this purpose. As he had blessed Adam when he created him and had commanded that he be fruitful and multiply, so now at the beginning of a new world he blessed Noah and bade him be fruitful. He also laid injunctions on the head of the new race; but of the 7 precepts of Noah, as they are called, which were regarded by the Jews as antecedent to the Law and the observance of which was required of all proselytes, 3 only are expressly mentioned here: the abstinence from blood, the prohibition of murder, and the recognition of the civil authority (Gen. 9:4–6). The remaining 4, the prohibition of idolatry, blasphemy, incest, and theft, rested on the general sense of mankind. God further, in revealing his purpose not to curse the ground again for man's sake, pledged himself not to cut off all flesh again by the waters of a flood, and adopted the rainbow as the sign of the engagement by which he had bound himself (vs. 8–17).

Noah naturally devoted himself to agriculture. Among other works he planted a vineyard, and he drank himself drunk on the wine.

His son Ham mocked at his disgrace, but the other sons sought to protect their father. When Noah recovered and learned what had occurred, with insight into character, and with that knowledge which he had derived before the Flood of God's ordination that the evil propensities of parents descend to children and that God blesses the righteous in their generations (Ex. 20:5, 6), he foretold degradation among the posterity of Ham, for some reason singling out only 1 of Ham's sons, predicted the subjection of this branch of the tribe to the descendants of the high-minded and godly brothers, pronounced the divine blessing on the families of Shem and Japheth, and announced especially their united service of Jehovah, God of Shem (Gen. 9:20–27); see CANAAN 1, JAPHETH, and SHEM.

Noah lived, or the family which he represented continued its leadership, for 350 years after the Flood (Gen. 9:28). Then the Semites, as distinguished from the other descendants of Noah, became the leading family and the line in which the Church descended. Isaiah (ch. 54:9) and Ezekiel (ch. 14:14) both allude to Noah. Our Lord compares the days of Noah to those which should precede his own Second Coming (Matt. 24:37); the patriarch's faith is commended in Heb. 11:7, and Peter twice alludes to the 8 saved from the Deluge when it overwhelmed the ungodly (I Peter 3:20; II Peter 2:5). The Greeks and Romans had a story about a flood from which only 2 people were saved, Deucalion and his wife Pyrrha; Deucalion may be Noah under a different name. However this may be, the Babylonians at any rate preserved a tradition of the same flood of which the Hebrews had knowledge. See FLOOD.

No'ah, II (nō'á) [a quivering, trembling]. A daughter of Zelophehad (Num. 26:33; 27:1; 36:11; Josh. 17:3).

No'-a'mon (nō'ā'mŏn). See No.

Nob (nŏb). A town of the priests (I Sam. 22:19), in the territory of Benjamin (Neh. 11:32), on the n. and apparently within sight of Jerusalem (Isa. 10:32). After the capture of the Ark, the tabernacle was for a time pitched at Nob, with Ahimelech as high priest. He was ignorant of the variance between Saul and David, and when the latter came to Nob, Ahimelech allowed him and his men to eat the showbread and gave him the sword of Goliath. This act was reported to Saul, who summoned the priests and had them slain, and smote Nob, men, women, and children, with the sword. Abiathar, however, escaped and told David (I Sam., chs. 21; 22). The place was inhabited after the Exile (Neh. 11:32). Robinson contents himself with locating the place "somewhere upon the ridge of the Mount of Olives, n.e. of the city." Père Abel locates it more definitely on Scopus at the point known as Rās Umm eṭ-Ṭala, the site of the Augusta-Victoria Stiftung.

No'bah (nō'bá) [barking]. 1. A Manassite, presumably, who captured the town of Kenath, on the w. slope of the Jebel Hauran, and gave it his own name (Num. 32:42). The old name was probably ere long restored. See KENATH.

2. A town mentioned in connection with the Gadite town of Jogbehah. A road leading to the country of the nomads passed on the e. (Judg. 8:11). The site of Nobah is a tell near Ṣāfūt.

No'bai (nō'bī), in A.V. and marg. of R.V. Ne'bai, which is the kere. One of the chiefs of the people who with Nehemiah sealed the covenant (Neh. 10:19).

Nod (nŏd) [wandering, exile]. A district on the e. of Eden to which Cain went and there abode (Gen. 4:16).

No'dab (nō'dăb) [probably, generosity, nobility]. An Arab tribe of the Syrian desert, to judge from their allies (I Chron. 5 :19).

No'e (nō'ê). See NOAH, I.

No'gah (nō'gȧ) [brilliance]. A son of David (I Chron. 3 :7 ; 14 :6).

No'hah (nō'hȧ) [rest]. The 4th son of Benjamin (I Chron. 8 :2), who, however, did not give rise to a tribal family. He is not mentioned among those who accompanied Jacob into Egypt, probably because he was born after the migration into Egypt. Keil offers a different explanation. He supposes that Nohah either is another name for Shephupham (Num. 26 :39, R.V.), or else was a celebrated chief who was descended from Shephupham and whose name supplanted Shephupham as the designation of the family.

Non (nŏn). See NUN.

Noph (nŏf). See MEMPHIS.

No'phah (nō'fȧ) [possibly, a breeze]. A Moabite town (Num. 21 :30), not elsewhere mentioned. The text is open to question ; the LXX reads, "And the women besides [yet] kindled a fire at [against] Moab."

Nose Jew'el. A jewel inserted, generally by means of a ring, into the side of the nostril for an ornament (Isa. 3 :21).

Nose Ring. A ring worn as an ornament, especially by women (R.V. of Gen. 24 :47;

Nose Rings

Ezek. 16 :12). It was inserted through the partition between the nostrils or in the side of the nose.

Num'ber and Nu'mer-al. There is no evidence that the ancient Hebrews used figures to denote numbers. The numerals which occur in the present text of the Heb. Scriptures, in the Siloam inscription, and on the Moabite stone are spelled in full. The Hebrews employed the letters of the alphabet to represent numerals as early as Maccabaean times, using *aleph* for 1, *beth* for 2. In the Elephantine papyri (mostly 5th century B.C.) the numerals are generally represented by signs. In the Nabataean inscriptions of the 1st century the numerals are generally spelled, but they are occasionally represented by signs, upright strokes for the smaller units, a figure like 5 without the upper horizontal arm for 5, and other marks. In the Aramaic inscriptions of the same period at Palmyra signs are also used. On the lion weights, which were used by Aramaean traders in Nineveh in the 8th century B.C., the weight is indicated by upright strokes for the units and a horizontal stroke for 10. In yet earlier centuries the Assyrians and Babylonians used cuneiform signs to indicate number.

Numbers were used symbolically and conventionally. Three had apparently no symbolism ; but emphasis was conventionally expressed by it ; as "The temple of the Lord, the temple of the Lord, the temple of the Lord, are these" (Jer. 7 :4), "O earth, earth, earth" (ch. 22 :29), "I will overturn, overturn, overturn it" (Ezek. 21 :27), "Holy, holy, holy" (Isa. 6 :3), and the triple blessing (Num. 6 :

24–26). The threefold character of the baptismal formula and the apostolic benediction resulted from the doctrine of the Trinity (Matt. 28 :19 ; II Cor. 13 :14). Four does not play an important part. Four corners or quarters of the earth were recognized, n., s., e., and w. (Isa. 11 :12), and hence 4 winds (Dan. 7 :2), and 4 chariots (Zech. 6 :1, 5). Seven was early a sacred number among the Semites (Gen. 2 : 2 ; 4 :24 ; 21 :28). It did not derive its character from the fact that it was equal to 3 plus 4. Not arithmetical, but religious considerations were involved ; see SABBATH. Ten was recognized as a complete number, and was constantly used as such ; there were 10 commandments (Ex. 34 :28), 10 antediluvian and 10 postdiluvian patriarchs (see CHRONOLOGY). Twelve was the basis of the duodecimal system of the Babylonians, and as a result found employment in common life. Something of it was probably inherited by the Hebrews, and was enhanced by the fact that the tribes of Israel were 12. Forty was a round number much in vogue (Ex. 24 :18 ; I Kings 19 :8 ; Jonah 3 :4 ; Matt. 4 :2 ; see CHRONOLOGY, III.

Num'bers. The 4th book of the Pentateuch. In the Heb. Scriptures it is named "In the wilderness" (see Num. 1 :1). Its modern designation originated with the Gr. translators, and was chosen on account of the 2 enumerations of the people which the book relates : the 1st at Sinai in the 2d year of the Exodus, the 2d on the Jordan in the 40th year. It may be divided into 3 main sections :

I. *In the wilderness at Sinai* (Num. 1 :1 to 10 :11). Census of the people, exclusive of the Levites, with assignment of a place for each tribe in the encampment (chs. 1 ; 2) ; census of the Levites, their location in the camp and specific duties (chs. 3 ; 4). The unclean removed from the camp (ch. 5 :1–4). Law that the restitution for a trespass go to the priest in case the person wronged, to whom it ordinarily went, has died and is without heirs (vs. 5–10). Laws about jealousy and Nazirites and form of the priest's blessing (chs. 5 :11 to 6 :27). Offering of the princes at the dedication of the tabernacle (ch. 7), The place of the 7 lamps (ch. 8 :1–4). Consecration of the Levites (vs. 5–22), and the age of entering service (vs. 23–26) ; see LEVITES. Observance of the passover and law of the supplementary celebration (ch. 9 :1–14). The guiding pillar of cloud (vs. 15–23) and silver signal trumpets (ch. 10 :1–10).

II. *On the way from Sinai* to the Jordan (chs. 10 :11 to 21 :35). Order of march (ch. 10 :11–28). Hobar invited to go with Israel (vs. 29–32). A stage of the journey (vs. 33,34). Words used when the Ark set forward and when it rested (vs. 35, 36). Murmurs against the manna, 70 elders to aid Moses, descent of quails (ch. 11). Miriam's leprosy (ch. 12). At Kadesh : the spies and their report, the people faithless and condemned to die in the wilderness (chs. 13 ; 14). Supplementary legal specifications (ch. 15). Rebellion of Korah, Dathan, and Abiram, and related events (chs. 16 ; 17) ; in consequence, duties and privileges of the priests and Levites affirmed (ch. 18). Law for purification of those defiled by contact with a dead body (ch. 19). Return to Kadesh : death of Miriam, sin of Moses and Aaron, embassy to Edom (ch. 20 1–21). Death of Aaron, journey from Mount Hor around Edom to plains of Moab, fiery serpents, conquest of the country e. of the Jordan (chs. 20 : 22 to 21 :35).

III. *At Shittim opposite Jericho* (chs. 22 : 1 to 36 :13). Balaam (chs. 22 to 24). Sin of Baal-peor (ch. 25). Census of the new generation (ch. 26). Laws regarding inheritance by daughters (ch. 27 : 1–11). Public announcement of Joshua as Moses' successor (vs. 12–

23). Further regulation of the daily offerings and of vows (chs. 28 to 30). War with Midian (ch. 31). Assignment of the conquered country e. of Jordan to the Reubenites, Gadites, and half tribe of Manasseh (ch. 32). Itinerary from Egypt to Shittim (ch. 33). Boundaries of the land and a commission on allotment (ch. 34). Laws of the cities of refuge (ch. 35). Supplementary law concerning inheritance by daughters (ch. 36).

Nu·me′ni·us (nū-mē′nĭ-ŭs) [Lat. from Gr., pertaining to new moon]. A Jew, son of Antiochus and a member of the senate (Jos. *Antiq.* xiii. 5, 8), sent as ambassador to Rome and Sparta in 144 B.C. by Jonathan Maccabaeus, and dispatched a 2d time to Rome by Simon in 140 B.C. (I Macc. 12 :16 ; 14 :24 ; 15 :15).

Nun (nŭn), in A.V. and Heb. text once **Non** (I Chron. 7 :27) [fish]. 1. Father of Joshua, the military leader (Ex. 33 :11 ; Josh. 1 :1), descended through Tahan and perhaps Beriah from Ephraim (I Chron. 7 :27).

2. The 14th letter of the Heb. alphabet; it represents the same sound as Eng. *n*. It heads the 14th section of Psalm 119, in which section each verse of the original begins with this letter.

Nurse. 1. A wet nurse, *mēneḳeth,* employed to suckle an infant (Ex. 2 :7–9 ; II Kings 11 : 2). Deborah, who had nursed Rebekah, remained an honored servant in the family (Gen. 24 :59 ; 35 :8), as was frequently the case (Homer *Odyssey* xix. 15, 251).

2. A male (*′ōmēn*) or female (*′ōmeneth*) attendant, who acted as nurse, i.e., had the care of small children, either when infants (Num. 11 :12 ; Ruth 4 :16) or when older but still helpless (II Sam. 4 :4).

Nuts. 1. The rendering of Heb. *boṭnim,* pistachio nuts (Gen. 43 :11, R.V. marg.). The true pistachio tree (*Pistacia vera*) belongs to the order *Anacardiaceae.* Its fruit, which is a little less than an inch in diameter, consists of a bony shell surrounded by a dry covering and enclosing a sweet, somewhat oily kernel. The nuts are eaten like almonds or used for making confectionery. It is a native of w. Asia, from which it has been introduced into s. Europe. It is not now common in Palestine. Jacob sent some of its fruit, with other vegetable produce, as a present to the Egyptian prime minister (Gen. 43 :11).

2. The rendering of the Heb. word *′ĕgōz,* walnut (S. of Sol. 6 :11). The walnut tree (*Juglans regia*), in America distinguished as the English walnut, is native from the Caucasus to the mountains of n. India. It is cultivated in Galilee and along the slopes of Lebanon and of Hermon.

Nym′phas (nĭm′făs) [Gr., sacred to the nymphs]. A Christian at Laodicea or Colossae, to whom Paul sent salutation (Col. 4 :15). Note form Nympha in R.V. marg.

O

Oak. 1. A rendering of Heb. *′ēlāh.* The Heb. word occurs in 15 passages of the O.T. In 3 of these it serves as a geographical designation and is treated as a proper name, valley of Elah (I Sam. 17 :2, 19 ; 21 :9 ; R.V. marg., terebinth). In 2 passages, where it is associated with another word, *′allōn,* which is rendered oak, it is translated terebinth in R.V., but teil tree and elms in A.V. (Isa. 6 :13 ; Hos. 4 :13). In the remaining 10 passages it is rendered oak, with terebinth in the marg. of R.V.

2. The rendering of Heb. *′ēlōn,* in the text of 9 passages of the R.V., terebinth being placed in the marg. The A.V., following the Targums and Vulgate (place, plain), uni-

formly renders *′ēlōn* by plain, but in the marg. of Judg. 9 :6 it substitutes oak. There were the oak of Moreh (Gen. 12 :6 ; Deut. 11 :30), the oak of Mamre (Gen. 13 :18 ; 14 :13 ; 18 :1), the oak in Zaanannim (Judg. 4 :11), the oak of the pillar that was in Shechem (ch. 9 :6), the oak of the augurs (ch. 9 :37, R.V. marg.), and the oak of Tabor (I Sam. 10 :3).

3. The rendering of Heb. *′ēl* in Isa. 1 :29.

4. The uniform and doubtless correct rendering of Heb. *′allōn.* It occurs in 8 passages, and was a species of oak associated with Bashan (Isa. 2 :13 ; Zech. 27 :6 ; Zech. 11 :2). Under a tree of this species near Beth-el Deborah, Rebekah's nurse, was buried (Gen. 35 :8). It was probably the prickly oak (*Quercus coccifera*).

5. The rendering of Heb. *′allāh* (Josh. 24 :26).

Oak is the meaning of *′allōn,* for it was a characteristic tree of Bashan. *′Elāh* differed from it (Isa. 6 :13 ; Hos. 4 :13), and hence is probably the terebinth; and the 3 related words, *′ēlāh, ′ēl,* and *′ēlōn,* may denote 3 kinds of terebinth. They may, however, designate any large tree, and not specify the terebinth in particular. Several species of oak grow in Palestine. *Quercus sessiliflora* grows high up on Lebanon and in the Hauran. Four varieties of the prickly evergreen oak (*Q. coccifera*) occur : one is *Q. pseudococcifera,* and is found on Carmel, in Gilead, and in Bashan, often being of magnificent growth ; another is *Q. calliprinos,* which is found in Lebanon, on Tabor, and in Gilead. Valonia oak (*Q. aegilops*) is deciduous. It is common in Galilee and Gilead.

Oath. An appeal to God in attestation of the truth of a statement or of the binding character of a promise (Gen. 21 :23 ; 31 :53 ; Gal. 1 :20 ; Heb. 6 :16). Its violation was an offense against God (II Chron. 36 :13 ; Ezek. 17 :13, 18). Sometimes the appeal was to the sovereign or other sacred object (Gen. 42 :15 ; II Sam. 11 :11 ; Matt. 5 :33 ; 23 :16–22). Jehovah condescended to confirm his promise to the patriarch by an oath, swearing by himself (Gen. 22 :16 ; Heb. 6 :13–20). An oath was commonly made by lifting the hand unto God (Gen. 14 :22 ; Ezek. 20 :5, 6 ; Rev. 10 :5), but it was sometimes made by placing the hand under the thigh of the person to whom the promise was made (Gen. 24 :2 ; 47 :29), probably as an invocation of the posterity, which should proceed from the loins, to guard the oath and avenge its violation. The oath was occasionally taken before the altar (I Kings 8 :31). Abraham gave Abimelech 7 ewe lambs as witness of the oath (Gen. 21 :27–31). An oath was sometimes intensified by slaying an animal, dividing it into 2 parts, and passing between the pieces (ch. 15 :8–18). Each party to the oath invoked upon himself the fate of the victim if he broke the covenant. By the Mosaic Law, in certain judicial investigations, a man to clear himself was required to swear an oath of the Lord (Ex. 22 :11 ; Num. 5 :19–22). Any man swearing an oath or making a vow to God was required to carry out his promise, as was a woman, if while she was a virgin her father did not disallow her oath, or after her marriage her husband did not interfere ; if she was a widow, or had been divorced, her oath stood (Num., ch. 30). If anyone swore falsely by the name of the true God, he profaned the divine name (Lev. 6 :3 ; 19 :12 ; cf. Isa. 48 :1 ; Jer. 12 :16 ; Mal. 3 :5) ; and no one was under any circumstances to swear by a false god (Josh. 23 :7). The man is commended in Ps. 15 :4 who does not change, although he has sworn to his hurt. Our Lord condemned the use of oaths, even when taken with the best intention, declaring that whatever went beyond "yea, yea; nay, nay," was of the Evil One (Matt. 5:33–37). He was delivering the Sermon on the Mount and correcting various perversions of the Law which the scribes had introduced; and among other evils he condemned swearing in ordinary communications between man and man. But the judicial oath is lawful; for it was enjoined by God (Ex. 22:11). The oath was recognized as lawful by the apostles also, for they called on God to witness to the truth of what they said (II Cor. 11:31; Gal. 1:20). The mischief which may arise from a rash oath was well illustrated in that of Herod the tetrarch, which made him against his will the murderer of John the Baptist (Matt. 14:3–12).

O'ba·dī'ah (ō'bȧ-dī'ȧ) [servant of Jehovah]. 1. A man of Issachar, family of Tola, house of Uzzi (I Chron. 7:3).

2. A Gadite hero who joined David at Ziklag (I Chron. 12:9).

3. Father of the chief of the Zebulunites in David's reign (I Chron. 27:19).

4. A descendant of Jonathan (I Chron. 8:38; 9:44).

5. The governor of Ahab's palace, who during the persecution of Jehovah's prophets by Queen Jezebel, had 100 prophets, in 2 companies of 50, in a cave (I Kings 18:3, 4). He was sent by his royal master to look for grass for the horses and mules during the great drought, and while so engaged fell in with Elijah, who persuaded him to announce to the king the presence of the prophet (vs. 5–16). Elijah's interview with the king led to the contest at Carmel, which was followed by the slaughter of Baal's prophets.

6. One of the princes sent by Jehoshaphat to teach in the cities of Judah (II Chron. 17:7).

7. A prophet of Judah (Obad. 1). Josephus believed that he was the God-fearing Obadiah of Ahab's palace, but the prophet probably lived at least a century after Ahab.

The Book of Obadiah is the 4th of the Minor Prophets. It consists of one chapter, and foretells the destruction of Edom (vs. 1–9) and the reason of it, namely, Edom's unbrotherly attitude toward the children of Jacob (vs. 10, 11), warns Edom accordingly not to exult over the children of Judah in their distress (vs. 12–16), and predicts the deliverance and enlargement of Israel (vs. 17–21). The entire prophecy derives its incentive and strength from the great truth, clearly discerned by other holy men of God as well as by Obadiah, that the day of Jehovah is coming upon all nations (v. 15) to the destruction of every foe, native and foreign, of God's rule on earth; and the Kingdom shall be Jehovah's (v. 21; cf. Isa. 2:12, 17, 20, 21; 10:12–19; Joel 3:12–21; Amos 5:18; 9:8–15; Micah 4:11–13).

Much uncertainty exists as to the date of the prophecy.

I. *It is very generally ascribed to the Chaldean period,* when Jerusalem was alternately subject to the king of Egypt and the king of Babylon, and was finally captured by Nebuchadnezzar in 586 B.C., razed to the ground, and its inhabitants carried into captivity. This view is based on the description of Judah's calamity (Obad. 10–16), and the fact is appealed to that Edom gave its sympathy to Babylon at this crisis (Ps. 137:7) and prophets of the time severely denounced Edom (Jer. 49:7–22; Ezek. 25:12–14; ch. 35). According to this view the place of the book in the Minor Prophets has no relation to the date of composition; the reference to Edom in Amos 9:12 may have been the occasion for placing Obadiah directly after Amos. Some critics, however, date vs. 1–14, 15b, a little before or after 460 B.C. and vs. 15a, 16–21, about 400 B.C.

II. *The prophecy may, however, be much earlier,* for: 1. No allusion is made to the strik-

ing features of the fall of Jerusalem, the burning of the Temple, the razing of the walls, and annihilation of the city. 2. The relation of verses 1–9 to Jer. 49:7–22. On account of this common element it may be supposed that one borrowed from the other. It seems that this prophecy is in its more original form in Obadiah. It may be better, however, to assume that both prophets had access to an older prophecy which Obadiah incorporated with less alteration, while Jeremiah treated it with greater freedom. 3. The hostile attitude of Edom was of long standing (Ezek. 35:5), and the feeling against Edom expressed by Obadiah was voiced by Amos more than a century before the Chaldean invasion (Amos 1:6, 9, especially vs. 11, 12; 9:12; cf. Joel 3:19). 4. Particular historical conditions, which are presupposed by the prophet, existed as early as the reign of Amaziah. Jerusalem had been plundered by Egyptians in the time of Rehoboam (I Kings 14:25, 26), by Arabians and Philistines in the reign of Jehoram (II Chron. 21:16, 17); and in the reign of Amaziah, who slaughtered the Edomites, the king of Israel entered Jerusalem, broke down the n. wall of the city, plundered the Temple and palace, and carried off hostages (II Kings 14:14, 17; II Chron. 25:11, 12, 23, 24). These events may well have called forth those manifestations of Edom's unbrotherly spirit, which Obadiah rebukes. In that case the prophecy would date from the early part of the 8th century B.C., and antedate Joel (cf. Obad. 17; Joel 2:32; see JOEL 13); according to this view its position after Joel cannot be taken as indicating the exact chronological order of the Minor Prophets.

III. *The book may, however, be approximately in its proper chronological place,* and accordingly date from the time of Ahaz. For calamities befell Judah in the reign of Ahaz: the king of Damascus wrested Edom from Judah, the king of Israel ravaged to the gates of Jerusalem, the Philistines took the cities of the lowland, and Ahaz stripped the Temple of its treasures to buy aid from the king of Assyria, did homage to this foreigner, and made Judah a vassal state, Israelites also were carried into captivity (Obad. 20; Amos 1:6, 9; cf. I Chron. 5:26); then the Edomite did violence to his brother Jacob, refrained from extending aid, and became as one of Judah's enemies (II Chron. 28:17; II Kings 16:6, R.V. marg.; Obad. 10, 11). The year 731 B.C. or slightly earlier, in the reign of Ahaz when Judah was so deeply humiliated, was an appropriate time for Obadiah to take up his prophecy against the Edomites, rebuke them for their indifference to Judah's woes and for their open hostility in the past and present, and warn them not to exult over Judah's present distress for their own time of punishment was coming.

8. A Levite, one of the overseers over the workmen who repaired the Temple in the reign of Josiah (II Chron. 34:12).

9. Founder of a family, presumably of the lineage of David (I Chron. 3:21).

10. A descendant of Joab. He came from Babylon with Ezra (Ezra 8:9).

11. A priest who, doubtless in behalf of a father's house, sealed the covenant made in the time of Nehemiah (Neh. 10:5).

12. A Levite, apparently founder of a family of porters (Neh. 12:25). He seems to have been the Levite Obadiah, son of Shemaiah (I Chron. 9:16), called Abda in Neh. 11:17.

O'bal (ō'bȧl) [cf. Arab. *'abila,* to be thick]. A people descended from Joktan (Gen. 10:28). 'Abil is the name of one of the oldest tribes of Arabia (Delitzsch) and of a district in Yemen (Halévy). Bochart suggests Pliny's Avalitae on the African coast, near the straits of Bab el-Mandeb. In I Chron. 1:22 the name is written Ebal, *yodh* (*jod*), being used instead of *vav* (*vau*). These letters were often confused by copyists.

O'bed (ō'bĕd) [server, worshiper]. 1. Son of Ephlal, of the house of Jerahmeel, tribe of Judah (I Chron. 2:37).

2. Son of Boaz and Ruth, and grandfather of David (Ruth 4:17, 21, 22).

3. One of David's mighty men (I Chron. 11:47).

4. A Levite, one of the doorkeepers, son of Shemaiah, house of Obed-edom (I Chron. 26:7).

5. The father of a certain Azariah, in the time of Athaliah (II Chron. 23:1).

O'bed-e'dom (ō'bĕd-ē'dŏm) [serving Edom, or Edom is serving]. 1. A Gittite, that is, a native either of the Philistine Gath, and, if so, probably a member of David's bodyguard, or else of the Levitical city of Gath-rimmon in Dan. He lived between Kiriath-jearim and Jerusalem, near the spot where Uzzah was struck dead for touching the Ark. The Ark was therefore taken to Obed-edom's house by David's order, where it remained 3 months, blessings attending him and his family for giving it accommodation (II Sam. 6:10–12; I Chron. 13:13, 14; 15:25). If a Levite, he is doubtless identical with Obed-edom the Korahite (see 3). The Korahites were a division of the Kohathite family to which Gath-rimmon was assigned, and the statement that God blessed him (I Chron. 26:5) seems to refer to I Chron. 13:14 and II Sam. 6:11.

2. A Levite of the 2d degree, who with others acted as doorkeeper for the Ark, and was moreover a musician who played the harp at the removal of the Ark to Jerusalem, and afterward as a regular duty in the tent erected for the Ark (I Chron. 15:18, 21; 16:5).

3. A Levite, who as doorkeeper marched in front of the Ark at its removal to Jerusalem (I Chron. 15:24). He is probably also with Obed-edom, son of Jeduthun, a doorkeeper for the Ark in the tent at Jerusalem (ch. 16:38), and who is generally, though on uncertain grounds, held to be the person mentioned in the preceding clause of the verse. He appears to be Obed-edom the Korahite (ch. 26:1, 4; cf. v. 10 with ch. 16:38), whose sons and grandsons, with their brethren, 62 in number, were among the 93 of whom the courses were formed in David's reign (ch. 26:8). Their station was at the s. gate (v. 15). The family was still on duty in the reign of Amaziah (II Chron. 25:24).

O'bil (ō'bĭl) [perhaps, camel driver]. An Ishmaelite who had charge of David's camels (I Chron. 27:30).

Ob·la'tion. See OFFERINGS.

O'both (ō'bŏth) [water skins]. A station of the Israelites before their arrival in the desert e. of Moab (Num. 21:10, 11; 33:43, 44); the oasis el-Weiba.

Och'ran (ŏk'răn), in A.V. **Oc'ran** (ŏk'răn) [troubled]. An Asherite, father of Pagiel (Num. 1:13).

O'ded (ō'dĕd) [he has restored; or perhaps, seer, prophet]. 1. Father of the Prophet Azariah (II Chron. 15:1). In v. 8 the text is evidently corrupt.

2. An Israelite prophet in the reign of Pekah. Meeting the army of the Northern Kingdom returning from battle with many captives of Judah, the prophet remonstrated with them on their unbrotherly conduct, and in the name of Jehovah called on them to send the captives home. His words produced a great effect. Some of the leading men in Samaria, persuaded by him as to the path of duty, refused to allow the army to bring the prisoners inside the city. They then clothed the naked, fed the hungry, and, mounting the feeble on asses, took them to Jericho and handed them over to their countrymen (II Chron. 28:9–15).

Od·o·me'ra (ŏd-ŏ-mē'rà), in A.V. **Od'o·nar'·kes** (ŏd'ŏ-när'kēz). Chief of a nomad tribe, or possibly an officer under Bacchides, whom Jonathan Maccabaeus smote (I Macc. 9:66).

Of'fer·ings. Offerings to God of various kinds can be traced from the dawn of human history. In the O.T. alone there are mentioned among others of early times the vegetable offering (Gen. 4:3), the sacrifice of the firstling of the flock (ch. 4:4), the burnt offering (Gen. 8:20; Ex. 10:25), the sacrificial meal (Gen. 31:54), and the drink offering (ch. 35:14). An elaborate ritual of sacrifice existed among the great nations of antiquity, notably in Babylonia and Egypt, long before the days of Moses.

Offerings of many kinds to God, or oblations, constituted a marked feature of the Israelitish worship. Extended information on the subject is found in Lev., chs. 1 to 7, but not there exclusively. Offerings were of 2 classes, public and private, according as they were offered at the expense of the nation or of an individual, and they were of 3 kinds: drink offerings, vegetable or meal offerings, and animal offerings or sacrifices.

The drink offering was not independent under the Law. It was made only in connection with the meal offering which accompanied all burnt offerings, except perhaps that of Lev. 12:6, and all peace offerings which were Nazirite, votive or freewill (Num. 6:17; 15:1–12). It was excluded from sin and trespass offerings.

The vegetable offering, called meat offering in A.V. and meal offering in R.V., consisted of white meal, or of unleavened bread, cakes, wafers, or of ears of grain roasted, always with salt and, except in the sin offering, with olive oil (Lev. 2:1, 4, 13, 14; 5:11). It might form an independent offering: and part might be placed on the altar and the rest belong to the priest, as in private voluntary offerings (ch. 2), and when accepted as a sin offering from the very poor in lieu of an animal (ch. 5:11–13); or else the whole might be consumed on the altar. In this latter case it corresponded to the burnt offering, and was made at the consecration of the high priest and at the cleansing of the leper (chs. 6:19–23; 14:10, 20). Or the vegetable offering might be subordinate, an accompaniment of a sacrifice. It was thus the invariable concomitant of the burnt offering, except perhaps that of Lev., ch. 12, and of peace offerings, except those obligatory at the feast of weeks. In these cases, according to tradition, it was entirely consumed on the altar. In other cases, part was placed on the altar and the rest went to the priest; namely, the wafers at the consecration of priests (ch. 8:26–28), in the thank offering (ch. 7:12–15), and at the release of the Nazirite (Num. 6:13–20).

Animal offerings or sacrifices called for cattle, sheep and goats of both sexes, rarely for doves. The animal was required to be free from blemish and at least 8 days old. Sacrifices were of 3 kinds, in each of which the blood made atonement (Lev. 1:4; 17:11): 1. The burnt offering, for which a male lamb, ram, goat, or bullock was prescribed. The case in I Sam. 6:14 was extraordinary. The blood was sprinkled round about upon the altar, and the entire animal was consumed on the altar. It was expressive of the entire self-dedication of the offerer to Jehovah. 2. The sin offering and the trespass or guilt offering; for the former of which a bullock, a male or female goat, a female lamb, a dove, or a pigeon was used (Lev. 4:4, 23, 28, 32; 5:7), while for the latter a ram was prescribed or, in the case of the leper and the Nazirite, a male lamb (Lev. 6:6; 14:12, 21; Num. 6:12). The blood was symbolically displayed, but in different ways. In the sin offering a portion of the blood was sprinkled before the Lord and smeared on the horns of the altar of incense, and the rest was poured out at the base of the altar of burnt offering, when the sin had been committed by the high priest or the nation; but in the case of other sinners, a part was put on the altar of burnt offering and the rest was poured out as before (Lev. 4:6, 7, 17, 18, 25, 30, 34). In the trespass offering all the blood was scattered over the altar. The fat only was burnt on the altar. The flesh of those sin offerings of which the blood was taken into the sanctuary was burnt without the camp, whereas the flesh of other sin offerings and of trespass offerings belonged to the priests (Lev. 6:26, 30; 7:6, 7; cf. Ex. 29:14; Lev. 4:3, 12, 13, 21; 16:27; Heb. 13:11, 12). No part of these offerings was eaten by the offerer, as in the peace of-

Altar of Burnt Offering

ferings; for the sacrificer came as one unworthy of communion with God, and these offerings were for purposes of expiation. The sin offering was made for sins of which the effect terminates primarily on the sinner; the trespass offering for sins of which the effects terminate primarily on another, and for which, in addition to the sacrifice, restitution was made through the hands of the priest to the person injured or, in case of his death without heirs, to the priest (Lev. 5:16; 6:5; Num. 5:7, 8). But sins committed deliberately and for which the penalty was death could not be expiated (Num. 15:30, 31). Atonement could be made for unintentional sins; for non-capital sins, like theft, for which punishment had been endured and restitution made; and for sins which the guilty one voluntarily confessed and for which he made compensation when possible. 3. The peace offering. Three kinds are distinguished: the thank offering in recognition of unmerited and unexpected blessings; the votive offering, in payment of a vow; and the freewill offering, probably not in gratitude for a special favor but as an expression of irrepressible love for God (Lev., ch. 3). Peace offerings might also be prompted by the felt need of renewing peaceful communion with God (Judg. 20:26; 21:4; II Sam. 24:25). Any animal authorized for sacrifice, of either sex, might be used, but no bird. The blood was

sprinkled; the fat was consumed on the altar; and, when the offering was private, the breast and shoulder went to the priests and the rest of the flesh was eaten by the offerer and his friends before the Lord at the place of the sanctuary (Lev., chs. 3; 7:11–21; cf. ch. 7:22–27; Ex. 29:20–28; Deut. 12:7, 18; I Sam. 2:15–17); see WAVE OFFERING. The meal before Jehovah was a eucharistic feast. It signified that Jehovah was present as a guest.

The sacrificial acts were five: 1. Presentation of the sacrifice at the door of the sanctuary by the offerer himself as his personal act. 2. Laying on of hands. The offerer placed his hands on the victim's head, thereby dedicating it to God and making it his own representative and substitute (cf. Lev. 16:21); see LAYING ON OF HANDS. 3. Slaying the animal by the offerer himself, who thus symbolically accepted the punishment due for his sin. In later times the priests slew the animal. 4. Symbolic application of the blood. The priest sprinkled or smeared it on the altar and poured it out at the base. In specified cases a part was put on the offerer, or it was sprinkled before the veil of the sanctuary (Lev. 4:6), or carried into the Holy Place (ch. 6:30), or even into the Holy of Holies (ch. 16:14). 5. Burning the sacrifice, the whole of it or its fat only, on the altar of burnt offering, whereby its essence and flavor ascended to God.

Og (ŏg). A king of the Amorites of Bashan (Deut. 3:1, 8), whose rule extended from the Jabbok to Mount Hermon (Deut. 3:8, 10; cf. Num. 21:23, 24). He had residences at both Ashtaroth and Edrei (Josh. 12:4, 5; 13:12). He was huge of stature, the last of the Rephaim, and had an iron bedstead or sarcophagus of ironstone, 9 cubits long by 4 broad, of course longer and wider than its occupant. This relic was preserved in Rabbath Ammon (Deut. 3:11). After the Israelites had conquered Sihon, they left their families and their cattle at the secure camp at Pisgah and marched against Og. They defeated and slew him at Edrai and took possession of his country (Num. 21:32–35; Deut. 3:14). This territory was given to the half tribe of Manasseh (Deut. 3:13).

O'had (ō'hăd). A son of Simeon (Gen. 46:10; Ex. 6:15). He did not found a tribal family.

O'hel (ō'hĕl) [a tent]. A son of Zerubbabel (I Chron. 3:20).

O·ho'lah (ŏ-hō'lȧ), in A.V. **A·ho'lah** [(her?) tent]. Samaria and the Kingdom of Israel personified as a woman of bad character (Ezek. 23:1–49). Her name typified her infidelity to Jehovah.

O·ho'li·ab (ŏ-hō'lĭ-ăb), in A.V. **A·ho'li·ab** [father's tent; or a tent (protection) is the father]. An artificer of the tribe of Dan, who assisted Bezalel in making furniture for the tabernacle (Ex. 31:6; 35:34, 35).

O·hol'i·bah (ŏ-hŏl'ĭ-bȧ), in A.V. **A·hol'i·bah** [tent in her; or my tent is in her]. Jerusalem and the Kingdom of Judah personified as a woman of bad character (Ezek. 23:1–49), although possessing Jehovah's tent.

O·hol'i·ba'mah (ŏ-hŏl'ĭ-bā'mȧ), in A.V. **A·hol'i·ba'mah** [my tent is a high place; or, tent of the high place]. A wife of Esau, daughter of Anah the Hivite (Gen. 36:2). She gave name to an Edomite family, organized under a chief (v. 41). She was also called Judith, the praiseworthy (ch. 26:34; see ANAH 1).

Oil. The oil used by the ancient Hebrews was chiefly olive oil. The fruit of the olive ripens in the autumn. It was, and is still, obtained by shaking the tree or beating it (Deut. 24:20; and Isa. 17:6; 24:13, R.V. text and marg.). The oil was pressed from the olives by treading them with the foot (Deut. 33:24; Micah 6:15), often in a shallow cavity hewn in the native rock, or by crushing them in a basin or circular trough under a wheel, collecting the outflowing oil, and then, in order to secure every drop that they contained, squeezing the pulp in a press constructed for the purpose. The expressed oil was collected in a rock-hewn vat or in a jar, and the impurities were allowed to settle. The fresh oil was specifically known to the Hebrews as *yiṣhār* (cf. Joel 2:24, Heb. text). Pure beaten olive oil (Ex. 27:20; 29:40) was the finest in quality. Leaves, twigs, and dirt having been removed, the olives were beaten to pieces and crushed and put into a basket, and the oil was allowed to flow out of itself. It was a sort of first fruit, obtained before the pulp was placed under the press.

Oil was so important a product of Palestine that oil and wine are frequently mentioned, with or even without grain, as the chief harvest gain (Num. 18:12; Deut. 7:13; Neh. 10:39; 13:5; etc.). Oil was used for illuminating purposes, being burned in lamps (Ex. 25:6; Matt. 25:3). Pure beaten olive oil was prescribed for the continual light in the sanctuary (Ex. 27:20). Oil was used for food (I Chron. 12:40; Ezek. 16:13). It was mixed with meal and made into bread (I Kings 17:12); and cakes of fine flour mingled with oil, or with oil poured upon them, were part of the meal offering (Lev. 2:1, 4–7), the oil being prescribed probably on account of its common use in food. Oil was used in medicine for mollifying wounds (Isa. 1:6; Mark 6:13). Sometimes wine was added to the oil, as was done by the Good Samaritan in the case of the wounded Israelite (Luke 10:34). Herod was put in a bath of warm oil in the hope of alleviating his disease (Jos. *War* i. 33, 5). Oil was used for anointing the body, especially after a bath, and for rendering the hair smooth (II Sam. 14:2; Ps. 23:5; 104:15). Olive oil was used for anointing kings (I Sam. 10:1; 16:1, 13; I Kings 1:39; II Kings 9:1, 6); and was called holy because employed in behalf of God (Ps. 89:20). A holy oil of composite and expensive character was used for the anointing of high priests. The tabernacle, the Ark, the table, the candlestick, the altar, the laver and its foot were also anointed with the same precious compound (Ex. 30:22–33).

Oil Tree. The literal rendering of Heb. *ēṣ shemen*, tree of oil, in Isa. 41:19. The words are translated olive wood (I Kings 6:23; in A.V. olive tree) and wild olive (Neh. 8:15; in A.V. pine branch). From its wood the 2 cherubim in the oracle of Solomon's Temple were made, each of which was 10 cubits high (I Kings 6:23, 26), and also the doors of the oracle and the door posts for the entrance of the Temple (vs. 31–33). It is generally believed to be the oleaster (*Elaeagnus hortensis*), a name formerly applied to wild olive. The oleaster is a shrub with sweet-smelling white flowers and silver-gray-green leaves. It yields an oil, but much inferior to that of the olive. It is abundant in Palestine, especially near Hebron, Samaria, and Mount Tabor. It is difficult to see how a shrub like the oleaster could fulfill the conditions required in the preceding references in I Kings. G. E. Post may be right in identifying the oil tree with a pine; in that case the resin could be regarded as oil or fat.

Oint'ment. Fragrant ointments were highly prized among the Hebrews. They were used in dressing the hair and in purifying and perfuming the skin (Esth. 2:12; Eccl. 9:8), and

Jesus was several times anointed with ointment brought by women who regarded him with adoration (Matt. 26:6–13; Luke 7:36–50). Ointments, with other spices, were employed on the dead body and in embalming (Luke 23:56). Balm of Gilead and eye salve were used in medicine (Jer. 8:22; Rev. 3:18). In the ritual an ointment or holy oil was used, composed of myrrh, cassia, cinnamon, calamus, and olive oil (Ex. 30:25). In Palestine the usual ointment consisted of perfumed olive oil. The Heb. word for oil is sometimes rendered ointment in A.V. (cf. II Kings 20:13; Prov. 27:9; Eccl. 7:1; 9:8; 10:1; S. of Sol. 1:3; 4:10; Isa. 57:9; Amos 6:6, where A.R.V. has oil). See PERFUMERY.

Old Tes'ta·ment. The 1st of the 2 portions into which the Bible is naturally divided. The title was borrowed from the Apostle Paul, who in II Cor. 3:14, says: "For until this day remaineth the same vail untaken away in the reading of the old testament [in R.V. covenant]." The O.T. consists of 39 books which, in the order in which they stand in the English Bible, naturally divide into 3 classes: 17 historical books (Genesis to Esther), 5 poetical books (Job to Song of Solomon), and 17 prophetical books. Poems and fragments of poems occur in the historical books (Gen. 4:23, 24; 9:25–27; 49:2–27; Ex. 15:1–18; Judg., ch. 5); prophecy also is found in the historical books (Gen. 3:15; 9:11–16; II Sam., ch. 7) and history in the prophetical books (Isa., ch. 7; Jer., chs. 26; 37:11 to 39:14; 40:7 to 43:8); and poetry abounds in the prophetical books. The Hebrew Bible contains all these books and no more; but there is a difference in the arrangement and in the classification. See CANON. The English Bible has adopted the arrangement of the Vulgate, which partly follows that of the LXX.

The whole of the O.T. was originally written in Heb., except Ezra 4:8 to 6:18; 7:12–26; Jer. 10:11; Dan. 2:4 to 7:28, which are in Aram. The letters of the Heb. and Aram. alphabets were similar. A primitive form of them was in use in Phoenicia as far back as c. 1500 B.C. An early form is seen on the Moabite stone, in the Siloam inscription, and on Maccabaean coins. They passed through various changes of form until they ultimately became the familiar square characters of the extant Hebrew MSS. and printed editions of the Hebrew Bible. The books of the O.T. were written in the older script, but, in the course of their multiplication by manuscript copies, the older characters were gradually transliterated into the square.

In writing the Hebrews originally made use of consonants only, leaving the vowels to be supplied by the reader. But by c. A.D. 700 Jewish scholars, resident chiefly at Tiberias in Palestine, had supplied vowel points which indicated the proper vocalization and followed the traditional pronunciation. Thus Aaron ben-Asher (the son of Moses ben-Asher) not only prepared the MS. of the O.T. marked with vowels and accents which became standard, but also prepared a number of Masoretic and grammatical manuals. These vowel signs gave greater fixity to the meaning of the texts. These Jewish scholars are called Masoretes or Massoretes, from Heb. *māsōreth, massōreth,* tradition; and the text, as supplied with vowels and otherwise improved, is known as the Masoretic (Massoretic) text. They also added a system of accents to indicate the proper accentuation of the words and the manner in which they are to be conjoined or disjoined. In the Jewish schools of Babylonia a different method of indicating the vowels was in vogue. The Babylonian punctuation was written above the lines of the text and was not as convenient as the Palestinian system, which became the prevailing one.

The Jews have divided the Hebrew text of the books of Moses into 54 sections or pericopes, for reading on the Sabbaths of the year. For example, the 1st section extends from Gen. 1:1 to 6:8; and the 2d from chs. 6:9 to 11:32. These larger sections are broken into smaller ones of 2 kinds, main divisions and subdivisions, technically called open and closed, and indicated in some printed editions by the letters *pe* (p) and *samech* (s) respectively. In the oldest and best MSS. as well as in Ginsburg's editions these letters are not used. Immediately before an open section the previous line is unfinished, the vacant space being that of 3 triliteral words. Or, if the previous section fills up the last line, an entire blank line precedes the open section. A closed section is indicated by its beginning with an indented line, the previous one being

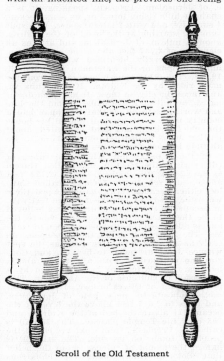

Scroll of the Old Testament

finished or unfinished. If the foregoing section ends in the middle of the line, there is left the prescribed vacant space, and the next closed section begins in the same line. Thus in the 2d pericope 1 open section contains the narrative of the Flood (chs. 6:9 to 9:17), which is subdivided into the 4 closed sections, ch. 6:9–12, introduction; chs. 6:13 to 8:14, the ark and the Flood; chs. 8:15 to 9:7, Noah leaves the ark, sacrifices, and receives God's blessings and commands; ch. 9:8–17, the covenant of the rainbow. Another open section contains the generations of Shem and Terah (ch. 11:10–32). Its closed sections are closely followed by the R.V. in paragraphing the English text. The verses were first numbered in the Hebrew Bible in Bomberg's edition of 1547, in which the number was noted on the marg. opposite every 5th verse by the appropriate letter of the Heb. alphabet used numerically. Arias Montanus, in his Hebrew Bible with interlinear Lat. translation, pub-

lished at Antwerp in 1571, was the first actually to break up the Heb. text into chapters. To number the verses, he added the Arab. numerals in the marg. See BIBLE.

The Hebrew text of the O.T. has come down practically unchanged since at least the 1st half of the 2d century of the Christian era. From this form all existing MSS. are derived. The preservation of this standard text, in its integrity and with freedom from errors, during its transmission has been due to the existence of professional scribes to whom its copying, pronunciation, and interpretation were entrusted and to the elaborate rules adopted for their guidance which rendered mistakes in copying unlikely to occur and made the detection of a chance error almost certain. In the early part of the 10th century Aaron ben-Asher and Ben-Naphtali were 2 rival textual critics. Of the latter nothing is known, and no MS. which he edited has come to light; his readings are known only from official lists of the variations of the 2 scholars. Moses ben-Asher copied and edited a MS. (c. A.D. 890–895), now in the possession of the Karaite community at Cairo; it contains only the Former and Latter Prophets. His son Aaron ben-Asher (c. A.D. 900–940) continued his father's studies; a MS. based on his work and including the whole O.T. is in possession of the Jewish community at Aleppo. A copy of this MS. made A.D. 1009 is now in Leningrad.

It is believed that the original MSS. of the O.T. books were written on skins; see BOOK. That many of them were is certain (Ps. 40:7; Jer. 36:14, 23). The existing MSS. are usually of parchment or, in the East, of leather. They are not old. In the British Museum is an undated MS. of the Pentateuch, probably written c. A.D. 820–850; reference has already been made to the MS. of the elder Ben-Asher in the Karaite synagogue at Cairo as well as to that based on the work of Aaron ben-Asher. The oldest extant MS. of which the date (A.D. 916) can be affirmed with certainty is a copy of the Latter Prophets (Major and Minor). Although it is written with the supralinear (Babylonian) punctuation, it is a mixed text and embodies both the e. and the w. readings before they were definitely separated. It is now at Leningrad. The MS. of the entire O.T. dated A.D. 1009, now at Leningrad, has been noted above. The scarcity of ancient Heb. MSS. is to a large extent due to the practice of the Jews, which is alluded to in the Talmud, of burying all sacred MSS. which became defective through wear or were otherwise faulty.

After the invention of printing, the book of The Psalms was put in type and published in 1477. Eleven years later, in 1488, the whole printed Heb. Bible was issued in folio from a press at Soncino in the duchy of Milan. In 1492 there appeared at Brescia an octavo volume containing the Pentateuch, the Five Megilloth, and the Haphtaroth (lessons from the Prophets); the companion volume containing the Prophets and the Hagiographa (except the Megilloth) was printed at the same place in 1494. Luther used this edition in making his translation. The great Rabbinic Bible of Jacob ben Hayyim, published by Daniel Bomberg at Venice in 1524–1525 in 4 volumes, is based upon a careful collation of MSS. and faithfully reproduces the standard text of the scribes at Tiberias. Van der Hooght's edition of the Heb. text was first published at Amsterdam in 1705. It has held its ground on account of its accuracy, being reprinted with minor corrections by Aug. Hahn in 1831 and by C. G. G. Theile in 1849. It has about 1,000 marginal readings, most of them of considerable antiquity. Yet more important is the edition of the Masoretic text, with critical and Masoretic appendixes, prepared by S. Baer and Franz Delitzsch. Genesis appeared in 1869, and various other books have followed at intervals. This edition and that of Ginsburg issued at London in 1894 are revisions of the text of Jacob ben Ḥayyim, designed to conform it more closely to the teachings of the Masora. A 2d edition in 4 volumes by Ginsburg, with a large critical apparatus, was published in London, 1926. Kittel's edition, printed at Leipzig, 1906, reproduces the text of Jacob ben Ḥayyim, and gives in footnotes the more important variants of the MSS. and versions; a 2d edition appeared, 1909, 1912–1913. The 3d edition by Kittel, Kahle, Alt, and Eissfeldt was published at Stuttgart in 1937; the text is based on the Leningrad MS. (A.D. 1009), and thus an attempt was made to reproduce the work of Ben-Asher. The variants in different Hebrew MSS. were collected and published by Bishop Kennicott (1776–1780) and de Rossi (1784–1788; 1798).

Ol'ive. A tree largely cultivated in Palestine in olive yards (Ex. 23:11; Josh. 24:13; Judg. 15:5; I Sam. 8:14). It grew also in Assyria (II Kings 18:32). Strabo mentions it among the trees of Armenia, and it is supposed to be indigenous in n. India and other temperate regions of Asia. The wood was used for timber (I Kings 6:23, 31–33). A valuable oil was obtained from the fruit, and had extensive use; see OIL.

Plants grown from the drupe or from slips cut from below the grafted branches, and the shoots which spring up around the trunk, are of the wild variety and require grafting. A good, fruitful olive tree, if its cultivation is neglected, deteriorates and becomes wild. The wild olive is a shrub or low tree; and any berries which it may produce are small and of no value. The process of grafting a cutting from the wild olive tree into one of the cultivated kind is alluded to in Rom. 11:17, 24 to illustrate the grafting of the Gentile converts on what hitherto had been the Jewish Church. In gardening the process was different; it was the grafting of a cutting from the cultivated tree into a stock of the wild olive to alter and improve its nature.

From an olive tree the dove plucked the leaf when the Flood was subsiding (Gen. 8:11). An olive branch is now an emblem of peace. The olive was also a symbol of prosperity and divine blessing, of beauty and strength (Ps. 52:8; Jer. 11:16; Hos. 14:6). The aged olive tree is often surrounded by young and thrifty shoots (Ps. 128:3). Women sometimes adorned themselves with garlands of olives on festal occasions (Judith 15:13), and at the Olympic games in Greece the victor's crown was composed of olive leaves.

The olive tree of Palestine is the common *Olea europaea*. It has lanceolate, entire, leathery, evergreen leaves of a dusty color, and small whitish, monopetalous flowers. The olive is still cultivated through nearly every part of Palestine.

Ol'ives (ŏl'ĭvz), **Mount of,** and **Ol'i·vet** [Lat. *olivetum*, olive grove; cf. Vulgate, Matt. 21:1; 26:30; Acts 1:12]. A hill which is before Jerusalem on the e. (Zech. 14:4), separated from it by the valley of the Kidron (II Sam. 15:14, 23, 30). Its summit with the farther slope was reckoned as a Sabbath-day's journey from the city (Acts 1:12), or, according to Josephus, at 5 or 6 stades (Jos. *Antiq.* xx. 8, 6; *War* v. 2, 3). David, barefoot and with covered head, went up its ascent when he fled from Absalom. On its summit God was wont to be worshiped (II Sam. 15:32). The glory of the Lord appeared there to Ezekiel in a vision (Ezek. 11:23), and Zechariah prophetically portrayed Jehovah standing on the mountain to interpose in behalf of his people (Zech. 14:4). Jesus went often to the

Mount of Olives (Luke 21:37; 22:39; John 8:1). He was descending its slope when the multitude welcomed him to the city with hosannas (Luke 19:37, 38). He had crossed its summit when Jerusalem burst into full view, and he wept over the fate which he knew awaited the city (vs. 41–44). He was sitting on the mount with his disciples, gazing across the valley at the splendid Temple and the city, when he prophesied the destruction of both (Matt. 24:3; Mark 13:3). After his last passover he retired to the Mount of Olives (Matt. 26:30; Mark 14:26). The Garden of Gethsemane was w. of it, either at its base or some short distance up its ascent. Bethany and Bethphage were on the e. side (Matt. 21:1; Mark 11:1; Luke 19:29). It was near the former of these villages that our Lord's ascension took place (Luke 24:50). The Mount of Olives is unquestionably the eminence now called by the Arabs Jebel eṭ-Ṭūr, e. of Jerusalem. Properly speaking, it is a chain of hills rising into 3 or, as some reckon, 4 summits, and with 2 lateral spurs. One spur runs w., starting at the bend of the Kidron, about a mile n. of Jerusalem, and attains an elevation of 2,737 feet above the sea. This n. spur is generally identified with Josephus' hill of Scopus, or the watchman (Jos. *War* ii. 19, 4). The other spur is separated from the main ridge by the Kidron. It also runs w., and faces the city on the s. It has been designated the hill of Evil Counsel, from the late and worthless tradition that Caiaphas had a country place on its summit and in his house the chief priests met and consulted about putting Jesus to death (John 11:47–53). Its altitude is 2,549 feet.

Of the 4 peaks into which the range of Olivet rises, the most n. one, called Karem eṣ-Ṣayyād, is the highest, being 2,723 feet above sea level. It was formerly called Galilee, either because Galileans encamped there when they came to Jerusalem to the festivals, or because in the 14th century it was believed to be the place of the ascension, where the angels addressed the disciples as men of Galilee. The 2d peak is called the Ascension. As early as A.D. 315 it was regarded as the spot whence Jesus ascended to heaven, and Constantine crowned it with a rotunda and a basilica. The latter has been replaced by a succession of churches of the Ascension. This is the Mount of Olives proper. It stands directly opposite to the e. gate of Jerusalem, and rises to 2,643 feet above the level of the ocean, 371 above the bed of the Kidron, and 208 over the Temple plateau. The 3d hill is called the Prophets', from what are called the prophets' tombs on its side. The 4th hill is named the mount of Offense, from the belief that Solomon there built the idolatrous shrines for his heathen wives. The Ascension hill and the hill of the Prophets are so slightly dissevered that some reduce the 4 summits to 3.

At the foot of the Mount of Olives proper, at the traditional site of Gethsemane, the road forks, including the Garden in its crotch. One branch runs s., rises by a gradual ascent, winds round the s. shoulder of the mountain, and continues on to Bethany and Jericho. It was built in the 7th century A.D. by the caliph 'Abd al-Malik. The n. fork runs e., and at the distance of about 50 yards divides into 3. The middle one, steep and rugged, leads up the face of the mountain, crosses it near the summit, and goes on past the so-called stone of Bethphage to Bethany. As early as the 4th century the Christians of Jerusalem, when celebrating the triumphal entry of Jesus into the city, used to come in procession over this road. The 2 branches on either side of this steep middle road also reach the top of the mountain, but they follow a more gradual

THE MOUNT OF OLIVES

ascent. Farther up the Kidron valley a Roman road to the Jordan climbed the w. slope of the ridge near 'Ain eṣ-Ṣuwan, crossed the crest about half a mile n. of the top of Olivet, in the depression n. of Karem eṣ-Ṣayyād, descended into the wadi and crossed it near the ruin Bukei'dan and, keeping the wadi Rawā-beh hard by on the n., continued on to the Jordan.

Ol'i·vet (ŏl'ĭ-vĕt). See OLIVES, MOUNT OF.

O·lym'pas (ō-lĭm'păs). A Roman Christian to whom Paul sent his salutation (Rom. 16:15).

O'mar (ō'mēr). A descendant of Esau through Eliphaz (Gen. 36:11), and chieftain of a tribe of the name (v. 15).

O·me'ga (ō-mē'gà). The last letter of the Gr. alphabet, hence used figuratively for the last or for the end (Rev. 1:8, 17; 21:6; 22:13).

O'mer. A measure for dry articles. It contained a 10th part of an ephah (Ex. 16:36), and was therefore 100th of a homer (Ezek. 45:11). The omer contained 3.36 quarts. See MEASURE, III.

Om'ri (ŏm'rī) [Cf. Arab. 'Umar, 'Omar].
1. A man of Benjamin, family of Becher (I Chron. 7:8).
2. A man of Judah, family of Perez (I Chron. 9:4).
3. Son of Michael and prince of the tribe of Issachar in David's reign (I Chron. 27:18).
4. A king of Israel. Before gaining the throne he was commander of the Israelite army in the reign of Elah and not unlikely in that of Baasha also; and he may have subjugated Moab at this time (Moabite Stone, 7, 8; see MOABITE STONE). He was conducting the siege of Gibbethon, which belonged to the Philistines, when news arrived that Zimri had murdered Elah and usurped the throne. The army at once proclaimed Omri king of Israel. He accepted the honor and led his troops against the town of Tirzah, the national capital, where Zimri was. The latter, despairing of his ability to hold the throne, committed suicide (I Kings 16:15–20). But the nation was divided. One half adhered to Omri and the other half supported the claims of Tibni; and it was not until the death of Tibni 5 years later that Omri became the undisputed sovereign of all Israel (vs. 21–23). The statement of v. 23, "In the thirty and first year of Asa king of Judah began Omri to reign over Israel" (in Heb. simply "Omri reigned"), refers, not to the time of his proclamation by the soldiery and his assumption of the royal title (although the 12 years of his reign are counted from this event), but to his attainment of the sole authority in the kingdom (cf. vs. 15, 29). He transferred the seat of government from Tirzah to Samaria, which he built for the purpose (v. 24). He followed the idolatries of Jeroboam and acted in other respects more wickedly than any of his predecessors on the throne of the 10 tribes (I Kings 16:26; Micah 6:16). He died about 874 B.C. and was buried in Samaria. His son Ahab succeeded him on the throne (I Kings 16:28). Omri made an impression on history outside of Israel. Not only did the Moabites remember his name, but after his death and the annihilation of his family the Assyrians for a time still attached his name, which they wrote Humri, to the reigning monarch and land of Israel.

On, I (ŏn) [strength]. A Reubenite chief who took part in the rebellion of Korah (Num. 16:1); see KORAH 4.

On, II (ŏn) [Heb. 'ōn, from Egypt. iwnw; cf. Coptic ōn]. An old and renowned city of Lower Egypt, on the e. of the Nile, in the Delta, several miles from the river and 19 miles n. of Memphis. It was the principal seat of the worship of the sun; hence called Heliopolis by the Greeks (cf. Ex. 1:11, LXX) and Beth-shemesh by Jeremiah (Jer. 43:13). It is not certain whether Isaiah had this city in mind; a slight change in the 1st letter of the name (ḥeres, sun; ḥeres, destruction) would turn city of the sun into city of destruction, to denote the overthrow of idolatry

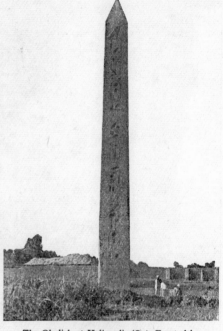

The Obelisk at Heliopolis (On), Erected by Senwosret (Sesostris) I, Second King of Dynasty XII

(Isa. 19:18; cf. marg.). With the temple of the sun were connected a training school for priests and a medical school, and these institutions were visited by all the Greek philosophers who went to Egypt to study. In Herodotus' day the priests of On were esteemed the most learned in history of all the Egyptians (Herod. ii. 3). It was the daughter of a priest of On whom Pharaoh gave to Joseph to wife (Gen. 41:45, 50; 46:20).

O'nam (ō'năm) [strong, wealthy]. 1. A Horite (Gen. 36:23; I Chron. 1:40).
2. A man of Judah, house of Jerahmeel (I Chron. 2:26, 28).

O'nan (ō'năn) [strong]. A son of Judah by a Canaanitess. That his brother might have no heir, he sinned; but he himself died without male issue (Gen. 38:4–10; 46:12).

O·nes'i·mus (ō-nĕs'ĭ-mŭs) [Gr., useful, profitable]. A slave of Philemon, whom Paul was the means of converting at Rome, and whom he sent back to his Christian master requesting that he might be received, not as a servant, but as a brother beloved (Philemon 10–19). He was a man of Colossae, and with Tychicus carried from Rome to that city the epistles to the Colossians and to Philemon (Col. 4:7–9).

On·e·siph'o·rus (ŏn·ĕ-sĭf'ō-rŭs) [Gr., profit bringer]. A Christian whose home was probably at Ephesus (II Tim. 1:16–18). When he was at Rome he sought out the Apostle Paul, then a prisoner, and showed him great kindness. The members of his household were with Timothy, and Paul sent them his salutations (ch. 4:19).

O·ni′as (ō-nī′ăs), in A.V. once **O·ni′a·res** (ō-nī′á-rēz) (I Macc. 12:19). The form Oniares is an old corruption, in which the 2 names Onias Arius are blended (cf. Jos. *Antiq.* xii. 4, 10). A high priest of the Jews, who held office from c. 323–300 B.C. He was a contemporary of Arius, king of Sparta, who reigned from 309 to 265 B.C. (I Macc. 12:7, in A.V. Darius, a corruption of Arius, vs. 19, 20). Onias succeeded Jaddua, and was the father and predecessor of Simon the Just (Jos. *Antiq.* xi. 8, 7; xii. 2, 5). He is probably referred to in Ecclus. 50:1. Josephus errs in regarding Onias III, a later pontiff, as the recipient of the letter from Arius.

For others of the name, see HIGH PRIEST.

On′ion. A plant, the bulbous root of which was much used in Egypt as an article of food (Num. 11:5; Herod. ii. 125). It is *Allium cepa*, called in Heb. *bāṣāl*. It has been cultivated from an early period in Egypt and other parts of the East.

O′no (ō′nō) [strong]. A town of Benjamin (Neh. 6:2; 11:35), built or rather rebuilt by a Benjamite called Shamed (I Chron. 8:12). Some of its inhabitants returned from the Babylonian Captivity (Ezra 2:33; Neh. 7: 37). It is considered to have been at Kefr 'Ana, about 7 miles inland e. by s. from Joppa.

On′y·cha. The rendering of Heb. *sheḥēleth* (Ex. 30:34). It was 1 of the ingredients in a perfume made for the service of the tabernacle. It is believed to have been the operculum (lid) of a shell mollusk called stromb or wing-shell, which being burned gave out a certain perfume.

On′yx [Lat. from Gr., finger nail, onyx]. The rendering of Heb. *shōham*. The Heb. word denotes a precious stone (Job 28:16, R.V. marg. beryl; Ezek. 28:13) which was found in the land of Havilah (Gen. 2:12). Two of these stones, each graven with the names of 6 Israelite tribes, were put on the shoulder pieces of the high priest's ephod (Ex. 28:9, 12), and another was the 2d stone in the 4th row on his breastplate (ch. 28:20). David gathered such stones for the service of the future Temple (I Chron. 29:2). The onyx is a cryptocrystalline variety or subvariety of quartz. It is in layers of different colors, which alternate with each other and bear some resemblance to the white and flesh-colored bands of the finger nail.

O′phel (ō′fĕl) [swelling, bulge, hill]. The s. part of the e. hill at Jerusalem, enclosed by the city wall; perhaps originally a massive circular tower or projection in the fortifications at this point. The general locality is indicated by the proximity of the pool of Shelah, i.e., doubtless Siloam, the court of the guard, the water gate, and the horse gate (Neh. 3:15–27; see JERUSALEM, II. 3); the pool of Siloam, the e. court of the Temple, and the Kidron valley (Jos. *War* v. 4, 1 and 2; 6, 1). Jotham built much on its walls, and Manasseh increased their height (II Chron. 27:3; 33:14). After the Exile, if not before, the Nethinim had their residence in this quarter, because of its convenience to the Temple (Neh. 3:26; 11:21). At the ophel, or hill, in Samaria Gehazi deposited the goods got by deceit from Naaman (II Kings 5:24, R.V. marg.); and in a city of Moab Mesha built the wall of the ophel (*Moabite Stone*, 22; see MOABITE STONE).

O′phir (ō′fēr). A tribe descended from Joktan (Gen. 10:29; I Chron. 1:23), and the country which it inhabited. This region was celebrated for its gold (I Chron. 29:4; Job 22:24; 28:16; Ps. 45:9; Isa. 13:12), to obtain which, Hiram, in conjunction with Solomon, sent a navy from Ezion-geber (I Kings 9:28). The ships brought back algum or almug trees as well as gold (ch. 10:11), and probably also silver, ivory, apes, and peacocks (v. 22; cf. ch. 22:48). Jehoshaphat attempted to imitate the enterprise, but his ships were wrecked at Ezion-geber (ch. 22:48). As this port was on the Gulf of 'Aḳabah, the route to Ophir was by the Red Sea and not by the Mediterranean. The voyage out and back in the ships of that day, with the peculiar winds of the Red Sea, and including the lying in port, lasted, it may be judged, 3 years (ch. 10:22; cf. ch. 22:48); see RED SEA.

It is not certain where Ophir was. Josephus says that it was the Golden Land in India (Jos. *Antiq.* viii. 6, 4), perhaps on the river Cophen (i. 6, 4); and hence it has been conjecturally located at the mouth of the Indus, in the region of the Abhīra. Punt and s. Arabia have also been suggested, as well as e. Arabia on the Persian Gulf; it may have been on the African coast in the general region of Somaliland.

Oph′ni (ŏf′nī). A village of Benjamin (Josh. 18:24). Robinson suggests its identity with Gophna, on the highway from Samaria to Jerusalem, a day's march n. of Gibeah (Jos. *War* v. 2, 1); the modern Jifnā, 3 miles n.w. by n. of Beth-el. This identification assumes that the boundary of Benjamin turned n. near Beth-el, for Beth-el was on the n. boundary.

Oph′rah (ŏf′rá) [hind]. 1. A son of Menothai, of the tribe of Judah (I Chron. 4:14).

2. A town of Benjamin (Josh. 18:23), evidently n. of Michmash (I Sam. 13:17). According to the Onomasticon, of the 4th century A.D., it was a village then called Ephraim, 5 miles to the e. of Beth-el. Robinson identified it with eṭ-Ṭaiyibeh, about 4 miles n.e. by e. of Beth-el, with a splendid view from its summit. His opinion has been widely accepted.

3. A village w. of the Jordan, occupied by the Abiezrites, a family of Manasseh (Judg. 6:11, 15; cf. Josh. 17:1, 2). It was the home of Gideon, where he was called to his mission and built an altar, where he made an ephod to the ensnaring of Israel, and where he was buried (Judg., chs. 6 to 8). It may possibly be identified with eṭ-Ṭaiyibeh, s. of Ṭūl-karem.

Or′a·tor. 1. The rendering of Heb. *laḥash*, an incantation, preceded by *nebōn*, skillful in enchantment (Isa. 3:3). The R.V. accurately translates the phrase by "skillful enchanter."

2. The rendering of Gr. *rhētōr*, public speaker, pleader, in Acts 24:1, applied to Tertullus. He was a professional advocate engaged by Paul's Jewish enemies to prosecute the apostle before the Roman procurator.

Or′chard. See GARDEN.

O′reb (ō′rĕb) [a raven]. 1. One of 2 Midianite princes defeated, captured, and put to death by Gideon. He was slain at a rock, which came to be called in consequence the rock of Oreb (Judg. 7:25; 8:3; Ps. 83:11; Isa. 10:26).

2. A rock on which the Midianite prince Oreb was killed by Gideon (Judg. 7:25; Isa. 10:26); doubtless it was w. of the Jordan near the river (Judg. 7:25; 8:4).

O′ren (ō′rĕn) [a species of fir or cedar tree]. A man of Judah, house of Jerahmeel (I Chron. 2:25).

Or′gan. See PIPE 2.

O·ri′on (ō-rī′ŏn). A constellation (Job 9:9; 38:31; Amos 5:8), in Heb. *kesīl*, stupid fellow, fool; in religious sense, impudent, defiant, godless. The Targums and the Peshitta render the word by giant; the LXX and Vulgate employ the name Orion. In classical mythology Orion is represented as a man of great strength, celebrated as a worker in iron and as a hunter. Being killed by the goddess Diana, he was transferred to the heavens and bound to the sky (cf. Job 38:31), and became the constellation Orion.

The constellation is visible in all latitudes. It disputes with the Great Bear the distinction of being the finest constellation of the sky. Two of its stars—Betelgeuse at the upper part of his right arm as he faces the spectator, and Rigel at his uplifted left foot—are of the 1st magnitude. About 100 stars in the constellation are visible to the naked eye, and 2,000 or more may be seen under the telescope.

Or'na·ments. Orientals adorn themselves with ornaments to an extent deemed excessive by Occidental taste. It has ever been so. Hebrews, Egyptians, Midianites, Syrians, both men and women, were fond of wearing ornaments (Gen. 24:22; Ex. 3:22; 11:2; 32:2; Num. 31:50). Women wore beads and pearls, and articles of gold, silver, and brass (S. of Sol. 1:10, 11; I Tim. 2:9); earrings, nose rings, pendants, necklaces, chains, brazen mirrors, armlets, bracelets, finger rings, anklets (Gen. 24:22, 47; 35:4; Ex. 35:22; Num. 31:50; Isa. 3:18–23). Men of all classes except the poorest wore seal rings (Gen. 38:18), which were useful in business as well as ornamental. Nor did they regard rings for the arms as effeminate. Saul, like the kings of Assyria, wore a ring about the arm or wrist (II Sam. 1:10). It was a national custom with the Ishmaelites for the men to wear earrings (Judg. 8:25, 26), and men among the Hebrews sometimes did so (Ex. 32:2). Men of high rank wore a gold chain as badge of office (Gen. 41:42; Dan. 5:29).

Ornaments were laid aside in time of mourning (Ex. 33:4–6).

Or'nan (ôr'năn). See ARAUNAH.

Or'pah (ôr'pä) [neck, i.e., stubbornness]. The wife of Chilion, and the sister-in-law of Ruth. She consented to remain in her native country, Moab, when Ruth, drawn by affection to her mother-in-law Naomi, insisted on accompanying her to Palestine (Ruth 1:4, 14, 15; cf. ch. 4:10).

Or'tho·si'a (ôr'thô-sī'à), in A.V. **Or'tho·si'as** (ôr'thô-sī'ăs). A city of Phoenicia, between Tripoli and the river Eleutherus (I Macc. 15:37).

Os·nap'par (ŏs-năp'ẽr), in A.V. **As·nap'per** [Biblical Aram. 'āseⁿappar]. A high Assyrian dignitary called great and noble who settled various foreign tribes in Samaria (Ezra 4:10). Formerly it was supposed that he was either Esarhaddon or 1 of his officials (cf. vs. 2, 10). Scholars now identify him with Ashurbanipal, the son of Esarhaddon, who from c. 673 B.C. was his heir apparent; in 669 he became his successor on the Assyrian throne, and reigned until 626 B.C. Ashurbanipal records that he penetrated Elam, took Susa the capital, and carried off many of the inhabitants to Assyria (cf. Ezra 4:9, 10). His father, Esarhaddon, had conquered Egypt in 671. Rebellion occurred among the petty rulers, and assistance was rendered them by the able Tirhakah. To suppress this revolt, Ashurbanipal conducted 2 campaigns, in which on the whole he was successful, though Egypt was finally lost. In the later campaign, about 663 B.C., Thebes, then known as No, was captured and plundered (cf. Nahum 3:8–10). He had relations first friendly, but afterward the reverse, with Gyges, the usurping king of Lydia; see GOG 2. He had to crush a rebellion of Shamash-shum-

ukin, his own brother, the viceroy of Babylon. By the Greeks, who called him Sardanapalus, he was considered effeminate. Modern scholars regard his memory with gratitude on account of the splendid library that he brought together. He had copyists incessantly at work, not merely transcribing Assyrian books, but also copying and translating works of value from Sumerian and Akkadian. Part of this library has been recovered, and it is from it that we derive most of our acquaintance with the Assyrian Empire and its kings.

Os'pray, obsolete form of **Os'prey.** The rendering of Heb. 'ozniyyāh (Lev. 11:13; Deut. 14:12), an unclean bird. The LXX translates it haliaietos, that is, Pandion haliaëtus. It is a dark brown eagle widely distributed throughout the world, frequenting seacoasts and living on fish. In Palestine it occurs along the Mediterranean, especially in the lagoons at the mouth of the Kishon.

Os'si·frage [Lat., bone breaker]. The rendering in A.V. of Heb. peres, breaker. It was an unclean bird (Lev. 11:13; and Deut. 14:12). The R.V. translates it gier eagle. It is believed to be the lammergeier, or bearded eagle (Gypaëtus barbatus). The Eng. ossifrage and Heb. peres both refer to the fact that the bird delights in bones, snakes, and tortoises, which it breaks. This it sometimes does by taking them up to a great height in the air and dropping them on a stone. The ossifrage is 3½ feet high; the expansion of its wings is about 9 feet. Its claws are not adapted for carrying off living prey, and its disposition is cowardly. In Palestine the ossifrage is rare and tending to extinction, its chief haunts being the ravines of the Arnon, e. of the Dead Sea.

Os'trich. 1. The rendering of Heb. yā'ēn, fem. ya'ănāh, probably the voracious bird. It was ceremonially unclean (Lev. 11:16; Deut. 14:15), makes a mournful sound (Micah 1:8), inhabits the wilderness (Isa. 13:21; 34:13), and was believed to forsake its eggs (Lam. 4:3). The A.V. translates the masc. form by ostrich, the fem. form by owl.

2. The rendering of Heb. pl. reⁿānīm, utterers of tremulous sounds (Job 39:13, in A.V. peacock). The female deposits her eggs on the ground to be warmed in the dust; and it was popularly supposed that she abandoned them to their fate, forgetting that the foot might crush them or that the wild beast might trample them (vs. 14, 15). The speed of the ostrich is such that it distances a man on horseback (v. 18).

3. The A.V. inaccurately renders Heb. nōṣāh by ostrich in Job 39:13b. It means a feather, as in Ezek. 17:3, 7.

Ostrich

The ostrich (*Struthio camelus*) belongs to the aberrant subclass or division called *Ratitae*, or struthious birds. It is among the largest in size of the class, but are not able to fly, the deprivation being compensated by great power of running. The common ostrich is 6 or 8 feet high. The bird prepares a nest by rolling in the sand and scooping out a hole about 6 feet in diameter. An egg is laid every other day, until the eggs number 10, 12, or more. Each egg is about 3 pounds in weight. They appear to be hatched partly by the heat of the sun, but mainly by incubation, the male bird sitting on them for about 20 hours to the hen's 4. The male takes charge of the young brood. At night the bird utters a hoarse, complaining cry, alluded to in Micah 1:8. The ostrich is diffused over the greater part of Africa. It still occurs in Arabia, but its area there seems to have diminished since O.T. times.

Oth'ni (ŏth'nī) [abbreviation of Othniel]. A porter, the son of Shemaiah (I Chron. 26:7).

Oth'ni·el (ŏth'nĭ-ĕl) [perhaps, God is might]. A son of Kenaz and brother or half brother of Caleb, son of Jephunneh the Kenizzite (Josh. 15:17; I Chron. 4:13); see CALEB 2. Caleb promised to give his daughter Achsah in marriage to any hero who took the town of Debir or Kiriath-sepher. Othniel effected its capture and received Achsah (Josh. 15:15–17; Judg. 1:11–13). He subsequently delivered the Israelites from the tyranny of Cushan-rishathaim, king of Mesopotamia, and became judge, and the land had rest 40 years (Judg. 3:8–11).

Ov'en. See BREAD.

Owl. 1. The rendering of Heb. *bath hayya'ănāh* (Lev. 11:16, A.V.). See OSTRICH 1.
2. The rendering of Heb. *kōs*, a cup, an owl. The owl was ceremonially unclean (Lev. 11:17; Deut. 14:16, little owl), and frequented waste places (Ps. 102:6). Probably the s. little owl (*Athene glaux*) is intended, which is universally distributed through Palestine, occurring in olive yards, rocks, thickets, and among ruins and tombs.
3. The rendering of Heb. *yanshūph.* It was ceremonially unclean (Lev. 11:17; Deut. 14:16, great owl) and frequented waste places (Isa. 34:11; R.V. marg., bittern). It is rendered ibis in the LXX and Vulgate, and owl in the Targums and the Peshitta. Tristram believes that the species was the Egyptian eagle owl (*Bubo ascalaphus*). It lives in caves and among ruins, and is common about Petra and Beer-sheba.
4. The rendering of Heb. *tinshemeth* (Lev. 11:18; in A.V. swan). The LXX renders it purple coot or water hen, and the Vulgate swan.
5. The rendering of Heb. *lilith*, nocturnal specter (Isa. 34:14; in A.V. screech owl, in R.V. night monster). The screech or barn owl (*Strix flammea*) is found in Palestine frequenting ruins.
6. The rendering of Heb. *kippōz* (Isa. 34:15; in R.V. dart-snake).

Ox. The male of the species *Bos taurus*, though ox frequently signifies any animal of the kind, without respect to sex (Ex. 20:17), and the pl. oxen is often synonymous with cattle. The ox was early domesticated. Abraham had sheep and oxen (Gen. 12:16; 21:27); so had his contemporary Abimelech (ch. 20:14), and the Egyptians at the time of the 10 plagues (Ex. 9:3). The ox was used for plowing (I Kings 19:19), for dragging carts or wagons (Num. 7:3; II Sam. 6:6; etc.), and for treading out grain (Deut. 25:4). They were eaten (I Kings 1:25; cf. Matt. 22:4), and were largely sacrificed, especially in connection with the burnt offerings (Num. 7:87, 88; II Sam. 24:22; II Chron. 5:6; 7:5; etc.). A yoke of oxen was 2 oxen designed to be yoked together for the plow, for a cart, or for anything similar. Tristram says that the common cattle of s. and central Palestine are small in

Egyptian Oxen Treading Out Grain

size, those of n. Palestine are larger. The largest herds are now beyond the Jordan.

The word *te'ō*, rendered wild ox (Deut. 14:5, A.V.) and wild bull (Isa. 51:20, A.V.), is translated in R.V. by antelope (*q.v.*). See UNICORN.

Ox'goad'. See GOAD.

O'zem (ō'zĕm) [cf. Arab. *'adam*, anger].
1. A son of Jesse (I Chron. 2:15).
2. A son of Jerahmeel (I Chron. 2:25).

O·zi'as (ō-zī'ăs). See UZZIAH.

Oz'ni (ŏz'nī) [Jehovah has given ear; cf. Azaniah]. A son of Gad, and founder of a tribal family (Num. 26:16). He was either called also Ezbon (Gen. 46:16), or else on Ezbon's death he took his place and founded a tribal family, as did Hezron and Hamul in Judah (Num. 26:19–21).

P

Pa'a·rai (pā'á-rī). One of David's mighty men (II Sam. 23:35, most probably a diverse reading of I Chron. 11:37).

Pad'dan (păd'ăn) and **Pad'dan-a'ram** (păd'ăn-ā'răm), in A.V. **Pa'dan** (pā'dăn) and **Pa'dan-a'ram** (pā'dăn-ā'răm) [plain, plain of Aram, i.e., Syria]; see ARAM 2 (1).

Pa'don (pā'dŏn) [ransom, redemption]. Founder of a family of Nethinim, members of which returned from captivity (Ezra 2:44; Neh. 7:47).

Pa'gi·el (pā'gĭ-ĕl) [perhaps, a meeting with God]. Head of the tribe of Asher in the wilderness (Num. 1:13; 2:27; 7:72, 77; 10:26).

Pa'hath-mo'ab (pā'hăth-mō'ăb) [governor of Moab]. Founder of a family, members of which returned from the Babylonian Captivity (Ezra 2:6; 8:4; Neh. 7:11). Some of them married heathen wives, from whom Ezra persuaded them to separate (Ezra 10:30). The representative of the family signed the covenant (Neh. 10:14), and Hashub, a member of the family, rebuilt or replaced part of the wall of Jerusalem (Neh. 3:11).

Pa'i (pā'ī). See PAU.

Paint. In ancient Egypt and Assyria the custom of painting a black rim around the eyes prevailed among the women. The Hebrews seem to have regarded the practice as a meretricious art, unworthy of a woman of high character (II Kings 9:30; Jer. 4:30; Ezek. 23:40; Jos. *War* iv. 9, 10). Doubtless various dye stuffs were used for the purpose. Antimony, burned to blackness and pulverized, was employed. Probably lead also was used, as it is in Persia. The ordinary kohl used by women in Egypt is a powder obtained from almond shells or by burning a fragrant resin. The powder was kept in small, covered jars and was applied, both dry and moistened with oil, by means of a probe made of wood, silver, or ivory, blunt at the end.

For cosmetics applied to other parts of the body, see HENNA; and for pigments used to color walls and other objects, see COLORS.

Pal'ace. David occupied a royal residence at Jerusalem (II Sam. 5:9; 7:1, 2), but Solomon's commodious and magnificent abode was the first in Jerusalem to be constructed on a grand scale (I Kings 7:1–12). It was 13 years in course of erection, whereas the Temple was completed in 7 years (chs. 6:38; 7:1). It contained the house of the forest of Lebanon (vs. 2–5), which took its name from its numerous cedar pillars. This house was 100 cubits or 150 feet long, 50 cubits wide, and 30 cubits high. Its walls were of solid masonry. Within were 4 rows of cedar pillars. Probably 1 row ran parallel with each wall, and the 4 rows formed the 4 sides of a rectangular court, about 30 by 80 cubits in dimension; or else the pillars were disposed in 2 double rows parallel to the long sides of the building and left a court in the center. Beams extended from the pillars to the walls and supported 3 tiers of chambers. These chambers looked down into the court. This building was at once armory and treasure house (I Kings 10:17, 21; Isa. 22:8), and may have served other purposes as well. A hall of pillars was the reception and waiting room of the palace (I Kings 7:6). It was 50 cubits in length and 30 cubits in breadth, and had a portico in front of its portal. This portico was not unlikely the main entrance to the palace. Next came the hall of judgment (v. 7), open in front, but probably closed on the other 3 sides by solid walls pierced by doors only. It was the throne room. The great ivory throne overlaid with gold stood there (ch. 10:18–20). These 3 buildings probably opened on a rectangular court, the sides of which were the portal in the central part of the inner long wall of the house of the forest of Lebanon, the inner doors and wall of the hall of pillars, and the open front of the throne room. Behind the throne room was the inner court where the king dwelt. The principal entrance to it was probably through the throne room, so that the king pronounced judgment and granted audiences in the gate of his palace. This court was, of course, adorned with flowers and fountains, and surrounded by cloisters. The palace of Pharaoh's daughter (ch. 7:8) was next to the throne room, according to Josephus (Jos. Antiq. viii. 5, 2). Solomon's palace was constructed on the general model which prevailed in w. Asia, and which is now familiar from the remains of the royal abodes unearthed in Assyria, Babylonia, and Persia. Some conception of its elegance and beauty may be formed from casual references in The Book of Esther to the palace of the Persian king at Shushan (Esth. 1:5, 6, 9; 2:3, 14; 5:1, 2; 7:7). See HOUSE; HASMONAEANS, PALACE OF THE; HEROD, PALACE OF; and PRAETORIUM.

Pa'lal (pā'lăl) [(God) has judged, decided]. A son of Uzai. He helped to rebuild the wall of Jerusalem (Neh. 3:25).

Pal'an·quin'. A covered conveyance, arranged both for sitting and reclining, and carried by means of poles on the shoulders of 2, 4, or 6 men or borne as a litter between 2 camels, horses, or mules. The royal palanquin, provided by Solomon for his bride, consisted of a frame made of cedar, with small ornamental pillars of silver, a bottom of gold, costly coverings of purple for the seat, and perhaps embroideries lovingly made by the daughters of Jerusalem (S. of Sol. 3:9, in A.V. chariot).

Pal'es·tine (păl'ĕs-tīn) (Joel 3:4) and **Pal'es·ti·na** (păl'ĕs-tī-nà) (Ex. 15:14; Isa. 14:29, 31), in R.V. always **Phi·lis'ti·a.** In the O.T. the name denotes the country of the Philistines (cf. Herod. vii. 89). The name now designates a country in the s.w. corner of Asia, constituting the s. portion of Syria; for a long time it was in the possession of the Hebrews. That portion of this territory which lies w. of the Jordan the ancient Hebrews called Canaan as distinguished from the land of Gilead e. of the river. After the Conquest the entire country became known as the land of Israel (I Sam. 13:19; I Chron. 22:2; Matt. 2:20), but after the division of the kingdom this name was often given to the Northern realm. In The Epistle to the Hebrews (Heb. 11:9) it is called the Land of Promise. Soon after the beginning of the Christian era Greek and Latin writers denominate it Palaestina. In the Middle Ages it became known as the Holy Land (cf. Zech. 2:12; II Macc. 1:7).

1. *Boundaries and extent of Palestine.* The Hebrews occupied the region from Kadeshbarnea and Wadi el-'Arīsh on the s. to Mount Hermon on the n., and from the Mediterranean Sea on the w. to the desert on the e., except the plain of the Philistines and the country of Moab. In prosperous reigns powerful kings extended their sway beyond these limits and held dominion over Hamath and Damascus and beyond, as far as the river Euphrates, and over Ammon, Moab, and Edom. The Hebrews themselves were accustomed to say that their country extended from Dan to Beer-sheba, a distance of 150 miles. The s. boundary was then Wadi el-Fiḳrah and the river Arnon. These limits included the thickly populated portion of the land. Taking the smaller limits, which exclude most of the territory occupied by the tribe of Simeon and part of that occupied by Naphtali, the boundaries form a parallelogram, the altitude of which, measured by the latitudes of Dan and the s. extremity of the Dead Sea, is 145 miles, and the base 70 miles. The area is 10,150 square miles. This includes the Philistine country, which, at its utmost extent from Carmel to Beer-sheba, had an area of 1,765 square miles, leaving 8,385 square miles as the territory occupied by the Hebrews. The survey assigns to e. Palestine, from Hermon to the Arnon, about 3,800 square miles; and to w. Palestine, as far s. as Beer-sheba and including Philistia, 6,040 square miles.

2. *Population of Palestine.* The Hebrews at the time of the Conquest numbered 600,000 men, or else 600 clans (see THOUSAND). If the men alone numbered 600,000, the population was about 2,000,000, in a territory of 8,300 square miles. Massachusetts, with an area of 8,315 square miles, had a population of 4,312,-332 in 1940, and New Jersey, with an area of 7,815 square miles, had a population of 4,148,-562. David took the census of a much larger region. Modern Palestine (1940) with an area of 10,429 square miles has a population of 1,466,536. That it was formerly a populous country is evident from the statements of the Bible and Josephus, and from the numerous ruins of former towns. Scarcely a hilltop of the multitude always in sight but is crowned with a city or village, inhabited or in ruins.

3. *The geology of Palestine.* A band of Nubian or Petra sandstone extends along the e. coast of the Dead Sea and along part of the wall of rock flanking the Jordan Valley on the e., and appears on the w. slopes of Lebanon and Anti-Lebanon. It is generally of a dark red or blackish color. Above this lies the most important geological formation in Palestine, the cretaceous limestone which constitutes the main part of the tableland of the country both e. and w. of the Jordan. At Jerusalem there are 2 beds of the limestone, an upper or

harder layer, called by the inhabitants *mazi*, and an inferior soft one, denominated *malaki*. The reservoirs, sepulchers, and cellars under and around the city have been excavated in the soft *malaki*, while the foundations of the buildings are on the hard *mazi*. The large quarries near the Damascus gate are in the *malaki*. From them came the stone of which the Temple walls were constructed. These beds of cretaceous limestone underlie a newer series which, commencing at Mount Carmel, runs nearly s. to Beer-sheba, from which it then curves in a s.w. direction parallel to the Mediterranean. Outliers of it exist also n.e., e., and s.w. of Jerusalem and around Shechem. From the abundance in them of the little *foraminifera* called nummulites, the beds are named the nummulitic limestone. They belong to the Eocene Tertiary, and probably to the Middle Eocene. This rock is so connected with the cretaceous limestone that the 2 are generally held to constitute but a single formation, called the cretaceo-nummulitic series. Flanking the nummulitic limestone on the w. a long continuous band of calcareous sandstone extends through the Philistine country and appears in scattered patches farther n., to near Mount Carmel. As a rule, it is porous and soft, and since it easily weathers away, it exposes the harder limestone of the tableland which dips beneath it, and makes the descent from the uplands to the lowlands of Judea and Samaria more abrupt than it otherwise would be. Between this sandstone and the Mediterranean lie raised beaches belonging to the upper Pliocene, or to recent times. All these are sedimentary beds. A few igneous rocks, however, exist in the land. A minute patch of very old igneous rocks, an outlier of the great mass of granite, porphyry, diorite, and felsite, which occurs farther s. in the 'Arabah and especially at Sinai, is combined with the carboniferous rocks. On the e. side of the Jordan, nearly all the way from the roots of Mount Hermon to s. of the Sea of Galilee, and e. and s.e. to the Hauran, beyond the limits of Palestine, the country is overspread by an immense mass of volcanic material, basalt, dolerite, felsite, none of it older, and some of it apparently more recent, than the Pliocene Tertiary. There are detached portions of the same volcanic rocks in w. Palestine, w. and n.w. of the Sea of Galilee, with fragments in other quarters. Along the Mediterranean coast of Palestine, wherever the ground is low and level, there is a row of sand dunes, some rising 200 feet in height. Those on the s.w. of the country may have been at least partly formed by the blowing of sand from the Egyptian and Sinaitic deserts. Those farther n. obtained the sand from the weathering of the calcareous sandstone of Philistia. They tend to encroach upon the cultivated parts adjacent, the wind continually blowing particles from them inland. Palestine lies in one of the lines in which earthquake action is potent ; and both in ancient times and more recently portions of the country have been seriously convulsed. To recapitulate, the geological structure of Palestine consists of a layer of red sandstone over the primitive rocks ; then comes the chalky limestone which forms the mass of the country, overlaid with nummulite limestone and alluvial soil ; and lastly in the n.e. appear colossal erupted masses of volcanic rock.

4. *The physical geography of Palestine.* The physical divisions of Palestine are 5 : the Maritime Plain, the Low County or Shephelah, the Central or Western Mountain Range, the Jordan Valley, and the Eastern Range. These form parallel zones, and with certain modifications extend through the entire length of the country from n. to s. In Samaria the Central Range falls directly into the Maritime Plain, which is called Sharon. These zones are broken by the Plain of Esdraelon, which lies athwart the mountain range and connects the seacoast with the Jordan Valley. 1. The Maritime Plain lies along the coast of the Mediterranean Sea for the entire length of the country, being broken only by Mount Carmel. N. of Carmel it is quite narrow, but s. of that mountain it is 6 miles wide and increases in width s. It is an undulating plain 100 to 200 feet above sea level, and very fertile. Between Carmel and the 'Aujah, which empties into the sea n. of Joppa, it was called Sharon ; s. of Joppa it was occupied by the Philistines. 2. The Low Country or Shephelah is a region of low hills situated between the Maritime Plain s. of Carmel and the high Central Range. It forms a terrace with an elevation of about 500 feet above the sea level. The name is applied almost exclusively to that part of the low hilly country which extends from the latitude of Joppa s. to Beer-sheba, and which is sharply separated from the Central Range by a series of valleys running n. and s. 3. The Central Mountain Range is a continuation of the Lebanon Mountains. S. of the river Leontes the lofty ridge drops to a high plateau which reaches s. as far as the n. end of the Sea of Galilee and Acre. This is Upper Galilee. It contains a number of hills between 2,000 and 3,000 feet in elevation ; while several rise considerably above that height, like Jebel Jermuk which is 3,934 feet. Lower Galilee is triangular, having the Sea of Galilee and the Jordan as far as Beth-shean on its e. side and the Plain of Esdraelon on the s.w. side. It consists of a series of low ridges running e. and w. Its elevation is considerably less than that of Upper Galilee, many of its hills being only 400, 500, or 600 feet high, though there are a few loftier peaks immediately w. of the Sea of Galilee. Southwest of the sea is Mount Tabor, 1,843 feet high ; and farther s. Mount Gilboa, with one peak 1,698 feet and another 1,648 feet. The s. part of Lower Galilee descends into the Plain of Esdraelon, most of the places in which do not exceed 200 or 300 feet in height. South of the Plain of Esdraelon the range is broken by many wadies, mountains are scattered into groups, and its inner recesses are accessible from the Maritime Plain, Esdraelon, and the Jordan Valley. Carmel is thrust out as a spur toward the n.w. The average watershed is 2,000 feet high. But Mount Ebal rises 3,077 feet and its companion Gerizim 2,849. This was Samaria. From Beth-el to Hebron and almost to Beer-sheba, a distance of about 45 miles, the range forms 1 compact mass with precipitous sides on the e. and w. and with an average height of 2,200 feet. Beth-el, however, has an elevation of 2,930 feet above sea level, the highest part of Jerusalem 2,598, Bethlehem 2,550, and Hebron 3,040. About 15 miles s. of Hebron it slopes down to the desert of the wandering. The summit of the range is the narrow tableland which was occupied by the tribes of Benjamin and Judah. 4. The Jordan Valley is a remarkable chasm which begins near Ḥasbeya at the w. foot of Mount Hermon, 1,700 feet above sea level, but with lofty mountains on each side, and grows rapidly deeper as it goes s. until at the surface of the Dead Sea it is 1,290 feet lower than sea level ; see DEAD SEA and JORDAN. Though not an impassable barrier, it prevented free intercourse between the peoples who dwelt e. of it s. of the Jabbok as far as Edom, and the tribes of Judah and Benjamin on the w. 5. The Eastern Range is a great fertile tableland, much of it more than 3,000 feet in elevation, stretching from the bluffs which overlook the Jordan Valley to the Syrian desert. It is divided by the gorge of the Jabbok and the n. portion is further cleft by the Yarmūk, immediately s. of the Sea of Galilee.

5. *The principal roads of Palestine.* The physical structure determined the course of travel. The great commercial and military highway between Egypt and the empires of the East passed through Palestine. It crossed Wadi el-'Arîsh near its mouth, followed the seacoast to Gaza, where it was met by a road from Elath and Arabia, and continued through the plain of the Philistines to Ashdod. Beyond Ashdod it forked. One branch followed the coast by Joppa and Dor, and avoided Mount Carmel by keeping to the seashore at the base of the headland; but the way is only 600 feet wide under the headland, and is broken by rocks. The other branch, and the main line of travel, continued from Ashdod through Ekron and Lod and crossed the mountains to the Plain of Esdraelon by 1 of 3 passes. The w. road emerged by Tell Keimun and led to Acre, Tyre, Sidon, and the n. The central road crossed to el-Lejjun (Megiddo), traversed the Plain of Esdraelon and Lower Galilee to the plain of Gennesaret, followed the Jordan n., and by one branch entered the valley of the river Litany between Lebanon and Anti-Lebanon, and led to Hamath and the n. The other branch crossed the Jordan between the Lake of Ḥûleh and the Sea of Galilee, and went n.e. to Damascus. The 3d and most frequented route from the Maritime Plain passed through the plain of Dothan to En-gannim, where it divided, one branch joining the aforementioned road across Lower Galilee, and the other leading to Beth-shean, and, dividing again, continuing to Gilead or to Damascus. By any of the n. routes Carchemish on the Euphrates might be reached.

There was another road from the Plain of Esdraelon to Egypt. It traversed the hill country, passing by Samaria, Shechem, Beth-el, Jerusalem, Bethlehem, Hebron, and Beer-sheba. At this point the road branched, and there was a choice of routes; the highway along the seacoast might be gained by diverging to the w., or the journey might be continued by way of Rehoboth and 'Ain Muweileh, and thence across the desert to Egypt. A route from Beth-shean to Edom, which was also used by travelers to Jerusalem, passed down the Jordan Valley to Jericho, where persons going to Jerusalem took the steep road up the mountains to the capital. From Jericho the road continued along the w. shore of the Dead Sea to En-gedi, where it was joined by a road from Jerusalem and Bethlehem, and thence continued to Edom and Elath at the head of the Red Sea, where it joined the caravan routes from Egypt and Gaza to s. Arabia.

East of the Jordan a caravan route led from Damascus along the edge of the desert s. to Arabia; see DECAPOLIS. It was joined by roads running from Beth-shean across Gilead; by a road from Shechem down Wadi Fār'ah to the ford of the Jordan below the mouth of the Jabbok, and thence across Gilead to Rabbath Ammon; and by another from the ford at Jericho by way of Heshbon. West of the Jordan Galilee was crossed by a road running almost due e. from Acre, which joined the road to Damascus near the point where it crossed the Jordan, midway between the waters of Merom and the Sea of Galilee. The high tableland occupied by the tribes of Benjamin and Judah was not easy of access from the Maritime Plain. A way, however, led from the plain of Sharon and the Nahr el-'Aujah at Ras el-'Ain (Antipatris) s.e. into the hill country, and joined the road from Samaria to Jerusalem at a point 2 miles s.w. of Beth-el. From the seaport of Joppa a road led to Jerusalem by the valley of Aijalon and Beth-horon. From Ashdod the capital was most readily reached by Wadi eṣ-Ṣarār and Beth-shemesh; but a route to Jerusalem and also to Bethlehem was afforded by Wadi es-Sanṭ past Socoh.

Access to the hill country in the vicinity of Hebron was had through Wadi el-'Afranj by Beit Jibrin, and by Wadi el-Ḥasi by Tell el-Ḥasi.

6. *The meteorology of Palestine.* The great contrasts in physical features have given Palestine a remarkable range of climate, from the perpetual snow on Mount Hermon to the tropical heat of the Jordan Valley at Jericho and En-gedi. The average temperature at Jerusalem in January, which is the coldest month, is about 49.4° F., and the greatest cold 28°. In August the average is 79.3°, and the greatest heat is 92° in the shade. At Jericho the temperature in July is over 100° F., and it rises as high as 118° in August. See also YEAR.

7. *The botany of Palestine.* In consequence of the great diversity of surface and climate, the flora is extensive and plants of many latitudes flourish. Tristram showed that of 3,002 flowering plants and ferns known to exist in Palestine, a large number for so small a country, 2,563 are Palaearctic, and most of them belong to its Mediterranean section; 161 are Ethiopian, 27 Indian, and 251 peculiar. In the region which lies between the Taurus Mountains and the s. point of the peninsula of Sinai, and between the Mediterranean Sea and the Syrian desert, Dr. Post has found 850 genera and about 3,500 species.

8. *The zoology of Palestine.* The distribution of the several species of animals essentially agrees with that of the Palestinian plants. Of 113 mammalia known to occur in Palestine, Tristram found 55 to belong to the Palaearctic region, the same to which our European species belong; 34 were Ethiopian, 16 Indian, and 13 peculiar to the land. The same species sometimes belongs to 2 regions. Of 348 species of birds, 271 were Palaearctic, 40 Ethiopian, 7 Indian, and 30 peculiar. Of the 91 reptiles and amphibians, 49 were Palaearctic, 27 Ethiopian, 4 Indian, and 11 peculiar. Of 43 fresh-water fishes, 8 were Palaearctic, 2 Ethiopian, 7 Indian, and 26 peculiar. In the case of both plants and animals, the African and Indian types come chiefly from the lowlying region around the Dead Sea, and to a less extent from the low valley of the Jordan.

9. *The ethnology of Palestine.* The aboriginal inhabitants of Palestine were a tall, stalwart race, consisting of Anakim (Josh. 11:21, 22), Rephaim (Gen. 14:5), Emim, Zamzummim, and Horites (Deut. 2:10–23). Traces of the primitive population continued to exist as late as the time of the monarchy (II Sam. 21:16–22). When Abraham arrived, the country was occupied chiefly by the Amorites and other smaller tribes of Canaanites, but Philistines (an autochthonous group, not to be identified with those from Caphtor) and Phoenicians were settled on the seacoast and Hittites dwelt on the n. border and at Hebron. The Philistines came from the w., probably from Crete, about the 12th century B.C. The Canaanites, including the Phoenicians, spoke a Semitic language. These various peoples were conquered, but not utterly exterminated, by the Hebrews under the leadership of Moses and Joshua. The occasional introduction of Edomites, Ammonites, and Moabites by conquest and immigration did not bring a new strain into the blood, for these peoples were Semitic and like the Hebrews descended from Abraham. The conquest of Aramaean tribes, so far as it resulted in adding foreigners to the commonwealth of Israel, added Semites. After the fall of Samaria, the Assyrians deported the n. and e. tribes of the Israelites and introduced colonists from Hamath, Babylonia, and Elam (II Kings 17:24; Ezra 4:9). They were largely Semites and Aryans. A large immigration of Greeks followed in the wake of the conquest of Alexander the Great, colonized Ptolemaïs, built the Greek towns of the Decap-

olis, and introduced the Greek language, customs, and culture. Later, Roman officials and a Roman army of occupation were in the country, and ultimately Roman colonists came. Between A.D. 633 and 640 the country was subjugated by the Moslems. The decisive battle was fought at the Yarmūk (636); Jerusalem fell in 638. See JERUSALEM, III. 3. Since 1920 Palestine has been governed by Great Britain under a mandate from the League of Nations (approved July 24, 1922).

10. *The history of Palestine.* The early history of Palestine, before the arrival of Abraham, is involved in obscurity. The succession of races who inhabited the country may be gathered from the Hebrew records, as already pointed out. The kings of Babylonia early began their invasions of the w., and the campaign of Chedorlaomer in e. Palestine in the time of Abraham is described in Gen., ch. 14. The Babylonians impressed their culture, including the cuneiform script and their language as a medium of international communication, upon the inhabitants. After the expulsion of the Hyksos from the country of the Nile, the great Pharaohs of Dyn. XVIII extended their sway far into Asia. Thutmose (Thothmes) III conquered Canaan and exacted tribute from the nations dwelling as far as the Euphrates. During the reigns of Amenhotep (Amenophis) III and IV, who succeeded him after an interval, Canaan was garrisoned by Egyptian troops and governed by Egyptian officials. But in the latter reign the grasp of Egypt was evidently weakening. The Hittites were threatening the n. frontier, lawlessness prevailed in various parts of the land, travel was insecure, individual states were in a foment of discontent or in rebellion, and various tribes were extending their territory at the expense of Egypt. Under the succeeding dynasty Sethi I passed through Palestine and waged war with the Hittites on the Orontes; Ramesses II invaded Palestine, but in 1272 B.C. he made a treaty with the Hittites on terms of equality. There were revolts at the death of Ramesses II, but Merneptah once more pacified the country. For the Exodus, see EGYPT, III. 8. Under the leadership of Moses, the Israelites conquered the region e. of the Jordan; and in the following year, under Joshua, they crossed the river, and after repeated campaigns took possession of Canaan. From this time onward, until the fall of Jerusalem in the 1st century of the Christian era, the history of Palestine is largely the history of the Hebrew people. See HISTORY.

11. *The topography of Palestine.* As nearly as can be estimated, 622 towns w. of the Jordan are mentioned in the Bible and the Apocrypha. Of special importance for locating Palestinian places are the names of places recorded in the lists of Thutmose III, Sethi I, Ramesses II, and Sheshonk (Shishak) I at Karnak. They throw light on the topography of Palestine and The Book of Joshua. References to towns of Palestine in the time of Amenhotep (Amenophis) III and IV occur in the Tell el-Amarna letters. Later references are found in contemporary records of Assyria, especially in documents which relate to campaigns conducted in Palestine. Eusebius, bishop of Caesarea in the 1st half of the 4th century of the Christian era, wrote a tract concerning the names of places in the Scriptures. It was translated and enlarged by Jerome, resident at Bethlehem a century later. The work is commonly known as the Onomasticon of Eusebius and Jerome. The notices regarding the situation of ancient places in Palestine, according to the information possessed by the learned authors, are often valuable, sometimes absurd.

The information gathered by Reland and published by him in 1714, and the travels of Seetzen and Burckhardt, especially e. of the Jordan, in the beginning of the 19th century, prepared the way for the systematic, scientific investigation conducted by Dr. Robinson. He visited Palestine in 1838, accompanied by a former pupil of his, Rev. Eli Smith, American missionary at Beirut, who greatly aided the inquiry by his knowledge of Arabic. They found by asking the natives what certain ruins or yet inhabited villages were called, that they often bore the old Hebrew names in modified form in modern Arabic. Their discoveries in the topography of Palestine were very important, and were given to the world by Prof. Robinson in 1841 in 3 octavo volumes. Returning from America, Dr. Robinson resumed his researches in Palestine in 1852, accompanied again by Rev. Eli Smith and others. He made fresh discoveries, embodied in his *Later Biblical Researches,* 1856. Dr. Robinson brought to bear on his inquiry not merely keen observation and sound judgment, but great learning; and many of his conclusions have been accepted. In 1848 Lieut. William F. Lynch was commander of the United States expedition to explore the Jordan River and the Dead Sea.

On June 22, 1865, a society, named The Palestine Exploration Fund, was formed in England to prosecute in a scientific spirit all branches of inquiry regarding the Holy Land. Since then it has conducted an ordnance survey of a great part of Palestine, and constructed a superb map of the country in 26 sheets. This result is a permanent and splendid achievement. The society has also carried on various excavations.

In 1895 Prof. Thayer in his presidential address to the Society of Biblical Literature and Exegesis made an appeal for the establishment of an American School of Oriental Study and Research in Palestine. Within 5 years Dr. Charles C. Torrey, of Yale, went forth as the 1st director. In 1921 a similar school was founded at Baghdad. The 2 institutions are now incorporated under the name of the American Schools of Oriental Research. In its 1st year the Jerusalem school excavated some Phoenician tombs at Sidon, and since that time it has excavated various places in Palestine. The American Schools of Oriental Research have issued regularly a series of scholarly publications: *The Annual, The Bulletin,* and *The Biblical Archaeologist.*

Pal'lu (păl'ū), in A.V. once **Phal'lu** (Gen. 46:9) [distinguished]. A son of Reuben, and founder of a tribal family (Gen. 46:9; Ex. 6:14; Num. 26:5).

Palm. A tree, called in Heb. *tāmār* and *tomer,* and in Gr. *phoinix.* It is a tall tree (S. of Sol. 7:7, 8), straight and upright (Jer. 10:5). It is a fruit tree (Joel 1:12), and sufficiently ornamental to have been carved in various parts of Solomon's Temple and other sanctuaries (I Kings 6:29, 32, 35; Herod. ii. 169). Its great leaves were used as tokens of victory and peace (I Macc. 13:51; II Macc. 10:7; John 12:13; Rev. 7:9; imitated in II Esdras 2:43–47). These leaves are often popularly called branches; and this designation is employed in the Eng. versions (Lev. 23:40; Neh. 8:15; John 12:13), but is not botanically correct. Scarcely any palms have branches at all; and the date palm, the species grown in parts of Palestine, is not one of the few exceptions to the rule. The leaves are large and feathery, from 4 to 6 feet in length; they are quite accessible, as there are generally a number of young plants around the foot of the parent stem. Palm trees flourished on the banks of the Nile. They grew at Elim, in the wilderness near the Red Sea (Ex. 15:27), and in Edom (Virgil *Georg.* iii.

12). They grew in various parts of Judea, as in the valley of the Jordan, at Jericho, and En-gedi, and on the coast of the Sea of Galilee (Gen. 14:7, in the proper name; Deut. 34: 3; Ecclus. 24:14; Jos. *Antiq.* ix. 1, 2; *War* i. 6, 6; iii. 10, 8); in the s. of Judah (Josh. 15: 31, 49, in the names Sansannah and Kiriath-sannah, *q.v.;* in Mount Ephraim near Beth-el (Judg. 4:5; 20:33), near Jerusalem (Neh. 8: 15; John 12:13). They grew also in the desert e. of Damascus, at the town named from them, Tadmor, Tamar, and Palmyra. They flourished also in the lower valleys of the Tigris and Euphrates (Herod. i. 193). The tree was regarded by the Greeks and Romans as peculiarly characteristic of Palestine and the neighboring regions. Phoenicia took its name in Greek from the date palm; and the coin struck at Rome to commemorate the capture of Jerusalem represented a woman, emblem of the country, sitting disconsolate under a date palm. The tree which was once so

Date Palm

common has almost disappeared from Palestine, except in the Maritime Plain of Philistia and in the neighborhood of Beirut, but it is being cultivated anew near Jericho.

The palm tree in Scripture almost always means the date palm (*Phoenix dactylifera*), which grows about 60 or 80 feet high, having a single upright stem of uniform thickness through its entire length and marked by the scars of fallen leaves. The stem terminates above in a circle of great feathery leaves, perennially green. It is believed to attain a great age, from 100 to 200 years. The domestic uses of the palm are numerous. The leaves are employed for covering the roofs and sides of houses, for fences, mats, and baskets. When the tender part of the spathe is pierced, a sweet juice exudes, from which sugar is obtained by evaporation, and a strong drink called arrack by fermentation or distillation (Jos. *War* iv. 8, 3; Herod. i. 193). The fruit, which it produces annually in numerous clusters and great abundance, constitutes its chief value, being largely used as an article of food. Even the stony seeds are ground, and yield nourishment to the camel of the desert.

Palm'er Worm. The rendering of Heb. *gāzām,* devourer, an insect which devoured vines, fig trees, olive trees, and the produce of the gardens and fields generally (Joel 1: 4; 2:25; Amos 4:9). Probably a kind of locust, or a locust in a certain stage of its growth (Joel 1:4, R.V. marg.). When the A.V. was made, palmer worm denoted a sort of hairy caterpillar which has no fixed abode, but wanders like a palmer or pilgrim from place to place.

Pal'sy. A partial or total loss of sensibility, voluntary motion, or both, in 1 or more parts of the body (Mark 2:3, 9–12; Acts 9:33–35). It is produced by disease of the brain, the spinal cord, or particular nerves. Under this term the ancients included a variety of diseases affecting the muscles.

Pal'ti (păl'tī, in A.V. once **Phal'ti** (I Sam. 25:44) [abbreviation of Pelatiah]. 1. The representative spy from the tribe of Benjamin (Num. 13:9).
2. The man to whom Saul married Michal, David's wife, and from whom she was later wrested away and restored to David (I Sam. 25:44; II Sam. 3:15, where the unabbreviated form is used).

Pal'ti·el (păl'tī-ĕl), in A.V. once **Phal'ti·el** (II Sam. 3:15) [God has delivered]. 1. Prince of the tribe of Issachar and a contemporary of Moses (Num. 34:26).
2. The same as Palti 2 (II Sam. 3:15).

Pal'tite (păl'tīt). Probably one from Beth-pelet, a town in the extreme s. of Judah. To judge, however, from II Sam. 23:26 compared with I Chron. 27:10, the Paltites belonged to Ephraim. See PELONITE.

Pam·phyl'i·a (păm-fĭl'ĭ-á). A stretch of coast land in Asia Minor. It was bounded on the n. by Pisidia; on the s. by a gulf of the Mediterranean, called the sea of Pamphylia, across which Paul sailed (Acts 27:5); on the e. by Cilicia; and on the w. by Lycia. Pamphylia contained Jewish communities (ch. 2: 10). Its towns, Perga and Attalia, were visited by Paul on his First Missionary Journey (chs. 13:13; 14:24, 25; 15:38).

Pan'nag. A product of Palestine which the Tyrians purchased (Ezek. 27:17). The R.V., following the Jewish Targum, suggests that perhaps it was a kind of confection. In Akkadian *pannigu* is a kind of cake.

Pa'per. See PAPYRUS.

Pa'per Reed. Papyrus; the rendering in the A.V. of Heb. *'ārāh,* bare place (Isa. 19:7); see PAPYRUS. R.V. renders by "meadow."

Pa'phos (pā'fŏs). A town (modern Kuklia) at the s.w. extremity of Cyprus, near Cape Zephyrion. It was called Old Paphos to distinguish it from the newer seaport town about 10 miles to the n.w. New Paphos was the capital of the Roman province of Cyprus, and the residence of the proconsul. In its vicinity was a celebrated temple of the Cyprian Aphrodite (Homer *Odyssey* viii. 362). The town was visited by Paul (Acts 13:6–13). The modern name of New Paphos is Baffo.

Pa·py'rus [Lat. from Gr., probably from Egypt. *p¦pr-'¦,* that of the Pharaoh; meaning perhaps, the royal plant, or rather referring to the royal manufacture of writing material from the papyrus plant]. The rendering of Heb. *gōme';* a plant which grows in mire (Job 8:11, R.V. marg.; in Isa. 35:7 rendered rush), and of which the tiny ark of Moses (Ex. 2:3, R.V. marg.; in text, bulrushes) and also larger boats (Isa. 18:2, R.V.) were made. The plant referred to is the paper reed (*Papyrus antiquorum*). But the papyrus is not a grass, as the word reed might suggest; nor is it a rush. It is a giant sedge, with a triangular stock 8 or 10 feet high, terminating in a tuft of flowers. It grows in the plain of Sharon, near the Sea of Galilee, and in the waters of the Ḥûleh, commonly thought of as Merom; and it formerly flourished on the Nile, though now almost extinct upon that river. Its use was widespread (II Esdras 15:2; III Macc. 4:20). The Egyptians made shoes, baskets, boats, and other articles of it; and used sheets, formed of strips of the pith, as writing paper. On such material, called in Gr. *chartēs*, the Apostle John wrote his 2d Epistle (II John 12).

Of special importance for the Biblical student is the use of papyrus as writing material, which goes back in Egypt as far as the 3d millennium B.C., if not earlier. The pith of the papyrus plant was cut into thin strips, which were laid down in layers at right angles to one another so that the fibres were horizontal on one side and vertical on the other. In the finished product the side on which the fibres are horizontal is called the recto; the other, the verso. The 2 layers were fastened together by pressure and glue. In this way sheets were formed which could be attached to each other so as to form a roll. Some rolls are 15 inches high, but for literary work those of 10 inches were generally used. Some Egyptian liturgical rolls have a

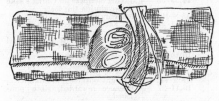

Papyrus Letter, Folded and Sealed

length of 50 feet and more, while one is known of 133 feet. From the early part of the 2d century the Christians began to use papyrus in the *codex* form (the ancestor of the modern book), with leaves arrayed in quires or gatherings. To produce these a sheet of papyrus was taken and folded in the middle.

To the dry climate and sands of Egypt we owe the preservation of many papyri. The Nash papyrus, now at Cambridge University, is a small Hebrew fragment of the 2d century B.C. Of the same century are the small Greek fragments of Deuteronomy in the John Rylands Library. Reputed sayings (logia) of our Lord recorded on papyri were found at Oxyrhynchus. A papyrus in the John Rylands Library, the oldest extant MS. of any part of the N.T., contains John 18:31-33, 37, 38 and can be confidently assigned to the 1st half of the 2d century. See John, Gospel According to. The Freer Greek MS. at Washington contains portions of the Minor Prophets. The Chester Beatty papyri include portions of the Greek O.T. and N.T. The John H. Scheide Biblical papyri (Ezek., chs. 19:12 to 39:29, with some losses, in Greek), dating from the late 2d or early 3d century A.D., are now deposited at Princeton University; they have been edited and published by A. C. Johnson, H. S. Gehman, and E. H. Kase. The Elephantine papyri are Aramaic documents of various kinds, mostly of the 5th century B.C., of a Jewish garrison colony at Elephantine and Syene, where it was stationed from the 6th century to c. 400 B.C. for defending the s. frontier of Egypt.

Par′a·ble. A method of speech in which moral or religious truth is illustrated from the analogy of common experience. The comparison may be expressed, as by the word like, or be implied. The limits between the parable and simile and metaphor are not well defined. Often there is scarcely any difference, except that the simile and metaphor are short and the parable comparatively long. "Ye are the light of the world" is a metaphor; "as a lamb before his shearer is dumb" is a simile; but "the kingdom of heaven is like unto leaven, which a woman took, and hid in three measures of meal, till it was all leavened," is a parable (Matt. 13:33). The parable has certain advantages. One is, that this means of conveying truth makes it adhere to the memory much more than a plain didactic statement would do. For instance, no didactic statement as to the willingness of our Lord to receive penitent sinners would have had an effect at all equal to that produced by the parable of the Prodigal Son (Luke 15:11–32). A 2d advantage in a parable is that when it is needful for a prophet or a preacher to censure a powerful personage, who will not allow himself to be directly found fault with, it is possible by a skillfully framed parable to make him not merely listen patiently, but condemn himself before he discovers that it is himself he is condemning. This was done with much skill by the Prophet Nathan when he went to reprove David for his great sin in the matter of Uriah the Hittite.

The following are the chief parables in the O.T.: the Trees Anointing a King (Judg. 9:8–20), the Ewe Lamb (II Sam. 12:1–14), the Widow, one of whose 2 sons slew the other (II Sam. 14:4–20), the Soldier, who let his captive escape (I Kings 20:35–42), the Thistle, which asked for the cedar's daughter as a wife for his son (II Kings 14:9–11), the Vineyard (Isa. 5:1–7), the Two Eagles and a Vine (Ezek. 17:1–10), the Lion's Whelps (Ezek. 19:1–9), Oholah and Oholibah (Ezek. 23:1–49), the Boiling Pot (Ezek. 24:1–14).

An important part of our Lord's teaching was by means of parables; and when Scripture parables are spoken of, generally those of Jesus are meant. Christ used the parabolic form of teaching at every period of his public ministry (Mark 3:23; Luke 6:39; 7:40–50), but there came a time when a distinct change took place and he gave a larger place to parables in his public instruction (Matt. 13:3; Mark 4:2). Two reasons are assigned why he adopted this method of teaching to such an extent. One given by Matthew is that it was prophesied (Matt. 13:34, 35; cf. Ps. 49:4; 78:2, 3). The other, emanating from our Lord, explains the former. He used parables because it was not given unto his auditors to know the mysteries of the Kingdom of heaven, since seeing they saw not and hearing they did not understand (Matt. 13:10–16). This statement of Jesus has been interpreted to mean that he clothed the truths of the Kingdom in images in order to make them more intelligible to his hearers and to impress them indelibly on their memory. But this was true of a certain class of hearers only and in many cases, even in respect to them, only after the parable had been explained. Jesus rather meant that his auditors generally were unprepared to hear and heartily believe the spiritual truths of the Kingdom; and while the time had come to teach these doctrines to his followers who were to carry on his work after his departure (Mark 4:33, 34), the truth was henceforth hidden from those who had heard without repentance, was cautiously uttered in the hearing of obdurate enemies who were watching to seize upon his words and employ them against him, and was veiled from the fickle multitude who would refuse to listen to his words if they perceived the full import of them (Mark 4:11, 12).

PARABLES OF OUR LORD

Parables	Matt.	Mark	Luke	General Teaching
I. RECORDED IN ONE GOSPEL ONLY				
The Tares.....................	13:24–30	....	....	Good and evil in life and judgment
The Hidden Treasure..........	13:44	....	....	Value of the gospel
The Pearl of Great Price......	13:45 *seq.*	....	....	Seeking and finding salvation
The Dragnet..................	13:47–50	....	....	The visible Church a mixed group
The Unmerciful Servant........	18:23–35	....	....	The injunction of forgiveness
The Laborers in the Vineyard...	20:1–16	....	....	Precedence or length of service no claim for priority in reward
The Two Sons.................	21:28–32	....	....	Insincerity and repentance
The Marriage of the King's Son.	22:2–14	....	....	Necessity of the robe of righteousness
The Ten Virgins..............	25:1–13	....	....	Spiritual preparation and careless security
The Talents..................	25:14–30	....	....	Profiting by opportunities and advantages
The Seed Growing Secretly.....	....	4:26–29	....	The law of growth in religion
The Absent Householder........	....	13:33–37	....	Watchfulness
The Two Debtors..............	....	....	7:41–43	Gratitude for pardon
The Good Samaritan...........	....	....	10:30–37	Neighborliness shown in active benevolence
The Importunate Friend.......	....	....	11:5–13	Perseverance in prayer and the results
The Rich Fool...............	....	....	12:16–21	Worldly-mindedness
Servants Watching...........	....	....	12:35–40	Watchfulness and expectancy of our Lord's return
The Faithful Steward.........	....	....	12:42–48	Conscientiousness in trust
The Barren Fig Tree..........	....	....	13:6–9	Unprofitableness under grace
The Great Supper............	....	....	14:16–24	Universality of the divine call
Building a Tower and a King Going to War..............	....	....	14:25–35	Making sacrifices for Christ's sake and counting the cost
The Lost Coin...............	....	....	15:8–10	Heavenly joy over penitence
The Prodigal Son............	....	....	15:11–32	The Father's welcome to the returning sinner
The Unjust Steward..........	....	....	16:1–13	Faithfulness to trust and spiritual aggressiveness
The Rich Man and Lazarus.....	....	....	16:19–31	Hopeless future of the unfaithful
Unprofitable Servants.........	....	....	17:7–10	God's claim on all our service
The Unrighteous Judge........	....	....	18:1–8	Power of persistent prayer
The Pharisee and the Publican.	....	....	18:9–14	Self-righteousness and humility
The Pounds..................	....	....	19:11–27	Diligence rewarded, sloth punished
II. RECORDED IN TWO GOSPELS.				
House on Rock and House on Sand, or the Two Builders ...	7:24–27	....	6:47–49	Wisdom and folly in laying a foundation of life
The Leaven..................	13:33	....	13:20 *seq.*	Transforming power of Christianity
The Lost Sheep..............	18:12–14	....	15:3–7	Heavenly joy over penitence
III. RECORDED IN THREE GOSPELS.				
Candle Under a Bushel........	5:14–16	4:21 *seq.*	8:16 *seq.* 11:33–36	Dissemination of the truth by radiant living
New Cloth on Old Garment....	9:16	2:21	5:36	New teaching cannot simply patch up old customs or beliefs
New Wine in Old Bottles.......	9:17	2:22	5:37 *seq.*	Outworn customs incompatible with new life
The Sower..................	13:3–23	4:2–20	8:4–15	Various classes of hearers
The Mustard Seed............	13:31 *seq.*	4:30–32	13:18 *seq.*	Growth of the Kingdom of God
The Wicked Husbandmen......	21:33–45	12:1–12	20:9–19	Rejection of Christ by his people
The Fig Tree (and all the trees)	24:32–44	13:28–32	21:29–33	Signs of our Lord's return

H.S.G.

In interpreting the parables, rigid inquiry should be made into the circumstances under which each was delivered at first, and the doctrine or argument it was intended primarily to convey. This done, it is at once seen that the teaching of the parable is of universal application, suited for all analogous circumstances and for all succeeding time.

Par'a·clete (păr'a̍-klēt) [Gr. *paraklētos,* counsel for defense, advocate, intercessor]. The word occurs in R.V. in the marg. of John 14:16, 26; 15:26; 16:7, where helper or advocate is given as the English equivalent. In the text of these passages the translation is comforter, but in I John 2:1 it is advocate. It is applied to:

1. The Lord Jesus Christ. He was the advocate, by implication in John 14:16, who guided, counseled, and strengthened the disciples while he was present with them, and he is now the Christian's advocate with the Father, and pleads the believer's cause with

God (I John 2:1) as he did while on earth (Luke 22:31, 32; John, ch. 17).

2. The Holy Spirit, who is Christ's advocate with the believer, glorifying Christ and declaring him (John 15:26; 16:14), vindicating him from man's unworthy thoughts, and exhibiting him as man's great need; and he is the Spirit of truth, who teaches the believer and guides him into the truth (chs. 15:26; 16:13, 14), convicting of sin, righteousness, and judgment (v. 8), who teaches to pray and makes intercession with groanings that cannot be uttered (Rom. 8:26, 27).

Par'a·dise (păr'a̍-dīs) [Lat. *paradisus,* Gr. *paradeisos* (park, pleasure ground), from Avestan *pairi-daēza* (enclosure)]. A pleasure ground, orchard, or park, in Heb. *pardēs* (Eccl. 2:5; S. of Sol. 4:13, R.V. marg.; in Neh. 2:8 rendered forest). Solomon's gardens at Etham and the hanging gardens in Babylon are called paradises in the Gr. text of Josephus (*Antiq.* viii. 7, 3; *Apion* i. 20), and the garden of Eden is called a paradise in Eden in the LXX (Gen. 2:8).

Paradise was the region of bliss which man had lost, and it naturally came to be a designation for the place of the righteous dead. The later Jews distinguished between a supernal and an infernal paradise, the former being a part of heaven, the latter a division of Hades assigned to the souls of the just.

In the N.T. paradise means heaven in 2 instances (II Cor. 12:4; cf. v. 2; Rev. 2:7; cf. 22:2); see HEAVEN. Accordingly it naturally denotes heaven in the remaining instance (Luke 23:43).

Pa′rah (pā′rá) [heifer, young cow]. A village of Benjamin (Josh. 18:23), identified with the ruins Fārah in Wadi Fārah, 5½ miles n.e. of Jerusalem.

Pa′ran (pā′răn). A wilderness between Mount Sinai, or more exactly between Hazeroth, several days' march from Sinai, and Canaan (Num. 10:12; 12:16). It was on the s. of Judah (I Sam. 25:1–5). Kadesh was situated in it (Num. 13:26), and apparently also Elath on the Red Sea (Gen. 14:6; see EL-PARAN). It lay e. of the wildernesses of Beersheba and Shur (Gen. 21:14, 21; cf. chs. 25:9, 12–18; 28:9). It included the wilderness of Zin, or insensibly merged itself in it without a sharply defined boundary (cf. Num. 13:26 with ch. 20:1). These data indicate the plateau or mountain land (Deut. 33:2; Hab. 3:3), lying s. of Canaan, and bounded on the other sides by the wilderness of Shur, the curved range of mountains known as Jebel et-Tīh, and the Arabah. It is the wilderness where the Israelites wandered 38 years. Most of it is from 2,000 to 2,500 feet above sea level. There is a wadi, or valley, in the Sinaitic Peninsula, called Wadi Feiran, which looks very much like Paran altered. Niebuhr thought that they might be identified; but it is so difficult to harmonize the Scripture location of the place with this view that Robinson, Stanley, and most inquirers decline to accept the identification. Wadi Feiran is between Mount Sinai and the Red Sea. Paran is not reached till after the departure from Sinai in the opposite direction.

Par′bar (pär′bär) [probably, colonnade]. A precinct on the w. side of the outer court of the Temple (I Chron. 26:18). It contained chambers for officials and stalls for cattle (II Kings 23:11, where the pl. is rendered "suburbs" and "precincts").

Parched Corn. Roasted grain used as food (Lev. 23:14; Ruth 2:14; I Sam. 17:17). Thomson describes the method of preparing it. A number of the best ears of grain, not too ripe, are plucked, with the stalks attached. They are tied in small parcels and a blazing fire of dry grass and thorn bushes is kindled under them, which burns off the chaff and roasts the grain.

Parch′ment. The skin of sheep or goats prepared for use as a writing material or for other purposes. The skin is first soaked in lime to remove the hair, and is then shaved, washed, dried, stretched, and smoothed. Herodotus relates that the ancient Ionians used the skins of goats and sheep because of the scarcity of papyrus (Herod. v. 58). In Herodotus' own time papyrus was the common writing material. According to tradition parchment was 1st obtained at Pergamum; and when Ptolemy forbade the export of papyrus, Eumenes II, king of Pergamum (197–160/159 B.C.), adopted parchment for the books of his great library, and such skins became known as *chartae pergamenae*, whence the word parchment is derived. Some documents on vellum or parchment, however, were found in 1923 at Dura on the Euphrates,

which bear dates equivalent to 196–195 and 190–189 B.C.; thus we know that the material was also in use at a place far distant from Pergamum. In the time of Josephus and earlier, parchment was used by the Jews for the MSS. of their sacred writings (Jos. *Antiq.* xii. 2, 11); and it was a provision of the Talmud that the Law should be written on the skins of clean animals, tame or wild, and even of clean birds. Papyrus was a common writing material (II John 12, paper), but Paul refers to parchments of his, about which he is especially solicitous (II Tim. 4:13).

Par′ents. The Fifth Commandment inculcates upon children the duty of reverencing their parents and attaches a promise to its fulfillment (Ex. 20:12; Deut. 5:16; Eph. 6:1, 2). Upon the parents rests the obligation of bringing up the children in the fear of the Lord, and not provoking them to wrath (Gen. 18:19; Deut. 6:7; Eph. 6:4). According to the Mosaic Law, a son that smote father or mother, or cursed them, was punished with death (Ex. 21:15, 17; Lev. 20:9; Deut. 27:16); and as an extreme measure, parents were enjoined to bring a stubborn and rebellious son before the elders for trial and execution (Deut. 21:18–21). The Mosaic Law thus regulated the power of parents. According to Roman law, as set forth in the 12 tables, the life and liberty of children were in the father's hands. In Hebrew law the right of life and death did not rest with the parents, but was vested in the judicial body. Custom permitted an impoverished parent to sell a daughter to be a maidservant, but the Mosaic Law carefully guarded her rights (Ex. 21:7–11). Israelitish custom further permitted a creditor to seize a bankrupt debtor and enslave his wife and children (II Kings 4:1; Neh. 5:5; Isa. 50:1; Matt. 18:25); and in cases of grave sin the entire family was involved in the extermination of the offender (Josh. 7:24).

Par′lor. Eglon's summer parlor was an upper chamber exposed to the cool breezes (Judg. 3:20, cf. A.V. and R.V.). See HOUSE.

Par·mash′ta (pär-mäsh′tá) [Old Pers., the very first]. A son of Haman (Esth. 9:9).

Par′me·nas (pär′mē-năs) [Gr., probably, steadfast]. One of the 7 men elected to look after the Greek-speaking widows and, apparently, the poor and financial affairs generally in the Apostolic Church (Acts 6:5).

Par′nach (pär′năk). A Zebulunite (Num. 34:25).

Pa′rosh (pā′rŏsh), in A.V. once **Pha′rosh** (Ezra 8:3) [a flea]. Founder of a family, members of which returned from the Babylonian Captivity (Ezra 2:3; 8:3). One of the clan was called Pedaiah (Neh. 3:25). Other members of it married foreign wives, whom Ezra induced them to put away (Ezra 10:25).

Par′shan·da′tha (pär′shăn-dā′thá) [Old Pers., given to questions, inquisitive]. A son of Haman (Esth. 9:7).

Par′thi·ans (pär′thĭ-ănz). A people who, when first heard of, occupied a region nearly corresponding to the modern Persian province of Khorasan, a considerable distance s.e. of the Caspian Sea. The length of Parthia proper was about 300 miles, its breadth from 100 to 120, its area about 33,000 square miles, or slightly more than that of Scotland and nearly that of Indiana. The first mention of the Parthians is in the inscriptions of Darius Hystaspis. They revolted against the Persians, 521 B.C., but were soon subdued again. From the Persians they passed to Alexander the Great, and then to his e. successors, the Seleucidae. About 255 B.C. Bactria successfully revolted against Seleucidan domination, and Parthia, under Arsaces I, immediately followed the example. His successors are generally known as the Arsacidae; the year 247 B.C. marks the era of Parthia, the year of its independence. Mithridates I, who reigned from c. 174 to c. 138 B.C., raised the kingdom founded by Arsaces into an empire, stretching 1,500 miles from c. to w., with a varying breadth from n. to s. of 100, 300, or 400 miles. It extended from the Caspian Sea to the Persian Gulf. The w. boundary was the Euphrates. The chief city was Ctesiphon on the Tigris, opposite Seleucia. After ridding themselves of the Macedonian-Greek domination, the Parthians came into frequent collision with the Romans, one standing bone of contention between them being the possession of Armenia. From 64 B.C. to A.D. 226 they set limits to the Roman Empire in the East. In 40–37 B.C. their armies overran Asia Minor and Syria, took and plundered Jerusalem, and placed Antigonus, the last of the Hasmonaeans, on the throne (Jos. *Antiq.* xiv. 13, 3; *War* i. 13, 1). Jews from Parthia were present at Jerusalem on the Day of Pentecost (Acts 2:9), and may have carried the gospel to Parthia when they returned home. After wielding power for nearly 500 years, the Parthians became enervated by luxury, and the Persians, under the leadership of Ardashir, family of Sassan, terminated the Parthian dominion, substituting the 2d Persian or Sassanian empire in its stead (A.D. 226). See PERSIA.

Par′tridge. A wild bird, called in Heb. *ḳōrē′*, the crier or caller, in Gr. *perdix*, which was hunted on the mountains of Palestine (I Sam. 26:20). The caged partridge was used as a decoy bird (Ecclus. 11:30). Jeremiah compares the amasser of ill-gotten wealth to the partridge which, according to the belief of the Israelites of his time, gathers young which it has not brought forth, or sits on eggs which it has not laid (Jer. 17:11, R.V. text and marg.). Two species are found in Palestine, the desert or Hey's sand partridge (*Ammoperdix heyi*), which is the only species at

Partridge

En-gedi, in the wilderness where David was when he compared himself to a hunted partridge; and the chukar partridge (*Caccabis chukar*), which is abundant in all the hilly parts of Palestine. It has richly barred feathers on the flanks, deep red legs and bill, and deep black gorget. It is a large and fine bird, a variety of the Greek partridge (*Caccabis saxatilis*), but larger, and it exceeds the chukar partridge of India in size.

Pa·ru′ah (pȧ-rōō′ȧ) [sprouting, blooming]. The father of Solomon's purveyor in Issachar (I Kings 4:17).

Par·va′im (pär-vā′ĭm). The place from which came gold for the ornamentation of Solomon's Temple (II Chron. 3:6). Glaser identified it with Sǎk el-Farwain near Jebel Shammar in e. Arabia.

Pa′sach (pā′sȧk) [perhaps Aram., divider]. An Asherite, of the family of Beriah (I Chron. 7:33).

Pas′-dam′mim (pǎs′dăm′ĭm). See EPHES-DAMMIM.

Pa·se′ah (pȧ-sē′ȧ), in A.V. once **Pha·se′ah** (Neh. 7:51) [lame, halting]. 1. A man of Judah, descended from Chelub (I Chron. 4:12).
2. The father of a certain Jehoiada, who repaired the old gate of Jerusalem (Neh. 3:6). He was the founder of a family of Nethinim, members of which returned from captivity (Ezra 2:49; Neh. 7:51).

Pash′hur (păsh′hĕr), in A.V. **Pash′ur.** (păsh′ĕr) [perhaps Egypt., portion of Horus]. 1. Son of Malchijah, and one of several officials who had influence with King Zedekiah and bitterly opposed the Prophet Jeremiah (Jer. 21:1; 38:1, 4; cf. ch. 21:9 with ch. 38:2). It is natural to suppose that his father is the Malchijah mentioned in ch. 38:6, a royal prince into whose dungeon the prophet was cast. His identity with the priest Pashhur, the son of Malchijah (I Chron. 9:12) is doubtful; especially since to his companion, but not to him, is given the priestly title (Jer. 21:1).
2. A son of Immer, a priest. He put Jeremiah in the stocks on account of his discouraging predictions (Jer. 20:1–6).
3. The father of an opponent of Jeremiah named Gedaliah (Jer. 38:1).
4. The founder of a priestly family, members of which returned from the Babylonian Captivity (Ezra 2:38; Neh. 7:41, and perhaps I Chron. 9:12). Some of his descendants married foreign wives, whom Ezra induced them to put away (Ezra 10:22).
5. A priest, doubtless head of a father's house, who, with others, sealed the covenant, made in the days of Nehemiah, by which it was agreed to forbid the intermarriage of their children with foreigners and to keep the Law of God (Neh. 10:3).

Pas′sa·ges, The. See ABARIM.

Pas′sion [Lat., *passio*, suffering]. The expression, "After his passion" (Acts 1:3), is a paraphrase of the Gr., "After he had suffered"; it is based on the Vulgate *post passionem suam*, and in Eng. goes back to Wycliffe. In this sense the term denotes the sufferings of Christ upon the cross, but more specifically it is applied to his sufferings subsequent to the Last Supper. Sometimes it is distinguished from those of the crucifixion, as in the Litany in *The Book of Common Prayer:* "By thy Cross and Passion." More properly the Passion of Christ includes his sufferings beginning with his agony in the Garden of Gethsemane and ending with his death upon the cross.

Pass′o′ver (pȧs′ō′vẽr) [Heb. *pesaḥ* from *pāsaḥ* (to pass over, in sense of sparing); cf. Ex. 12:13, 23, 27; Isa. 31:5]. 1. The 1st of the 3 annual festivals at which all the men were required to appear at the sanctuary (Ex. 12:43; Deut. 16:1), known also as the feast of unleavened bread (Ex. 23:15; Deut. 16:16). It was instituted in Egypt to commemorate the culminating event in the redemption of the Israelites (Ex. 12:1, 14, 42; 23:15; Deut. 16:1, 3). That night was to be much observed unto the Lord, when he smote all the firstborn in the land of Egypt, but passed over the houses of the Israelites where the blood had been sprinkled and the inmates were standing, staff in hand, awaiting the deliverance promised by the Lord. The festival began on the 14th of Abib at evening, that is, in the beginning of the 15th day, with the sacrificial meal (Lev. 23:5 *seq.*). A lamb or kid was slain between the evenings, that is, toward sunset (Ex. 12:6; Deut. 16:6; cf. between the 9th and 11th hours, Jos. *War* vi. 9, 3). It was roasted whole, and was eaten with unleavened bread and bitter herbs (Ex. 12:8). The shed blood denoted expiation, the bitter herbs symbolized the bitterness of Egyptian bondage, the unleavened bread was an emblem of purity (cf. Lev. 2:11; I Cor. 5:7, 8). The Israelites pleading the blood, mindful of the afflictions from which they awaited deliverance, and putting away wickedness, were the people of the Lord in holy, glad communion before him. The supper was partaken of by the members of every household. If the family was small, neighbors joined until the company was large enough to consume the entire lamb (Ex. 12:4). The head of the household recited the history of the redemption.

At the first institution the participants stood; in later times they reclined. Other minor features were introduced: 4 successive cups of wine mixed with water, to which there is no reference in the Law; singing of Psalms 113 to 118 (cf. Isa. 30:29; Ps. 42:4); a dish of fruits reduced with vinegar to the consistency of lime as a reminder of the mortar used during the Egyptian bondage. The paschal supper was the introductory ceremony and chief feature of the festival, which lasted until the 21st day of the month (Ex. 12:18; Lev. 23:5, 6; Deut. 16:6, 7). That the event was to be commemorated by a festival of 7 days' duration (Ex. 12:14-20) was not communicated to the people until the day of the flight (ch. 13:3-10). They were directed regarding 1 evening only (eh. 12:21-23), and informed that the service was to be kept perpetually (vs. 24, 25). The attendance of the pilgrims was required at the supper only. They were at liberty to depart on the morrow (Deut. 16:7).

The 1st day, that is the 15th, was kept as a Sabbath and likewise the 7th; no work was done and there was a holy convocation (Ex. 12:16; Lev. 23:7; Num. 28:18, 25, of which only the last is emphasized in Ex. 13:6; Deut. 16:8). On the morrow after the Sabbath, that is, on the 2d day of the festival, a sheaf of the first-ripe barley was waved by the priest before the Lord to consecrate the opening harvest (Lev. 23:10-14; cf. Josh. 5:10-12, R.V.; LXX of Lev. 23:7, 11; Jos. *Antiq.* iii. 10, 5); see WEEKS, FEAST OF. This was an incidental feature: the act consecrated the opening harvest, but it held a subordinate place; the 2d day, when it was performed, was not observed as a Sabbath; and altogether the relation of the passover to the agricultural year was less marked than in the festivals of weeks and tabernacles. During the passover day by day continually, in addition to the regular sacrifices of the sanctuary, 2 bullocks, 1 ram, and 7 lambs were offered as a burnt offering, and a he-goat as a sin offering (Lev. 23:8; Num. 28:19-23). During the 7 days also unleavened bread was eaten. The people had no leaven in their houses the night of the passover, and consequently the dough that they seized in their hurried flight was unleavened (Ex. 12:8, 34, 39). It was baked thus. Henceforth unleavened bread was associated in their minds, not only with the thought of sincerity and truth, which was the essential idea, but also with that of the hurried flight from Egypt (Deut. 16:3). It appears that originally the passover and the feast of unleavened bread were 2 distinct festivals: probably they were combined through their contiguity of time. The feast of unleavened bread is an agricultural festival, falling into line with the feasts of Pentecost and tabernacles.

Celebrations of the passover are recorded at Sinai (Num. 9:1-14), on entering Canaan (Josh. 5:11), under Hezekiah (II Chron. 30:1-27; with reference to Solomon in vs. 5, 26), under Josiah (II Kings 23:21-23; II Chron. 35:1-19), in the days of Ezra (Ezra 6:19-22). See also Matt. 26:17 *seq.;* Mark 14:12 *seq.;* Luke 22:7 *seq.;* John 18:28; Jos. *Antiq.* xvii. 9, 3; xx. 5, 3; *War* vi. 9, 3.

2. The lamb or kid killed at the festival of the passover (Ex. 12:21; Deut. 16:2; II Chron. 30:17). Christ is our passover (I Cor. 5:7). Like the paschal lamb, he was without blemish (cf. Ex. 12:5 with I Peter 1:18, 19), not a bone was broken (cf. Ex. 12:46 with John 19:36), his blood was a token before God (Ex. 12:13), and the feast was eaten with unleavened bread (cf. Ex. 12:18 and I Cor. 5:8).

Pat'a·ra (păt'à-rà). A maritime city of s.w. Lycia. Paul took ship there for Phoenicia on his last voyage to Palestine (Acts 21:1). It possessed a famous oracle of Apollo.

Path'ros (păth'rŏs) [Egypt., Southland]. The country of s. or Upper Egypt. It is mentioned between Egypt and Cush (Isa. 11:11). It was the original seat of the Egyptians themselves (Ezek. 29:14); and the 1st historical king of Egypt, Menes, is reported to have resided in Upper Egypt, in whose time all the lower country n. of Lake Moeris was a swamp (Herod. ii. 4, 15, 99). Isaiah foretold the dispersion of Israel to the remotest regions and their eventual return, among other places from Pathros (Isa. 11:11; cf. ch. 7:18). After the capture of Jerusalem by Nebuchadnezzar, Jews, probably refugees, were dwellers in Pathros (Jer. 44:1, 2, 15).

Path·ru'sim (păth-rōō'sĭm). One of 7 peoples proceeding from Mizraim. They are the inhabitants of Pathros (Gen. 10:14; I Chron. 1:12).

Pat'mos (păt'mŏs). An island to which the Apostle John was banished for the word of God, and for the testimony of Jesus Christ, and where he saw the visions recorded in the book of Revelation (Rev. 1:9). It is a small, rocky island, one of the Sporades, in the Greek Archipelago, and is now called Patino. It lies off the s.w. coast of Asia Minor, about 30 miles s. of Samos; and is about 10 miles long and 6 wide, and generally barren.

Pa'tri·arch [Gr., the father or head of a family, tribe, or race]. The father or chief of a race; a name given in the N.T. to the founders of the Hebrew race and nation. It is applied to Abraham (Heb. 7:4), to the 12 sons of Jacob (Acts 7:8, 9), and to King David (Acts 2:29). The title is commonly given to the godly men and heads of families, whose lives are recorded in the O.T. previous to the time of Moses, as the antediluvian patriarchs whose lineage is given in Gen., ch. 5. In the patriarchal system the government of a clan is regarded as the paternal right. It resides in the 1st instance in the progenitor of the tribe, and descends from him to the first-born son or eldest lineal male descendant. The head of each several family, into which the increasing tribe expands, exercises a similar government within his own limited sphere.

The patriarchal dispensation was the period before the establishment of the theocracy at Sinai, when each patriarchal head of a family was the priest of his own household, and God communed with him as such.

Pat'ro·bas (păt'rŏ-bàs). A Christian at Rome, to whom Paul sent salutations (Rom. 16:14).

Pa'u (pā'ù) [groaning, bleating]. A town of Edom, the city of King Hadar (Gen. 36:39).

Called in I Chron. 1:50 Pai, *waw* or *vau* (w) and *yodh* or *jod* (y) being interchanged.

Paul (pôl) [Gr., *Paulos,* from Lat. *Paulus,* little].

1. *Name and family.* The great apostle to the Gentiles. His Jewish name was Saul (Heb. *Shā'ūl,* Gr. *Saulos*). He is so called in The Acts until after the account of the conversion of Sergius Paulus, proconsul of Cyprus, from which point in the narrative (Acts 13:9) the name Paul alone is given him. In his epistles the apostle always calls himself Paul. It is not strange that some have supposed that he took the name Paul from the proconsul. But this is in reality quite improbable in itself and fails to observe the delicacy with which Luke introduces the apostle's Gentile name when his work among the Gentiles, by whom he was known as Paul, began. It is more probable that, like many Jews (Acts 1:23; 12:12; Col. 4:11), and especially in the Dispersion, the apostle had from the beginning both names. He was born in Tarsus, the chief city of Cilicia (Acts 9:11; 21:39; 22:3), and was of the tribe of Benjamin (Phil. 3:5). It is not known how the family came to reside in Tarsus, though 1 ancient tradition represents it as having removed there from Gischala in Galilee after the latter place had been captured by the Romans. It is possible, however, that the family had at an earlier time formed part of a colony settled in Tarsus by one of the Syrian kings, or they may have voluntarily migrated, as so many Jews did, for commercial purposes. Paul seems, however, to have had a large and even influential family connection. In Rom. 16:7, 11 he salutes 3 persons as his kinsmen, 2 of whom, Andronicus and Junias (R.V.), are said to have been "of note among the apostles," and to have become Christians before Paul did. From Acts 23:16 we learn that his "sister's son," who seems to have resided, perhaps with his mother, in Jerusalem, gave information to the chief captain of the plot to kill Paul, from which it may be inferred that the young man was connected with some of the leading families. This is also confirmed by the prominence of Paul, though himself a young man, at the time of Stephen's death. He was apparently already a member of the council (Acts 26:10), and soon afterward the high priest entrusted to him the work of persecuting the Christians (chs. 9:1, 2; 22:5). His language in Phil. 3:4–7 further implies that he occupied originally a position of large influence, and that opportunities of honor and gain had been open to him. His family connections, therefore, cannot have been obscure. Though he was brought up in the strict observance of the Hebrew faith and traditions, his father having been a Pharisee (Acts 23:6), he was born a free Roman citizen. We do not know by what means his ancestor obtained citizenship. It may have been for service to the state or possibly by purchase. Its possession may have had some connection with the apostle's Roman name Paulus. But, however acquired, his Roman citizenship became of great importance in the prosecution of his Christian work and more than once saved his life.

2. *Education.* Tarsus was one of the intellectual centers of the East, and the seat of a famous school of learning in which Stoicism was the dominant philosophy. It is scarcely probable, however, that Paul came under these influences when a boy, for his parents were strict Jews, and he was early sent to Jerusalem to be educated. Like other Jewish boys he was taught a trade, which in his case was the manufacture of tents, such as were used by travelers (Acts 18:3). But, as he himself says (ch. 22:3), he was brought up in Jerusalem. He must, therefore, have been sent there when quite young. And his education in Jerusalem tended to deepen the hold upon him of his inherited Pharisaic traditions. He was instructed "according to the strict manner of the law of our fathers" (*ibid.*). He had for his teacher one of the most learned and distinguished rabbis of the day, Gamaliel, who was the grandson of the famous Hillel. It was this Gamaliel whose speech, recorded in Acts 5:34–39, prevented the sanhedrin from attempting to slay the apostles. Gamaliel, indeed, had some leaning toward Greek culture, and his speech in The Acts shows the reverse of a bitter, persecuting spirit. But he was famous for rabbinical learning, and at his feet the young man from Tarsus became versed not only in the teaching of the O.T., but in the subtleties of rabbinical interpretation, while it is plain also that his zeal for the traditions of the fathers and his narrow Pharisaism burned with the fiery intensity of youth. Thus the future apostle grew up an ardent Pharisee, trained in the religious and intellectual ideas of his people, and from his personal qualities, and probably his family connections prepared to take a high position among his countrymen.

3. *Persecution of Christians.* He first appears in Christian history as the man at whose feet the witnesses who stoned Stephen laid their garments (Acts 7:58). He is described as being then a young man. The position he is here said to have occupied was not an official one. It seems to imply, however, especially when taken with the statement (Acts 8:1) that he "was consenting unto his death," that Paul was active in the persecution of the 1st Christian martyr. He was doubtless 1 of the Hellenists, or Greek-speaking Jews, mentioned in Acts 6:9 as the original instigators of the charge against Stephen. We cannot be wrong in supposing that Paul's hatred of the new sect had already been aroused; that he not only despised their crucified Messiah, but regarded them as being both politically and religiously dangerous; and that he was already prepared, with bitter but conscientious fanaticism, to oppose them to the death. So we find him, immediately after Stephen's death, taking a leading part in the persecution of the Christians which followed (Acts 8:3; 22:4; 26:10, 11; I Cor. 15:9; Gal. 1:13; Phil. 3:6; I Tim. 1:13). He did this with the fierceness of a misguided conscience. He was the type of the religious inquisitor. Not content with waging the persecution in Jerusalem, he asked of the high priest letters to the synagogues in Damascus that he might bring from there any Christian Jews whom he might find (Acts 9:1, 2). Large powers of internal administration were granted to the Jews even by the Romans, and in Damascus, which was under the control of Aretas, king of the Nabateans, the governor was particularly favorable to them (Acts 9:23, 24; II Cor. 11:32), so that Paul's persecution of the Christians is not in the least incredible. The important thing to observe, however, is that according to the express testimony of Luke and of Paul himself, he was filled with fury against them up to the very moment of his conversion, and believed that in persecuting them he was rendering the highest service to God.

4. *Conversion.* It was on the way to Damascus that his sudden conversion occurred (Acts 9:1–19). Paul and his companions, probably on horseback, had been following the usual road across the desert from Galilee to the ancient city. Damascus had been nearly reached. It was the hour of noon and the sun was blazing in the zenith (Acts 26:13). Sud-

454

denly a light from heaven, brighter than the sun, streamed round about them, and, overcome by its blinding brilliance, Paul fell upon the ground. His companions, too, fell to the ground (v. 14), though they appear afterward to have arisen while he remained prostrate (ch. 9:7). Out of the light he heard a voice, saying in the Hebrew language: "Saul, Saul, why persecutest thou me? it is hard for thee to kick against the goad" (ch. 26:14, R.V.). He replied: "Who art thou, Lord?" He heard in answer: "I am Jesus whom thou persecutest" (v. 15). "Arise, and go into the city, and it shall be told thee what thou must do" (chs. 9:6; 22:10). His companions heard the sound of the voice (ch. 9:7), but did not understand what was said (ch. 22:9). Paul, however, was found to be blinded by the light, so they led him by the hand into Damascus, where he lodged in the house of a certain Judas (ch. 9:11). For 3 days he remained blind and fasting, praying (vs. 9, 11) and meditating on the revelation which had been made to him. On the 3d day the Lord commanded a certain Jewish Christian, named Ananias, to go to Paul and lay his hands on him that he might receive his sight. The Lord assured Ananias, who was afraid of the persecutor, that the latter had already seen him in a vision coming to him. Thereupon Ananias obeyed. Paul confessed his faith in Jesus, received his sight, accepted baptism, and forthwith, with his characteristic energy and to the astonishment of the Jews, began to preach in the synagogues that Jesus was the Christ, the Son of God (ch. 9:10–22).

Such is the narrative of the conversion of Saul of Tarsus. Three recitals of it are given in The Acts; one by Luke (ch. 9:3–22); one by Paul himself before the Jews (ch. 22:1–16); again by Paul before Festus and Agrippa (ch. 26:1–20). The 3 accounts entirely agree, though in each of them particulars are dwelt on that are not found in the others. The story in each case is told with special regard to the purpose of the narrator. Paul in his epistles also frequently alludes to his conversion, attributing it to the grace and power of God, though he does not describe it in detail (I Cor. 9:1, 16; 15:8–10; Gal. 1:12–16; Eph. 3:1–8; Phil. 3:5–7; I Tim. 1:12–16; II Tim. 1:9–11). The fact, therefore, is supported by the strongest possible testimony. It is certain also that Jesus not only spoke to Paul but visibly appeared to him (Acts 9:17, 27; 22:14; 26:16; I Cor. 9:1). While the form in which he appeared is not described, we may be sure that it was a glorious one; so that Paul realized at once that the crucified Jesus was the exalted Son of God. He himself describes it as "the heavenly vision" (Acts 26:19), or spectacle, a word used in Luke 1:22 and 24:23 to describe the manifestation of angelic beings. There is no ground, therefore, for the allegation that it was an illusion of any kind. At the same time the mere appearance of Christ did not convert Paul. This was the work of the Spirit in his heart, enabling him to apprehend and accept the truth which had been revealed to him (see especially Gal. 1:15 seq.). Ananias also was evidently made use of in order to connect Paul's new life with the already existing Church.

The various rationalistic attempts that have been made to explain Paul's conversion without acknowledgment of the objective and supernatural interposition of the Lord are wrecked upon the testimony of Paul himself, that he had thought up to the time of his conversion that it was his religious duty to persecute Christianity, and that his change was due to the sovereign exercise of God's power and grace. The expression, "It is hard for thee to kick against the goad," does not imply that he had been an unwilling persecutor or that he already believed that Christianity might be true, but describes the folly of any resistance to the purpose of God. At the same time his previous history had been an unconscious preparation for his future work. His Roman citizenship, his rabbinical training, as well as his natural qualities of mind fitted him for his life task. There is reason to believe also that with all his zeal he had not found spiritual peace in Judaism (Rom. 7:7–25). If so, the manner of his conversion must have made him realize vividly that salvation is alone through the grace of God in Christ. His religious experience, therefore, was also part of his preparation to become the great expounder of the gospel as providing justification for the sinner on the ground of Christ's merits received through faith alone.

As soon as he was converted Paul began evangelistic work. This was partly due to his natural energy, but also to the fact that it had been revealed to him that God's purpose in calling him was to make him a missionary and apostle (Acts 9:15; 26:16–20; Gal. 1:15, 16). He began work in the synagogues of Damascus and pursued it with success. This raised against him persecution from the Damascene Jews, who were aided by the governor of the city; so that he was compelled to flee secretly, being let down by his disciples in a basket from a window in the city wall (Acts 9:23–25; II Cor. 11:32, 33). Instead of returning to Jerusalem, however, he went to Arabia and afterward returned to Damascus (Gal. 1:17). We do not know where he went in Arabia, nor how long he stayed, nor what he did there. It is not improbable that the time was mainly spent in meditation upon the great change which had come over his life and the truth as it had now been revealed to him. But 3 years after his conversion he determined to leave Damascus and visit Jerusalem again. He tells us (Gal. 1:18, 19) that his main purpose was to visit Peter; that he remained in Jerusalem only 15 days; and that of the apostles he saw Peter only, though he mentions that he also saw James, the Lord's brother. Luke, however (Acts 9:26–29), gives further particulars.

It appears that the Christians in Jerusalem were afraid of him because of his former reputation and did not believe he was really a disciple; but that Barnabas, with that generosity of mind which was ever characteristic of him, took Paul to the apostles and related the story of his conversion and subsequent changed life. We are also told that Paul preached as fearlessly in Jerusalem as he had done at Damascus and directed his efforts especially toward his old friends, the Greek-speaking Jews (ch. 9:28, 29). These plotted at once against his life. The threatening danger caused the brethren to send him away, so they took him to Caesarea and sent him from there to Tarsus (Acts 9:29, 30; Gal. 1:21). He departed the more willingly because in the Temple the Lord had appeared to him in a vision bidding him go and telling him distinctly that his mission was to the Gentiles (Acts 22:17–21). The accounts in The Acts and the Epistle to the Galatians of this visit to Jerusalem have sometimes been thought inconsistent, but they may be naturally harmonized. It is highly probable that Paul would want to visit Peter in order that his work might proceed in unison with that of the original apostles, of whom Peter was the most prominent. It is equally natural that the Jerusalem Christians should be at first afraid of him; and the conduct of Barnabas, who was, like Paul, a Hellenistic Jew, is in keeping with his action throughout the whole history. Fifteen days, moreover, are not too short a time for the events described in The

Acts. It is, in fact, confirmed by the Lord's command to Paul to depart quickly (Acts 22:18). Nor is Luke's statement that Barnabas brought Paul "to the apostles" inconsistent with Paul's statement that he saw Peter only, together with James. The reception of the new convert even by Peter alone, not to speak of James, who occupied almost an apostolic position (Gal. 2:9), was equivalent to apostolic recognition of him, and this is all that Luke's expression was meant to describe. It is further worthy of remark that it was now realized fully, by both Paul and the leaders in Jerusalem, that the new convert was a chosen apostle of Christ, and that his mission was to the Gentiles. At the same time the question does not appear to have been raised of what would be the relation of Gentile converts to the Mosaic Law. Neither did any foresee how important Paul's mission was to become. His commission, however, was admitted, and he was sent forth to Tarsus to engage in such work as might open before him.

Paul's stay in Tarsus is nearly a blank to us. It probably lasted 6 or 7 years; see the following "chronology of Paul's life." No doubt he engaged in missionary work, and probably founded the churches of Cilicia, which are mentioned incidentally in Acts 15:41. If at any time he felt the intellectual influences of Tarsus, this must have been the period. As already remarked, Tarsus was one of the centers of the Stoic philosophy, and Paul's appreciation of Stoicism plainly appears in his speech at Athens. While doubtless not inactive, Paul was waiting for the Lord by his providence to make plain the way in which his chosen ambassador was to go.

At length, however, the purpose of God began to appear. Some of the Greek-speaking Jewish Christians, who had been driven from Jerusalem by the persecution which followed Stephen's death, came to the great city of Antioch in Syria. It was situated on the Orontes, n. of the Lebanon range, had been the capital of the Syrian kingdom, and was then the residence of the Roman governor of the province. It was rated as one of the chief cities of the empire. Its mixed population and extensive commerce made it a center of wide influence. Lying just outside Palestine and at the entrance to Asia Minor, connected also by traffic and politics with the whole empire, it formed a natural base of operations from which the new faith, if it was to be separated from Judaism, could go forth to the conquest of the world. In Antioch the Christian refugees began, we are told (Acts 11:20), to preach to the Gentiles (A.V. Grecians; R.V. Greeks). There is a difficult question of the text in the original; but the context leaves no room for doubt that the work was among Gentiles. Many were converted, so that a distinctively Gentile church sprang up in the metropolis of Syria. When the fact was reported at Jerusalem, Barnabas was sent to investigate. With noble breadth of view he saw the Lord's hand in the new development in spite of the fact that the converts were uncircumcised. He seems also to have realized that this was the divine opening for Paul, for he went to Tarsus to seek him and brought him to Antioch. Together they labored for a year in Antioch. Many more Gentiles were converted, and the non-Jewish character of the Church was signalized by the fact that to the disciples in Antioch the name Christians was first given, evidently by their heathen neighbors. Thus began Paul's connection with Antioch. Thus also arose on the page of church history the first Gentile Christian organization. It was to be the starting point for Paul's mission to the pagan world.

While Paul was at Antioch, a prophet from Jerusalem, named Agabus, predicted in the Christian assembly that a famine was soon to occur. This was seized upon by the brethren at Antioch as an occasion for evincing their love to and fraternity with the Christians of Judea. The fact is a remarkable proof of the sense of obligation which these Gentiles had to those from whom they had received their new faith, as well as of the extent to which the gospel broke down at once the barriers which had existed between races and classes. Contributions for the relief of the Judean Christians were made at Antioch, and the same were sent to the elders at Jerusalem by the hands of Barnabas and Paul (Acts 11:29, 30). This visit of Paul to Jerusalem probably occurred in A.D. 44, or shortly after. It is not mentioned by Paul in Galatians, no doubt because he did not see any of the apostles. Some writers indeed have tried to identify it with the visit recorded in Gal. 2:1–10; but that plainly occurred after the dispute concerning the circumcision of Gentiles had sprung up, and Luke distinctly assigns the rise of that controversy to a later date (Acts 15:1). The purpose of Paul in Galatians was to recount the opportunities he had had of obtaining his gospel from the older apostles; and if on this occasion, as Luke intimates (Acts 11:30), he met only the elders of the church, and if the brief visit was purely on a matter of charity, his argument in Galatians did not require him to mention the journey. Barnabas and Paul soon returned to Antioch, taking with them John Mark (Acts 12:25).

5. *First Missionary Journey.* The time had at length arrived when Paul's historic missionary work to the Gentiles was to begin. It was indicated by the Spirit to the prophets belonging to the church in Antioch (Acts 13:1–3). They were directed to set apart 2 of their number, Barnabas and Paul, for the work to which God had called them. Thus by divine direction and under the auspices of the church at Antioch, the apostle's First Missionary Journey began. Its exact date is uncertain. We can only assign it to the years between A.D. 45–50; perhaps, 46–48. Neither is there any clear indication how long a time it occupied. Barnabas, who was the older, is mentioned as the leader; but Paul soon took the chief place. John Mark also went as their helper. The party went from Antioch to Seleucia, at the mouth of the Orontes, and thence sailed to Cyprus, the original home of Barnabas. Landing at Salamis, on the e. coast of Cyprus, they began work, as was natural, in the Jewish synagogues. Then they moved through the island from place to place until they reached Paphos on the s.w. coast. Here they attracted the notice of Sergius Paulus, the Roman proconsul, and were violently opposed by a Jewish sorcerer, Bar-Jesus, who called himself Elymas and who had previously won the patronage of the proconsul (Acts 13:6, 7). Paul, with much indignation, rebuked the sorcerer and smote him with blindness; and the effect of the miracle and of the missionaries' teaching was the conversion of Sergius (vs. 8–12).

Then leaving Cyprus, the party, of whom Paul was now the recognized head (v. 13), sailed n. toward Asia Minor and came to Perga in Pamphylia. There John Mark, for some unexplained reason, left them and returned to Jerusalem. Nor do Paul and Barnabas appear to have remained in Perga, but journeyed n. into Phrygia until they reached Antioch, called Pisidian because it lay toward Pisidia. This was the chief city of the Roman province of Galatia. There they entered the Jewish synagogue and, on invitation of the rulers of the synagogue, Paul made the great address recorded in Acts 13:16–41, the 1st recorded specimen of his preaching. After rehearsing the divine leading of Israel with a view to the coming Messiah, he related the testimony of the Baptist and the rejection of Jesus by the Jewish rulers, but declared that God had raised him from the dead, that in him the ancient promises to Israel were being fulfilled, and that only through faith in him could men be justified. He also warned the Jews not to repeat the crime of their rulers in Jerusalem. The speech aroused the enmity of the leading Jews; but it made an impression on some others, and yet more on those Gentiles who were already under the influence of the synagogue and who ever formed the connecting link for Paul between the synagogue and the pagan world. The next Sabbath the break took place between the missionaries and the synagogue, and the former began to address their work directly to the Gentiles. The chief people of the city, however, were excited by the Jews against the Christians, and Paul and Barnabas were expelled (Acts 13:50). From Antioch they went to Iconium, another city of Phrygia, where many converts, both Jewish and Gentile, were made (v. 51). But the Jews again succeeded in raising persecution, and the missionaries passed on to Lystra and Derbe, important cities of Lycaonia (ch. 14:1-6). At Lystra the miraculous cure of a lame man by Paul led to an attempt on the part of the heathen populace to offer worship to the missionaries, calling them Jupiter and Mercury; and this occasioned the 2d recorded speech of Paul (vs. 15-18), in which he reasoned against the folly of idolatry. At Lystra Timothy was probably converted (Acts 16:1; II Tim. 1:2; 3:11). The brief popularity of the apostle was, however, soon followed by renewed persecution under Jewish instigation (Acts 14: 19), so that he was stoned, dragged out of the city, and left for dead. When he revived he departed with Barnabas to Derbe, which was probably at the s.e. limit of the province of Galatia (v. 20). It would have been possible for the missionaries to cross the mountains into Cilicia and so go directly, by way of Tarsus, back to Syrian Antioch. Their route had followed a rough circle. But they would not return until they had placed the new churches on a firm basis. Hence they returned from Derbe to Lystra, from Lystra to Iconium, from Iconium to Pisidian Antioch, and from Antioch to Perga, in each place organizing the Church and encouraging the disciples. At Perga they preached, as they had seemingly not done at the former visit; then, going to its seaport, Attalia, they returned to Antioch in Syria (Acts 14:21-26). Thus the First Missionary Journey of the apostle was completed. It covered the regions next toward the w. of those already occupied by the gospel. His method was to offer the gospel 1st to the Jews and then to the Gentiles. He found a large number of the latter already influenced by Judaism, and therefore somewhat prepared to receive Christianity. His method was to found churches in the principal cities, and his journeys were facilitated by the fine roads that the Roman government had made between the military posts. The Greek language also was everywhere understood. Providence had thus prepared the way for the prepared herald of the gospel to the world.

The success of Paul's work among the Gentiles led, however, to controversy within the Church. Certain strict Jewish Christians from Jerusalem went to Antioch and declared that unless the converted Gentiles were circumcised, they could not be saved (Acts 15:1). Some years before this time God had revealed to the Church through Peter that Gentiles were to be received without observ-

ance of the Mosaic Law (Acts 10:1 to 11:18). But the strict Jewish party, made up mostly of converted Pharisees (ch. 15:5), would not abide by this teaching; and the announcement of their doctrines in Antioch so disturbed the Church there that the brethren determined to send Paul and Barnabas, with others, to Jerusalem to consult with the apostles and elders about this question. This is the visit described in Acts, ch. 15, and Gal. 2:1-10. Both accounts are entirely harmonious, though written from different points of view. Paul tells us that a revelation from God directed him to go (Gal. 2:2). It was a great crisis. The whole future of the new religion was depending on the issue. But the result was a triumph of Christian loyalty and charity. Paul and Barnabas proclaimed to the mother church what God had done through them. When the strict Jewish Christians opposed them, a council was held of the apostles and elders (Acts 15:6-29). Peter reminded the church of God's will as shown in the case of Cornelius; Paul and Barnabas related the mighty attestations which God had given to their mission; James, the Lord's brother, pointed out that prophecy had foretold the calling of the Gentiles. It was resolved to recognize heartily the uncircumcised converts as brethren, but to direct them to avoid certain practices which were specially offensive to the Jews.

Paul tells us in Galatians that the church in Jerusalem stood by him against the "false brethren"; and also that James, Peter, and John gave him the right hand of fellowship, he to go to the Gentiles, they to the Jews. Thus Paul retained fellowship with the other apostles while at liberty to go on his own divinely appointed mission. How bitter the controversy was on the part of the Judaizers is shown by their subsequent hatred and hostility to Paul. But he had gained his point. The unity of the Church was preserved. The liberty of the Gentiles was preserved. A practical adjustment was made by which reasonable Jewish prejudice was conciliated, while the way was open for the carrying of the gospel to all peoples, unencumbered by Jewish ceremonialism. A brief reminder of the controversy occurred indeed soon after in Antioch, which ought to be mentioned (Gal. 2:11-21). Peter had gone there and, being in entire agreement with Paul, had lived in free association with the Gentiles. But when Jews from Jerusalem came to Antioch, Peter and even Barnabas withdrew from this association. This led Paul publicly to rebuke Peter, and in his rebuke he outlined the doctrinal ground on which he rested the rights of the Gentiles in the Church. Salvation is by faith alone, he said, because the believer has died with Christ to the Law; i.e., Christ by dying has met all the obligations of the Law for his people, and therefore nothing more than faith in Christ can be made the condition of anyone's becoming a Christian. We thus see that the rights of the Gentiles in the Church involved for Paul much more than a question of church unity. He saw that it involved the essential principle of the gospel. By his defense of this principle, as well as by his missionary work, Paul was the chief agent in the establishment of universal Christianity.

6. *Second Missionary Journey.* The council at Jerusalem was probably held in A.D. 50; see the chronology below. Not long after it Paul proposed to Barnabas a Second Missionary Journey (Acts 15:36). He was unwilling, however, that John Mark should again go with them, and this led to the final separation of the 2 great missionaries. Paul thereupon took with him Silas; see SILAS. They 1st visited the churches of Syria and Cilicia, and then passed n., through the Taurus Moun-

tains, to the churches which had been founded on Paul's First Journey. They thus came first to Derbe, then to Lystra. At the latter place Paul determined to take Timothy with him, and circumcised him to prevent giving offense to the Jews, for Timothy's mother was a Jewess. Paul thus showed willingness to conciliate Jewish prejudice ; though he would not yield an inch when the principles of the gospel were at stake.

From Lystra they appear to have gone to Iconium and Pisidian Antioch. Their movements here, however, are much disputed by scholars. Ramsay and others, who believe that the churches of the First Journey were the "churches of Galatia" to which the epistle with that name was afterward written (see GALATIA, GALATIANS, EPISTLE TO THE), hold that Paul went directly n. from Pisidian Antioch through the Roman province of Asia, but without preaching, since he was "forbidden of the Holy Ghost to preach the word in Asia" (Acts 16 :6) ; that when they came "over against Mysia" (v. 7) they attempted to go into Bithynia, but were again forbidden ; then passing by (or, as the original may mean, neglecting) Mysia they turned w. through or alongside of Mysia to Troas. The commoner view is that from Pisidian Antioch the travelers moved n.e. into Galatia proper ; that on the way Paul was for a while disabled by sickness, and that this led him to improve the opportunity, sick though he was, of preaching in Galatia and so of founding the "churches of Galatia" (Gal. 4 :13-15) ; that this movement to the n.e. from Pisidian Antioch was due to the command not to preach in Asia ; that when his work in Galatia proper was done, he attempted to enter Bithynia, but was again forbidden ; and so, as on the former theory, he turned w. through or alongside of Mysia to Troas. This whole period is very briefly described by Luke. The Spirit was directing the missionaries to Europe, and Luke's narrative likewise hastens forward.

At Troas there appeared the vision of the man of Macedonia (Acts 16 :9), in response to whose call the missionaries, now joined by Luke himself (cf. "we"), took ship for Europe, and, landing at Neapolis, went forward to the important city of Philippi. Here a church was founded (ch. 16 :11-40), which ever remained specially dear to the apostle's heart (see Phil. 1 :4-7 ; 4 :1, 15). Here, too, Paul first came into conflict with Roman magistrates and found that his citizenship was a protection for his work (Acts 16 :20-24, 37-39). From Philippi, where Luke remained, Paul, Silas, and Timothy went on to Thessalonica. The brief account in Acts 17 :1-9 of the work done there is supplemented by the allusians made to it in his two epistles to that church. He had much success among the Gentiles ; he laid with great care the foundations of the Church ; and he gave the example of industry and sobriety by supporting himself by his trade while preaching the gospel (I Thess., ch. 2 ; etc.). But persecution arose, instigated by the Jews, so the brethren sent Paul to Berea, and from there, after marked success even in the synagogue, to Athens. His sojourn at Athens was rather disappointing, and is memorable chiefly for the address before the philosophers on Mars' Hill (Acts 17 : 22-31), in which Paul showed his appreciation of the truths which the gospel had in common with Stoicism, while he yet faithfully proclaimed to the members of a critical audience their duty to God and what God required them to believe.

At Corinth, on the contrary, to which he next went, he remained 18 months, and his work was most successful. Here he made the acquaintance of Aquila and Priscilla and

abode with them (Acts 18 :1-3). At first he preached in the synagogue, but afterward, because of the opposition of the Jews, in the house of a Gentile, Titus Justus, who lived next to the synagogue (vs. 5-7). In both Acts (ch. 18 :9, 10) and I Cor. (ch. 2 :1-5) there are allusions to the great anxiety of mind with which the apostle prosecuted his mission in Corinth, and to his earnest determination to proclaim in Greece as elsewhere the simple gospel of the Crucified ; while I Cor. amply testifies both to his success and to the many temptations to which the Christians of Corinth were exposed, and which from the beginning occasioned the apostle special solicitude. The needs of other churches also pressed upon him, so that from Corinth he wrote the 2 epistles to the Thessalonians for the purpose of warning against certain doctrinal and practical perils by which that church was threatened. The hostility of the Jews also did not cease, and, on the coming to Corinth of the new proconsul, Gallio, they accused Paul of violation of the law. But the proconsul properly decided that the matter pertained to the synagogue itself and that the apostle had broken no law of which the government could take cognizance. The empire thus at this period protected the Christians from Jewish violence by identifying them with the Jews, and Paul was permitted to continue his work unmolested. His mission to Corinth was one of the most fruitful in the history of the Early Christian Church. At length, however, Paul turned his face again to the e. From Corinth he sailed to Ephesus. He did not remain there, however, but, promising to return, sailed to Caesarea, made apparently a hasty journey to Jerusalem, and, having saluted the church there, returned to Antioch, whence he had originally started (Acts 18 :22). Thus was completed his Second Missionary Journey. Its result had been the establishment of Christianity in Europe. Macedonia and Achaia had been evangelized. The gospel had thereby taken a long step forward toward the conquest of the empire.

7. *Third Missionary Journey.* After remaining some time at Antioch, Paul, probably in A.D. 54, began his Third Journey. He first traversed "the region of Galatia and Phrygia, in order, establishing all the disciples" (Acts 18 :23), and then settled in Ephesus. It thus appears that the previous divine prohibition to preach in the province of Asia had been removed. Ephesus was the capital of Asia and one of the most influential cities of the East. Hence the apostle for 3 years made it his center of operations (Acts 19 :8, 9 ; 20 : 31). For 3 months he taught in the synagogue (ch. 19 :8), and then for 2 years in the school or lecture hall of a certain Tyrannus (v. 9). His work in Ephesus was marked by great thoroughness of instruction (ch. 20 : 18-31) ; by the exercise of astonishing miraculous power (ch. 19 :11, 12) ; by great success, so that "all they that dwelt in Asia heard the word of the Lord" (v. 10), and even some of the chief officers of Asia became Paul's friends (v. 31) ; yet also by constant and fierce opposition (Acts 19 :23-41 ; I Cor. 4 :9-13 ; 15 :32) ; and finally, by the care of all the churches (II Cor. 11 :28). This period of the apostle's life is especially rich in incidents. Much occurred of which The Acts tells nothing. Here Paul heard of attacks made on him and his doctrine by Judaizing teachers in Galatia ; and in reply he wrote the famous Epistle to the Galatians, in which he defends his apostolic authority, and gives the 1st formal statement and proof of the doctrine of grace. The condition of the Corinthians also occasioned him much anxiety. In reply to inquiries from Corinth he wrote a letter, now lost, concerning the relations of believers

to the pagan society about them (I Cor. 5:9). But later reports showed that more serious troubles had arisen. Hence our I Cor. was written, an epistle which finely exhibits the apostle's practical wisdom in the instruction and discipline of the infant churches. Even so, however, the seditious elements in the Corinthian church would not yield. Many think that Paul, after writing I Cor., himself made a hurried visit to Corinth for disciplinary purposes (cf. II Cor. 12:14; 13:1). At any rate, before leaving Ephesus he sent Titus to Corinth, probably with a letter, to secure the discipline of a refractory member of the church. Titus was to rejoin him in Troas. When he failed to do so, Paul passed on in much anxiety to Macedonia, whither Timothy and Erastus had preceded him (Acts 19:22). At length, however, Titus rejoined him (II Cor. 2:12–14; 7:5–16), with the good news that the Corinthian church had obeyed the apostle and were loyal in their love for him. Whereupon Paul wrote our II Cor., the most biographical of all his epistles, in which he rejoices in their obedience, gives directions concerning the collection he was making for the Judean saints, and once more defends his authority as an apostle of Christ. From Macedonia he himself went to Corinth and passed the winter of A.D. 57–58 there. No doubt he completed the discipline and organization of the Corinthian church; but the visit is most memorable because he then wrote the Epistle to the Romans. In it he states most completely the doctrine of the way of salvation. He evidently regarded Rome as the place where his labors should culminate. He could not, however, go there at once, because he felt it necessary to return to Jerusalem with the gifts of the Gentile churches to the mother church. Christian work had already been begun at Rome and was being carried on mainly by Paul's own friends and disciples (cf. Rom., ch. 16). Hence, he sent the epistle from Corinth that the Christians of the capital might possess complete instruction in the gospel which Paul was proclaiming to the world.

Paul now set out on his last journey to Jerusalem. He was accompanied by friends who represented various Gentile churches (Acts 20:4). The apostle's work among the Gentiles had been much opposed by Judaizers, and even the ordinary Jewish Christians often regarded him and it with distrust. Hence arose his scheme of proving the loyalty of the Gentile churches by inducing them to send a liberal offering to the poor Christians of Judea. It was to carry this offering that he and his friends left Corinth for Jerusalem. His plan had 1st been to sail direct to Syria, but a plot of the Jews led him to change his route and to return by way of Macedonia (ch. 20:3). He lingered at Philippi while his companions went on to Troas, but he was rejoined at that place by Luke (v. 5). After the passover he and Luke went on to Troas, where the others were waiting for them and where all remained 7 days (v. 6). A church had grown up at Troas, and an interesting account is given by Luke of the events of the apostle's interview with it on the day and night before he left it (vs. 7–12). From Troas Paul went by foot about 20 miles to Assos, whither his companions had already gone by boat (v. 13). Thence they sailed to Mitylene, on the e. shore of the island of Lesbos, and then, coasting s., they passed between the mainland and the island of Chios, touched the next day at the island of Samos, and the day following reached Miletus (vs. 14, 15). The A.V. states (Acts 20:15) that they "tarried at Trogyllium" after leaving Samos; see TROGYLLIUM. The R.V. with the best MSS. omits this clause. Miletus was about 36 miles from Ephesus, and as Paul

was in haste, he determined not to go to Ephesus, but to send for the elders of the church. At Miletus he took leave of them in the affectionate address recorded in Acts 20:18–35. No words could more strongly exhibit the apostle's devotion to his work, his love for his converts, and his realization of the spiritual perils to which they would be exposed. Leaving Miletus, the ship went with a straight course to Cos (Acts 21:1, in A.V. Coos), an island about 40 miles to the s.; then, the next day, Rhodes, an island and city about 50 miles s.e. of Cos, was reached; and from Rhodes the course lay e. to Patara, on the coast of Lycia (Acts 21:1). At Patara a ship for Phoenicia (Syria) was found and the party went on board (v. 2), and, passing w. of Cyprus, reached Tyre (v. 3). There they remained a week, and the disciples of Tyre urged Paul not to go to Jerusalem (v. 4); but after an affectionate farewell he sailed (vs. 5, 6) to Ptolemais, the modern Acre, and came the next day to Caesarea (vs. 7, 8). At Caesarea the company abode with Philip the evangelist. There too the Prophet Agabus, who at an earlier time had foretold the famine (ch. 11:28), bound his own hands and feet with Paul's girdle and predicted that so would the Jews bind Paul and deliver him to the Gentiles. But in spite of this warning and the lamentation of the brethren, Paul insisted on going forward (ch. 21:11–14). So, in company with a number of the disciples, he went on to Jerusalem, thus completing what is known as his Third Missionary Journey.

8. *Paul in Jerusalem.* The prediction of Agabus was soon fulfilled. Paul was at first indeed well received by the brethren in Jerusalem, and on the day following his arrival went to James, the Lord's brother, and the elders of the Church. When he had related his work among the Gentiles, they glorified God. At the same time they reminded him that many of the Jewish Christians had heard evil reports about him and doubted his fidelity to Moses. It was proposed, therefore, that he should give an ocular proof that he still held the Jewish customs in honor. He was to join with 4 men, who at that time were performing a Nazirite vow in the Temple. To this Paul assented, for he was ever anxious not to give needless offense to the Jews, and the observance proposed was probably little more than what he had done of his own will at Corinth (Acts 18:18). While Paul insisted that no Gentile should observe the Mosaic Law, and while he maintained that no Christian Jew was bound to observe it, he found no fault with Jews who chose to observe it, and held himself at liberty to observe its regulations or not as circumstances might seem to make expedient. His assent to this proposal, therefore, was not inconsistent with his action on other occasions. But the expedient proved unavailing for the purpose for which it was intended. Certain Jews from Asia saw him in the Temple and raised a tumult. They falsely charged him with having brought Gentiles into the Temple, and declared to the populace that he had everywhere taught men to dishonor both the Temple and the Law (ch. 21:27–29). A riot speedily ensued in which Paul would probably have been slain, had not the commander of the Roman garrison, Claudius Lysias, hastened with soldiers to quell the uproar. He was leading Paul, bound with 2 chains, into the castle for examination and the Jews were following with many outcries, when the apostle desired liberty to speak. The commander was surprised that the prisoner could use Greek, for he had supposed him to be an Egyptian insurrectionist who had recently given trouble to the government (v. 38). When Paul explained that he was a Tarsian

Jew, Lysias allowed him to address the multitude. He did so in the Hebrew (Aramaic) tongue (ch. 22:2). He related his early life and the story of his conversion. They heard him till he uttered the word Gentiles, when the uproar was renewed, and Lysias withdrew him into the castle for safety and further examination. The examination would have been by scourging had not Paul remarked to the centurion that he was a Roman citizen (v. 25). When this was reported to Lysias, he unbound Paul and, feeling that the matter was a serious one, directed the priests to convoke the sanhedrin on the following day that the prisoner might be tried.

The appearance of Paul before the council led, however, to another tumult (Acts 23:1-10). The apostle was now fighting for his life. He had no hope of justice and, should the council condemn him, Lysias might give him over to execution. With much shrewdness he succeeded in dividing his enemies. He claimed to be a Pharisee and to be on trial for teaching the doctrine of the resurrection of the dead. This was true, as far as it went, and it served Paul's purpose. The hatred of the Pharisees and Sadducees for each other was greater than their hostility to Paul, and the 2 sects quickly arrayed themselves on opposite sides. The commander feared that Paul would be pulled to pieces between his defenders and his opponents, so by his orders the soldiers removed the prisoner again to the castle.

9. *Paul a prisoner in Caesarea.* That night the Lord appeared to Paul in a vision and bade him be of good cheer, since he was certainly to bear his testimony at Rome (Acts 23:11). This consummation was to be effected, however, in an unexpected way. Some of the Jews formed a plot to kill Paul and, to accomplish this, it was determined to request the commander to bring the prisoner once more before the council. But Paul's nephew heard of the plot and managed to inform his uncle and the commander (vs. 12-22). Thereupon Lysias sent Paul under a strong guard to Caesarea with a letter to Felix, the procurator, referring the case to him. When Felix learned that the accused was from Cilicia, he declared that he would wait until the accusers came, and meanwhile placed Paul for safe keeping in Herod's palace, which was used as the praetorium or residence of the procurator. Then followed 2 years of imprisonment in Caesarea. When the Jews appeared before Felix, they made a general accusation against Paul of sedition and especially of profanation of the Temple, complaining of the violence with which Lysias had taken their prisoner out of their hands (ch. 24:1-9). To this Paul replied by an explicit denial and a demand that witnesses should be produced against him (vs. 10-21). Felix appears to have been sufficiently acquainted with the matters in dispute to perceive that Paul had not committed any crime worthy of punishment. He dismissed the accusers on the plea that he must learn further particulars from Lysias, and directed that Paul should be kept in confinement, but that his friends should be allowed to visit him freely. Felix and his wife Drusilla were also much impressed by what Paul had said and "heard him concerning the faith in Christ" (v. 24). In fact, the apostle seems to have exercised a strange fascination over the procurator, who trembled before his solemn preaching and promised to send for him again. He hoped also that Paul would pay for his liberty (vs. 25, 26). But the apostle would not bribe the procurator, and the latter deferred decision of the case, so that when, after 2 years, Porcius Festus succeeded Felix, Paul was still a prisoner (v. 27).

The Jews hoped that the new governor would prove more favorable to their desires than Felix had been. But Festus refused to send Paul to Jerusalem for trial, and required his accusers to confront him again in Caesarea (Acts 25:1-6). Again, however, they were unable to prove any crime against him, while he persistently maintained his innocence (vs. 7, 8). Festus, however, willing to please the Jews, asked Paul if he would go to Jerusalem to be tried. Paul knew that such a course would probably prove fatal to him. He availed himself, therefore, of his right as a Roman citizen and appealed unto Caesar (vs. 9-11). This took the case out of the procurator's hands and necessitated the prisoner's transmission to Rome. Before he could be sent, however, Agrippa II and his sister Bernice came to visit Festus, doubtless to congratulate him on his accession to office; and the procurator, who was not well versed in Jewish disputes and yet was bound to send to the emperor a full account of the case, related the matter to Agrippa, who expressed his desire to hear what the prisoner had to say. Forthwith it was arranged that Paul should state his case before the assembled company. Agrippa's familiarity with Jewish affairs would be of service to the procurator in preparing his report to the emperor (vs. 12-27).

Paul's defense before Agrippa forms one of his most notable speeches. In it he displayed the courtesy of a gentleman, the eloquence of an orator, and the fearlessness of a Christian. He reviewed his life in order to show that he had been governed only by the wish to obey the God of Israel, and maintained that his course as a Christian had not only been determined by God's direction, but had been the fulfillment of the Hebrew prophecies themselves (Acts 26:1-23). When Festus interrupted him with the exclamation that he was mad, Paul appealed earnestly to Agrippa. But the king was not disposed to be more than an observer and critic of what he deemed a new fanaticism. He replied with some contempt, "With but little persuasion thou wouldest fain make me a Christian" (v. 28, R.V.). Nevertheless he admitted that Paul had done no crime, and might have been set at liberty if he had not appealed unto Caesar (vs. 31, 32).

10. *Journey to Rome.* In the autumn of the same year, A.D. 60 (see following chronology), Paul was sent to Rome. He was committed, with other prisoners, to the care of a centurion, Julius, of the Augustan band or cohort. He was accompanied by Luke and Aristarchus, a Thessalonian (ch. 27:1, 2). The account of the voyage is related by Luke with singular detail and accuracy. The apostle was treated with notable courtesy by the centurion. Leaving Caesarea in a coasting ship of Adramyttium, they touched at Sidon and then sailed to Myra in Lycia. There they were transferred to an Alexandrian merchant ship bound for Italy. The wind, however, was not favorable. They were compelled at first to keep coasting n.w. until over against Cnidus on the coast of Caria. Then putting s., they rounded with difficulty Cape Salmone, on the e. extremity of Crete, and managed to reach Fair Havens, a port on the s. shore of the same island (Acts 27:3-8). It was now after the Fast, i.e., the 10th of Tishri or Day of Atonement (v. 9), when the season of navigation was drawing to a close. The weather also continued threatening. Paul counseled against sailing farther, but the centurion followed the advice of the master and the owner of the ship, who wished to go on to Phoenix, farther w. on the coast of Crete, where there was a better harbor (vs. 9-12). But when they had left Fair Havens, a fierce n.e. wind came down upon them and drove

them to the s. Passing s. of Cauda (or Clauda, A.V., the modern Gozzo), and having lightened the ship, they were driven for 14 days before the gale in a w. direction. Paul alone maintained his courage and that of the rest, for an angel of the Lord assured him that no life would be lost (vs. 13–26). On the 14th night the sounding lead told of their approach to land; and, casting 4 anchors, they waited for the day. When daylight came, they perceived in the unknown land a small bay with a beach; so, cutting off their anchors, they hoisted the foresail to the wind and made for the beach (vs. 27–40). The ship, however, grounded, and soon began to break up under the violence of the waves. Thereupon the whole company cast themselves overboard and, as Paul had predicted, all reached land in safety (vs. 41–44). In this thrilling adventure, which Luke relates with so much detail, the conduct of Paul beautifully illustrates the courage of the Christian and the influence over others which a man of faith can exercise in times of peril.

The land on which they had been cast was the island of Melita, the modern Malta, which lies 58 miles s. of Sicily. The inhabitants kindly received the shipwrecked company, and Paul by his miracles gained special honor among them (Acts 28:1–10). After 3 months, however, the party were put on board another Alexandrian ship, which had wintered in the island, and, after touching at Syracuse and Rhegium, arrived at Puteoli, a harbor of s.w. Italy. There Paul found Christian brethren with whom he tarried 7 days (vs. 11–14). Meanwhile word of his arrival had reached the Christians in Rome, so that some of them went to meet him at the Market of Appius and The Three Taverns, 2 places distant from Rome about 43 and 33 miles respectively (v. 15). According to the A.V. (v. 16) the centurion delivered his prisoners to the captain of the guard, and this has been usually understood to mean the prefect of the Praetorian Guard, who at this time, A.D. 61, was the celebrated Burrus. The R.V., however, with the best MSS. omits this statement. Mommsen, followed by Ramsay, thinks that the prisoners were delivered to the captain of another corps, to which Julius the centurion himself belonged, and whose duty it was to superintend the transportation of grain to the capital and to perform police duty. We really cannot tell into whose custody Paul was delivered. We know only that he was held in military confinement, chained to a soldier (Acts 28:16; Phil. 1:7, 13), but allowed to lodge by himself. Appeals to Caesar were slow processes. Paul soon hired a dwelling and continued in it for 2 years (Acts 28:30).

11. *First imprisonment in Rome.* The Acts closes with an account of how after 3 days he summoned the chief of the Jews, related the reason of his presence in the capital, and on an appointed day expounded to them the gospel; but that when they, like their countrymen elsewhere, disbelieved, Paul again declared that he would turn to the Gentiles. His imprisonment, therefore, did not prevent his missionary activity. The last verses of The Acts relate that for 2 whole years he received all who came to him and preached the Kingdom of God and the things concerning the Lord Jesus Christ without hindrance from the authorities (Acts 28:17–31). But still more light is thrown on this period of Paul's life by the epistles which he wrote during it. They are those to the Colossians, to Philemon, to the Ephesians, and to the Philippians. The first 3 were probably written in the earlier part of the period and that to the Philippians toward its close. These epistles show that the apostle in Rome had many faithful friends working with him. Among these were Timothy (Col. 1:1; Phil. 1:1; 2:19; Philemon 1), Tychicus (Eph. 6:21; Col. 4:7), Aristarchus (Col. 4:10; Philemon 24), John Mark (Col. 4:10; Philemon 24), and Luke (Col. 4:14; Philemon 24). His friends had unhindered access to him; they acted as his messengers to the churches and also as his co-workers in Rome; and they made the imprisoned apostle the center and head of the Gentile Christian work throughout the empire. The epistles further show the personal activity of the apostle's life. With great zeal and success, in spite of his bonds, did he preach the gospel. He was an ambassador in bonds (Eph. 6:20). He desired his friends to pray that God would open for him a door of utterance (Col. 4:3). In Onesimus, the runaway slave, we see an example of the fruit of his labors (Philemon 10). As time went on the success of his work increased. He wrote to the Philippians (Phil. 1:12, 13, R.V.) that the things which had happened to him had fallen out unto the progress of the gospel, so that his bonds were manifest in Christ throughout the whole Praetorian Guard and to all the rest. He sent greetings also (ch. 4:22) from "them of Caesar's household." At the same time he was opposed even by some of the Christians, probably of the Jewish Christian type (ch. 1:15–18). But he regarded their opposition with equanimity, and was confident that he would finally be released (Phil. 1:25; 2:17, 24; Philemon 22). His imprisonment was only God's way of enabling his ambassador to fulfill to the uttermost his chosen mission. Finally, the epistles testify to the apostle's continued superintendence of the churches throughout the empire. New heresies had arisen in Asia. In the epistles of the imprisonment Paul gave his ripest instructions concerning the Person of Christ and the eternal purpose of God revealed in the gospel, while the practical directions which they contain disclose the breadth of his grasp on Christian duty and the fervor of his own Christian life.

12. *Release from first Roman imprisonment.* Although the book of The Acts leaves Paul a prisoner at Rome, there is reason to believe that he was released after 2 years' confinement and resumed his missionary journeys. The evidence for this may be summarized as follows: (1) The closing verse of The Acts accords better with this view than with the supposition that the imprisonment which has been described ended in the apostle's condemnation and death. Luke emphasizes the fact that no one hindered his work, thus certainly giving the impression that the end of his activity was not near. Moreover (2) Paul fully expected to be released (Phil. 1:25; 2:17, 24; Philemon 22), and this expectation was fully justified by the treatment which he had always received at the hands of Roman officials. It should be remembered that Nero's persecution of the Christians had not yet begun; that it was a sudden outbreak, preceded by no official ill-treatment of them; and that in the view of Roman law the Christians were as yet only a sect of the Jews, whose liberty to maintain their religion was fully recognized. It is therefore altogether probable that, when Paul's case came before the imperial tribunal, he was acquitted of any crime of which Roman law could take cognizance. No doubt, also, the report of Festus was a favorable one (see Acts 26:31); nor do the Jews appear to have sent any accusers to Rome to appear against him (ch. 28:21). (3) The tradition that he was released and resumed his journeys, and was again arrested dates from an early period. Clement of Rome, A.D. 96, seems clearly to imply that Paul went to

Spain, for he says that in his journeys "he reached the limit of the West." His journey to Spain is also mentioned in the so-called Muratori Fragment, A.D. 170. The first 3 chapters of the Gnostic *Acts of Peter* (written not later than A.D. 200, probably by a resident of Asia Minor) relate in detail the preparations in Rome for Paul's journey to Spain. With the foregoing agrees Eusebius (*H. E.* ii. 22, 2), A.D. 324, who reports, as the common tradition, that "after he [Paul] had made his defense, the apostle was sent again on the ministry of preaching, and a second time having come to the same city [Rome], he suffered martyrdom." It must be admitted that this traditional evidence is not sufficiently strong to be absolutely demonstrative; but it is early and strong enough to confirm the rest of the evidence, and no sufficient counterevidence can be adduced. (4) The Epistles to Timothy and to Titus are most probably, on the basis of internal and external evidence, to be attributed to Paul. No place for them, however, can be found in the history of Paul related in The Acts. They must, therefore, have been written later, and that fact compels us to accept the tradition given by Eusebius.

13. *Later missionary activities.* We must, therefore, believe that Paul's appeal from Festus to Caesar resulted in his release. His subsequent movements can be inferred only from the allusions contained in the Epistles to Timothy and to Titus and from tradition. We may suppose that after his release he went, as he had intended (Phil. 2:24; Philemon 22), to Asia and Macedonia. From I Tim. 1:3 we learn that he had left Timothy in charge of the churches about Ephesus when he himself went to Macedonia. Where he was when he wrote I Tim. is not clear, but he hoped soon to be able to return to Ephesus (I Tim. 3:14). From Titus we learn that he had left Titus in charge of the churches of Crete, and expected to winter in Nicopolis (Titus 3:12). Though there were several cities by that name (see NICOPOLIS), it is probable that Nicopolis in Epirus was the one referred to. If we accept the early tradition that Paul went to Spain (see above), we may suppose that he did so after having been in Asia and Macedonia; that after that, on his return from Spain, he stopped at Crete and left Titus on that island; that then he returned to Asia, from which place he doubtless wrote the Epistle to Titus. We learn from II Tim. 4:20 that he had passed through Corinth and Miletus, the one in Greece, the other in Asia. There is nothing to show whether he carried out his intention of wintering in Nicopolis. Many suppose, however, that he did go to Nicopolis in Epirus, and was there rearrested and sent to Rome. But while the apostle's movements during this closing period of his life are somewhat uncertain, the epistles then written show that he occupied himself, in addition to evangelizing new regions, with the perfecting of the organization of the already existing churches. He evidently felt that his career must soon close, and that the churches would be exposed to new dangers, from both without and within. Hence the Pastoral Epistles, as they are called, round out the apostle's instruction of the churches by solidifying their organization and practically equipping them for their future work.

14. *Final imprisonment and death.* The release of Paul from his 1st Roman imprisonment probably occurred in A.D. 63, and his subsequent activity lasted about 4 years. According to Eusebius, his death took place in A.D. 67; according to Jerome, in A.D. 68. How he came to be rearrested we do not know. There are a few slight hints furnished, how-

ever, by the Second Epistle to Timothy, which was written from Rome shortly before Paul's death. We should remember, moreover, that in A.D. 64 Nero's persecution of the Christians in Rome broke out; and it was doubtless followed by sporadic outbreaks against them in the provinces (I Peter 4:13–19). It may be, as some have supposed, that Paul was informed against as a leader of the now proscribed sect by the Alexander mentioned in II Tim. 4:14. At any rate, and wherever he was arrested, he was sent to Rome for trial, either because, as before, he appealed to Caesar, or because he was charged with a crime committed in Italy, perhaps with complicity in the burning of Rome, or because the provincials wished to gratify Nero by sending so notable a prisoner to the capital. Only Luke, of his former friends, was with him when II Tim. was written (II Tim. 4:11). Some had even deserted him (II Tim. 1:15; 4:10, 16), while others had gone away on various errands (ch. 4:10, 12). Yet when arraigned before the tribunal he was at first not condemned (ch. 4:17), though he continued to be held on some other charge. Possibly he was able to disprove a charge of criminal conduct, but was retained in custody because he was a Christian. He speaks of himself as a prisoner (II Tim. 1:8) in bonds (v. 16), as if an evildoer (ch. 2:9), and regards his fate as sealed (ch. 4:6–8). No doubt he was finally condemned to death simply because he was a Christian, in accordance with the policy begun by Nero in A.D. 64. Tradition relates that the apostle was beheaded, as became a Roman citizen, on the Ostian Way.

15. *Character, contributions, and theology of Paul.* In giving this outline of the life of the Apostle Paul, we have necessarily followed the express testimony of The Acts and his epistles. But it should not be forgotten that many other events occurred in his active and checkered career. To some of these allusions are made in his epistles (Rom. 15:18, 19; II Cor. 11:24–33). Yet the well-known events of his life, taken with his epistles, make plain the character of the man and the supreme value of his work. It is difficult to gather into one picture the many features of his versatile character. He was by nature intensely religious and his religion controlled his whole being. This was true of him even as a Jew, and much more so after his conversion. Keenly intellectual, he grasped truth at its full value and logically wrought out its implications. Yet truth possessed his heart equally with his intellect, and his emotions were as fervid as his logical processes were vigorous. At the same time the practical aspects of truth were seen by him no less than the theoretical side. If on the one hand he fully wrought out dialectically the content of his doctrinal ideas, on the other hand he applied Christianity to life with the wisdom and completeness of a practical man of affairs. He was intense in his affections, at times ecstatic in his religious experiences, ever progressive in his statements of truth, capable of soaring to the loftiest heights of religious thought, and of embodying in action the truth for which he stood. This versatility, intensity, purity, breadth of mental and spiritual life, when used by the all-controlling Spirit of God, fitted Paul for the work for which the providence of God intended him.

And that work consisted in authoritatively interpreting to the Gentile world, in action and in written statement, the mission and message of Christ. How Paul did this in action is narrated in the book of The Acts. Through his agency the universalism of Christianity, its independence of the Jewish ritual, its adaptation to all mankind, was historically established. Other men also contributed to the result. But it was Paul's divinely given task to bear the burden of this achievement, and to him, as to no other man, Christianity owes its possession of a world-wide destiny. All this was done, of course, in accordance with the purpose of Christ and under his direction. But the student of Christian history must recognize in Paul the principal agent used to accomplish the result. On the other hand, the epistles of Paul disclose in written statement the doctrinal and ethical interpretation of Christ's word and work, which accompanied Paul's missionary activity and made it profound and permanent. It is, therefore, to Paul as a theologian that we rightly look with the greatest admiration. His theology took shape from the peculiar experience of his own conversion. By that sudden transition he was made to realize the impossibility of man's saving himself, the dependence of the sinner on the sovereign grace of God, and the completeness of the redeeming work which Jesus, the Son of God, had done through his death and resurrection. It followed that only by union with Christ through faith can any man be saved. Salvation consists in justification of the sinner by God on the ground of Christ's obedience, and when thus justified the sinner, being united to Christ, is made to partake of all the spiritual benefits, external and internal, in heaven and on earth, which Christ has purchased for him. The Spirit inspired Paul to set forth on this foundation the truth of Christ's whole work and person. In the Epistles to the Galatians and to the Romans the way of salvation itself is most fully elaborated, while in the epistles of the imprisonment the exalted dignity of Christ and the whole breadth and end of God's eternal purpose of grace in Christ and his Church find their full expression. Besides these principal themes, almost every phase of Christian truth and duty is touched upon in Paul's epistles. His is emphatically the theology of grace. He sounded the depths of this truth. He interpreted the Hebrew Messiah to the Gentile world. He was raised up to explain to the world the Saviour in whom it was invited to believe and the work which the Saviour had done. Paul was pre-eminently the theologian of the apostles as well as the most aggressive missionary. It is not possible to understand Christianity unless we unite with the teaching and work of Jesus Christ the interpretation thereof furnished by his apostle Paul.

16. *Chronology of Paul's life.* While the order of events in Paul's life and the relative dates of his epistles are in the main quite clear, there is some dispute concerning the precise years to which both events and epistles are to be assigned. In the book of The Acts 2 dates may be regarded as certain, viz., the ascension of Christ in A.D. 30 (though some scholars assign this to A.D. 29) and the death of Herod Agrippa (Acts 12:23), which all admit to have taken place in A.D. 44. Neither of these dates, however, is of much assistance in determining the absolute chronology of Paul's life. That depends mainly on the date assigned to the accession of Festus as procurator of Judea. According to the common and most probable opinion, Festus became governor (Acts 24:27) in A.D. 60. Josephus assigns nearly all the events during the governorship of Felix to the reign of Nero, which began in October, A.D. 54, and Paul (ch. 24:10) speaks of Felix as having been "of many years a judge unto this nation." It is hardly possible, therefore, to assign Paul's arrest when he appeared before Felix to a date earlier than A.D. 58. Then

Paul was kept 2 years in confinement in Caesarea, which would make the accession of Festus, who then succeeded Felix, to have taken place in A.D. 60. It can hardly have been later, since Festus was succeeded by Albinus in A.D. 62, and the events recorded of him imply that he was governor for more than a year. But if Festus became governor in A.D. 60, Paul was sent to Rome in the autumn of that year, and arrived at Rome in the spring of A.D. 61, having spent the winter on the way. Then the close of The Acts, and probably the apostle's release from his first Roman imprisonment, are to be dated in A.D. 63 (Acts 28:30).

For the earlier events of Paul's life, we date back from the accession of Festus. Assuming the latter to have been in A.D. 60, then Paul's arrest, which occurred 2 years before (Acts 24:27), was in A.D. 58. This was at the close of his Third Journey. The winter preceding his arrest he had spent in Corinth (ch. 20:3), the preceding autumn in Macedonia (v. 2), and before that, for 3 years, he had been in Ephesus (v. 31), to which he had gone from Antioch after a rapid tour through Galatia and Phrygia (ch. 18:23). Hence 4 years must be allowed for the Third Journey. If he was arrested in Jerusalem in the spring of A.D. 58, he must have begun this journey in the spring of A.D. 54. The Third Journey followed the Second by a moderate interval (ch. 18:23), and for the latter at least 2½ years must be allowed, since 18 months were spent at Corinth (v. 11), and the preceding events of the tour may fairly be supposed to have occupied a year more (chs. 15:36 to 17:34). If, therefore, the Second Journey closed in the autumn of A.D. 53, it probably began in the spring of A.D. 51. The Second Journey in turn began some days (ch. 15:36) after the council of Jerusalem. This latter epoch-making event may, therefore, be assigned to the year A.D. 50. The First Missionary Journey can be located only roughly between A.D. 44, the date of Herod's death (ch. 12), and A.D. 50, the date of the council (ch. 15). We may probably assign it to the years A.D. 46-48, though it is not possible to say how long a time it consumed.

For the date of Paul's conversion, we must combine the results given above with his statements in the Epistle to the Galatians. In Gal. 2:1 he says: "Then after . . . fourteen years I went up again to Jerusalem with Barnabas." This visit is probably the one to the council which we have located in A.D. 50. But from what event are these 14 years to be counted? According to some commentators, they are to be reckoned from his conversion mentioned in Gal. 1:15. If so, his conversion was in A.D. 36 or 37, according as we count the 14 years exclusively or inclusively of the first of them. But in Gal. 1:18 Paul notes that he first visited Jerusalem 3 years after his conversion. Hence it is more natural to date the 14 years of Gal. 2:1 from the close of the previously mentioned 3 years. In that case, according as we reckon exclusively or inclusively, his conversion was in A.D. 33 or 35. It is most in accordance with Hebrew custom to reckon inclusively. Hence we may assign his conversion to A.D. 35, his 1st subsequent visit to Jerusalem (Gal. 1:18) to A.D. 37, and the 14 years after (ch. 2:1) to A.D. 50. As already remarked, all these dates are disputed. Some assign the accession of Festus to A.D. 55, and therefore push back all the other dates 5 years earlier than those given above. Other scholars vary on special points. Some assign Paul's death to A.D. 64, supposing that he died in the 1st year of Nero's persecution. But the dates given above appear to be by far the most probable. They yield, with some other details, the following table:

Death, resurrection, and ascension of Christ A. D.	30
Conversion of Paul.	" 35(?)
First subsequent visit to Jerusalem (Gal. 1: 18).	" 37
Paul at Tarsus	" 37–43
Visit to Jerusalem with the gifts from Antioch (Acts 11: 30)	" 44 or 45
First Missionary Journey	" 46–48(?)
Council at Jerusalem.	" 50
Second Missionary Journey	" 51–53
I and II Thessalonians	" 52–53
Third Missionary Journey	" 54–58
Galatians	" 55
I Corinthians	" 56 or 57
II "	" 57
Romans	" 57–58
Arrest	" 58
Imprisonment in Caesarea	" 58–60
Accession of Festus.	" 60
Paul arrives at Rome.	" 61
First Roman imprisonment	"61–63 or 64
Colossians, Philemon, Ephesians.	" 62
Philippians	" 63
Release from first Roman imprisonment	" 63–64
I Timothy	" 64 or 65
Titus.	" 65 or 66
II Timothy	" 67
Death of Paul.	" 67–68

G. T. P. (rev., H. S. G.)

Pave′ment. See GABBATHA.

Pe (pā). The 17th letter of the Heb. alphabet. It was pronounced like *p*, but single *pe* after a vowel is pronounced as *ph*. It heads the 17th section of Psalm 119, in which section each verse of the original begins with this letter.

Peace Of′fer·ing. See OFFERINGS.

Pea′cock′. 1. The rendering of Heb. *tuk-kiyyim;* along with ivory and apes, *tukkiyyim* were imported by Solomon in ships of Tarshish (I Kings 10:22; II Chron. 9:21). Now the words for ivory and ape are of Indian origin, and *tukkī* also finds a satisfactory origin in Malabar *tōgai, tōghai,* Old Tamil *tokei, togei,* a peacock. The peacock (*Pavo cristatus*) is a native of India, where it may be found in the jungles, generally running rapidly away when disturbed. Since the natives do not allow it to be molested, it often makes its way into the villages.

Another interpretation is from Egypt. *t.ky* (monkey); the letter *t* is the fem. article; this rendering implies 2 kinds of monkeys as is the case in certain Egyptian records, and also favors an African origin of the animal as well as an African location for Ophir.

2. See OSTRICH 2.

Pearl. A precious article of commerce (Matt. 13:45, 46; Rev. 21:21; also Job 28:18, in R.V. crystal), used as an ornament by women (I Tim. 2:9; Rev. 17:4). Pearls are found inside the shells of several species of *Mollusca.* They consist of carbonate of lime interstratified with animal membrane, and are formed by the deposit of the nacreous substance around some foreign body within the mantle lobes, such as a grain of sand, which acts as an irritant and serves as a nucleus. This substance is the same as the mother-of-pearl which forms the lustrous inner lining of the shell. Pearls of large size and fine quality are yielded by the pearl oyster (*Pinctada margaritifera*), which abounds in the Indian seas, especially in the Persian Gulf and near Ceylon.

Ped′a·hel (pĕd′a-hĕl) [God has ransomed]. A prince of the tribe of Naphtali in the wilderness (Num. 34:28).

Pe·dah′zur (pê-dă′zẽr) [the Rock (God) has ransomed]. Father of the prince of Manasseh in the wilderness (Num. 1:10; 2:20).

Pe·da′iah (pê-dā′yȧ) [Jehovah has ransomed]. 1. The father of Joel, prince of Manasseh (I Chron. 27:20).

2. A citizen of Rumah and maternal grandfather of King Jehoiakim (II Kings 23:36).

3. A brother of Shealtiel or possibly, though

not probably, his son (I Chron. 3:18, 19). See ZERUBBABEL.

4. A descendant of Parosh. He rebuilt and repaired part of the wall of Jerusalem (Neh. 3:25).

5. One of those, probably priests, who stood on Ezra's left hand when he addressed the people (Neh. 8:4).

6. A Benjamite of the family of Jeshaiah (Neh. 11:7).

7. A Levite; one of those appointed by Nehemiah over the treasures (Neh. 13:13).

Pe′kah (pē′kä) [(God) has opened (the eyes), sees]. Son of Remaliah. He was a captain under Pekahiah; but he conspired against his king, slew him, and reigned in his stead. He adhered to the calf worship of Jeroboam I (II Kings 15:25–28). When Jotham's reign was drawing to a close, Pekah entered into an alliance with Rezin, king of Syria, against Judah. They purposed to dethrone the king and place the crown on a creature of their own. The allied kings began their great invasion of Judah just as the reins of government passed from Jotham into the hands of Ahaz. The Syrians advanced through the country e. of the Jordan to Elath, intending to meet at Jerusalem. Pekah led his army directly toward the capital of Judah, burning and pillaging as he went. The inhabitants of Jerusalem were greatly alarmed. Isaiah, however, was directed to encourage the king and the people with the assurance that the plan of the enemy would fail, and to exhort them to put their trust in Jehovah. Ahaz spurned the advice, preferring to trust to the king of Assyria, and purchased the aid of Tiglath-pileser III. The advance of the Assyrian army through Galilee (II Kings 15:29) to Philistia, in 734 B.C., compelled the allied kings to withdraw their troops from Judah in order to protect their own dominions. Pekah carried off a multitude of captives as he departed; but on the remonstrance of the Prophet Oded, he clothed and fed them and sent them home (II Kings 16:5–9; II Chron. 28:5–15; Isa. 7:1–13). In 730 B.C. Hoshea murdered Pekah and ascended the throne in his stead (II Kings 15:30). This deed was accomplished with the connivance of Tiglath-pileser III. The present Heb. text assigns 20 years to the reign of Pekah (II Kings 15:27). It is impossible that he occupied the throne of Samaria during all these years, for Menahem, a predecessor of his, was on the throne about 738 B.C., in the reign of Tiglath-pileser III (II Kings 15:19). Critics of all schools accordingly admit that 20 years is much too long. There is a bare possibility, however, that the Hebrew writer, when he summarizes the reign of Pekah, and states that "in the fifty-second year of Uzziah Pekah reigned over Israel in Samaria—twenty years," does not mean that Pekah reigned all these 20 years in Samaria. Pekah was associated with Gileadites (II Kings 15:25). It is possible that he set up his authority in n. Gilead and Galilee in 749 B.C., during the confusion which accompanied the death of Jeroboam II, and maintained his power during the greater part of Menahem's reign, being the cause of Menahem's feeling of insecurity until Tiglath-pileser III invaded the n. and established Menahem's sway over the whole country (II Kings 15:19). Then Pekah probably abandoned opposition, professed loyalty, and was given a high military position in the service of the king to whom he had hitherto refused obedience. After Menahem's death and in the absence of Tiglath-pileser III, and perhaps backed by Rezin, Pekah seized the throne in the 52d year of Uzziah and again reigned. See CHRONOLOGY, IV.

Pek′a·hi′ah (pĕk′a-hī′a) [Jehovah has opened (the eyes), sees]. Son and successor of Menahem in the Kingdom of Israel. He came to the throne c. 735 B.C., and reigned 2 years, adhering to the calf worship of Jeroboam I. He was assassinated in his palace at Samaria by Pekah, a captain of his, who then usurped the throne (II Kings 15:23-26).

Pe'kod (pē'kŏd). The Puḳūdu, a powerful Aramaean tribe inhabiting the plain e. of the Tigris, not far from its mouth. In Ezekiel's time they belonged to Nebuchadnezzar's empire (Jer. 50:21; Ezek. 23:23).

Pe·la'iah (pē-lā'yȧ) [Jehovah is wonderful]. 1. One of the Levites who with Ezra caused the people to understand the Law (Neh. 8:7) and sealed the covenant (ch. 10:10).
2. A man of Judah, descended from Shecaniah (I Chron. 3:24).

Pel'a·li'ah (pĕl'ȧ-lī'ȧ) [Jehovah has judged]. A priest descended from Malchijah (Neh. 11:12).

Pel'a·ti'ah (pĕl'ȧ-tī'ȧ) [Jehovah has set free]. 1. One of the Simeonite captains in the successful war between that tribe and the Amalekites (I Chron. 4:42).
2. A prince of Israel, and son of Benaiah. He misled the people. In vision Ezekiel saw him, and he prophesied against him, and Pelatiah suddenly died (Ezek. 11:1-13; cf. chs. 8:1, 3; 11:24).
3. A son of Hananiah, and a grandson of Zerubbabel (I Chron. 3:21). Perhaps he was the person of this name who was a chief of the people and with Nehemiah sealed the covenant (Neh. 10:22).

Pe'leg (pē'lĕg), in A.V. (Luke 3:35) **Pha'lec** [division]. A son or descendant of Eber (Gen. 10:25; 11:16). He takes his name from the fact that in his days the earth was divided. The division alluded to may be the separation of the descendants of Arpachshad from the Joktanide Arabs (ch. 10:24-29); or it may refer to the scattering of the descendants of Noah.

Pe'let (pē'lĕt) [(God) has set free]. 1. A son of Jahdai, of the tribe of Judah (I Chron. 2:47).
2. A Benjamite who joined David while he was at Ziklag (I Chron. 12:3).

Pe'leth (pē'lĕth) [cf. Arab. *fulat*, swift (of a horse)]. 1. A Reubenite, father of that On who joined in Korah's rebellion (Num. 16:1).
2. A man of Judah, family of Hezron, house of Jerahmeel (I Chron. 2:33).

Pel'e·thites (pĕl'ē-thīts). Certain members of David's bodyguard. Apparently they were from the Philistine country, as were the Cherethites and the men of Gath, who were their comrades in arms. They were faithful to David during the calamities of his later years and took a prominent part in the war in which Absalom lost his cause and his life (II Sam. 15:18-22). They also helped in the fight with Sheba (ch. 20:7). The name which they bear is doubtless a gentilic adjective, and some scholars regard it as a var. form of *Pelishtī*, Philistine. See CHERETHITES.

Pel'i·can. The rendering of Heb. *ḳā'ath*, the vomiter. The word is twice translated cormorant in the text of A.V. (Isa. 34:11; Zeph. 2:14); but elsewhere pelican, as everywhere in R.V. The bird was ceremonially unclean (Lev. 11:18; Deut. 14:17), lived in the wilderness (Ps. 102:6), and frequented ruins (Isa. 34:11; Zeph. 2:14). It is probably the common or roseate pelican (*Pelecanus onocrotalus*), though rivers and lakes, rather than ruined cities, unless the ruins are interspersed with marshes, are its appropriate place of abode. Its 4 toes, being all connected by large

webs, adapt it for aquatic life. It sometimes, however, perches on trees. Its bill is large and furrowed and has under it a large pouch in which the bird carries the fish on which its young feed. Its height is from 5 to 6 feet; the expansion of its wings 12 or 13. A few individuals are found on the Sea of Galilee; a much larger number on the shallow lakes of Egypt and on the Nile.

Pel'o·nite (pĕl'ō-nīt). A word in I Chron. 11:27; 27:10 corresponding to Paltite in II Sam. 23:26, and in I Chron. 11:36 apparently to Gilonite in II Sam. 15:12; 23:34. In I Chron. 27:10 the person who is designated by this epithet is further said to be of the children of Ephraim. No person or place is known from which this adjective could be derived; certainly not from Pallu, who was a Reubenite and whose descendants were called Palluites (Num. 26:5). In view of these circumstances, Pelonite is not unreasonably believed to be a corruption of the text. Hebrew *pelōnī*, however, means "such and such a one" (e.g., I Sam. 21:2), and it may have been inserted in the passages mentioned by a scribe who could not read the original word in the text which he was copying.

Pen. 1. A stylus or graving tool made of iron and used by writers for cutting letters on stone (Job 19:24; Ps. 45:1; Jer. 8:8; 17:1). In Heb. it is called *'ēṭ* and once *ḥereṭ* (Isa. 8:1).
2. A reed pen used for writing with ink on papyrus (III John 13; cf. II John 12). The mention of a penknife or knife of a writer in Jer. 36:23, and of a roll in which the prophet's words were written, imply that reed pens had been introduced among the Israelites by the time of Jehoiakim.
The Heb. words rendered "pen of the writer" in Judg. 5:14, A.V., mean literally "staff of a marshal" or scribe (R.V.).

Pe·ni'el (pē-nī'ĕl). See PENUEL 1.

Pe·nin'nah (pē-nĭn'ȧ) [coral]. One of Elkanah's 2 wives, the other being Hannah (I Sam. 1:2-6).

Pen'ny. The rendering of Gr. *dēnarion*. It was the denarius, a silver coin of the Romans (Matt. 22:19-21), worth about 17 cents in the time of Christ (ch. 18:28, R.V. marg.). See MONEY. It was the ordinary pay of an agricultural laborer for a day (Matt. 20:2, 9, 13). Two were given to the innkeeper by the Good Samaritan for looking after the wounded Jew, though he promised to supplement this sum if the expense should exceed it (Luke 10:35). The apostles calculated that 200 would be needed to buy sufficient bread to feed 5,000 people (Mark 6:37). This would be 1 denarius for each 25, or ⅔ of a cent to each person. The prices in Rev. 6:6 were those asked during a dearth.

Pen'ta·teuch (pĕn'tȧ-tūk) [Gr. *pentateuchos*, consisting of 5 books]. The first 5 books of the O.T., viz., Genesis, Exodus, Leviticus, Numbers, and Deuteronomy. The word nowhere occurs in Scripture, the Israelites calling these books collectively the Law (Josh. 1:7; Matt. 5:17), the Law of Moses (I Kings 2:3; Ezra 7:6; Luke 2:22), the Law of the Lord (II Chron. 31:3; Luke 2:23), the Book of the Law (Josh. 1:8), the Book of Moses (II Chron. 25:3, 4), the Book of the Law of Moses (Josh. 8:31), the Book of the Law of God (Josh. 24:26), the Book of the Law of the Lord (II Chron. 17:9). This fact suggests that the 5 books were considered as 1; and they still are so in Heb. MSS., though severally cited by their opening words. The division into 5 distinct books is mentioned by Josephus (Jos. *Apion* i. 8). It may have originated with the Greek translators or been ancient. But whether or not the LXX translators adopted or originated this fivefold division, from them at least emanated the modern names Genesis, Exodus, Leviticus, Numbers, and Deuteronomy.*

According to the traditional view, the events recorded in the 1st book of the Pentateuch were transmitted until the time of Moses, as is now known, by tradition oral and written ; the

Pentateuch (12th Century), Numbers 6:3–6
Each verse of the Hebrew is followed by the corresponding verse from the Targum of Onkelos

subsequent occurrences fell under Moses' own observation, and he was himself an actor in the most stirring events. Writing was practiced long before the time of Moses. In the 4th millennium cuneiform was used by the Sumerians in Babylonia, and hieroglyphs by the Egyptians. The Proto-Sinaitic inscriptions

may be dated in the 19th century B.C. ; the Ras Shamra cuneiform alphabet was in use in the 16–14th centuries B.C. Akkadian was the international written language in the Tell el-Amarna period in Palestine and Syria. And the various forms of literature represented in the Pentateuch were familiar literary conceptions of Moses' time (see MOSES). Though the 5 books themselves are not attributed as a whole to Moses in any verse which they contain, yet the Pentateuch testifies expressly to the Mosaic authorship of its contents. Two passages of the narrative portion are attributed to his pen : the account of the victory over Amalek (Ex. 17:14), and the itinerary of the march of the Israelites from Egypt to the plains of Moab opposite Jericho (Num. 33:2). A didactic song, reciting the dealing of the Most High with Israel, is declared to have been written and uttered by Moses (Deut. 31: 19, 22, 30 ; 32:44) ; and a hymn of praise, evoked by the deliverance from Pharoah at the Red Sea, is recorded as sung by Moses (Ex. 15:1–18 ; cf. v. 21). The legal portion consists of 3 distinct bodies of law. The 1st is entitled the Book of the Covenant, and comprises the Ten Commandments, which formed the fundamental law of the nation, and specific regulations based on them (Ex., chs. 20 to 23). This book Moses is expressly said to have written (Ex. 24:4). The 2d body of laws pertains to the sanctuary and service (Ex., chs. 25 to 31 ; 35 to 40 ; Leviticus ; and major legal part of Numbers). This legislation is constantly declared to have been revealed by the Lord to Moses (Ex. 25:1, etc.). The 3d body of legislation expressly and repeatedly claims to be the address of Moses to the new generation of people on the eve of their entrance into Canaan. It contains a brief rehearsal of the way in which God has led them and then repeats sundry portions of the Law with the special object of exhibiting its spirituality, emphasizing the features which are of vital religious importance in the new circumstances in which the people will soon be placed, and modifying details to adapt the laws to the new requirements of the settled life in Canaan. Moses wrote this address and delivered it into the custody of the Levites (Deut. 31:9, 24–26). These are the explicit claims, scattered throughout the Pentateuch itself, to its Mosaic authorship.

The remainder of the O.T. refers to the Law as the work of Moses and written in a book (Josh. 1:7, 8 ; Ezra 6:18 ; Neh. 8:1, 18), and abounds in explicit references to the Law of Moses (Josh. 1:7, 8 ; 8:31–35 ; Judg. 3:4 ; I Kings 2:3 ; II Kings 18:6, 12 ; cf. Deut. 24: 16 ; II Kings 21:7, 8 ; Dan. 9:11, 13 ; Ezra 3: 2 ; 6:18 ; 7:6 ; Neh. 8:1, 18 ; Mal. 4:4). One feature of this law, namely, the law of the one altar, was in abeyance during the captivity and seclusion of the Ark after the Lord had forsaken Shiloh (I Sam. 4:11, 21, 22 ; 6: 1 ; 7:2 ; Ps. 78:60 ; Jer. 7:12–15 ; 26:6). During this period the people under the leadership of Samuel sacrificed where they could (I Kings 3:2–4), as their fathers had done in the olden time before the covenant had been entered into between Jehovah and the Israelites, of which the Law and the Ark were the sign and pledge. Once again this specific law was in abeyance. The pious Israelites of the Northern Kingdom were prevented from going up to Jerusalem to worship. They had to choose between refraining from sacrifice altogether or worshiping God as did Abraham, Isaac, and Jacob. They properly chose the latter alternative. All other cases of sacrifice offered elsewhere than at the central sanctuary were strictly in accord with the law which expressly provided that wherever Jehovah manifested his name there sacrifice was fitting (Ex. 20:24 ; cf. Judg. 2:

*The division of the Law of Moses into 5 books furnished the model, it is thought, for the similar division of the Psalter. If it did, it is ancient; for the Psalter was early divided into 5 books. Proof that it did is sought in the alleged discovery that the contents of each book are so arranged that the opening psalm shall correspond to the respective book of the Pentateuch. Psalm 1, with its comparison of the righteous to a tree planted by the rivers of water, is a reminder of the garden of Eden in the 1st book of the Pentateuch. Psalm 42, with which the 2d book of the Psalter opens, is the cry of a man in distress, oppressed by the enemy and thinking himself forgotten by God, but anticipating deliverance out of all his trouble. It recalls the affliction of Israel in Egypt and the deliverance as related in Exodus. In Psalm 73, with which the 3d book begins, the doubts of the psalmist regarding the justice of God's dealing with men vanish when he considers the end of the wicked. The psalm is supposed to reflect gratitude for God's goodness in giving the law of Leviticus, which was an abiding mercy. Psalm 90, a prayer of Moses, in which God is besought to teach us to number our days, corresponds to Numbers. Psalm 107, which begins the 5th book, speaks of the goodness of the Lord in the days of trouble, and is thus like Deuteronomy, which recapitulates the instances of God's loving-kindness to Israel. It must be confessed that the correspondence is rather fanciful; and if an editor set about securing correspondence, it is strange that he did not adopt a more appropriate arrangement. Psalm 8, with its reference to the heavens, the work of God's fingers, to the moon and stars which he ordained, and to man whom he made and to whom he gave dominion over all creatures, would have better corresponded with Gen., ch. 1. Psalm 66 of the 2d book, which tells of the works of God, how he turned the sea into dry land for the people to pass through, and how he tried the Israelites, laid sore burdens on them, and caused men to ride over their heads, and then brought them out into a wealthy place, should have opened the book. It has an obvious reference to the events recorded in Exodus, whereas Psalm 42 has not. Psalm 76 or 78 should form the opening of the 3d book in order to correspond appropriately to Leviticus.

1, 5; 6:19–24; 13:15–22; see ALTAR). The Law of Moses was known and its authority acknowledged even in the Northern Kingdom. The prophets Hosea and Amos, who labored among the 10 tribes of the North, although they do not mention the name of Moses, frequently refer to the laws recorded in the Pentateuch. At a still later time the Temple copy of the Book of the Law was unused and cast aside during the half century of Manasseh's reign when the religion of Jehovah was neglected; but when the Temple was being repaired, preparatory to the restoration of Jehovah's worship, this book was found, or so much of it at least as contained Deuteronomy (II Kings 22:8; 23:25); or, less likely, the book which the high priest found was a copy of the Law of God which had been embedded in the wall of the Temple as a record at the time of building the sanctuary. Daniel, Ezra, and Nehemiah allude to the written Law of Moses. That Moses was the author of the Pentateuch was the opinion of the Jews of Christ's time (Mark 12:19; John 8:5; Jos. *Antiq.*, preface 4; *Apion* i. 8). Christ and the Evangelists call the Pentateuch Moses and the Book of Moses (Mark 12:26; Luke 16: 29; 24:27, 44), and speak of its having been given by Moses and committed to writing by Moses (Mark 10:5; 12:19; John 1:17; 5:46, 47; 7:19).

The Mosaic authorship of the Pentateuch, however, is not generally accepted by critics. The principal objections formerly urged against it were several verses in which reference has been found to times subsequent to the death of Moses: 1. In Gen. 12:6 we read: "And the Canaanite was then in the land" (cf. ch. 13:7). The meaning assigned to these words is that the Canaanites had ceased to be there when the writer lived. The words, however, actually state only that the Canaanites were in the country when Abraham was there, and were occupying the land promised to him. 2. In Gen. 14:14 we read that Abraham pursued the defeated confederates to Dan. In the patriarch's time, however, the place was called Laish, the name Dan not having been given it till the time of the Judges (Judg. 18:29). The question is, however, whether Dan in Genesis is the place mentioned in The Book of Judges. If it is, the more familiar name may have been substituted in the place of Laish in the course of repeated transcription for the sake of clearness. 3. In Gen. 36:31 the words occur: "Before there reigned any king over the children of Israel," as if the Hebrew monarchy under Saul had already been established when the author wrote. But the kings of Edom, mentioned in vs. 32–43, reigned before Moses; and Moses notes that the descendants of Esau already had kings, although the Israelites, to whom the promise had been given that kings should arise among them (Gen. 17:6, 16; 35:11), as yet had none. 4. Moses is said to be beyond Jordan, meaning e. of the river, as though the writer himself were in Canaan (Deut. 1:1). The expression, however, does not necessarily imply this. Canaan was the land that had been promised to Abraham, Isaac, and Jacob and which the Israelites accordingly regarded as their proper home. From his point of view the land e. of the river was "beyond Jordan." Moses was still beyond Jordan. No matter on which side of the river the people were, they designated the mountains e. of the Dead Sea Abarim (those beyond) and in later times they called the country between the Jabbok and the Arnon Perea (region beyond). 5. It is universally admitted that Deut. 34:5–12, in which the death of Moses is recorded and comparison made between him and prophets subsequently raised up (vs. 5, 10, etc.), cannot have been from his pen. But an addition of this sort does not militate against the Mosaic authorship of the Pentateuch as a whole.

The orthodox theologian and commentator Vitringa expressed the opinion in 1707, in the interest of the credibility of Genesis, that Moses edited and supplemented records left by the fathers and preserved among the Israelites. In 1753, Jean Astruc, a French physician of ability, but profligate, attempted to distinguish 2 leading authors in Genesis, whose writings Moses used and who are distinguished by their employment respectively of the words Elohim, that is God, and Jehovah. Besides the writings of these 2, he thought he could detect 10 minor documents relating chiefly to foreign nations and in which no name of God is found. This hypothesis was adopted by Eichhorn and elaborated with learning and ingenuity. He steadfastly insisted that Moses compiled Genesis and was the author of the rest of the Pentateuch. It was soon discovered, however, that the principles which govern the partition of Genesis were capable of being applied with similar results to the entire Pentateuch; and if so, the original documents covered the history of Moses' own time and were scarcely put together by Moses to form the present Pentateuch. In fact critics have applied the same principles to The Book of Joshua that they join to the Pentateuch, thus forming the Hexateuch. The grounds on which the partition is made are chiefly 4: 1. The alternate use of the divine names God and Jehovah in successive paragraphs or sections. 2. The continuity of each so-called document when taken separately. 3. The diversity of style, diction, and ideas in the different documents. 4. Repetitions or parallel passages, often contradictory, indicative of distinct documents. Starting in simple form, the hypothesis underwent constant modification under careful criticism in order to remove the difficulties that beset it.

The documentary theory of the formation of the Pentateuch is generally known as the Graf-Wellhausen or simply as the Wellhausen hypothesis. It represents the accumulation of the work of various men, among whom may be mentioned Spinoza (1670), Hobbes (1651), R. Simon (1678), H. B. Witter (1711), Astruc (1753), J. G. Eichhorn (1780–1783), DeWette (1806), W. Vatke (1835), H. Hupfeld (1853), K. H. Graf (1866), A. Kuenen (1861–1870), and J. Wellhausen (1876–1884). Many others published on the same theme both before and after the days of Wellhausen. We can hardly expect to find uniformity among the critics, but a popular form of the documentary hypothesis may be set forth in outline as follows. (There are, however, numerous disagreements among scholars on various points which cannot be discussed here.) The writer J or the author of the document J (so called because he refers to God as Jehovah) is supposed to have lived in Judah c. 950–850 B.C. Some, however, would divide J into J^1 and J^2 (or L, lay document, and J respectively). The language of J is free, flowing, and picturesque. E or the writer of the E document (here God is called Elohim, whence the designation E) is supposed to have lived c. 750 B.C. E is said to reflect a more advanced civilization, a more refined environment, a more thoughtful age, and a higher ethical standard than J. Sometime the Decalogue (Ex. 20:1–17) and the Book of the Covenant (chs. 20:22 to 23:33) were set within the E document. The next important step is the combination of J and E after the fall of Samaria (722 B.C.) by a redactor c. 650 B.C. The resultant document is JE. The critics maintain that the strata J and E can be detected, because the redactor did not rewrite his sources, but dovetailed selected material from the 2 documents. The greater part of

Deuteronomy (chs. 5 to 26; 28) or D is assigned to the year 621 B.C., or perhaps rather a half century earlier (II Kings 22:8 seq.); on this document was based the reformation of Josiah or the Deuteronomic reformation (621 B.C.). The Law in Deuteronomy (cf. chs. 5:14 seq.; 15:12–18; 23:15 seq.; 24:19–22) receives a more sympathetic attitude and a more humane emphasis than in the Book of the Covenant. The Book of Deuteronomy would then represent the final result of a series of editorial expansions of D. From the point of view of the documentary hypothesis the 2d important growth of the Pentateuch was the addition of D to JE. In 597 B.C. Ezekiel was taken as an exile to Babylonia. The Holiness Code (Lev., chs. 17 to 26), known as H, may have been compiled after Ezekiel's work, about the middle of the 6th century. This code is supposed at some uncertain date to have been incorporated into P (the Priestly Code), the latest document of the Pentateuch, which is supposed to have been composed during the Babylonian Exile. P seems to have been based on written documents and represents a priestly point of view. It is exact in dates and genealogies; it is precise in cataloguing persons and things; it is punctilious and elaborate in dealing with essential details and is written in a stereotyped style. P begins with the creation of heaven and earth and includes an abstract of history to the time of Joshua; it calls God Elohim. Its aim is to give a systematic view of the origin and chief institutions of the Israelitish theocracy. Ezra returned to Jerusalem in 458 B.C., and Nehemiah in 444. According to the critics the 3d main stage in the growth of the Pentateuch was the joining of P to JED. Again the redactor did not rewrite but combined the various sources; thus the critics believe that they can detect the original underlying documents and the points of juncture. The general view of critics is that P was the foundation document of the Pentateuch and that it was supplemented by an editor by the addition of JED and possibly other elements. While it may be taken for granted that Ezra used the entire Pentateuch, it is generally assumed that he read P (Neh. 8:1–8) and that the final redaction of the Pentateuch took place later, probably shortly before 400 B.C. It is evident that there is much uncertainty as well as conjecture in this theory.

Objections may be raised: 1. This theory involves the denial of the truth of the historical narrative in the O.T., not the assertion of occasional or minute inaccuracies, but the rejection of the credibility of the O.T. narrative almost as a whole. Wellhausen makes no concealment of the fact. 2. Furthermore, to date the so-called documents so late is forbidden by the fact of the development of doctrine. In the Pentateuch the conceptions entertained and the doctrine taught concerning the future state, divine retribution, the spiritual character of true worship, angels, and the Messiah are rudimentary. They appear in developed form in late books, in Job, The Psalms, and the prophets. This is a strong argument that the writer of the Pentateuch lived at an earlier age and in a different intellectual environment. Dillmann, while accepting the existence of documents, opposed Wellhausen's arrangement, insisting that history required the existence of the Levitical legislation before that of Deuteronomy, and so far he is more in accord with the teaching of Scripture. 3. The early existence of the laws and institutions of the Pentateuch is attested by the traces of them in the writings of the early prophets. Now, it is possible to admit the genuineness of the passages where these traces are found, but to deny that they

were derived from Deuteronomic or priestly documents by assuming that the prophets were acquainted with old customs and unwritten laws which traditionally went back to Mosaic times. Furthermore the concession that the Pentateuchal law and organization were in existence in the 8th century B.C. is avoided by declaring that these references are late interpolations in the genuine writings of the prophets. As a rule no proof for such a declaration is offered. Believers in the Mosaic authorship of the Levitical and Deuteronomic law point with confidence to the evident indissolubleness of these references from the context and their inseparable connection with the original argument, which show that they are not interpolations, but an essential part of the discourse of the prophets of the 8th century. 4. The theory of the late origin of Israel's institutions asserts, as a fundamental postulate, that the Law and the elaborate ritual of Israel were the result of a gradual development. The Wellhausen hypothesis was formed under the influence of Hegelian philosophy and assumes 3 stages of evolution: pre-prophetic, prophetic, and legal. As in nature, so in art, law, and ritual, the simple ever precedes the complex, and the rude the refined. The thesis, as a general principle, is demonstrable and is universally accepted; and it is true also in the case of the civil law and the worship of Israel. But there is another truth, to speak of but one, namely, that Israel was the heir of the ages. When Wellhausen published his *Prolegomena* in 1878, archaeology had shed practically no light upon the Bible. Now the science of archaeology has vastly extended our knowledge of ancient history and the milieu in which lived the Israelites. The social psychology and thought patterns of the ancient Egyptian and Mesopotamian world stand in striking contrast to those of Israel as postulated and reconstructed by the followers of the Wellhausen school. Development in law and in the ritual of divine worship had been going on for centuries. The Israelites did not begin with nothing, any more than do the founders of a modern state or the framers of a modern constitution. Under Moses they appropriated the mature fruits of man's labor and man's experience. Among the nations with whom they were in close touch in the Mosaic era, among the Babylonians from the midst of whom their forefathers had emigrated and the Egyptians with whom they had sojourned, the development of the forms of worship had reached maturity in an elaborate refinement; and the legal sense of the Semites had developed so far as to discern a unity underlying manifold laws and to adopt the principle of codification. The statutes organized as a body of law and incorporated in the Book of the Covenant, the sanctuary as described in Exodus, and the ritual that is outlined in Leviticus were not strange novelties to the people assembled at Sinai, but were familiar conceptions and already full of significance, appealing to the sense of justice and appreciation for the rights of the lowly and helpless which the Semites possessed long before the days of Moses, representing types of sacred architecture and ritual approved by the most refined contemporary peoples, embodying lofty ideals possessed in common with the ethnic religions of the day, employing a symbolism that was, as it were, the universal religious speech among the men of that age, and giving expression to the common innate sense of propriety in the worship of God. The whole was molded and dominated by the truth of only one God, holy, gracious, and spiritual. The civil law of Israel and the sanctuary, priesthood, and ritual, rich, refined, elaborate, are not things new under the sun; but Moses, a statesman and religious leader, in long and intimate communion with God and under direct divine teaching and control, selected suitable materials from the legal and ritualistic wealth of the age and organized them into a vehicle that was a perfect expression of God's will for quickening, fostering, disciplining, and guiding the moral and religious consciousness of Israel and giving a proper and intelligible display of those great truths concerning God which Israel held and for which Israel was to bear witness among men. The law and worship of Israel as exhibited in the legislation at Sinai, however long the period of development may have been that preceded them, were timely, in entire harmony with the conceptions of the Mosaic age. If the documentary hypothesis be accepted without qualification, it involves a reversal of the facts of history by placing the prophets before the Pentateuch. See MOSES, ALPHABET, ALTAR, HAMMURABI, PRIEST, TABERNACLE, THEOCRACY.

Turning to the literary aspect of the question, what are the objections to the theory of documents? 1. The impossibility of separating the documents from each other in strict adherence to the principle that certain words are characteristic of the several writers. To take an example from the use of different divine names, which is the starting point of the hypothesis and the phenomenon most evident to English readers, the name Jehovah, which in A.V. is generally translated LORD, betokens J, and should not occur, according to the theory, in the book of Genesis in the documents E and P. But the critics maintain that the divine names are not the sole criterion in determining the documents. Thus Jehovah occurs in P (Gen. 17:1; 21:1b); in E (chs. 21:33; 22:11, 14; 28:21); also Elohim (God) is found in J (chs. 4:25; 6:2, 4; 7:9; 9:27; 33:5, 11). Here are a few instances in Genesis alone where the critical principle fails in respect to but 2 characteristic words. The compiler is said to have introduced the awkward words arbitrarily or from another document. In some cases J is said to have used the name God discriminatingly, but this seems to be a virtual abandonment of the theory. If the writer used the divine name discriminatingly in some cases, he may have done so in all, as the defenders of the Mosaic authorship maintain. On the theory of the Mosaic authorship, these words are in place; and it is ordinarily apparent that they are discriminatingly employed. Elohim (God) denotes the divine being in his relation to the universe at large as creator, preserver, and governor of all his creatures and all their actions. Jehovah denotes God as he reveals himself to man, especially in grace. 2. The continuity of the documents is frequently interrupted. Thus Gen., ch. 5, is a P chapter, but v. 29 is assigned to J; in ch. 7, vs. 1–5 belong to J, but v. 6 is P. J is resumed in v. 7 and continues to the end of v. 10, but in v. 9 "two and two," "male and female," and "God" belong to P. Verse 11 is P, but "six hundredth year," "second month," "seventeenth day of the month" belong to J; v. 12 belongs to J. Verses 13–16a are P, but 16b is J. Verse 17a is P, but "forty days" is J; 17b is J. Verses 18–21 are P; vs. 22, 23 are J, and v. 24 is P. J's narrative embraces chs. 10:21, 24–30; 11: (1–9) 28–30; 12:1–4a. P narrated chs. 1:1 to 2:4a, concluding with the emphatic declaration that "God saw everything that he had made, and, behold, it was very good." Then after listing the genealogy of Adam (ch. 5:1–28, 30–32), he suddenly writes: "And the earth was corrupt before God" (ch. 6:9–22). Again, P's narrative of the early history of Abraham appears as follows: chs. 11:27, 31, 32; 12:4b, 5; 13:6, 11b, 12a; 16:1a, 3, 15, 16; 17. What is not P in those chapters is assigned to J. Over

against this complication in the hypothetical documents, believers in the Mosaic authorship are able to show unity of theme, unbroken continuity of thought, balanced treatment of the parts, and progressive narrative. See GENESIS. 3. The theory that there are parallel accounts marked by difference of style fails as a trustworthy principle in the only case where it can be tested by external evidence. It is asserted that in the narrative of the Flood the storm which produced the Deluge is described twice in 3 successive verses: "The same day were all the fountains of the great deep broken up, and the windows of heaven were opened" (ch. 7:11, P), and "It came to pass after the seven days, that the waters of the flood were upon the earth, . . . and the rain was upon the earth forty days and forty nights" (vs. 10, 12, J). It is urged also that there are 2 literary styles apparent here: the former exuberant, vivid, poetic, the latter a bald statement of the facts in simple prose. On the theory of Mosaic authorship, there is no difficulty in accounting for difference of style. Different themes require different statement. Dates, genealogies, and the like do not call the imagination into exercise. Vivid and picturesque description belongs to the narration of lively and vivid incidents. 4. The critical theory that there are parallel accounts of the same event which are marked by contradictions likewise fails to stand the test of external evidence. It is contended that according to P God forewarns Noah of an impending destructive flood of waters, but does not reveal to him whether it will be caused by melting snows or continuous rains or tidal wave; and thus P contradicts J, who states that the Lord bade Noah enter into the ark, because in yet 7 days he would cause it to rain upon the earth. But again the Babylonian account shows that the Hebrew narrative does not embody 2 divergent accounts but is the record of successive progressive events. For according to it, as in Genesis, man was first warned of coming destruction and bidden to build a boat. The ruin was, accordingly, to be wrought by a flood of water, but whether the deluge would be due to rain, or a freshet, or the inflowing sea was not disclosed. When the appointed time approached, however, the prophecy became definite and foretold rain. The Hebrew account, with its present material and the present arrangement of that material, is essentially the ancient account handed down from the fathers. Nor can ch. 7:12 (J) and ch. 7:24 (P) be shown to be contradictory. According to those who hold to the traditional Mosaic authorship, the criticism which distributes the narrative among different writers on the ground of differences of style or alleged contradictions is demonstrably invalid.

The present trend in O.T. studies is away from the earlier and rather hypothetical criticism. Wellhausen lived before the time of archaeological contributions to the study of the O.T.; in consequence his point of view is antiquated and his picture of the development of Israelitish institutions sadly distorted. The old and fast literary criticism is now receiving severe blows; it was too formal and assumed an exactness that did not correspond to the situation in life. In 1921 R. Kittel said that the building lacked a foundation and that the architects were without standards. In 1931 Pedersen of Copenhagen stated that the beautiful and methodical regulation of the various strata as presented by Wellhausen and his generation rests upon an illusion. Yet there is no harm in subjecting the Pentateuch to the same methods that are applied to other literature. When the Pentateuch is studied in the light of all our historical, linguistic, archaeological, and critical knowledge, our understanding of it is bound to be increased, and our appreciation of it is enhanced.

A belief in the Mosaic origin of the Pentateuch, however, does not necessarily require that the Pentateuch come from the hand of Moses in its present form. The development and changes of languages are well-known, and from our knowledge of Semitic and other tongues it is hardly probable that the Hebrew of Moses' day was like that of Biblical Hebrew. Yet if Hebrew scribes "modernized" the language of Moses, the Pentateuch as a work would still remain Mosaic. It cannot be emphasized too strongly that there is hardly any evidence at all in the ancient Near East for documentary or literary fabrications. Sacred and profane documents in that region were transcribed with greater care than is true of copying in Greco-Roman times. Another important observation is that in the ancient Near East the scribes did not leave obvious archaisms in spelling or grammar, but they revised ancient literary and other writings periodically. There was a tendency among ancient Oriental scribes and compilers to add rather than to subtract. Thus if there be documents like J and E, the divergencies between them should be considered not as average variation, but rather as *maximum* variation. As is well-known, the power of the Oriental memory is prodigious; it is possible that many of Moses' decisions and statements were handed down for generations by memory. If they were recorded in later times and added to Moses' written works, they would in reality be a part of the work of Moses. Probably oral composition and transmission of literature played a far greater role in antiquity than is generally supposed. A study of the code of Hammurabi and other legal codes of the ancient Near East shows the antiquity of the Mosaic laws. Several types of laws are recognized in the Pentateuch: testimonies, statutes, ordinances, and commandments. According to Jirku (1927) there is nothing to oppose the view that Moses composed and promulgated a code of laws by using existing laws and following an ancient Oriental genre. For the solemn proclamation of the Law, cf. Deut. 27:1–4; 31:10–12; Josh. 8:33 *seq.*; apparently there were assemblies every 7 years where the Law was read. According to Alt (1934) nothing contradicts the view that the first of these assemblies coincided with the conclusion of the Mosaic covenant in the wilderness. The constitutional law of Israel is of necessity Jehovistic; so we must go back to Moses and his work with the tribes in the wilderness.

Many scholars, however, continue to recognize the 4 main documents JEDP, but they give them a different interpretation from what was implied in the Wellhausen theory of development. They would accept the antiquity of the contents by regarding the material as considerably older than the time of composition of JEDP. Some would assign these documents to schools rather than to individual writers; thus these documents might be considered as recensions of Mosaic material in vogue in various centers in Palestine, as Kadesh, Shechem, Shiloh, and Jerusalem. Duplications and various points of view within the Pentateuch could then be explained as being due to editors who later placed together documents which represent various recensions of the work of Moses. W. F. Albright (1940) places the Deuteronomic movement in the late 7th century B.C., but he arrives at this date without following the paths of Wellhausen. He considers the Deuteronomic reaction not as exclusively a local phenomenon, but as part of a movement throughout the ancient Near East; he refers to the imitation of the past in the Saïte Dynasty in Egypt and the copying of ancient Babylonian tablets for Ashurbanipal's library at Nineveh. In the same way he supposes that the book of Deuteronomy represents an attempt to return to the spirit of Moses. This principle could be applied to various parts of the Pentateuch by regarding additions to the original work of Moses as being made in the spirit of the founder of the code. Such a view allows for normal legal development from a Mosaic nucleus after the settlement in the Land of Canaan; in such a case the development of the Mosaic Law would be analogous to what is found in other lands.

The development of the religion of Israel demands that the Pentateuch precede the prophets, and such is the Biblical presentation. In order to understand the religious history of Israel it is necessary to retain the view of the Pentateuch that Moses was a monotheist and that his God was Jehovah. Moses was the framer of the religious system of Israel and the founder of the Hebrew commonwealth, and he remains, whether in a direct or more or less indirect sense, the author of the Pentateuch. Even though various scholars find documents or strata in the Pentateuch (and their views are far from agreeing on this point), archaeological, philological, and historical studies support the verisimilitude of the Pentateuch.

Pen·te·cost (pĕn'tē-kŏst). See WEEKS, FEAST OF.

Pe·nu'el (pē-nū'ĕl) and once **Pe·ni'el** (Gen. 32:30) [face of God]. 1. Originally an encampment e. of the Jordan, first named by Jacob because he had there seen God face to face, yet his life had been preserved (Gen. 32:30, 31). In the time of the Judges there was a tower there, which Gideon broke down, and a city, the inhabitants of which he slew (Judg. 8:8, 9, 17). It was fortified by Jeroboam I (I Kings 12:25).

2. A man of Judah, and the ancestor of the inhabitants of Gedor (I Chron. 4:4).

3. A Benjamite, family of Shashak (I Chron. 8:25).

Pe'or (pē'ŏr) [an opening, a cleft]. 1. A mountain in Moab looking toward the desert, or Jeshimon (Num. 23:28). From it the camp of Israel at Shittim was in full view (ch. 24:2). A mountain still bore the name in the time of Eusebius and Jerome. It stood opposite Jericho, on the road to Heshbon, above or to the e. of Livias, now Tell er-Rāmeh. Accordingly Peor was a peak of the Abarim range near Wadi Ḥesbân.

2. A Moabite divinity worshiped in Mount Peor, and often called Baal-peor; cf. Num. 25:18; 31:16; Josh. 22:17. See BAAL-PEOR.

Pe·rae'a (pē-rē'á) or **Pe·re'a** (pē-rē'á) [Gr., the land beyond]. The region between the Jabbok and the Arnon, beyond Jordan (Jos. *War* iii. 3, 3); cf. signification and location of Abarim. The name was, however, used in a wider sense; for Josephus calls Gadara, on the banks of the Yarmūk, the capital of Perea (Jos. *War* iv. 7, 3).

Per'a·zim (pĕr'á-zĭm). See BAAL-PERAZIM.

Pe'res (pē'rĕs). See MENE.

Pe'resh (pē'rĕsh) [distinction, separation, dung]. A man of Manasseh (I Chron. 7:16).

Pe'rez (pē'rĕz), in A.V. of O.T. **Pha'rez** except thrice (I Chron. 27:3; Neh. 11:4, 6); in A.V. of N.T. **Pha'res** [a breach]. A son of Judah, 1 of twins whom Tamar bore (Gen. 38:24–30). He became the founder of a tribal family which took its name from him, and of 2 other tribal families which sprang from his sons and were named from them (Num. 26:

20, 21; I Chron. 2:4, 5). He was an ancestor of David and consequently of Christ (Ruth 4:12-18; Matt. 1:3).

Pe'rez-uz'za (pē'rĕz-ŭz'ȧ) and **Pe'rez-uz'zah** (pē'rĕz-ŭz'ȧ) [breach of Uzza]. The name given by David to the place where Uzza was struck dead for touching the Ark (II Sam. 6:8; I Chron. 13:11). Exact situation unknown.

Per·fum'er·y. Spices of various kinds, such as aloes, cassia, cinnamon, myrrh, frankincense, spikenard, which were raised in the Jordan Valley or imported from Arabia and elsewhere, formed the basis of perfumery (Ecclus. 24:15). The spice was compelled to yield its fragrance by at least 4 different methods. It was tied in a bundle or enclosed in a bag (S. of Sol. 1:13); it was reduced to powder and burned as incense (ch. 3:6); its aromatic matter was separated by boiling, and the extract was carried as scent in smelling-bottles suspended from the girdle, or was mixed with oil and used as an ointment (S. of Sol. 1:3; Isa. 3:20; John 12:3). Frequently several spices were compounded (Ex. 30:23, 24; John 19:39). Perfumery was applied to the person and garments and furniture (Ps. 45:8; Prov. 7:17; S. of Sol. 4:11). It was used in the Temple service both as incense and as ointment (Ex. 30:22-38).

Per'ga (pûr'gȧ). A town in Pamphylia, and under the Romans the capital of the province, on the right bank of the river Cestrus, 7½ miles from the mouth. Paul and Barnabas visited the town on the First Missionary Journey, both going and returning (Acts 13:13, 14; 14:25). In the vicinity was a celebrated temple of the goddess Artemis of the Asiatic type (see DIANA), who was known as the queen of Perga.

Per'ga·mum (pûr'gȧ-mŭm), in A.V. **Per'ga· mos** (pûr'gȧ-mŏs). The most important city of Mysia, situated 3 miles n. of the river Caicus, about 15 miles from the sea. It was once the capital of a wealthy kingdom ruled over by a dynasty of kings, several of them called Attalus. The first of these kings, Attalus I, came to the throne in the year 241 B.C. He defeated the Gauls and settled them in the district henceforth known as Galatia. His son Eumenes, who succeeded him, 197 B.C., adorned the city and founded a celebrated library, which ultimately was 2d only to that of Alexandria. Attalus III, who died in the year 133 B.C., bequeathed his property to the Romans, but granted independence to Pergamum and some of the surrounding country. The Romans erected the kingdom into the province of Asia (129-126 B.C.) and made Pergamum the capital. Mark Antony gave the library of 200,000 volumes to Cleopatra and had it removed to Egypt, where it was added to the renowned Alexandrian library. The acropolis of Pergamum crowned a steep hill that rose 1,000 feet above the plain. Near the summit stood an immense altar to Zeus, erected by Eumenes II to commemorate the victory won by his father over the Gauls; and at a short distance from this altar there was an elegant temple of Athene. In the Roman period a temple to the divine Augustus was also built on the acropolis. Outside the city was a famous shrine of Asklepios (Æsculapius), god of medicine, to which people from all quarters flocked for healing. Parchment, called in Lat. *pergamena,* and in Gr. *pergamēnē,* was so named because it was first obtained at Pergamum. The 3d of the 7 churches of Asia addressed in the book of Revelation was that at Pergamum. It is said that Satan's seat was there, and that a faithful martyr, Antipas, had been put to death in the place. It must, therefore, have been a

stronghold of anti-Christian idolatry (Rev. 1:11; 2:12-17). It is now called Bergama.

Pe·ri'da (pē-rī'dȧ). See PERUDA.

Per'iz·zites (pĕr'ĭ-zīts) [dwellers in the open country]. An important section of the Canaanites, often enumerated as one of the tribes of Palestine (Gen. 15:20; Ex. 3:8; Josh. 9:1), and perhaps, like the Rephaim, an aboriginal people who were of different race from the Canaanites and in the land before them (cf. Gen. 13:7; Josh. 17:15; and the omission of them in Gen. 10:15 *seq.*). They were in the country as early as the days of Abraham and Lot (Gen. 13:7). In Joshua's time they inhabited the mountain region (Josh. 11:3), dwelling in the territory afterward given over to the tribes of Ephraim, Manasseh (Josh. 17:15), and Judah (Judg. 1:4, 5). They were not extirpated, but, contrary to the Law of Moses (Deut. 7:3), allowed to enter into marriage alliances with their conquerors, seducing them into idolatry (Judg. 3:5, 6). Solomon imposed upon these Perizzites a yoke of bondservice (I Kings 9:20, 21; II Chron. 8:7).

Per'seus (pûr'sūs). Son and successor of Philip III, and last king of Macedon. In 171 B.C. he resumed the war with the Romans which his father had waged; but, after 3 years of desultory fighting and occasional success, he was completely defeated (I Macc. 8:5) by L. Aemilius Paulus in the battle of Pydna (168 B.C.), which ended the Macedonian monarchy.

Per'sia (pûr'zhȧ). Persia proper, the seat of the Persians when they first became known to the Western nations as a settled people, lay s.e. of Elam and nearly corresponded to the province of modern Persia called Fars, or Farsistan, a modification of the original native name Pārsa. Persia, in this limited sense, was bounded on the n. by Great Media (Media Magna), on the s.w. by the Persian Gulf, on the e. by Carmania (now called Kerman), and on the n.w. by Susiana. Its length was at most about 250 miles; its average breadth about 200; its area considerably less than 50,000 square miles. In looser usage, the term Persia denoted the plateau of Iran, the region bounded by the Persian Gulf, the valleys of the Tigris and the Cyrus, the Caspian Sea, the rivers Oxus, Jaxartes, and Indus (I Macc. 6:1; II Macc. 1:19). But when the Persian Empire was at the height of its power, it stretched from the empire of India on the e. to the Grecian Archipelago on the w.; and from the Danube, the Black Sea, the Caucasus, and the Caspian Sea on the n., to the Arabian and Nubian deserts on the s. (Esth. 1:1; 10:1); and it was nearly 3,000 miles long, with a varying breadth of 500 to 1,500 miles. It had an area of 2,000,000 square miles, half that of Europe. The race inhabiting Persia proper was Aryan, closely related to the Median race.

The Persians are not mentioned in the table of nations (Gen., ch. 10). About 700 B.C. Persia, was one of the allies of Elam. But soon Teispes, a chief of the tribe and a member of the family of the Achaemenidae, conquered Elam and established himself as king in the district of Anshan. His descendants branched into 2 lines, 1 reigning in Anshan and the other remaining in Persia. His greatgrandson, Cyrus II, became king of Anshan (c. 558); united the divided power; conquered Media c. 550 B.C., Lydia in Asia Minor in 546, and Babylonia in 539. He allowed the Hebrew exiles to return to their own land; see CYRUS. Dying in 529 B.C., he was succeeded by his son Cambyses, who became jealous of his brother Smerdis (Bardiya) and had him privately put to death. In 525 the king conquered Egypt and remained there for 3 years. In the meanwhile a Magian, Gaumāta by name, personating Smerdis made himself king and ruled for 7 months, 522 B.C., the year in which Cambyses died. It is not certain whether the latter committed suicide. Gaumāta was slain in the autumn of 522. Darius I, son of Hystaspes, apparently the next heir to the throne when the family of Cyrus became extinct, began to reign in 521 B.C. The accession of the new king was the signal for a general revolt of the provinces, but the insurrection was suppressed, and Darius organized a new empire which extended from India to the Grecian Archipelago and the Danube; he divided it into 20 satrapies. It was under Darius that the Temple at Jerusalem was rebuilt. He died 486 B.C.; see DARIUS 2. His son and successor was Xerxes I, the Ahasuerus of the Book of Esther and probably of Ezra 4:6. He reconquered the Egyptians; and he attempted an invasion of Greece, but was repulsed with great loss to the Persians; see AHASUERUS 2. After a reign of 21 years, he was assassinated in 465 B.C. His son and successor, a much more respectable character, but still fickle and feeble, was Artaxerxes (I) Longimanus. He was not unfriendly to the Jews. He allowed Ezra to lead a large number of them back to Jerusalem, and he permitted Nehemiah to rebuild the walls of the city; see ARTAXERXES. He reigned 40 years, dying in 424 B.C. His successors were Xerxes II, 424; Sogdianus, 424; Darius (II) Nothus (the Illegitimate), 423–404; Artaxerxes (II) Mnemon (of good memory), 404–359/8; Artaxerxes (III) Ochus, 359/8–338/7; Arses, 338/7–336/5; and Darius (III) Codomannus, 336/5–331. The last king was conquered by Alexander the Great in 331 B.C., and with him the first Persian empire passed away. See DARIUS 3.

The royal residences were Persepolis (II Macc. 9:2), Susa, i.e., Shushan (Neh. 1:1; Esth. 1:2), Ecbatana, i.e., Achmetha (Ezra 6:2; Jos. Antiq. x. 11, 7), and to an extent Babylon (Ezra 6:1).

When Cyrus the Great allowed the Jews to return to their own land, 538 B.C., he did not grant them their independence. They were placed under governors appointed by the Persian emperor (Neh. 3:7), and formed part of the satrapy Beyond-the-river (Ezra 8:36) which consisted of Syria, Palestine, Phoenicia, and Cyprus (Herod. iii. 91). They were subjects of Persia for 207 years, from 539, the year in which Cyrus entered Babylon, to 332, that in which Alexander the Great completed the conquest of Palestine.

The religion of the empire was a dualism, Zoroastrianism, so named after its founder Zarathustra (Zoroaster); no effort, however, was made to enforce it on the subject peoples. It was a spiritual religion, recognizing the distinction between God and nature, between spirit and matter, and consequently being averse to images of God. Its fundamental ethical principle was the essential contradiction between good and evil, light and darkness. It conceived of 2 realms of spirits: 1 with a hierarchy of angels and archangels, where Ahuramazda or Ormazd the all-wise lord, God in the fullest sense, presides over the 7 holy spirits, who are his ministers and the expression of his attributes, and over thousands of worthy ones; and another realm of evil spirits ruled over by Ahriman, the spiritual enemy. It taught the duty of man to eradicate evil and cultivate good, and to strive after holiness in thought, word, and deed, which will be rewarded by immortality and heaven. Fire, air, earth, and water are considered the creation of Ahuramazda and consequently are holy. See MAGI. Later Judaism shows traces of Persian influence.

What once had been Persia passed first to the Macedonian Greeks and their successors of the same race. Then it became part of the Parthian Empire. In A.D. 208 Ardashir laid the foundations of a new Persian sovereignty, ruled by a dynasty called after his family Sassanian. In 224 he defeated and slew Artabanus V, the last Parthian king. In A.D. 226 Ardashir took the title of King of Kings of Iran. The Sassanian dynasty became powerful, met the Roman armies on equal terms, and set limits to the extension of their sway in the East. In A.D. 637 and 641, Yazdagird III, the last of the dynasty, was defeated by the Moslems, and Persia came under Mohammedan rule, which has continued till now. Some of the bolder spirits refused to submit to Mohammedan domination, and fled to the deserts and the mountains. Finally, a number of Persian refugees in the 8th century found a home in India. Their successors constitute a limited but important section of the Indian community. They are called Parsees. The modern name of Persia is Iran.

Per'sis (pûr'sĭs) [Gr., Persian]. A Christian at Rome who labored diligently in the Lord, and to whom Paul sent his salutation (Rom. 16:12).

Pe·ru'da (pē-rōō'dá), **Pe·ri'da** [divided, separated]. A subdivision of the children of Solomon's servants who returned from captivity (Ezra 2:55; Neh. 7:57).

Pes'ti·lence. An infectious or contagious disease, a plague. While the sending of pestilence is frequently mentioned as from God (Ex. 9:15; Lev. 26:25; Deut. 28:21), he very often, if not in all cases, uses secondary causes for its production. The punishment which is threatened is often described as the sword, the famine, and the pestilence, and these words tend to stand in this order (Ezek. 6:11). There is reason for this order. War breaks out. The people of the invaded country cannot cultivate their fields, or, if they do, they find their crops reaped or destroyed by the enemy. Besiegers invest the cities and intentionally cut off supplies with the object of forcing a surrender. Famine ensues in country and town. The starvation, the carnage, and the unsanitary condition of the cities crowded during the siege bring a pestilence.

Pe'ter (pē'tẽr) [Lat. Petrus, from Gr. Petros, a rock]. A translation of Aram. Cephas, a rock (John 1:42; I Cor. 1:12; 3:22; 9:5; 15:5; Gal. 1:18; 2:9, 11, 14), which Christ bestowed upon Simon or, more properly, Symeon or Simeon (Acts 15:14; II Peter 1:1, R.V. marg.) on his first appearance before him (John 1:42), and afterward explained more fully in its prophetic import (Matt. 16:18 seq.; Mark 3:16). Simon was the son of a certain John (John 1:42, R.V.; 21:15, 16, 17, R.V.) or Jona (Matt. 16:17, probably an equivalent of John), who, with his sons, Andrew and Peter, followed the trade of a fisherman on the Sea of Galilee in partnership with the sons of Zebedee (Matt. 4:18; Mark 1:16; Luke 5:3 seq.). He was a native of Bethsaida (John 1:44), and subsequently dwelt with his family at Capernaum (Matt. 8:14; Luke 4:38).

Peter was probably a disciple of John the Baptist, and was in the 1st instance brought to Jesus by his brother Andrew, who was 1 of the favored 2 disciples of John whom he pointed to Jesus immediately after his return from the temptation in the wilderness. With prophetic insight into Simon's character, Jesus at once conferred upon him the surname of Cephas, or Peter, that is, "Rock" (John 1:35–42). In common with the earliest followers of Jesus, Peter received 3 separate calls from his Master: 1st, to become his disciple; 2d, to become his constant companion (Matt. 4:19; Mark 1:17; Luke 5:10); and, 3d, to be his apostle (Matt. 10:2; Mark 3:14, 16; Luke 6:13, 14). Peter's ardor, earnestness, courage, vigor, and impetuosity of disposition marked him from the first as the leader of the disciples of Jesus. He is always named 1st in the lists of the apostles (Matt. 10:2; Mark 3:16; Luke 6:14; Acts 1:13). In the more intimate circle of the most favored disciples, he is likewise always named 1st (Matt. 17:1; Mark 5:37; 9:2; 13:3; 14:33; Luke 8:51; 9:28). He was the natural spokesman of the apostolic band. He was the 1st to confess Jesus as the Christ of God, but was equally forward to dissuade him from his chosen path of suffering, receiving from Christ the appropriate praise and blame (Matt. 16:16–23; Mark 8:29–33).

Peter's life exhibits 3 well-marked stages. 1. The period of training, as exhibited in the Gospel narrative. During these years of personal association with Christ, he learned to know both Christ and himself. And though he brought them to an end in a threefold denial of the Master whom he had boasted that he at least would never forsake (Matt. 26:69 seq.; Mark 14:66 seq.; Luke 22:54 seq.; John 18:15 seq.), Jesus closed them with a loving probing of his heart and restoration of his peace and confidence (John 21:15 seq.). 2. The period of leadership in the Church, as exhibited in the earlier chapters of The Acts. During these years Peter justified his surname, and fulfilled the prophecy that on him should the edifice of the Church be raised (Matt. 16:18). It was by his bold and strong hand that the Church was led in every step. It was he who moved the disciples to fill up the broken ranks of the apostolate (Acts 1:15); it was he who proclaimed to the assembled multitudes the meaning of the Pentecostal effusion (ch. 2:14); he was the leader in the public healing of the lame man and in the subsequent sermon and defense (chs. 3:4, 12; 4:8); it was by his voice that Ananias and Sapphira were rebuked (ch. 5:3, 8). Above all, it was by his hand that the door of salvation was opened alike to the Jews in the great sermon at Pentecost (ch. 2:10, 38) and to the Gentiles in the case of Cornelius (ch. 10). 3. The period of humble work in the Kingdom of Christ, exhibited in the Epistles of the N.T. When the foundations of the Church had been laid, Peter took a subordinate place, and in humble labors to spread the boundaries of the Kingdom disappeared from the page of history. In the Church at Jerusalem James takes henceforth the leading place (Acts 12:17; 15:13; 21:18; Gal. 2: 9, 12). The door had been opened to the Gentiles, and Paul now becomes the apostle to the Gentiles (Gal. 2:7). As the apostle to the circumcision (Gal. 2:8), Peter prosecuted henceforth his less brilliant work, wherever Jews could be found, and contentedly left Jerusalem to James and the Gentile world to Paul. The book of The Acts closes its account of him at the meeting at Jerusalem (ch. 15), when his policy of breaking down the barriers for the Gentiles met with universal acceptance. We hear of him afterward at Antioch (Gal. 2:11), possibly at Corinth (I Cor. 1:12), and certainly as prosecuting his work through missionary journeys, taking his wife with him (I Cor. 9:5). Finally he glorified God by a martyr's death (cf. John 21:19). Beyond this, Scripture tells us nothing of his fortunes, labors, sufferings, or successes, except what can be learned from his 2 epistles. In them he stands before us in a singularly beautiful humility, not pressing the recognition of personal claims to leadership upon the Christian community, but following up the teaching of Paul or of Jude with his own,

and exhorting his readers to hold fast to the common faith.

Few characters in Scripture history are drawn for us more clearly or strongly than Peter's. In the Gospels, in The Acts, and in the Epistles it is the same man who stands out before us in dramatic distinctness. Always eager, ardent, impulsive, he is pre-eminently the man of action in the apostolic circle, and exhibits the defects of his qualities as well as their excellences throughout life (Matt. 16: 22; 26:69–75; Gal. 2:11). His virtues and faults had their common root in his enthusiastic disposition; it is to his praise that along with the weed of rash haste there grew more strongly into his life the fair plant of burning love and ready reception of truth. He was treated with distinguished honor by his Lord: he was made the recipient of no less than 3 miracles in those early days of the Gospels; he was granted a special appearance after the resurrection (I Cor. 15:5); Jesus could find time in his Passion and while saving the world to cast on him a reminding glance and to bind up his broken heart. Accordingly the life of Peter is peculiarly rich in instruction, warning, and comfort for the Christian, and his writings touch the very depths of Christian experience and soar to the utmost heights of Christian hope.

Authentic history adds but little to our knowledge of Peter's life beyond what we glean from the N.T. Conformably to the prophecy of his martyrdom in John 21:19, we are credibly told that he died by crucifixion about the time of Paul's death by the sword, that is about A.D. 68. The place of his death is not incredibly witnessed to be Rome. Legend was early busy with his life; the Roman legend of his 25 years' episcopate in Rome has its roots in early apocryphal stories originating among the heretical Ebionites, and is discredited not less by its origin and manifest internal inconsistencies than by all authentic history.

The First Epistle of Peter

The author of this epistle announces himself as the Apostle Peter (ch. 1:1); and the whole internal character of the letter as well as exceptionally copious historical attestation bears out the assertion. It is addressed "to the elect who are sojourners of the Dispersion in Pontus, Galatia, Cappadocia, Asia, and Bithynia" (ch. 1:1), which evidently refers to the whole body of Christians inhabiting the region comprised in modern Asia Minor. That the readers in the mind of the author were largely of Gentile origin is clear from such passages as chs. 1:14; 2:9, 10; 3:6; 4:3. These were churches founded and nurtured in large part by the Apostle Paul, and to them Paul had written his letters to the Galatians, Ephesians, and Colossians; Peter writes to them as those who owed their conversion to others than himself (ch. 1:12, 25), and in order to testify that the gospel they had received was "the true grace of God" and to exhort them to "stand . . . fast therein" (ch. 5:12). Thus he publishes his hearty agreement with the Apostle Paul and at the same time pens what is pre-eminently the epistle of hope. The place of its composition was probably Rome, for Babylon (ch. 5:13) according to early patristic tradition was a mystic name of the new center of persecution of the people of God. Its date is set by its copious use of The Epistle to the Ephesians on the one side, and the death of Peter on the other, as between A.D. 63 and A.D. 67; it is most probable that it was written about 64 or 65. Allusion is made to the epistle as being Peter's in II Peter 3:1 (cf. ch. 1:1); it is unmistakably quoted by Polycarp, a disciple of the Apostle John; it is definitely quoted also as the writing of the Apostle Peter by Irenaeus and Tertullian in the closing decades of the 2d century; and from the very beginning it has always held a secure place in the Christian Bible in every part of the world, and has always been in the fullest use by Christians of every land.

The style in which the letter is written is at once simple, striking, and forcible, abounding in sudden and abrupt transitions and admirably reflecting the character of the writer. The whole mode of presentation of its matter is special and characteristic, though the doctrine presented is distinctly the same as that of the epistles of Paul, set forth here with prevailing reference to the grace of God and the future hope.

The epistle is filled to a remarkable degree with reminiscences of earlier Christian writings, particularly of the Epistles to the Romans and to the Ephesians and The Epistle of James (cf. I Peter 2:6, 8 with Rom. 9:32, 33; I Peter 2:5; 3:8, 9; 4:7–11 with Rom. 12:1, and vs. 16, 17, and vs. 3, 6; I Peter 2:18 and ch. 3:1–7 with Eph. 6:5 and ch. 5:22, 23; I Peter 1:1, 6, 7, 23 and ch. 5:6 with James 1:1, 2, 3, 18 and I Peter 4:10). It is remarkable for the combined depth and beauty of its Christian teaching. After the greeting (I Peter 1:1, 2) there follows an introductory section (ch. 1:3–12) in which God is praised for the blessings of salvation. The body of the letter (chs. 1:13 to 5:11) consists of: (1) a series of exhortations to a diligent Christian walk, correspondent to the teaching its readers had received (chs. 1:13 to 2:10); (2) a number of particular directions for the special relationships of life (chs. 2:11 to 4:6; and (3) some closing instructions for the present needs of the readers (chs. 4:7 to 5:11). It ends with salutations and announcements (ch. 5:12–14).

THE SECOND EPISTLE OF PETER

Critics are not agreed concerning the date and authorship of this epistle. The author describes himself as "Symeon Peter, a bondservant and apostle of Jesus Christ" (II Peter 1:1, R.V. marg.), and represents himself as having been present at Christ's transfiguration (ch. 1:16), and as having received from him a prediction regarding his death (ch. 1:14; cf. John 21:19), and also as standing on an equality with the Apostle Paul (II Peter 3:15). Yet many difficulties confront the acceptance of this testimony. In the first place, a lack of simplicity in the style and of ease in expression exhibited in II Peter is in striking contrast with the simplicity of style in I Peter. As early as Jerome's time this difference was made an argument for diversity of authorship. Furthermore, many scholars are loath to believe that in the lifetime of Peter the epistles of Paul could have been put on a par with the O.T. Scriptures (II Peter 3:15 seq.). Moreover, the uncertainty in some quarters of the Early Church regarding its authenticity (cf. Eusebius H.E. iii. 3, 1–4; vi. 25, 8) and the fact that the Syrian Church did not receive it into the canon until early in the 6th century deserve serious consideration. Calvin entertained doubts as to its genuineness, and most modern scholars regard it as the work of an unknown author, who c. A.D. 150 wrote in the name of the great Apostle Peter in order to secure a wider hearing.

In defense of its Petrine authorship, however, a few first-class scholars explain the difference in style by supposing that II Peter reflects the rugged diction of the apostle himself, while I Peter was freely composed by an amanuensis, Silvanus (I Peter 5:12), albeit under Peter's supervision. Moreover these scholars point out certain similarities between

the two epistles: both manifest a fondness for the pl. of abstract nouns, and there is noticeable in each the habit of presenting both the negative and positive aspect of a thought (e.g., I Peter 1:12, 14 seq., 18 seq.; and II Peter 1:16, 21; 2:4 seq.; 3:9, 17). These men furthermore interpret the doubts entertained in the Early Church concerning the authorship of II Peter as evidence of the strictness which was maintained in refusing to admit as canonical any writing that was not definitely apostolic; that it was finally approved by the Church is a token of its genuineness. In conclusion, while perplexing doubts arise still there is sufficient evidence for believing that II Peter is genuine.

The form of its address is quite general: "to them that have obtained a like precious faith with us" (II Peter 1:1); but ch. 3:1 shows that the same readers, or some one territorial group among them, are the ones to whom I Peter had been sent. The place from which it was written cannot be confidently ascertained; if the allusion in ch. 1:14 implies that Peter was on the verge of his martyrdom, we may think of Rome. In that case the letter should be dated in A.D. 68; and the nature of the errors rebuked in it, and its probable use of The Epistle of Jude as well as its allusion to I Peter, will accord with this date.

Its object, as is declared in II Peter 3:1, 17, 18, was to stir up the minds of its readers to remember what had been taught them, to the end that they might be saved from the errors now becoming prevalent and might grow in grace and the knowledge of the Lord and Saviour Jesus Christ. It was written, in other words, to rebuke the nascent Gnosticism creeping into the churches, and to build up Christians in true knowledge and purity. The contents of the letter are in full accord with its object. After the usual apostolical greeting (ch. 1:1, 2), it passes insensibly into an earnest exhortation to growth in grace and knowledge (vs. 3–11), and thence into a reminder of the grounds on which this knowledge, itself the basis of piety, rests (vs. 12–21), and a denunciation of the false teachers (ch. 2:1–22). The readers are then reminded of the nature and surety of the teaching given them as to the 2d advent and the end of the world (ch. 3:1–13); and the letter closes with an exhortation to them to make their calling and election sure, including a commendation of Paul's letters, and concludes with a doxology (vs. 14–18).

B. B. W. (rev., H. S. G.)

Peth'a·hi'ah (pĕth'a-hī'a) [Jehovah opened (the womb)]. 1. A descendant of Aaron whose family became the 19th course of priests (I Chron. 24:16).

2. A Levite who was induced by Ezra to put away his foreign wife (Ezra 10:23). He was probably the Levite of the name who assisted Ezra in his religious work (Neh. 9:5).

3. A man of Judah, family of Zerah, and an official of the Persian king for all matters concerning the people (Neh. 11:24).

Pe'thor (pē'thôr). A town near the Euphrates (Num. 22:5), by the mountains of Aram or Mesopotamia (Num. 23:7; Deut. 23:4). The town was captured by Shalmaneser II of Assyria from the Hittites, who called it Pitru; long before that time it appears in Thutmose III's list of Syrian towns. It was situated on the w. bank of the Euphrates, near the river Sagura, now Sajur, a few miles s. of Carchemish.

Pe·thu'el (pē-thū'ĕl). Father of the Prophet Joel (Joel 1:1).

Pe'tra (pē'trȧ). See SELA.

Pe•ul'le•thai (pê-ŭl'ê-thī), in A.V. Pe•ul'thai (pê-ŭl'thī) [Jehovah is a reward, or reward of Jehovah]. A Levite, a doorkeeper, son of Obed-edom (I Chron. 26:5).

Pha'lec (fā'lĕk). See PELEG.

Phal'lu (făl'ōō). See PALLU.

Phal'ti (făl'tī). See PALTI.

Phal'ti•el (făl'tī-ĕl). See PALTIEL.

Pha•nu'el (fá-nū'ĕl) [Gr. from Heb., face of God]. An Asherite, the father of Anna (Luke 2:36).

Phar'aoh (fâr'ō) [Egypt. *pr-'}*, great house]. A title used as the general designation of the sovereign of Egypt, both with and without the personal name attached.

Of the Pharaohs mentioned in the Bible, several, among whom are the Pharaohs of

Statue of Ramesses II, One of the Pharaohs

Abraham and Joseph, cannot be identified with any degree of certainty. For the Pharaoh of the oppression and the one of the Exodus, see EGYPT, III. 8.

1. SHISHAK. Called in Egyptian Sheshenk or Sheshonk, the 1st ruler of Dyn. XXII, the 1st of the Libyan period. An account of his expedition into Palestine (I Kings 14:25, 26; II Chron. 12:2–9), with the usual embellishments and exaggerations, is found on the s. wall of the temple at Karnak. He was probably an able statesman, since he was able to avoid a rupture with Solomon while keeping Solomon's enemy as a guest (I Kings 11:40). He shrewdly took advantage of the unsettled state of affairs in Palestine after the division of the kingdom, to make his invasion at that time when resistance to an enemy was necessarily weakened by dissensions at home. Jeroboam took refuge at his court some time after the 25th year of Solomon (I Kings 6: 38; 7:1; 9:10, 24; 11:27), and the invasion of Judah took place in the 5th year of Rehoboam. Shishak reigned from 945 to 924 B.C.

2. ZERAH the Cushite, who undertook an expedition against Judah in the reign of Asa, leading an army composed of Ethiopians and Libyans, doubtless in addition to the Egyptian troops. His forces were routed at Mareshah (II Chron. 14:9–15; 16:8). The monuments do not mention this military expedition, as it is their custom to pass over in silence their own defeats. Zerah is commonly identified with Osorkon I (924–895 B.C.), successor of Shishak in Dyn. XXII, or Bubastite Dynasty. Some scholars regard this identification as absurd and connect him with Arabia. The name occurs in S. Arabic inscriptions, and we may have here a reference to an Arabian invasion. Cush was the ancestor of Sheba and other Arabian divisions (cf. Gen. 10:7; II Chron. 21:16).

3. So, contemporary of Hoshea, king of Israel (II Kings 17:4); see So.

4. TIRHAKAH (Taharka in Egypt.), 3d and last king of Dyn. XXV, or Ethiopian Dynasty. As a youth of 20 he went n. from Napata, the capital of Ethiopia, with a king, probably his uncle Shabaka, when the latter invaded Egypt. A decade later this nephew was in command of the Egyptian and Ethiopian forces which were marching against the Assyrians. Sennacherib, king of Assyria, advancing through Philistia in the direction of Egypt in 701 B.C., heard a report that Tirhakah, king of Ethiopia, was coming against him (II Kings 19:9). In his own account of the affair Sennacherib, without mentioning their personal names, says that the kings of Egypt and the archers, chariots, and horses of the king of Ethiopia met him in battle at Eltekeh. About 688 B.C. Tirhakah became the Pharaoh. In 671 B.C. Sennacherib's son, Esarhaddon, king of Assyria, penetrated into the midst of the country, defeated Tirhakah, whom he calls king of Ethiopia, took Memphis, and made Tirhakah's son a captive. Tirhakah found refuge in Ethiopia, and on Esarhaddon's death in 669 B.C., returned to Egypt. Ashurbanipal sent an army against him, styling him king of Egypt and Ethiopia, and defeated his troops at Karbanit, near the mouth of the Canopic branch of the Nile. Tirhakah retired to Thebes. He still had the support of several minor kings of Egypt, among whom was Necho. Ashurbanipal afterward pursued him thither and took Thebes. This event occurred about 663 B.C.

5. NECO, also called Pharaoh-necoh, Pharaoh-neco, A.V. Necho, Pharaoh-nechoh, son of Psamtik (Psammetichus) I. He was the 2d ruler of Dyn. XXVI and reigned from 609 to 593 B.C. He attempted to complete a canal connecting the Red Sea with the Nile, and sent a successful expedition to circumnavigate Africa (Herod. ii. 158; iv. 42). He slew King Josiah at Megiddo (608) as the latter opposed his march toward Assyria. On Josiah's death the people set up his son Jehoahaz, but Pharaoh dethroned him and carried him off to Egypt, setting up in his stead his elder brother, Jehoiakim (II Kings 23:29–34; II Chron. 35:20 to 36:4). Necho seems to have left his army at Carchemish and gone back to Egypt. In 605 B.C. he returned to his army, the object being to protect the interests of Egypt w. of the Euphrates. But he found himself opposed by Nebuchadnezzar; he was utterly routed by him, and lost all of Egypt's Asiatic possessions (II Kings 24:7).

6. PHARAOH-HOPHRA, the Ha'abrē' of the Egyptians, the Ouaphris of Manetho, and the Apries of Herodotus. He was the 2d successor of Necho, separated from him by the short reign of Psamtik II. He reigned 19 years, from 588 to 569 B.C. He was on the throne while Jeremiah and his fellow fugitives from Palestine still lived. The prophet

intimated that Pharaoh-hophra should be given into the hands of his enemies, as Zedekiah, the last king of Judah, had been (Jer. 44:30). He was a warrior and appears to have conquered the combined fleets of Cyprus and Tyre, and he took Sidon. He failed at last in an attack on the Greek colony of Cyrene. He was killed in a revolt and was succeeded by Amasis (Ahmose II).

Phar'a·thon (făr'ȧ-thŏn). See PIRATHON.

Pha'res (fā'rēz) and **Pha'rez** (fā'rēz). See PEREZ.

Phar'i·sees (făr'ĭ-sēz) [Gr. from Aram. perīshā, separated]. One of the 3 chief Jewish parties, the others being the Sadducees and the Essenes. It was the straitest group (Acts 26:5). In all probability the Pharisees originated in the period before the Maccabaean war, in a reaction against the Hellenizing spirit which appeared among the Jews and manifested itself in the readiness of a part of the people to adopt Greek customs. Those who regarded these practices with abhorrence and their spread with alarm were incited to strict and open conformity to the Mosaic Law. They were drawn yet more closely together as a party by the fierce persecution which Antiochus Epiphanes, 175–163 B.C., set on foot against the faithful Israelites who would not abandon Judaism and accept the Greek faith, when he attempted to destroy the holy Scriptures, and commanded that whosoever was found with any Book of the Covenant or consented to the Law should be put to death (I Macc. 1:56, 57). The Hasidim (the Pietists) or Hasidaeans, who were mighty men of Israel, even all such as were voluntarily devoted unto the Law (ch. 2:42; cf. ch. 1:62, 63), participated in the Maccabaean revolt as a distinct party. They probably were the forerunners of the Pharisees, although they did not bear that name. When the war ceased to be a struggle for religious liberty and became a contest for political supremacy, they ceased to take an active interest in it. They are not mentioned during the time that Jonathan and Simon were the Jewish leaders, 160–135 B.C. The Pharisees appear under their own name in the time of John Hyrcanus, 135–105 B.C. He was a disciple of theirs, but left them and joined the Sadducees (Jos. Antiq. xiii. 10, 5 and 6); and his son and successor, Alexander Jannaeus, endeavored to exterminate them by the sword. But his wife, Alexandra, who succeeded him in 78 B.C., recognizing that physical force is powerless against religious conviction, favored the Pharisees (Jos. Antiq. xiii. 15, 5; 16, 1). Thenceforth their influence was paramount in the religious life of the Jewish people.

The Pharisees held the doctrine of foreordination and considered it consistent with the free will of man. They believed in the immortality of the soul, in the resurrection of the body, and in the existence of spirits; that men are rewarded or punished in the future life, according as they have lived virtuously or viciously in this life; that the souls of the wicked shall be detained forever in prison under the earth, while those of the virtuous rise and live again, removing into other bodies (Acts 23:8; Jos. Antiq. xviii. 1, 3; War ii. 8, 14). These doctrines distinguished them from the Sadducees, but did not constitute the essence of Pharisaism. Pharisaism is the final and necessary result of that conception of religion which makes religion consist in conformity to the Law and promises God's grace only to the doers of the Law. Religion becomes external. The disposition of the heart is less vital than the outward act. The interpretation of the Law and its application to the details of ordinary life ac-

cordingly became a matter of grave consequence, lawyers acquired increased importance, and expositions of the Law by recognized authorities grew to a body of precepts of binding force. Josephus, who was himself a Pharisee, describes them as not merely accepting the Law of Moses, and interpreting it more skillfully than others, but adds that they had delivered to the people a great many observances by succession from the fathers which are not written in the Law of Moses (Jos. Antiq. xiii. 10, 6), these being the traditional interpretations of the elders, which our Lord pronounced to be of no binding authority (Matt. 15:2, 3, 6).

At first, when one incurred great danger in joining the party, the Pharisees were men of strong religious character; they were the best people in the nation. Subsequently Pharisaism became an inherited belief, the profession of it was popular, and men of character very inferior to that of the original members joined its ranks. With the lapse of time also the essentially vicious element in the system developed and laid the Pharisees, as commonly represented by the members of the party, open to scathing rebuke. John the Baptist called them and the Sadducees a generation of vipers; and it is well-known how severely our Lord denounced them for their self-righteousness, their hypocrisy, their inattention to the weightier matters of the Law, while being very particular as to minute points, with other faults (Matt. 5:20; 16:6, 11, 12; 23:1–39). They became a cunning body of men (Jos. Antiq. xvii. 2, 4). They took a prominent part in plotting the death of Christ (Mark 3:6; John 11:47–57). Yet they always numbered in their ranks men of perfect sincerity and the highest character. Paul in his early life was a Pharisee and was accustomed to bring forward the fact when he was reasoning with his countrymen (Acts 23:6; 26:5–7; Phil. 3:5). His teacher, Gamaliel, was of the same sect (Acts 5:34).

Pha'rosh (fā'rŏsh). See PAROSH.

Phar'par (fär'pär) [cf. Arab. farfar, haste]. Presumably the less important of the 2 rivers of Damascus, for Naaman mentions it only 2d (II Kings 5:12). According to the local tradition, which can be traced back to the middle of the 16th century, the Pharpar is the Taura, 1 of 7 canals which are drawn off from the Barada as it nears Damascus. It is more common, however, outside of Damascus, to identify the Pharpar with the A'waj, the only independent stream except the Barada within the territory of Damascus, but distant a ride of 3 hours from the city. It is formed by the confluence of several streams which take their rise in Mount Hermon. It pursues a tortuous course through the plain to the s. of the city and finally enters the most s. of 3 inland lakes. In dry weather its waters are sometimes absorbed before they even enter the lake.

Pha·se'ah (fȧ-sē'ȧ). See PASEAH.

Pha·se'lis (fȧ-sē'lĭs). A city of Lycia, on the gulf of Pamphylia, with 3 excellent harbors. It enjoyed considerable commerce in early times (Herod. ii. 178). It was independent (I Macc. 15:23) until the war of 78–75 B.C., when the Romans destroyed it because it had become a center of organized piracy. It was rebuilt, but did not rise to importance again. It was a bishopric in the Byzantine period.

Phas'i·ron (făs'ĭ-rŏn). A Bedouin chief, or rather a Nabataean tribe (I Macc. 9:66).

Phe'be (fē'bê). See PHOEBE.

Phe·ni'ce. See PHOENICIA and PHOENIX.

Phe·ni'ci·a (fê-nĭsh'ĭ-*à*). See PHOENICIA.

Phi'col (fī'kŏl), in A.V. **Phi'chol** (fī'kŏl). The captain of the army of Abimelech, king of Gerar; present when treaty was made between Abimelech and Abraham, and between Abimelech or his successor with like title and Isaac (Gen. 21:22; 26:26).

Phil'a·del'phi·a (fĭl'*à*-dĕl'fĭ-*à*) [Gr., brotherly love]. 1. A city of Lydia, in Asia Minor, 28¼ miles s.e. of Sardis, in the plain of the Hermus. It was built by Attalus Philadelphus, on a part of Mount Tmolus. In A.D. 17 it was destroyed by an earthquake, but was soon rebuilt. It was the seat of 1 of the 7 churches of Asia addressed in the book of Revelation (chs. 1:11; 3:7-13). Unlike most of the 7, it receives commendation and encouragement, unmixed with censure. It is now called Ala-Sheher.
2. A later name of Rabbah of the Ammonites. See RABBAH 1.

Phi·le'mon (fī-lē'mŏn) [Gr., loving]. A convert of the Apostle Paul's (Philemon 19), who resided in the same city with Archippus and from which Onesimus had come, viz., Colossae (cf. Philemon 2 with Col. 4:17; and Philemon 10 with Col. 4:9). There was a church in his house (Philemon 2). Paul calls him a fellow worker (v. 1) and speaks of his kindness to the saints (vs. 5-7). As Paul had never been in Colossae (cf. Col. 2:1), we may suppose that Philemon was converted in Ephesus during the apostle's ministry there (cf. Acts 19:10). It is not improbable that Archippus was Philemon's son and Apphia his wife (Philemon 2).

The Epistle of Paul to Philemon is the brief letter sent by Paul, in conjunction with Timothy, to Philemon. The latter's slave, Onesimus, had run away, perhaps taking with him some of Philemon's money (vs. 18, 19); and, having made his way to Rome, had there been converted through the instrumentality of the apostle (v. 10). Paul would gladly have retained him as a free attendant, but did not feel at liberty to do so without Philemon's consent (vs. 13, 14). He doubtless felt too that Onesimus, as a Christian, ought to seek the forgiveness of his master; and he was equally anxious that Philemon should both forgive and receive the converted wrongdoer. So he sent Onesimus back to Philemon, urging the latter to receive him as a brother beloved (v. 16), telling of the love he himself bore toward the convert (vs. 10, 12), and offering to repay Philemon for whatever loss Onesimus had caused him (vs. 18, 19). The letter is an exquisite production. It reveals the delicacy of Paul's feeling and the graciousness of his relations with his friends. It also illustrates the effect of Christianity on social relationships generally, the spirit of love and justice which were destined to reorganize society. When Onesimus carried this letter to Philemon, he accompanied Tychicus, who also bore the Epistle to the Colossians (Col. 4:7-9) and that to the Ephesians (Eph. 6:21, 22). All 3 epistles were written at the same time, probably c. A.D. 62, and from Rome.

G. T. P. (rev., H. S. G.)

Phi·le'tus (fī-lē'tŭs) [Lat. from Gr., worthy of love]. One who joined with Hymenaeus in propagating the error that the resurrection is already past (II Tim. 2:17, 18).

Phil'ip (fĭl'ĭp) [Gr., fond of horses]. 1. Father of Alexander the Great of Macedon (I Macc. 1:1). He took charge of the government in 359 B.C., as regent for Amyntas, the son of his brother Perdiccas, and by skillful negotiations and successful war delivered the country from the danger which beset it by reason of the hostility of the Paeonians, Illyr-

ians, and Athenians. In view of these difficulties the Macedonians obliged him to take the monarchy himself. He captured Amphipolis and annexed it to his dominions in 357, and crossing the river Strymon, he took possession of Thracian territory and occupied Crenides, which he renamed Philippi (356). These achievements marked only the beginning of his unchecked career of conquest in Greece, by which he raised Macedonia from an obscure state to be the dominant power in Greek affairs. He was assassinated in 336 B.C., and was succeeded by Alexander.
2. Another king of Macedon, and 5th of the name. He entered into an alliance with Hannibal against the Romans in 215 B.C., but they held him in check with the co-operation of the Aetolians, who in 206 made a separate peace with him. In 200 B.C. the Romans invaded his kingdom. He successfully resisted them for 2 years, but in 197 he was completely defeated (I Macc. 8:5) by the Roman general Flaminius at Cynocephalae in Thessaly, and forced to conclude a humiliating peace. He died in 179 B.C.
3. Foster brother of Antiochus Epiphanes (II Macc. 9:29), and 1 of his privileged friends (I Macc. 6:14). When Antiochus was in Persia, nigh unto death, he appointed Philip regent during the minority of the young Antiochus (v. 15). Lysias, however, who was in Syria, usurped the position (v. 17). Philip returned in haste and obtained temporary possession of Antioch, the capital (vs. 55, 63). But Lysias succeeded in capturing the city. According to Josephus (Jos. *Antiq.* xii. 9, 7) Philip was executed, but perhaps he escaped and fled to Egypt before the city fell (II Macc. 9:29).

It has been conjectured, on insufficient grounds, that he is identical with Philip, the Phrygian who was made governor of Judea by Antiochus (II Macc. 5:22), and that he was the master of the elephants at the battle of Magnesia (Livy xxxvii. 41).
4. A son of Herod the Great, and the 1st husband of Herodias and brother or half-brother of Herod Antipas (Matt. 14:3; Luke 3:19). He is not called the tetrarch, and there is reason to believe that he was a different person from Philip the tetrarch, half-brother of Herod Antipas. In giving the genealogy of a portion of Herod the Great's family, Josephus states that Herodias married Herod, son of Herod the Great by Mariamne, daughter of the high priest Simon; that she left him to live with Antipas his half-brother; and that her daughter Salome married Philip the tetrarch, son of Herod the Great by Cleopatra of Jerusalem, and after Philip's death took another husband (Jos. *Antiq.* xviii. 5, 4). Thus, according to Josephus, the 1st husband of Herodias was a different person from Philip the tetrarch. The writers of the N.T. agree with Josephus in that they make Herodias' 1st husband a brother of Herod Antipas the tetrarch, and do not identify him with Philip the tetrarch, whom they also know (Luke 3:1). They differ as to his name. It is commonly believed that both authorities are right, and accordingly the 1st husband of Herodias is often designated Herod Philip. For among the children of Herod the Great 2 sons, born of different mothers, were named after Herod's father Antipas or Antipater. Three of his sons, born of 3 different mothers, were called Herod; one of whom, however, had a 2d name Antipas, and was spoken of indifferently either as Herod or Antipas (Jos. *Antiq.* xvii. 1, 3; xviii. 5, 1; 6, 2). One of the sons whom his wife Cleopatra of Jerusalem bore was called Philip; and it is probable that Mariamne's son, who is called Herod by Josephus, had the name of Philip also. Herod Philip

after the execution of his half-brothers Alexander and Aristobulus, was next in order of birth to Antipater, Herod the Great's firstborn, and for a time he was recognized as next in succession to the throne (Jos. *Antiq.* xvii. 3, 2) ; but he was passed over in Herod's later wills.

5. Philip the tetrarch. One of the 2 sons of Herod the Great and Cleopatra of Jerusalem. He was brought up at Rome with his half-brothers Archelaus and Antipas (Jos. *Antiq.* xvii. 1, 3 ; *War* i. 28, 4). In A.D. 4 he advocated the claims of Archelaus to succeed their common father, and was himself appointed by the emperor Augustus to be over Batanea, Trachonitis, Auranitis, and certain parts of Zeno's house about Jamnia (Jos. *War* ii. 6, 1–3 ; cf. *Antiq.* xvii. 11, 4). He was still tetrarch of the region of Ituraea and Trachonitis in the 15th year of Tiberius Caesar when John the Baptist began his public life (Luke 3 :1). He married Salome, the daughter of Herod, Mariamne's son, and Herodias (Jos. *Antiq.* xviii. 5, 4). He enlarged the town of Paneas, at the source of the Jordan, and named it Caesarea. It was afterward often spoken of as Caesarea Philippi (Matt. 16 :13), to distinguish it from Caesarea on the sea. He also raised the village of Bethsaida to the dignity of a city and called it Julias, in honor of Julia, daughter of Augustus and wife of Tiberius (Jos. *Antiq.* xviii. 2, 1 ; *War* ii. 9, 1). He reigned from 4 B.C. to A.D. 34, dying in the 20th year of Tiberius Caesar. His character was excellent, and his rule was mild and just (Jos. *Antiq.* xviii. 4, 6). His dominions were annexed to the province of Syria, but in A.D. 37 were assigned to Herod Agrippa I, who in A.D. 41 absorbed them into his larger Jewish kingdom.

6. Philip the apostle. One of the 12 apostles (Matt. 10 :3). His home was in Bethsaida, on the Sea of Galilee, and he was a fellow townsman of Andrew and Peter. Jesus met him at Bethany beyond the Jordan, where John was baptizing, won his faith, and called him to be a disciple. He found Nathanael and brought him to Jesus, in the conviction that an interview with the Master would convince Nathanael that Jesus was the Messiah. His confidence was justified (John 1 :43–48). A year later Jesus chose him to be an apostle. When our Lord was about to perform the miracle of feeding the 5,000, he first proved Philip, and awoke a conception of the magnitude of the miracle by asking Philip: "Whence are we to buy bread, that these may eat?" (John 6 :5, 6). On the day of the triumphal entry into Jerusalem, certain Greeks desired to see Jesus, and applied to Philip, who put them in communication with Jesus (John 12 :20–23). In making the acquaintance of Christ, the disciples had been making acquaintance with the Father; but when Christ spoke to them about their having known and seen the Father, Philip appeared not to understand and said: "Show us the Father, and it sufficeth us" (John 14 :8–12). He is named after the resurrection as one of the apostles who met in the upper chamber (Acts 1 :13). This is the last authentic notice we have of him.

7. Philip the evangelist. He was 1 of the 7 men of good report, full of the Spirit and of wisdom, chosen to be deacons to look after the interests of the Greek-speaking widows and probably the poor generally in the church at Jerusalem, and is mentioned next in order to the martyr Stephen (Acts 6 :5). Persecution followed the death of Stephen, and the Christians were scattered abroad. Philip became an evangelist. He visited Samaria, preached the gospel, wrought miracles, and made many converts (chs. 8 :4–8 ; 21 :8) ; among them was Simon the sorcerer, popu-

larly known as Simon Magus (ch. 8 :9–25). Afterward, by direction of an angel, Philip went along the road from Jerusalem to Gaza, on which, after a time, he met, preached to, and baptized the Ethiopian eunuch (ch. 8 :26–39). He afterward visited Azotus (Ashdod), and then went on preaching till he reached Caesarea (v. 40). He was still in that city years afterward when Paul passed through it on his last journey to Jerusalem. The fact is noted that Philip had 4 virgin daughters who had the gift of prophecy (ch. 21 :8, 9).

Phi·lip'pi (fĭ-lĭp'ī). A Macedonian city, called originally Crenides (Krenides, place of small fountains). It was within the limits of ancient Thrace, but in 356 B.C. Philip II of Macedon annexed the country as far as the river Nestus and thus took in the town, which he enlarged and strengthened and called after his own name. In its vicinity were rich gold and silver mines, the produce of which greatly aided Philip in carrying out his ambitious projects. In 168 B.C. the Roman consul Aemilius Paullus inflicted at Pydna a decisive and very sanguinary defeat on Perseus, the last of the Macedonian kings; and Philippi, with the rest of the territory, fell into the hands of the victors. In 42 B.C. 2 decisive battles took place in the neighborhood between Brutus and Cassius, 2 of Caesar's leading assassins, and Octavian and Antony, his chief avengers. After Octavian had become Augustus Caesar he took an interest in the place where he had gained the victory, and sent a Roman colony to Philippi. Luke refers to it as a colony (Acts 16 :12). It was the 1st city of the district ; not the capital, which was Amphipolis, but either the place of 1st importance or the 1st city reached by a traveler from the sea. About A.D. 52 Paul visited the city, making various converts, of whom the chief were Lydia of Thyatira, the damsel possessed with the spirit of divination, and the Philippian jailer (Acts 16 :12–40). The 2d of these successes had brought on persecution and imprisonment of the evangelists or they would not have had access to the jailer to do him spiritual good (I Thess. 2 :2). Paul had to leave the place abruptly on this occasion, but he visited it again at a future period, sailing thence en route to Syria (Acts 20 :3–6).

Philippi lies inland about 10 miles n.w. of its seaport Neapolis, the 2 being separated by a mountain range, the pass over which is about 1,600 feet above the sea level. The 2 towns were connected by a part of the great Egnatian Road. At first Philippi was confined to a small hill rising from the midst of a plain; an immense marsh lay directly s. of the town, fed by springs which gave it the older name of Crenides. The plain is connected with the basin of the Strymon in the valley of the Gangites, now called Angista.

Phi·lip'pi·ans (fĭ-lĭp'ĭ-ănz). The natives or inhabitants of Philippi (Phil. 4 :15). The Epistle of Paul to the Philippians was written by Paul, associating also Timothy with him, "to all the saints in Christ Jesus that are at Philippi, with the bishops and deacons" (Phil. 1 :1) ; a Christian community of which Paul himself had gathered the nucleus, and the first of the churches which he had founded in Europe. When Paul wrote the epistle, he was a prisoner (ch. 1 :7, 13, 14, 16). But where, in Caesarea, or Ephesus, or Rome? He was apparently in the custody of the Praetorian Guard (ch. 1 :13, R.V.), and he sends salutations from the saints that are of Caesar's household (ch. 4 :22). Many about him were actively engaged in propagating Christianity (ch. 1 :14–18). These references, as well as the whole tone of the letter, make it probable that the epistle was written from Rome during the apostle's first Roman imprisonment; see PAUL. It is also most probably to be dated toward the close of that period, in A.D. 63. This follows from several facts: 1. He had been for some time at the place of composition, probably in Rome (ch. 1:12 *seq.*). 2. He was expecting his release (chs. 1:25; 2:23, 24). 3. The Philippians had sent him a gift (ch. 4:10) by the hands of Epaphroditus (ch. 2:25); Epaphroditus, however, had been taken sick in Rome, the Philippians had heard of it, and Epaphroditus had learned of their sorrow over his illness (ch. 2:26). A considerable time, therefore, had elapsed since Paul had reached the capital.

The epistle was written primarily to acknowledge the gift which the Philippians had sent to Paul. Contrary to his custom, he had more than once received such gifts from them (ch. 4:15). But the apostle also seized the opportunity to tell them about himself and to warn them against error. It is the letter of a pastor to his flock. It was not called forth, like many of his epistles, by any crisis in the Church. It abounds in spiritual advice for the Christian life. At the same time it is valuable for the light it throws on Paul's situation in Rome. It was sent by the hand of Epaphroditus (ch. 2:25, 30) who, having recovered from his illness, was about to return to Philippi. It may be divided into the following sections: 1. Introduction (ch. 1:1, 2). 2. Gratitude for their fidelity; expression of his love for them; prayer for their sanctification (ch. 1:3–11). 3. Account of how God had used him, though a prisoner, to extend the gospel; of the opposition to him on the part of some, but of his own contentment; of his wish at times to die, but of his devotion to them and confidence that he would be spared to them; and of his earnest desire that they might stand firm (ch. 1:12–30). 4. Appeal to them for spiritual unity, through self-forgetfulness and love, after the example of Christ, that they may perfect the work of service which he had ever set before them (ch. 2:1–18). 5. Promise to send to them Timothy and, if possible, to go himself shortly; meanwhile he will send Epaphroditus (ch. 2:19–30). 6. Exhortation to pursue with joy the Christian life, based on his own joy in self-surrender to Christ and in the eager pursuit of the reward which Christ offers; to which he adds a warning against those who misuse the freedom of the gospel that they may indulge their fleshly appetites (ch. 3). 7. Concluding exhortations to individuals and to all, the keynotes of which are joy, contentment, holiness (ch. 4:1–9). 8. Final acknowledgment of the gift they had sent him and of his joy in their love, with a few parting salutations (ch. 4:10–23).

Some scholars interpret the sharp break in thought in ch. 3 between vs. 1 and 2 as evidence for the hypothesis that 2 letters have been joined together. An informal letter like Philippians, however, must not be dealt with as if it were a treatise constructed in accord with strict logic. In writing down his ideas as they came to him, Paul may well have turned abruptly from one subject to another. The epistle as it stands yields a satisfactory analysis, and there is no need for a partition theory.   G. T. P. (rev., H. S. G.)

Phi·lis'ti·a (fĭ-lĭs'tĭ-*à*). A word occurring in poetical passages of the O.T. (Ps. 60:8; 87:4; and R.V. of Isa. 14:29), and meaning the land of the Philistines. It was mainly that part of the Maritime Plain of Canaan which lies between Joppa and Gaza, approximately 50 miles in length and 15 in breadth. The greater portion is very fertile, bearing heavy crops of grain, as well as oranges, figs, olives, and other fruits. The coast line has a

row of sand dunes, and the sand continually encroaches on the cultivated districts. Of the 5 dominant towns (Josh. 13:3; I Sam. 6:17) 3, Gaza, Ashkelon, and Ashdod, were on the coast, Ekron about 6 miles inland, and Gath was situated among the hills of the lowland. All were walled.

Phi·lis'tines (fĭ-lĭs'tĭnz). A people mentioned in Gen. 10:14, and tabulated with descendants of Mizraim; this connection with Egypt is political rather than racial. They went forth from Casluhim, and were a remnant of the isle or seacoast of Caphtor (Jer. 47:4; Amos 9:7); see CAPHTOR. Apparently they came from Crete in the 1st quarter of the 12th century B.C. The country near Gaza was inhabited first by the Avvim, but settlers from Caphtor destroyed these aborigines and dwelt in their room (Deut. 2:23). Philistines were in the region about Gerar and Beersheba as early as the time of Abraham (Gen. 21:32, 34; 26:1, unless, as seems more probable, the name is here used proleptically). In 1194 B.C. Ramesses III defeated at the Delta an attack of the "Peoples of the Sea"; in c. 1190 he repelled from Syria a land and sea attack of these invaders, among whom were the Pulesati (Philistines) and others apparently identified with the Carians, Lycians, Achaeans, and groups with Greek affinities. The Philistines probably are Mediterraneans of Lycian-Carian origin (s.w. Asia Minor), who invaded Minoan Crete and settled for a

Philistines, from a Relief on the Palace of
Ramesses III

while in the e. part of the island. Thence they took part in the great movement which ended in defeat by Ramesses III, but some of the invaders remained in Syria and eventually reached Philistia. Or there may have been a peaceful migration of Cretans and Philistines to Palestine.

For travelers leaving Egypt the shortest way into Canaan was along the coast; but after the desert was passed the road was flanked by the fortified towns of Gaza, Ashkelon, Ashdod, and Ekron. At the Exodus from Egypt the tribes of Israel, migrating with their women, children, and cattle, were ill prepared for war and might well hesitate to fight their way; and they were directed to go by another route (Ex. 13:17, 18). A generation later Joshua, with an army under his command, did not attack the cities on the coast or Gath in the lowland (Josh. 13:2, 3; Judg. 3:3). But the tribe of Judah, when it settled in its allotted territory, took Gaza, Ashkelon, and Ekron (Judg. 1:18). Shamgar slew 600 Philistines with an oxgoad (ch. 3:31). Not long after this Israel, on account of its idolatries, was given into the hands of the Philistines (ch. 10:6, 7). It was delivered (v. 11), but sinning again came under the same domination for 40 years. From this they were delivered by Samson, but the Philistines ultimately proved his ruin (chs. 14 to 16). Early in Samuel's public life they defeated the Israelites, slaying, among others,

Hophni and Phinehas, Eli's sons, and capturing the Ark of God (I Sam., chs. 4 to 6). Twenty years later Samuel defeated them in battle at the same place, which he called Ebenezer, the stone of help, because Jehovah had helped him there (ch. 7:3–12). It was an overwhelming defeat. The Israelites had recovered their border from Ekron to Gath, regaining possession of the Shephelah or lowland, and the Philistines did not again dispossess them (ch. 7:13, 14).

The Philistines had control of the manufacture of iron tools and weapons (I Sam. 13:19–21). Iron was just coming into general use in the 11th century B.C., and the iron monopoly was not only an aid to Philistine superiority in arms, but also a commercial advantage. The power of the Philistines was formidable during the reign of Saul (chs. 10:5; 12:9; 14:52), but he and his son Jonathan smote them at Geba and Michmash (chs. 13:1 to 14:31). They soon appeared again within the territory of Judah, near Socoh; but fled when their champion Goliath was slain (chs. 17:1–58; 18:6; 19:5; 21:9; 22: 10). Saul and David had various encounters with them (chs. 18:27, 30; 19:8; 23:1–5, 27, 28); but at length to escape Saul David twice sought refuge in their country (chs. 21:10–15; 27 to 29; Psalm 56, title). On the 2d occasion the king of Gath placed the town of Ziklag under David's authority (I Sam. 27:6). The Philistines had penetrated to the very heart of Canaan when they defeated the Israelites on Mount Gilboa and slew Saul and his sons (I Sam. 28:4; 29:11; 31:1–13; I Chron. 10:1–14). David, when king, repelled invasions of the Philistines and also fought against them in their own country (II Sam. 3:18; 5:17–25; 8:1; 19:9; 21:15–22; 23:9–17; I Chron. 11:13; 18:1; 20:4, 5). After his death the Philistines are less frequently mentioned, as if their power was waning. Under Nadab, the son of Jeroboam I, and some other short-lived kings, the Israelites besieged Gibbethon, a Philistine city (I Kings 15:27; 16:15). The Philistines sent presents to Jehoshaphat (II Chron. 17:11); but they invaded Judah in the reign of his successor, Jehoram (ch. 21:16), and also in that of Ahaz (ch. 28:18). Uzziah and Hezekiah successfully invaded Philistia (II Kings 18:8; II Chron. 26:6, 7). Judgment against them is frequently threatened by the prophets (Isa. 11:14; Jer. 25:20; 47:1–7; Ezek. 25:15–17; Amos 1:6–8; Obad. 19; Zeph. 2:4, 5; Zech. 9:5–7). Many Philistines accompanied Gorgias, the Syrian general of Antiochus Epiphanes, in his invasion of Judah (I Macc. 3: 41). Judas Maccabaeus afterward captured Azotus (Ashdod) and other Philistine cities (ch. 5:68). Jonathan Maccabaeus burned Azotus, with the temple of Dagon, and the city of Ashkelon (ch. 10:83–89). He also burned the suburbs of Gaza, but took no further hostile measures, as the city itself was surrendered on his demand (ch. 11:60, 61). The Philistines are not mentioned by name in the N.T., and seem ultimately to have merged in the Jewish nation.

The Mediterranean is once called the sea of the Philistines (Ex. 23:31).

Phi·lol'o·gus (fĭ-lŏl'ō-gŭs) [Gr., fond of learning]. A Christian at Rome, apparently the head of a Christian household (Rom. 16:15).

Phi·los'o·phy [Gr., love of wisdom]. The spirit of pure philosophy, which seeks to penetrate to the essence of things in themselves, is foreign to the Eastern mind. The great distinction between Eastern and Western philosophy historically has been that Oriental reasoning remained in the sphere of religion and was never divorced from religious axioms, while Occidental investigation came to be conducted, even by profoundly religious minds, in a far wider sphere than religion and by the reason unassisted by the postulates of religion. Moral philosophy has characterized the East, metaphysics the West. For the Biblical student the contrast between Greek and Hebrew thought, their separate development, their eventual contact, and their mutual influence are important.

The Hebrew mind reflected on the view of the world which is presented by revelation. It drew wisdom from the experience of former generations, which was handed down by the ancients, from observation of human life and the results of conduct, and from the study of the adaptations of nature to an end. It thus gained true principles for the government of conduct, it sought to discover to what extent religious truth was approved by the test of human experience, and it wrestled with the paradoxes of the moral government of God, especially with the question of the sufferings of the righteous and the prosperity of the wicked. From these varied sources and manifold investigations the Hebrew wise man was confirmed in the conviction that the fear of God is the beginning of wisdom. Hebrew philosophy, or wisdom as the Bible calls it, received a great impulse through the interest of Solomon, who both gathered the maxims of other men and out of his own shrewd observation and varied experience gave utterance to new proverbs. The proverbs of Solomon largely concern conduct in relation to the individual and to God, such as chastity, temperance in meat and drink, self-control, honesty, suretyship, behavior in the presence of the mighty. From these things Hebrew thought proceeded to view morality in larger relations. From the consideration of apparent exceptions to its conclusions, it advanced to moral questions, and looked upon events not in their immediate personal results, but in the light of their effect upon posterity and of divine retribution in time to come. The Hebrew philosopher further studied nature, and saw that a divine purpose exists everywhere (Ps. 104:24). Everywhere is the impress of thought. Intelligence is involved in the creation and preservation of the universe (Prov. 3:19). He found wisdom to be an attribute of God, which is everywhere revealed in nature. It existed before God proceeded to create. He personified wisdom (Prov. 1:20–33; 8:12), and represented it as existing from everlasting, as brought forth before the creation of the world, as present with God when he established heaven and earth, and ordained to rule in the created universe (Prov. 8:22–31; Job 28:12–27). Wisdom was not itself a person, but it was looked upon as objective to God, as "the reflection of God's plan of the world," as the principle which God ordained for the world. By later writers the thought was developed and wisdom was still further distinguished from God (Wisd. of Sol. 7:22 to 8:5; 9:4, 9); see WISDOM.

Greek philosophy is usually said to begin with Thales about 640 B.C. Three main periods are distinguished: 1. The pre-Socratic schools which arose among the Greek colonies of Asia Minor. The great subject of inquiry was the constitution of the universe. Is there one underlying element, such as moisture, or the subtle and all-pervading air, or one eternal, infinite, immovable, unchangeable Being, or the instantaneous balance of power? 2. The Socratic schools represented by Socrates, Plato, and Aristotle, 469–322 B.C. Athens was the center of philosophic thought, and inquiry was directed to ideas, form (or essence) of things. But it was not a barren metaphysics that was cultivated; a lofty morality was inculcated. Socrates used inductive reasoning by which he sought to discover the permanent element underlying the changing forms of appearances and opinions; and the truth which he thus discovered he attempted to fix by a general definition or statement. Aristotle allowed absolute authority to the reason alone, and accepted nothing which he could not prove by logic. 3. The post-Socratic schools. Philosophy had culminated in Aristotle, and discussion reverted to ethics founded on metaphysics. Epicurus (342–270 B.C.) declared that the character of actions is determined by their result, and that permanent pleasure is the highest good. Zeno the Stoic (c. 336–264 B.C.) taught that moral character resides in the act itself, independent of the result, and inculcated the obligation of absolute obedience to the commands of duty. The Skeptics taught that certainty is not attainable in human knowledge; and early members of the school held that when we are convinced that we can know nothing, we cease to care, and in this way attain happiness.

Alexander the Great died in 323 B.C. and Aristotle in 322. Thus when Greek philosophy had reached its climax, Greek culture began to be introduced into Palestine and among the Jews of the Dispersion. Epicureanism and Stoicism were developed in Greece during the period of the first close contact of Greek and Hebrew, but they exercised little influence on Hebrew thought compared with the power exerted by Plato and Aristotle. The influence of the Socratic schools was seen in the Sadducees perhaps, who seem like Aristotle to have rejected everything which unaided reason did not teach, although they professed to be governed by a different principle. The influence of the Socratic schools was seen in the Alexandrian school of Jewish thinkers, whose prominent representative was Philo, a contemporary of Christ. They held to the teaching of Moses; but at the same time they took what they approved of in Greek philosophy, learning especially from divine Plato, and endeavored to show that it was already taught in the O.T. They combined the doctrines of the Greek sage and of Moses into a new system, and removed inconsistencies by arbitrarily allegorizing Scripture, even down to its geography. The influence of the Greek philosophy was seen in the improved methods and enlarged scope of debate. Paul advances a formal philosophic argument in his address in the midst of the Areopagus and in the beginning of his Epistle to the Romans (Acts 17:30; Rom. 1:19, 20). The influence of Greek philosophy was seen further in borrowed ideas, such as the pre-existence of the soul (Wisd. of Sol. 8:19, 20); in new words and new content of words, as in the use of the word form in the Aristotelian sense of essence or sum total of attributes (Phil. 2:6); and in nice discrimination of thought and precision of definition. Gnostic speculations later came from the East; and the attempt to combine Gnosticism with Christianity led Paul to combat it by presenting the true relation of Christ to God and the world in the Epistle to the Colossians.

Phin′e·has (fĭn′ē-ăs), in A.V. of I Macc. **Phin′e·es** (fĭn′ē-ĕs) [Egypt. *p}-nḥśy*, the Nubian]. 1. Son of Eleazar, and grandson of Aaron (Ex. 6:25). He ran a spear through an Israelite and a Midianite woman who had come into the camp at Shittim together, this summary punishment terminating a plague which was then raging as a judgment against the idolatries and impurities into which the Midianitish women were leading the Hebrews. An everlasting priesthood was therefore promised to him and his descendants (Num.

25:1–18; Ps. 106:30; I Macc. 2:54). With a short interruption when the house of Eli, of the lineage of Ithamar, officiated as high priests, Phinehas and his sons held the office until sacrifice ceased with the destruction of Jerusalem and the Temple by the Romans in A.D. 70. Phinehas went as priest with the army on the punitive expedition against the Midianites (Num. 31:6), and was sent with 10 princes to remonstrate with the tribes e. of the Jordan on their erection of an altar, erroneously supposed to be for schismatic worship (Josh. 22:13). He received as his share of the Promised Land a hill in Mount Ephraim (Josh. 24:33). Through him the Israelites inquired of the Lord whether they should attack the Benjamites for condoning the sin of the inhabitants of Gibeah (Judg. 20:28).

2. The younger of Eli's 2 degenerate sons. He was killed in the battle with the Philistines in which the Ark of God was taken; and when the news of the catastrophe arrived, it so affected the feelings of his wife that the pains of premature childbirth came upon her and she died (I Sam. 1:3; 2:34; 4:11, 19–22).

3. Father of a certain Eleazar (Ezra 8:33), evidently a priest.

Phle′gon (flē′gŏn) [Gr., burning, scorching]. A Christian at Rome to whom Paul sent his salutation (Rom. 16:14).

Phoe′be (fē′bē), in A.V. **Phe′be** [Gr., pure, bright, radiant]. A servant or deaconess of the church at Cenchreae, the e. port of Corinth. On her removing to Rome, Paul cordially commended her to the Christians there; for she had been a helper or patron of many, a term which may imply that she made it a duty to stand by foreigners in their civic helplessness (Rom. 16:1, 2). See DEACONESS.

Phoe·ni′ci·a (fē-nĭsh′ĭ-á), in A.V. once **Phe·nic′i·a** (fē-nĭsh′ĭ-á) (Acts 21:2), and twice **Phe·ni′ce** (fē-nī′sē) (chs. 11:19; 15:3) [from Gr., *phoinix*, purple-red, purple, or crimson]. A narrow strip of territory between the Mediterranean Sea on the w. and on the e. the crest of the Lebanon range and the detached hills running s. from it. The n. limit may be regarded as Arvad. Southward, after the settlement of the Hebrews on the coast, Phoenicia practically terminated at the Ladder of Tyre, about 14 miles s. of Tyre, although Phoenicians still dwelt in Achzib and Acco (Judg. 1:31). In the time of Christ Phoenicia extended s. as far as Dor, about 16 miles s. of Carmel. The distance from Arvad to the Ladder of Tyre is about 125 miles. The chief cities were Tyre and Sidon, of which Sidon was the first to rise to celebrity. Phoenicia was called Canaan by the ancient Hebrews (Isa. 23:11), and its inhabitants were reckoned as Canaanites (Gen. 10:15). According to their own tradition, they had migrated from the Erythraean Sea, by way of Syria, to the coast of Canaan (Herod. i. 1; vii. 89). According to Arabian authors, the migration was across the n. Arabian desert. The Phoenicians thus traced their origin to the neighborhood of the Persian Gulf; in other words they came from Arabia, the cradleland of the Semites.

The territory which the Phoenicians inhabited had good natural harbors; Mount Lebanon afforded them an almost inexhaustible supply of timber, with which ships were constructed, and they became the most skillful navigators known to antiquity. They not merely traded with distant countries accessible by Mediterranean routes, but they colonized spots favorable for commerce, some of which afterward rose to importance. Their most celebrated colony was Carthage, on the

African coast, near modern Tunis, which was long a rival of Rome, by which it was at last destroyed. Of the Carthaginian leaders who figured in the Punic wars, some, if not all, had names purely Phoenician, which is very close to Hebrew. Thus, Hannibal means "the grace of Baal," and Hasdrubal, "a help is Baal." When our Lord visited the coasts of Tyre and Sidon, he was within the Phoenician territory (Matt. 15:21; Mark 7:24, 31). Various Christians who were scattered abroad, owing to the persecution which followed the martyrdom of Stephen, found their way to Phoenicia (Acts 11:19). Paul and Barnabas went through it on their way from Antioch to Jerusalem (ch. 15:3). Paul, on his last voyage to Jerusalem, sailed in a Phoenician vessel, which brought him to Tyre (ch. 21:2, 3). See ALPHABET, TYRE, BAAL, ETHBAAL, JEZEBEL, and HIRAM.

Phoe'nix (fē'nĭks), in A.V. **Phe'nice** (fē'nĭs) [Gr., date palm]. A haven in Crete (Acts 27:12), safe throughout the year because the entrance to its harbor opens toward the n.e. and s.e. (R.V., cf. text and marg.). It is now called Loutro, and is the only harbor on the s. of Crete which is safe at every season of the year.

Phryg'i·a (frĭj'ĭ-á). A large and important province of Asia Minor, which, after its original boundaries were curtailed by the disseverance from it of Galatia, was bounded on the n. by Bithynia; on the s. by Lycia, Pisidia, and Isauria; on the e. by Lycaonia and Galatia; and on the w. by Caria, Lydia, and Mysia. The region is a high tableland between the chain of Taurus on the s., Olympus on the n., and Temnus on the w. Of its towns, 4 are mentioned in the N.T., Laodicea, Colossae, Hierapolis, and Antioch of Pisidia. At this period Phrygia had ceased to be a province and was merely a local name. Antiochus the Great settled 2,000 Jewish families from Babylonia and Mesopotamia in Lydia and Phrygia (Jos. *Antiq.* xii. 3, 4), and Jews from Phrygia were present at Jerusalem on that Day of Pentecost signalized by the descent of the Holy Spirit (Acts 2:10). Phrygia was traversed by Paul on his Second and Third Missionary Journeys (chs. 16:6; 18:23).

Phu'rah (fū'rá). See PURAH.

Phut (fŭt). See PUT.

Phu'vah (fū'vá). See PUVAH.

Phy·ge'lus (fī-jē'lŭs), in A.V. **Phy·gel'lus** (fī-jĕl'ŭs). A Christian in the province of Asia who, with others, deserted the Apostle Paul in the latter part of his life (II Tim. 1:15).

Phy·lac'ter·y [Gr., safeguard, amulet; so called because it was supposed to guard the wearer against malign influences]. A prayer band consisting of short extracts from the Law of Moses, and worn on the forehead or on the arm (Matt. 23:5). The phylactery eventually assumed the form of a small case, made of parchment or black sealskin. The one for the forehead contained 4 compartments, in each of which was placed a strip of parchment inscribed with a passage of Scripture. The 4 passages were Ex. 13:1–10, 11–16; Deut. 6:4–9; 11:13–21. It was fastened with straps on the forehead, just above and between the eyes. The other case, which was bound on the left arm, contained but 1 compartment, in which a strip of parchment was placed bearing the same 4 quotations from the Law. The first 3 of these were interpreted as enjoining the custom, but are rather to be understood figuratively (see FRONTLET). Phylacteries are worn by every male Jew dur-

ing the time of morning prayer, except on the Sabbath and festivals, which days are themselves signs and render phylacteries unnecessary (cf. Ex. 13:9).

Phylacteries

Phy·si'cian. See MEDICINE.

Pi·be'seth (pī-bē'sĕth) [Egypt., *pr-b'ṣ.t.t*, house of the goddess Bast]. An Egyptian city (Ezek. 30:17), in Gr. form written Bubastos or Bubastis (Herod. ii. 59, 137). It is now called Tell Basta, and is on the Delta near Zagazig, on the w. side of the Pelusiac branch of the Nile. It is about 45 miles n.e. by n. of modern Cairo, and 30 s.w. by s. of ancient Zoan. Among the ruins are the remains of a once splendid temple of red granite, dedicated to the cat-headed goddess Bast.

Piece. In the O.T., when piece refers to money and is not italicized, it denotes a certain amount of precious metal, whether coined or uncoined (Gen. 33:19; I Sam. 2:36). The word piece was chosen by the translators because it is vague, and they did not know the value of the money indicated by the several Hebrew words. Piece is also employed by the translators where the unit of weight or the coin is not expressly mentioned by the Hebrew writer, but where he ordinarily means a shekel (Judg. 17:2; II Sam. 18:11, in A.V. shekel; cf. Deut. 22:19; I Kings 10:29, where both versions have shekel). In the N.T. also a piece of silver commonly denotes the shekel or its equivalent (cf. Matt. 26:15 with Matt. 27:9 and Zech. 11:12); but in Luke 15:8 it is a drachma, worth about 16 cents.

Pi'e·ty. Filial piety, dutifulness in the family (I Tim. 5:4).

Pi'geon. See DOVE.

Pi'-ha·hi'roth (pī'há-hī'rŏth). The last station of the Israelites on leaving Egypt, near Baal-zephon and Migdol, and on the sea (Ex. 14:2, 9; Num. 33:7, 8). The site is uncertain, but Père Abel locates it in the swamps of Jeneffeh at the edge of the pass between the mountain and the Great Bitter Lake.

Pi'late (pī'lát) [Lat., armed with a javelin, or wearing the *pilleus* or felt cap which was worn by a manumitted slave as the emblem of liberty]. Pontius Pilate, 5th Roman procurator in Judea after the deposition of Archelaus in A.D. 6. See PROCURATOR. Through the influence of Sejanus he was appointed by the emperor Tiberius procurator of Judea about

A.D. 26, in succession to Valerius Gratus. He arrived in Judea the same year. He was accompanied by his wife (Matt. 27:19). For a long time it was illegal for a Roman governor who was appointed to a dangerous province to take his wife with him, but since the time of Augustus it had been permitted (Tacitus *Ann.* iii. 33).

Pilate sent a detachment of troops into Jerusalem by night, carrying with them their ensigns, which had hitherto always been left outside the city. On these ensigns were silver eagles and small images of the emperor, and they gave great offense to the Jews. Deputations of Jews went to Caesarea, the official residence of the procurators, to urge the removal of the ensigns, and Pilate, after vainly attempting to intimidate the petitioners, was obliged at last, upon seeing their willingness to die, to comply with their request (Jos. *Antiq.* xviii. 3, 1; *War* ii. 9, 2 and 3). Some time afterward, taking the sacred money called Corban, he began to expend it in making an aqueduct to bring water into Jerusalem from the uplands s. of the capital. The Jews considered that this was applying to secular uses money which had been dedicated to God; and on Pilate's visiting Jerusalem they beset his tribunal with much clamor and tumult. Having been told beforehand that such an occurrence was likely to happen, he had taken the precaution of mingling his soldiers in disguise among the multitude, armed with sticks, if not with concealed daggers. When the tumult was at its height he gave them a signal to attack the rioters with the sticks, which they did so vigorously that some were killed and the rest, fleeing in panic, trampled many of their number to death. The riot seems not to have been renewed, and the aqueduct was made; but the affair increased the disfavor with which the people regarded Pilate (Jos. *Antiq.* xviii. 3, 2; *War* ii. 9, 4). Pilate attempted to dedicate some gilt shields in honor of the emperor Tiberius and place them within Herod's palace at Jerusalem. They were inscribed with the imperial name but were without the imperial portrait. Still they gave offense. The people appealed to him in vain to forbear. Then the influential men of the city forwarded a petition to the emperor, who ordered Pilate to take the shields back again to Caesarea (Philo *Legat. ad Gaium* xxxviii.). In narrating this event, Philo, or rather Agrippa I, in a letter which Philo cites, describes Pilate as a man of inflexible disposition, and merciless as well as obstinate. He also says that he feared they might complain to the emperor about Pilate in respect to his corruption and his acts of violence, and his habit of insulting people, and his cruelty, and his continual execution of people untried and uncondemned, his never-ending and gratuitous and most grievous inhumanity. Pilate was in office when John the Baptist and our Lord began their respective ministries (Luke 3:1). It was the custom of the procurators to go up to Jerusalem when the immense gatherings took place at the leading Jewish festivals. On these occasions they took up their residence in the palace of Herod. It was probably at one of these that Pilate fell upon the Galileans, and mingled their blood with their sacrifices (Luke 13:1, 2). The Galileans were a turbulent class of men, prone to misbehave when they came up to the festivals (Jos. *Antiq.* xvii. 10, 2 and 9). There is no reason to believe that Pilate would have treated them as he did unless they had first broken out into riot. It is probable that Herod Antipas took offense at the summary way in which his subjects were slain by Pilate on this occasion; but whatever may have been the origin of the variance

between the 2, Herod's ill-will was appeased by Pilate's acknowledgment of the tetrarch's jurisdiction in Galilean affairs (Luke 23:6–12) on the day when our Lord was put to death.

The character of Pilate, which these various incidents of his official career reveal, is seen in his treatment of Jesus also. Pilate was a worldling, willing enough to act justly if this could be done consistently with his interests, and to avoid criminal acts provided that this could be done at small cost; but if heavy payment were needed, Pilate was not the man to give it. His secret question to himself was not, What is my duty? but, What is my interest? He acquitted our Lord of evil, was desirous of releasing him, and was aware that justice required that this should be done, but he knew also that it would further increase his unpopularity; so to please the Jewish people he gave orders to scourge Him in whom he had just before declared that he had found no crime. He allowed the Roman soldiers, whom a single word from him would have restrained, to inflict new tortures on the already lacerated body of Jesus, and, after many more insults and injuries to the uncomplaining sufferer, finally answered the Jewish clamors for the crucifixion of the Son of God by giving sentence that it should be as they required (Matt., ch. 27; Luke, ch. 23).

Pilate's government ended abruptly. A Samaritan impostor promised his countrymen that, if they would go to the top of Mount Gerizim, he would show them where Moses had hidden certain golden vessels of the tabernacle. Moses never was at Mount Gerizim; he had not crossed the Jordan; yet a deluded multitude gathered at a village at the foot of the mountain in order to go up. Unfortunately they carried arms. Pilate, therefore, seized all the ways to Gerizim with horsemen and foot soldiers, attacked the mass of the professed treasure-seekers, slew many, and made prisoners of others and sent them to execution. The Samaritans forwarded a complaint against Pilate to his immediate superior, Vitellius, the legate of Syria. Vitellius appointed a new procurator and ordered Pilate to proceed to Rome to answer to the emperor for his conduct. Before Pilate arrived Tiberius had died, March 16, A.D. 37 (Jos. *Antiq.* xviii. 4, 1 and 2). It is reported that Pilate was banished to Vienne, on the Rhone, in the s. of France, and ultimately committed suicide.

Various *Acta Pilati*, Acts of Pilate, are extant, but no 2 of them agree, and all are considered to be spurious.

Pil'dash (pĭl'dăsh). A son of Nahor and Milcah (Gen. 22:22).

Pil'ha (pĭl'hä), in A.V. **Pil'e•ha** (pĭl'ē-hä) [millstone; plowing]. One of those who with Nehemiah sealed the covenant (Neh. 10:24).

Pill. To take the skin or rind off, to peel (Gen. 30:38, R.V., peel).

Pil'lar. 1. A stone erected as a sign of the holiness of a place (Gen. 28:18), as a memorial of some person or event (Gen. 31:45; Josh. 4:5–9; I Sam. 7:12; II Sam. 18:18; and see GARRISON), or as a representative of parties present (Ex. 24:4). Isaiah prophesied that the time is coming when the converts to the true faith in Egypt shall erect an altar and a pillar to the Lord (Isa. 19:19), as Abraham and Jacob did of old in Canaan. The pillar was used by the heathen. The Canaanites erected pillars in connection with the worship of Baal. The Israelites were strictly enjoined, in the oldest legislation, to break them and overthrow the altars (Ex. 23:24, R.V.), and they were forbidden to erect similar pillars beside the altar of the Lord (Deut. 16:22, R.V.). Pillars, however, found favor among the apostate Israelites of the Northern Kingdom (Hos. 3:4; 10:1, 2, R.V.), and even in Judah (Micah 5:13, R.V.).

2. A support, much used in ancient architecture for upholding roofs and curtains (Ex. 26:32; Judg. 16:26). The earth and the heavens were often spoken of poetically as supported by pillars (I Sam. 2:8; Job 9:6; 26:11). Strong men and fundamental principles are figuratively called pillars (Gal. 2:9; I Tim. 3:15).

Pil′low. See BOLSTER.

Pil′tai (pĭl′tī) [deliverance]. A priest, head of the father's house of Moadiah in the days of the high priest Joiakim (Neh. 12:17).

Pim (pĭm) [Heb. *payim,* dual of *peh* (mouth, in sense of part), two thirds. Or it may be derived from Akkad. *šinipū* (from Sumerian *šanabi*), two thirds. If Akkad. *šinipū* were wrongly analyzed as *šinā* (two)+ *pū*, **pū* would be understood as third, whence the Heb. dual *payim,* two thirds]. The word occurs in J.V., I Sam. 13:21, "And the price of the filing was a pim for the mattocks, and for the coulters, and for the forks with three teeth, and for the axes; and to set the goads." The pim (or *payim*) was ⅔ of a shekel. Some of these weights in cubic form have been found in Palestine; one weighed 117.431 grains, and another 114.81 grains. Apparently the standards were not exact.

Pine and **Pine Tree.** 1. The rendering of Heb. *tidhār,* the name of a tree in Lebanon (Isa. 41:19; 60:13).

2. The rendering of *'ēṣ shemen,* oil tree (Neh. 8:15, in R.V. wild olive). See OIL TREE.

Pin′na·cle. A part of the Temple, the edge of which was at a great height above the ground (Matt. 4:5). Exact identification is impossible. The Gr. word *pterygion,* like pinnacle which is used to translate it, literally means a little wing; and it denotes in the LXX the fin of a fish, the border of a garment, or the end of the breastplate (Lev. 11:9; Num. 15:38; Ex. 39:19 = LXX, Ex. 36:27). It may be simply the edge of the roof or court. Lightfoot, influenced by the meaning of the Gr. word, suggested the porch which projected on each side of the Temple like wings (Jos. *War* v. 5, 4). Others have thought of the royal porch which adjoined the Temple and towered 400 cubits above the valley of the Kidron (Jos. *Antiq.* xv. 11, 5; xx. 9, 7). The golden spikes which were erected on the roof of the Temple to prevent birds from alighting, have been thought of also as most nearly resembling slender towers or pinnacles in the modern sense; but they were many, and the Evangelists speak of the pinnacle as if there were but one (R.V.).

Pi′non (pī′nŏn). A chieftain of Edom (Gen. 36:41; I Chron. 1:52), probably catalogued by the name of his town (Gen. 36:40); see PUNON.

Pipe. 1. A wind instrument, called in Heb. *ḥālīl,* pierced instrument, and in Gr. *aulos.* It is possible that *ḥālīl* is a general term for a wood-wind and may include the double clarinet. The single pipe or reed was held vertically and blown by a mouthpiece at the end. A different kind was held and blown like a flute. The double pipe consisted of right and left tubes, which were blown at the same time and played each with the corresponding hand. The *ḥālīl* probably was a double oboe; the word means flute in modern Heb. It was used in orchestra or was played alone (I Sam. 10:5; I Kings 1:40), and it accompanied merry song, religious praise, and the funeral dirge (Isa. 5:12; 30:29; Matt. 9:23; 11:17). See MUSIC.

2. A wind instrument of ancient origin, called *'ūgāb* (Gen. 4:21), which was used in merrymaking (Job 21:12; 30:31), and was deemed worthy of employment in the praise of God (Ps. 150:4). According to the Targums it was a pipe. The Vulgate and, in Psalm 150, the LXX explain it as a wind in-

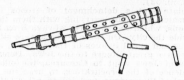

Palestinian Shepherd's Pipe

strument, the *organon.* The A.V. always translates it organ, doubtless in the sense of mouth organ or set of pipes. The R.V. uniformly renders it pipe.

It is uncertain whether *neḳeb* (Ezek. 28:13) denotes a pierced instrument (E.V. pipe) or a perforated gem.

Pi′ram (pī′răm) [probably, wild ass]. A Canaanite king of Jarmuth, one of those defeated by Joshua before Gibeon (Josh. 10:3).

Pir′a·thon (pĭr′á·thŏn), in R.V. of I Macc. 9:50 **Phar′a·thon** [height; cf. Arab. *far',* summit]. In A.V. of I Macc. the adjective Pharathoni is used. A town in the mount of the Amalekites, in the Ephraimite territory. Abdon, the judge, and Benaiah, the military official, were Pirathonites (Judg. 12:13–15; II Sam. 23:30; I Chron. 27:14). It was fortified by Bacchides (I Macc. 9:50; cf. Jos. *Antiq.* xiii. 1, 3). Robinson identified it plausibly with Fer′ata, on a hill about 7½ miles w. by s. of Shechem.

Pis′gah (pĭz′gá) [a part, piece, division]. That part of the Abarim range of mountains near the n.e. end of the Dead Sea (cf. Deut. 34:1 with chs. 3:27; 32:49). The Dead Sea was under its slopes (Deut. 3:17). Its top looked down upon the desert (Num. 21:20). The field of Zophim on its top was visited by Balaam and Balak (Num. 23:14). From its summit, called Nebo, a large part of Canaan w. of the Jordan was visible, and from it Moses viewed the Promised Land (Deut. 3:27; 34:1–4); see NEBO 2. It was on the s. border of the realm of Sihon, king of the Amorites (Josh. 12:2, 3). As late as the time of Eusebius, the mountainous country adjacent to Mount Peor was called Phasgō. The name Ashdoth-Pisgah occurs in A.V. (Deut. 3:17; Josh. 12:3; 13:20).

Pi′shon (pī′shŏn). See EDEN 1.

Pi·sid′i·a (pĭ·sĭd′ĭ·á). A district of Asia Minor, bounded on the n. by Phrygia, on the s. by Lycia and Pamphylia, on the e. by Lycaonia, and on the w. by Caria. On the e. it ran in a vague and indefinite way into Isauria. It formed a part of the Roman province of Galatia. The mountain chain of Taurus runs through it, and its turbulent inhabitants were so brave that they were never entirely subdued either by the Persians or by the Romans. Its chief town was Antioch, visited by Paul (Acts 13:14).

Pi′son (pī′sŏn). See EDEN 1.

Pis′pa (pĭs′pä), A.V. **Pis′pah** (pĭs′pä). An Asherite, son of Jether (I Chron. 7:38).

Pit. A large deep hole in the ground. It may be either natural or artificial (Gen. 14:10; 37:20, 24).

Figuratively it is used for the grave or death (Job 33:18, 24), and it is employed thrice to render *she'ōl* (Num. 16:30, 33; Job 17:16); see HELL 1 and ABYSS.

Pitch. 1. The rendering of Heb. *kōpher* (cf. Akkad. *kupru,* asphalt). The ark of Noah was daubed over with it to render the junction of wooden planks impervious to water (Gen. 6:14). It was probably asphalt from Hit, in Babylonia. See BITUMEN.

2. The rendering of Heb. *zepheth,* liquid. The ark of Moses was covered over with it (Ex. 2:3). The streams in the land of Edom were to become pitch of this character (Isa. 34:9). The last passage suggests that it also was asphalt from some locality. See BITUMEN.

Pitch'er. A water jar of earthenware (cf. Judg. 7:19), in the East generally having 1 or 2 handles. See JAR.

Pi'thom (pī'thŏm) [Egypt. *pr-itm,* house of Atum (Tum, Tem), who was an Egyptian god, the setting sun; Coptic, *Pethom, Peithom;* Gr. *Patoumos*]. One of the 2 store cities which the Israelites while in bondage in Egypt built for Pharaoh (Ex. 1:11). Excavations, made under the auspices of the Egyptian Exploration Fund, by Edouard Naville at Tell el-Maskhûṭah, led to identifying this with ancient Pithom. It is on the s. side of the sweet-water canal which runs from Cairo to Suez through Wadi Tumilat. There seems to have been at the spot an ancient shrine dedicated to Atum, and the antiquity of the place is confirmed by inscriptions from Dyn. VI and fragments from Dyn. I. Inscriptions dug up indicate, however, that the city and fortifications did not come into existence till the time of Ramesses II. To the n.e. of the temple of Tum are extensive subterranean buildings. The walls are 9 feet thick, built of crude bricks joined by thin layers of mortar. A most interesting observation was made that some bricks had been manufactured without straw (cf. Ex. 5:10–12). The walls enclosed a number of rectangular chambers not communicating with each other, the only access to them being from above. Naville believes that they were storehouses or granaries, into which the Pharaohs gathered the provisions necessary for armies or even for caravans about to cross the desert into Syria. In the Ptolemaic period Pithom received the new name of Heroonpolis, city of heroes, which may be a Gr. popular ety. derived from Egypt. *ḥꜣr* (container or measure of corn). It was in the land of Goshen; for Goshen the LXX substitutes Heroonpolis, into the land of Ramessē (Gen. 46:28). More recently an identification with Tell Retabeh has been favored. See SUCCOTH 2.

Pi'thon (pī'thŏn). A descendant of Jonathan (I Chron. 8:35; 9:41).

Plague. An infliction sent by God as a punishment for sin. In most of the cases mentioned in the Bible the infliction is an epidemic or other disease, but it may also be a judgment of a different character. A disease to be a plague need not be miraculous. The particular disease which God has attached as a penalty for the violation of this or that physical or mental law may be properly called a plague, if the act has moral quality. And even a disease which arises from ignorance of sanitary laws and from a violation of nature in no wise criminal, and which in itself is without moral significance, may become in God's hands an instrument for the punishment of evildoers, God predetermining and arranging for the time and place of its outbreak with this end in view. What is called in English by way of emphasis the plague is a highly malignant form of typhus fever, due to neglect of sanitary precautions, which has frequently originated at Cairo, in Egypt, and spread to Syria, Asia Minor, and adjacent regions. It is probable

that it has been used in times past as a chastening rod.

The first plague mentioned in Scripture was that sent on Pharaoh, Abraham's contemporary, for the protection of Sarah, the patriarch's wife (Gen. 12:17). The next plagues in point of time were the 10 inflicted on Egypt. They were not phenomena with which the Egyptians were previously unacquainted; but in most cases, if not in all, they were distresses common to the country. Yet they were not mere natural phenomena in aggravated form; they exhibited unmistakably miraculous features; see EGYPT, III. 6. The 1st consisted in the change of the river water into blood or something like it (Ex. 7:14–25); the 2d, in the vast multiplication of frogs (ch. 8:1–15); the 3d, in lice, sand flies, or fleas, produced from the dust (vs. 16–19); the 4th, in swarms of flies (vs. 20–32); the 5th, in murrain on the cattle (ch. 9:1–7); the 6th, in boils and blains on man and beast (vs. 8–12); the 7th, in a destructive hailstorm (vs. 13–35); the 8th, in locusts brought by the e. wind (ch. 10:1–20); the 9th, in dense darkness (vs. 21–29); and the 10th, in the death of all the first-born (chs. 11:1 to 12:30). A plague was sent upon the Israelites for making and worshiping the golden calf (Ex. 32:35); and another for murmuring against the sustenance provided for them by God (Num. 11:33, 34); another slew the spies who had brought up "an evil report of the land" (Num. 14:37); another raged among the people for murmuring at the righteous punishment of the rebels Korah, Dathan, and Abiram. In this visitation 14,700 perished (Num. 16:46–50). In another plague sent upon the people on account of the idolatries and impurities at Baal-peor 24,000 died (Num. 25:9; Josh. 22:17; Ps. 106:28–30). The infliction of the emerods, or piles, upon the Philistines is called a plague (I Sam. 6:4). A plague or pestilence, in which 70,000 perished, followed on David's numbering the people (II Sam. 24:13–25; I Chron. 21:12–30). A plague was threatened against Jehoram, king of Judah, and his people (II Chron. 21:14, 15).

Sometimes the word plague is used for diseases which are not epidemic; it is applied, for instance, to an issue of blood (Mark 5:29, 34, literally scourge), to leprosy in individuals (Lev. 13:3–6), and even to the spreading of some inferior forms of vegetation on the walls of presumably damp houses (Lev. 14:35).

Plain. In the A.V. 7 different words are rendered "plain." Three of these deserve special notice, *shephēlāh, kikkār,* and *'ărābāh.* The term *shephēlāh,* or lowland, as R.V. renders it, was the technical designation for the districts of s. and in part of central Palestine, between the higher hills on the e. and the low-lying plain along the Mediterranean on the w. In Josh. 15:33–47, 42 towns of Judah, with their villages, are enumerated as being within its bounds. Joshua 15:33–36 gives a total of 14, but lists 15 names; LXX, with a slightly different text, reads: "Gederah and its farm houses [farms, or camps]"; thus it lists only 14 names. The totals in the Hebrew text accordingly are correct. Some of these were, however, generally in Philistine hands, and hence Obad. 19 mentions the lowland of the Philistines. See LOWLAND.

Kikkār, which means circle, circuit, was applied especially to the plain of the Jordan from at least Succoth on the n. to Sodom and Gomorrah on the s. (Gen. 13:10–12; 19:17, 28; Deut. 34:3; II Sam. 18:23; II Chron. 4:17). The valley as far n. as the Sea of Galilee was probably included in the designation (Jos. *War* iv. 8, 2).

The word '*ărābāh*, which is rendered plain in A.V. of Deut. 2:8; 3:17; etc., is generally left untranslated in R.V. See ARABAH 1.

Plane. The rendering of Heb. '*armōn*, naked or bare (Gen. 30:37; Ezek. 31:8). So R.V. and the ancient versions, except that the LXX in Ezekiel renders it "pine." The A.V., following the rabbinical interpretation, calls it chestnut. The Oriental plane tree (*Platanus orientalis*) grows from 70 to 90 feet high. It has palmately lobed leaves, resembling those of the sycamore maple, which is the reason why the latter tree is sometimes called a plane, and has the name *Acer pseudo-platanus*. The Oriental plane is indigenous in s. Europe and w. Asia. In Palestine it is wild by the side of mountain streams, besides being cultivated in many places.

Plas'ter. See MORTAR, II.

Pledge. See LOAN.

Ple'ia·des (plē'yȧ-dēz). Hebrew *Kīmāh* is the name of a brilliant star or constellation (Job 9:9; 38:31; Amos 5:8, in A.V. the 7 stars), and in the opinion of the majority of ancient writers it denotes the Pleiades.

The Pleiades are a cluster of stars in the constellation Taurus (the Bull), in the shoulder of the animal. For some unknown reason they were anciently said to be 7; and since only 6 were usually seen, the notion arose of a lost Pleiad. Six stars are visible to the naked eye on ordinary nights, but more may be seen by persons of very good sight. With the aid of a telescope 100 stars may be counted. Josephus uses the setting of the Pleiades as a note of time (Jos. *Antiq.* xiii. 8, 2).

Plow. In Palestine the plow is of primitive character. It consists of a pole or the branch of a tree, to one end of which the yoke is attached, while from the other end a small branch projects or else through the end a beam is thrust which is sheathed in a thin plate of iron and forms the share (Isa. 2:4). In the Bronze Age the plowshare was of wood. It is possible that the Philistines introduced iron plowshares (I Sam. 13:20). The plow was dragged by oxen or cows, and was guided by the hand (Job 1:14; Ecclus. 38: 25, 26; Luke 9:62). Such an implement can do little more than scratch the surface of the ground. When Elisha was plowing with 12 yoke of oxen there were probably 12 plows, each with its pair of bullocks and its man, Elisha being the last of the 12 (I Kings 19: 19, 20).

Poch'e·reth-haz'ze·ba'im (pŏk'ē-rĕth-hă'zē-bā'ĭm) [binder (fem.) of the gazelles]. Name of a division of Solomon's servants, members of which returned from Babylon (Ezra 2:57; Neh. 7:59). The A.V. divides the name, makes the latter part a place, and calls the man Pochereth of Zebaim.

Po'et·ry. Poetry is one of the earliest forms in which the literary taste of a people begins to express itself. It is rhythmical and regular in form, like the motions of the dancer which it so frequently accompanied in ancient times (Ex. 15:20, 21). It is naturally born of the emotions, and is called forth by individual or national joy or sorrow or deep concern. The imagination also and the habit of expressing thought in vivid language borrowed from nature, which are vital elements in poetry, come to manifestation during the childhood of a people. The Hebrews formed no exception to the rule. The words of Sarah at the birth of her son have the poetic ring (Gen. 21:6, 7). The blessing which Jacob bestowed on his sons as the time of his death approached was couched in the sententious and picturesque form of Semitic poetry (Gen., ch. 49). The song of Moses and Miriam (Ex. 15:1–21), when they beheld the overthrow of Pharaoh's host in the sea and discerned the moral effect which it would have on the nations of Canaan, was also an utterance born of strong feeling and cast into the simple form of Hebrew poetry.

Ancient Semitic poetry does not rhyme. Poems have been discovered which show a certain caesural arrangement, but this feature is not essential. Assonance, alliteration, and rhyme, so common in Occidental poetry, occasionally occur in Hebrew poetry, but they also are not essential and they are extremely rare. Nor is there a regular recurrence of long and short syllables or feet; but the rhythmical tendency was strongly felt and unconsciously led to producing lines of nearly the same number of words or word-groups, or, to state the matter somewhat differently, the same number of main accents, including at times a secondary accent. The line, moreover, was made to end at a break in the sense except in extremely rare cases, such as Ps. 96:12.

The essential formal characteristic of Hebrew poetry is parallelism. By this is meant that the sentiment of one line is echoed in the next. The name was given to this feature by Bishop Robert Lowth in 1753, who investigated the phenomenon and drew attention to synonymous, antithetic, and synthetic parallelism. Parallelism is of various kinds:

1. *Synonymous*, when the thought of the 1st line is repeated in other words in the 2d line, as in Gen. 4:23:

Adah and Zillah, hear my voice;
Ye wives of Lamech, hearken unto my
speech.

The couplet:

For I have slain a man to my wounding
[or, for wounding me],
And a young man to my hurt [or, for
bruising me],

likewise exhibits synonymous parallelism; and at the same time it shows the exegetical

Plowing and Sowing in Ancient Egypt

importance of an acquaintance with this principle, for Lamech must not be understood to speak of 2 murders. He mentions killing but 1 man. This principle also enables the expositor of Scripture to interpret ambiguous words; for example, in Ps. 22:20:

Deliver my soul from the sword,
My darling from the power of the dog,

the parallelism determines that the darling referred to is not a dear friend, but means the psalmist's soul or his life (cf. R.V. marg.).

2. *Progressive,* in which the 2d line expresses a new idea more or less closely related to the 1st; as in Job 3:17:

There the wicked cease from troubling;
And there the weary are at rest.

3. *Synthetic or constructive,* in which there is parallelism of structure only, while the thought of one line serves as the foundation upon which to build a new thought; as Ps. 25:12:

What man is he that feareth Jehovah?
Him shall he instruct in the way that he
shall choose;

or Prov. 26:4:

Answer not a fool according to his folly,
Lest thou also be like unto him;

or Ps. 24:9:

Lift up your heads, O ye gates;
Yea, lift them up, ye everlasting doors:
And the King of glory will come in.

4. *Climactic,* in which the characteristic words are repeated and form the ladder on which the thought climbs to completion or to emphatic reiteration; as in Ps. 29:5:

The voice of Jehovah breaketh the cedars;
Yea, Jehovah breaketh in pieces the cedars
of Lebanon;

and in Ps. 121:3, 4:

He will not suffer thy foot to be moved:
He that keepeth thee will not slumber.
Behold, he that keepeth Israel
Will neither slumber nor sleep.

5. *Antithetic,* in which the thought is made more clear by contrast; as in Prov. 10:1:

A wise son maketh a glad father;
But a foolish son is the heaviness of his
mother;

and in Matt. 8:20:

The foxes have holes,
And the birds of the heaven have nests;
But the Son of man hath not where to lay
his head.

6. *Comparative,* in which the thought is explained by comparison with something else that is familiar; as in Ps. 42:1:

As the hart panteth after the water brooks,
So panteth my soul after thee, O God.

The parallelism usually yields a distich, but tristichs are not uncommon, as may be seen from the examples already cited. Tetrastichs and pentastichs also occur (Ps. 1:3; 27:4, 9; 37:7, 14, 20, 25, 28, 34, 40). The stanza is not essential to Hebrew poetry. It is used, however, in Psalms 42; 43, which form 1 poem, divided into 3 equal parts by a recurring verse. Psalm 46 consists of 3 groups of 3 verses each, the conclusion of each group being marked by Selah, and the last 2 groups closing with a refrain. There are also alphabetical psalms, in which in the Hebrew the principle is more or less fully observed of beginning the successive verses with the letters of the alphabet in consecutive order (Psalms 25; 34; 37). Psalm 119 consists of 22 groups

of 8 verses each. The number of groups equals the number of letters in the Heb. alphabet, and the initial letter of each verse in a group is in the original that letter of the alphabet which numerically corresponds to the group. The book of Lamentations is constructed on a similar alphabetical plan; see LAMENTATIONS.

Poetry is usually classified as epic, dramatic, lyric, and didactic. Neither the epic nor the drama is found in the Bible; but The Book of Job has a semi-dramatic form, for there is action, which forms the basis of drama, in the prologue and epilogue, and there is a regular alternation of speakers throughout. See also SONG OF SOLOMON. The lyrics are the most numerous poems. No period of Israelitish history after the Exodus is without them. They consist of triumphal odes which celebrate the deliverance wrought by Jehovah, like the song of Moses at the Red Sea and the song of Deborah; psalms of the penitent suing for mercy or expressing the joy of forgiveness (Psalms 32; 51), and of the poor and needy crying out in distress, calm in faith, or praising God for succor (Psalms 38; 3; 23; Hab., ch. 3; and I Sam. 2:1–10; Isa. 38:10–20; Luke 1:46–55); and plaintive elegies, as the lament of David over Saul and Jonathan, the songs of mourning for Judah, and the lamentations (II Sam. 1:17–27; Psalms 44; 60; 74).

Poi'son. Any substance, vegetable, animal, or mineral, which produces a morbid or deadly effect when introduced into the animal organism (II Kings 4:39, 40; Rom. 3:13). The venom of serpents is denoted in Heb. either by *ḥēmāh*, heat (Deut. 32:24, 33; Ps. 58:4), a general word which is also used for hot passion and the heat produced by wine, or by *rō'sh* (Deut. 32:33; Job 20:16), which also signifies a bitter herb; see GALL 2. The custom of anointing arrows with the poison of snakes is probably alluded to in Job 6:4. It was a practice of great antiquity and considerable extent (Homer *Odyssey* i. 261, 262; Pliny *Hist. Nat.* xi. 115; xviii. 1). Vegetable poison was also employed for this purpose, as that obtained from the yew tree (*Hist. Nat.* xvi. 20). The Gauls used a poisonous herb called *limeum,* perhaps leopard's bane (*Hist. Nat.* xxvii. 76).

The suicide of Ptolemy Macron by poison, the alleged murder of Pheroras by poisoned food, and the fame of Arabian women for skill in preparing poisonous potions (II Macc. 10:13; Jos. *Antiq.* xvii. 4, 1), serve to show that the crimes prevalent at that time in Rome were not left uncommitted in Judah and the East (cf. Mark 16:18); but the absence of direct mention of them in the Bible indicates that they were not common among the Jews.

Pol'lux (pŏl'ŭks). See CASTOR AND POLLUX.

Pome'gran'ate. The pomegranate (*Punica granatum*), in Heb. called *rimmōn,* is a tree from 12 to 15 feet high, having oblong-oblanceolate entire leaves, without dots. Here and there on the branches occasional thorns are found. The flowers generally have scarlet petals proceeding from a large leathery calyx. The fruit is about the size of an orange, and has a hard, red rind, filled with numerous seeds enveloped in bright red pulp. The pulp is most refreshing to the taste. The pomegranate is wild in n. Africa and w. Asia, and possibly so in Gilead. It was largely cultivated in Palestine in Biblical times (Num. 13:23; 20:5; Deut. 8:8; I Sam. 14:2; S. of Sol. 4:3, 13; 6:7, 11; 8:2; Joel 1:12; Hag. 2:19). The expressed juice of the fruit made a pleasant drink (S. of Sol. 8:2). Pomegranates of blue, purple, and scarlet stuff alternating with bells made of gold were put along the skirts of the robe connected with the high priest's ephod (Ex. 28:33, 34; 39:26). Each of the chapiters of the 2 pillars at the porch of Solomon's Temple had around it two rows of 100 pomegranates each (I Kings 7:20; II Kings 25:17; II Chron. 3:16). The fruit is still much cultivated in Palestine.

Pomegranate Branch

Pom'mel. Rounded portion or bowl of a chapiter (capital) (II Chron. 4:12, 13; in R.V. and in I Kings 7:41, 42, bowl).

Pon'tius (pŏn'shŭs). See PILATE.

Pon'tus (pŏn'tŭs) [Gr. and Lat., the sea]. The e. half of the coast of Asia Minor on the Pontus Euxinus, or Black Sea, from the 1st word of which the name of the province was derived. It may be described as reaching from the valley of the Phasis in Colchis to the river Halys, and extending inland s. across the mountains to Cappadocia. Six of its successive kings were called Mithridates; the founder of the dynasty ruled in Cius on the Propontis (337–302 B.C.). The last of them maintained (121–63 B.C.) a fierce struggle with the Romans, who reduced the kingdom to the position of a protected state, united it with Bithynia, and formed the province of Bithynia and Pontus (I Peter 1:1). Jews resided in Pontus (I Peter 1:1). Jews from Pontus were at Jerusalem during the Pentecostal effusion of the Holy Spirit (Acts 2:9). Aquila the Jew was born in the province (ch. 18:2).

Pool. A reservoir for water, supplied by rain or else by springs, like the pool of Siloam. From the pool the water was sometimes conducted in channels to town and garden (Eccl. 2:6; Ecclus. 24:30). The pools of Bethesda, Siloam, and Gihon were at Jerusalem, and water was also conducted to the city from the reservoirs at Etam; and there were pools at Gibeon, Hebron, Samaria, and Heshbon (II Sam. 2:13; 4:12; I Kings 22:38; S. of Sol. 7:4). The king's pool (Neh. 2:14; 3:15; II Kings 20:20) is probably identical with the pool of Siloam (John 9:7). Near by was the king's garden (II Kings 25:4; Jer. 39:4; 52:7), which was in all probability just outside the walls and irrigated by overflow water from the pool of Siloam.

Poor. The unequal distribution of the blessings of life is not ideal in the sight of God. Now God gave Canaan to his people (Ex. 6:4, 8). Accordingly the Mosaic Law provided for a general participation of the peo-

ple in the ownership of the land; and while it permitted freedom of sale, it secured a readjustment of property and a return to each family of its inheritance in Canaan every 50 years (Lev. 25:13, 23). But notwithstanding all that law and instruction can do, the poor are always present, sometimes through sins of their own or their ancestors, sometimes through the inscrutable but wise providence of God. The poverty which springs from indolence or personal crime was theoretically excluded from Israel, the kingdom of God; and its poor were regarded from the standpoint of the theocracy as the unfortunate and chastened but beloved children of God. All the poor, especially widows, orphans, and strangers, enjoyed the care of God and the godly, and all were specially favored by the Law. Every hungry person had the right to pluck and eat for present need in the vineyard or grainfield of another (Deut. 23:24, 25). Every poor person was authorized at harvest to glean after the reapers, to cut the grain that was left standing at the edge of the field, and to take any forgotten sheaf which remained in the field when the harvest was over. At the vintage and in fruit-picking time what was left hanging on the branches belonged to the poor (Lev. 19:9, 10; 23:22; Deut. 24:19–21). In the 7th year and 50th year the land was not tilled, and what grew of itself was not harvested, but was free to all to eat (Lev. 25:4–7, 11, 12). The poor man in his extremity might sell his services to a master for a term of years, but regained his freedom in the year of release (vs. 38–42). If a loan were required by a poor man, it was to be bestowed, even though the near approach of the release of the 7th year would soon give him the legal right of not repaying the debt (Deut. 15:7–10). The poll tax, which each man had to pay for the ransom of his soul or life on the taking of a census, was the same in amount for both rich and poor, being half a shekel; but in offerings presented at the tabernacle or Temple, a cheaper form of gift was sometimes prescribed for the poorer worshiper (Lev. 12:8; 14:21; 27:8). The prosperous were encouraged to invite the poor to the sacrificial feasts and to remember them on other joyous occasions (Deut. 16:11, 14). There are many beautiful examples of kindness shown to the needy (Job 31:16–22). There were also warnings in the Law against the oppression of the poor (Ex. 22:21–27). At the same time, justice must not be violated. A judge must not give a verdict in favor of a man because he was poor; the claims of justice were to be paramount over every other consideration (Ex. 23:3; Lev. 19:15). The kindly provisions of the Law, however, were frequently ignored in times of religious declension, and the prophets had occasion to rebuke hard-heartedness and injustice toward the poor (Isa. 1:23; 10:2; Ezek. 22:7, 29; Mal. 3:5). There were also abuses of the good Law itself. There were those who obeyed the letter, but not the spirit, who bestowed alms to be seen of men (Matt. 6:1). Many gracious promises are made to the pious poor, and the divine procedure to them is shown to be that of loving care (I Sam. 2:8; Job 5:15; 34:28; 36:15; Ps. 9:18; 10:14; 12:5; 34:6; 35:10). Blessings are also promised to the man who pities the poor (Ps. 41:1; Prov. 14:21, 31; 29:7; etc.). Our Lord in the course of his ministry showed his great love for the poor (Matt. 19:21; Luke 18:22; John 13:29; etc.), and it was a special characteristic of his ministry that to the poor the gospel was preached (Matt. 11:5; Luke 14:21–23). The Early Church considered it one of its most sacred duties to look after its poor and, as far as its limited resources would allow, the poor also outside its communion

(Acts 2:45; 4:32; 6:1–6; 11:27–30; 24:17; I Cor. 16:1–3; Gal. 2:10; I Thess. 3:6).

The poor in spirit are the humble, whether rich or poor in this world's goods (Matt. 5:3).

Pop'lar. The rendering of Heb. *libneh*, white, applied to a tree (Gen. 30:37). It ranked with trees of which the shadow is good (Hos. 4:13). If it is the poplar, the species is *Populus alba*, a tall tree with white wood, and the leaves white and cottony on the lower side. In the 1st passage the R.V., following the LXX, has storax-tree in the marg., referring to *Styrax officinalis*, sometimes called *libna* in Arab., a resinous shrub from 10 to 20 feet high, a native of the Levant; see STACTE. The LXX understands the white poplar to be meant in Hos. 4:13.

Po•ra'tha (pō-rā'thả) [Old Pers., giving much, liberal]. One of Haman's sons (Esth. 9:8).

Porch. A walk protected by a roof supported by pillars; a colonnade; a portico. There were often porches of this character in royal or other mansions (I Kings 7:6, 7), and there was a notable one on the e. front of Solomon's Temple (I Kings 6:3; Ezek. 8:16; Joel 2:17). Sometimes there was a colonnade on an upper floor (Judg. 3:23). The porches of the pool of Bethesda, and Solomon's porch connected with the 2d Temple, were also colonnades (John 5:2; 10:23), called in Gr. *stoa*. The porch where Peter's 2d denial took place was doubtless the passage from the street to the court of the house; and in the parallel passage it is styled the fore-court (Matt. 26:71; Mark 14:68, R.V. marg.).

Por'ci•us (pôr'shĭ-ŭs). See FESTUS.

Por'cu•pine. The rendering of the R.V. in Isa. 14:23; 34:11; Zeph. 2:14 of Heb. *ḳippōd*, the one rolling itself together. The corresponding word in other Semitic dialects denotes both the hedgehog and the porcupine. The European porcupine (*Hystrix cristata*) is common in Palestine, especially in the gorges leading down to the valley of the Jordan. A brush-tailed porcupine (*Atherura hirsutirostris*) has also been found in Judea. The A.V. translates *ḳippōd* by bittern, and this is retained by J.V.

Por'poise. The rendering of *taḥash* in R.V. marg. of Ex. 25:5 and elsewhere where the text has seal and A.V. has badger. This marginal rendering is based on Arab. *tukhas* (dolphin). It may, however, be a loan word from Egypt. *tḥś* (leather).

Pos•ses'sion. See DEMONIAC.

Por'ter. A gate keeper (I Chron. 9:22–24; 16:38, in R.V. doorkeeper). Keepers were stationed at the city gate (II Sam. 18:26; II Kings 7:10), at the doors of the Temple (I Chron. 9:22), at the entrance of private houses (Mark 13:34). When David organized the Levites for the service of the tabernacle, he assigned the duty of acting as doorkeepers to a large section of them, 4,000 in number. They were not all needed at once, so he distributed them into courses, officiating in succession (I Chron. 23:5; 26:1–19).

Post. 1. The upright timber at the side of a door (I Kings 6:33, door-post, R.V.). A stone pillar sometimes took the place of wood. A Hebrew slave who did not desire to embrace the opportunity of freedom afforded by the arrival of the 7th year, but preferred to remain permanently in the master's house, allowed an awl to be thrust through his ear into the door or door-post (Ex. 21:6; Deut. 15:17) as a sign of attachment to the house. 2. A courier (Esth. 3:13; Job 9:25).

Pot. The most frequent word is Heb. *sir*, a vessel made in various sizes, large and small (II Kings 4:38), and of different ma-

terials, earthenware and metal (Ex. 38:3), and used for manifold purposes, such as for boiling flesh (Ex. 16:3; II Chron. 35:13; Job 41:31; Ezek 24:3–5, in R.V. caldron), for washing (Ps. 60:8), for refining metals (Prov. 27:21). The term *dûd* might also designate a similar pot (Job 41:20; in I Sam. 2:14 rendered kettle; in II Chron. 35:13 rendered caldron); so also might *ḳallaḥath*, which is rendered caldron (I Sam. 2:14; Micah 3:3). In Job 41:20 the word translated caldron in A.V. should be rushes. Water for domestic purposes was kept in earthen pots (John 2:6).

Pot'i•phar (pŏt'ĭ-fẽr) [Egypt., that one whom Re (the sun-god) has given]. The captain of Pharaoh's guard and owner of Joseph. His wife attempted to seduce the young slave from the path of virtue, and when she failed she induced Potiphar to imprison him on a charge which she knew to be false (Gen. 39:1–20).

Po•tiph'er•a (pō-tĭf'ẽr-ả) in A.V. **Po•tiph'•er•ah** (pō-tĭf'ẽr-ả) [see Potiphar]. A priest of On, or Heliopolis, the city of the sun. He was the father of Asenath, who was given in marriage to Joseph (Gen. 41:45–50; 46:20).

Pot'ter. One who makes earthenware pots and similar vessels. The clay was trodden by foot of man to reduce it to a paste (Isa. 41:

Potters at the Kiln in Ancient Egypt

25; Wisd. of Sol. 15:7). It was then placed on a horizontal wheel, before which the potter sat, turning the wheel with his hand as he shaped the vessel, or keeping the wheel in motion with his foot, while he fashioned the revolving clay with his hand and arm. The finished work was glazed and baked in a furnace (Jer. 18:3, 4; Ecclus. 38:29, 30). The ability of the potter to mold the clay into any shape he desired is used in Isa. 45:9; Jer. 18:5–12; Rom. 9:20–25 to illustrate God's sovereignty over man. God, of course, in the exercise of sovereignty acts only in accordance with his infinite perfections of wisdom, justice, goodness, and truth.

Pot'ter's Field. See AKELDAMA.

Pound. See MONEY and WEIGHTS.

Pow'der. The fine particles into which any substance is crushed or ground (Ex. 32:20). Pulverized spice of any kind, intended to be burned as incense (S. of Sol. 3:6).

Prae'tor [Lat., one going before]. One of the chief civil magistrates in a Roman colony, in Gr. commonly designated *stratēgos* (Acts 16:12, and vs. 20, 35, R.V. marg.). There were usually 2 (Lat. *duoviri*) elected annually by the colonists. Two lictors attended each praetor, cleared the way before him, saw that due respect was shown him by the public, and executed his orders (Acts 16:35, 38, R.V. marg.).

Prae·to'ri·um [Lat., pertaining to a praetor]. The tent of a general; the official residence of a provincial governor; a palace. In the N.T. it denotes:
1. The palace occupied by Pontius Pilate at Jerusalem, in which his judgment seat was erected (Mark 15:16; and marg. of R.V. of Matt. 27:27; John 18:28, 33; 19:9, cf. v. 13). Some have taken it to be the castle of Antonia; but Herod's palace was the building occupied by the procurators. See HEROD, PALACE OF.
2. Herod's palace at Caesarea, in which Paul was confined (Acts 23:35, R.V. marg.; in text, palace; in A.V., judgment hall).
3. The Praetorian Guard at Rome, the duty of which was to guard the imperial palace and its occupant, the emperor (Phil. 1:13; A.V., palace; A.V. marg., Caesar's court).

Prayer. Prayer is communion with God. It implies that God is a person, able and willing to hear us, who has created the universe and still preserves and governs all his creatures and all their actions. He is not the slave of his own laws. He can produce results by controlling the laws of nature or cooperating with them as readily as a man can; in fact, more so, since he is God. He can influence the hearts and minds of men more readily than even a man can induce his fellow men to action. God has foreordained both the prayer and its answer. He has had a plan from the beginning; and he accomplishes this plan both by the manner in which he established the universe and the laws which he set in operation, and also by his constant presence in the universe, upholding it and controlling it.

Prayer is instinctive with man. In his extremity of need he cries out to God. And God requires prayer of all men; but to pray to God implies a right relation to him. Acceptable prayer can be offered unto God by the righteous only. The prayer of the wicked is abomination unto him (Prov. 15:29; 28:9). Only those who have forsaken sin are authorized to draw nigh unto God in prayer. Those who have rebelled against the authority of God can approach him only with renunciation of their rebellion and a petition for pardon. Prayer is the communion of the child of God with his Father in heaven. It consists of adoration, thanksgiving, confession, and petition (Neh. 1:4–11; Dan. 9:3–19; Phil. 4:6). It has been engaged in by God's people from the beginning.

Prayer is thus the natural expression of the religious feelings; and God's blessings are given in answer to prayer (I Kings 9:3; Ezek. 36:37; Matt. 7:7). God is attentive to every prayer that is rightly offered to him. He hears the young ravens when they cry; and God's people have the promise that he will answer their prayers (Ps. 65:2). James. citing history, says, "The supplication of a righteous man availeth much in its working" (James 5:16). Christ speaking to his disciples said, "Whatsoever ye shall ask in my name, that will I do" (John 14:13). God's people present their petitions to God and leave it to him to decide whether it is wise to grant the request or not. They know that God alone can tell whether the granting of the prayer would be for their own good or for the welfare of the Kingdom of God or for God's glory. The Apostle John, writing to believers, states the doctrine of prayer with its necessary condition when he says, "This is the boldness which we have toward him, that, if we ask anything according to his will, he heareth us" (I John 5:14). "The answer will be such as we, if duly enlightened, would ourselves desire." God often blesses his children best when he denies their requests. And when they pray they desire him to deny their requests if in his sight it is best to do so.

We must pray in the name of Christ, because sinful man cannot approach God. We must draw near, not claiming any inherent right of our own to come, but in the name of him who hath washed us from our sins in his blood and made us to be priests unto God.

Prayer is addressed to God in his fullness, as the triune God. Prayer to each of the 3 persons in the Godhead, Father, Son, and Holy Ghost, is involved in the apostolic benediction: "The grace of the Lord Jesus Christ, and the love of God, and the communion of the Holy Spirit, be with you all" (II Cor. 13:14). Prayer was addressed to the risen Christ. Christians called upon his name (I Cor. 1:2). Stephen petitioned him, Paul besought him and rendered thanks to him, the redeemed ascribe glory and dominion to him (Acts 7:59, 60; II Cor. 12:8, 9; I Thess. 3:11; I Tim. 1:12; Rev. 1:5, 6).

Prep'a·ra'tion. The day before the Sabbath (Mark 15:42; John 19:31; Jos. *Antiq.* xvi. 6, 2; cf. Judith 8:6). The preparation for the Sabbath of the passover was the eve of a peculiarly high day (John 19:14, 31).

Pres'by·ter'y [Gr. *presbyterion*]. The whole body of *presbyteroi*, elders in a church (I Tim. 4:14). See ELDER, LAYING ON OF HANDS.

Pres'ents. See GIFTS.

Priest [contracted from Lat., *presbyter*, Gr. *presbyteros*, elder]. An authorized minister. It sometimes denotes a minister of state or responsible adviser of the king (II Sam. 8:18; see R.V. marg.). In II Sam. 20:26 the official is described as priest to David (see R.V. marg.), and in I Chron. 18:17 as chief about the king. In I Kings 4:5 the title is qualified and explained by "friend of the king" (see FRIEND OF THE KING). Very frequently the ministers at the sanctuary are described as Levitical priests, as though the designation *kōhēn*, minister, priest, rather needed descriptive qualification.

An authorized minister of a deity who, on behalf of a community, officiates at the altar and in other rites. The essential idea of a priest is that of a mediator between man and God. The priests formed a distinct class in the nations of antiquity generally; as in Egypt, Midian, Philistia, Greece, Rome (Gen. 47:22; Ex. 2:16; I Sam. 6:2; Acts 14:13).

In the absence of a regularly organized priesthood, priestly functions were exercised from time immemorial by private individuals, as Cain, Abel; and by patriarchs in behalf of a family or tribe, as Noah, Abraham, Isaac, Jacob, Job. The natural head of a body of people acted as priest. There were those among the Israelites at the time of the Exodus who possessed this prerogative by natural right, and who had been influenced by the pressure of increasing priestly duties, arising from the growth of the Hebrew population, and by the spectacle of the Egyptian priesthood, to devote themselves professionally to priestly functions (Ex. 19:22). Even after the organization of the Levitical priesthood priestly prerogatives existed outside of that order. When God himself dispensed with the mediation of the ordained priests and manifested himself immediately to a man, that man recognized his right to offer sacrifice at once without the intervention of the regularly constituted mediators (Judg. 6:18, 24, 26; 13:16); and when for political reasons it became impossible for those in the Northern Kingdom who feared God to avail themselves of the offices of the Levitical priests, the primitive law was recalled and the father of the family or other person indicated by ancient custom erected the altar and offered sacrifices to Jehovah (I Kings 18:30).

When the Hebrew nation was organized at Sinai, a national sanctuary and service were projected on a noble scale, such as became the essential dignity of Jehovah, and appeared to no disadvantage when brought into comparison with the purest worship of the most cultured nations of that age. Priests were needed for its altar. Aaron and his sons were appointed to that office, and the priesthood was made hereditary in the family and restricted to it (Ex. 28:1; 40:12–15; Num. 16:40; chs. 17; 18:1–8; and cf. Deut. 10:6; I Kings 8:4; Ezra 2:36 seq.). All the sons of Aaron were priests unless debarred by legal disabilities (Lev. 21:16 seq.). Accordingly when they are referred to as a class, they are mentioned either simply as the priests or as the priests the sons of Aaron, in allusion to their descent as a family (Lev. 1:5; II Chron. 26:18; 29:21; 35:14; cf. Num. 3:3; 10:8; Josh. 21:19; Neh. 10:38), or as the priests the Levites, in allusion to the tribe to which they belonged (Deut. 17:9, 18; 18:1; Josh. 3:3; 8:33; II Chron. 23:18; 30:27; Jer. 33:18, 21; cf. Ex. 38:21), or later as the priests the Levites the sons of Zadok, as designation of a branch of the family (Ezek. 44:15; cf. 43:19). This method of designating the priests, as will be seen from the passages cited, was in vogue at a time when beyond all question the distinction between priest and Levite was firmly established. The distinction is recognized in history: the ministers at the altar of the tabernacle and Temple and the users of Urim and Thummim always belonged to the family of Aaron.

The duties of the priests were mainly 3: to minister at the sanctuary before the Lord, to teach the people the Law of God, and to inquire for them the divine will by Urim and Thummim (Ex. 28:30 and Ezra 2:63; Num. 16:40; 18:5; II Chron. 15:3; Jer. 18:18; Ezek. 7:26; Micah 3:11). The priest was subject to special laws (Lev. 10:8 seq.); and in respect to marriage, he could take to wife only one of his own nation, a virgin or a widow who had not been divorced, and her genealogy in the ancient records must be as regular as that of the priest himself (Lev.

21:7; Ezra 10:18, 19; Jos. *Apion* i. 7). His dress when on duty consisted of: 1. Short breeches, reaching from the hips to the thighs. 2. A coat fitting close to the body, woven in 1 piece without seam, and, at least in later times, extending to the ankles. It was gathered about the loins with a symbolically ornamented girdle. 3. A cap shaped like a cup. These several articles were made of white linen (Ex. 28:40–42; Jos. *Antiq.* iii. 7, 1–3). Priests and others officially connected with the solemn service often wore a linen ephod; but it was not prescribed and it was not made of varied and costly materials like that worn by the high priest (I Sam. 2:18; 22:18; II Sam. 6:14).

On the Conquest of Canaan, in view of the present needs of the descendants of Aaron, who were then doubtless in the 3d generation, but more especially with a view to future demands, 13 towns were designated where residence and lands for pasturing cattle were legally the priests' (Josh. 21:10–19). In the course of centuries they increased to a numerous body. Accordingly David divided them into 24 courses. Except during the great festivals, when all the courses were employed, each course officiated for a week at a time, the change being made on the Sabbath before evening sacrifice (I Chron. 24: 1–19; II Kings 11:5, 9; Jos. *Antiq.* vii. 14, 7). Four only of these courses appear to have returned from Babylon with Zerubbabel (Ezra 2:36–38); but the old number was eventually reconstructed (cf. Luke 1:5, 9). There were distinctions in rank among the priests. The supreme pontiff was the high priest (*q.v.*). Next to him stood the 2d priest (II Kings 25:18), who was probably the same as the ruler of the house of God (II Chron. 31:13; Neh. 11:11) and the captain of the Temple (Acts 4:1; 5:24). The chief priests who are mentioned in the N.T. were the officiating high priest, former high priests still alive, and members of their families. They were an anomaly of the times. The law which regulated the succession to the high priesthood had come into abeyance through political confusion and foreign domination. High priests were made and unmade at the will of the rulers.

Prince. A person of chief rank or authority in any official relation; as the king of a nation (I Kings 14:7), satrap over a province (Dan. 3:2, A.V.), head of a tribe (Num. 1: 16) or of a tribal family (Num. 24:14), a sheik (Gen. 23:6), a chief officer over the servants of a king (Dan. 1:7). "Prince" is the rendering of various Heb. and Gr. words.

Seven princes of Media and Persia had access to the king's presence and held the highest official position after the throne (Esth. 1:14). Apparently they were the 7 counselors of the king (Ezra 7:14). In the year 521 B.C. an event occurred which perhaps explains the origin of these privileges. Seven men of the 1st rank in Persia (Herod. iii. 77), having slain the false Smerdis, entered into a compact with one another, as they were about to choose 1 of their number to be king, that each of the 7 should have liberty to enter the palace without being announced, and that the king should not be allowed to marry outside of these 7 families (Herod. iii. 84).

Pris′ca (prĭs′kà) and **Pris·cil′la** (prĭ-sĭl′à) [Lat., old woman and little old woman]. The wife of Aquila, who went with him in his wanderings and showed at least equal zeal with her husband in advancing the Christian cause. Paul's estimate of her was high (Acts 18:1–3, 18, 26; Rom. 16:3; II Tim. 4:19), and in 3 out of 5 verses she is named before her husband. See AQUILA.

Pris'on. A special place was set apart in Egypt for the confinement of criminals. It was under the charge, and in the house, of a military officer, and the prisoners were often bound as well as kept in ward (Gen. 40:3, 4; 42:16, 17). The prison was an institution among the Philistines also; Samson was imprisoned, blinded, bound with fetters, and compelled to labor (Judg. 16:21).

Among the Hebrews there was a prison in Samaria in the reign of Ahab, which was under the charge of the governor of the city (I Kings 22:27). Later there is notice of the detention of prisoners at Jerusalem in the court of the guard (Jer. 37:21), and in the dry cistern that was in the court (ch. 38:6); but private houses were also used for the purpose (ch. 37:15). The prison fare was bread and water (I Kings 22:27). In the Roman period the procurator's palace at Caesarea on the sea, the castle of Antonia, and doubtless the palace of Herod at Jerusalem, had rooms where accused persons were confined (Acts 23:10, 35). The prison at Jerusalem into which Herod Agrippa I cast Peter was protected by iron gates, and important prisoners were bound with chains and guarded by soldiers in the cell, while other soldiers kept watch before the door (Acts 12:6, 10).

The Mamertine Prison at Rome, where Jugurtha was left to starve to death, and where according to tradition Peter was confined, is on the slope of the Capitoline Hill toward the Forum. It dates from the earliest ages of the city. It consists of 2 cells, 1 over the other. The lower one is 19 feet long, 10 wide, and 6½ high. It is entirely underground. It is vaulted, the walls gradually contracting. To judge by the slope of the walls, the chamber was originally about 10 feet in height, and was closed by a conical vault, similar in shape, but not constructionally an arch. Entrance to it was originally obtained only through a hole in the ceiling, through which criminals were let down. The floor is the native rock, from which a spring bursts, said in the legend to have been miraculously caused to flow by Peter in order to baptize his jailers.

Proch'o·rus (prŏk'ō-rŭs) [Gr., leader in a choric dance]. One of the 7 men elected to look after the Greek-speaking widows and probably the Christian poor at Jerusalem (Acts 6:5).

Pro·con'sul [Lat., one acting for a consul]. The governor of a Roman province which was administered by the senate (Acts 13:7; 18:12; 19:38, R.V.). He was appointed for 1 year, exercised in this province all the powers of a consul, and was attended by quaestors, who collected the revenues and paid them into the treasury managed by the senate.

Proc'u·ra'tor [Lat., manager, administrator]. The agent of the Roman emperor, who resided in imperial (as distinct from senatorial) provinces, received the revenues and paid them into the emperor's private exchequer. The military governor and chief magistrate was called propraetor or legate; but in the smaller imperial provinces and sometimes in parts of larger ones the office of legate was dispensed with, and the entire government civil and military was intrusted to a procurator. Such was the case in Judea. When Archelaus was deposed by the emperor Augustus in A.D. 6, Judea, Samaria, and Idumaea were erected into a division of the prefecture of Syria, called the province of Judea, and placed under procurators (Jos. Antiq. xvii. 11, 4; 13, 5; Tacitus Ann. xii. 23; Hist. v. 9). They were successively Coponius (Jos. Antiq. xviii. 1, 1; 2, 2; War ii.

8, 1); Marcus Ambivius; Annius Rufus, in whose time the emperor Augustus died; Valerius Gratus, who held office 11 years (Jos. Antiq. xviii. 2, 2); Pontius Pilate, who was appointed by the emperor Tiberius, deposed after 10 years, and arrived at Rome just after the death of Tiberius, which occurred in March, 37 (Jos. Antiq. xviii. 2, 2; 4, 2; 6, 5; War ii. 9, 2; Tacitus Ann. xv. 44; Luke 3:1); Marullus, appointed by the emperor Caius (Jos. Antiq. xviii. 6, 11), and after an interval which concluded with the 3-year reign of Herod Agrippa over Judea (Acts 12:1–23); Cuspius Fadus, who was appointed by the emperor Claudius; Tiberius Alexander (Jos. Antiq. xix. 9, 2; xx. 1, 2; 5, 2; War ii. 11, 6); Cumanus, appointed after the death of Herod, king of Chalcis and later recalled by the emperor Claudius (Jos. Antiq. xx. 5, 2; 6, 2 and 3; War ii. 12, 1 and 6); Felix, appointed by Claudius (Jos. Antiq. xx. 7, 1; War ii. 12, 8; Tacitus Hist. v. 9); Porcius Festus, sent out by Nero (Jos. Antiq. xx. 8, 9; War ii. 14, 1; Acts 24:27); and on the death of Festus, Albinus (Jos. Antiq. xx. 9, 1; War ii. 14, 1); and finally Gessius Florus, appointed by Nero shortly before the 12th year of his reign (Jos. Antiq. xx. 11, 1; War ii. 14, 2 seq.; Tacitus Hist. v. 10).

As appears from the cited passages and their context, these procurators were subject to the governor of Syria; but in Judea itself their authority was supreme. The Roman garrison stationed in the province stood at their command; all important matters came before their judgment seat; they had the power of life and death (Jos. War ii. 8, 1); and their sentence was executed by the soldiers. They commonly resided at Caesarea by the sea; but they were wont to go up to Jerusalem at the feasts and sometimes to winter there (Jos. Antiq. xviii. 3, 1), and they visited various cities of their dominion as occasion required. When in Jerusalem, they were accustomed to occupy the palace of Herod. See HEROD, PALACE OF.

Proph'et. An authoritative and infallible teacher of God's will; cf. the expression, "Thus saith the Lord." Speaking of the order of prophets conceived of as a unity, God promised to raise them up from among the chosen people, qualify them by putting his words into their mouth, enable them to speak all that he commanded them, and maintain the authority of his word which they should speak (Deut. 18:18, 19). Every prophet of God, and pre-eminently Christ, was like unto Moses (Deut. 18:18; Acts 3:22, 23), in similarity of enduement, of doctrine, of attitude toward the Law, of didactic work. The same authoritative and representative character of the prophet is referred to by Zechariah. Words are given to the prophet by God, and the prophet cannot resist the Spirit (Jer. 20:7–9; Amos 3:3–8; cf. Balaam, Num., chs. 22 to 24). The words are sent by his Spirit to the prophets, are given to be taught to the people, and have been accredited in the past by their fulfillment (Zech. 1:6; 7:12; also Neh. 9:30). The same facts regarding the prophet are abundantly illustrated in individual instances. The prophets did not inherit the office, nor receive it by human appointment, but were chosen, prepared, and called of God; and the call was often soul-searching (Ex. 3:1 to 4:17; I Sam. 3:1–20; Jer. 1:4–10; Ezek. 1:1 to 3:15). The word of the Lord came to them in various ways. They were commanded to proclaim it. They were accredited by signs, by the fulfillment of their predictions, and by the conformity of their teaching to the Law. And God held man accountable for obedience to their word (Deut. 13:1–5; 18:18–20).

But there were also false prophets. Besides heathen prophets who spoke in the name of an idol (Deut. 18:20; I Kings 18:19; Jer. 2:8; 23:13), there were false prophets who spoke in Jehovah's name (Jer. 23:16–32). They were of 2 classes: 1st, conscious impostors, enticed to claim the gift by the consideration and influence which true prophets enjoyed, and courted on account of their smooth words (I Kings 22:5–28; Ezek. 13: 17, 19; Micah 3:11; Zech. 13:4); and probably, 2d, sincere and even godly men, whose doctrine might be based on the Law of God, but who were self-deceived in that they had not been called to the prophetic office by God and were not infallible religious guides. Tests were therefore established for distinguishing the true from the false. The true prophet was recognized: 1. By signs (Ex. 4:8; Isa. 7: 11, 14). But signs alone were not sufficient, for they might occasionally come to pass accidentally or be wrought by artifice (Deut. 13:1, 2; cf. Ex. 7:11, 22; II Thess. 2:9). 2. By the fulfillment of his predictions (Deut. 18: 21, 22). This credential gains in evidencing power as time goes on and the historic events and developments take place which the prophet foretold of old. 3. By his teaching (Deut. 13:1–5; Isa. 8:20). If the doctrine taught by the claimant of a call from God led men away from the Ten Commandments, the speaker was manifestly not a man of God. The true prophet's teaching was found to agree with the doctrine of the Law concerning God, his nature, character, and worship, and concerning the conduct of man. But there was more than mere servile agreement with the Law of God. Planting themselves on the doctrines of the Law, the prophets unfolded its principles in their application to human conduct and in their revelation of God. And among the sages of all history the prophets whom Israel accepted tower aloft and stand alone in the purity, value, and fitness of their teaching.

Prophecy included the prediction of future events (Isa. 38:5, 6; 39:6, 7; Jer. 20:6; 25: 11; 28:16; Amos 1:5; 7:9, 17; Micah 4:10). Prediction was an important part of the prophet's work, but more important still the prophet had to deal with the present and the past, and to instruct men in God's ways (Isa. 41:26; 42:9; 46:9). The use of the Eng. word prophet must not be permitted to emphasize unduly the predictive side of prophecy. The Eng. word is derived from the Gr. *prophētēs*. In classical Gr. *mantis* is the ecstatic announcer of oracles, and *prophētēs* is their sober-minded interpreter, who makes the dreams, visions, or enigmatic utterances of the frenzied *mantis* intelligible. The *prophētēs*, accordingly, is not a predictor, but one who speaks forth that which he has received from the divine Spirit. The prefix *pro* is not temporal. The prophet speaks for, or in behalf of, another; he is the mouthpiece or the spokesman of God. He is a forthteller rather than a fore-teller.

The Heb. word *nābi'*, which is translated prophet, means one who announces. It seems to have been a comprehensive general term at first. In the Hebrew Scriptures Abraham is called a prophet (Gen. 20:7). Between him and God there was direct personal intercourse, with him was the secret of the Lord, to him God revealed himself and his purposes (Gen. 15:1–18; 18:17), he was able to teach his descendants the true knowledge of God (ch. 18:19), and he had power of intercession with God (vs. 23–32). Miriam, who expressly claims that the Lord had spoken by her, was a prophetess (Ex. 15:20; Num. 12: 2, 6). Aaron as the spokesman of Moses is called his prophet (Ex. 7:1; cf. ch. 4:16).

The *nābi'*, or prophet, was a person qualified by God to be his spokesman to men. And this is the fundamental idea which underlies the term as used in Deut. 18:18.

One of the qualifications was prophetic vision (I Sam. 3:1). Looked at in this aspect, the prophet was sometimes called a seer (I Sam. 9:9, in Heb. *rō'eh;* Isa. 30:10, in Heb. *hōzeh*). And when this was the main aspect in which he was regarded by the people, and this qualification was the one of highest value in popular estimation, seer was the designation in vogue among the people. This was the case for a considerable period in the early history of Israel. Samuel and Gad and Iddo were known by this title. But Samuel ceased to be merely a seer to whom the people resorted when they would inquire of the Lord, desiring to know God's will as to duty, or seeking direction in national affairs, or craving light upon private matters. Samuel went out among men as an authoritative teacher of the nation sent by God, and this public proclamation was the distinctive idea in prophecy (I Sam. 10:10–13; 19:20). The teaching function, as seen in Moses, became prominent again; and beginning with Samuel and his followers, and with renewed force several centuries later, the prophet became a constant presence in the national life, an ambassador of heaven to the kingdom of Israel, an authoritative preacher of righteousness, an interpreter of past and present history on its moral side, an admonisher of the consequences which God the Judge has annexed to conduct, a forewarner of the certainty of the divine judgment on sin, and a fosterer of fidelity toward Jehovah. To foretell the future and make known the secret counsel of God, as did Nathan when he forbade David to build the Temple and announced God's purpose to establish David's throne forever, remained functions of the prophet; but they became a comparatively small part of his work.

With Samuel, however, we have a step forward in the history of prophecy. We have a new beginning in an ancient institution (I Sam. 9:9). Samuel was called a seer by his contemporaries, but his great successors, whom God raised up and inspired to teach the nation, were commonly designated prophets by the men of their generation. Seer was not banished from use, but the title of prophet, which had never been entirely disused (Judg. 4:4; I Sam. 10:10–13; 19:20), was raised again to its former prominence (I Sam. 3:20). Amos had prophetic vision (Amos 1:1; 8:1; 9:1) and was derisively called a seer by Amaziah, the priest of Beth-el (ch. 7:12); but he had a call from God to prophesy, and he did so (ch. 7:15).

Referring to the prophet's special endowment from on high, he was called a man of the Spirit (Hos. 9:7). In common with other ministers of God, official or private, he is a man of God, a servant of God, a messenger of the Lord, a shepherd of God's people, a watchman, an interpreter.

That the prophet was to be raised up from the people of Israel alone did not prevent God, who worketh when and where he will, in caring for his Kingdom to send a dream to a Philistine, an Egyptian, a Midianite, a Chaldean, a Roman (Gen. 20:6; 41:1; Judg. 7:13; Dan. 2:1; Matt. 27:19). Even Balaam, who was a soothsayer, and as such was invited by the king of Moab to curse Israel, was temporarily used by God. These foreigners were in momentary contact with the Kingdom of God. In the case of Balaam we see a man acting as the mouthpiece of God (Num., chs. 22 to 24).

The prophets were taught of the Spirit of God (I Kings 22:24; II Chron. 15:1; 24:20;

Neh. 9:30; Ezek. 11:5; Joel 2:28; Micah 3: 8; Zech. 7:12; I Peter 1:10, 11). In this God worked in accordance with the psychological nature of man. An audible voice or an angelic messenger occasionally came (Num. 7:89; I Sam. 3:4; Dan. 9:21), but the instruction was ordinarily imparted by dreams, visions, and inward suggestions recognized by the prophets as not of themselves. They were not under the permanent influence of the Spirit. The word of the Lord came unto them. They waited for revelation (Lev. 24:12). And their natural mental discernment is distinguished from the divine word which came to them. Samuel's private thought is distinguished from God's (I Sam. 16:6, 7). Nathan at first approved of David's purpose to build a temple for the Lord, but afterward told the king that God had forbidden its construction (II Sam. 7:3). The prophets did not exercise the prophetic power at all times, but when God told them to speak.

From the time of Samuel the office was regularly transmitted. Though the prophets who are mentioned by name are few, there were many anonymous ones (I Kings 18:4; II Kings 2:7–16). The office seems not to have ceased until the death of Malachi. At the approach and Advent of Christ the tongue of prophecy was again loosed (Luke 1:67; 2: 26–38). In the Church of the N.T. also there were prophets (I Cor. 12:28). They were not an order, like apostles and elders. They were men and women (Acts 21:9), and they were specially illumined expounders of God's revelation. They spoke by the Spirit, occasionally foretold the future (Acts 11:27, 28; 21:10, 11), and taught and exhorted to great edification (I Cor. 14:3, 4, 24). Paul ironically gives the title to a heathen writer, who so correctly described the immoral character of the Cretans that he had proved himself to that extent a mouthpiece of the truth (Titus 1:12).

The call of the prophets came immediately from God himself (Amos 7:15). The prophet was aware of a definite moment when the call came. Moses was called at the bush to his comprehensive work (Ex. 3:1 to 4:17). Samuel had a special revelation in his youth (I Sam. 3:1–15), which was the beginning of his reception of revelation (chs. 3:19 to 4:1). Elisha knew when he was called to the office, and also when he was qualified for the work (I Kings 19:19, 20; II Kings 2:13, 14). The vision seen by Isaiah in the year that Uzziah died (Isa., ch. 6) is generally supposed to have been his original call. Elijah's inaugural call is not mentioned, but he was afterward commissioned at Horeb for a special work (I Kings, ch. 19). Jeremiah knew when he was called, and interposed objections (Jer. 1:4–10). Hosea refers to the time when Jehovah spoke at the first by him (Hos. 1:2). In the call of the prophets human instrumentality is mentioned but once, namely, in the case of Elisha (I Kings 19:16, 19). Evidence that the prophets were anointed with oil and inducted into office has been sought in Ps. 105:15, but the psalmist is speaking of the patriarchs. He speaks in the name of God, and uses the language of his own time in alluding to them as prophets, who were anointed with the Spirit. Accordingly the term is applied to the patriarchs as bearing the seal of a divine consecration in virtue of which their persons were sacred and inviolable. The anointing referred to in Isa. 61:1 is the unction of the Spirit. The case of Elisha has also been appealed to (I Kings 19:16), where Elijah is told to anoint Elisha to be prophet in his stead. But there is no evidence that even Elisha was ever anointed with oil. Elijah carried out the command by

casting his cloak upon Elisha. Figuratively speaking, he anointed Elisha when he cast his mantle upon him (cf. I Kings 19:15 with II Kings 8:13, where the command to anoint is fulfilled by speaking a word). The prophet's cloak was the sign of the prophet's vocation (II Kings 1:8; 2:9, 13–15), so that throwing it to him was a symbol of the call to the prophet's office.

To the prophets' mode of life there is only incidental allusion. Evidently in most respects it was like that of other men. As an appropriate dress for their work a garment of hair was frequently worn by them (II Kings 1:8; Zech. 13:4; cf. Matt. 3:4); not as an ascetic's habit, but as a mourner's garb, symbolic of mourning for the sins of the people. Sackcloth also was worn for the same purpose (Isa. 20:2). The rough garment was not worn next to the skin, after the manner of ascetics, but as a mantle, cast about the shoulders over other raiment. For the subsistence of the prophets wild fruits were at their disposal (II Kings 4:39; Matt. 3:4). Contributions were made for their support (I Sam. 9:8; I Kings 14:2, 3; II Kings 4:42). Hospitality was shown them (I Kings 17:9; 18:4; II Kings 4:8, 10). Some were Levites, and shared in the Levitical revenues. Some had private means, as Elisha and Jeremiah (I Kings 19:19, 21; Jer. 32:8–10). Perhaps some were supported at court by royal bounty, like Gad, the king's seer, and others who bore the same title (II Sam. 24:11; I Chron. 25:5; II Chron. 35:15). The prophets usually dwelt in houses like other men (I Sam. 7:17; II Sam. 12:15; I Kings 14:4; II Kings 4:1, 2; 5:9; 22:14; Ezek. 8:1). See also PROPHETIC ASSOCIATIONS.

Literary activities and duties devolved upon the prophets, as historians and writers of prophecy. The events of the reigns of David and Solomon were recorded in the histories of Samuel the seer, Nathan the prophet, and Gad the seer, and in the prophecy of Ahijah (I Chron. 29:29; II Chron. 9:29). Events of the reign of Rehoboam were written in the histories of Shemaiah the prophet and Iddo the seer (II Chron. 12:15), and of Jeroboam in the vision of Iddo the seer (ch. 9:29), of Abijah in the commentary of Iddo the prophet (ch. 13:22), of Jehoshaphat in the history of Jehu, son of Hanani (cf. ch. 20:34 with ch. 19:2), of Uzziah first and last and of Hezekiah in the writings of Isaiah (Isa. 26:22; 32:32). The 4 great historical works, the books of Joshua, Judges, Samuel, and Kings, were classed by the Jews as the Former Prophets in the canon. In the time of Amos, Hosea, and Isaiah the prophets entered upon their great careers as writers of prophecy. They committed their prophetic utterances in summary, or in considerable detail, or as isolated and individual prophecies, to writing.

Spiritually the prophets were prepared to receive divine communications. They were holy men, men who were surrendered to God's service and who lived in communion with God, men of habitual prayer (like Samuel, I Sam. 7:5; 8:6; 12:23; 15:11), who retired at times to their watchtower, that is, composed their minds and gave themselves up to quiet contemplation, in order to wait for revelation (Isa. 21:8; Hab. 2:1). Moses withdrew for 40 days and nights into the quiet and solitude of Mount Sinai for communion with God (Ex. 24:18). Occasionally, in the early period, music was employed to stimulate devotion and awaken religious feeling (I Sam. 10:5), or to soothe the mind and attune the heart for meditation, when the will of the Lord was sought (II Kings 3:15). It was perhaps not accidental that the prophets were sometimes by a river's side and soothed by the steady flow or the placidness of the stream, when the communication came (Ezek. 1:1, 3; Dan. 10:4), and that Samuel heard the Lord speak when night had fallen (I Sam. 3:2–10). By these various means the prophet's soul was kept or made ready for the operation of the Holy Spirit. God in holding communication with men worked in accordance with the laws of man's mind.

There were men who possessed and exercised the prophetic gift who were not officially prophets. We notice a prophetic spirit in various parts of the Pentateuch and also in The Psalms. Daniel had the gift of prophecy in an eminent degree; but he did not devote his life to teaching the people; he was officially a statesman and governor under Chaldean (Neo-Babylonian) and Persian kings. His writings, like those of David, were placed among the Hagiographa or sacred writings, and not with the works of official prophets. See CANON.

The term Former Prophets is applied in the Hebrew canon to the historical books of Joshua, Judges, I and II Samuel, I and II Kings; the strictly prophetical books beginning with Isaiah are called the Latter Prophets. The designation does not refer to the time when the books were composed, but to the respective places of these 2 groups of books, Kings, for example, being written after Isaiah, but holding a place among the Former Prophets. There were great prophets, like Elijah and Elisha, who did not commit their discourses to writing. They are termed oral prophets by modern scholars. The literary productions of other prophets who recorded their prophecies are cited, excerpted from, and incorporated in the books of the Former Prophets and other Scripture.

Of the Latter Prophets, Hosea, Amos, and Jonah (in addition to Nineveh, II Kings 14:25) labored in the Northern Kingdom; the rest exercised their office among the people of Judah and Benjamin, either in Palestine or in the land of exile. Classed chronologically, and including Daniel, they are: 1. In the Assyrian period, from shortly before the accession of Tiglath-pileser, 746/5 B.C., to the decay of the Assyrian power, about 625 B.C., Hosea, Amos, and Jonah in the n., and Isaiah, Micah, and Nahum in Judah. 2. During the Chaldean or Neo-Babylonian period in Judah, from 625 B.C. to the fall of Jerusalem, in 586 B.C., Jeremiah, Habakkuk, and Zephaniah. 3. During the Exile in Babylonia, Ezekiel and Daniel. 4. During the period of the restoration, Haggai, Zechariah, and Malachi. The dates of Obadiah and Joel (q.v.) are uncertain.

Proph′et·ess. 1. A woman called of God to the prophetic office. Miriam was a prophetess (Ex. 15:20, 21; Num. 12:2; Micah 6: 4). So was Deborah (Judg. 4:4). The Israelites resorted to her for judgment, and the Lord revealed his will through her to the nation (Judg. 4:5, 6, 14). So was Huldah. She was consulted by the high priest at the command of the king in regard to the teaching of Deuteronomy, and she declared the counsel of the Lord (II Kings 22:12–20). Four virgin daughters of Philip the evangelist prophesied (Acts 21:9).

2. A prophet's wife, as is probably meant in Isa. 8:3.

Pro·phet′ic As·so·ci·a′tions. The presence of a company of prophets at Gibeah of God, the home of Saul, is mentioned in I Sam. 10: 5. Whether they were a wandering band of prophets, going from town to town, or formed a community of prophets resident at Gibeah, cannot be determined. The designation of the place as the hill of God was probably derived, not from the abode of these prophets,

but from the high place of worship that was upon it (I Sam. 10:5). The word rendered company in A.V., band in R.V., is *ḥebel;* the word translated company in ch. 19:20 is *lahăḳāh;* the phrase is not definite, but is merely "a band of prophets."

Samuel dwelt at Ramah (I Sam. 7:17; 28: 3), where he was the head of a company of prophets (ch. 19:18–20). More definitely, he was at Naioth, in Ramah, a building or locality in the town of Ramah inhabited by this community of prophets (see NAIOTH). Jewish tradition is represented by the Targum of Jonathan, which renders the word Naioth by "house of instruction"; and this translation has given rise to the phrase "school of the prophets." The prophets who gathered together naturally employed their leisure hours in the study of things pertaining to God; but there is no hint in the narrative that they were at school or were novitiates in training for the prophetic office. The word and the narrative indicate that there was at Ramah a community of men already endowed with the prophetic gift and with power, in co-operation with God, spiritually to affect those who came in contact with them (I Sam. 10:10; 19:20–23); who dwelt together at or round about Samuel's house; under his conduct engaged in worship, giving utterance in praise and exhortation to their exalted religious feelings and apprehension of truth (cf. prophesying, I Sam. 10:5; I Chron. 25:1–3), and doubtless standing likewise under his direction in whatever other religious duties devolved upon them as prophets. The situation may be conceived thus: Shiloh, the religious meeting place of Israel, had been forsaken of God. The prophets gathered about God's great representative and the chief spiritual force of the time in order to cultivate their own spiritual life in common worship, to praise God together as the Spirit gave them utterance (I Sam. 19:20), to engage in united prayer in behalf of the nation (chs. 12:23; 15: 11, 35; 16:1), and to go forth in companies for the revival and instruction of the people (ch. 10: 5, 10). They sought on the one hand to benefit themselves by religious fellowship, holding prolonged communion with God amidst favorable surroundings, and thereby not only to satisfy their spiritual longings, but also to quicken their spiritual apprehension and to qualify themselves for God's use of them as his spokesmen; and they sought on the other hand to afford a center of reformation in the midst of great apostasy.

Two hundred years later, in the Northern Kingdom, prophetic communities made their appearance for a brief while. They were probably founded by Elijah, on the model of the earlier society under the presidency of Samuel. The members were designated "sons of the prophets." The name denotes that they belonged to the prophetic order; just as a son of the apothecaries was one who followed the trade of an apothecary, a son of the goldsmiths was a professional practitioner of the goldsmiths' art, and sons of the singers were members of the singers' guild (Neh. 3:8, 31; 12:28). The members of the prophetic order were called prophets and sons of the prophets indifferently, and the word of the Lord was revealed to them (I Kings 20:35–38, 41; II Kings 2:3, 5; 9:1). The associations which they formed were comparatively large (II Kings 2:7, 16; 4:42, 43), occupied a common building or compound (chs. 4:38; 6: 1–4), and were located at Beth-el, Jericho, and Gilgal (chs. 2:3, 5; 4:38). Beth-el was a prominent seat of idolatrous worship, and Jericho was hard by another such place; and the establishment of an organized society of prophets at them shows that the founder intended the prophetic community to be a counterpoise to apostate worship and a center of reformation. Elijah, and after him Elisha, stood at the head of these communities, visited them in turn (chs. 2:1, 2, 4; 4:38), was looked up to with respect and called master (ch. 6:5). Elisha was regarded with peculiar affection; they desired his presence with them, sat before him as having him for their president (and perhaps teacher), referred their plans and their difficulties to him, and were sent forth by him to perform prophetic functions (chs. 4:38, 40; 6:1–7; 9:1). Though not without revelation themselves they could learn much of the will of God from the greater prophet, as Miriam and Aaron did from Moses (chs. 2:15–18; cf. sitting before a prophet as equivalent to inquiring of God, Ezek. 8:1; 14:1–7; 20:1). The spiritual condition even of prophets could be promoted by the use of the means of grace, and meditation on God's Law could benefit even inspired men of God.

There is no evidence either in Isa. 8:16 or in Amos 7:14, that these societies existed after the time of Elisha. Huldah the prophetess was not connected with such a society; she did not dwell in the college, as the A.V. renders, but in the 2d quarter of the city (II Kings 22:14, R.V.).

Pros'e·lyte. In the N.T., a convert to Judaism. The Pharisees were very zealous to make 1 proselyte (Matt. 23:15). The Roman poet Horace mentions the trait as characteristic of the Jews (Horace *Sat.* i. 4, 142 and 143). Proselytes were present when the Pentecostal effusion took place (Acts 2:10). One of the men chosen to look after the poor in the Early Christian Church was Nicolaüs, a proselyte of Antioch (Acts 6:5). Proselytes were quite numerous in Antioch (Jos. *War* vii. 3, 3). At Damascus great numbers of women were converts to Judaism (Jos. *War* ii. 20, 2). The chamberlain of Queen Candace was evidently a convert (Acts 8:27), and the royal family of Adiabene, e. of the Euphrates, adopted the Jews' religion (Jos. *Antiq.* xx. 2–4). At Antioch, in Pisidia, many proselytes followed Paul and Barnabas (Acts 13:43). The rabbis recognized 2 orders of proselytes. One was proselytes of righteousness. They consented to be circumcised and baptized and to offer sacrifice. They adopted Judaism in its entirety. The proselytes of the gate or of sojourning were much less advanced. They agreed to observe what were called the 7 precepts of Noah (see NOAH), but declined to be circumcised or to embrace Judaism.

Prov'erbs, The. A poetical book on practical piety. The Heb. word *māshāl*, which has been rendered proverb, embraces more than a maxim. It includes also the fable, the riddle, the satire, the parable (Num. 23:7; Judg. 14:14, 18; Isa. 14:4; Ezek. 16:44; 17:2). The several parts of the book of The Proverbs are:

I. *Title*, Prov. 1:1–6, descriptive of the entire book; declaring the purpose of the collection to be "to know wisdom and instruction; . . . the words of the wise, and their dark sayings," and designating it the proverbs of Solomon, son of David, king of Israel. This title, however, does not affirm that the book in all its parts is from Solomon (cf. Ps. 72:20, although each psalm in the book is not thereby ascribed to David; see titles of Psalms 42 to 50).

II. *Main contents*. 1. Praise of wisdom, Prov. 1:7 to 9:18; a didactic poem in the form of addresses by a father to his son, and specially designed for young men. 2. The proverbs of Solomon, chs. 10 to 22:16; maxims arranged in no precise order and consisting in each case mostly of 2 contrasted sentences. 3. Without formal superscription, but which may be called from the opening verse, compared with ch. 24:23, the words of wise men, chs. 22:17 to 24:22. Among these words is a poem on the drunkard's woes, supplemented by the sayings of the wise, ch. 24:23–34, including an ode on the sluggard. 4. Proverbs of Solomon copied out by the men of Hezekiah, chs. 25 to 29; having all the characteristics of the popular proverb, and consisting of pithy sentences not only of 2, but also of 3, 4, or 5 parallel clauses each.

III. *Three appendixes*—as follows: 1. The words of Agur, ch. 30; enigmatical sayings in which numbers play a significant part. 2. The words of King Lemuel, ch. 31:1–9; maxims on practical life addressed to him by his mother. 3. Praise of the virtuous woman, ch. 31:10–31; a poem in which each of the 22 verses begins with a letter of the Heb. alphabet in regular order.

The particular ascription of certain sections of the book of Solomon, and of other sections apparently to other authorship, indicates that Solomon was not the author of the entire work; and the title of the 4th section, "These also are proverbs of Solomon, which the men of Hezekiah king of Judah copied out," is valid evidence that the book of The Proverbs did not receive its present shape before the reign of Hezekiah. The brief introduction (ch. 1:1–6) fittingly describes the entire book, and the poem in praise of wisdom (chs. 1:7 to 9:18) is not ascribed to Solomon, and forms the preface to the proverbs of Solomon, which immediately follow, or more probably to all the maxims of wisdom which constitute the remainder of the book. The introduction and poem may, therefore, be safely attributed to the hand and brain of another literary man than Solomon, and dated not earlier than the reign of Hezekiah. The 2d and 4th sections, chs. 10:1 to 22:16 and chs. 25 to 29, or nearly ⅔ of the book, are ascribed to Solomon. The absence of a polemic against idolatry has been urged as evidence that the proverbs in these sections originated or were collected after the cessation of the great struggle which the prophets carried on with encroaching heathenism. It may with equal justice be advanced as proof that these sections antedate that struggle. If the absence of polemic proves anything, it affords evidence that these proverbs were collected either before the division of the kingdom and the encroachments of idolatry, or after the Exile, when idolatry had lost its attractiveness. The language of these sections favors, though it does not establish, the ascription to Solomon, for it is pure Hebrew. It is free from foreign orthography and forms, such as are found in some books which were written immediately before the Exile or subsequently to it. Furthermore, proverbial literature is very ancient. It appeared early among the Hebrews also (I Sam. 24:13; 18:7). That Solomon composed and collected proverbs has early attestation (Prov. 25:1; I Kings 4:32; 10:1 *seq.*; Ecclus. 47:13–17). The titles, therefore, which attribute the maxims in these 2 sections of the book of The Proverbs, may safely be regarded as authentic.

Prov'ince. The rendering of Heb. and Aram. *medīnāh*, jurisdiction, and Gr. *eparcheia*, government. The young men or servants of the princes of the provinces, who fought under Ahab against Ben-hadad (I Kings 20:14), were not Israelites (v. 15). They probably served the chieftains who ruled various districts in Gilead and the Hauran, and made common cause with Israel in resisting the encroachment of the Syrians upon the country s. of Damascus.

The provinces of the Babylonian and Persian Empires were divisions of the realm for administrative purposes (Dan. 2:49; 3:3). Darius the Great, who as king of Persia had dominion from India to Ethiopia (Herod. iii. 90–94), divided this great empire into 20 governments called satrapies (i. 192; iii. 89); see SATRAP. These satrapies or large provinces were subdivided into smaller governmental districts, which the Jews designated likewise by the general term province (Ezra 8:36; Neh. 2:7, 9; Esth. 3:12; 8:9; cf. Herod. iii. 120, 128; vi. 42; with iii. 127; v. 11, 27, 30; see also DARIUS 2). In the days of Ahasuerus these minor provinces numbered 127 (Esth. 1:1). During the Persian period Judah was at first under the jurisdiction of the governor "beyond the River" (Ezra 5:3, 6), but by royal decree it was made a separate province and granted a governor of its own (chs. 2:63; 5:8).

The provinces of the Roman Empire were of 2 classes, imperial and senatorial. The imperial provinces were under the direct and sole control of the emperor; they comprehended all the frontier provinces which were supposed to need the presence of an army of occupation to hold them in subjection; they were governed by a military officer called a legate, who was appointed by the emperor; their revenues were received by imperial agents termed procurators and were paid into the private exchequer of the emperor. The smaller imperial provinces, and parts of larger ones like the subprovince of Judea, were ruled by a procurator only, the presence of a legate not being deemed necessary. Cilicia (Acts 23:34), Galatia, and Syria, of which Judea was a part, were imperial provinces. The senatorial provinces were administered by the senate; they did not require to be kept under control by military force; their governor was styled a proconsul. He was attended by quaestors, who received the revenues and paid them into the public treasury, which was managed by the senate. Cyprus (Acts 13:4, 7), Macedonia (ch. 16:12), Achaia (ch. 18:12), and Asia (ch. 19:10) were senatorial provinces.

Psalms, The. A collection of religious poems which were specially employed in the public worship of the God of Israel. In Hebrew it is called Book of Praises. The title in the English version is borrowed from the Greek translation (cf. Luke 20:42). The general designation Psalms of David is derived from the number of psalms, 73 in all, expressly ascribed to David in the Hebrew titles (cf. Heb. 4:7).

The psalms number 150. They are divided into 5 books, in imitation, it is thought, of the fivefold division of the Pentateuch; this division is ancient. It is indicated in the LXX, and is marked by headings in the Hebrew text. These books begin respectively with Psalms 1; 42; 73; 90; 107. Each book is arranged to close with a doxology. In the 1st book all the psalms are attributed to David except 4 (Psalms 1; 2; 10; 33). These are so-called orphan psalms; that is, they are anonymous. In the LXX all except Psalm 1, which is introductory, and Psalm 2 are ascribed to David, Psalm 10 being united to Psalm 9 and Psalm 33 bearing the title "To David." The divine name Jehovah is generally employed in the psalms of this book. In the 2d book, of the 31 psalms the first 8 are a collection of songs of the sons of Korah. Seven are expressly ascribed to them; and Psalm 43, whether written by them or not, was composed as the conclusion of Psalm 42. This group is followed by a psalm of Asaph. Then comes a group of 20 psalms attributed to David with the exception of 2 (Psalms 66;

67). Of the 2 exceptions, however, Psalm 67 is ascribed to David in the LXX. The book closes with an anonymous and a Solomonic psalm (Psalms 71; 72). In this book the divine name is prevailingly Elohim, God; and 2 psalms duplicate 2 of the 1st book, substituting the word God for Jehovah (Psalms 53; 70; cf. Psalms 14; 40:13–17). The 3d book contains 17 psalms. The first 11 are attributed to Asaph, 4 to the sons of Korah, and 1 each to David and Ethan. This collection of psalms was gathered after the destruction of Jerusalem and burning of the Temple (Ps. 74:3, 7, 8; 79:1). The 4th book likewise contains 17 psalms. The 1st is ascribed to Moses, 2 to David; and the remaining 14 are anonymous. The LXX gives 11 to David, leaving only 5 anonymous (Psalms 92; 100; 102; 105; 106). The 5th book has 28 anonymous psalms, while 15 are assigned to David and 1 to Solomon. The ascriptions differ considerably in the LXX. This collection was made late, for it includes psalms which refer to the Exile (Psalms 126; 137). It will be seen that the composition of the psalms ranges over a long period of time. That David was the author of psalms is supported by abundant early testimony, direct and indirect. See DAVID.

The titles of the psalms are ancient. They were not only in their place when the Greek version was made, but they were old at that time, for musical and other terms which occur were not understood by the translators. As they stand, they are not infallible, Psalm 88, for example, having 2 titles. The titles have been exposed, like the rest of the text of the Old Testament, to the ordinary vicissitudes of transmission, and errors have doubtless crept in during the process of copying which must be discovered and removed by textual criticism. In the titles the Heb. preposition l^e constantly occurs. It is translated "to" in the phrase "to the chief musician" (Psalm 4, title, in R.V. for), and "of" in such expressions as a "psalm of David" (Psalm 3), a "Michtam of David" (Psalm 16), "a psalm of the sons of Korah" (Psalm 47), "a psalm of Asaph" (Psalm 50), "a song of David" (Psalm 65), "a prayer of Moses the man of God" (Psalm 90), "a prayer of the afflicted" (Psalm 102), and "a psalm of David" (Psalm 11), "a psalm of the sons of Korah" (Psalm 44), "a psalm of Solomon" (Psalm 72), and simply "of David" (Psalm 122), "of Solomon" (Psalm 127); and "for" in "a song for the Sabbath day" (Psalm 92), "a psalm for the thank-offering" (Psalm 100, R.V. marg.). The force of this preposition in Hebrew was manifold. In the titles prefixed to poems 3 important meanings must be borne in mind by the interpreter. It may denote : 1. Possession, belonging to (Ps. 24:1, represented by the possessive case). 2. Authorship (Hab. 3:1). 3. Intended purpose. When the preposition is employed several times in a title, it may, of course, be used each time in a different sense (Psalm 4, rendered "for . . . of," in A.V. "to . . . of"; Psalm 18, "for . . . of . . . unto"; Isa. 5:1, "for" or "of," and "touching"). The simple phrases "of David" (Psalm 11), "of Asaph" (Psalm 81), and the Hebrew order of the words "of David, a psalm" (Psalm 24), "of the sons of Korah, a Maschil" (Psalm 44), "of the sons of Korah, a psalm" (Psalm 47), suggest that the word psalm or Michtam or prayer (Psalms 4; 16; 17) is an epithet descriptive of the poem, and in these and similar cases might be separated by a comma or other punctuation from the prepositional phrase that follows, thus "a psalm; of David," "a song; for the Sabbath day." Further, the preposition seems often to refer to a collection to which the particular psalm originally belonged, as in the phrase "of the sons of

Korah." This clue leads to the belief that the similar phrase "of David" refers to a collection prepared by David.

The book of The Psalms, as at present constituted in the O.T., was the hymn book of the 2d Temple. Its rich devotional songs were also sung in private gatherings for the worship of God (Matt. 26:30; see PASSOVER 1). Like modern hymn books, it was composed of the hymns of the ages, and in many cases the source from which these psalms were derived is stated in the titles. From these it appears that there were collections in use before the present Psalter was compiled. 1. The collection of David. Seventy-three psalms of the completed Psalter belonged originally to this earlier book of praise, according to the notes in the Hebrew text (Psalms 3 to 9; 11 to 32; 34 to 41; 51 to 65; 68 to 70; 86; 101; 103; 108 to 110; 122; 124; 131; 133; 138 to 145). In the Greek version the note is not found with Psalms 33; 43; 67; 71; 91; 93 to 99; 104; 137, in addition to the psalms provided with it in the Hebrew text. In this collection a number of psalms were provided with a prose introduction stating the occasion; and all that had this preface, or at least 13 of them, were taken over into the completed book of The Psalms (Psalms 3; 7; 18; 34; 51; 52; 54; 56; 57; 59; 60; 63; 142). No psalm of the completed Psalter has an introduction of this kind, except those that are marked "of David." To judge from the name, from the definite ascription of the authorship to David by means of a relative clause in the title of certain psalms thus marked (Psalms 7; 18), from David's known possession of poetic gifts, and from the ancient testimony to his interest in the musical service of the sanctuary (see DAVID), this collection was formed by David, and was the psalm book of the Temple in pre-exilic times. Probably it contained both sacred poems of David's own composition and psalms selected by him from various sources; and it would be quite in accordance with the history of hymnody if this collection of sacred songs, used by many generations in public and private worship, received additions of appropriate hymns as time went on, yet retained its original title of Prayers of David (Ps. 72:20). The present book of The Psalms, although it contains sacred poems written after the destruction of Jerusalem by the Babylonians, nevertheless is often entitled the Psalms of David. When the contents of this Davidic collection were combined with other collections, each of its psalms was marked as taken from the book of David. Writings of prophets, priests, and poets who lived before the Babylonian Exile survived that calamity, and it is not surprising that a body of religious songs should have outlived the catastrophe and been ultimately incorporated in the new hymnal. 2. A collection used by the sons of Korah, a family some of whom were officially connected with the sanctuary as singers (see KORAHITE). Eleven psalms are attested as having belonged to this collection (Psalms 42; 44 to 49; 84; 85; 87; 88). 3. A collection arranged by Asaph or members of his family, who were official musicians and singers at the sanctuary (see ASAPH 1). Twelve psalms are known to have belonged to this body of hymns, and in all the divine name kept prominent is God (Psalms 50; 73 to 83). Besides these 3 collections there were many fugitive hymns which in course of time received the approval of the religious authorities for use in public worship. But the 3 primary collections supply ⅔ of the psalmody admitted into the completed Psalter.

After these collections had been formed 3 minor groupings of psalms came into existence: 1. By culling mainly from the 3 primary collections a group of psalms was assembled in which the prominent thought is God in the fullness of his attributes (Psalms 42 to 83). Because the word God, in Heb. Elohim, predominates, these psalms are sometimes designated as Elohistic. The group contained the collection of Asaph, perhaps the whole of it, consisting of 12 numbers, 7 Korahite psalms, about a score from the psalter of David, and 1 from a book of Solomon's. It was made for the purpose of meeting a felt need in the worship; and it included, 1st, psalms that were written originally in adoring contemplation of God, in the fullness of the conception; and, 2d, psalms in which the divine name, if it was not originally God, was Jehovah, and was changed to God or Lord in order to adapt the psalm to the special use (cf. Psalm 14 with Psalm 53, and Ps. 108: 1-5 with Ps. 57:7-11; Jehovah being changed to God or Lord or *vice versa*). Scarcely an Elohistic psalm is found in the Psalter outside of this group. The group was given a place as a whole, and, so far as known, without diminution of number, in the completed Psalter; but the division of the Psalter into 5 books cut this section in two. 2. A collection of 15 psalms was formed from various sources, mostly from fugitive pieces, and entitled Songs of Ascents (Psalms 120 to 134). It, too, was kept intact in the final arrangement of the Psalter. 3. Further, and mainly from the 3 primary collections, a selection was made by the chief musician. It contained 55 psalms which appear in the completed Psalter; namely, 39 from the collection of David, 9 from that of the sons of Korah, and 5 from that of Asaph, with 1 or 2 from anonymous sources (Psalms 66; 67, unless the latter is Davidic, see Codex Vaticanus). To these 55 the LXX adds Psalm 30, from David's collection. The prayer of Habakkuk was also included (Hab. 3:19). All the psalms in the present Psalter that are provided with musical directions once belonged to this collection. Not all the psalms that once had a place in it, however, have musical notes. This latter fact, rather than the former, indicates a collection, since the musical notes might conceivably be mere instructions to the director of the Temple music and account for the mention of him. The fact that a psalm had belonged to the chief musician's collection is noted in connection with it in the completed Psalter.

Internal evidence for the date of a psalm may come from several sources: 1. Diction and grammatical constructions. The inquiry along these lines demands caution in view of the limited amount and scope of the literature available for comparison, the draughts upon the common Semitic stock of words enforced on the poet by the insistent call for synonyms in the parallelism of Hebrew verse (cf. Ps. 19:2-4), the vocabulary of poetry, which is characteristically rich in unusual words and constructions, and the dialects among the Hebrews in Palestine with their different content of words and forms (cf. Judg., ch. 5; I Kings, ch. 17, to II Kings, ch. 8; Hosea; Jonah). 2. Historical events and conditions reflected in the psalm. Unless an occurrence of known date is explicitly mentioned (Psalm 137), the evidence is inconclusive; for a suitable occasion which is familiar to the modern interpreter (as for Psalm 46, the deliverance from Sennacherib) may not have been in the mind of the psalmist at all. The critical question must ever be: Are the terms of the description so specific as to determine the event with certainty and render negligible the consideration of other similar crises? 3. The stage of religious development which the psalm reveals. The argument from this source is apt to turn on theories regarding the date of the documents contained in the Pentateuch or other O.T. literature, or on opinions about the insight into spiritual things and the depth of religious experience possessed by earnest men in the early days of the monarchy. There are writings, however, which are acknowledged by scholars to be earlier than David, others contemporary with him, and yet others not later than the 8th century. These writings afford a common though limited ground on which to discuss the extent of the religious knowledge and experience of individual men. 4. The fact that the speaker in the psalm, who uses the pronoun of the first person sing. or pl., in many instances represents the community, and is not the psalmist voicing his own personal emotions. The individualization of the nation, however, was common from the earliest times to the latest in Israel. It is found in the Ten Commandments and their preface, and frequently in the prophets. Hence its employment in a psalm is practically no aid toward determining the date of composition (cf. first person sing., Deut. 7:17; 8:17; 9:4; Isa. 12:1, 2; Jer. 3:4; 10:19, 20; 31:18, 19; Hos. 8:2; 12:8; 13:10; Micah 2:4). Moreover, these various criteria determine the date of those sections only to which they apply (Ps. 19: 7–14; 51:18, 19), and do not necessarily fix the date of the entire psalm. The cautious investigator discovers that in many cases a negative result only is attainable, namely, that sufficient reason does not exist for denying the authenticity of the title; or the outcome of the inquiry, stated positively, may be that the contents of the psalm are suitable to the occasion attested by the title.

Technical terms used are Neginah, a stringed instrument, and its pl. Neginoth; and Nehiloth, wind instruments (Psalms 4; 5; 61). Terms probably musical: Alamoth, maidens, perhaps maiden or treble voices (Psalm 46; I Chron. 15:20); Gittith, probably a vintage song, or perhaps a cither of Gath, or a march of the Gittite guard (Psalms 8; 81; 84); Selah, an orchestral interlude or a change from *piano* to *forte* (Ps. 3:2); Sheminith, the eighth (Psalms 6; 12; I Chron. 15:21). Terms indicative of the character of the psalm: Maschil, a didactic or reflective poem (Psalm 32, and 12 others); Michtam, perhaps epigrammatic (Psalms 16; 56 to 60); Mizmor, a lyric poem, regularly translated psalm (Psalm 3, *et passim*); Shiggaion, probably a wild dithyrambic (Psalm 7; Hab. 3:1, Shigionoth). Other terms are understood to indicate familiar melodies: Aijeleth hash-Shahar, "hind of the dawn" (Psalm 22); Jonath elem rehokim, "the silent dove of them that are afar off," or, changing the pronunciation of the 2d word, "the dove of the distant terebinths" (Psalm 56); Mahalath, "sickness" (Psalms 53; 88); Muth-labben (Psalm 9); Shoshannim (Shoshanim, Psalm 45) and Shoshannim Eduth and Shushan Eduth (Psalms 45; 60; 80, cf. R.V. marg.). The songs of ascents or degrees were probably designed for pilgrims going up to Jerusalem.

Psal'ter·y. The usual rendering of Heb. *nebel,* when a musical instrument is intended. In 4 passages it is translated viol (Isa. 5: 12, in R.V. lute; 14:11; Amos 5:23; 6:5). *Nebel* became the Gr. *nabla,* which was reputed to be of Sidonian origin; and it is usually translated by this Gr. word in the LXX (I Sam. 10:5; II Sam. 6:5; I Chron. 13:8; 15:16, 20). The body of the instrument was made of wood (II Sam. 6:5; II Chron. 9:11), or, later, of metal (Jos. *Antiq.* viii. 3, 8). The strings were of gut and their

number in the common instrument is unknown, but in a special variety they were 10 (Ps. 33:2; 92:3). The psaltery was tuned to the soprano register (I Chron. 15:20). It could be carried about while it was played (I Sam. 10:5). The name psaltery, which is occasionally given to this instrument in the LXX (Ps. 33:2; 57:8), has been thought to identify it with the *santîr* of the Arabs; but the history of the *santîr* and its name seems to be as follows: The Assyrians used a musical instrument consisting of a long, low, horizontal body over which strings were strung. It was played with a plectrum. The Greeks adopted it as the 20-stringed *magadis* and the 40-stringed *epigoneion.* Later the *magadis* received the name *psalterion,* and was apparently borrowed with its new name from the Greeks by the Aramaeans (Dan. 3:5, *pᵉsantērîn*) and by the Arabs. By the latter it was called *santîr.* In the light of this probable history of the *santîr,* the identity of its name with psaltery is seen not to identify it with the Heb. *nebel.* The tradition regarding the *nebel* indicates that it was a kind of harp. Josephus says that the difference between the *kinura* [Heb. *kinnôr,* lyre (harp)] and the *nabla* was that the former had 10 strings and was played with the plectrum, while the latter had 12 notes and was played with the fingers (Jos. *Antiq.* vii. 12, 3). According to Eusebius, the *psalterion* was called *nabla* by the Hebrews and had the metallic sounding-board above; and Augustine on Psalm 42 describes it as having the sounding-board above the strings, and not below as in the cither, the strings of the psaltery being stretched between a curved arm and the drum or resonance box in which it terminates above. Isidorus and Cassiodorus describe the psaltery as triangular in shape, like the Gr. letter *delta.* If they do not confound it with the *trigônon,* which had a triangular frame, and if they correctly give the shape of the psaltery, it appears to have resembled the upright harp which Assyrian musicians carried while they played it. The original form of the sounding-board and the arm probably bore resemblance to a skin bottle and its neck, and obtained for the musical instrument its name of *nebel,* bottle. It was one of the instruments which the company of prophets whom Saul met were playing when he came in their way (I Sam. 10: 5), and one of those used at David's removal of the Ark to Jerusalem (II Sam. 6:5). When David permanently organized the instrumentalists into an orchestra for the sanctuary, some were appointed to perform on the psaltery (I Chron. 15:16, 20, 28; 16:5; 25:1, 6); and it was subsequently in continual use for divine worship (II Chron. 5:12). It was played also at festive gatherings (Isa. 5:12; Amos 6:5). It was often combined with the harp (I Sam. 10:5; II Sam. 6:5; II Chron. 9:11; Ps. 81:2; 108:2). For its use in the sanctuary, see MUSIC.

Ptol'e·ma'is (tŏl′ê-mā′ĭs). See ACCO.

Ptol'e·my (tŏl′ê-mĭ). The name borne by all the male rulers of Egypt of the house of Lagus, which began with Ptolemy Soter (died 283 B.C.), one of the generals of Alexander the Great, and lasted until the Roman conquest of Egypt and the death of Cleopatra. The next 2 were Ptolemy (II) Philadelphus (285–246), coregent for 2 years, and Ptolemy (III) Euergetes I (246–221). The early Ptolemies, especially the first 3, were wise and efficient rulers and raised Egypt to a high position of power and influence. They held many foreign possessions, among which were Phoenicia, Coelesyria, Cyprus, and Cyrenaica, and for a while Palestine. They patronized art, letters, and science, and raised Alexandria, their capital, to be the leading university center of Greek culture. They were friendly to the Jews, encouraging them to settle in Alexandria, granting them special privileges, and giving to many of them high civil and military positions.

The later rulers of this house were, however, weak and wicked. Wars with their neighbors were frequent, revolts on the part of their people at home became common, incest and the murder of relatives were well known in the palace, and the loss of all the foreign possessions heralded the loss of the throne itself.

Three of the rulers of this line and several men of humbler rank are mentioned in the Books of the Maccabees:

1. PTOLEMY IV, called Philopator (221–203 B.C.). He was suspected of causing the death of his father, and his 1st act on coming to the throne was the murder of his mother and younger brother. His whole reign was a series of debaucheries and crimes. Encouraged by the weakness and profligacy of Ptolemy, Antiochus III, king of Syria, made war on him with a view to wresting Phoenicia from

Ptolemy Philopator

Egypt, but was utterly defeated by the Egyptian army at the battle of Raphia, 217 B.C. (III Macc. 1:1–5). After this battle, Ptolemy sacrificed in Jerusalem, but being prevented from entering the Holy of Holies, attempted to assassinate all the Jews in Alexandria in revenge. A somewhat fanciful account of this is found in the Third Book of Maccabees.

2. PTOLEMY VI, called Philometor (181/0–145), began to reign at the age of 7, under the regency of his mother, Cleopatra. He reigned for some years alone and for some years conjointly with his brother, Physcon, called Ptolemy VII. Later the kingdom was divided between them, Physcon ruling over Cyrene and Libya, and Philometor over Egypt and Cyprus. His generals invaded

Ptolemy Philometor

Syria and so came into contact with Antiochus Epiphanes, by whom they were completely defeated at Pelusium 169 B.C. Cyprus also was taken by Antiochus, and Alexandria would doubtless have fallen but for the interference of the Romans, who began at that time to exercise a quasi protectorate over Egypt. Philometor interfered frequently in the affairs of Syria, siding one time with the pretender Alexander Balas (I Macc. 10:51–

57) and afterward with Alexander's rival, Demetrius Nicator (ch. 11:1–18). While engaged in battle in Syria, he fell from his horse, and died shortly afterward from the effects of the injury, 145 B.C. Ptolemy showed special favor to the Jews. It was by his permission that Onias built a Jewish temple at Leontopolis copied after the Temple at Jerusalem.

3. PTOLEMY VII, Physcon, also called Euergetes II, was first co-regent with his brother Philometor, 169–164 B.C., but after the death of the latter reigned alone, 145–116 B.C. The early part of his reign was a series of crimes against his own family and such debauchery as alienated and disgusted his subjects, who revolted several times. Like his predecessors, he interfered in the affairs of Syria. He is mentioned (I Macc. 15:16) as in correspondence with Rome, and it is probably he who is meant in I Macc. 1:18.

4. PTOLEMY, a general of Antiochus Epiphanes (II Macc. 4:45; 6:8; 8:8). He took part in the expedition which Lysias organized against Judas Maccabaeus (I Macc. 3:38). It is possible that he is identical with Ptolemy Makron (II Macc. 10:12), who first served Ptolemy Philometor in Cyprus, then passed into the service of Antiochus Epiphanes and later into that of Antiochus Eupator. Falling into disfavor with the latter, he ended his life by taking poison, 164 B.C.

5. PTOLEMY, son-in-law of the high priest Simon. He murdered his father-in-law and 2 of his brothers-in-law in the stronghold of Dok, near Jericho (I Macc. 16:11 seq.).

Pu'a (pū′á). See PUVAH.

Pu'ah (pū′á). One of the Hebrew midwives who disobeyed the command of the Egyptian king to kill the male children at their birth (Ex. 1:15).

For others called Puah in the Eng. versions, but which is a different word in Heb., see PUVAH.

Pub'li·can [Lat., pertaining to public revenue]. A farmer of the Roman taxes and customs. In place of appointing revenue officers to raise fixed taxes from the community, the Romans and their deputy princes like the Herods were accustomed to put up to auction the privilege of farming the public revenues, or some specified part of them, in the several provinces, cities, towns, and districts. Those who bid at the auction were necessarily wealthy men, or representatives of wealthy companies; for they undertook to pay a given sum into the treasury, and they were obliged to give security to the government for the sums they promised to pay. In some cases they in turn sold the right of farming portions of the revenue to subcontractors, in others they engaged a number of subordinate agents to do the actual work of collecting the taxes. They themselves were generally Romans of equestrian rank, while their subordinates, of course, were of inferior dignity. The subordinates or actual collectors of the taxes and customs are called publicans in the Eng. version of the N.T. It was understood that the farmers were to repay themselves for their labor and the risk they had undertaken by taking from the taxpayers a fraction more than they paid over to the government. No proper means were adopted to prevent that fraction from assuming great proportions. With a few honorable exceptions, the publicans, great and small, were extortioners (cf. Luke 3:12, 13; 19:8). They were unpopular among all classes in the provinces, except, perhaps, with the Roman governors, who often received part of the plunder for conniving at the oppressions practiced. Sometimes the subcontractors, and in most cases the subordinate taxgatherer, in the conquered countries belonged to the native population. Thus Zacchaeus, a Jew, seems to have been a subcontractor for the revenues of Jericho (Luke 19:1, 2), and Matthew, or Levi (also a Jew), apparently a tax collector paid by the farmer for the ¬¬venues of Capernaum (Matt. 9:9; Mark 2: ¬.; Luke 5:27). It added to the unpopularity of the Jews who accepted office as the agents of the Roman publicans, or themselves became farmers of the revenue from particular towns, that they raised taxes for a foreign and heathen government. They were not admitted into society; in fact, it was considered disreputable for anyone to be their friend and associate. It was one of the charges brought against our Lord that he ate with publicans and sinners (Matt. 9: 10–13) and that he was their friend (ch. 11: 19). He honored them by choosing one of their number as an apostle (chs. 9:9; 10:3). Quite agreeing with popular opinion as to the low moral state of the average publican (chs. 5:46, 47; 18:17), he still invited them as freely as he did others into the Kingdom of God. His kindness touched their hearts, and not a few of them were baptized (Matt. 21:31, 32; Luke 3:12; 7:29). He introduced a penitent publican into his parable of the Pharisee and the Publican (Luke 18:9–14).

Pub'li·us (pŭb'lĭ-ŭs). The chief man and a land owner on the island of Melita, when Paul was there. He entertained the apostle and his companions for 3 days. He was rewarded; for Paul by prayer and the laying on of hands cured the father of Publius of fever and dysentery (Acts 28:7, 8). His name suggests that he was a Roman; and his title, which is also found in inscriptions relating to Malta, seems to mean that he was the highest Roman official on the island.

Pu'dens (pū'dĕnz) [Lat., bashful, modest]. A Christian at Rome who joined Paul in sending salutations to Timothy (II Tim. 4: 21).

Pu'hites (pū'hīts). See PUTHITES.

Pul (pŭl). 1. An African country and people. The latter are coupled with Tarshish and Lud, apparently all 3 being skillful in archery (Isa. 66:19). One opinion is that Pul is the island of Philae on the Nile in Upper Egypt on the confines of Ethiopia. It is, however, more probably a copyist's error for Put (q.v.); cf. LXX, Phoud.
2. A king of Assyria; see TIGLATH-PILESER.

Pulse. Leguminous plants or their seeds, specially peas and beans, which are eminently nourishing. On these Daniel and his companions desired to be fed (Dan. 1:12, 16, R.V. marg., herbs). Parched pulse is mentioned in II Sam. 17:28, but the word pulse is plausibly supplied by the translators; it is not in the original.

Pun'ish·ment. The penalty due for sin inflicted for the satisfaction of justice. So Adam, Eve, and Cain were punished by God. Punishment is not inflicted for the good of the offender, but the idea may be present incidentally. The destruction of the men of Sodom for their wickedness was not intended to benefit them. The execution of the murderer does not aim at his reformation. Chastisement, on the other hand, is intended to reform the offender. Nor is punishment primarily inflicted with a view to the prevention of crime, although this is a great end. The civil authority enforces law by penalty for the protection of the state, since purely moral considerations, such as the inherent righteousness of an act or the sense of justice, fail to prevent men from violating the

rights of others. One object in the infliction of punishment in the Mosaic code was to restrain the wicked, but it was not the principle on which the Law was based (Deut. 13:11; 17:13; 19:20; 21:21). Yet the chief end of punishment is not to restrain the criminal from further crime, nor to deter others from doing similar acts of violence. Sin ought to be punished irrespective of the effect which the punishment may have in preventing others. The indignation which men feel toward the offender himself, when they witness a flagrant act of wrongdoing, such as murder, oppression, or cruelty, and the demand which they instinctively make for his punishment show that they discern guilt in the sinner and that they do not think in the first instance of the need of deterring others from the commission of like crimes. The wrongdoer is punished because he deserves to be. So, under the Mosaic Law, the state must execute justice and punish the offender, or be held guilty of participating in and condoning the crime (Lev. 20:4, 5; Num. 25:4, 11; Deut. 21:8; Josh. 7:11–15). The people must cleanse Jehovah's land from the blood of murder. The execution of the murderer was an expiation of the land (Num. 35:33, 34; Deut. 21:8 seq.).

The majesty of the law is maintained only when the punishment bears an adequate proportion to the crime committed, neither too little nor too much. The penalty need not be, and seldom is, an exact equivalent. The penalty for theft is not the restitution of the stolen property or its exact value in money. Enforced restitution does not clear the thief. Law has been violated, guilt incurred, and punishment is demanded.

The laws of the Hebrews were stern, but the punishments were not cruel. In rare cases the family of the criminal was extirpated by the immediate act of God or by his express command (Num. 16:32, 33; Josh. 7: 24, 25; II Kings 9:25, 26); but this extent of punishment was recognized as extraordinary; it was not appointed by the Law as the prescribed penalty for any crime, and the Law expressly forbade that fathers should be punished for the children (Deut. 24:16). For a special case of impurity, the heinousness of which was aggravated by the relation of the party concerned to the sanctuary of God, and for incestuousness of peculiar abhorrence, the penalty was burning with fire (Lev. 20:14; 21:9; cf. Gen. 38:24). But there was no cruelty involved. The guilty ones were not burned alive; they were first stoned to death, and then their bodies were consumed by fire (cf. Josh. 7:15, 25). The hand of a woman who had used it in a shameless act to assist her husband in his struggle with an adversary was cut off (Deut. 25:11, 12). Retaliation for bodily injury, when inflicted willfully and not in a quarrel, eye for eye, tooth for tooth, was legalized. So it was by ancient Greek law and by the Roman laws of the 12 tables. In the later Jewish law (Jos. Antiq. iv. 8, 35), and perhaps in the earlier law as well, a ransom in lieu of the maiming might be accepted by the injured person. This exemption was based on Ex. 21:29, 30 on the principle that, since in so great a matter as the infliction of death by one's ox, a fine might take the place of the surrender of the owner's life, in all lesser cases of injury a fine might also be accepted. In its humanity the Hebrew administration of justice compares favorably with Roman methods. Unlike Roman law, the Hebrew penal code did not authorize the punishment of the parricide by scourging him to the effusion of blood and then sewing him up in a sack and drowning him; nor did it sanction the torture of witnesses, who were slaves, and of accused persons to extract testimony (Acts 22:24 *seq.*); the punishment of the condemned by stocks and cruel scourging (Matt. 27:26; Acts 16:24; Jos. *War* ii. 14, 9), the mockery of those about to be executed (Matt. 27:27–31), crucifixion (Matt. 27:26, 32, 44; Jos. *Antiq.* xvii. 10, 10), condemnation of criminals to fight with each other as gladiators or with wild beasts (I Cor. 15:32; Jos. *War* vi. 9, 2; vii. 2, 1), scourging to death, starving to death (see PRISON), and burning to death, not infrequently by clothing the victim in a shirt steeped in pitch and setting it on fire.

The Hebrew law did not rudely abolish established usage, even when custom fell short of the standard erected by God (see SLAVE, CONCUBINE, DIVORCE); it recognized the people's hardness of heart (Mark 10:5); but it brought custom under law, checked excesses, reformed abuses; it took solemn account of man's conception of right and justice as prevalent in that age, guarded against vengeance and vindictiveness, satisfied the sense of justice, and thus maintained the august majesty of law; and it set higher standards before man and was a distinct advance toward perfection. The form of punitive justice was further determined by the essential idea of the theocracy, which required that not only crimes against the state and society, but also violations of religious ordinances should be punished. The relation of the Israelites to their divine King resulted in God's punishing sin when man failed to do so, and in God's reserving to himself the right to punish certain specified sins, e.g., to inflict childlessness (Lev. 20:4–6, 20, 21). Furthermore, the administration of justice was a matter in which the entire community was concerned, and consequently the people participated in its execution. The people stoned the criminal condemned to death.

The offenses mentioned in the penal law were:

1. *Violation of the religious duties* of the covenant. There were: 1. capital offenses, which the human tribunal punished with death. They were 5: sacrifice to idols (Ex. 22:20; Lev. 20:2; Deut. 13:6–17; 17:2–7); sorcery, professed intercourse with a familiar spirit, soothsaying (Ex. 22:18; Lev. 20:27); profanation of the Sabbath (Ex. 31:14, 15; 35:2); blasphemy (Lev. 24:10–16); and false prophecy, whether uttered in behalf of heathen deities or in the name of Jehovah (Deut. 13:1–5; 18:20). The penalty was death by stoning. Instances of the infliction of the death penalty on persons charged with these offenses are recorded in history: for sacrificing to idols (II Kings 10:18–25; 11:18; 23:5, 20), for exorcising the dead (I Sam. 28:3, 9), for profaning the Sabbath (Num. 15:32–36), for blasphemy (I Kings 21:13), for uttering false prophecy (I Kings 18:40; 20:27, 28). 2. Offenses punishable by cutting off the offender from his people. They endangered covenant institutions and the fundamental ordinances of worship. They were refusal to receive circumcision, the sign of the covenant (Gen. 17:14), neglect of the passover, the covenant sacrifice, and consumption of leavened bread during the feast of unleavened bread (Ex. 12:15; Num. 9:13), performance of work and refusal to fast on the Day of Atonement (Lev. 23:29, 30), use of blood or fat for food, since they belonged to sacrifice and atonement (Lev. 7:25–27; 17:14), offering elsewhere than at the sanctuary (ch. 17:4), slaughtering sacrificial animals without making a peace offering, and eating the peace offering after the prescribed limit (Lev. 7:18; 17:9; 19:8), use of the holy anointing oil and the incense for common purposes (Ex. 30:33, 38), neglect to purify one's self from defilement, and eating sacrifice in an unclean condition (Lev. 22:3; Num. 19:20). The punishment of cutting off is in some instances accompanied by the death penalty or by threat of divine judgment. When accompanied by the death penalty, the execution of the offender was committed to man. The threat of divine judgment reserved the infliction to God himself. The question whether the punishment of cutting off in all cases implied death, even when the death penalty was not expressly annexed, has given rise to much debate. The phrase has been interpreted to mean excommunication, as rabbinical writers understand; or loss of the rights belonging to the covenant; or death, which in breaches of the ritual was intended to be commuted to banishment or deprivation of civil rights, or death in all cases, either invariable and without remission, or else voidable by repentance and use of the means of propitiation for ceremonial defilement. It probably means expulsion from the fellowship of Israel or, as is otherwise stated, the congregation of Israel (Ex. 12:15, 19; Num. 16:9; 19:13), and, whether specifically stated or not, includes divine intervention for the extermination of the evildoer (cf. Gen. 17:14 with Ex. 4:24; Lev. 17:10; 20:3, 5, 6; 23:30). Accidental breach or mere neglect did not involve this dire punishment (Num. 15:27 *seq.;* Lev., ch. 4). Only when a person offended with high hand and showed bold contempt for the law was he cut off from his people (Num. 15:30, 31).

2. *Unchastity.* 1. Abominations that defile the people and the land. The penalty was death. They were adultery and the seduction of a betrothed virgin, not a slave girl (Lev. 20:10; Deut. 22:21–27), unnatural lust, both bestiality and sodomy (Ex. 22:19; Lev. 20:13, 15, 16), incestuous relations with mother-in-law or daughter-in-law (Lev. 20:11, 12, 14). Unchastity on the part of a priest's daughter, since it defiles at the same time the father who was set apart to holy service, was punished not only by death, but also by burning the body (Lev. 21:9). 2. Unclean, but less repugnant, conjugal relations were punished by cutting the offenders off from their people or by childlessness (Lev. 20:17–21). 3. The hand of a woman which was used in a shameless and unchaste act to distress the adversary of her husband, was to be cut off (Deut. 25:11, 12). 4. Unchastity which is neither adulterous, unnatural, nor incestuous. The seduction of a virgin entailed marriage, the payment of the usual price for a wife, and in certain cases a fine (Ex. 22:16, 17); and the ravisher was obliged to marry the maid and pay her father 50 shekels, and forfeited the right of divorce (Deut. 22:28, 29).

3. *Insubordination* to the constituted authorities. The penalty was death. 1. Impiety toward parents: striking or cursing father or mother (Ex. 21:15, 17; Lev. 20:9), incorrigibility coupled with habitual drunkenness (Deut. 21:18–21). 2. Refusal to submit to the decree of the priest or judge (Deut. 17:12). 3. Treason, which is not treated in the law, but, according to history, was punished by death and confiscation of property (I Sam. 20:31; 22:16; II Sam. 16:4; 19:29; I Kings 2:8, 9; 21:13, 15).

4. *Crimes* against the person, life, character, and property of another. 1. Willful murder and man-stealing were punished by death (Ex. 21:12, 16; Deut. 24:7); see MURDER. 2. Bodily injury, inflicted intentionally or through carelessness, was punished according to circumstances by compensation or retaliation, an eye for an eye, a tooth for a tooth (Ex. 21:18–36). 3. A false witness in-

curred the penalty of the crime for which the accused was on trial (Deut. 19:16, 19), and a false accusation against a young wife's honor was punished by chastisement, a fine of 100 shekels, and forfeiture of the right of divorce (Deut. 22:13–19). 4. For injury to property the law required, according to circumstances, either simple compensation or a fine paid to the owner and amounting to several times the value of the stolen goods (Ex. 22:1–15).

The punishments recognized by the Mosaic Law were death, chiefly by stoning, and in extreme cases the burning or hanging of the body; chastisement, the stripes not to exceed 40 (Deut. 25:3); retaliation, compensation, which is scarcely a punishment, and fine; forfeiture of rights; and in a special case the loss of a hand. Death was sometimes inflicted by the sword, spear, or arrow, but without the forms of Hebrew law and in extraordinary cases (Ex. 19:13; 32:27; Num. 25:1–8; I Kings 2:25). The sword of the magistrate did not symbolize Hebrew judicial authority. Imprisonment, chains, and stocks were used by the authority of priests and kings, but they were not an institution of the early days of the Hebrew nation (Ezra 7:26; Jer. 20:2; Acts 5:40). See LAW, SIN, I.

Pu'non (pū'nŏn). A station of the Israelites in the wilderness not long before their arrival in Moab (Num. 33:42, 43). Identified with Feinan, on the e. side of the Arabah, about 5¼ miles s.s.e. of Khirbet Nahas and about 4⅓ miles s.s.e. of Khirbet Neḳeib Aseimer; it is in a region where copper and iron were mined. See PINON.

Pu'rah (pū'rá), in A.V. **Phu'rah**. The servant, doubtless armor-bearer, of Gideon (Judg. 7:10, 11).

Pu'ri·fi·ca'tion. Under the Mosaic Law these were of 4 kinds:

1. *Purification from uncleanness* contracted by contact with a corpse (Num., ch. 19; cf. ch. 5:2, 3), not a carcass (Lev. 5:2). For this purpose the ashes of a heifer were required, a female animal as in the case of the sin offering for the common people. It was necessary for the heifer to be red, the color of blood in which the life resides, to be without blemish, and never to have been used in the service of man. It was slain without the camp, its blood was sprinkled toward the sanctuary, and the carcass was burned together with cedar, hyssop, and scarlet. The ashes were gathered and preserved without the camp. When needed, they were mingled with living water; and a clean person, with a bunch of hyssop, sprinkled them upon the unclean on the 3d and 7th day. It only remained for the defiled to wash his clothes and bathe, in order to be ceremonially clean. The defilement of a Nazirite, whose consecration had been interrupted by contact with a corpse, was of greater moment, for he was specially dedicated to ceremonial purity. After a week's separation, on the 7th day he shaved off his hair, the sign of his vow. On the 8th day he brought the same offerings as a man who had been defiled by an issue or as a mother might after childbirth (Num. 6:9–12). A guilt offering followed (v. 12), preparatory to his reinstatement as a Nazirite; cf. the guilt offering of the leper.

2. *Purification from uncleanness due to an issue* (Lev., ch. 15; cf. Num. 5:2, 3). On the 7th day after recovery, the unclean person after bathing in living water and washing the raiment was clean; and on the 8th day he repaired to the sanctuary and offered 2 doves or young pigeons, 1 for a sin offering, the other for a burnt offering. Uncleanness

due to contact with a person having an issue, or with anything rendered unclean by such a person, was in ordinary cases cleansed by a bath, the uncleanness remaining until evening (Lev. 15:5–11).

3. *Purification of a mother* after childbirth. After the days of uncleanness, which were 7 for a man child and 14 for a female child, were over, those of purification followed, during which she touched no hallowed thing, lest she defile it, and for the same reason was forbidden access to the sanctuary. For a son these were to continue 33, and for a daughter 66 days, after which she brought a lamb of the 1st year or, in case of poverty, 2 pigeons or 2 doves for a burnt offering and a young pigeon or dove for a sin offering (Lev. 12:8; Luke 2:21–24).

4. *Purification of the leper* (Lev., ch. 14). The candidate for purification presented himself on the appointed day at the gate of the camp, later at that of the city. The priest killed a clean bird, holding it so that the blood flowed into an earthen vessel of living water. He made a sprinkler by binding a bunch of hyssop with a scarlet cord on a cedar handle, and dipped the sprinkler and a living bird into the bloody water, sprinkled the person undergoing purification, and released the bird; see AZAZEL. This much of the ritual was also performed in purifying a house of leprosy. The candidate was then pronounced clean; and having washed his clothes, shaved off all his hair, and bathed, he might enter camp or city, but must remain outside his habitation 7 days. On the 7th day he again washed his raiment, shaved and bathed, and was clean. On the 8th day he appeared at the sanctuary with 2 male lambs and a ewe lamb of the 1st year or, if his means were limited, with 1 lamb and 2 doves or pigeons, together with a meal offering and a measure of oil. One he-lamb was taken for a guilt offering. The priest put some of its blood on the candidate's right ear, right thumb, and right great toe. He did likewise with some of the oil, after sprinkling a little of it before the Lord, and poured the rest on the candidate's head. The ceremony was completed by offering the remaining lambs or pigeons for a sin offering and a burnt offering.

Pu'rim (pū'rim) [Heb. *pūr* (pl. *pūrīm*), lot; cf. Akkad. *pūrum*, lot; and also Akkad. *purrurum*, to destroy]. A Jewish festival, instituted to celebrate the deliverance of the exiles in Persia from the wholesale massacre of their race planned by Haman. He had cast *pur* (a lot) to ascertain a favorable day for carrying out his scheme. The festival was kept on the 14th and 15th days of the month Adar, approximately February (Esth. 9:20–28). In II Macc. 15:36 it is called the day of Mordecai. Josephus mentions that in his time all the Jews of the inhabited world kept the festival (Jos. *Antiq.* xi. 6, 13). Some have thought that the feast of the Jews mentioned in John 5:1 was that of Purim; but the statement that Jesus went up to Jerusalem is opposed to this view, for Purim was celebrated throughout the land, and only at 3 great feasts was a visit to Jerusalem compulsory. Purim was not one of the 3. From the time of its institution it has enjoyed great popularity among the Jews. The celebration has assumed a fixed form. The 13th of Adar they keep as a fast day. In the evening, which is the beginning of the 14th day, they assemble in their synagogues. After the evening service the reading of The Book of Esther is begun. When the name of Haman is reached, the congregation cry out, "Let his name be blotted out," or "The name of the wicked shall rot," while the youthful worshipers spring rattles. The names of Haman's sons are all read in a breath, to indicate that they were hanged simultaneously. Next morning the people repair again to the synagogue and finish the formal religious exercises of the festival. They then devote the day to mirth and rejoicing before the Lord, the wealthy giving gifts to the poor. The keeping of the Purim festival on the 14th of Adar from age to age is a strong argument for the historic character of the incidents recorded in The Book of Esther. Attempts at finding a Babylonian or Persian origin of the festival have not been convincing. See ESTHER.

Pur'ple. A color which in ancient and modern usage comprehends violet and all the hues intermediate between violet and crimson. In ancient times it included crimson and other reds (Pliny *Hist. Nat.* ix. 61, 62; cf. Mark 15: 17 with Matt. 27:28). Purple raiment was costly, and consequently its use was the privilege of the rich exclusively. It was worn by persons of wealth and high official position (Esth. 8:15; cf. Mordecai's elevation to office, Esth. 8:2; Prov. 31:22; Dan. 5:7; I Macc. 10:20, 62, 64; II Macc.

Murex trunculus

4:38; cf. v. 31; Luke 16:19; Rev. 17:4), and especially by kings, as by the kinglets of Midian (Judg. 8:26). It was a sign of royalty (I Macc. 8:14; Homer *Iliad* iv. 141-145), and was put on Jesus in mockery of his claims. Rich cloths of purple were used as coverings for the seats of princely palanquins (S. of Sol. 3:10), awnings for the decks of luxurious ships (Ezek. 27:7), and drapery for idols (Jer. 10:9). Purple was largely employed in the hangings of the tabernacle (Ex. 25:4; 26:1, 31, 36), and in the garments of the high priest (Ex. 28:5, 6, 15, 33; 39:29). The Jews interpreted the color symbolically (Jos. *War* v. 5, 4).

Purple dye was obtained from various kinds of shell fish (I Macc. 4:23; Jos. *War* v. 5, 4), and was yielded by a thin fluid, called the flower, secreted by a gland in the neck. The amount yielded by each fish was very small, much labor was required to collect it in quantity, and the price was correspondingly great. The larger purples were broken at the top to get at the gland without injuring it, but the smaller ones were pressed in mills (Pliny *Hist. Nat.* ix. 60). Two species of *Murex* were used by the ancient Tyrians, *Murex trunculus* and *Murex brandaris*, and yielded crimson. The *Murex* is common

throughout the Mediterranean Sea, but the shade of color varies with the coast. *Murex* shells were found at Minet el-Beida, the seaport of ancient Ugarit (Ras Shamra), showing that purple was made there in the 2d millennium B.C.

Purse. A bag for carrying money (Luke 10:4; 12:33; 22:35), which, however, was not a necessity, as money was often carried in the girdle (Matt. 10:9, R.V. marg.). The purse or common treasury of the disciples was in charge of Judas (John 12:6; 13:29, R.V. marg., box); the same word was used to describe it as that which designated the chests for offerings at the Temple. Before coins came into use, pieces of silver and gold of various sizes and shapes were tied in a bag or in the girdle, or rings of the precious metal were strung on a cord (Gen. 42:35; Prov. 7:20), and weights and scales were carried for weighing out the desired quantity (Deut. 25:13; Micah 6:11).

Put (pŭt), in A.V. **Phut** (Gen. 10:6; Ezek. 27:10; 38:5 marg.). A people related to the Egyptians (Gen. 10:6), and the country inhabited by them. Put is mentioned in association with Egypt and other African countries, especially with Lubim (Nahum 3:9) and Lud (Ezek. 27:10; and Isa. 66:19 in LXX; between Cush and Lud, Jer. 46:9; Ezek. 30:5); it is rendered Libyans by the LXX in Jeremiah and Ezekiel; it is also identified with Libya by Josephus (Jos. *Antiq.* i. 6, 2); but Put is distinguished from the Libyans (Nahum 3:9). The latest view connects Put with Punt. Punt lay s. or s.e. of Cush, and is commonly identified with Somaliland in Africa. According to Glaser the name first referred to E. Arabia, was then transferred to the S. Arabian incense coast, and was eventually applied to the African coast of Somaliland.

Pu·te'o·li (pū-tē'ō-lī) [Lat., little wells]. A seaport in Italy which Paul's vessel reached the day after it had been at Rhegium. The apostle found Christians there, and enjoyed their hospitality (Acts 28:13). Founded in the 6th century B.C., it was originally called Dicaearchia, and was the ordinary landing place of travelers to Italy from Egypt and the East (Jos. *Antiq.* xvii. 12, 1; xviii. 7, 2; *Life* 3). It was on the n. shore of the Bay of Naples, near the site where the modern city of that name now stands. Its old name of Puteoli still exists, little changed, as Pozzuoli. The whole region round is volcanic, and the crater of the Solfatara rises behind the town.

Pu'thites (pū'thīts), in A.V. **Pu'hites.** A family in Kiriath-jearim (I Chron. 2:53).

Pu'ti·el (pū'tĭ-ĕl) [ety. uncertain, afflicted by God; or perhaps with first component Egypt., he whom God gave]. Father-in-law of Eleazar, Aaron's son (Ex. 6:25).

Pu'vah (pū'và) and **Pu'ah**; instead of first form A.V. has **Phu'vah** (Gen. 46:13), **Pu'a** (Num. 26:23). 1. A son of Issachar and founder of a tribal family (Gen. 46:13; Num. 26:23; I Chron. 7:1).

2. A man of Issachar, son of Dodo, and father of the judge Tola (Judg. 10:1).

Py'garg. The rendering of Heb. *dishōn*, the name of a clean animal (Deut. 14:5). The pygarg of the ancients was a white rumped antelope. It seems to have been the addax (*Antilope addax*, or *Addax nasomaculatus*). The horns, which exist in both sexes, are twisted and ringed. It has a white patch on the forehead, and the hinder parts are grayish-white. It is about the size of a large ass. It is a native of n.e. Africa (cf. Herod.

iv. 192), but its range extends to the s.e. frontier of Palestine.

Pyr'rhus (pir'ŭs) [Gr., flame-colored, red]. The father of Sopater (Acts 20:4, R.V.).

Q

Qoph (kōf). See KOPH.

Quail. A bird which the Children of Israel twice during their journeying near Sinai providentially had for food in great abundance. In the wilderness of Sin the birds covered the camp on one evening (Ex. 16: 12, 13); at Kibroth-hattaavah they were driven in by the s.e. wind from the sea, and fell in vast quantities in and around the camp, lying in places 3 feet deep (Num. 11: 31–34; Ps. 78:26–31). Each time it was the spring of the year. The bird was called in Heb. *ṡelāw*, and the similarity between the Heb. word and Arab. *salway*, a quail, proves that to be the bird intended. It is the quail of Europe, not of America, is called *Coturnix dactylisonans*, or *communis*, and is placed in the *Tetraonidae* or grouse family, and the *Perdicinae*, or partridge subfamily. It is the smallest species of the partridge type, being only about 7½ inches long. Its general color is brown, with buffy streaks above and buff below. It is migratory, arriving in Palestine from the s. in immense numbers in March, and going s. again at the approach of winter. Quails fly rapidly and well, and take advantage of the wind; but if the wind changes its course, or the birds become exhausted from long flight, the whole immense flock is apt to fall to the ground, where the birds lie stunned (cf. Jos. *Antiq.* iii. 1, 5). In this condition they are captured in great quantities on the coasts and islands of the Mediterranean Sea. The Israelites spread the quails, which they could not eat at once, round about the camp (Num. 11:32) in order to dry them in the sun and air, as the Egyptians did with fish (Herod. ii. 77).

Quar'tus (kwôr'tŭs) [Lat., fourth]. A Corinthian Christian who joined with Paul in sending a salutation to the church of Rome (Rom. 16:23).

Qua·ter'ni·on. Four united persons or things; a guard of 4 soldiers (Acts 12:4). Four quaternions, i.e., 4 companies, each of 4 soldiers, 16 in all, were set to look after Peter when he was in prison at Jerusalem, each quaternion discharging the duty for 1 watch of 3 hours. During the night watches, 2 soldiers slept with the apostle in his cell, while the other 2 mounted guard before the door.

Queen. The consort of a king, or a woman who reigns by her own right. Vashti and Esther were queen consorts (Esth. 1:9; 2: 22). Even after the death of the king her husband, the queen, especially if mother of the new monarch, retained respect and influence (II Kings 10:13); for the practice of polygamy made the position of even the chief wife precarious, and at any time the king might capriciously promote over her head some one of her rivals; but the queen mother, i.e., the mother of the king, had an unalterable relation to the monarch, and was often the most potent female personage (cf. I Kings 2:19; 15:13; II Kings 24:8, 15). Three queens regnant or women who occupied the throne are mentioned in Scripture: Athaliah, who, after perpetrating a massacre of the seed royal, usurped the throne of Judah; the queen of Sheba (I Kings 10:1–13; II Chron. 9:1–12); and Candace, queen of the Ethiopians (Acts 8:27). The last 2, it is believed, came to their high dignity in a perfectly legitimate way.

The queen of heaven was a false divinity in honor of whom the Jews in Jeremiah's time made cakes, burnt incense, and poured out drink offerings (Jer. 7:18; 44:15–30). She was probably the Phoenician goddess Ashtoreth (*q.v.*), or a mother-goddess, whose figurines have been found in Palestine.

Quick'sand'. A sandbank which moves, quick being used in the sense of living. The quicksands of which the sailors on board Paul's ships were afraid (Acts 27:17), and which were the terror of ancient mariners, were 2 in number, the Greater and the Lesser Syrtis, the former constituting the s.e., and the latter the s.w. part of that great indentation in the n. African coast s. of Sicily. The Greater Syrtis, now called the Gulf of Sidra, curves inward on the African coast for about 126 miles, and measures 264 miles between the 2 promontories at its mouth. It is shallow and full of quicksands. The Lesser Syrtis does not run so far inland. At its mouth it measures about 69 miles from the island of Kerkenna on the n. to that of Jerba on the s. It is dangerous to navigate, owing to its winds and tides. It is now called the Gulf of Cabes.

Qui·rin'i·us (kwī-rĭn'ĭ-ŭs), in A.V. **Cy·re'· ni·us**; the former being the original Lat. name, the latter its modification in Gr. A Roman who was governor (*legatus Augusti*) of Syria in A.D. 6 (Jos. *Antiq.* xviii. 1, 1) and who may have exercised authority over Syria as governor or as military commander prior to 2 B.C. According to Luke (ch. 2:1– 5) an enrollment was made which led Joseph to go with Mary his espoused wife to Bethlehem. This visit to Bethlehem took place in the reign of Herod the Great, at the close of the year 5, or beginning of 4, B.C. The enrollment was not a local affair but was made in pursuance of a decree of the Roman emperor Augustus that all the world should be taxed. "This was the first enrollment made when Quirinius was governor of Syria."

Luke's account has presented historians with serious problems. Archaeology has solved certain of them: e.g., it now is known that during the 1st century of our era a census was taken in the Roman Empire every 14 years, that this system was certainly in operation as early as A.D. 20 and probably still earlier, and that it was customary (at least in Egypt) for people to go to their ancestral homes for enrollment. The most troublesome problem which remains involves Luke's chronology, for it makes Quirinius governor of Syria during the lifetime of Herod. From evidence derived from contemporary coins and from the historians Josephus (*Antiq.* xvii. 5, 2, etc.) and Tacitus (*Hist.* 5, 9), it is learned that Sentius Saturninus governed Syria 9–6 B.C. and that Quintilius Varus was in office from 6 B.C. to after the death of Herod (April, 4 B.C.), since he put down a sedition which arose when Herod died. Thus apparently no time is left for the governorship of Quirinius prior to the birth of Jesus in 5 or 4 B.C.

Conservative scholars adopt 1 of 2 theories, each of which is closely connected with a fragmentary Lat. inscription from Tivoli. This fragment, which refers to but does not preserve the name of a legate of Syria, is restored by some first-class scholars (including Mommsen, Ramsay, and Roos) to refer to Quirinius as governor of Syria in 3–2 B.C. Then Luke 2:1 is substantially accurate and is to be interpreted to mean that the command for the enrollment was issued prior to Herod's death (i.e., while Varus was governor) but was actually brought to completion while Quirinius was governor of Syria. The other theory which is favored by most conservatives supposes that while Quirinius was military commander of the troops of Syria (and it is known that some time after c. 11 B.C. he carried on a war with the Homonadenses of Cilicia), he also shared civil duties and prerogatives with Varus. It is further supposed that Quirinius was commissioned by Varus to conduct a census in his (Varus') province. But it must be admitted that this involves assumptions regarding an overlapping of authority that do not possess high probability.

Many scholars believe that Luke mistakenly antedates the enrollment made under Quirinius A.D. 6–7 after Judea had been incorporated into the Roman Empire, an act which was resented as a mark of servitude and occasioned disturbances stirred up by Judas, a Galilean (Acts 5:37; Jos. *Antiq.* xvii. 13, 5; *War* ii. 8, 1). But since Luke's accuracy has been many times vindicated, it is doubtless wisest to await further light from discoveries that may solve the difficulties.

Quiv'er. A case for containing arrows (Isa. 49:2; Lam. 3:13). The Assyrian archers on foot carried the quiver on the back, with the opening usually at the right shoulder, but archers who fought from chariots hung the quiver at the side of the vehicle. The Egyptians also slung the quiver across the back, but they seem to have allowed it to hang horizontally and to have drawn out the arrows from beneath the left arm.

R

Ra'a·mah (rā'a̯-ma̯), in R.V. once **Ra'a·ma** (rā'a̯-ma̯) (I Chron. 1:9), the Heb. spelling in this instance [cf. Arab. *raghama,* to constrain, humiliate]. Collective name for a Cushite people, associated with Sheba (Gen. 10:7; I Chron. 1:9). Men of the 2 tribes brought precious stones and gold to the markets of Tyre (Ezek. 27:22). Raamah is mentioned in inscriptions of Sheba as a place near Ma'īn, in s.w. Arabia; called Regma in LXX and Vulgate.

Ra'a·mi'ah (rā'a̯-mī'a̯) [perhaps, Jehovah has thundered]. See REELAIAH.

Ra·am'ses (ra̯-ăm'sēz). See RAMESES.

Rab'bah (răb'a̯), in A.V. twice **Rab'bath** (Deut. 3:11; Ezek. 21:20), the Heb. form when joined with a following word [great, i.e., the capital]. 1. A city at the headwaters of the Jabbok, 23 miles e. of the Jordan. It was the chief city of the Ammonites. When David was king, the Ammonites defied Israel, prepared for war, and hired auxiliaries from the Aramaeans. The hired army marched to the town of Medeba (I Chron. 19:7; or perhaps "waters of Rabbah"). Joab and the Israelites were encamped before the gate of Rabbah, and presently the Aramaeans pitched camp behind them in the open field. The Israelites were beset before and behind (II Sam. 10:8, 9; I Chron. 19:9). By dividing his forces Joab met and defeated both enemies (II Sam. 10:13, 14). The next spring Joab besieged Rabbah again. During a sally from the gate, Uriah the Hittite was killed. That part of the city lying between the citadel and the river, and called the city of waters, fell into the hands of Joab, but the citadel held out. David was sent for to complete the conquest and associate it with his name. He came, took the city, and condemned the inhabitants to forced labor (II

Sam. 11:1; 12:26–31; I Chron. 20:1–3). In time the Ammonites recovered the city. Judgments were denounced against it by Jeremiah (Jer. 49:2–6) and Ezekiel (Ezek. 21:20). It was embellished by Ptolemy Philadelphus (285–246 B.C.), and in his honor named Philadelphia. This city was the e. limit of Perea (Jos. *War* iii. 3, 3), and the most s. of the 10 cities of the Decapolis. The commercial highway between Damascus and Arabia which skirted the desert passed through it, and there was also a trade road from Philadelphia by way of Gerasa and Pella to Scythopolis. The modern name is 'Ammān, an echo of Ammon.

2. A city, with dependent villages, in the hill country of Judah (Josh. 15:60); probably near Jerusalem and corresponding to Rubute of the Tell el-Amarna tablets.

Rab'bath (răb'ăth). See RABBAH.

Rab'bi, and **Rab·bo'ni.** A doctor, teacher, or master; a respectful term applied by the Jews to their spiritual instructors (Matt. 23:7; John 1:38). The later Jewish schools are said to have had 3 grades of honor: *rab* (master), the lowest; *rabbi* (my master), the 2d; and *rabboni* (my lord, my master), the highest of all. When John wrote, the first person suffix (-*i*) had lost its especial significance as a possessive pronoun, for John explains *rabbi* and *rabboni* as meaning simply master (John 1:38; 20:16).

Rab'bith (răb'ĭth) [multitude]. A frontier village of Issachar (Josh. 19:20). Conder identifies it with the present village of Rāba, among hills 8 miles s. of Mount Gilboa, and 7 s.e. of Jenīn.

Rab·bo'ni. See RABBI.

Rab'-mag (răb'măg). A title of high office, borne by Nergal-sharezer, a chief officer in Nebuchadnezzar's army (Jer. 39:3). The exact meaning is uncertain, but it is probably derived from Akkad. *rab-mugi,* and means great prince.

Rab'-sa·ris (răb'sa̯-rĭs) [probably from Akkad. *rab sha rēshu,* chief who is head, the latter 2 words being modified, to suit the Hebrew ear, into *sārīs,* eunuch]. An official title. A rab-saris accompanied the armies of Sennacherib and Nebuchadnezzar (II Kings 18:17; Jer. 39:3). The officer at Nebuchadnezzar's court who is called master of the eunuchs in the Eng. version and whose title is given in Heb. as *rab sārīsīm* perhaps held the same office (Dan. 1:3).

Rab'sha·keh (răb'sha̯-kĕ) [Akkad. *rab-shākū,* chief cupbearer, head officer, general]. Title of a military official, associated with the tartan and the rab-saris of Sennacherib in command of an expedition against Jerusalem (II Kings 18:17). On this occasion he conducted the parley with the officials of Hezekiah (vs. 19, 26, 27, 37), and was perhaps head of the expedition (ch. 19:8).

Ra·ca' (ra̯-kä') [Aram. *rēḳā,* empty, worthless, good-for-nothing]. An expression of contempt (Matt. 5:22).

Ra'cal (rā'căl), in A.V. **Ra'chal** [trade, commerce]. A place in Judah to which David sent some of the recovered spoil of Ziklag (I Sam. 30:29).

Race. See GAMES.

Ra'chab (rā'kăb). See RAHAB, II.

Ra'chal (rā'kăl). See RACAL.

Ra'chel (rā'chĕl), in A.V. once **Ra'hel** (Jer. 31:15) [ewe]. The younger daughter of Laban. She was possessed of much personal beauty, and Jacob fell in love with her at first sight, when he met her at the well near Haran, in Mesopotamia, where she was watering her flock. Since he possessed no property and it was customary to pay the parents a price for the bride, he served her father 7 years for her, and then, being cheated by the substitution of the elder sister Leah, who was much less highly favored, he served another 7 for the younger maiden, the only one who had gained his affections. He married her also (Gen. 29:1–30), and she became the mother of Joseph (ch. 30:22–25) and Benjamin, dying when the latter was born (chs. 35:16–20; 48:7). She was buried a little to the n. of Ephrath, better known as Bethlehem. The grave was situated at a place which a traveler from Beth-el would reach before he came to Bethlehem. Jacob erected a pillar to mark the spot. This pillar long remained. It was near Zelzah (I Sam. 10:2). The reputed site was alluded to by Jerome and the Bordeaux pilgrim in the 4th century, and is accepted as correct by Jews, Christians, and Mohammedans. The erection called Ḳubbat Raḥîl (Dome of Rachel) is a small building like a mosque, with a dome. It has an open apartment toward the e. and a small enclosure toward the w. The present structure is of no great antiquity; it is located about 4 miles s. of Jerusalem and 1 mile n. of Bethlehem.

It seems, however, that there is a double tradition of the burial place of Rachel. Beth-el is about 11 miles n. of Jerusalem (cf. Gen. 35:16; 48:7), and according to I Sam. 10:2 Rachel's tomb is in the border of Benjamin. About 4 miles n. of Jerusalem lies Ramah, and it seems that Jeremiah (Jer. 31:15) favors the location of the tomb in that region. Matthew (Matt. 2:18), however, makes application of the s. tradition, which places the tomb in the neighborhood of Bethlehem.

The Prophet Jeremiah represents Rachel as weeping for her children, the descendants of her son Joseph, the people of Ephraim and Manasseh who were in captivity (Jer. 31:15; cf. vs. 9, 18). At Ramah was her voice heard; not so much because the prophet foresaw that the captives of Judah and Benjamin would be brought to Ramah after the fall of Jerusalem before being led into exile (ch. 40:1), but either because a town called Ramah was perhaps near Rachel's grave (cf. I Sam. 10:2; see RAMAH 2), or more probably because Ramah was a height in the territory of Rachel's remaining children, the descendants of Benjamin, and near the border of depopulated Ephraim, whence the desolation of the land was visible. This picture which the prophet drew of weeping Rachel found fulfillment in the slaughter of the innocents at Bethlehem in the land of Judah (Matt. 2:18), although the descendants of Leah, not Rachel, wept. Rachel looking on the wasted land of Ephraim, and bewailing her slain and exiled children, was witness that the process had begun which terminated in the possession of the Promised Land by foreigners, the occupation of the throne by an Edomite, and the slaughter of Leah's children in the endeavor to slay the legitimate king and destined Saviour of all Israel, Ephraim, Benjamin, and Judah alike. The picture of Rachel found more than a counterpart in the sorrow of the women of Bethlehem. It found completion, and it found renewed realization. Rachel wept again, this time with Leah. Rachel's hope for the return of her children to the Lord their God and David their king (Jer. 30:9) was bound up in Leah's yearning for that son of David in whose days Judah should be saved and Israel dwell in safety (ch. 23:6). Rachel's cry was the first wail of that lamentation which continued through the centuries and was heard at Bethlehem when a foreign king, in hostility to the son of David, legitimate king of the Jews, was able to send armed men to the city of David and slay the children. The process begun when Rachel first wept was being completed. The prophetic picture was finding final fulfillment.

Rad'dai (răd'à-ī) [perhaps, Jehovah has subdued]. A son of Jesse, and brother of David (I Chron. 2:14).

Ra'gau (rā'gō). See REU.

Ra·gu'el (rȧ-gū'ĕl). See REUEL.

Ra'hab, I (rā'hăb) [Heb. rahab, storm, insolence]. A poetical name for Egypt (Ps. 87:4; 89:10; Isa. 30:7, R.V.; 51:9). In Isa. 51:9 it is parallel with dragon; see DRAGON. In Job 9:13; 26:12, R.V., especially, some interpreters understand a sea monster, and some even discern an allusion to the Semitic myth of the sea monster Tiamat who attempted to reduce the ordered universe to chaos but was subdued by the sun-god Marduk. This interpretation is not necessary, but it is possible. The inspired poets and prophets might borrow the creations of fancy to illustrate truth; see LEVIATHAN.

Ra'hab, II (rā'hăb), in A.V. of N.T. once **Ra'chab** (rā'chăb) [Heb. rāḥāb, broad]. A harlot whose house was on the wall of Jericho. She harbored the spies sent by Joshua to explore the city, hid them when they were searched for, and, finally, let them down by a cord on the outer side of the wall, so that they escaped to the Israelite camp (Josh. 2:1–24). When Jericho was taken, Rahab and her family were spared and incorporated with the chosen people (Josh. 6:22–25; Heb. 11:31; James 2:25). It was probably she who became the wife of Salmon and the mother of Boaz, and a link in the chain of ancestry both of King David and of our Lord (Matt. 1:5).

Ra'ham (rā'hăm) [(God) has been compassionate]. A man of Judah, family of Hezron, house of Caleb (I Chron. 2:44).

Ra'hel (rā'hĕl). See RACHEL.

Rain. See YEAR.

Rain'bow'. A bow appearing in the part of the heavens opposite to the sun, consisting of the prismatic colors, and formed by the refraction and reflection of the sun's rays from drops of rain. After the Flood God selected the rainbow, which had often before been seen in the sky, and appointed or consecrated it as the token of the promise that he would not again destroy the earth by a flood (Gen. 9:12–17). It became the symbol of God's faithfulness and of his beneficence toward man (Rev. 4:3).

Rai'sin. See VINE.

Ra'kem (rā'kĕm) [variegated]. The Heb. pausal form of Rekem. A Manassite (I Chron. 7:16); J.V., Rekem.

Rak'kath (răk'ăth) [Aram., bank, shore]. A fenced city of Naphtali, on the w. shore of the Sea of Galilee (Josh. 19:35). The rabbis place it where Tiberias now stands, but it probably is to be located at Tell Eḳlātiyeh, s. of Magdala (el-Mejdel).

Rak'kon (răk'ŏn) [perhaps, shore]. A village of Dan (Josh. 19:46). Conder suggests as its site Tell er-Reḳḳeit, 2½ miles n. of the mouth of the 'Aujah, and 6 n. of Joppa. The name does not occur in the LXX, and so many consider it a textual corruption of Mejarkon which immediately precedes.

Ram, I. 1. The male of the sheep (Ezek. 34:17). It was used as food (Gen. 31:38), might be brought as a burnt offering or a peace offering (Gen. 22:13; Lev. 1:10; 8:18; and chs. 3:6; 9:4), and was appointed for a guilt or trespass offering (chs. 5:15; 6:6). Rams' skins dyed red were used, with other appliances, as coverings of the tabernacle (Ex. 26:14), and rams' horns as war and apparently jubilee trumpets in the time of Joshua (Josh. 6:4–6, 8, 13). The 2-horned ram seen by Daniel in prophetic vision was the Medo-Persian power, the 1st or smaller horn that came up being the empire of the Medes, the 2d or greater horn which rose at a later period that of the Persians (Dan. 8:3–7, 20).

2. The battering-ram was an instrument of war, used to beat down the gates and walls of a besieged city (Ezek. 4:2; 21:22; Jos. *War* v. 6, 4). It consisted of a log of wood, iron-pointed, swung by ropes from a support above and generally within a tower (Jos. *War* v. 11, 5). In attacking a fort or city, it was often necessary to throw up a mound of earth

called Ramathaim-zophim (cf. ch. 1:1 with v. 19; etc.). The town cannot be located with certainty. 1. It has been identified with Ramah of Benjamin. On this theory the place is rightly described, so it is contended, as situated in the hill country of Ephraim (I Sam. 1:1), and it is different from the unnamed town in the land of Zuph where Saul first met Samuel (ch. 9:5 *seq.*). Robinson called this identification in question, and probably justly, although his opinion has not been followed by all authorities. 2. It lay s. of Benjamin, for (*a*) the passage I Sam. 1:1 does not clearly locate Ramathaim in the hill country of Ephraim, but rather states that a certain man of the family of Zuph dwelt in Ramathaim, a city of the Zophites, who were a branch of the Kohathite Levites, and were called Ephraim-

Attack on a City by Means of Battering-ram and Archers

to serve as an inclined plane and enable the besiegers to bring the battering-ram and other military engines against the walls (Ezek. 4:2).

Ram, II (răm), in A.V. of N.T. **A'ram**, in imitation of the Gr. form [high]. The name assumes various Gr. forms, as Aram, Arran, Arni. 1. A man of Judah, a son of Hezron, and brother of Jerahmeel (Ruth 4:19; I Chron. 2:9; Matt. 1:3; Luke 3:33, R.V., text and marg.).

2. A man of Judah, family of Hezron, house of Jerahmeel (I Chron. 2:25, 27).

3. A descendant of Buz, founder of a family of the Buzites, and an ancestor of Elihu (Job 32:2). He has sometimes been identified with Aram of Gen. 22:21; but Aram was not descended from Buz (nor *vice versa*), and Aram and Ram are different names in Heb.

Ra'mah (rā'má), in A.V. of N.T. **Ra'ma** (rā'má), in imitation of the Gr. [a height]. 1. A town in Benjamin (Josh. 18:25), not far from Gibeah, Geba, and Beth-el (Judg. 4:5; 19:13, 14; Isa. 10:29). It was fortified by Baasha, king of Israel, to keep the people of Judah from making military excursions n. (I Kings 15:17, 21, 22; II Chron. 16:1–6); hence apparently s. of Beth-el. It seems to have been the place where the captives of Judah were massed together before their deportation to Babylon (Jer. 40:1). The town was reoccupied after the Captivity (Ezra 2:26; Neh. 11:33). According to Josephus, Ramah was distant 40 stades from Jerusalem (Jos. *Antiq.* viii. 12, 3). Robinson located it at er-Râm, on a height 5 miles n. of Jerusalem.

2. A town where the parents of Samuel lived (I Sam. 1:19; 2:11; cf. ch. 1:1), where he himself was born and had his residence (chs. 7:17; 8:4; 15:34; 16:13; 19:18, 19, 22, 23; 20:1), and where he was buried (chs. 25:1; 28:3). For the sake of distinction from other towns of similar name it was

ites because their assigned home was in the hill country of Ephraim, whence they had migrated (cf. Josh. 21:5; I Chron. 6:22–26, 35, 66 *seq.*). (*b*) If this be the true interpretation, then the unnamed city where Saul met Samuel is doubtless Ramathaim-zophim, for it is in the land of Zuph. This district lay outside the borders of Benjamin (I Sam. 9:4–6), and s. of Benjamin, i.e., in such a situation that a person going from a city in or quite near to it to Gibeah of Benjamin came to Rachel's sepulcher on the borders of Benjamin (I Sam. 10:2), between Beth-el and Bethlehem (Gen. 35:16, 19). (*c*) It is now plain why Saul did not know the Prophet Samuel by sight, which could scarcely have been the case had the prophet resided at Ramah of Benjamin, only 2½ miles from Saul's home (cf. also I Sam. 8:1, 2). 3. Another location for Ramathaim may be sought in the territory of Ephraim (Jos. *Antiq.* v. 10, 2) where the Zophites dwelt; but not in Benjamin and not the nameless town of I Sam. 9:5. Beit Rima, 13 miles n.e. of Lydda, has been suggested. Compare with caution RAMATHAIM.

3. A town on the boundary line of Asher (Josh. 19:29). If it is not the same town as Ramah of Naphtali (v. 36), its site may be at Râmeh, about 13 miles s.e. by s. of Tyre.

4. A fenced city of Naphtali (Josh. 19:36). It is believed to have been situated at er-Râmeh, about 5 miles s.w. of Safed and 17 e. of Acre.

5. Ramoth-gilead (cf. II Kings 8:28 with v. 29, and II Chron. 22:5 with v. 6).

6. A village in Simeon (Josh. 19:8; A.V., Ramath). It is doubtless the same as Ramoth of the South (I Sam. 30:27); and was also known as Baalath-beer (*q.v.*).

Ra'math (rā'măth) [height], the Heb. form of Ramah when joined to a following word. A village of Simeon (Josh. 19:8, in R.V. Ramah), known also as Ramoth of the South (I Sam. 30:27). See RAMAH 6.

Ra'ma·tha'im (rā'má-thā'ĭm), in A.V. **Ram'·a·them** (răm'á-thĕm) [twin heights]. A town which gave name to 1 of 3 governmental districts which were detached from Samaria and added to Judea (I Macc. 11:34; cf. ch. 10: 30, 38). Its location must be sought near the s. border of Ephraim.

Ra'ma·thaim-zo'phim (rā'má-thā'ĭm-zō'fĭm) [the twin heights (of the) Zophites]. The residence of Samuel's father (I Sam. 1:1); see RAMAH 2.

Ra'math·ite (rā'măth-īt). A native or inhabitant of any town called Ramah (I Chron. 27:27). Which of them is referred to in the passage is not known.

Ra'math-le'hi (rā'măth-lē'hī). See LEHI.

Ra'math-miz'peh (rā'măth-mĭz'pĕ). See MIZPAH 2.

Ram'e·ses [from Egypt. *R'-ms-św*, (the sun-god) Re is the one who has begotten him]. A town of Egypt. It was in the most fertile district of the country (Gen. 47:11), the land of Goshen (v. 6), the region where Pharaoh bade Joseph locate his father and brothers. Ramesses II built a town on the e. frontier of Egypt and gave it his own name. Perhaps it was the same as the store city Raamses, which the Israelites built for Pharaoh (Ex. 1:11); see EGYPT, III. 8. At the Exodus the Israelites marched from Rameses to Succoth (ch. 12:37); Avaris, Rameses, and Tanis were all successive phases of the same city and are to be located at Șan el-Ḥagar. See ZOAN.

Ra·mi'ah (rá-mī'á) [exalted is Jehovah]. A son of Parosh, induced by Ezra to put away his foreign wife (Ezra 10:25).

Ra'moth (rā'mŏth) [high places, height]. 1. A son of Bani, induced by Ezra to put away his foreign wife (Ezra 10:29). The R.V. reads Jeremoth in the text, and relegates Ramoth to the marg.
2. A town of Issachar, assigned for residence to the Gershonite Levites (I Chron. 6: 73); see JARMUTH 2.
3. A town in Gilead; see RAMOTH-GILEAD.
4. A town of the South (I Sam. 30:27); see RAMAH 6.

Ra'moth-gil'e·ad (rā'mŏth-gĭl'ê-ăd) [heights of Gilead]. See MIZPAH 2.

Ram'ses (răm'sēz). A method of Anglicizing the name of the Egypt. Pharaoh *R'-ms-św;* now generally called Ramesses. See EGYPT II. 3 (4) and RAMESES.

Ra'phah (rā'fá) and **Ra'pha** (rā'fá) [he (God) has healed]. 1. A son of Benjamin (I Chron. 8:2); but he is not enumerated with those who accompanied Jacob into Egypt (Gen. 46:21), and was probably born after the descent into Egypt. He did not found a tribal family; his descendants, if there were any, were included in other families of the Benjamites.
2. A descendant of Jonathan (I Chron. 8: 37). Called in ch. 9:43 Rephaiah, a synonymous name.

Ra'phon (rā'fŏn). A town of Gilead, besieged by the Ammonites, but relieved by Judas Maccabaeus (I Macc. 5:37). It was apparently not far from Carnaim (v. 43). It probably is Raphana, which was one of the original cities constituting the Decapolis, and was situated s. of the Sea of Galilee and e. of the Jordan.

Ra'phu (rā'fū) [healed, cured]. A Benjamite, father of Palti (Num. 13:9).

Ras Sham'ra (räs shäm'rá) [Arab., Fennel Head]. Ras Shamra (ancient Ugarit) is on the Mediterranean about 10 miles n. of Lata-

kia and about 25 s.w. of Antioch; it lies directly opposite the extreme e. point of Cyprus. Here were found between 1929 and 1939 several hundred clay tablets and fragments written in a cuneiform alphabet. The language, known as Ugaritic, is a Canaanite dialect and is closely related to proto-Hebrew. Among the literature are several Canaanite epics relating to Baal and Anath, Dan'el and Akhat, Keret, etc. Some of the tablets contain hymns, liturgies, rituals, and documents concerning temple administration. The date of these records of Canaanite religion and mythology is c. 1400 B.C., but the original compositions are much older and probably were handed down orally for a long time before they were reduced to writing. These tablets are of special importance for the light they shed on Canaanite religion and the many parallels they offer to the O.T. in vocabulary and poetic style.

Ra'ven. A bird, black in color (S. of Sol. 5:11), omnivorous, feeding even on carrion (Prov. 30:17), and hence ceremonially unclean (Lev. 11:15). Noah sent 1 forth from the ark. It did not return to him, finding, doubtless, floating carcasses on which it was able to feed (Gen. 8:7). It frequents valleys (Prov. 30:17), and makes its nest in solitary places (Isa. 34:11). By divine providence ravens fed Elijah with bread and flesh morning and evening at the brook Cherith during the drought and famine (I Kings 17:2–7). The consonants of the words for ravens and Arabs are the same in Heb.; and when the text is written without vowels, as originally, it is impossible to determine, if the context does not decide, whether Arabs or ravens are meant. It is generally admitted now that the LXX and Vulgate are right, and that the Hebrew writer intends to state that Elijah was fed by ravens. The bird referred to in Scripture is undoubtedly the common raven (*Corvus corax*), which is found in every part of Palestine. It is black, with steel-blue and purple iridescence, and is about 26 inches long. The name is broad enough, however, to include other *Corvidae*. Another species (*Corvus umbrinus*) occurs in s. Palestine and in the valley of the Jordan.

Ra'zor. A sharp instrument for removing the beard or hair (Isa. 7:20; Ezek. 5:1). See KNIFE, BEARD, HAIR.

Re·a'iah (rê-ā'yá), in A.V. once **Re·a'ia** (rê-ā'yá) (I Chron. 5:5) [Jehovah has seen, or provided for]. 1. A son of Shobal, and descended from Judah through Hezron (I Chron. 4:2), called in ch. 2:52 Haroeh, i.e., the seeing One.
2. A Reubenite (I Chron. 5:5).
3. Founder of a family of Nethinim, members of which returned from captivity (Ezra 2:47; Neh. 7:50).

Re'ba (rē'bá) [perhaps, a 4th part or quarter]. One of the 5 Midianite kings, allies or vassals of Sihon, slain by the Israelites in the war waged by Moses against Midian, because they seduced Israel to licentious idolatry (Num. 31:8; Josh. 13:21).

Re·bek'ah (rê-bĕk'á), in N.T. **Re·bec'ca** (rê-bĕk'á) (Rom. 9:10) [cf. Arab. *rabaķa*, to tie, bind; *rabķah, ribķah,* loop of a rope. Perhaps by metathesis of *r*; cf. Arab. *baķarah*, cow; Heb. *bāķār*, cattle]. A daughter of Bethuel. When she came with her pitcher to a well near the city of Nahor, in Mesopotamia, the servant of Abraham, who had been sent to obtain a wife for Isaac, presented himself and asked permission to drink from her pitcher. She not only granted his request but volunteered to draw water for his camels. He had asked God for this very sign; her conduct showed that she was of a generous disposition; he saw that she was beautiful; and he at once gave her expensive presents, as for a future bride. He did not at the time know her name, but asked what it was, and then added the inquiry whether he might lodge at her father's house. When her brother Laban's consent had been obtained, the delegate took up his temporary residence in their dwelling, and explained the object of his journey to Mesopotamia. He ended by petitioning that Rebekah should accompany him to Canaan and become the wife of Isaac. Laban gave his consent, and the maiden, adding hers, went with the servant, married Isaac, and became the mother of Esau and Jacob (Gen. 24:1–67). She preferred Jacob to Esau; and although she had the prophecy that Jacob should have the pre-eminence, she did not leave the matter in God's hands, but suggested a deceit by which the younger obtained the blessing belonging by birth to the elder (chs. 25:28; 27:1 to 28:5). She died apparently while Jacob was in Mesopotamia, and was buried in the cave of Machpelah (ch. 49:31).

Re'cah (rē'kà), in A.V. **Re'chah**. An unknown place in the tribe of Judah (I Chron. 4:12).

Re'chab (rē'kăb) [horseman, charioteer].
1. A son of Rimmon, a Beerothite. He was a captain of a band under Ish-bosheth and one of Ish-bosheth's murderers (II Sam. 4:2, 6).
2. A Kenite (I Chron. 2:55), father of that Jehonadab who was invited by Jehu to mount his chariot and see his zeal for the Lord (II Kings 10:15, 16, 23), and who placed his tribe under a rule of life. See RECHABITES.
3. Father of Malchijah, the ruler of Beth-haccherem (Neh. 3:14).

Rech'ab·ites (rĕk'à-bīts). A Kenite tribe, which dwelt among the Israelites. Their chief Jonadab, son of Rechab, commanded them to abstain from wine and all intoxicating liquor, not to live in houses, or plant or possess vineyards, but to dwell in tents. The object of these regulations was the preservation of primitive simplicity of manners. When Jeremiah tested their obedience years later, he found them faithful. A promise was therefore given them that they should never want a man to represent them in all succeeding time (Jer. 35:1–19). Professed descendants of the sect still exist in Mesopotamia and Yemen.

Re'chah (rē'kà). See RECAH.

Re·cord'er. An official of high rank in the Hebrew government from the time of David onward. He was called *mazkîr*, one who brings to mind, or remembrancer, and probably derived his title from his official duty of recording important events and advising the king respecting them. At any rate he held one of the highest offices of state. He was numbered among the chief officials of David and Solomon (II Sam. 8:16; I Kings 4:3). The prefect of the palace, the scribe, and the recorder represented Hezekiah in public business (II Kings 18:18, 37); and in the reign of Josiah the scribe, the governor of the city and the recorder were placed in charge of the repairs of the Temple (II Chron. 34:8).

Red Sea. The sea called by the Hebrews *yam sûph*, or sea of reeds. The Gr. term, of which Red Sea is the literal translation, is *erythra thalassa*, used by Herodotus (ii. 8), the LXX (Ex. 15:4, 22), Josephus (*Antiq.* ii. 11, 1; 15, 1), but the origin of the term is uncertain. The Greeks derived the name from Erythras, a fabulous king who reigned in the adjacent country (Strabo xvi. 3, 5; 4, 20; Pliny *Hist. Nat.* vi. 23). He possibly corresponds to Edom, or represents the red- or copper-skinned people, including Edomites, Himyarites, and original Phoenicians. Some would derive the name from reddish corals

which cover the floor or line the shores of this sea. "The Eocene and Cretaceous limestones assume by weathering a rich reddish-brown hue, and under the evening sun the eastern range glows with a ruddy radiance, which in the morning is equally seen on the western cliffs, while these colors contrast with the clear greenish-blue of the sea itself. Such an appearance would naturally suggest to early voyagers the name Red Sea" (Dawson, *Egypt and Syria*, 59). In I Kings 9:26, by reading Heb. *sûph* (sedge, reeds) as *sôph* (end), the LXX renders the name as the Uttermost Sea.

By the Erythraean Sea, the ancients understood not merely the Red Sea as limited by modern geographers, but also the Indian Ocean and ultimately the Persian Gulf. In the restricted sense in which the term is used in modern geography, the Red Sea is about 1,490 miles long, with an average breadth of about 150 miles. At its n. part it terminates in 2 gulfs, Suez and 'Akabah, which enclose between them the Sinaitic Peninsula. The Gulf of 'Akabah lies on the e., and is about 100 miles long by 15 broad. At its n. end stood the towns of Elath and Ezion-geber. The Gulf of Suez, on the w. of the peninsula, is about 180 miles long by 20 broad; but it formerly extended farther n. and included, in prehistoric times at least, Lake Timsah and the Bitter Lakes. The shores of both lakes abound in reeds, and this feature sufficiently accounts for the Heb. designation, "sea of sedge." The Heb. term *yam sûph* denotes the Red Sea of modern geography, or at least so much of it as embraces the peninsula of Sinai; for it lay to the e. of Egypt (Ex. 10:19), on it was an encampment of the Israelites not far from Sinai (Num. 33:10, 11), by taking the way of the *yam sûph* the Israelites compassed the land of Edom (ch. 21:4), and Ezion-geber in the land of Edom was on this sea (I Kings 9:26). The *yam sûph* was crossed by the Israelites, and the pursuing Egyptian hosts sank into its depths (Ex. 15:4, 22). The general opinion, based on constant Scripture representation, is that the sea crossed by the Israelites was the Gulf of Suez, probably at a point immediately n. or just s. of the Bitter Lakes.

The navigation of the sea is at all times somewhat perilous, from the sudden changes of the wind and the strength with which it often blows. The voyage from end to end was rendered slow by the prevalent wind in the n. part of the sea blowing toward the s. during 9 months of the year, and in the s. part blowing n. during the same period. Besides this, the mariner has to be on his guard against coral reefs and small islands, which in many places rise above the surface of the sea.

Reed. 1. Any tall, broad-leaved grass growing in a wet place. It is called *ḳâneh* in Heb., *kalamos* in Gr. (cf. Isa. 42:3 with Matt. 12:20). It grows or grew in the Nile and elsewhere in the water (I Kings 14:15; Isa. 19:6; 35:7), and is so tall and in such abundance that it helps to furnish shelter and concealment even for the bulky hippopotamus (Job 40:21). It is easily shaken by the wind (I Kings 14:15), and so fragile that if one leans upon it, it will break into a ragged fracture, the projecting points entering and piercing the hand (II Kings 18:21; Isa. 36:6; Ezek. 29:6, 7). In this last respect it affords a lively picture of the treatment Egypt had given to the Israelites when they leaned upon that power in seasons of emergency. It was a reed which the persecutors of our Lord thrust into his hand for a scepter, and with which they afterward struck him on the head; and it was to this or another stem of the same plant that the sponge was affixed which they dipped in vinegar and put to his lips (Matt. 27:29, 30, 48). The plant referred to is probably *Arundo donax*, which grows in the Nile and is common throughout Palestine, is at least 10 feet high, and has leaves as long and as broad as those of a sword. It is cultivated in France, where its long, straight, and light stems are made into fishing rods, arrows, fences, poles for vines.

A reed stalk was used as a measuring rod, and came to denote a fixed length of 6 long cubits (Ezek. 40:5; 41:8). Likewise in Babylonia 6 cubits made a reed or *ḳanu*.

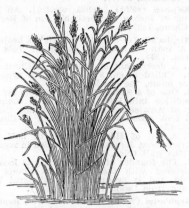

Reed (*Arundo donax*)

2. The rendering, by metonomy, in Jer. 51:32 of Heb. *'ăgam*, a marsh. R.V. marg. renders it marshes; J.V., castles.

Re'el·a'iah (rē'ĕl-ā'yȧ) [perhaps, Jehovah has shaken]. One of the leading men who accompanied Zerubbabel and Jeshua from Babylon (Ezra 2:2). Called Raamiah in Neh. 7:7.

Re·fin'er. One who refines the precious metals, as silver or gold, by causing them to pass repeatedly through the furnace till their dross is taken away (Zech. 13:9; cf. Ps. 12:6). It is said that the refiner knows when the process is complete by seeing his image reflected in the precious metal purified. God is compared to a refiner of silver, by which is meant that he casts his people into the furnace of affliction till they are refined and purified (Mal. 3:2, 3). Then they clearly reflect his image in their souls.

Ref'uge. See CITY OF REFUGE.

Re'gem (rē'gĕm) [ety. uncertain; cf. Arab. *ragm*, friend]. A man of Judah, a son of Jahdai (I Chron. 2:47).

Re'gem-me'lech (rē'gĕm-mē'lĕk) [perhaps, friend of king]. A man sent from Beth-el with companions to put a question to the priests regarding fasting (Zech. 7:2); the Peshitta reads *Rab-māg* (cf. Jer. 39:3, 13).

Re·ha·bi'ah (rē'hȧ-bī'ȧ) [Jehovah is comprehensive, or has extended]. Son of Eliezer, and grandson of Moses (I Chron. 23:17; 24; 21; 26:25).

Re'hob (rē'hŏb) [open space, broad street]. 1. A place situated toward Hamath; see BETH-REHOB.
2. A town on the boundary line of the territory of Asher (Josh. 19:28), probably to be identified with Khirbet el-'Amri. The Rehob which belonged to Asher (Josh. 19:30) is probably to be identified with Tell Berweh. From Rehob the Canaanites were not expelled

(Judg. 1:31). Rehob was assigned to the Levites (Josh. 21:31; I Chron. 6:75).
3. Father of Hadadezer, king of Zobah (II Sam. 8:3, 12).
4. A Levite who sealed the covenant (Neh. 10:11).

Re'ho·bo'am (rē'hô-bō'ăm), in A.V. of N.T. **Ro·bo'am** [the people is enlarged; or perhaps, the (divine) uncle or kinsman has enlarged]. Son of King Solomon by Naamah, an Ammonitess, one of his wives (I Kings 14:31). Although son of a wise father, he was himself a man of small mind. On the death of Solomon about 931 B.C., representatives of all the 12 tribes promptly assembled at the central city of Shechem to make Rehoboam, who was his lawful successor, king. Various causes more or less remote had led to jealousy and a growing coldness between Judah and the tribes to the n. and e.; see HISTORY, III. 3. Recently the people had suffered under heavy taxation levied to support Solomon's splendor, and opportunity was taken to lay this grievance of the people before the future ruler. The spokesman was Jeroboam, an able man who had been an official under Solomon and had been told by the Prophet Ahijah that he should become king of 10 tribes. The popular demand was that taxation might be lightened. Rehoboam asked 3 days for deliberation. He consulted the old men who had till lately been counselors of his father; they advised him to accede to the request and speak good words to the petitioners, and assured him that the people would then be his servants forever. He next consulted the young men who had grown up with him, and they urged him to say to the people: "My little finger is thicker than my father's loins. And now whereas my father did lade you with a heavy yoke, I will add to your yoke: my father chastised you with whips, but I will chastise you with scorpions." It indicated the mental caliber of Rehoboam that he rejected the counsel of the sages and uttered the words of folly which his young companions had put into his mouth. At once 10 out of the 12 tribes renounced their allegiance to Rehoboam, departed to their homes, and were forever lost to the house of David. The king sent after them Adoram, who was over the tribute, but they stoned him to death, and the king, fearing that the next missiles would be directed against himself, hastily mounted his chariot and drove to Jerusalem (I Kings 12:1-20; II Chron. 10:1-19). Judah and a large part of Benjamin, together with the Simeonites, were left him. He mustered the entire militia of his kingdom to attempt the subjugation of the revolted tribes, but the Prophet Shemaiah forbade the enterprise (I Kings 12:21-24; II Chron. 11:1-4). He therefore contented himself with fortifying a number of cities in Judah and Benjamin and provisioning the garrisons (II Chron. 11:5-12). The erection of the golden calves by his rival at Beth-el and Dan drove s. almost the whole body of the priests and Levites, which greatly increased the strength of the kingdom of Rehoboam; but after 3 years he himself lapsed into idolatry (I Kings 14:21-24; II Chron. 11:13-17; 12:1). In the 5th year of his reign, Shishak, king of Egypt, invaded his kingdom, capturing some of the fenced cities, ultimately taking Jerusalem itself and plundering the Temple and the palace (I Kings 14:25-28; II Chron. 12:2-12); see PHARAOH 1. Rehoboam had 18 wives and 60 concubines, 28 sons and 60 daughters (II Chron. 11:21). Abijah his son claimed that at the time of his great mistake he was young and tenderhearted (ch. 13:1-12); in reality, he was at that time 41 years old. He reigned 17 years, and died about 915 B.C., leaving his son, Abijah, to ascend the throne (I Kings 14:21, 31; II Chron. 12:13, 16).

Re•ho'both (rê-hō'bŏth) [broad places, streets]. 1. A well dug by Isaac in the valley of Gerar. Since the Philistine herdsmen did not claim it, as they had its 2 predecessors, he named it Rehoboth, meaning room (Gen. 26:22). Robinson identified the valley as Wadi Ruḥaibeh, about 19 miles s.w. of Beersheba.

2. A suburb of Nineveh (Gen. 10:11); see REHOBOTH-IR.

3. A town "by the River" (Gen. 36:37; I Chron. 1:48). "The River" commonly denotes the Euphrates, but since the reference is to Edom, the river here must be used in a different sense. The river probably is the Sail el-Ḳerāḥi, which flows into the Dead Sea near its s.e. extremity. There is a place of slight importance Khirbet Riḥāb, but on Jebel Riḥāb about 3 miles to the w. is Khirbet Musrab, which probably corresponds to Rehoboth; the military post may be placed farther w.n.w. in the direction of the extremity of the Dead Sea, at Khirbet Bīr Meliḥ.

Re•ho'both-Ir (rê-hō'bŏth-ĭr) [broad places of the city]. A city which formed part of the great city of Nineveh or, as we would say, Greater Nineveh (Gen. 10:11; in A.V. the city Rehoboth).

Re'hum (rē'hŭm) [beloved]. 1. A chancellor of Persia in the country beyond the River, who in the time of Artaxerxes complained against the Jews for rebuilding the Temple (Ezra 4:8, 9).

2. One of the principal men who returned with Zerubbabel from Babylon (Ezra 2:2); called Nehum in Neh. 7:7, probably through a copyist's error.

3. A chief of the priests, who returned with Zerubbabel from Babylon (Neh. 12:1–7). In the next generation a father's house, occupying the corresponding position in the enumeration, bears the name Harim (v. 15). One of these names has probably been miswritten by transposing the Heb. letters.

4. One of those who with Nehemiah sealed the covenant (Neh. 10:25).

5. A Levite, son of Bani. He repaired part of the wall of Jerusalem (Neh. 3:17).

Re'i (rē'ī) [friendly, sociable]. One who did not join in Adonijah's attempt to usurp the throne (I Kings 1:8).

Reins. The kidneys. They were supposed by the ancient Hebrews and others to be the seat of the innermost emotions (A.V. and R.V. marg. of Ps. 7:9; 26:2; 73:21; Prov. 23:16; Jer. 12:2).

Re'kem (rē'kĕm) [variegation]. 1. One of the 5 kings of Midian, allies or vassals of Sihon, slain in the war waged by Moses against the Midianites because they had seduced Israelites to licentious idolatry (Num. 31:8; Josh. 13:21).

2. A son of Hebron, a descendant of Caleb (I Chron. 2:43).

3. A city of the Benjamites (Josh. 18:27); probably to be located at Ḳalandiyeh.

Rem•a•li'ah (rĕm'á-lī'á) [S. Arab., soothsayer of Jehovah]. Father of King Pekah (II Kings 15:25).

Re'meth (rē'mĕth) [probably, a high place]. A frontier town of Issachar (Josh. 19:21). See JARMUTH 2.

Rem'mon (rĕm'ŏn) and **Rem'mon-meth'o•ar** (rĕm'ŏn-mĕth'ō-är). See RIMMON, I. 2 and 3.

Rem'nant. The portion of the people that survives the judgment sent to remove the dross from the Kingdom of God (Ezra 9:8; Zech. 14:2). Because of Jehovah's love for his people, this godly remnant shall be gathered from the nations among which Israel has been scattered and form the nucleus of a new Israel, holy, living in accordance with Jehovah's Law, loyal to him, and defended and blessed by him (Isa. 1:26; 4:2–6; 6:13; 10:20–23; 11:11 to 12:6; Jer. 23:3; 32:36–44; Amos 9:8–15; Micah 4:6–8; 5:7, 8; Zeph. 3:13; Zech. 8:12; 13:9).

Rem'phan (rĕm'făn). See REPHAN.

Re'pha•el (rē'fá-ĕl) [God has healed]. A Levite, son of Shemaiah, of the family of Obed-edom, and a doorkeeper of the sanctuary (I Chron. 26:7).

Re'phah (rē'fá) [riches, wealth]. An ancestor of Joshua and probably son of Beriah (I Chron. 7:25).

Re•pha'iah (rē-fā'yá) [Jehovah has healed]. 1. A man of Issachar, family of Tola (I Chron. 7:2).

2. A descendant of Jonathan (I Chron. 9:43). Called in ch. 8:37 Raphah, a synonymous name, "he has healed."

3. One of 4 Simeonite captains who led an expedition into Edom, destroyed a community of Amalekites who were dwelling there, and took possession of their land (I Chron. 4:42, 43).

4. A son of Hur and ruler of half the district about Jerusalem, who aided in repairing the wall (Neh. 3:9).

5. The founder of a family that is loosely registered with the royal descendants of David and is presumably a collateral line sprung from David (I Chron. 3:21).

Reph'a•im (rĕf'á-ĭm), in A.V. twice **Reph'a•ims** (rĕf'á-ĭmz) (Gen. 14:5; 15:20) [shades of the dead, spirits of the departed, extinct aborigines, giants]. 1. A people of large stature who in ancient times, even before the arrival of Abraham, dwelt in Palestine, e. and w. of the Jordan (Gen. 14:5; 15:20; Deut. 2:11, 20; 3:11; Josh. 17:15). A remnant of them appears to have taken refuge among the Philistines, when the Hebrews entered Canaan (II Sam. 21:16, 18, 20, 21, R.V. marg.).

2. A valley near Jerusalem and Bethlehem (Jos. *Antiq.* vii. 4, 1; II Sam. 23:13, 14), s.w. of Jerusalem and the valley of Hinnom (Josh. 15:8; 18:16); quite fertile (Isa. 17:5); presumably once inhabited by the Rephaim. The Philistines were twice defeated there by David (II Sam. 5:18–22; 23:13; I Chron. 11:15; 14:9). It is probably the broad valley called Baḳā', about 3 miles long, lying s.w. of Jerusalem, beginning beyond the ravine that bounds the city on the s. and w., and extending halfway to Bethlehem. It declines rapidly toward the w. and is stony but fertile.

Re'phan (rē'făn), in A.V. **Rem'phan**. A god who has a star associated with him, and who was worshiped by the Israelites in the wilderness (Acts 7:43). The passage is quoted from the O.T. The name represents *Raiphan*, a corrupt transliteration in the LXX of *Kaiwān* (*Kēwān*), which is the same as *Kaimānu*, Akkad. name of Saturn and was understood to be the god Chiun (Amos 5:26, A.V. and J.V.). See CHIUN, SICCUTH.

Reph'i•dim (rĕf'ĭ-dĭm) [expanses, stretches]. A camping ground of the Israelites in the wilderness between the wilderness of Sin and Sinai (Ex. 17:1; 19:2; Num. 33:12–15). There was no water obtainable, and the people murmured till Moses, accompanied by elders, went forward to Horeb by divine command and smote a rock, from which water at once issued (Ex. 17:5, 6). The water flowed down the wadi to the camp of the Israelites and supplied them during their sojourn at Mount Sinai also. Rephidim was the scene of the battle with Amalek, when Moses with uplifted hand pointed to Jehovah as the ensign under which Israel fought (Ex. 17:8-16). The site is not properly determined. The place probably is to be located on Wadi Refâyied, n.w. of Jebel Mûsa. Wadi Redwa, a stream of cold water, joins Wadi Refâyied, which has an oasis at the foot of Jebel Refâyied.

Re'sen (rē'sĕn). A city of Assyria, a suburb of Nineveh, a part of the complex of towns known as the great city. It was situated between Nineveh and Calah (Gen. 10:11, 12).

Resh (rĕsh). The 20th letter of the Heb. alphabet. English *r* comes by way of Gr. *rho* from the same source, and represents it in Anglicized Heb. names. It heads the 20th section of Psalm 119, in which section each verse of the original begins with this letter.

Copyists sometimes had difficulty in distinguishing *resh* from *daleth* (*q.v.*).

Re'sheph (rē'shĕf) [a flame]. A descendant of Ephraim and probably son of Beriah (I Chron. 7:25).

Re·turn'. See HISTORY, III. 4, and CHRONOLOGY, V, beginning with the year 539 B.C.

Re'u (rē'ū), in A.V. once **Ra'gau** (Luke 3:35) [one exercising oversight, shepherd, friend]. A descendant of Eber and an ancestor of Abraham (Gen. 11:18-26).

Reu'ben (rōō'bĕn) [behold a son; but cf. S. Arab. *Ra'bān*, chief]. 1. Jacob's eldest son, the 1st by his wife Leah (Gen. 29:31, 32; 35:23; 46:8; I Chron. 2:1; 5:1). Reuben was guilty of gross misconduct (Gen. 35:22); but when his brothers plotted to kill Joseph, Reuben came forward with the proposal to cast him into a pit, designing to restore him eventually to his father. He was not with them when Joseph was sold to the Midianite Ishmaelites, and was greatly moved when, visiting the pit, he found it empty (Gen. 37:21-29). When the brothers found themselves in trouble in Egypt 20 years later, Reuben was quick to remind his brothers that he had not concurred in their plot to take Joseph's life (ch. 42:22-24). When Jacob was reluctant to send Benjamin to Egypt, Reuben offered 2 of his sons as pledge that he would bring Benjamin home again in safety (ch. 42:37). Reuben had 4 sons in all: Hanoch, Phallu, Hezron, and Carmi (Gen. 46:8, 9; Ex. 6:14; I Chron. 5:3). Jacob, when about to die, pronounced Reuben to be unstable as water and declared that he should not have pre-eminence. By his heinous deed he had forfeited the birthright (Gen. 49:3, 4).

2. The tribe formed by descendants of Reuben, and the territory in which they dwelt. The tribe was divided into 4 great tribal families, the posterity of Reuben's 4 sons (Num. 26:5-11). Its prince at the beginning of the sojourn in the wilderness was Elizur (Num. 1:5; 2:10; 7:30-35; 10:18). At that time the tribe numbered 46,500 fighting men (ch. 1:20, 21); at the 2d census 38 years later, they had decreased to 43,730 (ch. 26:7). The Reubenite chief was head of the camp made up of the 3 tribes, Reuben, Simeon, and Gad, the aggregate military strength of which was 151,450 (Num. 2:10, 16). The spy from the tribe was Shammua, son of Zaccur (ch. 13:4). Dathan, Abiram, and On, who joined the Levite Korah in revolt against Moses and Aaron, were Reubenites (Num. 16:1-50; 26:9; Deut. 11:6); see KORAH 4. After the battles with Sihon and Og, the Gadites and Reubenites, with whom half the tribe of Manesseh joined, being rich in cattle, petitioned Moses to be allowed to settle e. of the Jordan, that region being well adapted for flocks and herds. Their request was granted on condition that they would send the greater number of their warriors across the Jordan

to help their brethren in the war with the Canaanites (Num. 32:1-42; Josh. 18:7). They did so, and took part in all of Joshua's wars in Canaan (Josh. 4:12). Afterward they returned with honor to their own territory. But the erection of a memorial altar by them and their Israelite brethren e. of Jordan led to a temporary misunderstanding which nearly involved them in civil war (Josh. 22:1-34). The Reubenites took no part in the contest with Sisera and were referred to reproachfully in Deborah's song (Judg. 5:15, 16). They made war against the Hagarites, in which they prevailed; the victors made a great slaughter of the enemy and lived in their territory to the time of the Captivity (I Chron. 5:18-22). Ezekiel allotted them a place in the reoccupied Canaan (Ezek. 48:6, 7), and named a gate after them in the restored Jerusalem (v. 31). When the book of Revelation records the sealing of the 144,-000, it assigns Reuben a quota of 12,000 (Rev. 7:5). The boundary of the territory of Reuben was on the e. the country of the Ammonites, on the s. the river Arnon (Num. 21:24), on the w. the Dead Sea and the river Jordan (Josh. 13:23), while on the n. the boundary line ran from the Jordan s. of Beth-nimrah to Heshbon (Josh. 13:17, 26; 21:37; and Num. 32:36; Josh. 13:27). Included in these limits were Aroer, on the edge of the valley of Arnon, and the city in the middle of the valley, all the plain by Medeba, Heshbon and its subordinate towns, Dibon, Bamoth-baal, Beth-baal-meon, Jahaz, Kedemoth, Mephaath, Kiriathaim, Sibmah, Zereth-shahar, Beth-peor, the slopes of Pisgah, Beth-jeshimoth; in short, the s. part of the Ammonite kingdom which had been ruled over by Sihon (Josh. 13:15-23). The 4 cities of Bezer, Jahaz, Kedemoth, and Mephaath, with their suburbs, were assigned to the ¡Merarite Levites (Josh. 21:7, 36, 37; I Chron. 6:63, 78, 79); the 1st of these, Bezer, was a city of refuge (Josh. 20:8; I Chron. 6:78). The Reubenites had an exposed position, the Moabites being in their immediate vicinity, while desert marauders could invade their territory both from the e. and the s. If the list of Reubenite cities given in this section is compared with those in Moabite possession incidentally mentioned in Isa., chs. 15; 16; Jer., ch. 48, and on the Moabite stone, it will be seen that in the times of Mesha and these prophets Reuben had its limits greatly curtailed by Moabite conquest. The whole territory is a tableland quite capable of cultivation.

Reu'el (rōō'ĕl), in A.V. once **Ra·gu'el** (Num. 10:29) in imitation of the Gr. form [God is a friend, or friend of God]. 1. A descendant of Esau and also of Ishmael (Gen. 36:2-4).

2. Moses' father-in-law (Ex. 2:18). See JETHRO.

3. A Benjamite, a son of Ibnijah (I Chron. 9:8).

4. A Gadite, father of Eliasaph (Num. 2:14); see DEUEL.

Reu'mah (rōō'mȧ) [exalted]. A concubine of Nahor, Abraham's brother (Gen. 22:24).

Rev·e·la'tion [Lat. *revelatio*, unveiling; hence to reveal, to expose to sight, and, metaphorically, to disclose to the mind truth otherwise unknown; Gr. *Apokalypsis*, whence Eng. Apocalypse]. In the O.T. the noun revelation does not occur; but the verb reveal is used in the sense of making known secrets (e.g., Prov. 11:13) and then of God's disclosure of his will to man (e.g., Deut. 29:29; Isa. 22:14; Dan. 2:19, 22, 28; Amos 3:7). In the N.T. revelation is used for the disclosure by God or Christ or the Spirit of truth concerning divine things previously unknown (e.g.. Rom. 16:25; I Cor. 14:6, 26; II

Cor. 12:1; Gal. 1:12; Rev. 1:1) or of duty specially required (Gal. 2:2), and then for the manifestation or appearance of persons or events previously concealed from sight (e.g., Rom. 2:5; I Peter 1:13). In theology revelation means the communication of truth by God to man, and is usually applied to such communications as have been conveyed through supernatural agencies.

The Revelation of John is the last book of the N.T., also called, from the Gr., the Apocalypse. The name is given to it because, as its opening words state, it is a disclosure of the future, and, therefore, pre-eminently a revelation. Its author describes it as a communication concerning "things which must shortly come to pass," which God gave to Jesus Christ, and which Christ gave by his angel to his servant John, to be communicated in turn to the Church (Rev. 1:1-3). The work is addressed to 7 churches of the Roman province of Asia: Ephesus, Smyrna, Pergamum, Thyatira, Sardis, Philadelphia, and Laodicea (vs. 4, 11), the number 7 being selected probably because, as the sacred number, it signified completeness, and thus indicated that the book was really addressed to the whole Church. The author calls himself, after the manner of the Hebrew prophets (cf. Isa. 1:1; Joel 1:1; Amos 1:1, etc.), simply John (Rev. 1:1, 4, 9; 22:8), and relates that the visions of the book were seen by him when he was in the island of Patmos "for the word of God and the testimony of Jesus" (ch. 1:9). Patmos lies off the s.w. coast of Asia Minor, and John had been banished to it because he was a Christian. This points to a period of persecution by the Roman government. The opening vision was of the exalted Christ, who is represented in a symbolic portraiture as standing in the midst of 7 golden candlesticks which represent the 7 churches (ch. 1:10-20). Christ gives to the seer messages to the 7 churches, and after that follows a succession of other visions. The revelation is said to have been given on the Lord's Day (ch. 1:10), by which we are doubtless to understand the 1st day of the week. See LORD'S DAY. The visions described are of a highly symbolical character. Many of the figures and much of the language are taken from the O.T. prophets, especially from Daniel and Ezekiel, and the meaning cannot be understood without constant reference to them.

Examining the book more closely, we find that after the introduction (ch. 1:1-3) and salutation (vs. 4-8), it consists of 7 chief divisions, extending to ch. 22:7, after which the book closes with an epilogue (vs. 8-21). These divisions constitute in fact 7 visions, or series of visions, and are themselves subdivided usually into 7 parts. Each series opens with a vision, which presents as a whole the idea of the series, and this is then followed in most instances by a sevenfold representation of its elements. These visions are probably not to be understood as representing events which were to follow one another in history in the order of time, but as symbolical portraitures of certain religious truths or principles which were to be realized in the experience of the Church. The whole is intended for the Church's comfort and warning amid the conflicts of time and in preparation for the Second Coming of her Lord (chs. 1:7, 8; 22:7, 10, 17, 20). The 7 series of visions, which show the analysis of the book, are the following:

1. The vision of the glorified Christ amid his Church, followed by 7 messages to the 7 churches of Asia (Rev. 1:9 to 3:22). Here the main thought is of instruction, warning, and encouragement for the Church in her present condition.

2. The vision of God, presiding over the destinies of the universe and adored by all creation, and of the exalted, but redeeming, Lamb of God, who holds in his hand the sealed book of the divine decrees (chs. 4; 5), followed by the breaking of the seals in 7 visions, whereby is portrayed the sevenfold purpose of God from the going forth of Christ to conquer unto the Last Judgment (chs. 6:1 to 8:1). Between the 6th and 7th seals an episode is introduced which shows the safety of the people of God amid the judgment which befalls the world (ch. 7).

3. The vision of the trumpets (chs. 8:2 to 11:19). It opens with the vision of an angel offering the prayers of the saints to God (ch. 8:2-6). Then each trumpet is followed by a vision of destruction upon the sinful world, ending again with the Last Judgment. Between the 6th and 7th trumpets an episode again is introduced, descriptive of the preservation of the witnessing Church (chs. 10:1 to 11:14). The main thought here appears to be that in reply to the prayers of the saints for God to vindicate his truth they are shown the desolations which befall the sinful world amid which they are to bear their testimony.

4. The vision of the Church, under the figure of a woman, bringing forth the Christ, against whom the dragon, or Satan, wages war (ch. 12), followed by visions of the beasts, which Satan will use as his agents (ch. 13), of the militant Church (ch. 14:1-5), and of the advancing stages of Christ's conquest (vs. 6-20). This may be called the vision of conflict.

5. The vision of the vials, or bowls, containing the last plagues, or judgments of God (chs. 15; 16). The opening vision (ch. 15) depicts the triumph of the saints, while the 7 bowls represent the sevenfold judgment of God on a wicked world (ch. 16).

6. The vision of the harlot city, Babylon (ch. 17), followed by the victory of Christ over her, and over his enemies in league with her, ending again in the Last Judgment (chs. 18:1 to 20:15). Between the 6th and 7th scenes of this triumph an episode is introduced (ch. 20:1-10), which is probably descriptive of the complete safety and spiritual deliverance of Christ's people throughout the whole period of the age-long battle. Some scholars, however, place the division between the 6th and 7th series of visions at ch. 19:11.

7. The vision of the ideal Church, the bride of Christ, or New Jerusalem (ch. 21:1-8), followed by a description of her glory (chs. 21:9 to 22:7).

General agreement prevails among both critical and devotional students of The Revelation that the book as it stands has unity. Structural unity is apparent in its having a framework consisting of 7 groups of usually 7 episodes and in a general grammatical and linguistic similarity. The strongly Semitic coloring of the Gr. of this book can be explained either by supposing that the author was accustomed to think in Aramaic or by postulating a written Aramaic (or possibly Hebrew) document from which the present Greek text was translated.

The author of The Revelation was a Jewish Christian with a noble universalistic outlook, thoroughly conversant with the contents of the O.T. and with its literary forms, and able to mold characteristic prophecies of Daniel and Ezekiel into his own picture of the Church's conflict and final glory (see DANIEL, EZEKIEL). His name was John (Rev. 1:1, 4, 9; 22:8). That he was John the apostle has been the tradition of the Church from the earliest time, being specifically so stated by Justin Martyr in the middle of the 2d century. But some scholars feel that the writer can scarcely be the author of the Fourth Gospel and the Johannine epistles. As Dionysius, bishop of Alexandria (A.D. 247–265) pointed out (Eusebius *H.E.* vii. 25), the Apocalypse differs markedly from the other Johannine writings in style, language, and recurring ideas. Proponents of the traditional common authorship of all 5 documents maintain that the divergencies can be explained on the basis of diversity of subject matter and the different dates of writing, and they push The Revelation back to the end of Nero's reign, c. A.D. 68. Thus it is supposed that the terrors of the fall of Jerusalem combined with those of the Neronian persecution provide many of the lurid figures used by the seer. The number 666 (Rev. 13:18) has been explained as being the total of the numerical values of the Heb. or Aram. letters in the name Nero Caesar (*nrwn ḳsr*); yet even if this is the true solution of the cryptogram, it does not necessarily prove that John wrote in Nero's time. N.T. scholarship of various schools quite generally favors the traditional date of the Apocalypse, voiced by Irenaeus as early as c. A.D. 180, which assigns it to the close of Domitian's reign, c. A.D. 96. The condition of the churches is later than Paul's time, as is seen in the references to the deterioration of the churches in Ephesus and Laodicea; furthermore the Nicolaitans are denounced, who favored a compromise between the claims of Christianity and that of the state religion (Rev. 2:1–6, 15; 3:14–19). Nero's persecution was confined to Rome; that of Domitian extended to Asia. The background seems to be the time when the emperor's demands for divine honors, his widespread use of informers, and his fiendish fury against the Christians established a reign of terror in his later years. Whoever was the author of the Gospel and the epistles of John, the testimony is strong that the Apostle John wrote the Apocalypse.

The Church was slow in recognizing the canonicity of this book. During the first 5 centuries, the Peshitta, the common Bible of the Syrian church, did not include the Apocalypse, nor do the mediaeval lectionaries of the Orthodox Catholic Church contain lessons from it.

The interpretations of The Revelation have been innumerable. Four general classes of interpretation may, however, be distinguished. 1. The praeterist interpretation, which regards the work as a description of what was taking place when the book was written. This view destroys its prophetic character, and is certainly to be rejected. 2. The futurist interpretation, which sees in the book predictions of events yet to be fulfilled. This view is met by the difficulty that all prophecy, and this one in particular, closely connects itself with the situation of the Church and prophet to whom it was given. 3. The historico-prophetical interpretation, which sees in the visions a successive portrayal of the events of Christian history. The difficulty with this view is that few expositors can agree on the details of the fulfillment, and that it disregards the contemporaneous character of the 7 series of visions. 4. The spiritual, symbolic interpretation, which regards the visions as figurative portraitures of certain truths or principles, destined to find their place in the history of the Church, and the contemplation of which in pictorial representation is intended to encourage and comfort Christ's people until he comes again in glory and to judgment. While no expositor can feel sure that he has understood the meaning of all the contents of The Revelation, the last method of interpretation has the advantage of directing the attention of readers to certain large and important

truths, under the form of pictures, thus making this most mysterious book of Scripture practically helpful.   G. T. P. (rev., H. S. G.)

Re·ven'ger. See AVENGER OF BLOOD.

Re'zeph (rē'zĕf) [glowing stone or coal]. A place which the rabshakeh boasted that the Assyrians had destroyed (II Kings 19:12; Isa. 37:12), doubtless the town Raṣappa, long residence of an Assyrian governor. Probably it is the modern Ruṣāfah, some miles w. of the Euphrates on the route to Palmyra.

Re·zi'a (rê-zī'á). See RIZIA.

Re'zin (rē'zĭn) [cf. Syriac *rāṣīnā*, brooklet]. 1. A king of Damascus. About 738 B.C. he paid tribute to Tiglath-pileser, king of Assyria. Four years later, in the time of Ahaz, he joined with Pekah, king of Israel, in an effort to capture Jerusalem and place a creature of their own upon the throne of David. They failed, after eliciting from Isaiah a celebrated prophecy (Isa. 7:1 to 9:12). On this campaign, before attempting to unite his troops with those of Pekah, Rezin marched to Elath on the Gulf of 'Aḳabah and took the town from Judah (II Kings 16:6). The aid of Tiglath-pileser had been purchased by Ahaz; and the Assyrian king, after chastising the Philistines for their participation in the hostilities against Judah, marched against Damascus, besieged it during the years 733 and 732 B.C., ravaged the surrounding district, finally captured the city, and slew Rezin (II Kings 16:7–9; and Assyrian inscriptions). 2. Founder of a family of Nethinim, members of which returned from the Captivity (Ezra 2:48; Neh. 7:50).

Re'zon (rē'zŏn) [prince, potentate]. A son of Eliada, and a subject of Hadadezer, king of Zobah. When David captured Zobah, Rezon gathered a band of men, seized Damascus, and founded the Syrian kingdom, with which, while it lasted, the Israelites had continual relations, hostile or friendly (I Kings 11:23–25).

Rhe'gi·um (rē'jĭ-ŭm). A city of Greek origin on the coast of Italy, opposite to Messina in Sicily. Paul's vessel touched at Rhegium after having made a circuit from Syracuse (Acts 28:13). Rhegium is now called Reggio.

Rhe'sa (rē'sá). A descendant of Zerubbabel, and an ancestor of Christ (Luke 3:27).

Rho'da (rō'dá) [Gr. *Rhodē*, a rose bush]. A servant girl of Mary, the mother of Mark. When Peter, after having been miraculously released from prison, knocked at the door of the gate of Mary's house, Rhoda was sent to see who was there. On hearing Peter's voice she was filled with joy and, forgetting in her excitement to let him in, ran back to tell that it was Peter. The apostle had to continue the knocking for some time before he could gain admittance (Acts 12:13–16).

Rhodes (rōdz), in A.V. of I Macc. 15:23 **Rho'dus** (rō'dŭs). An island off the coast of Caria, in the s.w. of Asia Minor. It is about 45 miles long by 20 broad, and is remarkable for its orange and citron groves. The island was at the junction of great commercial routes for coasting vessels, and became a commercial center which ranked with Alexandria and Carthage. Its capital, also called Rhodes, was famed for its Colossus, a great lighthouse, said to have been 70 cubits, or about 105 feet, high. It was erected between 300 and 288 B.C. The Rhodians were semi-independent under the Romans (I Macc. 15:23), except during 9 years in the reign of Claudius, beginning A.D. 44, and again in the time of Vespasian. The vessel in which Paul sailed to Palestine from Assos touched at

Rhodes (Acts 21:1), which was then a splendid city. As the Rhodians long remained unsubdued by the Romans, so, led by the Knights of St. John, who in A.D. 1310 had possessed themselves of the island, they defied the power of the Turks till 1522, when they had to surrender on terms, the knights being allowed to transfer themselves to the isle of Malta.

Ri'bai (rī'bī) [Jehovah strives]. A Benjamite of Gibeah, and the father of Ittai, one of David's mighty men (II Sam. 23:29; I Chron. 11:31).

Rib'lah (rĭb'là) [cf. Arab. *rabala*, to multiply]. A town in the land of Hamath (II Kings 23:33; 25:21). The Egyptians were encamped there when Jehoahaz was brought in as a prisoner (II Kings 23:33). When Zedekiah was captured after his escape from Jerusalem, he was brought to Nebuchadnezzar, then encamped at Riblah, who put out his eyes and had him bound to be carried to Babylon. His sons and the princes of Judah were also slain at Riblah (II Kings 25:6, 7, 21; Jer. 39:5–7; 52:9–11, 27). Buckingham, in 1816, met with ruins at a place called by him Rubla, but now more generally spelled Ribleh, on the right bank of the Orontes, about 36 miles n. by e. of Ba'al-bek, in the midst of the great plain of Coelesyria, very suitable for the encampment of a great army, and with easy access s. or n. if commotion arose. The ruins consist of low mounds surrounded by the remains of old buildings. It is hardly identical with Riblah on the n. boundary of Palestine, e. of Ain (Num. 34:11) for which no satisfactory identification has been found.

Rid'dle. In Biblical usage, any dark saying, of which the meaning is not at once clear and must be discovered by shrewd thought (Num. 12:8, dark speeches; Prov. 1:6, R.V. marg.). It may be a parable (Ps. 49:4; 78:2, dark sayings) and be proposed merely in order to arouse attention and start inquiry and to make the truth more vivid and impressive, the propounder intending to give an explanation immediately (Ezek. 17:2–24); or the riddle may be set forth for men to guess, as the riddle of Samson and those of Solomon and Hiram to which Josephus refers (Judg. 14:12–19; Jos. *Antiq.* viii. 5, 3). The riddle of Samson was proposed in verse. It was not properly a riddle at all, since the discovery of its meaning was not within the realm of possibility for the Philistines. It could not be guessed, for they were not acquainted with the facts on which it was based.

The Greeks and Romans were fond of the riddle or enigma. One of the most celebrated was put into the mouth of the monster named the sphinx, which had been sent to ravage the territory of Thebes. She asked: "What animal goes on four feet in the morning, two at noon, and on three in the evening?" After many had failed, Oedipus answered that it was man, who in infancy creeps on all fours, at maturity walks on 2 feet, and in old age uses a staff. Thereupon the sphinx flung herself to the ground and perished.

Rie, obsolete spelling of rye. See SPELT.

Rim'mon, I (rĭm'ŏn), in A.V. twice **Rem'·mon** (Josh. 19:7, 13); in R.V. once **Rim'·mo·no** (I Chron. 6:77) [a pomegranate]. 1. A Benjamite, whose 2 sons were captains under Ish-bosheth, and became his murderers (II Sam. 4:2).

2. A town in the s. of Judah near Ain (Josh. 15:32; I Chron. 4:32; Zech. 14:10), so near indeed as to form, apparently, one community with it (Neh. 11:29). It was soon transferred with Ain and other towns to Simeon (Josh. 19:7). It is identified with the ruin Umm er-Rumāmīn, about 9 miles n. of Beer-sheba.

3. A border town of Zebulun, but assigned to the Levites (Josh. 19:13; I Chron. 6:77; and Josh. 21:35, where Dimnah is doubtless a misreading, *resh* being mistaken for *daleth, q.v.*). Methoar in A.V. of Josh. 19:13 is improperly regarded as part of the name; whereas it describes the boundary as "stretching" to Neah. The name of the town is preserved in Rummāneh, a village 6 miles n., slightly e., of Nazareth.

4. A rock near Gibeah, where 600 vanquished Benjamites took refuge and remained 4 months (Judg. 20:45–47; 21:13). It is probably the detached limestone eminence 3½ miles e., slightly n., of Beth-el. It is separated from all approach on the s., the n., and the w. by ravines, and has caverns in which the refugees may have lived. The name still lingers in Rammūn, a village on the summit.

Rim'mon, II (rĭm'ŏn) [Akkad., thunderer]. A Syrian god, who had a temple at Damascus, in which Naaman and his royal master were accustomed to bow themselves for worship (II Kings 5:18). In Assyria Rimmon, or Rammān as his name was pronounced there, was numbered among the 12 great deities. He was the god of rain and storm, lightning and thunder. Sometimes he was dreaded as the destroyer of crops and the scatterer of the harvest, and at others was adored as the lord of fecundity. He was identical with Hadad, the supreme god of the Syrians. The 2 names are combined in Hadad-Rimmon.

Rim'mo·no (rĭm'ō-nō). See RIMMON, I.

Rim'mon-pe'rez (rĭm'ŏn-pē'rĕz), in A.V. **Rim'mon-pa'rez** (rĭm'ŏn-pā'rēz) [pomegranate of the breach or cleft]. A camping ground of the Israelites in the wilderness (Num. 33:19, 20); probably at Naḳb el-Biyâr.

Ring. See ORNAMENTS and SEAL 2.

Rin'nah (rĭn'á) [a ringing cry]. A man of Judah, a son of Shimon (I Chron. 4:20).

Ri'phath (rī'făth) [A people descended from Gomer (Gen. 10:3; in I Chron. 1:6 Diphath; see DALETH). Josephus identifies them with the Paphlagonians (Jos. *Antiq.* i. 6, 1). The name is perhaps preserved in the Riphaean Mountains, which were supposed by the ancients to skirt the n. shore of the world.

Ris'sah (rĭs'á) [a ruin; dew or rain]. A camping ground of the Israelites in the wilderness (Num. 33:21, 22), probably at Kuntilet el-Jerâfi between Kossaima and 'Aḳabah n.w. of the mountain Rueisset el-Nejin.

Rith'mah (rĭth'má) [broom plant]. A camping ground of the Israelites in the wilderness (Num. 33:18, 19).

Riv'er. Of several words translated river, only 3 require mention here: 1. *Nāhār*, a stream, in Gr. *potamos*, applied to the largest rivers known to the Hebrews, as the Tigris and Euphrates (Gen. 2:14; Rev. 9:14), the Abana and Pharpar (II Kings 5:12), the Jordan (Mark 1:5), and the affluents of the Upper Nile (Zeph. 3:10). The river or the great river usually denotes the Euphrates (Gen. 15:18; 31:21). 2. *Naḥal*, sometimes a perennial stream like the Jabbok (Deut. 2:37), but usually a winter torrent, the bed of which is dry in summer; a wadi. See BROOK. 3. *Ye'ōr*, a stream, used almost exclusively of the Nile and its mouths, and sounding much like the native Egyptian name of that river (Gen. 41:1; II Kings 19:24; Ezek. 29:3). It once denotes the Tigris (Dan. 12:5–7; cf. 10:4, R.V. marg.).

Riv′er of E′gypt (ē′jĭpt). 1. The Nile, and specifically its most e. channel, the Pelusiac branch (Gen. 15:18) ; see SHIHOR. In this passage the 2 great rivers, the Nile and the Euphrates, are named broadly as the boundaries of the Promised Land. The brook of Egypt or Wadi el-'Arīsh was commonly regarded as the s.w. limit of Palestine ; but the country between this wadi and the e. branch of the Nile was mainly desert, and the Nile was virtually on the boundary of Egypt. The passage means that the descendants of Abraham should possess the land as far as Egypt. The distinction between the Nile and Wadi el-'Arīsh is well established ; for the former is a *nāhār* and the latter a *nahal*.

2. A great wadi or *nahal*, uniformly called in the R.V. the brook of Egypt. It was the s.w. border of Canaan (Num. 34:5 ; I Kings 8:65 ; II Kings 24:7), and the limit in the same direction of the tribe of Judah (Josh. 15:4, 47). It was known to the Assyrians by the same name as to the Hebrews, and likewise as a boundary. It is Wadi el-'Arīsh, a watercourse nominally dry, but which after heavy rains runs n. from the desert, being fed by tributaries, one of which passes Kadesh-barnea. It falls into the Mediterranean about 50 miles s. of Gaza.

Ri·zi′a (rĭ-zī′á), in A.V. **Re·zi′a** [pleasant]. An Asherite, a son of Ulla (I Chron. 7:39).

Riz′pah (rĭz′pä) [a hot stone, hot coal]. A daughter of Aiah and concubine of Saul. On her account the quarrel arose between Ishbosheth and Abner which resulted in Abner's going over to David (II Sam. 3:6–8). Her children, Armoni and Mephibosheth, were put to death during the famine which arose in David's reign on account of Saul's treatment of the Gibeonites (II Sam. 21:8–11).

Road. An inroad, a raid, an incursion into an enemy's country (I Sam. 27:10, in R.V. raid). This sense is now obsolete in ordinary language. When a road in the modern sense is intended, the A.V. and R.V. generally use the term "way," or sometimes "path."

Rob′ber. See THIEF.

Ro·bo′am (rō-bō′ăm). See REHOBOAM.

Rock. Rocks were found nearly everywhere in the hilly and mountainous districts of Palestine. Some had definite names, as the rock of Oreb (Judg. 7:25), the rock of Etam (ch. 15:8). See OREB 2, ETAM 2.

Rock Badg′er. The rendering of Heb. *shāphān*, in the marg. of the R.V. (Lev. 11:5), where "coney" appears in the text. The animal intended by the Heb. word is small and wary, dwells among the rocks (Ps. 104:18 ; Prov. 30:24, 26), and chews the cud, but does not part the hoof (Deut. 14:7). The corresponding name in the dialect of s. Arabia denotes the *Hyrax syriacus*, the so-called rock badger. The hyrax looks like a rabbit or badger, but has more affinity to the rhinoceros and the tapir ; indeed, its structure is so anomalous that it has been given a whole order, *Hyracoidea*, to itself. It moves its jaws as if it were chewing the cud, but it does not really ruminate. The species *syriacus* is found in the peninsula of Sinai, n. Palestine, and the region round the Dead Sea. Its fur is tawny, with a yellow spot on the back. It lives in clefts of rocks, but does not scoop out a hole. Small parties meet together, with a sentinel on some eminence to give warning of danger. It is rarely seen except in the morning and evening, when it comes forth to feed.

Rod′a·nim (rŏd′à-nĭm). A people descended from Javan (Heb. text of I Chron. 1:7 ; and LXX and Samaritan text of Gen. 10:4). If Rodanim is the correct reading, the people of Rhodes and of the neighboring islands of the Aegean Sea are probably intended. See DODANIM.

Roe. A deer (*Capreolus capraea,* the *Cervus capraea* of Linnaeus) which is described under ROEBUCK 2 (II Sam. 2:18 ; I Chron. 12:8, in Heb. *ṣᵉbî;* and Prov. 5:19, A.V., in Heb. *ya'ălāh*) ; see GAZELLE and DOE.

Roe′buck′. 1. The rendering in A.V. of Heb. *ṣᵉbî* in Deut. 12:15, 22 ; 14:5 ; 15:22 ; I Kings 4:23. R.V. substitutes gazelle (*q.v.*).

2. The rendering in R.V. of Hebrew *yaḥmūr*. The animal was ceremonially clean and used for food (Deut. 14:5 ; I Kings 4:23, in A.V. fallow deer). Etymology indicates that its color was reddish. According to Arabian authorities, it casts its horns every year, which is characteristic of deer. In n. Galilee the name *yaḥmūr* is still given to the roebuck (*Capreolus capraea,* or *Cervus capreolus*). In Europe it is a small deer about 2 feet high at the shoulder, but in Asia it attains to a larger size. In summer it is dark reddish-brown, in winter yellowish-gray. It has a large patch of white on the rump. The antlers are about a foot long, with 3 points. It is wild over a great part of Europe and Asia. In Palestine it is found on Mount Carmel and Mount Lebanon.

By many, however, the *yaḥmūr* is identified with the bubale, one of the bovine antelopes. It is about the size of a large stag, has a long head, a narrow forehead, and reddish or pale brown hair. Its flesh is most savory.

Ro′ge·lim (rō′gē-lĭm) [fullers ; or spies]. A town in Gilead where Barzillai lived (II Sam. 17:27 ; 19:31) ; probably on Wadi er-Rujeileh, near Irbid.

Roh′gah (rō′gá) [cf. Arab. *rahj*, dust, tumult]. An Asherite, family of Beriah, house of Heber (I Chron. 7:34).

Roll. The sheet of papyrus or the parchment on which documents were frequently written in ancient times was rolled up or wound around a stick, like a modern map, and thus constituted a roll (Jer. 36:2), or a volume in the original sense of the term (Ps. 40:7, A.V.) ; see BOOK. The word *gillāyōn* rendered "roll" in Isa. 8:1, A.V., should be translated "tablet."

Ro·mam′ti-e′zer (rō-măm′tĭ-ē′zẽr) [I have exalted help]. A singer, a son of Heman (I Chron. 25:4). He obtained the 24th lot among the courses of the singers (v. 31). See GIDDALTI.

Ro′mans (rō′mănz). 1. Inhabitants of Rome (I Macc. 8:1 ; Acts 2:10, "sojourners from Rome," R.V.).

2. Those who represent the Roman government (John 11:48 ; Acts 25:16 ; 28:17).

3. Those, wherever born or of whatever race, who possessed the rights of citizenship in the Roman Empire (Acts 16:21, 37, 38 ; 22:25, 26, 27, 29). By the Valerian and Porcian Laws it was declared that no magistrate had the right to bind, scourge, or kill a Roman citizen. The life of one so privileged could not be taken away except by a decision of the whole people met in the *comitia centuriata,* a general assembly of the people, voting in divisions called centuries. If a magistrate or ruler of any kind gave orders to scourge one entitled to the protection of these laws, the latter had only to utter the words, "I am a Roman citizen," and all procedure was stayed till the people had decided on his case. When the power formerly possessed by the people was transferred to the emperor, it was to him that the right of appeal lay. The privileges of Roman citizenship were first limited to residents in Rome itself ; then they were extended to various Italian tribes and cities ; then to the greater part of Italy ; then

to places beyond the Italian peninsula; and so on and on till, it is said, Caracalla (A.D. 211–217) conferred them on every inhabitant of the Roman Empire. During the transition period individuals who had rendered service to Rome might be declared citizens, or the privilege might be purchased for money, even in towns or districts that were not as yet enfranchised. Sometimes also manumitted slaves were granted citizenship. These explanations make it easy to understand how Paul, though of Jewish descent (Phil. 3:5), could still be a Roman citizen; and how Claudius Lysias thought it worth his while to purchase the privilege for a great sum of money (Acts 22: 28); and how, when he had given orders that Paul should be scourged, and was informed by the centurion that the apostle was a Roman citizen, procedure was immediately stopped (Acts 22:25–29). One can also understand the alarm of the authorities at Philippi when they had taken the responsibility of having Paul and Silas openly beaten, and, to make matters worse, uncondemned, without first taking means to ascertain whether or not they were Roman citizens (ch. 16:36–38). It will appear also that Paul simply exercised his legal right when he took his appeal to Caesar; that is, to the Roman emperor (ch. 25:11).

Ro'mans (rō'mănz), **The E·pis'tle of Paul to the.** The first of Paul's epistles according to the order in which they are placed in our N.T. In order of composition, however, it was the 6th, since it was written from Corinth, as appears from the salutations (cf. Rom. 16: 23 with I Cor. 1:14 and II Tim. 4:20), and from the fact that it was probably carried to Rome by Phoebe, a servant or deaconess of the church at Cenchreae (Rom. 16:1), which was near Corinth (Acts 18:18); and, if so, it must have been written during the visit to Greece mentioned in Acts 20:2, 3. That was in the winter of A.D. 57–58. The apostle had long wished to visit Rome (Rom. 1:10–12; 15:23), and it was his purpose, his work in the e. having been finished (ch. 15:23), to visit the capital on his way to Spain (v. 28). Before doing so, however, he was determined to return to Jerusalem to present the gifts of the Gentile churches (v. 25, 26). Not knowing, however, what might be his fate on this dangerous journey (Rom. 15:30–32; Acts 20: 22), he sent this letter to the Christians at Rome, where he had many friends (cf. Rom., ch. 16), for, as the apostle of the Gentiles, he considered the church at Rome to be under his care (ch. 15:15, 16), although he had never visited it. The theme of the epistle, which is one of the most elaborate ever written by him, was naturally determined by the controversies through which he had passed and by the need of stating, formally and completely, the gospel which he preached among the Gentiles. It is a full presentation, therefore, of the way of salvation; hence its supreme importance. That he addressed it to the Christians at Rome indicates, no doubt, his appreciation of the influence which the church of the world's metropolis would exert, and the consequent necessity of establishing it in the faith that it might resist the assaults of error.

Whereas The Epistle of Paul to the Galatians is the Magna Charta of universal Christianity, The Epistle of Paul to the Romans is its constitution. The epistle may be analyzed as follows: After the salutation (ch. 1:1–7) and statement of his interest in the people addressed (vs. 8–15), he epitomizes the character of his gospel and, in doing so, gives the theme of the epistle: "The gospel . . . is the power of God unto salvation to every one that believeth. . . . For therein is revealed a

righteousness of God from faith unto faith" (vs. 16, 17).

He then proves the universal need of righteousness (chs. 1:18 to 3:20). He first shows that the Gentile world is in a state of sin and just condemnation (ch. 1:18–32), and then that the Jewish world is no exception, but is likewise guilty before God (ch. 2). To the objection that this destroys the privileges of the Jew, he replies by showing that their privilege consisted in being the trustees of revelation, but that their own Scriptures declared them to be sinful (ch. 3:1–19), so that there is no exception to the universal guilt. In fact, the Law only increases the consciousness of sin (v. 20).

He then states the righteousness which God has provided for every believer through the redemptive and sacrificial work of Christ (ch. 3:21–30), and proves that this way of salvation is that taught in the O.T. (chs. 3:31 to 4:25), that it is the basis of Christian experience (ch. 5:1–11), and that it proceeds upon the same principle of moral government on which God acted when he dealt with mankind in the person of its first head and representative, Adam (ch. 5:12–21).

The apostle then refutes 3 objections which would be brought against his doctrine of salvation by the work of Christ for us received through faith alone. The 1st objection is that on this doctrine men may continue in sin and yet be saved, to which he replies no, because faith in Christ involves vital union with him, whereby the believer rises with Christ into a new moral life (ch. 6:1–14). The 2d objection is that Paul's doctrine of deliverance from the Law released men from moral obligation, to which he replies no, because the believer accepts a new and higher obligation, whereby he devotes himself to the will of God (chs. 6:15 to 7:6). The 3d objection is that Paul's doctrine makes the Law of God an evil thing, to which he replies no, for the reason that the Law cannot save is not that the Law is evil, but that man is sinful and cannot keep it (ch. 7:7–25).

Having refuted objections, he shows (ch. 8) that on the basis of Christ's redemptive work provision is made for the spiritual renewal, complete sanctification, and final glorification of those who are in Christ, and who, being chosen and called by God, will certainly enjoy the perfect fruition of God's love. Having thus stated the gospel way of salvation, the apostle proceeds to adjust it to the fact that Israel, the chosen people, had as a nation rejected it. He does this by teaching that the saving promise of God had never been made to the Jews as a nation, but only to the "election," the true seed of Abraham, whom God had chosen (ch. 9:1–13), and he justifies from Scripture this doctrine of sovereign election (vs. 14–29); then, further, that the rejection of the Jews was due to their refusal of the very way of salvation taught by their own Scriptures (chs. 9:30 to 10:21), yet that the rejection of Israel was not complete, for the promised remnant, the election, did believe (ch. 11:1–10), and, finally, that in the end the Jews will be converted and with the Gentiles trust in the promised Redeemer (vs. 11–36).

The rest of the epistle consists of an exhortation to Christian living (ch. 12), to the performance of civil and social duties (ch. 13), and to Christian charity and unity (chs. 14:1 to 15:13), ending with personal messages and salutations (chs. 15:14 to 16:27).

The question has been raised whether or not the Epistle to the Romans in early days ever existed in a shorter form than at present. In view of certain phenomena 2 theories especially have attracted attention. They have literary interest but no doctrinal importance. According to one theory, an abridgment of the epistle was prepared for general circulation, being shortened by the omission of local references, such as "in Rome" (Rom. 1:7) and chs. 15 and 16, but retaining the entire doctrinal instruction and the essence of the practical appeal. Evidence for the existence of the epistle in this shorter form is sought in the presence of the doxology (ch. 16:25–27) in some MSS. at the end of ch. 14, or both there and at the end of ch. 16; in the lack of quotations from chs. 15 and 16 in the writings of Tertullian, Irenaeus, and Cyprian; and in the apparent omission of these chapters by Marcion. The lack of citation from these chapters is without significance, however, in view of their character. They have never been much quoted. The salutations especially do not lend themselves to quotation. The theory of an abridged edition of the epistle must rest mainly on the occurrence of the doxology at the end of ch. 14 in some MSS. This is a frail support; and it is especially weak in view of the fact that no extant MS. is an abridgment, but all MSS. of the epistle without exception contain chs. 15 and 16.

The other theory, and one widely held, is that ch. 16 did not form a part of the epistle originally, but constituted a brief note commending Phoebe to the church at Ephesus. For ch. 15 is not easily separated from ch. 14, but follows it naturally, and simply develops the appeal that is made in ch. 14 to the spirit of Christian self-sacrifice on the part of those who are strong in conscience. Moreover, ch. 15 closes, in v. 33, with a benediction such as occurs at the end of other letters written by Paul (II Cor. 13:11; I Thess. 5:23; II Thess. 3:16; Phil. 4:9), and forms the natural conclusion to the Epistle to the Romans. Moreover the Chester Beatty papyrus of the Pauline epistles (copied during the 1st part of the 3d century) puts the doxology (Rom. 16:25–27) after ch. 15:33. Chapter 16 would, therefore, seem to be appended. That the latter chapter was originally a letter commending Phoebe to the church at Ephesus, not to the Christians in Rome, may be gathered, it is argued, from the following considerations: 1. It is intended to accredit Phoebe (ch. 16:1). 2. Aquila and Priscilla, to whom salutations are sent (ch. 16:3), were certainly living in Ephesus about 3 years before the Epistle to the Romans was written, and they were not in Rome when Paul wrote the 2d letter to Timothy (II Tim. 4:19). 3. The reference to Epaenetus, "the firstfruits of Asia" (Rom. 16:5, R.V.), would be more natural in a letter to Ephesus than to Rome. 4. It is unlikely that Paul would have as many acquaintances in a church he had not visited as he salutes in ch. 16.

The objections to this theory that ch. 16 is a brief note to the church at Ephesus are: 1. Salutations were occasionally added, as here, after a doxology or a benediction, even when followed by Amen (Phil. 4:20; II Thess. 3:16; cf. II Tim. 4:18). 2. The fact that ch. 16 forms part of the epistle in all extant MSS. 3. Aquila and Priscilla migrated from place to place a great deal. They were residing in Rome when all Jews were notified to leave the city; they lived at Corinth for about 1½ years and accompanied Paul to Ephesus. In this place they actively worked for Christianity and remained at least until he returned from a trip to Jerusalem. It would not be strange if they went back to Rome, especially in connection with the apostle's plan to visit the city and introduce the Christian religion (Acts 19:21). 4. That Epaenetus, a convert of the province of Asia, found his way to Rome occasions no surprise; for Christians, Jews, and Gentiles were constantly going to the imperial capital for various reasons from all parts of the world, for example, Epaphras of Colossae and Aquila of Pontus and Herod the tetrarch. 5. The persons saluted in ch. 16 bear names that are proved to have been current in Rome, and some of them were common among the early Christians of the city. 6. It is not necessary to assume that the people to whom he sends greetings were in every case personal acquaintances of the apostle; it is enough that they were known to him as earnest, active Christians through references to them in letters from Aquila, Priscilla, and others concerning affairs in Rome.

G. T. P., supplemented (rev., H. S. G.)

Rome (rōm). The date 753 B.C. is accepted by the best authorities for the traditional founding of Rome by Romulus, who became its first king. The little kingdom grew in size and importance, absorbing its immediate neighbors through the reigns of 7 kings, until the tyranny of Tarquinius Superbus drove the people to take the government into their own hands and establish a republic. In the beginning the power was entirely in the hands of a few patrician families, the plebeians merely acquiescing in measures taken. The plebs, however, demanded and obtained privilege after privilege until every Roman citizen had a voice in the government. During the period of the republic Rome extended its boundaries at first over all Italy, and finally over the whole Mediterranean world.

Rome's first contact with Asia occurred 190 B.C., when the Roman army defeated Antiochus the Great, king of Syria, at the battle of Magnesia, and Rome assumed a protectorate over certain cities in Asia Minor (cf. I Macc. 1:10). Most of Rome's conquests after this were of a peaceful nature, other nations willingly acknowledging its superiority.

In 63 B.C. Judea became formally subject to Rome, being taken by Pompey after he had reduced the Seleucidan kingdom to the level of a province. It was required to pay tribute, but was left for a time under native rulers.

Meantime, several parties jealous of each other had been growing up in the state. As the result of an internal political struggle, the triumvirate of Caesar, Pompey, and Crassus was formed to rule, but by the death of Crassus, and the defeat of Pompey in a civil struggle, the power fell into the hands of Caesar alone. This did not last long. Caesar was murdered by his enemies in 44 B.C., civil war again broke out, a 2d triumvirate was formed by Antony, Octavian, and Lepidus, and, like the 1st, was soon reduced to 1 man, Octavian (31 B.C.). Full of ambition, Octavian had himself proclaimed emperor with the title of Augustus, and the Roman Empire began.

It was during the reign of Augustus that Christ was born; during that of his successor Tiberius, that the crucifixion took place. The martyrdom of James the brother of John took place in the reign of the emperor Claudius (Acts 11:28; 12:1, 2). It was to the emperor Nero that Paul appealed (ch. 25:11). The destruction of Jerusalem prophesied by our Lord (Matt., ch. 24; Mark., ch. 13; Luke 19:41–44; 21:5–36) was accomplished in the year A.D. 70 by Titus, who afterward became emperor. See CAESAR.

In the days of Augustus the empire was bounded by the Rhine and the Danube, the Euphrates, the African desert, the Atlantic, and the North Sea. The conquest of a part of Britain took place under Claudius, and Trajan expanded beyond the Euphrates. The Roman Empire covered practically the whole civilized world.

Weakened by excesses and corruption within, and attacked by enemies without, the empire in course of time began to fail. The last emperor of the whole Roman Empire was Theodosius (A.D. 379–395); at his death it was divided between his 2 sons and was never again united. The w. part disintegrated and finally Rome fell (476), when Odoacer, a German leader, became ruler of Italy.

During the decline of Rome's civil power the Christians there were growing in power and influence. Although it had been the policy of Rome to tolerate the religions of its conquered peoples, the Christians were persecuted almost from the first. This was due mainly to 2 causes: their uncompromising attitude toward all heathen rites and religions, and their unceasing efforts to make converts. The persecutions were especially severe under Nero, who attempted to throw on the Christians the blame for some of his own nefarious deeds. Persecutions were also very severe under Domitian, but notwithstanding constant imprisonment and death the Christians continued to grow in numbers and influence until the church in Rome and the bishop of Rome became no inconsiderable factor in the general growth of Christianity. The Christian religion was officially adopted and declared the religion of the state by the emperor Constantine early in the 4th century.

Roof. See HOUSE.

Room. 1. A chamber or other apartment in a house (Acts 1:13). See HOUSE.

2. In A.V. room is also used in the sense of place or position in society, a meaning which is now obsolete (Matt. 23:6; Luke 14:7, 8; 20:46). "Uppermost [or chief] room" is the translation of Gr. *prōtoklisia*, the chief (most honorable) reclining place; see MEALS. The scribes and Pharisees were censured for seeking the place of honor at feasts, desiring to recline on the most important couch. R.V. substitutes "place [or seat]" for "room," when used in this obsolete sense.

Rose. The rendering of Heb. *hăbaṣṣeleth* (S. of Sol. 2:1; Isa. 35:1), in the Eng. versions and by several Jewish scholars of the Middle Ages. Modern interpreters are divided in opinion. The most important suggestions are the following: 1. Some expositors, including Tristram, following the Targum of S. of Sol. 2:1, and sometimes appealing to a doubtful ety., understand the beautiful, white sweet-scented narcissus (*Narcissus tazetta*), common in spring in the plain of Sharon and in the hill country. 2. Syriac *hamṣalāytā*, cognate to the Heb. name, denotes colchicum and the crocus, which are strikingly alike and which, when the rainy season sets in, carpet the fields with bright flowers. The prevalent opinion, perhaps represented by R.V. marg., is that meadow saffron (*Colchicum autumnale*) is meant, with its pale lilac flowers. 3. Akkad. *ḫabaṣillatu* refers to marsh plants, so that the Heb. has been understood by some interpreters of late to denote *Cyperus syriacus*, known also as *Cyperus papyrus*, which grows on the Nahr el-'Aujah in the plain of Sharon and in other marshy districts of Palestine. It flowers toward the end of autumn.

The true rose is a native of Media and Persia. It was early transplanted to the countries on the Mediterranean, and grows on the mountains of Palestine. The maid who recognized the voice of Peter at the gate was named Rhoda, a rose (Acts 12:13); and the true rose is probably intended in Wisd. of Sol. 2:8; Ecclus. 24:14; 39:13; 50:8, where the Gr. word is used. Tristram, however, judges from its growing at Jericho and by the waters that the oleander is meant in these passages.

Rosh (rŏsh) [head, chief, prince]. 1. A son of Benjamin, who went down to Egypt with Jacob and his sons (Gen. 46:21). He did not give rise to a tribal family (Num. 26:38), because probably, like Er and Onan of Judah, he died without issue.

2. A n. people mentioned with Meshech and Tubal (Ezek. 38:2; 39:1, both R.V. text). The text of the A.V. and J.V., and the marg. of the R.V. render Rosh "chief prince," in which case Rosh as a proper name disappears.

Ru'by. 1. The pl., rubies, is the rendering of Heb. *peninim*, which occurs only in the pl. The marg. of the R.V. has coral, red coral, or pearls. The name may signify branches and thus aptly describe coral; but this signification is not established. It was ruddy in hue (Lam. 4:7), and was precious (Job 28:18; Prov. 3:15). The color is a good reason for not regarding it as a pearl. The true or Oriental ruby is, like the sapphire, a variety of corundum. It is a clear, bright gem, rich red in color. The spinel ruby is a deep red, and the balas ruby a rose-red, variety of spinel.

2. The marginal rendering of Heb. *'ōdem*, red gem (Ex. 28:17; Ezek. 28:13). In the text it is translated sardius, which is the better rendering.

Rue. A plant, in Gr. *pēganon,* of which the Pharisees, careful about minute points, were scrupulously accurate in paying tithes (Luke 11:42). It is *Ruta graveolens,* a half shrubby plant, 2 or 3 feet high, with pinnate bluish-green leaves, all dotted over with odoriferous

Rue

glands and yellowish corymbose flowers, mostly with 8 stamens. Its odor is very powerful. It is a native of the Mediterranean region. It was cultivated in Palestine as a medicine, and perhaps as a condiment for food. Had it been wild it would not have been a tithable plant.

Ru'fus (rōō'fŭs) [Lat., red]. A son of that Simon of Cyrene who was compelled to bear the cross of Christ (Mark 15:21). He may have been the same as the Rufus at Rome to whom Paul sent a salutation (Rom. 16:13), but there is nothing to prove that such a conjecture is correct.

Ru·ha'mah (rōō-hä'má) [she has obtained mercy]. One of the symbolical names with which the children of Judah and Israel shall eventually greet each other (Hos. 2:1).

Rul'er. In a general sense, anyone who exercises authority. More particularly: 1. Officer of a synagogue (Luke 8:41). See SYNAGOGUE.

2. Member of the sanhedrin, whether priest or layman (John 3:1; 7:26; cf. Acts 4:5 with vs. 8 and 15; cf. ch. 23:5).

3. Archon or civil magistrate of a city (Acts 16:19). In Macedonia and regions under Macedonian influence such officials were technically called politarchs or rulers of the city (ch. 17:6, 8).

4. The governor of a feast, who prepared it and had the direction of it, but was not the host (Ecclus. 32:1; II Macc. 2:27; and John 2:8, but marg. "steward").

Ru'mah (rōō'mà) [height, high place]. The home of a grandfather of Jehoiakim (II Kings 23:36); perhaps Arumah near Shechem (cf. Jos. *Antiq.* x. 5, 2), or Rumah in Galilee (Jos. *War* iii. 7, 21), represented by Khirbet Rumeh, 6 miles n. of Nazareth.

Run'ners. A class of soldiers who served as a bodyguard of the king (I Sam. 22:17, in A.V. footmen, R.V. guard), were posted at the door of the royal palace at Jerusalem (I Kings 14:27; II Kings 11:19), had their own guard room (I Kings 14:28), escorted the king to the Temple (v. 28), and executed the king's commands (I Sam. 22:17; II Kings 10:25). In each instance, see R.V. marg. Perhaps they ran before the royal chariot (see FORERUNNER).

Rush. See PAPYRUS.

Rust. A corrosive or disfiguring accretion, in Gr. *ios*, which denotes the rust of iron, the verdigris of brass, the tarnish on gold and silver (James 5:3). The Gr. word *brōsis*, eating, corrosion, is used in Matt. 6:19, 20.

Ruth (rōōth) [ety. uncertain; perhaps, sightly, comely]. A Moabitess married first to Mahlon of Bethlehem, who was sojourning in Moab with his parents and brother because of a famine in Judah. The 3 men died. Ruth left her native land and accompanied her mother-in-law Naomi to Bethlehem. While gleaning in the field of Boaz, a kinsman of Naomi's deceased husband, she found favor in his eyes. Custom required a kinsman of Mahlon to marry Ruth; and Boaz took her to wife, after one nearer of kin than he had refused. By this marriage Ruth became an ancestress of David. The transaction between Boaz and Ruth was not a levirate marriage (Deut. 25:7-10; cf. Ruth 1:11-13), for Boaz was not a brother of Ruth's deceased husband. Custom required that, when the widow of a childless man desired to sell his estate, if there was no brother, then the nearest of kin and heir to the deceased should buy or redeem it of the widow (Ruth 4:3, 4, 9). The property was thereby retained in the family. Custom was also urgent that the kinsman voluntarily assume levirate duties or take the woman to wife, if he would not thereby endanger his own inheritance (chs. 3:9; 4:5, 6). It was considered magnanimous to do so, and a mark of loyalty to the family. A son born of such union was legally the son of the deceased (ch. 4:5, 10, 14, 17); and doubtless ultimately received the first-born's right in the estate.

In the Hebrew collection The Book of Ruth is placed among the Megilloth (scrolls), which are publicly read on specified anniversaries; since its scenery is the harvest field, it is read at Pentecost, the harvest festival. In the LXX and in Josephus' enumeration of the canonical books it stands immediately after Judges, as in the English version. The events recorded occurred in the

days of the Judges (Ruth 1:1), 60 years or more before David's birth (ch. 4:21, 22). The marriage of a pious Israelite with a Moabitess is recounted, and the issue of the marriage is an ancestor of David. After the Exile such a marriage would have been regarded as discreditable, and would not have been invented. The narrative is, accordingly, historical. Its historical character receives confirmation from the appropriateness of the event to the period, for about that time friendly intercourse prevailed between Israel and Moab (I Sam. 22:3, 4). The event is related without disapprobation and without explanation or apology, an indication that it was committed to writing before the Exile. The language is also as pure as admittedly early writings, such as Judges, ch. 5. The book did not receive its final literary form until a considerable time after the event; for it explains the drawing off of the shoe in matters of attestation as a custom of former times (Ruth 4:7), and it brings down the genealogy to David.

Rye. See SPELT.

S

Sab'a•oth (săb'â-ŏth) [hosts, armies]. The Lord of Sabaoth is the same as Lord of hosts, the 2d part of the title being left untranslated (cf. Rom. 9:29 with Isa. 1:9; James 5:4). See HOST.

Sa'bat (sā'băt). See SHEBAT.

Sab'bath (săb'áth) [rest]. The divinely instituted day of rest, ordained for all men. God having completed the work of creation in 6 days ceased from creative work on the 7th day. "And God blessed the seventh day, and hallowed it; because that in it he rested from all his work" which he had made in a creative manner (Gen. 2:1–3); see CREATION. The next reference to a division of time into periods of 7 days occurs in the account of the Flood, when Noah was forewarned of the imminence of the storm a week before it broke in its fury, and again when he sent forth the birds at intervals of 7 days to discover through them the stage of water (Gen. 7:4; 8:10, 12). But it is not only in this express mention of the week, but also in the entire chronology of the Flood, when interpreted according to its own principles, that the hebdomadal division of time is found to have existed at that early date. The events are measured by intervals of the week both in the Hebrew narrative and in the Babylonian account. And what is more, there is repeated evidence that the 7th day was regarded as a season of divine benevolence toward man. According to both accounts, and reckoning from the day when the Flood began, the divine power which caused the storm was restrained at the close of a 6th day, and the 1st day that dawned fair and beautiful was a 7th day; and the day when the inmates of the ark were permitted to disembark, and when they offered sacrifices of thanksgiving, was likewise a 7th day. A glance at the chronology will show that not improbably Noah dispatched the birds in connection with the conventional 7th day because it was a day of divine favor.

From the days of Noah until the Exodus there is no express mention in the Hebrew records of a sanctification of the 7th day by rest from labor and by religious worship. There is no reason why there should be. There was no event specially to emphasize the day. And probably in that age the Sabbath was somewhat less sharply marked off from the other days of the week, even among the people of God, than it was later; for the nomad shepherds had certain labors which must be performed, and the Israelites in Egypt were not their own masters and could not rest on the 7th day. But when the nation was organized at Sinai a different mode of life was adopted, the people were able to frame their own laws, they formed an independent community, they led camp life in the wilderness and exchanged it for the settled life of agriculturists and traders, and as a natural result rest on the Sabbath made a greater outward difference than it had done before. Still, in both the Hebrew and Babylonian literature relating to the period before the Exodus there are incidental references to a period of 7 days (Gen. 29:27, 28). These are doubtless to be understood in the sense in which we use the term week, reckoning 7 days from any date we please. At any rate time was frequently measured by periods of 7 days. Several causes doubtless contributed to make this custom general, among others the phasing of the moon. But over and beyond the appropriateness of a lunar subdivision of the lunar month, there was the conception, traceable in the narrative of the Flood, that the 7th day was one of divine rest and favor toward men.

The Sabbath is Jehovah's day par excellence and does not have a Babylonian origin. A Babylonian tablet rendered freely, goes as follows: "The seventh day is the feast of Marduk and Zarpanit. The shepherd of the great people shall not eat flesh cooked on the coals. The garment of his body he shall not change; clean clothing he shall not put on. A sacrifice he shall not offer. The king in a chariot shall not ride. Commanding, he shall not speak. In a secret place a seer shall not give an oracle. A physician shall not lay his hand on the sick. The day is not fitting for carrying out an intention. At night (i.e., at the end of this day) the king shall bring his gift to the great gods; his offering he shall offer. Then his prayer is acceptable with god." These prohibitions apply to the 7th, 14th, 19th, 21st, and 28th days of the month, which apparently were *dies nefasti,* on which certain things were to be avoided; the king was especially restricted. There is an Akkad. word *shabattu,* the 15th day of the month or full moon, etymologically related to Heb. *Shabbāth* (Sabbath), but it is not applied to the series of days listed above. A comparison of the Heb. Sabbath with the Babylonian *dies nefasti* sets its peculiarity into a clear light. Now there may originally have been some connection with the phases of the moon, but it is entirely independent of the courses of that heavenly body, since the 7-day week, which is bounded by the Sabbath, regularly pursues its course through the year without any consideration of the lunar month. Thus it is entirely independent of the astrology of the heathen of antiquity; we cannot trace any connection with the heathen *dies fasti* and *dies nefasti.* The Sabbath is praised as the will of the sovereign God of creation at the foundation of the world (Gen. 2:2 *seq.*; Ex. 20:11; 31:15–17). Among the Hebrews it was not the 7th day only which was sacred, but the day which began and which consecrated the 7th month, and the entire 7th year, and the completion of the 7th year. And these seasons were all associated with the idea of rest, of worship, of liberty, of good will to man, and of divine favor.

The first occurrence of the name Sabbath in the Hebrew records is in Ex. 16:23. The Israelites had not reached Mount Sinai, nor had the Ten Commandments been spoken from its summit, but in the wilderness of Sin, when manna began to be given a double amount fell on the 6th day; and Moses said: "This is that which the Lord hath spoken,

To-morrow is a solemn rest, a holy sabbath unto the Lord: bake that which ye will bake, . . . and all that remaineth over lay up for you to be kept until the morning." None fell on the morrow, and Moses said in regard to what had been kept over: "Eat that to-day; for to-day is a sabbath unto the Lord: to-day ye shall not find it in the field. Six days ye shall gather it; but on the seventh day is the sabbath, in it there shall be none" (vs. 23–26; cf. v. 5).

Shortly afterward the commandment requiring the Sabbath to be kept was promulgated with 9 other laws by Jehovah at Sinai, and afterward written by the finger of God on tables of stone (Ex. 31:18; Deut. 9:10). Like its companion laws, it was of perpetual obligation. It commences, "Remember the sabbath day, to keep it holy," the word remember being appropriately used, since the people did not now for the first time learn that the Sabbath existed. In repeating the laws 40 years later at Shittim, Moses recalls the fact that the Lord their God had commanded them to observe the day; and then instead of stating the reason for the ordination of the Sabbath, he assigns Jehovah's deliverance of his people from bondage or labor in Egypt as the reason why Israel specially is under obligation to keep the day of rest instituted by God (Deut. 5:15). The Sabbath was to be kept by a holy convocation for the worship of the Lord (Lev. 23:3; cf. Ezek. 46:3), and should be a sign showing that God was their sanctifier (Ex. 31:13). The doctrine clearly was that the day was ordained by God; that it was established as a day of physical rest and refreshment for man; that the obligation to keep it arises from God's own example, his connecting a blessing with it, and his explicit command, and that his redemption of his people lays them under special obligation to set the day apart; that it is to be observed by God's people as a Sabbath unto him, and is to include a holy assemblage for worship. It was a reminder of God's complacency in the contemplation of his finished work, and of Jehovah's redemption of his people from Egyptian service.

In the tabernacle and Temple worship the pre-eminence of the Sabbath over the other days of the week was shown by the offering upon it of 2 lambs, while 1 was sacrificed on an ordinary week day (Num. 28:9, 19). The 12 cakes of showbread were also to be presented on that day (Lev. 24:5–8; I Chron. 9:32). In enforcing the law, no fire was allowed to be lit by an Israelite in his habitation on the Sabbath day; anyone doing work on it was to be put to death; and one who gathered sticks on the Sabbath in the wilderness was in fact stoned to death (Ex. 35:3; Num. 15:32–36); see PUNISHMENT. Isaiah (chs. 56:2–6; 58:13) and Jeremiah (ch. 27:21–27) strongly counseled the keeping of the day. A psalm or song was composed for the Sabbath, in which delight is expressed in the worship of Jehovah and thought is directed to God's works of creation (Psalm 92). Ezekiel complains that the Sabbaths had to a large extent been profaned or polluted (Ezek. 20:12, 24; 22:8, 26; 23:38). In Nehemiah's time traders, especially those of Tyre, continually brought merchandise to Jerusalem for sale on the sacred day, till Nehemiah peremptorily forbade the practice to be continued and took strong measures against those who attempted to disregard his directions (Neh. 10:31; 13:15–22).

At the commencement of the war of independence under the Maccabee family, the Jews were of opinion that they had no right to defend themselves on the Sabbath if they were attacked by an enemy. The campaign therefore began with the slaughter of 1,000 unresisting Jews, consisting of patriots and their families. The survivors resolved in future to defend themselves if they were directly attacked on the sacred day, but not to engage in offensive operations (I Macc. 2:31-41). Even then they were at a disadvantage with the Gentiles, who labored under no such restriction. The latter pushed on siege and other operations on the Sabbath unmolested, provided they abstained from directly attacking the Jews. Pompey raised his banks and mounted his battering-rams against Jerusalem on the Sabbath without any interference from the inhabitants, but delayed the effort to breach the walls till the sacred day was over (Jos. *Antiq.* xiv. 4, 2 and 3). In the time of our Lord the Pharisees applied the law to the most trivial acts, and forbade many works of necessity and mercy. They denounced Jesus because he healed sick people on the Sabbath, though if ox, or ass, or sheep fell into a pit on that day, they did not consider it at all unlawful to take it out without delay. They also led forth the animals to be watered just as on ordinary week days (Matt. 12:9-13; Luke 13:10-17). It was not merely to healing on the Sabbath that they objected. When the disciples of Jesus, passing on the Sabbath through the grain fields, plucked some of the ears, and, rubbing them in their hands, ate them, being hungry, the Pharisees denounced this as if it were in essence the same as reaping, threshing, and grinding. Our Lord made a notable reply, "The sabbath was made for man, and not man for the sabbath: so that the Son of man is lord even of the sabbath" (Mark 2:23-28). The Sabbath was instituted for the benefit of mankind; its obligation lasts as long as man has the same needs as at creation; the Son of Man is not the slave of the Sabbath, but its Lord.

The day for synagogue worship was the 7th day of the week, Saturday (Matt. 12:9, 10; Acts 13:14). The Apostolic Christian Church from the beginning held assemblages for worship on the 1st day of the week, which was the day on which Christ rose from the dead for our justification (Acts 2:1, probably; 20:7). On that day the Apostle Paul directed the Christians of Galatia and Corinth to make their weekly contribution to the charities of the Church (I Cor. 16:1, 2). It was designated the Lord's Day (Rev. 1:10); see LORD'S DAY. This day, like the former appointment of the 7th day, sets apart 1 day in 7 to be a Sabbath unto the Lord. It is equally a reminder of the Lord's redemption of his people. It is accompanied by the same evidence of divine favor in the form of physical and spiritual blessings.

The Sabbath of the land was a year in which the land of Canaan had a solemn rest. It came round once every 7 years. In it the ground was not sown or reaped, nor the vineyard pruned, nor its fruits gathered in. The spontaneous growth of field and orchard was free to all. In the Sabbatic year also the creditor released the Hebrew debtor from his obligation and freed the Hebrew slave (Ex. 23:10, 11; Lev. 25:3-7; Deut. 15:1-18; Neh. 10:31). On the completion of 7 such Sabbatic years, that is, at the end of 49 years, the trumpet was blown to proclaim liberty throughout the land, and the year of jubilee was ushered in (Lev. 25:8-10); see JUBILEE. Reliable historical notices of the observance of the Sabbatic year are the covenant of Nehemiah's time (Neh. 10:31), the 150th year of the Seleucidan era or 164-163 B.C. (I Macc. 6:49, 53; cf. Jos. *Antiq.* xii. 9, 5), the 178th Seleucic year or 136-135 B.C. (Jos. *Antiq.* xiii. 8, 1; *War* i. 2, 4), the decree issued by Caesar exempting the Jews

from tribute during the Sabbatic year (Jos. *Antiq.* xiv. 10, 6; cf. Tacitus *Hist.* v. 4), the year 38-37 B.C. (Jos. *Antiq.* xiv. 16, 2; xv. 1, 2), and the year before the fall of Jerusalem, A.D. 68-69 (Talmud). See also Jos. *Antiq.* xi. 8, 5, for time of Alexander the Great. If the Israelites disobeyed God's laws, they were to be carried into captivity, the land lying desolate, having rest and being left to enjoy its Sabbaths, or the rest which the Israelites had not allowed it on their weekly and septennial Sabbaths (Lev. 26:34-43). Jeremiah prophesied that the people should be punished for their idolatry by the desolation of their land and their bondage to the Babylonians for 70 years (Jer. 25:7-11). The Chronicler also connects the Captivity with the disobedience of the people and the pollution of the Temple; and he adds that they were servants unto the Babylonians for 70 years, as Jeremiah had foretold they should be, until the land had enjoyed its Sabbaths; for as long as it lay desolate it kept Sabbath, to fulfill threescore and ten years (II Chron. 36:14, 16, 20, 21). It must not be inferred from these words that the people had ignored the Sabbatic year exactly 70 times, or that the neglected Sabbatic years were continuous; and it is not stated that the Sabbatic year was neglected. Doubtless it had been neglected sometimes, for an idolatrous and disobedient people would scarcely obey an injunction when obedience would apparently involve pecuniary loss.

Evidently any period of time which was kept as a Sabbath could be called a Sabbath. Not only were the 7th day and the 7th year Sabbaths, but also the Day of Atonement on the 10th day of the 7th month (Lev. 23:32).

Sab′bath Day′s Jour′ney. A Sabbath-day's journey was a journey of limited extent proper, in the estimation of the scribes, on a Sabbath day. The expression occurs in Acts 1:12, where this is stated to be the distance between Mount Olivet and Jerusalem, or from Jerusalem to a place on the mountain from which Bethany was visible (Luke 24:50). If the measurement be made from the e. gate of Jerusalem (the Jewish method of reckoning) to the site of the Church of the Ascension, crowning the Mount of Olives, the distance, as the crow flies, will be about 2,250 English feet; but in actual travel it will be considerably more. According to Josephus, the mount was distant 5 or 6 stades from the city (Jos. *Antiq.* xx. 8, 6; *War* v. 2, 3). The regulation of the Sabbath-day's journey had its origin in the injunction not to leave the camp on the Sabbath (Ex. 16:29). It was reckoned at 2,000 cubits, partly on an interpretation of Num. 35:5, according to which the district pertaining to a Levitical city extended 2,000 cubits from the wall on every side, and partly on the belief, derived from Josh. 3:4, that the camp of the Israelites was 2,000 cubits from the tabernacle, to which of course they might go on the Sabbath. A man might travel on the Sabbath within the city where he resided as far as its limits allowed, be the city never so large. Rabbinic casuistry, however, found means of evading this strict regulation. A man could, previous to the Sabbath, establish a residence by depositing food for 2 meals at or within the 2,000-cubit limit; he could then go 2,000 cubits beyond that point on the Sabbath without transgressing the law.

Sab·bat′l·cal Year. See JUBILEE, SABBATH.

Sa·be′ans (să-bē′ănz). The people of Sheba (Isa. 45:14), a nation far off (Joel 3:8); also the people of Seba (Isa. 45:14; cf. Ezek. 23:42, A.V., which follows the kere). See SEBA, SHEBA, I.

Sab′tah (săb′tá) and **Sab′ta** (săb′tá). A
Cushite people (Gen. 10:7; I Chron. 1:9),
probably of s. Arabia; generally identified
with Shabwat, the ancient metropolis of
Hadramaut.

Sab′te·ca (săb′tē-ká), in A.V. **Sab′te·cha**
(săb′tē-ká) and **Sab′te·chah** (săb′tē-ká). A
Cushite people (Gen. 10:7; I Chron. 1:9),
probably of s. Arabia.

Sa′car (sā′kär) [hire, wages]. 1. A Hararite, father of one of David's mighty men
(I Chron. 11:35). In II Sam. 23:33 Sharar.
2. A son of Obed-edom (I Chron. 26:4).

Sack′but. A medieval wind instrument,
having a long bent tube of brass with a
movable slide for changing the pitch of the
tone, as in the trombone. The instrument referred to by this name in the English version
of Dan. 3:5 belonged to an entirely different
class. It was a stringed instrument, and the
English translation is erroneously a sound
equivalent of the original. It is called in
Aram. *śabbᵉkā*, which is evidently identical
with Gr. *sambykē*, which was an instrument
of music somewhat like the harp or lyre, but
with only 4 strings. Strabo affirms that the
Gr. word is of barbarian origin; and Athenaeus states that the instrument was invented by the Syrians.

Sack′cloth′. A coarse cloth, of a dark color,
usually made of goat's hair (Rev. 6:12). It
was called in Heb. *śak̠*, from which the Eng.
word is derived. It was worn customarily by
mourners (II Sam. 3:31; II Kings 19:1, 2),
often, if not habitually, by prophets (Isa.
20:2; Rev. 11:3), and by captives (I Kings
20:31; cf. Isa. 3:24). The garment of sackcloth probably resembled a sack, with openings made for the neck and arms, and slit
down the front. It was cast about the loins
(Gen. 37:34; I Kings 20:31) and girded on
(II Sam. 3:31; Ezek. 7:18; Joel 1:8); and
was usually worn over other raiment (Jonah
3:6; cf. II Sam. 21:10), but sometimes next
to the skin (I Kings 21:27; II Kings 6:30;
Job 16:15; Isa. 32:11).

The cloth was also used for making sacks,
which were known by the same name as the
material (Gen. 42:25; Josh. 9:4).

Sac′ri·fice. See OFFERINGS.

Sad′du·cees (săd′ū-sēz) [Lat. *Sadducaei*,
Gr. *Saddoukaioi*]. A Jewish party, the opponents of the Pharisees (Jos. *Antiq.* xiii. 10, 6).
They were comparatively few in number, but
they were educated men, and mostly wealthy
and of good position (*ibid.*; xviii. 1, 4). The
name, judged by the orthography, is derived
from Zadok, which was often written Sad-
douk in Greek. The rabbis say that the party
took its name from its founder Zadok, who
lived c. 300 B.C.; but since it appears that
the members and adherents of the highest
priestly aristocracy constituted the party, it
is now generally believed that the name refers to the high priest Zadok, who officiated
in David's reign and in whose family the
high priesthood remained until the political
confusion of the Maccabaean times, his descendants and partisans being Zadokites or
Sadducees.

In opposition to the Pharisees, who laid
great stress on the tradition of the elders,
the Sadducees limited their creed to the doctrines which they found in the sacred text
itself. They held that the word of the written Law was alone binding (Jos. *Antiq.* xiii.
10, 6). They maintained the right of private
interpretation (Jos. *Antiq.* xviii. 1, 4). They
held to the letter of Scripture, even when it
led to severity in the administration of justice (Jos. *Antiq.* xx. 9, 1). In distinction
from the Pharisees, they denied: 1. The res-

urrection and future retribution in Sheol, asserting that the soul dies with the body
(Matt. 22:23–33; Acts 23:8; Jos. *Antiq.* xviii.
1, 4; *War* ii. 8, 14). 2. The existence of angels and spirits (Acts 23:8). 3. Fatalism:
contending for the freedom of the will, teaching that all our actions are in our own power,
so that we are ourselves the causes of what
is good and receive what is evil from our own
folly, and affirming that God is not concerned
in our doing good or not doing what is evil
(Jos. *Antiq.* xiii. 5, 9; *War* ii. 8, 14). In denying immortality and the resurrection, they
were relying on the absence of an explicit
statement of these doctrines in the Mosaic
Law, and they failed to hold the faith of the
Patriarchs regarding Sheol, which, though it
was undeveloped, yet contained the germs of
the later Biblical doctrine of the resurrection
of the body and a future retribution. The
Patriarchs unquestionably believed in the
continued existence of the soul after death.
In affirming that there is neither angel nor
spirit, the Sadducees were setting themselves
against the elaborate angelology of the Judaism of their time; but they went to the other
extreme, and again fell short of the teaching
of the Law (Ex. 3:2; 14:19). They probably
at first emphasized the truth that God directs
affairs with respect to man's conduct, punishing or rewarding in this life according as
man's deeds are good or evil. If they actually taught, as Josephus affirms they did,
that God is not concerned in our doing good
or refraining from evil, they rejected the
clear teaching of the Mosaic Law which they
professed to believe (Gen. 3:17; 4:7; 6:5–7).
It is probable that they began by denying
what is not expressly taught in the letter of
Scripture; but as they yielded more fully to
Greek influence, they adopted the principles
of the Aristotelian philosophy, and refused to
accept any doctrine which they could not
prove by pure reason.

As to the origin and growth of the Sadducees, Schürer suggests that the priestly house
of Zadok, which was at the head of affairs
in the 4th and 3d centuries B.C. under the
Persian and Grecian kings, began, unconsciously perhaps, to place political above religious considerations. In the time of Ezra
and Nehemiah the family of the high priest
was worldly and inclined to resist the strict
separation of Jew from Gentile. See ELIA-
SHIB 5. In the time of Antiochus Epiphanes
(175–163 B.C.) a large number of priests were
friendly to Greek culture (II Macc. 4:14–16),
and the high priests Jason, Menelaus, and
Alcimus were pronounced Hellenizers. The
people took a determined stand under the
Maccabees for purity of Israel's religion; and
when this party triumphed and the Maccabees secured the high priesthood, the Zadokites were forced into retirement and driven
to politics, and they continued to be ready to
neglect the customs and traditions of the
elders and favor Greek culture and influence.
John Hyrcanus, Aristobulus, and Alexander
Jannaeus (135–78 B.C.) favored the Sadducees, and the conduct of political affairs was
largely in their hands under the Romans and
the Herods, for the high priests of this period
were Sadducees (Acts 5:17; Jos. *Antiq.* xx.
9, 1). The Sadducees, as well as the Pharisees, who visited John the Baptist in the
wilderness, were addressed by him as a generation of vipers (Matt. 3:7). They joined
with the Pharisees in demanding from our
Lord a sign from heaven (Matt. 16:1–4), and
Jesus warned his disciples against both (vs.
6–12). The Sadducees attempted to embarrass
him by putting to him an ensnaring question
regarding the resurrection, but he refuted
their arguments, and reduced them to silence
(Matt. 22:23–33). They joined with the

priests and the captain of the Temple in persecuting Peter and John (Acts 4:1–22). Both Pharisees and Sadducees were in the sanhedrin which tried Paul, and the apostle, taking note of the fact, cleverly set them at variance with each other (Acts 23:6–10).

Sa'doc (sā'dŏk) [ṣādōḳ, just, righteous]. An ancestor of Christ, who lived after the Exile (Matt. 1:14).

Saf'fron. A fragrant plant (S. of Sol. 4: 14), called in Heb. karkôm, in Arab. kurkum. It is the saffron crocus (Crocus sativus), a native, apparently, of n. Italy and of w. Asia. From a remote period of antiquity it has been largely cultivated in s. Europe and Asia. The flowers are light violet in color, veined with red. The dried stigmas, pulverized or pressed, yield a yellow dye. Clothing and rooms were sprinkled with water scented with saffron; olive oil perfumed with it was used as an ointment; food was spiced with it; and it was employed in medicine.

Sa'la (sā'lá) and **Sa'lah** (sā'lá). See SHELAH, I.

Sal'a·mis (sǎl'á-mǐs). A city on the e. or s.e. coast of Cyprus, traditionally reported to have been built by Teucer, from the island of Salamis, off the coast of Greece. It contained synagogues of the Jews, in which Paul on his First Missionary Journey preached (Acts 13:4, 5). The place is now called Famagusta.

Sa·la'thi·el (sá-lā'thǐ-ĕl). See SHEALTIEL.

Sal'e·cah (sǎl'ê-ká) in A.V. **Sal'cah** (sǎl'ká) and **Sal'chah** (sǎl'ká) [cf. Arab. salaka, to go along a road]. A city of Bashan, near Edrei (Deut. 3:10; Josh. 12:5; 13:11). It was on the boundary of Og's kingdom, and afterward constituted the n. limit of the Gadites (I Chron. 5:11). It is now known as Salkhad, 35 miles e. of Edrei, and 66 e., very slightly n. of the Jordan, opposite to Beth-shean, in Samaria.

Sa'lem (sā'lĕm)[complete, peaceful, peace]. A natural abbreviation of the name Jerusalem, the city or foundation of peace (Ps. 76:2; and probably Gen. 14:18). See MELCHIZEDEK, SHALEM.

Sa'lim (sā'lǐm) [perhaps, Aram. shelǐm, completed]. A place near which were the waters of Aenon (John 3:23); see AENON.

Sal'la·i (sǎl'á-ī) [cf. Arab. sala'a, to pay promptly; but in S. Arab., to consecrate, offer]. 1. A chief of a family of Benjamites who resided at Jerusalem (Neh. 11:8). 2. A father's house among the priests after the Captivity (Neh. 12:20); see SALLU 2.

Sal'lu (sǎl'ū) [cf. Sallai]. 1. A Benjamite, a son of Meshullam and a chief of a family resident at Jerusalem (I Chron. 9:7; Neh. 11:7). 2. A chief of the priests who came from Babylon with Zerubbabel (Neh. 12:7). In the next generation a father's house, which occupies the same position in the corresponding catalogue, bore the name Sallai (v. 20). One of the 2 names has probably been misread, the difference being merely that between a yodh (jod) and a waw (vav), q.v.

Sal'ma (sǎl'má). See SALMON.

Sal'mai (sǎl'mī), in A.V. **Shal'mai** (sǎl'mī) of Ezra 2:46 **Sham'lai** (shăm'lī); the forms being confused in the Heb. text itself. Founder of a family of Nethinim, members of which returned from captivity with Zerubbabel (Ezra 2:46; Neh. 7:48).

Sal'mon (sǎl'mŏn) or **Sal'mah** (sǎl'má) or **Sal'ma**. Father of Boaz. He was a man of Judah, descended through Perez, Hezron, and Ram (Ruth 4:18–21; Matt. 1:4; Luke 3:32).

In the Hebrew text of Ruth 4:20, not 21, the form Salmah is used, of which Salma is the later orthography (I Chron. 2:11). He has sometimes been thought to have been the ancestor of the inhabitants of Bethlehem, mentioned in I Chron. 2:51, 54. But the genealogy of Salma, ancestor of the Bethlehemites, is traced back by the line of Caleb, not of Ram. The different lineage probably indicates a different person; though, of course, genealogies may intertwine. For Salmon of Ps. 68:14, see ZALMON.

Sal·mo'ne (săl-mō'nê). A promontory, constituting the e. extremity of Crete (Acts 27: 7). It is now known as Cape Sidero.

Sa'lom (sā'lŏm). See SALU.

Sa·lo'me (sá-lō'mê) [fem. of Solomon]. 1. The wife of Zebedee, and the mother of James and John (cf. Matt. 27:56 with Mark 15:40; 16:1). She was one of the women who from a distance saw the crucifixion (Matt. 27:56), and who went to the sepulcher of our Lord on the resurrection morning with sweet spices to anoint his body (Mark 16:1). 2. The daughter of Herodias, who danced before Herod the tetrarch and received the head of John the Baptist (Matt. 14:3–11; Mark 6:17–28). For her name, see Jos. Antiq. xviii. 5, 4.

Salt. Salt of poor quality could be scraped up on the shore of the Dead Sea, when the salty water had evaporated, or be cut from the neighboring cliffs. It was used in Canaan and the adjacent regions as a condiment and preservative for animal food (Job 6:6; Ecclus. 39:26). Under the Law, it was presented with offerings of all kinds (Lev. 2:13; Ezek. 43:24; Jos. Antiq. iii. 9, 1). Salt land is unfruitful (Job 39:6), and when a captured city was doomed to utter destruction the final step sometimes was to sow it with salt. Abimelech thus treated Shechem (Judg. 9:45). Salt preserves from corruption and renders food palatable, and is therefore used figuratively for the true disciples of Jesus, who by their precepts and example raise the moral tone of society (Matt. 5:13; Mark 9: 50; Luke 14:34). Salt is also used for wholesome character and speech (Mark 9:50; Col. 4:6). The impure salt of Syria, when exposed to the rain and sun or stored in damp houses, is apt to lose its taste and become useless. It cannot be used like much other refuse as a fertilizer, for it is good for nothing (Matt. 5:13; Luke 14:35). During the convulsion in which the guilty cities of the Plain were destroyed, Lot's wife, lingering in the doomed region, perished, and was transformed into a pillar of salt (Gen. 19:26; Wisd. of Sol. 10:7; Jos. Antiq. i. 11, 4).

A covenant of salt was a covenant of permanent continuance and perpetual obligation (Lev. 2:13; Num. 18:19; II Chron. 13:5).

Salt, Cit'y of. A city in the wilderness of Judah. It is mentioned along with En-gedi on the shore of the Dead Sea, from which, presumably, it was not far distant (Josh. 15:62).

Salt, Val'ley of. A valley in which the army of David slew 18,000 men of Aram (II Sam. 8:13) or rather Edom (II Sam. 8:14; I Chron. 18:12; cf. I Kings 11:15–17; Psalm 60, title); see DALETH. Amaziah, king of Judah, slew 10,000 Edomites in the Valley of Salt, and then took their capital, Sela (II Kings 14:7; II Chron. 25:11). The site of the Valley of Salt was formerly placed at the s. end of the Dead Sea, where there is a range of hills 5 miles in length, consisting of layers of salt, and between this chain and the sea is a valley 6 or 8 miles long. East of Beer-sheba, however, there is Wadi el-Milḥ (salt), which flows by the foot of Tell el-

Milḥ, and this seems to be the scene of the defeat of the Edomites.

Salt Sea. The name given in the O.T. to what is now generally called the Dead Sea (Gen. 14:3; Num. 34:3, 12; Deut. 3:17; Josh. 15:2, 5). See DEAD SEA.

Salt'wort'. The rendering of Heb. *mallûaḥ*, saline plant (Job 30:4; in A.V. mallows). It was used as food by the very poor. Two genera of plants are commonly so designated, *Salicornia* and *Salsola*, but neither is suitable for food. The plant intended is probably some other chenopod, as spinach or, better, sea purslane (*Atriplex halimus*). This latter is a bush. It grows abundantly in salt marshes along the Mediterranean and on the shores of the Dead Sea. Its small, thick, sour leaves would, in extreme need, furnish a miserable food.

Sa'lu (sā'lū) [passive participle of root *sala'a;* see SALLAI]. A Simeonite, father of Zimri whom Phinehas slew (Num. 25:14; in A.V. of I Macc. 2:26 Salom).

Sal'u·ta'tion. Among the Hebrews salutation on meeting consisted in the expression of good wishes or a solemn blessing. The forms most prevalent were : 1. "Blessed be thou of the Lord," or "God be gracious unto thee," or the equivalent (Gen. 43:29; Ruth 3:10; I Sam. 15:13). 2. "The Lord be with thee," to which the rejoinder was, "The Lord bless thee" (Ruth 2:4). 3. "Peace be unto thee," or "Peace be upon thee," peace meaning welfare (Luke 24:36). This was the most common salutation, and is still in use among the Jews. The reply is, "Upon thee be peace." If the occasion made the words appropriate, the form was: "Peace be unto thee, and peace be to thy house" (cf. I Sam. 25:6; Luke 10:5). 4. "Hail!" a common salutation in the Greek period (Matt. 26:49; 27:29; 28:9; Luke 1:28). 5. "Let the king live for ever" was the salutation addressed by a subject to the Hebrew monarch (cf. I Kings 1: 31), and was employed in the Babylonian and Persian courts (Neh. 2:3; Dan. 2:4; 5:10; 6:6, 21).

At parting a blessing was invoked (Gen. 24:60; 28:1; 47:10; Josh. 22:6), which eventually assumed the conventional form, "Go in peace," or "Farewell" (I Sam. 1:17; 20: 42; II Sam. 15:9; Mark 5:34; Acts 16:36); and the rejoinder to a superior might be, "Let thy handmaid find favor in thy sight" (I Sam. 1:18).

Abraham and Lot rose up to meet passing strangers, bowed before them to the earth, and pressed hospitality upon them (Gen. 18: 2; 19:1); Boaz exchanged greeting with his reapers (Ruth 2:4); travelers on the road saluted workmen in the field (Ps. 129:8). The salutation was often withheld from men of a different religion (Matt. 5:47); and rightly so, when it was apt to lead to fellowship and to imply a wish for the success of a bad cause (II John 11). Messengers might be charged to salute no man by the way (II Kings 4:29; Luke 10:4), for the formality incident to offering a greeting and receiving a response involved delay. The bow was not a mere nod, but profound obeisance or prostration; and in deferential greetings, a rider dismounted from his beast or left his chariot (I Sam. 25:23; II Kings 5:21).

Letters in Palestine, before the conquest of the country by the Hebrews, and in Egypt, always began with salutations. The greetings are all framed on the same model. A son begins a letter to his father thus: "To Dûdu, my lord, my father, thus speaketh Aziri thy son, thy servant. At the feet of my father I prostrate myself. Upon my father be peace [welfare]." A subject addresses his liege, the king of Egypt, after this manner: "To the king my lord, my gods, my sun, thus speaketh Yapaḥi thy servant, the dust of thy two feet. At the feet of the king my lord, my gods, my sun, seven times and seven times I prostrate myself." The governor of a district writes to his equals: "To the kings of Canaan, servants, my brothers, thus the king." And Pharaoh begins a letter to a Kassite monarch with the words: "To Kadashman-Enlil, king of Karduniash [Babylonia], my brother, thus saith Nibmuaria [Amenhotep III] the great king, king of Egypt, thy brother. To me is peace [welfare]. May peace [welfare] be to thee! To thy house, thy wives, thy children, thy chief men, thy horses, thy chariots, in the midst of thy lands, may it be very well!"

The usual epistolary salutation in the Greco-Roman period in Palestine was briefer, more direct, more businesslike, and in it the name of the writer commonly stands first. "King Alexander to his brother Jonathan, greeting" (I Macc. 10:18). "King Demetrius unto the nation of the Jews, greeting" (I Macc. 10:25; and so Acts 15:23; 23:26; James 1:1). The letter was frequently concluded with a salutation, derived from Latin usage, "Fare ye well" (Acts 15:29). To the brief salutation after the Latin manner, the Hebrews, following their own customs, often added a prayer for peace (II Macc. 1:1). Their salutation also was often elaborate (vs. 1–5), and the old order was frequently observed (ch. 9:19, 20). The salutations with which Paul begins his letters are equally manifold (Rom. 1:1–7). In the epistles to Timothy he wishes his true child in the faith, grace, mercy, and peace; but his usual greeting is, "Grace to you and peace," and he was apt to close his letters with salutations from himself and others (I Thess. 1:1; 5:26–28, his first letter).

Sa·mar'i·a (sȧ-mâr'ĭ-ȧ) [Lat. *Samaria* from Gr. *Samar(e)ia*, from Aram. *Shāmerayin;* for Heb. see below]. 1. The capital of the 10 tribes during the longest period of their history; the site had been occupied in the early Bronze period. The city was built or commenced by Omri, king of Israel, on a hill purchased for 2 talents of silver, which may be the equivalent of about $3,900. The former owner's name was Shemer; and since it expressed the idea of watching, guarding, keeping, it suggested an appropriate designation for a city on a hill. Accordingly Omri called the city Shōmerōn, place of watch (I Kings 16:24); it was actually protected by a strong watchtower on the s.w. The eminence which the city crowned was sometimes denominated the mountain of Samaria (Amos 4:1; 6:1). It stood in the midst of a fertile valley (Isa. 28:1). The site was so well chosen that the city continued to be the capital of the Northern Kingdom to the captivity of the 10 tribes, the successive sovereigns reigning, and at their death being buried, there (I Kings 16: 28, 29; 20:43; 22:10, 37, 51; etc.). Scarcely was Samaria built before hostilities arose between Ben-hadad I, king of Syria, and Omri. The former, if his son spoke the truth, had the advantage, and, to please the victor, Omri had to make streets in Samaria for Syrian merchants (I Kings 20:34). During the reign of Ahab, Omri's son and successor, the city, which was surrounded by a wall, was unsuccessfully besieged by Ben-hadad II (vs. 1–21). On the n. was a pool or reservoir which was cut in the rock and cemented; at the side of it the royal attendants washed the blood-stained chariot in which Ahab's body was brought home from Ramoth-gilead (I Kings 22:38). The excavation of Ahab's palace has revealed furnishings with ivory inlay (cf. v.

Sebastiyeh, the Site of Ancient Samaria

39); in an adjacent building were found a number of ostraca inscribed in Hebrew. It was probably in the days of Joram when the capital was unsuccessfully besieged by Ben-hadad II (II Kings 6:8 to 7:20). The elders of Samaria, afraid of displeasing Jehu, obeyed his order to murder Ahab's 70 sons (ch. 10:1–10).

From the very beginning Samaria had been a city notorious for its idolatry. Ahab had led the way in this heathen worship by rearing a temple and an altar to Baal (I Kings 16:32); and since in his reign reference is made to 400 prophets of the Asherah who ate at Jezebel's table (ch. 18:19), it is probable that the idol so named remained till Jehu's reign (II Kings 13:6). Attendant on this idolatry was great corruption of morals (Hos. 7:1–8; Amos 4:1; 8:14). Against these idolatrous practices Elijah worked (I Kings, ch. 18). Elisha made the city his headquarters (II Kings 5:3–9; 6:32); and doubtless Hosea labored there. Samaria and the kingdom were threatened with judgment by many prophets (Isa. 7:9; 8:4; Jer. 31:5; Ezek. 16:46, 51, 53, 55; 23:33; Hos. 8:5, 6; 13:16; Amos 3:12; Micah 1:5–9).

At length the disaster came upon the city. The siege was begun by the Assyrians under Shalmaneser, 724 B.C., and in 722, or early in

721, the city was captured by the king of Assyria (II Kings 17:3–6). The glory of the capture is claimed by Sargon, Shalmaneser's successor, who in that year ascended the throne; see SARGON. The conquerors repeopled the town with foreigners (v. 24); see SAMARITAN. In 332 or 331 B.C. Alexander the Great took Samaria and transferred its inhabitants to Shechem, placing Syro-Macedonians in their place. About the year 108 B.C. Samaria was besieged by John Hyrcanus, who drew around it a wall of circumvallation 80 stades, or about 9 miles, in extent. The city held out for a year but was ultimately forced by famine to surrender. The victor demolished it, attempting to efface all proofs that a fortified city had ever stood on the hill (cf. Micah 1:6; Jos. *Antiq.* xiii. 10, 2 and 3; *War* i. 2, 7 and 8). It was again inhabited in the time of Alexander Jannaeus. Pompey annexed it to the province of Syria. Gabinius fortified it anew (Jos. *Antiq.* xiv. 4, 4; 5, 3). It was rebuilt and refortified by Herod the Great, who called it Sebaste, a Gr. fem. of *Sebastos,* the Gr. for Lat. Augustus, the title of his patron, the first Roman emperor (Jos. *Antiq.* xv. 8, 5). The evangelist Philip labored there with success; among others Simon Magus believed and was baptized (Acts 8:5–13). To carry on this work Peter and John were sent from Jerusalem (vs. 14–25). The site of Samaria is the hill, 5½ miles n.w. of Shechem, on which the village of Sebastiyeh stands. The sides are steep, the summit a tableland about a mile from e. to w.

2. The territory occupied by the 10 tribes, or the Kingdom of Israel personified (I Kings 21:1; II Kings 17:24; Isa. 7:9; Jer. 31:5; Ezek. 16:46). See ISRAEL.

3. The district of Samaria, occupying central Palestine, between Galilee on the n. and Judea on the s. (I Macc. 10:30). Josephus' description of its limits (Jos. *War* iii. 3, 4, and 5) is not very intelligible, but he makes it plain that the n. limit passed through "a village that is in the great plain called Ginea." This is apparently En-gannim (Josh. 19:21; 21:29), at the s. angle of the Plain of Esdraelon. The s. limit was the toparchy Acrabattene, some 6 or 7 miles s. of Shechem. Samaria extended to the Jordan on the e., but did not reach the Mediterranean on the w. Acco belonged to Judea. The Talmud makes Antipatris the w. limit. It comprehended the old territories of Manasseh w. of the Jordan, and of Ephraim, with a portion of Issachar and Benjamin. Pompey, in 63 B.C., attached it to the province of Syria (Jos. *Antiq.* xiv. 4, 4). In A.D. 6 the emperor Augustus erected Judea, Samaria, and Idumaea into a division of the prefecture of Syria, called the province of Judea, and placed it under procurators (Jos. *Antiq.* xvii. 13, 5; cf. 11, 4), and this arrangement obtained in the time of our Lord.

Sa·mar'i·tan (să-măr'ĭ-tăn). In the only passage in which the word is found in the O.T. (II Kings 17:29) it means an individual belonging to the old kingdom of Northern Israel. In later Hebrew literature it signifies an inhabitant of the district of Samaria in central Palestine (Luke 17:11). When Sargon captured Samaria (722/1 B.C.), he carried into captivity, by his own account, 27,280 people. That he left many Israelites in the land is evident. Finding that the remaining Israelites were rebellious, he began a systematic course for their denationalization. He introduced colonists from Babylonia and Hamath (II Kings 17:24) and Arabia, who continued to practice idolatry in their new home. The population of the country had been thinned, and the cultivation of the soil interrupted, by these wars, so that oppor-

tunity was afforded for wild beasts to multiply, which God used as a scourge. Lions killed some of the idolaters. The newcomers concluded that they did not understand how to worship the particular god of the country, and they informed the king of Assyria. He sent them a priest from among the captive Israelites, who took up his residence at Beth-el and began to instruct the people regarding Jehovah. He was unable to persuade them to abandon their ancestral idolatry. They erected images of their gods on the high places of the Israelites, and combined their idolatries with the worship of Jehovah (II Kings 17:25–33). This dual worship they kept up until after the fall of Jerusalem (vs. 34–41). Esarhaddon continued the policy of his grandfather, Sargon (Ezra 4:2), and finally Asnapper (Osnapper), probably Ashurbanipal, completed the work by adding to the population people from Elam and elsewhere (vs. 9, 10).

The new province of the Assyrian empire was weak, and Josiah or his agents traversed its whole extent, everywhere destroying the high places with which it abounded (II Chron. 34:6, 7). The idols were still on these high places, but it is probable that idolatry was decreasing under the influence of the Israelites who remained in the land and through the teaching of the priests. And this act of Josiah's was another blow to it. Several decades later some among the Samaritans were in the habit of visiting the Temple at Jerusalem for worship (Jer. 41:5). When Zerubbabel led back his band of exiles from Babylonia to Jerusalem, the Samaritans asked permission to participate in the erection of the Temple on the ground that they had worshiped the God of Israel ever since the time of Esarhaddon (Ezra 4:2).

There was early a repugnance on the part of most of the Jews to social and religious association with the Samaritans, and this feeling developed into intense antipathy as years rolled on (Ezra 4:3; Ecclus. 50:25, 26; Luke 9:52, 53; John 4:9). The Samaritans were neither of pure Hebrew blood nor of uncontaminated worship. Josephus (*Antiq.* ix. 14, 3) says that when the Jews were in prosperity, the Samaritans claimed that they were allied to them in blood; but when they saw them in adversity, they declared that they had no relationship to them, but were descended from the Assyrian immigrants. When the offer of the Samaritans to assist in rebuilding the Temple was rejected by Zerubbabel, Jeshua, and their associates, the Samaritans made no further efforts at conciliation but did their best with other adversaries to prevent the completion of the work (Ezra 4:1–10); they also opposed the rebuilding later on of the walls of Jerusalem by Nehemiah (Neh. 4:1–23). Their leader on the latter occasion was Sanballat, the Horonite. It was he whose son-in-law was put out of the priesthood by Nehemiah; and the father-in-law probably founded the Samaritan temple on Mount Gerizim; see SANBALLAT. Henceforward fugitives from discipline at Jerusalem were accustomed to go to the rival edifice on Mount Gerizim where they were sure of obtaining a warm welcome (Jos. *Antiq.* xi. 8, 7). During the persecution under Antiochus Epiphanes they declared that they were not of the same race as the Jews, and gratified the tyrant by expressing a desire that their temple on Mount Gerizim might in future be dedicated to Jupiter, the defender of strangers (II Macc. 6:2). About 128 B.C. John Hyrcanus took Shechem and Gerizim, destroying the Samaritan temple (Jos. *Antiq.* xiii. 9, 1); but the worshipers continued to offer their adorations on the summit of the hill where the sacred edifice had stood. They did so when our Lord was on earth (John 4:20, 21).

In the time of Christ their theological tenets did not essentially differ from those of the Jews, and especially of the Sadducean sect. They shared with them the expectation of a coming Messiah (John 4:25). They, however, accepted no more of the O.T. than the Pentateuch. The main cause for the Samaritans' receiving the gospel so gladly when Philip preached to them was the miracles which he wrought (Acts 8:5, 6); but another undoubtedly was that, unlike Judaism, Christianity followed the example and teaching of its founder and admitted Samaritans within its pale and to the same privileges as those possessed by the Jewish converts (Luke 10: 29–37; 17:16–18; John 4:1–42). A small community of Samaritans still exists at and around Nablus, the ancient Shechem.

Sa·mar'i·tan Pen'ta·teuch (să-măr'ĭ-tăn pĕn'-tȧ-tūk). The Samaritans possessed the Pentateuch in Hebrew. It was quoted by Jerome, Eusebius, and other Christian fathers. In A.D. 1616 Pietro della Valle purchased a copy from the Samaritans of Damascus, which was placed in 1623 in the library of the Oratory in Paris. By the end of the 18th century 15 other copies, more or less complete, had reached Europe, and the number has since been increased. Morinus, who published the Samaritan Pentateuch in 1632, considered the Samaritan text vastly superior to that of the Masoretes. Controversy on the subject went on, with occasional intervals, for nearly 2 centuries, till, in 1815, the great Hebrew scholar Gesenius, who had made a very careful examination of the Samaritan text, considered it to be far inferior to that of the Hebrew Masoretes, and of small critical value. Most of the Samaritan rolls, containing the whole or a part of the Pentateuch, are supposed not to be older than the 10th century of the Christian era, though there is 1 whose oldest portions claim A.D. 656 as the date. The Samaritan community at Nablus possesses a MS. said to have been copied in the 13th year after the Conquest of Canaan, but scholars consider the hand of a 13th century type. The several rolls are in the Samaritan character, that on the Maccabaean coins, which was also that of the Hebrews before they introduced the present square letters.

The Samaritan text in about 6,000 places differs from the Hebrew text of the Masoretes. In Deut. 27:4, 8, we read that Moses directed the people when they passed the Jordan to set up certain stones in Mount Ebal, plaster them, and write on them the Law. Here the Samaritans have substituted Gerizim for Ebal, to increase the veneration for their sacred mountain. There are various other less important variations; see CHRONOLOGY. Most of them are manifestly due to the haste of the scribes or to alterations which they deliberately made. In about 1,900 places the text agrees with that of the LXX against the Hebrew readings, which indicates that the Greek translators used a Hebrew text much like that possessed by the Samaritans; but the great majority of these are of trifling consequence. Yet where it agrees with the LXX, we have one tradition of the Hebrew text preserved. Probably the Samaritan Pentateuch goes back to the time when Manasseh, the grandson of Eliashib the high priest and son-in-law of Sanballat, was expelled from Jerusalem (Neh. 13:23–30; Jos. *Antiq.* xi. 7–8). He took refuge with the Samaritans, and a rival temple was built upon Mount Gerizim. If the Pentateuch was canonized c. 400 B.C., the Samaritan Pentateuch was no longer influenced by that of the Jews

after that date. Apparently the rift between the Jews and Samaritans occurred before the canonization of the Prophets.

The Samaritan Pentateuch must not be confounded with the Samaritan version of the Pentateuch made into the dialect of the Samaritans early in the Christian era. They possess an Arabic translation also, made in the 11th or 12th century, a book of Joshua, founded on the canonical book of the same name and written about the 13th century A.D., and some other literature.

Sa'mekh (sä'mĕk), in A.V. **Sa'mech** (sä'-mĕk). The 15th letter of the Heb. alphabet. It is represented by *s* in Anglicizing Hebrew names which contain it, as Joseph. It heads the 15th section of Psalm 119, in which section each verse of the original begins with this letter.

Sam'gar·ne'bo (săm'gär-nē'bō) [perhaps Akkad. *Shumgir-Nabū*, be gracious, Nebo]. One of Nebuchadnezzar's princes who entered Jerusalem (Jer. 39:3).

Sam'lah (săm'lȧ) [a garment]. A king of the Edomites, a native of Masrekah (Gen. 36:36, 37).

Sa'mos (sā'mŏs) [Gr., a height by the seashore]. An island about 80 miles in circumference off the coast of Asia Minor, s. by w. of Ephesus, and nearly opposite to the promontory of Trogyllium. After the defeat of Antiochus the Great by the Romans at Magnesia, in 190 B.C., it was independent (I Macc. 15:23); but it was under the influence of Pergamos, and along with Pergamos it passed into the hands of the Romans in 133 B.C. At the time Paul reached it (Acts 20:15), it still enjoyed the autonomy conferred upon it by the Romans in 17 B.C. Its inhabitants were noted for commercial enterprise.

Sam'o·thrace (săm'ō-thrās), in A.V. **Sam'o·thra'ci·a** (săm'ō-thrā'shĭ-ȧ) [Gr., Samos of Thrace]. An island in the archipelago off the coast of Thrace and opposite the mouth of the Hebrus. It has an area of about 30 square miles, and has in it a mountain 5,000 feet high. Paul's vessel made a straight course to the island from Troas, in Asia Minor (Acts 16:11).

Samp'sa·mes (sămp'sȧ-mēz). A country, rather than a king, which was friendly to Rome (I Macc. 15:23). Not identified.

Sam'son (săm's'n) [little sun, solar]. One of the most eminent of the Hebrew Judges. He was the son of a Danite called Manoah, was born at Zorah, within the limits of the s. territory of Dan, and had his birth and his subsequent career announced beforehand to his parents by the angel of the Lord. He was a Nazirite from his birth, no razor coming upon his head, and no wine or strong drink entering into his mouth. As long as he submitted to these restrictions he was capable of heroic achievements against the Philistines (Judg. 13:1–24). Circumstances conspired at this time to separate Judah and Dan from the rest of the Hebrews and to compel these 2 tribes to act alone. They were at the mercy of the Philistines, who had promptly embraced the opportunity to oppress them. Isolated, Judah was able to do little more than harass the oppressors by bold deeds and stratagems. The Spirit of the Lord early moved Samson to commence his lifework in the camp of Dan (Judg. 13:25); but almost from the outset he showed one conspicuous weakness in his character: he was the slave of passion. He was betrothed to a Philistine woman, a native of Timnath; but she married another man, and in revenge Samson, aided perhaps by his friends, caught 300 jackals or foxes, tied them together in pairs by the tails, with a burning torch between, and turned them loose amidst the ripened grain of the Philistines (chs. 14:1 to 15:5). The Philistines invaded Judah and demanded that Samson be delivered unto them. He permitted his craven countrymen to bind him in whom they failed to perceive their deliverer. But when he was about to be surrendered to the uncircumcised Philistines, the Spirit of the Lord came mightily upon him and he snapped the ropes asunder. The Philistines, amazed at his display of strength, feared him. He seized the jawbone of an ass and, as the Philistines turned to flee, pursued them and slew a thousand men (in round numbers). They fell in several heaps. Samson acknowledged that the work was of God and confessed his own need of help lest he die of thirst. God in his providence caused a spring to give forth its water. The men of Judah now recognized Samson as their deliverer (ch. 15:6–20).

Afterward Samson fearlessly went to Gaza, and there he fell into sin. The Gazites thought that their opportunity had come to seize him, but at midnight he came to the gate and, finding it closed, laid hold of its doors and the two posts, and plucked them up, bar and all, and carried them to the top of a hill in the direction of Hebron. An entanglement with the woman Delilah, from the valley of Sorek, caused his ruin. By direction of her countrymen, she importuned him to tell her in what his great strength lay. At first he gave her deceitful answers, but at last he revealed the secret. If his head were shaved, he would become weak as another man. The Philistines at once shaved his head and found that his strength had departed. They therefore put out his eyes and made him grind in the prison house at Gaza. They brought him out to exhibit him to the people on occasion of a great festival and public sacrifice to their god Dagon. His hair had by this time begun again to grow, and he was again fulfilling his Nazirite vow. The great temple was full of people, and some 3,000 more were on the roof. Samson knew the structure of the building, for he had been in Gaza before when he possessed his sight. He asked the lad who attended him to let him rest himself against the 2 middle pillars on which the roof was supported, and grasping them he prayed to God for one more manifestation of favor and the gift of strength that he might be avenged on the Philistines. He then tore the pillars from their position, brought down the roof, and perished with a multitude of his foes (ch. 16:1–31). Notwithstanding the defects in his character, the N.T. names him with those Hebrew heroes whose animating principle was faith (Heb. 11:32).

Samson had the strength of a man in a preternatural degree. When the Spirit of the Lord impelled him from time to time, he accomplished his great deeds. His strength did not reside in his long hair. His unshorn locks were the external evidence of his relation to God, a public profession that he was acting as the servant of the Lord. When he informed Delilah that he was a Nazirite and allowed her to take advantage of him and to have his hair cut, he broke his vow, and it is significantly said that the Lord abandoned him. His marvelous strength failed when God left him, and it returned when God granted his prayer. His preternatural strength was a sign, testifying to the men of Judah that this Nazirite was indeed called of God to deliver them from their enemies, and bearing witness among the Philistines to the superiority of the servant of Jehovah.

Various attempts have been made to group the deeds of Samson. Ewald, led by a favorite theory of his, thought he could discover a drama in 5 acts. In fact the narrative itself

describes 5 groups of related deeds: 1. Those that resulted from his wooing of the woman of Timnath; namely, his rending the lion, slaughter of 30 Philistines at Ashkelon, release of the jackals bearing burning torches among the ripened grain of the Philistines, and a defeat of the Philistines who had burned the woman. 2. The events at the rock of Etam, when his fellow countrymen asked permission to deliver him into the hands of the Philistines, and he broke his bonds of rope in the presence of the uncircumcised, slew a thousand of their number with the jawbone of an ass, and by prayer obtained water to quench his thirst. 3. The visit to Gaza, when he carried off the doors of the city gate. 4. His passion for the Philistine woman Delilah, when he broke the 7 green withes wherewith she had bound him and then the 9 cords with which she next bound him, and tore away the web with which she had woven his locks. 5. A blind slave at Gaza, when he pulled down the pillars on which the roof of Dagon's temple rested. The particular achievements in the 5 groups are 12 as enumerated.

Samson's name may be interpreted as meaning solar or little sun, and a strenuous effort has been made by Roskoff, Steinthal, and others like-minded, to connect his achievements with the 12 labors of Hercules or with the Babylonian Gilgamesh or otherwise with the sun-god Shamash. Hercules wandered in search of adventures, slew a lion, slept, was sold as a slave, immolated himself voluntarily. Gilgamesh overcame the bull, rejected the advances of Ishtar, the goddess of love. Hercules is a sun myth. The story of Gilgamesh is the history of an ancient king of Erech embellished with legend and wrought out into an epic in 12 parts; see NIMROD. But with neither the sun-god nor the king of Erech is Samson to be identified; for: 1. The ancient Hebrews themselves assigned Samson to a time well within their historical period, in the generation before Samuel and Saul. 2. The Hebrew account of Samson states definitely the place of his birth and his deeds, and gives the location of his grave. 3. The enumeration of 12 labors is a matter of some importance to those who would identify Samson with Hercules or Gilgamesh, but in itself the number is not of consequence. And the number 12 is not so readily made out. The cry of Samson to God for drink can scarcely be called a labor of Samson's. The narrative speaks of other deeds of Samson which it does not specify (Judg. 13:25), showing that the narrator did not think of 12 achievements only. 4. While the strength which Samson exercised was the gift of God and was not inherent in him as a man, while it failed when he was left to himself, yet it was preternatural in the sense that what he accomplished by it might have been a work of nature but was not. There are parallels in the O.T. David without a weapon slew a lion and a bear; Jonathan and his armor-bearer, and Eleazar and Shammah and Abishai each singlehanded performed prodigies of valor equal to Samson's (I Sam. 14:1–17; II Sam. 23:9–12, 18).

Sam'u·el (săm'ủ-ĕl), in A.V. once She'mu·el (shĕm'ủ-ĕl) (I Chron. 6:33) [name of God, or his name is El (God)]. The earliest of the great Hebrew prophets after Moses and the last of the Judges. His father, Elkanah, was a Levite, family of Kohath, house of Izhar (see ELKANAH 4); he was a Zophite, because descended through Zophai or Zuph (I Sam. 1:1; I Chron. 6:26, 35); and he was a man of the hill country of Ephraim or an Ephraimite, because the family had been assigned residence in that tribe (Josh. 21:5; I Chron. 6: 66). Elkanah lived in Ramah or, as it was called to distinguish it from other towns of the name, Ramathaim of the Zophites (I Sam. 1:1, 19; 2:11). He had 2 wives, Peninnah and Hannah. Hannah had no child and prayed earnestly to God that she might give birth to a boy, vowing that if her prayer were answered the infant should be devoted for life to Jehovah, apparently as a Nazirite, for she added, "There shall no razor come upon his head" (cf. Num. 6:1–5). Her petition was granted. She named the boy Samuel; and when he was weaned she brought him to the tabernacle at Shiloh, and put him in charge of the high priest, Eli, to train him for his sacred duties (I Sam. 1; 2:1–11).

While yet a child Samuel ministered before God, clad in the simple linen ephod which was worn by ordinary priests when engaged in the sanctuary and even by laymen (I Sam. 2:18). He lived at the tabernacle, sleeping in some chamber connected with it, opened the doors of the sanctuary in the morning, and otherwise assisted Eli in his ministrations (ch. 3:1, 3, 15). He had not advanced beyond early boyhood when Jehovah revealed to him the approaching doom of Eli's house for the foolish indulgence which the father had shown to his unworthy sons (ch. 3:1–18). Josephus says that Samuel was 12 years old at this time (Jos. Antiq. v. 10, 4). His statement is about right; but his authority for it is unknown. By the time that the child had reached manhood all Israel, from Dan even to Beer-sheba, knew that he was established to be a prophet of the Lord, for the Lord revealed himself to Samuel in Shiloh (I Sam. 3:20, 21). Soon afterward the judgment threatened against Eli and his house began by the death of Eli's 2 sons in battle, the capture of the Ark by the Philistines, and the death of Eli on hearing the fatal news (ch. 4:1–22). The Ark was soon restored to the Israelites; but it was kept in seclusion and placed for safe keeping with a proper guardian at Kiriath-jearim until the people should be spiritually prepared to receive it.

Samuel was an accredited prophet and, after the death of Eli, the chief religious authority in the land. He addressed himself to the work of reforming the people. Twenty years after the restoration of the Ark he found the moral condition of the nation improved, and he convoked an assembly at Mizpah, near the place where the Ark had been lost, to make confession of sin, to fast before the Lord, and to beseech a return of his favor. The Philistines gathered their forces to battle when they heard of this assembly; but Samuel exhorted the people to pray for deliverance, and he himself besought the Lord for Israel. A thunderstorm discomfited the Philistines, the Israelites discerned the hand of God, embraced the opportunity, pursued the enemy, and gained such a victory over the Philistines as deterred those pertinacious foes from again invading the land while Samuel was at the head of affairs (I Sam. 7:3–14); see PHILISTINES and SAMUEL, BOOKS OF. This signal deliverance indicated that God had raised up Samuel to be judge, in the usual sense of defender and director. Like Deborah, and more fully like Moses, Samuel was accredited prophet and judge. In the discharge of his duties he went annually in circuit to Beth-el, Gilgal, and Mizpah; but his residence was at Ramah, where a company of prophets gathered about him to be at his service in the work of reform (chs. 7:15–17; 19:18–20). Here he built an altar to the Lord; for God had forsaken Shiloh, the Ark was in necessary seclusion, the covenant was in abeyance because the Israelites had broken it by their idolatries and sacrilege, and Samuel was Jehovah's representative; see ALTAR. During the years of Samuel's vigorous administration the land enjoyed freedom from foreign domination. When he was old he made his 2 sons judges at Beer-sheba. They proved themselves unworthy of their high trust, taking bribes and perverting justice. Their misconduct and the threatening attitude of the surrounding heathen nations produced the request on the part of the Israelite elders and people for the institution of kingly government; and Samuel was divinely commissioned to anoint first Saul, and, when he was rejected, David; see the detailed account in SAMUEL, BOOKS OF. Samuel died while David was a fugitive from Saul in the wilderness of En-gedi. He was buried in his house at Ramah, all Israel lamenting his loss (ch. 25:1). On the night before the battle of Gilboa, Saul desired the woman with the familiar spirit at En-dor to call up Samuel from Sheol (ch. 28:3–25); see SAUL 2. Heman, one of David's singers, was a grandson of Samuel (I Chron. 6:33, R.V.; cf. v. 28). Samuel is in the list of O.T. heroes whose animating principle was faith (Heb. 11:32).

Sam'u·el (săm'û-ĕl), **Books of.** Two books of the O.T. They were originally one, as appears from the Masoretic note to I Sam. 28:24, which states that this verse is the middle of the book. They are treated as one by Josephus in his enumeration of the books of the O.T., and in Heb. MSS. The division was introduced into the Rabbinic Hebrew Bible printed by Bomberg at Venice, 1516–1517, and was derived from the LXX and Vulgate. Since Samuel is the leading person during the first half of the period covered, and since he was one of the greatest of the prophets that Israel ever had, the organizer of the kingdom, the agent in the selection of both Saul and David for the throne, and the coadjutor of Saul as long as the king remained faithful to his theocratic obligations, the book appropriately bears his name. Since it contains the history of the first 2 kings, it is divided in the LXX into 2 books, and called First and Second of Kingdoms; and the 2 books which continue the history, and are known in the Eng. version as First and Second Books of the Kings, are called Third and Fourth of Kingdoms in the LXX. Jerome substituted Book of Kings for Book of Kingdoms in his Lat. version.

The work is divisible into 3 sections: 1. Samuel, the prophet and judge (I Sam., chs. 1 to 7), including his birth and early life, the causes which led to his call to the prophetic office (ch. 3:20), and which left him as prophet in possession of the sole authority and opened the way for his judicial administration (ch. 4), his reformatory work, and the attestation of his right to the judgeship, which was afforded by the deliverance of Israel from Philistine oppression by his hand (ch. 7:1–12). Summary of his administration (vs. 13–17). 2. Saul the king (chs. 8 to 31), including (a) the popular demand for a king in Samuel's old age and Samuel's promise to accede to it (ch. 8), the interview between Samuel and Saul and the anointing of Saul in private (chs. 9:1 to 10:16), the public assembly called by Samuel at Mizpah, and the selection of Saul by lot (vs. 17–26), the dissatisfaction of a portion of the people (v. 27), the occasion which won the people for their divinely appointed king and his induction into office (ch. 11), Samuel's farewell address (ch. 12). (b) Revolt against the Philistines, and Saul's failure to observe his theocratic obligations (ch. 13), the feat of Jonathan, leading to the rout of the Philistines (ch. 14:1–46), summary of Saul's wars (vs. 47, 48), his family (vs. 49–51), the particulars of one of these wars, that with Amalek, in which Saul again and in aggravated manner shows his contempt for his theocratic obligations (ch. 15). Then follows (c) an account of the latter years of Saul's reign, with special reference to the relations between the king and David (chs. 16 to 31): Saul having been rejected by God, Samuel by divine direction anoints David (ch. 16:1–13), Saul troubled by an evil spirit summons David as harpist to his court (vs. 14–23), David slays Goliath and becomes a permanent attaché of Saul's court (chs. 17:1 to 18:5), jealousy of Saul and his attempts on David's life (chs. 18:6 to 19:17), flight of David from court and his wandering life (chs. 19:18 to 27:12), invasion of the Philistines and Saul's inquiry of the woman with the familiar spirit (ch. 28), David, expelled from the Philistine camp, pursues a marauding band of Amalekites (chs. 29; 30), battle of Gilboa and death of Saul (ch. 31). 3. David the king (II Sam., chs. 1 to 24). Announcement of Saul's death to David (ch. 1), contest for the throne between David, supported by the men of Judah, and Ish-bosheth as head of the other tribes (chs. 2 to 4), David made king by all Israel (ch. 5:1–3), his reign (chs. 5:4 to 24:25). See DAVID.

The double book of Samuel is placed among the Former Prophets in the Hebrew canon. The work owes its title to the fact that Samuel is the prominent figure both at its opening and for some time subsequently. Samuel wrote a book and laid it up before the Lord (I Sam. 10:25), and part of the double book may be derived from the History of Samuel the Seer (I Chron. 29:29); but scarcely half of the book could have come from his pen, for he died before the end of Saul's reign (I Sam. 25:1). It was written after David's death (cf. II Sam. 5:5). An allusion to the kings of Judah probably indicates that the book was not completed until after the division of the Israelites into the kingdoms of Judah and Israel (I Sam. 27:6), but the distinction between Israel and Judah existed in the time of David (I Sam. 11:8; 17:52; II Sam. 3:10; 24:1).

There were several documents relating to the period treated in the books, such as the History of Samuel the Seer, the History of Nathan the Prophet, and the History of Gad the Seer (I Chron. 29:29), but the author or redactor does not mention the sources whence he derived his information, as do the authors of Kings and Chronicles.

Critics generally have come to the conclusion that the books of Samuel comprise at least 2 principal sources, an early one and a late one. It appears that, speaking relatively, the latest passages are I Sam. 2:1–10, 27–36; 7:2 to 8:22; 10:17–27a; 11:14; chs. 12 and 15; II Sam., ch. 7. Most of these passages in their present form have some affinities in thought and expression with Deuteronomy, but less so than is the case in the books of Kings. They probably are pre-Deuteronomic and are hardly later than c. 700 B.C. Driver supposes that I Sam., chs. 7; 8; and 12, may have been in parts expanded by a Deuteronomic hand. The rest of the material in the books of Samuel is probably earlier than the passages quoted (i.e., it is from the early source), but apparently it is not throughout the work of one writer; the following passages especially seem to come from a different hand: I Sam., chs. 1 to 4:1a; 17:1 to 18:5; 19:18–24; 24; 26; II Sam. 5:17–25. One section of the early source (I Sam. 4:1b to 7:1) begins by continuing the history of the conflict with the Philistines as narrated in Judges, chs. 13 to 16. One section (II Sam., chs. 9 to 20) is nearly contemporary with the events recorded and clearly appears to be the work of one writer. Many parts of the preceding history of David (I Sam., ch. 15 to II Sam., ch. 5) form a continuous narrative and probably come from one writer, though it cannot be determined whether he is the same

as the one who wrote II Sam., chs. 9 to 20.

Who the author of the early source is remains unknown, but some have conjectured Ahimaaz. Robert H. Pfeiffer, in writing of this early historian, says he "is the 'father of history' in a much truer sense than Herodotus half a millennium later. As far as we know, he created history as an art, as a recital of past events dominated by a great idea. . . . Without any previous models as guide, he wrote a masterpiece, unsurpassed in historicity, psychological insight, literary style, and dramatic power."

It has been suggested that the addition of the 2d or late document to the earlier work made it unnecessary for the Deuteronomists, who according to the critics edited the books from Genesis to Kings c. 550 B.C., to subject the books of Samuel to a thorough revision.

San·bal'lat (săn-băl'ăt) [Akkad., Sin (the moon-god) has given life]. An influential Samaritan (Neh. 2:10). He was a Horonite. This designation scarcely means a native of Horonaim in Moab, but rather describes him as a man of Beth-horon (cf. chs. 4:2; 6:2). He was opposed to the rebuilding of the wall of Jerusalem by Nehemiah and tried, unsuccessfully, to stop it (ch. 4:7, 8). Next he plotted with others to invite Nehemiah to a conference and assassinate him (ch. 6:1–4). This new device failing, he tried intimidation, but in vain (vs. 5–14).

Sanballat the Horonite was a contemporary of the high priest Eliashib, great-grandfather of Jaddua; was associated with Tobiah the Ammonite; and opposed the rebuilding of the wall of Jerusalem by Nehemiah in the 20th year of Artaxerxes (Neh. 3:1; 4:7). He was governor of Samaria shortly before 407 B.C., the 17th year of Darius Nothus (Elephantine papyri). A son of Joiada, who was the son of Eliashib the high priest, took Sanballat's daughter to wife, and for this offense was expelled by Nehemiah (ch. 13:4, 28). Josephus mentions one Sanballat, a Cuthean by birth, whom Darius, the last king (of Persia, 336/5–331 B.C.) sent to Samaria as governor, but who, on the defeat of Darius, went over to Alexander the Great, 331 B.C. His daughter Nicaso was taken to wife by Manasseh, brother of the high priest Jaddua. This foreign marriage offended the Jewish authorities, and they drove Manasseh from the altar at Jerusalem; but Sanballat, with the approbation of Alexander, built a temple on Mount Gerizim and made his son-in-law its priest (Jos. *Antiq.* xi. 7, 2; 8, 2 and 4). These statements of the Jewish historian do not accord with the facts of Sanballat's history already recited. The older commentators thought that Josephus speaks of a later Sanballat. Josephus, however, doubtless has in mind Sanballat the Horonite and the marriage referred to in Neh. 13:28; but he has probably lowered the date of Sanballat 100 years to conform the facts to his belief that the son-in-law of Sanballat not only founded or greatly promoted the Samaritan religion, but also built the temple on Gerizim, and that this temple was erected after Alexander's conquest of the country (Jos. *Antiq.* xiii. 9, 1), 200 years before 128 B.C. or thereabout, and that Alexander and the high priest Jaddua were contemporaries (Jos. *Antiq.* xi. 8, 5). Josephus assigns a false date here; as he also does when he dates Nehemiah's commission in the 25th year of Xerxes, who reigned but 21 years (Jos. *Antiq.* xi. 5, 7), instead of in the 20th year of his successor, Artaxerxes (Neh. 2:1), and when he dates the arrival of Ezra in Jerusalem in the 7th year of Xerxes (Jos. *Antiq.* xi. 5, 2), instead of 21 years later, in the 7th year of Artaxerxes (Ezra 7:1, 8), and when he confounds Onias I with Onias

III, who lived a century later (I Macc. 12 :7, 20 ; Jos. *Antiq.* xii. 4, 10).

San'dal. See CLOTHING, SHOE.

San·he·drin (săn'hĕ-drĭn) and **San'he·drim** (săn'hĕ-drĭm) [Talmudic Heb., from Gr. *synedrion*, a council]. The name generally given by writers on Jewish antiquities and history to the highest Jewish assembly for government in the time of our Lord. The English version uses the more familiar word council ; see COUNCIL 1.

San·san'nah (săn-săn'à) [a palm branch]. A town in the extreme s. of Judah (Josh. 15 : 31) ; identified with Khirbet esh-Shamsāniyāt, between Khirbet er-Rās and Tātreiṭ, about 10 miles n.n.e. of Beer-sheba.

Saph (săf) [a basin, threshold]. A Philistine giant, slain by Sibbecai in a battle at Gob (II Sam. 21 :18). Called in I Chron. 20 :4 Sippai.

Sa'phir (sā'fẽr). See SHAPHIR.

Sap·phi'ra (să-fī'rà) [Aram., beautiful]. The wife of that Ananias who was struck dead for having lied unto God. She shared her husband's sin and its penalty (Acts 5 :1–10).

Sap'phire. A precious stone, called in Heb. *sappîr*, in Gr. *sappheiros*. It was the middle gem in the 2d row of the high priest's breastplate (Ex. 28 :18), and adorned the 2d foundation of the New Jerusalem (Rev. 21 :19). The sapphire is 1 of the 3 varieties of corundum, the others being corundum proper and emery. It is of a bluish color, and transparent or translucent (cf. Ex. 24 :10). It is inferior in hardness only to the diamond, and is still greatly prized. The ancients obtained it from India and Ethiopia. Fine specimens are brought from Ceylon.

Sar'ah (sâr'à), in A.V. of N.T. twice **Sar'a** (sâr'à) (Heb. 11 :11 ; I Peter 3 :6) [a princess]. 1. The wife of Abraham, 10 years his junior, married to him in Ur of the Chaldees (Gen. 11 :29–31 ; 17 :17). She was also his half sister, being the daughter of his father, but not of his mother (Gen. 20 :12). Her name was originally Sarai. When Abraham departed from Haran to go to Canaan, Sarai was about 65 years old (ch. 12 :4). Evidently she was a well-preserved woman, for she lived to be 127 years old ; and shortly after leaving Haran, when about to enter Egypt, Abraham feared lest her beauty should attract the Egyptians and lead to his murder, and he represented that she was his sister, keeping back the fact that she was his wife (ch. 12 : 10–20). Years later he did so again at the court of Abimelech, king of Gerar (ch. 20 :1–18). Why he did so is not stated, nor is it said that Abimelech was influenced by her beauty. The king of Gerar may have thought of the desirability of an alliance with the powerful Hebrew chieftain and, with this end in view, determined to take a woman of the immediate family of Abraham into his harem, as was frequently done by princes of that period when they concluded alliances. Sarai was childless ; and when about 75 years old concluded that she was an obstacle to the promise made to Abraham of numerous posterity, and persuaded her husband to take Hagar, her handmaid, as secondary wife. He did so, and became the father of Ishmael (ch. 16 :1–16). Afterward Sarai, when about 89, received a promise from God that she should herself bear a son, and in the course of a year gave birth to Isaac, the child of promise. It was when this promise was made to her that God changed her name to Sarah, meaning princess (chs. 17 :15–22 ; 18 :9–15 ; 21 :1–5). When Isaac was weaned, his parents made a great feast, at which Sarah saw Ishmael,

Hagar's son, mocking. She insisted that both mother and son should be sent away (ch. 21 : 9–21). Sarah died at Kiriath-arba (Hebron) at the age of 127 (ch. 23 :1, 2), and was buried in the cave of Machpelah, which Abraham purchased at that time for a family sepulcher.

2. For Sarah of Num. 26 :46, A.V., a different word in Heb., see SERAH.

Sa'rai (sā'rī). See SARAH 1.

Sar'a·mel (săr'à-mĕl). See ASARAMEL.

Sa'raph (sā'răf) [burning ; or, serpent]. A descendant of Shelah, the son of Judah. At one time he exercised dominion in Moab (I Chron. 4 :22).

Sar'dine. See SARDIUS.

Sar'dis (sär'dĭs). A city, first of the Maeonians and then of the Lydians, situated at the foot of Mount Tmolus, on the e. bank of the river Pactōlus, in the midst of a fertile region, about 50 miles e. of Smyrna. The acropolis crowned a hill, 950 feet high, a spur of the mountain. The Lydian town lay at its foot on the w., between the acropolis and the river ; but the Romans eventually built to the n. of the acropolis. In 546 B.C. Cyrus the Great took the city, which was the capital of Croesus, the rich Lydian king, and it became the seat of a Persian satrap. The Athenians burned it in 499 B.C., and thereby brought on the Persian invasions of Greece in the reigns of Darius and Xerxes. In 334 B.C. it surrendered to Alexander the Great, after his victory at the Granicus. In 214 B.C. it was taken by Antiochus the Great, but he lost it on being defeated by the Romans at Magnesia in 190 B.C. The Romans annexed it to the kingdom of Pergamos ; but when in 129 B.C. they erected the province of Asia, Sardis fell within its bounds. In A.D. 17, when it was destroyed by an earthquake, the emperor Tiberius remitted the taxes of the citizens and rebuilt the city. Jews dwelt in the city (Jos. *Antiq.* xiv. 10, 24), and a Christian community early grew up there (Rev. 1 :11 ; 3 :1, 4). Sardis is a small village ; but on the site of the Lydian town are the remains of a magnificent temple of Artemis, built in the 4th century B.C. to replace an older structure, and a temple of Zeus, said to stand above the foundations of Croesus' palace. Immediately outside the temple of Artemis, at the e. end, the walls of a Christian church are still standing, which were erected before the 4th century A.D.

Sar'di·us, in A.V. of Rev. 4 :3 **Sar'dine.** A variety of chalcedony, which the Greeks called *sardios* and *sardion*. It was a precious stone (Rev. 4 :3), and constituted the 6th foundation of the wall about the New Jerusalem (ch. 21 :20). Two sorts, distinguished by their color, were known by the name of sardius : the transparent red being our carnelian and the brownish red being the variety of carnelian to which we restrict the name sardius. According to Pliny, it was found near Sardis, whence it derived its name, but the finest qualities were brought from Babylon. The best carnelians now come from India ; some also occur in Arabia, whence the ancient Hebrews may have obtained them.

In the O.T. sardius is the rendering of Heb. *'ōdem*, reddish gem. It was the 1st stone in the 1st row on the high priest's breastplate (Ex. 28 :17), and was 1 of the stones with which Tyre adorned itself (Ezek. 28 :13). The marginal reading is ruby, but the LXX renders *'ōdem* by *sardion*.

Sar'do·nyx. A variety of chalcedony, called by the Greeks *sardonyx*. It forms the 5th foundation of the wall surrounding the New Jerusalem (Rev. 21 :20). It is like the onyx in structure, but includes layers of carnelian along with others of white, whitish-brown, or sometimes of black. It was obtained chiefly in India and Arabia.

Sa·rep'ta (sȧ-rĕp'tȧ). See ZAREPHATH.

Sar'gon (sär'gŏn) [Heb. for Akkad., the constituted king]. A king of Assyria, mentioned by name in Scripture in Isa. 20:1 only; he, succeeded Shalmaneser V. He was perhaps of royal blood, as he claims; but it is believed that he usurped the throne, assuming the name of Sargon, an ancient and celebrated Akkadian king. He either secured the throne and then completed the siege of Samaria, which Shalmaneser had begun in 724 B.C., or else he ascended the throne immediately after the fall of Israel's capital and, perhaps as the general who had brought these military operations to a successful termination, claimed the capture as an act of his accession year. The Biblical record is not clear (II Kings 17:1–6). The Hebrew writer relates that Shalmaneser came against Hoshea, and proceeds by saying that "the king of Assyria found conspiracy in Hoshea" and cast him into prison, and that the king of Assyria besieged Samaria 3 years, and in the 9th year of Hoshea took the city. Until the claim of Sargon to have captured Samaria came to light, readers of the Hebrew narrative inferred that Shalmaneser was the conqueror of Samaria. But the inference was not warranted, for the writer continues to speak of the king of Assyria, where it is probable that he does not mean the conqueror of Samaria (II Kings 17:24, 27). He does not specify the particular king, but uses the general title; and when he recurs to the siege, he names Shalmaneser as the besieger, but continues by saying, "They took it" (ch. 18: 9, 10). At any rate, Samaria fell in 722 or the early months of 721 B.C., and Sargon ascended the throne on the 12th of Tebet, the 10th month, of that year. Immediately after his accession the Babylonians, assisted by the Elamites, revolted and Sargon was for a time unable to reduce them to subjection. In 720 the remaining Israelites of Samaria in alliance with the men of Hamath rebelled, but Sargon subdued them, and placed captive Hamathites as colonists in Samaria. In the same year he defeated the allied forces of Ḥanunu, king of Gaza and Sib'e, better known to readers of the Bible as So, the tartan of Egypt, in a battle fought at Raphia. Sargon took Carchemish, the capital of the Hittites, in 717, and with the capture of their capital the empire of the Hittites fell. In 716 his armies waged war in Armenia, in 715 they were still engaged in war in Armenia, and were carrying on operations in Media. In this year also Arab tribes were planted as colonists in Samaria by Sargon's orders, and he received tribute from Pharaoh of Egypt. He boasted of having subjugated Judah. The tablet on which this boast appears was inscribed before the close of 714, to judge from its contents. The combined Assyrian and Hebrew data point to the end of 715 or the beginning of 714 as the date when Hezekiah acknowledged the suzerainty of Assyria by beginning to pay tribute. Merodach-baladan incited the nations from Elam to the Mediterranean Sea to revolt from Assyria. In 712, therefore, Sargon dispatched troops against Ashdod, and in 710 he captured Babylon and assumed the title of king of Babylon. He began to erect a new palace and town 10 miles n.e. of Nineveh in 712 and named it Dur-sharrukin (Sargonsburg). The ruins are known as Khorsabad; see NINEVEH. He was murdered in 705 and was succeeded by his son Sennacherib.

Sa'rid (sā'rĭd) [survivor]. A village on the s. frontier of Zebulun (Josh. 19:10, 12); Tell

Shadūd in the n. part of the Plain of Esdraelon, 5 miles s.w. of Nazareth.

Sa'ron (sā'rŏn). See SHARON.

Sar'se·chim (sär'sē-kĭm). One of Nebuchadnezzar's princes who entered Jerusalem (Jer. 39:3).

Sa'ruch (sā'rŭk). See SERUG.

Sa'tan (sā'tăn) [śāṭān, adversary]. The Devil (cf. Matt. 4:1 with vs. 10, 11; Mark 1: 13); pre-eminently "the Adversary" (Job 1:6 marg.; Zech. 3:1 marg.), because animated by a disposition hostile to all goodness and the chief opponent of God and man (Job 2:3; Luke 22:3; cf. I Chron. 21:1 and Ps. 109:6, but see R.V.), aiming to undo the work of God (Mark 4:15), seeking to persuade men to sin, desirous of leading them to renounce God (Job 2:5; Matt. 4:9, 10), and endeavoring to prevent their acceptance and salvation by God (Zech. 3:1, 2). He is sometimes influential in bringing about pecuniary loss, physical sickness, bereavement (Job 1:10–22; 2:4– 7; Luke 13:16). He is, however, under the control of God. Only by God's permission can he pursue his malicious designs (Job 1:12; 2:5, 6; Luke 22:31, 32). When permission is granted him to carry out his evil plots, it is only that he may become an instrument in furthering the divine plan. In Job's case, the vain efforts of Satan to induce the patriarch to sin resulted in disciplining Job's character and maturing his faith in God. In the fully revealed doctrine of Satan, which is seen in the N.T., he is the demon of this world who has access to the hearts of men, deceives them, and receives their witting or unwitting obedience (Acts 5:3; 26:18; II Cor. 4:4; II Thess. 2:9; Rev. 12:9). He is the ruler of a kingdom, having principalities, powers, and demons under him (Matt. 12:24, 26; Luke 11:18; Rev. 12:7).

Satan was the seducer of Adam and Eve (II Cor. 11:3; Rev. 12:9). This fact may have become known to them. If not, it was discerned as soon as the existence of the Devil and his work became known, for the temptation of Eve came from without through the persuasions of the serpent. The malignant spirit behind the serpent, hostile to good, seeking to undo the work of God, and supernaturally lending speech to the reptile, or communicating with the mind of the woman so that she thought she heard articulate speech, was evidently Satan. This doctrine went hand in hand with the doctrine concerning the Devil, and received the highest sanction (Wisd. of Sol. 2:24; John 8:44; Rom. 16:20); see SERPENT 1. Satan produced demoniacal possession (Matt. 12: 22–29; Luke 11:14–23). He approached Jesus with temptation (Matt. 4:1–11). He steals the word from the heart of the ignorant or inattentive hearer (Mark 4:15). He entered into the heart of Judas before the commission of the great crime (John 13:27). He had to do with Peter's fall (Luke 22:31). It was under temptation by Satan that Ananias and Sapphira lied to the Holy Spirit (Acts 5:3). He hindered Paul in his ministry (I Thess. 2:18), having previously sent a messenger to buffet him (II Cor. 12:7). Pergamos, where a faithful Christian, Antipas, suffered martyrdom, was a place where Satan dwelt (Rev. 2:13). Men with hearts unchanged are under Satan's power (Acts 26:18). An assembly of those who have grievously erred from the faith, and perhaps from morality, is the synagogue of Satan (Rev. 2:9; 3:9; cf. I Tim. 5:14, 15). Those who are expelled from the Church are said to be delivered to Satan; but this is designed to produce their reformation and not their destruction (I Cor. 5:5; I Tim. 1:20). There are depths in Satan which inexperienced Christians fail to fathom (Rev. 2:24). He is, moreover, so plausible that he seems to be an angel of light (II Cor. 11:14). He sometimes gains advantages over Christians (II Cor. 2:11), but he shall ultimately be bruised under their feet (Rom. 16:20). He is the real agent in the operations carried on by the man of sin (II Thess. 2:1–12), but the day will come when, after a temporary triumph, Satan shall be expelled from the earth and, being bound, shall be cast into the abyss (Rev. 12:9; 20:1, 2). See DEVIL 2.

Simon Peter was called Satan when he took it upon himself to contradict Christ's prophecy of his death and resurrection, for he was a stumbling-block to Christ, opposed him, and minded not the things of God (Matt. 16:23; Mark 8:33).

Sa'trap [Gr. from Old Pers. *xshathra-pāvan*, protector of the land]. The official title of the viceroy who, in behalf of the Persian monarch, exercised the civil and military authority in several small provinces combined in one government. Each of these provinces had its own governor (Ezra 8:36; Esth. 3:12, in A.V. lieutenant). The title is used in Aramaic historical documents written after the Persian conquest, in referring to high officials of the Babylonian empire and of the kingdom ruled by Darius the Mede (Dan. 3:2; 6:1, in A.V. prince).

Sat'yr. A sylvan god of the Greeks and Romans, a companion of Bacchus. At first he was represented with long-pointed ears, snub nose, and goat's tail. At a later period goat's legs were added. He was supposed to possess a half brutal and lustful nature. In A.V. satyr is the rendering of Heb. *śā'îr*, and is applied to wild animals or demons which should dance among the ruins of Babylon (Isa. 13:21) and of the Edomite cities (ch. 34:14). The word commonly signifies a he-goat. In 2 passages it denotes an object of idolatrous worship (Lev. 17:7; II Chron. 11: 15, both R.V.). In the latter place it is mentioned with calf idols, suggesting that it refers to idols having the likeness of goats. In Isa. 13:21, 22 it is associated with wild animals; in ch. 34:14 with a creature of the night also, which may be either some nocturnal animal (in A.V. the screech owl) or a nocturnal demon; see NIGHT MONSTER. In the adaptation of Isaiah's words in The Revelation, the language is quoted from the LXX and the word demons is used (Rev. 18:2, R.V.). Accordingly, interpreters dispute whether the Hebrew prophet meant that wild goats, ostriches, wolves, jackals, and other beasts of the desert should wander among the forsaken ruins, or whether he introduced into the imagery of his poetic description a popular belief in demons which appeared in the form of goats and haunted desert places.

Saul (sôl) [asked (of God); or lent (to God)]. A king of Edom, from Rehoboth, on the Euphrates (Gen. 36:37, 38, in R.V. Shaul).

2. The first king of Israel, son of Kish, a Benjamite; see KISH 2. The Prophet Samuel had grown old; his sons showed by their conduct that they did not possess his upright character and could not carry on his work; and the surrounding nations were evidently ready to harass and oppress Israel (I Sam. 8:1, 3, 20; 12:12). The elders of Israel accordingly came to Samuel and demanded that the form of government be changed and that a visible king be set over them, so that they might be like the well-organized nations about them and have one who could lead them to victory over their foes (ch. 8:4, 5, 19, 20). Although the ultimate organization of the Hebrews as a kingdom, with an earthly

monarch as the representative of Jehovah, had long been contemplated (Gen. 17:6, 16; 35:11; Deut. 17:14–20), yet the spirit of the people in demanding a king at this crisis was irreligious. They lacked abiding faith in God, without which the rule of Jehovah as theocratic king was impossible. They were turning from faith in the invisible God to put confidence in a visible king. By divine direction Samuel informed the elders what the people would have to endure from a king, but on their persisting in their demand, he promised to do as they desired and dismissed them.

The elevation of Saul to the throne. About this time the asses of Kish, a Benjamite, went astray, and his son, Saul, was sent to seek them. Saul was at the time a young man, perhaps 35 years old; and he was head and shoulders taller than any of the people. Not finding the asses after 3 days' search, he was about to give up the quest and return home. His servant, however, suggested one further effort. Persons of whom the servant made inquiry concerning the asses probably told him that there was a man of God in the neighboring city who might give the desired information, and he persuaded Saul to go to him. The man of God was Samuel, who had been told by God to expect a Benjamite and to anoint him prince over Israel. Saul and his family in Gibeah knew Samuel well by report (I Sam. 10:14–16), but Saul seems not to have met the prophet before and not to have understood that Samuel was the man of God of whom the people spoke. He refers to him as "the man" (ch. 9:7), and on meeting him at the city gate does not know him (vs. 18, 19). Samuel informed Saul that the asses had been recovered, intimated to him that he would be chosen king, and put him in the place of honor at the sacrificial feast which he was about to celebrate. Next morning, as the guest was leaving the town, the prophet took a vial of oil, poured it upon his head, and having kissed him, said, "Is it not that Jehovah hath anointed thee to be prince over his inheritance?" and charged him not to disclose the secret, to go to Gilgal at the proper time and tarry there 7 days, until he himself should come and offer sacrifice and give instruction (chs. 9:20 to 10:16). Samuel soon summoned the people to Mizpah. The choice was left to God. The lot was cast, and Saul was chosen. But he had hidden himself. When he was brought from his hiding place and stood forth, towering above the multitude, he was received with enthusiasm. God had selected a man of fine appearance in order to win the admiration and confidence of all the Israelites, and a man of the tribe of Benjamin, which stood on the border between Ephraim and Judah, in order to satisfy both n. and s. Samuel had committed the choice to God in order to secure the allegiance of the godly men for the king. A large company of men, obedient to God, escorted Saul home; but certain men of Belial were nevertheless dissatisfied, and Saul retired to private life until private jealousies should be overcome. He devoted himself to the cultivation of his father's fields. A month later (ch. 10:27, LXX) the town of Jabesh in Gilead was straitly besieged by the Ammonites. At the request of the citizens, the besiegers scornfully granted a truce of 7 days in order that the townspeople might invoke the aid of their fellow countrymen. The messengers, or some of them, came to Gibeah with their mournful story. Saul heard it when he returned from the field. The Spirit of God stirred him. He sent summons to the tribes to follow him and Samuel to the rescue of their imperiled brethren. Jabesh was relieved. The people asked where were they who had refused to recognize Saul as king, and they carried Saul to Gilgal, the nearest place of customary sacrifice, where he was inducted into office and Samuel laid down his judgeship (chs. 11:1 to 12:25); see SAMUEL, BOOKS OF.

The reign of Saul. The age of Saul when he began to reign is unknown, since the Heb. text of I Sam. 13:1 is defective, the numeral being omitted. The number 30 is derived from some LXX MSS. He was at any rate old enough to have a son capable of holding a military command. Saul established a small standing army of 3,000 men; 2,000 of these were with him at Michmash and Beth-el, and 1,000 were stationed with Jonathan at Gibeah (ch. 13:2). Jonathan smote a Philistine garrison, or rather deputy, at Geba (ch. 13:3); see GARRISON. The Philistines heard thereof and held the Israelites in abomination. The Israelites, learning of their danger, responded to Saul's summons to assemble at Gilgal (ch. 13:3, 4), whither Samuel had promised to come in this emergency and entreat the favor of the Lord (chs. 13:8, 11, 12; 10:8). A Philistine army advanced into the land of Israel and pitched at Michmash. Great fear seized the Israelites, Samuel intentionally delayed to appear, the people began to scatter and leave the king, and a descent of the Philistines upon Saul and his decreasing forces seemed imminent (ch. 13:8, 11, 12); and therefore Saul presumed to conduct the sacrifice. But Samuel came, rebuked the king for transgressing God's command, and declared that Saul on account of his disobedience should not found a dynasty (ch. 13:13, 14). Samuel went to Gibeah (v. 15). Saul and Jonathan took post at Geba of Benjamin, while the Philistines lay encamped at Michmash (v. 16). By a feat of valor, Jonathan started a panic in the garrison of the Philistines, which spread to their camp and to their prowling bands. Saul took advantage of it, and secured a victory (chs. 13:15 to 14:46). Afterward Samuel directed Saul to wage a war of extermination against the Amalekites. Saul undertook the war, but he spared the best of the cattle to sacrifice to the Lord at Gilgal, and also saved their king. For this 2d act of disobedience, by which he showed that he could not be trusted to act as God's instrument, but desired to assert his own will in God's kingdom, he was rejected from being king (ch. 15:1–35); see SAMUEL, BOOKS OF. Samuel, therefore, was sent to Bethlehem to anoint David king (ch. 16:1–13).

The Spirit of the Lord now departed from Saul, and he began to be troubled by an evil spirit. A harper was required to charm away his melancholy madness, and David was selected to discharge the duty (I Sam. 16:14–23). The plaudits with which the youthful son of Jesse was welcomed on returning from his great victory over Goliath so excited Saul's jealousy that before long the hero was a fugitive, pursued with relentless fury by the now vindictive monarch (chs. 17 to 30); see DAVID. At last the end came. The Philistines, invading the Israelite territory, pitched in Shunem, near the valley of Jezreel. Saul, following to give them battle, established his headquarters on the slope of Mount Gilboa. Sad forebodings of his fate troubling him, he made a night journey quite close to the Philistine camp, to En-dor, where lived a woman who was reputed to have the power of calling up even the dead, and he was there informed that he and his sons should perish on the morrow (ch. 28:1–25). The morrow came, and the battle began. The Philistine archers slew many in the Israelite ranks. They slew 3 of Saul's sons, including the eldest, the unselfish and heroic Jonathan. They seriously wounded Saul himself, on which he called to

his armor-bearer to thrust him through. The young man declined the responsibility, whereupon the erring monarch fell upon his sword and died. The victorious Philistines, finding his corpse, severed the head from the body and affixed the latter, with the bodies of his sons, to the wall of Beth-shean, whilst they sent his armor as a trophy to be kept in the temple of Ashtaroth. The men of Jabeshgilead, whom Saul had saved in the early part of his reign, feeling gratitude for their deliverance, crossed the Jordan by night to Beth-shean, took down the bodies, and gave them honorable interment, while David mourned the fate of the Lord's anointed and the beloved Jonathan in plaintive poetry (I Sam., ch. 31; II Sam., ch. 1). The length of Saul's reign is not stated in the O.T., but both Paul and Josephus are able to assign it 40 years (Acts 13:21; Jos. *Antiq.* vi. 14, 9).

Saul and the woman of En-dor. The old man covered with a robe, who figures in the interview between the woman of En-dor and Saul (I Sam. 28:3–19), has been explained in 3 different ways. He was the woman's accomplice, and when he appeared she uttered a loud cry, and she pronounced the man who had come to seek her aid to be Saul. The loud cry was her customary trick. She knew that the king was in the neighborhood, and she had at once detected that her visitor was he, in his tall stature, in his bearing, in his words, and in the manner of his attendants. Or else the appearance was a spirit, quite unexpected by her, at which she uttered a loud cry because she was really startled. If an unexpected appearance, it was either the Devil, as Luther and Calvin believed, and as those understand who think that certain phenomena of ancient sorcery and modern spiritualism are due to Satanic agency (see DEVIL and DEMONIAC), or else Samuel, reappearing as did Moses and Elijah on the Mount of Transfiguration, as do most of the evangelical interpreters since the Reformation. The basis for the opinion that Samuel appeared is that the narrator refers to the person as though he is Samuel (I Sam. 28:14, 15, 16, 20), and that the words spoken by him were fulfilled. The Biblical recorder simply describes what occurred. It is to be noted that the woman was a lawbreaker, and was also condemned by the religion of Jehovah. Moreover, she alone saw the apparition, and she described the appearance in most vague terms —an old man rising from the earth and covered with a robe. This description would apply to any aged person, but Saul concluded that Samuel had really appeared. The words which were uttered by the robed figure boldly forecast the future as a fortune teller does or else predicted it with full knowledge. The words came true, but they were in part fulfilled by Saul's own deliberate act. If Samuel himself appeared, then this is the sole instance recorded in Scripture where the spirit of a departed saint has returned to earth and conversed with men, since the case of Moses and Elijah in converse with the transfigured Christ is not analogous. Moreover, it would be strange, indeed, if, after God had refused to answer Saul, either by dreams or by prophets, his servant Samuel should appear, and especially if he should appear at an interview strictly forbidden by God and at the behest of a woman who was condemned alike by the law of the land and by the Law of God (Ex. 22:18; Lev. 20:27; Deut. 18:10–14; I Sam. 28:3, 9; I Chron. 10:13; Ecclus. 46:20).

3. The original name of the Apostle Paul (Acts 7:58; 13:9).

Sav'iour. One who saves from any evil or danger (II Kings 13:5; Neh. 9:27). In the

O.T. it is specially used of God, Jehovah, viewed as the deliverer of his chosen people Israel (II Sam. 22:3; Ps. 106:21; Isa. 43:3, 11; 45:15, 21; 49:26; 63:8; Jer. 14:8; Hos. 13:4). The Gr. word *sōtēr* (preserver, deliverer) is used by the classical writers specially of their gods, though sometimes a king assumed the title, as did Ptolemy Soter and Demetrius I. In the N.T. it is used of God the Father (I Tim. 1:1; 4:10; Titus 1:3; 3:4; Jude 25), but especially of Jesus Christ the Son, who saves his people from their sins (Matt. 1:21), delivering them out of their sinful condition and misery, from guilt, the wrath of God, the power of sin and the dominion of Satan, and bringing them into a state of salvation in blessed communion with God (Luke 19:10; Acts 5:31; Rom. 5:8–11; Phil. 3:20, 21; I Tim. 1:15; II Tim. 1:10; Titus 2:13, 14; Heb. 7:25).

Saw. A toothed tool for cutting wood and for shaping stone (I Kings 7:9; Isa. 10:15). Victims of persecuting rage were sometimes sawn asunder (Heb. 11:37). If David cut the Ammonites of Rabbah, and other towns which fell into his hands, with saws, harrows, and axes (II Sam. 12:31; I Chron. 20:3), it was an act of exceptional severity on his part and foreign to all else that is known of his character. A change of *resh* (r) to *mem* (m) in the verb used in Chronicles, and of *resh* (r) to *daleth* (d) in the verb in Samuel, would make the record state that David exacted labor from the captives (II Sam. 12: 31, R.V. marg.).

The saws used by the ancient Egyptians had, so far as known, but 1 handle. The blade was usually of bronze, let into the handle or bound to it by thongs. The teeth commonly inclined toward the handle. The wood was placed perpendicularly in a frame and was sawed downward. The Assyrians used a double-handled saw also, with a blade of iron.

Scape'goat'. See AZAZEL.

Scar'let. A bright, rich crimson, not the hue of recent origin known as scarlet. The coloring matter was obtained by the Israelites from an insect (*Coccus ilicis*), called *ḳirmiz* by the Arabs, whence the Eng. word crimson is derived. The insect abounds in Palestine on the holm oak (*Quercus coccifera*). The female alone yields the coloring matter. She attains the form and size of an ordinary pea, is violet-black in color, covered with a whitish powder, and wingless. Filled with eggs containing red matter, she adheres to the leaves and twigs of the oak, and feeds on its juices. From the resemblance of the insect to a berry, the Greeks called it *kokkos*, berry. It is related to the cochineal insect of Mexico (*Coccus cacti*), but it yields a much less valuable dye and has been supplanted commercially by its Mexican congener. The color was called in Heb. *shānī*, "brightness," "crimson," *sheni tōla'ath*, "brightness of the worm," "worm crimson," *tōla'ath shānī*, "worm of brightness," "crimson worm," *tōla'*, "worm," and in Gr. *kokkinos*, "pertaining to the coccus."

The color and the method of obtaining it were early known. It was much used in the hangings of the tabernacle and in the high priest's vestments. It was employed in the ceremony attending the purification of the leper, and in the preparation of the water of separation (Lev. 14:4; Num. 19:6; Heb. 9: 19).

Scep'ter. A rod held in the hands of kings as a token of authority (Ps. 45:6; Amos 1:5; Wisd. of Sol. 10:14; Heb. 1:8). It has been used from time immemorial. The staff was not, however, a symbol of royal sovereignty exclusively. It might be carried by any leader (Judg. 5:14, R.V.; Baruch 6:14); among the Greeks by kings, judges, heralds, and speakers given the floor by the herald (Homer *Iliad* i. 238; ii. 100; vii. 277; xxiii. 568). Nor is the Heb. name *shebeṭ* a specific term, but it denotes any rod, such as the walking stick, which was often carried as a mark of dignity (Gen. 38:18), the shepherd's staff (Lev. 27: 32; Ps. 23:4; Micah 7:14), or the rod used in threshing cummin (Isa. 28:27). The royal scepter was doubtless often of wood. The scepter of Ahasuerus was made of gold (Esth. 4:11). A reed was placed in Christ's hand when he was mocked as king (Matt. 27:29).

Sce'va (sē'và). A certain Jew, belonging to a high-priestly family; his 7 sons were exorcists (Acts 19:14).

School. There were no schools for children in ancient Israel, but instruction was not lacking. Parents gave their children religious instruction (Gen. 18:19; Deut. 6:7; Susanna 3; II Tim. 3:15). The older people had opportunity for obtaining further knowledge from the priests and Levites, who could be found at the sanctuary and in the towns assigned to them throughout the land, and who occasionally itinerated for the purpose of publicly teaching the statutes of the Law (Lev. 10:11; II Chron. 17:7–9; Hag. 2:11). Every 7 years, at the feast of tabernacles, the Law was read publicly in the audience of assembled Israel (Deut. 31:10–13). The great festivals themselves, and songs written for the purpose (Deut. 31:19, 30; 32:1–43), kept alive the knowledge of those events at the birth of the nation which obligated the Israelites as a people to serve Jehovah, their redeemer and bountiful benefactor. The prophets by their public preaching spread religious knowledge and quickened religious life. Business negotiations and legal processes were conducted in the open street, affording constant instruction to the public through eye and ear. Reading and writing were perhaps not uncommon among the young (Judg. 8: 14 marg.; Isa. 10:19).

In the Greco-Roman period the education of the young was carefully attended to (Jos. *Apion* i. 12; ii. 19). Elementary schools were established in connection with the synagogues, where the children were taught to read from the Scriptures, to write, and to cipher. About 75 B.C. attendance upon this primary instruction was made compulsory, and under Gamaliel the age for attendance was fixed at 6 years. Slaves and others were employed as tutors by the wealthy (Jos. *Antiq.* xvi. 8, 3). The scribes also imparted advanced instruction. The subject which they discussed was the Law. Chambers connected with the outer court of the Temple, and outside of Jerusalem a room in the synagogue, were used as lecture rooms (Luke 2:46). The instruction was nominally free, but it is said that in the time of Herod the Great the porter collected entrance money. Not only was instruction imparted directly to the pupils in these schools, but learned men held public disputations with each other there in the presence of the scholars.

School'mas'ter. The rendering in Gal. 3:24, 25, A.V., of Gr. *paidagōgos* (one who leads a boy, a pedagogue). It is translated "tutor" in the R.V. of this passage and I Cor. 4:15. The *paidagōgos*, or pedagogue, in a Greek household was a trusted slave, to whose care the children were committed (Jos. *Life* 76; Herod. viii. 75). He always accompanied them when they were out of doors. He was responsible for their personal safety, guarded them from physical evil and bad company, and led them to and from school. The Law as a pedagogue led us to Christ. It prepared us to receive him as our Redeemer. It displayed the justice of God and convinced us that we were unrighteous; its threatenings pressed us to seek refuge from the wrath and curse of God; it made apparent the inability of man to obtain salvation by the works of the Law; it exhibited the plan of salvation in types and ceremonies and excited to faith in the coming Redeemer (Gal. 3:24; Rom. 3:19–21; 4:15; 7:7–25).

Sci'ence. The rendering of Heb. *maddā'* and Gr. *gnōsis* in Dan. 1:4 and A.V. of I Tim. 6:20. The word is not used in its modern sense. It does not denote knowledge gained by observation of phenomena and systematized. The Heb. and Gr. words mean simply knowledge. The false knowledge spoken of by Paul is the teaching of Judaizing and mystic sects in the Apostolic Age, which they boastfully claimed to be certain (cf. Col. 2:8), against which Paul urgently warns men (I Cor. 8:1, 7), and which counterfeits the true knowledge which he praised and in which he desired Christians to grow (I Cor. 12:8; 13:2; Phil. 1:9).

Scor'pi·on. A small animal with a tail armed with a sting which inflicts great pain (Rev. 9:5, 10). It was called *'akṛāb* by the Hebrews, and *skorpios* by the Greeks. It abounds in Palestine, and is common in the wilderness s. of Judah (Deut. 8:15); see AKRABBIM. Rehoboam threatened to chastise his subjects, not with whips, but with scorpions (I Kings 12:11; II Chron. 10:14), which probably are whips armed with sharp points to make the lash more severe. The scorpion is a small invertebrate animal of the order *Arachnida*. It is closely akin to the higher spiders, having, like them, 8 legs; but it differs in shape, and in having the poison bag not in proximity to the jaws, but at the extremity of the tail. It has a pair of nippers like the lobster. The tail is long and jointed and capable of being curled up over the back. The last joint is swollen, contains the venom gland, and is armed with a per-

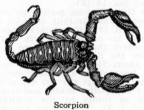

Scorpion

forated sting by means of which the poison is discharged. The scorpion feeds principally on beetles and locusts, which it seizes with its nippers and stings to death. Some 8 or more species exist in Palestine. The largest is about 8 inches long, and black.

Scourge and **Scourg'ing.** Scourging is severe punishment or torture by lashing. The Law authorized beating, when the culprit lay down and was smitten on the back (Deut. 25:2, 3). Scourging is perhaps alluded to by Rehoboam as a known punishment (I Kings 12:11, 14), and it was employed by Antiochus Epiphanes to drive the Jews by its tortures to eat swine's flesh (II Macc. 6:30; 7:1). As a legal penalty it was recognized by the later Jewish law, which prescribed beating or scourging for ecclesiastical offenses, such as transgression of ceremonial ordinances for which the Mosaic Law did not specify the punishment, disobedience of the orders of the sanhedrin, and heresy. Rods were used for beating (II Cor. 11:25); and for scourging a whip was employed, which consisted of 3 thongs, 1 of ox hide and 2 of ass's hide. The

number of stripes ranged from a few blows up to 39, this limit being set in order to avoid all danger of exceeding the 40 blows allowed by the Mosaic Law in corporal punishment (Deut. 25:2, 3). When the punishment was inflicted in the synagogue (Matt. 10:17; 23:34), it was administered by the *ḥazzān* (overseer, officer); but culprits were also beaten before the sanhedrin (Acts 5:40).

The Romans used a scourge of cords or thongs, made more painful by various expe-

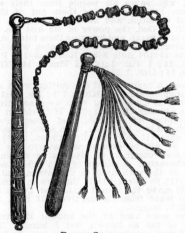

Roman Scourges

dients which cruelty suggested. Pieces of lead or brass, or small, sharp-pointed bones, were attached to the lashes. The Romans employed scourging as a punishment or as torture to extract confession or testimony. After the Porcian law and the Valerian law, Roman citizens were exempted from scourging (Livy x. 9); but free persons not Roman citizens might be beaten and slaves scourged. Lawless governors, however, did not scruple to scourge free provincials and even Roman citizens (Jos. *War* ii. 14, 9). Criminals condemned to crucifixion were ordinarily scourged before being executed (Livy xxxiii. 36); this took place in the case of Jesus and of many of the Jews before the revolt and after the siege of Jerusalem by the Romans (Matt. 27:26; Jos. *War* v. 11, 1). The victim was stripped to the waist, and bound in a stooping position, with the hands behind the back, to a post or pillar. The suffering under the lash was intense. The body was frightfully lacerated. The Christian martyrs at Smyrna about A.D. 155 were so torn with the scourges that their veins were laid bare, and the inner muscles and sinews, and even the entrails, were exposed (Eusebius *H.E.* iv. 15).

Screech Owl. The rendering of Heb. *lilith*, a nocturnal being (Isa. 34:14; in R.V. night monster). It frequents the ruins of cities. Tristram believes it to be the tawny owl (*Syrnium aluco*) which is found in Gilead, Bashan, Lebanon, and the valley of the Jordan, breaking in on the stillness of night with its hooting. See NIGHT MONSTER, SATYR.

Scribe. 1. A public writer who was employed as an amanuensis to write at dictation (Jer. 36:4, 18, 32) and to draw up legal documents (ch. 32:12, probably). For a description of the ancient scribe, see Ezek. 9:2. In the Hymn to Gilgamesh is a reference to "the mighty one who has the writing tablet in the girdle of his loins." Representations of the god Nabū, the writer of the book of fate, with a stylus in his hand are specially frequent in the Neo-Babylonian period. In Egyptian religion Thot exercises the same functions as the Babylonian Nabū. Public scribes still frequent the streets of cities in the Near East.

2. A secretary; a government or other clerk (II Kings 12:10; Ezra 4:8). Levites were employed as scribes for the business of repairing the Temple (II Chron. 34:13).

3. A copier of the Law and other parts of the Scriptures (Jer. 8:8). The most noted of these earlier scribes was the priest Ezra, who was a ready scribe in the Law of Moses and had set his heart to seek the Law of the Lord and to do it, and to teach in Israel statutes and judgments (Ezra 7:6, 10). In this latter respect he is the prototype of the scribes of later times, who were professional interpreters of the Law. In the N.T. they are called *grammateis*, or more exactly *nomikoi*, rendered "lawyers," and *nomodidaskaloi*, "teachers of the Law." They devoted themselves: (1) To the study and interpretation of the Law, which it will be remembered was both civil and religious; and to determining its application to the details of daily life. The decisions of the great scribes became the oral law or tradition. (2) To the study of the Scriptures generally in regard to historical and doctrinal matters. (3) To teaching, each noted scribe having a company of disciples about him; see SCHOOL. The profession of scribe received a great impulse after the Return of the Jews from the Exile, when prophecy had ceased and it only remained to study the completed Scriptures and make them the basis of the national life. The scribes were becoming numerous in the Maccabaean period (I Macc. 7:12) and at the time of Christ had attained paramount influence among the people. The sanhedrin counted many of them among its members (Matt. 16:21; 26:3). Though there were among them some who believed in Christ's teaching (Matt. 8:19), the majority of them were hopelessly prejudiced against him. They murmured at or found fault with much that he and his disciples said or did (Matt. 21:15), and they had a large share in the responsibility for his death. They were also associated with the rulers and elders in the persecution of Peter and John (Acts 4:5; etc.), and in that which led to the martyrdom of Stephen (ch. 6:12); but the scribes of the Pharisees took Paul's part with respect to the resurrection (ch. 23:9).

Scrip. A bag or wallet for carrying provisions or articles required on a journey (Matt. 10:10, in R.V. wallet). The scrip of modern Palestine is made of the skin of a kid stripped off whole from the carcass and tanned, and slung from the shoulder by straps. Every shepherd and farmer has such an article. David when a shepherd carried one (I Sam. 17:40).

Scrip'ture. A writing, a narrative or other matter committed to writing (Dan. 10:21, in R.V. writing); especially the sacred writings of the Hebrews, viewed either collectively or individually, or even a single passage or quotation from them, as in Mark 12:10; Luke 4:21; John 19:37. When this collection of sacred documents is thought of as forming 1 book, the word is sing., the Scripture (John 7:42; 10:35; 17:12; 19:28; Gal. 3:22). More frequently the many documents from different authors which constitute the O.T. are in mind and the pl. is used, the Scriptures (Matt. 21:42; Luke 24:27; John 5:39; Rom. 1:2; II Tim. 3:15–17). The epistles of Paul at once took their place with the other Scriptures as authoritative (II Peter 3:16). See BIBLE, CANON, INSPIRATION.

Scyth'i·an (sĭth'ĭ-ăn). A native of Scythia. This name was applied originally to the region immediately n. of the Black Sea and e. of the Carpathian Mountains. When the conquests of Alexander the Great revealed the existence of men in Asia like the European Scythians in race, an Asiatic Scythia began to be recognized; and finally, all n.e. Europe and central and n. Asia were supposed to be traversed by the nomad Scythian race. They were far behind in civilization; so that at last the name Scythian was used as we now use Tartar, or the Greeks and Romans used the term Barbarian (II Macc. 4:47; Col. 3:11); see BETH-SHEAN.

Sea. 1. The ocean or general gathering of the waters, as distinguished from the dry land of the globe (Gen. 1:10; Ps. 8:8; Rev. 7:1–3; 21:1).

2. A more or less detached portion of that ocean (Gen. 49:13; Acts 10:6), or a large inland lake of fresh or salt water (Num. 34:11, 12; Matt. 4:18). The chief seas with which the Israelites had to do were the Mediterranean, the Red Sea, the Dead Sea, and the Sea of Galilee. The Mediterranean was referred to as the sea, or was called the great sea, the sea of the Philistines, the hinder or w. sea, the utmost and uttermost sea; see MEDITERRANEAN SEA. The Dead Sea was variously known as the Salt Sea, the Eastern Sea, Sea of the Arabah or the Plain, and according to A.V. of Zech. 14:8, the former sea; see DEAD SEA. The Sea of Galilee was also named the Sea of Chinnereth, Lake of Gennesaret, and Sea of Tiberias; see GALILEE, SEA OF.

3. A large river with its network of branches, channels, and irrigating canals, as the Euphrates (Jer. 51:36, 42) and the Nile (Nahum 3:8).

4. The large basin in Solomon's Temple where the priests washed their hands and feet preparatory to ministering in the sanctuary or at the altar (I Kings 7:39); see MOLTEN SEA.

Sea Mew. The rendering in R.V. of Lev. 11:16 and Deut. 14:15 of the Heb. noun *shaḥaph* (perhaps suggesting leanness), a bird ceremonially unclean. The A.V. makes it the cuckow (cuckoo). The LXX and Vulgate regard it as a sea mew or gull. Sea mew is an indefinite term, broad enough to include gulls, terns, and petrels, all of which abound on the shore and lakes of Palestine. If any single species is meant, perhaps it is the *Sterna fluviatilis*, the common tern, or sea swallow. This bird, which looks lean, might be included under the designation sea mew, for the *Sterninae*, or terns, are a sub-family of the *Laridae*, or gulls. It is plentiful along the shores of Palestine. .

Sea Mon'ster. Any great fish of the sea (Gen. 1:21; Job 7:12; in A.V. whale), called in Heb. *tannin*. See DRAGON. In Lam. 4:3, Heb. *tannin*, although it is sing. number, stands in Heb. before a pl. verb. It is doubtless a copyist's error for *tannim* (jackals). This reading is adopted by the R.V.

Seal. 1. The rendering of Heb. *taḥash* in R.V., with porpoise in the marg. (Ex. 26:14; Ezek. 16:10) in A.V. badger. Its skin was used for the outer covering of the tabernacle and for sandals. *Taḥash* corresponds to Arab. *tuḥas*, which embraces seals and specially denotes the dugong (*Halicore hemprichii*). The latter belongs to the order *Sirenia*, of which the nearest allies are mammals of the whale order. It is generally 10 to 12 feet long, with a round head, breasts for suckling its young, and a fish-like tail. The color is slaty above and white below. It is believed to be 1 of the animals, if not indeed the animal, which gave rise to the fabled mermaid, half woman, half fish. It is common among the coral banks of the Red Sea, whence it extends as far as the coasts of Australia.

2. A signet ring or cylinder, engraven with the owner's name or some design or both (Ex. 28:11; Esth. 8:8). In Babylonia the cylinder seal and writing go back to the Uruk or Warkan period; the cylinder seals of the 3d quarter of the 4th millennium B.C. show a remarkable development in art. The seal was worn on the finger, if a ring, or was strung on a cord and hung around the neck (Gen. 38:18, R.V.; Jer. 22:24). Men affixed their seal as signature to letters or other documents (I Kings 21:8; Neh. 9:38; Esth. 8:8; Jer. 32:10, 44; John 3:33). These were usually written on clay, and the seal was pressed on the soft material and left its mark (Job 38:14). A large number of seals and seal impressions have been found in Palestine, dating between the 8th and 5th centuries B.C., which bear the personal names of their owners. Chests, boxes, tombs, or anything which required to be guarded from being opened, were sealed with the signet of the person who had authority to prohibit intrusion (Job 14:17; 41:15; Dan. 6:17; Matt. 27:66; Rev. 5:1).

Se′ba (sē′bȧ). A people in the Cushite genealogy (Gen. 10:7), who dwelt in s. Arabia. Seba is a dialectic variation of Sheba, giving the Arab. pronunciation. According to the Assyrian inscriptions this people was in n.w. Arabia in the 8th century B.C. Seba is associated with Sheba as a remote s. country (Ps. 72:10); and with Egypt and Ethiopia as if in Africa, whither many Cushites migrated (Isa. 43:3; 45:14). Josephus identifies Seba with the isle of Meroë (Jos. *Antiq.* ii. 10, 2). The region so named is situated between the Nile and its affluent, the Atbara. It is about 400 miles long by 200 broad. But this district was known to the Hebrews as Cush. According to Strabo (xvi. 4, 8–10) there were on the w. coast of the Red Sea the harbor Saba and the town Sabai.

Se′bam (sē′băm), in A.V. **She′bam.** See SIBMAH.

Se′bat (sē′băt). See SHEBAT.

Se·ca′cah (sē-kā′kȧ) [thicket, cover]. A village in the wilderness of Judah (Josh. 15:61). Conder places it doubtfully at Khirbet Sikkeh or Dikkeh, about 2 miles e. of Bethany.

Se′cu (sē′kū), in A.V. **Se′chu** (sē′kū) [probably, lookout place]. A village near Samuel's town of Ramah (I Sam. 19:22), probably in the direction of Gibeah (v. 9). Conder doubtfully suggests as its site Shuweikeh, about 3 miles n.w. by n. of er-Rām; see RAMAH 1.

Se·cun′dus (sē-kŭn′dŭs) [Lat., second]. A man of Thessalonica who accompanied Paul from Macedonia into Asia Minor (Acts 20:4).

Se′er. See PROPHET.

Se′gub (sē′gŭb) [exalted]. 1. The youngest or younger son of Hiel. He died when his father set up the gates of Jericho, which he was then fortifying (I Kings 16:34), completing the fulfillment of the curse pronounced by Joshua (Josh. 6:26).

2. Son of Hezron, by a daughter of Machir (I Chron. 2:21, 22).

Se′ir (sē′ĭr) [hairy, shaggy; i.e., covered with brushwood]. 1. A land and its inhabitants. Seir was the mountain range of Edom (Gen. 36:21; Num. 24:18; Ezek. 35:15). The original inhabitants of these mountains were Horites (Gen. 14:6). Seir is elsewhere used collectively for the people (Ezek. 25:8). Esau took up his abode in Mount Seir (Gen. 32:3),

and his descendants dispossessed the Horites (Deut. 2:12; Josh. 24:4). A remnant of the Amalekites took refuge in these mountain fastnesses, but were finally destroyed by the Simeonites (I Chron. 4:42, 43).

2. A ridge on the border line of the territory of Judah w. of Kiriath-jearim (Josh. 15:10); generally identified with the rocky point on which the village of Saris stands, s.w. of Kiriath-jearim.

Se·i′rah (sē-ī′rȧ), in A.V. **Se·i′rath** (sē-ī′răth) [see SEIR]. A locality in Mount Ephraim, probably in the s.e. part, to which Ehud escaped after murdering Eglon (Judg. 3:26).

Se′la (sē′lȧ), in A.V. once **Se′lah** (sē′lȧ) (II Kings 14:7) [rock]. A place in Edom taken by Amaziah, king of Judah, and named by him Joktheel (II Kings 14:7). It is hardly referred to in Judg. 1:36; but probably in II Chron. 25:12; Isa. 42:11; Obad. 3; and perhaps in Isa. 16:1 (R.V., Selah). The inhabitants dwelt high, among clefts (Obad. 3). These indications point to the ravine called by the Greeks Petra, which is simply a translation of the Heb. Sela. About 300 B.C. Petra passed from the Edomites to the Nabataean Arabs. The dynasty which now began to rule in Petra contained several kings of the name of Aretas, 1 of whom is mentioned in II Cor. 11:32. The kingdom of the Nabatae-

The Treasury at Petra

ans came to an end in A.D. 105 and Arabia Petraea was made a province of the Roman Empire. See NABATAEANS. The place was rediscovered by Burckhardt in 1812 and has since been visited by various travelers. It lies in the nook of a deep chasm excavated by water on the n.e. flank of Mount Hor. The valley, with branching side valleys, is about 4,500 feet long by 740 to 1,500 broad, and is surrounded on all sides by precipitous sandstone cliffs. The main gorge is called Wadi Mūsa, the valley of Moses, though probably he was never there. A rivulet traverses it through its whole length. The variegated colors of the rock—red, brown, purple, yellow—add to the beauty of the spot. There are tombs, remains of temples, an amphitheater, a triumphal arch, etc., most of them apparently of Roman times. Besides these, there are tombs and dwelling houses in the adjacent cliffs, some of which may be of older date. On the height above, overlooking the ancient city, is the great high place; and yet other altars stand on neighboring lofty sites.

Se'lah (sē'lȧ) [Heb. *sălal*, to lift up; cf. Akkad. *sullû*, prayer]. A word occurring 71 times in The Psalms, as well as in Hab. 3: 3, 9, 13. It is universally agreed that this word is a musical or liturgical sign of some kind, but the exact meaning has not been determined: 1. The LXX renders it by *diapsalma*, which may imply the intervention at the particular place by a musical symphony. In this case, the meaning may be "Lift up! Loud!" a direction to the orchestra. The singers' voices would cease, and then the instruments would be heard with full effect (cf. *forte, fortissimo*). 2. The Targum, Aquila, and Jerome render it "for ever," but this interpretation has no known ety. and is unsuitable in the majority of passages. 3. Jacob of Edessa (640–708) compares it with the Christian Amen sung by the people after the Gloria. It may therefore mean "Lift up your benedictions" and may refer to a doxology sung after every psalm or section of a psalm which for any liturgical reason was separated from a following section. It probably was introduced in the late Persian period in connection with the liturgical use of the psalms and indicated the place of benedictions.

Se'la·ham·mah'le·koth (sē'lȧ-hă-mä'lĕ-kŏth) [rock of divisions or escapes]. A cliff in the wilderness of Maon. It was so called because David on 1 side of the eminence eluded Saul on the other (I Sam. 23:28). Conder points out that about 8 miles e.n.e. of Maon there is a cliff at Wadi el-Malāḳi, a narrow but deep chasm, impassable except by making a circuit of many miles. Saul might here have come near enough to see David and yet not have been able to reach the place where David was except by making a long detour.

Se'led (sē'lĕd) [exultation]. A man of Judah, family of Jerahmeel (I Chron. 2:30).

Se·leu'ci·a (sė-lū'shĭ-ȧ). A city on the seacoast of Syria (I Macc. 11:8), 5 miles n. of the mouth of the Orontes. It was built on the site of an earlier town by Seleucus Nicator, founder of the kingdom of Syria, and was the seaport of Antioch, which lay about 16 miles farther up the river. Pompey made the city free. Paul and Barnabas sailed thence for Cyprus (Acts 13:4).

Se·leu'cus (sė-lū'kŭs). A king of Syria (I Macc. 7:1; II Macc. 3:3), called Philopator. He was son and successor of Antiochus the Great, and reigned from 187–175 B.C., when

Seleucus Philopator

he was murdered by Heliodorus, one of his courtiers. He was followed on the throne by Antiochus Epiphanes; see ANTIOCHUS 1 and 2. During his father's reign he fought in the

disastrous battle of Magnesia. During his own administration he sought to strengthen his kingdom, and was conciliatory toward the Jews; although it is said that he attempted to plunder the Temple (II Macc. 3: 4–40), possibly to help to raise the enormous tribute which he was compelled to pay the Romans.

Sem (sĕm). See SHEM.

Sem'a·chi'ah (sĕm'ȧ-kī'ȧ) [Jehovah has sustained]. A Levite, descendant of the doorkeeper Obed-edom (I Chron. 26:7).

Sem'e·in (sĕm'ė-ĭn), in A.V. **Sem'e·i** (sĕm'ė-ī) [Gr. for Heb. *Shim'ī*, Shimei]. An ancestor of Christ, who lived after the time of Zerubbabel (Luke 3:26).

Se·mit'ic (sė-mĭt'ĭk) [Lat. *Semiticus* from *Sem*, Gr. *Sēm*, from Heb. *Shēm*, Shem]. The languages which, speaking broadly, were or are vernacular to the descendants of Shem are called Semitic. They are inflectional, and together with Egyptian, which is a Semitico-Hamitic tongue, the Semitic languages have the longest recorded history. They constitute one of the leading families of languages. Many scholars accept a common parentage for the Hamitic and Semitic tongues, but the connection with the Indo-European through the Indo-Hittite is very remote. According to this theory the Hamites were in n. Africa, where the Hamitic languages grew up; the Semites were in Arabia, where their language developed its special characteristics and diverged from that of the Hamites. Thus it is supposed that there was at first 1 primitive Semitic language, but the separation of the tribes speaking it led ultimately to its divergence into several languages. No doubt dialects occurred in Arabia before the Semitic migrations into the Fertile Crescent. In each the roots of the words are nearly always triliteral, the 3 radical letters being 3 consonants. Many triliterals appear to be based on pre-existing biliterals; and it is even supposed by some that originally there were but 2 radical consonants. The various modifications of meaning were produced from these roots by the use of vowels, of which 3 only, *a, i,* and *u,* were originally employed: thus the 3 consonants ḳ, ṣ, r suggest the idea of cutting off, and *ḳaṣar* means he reaped, *ḳeṣôr* reap, *ḳôṣēr* reaper, *ḳāṣîr* harvest, *ḳāṣur* reaped. The meaning was also modified by laying stress on certain of the consonants and by means of affixes: thus *gādal* he became large, *giddal* he magnified, *gaddēl* magnify, *migdāl* a tower.

The Semitic languages are arranged under 4 groups: 1. The eastern consists of Akkadian, Babylonian, Assyrian, and Neo-Babylonian. The name Akkadian is generally applied in a comprehensive sense to the whole group. 2. The northern embraces the Amorite and Aramaic. Western Aramaic includes Old Aramaic, Biblical and Palestinian Aramaic, the language of the Elephantine papyri, that of the Targums, Palmyrene, and Nabataean. In eastern Aramaic are the Aramaic of the Babylonian Talmud, Mandaic, Syriac, and Modern Aramaic. 3. The western includes Ugaritic, Canaanite, Moabite, Phoenician and Punic, and Hebrew (Biblical, Mishnaic, Rabbinic, and Modern). 4. The southern is divided into Arabic and Ethiopic. Under Arabic we have N. Arabic, which includes Classical Arabic, Modern Arabic, and Maltese; under S. Arabic are listed Minaean, Sabaean, Himyarite, and modern dialects (Mahri-Sokotri). The Ethiopic group consists of Ethiopic or Ge'ez, Amharic, Tigré, and Tigriña.

Semitic writing is in most of the languages from right to left: that is, in the other direction from English. Hence the title-page in the Hebrew Bible is at what looks like the end of the volume. From this it reads backward, till it ends at what, if it were English, would be called the beginning of the book.

The intellectual ability of the Semitic race is shown by the place which the Jews have taken in Christian countries and by the role played by the Arabs in the Middle Ages.

Se·na'ah (sē-nā'à). See HASSENAAH.

Se'neh (sē'nĕ) [thorn bush, bramble]. A sharp rock, 1 of 2 which flanked a pass running e. and w. between Michmash and Gibeah. It was the more s. of the cliffs, and nearer Gibeah than Michmash. It was between these 2 rocks that Jonathan and his armor-bearer passed when they were going to surprise the Philistine garrison (I Sam. 14:4, 5). It overlooked Wadi Suweinit, about 3½ miles s.e. by s. of Michmash.

Se'nir (sē'nĭr), in A.V. twice **She'nir** (Deut. 3:9; S. of Sol. 4:8) [perhaps, mount of light, but cf. SIRION]. The Amorite name of Hermon (Deut. 3:9). In S. of Sol. 4:8 Senir and Hermon are distinguished, each probably being a distinct peak of the giant mountain. Fir timber was obtained on Senir (Ezek. 27:5).

Sen·nach'er·ib (sē-năk'ĕr-ĭb) [Akkad., Sin (the moon-god) has increased the brothers]. A son of Sargon, who succeeded to the Assyrian throne on the murder of his father, in the year 705 B.C. Though a warrior, he was inferior to Sargon in ability. He was boastful, cruel, and not wise enough to perpetuate his conquests by conciliating those whom he had vanquished. On his accession Merodach-baladan of Babylon attempted to throw off the Assyrian yoke. Sennacherib defeated him and his ally, the king of Elam, placed Bel-ibni on the Babylonian

Sennacherib on His Throne at Lachish

throne, and returned in triumph to Nineveh, laden with captives and spoil. Discontent and rebellion manifested themselves in the w. also, among the peoples who had submitted to Sargon. To quell this revolt, Sennacherib in 701 appeared in Phoenicia, capturing Great and Little Zidon, Zarephath, Achzib, and Acco, but Tyre appears to have held out. Neighboring states hastened to announce their submission. Proceeding to the Philistine country, he took Ashkelon, Beth-dagon, and Joppa. Next he invested and captured Lachish, sent a detachment of his troops to Jerusalem, secured the release of the dethroned king of Ekron from Jerusalem,

defeated the combined armies of Egypt and Ethiopia at the battle of Eltekeh, and added Ekron to his conquests. On this campaign he not only took Lachish and Eltekeh, cities of Judah, but by his own account took 46 fortified towns of Judah, carried away 200,-150 people captive, and seized multitudes of horses, mules, asses, camels, and sheep. His career of conquest was cut short by the plague, which devastated his army and compelled him to return to Nineveh. No express mention is, of course, to be expected in the Assyrian inscriptions of his failure to possess himself of Jerusalem; but it is clearly implied, for he is unable to tell of the capture of the city, and he apparently covers up the inglorious conclusion of the campaign by placing at the close of his narrative the account of the tribute which he received from Hezekiah. Here is his own account of the matter: "Hezekiah himself I shut up like a caged bird in Jerusalem, his royal city. I erected beleaguering works against him and turned back by command every one who came out of his city gate. I severed his towns, which I plundered, from his dominions and gave them to Mitinti, king of Ashdod, Padi, king of Ekron, and Ṣillibaal, king of Gaza. Thus I diminished his land. In addition to the former tribute, their yearly tax, I added a tax as the impost of my overlordship and laid it upon them. As for Hezekiah, the fear of the glory of my sovereignty overwhelmed him, and the Urbi and his favorite soldiers, whom he had brought in to strengthen Jerusalem, his capital city, deserted. With thirty talents of gold, 800 talents of silver, precious stones, rouge, *dakkasi*, lapis lazuli, great *angugmi*-stones, beds of ivory, stationary ivory thrones, elephants' hide, ivory, *ushu*-wood, *ukarinnu*-wood, all sorts of objects, a heavy treasure; also his daughters, the women of his palace, male and female musicians he sent after me to Nineveh, my capital city, and sent his messenger to present the gift and to do homage." A story was told the Greek historian Herodotus by the Egyptian priests that Sennacherib advanced against Egypt and had reached Pelusium, when immense numbers of field mice destroyed the bowstrings of the Assyrians, who next morning commenced their flight from the country. For the series of historic events in which Sennacherib and Hezekiah figure as antagonists, see HEZEKIAH. Sennacherib's failure against Jerusalem was in 701 B.C.

In the meantime new troubles for Sennacherib arose in Babylonia; and in the 3d year of Bel-ibni, in 700 B.C. the Assyrian king marched to the s., removed Bel-ibni, and placed his own son Ashur-nadin-shum on the throne 699. Freed from concern for the s. Sennacherib next turned his attention to the n.w. and brought Cilicia under the Assyrian yoke. In 694 he made a novel expedition by ship and attempted to root out the followers of Merodach-baladan from their last refuge at the mouth of the Ulai. The campaign was in a measure successful; but the Elamites invaded Babylonia, seized Ashur-nadin-shum, and placed a Babylonian king on the throne, who held the country for 1½ years. But though Sennacherib took Erech, captured the Babylonian king, and devastated Elam, yet another Babylonian king ascended the throne, and the Assyrians did not succeed in finally chastising Babylonia until 689. Then Sennacherib advanced against Babylon, captured and plundered the city, massacred the inhabitants, fired the buildings, razed the walls and temples, and flooded the ruins with water from the Euphrates and its canals.

The last 8 years of his reign were mostly peaceful. He had some time before surrounded Nineveh with a wall 8 miles in circumference. About 695 B.C. he finished a great palace which he had built for himself in the n.w. part of Nineveh. It was 1,500 feet long and 700 broad, with great courts, halls, and chambers. He res.ored another palace and constructed a system of canals by which he brought good drinking water to the city. After a reign of 24 years and 5 months, he was assassinated in the year 681. The deed was done by 2 of his sons, Adrammelech and Sharezer, who were excited against him because his favorite in the family was another brother, Esarhaddon (II Kings 19:37; II Chron. 32:21).

Se·nu'ah (sĕ-nū'à). See HASSENUAH.

Se·o'rim (sĕ-ō'rĭm) [barley]. A descendant of Aaron. His family had grown to a father's house in the time of David, and cons.ituted the 4th course when David distributed the priests into divisions (I Chron. 24:1–8).

Se'phar (sē'fär) [numbering]. A place which formed the limit in 1 direction of the territory settled by the descendants of Joktan (Gen. 10:30). It was probably in s. Arabia.

Se·pha'rad (sĕ-fā'răd). This place of captivity of people of Jerusalem (Obad. 20) may be Sardis in Asia Minor. Sparda, a district frequently mentioned in Persian inscriptions along with Ionia, Armenia, and Cappadocia, may be Sardis and so stand for Lydia. The name occurs in Assyrian inscriptions as early as the time of Esarhaddon, 681–669 B.C. Perhaps happier is the identification with Sharparda, which Sargon, who transported Israelites to the cities of the Medes (II Kings 17:6), and boasts of having subjugated Judah, mentions as a district of s.w. Media.

Seph'ar·va'im (sĕf'är-vā'ĭm). A place from which the Assyrians brought colonists to inhabit Samaria (II Kings 17:24, 31). Not improbably the same town is referred to in chs. 18:34; 19:13. Formerly it was identified with Sippar on the e. bank of the Euphrates, above Babylon. It may, however, be Sabarim, a Syrian city (cf. Sibraim, Ezek. 47:16), which was destroyed by Shalmaneser V in 727 B.C.

Se'phar·vites (sē'fär-vīts). Natives or inhabitants of Sepharvaim (II Kings 17:31).

Se·phe'la (sĕ-fē'là). See SHEPHELAH.

Sep'tu·a·gint (sĕp'tû-à-jĭnt). See VERSIONS, I. 1.

Sep'ul·cher. The Hebrews, as a rule, buried their dead in caverns, natural or artificial (Gen. 23:9; Isa. 22:16; Matt. 27:60; John 11:38), natural caves being often extended by excavation (Gen. 50:5). The cliffs near Jerusalem are full of such sepulchers. The entrance to the cavern or its chambers was closed by a stone (Matt. 27:60) to exclude jackals and other beasts that prey upon dead bodies. It was desirable that the sepulchers should be at a distance from human habitations. They might be in gardens attached to dwellings (II Kings 21:18, 26), or within the city walls (I Kings 2:10); but they were generally outside the town. Even then trees or gardens might surround them (John 19:41). Often, however, they were excavated high up in the face of a precipitous cliff, with their entrance far above the ground. Frequently the tomb was whitewashed (Matt. 23:27), not only for cleanliness and beauty, but also that it might be clearly seen and not touched, for the touch brought defilement. Inside the sepulcher the individual grave was sunk in the floor and covered by a slab of stone, or was cut as a niche in the wall, or driven as a shaft into the side of the

cavern and closed by a flat stone or door, or a shelf for bodies was hewn around the chamber. Some imes there were double tiers of niches or shafts. Coffins were not necessary; but occasionally among the wealthy the body was inclosed in a stone sarcophagus and placed in the tomb. The entrance was sometimes richly ornamented. Sometimes a monument was erected. It might consist of a simple pillar (II Kings 23:17, R.V.), or it might assume the form of a mausoleum (I Macc. 13:27). The Hebrews and their neighbors were fond of family burial places, and the sepulcher with its chambers and niches was adapted to this purpose (Gen. 49:29–31; II Sam. 2:32; I Kings 13:22; I Macc. 9:

Sealed Stone at Entrance of a Tomb

19; 13:25). Public burial places were used by the poor and were provided for strangers (II Kings 23:6; Jer. 26:23; Matt. 27:7). See GRAVE.

Sep'ul·cher, Ho'ly. See CALVARY.

Sep'ul·chers of the Kings, or of Da'vid (dā'vĭd). The royal burial place in the city of David, not far from the king's garden and the pool of Shelah (I Kings 2:10; II Chron. 21:20; Neh. 3:15, 16), and doubtless in the field of burial which belonged to the kings (II Kings 15:7; II Chron. 26:23). Theodoret quotes Josephus as saying that the tomb is near Siloam, is in fashion like a cave, and reveals the royal lavishness. It consisted of several chambers (Jos. *Antiq.* vii. 15, 3). It was robbed of large treasure by John Hyrcanus; and the report of the sum which that prince had obtained led Herod the Great to search it in the hope of securing additional plunder; but he became frightened, abandoned the search, and erected a propitiatory monument of white stone at its mouth (Jos. *Antiq.,* xiii. 8, 4; xvi. 7, 1; *War* i. 2, 5). It was extant in the time of Christ (Acts 2:29). All the kings from David to Hezekiah inclusive were buried in the city of David. The common royal sepulcher was by implication ordinarily used; but Asa and probably Hezekiah had tombs of their own (II Chron. 16:14; 32:33, R.V.), and Jehoram, Joash, Uzziah, and Ahaz were not admitted to the royal sepulcher (chs. 21:20; 24:25; 26:23; 28:27). Manasseh, Amon, and Josiah were buried at Jerusalem in their own tombs (cf. II Kings 21:18, 26; 23:30 with II Chron. 35:24). Jehoahaz died in Egypt, and Jehoiachin and Zedekiah doubtless in Babylonia. Jehoiakim was probably left unburied.

The caverns of the kings, which are referred to by Josephus (Jos. *War* v. 4, 2), may be what is now known as the Grotto of Jeremiah.

Se′rah (sē′rȧ), in A.V. once **Sar′ah** (Num. 26:46) [cf. S. Arab. *Shârih*, the one who opens or explains]. A daughter of Asher (Gen. 46:17; I Chron. 7:30).

Se·ra′iah (sē-rā′yȧ) [Jehovah has striven, or ruled]. 1. A son of Kenaz (I Chron. 4:13).
2. A scribe who had held office under David (II Sam. 8:17); see SHAVSHA.
3. A Simeonite, son of Asiel (I Chron. 4: 35).
4. One of those sent to arrest Baruch the scribe and Jeremiah the prophet (Jer. 36:26).
5. The chief priest when Nebuchadnezzar captured Jerusalem. He was put to death by Nebuchadnezzar at Riblah (II Kings 25: 18–21; Jer. 52:24–27). He was the father of Jehozadak, who was carried into captivity; and the grandfather of Jeshua, who was high priest immediately after the Exile; and he was also an ancestor of Ezra, the scribe (I Chron. 6:14, 15; Ezra 3:2; 7:1).
6. The son of Neriah; he was "quartermaster" (R.V. marg.; J.V.); "chief chamberlain" (R.V.); "a quiet prince" (A.V.). The 1st translation is preferable. He was carried captive to Babylon (Jer. 51:59–64).
7. The son of Tanhumeth, a Netophathite (II Kings 25:23; Jer. 40:8).
8. One of those who accompanied Zerubbabel from Babylon (Ezra 2:2). Called in Neh. 7:7 Azariah.
9. A chief of the priests who returned from Babylon with Zerubbabel (Neh. 12:1, 7). A father's house bore his name in the next generation (v. 12). Possibly the same as number 8.
10. A priest, doubtless head of a father's house and probably of the father's house just mentioned, who with Nehemiah signed the covenant to keep separate from the heathen and observe the Law of God (Neh. 10:2). Probably also he is identical with the following.
11. A priest, son of Hilkiah and ruler of the house of God after the Exile (Neh. 11: 11; cf. the preceding). The name Azariah occurs in the corresponding place in I Chron. 9:11. Different persons are probably intended, of whom Azariah lived before and Seraiah after the Exile. Possibly, however, different persons are intended, each of whom lived after the Exile, Azariah being a predecessor of Seraiah. Or the text may be corrupt; in 1 of the passages the name may

have been misread by a copyist; or as both names belong to the high-priestly genealogy and succeed each other there (I Chron. 6: 12–15), something may have slipped from the text, as, for example: "Seraiah, son of" may have been lost before Azariah in Chronicles, or "son of Azariah" after Seraiah in Nehemiah.

Ser′a·phim (sĕr′ȧ-fĭm), in A.V. **Ser′a·phims** (sĕr′ȧ-fĭmz). Celestial beings who stood before the enthroned Lord when he appeared in vision to Isaiah. "Each . . . had six wings; with twain he covered his face, and with twain he covered his feet, and with twain he did fly. And one cried unto another, and said, Holy, holy, holy, is Jehovah of hosts: the whole earth is full of his glory" (Isa. 6: 2, 3). The prophet having confessed his sinfulness, one of the seraphim flew unto him, "having a live coal in his hand, which he had taken with the tongs from off the altar"; and he touched the prophet's mouth with it, and said: "Lo, this hath touched thy lips; and thine iniquity is taken away, and thy sin forgiven."
Scripture affords no further information regarding the seraphim. They are mentioned in this 1 passage only. Various suggestions have been proposed: 1. Gesenius derives their name from Arab. *sharafa*, "to surpass in glory or rank." The Arab. root would regularly be *sâraph* in Heb. 2. Cheyne conjectures that the seraphim are the serpent-like lightning, referring to the fact that *sârâph* and *s͏erâphîm* denote the fiery serpents in the wilderness (Num. 21:6, 8; Isa. 14:29; 30:6). But even if the words seraphim and fiery serpent have the same form in the sing. number, and if they are from the same Semitic root, which is probable, they yet need not signify the same beings or similarly shaped beings. Shape is not denoted by the name. The common characteristic, which finds expression in the word, is burning, in the transitive sense; this would accord with the idea of making the seraphim agents of purification by fire (Isa. 6:6, 7). But the seraphim do not resemble serpents outwardly, for they have hands, feet, and wings. So if the root *sâraph* (to burn) is taken, the idea of serpent must be excluded. Cheyne admits that Isaiah did not regard them as animals in form. 3. The seraphim are identical with the Egyptian griffins, *seref,* and were borrowed

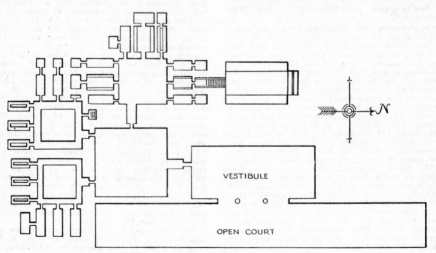

VESTIBULE

OPEN COURT

Plan of the So-called Tombs of the Kings

544

by the Israelites. If so, they were personifications of natural objects or phenomena; and in the vision of Isaiah they symbolically represent the powers of nature attendant upon nature's Lord (cf. Zech. 6:1–8, R.V.). There is little support for these theories. 4. They are an order of angels. So the Jews understood. The Targum inserts the word in Ezek. 1:8; Zech. 3:7. They are consuming beings, who cry, "Holy, holy, holy," who are most impressed with the attribute of holiness in God, worship him most fondly in that character, and execute his purposes of holiness in the world. The conclusive argument in favor of this theory against the 3d is that their adoration of holiness in God and their employment in the ministry of atonement indicate moral beings and not physical powers personified.

Se'red (sē'rĕd) [cf. Syr. *serad*, to be terrified]. A son of Zebulun, and founder of a tribal family (Gen. 46:14; Num. 26:26).

Ser'gi·us Pau'lus (sûr'jĭ-ŭs pô'lŭs). The proconsul of Cyprus, which constituted a senatorial province in Paul's time (Acts 13:5–12); see CYPRUS. The inscription on a coin found at ancient Soli, on the n. coast of the island, mentions "Paulus proconsul."

Se'ron (sē'rŏn). Commander of the army of Syria (I Macc. 3:13) in the reign of Antiochus Epiphanes. He attempted to suppress the revolt of the Jews, but was defeated by Judas Maccabaeus near Beth-horon in 166 B.C. (vs. 14–24). Josephus states that Seron lost his life in the battle (Jos. *Antiq.* xii. 7, 1).

Ser'pent. 1. An animal which creeps on its belly (Gen. 3:1, 14); having head, tail, and body (Gen. 3:15; Ex. 4:4), but no limbs. It is generically called *nāḥāsh* in Heb., *ophis* in Gr. (cf. Gen. 3:13 with II Cor. 11:3; Num. 21:9 with John 3:14). As it wriggles along, its mouth is apt to come in contact with the dust, which it licks (Micah 7:17; cf. Gen. 3:14). The bite of some species infuses fatal poison into the wound (Num. 21:6; Ps. 58:4; Prov. 23:32). Some can be charmed (Eccl. 10:11). The serpent is found in the wilderness and in inhabited districts, by the road, in hedges, on rocks, in walls (Gen. 49:17; Num. 21:6; Prov. 30:19; Eccl. 10:8; Amos 5:19).

The fiery serpents which bit the children of Israel in the wilderness and caused death were a kind of snake found in Arabia and elsewhere whose bite produces the fiery burning of inflammation and thirst. See BRAZEN SERPENT.

The serpent of the temptation was an ordinary snake, one of the beasts of the field, comparable with them in subtlety and skill in securing prey, and, after it was involved in the temptation of man, cursed among them (Gen. 3:1, 14). Perhaps Eve saw nothing more than a snake; but the Devil was in this serpent, as afterward the demons were in men and in the swine, controlling it, lending it supernatural subtlety, and using it as a means by which to approach Eve (Wisd. of Sol. 2:24; Rom. 16:20; II Cor. 11:3; Rev. 12:9); see SATAN. It suffered in the punishment, as did other innocent animals when made the instruments of sin (Lev. 20:15, 16). Its mode of locomotion was not new: it had beyond doubt always crept, but now its groveling on the earth is made the memorial of its degradation. It does not suffer thereby, save as it is loathed and killed by man. But the more distinctly man recognizes that the evil spirit was the serpent's master, the more does man transfer his enmity to the Archfiend.

2. A species of serpent, in Heb. *pethen* (Ps. 91:13, adder). See ASP.

Se'rug (sē'rŭg), in A.V. of N.T. **Sa'ruch** [perhaps, shoot, branch]. Son of Reu, father of Nahor, and ancestor of Abraham (Gen. 11:20–23; I Chron. 1:26; Luke 3:35). There was a city by this name near Haran.

Serv'ant. One who serves, in Heb. usually *'ebed*. It is a general term, including voluntary and involuntary service, and embracing all who are under obligation of any kind to render service to another, from the slave captured in war or purchased at a price, to the envied official of a king and the willing worshiper of God (cf. Gen. 39:1 with chs. 41:12; 40:20; Ex. 32:13; Acts 16:17). It is systematically employed by Orientals when addressing a superior, whether man or God (Gen. 32:4, 20; 50:18; Deut. 3:24; II Sam. 9:2; Luke 2:29; Acts 4:29); and is applied to conquered nations compelled to pay tribute to their conqueror (II Sam. 8:2). God also designates his worshipers servants (Gen. 26:24; Num. 12:7; II Sam. 7:5). See MINISTER, SLAVE.

Serv'ant of Je·ho'vah (jĕ-hō'và). 1. One who acknowledges Jehovah as his God and, by implication of the term, faithfully performs his will; as Abraham (Ps. 105:6), Moses (v. 26), David (Ps. 132:10), Isaiah (Isa. 20:3).

2. The prominent figure in Isa., chs. 40 to 66 (cf. especially chs. 42:1–7; 49:1–6; 50:4–9; 52:13 to 53:12). The view most widely entertained by modern commentators is that the servant of the Lord in these chapters is Israel, the eye of the prophet being fixed sometimes on the nation as a whole, sometimes on the godly portion, sometimes on a perfect representative of Israel: that individual is Christ. Against other views there may be urged: 1. The servant of chapter 53 is interpreted by the Targum as Messiah. 2. The Prophet Zechariah apparently identifies the branch, a familiar designation of Messiah, with the servant whereby the iniquity of the land is taken away (Zech. 3:8–10; cf. Jer. 23:5–8). 3. The description of the suffering servant of Isa., ch. 53 actually finds its counterpart in Christ.

The interpreter of Isa., ch. 53 must be ever mindful of certain controlling facts: 1. When this chapter was penned, the Hebrews were fully acquainted with the sense of guilt (Gen. 39:9; II Sam. 12:5–13; Isa. 6:5–7; cf. Psalms 32; 51). 2. The godly among the Israelites recognized themselves as sinful and as involved in the guilt of the nation, in its disobedience to God's Law and in its failure to fulfill the purpose of its selection to be God's servant among men. Israel's best men felt this truth keenly (Neh. 1:6, 7; Dan. 9:5–11, 20). Israel was a unit, a solidarity: the sin of a part of the people involved all in guilt (Deut. 21:1, 7, 8; Josh. 7:1, 11, 13, 15, 25; Judg. 20:6, 10, 13). 3. When this chapter, Isa., ch. 53, was written, the Israelites were familiar with the symbolism of atonement. The prophecy was uttered when the truths were well known that God might pardon after sufficient punishment had been inflicted (Isa. 40:2), yet the mere punishment of sin or compensation for an injury does not cleanse the sinner. Punishment and restitution and cleansing are required (Isa. 4:3, 4; 6:6, 7; 53:10; Lev. 5:14–16; Num. 5:5–8; Ps. 51:2, 7). 4. The doctrine of substitution was also known. It pervades the chapter (Isa. 53:5, 6, 11, 12). It was publicly illustrated on the annual Day of Atonement (Lev. 16:20–22). 5. To fulfill these conditions and satisfy the creed of Israel, the servant of Jehovah must be of sufficient worth to be substituted for Israel, must be identical with Israel in order that he may really represent Israel before God and that it may be said that Israel has actually met its obligations in him; and yet the servant must be distinct from Israel so as not to be involved in Israel's guilt and to have no obligation of service to discharge for himself. These doctrinal requirements point not obscurely to the need of divinity in him who fills the office assigned to the Lord's servant in Isa., ch. 53.

Seth (sĕth), in A.V. once **Sheth** (I Chron. 1:1) [appointed, substituted]. A son of Adam. He was born after the murder of Abel, for whom to a certain extent he became a substitute (Gen. 4:25; 5:3). He became the father of Enos, and died at the age of 912 (Gen. 5:6–8; Luke 3:38).

Se'thur (sē'thẽr) [hidden]. The representative spy from the tribe of Asher (Num. 13:13).

Sev'en. Seven is an ordinary numeral, and it was commonly used without religious significance; but it was also a sacred number among the Hebrews and other Semites, and also among the Aryans of Persia and even of Greece. Its sacredness is traceable to remote antiquity. It is seen in the 7 pillars of wisdom's house (Prov. 9:1), the 7 locks into which Samson, who was consecrated to God, braided his hair (Judg. 16:13, 19), the 7 victims to atone for the broken covenant (II Sam. 21:6, 9), the 7 stones of the ancient Arabs smeared with the blood of the covenanting parties (Herod. iii. 8), the 7 lambs to attest the conclusion of a treaty (Gen. 21:28–30), the Hebrew words for oath and taking an oath, which incorporate the number 7, and the sacredness of the 7th portion of time. The idea that 7 derived its sacred character from the fact that 3 plus 4 make 7 is pure fancy. It was held sacred because men believed that God recognized the number. He placed 7 luminaries in the sky: sun, moon, and 5 planets. The moon has its phases every 7 days. These phenomena, however, were but confirmatory and served as reminders of a greater recognition. God had blessed the 7th day and hallowed it. Far more was needed than the signs of the sky to originate the sacredness of 7. Twelve did not become a sacred number, although there are 12 months in the year and 12 signs in the zodiac. Man noted these phenomena in the earliest times, adopted them into his daily life and language, and celebrated certain of them with religious festivals. In Babylonia 12 was made the basis of an arithmetical system (the duodecimal), and in Assyria the pantheon contained 12 great gods. Notwithstanding all this, 12 did not become a sacred number; but 7 did become a sacred number, and the 7th portion of time a sacred season; and not merely was the recurring 7th portion of time sacred, but it involved a benediction. It was cherished in hoary antiquity as a season of divine favor toward man, when the manifestation of God's good will was to be expected. See SABBATH.

Se·ve'neh (sĕ-vē'nĕ), in A.V. **Sy·e'ne.** A town constituting the extreme limit of Egypt in 1 direction. Which direction depends on the translation of Ezek. 29:10; 30:6. The preferable rendering is that of the marg., "from Migdol to Syene," and so it is in J.V. The town of Seveneh is in the s. of Egypt, on the borders of Ethiopia, and is the Roman Syene, the modern Aswān, on the Egyptian side of the First Cataract, where a few remains of the ancient city exist. Here, or on the island hard by, the border garrison was stationed (Herod. ii. 30). On the island, as early as the time of the Persian conquest of Egypt, a Jewish colony maintained a temple to Jehovah (Elephantine papyri); see ALTAR.

Sev'en Words, The. These words were spoken by Jesus from the cross. The progressive stages by which they are characterized may be interpreted as showing a gradual unfolding of the will and purpose of God for the redemption of mankind. They are as follows: (1) "Father, forgive them; for they know not what they do" (Luke 23:24); (2) "Verily I say unto thee, To-day shalt thou be with me in Paradise" (Luke 23:43); (3) "Woman, behold, thy son! . . . Behold, thy mother!" (John 19:26, 27); (4) "Eli [Eloi], Eli [Eloi], lama sabachthani? . . . My God, my God, why hast thou forsaken me?" (Matt. 27:46; Mark 15:34); (5) "I thirst" (John 19:28); (6) "It is finished" (John 19:30); (7) "Father, into thy hands I commend my spirit" (Luke 23:46).

Sha·al'bim (shā-ăl'bĭm), once **Sha'a·lab'bin** (shā'ȧ-lăb'ĭn) (Josh. 19:42) [cf. Arab. tha'lab, fox]. An Amorite city within the territory of Dan (Josh. 19:42), which the Amorites did not yield (Judg. 1:35) until some time after the settlement of the Hebrews in the land (I Kings 4:9). It may be Selbît, 3 miles n.w. of Aijalon and 8 miles n. of Bethshemesh.

Sha'al·bo'nite (shā-ăl-bō'nīt). A native or inhabitant either of an unknown town called Shaalbon, or more probably of Shaalbim (II Sam. 23:32; I Chron. 11:33).

Sha'a·lim (shā'ȧ-lĭm), in A.V. **Sha'lim** [perhaps, foxes]. A district apparently in Ephraim, through which Saul, on leaving the land of Shalishah, passed in quest of his father's asses (I Sam. 9:4).

Sha'aph (shā'ăf) [Aram., balsam]. 1. A son of Jahdai, included in the registry of Caleb (I Chron. 2:47).
2. A son of Caleb by his concubine Maacah. He was ancestor of the inhabitants of Madmannah (I Chron. 2:49).

Sha'a·ra'im (shā'ȧ-rā'ĭm), in A.V. once **Sha·ra'im** [two gates]. 1. A town in the lowland of Judah (Josh. 15:36), apparently w. of Socoh and Azekah (cf. I Sam. 17:52 with v. 1). Sa'ireh among the hills, 5 miles n.e. by n. of Socoh, has not the proper location; it may be near Tell eṣ-Ṣāfi.
2. A town of Simeon (I Chron. 4:31); see SHARUHEN.

Sha·ash'gaz (shā-ăsh'găz). A chamberlain of King Ahasuerus (Esth. 2:14).

Shab'be·thai (shăb'ĕ-thī) [born on the Sabbath]. A chief Levite, prominent in Ezra's time (Ezra 10:15; Neh. 8:7; 11:16).

Sha·chi'a (shȧ-kī'ȧ) [Jehovah has hedged about]. A Benjamite, son of Shaharaim (I Chron. 8:10).

Sha'drach (shā'drăk) [perhaps, Akkad. Shudur (command of)+Sumerian Aku (the moon-god); but it may be merely a perversion of Marduk]. The name given by the prince of the eunuchs at Babylon to Hananiah, 1 of the 3 faithful Hebrews afterward miraculously saved from the fiery furnace (Dan. 1:7; 3:12–30).

Sha'gee (shā'gē), in A.V. **Sha'ge** (shā'gē) [wandering]. A Hararite, the father of one of David's mighty men (I Chron. 11:34). Some expositors would read Agee instead of Shage, on the ground of II Sam. 23:11. The more appropriate comparison with II Sam. 23:32, 33, and the reading of Lucian's recension of the LXX render more probable the conjecture that the name is really Shammah; see SHAMMAH 3.

Sha·ha·ra'im (shā'há-rā'ĭm) [the double dawning]. A Benjamite, who had numerous descendants (I Chron. 8:8).

Sha·ha·zu'mah (shā'há-zoo'má), in A.V. **Sha·ha·zi'mah** (shā'há-zī'má), as in Heb. marg. [perhaps, lofty places]. A town on the border of Issachar between Tabor and the Jordan (Josh. 19:22); identified with Tell el-Mekarkash (Mukarkash), at the junction of Wadi Sherrār and Wadi Tuffāḥ.

Sha'lem (shā'lĕm) [entire, safe]. A town near Shechem (Gen. 33:18), according to the Gr., Lat., and Syriac versions, followed by A.V. It is scarcely Salem (Gen. 14:18), for that town is probably Jerusalem; nor Salim, 4 miles e. of Shechem, which is not mentioned in the O.T. The word is probably a common noun, to be rendered, with R.V., "in peace or safety."

Sha'lim (shā'lĭm). See SHAALIM.

Sha·li'shah (shá-lī'shá), in A.V. **Sha·li'sha** (shá-lī'shá) [a third part]. A district apparently in the hill country of Ephraim, traversed by Saul in quest of his father's asses (I Sam. 9:4); probably n.e. of Lydda on the w. slope of the range. It does not seem to be the same as Baal-shalishah.

Shal'le·cheth (shăl'ĕ-kĕth) [casting out]. A gate of Solomon's Temple on the w. (I Chron. 26:16).

Shal'lum (shăl'ŭm) [recompense]. 1. A son of Naphtali (I Chron. 7:13); see SHILLEM.

2. A descendant of Simeon through Shaul (I Chron. 4:24, 25).

3. A descendant of Judah through Sisamai (I Chron. 2:40, 41).

4. The chief porter at the sanctuary (I Chron. 9:17, 18). If before the Exile, as is probable, he is mentioned by Jeremiah (Jer. 35:4). He was a son of Kore, a Korahite, and he and his family were keepers of the gates of the sanctuary (I Chron. 9:19). The name Shallum may be equivalent to Meshelemiah or Shelemiah (ch. 26:1, 14), according to whether the registry of ch. 9 is referred to the time before or after the Exile. A comparison of ch. 9:21 with ch. 26:2 raises a strong presumption against the identification. If notwithstanding this the registry be regarded as postexilic and Shallum be identified with Shelemiah, then Shallum is not the name of a person, but of the family, in the registry.

5. A son of Jabesh, who murdered King Zechariah and reigned in his stead over the 10 tribes, but in a month was himself assassinated by Menahem (II Kings 15:8-15).

6. Father of a certain Jehizkiah (II Chron. 28:12).

7. A member of the high-priestly family of Zadok, and an ancestor of Ezra. He lived several generations before the capture of Jerusalem by Nebuchadnezzar (I Chron. 6:12-15; Ezra 7:2). Called Meshullam in I Chron. 9:11; see MESHULLAM 4.

8. A son of Tikvah, and the husband of Huldah, the prophetess, and in the reign of Josiah the officer who had charge either of the priests' garments which were kept in the Temple or of the king's wardrobe (II Kings 22:14; II Chron. 34:22).

9. Uncle of Jeremiah, and the father of Hanameel (Jer. 32:7, 8). He was not a member of the high-priestly family, as some have thought; for his son lived at Anathoth, a town where priests of Ithamar's line represented by Abiathar dwelt (I Kings 2:26), and the high priests of this time belonged to the line of Eleazar.

10. Another name for Jehoahaz, son of Josiah, king of Judah (II Kings 23:30; Jer. 22:11); see JEHOAHAZ 3.

11 and 12. A porter of the Temple, and a son of Bani, each of whom was induced by Ezra to put away his foreign wife (Ezra 10:24, 42).

13. A son of Hallohesh, ruler of half the district of Jerusalem. With his daughters, he repaired part of the wall of Jerusalem (Neh. 3:12).

Shal'lun (shăl'ŭn) [perhaps, same as Shallum]. A ruler of part of Mizpah, who repaired the gate of the fountains at Jerusalem (Neh. 3:15).

Shal'mai (shăl'mī). See SALMAI.

Shal'man (shăl'măn). Tiglath-pileser mentions Salamanu of Moab among the various princes who were tributary to him, and Schrader believes that this person is Shalman, the destroyer of Beth-arbel, to whom Hosea refers (Hos. 10:14), and that Beth-arbel is the town of that name e. of the Jordan, near Pella. These identifications may be correct, but they are unsupported. It is not known that Salamanu of Moab invaded the land of Israel, but it is known that Shalmaneser of Assyria did. In the light of present knowledge, it is more natural to regard Shalman as an abbreviation of Shulmanu-asha= aridu (shortened in II Kings to Shalmaneser), and to think of Beth-arbel as being the town of Galilee, from which Shalmaneser's army was certainly not far distant. See SHALMANESER 3.

Shal'man·e'ser (shăl'măn-ē'zēr) [Assyrian *Shulmanu-asharidu*, god Shulman is chief]. The name of several Assyrian kings: 1. Shalmaneser I, the builder, or rather rebuilder, and fortifier of the town of Calah (*q.v.*). He reigned 1280-1260 B.C.

2. Shalmaneser III, the son of Ashur-nasir-pal. He reigned from c. 860 to 825 B.C., and was the 1st Assyrian king who came into conflict with the Israelites. He was energetic and persistent in purpose. He crossed the Euphrates with hostile intent as early as his 1st year and wasted the Hittite country as far as the Mediterranean; and he repeatedly crossed the river later, besides waging war in the countries n., e., and s., of Nineveh. To resist him in the w., the Syrian league was formed, which included Damascus, Hamath, and the 12 kings of the coast, and was at times re-enforced by the soldiers of the neighboring nations. Thus, for instance, the army of Ahab of Israel was found fighting side by side with the men of Damascus against the common Assyrian foe at Karkar, (854) 853 B.C.; see AHAB 1, BEN-HADAD 2. Shalmaneser claims to have won the battle of Karkar; but he gained nothing if he did, and at once led his army back to Nineveh. After 3 years he returned, but his onward course was again stopped by the allies. The following year, the 11th of his reign, he crossed the Euphrates and plundered many towns of the kingdom of Hamath, but he was again checked. In his 14th year he returned and conquered. In his 18th year, 842 B.C., he defeated Hazael of Damascus at Mount Hermon. The kings of Tyre and Sidon, and Jehu of Israel, in dismay hastened to make submission by sending tribute.

3. Successor of Tiglath-pileser. He reigned from 728/7 B.C., to 722 B.C. In 725 he undertook an expedition to foreign parts. According to the Syrian annals cited by Josephus, Shalmaneser overran Phoenicia. On the approach of the Assyrians, Sidon, Acre, and Tyre on the mainland revolted from the dominion of island Tyre and acknowledged the suzerainty of the invader. The Assyrian king thereupon withdrew. He returned, however, to war against the island. His ships, manned by his Phoenician subjects, were scattered by the Tyrians in a naval engagement. After this defeat Shalmaneser marched away, leav-

Cast of the Black Obelisk of Shalmaneser III

ing troops enough to maintain a siege of the city, which was sustained for 5 years (Jos. *Antiq.* ix. 14, 2), when Tyre submitted to Sargon. When Shalmaneser arrived in the w., Hoshea paid him tribute, as he had done to his predecessor, but he soon stopped his pay-

ments, relying upon So of Egypt to aid him in fighting the Assyrians and perhaps encouraged by the stern resistance of Tyre. Shalmaneser promptly had him seized and imprisoned. After seizing the king, whether at Arbela in Galilee or elsewhere, Shalmaneser laid siege to the capital. Samaria stood this siege for 3 years and then fell into the hands of the Assyrians (II Kings 17:1–6; 18:9, 10). See SARGON.

Sha′ma (shā′mȧ) [he (God) has heard]. A son of Hotham, the Aroerite. He was one of David's mighty men (I Chron. 11:44).

Sham′a·ri′ah (shăm′ȧ-rī′ȧ). See SHEMARIAH.

Sha′med (shā′mĕd). See SHEMED.

Sha′mer (shā′mẽr). See SHEMER.

Sham′gar (shăm′gär) [probably Hurrian, *Shimig-ar(i)*, (the god) Shimike gave]. A son of Anath (Judg. 3:31). Shortly before the time of Deborah, for fear of the Philistines, travelers avoided the highways and crept along by-paths (ch. 5:6). But Shamgar fought single-handed with the oppressors. Their dead, slain from time to time by his oxgoad, at length amounted to 600. He thus saved Israel (ch. 3:31); but he is not called a judge, and no years are assigned him in the chronology.

Sham′huth (shăm′hŭth) [desolation, appallment]. An Izrahite, David's captain for the 5th month (I Chron. 27:8). Perhaps identical with Shammah, one of David's mighty men. See SHAMMAH 4.

Sha′mir (shā′mẽr) [thorn, flint]. 1. A town in the hill country of Judah (Josh. 15:48); the name is represented by the ruin Sōmerah, about 13 miles w.s.w. of Hebron, but the old site was probably at el-Bîreh.

2. A town in Mount Ephraim, which the judge Tola, though a man of Issachar, made his residence, and where he was buried (Judg. 10:1, 2). Sanûr between Samaria and Engannim has been suggested, but Codex Alexandrinus has Samaria.

3. A Levite, a son of Micah (I Chron. 24:24).

Sham′ma (shăm′ȧ) [desolation, appallment]. An Asherite, a son of Zophah (I Chron. 7:37).

Sham′mah (shăm′ȧ) [desolation, appallment]. 1. A descendant of Esau and also of Ishmael (Gen. 36:3, 4, 13, 17). He became a chief of Edom (v. 17).

2. Third son of Jesse, and brother of David (I Sam. 16:9; 17:13). See SHIMEA 3.

3. One of David's first 3 mighty men, a son of Agee, a Hararite (II Sam. 23:11). Shammah the Hararite is named in v. 33; and, in view of I Chron. 11:34 and textual considerations, is reasonably believed to be this person mentioned again as father of Jonathan. The words in Samuel and Chronicles are to be read: "Jonathan, son of Shammah the Hararite." See SHAGEE.

4. A Harodite, also one of David's mighty men (II Sam. 23:25). In I Chron. 11:27 the pl. form Shammoth is used. Shamhuth of I Chron. 27:8 is perhaps another external and unessential variation of this man's name.

Sham′ma·i (shăm′ȧ-ī) [perhaps, (Jehovah) has heard]. 1. A son of Onam, house of Jerahmeel, tribe of Judah (I Chron. 2:28).

2. A son of Rekem, house of Caleb, tribe of Judah (I Chron. 2:44).

3. A son of a certain Ezrah, registered with the tribe of Judah (I Chron. 4:17).

Sham′moth (shăm′ŏth) [desolations]. See SHAMMAH 4.

Sham·mu′a (shȧ-mū′ȧ), in A.V. once **Sham-mu′ah** (shȧ-mū′ȧ) (II Sam. 5:14) [heard (by God)]. 1. The representative from the tribe of Reuben sent to spy out the Land of Canaan (Num. 13:4).

2. A son of David by Bath-sheba, born at Jerusalem (II Sam. 5:14; I Chron. 3:5); see BATH-SHUA 2. He bore an uncle's name (R.V., I Chron. 2:13). In I Chron. 3:5 he is called Shimea, an unessential variant, having the same meaning as Shammua.

3. A Levite descended from Jeduthun (Neh. 11:17).

4. A priest in the days of the high priest Joiakim. He was head of the father's house of Bilgah (Neh. 12:18).

Sham′she·rai (shăm′shê-rī). A Benjamite, a son of Jeroham (I Chron. 8:26).

Sha′pham (shā′făm). A Gadite dwelling in Bashan (I Chron. 5:12).

Sha′phan (shā′făn) [hyrax, rock badger]. A scribe in the reign of Josiah. When Hilkiah found the Book of the Law, he gave it to Shaphan, who read it at first privately, and then to the king. Afterward he was one of those who went to Huldah, the prophetess, to consult her regarding the threatenings contained in the book (II Kings 22:8–14). He was the father of Ahikam (Jer. 26:24; 39:14), Elasah (Jer. 29:3), Gemariah (Jer. 36:10), and Jaazaniah (Ezek. 8:11), and the grandfather of Gedaliah (II Kings 25:22).

Sha′phat (shā′făt) [he has judged]. 1. The representative from the tribe of Simeon who was sent to spy out the Land of Canaan (Num. 13:5).

2. A Gadite in Bashan (I Chron. 5:12).

3. Son of Adlai, and David's overseer of the herds that were in the valleys (I Chron. 27:29).

4. Father of the Prophet Elisha (I Kings 19:16).

5. A son of Shemaiah, registered with the descendants of David (I Chron. 3:22).

Sha′pher (shā′fēr). See SHEPHER.

Sha′phir (shā′fēr), in A.V. **Sa′phir** [beautiful]. A town in Judah (Micah 1:11); not identified. Robinson and others locate it at es-Suwâfir, 3½ miles s.e. of Ashdod.

Sha·ra′i (shȧ-rā′ī) [perhaps, (Jehovah has set) free]. A son of Bani, induced by Ezra to put away his foreign wife (Ezra 10:40).

Sha·ra′im (shȧ-rā′ĭm). See SHAARAIM.

Sha′rar (shā′rēr) [Aram., firm]. A Hararite, father of one of David's mighty men (II Sam. 23:33). Called in I Chron. 11:35 Sacar.

Sha·re′zer (shȧ-rē′zēr), in A.V. **She·re′zer** in Zech. 7:2 [Akkad., protect the king]. 1. A son of Sennacherib. With one of his brothers he murdered his father (II Kings 19:37; Isa. 37:38).

2. A man sent from Beth-el to the priests at Jerusalem to inquire whether the fasts should be kept now that the cause for them no longer existed (Zech. 7:2).

Shar′on (shăr′ŭn), in A.V. of N.T. **Sa′ron** (Acts 9:35) [a plain]. 1. The seacoast between Joppa and Carmel, and extending back to the hills of Samaria. It was a fertile region (Isa. 35:2), a pasture land for flocks (I Chron. 27:29; Isa. 65:10); but like a desert when devastated (Isa. 33:9). Among its flowers, lilies and anemones are prominent; see LILY, ROSE. Lydda was at its s. limit (cf. Acts 9:35). Its length is about 50 miles, its breadth 9 or 10. It is not flat, but agreeably undulated, with here and there groves of oak, and with excellent pasturage, except that in places thorns and thistles too much abound.

2. A pasture region e. of the Jordan (I Chron. 5:16). One suggestion is that Sharon is a corruption of Sirion (Hermon), and accordingly it would be the pasture lands of Hermon. Another view is that the *mishôr* or

tableland of Gilead between the Arnon and Heshbon is meant (cf. Deut. 3:10).

Sha·ru′hen (shȧ-rōō′hĕn). A village in the territory of Simeon (Josh. 19:6), apparently the place called Shaaraim (I Chron. 4:31) and Shilhim (Josh. 15:32); identified with Tell el-Fâr′ah, about 15½ miles s.s.e. of Gaza.

Sha′shai (shā′shī) [perhaps, whitish, pale]. A son of Bani, induced by Ezra to put away his foreign wife (Ezra 10:40).

Sha′shak (shā′shăk). A Benjamite, a son of Elpaal (I Chron. 8:14, 25).

Sha′ul (shā′ŭl) [asked (of God)]. 1. A king of Edom, from Rehoboth on the Euphrates (Gen. 36:37, in A.V. Saul; I Chron. 1:48).

2. A son of Simeon by a Canaanitish woman (Gen. 46:10; Ex. 6:15; I Chron. 1:48). He founded a tribal family (Num. 26:13).

3. A Kohathite Levite, descended through Korah, Abiasaph, and Tahath (I Chron. 6:24).

Sha′veh (shā′vĕ) [a plain]. A valley, afterward called the king's dale, near Salem, in which the king of Sodom met Abraham after the defeat of Chedorlaomer (Gen. 14:17, 18). Absalom reared a memorial pillar for himself there (II Sam. 18:18), which according to Josephus stood about a quarter of a mile from Jerusalem (Jos. *Antiq.* vii. 10, 3).

Sha′veh-kir′i·a·tha′im (shā′vĕ-kĭr′yȧ-thā′ĭm), in A.V. **Sha′veh Kir′ia·tha′im** (shā′vĕ kĭr′yȧ-thā′ĭm) [plain of Kiriathaim]. A plain near the city of Kiriathaim, in the territory afterward assigned to Reuben. It was at first inhabited by Emim (Gen. 14:5). Exact situation unknown.

Shav′sha (shăv′shȧ) and **Shi′sha**. A scribe of David and afterward of Solomon (I Chron. 18:16; I Kings 4:3). Probably identical with the scribe Seraiah (II Sam. 8:17) and doubtless with the scribe Sheva (II Sam. 20:25).

She′al (shē′ăl) [asking]. A son of Bani induced by Ezra to put away his foreign wife (Ezra 10:29).

She·al′ti·el (shē-ăl′tĭ-ĕl), in A.V. of I Chron. 3:17 and of N.T. **Sa·la′thi·el**, the Gr. form [I have asked God]. A son of King Jeconiah (I Chron. 3:17; Matt. 1:12) and also of Neri (Luke 3:27); identified with the father of Zerubbabel (Ezra 3:2; etc.), and yet apparently his uncle, or possibly, though not probably, his grandfather (I Chron. 3:17–19). The explanation probably is that, while neither the son of Jeconiah nor the father of Zerubbabel after the flesh, he was the legitimate successor of Jeconiah to the royal title, and on his own death the right to the throne passed to Zerubbabel. He is the link in the royal succession connecting Jeconiah with Zerubbabel. See ASSIR 3, ZERUBBABEL, and GENEALOGY, II.

She′a·ri′ah (shē′ȧ-rī′ȧ) [Jehovah has esteemed]. A descendant of Jonathan (I Chron. 8:38).

Shear′ing House. The place where Jehu slew the 42 brethren of Ahaziah, king of Judah, who were going to Ahaziah at Samaria while he was on a visit to the wounded king of Israel (II Kings 10:12–14). It took its name either from the fact that shepherds there bound the sheep which they were about to shear, or because they were in the habit of meeting there (Targum; R.V. marg.). The Heb. name is *Bêth 'êḵed hārō'īm*, and is probably to be identified with Beit Ḳâd, about 3 miles e. by n. of En-gannim, and about 16 n.e. by n. of Samaria.

She′ar·ja′shub (shē′är-jä′shŭb) [a remnant shall return]. A son of Isaiah. His name was designed to embody a prophecy (Isa. 7:3; cf. ch. 10:21).

She'ba, I (shē'bȧ) [Heb. *Sheḇā'*]. A people of Cushite genealogy descended through Raamah and closely related to Dedan (Gen. 10:7), but also classed as a Semitic people descended through Joktan (v. 28) and, like Dedan, from Abraham through Jokshan (ch. 25:3). So far as connected with Abraham, they migrated e. (Gen. 25:6; cf. Job 1:15; 6:19). See ARABIA. They dwelt in the s. (Matt. 12:42), and traded in gold, incense, and precious stones (I Kings 10:1 *seq.;* Ps. 72:10; Isa. 60:6; Jer. 6:20; Ezek. 27:22; 38:13). Sheba was a country and people of s.w. Arabia, well known from its own records and classical geographers. Its capital was Marib, where was the famous great dam, which after various earlier breaks and repairs finally broke sometime between A.D. 542 and 570. The Sabeans were a great commercial people. They traded not only in the products of their own land, but also in those of India and Ethiopia. Their language was s. Arabic. They spread widely and were in n.w. Arabia in Assyrian times (8th century B.C.), and in the n. desert along with the Nabataeans. It is readily conceivable that in their dispersion they became mingled with other tribes by intermarriage or attached to them by political relations, and hence they might trace their descent by different lines and be classed variously in a genealogy.

She'ba, II (shē'bȧ) [Heb. *sheba'*, seven, an oath]. 1. A Simeonite town, mentioned after Beer-sheba (Josh. 19:2). Three views are entertained regarding it: (1) Its site may be Tell es-Seb'a, 3 miles e. of Beer-sheba. (2) It is a corruption of Shema (cf. LXX and Josh. 15:26). (3) Since it is lacking in I Chron. 4:28, and this agrees with the summation in Josh. 19:6, it is an abbreviated form of Beer-sheba (see R.V.) or accidentally introduced into the text by dittography.

2. A Benjamite, a son of Bichri. After the collapse of Absalom's rebellion and the concurrence of the 10 tribes with Judah in restoring David to his throne, Sheba blew a trumpet, and summoned the 10 tribes to renounce their allegiance. He was besieged in Abel of Beth-maacah and lost his life there, for the inhabitants cut off his head and threw it over the wall to Joab (II Sam. 20:1–22).

3. A Gadite dwelling in Gilead in Bashan (I Chron. 5:13, 16).

She'bah (shē'bȧ). See SHIBAH.

She'bam (shē'băm). See SIBMAH.

Sheb'a·ni'ah (shĕb'ȧ-nī'ȧ) [perhaps, Jehovah has brought me back]. 1. A Levite who was a trumpeter in David's time (I Chron. 15:24).

2. A father's house among the priests in the generation after the Exile (Neh. 12:14); see SHECANIAH 3. Its representative set his seal to the covenant (Neh. 10:4).

3. A Levite who assisted at the feast of tabernacles in Ezra's time (Neh. 9:4, 5), and in behalf of his house sealed the covenant (ch. 10:10).

4. Another Levite who sealed the covenant (Neh. 10:12).

Sheb'a·rim (shĕb'ȧ-rĭm) [breakings; perhaps, quarries]. A locality near Ai (Josh. 7:5). Site unknown.

She·bat' (shĕ-băt'), in A.V. Se'bat, and I Macc. 16:14, A.V. Sa'bat, R.V. Se'bat [Heb. *sheḇāṭ* from Akkad. *shabāṭu*]. The 11th month of the year (Zech. 1:7); see YEAR.

She'ber (shē'bẽr) [cf. Arab. *sabr*, lion; Aram. *shabrā*, childish, simple]. A son of Caleb, by his concubine Maacah (I Chron. 2:48).

Sheb'na (shĕb'nȧ), twice **Sheb'nah** (shĕb'nȧ) (II Kings 18:18, 26) [perhaps, short form of Shebaniah]. The steward of the king's house under Hezekiah (Isa. 22:15), a man of great influence, apparently a foreigner, and fond of display (vs. 16, 18). As was customary among the wealthy, he built himself a sepulcher in his lifetime (v. 16). Isaiah rebuked him, calling him the shame of his lord's house, and predicted his fall and his retirement from Judah, and the elevation of Eliakim to his place (vs. 17–25). Probably later, in 701 B.C., Eliakim held the position of house steward, while Shebna was only Hezekiah's scribe or secretary (II Kings 18:18, 26, 37; 19:2).

She·bu'el (shē-bū'ĕl), in LXX and Lucian everywhere Shu'ba-el [return, O God]. 1. A son of Gershom, and a grandson of Moses (I Chron. 23:16; 26:24; in ch. 24:20 Shubael).

2. A son of Heman, in David's time (I Chron. 25:4; in v. 20 Shubael).

Shec'a·ni'ah (shĕk'ȧ-nī'ȧ), in A.V. Shech'a·ni'ah (shĕk'ȧ-nī'ȧ) except I Chron. 24:11; II Chron. 31:15 [Jehovah hath dwelt]. 1. A descendant of Aaron. His family had grown to a father's house in the time of David, and became the 10th of the 24 courses into which David divided the priests (I Chron. 24:1, 6, 11).

2. A Levite in King Hezekiah's reign (II Chron. 31:15).

3. A chief of the priests, who returned with Zerubbabel from Babylon (Neh. 12:3, 7). In the next generation a father's house probably bore his name, although it is written Shebaniah (v. 14); for the possibility of misreading *kaph* (k) as *beth* (b) cf. these letters in the table under ALPHABET. See SHEBANIAH 2.

4. Founder of a family, presumably a descendant of David, but not in the line of succession to the throne (I Chron. 3:21, 22), for he is loosely registered, his kinship with Zerubbabel not being given. Perhaps his was the family of which the representative returned from Babylon with Ezra (Ezra 8:3). The name of this representative has probably fallen out of the Hebrew text between Shecaniah and the words "of the sons of Parosh." The parallel passage, I Esdras 8:29, R.V., has: "Of the sons of David, Attus the son of Sechenias." This agrees indeed with the fact that Hattush was a grandson of Shecaniah (I Chron. 3:22), but it is not supported by either the LXX or Hebrew of Ezra 8:3.

5. A son of Jahaziel and descendant of Zattu, who returned from Babylon with Ezra (Ezra 8:5, LXX; I Esdras 8:32).

6. A son of Jehiel, one of the sons of Elam. He confessed the guilt of himself and his brethren who had married foreign wives, and proposed to Ezra that they should put them away (Ezra 10:2, 3).

7. Father of Shemaiah, the keeper of the e. gate in Nehemiah's time, and probably a Levite (Neh. 3:29), and not the man of Judah (I Chron. 3:22).

8. Father-in-law of Tobiah, the Ammonite. He was the son of Arah (Neh. 6:18).

She'chem (shē'kĕm), in A.V. once Si'chem (Gen. 12:6), twice Sy'chem (Acts 7:16), Gr. forms [shoulder]. 1. A walled town (Gen. 33:18; cf. ch. 34:20), by Mount Gerizim (Judg. 9:7), in the hill-country of Ephraim (Josh. 20:7). Abraham camped near it (Gen. 12:6). He found Canaanites in the land, but Jehovah told him that this was the land promised him for his descendants. Jacob, coming back to the Promised Land, found a tribe of Hivites inhabiting Shechem (Gen. 34:2). He bought a parcel of ground from them (Gen. 33:18, 19), where Joseph's body was eventually buried (Josh. 24:32; in Acts 7:16 confused by Stephen with Abraham's purchase of Machpelah). On account of the mistreatment of their sister, Simeon and Levi broke treaty and massacred the male inhabitants, and the sons of Jacob pillaged the town (Gen. 34:25–29; 48:22). Jacob condemned the deed (chs. 34:30; 49:5–7). Joseph's brothers for a time fed their flocks near Shechem (ch. 37: 12, 13). The town fell into the hands of the Habirū in the 15th century B.C. (Tell el-Amarna letters). In the vale of Shechem the tribes assembled solemnly to assume obligation to the Law of Jehovah (Josh. 8:30). The boundary between the tribes of Ephraim and Manasseh passed near it (Josh. 17:7), and it was one of the cities of refuge and a Levitical city (chs. 20:7; 21:21). Joshua summoned the tribes thither to hear his farewell address (ch. 24:1). In the time of the Judges, a temple of Baal-berith was maintained in the town (Judg. 8:33; 9:4). Gideon's concubine lived there; and her son, Abimelech, was for a time assisted in his political designs by its citizens

cupies the bottom of the valley, at its narrowest point, where the 2 mountains are only 100 yards apart, and climbs the slope of Gerizim to the foot of the cliffs. There is still a small community of Samaritans at and around Nablus.

2. The son of Hamor, the Hivite, who was prince of Shechem (Gen., ch. 34).

3. A son of Gilead, and the founder of a tribal family (Num. 26:31; Josh. 17:2).

4. A Manassite, a son of Shemidah (I Chron. 7:19).

Shed′e•ur (shĕd′ē-ēr) [Shaddai (the One of the mountains) shines (shows favor to me)]. Father of Elizur, the Reubenite chief in the wilderness (Num. 1:5; 2:10).

Sheep. Sheep were early domesticated (Gen. 4:2). They were herded by the Hebrew Patriarchs (Gen. 12:16), and by their descendants when sojourning in Egypt and when settled

The Village of Nablus, the Ancient Shechem

(Judg. 9:1, 3, 6), but they turned against him and he destroyed the town (vs. 23, 45). At Shechem the 10 tribes rejected Rehoboam and made Jeroboam king (I Kings 12:1–19); Jeroboam fortified the town, and occupied it for a time as his capital (v. 25). It continued in existence after the fall of the Northern Kingdom (Jer. 41:5); and became the chief city of the Samaritans (Ecclus. 50:26; Jos. Antiq. xi. 8, 6). It was captured by John Hyrcanus (Jos. Antiq. xiii. 9, 1). Shechem, or Nablus, is about 31½ miles n. of Jerusalem and 5½ s.e. of Samaria. It lies in the upland valley bounded by Mount Ebal on the n., and Mount Gerizim on the s. The valley was known as Mabartha, the defile, being a pass from the seacoast to the Jordan; and Vespasian, leading his army from Emmaus to Jericho, camped at Shechem for a night (Jos. War iv. 8, 1). After the war Shechem was rebuilt, and the new town was named Flavia Neapolis in honor of Flavius Vespasian, then Roman emperor. This name still persists in the form Nablus. The original settlement was probably at the e. end of the valley, at Tell Balâṭa, which hides walls of great strength and thickness. The town today stands at the w. end of the pass, at the watershed, 1,870 feet above sea level. It oc-

in Canaan (Ex. 10:9; 12:32, 38; I Chron. 27: 31), even down to the latest times (Luke 2:8). The wilderness of Judea and the s. country, and the plateau of Moab, were pasture lands (Num. 32:1; Judg. 5:16; I Sam. 16:11; 25:2; and so was the country around Haran (Gen. 29:2), and the land of Midian (Ex. 2:16), and of Uz and the Hagarenes (Job 1:3; I Chron. 5:20, 21), and of the tribes of Kedar and Nebaioth (Isa. 60:7; Ezek. 27:21; cf. I Sam. 15:7, 9). In these regions the sheep, owing to the heat and dryness of the climate, require water daily (Gen. 29:7–10; Ex. 2:16–19). The sheep was a clean animal and used for food; its flesh was eaten (I Sam. 14:32; 25:18; II Sam. 17:29; I Kings 4:23), and the rich milk of the ewes was drunk (Deut. 32:14; Isa. 7:21, 22; I Cor. 9:7). The skin served as rude clothing (Heb. 11:37; cf. Zech. 13:4; Matt. 7:15), and it was sometimes used in covering tents (Ex. 26:14). From the wool, cloth was woven (Lev. 13: 47, 48; Job 31:20; Prov. 27:26; Ezek. 34:3); hence wool was a valuable commodity, and was rendered as tribute (II Kings 3:4; Isa. 16:1). Sheepshearing was made a time of feasting and frolic (Gen. 38:12; I Sam. 25:4, 11, 36; II Sam. 13:23). The horns of rams served as flasks and trumpets (Josh. 6:4; I

Sam. 16:1). As the sheep was a clean animal, it was used in sacrifice by the Hebrews and other peoples (Ex. 20:24; Num. 22:40; John 2:14). An animal of the flock might be taken for a burnt offering (Lev. 1:10), a sin offering of the common people (ch. 4:32), a guilt and a trespass offering (chs. 5:15; 6:6), and a peace offering (ch. 22:21); see LAMB, RAM, I. 1. The sheep was known for its affection (II Sam. 12:3), docility (John 10:3, 4), meekness and submissiveness (Isa. 53:7; Jer. 11:19), helplessness when left to itself (Micah 5:8; Matt. 10:16), and its need of guidance (Num. 27:17; Ezek. 34:5; Matt. 9:36; 26:31). The sheep of Palestine and the adjacent regions are usually white (Ps. 147:16; Isa. 1:18; Ezek. 27:18), but occasionally they are black or brown, or piebald, either white and tawny or white and black (Gen. 30:32). Two breeds of sheep are found in Palestine. In the n. districts a short-wooled variety is raised, of which both the rams and ewes are horned. But the broad-tailed sheep (*Ovis laticaudata*) is more general. It has been bred since early ages in Arabia and Palestine (Herod. iii. 113; cf. Ex. 29:22; Lev. 3:9; 7:3; 8:25). The tails which are offered for sale in the markets ordinarily weigh 10 or 15 pounds; but when the sheep is well fattened, the tail grows to an enormous size. The Arabs regard it as a delicacy, frying it in slices.

Sheep'fold' and **Sheep'cote'.** An enclosure for sheep (Jer. 23:3; Ezek. 34:14), whither the flock was ordinarily driven for the night. Many were permanent pens, surrounded by a stone wall (cf. Num. 32:16) and entered by a gate (John 10:1). The wall was often surmounted with branches of thorny shrubs. The sheep lay in the yard under the open sky; but doubtless there were in former days, as there are now, low, flat buildings on the sheltered side of the area, in which the flocks were shut up on cold nights. It was common for several flocks to pass the night in one fold under the care of an undershepherd, who guarded the door. The shepherds came in the morning, and were admitted by the undershepherd. Each shepherd knew the sheep of his own flock and was known by them (John 10:2–5). Less substantial inclosures were hastily formed of tangled thorn branches for temporary use on pastures remote from home, and caves and other natural shelters were also taken advantage of for protecting the sheep at night, the shepherds camping with their flocks. On ranges exposed to the raids of robbers or hostile tribes, towers were erected, about which the flocks and herds were pastured and at night folded (II Chron. 26:10; Micah 4:8).

Sheep Gate. See JERUSALEM, II. 3.

Sheep Mar'ket, in R.V. **Sheep Gate.** See JERUSALEM, II. 3.

She'e·rah (shē'ē-rá), in A.V. **She'rah** [consanguinity, a female relative]. A daughter of Ephraim, or perhaps of Beriah. She or rather her descendants built upper and nether Bethhoron and Uzzen-sheerah (I Chron. 7:24). She may have married Becher and given rise to the tribal family of the Becherites.

She·ha·ri'ah (shē'há-rī'á) [Jehovah is the dawn]. A Benjamite, son of Jeroham (I Chron. 8:26).

Shek'el [weight]. A weight used for metals (Gen. 24:22; I Sam. 17:5, 7); see WEIGHTS. At an early period this quantity of silver, uncoined, was a recognized standard in financial transactions (Gen. 23:15, 16). Half a shekel was to be given by each man as a ransom for his life when a census was taken (Ex. 30:14, 15). The standard shekel weighed 11.46 grams (metric system), or 176.85 grains.

There are 437½ grains in one ounce avoirdupois, and thus 2½ shekels would be slightly heavier than one ounce avoirdupois. Discoveries at Kiriath-sepher now prove what scholars had concluded inductively concerning the weight of the shekel. It is important that we do not identify this weight with the coin bearing the same name. See MONEY, WEIGHTS.

She·ki'nah (shē-kī'ná) [the earthly presence (dwelling) of God]. See THEOPHANY.

She'lah, I (shē'lá), in A.V. of Genesis **Sa'lah**, of N.T. **Sa'la**, in imitation of Gr. form [a shoot, a sprout]. 1. The son of Arphaxad (Gen. 10:24; 11:12–15; I Chron. 1:18).
2. A pool at Jerusalem, near the king's garden, erroneously translated in A.V. Siloah (Neh. 3:15). See SHILOAH, SILOAM.

She'lah, II (shē'lá). The 3d son of Judah by a Canaanite woman. He was the founder of a tribal family (Gen. 38:2, 5, 11, 14, 26; Num. 26:20).

Shel'e·mi'ah (shĕl'ē-mī'á) [Jehovah has recompensed]. 1. A doorkeeper of the sanctuary in David's time (I Chron. 26:13, 14). See MESHELEMIAH.
2. Son of Cushi (Jer. 36:14).
3. Son of Abdeel (Jer. 36:26).
4. Son of Hananiah (Jer. 37:13).
5. Father of Jucal (Jer. 38:1).
6, 7. Two men, descendants of Bani, each of whom was induced by Ezra to put away his foreign wife (Ezra 10:39, 41).
8. Father of that Hananiah who helped to rebuild the wall of Jerusalem (Neh. 3:30).
9. A priest whom Nehemiah appointed as one of 3 treasurers who were commissioned to distribute the tithes among the Levites (Neh. 13:13).

She'leph (shē'lĕf) [cf. Arab. *salafa*, to till]. A Semitic people descended through Joktan (Gen. 10:26; I Chron. 1:20), and doubtless dwelling in s. Arabia. The name is a common one in Yemen.

She'lesh (shē'lĕsh) [triad; but cf. Arab. *salis*, obedient, meek]. An Asherite, son of Helem (I Chron. 7:35).

She·lo'mi (shē-lō'mī) [at peace, complete, perfect]. Father of Ahihud, who was prince of Asher in the latter part of the wilderness wanderings (Num. 34:27).

She·lo'mith (shē-lō'mĭth) [fem. of Shelomi]. 1. A Danite, a daughter of Dibri, and mother of the Israelite who was put to death in the wilderness for blasphemy (Lev. 24:11).
2. A Levite, family of Kohath, house of Izhar (I Chron. 23:18). Called Shelomoth in ch. 24:22.
3. A descendant of Moses through Eliezer. He and his brethren were appointed by David over the dedicated treasures (I Chron. 26:25, 26, in R.V., following the Heb. text, Shelomoth; cf. ch. 23:15–17).
4. A Gershonite Levite, son of Shimei (I Chron. 23:9, in R.V. Shelomoth).
5. A son or daughter of Rehoboam (II Chron. 11:20).
6. Son of Josiphiah (Ezra 8:10). The Heb. text is faulty. The LXX shows that he was a member of the family of Bani: "Of the sons of Baani, Salimouth, son of Iōsephia."
7. A daughter of Zerubbabel (I Chron. 3:19).

She·lo'moth (shē-lō'mŏth). See SHELOMITH 2.

She·lu'mi·el (shē-lū'mĭ-ĕl) [El (God) is welfare, peace]. The prince of the tribe of Simeon early in the wilderness wanderings (Num. 1:6; 2:12; 7:36, 41; 10:19).

Shem (shĕm), in A.V. of N.T. **Sem** [name, renown]. One of the 2 elder sons of Noah (Gen. 10:1, 21; cf. ch. 9:24), and probably the first-born (ch. 5:32). For explanation of ch. 11:10, see CHRONOLOGY, I. 3, section relating to the period from the Creation to Abraham. With his descendants, he is mentioned last in the catalogue of Gen., ch. 10 in accordance with the author's custom of disposing of subordinate genealogies before presenting the main line of the people of God. He was born about the 500th year of Noah's life (see NOAH, I). At the time of the Deluge he was married, but had no children (Gen. 7:7; I Peter 3:20). After that catastrophe, he acted with filial respect to his father when the latter committed his great sin. Shem in consequence received a blessing, the wording of which implied that God would bless Shem and that the worship of the true God should continue in his family (Gen. 9:23, 27). He was progenitor of the people who inhabited or perhaps in some cases held in subjection Elam, Asshur, Arpachshad, Lud, and Aram (ch. 10:21, 22).

She'ma (shē'må) [report, fame; or he (God) has heard]. 1. A town in the extreme s. of Judah (Josh. 15:26); see SHEBA, II. 1.

2. A son of Hebron, belonging to the tribe of Judah (I Chron. 2:43, 44); see MARESHAH 2.

3. A Reubenite, a son of Joel (I Chron. 5:8; cf. v. 4).

4. A Benjamite, head of a father's house in Aijalon (I Chron. 8:13). Called in v. 21 Shimei, in A.V. Shimhi.

5. One of the men, probably priests, who assisted Ezra at the public reading of the Law (Neh. 8:4).

She·ma'ah (shē-mā'å) [report, fame]. A Benjamite of Gibeah, who joined David at Ziklag (I Chron. 12:3).

She·ma'iah (shē-mā'yå) [Jehovah has heard]. 1. A Simeonite (I Chron. 4:37).

2. A Reubenite, a son of Joel (I Chron. 5:4).

3. A Levite, chief of the sons of Elizaphan, who to the number of 200 took part in the ceremonies attendant on the removal of the Ark from the house of Obed-edom to Mount Zion (I Chron. 15:8–11).

4. A Levite, a son of Nethanel. He was a scribe in the time of David, and noted down the 24 divisions then made of the priests (I Chron. 24:6).

5. Eldest son of Obed-edom (I Chron. 26:4). He was the father of various valiant sons who, with him, were doorkeepers of the tabernacle (vs. 6–8).

6. A prophet in the reign of Rehoboam, who forbade the king to attempt the conquest of the revolted 10 tribes (I Kings 12:22–24; II Chron. 11:2–4). Five years later, when Shishak invaded the land, he declared that the invasion was permitted as a punishment for sin. Thereupon the princes humbled themselves, and the affliction was made lighter (II Chron. 12:5–8). Shemaiah wrote a history of Rehoboam's reign (v. 15).

7. One of the Levites sent by Jehoshaphat to teach the people (II Chron. 17:8).

8. A Levite, descendant of Jeduthun. He helped to cleanse the Temple in Hezekiah's reign (II Chron. 29:14, 15). He is, perhaps, the Levite mentioned in I Chron. 9:16, and he may be the person called Shammua in Neh. 11:17.

9. A Levite in Hezekiah's reign who, with others, had to distribute the firstlings, tithes, and gifts to the Levites in the cities (II Chron. 31:15).

10. A chief Levite in Josiah's reign who, with others, was liberal in his donations of animals for the passover services (II Chron. 35:9).

11. Father of Urijah, of Kiriath-jearim, who was put to death by King Jehoiakim for the true prophecies he had uttered (Jer. 26:20–23).

12. Father of Delaiah, the latter being a prince in the reign of Jehoiakim (Jer. 36:12).

13. A Nehelamite, a false prophet among the exiles in Babylonia, who prophesied a speedy return from captivity. He wrote to the people of Jerusalem and the priest who had oversight of the Temple, and complained that Jeremiah, who declared that the Exile would be long, remained unpunished. When Jeremiah heard the complaint, he foretold that Shemaiah should leave no posterity and not live to see the Return (Jer. 29:24–32).

14. A chief of the priests who returned from Babylon with Zerubbabel (Neh. 12:6, 7). In the next generation a father's house bore this name (v. 18).

15. A son of Adonikam, and one of the chief men who accompanied Ezra from the land of the Captivity to Canaan (Ezra 8:13).

16. A chief man whom Ezra sent with others to Iddo to obtain Levites who were lacking in the party leaving the land of the Captivity for Canaan (Ezra 8:16).

17 and 18. Two men, 1 descended from the priest Harim, and the other from the layman Harim, each of whom was induced by Ezra to put away his foreign wife (Ezra 10:21, 31).

19. A son of Shecaniah (I Chron. 3:22); see SHECANIAH 4.

20. Keeper of the e. gate, and probably a Levite. He repaired part of the wall of Jerusalem in Nehemiah's time (Neh. 3:29); see SHECANIAH 7.

21. A Levite, descended from Bunni. He was an overseer of the business of the house of God in Nehemiah's time (Neh. 11:15; cf. I Chron. 9:14).

22. A false prophet, son of Delaiah, son of Mehetabel. He was hired by Tobiah and Sanballat to frighten Nehemiah into going with him into the Temple and shutting the doors to avoid assassination (Neh. 6:10–13). In carrying out his plan, he shut himself in his house and pretended to fear for his life.

23. A priest who, doubtless in behalf of a father's house, sealed the covenant in the days of Nehemiah (Neh. 10:8).

24. A prince of Judah who took part in the ceremonies at the dedication of the wall of Jerusalem (Neh. 12:34).

25. A Levite of the lineage of Asaph (Neh. 12:35).

26. One of the company of Levite musicians at the dedication of the wall of Jerusalem (Neh. 12:36).

27. A priest who blew a trumpet on the same occasion (Neh. 12:42).

Shem'a·ri'ah (shĕm'å-rī'å), in A.V. once **Sham'a·ri'ah** (II Chron. 11:19) [Jehovah has kept, preserved]. 1. A Benjamite who joined David at Ziklag (I Chron. 12:5).

2. A son of Rehoboam (II Chron. 11:19).

3 and 4. A son of Harim and a son of Bani, each of whom was induced by Ezra to put away his foreign wife (Ezra 10:32, 41).

Shem·e'ber (shĕm-ē'bĕr). The king of Zeboiim, defeated, with the other kings ruling over the cities of the Plain, by Chedorlaomer and his confederates (Gen. 14:2, 8, 10).

She'med (shē'mĕd), in A.V. **Sha'med**, the pausal form [destruction]. A Benjamite, descended from Shaharaim through Elpaal. He was a rebuilder of Ono and Lod, with their dependent villages (I Chron. 8:12).

She'mer (shē'mĕr), in A.V. of Chronicles **Sha'mer**, the pausal form [guard, watcher]. 1. The man from whom Omri purchased the hill on which to build Samaria (I Kings 16:24).

2. A Merarite Levite, the son of Mahli (I Chron. 6:46).

3. An Asherite (I Chron. 7:34). The same as the Shomer of v. 32.

She·mi′da (shê-mī′dȧ), in A.V. once **She· mi′dah** (I Chron. 7:19) [the name (posterity) has known]. A son of Gilead, and founder of a tribal family (Num. 26:32; Josh. 17:2).

Shem′i·nith (shĕm′ĭ-nĭth) [eighth]. A musical term (I Chron. 15:21; and Psalms 6 and 12, titles). Perhaps, in contrast with alamoth, it means an octave lower, or, on the lower octave: tenor or bass (cf. I Chron. 15:19–21).

She·mir′a·moth (shê-mĭr′ȧ-mŏth) [perhaps, name of heights]. 1. A Levite and singer in the reign of David (I Chron. 15:18, 20).

2. A Levite, one of those employed by Jehoshaphat to teach the people (II Chron. 17:8).

Shem·it′ic (shĕm-ĭt′ĭk). See SEMITIC.

She·mu′el (shê-mū′ĕl). The same Hebrew name as that commonly rendered Samuel (*q.v.*). 1. A son of Ammihud. He was appointed as the representative for the tribe of Simeon on the commission to divide Canaan (Num. 34:20).

2. A man of Issachar, family of Tola, and head of a father's house (I Chron. 7:2).

3. The Prophet Samuel (I Chron. 6:33, A.V.).

Shen (shĕn) [a tooth, a jagged rock]. A spot a little on one side of the place where Samuel set up the stone which he called Ebenezer (I Sam. 7:12). The text is suspicious. The Greek and Syriac versions indicate Jeshanah. See JESHANAH.

She·naz′zar (shê-năz′är), in A.V. **She·na′zar** (shê-nā′zär) [Akkad., O Sin (moon-god), protect]. A son or descendant of Jeconiah (I Chron. 3:18).

She′nir (shē′nẽr). See SENIR.

She′ol (shē′ŏl). See HELL 1.

She′pham (shē′făm). A place on the n.e. border of Canaan, near Riblah (Num. 34:10, 11).

Sheph·a·ti′ah (shĕf′ȧ-tī′ȧ), in A.V. once erroneously **Sheph·a·thi′ah** (shĕf′ȧ-thī′ȧ) (I Chron. 9:8) [Jehovah has judged]. 1. A Haruphite, one of the Benjamites who joined David at Ziklag (I Chron. 12:5).

2. A son born to David at Hebron by one of his wives, Abital (II Sam. 3:4; I Chron. 3:3).

3. Son of Maacah and head of the Simeonite tribe in David's reign (I Chron. 27:16).

4. The father of a Benjamite who dwelt at Jerusalem (I Chron. 9:8).

5. A son of King Jehoshaphat (II Chron. 21:2).

6. A prince, son of Mattan. He was one of those who advised Zedekiah to put the Prophet Jeremiah to death, as his unfavorable prophecies were discouraging the defenders of Jerusalem during its siege by Nebuchadnezzar's army (Jer. 38:1).

7. Founder of a family, 372 members of which returned from captivity with Zerubbabel (Ezra 2:4; Neh. 7:9), and 81 more with Ezra (Ezra 8:8).

8. A man of Judah, family of Perez. He evidently lived before the Exile (Neh. 11:4).

9. A man whose descendants, classified with Solomon's servants, came from Babylon with Zerubbabel (Ezra 2:57; Neh. 7:59).

She·phe′lah (shê-fē′lȧ) [low land]. A well-known name in the geography of Palestine, used, however, in the English versions only in I Macc. 12:38, A.V., and then in the form Sephela. See LOWLAND.

She′pher (shē′fẽr), in A.V. **Sha′pher** [beauty, elegance]. A mountain constituting an encampment of the Israelites in the wilderness (Num. 33:23, 24).

Shep′herd. One whose occupation it is to take charge of a flock of sheep. Abel was a keeper of sheep (Gen. 4:2). The occupation of the Patriarchs from Abraham to Jacob and his sons was pastoral (ch. 13:1–6). There were nomad shepherds who owned flocks and herds, dwelt in tents, and moved from place to place to find pasture for their cattle and afford them protection, like Jabal, Abraham, and the Rechabites (Gen. 4:20; cf. ch. 13:2, 3, 18 with ch. 20:1; Jer. 35:6–10). There were also wealthy sheep owners who dwelt in towns while their flocks were driven from pasture to pasture by their servants (I Sam. 25:2, 3, 7, 15, 16; cf. Gen. 37:12–17). Then there was the settled shepherd, who led the flock from the permanent fold to the pasture in the morning, and in the evening brought it home again (John 10:1–4); see SHEEPFOLD. The care of the flock was often committed to a son (Gen. 37:2; I Sam. 16:11, 19), or a daughter (Gen. 29:9; Ex. 2:16, 17), or a hired servant (Gen. 30:31, 32; Zech. 11:12; John 10:12). The shepherd was ordinarily responsible to the owner for any loss of sheep (Gen. 31:39). The Mosaic Law relieved him of responsibility if he could prove that the loss was not due to his neglect (Ex. 22:10–13).

In the morning the shepherd went to the fold, where several flocks were lying, and called. His own sheep knew his voice and followed him. The sheep which belonged to other owners or were under the care of other keepers paid no attention to the strange voice (John 10:2–5). The shepherd led his own sheep to pasture, spent the day with them there, and sometimes the night also (Gen. 31:40; S. of Sol. 1:7; Luke 2:8); defended them from wild beasts and robbers (I Sam. 17:34, 35; Isa. 31:4); kept the restless sheep from trespassing on cultivated ground, searched for the strayed sheep, and brought them back (Ezek. 34:12; Luke 15:4); and tenderly cared for the delicate and the weak (Isa. 40:11; Ezek. 34:3, 4, 16; Zech. 11:9). The sheep which kept near the shepherd had each a name and answered to it, and were the recipients of many little kindnesses. Such is still the case in the Orient.

The shepherd carried a garment in which to wrap himself in inclement weather, a pouch for food, and some defensive weapon (I Sam. 17:40; Jer. 43:12). A long rod, doubtless generally in ancient times as now with a crook at the upper end, was used to manage the flock, keep it together, guide it, defend it, and chastise the disobedient (Ps. 23:4; Micah 7:14; Zech. 11:7). The shepherd was aided by dogs (Job 30:1); not intelligent, faithful dogs, but lazy, mean brutes, which loitered behind the flock, but were of service; they gave warning of danger by their bark.

Jehovah was the Shepherd of Israel, and especially of the faithful section of the people (Gen. 49:24).

Christ is the Good Shepherd, entering into the sheepfold by the door, calling out his own sheep by name, and so possessing their confidence and affection that they follow him while they refuse to follow any other. He satisfactorily met the test of supreme devotion to his flock and to his duty by laying down his life for the sheep (John 10:1–18).

All who had responsible positions in the theocracy, prophets, priests, and kings, were looked on as pastors of the Israelitish people. They were undershepherds, aiding Jehovah, and their unfaithfulness was frequently pointed out (Isa. 56:11). And in the Chris-

A SHEPHERD OUTSIDE HEROD'S GATE, JERUSALEM

tian Church, the elders or bishops are pastors or shepherds, under Christ, the chief Shepherd, appointed to tend the flock of God (I Peter 5:1–4).

She'phi (shē'fī) and **She'pho** (shē'fō) [bareness]. A son or tribe of Shobal, descended from Seir, the Horite (Gen. 36:23); for the 2 forms, see VAV.

She·phu'pham (shĕ-fū'făm) and **She·phu'·phan** (shĕ-fū'făn). A son or remoter descendant of Benjamin and founder of a tribal family (Num. 26:39; in A.V. Shupham). In the same verse his name appears as Shupham (in Shuphamites). He is also called Muppim (Gen. 46:21) and Shuppim (I Chron. 7:12, 15). The letters m and s or sh were very much alike in the old Heb. alphabet. He was perhaps known also as Shephuphan (I Chron. 8:5). In this passage Shephuphan is probably listed as a descendant of Bela, although it is not impossible that the enumeration of Bela's sons closes with Gera and that Shephuphan is registered as a son of Benjamin. In ch. 7:12 Shuppim is catalogued among the sons of Benjamin, but it is not clear whether he is enrolled as a son in the strict sense or as descended from Benjamin's son Bela through Ir or Iri (v. 7). In the latter case he was born after the descent of Jacob's family into Egypt, but is enumerated with those who went down into Egypt because he founded a tribal family.

She'rah (shē'rȧ). See SHEERAH.

Sher'e·bi'ah (shĕr'ē-bī'ȧ) [Jehovah has sent burning heat]. 1. A Levite, head of a family, who came from Babylon with Zerubbabel (Neh. 12:8). The representative of the family sealed the covenant (ch. 10:12). It was a family of singers (ch. 12:24).
2. Head of a family of Levites who returned with Ezra from Babylon (Ezra 8:18). He was perhaps the representative of a part of the aforementioned family which had remained behind when the exiles returned with Zerubbabel, and as representative he officially bore the family name. He is probably intended in v. 24, although the present text describes him as a priest, and was one of the men to whose custody during the journey Ezra committed the gifts for the Temple.
3. One of the Levites who assisted Ezra, reading the Law to the people, and giving the sense, so that the listeners might understand what they heard (Neh. 8:7). He took part in the public confession of sin after the feast of tabernacles (ch. 9:4).

She'resh (shē'rĕsh) [perhaps, root or sprout]. A man of Manasseh, family of Machir (I Chron. 7:16).

She·re'zer (shē-rē'zēr). See SHAREZER.

She'shach (shē'shăk). According to ancient tradition, a cypher for Babel (Jer. 25:26; 51:41), constructed on the system known as Athbash. The letters of the alphabet were numbered both in their regular order of sequence and in the reverse order; and when the cypher of a name was desired, its consonants were replaced by those which have the same numbers in the reverse enumeration. B is the 2d letter of the Heb. alphabet and s or sh is the 2d from the end, l is the 12th letter from the beginning and k is the 12th from the end; hence the cypher for Babel was Sheshak. There may be a wordplay here; shēshak may have suggested the Heb. root shākak (to sink, bow) and thus implied the humiliation or punishment of Babylon.

She'shai (shē'shī) [probably, whitish]. A son or family of Anak, resident at Hebron, and driven thence by Caleb (Num. 13:32, cf. v. 33; Josh. 15:14).

She'shan (shē'shăn) [perhaps, whitish]. A man of Judah, family of Hezron, house of Jerahmeel (I Chron. 2:31). He had no sons, but only daughters, one of whom he gave in marriage to an Egyptian slave (vs. 34, 35). See AHLAI.

Shesh·baz'zar (shĕsh-băz'ēr) [Akkad., perhaps, O sun-god, protect the lord (or the son)]. A prince of Judah whom Cyrus made governor, to whom he restored the sacred vessels which had been carried to Babylon by Nebuchadnezzar, and who returned to Jerusalem and laid the foundation of the Temple (Ezra 1:8, 11; 5:14, 16). Sheshbazzar may have been the Babylonian name of Zerubbabel, as Belteshazzar was that of Daniel.

Sheth, I (shĕth) [compensation]. A son of Adam (I Chron. 1:1). See SETH.

Sheth, II (shĕth) [tumult]. A designation of the Moabites as makers of war and tumult (Num. 24:17, A.V.).

She'thar-boz'e·nai (shē'thär-bŏz'ē-nī), in A.V. **She'thar-boz'nai** (shē'thär-bŏz'nī). A Persian official who with others attempted to prevent the returned Jewish exiles from rebuilding the Temple (Ezra 5:3, 6; 6:6).

She'va (shē'vȧ) [vanity; but cf. Arab. sawā', equal, similar]. 1. A man of Judah, family of Hezron, house of Caleb. He was the ancestor of the inhabitants of Machbena and Gibea (I Chron. 2:49).
2. A scribe in David's reign (II Sam. 20:25). See SHAVSHA.

Shew'bread'. See SHOWBREAD.

Shi'bah (shī'bȧ), in A.V. **She'bah** [seven, an oath]. Fem. form of Sheba. A well at Beersheba which Isaac's servants redug, and which Isaac named Shibah on account of the covenant he had just made with Abimelech (Gen. 26:33).

Shib'bo·leth (shĭb'bō-lĕth) [an ear of grain, or a stream]. The local dialect of the Ephraimites was characterized by the absence of sh at the beginning of a word and the use of s in its stead. When Jephthah, at the head of the Gileadites, had vanquished the Ephraimites and seized the fords of the Jordan, many of the defeated tribe came to the river desiring to pass. On being asked if they were Ephraimites, and denying the fact, they were required to pronounce the word Shibboleth, and if they called it Sibboleth, were slain without further ceremony (Judg. 12:5, 6). The word has entered the English language, and is used to mean a test word or the watchword or pet phrase of a party or sect.

Shib'mah (shĭb'mȧ). See SIBMAH.

Shic'ron (shĭk'rŏn). See SHIKKERON.

Shield. See ARMOR.

Shig·ga'ion (shĭg-gā'yŏn) and pl. **Shig'i·o'·noth** (shĭg'ĭ-ō'nŏth) [wandering, irregular]. A musical term (Psalm 7, title; Hab. 3:1). Probably a dithyrambic ode, erratic, wild, enthusiastic.

Shi'hon (shī'hŏn). See SHION.

Shi'hor (shī'hŏr), in A.V. **Si'hor** (sī'hŏr), except I Chron. 13:5 [Egypt. Shi-ḥrw, lake or pool of Horus; this suggests Heb. shāḥōr, black]. The river Nile (Isa. 23:3; Jer. 2:18, see R.V. marg.). Its e. or Pelusiac branch was on the boundary of Egypt toward Canaan (Josh. 13:3; I Chron. 13:5); see RIVER OF EGYPT 1. The R.V., however, and many commentators regard the Shihor in the last 2 passages as a title of the brook of Egypt, the wadi el-'Arish (Josh. 13:3, R.V. marg.). According to Brugsch, the name belonged in the 1st instance to a canal on the e. boundary of Egypt, parallel to the course of the Pelusiac branch.

Shi′hor-lib′nath (shī′hōr-lĭb′năth) [turbid stream of Libnath]. A small river at the s.w. corner of Asher (Josh. 19:26) and apparently near Carmel. It is now commonly believed to be the Zerkā, 6 miles s. of Dor, a town of Asher.

Shik′ke·ron (shĭk′ē-rŏn), in A.V. Shic′ron [drunkenness]. A town on the n. border of the tribe of Judah (Josh. 15:11).

Shil′hi (shĭl′hī) [perhaps, Jehovah has sent]. Father of Azubah, Jehoshaphat's mother (I Kings 22:42).

Shil′him (shĭl′hĭm) [missiles, sprouts]. A town in the extreme s. of Judah (Josh. 15:32). The name may be in Khirbet Shalḥa, 5 miles w. of Beit Jibrīn; see SHARUHEN.

Shil′lem (shĭl′ĕm) [he (God) has made compensation]. A son of Naphtali, and founder of a tribal family (Gen. 46:24; Num. 26:49). Called Shallum, a synonymous and more common name, in I Chron. 7:13.

Shil′ling. See PENNY.

Shi·lo′ah (shĭ-lō′à) [a sending of waters, an aqueduct]; see SILOAM.

Shi′loh (shī′lō) [tranquillity, rest]. A town n. of Beth-el, s. of Lebonah, and on the e. side of the highway connecting Beth-el with Shechem (Judg. 21:19), and hence within the territory of Ephraim. It has been identified with Seilūn, about 10 miles n.n.e. of Beth-el. There the Israelites under Joshua set up the tabernacle (Josh. 18:1), and divided by lot the, as yet, unappropriated parts of Canaan (Josh. 18:8–10; 19:51; 22:9). When the w. tribes were convened to call the tribes e. of the Jordan to account for their building of an altar, it was at Shiloh that the gathering took place (Josh. 22:12). In the times of the Judges there was there an annual feast of Jehovah (Judg. 21:19; I Sam. 1:3), at which the Benjamites on 1 occasion obtained wives by capture (Judg. 21:16–23). The tabernacle, with the Ark, was still there in the time of Eli and during the early years of Samuel (Judg. 18:31; I Sam. 1:9, 24; 2:14, 22; 3:3, 21; 4:3, 4; 14:3). The capture of the Ark was understood to mean that God had forsaken Shiloh (Ps. 78:60; Jer. 7:12, 14; 26:6, 9). The covenant made at Sinai, of which the Ark and the ritual were the outward sign and privilege, was suspended. When the Ark was returned by the Philistines, it was not taken again to Shiloh (I Sam. 6:21; 7:1, 2; II Sam. 6:2, 11, 17), but the work of reviving true religion, preparatory to the restoration of covenant privileges, was begun by Samuel. Ahijah the prophet, who told Jeroboam of his approaching greatness, lived at Shiloh, and it was thither that the king's consort repaired to inquire about the issue of their sick child's malady (I Kings 14:2, 4). It continued to be inhabited at least as late as the time of Jeremiah (Jer. 41:5).

There are 3 main interpretations of Shiloh in the difficult passage Gen. 49:10, each of which receives recognition in R.V.: 1. Shiloh is a proper name, which designates the Messiah and refers to the peacefulness of his disposition and his reign. 2. Shiloh, place of tranquillity, is the town in central Palestine where the tabernacle was placed immediately after the conquest of Canaan by Joshua (Josh. 18:1). 3. Shiloh is not a proper name, nor is it a simple word. It is a compound, composed of the relative pronoun she, the preposition le, and the pronominal suffix of the 3d person masc. ōh. The same form of the suffix occurs twice in the following verse. This phrase has been interpreted as meaning "that which is his," "whose it is," or "his own one." The 2d of these 3 meanings would happily correspond to Ezek 21:27,

but the omission of the subject is a serious syntactic difficulty; and the 1st regarded as objective, "he shall come to that which is his," is grammatically difficult, for a relative clause with indefinite antecedent used as an accusative is preceded by a preposition or the sign of the accusative. This conception of the word as a phrase is old, having been entertained by the ancient versions, namely, LXX, Targums of Onkelos and Jonathan, Syriac, and Jerome.

On the 1st interpretation and commonly on the 3d the Messiah is expressly referred to. In the 2d the reference is to the covenant blessing, which the prophets of a later age discerned to belong in its fullness to Messianic times. Reuben had forfeited his birthright by misconduct (Gen. 49:4; 35:22), Simeon and Levi had incurred their father's just censure (chs. 49:5–7; 34:30), and Judah was consequently assigned the place of the first-born, and became the representative of the tribe and the peculiar possessor of the blessing covenanted to Abraham and his seed (ch. 49:8). The promise of victory to the woman's seed (ch. 3:15), the blessing of God's favor centered in Shem (ch. 9:26, 27), the further centralization of the covenant blessing in the family of Abraham (ch. 17), belonged thenceforth pre-eminently to Judah, the possessor of the birthright. By him, according to the 1st and 3d interpretations, the prerogative shall be held until one who is his, one of his tribe, the man of peace comes, to whom shall be the obedience of the peoples, and in whom the covenant blessing shall be still further centered. This interpretation, with many modifications of detail, according as the scepter is thought of restrictedly as the emblem of royalty or is regarded as the symbol of leadership in general, is represented in the text of the English versions. And it is argued that this essentially must be the true interpretation, because the town of Shiloh does not fulfill the historical conditions, for neither is there any reason why Jacob, apart from special revelation, should think of Shiloh as the future place of worship, nor did Judah occupy pre-eminence among the tribes before the tabernacle was pitched in Shiloh, save somewhat in numbers and in being permitted to lead the van, while the people were marching to Canaan, and to pitch their tents in front of the tabernacle. The leadership was at first in the hands of Moses, of the tribe of Levi, which excited the jealousy of the princes of Reuben, and after Moses' death, and until the tabernacle was pitched at Shiloh, the authority was exercised by Joshua, of the tribe of Ephraim.

But it is more natural to regard Shiloh in this passage as the name of the town, for it is such everywhere else, and on this interpretation the words of Jacob are at once intelligible. This view is commonly entertained by those who deny that Jacob uttered the words, and who affirm that the address is a prophecy after the event. But the address is not the utterance of a late prophet, commenting on the past history of the 12 tribes and putting his reflections in the mouth of their common ancestor Jacob, for the descriptions do not fit the actual state of things at any period of the national history; see, for example, Gen. 49:13 and ZEBULUN. Believers in the genuineness of the address hold that the town of Shiloh is meant and they are able fairly to explain how Jacob came to use the name, and how Moses the Levite and Joshua the Ephraimite could lead the people while yet the scepter was acknowledged as belonging to Judah. The argument of Delitzsch may be amplified. Shiloh doubtless existed in the days of the Patriarchs; and Jacob, who looked for the ultimate return of his people to Canaan (Gen. 15:13–16; 46:3, 4; 48:21), employs this name, "place of tranquillity," as an omen of the future, playing upon it as Esau played upon the name Jacob and Micah upon the names of the towns of Judah. It made no difference that God raised up men from other tribes to meet special emergencies: the birthright and its accompanying privileges belonged to Judah. It was accorded to him by the position assigned him at the head of the marching host and in camp in front of the tabernacle. It was accredited to him by God's multiplication of his descendants, so that his tribe was much larger than any single tribe during the 40 years in the wilderness. It was confirmed by the lot's falling 1st to his tribe when the conquered land was distributed at Gilgal. The actual coming to the town of Shiloh was not contemplated as necessary by Jacob. The fulfillment of his words was more literal than his expectation. He had merely the peaceable possession of the Promised Land in view.

The erection of the tabernacle at Shiloh, a town which Joshua may have been led to choose by having knowledge of Jacob's words, marked the 1st stage in the realization of the promise. A new period had been reached in Israel's history. The conquest was completed, the inheritance was theirs, possession had begun, rest had been won. Judah, the possessor of the birthright, had come to a place of tranquillity in Canaan, having obtained the obedience of the peoples, and being now ready to occupy and enjoy his conquered possession (Gen. 49:10–12). The words do not mean that when he should come to Shiloh the scepter should depart. They are to be understood as the similar language in Isa. 42:4: "He will not fail nor be discouraged, till he have set justice in the earth." This does not mean that the servant will then fail and lose courage. So Jacob meant that the privilege conferred by the birthright, which centered in the Abrahamic covenant, should not be transferred until Judah had obtained the promised blessing, the possession of Canaan, when he would enter upon its enjoyment. A new period opens to him. He was still accorded by God the 1st position among the tribes, being called to go up 1st against the Canaanites still in the allotted land. He was called to go up 1st against the Benjamites in the war against that tribe to punish national sin. And the 1st and only deliverer of all Israel during the period of the Judges proper sprang from Judah (Judg. 3: 7–11). Saul, a Benjamite, was raised up like the Judges to deliver Israel (I Sam. 9:16; 10:6), and might have retained the throne in his family (chs. 13:13, 14; 15:23, 26, 28), but he lost the opportunity through sin, as Reuben had lost the birthright, and the permanent royal line was taken from Judah. The obedience of the peoples was but the foretaste, and the possession of the land and enjoyment of its fertility were but a type, of the Messianic triumphs and peace involved in the covenanted mercies. As time went on, the fullness of meaning was revealed in the words of the prophets. (See Isa. 2:2–4; Micah 4:1–5; Joel 3:9–21.)

Shi·lo′ni (shĭ-lō′nī) [a Shilonite]. According to the A.V., a man of the tribe of Judah (Neh. 11:5, A.V.). But the word is preceded by the definite article in the Hebrew text, and hence is not a proper name. The R.V. correctly translates it "the Shilonite," and Shiloni, as a man, disappears. See SHILONITE 2.

Shi′lo·nite (shĭ′lō-nīt). 1. A native or inhabitant of Shiloh (I Kings 11:29).
2. A member of the tribal family of Shelah (Neh. 11:5, in A.V. Shiloni).

Shil′shah (shĭl′shä) [triad]. An Asherite, son of Zophah (I Chron. 7:37).

Shim′e·a (shĭm′ê-ȧ), once **Shim′e·ah** (shĭm′ê-ȧ) (II Sam. 13:3) [he (God) has heard].
1. A Levite, family of Merari, house of Mahli (I Chron. 6:30).
2. A Levite, family of Gershom (I Chron. 6:39–43).
3. A brother of King David (II Sam. 13:3; I Chron. 20:7). In A.V. of I Chron. 2:13 he is incorrectly called Shimma, the Heb. having Shimea. In I Sam. 16:9; 17:13 his name appears as Shammah.
4. A son of David; see SHAMMUA 2.
5. Another Shimeah, whose name in Heb. has 'aleph instead of 'ayin as the 3d radical; thus it is different from the foregoing (I Chron. 8:32); see SHIMEAM.

Shim′e·am (shĭm′ê-ăm). A Benjamite, a son of Mikloth, resident in Jerusalem (I Chron. 9:38). In ch. 8:32 he is called Shimeah, a synonymous name.

Shim′e·ath (shĭm′ê-ăth) [report]. An Ammonitess, mother of one of King Joash's assassins (II Kings 12:21).

Shim′e·ath·ites (shĭm′ê-ăth-īts). A Kenite family of scribes, descended through a certain Shimeah from the founder of the house of Rechab and resident at Jabez (I Chron. 2:55).

Shim′e·i (shĭm′ê-ī), in A.V. once **Shim′i** (Ex. 6:17), once **Shim′hi** (I Chron. 8:21) [(Jehovah) has heard]. 1. A son of Gershon, and a grandson of Levi. He founded a subdivision of the tribal family of Gershon (Ex. 6:17; Num. 3:18, 21; I Chron. 23:7, 10; Zech. 12: 13).
2. A Levite, family of Merari, house of Mahli (I Chron. 6:29).
3. A Simeonite, probably of the family of Shaul. He had 16 sons and 6 daughters (I Chron. 4:24–27).
4. A Levite, son of Jahath, of the family of Gershom (I Chron. 6:42).
5. A Benjamite, head of a father's house in Aijalon (I Chron. 8:21, in A.V. Shimhi). Called Shema in v. 13.
6. A Levite, family of Gershon, and head of one of the subdivisions of Ladan, which latter was apparently a division of the house of Libni (I Chron. 23:9).
7. A Levite, head of the 10th course of singers in David's reign, and evidently a son of Jeduthun, for his name is needed to make out the 6 spoken of in I Chron. 25:3 (v. 17).
8. A Ramathite, who was over David's vineyards (I Chron. 27:27).
9. A Benjamite, the son of Gera. He was of Saul's family, which had lost the throne. When he saw David, with his attendants, descending the e. slope of the Mount of Olives, while Absalom was in possession of Jerusalem, he thought it safe to insult the fallen king, which he did in gross language. He was forgiven by David, but was afterward put to death by Solomon for disobeying a command of the latter (I Kings 2:44–46).
10. An adherent of David and Solomon during Adonijah's usurpation (I Kings 1:8). He was probably the son of Ela, who became Solomon's purveyor in the territory of Benjamin (ch. 4:18).
11. A Reubenite (I Chron. 5:4).
12. A Levite, a son of Heman, who helped to purify the Temple in Hezekiah's reign (II Chron. 29:14–16). He may be identical with the following.
13. A Levite, brother of Conaniah, in Hezekiah's reign. He was one of those who looked after the tithes (II Chron. 31:12).
14. A Benjamite, son of Kish and an ancestor of Mordecai (Esth. 2:5).

15. A man belonging to the royal family of Judah, and a brother of Zerubbabel (I Chron. 3:19).

16, 17, 18. Three men, 1 a Levite, 1 a son of Hashum, and 1 a son of Bani, each of whom was induced by Ezra to put away his foreign wife (Ezra 10:23, 33, 38).

Shim'e·ites (shĭm'ê-īts). See SHIMEI 1.

Shim'e·on (shĭm'ê-ŭn) [a hearkening, answering (of prayer)]. A son of Harim, induced by Ezra to put away his foreign wife (Ezra 10:31).

Shim'hi (shĭm'hī). See SHIMEI 5.

Shim'i (shĭm'ī). See SHIMEI 1.

Shim'ma (shĭm'ȧ). See SHIMEA 3.

Shi'mon (shī'mŏn). A man who had his registry with the tribe of Judah (I Chron. 4:20).

Shim'rath (shĭm'răth) [watching, guarding]. A Benjamite, son of Shimei of Aijalon (I Chron. 8:21).

Shim'ri (shĭm'rī), in A.V. once **Sim'ri** (I Chron. 26:10) [(Jehovah) has watched, protected]. 1. A Simeonite, son of Shemaiah (I Chron. 4:37).

2. Father of one of David's mighty men (I Chron. 11:45).

3. A Merarite Levite, a son of Hosah (I Chron. 26:10).

4. A Levite, who lived in the reign of Hezekiah. He was a son of Elizaphan of the family of Kohath, house of Uzziel (II Chron. 29:13).

Shim'rith (shĭm'rĭth) [vigilant]. A Moabitess, mother of one of King Joash's assassins (II Chron. 24:26). Called in II Kings 12:21 Shomer.

Shim'ron (shĭm'rŏn), in A.V. once **Shim'rom** (shĭm'rŏm) (I Chron. 7:1) [watching, a guard]. 1. A son of Issachar, and founder of a tribal family (Gen. 46:13; Num. 26:24).

2. A border town of Zebulun (Josh. 11:1; 19:15).

Shim'ron·me'ron (shĭm'rŏn-mē'rŏn). A Canaanite town, whose king was vanquished and slain by Joshua (Josh. 12:20). Probably the full name of Shimron.

Shim'shai (shĭm'shī) [sunny, sun-child]. A scribe, one of those who complained to Artaxerxes Longimanus that the Jews were rebuilding the Temple (Ezra 4:8).

Shin (shēn). The 21st letter of the Heb. alphabet. English s comes from the same source, and with sh represents it in Anglicized Hebrew names; as in Simeon, Shimea, Ishmael. It heads the 21st section of Psalm 119, in which section each verse of the original begins with this letter.

Shi'nab (shī'năb). The king of Admah, who was defeated by Chedorlaomer (Gen. 14:2, 8, 10).

Shi'nar (shī'när). A country in which the cities of Babel, Erech, Accad, and Calneh were situated (Gen. 10:10; 11:2; Dan. 1:2). Hence, in Hebrew usage, Shinar comprehended the alluvial plain of Babylonia; ancient Sumer was in the lower part of this region. In the days of Abraham, Amraphel was king of the whole or a large part of it (Gen. 14:1, 9). Some of the Jews were to be carried thither as captives (Isa. 11:11; Zech. 5:11).

Shi'on (shī'ŏn), in A.V. **Shi'hon** [destruction, ruin]. A town of Issachar (Josh. 19:19). The site is perhaps at 'Ayûn esh-Sha'īn, 3 miles w.n.w. of Mount Tabor.

Ship. As early as 3000 B.C. men had learned to navigate both the Nile and the Euphrates. Little boats were used for going from the

upper Euphrates to Babylon (Herod. i. 194). They were circular in form. The ribs were made of willow, over which hides were stretched as a covering. They were steered by 2 men who stood upright, each with a spar which they thrust alternately. The largest vessels carried 5,000 talents. On the Nile boats built of acacia wood were used (Herod. ii. 96).

Boats were doubtless used on the Sea of Galilee in O.T. times, but they are not mentioned. In the Roman period the sea was alive with small fishing vessels (Luke 5:2; John 6:22, 23; Jos. *War* ii. 21, 8; iii. 10, 9; *Life* 33). They were propelled by oars; but some, at least, had both oars and sails (cf. Mark 4:38 with Luke 8:23); they carried an anchor and a pilot (Jos. *Life* 33).

The Israelites were not a seafaring people; although shipbuilding was far advanced among the Egyptians and doubtless among the Phoenicians before the Exodus, and the Hebrews had the spectacle of ships on the Mediterranean before their eyes during the whole period of their national history. Solomon conducted commercial enterprises, and Jehoshaphat attempted to imitate him; but these were transient efforts and were more or less dependent upon Phoenician sailors.

Phoenician Ship

The rafts of cedar and fir destined for Solomon's Temple were floated to Joppa by Tyrians (I Kings 5:9; II Chron. 2:16), and the timber for the 2d Temple was likewise brought by sea to Joppa by Phoenicians (Ezra 3:7). The crew of the vessel in which Jonah sailed from Joppa was also composed of foreigners (Jonah 1:5). In the Roman period, piratical expeditions by Jews are reported (Jos. *Antiq.* xiv. 3, 2; *War* iii. 9, 2 and 3).

Both merchant vessels and war ships were used on the Mediterranean (Num. 24:24; Dan. 11:30; Jonah 1:3; I Macc. 11:1). In war, vessels were employed for transporting troops (I Macc. 15:3, 4; II Macc. 14:1) and for fighting at sea (I Macc. 8:23, 32; Jos. *Antiq.* ix. 14, 2; cf. *War* iii. 10, 1). Some ships were equipped with a sharp, pointed ram in front, which was employed in sinking another ship in battle. Some of these seagoing vessels were propelled by sails alone; others by both sails and oars. A gallant merchantman of Tyre was built of planks and calked (Ezek. 27:5, 9); had masts, linen sails, and tackling (Ezek. 27:7; Isa. 33:23), benches of boxwood, and oaken oars (Ezek. 27:6, R.V.). It was manned by sailors and guided by a pilot (vs. 8, 27). When luxuriously furnished, the sails were embroidered and a rich awning was spread (v. 7). Such vessels made the voyage to Tarshish (Jonah 1:3, 5, 6, 13), and even navigated the Atlantic Ocean from Spain to England; see TIN. The ship of Alex-

andria, in which Paul was conveyed from
Myra to Malta, was large enough to accommodate a crew and passengers numbering
276 persons, besides a cargo of wheat (Acts
27:37, 38). The vessel in which Josephus was
wrecked had 600 persons on board (Jos. *Life*
3). The Alexandrian wheat ship, described
by Lucian as driven into the port of Athens
by rough weather, was 120 cubits, or 180 feet,
in length, doubtless including the projection
at each end, and 45 feet in breadth. Its size
attracted attention. Its capacity is supposed to have been about 1,200 or 1,300 tons.
The exceptionally large war galley of Ptolemy

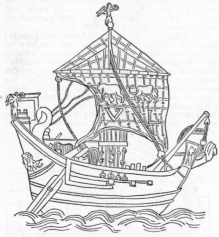

Roman Ship, from a Relief

Philopator measured, according to Athenaeus,
420 feet in length and 57 feet in breadth.
Paul's ship was in charge of a master and
the owner (Acts 27:11), and was managed
by a crew (v. 30). It was built of planks
(v. 44), carried a foresail, which could be
raised and lowered (v. 40, R.V.), and by
implication a foremast and a mainmast, and
was steered by rudders, doubtless 2 (v. 40).
Four anchors were stowed at the stern and
several forward (vs. 29, 30), and a small
boat was towed behind, which could be raised
by ropes or davits to the deck (vs. 16, 17, 30,
32). Soundings were taken (v. 28). It was
customary for ships to have an eye painted
or carved on each side of the stem. Paul's
vessel was unable to face the gale, literally
to keep the eye to the wind (v. 15).

A ship of Paul's time, depicted at Pompeii,
shows a foremast inclined like a bowsprit,
but intended to carry a square sail, and 1
large mast with 1 square sail fitted to a yard
of great length. The yard was composed of
2 spars spliced together, and was placed with
its center against the mast. The sail was
strengthened by ropes sewed across it vertically and horizontally; and if torn, the rent
was confined to the square in which it occurred. The sail was furled by being drawn
up to the yard. The deck was protected by a
rail. The stern post, and in many vessels the
stem post also, rose in a curve. It was customary, as in this ship, for the stern post at
least to terminate in the head of a water
fowl. The sign of the ship (Acts 28:11) was
painted or carved on each side of the prow.
The vessel was steered by 2 broad oars or
paddles, 1 on each quarter and acting through
a porthole. The anchors were similar to
those in modern use, except that they had no
flukes. To prevent the starting of the planks

in a storm, cables or chains, called helps or
undergirders (Acts 27:17), were passed
around the vessel at right angles to its length
and made tight.

Shi'phi (shī'fī) [abounding, abundant]. A
Simeonite, son of Allon (I Chron. 4:37).

Shiph'mite (shĭf'mīt). A native or inhabitant probably of Siphmoth (I Chron. 27:27).

Shiph'rah (shĭf'rȧ) [splendor, beauty]. One
of the Hebrew midwives in Egypt who declined to kill the male babes (Ex. 1:15).

Shiph'tan (shĭf'tăn) [(God) exercises
judgment]. An Ephraimite, father of Kemuel (Num. 34:24).

Shi'sha (shī'shȧ). See SHAVSHA.

Shi'shak (shī'shăk). See PHARAOH 1.

Shit'rai (shĭt'rī). A Sharonite, who looked
after David's herds on the plain of Sharon
(I Chron. 27:29).

Shit'tah (shĭt'ȧ) **Tree** and **Shit'tim** Wood.
A tree (Isa. 41:19). The R.V. renders the
word by acacia tree or wood. It grew in the
Jordan Valley, from the Sea of Galilee to the
Dead Sea (see BETH-SHITTAH and SHITTIM).
It was plentiful in the wilderness of Sinai,
and its timber was largely used in the tabernacle, for the woodwork of the Ark, the altars and their staves, the table, the boards,
bars, and pillars (Ex. 25:5, 10, 13, 23; 26:
15, 26, 32; 27:1, 6; 30:1, 5). The wood was
used in Egypt in boat building (Herod. ii.
96), and Josephus speaks of its strength and

Shittah (*Acacia seyal*)

durability (Jos. *Antiq.* iii. 6, 5). Arabic *sanaṭ*,
sanṭ is the same word as the Heb. *shittāh*,
and denotes the acacia. There are several
species. *Acacia seyâl* and *tortilis* are found
in the valleys about the Dea Sea and s., and
Acacia nilotica grows in the s. part of the
peninsula of Sinai and in Egypt. Other species are found in various parts of Palestine.
The genuine acacias are generally small
trees, growing from 15 to 25 feet high, thorny,
with bipinnate leaves, and pods with several
seeds. The wood is hard and close-grained.
Certain species yield the gum arabic of commerce.

Shit'tim (shĭt'ĭm) [acacias]. 1. An important encampment of the Israelites in the plains of Moab, e. of Jordan, opposite Jericho (cf. Num. 22:1 with ch. 25:1). The camp had been removed from Pisgah on the mountains of Abarim and pitched at Shittim after the conquest of Sihon and Og (chs. 21:20; 22:1; 33:47, 48). It was located on a tableland, the topmost of the 3 terraces which at this point form the valley of the Jordan, and among the long groves of acacia trees. It extended "from Beth-jeshimoth even unto Abel-shittim" (ch. 33:49; cf. ch. 23:28), a distance of 3 miles and more. It was arranged in an orderly manner, the Israelites dwelling according to their tribes (ch. 24:2, 5, 6); see CAMP. The sojourn at Shittim was eventful. While the Israelites were encamped there, Balaam attempted to curse them (chs. 22 to 24), the people committed sin with the daughters of Moab and Midian at Baal-peor, and were plagued in consequence (ch. 25), the 2d census was taken (ch. 26), occasion arose for enacting laws regarding the inheritance of daughters (ch. 27:1–11), Joshua was publicly proclaimed the successor to Moses (vs. 12–23), daily offerings and vows were further regulated (chs. 28 to 30), war was waged with the 5 Midianite tribes of the neighborhood on account of the deliberate attempt which they had recently made to seduce the Israelites into licentious idolatry at Baal-peor (ch. 31), Reuben and Gad, at their own request, received inheritance e. of the Jordan (ch. 32). Measures were also taken for the occupation of Canaan: in view of recent events, the expulsion of the Canaanites and the destruction of their altars and idols were urgently commanded anew; the boundaries of the land were defined, and a commission was appointed to superintend the allotment of territory to the tribes; and it was ordered that cities be assigned to the Levites, and that 6 cities of refuge be designated for the unintentional murderer (chs. 33: 50 to 35:34). The matter of the inheritance of daughters was further regulated (ch. 36). Then Moses delivered his farewell address (see DEUTERONOMY), Joshua received a solemn charge, and Moses ascended Nebo and died. After the death of Moses, Joshua sent forth 2 spies from Shittim to examine and report on the defenses of Jericho (Josh., ch. 2). Then camp was broken at Shittim, and the people crossed the Jordan (ch. 3).

2. A valley, dry and comparatively unfruitful, where only the acacia or shittah tree grows (Joel 3:18). If a particular valley is in the prophet's mind, it may be the Kidron Wadi, which under the name of Wadi el-Jōz starts a little n.w. of Jerusalem, bends round so as to run e. of the city, separating it from the Mount of Olives, and then as a deep rocky gorge (Wadi en-Nār) runs s.e. toward the Dead Sea, which it joins at about 10 miles from its n. end. Or it may be simply the Arabah about the Dead Sea (cf. Ezek. 47:1–12). The prophet names it from the encampment of the Israelites at Shittim, and he selects it as a type because the waters of its sea were practically lifeless, and its s. portion consisted of barren rocks and cliffs of salt. After Jehovah has judged all nations, the Kingdom of God shall flourish and the kingdoms of the world become waste (Joel 3:9–21). The mountains of Judah shall drop down new wine, its hills flow with milk, its wadies be brooks of water, and from the house of the Lord shall go forth waters that shall make glad the valley of acacias. In other words, the desert shall blossom as the rose; spiritual life shall proceed from the Lord God and shall supply the needs of his Kingdom (cf. Rev. 22:1, 2).

Shi'za (shĭ'zȧ). A Reubenite, father of one of David's heroes (I Chron. 11:42).

Sho'a (shō'ä). A country and its inhabitants, mentioned in connection with the Babylonians, Chaldeans, and Assyrians (Ezek. 23: 23); probably the Sutū, who were nomads in the Syrian desert at the time of the Amarna letters. In the 11th century they entered Babylonia and then were forced into the plains e. of the Tigris. In alliance with Aramaean tribes they were constantly at war with Assyria and never completely conquered.

Sho'bab (shō'băb) [backsliding, apostate]. 1. A man of Judah, family of Hezron, house of Caleb. His mother was Azubah (I Chron. 2:18).
2. A son of David, born to him at Jerusalem (II Sam. 5:14).

Sho'bach (shō'băk) [one who pours out]. Commander-in-chief under Hadarezer, king of Zobah (II Sam. 10:16). Called in I Chron. 19:16, 18, Shophach.

Sho'bai (shō'bī) [perhaps, one who leads captive]. A Levite, founder of a family of doorkeepers, members of which returned with Zerubbabel from captivity (Ezra 2:42).

Sho'bal (shō'băl). 1. A tribe of Horites (Gen. 36:20), consisting of several families (v. 23), and ruled by a chieftain (v. 29).
2. A son of Hur, a man of Judah, family of Hezron, house of Caleb. He was ancestor of the inhabitants of Kiriath-jearim (I Chron. 2:50; 4:1, 2, 4).

Sho'bek (shō'běk) [cf. Arab. sābiḳ, one who precedes, victor]. One of the Jewish chiefs who with Nehemiah sealed the covenant (Neh. 10:24).

Sho'bi (shō'bī) [perhaps, one who leads captive]. Son of a resident in Rabbah of the Ammonites named Nahash (II Sam. 17:27). Shobi brought food and other necessaries to David at Mahanaim.

Sho'cho (shō'kō), Sho'choh (shō'kō), Sho'co (shō'kō). See Soco.

Shoe. Hebrew shoes were, as a rule, simply leather sandals affixed to the foot by straps known as latchets; see CLOTHING. Shoes were not worn in the sitting room or at the table (cf. Luke 7:38); and in well-appointed houses a servant stood ready to unloose the latchet and remove the shoe of the guest (cf. Mark 1:7). Shoes were also removed when one was about to tread holy ground (Ex. 3:5; Josh. 5:15); and the absence of shoes in the description of the

Sandals

priests' garments is supposed to indicate that the priests performed their duties in the Temple barefoot. To be without shoes and stripped of superfluous raiment might betoken the captive's plight (Isa. 20:2), and was a customary sign of mourning (II Sam. 15:30); while to wear shoes in time of sorrow, and attire the head, was a concealment of grief (Ezek. 24:17, 23). In the olden time in Israel, in matters of redemption and exchange, a man drew off his shoe (sandal) and gave it to him with whom he had concluded the agreement, as confirmation of the transaction (Ruth 4:7, 8); and the shoe of the man who refused to take his deceased brother's wife was loosed, with other insult (Deut. 25:9, 10). To cast the shoe upon a place symbolized the act of taking possession or, possibly, of treating it as a slave upon whom as a task the master flings his shoes in order that they may be carried or cleaned (Ps. 60:8). The Assyrian soldier's boot (Isa. 9:5, R.V. marg.; J.V.) was not in use in Judah.

Sho'ham (shō'hăm) [a beryl or onyx]. A Levite, son of Jaaziah (I Chron. 24:27).

Sho'mer (shō'mẽr) [keeper, watchman]. 1. An Asherite, son of Heber (I Chron. 7:32). See SHEMER 3.

2. A Moabitess, mother of one of King Joash's assassins (II Kings 12:21). See SHIMRITH.

Sho'phach (shō'fäk). See SHOBACH.

Sho'phan (shō'făn). See ATROTH-SHOPHAN.

Sho·shan'nim (shō-shăn'ĭm) [lilies]. A word occurring in the titles of Psalms 45 and 69. Three opinions exist as to its meaning: symbolical of the contents of the psalm, a musical instrument resembling a lily, a familiar melody. It doubtless indicates a popular air. This appears from the combinations Shoshannim Eduth, "Lilies a testimony" (Psalm 80, title), and Shushan Eduth, "Lily a testimony" (Psalm 60, title).

Show'bread', in A.V. **Shew'bread'**. Literally "bread of the presence." It consisted of 12 loaves of bread, laid in 2 rows and displayed on a table in the Holy Place before the Lord continually. The bread was changed every Sabbath, and the old loaves were eaten by the priests in the Holy Place (Ex. 25:30; Lev. 24:5-9; I Sam. 21:6; Matt. 12:4). The bread was also known as "the continual bread" (Num. 4:7, where the name "showbread" is also used); and "continual row," or arrangement (II Chron. 2:4, translated "showbread") or "the bread of the row," or arrangement (I Chron. 9:32, translated "showbread"), because arranged in rows or columns (Lev.

Showbread Table of Herod's Temple, Based on the Relief on the Arch of Titus

24:6). Josephus says the bread was unleavened (Jos. *Antiq.* iii. 6, 6). Each loaf contained ²⁄₁₀ of an ephah of fine flour, such as was used for honored guests and for the king's table (Gen. 18:6; I Kings 4:22), and was employed in various offerings (Lev. 2:1; 5:11; etc.). The 12 loaves represented the 12 tribes of Israel (cf. Lev. 24:7 with Ex. 28:10-12; also Ex. 24:4; 28:21). These 12 loaves set in the presence of Jehovah probably signified the constant communion of his people with him in those things which his bounty provided and they enjoyed in his presence and used in his service. The Kohathites had charge of the showbread (I Chron. 9:32).

The table of showbread was made of acacia wood overlaid with gold. It was bordered by a golden crown, and had a ring at each corner for the rods by which it was carried. It measured 2 cubits long, 1 broad, and 1½ high (Ex. 25:23-29); for its transportation, cf. Num. 4:7, 8). It stood in the Holy Place, by the n. wall, that is, to the right of one entering the tabernacle (Ex. 40:22). In Solomon's Temple there were 10 tables for showbread, corresponding to the 10 candlesticks, although like the candlesticks apparently only 1 was in use at a time (I Chron. 28:16; II Chron. 4:8, 19; 13:11; Jos. *Antiq.* viii. 3, 7); hence only 1 is mentioned in I Kings 7:48; II Chron. 29:18. The table which belonged to the 2d Temple was carried off by Antiochus Epiphanes, but a new one was provided by Judas Maccabaeus (I Macc. 1:22; 4:49). Titus carried it to Rome (Jos. *War* vii. 5, 5).

Shu'a (shoo'à), in A.V. twice **Shu'ah** (Gen. 38:2, 12) [wealth]. 1. A Canaanite, whose daughter became Judah's wife or concubine, and the mother of his sons, Er, Onan, and Shelah (Gen. 38:2, 12; I Chron. 2:3).

2. An Asherite, a daughter of Heber (I Chron. 7:32).

Shu'ah (shoo'à) [depression]. A son of Abraham by Keturah (Gen. 25:2), that is, an Arab tribe descended from them, doubtless the Shuhites who dwelt near the land of Uz (Job 2:11). Their land is plausibly identified with a district of the same name, in Assyrian Suḫu, on the w. of the Euphrates, near the mouths of the Balikh and Khabur. For others whose name is rendered Shuah in A.V., see SHUA and SHUHAH.

Shu'al (shoo'ăl) [a fox or jackal]. 1. An Asherite, son of Zophah (I Chron. 7:36).

2. A district near Ophrah, to the n. of Michmash (I Sam. 13:17).

Shu'ba·el (shoo'bà-ĕl). See SHEBUEL.

Shu'hah (shoo'hà), in A.V. **Shu'ah** [depression]. A man of Judah (I Chron. 4:11).

Shu'ham (shoo'hăm). The son of Dan, and founder of the tribal family (Num. 26:42). Called in Gen. 46:23 Hushim.

Shu'hite (shoo'hīt). See SHUAH.

Shu'lam·mite (shoo'lăm-īt), in A.V. **Shu'·lam·ite** (shoo'lăm-īt). A young woman mentioned in the Song of Solomon (ch. 6:13). The name has been derived from that of the town of Shunem. The LXX translates it by *Soumaneitis,* i.e., Shunammite; the town of Shunem was known in the time of Eusebius as Shulem, and today bears the name Sōlem or Sūlam. The form Shulammite may have been preferred to Shunammite because of its assonance with Solomon, in Heb. *Shᵉlōmōh;* in fact, it may be a fem. of Solomon, not as a proper name, but as a sort of title.

Shu'math·ites (shoo'măth-īts). One of the leading families in Kiriath-jearim (I Chron. 2:53).

Shu'nam·mite (shoo'năm-īt). A native or inhabitant of Shunem; as Abishag (I Kings 1:3), and she whose son Elisha restored to life (II Kings 4:8, 12; 8:1).

Shu'nem (shoo'nĕm). A town of Canaan, taken by Thothmes III, in the territory of Issachar (Josh. 19:18), opposite Mount Gilboa (I Sam. 28:4). The Philistines encamped there before the battle with Saul. The site is at Sōlem or Sūlam, on the w. slope of a hill 3½ miles n. by e. of Jezreel, 5 n. of the w. end of Mount Gilboa, and about 16 miles from Carmel, whither the Shunammite woman went to find Elisha (II Kings 4:25).

Shu'ni (shoo'nī). A son of Gad, and founder of a tribal family (Gen. 46:16; Num. 26:15).

Shu'pham (shōō'făm). See SHEPHUPHAM.

Shup'pim (shŭp'ĭm). 1. A Benjamite (I Chron. 7:12, 15); see SHEPHUPHAM.

2. A Levite, who served as a doorkeeper at the sanctuary (I Chron. 26:16). The Hebrew text is doubtless corrupt. Perhaps the name crept in from the preceding verse, which ends with a word very like Shuppim.

Shur (shōōr) [wall, fortification]. 1. A locality in the wilderness, s. of Palestine, or more exactly s. of Beer-lahai-roi, and e. of Egypt (Gen. 16:7; 25:18). It has not been identified, but was doubtless connected with the frontier fortresses of Egypt. It gave name to the wilderness through which the Israelites marched for 3 days immediately after crossing the Red Sea (Ex. 15:22). This waste was also sometimes called the wilderness of Etham (Num. 33:8).

Shu'shan (shōō'shăn). A city and royal residence in the Persian empire (Neh. 1:1; Esth. 1:2), in the province of Elam, on the river Ulai (Dan. 8:2). It was also a royal treasure city (Herod. v. 49). The place referred to in these passages is Susa. Ashurbanipal captured the city in a campaign c. 642–639 B.C., and later it became subject to the Chaldean kings. The royal family to which Cyrus, who conquered Babylon, belonged ruled over Anshan, which appears to have been a district of e. Elam. When Cyrus, by his military achievements, established the Persian empire, Susa was elevated to the rank of a capital of the empire, sharing this distinction with Ecbatana and Babylon. When Alexander the Great entered Susa, in 331 B.C., it had in it immense treasures, of which he took possession. In 317 B.C. it was occupied by Antigonus. After this it began to decline, but was still defensible when the Moslems conquered Persia. The site of the city is at Sus, in latitude 32° 10″ n., longitude 48° 26″ e., between the river Eulaeus (the Roman name for Daniel's Ulai) and the Shahpur, and about 100 miles from the Persian Gulf. The chief ruins are found within an area of about 6,000 feet long by 4,500 broad, the circumference being about 3 miles; but if scattered remains be taken in, the 3 miles may become 6 or 7. They consist of a series of mounds, in one of which the explorers laid bare the ruins of a palace, doubtless that begun by Darius, and in which Xerxes held his court. It seems to have been there that Esther's Ahasuerus held his feasts and his banquets (Esth. 1:2, 3, 9; 2:18; etc.).

Shu·shan'chites (shōō-shăn'kīts), in A.V. **Su·san'chites.** Natives or inhabitants of the Persian Susa, the Shushan of the O.T. Shushanchites were brought, with others, to central Palestine to supply the place of the 10 tribes carried into captivity (Ezra 4:9).

Shu'shan E'duth (shōō'shăn ē'dŭth). See SHOSHANNIM.

Shu·the'lah (shōō-thē'lȧ). 1. A son of Ephraim, and founder of a tribal family (Num. 26:35, 36; I Chron. 7:20).

2. Another descendant of Ephraim in the same line (I Chron. 7:21).

Si'a·ha (sī'ȧ-hȧ) and **Si'a** (sī'ȧ) [assembly]. A family of Nethinim, members of which returned with Zerubbabel from the Captivity (Ezra 2:44; Neh. 7:47).

Sib'be·cai (sĭb'ē-kī), in A.V. twice **Sib'be·chai** (sĭb'ē-kī) (II Sam. 21:18; I Chron. 20:4). A Hushathite, one of David's mighty men (I Chron. 11:29). He won renown by slaying the Philistine Saph, one of the sons of the giant (II Sam. 21:18). He commanded the division of the army for the 8th month (I Chron. 27:11). He is called in II Sam. 23:27 Mebunnai (*q.v.*).

Sib'bo·leth (sĭb'ō-lĕth). See SHIBBOLETH.

Sib'mah (sĭb'mȧ), in A.V. once **Shib'mah** (shĭb'mȧ) (Num. 32:38) [cf. Arab. *shabima*, to be cold]. A town assigned to Reuben (Num. 32:38; Josh. 13:19), which afterward reverted to Moab. It was celebrated for its vines (Isa. 16:8, 9; Jer. 48:32). The masc. form of the name is Sebam (Num. 32:3; in A.V. Shebam). According to Jerome, it was situated scarcely half a mile from Heshbon; it might be identified with Ḳurn el-Kibsh, between Ḥesbān and Nebo, about 3 miles e.n.e. of Siāgha, upon Wadi Salma.

Sib·ra'im (sĭb-rā'ĭm) [perhaps, hope]. A place on Ezekiel's n. boundary of Canaan (Ezek. 47:16); perhaps to be identified with Shomeriyeh, e. of Lake Ḥomṣ. See SEPHARVAIM.

Sic'cuth (sĭk'kōōth). A word occurring in Amos 5:26, E.R.V. and J.V.; but in A.V. and A.R.V. translated tabernacle (cf. the word Succoth). Regarded as a proper name, it corresponds to Sakkut, a designation given by the Babylonians to the planet Saturn. Another designation which they had for the planet was *Kaimānu*, or in modified pronunciation *Kaiwānu* (see CHIUN; Amos 5:26, A.V., E.R.V., and J.V.). It seems that the Masoretes gave Sakkut the vocalization of *shikkūṣ* (a detestable thing), whence Siccuth. See REPHAN.

Si'chem (sī'kĕm). See SHECHEM.

Sic'y·on (sĭsh'ĭ-ŏn). A Dorian town in the Peloponnesus (Herod. viii. 43), on the Gulf of Corinth, 10 miles n.w. of the city of Corinth. The old town at the harbor was abandoned in 303 B.C., and the populace removed to the new town, about 2 miles inland, which occupied a strong natural position. The city became a member of the Achaean league in 251 B.C. Half a century later it began to show friendliness to the Romans, and continued to do so during the 50 years that followed; and in 146 B.C., on the destruction of Corinth by the Roman general, Mummius, it was rewarded with a large portion of the conquered territory and with the management of the Isthmian Games. It held this distinction for a century, until Corinth was founded again and made a Roman colony. The Roman senate addressed the letter to Sicyon mentioned in I Macc. 15:23, about 139 B.C.

Sid'dim (sĭd'ĭm) [probably, salt flats, from Hittite *siyanta*, salt]. A valley, full of bitumen pits, in the region of the Salt or Dead Sea. There Chedorlaomer defeated the king of Sodom and his allies (Gen. 14:3, 8, 10).

Si'de (sī'dē). A maritime town of e. Pamphylia in Asia Minor. It maintained close commercial relations with Aradus in Phoenicia, gave the title Sidetes to Antiochus VII, who was brought up in the town, and was one of the places to which the Roman senate sent letters in favor of the Jews (I Macc. 15:23).

Si'don (sī'dŏn) and **Zi'don**; in A.V. usually **Zi'don** in O.T.; in A.V. and R.V. always **Si'don** in N.T. [a fishery]. An ancient city of the Canaanites (Gen. 10:15, 19), on the seacoast, 22 miles n. of Tyre. It was subject to Egypt in the 15th century B.C. Its importance is attested by Homer, who often mentions Sidon, but never Tyre, and who uses Sidon and Sidonian as synonymous with Phoenicia and Phoenician. It was the n. limit of the Canaanites, in the narrow sense (Gen. 10:19). Its territory was near Zebulun (ch. 49:13) and the boundary of Asher reached it (Josh. 19:28, where and in ch. 11:8 it is called Great Sidon). The tribe of Asher, however, failed to expel the Canaanite inhabitants (Judg. 1:31). In the period of the Judges the

Sidonians oppressed the Israelites (Judg. 10: 12), and the latter people are accused of worshiping the gods of Sidon (v. 6). Of these gods, Baal was doubtless the chief (I Kings 16:31); the principal object of worship, however, was Ashtoreth, a goddess of fertility (I Kings 11:5, 33; II Kings 23:13). Ethbaal, a king of Sidon, was the father of Jezebel (I Kings 16:31). Isaiah predicted that it would be visited with judgment which would make its inhabitants pass to Kittim, that is, Cyprus (Isa. 23:12). It was for a time subject to the neighboring city of Tyre (Jos. *Antiq.* ix. 14, 2). In 701 B.C., it submitted to Sennacherib, king of Assyria. In 677 B.C. it was destroyed by Esarhaddon. Jeremiah predicted its subjugation by Nebuchadnezzar, king of Babylon (Jer. 27:3, 6). Ezekiel denounced judgment against it because it had been "a pricking brier unto the house of Israel" (Ezek. 28:21, 22). Joel charges the Sidonians and others with having helped to plunder Jerusalem, carrying off silver and gold, and selling its inhabitants for slaves (Joel 3:4–6). About 526 B.C. Sidon submitted to Cambyses, son of Cyrus, king of Persia. The Sidonians sold cedar timber to the Jews for the Temple which Zerubbabel was building (Ezra 3:7). It revolted against Artaxerxes Ochus, king of Persia (c. 351 B.C.), but was retaken and destroyed (345 B.C.). To get rid of the Persians, in 333 B.C. it opened its gates to Alexander the Great. From his successors it passed, in 64 B.C., to the Romans. People from Sidon came to Galilee to attend on the preaching of Jesus and to witness his miracles (Mark 3:8; Luke 6:17; etc.). He once visited the region, and probably the city (Matt. 15:21; Mark 7:24, 31). Herod Agrippa II was highly displeased with the people of Tyre and Sidon, but they made peace with him "because their country was fed from the king's country" (Acts 12:20). Paul touched at the port (Acts 27:3). Since N.T. times Sidon has seen many vicissitudes. The modern city, called Saida, lies on the n.w. slope of a small promontory jutting out into the sea. The ancient harbor was formed by a ridge of rocks parallel to the shore. It was partly filled up with stones and earth by Fakhr ed-Din, the ruler of the Druses, in the 17th century. There is a wall protecting the land side of the city. The highest ground, which is crowned by the citadel, is on the s. side. Sidon has in and around it a few broken granite columns; and various sarcophagi, including the celebrated one of Eshmunazar, were brought from tombs in its vicinity.

Si·do'ni·ans (sī-dō'nǐ-ǎns), in A.V. frequently **Zi·do'ni·ans** (zǐ-dō'nǐ-ǎnz).

Siege. See WAR.

Sig'net. See SEAL 2.

Si'hon (sī'hŏn). A king of the Amorites, whose capital was Heshbon. He drove the Moabites from the country between Heshbon and the Arnon and took possession of it (Num. 21:26–30). Five Midianite tribes were his vassals (Josh. 13:21). When the Israelites arrived in the wilderness on the s.e. of the Arnon, Moses sent messengers to him to ask permission to cross his territory (Num. 21:21, 22; Deut. 2:26). Upon his refusal, the Israelites entered his domains under the necessity of fighting their way to the Jordan. Sihon gathered his army together at Jahaz and opposed the invaders, but he was defeated and his kingdom taken possession of by the Israelites (Num. 21:21–32; Ps. 135:11). The country thus seized was included between the Jordan, the Jabbok, and the Arnon (Num. 21:24, 32; Deut. 2:36; Judg. 11:22). The camp of Israel was pitched at Pisgah, a secure position on the mountains of Abarim,

nearly in the center of the conquered district, preparatory to the campaign against Bashan (Num. 21:20; cf. chs. 22:1; 33:47). Sihon's kingdom was afterward assigned to the tribes of Reuben and Gad, who desired it because it afforded good pasturage (Num. 32:1–4, 33–38).

Si'hor (sī'hōr). See SHIHOR.

Si'las (sī'lás) [Gr. for Aram. *She'ila* (= Saul)]. A distinguished member of the Apostolic Church at Jerusalem. He was sent with Paul to communicate the decision of the council held at that city to the Christians at Antioch (Acts 15:22, 27, 32). When Paul declined to take John Mark with him on the Second Missionary Journey, and parted with Barnabas, he chose Silas as his companion (v. 40), and the 2 were imprisoned together at Philippi (ch. 16:19, 25, 29). Silas was with Paul during the riot at Thessalonica (ch. 17: 4), and was sent away with him to Berea, remaining there with Timothy after the apostle had been obliged to depart (v. 14). The 2 were, however, soon directed to follow Paul to Athens (v. 15). They started to join him, but do not seem to have come up with him till after his arrival at Corinth (ch. 18:5). In this city Silas was an esteemed co-worker of Paul's (II Cor. 1:19). The same individual who in The Acts is familiarly named Silas is unvaryingly called Silvanus in the Epistles. As the Apostle Paul was known by two names, so Silas had also a Latin appellation, Silvanus (sylvan), which resembles his Aramaic name. He was associated with Paul and Timothy in sending the 2 letters to the Thessalonians (I Thess. 1:1; II Thess. 1:1). He is probably the Silvanus who carried to its destination The First Epistle of Peter (I Peter 5:12).

Silk. A fine, soft thread produced by various species of caterpillars, and a fabric woven from the thread. Silk reached the markets of the West shortly after the conquest of Alexander the Great. It was known to the Greeks as *sērikon*, pertaining to the Seres, who are generally identified with the Chinese. It was a choice article of merchandise (Rev. 18:12), fit for the clothing of Roman emperors (Jos. *War* vii. 5, 4). As late as the reign of the emperor Aurelian, A.D. 270–275, unmixed silk goods were sold for their weight in gold. The fine raiment referred to in Ezek. 16:10, 13 by the term *meshī* was probably silk, as the rabbinical interpreters understood and as it is rendered in English.

Sil'la (sĭl'á). An unknown place near Millo (II Kings 12:20).

Si·lo'ah (sĭ-lō'áh), an erroneous transliteration of Shelah in A.V. of Neh. 3:15. See SILOAM.

Si·lo'am (sĭ-lō'ăm) [sent, or conducted; a sending of water through an aqueduct]. A pool at Jerusalem (John 9:7); identical with Shiloah, the waters of which "go softly" (Isa. 8:6), and the pool of Shelah, which was by the king's garden (Neh. 3:15). Josephus says that it was situated at the extremity of the valley of cheesemongers, near a bend of the old wall beneath Ophlas, i.e., Ophel (Jos. *War* v. 4, 1 and 2). The name is preserved in the Birket Silwân, which occupies the general site of the ancient pool. It is a rectangular reservoir, 58 feet long, 18 broad, and 19 deep, built of masonry, the w. side of which has considerably broken down. The fountain is a small upper basin excavated in the rock. It is really the termination of the tunnel which was cut to conduct the water from the Fountain of the Virgin. From the lower reservoir, the water flows in a small rill across the road and irrigates gardens in the Kidron Valley.

In 1880 an inscription of 6 lines was discovered on the walls of this tunnel by a youth who had entered from the Siloam end. It proved to be written in pure Hebrew, and is supposed to date from the time of Ahaz or Hezekiah. A portion of the first 3 lines has been destroyed by the wearing away of the rock, and occasionally a letter cannot be made out with certainty. Still the sense is plain. It describes how the workmen, who had excavated toward each other from the 2 ends of the tunnel, met. It is as follows, as nearly as possible. ". . . the boring through ! And this was the manner of the boring through. While yet [the miners were lifting up] the pick one toward another, and while there were yet three cubits to be [cut through, there was heard] the voice of each calling to the other ; for there was a split in the rock on the right hand . . . . And on the day of the boring through, the miners struck the one so as to meet the other, pick against pick. And the water flowed from the source to the pool, 1200 cubits ; and 100 cubits was the height of the rock over the head of the miners."

The tower in Siloam which fell (Luke 13 : 4) was probably one on the Ophel ridge, near Siloam.

Sil·va'nus (sĭl-vā'nŭs). See SILAS.

Sil'ver. A precious metal. Its ore was mined from the earth (Job 28 :1) and melted in a furnace, by which process the dross was separated from the richer metal (Ps. 12 :6 ; Prov. 17 :3 ; 25 :4 ; Ezek. 22 :22). It was obtained in Arabia (II Chron. 9 :14; cf. I Kings 10 :22, 27) and Tarshish (Jer. 10 :9 ; Ezek. 27 :12), Spain being a large producer (I Macc. 8 :3). It was used as a medium of exchange from remotest antiquity (Gen. 23 :16 ; 37 :28). The amount required was weighed out (Job 28 :15 ; Isa. 46 :6), for silver was not coined until late, among the Jews not until long after the Exile (I Macc. 15 :6) ; see MONEY. Personal ornaments (Gen. 24 :53 ; Ex. 3 :22 ; S. of Sol. 1 :11), crowns (Zech. 6 :11), musical instruments, as trumpets (Num. 10 :2), and household utensils of the wealthy, like Joseph's drinking cup (Gen. 44 :2) were made of silver. Large quantities of the metal were used in the tabernacle and Temple for sockets (Ex. 26 :19), hooks, chapiters and fillets of the pillars (Ex. 27 :10 ; 38 :19), platters and bowls (Num. 7 :13 ; I Chron. 28 :17 ; Ezra 1 :9, 10), cups (II Kings 12 :13), candlesticks, and tables (I Chron. 28 :15, 16). Idols and models of idol shrines were constructed of silver (Ps. 115 :4 ; Acts 19 :24).

Sil'ver·ling. The rendering of Heb. *keseph*, silver, in Isa. 7 :23, which is elsewhere translated by shekel or piece of silver.

Si'mal·cu'e (sī'măl-kū'ē). See IMALCUE.

Sim'e·on (sĭm'ē-ŭn), in R.V. of N.T. **Sym'·e·on**, in imitation of a Gr. form, when the persons are not mentioned in O.T. (Luke 3 :30 ; Acts 13 :1 ; 15 :14) [hearing]. 1. The second-born son of Jacob by Leah (Gen. 29 : 33). In conjunction with his brother Levi, he massacred the Hivite inhabitants of Shechem on account of the injury done by one of their number to Dinah (ch. 34 :24–31) ; see DINAH. When one of Jacob's sons was to be kept a prisoner in Egypt as security for return of the rest, Joseph took Simeon and bound him (ch. 42 :24). The prediction of Simeon's future by the dying Jacob returns to the subject of the massacre, and threatens Simeon as well as Levi that they will be scattered in Israel (ch. 49 :5–7).

2. The tribe of which Simeon, the son of Jacob, was the progenitor. He had 6 sons: Jemuel or Nemuel, Jamin, Ohad, Jachin or Jarib, Zohar or Zerah, and Shaul. With the exception of Ohad, all these founded tribal families (Gen. 46 :10 ; Num. 26 :12–14 ; I Chron. 4 :24). The prince of the tribe in the early times of the wilderness wanderings was Shelumiel, son of Zurishaddai (Num. 1 :6 ; 2 : 12 ; 7 :36, 41 ; 10 :19), and at a later period Shemuel, son of Ammihud (ch. 34 :20). At the 1st census in the wilderness the tribe numbered 59,300 fighting men (chs. 1 :23 ; 2 :13), at the 2d, 22,200 (ch. 26 :12–14). Shaphat, son of Hori, was the spy from the tribe (ch. 13 :5). Moses, before his departure, blessed the tribes, but omitted to mention Simeon explicitly (Deut., ch. 33). This omission is probably due to the artificial construction of the poem. Moses wanted 12 for the number of the tribes. He formed 2 groups, departing from the order of birth, and placing the children of Jacob's 2 wives in the 1st group and those of the 2 maids in the 2d.

Leah 3	Leah's maid 1
Rachel 3	Rachel's maid 2
Leah 2	Leah's maid 1

The 1st group contains 8, Simeon being omitted, and the 2d group contains just half as many. The 1st group is subdivided into 3 minor groups, beginning with 3 of the elder children of Leah and closing with Leah's youngest 2, and having Rachel's 3 in the center ; the number 3 for Rachel is obtained by counting Joseph as 2, i.e., Ephraim and Manasseh. The 2d group is made to correspond to this arrangement. It begins with Leah's first-born by her maid and closes with her 2d son by the same maid, and the 2 sons of Rachel by her maid are placed between. The blessings pronounced upon these tribes are framed within a benediction upon all Israel (Deut. 33 :2–5, 26–29). The tribe of Simeon could best be omitted from the particular enumeration because it was to be scattered in Israel (Gen. 49 :5–7). The same punishment also awaited Levi, but recent deeds had partly atoned for the past and given the tribe of Levi a position of honor among the people of God. After Moses' death the tribe of Simeon was not assigned a self-contained territory, but was granted possession in the midst of Judah. The Simeonites, however, although not explicitly mentioned, were not excluded from the blessings invoked on the tribes. They were included in the general benediction upon Israel as a whole, with which the poem opens and closes. The tribe of Simeon was one of those who stood at the foot of Mount Gerizim to pronounce blessings (Deut. 27 :12).

When the Land of Canaan was distributed by lot, the 2d lot taken at Shiloh came forth for the tribe of Simeon, and land was assigned them in the extreme s. of Canaan, in the midst of the inheritance of the children of Judah (Josh. 19 :1–9), and the 2 tribes made common cause against the Canaanites (Judg. 1 :1, 3, 17). Among the Simeonite cities were Beer-sheba, Ziklag, and Hormah (Josh. 19 :1–9), in the s. part of Judah. In the reign of Hezekiah the Simeonites smote the people of Ham and the Meunim who dwelt in the valley of Gedor ; 500 of them also slaughtered the Amalekites of Mount Seir ; in both cases occupying the territory of the vanquished tribes (I Chron. 4 :24–43). It is believed that ultimately a great part of the tribe disappeared, but it was recognized by Ezekiel in his prophecies of the future Canaan (Ezek. 48 :24, 25, 33), and in the apocalyptic vision there were sealed 12,000 Simeonites (Rev. 7 :7).

3. An ancestor of Christ, who lived after David but before Zerubbabel (Luke 3 :30).

4. A priest of the family of Joarib, and an ancestor of the Maccabees (I Macc. 2 :1).

5. A righteous and devout man, to whom

it had been revealed by the Holy Spirit that he should not see death till he had seen the Lord's Christ. Coming into the Temple when Joseph and Mary had just brought in the infant Jesus, Simeon recognized him as the promised Messiah, expressed his willingness now to depart in peace, and made a prophetic address to Mary with respect both to her and to her child (Luke 2:25-35).

6. Simon Peter (Acts 15:14); see PETER.

7. A Christian prophet or teacher at Antioch. He was surnamed Niger, black, and may perhaps have been of African race (Acts 13:1).

Si'mon (sī'mŭn) [hearing]. Simon and Symeon represent Gr. for Heb. *Shim'ōn*, Simeon. 1. Second son of the priest Mattathias. He was called Thassi, which may perhaps mean director or guide (I Macc. 2:3, in Syriac Tharsi). With his brothers he sympathized with his father in the revolt against the religious intolerance of the Syrians (v. 14). Regarding him as the wisest of the sons, his father, when about to die, appointed him the adviser of the family, but gave the military authority to Judas, a younger brother (vs. 65, 66). Simon held a military command under Judas and led a detachment of troops to the aid of the Jews in Galilee (ch. 5:17, 20-23). After the death of Judas, Jonathan was chosen leader. He made Simon commandant of the entire coast (chs. 11:59; 12:33, 34). When Jonathan was seized and held prisoner by Tryphon, the conduct of the war devolved on Simon, as the last remaining brother of the Maccabee family (ch. 13:1-9). He at once completed the fortifications of Jerusalem and secured possession of Joppa (vs. 10, 11). When Tryphon invaded Judea, Simon dogged his army (v. 20), and when Tryphon withdrew from the country, Simon rebuilt and provisioned the strongholds of Judea (v. 33). He also allied himself with Tryphon's rival, Demetrius II, and obtained from him the recognition of the independence of Judea, 142 B.C. (vs. 34-42). Thereupon he besieged and captured Gezer (vs. 43-48, in A.V. Gaza). In the spring of 141 he reduced the Syrian citadel at Jerusalem (vs. 49-52). A season of peace followed, during which Simon devoted his energies to internal administration and the encouragement of commerce and agriculture (ch. 14:4-15). He embellished the family tomb at Modin, in which he had placed the remains of his brother Jonathan (ch. 13:25-30). The Spartans and Romans renewed the league with him (chs. 14:16-24; 15:15-24). He was acknowledged by the Jews as high priest and captain and leader (chs. 13:42; 14:41, 42, 47; 15:1, 2), and in 140 B.C. was authorized to wear the purple (ch. 14:43, 44). Antiochus Sidetes, when on the eve of coming to Syria to help to defend the cause of the absent Demetrius against Tryphon, made concessions to Simon and gave him authority to coin money (ch. 15:6), but afterward became estranged from him and demanded the surrender of Joppa, Gezer, and the citadel at Jerusalem (vs. 26-31). Simon refused, and war ensued, 138-7 B.C., but the Syrians were worsted. In the early spring of 135 B.C., while on a tour of visitation to the cities of his dominion, he was treacherously murdered in the castle of Dok, near Jericho, by his son-in-law (ch. 16:14-16).

2. Father of Judas Iscariot (John 6:71). He too bore the designation Iscariot (*ibid.* and ch. 13:26, R.V.).

3. Simon Peter (Matt. 10:2); see PETER.

4. Simon the Zealot, one of the 12 apostles (Luke 6:15; Acts 1:13); see CANANAEAN.

5. One of the Lord's brethren (Matt. 13:55; Mark 6:3); see BRETHREN OF THE LORD.

6. A Pharisee, at whose house our Lord once ate, on which occasion a woman, who was a sinner, anointed his feet (Luke 7:36-50).

7. A householder in Bethany. He had been a leper and not improbably had been cured by Christ. When our Lord was at meat in his house, Mary, the sister of Lazarus, anointed his feet with precious ointment (Matt. 26:6-13; Mark 14:3-9). Martha served, and Lazarus was one of those who ate. The presence of the brother and 2 sisters, and the active part taken by the sisters, as well as the fact that Simon's house was in the town of Lazarus and his sisters, makes it evident that Simon was a relative or intimate friend of theirs. But there is no reason to believe that he was their father or the husband of Mary. He may have been the husband of Martha; see MARTHA.

8. The Cyrenian who was compelled to bear the cross of Christ. He was the father of Alexander and Rufus (Matt. 27:32).

9. A sorcerer (now popularly called Simon Magus, i.e., Simon the magician) who so amazed the people of Samaria with his arts that they said, "This man is that power of God which is called Great." He was apparently converted through the instrumentality of Philip the evangelist, by whom he was baptized. Having subsequently offered to buy with money the privilege of conferring the Holy Spirit on anyone he wished by the imposition of hands, he was sternly rebuked by Peter, who declared that his heart was not right with God, and that he was still in the gall of bitterness and in the bond of iniquity. He took the reproof meekly and begged the apostle to pray for him that none of the evils threatened might be allowed to befall him (Acts 8:9-24). He was afraid, but there is no evidence that he was penitent. Ecclesiastical tradition makes Simon recommence his sorceries and become the persistent antagonist of the Apostle Peter, following him about from place to place and seeking encounters with him, but only to be signally defeated. He is said to have helped to originate Gnosticism.

10. A tanner at Joppa, in whose house Peter lodged (Acts 9:43; 10:6, 17, 32).

Sim'ri (sĭm'rī). See SHIMRI.

Sin, I. "Any want of conformity unto, or transgression of any law of God, given as a rule to the reasonable creature" (Rom. 3:23; I John 3:4; Gal. 3:10-12). A sin of omission is the neglect to do what the Law of God commands; a sin of commission is the doing of anything which it forbids. See EVIL.

Sin, II (sĭn) [Heb. *Sin*]. 1. A wilderness through which the Israelites passed on their way from Elim and the Red Sea to Rephidim and Mount Sinai (Ex. 16:1; 17:1; Num. 33:11, 12). It probably is Debbet er-Ramleh, a tract of sand, in the interior of the peninsula at the foot of Jebel et-Tih, but the desert plain el-Markhah on the coast has also been suggested. If the latter, the Israelites on leaving it probably continued to journey along the coast and turned inland through Wadi Feirān.

2. A city and stronghold of Egypt (Ezek. 30:15, 16). The LXX in v. 15 reads Sais, which, however, was never an important fortress. The Vulgate renders it Pelusium, which was "the key of Egypt," strongly fortified, and necessary to be captured before an army could enter Egypt from the n.e. In v. 16 the LXX reads *Syēnē*, which is modern Assuan at the First Cataract; and the order of enumeration of Egyptian cities, from s. to n. (vs. 16-18) lends confirmation to this identification with Syene.

Si'nai (sī'nī), in A.V. of N.T. twice **Si'na** [sī'ná] (Acts 7:30, 38). A mountain, called also Horeb, at which the Israelites, traveling by way of Marah, Elim, and the Red Sea, arrived in the 3d month after their departure from Egypt (Ex. 19:1). It was distant from Kadesh-barnea 11 days' journey by way of Mount Seir (Deut. 1:2). A wilderness, sufficiently large for the camp of Israel, lay at its foot (Ex. 19:2); so close that the mountain could be touched (v. 12), and yet its upper part was visible from the camp (vs. 16, 18, 20). From this mountain the Law of the Ten Commandments was given, and at its base the covenant was ratified which made the Israelites a nation with Jehovah as king (Ex. 20:1 to 24:8). All the legislation contained in Ex., ch. 20 to Num., ch. 10 was enacted on or at the foot of Mount Sinai, according to repeated statement (Ex. 24:12; 31:18; 34:2; Lev. 1:1; 16:1; 25:1; 26:46; 27:34; Num. 1:1; 9:1). The only later visit to the mount recorded in Scripture is that of Elijah when he was threatened by Jezebel (I Kings 19:8).

A theory has found favor that Mount Sinai stood within the borders of Mount Seir, but the opinion prevails that Sinai is to be sought among the mountains in the interior of the Sinaitic peninsula. Tradition in favor of Mount Serbāl, on Wadi Feirān, is traceable as far back as the time of Eusebius, for Jebel Mūsa only to that of Justinian. But neither tradition is regarded as weighty. Serbāl is the more imposing of the 2. It is a solitary, majestic mountain, 6,712 feet high, visible from a great distance. But at its foot is no wilderness which could be called the wilderness of Sinai. Jebel Mūsa is part of a short ridge of granite formation, extending about 2 miles from n.w. to s.e. The ridge has 2 peaks: Rās eṣ-Ṣafṣāfeh, or peak of willows, at the n. end with an altitude of 6,540 feet; and Jebel Mūsa, the traditional Sinai, at the s. end rising to a height of about 7,363 feet. A plateau at the head of Wadi es-Sadad and almost due e. of Jebel Mūsa has been regarded by some scholars, including Tischendorf, as the site of the encampment of the Israelites, but its area is too limited to accommodate any considerable host. The base of Rās eṣ-Ṣafṣāfeh toward the n.w. consists of a precipitous cliff. At the bottom of the cliff lies the plain of er-Rāḥah, about 1 square mile in extent, and, with the adjacent wadies esh-Sheikh and ed-Deir, entirely suitable for a camping ground. The Biblical description makes it scarcely necessary, if not idle, to inquire whether the Law was given from Jebel Mūsa or Rās eṣ-Ṣafṣāfeh, and whether one peak or the other was known as the mount of God in distinction from the rest of the clump. See HOREB.

The monastery of St. Catherine, a convent of Greek monks, is situated on the e. slope of the mountain, at the foot of Jebel Mūsa, in the wadi ed-Deir, 5,014 feet above sea level. Surrounded by massive granite walls, it is, as it were, a fortress. Its foundation is ascribed to the emperor Justinian in A.D. 527, who is said to have built it around a tower erected long before by Helena, mother of Constantine; but this ascription is probably due to confusion with the fact that Justinian built a castle in 530 for the protection of the monks who dwelt in the region. The monastery is named after St. Catherine, who was tortured on the wheel and beheaded in Alexandria in A.D. 307, and whose body is said by the monks to have been carried by angels from Alexandria to the lofty summit of Jebel Katherîn, 2¼ miles s.w. of Jebel Mūsa. Her head and 1 hand are said to be contained in a marble sarcophagus in the chapel of the monastery. The monastery has often been destroyed and rebuilt.

The Church of the Transfiguration is an early Christian basilica with mosaics of the 7th or 8th century. The oldest part of it is probably the Chapel of the Burning Bush, at the back of the apse and on the reputed site of the event it commemorates. In the garden are fig, orange, olive, almond, apple, and apricot trees, grape vines, and a few lofty cypresses. The library is exceedingly valuable. It contains many MSS., predominantly Greek and Arabic, but also many others, including some written in Syriac and Ethiopic. Here, in 1844 and 1859, Tischendorf found the Codex Sinaiticus, which dates from about A.D. 400; see NEW TESTAMENT. Here also, in 1892, Mrs. Lewis discovered a MS. which contains the text of the Old Syriac Gospels; see VERSIONS.

Si'nim (sī'nĭm), **Land of.** A country cited to illustrate the promise that the scattered Israelites shall be gathered from the remotest regions of the earth. "Lo, these shall come from far; and, lo, these from the north and from the west; and these from the land of Sinim" (Isa. 49:12). Since the w. and n. have been mentioned, the land of Sinim is not to be sought there, but in the s. or e. Wherever the prophet was when he uttered these words, his words exclude the Sinites of Phoenicia (Gen. 10:17), for they were not a remote people. Besides this, they were an unimportant tribe. For the same reason, the people of Syene or Pelusium (cf. the name Sin in Ezek. 30:15, 16) are excluded. They were almost in the heart of the inhabited world, separated from the remote bounds of the earth by Ethiopia and Libya at least. The chief theories are: 1. The expression was chosen as a designation of the lands s. of Palestine, because in that direction lay the town of Sin (Pelusium or Syene), the wilderness of Sin (Ex. 16:1), and Mount Sinai. But this region was too near at hand to denote the remotest countries. Sheba and Cush, which are used to denote the utmost parts of the earth toward the s. lay far beyond. In favor of Syene, however, is the fact that there was a Jewish garrison colony at Elephantine and Syene, from the 6th century to c. 400 B.C., for defending the s. frontier of Egypt. 2. The Sinim were the Shinas, who have dwelt from ancient times at the foot of the Hindu Kush mountains. 3. It may refer to Elam, which in Old Akkadian was known as Si-nim (highland). 4. A widely held view is that the Chinese are meant. The prophet does not assert that Israelites were already living in China (if his words be restricted to a return of the exiles). They may have been; for the presence of Israelites in China is attested as early as the 3d century B.C., and it is not known how much earlier they migrated to that land. But the people were scattered far and wide, and yet wider dispersion was in prospect (Isa. 11:11). They should be recovered from the farthest bounds of earth where they are found. According to the Chinese records Chinese merchants visited foreign lands as early as the 12th century B.C., and foreign merchants entered China as early as the 10th century. It is probable that direct commercial relations existed between China and India, and hence indirectly at least with the countries farther w.

Si'nite (sī'nīt). A Canaanite tribe, mentioned between the Arkite and the Arvadite (Gen. 10:17). A place named Sin not far from Arka was known to Jerome, and Strabo mentions a fortress called Sinna on Mount Lebanon.

Sin Of'fer·ing. See OFFERINGS.

Si'on (sī'ŭn) [elevated, towering]. A name for Mount Hermon (Deut. 4:48). For Mount Sion at Jerusalem, a different word in Heb., see ZION.

Siph'moth (sĭf'mŏth). A haunt of David during his wanderings, to which he sent part of the spoils of Ziklag (I Sam. 30:28; cf. I Chron. 27:27).

Sip'pai (sĭp'ī). See SAPH.

Si'rah (sī'rà). A well or cistern 20 stades from Hebron (Jos. *Antiq.* vii. 1, 5) from which Abner was treacherously recalled to Hebron by Joab (II Sam. 3:26). It is probably 'Ain Sârah, 1½ miles n.w. of Hebron.

Sir'i·on (sĭr'ĭ-ŏn) [cuirass, coat of mail]. The name given by the Sidonians to Mount Hermon (Deut. 3:9; Ps. 29:6).

Sis'a·mai (sĭs'à-mī). See SISMAI.

Sis'er·a (sĭs'ēr-à). Commander of a Canaanite army which held northern Israel in subjection. Defeated on the Kishon and fleeing n., probably on his way to the overlord of the Canaanite king, he sought refuge with Heber the Kenite, who was at peace with the Canaanites. Heber's wife saw him coming, went forth, and invited him into her tent, but killed him while he slept (Judg., chs. 4; 5; I Sam. 12:9; Ps. 83:9); see JAEL. Probably those Nethinim who were known as the children of Sisera were descended from captives taken at this time (Ezra 2:53; Neh. 7:55).

Sis'mai (sĭs'mī), in A.V. **Sis'a·mai**. A man of Judah, family of Hezron, house of Jerahmeel (I Chron. 2:40).

Sis'ter. A kinswoman; a full sister or a half-sister (Gen. 20:12; Deut. 27:22; or a wife (S. of Sol. 4:9; Tobit 5:20; 7:16; 8:4); or a woman of the same tribe (Num. 25:18) or a woman fellow believer in Christ (Rom. 16:1; James 2:15).

Sis'trum. A musical instrument (II Sam. 6:5, R.V. marg.), consisting of several metallic rods in an oval metallic frame. The rods were either loosely inserted or loose rings were hung on them, so that the instrument would jingle when shaken.

Sith'ri (sĭth'rī), in A.V. **Zith'ri** [a hiding place is (Jehovah)]. A Levite, family of Kohath, house of Uzziel (Ex. 6:22).

Sit'nah (sĭt'nà) [accusation, enmity (cf. Satan)]. A well dug by Isaac in the Philistine country, not far from Gerar; but the inhabitants of the district disputed his right to it (Gen. 26:21). Palmer and Drake in 1870 found a small valley called Wadi Shuṭnet er-Ruḥeibeh. The first portion of the name corresponds to Sitnah, and Ruḥeibeh to Rehoboth, which was in the immediate vicinity of Sitnah (v. 22).

Si'van' (sē-vän') [Heb. *sīwān* from Akkad. *simānu*]. The 3d month of the Babylonian and Jewish year (Esth. 8:9), extending from the new moon of May to that of June. See YEAR.

Slave. Slavery existed in remote antiquity. Slaves were acquired: 1. By capture, especially in war (Num. 31:9; II Kings 5:2; Jos. *War* iii. 4, 1; vi. 9, 2). 2. By purchase from slave owners (Gen. 17:27; 37:28, 36; Ezek. 27:13; Joel 3:6, 8). 3. By birth from slaves owned (Gen. 17:12). 4. In payment of debt: thieves unable to make restitution, and, though contrary to the spirit of the Mosaic Law, a debtor, or his children, being sold as slaves (Ex. 22:3; II Kings 4:1; Neh. 5:5, 8; Amos 2:6; Matt. 18:25). 5. Among the Hebrews there was also the voluntary sale of one's self or one's daughter on account of poverty (Ex. 21:2, 7; Lev. 25:39, 47).

The price of a slave varied of course according to times and circumstances. It was reckoned in Hebrew judicial cases as averaging 30 shekels (Ex. 21:32). The Jewish slaves in Alexandria in the 3d century B.C.

brought about the same, 120 drachmas (Jos. *Antiq.* xii. 2, 3). Joseph at 17 years of age was purchased for 20 shekels (Gen. 37:28).

Among the Hebrews the legal status of a Hebrew slave was very different from that of the slave who was not an Israelite. The Hebrew slave had manumission after 6 years of service, if he chose; might not be harshly treated, nor sent away empty on his release; and, if owned by a foreign sojourner in Israel, had the privilege of redemption at a price legally regulated, the moment he could secure the necessary money (Ex. 21:2–6; Lev. 25:43, 47–55; Jer. 34:8–16). The rights of the Hebrew maid were the subject of further special legislation (Ex. 21:7–11). All Hebrew slaves, both those who had elected to remain with their masters when the 7th year had come and those who had not served 6 years, were released at the year of jubilee (Lev. 25:40). This provision was necessitated when the law regarding the restoration of every man's inheritance at the jubilee was enacted. The return of the slave to his inheritance was involved, whether he chose to go back to his master's family afterward or not. The slave also who was not an Israelite fared well among the Hebrews. The Mosaic Law recognized that he possessed rights. He might be whipped or beaten, but not maimed or killed (Ex. 21:20–27; Lev. 24:17, 22). In case a captive slave girl was taken to wife, she acquired new rights (Deut. 21:10–14). All these non-Hebrew slaves were regarded as members of the commonwealth of Israel (Gen. 17:10–14); and they were equal before God, participating in the religious festivals and sacrifices (Ex. 12:44; Lev. 22:11; Deut. 12:12, 18; 16:11, 14), and enjoying the rest of the Sabbath day (Ex. 20:10; 23:12). Another humane feature of the Mosaic Law gave an asylum to fugitive slaves. They were not to be surrendered, but were allowed to dwell in the land wherever they chose (Deut. 23:15, 16). It also forbade, on pain of death, the stealing of men and the selling or holding of them (Ex. 21:16; Deut. 24:7); and there is no evidence that slave markets ever existed in Israel. The Mosaic Law contrasts most favorably with the laws of contemporary heathen nations in its humanity toward slaves. The relationship between master and slave was often cordial (Gen., ch. 24). The slave was regarded as entitled to justice (Job 31:13–15); he sometimes inherited the property of his master (Gen. 15:2, 3), and was sometimes admitted into the family as son-in-law (I Chron. 2:34, 35).

Christianity avoided a sudden reversal of established usages (I Cor. 7:21), urged the slave to obey his master (Eph. 6:5–8; Col. 3:22–25; I Tim. 6:1, 2; I Peter 2:18–21), and sent the runaway slave voluntarily back to his Christian master (Philemon 10–16). But it also promulgated principles which improved the condition of slaves in the Roman Empire. It recognized the equality of slave and master in God's sight (I Cor. 7:21, 22; Gal. 3:28; Col. 3:11). It exhorted the master to treat his slaves considerately, reminding him that they had rights which God will maintain (Eph. 6:9; Col. 4:1).

Slime. See BITUMEN.

Sling. A simple weapon usually consisting of a piece of leather with 2 strings attached to its opposite sides and a stone inserted. It was whirled once or twice round the head and 1 string let go, whereby the stone was projected with great force. On the field of battle the stones were either carried in a bag by the slinger or piled at his feet (I Sam. 17:40).

It seems to have been used in warfare by practically all the peoples of antiquity; by the Egyptians, Syrians (I Macc. 6:51; 9:11), Assyrians, Persians (Xen. *Anabasis* iii. 3, 18), and in the far w. by Sicilians (Herod. vii. 158) and mercenaries in the Roman army. Among the Hebrews the Benjamites in the times of the Judges and in the reign of Saul were noted for their skill in its use,

Early Slingstones, Found in Palestine

being able to sling stones with the left hand (Judg. 20:16; I Chron. 12:2). David slew Goliath with a stone from a sling (I Sam. 17:48–50). Slingers served in the armies of Jehoram, Jehoshaphat, and Uzziah (II Kings 3:25; II Chron. 26:14), and were effective as late as the war with the Romans (Jos. *War* ii. 17, 5; iv. 1, 3).

Smith. An artificer who forges iron and brass into tools and weapons, a blacksmith (I Sam. 13:19; Isa. 44:12; 54:16), like Tubal-cain (Gen. 4:22); or one who refines

Egyptian Smith at His Furnace

and shapes the precious metals, a goldsmith (Isa. 40:19). The blacksmith used a charcoal furnace, bellows, tongs, anvil, and hammer (Ecclus. 38:28). See BELLOWS.

Smyr'na (smûr'na) [Gr., myrrh]. A city of great antiquity on the w. coast of Asia Minor. It was possessed by the Aeolian Greeks, and finally the Ionian Greeks admitted it into their confederacy. The Lydian king, Alyattes, destroyed it (c. 580 B.C.), and it lay waste for some 200 years, till the plan of rebuilding it was formed by Alexander the Great, and executed by his immediate successors, on a new site near by. It then became a large and flourishing commercial center, retaining its importance under the Romans. It became a part of the province of Asia, which was annexed in 133 B.C. and organized in 129–126 B.C. Its church was the 2d of the 7 addressed by John in the book of The Revelation. It escapes all censure, but it is exhorted to remain constant in the midst of persecution (Rev. 1:11; 2:8–11). Its bishop, Polycarp, suffered martyrdom by fire, near the stadion, probably in A.D. 169. In A.D. 178 Smyrna was destroyed by an earthquake, but was speedily rebuilt. Lying as it does at the extremity of a fine bay, in the track of trade, it is admirably adapted for commerce.

Snail. 1. The rendering of Heb. *ḥōmeṭ* (Lev. 11:30; in R.V. sand lizard).

2. The rendering of Heb. *shabbelūl* (Ps. 58:8), a genuine snail, especially of the shell-less family (*Limacidae*).

Snow. Snow occurs in the hilly country of Palestine, as at Sepphoris in Galilee, Naza-

reth, Jerusalem, Hebron (I Macc. 13:22; Jos. *War* i. 16, 2; iv. 8, 3). It may be expected in January or February, although the winter often passes wtihout it. It sometimes falls to the depth of a foot, but seldom lies longer than a day. On Mount Lebanon it is found lingering on the heights and in the ravines late in the summer, and it crowns the summit of Hermon the year round. It is frequently referred to in Scripture as the standard of whiteness and the emblem of purity (Ps. 51:7; Isa. 1:18; Lam. 4:7; Matt. 28:3). It is poetically described as stored by God in his treasury (Job 38:22), commanded by him to fall (Job 37:6; Ps. 147:16), and descending like wool or birds or a swarm of locusts (*ibid.;* Ecclus. 43:17). Its value as a source of moisture to the ground was recognized (Isa. 55:10). Men took advantage of it in summer to cool their beverages (cf. Prov. 25:13). Clean snow would yield pure water for washing purposes (Job 9:30).

So (sō). King of Egypt, whose aid against Assyria Hoshea, king of Israel, endeavored to secure about 724 B.C. (II Kings 17:4). As the Heb. consonants may be pronounced Sewe', he is commonly identified, and doubtless correctly, with Sib'e, tartan of Egypt, who in 720 B.C. in alliance with Ḥanunu, king of Gaza, met Sargon, king of Assyria, in battle at Raphia on the Mediterranean, about 20 miles s. of Gaza. The allies were routed, Sib'e fled, Ḥanunu was captured, and presently Pharaoh paid tribute to Assyria. It is doubtful whether Sib'e was Shabako, king of Egypt. At this time at least he was tartan rather than Pharaoh.

Soap. Not the composition famliiar in modern domestic use. The Heb. words *bōr* and *bōrith*, that which cleanses, denote an alkali. It was used for washing the person (Job 9:30, R.V. marg., lye; Jer. 2:22), for washing clothes (Mal. 3:2), and as a flux in smelting ores (Isa. 1:25, R.V. marg., lye). The Greek translators regarded it as a plant or obtained from a plant, for they represented it by the Gr. word *poa,* grass, grass-like plant. The root of the soapwort (*Saponaria officinalis*) is largely used in Palestine for washing linens, because it does not cause them to shrink. The employment of the alkali for smelting purposes indicates that it was in the form of ashes. It was doubtless obtained from such plants as the glasswort (*Salicornia fruticosa*) and the saltwort (*Salsola kali*), which are to this day reduced to ashes for the soda which they yield.

So'co (sō'kō) and **So'coh** (sō'kō), according to the alternate Heb. orthography; in A.V. variously spelled **So'coh**, **So'cho** (sō'kō), **So'choh** (sō'kō), **Sho'cho**, **Sho'choh**, **Sho'co** [thorn, hedge of thorns]. 1. A town in the Shephelah or lowland of Judah (Josh. 15:35). It stood on the hilly border of the valley of Elah, in a strong position isolated from the rest of the ridge. The Philistines pitched between it and Azekah just before Goliath stood forth as their champion (I Sam. 17:1). It was rebuilt or refortified by Rehoboam (II Chron. 11:7). It was captured, with the dependent villages, in the reign of Ahaz (ch. 28:18). Robinson successfully identified it with Khirbet Shuweikeh, 13 miles w. by s. of Bethlehem.

2. A town in the hill country of Judah (Josh. 15:48). Its site is found at another Khirbet Shuweikeh, 10 miles s.s.w. of Hebron.

It is doubtful which of the 2 towns is referred to in I Kings 4:10 and I Chron. 4:18.

So'di (sō'dī) [one in the secret or familiar council (of Jehovah)]. Father of the spy from the tribe of Zebulun (Num. 13:10).

Sod'om (sŏd'ŭm), in A.V. of N.T. once **Sod'o•ma** (sŏd'ō-má) (Rom. 9:29). One of the 5 cities in the Plain of the Jordan (Gen. 13:10). When Lot separated from Abraham, he chose it for his residence, though even then the place was notorious for its wickedness (vs. 11–13). It was plundered by Chedorlaomer (ch. 14:11), but the goods and captives were recovered by Abraham and restored (vs. 21–24). Subsequently it and at least 3 other cities of the Plain were destroyed by God on account of their wickedness. God probably effected his purpose by causing an eruption of burning asphalt and sulphur. Lot and his 2 daughters were spared (Gen. 19:1–29; Deut. 29:23; Isa. 1:9, 10; 3:9; 13:19; Jer. 49:18; 50:40; Lam. 4:6; Ezek. 16:46–56; Amos 4:11; Zeph. 2:9; Matt. 10:15; 11:24; Luke 10:12; 17:29; Rom. 9:29; II Peter 2:6; Jude 7). In the Apocalypse the great city of sin is spiritually called Sodom and Egypt (Rev. 11:8).

The exact site of Sodom is unknown. Two arguments may be advanced for the n. end of the Plain: 1. From a point near Beth-el, Abraham and Lot could see all the Plain of Jordan (cf. Gen. 13:3 with v. 10). Care must be exercised, however, in interpreting the word "all." 2. Chedorlaomer, coming from the s., had smitten the Amorites of Hazezon-tamar, i.e., En-gedi, before he was opposed by the king of Sodom and his allies (ch. 14:7, 8), a fact which seems to indicate that the meeting took place between En-gedi and the n. end of the sea. On the other hand, scholars favor the s. end, for which there are 3 weighty arguments: 1. Asphalt is found in large quantities only at the s. end of the Dead Sea (cf. Gen. 14:10). 2. Assuming that the sea covers the site (cf. ch. 14:3), the cities might have been situated at the s. end, where the water of the bay has a depth of from 2 to 20 feet, but could not have been in the n. part, where the sea is from 600 to 1,000 feet deep. The shallow s. basin of the Dead Sea has been encroaching on its shores steadily for the past century, during which its area has increased fully ⅓. 3. Zoar, 1 of the cities (ch. 13:10), lay at the s. end of the sea (Jos. *War* iv. 8, 4).

For the vine of Sodom, see VINE OF SODOM.

Sod'om•ite (sŏd'ŭm-īt). A person guilty of sodomy, the unnatural vice of Sodom (Gen. 19:5). The word renders Heb. *ķādēsh*, one consecrated, a man dedicated to impure heathen worship. A woman thus dedicated practiced uncleanness as a priestess in the service of Ashtoreth or Asherah in Canaan, of Ishtar in Babylonia (Gen. 38:21, 22; Hos. 4:14). Sodomy was forbidden by the Mosaic Law (Deut. 23:17); but sodomites were found in Judah during the reign of Rehoboam (I Kings 14:24); Asa and Jehoshaphat cut them off (chs. 15:12; 22:46); but others arose in their place, and Josiah, to rid the land of them, broke down their houses (II Kings 23:7).

So•journ'er, in A.V. and sometimes in R.V. **Stran'ger.** See STRANGER.

Sol'o•mon (sŏl'ō-mŭn) [peaceable]. David's youngest son, at least by Bath-sheba (II Sam. 12:24; I Chron. 3:5; and cf. Jos. *Antiq.* vii. 14, 2). He was born at Jerusalem. David named him Solomon, "peaceable," in anticipation of the peace and quietness of his reign in contrast with his own stormy life (I Chron. 22:9); but through the Prophet Nathan he was divinely honored with the name Jedidiah, "beloved of Jehovah" (II Sam. 12:25). When David was old and feeble, Adonijah, one of his sons born at Hebron, and probably the eldest now that Amnon and Absalom were dead, planned to rule independently of his father's sanction; but the design was thwarted by the Prophet Nathan with the aid of Zadok the priest and Benaiah the military commander, supported by David's bodyguard. Solomon was proclaimed king (I Kings 1:5–40), and the party of Adonijah at once collapsed. David soon afterward died, and Solomon began his sole reign about the year 970 B.C., being at the time probably about 20 years old. Obedient to the dying charge of his father, he dealt out justice to Abiathar and Shimei; and when Adonijah began anew to plot against the king, he put him to death and ordered the execution of Joab likewise, who was implicated in the conspiracy (ch. 2:1–46). The young king soon brought to Jerusalem Pharaoh's daughter (ch. 3:1) as his queen. At that time the worship at the sanctuary, which had been broken up when the Lord forsook Shiloh, was still interrupted. The tabernacle was at Gibeon and the Ark at Jerusalem. The people worshiped at high places. Solomon went to Gibeon to sacrifice. There God appeared to him in a dream by night and bade him ask for anything he chose. He asked for an understanding heart, that he might be able justly to judge the people of God, for it was part of a king's duty in those days to administer justice. His request was granted, as he soon afterward showed by the skillful manner in which he disentangled truth from falsehood when he decided between the 2 women, each of whom claimed the living babe as her own (I Kings 3:2–28; II Chron. 1:3–12). Twenty or more years later the Lord appeared to him again, conditionally promised to continue the throne in Solomon's own line, and gave him solemn warning (I Kings 9:1–10; II Chron. 7:12–22).

His father had subdued the neighboring nations. Against Hamath only is it recorded that Solomon went to war. He was obliged to control that city in order to secure the n.e. portion of his dominions. Hadad the Edomite and Rezon of Damascus were hostile to Solomon, but the Hebrew monarch probably gave himself but little concern about them. He fortified Hazor at the crossing of the upper Jordan and built a tower in Lebanon, in order to hold Damascus in check, and saw to it that the road by Edom to Ezion-geber was open and safe. Otherwise Solomon's relations with neighboring kings were friendly, and he was able to devote himself to the organization of his kingdom and to the arts of peace.

David had amassed a great store of precious metals for the construction of a magnificent temple to Jehovah. Solomon took up the work, and with Tyrian help finished the Temple in 7 years (I Kings, chs. 5; 6). Then, after furniture had been made for it, it was dedicated (I Kings 7:13 to 8:66; II Chron., chs. 2 to 7). Next, the monarch erected a palace for himself, which took 13 years in building (I Kings 7:1–12); see PALACE. He also fortified and built cities in various parts of the country (ch. 9:17–19, R.V.; II Chron. 8:4–6, R.V.).

Solomon showed sagacity in government. He surrounded himself with eminent officials, among whom the son of the high priest held the 1st place (I Kings 4:2–6). He maintained the army at full strength. For administrative purposes he divided the kingdom into 12 districts, entirely independent of the old tribal lines (vs. 7–19). Nor did he fail to take a prominent part in the religion of the state. He led the nation in prayer at the dedication of the Temple, and invoked the divine blessing upon the assembled multitude.

Commerce flourished in his kingdom, and brought wealth (I Kings 10:14–29; II Chron. 9:13–27); and voyages were successfully made to Ophir and traffic was conducted with India (I Kings 10:22, 23; II Chron. 9:10–22). For the protection and fostering of trade, he built store cities, among others Palmyra, in the desert midway between Damascus and the Euphrates.

Solomon was interested in literary pursuits: he was a naturalist and wrote treatises on plants, "from the cedar that is in Lebanon even unto the hyssop that springeth out of the wall: he spake also of beasts, and of birds, and of creeping things, and of fishes" (I Kings 4:33). He collected and composed many proverbs, some of which constitute part of the O.T.; see PROVERBS, THE. Two psalms (Psalms 72; 127) are attributed to him by their titles. See also ECCLESIASTES and SONG OF SOLOMON.

The splendor of his court, the magnificence of his table, and his pomp when on excursions corresponded to his wealth and political power (I Kings 10:4, 5, 21). People came from all parts to hear his wisdom (I Kings 4:34; 10:23–25). The report of his wisdom was carried even to s. Arabia, and the queen of Sheba journeyed to Jerusalem to test it and to see his magnificence (ch. 10:1–13).

Solomon erred in 2 respects. He established a harem, which included from 1st to last about 1,000 members. Doubtless not a few of these were hostages, princesses given him as pledges of political amity. Now many of these women were foreigners by birth and idolatrous in their religion, and he allowed himself to be persuaded by them to erect idol shrines (I Kings 11:1–8). For this apostasy Solomon was punished. The kingdom in its great extent and power was taken from the dynasty and only a fragment of it left to the family (vs. 9–13). The example of Solomon's disloyalty to Jehovah had direct influence in producing this penal result. Also influential to this end was the announcement by the Prophet Ahijah to Jeroboam that God would rend 10 tribes from Solomon and give them to him (vs. 28–39). Jeroboam became a recognized opponent of the king; but not until Solomon's son Rehoboam ascended the throne did Jeroboam secure a kingdom. A 2d less obvious yet an important error was Solomon's luxury, which imposed a burden on his overtaxed subjects, shook their loyalty to the throne, and sowed the seeds of future rebellion. See REHOBOAM.

Solomon reigned 40 years, dying about 931 B.C. The events of his life and reign were recorded in the Book of the Acts of Solomon, the History of Nathan the Prophet, the Prophecy of Ahijah the Shilonite, the Visions of Iddo the Seer (I Kings 11:41–43; II Chron. 9:29–31).

Sol'o·mon's (sŏl'ô-mŭnz) **Porch.** A splendid colonnade, reputed to have been built by Solomon, on the e. side of the Temple area, on an artificial embankment built up from the valley of the Kidron (Jos. *Antiq.* xx. 9, 7; *War* v. 5, 1). It is once mentioned that Christ walked in it (John 10:23); and the apostles were not infrequently there (Acts 3:11; 5:12).

Sol'o·mon's Serv'ants. Certain persons whose descendants were associated with the Nethinim, 390 or 392 of the 2 classes combined returning with Zerubbabel from the Captivity (Ezra 2:55–58; Neh. 7:57–60). Some of their names have a foreign aspect. They seem to have been the descendants of those Canaanites of various tribes from whom Solomon exacted bond service for the sake of the Temple and other magnificent buildings (I Kings 5:13–18; 9:21). See NETHINIM.

Sol'o·mon's Song. See SONG OF SOLOMON.

Sol'o·mon, Wis'dom of. See APOCRYPHA.

Son. 1. A male child; an immediate male descendant (Gen. 27:1). Other prominent significations follow.

2. A remoter male descendant. For instance, Jehu, son of Nimshi, was really Nimshi's grandson, for he was the son of Jehoshaphat, the son of Nimshi (cf. II Kings 9:20 with v. 2). The Israelites were known as sons or children of Israel or Jacob centuries after the death of the Patriarch (Mal. 3:6; Luke 1:16).

3. A person received into filial relation by adoption or marriage (Ex. 2:10).

4. A kindly form of address used by an elderly man to a younger friend (Josh. 7:19; I Sam. 3:6, 16; 4:16; II Sam. 18:22).

5. Member of a guild or profession, as son of the apothecaries (Neh. 3:8, in R.V. one), sons of the singers (ch. 12:28), sons of the prophets (II Kings 2:3, 5; cf. Amos 7:14). Worshiper of a god, as the sons of Chemosh (Num. 21:29).

6. Inhabitant of a city or country, as sons of Zion (Lam. 4:2), sons of Javan (Gen. 10:4).

7. Possessor of a quality, as son of Belial or worthlessness (I Sam. 25:17, A.V.), son of strength, i.e., a valiant man (I Sam. 14:52), son of peace (Luke 10:6).

Son of God. A title of the Messiah (Ps. 2:7; John 1:49); in its deepest sense expressive of the mysterious relation existing between the eternal Father and the eternal Son. In the Revised Version of the New Testament the designation Son of God is used about 45 times, in about 44 unequivocally denoting our Lord (Matt. 4:3, 6; 16:16; 26:63; 27:43; Mark 1:1; etc.), and in the remaining 1 characterizing Adam (Luke 3:38). In John 3:18 Christ is called the only begotten Son of God. Two reasons are suggested for the appellation: his eternal generation (Heb. 7:3), and his miraculous birth by the operation of the Holy Spirit (Luke 1:35). As Son of God, Christ is God with all the infinite perfections of the divine essence (John 1:1–14; 10:30–38; Phil. 2:6), and is equal with God (John 5:17–25). He is subordinate in mode of subsistence and operation; that is, he is of the Father, is sent by the Father, and the Father operates through him (John 3:16, 17; 8:42; Gal. 4:4; Heb. 1:2). Accordingly, the word "Son" is not a term of office, but of nature. He has the same nature, a fact which includes equality with God.

The claim was put forth by our Lord (Luke 22:70, R.V. marg.; John 5:17–47; 10:36; 11:4), and urged by the apostles (Acts 9:20; Gal. 2:20; I John 3:8; 5:5, 10, 13, 20), and it was for maintaining it that he was condemned by the sanhedrin on a charge of blasphemy (Matt. 26:63–66; Mark 14:61–64); but the justice of his claim had been acknowledged on the occasion of his baptism by the descent upon him of the Holy Spirit, accompanied by an audible utterance from his heavenly Father (Matt. 3:16, 17; Mark 1:10, 11; Luke 3:22; John 1:32–34). It was similarly acknowledged at the transfiguration (Matt. 17:5; Mark 9:7; Luke 9:35; II Peter 1:17). It was sustained by his character and by his works (John 1:14; 10:36–38; Heb. 1:3). And he "was declared to be the Son of God with power, according to the spirit of holiness, by the resurrection from the dead" (Rom. 1:4), and by his ascension (Heb. 1:3).

In 1 passage of the O.T. the expression Son of God appears (Dan. 3:25, A.V.), but the R.V. alters this to a son of the gods. The speaker was a Babylonian heathen.

For the title "sons of God" applied to men, see SONS OF GOD.

Son of Man. A person possessed of humanity in distinction from divinity and the brute nature; a human being, with the emphasis on human (Num. 23:19; Job 25:6; Ps. 8:4; Isa.

51:12) ; see Son 7. When Daniel fell frightened on his face before the heavenly messenger, Gabriel addressed him as son of man (Dan. 8:17). When Ezekiel had seen the vision of Jehovah and fallen upon his face, a voice said: "Son of man, stand upon thy feet" (Ezek. 2:1), and thenceforth the prophet is constantly addressed as son of man. It was foretold (Dan. 7:13, 14, R.V.) that the hostile worldly power, represented by beasts, shall succumb before the Ancient of Days, and "one like unto a son of man," coming with the clouds of heaven, shall receive dominion and a kingdom, that all the peoples, nations, and languages shall serve him ; "his dominion is an everlasting dominion, which shall not pass away, and his kingdom \that which shall not be destroyed." This figure seen in vision, a human being in contrast with the beasts that typified the kingdoms of the world, symbolized the saints of God in their corporate aspect, to whom universal and everlasting dominion shall be given (cf. v. 14 with v. 27).

The title was adopted by our Lord, evidently with reference to Dan. 7:13, 14, 27 (Matt. 24:30; Mark 14:62). He is recorded in the Gospels as having applied it to himself 78 times. It is also used of him by Stephen (Acts 7:56); cf. Heb. 2:6; Rev. 1: 13 ; 14:14. Christ did not choose the title to assert that he had a fellow feeling for man and was a brother to all men ; nor did he employ it to denote that he was a mere man and not divine, for he constantly claimed divine attributes (Luke 5:24). He chose a title which, by reason of its several possible interpretations, until fully defined by Jesus himself, could not be used against him by his foes. By it: 1. He identified himself with that human being in Daniel's vision who receives a universal and everlasting dominion (Dan. 7:14 ; cf. Matt. 16:28 ; 28:18). 2. He identified himself with the saints of the Most High, regarded collectively as a people, which the human figure in the vision symbolized, making himself their embodiment and their representative before God (Dan. 7:13, 27 ; cf. Matt. 25:31, 40 ; Mark 10:45 "a ransom for many" ; Luke 12:8, 9). 3. He assumed for himself the sufferings and the glory that should follow which were predicted for that human kingdom in its efforts to establish itself and overcome the world (Dan. 7:21, 22, 25 ; cf. Matt. 17:22, 23 ; Luke 9:26 ; 18: 31–33). 4. He implied that he will come with the clouds of heaven to receive the Kingdom (Dan. 7:13 ; cf. Matt. 24:30 ; 26:64). 5. He emphasized the human and humane in contrast with the brutal and bestial (Dan. 7:3– 9, 13 ; cf. Matt. 25:31 with vs. 35, 36 ; Mark 10:45 "minister, and to give his life" ; Luke 19:10).

Son of Man and Son of God are united in the same person. "Who do men say that the Son of man is? . . . Simon Peter answered and said, Thou art the Christ, the Son of the living God. And Jesus answered and said unto him, Blessed art thou, Simon Bar-Jonah: for flesh and blood hath not revealed it unto thee, but my Father who is in heaven" (Matt. 16:13, 16, 17). "The high priest said unto him, I adjure thee by the living God, that thou tell us whether thou art the Christ, the Son of God. Jesus saith unto him, Thou hast said: nevertheless I say unto you, Henceforth ye shall see the Son of man sitting at the right hand of Power, and coming on the clouds of heaven" (Matt. 26:63, 64).

Song. A poetical composition, generally brief, capable of being set to music and sung, whether or not it was intended for singing or was ever actually sung (Ex. 15:1–18 ; Deut. 31:30 to 32:44). It was often sung to the

accompaniment of music (Ex. 15:20, 21 ; Isa. 38:20). It might be secular or religious (Gen. 31:27 ; Num. 21:17, 18 ; Psalm 92, title; 137:3, 4) ; in praise of men or of God (I Sam. 18:6, 7 ; Ps. 28:7) ; the expression of light-heartedness or deep emotion ; the utterance of innocent mirth or the outcome of a bacchanalian revel (Ps. 69:12).

Song of Sol'o·mon (sŏl'ō-mŭn), **The.** The last of the 5 poetical books of the O.T. in our present English Bible, an arrangement derived from the LXX. In the Hebrew Scriptures the Song stands between Job and Ruth, in the Writings (Hagiographa), or 3d section of the canon, and is the 1st of the 5 smaller rolls (Megilloth), which formed a group by themselves because they had come to be read on the 5 great anniversaries. The Song was read on the 8th day of the passover festival, the book being allegorically interpreted with reference to the history of the Exodus. The Song of Solomon is more fully called "The Song of songs, which is Solomon's" (S. of Sol. 1:1). The reduplication of the word song has superlative force, like servant of servants, Lord of lords, heaven of heavens, vanity of vanities (Gen. 9:25 ; Deut. 10:17 ; I Kings 8:27 ; Eccl. 1:2), and intimates that the production is a song of the highest character. In the Vulgate the title is literally translated *Canticum Canticorum,* from which the name Canticles is derived.

Several speakers take part in the dialogue. The distinction between them is quite clear in the Hebrew original, because the grammatical forms indicate gender. The R.V. marks change of speaker by space between the verses or sections. How many prominent personages are there in the poem? Are there 2, besides the daughters of Jerusalem, who resemble the chorus in a Greek play ; or are there 3, either actually speaking or introduced in the remarks of the Shulammite maid? According to the latter view, or shepherd theory, in its general form, the 3 chief speakers are a country maid, her rustic lover, and Solomon. The maid is betrothed to her country swain ; but she is noticed by Solomon and his companions during some journey to the n. (ch. 6:10–13), brought to Jerusalem, and there, surrounded by the women of the palace, wooed by the king in the hope of gaining her affections. But the maid resists all enticements. When Solomon praises her, she responds by praising her rustic lover. She longs for him by day, and dreams of him by night. She sustains her devotion to him by recalling his speeches. She is true to him and to her vows. At length the parted lovers are reunited (ch. 8:5–7), and she is praised by her brothers for resisting all allurements. Throughout Solomon appears in an unfavorable light. He attempts to persuade the maid to forsake her proper allegiance (ch. 7:1–9). The poem, according to this view, celebrates a pure affection, which holds out against the temptations of a court, and is strong enough to resist the seductive arts of a king.

Many scholars have regarded the book as a collection of nuptial songs. In 1861 Wetzstein studied the marriage customs of a tribe living n. of Damascus. There in the first 7 days after their marriage the peasant couple play the part of king and queen, and they are treated as such by the community. These weddings generally are held in March. The threshing board is turned into a mock throne ; songs are sung by the friends of the bride and groom, in which a description of the physical beauty of the couple holds a prominent place. While numerous parallels are apparent, there are difficulties in the theory, and it does not explain the unity of the poem.

Instead of regarding the Shulammite as a country girl, some interpreters see in her the daughter of Pharaoh whom Solomon married. She is a stranger, dark of complexion, and a prince's daughter (chs. 1:5; 7:1). The blackness of skin, however, was due to sunburn (ch. 1:6), and the title of prince's daughter probably does not indicate her birth, which was apparently lowly, but her present high rank to which she has been raised (cf. ch. 6:12). According to this view the poem occupies an intermediate position between the dramatic and lyric conceptions of the book.

The Song has been regarded as a drama by many interpreters, but few have imagined that it was designed for presentation on the stage. It has been thought to consist of 4 acts (Ewald at 1st, Friedrich), or of 5 acts containing from 13 to 15 scenes (Ewald, Böttcher, and others), or of 6 acts with 2 scenes each (Delitzsch, Hahn). Bossuet discovered 7 acts, each filling a day, concluding with the Sabbath, inasmuch as the bridegroom on this day does not, as usual, go forth to his rural employments. His several days are: chs. 1:1 to 2:6; 2:7–17; 3:1 to 5:1; 5:2 to 6:9; 6:10 to 7:11; 7:12 to 8:3; 8:4–14.

Delitzsch follows the traditional view that there are but 2 main characters by whom the dialogue is sustained: Solomon and the Shulammite maiden; his scheme is as follows: Act I. Mutual passion of the lovers (chs. 1:2 to 2:7), concluding with "I adjure you, O daughters of Jerusalem." The scene is laid in the palace of Solomon. Scene 1. Dialogue between the Shulammite maid and the court ladies, daughters of Jerusalem (ch. 1:2–8). Scene 2. Enter Solomon: dialogue between him and the maiden, who is not yet his bride (chs. 1:9 to 2:7). Act II. Mutual seeking and finding (chs. 2:8 to 3:5), concluding with "I adjure you." The scene is the Shulammite's country home. Scene 1. She relates a rapturous meeting with Solomon (ch. 2:8–17). Scene 2. She relates a dream, in which she thought she had lost her beloved, but found him again (ch. 3:1–5). Act III. Bringing the betrothed to the capital and the marriage (chs. 3:6 to 5:1), with the introduction, "Who is this?" and the conclusion, "Eat, O friends; drink, yea, drink abundantly, O beloved." Scene 1. Procession to the palace (ch. 3:6–11). Scene 2. Dialogue between Solomon and his betrothed (ch. 4:1–16). The wedding must be supposed to follow; and then ch. 5:1, Solomon's morning greeting to his bride, and afterward his exhortation to the guests. Act IV. Love disdained, but regained (chs. 5:2 to 6:9). Scene 1. Shadows fall on the married life. The Shulammite dreams of seeking her beloved, but finding him not (chs. 5:2 to 6:3). Scene 2. She has found her beloved again (ch. 6:4–9). Act V. The Shulammite the beautiful but humble princess (chs. 6:10 to 8:4), with the introduction, "Who is she?" and the conclusion, "I adjure you." Scene 1. In the royal gardens; dialogue between the Shulammite and the daughters of Jerusalem (chs. 6:10 to 7:5). Scene 2. In the palace; Solomon and the Shulammite alone (chs. 7:6 to 8:4). Act VI. The confirmation of love's bond in the Shulammite's old home (ch. 8:5–14), beginning "Who is this?" Scene 1. Solomon and his bride appear in the presence of her kinsfolk (ch. 8:5–7). Scene 2. The Shulammite in her paternal home; dialogue between her and her brothers and the king (vs. 8–14).

A later and more probable view, accepted by the majority of modern critics and commentators, is that there are 3 principal characters: Solomon, a beautiful Shulammite maiden, and her shepherd-lover. This was developed by Ewald and appears in outline

as follows: Act I. Scene 1. The Shulammite, longing for her absent shepherd-lover, complains that she is detained in the royal palace against her will (ch. 1:2–7). Ironical reply of the court ladies (v. 8). Scene 2 (chs. 1:9 to 2:7). Solomon seeks to win the Shulammite's love. In ch. 2:5, 6 she sinks down in a fit of half-delirious sickness; in v. 7 she reminds the court ladies that love is a spontaneous affection and entreats them not to excite it in Solomon's favor. Act II. Scene 1 (ch. 2:8–17). The maiden recounts a scene from her past life, when her shepherd-lover visited her in her rural home. In vs. 16, 17 she declares her present unaltered devotion to him and expresses the hope that the separation may soon be at an end. Scene 2 (ch. 3:1–5). The Shulammite narrates a dream which she recently had in the royal palace; she had gone in search of her absent lover through the city and found him. Verse 5 repeats the refrain of ch. 2:7. Act III. Scene 1 (ch. 3:6–11). Citizens of Jerusalem assembled in front of one of the gates; in the distance a royal pageant is seen approaching. Solomon is in the palanquin, wearing the crown which his mother gave him on his wedding day. The purpose is to dazzle the rustic maiden with the sense of the honor of becoming the king's bride. Scene 2 (ch. 4:1–7). Solomon, the maiden, and the court ladies. Solomon seeks to win the maiden's love. Scene 3 (chs. 4:8 to 5:1). The Shulammite and the ladies. The maiden and her lover in ideal interview. Scene 4 (ch. 5:2–8). The maiden's 2d dream. This time she sought him in vain in the city, and with the memory of her dream she makes a fresh avowal of her love. Act IV. Scene 1 (chs. 5:9 to 6:3). The court ladies are surprised at the Shulammite's persistent rejection of Solomon's advances and her devotion to one absent. Scene 2 (ch. 6:4–13). The king's renewed endeavor to win the maiden's affection; he praises her beauty and describes the honor in store for her. Scene 3 (ch. 7:1–9). Solomon's final endeavor to gain the Shulammite's heart. Scene 4 (chs. 7:10 to 8:4). Heedless of the king's admiration, the maiden declares her unswerving devotion to her shepherd-lover. Act V. (ch. 8:5–14). The shepherds of Shulem see the maiden leaning on her lover's arm. She declares that she has fulfilled her brothers' best expectations. In v. 13 the shepherd asks his love for a song; she responds in v. 14, inviting him to join her over the hills.

But the opinion that the Song is a drama, although widely entertained in modern times and unobjectionable in itself, has not failed to meet with decided opposition. The Song does not naturally conform to the rules of dramatic unity. A regular plot is not yielded by the poem itself. A consecutive narrative can be made out only by supplying connecting links of which the poem gives no indication. The several parts have been made to tell very different continuous tales, according as interpreters have supplied this or that connecting link. The several scenes are grouped rather than linked, and the transitions are abrupt. The arrangement may not be pleasing to the Occidental mind, which loves order and logical sequence, but the structure of the poem is in entire harmony with Oriental methods of literary composition. On account of the variety of subjects and situations, repetitions and parallels and lack of logical order some critics consider the book an anthology of love lyrics and related poems rather than a collection of songs for a specific purpose, or a single lyrical or dramatic poem.

Three leading methods of interpretation have been adopted, and all still find advocates: the allegorical, the literal, and the typical methods. The Jews, who have always greatly prized The Song of Solomon, have generally regarded it as a spiritual allegory. Its sole intention was to teach God's love for ancient Israel. He is the Lover, and it the one beloved. The allegorical interpretation was introduced into the Christian Church by Hippolytus of Rome in his commentary written early in the 3d century A.D. Origen, who lived in Palestine, a somewhat younger contemporary of Hippolytus, is the classic Christian commentator on the Song, having left a commentary in 5 books. Christ became the Lover, and his Church or the individual soul the beloved one. The details of this scheme may be learned from the headings of the several chapters in the A.V. The mystical or allegorical interpretation has found support among scholars who noted parallels in the Sufic literature in Islam. On the literal interpretation the poem is a historical tale, a true story of Solomon's love for the Shulammite. The typical interpretation, to a certain extent, harmonizes the other two. The pure, spontaneous, mutual love of a great king and a humble maid was seen to exemplify the mutual affection between Jehovah and his people, and the story was told, not merely because it was beautiful, but chiefly because it was typical of this great religious truth. The Song of Solomon is thus analogous to Messianic psalms, which are based on the personal experiences or official position of David or Solomon, and exhibit truths regarding the great king. The comparison of the mutual love between the Church and its divine Head to that of a bride and a bridegroom frequently occurs in the N.T. (Eph. 5:25–33; Rev. 19:7–9; 21:9; etc.).

During the years 1922–1924, however, the allegorical interpretation was revived in a pagan guise by attempting to find in the book remnants of an early fertility cult taken over by the Hebrews from the agricultural Canaanites on their settlement in Canaan. Such a view supposes that the Song consists of songs written originally in the cult language of the liturgies used in the worship of Tammuz (Adonis), that they were reinterpreted by the Hebrews, and that thus their original pagan significance was lost. According to this interpretation the poem would be one of the earliest of Hebrew compositions.

Regarding the date and authorship of the Song, it will be perceived at once that the shepherd theory disposes of the possibility that the poem proceeded from the pen of Solomon. This hypothesis requires the assumption of another and a later author than Solomon. Turning to the marks of authorship and date found in the poem, the title reads: "The Song of songs, which is Solomon's" (ch. 1:1). The words are ambiguous, according to the Hebrew idiom; they may mean either that Solomon was the author of the Song (cf. Hab. 3:1, Heb.), or that the Song is about Solomon (cf. Isa. 5:1, Heb.). The ambiguity is admitted, but tradition has attributed the poem to Solomon.

The Solomonic authorship, however, is no longer held even by conservative scholars; it is assumed that, at a time when the true origin of the Song was forgotten, it was attributed to Solomon because of references to him in the poem. The diction exhibits several peculiarities in the use of the relative *she*, which occurs also, among other places, in the song of Deborah. From the way in which Tirzah and Jerusalem are mentioned (S. of Sol. 6:4) Ewald and Hitzig concluded that it was written during the time that Tirzah was the capital of the Northern Kingdom (I Kings 14:17 to 16:24), i.e., in the 10th century B.C. But we find Tirzah mentioned afterward (II Kings 15:14, 16), and so this argument is not conclusive. The use of Tirzah may be only a literary reminiscence. The Aramaisms in the book may indicate that the work is late (postexilic). On the other hand, it may be early; in that case it would stem from northern Israel, the language of which differed dialectically from that of Judah. The purity and brightness of the style as well as the author's acquaintance with places in n. Palestine also suggest an early date. The foreign words, chiefly names of plants or articles of commerce, might have reached Palestine through Solomon's commercial relations with the East. It seems that the recollection of Solomon and of the pomp of his court are relatively fresh. If the poem was built upon a basis of fact, the dramatic form and the idyllic imagery were supplied by the poet.

Two words require special mention: *pardēs* (orchard, park, paradise) in S. of Sol. 4:13 is of Pers. origin (cf. Avestan *pairi-daēza*, an enclosure); *'appiryōn* (palanquin) in ch. 3:9 suggests Gr. *phoreion* (litter, palanquin). If these words are not editorial additions to an earlier work, the book would probably date from the Greek period, c. 300, or perhaps the first half of the 3d century B.C. On account of the Aramaisms and these 2 words many critics favor the late date. It should be borne in mind, however, that most of the book may have an early origin and that it may have received its final form from editors at a late date. At any rate the evidence for dating the poem is far from conclusive, and the spontaneity of the diction rather suggests an early date.

The Song of Solomon is a gem of literature; it became an authoritative thesaurus of word and thought for the mystic's vocabulary, and its place in the canon has approved itself to those souls who have known how to use it in an allegorical and mystical sense.

Sons of God. Worshipers and beneficiaries of God; there is reason to believe that this is its signification in the celebrated passage where it first appears in the Bible. "It came to pass, when men began to multiply on the face of the ground, and daughters were born unto them, that the sons of God saw the daughters of men that they were fair; and they took them wives of all that they chose" (Gen. 6:1, 2). Many commentators regard Gen. 6:1–4 as a kind of preface to the narrative of the Flood and consider it as an isolated survival of early Hebrew mythology. Accordingly in the infancy of the human race marriages were formed between supernatural beings and mortal women, and thus there arose heroes or demigods. The implication is (v. 4) that such beings, intermediate between the divine and the human, introduced an element of disorder into the world which had to be checked by the special intervention of Jehovah (v. 3).

Three well-known interpretations have been proposed. The sons of God are: 1. The great and noble of the earth, and the daughters of men are women of inferior rank (Samaritan version; Greek translation of Symmachus; Targums of Onkelos and Jonathan). 2. Angels, who left their first estate and took wives from among the children of men (certain MSS. of LXX, Book of Enoch, Philo, Josephus, Justin Martyr, Clement of Alexandria, Tertulian). 3. Pious men, worshipers of God, who were especially represented by the descendants of Seth. They were attracted by the beauty of women who did not belong to the godly line, married with them, and became secularized (Julius Africanus, Chrysostom, Cyril of Alexandria, Augustine, Jerome). The 1st interpretation no longer has any advocates. In favor of the 2d, it is asserted that the term denotes angels everywhere else in the O.T. (Job 1:6; 2:1; 38:7; cf. a similar expression Ps. 29:1; 89:6; R.V. marg.; but not Dan. 3:25); that the designation describes angels according to their nature, whereas the ordinary word for angels, mal'ăkim, messengers, refers to their official employment; and that this interpretation is confirmed by Jude 6 and II Peter 2:4. But that the term relates to the nature of angels lacks proof; it is quite as natural that it should describe angels as worshipers of God. As to the passages in Jude and Peter, to cite them is begging the question, since exegetes point out other references, as Isa. 24:21-23; moreover in Jude the word "these" in v. 7 and elsewhere does not refer to angels that kept not their own principality (v. 6, R.V.), but to certain ungodly men (v. 4). And unless the title be restricted to the special form which it has in the passage under discussion, it is not true that the term denotes angels in all other places where it occurs in the O.T. The worshipers of the heathen deity Chemosh are called the people of Chemosh, and his sons and daughters (Num. 21:29; Jer. 48:46). When the men of Judah, professed worshipers of Jehovah, took heathen women to wife, Judah was said to have married the daughter of a strange god (Mal. 2:11). Moses was directed to say to Pharaoh: "Thus saith the LORD, Israel is my son, . . . Let my son go" (Ex. 4:22, 23). Other passages are: "Ye are the children [or sons] of the LORD your God" (Deut. 14:1). "They have dealt corruptly with him [Jehovah], they are not his children [or sons]." "Is not he [Jehovah] thy father?" "The LORD saw it, and abhorred them, Because of the provocation of his sons and his daughters" (Deut. 32:5, 6, 19). "Ye are the sons of the living God" (Hos. 1:10). "When Israel was a child, . . . I . . . called my son out of Egypt" (Hos. 11:1). "Bring my sons from afar, and my daughters from the end of the earth; every one that is called by my name, and whom I have created for my glory" (Isa. 43:6, 7). The pious are the generation of God's children (Ps. 73:15), and Ephraim is his dear son (Jer. 31:20). Taking a broader survey, and examining Semitic literature other than Hebrew, one observes the same fact. Many a Babylonian styled himself the son of the god whom he worshiped and upon whom he relied for protection and care.

The interpretation that the sons of God in Gen. 6:2 were pious people, the worshipers of the true God, more especially that they were the godly descendants of Adam through Seth, whose genealogy is given in Gen., ch. 5, is not only in accordance with Semitic, and particularly Biblical, usage of the designation, as already shown, but it is consistent with the context. The sons of God are contrasted with the daughters of men, that is, of other men. So Jeremiah says that God set signs in Israel and among men; and the English version supplies the word "other" before men, in order to bring out the sense (Jer. 32:20). Likewise the psalmist says that the wicked "are not in trouble as men; neither are they plagued like men"; and again the English version supplies the word "other" (Ps. 73:5). After the same manner Gen. 6:1, 2 may perhaps be understood: "When mankind began to multiply on the face of the ground, and daughters were born unto them, the sons of God saw the daughters of other men that they were fair; and they took them wives of all that they chose." The meaning of the writer is that when men began to increase in number, the worshipers

of God so far degenerated that in choosing wives for themselves they neglected character, and esteemed beauty of face and form above piety. The offspring of these marriages were perhaps stalwart and violent (v. 4). Mixture of race in marriage often produces physical strength in the descendants, and lack of religion in the parents is apt to be reproduced in the children. The intermarriage of the sons of God and the daughters of men was offensive in the sight of God. Sentence was pronounced against the wrongdoers (v. 3). The penalty is not denounced against angels, who were not only implicated, but were the chief sinners, if the sons of God were angels. The punishment is pronounced against man only. Man, not angels, had offended.

Sons of God means the worshipers and beneficiaries of God, both among mortal and immortal beings. But the content of this idea did not remain the same through the ages. It became larger with increasing knowledge of the riches of God. It enlarged, for example, at the time when the Israelites were delivered from Egypt. God said: "I have surely seen the affliction of my people" (Ex. 3:7); and again: "Say unto Pharaoh, . . . Israel is my son, my firstborn"; this implies that Israel is as dear to God as Pharaoh's first-born is to him (cf. ch. 4:22 with v. 23); and again: "I will take you to me for a people, and I will be to you a God" (ch. 6:7). Heretofore the title had emphasized a filial relation of men to God, their dependence upon him for protection and care, and their duty of reverence and obedience. Now God formally accepts the obligations which implicitly devolve on him. The content of the title was further enlarged through the teaching of Jesus Christ. He took truths already known, shed light on them, and connected them with this designation. He exhibited the fact that God is an actual father and that his people are actual children of God. They are such by the new birth (John 3:3, 5, 6, 8), begotten of God (John 1:12, 13; 5:21; and so Eph. 2:5; James 1:18; I Peter 1:23), made partakers of the divine nature through the mediation of the indwelling Spirit (John 6:48-51; 15:4, 5), and possessing a like character with God, resembling him in holiness, love, and elevation above the illusions of earth (I John 3:9; 4:7; 5:4), although falling far short of the divine character in this life. They have been adopted as sons (Gal. 4:5), are taught by the Spirit to say "Abba, Father" (Gal. 4:6; Rom. 8:15), and are led by the Spirit (Rom. 8:14).

Sons of the Proph'ets. See PROPHETIC ASSOCIATIONS.

Sooth'say'er. A diviner (cf. Josh. 13:22, with Num. 22:7), one who prognosticates future events (Jer. 27:9, R.V.). As rendering of the Aram. gāzᵉrin, it denotes one who professed to be able to interpret dreams (Dan. 4:7) and explain dark sentences (chs. 4:9; 5:11, 12), and to whom men in desperation resorted to obtain, if possible, the revelation of secrets (ch. 2:27).

So'pa·ter (sō'pȧ-tẽr) [Gr., of sound parentage]. A Christian of Berea, and one of Paul's companions from Greece as far as the province of Asia, when the apostle was returning from his Third Missionary Journey (Acts 20:4). He was son of Pyrrhus (R.V.).

So·phe'reth (sō-fē'rĕth), in R.V. of Ezra Has·so·phe'reth, with the Heb. article [secretariat]. The name, probably denoting an office, belonging to a certain class of Solomon's servants. Members of it returned from captivity with Zerubbabel (Ezra 2:55; Neh. 7:57).

Sor'cer·er. One who practices sorcery, uses potions that derive a supposed efficacy from magical spells, and professes to possess supernatural power or knowledge, gained in any manner, especially through the connivance of evil spirits (Ex. 7:11; Jos. *Life* 31). Sorcerers were found in Egypt, Assyria (Nahum 3:4), Babylonia (Isa. 47:9; Dan. 2:2), and other heathen lands; but were strictly forbidden in Israel (Ex. 22:18), and warning was uttered against their deception (Jer. 27:9), and their punishment was foretold (Micah 5:12; Mal. 3:5; Rev. 21:8). The Heb. and Gr. words for sorcerer and sorcery are sometimes rendered witch and witchcraft. Simon, called Magus or magician, and Bar-Jesus were prominent sorcerers in apostolic history (Acts 8:9–24; 13:6–12). A sorceress, and likewise the sorcerer and the practicer of other forms of the black art, was not to be permitted to live (Ex. 22:18; Lev. 20:27; Deut. 18:10–12). God's own attitude toward such persons and those who consulted them was also one of destruction (Lev. 20:6, 23; Wisd. of Sol. 12:4–6).

So'rek (sō'rĕk) [a choice vine]. A valley in which Delilah lived (Judg. 16:4). It is doubtless Wadi eṣ-Ṣarār, which commences about 13 miles w., slightly s., of Jerusalem, and pursues a tortuous course in a n.w. direction toward the Mediterranean Sea. It is traversed by a stream which falls into the sea about 8½ miles s. of Joppa. The name Sūrik is still borne by a ruin n. of the valley, 2 miles from Zorah, Samson's birthplace.

So·sip'a·ter (sō-sĭp'ȧ-tẽr) [Gr., saving a father]. A Christian who joined with Paul in sending salutations (Rom. 16:21).

Sos'the·nes (sŏs'thĕ-nēz) [Gr., of sound strength]. A ruler of the Jewish synagogue at Corinth when Paul was there. In the outbreak which Paul's preaching excited, the crowd seized Sosthenes and beat him before the judgment seat of Gallio (Acts 18:17). Perhaps he became a Christian, for one Sosthenes is associated with Paul as a brother Christian in the salutation to the Corinthians (I Cor. 1:1).

So'tai (sō'tī). One of the class known as Solomon's servants. He founded a family, members of which returned with Zerubbabel from captivity (Ezra 2:55; Neh. 7:57).

Soul. In ordinary English usage, a spirit is an immaterial, incorporeal being, which may or may not be associated with a body, as "God is a Spirit," "My spirit hath rejoiced in God my Saviour" (John 4:24; Luke 1:47). A soul is also a spirit that is or at least has been embodied, as the souls of them that had been slain (Rev. 6:9).

Theologians entertain 2 main views as to the soul, and consequently as to the nature of man and irrational animals. One is embraced under the doctrine of trichotomy. Trichotomists differ considerably among themselves; but according to the doctrine, in its general outlines, man consists of 3 parts or essential elements, body, soul, and spirit (I Thess. 5:23). The body is the material part of man's constitution. The soul, in Heb. *nephesh*, in Gr. *psychē*, is the principle of animal life: man possesses it in common with the brutes; to it belong understanding, emotion, and sensibility, and it ceases to exist at death. The spirit, in Heb. *rūaḥ*, in Gr. *pneuma*, is the mind, the principle of man's rational and immortal life, the possessor of reason, will, and conscience. God created man by giving life to inorganic matter formed into a body, and then creating a rational spirit and infusing it (Gen. 2:7); at death the dust or body returns to the

earth as it was, and the spirit returns unto God who gave it (Eccl. 12:7). The soul of life (Heb. *nephesh ḥayyāh*, living soul), in the instance of the animal (Gen. 1:21, 24), is only the animal soul, which is physical and material in its nature, and perishes with the body of which it is the vital principle; but the soul of life in the instance of man (ch. 2:7) is a higher principle, the rational soul, which was inbreathed by the Creator and made in his image. Usually the Biblical writers do not distinguish the *psychē* or animal soul, which is the lower side of the human soul, from the *pneuma* or rational soul, the higher side, since they constitute one soul, *psychē*, in distinction from the body, and they are sometimes designated in their unity by *pneuma*, and sometimes by *psychē*. Commonly the sacred writers speak of man as constituted of body and soul, or body and spirit, and not of body, soul, and spirit; but in I Cor. 15:44, as in I Thess. 5:23 and Heb. 4:12, Paul requires the distinction between the animal and the rational soul for the purposes of his discussion, and he accordingly makes it.

According to dichotomy, on the other hand, there are only 2 essential elements in the constitution of man: the body formed from the dust of the earth, and the soul or principle of life (Gen. 2:7). The soul is the principle of the whole life of whatever subject is spoken of, whether man or beast. It is the principle of all life, physical, intellectual, moral, religious. There is not one substance, the soul, which feels and remembers, and another substance, the spirit, that has conscience and the knowledge of God. The soul of the brute is the living principle in the brute: it is conscious of the impressions which are made by external objects on the organs of sense belonging to the body; it is endowed with that measure of intelligence which experience shows the lower animals to possess, but it is irrational and mortal. Brutes perish because God does not will that the living principle in them should continue. The soul of man is the same in kind with that of the brute, but it differs in being of a higher order: in addition to the attributes of sensibility, memory, and instinct, it has the higher powers which pertain to the intellectual, moral, and religious life, and it has continued existence after the death of the body, not because of its inherent nature, but because God wills to preserve it. It is argued from the usage of words in Scripture in defense of this dualism that: 1. Living soul, *nephesh ḥayyāh*, means simply animate existence, a being in which there is a living soul, and there is no authority to make it mean one thing in the case of a brute and quite another thing in the case of a man. 2. The Bible does not ascribe a *psychē* only, and both a *psychē* and *pneuma* to man. The living principle in brutes is called spirit, *rūaḥ*, as well as soul, *nephesh*, *psychē*. "Who knoweth the spirit of man, whether it goeth upward, and the spirit of the beast, whether it goeth downward to the earth?" (Eccl. 3:21; cf. v. 19, R.V. marg.; Gen. 7:15). 3. No distinction is observed in the use of the words soul and spirit. The souls of them that were slain for the word of God are in heaven (Rev. 6:9; 20:4), and likewise the spirits of just men made perfect (Heb. 12:23).

Trichotomists quote I Thess. 5:23: "The God of peace himself sanctify you wholly; and may your spirit and soul and body be preserved entire, without blame at the coming of our Lord Jesus Christ" (cf. Heb. 4:12), as evidence that Paul distinguishes the animal soul from the rational spirit. But dichotomists reply that Paul's language is quite analogous to that employed in the command, "Thou shalt love the Lord thy God with all thy heart, and with all thy soul, and with all thy mind, and with all thy strength" (Mark 12:30; cf. Luke 1:46, 47). The intention in the demand for love, and in the prayer for preservation, is simply to lay stress on the whole man, and the description is accordingly plethoric. As heart, soul, strength, and mind are not so many essential elements in man's constitution, so there is no proof that body, soul, and spirit are. The main passage relied upon to support the trichotomist position is I Cor. 15:44: "It is sown a natural body; it is raised a spiritual body. If there is a natural body, there is also a spiritual body." Trichotomists interpret the *sōma psychikon* or natural body as one marked by the qualities of the *psychē* or animal soul; namely, by physical appetites and passions, such as hunger, thirst, and sexual appetite. These are founded in "flesh and blood," or that material substance of which the present human body is composed. The resurrection, or spiritual body, on the other hand, will be marked by the qualities of the *pneuma* or rational soul. It will not be composed of flesh and blood, but of a substance which is more like the rational than the animal soul. There is, however, another interpretation, not only in harmony with the doctrine of the dual constitution of man, but in accord with the general usage of the words *psychikos* and *pneumatikos*, natural and spiritual. The resurrection body of the redeemed will not be marked by the qualities of ordinary animal life, right and proper though that life is, but the resurrection body will be opposed to everything carnal, and will be characterized by the qualities which belong to the Spirit-led man. This appears from a study of the words. In established usage among the Greeks *psychē* was the common word for the vital principle; which, however, might be thought of as a disembodied soul, the immortal part of man, and the organ of thought and judgment (Herod. ii. 123; Plato *Timaeus*, 30B), hence *psychikos* referred primarily to the ordinary animal life, and is so used by Paul, James, and Jude (I Cor. 2:14; James 3:15; Jude 19). *Pneumatikos*, on the other hand, almost exclusively has reference in Scripture to the *Pneuma Hagion*, the Holy Spirit. It is opposed to carnal and fleshly, to human nature deprived of the Spirit of God; it refers to possession and control by the Holy Spirit as contrasted with the domination of the flesh (I Cor. 3:1); it denotes what is effected by the Spirit and pertains to the Spirit (Rom. 1:11; I Cor. 2:13; 12:1). Hence a spiritual body, contrasted with a natural body, is a body not only free from fleshly lusts, but elevated above the physical passions and appetites which are natural to man (Matt. 22: 30), in vital union with the Spirit of God, and marked by the qualities which characterize the Spirit-led man.

South, The. See NEGEB, THE.

South Ra'moth (rā'mŏth). See RAMAH 6.

Sow. See SWINE.

Sow'er and **Sow'ing.** Sowing began with the rain of October; see YEAR. The seed was required to be ceremonially clean (Lev. 11:37, 38). The sower held the vessel containing the seed in the left hand and scattered the seed with his right. When the soil was favorable, he seems sometimes to have cast in front of the plow, which then served the purpose of a harrow to cover the seed. Wheat was best sown, it was thought, in rows (Isa. 28:25, R.V.). The sowing of mixed seed was forbidden (Lev. 19:19; Deut. 22:9), as being

contrary to nature as established by the Creator; but the planting of several kinds of seeds in different sections of the same field was permitted.

Sowing the Seed

Spain (spān). The well-known country in the s.w. portion of Europe. Its mines yielded gold and silver (I Macc. 8:3). Paul desired to visit it (Rom. 15:24, 28), and probably carried out his intention, for Clement of Rome, writing from Italy about A.D. 96, says that Paul "reached the bounds of the west," and the Muratorian fragment, written about A.D. 170, states explicitly that he went to Spain. This visit must have taken place after Paul's imprisonment at Rome which is recorded in The Acts. See TARSHISH 1.

Spar'row. The rendering of Heb. *ṣippōr*, in Ps. 84:3; 102:7; and R.V. of Prov. 26:2. The word is more frequently translated bird; in fact, it is often employed as a general term for bird or fowl (Ps. 8:8; 148:10; Ezek. 17:23). It may be a bird of prey (Jer. 12:9; Ezek. 39:17), such as the raven and crow, which are passerine birds, although they feed on carrion; or it may be a bird ceremonially clean and large enough to be eaten as food (Lev. 14:4; Neh. 5:18). It may live in the mountains or in the town (Ps. 11:1; 84:3), and may build its nest in trees or on the ground or about human habitations (Deut. 22:6; Ps. 84:3). The term includes doves and pigeons (Gen. 15:9, 10), and the ety. indicates that in the first instance it designates chirping birds, like the sparrow and the finch. In the N.T. sparrow is the rendering of Gr. *strouthion*. It was sold and eaten (Matt. 10:29; Luke 12:6, 7).

The house sparrow (*Passer domesticus*), familiarly known as the English sparrow, is found through Europe, n. Africa, and w. Asia, and is common in the coast towns of Palestine. Two species of s. Europe, closely allied to it, the Italian sparrow (*Passer italiae*) and the marsh sparrow (*Passer hispaniolensis*), also occur, the latter chiefly in the Jordan Valley, where it breeds in vast numbers in the thorn trees. The tree sparrow (*Passer montanus*) is a near relative of the house sparrow, and perhaps in Palestine should not be separated from it; but the sparrows which frequent the sacred precincts on the Temple hill and are common on the Mount of Olives have sometimes been spoken by writers of authority as tree sparrows. Another sparrow (*Passer moabiticus*) is found in the vicinity of the Dead Sea, but is rare. The rock or

foolish sparrow (*Petronia stulta*) is common
on the central ridge of Palestine. It never
resorts to inhabited dwellings. Thomson says
that a sparrow which has lost its mate is
often seen sitting alone on the housetop,
lamenting its fate (cf. Ps. 102:7). Tristram
is inclined to see in this passage a reference
to the blue thrush (*Monticola cyanus*), a
solitary bird which perches on the housetop,
uttering meanwhile a monotonous and plaintive note.

Spar'tans (spär'tănz). Inhabitants of the
celebrated city of Sparta in Greece. It was
known also as Lacedaemon. Jonathan Maccabaeus refers to an ancient friendship which
existed between the Spartans and the Jews in
the days of King Arius and the high priest
Onias, about 300 B.C. (I Macc. 12:7, 19–23;
in A.V. Lacedemonians); and he sent letters
to them, when he sent an embassy to Rome,
to renew the friendship with them (vs. 2, 5).
Jonathan did not live to hear their answer,
but Simon received cordial letters from them
(ch. 14:16, 20–23).

Spear. The spear, called in Heb. *ḥănīth*,
consisted of a metallic head on a shaft (I
Sam. 13:19; 17:7; Isa. 2:4). It could be carried in the hand; stuck in the ground when
not wanted; and, though used for thrusting,
could be hurled (I Sam. 18:10, 11, in A.V.
javelin; 26:7, 8; II Sam. 2:23; John 19:34).

A long spear was used (Judg. 5:8; I Chron.
12:8, 24; Neh. 4:13; Jer. 46:4). It was called
rōmah by the Hebrews, and was used for
thrusting (Num. 25:7, 8, R.V.), not for
throwing. In R.V. it is once rendered lance
(I Kings 18:28); in A.V. lancet.

Spear'men. The rendering of the pl. of Gr.
Dexiolabos or, as in Codex Alexandrinus,
Dexiobolos in Acts 23:23, a body of troops
distinguished from the legionary soldiers and
the cavalry. In the only other passage where
the word occurs, which is late, they are distinguished from archers and targeteers. Evidently they were light-armed soldiers who
carried a weapon in the right hand.

Spelt. The revised rendering of Heb. *kussemeth* (Ex. 9:32 and Isa. 28:25, in A.V. rie;
Ezek. 4:9, in A.V. fitches). Spelt is an inferior kind of wheat, the chaff of which
slightly adheres to the grain. It was sown in

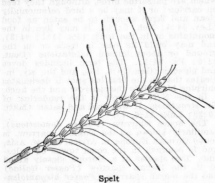

Spelt

Egypt, springing up after the barley. The
Egyptians made their bread of it (Herod. ii.
36). Rye is a n. plant, and is not grown in
Egypt and Palestine.

Spice. 1. The rendering of Heb. *bōšem*,
bešem, and its pl. *bešāmim*, which are used
generically for fragrant stuff, spice, spicery
(Ex. 25:6; I Kings 10:10; S. of Sol. 4:10, 14).
Spice is a vegetable substance possessing aromatic and pungent qualities (S. of Sol. 4:16).

The chief spices were myrrh, cinnamon, calamus, and cassia or costus (Ex. 30:23, 24).
Southern Arabia was the great, but not exclusive, producer of them (I Kings 10:2;
Ezek. 27:22). *Bōšem* in S. of Sol. 5:13; 6:2,
and *bāšām* in ch. 5:1, are probably applied
specifically to balsam or balm of Gilead (R.V.
marg.).

2. *Neꝉkō'th* (Gen. 37:25; 43:11) is probably
a specific term for tragacanth or storax (R.V.
marg.). A form of this word is perhaps used
in II Kings 20:13; Isa. 39:2 for spices in
general.

3. *Sammim*, fragrant odors, were aromatic
substances used in the preparation of incense
(Ex. 30:7). Three are specified: stacte or
opobalsamum, onycha, and galbanum (v. 34).

4. The rendering of Gr. *arōma*, a generic
term (Mark 16:1), including myrrh and aloes
(John 19:40).

Spice Mer'chant. The rendering of Heb.
rōkēl in I Kings 10:15. It means simply, as
the R.V. makes it, a merchant; and A.V.
renders it so elsewhere, e.g., Ezek. 27:13.

Spi'der. An animal of the class *Arachnida*,
called in Heb. *'akkābish*. It weaves a web
(Job 8:14; Isa. 59:5). The number of species
in Palestine amounts to 600 or 700. In A.V.
spider is the rendering of Heb. *semāmith*
(Prov. 30:28, in R.V. lizard).

Spike'nard. A fragrant plant, in Heb. *nērd*
(S. of Sol. 4:13, 14), from which an aromatic
ointment was made, called *nardos* in Gr.
(Mark 14:3). It is believed to be *Nardo-*

Spikenard (*Nardostachys jatamansi*)

stachys jatamansi, a plant of the Valerian
family, with fragrant roots, growing in the
Himalaya Mountains at an elevation of 11,000
to 17,000 feet. It was used by the Hindus as
a medicine and perfume from remote antiquity, and was early an article of commerce.
The long distance which it had to be brought
to Palestine rendered it on its arrival very
precious. The alabaster cruse of it, which was
poured over the head of Jesus, was worth 300
denarii (Mark 14:3, 5). In Mark 14:3; John
12:3 (see R.V. marg.), the spikenard is described by the Gr. adjective *pistikos*, a variant of *pistos*, genuine; less likely is the derivation from *pistos*, liquid. Some interpreters,

however, think that the adjective denotes the place where this variety was obtained.

Spin'ning. Spinning was the work of the women (Ex. 35:25). The wheel was unknown, and spinning was done by hand. Distaff and spindle were used (Prov. 31:19). The flax or wool was wound on the distaff, which was held under the arm or stuck upright in the ground, and the thread was drawn out by hand. To the end of this thread the spindle, with a circular rim to steady it when revolving, was attached and by rotating it the spinner twisted the thread.

Spir'it. See SOUL and HOLY SPIRIT.

Spring. See FOUNTAIN.

Sta'chys (stā'kĭs) [Gr., an ear of grain]. A Christian at Rome to whom the Apostle Paul sent a salutation (Rom. 16:9).

Stac'te. The rendering of Heb. *nāṭāph*, a drop. It denotes a sweet spice, which was used for incense (Ex. 30:34; cf. Ecclus. 24:15). The LXX interprets *nāṭāph* by *staktē*, which likewise signifies a drop or exudation, and was employed for the oil which trickles from fresh myrrh or cinnamon. It is believed, however, that *nāṭāph* is the gum of the storax tree, or else opobalsamum (R.V. marg.).

The storax (*Styrax officinalis*) is a resinous shrub or small tree, from 10 to 20 feet high,

Stacte (*Styrax officinalis*)

with flowers resembling those of the orange in color, size, and fragrance, and mostly growing in spikes of 4 or 5. The tree is very showy when in bloom. It is native in Asia Minor and Syria, and abounds in Galilee. The official storax is the inspissated juice of the bark; it is used medicinally as an expectorant, and also in perfumery. The liquid storax of commerce is the product of an entirely different plant.

Opobalsamum (R.V. marg.) is a resinous juice, also called balm and balm of Gilead (*q.v.*).

Star. The number of the stars and their grouping in constellations early attracted man's attention (Gen. 22:17). Orion, Pleiades, the Bear, the zodiac were pointed out (Job 9:9; 38:31, 32), planets were known and

named (see CHIUN, LUCIFER), perhaps meteors or comets are referred to (Jude 13), the position of certain stars served as dates (Jos. *Antiq.* xiii. 8, 2), and in Egypt the successive rising of 36 constellations marked off an equal number of 10-day periods in the year; see WEEK. The stars were recognized in Israel as the handiwork of God (Gen. 1:16; Ps. 8:3), and as under his control (Isa. 13:10; Jer. 31:35).

But among the heathen and the degenerate Israelites the stars became objects of worship (Deut. 4:19; II Kings 17:16); altars were reared, and incense was burnt to them (II Kings 21:5; 23:5). They were believed to exercise influence, not only in the ordinary economy of nature (cf. Job 38:31, A.V.; R.V. marg.), but also over the affairs of men. This belief was widespread among the heathen. Deborah may perhaps be using a phrase of current speech, in which a reminiscence of heathen notions lingers, when she poetically describes the stars from their courses fighting against Sisera (Judg. 5:20); but Bertheau is probably correct in understanding her to speak poetically of divine assistance (ch. 4:15), as if heaven or, to use her own words, as if the stars, forsaking their usual orbits, had fought against Sisera (cf. Ps. 18:9). A reference has also been seen in her words to a providential storm which discomfited the Canaanites; and Judg. 5:21 and Josephus (*Antiq.* v. 5, 4) are cited in confirmation: but Josephus probably deduces this storm from the analogy of Josh 10:10, 11 and I Sam. 7:10. The stars were also supposed by the heathen to portend coming events, and they were observed with a view to prognostication (Isa. 47:13). See ASTROLOGERS 1.

J. D. D. (rev., H. S. G.)

Several stars mentioned in the N.T. require particular notice:

1. *The day-star* (II Peter 1:19) is probably a figurative description of the signs immediately preceding the Second Advent. Others understand it as the Spirit's illumination of the believer's heart.

2. *The morning star* (Rev. 2:28). This obscure symbol is perhaps derived from the familiar apocalyptic saying that in the Messianic Kingdom the righteous shall shine as the stars (cf. Dan. 12:3; II (IV) Esdras 7:97; Enoch 104:2). It refers to the glory which will be given to the victor, whose share in the Messiah's conquest over his enemies may suggest the glory that is to follow. "The bright, the morning star" (Rev. 22:16, R.V.) probably refers to Christ as the herald to his people of the eternal day. See LUCIFER.

3. *The star of the Wise Men;* see MAGI. The usual view has been that this was a purely supernatural phenomenon, a starlike object which appeared to the Magi in their e. sky, and suggested to them, perhaps through their acquaintance with the prophecy of Balaam (Num. 24:17) or other predictions, that the king of the Jews was born. Afterward it reappeared, as they journeyed from Jerusalem to Bethlehem, and guided them on their way until it rested over the house in which Jesus was. Others, however, consider it a natural phenomenon providentially used to direct the Magi. In Dec., 1603, the astronomer Kepler noted a conjunction of Jupiter and Saturn, joined in March, 1604, by Mars, and in Oct., 1604, by a brilliant new star, which gradually faded and vanished in Feb., 1606. Kepler calculated that the planets were in conjunction in 7 and 6 B.C., and, supposing that the new or variable star had followed the conjunction then as it did in 1604, believed it to be the star of the Magi. Others have identified the Magi's star with the planetary conjunction itself, and the calculations of Kepler have been corrected by Ideler, Pritch-

ard, and Encke, with the result that we know that in 7 B.C. there were 3 conjunctions of Jupiter and Saturn, in May, September, and December. Hence, it has been supposed that the Magi saw the heavenly spectacle in May; connected it, through their astrology and knowledge of Hebrew prophecy and expectation, with the birth of a Jewish king; and, when going from Jerusalem to Bethlehem in December, saw again the conjunction overhead. But the word star can hardly mean a conjunction, and this view would place Christ's birth earlier than other considerations warrant. If we can believe that Kepler's variable star followed the conjunction, as he supposed, it would answer the conditions better than the conjunction itself. It is on some accounts more probable that the event was a natural rather than a supernatural phenomenon. The Magi were doubtless astrologers and would attach special ideas to the positions and variations of the stars. The star did not go before them to Judea, but only, after its reappearance, did it seem to lead them from Jerusalem to Bethlehem. On the other hand, many think that Matt. 2:9 cannot fairly be understood of anything but a supernatural phenomenon; nor can the astronomical calculations above described safely be held to have identified the star, even if it be regarded as a natural object.

A. T. Olmstead (1942), who sees here Babylonian, not Jewish lore, maintains that the Gr. verb for "appeared" (Matt. 2:7) is a literal and technical equivalent of Akkad. *ereshu*, which refers to the heliacal rising of a planet. Accordingly, the Magi reported that the star was seen, not "in the east," but "at its rising." In other words, the star made its first appearance in the e. sky exactly at sunrise. The expression that the star went before them (ch. 2:9) refers to its nightly shift of apparent position in the heavens. The star "stood over where the young child was" represents Akkad. *izazu* (stand still); this denotes the 2 periods of opposition when to the naked eye for about 4 days the planet does not appear to change its position in the celestial vault. Striking parallels to Matthew's account may be read in letters from the latter days of Esarhaddon when his sons Shamash-shum-ukin and Ashurbanipal were contending for the succession. There was accordingly the rising of Jupiter accompanied by that of the sun, Saturn, and Mars.

G. T. P. (rev., H. S. G.)

Sta'ter. A shekel; cf. Matt. 17:27, R.V. marg. See MONEY.

Steel. A modified form of iron, resulting in elasticity and hardness. The earliest known and simplest method of reducing iron from its ore was capable of yielding steel. The Chalybes in Pontus were celebrated for hardening iron, and their name was used by the Greeks for steel. Hebrew *pᵉlādāh* in Nahum 2:3 apparently means steel (R.V., in A.V. torches).

Where steel occurs in A.V., brass is correctly substituted in R.V.

Steph'a·nas (stĕf'á-năs) [Gr., crowned]. A Christian convert at Corinth. His household was the first fruit of Paul's labors in the province of Achaia. The apostle himself baptized its members, and they set themselves to minister unto the saints. Stephanas also visited the apostle, bringing him aid, and was with him when the First Epistle to the Corinthians was penned (I Cor. 1:16; 16:15, 17).

Ste'phen (stē'vĕn) [Gr., wreath or crown]. The first Christian martyr. He is first mentioned as 1st in the list of the 7 men chosen by the Jerusalem Christians, at the sugges-

tion of the apostles, to superintend the distribution of the Church's alms (Acts 6:5). Since the appointment of these 7 men, usually regarded as the first deacons, arose from the complaints made by the Greek-speaking or Hellenistic Jewish Christians that their widows were neglected in the daily ministration, and since Stephen is itself a Greek name, and since the subsequent persecution of Stephen arose among the Greek-speaking Jews of Jerusalem, it is probable that Stephen himself was a Hellenist, and perhaps had come from abroad. He was a notable man, who after his appointment became more than ever conspicuous as a preacher and worker of miracles (v. 8). His activity occasioned for the first time opposition to the Church among the foreign Jews, who had synagogues in Jerusalem. The trouble originated particularly when there disputed with Stephen "certain of them that were of the synagogue called the synagogue of the Libertines [or, Freedmen], and of the Cyrenians, and of the Alexandrians, and of them of Cilicia and Asia" (v. 9). These charged Stephen with blaspheming Moses and God, and, more especially, with declaring that Jesus would destroy the Temple and change the customs derived from Moses (vs. 11–14). Luke states that the witnesses produced against Stephen were suborned and false, as those against Christ had been; but Stephen must have said something which could be thus perverted. He was brought before the sanhedrin, and from his defense, reported in Acts 7:2–53, we can understand his position. He first recited God's early choice and guidance of the Patriarchs (vs. 2–22), apparently to bring out the fact that God from the beginning had been leading Israel to a definite goal; then, continuing the history, he showed that the Hebrews had repeatedly resisted God's purpose with them, both in the days of Moses and subsequently (vs. 23–43), and had failed to see the temporary and typical character of both tabernacle and Temple (vs. 44–50). Then, suddenly stopping his argument, he bitterly charged them with resisting, as their fathers had done, the Holy Spirit, with having slain the Christ as their fathers had slain the prophets, and with failing to keep in reality their own Law (vs. 51–53). At this point the listeners gnashed upon him with their teeth and prepared to rush upon him. A vision was given him of the Son of Man standing (as though to receive him) at the right hand of God; and, when he declared it, they seized him, cast him out of the city, and stoned him. It was not lawful for them to put anyone to death without permission from the Romans, but the martyrdom was evidently the result of an uncontrollable outbreak. The speech and death of Stephen mark the transition of Christianity from its earliest Jewish form to its extension among the Gentiles. Peter preached Christianity as the fulfillment of prophecy; Stephen preached it as the goal of Hebrew history. Yet while Stephen declared that Christianity could not be limited by Judaism, he did not set forth, like Paul afterward, its Gentile mission or its deliverance, by the doctrine of salvation by faith alone, from its Jewish environment. He marks, therefore, the transition from Jewish to Gentile Christianity. Moreover, the persecution which followed his martyrdom led to the dispersion of the disciples, and so in fact to the carrying of the gospel to the Samaritans and then to the Gentiles. Stephen's personal character also was very beautiful. As a man he was "full of faith and of the Holy Spirit" (ch. 6:5); as a preacher, "full of grace and power" (v. 8); before the council, his enemies "saw his face as it had been the face of an angel" (v. 15); and his last words were:

"Lord, lay not this sin to their charge" (ch. 7:60).   G. T. P. (rev., H. S. G.)

Stocks. An instrument of punishment, called in Heb. *sad*, consisting of a wooden frame, hence called *xylon* in Gr., in which the feet were put and firmly held (Job 13:27; 33:11; Acts 16:24). The prisoner remained in a sitting posture. A special form of the apparatus, apparently, was called in Heb. *mahpeketh*, turning, torsion, because the body was forced into an unnatural position (II Chron. 16:10, R.V. marg.; Jer. 20:2). It included shackles or rather a collar; at least these could be used on the prisoner at the same time (Jer. 29:26, R.V.), so that his neck, arms, and legs could all be held fast together.

Sto'ics (stō'ĭks) [Gr. *stoikos*, pertaining to the porch]. A sect of philosophers, 1 of 2 which Paul encountered at Athens (Acts 17:18). Their founder was Zeno of Citium in Cyprus, who must not be confounded with an earlier philosopher, Zeno of Elea, in Italy. The Cyprian Zeno was born c. 336 and died c. 264 B.C. Removing from his native place to Athens, he taught for about 58 years in the *stoa*, or porch, on the public market place. His doctrine was essentially pantheistic. The Stoics distinguished matter and force as the ultimate principles in the universe; and the force working everywhere they called reason, providence, God, and regarded it as conscious and thinking, yet dependent and impersonal, a breath or a fire which forms, permeates, and vivifies all things, and which in accordance with inexorable necessity calls beings and worlds into existence and destroys them again, so that at the end of a cosmical period the universe is resolved into fire in a general conflagration, and the evolution of the world begins again, and so on without end. The human soul is a spark or emanation of this conscious but impersonal deity. It survives the body, but lives only for a cosmical period, and is reabsorbed at last into the source from which it came. The Stoics classed themselves among the followers of Socrates, and resembled him in their theory of life. They rigidly severed the morally good from the agreeable. They declared that an act is good or evil in itself, and that pleasure should never be made the end of an action. The highest good is virtue. Virtue is a life conformed to nature, or the agreement of human conduct with the law of the universe, and of the human with the divine will; it is especially resignation in respect to fate. The cardinal virtues are practical wisdom as to what is good and evil, courage, prudence or self-restraint, and justice. Zeno encouraged his followers to hold their feelings in rigid control, so as to be as much as possible independent of all disturbing influences, whatever occurrences might take place. Stoicism made noble characters. It continued as a power for about 400 years, its most eminent professors being the slave Epictetus, the philosopher Seneca, and the emperor Marcus Aurelius.

Stom'ach·er. A part of dress, once worn by women, covering the pit of the stomach and the breast, and often highly ornamented. It is the rendering adopted in Isa. 3:24 of Heb. *pethigil*, applied to an article of female attire. The meaning of the Heb. word is uncertain. A.R.V. renders it "robe"; Luther, "wide mantle."

Stone. Palestine is a stony country, and it was often necessary to clear a field of stones preparatory to its cultivation (Isa. 5:2). An enemy's fields were marred by throwing stones on them, and his wells were choked with stones (II Kings 3:19, 25).

Stones were put to various uses: 1. For moles, quays (Jos. *War* i. 21, 6), city walls

(Neh. 4:3); for dwellings (Lev. 14:45; Amos 5:11), palaces (I Kings 7:1, 9), fortresses, temples (I Kings 6:7); for the pavement of courtyards and for columns (Esth. 1:6), and in Herodian times at least for paving streets (see STREET); and for aqueducts, reservoirs, bridges; dykes about vineyards (Prov. 24:30, 31). In building altars the Israelites used unhewn stones (Ex. 20:25), likewise for an ordinary dyke, and when heaps of stones were made to commemorate an event (Gen. 31:46) or to mark the grave of a notorious offender (Josh. 7:26; 8:29; II Sam. 18:17), a custom still in vogue in Syria and Arabia, but not restricted to the graves of evildoers. But for some purposes the stones were sawed and hewn (I Kings 7:9–11); and, where suitable, stones of enormous size were used, as in the walls of the Temple and the mole at Caesarea.

2. Single stones were used to close the mouth of cisterns and wells, and the entrance of tombs (Gen. 29:2; Matt. 27:60; John 11:38), to mark boundaries (Deut. 19:14), and probably as way marks (Jer. 31:21). In Roman times milestones were erected along the chief public highways, as, for example, on the road between Tyre and Sidon and between Pella and Gerasa, where they are still to be seen. Stones were set up to mark graves and to commemorate events (Gen. 31:45; 35:14, 20; II Sam. 18:18), and were sometimes inscribed with a record of deeds (Herod. ii. 106; see MOABITE STONE). Stones, both in their natural state and graven, served as idols (Lev. 26:1; Deut. 29:17; II Kings 19:18; cf. Isa. 57:6). Certain small stones, called in Gr. *baituloi* and *baitulia*, which were often, if not always, meteorites and held sacred because they fell from heaven, played a part in Gentile superstition. They were said to move, talk, and guard from evil. The Greek name, which is doubtless of Semitic origin, is akin to *beth'ēl* and may indicate that the stone was regarded as the abode of a supernatural power, spirit, or god. The Israelites sometimes consecrated a single stone as a memorial to God (Gen. 28:18–22; I Sam. 7:12; Isa. 19:19), and they might give a religious name to the place (Gen. 35:7) or even to the stone, just as they sometimes called an altar by God's name (Gen. 33:20; Ex. 17:15; cf. Gen. 35:7); but in the recorded cases they did not regard deity or power as resident in the stone or altar and did not pay it divine honor. If they worshiped, they worshiped God apart from the memorial stone (Gen. 31:54; 35:1, 7; I Sam. 7:9).

3. Stones were hurled by slings and catapults (Judg. 20:16; I Sam. 17:40; II Chron. 26:15; Wisd. of Sol. 5:22; I Macc. 6:51), and were a means of putting criminals to death (see STONING). Flints were used for striking fire (II Macc. 10:3), and were shaped into rude form to serve as knives (Josh. 5:2). Weights for scales were often cut out of stone (Deut. 25:13; see WEIGHTS), and tablets of stone were employed for written documents (Ex. 24:12). Vessels for holding water were hewn from stone (Ex. 7:19; John 2:6), tables also (Ezek. 40:42). A rounded stone, of 30 pounds' weight or so, was rolled back and forth over grain to crush it to flour, or 2 stones were formed into a mill for grinding (Deut. 24:6).

The white stone mentioned in Rev. 2:17 has been variously interpreted, but the idea underlying this figure of speech is that of an amulet containing as its secret inscription the victor's name; through this he will have power against every enemy. The symbol is derived from familiar beliefs and practices regarding spiritual means of defense. The victor's new name characteristic of his new state will be given him on a pebble, whose color befits his victory and glory, but none save himself will know that name written on the stone. According to the best interpretation the writer has in mind a small stone, a common writing material, white to symbolize the heavenly character of the victorious believer, and marked with the name bestowed as sign and seal of his future glory.

Figuratively stone denotes hardness or insensibility (I Sam. 25:37; Ezek. 36:26), firmness or strength (Job 6:12; 41:24). A living stone is a stone in its natural condition, sound and not disintegrating. The followers of Christ are living stones built into the spiritual temple, of which Christ himself is the chief corner stone (Eph. 2:20–22; I Peter 2:4–8).

Stones, Pre′cious. All the precious stones referred to in the canonical Scriptures, except 3, are enumerated in R.V. of Ex. 28:17–20 and Rev. 21:11, 19–21, text and marg. The 3 remaining ones are adamant (Ezek. 3:9), and ligure and sardine (Ex. 28:19; Rev. 4:3, both A.V.), and of these at least 2 are merely other names for 2 of those already mentioned. The precious stones are adamant, agate, amber, amethyst, beryl, carbuncle, chalcedony, chrysolite, chrysoprase or chrysoprasus, crystal, diamond, emerald, jacinth or hyacinth, jasper, lapis lazuli, ligure, onyx, pearl, ruby, sapphire, sardius or sardine, sardonyx, and topaz.

Ston′ing. The ordinary mode of capital punishment prescribed by Hebrew law (Lev. 20:2); see PUNISHMENT. It was an ancient method; and it was not confined to the Hebrews, but was practiced by the Macedonians and Persians as well. The execution took place outside the city (Lev. 24:14; I Kings 21:10, 13; Acts 7:58). The witnesses placed their hands on the head of the criminal in token that the guilt rested on him. They laid aside any clothing that might impede them in their solemn duty. In cases of idolatry, and apparently in other cases also, the witnesses hurled the first stones (Deut. 13:9; 17:7; cf. John 8:7). The rabbis state that the culprit was stripped of all clothing except a cloth about the loins, and was thrown to the ground from a scaffold about 10 feet high by the 1st witness; the 1st stone was cast by the 2d witness, on the chest over the heart of the criminal, and if it failed to cause death, the bystanders completed the execution. Sometimes the body was afterward suspended until sundown or burned (Deut. 21:23; Josh. 7:25; Jos. Antiq. iv. 8, 24), and according to late Jewish law was not buried in the family grave.

Stool. See BIRTHSTOOL. A chair of peculiar form, upon which the patient sat during parturition. It was denominated 'obnāyim, double stones, by the Hebrews (Ex. 1:16).

Stork. A bird called in Heb. ḥăsîdāh, affectionate, on account of its love for its young. It was ceremonially unclean (Lev. 11:19; Deut. 14:18), dwelt in fir trees (Ps. 104:17), and was migratory (Jer. 8:7). It is the Ciconia alba, a white heronlike bird, which spends its winter in central and s. Africa, but in spring visits continental Europe, Palestine, and n. Syria in large numbers. It is about 4 feet high, with long red bill and legs, white plumage, and glossy black wings. It feeds on frogs and small reptiles or, lacking these, on offal, and hence was ceremonially unclean. It is regarded as a sacred bird, and in most places is unmolested, so that it fearlessly visits the haunts of man. The black stork, Ciconia nigra, named from the color of its back and neck, is also found in Palestine, being common in the valley of the Dead Sea; it breeds in trees.

Stran′ger, in R.V. generally **So·journ′er.** A stranger in the Mosaic Law, and in the O.T. generally, means one not of Israelitish descent dwelling with the Hebrews, as distinguished from a foreigner temporarily visiting the land (Ex. 20:10; Lev. 16:29; 17:8; II Sam. 1:13; Ezek. 14:7). The stranger was not a full citizen, yet he had recognized rights and duties. He was under the protection of God, and the Israelites were charged to treat him kindly (Lev. 19:33, 34; Deut. 10:18, 19). His rights were guarded by injunctions in the Law (Ex. 22:21; 23:9). When poor, he enjoyed the same privileges as the Hebrew poor (Deut. 24:19, 20). The prohibitions that rested on an Israelite rested on him (Ex. 12:19; Lev. 16:29; 17:10; 18:26; 20:2; 24:16; and 17:15, which was modified later by Deut. 14:21); but he was not obligated to all positive religious duties which devolved on the Israelite. He was exempt, if he chose to be and if he was a free man, from circumcision and barred from participation in the passover (Ex. 12:43–46). The Israelites were encouraged to invite him to the sacrificial meals (Deut. 16:11, 14). He was allowed to sacrifice to the Lord, he shared in the atonement made for the sin of the congregation on account of sin unwittingly committed, he had the privilege of a sin offering for aught done unwittingly by himself, and the city of refuge offered him asylum in case of need (Lev. 17:8; Num. 15:14, 26, 29; 35:15). In case he contracted uncleanness he was required to employ the rites of purification (Lev. 17:15; Num. 19:10). If he accepted circumcision for his household, he was admitted to the passover (Ex. 12:48, 49). The chief disability under which he labored was that in case he became a bondman, the year of jubilee did not bring him release; he could be bought and made an inheritance for the purchaser's children (Lev. 25:45, 46).

Ammonites and Moabites formed an exceptional class among the strangers. They were not allowed membership in Israel even by circumcision (Deut. 23:3), but the son of an Israelite and a Moabitess might be admitted (cf. JESSE and REHOBOAM). Intermarriage with the idolatrous Canaanites who were in the land at the time of the Conquest was strictly forbidden (Deut. 7:3), but the remnant who were left after the Conquest eventually became to a large extent proselytes. In Solomon's reign the census revealed 153,600 strangers in the realm (II Chron. 2:17).

In the N.T. the word stranger does not have this technical signification, but denotes one who is unknown (John 10:5), an alien (Luke 17:16, 18), a sojourner away from home (Luke 24:18; Acts 2:10), an Israelite dwelling in the Dispersion (I Peter 1:1, A.V.).

Straw. Wheat and barley straw, ground and cut to small pieces in the process of threshing, and doubtless often mixed with beans or barley, was used by the ancient Hebrews as fodder for their cattle, camels, asses, and horses (Gen. 24:25, 32; Judg. 19:19; I Kings 4:28; Isa. 11:7). The Egyptians, in making bricks, mixed it with clay to render them more compact and to prevent their cracking. When Pharaoh withheld the chopped straw, the Hebrew slaves were compelled to go forth into the field and gather stubble, or rather stalks, for themselves, and chop their own straw (Ex. 5:7, 12, 16). Straw was probably not used by the ancient Hebrews as a litter in the stall. In Palestine today dried dung serves for this purpose.

Stream. See RIVER.

Street. The streets of Oriental towns were generally narrow, tortuous, and dirty (Jos. Antiq. xx. 5, 3; War ii. 14, 9; 15, 5). They were seldom wide enough to permit 2 laden camels to pass each other; but some were sufficiently broad for chariots to be driven through them (cf. Jer. 17:25; Nahum 2:4). Great cities were sometimes adorned by a grand avenue or even by several, as Alexandria and Babylon. In Damascus the street called Straight was a magnificent thoroughfare, 100 feet broad and divided into 3 avenues by rows of columns. Many streets were flanked by blank walls, seldom pierced except by doors, the windows of the houses opening on interior courts. The streets devoted to stores were lined by salesrooms with open fronts; and bazaar streets, each surrendered to 1 kind of business, were features of the ancient city (Jer. 37:21; Jos. *War* v. 8, 1). The intersections of the streets were centers of concourse and display (Prov. 1:21; Matt. 6:5; cf. Luke 13:26). At the gates were broad, open places where business was transacted. There is no evidence that the streets were paved in ancient times; but Josephus affirms that Solomon paved the roads leading to Jerusalem with black stones (Jos. *Antiq.* viii. 7, 4); and at the time of the Herods pavements were laid (Jos. *Antiq.* xvi. 5, 3; xx. 9, 7), and efforts were in some instances made toward keeping the streets clean (Jos. *Antiq.* xv. 9, 6).

Stripes. See Scourge.

Strong Drink. Intoxicating liquor, in Heb. *shēkār* (I Sam. 1:13–15; Prov. 20:1; Isa. 29:9); cf. Eng. slang from Yiddish *shicker*, *shickered* (drunk). Wine and strong drink were forbidden to the priest when about to enter the sanctuary (Lev. 10:9; cf. Ezek. 44: 21), and kings and princes were warned against its use, lest it lead to perversion of judgment (Prov. 31:4, 5); yet Isaiah was compelled to point to the sad spectacle of priests and prophets, even in Judah, scandalously failing in duty through wine and strong drink (Isa. 28:7). Wine, strong drink, vinegar, any liquor of grapes, and even fresh grapes were forbidden the Nazirite (Num. 6:3; cf. Judg. 13:4; Luke 1:15); see Nazirite. Both wine and strong drink were allowed at the feast spread by the bringer of tithes (Deut. 14:26). On the basis of the exhortation, "Give strong drink unto him that is ready to perish" (Prov. 31:6), kindhearted women of Jerusalem provided stupefying draughts for criminals condemned to death (Mishnah; cf. Mark 15:23).

Stub'ble. See Straw.

Su'ah (sū'ȧ) [sweepings]. An Asherite, a son of Zophah (I Chron. 7:36).

Su'cath·ite (sū'kăth-īt), in A.V. **Su'chath·ite**. A native or an inhabitant of an unknown place called Sucah or Socah (I Chron. 2:55).

Suc'coth (sŭk'ŏth) [booths or huts]. 1. A place e. of the Jordan (Judg. 8:4, 5), at which Jacob, on his return from Mesopotamia, after crossing the Jabbok (Gen. 32:22), built himself a house, with booths for his cattle, giving the spot from the latter circumstance the name of Succoth (ch. 33:17). He journeyed thence to Shechem (v. 18). It was in the valley of the Jordan, near Zarethan (I Kings 7:46; Ps. 60:6; 108:7), and was assigned to the Gadites (Josh. 13:27). In the time of Gideon it was an important town, ruled by 77 elders. They refused him assistance when he was pursuing Zebah and Zalmunna, and were in consequence punished by him when he returned a victor (Judg. 8:5–16). The site is at Tell Aḥṣāṣ, about 1¼ miles n. of Nahr ez-Zerḳā (Jabbok) and about 9 miles n.e. of Dāmiyeh; it is about 426 feet w. of Deir 'Alla (Tar'alah, Dar'alah), which the Talmud identifies with Succoth.

2. The first camping ground of the Israelites after leaving Rameses (Ex. 12:37; 13:

20; Num. 33:5, 6); by some identified with Thuku, the civil city surrounding the sacred buildings at Pithom. More recently it has been identified with Tell el-Maskhûṭah. See Pithom.

Suc'coth-be'noth (sŭk'ŏth-bē'nŏth). An idol which the Babylonian colonists set up in Samaria (II Kings 17:30). The tutelary deity of Babylon was Marduk, and his consort was Zarpanitum, although numerous other deities were worshiped in the city. The historian Rawlinson, followed by Schrader, proposed to identify Succoth-benoth with Zarpanitum, the latter part of the 2 names being essentially the same. Friedrich Delitzsch regards Succoth-benoth as a Hebraization of the Akkad. words *sakkut bĭnūti*, supreme judge of the universe, and he considers it to have been in this instance a title of Marduk.

Su'chath·ite (sū'kăth-īt). See Sucathite.

Suk'ki·im (sŭk'ĭ-ĭm), in A.V. **Suk'ki·ims** (sŭk'ĭ-ĭmz). One of the peoples furnishing soldiers to the army of Shishak, king of Egypt, when he invaded Palestine. They were evidently an African race (II Chron. 12:3).

Su'mer (sū'mēr). See Babylonia.

Sun. The luminary of the day, created by God (Gen. 1:16), preserved by God (Jer. 31: 35; Matt. 5:45), and subject to God (Ps. 104:19); influential in promoting vegetation (Deut. 33:14; I Sam. 23:4), and also burning it with its heat. It is spoken of as rising and setting; is poetically described as occupying a tent in the heavens; its rising in the morning with vigor and joy is likened to a bridegroom coming forth from his chamber (Ps. 19:4–6). Death in the meridian of one's days, and the sudden loss of prosperity, are likened to the setting of the sun at midday (Jer. 15:9; Amos 8:9; Micah 3:6). The sun was worshiped by the nations contemporary with the Hebrews, notably by the Babylonians at Sippar and Larsa, and by the Assyrians under the name of Shamash, and by the Egyptians under that of Re. The Hebrews were warned against all such heathenism, but sun worship nevertheless found entrance among them. Altars were erected to all the host of heaven (II Kings 21:5), incense was burned to the sun and horses were dedicated to it (II Kings 23:5, 11; cf. the Persian worship, Herod. vii. 54), and kisses were thrown to it with the hand (Job 31:26, 27).

Joshua commanded the sun to stand still. The older commentators referred the words of Hab. 3:11 to this event, but the Heb. construction and the context are against it. Sun and moon withdraw into their habitation. Dread before the presence of the Lord seizes all nature and reveals itself in the trembling of the mountains, in the raging of the sea, and in the withdrawal of their light by sun and moon (vs. 10, 11). The first reference to the astronomical lengthening of the day at Beth-horon is found in Ecclesiasticus, and its author evidently believed that the sun and moon were checked in their courses. "Did not the sun go back by his hand? And did not one day become as two" (Ecclus. 46:4). Josephus also understood that the day was lengthened (Jos. *Antiq.* v. 1, 17). Unquestionably God could work this wonder, with all that it involved. The circumstances, however, scarcely afforded an adequate occasion for so stupendous a miracle. Another interpretation has much in its favor. It is certain that Josh. 10:12b and 13a are poetry. Verses 12–15 in all probability form a paragraph by themselves (cf. the repetition, v. 15 and v. 43), and are quoted from The Book of Jashar, a collection of poems with introductory and perhaps concluding remarks in prose (see Jashar; cf. Job with its prose introduction and conclusion; cf. the position of the quoting clause in Josh. 10:13 and II Sam. 1:18). Joshua's words are the impassioned utterance of a general inspiring his army on the field of battle. Desirous that Israel may have time completely to overthrow the foe, he apostrophizes sun and moon. In fervent, imperious words, he demands time. "Sun, stand thou still upon Gibeon; and thou, Moon, in the valley of Aijalon." God granted his wish. Before the light of day failed, the people had avenged themselves on their enemies. A hailstorm assisted the Israelites, and they drove the enemy to Azekah and Makkedah and made a great slaughter. This event, it seems, was worked up poetically in The Book of Jashar, and must be interpreted as poetry, as one interprets the psalmist when, telling of the gift of manna, he says: "He commanded the skies above, and opened the doors of heaven; and he rained down manna upon them to eat, and gave them of the corn of heaven" (Ps. 78:23, 24); or as one understands the poet who, after relating the passage of the Red Sea and the Jordan, adds: "The mountains skipped like rams, and the little hills like lambs" (Ps. 114:6); or as one understands the Prophet Habakkuk when he pictures Jehovah as a warrior and says: "Thou didst ride upon thine horses, upon thy chariots of salvation" (Hab. 3:8).

R.V. translates Heb. *ḥammānim* as sun-images (Lev. 26:30; II Chron. 14:5; 34:4, 7; Isa. 17:8; 27:9; Ezek. 6:4, 6). There was found at Palmyra an altar inscribed with its name, a cognate of the above Heb. noun, and accordingly the term sun-images must be understood as altars of incense (cf. Hos. 4:13). Altars of incense were found at Megiddo which antedate the middle of the 10th century B.C.; they belong to the religion of Baal and not to orthodox Israelite worship.

For the recession of the sun's shadow on the dial of Ahaz, see DIAL.

Suph (sōōf) [reeds]. A locality (Deut. 1:1, R.V.), situation unknown; there is a Khirbet Sufa 3¾ miles s.s.e. of Medaba. The A.V., following the Vulgate and the LXX, assumes that the Heb. word for sea has fallen out of the text. On this assumption the text originally was *yām sūph*, Red Sea, and the reference was to that part of the sea known as the Gulf of 'Aḳabah.

Su'phah (sōō'fȧ). Probably a proper name, denoting the region in which Vaheb was situated (Num. 21:14, R.V.). See SUPH.

Sup'per. See MEALS.

Sure'ty. A person who makes himself liable for the obligations of another (Prov. 22:26, 27). A surety was sometimes offered for a service to be rendered (Gen. 44:32); and, when commercial transactions were common, a surety was often required to be found before credit was given. The formalities consisted in giving the hand, in the presence of witnesses, to the person to whom the debt was due, and promising to discharge the obligation in case the debtor defaulted (Prov. 6:1, 2; 17:18). The folly of becoming surety, especially in behalf of a stranger, was proverbial (Prov. 11:15; 17:18; 20:16); but it was regarded as proper under circumstances and for a moderate amount, and as a neighborly act (Ecclus. 8:13; 29:14, 20); yet its grave dangers and its liability to abuse by a dishonest client were recognized (Ecclus. 29: 16–18).

Su'sa (sōō'sȧ). See SHUSHAN.

Su·san'chite (sū-săn'kīt). See SHUSHAN-CHITES.

Su·san'na (sū-zăn'ȧ) [Gr. from Heb., a lily]. One of the women who ministered to Jesus of their substance (Luke 8:3).

Su'si (sū'sī) [horseman]. Father of Gaddi, the spy from the tribe of Manasseh (Num. 13:11).

Swad'dling Band. A cloth in which infants were wrapped (Job 38:9; Ezek. 16:4; Luke 2:7, 12). The babe was laid diagonally on a square piece of cloth and 2 corners were turned over its body, 1 over its feet, and 1 under its head. The whole was then fastened by bands wound around the outside.

Swal'low. 1. A bird, in Biblical and Talmudic Heb. *dᵉrôr*, shooting straight out or freedom. It frequented the sanctuary at Jerusalem, and nested there (Ps. 84:3), and it was found in company with other small birds, like the sparrow (*ibid.*; Prov. 26:2). The barn swallow of Great Britain (*Hirundo rustica*) is abundant in Palestine from March to the approach of winter. Several other species also occur, but are less common.

2. The rendering in the R.V. of Heb. *sûs* or *sîs*, a bird with a chattering note (Isa. 38: 14) and migratory (Jer. 8:7). Swallow is the rendering adopted by the LXX, Vulgate, and Syriac versions, but the A.V., following the rabbis, translates it crane. Tristram believes that the swift is intended. He says that the common swift (*Cypselus apus*) is called *sîs* in the vernacular Arabic. It visits Palestine in immense numbers in its migrations, remaining from April to November, and building in the interval. Two other species of the genus occur in Palestine, the white-bellied swift (*Cypselus melba*) and the white-rumped swift (*Cypselus affinis*).

3. The rendering in A.V. of Heb. *'āgûr* (Isa. 38:14; Jer. 8:7). The R.V. in both passages renders it crane.

Swan. The rendering of Heb. *tinshemeth*, a name applied to an unclean bird (Lev. 11:18, R.V. marg.; Deut. 14:16; text of A.V.). The R.V. text makes it the horned owl. The same name belonged to a reptile classed with the lizards (Lev. 11:30, in R.V. chameleon, in A.V. mole). Tristram thinks that the bird was probably either the purple gallinule (*Porphyrio caeruleus*) or the glossy ibis (*Ibis falcinellus*).

Swear'ing. See OATH.

Sweat. It is a common occurrence for perspiration to break out suddenly over the body when the individual is under the influence of strong mental excitement. Well-authenticated cases have been recorded in which this perspiration has been colored with blood. The phenomenon is recognized in medical science, and is called *diapedesis*, or the oozing of the blood corpuscles through the walls of the blood vessels without rupture. During Christ's agony in Gethsemane his sweat became as it were great drops of blood falling down upon the ground (Luke 22:44).

Swine. The swine was a ceremonially unclean animal (Lev. 11:7; Deut. 14:8). It is dirty, does not refuse to eat offal and carrion, and the use of its flesh for food in hot countries is supposed to produce cutaneous diseases. It was not raised by the Arabs (Pliny *Hist. Nat.* viii. 78), and was regarded as unclean by Phoenicians, Ethiopians, and Egyptians. In Egypt, however, a pig was sacrificed and eaten on the annual festival of the moon-god and Osiris (Bacchus); nevertheless, a man who accidentally touched a pig at once washed, a swineherd was not allowed to enter a temple and was compelled to find a wife among the people of his own occupation, as no other man would give a daughter to him in marriage (Herod. ii. 47). To the Jews swine's flesh was abominable, the pig was the emblem of filth and coarseness (Prov. 11:22; Matt. 7:6; II Peter 2:22), and to feed swine was the lowest and most despicable occupation to which a Jew could be reduced (Luke 15:15). Yet pork found entrance to the idolatrous feasts of degenerate Hebrews (Isa. 65: 4; 66:17). In the reign of Antiochus Epiphanes the command to a Jew to offer or to taste swine's flesh was used as a means of determining whether he was loyal to the religion of his fathers or was willing to accept the worship favored by his conquerors (I Macc. 1:47, 50; II Macc. 6:18, 21; 7:1, 7). But many Jews affected Grecian manners, and John Hyrcanus some years later found it advisable to issue an edict that no one should keep swine. In the time of Christ one large herd of swine at least was pastured in the Decapolis (Mark 5:11–13), a region colonized by Greeks, among whom the swine was highly esteemed as an article of food. There is no reason to suppose that Jews owned either these swine or those in the far country fed by the Prodigal Son (Luke 15:15). See BOAR.

Sword. A weapon with which an adversary was cut by being struck or was thrust through (I Sam. 17:51; 31:4; II Sam. 2:16; Matt. 26:51). It had hilt and blade (Judg. 3:22), was carried in a sheath (I Sam. 17: 51; Jer. 47:6), and girded on the loins (Ex. 32:27; II Sam. 20:8), usually at the left side (cf. Judg. 3:16 with vs. 15, 21). The hilt was often highly ornamented, at least among the Egyptians, Babylonians, and Assyrians. The blade was commonly made of iron (Isa. 2:4), perhaps also of bronze, as not seldom in Egypt. It was straight or slightly curved, long or short (Judg. 3:16, a cubit long), single or double-edged (*ibid.*; Ps. 149:6).

In the Roman period a short, slightly curved dagger was worn under the clothing by the Jewish *sicarii*, or assassins (Jos. *Antiq.* xx. 8, 10; *War* ii. 13, 3). Roman infantry wore the sword on the left side and the dagger on the right, but the cavalry wore the sword on the right (Jos. *War* iii. 5, 5). This, however, was not an invariable rule.

Syc'a·mine Tree. The mulberry tree, called in Gr. *sykaminos* (Luke 17:6). The black mulberry (*Morus nigra*), a tree 20 or 30 feet high, is the species commonly cultivated for its leaves and fruit. The silkworm feeds on the leaves. The fruit is dark red or black, with an uneven surface. The tree has been planted extensively in Palestine.

Sy'char (sī'kär). A town of Samaria, in the vicinity of the land given by Jacob to his son Joseph, near Jacob's well (John 4:5; cf. Gen. 48:22). Formerly it was supposed to be a Gr. corruption of Shechem; in the Old Syriac Gospels the reading is Shechem. It is now believed to be the village of 'Askar, on the e. declivity of Mount Ebal, 1¾ miles e.n.e. from Nablus (Shechem) and a little over ½ mile n. of Jacob's well.

Sy'chem (sī'kĕm). See SHECHEM.

Syc'o·more. A fig tree, called in Heb. *shiḳ-māh*, in Gr. *sykomoros, sykomorea*. It was abundant in the lowland of Judah (I Kings 10:27; I Chron. 27:28; II Chron. 1:15; 9:27), grew in the Jordan Valley (Luke 19:4), and was cultivated in Egypt (Ps. 78:47). Its timber was much used, although less durable than cedar (Isa. 9:10). The tree is the *Ficus sycomorus*, a fig tree, 25 to 50 feet high and 60 feet broad, with persistent, heart-shaped leaves downy beneath. It is often planted by the wayside on account of its grateful shade (cf. Luke 19:4). The fruit grows in clusters on twigs which spring directly from the trunk and larger branches, but cannot be eaten until it has been punctured and the insect that infests it has been allowed to escape (cf. Amos 7:14).

This tree must not be confounded with our sycamore (*Platanus occidentalis*), although the modern spelling is sycamore.

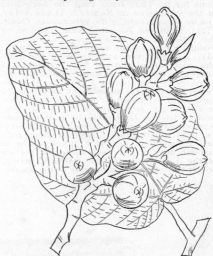

Leaf and Fruit of the Sycamore
(*Ficus sycomorus*)

Sy·e'ne (sī-ē'nē). See SEVENEH.

Sym'e·on (sĭm'ē-ŭn). See SIMEON.

Syn'a·gogue [Gr., assembly, place of meeting, synagogue]. A Jewish place of worship. The building served also for local law court and school. Previous to the Captivity, worship of the highest kind could be performed only at the Temple at Jerusalem. Of course, the Scriptures could be publicly read elsewhere (Jer. 36:6, 10, 12–15), and the people could resort to the prophets anywhere for religious instruction (II Kings 4:38). Worship at Jerusalem was impossible when the people were in captivity in Babylon, and it seems to have been then and there that synagogues first arose. They were designed to be places, not of sacrifice, but of Scriptural instruction and prayer. The Eng. word synagogue occurs only once in the O.T. (Ps. 74: 8). The marg. of R.V. has "places of assembly" instead of synagogues, and the LXX renders by *heortē* (a feast, a festival, a holiday). It is not, therefore, certain that there is any reference to a synagogue in the O.T. In the 1st century they were found wherever Jews dwelt. Even small communities of Jews in the lesser cities outside of Palestine had their synagogues; as in Salamis in Cyprus (Acts 13:5), Antioch of Pisidia (v. 14), Iconium (ch. 14:1), Berea (ch. 17:10). In large cities synagogues were often numerous; as in Jerusalem (ch. 6:9) and Alexandria. These religious communities maintained an existence separate from the state and managed their own religious and civil affairs, subordinate, of course, to the law of the land (Jos. *Antiq.* xix. 5, 3). A board of elders managed the affairs of the synagogue and of the religious community which it represented (Luke 7:3–5). The special officers, who directed the worship, maintained order, and looked after the temporalities, were: 1. The ruler of the synagogue (Acts 18:8). In some synagogues several rulers were in office (Mark 5:22). The ruler presided at the service; appointed or permitted suitable members to pray, read the Scriptures, and exhort; and was responsible for the proprieties (Luke 13:

14). The services were not conducted by permanent officers set apart for the duty, but by private members who had shown qualifications for it. Thus Jesus read the Scriptures in the synagogue at Nazareth (Luke 4:16), and he often taught in the synagogues (Matt. 4:23). Paul and Barnabas were called on by the rulers of the synagogue at Antioch of Pisidia for words of exhortation (Acts 13: 15). 2. One or more attendants for the humbler and menial duties. They brought the Scriptures to the reader and replaced the roll in its depository (Luke 4:20), and they inflicted the corporal punishment to which the authorities sentenced a member. 3. Dispensers of alms (cf. Matt. 6:2). 4. Wealthy men of leisure, if possible 10 or more, who represented the congregation at every service. The congregation assembled every Sabbath for worship (Acts 15:21), and on the 2d and 5th days of the week to hear a portion of the Law read. At the Sabbath service prayer was offered by a member of the congre-

a mixture of Corinthian and Ionic. The faces of the lintels over the gateways have as a frequent ornament the representation of a scroll of vine leaves with bunches of grapes. At Nebartein there is a figure of the 7-branched candlestick, with an inscription; at Kefr Bir'im what is intended apparently for the paschal lamb; while at Tell Hum there are both the lamb and the pot of manna. The synagogue at Dura-Europus (on the right bank of the Euphrates on the road from Aleppo to Baghdad) was excavated in 1934. It is dated by an inscription of the year A.D. 245; it contains a remarkable variety of frescoes illustrating Biblical scenes and marks an epoch in the origins of Christian art.

The assembly room was provided with a reading desk, a chest or closet for the Scriptures, and seats for at least the elders and richer members (Matt. 23:6; James 2:2, 3). The more honorable seats were near the place where the Scriptures were kept. The congregation was divided: the men on one side, the

Remains of the Synagogue at Capernaum (Tell Hum)

gation. It consisted chiefly in reading Deut. 6:4-9; 11:13-21; Num. 15:37-41; and offering some or all of the 18 prayers and benedictions. The people were accustomed to stand during this prayer (Matt. 6:5; Mark 11:25), and united in saying "Amen" at its close. A lesson from the Law was read (Acts 15:21) by several members, each taking a short paragraph in turn. This reading was prefaced and concluded by thanksgiving. Then came a lesson from the Prophets, read by the person who had opened the service with prayer. The reading was followed by an exposition and an exhortation given by the reader or some other person (Luke 4:16-22; Acts 13:15). The service was concluded by a benediction, which was pronounced by a priest, if one were present, and the congregation said, "Amen." The synagogue was called by the Jews in their own language "assembly house." Ruins of these buildings still exist in Galilee at Tell Hum, which is perhaps the site of Capernaum, at Irbid, Kefr Bir'im, Nebartein, and some other places. These were rectangular structures. All lay n. and s., and had a large middle portal and 2 smaller side doors on the s. side. The interior was divided into 5 aisles by 4 rows of columns, and the 2 n. corners were formed by double-engaged columns. At Tell Hum there are Corinthian capitals; at Irbid

women on the other. Punishment ordered by the authorities of the synagogue was inflicted in the building, possibly in some chamber (Matt. 10:17; Acts 22:19).

The Great Synagogue denotes a council, said to have been organized by Nehemiah about 410 B.C. It consisted of 120 members (Megilloth, 17, 18). Ezra was its president. To this body the prophets transmitted the Law of Moses (Pirke Aboth i. 1). Simon the Just, who died about 275 B.C., was one of the last of its members. It was succeeded by the sanhedrin (Aboth x. 1). Its special work was to reorganize religious worship among the returned captives and to gather together the canonical books. Such is the Jewish tradition. The existence of the Great Synagogue has been doubted, since there is no mention of any such body in the Apocrypha, in Josephus, or in Philo. Nor does the name appear anywhere in Scripture. But the tradition is not to be wholly rejected. The Great Synagogue was probably a council of scribes for the decision of theological questions, contained from first to last, during an existence of a little more than a century and a half, about 120 prominent members, and numbered among them all the leading scribes from Ezra to Simon the Just.

Syn'ty·che (sĭn'tĭ-chē) [Gr., fortunate]. A woman in the Philippian church whom Paul exhorted (Phil. 4:2).

Syr'a·cuse (sĭr'à-kūs). A celebrated city on the e. coast of Sicily, founded about 735 B.C. by a colony of Corinthians and Dorians, led by Archias of Corinth. It greatly flourished and in 413 B.C. defeated and destroyed an Athenian fleet of 200 vessels. In 212 B.C. it was taken by the Romans. Paul saw it on his voyage to Rome (Acts 28:12). It was taken by the Moslems in A.D. 878.

Syr'i·a (sĭr'ĭ-à). A country along the e. coast of the Mediterranean and extending far inland. It comprehended most of the regions known in O.T. times as Canaan and Aram. The name is sometimes used as a translation of Aram, but inaccurately, being much too broad a term. The word Syria is an abbreviated form of Assyria, and became current after the conquests of Alexander the Great. Syria formed the most important province, both commercially and from a military point of view, of the kingdom of the Seleucidae, whose capital was at Babylon. It soon became apparent that w. Asia required a government of its own, more in the Greek spirit than was the system suitable for the far east. For this purpose Antioch was founded as a royal city about 300 B.C. (cf. I Macc. 3:37). The kingdom of the Seleucidae was gradually reduced by the encroachment of its foes, until at the close of the 2d century B.C. only Syria was left. With the Roman conquest in 64 B.C., the kingdom was erected into the province of Syria, with a Roman governor resident in Antioch. The name Syria was limited to this province, which included the country w. of the Euphrates from the Taurus Mountains to the borders of Egypt. From the time of Augustus it was governed by a consular legate of the emperor. In A.D. 70 Judea was separated from Syria and made a distinct province under an imperial legate.

Syr'i·ac (sĭr'ĭ-ăk) **Ver'sions.** See VERSIONS, II. 1.

Syr'i·an (sĭr'ĭ-ăn). One of the Syrian race, or an inhabitant of Syria. In O.T. times the word Syria was not in use; and where Syrian occurs in the E.V. of the O.T. it denotes a native of Aram, properly called an Aramaean (Gen. 28:5); see ARAM, DAMASCUS, and for the period after the conquests of Alexander the Great, SYRIA.

Sy'ro·phoe·ni'cian (sī'rô-fê-nĭsh'ăn), in A.V. **Sy'ro·phe·ni'cian** (sī'rô-fê-nĭsh'ăn). A Phoenician of Syria in distinction from the Libyphoenicians of n. Africa (Mark 7:26; cf. Matt. 15:22). A new distinction arose toward the end of the 2d century of the Christian era, when the province of Syria was divided into Syria Magna and Syria-Phoenice.

Syr'tis (sûr'tĭs). See QUICKSAND.

T

Ta'a·nach (tā'à-năk), in A.V. once **Ta'nach** (Josh. 21:25). A Canaanite city, mentioned about 1600 B.C. in connection with the advance of Thothmes III against Megiddo. Its king was defeated and slain by Joshua (Josh. 12:21). It lay within the limits of Issachar, but was nominally possessed by the Manassites (Josh. 17:11; I Chron. 7:29). Residence in it was assigned to the Kohathite Levites (Josh. 21:25). The Manassites failed to expel the Canaanite inhabitants, but ultimately rendered them tributary (Judg. 1:27). The great battle between Barak and Sisera was fought near Taanach (Judg. 5:19). The place was important in Solomon's reign (I Kings

4:12). Tell Ta'annak, the site of the ancient city, is situated among the low hills on the s. edge of the plain of Jezreel, 5 miles to the s.e. of ancient Megiddo.

Ta'a·nath-shi'loh (tā'à-năth-shī'lō) [approach to Shiloh]. A town on the border between Ephraim and Manasseh (Josh. 16:6). It is Khirbet Ta'na, 7 miles s.e. by e. of Shechem.

Tab·ba'oth (tă-bā'ŏth) [rings]. A family of Nethinim, represented in Zerubbabel's colony (Ezra 2:43; Neh. 7:46).

Tab'bath (tăb'àth). A place near Abelmeholah (Judg. 7:22); located at Rās Abū Ṭābāt.

Ta'be·al (tā'bê-ăl), A.V.; in R.V. **Ta'be·el** [good-not; a scornful modification of Tabeel]. A man whose son the allied kings, Rezin of Damascus and Pekah of Israel, attempted to place on the throne of David as their puppet king of Judah (Isa. 7:6).

Ta'be·el (tā'bê-ĕl) [Aram., God is good].
1. Probably the original pronunciation of Tabeal (q.v.).
2. A Persian petty governor, probably of Syrian descent, one of those who complained to Artaxerxes Longimanus that the wall of Jerusalem was being rebuilt (Ezra 4:7).

Tab'e·rah (tăb'ê-rà) [burning]. A place where the Israelites murmured, and the fire of the Lord burned among them in the uttermost part of the camp. The burning abated at the intercession of Moses. The event perhaps occurred at no formal encampment, but in the uttermost part of the camp at Kibrothhattaavah (Num. 11:1–3, 35; Deut. 9:22).

Ta'ber·ing. Beating, as on a tabor, tabret, tamborine, or timbrel (Nahum 2:7, A.V.).

Tab'er·nac'le. 1. A provisional tent where the Lord met his people (Ex. 33:7–10); see TENT OF MEETING 1.
2. The movable sanctuary in the form of a tent which God directed Moses at Sinai to make, that God might dwell as king among his people (Ex. 25:8, 9). Hence it was called "the dwelling" (chs. 25:9 marg. of R.V.; 26:1), and, as the place where Jehovah met his people, "the tent of meeting" (Ex. 40:34, 35, R.V.), and as the depository of the tables of the Law or testimony, "the tabernacle of the testimony" (Ex. 38:21; cf. ch. 25:21, 22; Num. 9:15). It was also known by the general designation "house of Jehovah" (Ex. 34:26; Josh. 6:24). The materials for its construction were largely obtained in the vicinity: the acacia wood of the wilderness, hair and skins of the flocks, skin of the tachash, a porpoise or similar creature, from the Red Sea. Gold, silver, brass, and linen, or perhaps muslin, were liberally furnished by the people, who gave their ornaments for the work (Ex. 35:21–29). The lavish expenditure of precious metals for this temporary structure and its furniture was justified, since none of this wealth would be lost when the movable tent gave place to a permanent edifice. The sacred vessels might serve in a new sanctuary or be wrought into new forms.

The architectural specifications for the tabernacle are drawn up systematically, and begin with the Ark, which was the central and essential feature of the appointed meetingplace between Jehovah and his people (Ex. 25:22):

I. *The essential and permanent features:* the Ark, table of showbread, and candelabrum (Ex. 25:10–40), which were symbols of heavenly things (Heb. 9:23). Their housing (Ex. ch. 26). The altar of burnt offerings (ch. 27: 1–8). The court (vs. 9–19). Continual testimony to be borne by the maintenance of light from pure beaten oil (vs. 20, 21). No such specifications for the showbread were required; the ordinance of ch. 25:30 sufficed, since the finest flour was always used in offerings.

II. *The means of approach.* A priesthood: authorized and appointed (ch. 28:1), garments (vs. 2–43), and consecration (ch. 29: 1–35). After mediating priests have been provided, atonement of the altar is specified (vs. 36, 37) and the continual sacrifice (vs. 38–42).

III. *When the way of approach has been opened,* the specifications advance to the altar of incense (ch. 30:1–10), symbolical of the adoration of God by his people cleansed of sin. Only here is the altar of incense mentioned apart from the other furniture in a description of the tabernacle. It is ordered in its logical place in the worship of God by his people. Elsewhere it is named with the other furniture in the unvarying order of Ark, table, candlestick, altar of incense, altar of burnt offering; as in the account of the manufacture of the furniture (ch. 37:25–28), in the enumeration of the completed furniture (ch. 39:38), in the directions for the erection of the tabernacle (ch. 40:5), and in the record of its erection (v. 26).

IV. *Provision for the needs of the service:* the half shekel atonement money (Ex. 30:11–16), the laver (vs. 17–21), the holy anointing oil (vs. 22–33), and the incense (vs. 34–38).

The tabernacle formed a rectangle, 30 cubits long by 10 broad, with the entrance at the e. end. The rear end and the 2 sides were made of boards, 48 in number, 20 on each side and 8 in the rear, of which 2 formed the posts at the angles. Each plank was 10 cubits long by 1½ cubits broad, and was overlaid with gold. They were hardly cut from the log in a single piece, but were probably framed of several pieces. They were set on end and were held in place at the bottom by tenons sunk in sockets of silver, 2 to each plank, and they were bound together laterally by transverse bars of acacia wood, which were arranged 5 on a side externally and thrust through rings attached to each plank (Ex. 26:15–30). The entire front was left as an entrance. This portal consisted of a row of 5 pillars overlaid with gold, resting in sockets of brass and supporting a curtain. The interior was divided into 2 apartments by 4 similar pillars sunk in sockets of silver and hung with a curtain (vs. 32, 37). These rooms were respectively the w., called the Holy of Holies, measuring 10 cubits in every direction, and the sanctuary or Holy Place, which was 20 cubits long by 10 cubits in breadth and height (cf. Ex. 26:16 for height; vs. 16, 18 for length; v. 16 with vs. 22–24 for width; Jos. *Antiq.* iii. 6, 4). The hangings were 4: 1. The ceiling and apparently the walls were hung with a curtain of white twined linen, blue, purple, and scarlet, and figured with cherubim. This curtain was made in 10 pieces, each 28 cubits by 4, sewed together in 2 sheets. These sheets were then looped together. One formed the ceiling and 3 sides of the Holy of Holies, and the other the ceiling and 2 sides of the sanctuary (Ex. 26:1–6). 2. The main external covering was of goats' hair, and consisted of 11 narrow curtains, each 30 cubits by 4; that is, 2 cubits longer than the under curtain of linen (cf. v. 13). These strips were united into 2 great curtains, which were looped together. The smaller one, which was made of 5 strips, covered the top and 3 sides of the Holy of Holies; the larger one covered the top and sides of the sanctuary, and had 1 breadth depending over the portal in front (vs. 7–13). 3. Over this covering of goats' skins a double roof of red-dyed rams' skins and *taḥash* (perhaps porpoise) skins was thrown (v. 14). 4. Two

veils were hung, one at the entrance to the sanctuary and the other in front of the Holy of Holies. Each was wrought of blue, purple, scarlet, and fine twisted linen; but on the inner veil, which separated the Holy of Holies, were figures of cherubim, in token of the presence and unapproachableness of Jehovah, while the outer veil, which was passed by the priests when they entered the sanctuary to minister, lacked symbols to prevent man's ingress (vs. 31–37).

The tabernacle stood in a courtyard, like itself rectangular in form; its longer sides,

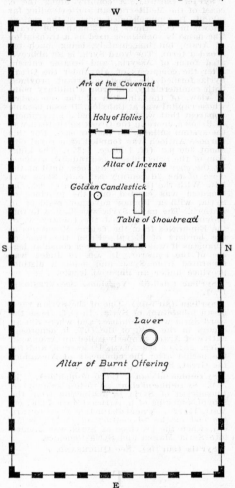

W

Ark of the Covenant

Holy of Holies

Altar of Incense

Golden Candlestick

Table of Showbread

S   N

Laver

Altar of Burnt Offering

E

Plan of the Tabernacle

running e. and w., were 100 cubits, while the shorter 2, running n. and s., were 50. The court was inclosed by a fence, 5 cubits high, formed of pillars filleted with silver, resting in sockets of brass, placed 5 cubits apart, and hung with fine twisted linen. The entrance was at the e. It was 20 cubits wide and was closed by a curtain of blue, purple, scarlet, and fine twisted linen, hung on 4 pillars (Ex. 27:9–18). The tabernacle was pitched in the w. half of this area, the laver and the altar of burnt offering being erected in the open e. half. The Ark was the central feature. It stood in the Holy of Holies. In the sanctuary, immediately in front of the veil that separated it from the Holy of Holies, stood the altar of incense, which however belonged to the oracle (I Kings 6:22, R.V.; Heb. 9:3, 4). In this apartment also were the table of showbread on the right hand and the golden candlestick on the left. In the court stood the laver and the altar of burnt offering. For the description of these objects and their symbolism, see the several articles.

The tabernacle was dedicated on the 1st day of the 2d year after the departure of the Israelites from Egypt. A cloud rested on it by day and a pillar of fire by night during all the period of the wandering. When the people broke camp, the Levites took the structure to pieces and put it together again at the new camping ground (Ex. 40:34–38). During the Conquest of Canaan the Ark remained in the camp at Gilgal. After the settlement of the Israelites, Joshua set up the tabernacle at Shiloh, where it remained during the period of the Judges (Josh. 18:1). Apparently with the lapse of time chambers for the occupancy of the priests and for the storing of gifts came to cluster about it (I Sam. 3:3; cf. the encampment of the Levites about it, Num. 3:23, 29, 35), and not unlikely the court was surrounded by a more substantial structure than hangings of linen. It was spoken of as a tent (II Sam. 7:6), the tent of meeting (Josh. 19:51; I Sam. 2:22), Jehovah's dwelling (Josh. 22:19, 29, translated tabernacle); Jehovah's house (Judg. 19:18; I Sam. 1:7, 24; 3:15), and as the abode of Israel's king, Jehovah's residence or palace (I Sam. 1:9; 3:3, translated temple). By the capture of the Ark by the Philistines, the tabernacle lost its glory and its value (Ps. 78:60). In the reign of Saul it was at Nob (cf. I Sam. 21:1 with Mark 2:26). During the greater part of David's reign, and in that of Solomon until the building of the Temple, the tabernacle was at the high place of Gibeon (I Chron. 16:39; 21:29). Afterward Solomon laid it up in the Temple (I Kings 8:4; II Chron. 5:5), which was constructed on the same model, but in every part was of dimensions twice as great.

Tab·er·nac'les, Feast of. The last of the 3 great annual festivals at which every man of Israel was required to appear before the Lord at the sanctuary, and the 2d of the harvest festivals (Deut. 16:16; II Chron. 8:12, 13; cf. I Kings 9:25; 12:32, 33; Zech. 14:16). It took its name from the custom of dwelling in booths during its celebration (Lev. 23:40–42), which, after the establishment of the sanctuary at Jerusalem, were erected in the open places of the city, on the roofs and in the courts of the houses, in the precincts of the Temple (Neh. 8:16), and in the open country outside the walls. It was the culminating festival of the year; and while preeminently and essentially agricultural, it combined a historical association, the reverse in this respect of the passover (Lev. 23:39, 43). It was kept in the 7th month, which by reason of the number was sacred, at the close of the agricultural season, when all the products of the year from grainfield, oliveyard, and vineyard were garnered. Hence the name "feast of ingathering," under which it was instituted (Ex. 23:16; 34:22; Lev. 23:39; Deut. 16:13–15). It began on the 15th day of the month, and was celebrated during 7 days. The special burnt offering amounted to 70 bullocks, distributed on a decreasing scale over the week, together with 2 rams and 14 lambs daily; and as a sin offering a he-goat was daily sacrificed (Num. 29:12–34; cf. Lev. 23:36; Ezra 3:4). The booths made of the boughs of trees suggested the vintage life;

but they were also made a reminder of the march from Egypt through the wilderness (Lev. 23:43; cf. Hos. 12:9). Every 7 years the Law of Moses was publicly read, the year of reading coinciding with the year of release, when there was no occasion to celebrate an ingathered harvest (Deut. 31:9–13). The festival occurred almost immediately after the Day of Atonement. The people, purged ceremonially from their sinfulness, could keep the feast with a glad sense of their fitness to commune with the bountiful God. The needy were remembered (Deut. 16:14). An 8th day of solemn assembly was added to the festival. It was distinct from the festival; the requirement to dwell in booths did not extend to it, and its offerings stood in no relation to those of the festival proper (Lev. 23:36, 39; Num. 29:35–38). It was not intended to conclude the feast of tabernacles, but only to bring the annual cycle of festivals to a fitting close. Later, however, the festival was spoken of as continuing for 8 days (II Macc. 10:6; Jos. Antiq. iii. 10, 4). It is disputed whether the 7th or the 8th day was the great day referred to in John 7:37. Splendid ceremonies were subsequently added to those prescribed in the Law for the festival. At the time of the morning sacrifice the people took branches of palm, myrtle, and willow intertwined and fruit in their hands, repaired to the Temple, and marched around the altar of burnt offering once daily and 7 times on the 7th day (Jos. Antiq. iii. 10, 4; xiii. 13, 5; cf. II Macc. 10: 6, 7). Another custom, possibly also in vogue in Christ's day, was that daily during the festival, at the time of the morning and evening oblation, a priest filled a golden vessel with water at the pool of Siloam and carried it to the Temple, where it was received with trumpet blast and the words of Isa. 12:3: "Therefore with joy shall ye draw water out of the wells of salvation." It was mixed with the wine of the sacrifices and, while priests blew trumpets and Levites played on instruments and sang psalms, was poured out beside the altar, whence it was conducted by a sewer into the Kidron Valley. It was also customary in the evening following the 1st day of the festival, and perhaps on the subsequent evenings, to illuminate the Court of the Women from 2 lofty stands, each supporting 4 immense lamps, which threw their light not only into the courts of the Temple, but far and wide over the city. The wicks were made of the cast-off linen of the priests. Levites, stationed on the steps of the court, rendered instrumental music and sang psalms; and a dance was performed by prominent laymen and priests.

Jews who were unable to attend the celebration at Jerusalem on account of the distance of the city from their home, especially Jews dwelling in foreign countries, kept the festival at the synagogue of the town where they lived, but of course without the offering of sacrifices.

Tab'i·tha (tăb'ĭ-thȧ). See DORCAS.

Ta'bor (tā'bẽr). 1. A mountain on the boundary of the territory of Issachar (Jos. Antiq. v. 1, 22; perhaps Josh. 19:22), situated inland among the mountains (Jer. 46:18). It is a notable mountain (Ps. 89:12), though vastly inferior in size to Hermon. The forces of Issachar and Zebulun assembled there preparatory to fighting with Sisera (Judg. 4:6, 12, 14). In 218 B.C., Antiochus the Great captured a town on its summit and fortified the place (Polybius v. 70, 6). Josephus encircled the top with a wall for defense (Jos. Life 37; War iv. 1, 8). Tabor, now called Jebel eṭ-Ṭūr, is a detached hill of limestone, rising 1,843 feet above the level of the Mediterranean, in the n.e. part of the plain of Jezreel, about 12 miles n. of Mount Gilboa, 5½ e. by s. of Nazareth, and 12 w. by s. of the s. curve of the Lake of Gennesaret. From the w.n.w. it looks like a truncated cone, and from the s.w. the segment of a sphere. The sides are steep. The n. side is covered with thickets of oak and terebinth. The top is flat and elliptical. In the 2d century the opinion was current that Tabor was the scene of the transfiguration, and ecclesiastical buildings in commemoration were erected from time to time on the summit. The theory is beset by the difficulty that there was a town on the summit in the days of Christ.

2. A town of Zebulun, given to the Merarite Levites (I Chron. 6:77), perhaps the place on the border of Issachar (Josh. 19:22). The latter is scarcely identical with the border town Chisloth-tabor (Josh. 19:12), which rather corresponds with Chesulloth (v. 18). It may be identified with Khirbet Dabûra, which is situated on the ridge joining Mount Tabor to the hill of Nazareth.

3. The oak or terebinth of Tabor (I Sam. 10:3; not "plain," as in A.V.), apparently in the territory of Benjamin.

Tab'ret. A musical instrument (I Sam. 10: 5), a timbrel (*q.v.*).

Tab'rim·mon (tăb'rĭm-ŏn), in A.V. **Tab'rimon** (tăb'rĭ-mŏn) [Aram., Rimmon is good]. A son of Hezion, and father of Ben-hadad I, king of Syria (I Kings 15:18).

Tache. A catch for taking hold or holding together. It was used about the tabernacle for coupling curtains together (Ex. 26:6, 11, in R.V. clasp).

Tach'mo·nite (tăk'mô-nīt). See TAHCHEMONITE.

Tad'mor (tăd'môr) [cf. Heb. *tāmār*, a palm tree]. A town in the desert (II Chron. 8:4). It was fortified by Solomon, doubtless to control the caravan route across it. In the parallel passage (I Kings 9:18, R.V.) it is called "Tamar in the wilderness," and described as being not only in the desert, but also "in the land." This latter phrase is probably broad enough to denote the extensive kingdom of Solomon (I Kings 9:19; 4:21, 24). The suggestion has been made that the town may be identical with Tamar at the s.e. corner of the promised boundaries of the land (Ezek. 47:19; 48:28), probably on the road from Hebron to Elath; see TAMAR 5. This identification is in itself suitable, and may include or correct Tadmor in II Chron. 8:4, which has been proposed in explanation of I Kings 9:18. But the text of Kings is suspicious; for the phrase "in the land" is superfluous, since all the towns mentioned were in the land, and the text departs from the parallel enumeration in Chronicles in failing to locate in Hamath the store cities of Solomon. Perhaps the original text was "Tamar in the wilderness, in the land of Hamath all the store cities." Tadmor eventually became subject to the Romans, who called it by its Greek name Palmyra (cf. Jos. *Antiq.* viii. 6, 1). Between A.D. 251 and 273 it was at first partially, and then for a time totally, independent. The place is called Tadmur in modern Arabic. It is in an oasis about 140 miles e.n.e. of Damascus, and about 120 from the Euphrates. It is now a ruin, stretching more than a mile and a half. It has long rows of Corinthian columns and a few of the Ionic order, with a number of towerlike tombs.

Ta'han (tā'hăn). A descendant of Ephraim, and founder of a tribal family (Num. 26:35). His descent was probably through Telah, Rephah, and Beriah to Ephraim (I Chron. 7:25).

Ta·hap'a·nes (tà-hăp'à-nēz). See TAHPANHES.

Ta'hash (tā'hăsh), in A.V. **Tha'hash** (thā'-hăsh) [porpoise, dolphin]. A son of Nahor by his concubine Reumah (Gen. 22:24).

Ta'hath (tā'hăth) [that which is beneath]. 1. A station of the Israelites in the wilderness (Num. 33:26, 27).

2. A Levite, family of Kohath, house of Izhar, and of the line of Korah and Abiasaph (I Chron. 6:24, 37). From him 2 families branched, those of Uriel and Zephaniah.

3. An Ephraimite, son of Bered, family of Shuthelah (I Chron. 7:20).

4. A son of Eleadah, and a descendant of Tahath, son of Bered (I Chron. 7:20).

Tah'che·mo·nite (tä'kĕ-mô-nīt), in A.V. **Tach'mo·nite.** A word found in II Sam. 23:8. It is probably a corruption, in the Heb. text, of "the Hachmonite," a copyist having mistaken Heb. *h* for *t*. See HACHMONI.

Tah'pan·hes (tä'păn-hēz), and once **Te·haph'ne·hes** (Ezek. 30:18); in A.V. once also **Ta·hap'a·nes** (Jer. 2:16). An Egyptian city (Ezek. 30:18), to which Jews fled to escape Babylonian vengeance after the murder of Gedaliah (Jer. 43:7–9). Jews seem to have become permanent residents there (Jer. 44:1; 46:14). The LXX renders the name Taphnas, obviously the same as Daphne, a fortified city on the Pelusiac channel of the Nile (Herod. ii. 30, 107), probably marked by Tell Defenneh, 12 miles n. of Pithom.

Tah'pe·nes (tä'pē-nēz). A queen of Egypt in the time of Solomon (I Kings 11:19, 20).

Tah're·a (tä'rē-à). See TAREA.

Tah'tim-hod'shi (tä'tĭm-hŏd'shī). A region visited by David's census takers in connection with Gilead, before they came to Danjaan and roundabout to Zidon (II Sam. 24: 6). The name is elsewhere unknown, and perhaps stands for "the Hittites toward Kadesh"; see KADESH 2.

Tal'ent. A weight used both for ordinary commodities and for the precious metals; see WEIGHTS. Naturally the talent as a money unit was not coined. From the parable of the Talents, in which a master distributes talents among his servants, according to their several abilities, to be put to profitable use (Matt. 25:14–30), is derived the English figurative use of the word talent.

Tal'i·tha cu'mi (tăl'ĭ-thà kōō'mĕ) [Aram., maiden arise] (Mark 5:41).

Tal'mai (tăl'mī) [pertaining to furrows, plowman; but perhaps from Hurrian *talma*, big]. 1. A son of Anak, and probably founder of a family of Anakim (Num. 13:22), driven from Hebron by Caleb (Josh. 15:14; Judg. 1:10).

2. A king of Geshur, whose daughter Maacah was one of David's wives, and Absalom's mother (II Sam. 3:3; 13:37).

Tal'mon (tăl'mŏn). A porter (a Levite), and the family which he founded (I Chron. 9:17). Members of the family returned from exile with Zerubbabel (Ezra 2:40, 42; Neh. 7:45), and served as porters at the new Temple (Neh. 11:19; 12:25).

Ta'mah (tā'mà). See TEMAH.

Ta'mar (tā'mēr), in A. V. of N.T. **Tha'mar** [palm tree]. 1. The wife of Er, son of Judah. When left a widow, she became the mother of Perez and Zerah by Judah (Gen. 38:6–30), and thus the ancestress of several tribal families (Num. 26:20, 21).

2. Absalom's beautiful sister, abused by her half-brother Amnon (II Sam., ch. 13; I Chron. 3:9).

3. A daughter of Absalom, named doubtless after his sister (II Sam. 14:27). Perhaps she became Uriel's wife and the mother of Maacah, Rehoboam's wife (II Chron. 13:2; Jos. *Antiq.* viii. 10, 1). See MAACAH 9.

4. A town in the desert (I Kings 9:18). The Heb. kere, the A.V., the marg. of the R.V., and II Chron. 8:4 have Tadmor; see TADMOR.

5. A place at the e. end of the promised s. frontier of Palestine (Ezek. 47:19; 48:28). It would lie s. of the Dead Sea; and perhaps is identical with the village Thamara, which had a Roman garrison, on the road between Hebron and Elath.

Tam'a·risk Tree. The tamarisk (*Tamarix articulata*) is called '*athl* in Arab., '*athlā* in Aram.; and accordingly the cognate Heb. word '*ēshel* doubtless likewise denotes the tamarisk. Abraham planted 1 in Beer-sheba (Gen. 21:33; in A.V. grove), Saul dwelt beneath 1 in Ramah (I Sam. 22:6; in A.V. a tree), and the bones of Saul and his sons were buried beneath 1 in Jabesh-gilead (I Sam. 31:13; in A.V. a tree). The Chronicler states that the bones of the king and his sons were interred beneath the '*ēlāh* in Jabesh (I Chron. 10:12, oak; J.V. and R.V. marg. terebinth). He may, however, use the term '*ēlāh* in its broad signification of strong tree; see OAK. The tamarisk is a small tree, with durable wood, deciduous branches, and minute, scale-like, evergreen leaves. Nine species occur in Palestine. The most widely distributed is *Tamarix pallasii*, which attains a height of from 10 to 20 feet. The largest species is *Tamarix articulata*, from 15 to 30 feet. It is found along the w. border of the desert of the wandering. *Tamarix mannifera*, from 10 to 15 feet in height, growing in ancient Moab, Edom, and the peninsula of Sinai, yields the substance popularly known as manna; see MANNA.

Tam'muz (tăm'ŭz). A deity of the Babylonians, called by them *Dumu-zi;* his full name in Sumerian was *Dumu-zid-abzu* (the faithful son of the Subterranean [freshwater] Ocean), but he is also called in late Sumerian liturgies *Sataran* (lord of healing). The Tammuz literature was transmitted orally for many centuries before it was reduced to writing in Sumerian in the late 3d millennium. Tammuz was worshiped throughout Babylonia, and in Assyria, Phoenicia, and Palestine; and he gave name to the 4th month of the Semitic year; see YEAR. He was the husband of his sister, the goddess Ishtar, and king of the nether world. He was also god of the pasture, the patron of flocks and their keepers, and hence was himself entitled shepherd. He was represented as dying annually and returning to life with each recurring year. While Tammuz was in the underworld, all life on earth languished and died. Ishtar penetrated into the nether world and recovered him. The story is clearly a nature myth. However its details may be explained, it symbolizes more or less the alternation of summer heat and the spring inundation, the death and revival of vegetation. Ezekiel in vision saw the worship of Tammuz in favor among the Jews, and women sitting at the n. gate of the Temple weeping for the god (Ezek. 8:14). This is significant, since the cult of the Sumero-Akkadian Tammuz can scarcely have become popular in s. Palestine before the 7th century B.C. Cyril of Alexandria and Jerome identified him with the Phoenician Adonis. Jerome says that the Syrians celebrated an annual solemnity to Adonis in June, when he was lamented by the women as dead, and afterward his coming to life again was celebrated with songs. From other sources it ap-

pears that Byblos in Phoenicia was the headquarters of the Adonis worship. The annual feast in his honor was held at the neighboring temple of Aphrodite in Mount Lebanon, and lasted 7 days. It began with a commemoration of the disappearance of the god. Vessels filled with mold and containing stalks of wheat, barley, lettuce, and fennel, and called gardens of Adonis, were exposed to the heat of the sun. The withering of the plants symbolized the slaughter of the youth by a wild boar, which in later versions was said to have been sent by Ares (Mars). Then followed a search for Adonis by the women. At length his image was found in one of the gardens. The finding was celebrated by lewdness and song. The image was then coffined, and the wound made by the boar which slew the young god was shown on his body. The people sat on the ground around the bier with their clothes rent, and the women raised loud lamentation. Sacrifice was offered for the dead god, and the image was buried.

Ta'nach (tā'năk). See TAANACH.

Tan·hu'meth (tăn-hū'mĕth) [consolation]. A Netophathite (II Kings 25:23; Jer. 40:8).

Tan'ner. A dresser of hides (Acts 9:43), who removes the hair by means of lime or other agent, steeps the skins in an infusion of bark, especially of oak bark, in order to impregnate them with the acid juice of the plant and render them firm, pliable, and durable, and thus converts the hide into leather. At Joppa Peter lodged with a tanner (Acts 10:5, 6). See LEATHER.

Ta'phath (tā'făth) [a drop]. A daughter of Solomon, and wife of Abinadab's son (I Kings 4:11).

Ta'phon (tā'fŏn). See TEPHON.

Tap·pu'ah (tăp-pū'ȧ) [apple]. 1. A town in the lowland of Judah (Josh 15:34), probably Beit-Nettif, formerly Beth-letepha, a corruption of Beth le-Taphua.

2. A town of Ephraim w. of Shechem and on the boundary of Ephraim (Josh. 16:8; 17:7, 8), probably to be identified with Sheikh Abu Zarad, near the modern Jāsūf, about 8 miles s. of Shechem.

3. A son of Hebron (I Chron. 2:43).

Ta'rah (tā'rȧ). See TERAH.

Tar'a·lah (tăr'ȧ-lä). A city of Benjamin (Josh. 18:27).

Ta're·a (tā'rê-ȧ). A descendant of King Saul through Jonathan (I Chron. 8:35; Tahrea, ch. 9:41).

Tares. The rendering of Gr. *zizanion* in Matt. 13:25–27, 29, 30; R.V. marg. darnel. The tare (*Vicia sativa*), a vetch, with pinnate and purple-blue or red papilionaceous flowers, would be easily distinguished from the wheat. The Gr. word *zizanion*, which is probably of Semitic origin, corresponds to

Bearded Darnel

Arab. *zuwān*, which denotes *Lolium*, and to Talmudic *zōnīn*. The bearded darnel (*Lolium temulentum*) is a poisonous grass, almost indistinguishable from wheat while the 2 are only in blade, but which can be separated without difficulty when they come into ear (cf. vs. 29, 30).

Tar'get. See ARMOR.

Tar'gums (tär'gŭmz). See VERSIONS, I. 3.

Tar'pel·ites (tär'pĕl-īts). An unidentified people settled by the Assyrians in the cities of Samaria; the Tibareni of the coast of Pontus and Tripolis of n. Phoenicia have been conjectured. Some have supposed that the word is no ethnic name, but is the title of certain Persian officials in Samaria (Ezra 4:9).

Tar'shish (tär'shĭsh), in A.V. 4 times **Thar'shish** (I Kings 10:22; I Chron. 7:10) [Phoenician, from Akkad., smelting plant, refinery]. 1. A people descended from Javan (Gen. 10:4) and their country. Since Jonah (Jonah 1:3) entered a ship at Joppa in order to flee thither, the route to it was evidently across the waters of the Mediterranean. It was a distant land (Isa. 66:19). The imports from Tarshish were silver beaten into plates (Jer. 10:9), and iron, tin, and lead (Ezek. 27:12). It is believed that Tarshish was Tartessus, in s. Spain, near Gibraltar (Herod. iv. 152). The mineral wealth of the region attracted the Phoenicians, who established a colony there. Spain has long been noted for its mineral wealth.

Ships of Tarshish were originally ships trading to and from Tarshish, but ultimately ships of first-rate magnitude to whatever place their voyages may have been made (Ps. 48:7; Isa. 2:16; 23:1, 14; 60:9; Ezek. 27:25). Such vessels, built by Jehoshaphat to go to Ophir, lay in the harbor at Ezion-geber on the Red Sea (I Kings 22:48). The term Tarshish ship is paraphrased as "ship going to Tarshish" (II Chron. 9:21, Heb. text; cf. I Kings 10:22) and "ship to go to Tarshish" (II Chron. 20:36); on the other hand, it is possible that the term originally meant refinery ship, so called after similar ships which plied the Mediterranean, connecting the mines and refineries of Sardinia and later those of s. Spain with Phoenicia.

2. A Benjamite, son of Bilhan (I Chron. 7:10).

3. One of the 7 highest princes of Persia (Esth. 1:14).

Tar'sus (tär'sŭs). The chief city of Cilicia, in the e. part of Asia Minor. It was situated on both banks of the river Cydnus, about 12 miles from the sea. About 833 B.C. it is mentioned by Shalmaneser, king of Assyria. When the Romans formed the province of Cilicia in 64 B.C., they made Tarsus the residence of the governor. For its allegiance to Julius Caesar, Cassius ordered it to be plundered, but in compensation, Mark Antony granted it municipal freedom and exemption from taxation. It was famed for its schools, which almost rivaled those of Athens and Alexandria. It was the birthplace of the Apostle Paul (Acts 21:39; 22:3), and he revisited it at least once after his conversion (chs. 9:30; 11:25).

Tar'tak (tär'tăk). An idol set up by the Avvites in Samaria (II Kings 17:31).

Tar'tan (tär'tăn). The title of the commander-in-chief of the Assyrian army (II Kings 18:17; Isa. 20:1). The name was pronounced by the Assyrians both *tartānu* and *turtānu*.

Tat'te·nai (tăt'ê-nī), in A.V. **Tat'nai** (tăt'-nī). A Persian governor w. of the river Euphrates, who opposed the rebuilding of the Temple (Ezra 5:3; 6:6; in I Esdras 6:3; etc., Sisinnes).

Tau (tō, tou), in A.R.V. **Tav** (tō, tou). [Heb. *tāw*]. The 22d and last letter of the Heb. alphabet, pronounced *t*; or *th*, when followed by a vowel. English *T* comes from the same source, and with *th* represents it in Anglicized Hebrew names; as Tamar, Nathan. It heads the 22d section of Psalm 119, in which section each verse of the original begins with this letter.

Tax'es. Under the Judges the regular payments obligatory on the Israelites were for the worship of Jehovah. There was as yet no army and no royal court to support. But there was a tabernacle and a priesthood, and these were maintained by the tithes and other offerings, and by the land which was permanently placed at the disposal of the Levites.

After the establishment of the kingdom, revenue for its support was obtained from various sources: 1. Taxes in kind were levied by Solomon on the produce of the field and the flock (I Kings 4:7–28; cf. Amos 7:1). 2. Tribute was rendered by subject peoples (II Sam. 8:6, 14; I Kings 10:15; II Kings 3:4), and service was exacted of the Canaanites who dwelt in the midst of Israel (Judg. 1:28, 30; I Kings 9:20, 21). When the Hebrews were subject to a foreign prince, they

St. Paul's Gate, Tarsus

had to pay tribute to him in addition to taxes for the support of their own government. 3. Duties were paid by tradesmen and merchants (I Kings 10:15). Without levying taxes in money or produce, and with little expense to himself, David attained the object of a standing army by dividing the men of military age into brigades of 24,000 men, and requiring each brigade in turn to hold itself in readiness during 1 month for instant service (I Chron. 27:1). Under Solomon the people were oppressed by taxation, and this grievous burden was an immediate cause of the disruption of the kingdom (I Kings 12:4).

Under the Persian empire, by decree of Darius Hystaspis the satraps of each province paid a fixed sum into the royal treasury (Herod. iii. 89). The inhabitants had to provide for the maintenance of the governor's household also. This provision was called the bread of the governor, and so far as Judah was concerned included food and 40 shekels daily in money (Neh. 5:14, 15). The revenue was derived from tribute, customs, and toll (Ezra 4:13). Priests, Levites, and Nethinim were exempted from these taxes in Judah (Ezra 7:24); but the burdens pressed heavily on the great body of the people, who had the sanctuary likewise to support, and many were forced to mortgage their fields and vineyards to raise money for the tribute (Neh. 5:4; 9:37).

Under the Ptolemies and the Seleucidae, instead of a fixed amount being levied by the crown on the people, the privilege of collecting the taxes of a district was put up at auction and sold to the highest responsible bidder. The party who promised the most revenue from a province was authorized to collect it and was furnished with military power sufficient to enable him to enforce his demands (Jos. Antiq. xii. 4, 1–5). The Syrian kings imposed a poll tax and a duty on salt, exacted a sum of money in lieu of the annual present of a crown of gold, which it had become customary to demand, took ⅓ of the grain and ½ of the fruit, and in addition levied on the tithes and tolls paid into the Temple at Jerusalem (I Macc. 10:29–31; 11: 34, 35; 13:37, 39; Jos. Antiq. xii. 3, 3).

When the Romans under Pompey took Jerusalem in 63 B.C., tribute was imposed on the Jews which in a short time amounted to more than 10,000 talents (Jos. Antiq. xiv. 4, 4 and 5). Julius Caesar decreed that the tribute should not be farmed, that it should not be levied in a Sabbatic year, and that in the year following a Sabbatic year only ¼ the usual amount should be collected (Jos. Antiq. xiv. 10, 5 and 6); Herod the Great taxed the produce of the field (xv. 9, 1), and levied duties on commodities bought and sold (xvii. 8, 4). When Judea was placed under procurators, the financial system of the empire was introduced. The revenues were farmed; see PUBLICAN. There were levied: 1. Tribute of the soil, paid either in kind or in money. 2. A poll tax (Matt. 22:17) and, under the same name, a tax on personal property. 3. Export and import duties, collected at seaports and at the gates of cities. In Jerusalem a house duty was paid by the inhabitants (Jos. Antiq. xix. 6, 3).

After the Exile a Temple tax of half a shekel was imposed on every Israelite who had reached the age of 20 years (Matt. 17: 24). The collectors visited each town of Judea annually at a fixed time, and in foreign countries places were designated where it might be paid. See TRIBUTE 2.

Tax'ing. An enrollment, ordered by the Roman emperor Augustus, which in the providence of God brought Joseph and Mary to Bethlehem, and led to the fulfillment of the ancient prophecy that the Messiah should be born in that town (Micah 5:2; Matt. 2:5, 6; Luke 2:1–20). A later enrollment led to tumults among the Jews (Acts 5:37). See QUIRINIUS.

Te'bah (tē'bả) [slaughter]. A son of Nahor by Reumah, his concubine (Gen. 22:24), and the tribe descended from him. The name is found in II Sam. 8:8, in the Peshitta as Ṭᵉbaḥ, and the Lucianic reading Matebak suggests the same name; in I Chron. 18:8 in the form Ṭibḥath, it denotes a town of Aram-zobah.

Teb'a·li'ah (tĕb'á-lī'á) [Jehovah has immersed, i.e., ceremonially purified]. A Merarite Levite, the 3d son of Hosah (I Chron. 26:11).

Te'beth (tē'bĕth) [Akkad. ṭebētu, month of sinking in, muddy month]. The 10th month of the Semitic calendar (Esth. 2:16). See YEAR.

Te·haph'ne·hes (tê-hăf'nê-hēz). See TAH-PANHES.

Te·hin'nah (tê-hǐn'á) [grace, supplication]. A man of Judah, descended from Chelub, and ancestor of the inhabitants of Ir-nahash (I Chron. 4:12).

Teil Tree. The linden, a tree of the genus Tilia. The Heb. word 'ēlāh is once translated thus in A.V. (Isa. 6:13; in R.V. terebinth); see OAK 1 and TEREBINTH. The teil tree does not grow in Palestine.

Te'kel (tē'kĕl) [Aram. tᵉḳal = Heb. shāḳal, to weigh; cf. Aram. tᵉḳēl = Heb. sheḳel, shekel]. See MENE.

Te·ko'a (tê-kō'á), in A.V. thrice **Te·ko'ah** (tê-kō'á) (II Sam. 14:2, 4, 9), and so in R.V. of I Macc. 9:33, where A.V. has **The·co'e.** A town in Judah (I Chron. 2:24; 4:5; LXX, Josh. 15:60), in the wilderness toward Engedi (II Chron. 20:20). It was fortified by Rehoboam (II Chron. 11:6). It was the home of the Prophet Amos (Amos 1:1). In Nehemiah's time the common people of Tekoa helped to rebuild the wall of Jerusalem, while the nobles of the place showed indifference to the work (Neh. 3:5, 27). The name still lingers as Ṭaḳū'a, a ruined village 6 miles s. of Bethlehem. It is on a hill broad at the top, where are found the remains of the foundations of houses, often with beveled stones, the whole occupying an area of 4 or 5 acres.

Te·ko'ite (tê-kō'ĭt). A native or inhabitant of Tekoa (II Sam. 23:26).

Tel'-a'bib (tĕl'ã'bĭb) [heap, or hill of ears of grain]. A place in Babylonia, near the river Chebar. Jewish exiles were located there (Ezek. 3:15).

Te'lah (tē'lá) [fracture]. A descendant of Ephraim, probably through Beriah (I Chron. 7:25).

Te·la'im (tē-lā'ǐm) [little lambs]. A place where Saul assembled his army to war against the Amalekites (I Sam. 15:4; cf. ch. 27:8, in some MSS. of the LXX). It may be Telem of Josh. 15:24; but the 2 names as traditionally pronounced have a different meaning.

Te·las'sar (tê-lăs'ẽr), in A.V. once **The·la'·sar** (II Kings 19:12) [probably, hill of Asshur]. A place inhabited by the children of Eden (II Kings 19:12; Isa. 37:12); it may have been one of the cities of Bit-Adini, a small kingdom on the upper Euphrates.

Te'lem (tē'lĕm). 1. A town in the extreme s. of Judah (Josh. 15:24). See TELAIM.

2. A porter, whom Ezra induced to put away his foreign wife (Ezra 10:24).

Tel'-har'sha (tĕl'här'shȧ), in A.V. **Tel'-har'sa** (tĕl'här'sȧ) and **Tel'-ha·re'sha** (tĕl'hȧrē'shȧ) [mound of the artificer's work, of silence, or of enchantment, incantation]. A place in Babylonia whence certain people who claimed to be Israelite exiles returned with Zerubbabel to Jerusalem (Ezra 2:59; Neh. 7:61).

Tell' el-A·mar'na (tĕl' ĕl-ä-mär'nȧ). Amenhotep IV (Akhnaton), who was Pharaoh from c. 1387 to c. 1366 B.C., built a new capital, which he named Akhetaton. It was situated on the east bank of the Nile River, about 160 miles above the Delta and nearly 300 below Thebes; the modern name is Tell el-Amarna. Here were found in the year 1887 more than 350 clay tablets. They were written in Akkadian, the international language of the 15th and 14th centuries B.C., and proved to be the correspondence of the vassal princes and governors in Syria and Palestine with their overlords, Amenhotep III and IV. Nearly all of them were written in Syria and Palestine, and accordingly they are of first-hand value for the light they shed on conditions in Palestine of that period. Whether they reflect the conditions of about the time of the conquest by Joshua or of about a century and a half before the Israelite conquest of Palestine depends upon the date of the Exodus. See EGYPT, III. 8.

Tel'-me'lah (tĕl'mē'lȧ) [hill of salt]. A place in Babylonia, whence certain people who claimed to be Israelite exiles came to Jerusalem with Zerubbabel (Ezra 2:59; Neh. 7:61).

Te'ma (tē'mȧ). A tribe of Ishmaelites and the district they inhabited (Gen. 25:15; Isa. 21:14). Their caravans were well known (Job 6:19). Tema denotes Taima (Taymā') in Arabia, midway between Damascus and Mecca and equidistant from Babylonia and Egypt.

Te'mah (tē'mȧ), in A.V. **Ta'mah** and **Tha'·mah**. Founder of a family of Nethinim, members of which returned with Zerubbabel from the Captivity (Ezra 2:53; Neh. 7:55).

Te'man (tē'măn) [on the right hand, southern]. A tribe descended from Esau and the district it inhabited (Gen. 36:11, 15, 34). The territory was in Edom (Jer. 49:20; Amos 1:12), apparently in the n. part (Ezek. 25:13). Its inhabitants were noted for their wisdom (Jer. 49:7).

Te'man·ite (tē'măn-īt), in A.V. once **Tem'·a·ni** (tĕm'ȧ-nī). A member of the tribe of Teman (Gen. 36:34), or of Tema. It is not certain in which sense Eliphaz, Job's friend, was a Temanite (Job 2:11).

Tem'e·ni (tĕm'ē-nī). A son of Ashhur (I Chron. 4:5, 6).

Tem'ple. A building dedicated to the worship of a deity (Joel 3:5; cf. Ezra 5:14 with ch. 1:7; Acts 19:27). In 3 passages it is applied to the tabernacle (I Sam. 1:9; 3:3; II Sam. 22:7; cf. Rev. 15:5); but generally the reference is to some one of the temples successively erected to Jehovah at Jerusalem.

1. *Solomon's Temple.* The erection of a permanent house of the Lord, instead of the movable tabernacle, was proposed by David, and the necessary materials were largely amassed by him (II Sam., ch. 7; I Kings 5:3–5; 8:17; I Chron., chs. 22; 28:11 to 29:9). He gathered 100,000 talents of gold and 1,000,000 talents of silver for the prospective structure and its furnishings (I Chron. 22:14), and added from his own private fortune 3,000 talents of gold and 7,000 talents of silver, and the princes contributed 5,000 talents of gold, 10,000 darics of gold, and 10,000 talents of silver (ch. 29:4, 7), making a total

of 108,000 talents of gold, 10,000 darics of gold, and 1,017,000 talents of silver. It should also be borne in mind that the purchasing power of money was greater in those times than now. This large amount is perhaps not incredible, in view of the booty which David brought home from his wars and received as tribute. Still the sum is very large, and it is well to admit the probability of the text's being corrupt. This store of precious metals was placed at the disposal of Solomon for the use of the Temple, but it was not all expended (I Kings 7:51; II Chron. 5:1).

Solomon began the work in the 4th year of his reign, and it was completed in 7 years and 6 months (I Kings 6:1, 38). The alliance with Hiram, king of Tyre, rendered it easy to obtain timber from Lebanon, and skilled Phoenician artificers. 30,000 Israelites were levied and sent in detachments of 10,000 for a month to the Lebanon Mountains (I Kings 5:13, 14), and the remnant of the Canaanites was impressed to the number of 150,000 to serve as hewers of stone and carriers (I Kings 5:15; 9:20, 21; II Chron. 2:2, 17, 18). Overseers were appointed, apparently 550 chiefs and 3,300 subordinates (I Kings 5:16; 9:23), of whom 3,600 were Canaanites and 250 Israelites (II Chron. 2:18; 8:10). The building was erected on Mount Moriah, at the spot where the threshing floor of Ornan, or Araunah, the Jebusite, had stood (II Chron. 3:1). Its general plan was that of the tabernacle, but the dimensions were double and the ornamentation was richer. The interior of the edifice measured 60 cubits in length, 20 in breadth, and 30 in height, in this last particular deviating from the proportions of the tabernacle (I Kings 6:2). The walls were built of stone made ready at the quarry (v. 7). The roof was constructed of beams and planks of cedar (v. 9), the floor was laid with fir (cypress), and the walls from the floor to the ceiling were lined with cedar (v. 15). The whole interior was overlaid with gold (I Kings 6:20, 22, 30; II Chron. 3:7 *et passim*), and its walls were carved not only with cherubim, but also with palm trees and flowers.

The Holy of Holies was a cube. Each side measured 20 cubits (I Kings 6:16, 20). The space, nearly 10 cubits high, between its ceiling and the roof was probably occupied by upper chambers, gold-lined (I Chron. 28:11; II Chron. 3:9). In the Holy of Holies itself was placed the Ark (I Kings 8:6), under the wings of 2 colossal cherubim of olive wood overlaid with gold. Each cherub was 10 cubits in height, and had wings 5 cubits long. With the tip of 1 wing it touched a side wall, and with the other wing it reached forward to the center of the room and touched the corresponding wing of its companion. The 4 wings thus extended across the width of the house, while the cherubim turned their faces toward the sanctuary (I Kings 6:23–28; II Chron. 3:13). Under their wings the Ark was placed (I Kings 8:6). The partition between the Holy and the Most Holy Place was of cedar boards, overlaid on both sides with gold, and it had 2 doors of olive wood, decorated with palm trees, flowers, and cherubim, and overlaid with gold; see LEAF 2. There were hung, toward the sanctuary, chains of gold and a curtain patterned after that of the tabernacle (I Kings 6:16, 21, 31, 32; II Chron. 3:14; cf. Jos. *Antiq.* viii. 3, 3 and 7).

The Holy Place or sanctuary was 40 cubits long, 20 wide, and 30 high. Its walls were pierced by latticed windows, probably near the roof, for ventilation and the escape of smoke (I Kings 6:4). The altar of incense was made of cedar, instead of acacia, and overlaid with gold (chs. 6:20, 22; 7:48). It belonged to the Holy of Holies (I Kings 6: 22, R.V.; Heb. 9:3, 4), but stood in the Holy Place, doubtless because the priest, who might enter the Holy of Holies but once in the year, had occasion to offer incense daily. There were 10 golden candlesticks instead of 1, and likewise 10 tables, although doubtless the showbread was displayed on but 1; see CANDLESTICK and SHOWBREAD. The entrance to the sanctuary from the court had doors of fir wood (I Kings 6:33, 34).

Against the 2 exterior sides and the rear of the Temple a 3-story building was erected, containing chambers for officials and for storage (I Kings 6:5–10). Before the front entrance a portico was built, 10 cubits wide, 20 long, and 120 or, more probably, 20 high (I Kings 6:3; II Chron. 3:4; cf. LXX; Syriac). By it stood the 2 brazen pillars, Boaz and Jachin, each 18 cubits high and richly ornamented (I Kings 7:15–22; II Chron. 3:15–17).

The courts of the Temple were 2: the inner, upper Court of the Priests, and the Great Court (II Kings 23:12; II Chron. 4:9; Jer. 36:10). They were separated from one another, both by the difference of level and by a low wall, consisting of 3 courses of hewn stone and 1 course of cedar beams (I Kings 6:36; 7:12). In the Court of the Priests were a brazen altar for sacrifice (I Kings 8:64; II Kings 16:14; II Chron. 15:8), in size nearly 4 times that used at the tabernacle (II Chron. 4:1), and a brazen sea and 10 brazen lavers (I Kings 7:23–39). The sea contained water for the priests to wash themselves; the lavers were for washing such things as belonged to the burnt offering (II Chron. 4:6); see ALTAR, MOLTEN SEA, LAVER. The Great outer Court was for Israel (cf. I Kings 8:14). It was paved (II Chron. 7:3); and it was surrounded by a wall, for it had gates (II Chron. 4:9; cf. Ezek. 40:5).

This Temple was plundered and burned by the Babylonians when they captured Jerusalem in 586 B.C. (II Kings 25:8–17).

2. *Zerubbabel's Temple.* Cyrus authorized the erection of a temple 60 cubits in breadth and height (Ezra 6:3; Jos. *Antiq.* xi. 4, 6; cf. xv. 11, 1). It was begun in the 2d year after the return from captivity; and, after much opposition from the inhabitants of Samaria, it was renewed the 2d year of Darius (520) and completed in the 6th year of Darius, 515 B.C. (Ezra 3:8; 6:15). The dimensions of the several parts are not known. The plan of Solomon's Temple was, however, followed; though the new building was projected on a scale of far less magnificence. In the construction of the house, cedar from Lebanon was used (Ezra 3:7); and precious metals which were provided, as in the wilderness, by the freewill offerings of the people (chs. 1:6; 2:68, 69). Many of the vessels used in the former Temple were restored (ch. 1:7–11). The interior walls were overlaid with gold; and the house was divided, as usual, into the Holy of Holies and the sanctuary, apparently separated from each other by at least a veil (I Macc. 1:21, 22; 4:48, 51). The Holy of Holies was empty, for the Ark of the Covenant had disappeared (Tacitus *Hist.* v. 9; cf. Cicero *Pro Flac.* 28). The sanctuary was furnished with an altar of incense, and, like the tabernacle, with only 1 candlestick and 1 table for showbread (I Macc. 1:21, 22; 4:49). Exterior chambers were attached to the building (Neh. 10:37–39; 12:44; 13:4; I Macc. 4:38); and the whole was surrounded with courts (Neh. 8: 16; 13:7; Jos. *Antiq.* xiv. 16, 2). A brazen sea (Ecclus. 50:3) and an altar for sacrifice were used (Ezra 7:17). The altar was built of stones (I Macc. 4:44–47). The Court of the Priests was eventually separated from the

Outer Court by a wooden railing (Jos. *Antiq.* xiii. 13, 5). The Temple and its precincts were closed by doors and gates (Neh. 6:10; I Macc. 4:38).

3. *Herod's Temple* superseded Zerubbabel's. It is fully described by Josephus, who was thoroughly familiar with the building (Jos. *Antiq.* xv. 11; *War* v. 5), and in the Mishnah (*Middōth*). The materials were brought together before the old structure was taken down. Work was commenced in the 18th year of Herod's reign, 20–19 B.C. The main edifice was built by priests in a year and a half, and the cloisters were finished in 8 years; but the work on the entire complex of courts and buildings was not completed until the procuratorship of Albinus, A.D. 62–64 (Jos. *Antiq.* xv. 15, 5 and 6; xx. 9, 7; cf. John 2:20). The old area was enlarged to twice its former dimensions (Jos. *War* i. 21, 1). The Temple proper stood upon the highest ground in the inclosure. It was built of great blocks of white stone. Its interior had the length and breadth of Solomon's Temple; but a height of 40 cubits, exclusive of an upper chamber, instead of 30 cubits. It was divided into the Holy of Holies and the sanctuary on the customary lines. The Holy of Holies was empty. It was separated from the Holy Place by a veil (Jos. *War* v. 5, 5). The rending of this veil by an earthquake at the death of Christ signified that the way to the mercy seat is no longer closed to all save the mediating high priest, but is at all times open to the sincere worshiper (Matt. 27:51; Heb. 6:19; 10:20). The Holy Place contained, as usual, a golden altar for incense, a table for showbread, and a candlestick. It was entered from the e. by a great doorway closed by golden doors, each 55 cubits high and 16 broad; hung with a veil of blue, purple, scarlet, and fine linen; and encompassed on the outer or court side by a golden vine from which depended immense clusters of golden grapes. Against the 2 sides and rear of the Temple, a 3-story building, 40 cubits high, containing chambers, was constructed (cf. Jos. *War* vi. 4, 7), and in addition 2 wings, 1 containing winding stairs, sprang from the front corners. The building measured externally 100 cubits in length and 54 or, including the 2 wings at the front, 70 cubits in width. Over the Holy Place and the Holy of Holies was an attic, which had the same dimensions as the sacred apartments beneath. This attic, together with its floor and the roof, increased the height of the sacred edifice to over 90 cubits. A vestibule or porch ran along the entire front of the house, 100 cubits long and high and 20 broad. Its portal was 70 cubits high by 25 broad (or, according to the Mishnah, 40 and 20), without doors, allowing the great doorway of the sanctuary to be seen from without. Above this porch, over the great gate of the Temple, Herod erected the celebrated golden eagle (Jos. *Antiq.* xvii. 6, 2 and 3; *War* i. 33, 2 and 3). Twelve steps descended from the vestibule to the Court of the Priests. This court surrounded the sacred edifice. It contained the altar for burnt offerings, of which the height was 15 cubits, and the base a square measuring 50 cubits to the side. According to the Mishnah, it was built of unhewn stones; and contracted from a base 32 cubits square to a top 24 cubits square. It was reached by an inclined plane. A brazen sea or laver was also in use (Mishnah). This court was encompassed by a wall or coping about a cubit in height. All around the Court of the Priests lay, as of old, the Great Court, now double. It was inclosed by a wall, whose top was 25 cubits higher than the pavement. Against the inner side of this wall storage chambers were built (Jos. *War* vi. 5, 2), and in front of these, that is, on the Temple side, ran a covered

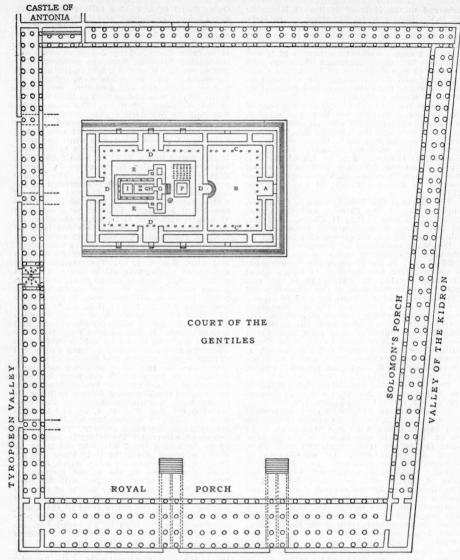

CASTLE OF ANTONIA

COURT OF THE

GENTILES

TYROPOEON VALLEY

SOLOMON'S PORCH

VALLEY OF THE KIDRON

ROYAL   PORCH

APPROXIMATE PLAN OF HEROD'S TEMPLE AND ITS COURTS

A. Beautiful Gate (Gate of Nicanor)
B. Court of the Women
C. Women's Gallery
D. Court of Israel
E. Court of the Priests

F. Altar of Burnt Offering
G. Porch
H. Holy Place
I. Holy of Holies

colonnade. This court was divided into 2 parts by a wall. The w. portion, that encompassing the Court of the Priests, was the Court of Israel. Only the men of Israel were allowed within it. The Court of the Women was the e. and lower portion. It was reached from the Court of Israel through a great gate in the center of the partition wall and by a descent of 15 steps. Only Israelites might enter this court, and women might not advance farther. These 3 courts and the Temple were embraced in the sacred inclosure. The inclosing barrier was triple: the wall of

the Courts of Israel and the Women, which has been already mentioned, and which was very thick, like the walls of a fortress (cf. Jos. *War* vi. 4, 1) ; a terrace, of which the top was level and 10 cubits broad; and at the foot of the terrace a wall 3 cubits in height, surmounted by pillars, on which were inscriptions forbidding all persons save those of the commonwealth of Israel from entering the inclosure. "Let no foreigner," so ran the Greek inscription, "enter inside of the barrier and the fence around the sanctuary. Whosoever is caught will be the cause of death following as a penalty (upon himself)." This triple wall of partition (Eph. 2:14) was pierced by 9 gates. These tower-like structures were sheathed with gold and silver. Four were on the n., and 4 on the s. side. Of these, 1 on each side led into the Court of the Women and 3 into that of Israel. The 9th was the great e. gate, the only one on that side, probably the gate Beautiful (Acts 3:2, 10). The difference of level between the vestibule of the Temple within the inclosure and the Court of the Gentiles without appears to have been about 15 cubits. From the vestibule to the Court of the Priests were 12 steps; from the Court of Israel to that of the Women 15; thence to the terrace 5; and thence to the Court of the Gentiles 14. This Court of the Gentiles occupied the remainder of the Temple yard and completely surrounded the sacred inclosure. It was foursquare (Jos. *War* vi. 5,

known by the name of Huldah. In the e. wall was the Shushan gate. One is mentioned in the n. wall (Jos. *War* vi. 4, 1).

During the siege of Jerusalem by the Romans in A.D. 70, the Jews themselves, who were using the Temple yard as a fortress, set fire to the outer cloisters; but the Temple itself was fired by a Roman soldier contrary to the orders of Titus, and all that was combustible was destroyed (Jos. *War* vi. 3, 1; 4, 5; cf. 5, 1; 9, 2). Afterward the conquerors threw down the walls (Jos. *War* vii. 1, 1). On its site the emperor Hadrian dedicated a temple to Jupiter Capitolinus in A.D. 136 or earlier. In A.D. 363 the emperor Julian, in order to defeat the prophecy of Christ (Matt. 24:1, 2), undertook to rebuild the Temple; but his plans were frustrated by flames which burst from the foundation. In A.D. 691 'Abd-al-Malik built on the site of the Temple of Solo-

Warning Tablet of Herod's Temple

4), and measured fully 6 stades, or ¾ of a mile, in circuit (Jos. *War* v. 5, 2). It was paved throughout. At the n.w. corner stood the castle of Antonia. Except perhaps at that point, it was bordered on all sides by magnificent, covered colonnades or cloisters (Jos. *Antiq.* xvii. 10, 2; cf. *War* vi. 3, 2). Those on the s. were the finest. They contained 162 columns, arranged in 4 rows, forming 3 aisles. Each column was a monolith of white stone, 25 cubits high. The roof was ceiled with cedar, curiously carved and carefully polished. The other colonnades consisted of 2 rows of columns. That along the e. side of the court was regarded as a remnant of the 1st Temple, and was called Solomon's Porch (John 10:23; Acts 3:11; Jos. *Antiq.* xx. 9, 7; *War* v. 5, 1). It was this court which was so far abused that money changers were allowed to set up their tables and traders were permitted to expose cattle for sale there (Matt. 21:12; John 2:14). Finally the sacred area was surrounded by massive walls. The w. wall was pierced by 4 gates: the 2 more n. ones led to the suburbs; the 3d led to a way that crossed the Tyropoeon Valley at a point now marked by Wilson's Arch; and the 4th, still farther s., opened into the valley and was reached by steps from the Temple yard (Jos. *Antiq.* xv. 11, 5). In the s. wall were 2 gates,

mon the Dome of the Rock, wrongly called the "Mosque of Omar."

Ten Com·mand'ments. The fundamental laws of the Hebrew state; see THEOCRACY. The Hebrews called them the 10 words (R.V. marg. of Ex. 34:28; Deut. 4:13; 10:4). They were spoken by God at Sinai, and written on 2 tables of stone (Ex. 31:18). The engraving was on both front and back surfaces (ch. 32: 15). The laws appear in 2 forms: the original form, contained in Ex. 20:1–17, and the free citation of the words in Deut. 5:6–21. The principal difference is that the law of the Sabbath is enforced, in the original Law, by reference to God's resting on the 7th day from the work of creation; whereas when Moses cites the Law in his public address, he omits this fundamental basis of the command and urges the deliverance from Egypt as the reason why Israel should remember the day. Another difference, and one upon which undue stress has been laid, is that when Moses repeats the Tenth Commandment, he uses the word covet in 1 clause only and employs "desire" instead of "covet" in reference to a neighbor's house, field, etc. (R.V.). These differences are not contradictions, and they are fully explained by the character of Deuteronomy. See DEUTERONOMY, SABBATH.

597

The Ten Commandments are not individually numbered in the Bible. Later Jews regarded the words "I am the Lord thy God, which have brought thee out of the land of Egypt, out of the house of bondage" (Ex. 20:2) as the First Commandment. These words, however, are not in the form of a command. They constitute the preface to the 10 laws which follow. Omitting the preface, there are 2 methods of enumeration: 1. According to the received teaching of the Roman Catholic and Lutheran Churches, based on Augustine, the 1st table contains 3 commandments and the 2d table 7. Augustine adopted this classification because it exhibits the symbolical numbers 3, 7, 10, and represents a real difference in the nature of the commands, the first 3 being duties toward God and the last 7, duties toward man. The 1st division included the command to remember the Sabbath; and to make out 3 commands in this table, Augustine joined into 1 the commands to have no other gods and to make no graven image; and to secure 7 in the 2d table he divided the command against covetousness into 2 laws. He followed the text of Deuteronomy, and made the command not to covet a neighbor's wife the Ninth Commandment, and that against desiring a neighbor's property the Tenth. The Lutheran Church follows the text of Exodus, and makes the command not to covet a neighbor's house the Ninth, and that against coveting a neighbor's wife, manservant, etc., the Tenth. The great objections to this method of enumeration are that it makes no distinction between polytheism and idolatry, and introduces an arbitrary distinction regarding kinds of covetousness. 2. The division which numbers the command against polytheism as the First, that against idolatry as the Second, and that against covetousness as the Tenth. This division is the oldest that is known. It was recognized by Josephus (Antiq. iii. 5, 5), by Philo (Decalogue), and by Origen; and it was adopted by the Reformed Churches at the Reformation. But there are 2 methods of distributing the 10 between the 2 tables: 1. They are ordinarily grouped as 4 relating to man's duty toward God and 6 to his duty to his fellows. This division is simple enough, and it is ethically correct; but it lacks symmetry. 2. Five are assigned to each table (Jos. Antiq. iii. 5, 8). This arrangement preserves the grouping of laws into decads, subdivided into pentads, which characterizes much of the legislation. And from the Jewish point of view, doubtless, the division is ethically correct; for the 1st table includes duties of piety, which imply no corresponding rights, and the 2d table embraces duties of justice, which involve rights. The duty of honoring parents, to the extent of maintaining them if need be, was regarded as absolute and unconditional (Mark 7:10–13). It was a pious duty, a religious duty, and properly belonged to the 1st table. Paul is sometimes cited as lending countenance to this division; for when summing up the duties which are comprehended in the command to love one's neighbor as one's self, he enumerates the last commandments, and makes no mention of honoring parents (Rom. 13:9). But Paul's enumeration is not intended to be complete. He omits the Ninth Commandment. Jesus placed the Fifth Commandment in the same group with the last 5 (Mark 10:19).

Tent. 1. A movable habitation; such as is used by nomads, shepherds, and soldiers (Gen. 4:20; 25:27; Judg. 8:11). The tent was frequently made of black cloth woven from goats' hair (S. of Sol. 1:5), fastened with cords and stakes (Ex. 35:18; Isa. 54:2). There were both round and tapering tents; and flat, oblong tents.

2. A habitation generally (Gen. 9:27; I Kings 8:66; II Kings 13:5; Job 8:22, R.V.; Ps. 84:10; Jer. 30:18; Lam. 2:4, R.V.; Zech. 12:7; Mal. 2:12, R.V.).

Tent of the Con′gre·ga′tion. See following article.

Tent of Meet′ing, in A.V. **Tent or Tab′er·nac′le of the Con′gre·ga′tion** [tent where Jehovah meets his people]. 1. A provisional tent where Jehovah met with his people (Ex. 33: 7–11; cf. ch. 34:34, 35). After the golden calf was made, Jehovah refused to acknowledge Israel any longer as his people and to dwell in their midst. He was estranged and distant. Because of this fact and to symbolize it, Moses used to pitch the tent outside the camp (ch. 33:7, R.V.), probably until God again promised to go in the midst of Israel (ch. 34: 9). What tent this was is uncertain. But a tent unquestionably formed the headquarters of the camp. It was the place of judicial proceedings, where Moses sat to judge the people (Ex. 18:13). And it was the high tribunal after the administration of justice had been organized (vs. 21–26). Probably it was for the time being the depository of the Book of the Covenant (chs. 20 to 23), which was at once a sacred volume of the statutes of God (ch. 18:16) and the book containing the civil laws for the government of Israel. Moses called this tent the tent of meeting: (1) because it was the tribunal of justice, whither everyone went who sought the Lord (ch. 33: 7); for the matter in dispute or doubt was laid before God or, to use their phrase, the party sought Jehovah's face (II Sam. 21:1, R.V.), inquired of God (Ex. 18:15), brought the cause to God (Ex. 18:19; Num. 27:5), came unto God or came before him (Ex. 21:6; 22:9, R.V.), stood before Jehovah (Deut. 19:17); and (2) because it was a place of revelation: there Jehovah met his people in their representative, when the pillar of cloud descended to the door of the tent (Ex. 33:9). It may have borne its appropriate name from the first; if not, Moses borrowed the name from the instructions which he received regarding the permanent tabernacle, since it represented the same truth (Ex. 27:21). An altar may have stood near it (ch. 18:12), but the tent was not a national sanctuary, did not contain an ark or appointments for worship, and did not possess a priesthood. This tent was cared for by Joshua (Ex. 33:11); the tabernacle by Aaron (Deut. 10:6). The cloud descended upon this tent when Moses entered it to inquire of God; but the cloud abode on the permanent tabernacle and the glory of the Lord filled it, and Moses could not enter it (Ex. 40: 34, 35, 38).
2. The tabernacle (q.v.).

Tent of the Tes′ti·mo′ny (Num. 9:15). See TABERNACLE 2.

Te′phon (tē′fŏn), in A.V. **Ta′phon.** A town of Judea fortified by Bacchides (I Macc. 9: 50). Tephon is perhaps a modification of Tappuah, a name which was borne by several towns.

Te′rah (tē′rȧ), in A.V. twice **Ta′rah** (Num. 33:27, 28) once **Tha′ra** (Luke 3:34) [cf. Akkad. turāḫu, ibex]. 1. The son of Nahor, and the father of Abraham, another Nahor, and Haran. He was a resident at Ur of the Chaldees during the greater part of his life; serving other divinities than Jehovah (Josh. 24:2), probably among the rest the moon-god, who had a celebrated temple at Ur. With Abraham and Lot, he removed to Haran, where he died at the age of 205 (Gen. 11:25–32).
2. An encampment of the Israelites in the wilderness (Num. 33:27, 28).

Ter′a·phim. Images of household gods, which varied in size from such as were small enough to be easily carried in hasty flight and concealed in the saddle of a camel (Gen. 31: 19, 30, 34, R.V.) to one apparently large enough to represent a man (I Sam. 19:13, R.V.). Archaeology, however, has discovered no large teraphim. They were probably regarded as bringers of good luck. They were consulted with respect to the advisability of proposed actions (Ezek. 21:21; Zech. 10:2, both R.V.). The word, like the usual word for God, is pl. in form, but may be sing. in signification (I Sam. 19:13). Teraphim were employed in Babylonia. Laban used them in Haran, and his daughter Rachel stole them and carried them with her to Canaan (Gen. 31:19, 34). This was done without Jacob's knowledge (v. 32); according to Hurrian law the possession of the teraphim ensured title to her father's property for her husband. When Jacob reached Shechem, he demanded the surrender of all the strange gods which members of his company had brought with them, and he removed them from his people (ch. 35:2–4). In the days of the Judges Micah of Mount Ephraim had a private sanctuary with priest, ephod, and teraphim and a molten image and a graven image (Judg. 17:4, 5; 18: 14). Through them probably the Lord was consulted (vs. 5, 6). All these idols were carried off by a band of Danites (vs. 17–20). Samuel the prophet classed teraphim with witchcraft and rebellion (I Sam. 15:23, R.V.); nevertheless, there was one in David's house, doubtless belonging to his wife (ch. 19:13, R.V.). Teraphim figured largely in the corrupt religion of the northern Israelites (Hos. 3:4). The teraphim were condemned with other idols as abominations, and were destroyed by Josiah in his work of reformation (II Kings 23:24, R.V.); but they still found favor with a part of the people after the Exile (Zech. 10:2).

Ter′e·binth. The rendering of Heb. ′ēlāh, a robust tree, in the R.V. marg. with oak in the text. Twice, when it is associated with ′allōn, which is rendered "oak," it appears in the text of the R.V. (Isa. 6:13; Hos. 4:13). See TEIL TREE. ′Elāh is probably the tere-

Terebinth

binth. The terebinth or turpentine tree (*Pistacia terebinthus*) is a small tree with pinnate leaves, inconspicuous flowers, with the sexes separated, and little roundish dark-purple fruit; it reaches the height of 15 to 17, rarely 20, feet. It is a native of s. Europe, n. Africa, and w. Asia, including Palestine. The turpentine is obtained by making incisions in the trunk. It merges into *Pistacia palaestina*, which is also found in Palestine, and is but a variety of the species.

Te′resh (tē′rĕsh) [cf. Avestan *tarshav*, dry, firm]. A chamberlain who kept a door in the palace of King Ahasuerus, and plotted the murder of his master and king, a crime for which he and an accomplice were executed (Esth. 2:21–23; 6:2).

Ter′ti·us (tûr′shĭ-ŭs) [Lat., third]. Paul's amanuensis, who wrote for him the Epistle to the Romans (Rom. 16:22).

Ter·tul′lus (tĕr-tŭl′ŭs) [Lat., diminutive of Tertius]. A Roman advocate, employed by the Jewish authorities to prosecute Paul before the tribunal of Felix, the Roman procurator. His rhetorical address is thoroughly in the style affected by Roman advocates of the time (Acts 24:1–8).

Tes′ta·ment. The rendering of Gr. *diathēkē*, a will, a covenant. In Heb. 9:16, 17 *diathēkē* is clearly a will. But in chs. 8:6–10, 13; 9:1, 4 the meaning is evidently covenant, and the term is so translated in the text. The Old Covenant and the New Covenant would be more accurate designations of the 2 parts of the Bible than the Old Testament and the New Testament. See NEW TESTAMENT, OLD TESTAMENT.

Teth (tāth). The 9th letter of the Heb. alphabet. Greek *theta* comes from the same source; but the Gr. versions represent it in Heb. names by *tau*, reserving *theta* for the aspirated Heb. *tau*. In the Eng. versions *teth* is represented by *t*. It stands at the beginning of the 9th section of Psalm 119, in which section each verse begins with that letter.

Te′trarch. One who rules over the 4th part of a kingdom or province. Philip of Macedon divided Thessaly into 4 districts called tetrarchies. Eventually the word tetrarch was used loosely for a petty subject prince, even though the land was not divided among 4 such rulers. The Romans adopted the term and used it as a convenient title for a prince to whom they granted a small territory only, and whom they were unwilling to dignify with the authority and rank of a king. The N.T. names 3 of these petty dignitaries: Herod, tetrarch of Galilee, Philip, tetrarch of Ituraea and Trachonitis, and Lysanias, tetrarch of Abilene (Luke 3:1). In the case of the tetrarchs Herod Antipas and Philip the title was appropriate, even in its original sense, for Augustus gave ½ of the kingdom of Herod the Great to Archelaus, with the title of ethnarch, and divided the remainder into 2 tetrarchies, which he gave to them (Jos. *Antiq.* xvii. 11, 4; *War* ii. 6, 3). A tetrarch was sometimes in courtesy called a king (cf. Matt. 14:1 with v. 9; Mark 6:14).

Thad·dae′us (thă-dē′ŭs). See JUDAS 8.

Tha′hash (thā′hăsh). See TAHASH.

Tha′mah (thā′má). See TEMAH.

Tha′mar (thā′mär). See TAMAR.

Tham′na·tha (thăm′ná-thá). See TIMNAH.

Thank Of′fer·ing. See OFFERINGS.

Tha′ra (thā′rá). See TERAH.

Thar′shish (thär′shĭsh). See TARSHISH.

The′a·ter. A place where dramatic performances are given. The theater, with its auditorium, orchestra, and stage, and capable of seating immense throngs (see EPHESUS), was admirably adapted for large public meetings and the transaction of public business, and in Greek cities was often put to that use (Acts 19:29, 31; Jos. *Antiq.* xix. 8, 2).

Thebes (thēbz). See No.

The'bez (thē'bĕz) [perhaps, brightness or splendor]. A town near Shechem, having in it a strong tower, in besieging which Abimelech was killed (Judg. 9:50–55; II Sam. 11:21). It continues to exist in the large village of Ṭūbās, 10 miles n.e. of Shechem, on the road to Beth-shean.

The•co'e (thē-kō'ê). See TEKOA.

The•la'sar (thē-lā'sẽr). See TELASSAR.

The•oc'ra•cy. Josephus coined the word theocracy to describe the government instituted at Sinai. "Our legislator . . . ordered our government to be what I may call by a strained expression a theocracy, attributing the power and the authority to God" (Jos. *Apion* ii. 16). Jehovah was the head of the nation, dwelling in its midst between the cherubim (Ex. 25:22). In him all the powers of the state, legislative, executive, judicial, were united. As legislator, he announced the fundamental law of the state in the hearing of the congregation. After that immediate presentation of himself to the nation, he exercised his governmental offices for the most part through men whom he raised up. Like all potentates, he delegated the judicial function for the most part to judges; only the most difficult matters were referred to Jehovah (Ex. 18:19); see URIM AND THUMMIM. His legislative function he exercised through Moses and through prophets (Deut. 18:15–19). Legislation was intermittent; the given body of laws was a sufficient rule, and seldom required modification or enlargement. The executive function was likewise exercised for many years intermittently through leaders, called Judges, who were raised up from time to time, and who, accredited by the great deeds which were wrought by their hands, secured public confidence and became the acknowledged head in state affairs.

The theocratic government was proposed by God at Sinai on condition of obedience (Ex. 19:4–9). The terms were accepted by the elders of the people (vs. 7, 8). The Ten Commandments, which formed the basis of the covenant, were proclaimed by Jehovah himself in such a manner that all the people could hear (Ex. 20:1, 19, 22; Deut. 4:12, 33, 36; 5:4, 22), in order that they might believe (Ex. 19:9). At the people's request the remaining laws, which are a practical application and interpretation of the Ten Commandments, were not spoken directly to them, but through Moses (ch. 20:18–21). Then the covenant was ratified. Moses wrote all the words of the Lord, erected an altar and 12 pillars, ordered a sacrifice, and sprinkled the altar with half the blood. He read the Book of the Covenant in the audience of the people, and, on their formal acceptance of it, sprinkled the remaining portion of the blood upon the people, saying: "Behold the blood of the covenant, which the Lord hath made with you concerning all these words." Finally the covenant meal was eaten by the representatives of Israel, and thus the theocracy was established (ch. 24:3–11).

This Book of the Covenant contains the constitution and earliest laws of Israel. The Ten Commandments formed the fundamental law of the state. In Hebrew conception and as a matter of fact, they were a covenant between God and the nation. There was a treaty, not between several communities, but between the community and God. Being fundamental law, they were engraven on stone,

and deposited in the Ark; they were known as the covenant (Deut. 4:13; 9:9, 11; I Kings 8:9–21; cf. Num. 10:33; Judg. 20:27; I Sam. 4:3); or the testimony (Ex. 31:18; 32:15). The laws which follow the Ten Commandments are by-laws or statutes. They are constitutional, involving no principle contrary to the organic law of the state; they are expository, being the application of the doctrines of the constitution to the affairs of daily life; they are temporary, liable to abrogation and amendment and numerical increase to meet the new conditions and peculiar needs of each age. They are presented in the form of a code; they are not a loose aggregation of statutes, but are disposed in orderly arrangement, mostly in groups of 10 or 5, and are usually introduced by the word "if." 1. Laws relating to the form of worship (Ex. 20:23–26). 2. Laws to protect the rights of man. (*a*) To protect liberty (ch. 21:2–11). (*b*) Concerning injury of person (vs. 12–32). (*c*) Concerning property rights (chs. 21:33 to 22:15). 3. Laws to govern personal conduct (chs. 22:16 to 23:9). 4. Laws concerning sacred seasons and sacrifice (vs. 10–19). 5. The promise annexed (vs. 20–33). Regarding the antiquity, character, and codification of these laws, see HAMMURABI and MOSES; and for the process of annulment and enactment during the ensuing 40 years, see ZELOPHEHAD and DEUTERONOMY.

At the institution of the theocratic government at Sinai, the idea before the people was simply that God was Ruler and Moses his accredited representative through whom he exercised the legislative, judicial, and executive offices. Moses already had subordinate judges to assist him (Ex. 18:21–26). The expectation was also entertained by Moses that God would appoint leaders to succeed him, and that eventually, on account of the people's lack of faith, a king would be needed as earthly, visible representative of the executive power when the people should be settled in Palestine. Accordingly a general law of the king was framed (Deut. 17:14–20).

The stability of the state under the theocratic form of government depended in the first instance and ultimately on the faithfulness of God to his election and his promises; but the success of the theocracy at any given period was conditioned by the attitude of the people toward God and toward the provisions of the covenant. Their obedience to God and reliance on him were requisite. The theocracy was based on the conception of Israel as a community, and it is well to note the weakness of the bond which at the first bound Israel into a community. The Children of Israel were divided into 12 tribes; they were bound together by common blood and common language, by common misfortune and common need. They were held together in pursuit of a great end by the enthusiasm and expectation which 1 man had awakened, by the hope of freedom and a country, by the promise and evidence of God's protection. They were kept together by Providence. All these unifying elements save the last were weak. They were bonds that might easily be, and constantly were, broken. This lack of communal strength was an obstacle to the theocracy, which even the establishment of the monarchy did not rectify.

The•oph'a•ny. A manifestation of God to man by actual appearance. It was not an immediate revelation of God the Father (John 1:18; I Tim. 6:16), but a manifestation of Jehovah in the person of the angel of the Lord (Gen. 16:7), the angel of the presence or the Lord's presence (Ex. 32:34; 33:14), the angel (messenger) of the covenant (Mal. 3:1), or Christ. A common classification is : 1. The O.T. theophany, an epiphany of the future Christ. 2. The incarnation of Christ, as the revelation of God in the flesh. 3. The Second Coming of Christ.

The O.T. theophanies were transient manifestations and became permanent localization. They were temporary manifestations to the Patriarchs, and became abiding in the Shekinah. The theophanies which were granted to the Patriarchs may have been unsubstantial manifestations, incorporeal and merely the appearance of the human form. Some interpreters, like Tertullian, believe that occasionally at least there was actual flesh, not putative flesh ; but real and solid human substance. If the angel of the Lord assumed an actual body, he did so miraculously, and also again disappeared miraculously from men's sight. In the O.T. theophany the angel of the Lord ate actual food (Gen. 18 :1–8). Does this prove that the angel had assumed an actual body ? 1. Josephus interprets the eating as mere appearance (Jos. *Antiq.* i. 11, 2) ; so also Philo (*Op.* ii. 18) and the writer of Tobit (Tobit xii. 19). 2. Justin Martyr speaks of the angel as consuming food "as fire consumes" (*Dial c. Tryph.* xxxiv.). The angel of the Lord who appeared to Manoah touched the food, and it was burned. "The thirsty earth absorbs water in one manner, the hot ray of the sun in another" (Augustine).

The transient manifestations gradually gave place to the permanent localization. The Shekinah was the visible majesty of the divine presence, especially when dwelling between the cherubim in the tabernacle and Temple in the midst of God's people Israel. It first appeared at the Exodus. The Lord went before the Israelites in a pillar of cloud by day, and by night in a pillar of fire to give them light (Ex. 13 :21, 22). A thick cloud rested upon Mount Sinai, and the whole mountain smoked, because the Lord descended upon Mount Sinai in fire (ch. 19 : 16, 18). Later the glory of the Lord abode on Mount Sinai, and the cloud covered it 6 days ; and the 7th day he called unto Moses out of the midst of the cloud, and the appearance of the glory of the Lord was like devouring fire on the top of the mount in the eyes of the children of Israel (ch. 24 :16, 17). When Moses entered the 1st tent of meeting, the cloud descended and hovered at the door, and the Lord talked with Moses face to face (Ex. 33 :10, 11 ; cf. Deut. 5 :4). When the tabernacle was erected, the Lord took possession of it. The cloud, dark by day and luminous by night, covered the tent, and the glory of the Lord filled it (Ex. 40 :34, 35 ; Num. 9 :15, 16). When Moses appeared before the Lord in the tabernacle, he heard the voice of one speaking unto him from off the mercy seat (Num. 7 :89 ; cf. Ex. 25 :22 ; Lev. 16 :2). Probably the glory was not seen constantly but gleamed forth occasionally from the cloud which concealed it (Ex. 16 :7, 10 ; Lev. 9 :6, 23 ; Num. 14 :10 ; 16 :19, 42 ; 20 :6). From frequent references it seems, however, that God continued to manifest his presence between the cherubim on the Ark. At length, when the Temple of Solomon was dedicated, the cloud filled the house of the Lord, so that the priests could not stand to minister by reason of the cloud ; for the glory of the Lord filled the house (I Kings 8 :10, 11).

The temporary manifestations had given place to the abiding presence in the tabernacle and Solomon's Temple : and finally the Word became flesh and dwelt among men ; and men "beheld his glory, glory as of the only begotten from the Father" (John 1 :14). The latter glory of the house was greater than the former (Hag. 2 :9, R.V.). The divine presence dwelt in Christ's body as in the Temple.

The·oph'i·lus (thê-ŏf'ĭ-lŭs) [Gr., loved by God]. The Christian to whom Luke addressed his Gospel (Luke 1 :3) and The Acts (Acts 1 :1). See ACTS, THE.

Thes'sa·lo'ni·ans (thĕs'à-lō'nĭ-ănz), **The E·pis'tles of Paul to the.** The First Epistle of Paul to the Thessalonians is the earliest of Paul's epistles. It was written by the apostle in conjunction with Silvanus (Silas) and Timothy, to the church at Thessalonica. Paul had founded this church on his Second Missionary Journey, and had been driven from Thessalonica to Berea and from Berea to Athens by the persecuting Jews ; see PAUL 6. The epistle contains allusions (I Thess., ch. 2) to his life at Thessalonica. It also relates that, when at Athens, he had sent Timothy back to Thessalonica to encourage the Christians amid their persecutions (ch. 3 :1–3) and that Timothy had recently brought him good news of their steadfastness. In Acts 18 :5 we learn that Silas and Timothy rejoined the apostle at Corinth. Hence the epistle was written from that city, probably in the year A.D. 52. The allusions which the epistle contains to Paul's life in Thessalonica and to the distress felt by the Thessalonians over the death of their friends, as well as the elementary character of the instruction given, confirm this date. There appear to have been 3 special features in the condition of the Thessalonians which occasioned anxiety to the apostle and led him to write this epistle : (1) a tendency to neglect their daily work, probably under the idea that the Second Advent would soon take place, and with this was sometimes found a failure to preserve moral purity of life ; (2) distress lest their Christian friends who died would fail to enjoy the glories of the Kingdom which the returning Christ was to establish (3) friction between the regular officers of the Church and those who possessed miraculous endowments of the Spirit. Hence the analysis of the epistle : 1. A grateful statement of their Christian earnestness, their endurance of trial, and the influence they had already exerted over others (I Thess., ch. 1). 2. A reminder of the uprightness and industry with which he had lived among them, and of the enthusiasm with which they had received his preaching even in the face of persecution from the Jews (ch. 2). 3. A recital of the joy he had had in Timothy's good report of their condition (ch. 3). 4. Instruction on special points (chs. 4 :1 to 5 :24 : (*a*) Concerning purity in the relation of the sexes (ch. 4 :3–8). (*b*) Concerning a life of mutual love and orderliness (vs. 9–12). (*c*) Concerning dead believers, declaring that at the Advent they will rise first and be caught up with the living to meet the Lord in the air, and thus will not fail of their reward (vs. 13–18). (*d*) Concerning watchfulness and sobriety of life (ch. 5 :1–11). (*e*) Concerning respect for officers of the Church, consideration for those in need, cultivation of spiritual gifts, and other duties of the Christian life (vs. 12–24). 5. Closing words (vs. 25–28).

The epistle strikingly illustrates the difficulties natural to a newly formed Gentile church and the breadth and practical wisdom of the apostle's instructions.

The Second Epistle of Paul to the Thessalonians evidently followed the First after but a short period. It too, therefore, is to be assigned to c. A.D. 52, and was written from Corinth. We learn from it that the difficulties of the Thessalonians had become more serious, but were still of the same general character as those dealt with in the First Epistle. Like the First, this was written by Paul in conjunction with Silvanus (Silas) and Timothy ; it deals largely with the Second

Advent and misconceptions about it; and refers again to the tendency of some to disorderly living (II Thess. 3:6–12). If, however, the First Epistle treated of the relation of the Advent to believers, the Second treats of its relation to the wicked (ch. 1:5–10). Further, the apostle warns them not to suppose that "the day of the Lord is just at hand" (ch. 2:2, R.V.), and that the visible Advent would therefore soon come; for, before that happens, there must be the apostasy (predicted by Christ, cf. Matt. 24:9–12; and referred to by Paul in Acts 20:29, 30; Rom. 16:17–20; II Cor. 11:13–15; I Tim. 4:1) and the revelation of the man of lawlessness (II Thess. 2:3, 4, R.V.; Dan. 7:25; 11:36; I John 2:18; see ANTICHRIST), whom the Lord will destroy at his coming. He had, when with them, told them of these things (II Thess. 2:5).

The epistle may be divided as follows: 1. Thanksgiving for their fidelity amid persecution, and assurance that persecution should only make stronger their faith in the vindication of the saints and in the punishment of the ungodly which will take place at the Second Advent (ch. 1). 2. Warning against supposing that "the day of the Lord is just at hand," and description of the apostasy and rise of the man of lawlessness, which must precede the coming of the Lord (ch. 2:1–12). 3. Expression of his confidence in their election and fidelity (vs. 13–17). 4. Concluding exhortations: that they pray for him, that they avoid those who are disorderly, that they be industrious and faithful, that they all subject themselves to the authority which he as an apostle exercised, etc. (ch. 3). From ch. 2:2 it appears that a forged letter of Paul's had been circulated; hence in ch. 3:17 he appends his signature. We thus see also that from the beginning the same authority was attached in the Church to the apostle's letters as to his oral teaching. The statements concerning the apostasy and the man of lawlessness have been variously interpreted. We think it most probable that the apostasy was contemplated by Paul as arising within the Church; the man of lawlessness as the culmination of the apostasy in a personal Antichrist; and he or that which restrains (ch. 2:7) as either the civil power or else, and with much probability, the Holy Spirit.   G. T. P. (rev., H. S. G.)

Thes′sa·lo·ni′ca (thĕs′á-lô-nī′ká). A city on the Thermaic Gulf, now called the Gulf of Salonika. The city was first called Therme, or Therma, hot spring; but Cassander, 1 of the successors of Alexander the Great, made it his residence and renamed it Thessalonica, after his wife Thessalonike, a daughter of the conqueror of the Chersonesus and sister of the great Alexander. Under the Romans it was the capital of the 2d district out of 4 into which they had divided Macedonia. It was a military and commercial station on the Via Egnatia; and was made a free city in 42 B.C. Its civil magistrates were called politarchs, rulers of the city (Acts 17:6, Gr. text; inscription on arch in Thessalonica); see RULER 3. The Jews had a synagogue in the city. Paul preached there and made converts, who became the nucleus of a Christian church (Acts 17:1–13; cf. Phil. 4:16). To this church Paul sent 2 letters. Two of his co-workers, Aristarchus and Secundus, were men of Thessalonica (Acts 20:4; 27:2). The modern name is Salonika.

Theu′das (thū′dás). Gamaliel, in his speech before the sanhedrin, about A.D. 32, referred to Theudas, who gave himself out to be somebody, to whom a number of men, about 400, joined themselves: "who was slain; and all, as many as obeyed him, were dis-

persed, and came to nought," and after whom Judas of Galilee rose up in the days of the enrollment (Acts 5:36, 37). There can be no doubt that the Judas here spoken of was Judas the Gaulonite of Gamala, who, in the time of Quirinius, during the procuratorship of Coponius, raised an insurrection by opposing the enrollment (Jos. *Antiq.* xviii. 1, 1; *War* ii. 8, 1). Theudas accordingly arose sometime before A.D. 6. Now Josephus mentions a magician named Theudas, who, while Fadus was procurator of Judea, A.D. 44–c.46, persuaded a great part of the people to follow him to the river Jordan, for he told them that he was a prophet, and that at his command the waters would divide and allow them a passage. But Fadus sent a troop of horse against him, who fell upon the people unexpectedly, slew many and took many others alive, and secured Theudas, cut off his head and carried it to Jerusalem (Jos. *Antiq.* xx. 5, 1).

The question is whether Luke and Josephus refer to the same person. Some answer that they do, and accordingly say that either Luke or Josephus errs. Josephus scarcely is mistaken, for he gives details. But Luke has fully established his credibility as a historian, and it is a rash thing to accuse him of an error. Accordingly other interpreters conjecture that 2 persons by the name of Theudas, at a distance of 40 years or more from each other, laid themselves open to the just vengeance or justifiable suspicions of the Romans and were punished. It is not at all clear that Theudas the magician was an insurgent of the same class as Theudas whom Gamaliel cites. The one was an impostor, a pretended prophet, who, on the faith of the people in his supernatural powers, drew crowds of followers after him. The other made some sort of claim to greatness, gained a following of 400 men, and came to nought. Who then was Theudas to whom Gamaliel refers? He may have been one of the insurrectionary chiefs, who led belligerent bands in the closing year of Herod the Great. That year was remarkably turbulent. Josephus mentions 3 disturbers by name, and makes general allusion to others. Theudas was either: (1) one of these unnamed insurrectionists, whom Gamaliel cites to show that a bad cause and its leaders come to grief (Theudas was a common name and, within a period of half a century, might be borne by 2 persons of some prominence and somewhat similar careers. Analogously Josephus gives an account of 4 men named Simon, who followed each other within 40 years, and of 3 named Judas, within 10 years, who were all instigators of rebellion); or (2) one of the 3 insurgents who are named by Josephus. Two have been advocated by certain scholars as identical with Theudas: 1. Simon (Jos. *Antiq.* xvii. 10, 6; *War* ii. 4, 2), a slave of Herod, who attempted to make himself king when Herod died. Since it was quite common among the Jews to assume a new name on changing occupation or mode of life, it is possible that Gamaliel speaks of him as Theudas, the name he had borne longest, and by which he was best known in Jerusalem and to the members of the sanhedrin, while Josephus calls him by the name Simon, which he had adopted when appearing as king of the Jews and by which he was naturally known to the Roman government and people. 2. The man called Matthias by Josephus (Jos. *Antiq.* xvii. 6, 2; *War* i. 33, 2). Matthias is a Gr. form of Heb. *Mattanyăh*, gift of God, and is equivalent to the Gr. name Theudas, which possibly may be the same as *Theodas*, shortened from *Theodōros*, gift of God. However strongly these conjectures may commend themselves to their proponents, it must be admitted that we do not know enough to explain the historical difficulty in Acts 5:36, 37.

Thief. In a broad sense, anyone who appropriates what is not his own, as the petty pilferer (John 12:6), the robber or highwayman (Luke 10:30, R.V. robber), the burglar (Matt. 6:20). The highwayman was often a rebel against Roman rule and a fomenter of strife, like Barabbas (Mark 15:7), who was compelled by the exigencies of the case, as much as by the lust of plunder, to flee from the soldiers and adopt the wild robber life. Under the Mosaic Law a thief caught had to make restitution of twice the amount he had taken, and if he were unable, could be sold into temporary servitude till he had earned the requisite amount. If a thief entered a house and, coming into contact with the owner in the dark, was killed, the homicide was not to be charged with bloodguiltiness; but if the sun had risen, the householder was held to be guilty if he killed the intruder (Ex. 22:1–4). That the thieves on the cross were something far beyond petty pilferers is plain from the Gr. term (*lēistēs*) applied to them, the severity of their punishment (Jos. *War* ii. 13, 2), and the fact that one of them acknowledged the justice of the death penalty inflicted on him (Luke 23:41); he must have been a robber at the least (Matt. 27:38, R.V.), and quite possibly even a brigand. Both reviled Jesus on the cross (Matt. 27:44), but subsequently 1 was touched with awe at the meekness and forgiving spirit of Jesus, and, with the fear of God in his heart, the confession of the sinfulness of his past life, the acknowledgment that Jesus had done nothing amiss and was the true King and would reign in power after the death on the cross, turned to Jesus for acceptance after death (Luke 23:39–43).

Thim′na·thah (thĭm′nȧ-thä). See TIMNAH.

This′tle. See THORNS AND THISTLES.

Thom′as (tŏm′ȧs) [Gr., from Aram. *teʻōmā*, twin]. One of the 12 apostles (Matt. 10:3). He was also called Didymus, a Greek name, meaning, like Thomas, a twin. When the disciples were astonished that Jesus intended going again to Judea, where a little before the Jews had threatened to stone him (John 11:7, 8), Thomas, in devotion to Jesus, determined to share the peril, and said to his fellow disciples, "Let us also go, that we may die with him" (v. 16). When Jesus, in anticipation of his departure, spoke of going to prepare a place for them, and added that they knew whither he was going and the way, Thomas said, "Lord, we know not whither thou goest; how know we the way?" In reply Jesus spoke the well-known words: "I am the way, and the truth, and the life" (ch. 14:1–6). Thomas was not at the first meeting at which the privilege was granted of seeing the risen Lord, and when he heard that Jesus had been present he said, "Except I shall see in his hands the print of the nails, and put my finger into the print of the nails, and put my hand into his side, I will not believe" (ch. 20:24, 25). This incident has given rise to his designation, "doubting Thomas." But God turned the doubt of Thomas to the good of others. "He doubted that we might not doubt" (Augustine), and 8 days later Jesus gave him the evidence he required and elicited from him the adoring exclamation, "My Lord and my God" (vs. 26–29). He was on the Sea of Galilee with 6 other disciples when Jesus hailed them from the beach and told them where to cast the net (ch. 21:1–8); and was with the rest of the apostles in the upper room at Jerusalem after the ascension (Acts 1:13). Tradition makes Thomas afterward

labor in Parthia and Persia, dying in the latter country. At a later period India was named as the place where he had preached and suffered martyrdom, and a place near Madras is called St. Thomas' Mount.

Thorns and This′tles. In most passages where the words occur the terms are generic rather than specific. Thorny weeds, bushes, and small trees of various kinds are abundant in Palestine. Among them may be mentioned the thorny burnet (*Poterium spinosum*), which is burned as fuel in lime kilns and ovens; the thorny caper (*Capparis spinosa*), seen everywhere hanging from rocks and walls; the Jamestown or Jimson weed (*Datura stramonium*) by the roadside and in waste places; the artichoke (*Cynara syriaca*); and in the uplands the acanthus with its whitish flowers. The prickly pear (*Opuntia ficus-indica*), a cactus with yellow flowers, is the characteristic hedge plant of modern Syria; but it was introduced from America and was unknown in ancient times. For hedge purposes there are also used the box thorn (*Lycium europaeum*) and the bramble (*Rubus discolor*). Various hawthorns are found, *Crataegus azarolus, C. monogyna*, and e. of the Jordan *C. orientalis*. Numerous thistles grow in the fields and waste places: such as *Cirsium acarna*, with its leaves tipped with long, yellow spines; *Carthamus lanatus*, with yellow flowerets, *C. glaucus*, with purple, *C. caeruleus*, with blue, and *C. tinctorius*, with red flowerets, which are used as a red dye; *Carduus pycnocephalus* and *argentalus*; *Echinops viscosus*; the tall *Notobasis syriaca*, with pink flowers and powerful spines; cotton thistles (*Onopordon illyricum* and *cynarocephalum*); the milk thistle (*Silybum marianum*); sow thistles (*Sonchus oleraceus* and *glaucescens*); star thistles (*Centaurea calcitrapa* and *verutum*), the former with purple, the latter with yellow flowers. The cocklebur (*Xanthium*) is common, as is also teasel (*Dipsacus sylvestris*).

Several words rendered thorn or thistle appear to be used specifically, e.g., Heb. *dardar*, Gr. *tribolos*, which grows in fields (Gen. 3:18; Hos. 10:8; Matt. 7:16; all in E.V. thistle; and Heb. 6:8, in A.V. brier) is probably a species of *Tribulus*, perhaps *T. terrestris*, one of the plants called caltrop. It is common in the fields and by the roadside. The fruit is composed of bony cells armed with prickles on the back. It does not belong to the *Compositae*, as do the thistles.

See BRAMBLE, BRIER, NETTLE.

The crown of thorns, which was plaited by the Roman soldiers and placed on the head of Jesus to torture and insult him (Matt. 27:29), is generally believed to have been made of the *Zizyphus spina Christi*, a species of jujube or lotus tree, with soft, round, pliant branches, and with leaves resembling the ivy with which emperors and generals were wont to be crowned. See BRAMBLE.

The thorn in the flesh was some bodily pain or infirmity sent as a messenger of Satan to buffet the Apostle Paul and keep him humble amid all his spiritual triumphs (II Cor. 12:7). Its nature is unknown.

Thou′sand. A division of the tribe (Num. 31:5; Josh. 22:14); consisting nominally of 1,000 persons, but through birth and death ever varying and doubtless falling far short of the standard number; used for military and judicial purposes (Ex. 18:21, 25; Num. 31:14; I Sam. 8:12; 22:7; II Sam. 18:1); and practically, perhaps exactly, equivalent to the subdivision of the tribe which was technically known as a father's house (cf. Num. 1:2, 4 with v. 16, R.V.; Judg. 6:15, cf. R.V. marg.; cf. I Sam. 10:19 with v. 21).

A THRESHING FLOOR IN SAMARIA

Three Tav'erns. A small station on the Appian Way, about 10 miles from Appii Forum, and 30 miles from Rome, where a number of Roman Christians met Paul on his way to Rome (Acts 28:15).

Thresh'ing. The process of separating grain from the straw. Small quantities of grain were beaten out with a stick or flail (Judg. 6:11), and this was the customary method of hulling fitches and cummin (Isa. 28:27); but when much work was to be done, oxen and threshing floors were employed. The weather of Palestine permits the threshing floor to be under the open sky (Judg. 6:37). It is generally common to the whole village,

604

but may have a private owner (II Sam. 24: 16). If possible, it is the surface of a flat rock on the top of a hill, exposed to any wind that blows. If such a natural floor is not available, an artificial floor is laid out by the roadside, and soon assumes a circular shape, about 50 feet in diameter, and becomes firm and hard under the trampling of the oxen. The sheaves are loosened and arranged in a circle on the floor; or, if the straw is to be preserved whole, the ears are cut from the stock and cast on the floor. Oxen, which to this day are unmuzzled except by the niggardly (Deut. 25:4), are driven round and round to trample out the kernels; or else are made to drag a sled or cart, weighted by a heavy stone or the driver, to facilitate the operation. The sled is made of 2 heavy planks, curved upward at the front and fastened side by side. Sharp pieces of stone are fixed in holes bored in the bottom. The cart, at least as used in Egypt, consists of a frame containing 3 wooden rollers set with sharp iron knives. If there is any wind, the threshed grain is tossed high in the air with a shovel or a fork, when the chaff is blown away and the clean grain falls to the ground; but if there is no wind, a large fan is plied by one man, while another tosses the grain with his shovel (Isa. 30:24; Matt. 3:12; *Iliad* xiii. 588). The fan, however, is seldom used except to purge the floor of the refuse dust. Winnowing is done in the evening for the sake of the wind; and it is customary for the owner of the grain to spend the night at the floor during the time of threshing to prevent stealing (Ruth 3:2 *seq.*). The grain is finally passed through a sieve to cleanse it from dirt, after which it is ready for grinding (Amos 9:9).

Thresh'olds of the Gates. A building, in Heb. *'ăsuppîm* (stores), which was intended for the storage of Temple goods (Neh. 12: 25, A.V.); rendered "storehouses of the gates" in R.V. See ASUPPIM.

Throne. A chair of state, in Heb. *kissē'*, in Gr. *thronos*, which was occupied by a person of authority, whether high priest, judge, military leader, governor, or king (Gen. 41:40; II Sam. 3:10; Neh. 3:7; Ps. 122:5; Jer. 1: 15; Matt. 19:28). Royal thrones were often portable, like those of Ahab and Jehoshaphat (I Kings 22:10), and the one used by

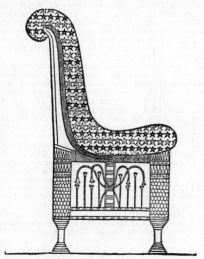

Ancient Egyptian Throne

Sennacherib at Lachish. Solomon's throne was an elevated seat reached by 6 steps. Its frame was probably made of cedar. It was inlaid with ivory, and elsewhere overlaid with gold; the back of it was arched or rounded off; it was furnished with arms and was provided with a footstool. A lion stood at each side, ornamenting the arms, and on each end of each of the 6 steps (I Kings 10: 18–20; II Chron. 9:17–19).

The king, arrayed in his royal robes, regularly sat on his throne when granting audiences, receiving homage, administering justice, or promulgating commands (I Kings 2: 19; 7:7; II Kings 11:19; Jonah 3:6).

The throne symbolized supreme power and authority, and is constantly attributed to Jehovah.

Thum'mim. See URIM AND THUMMIM.

Thun'der. The noise that follows a flash of lightning. It intensifies the awfulness of a terrific storm (Ex. 9:23). Thunder is an unusual event during the summer, which is the dry season in Palestine (Prov. 26:1); and hence, when it occurred at that time of year after prayer for it, it was an evident answer and served as a sign (I Sam. 12:17). It was often called simply *ḳōl*, voice, sound, noise; and was poetically described as the voice of Jehovah (Job 37:2–5; 40:9; Ps. 29:3–9), who sends and directs the storm (Job 28: 26). It accompanied manifestations of God's presence when he came in dread majesty (Ex. 19:16; Rev. 4:5); it was an indication of divine power at work in nature; and since thunder is a precursor of the destructive storm, it symbolized divine vengeance (I Sam. 2:10; II Sam. 22:14, 15; Ps. 77:18).

Thy'a·ti'ra (thī'á-tī'rá). A city of Asia Minor, in Lydia, near the boundary of Mysia; the name probably is Lydian, meaning "the town or citadel of Thya." It was on the road from Pergamos to Sardis. When Seleucus Nicator between 301 and 281 B.C. colonized it with Greeks, he gave it the name of Thyatira. It had already been known as Pelopia and Euhippia (Pliny *Hist. Nat.* v. 31), but these names may have been mere epithets. Its inhabitants were famed for their skill in dyeing purple; and Lydia, the seller of purple at Philippi, came from Thyatira (Acts 16:14). It contained one of the 7 churches in Asia (Rev. 1:11; 2:18–29). Traces of its existence remain in fragments of columns built into the streets and edifices of its modern successor Ak Hissar.

Thy'ine Wood. An article sold in the markets of the mystic Babylon (Rev. 18:12). It was the wood of *Callitris quadrivalvis,* a large tree of the cypress family. It is reddish-brown, hard, and fragrant, and was greatly prized by the Romans for ornamental purposes. They ran it up to a high price. The resin which exudes from the tree is gum sandarac.

Ti·be'ri·as (ti-bē'rĭ-ăs). A city on the Sea of Galilee (John 6:23), built by Herod the tetrarch, and named by him after the then reigning Roman emperor, Tiberius Caesar (Jos. *Antiq.* xviii. 2, 3; *War* ii. 9, 1). Tiberias was fortified by Josephus during the Jewish war (Jos. *Life* 8; *War* ii. 20, 6). It opened its gates to Vespasian, and a number of the inhabitants of Taricheae, a neighboring town, whom he had assured of their lives, were afterward slain in cold blood in the race course of Tiberias (Jos. *War* iii. 10, 1–10). After the destruction of Jerusalem and the expulsion of the Jews from Judea, consequent on the failure of Barcocheba's rebellion, Tiberias became the virtual metropolis of the Jewish nation, and coins of the city have been found, bearing the names of

Tiberius, Claudius, Trajan, Adrian, and Antoninus Pius. The sanhedrin was transferred to Tiberias about the middle of the 2d century, and the city became the center of Jewish learning. A celebrated school was established in it, which produced the volume of tradition called the Mishnah, about A.D. 190 or 220, and much of its supplement, the Gemara, was codified in the same place by the 4th century. The Masorah, or body of traditions which transmitted the details of the Hebrew text of the O.T. and preserved its pronunciation by means of vowel signs, originated in a great measure at Tiberias; see OLD TESTAMENT. The Jews regard Tiberias as one of their 4 sacred cities, Jerusalem, Hebron, and

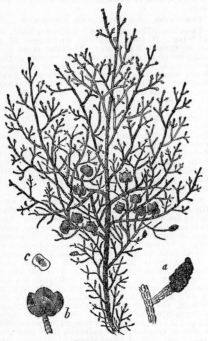

Thyine Wood

Safed being the others, in which prayer must be offered continually, or the world will instantly fall back into chaos. It still exists under the name of Tubarīya, on the w. shore of the Sea of Galilee, 11½ miles from the entrance and 6 from the exit of the Jordan. At that place the steep mountain ridge does not closely approach the lake, but leaves on its margin a narrow strip of undulating land, at the n. part of which Tiberias stands. It extends about half a mile along the shore, and is defended on the land side by a wall, towers, and a castle.

The Sea of Tiberias is more commonly called the Sea of Galilee (John 6:1; 21:1).

Ti·ber'i·us Cae'sar (tī-bẽr'ĭ-ŭs sē'zẽr). See CAESAR 2.

Tib'hath (tĭb'hăth) [slaughter]. A town of Aram-zobah (I Chron. 18:8). See BETAH and TEBAH.

Tib'ni (tĭb'nī) [cf. Arab. *tibn*, straw]. A son of Ginath, and the unsuccessful competitor for the throne of Israel with Omri (I Kings 16:21, 22).

Ti'dal (tī'dăl). King of Goiim and one of Chedorlaomer's confederates (Gen. 14:1, 9,

R.V.). The name may correspond to Hittite Tudḫalijash.

Tig'lath-pi·le'ser (tĭg'láth-pĭ-lē'zẽr), in Chronicles **Til'gath-pil·ne'ser** [Assyrian *Tukulti-apil-esharra*, my trust is the son of Esharra, i.e., the god Ninib]. A king of Assyria, who reigned from 746/5 to 728/7 B.C. Tiglath-pileser is but another name for Pul, as appears from the fact that where Ptolemy's list of Babylonian kings gives Poros, and the so-called dynastic tablets of the Babylonians give Pulu, the Babylonian chronicle gives Tiglath-pileser. Probably Pul was his original name, and when he secured the throne he assumed the grander title of Tiglath-pileser, which had already been made famous by a great king of the past. The military power of Assyria had suffered serious reverses, but a new era began with the accession of Tiglath-pileser III. In the 1st year of his reign he began a new order of administration for subject territory. He divided the empire into 4 administrative provinces over which he placed native Assyrian governors who were responsible for collecting tribute and maintaining order. He seated himself upon the Assyrian throne on the 13th day of the 2d month and in the 7th month was marching against Babylonia. He first became known to the Israelites as Pul.

During the years 743–740 his military headquarters were at Arpad in n. Syria, not far from the site of the later Antioch; but he found opportunity to send or lead expeditions and terrify the country within a radius of 100 miles or more. Among other places against which he came at that time or a little later was the land of Israel, but Menahem paid him tribute and the Assyrian confirmed the kingdom to Menahem and left the country (II Kings 15:19, 20); see PEKAH. Tiglath-pileser records the names of kings who about 738 B.C. paid him tribute, and among others the name of Menahem of Samaria. During the next few years he was conducting war first in the far east, and then in the country n. and n.w. of Nineveh; but in 734 he was again in the west. The alliance of Pekah and Rezin against Ahaz of Judah impelled Ahaz, contrary to the exhortation of the Prophet Isaiah, to turn for help to a human potentate. Tiglath-pileser was induced by large money (II Kings 16:7, 8), and by the favorable opportunity afforded him of extending his authority, to side with Ahaz. He marched against Philistia, capturing cities on the Phoenician coast as he proceeded; Gaza fell in 734. Thus were punished the Philistines, who had taken advantage of Judah's straits to pillage (II Chron. 28:18).

It was either during his advance s. or as he returned n. that he took Ijon, Abel-beth-maacah, Janoah, Kedesh, Hazor, Gilead, and Galilee, all the land of Naphtali, and carried them captive to Assyria (II Kings 15:29). At this time God "stirred up the spirit of Pul king of Assyria, and [or rather, as it may equally well be translated, even] the spirit of Tilgath-pilneser king of Assyria, and he carried them away, even the Reubenites, and the Gadites, and the half-tribe of Manasseh" (I Chron. 5:26). Thus there was an extensive deportation from the Northern Kingdom to Assyria before the fall of Samaria, 722 (721). Tiglath-pileser reports his reception of tribute from many kings, among others from the kings of Ammon, Moab, and Edom, and from Jehoahaz of Judah. This statement agrees with the Biblical record that King Ahaz went to Damascus to meet Tiglath-pileser (II Kings 16:10).

In 732 Damascus fell into his hands, and Assyria now controlled the west. Babylonia had been overrun by the Chaldeans, and so

Tiglath-pileser went in 731 to pacify that land. In 729 he was again in the country, and he was determined to make an end of ruling Babylonia by native princes. So he became an adopted son of the god Marduk by taking hold of the hands of his image, and accordingly was proclaimed king of Babylonia.

In 730 B.C., according to Biblical chronology, Hoshea revolted against Pekah. The revolt was instigated or assisted by Tiglath-pileser. Tiglath-pileser carried on extensive exchanges of populations in his colonizing schemes. His plan of planting colonies and of transporting captives had been tried by other Assyrian kings on a small scale, but it had never been adopted as a fixed and settled policy. He hoped thereby to break down national feeling, sever local ties, and make the empire homogeneous. He died in the 10th month, Tebeth, 728/7 B.C., after having occupied the throne for 18 years and having raised the Assyrian empire to a power and glory unknown to it under any of his predecessors.

Ti'gris (tī'grĭs). See HIDDEKEL.

Tik'vah (tĭk'vä) [hope, expectation]. 1. The father of Shallum, the husband of Huldah the prophetess (II Kings 22:14). In II Chron. 34:22 the name appears as Tokhath (in A.V. Tikvath), which suggests Arab. *waḳiha*, to obey, but the Heb. form is probably a corruption of Tikvah.
2. The father of a certain Jahaziah (Ezra 10:15).

Tik'vath (tĭk'văth). See TIKVAH.

Tile. A slab or tablet of baked clay. Tiles were the common writing material of Babylonia (Ezek. 4:1). The characters were impressed on the surface while it was yet soft, and the clay was then baked to render the writing indelible. Tiles were used in many countries as roofing material (Luke 5:19), but not, or not commonly, in Palestine. Probably Luke, accustomed to the tiled roofs of Greek houses, uses the expression "through the tiles" for through the roof, without reference to the material of the roof in question, or else in this particular house there was an opening in the roof to permit the inmates to ascend from the room to the coolness of the outer air. During the winter, however, this opening may have been closed with a frame and bricked over.

Til'gath-pil·ne'ser (tĭl'găth-pĭl-nē'zẽr). See TIGLATH-PILESER.

Ti'lon (tī'lŏn). A son of Shimon, whose registry was with the tribe of Judah (I Chron. 4:20).

Ti·mae'us (tī-mē'ŭs) [Gr., highly prized]. Father of the blind beggar of Jericho (Mark 10:46).

Tim'brel or **Tab'ret.** A kind of drum, probably a hand drum or tambourine, called *tōph* in Heb.; this term is used in Modern

A Timbrel

Hebrew for drum. It was much used in domestic festivities, was often played by women to accompany song and beat time for dances,

and was employed alone or in orchestra in the worship of God (Gen. 31:27; Ex. 15:20; Judg. 11:34; I Sam. 10:5; 18:6; I Chron. 13: 8; Job 21:12; Ps. 81:2; Isa. 5:12).

Tim'na (tĭm'nà), in A.V. twice **Tim'nah** (Gen. 36:40; I Chron. 1:51) [Heb. *Timna'*; cf. the same name in S. Arab., the capital of Ḳatabān, about 50 miles s.e. of Mārib]. 1. Daughter of Seir and sister of Lotan. She became a concubine of Eliphaz, Esau's eldest son, and the mother of Amalek (Gen. 36:12, 22; I Chron. 1:39). In interpreting these statements, it must be remembered that terms of relationship are used in describing tribes as well as individuals.
2. A duke of Edom (Gen. 36:40; I Chron. 1:51).

Tim'nah (tĭm'nà), in A.V. 8 times **Tim'nath** (Gen. 38:12–14; Judg. 14:1–5), once **Thim'·na·thah** (thĭm'nà-thä) (Josh. 19:43), and once **Tham'na·tha** (thăm'nà-thà) (I Macc. 9: 50, A.V.) [Heb. *timnāh*, allotted portion].
1. A town on the border line of the territory assigned to Judah, and not far from Beth-shemesh (Josh. 15:10). It was subsequently given over to the tribe of Dan (ch. 19:43). It was occupied by the Philistines in the days of Samson (Judg. 14:2), and was captured by them in the reign of Ahaz (II Chron. 28: 18). Its site is at Tibnah, about 3 miles w. by s. of Beth-shemesh, 15½ w. by s. of Jerusalem, and 16 e. of Ashdod.
2. A town in the hill country of Judah (Josh. 15:57), probably the place referred to in Gen. 38:12–14. It was near a certain Gibeah and is mentioned in connection with Adullam and Enaim. About 4 miles e. of Beit Nettīf is found a certain Tibnah on a slope which rises toward el-Khaḍer; near by to the s.e. is Jeba', and thus the Biblical data are fulfilled.
3. A town enumerated after Emmaus, Beth-horon, and Beth-el, and before Pharathon (I Macc. 9:50). It was fortified by Bacchides. The data point to Thamna, chief city of a toparchy (Jos. *War* iii. 3, 5), which bordered on the toparchies of Gophna, Lydda, and Emmaus (Jos. *War* ii. 20, 4), and lay between Antipatris and Lydda (Jos. *War* iv. 8, 1). Its site is probably marked by Khirbet Tibnah, 7½ miles w.n.w. of Jufna (Gophna), on the old road from Antipatris by way of Gophna to Jerusalem. See TIMNATH-SERAH.
4. An improper spelling, found in both versions, of the name of Timna, daughter of Seir.

Tim'nath (tĭm'năth). See TIMNAH.

Tim'nath-he'res (tĭm'năth-hē'rēz). See TIMNATH-SERAH.

Tim'nath-se'rah (tĭm'năth-sē'rà) [extra portion]. A village in the hill country of Ephraim, on the n. side of the hill of Gaash. It was given to Joshua as an inheritance, and there he was buried (Josh. 19:50; 24: 30). It is once written Timnath-heres, portion of the sun (Judg. 2:9), but heres is probably serah accidentally written backwards. It is probably Tibnah, which is 12 miles n.e. of Lydda and 8½ miles s. by w. of Kefr Hāris, where Samaritan tradition locates the graves of Joshua and Caleb. See TIMNAH 3.

Tim'nite (tĭm'nīt). A native or inhabitant of Timnah (Judg. 15:6).

Ti'mon (tī'mŏn) [Gr., deeming worthy]. One of the 7 men chosen to relieve the apostles from semisecular work in the primitive Church (Acts 6:5).

Ti·mo'the·us (tī-mō'thē-ŭs) [Gr., worshiping God]. 1. Leader of a large body of Ammonites, with whom Judas Maccabaeus fought several battles (I Macc. 5:6, 40).

2. Paul's convert and fellow worker. See TIMOTHY.

Tim·o·thy (tĭm'ô-thĭ), in A.V. usually **Ti·mo·the·us** [Gr., venerating or worshiping God]. The well-known companion and assistant of Paul. The terms which the apostle applies to him, "my beloved and faithful child in the Lord" (I Cor. 4:17), "my true child in faith" (I Tim. 1:2, etc.), seem to indicate not only the apostle's love for his youthful friend, but also that he had been the means of Timothy's conversion. At any rate it is clear (II Tim. 1:5) that when on his First Missionary Journey Paul visited Lystra in Lycaonia, Timothy's mother Eunice and grandmother Lois were led to Christ, and that Timothy was old enough to be instructed in the new faith which his mother had adopted. Though his mother was a Jewess, his father was a Gentile (Acts 16:1). On the one hand he had from a child been instructed in the O.T. (II Tim. 3:15); yet, on the other, he had not been circumcised (Acts 16:3). But, whether converted through Paul or afterward through the instruction of his mother, Timothy soon became active in Christian work, so that when, a few years later, Paul on his Second Journey again visited Lystra he found the young man well reported of by the brethren both at Lystra and Iconium (Acts 16:2). Already the voice of prophecy had indicated that Timothy was destined for special service (I Tim 1:18; 4:14). Paul therefore determined to take him with him; and the young man was set apart to the work of an evangelist by the laying on of the hands both of Paul and of the presbytery (I Tim. 4:14; II Tim. 1:6). In order also not to offend the Jews, Timothy was circumcised (Acts 16:3), the apostle thus indicating his wish, where no principle was involved, to conciliate those among whom in nearly every place he would have to begin work. Thereafter Timothy's fortunes were united with Paul's. He evidently accompanied the apostle through Galatia, then to Troas and Philippi, and then to Thessalonica and Berea, for it is mentioned (Acts 17:14) that he and Silas remained in Berea when Paul went on to Athens. Paul sent word for them to follow him to Athens speedily (Acts 17:15); but from I Thess. 3:1, 2 it appears that he sent Timothy back to Thessalonica, and that Silas and Timothy did not rejoin him until he had reached Corinth (Acts 18:5; I Thess. 3:6). Timothy then remained with Paul in Corinth (I Thess. 1:1; II Thess. 1:1) and probably, though his name is not mentioned, accompanied the apostle on his return voyage. We next hear of him during Paul's ministry in Ephesus. Paul informs us in I Cor. 4:17 that, before writing that epistle, he had sent Timothy to Corinth to correct abuses there. Yet for some reason, as I Cor. 16:10 intimates, there was a possibility that Timothy might not reach Corinth, and in fact we do not know whether he did so or not. At any rate he seems to have returned to Ephesus, for shortly before Paul left that city Timothy and Erastus preceded him into Macedonia (Acts 19:22), where Paul soon joined his young friend (II Cor. 1:1). Together they went to Corinth (Rom. 16:21), and Timothy is mentioned as one of the company who escorted the apostle on his return from the Third Journey toward Jerusalem (Acts 20:4). Whether Timothy went with the apostle to Jerusalem does not appear. No mention of him occurs during the imprisonment at Caesarea or the voyage to Rome. But in the epistles which were probably written from Rome his name occurs (Phil. 1:1; 2:19-23; Col. 1:1; Philemon 1). He had evidently followed the apostle to the capital and was his devoted co-worker. After the apostle's release, he

seems to have more than ever intrusted important duties to Timothy. In I Timothy we find that he had been left in charge of the church at Ephesus. It was a post of responsibility and difficulty, especially for one who was still a young man (I Tim. 4:12). False teachers were to be combated, officials were to be appointed, church customs were to be organized or regulated. The position of Timothy appears to have been that of an apostolic deputy, and it is not surprising that Paul wrote to him a special epistle with regard to his task. To Timothy he also wrote his last epistle shortly before his death (II Tim.). Almost alone, and with death impending, Paul desired ardently the presence of Timothy (ch. 4:9, 21), and to him he laid bare his whole heart. It is probable that Timothy reached Paul before the latter's death, but we do not know. The only further reference to him is Heb. 13:23. From it we learn that Timothy had suffered imprisonment, but had been set at liberty again. When this occurred, we do not know.

The First Epistle of Paul to Timothy probably was written after the apostle's traditional release from his 1st Roman imprisonment and resumption of missionary work (see above; also PAUL). Timothy had been left in charge of the church of Ephesus while Paul went into Macedonia (I Tim. 1:3). The epistle perhaps was written from Macedonia c. A.D. 64 or 65. It deals with the ecclesiastical difficulties that confronted Timothy, and gives him personal advice. It evinces the interest of the apostle in the practical working of the Church and his personal interest in Timothy's own welfare and success. Its contents may be arranged as follows: 1. Instructions concerning the Church (chs. 1 to 3); including warnings against false teachers (ch. 1), instructions concerning worship (ch. 2), instructions concerning church officers, closing with a brief statement of the dignity of the Church and the fundamental truths on which it rests (ch. 3). 2. Advice for Timothy's own guidance (chs. 4 to 6), with respect to the false doctrines and practical errors which he had to meet (ch. 4), and with respect to his treatment of various classes in the Church (chs. 5:1 to 6:2), followed by concluding exhortations partly of a personal character and partly to reinforce the previous instructions (ch. 6:3-21).

The Second Epistle of Paul to Timothy probably was written from Rome after the apostle had been arrested the 2d time, c. A.D. 67. He speaks of himself as a prisoner (II Tim. 1:8, 16; 2:9), charged with being an evildoer (ch. 2:9), and he expected soon to suffer martyrdom (ch. 4:6). Many of his friends had left him (chs. 1:15; 4:10, 12). Luke only, of his former friends, was with him (ch. 4:11), though other friends had gathered round him (v. 21). He had already had 1 trial, at which he had not been condemned (vs. 16, 17), but he was still held on some other charge. In his loneliness and danger his heart turned to Timothy, and this letter was written partly to encourage Timothy in his work as an evangelist and partly to urge him to hasten to Rome and to perform some personal services for the apostle. It may be divided as follows: 1. After a brief introduction, expressive of his wish to see Timothy and his confidence in him (ch. 1:1-5), he urges him to be courageous in spite of existing trials (vs. 6-12), and to be faithful to the truth he had received in spite of all opponents (vs. 13-18). 2. He charges Timothy to be strong, to secure the preservation of the truth, to be a good soldier, to bear in mind the imperishable foundation of fact and truth on which the gospel rests, to avoid false teaching, and to take heed to his own spiritual life (ch. 2). 3. He warns him that errors will increase, and bids him remember the example of steadfast endurance which Paul himself had shown him and the teaching of inspired Scripture in which he had been trained (ch. 3). 4. As his last direction, he bids Timothy preach the word and make full proof of his ministry (ch. 4:1-5), solemnly adding that he, Paul, on the verge of death, rejoiced that he had been able to do the same (vs. 6-8). The epistle then closes with some personal directions (vs. 9-22).

The epistles to Timothy and Titus are called, from their contents, the Pastoral Epistles. See PAUL.   G. T. P. (rev., H. S. G.)

Tin. A metal, in Heb. *beḏîl*, separated, dross, alloy. It was obtained from its ore by smelting. It was in use in Palestine and neighboring countries before the Exodus (Num. 31:22), in Egypt as early as Dyn. VI at least. Its principal use was in making bronze, which is an alloy of copper and tin. The Tyrians got their supply from Tarshish (Ezek. 27:12). Tin was obtained in Spain, but most of it came from islands in the w. ocean (Pliny *Hist. Nat.* xxxiv. 47; Herod. iii. 115). There is little doubt that these islands were the isles of Scilly, off the Cornwall coast, and that the mines of Britain were the chief source of supply to the ancient world, and that Phoenician mariners made direct voyages from Gades in Spain to Cornwall for the metal (Strabo iii. 175). Later it was transported across France to the mouth of the Rhone by a 30 days' journey (Diodorus Siculus v. 21, 22). The same word signifies the base metal existing in combination with silver in the ore (Isa. 1:25), and is supposed to denote the slag which separates from the lead when silver is being smelted from the ore.

Tiph'sah (tĭf'sȧ) [a passage, ford]. 1. A town at the extreme limit of Solomon's dominions, in the direction of the Euphrates (I Kings 4:24). It is generally identified with Thapsacus, on the right bank of the Euphrates, above the confluence of the Balikh. It was the most important crossing place in the middle course of the Euphrates; under the Seleucidae it was known as Amphipolis. The ford was used by the armies of Cyrus the Younger and Alexander the Great.

2. A place on the inhabitants of which Menahem inflicted barbarous cruelties (II Kings 15:16). It is mentioned in connection with Tirzah, from which it would seem not to have been far distant. Conder identifies it with the ruined village Ṭafsah, 6½ miles s.w. of Shechem. Many scholars follow Lucian's Gr. reading *Taphōe* and accordingly identify it with Tappuah (*q.v.*).

Ti'ras (tī'răs). A land and its inhabitants, who were a Japhetic people (Gen. 10:2). Ancient opinion identified it with Thrace (Jos. *Antiq.* i. 6, 1), from slight similarity of sound. The river Tyras, the modern Dneister, and the Tyritai, who dwelt on its banks (Herod. iv. 51), have also been suggested. The conditions are best met by the Tyrsenoi, an ancient Pelasgic people who occupied islands and coast lands of the Aegean Sea (Herod. i. 57, 94), probably the piratical Turusha who invaded Syria and Egypt in the 13th century B.C. *Tyrsēnos* is the Ionic and old Attic form of *Tyrrēnos*, Tyrrhenian.

Ti'rath·ites (tī'răth-īts). A family of scribes, Kenites from Tirah, dwelling at Jabez (I Chron. 2:55).

Tire. The rendering of Heb. *pe'ēr*, headdress, from root meaning to beautify, glorify. It means an ornamental headdress (Ezek. 24:17, 23). Aaron in his priestly capacity wore one of fine linen (Ex. 39:28; in A.V. bonnet). Women also wore it (Isa. 3:20; in A.V. bon-

net). The bridegroom decked himself with it (Isa. 61:10; in A.V. ornaments, R.V. garland; J.V. priestly diadem).

Tir'ha·kah (tûr'hȧ-kä). See PHARAOH 4.

Tir'ha·nah (tûr'hȧ-nä). A son of Caleb, the brother of Jerahmeel, by Maacah, his concubine (I Chron. 2:48).

Tir'i·a (tĭr'ĭ-ȧ). A son of Jehallelel (I Chron. 4:16).

Tir·sha'tha (tûr-shä'thȧ) [Heb. from Pers.; cf. Avestan *tarshta*, feared, revered]. The Persian title of the governor of Judah under the Persians, A.V.; R.V., "governor." It is borne by Zerubbabel (Ezra 2:63; Neh. 7:65, 70), and Nehemiah (Neh. 8:9; 10:1). In Neh. 12:26 the latter ruler is called *peḥâh*, or governor, to which Tirshatha, therefore, must have been practically equivalent.

Tir'zah (tûr'zȧ) [pleasantness, delightfulness]. 1. The youngest among the 5 daughters of Zelophehad (Num. 26:33; 27:1; Josh. 17:3).

2. A town noted for beauty (S. of Sol. 6:4), which belonged originally to the Canaanites, but was captured by Joshua (Josh. 12:24). Jeroboam I took up his residence in Tirzah (I Kings 14:17), and it became the capital of the 10 tribes (chs. 15:21, 33; 16:6, 8, 9, 15, 17) till Omri built Samaria (vs. 23, 24), after which it sank into a provincial but still important town (II Kings 15:14, 16). It is probably to be identified with the large mound of Tell el-Fār'ah, about 7 miles n.e. of Nāblus (Shechem) in a straight line.

Tish'bite (tĭsh'bīt). A member of the family, or native of the town, called Tishbeh or something similar (I Kings 17:1). A family of this name is unknown. Towns only claim attention. One is mentioned in the Book of Tobit (ch. 1:2): "Thisbe, which is on the right [i.e., south] of Kydiōs of Naphtali in Galilee above Asher"; Kydiōs is Kedesh, and is so rendered in R.V. Another is discerned by the LXX and Josephus in the text of I Kings 17:1, lying e. of the Jordan, in Gilead. The construct pl. before Gilead in the Heb. text, which is rendered sojourners in the E.V., the LXX regarded as a local name, and made it Thesbōn (Lucian, Thessebōn). Josephus writes: "from the city of Thesbōnē [Thessebōnē, Niese's text] in the country of Galaditis" (*Antiq.* viii. 13, 2).

Tish'ri (tĭsh'rē) [late Heb. from Akkad. *tashrētu, tashrītu, teshrētu*, beginning]. The 7th month, also called Ethanim. The name implies a calendar in which the year began with this month; the 1st day of Ethanim or Tishri is the Jewish New Year (cf. Num. 29:1).

Tithe. A 10th part of one's income consecrated to God. The separation of a certain proportion of the products of one's industry or of the spoils of war as tribute to their gods was practiced by various nations of antiquity. The Lydians offered a tithe of their booty (Herod. i. 89). The Phoenicians and Carthaginians sent a tithe annually to the Tyrian Hercules. These tithes might be regular or occasional, voluntary or prescribed by law. The Egyptians were required to give a 5th part of their crops to Pharaoh (Gen. 47:24). Before the days of Joseph and Pharaoh, Abraham, returning with spoil from his victory over the confederate kings, gave to Melchizedek, priest-king of Salem, a 10th part of all (Gen. 14:20). Jacob said that if God conferred on him certain specified benefits, he would surely give 1/10 of it to God (ch. 28:22). Under the Mosaic Law the fruits of the ground and cattle were subject to tithing (Lev. 27:30, 32). The tithe of grain and fruit need not be paid in kind. The owner might redeem it by purchasing it at ⅕ more than its market value (v. 31). But the tithe of the herd and flock might not be redeemed. This tithe was separated by causing the cattle to pass under the rod, and every 10th animal was taken, whether it was defective or without blemish. The choice had been committed to God, and the beast might not be exchanged (vs. 32, 33). Grain was threshed before it was tithed, and the fruit of vineyard and oliveyard was converted into wine and oil before $\frac{1}{10}$ of it was taken (Num. 18:27). All the tithe of Israel, which was offered as a heave offering, was given unto the Levites (vs. 21, 24). It was given to them as an inheritance in return for the service which they rendered at the sanctuary (v. 21), and as compensation for their lack of landed possessions. They paid a tithe of it to the priest (v. 26), and freely ate the rest anywhere (v. 31). On the eve of entering Canaan, where many of the Israelites would obtain homes far from the sanctuary, it was necessary to insist that the people should bring all prescribed sacrifices and freewill offerings, and all tithes, to the sanctuary (Deut. 12:5, 6, 11). They might not eat at home the tithe of their grain, wine, or oil, nor any offering, but before the Lord (vs. 17, 18). They must tithe all the increase of the field, and eat before the Lord the tithe of grain, wine, and oil, and the firstlings of flock and herd; but if the distance to the sanctuary was great, they might convert the offering into money, carry that to the sanctuary, and there buy what they chose for the eucharistic meal (ch. 14: 23-27). Every 3d year each man's tithe should be laid up in his town, and the Levite, the stranger, the widow, and the fatherless should go to the store and eat (vs. 28, 29). After tithing the tithe in this 3d year, which was distinguished as the year of tithing and reminded the people that the tithe was to be kept in the town, it was put at the disposal of those for whom it was intended (ch. 26:12). There were 2 third-year tithings between Sabbatic years, when there was no tithe.

Inconsistencies between these laws do not exist, although interpreters often force them into contradiction. The Israelites took the tithe to the sanctuary both during the sojourn in the wilderness and after the settlement in the land (Num. 18:24; Deut. 12:6). There a portion was eaten by the offerer and the Levites in a eucharistic feast, and the rest was given to the Levites. The law was slightly modified in anticipation of the settlement of Canaan, and the residence of Levites and producers in many cases far from the sanctuary. Every 3d year they should store the tithe in the town where they dwelt, dispense with the eucharistic meal, place all the tithe at the disposal of the Levites and other dependent persons, and make solemn protestation before the Lord to having done this (Deut. 26:12-15). This asseveration before the Lord may have been made in the town, or at the sanctuary on occasion of attending one of the annual festivals. It is sometimes asserted that Deuteronomy is peculiar in 2 respects: it prescribes vegetable tithes only, and it enjoins that they shall be eaten at the altar by the offerer and the Levites in company. If Deuteronomy does actually differ from the law of Leviticus and Numbers in these points, it is a modification of the law 40 years after its first enactment and in view of new circumstances. In the later history, even when the Levitical legislation was in full force, the vegetable tithe alone is often mentioned (Neh. 10:37; 12:44; 13:12). It was the more prominent, since agriculture and horticulture were the chief industries of the people. The tithe of the cattle is, however, referred to (II Chron. 31:6). It would be in itself natural,

if the eucharistic feast did not already exist, for Moses to introduce it in connection with tithes and firstlings, in view of the fact that the offerer frequently came from a distance and naturally required at least 1 meal at the sanctuary before returning. Still the omission of all mention of the feast in Leviticus and Numbers may be due to the feast's being regarded as a matter of course, a meal having been customary from time immemorial in connection with certain kinds of sacrifices and offerings. The tithe on agricultural and horticultural products alone is mentioned in Deuteronomy because, as regards tithes, it was only in connection with these tithes that a meal at the sanctuary was eaten, and the legislation in question is treating of eucharistic meals.

Another interpretation of the tithing laws requires mention. Not a few scholars have believed that the setting apart of $\frac{1}{5}$ for Pharaoh, to which the Israelites had been accustomed in Egypt, was perpetuated by the Mosaic Law as tribute to Jehovah. This $\frac{1}{5}$ was made up of 2 tithes. The 1st went to the Levites; the 2d was taken to the sanctuary and consumed there (Jos. *Antiq.* iv. 8, 8), but in the 3d year was given to the Levites in addition to their own tithe. Some interpreters have even thought of 3 tithes. They regard the tithing of the 3d year as additional to the 2 others. This interpretation is as old as Josephus at least (Jos. *Antiq.* iv. 8, 22), but it is unnecessary, and was scarcely the original intention of the law. The law is satisfied by the theory of 1 tithing.

In times of religious decline the people neglected to pay tithes. Hezekiah found it necessary to call authoritatively for their payment (II Chron. 31:4-12), and the Prophet Malachi was obliged to rebuke the people of his day for robbing God by withholding tithes and offerings (Mal. 3:7-12). The response of the people to Hezekiah's appeal was so hearty that he had to prepare chambers in the Temple precincts for storing the tithes (II Chron. 31:11). Whether he built additional quarters or cleared out old storehouses is not stated. The 2d Temple was likewise provided with storehouses (Neh. 13:10-14; Mal. 3:10), and Levites under the superintendence of a priest gathered the tithes into the towns and tithed them for the sanctuary (Neh. 10:37, 38). The payment of tithes continued (I Macc. 3:49; Luke 11:42; 18:12), but by the time of Christ changes had occurred. The tithe went to the priests (Jos. *Antiq.* xi. 5, 8; *Apion* i. 22; cf. Heb. 7:5), and was collected by them (Jos. *Life* 12, 15). Later the ordinary priests suffered from the cupidity of the chief priests, who forcibly took possession of the tithes (Jos. *Antiq.* xx. 8, 8; 9, 2).

Tit'tle. A point or small line used to distinguish one letter of the Heb. alphabet from another as ‫ב‬ (*beth*) from ‫כ‬ (*kaph*), ‫שׂ‬ (*sin*) from ‫שׁ‬ (*shin*), or ‫ר‬ (*resh*) from ‫ד‬ (*daleth*); hence a minute requirement of the Law (Matt. 5:18, in Gr. *keraia*, horn, projection).

Ti'tus (tī'tŭs). 1. A godly man of Corinth who was surnamed Justus (Acts 18:7, R.V.); see JUSTUS 2.

2. A trusted companion of Paul. He is not mentioned in The Acts, but is frequently referred to in Paul's epistles. He was born of Gentile parents (Gal. 2:3), and was one of the delegation from Antioch (Acts 15:2) who accompanied Paul and Barnabas to Jerusalem at the time of the council (Gal. 2:1, 3). It is possible that he was a native of Antioch, and, since Paul calls him "my true child after a common faith" (Titus 1:4, R.V.), he may have been converted through the instrumentality of the apostle. He was evidently also

much younger than Paul. His presence at the council gave offense to the Judaizers, but the Church refused to compel him to be circumcised, thus siding with Paul in his advocacy of the freedom of Gentiles from the Mosaic Law (Gal. 2:3–5). Titus next appears during and after Paul's residence in Ephesus. Titus had been sent to Corinth to correct certain abuses there which caused anxiety to the apostle (II Cor. 2:13; 7:6, 13; 8:6, 16; 12: 18). He and another (ch. 12:18) probably were dispatched after I Corinthians had been sent, on account of later reports which the apostle had received. His task was a delicate one, and Paul awaited his return with much solicitude. When the apostle left Ephesus, he expected to meet Titus at Troas (II Cor. 2:12, 13), and, failing in this, went to Macedonia. There Titus rejoined him with good news (ch. 7:6, 13, 14), and was forthwith sent back to Corinth with our Second Epistle to the Corinthians (ch. 8:6, 18, 23). We do not read again of Titus until after Paul's release from his 1st Roman imprisonment; see PAUL. The Epistle to Titus informs us that he had been left in Crete to superintend the organization of the churches in that island. He seems to have been, like Timothy in Ephesus, an apostolic deputy. His mission, however, was but a temporary one, and he was told to rejoin the apostle in Nicopolis. The only remaining notice of him is in II Tim. 4:10, where he is said to have gone to Dalmatia.

The Epistle of Paul to Titus probably was written after Paul's traditional release from his 1st Roman imprisonment and his resumption of missionary work. It may be assigned to A.D. 65 or 66. Titus had been left as superintendent of the churches in Crete, and the epistle, like the First Epistle to Timothy, was intended to direct him in the performance of his difficult task. It may be divided as follows: 1. Salutation, particularly describing the dignity of the apostolic message (ch. 1: 1–4). 2. Instructions concerning the character of those selected for bishops or elders, especially in view of the many false disciples whom Titus would be likely to meet and by whom he might be imposed upon (vs. 5–16). 3. Instructions which Titus should give to various classes in the Church, all to the effect that Christians should be "zealous of good works" (ch. 2). 4. Directions concerning the duty of Christians to society, bidding them emulate the love of man which God has shown in Christ (ch. 3:1–8). 5. Warnings against false teaching and heretics (vs. 9–11). 6. Personal directions and closing exhortation and benediction (vs. 12–15). The leading thought of the epistle is the importance of good works in all those representing or professing Christianity. On the Pastoral Epistles, see TIMOTHY and PAUL.   G. T. P. (rev., H. S. G.)

Ti'zite (tī'zīt). The designation of a certain Joha (I Chron. 11:45), probably derived from the place of which he was a native.

To'ah (tō'à) [cf. Akkad. *taḫū*, child]. A Kohathite Levite (I Chron. 6:34); see NAHATH 2.

Tob (tŏb) [good] A region e. of the Jordan, to which Jephthah fled when disowned by his brethren (Judg. 11:3, 5). Hanun, king of Ammon, who had given David just offense, drew soldiers from Tob among other places (II Sam. 10:6, R.V.), which indicates that it was beyond the borders of Israel. It was probably the district of Gilead known in Greek as the land of Tubias (I Macc. 5:13; cf. II Macc. 12:17). It may be eṭ-Ṭaiyibeh, 10 miles s. of Gadara (Mukeis or Umm Keis).

Tob'-ad'o·ni'jah (tŏb'ăd'ō·nī'jà) [good is Lord Jehovah]. One of the Levites sent by Jehoshaphat to teach in the cities of Judah (II Chron. 17:8).

To·bi'ah (tô-bī'à) [Jehovah is good]. 1. Founder of a family, members of which, coming to Jerusalem after the Captivity, failed to prove their descent (Ezra 2:60; Neh. 7:62). 2. An Ammonite servant who ridiculed the efforts of the Jews to rebuild the wall of Jerusalem (Neh. 2:10; 4:3, 7).

To'bie (tō'bĭ). See TUBIAS.

To·bi'jah (tô-bī'jà) [Jehovah is good]. 1. One of the Levites sent by Jehoshaphat to teach in the cities of Judah (II Chron. 17:8). 2. A Jew, one of those of the Captivity from whom the Prophet Zechariah obtained gold and silver to make crowns to put on the head of Joshua, the high priest (Zech. 6:10, 11, 14).

To'bit (tō'bĭt). See APOCRYPHA 3.

To'chen (tō'kĕn) [a weight, a measure]. A city belonging to the tribe of Simeon (I Chron. 4:32).

To·gar'mah (tô-gär'mà). A country of the far n. (Ezek. 38:6), inhabited by a people descended from Japheth through Gomer (Gen. 10:3). They traded in horses and mules (Ezek. 27:14). It is generally identified with Armenia. Friedrich Delitzsch, however, believes that the name appears in Til-garimmu, a city in the extreme e. of Cappadocia, mentioned in the Assyrian inscriptions.

To'hu (tō'hū) [cf. Akkad. *taḫū*, child]. A son of Zuph, an ancestor of Samuel (I Sam. 1:1); see NAHATH 2.

To'i (tō'ê) and **To'u**. A king of Hamath, probably a Hittite, who was at war with Hadadezer, king of Zobah, a Syrian. He sent to congratulate David on his victory over their common foe (II Sam. 8:9–12; I Chron. 18:9–11).

Tok'hath (tŏk'hăth). See TIKVAH 1.

To'la (tō'là) [worm, scarlet]. 1. A son of Issachar, and founder of a tribal family (Gen. 46:13; Num. 26:23; I Chron. 7:1). 2. Son of Puah, of the tribe of Issachar, who judged Israel 23 years. He lived, died, and was buried at Shamir, on Mount Ephraim (Judg. 10:1, 2).

To'lad (tō'lăd). See ELTOLAD.

Tomb. See SEPULCHER.

Tongue. 1. Besides signifying the organ of speech in the mouth, the word also denotes in a figurative sense speech or language (Gen. 10:5; cf. Acts 2:8 with v. 11). The descendants of Noah inherited and, for a long time after the Flood, spoke one language (Gen. 11:1). According to the Biblical account differences of speech were produced by divine judgment at Babel, which resulted in scattering abroad the people who had gathered there to all parts of the known world (vs. 2–9); see BABEL. In process of time the descendants of Noah came to speak several distinct languages and many different dialects. The Japhetic peoples largely used the languages now classed as Indo-European (ch. 10:2–5).

The Indo-European languages may be divided into: (1) Indo-Iranian: (a) Indic, including Sanskrit, Pali, Prakrit, Hindi (Hindustani, Urdu), (b) Iranian, including Avestan, Old Persian, Modern Persian; (2) Armenian; (3) Balto-Slavonic: (a) Slavic or Slavonic (Bulgarian, Serbo-Croatian, Slovenian, Russian with its dialects, Czech, Slovak), (b) Lithuanian, Lettish; (4) Greek; (5) Italic, which includes Oscan and Umbrian, and Latin with the Romance languages; (6) Celtic, including Welsh, Breton, Irish, Gaelic, Manx; (7) Germanic or Teutonic: (a) Gothic, (b) Scandinavian, which includes Swedish, Danish, Norwegian, and Icelandic, (c) West Germanic, including High German and Low German. (Under High German are grouped Old High German, Middle High German, and Modern German. Low German includes: on the one hand Plattdeutsch, Dutch and Afrikaans, Flemish, and Frisian; on the other hand, Anglo-Saxon, Middle English, and Modern English.)

The Semitic peoples generally spoke various dialects of the Semitic group (Gen. 10:21–31), embracing Akkadian (including Babylonian and Assyrian), Aramaic (v. 22), Arabic (vs. 26–29), Hebrew, and Ethiopic; see SE-MITIC. In a very broad sense of the term the descendants of Ham spoke Hamitic languages. The Semitic and Hamitic languages are rather closely related, but they form 2 different groups. Under Hamitic languages we have: (1) the North African, of which the Berber languages are modern representatives; (2) Ethiopian or Cushitic of Abyssinia and the region s., as Afar, Galla, Somali; (3) Ancient Egyptian, together with its descendant Coptic. Since Egyptian bears a closer relationship to the Semitic languages than do the other 2 Hamitic groups, it may be called a Hamito-Semitic or Semito-Hamitic language.

The gift of tongues was granted on the Day of Pentecost which followed the feast of the passover at which Jesus suffered. The disciples were all together when suddenly there came from heaven a sound like that of a rushing, mighty wind, and visible tongues, having the appearance of fire, were distributed to each, and they were all filled with the Holy Spirit (Acts 2:1–4). The Church was qualified and symbolically commissioned by the Spirit to declare the gospel to all men. Two general theories exist as to the nature of this gift: (1) The gift of tongues was manifested in ecstatic or elevated praise of God (Acts 10:46), which was unintelligible to man. The tongue was the organ of the Holy Spirit, and not of the person to whom the gift was given; and the words spoken were devotional and not for the instruction of the Church. In defense of this view it is urged that: (a) Paul makes no mention of foreign languages having been introduced at Corinth; and if tongues were referred to in I Cor., ch. 14 only, the impression would never have been made that they denote foreign languages. (b) Paul teaches that the understanding was not engaged (I Cor. 14:2). (c) The multitude could not understand them at Pentecost and accused the speakers of being drunken. It was necessary for Peter to interpret to the multitude what had taken place (Acts 2:13–17). Or if the disciples used foreign languages on the Day of Pentecost, this was a temporary form in which the gift of tongues was manifested and did not appear again. (2) The gift of tongues was manifested in intelligible discourse in tongues before unknown. (a) Luke's language clearly implies this (Acts 2:6–12). (b) Anybody could babble hysterically; only when the speakers used languages which they did not know before could the gift of tongues be recognized as miraculous. (c) The whole argument in I Corinthians assumes that the gift was speech in a foreign language, Paul contrasting speech and prayer in a foreign language uninterpreted with speaking and praying so as to be understood (I Cor. 12:10, 30; 14:13–16, 27, 28). Christians who had the gift should use it for missionary purposes and not exhibit their skill before their brethren, who did not understand what they said unless an interpreter were present.

Tongues were one of the signs that followed them that believed (Mark 16:17). They were a visible gift of the Holy Spirit bestowed in connection with the preaching of the apostles, or by the apostles through laying on of their hands (Acts 10:44–46; 19:1–7; cf. ch. 8:14–24). They were a phenomenon of the Apostolic Age, and gradually disappeared afterward. In the next century, perhaps 50 or 60 years after the death of the last apostle, Irenaeus could still report that he had heard many brethren who had prophetic gifts and spoke through the Spirit in all kinds of tongues (*Haer.* v. 6, 1).

2. A bar of gold (Josh. 7:21, 24, literally "tongue," but translated "wedge"). The Babylonians also spoke of tongues of gold, and a gold bar resembling a tongue has been found in the mound of ruined Gezer.

To'paz. A precious stone, called in Gr. *topazion,* and generally believed to be denoted by Heb. *piṭᵉdāh.* It was the 2d stone in the 1st row of the high priest's breastplate (Ex. 28:17; cf. the LXX and Jos. *Antiq.* iii. 7, 5). It was found in Ethiopia (Job 28:19) and on an island in the Red Sea (Diodorus Siculus iii. 38, 39; Pliny *Hist. Nat.* xxxvii. 9), and was known at Tyre (Ezek. 28:13). It adorns the 9th foundation of the New Jerusalem (Rev. 21:20). The topaz of the ancients was a yellow variety of corundum.

To'phel (tō'fĕl). A place, perhaps once a station of the Israelites in the wilderness (Deut. 1:1). Robinson and others have identified it with Ṭafîleh, about 14 miles s.e. of the s.e. curve of the Dead Sea. The consonants, however, are different, *teth* instead of *tau,* which raises a doubt as to the correctness of the identification.

To'pheth (tō'fĕth), in A.V. **To'phet** (tō'fĕt) (except II Kings 23:10) [ety. uncertain; spitting out, place of abhorrence; or perhaps originally from an Aram. word, place of burning]. Certain high places built in the valley of the son of Hinnom; on these the people of Jerusalem in the times of Isaiah and Jeremiah were accustomed to burn their sons and their daughters in the fire (Jer. 7:31) as offerings to Molech (II Kings 23:10). Apparently on the top of the high place there was a deep and large hole in which much wood was piled, ignition being produced by a stream of brimstone (Isa. 30:33). Josiah defiled it, and Jeremiah prophesied that such a number of people should be killed there that the name Topheth should disappear, and the valley where it stood be called the valley of slaughter (Jer. 7:32, 33; 19:6). A Topheth, apparently of the same type, was to be prepared for the king of Assyria. See HINNOM, VALLEY OF.

Torch. A flambeau, giving a flaring light, and often portable (Judg. 7:16, R.V.; Matt. 25:3, R.V. marg.; John 18:3; see LAPPIDOTH); primitively, merely a piece of resinous wood, or a bunch or twist of absorbent material soaked in oil and borne on a rod or carried by some other form of holder or incased in a narrow, conical clay wrapping or vase.

Tor'mah (tôr'må) [fraud]. A town in which Abimelech was once found (Judg. 9:31, R.V. marg.). More probably the word means craftily, as it is rendered in the R.V.; in which case the town of Tormah disappears.

Tor'men'tors. The jailers who were to keep the debtor safe and make his life miserable by chains, stocks, and doubtless other means of distress and torture until his debts were paid (Matt. 18:34). Torture was often applied to extort confessions (Acts 22:24; Jos. *Antiq.* xvi. 8, 4; 11, 6).

Tor'toise. See LIZARD.

To'u (tō'ōō). See TOI.

Tow'er. A lofty building, much higher than broad. A booth was sufficient to shelter the watchman placed to guard a vineyard (Isa.

1:8); but a tower, being more permanent and ornamental, indicated the owner's interest in his vineyard and his expectation of many seasons of fruitfulness (Isa. 5:2; Matt. 21:33; Mark 12:1). Stronger towers were built for defense. They were erected in the wilderness for the security of the shepherds and to keep marauders away (II Kings 17:9; II Chron. 26:10). They formed part of the defenses of fortified cities (II Kings 14:7; Neh. 3:1). They were erected beside the city gates, at the corners of the walls, and at intervals in the intervening space (II Chron. 26:9). Watchmen were stationed on them (II Kings 9:17), military engines for shooting arrows and stones were mounted on them (II Chron. 26:15), and the citizens found refuge in them when sore pressed by the enemy (Judg. 9:51, 52; Ps. 61:3). Within their massive walls the inmates were secure; their height allowed openings for light and air, out of reach of the adversary; and from their top missiles could be advantageously discharged at the foe.

Tow'er of Ba'bel (bā'bĕl). See BABEL.

Town Clerk. An official with the title of *grammateus* or scribe (Acts 19:35). Probably the duties of a *grammateus* originally were to record the laws and read them in public, but in course of time other functions were added to the office. Coins show that in the several cities of Asia Minor the town clerk presided in popular assemblies and was the virtual, or in some cases the actual, head of the municipal government.

Trach'o·ni'tis (trăk'ō-nī'tĭs) [Gr., rough, i.e., hilly region]. A region which at the appearance of John the Baptist as a preacher constituted, with Ituraea, a tetrarchy ruled over by Philip, the brother of Herod, the tetrarch of Galilee (Luke 3:1). It lay s. of Damascus (Strabo xvi. 2, 20), and comprehended the stretch of volcanic rocks now called al-Laja', and extended w. to Ulatha and Paneas, and s. to the borders of Batanea and Jebel Hauran (Jos. *Antiq.* xv. 10, 3; xvii. 2, 1 and 2).

Trag'a·canth. A gum (Gen. 37:25, R.V. marg.; 43:11), produced by several low, spiny shrubs of the genus *Astragalus*, especially from *Astragalus gummifer.* The plant is leguminous. Those from which gum is obtained are dwarf shrubs, protected by a dense mass of long thorns. The flowers are axillary and in most species are yellow, but in some are white or purple. Under the heat of the sun the gum exudes from the trunk, branches, thorns, and leaves, and is collected in Palestine by passing over the shrub a cloth or bunch of threads to which the viscous exudation adheres. It is used to impart firmness to pills, to marble books, and to stiffen crepes and calicoes.

Trance. A state in which the functions of the senses are suspended and the soul seems to be liberated from the body while it contemplates some extraordinary object; ecstasy. Peter on 1 occasion (Acts 11:5), and Paul on another, fell into such a trance (ch. 22:17). See VISIONS.

Tres'pass Of'fer·ing. See OFFERINGS.

Tribe. See EGYPT, III. 7.

Trib'ute. 1. Money, goods, or service exacted by a nation or king from foreign subjects (Deut. 20:11; R.V. marg., taskwork; Judg. 1:28, A.V.; Ezra 4:13; Neh. 5:4; Esth. 10:1; Matt. 17:25). The Pharisees endeavored to put Jesus in a dilemma by asking him whether it was lawful to pay tribute to the Roman emperor (Matt. 22:17). If he answered in the affirmative, he would offend the people, since with them independence was a matter of religion and they paid the foreign

tax with undisguised reluctance. The Pharisees expected him to declare that tribute to the Romans was unlawful, for they knew that he had publicly announced his claims to the throne of David; and an answer of this sort would justify a charge of rebellion against him. Jesus replied by calling for a coin. The coinage of money is the prerogative of the ruler. He pointed to the image of the Roman emperor which it bore, and his reply meant: "Give to the ruler whom you acknowledge whatever belongs to him, and to God whatever belongs to God." Jesus recognized the distinction between the 2 spheres of duty.

2. The didrachma or half shekel paid for the expenses of the Temple worship (Matt. 17:24; in R.V. half shekel). This payment was suggested at first by the half shekel which each male Israelite above 20 years of age paid as atonement money when he was numbered in the census (Ex. 30:11–16). In the time of Nehemiah the Israelites voluntarily assumed an annual payment of the 3d part of a shekel toward defraying the cost of the Temple service (Neh. 10:32, 33). Later the 3d part of a shekel was changed to half a shekel, and was made an annual tax collected from every Jew of 20 years of age and upward throughout the world (Jos. *Antiq.* xviii. 9, 1). The collector at Capernaum asked Peter whether his Master paid this half shekel, and Peter impulsively answered that he did (Matt. 17:24, 25). Jesus did indeed pay it; but it was incongruous for him to do so, and he drew Peter's attention to the matter. He pointed out to him that earthly kings exact tribute from aliens, not from their own children. Peter had recently confessed Jesus as the Son of God. It was for God's house and worship that this tax was levied, and it was scarcely proper for God's Son to be required to pay it. Such is the common interpretation of Christ's words on this occasion. After the fall of Jerusalem the Roman emperor Vespasian enjoined the Jews throughout the empire to bring to Jupiter Capitolinus in Rome the 2 drachmas which they had formerly paid to the Temple (Jos. *War* vii. 6, 6).

Tro'as (trō'ăs) [Gr., the Troad, region around Troy]. A seaport (Acts 16:11) of Mysia; where Paul saw in vision a man of Macedonia inviting him to Europe (Acts 16: 8–10; II Cor. 2:12). The apostle tarried there a week while returning from his Third Journey (Acts 20:6). On one occasion he left his cloak, books, and parchments there (II Tim. 4:13). It was founded by Antigonus, one of Alexander's successors, who called it Antigonia; but after his death his opponent Lysimachus, king of Thrace, altered its name to Alexandria, and Troas was added to distinguish it from Alexandria in Egypt. It was situated some distance s. of Homer's Troy, which furnished the name Troas to the district.

Tro·gyl'li·um (trō-jĭl'ĭ-ŭm). A town and a promontory on the w. coast of Asia Minor, opposite the island of Samos. Paul tarried there on the return to Jerusalem from his Third Journey (Acts 20:15; see R.V. marg.). An anchorage at the place is called St. Paul's Port.

Troph'i·mus (trŏf'ĭ-mŭs) [Gr., nourishing]. A Gentile Christian of Ephesus, who was with Paul for a time on his missionary travels, and whom he was falsely accused of having brought into the Temple in defiance of the Law (Acts 20:4; 21:29). The last we hear of him is that he was left by the apostle at Miletus sick (II Tim. 4:20, in A.V. Miletum).

Trum'pet. 1. A wind instrument, made of the horn of an animal or in imitation of it (Josh. 6:5; cf. Dan. 3:5, where *ḳeren*, horn, is rendered cornet), and called in Heb. *shōphār*. The latter word is rendered cornet in 4 passages where the *ḥăṣōṣᵉrāh* is mentioned with it and rendered trumpet (I Chron. 15:28; II Chron. 15:14; Ps. 98:6; Hos. 5:8). Its sound was loud, and audible at a great distance (Ex. 19:16, 19); and was well adapted to increase the noise of shouting (II Sam. 6:15; Ps. 98:6), but was ill-suited to be played with harps and pipes in an or-

Ancient Horns and Curved Trumpets

chestra. At the shout of the people and the blast of the trumpets the walls of Jericho came tumbling down (Josh. 6:1–20). It was used in war to assemble the army (Judg. 3:27; 6:34; I Sam. 13:3), to sound the attack (Job 39:24), to signal the cessation of the pursuit (II Sam. 2:28; 18:16), and to announce the disbanding of the army (II Sam. 20:1, 22). Watchmen blew it to sound the alarm (Jer. 6:1; Amos 3:6). Its blast proclaimed the accession of the king (II Sam. 15:10; I Kings 1:34; II Kings 9:13), and the commencement of the year of jubilee (Lev. 25:9). The 1st day of the 7th month was celebrated by solemn rest from ordinary labor, a holy convocation, and the offering of special burnt offerings (Lev. 23:24, 25; Num. 29:1–6), because the day marked a recurring 7th portion of time. It was a day or memorial of blowing of trumpets, designed to bring the people into remembrance before the Lord. The Jewish tradition is doubtless correct which states that the trumpet used was the *shōphār* (cf. Lev. 25:9).

2. The invariable rendering of Heb. *ḥăṣōṣᵉrāh*. Two were made of silver for use at the tabernacle (Num. 10:2); but the number was increased as time went on. One hundred and twenty were blown at the dedication of the Temple (II Chron. 5:12). The doubling of trumpets is noteworthy; 2 trumpets are shown on the Arch of Titus and likewise on Jewish coins. The priests often functioned in pairs, and 2 priests would need 2 trumpets. Probably they played in unison, but they may have given some passages antiphonally. The trumpets were a little less than a cubit in length. The tube was narrow, somewhat thicker than a flute, and ended in the form of a bell, like common trumpets (Jos. *Antiq.*

iii. 12, 6). They were used by the priests to announce festivals, to call the congregation, and on advancing to battle (Num. 10:1–10; 31:6). The trumpet was used to give the alarm in war (Hos. 5:8). Priests may have blown them at the coronation of Joash (II Kings 11:14; II Chron. 23:13). For their use in the Temple orchestra, see MUSIC.

3. Trumpet is expressed by the Gr. word *salpi(n)gx* in the N.T. It was used in war (I Cor. 14:8), and will announce the Second Advent of Christ (Matt. 24:31), and the resurrection of the dead (I Cor. 15:52). Seven trumpets were sounded to introduce as many apocalyptic visions (Rev., chs. 8 to 11). By *salpi(n)gx* the *ḥăṣōṣᵉrāh* or sacred trumpet is meant in Ecclus. 50:16; I Macc. 3:54; and probably chs. 4:40; 5:33; 16:8.

Try·phae′na (trĭ-fē′nȧ), in A.V. **Try·phe′na** (trĭ-fē′nȧ) [Lat. from Gr., delicate, dainty]. A woman at Rome to whom Paul sent his salutation, commending her for laboring in the Lord (Rom. 16:12).

Try′phon (trī′fŏn) [Gr., luxurious]. A general of Alexander Balas (I Macc. 11:39). He was a native of Casiana near Apamea in Syria, and originally bore the name of Diodotus (Strabo xvi. 2, 10). After the death of Balas and the recognition of Demetrius II as king of Syria, 145 B.C., Tryphon set up Antiochus VI, the infant son of Alexander Balas, as a rival to Demetrius (I Macc. 11:39, 40), and with the help of the Jews was rapidly conquering the country. His treachery to Jonathan Maccabaeus, however (chs. 12:39; 13:31, 32), caused his Jewish allies to go over to the side of Demetrius. Tryphon

Tryphon

meantime had murdered young Antiochus and declared himself king (ch. 12:31, 39). The capture of Demetrius by Arsaces, the Parthian king, left Tryphon to his own schemes for a while, but Demetrius' brother, Antiochus VII, opposed him and succeeded in besieging him, first in Dor on the Phoenician coast (ch. 15:10–14, 37), and afterward in Apamea, where Tryphon lost his life in 138 B.C. (Jos. *Antiq.* xiii. 7, 2).

Try·pho′sa (trĭ-fō′sȧ) [Gr., dainty, delicate]. A woman at Rome whose name is coupled with that of Tryphaena in the list of

Assyrian and Egyptian Trumpets

those Romans to whom Paul sent his salutation. They may have been sisters or fellow deaconesses. They are mentioned as laboring in the Lord (Rom. 16:12).

Tsa·dhe' (tsä-dā'), in A.V. **Tzad'di**; E.R.V. **Tza·de'** (tsä-dā') [Heb. *ṣādē*]. The 18th letter of the Heb. alphabet. No letter in the Eng. alphabet corresponds to it, but it is a strong *s* sound. In Anglicizing Hebrew names, *s*, *t*, or *z* is used to represent it. It heads the 18th section of Psalm 119, in which section each verse of the original begins with this letter.

Tu'bal (tū'băl). A tribe descended from Japheth (Gen. 10:2). It is mentioned with Javan (Isa. 66:19) and with Meshech as trading in the Tyrian markets with slaves and vessels of brass (Ezek. 27:13; 32:26). Gog was prince of Meshech and Tubal (chs. 38:2, 3; 39:1). The descendants of Tubal are the Tibareni or Tibarenoi of the classical writers. For their country and history, see MESHECH.

Tu'bal-cain' (tū'băl-kān') [Tubal, the smith]. A son of the Cainite Lamech by his wife Zillah. He was the forger of cutting instruments of brass and iron (Gen. 4:22). Tubal represents the Tibarenoi, who were iron workers, and so the name Tubal-cain looks like a doublet denoting the occupation of the smith.

Tu'bi·as (tū'bĭ-ăs), in A.V. **To'bie**. A district e. of the Jordan (I Macc. 5:13; cf. II Macc. 12:17), probably the land of Tob; see TOB.

Tur'ban. See DIADEM.

Tur'tle and **Tur'tle·dove'**. A species of pigeon. It is gentle and harmless, fit emblem of a defenseless and innocent people (Ps. 74:19). It is migratory (Jer. 8:7), and a herald of spring (S. of Sol. 2:12). Abraham sacrificed a turtledove and other victims when the Lord's covenant was made with him (Gen. 15:9). Under the Law it served as a burnt offering (Lev. 1:14) and for a sin offering; and 2 turtledoves were prescribed for these 2 sacrifices in case a poor person was obliged to make a guilt offering, and for the purification of a woman after childbirth if she was poor, of a man or woman with an issue, and of a Nazirite (Lev. 5:7; 12:6, 8; 15:14, 29, 30; Num. 6:10, 11). It was readily obtainable by the poor, for it abounds in Palestine and is easily trapped. Three species of turtledove are described by Tristram as occurring in Palestine. The most abundant is the common turtledove (*Turtur vulgaris*), which reaches Palestine from the s. in countless numbers at the beginning of March, and departs again at the approach of winter. The 2d is the collared turtledove (*Turtur risorius*). It is a summer migrant, breeding in Palestine in trees and bushes. The 3d species, the palm turtledove (*Turtur senegalensis*), does not migrate, but remains permanently in the Dead Sea Valley, which has a tropical climate.

Tu'tor. See SCHOOLMASTER.

Twin Broth'ers. See CASTOR AND POLLUX.

Tych'i·cus (tĭk'ĭ-kŭs) [Gr., fortuitous]. A Christian of the province of Asia who, with others, traveled on in advance of Paul from Macedonia to Troas, and awaited the apostle's arrival in that city (Acts 20:4). He was a beloved brother and faithful minister in the Lord, and was sent by Paul to carry to their destination the Epistles to the Ephesians and to the Colossians (Eph. 6:21; Col. 4:7). Paul proposed also to send him as a messenger to Titus in Crete (Titus 3:12). Afterward he was dispatched to Ephesus (II Tim. 4:12).

Ty·ran'nus (tī-răn'ŭs) [Lat. from Gr., an absolute sovereign, a tyrant]. A man at Ephesus who was either a teacher of philosophy or rhetoric, or else a Jewish scribe who gave instruction in the Law. In his school Paul disputed, with the view of making Christianity known after he no longer had access for this purpose to the Jewish synagogue (Acts 19:9).

Tyre (tīr), in A.V. often **Ty'rus** (tī'rŭs) [a rock]. An important city of Phoenicia. It was a place of great antiquity (Isa. 23:7; Jos. *Antiq.* viii. 3, 1); but it was founded or attained to importance after Sidon (Gen. 10:15; Isa. 23:12). The priests of Melkarth told Herodotus that it was founded 2,300 years before his visit, which would make the city come into existence about 2,750 B.C. (Herod. ii. 44). According to ancient testimony, Tyre originally stood on the mainland; but in course of time, for safety against besiegers, it was transferred to the neighboring rocky island which gave name to the locality. Ancient writers frequently allude to its situation in the sea (Ezek. 26:17; 27:32). The town on the mainland became known as Palaetyrus or Old Tyre. Tyre was nearer to the Israelites than Sidon, and this fact, with the increasing greatness of Tyre over Sidon, established the constant order observed in speaking of the 2 cities, Tyre and Sidon. Tyre was subject to Egypt in the 15th century B.C. (Tell el-Amarna tablets). In the time of Joshua it was a strong place (Josh. 19:29). It lay on the border of Asher, but was not assigned to that or any other tribe, nor do the Israelites appear to have possessed it at any period of their history. In the time of David it was regarded as a stronghold (II Sam. 24:7). Hiram, king of Tyre, was friendly with David and Solomon, and aided them with materials for the erection by the former of his palace (II Sam. 5:11; I Kings 5:1; I Chron. 14:1) and by the latter of the Temple and the other edifices which he built (I Kings 9:10–14; II Chron. 2:3–16). Another Hiram, a brass founder, who cast pillars and other work for the Temple, was of mixed Tyrian and Hebrew parentage (I Kings 7:13, 14, 40, 45). The taste of the Tyrians was not for war, but for manufacture, commerce, money-making, sea voyages, and colonization. They produced purple dyes, metal work, and glassware; and they trafficked even with remotest peoples (cf. I Kings 9:28). Their merchants were princes, the honorable of the earth (Isa. 23:8). In the 9th century B.C. a colony from Tyre founded Carthage, which became a formidable rival to Rome. Still, though by taste a commercial people, they were often forced into war. Early in the 9th century they purchased immunity from Ashur-nasir-pal, king of Assyria, and later were represented in the alliance, which included Ahab, formed to resist Ashur-nasir-pal's son and successor Shalmaneser. But at length Tyre with others paid him tribute. About 724 B.C. Shalmaneser V, king of Assyria, after receiving the submission of Old Tyre, laid siege to island Tyre, but he died in 722 without effecting its capture (Jos. *Antiq.* ix. 14, 2; cf. probably Isa., ch. 23). It yielded to his successor Sargon. The friendliness of the Tyrians toward Israel had ceased by this time. The prophets denounced the Tyrians for delivering Israelites to the Edomites (Amos 1:9), and despoiling them of goods, and selling them as slaves to the Greeks (Joel 3:5, 6). The city was not plundered, as were the neighboring towns by Sennacherib, but was besieged by Esarhaddon, and yielded on honorable terms to Ashurbanipal in 664 B.C. In the next century it enjoyed great commercial prosperity, and its merchants traded with all the countries of the known world (Ezek., ch. 27). Jeremiah prophesied Tyre's subjection (Jer. 27:1–11). The classic prophecy against Tyre, entering into more detail, is that of Ezekiel (Ezek. 26:1 to 28:19; 29:18–20). These prophecies of Jeremiah and Ezekiel refer largely to a siege of Tyre (585–573 B.C.) by Nebuchadnezzar, lasting 13 years (Jos. *Apion* i. 21). It is not certainly known whether he actually captured any part of the 2 cities (cf. Ezek. 29:18–20); if he did, it was probably only the one on the shore (ch. 26:7–11 and perhaps 12), and the result did not compensate the besiegers for their toil. However, Tyre finally made terms and acknowledged Nebuchadnezzar's suzerainty. In 332 B.C. Alexander the Great took the city on the island after a siege of 7 months, having made his way to it by building a mole from the mainland across the narrow strait. But it soon recovered considerable prosperity (cf. Isa. 23: 15–18).

Our Lord once visited the coasts of Tyre and Sidon (Matt. 15:21–28; Mark 7:24–31), and people from the region occasionally attended on his ministry (Mark 3:8; Luke 6: 17). He pointed out that the responsibilities of those heathen cities were much less than those of the places around the Sea of Galilee, which constantly heard his preaching and saw his miracles (Matt. 11:21, 22; Luke 10:13, 14). A Christian community existed there in the 1st century (Acts 21:3–6). The scholar Origen, who died about A.D. 254, was buried in the Christian basilica in Tyre. A larger and grander basilica was erected by the bishop Paulinus, and at its consecration in 323 the church historian Eusebius, bishop of Caesarea, preached the sermon.

In 638 the city was captured by the Moslems. The lives and property of the citizens were spared on the condition that no new churches be built, no bells be rung, no horses be ridden by Christians, no insults be offered to Islam. On the 27th of June, 1124, Tyre was taken by the Crusaders. The German emperor Barbarossa, who was drowned on his crusade in 1190, was buried in their cathedral. They lost the city again in March, 1291, when it was reduced almost to a heap of stones. Quantities of its stones have been carried away to Beirut, Acre, and Joppa, for building purposes. The walls are in ruinous condition and have in part disappeared or been covered with sand. Tyre had 2 harbors: the Sidonian on the n.e. part of the island, and the Egyptian on the s. end. The Sidonian was within the circumvallation of the city, and its entrance could be blocked by stretching a chain from one side to the other. The Egyptian was an open harbor, outside the fortifications, but adjoining them; it is now filled with sand and no longer used. Alexander's mole still remains; its breadth is nearly half a mile. Most of the ruins, including the cathedral, are of Crusader times. The fountains and reservoirs called Rās el-'Ain supplied the city with water by means of an aqueduct starting 15 or 20 feet above the level of the ground, so as to give a sufficient slope for its descent. Tyre was for a considerable period all but destitute of inhabitants. It has, however, slightly revived and is called Ṣūr, the old name in Arabic form. Its houses are chiefly on the e. part of what was once the island, but the former island has been converted by Alexander's mole and accumulated sand into a promontory jutting out from the shore. In its prime Tyre was as important in commerce as Jerusalem is for religion, Athens for philosophy, and Rome for law and government.

The Ladder of Tyre is a high mountain on the coast of Syria, 100 stades or about 11 miles n. of Ptolemais (Jos. *War* ii. 10, 2). This statement of distance and direction identifies it with a part or the whole of the massive, mountainous promontory, 7 miles in width, which thrusts itself into the sea and forms the natural boundary between Palestine and Phoenicia (I Macc. 11:59). At its s.w. angle Rās en-Nāḳūrah, a bold headland, projects, leaving no beach between its base and the water, and forcing the coast road to ascend and cross it. This part of the great promontory is commonly identified with the Ladder. Some travelers, however, localize the Ladder at the n.w. angle, where Rās el-'Abyaḍ, the white promontory, stands. A road is cut through its precipitous cliffs for about a mile; it overhangs the sea and rises at points to the height of 200 feet above the water.

Tzad′di (tsăd′ē; tsä-dē′). See TSADHE.

U

U′cal (ū′kăl) [I am strong]. One of 2 sons, pupils, or contemporaries, to whom Agur addressed his prophecy or proverbs (Prov. 30: 1). This interpretation represents the traditional Hebrew punctuation and derives support from v. 4, where a person is addressed and asked to answer if he knows. Another interpretation (I am consumed), which, however, rejects the Masoretic punctuation, is given in the margin of the R.V.

U′el (ū′ĕl) [will of God]. A son of Bani, induced by Ezra to put away his foreign wife (Ezra 10:34).

Uk′naz (ŭk′năz). The marginal reading of I Chron. 4:15, A.V.; but a Hebrew proper name would not begin as this word does. In the text it is properly regarded as 2 words, and the R.V. correctly renders it "and Kenaz."

U′lai (ū′lī). A river on the banks of which Daniel was in vision when he saw the prophetic ram, the he-goat, etc. (Dan. 8:2, 16). The Ulai is undoubtedly the Eulaeus. Among the 3 streams near Susa, the Ulai can best be identified with an artificial canal some 900 feet wide; it left the Choaspes at Pai Pul, about 20 miles n.w. of Susa, passed close to the town of Susa on the n. or n.e., and afterward joined the Coprates.

U′lam (ū′lăm) [first, leader; cf. Arab. *'awwal*, first]. 1. A Manassite (I Chron. 7: 16, 17).

2. A son of Eshek, a Benjamite descended from Saul through Jonathan (I Chron. 8: 39, 40).

Ul′la (ŭl′à). An Asherite (I Chron. 7:39), probably descended from Helem (v. 35).

Um′mah (ŭm′à) [juxtaposition]. A town of Asher (Josh. 19:30); not identified. Thomson proposes 'Alma, about 5 miles from the shore at Rās en-Nāḳūrah. Some considerations suggest that Akko may be the original text. *Kaph* (k) was not infrequently mistaken for *mem* (m).

Un′cle. The brother of one's father (II Kings 24:17, Heb.). The Heb. word is *dōd*, which is of broader meaning than uncle and denotes any kinsman on the father's side (Lev. 10:4; Amos 6:10); as a cousin (cf. Jer. 32:12 with vs. 8, 9), or a member of the same tribe (Num. 36:11).

Un·clean′ An′i·mals. A general distinction between clean and unclean meats was made by the nations of antiquity. Some animals were recognized as fit for food and sacrifice, while others were not. The distinction was based partly on the discovered unsuitableness or unwholesomeness of the flesh for food, partly on habits and prey, and partly on an inexplicable natural abhorrence to certain animals. Regard was paid in the Mosaic legislation to this customary attitude of the men of the age, and the distinction between clean and unclean meats was incorporated in the Law. Other animals were added to the list of the unclean, out of special considerations involved in the religion of the Israelites; in some cases no doubt ancient taboos were considered. Unclean animals were classified as follows: 1. Beasts that do not both part the hoof entirely and chew the cud (Lev. 11:3, 4), including all that go on 4 paws (v. 27). The Law accordingly allows only animals of the ox, sheep, and goat kind, and deer and gazelles (Deut. 14:4, 5). It excludes among other animals all carnivorous beasts. They eat blood or carrion, and were therefore intolerable to the Israelite. 2. Carnivorous birds, of which 20 or 21 are specially named (Lev. 11:13–19; Deut. 14:12–18). The enumeration included the bat, which was classed as a bird. They eat blood or carrion. 3. Winged insects which do not have in addition to the 4 legs 2 hind legs for leaping (Lev. 11:20–23). All insects are excluded except the locust (grasshopper). 4. Whatever in the water has not both fins and scales (vs. 9, 10). This prohibition left for use the most wholesome varieties of fish found in the waters of Palestine. It excluded eels and water animals which are not fish, such as crabs. Numa forbade the Romans to offer scaleless fish in sacrifice (Pliny Hist. Nat. xxxii. 10); and the modern Egyptians are said to regard such fish as unwholesome. Some of these scaleless and finless creatures were snakelike, and recalled the first sin and its curse. 5. Small creeping things (Lev. 11:29, 30); every creeping thing that goes upon its belly or upon all fours, or has many feet (vs. 41, 42). Some were unwholesome; others crept in the dust or through slime; still others were snakelike. Not improbably there was a religious repugnance to creeping things in general, because their mode of locomotion was a reminder of the serpent and the curse on the tempter.

These animals were unclean under any circumstance. But the flesh of even clean animals might become unclean. The Law forbade the eating of things offered in sacrifice to idols, things strangled or dead of themselves or killed by beast or bird of prey. Blood and fat of bird and beast were sacred to the Lord. None might eat of the blood, not even the stranger that sojourned in Israel (Lev. 17:10–14). The violator of the law respecting blood was cut off from his people (chs. 7:27; 17:10, 14). The offender against the laws regarding unclean animals was unclean until the evening (chs. 11:24, 40; 17:15). Animals that died of themselves might be sold to strangers and eaten by them (Deut. 14:21).

Un·clean'ness. The Law distinguished between clean and holy (Lev. 10:10); for example, animals are clean or unclean, not holy or unholy. Uncleanness, when not presumptuously incurred, was ceremonial, not moral defilement. It excluded man from the sanctuary (ch. 7:20, 21) and from fellowship with members of the commonwealth of Israel, but it did not interrupt spiritual communion with God in prayer. At the same time, the laws that defined uncleanness were in some cases enforced by the injunction, "Be ye holy; for I am holy" (ch. 11:44, 45). In keeping himself from the unclean, man had regard to the fact that he was set apart from a common to a sacred service, and that as a man of God he was holy unto the Lord and must be separate and touch no unclean thing. Furthermore, ceremonial uncleanness was typical of sin. Physical cleanliness also is different from ceremonial cleanness. The 2 were not synonymous, although the 2 conditions sometimes coincided. Comfort and the demands of society required bodily cleanliness on the part of the Hebrews. There were divers washings which had nothing to do with ceremonial purity. The laws of cleanliness which governed men in their intercourse with each other were instinctively observed by reverent persons in their approach to God, and found expression in commands and institutions (Ex. 19:12, 14; 30:18–21; Josh. 3:5). Ceremonial defilement, for which purification was provided, was incurred in a special manner and was restricted to certain acts and processes. It was acquired by: 1. Contact with a human corpse (Num. 19:11–22). This defilement was the gravest, for the effect of sin is revealed in strongest light in the death of man and the dissolution of the body. Uncleanness arising from this cause continued 7 days, and was removed by the water of separation. Even the necessary handling of the ashes of the red heifer, which were used to cleanse from defilement by contact with the dead, rendered unclean (vs. 7–10); and contact with the unclean person rendered the clean person unclean until evening (v. 22). 2. Leprosy in man, clothing, or building (Lev., chs. 13; 14). The leper was excluded from human society (ch. 13:46), and for his cleansing he required special ablution and sacrifice. 3. Natural and morbid issues from the generative organs (Lev., ch. 15), including puerperal uncleanness (ch. 12). Generation and parturition were not sinful in themselves; they were ordained by the Creator (Gen. 1:27, 28). The bodily issues connected with them, however, in man or woman, whether voluntary or involuntary, defiled; man's affinity to the lower animals is apparent in reproduction, for right though marriage is, in heaven they neither marry nor are given in marriage; and probably the divine judgment pronounced on Eve for sin was remembered in connection with childbirth. 4. Eating the flesh of an unclean animal, or contact with its carcass or with that of a clean animal not slain for food and which had thus become subject to the corruption of death (Lev., ch. 11). See UNCLEAN ANIMALS and PURIFICATION.

U'ni·corn. Any 1-horned animal, as the rhinoceros (Isa. 34:7, A.V. marg.; the word is rendered "wild-ox" in R.V.). The idea of the unicorn may have its origin in art, where the artist depicted the animal from 1 side so that the 2 horns were merged into 1. The Biblical animal, however, was 2-horned (Deut. 33:17, where the word is sing., and not pl., as in A.V.). It was possessed of great strength (Num. 23:22; 24:8), but was too untamable to bend its neck to the yoke or assist man in his agricultural labors (Job 39:9–12). It was frisky in youth (Ps. 29:6). It was not the wild buffalo, for this beast is quite tamable. The R.V. marg. (Num. 23:22) renders it by "ox-antelope," meaning the oryx (Antilope leucoryx); see ANTELOPE. This interpretation is supported by the analogy of Heb. re'ēm to Arab. rim, (white antelope or gazelle); but the oryx is timid and in ancient Egypt was frequently tamed and used in the plow. There is every reason to believe that the Heb. word signifies the wild ox (R.V.); for this animal is denoted by the corresponding Akkad. word rimu. Admirable representations of it by Assyrian artists show it to be the aurochs (Bos primigenius). Tiglath-pileser I (c. 1115–1102 B.C.) hunted it in the land of the Hittites, at the foot of Lebanon. It is now extinct, and its name has been transferred in Syria to another animal; but its previous occurrence on and around Lebanon is independently proved by the fact that Tristram discovered its teeth in the bone caves of Lebanon. It

Goat Statuette from the Royal Cemetery at Ur

is distinguished from its descendant, the common ox, by having a flatter forehead and large horns with double curvature.

Un'ni (ŭn'ī) [(Jehovah) has answered]. 1. A Levite of the 2d degree in David's reign,

who played the psaltery (I Chron. 15:18, 20). It is doubtful whether the word doorkeepers (v. 18) is intended to include him.
2. A Levite in the time of Zerubbabel (Neh. 12:9, A.V.); see UNNO.

Un'no (ŭn'ō), in A.V. **Un'ni** [the former is the kethib; the latter, the kere]. A Levite who was a contemporary of the high priest Jeshua (Neh. 12:9).

U'phar'sin (û-fär'sĭn). See MENE.

U'phaz (ū'făz). A place from which gold was brought (Jer. 10:9; Dan. 10:5). No such place is known, but it has been understood to refer to Ophir. But *paz* is Heb. for fine gold, and the word has accordingly been rendered by some commentators "and fine gold."

Ur, I (ûr). A city of ancient Sumer (later Babylonia, which finally was occupied by the Chaldeans or Chaldees), the birthplace of Abraham (Gen. 11:28, 31; 15:7; Neh. 9:7). Its site is now identified with Muḳayyar (Arab., bitumened, or pitched), in Lower Babylonia, on the w. bank of the Euphrates. It may have been settled somewhere around 4000 B.C., when settlers began to appear in the marshlands. It was a seat of the worship of the moon-god. See BABYLONIA.

Ur, II (ûr) [flame]. Father of one of David's mighty men (I Chron. 11:35). The transcriber perhaps made 2 heroes, Ur and Hepher, out of 1 whose name was Ahasbai or perhaps *'ūrīḥaph* (cf. II Sam. 23:34).

Ur·ba'nus (ûr-bā'nŭs), in A.V. **Ur'bane** (ûr'bān) [Lat., urbane, polite]. A Christian to whom the Apostle Paul sent his salutation (Rom. 16:9).

U'ri (ū'rī) [an abbreviation of Urijah, q.v.]. 1. Father of Bezalel, the craftsman (Ex. 31:2).
2. Father of Solomon's taxgatherer Geber (I Kings 4:19).
3. A porter whom Ezra induced to put away his foreign wife (Ezra 10:24).

U·ri'ah (û-rī'á), in A.V. of N.T. **U·ri'as** (û-rī'ăs) [Jehovah is a light]. The Hebrew name is often rendered Urijah. 1. A Hittite, one of David's mighty men (II Sam. 23:39; I Chron. 11:41), whom the king arranged to have placed at an exposed point in a battle

Excavating in the Royal Cemetery at Ur

with the Ammonites so that he would lose his life and thus be prevented from discovering an intrigue which his sovereign had been carrying on with the faithful soldier's wife (II Sam. 11:1–27; Matt. 1:6). It is possible that his name was Hurrian Ariya, which was transformed by popular etymology into Uriah.

2. A priest, 1 of 2 witnesses to a tablet written by Isaiah (Isa. 8:2); see URIJAH 1.

3. A prophet, the son of Shemaiah of Kiriath-jearim. He predicted that the Kingdom of Judah was about to be temporarily destroyed, which so enraged King Jehoiakim that he sought to kill the prophet of evil. Uriah fled to Egypt but was brought back and slain (Jer. 26:20–23; in A.V. Urijah).

4. A priest, father of a certain Meremoth (Ezra 8:33; Neh. 3:4, 21, in A.V. Urijah).

5. One of those, probably priests, who stood by Ezra while he addressed the people (Neh. 8:4, in A.V. Urijah).

U·ri·el (ū′rĭ-ĕl) [El (God) is a light]. 1. A Levite, family of Kohath, house of Izhar, descended through Korah, Abiasaph, and Tahath (I Chron. 6:24). He is probably a different person from Zephaniah (v. 36), and belonged to the collateral line which sprang from Tahath. The head of the Kohathite family in David's reign bore this name (ch. 15:5, 11) and is conceivably the same person.

2. A man of Gibeah whose daughter Micaiah was Abijah's mother (II Chron. 13:2).

U·ri′jah (ū-rī′jȧ) [Jehovah is a light]. 1. The high priest in Ahaz' reign who was directed to make an altar like that which caught the king's fancy at Damascus (II Kings 16:10–16). He was probably 1 of the 2 witnesses to the enigmatical inscription written by Isaiah (Isa. 8:2, in E.V. Uriah).

2. A prophet (Jer. 26:20, A.V.); see URIAH 3.

3. A priest (Neh. 3:4, 21, A.V.); see URIAH 4.

4. One who stood by Ezra while he addressed the people (Neh. 8:4, A.V.); see URIAH 5.

U′rim (ū′rĭm) **and Thum′mim** (thŭm′ĭm) [lights and perfections]. It should be observed that the 2 Heb. words begin with the 1st and last letters of the alphabet respectively. The order is once reversed (Deut. 33:8), and twice Urim alone is used (Num. 27:21; I Sam. 28:6). One or more objects belonging to the ephod of the high priest, put in the breastplate of judgment so as to be on the high priest's heart when he went in before the Lord (Ex. 28:30; Lev. 8:8; cf. Ecclus. 45:10). The receptacle was probably a fold of the breastplate or the space underneath it. In connection with the Urim and Thummim, the high priest learned the will of God in doubtful cases. This method was not adopted for inquiring the divine will concerning private individuals or private matters, but was employed only in behalf of the nation; hence the required place for the Urim and Thummim was in the breastplate of judgment, which bore the names of the 12 tribes of Israel on 12 precious stones. With the Urim and Thummim, the will of Jehovah, the Judge, concerning judicial matters, and the royal desire of Jehovah, the King, were learned (Num. 27:21; cf. Josh. 9:14; Judg. 1:1; 20:18, 23, 27, 28; I Sam. 10:22; 14:36–42; 22:10, 13; 23:9–12; 28:6; 30:7, 8; II Sam. 2:1; 5:19, 23, 24). The will of Jehovah was inquired with Urim and Thummim, not only in the sanctuary or where the Ark was (Judg. 20:27, 28; I Sam. 22:10), but in any place, provided the authorized priest with the ephod was present. The answer was usually quite simple, often a mere affirmation or denial, or a choice of 1 tribe or place out of several; but it was not always so (I Sam. 10:22; II Sam. 5:23, 24).

Occasionally, also, when sin had interrupted communion with God, no answer was granted (I Sam. 14:37; 28:6). There is no reference to the use of Urim and Thummim after the reign of David, and at the time of the Return from exile there was no priest with Urim and Thummim (Ezra 2:63; Neh. 7:65); hence Josephus is probably wrong in saying that the virtue or use ceased 200 years before his time (Jos. *Antiq.* iii. 8, 9). The use of this method was a prerogative of the high priest alone; and, since he belonged to the tribe of Levi, the possession of the Urim and Thummim was a glory of that tribe (Deut. 33:8).

Different explanations of the Urim and Thummim have been offered. For example, an analogue has been sought in the badge of office which the Egyptian high priest, as supreme judge, is reported by classical writers to have worn, consisting of an emblem of truth suspended from his neck on a golden chain; but the Egyptian high priest carried this official token during the judicial proceedings only, and hung it on the person in whose favor judgment was pronounced; and

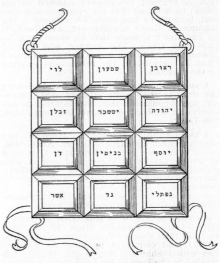

Breastplate of the High Priest

there is no evidence that it was ever used as a means for inquiring the divine will. Other interpreters have supposed that when to the high priest, clad in the ephod with the Urim and Thummim and offering prayer, an idea occurred, its divine origin and truth were confirmed by the unwonted gleaming of the gems in the breastplate. From this phenomenon was derived the name Urim, lights. It has been suggested that the answer was spelled out by the successive gleaming of the letters which composed the proper names on the stones; but, to say nothing of the fact that the complete alphabet is not yielded by these names, and that in several of the recorded responses letters occur which are not found on the stones, the whole idea smacks of the feigned miracles of Greek and Roman priests, and is foreign to the methods and conceptions of the Hebrew ritual.

Only 2 theories are important: 1. The Urim and Thummim probably were 2 appendages of the ephod and detachable, and were used as the lot, cast like dice, and by their fall somehow revealed the divine will. Support is sought for this theory in the fact that the casting of the lot is twice referred to in close association with seeking revelation through Urim and Thummim (I Sam. 10:19–22; 14: 37–42). In the latter case, Saul prayed, "Give a perfect lot" (ch. 14:41, R.V. marg.). The word *thâmîm* is used, which it is proposed to pronounce *thummim,* and thus make the Urim and Thummim to have been a kind of sacred lot. The text of the LXX favors this interpretation. While there is much uncertainty about Urim and Thummim in the sacred lot, some have supposed that they were flat stones, white on the one side and black on the other. If both fell white side up, the answer was in the affirmative; if black, then negative. But if one had the white side and the other the black side upwards, no reply was vouchsafed to the question. 2. The Urim and Thummim gave no outward manifestation, but served as a symbol. The high priest arrayed himself in the ephod with Urim and Thummim, which betokened his authority to obtain light and truth, as the name indicates, in order that he might seek counsel of Jehovah in the divinely appointed manner. He laid the matter humbly before God in prayer; the answer dawned in his mind; he believed that the response was correct, because he had made his request in the manner of God's appointment, and because he had God's promise that he should receive light and truth. The answer was inward illumination, without any external sign, and finds its parallel in the revelations granted to the prophets.

U'su·ry. Interest paid on borrowed money; the word is used in its primary sense, without any imputation that the interest is excessive in amount or above the legal rate. See LOAN.

U'thai (ū'thī) [probably, Jehovah has shown himself as surpassing; cf. Arab. *'atā,* to be proud, go beyond bounds]. 1. A man of Judah, family of Perez, and son of Ammihud. He was the head of the father's house to which he belonged, and dwelt at Jerusalem (I Chron. 9:4).
2. A descendant of Bigvai. He accompanied Ezra from Babylon (Ezra 8:14).

Uz (ŭz), in A.V. once **Huz** (Gen. 22:21). A tribe of the Aramaeans (Gen. 10:23), able to trace their descent partly from Nahor (ch. 22:21), and connected by blood or political ties with Dishan the Horite (ch. 36:28). Job resided in the land of Uz (Job. 1:1), and was exposed to attack from the Sabeans and Chaldeans (vs. 15, 17). At the time of Jeremiah, Edomites dwelt in the land of Uz (Lam. 4: 21). Josephus regarded Uz as the founder of Trachonitis and Damascus (Jos. *Antiq.* i. 6, 4). Ptolemy locates the Ausitai in the desert w. of the Euphrates. Uz, according to these data, was in the Syrian desert between the latitudes of Damascus and Edom.

U'zai (ū'zī) [perhaps, Jehovah has heard]. Father of one who helped to rebuild the wall of Jerusalem (Neh. 3:25).

U'zal (ū'zăl). A people of Arabia descended from Joktan (Gen. 10:27; I Chron. 1:21; Ezek. 27:19, R.V. marg.). The kindred name Azal was, according to Arabian tradition, the ancient name of Şan'â', the capital of Yemen, in Arabia.

Uz'za (ŭz'á) [(Jehovah is) strength]. 1. A Benjamite, a son or a descendant of Ehud (I Chron. 8:7).
2. The founder of a family of Nethinim, members of which returned from captivity (Ezra 2:49; Neh. 7:51).
3. A man known only as the original owner of a garden. This garden ultimately passed

into the hands of Manasseh, king of Judah, and was within the precincts of his palace. Both Manasseh and his son Amon were buried in it (II Kings 21:18, 26; cf. II Chron. 33:20). The garden was apparently at or near Jerusalem, but the exact spot is undetermined.

4 and 5. Two men otherwise called Uzzah.

Uz'zah (ŭz'á), and **Uz'za** in I Chron. 13:7–11 and A.V. of ch. 6:29 [(Jehovah is) strength]. 1. A son of Abinadab, of what tribe is unknown. When the Ark had reached the threshing floor of Nacon, or Chidon, on its way to the city of David, the oxen stumbled, and Uzzah, putting forth his hand to support the sacred symbol, was struck dead. The place was therefore called Perez-uzzah, breach of Uzzah, or breaking out against Uzzah, and long retained the name (II Sam. 6:3–11; I Chron. 13:7–14).
2. A son of Merari (I Chron. 6:29).

Uz'zen-she'e·rah (ŭz'ĕn-shē'ĕ-rá), in A.V. **Uz'zen-she'rah** (ŭz'ĕn-shē'rá). A village built by Sheerah, daughter of an Ephraimite named Ephraim (I Chron. 7:24). It is mentioned in connection with the 2 Beth-horons, and is considered to have been at Beit Şîrâ, 3 miles w. by s. of the nether Beth-horon, and 13 w. by n. of Jerusalem.

Uz'zi (ŭz'ī) [(Jehovah is) strength]. 1. A man of Issachar, family of Tola, and head of a father's house (I Chron. 7:2, 3).
2. A priest, son of Bukki, and father of Zerahiah, of the line of Eleazar (I Chron. 6: 5, 6, 51). He was an ancestor of Ezra (Ezra 7:4).
3. A Benjamite, family of Bela, and head of a father's house (I Chron. 7:7).
4. Another Benjamite, son of Michri, and father of Elah (I Chron. 9:8).
5. A Levite of the sons of Asaph. He was son of Bani, and overseer of the Levites at Jerusalem (Neh. 11:22).
6. A priest, head of the house of Jedaiah in the days of the high priest Joiakim (Neh. 12:19).
7. A priest, one of those who assisted at the dedication of the rebuilt wall of Jerusalem (Neh. 12:42).

Uz·zi'a (ŭ-zī'á) [Jehovah is strength]. A man from the town of Ashtaroth, and one of David's mighty men (I Chron. 11:44).

Uz·zi'ah (ŭ-zī'á), in A.V. of N.T. **O·zi'as** [Jehovah is strength]. 1. A Kohathite Levite, the son of Shaul (I Chron. 6:24).
2. The father of a certain Jehonathan in David's time (I Chron. 27:25).
3. A king of Judah (II Kings 15:13, 30–34; II Chronicles; Isaiah; Hos. 1:1; Amos 1: 1; Zech. 14:5; Matt. 1:9); called Azariah in II Kings 14:21; 15:1–8, 17–27; I Chron. 3:12 (see AZARIAH 11). He succeeded his father Amaziah about 785 B.C. during the latter's lifetime, a few years after the crushing defeat inflicted on Amaziah by the king of Israel. That he reigned during his father's lifetime is evident from the statement, made in connection with the record of his reign, that he built Elath after the death of the king (II Kings 14:22). He was 16 years old when he ascended the throne (v. 21). After conducting the government for 24 years, it is recorded, "In the twenty and seventh year of Jeroboam . . . began Azariah [Uzziah] . . . to reign" (ch. 15:1; the word "began" is not in the Heb. text). This statement "is most easily explained," says Kleinert, "by the assumption that in this year the kingdom of Judah had regained the full sovereignty"; freeing itself from vassalage to Jeroboam, in which it had been held since the overthrow of Amaziah, the capture and dismantlement of Jerusalem, and the enforcement of hos-

tages. Uzziah organized the army; and he improved the fortifications of Jerusalem and the weapons and military engines of his troops. He gained important victories over the Philistines and Arabs, razed the walls of Gath, Jabneh, and Ashdod, and received tribute from the Ammonites and other foes (II Chron. 26:6–8). Thus Judah became strong, and Uzziah promoted agriculture by building towers in the desert and digging wells. Uzziah himself worshiped Jehovah, but did not take away the high places at which his people sacrificed to other gods. At length, elated by his prosperity, he entered the Temple against priestly remonstrance and attempted to offer incense, and was struck with leprosy from which he never recovered. He had therefore to associate his son Jotham with him in the government. A notable earthquake occurred during his reign (Amos 1:1; Zech. 14:5); this event came, in the popular memory, to be connected with his attempt to invade the priest's office (Jos. *Antiq.* ix. 10, 4). His reign extended to 52 years. He died about the year 734 B.C. (II Kings 15:1–7; II Chron., ch. 26). Before his decease the prophets Isaiah, Hosea, and Amos had begun their public careers (Isa. 1:1; 6:1; Hos. 1:1; Amos 1:1).

4. A priest, son of Harim. He was induced by Ezra to put away his foreign wife (Ezra 10:21).

5. A man of Judah, family of Perez (Neh. 11:4).

Uz·zi'el (ŭ-zī'ĕl) [El (God) is strength]. 1. A Levite, son of Kohath, and founder of a tribal family (Ex. 6:18, 22; Num. 3:19, 27, 30). He was a kinsman of Aaron on the father's side (Lev. 10:4). Amminadab, the chief of the Uzzielites, and 112 of his brethren were organized by David for service when he brought up the Ark to the city of David (I Chron. 15:10).

2. A Benjamite, family of Bela (I Chron. 7:7).

3. A Levite, instrumentalist in David's reign (I Chron. 25:4). Called in v. 18 Azarel; see AZAREL 2.

4. A Levite, son of Jeduthun. He assisted King Hezekiah in his work of reformation (II Chron. 29:14).

5. A Simeonite captain, one of those who, in Hezekiah's reign, led a successful expedition against the Amalekites of Mount Seir (I Chron. 4:41–43).

6. A goldsmith, son of Harhaiah. He helped to rebuild the wall of Jerusalem (Neh. 3:8).

V

Va'heb (vā'hĕb). A place near the Arnon (Num. 21:14, 15, R.V.). See DI-ZAHAB.

Vai·za'tha (vī-zä'thȧ), in A.V. **Va·jez'a·tha** (vȧ-jĕz'ȧ-thȧ) [from Old Pers., son of the atmosphere; cf. Avestan *vaya* (air) + *zāta* (born)]. A son of Haman (Esth. 9:9).

Vale and **Val'ley.** The vale or the valley, *par excellence*, is in A.V. the Shephelah or lowland (*q.v.*).

Va·ni'ah (vȧ-nī'ȧ). A son of Bani, induced by Ezra to put away his foreign wife (Ezra 10:36).

Vash'ni (văsh'nī). According to I Chron. 6:28 (A.V. following the Heb. text), the eldest son of Samuel, in which case he would be the same as Joel of v. 33, and of I Sam. 8:2. But the text is corrupt. Joel has accidentally slipped out, the conjunction *waw* (*vav*, *vau*) before Abiah has crept in, and *vashni* should

be rendered "and the second" (R.V. following Syriac and I Sam. 8:2).

Vash'ti (văsh'tĭ) [Old Pers., the desired one, the beloved; cf. Avestan *vas* (wish, desire), past participle *ushta*. Cf. also Modern Pers. *vashti* (beauty). There may also be considered Avestan *vahishta* (best)]. The queen of the Persian sovereign Ahasuerus. For refusing to show herself to the king's guests at a feast celebrated in his 3d year, she was divorced and deposed (Esth. 1:3, 9 to 2:1). Amestris, daughter of Otanes, was the wife of Xerxes (Herod. vii. 61, 114). If she was Vashti, Vashti was ultimately restored to favor, for Amestris was the recognized wife of Xerxes sometime after the battle of Mycale, 479 B.C. (Herod. ix. 109).

Vav (văv), in A.V. and E.R.V. **Vau** (vō) [Heb. *wāw*]. The 6th letter of the Heb. alphabet. The Eng. *F*, through the Gr. *digamma* or *vau*, has the same origin. Where it is a consonant in Hebrew names it appears as *v* in the Anglicized form. In Heb. it is pronounced as Eng. *w*.

It stands at the head of the 6th section of Psalm 119 in the Eng. Bible, in which section each verse begins with this letter in the original Heb.

Ve'a·dar (vē'ȧ-där) [and Adar, i.e., the 2d or intercalary Adar]. In a cycle of 19 years Veadar is introduced 7 times in order to render the average length of the year nearly correct. This month falls in the latter part of March and the beginning of April. See YEAR.

Ve'dan (vē'dăn). A place with which Tyre traded (Ezek. 27:19, R.V.); possibly either Adin or Weddān, between Mecca and Medina. But the text may be corrupt. The A.V. has the rendering "Dan also," the first syllable being regarded as the Heb. conjunction *waw* (*vav*, *vau*), meaning "and."

Veil, in A.V. often **Vail**. See CLOTHING, TABERNACLE 2, and TEMPLE 3.

Ver·mil'ion. A red pigment obtained by grinding the mineral cinnabar (Pliny *Hist. Nat.* xxxiii. 38). It was called *shāshar* in Heb., *miltos* in Gr.; and was used to paint walls, mural decorations, and idols (Jer. 22:14; Ezek. 23:14; Wisd. of Sol. 13:14). Vermilion is a satisfactory translation of the word in these passages; but *miltos* was of broader meaning and denoted any red mineral coloring matter; as red lead, or clay mingled with the oxide of iron and known as ocher. Rude Africans bedaubed the body with it (Herod. iv. 191, 194), and certain tribes used it as war paint (Herod. vii. 69).

Ver'sions. Translations of the Bible or of any portions of it into vernacular tongues, for the benefit of those who understand the original imperfectly or not at all.

Versions are immediate or mediate, according as they are made directly from the original text or through the medium of other translations. Four ancient immediate versions of the O.T. have come down to modern times: the Septuagint (LXX), the Targums of Onkelos and Jonathan ben Uzziel, the Syriac Peshitta with a considerable portion of its predecessors, and the Latin Vulgate. They derive special critical value from the fact that they were made before the Hebrew text of the Masoretes was established.

The Samaritan Pentateuch is not a version; it is the Hebrew text written in Samaritan or old Hebrew characters, with various divergences from the Hebrew text of the Masoretes (see SAMARITAN PENTATEUCH); and the Samaritan version of the Pentateuch is a translation of this divergent text into the Samaritan dialect.

ANCIENT VERSIONS

Codex Sinaiticus (4th Century), Esther 2:6-8

The John H. Scheide Biblical Papyri
(Late 2d or Early 3d Century),
Ezek. 20:8-14

Ethiopic Octateuch (15th Century),
Gen. 29:11-16

Syriac Manuscript of the Bible (Peshitta, A.D.
464), Ex. 13:14-16

ENGLISH VERSIONS

Wycliffe's Bible, John 1:1–5

Anglo-Saxon Gospel (About A.D. 1000),
John 1:1–12

The xvi. Chaptcr.

Ꮋen cam to him the pharises with the saduces also / and dyd tēpte him / desyringe that he wolde shewe thē sōme sygne frō heven. He answered and saide vnto them: At even ye saye / we shall have fayre wedder. and that because the skye ys reed: ʒi the mornigte: ye saye / to daye shalbe foule wedder / z that because the skye is troblous and reed. O ye ypocryts / ye

Tyndale's New Testament (1525), Matt. 16:1–3

ᏁᎠ I sawe when the Lambe opened one of the seales, and I heard as it were the noise of thunder, one of the foure beastes, saying, Come and see.

2 And I saw, and behold, a white horse, and hee that sate on him had a bowe, and a crowne was giuen vnto him, and hee went foorth conquering, and to conquere.

3 And when hee had opened the second seale, I heard the second beast say, Come and see.

4 And there went out another

King James Bible (Authorized Version, 1611),
Rev. 6:1–4

623

I. ANCIENT VERSIONS OF THE O.T., MADE FOR THE USE OF JEWS.

I. 1. *The Septuagint.* The most celebrated Greek version of the Hebrew Scriptures and the oldest complete translation of them. It was called the Septuagint, commonly designated by LXX, after the 70 translators reputed to have been employed on the Pentateuch in the time of Ptolemy Philadelphus, 285–246 B.C. Originally the name was applied to the translation of the Pentateuch, but eventually to the whole Greek O.T. Aristobulus, a Jewish priest who lived in Alexandria during the reign of Ptolemy Philometor 181/0–145 B.C., and who is mentioned in II Macc. 1:10, is quoted by Clement of Alexandria and Eusebius as stating that while portions relating to Hebrew history had been translated into Greek previously, the entire Law was translated from the Hebrew in the reign of Ptolemy Philadelphus under the direction of Demetrius Phalereus. The same tradition, but considerably embellished, is contained in a letter purporting to have been written by Aristeas to his brother Philocrates. This letter is condemned by modern scholars as spurious. The same story as that told by Aristeas is repeated with slight variations by Josephus, who may have had the letter before him. Josephus relates that Demetrius Phalereus, librarian to Ptolemy Philadelphus, wished to add to the 200,000 volumes in the library a copy of the Hebrew books of the Law, and to have them translated into Greek, as they were unintelligible in the original. The king consented, and made application to Eleazar, the high priest at Jerusalem, for 72 aged and skillful interpreters, 6 from each tribe, to make the translation. They arrived in Alexandria, bringing the Law written in golden letters on books of parchment. They were hospitably received, were assigned a quiet house on the island of Pharos in the harbor of Alexandria, and transcribed and interpreted the Law in 72 days (Jos. *Antiq.* xii. 2, 1–13; *Apion* ii. 4).

These ancient reports concerning the origin of the LXX have great value, although reliance cannot be placed on the details, and the statements regarding the scope of the work are difficult of interpretation. It is, however, commonly agreed that the LXX originated in Egypt, that the Pentateuch was translated into Greek in the time of Ptolemy Philadelphus, that the other books followed gradually, and that the entire work was completed by 150 B.C. Reference to a Greek version of the Law, the Prophets, and the other books is made by Jesus, son of Sirach, as early as 132 B.C. (Ecclus., prologue). The version is the work of many translators, as differences in style and method show, and its quality is unequal in different parts; it is also much corrupted. The translation of the Pentateuch, except poetic portions (Gen., ch. 49; Deut., chs. 32; 33), is the best part of the work, and on the whole is well executed, although not literal. The translators of Proverbs and Job were masters of a good Greek style, but were imperfectly acquainted with Hebrew and handled the original arbitrarily. The translation of Proverbs is based on a Hebrew text that varied considerably from the present Masoretic text. The general sense of Psalms is fairly well reproduced. Ecclesiastes is rendered with slavish literalness. The translation of the Prophets is unequal in quality. That of Amos and Ezekiel is tolerably well done, but that of Isaiah is quite inferior. The version of Jeremiah was possibly made from a Hebrew text different from the Masoretic. In The Book of Daniel the early Christians, since the time of Irenaeus and Hippolytus, substituted for the Old Greek the version of Theodotion.

The quotations from the O.T. in the N.T. are usually citations from the LXX, either verbatim or with unimportant verbal changes; in other cases, the N.T. writers apparently themselves translated from the original Hebrew. The Ethiopian eunuch whom Philip met was reading the LXX (Acts 8:30–33).

Three main recensions of the LXX were made. One was issued c. A.D. 245, and the others previous to A.D. 311. They were that of Origen in Palestine, of Lucian in Antioch and Constantinople, and of Hesychius in Egypt. Codex Vaticanus (B) of the early 4th century, although not the original LXX, is acknowledged to exhibit *relatively* the most original text, and it probably descended from that upon which Origen based the text of the LXX given in the 5th column of his Hexapla. It should be noted, however, that there is no prominent Biblical MS. in which there occur such gross cases of misspelling, faulty grammar, and omissions, as in B; in proper names it is often very bad. The Chester Beatty and the John H. Scheide papyri (2d and early 3d centuries A.D.) yield further important evidence of the original LXX. Lucian's recension has been edited in part by Lagarde and by Oesterley. Lucian was a presbyter of Antioch, and died a martyr's death at Nicomedia in A.D. 311 or 312. He issued a revised text of the LXX based on a comparison of the common Greek text with the Hebrew text, which proves to have been a good text, but different from that of the Masoretes. Hesychius was bishop of Egypt, and suffered martyrdom A.D. 311; his text has been lost; but Codex Marchalianus (Q) of the 6th century, preserved in the Vatican library and containing the Prophets, is believed to show it for these books.

I. 2. *Minor Greek versions.* After the destruction of Jerusalem in A.D. 70, the LXX lost favor among the Jews, partly because of the successful use made of it by the Christians in establishing the claims of Jesus, and partly because they discovered that its style lacked elegance. Accordingly, 3 translations of the canonical books of the O.T. were made by Jews in the 2d century; they are known to us only in isolated fragments or citations. (1) The translation (c. A.D. 128) by Aquila, a native of Pontus and a proselyte to Judaism. He lived in the time of the emperor Hadrian, and he undertook to make a literal version of the Hebrew Scriptures in order to counteract the use of the LXX made by the Christians in advancing their doctrines. It was so slavishly literal as often to be unintelligible to readers who did not know Hebrew as well as Greek. (2) The revision of the LXX by Theodotion, a Jewish proselyte of Ephesus according to Irenaeus, and according to Eusebius an Ebionite, believing in the Messiahship, but not in the deity of Christ. We know next to nothing as to Theodotion's person and date; he may be placed in the first 3d of the 2d century A.D. and may even precede Aquila. In his revision of the LXX he made use of the Hebrew original. (3) The elegant, but periphrastic, translation toward the end of the 2d century A.D. by Symmachus, a Samaritan Ebionite. Origen knew also of 3 anonymous Greek versions known as the Quinta, the Sexta, and the Septima.

Origen (c. 185–c. 254) arranged the Hebrew text and 4 different versions in 6 parallel columns for purposes of comparison. In the 1st column he put the Hebrew text, in the 2d the Hebrew written in Greek letters, in the 3d the version of Aquila, in the 4th that of Symmachus, in the 5th the LXX or Old Greek, in the 6th the revision by Theodotion. From these 6 columns his work takes its name of Hexapla. In the column devoted to the LXX he marked with an obelus (— or ÷) words which were not in his Hebrew text. He emended the Greek text by supplying words lacking in it but found in the Hebrew. These he indicated with an asterisk (*). A metobelus (: or */. or ⊥) marked the conclusion of the passage to which the asterisk or obelus referred. The Hexapla was completed by c. A.D. 245, and was followed by a shortened edition, or Tetrapla, in which the 2 Hebrew columns were omitted. These 2 works were deposited in the library founded by Origen's disciple, Pamphilus, at Caesarea in Palestine. They were consulted by Jerome in the 4th century, and were still in existence in the 6th century. It is thought that they were destroyed when the Arabs took the town in A.D. 638.

Fragments of Origen's great work are preserved in quotations made by the fathers. The LXX column was separately published by Pamphilus and Eusebius, who supplied Constantine with 50 copies of that edition; and it was translated into Syriac (616–617) by Paul, bishop of Tella, who retained Origen's critical symbols. Origen pursued an unfortunate method when he conformed the text of the LXX to the Hebrew text of his day; since the great desideratum of scholars is the Greek text as it left the translators' hands, for that text would throw light on the Hebrew text which they used. Moreover, the obeli and asterisks, which Origen had so carefully used, were often neglected or carelessly employed by copyists; furthermore when the 5th column circulated separately, the interest in comparison with the Hebrew and the various Greek versions was lost. In this way Origen's critical studies unwittingly introduced chaos into the text of the original Greek version.

I. 3. *The Targums.* When the Jews returned from the Babylonian Exile, the Hebrew of their forefathers ceased to be their ordinary speech, and Aramaic, misnamed Chaldee, took its place. It soon became necessary at the public reading of the Scriptures for the reader or his assistant to translate the passage orally that the people might understand. The custom of explaining obscure words and phrases at the public reading was in vogue in Ezra's time (Neh. 8:8). The event referred to has been cited as evidence that the words read were translated; but this is more than the statement warrants, and depends upon the answer to the question of whether or not the Hebrews had adopted a foreign language during the Exile. The oral targum —that is, interpretation or translation— which became necessary, was at first a simple paraphrase in Aramaic, but eventually it became elaborate; and in order to fix it as a translation and render it authoritative as an interpretation, it was reduced to writing. These written Targums are a valuable aid in determining the text as read in the early synagogues and in discovering the meanings which the Jews attached to difficult passages. The principal Targums are the Targum of Onkelos on the Pentateuch and the Targum of Jonathan ben Uzziel on the Prophets. Onkelos is sometimes identified with the translator Aquila (see VERSIONS, I. 2), but the best opinion seems to be that this Targum was produced in its present form about the 3d century on the basis of an earlier paraphrase. It is quite literal. The Targum ascribed to Jonathan ben Uzziel, a pupil of Hillel, of the 1st century A.D., on the other hand, is periphrastic; it received its final form in Babylon about the 5th century.

II. ANCIENT VERSIONS OF A PART OR THE WHOLE OF THE BIBLE, AND INTENDED CHIEFLY FOR CHRISTIANS.

II. 1. *Syriac versions.*
(1) *The Diatessaron.* Tatian (fl., c. 160–c. 180), a native of the Euphrates Valley and a former disciple of Justin Martyr in Rome, wove into 1 narrative the material of the 4 Gospels. This harmony in Syriac, known by a Greek title, the Diatessaron, circulated widely among the churches of Syria from about the beginning of the 3d quarter of the 2d century to the 4th or 5th century. It is now extant only in translations into Arabic and Latin; we have also an Armenian translation of St. Ephraem's commentary on it. In 1933 a vellum fragment containing 14 imperfect lines of the Diatessaron in Greek was discovered among the ruins of a Roman fortress at Dura-Europos on the w. bank of the upper Euphrates.

(2) *The Old Syriac Gospels.* At the close of the 2d century the 4 Gospels circulated in Syria also in a separated form (*da-mepharreshē*). Two MSS. (with numerous losses) of this version were discovered, one in 1842 by William Cureton in a Syrian convent in the Nitrian desert s.w. of the Nile Delta, and the other in 1892 by Agnes Smith Lewis in the convent of St. Catherine on Mount Sinai. No doubt there was an Old Syriac version of the rest of the N.T. books accepted by the Syrian Church, but that has not been recovered.

(3) *The Peshitta.* Peshitta means "simple" or "vulgate." The O.T. was made directly from the Hebrew, probably in the 2d or 3d century A.D. At a later date it was revised by a comparison with the Greek. The N.T. owes its origin to the effort of Rabbula, bishop of Edessa (411–435), to establish a uniform text by revising divergent copies of the Old Syriac in accord with Greek MSS. of a later type of text. Since the Syrian Church did not accept as canonical the 4 minor Catholic Epistles (II Peter, II and III John, Jude) and the Apocalypse, the Peshitta did not include these 5 books.

(4) *The Philoxenian and Harclean Versions of the N.T.* About 508 Philoxenus, Jacobite bishop of Hierapolis in e. Syria, had a translation made of the entire N.T. For the first time the minor Catholic Epistles and the Apocalypse were included in a Syriac Bible. In 616 Thomas of Heraclea (Ḥarḳel) elaborately revised this version with the help of some MSS. in Alexandria. His work is literal in the extreme.

(5) *The Palestinian Syriac Version* probably originated in the late 5th or early 6th century. Nearly all the surviving MSS. are in the form of lectionaries, or church reading books. The version is remarkable in that it was the only Syriac version used by any considerable body of Syrian Christians which contained the *pericope de adultera* (John 7: 53 to 8:11).

II. 2. *Latin versions.*
(1) *The Old Latin.* Probably by the end of the 2d century A.D. a Latin version of the Scriptures was in circulation in n. Africa. Tertullian (c. 150–c. 220) shows that he was familiar with parts of it, and Cyprian (c. 200–258), bishop of Carthage, used it freely. The O.T. was not translated from the Hebrew, but was based upon the Old Greek (LXX). The earliest translation was made in n. Africa and is known as the Afra, while the Itala was rendered at a later date in Italy. From a study of the text of Ezekiel it appears that the Itala in that particular book is based upon a B-type of text; the Afra comes from a type related to the AQ-type and the Scheide papyri. The Old Latin is important for determining the pre-Origenian reading of LXX passages. A study of the Old Latin of Ezekiel furthermore indicates definitely a 3d stratum; Jerome apparently revised the Old Latin from a Q-type of text on the basis of the Itala or a Latin version which was translated from a B-type of Greek. Augustine (354–430) testifies, probably with reference to the N.T., that

anyone who thought that he had sufficient knowledge of Greek and Latin ventured to make a translation. Consequently there grew up a welter of diverse translations. Among them there gradually developed 3 types of text; Cyprian represents the African text, Irenaeus (c. 130–c. 202) of s. Gaul the European, and Augustine the Italian.

(2) *The Vulgate.* Amid this confusion of vernacular Latin texts a need was felt for a dignified and accurate Latin version. Damasus, bishop of Rome, urged Jerome, or Hieronymus (c. 340–420), the most learned Christian scholar of his day, to undertake a revision of the Latin N.T. In 384, Jerome published his work on the Gospels, having compared the Latin with the original Greek in order to correct gross errors. He also made 2 revisions of the Old Latin version of The Psalms by comparing it with the LXX. These are known as the Roman (384) and Gallican (387–390) Psalters, because they were introduced into Rome and Gaul respectively. In 387 Jerome took up his residence in a monastery at Bethlehem, and ultimately he made a version of the O.T. directly from the Hebrew, with constant reference to the Greek versions and with special respect for Symmachus. As a youth he had pursued the study of Hebrew, and after his removal to Bethlehem he resumed it with the aid of Jewish teachers; he began his work on the Vulgate c. 390, and the entire work was completed in 405. His own generation gave him abuse rather than gratitude for the very important service he had rendered it; and the eminent father, whose temper was none of the best, retorted by expressing the contempt which knowledge feels for blatant and aggressive ignorance. As the ages rolled forward his work, which was done not for one generation but for all succeeding time, was more and more appreciated. The Vulgate became the Bible of the whole Western Church in the Middle Ages and, notwithstanding vernacular translations, still remains the Bible of the Roman Catholic Church. Jerome's final revision of the Psalter from the Hebrew is known as the Hebrew Psalter, but it never attained to general use or popularity. The Roman Psalter is still in use in St. Peter's, Rome; the Gallican Psalter is in general use in the Roman Catholic Church in spite of the superior accuracy of the 3d edition or Hebrew Psalter. A recension of the text was made by Alcuin, at the instance of Charlemagne, about 802. The Latin Vulgate was the 1st book ever printed, having been issued from the press about 1455, soon after the invention of printing. On April 8, 1546, the Council of Trent made a decree which expressed the wish for a fresh revision. Scholars were dilatory about undertaking the duty, till a pontiff of iron will, Sixtus V, urged on the work and even took a personal part in its accomplishment. The revision was published in 1590. A different one came forth under the auspices of Pope Clement VIII in 1592; this became the standard edition of the Roman Catholic Church. In 1907 work on a critical edition of the Vulgate was begun, and since 1926 various books in quarto have been appearing. It is from the Vulgate that a large part of the technical language used in theology is derived. For instance, sacrament, justification, and sanctification are simply the Anglicized forms of *sacramentum, justificatio,* and *sanctificatio,* occurring in the Vulgate.

II. 3. *Coptic versions of the Bible.* These appear in several dialects, the most important of which are the Sahidic and the Bohairic. The Sahidic was the earlier, but the Bohairic became the accepted version of the Coptic Church. We cannot determine definite dates of translation. Probably portions of the N.T.

were translated into Sahidic and Bohairic before the close of the 2d century A.D. Perhaps the Sahidic Bible was complete in the 3d century; some make it c. A.D. 350. The Bohairic Bible is somewhat later, some dating it in the 6th century or even c. 650. In The Book of Daniel the Sahidic was translated from Theodotion with Origenian or Hexaplaric influence on an Egyptian or Hesychian background; the Bohairic is definitely Hexaplaric, and the text is specifically Egyptian or Hesychian.

II. 4. *The Ethiopic Version.* According to tradition Christianity was brought to Ethiopia in the time of Constantine the Great (324–337). Frumentius, a Syrian, was consecrated as bishop of Ethiopia before 370, perhaps c. 330, by Athanasius, the patriarch of Alexandria. About 340 'Ezānā, king of Axum, who had become a Christian, made his kingdom Christian. It is possible that Frumentius began the work of translating the Scriptures or had it done under his supervision. According to another tradition the Bible was turned into Ethiopic by the Nine Saints, who as Monophysites fled after the Council of Chalcedon in 451 from Syria to Egypt, whence they made their way to Abyssinia. Probably the translation was begun in the 2d half of the 4th century before the arrival of the Nine Saints, who, however, may have revised the original translation. In I Kings the Ethiopic Bible is based on a text like B (Codex Vaticanus) with a strong Lucianic influence; this may indicate the entrance of Christianity into Ethiopia from Alexandria and from Syria. In the 14th century and later the Ethiopic Bible was revised with the help of Arabic translations.

II. 5. *The Gothic Version* was made c. 350 by Ulphilas, bishop of the West Goths. It embraced the whole Bible except the books of Samuel and Kings, which the bishop omitted, because he thought it would be dangerous to place them, with their warlike spirit and opposition to idolatry, in the hands of the Goths. Most of the N.T. and a few fragments of the O.T. in this version are extant. It is the earliest surviving literature in any Teutonic language. The O.T. was made from Lucian's recension.

II. 6. *The Arabic Version.* The expansion of Islam beyond the limits of Arabia after the death of Mohammed (632) was followed by the translation of the Scriptures into Arabic. Partial translations probably were prepared in the 7th century for Christians in the Orient, but we have the definite record that in 724 a version was made in Spain by John, bishop of Seville, with the intention of helping the Christians and the Moors. Padre Juan de Mariana (1537–1624) says that copies of this translation were preserved until his day and seen in parts of Spain. In 946 Isaak Velásquez of Córdoba translated Luke (and presumably the other Gospels also) into Arabic. Saadia Gaon (892–942) rendered the O.T. from Hebrew into Arabic for the Jews. With the exception of the Pentateuch and Joshua none of the other books published in the Paris (1645) and the London (1657) Polyglots was rendered from the Hebrew. A study of the Arabic of Daniel in these two Polyglot Bibles shows that that book was rendered from the Greek and represents a Hexaplaric text of Constantinople in a recension superior to Codex A (Alexandrinus); it doubtless is the best representative of that group.

II. 7. *The Armenian and Georgian Versions.* An Armenian writer of the 5th century, Moses of Chorene, says that the 1st edition was translated from a Syriac text by Sahak (patriarch, 390–428). Koriun (5th century) records that by 411 Mesrop (the inventor of the Armenian alphabet, c. 406), with the aid of a Greek scribe, Rufinus, had translated the entire Bible from Greek, beginning with The Proverbs.

This may imply that the previous books had been rendered by unknown translators. After the Council of Ephesus (431) there was brought from Constantinople a Greek Bible, on the basis of which Sahak and Mesrop revised the Armenian Bible. Later Moses of Chorene and others were sent to Alexandria, and this visit had a decided influence upon the Armenian text. In general the Armenian version of the O.T. follows the Hexaplaric recension. In the case of The Book of Daniel it represents an Origenian-Constantinopolitan text, but it has decided agreements with the Hesychian group; the Syriac influence is also apparent. It seems that the Gospels were done from the Old Syriac. The Armenian is so well adapted to render the Greek literally without being literalistic that an Armenian codex has almost the same value for the critic as the Greek original on which it is based.

The Georgian Bible, aptly called "the twin sister of the Armenian," was completed by the end of the 6th century. The original version, made by several hands, had an Armenian-Syriac foundation, but discloses also some Greek influence.

II. 8. *The Slavonic Version* was made in the 9th century by Cyril and Methodius. Except for fragments embedded in the official Slavonic Bible, the original translation has perished. It seems in the O.T. to have been based on a Lucianic text, but in the present Bible some books are rendered from the Hebrew or the Vulgate.

III. ENGLISH VERSIONS.

III. 1. *Early English versions*. In Anglo-Saxon times portions of Scripture, especially The Psalms, the Ten Commandments, and portions of the Gospels, were translated into the vernacular tongue. After the language had been modified by the Norman Conquest, various portions of Scripture, especially the Gospels, were rendered into the language of the nation. But no effort was made similarly to treat the Bible as a whole.

III. 2. *Wycliffe and Purvey's Bible*. Of this there are 2 versions: the 1st apparently between 1382 and 1383, and the 2d about 1388. The 1st, which was robust and terse, but unpolished in language, was mainly Wycliffe's; the 2d, which was more refined and became better known, emanated chiefly from Wycliffe's disciple, John Purvey. Both versions were made from the Latin Vulgate. Wycliffe's version was the 1st extensive rendering of the Scriptures into any form of modern English; it helped to mold the language and also exerted great influence on the national life. It circulated in manuscript copies only, and the complete Wycliffe Bible was not printed until 1850.

III. 3. *Tyndale's Bible*. About 1526 there arrived in England from abroad a translation of the N.T. from the original Greek by the reformer William Tyndale, who had left his native England to escape persecution. It was published at Worms, and was made from the Greek of Erasmus, probably from the edition of 1519, although the edition of 1522 was consulted. Tyndale translated directly from the Greek, using the German N.T. of Luther and the Vulgate as aids. His work excited great opposition from the leading dignitaries of the then dominant Church, though many of the common people received it gladly. The book was pronounced full of pestilent errors, and was publicly burned at Paul's Cross. In 1530, and again in 1534, he published a translation of the Pentateuch, and in 1531 of The Book of Jonah. He made these directly from the original Hebrew, using Luther and the Vulgate as aids. In 1534 a fresh edition of his N.T. was issued from Antwerp. There is evidence that he translated other portions of the O.T. besides those already mentioned, most probably to the end of Chronicles with several prophetical books; but he did not live to publish them. He was arrested on May 23 or 24, 1535, at Antwerp, where he had permanently settled, and on Oct. 6, 1536, was strangled and burned as a heretic. But his work remained. It fixed the English standard of Bible translation, and its diction and style still live in the English version and lend it literary charm and character.

III. 4. *Coverdale's Bible*. This work was published in 1535, with no mention who the printer was nor from what city or town it issued; possibly Zürich is entitled to the honor. It was the 1st complete English Bible issued from the press. The N.T. and much of the O.T. are practically Tyndale's. Only the portion from Job to Malachi was translated independently by Miles Coverdale, and he used, not the original Hebrew, but the Vulgate and Pagninus' Latin Bible and 2 German versions, Luther's and the Zürich Bible. He describes the book as "translated out of Douche and Latyn in to Englishe." It was dedicated to Henry VIII, but not issued under royal license. Coverdale's version of The Psalms, virtually unchanged, is still used by the Church of England and the Protestant Episcopal Church in *The Book of Common Prayer*.

III. 5. *Matthew's Bible*. Thomas Matthew is believed to have been only a name assumed by John Rogers, an associate of Tyndale. In 1537 he printed an edition of the Bible, perhaps at Antwerp. It contains Tyndale's translations in their latest form. For books not translated by Tyndale, the text is taken from Coverdale's version. On the title page appear the words, "Set forth with the Kinges most gracyous lycence." This royal license was also extended to Coverdale's Bible, as appears on the title page of his quarto edition of 1537.

III. 6. *Taverner's Bible*. This was published in the year 1539 by Richard Taverner; it was a revision of Matthew's Bible.

III. 7. *The Great Bible;* called also *Cranmer's Bible*. The 1st name was given it on account of its size, the pages measuring 15 by 10 inches, and the 2d name came into use because Cranmer wrote the preface to the 2d and subsequent editions. It was undertaken by Coverdale at Cromwell's suggestion, was produced mainly by the revision of the text of Matthew's Bible, and appeared in 7 editions, 1539–1541. King Henry VIII gave to Cromwell the absolute right of licensing the publication of the Bible for 5 years. The edition of April, 1540, which was a revision of the one of 1539, had on the title page, "This is the Byble apoynted to the use of the churches."

III. 8. *The Geneva Bible*. This revision was the work of 3 exiles who had taken refuge in Geneva during the Marian persecution, Whittingham, Gilby, and Sampson. It was a revision of Tyndale, collated with the Great Bible. From the occurrence of the word "breeches" in Gen. 3:7, where the A.V. was subsequently to have "aprons," it is sometimes called the Breeches Bible. The N.T. appeared anonymously in 1557, and the whole Bible in 1560. These 2 editions were the 1st English translations to use the division into verses. The translators availed themselves of the aids furnished by the best Biblical scholarship of the age, and it is itself the most scholarly of the early English versions. It was a handy volume, being small quarto in size. It was well received among the common people, especially those of Puritan tendency, and for 75 years was the Bible in current use. It was provided with marginal notes, supplying a sound and helpful commentary along practical, expository, and doctrinal lines.

III. 9. *The Bishops' Bible*. The popularity of the Geneva Bible was not acceptable to the bishops, and in 1568 they issued one of their own. It borrowed from the Geneva version the division of the chapters into verses. In 1571 the Convocation of Canterbury pronounced in its favor and ordered copies to be placed in all the churches. It was founded chiefly on the Great Bible, though borrowing variations from the Geneva version. The work was of uneven value on account of the lack of editorial oversight and of co-ordination of the work of the churchmen who worked on the various books. The revision of 1572, in the 1602 edition, was used as the official basis of the A.V., but other translations were freely used when they were better.

III. 10. *The Rheims and Douay Bible.* This is the Roman Catholic version of the Scriptures in English. It was made from the Vulgate, and published, the N.T. at Rheims in 1582, and the O.T. at Douay in 1609-1610. Its language and style smack more of Latin than English; but it gave currency to many words borrowed from the Latin, and not a few of them, such as impenitent, propitiation, and remission, found a place in the A.V.

III. 11. *The Authorized Version.* The proposal to make this version came from Dr. Reynolds, president of Corpus Christi College, Oxford, during the discussion between the Anglicans and the Puritans at the Hampton Court Conference, on Jan. 16, 1604. King James I, whose interest in theology is well known, was pleased by the proposal, and on Feb. 10, 1604, he ordered, among other things, "that a translation be made of the whole Bible, as consonant as can be to the original Hebrew and Greek; and this to be set out and printed, without any marginal notes, and only to be used in all Churches of England in time of Divine Service." The king appointed 54 translators, but only 47 took part in the work. They were formed into 6 companies, 2 of which met at Westminster, 2 at Oxford, and 2 at Cambridge. The work was issued in 1611, with a fulsome dedication to King James. The title page of the 1611 edition bears the legend: "Newly Translated out of the Originall tongues: & with the former Translations diligently compared and reuised by his Maiesties Speciall Commandement. Appointed to be read in Churches." Although the promotion and preparation of this version was under a direct order of the king and his chief advisers, there is no record that its use was sanctioned or authorized as is implied on the title page. Yet the King James Version is known as the Authorized Version. It was not a new translation, but a scholarly revision on the basis of the original languages of Scripture; about 9/10 of the language of the N.T. is still that of Tyndale. It has endeared itself to all English-speaking Christians, and is the translation now in common use.

III. 12. *The Revised Version.* A revision of the A.V. became necessary because in the course of more than 2½ centuries, through the discovery of MSS. older than those used heretofore, a superior text of the N.T. had been provided. Greek and Hebrew scholarship had also made great advances during the same period. In February, 1870, the Convocation of the Province of Canterbury planned, not a new translation, but a fresh revision of the time-honored version. Two companies were formed for the purpose, 1 for each Testament. The O.T. group consisted originally of 37 members, but the O.T. was completed eventually by only 27; the N.T. group consisted of 28 at first, but for the greater part of the time of 24. About ⅔ of these belonged to the Church of England. Two companies of scholars in America co-operated, 15 for the O.T. and 19 (but only 15 took an active part) for the N.T., representing 9 different Protestant Churches. The work was begun on June 22,

1870. The N.T. took 10½ years, and was published in May, 1881. The revision of the O.T. was commenced on June 30, 1870, and was completed in 14 years, on June 20, 1884, and published in 1885. The American Revised Version is the Revised Version of 1881 and 1884 newly edited, the N.T. in the year 1900, and the O.T. in 1901. The American edition incorporates in the text the readings and renderings preferred by the 2 American committees, adds references to parallel and illustrative passages, provides a running headline to indicate the topics in the page, removes the verse numbers from the margin to the text, substitutes the name Jehovah for Lord and God, wherever *YHWH* (Jehovah) is found in the original, and uses Holy Spirit for Holy Ghost. It also increases the number of changes made for the sake of euphemism. The R.V. is inferior to the A.V. in felicity of expression, and the sentences are less perfect in their rhythm and their cadence. But as a work of exact scholarship it is an improvement on the A.V. Especially in the prophetical portions of the O.T. and in the Epistles of the N.T. has the true meaning been made clear. The orthography also of the proper names has been vastly improved. Nowhere does A.V. distinguish poetry from prose, but in R.V. much of the poetry is printed as poetry. Yet in many places, e.g., in the Prophets, J.V. indicates the poetry where R.V. has not done so.

A new Version of the American Standard Bible is in process of preparation.

III. 13. *The Jewish Version.* This translation of the O.T., the work of a committee of Jewish scholars with Max L. Margolis as editor in chief, was concluded in 1916; it bears the title of *The Holy Scriptures According to the Masoretic Text—a New Translation.* Although it was intended primarily for Jews, its many merits are recognized by a number of Christian scholars. The basis of the language is generally that of the A.V., but the translators consulted the R.V. as well as the older English versions.

IV. German Versions.

Between 1466 and 1518, 14 complete German Bibles were published; between 1480 and 1522 there appeared also 4 Bibles in Low German. The translation by Martin Luther, however, became the people's Bible. He began his work on the N.T. early in Dec., 1521, and it left the press Sept. 21, 1522. From that year until his death Luther's N.T. was reprinted 115 times, and often in large editions. It was based chiefly on Erasmus' Greek N.T., 2d edition, 1519. For the O.T. Luther used the Hebrew Bible published at Brescia, 1494. He began his work on the O.T. in 1522 before the N.T. had left the press, and the Pentateuch was published the following year. Other parts followed in due course until the publication of the Prophets in 1532. Revisions were continuously made, and finally the complete Bible was published at Wittenberg in 1534. Luther continued his revisions until the edition of 1545.

Because of delays in Luther's work there appeared 2 other translations of the Prophets, one at Worms, 1527, and one at Zürich, 1529. The preachers of Zürich had issued a complete Bible in 6 parts (1525–1529), turning Luther's work as far as available into Swiss German and adding their own rendering of the Prophets and that of the Apocrypha by Leo Juda. The 1st Zürich Bible in one volume appeared in 1530; the complete Worms Bible was published in 1529, and the Strassburg Bible in 1530. These German versions simply incorporated, or were based upon, Luther's Bible as far as it had appeared, while they added the other part or parts.

Vine. Any plant with a long, slender, prostrate or climbing stem, with tendrils, as a gourd (II Kings 4:39). The word usually denotes the common or grape vine (*Vitis vinifera*). It is believed to be indigenous in w. Asia s. of the Caspian Sea (cf. Gen. 9:20, 21). It was largely cultivated in Egypt (Gen. 40: 9–11; Ps. 78:47); and Egyptian sculptures of the Old Empire represent vineyards, vines laden with grapes, presses, and the manufacture of wine. The soil and climate of Palestine were favorable to the vine, and it was early cultivated in Canaan (Gen. 14:18; see the Egyptian *Tale of Sinuhe* for grapes and wine). It is incidentally referred to as growing in the lowland of Philistia, at Jezreel, and in the plain of Gennesaret (I Kings 21:1; Jos. *War* iii. 10, 8), and especially in the mountainous districts, as near Hebron, Shiloh, and Shechem (Num. 13:23; Judg. 9:27; 21:20; Jer. 31:5). Especial mention is made of the vines of Eshcol in the hill country of Judah (Num. 13:23), of En-gedi in the valley of the Dead Sea (S. of Sol. 1:14), of Heshbon, Elealeh, and Sibmah beyond Jordan (Isa. 16: 8–10; Jer. 48:32), and of Lebanon (Hos. 14: 7). There was great difference in value between the choicest, noble vines and the degenerate plant of a strange vine (Isa. 5:2; Jer. 2:21). Israel is compared to a vine (Ps. 80:8–16), and our Lord to the stem of a vine, and his true followers to the branches (John 15:1–8).

The vineyard was frequently on a hillside or peak (Isa. 5:1; Joel 3:18), which was terraced when necessary. It was surrounded by a hedge or a stone wall to keep out destructive animals (Num. 22:24; Ps. 80:8–13; Prov. 24: 30, 31; S. of Sol. 2:15; Isa. 5:5). The ground was cleared of stones, the vines were planted, a booth or tower was erected for the watchman, a press was constructed, and a vat was hewn in the rock (Isa. 1:8; 5:1–7; Matt. 21: 33–41). Laborers were sometimes hired to work in it (Matt. 20:1–16), for it was necessary to prune the vines, dig about them, and keep the ground free from weeds (Lev. 25:3; Prov. 24:30, 31; Isa. 5:6; John 15:2). The vines were allowed to spread on the ground, the stock not being supported, only the fruit-bearing branches being slightly raised from the earth (Isa. 16:8; Ezek. 17:6). Other vines were doubtless trained to trees; and yet others were probably planted, as at present in Palestine, in rows, 8 to 10 feet apart, the stock being allowed to grow 6 or 8 feet high and then fastened to stout stakes, and the branches trained from stock to stock.

The grapes ordinarily grown were red (Isa. 63:2; Rev. 14:19, 20); but at the present day a white variety is almost exclusively raised at Bethlehem and Hebron. The grapes began to ripen about August, in favored localities somewhat earlier. They were eaten both fresh and dried (Num. 6:3; Deut. 23:24). The dried grapes or raisins were preserved in clusters or pressed into cakes, and were esteemed as food (I Sam. 25:18; I Chron. 16:3). The juice of grapes was expressed, and was drunk fresh and fermented; see WINE.

The vintage began in the middle of September and continued into October. It was a season of festivity. In the vineyards there were singing and joyful noise, and the treaders in the press kept time by shouting as they trod the grapes (Judg. 9:27; Isa. 16:10; Jer. 25:30; 48:33).

Vine of Sod'om (sŏd'ŭm). A plant growing near Sodom, and bearing clusters of bitter fruit (Deut. 32:32). But the language may be figurative. Josephus describes fruits growing near the site of Sodom, which bear a color as if they are fit to be eaten but contain ashes, and if plucked with the hands, dissolve into smoke and ashes (Jos. *War* iv. 8, 4; cf. Tacitus *Hist.* v. 6). This fruit does not correspond to the grapes of gall and bitter clusters which apparently characterize the vine of Sodom. Excluding plants which are common elsewhere in Palestine, the principal claimants are: 1. What the Arabs call the *'ushar*, an asclepiadaceous plant (*Calotropis gigantea* or *procera*), a native of Upper Egypt, Arabia, and India. It grows at En-gedi and other parts of the tropical Dead Sea Valley, is a tree 10 or 15 feet high, and bears a fruit resembling an apple or orange, 3 or 4 of them in a cluster. They are pleasant to the eye and to the touch; but if pressed or struck they explode like a puffball, leaving only fragments of the rind and a few fibers in the hand. A formidable objection to the identification is the difficulty of seeing how the term vine can be applied to a small, erect tree. 2. The colocynth (*Citrullus colocynthus*), a trailing plant. Its fruit is "fair to look upon; but when fully ripe, merely a quantity of dusty powder with the seeds inside its beautiful orange rind" (Tristram); see GOURD, WILD.

Vin'e·gar. Wine or other strong drink turned sour by acetous fermentation (Num. 6:3). If vinous fermentation was pushed too far, or if the wine was kept too long, it became vinegar. Vinegar is acid, setting the teeth on edge (Prov. 10:26), and hardening soap or neutralizing its alkali (ch. 25:20). In itself it is unfit to drink (Ps. 69:21); but mingled with a little oil it is drunk by the common people in the East to quench thirst when fresh water is not obtainable; and it was used at meals in the heat of harvest, bread being dipped in it, since it brought grateful refreshment to the system (Ruth 2:14). The vinegar used by Boaz' reapers is, however, regarded by many interpreters as sour, not soured, wine. The Roman soldiers when in camp drank a thin, sour wine called *acetum*, vinegar, both in its pure state and diluted with water. It was probably a drink of this sort which the Roman soldier offered to Jesus on the cross to quench his burning thirst (Mark 15:36; John 19:29, 30). This draught, which Jesus accepted, was different from the sour wine, previously offered and refused, which was mingled with a bitter substance or more definitely with myrrh, which is astringent (Matt. 27:34; Mark 15: 23).

Vine'yard. See VINE.

Vine'yards, Plain of. See ABEL-CHERAMIM.

Vi'ol. See PSALTERY.

Vi'per. 1. The rendering of Heb. *'eph'eh*, a venomous serpent referred to as inhabiting the s. country (Job 20:16; Isa. 30:6; 59:5).

2. A poisonous reptile, in Gr. *echidna*, incidentally mentioned as found on the island of Melita (Acts 28:3) and familiar to the Jews (Matt. 3:7); probably the common viper (*Vipera communis* or *Pelias berus*), which is common on the Mediterranean coast.

Vi'sions. No sharp line of demarcation is discernible between visions and dreams (*q.v.*). The one shades into the other. The Bible recognizes: 1. Vain visions (Job 20:8; Isa. 29:7). 2. Visions of the prophets. These were for the most part private; they were apprehended by the individual, not by his companions. A natural cause sometimes co-operated in producing the vision: the vision of the great sheet let down from heaven, which Peter saw, and the voice heard saying, "Rise, Peter; kill and eat," stood in some relation to his bodily hunger, as the account in The Acts clearly intimates (ch. 10:9 *seq.*). Thus far the visions of the prophets have points in common with visions begotten of an abnormal mental condition, and to this extent are to be classed as mental phenomena. These facts are only additional proofs of what might be expected, namely, that God, in holding communication with men, works in accordance with the laws of man's mind. The visions of the prophets, however, form a unique class. With perhaps 1 exception (Num. 24:4), they were granted to holy men only, men who were surrendered to God's service, men between whom and their divine Sovereign there "had arisen an understanding." These visions, again, were clearly distinguished by those who saw them from ordinary visions and were recognized as proceeding from God. They were cautiously accepted by the Church; by law they were not received as genuine until their teaching and their credentials had been subjected to tests (Jer. 23:16, 21, 22, 27; cf. Isa. 8:20; Deut. 18:10 seq.). The visions recorded in the Bible stand alone, in the history of religions, for purity and righteousness. They are never vain, never meaningless vagaries or lying wonders. They always have a clearly discernible moral and didactic content. They were often predictive, upon which fulfillment has set the seal of truth. They belonged to an age of revelation and came to men who in manifold manner proved themselves to be vehicles of revelation.

Because there were genuine visions, false prophets feigned visions. These men are denounced and their destruction foretold (Jer. 14:14; 23:16; Ezek. 13:7 seq.).

Voph′si (vŏf′sī). Father of Nahbi, the Naphtalite spy (Num. 13:14).

Vow. A voluntary obligation to God, generally assumed on condition of his bestowing certain specified blessings. Man has shown a tendency during sickness or any other affliction, or in time of anxiety or earnest desire, to make a vow to God to be fulfilled when the calamity is over or the desired object obtained (Gen. 28:20–22; Num. 21:2; I Sam. 1:11; II Sam. 15:8). The vow sprang primarily from the consciousness of entire dependence on the will of God and of the obligation of thankfulness. Vows were taken by persons of every nation (Jonah 1:16), and not by the Jews only. The earliest mention of a vow in Scripture, and a typical case, is that of Jacob at Beth-el, who promised that if God would care for him and bring him again to his father's house, the place where he was should be a sanctuary and ⅒ of his income should be the Lord's (Gen. 28:18–22).

The Mosaic Law did not prescribe vows; it only regulated them. Three kinds were the subject of legislation: vows of devotion, of abstinence, and of devotion to destruction. 1. By the vow of devotion, any person or possession, not already set apart for sacred uses, or otherwise removed from the legal control of the devoter, might be devoted and turned over to the sanctuary; but anything thus devoted to the service of God was redeemable, except a sacrificial animal (Lev. 27:1–27), usually at ⅕ more than its assessed value. Devoted land sold by the owner, without having been first redeemed, was retained by the buyer, but at the year of jubilee did not return to the seller, but became the possession of the sanctuary (vs. 20, 21). Persons devoted to God served at the sanctuary (I Sam. 1:11, 24, 28), but were usually redeemed (II Kings 12:4), especially as the service of the Levites rendered such devotion as a rule useless. The price of redemption varied with age and sex. 2. The vow of abstinence involved a renunciation of some enjoyment, otherwise allowable, for the glory of God. It included such acts as fasting, in testimony of penitence, and such obligation as was assumed by the Nazirite. 3. It has been inferred from Ex. 22:20; Deut. 13:16, that only what was under judgment for idolatry

could be devoted by a vow of destruction. Nothing devoted by such a vow was redeemable (Lev. 27:28, 29).

General principles applying to vows were: 1. Vows were assumed voluntarily, but once made were regarded as compulsory (Num. 30:2; Deut. 23:21–23); only in exceptional cases, as in those of Samson, Samuel, and John the Baptist, who had special missions to fulfill, was the Nazirite vow prescribed. 2. A vow, especially a vow of abstinence, made by an unmarried daughter or a wife, was void if disallowed by the father or husband (Num. 30:3–16). 3. The produce of sinful traffic could not be devoted (Deut. 23:18); see Dog. 4. Vows must not be taken rashly. This principle was enforced by the example of Jephthah, and inculcated by proverb (Prov. 20:25).

Vul′gate (vŭl′gât). See Versions.

Vul′ture. A bird of prey, which has the head naked or but thinly covered with feathers, and feeds largely or wholly on carrion. It is employed in the A.V. to render Heb. ′ayyāh (Job 28:7, elsewhere kite; in R.V. always falcon), dā′āh (Lev. 11:14; in R.V. kite), and dayyāh (Deut. 14:13; Isa. 34:15; in R.V. kite). In the R.V. it is used to translate rāḥām (Lev. 11:18; in A.V. gier eagle); and frequently in the margin, where the text has eagle, to render Heb. nesher, Gr. aetos.

The great vulture (Lev. 11:13, R.V. marg.) is the fulvous or tawny vulture, generally called the griffon (Gyps fulvus). The neck and head are bald, covered with down. The whole of the body, the wings, and the back on to the tail are yellowish-brown. It is about 4 feet high. Its talons are not formidable, but its bill is. "The griffon," says Tristram, "is the most striking ornithological feature of Palestine. It is impossible in any part of the country to look up without seeing some of them majestically soaring at an immense height, and their eyries abound in great colonies in all the ravines of the country."

W

Wag′es. In early times and not infrequently at a comparatively late date wages were paid in kind (Gen. 29:15, 20; 30:28–34). In Egypt money or goods were given as hire at the time of the sojourn of the Israelites there (Ex. 2:9). By the Law of Moses, wages were to be paid each evening (Lev. 19:13; Deut. 24:14, 15), and the withholding of wages due was severely denounced by religious teachers (Jer. 22:13; Mal. 3:5; James 5:4). Tobit offered a drachma, or 16 cents, a day and food as wages (Tobit 5:14). When our Lord was on earth, the rate for a day's labor was a denarius, worth about 17 cents (Matt. 20:2, in A.V. penny). What the purchasing power of that amount was is, however, unknown; it was evidently great (cf. Luke 10:35). In the later days of the Roman republic, the usual pay of a Roman soldier was 10 asses, or about a dime, a day (Tacitus Ann. i. 17).

Wag′on. See Cart.

Wal′let. See Scrip.

War. Before engaging in aggressive war, the Israelites consulted God's will in the matter (Judg. 20:23, 27, 28; I Sam. 14:37; 23:2; I Kings 22:6) or, when conflict was unavoidable, invoked God's help by prayer and sometimes by sacrifice (I Sam. 7:8, 9; 13:12; II Chron. 20:5–12; I Macc. 3:47–54). The heathen had recourse to divination for the same purpose (Ezek. 21:21), and were careful to set forth on a day pronounced to be propitious. Frequently before entering a hostile country or engaging in battle spies were sent forward to obtain information regarding the country and the preparation for resistance (Num. 13:17; Josh. 2:1; Judg. 7:9-11; I Sam. 26:4); and, when captives were taken, they were questioned with the same intention (Judg. 8:14; I Sam. 30:11-15). When the host drew nigh unto battle, a priest or the commander encouraged the people by reminding them of God's presence and help; and the officers exempted from service those who were faint-hearted and those who had built a new house but not inhabited it, planted a vineyard but not enjoyed the fruit of it, betrothed a wife but not married her (Deut. 20:2-9; II Chron. 20:14-20; I Macc. 3:56; 4:8-11). Various stratagems were practiced, such as surprise, ambush, pretended flight, circumvention (Gen. 14:15; Josh. 8:2-7; Judg. 7:16-22; II Sam. 5:23). Occasionally when the opposing armies were drawn up in battle array, a champion was chosen by each party (I Sam., ch. 17). Otherwise the battle was joined. A trumpet sounded the attack, the blast being both a signal to advance and an appeal to God (Num. 10:9; Josh. 6:5; Judg. 7:20; II Chron. 13:12; I Macc. 4:13; 5:33). The host pressed forward with shouting (Josh. 6:5; I Sam. 17:52; Jer. 50:42; Ezek. 21:22; Amos 1:14), and engaged in hand-to-hand conflict. The pursuit was bloody. Like other nations of their time, the Israelites when victorious pillaged the camp of the enemy, robbed the dead (Judg. 8:24-26; I Sam. 31:9; II Chron. 20:25; I Macc. 4:17-23), and sometimes killed or mutilated the prisoners (Josh. 8:23, 29; 10:22-27; Judg. 1:6; 8:21; II Sam. 8:2), but more frequently reduced them to slavery.

When a city was besieged, the besiegers fortified their own camp against attack (Jos. War v. 2, 3); if possible, they cut off the water supply from the city (Judith 7:7). In order to bring their engines into play they cast up mounds in the direction of the city (II Sam. 20:15; Ezek. 4:2). The mound gradually increased in height until it was sometimes half as high as the city wall. Upon this inclined plane the battering-ram was rolled into position; from its roof and from the mound, archers and slingers discharged their missiles, and from the summit of the mound scaling-ladders were leaned against the wall. Sometimes fuel was laid against the gates and fired in order to burn them and afford ingress (Judg. 9:52); and often the defenders of the wall were attacked by archers posted, not on the mound, but at the base of the wall. The besieged were not idle: they prepared for the investment by protecting their water supply, and repairing and strengthening the fortifications (II Chron. 32:3-5); they harassed the enemy and attempted to drive them off by sallies; they repelled attack and hindered the besiegers in their aggressive operations by casting darts and stones and shooting arrows at them from the walls; and they destroyed or attempted to destroy the military engines by hurling burning torches at them and by undermining the banks on which the battering-rams stood (II Sam. 11:21, 24; II Chron. 26:15; I Macc. 6:31; Jos. War v. 2, 2 and 4; 6, 4; 11, 4). Captured cities were often destroyed and their inhabitants slaughtered, neither age nor sex being spared (Josh. 6:21, 24; 8:24-29; 10:22-27; II Kings 15:16). Victory was celebrated with song and dance (Ex. 15:1-21; Judg., ch. 5; I Sam. 18:6; II Chron. 20:26-28; I Macc. 4:24). See ARMY.

Wash'ing. See BATHING.

Watch. See NIGHT.

Wa'ter of Bit'ter·ness. Holy water in an earthen vessel, mingled with dust from the floor of the sanctuary (Num. 5:17), intended to reveal the innocence or guilt of a woman accused of adultery by her husband, when there were no witnesses. The charge was perhaps brought only when suspicion was aroused by the woman's being found with child. The accused woman, with loosened hair, sat before the Lord in the sanctuary, and held an offering of dry, unscented, barley meal in her hand (v. 18, R.V.). The priest, taking the water of bitterness, asked that it have no effect upon the woman if she were innocent, but that God would cause her body to swell and her thigh to fall away if she were guilty. The woman responded, Amen. The priest wrote the imprecation in a book, and washed it out into the water; and having waved the meal offering before the Lord and thrown a handful of it on the altar, he gave the water of bitterness to the woman to drink. If she was guilty, it became bitter within her and the curse went into effect; if innocent, the potion remained inoperative, and the woman was pronounced clean and received or retained ability to conceive. The essential part of this procedure was the oath: the ritual was symbolical; the effect was left to God. It is probable that this ordeal was an old custom which the Mosaic Law took up in order to regulate and elevate it.

Wa'ter of Sep'a·ra'tion. A.V. and E.R.V. (text); E.R.V. marg., "water of impurity"; A.R.V., "water for impurity" (Num. 19:9, 13, 20, 21; 31:23). It means water for the removal of impurity. Cf. PURIFICATION 1.

Wa'ter·pot'. See PITCHER, POT.

Wave Of'fer·ing. The rite of waving was regularly performed in connection with: 1. Peace offerings: the right thigh or shoulder of the animal sacrificed was heaved and the breast was waved before the Lord and, after having been thus consecrated, they were eaten by the priest. 2. The sheaf of first-ripe grain on the 2d day of the passover, whereby the harvest was consecrated to the Lord (Lev. 23:10, 11). 3. The 2 loaves made from the new grain and the 2 lambs for a peace offering at Pentecost, 50 days from the waving of the sheaf at the passover (Lev. 23:15, 20). 4. The guilt offering of the leper (Lev. 14:12, 21), whereby the offerer represented by it was consecrated again to the service of God. 5. The meal offering of jealousy (Num. 5:25).

When the peace offering was private, the wave breast and the heave shoulder or thigh went to the priest, and the rest of the flesh was eaten by the offerer and his friends before the Lord at the sanctuary (Lev. 7:30-34; 10:14, 15; Num. 18:18). Of the peace offering brought by the Nazirite, the sodden shoulder of the ram went to the priest, in addition to his regular perquisites (Num. 6:17-20). At Pentecost, the whole of the 2 lambs of the peace offering and the loaves went to the priests (Lev. 23:20), since they were offered in behalf of the nation.

In performing the rite the priest laid the matter to be waved upon the hands of the offerer, probably placed his own hands under the hands of the latter, and moved them (Ex. 29:24, 25; Num. 6:19, 20).

Waw (wou). See VAV.

Wea'sel. The rendering of Heb. ḥōled, applied to an unclean quadruped (Lev. 11:29). It is confessedly either a weasel or a mole. The corresponding word in Arab. and Syriac signifies a mole; but probably the former meaning is intended by the Heb. word, as it is rendered in the LXX and Vulgate. The A.V. and R.V. render it by "weasel"; in the Talmud the ḥuldāh is often mentioned as an animal that captures birds and creeping things, like the mouse, can run with such prey in its mouth, and can lap water out of a dish; and, finally, the typical mole genus

Talpa is not believed to occur in Palestine (see MOLE 2), while the weasel (*Putorius vulgaris*) and the polecat (*Putorius foetidus*) are found throughout the country.

Weav'ing. The Egyptians practiced the art of weaving before the arrival of the Israelites in their midst, producing woven goods such as linen (Gen. 41:42). The work was usually done by men (Herod. ii. 35), but not exclusively, for women appear at the loom in ancient Egyptian pictures. At the time of the Exodus the Hebrews understood both simple and elaborate weaving (Ex. 35:35). They produced various textures on the looms. Coarse kinds, such as tent cloth, and rough garments for the poor, were made of goats' and camels' hair (Ex. 26:7; Matt. 3:4); finer goods were woven of flax and wool (Lev. 13:47); chequered and figured patterns, as well as variegated stuffs, were made by the use of differently colored threads (Ex. 26:1; cf. ch. 28:39, R.V.; cf. Herod. iii. 47), and gold threads were even woven in (Ex. 39:3); cloth was also embroidered with figures or patterns (chs. 27:16; 38:23) with the needle; see EMBROIDERY. Many interpreters, however, believe that the Heb. word *rōḳēm*, rendered "embroiderer," denotes one who inweaves designs, a variegator. Among the Hebrews, the weaving as well as the spinning was usually

Week. The division of time into periods of 7 days appears in Scripture in connection with the institution of the Sabbath (Gen. 2:1–3), and according to both the Hebrew and Babylonian account was in vogue at the time of the Flood (chs. 7:4, 10; 8:10, 12); see FLOOD. In the Babylonian legend of Adapa it is mentioned that the wind ceased to blow for 7 days. There is reason to believe that the reference to its cessation for 7 days is more than the mere note of a chance fact. Gudea, prince of Lagash, celebrated the completion of a temple by a festival of 7 days' duration. Seven days was the conventional period for marriage festivities in Syria at the time of Laban and Jacob (Gen. 29:27, 28); and the same custom prevailed among the Philistines in the days of Samson (Judg. 14:12, 17). Funeral obsequies also, like those of Jacob and others, were conducted for 7 days (Gen. 50:10; I Sam. 31:13). Weeks constantly entered into all the arrangements of the ceremonial law (Ex. 12:15; 13:6, 7; 22:30; 29:30, 35, 37; Lev. 12:2; 13:5; 14:8; etc.). A week with a fixed beginning, which everybody reckoned as the 1st day, is, of course, not intended in all or even in the majority of these cases. The week of nuptial festivities, for example, began on the day of the wedding on whatever date it occurred. Nevertheless these numerous instances show that the 7-day period was

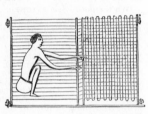 

Weaving and Spinning in Ancient Egypt

done by the women (II Kings 23:7; cf. I Sam. 2:19; Prov. 31:22, 24; Acts 9:39). Mantles and even tunics came from the loom ready for use; the latter, when thus woven complete, required no seam. Such tunics were prescribed for the priests (Ex. 28:6, 8; Jos. *Antiq.* iii. 7, 4); and one was worn by Jesus previous to his crucifixion (John 19:23).

The loom in Egypt was placed either vertically or horizontally. In Egyptian representations the frame is but slightly raised above the ground; the weaver squats at his work and apparently treads on the threads. The warp threads run in parallel relation and extend between the 2 beams to which they are attached; heddles of primitive sort, which separate the warp threads into 2 series and form a shed for the passage of the shuttle or other bearer of the woof threads, are next to him, between him and the woven cloth. With a reed he strikes the last thread which he shot through against the woof, pressing it close.

The Hebrew loom likewise had its beam and shuttle (I Sam. 17:7; II Sam. 21:19; Job 7:6). The pin of the beam, or rather weaving pin, for a different Heb. word is used from that elsewhere rendered "beam," may have been the sley or reed by which the thread of the woof was struck home (Judg. 16:13, 14). The web was cut off from the thrum (Isa. 38:12, R.V. marg.), or, to speak more generally, from the loom (R.V. text).

Wed'ding. See MARRIAGE.

Wedge. See TONGUE.

a standard in common use; and it is worthy of notice that the periods are consecutive in the narrative of the Flood (see FLOOD), as well as later, in determining the date of Pentecost. For the origin of the week, see SABBATH.

The ancient Hebrews named none of the days of the week except the 7th day, which they called the Sabbath. They numbered the days of the festivals, and the Babylonian narrator enumerates each of the 7 days during which the ark lay stranded. In the N.T. period the Hebrews numbered the days of the week (Matt. 28:1; Acts 20:7), and besides the 7th day named also the preceding day, which they called the preparation (Mark 15:42).

The week and the names of its days were introduced at a comparatively late period into the Roman Empire. The ancient Romans had a week of 8 days. The Greeks divided the month into 3 periods. The Egyptians, as early as the time when the pyramids were built, had periods of 10 days, each one of which began with the rising of 1 of 36 constellations in succession. Dio Cassius, who wrote in the 2d century A.D., speaks of the hebdomadal division of time being universal in his day in the Roman Empire, and a recent introduction. He represents it as borrowed from the Egyptians, and as based upon astrology. Of the 2 schemes, by one or the other of which he considers that the planetary names of the different days were fixed, only 1 has plausibility: each day in succession was assigned to one of the planets as regent, and the hours were also allotted to the planets. If the planets are arranged in the order of their distance from the earth, as believed at the time of Dio Cassius, Saturn, Jupiter, Mars, Sun, Venus, Mercury, Moon, and if, further, the 1st hour is allotted to Saturn, the 2d to Jupiter, and so on, the 25th hour, or the 1st hour of the morrow, will fall to the sun and on the following morning to the moon, and so on to Mars, Mercury, Jupiter, and Venus. If the planet to which the 1st hour of the day belongs be reckoned as the regent of the day, the days of the week will be, Saturn's day, Sun's day, Moon's day, and so on. This theory must be held with cautious reserve. There may be an entirely different reason from that given for the order of the planets. There are various orders of the arrangement of the sun, moon, and 5 known planets among the Babylonians, but our succession of the names of the days of the week does not correspond to any one of them. There was, however, among the Sabians of Haran in Mesopotamia a list, doubtless of Babylonian origin with modifications, which corresponds to the order and names used by the Romans: Shamash (Sun), Sin (Moon), Nergal (Mars), Nabu (Mercury), Marduk or Bel (Jupiter), Ishtar (Venus), and Ninib (Saturn). The names passed from Roman to later European use, both in their Latin form and also, when translated into the Germanic languages, with the names of Germanic deities substituted for the corresponding Roman ones. The names are of heathen origin, but no associations of any kind are now connected with the heathen divinities; the use of the names of the days of the week is simply a matter of convenience.

The Heb. word for week, *shābūa‘*, hebdomad, refers to a period of 7 days, and by extension the term is applied to a week of years; cf. the Sabbatic year and the Heb. word for week used by Daniel for a period of 7 years, as interpreters commonly understand (Dan. 9: 24–27; cf. Lev. 25 :8).

Weeks, Feast of. The 2d of the 3 annual festivals at which every male Israelite was required to appear before the Lord at the sanctuary, and the 1st of the 2 agricultural festivals (Ex. 34 :22, 23; II Chron. 8 :12, 13; cf. I Kings 9 :25). It was so called because its date was set 7 complete weeks after the consecration of the harvest season by the offering of the sheaf of the first-ripe barley (Lev. 23 :15, 16; cf. Deut. 16 :9, 10). This sheaf was waved on the morrow after the Sabbath (Lev. 23 :11). The Boethusians (associated with the Sadducees) interpreted this Sabbath as meaning the weekly Sabbath which occurred during the festival of unleavened bread; and some modern scholars have adopted this view. The opinion has even been held that it denoted merely the weekly Sabbath which fell immediately before the harvest. The older and better opinion is that it denotes the 1st day of the festival of unleavened bread. The Greek translators understood it so (Lev. 23 :7, 11, LXX), as did also those who directed the services of the 2d Temple (Jos. *Antiq.* iii. 10, 5); this 1st day was kept as a Sabbath: no work was done on it and there was a holy convocation; and such rest days, no less than the 7th day of the week, were called Sabbath (Lev. 23 :32; 25 : 2); on the morrow after the passover the new grain was used, which could not be eaten until the sheaf had been waved before the Lord (Lev. 23 :14; Josh. 5 :10, 11, R.V.). The festival fell on the 50th day after the waving of the sheaf, which gave rise to the name Pentecost or 50th day (Acts 2 :1). It was also called the feast of harvest or day of first fruits, because the first fruits of the wheat harvest, then ended in most districts, were presented (Ex. 23 :16; 34 :22; Num. 28 :26).

It celebrated the close of the grain harvest. It was bound up with the cycle of religious feasts by the number 7. It was observed as a Sabbath, ordinary labors were suspended, and there was a holy convocation (Lev. 23 : 21; Num. 28 :26); 2 loaves of leavened bread, such as was used in the household, representing the first fruits of the grain harvest, were offered to the Lord (Lev. 23 :17, 20; cf. Ex. 34 :22; Num. 28 :26; Deut. 16 :10); and with them 10 proper animals were sacrificed for a burnt offering, a kid for a sin offering, and 2 lambs for a peace offering (Lev. 23 :18, 19).

The sacrifices for the entire day were distributed into: 1. The regular daily burnt offering of 2 lambs (Num. 28 :3, 31). 2. The special sacrifices for the feast day (vs. 27– 30), which were the same as on the day of the new moon and each day of unleavened bread (vs. 11, 19). 3. The sacrifices connected with the offering of the loaves and the 2 lambs (Lev. 23 :17–19). Josephus correctly sums up the offerings additional to the daily burnt offering, except that he or his text as transmitted mentions 2 instead of 3 rams (Jos. *Antiq.* iii. 10, 6). As at the culminating agricultural festival, so at this the people were urged to remember the needy (Deut. 16 :11, 12). Pentecost came to be regarded in later times, especially in the early Christian centuries, as the commemoration of the giving of the Law on Mount Sinai; but there is no authority for this belief in the O.T., and it cannot be shown that the Law was given exactly 50 days after the passover.

The most notable Pentecost was the 1st which occurred after the resurrection and ascension of Christ (Acts, ch. 2). From it dates the founding of the Christian Church. The essential traits of an institution are seen in the history of its establishment. At the institution of the Church, the Holy Spirit descended into all believers, without distinction of age, sex, or class (Acts 2 :1–4, 14–21); see TONGUE. Life had been imparted. The Spirit had been given to men before, but now the Church entered upon what is characteristically the dispensation of the Spirit. The Spirit is now given in full measure to all believers without the intervention of prescribed rites. He had preserved a people of God on earth; in this new era of his power he devotes his divine energy to enlarging, perfecting, and edifying the Church.

Weights. The Hebrews used scales and weights (Lev. 19 :36), and they weighed money as well as other commodities (Jer. 32 : 10). The Hebrew denominations were talent (Gr. *talanton*, translation of Heb. *kikkār*, round, oval), mina (Gr. *mnā*) or maneh (Heb. *māneh*, from Akkad. *manū*; in both languages, the root means to count or reckon), shekel (weight), gerah (Heb. grain, bean; but probably from Akkad. *geru*, originally ¼₄ shekel), and beka (half [shekel]).

Exact weights are necessary in the economic life of a nation (cf. Deut. 25 :13–16; Prov. 11 :1; 20 :10). The inscriptions or marks on weights are doubtless more or less a guarantee of the exactness of the weight, and accordingly a few early inscribed Hebrew weights which have been found are important. It is highly probable that the inscribed ones were standard, but in general unmarked weights were used. The number of the latter is relatively much greater. Nearly all early Hebrew weights were of stone. There was found at Lachish a stone weight with the inscription *neṣeph*; it weighed 10.515 grams (.371 oz., avoirdupois). Ten other examples of weights of the same class range from 10.21 to 9.28 grams. Two stone weights from Lachish with the inscription *pym* (payim, pim) weighed 8.13 and 7.805 grams (.287 and .275

oz., avoirdupois, respectively); at the same place appeared also 2 stone weights with the inscription *beḳa'*, weighing 6.15 and 6.095 grams (.217 and .215 oz., avoirdupois, respectively). Most of the Lachish weights belong probably to the end of the 7th and the beginning of the 6th century B.C. From the varying weight of the same denomination we may infer that there were different local standards in Palestine and that they varied throughout the country and were subject to considerable fluctuations. There is a possibility that there were different standards analogous to our avoirdupois, troy, and apothecaries' weight. Furthermore ancient balances did not conform to modern standards in accuracy and sensitiveness.

In Babylonia and Assyria 60 shekels made a maneh. There were also a heavy talent, a heavy maneh, and a heavy shekel; they were exactly double the weight of the ordinary standards. By contrast the regular weights

merians. One such Babylonian maneh, a medium weight, consists of 505 grams, while in a series preserved in the British Museum the weights vary between 570.60 grams and 423 grams. On the basis of a mathematical analysis there have been distinguished among these weights 3 distinct standards of the Babylonian maneh: 491.14, 502.20, and 511.83 grams.

Various values may be determined for the shekel according to the weights from Lachish. On the basis of a weight marked *neṣeph*, one may assume a shekel of 10.515 grams (.371 oz., avoirdupois); on the basis of the *payim* (pim) one may calculate a shekel of 11.951 grams (.421 oz., avoirdupois); on the basis of weights marked *beḳa'*, a shekel of 12.245 grams (.432 oz., avoirdupois) may be assumed. There were also found at Lachish six weights marked with a sign ૪ accompanied by ૮; the latter probably is a numerical sign denoting 8. If this be the case, these weights

A Weight Found at Lachish; and Weights in the Form of a Lion and of a Duck, Which Were Used at Nineveh

are called light talent, light maneh, and light shekel.

In Palestine a maneh consisted of 50 shekels. At Ras Shamra (*q.v.*) the maneh of 50 shekels was in vogue during the 14th and 13th centuries B.C. The following is the Hebrew table of weights:

> 20 gerahs = 1 shekel
> 50 shekels = 1 maneh
> 60 manehs = 1 talent.

In this connection should be considered Ezek. 45:12, which gives a total of 60 shekels to the maneh. This may represent a theoretical reform to restore the original weight of the maneh for use in the sanctuary, since the maneh of the market place apparently had been reduced in weight. The series given by Ezekiel of 20, 25, 15 shekels (a total of 60) suggests an artificial scheme to attain a total of 60. If the maneh is reckoned at 60 shekels, we have the sequence 4/12, 5/12, 3/12, which when added together give one maneh. On the other hand, if we reckon the maneh at 50 shekels, we have the sequence 4/10, 5/10, 3/10, making a total of 12/10 of 50 shekels, or 60 shekels. In other words, if the maneh of 50 shekels was to have the value of 60 shekels, the weight of the shekel had to be increased. Many scholars, however, prefer the Greek reading of this passage according to Codex Alexandrinus: "Five shekels are five, and ten shekels are ten, and fifty shekels shall be your maneh." In other words, the current weights shall be neither more nor less than the standard value; just weighing shall prevail.

The pim (*q.v.*) was ⅔ of a shekel. See PIM, SHEKEL. Reckoning the shekel at 176.85 grains, a talent would weigh 75.793 lbs., avoirdupois, or 92.109 lbs., troy.

In Babylonia there were local standards existing beside the maneh (mina) of the Su-

are based on a unit averaging 11.389 grams or .402 oz., avoirdupois; this unit also may be regarded as a shekel. The weights found at Lachish agree substantially with evidence previously discovered at other places in Palestine. At Ras Shamra there was found a weight of about 470 grams, occupying a middle place between the Babylonian maneh of 505 and 491.14 grams on the one hand and the Egyptian maneh of 437 grams on the other. For practical purposes the shekel should be considered as 11.46 grams or 176.85 grains (.404 oz., avoirdupois; .368 oz., troy). See SHEKEL.

For the talent as a monetary value, see MONEY, TALENT. Sometimes it may be desirable to compare ancient values with modern money, but such comparisons are often misleading, especially since the purchasing power of money in antiquity was much higher than in the present era. If we should reckon the mina at about $16, the Attic talent would be worth approximately $960. This, however, is only a very rough approximation, and sometimes the statement is made that a talent in N.T. times was worth in round numbers $1,000. If such a parallel be considered, it should be clearly understood that such an equating is made only as a matter of convenience for visualizing ancient values and that it does not approach scientific accuracy. The talent was never coined.

Pound is the rendering of: 1. Heb. *māneh* (I Kings 10:17). 2. Gr. *mnā* (I Macc. 14:24; 15:18). 3. *Litra* (John 12:3; 19:39), equivalent to the Roman *libra*, of which 2½ equaled a Hebrew maneh of gold (Jos. *Antiq.* xiv. 7, 1). The Roman pound contained 327.45 grams.

Well. A pit sunk in the earth to reach a supply of water. It was called in Heb. *b'ēr*, a word often used in compound names like

Beer-sheba. The water reached was found collected in a depression, or slowly percolating through the sand on its way to a lower level, or flowing as an underground stream (cf. Gen. 16:7 with v. 14; ch. 24:11 with v. 13). Wells were often scooped in the sandy soil by those who knew of the presence of water. They were dug in the wadies and fed by an underflow, even when the bed of the torrent was dry, as at Beer-sheba and in the valley of Gerar (Gen. 21:30, 31; 24:19). They were sunk far and wide through the surface soil of the Philistine plain into the lower sand, where an inexhaustible stream makes its way to the sea. In hilly Palestine they were dug in the limestone rock. The well did not essentially differ in outward appearance from a cistern. To prevent accidents to man or beast the mouth was covered by a stone or plank (Gen. 29:2, 3; Ex. 21:33; II Sam. 17:19; Jos. *Antiq.* iv. 8, 37). When the well was shallow, steps were cut in the rock which led down to the water. Troughs of wood or stone were placed near the mouth for the benefit of the cattle (Ex. 2:16). The water was dipped with the pitcher (Gen. 24:16), or, when the well was deep, was drawn by a rope with bucket, jar, or waterskin attached (John 4:11). The rope was either dragged over the curb by the person getting the water, or perhaps an ox or ass was sometimes employed, as now, for the purpose, and occasionally a wheel was, as now, fixed over the well to assist in the work. See CISTERN, FOUNTAIN.

Whale. The word rendered "whale" in the A.V. of the O.T. denotes any great animal of the sea, except in Ezek. 32:2, where the Hebrew text must be emended and translated "dragon" (E.R.V., J.V., and A.V. marg.) or "monster" (A.R.V.). This interpretation is supported by 2 Heb. MSS., the LXX, and the Vulgate. Cf. also DRAGON.

The Gr. word *kētos,* which is used in Matt. 12:40, and rendered "whale," means any huge fish or other large animal of the sea, such as the dolphin, sea dog, and seal, and later whale. The LXX employs *kētos mega* in Jonah 1:17 (in LXX, ch. 2:1) to render the 2 words "great fish" of the Hebrew text, and thus the word *kētos* passed into Matt. 12:40.

Wheat. Wheat was cultivated in Babylonia (Herod. i. 193), in Mesopotamia (Gen. 30:14), in Egypt (Ex. 9:32), in Palestine (Ex. 34:22; Deut. 8:8; Judg. 6:11), and elsewhere, from a very early period.

In Palestine wheat was sown in November or December, after the rains began. The harvest was in April, May, or June in Palestine, varying according to the locality, the soil at the place, and the weather at the time; see YEAR.

The ordinary bread of the Hebrews was made of the flour of wheat (Ex. 29:2). The ears were also roasted and eaten (Lev. 2:14, 16; Ruth 2:14); see PARCHED CORN. The wheat, bruised and crushed, was also used as food. New wheat thus prepared, or else the fresh ear, is mentioned as eaten (Lev. 23:14; II Kings 4:42).

Egypt was the granary of the Mediterranean region, and vast quantities were shipped annually to Rome from Alexandria (Acts 27:6, 38). The best quality, according to Pliny, was grown in Upper Egypt, in the Thebaid (*Hist. Nat.* xviii. 47). The Egyptian wheat was a bearded variety, with many ears on the head (*Triticum compositum*). It is mentioned in Gen. 41:22, is depicted on the ancient monuments, and is still grown. The wheat generally cultivated in Palestine is the common variety, *Triticum vulgare,* with a simple head.

Wheel. See GARDEN, WELL.

Whore. See HARLOT.

Wid'ow. A widow from early times wore an appropriate garb (Gen. 38:14, 19); she laid aside her ornaments, clothed herself in sackcloth, let her hair hang unbound, and did not anoint her face (Judith 10:3, 4; 16:8). God shows special compassion to the more helpless classes, among whom he reckons widows (Deut. 10:18; Ps. 68:5; 146:9; Prov. 15:25; Jer. 49:11). Under the Mosaic Law, and subsequently, the Hebrews were enjoined to treat widows with justice and consideration, threatening judgment on those who did differently (Ex. 22:22; Deut. 14:29; 16:11, 14; 24:17–21; 26:12, 13; Isa. 1:17; Jer. 7:6; 22:3; Zech. 7:10; Mal. 3:5), as our Lord also did in his preaching (Mark 12:40). The Apostolic Church looked after poor widows (Acts 6:1;

Egyptian Wheat

James 1:27). In the churches under Timothy's care certain widows, who were widows indeed, and had neither children nor grandchildren to provide for them (I Tim. 5:4), were enrolled and cared for by the Church (v. 16). To obtain enrollment it was required that they be at least 60 years of age, have been married but once, and be well reported of for good works (vs. 9, 10). Here are the beginnings of an institution. From the end of the 2d century to the 4th they are mentioned by ecclesiastical writers as elder widows or the order of widows. Their duty was to serve the Church, and they had oversight over the women of the congregation, especially over widows and orphans. The office was abolished by the synod of Laodicea, A.D. 364.

For the enactment as to marriage in certain circumstances to a deceased husband's brother, see MARRIAGE.

Wife. See MARRIAGE.

Wild Ass, Bull, Goat, etc. See Ass and the other nouns; but for **Wild Ox,** see both Ox and UNICORN.

Wil'der·ness. See DESERT.

Wil'der·ness of the Wan'der·ing. 1. *Boundaries and extent of the wilderness.* Nature has defined a large inverted triangle, having for its base the s.e. shore of the Mediterranean Sea and the s. boundary of Palestine, for its w. side the depression in which the Gulf of Suez and the Bitter Lakes lie, and for its e. side the depression occupied by the Gulf of 'Akabah and the gorge of the Arabah. The base of this triangle measures 200 miles, and its area about 22,000 square miles. This district may be called the wilderness of the wandering; but this designation in Arabic, Bādiyat et-Tīh, is restricted to the tableland n. of Sinai. The region is barren, little desired by man; and the great nations of antiquity accordingly left it virtually to itself. The Israelites pushed their s. boundary but a short distance into its limits, and the Egyptians fortified a frontier for themselves where its sands began.

2. *Physical features of the wilderness.* The chief features of the territory are 4: a region of sand, or the n. and n.w. coast; a region of limestone, or the tableland; a region of sandstone, or the low mountains; and a region of granite, or the high mountains. (1) The region of sand extends in a broad band from Philistia along the shore of the Mediterranean Sea to the boundary of Egypt and beyond, bending to the s. and continuing in a strip about 10 miles wide past Suez to a point ⅓ the way down the coast. This sandy region is more or less coextensive with the wilderness of Shur. (2) The n. and central portion of the triangle is a sterile tableland of limestone, from 2,000 to 2,500 feet high; sloping down on the n. to the sandy region on the Mediterranean; swelling in the n.e. into a mountainous country; and confined on the other sides by an encircling chain of mountains, 4,000 and more feet high, now called Jebel et-Tīh. The middle of this desert is occupied by a long central basin, which is drained into the Mediterranean by Wadi el-'Arīsh and its tributaries. These water courses are dry most of the year, but filled by the rains they become raging torrents. West of this basin, other wadies run by themselves down to the sea. On the e. of the same central basin, between it and the Arabah, is another similar and parallel one, extending from Jebel et-Tīh nearly to Jebel 'Araif and the mountainous country of the n.e., and drained throughout by Wadi el-Jerāfi. The tableland proper, with its continuation in the adjacent clusters of mountains in the n.e. as far as the cleft of Wadi el-Fikreh, was the wilderness of Paran (Num. 10:11, 12; 13:26; I Sam. 25:1), in which the Israelites wandered for 38 years, and of which the portion lying between Horeb and Kadesh was remembered by them as "that great and terrible wilderness" (Deut. 1:19). This plateau is mostly naked of vegetation, and has a gravelly surface. The wadies, however, seldom fail to show vegetation of some sort, and after the rainy season are covered with a thin herbage. The springs are few, and generally send forth impure water; but in the region about Kadesh and along the border of the Arabah there are a considerable number of living fountains, and near Kadesh and even at other places in the very heart of the desert water is obtainable by digging. (3) The sandstone formation crosses the peninsula in a broad belt immediately s. of Jebel et-Tīh and extends nearly from shore to shore, separating the limestone tableland from the granite mountains. It is rich in mineral wealth. It may be compared to a dumbbell in shape; for it consists of 2 groups of mountains connected by a central plateau. This sandy tableland has an altitude of about 1,500 feet. (4) The region of granite consists of the groups of mountain ranges about Mount Sinai. The watershed runs n. and s. and lies just e. of Wadi esh-Sheikh.

3. *Possibility of a sojourn of forty years in the wilderness.* The Israelites numbered 600,-000 men from 20 years old and upward, according to the repeated testimony of the Hebrew records. According to statistics of population, which yield the proportion of 4 to 5 between those under and those above 20 years of age in a given community, the whole body of fugitives from Egypt numbered 2,100,000. The Bible, as well as exploration, teaches that this great host could not have survived for any great length of time in the wilderness save by the providence and miracles of God. Moses reminded the people that in the wilderness they had seen how that the Lord their God did bear them, "as a man doth bear his son," in all the way that they went (Deut. 1:31). The recorded miracles of sustenance are few. In the wilderness of Sin, at the beginning of their journey, manna was given to the Children of Israel and they continued to eat of this food for 40 years, until they came into the borders of Canaan (Ex. 16:1, 4, 14, 15, 35). This was the permanent provision for their needs. The occasional supplies were the quails, given at the same time as the manna, but apparently only as a sign and temporarily, for they are not again mentioned (Ex. 16:12, 13); the water provided shortly afterward from the rock near Rephidim (ch. 17:3–7); the quails given in the 2d year for a month (Num. 10:11; 11:4–6, 31); and the water caused to gush from the rock at Kadesh toward the end of the 40 years' sojourn (ch. 20:2–11). The Bible teaches further that, notwithstanding these miracles, certain periods of the sojourn remained a horrible memory (Deut. 1:19; 8:15); that though it could be said, "Thou hast lacked nothing" (ch. 2:7), yet the life in the wilderness was one of repeated privation and hardship. The water was insufficient at Rephidim and Kadesh (Ex. 17:1; Num. 20:2); the people were murmuring 3 days after leaving Sinai before reaching Hazeroth (Num. 10:33; 11:1, 35) and as they journeyed from Mount Hor toward the Red Sea (Num. 21:4, 5); and the wilderness was found to be terrible (Deut. 8:15).

It appears from the Biblical narrative that the manna sufficed as staple fare, though the people grew weary of it; and that the water supply, though scanty often to distress, was ordinarily sufficient. Food was furnished continuously. In regard to the supply of water in this region of desolation, there are 2 considerations of importance: (1) The ability of the people to alleviate the distress of the desert journey arising from the scarcity of water. The power of man and beast to endure thirst is great in these dry countries. The camel drivers of Egypt, both men and boys, escort travelers across scorching sands and under a burning sun without tasting a drop of water from early morning until after nightfall, because unable to obtain it. Dr. Robinson relates that his Arab guide spent a fortnight on the Sinaitic peninsula near Mount Serbāl pasturing his camels, without a drop of water for himself or them. He drank the milk of the camels; and they, as well as sheep and goats, when they have fresh pasture, need no water, sometimes going 3 or 4 months without it (*Researches* i. 150). Again, like other travelers in the desert, the Israelites undoubtedly carried a supply of water with them, which they replenished at every opportunity. It is evident from the narrative that at the beginning of their journey they provided water sufficient for a march of at least 3 days into the wilderness (Ex. 15:22). Again, the Israelites discovered hidden natural supplies. Frequently when the bed of the wadi or the surface of the plain is dry, a stream flows or water lies in a basin underground. According to the geologist Fraas, the so-called wells of Moses, which bubble up in the desert a short distance from Suez, are fed by a subterranean stream which flows from the mountains of er-Raḥah, 10 or 14 miles away. In Wadi Gharandel, which is commonly identified with Elim, there is a subterranean stream which the Arabs open when the upper watercourse is dry. Though the rains fail for 2 or 3 years, water is always to be found by digging a little below the surface (Robinson, *Researches* i. 69). Back of Tur, at Mabuk, at Kubab, and elsewhere, water collects beneath the surface and may be reached with slight effort (Ritter, *Erdkunde* xiv. 161, 185; Robinson, *Researches* i. 167). The Hebrews understood this fact and took advantage of it during their sojourn in the wilderness, as the song of the well testifies (Num. 21:17, 18). Again, if the manner of travel was like the migrations of other large bodies of people, the Israelites scattered in order to utilize for man and beast all the soil and herbage and water. Again, the Israelites husbanded the resources of water. The rainfall is considerable; the wadies bear evidence of the torrents which at times sweep down their courses. The early Christian monks who dwelt in the mountains of Sinai and the former inhabitants and cultivators of the district about Kadesh built dams across the ravines and dug cisterns, and thus secured water for themselves, their cattle, and their gardens. Abraham, Isaac, and Jacob, the forefathers of these Israelites of the Exodus, had likewise husbanded the rainfall, and the descendants of these Israelites dug trenches in the valleys and built reservoirs for a like purpose; and doubtless so did the Israelites during their sojourn of 38 years in the wilderness (Deut. 2:14). (2) A 2d important consideration is the evidence that the country was better wooded in former times. Charcoal has been made in the peninsula from the acacia tree for ages, but the improvident Arabs have never been wont to replace the destroyed timber by replanting. Bartlett in 1874 mentions seeing stumps where the Arabs had burned down the trees, and acacias with the boughs lopped off for the camels to eat (*From Egypt to Palestine*). Burckhardt, one of the earliest travelers to explore Sinai, in his journey across the country in 1812 came across charcoal burners (*Erdkunde* xiv. 183); and Rüppell in 1822 mentioned the burning of charcoal for sale in Egypt as an immemorial industry of the Bedouin, and ascribed the nakedness of the valleys to the neglect of the Arabs to replant the ground which they had denuded (*Erdkunde* xiv. 274, 342). But charcoal burning for domestic purposes and export has not been the only means whereby the peninsula has been impoverished of wood; mining and smelting have also caused the destruction of great quantities of timber. The ancient Egyptians worked copper mines in the sandstone mountains of the w. intermittently from a very early period, and were still operating them subsequently to the Exodus. Acacia wood was sometimes used as supports for the roofs of the mines (Palmer, *Desert of the Exodus* i. 205), and the smelting operations, which were of magnitude, demanded large quantities of timber for fuel

(*ibid.*, 26, 43, 231–235; *Erdkunde* xiv. 786, 787). One should recall the disappearance of the cedars of Lebanon and of wide stretches of forest in America. It is clear that, beginning long before the Exodus and continuing down to the present day, causes have been at work reducing the timber in the region traversed by the Israelites. This fact has a direct bearing on the question of the water supply in earlier times; for, the country being better wooded, there was a natural preservation of the rainfall. As always where there is vegetation, the rain fell more regularly; the water was admitted to the wadies more slowly and gently; soil and vegetation were less ruthlessly swept away; springs were more numerous and flowed more copiously; and streams endured longer into the dry season and were more frequently perennial.

Under an energetic, competent, and provident leader who was acquainted with the desert and its resources, by husbanding the supply, by extending the bounds of the encampment, and by scattering from the central camp in groups of various size, and with no failure of the annual rains, it is not to be doubted that a large host could have secured a sufficient though scant supply of water for man and beast.

4. *The route of the Israelites through the wilderness.* Certain sites have been identified: Succoth in Egypt at the beginning of the journey, the river Arnon which was reached at the close of the 40 years, when the wilderness was left, and the encampments beyond the Arnon which are mentioned in the itinerary, Kadesh, which has been identified with 'Ain Ḳadis, where the camp was twice pitched, and whence the Israelites expected to march directly into the Promised Land, and Eziongeber, where the camp was located just before the 2d march to Kadesh, and near which they afterward passed on their way to the Arnon. Mount Sinai is almost universally located in the peninsula, which is accordingly called the peninsula of Sinai. The camp at Moserah was hard by Mount Hor, on the border of Edom; and the wells of Bene-jaakan and Hor-haggidgad were also near the boundary of Edom. Punon was e. of Edom and n.e. of Petra. With a knowledge of the location of these places, one may readily trace the general route.

An itinerary covering the journey from Rameses and Succoth to the camp opposite Jericho was drawn up by Moses (Num., ch. 33). The encampments recorded in it after Sinai represent the movements of the tabernacle. The people were, however, doubtless often dispersed through the wilderness, tending their flocks wherever herbage and water were found. When they were collected and encamping in a body, their camp was very large and, in a settled country, covered the distance between several towns; hence the same encampment may be differently described or designated (cf. Num. 33:49 with ch. 25:1). Besides the itinerary there is the narrative of the journey (Ex., ch. 12, to Num., ch. 25), and there are also scattered allusions in the address of Moses to various incidents that occurred on the way. It is important to remember that each of these 3 recitals was prepared for a special purpose of its own. The itinerary records formal encampments and does not mention every halting place and every place of spending the night (Ex. 15:22; Num. 10:33). It is doubtful whether it omits a single encampment where the tabernacle was set up. In the address events are cited as illustrations or to enforce the argument; and of course they are chosen at random, without reference to chronological sequence, and they are frequently alluded to broadly and by comprehensive statement.

JOURNEY THROUGH THE WILDERNESS

ITINERARY	NARRATIVE	ALLUSIONS IN MOSES' ADDRESS
From Rameses to Mount Sinai		
Rameses, left in 1st month, 15th day . . . . Num. 33:3, 5	Night after 14th day of 1st month . . . . Ex. 12:18, 34, 37	. . . . Deut. 16:1
Succoth 5	 37	
Etham, on the edge of the wilderness 6	. . . . 13:20	
Pi-hahiroth 7	. . . . 14:2	
Passage of the Red Sea . . 8	 22	. . . . 11:4
Went 3 days' journey into the wilderness of Etham and pitched at	Went out into the wilderness of Shur, and went 3 days in the wilderness and came to	
Marah 8	Marah 15:23	
Elim 9	 27	
By the Red Sea 10		
Wilderness of Sin 11	2d month, 15th day . . . 16:1	
Dophkah 12		
Alush 13		
Rephidim, where was no water for the people to drink 14	. . . . 17:1-8	. . . . 6:16; 25:17
Wilderness of Sinai 15	before the Mount 19:2	. . . . 4:10, 11; 5:2
	in 3d month 1	
From Mount Sinai to Kadesh-barnea		
Wilderness of Sinai	. . . . Num. 10:12	Horeb
	in 2d year, 2d month, 20th day 10:11; cf. 1:1; 9:5	through all that great and
Kibroth-hattaavah 16	Three days' journey 10:33	terrible wilderness
	. . . the outermost part of the camp where the fire devoured being called Taberah 11:1, 3, 34	by the way to the hill
	Apparently remained 30 days 21	9:22 country of the
Hazeroth . . . . • . 17	Remained at least 7 days . 12:15	24:9 Amorites to
Rithmah 18	Kadesh, in the wilderness of Paran 12:16;13:26	Kadesh-barnea 1:19
		It is 11 days' journey from Horeb by the way of Mount Seir to Kadesh-barnea 2
	About the time of the first ripe grapes, i.e., in the latter part of the 5th month 13:20	 25
	Discouraged by the spies' report, the Israelites refused to advance. After being condemned to wander in the wilderness 40 years and ordered to turn back into the wilderness by the way to the Red Sea, the people attempted to enter Canaan, and went up into the mountain, but were smitten, even unto Hormah. Moses departed not from the camp . . 14:25, 33–45	. . . . 1:40–45; 9:23
From Kadesh to Ezion-geber and Return, until the men of that generation died.		
Rithmah	. . . .	At Kadesh many days . . . 1:46
Rimmon-perez 19		Turned and took their journey into the wilderness by the way to the Red Sea, as God had commanded . . 2:1
Libnah 20		
Rissah 21		
Kehelathah 22		
Mount Shepher 23	In the wilderness 15:32	
Haradab 24		
Makheloth 25		
Tahath 26		
Terah 27		
Mithkah 28		
Hashmonah 29	In the wilderness 16:13	
Moseroth 30		
Bene-jaakan 31		
Hor-haggidgad 32		Compassed
Jotbathah 33		
Abronah 34		Mount
Ezion-geber 35		
Wilderness of Zin, i.e., Kadesh 36	Wilderness of Zin at Kadesh, in 1st month [of 40th year] 20:1	Seir many
	Moses and Aaron sinned against God when smiting the rock 2-13	cf. 32:51
		3:26; 4:21 days 2:1, 2
	Messengers were sent to the king of Edom, asking permission for Israel to cross his territory 14-17	

JOURNEY THROUGH THE WILDERNESS—*Continued*

ITINERARY **From Kadesh to the Jordan**		NARRATIVE		ALLUSIONS IN MOSES' ADDRESS	
Kadesh		Kadesh	22		
		Journey toward Edom by the way of Atharim or the spies	21:1	Wells of Bene-jaakan	10:6
Mount Hor, in the edge of the land of Edom	37	Mount Hor, by the border of the land of Edom . . 20:22, 23		Moserah, 10:6	
In 40th year, 5th month, 1st day	38				
Aaron ascended the moun- tain and died	39	. . . .	24–29	where Aaron died 10:6	
The king of Arad heard of the coming of the Israel- ites	40	The king of Arad heard of their coming, fought against them, and took some of them captive . .	21:1	Close of the 40 years	
		At Mount Hor the Israelites probably received the an- swer of the king of Edom, and found his army drawn up to oppose them, where- fore Israel turned away from him 20:18–21			2:7; 29:5
		From Mount Hor they jour- neyed, by the way to the Red Sea, to compass the land of Edom	21:4	Gudgodah. 10:7 Jotbathah. 10:7	
				Crossed the s. end of Edom, near Elath and Ezion-geber, and turned	
Zalmonah	41	Fiery serpents hereabouts . .	6–9	Deut. 8:15	n., journeying
Punon	42				by the way
Oboth	43	. . . in the wilderness e. of	10		of the wil-
Iye-abarim, in the border of Moab	44	Moab	11	Moab 2:4,5,8	derness of
		Valley of Zered	12	Crossed the brook Zered 38 13 years after their condem- nation at Kadesh-barnea 14	
		In the wilderness on the other, i.e., the s. side of the [upper] Arnon	13	Crossed the [upper] Arnon, perhaps the tributary known as Seil es-Sfei, and so were in the neighbor- hood of the Ammonites 2:18,19 and on the borders of the Amorite kingdom . . . 24	
		Beer, in the wilderness . . .	16, 18	From the wilderness which took its name from Kede- moth, the Israelites sent messengers to Sihon . . 26	
		Sihon went against Israel into the wilderness, and the battle was fought at Jahaz	23	 32	
		Mattanah, not in the wilder- ness	18		
Dibon-gad, the camp prob- ably extending to Nahaliel	45	Nahaliel	19		
Almon-diblathaim and prob- ably to Bamoth	46	Bamoth	19		
In the mountains of Abarim, before Nebo	47	Valley at the top of Pisgah .	20		
Plains of Moab, opposite Jericho, from Beth-jeshi- moth to Abel-shittim .	48, 49	. . . .	22:1	In the valley over against Beth-peor 3:29; 4:46	
		at Shittim	25:1	In the 40th year, before the 11th month 1:3	

Wil'low, Wil'low Tree. 1. Any tree of the genus *Salix*, called *ṣaphṣāphāh* in Heb. (Ezek. 17:5). Several species are common in Palestine.

2. The rendering of Heb. *'ărābāh*. The Israelites were directed to take branches from it, as well as from other trees, to make booths at the feast of tabernacles (Lev. 23:40). It grew beside brooks or watercourses (Isa. 44:4), and afforded cover even to the bulky behemoth (Job. 40:22). It was the tree on which the Hebrews hung their harps when exiles at Babylon (Ps. 137:2). The LXX and Vulgate render the Heb. word by willow, and they are followed by the English version. It may have been the weeping willow (*Salix babylonica*), which is found abundantly on the Euphrates and is cultivated in Palestine. But leading interpreters, following Wetzstein, understand the Arab. *gharab*, and consequently its etymological Heb. equivalent, *'ărābāh*, to denote the Euphratean poplar (*Populus euphratica*).

Wil'lows, Brook of the. A brook in Moab (Isa. 15:7), the lower course of Wadi el-Hesā at the junction of the upper course of Seil el-Ḳerāhi, where there is a small plain covered with willow trees. It was at the boundary between Moab and Edom. It may be identical with the brook of the Arabah (Amos 6:14, R.V.).

Wim'ple. An article of woman's attire, made of silk or linen, and worn as a covering for the neck, chin, and sides of the face; it may have been a long pendulous kerchief. In A.V. of Isa. 3:22, it is the rendering of Heb. *mitpaḥath*, a shawl or mantle (*ibid.*; Ruth 3:15, both R.V.).

Wind. The Hebrews, who did not define direction with the minuteness customary in modern times, recognized 4 winds: the e., the w., the n., and the s. winds (Jer. 49:36; Ezek. 37:9; Rev. 7:1). God created the wind (Amos 4:13); and it stands at his summons, is under his control, and performs his pleasure (Job 28:25; Ps. 78:26; 107:25; 135:7; 148:8; Matt. 8:26). The wind that blew from the w., s.w., and n.w. brought rain to Palestine, and accompanied the storm (I Kings 18:43–45; Ps. 147:18; Prov. 25:23, R.V.; Ezek. 13:13). Wind was often destructive to houses and shipping (Job 1:19; Ps. 48:7; Matt. 7:27). The scorching wind dried up streams and blasted vegetation (Gen. 41:6; Isa. 11:15; Ezek. 19:12; Jonah 4:8); see EAST WIND. The s. and s.e. winds traversed the Arabian desert, and were dry and hot (Job 37:17; Luke 12:55). The n. wind was cooler (Ecclus. 43:20), and was favorable to vegetation (S. of Sol. 4:16). Wind was taken advantage of by the thresher to blow away the chaff and broken straw (Job 21:18; Ps. 1:4); see THRESHING. The mariner also availed himself of the wind (Acts 27:40). The words which are rendered "whirlwind" in English do not denote a rotary wind specifically, but signify a violent storm of any kind.

Win'dow. An aperture, especially in the wall of a building (Gen. 26:8; I Kings 6:4; Jer. 22:14), which was opened and closed at convenience by means of a movable shutter of some sort (Gen. 8:6; II Kings 13:17; Dan. 6:10), generally a lattice (Judg. 5:28; II Kings 1:2; Prov. 7:6; S. of Sol. 2:9); but a window on the ground floor, that looked into the street, was doubtless in ancient as in modern times small, high up in the wall, and strongly barred. In the better class of houses most of the windows faced the court. Houses that abutted on the town wall usually had windows looking toward the country (Josh. 2:15; II Cor. 11:33).

Wine. Wine was made from grapes. The ripe clusters were gathered in baskets (Jer. 6:9), carried to the press, and thrown into it. The press consisted of a shallow vat, built above ground or excavated in the rock (Isa. 5:2) and, through holes in the bottom, communicating with a lower vat also frequently excavated in the rock. An upper vat measuring 8 feet square and 15 inches deep had at times a lower vat 4 feet square and 3 feet deep. The grapes were crushed by treading (Neh. 13:15; Job 24:11), 1 or more men being employed according to the size of the vat. In Egypt, and probably in Palestine, the treaders held to ropes overhead to keep from falling; they sang at their work and shouted, doubtless to keep time (Isa. 16:10; Jer. 25:30; 48:33); and the red blood of the grapes flowed around them and stained their skin and their garments (Isa. 63:1–3). From the upper vat the juice trickled into the lower. From this receptacle the juice was put in bottles of skin (Job 32:19; Matt. 9:17), or in large earthenware jars, where it was allowed to ferment. When fermentation had proceeded far enough, the wine was drawn off into other vessels (Jer. 48:11, 12).

The juice of the grape when expressed was used in various conditions: as must, fresh from the press; as wine, which was produced by vinous fermentation; and as vinegar, which resulted when the fermentation was continued too long. Probably in ancient times, as at the present day, some of the must was reduced to a syrup or honey by boiling. As vinegar it was called *ḥōmeṣ*, in Gr., *oxos*; see VINEGAR. Various names were applied to it in the other states:

Hebrew *tīrōsh*, must, fresh or new wine; the R.V. sometimes renders this word by "vintage" (Num. 18:12; Neh. 10:37, marg.); and the attempt has been made by some interpreters to limit the meaning to this sense, and to deny that it ever signifies new wine or must. It means juice of the grape or must in Joel 2:24: "The floors shall be full of wheat, and the vats [A.V., fats] shall overflow with new wine and oil"; cf. ch. 3:13: "Put ye in the sickle; for the harvest is ripe: come, tread ye; for the winepress is full [of grapes], the vats [both of them] overflow." It also means juice of the grape or new wine, as it is rendered in Hos. 4:11: "Whoredom and wine and new wine take away the understanding." There is no need to depart from this meaning of *tīrōsh* anywhere and render it vintage; for example: 1. Isa. 62:8, 9: "Surely I will no more give thy grain to be food for thine enemies; and foreigners shall not drink thy new wine, for which thou hast labored: but they that have garnered it shall eat it, and praise Jehovah; and they

Treading the Wine Press in Ancient Egypt

that have gathered it shall drink it in the courts of my sanctuary." There is no need to give *tīrōsh* the meaning of vintage here, as the R.V. shows by placing wine in the text, as the A.V. did. It is said indeed to be gathered; but this is a proleptic form of speech, and elsewhere wine and oil are said to be gathered (Jer. 40:10; the Heb. word for wine being *yayin*). 2. Isa. 65:8: "As the new wine is found in the cluster, and one saith, Destroy it not, for a blessing is in it." Cheyne renders, "As when [a few good] grapes are found in the cluster, and one saith [to the other gleaners] destroy it not, for a blessing is in it." But the same meaning exactly is yielded by rendering, "As when the juice is found in the cluster," etc. 3. Micah 6:15: "Thou shalt sow, but shalt not reap; thou shalt tread the olives, but shalt not anoint thee with oil; and the vintage [A.V., sweet wine], but shalt not drink the wine." The Hebrews spoke of treading grapes (Amos 9:13) and of treading wine (Isa. 16:10, *yayin* being used). 4. Not even in those numerous passages where the fruits of the ground are mentioned comprehensively as corn, wine, and oil (Num. 18:12, R.V. vintage; Deut. 7:13; 11:14; 12:17; Hos. 2:8, 22; Joel 1:10; 2:19, in all 18 times). In many of these passages the tithe of the corn, wine, and oil is spoken of. Since *yiṣhār* denotes the oil which is found in the olive (II Kings 18:32; Zech. 4:12), *tirōsh* may denote the juice which is found in the grape; and as the grain was thought of as threshed, the *tirōsh* and the oil may be thought of as expressed. The only question then is: Were not first fruits and tithes brought from the other produce of the vineyard which was not reduced to wine? They were; but they are not specifically included in the threefold designation so often employed. The first fruits of all that was in the land were presented to the Lord, as is more explicitly stated in Num. 18:13; and mint and anise were tithed, although the threefold designation does not when interpreted literally embrace them.

Hebrew *'āsis*, something trodden out; hence grape juice, must (Isa. 49:26; Amos 9:13). It does not denote the expressed juice of the grape only, but of other fruits as the pomegranate.

Greek *gleukos* is used by Josephus in speaking of the grape juice squeezed into Pharaoh's cup (Gen. 40:11; Jos. *Antiq.* ii. 5, 2). It is explained by Hesychius as the juice that flowed spontaneously from the grapes before the treading commenced. It was drawn off and kept separate from the juice which flowed under pressure. It was with this that the apostles were accused of being filled on the Day of Pentecost (Acts 2:13).

Must was drunk; and, after fermentation had set in, was intoxicating (Hos. 4:11, *tirōsh*; Acts 2:13, *gleukos*; and probably Isa. 49:26, *'āsis*). But although must was used as a drink, the old wine was preferred (Ecclus. 9:10; Luke 5:39). Pliny regarded must as hurtful to the stomach (*Hist. Nat.* xxiii. 18).

Hebrew *yayin* is the cognate of the Semitic word from which are derived Gr. *oinos* and Lat. *vinum.* *Ḥamar* is the Aram. name for the same thing; and *ḥemer* is the etymological equivalent of the Aram. word, and is occasionally used in Hebrew poetry. When the Heb. word *yayin* first occurs in Scripture, it is the fermented juice of the grape (Gen. 9:21), and there is no reason to believe that it has a different meaning elsewhere. The Gr. *oinos* also means the fermented juice of the grape, except when it is qualified by the word new, and even then there are not 2 wines, 1 fermented and the other unfermented. New wine is must, which only becomes wine by fermentation. An argument for the use of the term wine for unfermented grape juice has been sought in the fact that wine was used in later times at the passover, and yet leaven was strictly forbidden during the 7 days of the paschal festival; hence the term wine, it has been argued, must have been applied to unfermented juice. But the reason is invalid. Vinous fermentation was not regarded as leaven. Wine was drunk at the passover (Mishnah, *Pesāḥim* x); at that season it was unlawful to put meal or flour into the *ḥārōseth* (a sauce made of fruits and spices with wine or vinegar), probably since the fermentation that ensued would be considered like the leaven of bread (Mishnah, *Pesāḥim* ii). There were numerous varieties of wine which differed in body and flavor, such as the wine of Lebanon, the wine of Helbon. See VINE.

"Fruit of the vine," the designation used by Jesus at the institution of the Lord's Supper (Matt. 26:29), is the expression employed by the Jews from time immemorial for the wine partaken of on sacred occasions, as at the passover and on the evening of the Sabbath (Mishnah, *Berākōth* vi. 1). The Greeks also used the term as a synonym of wine which was capable of producing intoxication (Herod. i. 211 f.). The juice of the grape that was ordinarily planted was red (Isa. 63:2; Rev. 14:18–20) and was called the blood of the grape (Gen. 49:11; Deut. 32:14; I Macc. 6:34; Ecclus. 50:15).

Mixed wine was known by the specific names of *mesek* (Ps. 75:8), *mimsāk* (Prov. 23:30; Isa. 65:11), and *mezeg* (S. of Sol. 7:2), each of which means mixture and denotes wine mixed with spices to give it a pleasant flavor (S. of Sol. 8:2; Pliny *Hist. Nat.* xiv. 19, 5), or with water to diminish its strength (cf. Herod. vi. 84).

Wine differed from *shēkār,* rendered "strong drink" in E.V., in that wine was made from the juice of the grape, and *shēkār* from the juice of other fruits and of grain. *Shēkār* was fermented, for it was capable of producing intoxication (Isa. 28:7; 29:9). It was prepared from barley (Herod. ii. 77), from honey, or from dates (i. 193; Jerome *Epist. ad Nepotianum*), or from the lotus (Herod. iv. 177). The drink made from dates is wholesome and refreshing, but in 1 day's heat it undergoes rapid fermentation, effervesces, and produces intoxication if taken immoderately. *Shēkār* is once used in a broad sense for strong drink generally in distinction from water, and refers to the drink offering, which consisted of wine exclusively (Num. 28:7).

Other words are *sōbe',* derived from a root which signifies to drink to excess (Isa. 1:22; Nahum 1:10); and *shemārim,* which strictly denotes the lees of wine and then is used for wine kept long on the lees, and hence, old.

Wine was employed medicinally (Prov. 31:6; Luke 10:34; I Tim. 5:23); was used in the service of God (Ex. 29:39–41; Lev. 23:13); and light wine was a staple article of diet in Palestine, as it has been in other Mediterranean lands from time immemorial (Num. 6:20; Deut. 14:26; II Chron. 2:15; Neh. 5:18; Matt. 11:19; I Tim. 3:8). According to the Egyptian Tale of Sinuhe wine was abundant in Palestine before and in Dyn. XII. Palestine was a country where meat was difficult to obtain and vegetables were rare; and wine supplied the lack. It would be a mistake, however, to suppose that wine was the invariable accompaniment of a meal; many a repast was doubtless partaken of without it. Still wine was in common use. Bread and wine signified the staples of life (Ps. 104:14, 15; Prov. 4:17). Wine was offered as an ordinary hospitality (Gen. 14:18) and was served at festivities (Job 1:13, 18; John 2:3). The Hebrew people were, as a rule, simple in their mode of living, and temperate; but the danger of excess in the use of even light wine, especially at feasts, was clearly discerned. Its use was accordingly forbidden to priests when ministering at the sanctuary (Lev. 10:9), and was declared to be improper for those about to sit on the judgment seat (Prov. 31:4, 5; cf. Eccl. 10:17; Isa. 28:7); and precautions were taken to guard all men against excess. The means employed to prevent the danger line from being crossed were: 1. The wine was weakened with water (II Macc. 15:39; cf. Herod. vi. 84). That this was done further appears, for example, in connection with the kettle of warm water and the servants to mix the wine, which were employed at the passover (Mishnah, *Pesāḥim* vii. 13; x. 2, 4, 7); hence in the Early Christian Church it was customary to mix the sacramental wine with water (Justin Martyr *Apol.* i. 65). 2. There was a governor of the feast (Ecclus. 32:1, 2; John 2:9, 10), one of whose duties, at least where Greek customs were observed, was to fix the proportion in which the wine and water should be mixed and to determine how much wine each guest might drink; see MEALS. 3. Warnings against the danger of lingering over the wine, of tampering with the cup when it delights the eye, and of making strong intoxicants were urgently given, and the degradation of the drunkard was pointed out by sad example (Gen. 9:21; Prov. 23:29-35; Isa. 5:22). 4. The folly of excess even from a worldly standpoint was emphasized and expressed in proverbs, and put on record in the religious literature of the people (Prov. 20:1; 21:17; 23:20, 21; Hab. 2:5; Ecclus. 31:25-31). 5. The sinfulness of drunkenness was earnestly taught and the condemnation of the drunkard by God was fully known (I Sam. 1:14-16; Isa. 5:11-17; I Cor. 5:11; 6:10; Gal. 5:21; Eph. 5:18; I Peter 4:3).

Wine Press. See WINE.

Win·now·ing. See THRESHING.

Wis'dom. One of the 3 departments of knowledge among the Hebrews, the other 2 being the law and prophecy. The law presents the commandments and claims of Jehovah to man; prophecy passes judgment on conduct in the light of God's revealed will and explains the object of God's dealings with men; wisdom seeks by observation, experience, and reflection to know things in their essence and reality as they stand related to man and God. The law and prophecy proceed directly from God, and in the highest sense are the word of God. Wisdom proceeds from man, and is the product of his own experience and observation. But while it is a human effort, it recognizes that a good understanding is the gift of God, and it postulates the fear of God and obedience to his commands as its first principle (Ps. 111:10; Prov. 9:10; Eccl. 12:13). In the earlier chapters of The Proverbs, in The Book of Job, and in The Wisdom of Solomon, wisdom is personified. See PHILOSOPHY.

The wise in counsel (Jer. 18:18) are met with from time to time during Israel's national history; as the wise woman of Tekoa (II Sam. 14:2), the wise woman of Abel-beth-maacah (II Sam. 20:18), the 4 celebrities Ethan, Heman, Calcol, and Darda (I Kings 4:31). Their utterances took the form of parable (II Sam. 14:4-11), precept (Prov. 24:27-29), proverb (vs. 23-26), riddle (ch. 1:6), the story of real life and its lesson (ch. 24:30-34); and it is customary to see specimens of their keen observation, method, and shrewd sayings in Jotham's fable (Judg. 9:7-20), Samson's riddle or dark saying (ch. 14:14), Nathan's parable and those enacted by the wise woman of Tekoa and a certain prophet (II Sam. 12:1-7; 14:4-17; I Kings 20:35-43), and the fable uttered by King Jehoash (II Kings 14:9, 10). But the great books of Hebrew wisdom are Job, Proverbs, Ecclesiastes, Ecclesiasticus, and The Wisdom of Solomon.

Wis'dom of Sol'o·mon (sŏl'ȯ-mŭn). See APOCRYPHA 6.

Wise Men. See MAGI.

Witch and **Witch'craft'.** See SORCERER.

Wit'ness. Evidence which could be appealed to in the future was secured by some tangible token or memorial, as a heap of stones (Gen. 31:46-52), or by calling in men to witness the event (ch. 23:10-18), by a written document, as a deed or a letter of divorce (Deut. 24:1, 3; Jer. 32:10).

The concurrent testimony of at least 2 witnesses was required under the Mosaic Law to establish guilt of a capital crime (Num. 35:30; Deut. 17:6; Heb. 10:28; cf. I Kings 21:10, 13; Matt. 26:60). This principle was a general rule in all judicial procedure (Deut. 19:15). The Mosaic Law did not sanction the use of torture to extract testimony; see PUNISHMENT. The witness, before his testimony was given, was adjured to tell the truth and to conceal nothing; and then it was sin for him to withhold evidence in his possession (Lev. 5:1; Prov. 29:24). False witness bearing was denounced in the Decalogue (Ex. 20:16), and when detected, it drew upon the false witness the same penalty that he had attempted to get imposed on the accused (Deut. 19:16, 19). The witnesses aided in executing a sentence of death; see STONING. Josephus asserts that women and children were excluded from giving testimony by the Mosaic Law (Antiq. iv. 8, 15). The Law itself says nothing on the subject; but the participation of the witnesses in the execution of the death penalty would make the exclusion of women and children from witness bearing expedient. Josephus' statement evidently represents the current interpretation of the Mosaic Law in his day.

The excellent principle involved in having at least 2 witnesses is capable of broad application in the dealings of man with man (Isa. 8:2; Matt. 17:1, 2; 18:16; John 8:17, 18; I Tim. 5:19).

Those who in the face of danger and distress testify to the truth of God are witnesses in the highest sense (Heb., chs. 10; 11; 12:1). Martyr is a Gr. word meaning witness, and it came to signify one who sealed his testimony with his blood, as Stephen and Antipas (Acts 22:20; Rev. 2:13).

Wiz'ard. A professed possessor of supernatural knowledge derived, in the form of wizardry referred to in the Bible, from the pretended ability to converse with the spirits of the dead (Isa. 8:19). The wizard chirped and muttered in imitation of the voice of the spirit (cf. Isa. 29:4). The wizard is never mentioned alone, but always in connection with them that have familiar spirits, because he belonged to the same class of questioners of the dead. The Canaanites consulted wizards (Deut. 18:9-12); so did the Egyptians (Isa. 19:3); but for a Hebrew to go to such an oracle defiled him, and was apostasy from Jehovah (Lev. 19:31; 20:6; Isa. 8:19). The offense of wizardry was punished with death (Lev. 20:27). Saul, and subsequently Josiah, put the law in force (I Sam. 28:3, 9; II Kings 23:24); while Manasseh violated it shamelessly (II Kings 21:6).

Wolf. 1. A carnivorous animal, wild and fierce (Isa. 11:6; Hab. 1:8), that kills sheep (Ecclus. 13:17; John 10:12), and is accustomed to remain in hiding by day and seek its prey in the evening (Zeph. 3:3). Benjamin was compared to the fierce and dreaded wolf (Gen. 49:9, 27; see the warrior ZEEB). But comparison with the wolf was not always intended as an honor. Violent princes who prey upon the helpless are likened to ravening wolves (Ezek. 22:27), and so are false teachers (Matt. 7:15; Acts 20:29) and enemies of the flock of God (Matt. 10:16). The wolf of Palestine is a variety of the European species (*Canis lupus*), and is found throughout the country. Owing to the ease with which food is obtained and the mildness of the winter, wolves do not hunt in packs, as in the colder n., but prowl alone.

2. The rendering of Heb. *'iyyĭm*, howling creatures (Isa. 13:22; 34:14; Jer. 50:39; in A.V. wild beasts of the islands). The wolf belongs to the same genus as the dog, but it cannot bark; it can only howl.

Wom'an. The counterpart of man, made to be "a help meet unto him" and his social equal (Gen. 2:21-24; see EVE). Monogamy, or the marriage of 1 man and 1 woman, was the Creator's intention; see MARRIAGE.

The younger women of the family, especially in the earlier times and among the nomads, tended the sheep (Gen. 29:6; Ex. 2:16), and they went to the harvest field and gleaned (Ruth 2:3, 8); but the main duties of women were concerned with the household. They brought water from the well (Gen. 24:

13; John 4:7), ground the grain for daily use (Matt. 24:41), prepared the meals (Gen. 18: 6; II Sam. 13:8; Luke 10:40), spun wool and made clothing (I Sam. 2:19; Prov. 31:13, 19; Acts 9:36–39), taught the children religious truth (Prov. 1:8; 31:1; cf. II Tim. 3:15), and directed the household (Prov. 31:27; I Tim. 5:14).

The Mosaic Law and also public opinion among the Hebrews secured to women the enjoyment of many rights; see CONCUBINE, DIVORCE, MARRIAGE. Marriage was regarded by the Hebrews as a sacred relation (Mal. 2:14–16). The wife was spoken of with respect, and accorded honor (Prov. 5:18; 18: 22; 31:10–12; Eccl. 9:9). To the mother honor was due, and her law had authority (Ex. 20:12; Prov. 1:8). The capable woman was highly praised (Prov. 31:10–31), and examples of noble womanhood were freely and purposely admitted to the sacred writings. The spirit of the N.T. was equally opposed to woman's degradation. It insisted that man and woman shall occupy their respective spheres as indicated by the Creator in mutual respect and dependence (Mark 10: 6–9; Eph. 5:31; I Tim. 2:12–15). The sanctity and permanence of the marriage relation were taught, and divorce was permitted only for extreme causes (Matt. 19:8, 9; I Cor. 7: 15; Eph. 5:22–33). Woman was made the recipient of the same grace as man, and heir of the same promises (Gal. 3:28); she was accorded honorable position in the Church, and her services in the cause of Christ were fully appreciated and acknowledged (Rom. 16:1–4, 6, 12). The practical precepts in the Epistles were calculated, whether addressed to saints generally or to woman in particular, to refine and ennoble her, and to bring her best qualities into exercise (I Tim. 2:9, 10; 3:11).

Wool. See SHEEP, SPINNING, WEAVING.

World. The world as known in the Mosaic age was small (Gen., ch. 10). On the s. it extended from the mountains e. of the Persian Gulf to the Nile, and on the n. from the Caspian Sea to the Grecian islands; in other words, it measured about 1,500 miles from e. to w., and 900, or including s. Arabia about 1,500, miles from n. to s. The area was about 2,250,000 square miles; but a large part of the surface was occupied by sea, so that, roughly speaking, the land was scarcely ⅔ the extent of the United States, excluding Alaska. The history which is recorded in the Bible, and the great events of the world's history, were enacted in the n. portion of this region, in an area about ⅓ that of the United States.

During O.T. times these limits remained essentially unchanged, although the geographical horizon widened a little. Media and Persia rose to importance before the close of this period, making themselves known as never before and taking the 1st place among the nations. India became a boundary (Esth. 1:1). The existence of the Sinim was known (Isa. 49:12). In the w., Africa was circumnavigated during the reign of Necho, but the navigators did not realize the meaning of their achievement. They had spent more than 2 years on the voyage, and what appeared most noteworthy to them was that in sailing round Libya (i.e., Africa) they had the sun on their right hand (Herod. iv. 42). In Italy and on the opposite coast of Africa population was increasing and civilization was slowly developing; but these facts seldom reached the ears of men in the e., and then only through the reports of traders. Almost at the close of the O.T. period Greece emerged from obscurity by the vigorous resistance which it offered to the Persians.

Alexander the Great conquered the world. He extended its e. limits, and added immensely to geographical knowledge, by carrying his arms across the Oxus, e. beyond the bounds of modern Afghanistan, and s. into n. India. The Romans followed him. In the time of Christ the world, as currently thought of by men, extended from Spain and Britain to the plateau of Iran and India, and from the desert of Sahara on the s. to the forests of Germany and the steppes of Russia and Siberia on the n. Knowledge of inhabited regions beyond these limits existed; but there was little contact with this outside world, it seldom engaged men's attention, and the ideas of its geography were confused.

"World" is frequently used for the inhabitants of the world (Ps. 9:8; Isa. 13:11; John 3:16; 7:7; Rom. 3:19), and in the N.T. for that which pertains to the earth and this present state of existence merely (I Cor. 7: 31; Gal. 6:14; Eph. 2:2; James 1:27; 4:4; I John 2:15).

Worm. Any small, creeping animal, whose body is boneless and consists of a number of movable joints or rings, and which has no limbs or only very short ones. It was generically called *tôlē'āh* or *tôla'ath* in Heb., *skōlēx* in Gr.; and it is mentioned as destroying grapes and the gourd vine (Deut. 28:39; Jonah 4:7), being bred over night in manna (Ex. 16:20), consuming the corpse (Isa. 14: 11; cf. ch. 66:24 with Mark 9:48), and causing death to the living (Acts 12:23). Man as feeble and despised is likened to a worm (Job 25:6; Isa. 41:14).

Specific worms referred to are:

1. Maggots, in Heb. a collective term *rimmâh*, putridity and the worm bred in it. They feed on corpses (Job 21:26; 24:20; Isa. 14: 11), and might be expected in putrid manna (Ex. 16:24). Man as very small and despicable is likened to the maggot (Job 25:6). In all these passages the E.V. uses the general term worm.

2. The larva of the moth, in Heb. *sās* (Isa. 51:8); see MOTH.

Wormwood (*Artemisia absinthium*)

3. The coccus worm, *tōla'ath shānī*, which, however, is not a worm, but an insect, according to modern classification; see SCARLET.

Hebrew *zāḥal*, the *ḳal* participle of which means creeper, denotes something that crawls on the ground, and is rendered by worm in A.V. (Micah 7:17), in R.V. crawling things (cf. Deut. 32:24).

Worm'wood'. A plant ranked with gall, having very bitter juice (Deut. 29:18; Prov. 5:4), unpalatable and, when exclusively drunk, noxious (Rev. 8:11); called in Heb. *la'ănāh*, in Gr. of N.T. *apsinthos*. It is used figuratively for injustice (Amos 5:7; 6:12; in latter passage rendered hemlock in A.V.), for sore punishment (Jer. 9:15), for bitter

Sam. 24:20), or worship rendered to God (Gen. 24:52, R.V.; Ps. 95:6), the same Heb. word being used in all these passages. The performance of this outward act to idols was strictly forbidden (Ex. 20:5).

For public worship in apostolic times see CHURCH.

Writ'ing. The Hebrews, or rather some of them, were able to write (Ex. 17:14; 24:4; Num. 33:2). The Sumerians invented in the Uruk period pictographic writing, out of which developed the cuneiform; in other words writing was in vogue in Babylonia centuries before Abraham left Ur of the Chaldees, and in Egypt centuries before the Israelites sojourned on the Nile. It was in use

Clay Tablet and Envelope, from About 1958 B.C.

suffering (Lam. 3:19) with which one is sated, not intoxicated (v. 15). It seems to be some species of the great composite genus *Artemisia*. About 180 species are known. Post enumerates 5 species and several varieties as occurring in Palestine or the adjacent regions. The type is the common wormwood (*Artemisia absinthium*) cultivated in gardens.

Wor'ship. Respect and honor shown to a person (Luke 14:10, in R.V. glory), but this sense of the word has become obsolete. Respect which implies that the object thereof possesses divine attributes (Matt. 14:33; 15:25; Rev. 14:7). Man is forbidden to give this worship to any but God alone (Ex. 34:14; Matt. 4:10; Acts 10:25; Rev. 19:10). The same outward act may be civility shown to man, as when people bowed down to Esau, to Joseph, or to the king (Gen. 33:3; 42:6; II

in the towns of Canaan before the conquest of the country by the Hebrews. It is recorded that the Hebrews at the time of the Exodus wrote documents (Deut. 31:24), inscribed the Law on the plaster of an altar (Ex. 27:4, 8; Josh. 8:32), and engraved words on gems and metallic plates (Ex. 39:14, 30). In the time of Gideon a young man of Succoth wrote down the princes and elders of Succoth, 77 men (Judg. 8:14, R.V. marg., and A.V. marg.). The ancient cuneiform inscriptions of Babylonia were impressed on soft clay, afterward baked; and were engraven on stone tablets, on the surface of stone statues, on metal, and on the gem of which the seal was made. The letters sent from Canaan to Pharaoh previous to the Exodus were written on clay tablets. The Egyptians, long before the sojourn of the Israelites among them, cut records in stone and wrote on papyrus. See

ALPHABET, BOOK, INKHORN, PAPYRUS, PARCH-
MENT, RAS SHAMRA, TELL EL-AMARNA, TILE.

Writings. Same as Hagiographa. See
CANON.

X

Xer'xes (zûrk'sēz). See AHASUERUS 2.

Y

Yah (yä). See JAH.

Yarn. See LINEN 6.

Year. The year of the Hebrews consisted
of 12 months (I Kings 4:7; I Chron. 27:1–
15). These appear to have been lunar (see
MONTH), and the year would accordingly contain 354 days, 8 hours, 48 minutes, 34 sec-
onds. The annual festivals were inseparably
connected with the agricultural seasons. A
strictly lunar year would cause these festivals, as fixed by the calendar, constantly to
recede from their appropriate season. It was
necessary to bring the lunar year into correspondence with the solar year of 365 days.
This was accomplished by the intercalation
of an additional month (Veadar, q.v.) every
leap year, although the custom is not mentioned in the Bible. Nineteen years constitute
a lunar cycle, of which the 3d, 6th, 8th, 11th,
14th, 17th, and 19th are leap years. The year
began with the month Abib or Nisan (Ex.
12:2; 23:15; Esth. 3:7), with the new moon
next before or next after the vernal equinox,
when the sun is in Aries (Jos. Antiq. iii. 8, 4;
10, 5); but there was from the earliest times
a civil, or rather agricultural, year which began in the autumn (cf. Ex. 23:16; 34:22;
Lev. 25:4, 9 seq.). It was convenient for a
people devoted to horticulture and agriculture
to begin the year with the season of plowing
and sowing, and to close it with harvest. In
practice they frequently preferred to indicate
the time of year by the particular harvest
or agricultural occupation rather than by the
number or name of the month (e.g., Num.
13:20; Ruth 1:22). Sometime after the Exile
the day of the new moon of the 7th month
came to be kept as new year's day. The custom was probably not started by the events
recorded in Ezra 3:6 and Neh. 8:2, although
in course of time they may have stimulated
such a trend.

Yodh (yōd), A.R.V.; in A.V. Jod. The 10th
letter of the Heb. alphabet. Eng. I and its
modification J come from the same source,
and both are used to represent it in Anglicizing Heb. names, as in Jechoniah. It stands at
the head of the 10th section of Psalm 119 in
several versions, in which section each verse
begins with this letter. It was often confused by copyists and readers with waw, vav,
vau (q.v.).

Yoke. A small transverse bar of timber,
generally with 2 portions of the lower surface
hollowed so as to rest on the necks of 2 oxen,
used to draw a cart or a plow (Num. 19:2).
Two oxen thus held together were also called
a yoke (I Kings 19:19), and so, figuratively,
was any burden imposed on one as a token
and means of subjection (I Kings 12:4;
Matt. 11:30; Acts 15:10).

Z

Za'a·na'im (zā'a-nā'ĭm). See ZAANANNIM.

Za'a·nan (zā'a-năn). A town (Micah 1:11),
perhaps the same as Zenan.

Za'a·nan'nim (zā'a-năn'ĭm), in A.V. once
Za'a·na'im (Judg. 4:11), where A.V. follows
the kethib instead of the kere. A frontier
town of Naphtali (Josh. 19:33), near Kedesh
(Judg. 4:11). It may be identified with Khān
et-Tujjār, about 3 miles n.n.e. of Mount
Tabor. Conder, however, follows the LXX
which has Besemiin, having made 1 word of
"in Zaanannim" (so Josh. 19:33, R.V. marg.),
and he believes it to have been probably near
Bessūm, on the tableland w. of the Sea of
Galilee, about 3 miles n.e. of Mount Tabor,
and about 5 miles w. of the s. end of the Sea
of Galilee.

Za'a·van (zā'a-văn), in A.V. once **Za'van**
[unquiet]. A son of Ezer the Horite (Gen.
36:27; I Chron. 1:42).

Za'bad (zā'băd) [S. Arab., he (God) has
given, or gift]. 1. A descendant of Ephraim,
family of Shuthelah (I Chron. 7:21).
2. A man of Judah, family of Hezron,
house of Jerahmeel, descended through Sheshan, and a great-grandson of Ahlai (I
Chron. 2:31, 34–37). Possibly he was David's
mighty man of this name (ch. 11:41).
3. Corrupt form of Jozacar (II Chron. 24:
26); see JOZACAR.
4, 5, 6. Three Hebrews, each of whom was
induced by Ezra to put away his foreign wife
(Ezra 10:27, 33, 43).

Zab'a·dae'ans (zăb'a-dē'ănz), in A.V. **Zab'a·**
de'ans (zăb'a-dē'ănz). An Arabian tribe which
dwelt between the river Eleutherus, Hamath,
and Damascus (I Macc. 12:30–32; cf. v. 25),
and hence probably occupied that part of the
Anti-Lebanon Mountains where the villages
of Zebedani and Zebad are situated, on the
route from Ba'al-bek to Damascus.

Zab'ba·i (zăb'ả-ī) [cf. S. Arab. Zabbay;
probably for Zabday, he (God) has given].
A son of Bebai. He was induced by Ezra to
put away his foreign wife (Ezra 10:28). He
was the father of a certain Baruch (Neh.
3:20).

Zab'bud (zăb'ŭd) [given (by God); cf.
ZABAD, ZABBAI, ZABDI]. Head of a family
among the sons of Bigvai, who accompanied
Ezra from Babylon (Ezra 8:14).

Zab'di (zăb'dī) [he (God) has given; probably of S. Arab. origin]. 1. A man of Judah,
family of Zerah, and founder of a house
(Josh. 7:1). Called in I Chron. 2:6 Zimri.
For the possibility of confusion of beth (b)
and mem (m), daleth (d) and resh (r), see
table of the alphabet, under ALPHABET.
2. A Benjamite (I Chron. 8:19).
3. A Shiphmite, David's officer over the increase of the vineyards for the wine cellars
(I Chron. 27:27).
4. A Levite, son of Asaph (Neh. 11:17);
see ZICHRI 5.

Zab'di·el (zăb'dī-ĕl) [S. Arab., El (God)
has given]. 1. Father of Jashobeam (I
Chron. 27:2).
2. Son of Haggedolim (Neh. 11:14), or one
of the great men (A.V. and marg. of R.V.).
3. An Arabian prince who treacherously
decapitated Alexander Balas and sent the
head to Ptolemy Philometor (I Macc. 11:17;
Jos. Antiq. xiii. 4, 8). He is possibly the
person referred to by Diodorus Siculus as
Diocles, ruler of Abae, to whose care Alexander committed his infant son. While Alexander was sojourning with Diocles, the former was murdered.

Za'bud (zā'bŭd) [given (by God)]. Son of
Nathan and chief minister in Solomon's reign
(I Kings 4:5).

Zab'u·lon (zăb'û-lŏn). See ZEBULUN.

Zac'ca·i (zăk'ả-ī) [probably contraction for
Zechariah]. Founder of a family, members

Month	Approximation	Festival	Season
1. Abib or Nisan. Ex. 23:15; Neh. 2:1; Jos. *Antiq.* i. 3, 3; iii. 10, 5. 30 days.	April.	1. New Moon.* 14. Passover in the evening, the beginning of the 15th day (Ex. 12:18, 19; 13:3–10), introducing 15–21. Feast of unleavened bread (Lev. 23:6). 16. Sheaf of first fruits of the harvest presented (Lev. 23:10–14; cf. Josh. 5:11; Jos. *Antiq.* iii. 10, 5).	Latter or spring rains. Flax harvest at Jericho (Josh. 2:6). Jordan at flood (Josh. 3:15; I Chron. 12:15; Ecclus. 24:26). Barley harvest in the Maritime Plain. Wheat ripe in hot Jordan Valley. Pods on the carob tree. Dry season begins, continuing to early October, with prevailing wind from the n.w.
2. Ziv or Iyar. I Kings 6:1, 37; Jos. *Antiq.* viii. 3, 1. 29 days.	May.	14. Passover for those who could not keep regular one (Num. 9: 10, 11).	Barley harvest in uplands (cf. Ruth 1:22). Wheat harvest in lowlands.
3. Sivan. Esth. 8:9. 30 days.	June.	6. Pentecost, or feast of weeks or of harvest, or day of first fruits. Loaves as first fruits of gathered harvest presented (Ex. 23:16, 19; 34:22; Lev. 23:15–21; Num. 28:26; Deut. 16:9, 10).	Apples on seacoast. Early figs general. Oleander in bloom. Almonds ripe. Intense heat (Jos. *War* iii. 7, 32).
4. Tammuz. 29 days.	July.		Wheat harvest in high mountains. First grapes ripe. Heat increases. Olives in lowlands.
5. Ab. Jos. *Antiq.* iv. 4, 7. 30 days.	August.	9. Fast day—destruction of Temple.	
6. Elul. Neh. 6: 15. 29 days.	September.		Dates and summer figs. Vintage general (cf. Lev. 26:5; Num. 13:23).
7. Ethanim or Tishri. I Kings 8:2; Jos. *Antiq.* viii. 4, 1. 30 days.	October.	1. Memorial of trumpet-blowing (Num. 29:1). Jewish New Year (Rosh Hashana). 10. Day of Atonement, or Yom Kippur (Lev. 16:29–31). 15–21. Feast of ingathering or tabernacles. First fruits of wine and oil (Ex. 23:16; Lev. 23: 34; Deut. 16:13). 22. Solemn Assembly (Lev. 23:36; Num. 29:35; Neh. 8:18; cf. John 7:37).	Pomegranates ripe. Season changing to the winter (Jos. *Antiq.* iii. 10, 4) or rainy season, with prevailing wind from w. and s.w. Former or early rains. Pistachio nuts ripe. Plowing.
8. Bul or Marheshvan (Marcheshvan). I Kings. 6:38; Jos. *Antiq.* i. 3, 3. 29 days in regular and defective year; 30 days, in perfect year.	November.		Barley and wheat sown. Olives gathered in n. Galilee.
9. Chislev (Kislev). Zech. 7:1; cf. Jos. *Antiq.* xii. 5, 4; 7, 6. 29 days in defective year; 30 days in regular and perfect year.	December.	25. Feast of dedication (I Macc. 4: 52; John 10:22).	Winter figs on trees. Rainfall increases (cf. Ezra 10:9, 13).
10. Tebeth. Esth. 2:16; Jos. *Antiq.* xi. 5, 4. 29 days.	January.		Hail; snow on higher hills and occasionally at Jerusalem. In lowlands grain fields and pastures green, wild flowers abundant.
11. Shebat. Zech. 1:7; I Macc. 16:14. 30 days.	February.		Almond trees in blossom. Appearance of blossom, or perhaps of young fruit, of the fig.
12. Adar. Esth. 3:7; Jos. *Antiq.* iv. 8, 49. 29 days; 30 days, in leap year. 13. Veadar, intercalary month in leap years.] 29 days.	March.	14, 15. Feast of Purim (Esth. 9: 21–28).	Carob tree in blossom. Oranges and lemons ripe in the lowlands. Storax blossoming and pomegranates showing their first flowers. Barley harvest at Jericho.

*In every month the new moon falls on the 1st day of the month.

of which returned with Zerubbabel from the Captivity (Ezra 2:9; Neh. 7:14).

Zac·chae′us (ză-kē′ŭs) [Gr. from Heb. *Zakkay* (Zaccai)]. A wealthy man of Jericho who farmed the revenue for the Roman government. He became a disciple of Christ (Luke 19:1–10).

Zac′cur (zăk′ûr), in A.V. once **Zac′chur** (zăk′ûr) (I Chron. 4:26) [remembered]. 1. A Reubenite (Num. 13:4).

2. A Simeonite, descended through Mishma (I Chron. 4:26).

3. A Merarite Levite, a son of Jaaziah (I Chron. 24:27).

4. A Gershonite Levite, a son of Asaph, and head of a course of musicians in David's reign (I Chron. 25:2, 10; Neh. 12:35). See ZICHRI 5.

5. A son of Imri, who helped to rebuild the walls of Jerusalem (Neh. 3:2).

6. A Levite, who sealed the covenant (Neh. 10:12).

7. Son of Mattaniah and father of Hanan (Neh. 13:13).

Zach′a·ri′as (zăk′á-rī′ás) twice **Zach′a·ri′ah** (zăk′á-rī′á) (Matt. 23:35; Luke 11:51) [Gr. form of Heb. *Zᵉkaryāh*, Jehovah has remembered]. 1. Father of the captain Joseph (I Macc. 5:18).

2. Father of John the Baptist. He was a priest of the course of Abijah (Luke 1:5); see ABIJAH 8. He and his wife were godly people, and she was related to Mary of Nazareth (vs. 6, 36). Their home was in the hill country of Judea (vs. 39, 40). It was customary to allot to the members of the course on duty at the sanctuary the several parts to be performed in the daily ministrations. When Zacharias' course assembled at Jerusalem, the lot fell to him to burn incense; and while he was discharging this service at the hour of prayer, an angel appeared to him and announced that his supplication was heard. His old prayer for a son, although long abandoned as denied by God (v. 18), and the prayer which he continually offered for the Advent of the Messiah (vs. 68–75), were heard; and he was told that his wife should bear a son who should go before the face of the Lord to make ready for the Lord a people prepared for him (vs. 13–17). Zacharias questioned the promise on account of the advanced age of himself and his wife, and asked for a sign. The sign was granted in the form of a punishment. Zacharias was smitten with dumbness until the promise was fulfilled (vs. 18–22, 62–64). When the child was born, not only was the tongue of Zacharias released from its speechlessness, but he himself was filled with the Spirit and prophesied in words of thanksgiving and praise (vs. 67–79).

3. A righteous man who was murdered in the court of the Temple, between the sanctuary and the house (Matt. 23:35; Luke 11:51); see ZECHARIAH 11.

Za′cher (zā′kẽr). See ZECHARIAH 1.

Za′dok (zā′dŏk) [just, righteous]. 1. A descendant of Eleazar, the son of Aaron (I Chron. 24:3). He was the son of Ahitub (II Sam. 8:17). He was doubtless the young man, mighty of valor, who went with the chief men of the tribes of Israel to David at Hebron to turn the kingdom of Saul to David (I Chron. 12:27, 28). Early in David's reign he was joint high priest with Abiathar (II Sam. 8:17). During the rebellion of Absalom the 2 colleagues joined in David's flight from Jerusalem, carrying with them the Ark, but the king desired them to return to the capital and there await the issue of the contest (II Sam. 15:24–29). After the death of Absalom a message, on which they acted,

was sent by David to Zadok and Abiathar, requesting them to suggest to the people that the king should be called back (II Sam. 19:11). When, in David's old age, Adonijah plotted to usurp the throne, Zadok remained faithful, while his colleague Abiathar went with the usurper (I Kings 1:7, 8). When the plot was made known to David, Zadok, with Nathan the prophet, received instructions immediately to anoint Solomon king (vs. 32–45). Abiathar was deposed from the priesthood, and Zadok was the sole occupant of the high office till his death, during the reign of the new monarch (ch. 2:26, 27; cf. ch. 4:4). The office of the high priest was thus restored to the line of Eleazar; see HIGH PRIEST.

2. A priest in the line of high priests, father of Shallum (I Chron. 6:12). He was descended from the 2d Ahitub (*ibid.*; Ezra 7:2) through the 2d Meraioth (I Chron. 9:11; Neh. 11:11).

3. Father of Jerusha, King Uzziah's mother (II Kings 15:33).

4. A son of Baaha. He repaired part of the wall of Jerusalem (Neh. 3:4), and was perhaps the person of the name who sealed the covenant (ch. 10:21).

5. A priest, son of Immer. He repaired the city wall opposite to his house (Neh. 3:29), and was perhaps the scribe who was made a treasurer (ch. 13:13).

Za′ham (zā′hăm) [foul, loathsome]. A son of Rehoboam (II Chron. 11:19).

Za′in (zä′ĭn). See ZAYIN.

Za′ir (zä′ĭr) [little]. A place in or near Edom, where King Joram, of Judah, encamped before making a night attack on the Edomites (II Kings 8:21; cf. the different text in II Chron. 21:9). It is probably to be identified with Ṣa·'îr or Ṣi·'îr, a village about 5 miles n.n.e. of Hebron, where is venerated the tomb of Esau. See ZIOR.

Za′laph (zā′lăf) [cf. neo-Heb., *ṣālāph*, caper-plant]. Father of a certain Hanun (Neh. 3:30).

Zal′mon (zăl′mŏn), in A.V. once **Sal′mon** (Ps. 68:14) [dark; cf. Arab. *ẓalima* and Ethiopic *ṣalma*, to be dark]. 1. An Ahohite, one of David's mighty men (II Sam. 23:28). Also called Ilai (I Chron. 11:29).

2. A wooded mountain near Shechem probably a branch of Gerizim (Judg. 9:48; cf. Ps. 68:14).

Zal·mo′nah (zăl-mō′ná) [dark, shady; cf. ZALMON]. An encampment of the Israelites (Num. 33:41, 42), probably e. of Jebel Hārūn, at Bîr Madhkûr.

Zal·mun′na (zăl-mŭn′á) [popular ety., shadow (protection) is withheld; but it may mean (the god) Ṣalm, i.e., the dark one, or Saturn, rules]. One of the 2 kings of Midian slain by Gideon (Judg. 8:4–28; Ps. 83:11).

Zam′bri (zăm′brī). See ZIMRI 2.

Zam·zum′mim (zăm-zŭm′ĭm), in A.V. **Zam·zum′mims** (zăm-zŭm′ĭmz) [murmurers, makers of noise; cf. Arab. *zamzama*, to hum, mumble]. A tribe of Rephaim, who in ancient times inhabited the region e. of the Jordan, afterward occupied by the Ammonites (Deut. 2:20); probably the same as the Zuzim.

Za·no′ah (zá-nō′á) [perhaps, stench]. 1. A town in the lowland of Judah (Josh. 15:34). It was inhabited after the Captivity (Neh. 11:30), and seems to have been the Zanoah whose inhabitants restored the valley gate of Jerusalem (ch. 3:13). It is Khirbet Zanū' or Zanuḥ, nearly 3 miles s.e. by s. of Beth-shemesh.

2. A town in the hill country of Judah (Josh. 15:56; and probably I Chron. 4:18). It is probably to be located about 1¼ miles n.w. of Yaṭṭā at a place called Khirbet Beit

'Amra on Wadi Abu Zenaḥ, a section of the long Wadi el-Khalil.

Zaph'e·nath·pa·ne'ah (zăf'ė-năth-pȧ-nē'ȧ), in A.V. Zaph'nath-pa'a·ne'ah (zăf'năth-pā'ȧ-nē'ȧ) [Egypt., food, sustenance of the land is the living one, or is this living one]. Joseph's name, given him by Pharaoh (Gen. 41:45). From the sound of the name the Jews guessed that it meant revealer of secrets (Targum Onkelos; Jos. Antiq. ii. 6, 1).

Za'phon (zā'fŏn) [north]. A town of the Gadites in the Jordan Valley (Josh. 13:27; cf. Judg. 12:1, R.V. marg.). The Talmud identifies it with 'Amatho, i.e., Amathus (Jos. Antiq. xiii. 13, 5; xiv. 5, 4), and its site would be Tell 'Ammatah, in the Jordan Valley, e. of the river and 8 miles n. by e. of the mouth of the Jabbok. It has been proposed to identify it with Tell es-Sa'idiyeh, which is situated near the confluence of Wadi Kafrinji with the Jordan, but Glueck (1943) locates it at Tell el-Ḳos.

Za'ra (zā'rȧ) and Za'rah (zā'rȧ). See ZERAH.

Za're·ah (zā'rė-ȧ). See ZORAH.

Za're·ath·ite (zā'rė-ăth-īt). See ZORATHITE.

Za'red (zā'rĕd). See ZERED.

Zar'e·phath (zăr'ė-făth), in A.V. of N.T. Sa·rep'ta (Luke 4:26). A town belonging to Sidon (I Kings 17:9; Luke 4:26; Jos. Antiq. viii. 13, 2). Thither Elijah repaired when the brook Cherith dried up. Trusting his word, spoken in the name of Jehovah, a widow of Zarephath gave him a home while the famine lasted. As a reward for her faith her oil and meal failed not, and her boy was brought back to life (I Kings 17:8–24). The town yielded to Sennacherib in 701 B.C. Its future possession by Israel is announced (Obad. 20). The name still lingers in the form of Ṣarafend, a village on a hill near the sea, 14 miles n. of Tyre, and 8 s. of Sidon. The ancient city was, however, on the shore, along which the ruins extend for a mile or more.

Zar'e·than (zăr'ė-thăn), in A.V. Zar'e·tan (zăr'ė-tăn) (Josh. 3:16), and Zar·ta'nah (I Kings 4:12), and Zar'than (I Kings 7:46). A village beneath Jezreel near the towns of Beth-shean and Adam (Josh. 3:16; I Kings 4:12); evidently in the territory of Manasseh. In clayey ground between Succoth, e. of the Jordan, and Zarethan, w. of the river, bronze work for the Temple was cast (I Kings 7:46). In II Chron. 4:17 the name is given as Zeredah. It is difficult to determine the exact site; many place it at Ḳarn Ṣartabah, which projects from the mountains of Ephraim into the valley of the Jordan opposite the mouth of the Jabbok. But it may be beyond the Jordan, n. of Rās Abū Ṭābāt, and Tell Sleiḥāt has been suggested. Glueck (1943) identifies it with Tell es-Sa'idiyeh.

Zar'hite (zär'hīt). See ZERAHITE.

Zar·ta'nah (zär-tā'nȧ). See ZARETHAN.

Zar'than (zär'thăn). See ZARETHAN.

Zat'tu (zăt'ū), in A.V. once Zat'thu (zăt'thū) (Neh. 10:14). Founder of a family, members of which returned from the Captivity (Ezra 2:8; Neh. 7:13). Some of them married foreign wives, but were induced to put them away (Ezra 10:27). The representative of the family sealed the covenant (Neh. 10:14).

Za'van (zā'văn). See ZAAVAN.

Za'yin (zā'yĭn) in A.V. Za'in. The 7th letter of the Heb. alphabet. English Z, which ultimately goes back to this letter, represents it in Hebrew names in the English version. It heads the 7th section of Psalm 119 in several versions, because each verse of the section begins with this letter.

Za'za (zā'zȧ) [cf. Arab. za'za'a, to move, frighten]. A man of Judah, family of Hezron, house of Jerahmeel (I Chron. 2:33).

Zeal'ot, in A.V. Ze·lo'tes [Gr., zealous one]; Gr. for Aram. Cananaean (q.v.). A member of a Jewish patriotic party (Jos. War iv. 3, 9; vii. 8, 1). Simon the apostle was distinguished from Simon Peter and others by this epithet (Luke 6:15; Acts 1:13). The party was a movement started by Judas the Galilean in the time of Cyrenius to resist Roman aggression. Its increasing fanaticism contributed to provoke the Roman war. Ultimately it degenerated into a body of mere assassins, called Sicarii (Jos. Antiq. xviii. 1, 1 and 6; War ii. 8, 1; 17, 8; iv. 3, 9 seq.).

Zeb'a·di'ah (zĕb'ȧ-dī'ȧ) [Jehovah has given; cf. ȤABAD, ZABBUD, ZABDI, ZABDIEL]. 1. A Benjamite, of the house of Beriah (I Chron. 8:15, 16).

2. A Benjamite, descended from Elpaal (I Chron. 8:17, 18).

3. A son of Jeroham of Gedor. He joined David at Ziklag (I Chron. 12:7).

4. Son of Asahel, who was Joab's brother (I Chron. 27:7).

5. A Korahite Levite, a son of Meshelemiah, in David's reign (I Chron. 26:1, 2).

6. One of the Levites sent forth by Jehoshaphat to teach the Law (II Chron. 17:8).

7. A prince of Judah, who was the chief judicial functionary for civil cases in the court which Jehoshaphat established at Jerusalem (II Chron. 19:11).

8. A descendant of Shephatiah. He was one of those who accompanied Ezra from Babylon (Ezra 8:8).

9. A priest of the house of Immer. He was induced by Ezra to put away his foreign wife (Ezra 10:20).

Ze'bah (zē'bȧ) [slaughter, sacrifice]. One of the 2 kings of Midian pursued and slain by Gideon (Judg. 8:4–28; Ps. 83:11).

Ze·ba'im (zė-bā'ĭm). See POCHERETH-HAZ-ZEBAIM.

Zeb'e·dee (zĕb'ė-dē) [Gr. form of Heb. Zᵉbadyāh, Jehovah has given]. The husband of Salome (q.v.), and father of James and John. Like his sons, he was a fisherman on the Sea of Galilee (Matt. 4:21, 22), and was a man of some substance, for he had hired servants (Mark 1:19, 20).

Ze·bi'dah (zė-bī'dȧ), in A.V. Ze·bu'dah, which follows the kere [given, bestowed]. A daughter of Pedaiah of Rumah, and mother of King Jehoiakim (II Kings 23:36).

Ze·bi'na (zė-bī'nȧ) [Aram., purchased]. A descendant of Nebo. He was induced by Ezra to put away his foreign wife (Ezra 10:43).

Ze·boi'im, I (zė-boi'ĭm) and Ze·bo'im (zė-bō'ĭm) (A.V., Gen. 10:19; Deut. 29:23; Hos. 11:8) [Heb. ṣᵉbōyim, gazelles]. One of the 5 cities of the Plain (Gen. 10:19). Its king was defeated by Chedorlaomer (Gen. 14:2, 8, 10). It was destroyed with the other cities of the Plain by fire from heaven (Gen. 19:17–29; Deut. 29:23; Hos. 11:8).

Ze·bo'im, II (zė-bō'ĭm) [Heb. ṣᵉbō'im, hyenas]. 1. A valley in the territory of Benjamin, between Michmash and the wilderness on the e. (I Sam. 13:16–18). The name is preserved in modern Arab.; Wadi Abu Dibā' (father of hyenas) is a s. tributary of Wadi el-Kelt. North of the latter wadi is a small branch valley called Shakk eḍ-Ḍibā' (ravine of the hyenas).

2. A town occupied by Benjamites after the Captivity (Neh. 11:34). It is evidently to be sought in the hills bordering the plain of Sharon, n. of Lydda.

Ze·bu'dah (zė-bū'dȧ). See ZEBIDAH.

Ze′bul (zē′bŭl) [habitation]. The governor of the city of Shechem in the time of Abimelech, to whom he showed unswerving fidelity (Judg. 9:28, 36–39).

Zeb′u·lon·ite (zĕb′ụ-lŭn-īt). See ZEBULUN-ITE.

Zeb′u·lun (zĕb′ụ-lŭn), in A.V. of N.T. **Zab′·u·lon** [habitation, dwelling]. 1. The 10th son of Jacob, and the 6th by Leah (Gen. 30:19, 20). He went down with his father into Egypt (Ex. 1:3). He had 3 sons: Sered, Elon, and Jahleel (Gen. 46:14). Jacob, in his farewell address, blessing his sons, pictured Zebulun as dwelling at the haven of the sea, being a haven of ships and having his border on Sidon (Gen. 49:13). This picture was realized in its essentials, but not in its details. Zebulun was allotted territory in the vicinity of the sea and enjoyed the markets of the towns on the coast; but it was itself separated from the Sea of Galilee by Naphtali and Issachar, and from the Mediterranean Sea and the city of Sidon by the tribe of Asher.

2. The tribe of which Zebulun was the progenitor. From his 3 sons sprang the great families into which the tribe was divided (Num. 26:26, 27). The prince of the tribe early in the wilderness wanderings was Eliab, son of Helon (chs. 1:9; 10:16), and at a later period Elizaphan, son of Parnach, was a prince (ch. 34:25). The spy from the tribe was Gaddiel, son of Sodi (ch. 13:10). At the 1st census it contained 57,400 fighting men (ch. 1:30, 31); at the 2d, 60,500 (ch. 26:27). It was 1 of the 6 tribes the representatives of which stood on Mount Ebal to pronounce curses on transgressors (Deut. 27:13; cf. Josh. 8:32–35). Moses before his departure, associating the 2 brothers, later sons of Leah, and with the prophecy of Jacob in mind, thus indicated their future history: "Rejoice, Zebulun, in thy going out; and, Issachar, in thy tents. They shall call the peoples unto the mountain; There shall they offer sacrifices of righteousness: For they shall suck the abundance of the seas, and the hidden treasures of the sand" (Deut. 33: 18, 19). In the mountain of Jehovah's inheritance (Ex. 15:17), where he will establish his chosen people, Zebulun and Issachar will bring rich offerings to their bountiful Benefactor. After the Conquest of Canaan, Zebulun was allotted territory in the n. part of the country. It lay n. of Issachar, e. of Asher, and s. and w. of Naphtali (Josh. 19: 27, 34). Its s. boundary ran by Daberath on the w. foot of Mount Tabor, passed Chisloth-tabor, and after skirting the Plain of Esdraelon and then crossing it reached the brook that is before Jokneam (vs. 10–12), probably Wadi el-Milh, a s. tributary of the Kishon. Its e. boundary went to Gath-hepher, which was probably 3 miles n. by e. of Nazareth, and on to Rimmon, 6 miles almost due n. of Nazareth (v. 13, R.V.). At the n.w. corner of the territory was the valley of Iphtah-el (v. 14), probably about 9 miles n. by w. of Nazareth, and leaving the fertile plain of el-Buṭṭauf within the bounds of Zebulun. Since Bethlehem, 7 miles w.n.w. of Nazareth, belonged to Zebulun (v. 15), the w. boundary was doubtless in part Wadi el-Khallaḍĩyeh. The region possessed by Zebulun was fertile. It embraced a part of the mountainous country of lower Galilee and the n.w. corner of the Plain of Esdraelon. The Zebulunites constituted an important part of Barak's force in the fight with Sisera (Judg. 4:6–10; 5:14, 18), and of Gideon's army in the war with Midian (ch. 6:35). According to Deborah, there were in the tribe they that handle the marshal's staff, or the staff of the scribe (Judg. 5:14, R.V. text and

marg.); she means the scribes who gathered and mustered the army (II Kings 25:19). The judge Elon was a member of the tribe, exercised his office, died, and was buried at Aijalon, within its territory (Judg. 12:12). Fifty thousand warriors of the tribe, with skillful and faithful commanders, went with the other tribes to Hebron to make David king (I Chron. 12:33, 40). Ishmaiah was the ruler of the Zebulunites in David's reign (ch. 27:19). The tribe with the rest of Galilee suffered severely during the Assyrian wars, but Isaiah prophesied that it would obtain compensatory blessings in Messianic times (Isa. 9:1, 2; Matt. 4:12–16). Some men of the tribe accepted Hezekiah's invitation to come to Jerusalem for his great passover (II Chron. 30:10, 11, 18). The Prophet Ezekiel assigns a gate for the Zebulunites in the Jerusalem which he describes (Ezek. 48:33), and of the tribe there were sealed in the apocalyptic vision the normal number 12,000 (Rev. 7:8).

Zeb′u·lun·ite (zĕb′ụ-lŭn-īt), in A.V. in Judges **Zeb′u·lon·ite** (zĕb′ụ-lŭn-īt). One belonging to the tribe of Zebulun, or resident within its territory (Num. 26:27; Judg. 12: 11, 12).

Zech′a·ri′ah (zĕk′ạ-rī′ạ), in A.V. 4 times **Zach′a·ri′ah** (II Kings 14:29; 15:8, 11; 18:2) [Jehovah has remembered]. 1. A Benjamite of the family of Jeiel (A.V., Jehiel) of Gibeon (I Chron. 9:35, 37); called in I Chron. 8:31 Zecher (A.V., Zacher). If the traditional vocalization is correct, Zecher is a synonymous name meaning memory. Probably, however, it was an abbreviation of Zechariah, as Ahaz is of Ahaziah, and was pronounced Zachar, meaning "he has remembered."

2. A Levite, family of Kohath, house of Izhar, descended through Ebiasaph. He was the eldest son of Meshelemiah. He was porter of the door of the tent of meeting in David's reign (I Chron. 9:21, 22; 26:2). He was a discreet counselor (ch. 26:14).

3. A Levite of the 2d degree who played a psaltery in the procession that escorted the Ark to Jerusalem, and afterward was permanently employed in the tabernacle which David pitched for the Ark (I Chron. 15:18, 20; 16:5). It is doubtful whether the word doorkeepers (ch. 15:18) is intended to include him.

4. A priest who blew a trumpet when the Ark was brought up from the house of Obededom (I Chron. 15:24).

5. A Levite, family of Kohath, house of Uzziel. He was a son of Isshiah and lived in the reign of David (I Chron. 24:25).

6. A Levite, family of Merari, and 4th son of Hosah. He was one of the doorkeepers in David's reign (I Chron. 26:10, 11).

7. A Manassite of Gilead and father of Iddo, who lived in David's reign (I Chron. 27:21).

8. A Levite, of the sons of Asaph, and hence of the family of Gershom (II Chron. 20:14).

9. One of the princes whom Jehoshaphat sent to teach the people of Judah (II Chron. 17:7).

10. Fourth son of King Jehoshaphat (II Chron. 21:2).

11. Son of Jehoiada, the high priest, and a righteous man like his father. He lived in the reign of King Joash of Judah. The Spirit of God came upon him and he remonstrated with the people on their apostasy from Jehovah which ensued on the death of Jehoiada. At the instance of the king he was stoned to death in the court of the Temple (II Chron. 24:20–22). It is commonly believed that he is referred to by our Lord

when speaking of the righteous blood shed on earth, "from the blood of Abel unto the blood of Zachariah, who perished between the altar and the sanctuary" (Luke 11:51). Zechariah, son of Jehoiada, is the only person mentioned in Scripture as being thus slain; his violent death was memorable and was familiar to succeeding generations; and he is the last of the righteous men wickedly slain, as Abel was the 1st, who are mentioned in the Hebrew Scriptures, Chronicles being the last book in the Hebrew Bible. He is called the son of Barachiah in the parallel passage (Matt. 23:35, in A.V. Barachias), which naturally identifies him with the well-known prophet who lived after the Exile. But this explanatory clause in Matthew is not improbably a gloss which was written on the margin by a reader and afterward crept into the text.

12. A man who had understanding in the vision of God, and gave wise counsel to King Uzziah, which for a time he followed (II Chron. 26:5).

13. A king of Israel and last ruler of the dynasty of Jehu. He came to the throne of Samaria in the 38th year of Azariah, king of Judah, and reigned 6 months. See CHRONOLOGY, IV. He was the son of Jeroboam II, and was murdered at Ibleam by Shallum, who succeeded him as king (II Kings 14:29; 15:10, Greek text of Lucian). By his occupancy of the throne the prediction was fulfilled that the 4th generation of Jehu's sons should sit on the throne (ch. 10:30).

14. A Reubenite chief (I Chron. 5:7).

15. Son of Jeberechiah. He was a witness that Isaiah wrote certain enigmatical words about a year before their meaning was explained by a prophecy (Isa. 8:2).

16. Maternal grandfather of Hezekiah (II Kings 18:1, 2).

17. A Levite descended from Asaph. He took part in the cleansing of the Temple during the reign of Hezekiah (II Chron. 29:13).

18. A Kohathite Levite, overseer of the workmen employed to repair the Temple in Josiah's reign (II Chron. 34:12).

19. A ruler of the house of God in Josiah's reign and doubtless a priest (II Chron. 35:8).

20. A man of Judah, family of Shelah (Neh. 11:5).

21. A man of Judah, family of Perez (Neh. 11:4).

22. A priest descended from Pashhur of the house of Malchijah (Neh. 11:12).

23. A descendant of Parosh. He returned from Babylon with a party along with Ezra (Ezra 8:3).

24. A son of Bebai who returned with Ezra (Ezra 8:11).

25. One of the chief men whom Ezra sent to secure Levites and Nethinim to accompany the returning exiles (Ezra 8:16).

26. One of the men, probably priests, who stood beside Ezra at the public reading of the Law (Neh. 8:4).

27. A son of Elam, induced by Ezra to put away his foreign wife (Ezra 10:26).

28. A Levite, son of Jonathan, and a descendant of Asaph. He led a division of Levitical musicians at the dedication of the rebuilt wall of Jerusalem (Neh. 12:35, 36).

29. A priest who blew a trumpet at the dedication of the rebuilt wall of Jerusalem (Neh. 12:41).

30. A priest, head of the father's house of Iddo in the days of the high priest Joiakim (Neh. 12:16). See the following.

31. A prophet, son of Berechiah, and grandson of Iddo (Zech. 1:1). His first recorded prophecy was delivered in the 2d year of Darius Hystaspis, 520 B.C. (ibid.; Ezra 4:24; 5:1). He was a contemporary of

Zerubbabel the governor, Jeshua (Joshua) the high priest, and Haggai the prophet (Zech. 3:1; 4:6; 6:11; Ezra 5:1, 2), and united with Haggai in exhorting the leaders of the Jewish colony to resume work on the house of God. It scarcely admits of question that he was born in Babylonia, for the exiles had been back in Palestine 18 years only and Zechariah hardly began to prophesy before he was 18. Not improbably Zechariah belonged to the tribe of Levi and, like Jeremiah and Ezekiel, was a priest as well as a prophet; for, according to Nehemiah (Neh. 12:1, 4, 7) Iddo was head of a priestly family and one who returned from Babylonia with Zerubbabel; and a descendant of his, Zechariah by name, was head of the priestly house of Iddo during the high priesthood of Joiakim, son of Jeshua (vs. 10, 12, 16). It is true that the lineage which is involved in Nehemiah's statements may be quite distinct from the genealogy of the prophet, although it contains the same names in the same order, but the theory which identifies the 2 has not a little confirmation: (1) Since Iddo had attained to the headship of a priestly family, he is rightly judged to have been an elderly man in the year of the Return, 538 B.C. His descendant, Zechariah, attained to the same position in the next generation, which would naturally involve his being of such an age in 520 B.C. that he could be called a young man. In fact the Prophet Zechariah is referred to by an angel as a young man in the year 520 B.C. (Zech. 2:4). (2) Assuming that the prophet's father Berechiah was the son of the priest Iddo and died prior to 520, without attaining to the headship of the family, then the Prophet Zechariah was left next in the line of succession, and this would lead Ezra to call him the son of Iddo, naming him both as descendant and successor of Iddo. But even if Berechiah were alive, his name might be omitted; for it was only necessary to name the father's house to which a man belonged in order to locate him among the tribes and families of Israel. The assumption of Berechiah's death would also account for the fact that in the generation after the Return, Zechariah was head of the father's house. (3) The theory that the Prophet Zechariah was a priest accounts for his familiarity with priestly functions and ideas (chs. 3; 4).

Another view is that favored by Kimchi. According to him, the term prophet in ch. 1:1, 7 refers to Iddo (for position of the title, cf. Ezra 7:5), and the latter is the seer who prophesied in the reign of Rehoboam (II Chron. 12:15; 13:22). The theory is improbable, but it is not to be rejected because 4 centuries intervened between the seer Iddo and the Prophet Zechariah.

The Book of Zechariah is the 11th of the Minor Prophets. It may be divided as follows:

I. *Introduction to the book* and a series of 8 visions. The introduction (ch. 1:1–6) strikes the keynote, not to these visions only, but to the whole book. Learn the lesson of the past: "Return unto me . . . and I will return unto you." Vision 1: Jehovah's horsemen (vs. 7–17), fleet, tireless messengers. By this picture it is shown that God is watching the events of earth; there is no sign of relief for God's people or of the punishment of their oppressors; the nations are at rest. Yet God is jealous for Zion and sore displeased with its oppressors; therefore, he is returned to Jerusalem with mercies; his house and his city shall be built; the land shall greatly prosper. The first vision is introductory to the 7 that follow. Vision 2: the 4 horns and the 4 smiths (vs. 18–21). The vision means that for each of the horns, i.e., nations that scattered Judah, destruction is appointed. Vision 3: the man with a measuring line (ch. 2). The comfortable message of the 1st vision is unfolded, namely, the rebuilding of the city. The idea is expanded, however. Jerusalem shall not be measured, as cities usually are, by the extent of its walls; for, enjoying unbounded prosperity, it shall spread abroad without walls. It will not be insecure, however; Jehovah will be a wall of fire about it. Vision 4: Joshua, the high priest, and Satan (ch. 3). The priesthood, although human and defiled, a brand being consumed in the fire of God's wrath, is by grace plucked forth, cleansed, and, on condition of obedience, promised continuance. The restored priesthood is a pledge of the approach of the Messianic Kingdom; the Messiah is called "my servant the Branch." Vision 5: the golden candlestick and the 2 olive trees (ch. 4). It seems as if the light of the Church, burning feebly after the Exile, must needs go out; but it is not so, for God has provided an abundant, unfailing, self-furnishing supply of oil. Vision 6: the flying roll (ch. 5:1–4). God has pronounced a curse for the destruction of wickedness. Vision 7: the departing ephah (vs. 5–11). This is the sequel of the 6th vision. Wickedness, personified as a woman in an ephah, is removed from the land. Vision 8: the 4 chariots issuing from the presence of the Lord of all the earth (ch. 6:1–8). The 4 chariots are declared to represent the 4 winds, which commonly denote the unseen power of God; and the vision is a promise that the entire plan outlined in the preceding series will be executed by the Lord of all the earth.

II. *Symbolic action:* crowning of the high priest (ch. 6:9–15). This procedure is expressly declared to belong to the future and to relate to the well-known branch who was the expected king of David's line.

III. *Deputation from Beth-el* to inquire whether the fasts shall still be kept, now that the disasters which they commemorated have been in part retrieved, and the prophet's 4 answers (chs. 7; 8): 1. Fasts terminate on the faster; they do not affect God; obedience is the 1 thing God requires (ch. 7:4–7). 2. Justice and truth are the will of God, which is to be obeyed. The desolation of the land and dispersion of the people were not a calamity to be bewailed; they were a punishment for disobedience and intended to work reform (vs. 8–14). 3. God returns to Zion in jealousy, and will secure truth and holiness (ch. 8:1–17). 4. The fasts will become festivals (vs. 18–23).

IV. *Burdens* naturally follow the visions which revealed God's purpose to destroy the oppressors of Judah and bring many nations into the Kingdom. Burden 1: Jehovah's overthrow of the enemies of God's Kingdom. Punishments are impending which shall bring the surrounding nations low. A remnant of Philistia, however, shall be incorporated in God's Kingdom; and Jerusalem shall be safe amid the widespread desolation, for God shall encamp about Judah and Judah's king shall come (ch. 9). Episode: exhortation to look to the Lord for promised blessings, and not to idols and soothsayers, who only cause the flock to err (ch. 10:1, 2). Resumption of the prophecy. The Lord, however, as already said, has visited his flock, and because of his wrath will make it as his goodly horse in battle, free Judah from all oppressors, gather both Judah and Ephraim, and make Ephraim joyful in his former habitation (vs. 3–12). These promised blessings, however, will not be enjoyed for some time to come. "Desolation to the land!" is the prophet's cry (ch. 11: 1–3). The reason for this desolation is explained by the parable of the rejected shep-

herd (vs. 4–17): because of the continued rejection of God's righteous government, the covenant with the nations is broken, and Israel is open to desolation; because of the same sin, the unity of Judah and Ephraim remains unaccomplished, and weakness, discord, and desolation result. Burden 2: the conflict and final triumph of the Kingdom of God. The nations of the earth are arrayed against Jerusalem and Judah, which at the time of the writer were coextensive with the visible Church of Jehovah; but Jehovah makes Jerusalem "a cup of reeling" and a burdensome stone to the nations, smiting the enemy with madness, and revealing the fact that the citizens of Zion are strong in the Lord (ch. 12:1–8). The preparation of Jerusalem (chs. 12:9 to 14:5): God will prepare Jerusalem, 1st, by gracious spiritual change wrought by himself (chs. 12:10 to 13:6); 2d, by purifying chastisement (chs. 13:7 to 14: 5a). The final triumph (vs. 5b–21). The Lord shall come; it shall be a time of darkness and judgment, both for the Church and the nations; but at a time appointed of God, at eventide there shall be light. The Church shall flourish, and a remnant of the nations shall go up from year to year to worship Jehovah, the king. Then shall the idea of the Kingdom of God be realized, the Church shall be holy.

The first to hint that The Book of Zechariah did not proceed in its entirety from the pen of the prophet whose name it bears was Joseph Mede, of Christ Church College, Cambridge, in 1653. He argued that chs. 9 to 11 were written by Jeremiah, because Matthew in quoting Zech. 11:13 refers it to Jeremiah (Matt. 27:9). This argument no longer has weight with critics. Some would say that the mention of Jeremiah is an error by Matthew, while others believe that it is probably an early corruption of Matthew's text. It has even been suggested that since the Hebrews in their arrangement of the Scriptures at one time began the latter prophets with Jeremiah, observing the sequence Jeremiah, Ezekiel, Isaiah, instead of the present order, Isaiah, Jeremiah, Ezekiel (see CANON, ISAIAH), this prophetic section was sometimes referred to as Jeremiah, just as Christ apparently refers to the Hagiographa by the name of the 1st book in that collection, The Psalms (Luke 24:44). In somewhat similar fashion we often refer to The Psalms and The Proverbs as the Psalms of David and the Proverbs of Solomon, although David was not the sole author of The Psalms nor Solomon of The Proverbs. Since Mede's day many critics have held that in the present Book of Zechariah there are the writings of 2, 3, or more prophets. The principal views are: 1. Chapters 9 to 11 were written shortly before the fall of Samaria in 722 (721) B.C., and chs. 12 to 14 shortly before the destruction of Jerusalem in 586 B.C. 2. Chapters 9 to 14 were written in the late Persian period more than a century and a half after the death of Zechariah, or in the Maccabaean period. 3. Chapters 9 to 14, as well as chs. 1 to 8, proceeded from Zechariah. The debate, it will be seen, does not affect the first 8 chapters, but concerns only chs. 9 to 14. The debated section contains the 2 burdens. What then is the date of these burdens? In regard to the 1st burden, when it was written the house of the Lord was standing (chs. 9:15; 11:13); but from this fact no argument as to the date of the burden can be drawn, for Solomon's Temple was standing down to the Exile, and the new Temple, built after the Return, was in use after the year 515 B.C. The reference in ch. 10:10, 11 has been cited to prove that Egypt and Assyria were great powers at the time that this prophecy was delivered, and it was delivered after Israel had been carried captive (ch. 10:6), hence after the capture of Samaria but before the fall of Nineveh, c. 612 B.C. But a prophet after the Exile, as well as a prophet of an earlier date, could foretell that the Israelites would be restored to the lands from which they had been carried, namely, from Egypt and Assyria; and although Assyria had succumbed to a later world empire, he could still say that the pride of Assyria, the power by which the Israelites were still kept in captivity, should be brought down; or Assyria may be used of a geographical region, including Babylonia, just as the term is employed by Ezra (Ezra 6:22), although the region was then under the government of Persia. Accordingly, the 1st burden may have been delivered either before the fall of Nineveh, while Assyria was still a power, or else after the Exile, when the Assyrian empire had given place to other empires, and, since the Temple is standing, after the 6th year of Darius, king of Persia. Another datum which contributes to the solution of this question is obtained from the statement that God will break the brotherhood between Judah and Israel (Zech. 11:14). The brotherhood existed until the reign of Rehoboam, when it was broken by the refusal of the Northern tribes to render further allegiance to the throne of David. It might also be said to have been broken when Samaria fell, and the Northern tribes were scattered. The brotherhood existed once more after the Babylonian Exile. Now this burden was pronounced after the fall of Samaria and the captivity of Ephraim (ch. 10:6); and therefore it properly dates from the time after the Exile, when the current conception was that Ephraim and Judah were reunited in the brotherhood. In point of fact they were reunited: many members of the 10 tribes had joined themselves to Judah; and the existing nation was universally regarded as the representative of the 12 tribes, and in Ezra's day accordingly 12 goats were offered as a sin offering at the dedication of the Temple, and a 2d sin offering of 12 bullocks was made for all Israel (Ezra 6:17; 8:35; cf. Matt. 19:28; Luke 2:36; Acts 4:36; 26:7; Phil. 3:5). It is true that the prophet frequently uses the old terms Judah and Ephraim, and this fact has been urged to prove that the prophecy was uttered long before the time of Zechariah, but many people living after the Exile used the old terms. Zechariah himself in the first 8 chapters employs them. He addresses the "house of Judah and house of Israel" (Zech. 8:13). It is to this postexilic period accordingly that the references to the brotherhood of Ephraim and Judah point. There is a further mark. It is declared that God will raise up Judah against the distant sons of Javan, or the Greeks (ch. 9:13). It will be observed that the Greeks are chosen for 2 reasons: 1. Because the prophet descries the conflict of the Church with the most distant nations of the world. Javan and the isles were at this time within the geographical horizon of the Hebrews, and they were used as types of the remotest heathen nations (Gen. 10:4, 5; Isa. 41:5; 59:18; 66:19; Ezek. 27:13). 2. The novel feature here is that Javan looms up as the world power of heathenism. The earliest date when the coming power of Greece became evident to observers in the Persian Empire was during the years from 500 to 479 B.C., and the coming greatness of Greece as the successful antagonist of Persia was clearly evident. Greece had successfully checked the advance of Persian arms, and the Grecian cities of Asia Minor were in open revolt against their Persian lords during the years 500 to 495 B.C.; the Persians were defeated at Marathon in 490 and, after their victory

at Thermopylae, were crushingly defeated by the Greeks at Salamis, 480, Plataea and Mycale, 479. Zechariah, there is reason to believe on considerable and varied evidence, was a young man, say 20 or 25, when in 520 B.C. he exhorted Zerubbabel to the work of rebuilding the Temple, and consequently these stirring events which revealed the unsuspected greatness of Greece and opened the prospect that it would successfully intermeddle in Oriental affairs occurred during the years which were Zechariah's prime of life.

The 2d burden, chs. 12 to 14, is also shown by its contents to belong to the postexilic period. The writer refers to the terror of the people when the earthquake in the days of Uzziah occurred. He refers to it as an event living vividly in the consciousness of the people. It was vivid to them either because of recent occurrence or because it had made a lasting impression on their minds. It certainly had made this lasting impression; it is treated as an epoch by the people of the generation in which it occurred (Amos 1:1), and in the 1st century of the Christian era it was still remembered as a solemn and striking event (Jos. Antiq. ix. 10, 4). There is another historical mark in this 2d burden, the reference to the mourning of Hadadrimmon in the valley of Megiddon (Zech. 12:11). The only natural reference here is to the killing of Josiah, who opposed Necho at Megiddo, and was mortally wounded there, and soon died; his death was mourned by the singing men and singing women, and a lamentation was composed by the Prophet Jeremiah. Accordingly the 2d burden was delivered not earlier than the eve of the Exile.

Not only do the historical references in the 2 burdens point to late times, but the literary characteristics of these burdens proclaim them to have proceeded from the same source as the first 8 chapters. This is strenuously denied by certain critics. It is urged that a difference of style is discernible between the burdens and the visions. This is true, but the style of an author may differ at various periods of his literary career, especially when he essays different forms of literature. Zechariah's style naturally underwent change during a period of 30 or 40 years and differed when he depicted visions and symbolic actions from the style in which he set forth solemn warnings. Still, in the parable or the symbolic representation of the good shepherd, there are traces of the same literary hand as that which portrayed the visions and the crowning of the high priest. And the more subtle marks of the same hand are seen in the unique usage of certain words and expressions which characterize the first 8 chapters in common with the last 6. These reasons may favor the view that Zechariah was the author of the entire book, and that his mature life was passed between the years 520 and 479 B.C.

On the other hand, the date of the 2d part of The Book of Zechariah (chs. 9 to 14) has caused many problems. Critics generally, however, hold the view that these chapters are not the work of Zechariah, mainly on account of the obscure historical allusions and apocalyptic eschatology of this part of the book which are in sharp contrast with the clear historical background of chs. 1 to 8. The 2d part of the book is divided into 2 sections: chs. 9 to 11, to which should be joined ch. 13:7-9 as a conclusion to ch. 11, and chs. 12 to 14 (minus ch. 13:7-9). It should furthermore be noted that the expression "the burden of the word of Jehovah" stands at the head of ch. 9 and of ch. 12. Accordingly some critics speak of the Deutero-Zechariah and the Trito-Zechariah, to whom these sections are respectively assigned. The same words are found in the heading of The Book of Malachi. Some scholars have consequently assumed that the editor of the Twelve Minor Prophets appended to the original book of Zechariah 3 anonymous works: Deutero-Zechariah, Trito-Zechariah, and Malachi. This view assumes that the word Malachi is not a proper name, but means simply "my messenger" (Mal. 3:1).

Chapters 9 to 14 of Zechariah are divided into sections. The 1st, chs. 9 to 11 plus ch. 13:7–9, consists of 3 prophetic poems (chs. 9:1–10; 9:11 to 10:2; 10:3 to 11:3) and a description of a symbolic action containing some poetic oracles (chs. 11:4–17; 13:7–9). The 2d section (chs. 12:1 to 13:6; 14) consists of 2 eschatological oracles dealing with the onslaught of the heathen on Jerusalem and the Messianic Age inaugurated after their destruction.

The date of chs. 9 to 14 is not easily settled. In chs. 1 to 8 the lifetime of Zechariah and the objects of his interest (the Temple and the affairs of the restored community) are very manifest, but the circumstances and interests of chs. 9 to 14 are very different. It is difficult to determine the date of these latter chapters, since the evidence points in several directions. In favor of a pre-exilic date have been cited references to the nations mentioned in ch. 9:1–7, to the Northern Kingdom (chs. 9:10; 11:14), and to Assyria and Egypt (ch. 10:10, 11). Accordingly a date toward the end of the reign of Jeroboam II has been favored. Chapter 10 has been placed somewhat later, since reference to the deportation of some of the N. tribes in 734 B.C. may be detected, while ch. 11:1–3 has been dated earlier as predicting the invasion of Tiglath-pileser III. It has accordingly been supposed that the author was a contemporary of Isaiah. On the other hand, certain passages have been interpreted as implying a postexilic date (chs. 9:11, 12; 10:6–9). In ch. 9:13 the Greeks (Javan) are mentioned not as an unimportant people as they would be in the 8th century or c. 520 B.C., but as a world power. Such a position was attained only after Alexander's victory at Issus (333 B.C.). Accordingly some critics date chs. 9 to 11 not earlier than 333 B.C. Stade prefers c. 280 B.C. As regards chs. 12 to 14, critics observe that they were written after the fall of the Northern Kingdom in 722 (721) B.C. or after the death of Josiah, but some think that they were written before the destruction of Jerusalem in 586 B.C. However, for these chapters also most critics favor a postexilic date.

The historical events behind the allegory of the shepherds (chs. 11:4–17; 13:7–9) are not clear to the critics; attempts to fix them either in the decline and fall of the Northern Kingdom or at the beginning of the Maccabaean revolt are not convincing. Pfeiffer writes (1941): "In view of the fact that no part of the book seems to be earlier than the time of Alexander the Great, it seems likely that the political disturbances, darkly alluded to in this allegory and in ch. 12:10, belong to the third century, during which the history of the Jews is for us a total blank; 11:4–17 is unquestionably influenced by Ezek. 34; 37: 16–28." He concludes that in dating Zech., chs. 9 to 14, in the 3d century justice is done to the general apocalyptic character of these oracles and to numerous clues of postexilic origin. In this connection there may be noted the reference to ritual observances (chs. 9: 11; 14:16–21), allusions to the Jews scattered among the nations (chs. 9:11, 12; 10:8–11), the decay of the prophetic movement (ch. 13:2–6), and the obvious imitation of parts of Ezekiel, Joel, and Deutero-Isaiah (cf. Zech. 12:1 with Isa. 42:5; 44:24). Jesus, the son of Sirach, knew the book of the Twelve

Prophets (Ecclus. 49:10). If the "Twelve" were complete in his day, it is improbable that additions were made to a canonical book after 200 B.C.

Ze'cher (zē'kẽr). See ZECHARIAH 1.

Ze'dad (zē'dăd). A place, probably a tower, on the n. boundary line of Palestine (Num. 34:8; Ezek. 47:15); identified with Ṣadad, s.e. of Ḥoms on the way from Riblah to Palmyra.

Zed'e·ki'ah (zĕd'ê-kī'á), in A.V. once **Zid-ki'jah** (Neh. 10:1) [Jehovah is righteousness, or righteousness of Jehovah]. 1. A son of Chenaanah. Having joined with other false prophets in encouraging Ahab to attempt the capture of Ramoth-gilead, and having predicted that Ahab would defeat the Syrians, he was so excited when Micaiah, a prophet of Jehovah, made a contrary prediction, that he struck the man of God upon the cheek, accompanying the blow with words of insult. Micaiah told him that he would have cause to acknowledge his error (I Kings 22:11–25).

2. A lying and immoral prophet, the son of Maaseiah. Jeremiah predicted that Nebuchadnezzar would roast him in the fire (Jer. 29: 21–23).

3. A son of Hananiah. He was a prince of Judah in the reign of Jehoiakim (Jer. 36:12).

4. The name given by Nebuchadnezzar to Mattaniah, one of Josiah's sons, on appointing him vassal-king of Judah in place of his nephew, Jehoiachin (II Kings 24:17; I Chron. 3:15). In II Chron. 36:9, 10 he is called Jehoiachin's brother, i.e., kinsman of the same ancestry; see BROTHER. He was the younger of Josiah's 2 sons by Hamutal (cf. II Kings 23:31 with ch. 24:18). He was 21 years old when he ascended the throne, and reigned 11 years, from c. 597 to 586 B.C. Neither he nor his people gave heed to the word of the Lord which was spoken by Jeremiah (II Chron. 36:12; Jer. 37:1, 2). The Temple was polluted with idolatry (II Chron. 36:14), and justice was not executed (Jer. 21:11, 12). A strong party in the state, assisted by false prophets, urged the king to throw off the foreign yoke (ch. 27:12–22). At the beginning of Zedekiah's reign (v. 1, R.V. marg.) messengers from Edom, Moab, Ammon, Tyre, and Sidon came to him in Jerusalem to plan a united revolt from the king of Babylon; but Jeremiah was divinely instructed to condemn the purpose (vs. 2–11). Zedekiah sent an embassy to Nebuchadnezzar, probably to assure the great king of his fidelity (ch. 29:3), and in his 4th year he himself visited Babylon (ch. 51:59). Ultimately he was rash enough to rebel. On the 10th day of the 10th month, in the 9th year of Zedekiah's reign, the Babylonian monarch took post against Jerusalem, and began to erect forts around the city. It was too strong to be taken by assault; and the Babylonians held it in siege. The advance of the Egyptians compelled the Babylonians to withdraw for a time (Jer. 37:5), but they soon returned. By the 9th day of the 4th month, in the 11th year of Zedekiah's reign, the food in the beleagured capital was exhausted. That night Zedekiah, with all the men of war, secretly quitted the stronghold and, passing as noiselessly as possible between the Babylonian forts, fled in an e. direction toward the Jordan. On learning that the king was gone, the Babylonian army pursued and overtook him in the plain of Jericho. He was brought a prisoner to Nebuchadnezzar, who had retired to Riblah, a little n. of Palestine. There, after he had been tried and condemned, his sons were put to death in his presence, and his own eyes put out; after which he was bound in fetters, carried to Babylon (II Kings 24:17–20; 25:1–7; II Chron. 36:11–21; Jer. 39:1–14), and put in

prison till the day of his death (Jer. 52:11). Jeremiah prophesied during the whole of Zedekiah's reign.

5. A son of Jeconiah (I Chron. 3:16); but some expositors assume that "son" is used here in the sense of successor.

6. A high official who set his seal to the covenant immediately after Nehemiah the governor (Neh. 10:1).

Ze'eb (zē'ĕb) [wolf]. A Midianite prince captured and put to death by Gideon. He was slain at a wine press, which was afterward called that of Zeeb (Judg. 7:25). See OREB.

Ze'la (zē'là), in A.V. **Ze'lah** (zē'là), and so once in R.V. erroneously (Josh. 18:28) [rib, side]. A town allotted to Benjamin (Josh. 18:28). It contained the sepulcher of Kish; and thither the bones of Saul and Jonathan were carried from Jabesh in Gilead and buried (II Sam. 21:14). Khirbet Ṣalaḥ, n.w of Jerusalem, has been suggested as a reasonable identification.

Ze'lek (zē'lĕk) [a cleft]. An Ammonite, one of David's mighty men (II Sam. 23:37; I Chron. 11:39).

Ze·lo'phe·had (zē-lō'fē-hăd) [shadow of the fear, i.e., protection against fear]. A Manassite, family of Machir, subfamily of Gilead, house of Hepher. He had no sons, but 5 daughters (Num. 26:33). This condition of affairs gave occasion for enacting the law that if a man die and leave no son the inheritance should pass to his daughter (ch. 27:1-8). The law was soon afterward developed by the addition of the provision that the daughter must marry within her father's tribe in order that no part of the tribal possession be transferred to another tribe (ch. 36:1-12). The inheritance of the family was e. of the Jordan (Josh. 17:1-6).

Ze·lo'tes (zē-lō'tēz). See ZEALOT.

Zel'zah (zĕl'zà). A frontier town of Benjamin, near Rachel's sepulcher (I Sam. 10:2).

Zem'a·ra·im (zĕm'à-rā'ĭm). 1. A town of Benjamin (Josh. 18:22), often identified with Khirbet es-Samrah about 3 miles w. of the river Jordan, and 4 n. of Jericho. A more likely conjecture places it at Rās ez-Zeimara in the mountain between eṭ-Ṭaiyibeh and Rammūn.

2. A mountain in the hill country of Ephraim, on which Abijah, king of Judah, stood to address the 10 tribes before encountering them in battle (II Chron. 13:4). Perhaps it was s. of Beth-el (v. 19). Probably it lay not far from the city of Zemaraim, from which its name apparently was derived.

Zem'a·rite (zĕm'à-rīt). A Canaanite tribe (Gen. 10:18; I Chron. 1:16). It is enumerated between the Arvadite and Hamathite, and inhabited Ṣumur, Ṣimirra (Gr. Simyra), modern Sumra, on the coast between Arvad and Tripolis.

Ze·mi'rah (zē-mī'rà), in A.V. **Ze·mi'ra** (zē-mī'rà) [cf. S. Arab. Zamr; Arab. zamūr, handsome and beardless young man, and zamīr, small in stature]. A Benjamite, family of Becher (I Chron. 7:8).

Ze'nan (zē'năn) [point or, perhaps, a place of flocks]. A town in or w. of the lowland of Judah (Josh. 15:37). Probably the same as Zaanan (Micah 1:11), and to be identified with 'Arāḳ el-Kharba.

Ze'nas (zē'năs) [Gr., contraction of Zēnodoros, gift of Zeus]. A lawyer, journeying in Crete with Apollos, whom Titus was enjoined by Paul to set forward on their journey (Titus 3:13).

Zeph·a·ni'ah (zĕf'à-nī'à) [Jehovah has hidden, treasured]. 1. A Levite of the family of

Kohath and house of Izhar (I Chron. 6:36-38).

2. A priest, the son of Maaseiah. He was one of those who carried messages between Zedekiah and Jeremiah (Jer. 21:1; 37:3). A certain false prophet who dwelt in Babylon, Shemaiah by name, having sent him letters directing him to punish Jeremiah for his discouraging predictions, he showed the missive to the prophet (ch. 29:24-32). He had the oversight of the Temple, and was 2d priest under the chief priest Seraiah. After the capture of Jerusalem by the Babylonians, Zephaniah was put to death at Riblah (II Kings 25:18-21; Jer. 52:24-27).

3. A man whose son Josiah lived in the days of Zerubbabel and the Prophet Zechariah (Zech. 6:10, 14).

4. A prophet, whose descent is traced through 4 degrees to Hezekiah (Zeph. 1:1; A.V. Hizkiah). This ancestor is probably the king, from the fact that so remote a descent is traced and because the time suits. The prophet himself lived and labored in the reign of Josiah (ibid.).

The Book of Zephaniah is the 9th among the Minor Prophets. The date given in its title (ch. 1:1) is confirmed by the omission of Gath in the enumeration of Philistine cities (ch. 2:4), by Nineveh's being still in existence (v. 13), and by the absence of all allusion to the Chaldeans. The basis of the prophecy is the great doctrine of God's universal judgment. (1) A universal judgment, like the Deluge in destructiveness (ch. 1:2, 3). Idolatry will be overthrown in Jerusalem (vs. 4-6), and the sinners of Judah visited with judgment, as if Jehovah conducted a great sacrifice (vs. 7-13); and it will be a day of wrath upon men because of their wickedness (vs. 14-18). At the approach of the Scythian hordes the prophet proclaims the imminent coming of the Day of the Lord (cf. Lat. hymn Dies irae, dies illa). (2) A call to repentance as the only possible means of escape (ch. 2:1, 2), especially a summons to the humble and Godfearing to seek Jehovah and perhaps obtain deliverance (v. 3); enforced by the certainty that God will punish other nations for their wickedness (vs. 4-15), and Jerusalem shall not escape, for she does not repent and the Lord in the midst of her is righteous (ch. 3:1-8). (3) The blessed result of the judgment. The nations shall turn to the Lord (vs. 9, 10), the remnant of Israel shall trust in the Lord and be holy (vs. 11-13), and the Lord shall reign gloriously and beneficently as king in the midst of his people (vs. 14-18), who shall be gathered from captivity and be "a praise" in the earth (vs. 19, 20).

It seems that the prophecy was delivered before the religious reformation inaugurated by Josiah in 621 B.C. (II Kings 22:3; II Chron. 34:8 to 35:19). Zephaniah was a contemporary of Habakkuk and prophesied a few years before him; his prophecies may be dated in the time of the Scythian invasion along the Mediterranean coast (between 630 and 624 B.C.).

Ze'phath (zē'făth) [watchtower]. A Canaanite town in the s. country toward the border of Edom, assigned to the tribe of Simeon. The Simeonites, assisted by their brethren of Judah, captured the place and changed its name to Hormah (Judg. 1:17); see HORMAH.

Zeph'a·thah (zĕf'à-thà) [watchtower]. A valley near Mareshah, in the tribe of Judah (II Chron. 14:10). Conder proposes Wadi Safiyeh, which, commencing about a mile n.e. of Mareshah, near Beit Jibrīn, runs for a short distance in that direction.

Ze'phi (zē'fī) and **Ze'pho** (zē'fō) [watch]. A son of Eliphaz, and grandson of Esau. He

founded a tribe (Gen. 36:11, 15; I Chron. 1:
36). The difference in spelling can be explained as a confusion of *waw* (w) and
yodh (y).

Ze′phon (zē′fŏn) [watching, expectation].
A son of Gad, and founder of a tribal family
(Num. 26:15). Called in Gen. 46:16 Ziphion.

Zer (zûr). A fortified city of Naphtali
(Josh. 19:35).

Ze′rah (zē′rá), in A.V. twice **Za′rah** (Gen.
38:30; 46:12); once **Za′ra** (Matt. 1:3) [dawning, shining]. 1. A duke of Edom descended
from Esau and also from Ishmael (Gen. 36:3,
4, 13, 17; I Chron. 1:37, and perhaps 44).

2. One of twins borne to Judah by Tamar,
and the founder of a tribal family (Num.
26:20; Josh. 7:1, 17).

3. A son of Simeon, and founder of a tribal
family (Num. 26:13). He is called in Gen.
46:10; Ex. 6:15 Zohar.

4. A Levite, of the family of Gershom (I
Chron. 6:21, 41).

5. An Ethiopian who led a vast army to
attack King Asa, but was defeated with great
slaughter in a battle at Mareshah (II Chron.
14:8-15). See PHARAOH 2.

Zer′a·hi′ah (zĕr′á-hī′á) [the Lord is risen
(cf. Isa. 60:1, 2)]. 1. A priest, son of Uzzi,
and a descendant of Phinehas (I Chron. 6:6,
51; Ezra 7:4).

2. One of the children of Pahath-moab
(Ezra 8:4).

Ze′ra·hite (zē′rá-hīt), in A.V. **Zar′hite.**
A person belonging to the family of Zerah.
There was a family of this name in the tribe
of Simeon and another in Judah (Num. 26:
13, 20; Josh. 7:17; cf. Josh. 7:1; I Chron.
27:11, 13).

Ze′red (zē′rĕd), in A.V. once **Za′red** (Num.
21:12). A brook and valley, which the Israelites crossed 38 years after being turned back
into the wilderness at Kadesh-barnea, and
which constituted the farthest limit of the
wanderings in the wilderness (Num. 21:12;
Deut. 2:13, 14). It was s. of the Arnon and
is probably to be identified with Wadi el-
Ḥesā (about 14 miles s. of Wadi el-Kerak),
an affluent of the Dead Sea. By some it has
been identified with Wadi es-Sulṭāni, a s.e.
affluent of a tributary of the Arnon.

Zer′e·dah (zĕr′ē-dá), in A.V. **Zer′e·da** (zĕr′-
ē-dá), **Zer′e·da′thah** (zĕr′ē-dā′thá) [cf. Arab.
ṣard, cold]. A village whence came Nebat, an
Ephraimite, the father of Jeroboam, and apparently also Jeroboam himself (I Kings 11:
26); but the village itself may have been elsewhere than in the territory of Ephraim (cf.
Josh. 16:9; 17:9). The exact equivalent of
the name is found in ′Ain Ṣeredah, the fountain of Khirbet Balāṭah, in Mount Ephraim,
15 miles s.w. of Shechem, at a bend of Wadi
Deir Ballūṭ (Albright). The LXX and Lucian,
however, invariably call the city and home of
Jeroboam Sareira, i.e., Zererah (I Kings, ch.
11, v. 26 LXX, v. 24 Luc.), and locate it in
Mount Ephraim (ch. 11, v. 43 LXX, v. 42
Luc.; ch. 12, v. 24b LXX, vs. 28, 29 Luc.; v.
24f LXX, v. 39 Luc.); perhaps confusing it
with Tirzah in ch. 14, v. 17 (Heb. and LXX,
and vs. 7, 10, 13 Luc.).

Zer′e·rah (zĕr′ē-rá), in A.V. **Zer′e·rath** (zĕr′-
ē-răth). A town in the Jordan Valley (Judg.
7:22, in the form *Ṣerērāthāh*), apparently the
same as Zarethan (I Kings 4:12), and, if so,
indicative that 2 r′s are blended in Zarethan
(q.v.).

Ze′resh (zē′rĕsh) [from the Avestan root
zarsh may be derived these senses: the ruffled
one, the one with dishevelled hair, the joyful
or elated one]. The wife of Haman (Esth.
5:10; 6:13).

Ze′reth (zē′rĕth) [perhaps, splendor]. A
son of Ashhur, of the tribe of Judah, by his
wife Helah (I Chron. 4:5-7).

Ze′reth-sha′har (zē′rĕth-shā′här), in A.V.
Za′reth-sha′har (zā′rĕth-shā′här) [brightness
of the dawn]. A town of Reuben, on a mountain which overlooks a valley, doubtless that
of the Dead Sea (Josh. 13:19). There has
been found no satisfactory identification. In
the neighborhood of Machaerus are hot
springs known as Ḥammat eṣ-Ṣara, which
may have an echo of this name.

Ze′ri (zē′rī). A son of Jeduthun (I Chron.
25:3). In v. 11 he is called Izri; the initial
yodh (y) may have been lost in course of
transcription.

Ze′ror (zē′rôr) [bundle or, perhaps, pebble].
A Benjamite, an ancestor of King Saul (I
Sam. 9:1).

Ze·ru′ah (zē-rōō′á) [smitten, leprous]. The
widowed mother of Jeroboam I (I Kings 11:
26).

Ze·rub′ba·bel (zē-rŭb′á-bĕl), in A.V. of N.T.
Zo·rob′a·bel [Heb. from Akkad. *zēru Bābili*,
seed of Babylon]. A son of Pedaiah, and heir
to the throne of Judah (I Chron. 3:17-19).
But he is constantly called the son of Shealtiel, who was the brother of Pedaiah, quite
improbably his son (Ezra 3:2, 8; Neh. 12:1;
Hag. 1:1, 12, 14; 2:2, 23; Matt. 1:12, 13;
Luke 3:27). Shealtiel doubtless died childless; and either his nephew was his legal heir,
and hence called his son (Ex. 2:10), or else
Pedaiah married his widow, in which case the
1st child would be considered that of the deceased brother (Deut. 25:5-10; etc.). When
Cyrus, after the conquest of Babylon, adopted
the wise political policy of allowing the Jews
to return to their own land, he appointed the
prince of Judah, whose name Sheshbazzar
was perhaps the name given to Zerubbabel by
the Babylonians and used when he was acting
as representative of Cyrus, to be governor of
the colony (Ezra 1:8, 11; 5:14). The returning exiles were led by Zerubbabel and the
high priest Jeshua (Joshua), with other
princes (Ezra 2:1-64; Neh. 7:5-7; 12:1-9),
and reached Jerusalem in 538 B.C. Arrived at
the ruined city, Jeshua as head of the priesthood and Zerubbabel as head of the civil administration, acting together, reared an altar
and restored the worship (Ezra 3:1-9). The
foundations of the Temple were next laid by
Sheshbazzar as Persian governor, acting in
his official name (chs. 1:2; 5:16; 3:6, 10-13).
But adversaries, failing to make Zerubbabel
stop proceedings, appealed to successive Persian kings, so that building operations ceased
until 520 B.C., the 2d year of Darius Hystaspis
(ch. 4). In this year, urged by the prophets
Haggai and Zechariah, Zerubbabel, now Persian governor under Darius, and Jeshua resumed the work; and under the constant encouragement of the prophets brought the
building to completion in the early spring of
515 B.C. (Ezra 6:14, 15; Hag., chs. 1; 2;
Zech., ch. 4). From the office Zerubbabel held
when the 2d Temple was built, and the personal interest he took in its erection, it is
often called Zerubbabel's Temple. His governorship continued at least till 515 B.C. How
much longer it lasted is unknown. Zerubbabel
was in his day the representative of the
Davidic monarchy (Hag. 2:20-23). He was
also in the direct line of ancestry of our Lord
(Matt. 1:12, 13; Luke 3:27).

Zer′u·i′a (zĕr′ōō-ī′á) [probably, one perfumed with storax]. A sister of David (I
Chron. 2:16), but probably, like her sister
Abigail, not a daughter of Jesse, but a daughter of David's mother by an earlier marriage
with Nahash (II Sam. 17:25). She was the

mother of Abishai, Joab, and Asahel (II Sam. 2:18; I Chron. 2:16).

Ze′tham (zē′thăm) [olive tree; cf. ZETHAN]. A Gershonite Levite, house of Ladan and son of Jehiel (I Chron. 23:8; 26:22).

Ze′than (zē′thăn) [olive tree]. A Benjamite, family of Jediael (I Chron. 7:10).

Ze′thar (zē′thär) [Old Pers. ǰaⁿtar; Avestan ǰantar, smiter, slayer]. A chamberlain at the court of Ahasuerus (Esth. 1:10).

Zi′a (zī′á) [perhaps, the trembler]. A Gadite, probably head of a father's house (I Chron. 5:13).

Zi′ba (zī′bá) [cf. Aram., branch, twig]. A servant or slave of King Saul. He had been set free (Jos. Antiq. vii. 5, 5), perhaps at the time of Saul's overthrow by the Philistines, and he was father of a large family and had acquired slaves (II Sam. 9:10). David made him and his sons and slaves servants to Mephibosheth, Saul's grandson, and ordered them to till Mephibosheth's lands (vs. 9–12). When David was compelled to flee from Jerusalem because of Absalom's rebellion, Ziba appeared with a couple of asses laden with provisions for the king and stated that Mephibosheth was expecting that Israel would restore Saul's kingdom to him. Thereupon David transferred Mephibosheth's estates to Ziba (ch. 16:1–4). After the death of Absalom, when the king was returning to Jerusalem, among those who went to the Jordan to welcome him back was Ziba with his sons and slaves (ch. 19:17). Mephibosheth also went to meet the king. He had neglected his person, as a sign of sorrow, during the king's absence, and now he declared that he had ordered his ass to be saddled in order to accompany David on his flight, but that Ziba had disobeyed his orders and had also slandered him to the king, and he asked David to do what seemed right. David replied somewhat crustily and ordered half the estates to be restored to Mephibosheth and the rest left in the possession of Ziba (vs. 24–30).

Zib′e•on (zĭb′ē-ŭn) [cf. Arab. ḍab′, hyena]. A Hivite (Gen. 36:2; if the text should not be amended to Horite), who perhaps migrated with his family to Mount Seir and became a Horite tribe (vs. 20, 24), organized under a chief (v. 29). He was ancestor of a wife of Esau (vs. 2, 25).

Zib′i•a (zĭb′ĭ-á) [gazelle]. A Benjamite, son of Shaharaim and head of a father's house (I Chron. 8:9).

Zib′i•ah (zĭb′ĭ-á) [gazelle]. A woman of Beer-sheba, wife of Ahaziah, and mother of Jehoash, king of Judah (II Kings 12:1).

Zich′ri (zĭk′rī) [mindful]. 1. A Levite, family of Kohath, house of Izhar (Ex. 6:21).

2. A Benjamite, son of Shimei (I Chron. 8:19).

3. A Benjamite, son of Shashak (I Chron. 8:23).

4. A Benjamite, son of Jeroham (I Chron. 8:27).

5. A Levite, son of Asaph (I Chron. 9:15). In all probability he is the person called Zaccur (from the same root), in I Chron. 25: 2, 10; Neh. 12:35; and also the person called Zabdi in Neh. 11:17. In the latter instance the letters kaph (k, Anglicized as ch) and resh (r) were misread as beth (b) and daleth (d) respectively.

6. A Levite, descended from Moses' son, Eliezer (I Chron. 26:25).

7. A Reubenite (I Chron. 27:16).

8. A man of Judah, and father of Amasiah, a captain in the army of Jehoshaphat (II Chron. 17:16), and quite possibly of Elishaphat who aided Jehoiada in overthrowing Athaliah (II Chron. 23:1).

9. A valiant Ephraimite in Pekah's army, who slew Maaseiah, a royal prince, and 2 of Ahaz' chief officers (II Chron. 28:7).

10. A Benjamite (Neh. 11:9).

11. A priest, head of the father's house of Abijah. He lived in the days of the high priest Joiakim (Neh. 12:17).

Zid′dim (zĭd′ĭm) [sides]. A fenced city of Naphtali (Josh. 19:35). The Talmud calls the place Kefar Ḥaṭṭya, which has led to locating it at Hattin, about 5½ miles w. by n. of Tiberias, and less than a mile n. of the celebrated Horns of Hattin.

Zid•ki′jah (zĭd-kī′já). See ZEDEKIAH.

Zi′don (zī′dŏn). See SIDON.

Zif (zĭf). See ZIV.

Zi′ha (zī′há). Founder or possibly only the head of a family of Nethinim, members of which returned from the Captivity (Ezra 2: 43; Neh. 7:46). If he was identical with Ziha, an overseer of the Nethinim, who is named in Neh. 11:21, the family was of recent origin among the Nethinim, and small, or else it was an older family named from its present chief.

Zik′lag (zĭk′lăg). A city in the extreme s. of Judah (Josh. 15:31), assigned to the Simeonites (Josh. 19:5; I Chron. 4:30). In the time of Saul it was in the hands of the Philistines, and at one time David held it as the vassal of their king, Achish (I Sam. 27:6; I Chron. 12:1–22). It was captured, plundered, and burnt by the Amalekites, but David pursued them, recovered the spoil, and sent portions of it to many other towns (I Sam. 30:1–31; II Sam. 1:1; 4:10). The connection of David with Ziklag detached it permanently from the Philistines and placed it under the kings of Judah (I Sam. 27:6). It was inhabited after the Captivity (Neh. 11:28). It is probably to be identified with Tell el-Khuweilfeh, about 10 miles e. of Tell esh-Sheri′a.

Zil′lah (zĭl′á) [shadow, i.e., protection]. One of Lamech's wives, and the mother of Tubal-cain (Gen. 4:19–23).

Zil′le•thai (zĭl′ē-thī), in A.V. **Zil′thai** [(Jehovah is) a shadow, protection]. 1. A Benjamite, son of Shimei (I Chron. 8:20).

2. A Manassite, captain of 1,000 men, who joined David at Ziklag (I Chron. 12:20).

Zil′pah (zĭl′pá) [cf. Arab., zulfah, dignity]. A maidservant, given by Laban to Leah on her marriage with Jacob (Gen. 29:24). At Leah's request, she became his secondary wife, and bore to him Gad and Asher (ch. 30: 9–13).

Zil′thai (zĭl′thī). See ZILLETHAI.

Zim′mah (zĭm′á) [probably, counsel, device]. A Gershonite Levite, son of Shimei, and grandson of Jahath (I Chron. 6:20, 42, 43; and perhaps II Chron. 29:12).

Zim′ran (zĭm′răn) [probably, antelope]. A son or rather tribe descended from Abraham and Keturah (Gen. 25:2; I Chron. 1:32). An echo of the name has been surmised either in Zabram, a town w. of Mecca, on the Red Sea (Ptol. vi. 7, 5), or in Zamareni, an Arabian tribe (Pliny Hist. Nat. vi. 32, 5).

Zim′ri (zĭm′rī) [pertaining to an antelope]. 1. Son of Zerah, and grandson of Judah (I Chron. 2:6); called in Josh. 7:1, 17, 18 Zabdi (q.v.).

2. A prince of the tribe of Simeon. He was slain at Shittim for participating with the Midianites in licentious idolatry (Num. 25: 14; I Macc. 2:26, in A.V. Zambri).

3. A Benjamite, a descendant of Jonathan, Saul's son (I Chron. 8:36; 9:42).

4. A military officer who commanded half the chariots of Elah, king of Israel, whom

he assassinated, fulfilling the denunciation against Baasha's house by extirpating it. Then he set himself up as king in Tirzah. Israel at once proclaimed Omri, the commander-in-chief, king. Omri marched against the usurper and captured his capital, Tirzah. When Zimri saw that the city was taken, he set the palace on fire and perished in the flames. His reign, which lasted only a week, fell within the year c. 885 B.C. (I Kings 16:8–20). It has been suggested that he may have been Saul's descendant (I Chron. 8:36), seeking to regain the throne.

5. A people (Jer. 25:25) not otherwise known. They may have been descended from Zimran, but there is no certainty in the case.

Zin (zĭn) [Heb. Ṣin]. A wilderness traversed by the Israelites on their way to Canaan. It was close to the s. boundary of that land (Num. 13:21). Kadesh-barnea was within its limits (Num. 20:1; 27:14; 33:36; Deut. 32:51). It constituted the limit of Edom on the w. and of Judah on the s.e. (Josh. 15:1–3). It was either a part of the wilderness of Paran or bordered on that wilderness at Kadesh. It is not the same place as the wilderness of Sin, the Heb. words for the two being quite different.

Zi'na (zĭ'nȧ). See ZIZAH.

Zi'on (zĭ'ŭn); in Maccabees **Si'on**, and so in A.V. of N.T. always, and in O.T. once (Ps. 65:1) [probably, citadel; cf. Arab. ṣâna and Eth. ṣawana, to protect, defend; Eth. ṣawan, safe place, refuge, fortification, castle, burg, citadel]. 1. One of the hills on which Jerusalem stood. It is 1st mentioned in the O.T. as the seat of a Jebusite fortress. David captured this stronghold and changed its name to the city of David (II Sam. 5:7; I Chron. 11:5). Hither he brought the Ark, and the hill from that time forth became sacred (II Sam. 6:10–12). The Ark was afterward removed by Solomon to the Temple which he erected on Mount Moriah (I Kings 8:1; II Chron. 3:1; 5:2). From the last 2 of these passages it is plain that Zion and Moriah were distinct eminences. For the question which hill was known as Zion, see JERUSALEM, II. 1.

2. After the building of the Temple on Mount Moriah and the transfer of the Ark to it, the name Zion was extended to comprehend the Temple (Isa. 8:18; 18:7; 24:23; Joel 3:17; Micah 4:7). This accounts for the fact that while Zion is mentioned between 100 and 200 times in the O.T., Mount Moriah is named only once (II Chron. 3:1), or at most twice (Gen. 22:2).

3. Zion is often used for the whole of Jerusalem (II Kings 19:21; Ps. 48; 69:35; 133:3; Isa. 1:8; 3:16; 4:3; 10:24; 52:1; 60:14).

4. In the Maccabaean period the hill on which the Temple stood, as distinct from the city of David (I Macc. 7:32, 33).

5. The Jewish Church and polity (Ps. 126:1; 129:5; Isa. 33:14; 34:8; 49:14; 52:8).

6. Heaven (Heb. 12:22; cf. Rev. 14:1).

Zi'or (zĭ'ôr) [smallness]. A town in the hill country of Judah, near Hebron (Josh. 15:54), identified with Ṣa'ir (Ṣi'ir), 5 miles n.n.e. of Hebron. See ZAIR.

Ziph (zĭf). 1. A town in the extreme s. of Judah (Josh. 15:24), identified with ez-Zeifeh, s.w. of Kurnûb.

2. A town in the hill country of Judah (Josh. 15:55), near a wilderness and a forest (I Sam. 23:14, 15). It was fortified by Rehoboam (II Chron. 11:8); it is identified with Tell Zîf, a conspicuous mound 2,882 ft. above sea level, 4 miles s. by e. of Hebron.

3. A man of Judah, house of Jehallelel (I Chron. 4:16).

Zi'phah (zĭ'fȧ). A man of Judah, house of Jehallelel (I Chron. 4:16).

Ziph'ims (zĭf'ĭmz). See ZIPHITES.

Ziph'i·on (zĭf'ĭ-ŏn). See ZEPHON.

Ziph'ites (zĭf'ĭts), in A.V. once **Ziph'ims** (zĭf'ĭmz) (Psalm 54, title). Natives or inhabitants of Ziph 2 (I Sam. 23:19; 26:1; Psalm 54, title).

Ziph'ron (zĭf'rŏn) [cf. Syriac zᵉphar, to stink]. A place on the n. boundary line of the Promised Land (Num. 34:9); probably to be identified with Za'ferâneh, s.e. of Restân.

Zip'por (zĭp'ôr) [bird; perhaps, sparrow]. Father of Balak, king of Moab (Num. 22:4, 10).

Zip·po'rah (zĭ-pō'rȧ) [bird; perhaps, sparrow]. A daughter of Jethro, priest of Midian. She became the wife of Moses (Ex. 2:21, 22). She evidently opposed the circumcision of their 2d son; but when the family was journeying to Egypt and her husband's life was in danger on account of that breach of the covenant, she acquiesced (ch. 4:18–26); see MOSES. She may have returned with her sons to her father at this time; but quite probably they accompanied Moses to Egypt, and after the Exodus, when the host of Israel was slowly approaching Mount Sinai, were sent forward to visit Jethro and inform him of all that God had done for Moses and for the Israelites, and how the Lord had brought Israel out of Egypt (ch. 18:1). Jethro returned with them to the camp at Rephidim (vs. 2–6).

Zith'ri (zĭth'rĭ). See SITHRI.

Ziv (zĭv), in A.V. **Zif** (zĭf) [splendor, bloom]. The 2d month of the Jewish year (I Kings 6:1, 37), approximately May. Later it was commonly called Iyar. See YEAR.

Ziz (zĭz) [brightness, shining thing, flower]. An ascent by which the Moabites and Ammonites ascended from En-gedi toward the wilderness of Jeruel and Tekoa (II Chron. 20:16; cf. vs. 2, 20). It is generally identified with Wadi Ḥaṣâṣa, which leads from the w. shore of the Dead Sea n. of En-gedi to the tableland of Judea.

Zi'za (zĭ'zȧ) [probably a reduplication derived from children's talk]. 1. A Simeonite, descended from Shemaiah (I Chron. 4:37).

2. A son of Rehoboam, by his queen Maacah (II Chron. 11:20).

Zi'zah (zĭ'zȧ) [See ZIZA]. A Levite, family of Gershom, house of Shimei (I Chron. 23:11). In v. 10 the name is mistranscribed Zina.

Zo'an (zō'ăn) [Heb. Ṣō'an from Egypt. D'n.t]. An Egyptian city of the e. part of the Delta, on the Tanitic branch of the Nile, near the 31st degree of n. latitude. It was built 7 years later than Hebron, which was in existence in Abraham's lifetime (Num. 13:22). Zoan existed at least as early as Dyn. VI. The earliest kings of Dyn. XII made it their capital in order to check invasions from the e. The Hyksos fortified it and retained it as the capital under the name of Avaris. After their expulsion the city was neglected, but it was re-established with great ceremony by Sethi I. Avaris (later known as Tanis) was the old home of the Egyptian god Seth. The Ramesside house traced its ancestry back to the Hyksos kings; the great-grandfather of Ramesses (Ramses) II apparently came from an old Tanite family, possibly of Hyksos origin, since his name was Sethos (Suta). In Sethi I's time the god Seth received a new temple, which was enlarged by Ramesses II, who took up his residence in the vicinity at Per-Re'emasese, that is, the city of Ramesses (Raamses, Ex. 1:11). Zoan was the place of meeting between Moses and Pharaoh (Ps. 78:12, 43). It was still an important city in the time of Isaiah and also of Ezekiel (Isa.

19:11, 13; cf. 30:4; Ezek. 30:14). Between the days of Isaiah and Ezekiel, it was captured by the Assyrians. The city was known to the Greeks as Tanis. It has lingered on to modern times, now being Ṣân el-Ḥagar. The famous "400 year" stele of Tanis, erected shortly before the accession of Ramesses I, 1320 B.C., commemorates the founding of the city or an important date in its earliest Hyksos history. See EGYPT, III. 8.

Zo'ar (zō'ẽr) [littleness (Gen. 19:20, 22)]. One of the cities of the Plain, and apparently the smallest of the 5 (Gen. 19:20, 22). The Plain was visible from Mount Nebo as far as Zoar (Deut. 34:3). Zoar's original name was Bela, and it had a king, one of those defeated by Chedorlaomer (Gen. 13:10; 14:2, 8). When threatened judgment was about to descend on the guilty cities, Lot successfully interceded for Zoar and fled thither from the catastrophe (ch. 19:20–23). A mountain (or at least high land) rose immediately behind it, with a cavern, in which Lot and his 2 daughters dwelt for a time (v. 30). Zoar still existed in the days of Isaiah and in those of Jeremiah, and, from their mentioning it in connection with Moab, it may be presumed that it was on the Moabite or e. side of the Dead Sea (Isa. 15:5; Jer. 48:34; cf. also Gen. 19: 37). In the Maccabaean period it belonged to an Arabian kingdom of which Petra was the capital (Jos. Antiq. xiii. 15, 4; xiv. 1, 4). It stood at the s. end of the Dead Sea (Jos. War iv. 8, 4). In the Middle Ages it was an important point on the road from Elath to Jerusalem, 3 days' journey from the latter city via Hebron. These data are satisfied by assuming that Zoar was situated near where the wadi el-'Aḥsy opens through the Moabite mountains into the Plain, about 2 miles from the s. end of the sea (Wetzstein), at the ruins el-Ḳeryeh. This was the later settlement, whither the people of Zoar moved and to which they gave the old name. The original site doubtless now lies beneath the waters of the sea.

Zo'bah (zō'bà), in A.V. twice Zo'ba (zō'bà) (II Sam. 10:6, 8); see ARAM 2 (3).

Zo·be'bah (zō-bē'bà) [cf. Arab. ḍabb, hatred, anger; lizard]. Son of Hakkoz, a man of Judah (I Chron. 4:8).

Zo'har (zō'här) [cf. Arab. and S. Arab. ṣaḥr, fawn color, gray on a red background; Heb. ṣāḥōr, white]. 1. Father of Ephron the Hittite (Gen. 23:8).
2. Son of Simeon (Gen. 46:10). Called also Zerah (Num. 26:13); see ZERAH 3.
3. A man of Judah (I Chron. 4:7, R.V. marg.); see IZHAR, II.

Zo'he·leth (zō'hē-lĕth) [a serpent or other creeper]. A stone beside En-rogel (I Kings 1:9). Clermont-Ganneau pointed out that the ledge of rocks on which the village of Silwan stands is called by the Arabs Zeḥwele or Zaḥweileh, which is like an altered form of Zoheleth. But it is questionable whether the term stone would have been applied to a cliff, and the distance of the ledge from En-rogel seems too great.

Zo'heth (zō'hĕth) [cf. neo-Heb. zaḥtān, proud]. A son of Ishi, registered with the tribe of Judah (I Chron. 4:20).

Zo'phah (zō'fà) [(bellied) jug or jar; cf. Arab. ṣaffaḥa, to make wide, and Eth. saphḥa, to extend]. An Asherite, son of Helem (I Chron. 7:35, 36).

Zo'phai (zō'fī). See ZUPH 1.

Zo'phar (zō'fẽr) [perhaps, chirper; cf. Arab. ṣafara, to whistle]. A Naamathite, one of Job's friends (Job 2:11; 11:1; 20:1; 42:9).

Zo'phim (zō'fīm) [watchers]. A field on the top of Pisgah, from which Balaam could see a part of the encampment of the Israelites at Shittim (Num. 23:14). Conder places it at Tal'at eṣ-Ṣufa, in the valley separating the s.e. point of Pisgah from Luhith.

Zo'rah (zō'rà), in A.V. once Zo're·ah (Josh. 15:33), once Za're·ah (Neh. 11:29) [perhaps, stroke, scourge, or hornet]. A town in the lowland of Judah (Josh. 15:33), inhabited by the Danites (ch. 19:41). Manoah, Samson's father, belonged to the place (Judg. 13:2), and Samson was buried near the town (ch. 16:31). Some of the 5 Danite spies and of the warriors who subsequently took Laish were from Zorah (ch. 18:2, 8, 11). The town was fortified by Rehoboam (II Chron. 11:10). It was inhabited after the Captivity (Neh. 11: 29). Its site is Ṣar'a, on the n. side of the valley of Sorek (Wadi eṣ-Ṣarār), about 14 miles w. of Jerusalem.

Zo'rath·ite (zō'răth-īt), in A.V. once Za're· ath·ite (I Chron. 2:53). A native or inhabitant of Zorah (I Chron. 2:53; 4:2).

Zo're·ah (zō'rē-à). See ZORAH.

Zo'rite (zō'rīt). Either the same as Zorathite, or a citizen of some unknown place (I Chron. 2:54).

Zo·rob'a·bel (zō-rŏb'à-bĕl). See ZERUBBABEL.

Zu'ar (zū'ẽr) [small, little]. Father of that Nethaneel who was prince of the tribe of Issachar in the wilderness (Num. 1:8; 2:5; 7:18, 23; 10:15).

Zuph (zŭf) [honeycomb]. 1. A Levite, descended from Kohath, and an ancestor of the Prophet Samuel (I Chron. 6:35). A variant form, of similar meaning, is Zophai (v. 26).
2. A district beyond the borders of Benjamin (I Sam. 9:4, 6). It may have received its name from the settlement of the family of Zuph there. See further in connection with RAMAH 2.

Zur (zŭr) [a rock]. 1. A king of Midian, ally or vassal of Sihon, and the father of the woman Cozbi (Num. 25:15). He was killed in the war of extermination waged by Moses against the Midianites for their seduction of the Israelites to licentious idolatry (Num. 25: 15, 18; 31:8; Josh. 13:21).
2. A Benjamite, son of Jeiel (I Chron. 8: 30).

Zu'ri·el (zū'rĭ-ĕl) [God is a rock]. A Levite, chief of the Merarites in the wilderness (Num. 3:35).

Zu'ri·shad'dai (zū'rĭ-shăd'ī) [the Almighty is a rock]. Father of the prince of the Simeonites in the wilderness (Num. 1:6; 2:12; 7:36, 41; 10:19).

Zu'zim (zū'zĭm), in A.V. Zu'zims (zū'zĭmz). A tribe occupying a district called Ham, e. of the Jordan, conquered by Chedorlaomer (Gen. 14:5). Apparently the same as Zamzummim.

WESTMINSTER
HISTORICAL MAPS OF
BIBLE LANDS

EDITED BY

G. ERNEST WRIGHT

Associate Professor of Old Testament
McCormick Theological Seminary

FLOYD V. FILSON

Professor of New Testament Literature and History
McCormick Theological Seminary

TABLE OF MAPS

MAP INDEX

1

4

WESTMINSTER

HISTORICAL MAPS OF
BIBLE LANDS

PLATE I

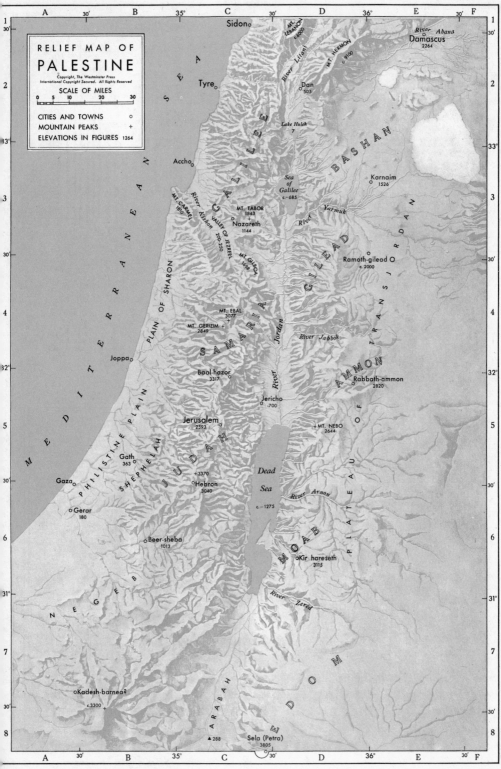

RELIEF MAP OF
PALESTINE

Copyright, The Westminster Press
International Copyright Secured. All Rights Reserved

SCALE OF MILES

0   5   10   20   30

CITIES AND TOWNS   o
MOUNTAIN PEAKS   +
ELEVATIONS IN FIGURES   1264

Sidon

Tyre

Accho

Damascus
2264

River Abana

MT. LEBANON
c.6000

River Litani

MT. HERMON
c. 9100

Dan
505

Lake Huleh
7

SEA

BASHAN

Karnaim
1526

Sea
of
Galilee
c.-685

MT. CARMEL
1810

River Kishon

VALLEY OF JEZREEL
200-250

MT. TABOR
1843
Nazareth
1144

GALILEE

River Yarmuk

River Jordan

GILEAD

Ramoth-gilead O
c. 2000

MT. GILBOA
1698

PLAIN OF SHARON

MT. EBAL
3077
MT. GERIZIM +
2849

SAMARIA

River Jabbok

TRANSJORDAN

AMMON

Joppa o

River Jordan

Baal-hazor
3317

Rabbath-ammon
2820

Jericho
-700

Jerusalem
2593

+ MT. NEBO
2644

MEDITERRANEAN

SHEPHELAH PLAIN

Gath
363

+3370
Hebron
3040

JUDAH

Dead
Sea
c. -1275

Gaza o

Gerar
180

River Arnon

PHILISTINE PLAIN

PLATEAU OF

Beer-sheba
1013

Kir hareseth
3115

MOAB

N E G E B

River Zered

Kadesh-barnea?
c. 3300 +

ARABAH

E   D   O   M

▲ 288

Sela (Petra)
3805

Cartography By G. A. Barrois and Hal & Jean Arbo

Edited By G. Ernest Wright and Floyd V. Filson

PLATE II

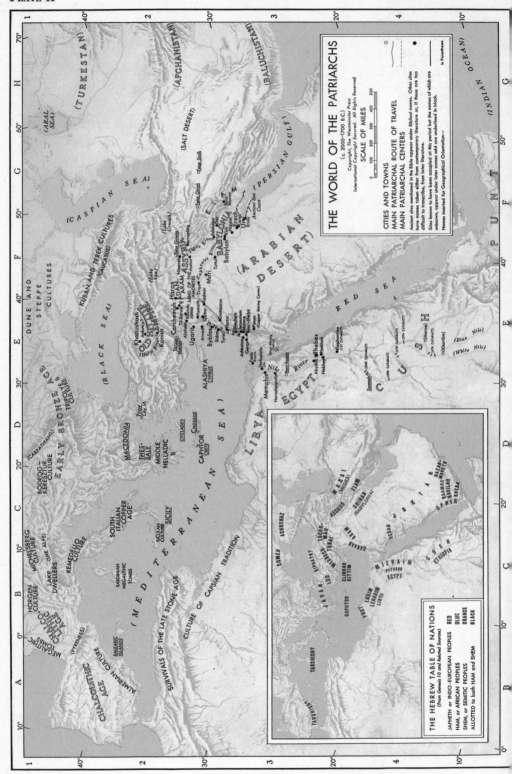

THE WORLD OF THE PATRIARCHS

(c. 2000-1700 B.C.)

Copyright, The Westminster Press
International Copyright Secured. All Rights Reserved.

SCALE OF MILES

0   100   200   300   400   500

CITIES AND TOWNS
MAIN PATRIARCHAL ROUTE OF TRAVEL
MAIN PATRIARCHAL CENTERS

Ancient sites mentioned in the Bible appear under Biblical names. Other sites
have names taken either from contemporary literature or, if these are too
difficult to transcribe, from later literatures.

Sites known to have been occupied at this period but the names of which are
unknown, appear under later names and are underlined in black.

Names inserted for Geographical Orientation—   in Parentheses

THE HEBREW TABLE OF NATIONS

(From Genesis 10 and Related Sources)

JAPHETH or INDO-EUROPEAN PEOPLES   RED
HAM, or AFRICAN PEOPLES   BLUE
SHEM, or SEMITIC PEOPLES   ORANGE
ALLOTTED to both HAM and SHEM   BLACK

PLATE III

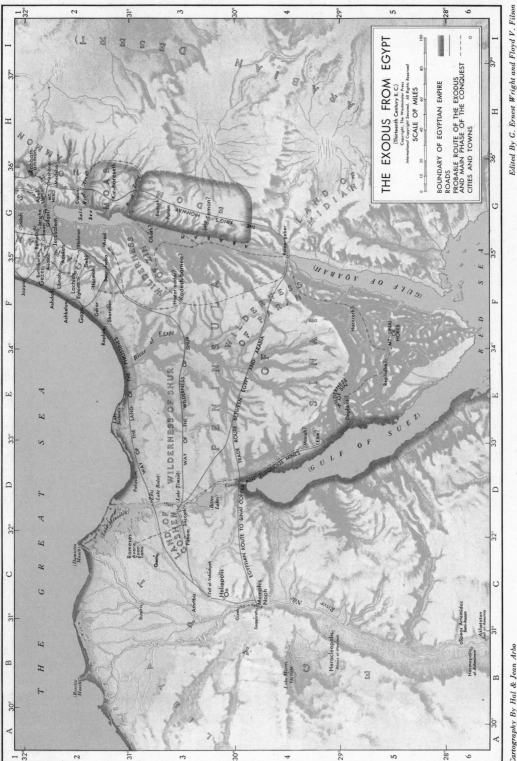

THE EXODUS FROM EGYPT
(Thirteenth Century B. C.)

SCALE OF MILES

BOUNDARY OF EGYPTIAN EMPIRE
ROADS
PROBABLE ROUTE OF THE EXODUS
AND MAIN PHASE OF THE CONQUEST
CITIES AND TOWNS

Edited By G. Ernest Wright and Floyd V. Filson

Cartography By Hal & Jean Arbo

Plate IV

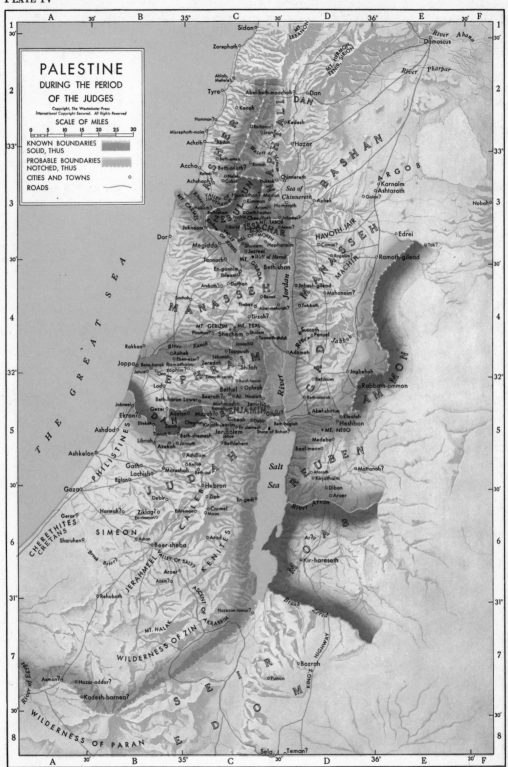

PALESTINE

DURING THE PERIOD

OF THE JUDGES

Copyright, The Westminster Press
International Copyright Secured. All Rights Reserved

SCALE OF MILES

0   5   10   15   20   25   30

KNOWN BOUNDARIES
SOLID, THUS

PROBABLE BOUNDARIES
NOTCHED, THUS

CITIES AND TOWNS   o

ROADS

Cartography By G. A. Barrois and Hal & Jean Arbo   *Edited By G. Ernest Wright and Floyd V. Filson*

PLATE V

THE EMPIRE OF DAVID
AND SOLOMON
(c. 1000-930 B.C.)
Copyright, The Westminster Press
International Copyright Secured. All Rights Reserved

SCALE OF MILES
0 10 20   40   60

BOUNDARY OF THE EMPIRE
INDEPENDENT PHILISTIA AND PHOENICIA
ADMINISTRATIVE DISTRICTS OF SOLOMON
TERRITORY CONQUERED BY DAVID
CITIES AND TOWNS

Map labels:
CYPRUS
THE GREAT SEA
Hamath
Arvad
Kadesh
Tadmor
Riblah
Chun
Zedad
Hazar-enan?
Byblos
Gebal
Berothai
ZOBAH
Helbon
Sidon
MT. LEBANON
Jion?
MT. HERMON
Damascus
Tyre
Abel
Dan
PHOENICIA
MAACHAH
IX
VIII
Accho
Cabul
GESHUR
Ashtaroth
Nobah
VI
Edrei
Salcah
Dor
IV
X
Megiddo
V
Ramoth-gilead
Mahanaim?
ISRAEL
VII
III
Shechem
Adamah
AMMON
Joppa
I
XII
Rabbath-ammon
Rabbah
Bethel
Ashdod
II
Jerusalem
XI
Heshbon
Ashkelon
Gath
Medeba
PHILISTIA
Lachish
Hebron
Dibon
Gaza
JUDAH
Salt Sea
Gerar
MOAB
Beer-sheba
Ar?
Kir-hareseth
(ARABIAN DESERT)
River of Egypt
Bozrah
Punon
Kadesh-barnea?
EDOM
Sela
Teman?
Ezion-geber

Cartography By Hal & Jean Arbo   Edited By G. Ernest Wright and Floyd V. Filson

PLATE VI

CYPRUS

Hamath

THE GREAT SEA

Arvad

Kadesh
Riblah
Chun
Zedad
Tadmor
Hazar-enan?

Byblos
Gebal

MT. AMANA
MT. LEBANON
PHOENICIA

Berothai

Helbon

Sidon

MT. HERMON
Ijon?
Abel
Dan

A R A M   (S Y R I A)
A S S Y R I A

Damascus

Tyre

Accho
Cabul

Ashtaroth

Nobah

Dor
Megiddo
Tishbeh?
Mahanaim?
Edrei
Ramoth-gilead
Salcah

(ARABIAN DESERT)

ISRAEL

Samaria

A M M O N

Joppa

Bethel
Jericho
Rabbath-ammon

Ashdod
Ashkelon
Gath
Lachish
Hebron
Jerusalem
Heshbon
Medeba

PHILISTIA

Gaza
Gerar
JUDAH
Salt Sea
Dibon
M O A B

Beer-sheba
Ar?
Kir-hareseth

River of Egypt

Bozrah
Punon

Kadesh-barnea?

E D O M

Sela
Teman?

Ezion-geber

THE KINGDOMS OF ISRAEL AND
JUDAH IN ELIJAH'S TIME
(c. 860 B.C.)
Copyright, The Westminster Press
International Copyright Secured, All Rights Reserved
SCALE OF MILES
0   10   20   40   60

KINGDOM OF ISRAEL
KINGDOM OF JUDAH
KINGDOM OF AMMON
KINGDOM OF ARAM (SYRIA)
PHILISTINE AND
PHOENICIAN TERRITORY
CITIES AND TOWNS   ○

Cartography By Hal & Jean Arbo   *Edited By G. Ernest Wright and Floyd V. Filson*

PLATE VII

THE KINGDOM OF JUDAH
IN ISAIAH'S TIME
(c. 700 B.C.)
Copyright, The Westminster Press
International Copyright Secured. All Rights Reserved

SCALE OF MILES
0 10 20 40 60

ASSYRIAN EMPIRE
KINGDOM OF JUDAH
KINGDOM OF EDOM
KINGDOM OF MOAB
KINGDOM OF AMMON
INDEPENDENT TYRE   *
ASSYRIAN PROVINCES   DU'RU
CITIES AND TOWNS   o

Cartography By Hal & Jean Arbo

Edited By G. Ernest Wright and Floyd V. Filson

PLATE VIII

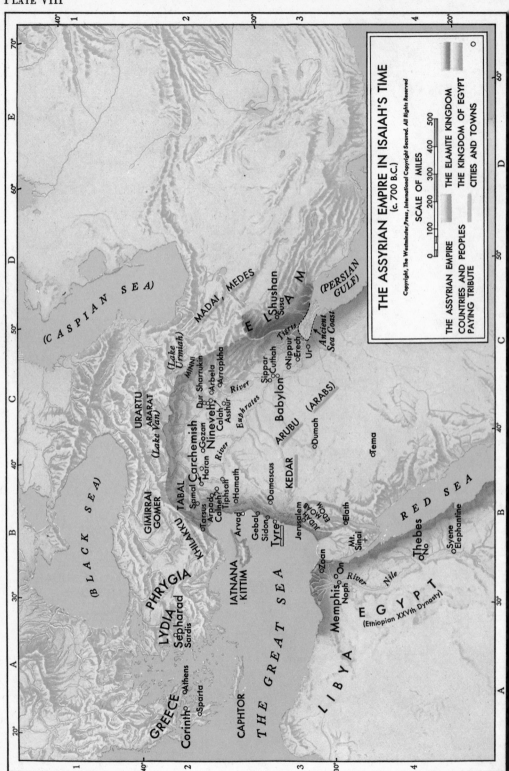

THE ASSYRIAN EMPIRE IN ISAIAH'S TIME
(c. 700 B.C.)

SCALE OF MILES

0   100   200   300   400   500

THE ASSYRIAN EMPIRE   THE ELAMITE KINGDOM
COUNTRIES AND PEOPLES   THE KINGDOM OF EGYPT
PAYING TRIBUTE   CITIES AND TOWNS

PLATE IX

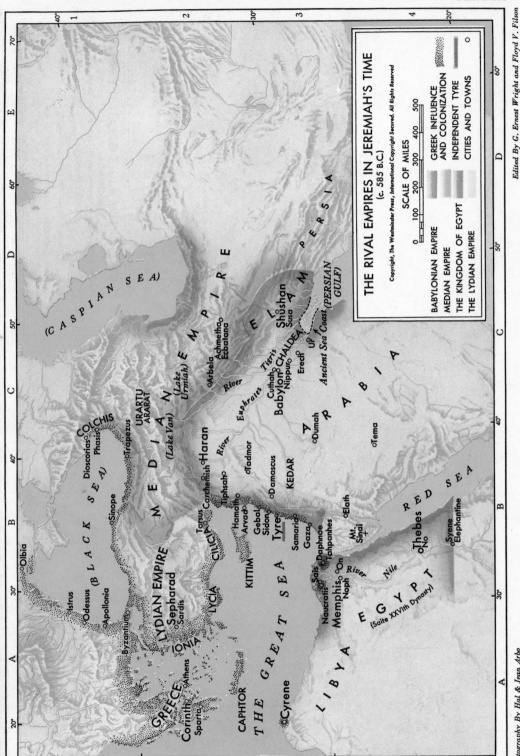

THE RIVAL EMPIRES IN JEREMIAH'S TIME
(c. 585 B.C.)

SCALE OF MILES

0   100   200   300   400   500

BABYLONIAN EMPIRE

MEDIAN EMPIRE

THE KINGDOM OF EGYPT

THE LYDIAN EMPIRE

GREEK INFLUENCE
AND COLONIZATION

INDEPENDENT TYRE

CITIES AND TOWNS

Edited By G. Ernest Wright and Floyd V. Filson

Cartography By Hal & Jean Arbo

PLATE X

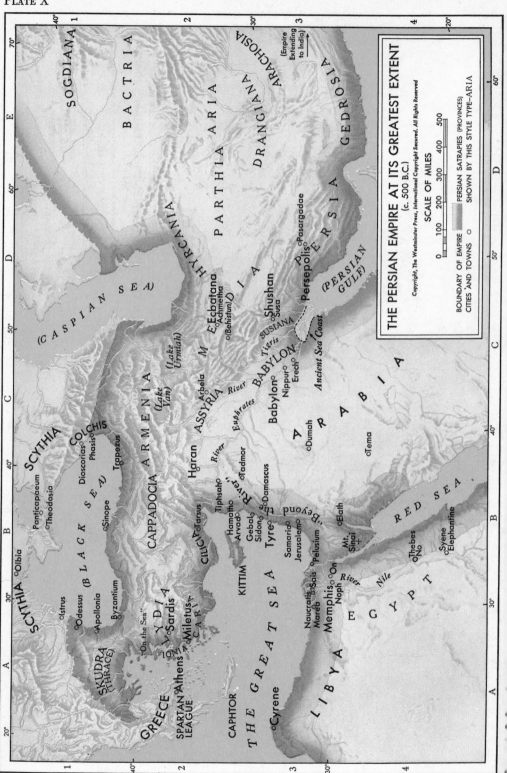

THE PERSIAN EMPIRE AT ITS GREATEST EXTENT
(c. 500 B.C.)

Copyright, The Westminster Press, International Copyright Secured. All Rights Reserved

SCALE OF MILES

0   100   200   300   400   500

BOUNDARY OF EMPIRE

CITIES AND TOWNS ○

PERSIAN SATRAPIES (PROVINCES)
SHOWN BY THIS STYLE TYPE–ARIA

PLATE XI

CYPRUS

34° A · 35° B · C · 36° D · 37° E · 38° F

Hamath

Arvad

ARVAD

HAMATH

Tadmor

THE GREAT SEA

Tripolis

TRIPOLIS

Riblah

Chun

Zedad

Hazar-enan?

Byblos
Gebal

BYBLOS

ROYAL PARK

MASSYAS

Berothai
MT. AMANA

Helbon

(ARABIAN DESERT)

Sidon

SIDON

Ijon?
MT. HERMON

Damascus

Tyre

TYRE

Abel
Dan

QARNAIM

Accho

GELIL

Ashtaroth

HA-GOIM

DOR

Nobah

HAURAN

Dor

Ramoth-
gilead

Edrei

Salcah

GILEAD

Samaria

SAMARIA

AMMON

Joppa

Bethel

Rabbath-ammon

Ashdod

ASHDOD

JUDAH

Jerusalem

Heshbon

Medeba

Ashkelon

Beth-zur

Gaza

Lachish

Hebron

Gerar

Salt
Sea

Beer-sheba

IDUMAEA

MOAB

ARABS

River of Egypt

Kadesh-barnea?

Elath?

THE PROVINCE OF JUDAH
IN NEHEMIAH'S TIME
(c. 444 B.C.)

Copyright, The Westminster Press
International Copyright Secured. All Rights Reserved

SCALE OF MILES

0 10 20   40   60

BOUNDARY OF THE
PERSIAN EMPIRE

PROVINCES OF THE
FIFTH PERSIAN SATRAPY

CITIES AND TOWNS   o

Cartography By Hal & Jean Arbo

Edited By G. Ernest Wright and Floyd V. Filson

PLATE XII

PALESTINE
IN THE
MACCABEAN PERIOD
(168-63 B.C.)

(MEDITERRANEAN SEA)

SEA)

PHOENICIA

MT. LIBANUS

MT. HERMON

Sidon

Tyre

Damascus

Cedes

Asor

Ptolemais

GALILEE

GAULANITIS

Seleucia

Raphon

Bosor

Carnaim

Cana

Asochis

Tarichaea

Arbela

Sepphoris

Hippos

Gamala?

Dion

MT. CARMEL

Philoteria

Gadara

Dora

SAMARIA

Scythopolis

GALAADITIS

Strato's Tower

Pella

Bosora
Bostra

Samaria

Asophon

Amathus

Gerasa

Apollonia

Pharathon?

Sichem

Ragaba

Antipatris

Corea

Joppa

Alexandrium

Jordan River

Philadelphia

PERAEA

Lydda

Modein

Gophna

Aphairema

Elasa

Berea

Jamnia

Gazara

Caphar-salama

Machmas

Dok

Cedron

Adasa

Jerichom

Accaron?

Massepha?

Adasa

Samaga

Azotus

Jerusalem

Hyrcania

Medeba

JUDAEA

Bethbassi

Ascalon

Bethzacharia

Libba

Anthedon

Marisa

Bethsura

Lemba

Gaza

Adoro

Adoreus

Hebron

Machaerus

IDUMAEA

(Dead

Sea)

MOABITIS

Raphia

Agala?

Alusa

Athone?

Thone?

Oronai?

Zoara

Zara

Oryba?

Orybda?

N

A

B

Petra

SCALE OF MILES
0 5 10 20 30

BOUNDARY LINE SHOWS MAXIMUM
EXTENT OF MACCABEAN KINGDOM
UNDER ALEXANDER JANNAEUS
(103-76 B.C.)

KINGDOM OF
ALEXANDER JANNAEUS

FREE CITY

CITIES AND TOWNS   o

Cartography By G. A. Barrois and Hal & Jean Arbo

Edited By G. Ernest Wright and Floyd V. Filson

PLATE XIII

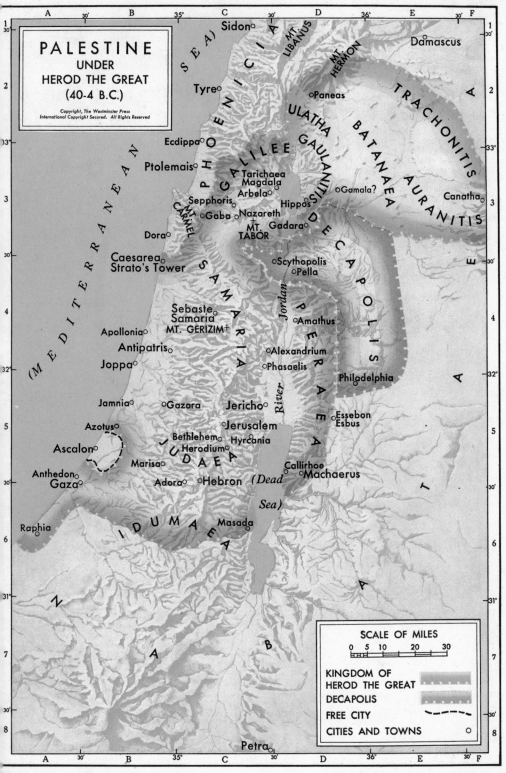

PALESTINE
UNDER
HEROD THE GREAT
(40-4 B.C.)

Copyright, The Westminster Press
International Copyright Secured. All Rights Reserved

SCALE OF MILES

0   5 10   20   30

KINGDOM OF
HEROD THE GREAT

DECAPOLIS

FREE CITY

CITIES AND TOWNS   ○

Cartography By G. A. Barrois and Hal & Jean Arbo

Edited By G. Ernest Wright and Floyd V. Filson

PLATE XIV

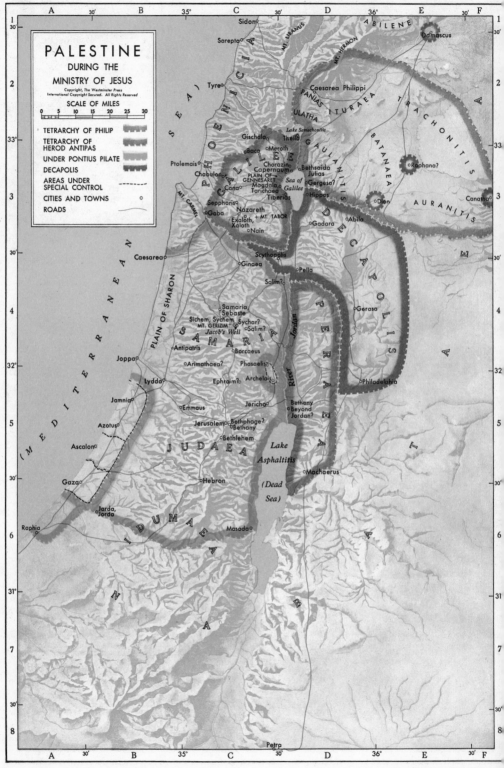

PALESTINE
DURING THE
MINISTRY OF JESUS

Copyright, The Westminster Press
International Copyright Secured. All Rights Reserved

SCALE OF MILES

0   5   10   15   20   25   30

TETRARCHY OF PHILIP
TETRARCHY OF HEROD ANTIPAS
UNDER PONTIUS PILATE
DECAPOLIS
AREAS UNDER SPECIAL CONTROL
CITIES AND TOWNS   o
ROADS

Cartography By G. A. Barrois and Hal & Jean Arbo

Edited By G. Ernest Wright and Floyd V. Filson

PLATE XV

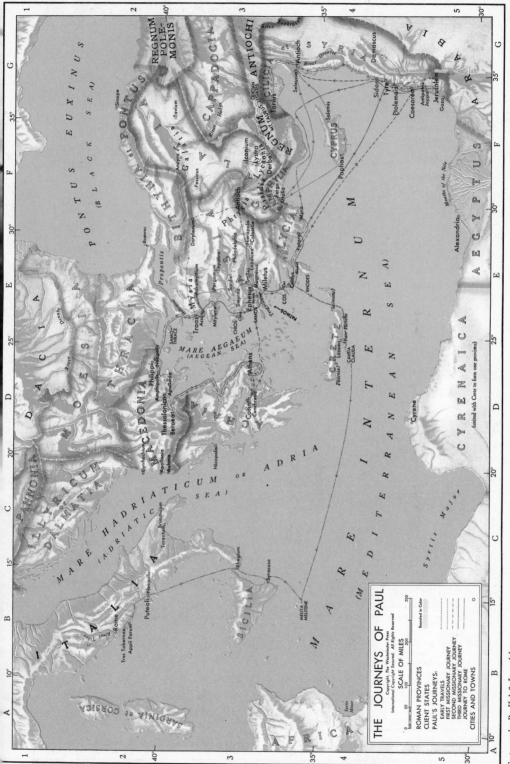

THE JOURNEYS OF PAUL

SCALE OF MILES

ROMAN PROVINCES

CLIENT STATES

PAUL'S JOURNEYS:

EARLY TRAVELS

FIRST MISSIONARY JOURNEY

SECOND MISSIONARY JOURNEY

THIRD MISSIONARY JOURNEY

JOURNEY TO ROME

CITIES AND TOWNS

Edited By G. Ernest Wright and Floyd V. Filson

Cartography By Hal & Jean Arbo

PLATE XVI

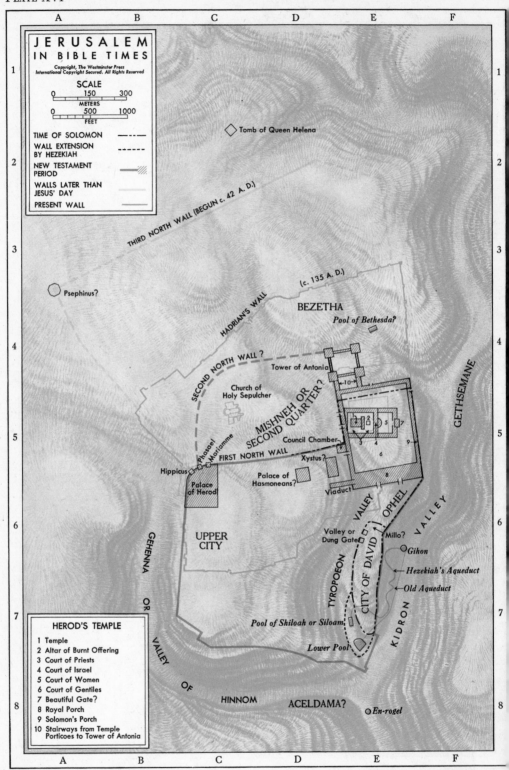

JERUSALEM
IN BIBLE TIMES

Copyright, The Westminster Press
International Copyright Secured. All Rights Reserved

SCALE

0   150   300
METERS
0   500   1000
FEET

TIME OF SOLOMON

WALL EXTENSION
BY HEZEKIAH

NEW TESTAMENT
PERIOD

WALLS LATER THAN
JESUS' DAY

PRESENT WALL

Tomb of Queen Helena

THIRD NORTH WALL (BEGUN c. 42 A.D.)

Psephinus?

(c. 135 A.D.)

HADRIAN'S WALL

BEZETHA

Pool of Bethesda?

SECOND NORTH WALL?

Tower of Antonia

Church of
Holy Sepulcher

MISHNEH OR
SECOND QUARTER?

Council Chamber

FIRST NORTH WALL

Phasael
Mariamme

Xystus?

Hippicus

Palace of
Hasmoneans?

Palace
of Herod

Viaduct

VALLEY

OPHEL

GETHSEMANE

UPPER
CITY

Valley or
Dung Gate

Millo?

Gihon

Hezekiah's Aqueduct

Old Aqueduct

TYROPOEON

CITY OF DAVID

KIDRON VALLEY

Pool of Shiloah or Siloam

Lower Pool

GEHENNA

OR

VALLEY

OF

HINNOM

ACELDAMA?

En-rogel

HEROD'S TEMPLE

1 Temple
2 Altar of Burnt Offering
3 Court of Priests
4 Court of Israel
5 Court of Women
6 Court of Gentiles
7 Beautiful Gate?
8 Royal Porch
9 Solomon's Porch
10 Stairways from Temple
  Porticoes to Tower of Antonia

Cartography By Hal & Jean Arbo

Edited By G. Ernest Wright and Floyd V. Filson